THE HOLY QUR'AN

قُرْاٰنٌ مَجِيْدٌ

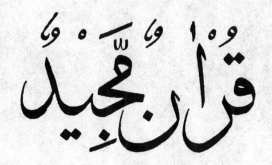

THE HOLY QUR'AN

ARABIC TEXT AND

ENGLISH TRANSLATION WITH COMMENTARY

Edited by Malik Ghulām Farīd

Published under the auspices of

HAZRAT MIRZA TAHIR AHMAD

Fourth Successor of the Promised Messiah
and Head of the Ahmadiyyah Movement in Islam

1988

ISLAM INTERNATIONAL PUBLICATIONS LTD.

First Published in 1969 in Pakistan by
The Oriental and Religious Publishing Corporation Ltd.
First Published in U. K. in 1981 by
The London Mosque, 16 Gressenhall Road,
London SW18 5QL

Present Edition Published by
ISLAM INTERNATIONAL PUBLICATIONS LTD.
ISLAMABAD, Sheephatch Lane, Tilford, Surrey, U. K. GU10 2AQ
and Printed in Great Britain at the Alden Press, Oxford.

British Cataloguing in Publication Data.
[Koran. English & Arabic].
The Holy Quran with English Translation
and Short Commentary.
I. Farid, Malik Ghulam
297'. 1224

ISBN 1-85372-007-0

CONTENTS

FOREWORD

Great is Allāh and great is His mercy. It is through His boundless grace and infinite mercy that we have been able to bring out an abridged edition of "The English Commentary" of the Holy Qur'ān. The preparation of "The English Commentary" was entrusted some years ago to a Board of Translators consisting of the late Maulawī Sher 'Alī, the late Mirzā Bashīr Aḥmad and the writer of these lines, Malik Ghulām Farīd; some spade work having previously been done by the late Maulawī Ṣāḥib. The "Commentary" took several years to be completed. Immediately after the Partition in 1947, Maulawī Sher 'Alī died and Mirzā Bashīr Aḥmad was called to other important duties when Explanatory Notes of only the first nine Chapters had been published and the writer of these lines was left alone to carry on and finish the work.

The "Commentary" covered about 3,000 pages with a very learned Introduction by the late Ḥaḍrat Mirzā Bashīr-ud-Din Maḥmūd Aḥmad, Second Successor of the Promised Messiah and his Promised Son, and was published in 1963 in three large volumes. Evidently, such a voluminous book could hardly be of regular daily use for the average reader and the need was keenly felt for an abridged edition. The present book is intended to meet that need. Fortunately, during the interval a masterly exposition of the meanings of the Qur'ān by the late Ḥaḍrat Khalīfatul Masīḥ II appeared in the form of "Tafsīr Ṣaghīr." The Editor has done his best to incorporate in the present book all that could be of use and interest in the "Tafsīr Ṣaghīr," especially for those upon whom modern thought and western sciences have exercised not altogether a healthy influence. He has also extensively revised the Translation of the Text of the 1954 Edition, printed in Holland, in the light of the Urdu Translation of the "Tafsīr Ṣaghīr."

The Editor is overwhelmed with feelings of deepest gratitude to the Almighty in that he was fortunate to have been vouchsafed ample opportunities to sit at the feet of the late Ḥaḍrat Khalīfatul Masīḥ II (of blessed memory) and for years listened to his speeches, discourses on various religious subjects, sermons, and highly enlightening lessons on the Qur'ān, in which were reflected those mysteries of Divine knowledge to which only the pure of heart are granted access. The present Abridged Edition is mainly based, as was "The Larger Edition" on the material culled and collected from his speeches and writings. "Introduction to the Study of the Holy Qur'ān" by the late Ḥaḍrat Khalīfatul Masīḥ, II, forms an integral part of this Abridged Edition, but in view of its volume and importance it has been printed as a separate book.

The Arabic Text of the book has been given side by side with the English Translation. A mere translation without the text is likely, in the long run, to endanger the purity of the text; besides depriving the reader of the opportunity of comparison.

The explanations of the important Arabic words and expressions in the Commentary are based on the standard lexicons of the Arabic language, such as the Lisān al-'Arab, the Taj al-'Arūs, the Mufradāt of Imām Rāghib, the Arabic English Lexicon by E. W. Lane and the Aqrab Al-Mawārid. As regards the Translation, our procedure has been to base the meaning of every word, first on the corroborative testimony of other parts of the Qur'ān and secondly on the context. The words printed in italics have been introduced to explain the meaning of the Text, there being no words corresponding to them in the original.

As regards Explanatory Notes or Commentary, every Note first derives its authority from the tenor and spirit of the Qur'ān as expressed at various other places. Next to the Qur'ān precedence is given to the Ḥadīth and then come the standard dictionaries of the Arabic Language. Last of all, recourse is had to the evidence of history which was necessary for the explanation of such verses as refer to well-known historical events.

In the course of the preparation of these Notes light has been thrown from time to time on the order which runs through the verses of each Chapter, the one following the other in natural sequence. By a careful perusal of these Notes the reader will realize that the Qur'ān forms a thoroughly coherent and consistent reading.

Special care is taken in the Notes to refute the principal objections raised against Islām by Christian writers. These objections are based either on ignorance or on deliberate misrepresentation of the true teachings of Islām on the part of these writers. Refutation of such objections helps to remove much bias and prejudice against Islām and to create an atmosphere for a better appreciation of its teachings.

A system of cross-references has been introduced. These cross-references have been placed below the Text and the Translation. They give at a glance the various places where the subject of a particular verse has been dealt with in the Qur'ān.

An Introduction is prefixed to each Chapter. It discusses the place and date of its revelation and gives a summary of its contents and the relation it has with the Chapters preceding or following it. It also provides sufficient material for the reader to understand and realize that not only the verses of the various Chapters but also the specific position of each Chapter itself is governed by an intelligent order.

In numbering the verses of the Qur'ān we have followed the system in vogue in the standard Editions of the Qur'an in Pakistan with this exception that in our numbering *Bismillāh* is counted as the first verse of every Chapter, while in other Editions the verse following *Bismillāh* is numbered as the first verse of the Chapter. Chapter 9, however, is an exception to this rule. It does not begin with *Bismillāh*, and therefore in this Chapter our numbering is identical with that of other Editions of the Qur'ān. Our numbering of the Notes is continuous. It does not end where a *Sūrah* ends but is continued into the next *Sūrah* to the end of the Book.

In references the figure on the left side of the colon shows the number of the Chapter, while that on its right the number of the verse. It should also be noted that when reference is to a Chapter of the Qur'ān, the word Qur'ān is invariably omitted for brevity's sake. Thus 20 : 8 refers to the 8th verse of the 20th Chapter of the Qur'ān; in references to other religious Scriptures, however, the name of the book is invariably mentioned, though generally in an abbreviated form. So Gen. 5 : 6 means the 6th verse of the first chapter of Genesis, the first Book of Moses.

The Editor would be failing in his duty if he does not acknowledge his deep debt of gratitude to Mirzā Mubārak Aḥmad, Vakīl A'lā, Taḥrīk Jadīd, without whose active and valuable support and useful guidance it would not have been possible for this Abridged Edition to see the light of the day. He also expresses his sincere thanks to Maulawi Muḥammad Aḥmad Jalīl and Ch. Muẓaffar Dīn, who helped him by very carefully reading the proofs of the whole manuscript and making meaningful suggestions and also to Maulawī Nūr-ud-Dīn Munīr, who has taken great pains in preparing an exhaustive Index.

The Editor
(Malik Ghulām Farīd).

BOOKS OF REFERENCE WITH THEIR ABBREVIATED TITLES

Some Commentators of the Qur'ān have given single letters or a group of letters as abbreviations for the authorities they have quoted. These are not of much help to the reader who has to turn to the list of abbreviations again and again in order to ascertain to which authority the letter refers. But it also seems cumbrous to give the names of the authorities in full. So we have followed a middle course and have given a shortened form of the name, which generally consists in a part of the name of the book or its author. Thus, for instance, instead of Al-Baḥr al-Muḥīṭ by Abū Ḥayyān, we have simply given the word 'Muḥīṭ,' and for Sīrat al-Nabī by Ibn Hishām, the abbreviated form 'Hishām' is given. These abbreviated names easily suggest to the reader the book of the author to which reference is made. No shortened form, however, has been used for the authorities that are not frequently quoted. In case of the books of the Bible, we have made use of the abbreviations that are generally used in Christian literature. Following is a list of well-known works of reference and other important books to which we have referred in this Commentary. We have taken special care to give the full name of each book and its author along with its abbreviated title.

Books Of Ḥadīth

Shortened form of the name		*Full name with the name of the Author*
Bukhārī	..	The Ṣaḥīḥ of Bukhārī by Abū 'Abd Allāh Muḥammad ibn Ismā'īl Bukhārī.
Muslim	..	The Ṣaḥīḥ of Muslim by Ḥāfiẓ Abu'l Ḥusain Muslim ibn Ḥajjāj al-Qashīrī.
Tirmidhī	..	The Jāmi' of Tirmidhī by Abū 'Īsā Muḥammad ibn 'Īsā Tirmidhī.
Dāwūd or Abū Dāwūd		Sunan of Abū Dāwūd by Ḥāfiẓ Sulaimān ibn Ash'ath Abū Dāwūd.
Mājah	..	Sunan of Ibn Mājah by Muḥammad ibn Yazīd Abū 'Abd Allāh ibn Mājah Qazwīnī.
Musnad	..	Musnad of Aḥmad ibn Ḥanbal by Imām Abū 'Abd Allāh Aḥmad ibn Ḥanbal.
Nasa'ī	..	Sunan of Nasa'ī by Ḥāfiẓ Abū 'Abd al-Raḥmān Aḥmad ibn Shu'aib Nasa'ī.
Mu'aṭṭa'	..	Mu'aṭṭa' by Imām Mālik.
Baihaqī	..	Sunan of Baihaqī by Abū Bakr Aḥmad ibn Ḥusain al-Baihaqī
'Ummāl	..	Kanz al'Ummāl fī Sunan al-Aqwāl wa'l Af'āl by Shaikh 'Alā al-Dīn 'Alī al-Muttaqī.
Quṭnī	..	Sunan of Dār Quṭnī by Ḥāfiẓ 'Alī ibn 'Umar al-Dār Quṭnī.
Qasṭalānī	..	Irshād al-Sārī by Aḥmad Muḥammad al-Khaṭīb Qasṭalānī.

Bārī	..	Fatḥ al-Bārī by Abu'l Faḍl Shihāb al-Dīn Aḥmad ibn 'Alī 'Asqalānī.
Ṣaghīr	..	Al-Jāmi' al Ṣaghīr fī Aḥādīth al-Bashīr al-Nadhīr.
'Asākir	..	Ibn 'Asākir by Abu'l Qāsim 'Alī ibn al-Ḥasan ibn 'Asākir.
Mardawaih	..	Mardawaih by Abū Bakr Aḥmad ibn Mūsā ibn Mardawaih.
Ṭaḥāwī	..	Sharḥ Ma'ānī al-Āthār by Abū Ja'far al-Ṭaḥāwī.
Manāwī	..	Al-Tafsīr, Exposition of al-Jāmi' al-Ṣaghīr by Imām 'Abd al-Ra'ūf al-Manāwī.

Commentaries Of The Qur'ān

Jarīr	..	Commentary of the Qur'ān by Imām Abū Ja'far Muḥammad ibn Jarīr Ṭabarī.
Kathīr	..	The Tafsîr of Abu'l Fidā Ismā'īl ibn al-Kathīr.
Kashshāf	..	Al-Kashshāf 'an Ghawāmiḍ al-Tanzīl by Imām Maḥmūd ibn 'Umar Zamakhsharī.
Muḥīṭ	..	Al-Baḥr al-Muḥīṭ by Athīr al-Dīn Abū 'Abd Allāh Muḥammad ibn Yūsuf of Granada (Spain), *alias* Abū Ḥayyān.
Manthūr	..	Durr Manthūr by Ḥāfiẓ Jalāl al-Dīn 'Abd al-Raḥmān Sayūṭī.
Ma'ānī	..	Rūḥ al-Ma'ānī by Abu'l Faḍl Shihāb al-Dīn Maḥmūd al-Baghdādī.
Baiḍāwī	..	Anwār al-Tanzīl by Qāḍī Naṣīr al-Dīn Abū Sa'īd Baiḍāwī.
Qadīr	..	Fatḥ al-Qadīr by Muḥammad ibn 'Alī al-Shaukānī.
Fatḥ	..	Fatḥ al-Bayān Abū'l-Ṭayyib Ṣiddīq ibn Ḥasan.
Rāzī	..	Tafsīr Kabīr by Imām Muḥammad Fakhr al-Dīn Rāzī.
Bayān	..	Rūḥ al-Bayān by Ṣhaikh Ismā'īl Ḥaqqī.
Tafsīr	..	Tafsīr Kabīr by Ḥaḍrat Mirzā Bashīr-ud-Dīn Maḥmūd Aḥmad.
Tha'labī	..	Al-Jawāhir al-Ḥisān fī Tafsīr al-Qur'ān by Shaikh 'Abd al-Raḥmān Tha'labī.
Qurṭubī	..	Qurṭubī Abū 'Abd Allāh Muḥammad ibn Aḥmad al-Qurṭubī, Cordova (Spain).
Wherry	..	Commentary on the Qur'ān by Rev. E. M. Wherry, M.A.

Lexicons, Encyclopaedias And Periodicals

Biḥār	..	Majma' Biḥār al-Anwār by Shaikh Muḥammad Ṭāhir of Gujrāt.
Kulliyyāt or Baqā'	..	Al-Kulliyyāt by Abu'l Baqā' al-Ḥusainī.
Mufradāt	..	Al-Mufradāt fī Gharā'ib al-Qur'ān by Shaikh Abu'l Qāsim Ḥusain ibn Muḥammad al-Rāghib.

Lisān	..	Lisān al-'Arab by Imām Abu'l Faḍl Jamāl al-Dīn Muḥammad ibn Mukarram.
Tāj	..	Tāj al-'Arūs by Abu'l Faiḍ Sayyid Muḥammad Murtaḍā al-Ḥusainī.
Lane	..	Arabic-English Lexicon by E. W. Lane.
Qāmūs	..	The Qāmūs by Shaikh Naṣr Abu'l Wafā'.
Ṣiḥāḥ	..	The Ṣiḥāḥ by Abu'l Naṣr Ismā'īl Jauharī.
Aqrab	..	Aqrab al-Mawārid by Sa'īd Al-Khaurī al-Sharṭūṭi.
Miṣbāḥ	..	Al-Miṣbāḥ al-Munīr by Aḥmad ibn Muḥammad al-Fayūmī.
Gesenius	..	The Hebrew-English Lexicon by Gesenius.
Enc. Bri.	..	Encyclopaedia Britannica, 14th Edition.
Enc. Rel. Eth.	..	Encyclopaedia of Religions and Ethics.
Jew. Enc.	..	Jewish Encyclopaedia.
Enc. Bib.	..	Encyclopaedia Biblica.
Enc. Islām	..	Encyclopaedia of Islām.
Rev. Rel.	..	The Review of Religions.
Cruden	..	Cruden's Complete Concordance to The Old and The New Testaments and Apocrypha.

History And Geography

Ṭabarī	..	Tārīkh al-Rusul wa'l-Mulūk by Abū Ja'far Muḥammad ibn Jarīr Ṭabarī.
Isḥāq	..	Ibn Isḥāq.
Sīrat	..	Sīrat Khātam al-Nabiyyīn by Mirzā Bashīr Aḥmad, M.A., Rabwah.
Muir	..	Life of Muḥammad by Sir William Muir, K. C. S. I. (1923).
The Caliphate	..	The Caliphate, Its Rise, Decline and Fall by Sir William Muir, K. C. S. I.
Hishām	..	Sīrat al-Nabī by Shaikh Abū Muḥammad 'Abd al-Mālik ibn Hishām.
Futūḥ	..	Futūḥ al-Buldān by Balādharī.
Ṭabaqāt	..	Ṭabaqāt al-Kabīr by Muḥammad ibn Sa'd.
Khamīs	..	Tārīkh al-Khamīs by Shaikh Ḥusain ibn Muḥammad al-Diyār al-Bakrī.
Zurqānī	..	Sharḥ Zurqānī by Imām Muḥammad ibn 'Abd al-Bāqī al-Zurqānī.
Ghābbah	..	Usud al-Ghābbah fī Ma'rifat al-Ṣiḥābah by Ḥāfiẓ Abu'l Ḥasan 'Alī ibn Muḥammad.
Ma'ād	..	Zād al-Ma'ād fī Hadyi Khair al-'Ibād by Muḥammad ibn Abū Bakr ibn Ayyūb al-Dimashqī.

Buldān .. Mu'jam al-Buldān by Abū 'Abd Allāh Yāqūt ibn 'Abd Allāh al-Baghdādī.

Dhahab .. Murūj al-Dhahab wa Ma'ādin al-Jauhar by 'Allāmah Abu'l Ḥasan 'Alī ibn Ḥusain al-Mas'ūdī.

Athīr .. Kāmil ibn Athīr by Abu'l Ḥasan 'Alī ibn Abū'l Karam *alias* ibn al-Athīr.

Mawāhib .. Mawāhib al-Ladunniyyah by Shihāb al-Dīn Aḥmad Qasṭalānī.

Khaldūn .. Tārīkh al-Umam by 'Abd al-Raḥmān ibn Khaldūn al-Maghribī.

Ḥalbiyyah .. Sīrat al-Ḥalbiyyah by 'Alī ibn Burhān al-Dīn al-Ḥalbī.

Taṣawwuf And 'Aqā'id

Futūḥāt .. Futūḥāt Makkiyyah by Muḥyī al-Dīn ibn al-'Arabī.

'Awārif .. 'Awārif al-Ma'ārif by Abū Ḥafṣ 'Umar ibn Muḥammad.

Zāhirī .. Dawūd Zāhirī.

Malā'ikah .. Malā'ikat Allāh by Ḥaḍrat Mirzā Bashīr ud-Dīn Maḥmūd Aḥmad.

Science Of Philology And Polite Literature

Mubarrad .. Kitāb al-Kāmil by Abu'l 'Abbās Muḥammad ibn Yazīd al-Mubarrad.

Mu'allaqāt .. Sab' Mu'allaqāt, the seven well-known poems by seven eminent pre-Islamic poets.

Grammar

Sībawaih .. Sībawaih by Abu'l Bashr 'Amr Sībawaih.

Wright .. A Grammar of the Arabic Language by W. Wright, LL.D.

Jurisprudence

Mūḥallā .. Al Mūḥallā by Imām Abū Muḥammad 'Alī ibn Aḥmad ibn Sa'īd ibn Ḥazm.

Mardawaih .. Ibn Mardawaih.

Ma'ānī

Mukhtaṣar .. Mukhtaṣar al-Ma'ānī by Mas'ūd ibn 'Umar *alias* Sa'd Taftāzānī.

Muṭawwal .. Al-Muṭawwal by Mas'ūd ibn 'Umar *alias* Sa'd Taftāzānī.

Works Of The Promised Messiah

Tauḍīḥ .. Tauḍīḥ al-Marām.

Ā'īnah .. Ā'īnah Kamālāt Islām.

Ḥaqīqat .. Ḥaqīqat al-Waḥy.

Izālah .. Izālah Auhām.

Teachings .. The Teachings of Islām.

Barāhīn .. Barāhīn Aḥmadiyyah.

Miscellaneous

Among other works which are not included in the above list but which have been consulted in the course of the preparation of this Commentary may be mentioned as follows (the list is by no means exhaustive) :

Asās .. .. Ḥaqīqat al-Asās.
Māwardī .. .. Al-Māwardī.
Izālat al-Khifā' 'an Khilāfat al-Khulafā' by Ḥaḍrat Shāh Walī Allāh of Delhi.
The Al-Ḥakam.
The Al-Faḍl.
The Tomb of Jesus by Dr. M. M. Ṣādiq, Rabwah (formerly of Qadian).
The Old and The New Testaments.
The Zend-Avesta.
The Dasātīr.
The Jāmāspī by Jāmāsap, First Successor of Zoroaster.
Dictionary & Glossary of the Qur'ān by John Penrice.
Historians' History of the World.
History of the Arabs by P. K. Hitti.
Abbot's Life of Napoleon.
Renan's History of the People of Israel.
Josephus : History of the Jewish Nation.
Hutchinson's History of the Nations.
The Apocrypha.
The Dawn of Conscience by James Henry Breasted.
Moses and Monotheism by Sigmund Freud.
Decline and Fall of the Roman Empire by Edward Gibbon.
Biblical Cyclopaedia by J. Eadie.
Diodorus Siculus (Translation by C. M. Oldfather, London, 1935).
The Pilgrimage by Lieut. Burton.
The Jewish Foundation of Islām.
Scoffield Reference Bible.
Cyclopaedia of Biblical Literature (New York, 1877).
Leaves from Three Ancient Qur'āns, Edited by Rev. A. Mingana, D.D.
Translation of the Targum by J. W. Etheridge.
Capital Punishment in the Twentieth Century by E. Roy Calvert.
Lalita Vistara (Sk.).
Buddha-Charita (Sk.).
The Making of Humanity by Robert Briffault.
On Heroes And Hero-Worship by Thomas Carlyle.
History of Palestine and the Jews by John Kitto (London, 1844).
American Medical Journal.
Indo-Aryans by R. Mitra, LL.D., C.I.E.
The Talmud (Selections by H. Polano).
Commentary of the Bible by C. J. Ellicott, Lord Bishop of Gloucester.
Commentaries on The Old and The New Testaments, published by Society for Promoting Christian Knowledge, London.
Sharḥ al-Sunnah by Abū Muḥammad al-Ḥusain ibn Mas'ūd al-Baghwī.
Faṣl al-Khiṭāb by Ḥaḍrat Maulawī Nūr-ud-Dīn Khalīfatul-Masīḥ I.

Khuṭabāt Aḥmadiyyah by Sir Sayyid Aḥmad Khan, K.C.S.I.
Everyman's Encyclopaedia.
Story of Rome by Norwood Young.
Decline of the West by Spengler.
A Study of History by Toynbee.
The Universe Surveyed by Harold Richards.
The Nature of the Universe by Fred Hoyle.
Commentary on the Bible by Dr. Peake.
Rise of Christianity by Bishop Barns.
Marvels and Mysteries of Science by Allison Hox.
Once to Sinai by H. F. Prescott.
Emotion as Basis of Civilization.

SYSTEM OF TRANSLITERATION

In transliterating Arabic words we have followed the system adopted by the Royal Asiatic Society.

ا at the beginning of a word, pronounced as *a, i, u* preceded by a very slight aspiration, like *h* in the English word 'honour'.

ث *th*, pronounced like *th* in the English word 'thing'.
ح *ḥ*, a guttural aspirate, stronger than h.
خ *kh*, pronounced like the Scotch *ch* in 'loch'.
ذ *dh*, pronounced like the English *th* in 'that'.
ص *ṣ*, strongly articulated s.
ض *ḍ*, similar to the English *th* in 'this'.
ط *ṭ*, strongly articulated palatal t.
ظ *ẓ*, strongly articulated z.
ع ', a strong guttural, the pronunciation of which must be learnt by the ear.

غ *gh*, a sound approached very nearly in the *r'grasseye'* in French, and in the German *r*. It requires the muscles of the throat to be in the 'gargling position whilst pronouncing it.

ق *q*, a deep guttural *k* sound.
ء ', a sort of catch in the voice.

Short vowels are represented by *a* for َ (like *u* in 'bud'); *i* for ِ (like *i* in 'bid'); u for ُ (like *oo* in 'wood'); the long vowels by *ā* for ـَا or آ (like *a* in 'father'); *ī* for ِي (like *ee* in 'deep'); *ai* for َي (like *i* in 'site'); *ū* for ُو (like *oo* in 'root'): *au* for, َو (resembling *ou* in 'sound').

The consonants not included in the above list have the same phonetic value as in the principal languages of Europe.

CHAPTER 1

AL-FĀTIḤAH

(*Revealed before Hijrah*)

Place and Time of Revelation

As reported by many traditionists, the whole of this *Sūrah* was revealed at Mecca, and from the very beginning formed part of the Muslim Prayer. The *Sūrah* has been referred to in the Quranic verse, *We have indeed given thee the seven oft-repeated verses and the great Qur'ān* (15 : 88), which was admittedly revealed at Mecca. According to some reports, the *Sūrah* was also revealed a second time at Medina. The time of its first revelation, however, may be placed very early in the Prophet's ministry.

Names of the Sūrah and their Significance

The best-known title of this short *Sūrah, i.e., Fātiḥat al-Kitāb*, (Opening Chapter of the Book) is reported on the authority of several reliable traditionists (Tirmidhī & Muslim). The title was later abbreviated into *Sūrah Al-Fātihah*, or simply *Al-Fātiḥah*. The *Sūrah* is known by quite a number of names, the following ten are more authentic, *viz., Al-Fātiḥah, Al-Ṣalāt, Al-Ḥamd, Umm al-Qur'ān, Al-Qur'ān al-'Aẓīm, Al-Sab' al-Mathānī, Umm al-Kitāb, Al-Shifā', Al-Ruqyah* and *Al-Kanz*. These names throw a flood of light upon the extensive import of the *Sūrah*.

The name *Fātiḥat al-Kitāb* (Opening Chapter of the Book) signifies that the *Sūrah* having been placed in the beginning serves as a key to the whole subject-matter of the Qur'ān. *Al-Ṣalāt* (The Prayer) signifies that it forms a complete and perfect prayer and constitutes an integral part of the institutional Prayers of Islām. *Al-Ḥamd* (The Praise) signifies that the *Sūrah* brings to light the lofty purpose of man's creation and teaches that the relation of God to man is one of grace and mercy. *Umm al-Qur'ān* (Mother of the Qur'ān) signifies that the *Sūrah* forms an epitome of the whole of the Qur'ān, containing in a nutshell all the knowledge that has a bearing on man's moral and spiritual development. *Al-Qur'ān al-'Aẓīm* (The Great Qur'ān) signifies that although the *Sūrah* is known as *Umm al-Kitāb* and *Umm al-Qur'ān*, it nevertheless forms part of the Holy Book and is not separate from it, as mistakenly considered by some. *Al-Sab' al-Mathānī* (The Oft-repeated Seven Verses) signifies that the seven short verses of the Chapter virtually fulfil all the spiritual needs of man. It also signifies that the Chapter must be repeated in every *Rak'at* of Prayer. *Umm al-Kitāb* (Mother of the Book) signifies that the prayer contained in the Chapter was the cause of the revelation of the Quranic Dispensation. *Al-Shifā'* (The Cure) signifies that it provides remedy for all the legitimate doubts and misgivings of man. *Al-Ruqyah* (The Charm) signifies that it is not only a prayer to ward off disease but also provides protection against Satan and his followers, and strengthens the heart of man against them. *Al-Kanz* (The Treasure) signifies that the *Sūrah* is an inexhaustible store-house of knowledge.

Al-Fātiḥah Referred to in a Prophecy of the New Testament

The best-known name of the *Sūrah*, however, is Al-Fātiḥah. It is interesting to note that this very name occurs in a prophecy of the New Testament: "I saw another mighty angel come down from heaven ... and he had in his hand a little *book open* : and he set his right foot upon the sea and his left foot on the earth" (Rev. 10 : 1-2). The Hebrew word for 'open' is *Fatoah* which is the same as the Arabic word *Fātiḥah*. Again, "And when he (the angel) had cried, seven thunders uttered their voices (Rev. 10 : 3-4). "The seven thunders" represent the seven verses of this Chapter. Christian scholars say that the prophecy refers to the second advent of Jesus Christ, and this has been established by actual facts. The Holy Founder of the Aḥmadiyya Movement, Ḥaḍrat Mirzā Ghulām Aḥmad, in whose person the prophecy relating to the second advent of Jesus has been fulfilled, wrote commentaries on this Chapter and deduced arguments of the truth of his claim from its contents and always used it as a model prayer. He deduced from its seven short verses Divine realities and eternal verities which were not known before. It was as if the Chapter had been a sealed book until its treasures were laid bare by Ḥaḍrat Aḥmad. Thus was fulfilled the prophecy contained in Rev. 10 : 4: " And when the seven thunders had uttered their voices, I was about to write and I heard a voice from heaven saying unto me,"Seal up those things which the seven thunders uttered and write them not." The prophecy referred to the fact that *Fatoah* or *Al-Fātiḥah* would, for a time, remain a closed book, but that a time would come when treasures of spiritual knowledge contained in it would be laid bare. This was done by Ḥaḍrat Aḥmad.

Connection With the Rest of the Qur'ān

The *Sūrah* forms, as it were, an introduction to the Qur'ān. It is, in fact, the Qur'ān in miniature. Thus at the very beginning of his study, the reader becomes familiar in broad outline with the subjects he should expect to find in the Holy Book. The Holy Prophet is reported to have said that *Sūrah* Al Fātiḥah is the most important Chapter of the Qur'ān (Bukhārī).

Subject-Matter

The *Sūrah* contains the essence of the entire Quranic teaching. It comprises, in outline, all the subjects dealt with at length in the body of the Qur'ān. It starts with a description of the fundamental attributes of God, which form the pivot round which all the other Divine attributes revolve, and the basis of the working of the universe and of the relation between God and man. The four principal Divine attributes, *Rabb* (Creator, Sustainer and Developer), *Raḥmān* (Gracious), *Raḥīm* (Merciful) and *Māliki Yaum al-Dīn* (Master of the Day of Judgment) signify that after having created man, God endowed him with the best natural capabilities and provided the means and material needed for his physical, social, moral and spiritual development. Further, He made a provision that man's strivings and endeavours should be amply rewarded. The *Sūrah* goes on to say that man has been created for *'Ibādah, i.e.*, the worship of God and the attainment of His nearness and that he constantly needs His help for the fulfilment of this supreme object. The mention of the four Divine attributes is followed by a comprehensive prayer in which all the urges of the human soul find full expression. The prayer teaches that man should always seek and invoke the assistance of God that He may provide him with the means required for success in this life and in the life to come. But as man is apt to derive strength and inspiration from the good example of those noble and great souls of the past, who achieved the object of their life, he is taught to pray that like them God should open up for him also avenues of unlimited moral and spiritual progress. Finally, the prayer contains a warning lest after having been led to the right path he should stray away from it, lose sight of his goal and become estranged from his Creator. He is taught to remain always on his guard and constantly to seek God's protection against any possible estrangement from Him. This is the subject, which is put in a nutshell in *Al-Fātiḥah* and this is the subject with which the Qur'ān deals fully and comprehensively, citing numerous examples for the guidance of the reader.

Believers are enjoined that before reading the Qur'ān they should solicit God's protection against Satan: *When thou recitest the Qur'ān, seek refuge with Allāh from Satan, the rejected* (16 : 99). Now, refuge or protection implies ; (1) that no evil should befall us; (2) that no good should escape us; and (3) that after we have attained goodness, we may not again relapse into evil. The prescribed words of the prayer are: "I seek refuge with Allāh from Satan, the rejected," which must precede every recitation of the Qur'ān.

A Chapter of the Qur'ān—and there are 114 of them—is called a *Sūrah.* This word, rendered into English as 'Chapter,' means, (1) rank and eminence; (2) a mark or sign; (3) an elevated and beautiful edifice; and (4) something full and complete (Aqrab & Qurṭubī). The Chapters of the Qur'ān are called *Sūrahs* because (a) one is exalted in rank by reading them and attains to eminence through them; (b) they serve as marks for the beginning and the end of the different subjects dealt with in the Qur'ān; (c) they are each like a noble spiritual edifice and (d) each one of them contains a complete theme. The name *Sūrah* for such a division has been used in the Qur'ān itself (2 : 24 & 24 : 2). It has been used in the Ḥadith also. Says the Holy Prophet : "Just now a *Sūrah* has been revealed to me and it runs as follows" (Muslim). From this it is clear that the name *Sūrah* for a division of the Qur'ān has been in use from the very beginning of Islām and is not a later innovation.

سُورَةُ الْفَاتِحَةِ مَكِّيَّةٌ

1. [a]In[1] the name[2] of Allāh,[3] the Gracious, the Merciful.[4] بِسْمِ اللّٰهِ الرَّحْمٰنِ الرَّحِيْمِ ①

[a]Placed before every Chapter except Chapter 9; also in 27 : 31. See also 96 : 2.

1. *Bā'* is a particle used to convey a number of meanings, the one more applicable here being 'with.' The compound word *Bism*, therefore, would mean 'with the name of.' According to Arab usage, the words *Iqra'* or *Aqra'u* or *Naqra'u* or *Ishra'* or *Ashra'u* or *Nashra'u* would be taken to be understood before *Bismillāh* which expression would thus mean, 'begin with the name of Allāh' or 'recite with the name of Allāh,' or 'I or we begin with the name of Allāh,' or 'I or we recite with the name of Allāh.' In the translation the expression *Bismillāh* has been rendered as 'in the name of Allāh' which is a more familiar form (Lane).

2. *Ism* means, a name or attribute (Aqrab). Here it is used in both senses. It refers to Allāh which is the substantive name of God ; and to *Al-Raḥmān* (The Gracious) and *Al-Raḥīm* (The Merciful) which are His attributive names.

3. *Allāh* is the name of the Supreme Being Who is the Sole Possessor of all perfect attributes and is completely free from all conceivable defects. In the Arabic language, the word Allāh is never used for any other thing or being. No other language has a distinctive or proper name for the Supreme Being. The names found in other languages are all attributive or descriptive and are often used in the plural, but the word "Allāh" is never used in the plural number. It is a simple substantive, not derived and is never used as a qualifying word. In the absence of a parallel word in the English language, the original name "Allāh" has been retained throughout the Translation. This view is corroborated by eminent authorities of the Arabic language. "Allāh," according to the most correct of the opinions respecting it, is a proper name, applied to the Being Who exists necessarily by Himself, comprising all the attributes of perfection, the *al* being inseparable from it (Lane).

4. *Al-Raḥmān* (The Gracious) and *Al-Raḥīm* (The Merciful) are both derived from the same root *Raḥima* meaning, he showed mercy; he was kind and good; he forgave. The word *Raḥmah* combines the idea of *Riqqah*, *i.e.*, 'tenderness' and *Iḥsān*, *i.e.*, 'goodness' (Mufradāt). *Al-Raḥmān* is in the measure of *Fa'lān* and *Al-Raḥīm* in the measure of *Fa'īl*. According to the rules of the Arabic language, the larger the number of letters added to the root-word, the more extensive or more intensive does the meaning become (Kashshāf). The measure of *Fa'lān* conveys the idea of fullness and extensiveness, while the measure of *Fa'īl* denotes the idea of repetition and giving liberal reward to those who deserve it (Muḥīṭ). Thus, whereas the word *Al-Raḥmān* would denote "mercy comprehending the entire universe," the word *Al-Raḥīm* would denote "mercy limited in its scope but repeatedly shown." In view of the above meanings *Al-Raḥmān* is One Who shows mercy gratuitously and extensively to all creation without regard to effort or work, and *Al-Raḥīm* is One Who shows mercy in response to, and as a result of, the actions of man but shows it liberally and repeatedly. The former is applicable to God only, while the latter is applied to man also. The former extends not only to believers and disbelievers but also to the whole creation; the latter applies mostly to believers. According to a saying of the Holy Prophet, the former attribute generally pertains to this life, while the latter attribute generally pertains to the life to come (Muḥīṭ), meaning that as this world is mostly the world of actions and the next world is the world where actions will be particularly rewarded, God's attribute *Al-Raḥmān* provides man with material for his works in this life, and His attribute *Al-Raḥīm* brings about results in the life to come. All things that we need and on which our life depends are purely a Divine favour and are provided for us before we do anything to deserve them or even before we are born, while the blessings in store for us in the life to come will be given to us as a reward of our actions. This shows that *Al-Raḥmān* is the Bestower of gifts which precede our birth, while *Al-Raḥīm* is the Giver of blessings which follow our deeds as their reward.

Bismillāh al-Raḥmān al-Raḥīm is the first verse of every Chapter of the Qur'ān except Al-Barā'ah which, however, is not an independent Chapter but a continuation of the Chapter

2. [a]All[5] praise[5A] belongs to Allāh *alone*, Lord[6] of all the worlds,[6A]

اَلْحَمْدُ لِلّٰهِ رَبِّ الْعٰلَمِيْنَ ۝۲

[a]6 : 2; 6 : 46; 10 : 11; 18 : 2; 29: 64; 30:19; 31:26; 34:2; 35:2; 37: 183; 39:76; 45:37.

Al-Anfāl. There is a saying, reported by Ibn ʻAbbās, to the effect that whenever any new *Sūrah* was revealed, *Bismillāh* was the first verse to be revealed, and without *Bismillāh* the Holy Prophet did not know that a new *Sūrah* had begun (Dāwūd). This saying shows that (1) the verse *Bismillāh* is a part of the Qur'ān and not something supernumerary, and (2) that the Chapter Barā'ah is not an independent Chapter. It also refutes the belief expressed by some that *Bismillāh* forms a part only of *Sūrah* Al-Fātiḥah and not of all the Quranic Chapters. The Holy Prophet is reported to have further said that the verse *Bismillāh* is a part of all the Quranic Chapters (Bukhārī & Quṭnī). Its place in the beginning of every Chapter has the following significance:

The Qur'ān is a treasure of Divine knowledge to which access cannot be had without the special favour of God: *None shall touch it but the purified* (56:80). Thus *Bismillāh* has been placed at the beginning of every Chapter to remind a Muslim that in order to have access to, and benefit by, the treasures of Divine knowledge, contained in the Qur'ān, he should not only approach it with a pure heart but should also constantly invoke the help of God. The verse *Bismillāh* also serves another important purpose. It is a key to the meaning of each individual Chapter, as all questions affecting moral and spiritual matters are related in one way or the other to the fundamental Divine attributes. *Raḥmāniyyah* (grace) and *Raḥīmiyyah* (mercy). Thus each Chapter, in fact, forms a detailed exposition of some aspects of the Divine attributes mentioned in the verse. It is contended that the formula *Bismillāh* was borrowed from earlier Scriptures. Whereas Sale says that it was borrowed from Zend-Avesta, Rodwell is of the opinion that the pre-Islamic Arabs borrowed it from the Jews and subsequently it became incorporated in the Qur'ān. Both these views are obviously wrong. First, it has never been claimed by Muslims that the formula in this or similar form was not known before the revelation of the Qur'ān. Secondly, it is wrong to argue that because the formula, in an identical or a similar form, was sometimes used by pre-Islamic Arabs even before it was revealed in the Qur'ān, it could not be of Divine origin. As a matter of fact, the Qur'ān itself states that Solomon used the formula in his letter to the Queen of Sheba (27:31). What Muslims claim—and this claim has never been refuted — is that the Qur'ān was the first revealed Scripture to use it in the way it did. It is also wrong to say that the formula was in vogue among pre-Islamic Arabs, for it is a known fact that the Arabs had an aversion for the use of the name *Al-Raḥmān* for God. Again, if such formulae were known before, it only corroborates the truth of the Quranic teaching that there has not been a people to whom a Teacher has not been sent (35:25) and that the Qur'ān is a repository of all permanent truths contained in the previous revealed Books (98 : 5). It adds much more, of course, and whatever it takes over, it improves in form or use or in both.

5. In Arabic *al* corresponds to the definite article "the" in English. It is used to denote comprehensiveness, that is to say all aspects or categories of a subject, or to denote perfection, which is also an aspect of comprehensiveness, inasmuch as it includes all degrees and grades. It is also used to indicate something which has already been mentioned, or a concept of which is present in the mind.

5A. In Arabic two words *Madḥ* and *Ḥamd* are used in the sense of praise and thankfulness; but whereas *Madḥ* may be false, *Ḥamd* is always true. Again *Madḥ* may be used about such acts of goodness over which the doer has no control, but *Ḥamd* is used only with respect to such acts as are volitional (Mufradāt). *Ḥamd* also implies admiration, magnifying and honouring of the object of praise; and lowliness, humility and submissiveness in the person who offers it (Lane). Thus *Ḥamd* is the most appropriate word to be used here, where a reference to the intrinsic goodness and truly merited praise and glorification of God is intended. In common usage the word *Ḥamd* has come to be applied exclusively to God.

6. The verb *Rabba* means, he administered the affair; he increased, developed, improved and completed the matter; he sustained and looked after. Thus *Rabb* means, (a) Lord, Master, Creator; (b) One Who sustains and develops; (c) One Who brings to perfection by degrees (Mufradāt & Lane). When used in combination with another word, it may be used for persons or beings other than God.

6A. *Al-ʻĀlamīn* is the plural of *al-ʻĀlam* from the root *ʻIlm* meaning 'to know.' The word has come to be applied to all beings or things by means of which one is able to

3. [a]The Gracious, [b]the Merciful,[7] الرَّحۡمٰنِ الرَّحِيۡمِ ۙ﴿۳﴾

4. [c]Master[8] of the [d]Day[9] of Judgment.[10] مٰلِكِ يَوۡمِ الدِّيۡنِ ؕ﴿۴﴾

[a]25:61; 26:6; 41:3; 55:2; 59:23. [b]33 : 44; 36:59. [c]48 : 15. [d]51:13; 74 : 47; 82 : 18, 19 ; 83 : 7.

know the Creator (Aqrab). It is applied not only to all kinds of the created beings or things but also to their classes collectively, so that one says *'Ālam al-Ins, i.e.*, the world of mankind, or *'Ālam al-Ḥayawān, i.e.*, the animal kingdom. The word *al-'Ālamīn* is not used to denote rational beings—men and angels—only. The Qur'ān applies it to all created things (26 : 24-29 & 41 : 10). Sometimes, of course, it is used in a restricted sense (2 : 123). Here it is used in its widest sense and signifies 'all that is besides Allāh,' *i.e.*, animate and inanimate things including heavenly bodies—the sun, the moon, the stars, etc.

The expression "All praise belongs to Allāh alone" is much wider and deeper in significance than "I praise Allāh," because man can praise God only according to his knowledge, but the clause "all praise belongs to Allāh" comprises not only the praise which man knows, but also the praise which he does not know. God is worthy of praise at all times, independently of man's imperfect knowledge or realization. Moreover, the word *al-Ḥamd* is an infinitive and as such can be interpreted both as a subject and as an object. Interpreted as a subject, *al-Ḥamdu Lillāhi* means, God alone has the right to bestow true praise. Interpreted as an object, it signifies that all true praise and every kind of praise in its perfection is due to God alone. For the particle *al* see 5.

The verse points to the law of evolution in the world, *viz.*, that all things undergo development and that this development is progressive and is brought about in stages, *Rabb* being One Who makes things grow and develop by stages. It also points out that the principle of evolution is not inconsistent with belief in God. But the process of evolution referred to here is not identical with the Theory of Evolution as generally understood. The words have been used in a general sense. Further, the verse points to the fact that man has been created for unlimited progress, because the expression *Rabb al-'Ālamīn* implies that God develops everything from a lower to a higher stage and this is possible only if after every stage there is another stage in a never-ending process.

7. In the expression *Bismillāh* the attributes *Al-Raḥmān* and *Al-Rahīm* serve as a key to the meaning of the whole *Sūrah*. Their mention here serves an additional purpose. They are used here as a link between the attribute *Rabb al-'Ālamīn* and *Mālik Yaum al-Dīn*.

8. *Mālik* means, master, or one who possesses the right of ownership over a thing and has the power to deal with it as one likes (Aqrab).

9. *Yaum* means, time absolutely; day from sunrise to sunset; present time (Aqrab).

10. *Dīn* means, recompense or requital; judgment or reckoning; dominion or government; obedience; religion, etc. (Lane).

The four attributes of God, *viz.*, "Lord of all the worlds," "Gracious," "Merciful" and "Master of the Day of Judgment" are fundamental attributes. The other attributes only explain and serve as a sort of commentary upon these four attributes, which are like four pillars on which the Throne of the Almighty rests.

The order in which these four attributes have been mentioned throws light on how God manifests His attributes to man. The attribute *Rabb al-'Ālamīn* (Lord of all the worlds) signifies that with the creation of man, God creates the necessary environment for his spiritual progress and development. The attribute, *Al-Raḥmān* (The Gracious), comes into operation next and through it God, so to speak, hands over to man the means and material, required for his moral and spiritual advance. And when man has made proper use of the means thus granted to him, the attribute *Al-Raḥīm* begins to operate to reward his works. Last of all, the attribute *Mālik Yaum al-Dīn* (Master of the Day of Judgment) produces the final

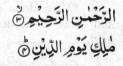

5. [a]Thee alone do we worship[11] and [b]Thee alone do we implore for help.[12]	إِيَّاكَ نَعْبُدُ وَإِيَّاكَ نَسْتَعِينُ ۝٥
6. Guide us in [c]the straight path,[13]	اِهْدِنَا الصِّرَاطَ الْمُسْتَقِيمَ ۝٦

[a]11 : 3; 12 : 41; 16 : 37; 17 : 24; 41 : 38. [b]2 : 46, 154; 21 : 113. [c]19 : 37; 36 : 62; 42 : 53, 54.

and collective results of man's labours; and the process finds consummation. Though the last and perfect reckoning will take place on the Day of Judgment, the process of requital is going on even in this life with this difference that in this life human actions are often judged and rewarded by other men, kings, rulers, etc.; and there is, therefore, always the possibility of error. On the Day of Judgment, however, the mastery of God will be exclusive and absolute and the work of requital will lie entirely in His hands. There will be no error, no undue punishments, no undue rewards. The use of the word "Master" is also intended to point to the fact that God is not like a judge who is bound to give his judgment strictly in accordance with a prescribed law. Being Master, He can forgive and show mercy wherever and in whatever manner He may like. Taking *Dīn* as meaning 'religion' the words "Master of the time of religion" would signify that when a true religion is revealed, mankind witnesses an extraordinary manifestation of Divine power and decrees and when it declines, it looks as if the universe is running mechanically without control or regulation by a Creator and Master.

11. '*Ibādah* signifies, complete and utmost humility, submissiveness, obedience and service. It also implies belief in God's Unity and declaration of it. The word also signifies, the acceptance of the impress of a thing. In this sense '*Ibādah* would mean, receiving the impress of Divine attributes and imbibing and reflecting them in one's own person.

12. The words, *Thee alone do we worship*, have been placed before the words, *Thee alone do we implore for help* to signify that after man becomes aware of God's great attributes, his first impulse is to worship Him. The idea of invoking God's help comes after the impulse to worship. Man wishes to worship God but he finds that for doing so he needs God's help. The use of the plural number in the verse directs attention to two very important points; (a) that man is not alone in this world but is part and parcel of the society that surrounds him. He should, therefore, seek not to go alone but to carry others also with him on the path of God; (b) as long as man does not reform his environment, he is not safe.

It is worthy of note that God is spoken of in the first four verses in the third person, but in this verse He is suddenly addressed in the second person. The contemplation of the four Divine attributes creates in man such an irresistible longing for seeing his Creator and such an intense desire to offer his whole-hearted devotion to Him that, in order to satisfy this longing of the soul, the third person used in the first four verses has been changed into the second in the present verse.

13. The prayer covers the entire field of man's needs—material and spiritual, present and future. The believer prays for being shown the straight path—the shortest path. Sometimes a man is shown the right and straight path but is not led up to it, or, if he is led up to it, he fails to stick to it and follow it to the end. The prayer requires a believer not to be satisfied with only being shown a path, or even with being led up to it, but ever to go on following it till he reaches the destination, this being the significance of *Hidāyah* which means, to show the right path (90:11), to lead to the right path (29:70) and to make one follow the right path (7:44), (Mufradāt & Baqā'). In fact, man needs God's help at every step and at every moment, and it is imperative that he should ever be offering to God the supplication embodied in the verse. Constant praying, therefore, is necessary. As long as we have requirements unfulfilled and needs unsatisfied and goals unattained, we stand in need of prayer.

7. The path of [a]those on whom Thou hast bestowed *Thy* favours,[14] those who have not [b]incurred *Thy* displeasure and those who have not [c]gone astray.[15]	صِرَاطَ الَّذِيْنَ اَنْعَمْتَ عَلَيْهِمْ ۙ۬ غَيْرِ الْمَغْضُوْبِ عَلَيْهِمْ وَلَا الضَّآلِّيْنَ ۝ ع

[a]4 : 70; 5 : 21; 19 : 59. [b]2 : 62, 91; 3 : 113; 5 : 61, 79. [c]3 : 91; 5 : 78; 18 : 105.

14. A true believer is not satisfied with only being guided to the right path or with doing certain acts of righteousness. He sets his goal much higher and tries to attain a position in which God begins to bestow His special favours upon His servants. He looks up to the examples of Divine favours bestowed upon God's Elect and receives encouragement from them. He does not stop even there, but strives hard and prays to be included among God's "Favoured Ones" and to become one of them. These "Favoured Ones" have been mentioned in 4:70. The prayer is general and not for any particular favour. The believer implores God to bestow the highest spiritual favour upon him and it rests with God to confer upon him the favour which He deems fit and which the believer deserves.

15. *Sūrah* Al-Fātiḥah reveals a beautiful order in the arrangement of its words and sentences. It is divided into two halves. The first half pertains to God, the second to man, and the different parts of each portion correspond to one another in a remarkable manner. Corresponding to the name "Allāh" which stands for the Being possessing all noble attributes in the first half, we have the words, *Thee alone do we worship*, in the second half. As soon as the devotee thinks of God as being free from all defects and possessing all perfect attributes, the cry, *Thee alone do we worship*, spontaneously rises from the depths of his heart. And corresponding to the attribute "Lord of all the worlds" are the words, *Thee alone do we implore for help*, in the second part. When a Muslim knows God to be the Creator and Sustainer of all the worlds and the Source of all development, he at once takes shelter in Him, saying, *Thee alone do we implore for help*. Then, corresponding to the attribute *Al-Raḥmān*, *i.e.*, the Giver of innumerable blessings and the Liberal Provider of our needs, occur the words, *Guide us in the straight path*, in the second; for the greatest of the blessings provided for man is guidance which God provides for him by sending revelation through His Messengers. Corresponding to the attribute *Al-Raḥīm*, *i.e.*, the Giver of the best rewards for man's works in the first part, we have the words, *The path of those on whom Thou hast bestowed Thy favours*, in the second, for it is *Al-Raḥīm* Who bestows merited blessings on His favoured servants. Again, corresponding to "Master of the Day of Judgment" we have, *Those who have not incurred Thy displeasure, and those who have not gone astray*. When man thinks of giving an account of his deeds, he dreads failure; so, pondering over the attribute, *Master of the Day of Judgment*, he begins to pray to God to be saved from His displeasure and from straying away from the right path.

Another special feature of the prayer contained in this *Sūrah* is that it appeals to the inner instincts of man in a perfectly natural manner. There are two fundamental motives in human nature which prompt submission, *viz.*, love and fear. Some people are touched by love, while others are moved by fear. The motive of love is certainly nobler but there may be—indeed there are—men to whom love makes no appeal. They only submit through fear. In Al-Fātiḥah an appeal has been made to both these human motives. First come those attributes of God which inspire love, "the Creator and Sustainer of the world," "the Gracious" and "the Merciful." Then in their wake, as it were, follows the attribute, "Master of the Day of Judgment," which reminds man that if he does not mend his ways and does not respond to love, he should be prepared to render account of his deeds before God. Thus the motive of fear is brought into play side by side with that of love. But as God's mercy far excels His anger, even this attribute which is the only fundamental attribute designed to evoke fear, has not been left without a reference to mercy. In fact, here too God's mercy transcends His anger, for it is implicit in this attribute that we are not appearing before a Judge but before a Master Who has the power to forgive and Who will punish only where punishment is absolutely necessary.

In short, Al-Fātiḥah is a wonderful store-house of spiritual knowledge. It is a short Chapter of seven brief verses, but it is a veritable mine of knowledge and wisdom. Aptly called "Mother of the Book," it is the very essence of the Qur'ān. Beginning with the name of Allāh, the Fountain-head of all blessings, the Chapter goes on to narrate the four fundamental attributes of God, *i.e.*, (1) The Creator and Sustainer of the world; (2) The Gracious, Who provides for all the requirements of man even before he is born and without any effort on his part for them; (3) The Merciful, Who determines the best possible results of man's labour and Who rewards him most liberally; and (4) Master of the Day of Judgment before Whom all will have to give an account of their actions, Who will punish the wicked but will not treat His creatures as a mere judge but as a master, tempering justice with mercy, and Who is eager to forgive whenever forgiveness is calculated to bring about good results. This is the portrait of the God of Islām as given in the very beginning of the Qur'ān— a God Whose power and dominion know no bounds and Whose mercy and beneficence have no limitations. Then comes the declaration by man that, his God being the Possessor of such lofty attributes, he is ready, nay eager, to worship Him and throw himself at His feet in complete submission; but God knows that man is weak and liable to err, so mercifully He exhorts His servant to seek His help at every step in his onward march and for every need that may confront him. Finally, comes a prayer—comprehensive and far-reaching —a prayer in which man supplicates his Maker to lead him to the straight path in all matters, spiritual or temporal, whether relating to his present or future needs. He prays to God that he may not only successfully stand all trials but, like His "Chosen Ones," do so with credit and become the recipient of His most bounteous favours; that he may for ever go on treading the straight path, pressing on nearer and yet nearer to his Lord and Master without stumbling on the way, as did many of those who have gone before. This is the theme of the Opening Chapter of the Qur'ān which is constantly repeated, in one form or another, in the main body of the Holy Book.

—o—

CHAPTER 2

AL-BAQARAH

(*Revealed after Hijrah*)

Title, Date of Revelation and Context

This, the longest *Sūrah* of the Qur'ān, was revealed at Medina in the first four years after the Hijrah and is known as Al-Baqarah. The name was used by the Holy Prophet himself. The *Sūrah* seems to have derived its title from vv. 68-72 where an important incident in the life of the Jewish nation is briefly mentioned. For a long time the Jews had lived in Egypt as serfs and slaves under the most cruel bondage of the Pharaohs who were cow-worshippers. As is generally the case with subject races, they had borrowed from, and slavishly imitated, many customs and habits of the Egyptians and consequently had come to possess a strong liking, bordering on adoration, for the cow. When Moses told them to sacrifice a particular cow which symbolised their object of worship, they made a great fuss about it. It is this incident to which vv. 68-72 refer. Besides Al-Baqarah, the *Sūrah* possesses another name—Al-Zahrā', and both this *Sūrah* and Āl 'Imrān are jointly known as Al-Zahrawān—The Two Bright Ones (Muslim). The Holy Prophet is reported to have said: 'Everything has its peak, and the peak of the Qur'ān is Al-Baqarah' (Tirmidhī). The *Sūrah* is placed next to Al-Fātiḥah because it embodies answers to all the important problems which at once confront the reader when he turns from Al-Fātiḥah to a study of the main Book. Though generally connected with all the other *Sūrahs*, Al-Fātiḥah possesses a special relationship with Al-Baqarah which constitutes the fulfilment of the prayer, 'Guide us in the straight path.................Thy displeasure.' Indeed Al-Baqarah with its discourses upon the Signs, the Book, the Wisdom and the Means of purification (2 : 130), constitutes an appropriate and comprehensive reply to that great prayer.

Subject-Matter

It is sometimes said that the Qur'ān starts with this *Sūrah* as its very opening verse, *viz.*, "This is a perfect Book; there is no doubt in it," shows; while Al-Fātiḥah being, as it were, the Qur'ān in miniature though forming its integral part, possesses an independent and peculiar position of its own (15: 88). The subject-matter of this long Chapter is epitomized in its 130th verse. This verse contains a prayer of the Patriarch Abraham in which he implores God to raise a Prophet among the Meccans who should (1) recite to them the Signs of God; (2) give the world a Scripture containing perfect laws of the *Sharī'ah*; (3) explain the wisdom underlying them ; and (4) should lay down principles and rules of conduct which should bring about complete spiritual transformation in their lives and should make them a great and powerful nation, fit to lead the whole world. The four great objects for which Abraham prayed have been dealt with in this Chapter in the same order in which he prayed for them. The "Signs" are discussed in the first 168 verses, the "Book" and "Wisdom" in vv. 169-243 and lastly "the Means of national progress in vv. 244-287. "The recital of the Signs" refers to the arguments about the truth of the Holy Prophet; "the teaching of the Book and Wisdom" to the laws of the *Sharī'ah* laid down in the *Sūrah* and the wisdom or philosophy which underlies them, and last of all in elucidation of the subject of the spiritual change spoken of in Abraham's prayer it refers to the principles that lead to national awakening.

The *Sūrah* has 40 sections and 287 verses. It opens with a statement of three fundamental beliefs—belief in God, Revelation and Life after death and two practical ordinances about Prayer and *Zakāt*, the rest being an extension and explanation of these principles and ordinances. In response to the prayer for guidance, the Qur'ān claims to present a perfect code of laws which comprises all the truths that were found in earlier revealed Scriptures, with much more that they did not contain, and claims also to guide man to the highest pinnacle of spiritual glory. The second section decries and deprecates mere verbal profession of faith which has no deep roots in the heart. The third section, however, lays down standards and criteria by which the truth of the Qur'ān can be tested and verified. And for this purpose it draws pointed attention to the process of evolution working in the physical universe. This process is to be seen in the spiritual realm also. Then mention is made of the first link in this spiritual chain—of Adam, the first man, to whom God revealed His Will. In the 4th section we are told that objections are being raised against the Holy Prophet.

But these objections cannot detract from his truth even as they could not detract from Adam's truth. The next twelve sections—5th to 16th—dispose of the objection, *viz.*, where was the necessity of a new revelation when God had already revealed Himself to Adam? It is stated that in harmony with progressive evolution in the spiritual system, God has been sending down His revelation in every age, every succeeding revelation being an improvement upon the preceding one. Moses was the Founder of a new *Sharī'ah*. He was followed by a galaxy of Divine Messengers who were opposed and persecuted by the Israelites. Persistent defiance of Divine commandments on the part of the Israelites and their iniquities made them lose their title to Divine grace. Hence Prophethood, in accordance with biblical prophecies, was transferred to the House of Ishmael and the Holy Prophet was raised in the barren and arid Valley of Mecca with the most perfect and complete Law. This filled the Israelites with rage though they had no right to fret and fume at their being deprived of Prophethood. They opposed the Holy Prophet and spared no pains to bring him to naught. But opposition to Divine purpose has never succeeded.

The next two sections dispense with the objections of the Israelites as to why the Holy Prophet has given up the *Qiblah* of all the former Prophets in favour of the Ka'bah. They are told that in the first place facing a certain direction in Prayers or fixing a particular place as the *Qiblah* cannot be an object to be sought after, it only serves to bring about and maintain unity among a people. Secondly, in the prayers which Abraham had offered for the sons of Ishmael, it was prophesied that Mecca would one day become a place of pilgrimage for them and the Ka'bah their *Qiblah*. In the 19th section it is mentioned that the Holy Prophet will meet strong opposition from disbelievers in the discharge of his onerous mission, and this opposition will continue till the Fall of Mecca. The 20th section draws attention to the supreme truth that all that is stated above is not an idle guess or conjecture; the very creation of the heavens and the earth, the alternation of day and night and other natural phenomena bear incontrovertible testimony to its truth inasmuch as, on the one hand, the law of nature points to the existence of a spiritual law and to a process of progressive evolution in it and, on the other, the whole universe seems to be working in support of the Holy Prophet. With the 21st section begins a description of the ordinances of the *Sharī'ah* and the wisdom underlying them; and first of all directions have been laid down for using lawful (*Halāl*) and wholesome (*Ṭayyib*) food, because human actions are governed by man's mental condition and his mental condition is strongly influenced by the food he eats. In the 23rd section substance of Islamic teaching is given which consists of belief in God, Life after death, revealed Scriptures and Divine Messengers. Doing good to others, worship and contributions to national funds are also mentioned as constituents of righteous conduct. To these, observance of patience under trials and fulfilment of solemn promises are added. Maintenance of justice, legitimate help of relatives and observance of social laws, of which the law of inheritance occupies a most prominent place, are also regarded as important. In the next section stress is laid on devotional exercises which purpose is fulfilled by the Islamic Fast. Sections 24th and 25th deal with rites and laws pertaining to Pilgrimage which plays a very important role in bringing about national unity and solidarity among Muslims. In section 26th light is shed on the philosophy of ordinances of the *Sharī'ah* which should be shown due regard because outward acts have a very potent effect on inward purity. Then it is stated that the laws of the *Sharī'ah* are disregarded because men generally do not like to spend their time and money in the cause of God and they adduce lame excuses to shirk their duty in this respect. In fact, no progress is possible without sacrifice and believers are exhorted to spend their hard-earned wealth in the way of Allāh so that full religious freedom may be established. In section 27th we are told that when religious freedom is interfered with, fighting becomes obligatory and sacrifice of life and money necessary. Then it is stated that, in order to while away their time and to seek mental relief, people indulge in drinking, and in order to collect money to meet the expenses of war, they have recourse to gambling. Islām condemns these evil practices. Next, we are told that war leaves behind many orphans who should be properly looked after, and in this connection Muslims are enjoined not to contract marriage with idolatrous women because it is calculated to disturb the harmony of their domestic life. In sections 28th, 29th, 30th and 31st, we are told not to have sexual intercourse with women in their monthly courses which is a sort of temporary separation. These instructions are followed by laws that govern divorce which is more or less a permanent separation and then by laws that concern suckling and also treatment of widows. Sections 32nd and 33rd deal with principles that have a special bearing on national awakening and by observing which alone a people can make real progress, and Muslims are told that a people who seek to occupy an honoured place among the powerful nations must be prepared to face death to promote the cause of truth and righteousness. In section 34th it is mentioned that man's stay on earth is but temporary and he should spare no effort to establish real connection with his Creator, and this is only possible by deep meditation on Divine attributes. Then in *Āyat al-Kursiyy* which the Holy Prophet has termed as one of the best and most exalted Quranic verses a brief but very comprehensive mention is made of God's attributes and it is said that no compulsion is needed to exhort a person to establish his connection with the Possessor of such noble and sublime attributes. Then in the 35th section it is stated that whereas moral righteousness takes place in an individual directly through God's own grace, moral transformation comes about among nations through the instrumentality of Divine Messengers, and hints that both these kinds of reformation are decreed to take place four times among the progeny of Abraham. Next, it is said that both collective effort and national co-operation are essential for moral transformation to take place on national scale; the results in this respect of the concerted and collective efforts and mutual co-operation of true believers are far in excess of their sacrifices. Then all transactions based on interest are strictly forbidden and the giving and taking of interest has been denounced as tantamount to waging war against God and His Prophet because transactions based on interest are against the spirit of mutual help and co-operation and of doing good to fellow beings. Muslims are further told that they should entertain no apprehension that no progress is possible without interest. God has decreed that eventually destruction will overtake nations which give or take interest. Next, it is stated that one way of rendering mutual help and co-operation is to advance money on loan but all transactions dealing with lending and borrowing money should be properly written down. The *Sūrah* ends on the beautiful note that whereas the above-mentioned directions are necessary for bringing about moral transformation among a people, the best, the safest and the surest means to raise their moral standard and to effect real and true righteousness and purity of character among them is that they should have firm faith in the Word of God, constantly keep in view, reflect and meditate upon His attributes and should seek Divine help by prayer sincerely offered to Him.

This is, in brief, a summary of the subject-matter of this longest of the Quranic *Sūrahs* and the moral is forcefully brought home directly to the disbelievers in general and to the People of the Book in particular that in the Holy Prophet is fulfilled the prayer of the Patriarch Abraham and thus if the Holy Prophet is rejected, Abraham will have to be regarded as a liar and an impostor and consequently the whole Mosaic Dispensation and Christianity also will be dubbed as tissues of lies and falsehoods. Indirectly, the truth of the Message of Islām has been made clear for the whole world to accept because the creation of man possesses a great and sublime object and that object can only be fulfilled by believing in the Message embodied in the Qur'ān which alone now contains the right *Sharī'ah* and sheds light on the wisdom and philosophy of its ordinances and by believing in and acting upon which alone can purity of the heart and Divine Realisation be attained.

—:o:—

رُكُوعَاتُهَا ٤٠ سُورَةُ البَقَرَةِ مَدَنِيَّةٌ (٢) ايَاتُهَا ٢٨٧

1. In the name of Allāh, the Gracious, the Merciful.	بِسْمِ اللّٰهِ الرَّحْمٰنِ الرَّحِيْمِ ① الجزء ١
2. Alif Lām Mīm.[16]	الٓمّٓ ②
3. This[17] is a perfect[17A] Book; [a]there is no doubt[18] in it; [b]*it is* a guidance for the righteous,[19]	ذٰلِكَ الْكِتٰبُ لَا رَيْبَ ۛۚ فِيْهِ ۚۛ هُدًى لِّلْمُتَّقِيْنَ ③

[a]2 : 24; 10 : 38; 32 : 3; 41 : 43. [b]2 : 186; 3 : 139; 31 : 4.

16. Abbreviations, like *Alif Lām Mīm*, are known as *al-Muqaṭṭa'āt* (letters used and pronounced separately), and occur in the beginning of not less than 28 *Sūrahs*, and are made up of one or more, to a maximum of five, letters of the Arabic alphabet. The letters out of which these abbreviations are constituted are fourteen in number: *Alif, Lām, Mīm, Ṣād, Rā, Kāf, Hā, Yā, 'Ain, Ṭā, Sīn, Ḥā, Qāf* and *Nūn*. Of these *Qāf* and *Nūn* occur alone in the beginning of *Sūrahs* Qāf and Qalam, the rest occur in combinations of two or more in the beginning of certain *Sūrahs*. The use of *Muqaṭṭa'āt* was in vogue among the Arabs. They used them in their poems and conversation. An Arab poet says: *Qulnā Qifī Lanā, Faqālat Qāf i.e.*, "We said to her, 'Stop for us for a while' and she said that she was stopping" the letter *Qāf* standing for *Waqaftu* (I am stopping). There is also a saying of the Holy Prophet as reported by Qurṭubī to the effect: *Kafā Bi'l-Saifi Shā, i.e.*, sufficient is sword as a remedy, *Shā* standing for *Shāfiyan*. In the modern West and in its imitation in Eastern countries also abbreviations are very popular and widespread. Every dictionary provides a list of them. The *Muqaṭṭa'āt* are abbreviations for specific attributes of God and the subject-matter of a *Sūrah* before which they are placed has a deep connection with the Divine attributes for which they stand. They have not been haphazardly placed at the beginning of different *Sūrahs*, nor are their letters combined arbitrarily. There runs a deep and far-reaching connection between their various sets, and the letters of which they are made also serve a definite purpose. The subject-matter of those Chapters which have no abbreviated letters is subordinate to, and follows the pattern of, the subject-matter of the preceding Chapters possessing them. Of the meanings ascribed to *Muqaṭṭa'āt* two seem to be more authentic: (a) That each letter has a definite numerical value (Jarīr). The letters *Alif Lām Mīm* have the numerical value 71 (*Alif* having the numerical value 1, *Lām* 30 and *Mīm* 40). Thus the placing of *Alif Lām Mīm* in the beginning of the *Sūrah* may signify that its subject-matter, *i.e.*, the special consolidation of early Islām, would take 71 years to unfold itself completely. (b) They are, as stated above, abbreviations for specific attributes of God and the *Sūrah* before which *Muqaṭṭa'āt* are placed is, in its subject-matter, connected with the Divine attributes for which the specific *Muqaṭṭa'āt'* stand. Thus the abbreviation *Alif Lām Mīm* placed here and in the beginning of the 3rd, 29th, 30th, 31st and 32nd Chapters of the Qur'ān signifies,"I am Allāh, the All-Knowing" which has the authority of Ibn 'Abbās and Ibn Mas'ūd, *Alif* standing for *Anā*, *Lām* for Allāh and *Mīm* for *A'lamu*; or according to some *Alif* stands for Allāh, *Lām* for Jibrīl and *Mīm* for Muḥammad, indicating that the central theme of the *Sūrah* is Divine knowledge which was given to Muḥammad by Allāh through Jibrīl. These abbreviated letters form an integral part of the Quranic revelation (Bukhārī).

17. *Dhālika* is primarily used in the sense of "that," but is also sometimes used in the sense of "this" (Aqrab). Sometimes it is used to indicate the high rank and dignity of the subject to which it refers. Here it signifies that the Book is, as it were, remote from the reader in eminence and loftiness of merit (Fatḥ).

17A. The particle *al*, like the definite article "the" in the English language, is used to denote a definite object known to the reader. In this sense the word *Dhālika al-Kitāb* would mean, this is *the* Book, or this is *that* Book—the promised Book. The particle is also used to denote the combination of all possible attributes in one individual. The expression thus means, this is a Book which possesses all those excellent qualities which a perfect book should possess. Or it means, this alone is a perfect Book.

18-19. See next page.

4. Who believe in [a]the unseen[20] and [b]observe Prayer[21] and [c]spend out of what We have provided[22] for them;

الَّذِيْنَ يُؤْمِنُوْنَ بِالْغَيْبِ وَيُقِيْمُوْنَ الصَّلٰوةَ وَمِمَّا رَزَقْنٰهُمْ يُنْفِقُوْنَ ﴿۳﴾

[a]5 : 95; 6:104; 21:50; 35:19; 36:12; 50:34; 57:26; 67:13. [b]2:44, 84; 1:11; 2:78; 5:56; 8:4; 9:71; 20:15; 27:4; 30:32; 31:5; 73:21. [c]2:196, 255, 263, 268; 3:93; 8:4; 9:34; 13:23; 14:32; 22:36; 28:55; 32:17; 42:39.

18. *Raib* means, disquietude or uneasiness of mind; doubt; affliction or calamity and evil opinion; false charge or calumny (Aqrab). The verse does not mean that nobody will ever entertain any doubt about the Qur'ān. It only means that its teaching is so rational that a right-thinking person, who approaches it with an unbiased mind, will find it a safe and sure guide.

19. *Muttaqī* is derived from *Waqā* which has the sense of guarding against that which harms or injures. *Wiqāyah* means, a shield and *Ittaqā bihī* (*Muttaqī* is in the nominative case of *Ittaqā*) means, he took him or it as a shield (Lane). Ubayy bin K'ab, a distinguished Companion of the Holy Prophet, aptly explains *Taqwā* by likening *Muttaqī* to one who walks through thorny bushes, taking all possible care that his clothes are not caught in, and torn by, their branches (Kathīr). A *Muttaqī*, therefore, is one who is ever on his guard against sins and takes God for his shield or shelter and is very regardful of his duty. The words, "a guidance for the righteous," mean that guidance contained in the Qur'ān knows no limit. It helps man to attain limitless stage of spiritual perfection and makes him more and more deserving of God's favours.

20. *Al-Ghaib* means, anything hidden or invisible ; anything unseen, absent or far away (Aqrab). God, the angels and the Last Day are all *al-Ghaib*. Moreover, the word as used in the Qur'ān does not mean imaginary and unreal things, but real and verified things, though unseen (32:7; 49:19). It is, therefore, wrong to suppose, as some Western critics of the Qur'ān do, that Islām forces upon its followers some mysteries of Faith and invites them to believe in them blindly. The word signifies things which, though beyond the comprehension of human senses, can nevertheless be proved by reason or experience. The supersensible need not necessarily be irrational. Nothing of " the unseen " in which a Muslim is called upon to believe is outside the scope of reason. There are many things in the world which, though unseen, are yet proved to exist by invincible arguments, and nobody can deny their existence.

21. The clause, "they observe Prayer," means, they perform their Prayers with all the prescribed conditions; *Aqāma* meaning, he kept the thing or the affair in a right state (Lane). Worship is the outer expression of the inner relationship of man to God. Moreover, God's favours surround the body as well as the soul. So, perfect worship is that in which body and soul both play their part. Without the two the true spirit of worship cannot be preserved, for though adoration by the heart is the substance and adoration by the body only the shell, yet the substance cannot be preserved without the shell. If the shell is destroyed, the substance is bound to meet with a similar fate.

22. *Rizq* means, anything bestowed by God on man, whether material or otherwise (Mufradāt). The verse lays down three directions and describes three stages for the spiritual well-being of man: (1) He should believe in the truths which are hidden from his eyes and are beyond his physical senses, for it is such a belief which shows that he is possessed of the right sort of *Taqwā* or righteousness. (2) When he reflects on the creation of the universe and the marvellous order and design which exist in it and when, as a result of this reflection, he becomes convinced of the existence of the Creator, an irresitsible longing to have a real and true union with Him takes hold of him. This finds consummation in the observance of Prayer. (3) Lastly, when the believer succeeds in establishing a living contact with his Creator, he feels an inward urge to serve his fellow-beings.

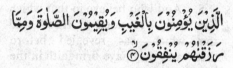

5. And who believe in that which has been [a]revealed to thee[23] and that which was revealed before thee[24] and they have firm faith in the [b]Hereafter.[25]

وَالَّذِيْنَ يُؤْمِنُوْنَ بِمَآ اُنْزِلَ اِلَيْكَ وَمَآ اُنْزِلَ مِنْ قَبْلِكَ ۚ وَبِالْاٰخِرَةِ هُمْ يُوْقِنُوْنَ ۝٥

6. It is they who [c]follow the guidance from their Lord and it is they [d]who shall prosper.

اُولٰٓئِكَ عَلٰى هُدًى مِّنْ رَّبِّهِمْ ۖ وَاُولٰٓئِكَ هُمُ الْمُفْلِحُوْنَ ۝٦

7. Those who have disbelieved—[e]it being alike to them whether thou warn them or warn them not—they will not believe.[26]

اِنَّ الَّذِيْنَ كَفَرُوْا سَوَآءٌ عَلَيْهِمْ ءَاَنْذَرْتَهُمْ اَمْ لَمْ تُنْذِرْهُمْ لَا يُؤْمِنُوْنَ ۝٧

8. Allāh [f]has set a seal[27] on their hearts and their ears, and over their eyes is a covering; and for them is a grievous chastisement.

خَتَمَ اللّٰهُ عَلٰى قُلُوْبِهِمْ وَعَلٰى سَمْعِهِمْ ۖ وَعَلٰٓى اَبْصَارِهِمْ غِشَاوَةٌ ۫ وَّلَهُمْ عَذَابٌ عَظِيْمٌ ۝٨

R. 2 9. And of the people there are some who say, [g]'We believe in Allāh and the Last Day;' while they are not believers *at all*.[28]

وَمِنَ النَّاسِ مَنْ يَّقُوْلُ اٰمَنَّا بِاللّٰهِ وَبِالْيَوْمِ الْاٰخِرِ وَمَا هُمْ بِمُؤْمِنِيْنَ ۝٩

[a]2 : 137, 286; 3 : 200; 4: 61, 137, 163· 5 : 60. [b]6 : 93; 27: 4; 31: 5. [c]2 : 158; 31 : 6. [d]23 : 2; 28 : 68; 31 : 6; 87 : 15; 91 : 10. [e]26 : 137; 36 : 11. [f]4 : 156; 6 : 26, 47; 7 : 102, 180; 10 : 75; 16 : 109; 45 : 24; 83 : 15. [g]2 : 178; 3 : 115. 4 : 40, 60; 6 : 93; 58 : 23.

23. Belief in the Holy Prophet is the central point so far as belief in the Prophets of God is concerned (2 : 286; 4: 66,137).

24. Islām makes it obligatory upon its followers to believe in the Divine origin of the teachings of all previous Prophets because God sent His Messengers to all peoples (13:8; 35:25).

25. *Al-Ākhirah* means, (a) the Last Abode, *i.e.*, the next life; (b) it may also signify the revelation which is to follow. This second meaning of the word finds further exposition in 62 : 3, 4 where the Qur'ān speaks of two advents of the Holy Prophet. His first advent took place among the Arabs in the 7th century of the Christian era when the Qur'ān was revealed to him; and his second advent was to take place in the Latter Days in the person of one of his followers. This prophecy found its fulfilment in the person of Aḥmad, the Promised Messiah and Founder of the Aḥmadiyya Movement.

26. The verse speaks of such disbelievers as become so indifferent to truth that it does not matter whether they receive a warning or not. Of these it is declared that as long as their present condition continues, they will not believe.

27. Organs which remain unused for a long time atrophy and become useless. The disbelievers mentioned here refused to employ their hearts and ears for the comprehension of truth, consequently their capacities for hearing and understanding were lost. It is only the natural consequence of wilful indifference which is described in the clause, *Allāh has set a seal.* As all laws proceed from God and every cause is followed by its natural effect under His Will, so the sealing of the hearts and the ears of disbelievers is ascribed to Him.

28. Only God and the Last Day are mentioned, other Islamic beliefs being left out, because God and the Last Day are respectively the first and the last items in the Islamic

10. They [a]would deceive[29] Allāh and those who believe, but they deceive none but themselves; only they perceive *it* not.

يُخٰدِعُوْنَ اللّٰهَ وَالَّذِيْنَ اٰمَنُوْا ۚ وَمَا يَخْدَعُوْنَ اِلَّآ اَنْفُسَهُمْ وَمَا يَشْعُرُوْنَ ۝١٠

11. [b]In their hearts was a disease, so Allāh has increased their disease;[30] and for them is a grievous punishment because they lied.

فِيْ قُلُوْبِهِمْ مَّرَضٌ ۙ فَزَادَهُمُ اللّٰهُ مَرَضًا ۚ وَلَهُمْ عَذَابٌ اَلِيْمٌ ۢ بِمَا كَانُوْا يَكْذِبُوْنَ ۝١١

12. And when it is said to them "Create not disorder in the earth,' they say, 'We are only promoters of peace.'

وَاِذَا قِيْلَ لَهُمْ لَا تُفْسِدُوْا فِي الْاَرْضِ ۙ قَالُوْٓا اِنَّمَا نَحْنُ مُصْلِحُوْنَ ۝١٢

13. Beware ! it is surely they who create disorder, but they do not perceive *it*.

اَلَآ اِنَّهُمْ هُمُ الْمُفْسِدُوْنَ وَلٰكِنْ لَّا يَشْعُرُوْنَ ۝١٣

14. And when it is said to them, 'Believe as *other* people have believed,' they say, 'Shall we believe as the fools have believed?' Remember! it is surely they that are the fools,[31] but they do not know.

وَاِذَا قِيْلَ لَهُمْ اٰمِنُوْا كَمَآ اٰمَنَ النَّاسُ قَالُوْٓا اَنُؤْمِنُ كَمَآ اٰمَنَ السُّفَهَآءُ ۭ اَلَآ اِنَّهُمْ هُمُ السُّفَهَآءُ وَلٰكِنْ لَّا يَعْلَمُوْنَ ۝١٤

15. And [d]when they meet those who believe, they say, 'We believe;' but when they are alone with their ring-leaders[32] they say, 'We are certainly with you; [e]we were only mocking.'

وَاِذَا لَقُوا الَّذِيْنَ اٰمَنُوْا قَالُوْٓا اٰمَنَّا ۚ وَاِذَا خَلَوْا اِلٰى شَيٰطِيْنِهِمْ ۙ قَالُوْٓا اِنَّا مَعَكُمْ ۙ اِنَّمَا نَحْنُ مُسْتَهْزِءُوْنَ ۝١٥

[a]4 : 143. [b]5 : 53; 9 : 125; 74 : 32. [c]2 : 28, 221. [d]2 : 77; 3 : 120; 5 : 62. [e]9 : 64, 65.

formula of faith and a profession of belief in them *ipso facto* implies profession of belief in the other items. Elsewhere, the Qur'ān states that belief in the Last Day implies belief in angels as well as in the Divine Books (6 : 93).

29. *Khāda'a-hū* means, he sought or desired to deceive him but did not succeed in his attempt. *Khada'a-hū* means, he succeeded in his attempt to deceive him; he forsook him or it (Baqā'). The former word is used about a man when he has not attained his desire and the latter when he has attained it (Lane).

30. God has shown so many Signs in support of Islām and it has become gradually so powerful that the hypocrites have become more and more afraid of Muslims and have consequently grown in their hypocrisy.

31. The hypocrites regarded the Muslims as a pack of fools in that they suffered, as the hypocrites thought, useless sacrifice of life and property for a lost cause. They themselves are fools, says the verse, as the cause of Islām is destined to make progress and to prosper.

32. *Shayāṭīn* means, ring-leaders (Ibn 'Abbās, Ibn Mas'ūd, Qatādah and Mujāhid). The Holy Prophet is reported to have said: 'A single rider is a *Shaiṭān*, a pair of riders is also

16. ^aAllāh will punish[33] their mockery and will ^blet them continue[33A] in their transgression, wandering blindly.[34]

اللّٰهُ يَسْتَهْزِئُ بِهِمْ وَيَمُدُّهُمْ فِيْ طُغْيَانِهِمْ يَعْمَهُوْنَ ۝

17. These are they who ^chave bartered away guidance for error;[35] but their traffic has brought them no gain, nor are they rightly guided.

اُولٰٓئِكَ الَّذِيْنَ اشْتَرَوُا الضَّلٰلَةَ بِالْهُدٰى ۖ فَمَا رَبِحَتْ تِّجَارَتُهُمْ وَمَا كَانُوْا مُهْتَدِيْنَ ۝

18. Their case is like the case of a person who kindled a fire,[36] and when it lighted up all around him, Allāh took away their light and ^dleft them in thick darkness;[37] they see not.

مَثَلُهُمْ كَمَثَلِ الَّذِى اسْتَوْقَدَ نَارًا ۚ فَلَمَّآ اَضَآءَتْ مَا حَوْلَهٗ ذَهَبَ اللّٰهُ بِنُوْرِهِمْ وَتَرَكَهُمْ فِيْ ظُلُمٰتٍ لَّا يُبْصِرُوْنَ ۝

19. *They are ^edeaf, dumb and* blind; so they will not return.[38]

صُمٌّ بُكْمٌ عُمْىٌ فَهُمْ لَا يَرْجِعُوْنَ ۝

---

^a9 : 79; 11:9; 21 : 42.   ^b6 : 111; 7 : 187; 10 : 12.   ^c2 : 87, 176; 3 : 178; 14 : 4; 16:108.
^d6:40, 123; 24:41.   ^e2:172; 6:40; 7:180; 8:23; 10:43; 11:25; 17:98;
21:46; 27:81; 30:53, 54; 43:41.

---

a pair of *Shaiṭāns*, but three riders are a body of riders (Dāwūd). The tradition lends support to the view that *Shaiṭān* does not *necessarily* mean a devil.

33. *Yastahzi'u bi-him* means, will punish them. In Arabic punishment for an evil deed is sometimes denoted by the word used for the evil itself. "The penalty for an evil deed is an evil the like thereof " (42 : 41). The famous Arab poet ʿAmr bin Kulthūm says : *Alā lā Yajhalan Aḥadun ʿAlainā, Fanajhal Fauqa Jahl al-Jāhilīnā, i.e.,* Beware ! none should dare employ ignorance against us, or we will show greater ignorance, *i.e.,* we will avenge his ignorance (Muʿallaqāt).

33A. The words do not mean that God grants the hypocrites respite to let them increase in their transgression. Such a meaning is contradicted by 35 : 38, where it is stated that God grants disbelievers respite that they should reform themselves.

34. *ʿUmyun* is the plural of *Aʿmā* which is derived from *al-ʿAmā. Al-ʿAmah* means, mental blindness and *al-ʿAmā* means, both mental and physical blindness (Aqrab).

35. (1) They have given up guidance and taken error instead; (2) both guidance and error were offered to them but they preferred error and refused guidance.

36. The word "fire" is sometimes used for war. "The kindler of fire" in the verse may signify either the hypocrites who conspired with disbelievers to wage war against Islām; or the Holy Prophet who under God's command kindled a Divine light. He is reported to have said : 'My example is like that of a person who kindles a fire' (Bukhārī).

37. The expression signifies that the hypocrites fomented wars in order to re-establish their lost influence but the actual result of these wars was the exposure of their hypocrisy and their consequent confusion and perplexity. The word *Zulumāt* has always been used in the Qur'ān in the plural, signifying moral and spiritual darkness. Sin and vice never exist in isolation. One vice attracts another and one misfortune draws another. The meaning is that the hypocrites are overtaken by manifold dangers and calamities.

38. As they turned a deaf ear to the Prophet's admonition and did not express their doubts to have them dispelled and had become insensitive to the progress that Islām was making before their very eyes, they are spoken of as deaf, dumb and blind.

20. Or *it is* like a heavy rain from the clouds,[39] [a]wherein is thick darkness and thunder and [b]lightning; they put their fingers into their ears because of the thunder-claps for fear of death,[40] and Allāh encompasses the disbelievers.

أَوْ كَصَيِّبٍ مِّنَ السَّمَآءِ فِيهِ ظُلُمٰتٌ وَّرَعْدٌ وَّبَرْقٌ ۚ
يَجْعَلُونَ أَصَابِعَهُمْ فِيٓ اٰذَانِهِمْ مِّنَ الصَّوَاعِقِ حَذَرَ
الْمَوْتِ ۗ وَاللّٰهُ مُحِيطٌۢ بِالْكٰفِرِينَ ﴿٢٠﴾

21. The lightning might well-nigh snatch away their sight; whenever it shines upon them, they walk therein; and [c]when it becomes dark to them, they stand still. And if Allāh had *so* willed, He could take away their hearing and their sight;[41] surely, Allāh has the power to do all that He wills.[41A]

يَكَادُ الْبَرْقُ يَخْطَفُ أَبْصَارَهُمْ ۖ كُلَّمَآ أَضَآءَ لَهُمْ مَّشَوْا
فِيهِ ۙ وَإِذَآ أَظْلَمَ عَلَيْهِمْ قَامُوا ۚ وَلَوْ شَآءَ اللّٰهُ لَذَهَبَ
بِسَمْعِهِمْ وَأَبْصَارِهِمْ ۚ إِنَّ اللّٰهَ عَلٰى كُلِّ شَيْءٍ قَدِيرٌ ﴿٢١﴾ ع ٢ ٢

R. 3 22. O ye men ![42] [d]worship your Lord Who created you and those who were before you, that you may guard against evil;

يٰٓأَيُّهَا النَّاسُ اعْبُدُوا رَبَّكُمُ الَّذِي خَلَقَكُمْ وَالَّذِينَ
مِنْ قَبْلِكُمْ لَعَلَّكُمْ تَتَّقُونَ ﴿٢٢﴾

[a]6 : 40, 123; 24 : 41. [b]13 : 13; 24 : 44; 30 : 25. [c]4 : 73, 74.
[d]4 : 2, 37; 5:73, 118; 16 : 37; 22:78; 51 : 57.

39. *Samā'* means, anything which hangs overhead and gives shade; the sky or the heaven; a cloud or clouds (Lane).

40. This and the preceding verses refer to two classes of hypocrites: (1) Disbelievers who posed as Muslims; and (2) believers, bad in faith and worse in works, with leaning towards disbelief. The purport of the verse seems to be that the condition of the latter class of hypocrites is like that of those timorous people who, at a mere shower of rain with thunder and lightning, become alarmed and fail to benefit by it.

41. The hypocrites, described as weak believers, are very near to losing their sight. They have not actually lost it, but if they are repeatedly confronted with situations demanding courage and sacrifice symbolized by lightning and thunder, they are very likely to lose it—their faith. But the mercy of God has so ordained that lightning is not always accompanied by thunderbolt. Often it is only a brilliant flash, which lifts the veil of darkness and helps the wayfarer to move on. In case Islām seems to make progress, these hypocrites make common cause with the Muslims. But when lightning is accompanied by thunder, *i.e.*, when the situation demands sacrifice of life or property the world becomes dark to them; they become dumb-founded and stand still, refusing to move on with the Faithful.

41A. *Shai'* signifies that which is willed or desired.

42. This verse contains the first commandment of God given in the Qur'ān. As the words show the commandment is addressed to all mankind and not to Arabs only, which indicates that Islām, from the very beginning, claimed to be a universal religion. It abolished the ideal of national religion and conceived mankind as one brotherhood.

23. [a]Who made the earth a bed for you, and[b] the heaven a roof,[43] and caused water to come down from the clouds and therewith brought forth fruits for your sustenance; so do not set up equals to Allāh, while you know.

الَّذِيْ جَعَلَ لَكُمُ الْاَرْضَ فِرَاشًا وَّالسَّمَآءَ بِنَآءً ۪
وَّاَنْزَلَ مِنَ السَّمَآءِ مَآءً فَاَخْرَجَ بِهٖ مِنَ الثَّمَرٰتِ
رِزْقًا لَّكُمْ ۚ فَلَا تَجْعَلُوْا لِلّٰهِ اَنْدَادًا وَّاَنْتُمْ تَعْلَمُوْنَ ﴿۲۳﴾

24. And if you are in doubt as to what We have sent down to Our servant, then [c]produce a chapter like it, and call upon your helpers beside Allāh, if you are truthful.[44]

وَاِنْ كُنْتُمْ فِيْ رَيْبٍ مِّمَّا نَزَّلْنَا عَلٰى عَبْدِنَا فَاْتُوْا
بِسُوْرَةٍ مِّنْ مِّثْلِهٖ ۪ وَادْعُوْا شُهَدَآءَكُمْ مِّنْ دُوْنِ
اللّٰهِ اِنْ كُنْتُمْ صٰدِقِيْنَ ﴿۲۴﴾

[a]20:54; 27:62; 43:11; 51:49; 71:20; 78:7. [b]51 : 48; 78:13; 79:28,29.
[c]10:39; 11:14; 17: 89; 52:35.

43. The expression suggests that just as a building or a roof is a means of protection for those living in or under it, similarly the remoter parts of the universe serve as a protection for our planet (earth); and those who have studied the science of the stars, the clouds and other atmospheric phenomena, know how the other heavenly bodies, running their courses through the boundless expanse rising high above the earth on all sides, make for its safety and stability. It is also hinted here that the perfection of the material world depends upon the co-ordination between earthly and heavenly forces.

44. The subject of the incomparable excellence of the Qur'ān has been dealt with at five different places, *i.e.*, in 2 : 24; 10 : 39; 11 : 14; 17 : 89 & 52 : 34, 35. In two of these five verses (2 : 24 & 10 : 39) the challenge is identical, while in the remaining three verses three separate and different demands have been made from disbelievers At first sight this difference in the form of the challenge at different places seems to be incongruous. But it is not so. In fact, these verses contain certain demands which stand for all time. The challenge is open even today in all the different forms mentioned in the Qur'ān as it was in the time of the Holy Prophet.

Before explaining the various forms of these challenges it is worth noting that their mention in the Qur'ān is invariably accompanied by a reference to wealth and power, except in the present verse which, as already stated, does not contain a new challenge but only repeats the challenge made in 10:39. From this it may be safely concluded that there exists a close connection between the question of wealth and power and the challenge for the production of the like of the Qur'ān or a part thereof. This connection lies in the fact that the Qur'ān has been held out to disbelievers as a priceless treasure. When disbelievers demanded material treasures from the Holy Prophet (11:13), they were told that he possessed a matchless treasure in the form of the Qur'ān; and when they asked, *Wherefore has not an angel come with him* (11:13), they were told in reply that angels did descend upon him, for their function was to bring the Word of God and the Divine Word had already been vouchsafed to him. Thus both the demands—for a treasure and for the descent of angels—have been jointly met by the Qur'ān which is a matchless treasure brought down by angels, and the challenge to produce its like has been put forward as a proof of its peerless quality.

Now, take the different verses containing this challenge separately. The greatest demand is made in 17: 89, where disbelievers are required to bring a book like the whole of the Qur'ān with all its manifold qualities. In that verse disbelievers are not required to represent their composition as the Word of God. They may bring it forward as their own composition and declare it to be the equal of, or, for that matter, better than, the Qur'ān. But as at the time when this challenge was made the whole of the Qur'ān had not yet been revealed, the disbelievers were not required to produce the like of the Qur'ān then and there; and the challenge thus implied a prophecy that they would never be able to produce the like of it,

25. But if you do *it* not—and never shall you do *it*—then guard against the Fire, [a]whose fuel[45] is men[46] and stones, *which is* prepared for the disbelievers.

فَإِنْ لَّمْ تَفْعَلُوْا وَلَنْ تَفْعَلُوْا فَاتَّقُوا النَّارَ الَّتِيْ وَقُوْدُهَا النَّاسُ وَالْحِجَارَةُ ۚ أُعِدَّتْ لِلْكٰفِرِيْنَ ﴿٢٥﴾

[a]3 : 11; 66 : 7.

neither in the form in which it then was, nor when it became complete. Again, the challenge was not confined to the disbelievers of the Prophet's time alone, but extended to doubters and critics of all time. The reason why the disbelievers in 11:14 have been called upon to produce ten *Sūrahs* and not the whole of the Qur'ān is that the question in that verse did not relate to the perfection of the whole of the Qur'ān in all respects, but to that of only a portion of it. The disbelievers had objected to some parts of it being defective. Hence they were not required to bring a complete book like the whole of the Qur'ān, but only ten *Sūrahs* in place of those parts of the Qur'ān which they deemed to be defective, in order that the truth of their assertion might be tested. As for the selection of the specific number 10 for this purpose, it may be noted that since in 17 : 89 the whole of the Qur'ān was claimed to be a perfect Book, its opponents were called upon to produce the like of the whole of it; but as in 11 : 14 the point was that certain portions of it were objected to, so they were asked to choose ten such portions as appeared to them to be most defective and then produce a composition even like those portions. In 10 : 39 disbelievers were called upon to produce the like of only one *Sūrah* of the Qur'ān. This is because, unlike the above-mentioned two verses, the challenge in that verse was in support of a claim made by the Qur'ān itself and not in refutation of any objection of the disbelievers. In 10 : 38 the Qur'ān claimed to possess five very prominent qualities. In support of this claim, verse 10 : 39 throws out a challenge to those who deny or doubt it to produce a single *Sūrah* containing these qualities in the same perfect form in which they are contained in the 10th *Sūrah*. The fifth challenge to produce the like of the Qur'ān is contained in the verse under comment (2:24) and here also, as in 10:39, disbelievers have been called upon to bring forward a single *Sūrah* like that of the Qur'ān. This challenge is preceded by the claim that the Qur'ān guides the righteous to the highest stages of spiritual progress. The disbelievers are told that if they are in doubt about the Divine origin of the Qur'ān, then they should bring forward a single *Sūrah* that may be comparable to it in the spiritual influence it exercises over its followers. See also The Larger Edition of the Commentary, pp. 58-62.

The above explanation will show that all these challenges calling upon disbelievers to produce the like of the Qur'ān are quite distinct and separate one from the other, and all of them stand for all time, none of them superseding or cancelling the other. But as the Qur'ān comprises sublime and lofty ideas, it was inevitable that a most beautiful diction and the chastest style should have been employed as the vehicle for the expression of those ideas; otherwise the subject-matter was liable to remain obscure and doubtful and the perfect beauty of the Qur'ān would have been marred. Thus, in whatever form and in whatever respect disbelievers have been challenged to produce a composition like the Qur'ān, the demand for beauty of style and elegance of diction comparable to that of the Qur'ān also forms a part of the challenge.

45. The word "fuel" may be taken in a figurative sense, meaning that the punishment of Hell is caused by idol-worship. So the idols are like fuel for hell-fire being a means of bringing it into existence. Or, "stones" mean idols which the idolaters worship as gods, the idea being that the idolaters will be humiliated by witnessing that their gods were cast into the fire.

46. The words *al-Nās* (men) and *al-Ḥijārah* (stones) may also be taken as indicating two classes of inmates of Hell; *al-Nās* may denote those disbelievers who retain something of the love of God, and *al-Ḥijārah* (stones), those who have no love left for God in their hearts. Such men are indeed no better than stones. The word is plural of *Ḥajar* which means, a stone; a rock; gold, and also one unequalled, *i.e.*, big man ; a leader (Lane).

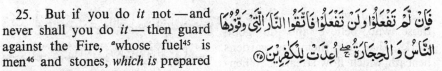

26. And give glad tidings to those who believe and do good works, that [a]for them are gardens beneath which flow streams. Whenever they are given a portion of fruit therefrom, they will say, 'This is what was given us before,' and gifts mutually resembling shall be brought to them. And they will have therein pure [b]mates,[46A] and therein will they abide.[47]

وَبَشِّرِ الَّذِيْنَ اٰمَنُوْا وَعَمِلُوا الصّٰلِحٰتِ اَنَّ لَهُمْ جَنّٰتٍ تَجْرِيْ مِنْ تَحْتِهَا الْاَنْهٰرُ ۗ كُلَّمَا رُزِقُوْا مِنْهَا مِنْ ثَمَرَةٍ رِّزْقًا ۙ قَالُوْا هٰذَا الَّذِيْ رُزِقْنَا مِنْ قَبْلُ ۙ وَاُتُوْا بِهٖ مُتَشَابِهًا ۗ وَلَهُمْ فِيْهَآ اَزْوَاجٌ مُّطَهَّرَةٌ ۙ وَّهُمْ فِيْهَا خٰلِدُوْنَ ﴿۲۶﴾

[a]3:16,134, 196, 199; 4:14, 58, 123; 5:13, 86; 7:44; 9:72, 89, 100; 10:10; 13:36; 22 : 15, 24; 25 : 11; 32 : 18; 47 : 16; 58 : 23; 61 : 13; 64 : 10. [b]3 : 16; 4 : 58.

46A. The Qur'ān teaches that every created thing stands in need of a mate for its full development. In Paradise righteous men and women will have pure mates for perfecting their spiritual development and completing their happiness. What kind of mates these will be, will be realized only in the Hereafter.

47. This verse gives a brief description of the rewards which the believers will have in the next world. Critics of Islām have raised all sorts of objections to this description. The criticism is based upon a complete misunderstanding of the Islamic teaching about heavenly blessings. The Qur'ān emphatically declares that it is beyond human mind to comprehend their nature (32:18). The Holy Prophet is reported to have said: "No eye has seen them, nor has any ear heard of them, nor can the mind of man conceive of them" (Bukhārī). The question naturally arises, why have the blessings of Heaven been given the names used for material things in this world? This is because the address of the Qur'ān is not merely to those people who are intellectually advanced. Therefore, it has used simple words which can be understood by all. While describing the heavenly blessings, the Qur'ān has used the names of things generally looked upon as good in this world, and believers are told that they would get all these things in a better form in the next world. It is to bring out this important contrast that familiar words have been used; otherwise there is nothing common between the joys of this world and the blessings of the next. Moreover, according to Islām, the next life is not spiritual in the sense that it will just consist of a mental state only. Even in the next life the human soul will have a kind of body, but that body will not be mateial. One can form some idea of this from the phenomenon of dreams. The scenes which a man witnesses in a dream cannot be called purely mental or spiritual, because in that state also he has a body and finds himself sometimes in gardens with streams, and eats fruits and drinks milk. It is difficult to say that the contents of dreams are only mental states. The milk enjoyed in a dream is no doubt a real experience, but no one can say that it is the material milk, found in this world which he drinks. The spiritual blessings of the next life will not be a mere subjective realization of the gifts of God which we enjoy in this world. What we have here is just a representation of the real and true gifts of God which man will find in the next world. Moreover, "gardens" represent faith; and "streams" good actions. Gardens cannot prosper without streams, nor can faith without good actions. Therefore, faith and actions are inseparable for the attainment of salvation. In the next world, gardens will remind the believers of their faith in this life and streams will remind them of their good works. They will know, then, that their faith and good works have not gone in vain. It is wrong to conclude from the words, *this is what was given us before*, that in Heaven the believers will be given such fruits as they had enjoyed in this world, because, as already explained, the two are not identical. The fruits of the next world will, in fact, be the images of the quality of their own faith. When they will eat them, they will at once recognize and remember that they are the fruits of the faith they had in this world; and it will be out of gratitude for this that they will say: *This is what was given us before.* This expression may also mean, 'what was promised us.'

27. Allāh [a]disdains not to [b]give an illustration[48]—*as small as* a gnat[48A] or even smaller.[48B] Those who believe know that it is the truth from their Lord, while those who disbelieve say, 'What does Allāh mean by such an illustration?' [c]Many does He adjudge by it to be in error[49] and many by it does He guide, and none does He adjudge thereby to be in error except the disobedient,

إِنَّ اللّٰهَ لَا يَسْتَحْيٖۤ اَنْ يَّضْرِبَ مَثَلًا مَّا بَعُوْضَةً
فَمَا فَوْقَهَا ؕ فَاَمَّا الَّذِيْنَ اٰمَنُوْا فَيَعْلَمُوْنَ اَنَّهُ الْحَقُّ مِنْ
رَّبِّهِمْ ۚ وَاَمَّا الَّذِيْنَ كَفَرُوْا فَيَقُوْلُوْنَ مَاذَاۤ اَرَادَ اللّٰهُ
بِهٰذَا مَثَلًا ۘ يُضِلُّ بِهٖ كَثِيْرًا ۙ وَّيَهْدِيْ بِهٖ كَثِيْرًا ؕ وَمَا
يُضِلُّ بِهٖۤ اِلَّا الْفٰسِقِيْنَ ۙ ﴿۲۷﴾

28. Who [d]break the covenant of Allāh after having established it, and cut asunder what Allāh has bidden to be joined, and create disorder in the earth; it is these that are the losers.

الَّذِيْنَ يَنْقُضُوْنَ عَهْدَ اللّٰهِ مِنْ بَعْدِ مِيْثَاقِهٖ ۠ وَ
يَقْطَعُوْنَ مَاۤ اَمَرَ اللّٰهُ بِهٖۤ اَنْ يُّوْصَلَ وَيُفْسِدُوْنَ
فِى الْاَرْضِ ؕ اُولٰۤئِكَ هُمُ الْخٰسِرُوْنَ ﴿۲۸﴾

---

[a]33 : 54. [b]14 : 25; 16 : 76,112; 47 : 4; 66 : 12. [c]6 : 118; 7 : 187; 13 : 28; 16 : 94; 40 : 35.
[d]2 : 101; 4 : 156; 5 : 14; 13 : 26.

The words "mutually resembling" refer to the resemblance between the acts of worship performed by believers in this world and the fruits thereof in Heaven. The acts of worship performed in this life will appear to believers as fruits in the next. The more sincere and the more appropriate a man's worship, the more will he enjoy his portion of the fruits in Paradise and the better in quality will they be. It, therefore, lies in one's own power to improve the quality of one's fruits as one likes. The verse also signifies that the spiritual food for believers in Heaven will be suited to the taste of each and every individual and to his stage of progress and degree of spiritual development.

The words, *they will abide*, signify that the believers in Heaven will not be subject to any change or decay. Man dies only when he cannot assimilate food or when someone kills him. But since the food of Paradise will be perfectly suited to every individual and since man will have pure and peaceful companions, death and decay will automatically disappear.

The Faithful will also have pure mates in Heaven. A good wife is a joy and a comfort. The Faithful try to have good wives in this world, and they will have good and virtuous mates in the next. Yet these joys of Heaven are not physical. For a fuller description of the nature and reality of the blessings of Paradise see also Chapters Al-Ṭūr, Al-Raḥmān and Al-Wāqi'ah.

48. *Ḍaraba al-Mathala* means, he gave an illustration or a description; he made a statement; he propounded a parable (Lane, Taj & 14 : 46).

48A. God has described Heaven and Hell in the Qur'ān in metaphors and similes. Metaphors and similes express depths of meaning which cannot adequately be expressed otherwise, and in things of the spirit they provide perhaps the only method by which ideas can be properly conveyed. The words used for describing Heaven may be as inadequate and insignificant as a gnat; which is considered by the Arabs and, in fact is, a very very weak creature. The Arabs say: *Aḍ'afu min Ba'ūḍatin, i.e.*, he is weaker than a gnat. Nevertheless they help to conjure up the picture. The believers know the words are only metaphorical and try to get to the depth of their meaning; but the disbelievers begin to find fault with them and increase in error and misguidance.

48B. *Fauq* means, above, and signifies both 'greater' and 'smaller' and is used in the sense which befits the context (Mufradāt).

49. *Aḍalla-hū Allāh* means, (1) God adjudged him to be in error; (2) God forsook or abandoned him so that he went astray (Kashshāf); (3) God found or left him in error or let him go astray (Lane).

29. How can you disbelieve in Allāh? You were without life[50] and [a]He gave you life,[51] and then will He cause you to die, then restore you to life,[52] and then to Him shall you be made to return.[53]

كَيْفَ تَكْفُرُوْنَ بِاللّٰهِ وَكُنْتُمْ اَمْوَاتًا فَاَحْيَاكُمْ ثُمَّ
يُمِيْتُكُمْ ثُمَّ يُحْيِيْكُمْ ثُمَّ اِلَيْهِ تُرْجَعُوْنَ ﴿۲۹﴾

30. [b]He it is Who created for you all that is in the earth; then [c]He turned[54] towards the heavens, and He perfected[55] them as seven[56] heavens; and He has perfect knowledge of all things.[56A]

هُوَ الَّذِيْ خَلَقَ لَكُمْ مَّا فِي الْاَرْضِ جَمِيْعًا ثُمَّ
اسْتَوٰٓى اِلَى السَّمَآءِ فَسَوّٰىهُنَّ سَبْعَ سَمٰوٰتٍ وَهُوَ
بِكُلِّ شَيْءٍ عَلِيْمٌ ﴿۳۰﴾ ع ٣ ٩

[a]19:34; 22:67; 30:41; 40:12; 45:27. [b]22:66; 31:21; 45:14. [c]7:55; 10:4; 41:10-13.

50. *Amwāt* is the plural of *Mayyit* which means, a thing dead, or without life. Thus the word is used both for a thing which so far has had no life and also for a thing which had life but is now dead and defunct. The word is also used about one who is dying or is nearing death but has not yet died (Lane).

51. *Ḥayāt* signifies, (1) the faculty of growth; (2) of sensation; (3) of intellect; (4) freedom from grief or sorrow; (5) everlasting life in the world to come; (6) advantage or profit or a means thereof; (7) state of activity and power (Lane).

52. The verse points to the supreme truth that man's life does not end with the extinction and dissolution of his physical body, as it is pregnant with too big an import to end with the latter's decay and death. If life had no great purpose God would not have created it and, after having created it, would not have made it subject to death unless there had been an after-life. If death were the end of all life, then the creation of man would have been "a mere sport and pastime" and this would have constituted a great reflection on the wisdom of God. The fact that God, the Source of all wisdom and intelligence, has done all this shows that He has not created man to return to dust after a life of merely 60 or 70 years. On the contrary, He has created him for a better, fuller and everlasting life which he must live after he has shed the encumbrances of his physical tabernacle.

53. After death the human soul does not go at once to Heaven or Hell. There is an intermediate state called *Barzakh* in which it is made to taste *some* of the good or bad results of its deeds; and Resurrection, which will herald a full and complete requital, will take place later.

54. *Istawā* means, he became firm or firmly settled. *Istawā ilā al-Shai'* means, he turned to a thing or he directed his attention to it (Lane).

55. *Sawwā-hu* means, he made it uniform or even, congruous or consistent in its several parts; he fashioned it in a suitable manner; he made it adapted to the exigencies, or requirements of its case; he perfected it; or he put it into a right or good state (Lane).

56. In Arabic "seven" is generally used as a symbol of perfection and the word along with "seventy" or "seven hundred" signifies a large number. All these three words have been used in this sense in the Qur'ān (9 : 80; 15:45). Elsewhere, the words "seven heavens" have been substituted by "seven stages" (23:18).

56A. The sun, the moon and other heavenly bodies are of immense benefit to man. Modern science has made many discoveries in this connection—and many more may yet be made—all of which testify to the truth and comprehensiveness of the Quranic teaching. Science also continues to find more and more the properties of things of this earth; many things which were formerly thought to be useless are now known to be highly serviceable to man.

R. 4 31. And when thy Lord said[57] to the angels,[57A] 'I am about to place a [a]vicegerent in the earth,' they said, 'Wilt Thou place therein such as will cause disorder in it, and shed blood?[58]—and we glorify[59] Thee with Thy praise and extol Thy holiness.'[60] He answered, 'I know what you know not.'[61]

وَإِذْ قَالَ رَبُّكَ لِلْمَلٰٓئِكَةِ إِنِّي جَاعِلٌ فِي الْأَرْضِ خَلِيفَةً ۖ
قَالُوٓا أَتَجْعَلُ فِيهَا مَنْ يُّفْسِدُ فِيهَا وَيَسْفِكُ الدِّمَآءَ ۚ
وَنَحْنُ نُسَبِّحُ بِحَمْدِكَ وَنُقَدِّسُ لَكَ ۖ قَالَ إِنِّيٓ أَعْلَمُ
مَا لَا تَعْلَمُونَ ﴿٣١﴾

[a]7:130; 10:15, 15:29; 24:56; 38:27.

57. *Qāla* is a common Arabic word meaning, he said. Sometimes, however, it is used in a figurative sense when, instead of a verbal expression, a state or condition amounting to a verbal expression is meant. The expression *Imtala'a al-Hauḍu wa Qāla Qaṭnī* (the tank became full and said, 'that will suffice') does not mean that the tank actually said so; only its condition implied that it was full.

The conversation between God and angels need not be taken in a literal sense as actually to have taken place. As stated above the word *Qāla* is sometimes used in a figurative sense to convey not actually a verbal expression, but simply a state or condition amounting to a verbal expression. The verse may thus simply mean that the angels by their state or condition implied a reply that has been here ascribed to them in words.

57A. *Malā'ikah* which is the plural of *Malak* is derived from *Malaka* which means, he controlled, or from *Alaka* meaning, he sent. The angels are called *Malā'ikah* because they control the forces of nature or because they bring Divine revelations to Heavenly Messengers and Reformers.

58. The angels did not object to God's purpose or claimed superiority over Adam. Their question was prompted by God's announcement of His plan to appoint a vicegerent. A vicegerent is needed when order has to be maintained and laws enforced. The seeming objection of the angels meant that there would be people on earth who would create disorder and shed blood. Man having been endowed with great powers to do good and evil, the angels spoke of the darker side of his character but God knew that he could rise to such moral heights as to become the mirror of Divine attributes. To this bright side of his character the words "I know what you know not" refer.

59. The question of the angels was not by way of finding fault with God's work, but by way of seeking greater knowledge of the nature and wisdom of the appointment. For the meaning of *Nusabbiḥu* see 2981.

60. Whereas *Tasbīḥ* (glorifying) is used with regard to God's attributes, *Taqdīs* (extolling His holiness) is used concerning His actions.

61. Adam, who lived about 6000 years ago, is popularly believed to be the first man created by God upon earth. This view, however, is not corroborated by the Qur'ān. The world has passed through different cycles of creation and civilization, and Adam, the progenitor of the present human race, is only the first link in the present cycle, and not the very first man in God's creation. Nations have risen and fallen, civilizations have appeared and disappeared. Other Adams may have gone before our Adam; other races may have lived and perished, and other cycles of civilization may have appeared and disappeared. Muhyī al-Dīn Ibn 'Arabī, the great Muslim mystic says that once he saw himself in a dream performing a circuit of the Ka'bah. In the dream a man who claimed to be one of his ancestors appeared before him. "How long is it since you died," asked Ibn 'Arabī. "More than forty thousand years," the man replied. "But this period is much more than what separates us from Adam," said Ibn 'Arabī. The man replied, "Of which Adam are you speaking? About the Adam who is nearest to you or of some other?" "Then I recollected," says Ibn 'Arabī, "a saying of the Holy Prophet to the effect that God had brought into being no less than a hundred thousand Adams, and I said to myself, "perhaps this man who claims to be an ancestor of mine was one of the previous Adams" (Futūḥāt, ii, b. 607).

It is not claimed that the race which lived before Adam was entirely swept away before he was born. Most probably, there had remained a small degenerated remnant of the old race and Adam was one of them. God then selected him to be the progenitor of a

32. And He taught Adam all[62] the [a]names,[62A] then He put *the objects of* these[62B] *names* before the angels and said, 'Tell Me the names of these, if you are right.'

وَعَلَّمَ اٰدَمَ الْاَسْمَآءَ كُلَّهَا ثُمَّ عَرَضَهُمْ عَلَى الْمَلٰٓئِكَةِ ۙ
فَقَالَ اَنْۢبِـُٔوْنِيْ بِاَسْمَآءِ هٰٓؤُلَآءِ اِنْ كُنْتُمْ صٰدِقِيْنَ ۝٣٢

33. They said, 'Holy art Thou! No knowledge have we except what Thou hast taught us; surely, Thou art the All-Knowing, the Wise.'[63]

قَالُوْا سُبْحٰنَكَ لَا عِلْمَ لَنَآ اِلَّا مَا عَلَّمْتَنَا ؕ اِنَّكَ اَنْتَ
الْعَلِيْمُ الْحَكِيْمُ ۝٣٣

[a]7 : 181; 17 : 111; 20 : 9; 59 : 24,25.

new race and the precursor of a new civilization. Created, as it were, out of the dead he represented the dawn of a new era of life. As *Khalīfah* means a successor, it is clear that men had existed and lived on earth before Adam whom he succeeded, and we cannot say whether the original inhabitants of America, Australia, etc., are the progeny of this last Adam or of some other Adam gone before him.

Much has been said about the place where Adam was born or where he was raised as a Reformer. The popular view is that he was placed in Paradise but was later expelled therefrom and put somewhere on the earth. But the words "in the earth" contradict this view and definitely show that Adam lived on the earth and it was on the earth that he was raised as a Reformer. Most probably he was first made to live in Iraq but was later directed to move down to a neighbouring land. See also The Larger Edition of the Commentary under this verse.

62. The word "all" used here does not imply absolute totality. It simply means *all that was necessary*. The Qur'ān uses this word in this sense elsewhere also (6:45; 27:17,24 ;28:58).

62A. *Asmā'* is plural of *Ism* which means, name or attribute; a mark or a sign of a thing (Lane & Mufradāt). Commentators differ as to what is here meant by the word *Asmā'* (names). Some think that God taught Adam the names of different things and objects, *i.e.*, He taught him the principles of language. There is no doubt that man needed language in order to become civilized and God must have taught Adam its principles, but the Qur'ān indicates that there are *Asmā'* (names or attributes) which man must learn for the perfection of his morals. They are referred to in 7 : 181. This shows that man cannot attain to Divine knowledge without a correct conception and comprehension of God's attributes and that they can be taught only by God. So it was necessary that God should have, in the very beginning, given Adam (man) knowledge of His attributes so that he should know and recognize Him and attain His nearness and should not drift away from Him. According to the Qur'ān, man differs from angels in that while the former can be an image or reflex of *al-Asmā' al-Ḥusnā*, *i.e.*, all the perfect Divine attributes, the latter represent only a few of them. Angels have no will of their own, but only passively perform the functions allotted to them by Providence (66:7). On the other hand, man, endowed with volition and free choice, differs from angels in that he possesses capabilities which make him a perfect manifestation of all Divine attributes. Briefly, the verse signifies that God first implanted in Adam free will and the needful capacity for the comprehension of various Divine attributes, and then gave him the knowledge of those attributes. *Asmā'* may also mean the qualities of the different things in nature. As man was to make use of the forces of nature, God endowed him with the capacity and power to know their qualities and properties.

62B. The pronoun *hum* (these) shows that the objects referred to here are not inanimate things; for in Arabic this form of pronoun is used only for rational beings. The meaning of the expression, therefore, would be that God granted to the angels a vision of the outstandingly righteous persons from among the progeny of Adam who were to become the manifestation of Divine attributes in the future, and were then asked whether they themselves could manifest the Divine attributes like them, to which they signified their inability. This is what is meant by the words, *Tell Me the names of these*, occurring in the present verse.

63. As the angels were conscious of their natural limitations, they frankly confessed that they were unable to reflect all God's attributes as man could do, *i.e.*, they could reflect only such of His attributes as He, in His eternal wisdom, had granted them the power to reflect.

34. He said, 'O Adam, tell them their names;' and when he had told them their names, He said, 'Did I not say to you, I know the secrets of the heavens and of the earth, and I know what you reveal and what you hide?'[64]

قَالَ يٰٓاٰدَمُ اَنْۢبِئْهُمْ بِاَسْمَآئِهِمْ ۚ فَلَمَّآ اَنْۢبَاَهُمْ بِاَسْمَآئِهِمْ ۙ قَالَ اَلَمْ اَقُلْ لَّكُمْ اِنِّيْٓ اَعْلَمُ غَيْبَ السَّمٰوٰتِ وَالْاَرْضِ ۙ وَاَعْلَمُ مَا تُبْدُوْنَ وَمَا كُنْتُمْ تَكْتُمُوْنَ ﴿۳۴﴾

35. And *remember the time* [a]when We said to the angels, 'Submit[65] to Adam,' and they *all* submitted. But[66] Iblīs[67] *did not.* He refused and deemed himself too big; and he was of the disbelievers.

وَاِذْ قُلْنَا لِلْمَلٰٓئِكَةِ اسْجُدُوْا لِاٰدَمَ فَسَجَدُوْٓا اِلَّآ اِبْلِيْسَ ؕ اَبٰى وَاسْتَكْبَرَ ٭ۤ وَكَانَ مِنَ الْكٰفِرِيْنَ ﴿۳۵﴾

[a]7:12,13; 15:29,33; 17:62; 18:51; 20:117; 38:72-77.

64. When the angels confessed their inability to manifest in themselves all the Divine attributes that Adam could manifest, the latter, in obedience to the Divine Will, manifested the different natural capabilities ingrained in him and revealed to the angels their extensive character. Thus Adam proved the necessity of the creation of a being who might secure from God the faculty of volition or the power of will by means of which he might voluntarily choose the way of goodness (or, of evil) and might thereby reveal the glory and greatness of God.

65. Adam having become an image of the attributes of God, and having attained the rank of a Prophet, God ordered the angels to serve him. The Arabic expression *Usjudū* does not mean—'fall prostrate before Adam,' because the Qur'ān definitely prohibits prostrating before anything but God (41:38) and a command to that effect could not have been given to angels. The command means, 'prostrate yourselves before *Me* as a mark of thanksgiving for My having created Adam.'

66. *Illā* (but) is used to signify 'exception.' In Arabic *Istithnā'* (exception) is of two kinds: (1) *Istithnā' Muttaṣil, i.e.*, an exception in which the thing excepted belongs to the same class or species to which the things from which an exception is sought to be made belong, (2) *Istithnā' Munqaṭi', i.e.*, an exception where the excepted thing belongs to a different class or species. In the verse under comment the word *illā* denotes the latter kind of exception, Iblīs not being one of the angels.

67. The word *Iblīs* is derived from *Ablasa* which means, (1) his good or virtue decreased; (2) he gave up hope or despaired of the mercy of God; (3) became broken in spirit; (4) was perplexed and unable to see his way; and (5) he was prevented from attaining his wish. Based on the root meaning of the word, Iblīs is a being which contains little of good and much of evil and which, on account of its having despaired of God's mercy owing to its disobedience, is left perplexed and confounded and unable to see its way. Iblīs is often considered identical with Satan, but is in some cases different from him. Iblīs, it must be understood, was not one of the angels, because, whereas he has been here described as disobeying God, the angels have been described as ever 'submissive' and 'obedient' (66:7). God was angry with Iblīs because he too was commanded to serve Adam but he disobeyed(7:13). Moreover, even if there were no separate commandment for Iblīs, the one for angels must be taken to extend to all beings because angels being the custodians of the different parts of the universe, the commandment given to them automatically extends to all beings. As stated above, Iblīs is really an attributive name given, on the basis of the root meaning of the word, to the Evil Spirit opposed to the angels. He has been so named because he possesses the attributes enumerated above, particularly the quality of being deprived of good and of being left bewildered in the way and of despairing of God's mercy. That Iblīs was not the Satan spoken of in 2:37 is apparent from the fact that the Qur'ān mentions the two names side by side wherever the story of Adam is given, but everywhere a careful distinction is observed between the two. Wherever it speaks of the being who, unlike the angels, refused to serve Adam, it invariably mentions the name Iblīs, and wherever it speaks of the being who beguiled Adam and became the means of his being turned out of "the garden" it mentions

36. And We said, 'O Adam, [a]dwell thou and thy wife in the garden,[68] and eat therefrom plentifully wherever you will,[68A] but approach not this tree,[69] lest you be of the wrongdoers.'

وَقُلْنَا يٰٓاٰدَمُ اسْكُنْ اَنْتَ وَزَوْجُكَ الْجَنَّةَ وَكُلَا مِنْهَا رَغَدًا حَيْثُ شِئْتُمَا وَلَا تَقْرَبَا هٰذِهِ الشَّجَرَةَ فَتَكُوْنَا مِنَ الظّٰلِمِيْنَ ۝

37. But Satan[70] caused them both to slip by means of it and drove them out of *the state* in which they were. And We said, [c]'Go forth hence; some of you are enemies of others and [d]for you there is an

فَاَزَلَّهُمَا الشَّيْطٰنُ عَنْهَا فَاَخْرَجَهُمَا مِمَّا كَانَا فِيْهِ ۪ وَقُلْنَا اهْبِطُوْا بَعْضُكُمْ لِبَعْضٍ عَدُوٌّ ۚ وَلَكُمْ فِي

[a]7:20,23; 20 : 117, 118. [b]7:21,28; 20:121. [c]7:25; 20:124. [d]7:25,26; 20:56; 77:26,27.

the name 'Satan.' This distinction, which is most significant and which has been maintained throughout the Qur'ān, in at least ten places (2:35,37; 7:12, 21; 15:32; 17:62; 18:51; 20:117,121; 38:75) clearly shows that Iblīs is different from the 'Satan' who beguiled Adam and who was one of Adam's own people. Elsewhere, the Qur'ān says that Iblīs belonged to a secret creation of God and, unlike the angels, was capable of obeying or disobeying God (7:12,13).

68. The word *Jannah* (garden) occurring in this verse does not refer to Heaven or Paradise but simply to the garden-like place where Adam was first made to live. It cannot refer to Heaven; first, because it was on the earth that Adam was made to live (2:37); secondly, Heaven is a place from which no one, who once enters it, is ever expelled (15:49), while Adam was made to quit the *Jannah* (garden) spoken of in this verse. This shows that the *Jannah* or garden in which Adam first dwelt was a place on this very earth which was given this name on account of the fertility of its soil and the abundance of its verdure. Recent researches go to show that the place was the Garden of Eden which lay near Babylon in Iraq or Assyria (Enc. Brit. under "Ur").

68A. The expression, *eat therefrom plentifully wherever you will,* indicates that the place where Adam lived had not yet come under anybody's jurisdiction and was what may be termed "God's land" which was given to Adam who was thus made, as it were, the lord of all he surveyed.

69. According to the Bible, the forbidden *Shajarah* (tree) was the tree of the knowledge of good and evil (Gen. 2:17). But according to the Qur'ān, after having eaten of the forbidden fruit, Adam and Eve became naked which signifies that, unlike knowledge which is a source of goodness, the tree was a source of evil, which made Adam exhibit a weakness. The Quranic view is evidently correct, because to deprive man of knowledge was to defeat the very purpose for which he had been brought into being. The Qur'ān and the Bible seem, however, to agree on the point that the tree was not a real one, but only a symbol, because no tree with either of the above characteristics, *i.e.,* making a man naked or giving him knowledge of good or evil, is known to exist on the face of the earth. So the tree must represent something else. *Shajarah* also means a quarrel. Elsewhere, the Qur'ān makes mention of two kinds of *Shajarah*: (1) *Shajarah Ṭayyibah* (good tree) and (2) *Shajarah Khabīthah* (evil tree) for which see 14:25 & 27. Pure things and pure teachings are likened to the former, and impure things and impure thoughts to the latter. In view of these explanations, the verse would signify, (1) that Adam was enjoined to avoid quarrels; (2) that he was warned against evil things.

70. The first two clauses of the verse mean that a satanic being enticed Adam and his spouse from the place in which they were placed and thereby deprived them of the comfort they enjoyed. As explained in 2:35 the being who beguiled and brought trouble on Adam was *Shaiṭān* and not Iblīs, who is spoken of as refusing to serve Adam. So *Shaiṭān* does not here refer to Iblīs, but to someone else from among the people of Adam's time who

abode in the earth[71] and a provision for a time.'

الْاَرْضِ مُسْتَقَرٌّ وَّ مَتَاعٌ اِلٰى حِيْنٍ ﴿۳۷﴾

38. Then Adam learnt from his Lord [a]certain words *of prayer*. So [b]He turned towards him with mercy. Surely, He is Oft-Returning *with compassion, and is* Merciful.

فَتَلَقّٰۤى اٰدَمُ مِنْ رَّبِّهٖ كَلِمٰتٍ فَتَابَ عَلَيْهِ ؕ اِنَّهٗ هُوَ التَّوَّابُ الرَّحِيْمُ ﴿۳۸﴾

39. We said, 'Go forth hence, all of you. And if [c]there comes to you guidance from Me, then whoso shall follow My guidance, on them *shall come* no fear[72] nor shall they grieve.'[73]

قُلْنَا اهْبِطُوْا مِنْهَا جَمِيْعًا ۚ فَاِمَّا يَاْتِيَنَّكُمْ مِّنِّىْ هُدًى فَمَنْ تَبِعَ هُدَاىَ فَلَا خَوْفٌ عَلَيْهِمْ وَلَا هُمْ يَحْزَنُوْنَ ﴿۳۹﴾

40. But [d]they who will disbelieve and treat Our Signs as lies, these shall be the inmates of the Fire; herein shall they abide.[74]

وَالَّذِيْنَ كَفَرُوْا وَكَذَّبُوْا بِاٰيٰتِنَاۤ اُولٰٓئِكَ اَصْحٰبُ النَّارِ ۚ هُمْ فِيْهَا خٰلِدُوْنَ ﴿۴۰﴾ ع

5 41. O Children of Israel![75] remember My [e]favours which I bestowed upon you, and fulfil your

يٰبَنِىْۤ اِسْرَآءِيْلَ اذْكُرُوْا نِعْمَتِىَ الَّتِىْۤ اَنْعَمْتُ عَلَيْكُمْ وَاَوْفُوْا

[a]7:24. [b]20 : 123. [c]7 : 36; 20 : 124. [d]7 : 37. [e]2 : 48,123; 5 : 21; 14 : 7.

was his enemy. The inference is further supported by 17:66 according to which Iblīs could have no power over Adam. The word *Shaiṭān* is of much wider significance than Iblīs, for whereas Iblīs is the name given to the Evil Spirit who belonged to the jinn and refused to serve Adam, thereafter becoming the leader and representative of the forces of evil in the universe, *Shaiṭān* is any evil or harmful being or thing, whether a spirit or a human being or an animal or a disease or any other thing. Thus Iblīs is a 'satan', his comrades and associates are 'satans', enemies of truth are 'satans,' mischievous men are 'satans,' injurious animals are 'satans' and harmful diseases are 'satans.' The Qur'ān, the Ḥadīth and Arabic literature are full of instances in which the word 'satan' has been freely used about one or all of these things.

71. The Qur'ān lends no support to the idea of anybody ascending to the heavens alive, for the verse clearly fixes the earth as the life-long abode of man and rejects the idea that Jesus or, for that matter, anybody else ever went up to the heavens alive.

72. *Khauf* denotes fear about the future.

73. *Ḥuzn* generally relates to the fear about what is past.

74. Islām does not believe in the eternity of Hell, but regards it as a sort of penitentiary where sinners will be made to live for a limited period for spiritual treatment and cure. See 1351.

75. "Israel" is another name of Jacob, son of Isaac. This name was bestowed on Jacob by God later in life (Gen. 32 : 28). The original Hebrew word is a compound one, made up of *Yasarā* and *Ail* and means : (a) God's prince, warrior or soldier (Concordance by Cruden & Hebrew-English Lexicon by W. Gesenius). The word Israel is used to convey three different senses : (1) Jacob personally (Gen. 32:28); (2) progeny of Jacob (Deut. 6:3,4); (3) any righteous and God-fearing person or people (Hebrew-English Lexicon).

covenant with Me, I will fulfil My covenant[76] with you, and Me alone should you fear.

بِعَهْدِىٓ أُوفِ بِعَهْدِكُمْ ۚ وَإِيَّاىَ فَارْهَبُونِ ﴿٤١﴾

42. And believe in what I have sent which [a]fulfils[77] that which is with you, and be not the [b]first to disbelieve therein, and barter not My Signs for a paltry price, and take protection in Me alone.

وَءَامِنُوا بِمَآ أَنزَلْتُ مُصَدِّقًا لِّمَا مَعَكُمْ وَلَا تَكُونُوٓا۟
أَوَّلَ كَافِرٍۭ بِهِۦ ۖ وَلَا تَشْتَرُوا بِـَٔايَٰتِى ثَمَنًا قَلِيلًا وَإِيَّٰىَ
فَاتَّقُونِ ﴿٤٢﴾

43. And [d]confound not truth with falsehood nor [e]hide the truth knowingly.[78]

وَلَا تَلْبِسُوا الْحَقَّ بِالْبَاطِلِ وَتَكْتُمُوا الْحَقَّ وَأَنتُمْ
تَعْلَمُونَ ﴿٤٣﴾

[a]2:90,98,102; 3:4.82; 4:48; 5:49. [b]7:102; 10:75. [c]2:80,175; 3:200; 5:45; 9:9; 16:96. [d]3:72. [e]2:147, 160; 6:92.

76. After Abraham the "covenant" was renewed with the Israelites. This second "covenant" is mentioned at several places in the Bible (Exod. ch. 20; Deut. chaps. 5, 18, 26). When the "covenant" was being made and the glory of God was being manifested on Mount Sinai, the Israelites were so terrified to see "the thunderings and the lightnings and the noise of the trumpet and the mountain smoking" (Exod. 20:18) that accompanied this manifestation that they exclaimed to Moses, saying: "Speak thou with us and we will hear; but let not God speak with us, lest we die" (Exod. 20:19). These impudent words sealed their fate; for thereupon God said to Moses that, in future no Law-giving Prophet, as he was, would appear from among them. Such a Prophet would in future appear from among the brethren of the Israelites, *i.e.*, the Ishmaelites. Thus in this verse God reminds the Children of Israel that He had made a "covenant" with Isaac and his seed after him to the effect that if they fulfilled their "covenant" with Him and obeyed all His commandments, He would continue to bestow His favours on them; but if they did not fulfil it, they would be deprived of His favours. Now, as the Israelites utterly failed to keep the "covenant," God raised the Promised Prophet from among the Ishmaelites as He had already promised, and henceforth the "covenant" was transferred to the followers of the new Prophet.

77. *Muṣaddiq* is derived from *Ṣaddaqa* which means, he held or declared him or it to be true (Lane). When the word is used in the sense of "holding a thing to be true," it is either followed by no preposition or by the preposition *bā'*. But when it is used in the sense of "fulfilling" as in the present verse, it is followed by the preposition *lām* (2:92 & 35:32). So here it means "fulfilling" and not "confirming" or "declaring to be true." The Qur'ān fulfils the prophecies that were contained in the previous Scriptures regarding the advent of a Law-giving Prophet and a universal Scripture. Wherever the Qur'ān speaks of itself as being *Musaddiq* of the previous Scriptures, it does not confirm their teachings but claims to have come in fulfilment of their prophecies. Nevertheless, it accepts the Divine origin of all the revealed Books before it. But it does not look upon all their present teachings to be true in their totality; for parts of them have been tampered with and much that was meant for a specific period has now become obsolete.

78. Here the Jews are forbidden (1) to mix the true with the false by quoting verses from their Scriptures and putting wrong interpretations on them; and (2) to suppress or hide the truth, *i.e.*, suppress such prophecies in their Scriptures as refer to the Holy Prophet.

44. And [a]observe Prayer and [b]pay the *Zakāt*, and bow down with those who bow.[79]

وَاَقِيْمُوا الصَّلٰوةَ وَاٰتُوا الزَّكٰوةَ وَارْكَعُوْا مَعَ الرّٰكِعِيْنَ ﴿٤٤﴾

45. [c]Do you enjoin others to do what is good[80] and forget your own-selves, while you read the Book?[81] Will you not then understand?

اَتَاْمُرُوْنَ النَّاسَ بِالْبِرِّ وَتَنْسَوْنَ اَنْفُسَكُمْ وَاَنْتُمْ تَتْلُوْنَ الْكِتٰبَ ۭ اَفَلَا تَعْقِلُوْنَ ﴿٤٥﴾

46. And [d]seek help with patience[82] and prayer;[83] and [e]this indeed is hard except for the humble in spirit,

وَاسْتَعِيْنُوْا بِالصَّبْرِ وَالصَّلٰوةِ ۭ وَاِنَّهَا لَكَبِيْرَةٌ اِلَّا عَلَى الْخٰشِعِيْنَ ﴿٤٦﴾

47. Who know for certain that [f]they will meet their Lord, and that to Him will they return.

الَّذِيْنَ يَظُنُّوْنَ اَنَّهُمْ مُّلٰقُوْا رَبِّهِمْ وَاَنَّهُمْ اِلَيْهِ رٰجِعُوْنَ ﴿٤٧﴾ ع

R. 6 48. O Children of Israel! [g]remember My favours which I bestowed upon you and that [h]I exalted you above the peoples[84] *of the time*.

يٰبَنِيْٓ اِسْرَآءِيْلَ اذْكُرُوْا نِعْمَتِيَ الَّتِيْٓ اَنْعَمْتُ عَلَيْكُمْ وَاَنِّيْ فَضَّلْتُكُمْ عَلَى الْعٰلَمِيْنَ ﴿٤٨﴾

[a]See 2:4. [b]2:84,111.178; 4:163; 5:56; 9:11; 21:74; 23:5. [c]26:227; 61:3-4. [d]2:154; 7:129. [e]4:143; 9:54. [f]2:224,250; 11:30 18:111; 29:6; 84:7. [g]See 2:41. [h]2:123; 3:34; 5:31; 6:87; 7:141; 45:17.

79. *Rāki'* means, one who bows down before God (Lisān). The Arabs used the word for one who worshipped God alone to the exclusion of idols (Asās).

80. *Birr* (good) means, behaving benevolently towards relations and others; truthfulness; fidelity; righteousness; obedience to God (Aqrab). The word also means extensive goodness or beneficence (Mufradāt).

81. 'Book' here refers to the Bible, but the clause, *while you read the Book*, does not imply that all the contents of the Bible have been accepted as true.

82. *Ṣabr* means, to adhere steadily to what reason and law command and to restrain oneself from what reason and law forbid and from manifesting grief, agitation and impatience (Mufradāt).

83. This verse along with the one that follows may be taken to be addressed either to the Jews or to the Muslims. In the former case, it constitutes a continuation of the address to the Israelites, meaning that they should not be hasty in rejecting the Holy Prophet but should try to find out the truth with patience and prayer. As taken to be addressed to Muslims it gives them a message of hope and encouragement. If they acted with patience and prayer, they need have no fear.

84. The verse signifies that the Israelites were superior to the peoples of only their own age. Where the Qur'ān desires to convey the idea of permanent superiority of a people over all nations, it uses other expressions such as in 3:111, where Muslims have been mentioned as "the best people."

49. And guard yourselves against the day [a]when no soul shall serve as a substitute for another soul at all, nor shall intercession[85] be accepted for it, [b]nor shall ransom[86] be taken from it, nor shall they be helped.

وَاتَّقُوْا يَوْمًا لَّا تَجْزِيْ نَفْسٌ عَنْ نَّفْسٍ شَيْـًٔا وَّ لَا يُقْبَلُ مِنْهَا شَفَاعَةٌ وَّ لَا يُؤْخَذُ مِنْهَا عَدْلٌ وَّ لَا هُمْ يُنْصَرُوْنَ ﴿۴۹﴾

50. And *remember the time* when We [c]delivered you from Pharaoh's[87] people[88] who afflicted you with grievous torment,[88A] [d]slaying your sons and sparing your women; and in that there was a great trial for you from your Lord.

وَ اِذْ نَجَّيْنٰكُمْ مِّنْ اٰلِ فِرْعَوْنَ يَسُوْمُوْنَكُمْ سُوْٓءَ الْعَذَابِ يُذَبِّحُوْنَ اَبْنَآءَكُمْ وَ يَسْتَحْيُوْنَ نِسَآءَكُمْ ؕ وَ فِيْ ذٰلِكُمْ بَلَآءٌ مِّنْ رَّبِّكُمْ عَظِيْمٌ ﴿۵۰﴾

[a]2:124; 31:34; 82:20. [b]2:124, 256; 19:88; 20:110; 21:29; 34:24; 39:45; 43:87; 53:27; 74:49. [c]14:7; 20:81; 44:31,32. [d]7 : 128, 142; 28:5.

85. *Shafā'ah* is derived from *Shafa'a* which means, he provided a thing which was alone with another; joined a thing to its like (Mufradāt). Thus the word has the significance of likeness or similarity; also it means, interceding or praying for a person that he may be shown favour and his sins may be passed over on the ground that he is connected with the intercessor, it being also implied that the petitioner is a person of higher position than the one for whom he pleads and also has deep connection with the person with whom he intercedes (Mufradāt & Lisān). *Shafā'ah* (intercession) is governed by the following conditions : (1) He who intercedes must have a special connection with the person with whom he wishes to intercede and enjoys his special favour, for without such connection he dare not intercede nor can intercession be fruitful. (2) The person for whom intercession is to be made must have a true and real connection with the intercessor, for none would think of interceding for a person unless the latter has real relationship with the former. (3) The person in whose favour intercession is sought must generally be a good person who has made an honest effort to win the pleasure of God (21:29), only he has fallen into sin in a moment of weakness. (4) Intercession can only be made with God's express permission (2 : 256; 10:4). *Shafā'ah* as conceived by Islām is, in fact, only another form of repentance, because *Taubah* (repentance) signifies reforming a broken connection or tightening up a loose one. So whereas the door of repentance becomes closed with death, the door of *Shafā'ah* remains open. Moreover, *Shafā'ah* is a means of the manifestation of God's mercy, and because God is not a judge but Master, there is nothing to stop Him from extending His mercy to whomsoever He pleases.

86. '*Adl* (ransom) means, equity or justice; equal compensation; fair and equitable ransom (Aqrab).

87. Pharaoh was not the name of a particular monarch. The rulers of the Nile Valley and Alexandria were called Pharaohs. Moses was born in the reign of Pharaoh Rameses II, and had to leave Egypt with the Israelites in the reign of his son, Merenptah II. Rameses II, is called the Pharaoh of the Oppression and his successor Merenptah II, the Pharaoh of Exodus (Enc. Bib. & Peake's Commentary on the Bible).

88. *Āl* (people) is derived from the verb *Āla* which gives the sense of returning or governing or exercising control. The word thus means, the family or party of a man, or followers of a leader, or subjects of a ruler to whom they constantly return or who governs or exercises control over them (Lane).

88A. Pharaoh had inflicted upon the Israelites grievous torments by imposing upon them hard and disgraceful labour. He also had given orders that their sons be slain and their daughters spared. In this way he sought to destroy not only their manhood but to kill in them manly qualities.

51. And *remember also the time* when We divided the sea[89] for you and saved you and [a]drowned Pharaoh's people, while you looked on.

وَإِذْ فَرَقْنَا بِكُمُ الْبَحْرَ فَأَنْجَيْنٰكُمْ وَأَغْرَقْنَآ اٰلَ فِرْعَوْنَ وَأَنْتُمْ تَنْظُرُونَ ﴿٥١﴾

[a]7:137; 8:55; 20:78,81; 26:64-67; 28 : 41; 44:25.

89. The incident mentioned in this verse relates to the time when, under God's command, Moses led the Israelites out of Egypt into Canaan. The Israelites left secretly by night and when Pharaoh learnt of their flight, he pursued them with his hosts and was drowned in the Red Sea. In order to appreciate fully the nature and significance of this incident which constituted a great Divine Sign, it is necessary to read the verse under comment along with other relevant verses such as vv. 20 : 78; 26 : 62-64; 44 : 25. The following facts emerge from these verses: (a) When Moses struck the sea with his rod as the Qur'ān says, or stretched out his hand over the sea as the Bible says, it was the time of the ebb-tide and the sea was receding, leaving a dry bed. (b) Moses was commanded by God to cross quickly the dry bed to the opposite bank, which he did. (c) But when the hosts of Pharaoh reached the sea, it was the time of high tide and in their zeal to overtake the Israelites they took no notice of it and at once jumped into the sea. (d) It seems that, being heavily equipped with big chariots and other heavy armaments the progress of the army of Pharaoh was greatly retarded so that while they were yet in the midst of the sea, the high tide returned and they were all drowned. The striking of the water of the sea with his rod by Moses had no cause and effect connection with the actual parting of the sea. It was merely a Sign or a Divine intimation for Moses that it was the time of the ebb-tide and that the Israelites should hasten to cross. God had so arranged that when Moses reached the sea the tide was about to recede, so that as soon as he struck the sea with his rod in obedience to Divine command, it began to recede and a dry path was made for the Israelites. The striking of the sea water with his rod by Moses and the recession of the sea coincided. This constituted a miracle because God alone knew when the sea would recede and He had commanded Moses to strike its waters at the time of recession.

Historians differ as to the exact place from where Moses crossed the Red Sea from Egypt into Canaan. Some are of the view that on his way from the territory of Goshen, which is also called the Valley of al-Tamthilāt or Wādī Tumilāt and where the capital of the Pharaohs was situated (Enc. Bib. vol. 4, col. 4012, under "Rameses"), Moses passed by the Gulf of Timsāḥ (Enc. Bib., cols. 1438 and 1439). Others think that he went much further to the north and going round Zoan crossed over to Canaan near the Mediterranean Sea (Enc. Bib., col. 1438). But what is most probable is the fact that from Tal Abī Sulaimān, which was the capital of the Pharaohs in Moses's time, the Israelites at first went to north-east to the Gulf of Timsāḥ but finding that a net of gulfs barred their way, they turned south and crossed the Red Sea near the town of Suez where it is hardly more than 2 to 3 miles wide, and started for Qadas (Enc. Bib., col. 1437). "The Israelites fled with him (Moses) across the Goshen marshes into the Sinaitic peninsula. The crossing of the "Red Sea" (*yam sūph*, "sea" or "lake of reeds") was probably the crossing of the southern end of a lake a few miles N.W. of what is now called the Red Sea. A wind laid bare a wide stretch of shore, and when an Egyptian force pursued the fugitives, their chariot-wheels stuck fast in the wet soil, and the water returned upon them when the wind shifted. Writers differ as to the route taken by the Israelites. Some think that they moved southward to the mountainous range of (the modern) Sinai, and then along the eastern arm of the Red Sea, now known as the Gulf of 'Akaba, to its northernmost point at Ezion-Geber. Others think that the evidence points to the route still taken by Mecca pilgrims, nearly due E. to Ezion Geber, and that thence they moved N.W. to the region of Kadesh (Barnea), to Mt. Sinai or southward along the E. side of the Gulf of 'Akaba to Mt. Horeb. The traditions differ and certainty is impossible" (Peake's Commentary on the Bible).

52. And when We made Moses[90] a [a]promise of forty nights,[91] then you [b]took the calf[92] *for worship* in his absence and you were transgressors.

وَإِذْ وٰعَدْنَا مُوسٰٓى أَرْبَعِينَ لَيْلَةً ثُمَّ اتَّخَذْتُمُ الْعِجْلَ
مِنْۢ بَعْدِهٖ وَأَنْتُمْ ظٰلِمُونَ ﴿٥٢﴾

53. Then [c]We forgave you thereafter, that you might be grateful.

ثُمَّ عَفَوْنَا عَنْكُمْ مِّنْۢ بَعْدِ ذٰلِكَ لَعَلَّكُمْ تَشْكُرُونَ ﴿٥٣﴾

54. And *remember* when [d]We gave Moses the Book[93] and [e]the "Discrimination,[94] that you might be rightly guided.

وَإِذْ اٰتَيْنَا مُوسَى الْكِتٰبَ وَالْفُرْقَانَ لَعَلَّكُمْ تَهْتَدُونَ ﴿٥٤﴾

55. And when Moses said to his people, 'O my people, you have indeed wronged yourselves by taking the calf *for worship*; turn ye therefore to your Maker, and kill your evil desires;[95] that is best for you in the sight of your Maker.' Then He turned towards you *with compassion*. Surely, He is Oft-Returning *with compassion and is* Merciful.

وَإِذْ قَالَ مُوسٰى لِقَوْمِهٖ يٰقَوْمِ إِنَّكُمْ ظَلَمْتُمْ أَنْفُسَكُمْ
بِاتِّخَاذِكُمُ الْعِجْلَ فَتُوبُوٓا إِلٰى بَارِئِكُمْ فَاقْتُلُوٓا أَنْفُسَكُمْ
ذٰلِكُمْ خَيْرٌ لَّكُمْ عِنْدَ بَارِئِكُمْ فَتَابَ عَلَيْكُمْ إِنَّهٗ هُوَ
التَّوَّابُ الرَّحِيمُ ﴿٥٥﴾

[a]7:143. [b]2:55,93; 4:154; 7:149,153; 20:89. [c]4:154. [d]2:88; 23:50; 32:24; 37:118; 40:54. [e]21:49.

90. Moses, the Founder of Judaism, who delivered the Israelites from the tyranny of Pharaoh, was the greatest Israelite Prophet. According to biblical data he lived about 500 years after Abraham and about 1,400 years before Jesus. He was a Law-giving Prophet; the other Israelite Prophets that came after him were only the followers of his system.

91. See 7:143.

92. Man generally is the slave of his environments. This is particularly true of a subject people, who generally imitate the manners and customs of their rulers. The Israelites had lived under the bondage of Pharaohs for a long time, and naturally had imbibed the idolatrous faith of the Egyptians. When they left Egypt with Moses and came across an idol-worshipping people on the way, they requested him to sanction a similar worship for them (7:139).

93. The "Tablets" on which the Ten Commandments given to Moses were written. See 7:146, 151, 155.

94. *Furqān* means, arguments; morning or dawn; support (Lane).

The verse means that God gave Moses not only the Book or the Commandments written on the Tablets, but also such clear Signs and arguments, and brought about such events, as led to clear discrimination between truth and falsehood.

95. *Anfusa-kum* (your evil desires) means, your kith and kin; your evil desires. *Nafs* which is the singular of *Anfus* also means, passion; desire. The Israelites were commanded to purge their souls of evil desires through mortification. The biblical statement that they were commanded 'to slay every man his brother, every man his companion and every man his neighbour' (Exod 32 : 27) is not supported by the Qur'ān according to which they were pardoned (4 : 154). Even their leader Sāmirī was not killed (20 : 98).

56. And *remember* when you said, 'O Moses, we will not believe thee [a]until we see Allāh face to face;' then the thunderbolt overtook you, while you witnessed *with your own eyes the consequences of your conduct.*

وَإِذْ قُلْتُمْ يٰمُوْسٰى لَنْ نُّؤْمِنَ لَكَ حَتّٰى نَرَى اللّٰهَ جَهْرَةً
فَاَخَذَتْكُمُ الصّٰعِقَةُ وَاَنْتُمْ تَنْظُرُوْنَ ﴿٥٦﴾

57. Then We [b]raised you up after your death,[96] that you might be grateful.

ثُمَّ بَعَثْنٰكُمْ مِّنْۢ بَعْدِ مَوْتِكُمْ لَعَلَّكُمْ تَشْكُرُوْنَ ﴿٥٧﴾

58. And We caused the clouds[97] to be a shade over you and [c]sent down on you Manna[98] and Salwā,[99] *saying*, [d]'Eat of the good things We have provided for you.' And they wronged Us not, but it was themselves that they wronged.

وَظَلَّلْنَا عَلَيْكُمُ الْغَمَامَ وَاَنْزَلْنَا عَلَيْكُمُ الْمَنَّ وَ
السَّلْوٰى ؕ كُلُوْا مِنْ طَيِّبٰتِ مَا رَزَقْنٰكُمْ ؕ وَمَا ظَلَمُوْنَا وَ
لٰكِنْ كَانُوْۤا اَنْفُسَهُمْ يَظْلِمُوْنَ ﴿٥٨﴾

59. And *remember the time* [e]when We said, "Enter this town[100] and eat therefrom—wherever you will—plentifully; and enter the gate submissively and say, '*God!* forgive us our sins.' We shall forgive you your sins and We shall give increase to those who do good."

وَاِذْ قُلْنَا ادْخُلُوْا هٰذِهِ الْقَرْيَةَ فَكُلُوْا مِنْهَا حَيْثُ شِئْتُمْ
رَغَدًا وَّادْخُلُوا الْبَابَ سُجَّدًا وَّقُوْلُوْا حِطَّةٌ نَّغْفِرْ لَكُمْ
خَطٰيٰكُمْ ؕ وَسَنَزِيْدُ الْمُحْسِنِيْنَ ﴿٥٩﴾

[a]4:154. [b]2:260; 6:123. [c]7:161. [d]7:161; 20:81. [e]7:162.

96. The verse may signify that this unreasonable demand of the Israelites so arrogantly expressed brought about their spiritual and not physical death. This significance finds corroboration in the next verse wherein God says: *Then We raised you up after your death, i.e.*, you regained respect and honour after you had lost it. *Maut* means, extinction of the power of growth (57 : 18); the loss of the feeling power (19 : 24); the loss of the power of reasoning (6 : 123); grief which embitters the life of a man (14 : 18); physical death (Lane).

97. See Exodus, 40 : 34-38.

98. *Mann* means a favour or gift; anything obtained without trouble or difficulty; honey or dew (Aqrab). The Manna has also been referred to in a saying of the Holy Prophet as : "The truffle is one of the things included in the Manna" (Bukhārī). See also Lane under "Turanjabīn."

99. *Salwā* is (1) a whitish bird resembling a quail and found in some parts of Arabia and the neighbouring countries; (2) whatever renders a person contented and happy; honey (Aqrab). The sending down of Manna and Salwā has been mentioned at three places in the Qur'ān,—in the present verse and in vv. 2:58 and 7:161, and at all these three places the fact has been followed by the injunction: 'Eat of the good things that We have provided for you.' This shows that whereas the food which was provided to the Israelites in the wilderness of Sinai was wholesome, palatable and of good taste, it consisted not of one but of several things; Manna (truffle) and Salwā (quails) forming the major part of them. See Exodus, 16:13—15.

100. "Town" need not refer to any particular town. It may signify any town on the way from Sinai to Canaan that may be near; or the nearest town. As the Israelites were

60. [a]The transgressors changed *it* for a word other than that which was said to them. So We sent down upon the transgressors a punishment from heaven, because they were disobedient.

فَبَدَّلَ الَّذِيْنَ ظَلَمُوْا قَوْلًا غَيْرَ الَّذِي قِيْلَ لَهُمْ
فَأَنْزَلْنَا عَلَى الَّذِيْنَ ظَلَمُوْا رِجْزًا مِّنَ السَّمَآءِ بِمَا
كَانُوْا يَفْسُقُوْنَ ﴿٦٠﴾ ع

R. 7 61. And *remember the time* [b]when Moses prayed for water for his people and We said, 'Strike the rock with thy rod;' and there gushed forth from it twelve springs,[101] *so that* every tribe knew their drinking place. *And they were told*, 'Eat and drink of what Allāh has provided, and commit not iniquity in the earth, creating disorder.'

وَإِذِ اسْتَسْقٰى مُوْسٰى لِقَوْمِهٖ فَقُلْنَا اضْرِبْ بِّعَصَاكَ
الْحَجَرَ ۭ فَانْفَجَرَتْ مِنْهُ اثْنَتَا عَشْرَةَ عَيْنًا ۭ قَدْ
عَلِمَ كُلُّ أُنَاسٍ مَّشْرَبَهُمْ ۭ كُلُوْا وَاشْرَبُوْا مِنْ رِّزْقِ
اللّٰهِ وَلَا تَعْثَوْا فِي الْأَرْضِ مُفْسِدِيْنَ ﴿٦١﴾

[a]7:163. [b]7:161.

eager to live in towns owing to the facilities and amenities of life they afforded and owing also to their previous mode of living, they were bidden to go to some neighbouring village where they would combine the life of the desert with that of a habitation and would be free to eat wherever they liked, as is usual in a desert place where there is no private ownership. But as this change was to bring them into contact with other people and was likely to affect their morals they were at the same time bidden to be careful about themselves and to be submissive to God.

101. That at present there is no trace of the springs at that spot is nothing to be wondered at, because it is not yet definitely known in what particular region Moses performed his journey. Moreover, it is a matter of common experience that springs sometimes cease to flow and their mouths become closed abruptly in the mountains. The event referred to here occurred thousands of years ago and it is well-known that sometimes a spring gushes forth, but soon the flow of water ceases and the spring runs dry. Often springs once flowing become so dry that no trace of them is left. Even as late as the end of the 15th century twelve springs actually flowed at this place. "The rock stands within the border of Arabia and some of his (the Prophet's) countrymen must needs have seen it if he himself had not, as it is most probable he had. And in effect he seems to be in the right. For one, who went into those parts in the end of the fifteenth century, tells us expressly that the water issued from twelve places of the rock, according to the number of the tribes of Israel" (Al-Koran by Sale, page 8). Moreover, as there were twelve Israelite tribes with Moses, God must have caused to flow as many springs for them. One spring could not meet their needs as their number was very large—according to the Bible they were 600,000 (Num. 1 : 46).

The miracle of Moses on this occasion did not lie in bringing about something against the known laws of nature, but in the fact that God revealed to him the specific spot where water was just ready to flow on a blow with his rod. It is within the experience of geologists that sometimes water flows at a small depth underneath hillocks or rocks and begins to gush forth the moment the rock is struck with something heavy or pointed.

The words *Iḍrib bi 'Asāka al-Hajara* may also mean: "Go forth or hasten with thy community to the rock," *'Aṣā* metaphorically meaning, " a community," and *Iḍrib* meaning,"go forth or hasten." They say, *Ḍaraba al-Arḍa* or *Ḍaraba fī al-Arḍi, i.e.*, he went forth or hastened in the land (Lane).

62. And *remember* when you said, 'O Moses, surely, we will not remain content with one *kind of* food; pray, then, to thy Lord for us that He may bring forth for us of what the earth grows—of its herbs and its cucumbers and its wheat and its lentils and its onions.' He said, 'Would you take in exchange that which is worse for that which is better? Go down to some town and there is for you what you ask.'[102] And [a]they were smitten with abasement and destitution, and [b]they incurred the wrath of Allāh; that was because they rejected the Signs of Allāh and sought to slay[103] [c]the Prophets unjustly; this was because they rebelled and transgressed.

وَإِذْ قُلْتُمْ يٰمُوْسٰى لَنْ نَّصْبِرَ عَلٰى طَعَامٍ وَّاحِدٍ فَادْعُ
لَنَا رَبَّكَ يُخْرِجْ لَنَا مِمَّا تُنْبِتُ الْاَرْضُ مِنْ بَقْلِهَا وَ
قِثَّآئِهَا وَفُوْمِهَا وَعَدَسِهَا وَبَصَلِهَا ؕ قَالَ اَتَسْتَبْدِلُوْنَ
الَّذِيْ هُوَ اَدْنٰى بِالَّذِيْ هُوَ خَيْرٌ ؕ اِهْبِطُوْا مِصْرًا فَاِنَّ
لَكُمْ مَّا سَاَلْتُمْ ؕ وَضُرِبَتْ عَلَيْهِمُ الذِّلَّةُ وَالْمَسْكَنَةُ ٭
وَبَآءُوْ بِغَضَبٍ مِّنَ اللّٰهِ ؕ ذٰلِكَ بِاَنَّهُمْ كَانُوْا يَكْفُرُوْنَ
بِاٰيٰتِ اللّٰهِ وَيَقْتُلُوْنَ النَّبِيّٖنَ بِغَيْرِ الْحَقِّ ؕ ذٰلِكَ بِمَا
عَصَوْا وَّكَانُوْا يَعْتَدُوْنَ ﴿٦٢﴾ ع

R. 8 63. [d]Surely, those who believe and the Jews and the Christians and the Sabians[104]—whichever *party from among these truly* [e]believes in Allāh and the Last Day and does good deeds, shall have their reward with their Lord, and [f]no fear *shall come* upon them, nor shall they grieve.

اِنَّ الَّذِيْنَ اٰمَنُوْا وَالَّذِيْنَ هَادُوْا وَالنَّصٰرٰى وَ
الصّٰبِـِٕيْنَ مَنْ اٰمَنَ بِاللّٰهِ وَالْيَوْمِ الْاٰخِرِ وَعَمِلَ
صَالِحًا فَلَهُمْ اَجْرُهُمْ عِنْدَ رَبِّهِمْ ۚ وَلَا خَوْفٌ عَلَيْهِمْ
وَلَا هُمْ يَحْزَنُوْنَ ﴿٦٣﴾

[a]3 : 113. [b]2 : 91; 3 : 113; 5 : 61. [c]2 : 88; 3 : 22, 113, 184; 5 : 71. [d]5 : 70; 22 : 18. [e]4 : 137; 6 : 93. [f]2 : 113, 278; 6 : 49; 10: 63.

102. Having lived for a long time in bondage and in a state of dependence, the Israelites had become cowardly and indolent. So God intended them to stay in the desert for some time and to live on game and wild herbs in order that they might shed their cowardice and indolence by living an independent life in the desert. Thus revitalized, they were to be led to the Promised Land and made rulers of Palestine. The Israelites, however, failed to understand the real purpose of God or, having understood it, failed to appreciate it and foolishly insisted upon living in a town. God wanted to prepare them for rule over the Promised Land but those unfortunate people hungered after husbandry. So they were told to go down to a town where they would get the desired things.

103. The word *Qatl* besides its primary sense of actual killing means, to attempt or intend to kill; to beat; to curse; to have nothing to do with, and to neutralise the blighting influence of a thing; and the expression *Yaqtulūn al-Nabiyyīn* does not signify that the Israelites actually slew the Prophets, because, up to the time of Moses no Prophet is known to have been slain by them. As a matter of fact, Moses was the first Prophet who was sent to the Israelites as a nation. He and his brother, Aaron, are the only persons to whom these words can be applied, but obviously they were not killed by the Israelites, although they were sometimes bent upon killing them (Exod. 17 : 4). Hence, the word *Qatl* in the verse cannot possibly mean "actual killing." It only means that they severely opposed the Prophets and would have killed them if they could. See also 3 : 22 & 40 : 29.

104. *Ṣābī* is one who forsakes his own religion for a new one. Technically, however, the word Sabians refers to certain religious sects that were found in parts of Arabia

64. And *remember the time* when ^a"We took a covenant from you and ^braised high above you the Mount,[105] *saying*, 'Hold fast that which We have given you and bear in mind what is therein, that you may be saved.'

وَاِذْ اَخَذْنَا مِيْثَاقَكُمْ وَرَفَعْنَا فَوْقَكُمُ الطُّوْرَ خُذُوْا مَا اٰتَيْنٰكُمْ بِقُوَّةٍ وَّاذْكُرُوْا مَا فِيْهِ لَعَلَّكُمْ تَتَّقُوْنَ ۝

65. Then you turned back there-after; and had it not been for Allāh's grace and His mercy[106] upon you, you would surely have been of the losers.

ثُمَّ تَوَلَّيْتُمْ مِّنْ بَعْدِ ذٰلِكَ فَلَوْلَا فَضْلُ اللّٰهِ عَلَيْكُمْ وَرَحْمَتُهٗ لَكُنْتُمْ مِّنَ الْخٰسِرِيْنَ ۝

66. And surely, you have known *the end of* those amongst you, who ^ctransgressed in the matter of the

وَلَقَدْ عَلِمْتُمُ الَّذِيْنَ اعْتَدَوْا مِنْكُمْ فِى السَّبْتِ

---

^a2 : 84, 94; 4 : 155.   ^b7 : 172.   ^c4 : 48, 155; 7 : 164; 16 : 125.

---

and countries bordering on it. The name was applied to (1) the star-worshipping people living in Mesopotamia (Gibbon's *Roman Empire*, *Murūj al-Dhahab* & Enc. Rel. Eth., viii under "Mandaeans"); (2) a people who lived near Mosul in Iraq and believed in one God and in all Divine Prophets but possessed no revealed Book. They claimed to follow the religion of Noah (Jarīr & Kathīr). They should not, however, be confused with the Sabians mentioned by certain commentators of the Bible as people living in ancient Yemen.

    The verse, as mistakenly understood, does not signify that belief in God and in the Last Day alone is sufficient for salvation. The Qur'ān emphatically declares that belief in the Holy Prophet is most essential (4 : 151, 152; 6 : 93) and forms an integral part of belief in God, and also that belief in the Hereafter includes belief in Divine revelation as well (4:151, 152; 6 : 93). Elsewhere, Islām alone has been unequivocally declared to be acceptable to God as a religion (3 : 20, 86). The Qur'ān here confines itself to a mention of belief in God and the Last Day, not because belief in revelation and in the Holy Prophet is not essential, but because the former two beliefs include the latter two, the four being essentially inseparable. In fact, the verse is intended to demolish the mistaken Jewish belief that they were "the favoured nation of God" and, therefore, were alone entitled to salvation. It signifies that it did not matter whether one was apparently a Jew, a Christian, a Sabian or, for that matter, a Muslim; if the faith was confined only to the lip, it was a dead thing, without life and without any motive power in it. The verse may also be taken as embodying a prophecy and as a safe criterion to test the truth of Islām. The prophecy is that Islām shall triumph because it is a true religion. The criterion lies in the fact that the prophecy was made at a time when Islām was fighting for its very life. The verse may also be taken as signifying that all those who claim to be believers whether they are Jews, Christians or Sabians or, for that matter, belong to any religion—if their faith in God and the Last Day is sincere and honest and they do good deeds which is the quintessence of a true religion, *i.e.*, Islām, no fear shall come upon them nor shall they grieve.

    105.   The words do not mean that Mount Sinai was physically lifted up to hang over the heads of the Israelites. They only mean that the covenant was taken at a time when the Israelites were standing at the foot of the Mount. They may also refer to the scene when the Mount Sinai was terribly shaken with an earthquake, while the Israelites were camping at its foot (Exod. 19 : 2). On such an occasion the shaking of a high mountain peak appears as it were hanging over the heads of those standing near it.

    106.   *Raḥmah* (mercy) in contrast to *Faḍl* (grace) is generally spoken in respect of such acts of God as relate to religious or spiritual matters.

Sabbath. So We said to them, [a]'Be ye apes, despised.'[107]

فَقُلْنَا لَهُمْ كُوْنُوْا قِرَدَةً خٰسِئِيْنَ ۝٦٦

67. Thus We made it an [b]example to those of its time and to those *who came* after it, and a lesson to those who fear *God*.

فَجَعَلْنٰهَا نَكَالًا لِّمَا بَيْنَ يَدَيْهَا وَمَا خَلْفَهَا وَ
مَوْعِظَةً لِّلْمُتَّقِيْنَ ۝٦٧

68. And *remember* when Moses said to his people, 'Allāh commands you to slaughter a cow,' they said, 'Dost thou make a jest of us?' He said, 'I seek refuge with Allāh lest I should be one of the ignorant.'

وَاِذْ قَالَ مُوْسٰى لِقَوْمِهٖٓ اِنَّ اللّٰهَ يَاْمُرُكُمْ اَنْ تَذْبَحُوْا
بَقَرَةً ؕ قَالُوْٓا اَتَتَّخِذُنَا هُزُوًا ؕ قَالَ اَعُوْذُ بِاللّٰهِ اَنْ اَكُوْنَ
مِنَ الْجٰهِلِيْنَ ۝٦٨

69. They said, 'Pray for us to thy Lord that He make plain to us what she is.' He answered, '*God* says, it is a cow, neither old nor young, full-grown, between the two; now do what you are commanded.'

قَالُوا ادْعُ لَنَا رَبَّكَ يُبَيِّنْ لَّنَا مَا هِيَ ؕ قَالَ اِنَّهٗ يَقُوْلُ
اِنَّهَا بَقَرَةٌ لَّا فَارِضٌ وَّلَا بِكْرٌ ؕ عَوَانٌ بَيْنَ ذٰلِكَ ؕ
فَافْعَلُوْا مَا تُؤْمَرُوْنَ ۝٦٩

70. They said, 'Pray for us to thy Lord that He make plain to us of what colour she is.' He answered, '*God* says, it is a cow of a dun colour, pure and rich *in tone*, delighting the beholders.'

قَالُوا ادْعُ لَنَا رَبَّكَ يُبَيِّنْ لَّنَا مَا لَوْنُهَا ؕ قَالَ اِنَّهٗ يَقُوْلُ
اِنَّهَا بَقَرَةٌ صَفْرَآءُ ۙ فَاقِعٌ لَّوْنُهَا تَسُرُّ النّٰظِرِيْنَ ۝٧٠

71. They said, 'Pray for us to thy Lord that He make plain to us what she is, for *all such* cows appear to us alike; and if Allāh please, we shall indeed be guided *aright*.'

قَالُوا ادْعُ لَنَا رَبَّكَ يُبَيِّنْ لَّنَا مَا هِيَ ۙ اِنَّ الْبَقَرَ تَشٰبَهَ
عَلَيْنَا ؕ وَاِنَّآ اِنْ شَآءَ اللّٰهُ لَمُهْتَدُوْنَ ۝٧١

[a]5 : 61; 7 : 167. [b]5 : 39.

107. The word "apes" has been used figuratively meaning that the Israelites became abject and mean like the monkeys, the transformation being not in body or form but in character and spirit. "They were not actually transformed into apes, only their hearts were changed" (Mujāhid). "God has used the expression figuratively" (Kathīr). Had the Qur'ān meant their physical transformation into apes the word *Khāsi'ah* would have been used and not *Khāsi'īn* which is used for rational beings. By the use of this word it is intended to point out that just as apes or monkeys are abject and despised animals, similarly the Jews will always remain humiliated in the world and, in spite of their great resources in wealth and education, will never be able to gain any stronghold on the earth; the root meaning of the word signifying abjectness and humiliation as well as grovelling in the dust. See also 764.

72. He answered, '*God* says, it is a cow [a]not broken to plough the earth or water the tilth; one without blemish; of one colour.' They said, 'Now hast thou brought the truth.' Then they slaughtered her, though they would rather not do it.[108]

قَالَ إِنَّهُ يَقُولُ إِنَّهَا بَقَرَةٌ لَّا ذَلُولٌ تُثِيرُ الْأَرْضَ وَلَا تَسْقِي الْحَرْثَ مُسَلَّمَةٌ لَّا شِيَةَ فِيهَا قَالُوا الْآنَ جِئْتَ بِالْحَقِّ فَذَبَحُوهَا وَمَا كَادُوا يَفْعَلُونَ ٧٢

R. 9 73. And *remember the time* when you killed[109] a person[109A] and differed among yourselves about it, and Allāh would bring to light what you were hiding.[109B]

وَإِذْ قَتَلْتُمْ نَفْسًا فَادَّارَأْتُمْ فِيهَا وَاللَّهُ مُخْرِجٌ مَّا كُنتُمْ تَكْتُمُونَ ٧٣

74. Then We said, 'Compare[110] this *incident* with some *other similar* ones' *and you will discover the truth*. Thus does [b]Allāh give life to the

فَقُلْنَا اضْرِبُوهُ بِبَعْضِهَا كَذَٰلِكَ يُحْيِي اللَّهُ الْمَوْتَىٰ

[a]67 : 16. [b]2 : 180.

108. The Israelites had lived for a long time among the Egyptians who had great veneration for the cow. Thus reverence for this animal had crept into their minds also. This is why, when they made an idol for themselves, they made it in the shape of a calf (Qur'ān 2 : 52 & Exod. 32 : 4). In order that their minds should have been purged of the feeling of veneration for the cow, they were repeatedly commanded to sacrifice it (Num. 19 : 1-9; Lev. 4 : 1-21; 16 : 3,11). It seems that they had a particular cow which served as a pet among them and they had a misgiving that the order pertained to it. So they repeatedly asked Moses to specify the cow which God meant to be slaughtered, and as a result of their questioning some conditions were added to specify the animal.

109. *Qataltum* means, you sought, attempted, claimed, or made up your mind, to kill (40:29), or you made him appear as dead; you almost killed him. They say *Qatala-hū*, *i.e.*, he rendered him like one killed physically or morally (Lane). The famous saying of 'Umar, *viz.*, *Uqtulū Sa'dan*, has been taken to signify, render Sa'd like one who is, to all intents and purposes, dead.

109A. *Nafsan* used as *Nakirah*, *i.e.*, in an undefined form, according to Arabic grammar may refer to a very important personage (Muṭawwal).

In the foregoing verses some of the evil practices and crimes of the Jews were mentioned. This verse refers to their crowning guilt, *i.e.*, they sought to kill Jesus on the Cross and thus to show that according to the Bible he was a false prophet (Deut. 21 : 23). In this nefarious attempt they utterly failed. Jesus was taken down from the Cross alive but like one dead. For the historical fact that Jesus did not die on the Cross but was taken down alive like one dead see 2000.

109B. The clause signifies that a time will come when the truth about Jesus's death will come to light and the mask which had so long been hanging over the incident will be lifted.

110. *Darb* meaning the like of a thing (Lane), the verb *Daraba* is used in different tenses in 13 : 18; 16:75 & 43: 58 as signifying "comparison." So the expression *Iḍribū-hu Bi-ba'ḍi-hā* may be interpreted as "compare the condition of Jesus in which he was taken down from the Cross as almost dead with the condition of persons who were considered dead while in reality they were not dead but only appeared as such; and you will discover the truth about the supposed death of Jesus."

dead[110A] and show you His Signs that you may understand.

وَيُرِيكُمْ اٰيٰتِهٖ لَعَلَّكُمْ تَعْقِلُوْنَ ﴿٧٤﴾

75. Then [a]your hearts became hardened[111] after that, till they were like stones or harder still; for of stones indeed there are some out of which gush forth streams, and of them there are some out of which flows water when they cleave asunder. And indeed of them there are some

ثُمَّ قَسَتْ قُلُوْبُكُمْ مِّنْۢ بَعْدِ ذٰلِكَ فَهِيَ كَالْحِجَارَةِ اَوْ اَشَدُّ قَسْوَةً ؕ وَاِنَّ مِنَ الْحِجَارَةِ لَمَا يَتَفَجَّرُ مِنْهُ الْاَنْهٰرُ ؕ وَاِنَّ مِنْهَا لَمَا يَشَّقَّقُ فَيَخْرُجُ مِنْهُ الْمَآءُ ؕ

[a]5 : 14; 6 : 44; 57 : 17.

110-A. The clause may signify: This is how God gave Jesus a new lease of life after he was almost dead, *Mautā* being the plural of *Mait* which means, one like dead or near death (Lane). Here the word *Mautā* would be taken in this sense because according to the Qur'ān those actually dead never come back to life (21 : 96 & 23 : 101).

The verse may also be rendered as : Then We said, "Smite him (the murderer) for a part of his offence. Thus doth Allāh give life to the dead and show you His Signs that you may understand." According to this meaning this and the preceding verse will refer to the murder of a Muslim by the Jews at Medina. On his arrival at Medina the Holy Prophet had entered into a treaty of peace and mutual good relations with the Jews. But the growing prosperity and success of Islām gradually roused their jealousy and some of their leaders, Ka'b bin Ashraf being foremost among them, began secretly to excite their people against Muslims. A short time after the Battle of Badr a Muslim lady happened to go to the shop of a Jew to make some purchases. The shop-keeper behaved very insultingly towards her. The helpless lady cried for help. A Muslim who happened to be nearby went to her help and in the scuffle which followed the shop-keeper was killed, whereupon the Jews fell upon him and murdered him. When the case came to be investigated none of the miscreants who had taken part in the heinous act would admit the guilt and every one of them sought to shift the responsibility for it to others. This murder of a Muslim was not an isolated mischievous act on the part of the Jews. Their behaviour daily had grown insulting and provocative and they were always on the look out to create fresh disturbances (Hishām), and also secretly plotted the assassination of the Holy Prophet himself (Iṣābah). K'ab bin Ashraf was the arch-enemy and the chief instigator of all these disturbances and plots. He had even gone to Mecca and with his powerful eloquence had made the Quraish, who were smarting under their ignominious defeat at Badr, take a solemn oath with the skirts of the Ka'bah in their hands, that they would know no rest until they had destroyed Islām and its Founder. K'ab also got widely circulated most scurrilous poems against the ladies of the Holy Prophet's family. So, for his repeated acts of treachery and mischief and as a punishment for the death of the innocent Muslim he was ordered to be put to death. The sentence of death was only a partial punishment of the offence, the rest of the punishment being reserved for the Hereafter. By using the word *Qataltum* in the plural number, the Qur'ān holds the entire Jewish community of Medina responsible for the murder. For the sentence of death, however, the ring-leader was marked out, the pronoun *hu* referring to Ka'b. According to this meaning of the verse the words, *Thus doth Allāh give life to the dead* signify that retaliation is an effective form of giving life to the dead, for in this way the would-be assassins are prevented from further murders. That retaliation is a most potent means of giving life to the dead is alluded to in 2 : 180. Moreover, the Arabs of the "Days of Ignorance" regarded a murdered person whose blood was not avenged as dead and regarded as living the person whose blood was fully avenged. Says the famous Arab poet Ḥārith bin Ḥilzah : "*In Nabashtum mā Baina Malḥata wa'l Ṣāqib, Fīhā al-Amwātu wa'l Aḥyā'ū, i.e.*, if you dig out the graves between Malḥah and Ṣāqib, you will find therein dead as well as living, *i.e.*, those whose murder has been avenged.

111. The murder of the innocent Muslim referred to in the preceding verses sealed the fate of the Medinite Jews who thereafter became more and more hardened, their hearts becoming like stones, even worse. The verse goes on to say that even lifeless things like

that humble themselves for fear of Allāh. And Allāh is not unmindful of what you do.[112]

وَإِنَّ مِنْهَا لَمَا يَهْبِطُ مِنْ خَشْيَةِ اللّٰهِ ۗ وَمَا اللّٰهُ بِغَافِلٍ عَمَّا تَعْمَلُونَ ﴿٧٥﴾

76. Do you expect that they will believe you when a party of them hear the Word of Allāh, then [a]pervert it after they have understood it, and they *well* know *the consequences thereof*.

أَفَتَطْمَعُونَ أَنْ يُؤْمِنُوا لَكُمْ وَقَدْ كَانَ فَرِيقٌ مِنْهُمْ يَسْمَعُونَ كَلَامَ اللّٰهِ ثُمَّ يُحَرِّفُونَهُ مِنْ بَعْدِ مَا عَقَلُوهُ وَهُمْ يَعْلَمُونَ ﴿٧٦﴾

77. And [b]when they meet those who believe, they say, 'We believe,' and when they meet one another in private, they say, 'Do you inform them (the believers) of what Allāh has unfolded to you, that they may thereby argue with you before your Lord. Will you not then understand?'[113]

وَإِذَا لَقُوا الَّذِينَ آمَنُوا قَالُوا آمَنَّا ۖ وَإِذَا خَلَا بَعْضُهُمْ إِلَىٰ بَعْضٍ قَالُوا أَتُحَدِّثُونَهُمْ بِمَا فَتَحَ اللّٰهُ عَلَيْكُمْ لِيُحَاجُّوكُمْ بِهِ عِنْدَ رَبِّكُمْ ۚ أَفَلَا تَعْقِلُونَ ﴿٧٧﴾

78. Do they not know that [c]Allāh knows what they keep secret and what they make known?

أَوَلَا يَعْلَمُونَ أَنَّ اللّٰهَ يَعْلَمُ مَا يُسِرُّونَ وَمَا يُعْلِنُونَ ﴿٧٨﴾

[a]3 : 79; 4 : 47; 5 : 14, 42. [b]2 : 15; 3 : 120; 5 : 62 [c]11 : 6; 35 : 39.

stones are of some use, but the Jews have become so depraved that, far from performing any act of virtue out of a desire to be virtuous, they have not even involuntarily done anything that might be called virtuous. They have become worse than stones, for even from stones there comes out water which people profit by.

112. The remarks do not apply to the whole Jewish nation; for some of the Israelites were, no doubt, swayed by the fear of God. Of these the Qur'ān says, *of them* (*the hearts*) *there are some that humble themselves for fear of Allāh*, the pronoun *hā* standing for *Qulūb* (hearts) and not for *Ḥijārah* (stones). The Qur'ān contains several instances of what is termed *Intishār al-Ḍamā'ir*, *i.e.*, similar pronouns occurring in the same verse standing for different nouns (48 : 10).

113. The verse mentions another class of Jews who always acted hypocritically. When they mixed with Muslims, they chimed in with them from worldly motives, confirming the prophecies contained in their Scriptures about the Holy Prophet. But when they mixed with their own people, other members of the community would reproach them for their enlightening the Muslims on what God had revealed to them, *i.e.*, for letting the Muslims know the prophecies about the Holy Prophet which were contained in their own Scriptures.

79. And some of them are illiterate;[113A] they know not the Book but *their own* false notions and they *do nothing* but conjecture.

وَمِنْهُمْ أُمِّيُّونَ لَا يَعْلَمُونَ الْكِتٰبَ إِلَّا أَمَانِيَّ وَإِنْ هُمْ
إِلَّا يَظُنُّونَ ﴿٧٩﴾

80. Woe, therefore, to those who write the Book with their own hands and then say, 'This is from Allāh,' that they may take for it [a]a paltry price. Woe, then, to them for what their hands have written, and woe to them for what they earn.[114]

فَوَيْلٌ لِّلَّذِينَ يَكْتُبُونَ الْكِتٰبَ بِأَيْدِيهِمْ ثُمَّ يَقُولُونَ
هٰذَا مِنْ عِنْدِ اللّٰهِ لِيَشْتَرُوا بِهِ ثَمَنًا قَلِيلًا فَوَيْلٌ
لَّهُمْ مِّمَّا كَتَبَتْ أَيْدِيهِمْ وَوَيْلٌ لَّهُمْ مِّمَّا يَكْسِبُونَ ﴿٨٠﴾

81. And they say, [b]'The Fire shall not touch us except for a *small* number of days.'[115] Say, [c]'Have you taken a promise from Allāh? Then, Allāh will never break His promise. Or, do you say of Allāh what you know not?'

وَقَالُوا لَنْ تَمَسَّنَا النَّارُ إِلَّا أَيَّامًا مَّعْدُودَةً قُلْ
أَتَّخَذْتُمْ عِنْدَ اللّٰهِ عَهْدًا فَلَنْ يُّخْلِفَ اللّٰهُ عَهْدَهُ
أَمْ تَقُولُونَ عَلَى اللّٰهِ مَا لَا تَعْلَمُونَ ﴿٨١﴾

82. Aye! whoso does evil and is encompassed by his sins—those are the inmates of the Fire; therein shall they abide.

بَلٰى مَنْ كَسَبَ سَيِّئَةً وَّأَحَاطَتْ بِهِ خَطِيئَتُهُ فَأُولٰئِكَ
أَصْحٰبُ النَّارِ هُمْ فِيهَا خٰلِدُونَ ﴿٨٢﴾

83. But they who believe and do good works—those are the dwellers of Heaven; therein shall they abide.

وَالَّذِينَ آمَنُوا وَعَمِلُوا الصّٰلِحٰتِ أُولٰئِكَ أَصْحٰبُ الْجَنَّةِ
هُمْ فِيهَا خٰلِدُونَ ﴿٨٣﴾

[a]2 : 175; 3 : 200. [b]3 : 25. [c]54 : 44.

113A. *Ummiyyūn* signifies those who follow no revealed Book. The word is plural of *Ummiyy* which means, one who cannot read or write.

114. There were Jews who composed books or parts thereof and then gave them out as the Word of God. This malpractice was common among the Jews. In addition, therefore, to the canonical Books of the Bible, there are a number of books which are supposed by the Jews to have been revealed, so that it has now become impossible to distinguish the revealed Books from those not revealed.

115. After recounting some malpractices of the Jews, the Qur'ān proceeds to explain the root cause of their arrogance and hard-heartedness. These evil practices of the Jews, the Qur'ān points out, are due to their wrong notion that they were immune from punishment (Jew. Enc. under 'Gehenna'), or, if they will at all be punished, the punishment will be very slight and of very short duration. At the time of the Holy Prophet, a section of the Jews thought that their punishment would not last more than forty days. Others reduced it to seven days (Jarīr, under 2 : 81). "It is a received opinion among the Jews at present that no person (from among the Jews), be he ever so wicked, or of whatever sect, shall remain in Hell above eleven months or at most a year, except Dathan and Abiram and atheists (from among the Jews) who will be tormented there to all eternity" (Sale).

R. 10 84. And *remember the time* when [a]We took a covenant from the Children of Israel: 'You shall worship none but Allāh and be kind to parents and to kindred and orphans and the poor, and speak to men kindly and [b]observe Prayer, and pay the *Zakāt*,'[116] then you turned away in aversion, except a few of you.

وَإِذْ أَخَذْنَا مِيْثَاقَ بَنِيْٓ إِسْرَآءِيْلَ لَا تَعْبُدُوْنَ إِلَّا
اللّٰهَ وَبِالْوَالِدَيْنِ إِحْسَانًا وَّذِي الْقُرْبٰى وَالْيَتٰمٰى
وَالْمَسٰكِيْنِ وَقُوْلُوْا لِلنَّاسِ حُسْنًا وَّأَقِيْمُوا الصَّلٰوةَ
وَاٰتُوا الزَّكٰوةَ ۭ ثُمَّ تَوَلَّيْتُمْ إِلَّا قَلِيْلًا مِّنْكُمْ وَأَنْتُمْ
مُّعْرِضُوْنَ ﴿٨٤﴾

85. And *remember* when We took a covenant from you: 'You shall not shed each other's blood nor turn your people out of your homes,'[117] then you confirmed *it*; and you have been witness *to it*.

وَإِذْ أَخَذْنَا مِيْثَاقَكُمْ لَا تَسْفِكُوْنَ دِمَآءَكُمْ وَلَا
تُخْرِجُوْنَ أَنْفُسَكُمْ مِّنْ دِيَارِكُمْ ثُمَّ أَقْرَرْتُمْ وَأَنْتُمْ
تَشْهَدُوْنَ ﴿٨٥﴾

86. Yet you are those who slay one another and turn out a section of your people from their homes, backing up their enemies against them in sin and transgression. And if they come to you as captives, you ransom them, while their expulsion itself was unlawful for you. Do you, then, believe in a part of the Book and disbelieve in another part? What is then the reward of such among you as do so, except disgrace in the present life; and on the Day of Judgment they shall be driven to a most severe chastisement; and surely, Allāh is not unmindful of what you do.[118]

ثُمَّ أَنْتُمْ هٰٓؤُلَآءِ تَقْتُلُوْنَ أَنْفُسَكُمْ وَتُخْرِجُوْنَ فَرِيْقًا
مِّنْكُمْ مِّنْ دِيَارِهِمْ تَظٰهَرُوْنَ عَلَيْهِمْ بِالْإِثْمِ
وَالْعُدْوَانِ ۭ وَإِنْ يَّأْتُوْكُمْ أُسٰرٰى تُفٰدُوْهُمْ وَهُوَ
مُحَرَّمٌ عَلَيْكُمْ إِخْرَاجُهُمْ ۭ أَفَتُؤْمِنُوْنَ بِبَعْضِ
الْكِتٰبِ وَتَكْفُرُوْنَ بِبَعْضٍ ۚ فَمَا جَزَآءُ مَنْ يَّفْعَلُ
ذٰلِكَ مِنْكُمْ إِلَّا خِزْيٌ فِي الْحَيٰوةِ الدُّنْيَا ۚ وَيَوْمَ الْقِيٰمَةِ
يُرَدُّوْنَ إِلٰٓى أَشَدِّ الْعَذَابِ ۭ وَمَا اللّٰهُ بِغَافِلٍ عَمَّا
تَعْمَلُوْنَ ﴿٨٦﴾

[a]4 : 155; 5 : 13. [b]2 : 44, 111; 4 : 78; 6 : 73; 22 : 79; 24 : 57; 30 : 32.

116. The verse does not refer to any particular covenant but to a general covenant enjoining the Jews to give up the vices which were rife among them at that time and to lead a virtuous life (Exod. 20 : 3-6, 12; Lev. 19 : 17,18; Prov. 3 : 27, 28, 30; Deut. 6 : 13 & 14 : 29). In this verse, as everywhere else in the Qur'ān, the sequence of words follows the natural order of importance of the works mentioned.

117. The reference may be to the covenant between the Holy Prophet and the Jews of Medina by which both sides undertook to help each other against a common enemy and all disputes were to be referred to the Holy Prophet for decision (Muir's 'Life of Mohammad' & 'Sīrat' by Mirzā Bashīr Aḥmad, M.A.).

118. There lived in Medina in the time of the Holy Prophet three Jewish tribes, the Banū Qainuqā', the Banū Naḍīr and the Banū Quraiẓah; and two pagan tribes, the Aus and the Khazraj. Two of the Jewish tribes, Banū Qainuqā' and Banū Quraiẓah, sided with

87. These are they who have preferred the present life to the Hereafter. Their punishment shall not, therefore, be lightened, nor shall they be helped *in any other way*.

أُولٰٓئِكَ الَّذِيْنَ اشْتَرَوُا الْحَيٰوةَ الدُّنْيَا بِالْاٰخِرَةِ فَلَا يُخَفَّفُ عَنْهُمُ الْعَذَابُ وَلَا هُمْ يُنْصَرُوْنَ ﴿٨٧﴾ ع

11 88. And verily [a]We gave Moses the Book and [b]caused Messengers to follow in his footsteps after him; and to Jesus, son of Mary, [c]We gave manifest Signs, and strengthened him with [d]the Spirit of holiness.[119] Will you, then, every time a Messenger comes to you with what you yourselves desire not, behave arrogantly and treat some as liars and slay others?

وَلَقَدْ اٰتَيْنَا مُوْسَى الْكِتٰبَ وَقَفَّيْنَا مِنْ بَعْدِهٖ بِالرُّسُلِ ۫ وَاٰتَيْنَا عِيْسَى ابْنَ مَرْيَمَ الْبَيِّنٰتِ وَاَيَّدْنٰهُ بِرُوْحِ الْقُدُسِ ؕ اَفَكُلَّمَا جَآءَكُمْ رَسُوْلٌۢ بِمَا لَا تَهْوٰٓى اَنْفُسُكُمُ اسْتَكْبَرْتُمْ ۚ فَفَرِيْقًا كَذَّبْتُمْ ۫ وَفَرِيْقًا تَقْتُلُوْنَ ﴿٨٨﴾

89. They said, [e]'Our hearts are wrapped up in covers.' Nay, Allāh has cursed them for their disbelief. Little is that which they believe.

وَقَالُوْا قُلُوْبُنَا غُلْفٌ ؕ بَلْ لَّعَنَهُمُ اللّٰهُ بِكُفْرِهِمْ فَقَلِيْلًا مَّا يُؤْمِنُوْنَ ﴿٨٩﴾

90. And when there came to them a Book from Allāh, [f]fulfilling that which is with them—and before that they had prayed for victory[120] over the disbelievers—yet when there came to them [g]that which they knew *to be the truth*, they rejected it. The curse of Allāh be on the disbelievers.

وَلَمَّا جَآءَهُمْ كِتٰبٌ مِّنْ عِنْدِ اللّٰهِ مُصَدِّقٌ لِّمَا مَعَهُمْ ۙ وَكَانُوْا مِنْ قَبْلُ يَسْتَفْتِحُوْنَ عَلَى الَّذِيْنَ كَفَرُوْا ۚ فَلَمَّا جَآءَهُمْ مَّا عَرَفُوْا كَفَرُوْا بِهٖ ۫ فَلَعْنَةُ اللّٰهِ عَلَى الْكٰفِرِيْنَ ﴿٩٠﴾

[a]See 2 : 54. [b]5 : 47; 57 : 28. [c]2 : 254; 3 : 185; 5 : 111; 43 : 64. [d]16 : 103. [e]4 : 156; 41 : 6. [f]2 : 42,92,98,102; 3 : 82; 4 : 48; 35 : 32; 46 : 13. [g]2 : 147.

the Aus, and Banū Naḍīr with the Khazraj. Thus, whenever these pagan clans were at war with each other, the Jewish tribes were automatically involved. But, if during a war any Jews were taken prisoner by the pagans, the former would collect money by subscription and ransom them. They considered it improper for a Jew to remain in bondage with a Gentile. The Qur'ān objects to this practice by saying that their Faith not only forbids the enslavement of Jews, but also prohibits mutual warfare and murder in which they openly indulged and there could be nothing worse than to accept a portion of a Scripture and reject the rest; for, when one accepts a portion of a Scripture, it is proof of the fact that one is convinced of the truth of the whole. Thus rejection of a portion is clear evidence of a perverted mind. For prohibition of enslavement of Jews, see Lev. 25 : 39—43, 47-49, 54, 55; Neh. 5 : 8.

119. It is commonly believed that the Spirit of holiness is another name of the angel Gabriel (Jarīr & Kathīr). *Rūḥ al-Qudus* also means, the holy or blessed Word of God.

120. The verse signifies that Jews used to disclose to the pagan Arabs the fact that there were prophecies in their Scriptures about the advent of a Prophet who would spread the

91. Evil is that for which they have sold their souls—that they should disbelieve in what Allāh has revealed, grudging that Allāh should send down His grace on whomsoever of His servants He pleases. So [a]they have incurred wrath upon wrath; and there is an humiliating chastisement for the disbelievers.

بِئْسَمَا اشْتَرَوْا بِهٖٓ اَنْفُسَهُمْ اَنْ يَّكْفُرُوْا بِمَآ اَنْزَلَ اللّٰهُ
بَغْيًا اَنْ يُّنَزِّلَ اللّٰهُ مِنْ فَضْلِهٖ عَلٰى مَنْ يَّشَآءُ مِنْ
عِبَادِهٖ ۚ فَبَآءُوْ بِغَضَبٍ عَلٰى غَضَبٍ ؕ وَلِلْكٰفِرِيْنَ عَذَابٌ
مُّهِيْنٌ ﴿٩١﴾

92. And [b]when it is said to them, 'Believe in what Allāh has sent down,' they say, 'We believe in what has been sent down to us;' and they disbelieve in what *has been sent down* after that, yet it is the Truth, fulfilling that which is with them. Say, [c]"Why, then, did you seek to slay the Prophets of Allāh before this, if you were believers?'

وَاِذَا قِيْلَ لَهُمْ اٰمِنُوْا بِمَآ اَنْزَلَ اللّٰهُ قَالُوْا نُؤْمِنُ بِمَآ
اُنْزِلَ عَلَيْنَا وَيَكْفُرُوْنَ بِمَا وَرَآءَهٗ ۚ وَهُوَ الْحَقُّ
مُصَدِّقًا لِّمَا مَعَهُمْ ؕ قُلْ فَلِمَ تَقْتُلُوْنَ اَنْۢبِيَآءَ اللّٰهِ
مِنْ قَبْلُ اِنْ كُنْتُمْ مُّؤْمِنِيْنَ ﴿٩٢﴾

93. And Moses came to you with manifest Signs, then [d]you took the calf *for worship* in his absence, and you were transgressors.

وَلَقَدْ جَآءَكُمْ مُّوْسٰى بِالْبَيِّنٰتِ ثُمَّ اتَّخَذْتُمُ الْعِجْلَ
مِنْۢ بَعْدِهٖ وَاَنْتُمْ ظٰلِمُوْنَ ﴿٩٣﴾

[a]3 : 113; 5 : 61. [b]2 : 171. [c]3 : 113, 182. [d]2 : 52; 4 : 154; 7 : 149, 153; 20 : 98.

truth all over the world (Deut 18 : 18 & 28 : 1-2). But when that Prophet actually appeared, even those of them who had seen the Signs of God being fulfilled in his person turned away from him. Or the meaning may be that before the advent of the Holy Prophet the Jews used to pray fervently to God to raise a Prophet who should cause the true Faith to triumph over false Faiths (Hishām, i. 150). But when the Prophet for whom they had prayed actually came and the ascendancy of truth over falsehood became manifest, they refused to accept him; consequently bringing on their heads the curse of God.

94. And *remember the time* when We took a covenant from you and raised high above you the Mount,[121] *saying*, 'Hold firmly to what We have given you and hearken;' they said,[121A] 'We hear and we disobey;' and their hearts were saturated with *the love* of the calf[122] because of their disbelief. Say, 'Evil is that which your faith enjoins on you, if you are believers.'

وَاِذۡ اَخَذۡنَا مِيۡثَاقَكُمۡ وَرَفَعۡنَا فَوۡقَكُمُ الطُّوۡرَ خُذُوۡا مَاۤ اٰتَيۡنٰكُمۡ بِقُوَّةٍ وَّاسۡمَعُوۡا ؕ قَالُوۡا سَمِعۡنَا وَعَصَيۡنَا وَاُشۡرِبُوۡا فِىۡ قُلُوۡبِهِمُ الۡعِجۡلَ بِكُفۡرِهِمۡ ؕ قُلۡ بِئۡسَمَا يَاۡمُرُكُمۡ بِهٖۤ اِيۡمَانُكُمۡ اِنۡ كُنۡتُمۡ مُّؤۡمِنِيۡنَ ۝

95. Say, [b]'If the abode of the Hereafter with Allāh is *solely* for you to the exclusion of *all* other people, then wish for death, if you are truthful.'[122A]

قُلۡ اِنۡ كَانَتۡ لَكُمُ الدَّارُ الۡاٰخِرَةُ عِنۡدَ اللّٰهِ خَالِصَةً مِّنۡ دُوۡنِ النَّاسِ فَتَمَنَّوُا الۡمَوۡتَ اِنۡ كُنۡتُمۡ صٰدِقِيۡنَ ۝

96. But [c]never shall they wish for it, because of what their own hands have sent on before *them*; and Allāh knows the wrongdoers well.

وَلَنۡ يَّتَمَنَّوۡهُ اَبَدًۢا بِمَا قَدَّمَتۡ اَيۡدِيۡهِمۡ ؕ وَاللّٰهُ عَلِيۡمٌۢ بِالظّٰلِمِيۡنَ ۝

97. And thou shalt surely find them, of all people, the most covetous of life, even more than those who set up equals *with God*.[122B] Every one of them wishes that he may be granted a life of a thousand years, but his being granted *such* life [d]shall not remove him further away from the punishment; and Allāh sees all that they do.

وَلَتَجِدَنَّهُمۡ اَحۡرَصَ النَّاسِ عَلٰى حَيٰوةٍ ۚۛ وَمِنَ الَّذِيۡنَ اَشۡرَكُوۡا ۚۛ يَوَدُّ اَحَدُهُمۡ لَوۡ يُعَمَّرُ اَلۡفَ سَنَةٍ ۚ وَمَا هُوَ بِمُزَحۡزِحِهٖ مِنَ الۡعَذَابِ اَنۡ يُّعَمَّرَ ؕ وَاللّٰهُ بَصِيۡرٌۢ بِمَا يَعۡمَلُوۡنَ ۝

---

[a]2 : 64; 4 : 155; 7 : 172.   [b]2 : 112;   62 : 7.   [c]62 : 8.   [d]62 : 9.

121. See 105.

121A. The words signify that they practically refused to obey. For the meaning of *Qāla* see 57.

122. The expression *Ushriba Fī Qalbihī Ḥubbu Fulānin* means, the love of such a person permeated his heart (Aqrab). The word is so used because love is like alcohol that intoxicates one who partakes of it. The words used in the text mean, the love of the calf had sunk deep into their hearts.

122A. The meaning is that if the Jews are convinced that they are justified in their claim that God will bestow His favours upon them alone, and that the Holy Prophet's claim is false, then they should invoke death and destruction upon the liar.

122B. The pagans were less cringingly attached to the present life than the Jews because unlike the Jews they did not believe in the life after death and therefore had no fear of punishment after death.

R. 2 98. Say, 'Whoever is an enemy to Gabriel[123] — for he it is who [a]has caused it to descend on thy heart by the command of Allāh, [b]fulfilling that *revelation* which precedes it, and is a guidance and glad tidings to the believers.

قُلْ مَنْ كَانَ عَدُوًّا لِّجِبْرِيْلَ فَإِنَّهُ نَزَّلَهُ عَلَى قَلْبِكَ
بِإِذْنِ اللّٰهِ مُصَدِّقًا لِّمَا بَيْنَ يَدَيْهِ وَهُدًى وَّبُشْرٰى
لِلْمُؤْمِنِيْنَ ﴿٩٨﴾

99. [c]"Whoever is an enemy to Allāh, and His angels, and His Messengers, and Gabriel, and Michael,[124] then, surely, Allāh is an enemy to *such* disbelievers.'[125]

مَنْ كَانَ عَدُوًّا لِّلّٰهِ وَمَلٰٓئِكَتِهٖ وَرُسُلِهٖ وَجِبْرِيْلَ
وَمِيْكٰىلَ فَإِنَّ اللّٰهَ عَدُوٌّ لِّلْكٰفِرِيْنَ ﴿٩٩﴾

100. And surely We have sent down to thee manifest Signs, and none disbelieves in them but the disobedient.

وَلَقَدْ أَنْزَلْنَآ إِلَيْكَ اٰيٰتٍۢ بَيِّنٰتٍ ۚ وَمَا يَكْفُرُ بِهَآ إِلَّا
الْفٰسِقُوْنَ ﴿١٠٠﴾

101. What! [d]every time they make a covenant, will a party among them throw it aside? Nay, most of them have no faith.

أَوَكُلَّمَا عٰهَدُوْا عَهْدًا نَّبَذَهٗ فَرِيْقٌ مِّنْهُمْ ۭ بَلْ
أَكْثَرُهُمْ لَا يُؤْمِنُوْنَ ﴿١٠١﴾

102. And *now* that there has come to them a Messenger from Allāh, [e]fulfilling that which is with them, a party of the people to whom the Book was given [f]have thrown the Book of Allāh behind their backs, as if they know *it* not.

وَلَمَّا جَآءَهُمْ رَسُوْلٌ مِّنْ عِنْدِ اللّٰهِ مُصَدِّقٌ لِّمَا
مَعَهُمْ نَبَذَ فَرِيْقٌ مِّنَ الَّذِيْنَ أُوْتُوا الْكِتٰبَ ۙ كِتٰبَ
اللّٰهِ وَرَآءَ ظُهُوْرِهِمْ كَأَنَّهُمْ لَا يَعْلَمُوْنَ ﴿١٠٢﴾

[a]26 : 194, 195. [b]See 2 : 90. [c]58 : 6. [d]3 : 188. [e]See 2 : 90. [f]3 : 188.

123. *Jibrīl* is a compound word, made up of *Jabr* and *Īl*, and means—a brave man of God, or a servant of God. *Jabr* in Hebrew is *Geber* which means, 'a servant, and *Īl* means 'the Mighty; the Powerful' (Hebrew English-Lexicon by William Geseneus; Bukhārī, chap. on Tafsir; and Aqrab). According to Ibn 'Abbās the other name of Jibrīl is 'Abd Allāh (Jarīr). Gabriel being the chief among the angels (Manthūr) was the bearer of the Quranic Revelation. See also The Larger Edition of the Commentary. According to Commentators of the Holy Qur'ān *Jibrīl* is synonymous with *Rūḥ al-Qudus* and *Rūḥ al-Amīn*. According to the Bible also the function of Gabriel is to convey Messages of God to His servants (Dan. 8 : 16; 9 : 21 & Luke 1 : 19). The Qur'ān, as the present verse points out, assigns the same function to Gabriel. But in some later Jewish writings he is described as "the angel of fire and thunder" (Enc. Bib. under Gabriel). In the Holy Prophet's time the Jews looked upon Gabriel as their enemy and as an angel of wars, calamities and hardships (Jarīr & Musnad).

124. *Mīkāl* is also one of the chief angels. The word is considered as being a combination of *Mīk* and *Īl* which means, who is like God, *i.e.*, there is none like God (Jew. Enc. & Bukhārī). The Jews looked upon Michael as their favourite angel (Jew. Enc.) and as the angle of peacc and plenty, rain and herbage (Kathīr) and is considered to be associated chiefly with the work of sustaining the world.

125. Angels constitute an important link in the spiritual chain and he, who breaks even one link of the spiritual chain or manifests ill-will against any single unit of the spiritual system, in fact, severs his connection with the whole system. Such a one deprives himself of the favours and blessings which are bestowed upon the true servants of God and renders

103. And they pursue[126] *the course* which was pursued by the rebellious *men* against[127] the Kingdom of Solomon. And Solomon did not disbelieve; but *it was* the rebellious ones *who* disbelieved. They taught people falsehood and deception.[128] And *they claim that they follow* what was revealed to the two[129] angels in Babylon, Hārūt and Mārūt.[130] But these two taught no one *anything* until they had said, 'We are but a trial, *from Allāh*, do not, therefore, reject *what we say*. So men learnt from them that by which they made a distinction between man and his wife, but they harmed no one thereby, except by the command of Allāh; *on the contrary*, these *people* (the opponents of the Holy Prophet) are learning that which would harm

وَاتَّبَعُوْا مَا تَتْلُوا الشَّيٰطِيْنُ عَلٰى مُلْكِ سُلَيْمٰنَ ۚ وَ
مَا كَفَرَ سُلَيْمٰنُ وَلٰكِنَّ الشَّيٰطِيْنَ كَفَرُوْا يُعَلِّمُوْنَ
النَّاسَ السِّحْرَ ۗ وَمَآ اُنْزِلَ عَلَى الْمَلَكَيْنِ بِبَابِلَ
هَارُوْتَ وَمَارُوْتَ ۗ وَمَا يُعَلِّمٰنِ مِنْ اَحَدٍ حَتّٰى
يَقُوْلَآ اِنَّمَا نَحْنُ فِتْنَةٌ فَلَا تَكْفُرْ ۗ فَيَتَعَلَّمُوْنَ مِنْهُمَا
مَا يُفَرِّقُوْنَ بِهٖ بَيْنَ الْمَرْءِ وَزَوْجِهٖ ۗ وَمَا هُمْ بِضَآرِّيْنَ
بِهٖ مِنْ اَحَدٍ اِلَّا بِاِذْنِ اللّٰهِ ۗ وَيَتَعَلَّمُوْنَ مَا يَضُرُّهُمْ

himself deserving of the punishment decreed for transgressors.

126. *Talautu-hū* means, I followed him (Lane).

127. *'Alā* gives the sense of *fī*, *i.e.*, "in" or "during" and "against" (Mughnī). The particle is also used in the Qur'ān in the sense of "in conformity with" (2 : 113); assigning a cause (2 : 186); in the sense of *fī* (28 : 16) and *min* (83 : 3). *Talā 'Alaihi* also means, he lied against him (Tāj, Muḥīṭ, & Raḍi).

128. *Siḥr* means, a crafty device ; mischief; enchantment; producing what is false in the form of truth ; any event of which the cause is hidden and which is imagined to be different from what it really is (Lane). Thus every falsehood, deceit or crafty device which is meant to hide the real object from public view is included in *Sihr*.

129.. The word "two angels" here signifies two holy men (12 : 32), because the two angels are here mentioned as teaching something to the people and angels do not live among men and do not have free intercourse with them (17 : 95 ; 21 : 8).

130. Hārūt and Mārūt are both descriptive names, the former being derived from *Harata*, (*i.e.*, he tore up —Aqrab) means, one who tears up; and the latter derived from *Marata*, (*i.e.*, he broke) means, one who breaks. These names signify that the object of the appearance of these holy men was to 'tear asunder' and 'break' the glory and power of the empire of the enemies of the Israelites. These holy men told the new members, at the time of initiation, that they were a sort of trial from God, serving to differentiate between the good and the bad. They confined the membership of their society to the males only. The verse signifies that the Jews in the time of the Holy Prophet indulged in the same mischievous devices and practices which characterized their forefathers in the days of Solomon. It further says that the mischief-mongers in Solomon's time were those rebellious men who called him a disbeliever. The verse clears Solomon of the accusation of disbelief. It adds that the mischief-mongers in Solomon's time taught their associates such signs as conveyed to them meanings quite different from those generally understood, for the purpose of deceiving people and concealing their real designs. The verse alludes to those secret plots which the enemies of Solomon hatched against him and by which they sought to break up his Empire. It is implied that the Medinite Jews are now resorting to the selfsame vile tactics against the Holy Prophet but they will never succeed in their evil designs.

them and do them no good.[130A] And they have certainly known that he who trafficks therein has no share *of good* in the Hereafter; and surely, evil is that for which they have sold their souls; if only they knew.

وَلَا يَنفَعُهُمْ ۚ وَلَقَدْ عَلِمُوا لَمَنِ اشْتَرٰىهُ مَا لَهُ فِي
الْاٰخِرَةِ مِنْ خَلَاقٍ ۚ وَلَبِئْسَ مَا شَرَوْا بِهٖ أَنفُسَهُمْ ۚ
لَوْ كَانُوا يَعْلَمُونَ ﴿١٠٣﴾

104. And [a]if they had believed and acted righteously, better surely, would have been their reward from Allāh, if only they knew.

وَلَوْ أَنَّهُمْ اٰمَنُوا وَاتَّقَوْا لَمَثُوبَةٌ مِّنْ عِندِ اللّٰهِ خَيْرٌ ۚ
لَّوْ كَانُوا يَعْلَمُونَ ﴿١٠٤﴾ ع ١٢ ١٢

R. 13 105. O ye who believe, [b]say not, *to the Prophet*, 'Rā'inā,'[131] but say 'Unẓurnā' and hearken unto him. And for the disbelievers is a painful punishment.

يٰٓأَيُّهَا الَّذِينَ اٰمَنُوا لَا تَقُولُوا رَاعِنَا وَقُولُوا انظُرْنَا
وَاسْمَعُوا ۗ وَلِلْكٰفِرِينَ عَذَابٌ أَلِيمٌ ﴿١٠٥﴾

[a]3 : 180; 5 : 66,67. [b]4: 47.

130A. When the Jews saw that the power of Islām was steadily expanding and opposition to it in Arabia had completely broken down and they could not arrest or retard its progress, they began to excite outsiders against it. Oppressed and persecuted by Christian rulers they had taken refuge in Persia and had shifted their religious centre from Judah to Babylonia (Hutchinson's History of the Nations, p. 550). Gradually, they came to exercise great influence at the court of the Persian Monarchs and began to hatch plots against Islām. When Chosroes II received a letter from the Holy Prophet inviting him to accept Islām, they succeeded in instigating him to issue orders to Bādhān, the Governor of Yemen, which was then a province of Persia, to arrest and send the Holy Prophet in chains to the Persian court. It is to these plots and machinations of the Jews in the Prophet's time that the verse alludes. Their attention is invited to the fact that their forefathers had also hatched plots first against Solomon when some members of their community set up against him societies in which secret signs and symbols were taught (I Kings, 11 : 29-32; I Kings. 11 : 14, 23, 26; II Chron. 10 : 2-4). The second occasion when they resorted to secret societies was during their captivity in Babylon in the time of King Nebuchadnezzar. The holy men referred to in the verse were Haggai, the Prophet, and Zechariah, the son of Iddo (Ezra, 5: 1). These holy men confined membership of their society to males and told the new members at the time of initiation that they were a sort of trial from God and that the Israelites should not, therefore, refuse to believe what they said. When Cyrus, King of Media and Persia, rose to power, the Israelites entered into a secret agreement with him which greatly facilitated his conquest of Babylon. In return for this service Cyrus not only allowed them to return to Jerusalem but also helped them in rebuilding the Temple of Solomon (Historians' History of the World, ii. 126). The verse hints that the efforts of the Jews on two previous occasions had met with different results. On the first occasion their conspiracy being directed against Solomon, had ended in the total loss of their prestige and finally in their banishment to Babylon. On the second occasion, they took a similar course under two inspired personages and were successful. Hence, in order to indicate whether the efforts of the Jews against the Holy Prophet would meet with failure, as they did in the days of Solomon, or with success as in Babylon, the Qur'ān says, *the opponents of the Holy Prophet are learning that which would harm them and do them no good*, hinting that they will not be successful as their forefathers were in Babylon.

131. The word *Rā'ınā* belongs to the measure of *Mufā'alah* which generally gives the sense of reciprocity, denoting two parties standing almost on the same level, and may mean, "have regard for us that we may have regard for you." Or being traced to the root *Rā'in* which means, a foolish or conceited fellow, the word signifies: 'O fool ' or 'O conceited fellow.' As this expression involved disrespect to the Holy Prophet, God forbids Muslims to

106. They, who disbelieve from among the People of the Book, or from among those who associate gods *with Allāh*, desire not that any good should be sent down to you from your Lord; but [a]Allāh chooses for His mercy whomsoever He pleases; and Allāh is Lord of exceeding bounty.

مَا يَوَدُّ الَّذِيْنَ كَفَرُوْا مِنْ اَهْلِ الْكِتٰبِ وَلَا الْمُشْرِكِيْنَ
اَنْ يُّنَزَّلَ عَلَيْكُمْ مِّنْ خَيْرٍ مِّنْ رَّبِّكُمْ ؕ وَاللّٰهُ يَخْتَصُّ
بِرَحْمَتِهٖ مَنْ يَّشَآءُ ؕ وَاللّٰهُ ذُو الْفَضْلِ الْعَظِيْمِ ﴿١٠٦﴾

107. [b]Whatever message[131A] We abrogate[132] or cause to be forgotten, We bring one better than that or the like thereof. Knowest thou not that Allāh has the power to do all that He wills ?

مَا نَنْسَخْ مِنْ اٰيَةٍ اَوْ نُنْسِهَا نَاْتِ بِخَيْرٍ مِّنْهَآ اَوْ
مِثْلِهَا ؕ اَلَمْ تَعْلَمْ اَنَّ اللّٰهَ عَلٰى كُلِّ شَیْءٍ قَدِيْرٌ ﴿١٠٧﴾

[a]3 : 75. [b]16 : 102.

use such words, and advises them to use language which is respectful and unequivocal, such as the word *Unẓurnā* meaning 'wait for us.' After mentioning the intrigues which the Jews of Arabia had carried on with outsiders to ruin the mission of the Holy Prophet, the Qur'ān proceeds to illustrate in this verse such of their machinations as they resorted to in order to belittle the Holy Prophet and sow dissension and discord among Muslims. An apparently minor illustration is selected to emphasize the fact that where the spirit of a people is concerned, sometimes very small things bring about dangerous results which undermine among them the spirit of discipline and respect for authority.

131A. *Āyah* means, message, sign, command or a verse of the Qur'ān (Lane).

132. It is mistakenly inferred from this verse that some verses of the Qur'ān have been abrogated. The conclusion is patently erroneous and unwarranted. There is nothing in this verse to indicate that the word *Āyah* refers to Quranic verses. Both in the preceding and the following verses, a reference is made to the People of the Book and their jealousies against the new Revelation which shows that the *Āyah* spoken of in this verse as being abrogated, refers to the previous Revelations. It is pointed out that the previous Scriptures contained two kinds of commandments : (a) Those which, owing to changed conditions and to the universality of the new Revelation, required abrogation. (b) Those containing eternal truths which needed resuscitation so that people might be reminded of the forgotten truth. It was, therefore, necessary to abrogate certain portions of those Scriptures and bring in their place new ones, and also to restore the lost ones. So, God abrogated some portions of the previous Revelations, substituting them with new and better ones, and at the same time re-introduced the missing portions by similar ones. This is the meaning which is consistent with the context and the general spirit of the Quranic teaching. The Qur'ān has abrogated all previous Scriptures; for, in view of the changed conditions of mankind, it has brought a new Law which is not only better than all the old Laws, but is also meant for all men for all times. An inferior teaching with a limited mission must give place to a superior teaching with a universal mission. In the verse the word *Nansakh* (We abrogate) relates to the word *Bi-Khairin* (one better) and the word *Nunsihā* (We cause to be forgotten) relates to the word *Bi-Mithlihā* (the like thereof), meaning that when God abrogates a certain thing He brings a better one in its place and when He causes a thing to be forgotten, He resuscitates it. It is admitted by Jewish scholars themselves that after the Israelites were carried away in captivity to Babylon by Nebuchadnezzar, the whole of the Pentateuch was lost (Enc. Bib.).

108. Knowest thou not that [a]the Kingdom of the heavens and the earth belongs to Allāh *alone*? And there is no protector or helper for you beside Allāh.

أَلَمْ تَعْلَمْ أَنَّ اللّٰهَ لَهُ مُلْكُ السَّمٰوٰتِ وَالْأَرْضِ ۗ وَ
مَا لَكُمْ مِّنْ دُوْنِ اللّٰهِ مِنْ وَّلِيٍّ وَّلَا نَصِيْرٍ ﴿١٠٨﴾

109. [b]Would you question[133] the Messenger sent to you as Moses was questioned before this? And whoever takes disbelief in exchange for belief has undoubtedly gone astray from the right path.

أَمْ تُرِيْدُوْنَ أَنْ تَسْـَٔلُوْا رَسُوْلَكُمْ كَمَا سُئِلَ مُوْسٰى مِنْ
قَبْلُ ۗ وَمَنْ يَّتَبَدَّلِ الْكُفْرَ بِالْإِيْمَانِ فَقَدْ ضَلَّ سَوَآءَ
السَّبِيْلِ ﴿١٠٩﴾

110. Many of the People of the Book wish, out of *sheer* envy from themselves, [c]that, after you have believed, they could turn you again into disbelievers after the truth has become manifest to them. But [d]forgive and overlook till [e]Allāh brings His decree. Surely, Allāh has the power to do all that He wills.

وَدَّ كَثِيْرٌ مِّنْ أَهْلِ الْكِتٰبِ لَوْ يَرُدُّوْنَكُمْ مِّنْ بَعْدِ
إِيْمَانِكُمْ كُفَّارًا ۚ حَسَدًا مِّنْ عِنْدِ أَنْفُسِهِمْ
مِّنْ بَعْدِ مَا تَبَيَّنَ لَهُمُ الْحَقُّ ۚ فَاعْفُوْا وَاصْفَحُوْا
حَتّٰى يَأْتِيَ اللّٰهُ بِأَمْرِهٖ ۗ إِنَّ اللّٰهَ عَلٰى كُلِّ شَيْءٍ قَدِيْرٌ ﴿١١٠﴾ الثلثة

111. And [f]observe Prayer and pay the *Zakāt*; and [g]whatever good you send on before you for yourselves, you shall find it with Allāh; surely, Allāh sees all that you do.

وَأَقِيْمُوا الصَّلٰوةَ وَاٰتُوا الزَّكٰوةَ ۗ وَمَا تُقَدِّمُوْا لِأَنْفُسِكُمْ
مِّنْ خَيْرٍ تَجِدُوْهُ عِنْدَ اللّٰهِ ۗ إِنَّ اللّٰهَ بِمَا تَعْمَلُوْنَ
بَصِيْرٌ ﴿١١١﴾

112. And they say, [h]'None shall ever enter Heaven unless he be a Jew or a Christian.'[134] These are their vain desires. Say, 'Produce your proof, if you are truthful.'

وَقَالُوْا لَنْ يَّدْخُلَ الْجَنَّةَ إِلَّا مَنْ كَانَ هُوْدًا أَوْ
نَصٰرٰى ۗ تِلْكَ أَمَانِيُّهُمْ ۗ قُلْ هَاتُوْا بُرْهَانَكُمْ إِنْ
كُنْتُمْ صٰدِقِيْنَ ﴿١١٢﴾

---

[a]3 : 190; 5 : 41; 7 : 159; 9 : 116; 43 : 86; 57 : 6. [b]4 : 154. [c]3 : 101, 150; 4 : 90. [d]5 : 14. [e]5 : 53 ; 16 : 34. [f]See 2 : 4. [g]73 : 21. [h]2 : 95; 62 : 7.

---

133. This verse mentions another artifice which the Jews employed to overthrow the mission of the Holy Prophet. They asked him absurd and silly questions as had no bearing on religion. This they did to inoculate Muslims with the spirit of stupid questioning, so that the dignity of faith should suffer and they may fall victim to doubts.

134. The Jews and The Christians both suffer from the delusion that only a Jew or a Christian could obtain salvation.

113. Nay, [a]whoever submits himself[135] completely to Allāh and he is the doer of good, shall have his reward from his Lord. [b]No fear *shall come* upon such, neither shall they grieve.

بَلٰى مَنْ اَسْلَمَ وَجْهَهٗ لِلّٰهِ وَهُوَ مُحْسِنٌ فَلَهٗۤ اَجْرُهٗ
عِنْدَ رَبِّهٖ ۪ وَلَا خَوْفٌ عَلَيْهِمْ وَلَا هُمْ يَحْزَنُوْنَ ﴿۱۱۳﴾ ع ۱۳

R.,14 114. And the Jews say, [c]'The Christians *stand* on nothing' and the Christians say, [d]'The Jews *stand* on nothing;'[136] while they *both* read the *same* Book. Even thus said those, who had no knowledge, like what they say. But Allāh shall judge between them on the Day of Resurrection concerning that wherein they disagree.

وَقَالَتِ الْيَهُوْدُ لَيْسَتِ النَّصٰرٰى عَلٰى شَيْءٍ ۪ وَّقَالَتِ
النَّصٰرٰى لَيْسَتِ الْيَهُوْدُ عَلٰى شَيْءٍ ۙ وَّهُمْ يَتْلُوْنَ الْكِتٰبَ ۭ
كَذٰلِكَ قَالَ الَّذِيْنَ لَا يَعْلَمُوْنَ مِثْلَ قَوْلِهِمْ ۚ فَاللّٰهُ
يَحْكُمُ بَيْنَهُمْ يَوْمَ الْقِيٰمَةِ فِيْمَا كَانُوْا فِيْهِ يَخْتَلِفُوْنَ ﴿۱۱۴﴾

115. And who is more unjust than he who prohibits the name of Allāh being glorified in [e]Allāh's temples and strives to ruin[137] them? It was not proper for such *men* to enter therein except in fear. For them is disgrace in this world; and theirs shall be a great punishment in the next.

وَمَنْ اَظْلَمُ مِمَّنْ مَّنَعَ مَسٰجِدَ اللّٰهِ اَنْ يُّذْكَرَ فِيْهَا
اسْمُهٗ وَسَعٰى فِيْ خَرَابِهَا ۭ اُولٰٓئِكَ مَا كَانَ لَهُمْ اَنْ
يَّدْخُلُوْهَآ اِلَّا خَآئِفِيْنَ ۥ لَهُمْ فِي الدُّنْيَا خِزْيٌ وَّلَهُمْ
فِي الْاٰخِرَةِ عَذَابٌ عَظِيْمٌ ﴿۱۱۵﴾

[a]4 : 126. [b]See 2 : 63. [c]5 : 69. [d]5 : 69. [e]9 : 17, 18 ; 22 : 26 ; 72 : 19, 20.

135. *Wajh* means, face; the thing itself; object and motive; deed or action to which a man directs his attention; the desired way; favour or countenance (Aqrab).

The verse alludes to the three important stages of perfect righteousness, *i.e.*, *Fanā'* (self-annihilation); *Baqā'* (regeneration); and *Liqā'* (union with God). The words, "submits himself completely to Allāh," mean that all our powers and organs and whatever belongs to us should be surrendered completely to God and devoted to His service. This state is known as *Fanā'* or death which a true Muslim must bring on himself. The second clause "and he is the doer of good" alludes to the state of *Baqā'* or regeneration, for when a man gets himself lost in the love of God and all his worldly designs and desires are extinguished, he is, as it were, granted a new life which may be called *Baqā'* or regeneration. He then lives for God and for the service of man. The concluding words describe the third and the highest stage of goodness—the stage of *Liqā'* or union with God which is also termed as "soul at rest," or *Nafs Muṭma'innah* in the Qur'ān (89 : 28).

136. *Shai'* means, a thing; anything good; concern; what is willed (Lane).

Nothing is more foreign to the whole spirit of Islām than opposition to truth. Islām teaches that all Faiths possess certain truths and a religion is called true not because it has a monopoly of truth but because it possesses the whole truth and is free from all forms of untruth. While claiming to be a perfect and complete religion, Islām frankly acknowledges the truths and virtues other Faiths possess.

137. The verse constitutes a strong indictment of those who carry their religious differences to such extremes that they do not even refrain from perpetrating outrages against

116. [a]To Allāh belong the East and the West;[138] so whithersoever you turn, there will be the face of Allāh. Surely, Allāh is Bountiful, All-Knowing

وَلِلّٰهِ الْمَشْرِقُ وَالْمَغْرِبُ ۚ فَأَيْنَمَا تُوَلُّوْا فَثَمَّ وَجْهُ اللّٰهِ ۚ إِنَّ اللّٰهَ وَاسِعٌ عَلِيْمٌ ﴿١١٦﴾

117. And they say, [b]'Allāh has taken *to Himself* a son.'[139] Holy is He! Nay, everything in the heavens and the earth belongs to Him. [c]To Him are all obedient.

وَقَالُوا اتَّخَذَ اللّٰهُ وَلَدًا ۙ سُبْحٰنَهٗ ۚ بَلْ لَّهٗ مَا فِي السَّمٰوٰتِ وَالْأَرْضِ ۚ كُلٌّ لَّهٗ قٰنِتُوْنَ ﴿١١٧﴾

118. He is [d]the Originator[140] of the heavens and the earth. When He decrees a thing, [e]He only says to it, 'Be,' and it is.

بَدِيْعُ السَّمٰوٰتِ وَالْأَرْضِ ۚ وَإِذَا قَضٰٓى أَمْرًا فَإِنَّمَا يَقُوْلُ لَهٗ كُنْ فَيَكُوْنُ ﴿١١٨﴾

[a]2 : 143; 26 : 29; 55 : 18. [b]4 : 172; 6 : 101, 102; 10 : 69; 17 : 112; 18 : 5; 19 : 36, 89, 90; 21 : 27; 25 : 3; 39 : 5; 43 : 82. [c]30 : 27. [d]6: 102. [e]3 : 48; 6 : 74; 16 : 41; 36 : 83; 40 : 69.

the places of worship belonging to other creeds. They hinder people from worshipping God in their sacred places and even go so far as to destroy their temples. Such acts of violence are denounced here in strong terms and a lesson of tolerance and broad-mindedness is inculcated. The Qur'ān recognizes for all men the free and unrestricted right to worship God in a place of worship, for a temple or a mosque is a place dedicated to the worship of God, and the person who prevents other men from worshipping Him in it, in fact, contributes to its ruin and desolation.

138. The verse embodies a prophecy that Islām will spread first in the East and then, in the Latter Days it will begin to penetrate in the West.

139. The words " son of God" metaphorically used in Jewish religious literature in the sense of "a beloved servant of God" or "a Prophet" subsequently came to bear a literal connotation (Luke 20 : 36 ; Matt. 5 : 9, 45, 48 ; Deut. 14 : 1 ; Exod. 4 : 22 ; Gal. 3 : 26 ; etc.). If God has a son, He must be subject to sexual desire and need a wife and be divisible, because the son is a part of the father's body. Again, He must be subject to death because the procreation of species, which attribution of a son to God implies, is the characteristic of perishable things. Islām repudiates all such ideas; for according to it God is holy and free from all defects.

140. This attribute not only constitutes a contradiction of the Christian dogma of the godhead of Jesus but also effectively repudiates the Hindu theory that soul and matter are primeval and eternal. God is the Creator of the heavens and the earth which means that He did not require the help of a son, and for that matter of anybody else, for creating the universe. (2) He is the Originator of the universe, *i.e.*, He created all things out of nothing, without a pre-existing model and without pre-existing matter. (3) He is All-Powerful, *i.e.*, whenever He decrees that a certain thing should come into being, it does come into being in conformity with His decree and design. The verse does not necessarily mean, as is sometimes erroneously understood, that when God decrees that a certain thing should come into being, it comes into being all at once. What it means is that when God decrees a thing, nothing can thwart His decree.

119. And those who have no knowledge say, 'Why does not Allāh speak to us, or [a]a Sign[141] come to us direct?' Likewise said those before them *what was* similar to their saying. Their hearts are all alike. We have certainly made the Signs plain for a people who firmly believe.

وَقَالَ الَّذِيْنَ لَا يَعْلَمُوْنَ لَوْلَا يُكَلِّمُنَا اللّٰهُ اَوْ تَاْتِيْنَآ
اٰيَةٌ ۗ كَذٰلِكَ قَالَ الَّذِيْنَ مِنْ قَبْلِهِمْ مِّثْلَ قَوْلِهِمْ ۘ
تَشَابَهَتْ قُلُوْبُهُمْ ۗ قَدْ بَيَّنَّا الْاٰيٰتِ لِقَوْمٍ يُّوْقِنُوْنَ ﴿١١٩﴾

120. We have sent thee with the Truth, [b]as a bearer of glad tidings and a Warner. And thou wilt not be questioned concerning the inmates of Hell.

اِنَّآ اَرْسَلْنٰكَ بِالْحَقِّ بَشِيْرًا وَّنَذِيْرًا ۙ وَّلَا تُسْئَلُ عَنْ
اَصْحٰبِ الْجَحِيْمِ ﴿١٢٠﴾

121. And the Jews will never be pleased with thee, nor the Christians, unless thou followest their creed. Say, 'Surely, Allāh's guidance alone is the *true* guidance,' And if thou follow their evil desires after the knowledge that has come to thee, thou shalt have from Allāh no friend nor helper.

وَلَنْ تَرْضٰى عَنْكَ الْيَهُوْدُ وَلَا النَّصٰرٰى حَتّٰى تَتَّبِعَ
مِلَّتَهُمْ ۗ قُلْ اِنَّ هُدَى اللّٰهِ هُوَ الْهُدٰى ۗ وَلَئِنِ
اتَّبَعْتَ اَهْوَآءَهُمْ بَعْدَ الَّذِيْ جَآءَكَ مِنَ الْعِلْمِ ۙ
مَالَكَ مِنَ اللّٰهِ مِنْ وَّلِيٍّ وَّلَا نَصِيْرٍ ﴿١٢١﴾

122. [d]They, to whom We have given the Book, follow it as it ought to be followed;[142] it is these that believe therein. And whoso believes not therein, these are they who are the losers.

اَلَّذِيْنَ اٰتَيْنٰهُمُ الْكِتٰبَ يَتْلُوْنَهٗ حَقَّ تِلَاوَتِهٖ ۗ اُولٰٓئِكَ
يُؤْمِنُوْنَ بِهٖ ۗ وَمَنْ يَّكْفُرْ بِهٖ فَاُولٰٓئِكَ هُمُ الْخٰسِرُوْنَ ﴿١٢٢﴾ ع

R. 15 123. O Children of Israel! [e]remember My favours which I bestowed upon you, and that [f]I exalted you above all the nations *of the time*.

يٰبَنِيْٓ اِسْرَآءِيْلَ اذْكُرُوْا نِعْمَتِيَ الَّتِيْٓ اَنْعَمْتُ عَلَيْكُمْ
وَاَنِّيْ فَضَّلْتُكُمْ عَلَى الْعٰلَمِيْنَ ﴿١٢٣﴾

---

[a]6 : 38; 20 : 135; 21 : 6; 43 : 54. [b]5 : 20; 6 : 49; 17 : 106; 33 : 46. [c]2 : 146; 13 : 38. [d]3:114. [e]See 2:41. [f]See 2:48.

---

141. It may be noted that whenever disbelievers are spoken of as demanding a Sign, the word "Sign" means either a Sign of their own devising or a Sign of punishment (21 : 6; 6 : 38; 13 : 28; 20 : 134, 135; 29 : 51).

142. The words refer to Muslims and not to Jews and Christians, because it is the Muslims who are the true and sincere followers of the Qur'ān and not the Jews or the Christians who refused to believe in it and rejected it as a piece of fabrication (Qatādah). This meaning of *Yatlūna* is supported by Ibn 'Abbās, 'Abd Allāh bin Mas'ūd, 'Aṭā, and 'Ikrimah.

124. And guard yourselves against the day when [a]no soul shall serve as a substitute for another soul at all, nor shall any ransom be accepted from it, [b]nor any intercession avail it, nor shall they be helped.

وَاتَّقُوْا يَوْمًا لَّا تَجْزِىْ نَفْسٌ عَنْ نَّفْسٍ شَيْئًا وَّ
لَا يُقْبَلُ مِنْهَا عَدْلٌ وَّلَا تَنْفَعُهَا شَفَاعَةٌ وَّلَا هُمْ
يُنْصَرُوْنَ ﴿١٢٤﴾

125. And *remember* when his Lord tried[142A] Abraham with certain commandments[142B] which he fulfilled, He said, [c]'I will make thee a leader[143] of men.' *Abraham* asked, 'And from among my offspring?' *God* said, 'My covenant does not embrace the transgressors.'

وَاِذِ ابْتَلٰۤى اِبْرٰهٖمَ رَبُّهٗ بِكَلِمٰتٍ فَاَتَمَّهُنَّ ؕ قَالَ اِنِّىْ
جَاعِلُكَ لِلنَّاسِ اِمَامًا ؕ قَالَ وَمِنْ ذُرِّيَّتِىْ ؕ قَالَ
لَا يَنَالُ عَهْدِى الظّٰلِمِيْنَ ﴿١٢٥﴾

126. And *remember the time* when We made the House a resort[144] for mankind and a place of security;[145] *We said*, [d]'Take ye the station of Abraham as a place of Prayer.' And We commanded Abraham and Ishmael, *saying*, 'Purify My House for those who perform the circuit and for those who remain *therein* for devotion and those who bow down and fall prostrate *in Prayer*.'

وَاِذْ جَعَلْنَا الْبَيْتَ مَثَابَةً لِّلنَّاسِ وَاَمْنًا ؕ وَاتَّخِذُوْا
مِنْ مَّقَامِ اِبْرٰهٖمَ مُصَلًّى ؕ وَعَهِدْنَاۤ اِلٰۤى اِبْرٰهٖمَ
وَاِسْمٰعِيْلَ اَنْ طَهِّرَا بَيْتِىَ لِلطَّآئِفِيْنَ وَالْعٰكِفِيْنَ
وَالرُّكَّعِ السُّجُوْدِ ﴿١٢٦﴾

---

[a]See 2:49. [b]See 2:49. [c]2:131; 16:121, 122; 60: 5. [d]3:98; 22:27.

142A. *Ibtilā'* implies two things, (a) the learning of the state or the condition of the object, and becoming acquainted with what was unknown of the case thereof; (b) the manifesting of the goodness or badness of the object (Lane).

142B. *Kalimāt* is the plural of *Kalimah* which means, a commandment (Mufradāt).

143. *Imām* means, any object that is followed, whether a man or a book (Mufradāt).

144. *Mathābah* signifies, a place paying a visit to which entitles one to reward; or resort of men (Mufradāt). The Ka'bah, as some traditions say and as hinted by the Qur'ān itself, was originally built by Adam (3:97) and was, for sometime, the centre of worship for his progeny. Then in the course of time people became separated into different communities and adopted different centres for worship. Abraham then rebuilt it and it continued to remain a centre of worship for his progeny through his son Ishmael. But with the lapse of time it became virtually converted into a house of idols which numbered as many as 360—almost the same as the number of days in a year. At the advent of the Holy Prophet, however, it was again made the centre of worship for all nations, the Holy Prophet having been sent as a Messenger to all mankind, to unite those, who had become separated after Adam, into one common human brotherhood.

145. The Ka'bah, and, for that matter, the town of Mecca, is declared to be a place of peace and security. Mighty empires have crumbled and large tracts of land laid

127. And *remember* when Abraham said, 'My Lord, [a]make this a town of peace and provide with fruits such of its dwellers as believe in Allāh and the Last Day. *Allāh* said, 'And on him *too* who believes not, will I bestow benefits for a little while; then will I drive him to the punishment of the Fire, and an evil destination it is.

وَإِذْ قَالَ إِبْرٰهٖمُ رَبِّ اجْعَلْ هٰذَا بَلَدًا اٰمِنًا وَّارْزُقْ
أَهْلَهٗ مِنَ الثَّمَرٰتِ مَنْ اٰمَنَ مِنْهُمْ بِاللّٰهِ وَالْيَوْمِ
الْاٰخِرِ ۭ قَالَ وَمَنْ كَفَرَ فَأُمَتِّعُهٗ قَلِيْلًا ثُمَّ اَضْطَرُّهٗٓ
اِلٰى عَذَابِ النَّارِ ۭ وَبِئْسَ الْمَصِيْرُ ﴿١٢٧﴾

128. And *remember the time* when Abraham and Ishmael raised[146] the foundations of the House, *praying*, 'Our Lord, [b]accept *this* from us; for Thou art the All-Hearing, the All-Knowing. ;

وَإِذْ يَرْفَعُ إِبْرٰهٖمُ الْقَوَاعِدَ مِنَ الْبَيْتِ وَإِسْمٰعِيْلُ ۭ
رَبَّنَا تَقَبَّلْ مِنَّا ۭ اِنَّكَ اَنْتَ السَّمِيْعُ الْعَلِيْمُ ﴿١٢٨﴾

[a]3 : 98; 14 : 36; 27 : 92; 28 : 58. [b]14:41.

waste since the dawn of history, but the peace of Mecca has never been materially disturbed. The religious centres of other Faiths have never claimed, and have, in fact, never enjoyed, such peace and immunity from danger. Mecca has, however, ever remained a place of security and safety. No alien conqueror has ever entered it. It has always remained in the hands of those who have held it in reverence.

146. ' /as Abraham the founder or only the rebuilder of the Ka'bah is a question that has given rise to much discussion. Some hold that Abraham was the first builder of the place, others trace its origin to Adam. The Qur'ān (3 : 97) and authentic Traditions favour the view that even prior to the erection of a building on this site by Abraham some sort of structure did exist, but it had fallen into ruins and only a trace of it had remained. The word *al-Qawā'id* in the verse shows that the foundations of the House were there which Abraham and Ishmael had raised. Moreover, Abraham's prayer at the time he had separated from the child Ishmael and his mother at Mecca, *viz., Our Lord, I have settled some of my children in an uncultivable valley near Thy Sacred House* (14: 38), shows that the Ka'bah had existed even before Abraham had settled his wife and son in the Valley of Mecca. The Ḥadīth also supports this view (Bukhārī). Historical records too lend support to the view that the Ka'bah is of antique origin. Historians of established authority and even some hostile critics of Islām, have admitted that the Ka'bah is an ancient place and has been held sacred from time immemorial. "Diodorus Siculus, Sicily (60 B.C.), speaking of the region now known as Hijāz, says that it was 'specially honoured by the natives' and adds, 'an altar is there built of hard stone and very old in years,............to which the neighbouring peoples thronged from all sides" (Translation by C. M. Oldfather, London, 1935, Book III, ch. 42 vol. ii. pp. 211-213)... 'These words must refer to the holy house of Mecca, for we know of no other which ever commanded the universal homage of Arabia.....Tradition represents the Ka'bah as from time immemorial the scene of pilgrimage from all quarters of Arabia.' See 'The Larger Edition of the Commentary,' pp. 180—182.'

129. 'Our Lord, make both of us submissive to Thee and make of our offspring a people submissive to Thee. And show us our ways of worship and turn to us with mercy; for Thou art Oft-Returning *with compassion*, *and art* Merciful;

رَبَّنَا وَاجْعَلْنَا مُسْلِمَيْنِ لَكَ وَمِنْ ذُرِّيَّتِنَآ أُمَّةً
مُّسْلِمَةً لَّكَ وَأَرِنَا مَنَاسِكَنَا وَتُبْ عَلَيْنَآ إِنَّكَ أَنْتَ
التَّوَّابُ الرَّحِيمُ ﴿١٢٩﴾

130. 'And, Our Lord, raise up among them [a]a Messenger from among themselves, who may recite to them Thy Signs and teach them the Book and Wisdom[147] and may purify them; surely, Thou art the Mighty, the Wise.'

رَبَّنَا وَابْعَثْ فِيهِمْ رَسُولًا مِّنْهُمْ يَتْلُوا عَلَيْهِمْ
آيٰتِكَ وَيُعَلِّمُهُمُ الْكِتٰبَ وَالْحِكْمَةَ وَيُزَكِّيهِمْ ط
إِنَّكَ أَنْتَ الْعَزِيزُ الْحَكِيمُ ﴿١٣٠﴾ ع ٨/١٥

[a]2:152; 3:165; 62:3.

147. The verse serves as a summary of the subject-matter of the entire *Sūrah* which constitutes not only its enlargement but treats the various subjects in exactly the same order in which they have been mentioned in this verse, *i.e.*, first come the Signs, then the Book, then the Wisdom of the Law, and last of all the Means of national progress (See Introduction to the *Sūrah*).

It may be of interest to note here that the Qur'ān speaks of two separate prayers of Abraham—one about the progeny of Isaac and the other about that of Ishmael. The former prayer is mentioned in 2:125 and the latter in the verse under comment. In his prayer about the progeny of Isaac, Abraham asks that *Imāms* or Reformers may be raised from among them, but he makes no mention of their special work or status—they are ordinary Divine Reformers who will follow one another for the reformation of the Israelites. In his prayer in the present verse, however, he prays to God to raise among his progeny a great Prophet with a specific mission. This difference indeed constitutes a marvellously true picture of the two branches of the House of Abraham. In making mention of the two prayers of Abraham in vv. 125-130 the *Sūrah* alludes to the fact that Abraham did not only pray for the prosperity of the children of Isaac but also for the posterity of Ishmael, his first-born. The offspring of Isaac lost the gift of Prophethood on account of their evil deeds. The Prophet promised and prayed for in the present verse must, therefore, belong to the other descendants of Abraham who were the children of Ishmael. In order to point out that the expected and promised Prophet was to be an Ishmaelite, the Qur'ān has quite appropriately made mention of the construction of the Ka'bah by Abraham and Ishmael and of the prayers offered by Abraham for the posterity of his eldest son. To this natural conclusion Christian critics generally bring forward two objections: (1) That the Bible makes no mention of any promise having been made by God to Abraham concerning Ishmael, and (2) that, admitting that God did make any such promise, there is no proof of the fact that the Prophet of Islām was descended from Ishmael.

As regards the first objection, even if the Bible be shown to contain no prophecy about Ishmael, it does not mean that such a prophecy was never made. Moreover, if the biblical evidence can be taken to establish the existence of a promise about Isaac and his sons, why should not the evidence of the Qur'ān and, for that matter, of the children of Ishmael, be accepted to establish the fact that promises were held out by God to Ishmael and his sons also. But the Bible itself does contain references to the future prosperity of the sons of Ishmael similar to those it contains about the sons of Isaac (Gen. 16:10—12; 17:6—10; 17:18—20). As a matter of fact, the promise made to Ishmael does not materially differ from that made to Isaac—they were both to be blessed, both were to be made fruitful, the descendants of both were to multiply exceedingly and both were to be made great nations, and kingdom and dominion are promised to the progeny of both. So when the nature of the promise

R. 16 131. And who will turn away from [a]the religion of Abraham but he who makes a fool[148] of himself. [b]Him did We choose in this world, and in the next he will surely be among the righteous.

وَمَنْ يَّرْغَبُ عَنْ مِّلَّةِ إِبْرٰهٖمَ إِلَّا مَنْ سَفِهَ نَفْسَهٗ ۚ وَلَقَدِ اصْطَفَيْنٰهُ فِي الدُّنْيَا ۚ وَإِنَّهٗ فِي الْاٰخِرَةِ لَمِنَ الصّٰلِحِيْنَ ﴿١٣١﴾

132. When his Lord said to him, 'Submit', he said, [c]'I have already submitted to the Lord of the worlds.'

إِذْ قَالَ لَهٗ رَبُّهٗٓ أَسْلِمْ ۙ قَالَ أَسْلَمْتُ لِرَبِّ الْعٰلَمِيْنَ ﴿١٣٢﴾

[a] 3:96; 4:126; 6:162. [b]2:125; 3:34; 16:121, 122; 60:5. [c]3:68; 4:126.

made to both the brothers does not substantially differ, the kind of reward granted to the children of Isaac will have also to be admitted for the children of Ishmael. This fact has been admitted by some very eminent Christian scholars (The Scofield Reference Bible, p. 25).

In reply to the second objection that even if the covenant be understood to include the sons of Ishmael, it has yet to be proved that the Holy Prophet belonged to the House of Ishmael, the following points may briefly be noted: (1) The Quraish, the tribe to which the Holy Prophet belonged, always believed and declared themselves to be the descendants of Ishmael and this claim was recognized by all the people of Arabia. (2) If the claim of the Quraish and, for that matter, that of other Ishmaelite tribes of Arabia, to Ishmaelite descent had been false, the real descendants of Ishmael would have protested against such a false claim; but no such objection is known to have ever been raised. (3) In Gen. 17:20 God had promised to bless Ishmael, to multiply his progeny, to make him a great nation and the father of twelve princes. If the people of Arabia are not his descendants, where is the promised nation? The Ishmaelite tribes of Arabia are indeed the only claimants in the field. (4) According to Gen. 21: 8-14 Hagar had to leave her home in order to satisfy the vanity of Sarah. If she was not taken to Ḥijāz, where are her descendants found, and which is the place of her banishment? (5) The Arab geographers are all agreed that Paran is the name given to the hills of Ḥijāz (Mu'jam al-Buldān). (6) According to the Bible the generations of Ishmael "dwelt from Havilah unto Shur" (Gen. 25:18), and the phrase "from Havilah unto Shur" designates the opposite extremes of Arabia (Bib. Cyc. by J. Eadie, London, 1862). (7) The Bible calls Ishmael 'a wild man' (Gen. 16:12) and the word A'rābī, *i.e.*, 'a dweller of the desert' conveys almost the same sense. (8) Even Paul has admitted Hagar's connection with Arabia (Gal. 4:25). (9) Kedar was a son of Ishmael and it is admitted that his descendants settled in the southern part of Arabia (Bib. Cyc. London, 1862). (10) Prof. C. C. Torrey says: "The Arabs were Ishmaelites according to the Hebrew tradition..........The 'twelve princes' (Gen. 17:20) subsequently named in Gen. 25 : 13ff, represent Arabian tribes or districts; notice especially Kedar, Duma (Dumat al-Jandal), Teima. The great nation is the people of Arabia" (Jewish Foundation of Islām, p. 83). 'The Arabs, from physical characteristics, language, the occurrence of native traditions ......and from the testimony of the Bible are mainly and essentially Ishmaelites' (Cyclopaedia of Biblical Literature, New York, p. 685). (11) 'Let us always blame the foul inclination of the sons of Hagar, and specially the people (the tribe) of Kuraish who are like animals' (Leaves from Three Ancient Qur'āns, edited by the Rev. Mingana, D.D., Intro. xiii).

148. The different forms of the word *Safiha*, *Safaha* and *Safuha* give different meanings, *Safiha* meaning, he was ignorant or foolish or light-witted. When the word is used with *Nafsa-hū* as its seeming object as in this verse, it does not actually become transitive but simply looks so (Lisān & Mufradāt). The words also mean: "Who has ruined his soul."

133. The same did Abraham enjoin upon his sons,—and Jacob *also*—*saying*, 'O my sons, truly Allāh has chosen this religion for you; [a]so let not death overtake you except when you are in a state of complete submission.'[149]

وَوَصّٰى بِهَآ اِبْرٰهٖمُ بَنِيْهِ وَيَعْقُوْبُ ؕ يٰبَنِيَّ اِنَّ اللّٰهَ اصْطَفٰى لَكُمُ الدِّيْنَ فَلَا تَمُوْتُنَّ اِلَّا وَاَنْتُمْ مُّسْلِمُوْنَ ﴿۱۳۳﴾

134. Were you present when death came to Jacob, when he said to his sons, 'What will you worship after me?' They answered, 'We will worship thy God, the God of thy fathers,[150] Abraham and Ishmael and Isaac, the One God; and to Him we submit ourselves.'[151]

اَمْ كُنْتُمْ شُهَدَآءَ اِذْ حَضَرَ يَعْقُوْبَ الْمَوْتُ ۙ اِذْ قَالَ لِبَنِيْهِ مَا تَعْبُدُوْنَ مِنْۢ بَعْدِيْ ؕ قَالُوْا نَعْبُدُ اِلٰهَكَ وَاِلٰهَ اٰبَآئِكَ اِبْرٰهٖمَ وَاِسْمٰعِيْلَ وَاِسْحٰقَ اِلٰهًا وَّاحِدًا ۚۖ وَّنَحْنُ لَهٗ مُسْلِمُوْنَ ﴿۱۳۴﴾

135. [b]Those are a people that have passed away, for them is that which they earned, and for you is what you earn, and you shall not be questioned as to what they did.

تِلْكَ اُمَّةٌ قَدْ خَلَتْ ۚ لَهَا مَا كَسَبَتْ وَلَكُمْ مَّا كَسَبْتُمْ ۚ وَلَا تُسْـَٔلُوْنَ عَمَّا كَانُوْا يَعْمَلُوْنَ ﴿۱۳۵﴾

136. And they say, [c]'Be ye Jews or Christians, then you will be rightly guided.' Say, 'Nay, but *follow ye* the religion of Abraham who was [d]ever inclined[152] *to* Allāh; he was not of those who associate gods *with Allāh*.'

وَقَالُوْا كُوْنُوْا هُوْدًا اَوْ نَصٰرٰى تَهْتَدُوْا ؕ قُلْ بَلْ مِلَّةَ اِبْرٰهٖمَ حَنِيْفًا ؕ وَمَا كَانَ مِنَ الْمُشْرِكِيْنَ ﴿۱۳۶﴾

[a]3:103. [b]2:142. [c]2:112. [d]3:68; 6:80; 16 : 124; 22:32.

149. As there is no time fixed for death, one should pass every moment of his life in complete submission to God. The verse may also mean that a true believer should always be so perfectly resigned to God's will and should so completely win His pleasure that God may, out of His limitless bounty, so arrange that death may come to him at a time when he is completely resigned to His will.

150. Ishmael was the uncle of Jacob, and yet the children of Jacob here include Ishmael among their "fathers" which shows that the word *Ab* (father) also sometimes means uncle. Jacob's sons, the Israelites, held Ishmael in great respect.

151. "At the time when our father Jacob quitted this world, he summoned his twelve sons and said to them, Hearken to your father Israel (Gen. 49 : 2). Have you any doubts in your hearts concerning the Holy One, blessed be He. They said, Hear, O Israel, our father, as there is no doubt in thy heart, so neither is there in ours. For the Lord is our God, and He is one" (Mider. Rabbah on Gen. par. 98, & on Deut. par. 2). Compare also Targ. Jer. on Deut. 6 : 4.

152. *Ḥanīf* means, (1) one who turns away from error to guidance (Mufradāt); (2) one who steadily follows the right faith and never swerves from it; (3) one inclining in a

137. Say ye, 'We [a]believe in Allāh and what has been revealed to us, and what was revealed to Abraham and Ishmael, and Isaac, and Jacob and *his* children,[153] and what was given to Moses and Jesus, and what was given to *all other* Prophets[154] from their Lord. [b]We make no distinction between any of them; and to Him we submit ourselves.'

قُوْلُوْٓا اٰمَنَّا بِاللّٰهِ وَمَآ اُنْزِلَ اِلَيْنَا وَمَآ اُنْزِلَ اِلٰٓى
اِبْرٰهٖمَ وَاِسْمٰعِيْلَ وَاِسْحٰقَ وَيَعْقُوْبَ وَالْاَسْبَاطِ
وَمَآ اُوْتِيَ مُوْسٰى وَعِيْسٰى وَمَآ اُوْتِيَ النَّبِيُّوْنَ مِنْ رَّبِّهِمْ ۚ
لَا نُفَرِّقُ بَيْنَ اَحَدٍ مِّنْهُمْ ۖ وَنَحْنُ لَهٗ مُسْلِمُوْنَ ﴿١٣٧﴾

138. And [c]if they believe as you have believed,[155] then are they rightly guided; but if they turn back, then they are *bent upon* creating a schism, and Allāh will surely suffice thee against them, for He is the All-Hearing, the All-Knowing.

فَاِنْ اٰمَنُوْا بِمِثْلِ مَآ اٰمَنْتُمْ بِهٖ فَقَدِ اهْتَدَوْا ۚ وَاِنْ
تَوَلَّوْا فَاِنَّمَا هُمْ فِيْ شِقَاقٍ ۚ فَسَيَكْفِيْكَهُمُ اللّٰهُ ۚ وَهُوَ
السَّمِيْعُ الْعَلِيْمُ ﴿١٣٨﴾

139. *Say*, '*We have adopted the* religion[156] of Allāh; and who is better than Allāh in *teaching* religion, and Him *alone* do we worship.'

صِبْغَةَ اللّٰهِ ۚ وَمَنْ اَحْسَنُ مِنَ اللّٰهِ صِبْغَةً ۫ وَّنَحْنُ
لَهٗ عٰبِدُوْنَ ﴿١٣٩﴾

[a]3.85. [b]2:286 ; 3:85 ; 4:153. [c]3 : 21.

perfect manner to Islām and continuing firm therein (Lane); (4) one who follows the religion of Abraham (Aqrab); (5) one who believes in all Prophets (Kathīr).

153. The word children here refers to the twelve tribes of Israel named after the twelve sons of Jacob— Ruben, Simeon, Levi, Judah, Issachar, Zebulun, Joseph, Benjamin, Dan, Naphtali, Gad and Asher (Gen. 35:23—26; 49:28).

154. It indeed redounds to the great credit of Islām that it is the only religion which recognizes the Prophets of all nations, whereas other religions confine Prophethood to their own respective spheres. Naturally, the Qur'ān mentions only the names of those Prophets who were known to the Arabs to whom the Message of Islām was first given; but it makes a general remark to the effect that, *there is no people to whom a Warner has not been sent* (35 : 25). The words, "We make no distinction between any of them," mean that a Muslim makes no difference between the different Prophets in respect of their Prophethood. The words should not be construed to mean that all the Prophets are of the same spiritual rank. Such an idea is against 2 : 254.

155. Muslims are here told that if Jews and Christians agree with them in holding that Religion is not an hereditary matter, but consists in accepting all revealed guidance, then there is no basic difference between them, otherwise their ways stand apart and a wide gulf separates them, responsibility for the schism and the resulting hostility in this case lying with Jews and Christians and not with Muslims.

156. *Ṣibghah* means, dye or colour; kind or mode or nature of a thing; religion; code of laws; baptism. *Ṣibghat Allāh* signifies God's religion; the nature with which God has endowed men (Aqrab). Religion is so called because it colours a man like a dye or colour. *Ṣibghah* is used here as an object of a verb which is understood. According to

140. Say, 'Do you dispute with us concerning Allāh, while He is our Lord and your Lord? And [a]for us are our works, and for you your works; and to Him *alone* we are sincerely devoted.'

قُلْ أَتُحَاجُّونَنَا فِي اللّٰهِ وَهُوَ رَبُّنَا وَرَبُّكُمْ وَلَنَا
أَعْمَالُنَا وَلَكُمْ أَعْمَالُكُمْ وَنَحْنُ لَهُ مُخْلِصُونَ ﴿١٤٠﴾

141. Do you say that [b]Abraham, and Ishmael, and Isaac, and Jacob, and *his* children were Jews or Christians?'[157] Say, 'Do you know better or Allāh and [c]who is more unjust than he who hides the testimony that he has from Allāh? And Allāh is not unaware of what you do.'

أَمْ تَقُولُونَ إِنَّ إِبْرٰهِمَ وَإِسْمٰعِيلَ وَإِسْحٰقَ وَ
يَعْقُوبَ وَالْأَسْبَاطَ كَانُوا هُودًا أَوْ نَصٰرٰى ۗ قُلْ
ءَأَنْتُمْ أَعْلَمُ أَمِ اللّٰهُ ۗ وَمَنْ أَظْلَمُ مِمَّنْ كَتَمَ
شَهَادَةً عِنْدَهُ مِنَ اللّٰهِ ۗ وَمَا اللّٰهُ بِغَافِلٍ عَمَّا
تَعْمَلُونَ ﴿١٤١﴾

142. [d]Those are a people that have passed away; for them is what they earned; and for you shall be what you earn;[158] and you shall not be questioned as to what they did.

تِلْكَ أُمَّةٌ قَدْ خَلَتْ ۚ لَهَا مَا كَسَبَتْ وَلَكُمْ مَّا
كَسَبْتُمْ ۚ وَلَا تُسْـَٔلُونَ عَمَّا كَانُوا يَعْمَلُونَ ﴿١٤٢﴾ ع ١٦ ١٦

PART II

R. 17 143. The fools among the people will say, 'What has turned them away from their *Qiblah* which they followed?' Say, 'To Allāh [e]belong the East and the West.[159] He guides whom He pleases to the right path.'

سَيَقُولُ السُّفَهَاءُ مِنَ النَّاسِ مَا وَلّٰهُمْ عَنْ الجزء
قِبْلَتِهِمُ الَّتِي كَانُوا عَلَيْهَا ۚ قُلْ لِلّٰهِ الْمَشْرِقُ وَ
الْمَغْرِبُ ۚ يَهْدِي مَنْ يَشَاءُ إِلٰى صِرَاطٍ مُّسْتَقِيمٍ ﴿١٤٣﴾

[a]28:56; 42:16; 109:7. [b]3 : 85; 4 : 164. [c]2 : 284. [d]2:135. [e]See 2:116.

Arabic Grammar, sometimes when it is intended strongly to induce a person to do a certain thing, the verb is omitted and only the object is mentioned. Therefore, words like *Nākhudhu* (we have adopted) or *Nattabi'u* (we have followed) will be taken as understood, and the clause would mean, "we have adopted or we have followed the religion which God wishes us to adopt or follow."

157. Jews and Christians have been indirectly told how Abraham and his children would fare, when as claimed by them salvation is their exclusive monopoly, because they belonged to pre-Mosaic period when Jewish and Christian religions had not yet come into existence.

158. Jews and Christians are again warned that their being the descendants of God's Prophets would do them no good. They will have to carry their own cross, because no one shall bear the burden of another (6:165).

159. In the foregoing several verses a pointed reference was made to the fact that in pursuance of a Divine plan the Patriarch Abraham had settled his wife Hagar and son Ishmael in the bleak and barren Valley of Mecca. When Ishmael grew up, Abraham rebuilt the Ka'bah with his assistance and while rebuilding it prayed to God to raise among the Arabs a great Prophet, who should be humanity's Guide and Leader for all time. When, however, in the fulness of time that great Prophet appeared, God's eternal plan came into operation and the Ka'bah was made the *Qiblah* for the whole of mankind. But while at Mecca, the Holy Prophet, in conformity with his old practice and also by Divine command, turned his face in Prayer to the Temple at Jerusalem which was the *Qiblah* of the Israelite Prophets. In Medina also he kept facing towards Jerusalem. But after a few months he was commanded by Divine revelation to turn his face towards the Ka'bah. This was objected to by the Jews.

144. And thus have [a]We made you an exalted[160] nation, [b]that you may be guardians over the people and the Messenger *of Allāh* may be a guardian[161] over you. And We did not appoint[162] the *Qiblah* which thou didst follow, except that We might know him who follows the Messenger *of Allāh* from him who turns upon his heels.[163] And this is indeed hard, except for those whom Allāh has guided. And Allāh would never let your faith go in vain; surely, Allāh is Compassionate *and* Merciful to the people.

وَكَذٰلِكَ جَعَلْنٰكُمْ اُمَّةً وَّسَطًا لِّتَكُوْنُوْا شُهَدَآءَ عَلَى
النَّاسِ وَيَكُوْنَ الرَّسُوْلُ عَلَيْكُمْ شَهِيْدًا ؕ وَمَا جَعَلْنَا
الْقِبْلَةَ الَّتِىْ كُنْتَ عَلَيْهَآ اِلَّا لِنَعْلَمَ مَنْ يَّتَّبِعُ الرَّسُوْلَ
مِمَّنْ يَّنْقَلِبُ عَلٰى عَقِبَيْهِ ؕ وَاِنْ كَانَتْ لَكَبِيْرَةً اِلَّا
عَلَى الَّذِيْنَ هَدَى اللّٰهُ ؕ وَمَا كَانَ اللّٰهُ لِيُضِيْعَ اِيْمَانَكُمْ ؕ
اِنَّ اللّٰهَ بِالنَّاسِ لَرَءُوْفٌ رَّحِيْمٌ ﴿۱۴۴﴾

[a]3 : 111. [b]22 : 79.

The verse under comment furnishes a reply to their objections and also sheds some light on the inwardness of the command for the change of the direction of the *Qiblah*. But the Qur'ān never abruptly gives any new commandment. It invariably begins by preparing the ground for its acceptance by giving arguments in its favour and anticipates and answers objections that are likely to arise against it. As the commandment regarding the change of the *Qiblah* was likely to disturb the mental poise of some people, so in this verse the ground is being prepared by making a general observation to the effect that the selection of a particular direction for worship does not really matter. What matters is the spirit of obedience to God and of unity among the Faithful. The clause, *To Allāh belong the East and the West*, signifies that the selection of the East or the West is not of much importance, and because the real object is God only, the adoption of a particular direction is primarily meant for the purpose of creating a sense of unity. The verse also implies that some day the Ka'bah will fall into the possession of the Muslims.

160. *Al-Wasaṭ* means, occupying the middle position; good and exalted in rank (Aqrab). The word is used here in the sense of good and exalted. In 3:111 also Muslims have been called the best people.

161. Muslims are here told that each generation of theirs should guard and watch over the next generation. Being the best people, it is incumbent upon them to be always on their guard against falling away from the high standard of life expected of them, and to see that each succeeding generation also follows the path pursued by those who enjoyed the ennobling company of the Holy Prophet. Thus, the Holy Prophet was to be a guardian over his immediate followers, while they in turn were to be guardians over their successors, and so on. The words may also mean that, as decreed, Muslims are to become the leaders of men and by their good deeds are to become recipients of God's special favours, and thus other people will be forced to the conclusion that they follow a true religion. In this way they (Muslims) will bear witness to the truth of Islām for other people, just as the Holy Prophet was a witness of its truth for them.

162. It appears from these words that the Holy Prophet had adopted the Temple at Jerusalem as his *Qiblah* by God's command; but as it was meant by God to be only a temporary *Qiblah* and was to be subsequently replaced by the Ka'bah which was to be the *Qiblah* for all mankind for all times, the command with regard to the temporary *Qiblah* was not included in the Qur'ān. This shows that all such commandments as possessed temporary application were not included in the Quranic revelation; only those of a permanent nature were included in it. The theory that the Qur'ān contains some verses that now stand abrogated is quite unfounded.

163. The Arabs were greatly attached to the Ka'bah, the ancient house of worship at Mecca. It was their national Temple which had come down to them from the days of Abraham. It, therefore, proved a severe trial for them when they were asked at the very

145. Verily, We see thee turning thy face *often* to heaven;[164] surely, then, will We make thee turn[165] to the *Qiblah* which thou likest. So, [a]turn thy face towards the Sacred Mosque; and wherever you be, turn your faces towards it.[166] And they to whom the Book has been given know that this is the truth from their Lord;[167] and Allāh is not unmindful of what they do.

قَدْ نَرٰى تَقَلُّبَ وَجْهِكَ فِي السَّمَآءِ ۚ فَلَنُوَلِّيَنَّكَ
قِبْلَةً تَرْضٰهَا ۖ فَوَلِّ وَجْهَكَ شَطْرَ الْمَسْجِدِ الْحَرَامِ ۖ
وَحَيْثُ مَا كُنْتُمْ فَوَلُّوْا وُجُوْهَكُمْ شَطْرَهٗ ۖ وَاِنَّ
الَّذِيْنَ اُوْتُوا الْكِتٰبَ لَيَعْلَمُوْنَ اَنَّهُ الْحَقُّ مِنْ رَّبِّهِمْ ۖ
وَمَا اللّٰهُ بِغَافِلٍ عَمَّا يَعْمَلُوْنَ ﴿١٤٥﴾

146. And even if thou shouldst bring every Sign to those who have been given the Book, [b]they would never follow thy *Qiblah* nor wouldst thou follow their *Qiblah*, nor would some of them follow the *Qiblah* of others.[168] [c]And if thou shouldst follow their desires after the knowledge that has come to thee, then thou shalt surely be of the transgressors.

وَلَئِنْ اَتَيْتَ الَّذِيْنَ اُوْتُوا الْكِتٰبَ بِكُلِّ اٰيَةٍ مَّا تَبِعُوْا
قِبْلَتَكَ ۚ وَمَآ اَنْتَ بِتَابِعٍ قِبْلَتَهُمْ ۚ وَمَا بَعْضُهُمْ بِتَابِعٍ
قِبْلَةَ بَعْضٍ ۖ وَلَئِنِ اتَّبَعْتَ اَهْوَآءَهُمْ مِّنْ ۢ بَعْدِ مَا
جَآءَكَ مِنَ الْعِلْمِ ۙ اِنَّكَ اِذًا لَّمِنَ الظّٰلِمِيْنَ ﴿١٤٦﴾

[a]2:150, 151. [b]109:3, 7. [c]6:57 ; 13:38.

inception of Islām to abandon it in favour of the Temple at Jerusalem which was the *Qiblah* of the People of the Book (Bukhārī & Jarīr) And later on at Medina the change of the *Qiblah* from the Temple at Jerusalem to the Ka'bah proved a great trial for both Jews and Christians. Thus the change proved a trial for both the "People of the Book" and the Muslims and also for the Meccan idolaters.

164. While at Mecca, the Holy Prophet under Divine command turned his face in Prayers towards the Temple at Jerusalem. But, as in his heart of hearts, he desired the Ka'bah to be his *Qiblah* and he also had a sort of intuition that eventually his wish will be satisfied, he generally chose such a place for worship where he could keep both the sacred Temple at Jerusalem and the Ka'bah before him. When, however, he emigrated to Medina, in view of the position of the town, he could only face towards the Temple at Jerusalem. With the change of the *Qiblah* his inner desire naturally became intensified, and though, out of deference to God's command, he did not actually pray for the change, yet he anxiously and eagerly looked towards heaven for a command to that effect.

165. *Nuwalliyannaka* also means, "We will make thee master and guardian." The expression embodied a double prophecy, *viz.*, that eventually the Ka'bah will become the *Qiblah* of all peoples and that its possession will also pass over to the Holy Prophet.

166. The words signify that though in ordinary circumstances, the Muslims are enjoined to turn their faces to the Ka'bah when saying their Prayers, yet direction is of secondary importance. The change was intended to bring about and maintain unity and uniformity in the Muslim brotherhood.

167. See Gen. 21:21; John 4:21. Isa. 45:13, 14 & Deut. 32:2.

168. This verse points to the hostility of Jews and Christians not only to Islām but also to one another. The Jews had Jerusalem as their *Qiblah* (Kings 8:22—30; Dan. 6 : 10; Ps. 5:7 & Jonah, 2:4), while the Samaritans, a disowned section of the Jews, who also

147. [a]Those to whom We have given the Book recognize it[169] even as they recognize[170] their sons, but surely, some of them [b]hide the truth knowingly.

الَّذِينَ آتَيْنَاهُمُ الْكِتَابَ يَعْرِفُونَهُ كَمَا يَعْرِفُونَ أَبْنَاءَهُمْ ۖ
وَإِنَّ فَرِيقًا مِّنْهُمْ لَيَكْتُمُونَ الْحَقَّ وَهُمْ يَعْلَمُونَ ﴿١٤٧﴾

148. [c]It is the truth from thy Lord; be not, therefore, of those who doubt.

الْحَقُّ مِن رَّبِّكَ فَلَا تَكُونَنَّ مِنَ الْمُمْتَرِينَ ﴿١٤٨﴾ ع

R. 18 149. And everyone has a goal to which he turns his *whole* attention. Then [d]vie with one another in good works.[171] Wherever you be, Allāh will bring you all together. Surely, Allāh has the power to do all that He wills.

وَلِكُلٍّ وِجْهَةٌ هُوَ مُوَلِّيهَا فَاسْتَبِقُوا الْخَيْرَاتِ ۚ أَيْنَ
مَا تَكُونُوا يَأْتِ بِكُمُ اللَّهُ جَمِيعًا ۚ إِنَّ اللَّهَ عَلَىٰ كُلِّ
شَيْءٍ قَدِيرٌ ﴿١٤٩﴾

150. And from wheresoever thou comest forth, [e]turn thy[172] face towards the Sacred Mosque; for that is indeed the truth[173] from thy Lord. And Allāh is not unmindful of what you do.

وَمِنْ حَيْثُ خَرَجْتَ فَوَلِّ وَجْهَكَ شَطْرَ الْمَسْجِدِ
الْحَرَامِ ۖ وَإِنَّهُ لَلْحَقُّ مِن رَّبِّكَ ۗ وَمَا اللَّهُ بِغَافِلٍ
عَمَّا تَعْمَلُونَ ﴿١٥٠﴾

[a]6:21. [b]2:175; 5:16; 6:92; [c]3:61; 6:115; 10:95. [d]3:134; 5:49; 35:33; 57:22. [e]See 2:145

followed the Mosaic Law, had adopted a certain mountain in Palestine, named Gerizim, as their *Qiblah* (Commentary on the New Testament by W. Walsham How, D.D.). The early Christians, followed the *Qiblah* of the Jews (Enc. Brit., 14th edition, v. 676 & Jew. Enc. vi. 53). The Christians of Najrān worshipped in the Holy Prophet's Mosque at Medina, with their faces turned to the East (Zurqānī, iv. 41). Thus the Jews, the Samaritans, and the Christians followed different *Qiblahs* owing to their mutual jealousy and enmity. In these circumstances it was vain to expect them to follow the *Qiblah* of the Muslims.

169. The pronoun it (or him) may be taken as referring either to the change of the *Qiblah* or to the Holy Prophet. The clause means that the People of the Book know on the basis of the prophecies found in their revealed Scriptures that a Prophet will appear among the Arabs who will have special relation with the Ka'bah.

170. *Ya'rifūna-hū* is derived from *'Arafa* which means, he knew or recognized or perceived a thing. Though the word is also used about such knowledge as is derived through the physical senses, it is particularly used of such knowledge as is obtained by pondering and meditating (Mufradāt).

171. The verse contains, in a few words, all the ingredients of a successful life: A Muslim should first fix for himself a definite goal. Then he should not only devote his whole attention to it and strain every nerve to attain it and vie with other Muslims in a spirit of healthy competition and try to excel them but should also help such of his comrades, as may happen to stumble, to rise up and continue the race. The word *Muwallī-hā* also means, "which he makes dominant over him," *i.e.*, a man first sets up an objective and then makes it a dominating factor in his life.

172 & 173. See next page.

151. And [a]from wheresoever thou comest forth, turn thy face towards the Sacred Mosque;[174] and wherever you be, turn your faces towards it that people may have no argument against you,[175] except those who are unjust—so [b]fear them not, but fear Me—and [c]that I may perfect My favour upon you,[176] and that you may be rightly guided.	وَمِنْ حَيْثُ خَرَجْتَ فَوَلِّ وَجْهَكَ شَطْرَ الْمَسْجِدِ الْحَرَامِ وَحَيْثُ مَا كُنْتُمْ فَوَلُّوا وُجُوهَكُمْ شَطْرَهُ لِئَلَّا يَكُونَ لِلنَّاسِ عَلَيْكُمْ حُجَّةٌ إِلَّا الَّذِينَ ظَلَمُوا مِنْهُمْ فَلَا تَخْشَوْهُمْ وَاخْشَوْنِي وَلِأُتِمَّ نِعْمَتِي عَلَيْكُمْ وَلَعَلَّكُمْ تَهْتَدُونَ ﴿١٥١﴾

[a]2 : 145, 150. [b]5 : 4. [c]5 : 4; 12 : 7.

172. When the Ka'bah was made the *Qiblah* it became essential for Muslims that they should have Mecca, in which it was situated, in their possession. They are enjoined in this verse to bend all their energies to its conquest and the Holy Prophet is commanded to keep his attention centred on this objective in all his campaigns, the word *Kharajta* also meaning "thou goest out for battle" (Lane). The word also signifies that the conquest of Mecca was the personal responsibility of the Holy Prophet. Moreover, whereas in v. 145 the command pertains to the change of the *Qiblah*, in 150-151 it refers to the conquest of Mecca, the infinitive *Khurūj* particularly meaning, to issue forth for battle.

173. The words imply that Mecca was sure to fall one day into the hands of the Muslims. Its conquest by the Muslims had also been predicted in the Qur'ān in 17 : 81, and 28:86. The prophecy contained in Deut. 33:2 was also fulfilled when the Holy Prophet entered Mecca as a conqueror at the head of ten thousand Muslims.

174. The Muslims were also enjoined never to lose sight of the supreme objective of conquering Mecca.

175. The words, *that people may have no argument against you*, mean that if the Muslims failed to conquer Mecca, the objection would quite legitimately be raised by the enemies of Islām that the Holy Prophet had not fulfilled the prayer of Abraham (2:130), and, therefore, he could not claim to be the Promised Prophet. Moreover, the House to which the Muslims were commanded to turn their faces in Prayers was, while under the control of the heathen Meccans, full of idols. If the idols had remained in the Ka'bah, the Muslims would have been accused of worshipping them. This objection could only be effectively answered if the Holy House, which had been originally dedicated to the worship of One God, had been cleared of idols. Hence the commandment to substitute the Ka'bah for the Temple of Jerusalem as the *Qiblah* was naturally followed by the injunction about the conquest of Mecca.

176. The words mean that with the taking of Mecca God's favour on the Muslims would become complete, for it would mean the subjugation of all Arabia and the entering of thousands of men into the fold of Islām. The result amply justified the above prophecy; for the conquest of Mecca was rapidly followed by the conversion to Islām of thousands of Arabs. Another reason why the conquest of Mecca was followed by a general influx of Arabs into Islām was that although the Arabs followed no revealed Book, yet the prophecy of Abraham that Mecca would not be conquered by the followers of any false Prophet, and any people attempting it would meet with destruction, was known to them. They had only recently seen a remarkable illustration of the fulfilment of that prophecy in the miraculous destruction of the Abyssinian invader, Abraha, and his powerful army.

152. Even as [a]We have sent to you a Messenger from among yourselves, who recites Our Signs to you, and purifies you, and teaches you the Book and Wisdom,[177] and teaches you that which you knew not.

كَمَآ اَرْسَلْنَا فِيْكُمْ رَسُوْلًا مِّنْكُمْ يَتْلُوْا عَلَيْكُمْ اٰيٰتِنَا وَ يُزَكِّيْكُمْ وَ يُعَلِّمُكُمُ الْكِتٰبَ وَ الْحِكْمَةَ وَ يُعَلِّمُكُمْ مَّا لَمْ تَكُوْنُوْا تَعْلَمُوْنَ ﴿۱۵۲﴾

153. Therefore, [b]remember[178] Me, *and* I will remember you; and be thankful to Me and do not be ungrateful to Me.

فَاذْكُرُوْنِيْٓ اَذْكُرْكُمْ وَ اشْكُرُوْا لِيْ وَ لَا تَكْفُرُوْنِ ﴿۱۵۳﴾

19 154. O ye who believe, [c]seek help through perseverance[179] and Prayer; surely, Allāh is with those who patiently persevere.[180]

يٰٓاَيُّهَا الَّذِيْنَ اٰمَنُوا اسْتَعِيْنُوْا بِالصَّبْرِ وَ الصَّلٰوةِ ؕ اِنَّ اللّٰهَ مَعَ الصّٰبِرِيْنَ ﴿۱۵۴﴾

155. And [d]say not of those who are slain in the way of Allāh that they are dead; nay, they are living,[181] only you perceive not.

وَ لَا تَقُوْلُوْا لِمَنْ يُّقْتَلُ فِيْ سَبِيْلِ اللّٰهِ اَمْوَاتٌ ؕ بَلْ اَحْيَآءٌ وَّ لٰكِنْ لَّا تَشْعُرُوْنَ ﴿۱۵۵﴾

[a]See 2:130. [b]2:204; 8:46; 62:11. [c]See 2:46. [d]3:170.

177. With a slight change in the arrangement of the words this verse refers to the work of the Holy Prophet in exactly the same words in which Abraham prayed to God about the appearance of a Prophet among the Meccans (2:130), which clearly shows that Abraham's prayer had found fulfilment in the person of the Holy Prophet.

178. Remembrance of God on the part of man means, to remember Him with love and devotion, to carry out His commands, to bear in mind His attributes, to glorify Him and offer prayers to Him. And remembrance of man on the part of God signifies, God's drawing man near to Himself, bestowing favours upon him and making provision for his welfare.

179. *Ṣabr* means, (1) to persevere in something; (2) to endure afflictions with fortitude and without complaint or murmur; (3) to hold fast to the Divine Law and the dictates of reason; (4) to refrain from doing what the Divine Law and reason forbid (Mufradāt).

180. The verse contains a golden principle of success. First, a Muslim should patiently persevere in his endeavours, never relaxing his efforts to achieve his object and never losing heart, at the same time avoiding what is harmful, and sticking fast to all that is good. Secondly, he should pray to God for success; for He alone is the Source of all good. The word *Ṣabr* (patient perseverance) precedes the word *Ṣalāt* (Prayer) in the verse in order to emphasize the importance of observing the laws of God which are sometimes flouted in ignorance. Ordinarily, Prayer can be effective only when it is accompanied by the use of all the necessary means created by God for the attainment of an object.

181. *Aḥyā'* is the plural of *Ḥayy* which, among other things, means: (1) One whose life-work does not go in vain; (2) one whose death is avenged. The verse comprises a great psychological truth which is calculated to exercise tremendous influence on the life and progress of a people. A people, who do not properly honour the memory of their martyrs and do not take steps to remove the fear of death from their hearts, seal their own fate.

156. And [a]We will try you with something of fear and hunger, and loss of wealth and lives and fruits;[182] but give glad tidings to those who patiently persevere.

وَلَنَبْلُوَنَّكُمْ بِشَيْءٍ مِّنَ الْخَوْفِ وَالْجُوْعِ وَنَقْصٍ مِّنَ
الْأَمْوَالِ وَالْأَنْفُسِ وَالثَّمَرٰتِ ۗ وَبَشِّرِ الصّٰبِرِيْنَ ﴿١٥٦﴾

157. Who, [b]when a misfortune overtakes them, say, [c]'Surely, to Allāh we belong and to Him shall we return.'[183]

الَّذِيْنَ إِذَآ أَصَابَتْهُمْ مُّصِيْبَةٌ ۙ قَالُوْٓا إِنَّا لِلّٰهِ وَإِنَّآ
إِلَيْهِ رٰجِعُوْنَ ﴿١٥٧﴾

158. It is these on whom descend blessings from their Lord and *also* mercy, and it is these who are rightly guided.

أُولٰٓئِكَ عَلَيْهِمْ صَلَوٰتٌ مِّنْ رَّبِّهِمْ وَرَحْمَةٌ ۗ وَ
أُولٰٓئِكَ هُمُ الْمُهْتَدُوْنَ ﴿١٥٨﴾

159. Surely, Al-Ṣafā and Al-Marwah[184] are among the [d]Signs of Allāh. It is, therefore, no sin for him who is on Pilgrimage to the House, or performs 'Umrah, to go around the two. And whoso does good beyond what is obligatory,[185] surely then, Allāh is Appreciative *of good deeds and* All-Knowing.

إِنَّ الصَّفَا وَالْمَرْوَةَ مِنْ شَعَآئِرِ اللّٰهِ ۚ فَمَنْ حَجَّ
الْبَيْتَ أَوِ اعْتَمَرَ فَلَا جُنَاحَ عَلَيْهِ أَنْ يَّطَّوَّفَ
بِهِمَا ۗ وَمَنْ تَطَوَّعَ خَيْرًا ۙ فَإِنَّ اللّٰهَ شَاكِرٌ
عَلِيْمٌ ﴿١٥٩﴾

[a]3:187. [b]22:36. [c]7:126; 26:51. [d]22:33.

182. This verse constitutes fitting sequel to the preceding one. Muslims should be prepared not only to lay down their lives in the cause of Islām but should also be prepared to suffer all sorts of afflictions which will be imposed on them as a trial.

183. God is the Master of all we possess, including our ownselves. If the Owner in His infinite wisdom deems fit to take away anything from us, we have no ground for complaint or demur. So every misfortune that befalls us should, instead of depressing us, spur us to make yet greater efforts to achieve still better results in life. Thus the formula contained in this verse is not a mere verbal incantation but a wise counsel and a timely warning.

184. Al-Ṣafā and Al-Marwah are the names of two hills near the Ka'bah in Mecca, the first-mentioned being the nearer of the two. These hills stand as a memorial to Hagar's great patience and extraordinary loyalty to God on the one hand and to God's special care of her and her son, Ishmael, on the other. A visit to these hills deeply impresses the pilgrim with the love, fidelity to and power, of God.

185. The words, *whoso does good beyond what is obligatory*, do not refer to *Ḥajj* (Greater Pilgrimage), which under certain conditions is obligatory on every Muslim once in a life-time, but to 'Umrah (Lesser Pilgrimage) which is not obligatory but only supererogatory. The words may also be considered to refer to any additional pilgrimage which a Muslim may perform, after he has performed the obligatory one.

160. Those who hide[186] what We have sent down of Signs and guidance after We have made it clear for the people in the Book, [a]it is these whom Allāh curses; and *so* curse them those who *have the right* to curse.

إِنَّ الَّذِينَ يَكْتُمُونَ مَآ أَنْزَلْنَا مِنَ الْبَيِّنٰتِ وَالْهُدٰى
مِنْ بَعْدِ مَا بَيَّنّٰهُ لِلنَّاسِ فِي الْكِتٰبِ ۙ أُولٰٓئِكَ يَلْعَنُهُمُ
اللّٰهُ وَيَلْعَنُهُمُ اللّٰعِنُوْنَ ﴿١٦٠﴾

161. But [b]they who repent and amend and openly declare *the truth*, it is these to whom I turn with forgiveness, and I am Oft-Returning *with compassion and* Merciful.

إِلَّا الَّذِينَ تَابُوا وَأَصْلَحُوا وَبَيَّنُوا فَأُولٰٓئِكَ أَتُوبُ
عَلَيْهِمْ ۚ وَأَنَا التَّوَّابُ الرَّحِيمُ ﴿١٦١﴾

162. Those who disbelieve and die while they are disbelivers, [c]on them shall be the curse of Allāh and of angels and of men all together.

إِنَّ الَّذِينَ كَفَرُوا وَمَاتُوا وَهُمْ كُفَّارٌ أُولٰٓئِكَ
عَلَيْهِمْ لَعْنَةُ اللّٰهِ وَالْمَلٰٓئِكَةِ وَالنَّاسِ أَجْمَعِينَ ﴿١٦٢﴾

163. [d]They shall remain under it. The punishment shall not be lightened for them, nor shall they be granted respite.

خٰلِدِينَ فِيهَا ۚ لَا يُخَفَّفُ عَنْهُمُ الْعَذَابُ وَلَا
هُمْ يُنْظَرُونَ ﴿١٦٣﴾

164. And [e]your God is One God;[187] there is no god but He, the Gracious, the Merciful.

ع وَإِلٰهُكُمْ إِلٰهٌ وَاحِدٌ ۚ لَا إِلٰهَ إِلَّا هُوَ الرَّحْمٰنُ الرَّحِيمُ ﴿١٦٤﴾

R. 20 165. [f]Verily, in the creation of the heavens and the earth and in the alternation of night and day, and in the ships which sail in the sea with that which profits men, and in the water which Allāh sends down from the sky and quickens therewith the earth after its death and scatters therein all kinds of beasts, and in the change of the winds

إِنَّ فِي خَلْقِ السَّمٰوٰتِ وَالْأَرْضِ وَاخْتِلَافِ الَّيْلِ وَ
النَّهَارِ وَالْفُلْكِ الَّتِي تَجْرِي فِي الْبَحْرِ بِمَا يَنْفَعُ
النَّاسَ وَمَآ أَنْزَلَ اللّٰهُ مِنَ السَّمَآءِ مِنْ مَّآءٍ فَأَحْيَا
بِهِ الْأَرْضَ بَعْدَ مَوْتِهَا وَبَثَّ فِيهَا مِنْ كُلِّ دَآبَّةٍ

[a]2:175. [b]3:90; 4:147; 5:40; 24:6. [c]3:88. [d]3:89. [e]2:256; 16:23; 22:35; 37:5; 59:23,24; 112:2. [f]3:191; 10:7; 30:23; 45:6.

186. The reference is to the Jews who concealed the prophecies contained in their Scriptures about the Holy Prophet.

187. As all sins spring from feebleness of faith, this verse fittingly refers to the Oneness of God, signifying that if people only believed in Divine Unity and refrained from setting up false gods, they would never deviate from the right path.

and the clouds pressed into service between the heaven and the earth—are indeed Signs for the people who use their understanding.[188]

وَتَصْرِيفِ الرِّيٰحِ وَالسَّحَابِ الْمُسَخَّرِ بَيْنَ السَّمَآءِ
وَالْاَرْضِ لَاٰيٰتٍ لِّقَوْمٍ يَّعْقِلُوْنَ ﴿١٦٥﴾

166. And there are some among men who take for themselves objects of worship[189] other than Allāh, loving them as they should love Allāh.[190] But believers are stronger in *their* love for Allāh. And if those who transgress could *now* see *the time* when they shall see the punishment, *they would realize* that all power belongs to Allāh and that Allāh is severe in punishing.

وَمِنَ النَّاسِ مَنْ يَّتَّخِذُ مِنْ دُوْنِ اللّٰهِ اَنْدَادًا
يُّحِبُّوْنَهُمْ كَحُبِّ اللّٰهِ ۗ وَالَّذِيْنَ اٰمَنُوْٓا اَشَدُّ حُبًّا
لِّلّٰهِ ۗ وَلَوْ يَرَى الَّذِيْنَ ظَلَمُوْٓا اِذْ يَرَوْنَ الْعَذَابَ ۙ
اَنَّ الْقُوَّةَ لِلّٰهِ جَمِيْعًا ۙ وَّاَنَّ اللّٰهَ شَدِيْدُ الْعَذَابِ ﴿١٦٦﴾

167. *Could they but see* [a]when those who were followed shall disown their followers and shall see the punishment and all their ties shall be cut asunder.[191]

اِذْ تَبَرَّاَ الَّذِيْنَ اتُّبِعُوْا مِنَ الَّذِيْنَ اتَّبَعُوْا وَرَاَوُا الْعَذَابَ
وَتَقَطَّعَتْ بِهِمُ الْاَسْبَابُ ﴿١٦٧﴾

[a]28 : 64, 65; 34 : 33, 34.

188. The Qur'ān takes the universe as a whole to prove its theme. The objects of nature taken individually do not furnish such conclusive evidence of the existence of God as the whole universe taken collectively. The earth may be said to owe its existence to a fortuitous concourse of atoms, and a similar reason may be given for the origin of the sun and the moon and so on. But when the universe as one united whole and the deep order that permeates it are taken into consideration, it becomes impossible for one to escape the conclusion, that this universe has not come into existence accidentally. Indeed, the consummate harmony that pervades it forcefully points to the fact that the whole system has been created and is being directed by One Intelligent Being Who is All-Powerful and All-Knowing. Moreover, by laying special emphasis on the study of the phenomena of nature, the attention of disbelievers is also drawn to the fact that they could not possibly hope to succeed in their designs against the Holy Prophet, because the whole universe is controlled by God and is working in his favour and in furthering his cause.

189. While dealing with the subject of idolatry the Qur'ān has used four words: *Nidd* (like or equal); *Sharīk* (co-partner or sharer); *Ilāh* (worthy of worship); and *Rabb* (sustainer). While the first two words are used only about objects of worship other than God, the last two are used about God also. The word *Nidd* (like or equal) refers to such objects of worship as are supposed to be like God or equal to Him, but are contrary or opposed to Him.

190. Love of God is the essence of all religious teaching and no religion has laid so much emphasis on Divine love as Islām has done. The Holy Prophet was so much engrossed in God that he was spoken of by the pagan Arabs as having fallen in love with Him. No other subject has been so completely and so repeatedly dealt with in the Qur'ān as God's beauty and beneficence and such of His attributes as create an irresistible love and longing in the human soul for the Supreme Being.

191. The verse constitutes a stern warning to those who blindly follow their leaders and, being led astray by them, reject God's Messengers.

168. And those who followed shall say, "If we could only return, we would disown them even as they have disowned us.' Thus will Allāh show them their works as anguish for them, and they shall not get out of the Fire.

وَقَالَ الَّذِيۡنَ اتَّبَعُوۡا لَوۡ اَنَّ لَنَا كَرَّةً فَنَتَبَرَّاَ مِنۡهُمۡ كَمَا تَبَرَّءُوۡا مِنَّاؕ كَذٰلِكَ يُرِيۡهِمُ اللّٰهُ اَعۡمَالَهُمۡ حَسَرٰتٍ عَلَيۡهِمۡؕ وَمَا هُمۡ بِخٰرِجِيۡنَ مِنَ النَّارِ ۠

R. 21

169. O ye men! eat of [b]what is lawful and good[192] in[c] the earth; and [c]follow not the footsteps of Satan,[193] surely [d]he is to you an open enemy.

يٰۤاَيُّهَا النَّاسُ كُلُوۡا مِمَّا فِى الۡاَرۡضِ حَلٰلًا طَيِّبًا ۖۗ وَّلَا تَتَّبِعُوۡا خُطُوٰتِ الشَّيۡطٰنِؕ اِنَّهٗ لَكُمۡ عَدُوٌّ مُّبِيۡنٌ ۞

170. He [e]enjoins upon you only what is evil and what is foul,[194] and that you say of Allāh what you do not know.

اِنَّمَا يَاۡمُرُكُمۡ بِالسُّوۡٓءِ وَالۡفَحۡشَآءِ وَاَنۡ تَقُوۡلُوۡا عَلَى اللّٰهِ مَا لَا تَعۡلَمُوۡنَ ۞

171. And [f]when it is said to them, 'Follow that which Allāh has sent down,' they say, 'Nay, we will follow that wherein we found our fathers.[195] What! even if their fathers had no sense *at all* and followed not the right path.

وَاِذَا قِيۡلَ لَهُمُ اتَّبِعُوۡا مَاۤ اَنۡزَلَ اللّٰهُ قَالُوۡا بَلۡ نَتَّبِعُ مَاۤ اَلۡفَيۡنَا عَلَيۡهِ اٰبَآءَنَاؕ اَوَلَوۡ كَانَ اٰبَآؤُهُمۡ لَا يَعۡقِلُوۡنَ شَيۡئًا وَّلَا يَهۡتَدُوۡنَ ۞

---

[a]23:100; 26:103.   [b]5:89; 8:70; 16:115.   [c]2:209; 6:143; 24:22.   [d]7:23; 12:6; 28:16; 35:7; 36:61.   [e]2:269; 24:22.   [f]5; 105; 10:79; 21:53, 54; 31:22.

192. Good actions must accompany true faith. With this verse begins a discussion of the second part of Abraham's prayer regarding the work of the Promised Prophet, *i.e.*, the teaching of the laws of the *Sharī'ah* and of the wisdom underlying them. Henceforward ordinances about Prayer, Fasting, Pilgrimage and *Zakāt* are given and so are the laws relating to social matters; and as food plays an important part in the formation of a man's character, regulations concerning it are mentioned first. All food according to Islām should be: (1) *Ḥalāl*, *i.e.*, allowed by the Law; and (2) it should also be *Ṭayyib*, *i.e.*, good, pure, wholesome and agreeable. Under the second condition sometimes even lawful things become forbidden.

193. The prohibition against following Satan, coming immediately after the commandment with respect to food, alludes to the influence which physical actions exercise on the moral and spiritual conditions of man. The use of unlawful and unwholesome food tends to impair man's moral faculties and impede his spiritual development. See also 23:52.

194. Satan first prompts man to do such deeds as do not appear to be manifestly bad and the influence of which is confined to the doer alone. Then step by step he makes him a hardened sinner, making him lose all sense of modesty.

195. See next page.

172. And the case of those who disbelieve is like the case of one who shouts to that which hears naught but a call and a cry.[196] *They are* deaf dumb *and* blind—so they do not understand.

وَمَثَلُ الَّذِيْنَ كَفَرُوْا كَمَثَلِ الَّذِىْ يَنْعِقُ بِمَا لَا يَسْمَعُ اِلَّا دُعَآءً وَّنِدَآءً صُمٌّ بُكْمٌ عُمْىٌ فَهُمْ لَا يَعْقِلُوْنَ ۝

173. *O ye who believe, eat of the good things[197] We have provided for you, and render thanks to Allāh, if it is He Whom you really worship.

يٰٓاَيُّهَا الَّذِيْنَ اٰمَنُوْا كُلُوْا مِنْ طَيِّبٰتِ مَا رَزَقْنٰكُمْ وَاشْكُرُوْا لِلّٰهِ اِنْ كُنْتُمْ اِيَّاهُ تَعْبُدُوْنَ ۝

174. *He has made unlawful to you only that which dies of itself, and blood and the flesh of swine,[198] and that on which the name of any other than Allāh has been invoked. But he who is driven by necessity, being neither disobedient nor exceeding the limit, it shall be no sin[199] for him. Surely, Allāh is Most Forgiving, Merciful.

اِنَّمَا حَرَّمَ عَلَيْكُمُ الْمَيْتَةَ وَالدَّمَ وَلَحْمَ الْخِنْزِيْرِ وَمَآ اُهِلَّ بِهٖ لِغَيْرِ اللّٰهِ فَمَنِ اضْطُرَّ غَيْرَ بَاغٍ وَّلَا عَادٍ فَلَاۤ اِثْمَ عَلَيْهِ اِنَّ اللّٰهَ غَفُوْرٌ رَّحِيْمٌ ۝

---

*See 2:19   *5:6;   16:115;   23:52;   40.65.   *5:4;   6:146;   16:116.

195. It is indeed strange, but nevertheless regrettable, that in matters of religion which so deeply concern his eternal life man is often content to follow blindly in the footsteps of his elders. But in worldly matters where only the interests of this life are at stake, and that too partially, he takes meticulous care to see that he adopts the right course, and does not blindly follow others.

196. The Holy Prophet delivered the Divine Message to disbelievers. He is the crier. They heard his voice but made no effort to grasp its meaning. His words fell, as it were, on deaf ears, with the result that their spiritual faculties became wholly vitiated and they stooped low to the level of animals and beasts (7:180; 25:45), which only hear the cry of the driver but do not understand what he says.

197. The injunction contained in the words, "eat of good, pure and wholesome things (*Ṭayyibāt*) indicates that Muslims are not allowed to use things which may, in any way, injure their physical or moral or spiritual health, though they may be allowed by the *Sharī'ah*.

198. The very name of this foul animal contains an allusion to the prohibition of its flesh. The word is a combination of *Khinz* and *Arā*; the first part meaning, 'very foul' and the second, 'I see,' meaning, 'I see it very foul'........In Hindi, this animal is known by the name *Sū'ar* which exactly means the same as the Arabic *Khinzīr, i.e.*, 'I see it very foul'.........In Hindi this animal is also known as *bad* meaning 'bad' or 'foul' which is probably a translation of the original Arabic word.

199. *Ithm* means, anything unlawful, *i.e,* a sin; anything which renders a person deserving of punishment (Aqrab); anything that pricks the mind as something evil (Mufradāt). The four things mentioned in this verse are not the only things prohibited in Islām. Islām prohibits the use of many other things also which are divided into grades or categories, some of them being "unlawful" and others *Mamnū'* (forbidden). The verse under

175. [a]Those who hide that which Allāh has sent down of the Book and [b]take in exchange for it a paltry price, they fill their bellies with nothing but fire.[200] [c]Allāh will not speak to them on the Day of Resurrection, nor will He purify them. And for them is a grievous punishment.

إِنَّ الَّذِينَ يَكْتُمُونَ مَا أَنْزَلَ اللّٰهُ مِنَ الْكِتٰبِ وَ
يَشْتَرُونَ بِهٖ ثَمَنًا قَلِيلًا أُولٰٓئِكَ مَا يَأْكُلُونَ فِي بُطُونِهِمْ
إِلَّا النَّارَ وَلَا يُكَلِّمُهُمُ اللّٰهُ يَوْمَ الْقِيٰمَةِ وَلَا يُزَكِّيهِمْ
وَلَهُمْ عَذَابٌ أَلِيمٌ ﴿١٧٥﴾

176. It is they [d]who have bought error for guidance and punishment for forgiveness. How great is their endurance[201] of the Fire !

أُولٰٓئِكَ الَّذِينَ اشْتَرَوُا الضَّلٰلَةَ بِالْهُدٰى وَالْعَذَابَ
بِالْمَغْفِرَةِ فَمَآ أَصْبَرَهُمْ عَلَى النَّارِ ﴿١٧٦﴾

177. That is because [e]Allāh has sent down the Book with the truth; and surely, they who disagree concerning the Book are *gone* far in enmity.

ذٰلِكَ بِأَنَّ اللّٰهَ نَزَّلَ الْكِتٰبَ بِالْحَقِّ وَإِنَّ الَّذِينَ اخْتَلَفُوا
فِي الْكِتٰبِ لَفِي شِقَاقٍ بَعِيدٍ ﴿١٧٧﴾

[a]See 2:147. [b]See 2:42. [c]2:160. [d]2:17; 3:178; 4:45. [e]17:106.

comment mentions only the "unlawful things." The forbidden things have been stated by the Holy Prophet and are mentioned in the Ḥadīth. The use of *Ḥarām* or an unlawful thing has direct bearing on the moral development of man but it is not so with a forbidden thing which stands on a lower level of importance, though both are prohibited. Among the things declared unlawful in this verse, the blood and the flesh of a dead animal as food are evidently injurious and have been recognized as such by most authorities on medicine. The flesh of swine has been proved to be injurious, besides man's physical health, to his moral and spiritual health. The swine eats filth and takes delight in living in dirty places. It has indecent habits and possesses the evil trait of sex-perversion. Tape-worms, scrofula, cancer and encysted trichina are known to be more prevalent among pork-eating peoples. The use of pork also causes trichinosis.

200. The words signify that as fire cannot satisfy thirst, but rather increases it, so the things of this world cannot bring peace of mind and contentment but rather the reverse of them.

201. The words mean that the disbelievers are, as it were, possessed of great endurance to bear the torment of the fire of Hell. These words have been used ironically.

R. 22 178. [a]It is not righteousness that you turn your faces to the East or the West, but *truly* righteous is he who believes in Allāh and the Last Day and the angels and the Book and the Prophets, and [b]spends his money out of love for Him,[202] on the kindred and the orphans and the needy and the wayfarer and those who ask *for charity*, and for *ransoming* the captives; and observes Prayer and pays the *Zakāt*; and those [c]who fulfil their promise when they have made one, and the patient in [d]poverty[202A] and afflictions and *the steadfast* in time of war; [e]it is these who have proved truthful and it is these who are *truly* God-fearing.[203]

لَيْسَ الْبِرَّ اَنْ تُوَلُّوْا وُجُوْهَكُمْ قِبَلَ الْمَشْرِقِ وَ
الْمَغْرِبِ وَ لٰكِنَّ الْبِرَّ مَنْ اٰمَنَ بِاللّٰهِ وَالْيَوْمِ الْاٰخِرِ
وَ الْمَلٰٓئِكَةِ وَ الْكِتٰبِ وَ النَّبِيّٖنَ ۚ وَ اٰتَى الْمَالَ عَلٰى
حُبِّهٖ ذَوِي الْقُرْبٰى وَ الْيَتٰمٰى وَ الْمَسٰكِيْنَ وَ ابْنَ السَّبِيْلِ ۙ
وَ السَّآئِلِيْنَ وَ فِي الرِّقَابِ ۚ وَ اَقَامَ الصَّلٰوةَ وَ اٰتَى
الزَّكٰوةَ ۚ وَ الْمُوْفُوْنَ بِعَهْدِهِمْ اِذَا عٰهَدُوْا ۚ وَ الصّٰبِرِيْنَ
فِي الْبَاْسَآءِ وَ الضَّرَّآءِ وَ حِيْنَ الْبَاْسِ ؕ اُولٰٓئِكَ الَّذِيْنَ
صَدَقُوْا ؕ وَ اُولٰٓئِكَ هُمُ الْمُتَّقُوْنَ ﴿۱۷۸﴾

179. O ye who believe! [f]*equitable* retaliation in *the matter of* the slain is prescribed for you; the free man for the free man, and the slave for the slave, and the female for the female. But for him who is granted any remission by his *injured* brother, pursuing *the matter for the realization of the blood-money* shall be done with fairness, and *the murderer* shall pay him the blood-money in a handsome manner. This is an alleviation from your Lord and a mercy.

يٰٓاَيُّهَا الَّذِيْنَ اٰمَنُوْا كُتِبَ عَلَيْكُمُ الْقِصَاصُ فِي الْقَتْلٰى ؕ
اَلْحُرُّ بِالْحُرِّ وَ الْعَبْدُ بِالْعَبْدِ وَ الْاُنْثٰى بِالْاُنْثٰى ؕ فَمَنْ
عُفِيَ لَهٗ مِنْ اَخِيْهِ شَيْءٌ فَاتِّبَاعٌ ۢ بِالْمَعْرُوْفِ وَ اَدَآءٌ
اِلَيْهِ بِاِحْسَانٍ ؕ ذٰلِكَ تَخْفِيْفٌ مِّنْ رَّبِّكُمْ وَ رَحْمَةٌ ؕ

[a]2:190. [b]76:9. [c]9:4; 13:21. [d]2:215; 6:43; 7:95. [e]49:16. [f]2:195; 5:46.

202. *'Alā Ḥubbi-hī* means, for love of God; notwithstanding love of money.

202A. *Al-Ba'sā'* and *al-Ba's* are both derived from *Ba'usa* and *Ba'isa, i.e.*; he was or became strong and valiant in war or fight; he was or became in a state of great want or poverty or distress. *Al-Ba'sā'* means, might or strength in war or fight; war or fight; fear; harm, etc., *al-Ḍarrā'* is especially that evil or affliction which relates to one's person as disease, etc., and *al-Ba'sā'* is that which relates to property, as poverty, etc (Lane).

203. The verse gives a gist of Islamic teaching. It begins with the basic Islamic beliefs and doctrines which are the source and basis of all actions and on the rightness of which depends the rightness of human actions — belief in God, in the Last Day, in angels, Revealed Books and Divine Prophets. After this some of the more important ordinances relating to man's actions are mentioned.

And whoso transgresses thereafter, for him there shall be a grievous punishment.[204]	فَمَنِ اعْتَدٰى بَعْدَ ذٰلِكَ فَلَهٗ عَذَابٌ اَلِيْمٌ ﴿۱۷۹﴾
180. And there is life for you in *the law of* retaliation, O men of understanding, that you may enjoy security.[204A]	وَلَكُمْ فِي الْقِصَاصِ حَيٰوةٌ يّٰاُولِي الْاَلْبَابِ لَعَلَّكُمْ تَتَّقُوْنَ ﴿۱۸۰﴾

204. The verse comprises a very important principle of civil law, *i.e.*, equality of man and necessity of awarding proportionate punishment to all offenders without distinction, unless an offender is forgiven by the relatives of his victim under circumstances that are calculated to lead to improvement and betterment of conditions.

The words "is prescribed for you" show that retaliation for the slain is obligatory. Failure to inflict the punishment prescribed by Law on the offender is tantamount to violation of the Divine commandment. The duty, however, of punishing the culprit devolves not on the heirs of the murdered person but, as the plural *'Alaikum* (for you) shows, on the authorities responsible for the maintenance of law and order. The former, however, have been given the option to forgive. So whereas on the one hand the concerned authorities are bound to punish the offender according to the requirements of law, having no right to pardon him of their own accord, on the other the heirs of the murdered person are not entitled to take the law into their own hands and inflict the punishment on the guilty person themselves. In awarding the punishment the verse makes no distinction between offenders. The words used are of a general nature and apply to all offenders who might be guilty of murder, no matter of what rank or station in life or of what religion. Any person, irrespective of his caste or creed and of his station, must be put to death for the murder of any other person, unless pardoned by the relatives of the victim and unless also the pardon has the sanction of the competent authorities. The sayings of the Holy Prophet are explicit on this point (Mājah, ch. on *Diyāt*). The Companions of the Holy Prophet are all agreed that a Muslim may be put to death for murdering a non-belligerent disbeliever (Ṭabarī, v. 44). The Holy Prophet himself ordered a Muslim murderer to be put to death for the murder of a non-belligerent non-Muslim (Quṭnī). The words, *the freeman for the freeman and the slave for the slave and the female for the female*, do not mean that a freeman should not be punished with death for the murder of a slave or that a woman should not be put to death for killing a member of the opposite sex, etc. The social position of a person or the sex of a party also cannot be considered a bar to the application of this law. The peculiar construction, *i.e.*, "the freeman for the freeman,........" has been adopted to refer to, and abolish, a certain custom of the Arabs whereby they used to take into consideration the sex and the social status of the murderer and the murdered person when determining punishment. The commandment contained in this verse seeks to abolish that obnoxious custom. In fact, the law of retaliation, as stated in this verse, is confined to the clause, *equitable retaliation in the matter of the slain is prescribed for you*, which forms a complete sentence in itself, giving a full and complete meaning. The ensuing expression, *the freeman for the freeman and the slave for the slave and the female for the female*, is something extra, not forming part of the law. It only contains a repudiation of the Arab custom referred to above and illustrates, by giving three instances, how the law is to be administered. Such an expression is known as *Jumlah Isti'nāfiah* in Arabic Grammar, and is technically introduced with a view to answering a question which is suggested by the preceding clause to which it is added without any intervening conjunction. The question answered in such an expression is often understood and not expressed (Mukhtaṣar). The Holy Prophet is reported to have said: "Whoever kills his slave shall be put to death" (Mājah). At another place he says: "The blood of all Muslims is alike in respect of the law of retaliation" (Nasaī').

204A. The Islamic law of retaliation provides a very effective means to put a stop to murder and safeguard human life. A man, who shows a callous disregard for human life loses all title to live as a member of human society. Pardon or remission is permissible only where the circumstances are such that it is likely to improve matters and bring about good results for all parties concerned (42:41). Thus, while, on the one hand, Islām has made due provision for the suppression of crime, it has, on the other, kept open the door for the display of the noble qualities of benevolence and mercy. The fact that, despite efforts to the

181. [a]It is prescribed for you, when death comes to any one of you, if he leave much wealth, *that he make* a will to parents and near relatives to act with fairness.[205] *This is* an obligation on those who fear God.

كُتِبَ عَلَيْكُمْ اِذَا حَضَرَ اَحَدَكُمُ الْمَوْتُ اِنْ تَرَكَ خَيْرًا ۖۚ الْوَصِيَّةُ لِلْوَالِدَيْنِ وَالْاَقْرَبِيْنَ بِالْمَعْرُوْفِ ۚ حَقًّا عَلَى الْمُتَّقِيْنَ ﴿۱۸۱﴾

182. And he who alters it after he has heard it, the sin thereof shall surely *lie* on those who alter it.[205A] Surely Allāh is All-Hearing *and* All-Knowing.

فَمَنْ بَدَّلَهٗ بَعْدَ مَا سَمِعَهٗ فَاِنَّمَآ اِثْمُهٗ عَلَى الَّذِيْنَ يُبَدِّلُوْنَهٗ ؕ اِنَّ اللّٰهَ سَمِيْعٌ عَلِيْمٌ ﴿۱۸۲﴾

183. But whoso apprehends from a testator a partiality or a wrong, and makes peace between them (the

فَمَنْ خَافَ مِنْ مُّوْصٍ جَنَفًا اَوْ اِثْمًا فَاَصْلَحَ بَيْنَهُمْ

[a]4:12,13,177; 5:107.

contrary, the death penalty is still found on the Statute books of most countries in one form or another, constitutes a sufficient proof of the wisdom of the Islamic ordinance. Even the most enthusiastic protagonists of the abolition of Capital Punishment have not yet been able to suggest a suitable alternative to it. They have had to admit that a long term of imprisonment as an alternative is "horrible" and is "not an ideal substitute" (Capital Punishment in the Twentieth Century by E. Roy Calvert, G. P. Putnam, London, 1930).

205. Verses 4 : 12, 13 fix the shares of all those persons who should succeed to a deceased person's property. These verses have been mistakenly understood by some Commentators to abrogate the verse under comment which, in fact, lays down an additional and very necessary provision, and refers only to bequests made in favour of individuals not legally entitled to a share in the testator's property, or for charitable purposes, or for war conditions. It does not refer to bequests made in favour of legal heirs which subject has been dealt with in 4:12-13. There is no question, therefore, of the abrogation of this verse by those verses which lay down the rules of inheritance and also recognise the validity of any bequests that may have been made. Each operates in its own sphere and draws strength from the other. The bequests thus made, however, should not exceed one third of the property left as is mentioned in a saying of the Holy Prophet related by Sa'd bin Abī Waqqāṣ (Bukhārī, *Kitāb al-Janā'iz*); this being the utmost limit to which the testator can exercise his discretion, and that only in case he leaves abundant wealth as the word *Khair* (much wealth) shows. Verse 5 : 107, according to which a dying Muslim could make a bequest and which was, by common consent, revealed after vv. 4 : 12-13, further supports the view that the verse under comment is not abrogated by vv. 4 : 12-13. In fact, the whole theory of abrogation has no foundation.

205A. This indicates that the previous verse contemplates some directions which are obligatory and a contravention of which would be sinful. Obviously, what is meant is a direction that the estate shall be administered in accordance with the law of inheritance. If the testator gives such a direction, then the sin of any contravention would lie on those who are guilty of the contravention.

ع ۲۲ فَلَآ اِثْمَ عَلَيْهِ ۭ اِنَّ اللّٰهَ غَفُوْرٌ رَّحِيْمٌ ﴿۱۸۳﴾

parties affected), it shall be no sin for him.[205B] Surely, Allāh is Most Forgiving *and* Merciful.

يٰۤاَيُّهَا الَّذِيْنَ اٰمَنُوْا كُتِبَ عَلَيْكُمُ الصِّيَامُ كَمَا كُتِبَ
عَلَى الَّذِيْنَ مِنْ قَبْلِكُمْ لَعَلَّكُمْ تَتَّقُوْنَ ﴿۱۸۴﴾

23 184. O ye who believe ! fasting is prescribed for you, as it was prescribed for those before you,[206] so that you may guard against evil.

اَيَّامًا مَّعْدُوْدٰتٍ ۭ فَمَنْ كَانَ مِنْكُمْ مَّرِيْضًا اَوْ عَلٰى
سَفَرٍ فَعِدَّةٌ مِّنْ اَيَّامٍ اُخَرَ ۭ وَعَلَى الَّذِيْنَ يُطِيْقُوْنَهٗ
فِدْيَةٌ طَعَامُ مِسْكِيْنٍ ۭ فَمَنْ تَطَوَّعَ خَيْرًا فَهُوَ خَيْرٌ
لَّهٗ ۭ وَاَنْ تَصُوْمُوْا خَيْرٌ لَّكُمْ اِنْ كُنْتُمْ تَعْلَمُوْنَ ﴿۱۸۵﴾

185. *The prescribed fasting is* for a [a]fixed number of days, but whoso among you is sick or is on a journey *shall fast* the same number of other days; and for those who are able to fast *only* with great difficulty[207] is an expiation—the feeding of a poor man. And whoso does good of his own accord it is better for him. And fasting is good for you, if you only knew.

---

[a]2 : 204.

205B. A will may comply with legal requirements and may yet be unfair in some of its provisions. For instance, if a person leaves a large number of heirs, it may entail a hardship on them if he wills away as much as the full one-third for charitable or other lawful purposes. Or, out of the permissible 1/3 the testator may have made unfair dispositions, neglecting or overlooking just claims. It would in such a case be permissible, indeed meritorious, to bring about a fair adjustment between the heirs and the legatees affected.

206. Fasting, as a religious institution, in whatever form or detail, is to be found in all Faiths. "By the greater number of religions, in the lower, middle and higher cultures alike, fasting is largely prescribed; and when it is not required it is nevertheless practised to some extent by individuals in response to the promptings of nature" (Enc. Brit). It is the common experience of saints and seers that a certain degree of severance from physical relations or worldly connections is essential for spiritual advancement and has a powerful purifying effect on the mind. Islām, however, has introduced a new orientation and a new spiritual significance in this institution. According to it fasting constitutes a symbol of complete sacrifice. One who fasts not only abstains from food and drink which are the chief means of sustenance and without which one cannot live, but also from going in unto one's wife which is the means of assuring one's progeny. Thus he who fasts really evinces his readiness, if need be, to sacrifice his all for the sake of his Lord and Creator.

207. This meaning of the Arabic expression in the text is supported by another reading of *Yuṭiqūna-hū* which is *Yuṭayyiqūna-hū* meaning, they can do so only with great difficulty (Jarīr). The verse mentions three classes of believers to whom concession is allowed: the sick ; those on a journey and those too weak to fast except with danger to their health. The expression may also mean: "Those who are unable to fast" (Lisān and Mufradāt). The whole sentence has also been taken to signify: "Those, who can afford, should, besides fasting, feed a poor man as an act of piety;" the pronoun *hū* in *Yuṭīqūna-hū* standing for "the feeding of a poor man."

186. The month of Ramaḍān[207A] is that in which the Qur'ān[207B] was revealed[208] as a guidance for mankind with clear proofs of guidance and [a]discrimination. Therefore, whosoever of you is present *at home* in this month let him fast therein. But whoso is *temporarily* sick or is on a journey, *shall fast* the same number of other days.[209] [b]Allāh desires ease for you, and He desires not hardship for you, and *He desires* that you may complete the number, and that [c]you may exalt Allāh for His having guided you and that you may be grateful.

شَهْرُ رَمَضَانَ الَّذِيْٓ اُنْزِلَ فِيْهِ الْقُرْاٰنُ هُدًى
لِّلنَّاسِ وَبَيِّنٰتٍ مِّنَ الْهُدٰى وَالْفُرْقَانِ ۚ فَمَنْ شَهِدَ
مِنْكُمُ الشَّهْرَ فَلْيَصُمْهُ ۗ وَمَنْ كَانَ مَرِيْضًا اَوْ عَلٰى
سَفَرٍ فَعِدَّةٌ مِّنْ اَيَّامٍ اُخَرَ ۗ يُرِيْدُ اللّٰهُ بِكُمُ
الْيُسْرَ وَلَا يُرِيْدُ بِكُمُ الْعُسْرَ ۫ وَلِتُكْمِلُوا الْعِدَّةَ
وَلِتُكَبِّرُوا اللّٰهَ عَلٰى مَا هَدٰىكُمْ وَلَعَلَّكُمْ تَشْكُرُوْنَ ۝١٨٦

[a]2:186; 3:4; 8:42; 21:49; 25:2. [b]2:287; 5:7; 22:79. [c]22:38.

207A. *Ramaḍān* is the ninth month of the lunar year. The word is derived from *Ramaḍa*. They say *Ramaḍa al-Ṣāi'mu, i.e.*, the inside of the man fasting became very hot with thirst owing to fasting (Lane). The month is so named because (1) fasting in this month produces heat and burning due to thirst; (2) worship in this month burns away the traces of sin in man ('Asākir & Mardawaih); and (3) because his devotions in this month produce in the heart of man the necessary warmth of love for his Creator and his fellow-beings. The name *Ramaḍān* is of Islamic origin, the former name of the month being *Nātiq* (Qadīr).

207B. *Al-Qur'ān* is derived from *Qara'a* which means, he read; he conveyed or delivered a message; he collected the thing. Thus Qur'ān means: (1) a book which is meant to be read. The Qur'ān is the most widely read book in the world (Enc. Brit); (2) a book or message which is meant to be conveyed and delivered to the world. The Qur'ān is the only revealed Book whose Message is absolutely unrestricted; for whereas all other revealed Books are meant for specific times and specific peoples, the Qur'ān is meant for all times and all peoples (34 : 29); (3) a book which comprises all truths; the Qur'ān is indeed a storehouse of knowledge which comprises not only all eternal truths contained in the previous revealed Books (98 : 4), but also all such truths as mankind may stand in need of at any time and in any circumstances (18 : 50).

208. It was on the 24th of Ramaḍān that the Holy Prophet received his first revelation (Jarīr); and the whole revelation was rehearsed every year to the Holy Prophet by the angel Gabriel in this month. This practice continued till the very last year of the Prophet's life when the whole of the Qur'ān was rehearsed to him twice by the Archangel Jibrīl in this month (Bukhārī). Thus in a way even the whole of the Qur'ān may be said to have been revealed in the month of Ramaḍān.

209. The sentence is not an unnecessary repetition; for whereas in the previous verse it formed part of the verse that was meant to prepare the ground for the commandment to fast, in this verse it forms part of the actual commandment. The Qur'ān, however, wisely refrains from defining the terms "sickness" and "journey," leaving them to be defined by the common usage of the people and the attending circumstances.

187. And when My servants ask thee about Me, *say*, [a]"I am near.[210] [b]I answer the prayer of the supplicant when he prays to Me. So they should hearken to Me and believe[211] in Me, that they may follow the right way.'

وَإِذَا سَأَلَكَ عِبَادِي عَنِّي فَإِنِّي قَرِيبٌ أُجِيبُ دَعْوَةَ
الدَّاعِ إِذَا دَعَانِ فَلْيَسْتَجِيبُوا لِي وَلْيُؤْمِنُوا بِي لَعَلَّهُمْ
يَرْشُدُونَ ﴿١٨٧﴾

188. It is made lawful for you to go in unto your wives on the night of the fast. They are a *sort of* garment[212] for you and you are a *sort of* garment for them. Allāh knows that you have been acting unjustly to yourselves, wherefore He has turned to you with mercy and afforded you relief.[213] So you may now go in unto them and seek what Allāh has ordained for you; and eat and drink until the white thread becomes distinct to you from the black thread of the dawn. Then complete the fast till nightfall[214] and do not go in unto them while you remain in the mosques[215] for devotion. These are the limits *set* by

أُحِلَّ لَكُمْ لَيْلَةَ الصِّيَامِ الرَّفَثُ إِلَىٰ نِسَائِكُمْ هُنَّ
لِبَاسٌ لَّكُمْ وَأَنتُمْ لِبَاسٌ لَّهُنَّ عَلِمَ اللَّهُ أَنَّكُمْ
كُنتُمْ تَخْتَانُونَ أَنفُسَكُمْ فَتَابَ عَلَيْكُمْ وَعَفَا
عَنكُمْ فَالْآنَ بَاشِرُوهُنَّ وَابْتَغُوا مَا كَتَبَ اللَّهُ لَكُمْ
وَكُلُوا وَاشْرَبُوا حَتَّىٰ يَتَبَيَّنَ لَكُمُ الْخَيْطُ الْأَبْيَضُ
مِنَ الْخَيْطِ الْأَسْوَدِ مِنَ الْفَجْرِ ثُمَّ أَتِمُّوا الصِّيَامَ
إِلَى اللَّيْلِ وَلَا تُبَاشِرُوهُنَّ وَأَنتُمْ عَاكِفُونَ فِي الْمَسَاجِدِ

[a]11 : 62; 34 : 51; 50 : 17. [b]27 : 63.

210. When the Faithful come to know of the blessings of the month of Ramaḍān and of fasting therein they naturally become eager to derive as much spiritual benefit from it as possible. It is to this hankering of the soul of a believer to which the verse supplies an answer.

211. The words, *believe in Me*, do not refer to belief in the existence of God; for, this idea is included in the preceding clause, *they should hearken to Me*, it being impossible that one should hearken to God and obey His commandments without believing in His existence. The words, *believe in Me*, therefore, refer to the belief that God hears and accepts the prayers of His servants.

212. How beautifully in these brief words the Qur'ān has described the rights and status of woman and the object and signif-ance of marriage and conjugal relations. The real object of marriage, the verse purports to say, is the comfort, protection and embellishment of the parties, for such are the uses of a garment (7 : 27 & 16 : 82). It definitely is not merely the satisfaction of sexual urge. Husband and wife also safeguard each other against evil and scandal.

213. The expression '*Afā Allāhu 'An-hu* means, God corrected his mistake and set right his affairs; bestowed honour upon him. It also means, God afforded him relief (Muḥīṭ).

214. At places where days and nights are unusually long (*e.g.* near the Poles) day and night should be calculated to be of twelve hours' duration (Muslim, ch. *Ashrāṭ al-Sā'ah*).

215. In *I'tikāf* which constitutes, as it were, the consummation of the spirit of fasting, intercourse with wives and preliminaries thereto are not allowed even at night time.

Allāh, so approach them not. Thus does Allāh make His commandments clear to men that they may become secure against evil.

تِلْكَ حُدُوْدُ اللّٰهِ فَلَا تَقْرَبُوْهَا ؕ كَذٰلِكَ يُبَيِّنُ اللّٰهُ اٰيٰتِهٖ لِلنَّاسِ لَعَلَّهُمْ يَتَّقُوْنَ ﴿۱۸۸﴾

189. And [a]do not devour your property[215A] among yourselves by false means[216] and offer it not *as bribe* to the authorities that you may devour a part of the wealth of *other* people wrongfully while you know.

وَلَا تَاْكُلُوْٓا اَمْوَالَكُمْ بَيْنَكُمْ بِالْبَاطِلِ وَتُدْلُوْا بِهَآ اِلَى الْحُكَّامِ لِتَاْكُلُوْا فَرِيْقًا مِّنْ اَمْوَالِ النَّاسِ بِالْاِثْمِ وَاَنْتُمْ تَعْلَمُوْنَ ﴿۱۸۹﴾ ع ٢٣ ٤

R. 24 190. They ask thee about the new moons. Say, [b]'They are means for measuring time,[217] for *the general convenience of* people and for the Pilgrimage.' And it is not righteousness that you come into houses by the backs[218] thereof; but [c]*truly* righteous is he who fears God. And you should come into houses by the doors thereof; and fear Allāh that you may prosper.

يَسْـَٔلُوْنَكَ عَنِ الْاَهِلَّةِ ؕ قُلْ هِيَ مَوَاقِيْتُ لِلنَّاسِ وَالْحَجِّ ؕ وَلَيْسَ الْبِرُّ بِاَنْ تَاْتُوا الْبُيُوْتَ مِنْ ظُهُوْرِهَا وَلٰكِنَّ الْبِرَّ مَنِ اتَّقٰى ۚ وَاْتُوا الْبُيُوْتَ مِنْ اَبْوَابِهَا ۠ وَاتَّقُوا اللّٰهَ لَعَلَّكُمْ تُفْلِحُوْنَ ﴿۱۹۰﴾

[a]4 : 30, 162; 9 : 34. [b]2 : 198; 9 : 36. [c]2 : 178.

215A. In order to emphasize communal or national unity the Qur'ān often refers to other Muslims' property as "your property." So here also other Muslims' property is spoken of as "your property."

216. The commandment relating to fasting enjoined Muslims to refrain from eating and drinking within specified periods with a view to attaining piety and righteousness. This was the most opportune time to remind them that unlawful eating, *i.e.*, unlawful acquisition of wealth, must all the more be scrupulously avoided. Incidentally, the verse forcefully condemns the practice of giving and taking bribe.

217. Islām has made use of both the lunar and solar systems for measuring time. Where worship is to be performed in different parts of the day the solar system of reckoning time is used, as in the five daily Prayers or for the beginning and the breaking of the daily fast; and where worship is to be completed within a particular month or part thereof, the lunar system is used, as in selecting the month of fasting or the appointment of the time of Pilgrimage, etc. Thus Islām has made use of both the systems ; so the solar system is as much Islamic as the lunar system.

218. The clause points to a very important principle that the real purpose in prescribing different acts of worship is the intrinsic usefulness thereof and not that every change of time should have attached to it an act of worship. Therefore the question, arising from the over-eagerness of the Faithful, that, like fasting, there may be prescribed other acts of worship in other months also, was like approaching a house not through its door but by "the back thereof." The primary thing is worship and time is only secondary, but those who put the question wanted to make time a primary, and worship merely a secondary thing. This was like putting the cart before the horse. The reference also seems to be to a practice of the pagan Arabs that when they had once started on Pilgrimage to

191. And *fight[219] in the way of Allāh against those who fight against you, but do not transgress. Surely, Allāh loves not the transgressors.

وَ قَاتِلُوْا فِىْ سَبِيْلِ اللّٰهِ الَّذِيْنَ يُقَاتِلُوْنَكُمْ وَ لَا تَعْتَدُوْا ۖ اِنَّ اللّٰهَ لَا يُحِبُّ الْمُعْتَدِيْنَ ۞

192. And slay *these transgressors*[220] wherever you meet them and drive them out from where they have driven[221] you out; for *persecution is worse than slaying. And fight them not *in and* near the Sacred Mosque until they fight you therein. But if they fight you, then fight them. Such is the requital for the disbelievers.

وَ اقْتُلُوْهُمْ حَيْثُ ثَقِفْتُمُوْهُمْ وَ اَخْرِجُوْهُمْ مِّنْ حَيْثُ اَخْرَجُوْكُمْ وَ الْفِتْنَةُ اَشَدُّ مِنَ الْقَتْلِ ۚ وَ لَا تُقَاتِلُوْهُمْ عِنْدَ الْمَسْجِدِ الْحَرَامِ حَتّٰى يُقَاتِلُوْكُمْ فِيْهِ ۚ فَاِنْ قَاتَلُوْكُمْ فَاقْتُلُوْهُمْ ۗ كَذٰلِكَ جَزَآءُ الْكٰفِرِيْنَ ۞

193. But *if they desist, then surely, Allāh is Most Forgiving, Merciful.

فَاِنِ انْتَهَوْا فَاِنَّ اللّٰهَ غَفُوْرٌ رَّحِيْمٌ ۞

194. And *fight them until there is no persecution, and religion is *professed only* for Allāh.[222] But if

وَ قٰتِلُوْهُمْ حَتّٰى لَا تَكُوْنَ فِتْنَةٌ وَّ يَكُوْنَ الدِّيْنُ لِلّٰهِ ۖ

---

*4 : 76; 8 : 40; 9 : 13; 22 : 40; 60 : 9,10. *2 : 218. *8 : 40. *8 : 40.

Mecca, if for any any reason they had to come back, they would enter their houses from their backs by scaling over the walls. The verse condemns such practices, pointing out that they do not constitute virtue which is a spiritual concept, and implies that appropriate means should be adopted for the achievement of one's objective (Bukhārī, ch. on Tafsīr).

219. This is one of the earliest verses in which permission to fight was given to Muslims, the very first verse revealed in this connection being 22 : 40. The verse under comment contains the gist of the conditions which should govern a religious war: (a) Such a war should be undertaken with the object of removing obstacles placed in the way of Allāh, *i.e.*, for the establishment of the freedom of religious belief and practice. (b) It is to be waged only against those who first take up arms against Muslims. (c) The Muslims should lay down arms as soon as the enemy desists from fighting.

220. This verse relates to conditions when war has actually broken out. Obviously, it enjoins Muslims to fight against only such disbelievers as are the first to take up arms against them.

221. The words signify that Mecca being the centre and the most sacred place of Islām, no non-Muslim should be allowed to remain in it.

222. This verse also shows that Muslims are allowed to fight in self defence only when war is inflicted upon them by the other party and to continue it till complete freedom of religion is established. The Holy Prophet could not have entered into a number of treaties of peace with disbelievers if the Divine commandment had been to continue fighting until all disbelievers had embraced Islām. For a detailed note on Jihād see 1956—1960.

they desist, then *remember* that no hostility[223] is *allowed* except against the wrongdoers.

فَاِنِ انْتَهَوْا فَلَا عُدْوَانَ اِلَّا عَلَى الظّٰلِمِيْنَ ﴿۱۹۴﴾

195. [a]The *violation of a* Sacred Month[224] *may be retaliated* in the Sacred Month; and for *all* sacred things there is *the law of* retaliation. So, whoso transgresses against you, punish[225] him for his transgression to the extent to which he has transgressed against you. And fear Allāh and know that Allāh is with those who fear *Him*.

اَلشَّهْرُ الْحَرَامُ بِالشَّهْرِ الْحَرَامِ وَالْحُرُمٰتُ قِصَاصٌ ؕ فَمَنِ اعْتَدٰى عَلَيْكُمْ فَاعْتَدُوْا عَلَيْهِ بِمِثْلِ مَا اعْتَدٰى عَلَيْكُمْ ۪ وَاتَّقُوا اللّٰهَ وَاعْلَمُوْٓا اَنَّ اللّٰهَ مَعَ الْمُتَّقِيْنَ ﴿۱۹۵﴾

196. And [b]spend in the cause of Allāh, and cast not yourselves into ruin with your own hands,[226] and do good; surely, Allāh loves those who do good.

وَاَنْفِقُوْا فِيْ سَبِيْلِ اللّٰهِ وَلَا تُلْقُوْا بِاَيْدِيْكُمْ اِلَى التَّهْلُكَةِ ۛۚ وَاَحْسِنُوْا ۚ اِنَّ اللّٰهَ يُحِبُّ الْمُحْسِنِيْنَ ﴿۱۹۶﴾

[a]See 2 : 179. [b]2 : 255; 14 : 32; 47 : 39; 57 : 11; 63 : 11.

223. '*Udwān* means, (1) hostility; (2) wrongful conduct; (3) punishment for wrongful conduct; and (4) approach to a person by way of justification or excuse against him (Mufradāt & Lane).

These four verses (191-194) embody the following rules about war : (a) War is to be resorted to only for the sake of God and not for any selfish motive, nor for aggrandisement or the advancement of national or other interests. (b) Muslims can go to war only against those who attack them first. (c) Even after the enemy has initiated the attack, they are enjoined to keep warfare within limits and not to extend it beyond the immediate objective. (d) They are to fight against only the regular army and not to attack or molest non-combatants. (e) During the course of fighting immunity is to be afforded to all religious rites and ceremonies. (f) To attack religious places or to do any kind of harm to them is absolutely forbidden, so that no fighting is allowed even in their neighbourhood. (g) If the enemy uses a place of worship as a base for attack, only then Muslims may return the attack in or near it. (h) Fighting is to continue only so long as interference with religious freedom lasts. See also 8 : 40; 9 : 4-6; 22: 40, 41; etc.

224. The Sacred Months are Dhu'l-Qa'dah; Dhu'l-Ḥijjah; Al-Muḥarram and Rajab. In these months all fighting is disallowed. The commandment is intended to safeguard the sanctity of the Ka'bah and the Sacred Months.

225. See 33.

226. As for the successful prosecution of war money is required, the believers are exhorted to spend freely in the cause of Allāh as any hesitancy to do so would result in national ruin.

197. And complete the Pilgrimage[227] and the 'Umrah[228] for the sake of Allāh; but [a]if you are kept back,[229] then *make* whatever offering is easily available; and do not shave your heads until the offering reaches its destination. And whoever among you is sick or has an ailment of the head, should make an expiation either by fasting or almsgiving or a sacrifice. But when you are safe, then he, who would avail himself of the 'Umrah together[230] with the Pilgrimage, *should make* whatever offering is easily obtainable. But such *of you* as cannot find *an offering* should fast three days during the Pilgrimage,[231] and seven when you return home; these are ten complete.

وَأَتِمُّوا الْحَجَّ وَالْعُمْرَةَ لِلّٰهِ ۚ فَإِنْ أُحْصِرْتُمْ فَمَا اسْتَيْسَرَ
مِنَ الْهَدْيِ ۚ وَلَا تَحْلِقُوا رُءُوسَكُمْ حَتّٰى يَبْلُغَ الْهَدْيُ
مَحِلَّهٗ ۚ فَمَنْ كَانَ مِنْكُمْ مَّرِيضًا أَوْ بِهٖٓ أَذًى مِّنْ رَّأْسِهٖ
فَفِدْيَةٌ مِّنْ صِيَامٍ أَوْ صَدَقَةٍ أَوْ نُسُكٍ ۚ فَإِذَآ أَمِنْتُمْ
فَمَنْ تَمَتَّعَ بِالْعُمْرَةِ إِلَى الْحَجِّ فَمَا اسْتَيْسَرَ مِنَ
الْهَدْيِ ۚ فَمَنْ لَّمْ يَجِدْ فَصِيَامُ ثَلٰثَةِ أَيَّامٍ فِي الْحَجِّ
وَسَبْعَةٍ إِذَا رَجَعْتُمْ ۭ تِلْكَ عَشَرَةٌ كَامِلَةٌ ۭ ذٰلِكَ لِمَنْ

[a]48 : 26.

227. With this verse begins the subject of *Hajj* (Pilgrimage). *Jihād* and *Hajj* seem to be correlated and both constitute a form of sacrifice which a true and sincere believer has to undergo in the way of Allāh, a subject which began with 2 : 178. The Pilgrimage is the last stage in the spiritual development of man, the other stages such as Prayer, Fasting and *Jihād* having already been discussed.

228. The 'Umrah or the Lesser Pilgrimage consists in entering into a stage of *Iḥrām* in the way mentioned above, circuiting the Ka'bah seven times, running between Ṣafā and Marwah and offering a sacrifice which, however, is not obligatory. The 'Umrah may be performed at any time of the year, whereas the *Ḥajj* or the Greater Pilgrimage is performed only during the month of Dhu'l-Ḥijjah.

229. The words, *if you are kept back*, refer to a state of affairs when a would-be pilgrim is prevented by disease, or a state of war, or by some other cause, from visiting the Ka'bah to perform the *Ḥajj* or the 'Umrah.

230. The 'Umrah and the *Ḥajj* may be combined in two ways : (a) The pilgrim who intends to perform the 'Umrah alone should enter into the state of *Iḥrām* and perform its rites and finish it. Then on the eighth day of *Dhu'l-Ḥijjah* he should again enter into the state of *Iḥrām* and perform the prescribed rites of *Ḥajj*. This form of combining the 'Umrah and the *Ḥajj* is technically called *Tamattu'* which literally means, "availing oneself of a thing." (b) The pilgrim may perform the 'Umrah and the *Ḥajj* simultaneously. He should, in this case, enter into the state of *Iḥrām* with that intention and should remain in that state till the end of the Pilgrimage. This combination of *Ḥajj* and 'Umrah is called *Qirān* which literally means, "the putting together of two things." In both *Tamattu'* and *Qirān* it is obligatory to offer the sacrifice. In the verse under comment the word *Tamattu'* is not used in the technical sense and covers *Qirān* also.

231. Fasting is mentioned in the clause, *should fast three days during the Pilgrimage*, is distinct and separate from the fasting mentioned above. The first-mentioned fasting is meant for those who cannot shave their heads while this fasting is meant for those who are unable to offer sacrifice in case of *Tamattu'*. The three days spoken of are preferably the 11th, 12th and 13th of *Dhu'l Ḥijjah*. The remaining seven fasts may be observed after one has returned home.

This is for him whose family does not reside near the Sacred Mosque.[232] And fear Allāh and know that Allāh is severe in punishing.

لَمْ يَكُنْ اَهْلُهٗ حَاضِرِي الْمَسْجِدِ الْحَرَامِ ۚ وَاتَّقُوا اللّٰهَ
وَاعْلَمُوْٓا اَنَّ اللّٰهَ شَدِيْدُ الْعِقَابِ ﴿١٩٧﴾ ع ۲۴ ۸

R. 25 198. [a]The months of the Pilgrimage are well known; so [b]whoever determines to perform the Pilgrimage in these months *should remember that* there is *to be* no foul talk,[233] nor any transgression, nor any quarrelling during the Pilgrimage. And whatever good you do, Allāh knows it. And furnish yourselves with *necessary* provisions *for your journey* and surely, the best provision is righteousness. And fear Me *alone*, O men of understanding.

اَلْحَجُّ اَشْهُرٌ مَّعْلُوْمٰتٌ ۚ فَمَنْ فَرَضَ فِيْهِنَّ الْحَجَّ
فَلَا رَفَثَ وَلَا فُسُوْقَ ۙ وَلَا جِدَالَ فِي الْحَجِّ ۗ وَمَا
تَفْعَلُوْا مِنْ خَيْرٍ يَّعْلَمْهُ اللّٰهُ ۗ وَتَزَوَّدُوْا فَاِنَّ خَيْرَ
الزَّادِ التَّقْوٰى ۫ وَاتَّقُوْنِ يٰٓاُولِي الْاَلْبَابِ ﴿١٩٨﴾

199. It is no sin for you that [c]you seek the bounty[234] of your Lord. But when you pour forth from 'Arafāt,[235] remember Allāh at Mash'ar al-Ḥarām,[236] and [d]remember Him as He has guided you; although, before this, you were of those gone astray.

لَيْسَ عَلَيْكُمْ جُنَاحٌ اَنْ تَبْتَغُوْا فَضْلًا مِّنْ رَّبِّكُمْ ۗ
فَاِذَآ اَفَضْتُمْ مِّنْ عَرَفٰتٍ فَاذْكُرُوا اللّٰهَ عِنْدَ الْمَشْعَرِ
الْحَرَامِ ۠ وَاذْكُرُوْهُ كَمَا هَدٰىكُمْ ۚ وَاِنْ كُنْتُمْ مِّنْ
قَبْلِهٖ لَمِنَ الضَّآلِّيْنَ ﴿١٩٩﴾

[a]2 : 190; 9 : 36. [b]3 : 98; 22 : 28. [c]62 : 11. [d]2 : 153, 204; 8 : 46; 62 : 11.

232. The words mean that the permission to combine *Ḥajj* and 'Umrah is meant not for the residents of Mecca but for those who come from outside. By some, however, the words "the Sacred Mosque" have been extended to include the whole of *Ḥaram, i.e.*, the sacred territory in and around Mecca.

233. *Rafath* includes all foul, immodest and lewd talk as well as acts relating to sex. *Fusūq* signifies transgression against the laws of God and disobedience of lawful authority, whether spiritual or temporal. And *Jidāl* means, disputes and quarrels with co-travellers, companions and neighbours.

234. As the object of Pilgrimage is that the greatest possible number of Muslims should take part in it, therefore, the Qur'ān permits pilgrims to engage in commerce and trade. Those, who cannot take hard cash with them, may carry merchandise and thereby earn money to meet the expenses of the journey.

235. 'Arafāt is a plain or valley near Mecca where pilgrims halt in the latter part of the ninth day of *Dhu'l Ḥijjah*. It is nine miles from Mecca, and the halt technically known as *Wuqūf* forms an important rite of the Pilgrimage. '*Arafāt* is a compound word meaning, the sacred place or means of perception or knowledge.

236. Mash'ar al-Ḥarām is a small hill in Muzdalifah, which lies between Mecca and 'Arafāt. Here the Holy Prophet said the evening and the night Prayers and remained engaged in prayer all night before the rising of the sun. The place is specially meant for meditation and prayer in Pilgrimage. It is about six miles from Mecca.

200. Then[237] pour forth from where the people pour forth,[238] and seek forgiveness from Allāh; surely, Allāh is Most Forgiving, Merciful.

ثُمَّ أَفِيضُوا مِنْ حَيْثُ أَفَاضَ النَّاسُ وَاسْتَغْفِرُوا
اللّٰهَ إِنَّ اللّٰهَ غَفُورٌ رَّحِيمٌ ﴿٢٠٠﴾

201. And when you have performed [a]the acts of worship prescribed for you, [b]celebrate the praises of Allāh as you *used to* celebrate the praises of your fathers, or with even greater devotion. And [c]of men there are some who say, 'Our Lord, grant us *good things* in this world; and such a one shall have no share in the Hereafter.

فَإِذَا قَضَيْتُمْ مَّنَاسِكَكُمْ فَاذْكُرُوا اللّٰهَ كَذِكْرِكُمْ
آبَاءَكُمْ أَوْ أَشَدَّ ذِكْرًا فَمِنَ النَّاسِ مَنْ يَّقُولُ
رَبَّنَا آتِنَا فِي الدُّنْيَا وَمَا لَهُ فِي الْآخِرَةِ مِنْ خَلَاقٍ ﴿٢٠١﴾

202. And [d]of them there are some who say, 'Our Lord, grant us good in this world as well as good in the world to come,[239] and save us from the torment of the Fire.'

وَمِنْهُمْ مَّنْ يَّقُولُ رَبَّنَا آتِنَا فِي الدُّنْيَا حَسَنَةً وَّ
فِي الْآخِرَةِ حَسَنَةً وَّقِنَا عَذَابَ النَّارِ ﴿٢٠٢﴾ النصف

203. For these there shall be a *goodly* share because of what they have earned. And Allāh is Swift at reckoning.

أُولٰٓئِكَ لَهُمْ نَصِيبٌ مِّمَّا كَسَبُوا وَاللّٰهُ سَرِيعُ الْحِسَابِ ﴿٢٠٣﴾

---

[a]2 : 129. [b]See 2 : 153. [c]4 : 135; 42 : 21. [d]42 : 21.

---

237. If *thumma* is taken to mean "and," and "the return" spoken of in this verse is taken to refer to the return from 'Arafāt, then *al-Nās* would mean "other people"; but if it is taken to mean "then" and "the return" spoken of here is taken to refer to the return from Mash'ar al-Harām, then *al-Nās* would signify "all people " and both these meanings are supported by rules of the Arabic language.

238. Before the advent of Islām the Quraish and the Banū Kinānah known as Ḥums did not accompany other pilgrims to 'Arafāt, but stopped short at Mash'ar al-Ḥarām, waiting to join other people returning from 'Arafāt. In this and the preceding verse, they are bidden not to stop short at Mash'ar al-Ḥarām but to go up to 'Arafāt and do as other people do. After returning from 'Arafāt to Mash'ar al-Ḥarām, pilgrims should proceed to Minā where sacrifices are offered and the state of *Iḥrām* comes to an end.

239. The verse mentions that class of men whose efforts and aspirations are not confined to this world only. They seek the good things of this world and also the good things of the next. *Ḥasanah* also means, success (Tāj). The prayer is very comprehensive and the Holy Prophet very often made use of it (Muslim).

204. And [a]remember Allāh during the appointed number of days,[240] but whoso hastens *to leave* in two days, it shall be no sin for him; and whoso stays behind, it shall be no sin for him *either*. *This direction is* for him who fears Allāh. So fear Allāh[241] and know that you shall *all* be brought together before Him.[242]

وَاذْكُرُوا اللّٰهَ فِيْٓ اَيَّامٍ مَّعْدُوْدٰتٍ ۭ فَمَنْ تَعَجَّلَ فِيْ
يَوْمَيْنِ فَلَآ اِثْمَ عَلَيْهِ ۚ وَمَنْ تَاَخَّرَ فَلَآ اِثْمَ عَلَيْهِ ۙ
لِمَنِ اتَّقٰى ۭ وَاتَّقُوا اللّٰهَ وَاعْلَمُوْٓا اَنَّكُمْ اِلَيْهِ تُحْشَرُوْنَ ﴿٢٠٤﴾

205. And [b]of men there is he whose talk[243] on this life would please thee, and he calls Allāh to witness as to that which is in his heart, and yet he is the most contentious of quarrellers.

وَمِنَ النَّاسِ مَنْ يُّعْجِبُكَ قَوْلُهٗ فِي الْحَيٰوةِ الدُّنْيَا
وَيُشْهِدُ اللّٰهَ عَلٰى مَا فِيْ قَلْبِهٖ ۙ وَهُوَ اَلَدُّ الْخِصَامِ ﴿٢٠٥﴾

[a]See 2 : 153. [b]63 : 5.

240. These are the 11th, the 12th and 13th day of *Dhu'l-Hijjah* during which the pilgrims are required, so far as possible, to stay at Minā and pass their time in glorifying God. They are called *Ayyām al-Tashrīq*, *i.e.*, the days of brightness and beauty.

241. The underlying object of the Pilgrimage is the attainment of *Taqwā* (righteousness), the very word with which the Qur'ān began its commandments about *Ḥajj* in 2 : 198, thus emphasizing that mere outward observance of certain rites is meaningless unless they are accompanied by the spirit of righteousness which should underlie all actions of man.

242. The different objects and places which play an important part in Pilgrimage are spoken of in the Qurā'n as *Sha'ā'ir Allāh* (2 : 159; 5 : 3; 22 : 33) or the Signs of God, which signifies that they are intended to serve only as symbols to impress upon the minds of pilgrims their inward significance. The Ka'bah round which thousands of pilgrims perform the circuit and towards which all Muslims turn while offering their Prayers wherever they may happen to be, recalls to their minds Divine Unity and the Majesty of God. It also reminds them of the unity of mankind. The act of running between Ṣafā and Marwah calls to the minds of pilgrims the story, full of pathos, of Hagar and Ishmael, reminding them how God provides for his helpless servants even in the solitude of a great wilderness. Minā, derived from *Umniyyah* (an object or a desire), reminds the pilgrim that he goes there with the "object" or the "desire" of meeting God. Mash'ar al-Ḥarām meaning, the sacred symbol, hints that the final stage is near. 'Arafāt reminds him that he has reached the stage of realisation, and *Iḥrām* reminds him of the Day of Resurrection. Like the shroud of a dead body, the pilgrim wears only two unsewn sheets, one for the upper part of the body and the other for the lower part; and he also remains bare-headed. This condition reminds him that he has, as it were, risen from the dead. The pilgrims gathered together at 'Arafāt present the spectacle of the Day of Resurrection—men suddenly risen from the dead in their white shrouds and assembled in the presence of their Lord. The sacrificial animals are reminders of the great sacrifice offered by Abraham of his son Ishmael, and the sacrifice embodies the lesson in symbolic language that man should ever be ready, not only to sacrifice himself but also his wealth and property and even his children, in the way of God.

243. There are persons whose eloquence and feigned love for fellow-beings would deceive the listener, but at heart they love and seek only their own interests and vehemently dispute with others for their smallest rights, supposed or real; not giving any proof of that spirit of sacrifice which is essential for real human progress.

206. And when he is in authority, he runs about in the land to create disorder in it and destroys the tilth[244] and the progeny of man; and Allāh loves not disorder.

وَإِذَا تَوَلّٰى سَعٰى فِي الْاَرْضِ لِيُفْسِدَ فِيْهَا وَيُهْلِكَ
الْحَرْثَ وَالنَّسْلَ ؕ وَاللّٰهُ لَا يُحِبُّ الْفَسَادَ ﴿۲۰۶﴾

207. And when it is said to him, 'Fear Allāh,' pride incites him to *further* sin.[245] So Hell[246] shall be his sufficient reward; and surely, it is an evil place of rest.[247]

وَإِذَا قِيْلَ لَهُ اتَّقِ اللّٰهَ اَخَذَتْهُ الْعِزَّةُ بِالْاِثْمِ فَحَسْبُهٗ
جَهَنَّمُ ؕ وَلَبِئْسَ الْمِهَادُ ﴿۲۰۷﴾

208. And of men there is he who would sell[248] himself to seek the pleasure of Allāh; and [a]Allāh is Compassionate to *His* servants.

وَمِنَ النَّاسِ مَنْ يَّشْرِيْ نَفْسَهُ ابْتِغَآءَ مَرْضَاتِ اللّٰهِ ؕ
وَاللّٰهُ رَءُوْفٌۢ بِالْعِبَادِ ﴿۲۰۸﴾

209. O ye who believe, come into submission all of you[249] and [b]follow not the footsteps of Satan; surely, he is your open enemy.

يٰٓاَيُّهَا الَّذِيْنَ اٰمَنُوا ادْخُلُوْا فِي السِّلْمِ كَآفَّةً ۪ وَلَا
تَتَّبِعُوْا خُطُوٰتِ الشَّيْطٰنِ ؕ اِنَّهٗ لَكُمْ عَدُوٌّ مُّبِيْنٌ ﴿۲۰۹﴾

[a]3 : 31: 9 : 117; 57 : 10. [b]See 2 : 169.

244. *Ḥarth* means, (1) a piece of land ploughed for sowing, or actually sown with some crop; (2) crop or produce of land whether field-crop or garden-crop; (3) gain, acquisition or earning; (4) reward or recompense; (5) worldly goods; (6) wife or wives, because a wife is like tilth in which seed is sown to produce crop in the form of children (Lane).

245. All his efforts are directed towards injuring the interests of other people and furthering his own.

246. Lexicographers agree that *Jahannam* has no root in Arabic. The word may have been derived from *Jahuma* which means, he became frowning or contracted or ugly in the face. If that be so the letter *nūn* in *Jahannam* would be something additional (Muḥīṭ). Thus *Jahannam* means, a place of punishment which is dark and waterless and which makes the face of its inmates ugly and contracted.

247. A false sense of dignity and prestige is his chief stumbling block, his vanity inciting him to further acts of sin, till it virtually encompasses him on all sides. Such a one paves his own way to Hell.

248. In contrast to the people mentioned in the previous verses there is a class of men whose sole concern is to seek the pleasure of Allāh as if they had given away their souls for that very purpose.

249. *Kāffah* means, (1) all together; (2) wholly or completely; (3) repulsing the enemy and (4) restraining oneself or others from sin and digression (Mufradāt).

210. But if you slip after the clear Signs that have come to you, then know that Allāh is Mighty *and* Wise.

فَإِنْ زَلَلْتُمْ مِّنْ بَعْدِ مَا جَآءَتْكُمُ الْبَيِّنٰتُ فَاعْلَمُوْٓا
اَنَّ اللّٰهَ عَزِيْزٌ حَكِيْمٌ ﴿۲۱۰﴾

211. [a]What do they wait for but that Allāh should come[250] to them in the coverings of the clouds[251] with angels,[252] and the matter be decided? And to Allāh do all things return.

هَلْ يَنْظُرُوْنَ اِلَّآ اَنْ يَّاْتِيَهُمُ اللّٰهُ فِيْ ظُلَلٍ مِّنَ
الْغَمَامِ وَالْمَلٰٓئِكَةُ وَقُضِيَ الْاَمْرُ ۭ وَاِلَى اللّٰهِ تُرْجَعُ
الْاُمُوْرُ ﴿۲۱۱﴾ ۲۵ ع۱۳ ۹

R. 26 212. Ask the Children of Israel [b]how many clear Signs We gave them. But whoso changes the gift of Allāh after it has come to him, surely then, Allāh is Severe in punishing.[253]

سَلْ بَنِيْٓ اِسْرَآءِيْلَ كَمْ اٰتَيْنٰهُمْ مِّنْ اٰيَةٍۢ بَيِّنَةٍ ۭ وَ
وَمَنْ يُّبَدِّلْ نِعْمَةَ اللّٰهِ مِنْۢ بَعْدِ مَا جَآءَتْهُ فَاِنَّ
اللّٰهَ شَدِيْدُ الْعِقَابِ ﴿۲۱۲﴾

213. [c]The life of this world is made to appear attractive to those who disbelieve; and they scoff at those who believe. But those who fear *God* shall be above them on the Day of Resurrection; and [d]Allāh bestows *His gifts* on whomsoever He pleases without reckoning.

زُيِّنَ لِلَّذِيْنَ كَفَرُوا الْحَيٰوةُ الدُّنْيَا وَيَسْخَرُوْنَ مِنَ
الَّذِيْنَ اٰمَنُوْا ۘ وَالَّذِيْنَ اتَّقَوْا فَوْقَهُمْ يَوْمَ الْقِيٰمَةِ ۭ
وَاللّٰهُ يَرْزُقُ مَنْ يَّشَآءُ بِغَيْرِ حِسَابٍ ﴿۲۱۳﴾

214. Mankind were one community,[254] *then they differed among themselves*, so Allāh raised Prophets

كَانَ النَّاسُ اُمَّةً وَّاحِدَةً ۣ فَبَعَثَ اللّٰهُ النَّبِيّٖنَ

---

[a]6 : 159; 16 : 34; 89 : 23. [b]17 : 102; 28 : 37. [c]3 : 15; 18 : 47; 57 : 21. [d]3 : 38; 24 : 39; 35 : 4; 40 : 41.

---

250. The phrase, "coming of God," is used by the Qur'ān elsewhere also (16 : 27; 59 : 3) and signifies God's punishment.

251. The word *al-Ghamām* has been used by the Qur'ān to express both mercy (7 : 161) and punishment (25 : 26).

252. The reference is to the Battle of Badr, when God helped the believers by sending down clouds and rain (Bukhārī), as was promised to them (25 : 26), and also sent down angels (8 : 10) who inspired the believers with courage and filled the hearts of the disbelievers with fear (8 : 13). Some of the disbelievers are reported to have actually seen the angels on that day (Zurqānī)

253. This does not mean that God is unnecessarily severe in punishment, but that Divine punishment is bound to be felt severely.

254. Before the advent of a Prophet all men are like one people in the sense that they are all unbelievers. But when a Prophet appears, they, in spite of their mutual differences, form one united front against him. The expression, "mankind were one community" or identical words have been used, besides the present verse, at seven places in the Qur'ān. In 10 : 20; 21 : 93 and 23 : 53 they signifiy "national unity" and in 5 : 49; 16 : 94; 42 : 9; 43 : 34 and in the verse under comment 'identity of ideas."

as [a]bearers of good tidings and as warners, and sent down with them the Book containing the truth that He might judge between the people wherein they differed. *But then they began to differ about the Book*, and none differed[255] about it except those to whom it was given, after clear Signs had come to them, out of envy towards one another. Now has Allāh, by His command, guided the believers to the truth in regard to which they (the unbelievers) differed; and Allāh guides whomsoever He pleases to the right path.

مُبَشِّرِينَ وَمُنذِرِينَ وَأَنزَلَ مَعَهُمُ الْكِتٰبَ بِالْحَقِّ
لِيَحْكُمَ بَيْنَ النَّاسِ فِيمَا اخْتَلَفُوا فِيهِ وَمَا اخْتَلَفَ
فِيهِ إِلَّا الَّذِينَ أُوتُوهُ مِن بَعْدِ مَا جَآءَتْهُمُ الْبَيِّنٰتُ
بَغْيًا بَيْنَهُمْ فَهَدَى اللّٰهُ الَّذِينَ اٰمَنُوا لِمَا اخْتَلَفُوا
فِيهِ مِنَ الْحَقِّ بِإِذْنِهِ وَاللّٰهُ يَهْدِي مَن يَشَآءُ
إِلٰى صِرٰطٍ مُّسْتَقِيمٍ ﴿٢١٤﴾

215. [b]Do you think that you will enter Heaven while there has not come to you the like of that *which came to* those who passed away before you? [256] [c]Poverty and afflictions befell them and they were violently

أَمْ حَسِبْتُمْ أَن تَدْخُلُوا الْجَنَّةَ وَلَمَّا يَأْتِكُم مَّثَلُ
الَّذِينَ خَلَوْا مِن قَبْلِكُم مَّسَّتْهُمُ الْبَأْسَآءُ وَالضَّرَّآءُ

[a]4 : 166; 6 : 49; 18 : 57. [b]3 : 143; 9 : 16. [c]See 2 : 178.

255. The "difference" referred to in the verse at two separate places signifies two different kinds of disagreement. Before the advent of a Prophet people differ among themselves about their idolatrous practices. But after his appearance, they begin to differ with regard to his claims. The Prophet does not create differences. The differences are already there; they merely assume a new form after his appearance. Before a Prophet appears, the people, in spite of their mutual differences, look like one people; they become divided into two distinct camps—believers and disbelievers,—after he appears. Viewed collectively, the verse describes five different stages through which mankind has passed. In the beginning there was unity among the people, all forming one community. With the increase in population and the extension of their interests and the complexity of their problems, they began to differ among themselves. Then God raised Prophets and revealed His Will. Every new revelation was made a cause of discord and differences, particularly by the people to whom the Divine Message was addressed. God finally raised the Holy Prophet with His last Book and a universal mission, calling upon all humanity to rally round his banner. Thus a circle was completed and the world which began with unity is designed to end in unity.

256. Acceptance of the Message of Islām was no bed of roses, and Muslims were warned that they would have to pass through fiery ordeals, trials and tribulations before they could hope to achieve their sublime ideal.

shaken [a]until [256A]the Messenger and those who believed along with him said, 'When *will* the help of Allāh *come*?'[257] Yea, surely the help of Allāh is nigh.

وَ زُلْزِلُوْا حَتّٰى يَقُوْلَ الرَّسُوْلُ وَ الَّذِيْنَ اٰمَنُوْا مَعَهٗ
مَتٰى نَصْرُ اللّٰهِ ؕ اَلَاۤ اِنَّ نَصْرَ اللّٰهِ قَرِيْبٌ ﴿۲۱۵﴾

216. They ask thee what they shall spend. Say, [b]'Whatever of good[258] and abundant wealth you spend should be for parents and near relatives and orphans and the needy and the wayfarer. And whatever good you do, surely Allāh knows it perfectly well.'

يَسْـَٔلُوْنَكَ مَاذَا يُنْفِقُوْنَ ؕ قُلْ مَاۤ اَنْفَقْتُمْ مِّنْ
خَيْرٍ فَلِلْوَالِدَيْنِ وَ الْاَقْرَبِيْنَ وَ الْيَتٰمٰى وَ الْمَسٰكِيْنِ
وَ ابْنِ السَّبِيْلِ ؕ وَ مَا تَفْعَلُوْا مِنْ خَيْرٍ فَاِنَّ اللّٰهَ بِهٖ
عَلِيْمٌ ﴿۲۱۶﴾

217. [c]Fighting is ordained for you, though it is repugnant[259] to you; but it may be that you dislike a thing while it is good for you, and it may be that you like a thing while it is bad for you. Allāh knows and you know not.

كُتِبَ عَلَيْكُمُ الْقِتَالُ وَ هُوَ كُرْهٌ لَّكُمْ ۚ وَ عَسٰۤى اَنْ
تَكْرَهُوْا شَيْـًٔا وَّ هُوَ خَيْرٌ لَّكُمْ ۚ وَ عَسٰۤى اَنْ تُحِبُّوْا
شَيْـًٔا وَّ هُوَ شَرٌّ لَّكُمْ ؕ وَ اللّٰهُ يَعْلَمُ وَ اَنْتُمْ لَا تَعْلَمُوْنَ ﴿۲۱۷﴾ ع

R. 27 218. They ask thee about fighting in the Sacred Month. Say, 'Fighting therein is a heinous thing, but to hinder *men* from the way of Allāh, and to be ungrateful to Him, and *to hinder men from* the Sacred Mosque, and to turn out its people therefrom, is more heinous in the sight of Allāh;[260] and

يَسْـَٔلُوْنَكَ عَنِ الشَّهْرِ الْحَرَامِ قِتَالٍ فِيْهِ ؕ قُلْ قِتَالٌ
فِيْهِ كَبِيْرٌ ؕ وَ صَدٌّ عَنْ سَبِيْلِ اللّٰهِ وَ كُفْرٌۢ بِهٖ وَ
الْمَسْجِدِ الْحَرَامِ ۗ وَ اِخْرَاجُ اَهْلِهٖ مِنْهُ اَكْبَرُ عِنْدَ

[a]12 : 111. [b]2 : 178 ; 4 : 37. [c]8 : 6.

256A. *Ḥattā* also means, "so that" (*Mughnī*). The word has also been used in this sense in 63 : 8.

257. The pathetic cry for help embodied in the words, *When will the help of Allāh come*, does not denote despair or despondency because an attitude of despair on the part of a Prophet of God and his followers is inconceivable, being inconsistent with true faith (12 : 88). The words in reality constitute a prayer—a way of earnestly beseeching God to expedite His help.

258. The verse signifies that whatever is spent should have been honestly acquired. What is spent must be good also in the sense that it should be acceptable to the receiver and should satisfy his need and that the object on which it is spent is also worthy and laudable.

259. Muslims hated war not because they were afraid of it, but because they did not like to shed human blood; also because they thought that a peaceful atmosphere was much more conducive to the spread and propagation of Islām than a state of war.

260. The believers were told that if disbelievers violated the sanctity of the Sacred Months, they should not hesitate to punish them in the Sacred Months, for thus alone could

[a]persecution is worse than killing.' And they will not cease fighting you until they turn you back from your Faith, if they can. And [b]whoso from among you turns back from his Faith and dies while he is a disbeliever, it is they [c]whose works shall be vain in this world and the next. These are the inmates of the Fire and therein shall they abide.

219. Those who believe and [d]those who emigrate and strive hard in the cause of Allāh, it is these who hope for Allāh's mercy; and Allāh is Most Forgiving, Merciful.

220. They ask thee concerning [e]wine[261] and games of chance.[262]

اللّٰهِ ؕ وَ الۡفِتۡنَةُ اَكۡبَرُ مِنَ الۡقَتۡلِ ؕ وَلَا يَزَالُوۡنَ
يُقَاتِلُوۡنَكُمۡ حَتّٰى يَرُدُّوۡكُمۡ عَنۡ دِيۡنِكُمۡ اِنِ اسۡتَطَاعُوۡا ؕ
وَمَنۡ يَّرۡتَدِدۡ مِنۡكُمۡ عَنۡ دِيۡنِهٖ فَيَمُتۡ وَهُوَ كَافِرٌ
فَاُولٰٓئِكَ حَبِطَتۡ اَعۡمَالُهُمۡ فِى الدُّنۡيَا وَالۡاٰخِرَةِ ۚ وَاُولٰٓئِكَ
اَصۡحٰبُ النَّارِ ۚ هُمۡ فِيۡهَا خٰلِدُوۡنَ ﴿۲۱۸﴾
اِنَّ الَّذِيۡنَ اٰمَنُوۡا وَالَّذِيۡنَ هَاجَرُوۡا وَجٰهَدُوۡا فِىۡ
سَبِيۡلِ اللّٰهِ ۙ اُولٰٓئِكَ يَرۡجُوۡنَ رَحۡمَتَ اللّٰهِ ؕ وَاللّٰهُ
غَفُوۡرٌ رَّحِيۡمٌ ﴿۲۱۹﴾
يَسۡـَٔلُوۡنَكَ عَنِ الۡخَمۡرِ وَالۡمَيۡسِرِ ؕ قُلۡ فِيۡهِمَاۤ اِثۡمٌ

[a]2 : 192. [b]3 : 87,91; 4 : 138; 5 : 55; 47 : 26. [c]3 : 23; 7 : 148; 18 : 106. [d]8 : 75; 9 : 20. [e]5 : 91,92.

the sanctity of a sacred thing be safeguarded (2 : 195). Commentators generally state, and in fact there are also traditions to this effect, that on one occasion the Holy Prophet sent 'Abd Allāh bin Jaḥsh to bring news about a party of the Quraish proceeding to Mecca. When 'Abd Allāh and his companions reached a place called Nakhlah, they met a small party. 'Abd Allāh attacked the party, killing one of them and capturing two. The date on which this happened was doubtful, some considering it to be one within the Sacred Month and others not. The news reached Mecca, the Quraish took advantage of the doubt and protested that the Muslims had violated the Sacred Month. The verse under comment was revealed on that occasion.

261. *Khamara al-Shai'a* means, he veiled or covered up or concealed the thing. Wine is called *Khamr* because it covers or obscures or affects the intellect or the senses, or because it agitates and excites the brain so as to make it lose its power of control. The word is specifically used for wine prepared from grapes but signifies all intoxicants (Lane). "Alcoholism is an important factor in the causation of disease; and in all diseases alcoholics are bad patients. In epidemics the mortality among drinkers is excessive; and the general power of resistance to disease, injury, and fatigue is diminished......Alcoholism lessens the chance of life; the English life-insurance companies found that the presumptive length of life of non-drinkers was about twice that of drinkers. The close relationship of alcoholism and crime is well-known; and the statistics of Baer, Kurella and Gallavardin and Sichart show that from 25 to 85 per cent of all malefactors are drunkards. ...... "The evil effects of alcoholism are evident in the drunkard's posterity.... Epilepsy, insanity, idiocy and various forms of physical, mental and moral degeneracy are very disproportionately prevalent among the offsprings of alcoholics" (Jew. Enc). "The effects of consumption of alcohol are almost all due to its action upon the nervous system. In the advanced stage of drunkenness, the intellectual processes of judgment and control are suspended." (Enc. Brit). "There is universal testimony as to the close relationship between excessive drinking and breaches of the moral law and the law of the State. This is a direct consequence of the paralysis of the higher faculties, intellectual and moral, and the resulting free play given to the lower inclinations" (Enc. Rel. Eth.).

262. *Aisara al-Rajulu* means, man became well off. *Maisar* is so called because the gambler seeks to become rich quickly and easily without undergoing the trouble of earning wealth by hard work. "The vicious tendency of gambling has never been called in

Say, 'In both there is great sin[263] *and harm* and also *some* advantages[264] for men; but their sin *and harm* are greater than their advantage.' And they ask thee what they should spend. Say, '*Spend* what you can spare.'[265] Thus does Allāh make His commandments clear to you that you may reflect

كَبِيْرٌ وَّمَنَافِعُ لِلنَّاسِ وَاِثْمُهُمَآ اَكْبَرُ مِنْ نَّفْعِهِمَا ؕ وَ
يَسْـَٔلُوْنَكَ مَاذَا يُنْفِقُوْنَ ؕ قُلِ الْعَفْوَ ؕ كَذٰلِكَ يُبَيِّنُ اللّٰهُ
لَكُمُ الْاٰيٰتِ لَعَلَّكُمْ تَتَفَكَّرُوْنَ ﴿۲۲۰﴾

221. Upon this world and the next. And they ask thee concerning [a]the orphans. Say, 'Promotion of their welfare is *an act of* great goodness.[266] And if you intermix with them, they are your brethren. And Allāh knows him who seeks to make mischief apart from him who seeks to promote the welfare *of the orphans*. And if Allāh had so willed, He would have put you to hardship. Surely, Allāh is Mighty *and* Wise.'

فِي الدُّنْيَا وَالْاٰخِرَةِ ؕ وَيَسْـَٔلُوْنَكَ عَنِ الْيَتٰمٰى ؕ قُلْ اِصْلَاحٌ
لَّهُمْ خَيْرٌ ؕ وَاِنْ تُخَالِطُوْهُمْ فَاِخْوَانُكُمْ ؕ وَاللّٰهُ يَعْلَمُ
الْمُفْسِدَ مِنَ الْمُصْلِحِ ؕ وَلَوْ شَآءَ اللّٰهُ لَاَعْنَتَكُمْ ؕ اِنَّ اللّٰهَ
عَزِيْزٌ حَكِيْمٌ ﴿۲۲۱﴾

[a]4 : 128; 89 : 18; 93 : 10; 107 : 3.

question. It is essentially anti-social; it sears the sympathies, cultivates hard egoism and so produces a general deterioration of character. It is a habit intrinsically savage......Its motive is carefully disguised covetousness. It is an attempt to get property without paying the price for it. It is a violation of the law of equivalents. It is a kind of robbery by mutual agreement just as duelling which is murder by mutual agreement. It is begotten of covetousness; it leads to idleness. It is, moreover, an appeal to chance. To make chance the arbiter of conduct is to subvert the moral order and stability of life. It concentrates attention upon lucre and thereby withdraws attention from worthier objects of life" (Enc. Rel. Eth.).

263. *Ithm* means, sin; punishment of sin; the harm that might result from sin (Lane).

264. It is characteristic of Islām that it never condemns a thing wholesale but freely and frankly admits even the smallest good that may be found in it. Islām prohibits certain things not because it considers them to be devoid of all good, for there is nothing in the world which is wholly bad, but because their evil outweighs their good. While prohibiting the use of intoxicants and games of chance because of their great harm, Islām has not failed to acknowledge the few advantages they possess.

265. '*Afw* means, (a) what exceeds or remains over and above one's requirements; and the spending of what does not cause hardship to the giver; (b) the best portion of a thing; (c) giving without being asked (Aqrab). Ordinary believers are required to spend what remains after their own legitimate needs have been met, and the higher class of believers are expected to spend the best portion of their possessions. If, however, the clause be applied collectively to all believers, it would mean that in times of war they should retain for themselves only such portion of their possessions as may suffice to meet their bare necessities of life.

266. The bringing up of orphans is a very delicate affair and also an important social duty. Orphans should be brought up in a manner most conducive to their physical, moral and spiritual welfare. They should be treated as members of the family—the exhortation being contained in the words, "they are your brethren."

222. And [a]marry not idolatrous women until they believe; *even* a believing bondwoman is better than an idolatress, although she may please you. And give not *believing women* in marriage to idolaters until they believe; *even* a believing slave is better than an idolater, although he may please you.[267] These call to the Fire, but Allāh calls to Heaven and to forgiveness by His Will. And He makes His Signs clear to the people that they may remember.

وَلَا تَنْكِحُوا الْمُشْرِكٰتِ حَتّٰى يُؤْمِنَّ ۚ وَلَاَمَةٌ مُّؤْمِنَةٌ
خَيْرٌ مِّنْ مُّشْرِكَةٍ وَّلَوْ اَعْجَبَتْكُمْ ۚ وَلَا تُنْكِحُوا الْمُشْرِكِيْنَ
حَتّٰى يُؤْمِنُوْا ۚ وَلَعَبْدٌ مُّؤْمِنٌ خَيْرٌ مِّنْ مُّشْرِكٍ وَّلَوْ
اَعْجَبَكُمْ ۚ اُولٰٓئِكَ يَدْعُوْنَ اِلَى النَّارِ ۖ وَاللّٰهُ يَدْعُوْٓا
اِلَى الْجَنَّةِ وَالْمَغْفِرَةِ بِاِذْنِهٖ ۚ وَيُبَيِّنُ اٰيٰتِهٖ لِلنَّاسِ
ع ۲۷ لَعَلَّهُمْ يَتَذَكَّرُوْنَ ﴿۲۲۲﴾

28 223. And they ask thee concerning menstruation. Say, 'It is a harmful thing, so keep away from women during menstruation, and go not in unto them until they are clean.[268] But when they have cleansed themselves, go in unto them as Allāh has commanded[269] you. Allāh loves those who keep themselves clean.'

وَيَسْـَٔلُوْنَكَ عَنِ الْمَحِيْضِ ۚ قُلْ هُوَ اَذًى ۙ فَاعْتَزِلُوا
النِّسَآءَ فِى الْمَحِيْضِ ۙ وَلَا تَقْرَبُوْهُنَّ حَتّٰى يَطْهُرْنَ ۚ
فَاِذَا تَطَهَّرْنَ فَأْتُوْهُنَّ مِنْ حَيْثُ اَمَرَكُمُ اللّٰهُ ۚ اِنَّ
اللّٰهَ يُحِبُّ التَّوَّابِيْنَ وَيُحِبُّ الْمُتَطَهِّرِيْنَ ﴿۲۲۳﴾

---

[a]60 : 11.

---

267. The question of marriage with "idolatrous women" is intimately connected with the subject of war, for it is during war that, being away from their homes for a considerable time, believers are liable to be tempted to contract marriages with such women. This, the Qur'ān positively prohibits, as also the giving of believing women in marriage to idolatrous men. The prohibition is based on religious as well as on moral and social grounds. An idolatrous husband is bound to exercise an extremely baneful influence, not only on his wife but also on the children born of this union; and an idolatrous wife is sure to ruin the up-bringing of the offspring. Moreover, when a believing man has an idolatrous wife or *vice versa*, their ideas, beliefs and outlook on life being widely different, there can possibly exist no harmony or concord between the two and consequently no peace in the family. In Islām slavery carries no stigma of inferiority; and a Muslim bondwoman would in every respect be a better spouse for a Muslim freemen than an idolatress and *vice versa*. Slaves commanded great respect in Muslim society for their faith and righteousness. Bilāl, Salmān and Sālim, very respected Companions of the Holy Prophet, were all freed slaves.

268. After laying down, in brief, the law about intermarriages, reference to marital relations and conjugal obligations became necessary.

269. The command implied in the words, *and seek what Allāh has ordained for you* (2 : 188), is that coitus with one's wife should be in a manner conducive to procreation.

224. Your wives are a *sort of* tilth[270] for you; so approach your tilth when and as[271] you like and send ahead *some good* for yourselves; and fear Allāh and know that you shall meet Him; and bear good tidings to those who believe.[272]

نِسَاۤؤُكُمْ حَرْثٌ لَّكُمْ فَاْتُوْا حَرْثَكُمْ اَنّٰى شِئْتُمْ وَ
قَدِّمُوْا لِاَنْفُسِكُمْ وَاتَّقُوا اللّٰهَ وَاعْلَمُوْٓا اَنَّكُمْ مُّلٰقُوْهُ
وَبَشِّرِ الْمُؤْمِنِيْنَ ﴿۲۲۴﴾

225. And make not Allāh a target[273] for your oaths that you may *thereby abstain* from doing good and acting righteously and making peace between men. And Allāh is All-Hearing, All-Knowing.

وَلَا تَجْعَلُوا اللّٰهَ عُرْضَةً لِّاَيْمَانِكُمْ اَنْ تَبَرُّوْا وَتَتَّقُوْا
وَتُصْلِحُوْا بَيْنَ النَّاسِ وَاللّٰهُ سَمِيْعٌ عَلِيْمٌ ﴿۲۲۵﴾

226. [a]Allāh will not call you to account for such of your oaths as are vain,[274] but He will call you to account for what your hearts have earned. And Allāh is Most Forgiving, Forbearing.

لَا يُؤَاخِذُكُمُ اللّٰهُ بِاللَّغْوِ فِيْٓ اَيْمَانِكُمْ وَلٰكِنْ يُّؤَاخِذُكُمْ
بِمَا كَسَبَتْ قُلُوْبُكُمْ وَاللّٰهُ غَفُوْرٌ حَلِيْمٌ ﴿۲۲۶﴾

[a]5 : 90

270. See 244.

271. *Annā* means, (1) how; (2) when; and (3) where. (Aqrab).

272. This verse constitutes an eloquent testimony to the inimitably pure and dignified language of the Qur'ān. An extremely delicate subject has been dealt with in a most decent and discreet manner and the whole philosophy of marriage and conjugal relations has been given in one brief sentence, *i.e.*, *Your wives are a sort of tilth for you.* A woman is indeed like a tilth in which the seed of progeny is sown. A wise husbandman selects the best soil, prepares the best tilth, secures the best seed, and chooses the best time and manner of sowing it. So should a believer do, for on the harvest which he is to reap in the form of children depends not only his own but also his community's entire future. It is to this supreme fact that the words so pointedly refer. Thus the likening of woman to tilth throws a flood of light on the morality of eugenics and sex.

273. The word *'Urḍah* meaning a butt or an obstacle, it is indeed an act of blasphemy that one should use the name of Allāh, Who is the Fountain-head of all goodness, to abstain from doing good deeds. Again, it is a gross violation of the sanctity of Allāh's name that it should be used as a butt or target for profane or purposeless oaths. This and the following verse serve as a sort of introduction to 2 : 227, in which the subject of swearing to keep away from one's wife has been pointedly stated.

274. Taking an oath is a serious matter, but some men are in the habit of swearing without meaning anything. Such oaths as are taken thoughtlessly or as a matter of habit or those taken in a sudden fit of anger do not call for expiation.

227. For those who vow *abstinence* from their wives, the *maximum* period of waiting is four months;[275] then if they go back *to their normal relationship*, surely, Allāh is Most Forgiving, Merciful.

لِلَّذِيْنَ يُؤْلُوْنَ مِنْ نِّسَآئِهِمْ تَرَبُّصُ اَرْبَعَةِ اَشْهُرٍ ۚ
فَاِنْ فَآءُوْ فَاِنَّ اللّٰهَ غَفُوْرٌ رَّحِيْمٌ ﴿٢٢٧﴾

228. And if they decide upon [a]divorce,[276] then surely Allāh is All-Hearing, All-Knowing.

وَاِنْ عَزَمُوا الطَّلَاقَ فَاِنَّ اللّٰهَ سَمِيْعٌ عَلِيْمٌ ﴿٢٢٨﴾

229. And [b]the divorced women shall wait concerning themselves for three courses;[277] and it is not lawful for them that they conceal what Allāh has created in their wombs, if they believe in Allāh and the Last Day; and their husbands have the

وَالْمُطَلَّقٰتُ يَتَرَبَّصْنَ بِاَنْفُسِهِنَّ ثَلٰثَةَ قُرُوْٓءٍ ۗ وَ
لَا يَحِلُّ لَهُنَّ اَنْ يَّكْتُمْنَ مَا خَلَقَ اللّٰهُ فِيْٓ اَرْحَامِهِنَّ
اِنْ كُنَّ يُؤْمِنَّ بِاللّٰهِ وَالْيَوْمِ الْاٰخِرِ ۗ وَبُعُوْلَتُهُنَّ اَحَقُّ

[a]2: 230; 33: 50; 65: 2. [b]2: 235; 65 : 5.

275. After the two introductory and intervening verses in which the subject of taking oaths has been dealt with, the Qur'ān now reverts to the original subject of conjugal relations. The verse speaks of those men who vow abstinence from their wives without actually divorcing them. It is, interesting to note that while approaching the subject of divorce, the Qur'ān first speaks of menstruation (2 : 223) which is a sort of temporary and partial, though unreal, separation. Then (as in the present verse) it speaks of real though indefinite separation. And then, in the succeeding verses, it speaks of real though revocable divorce. And finally (2 : 231) it speaks of irrevocable divorce. A really wonderful order designed to put as many obstacles as possible in the way of divorce which Islām recognizes and retains as a sort of necessary evil. Islām allows four months at the most to a person who swears not to approach his wife. During this period, he must either get reconciled to his wife and restore conjugal relations, or separation will be effected between the two. Islām would in no case permit indefinite separation without divorce, leaving the woman "suspended," as it were. *Īlā'* signifies an oath of separation according to which a woman in the "Days of Ignorance" would remain in a suspended state. She could neither marry another person nor could have conjugal relations with her husband.

276. With this verse begins the discussion of the Islamic law of divorce. According to this law, the husband possesses the right to divorce his wife, when legitimate necessity arises. But the right is to be exercised only on very rare occasions and in exceptional circumstances.

277. *Quru'* is plural of *Qur'* or *Qar'* which means, a time; menstruation; period or state of purity preceding and following a menstrual discharge, *i.e.*, the period between two menstruations; termination of a menstruation; the period of menstruation and that of purity taken together, *i.e.*, the whole month; the time or state when a woman leaves her state of purity and enters that of menstruation (Muḥīṭ & Mufradāt). Abū Bakr and 'Umar among the Companions of the Holy Prophet and Abū Ḥanīfah and Aḥmad bin Ḥanbal among the *Imāms* of Jurisprudence held the view that *Qur'* means menstruation and not the period of purity. On the contrary, 'Ā'ishah and Ibn 'Umar among the Companions, and Mālik and Shāfi'iy among the *Imāms* of Jurisprudence held the opposite view (Muḥīṭ). Opinions being so balanced, it is open to a Muslim to take either of the two views, but a collective survey of relevant arguments, which need not be stated here, leads one to the conclusion that of the two the first-mentioned view seems to be more akin to reason. If however, one would like to be on the safe side, it is open to him to take the word *Qur'* to signify the period of menstruation and purity taken together, *i.e.*, the whole month.

greater right to take them back during that period, provided they desire reconciliation.[278] And they (the women) have rights similar to those (of men) over them in equity; but [b]men have a degree *of advantage*[279] above them. And Allāh is Mighty *and* Wise.

بِرَدِّهِنَّ فِي ذَٰلِكَ إِنْ أَرَادُوٓا إِصْلَاحًا ۚ وَلَهُنَّ مِثْلُ
الَّذِي عَلَيْهِنَّ بِالْمَعْرُوفِ ۚ وَلِلرِّجَالِ عَلَيْهِنَّ دَرَجَةٌ ۗ
وَاللَّهُ عَزِيزٌ حَكِيمٌ ﴿٢٢٩﴾ ٢٨ ع ١٢

R. 29 230. *Such* [b]divorce may be *pronounced* twice; then [c]either retain *them* in a becoming manner or send *them* away with kindness.[280] And it

الطَّلَاقُ مَرَّتَانِ ۖ فَإِمْسَاكٌ بِمَعْرُوفٍ أَوْ تَسْرِيحٌ بِإِحْسَانٍ ۗ

[a]4 : 35. [b]See 2 : 228. [c]2 : 232; 4 : 130; 65 : 3.

278. In view of the fact that divorce is the most hateful of all lawful things in the sight of God (Dāwūd), it has been hedged round by many checks and limitations : (a) A husband can divorce his wife only when she is clean, *i.e.*, in a state of purity, and he has had no sexual knowledge of her in her period of purity. (b) After the pronouncement of divorce the wife must wait for three menstruations, *i.e.*, about three months, which period is called '*Iddat* or the period of waiting. This is because this period gives the husband sufficient time to consider all the implications of his action and to allow his love for her, if there is yet a dormant spark lying smouldering somewhere, to re-assert itself. (*c*) A divorced woman, if pregnant, must not conceal this fact from her husband, for the expected birth of a child is calculated to go a long way in bringing about reconciliation between the couple. (d) For complete and irrevocable separation there should be three divorces. After the pronouncement of the first as well as the second divorce and before the expiry of the period of waiting, the husband enjoys the privilege of taking his wife back, if he so desires. Even after the period of waiting is over, the couple can become re-united in the case of the first and second divorce by renewing the marriage tie.

279. As far as personal rights are concerned, the husband and the wife stand on a par, but as pointed out in 4 : 35 men have a supervisory authority on account of the physical advantage they possess and the financial responsibility that they carry for providing for the household.

280. This verse contains the fifth check on divorce. A man who seeks separation from his wife must pronounce divorce on three separate occasions, each in a separate period of purity when he has not gone in unto her during that period. The pronouncement of divorce twice or thrice at one and the same time is not permissible as is hinted in the word *Marratān* (twice) which signifies a thing happening on two separate occasions and not two things happening at one and the same time. The Holy Prophet treated such collective pronouncements, whatever their number, as only one divorce (Tirmidhī & Dāwūd). According to Nasa'ī, the Holy Prophet was extremely angry when one day he was told that a person had made all the three pronouncements of divorce at one and the same time and said, "Is the Book of God going to be made a plaything while I am yet among you?" After the pronouncement of the first two divorces, the husband can take back the divorced wife within '*Iddat,i.e.*, the period of waiting, with or without her consent; but after the period of waiting is over, he can take her back only with her consent and that after re-marrying her. After the third divorce, however, the husband forfeits this right and the couple are finally separated. A Companion of the Holy Prophet once asked him saying, "The Qur'ān has here spoken of two divorces only, whence comes in the third ?" The Holy Prophet referred him to the words, *or send them away with kindness*, meaning thereby that after the first two divorces the husband could retain and remarry her if she was also agreeable to the marriage; but if he wanted irrevocable separation, he should "send her away," *i.e.*, divorce her a third time (Jarīr and Musnad). The point is further made clear in the succeeding verse. Thus the word *Ṭasrīḥ* here signifies *Ṭalāq, i.e.*, divorce.

is not lawful for you that you take anything of what you have given them[281] (your wives) unless both fear that they cannot observe the limits *prescribed* by Allāh. But, if you fear that they cannot observe the limits *prescribed* by Allāh, then it shall be no sin for either of them in what she gives to get her freedom.[282] These are the limits *prescribed* by Allāh, so transgress them not; and whoso transgresses the limits *prescribed* by Allāh, it is they that are the wrongdoers.

وَلَا يَحِلُّ لَكُمْ اَنْ تَأْخُذُوْا مِمَّاۤ اٰتَيْتُمُوْهُنَّ شَيْئًا اِلَّاۤ اَنْ يَّخَافَاۤ اَلَّا يُقِيْمَا حُدُوْدَ اللّٰهِ فَاِنْ خِفْتُمْ اَلَّا يُقِيْمَا حُدُوْدَ اللّٰهِ فَلَا جُنَاحَ عَلَيْهِمَا فِيْمَا افْتَدَتْ بِهٖ تِلْكَ حُدُوْدُ اللّٰهِ فَلَا تَعْتَدُوْهَا وَمَنْ يَّتَعَدَّ حُدُوْدَ اللّٰهِ فَاُولٰٓئِكَ هُمُ الظّٰلِمُوْنَ ۞

231. And if he divorces[283] her *the third time*, then she is not lawful for him thereafter, until she marries another husband; and, if he *also* divorces her, then it shall be no sin for them to return to each other, provided they are sure that they would be able to observe the limits *prescribed* by Allāh. And these are the limits *prescribed* by Allāh which He makes clear to the people who have knowledge.

فَاِنْ طَلَّقَهَا فَلَا تَحِلُّ لَهٗ مِنْۢ بَعْدُ حَتّٰى تَنْكِحَ زَوْجًا غَيْرَهٗ فَاِنْ طَلَّقَهَا فَلَا جُنَاحَ عَلَيْهِمَاۤ اَنْ يَّتَرَاجَعَاۤ اِنْ ظَنَّاۤ اَنْ يُّقِيْمَا حُدُوْدَ اللّٰهِ وَتِلْكَ حُدُوْدُ اللّٰهِ يُبَيِّنُهَا لِقَوْمٍ يَّعْلَمُوْنَ ۞

---

281. When a person divorces his wife, he forfeits the dower-money he has given her; and if at the time of divorce he has not yet given her the dower-money, he must make the payment before the divorce becomes effective. Again, he is not allowed to take back anything he might have given her in the form of gifts and presents.

282. If, however, it is the wife who demands separation, technically known as *Khul'*, she must get it through a *Qāḍī* or judge as the words "you fear," in the plural number, hint. In this case she has to part with, in full or in part, her dowry as well as the gifts she might have received from her husband, as agreed upon by the parties or decided by the judge. The case of Jamīlah, wife of Qais bin Thābit, provides a good illustration of the exercise of the right of *Khul'* by women. She demanded separation from her husband, Qais, on the ground that she did not like him, *i.e.*, their temperaments being different she could not get on with him. She was granted *Khul'* by the Holy Prophet, but she had to return to her husband the orchard he had given her (Bukhārī).

283. This verse refers to the third and final divorce after which the husband loses all right of re-union with his wife unless the divorced woman marries another man and establishes conjugal relations with him, and is then formally divorced by him or he dies, leaving her free to marry another man. By the inclusion of this provision in the law of divorce Islām has, on the one hand, enhanced the sanctity of the marriage tie which must not be trifled with; and, on the other, it has afforded yet another, though extremely remote, opportunity to the couple who once had lived as husband and wife to become re-united if they so desire.

232. And when you divorce women and [a]they approach[283A] the end of their *appointed* period, then [b]either retain them in a becoming manner or send them away in a becoming manner;[284] but retain them not wrongfully so that you may transgress *against them.* And whoso does that, surely wrongs his own soul. And do not make a jest of the commandments of Allāh, and [c]remember the favour of Allāh upon you and the Book and the Wisdom which He has sent down to you, whereby He exhorts you. And fear Allāh and know that Allāh knows all things well.

وَاِذَا طَلَّقْتُمُ النِّسَآءَ فَبَلَغْنَ اَجَلَهُنَّ فَاَمْسِكُوْهُنَّ
بِمَعْرُوْفٍ اَوْ سَرِّحُوْهُنَّ بِمَعْرُوْفٍ وَّلَا تُمْسِكُوْهُنَّ
ضِرَارًا لِّتَعْتَدُوْا وَمَنْ يَّفْعَلْ ذٰلِكَ فَقَدْ ظَلَمَ نَفْسَهٗ
وَلَا تَتَّخِذُوْٓا اٰيٰتِ اللّٰهِ هُزُوًا وَّاذْكُرُوْا نِعْمَتَ اللّٰهِ عَلَيْكُمْ
وَمَآ اَنْزَلَ عَلَيْكُمْ مِّنَ الْكِتٰبِ وَالْحِكْمَةِ يَعِظُكُمْ
بِهٖ وَاتَّقُوا اللّٰهَ وَاعْلَمُوْٓا اَنَّ اللّٰهَ بِكُلِّ شَيْءٍ عَلِيْمٌ ﴿٢٣٢﴾

R. 30 233. And when you divorce women and they reach the end of their period, prevent them not from marrying their husbands,[285] if they agree between themselves in a decent manner. This is an admonition for him among you who believes in Allāh and the Last Day. It is more blessed for you and purer; and Allāh knows but you know not.

وَاِذَا طَلَّقْتُمُ النِّسَآءَ فَبَلَغْنَ اَجَلَهُنَّ فَلَا تَعْضُلُوْهُنَّ
اَنْ يَّنْكِحْنَ اَزْوَاجَهُنَّ اِذَا تَرَاضَوْا بَيْنَهُمْ بِالْمَعْرُوْفِ
ذٰلِكَ يُوْعَظُ بِهٖ مَنْ كَانَ مِنْكُمْ يُؤْمِنُ بِاللّٰهِ وَالْيَوْمِ
الْاٰخِرِ ذٰلِكُمْ اَزْكٰى لَكُمْ وَاَطْهَرُ وَاللّٰهُ يَعْلَمُ وَاَنْتُمْ
لَا تَعْلَمُوْنَ ﴿٢٣٣﴾

[a]2 : 229 ; 65 : 5. [b]See 2 : 230. [c]3 : 104.

283A. The expression *Balagha al-Ajala* means, he *approached* the end of the period; or he *reached* the end of, or completed, the period. According to consensus of scholarly opinion, the first meaning applies here (Qurṭubī).

284. As is apparent from the context, the divorce spoken of here refers to the revocable divorce. After such divorce has been pronounced there are only two courses open to the husband. He may either retain his wife and treat her with kindness or may part with her in a good and becoming manner. He is not allowed to maltreat her and keep her in a state of suspense.

285. The word "husbands" mentioned in this verse may refer either to former husbands or to prospective ones. In the former case, the clause, *and when you divorce women,* would be taken as referring to the first or second divorce. In case the word "husbands" stands for prospective husbands, the above phrase would refer to the third or final divorce. The guardian of a divorced woman cannot prevent her from re-marrying her former husband nor the former husband can prevent her from marrying a new husband.

234. And [a]mothers shall give suck to their children for two whole years ; *this is* for [b]those who desire to complete the *period of* suckling. And the man to whom the child belongs shall be responsible for their (the mothers') maintenance and clothing according to usage. [c]No soul is burdened beyond its capacity. Neither shall a mother be made to suffer[286] on account of her child, nor shall he to whom the child belongs[287] *be made to suffer* on account of his child and the same is *incumbent* on the *father's* heir.[288] If they both decide upon weaning *the child* by mutual consent and consultation,[288A] there is no blame on them. And if you desire to engage a wet-nurse for your children, there shall be no blame on you, provided you pay what you have agreed to pay in a fair manner. And fear Allāh and know that Allāh sees what you do.

وَالْوَالِدٰتُ يُرْضِعْنَ اَوْلَادَهُنَّ حَوْلَيْنِ كَامِلَيْنِ
لِمَنْ اَرَادَ اَنْ يُّتِمَّ الرَّضَاعَةَ ؕ وَعَلَى الْمَوْلُوْدِ لَهٗ
رِزْقُهُنَّ وَكِسْوَتُهُنَّ بِالْمَعْرُوْفِ ؕ لَا تُكَلَّفُ نَفْسٌ
اِلَّا وُسْعَهَا ۚ لَا تُضَآرَّ وَالِدَةٌۢ بِوَلَدِهَا وَلَا مَوْلُوْدٌ
لَّهٗ بِوَلَدِهٖ ۚ وَعَلَى الْوَارِثِ مِثْلُ ذٰلِكَ ۚ فَاِنْ اَرَادَا
فِصَالًا عَنْ تَرَاضٍ مِّنْهُمَا وَتَشَاوُرٍ فَلَا جُنَاحَ عَلَيْهِمَا ؕ
وَاِنْ اَرَدْتُّمْ اَنْ تَسْتَرْضِعُوْٓا اَوْلَادَكُمْ فَلَا جُنَاحَ
عَلَيْكُمْ اِذَا سَلَّمْتُمْ مَّآ اٰتَيْتُمْ بِالْمَعْرُوْفِ ؕ وَاتَّقُوا
اللّٰهَ وَاعْلَمُوْٓا اَنَّ اللّٰهَ بِمَا تَعْمَلُوْنَ بَصِيْرٌ ﴿۲۳۴﴾

[a]31 : 15 ; 46 : 16. [b]65 : 7. [c]2 : 287 ; 6 : 153 ; 7 : 43 ; 23 : 63 ; 65 : 8.

286. The expression, *lā Tudārra*, is both in the active and the passive voice ; the clause may, therefore, mean that : (1) the mother shall not make the father suffer on account of her child ; and (2) the mother shall not be made to suffer on account of her child ; and both meanings are equally applicable here.

287. The words *Maulūdun la-hū* (he to whom the child belongs) have been used here in preference to the simpler word *Wālid* (father), in order to point to the inherent right of the father to possess the child and to his natural responsibility for its maintenance.

288. One who inherits the property of a deceased person is in duty bound to bring up the children the latter may leave behind.

288A. The suckling of the child should last for two years at the maximum. But it is allowable to discontinue it before the end of this period, if the father and the mother both agree on this course. The verse also implies that the child is not to be weaned before the end of two years without the consent of its mother.

235. And *as for* ^athose of you who die and leave wives behind,^b these (wives) shall wait concerning themselves for four months and ten *days*. And when they have reached the end of their period,[289] no blame shall *attach* to you concerning anything that they do with regard to themselves[290] in a decent manner. And Allāh is Aware of what you do.

وَالَّذِيْنَ يُتَوَفَّوْنَ مِنْكُمْ وَيَذَرُوْنَ اَزْوَاجًا يَّتَرَبَّصْنَ بِاَنْفُسِهِنَّ اَرْبَعَةَ اَشْهُرٍ وَّعَشْرًا ۚ فَاِذَا بَلَغْنَ اَجَلَهُنَّ فَلَا جُنَاحَ عَلَيْكُمْ فِيْمَا فَعَلْنَ فِيْۤ اَنْفُسِهِنَّ بِالْمَعْرُوْفِ ۗ وَاللّٰهُ بِمَا تَعْمَلُوْنَ خَبِيْرٌ ۝

236. And there shall be no blame on you in throwing out a hint regarding a proposal of marriage to *these* women or in keeping *the desire* hidden in your minds. Allāh knows that you will think of them *in this connection*. But make not a contract with them in secret,[291] except that you say a fair word. And resolve not on the marriage tie until the prescribed period reaches its end. And know that Allāh knows what is in your minds; so beware of Him. And know that Allāh is Most Forgiving, Forbearing.

وَلَا جُنَاحَ عَلَيْكُمْ فِيْمَا عَرَّضْتُمْ بِهٖ مِنْ خِطْبَةِ النِّسَآءِ اَوْ اَكْنَنْتُمْ فِيْۤ اَنْفُسِكُمْ ۗ عَلِمَ اللّٰهُ اَنَّكُمْ سَتَذْكُرُوْنَهُنَّ وَلٰكِنْ لَّا تُوَاعِدُوْهُنَّ سِرًّا اِلَّاۤ اَنْ تَقُوْلُوْا قَوْلًا مَّعْرُوْفًا ۚ وَلَا تَعْزِمُوْا عُقْدَةَ النِّكَاحِ حَتّٰى يَبْلُغَ الْكِتٰبُ اَجَلَهٗ ۗ وَاعْلَمُوْۤا اَنَّ اللّٰهَ يَعْلَمُ مَا فِيْۤ اَنْفُسِكُمْ فَاحْذَرُوْهُ ۚ وَاعْلَمُوْۤا اَنَّ اللّٰهَ غَفُوْرٌ حَلِيْمٌ ۝

---

^a2 : 241.   ^b2 : 229.

289. The *'Iddat* or the period of waiting in the case of widows is four months and ten days, which roughly corresponds to four alternate periods of menstruation and purity combined. Islām has prescribed a longer period in the case of a widow as a mark of respect for her feelings at the death of her husband and has thus added to the dignity and sanctity of the marriage tie.

290. The words, *concerning anything that they do with regard to themselves*, obviously refer to re-marriage. Elsewhere the Qur'ān says, *And arrange marriages for your widows* (24 : 33)

291. It is forbidden to a man to make an open proposal of marriage to a widow within her prescribed period of waiting. He may drop a hint indirectly suggestive of his intention. But he must on no account make an open suggestion or a formal proposal or even a secret proposal concerning marriage. A widow, too, is prohibited from giving her consent to such a proposal within the prescribed period. She must patiently wait for four months and ten days, out of deference to the memory of her departed spouse and in order also that her possible pregnancy may become apparent, because a pregnant woman is not allowed to marry until she is delivered of the child.

R. 31 237. It shall be no sin for you if you divorce women while you have not touched them, nor settled for them a dowry. But provide[292] for them —the rich man according to his means and the poor man according to his means — a provision in a becoming manner. *This is* an obligation upon the virtuous.

لَا جُنَاحَ عَلَيْكُمْ إِنْ طَلَّقْتُمُ النِّسَآءَ مَا لَمْ تَمَسُّوْهُنَّ
أَوْ تَفْرِضُوْا لَهُنَّ فَرِيْضَةً ۚ وَّمَتِّعُوْهُنَّ عَلَى الْمُوْسِعِ
قَدَرُهٗ وَعَلَى الْمُقْتِرِ قَدَرُهٗ ۚ مَتَاعًا بِالْمَعْرُوْفِ ۚ حَقًّا
عَلَى الْمُحْسِنِيْنَ ﴿٢٣٧﴾

238. And if you divorce them before you have touched them, but have settled upon them a dowry, then half[293] of what you have settled *shall be due from you*, unless they remit, or he, in whose hand is the tie of marriage,[294] should remit.[294A] And that you should remit is nearer to righteousness. And do not forget to do good to one another. Surely, Allāh sees what you do.

وَإِنْ طَلَّقْتُمُوْهُنَّ مِنْ قَبْلِ أَنْ تَمَسُّوْهُنَّ وَقَدْ
فَرَضْتُمْ لَهُنَّ فَرِيْضَةً فَنِصْفُ مَا فَرَضْتُمْ إِلَّآ أَنْ
يَّعْفُوْنَ أَوْ يَعْفُوَا الَّذِيْ بِيَدِهٖ عُقْدَةُ النِّكَاحِ ۚ وَ
أَنْ تَعْفُوْٓا أَقْرَبُ لِلتَّقْوٰى ۚ وَلَا تَنْسَوُا الْفَضْلَ بَيْنَكُمْ ۚ
إِنَّ اللّٰهَ بِمَا تَعْمَلُوْنَ بَصِيْرٌ ﴿٢٣٨﴾

239. [a]Watch[295] over Prayers, and *particularly* the middle[296] Prayer, and stand before Allāh submissively.

حٰفِظُوْا عَلَى الصَّلَوٰتِ وَالصَّلٰوةِ الْوُسْطٰى ۚ وَقُوْمُوْا
لِلّٰهِ قٰنِتِيْنَ ﴿٢٣٩﴾

[a]23 : 10; 70 : 35.

292. This would be an exceptional case. But cases do sometimes happen where after a marriage contract has been completed, circumstances arise or become known which render the consummation and continuation of the marriage difficult or undesirable. This and the next verse make provision for such cases.

293. If the divorce occurs after the dowry has been fixed but before the husband has gone in unto his wife, the husband shall pay half of the fixed dowry.

294. The clause, *he in whose hand is the tie of marriage*, may signify either the husband or the guardian of the divorced woman, because whereas after marriage the tie of marriage is in the hands of the husband, before marriage the guardian of the woman holds it.

294A. *Ya'fū* may mean, "remits or increases." The wife (or her guardian) may remit the whole or a part of what is due to her, or the husband may pay more than what is due from him. But the husband is certainly desired to make a greater show of generosity.

295. After marriage one is apt to become a little lax in Prayers. Besides, family life multiplies the cares of both men and women. Hence, the necessity of urging married people to be more regular and punctual in their Prayers.

296. The view that it is *'Asr* Prayer is supported by some of the sayings of the Holy Prophet (Bukhārī). It seems to be the Prayer which happens to fall within busy hours, when one is in the middle of engrossing pre-occupations. But each Prayer in a sense is "the middle Prayer."

240. [a]If you are in a *state of* fear, then *say your Prayer* on foot or riding,[297] but [b]when you are safe, remember Allāh as He has taught you that which you did not know.

فَإِنْ خِفْتُمْ فَرِجَالًا أَوْ رُكْبَانًا ۚ فَإِذَآ أَمِنْتُمْ فَاذْكُرُوا
اللّٰهَ كَمَا عَلَّمَكُمْ مَّا لَمْ تَكُونُوا تَعْلَمُونَ ﴿٢٤٠﴾

241. And [c]those of you who die and leave behind wives shall bequeath to their wives provision for a year[298] without their being turned out. But if they *themselves* go out, then there shall be no blame upon you in regard to any proper thing which they do concerning themselves. And Allāh is Mighty *and* Wise.

وَالَّذِينَ يُتَوَفَّوْنَ مِنْكُمْ وَيَذَرُونَ أَزْوَاجًا ۚ وَصِيَّةً
لِّأَزْوَاجِهِمْ مَّتَاعًا إِلَى الْحَوْلِ غَيْرَ إِخْرَاجٍ ۚ فَإِنْ
خَرَجْنَ فَلَا جُنَاحَ عَلَيْكُمْ فِي مَا فَعَلْنَ فِيٓ أَنْفُسِهِنَّ
مِنْ مَّعْرُوفٍ ۗ وَاللّٰهُ عَزِيزٌ حَكِيمٌ ﴿٢٤١﴾

242. And for the divorced women *also* there should be a [d]provision[299] according to what is fair— an obligation on the God-fearing.

وَلِلْمُطَلَّقٰتِ مَتَاعٌ بِالْمَعْرُوفِ ۗ حَقًّا عَلَى الْمُتَّقِينَ ﴿٢٤٢﴾

243. Thus does Allāh make His commandments clear to you that you may understand.

ع ٣١ ١٥ كَذٰلِكَ يُبَيِّنُ اللّٰهُ لَكُمْ اٰيٰتِهٖ لَعَلَّكُمْ تَعْقِلُونَ ﴿٢٤٣﴾ ع

[a]4 : 102. [b]4 : 104. [c]2 : 235. [d]2 : 242; 65 : 8.

297. Observance of five daily Prayers is the most important commandment. In no circumstances should a Muslim neglect his Prayers as long as he is sane and conscious. Even when he is moving about in a state of extreme fear, he must not fail to say his Prayers and should perform them on horseback or on foot, whether running or sitting or lying, as the case may be.

298 The period of waiting laid down for a widow in 2 : 235 is four months and ten days in which time she can, as of right, claim residence and maintenance from the heirs of her deceased husband. The period of one year mentioned here is only a concession or a favour for a widow in addition to her right of residence and maintenance mentioned in 2 : 235. The concession forms no part of her share in the inheritance, nor is it an obligatory injunction.

299. Just as the preceding verse bestowed an additional favour on widows, the present one bestows an additional favour on divorced women. The injunction is particularly essential in the case of divorced women, because in moments of bitterness, which is the inevitable aftermath of a dissolved marriage, people are liable to be unjust and cruel towards their divorced wives.

R. 32 244. Hast thou not heard of those who went forth[300] from their homes, and they were thousands,[301] fearing death?[302] And Allāh said to them, [a]'Die';[303] then He brought them to life. Surely, Allāh is Gracious to men, but most men are not grateful.

أَلَمْ تَرَ إِلَى الَّذِينَ خَرَجُوا مِنْ دِيَارِهِمْ وَهُمْ أُلُوفٌ
حَذَرَ الْمَوْتِ فَقَالَ لَهُمُ اللّٰهُ مُوتُوا ثُمَّ أَحْيَاهُمْ
إِنَّ اللّٰهَ لَذُو فَضْلٍ عَلَى النَّاسِ وَلٰكِنَّ أَكْثَرَ
النَّاسِ لَا يَشْكُرُونَ ﴿٢٤٤﴾

245. And [b]fight[304] in the cause of Allāh and know that Allāh is All-Hearing, All-Knowing.

وَقَاتِلُوا فِي سَبِيلِ اللّٰهِ وَاعْلَمُوا أَنَّ اللّٰهَ سَمِيعٌ
عَلِيمٌ ﴿٢٤٥﴾

246. [c]Who is it that will lend[305] Allāh a goodly loan that He may multiply it for him manifold? And Allāh receives and enlarges, and to Him shall you be made to return.

مَنْ ذَا الَّذِي يُقْرِضُ اللّٰهَ قَرْضًا حَسَنًا فَيُضٰعِفَهُ
لَهُ أَضْعَافًا كَثِيرَةً ۚ وَاللّٰهُ يَقْبِضُ وَيَبْصُطُ وَ
إِلَيْهِ تُرْجَعُونَ ﴿٢٤٦﴾

[a]5 : 27. [b]2 : 191; 4 : 85. [c]57 : 12, 19; 64 : 18.

300. When, being persecuted by Pharaoh, the Israelites left Egypt and crossed over to Asia, Moses wanted them to enter the Promised Land, but they were afraid of the people that dwelt there and refused to march ahead (5 : 25).

301. The Bible represents the number of the Israelites migrating from Egypt as six hundred thousand. Recent researches favour the Quranic view according to which they were only several thousand (*History of the People of Israel*, by Ernest Renan. p. 145, 1888, and *History of Palestine and the Jews*, i. 174, by John Kitto). See also 2 : 61.

302. The Israelites left Egypt because their further stay in that country would have meant their total annihilation. Pharaoh had recourse to all sorts of means to destroy their manhood. See 2 : 50.

303. The reference is to the wandering in the wilderness of Sinai of the Israelites who had refused to march with Moses into Canaan until they perished in the wilderness and a new generation arose who, inspired with a new life, marched into the Promised Land under Joshua. Elsewhere the Qur'ān says, "Then we raised you up after your death" (2 : 57.)

304. The address is to the Muslims. They are told that a people who do not shed fear of death and are not prepared to sacrifice their all for the preservation of their national existence and honour, do not deserve to live. This is the secret of national progress which the Qur'ān inculcates.

305. The Qur'ān speaks of spending money in the cause of Allāh as giving a loan to Him, meaning thereby that money spent for the promotion of righteous causes should not be regarded as money wasted.

247. Hast thou not heard of the chiefs of the Children of Israel after Moses, when they said to a Prophet of theirs, 'Appoint for us a king that we may fight in the way of Allāh?' He said, [a]'Is it not likely that you will not fight, if fighting is prescribed for you?' They said, 'What reason have we that we should not fight[306] in the way of Allāh when we have been driven forth from our homes and our sons?' But when fighting was ordained for them, they turned back except a small number of them. And Allāh knows the transgressors well.

اَلَمْ تَرَ اِلَى الْمَلَاِ مِنْۢ بَنِيْۤ اِسْرَآءِيْلَ مِنْۢ بَعْدِ
مُوْسٰى ۘ اِذْ قَالُوْا لِنَبِيٍّ لَّهُمُ ابْعَثْ لَنَا مَلِكًا نُّقَاتِلْ
فِيْ سَبِيْلِ اللّٰهِ ؕ قَالَ هَلْ عَسَيْتُمْ اِنْ كُتِبَ عَلَيْكُمُ
الْقِتَالُ اَلَّا تُقَاتِلُوْا ؕ قَالُوْا وَمَا لَنَاۤ اَلَّا نُقَاتِلَ فِيْ
سَبِيْلِ اللّٰهِ وَقَدْ اُخْرِجْنَا مِنْ دِيَارِنَا وَاَبْنَآئِنَا ؕ
فَلَمَّا كُتِبَ عَلَيْهِمُ الْقِتَالُ تَوَلَّوْا اِلَّا قَلِيْلًا مِّنْهُمْ ؕ
وَاللّٰهُ عَلِيْمٌۢ بِالظّٰلِمِيْنَ ﴿٢٤٧﴾

248. And their Prophet said to them, 'Allāh has appointed for you Ṭālūt[307] as a king.' They said, 'How can he have sovereignty over us while we are better entitled to sovereignty than he, and he is not given abundance of wealth?' He said, 'Surely, Allāh has chosen him above you and has bestowed upon him abundant increase in knowledge and *in strength of* body. 'And [b]Allāh gives sovereignty to whom He pleases and Allāh is Bountiful, All-Knowing.

وَقَالَ لَهُمْ نَبِيُّهُمْ اِنَّ اللّٰهَ قَدْ بَعَثَ لَكُمْ طَالُوْتَ
مَلِكًا ؕ قَالُوْۤا اَنّٰى يَكُوْنُ لَهُ الْمُلْكُ عَلَيْنَا وَنَحْنُ
اَحَقُّ بِالْمُلْكِ مِنْهُ وَلَمْ يُؤْتَ سَعَةً مِّنَ الْمَالِ ؕ
قَالَ اِنَّ اللّٰهَ اصْطَفٰىهُ عَلَيْكُمْ وَزَادَهٗ بَسْطَةً فِي
الْعِلْمِ وَالْجِسْمِ ؕ وَاللّٰهُ يُؤْتِيْ مُلْكَهٗ مَنْ يَّشَآءُ ؕ
وَاللّٰهُ وَاسِعٌ عَلِيْمٌ ﴿٢٤٨﴾

[a]4 : 78. [b]3 : 27.

306. The incident mentioned indicates an improvement in the condition of the Israelites at the time to which this verse relates compared with the time of Moses himself. In 5 : 25 the Qur'ān relates that when Moses exhorted his followers to fight the enemy in the cause of Allāh, they replied, *Go thou and thy Lord and fight, and here we sit*. On the contrary, in the present verse they are reported to have said, *What reason have we that we should not fight in the cause of Allāh when we have been driven forth from our homes and our sons*. The improvement, however, was only verbal rather than real; for when the time of actual fighting came, many of them wavered and refused to fight. The incident thus serves as a grim warning to Muslims to beware of treading the same path.

307. Ṭālūt is the attributive name of an Israelite king who lived about two hundred years before David and about the same number of years after Moses. Some Commentators of the Qur'ān have wrongly identified Ṭālūt with Saul. The description of the Qur'ān fits in more with Gideon (Judg. chs. 6-8) than with Saul. Gideon lived in about 1250 B.C. and the Bible calls him a "mighty man of valour" (Judg. 6 : 12) which is the same as Ṭālūt. According to some Christian writers incidents related in this passage refer to two different periods

249. And their Prophet said to them, 'The sign of his sovereignty is that there shall be given you a heart[308] wherein there will be tranquillity from your Lord and a legacy[309] *of good* left by the family of Moses and the family of Aaron—the angels bearing it. Surely, in this there is a Sign for you if you are believers.'

وَقَالَ لَهُمْ نَبِيُّهُمْ إِنَّ آيَةَ مُلْكِهِ أَنْ يَأْتِيَكُمُ
التَّابُوتُ فِيهِ سَكِينَةٌ مِّنْ رَّبِّكُمْ وَبَقِيَّةٌ مِّمَّا
تَرَكَ آلُ مُوسَىٰ وَآلُ هَارُونَ تَحْمِلُهُ الْمَلَٰٓئِكَةُ إِنَّ
فِي ذَٰلِكَ لَآيَةً لَّكُمْ إِن كُنتُم مُّؤْمِنِينَ ﴿٢٤٩﴾ ٣٢ ع ٢ ١٦

which are separated from each other by the long interval of 200 years, and refer to this passage as an instance, as they say, of historical anachronisms to be found in the Qur'ān. The passage does indeed refer to two different periods, but there is no anachronism in it. The Qur'ān has here referred to both these periods. Its object in doing so is to show how the unification of the different tribes of Israel began in the time of Gideon, (*i.e.*, Ṭālūt), two hundred years before David, and was finally consummated in the time of David. The words "after Moses" in the preceding verse indicate that the incident belongs to an early period when the Israelites as a nation had just begun to take definite shape in history. For two hundred years after Moses they were divided into different tribes and had no king and no fighting force. In 1256 B.C., owing to their iniquity, God delivered them into the hands of the Midianites who plundered and ravaged them for seven long years, and they were compelled to take refuge in caves (Judg. 6 : 1-6). "Upon this they cried to God and He raised among them a Prophet; and an angel of the Lord appeared to Gideon, appointed him king and promised him Divine help. Then Gideon said to God, "Oh my Lord wherewith shall I save Israel? Behold, my family is poor in Manasseh, and I am the least in my father's house" (Judg. 6 : 15). This tallies with the description given in the verse under comment about Ṭālūt. What makes the identification of Ṭālūt with Gideon still more certain is the fact that it was in the time of Gideon and not that of Saul that the Israelites were tried by means of water, and the description of the trial as given in the Bible (Judg. 7 : 4-7) is the same as that of the Qur'ān. From Judg. 7 : 6,7, we learn that after the aforesaid trial there remained with Gideon only 300 men. It is interesting to note that a Companion of the Holy Prophet is reported to have said, " We were 313 men in the Battle of Badr, and this number corresponds to the number of men who followed Ṭālūt" (Tirmidhī, ch. on *Siyar*). The Ḥadīth lends support to the conclusion that Ṭālūt was no other than Gideon. What further confirms the identity of Ṭālūt with Gideon is the fact that this word is derived from a root which in Hebrew means "to fell" (Enc. Bib.) or "to hew" (Jew. Enc.). Thus Gideon means "one who cuts down his adversary and fells him to the ground" and the Bible itself speaks of Gideon as a "mighty man of valour" (Judg. 6 : 12). See also 'The Larger Edition of the Commentary.'

308. *Tābūt* means, (1) a chest or box; (2) chest or breast or bosom or the ribs with what they contain, as the heart, etc. (Lane); (3) the heart which is the store house of knowledge, wisdom and peace (Mufradāt). Commentators have differed about the significance of the word *Tābūt* and the Bible mentions it as an ark or chest, and the description given in the Qur'ān definitely shows that the word has been used here in the sense of "heart" or "bosom." The description of the *Tābūt* in the verse "wherein there will be tranquillity from your Lord" cannot apply to an ark; for, far from granting peace and tranquillity to others, the ark spoken of by the Bible could neither protect the Israelites against defeat nor could it protect itself, as it was carried away by the enemy. Even Saul who took with him the ark during his campaigns suffered crushing defeats, so much so that even the enemy pitied him and he met with an ignominious end. Such an ark could not be a source of tranquillity to the Israelites. What God bestowed upon them were hearts full of courage and perseverance, so that after the said tranquillity descended upon them, they successfully resisted the attacks of the enemy and inflicted heavy defeats on them.

309. Another favour which God conferred on the Israelites is referred to in the word "legacy." God imbued their hearts with the noble qualities which characterised their ancestors, the descendants of Moses and Aaron. The legacy left by the descendants of Moses and Aaron did not consist in any material things but meant the good moral qualities with which they were endowed as the heritage of their great ancestors.

R. 33 250. And when Ṭālūt set out with the forces, he said, 'Surely, Allāh will try you with a river. So he who drinks therefrom is not of me; and he who tastes it not is assuredly of me, save him who takes *only* a handful[310] of water with his hand.' But they drank of it, except a few of them. And when they crossed it—he and those who believed along with him—they said, 'We have no power today against Jālūt[310A] and his forces. But those, who knew for certain that they would *one day* meet Allāh, said, [a]'How many a small party has triumphed over a large party by Allāh's command! And Allāh is with the steadfast.'

فَلَمَّا فَصَلَ طَالُوتُ بِالْجُنُودِ قَالَ إِنَّ اللّٰهَ مُبْتَلِيكُمْ
بِنَهَرٍ فَمَنْ شَرِبَ مِنْهُ فَلَيْسَ مِنِّي وَمَنْ لَّمْ
يَطْعَمْهُ فَإِنَّهُ مِنِّي إِلَّا مَنِ اغْتَرَفَ غُرْفَةً بِيَدِهِ
فَشَرِبُوا مِنْهُ إِلَّا قَلِيلًا مِّنْهُمْ فَلَمَّا جَاوَزَهُ هُوَ
وَالَّذِينَ آمَنُوا مَعَهُ قَالُوا لَا طَاقَةَ لَنَا الْيَوْمَ
بِجَالُوتَ وَجُنُودِهِ قَالَ الَّذِينَ يَظُنُّونَ أَنَّهُمْ مُّلَاقُوا
اللّٰهِ كَمْ مِّنْ فِئَةٍ قَلِيلَةٍ غَلَبَتْ فِئَةً كَثِيرَةً بِإِذْنِ
اللّٰهِ وَاللّٰهُ مَعَ الصّٰبِرِينَ ﴿٢٥٠﴾

251. And when they issued forth to *encounter* Jālūt[311] and his forces, they said, 'O our Lord, [b]pour forth steadfastness upon us, and make our steps firm, and [c]help us against the disbelieving people.'

وَلَمَّا بَرَزُوا لِجَالُوتَ وَجُنُودِهِ قَالُوا رَبَّنَا أَفْرِغْ
عَلَيْنَا صَبْرًا وَّثَبِّتْ أَقْدَامَنَا وَانْصُرْنَا عَلَى الْقَوْمِ
الْكٰفِرِينَ ﴿٢٥١﴾

[a]3 : 124; 8 : 66. [b]3 : 148, 201; 7 : 127. [c]2 : 287; 3 : 148.

310. The exception of a handful of water was made with a twofold purpose: (1) To afford the marching force some essential physical relief by permitting them to moisten their parched throats, but at the same time to prevent them from drinking freely, which would have damped their spirits and made them negligent of the enemy; (2) To make the trial all the more tantalizing, for in many cases it is easier for a person to withhold himself from a thing altogether than to use it in a strictly limited measure. See Judg. 7 : 5-6. The word *Nahar* also means "plenty." In this sense of the word the verse signifies that they would be tried by "plenty;" those who succumbed to its temptations would no longer be fit to carry on God's work, but those who used it with restraint would achieve success.

310A. *Jālūt* is an attributive name meaning, a person or a people who are unruly and go about attacking and assaulting others. In the Bible the parallel name is Goliath (1 Sam. 17: 4) which means, "running, ravaging and destroying spirits," or "a leader" or "a giant" (Enc. Bib.;Jew. Enc.). The Bible uses tho name about one individual but really the word signifies a party of ruthless freebooters, though it may also be applied to certain individuals symbolizing the characteristics of the party. The Qur'ān appears to have used it in both these senses in the verses under comment.

311. Jālūt spoken of in this verse does not signify a person but a people, while the word "forces" points to the helpers and associates of these people. The Bible refers to Jālūt under the name of Midianites who pillaged and harassed the Israelites and destroyed their land for several years (Judg. 6 : 1-6). The Amalekites and all the eastern tribes assisted the Midianites in their raids (Judg. 6 : 3) and formed "the forces" referred to in the verse.

252. So they routed[312] them by the command of Allāh, and David slew Jālūt, and Allāh gave him sovereignty and wisdom and taught him of what He pleased. And [a]had not Allāh repelled *some* men by others, the earth would indeed be full of mischief.[313] But Allāh is Lord of grace to *all* peoples.

فَهَزَمُوْهُمْ بِاِذْنِ اللّٰهِ ۟ۙ وَ قَتَلَ دَاوٗدُ جَالُوْتَ وَ
اٰتٰىهُ اللّٰهُ الْمُلْكَ وَ الْحِكْمَةَ وَ عَلَّمَهٗ مِمَّا يَشَآءُ ؕ وَ
لَوْلَا دَفْعُ اللّٰهِ النَّاسَ بَعْضَهُمْ بِبَعْضٍ ۙ لَّفَسَدَتِ
الْاَرْضُ وَ لٰكِنَّ اللّٰهَ ذُوْ فَضْلٍ عَلَى الْعٰلَمِيْنَ ﴿۲۵۲﴾

253. These are the Signs of Allāh. We recite them unto thee with truth. Surely, thou art of the Messengers.

تِلْكَ اٰيٰتُ اللّٰهِ نَتْلُوْهَا عَلَيْكَ بِالْحَقِّ ؕ وَ اِنَّكَ لَمِنَ
الْمُرْسَلِيْنَ ﴿۲۵۳﴾

PART III

254. [b]These Messengers have We exalted some of them above others; [c]among them there are those to whom Allāh spoke; and [d]some of them He exalted in degrees of rank.[314] And [e]We gave Jesus, son of Mary, clear proofs and strengthened him with the Spirit of holiness. And if Allāh had *so* willed, those *that came* after them would not have fought with one another after clear Signs had come to them; but they did disagree. [f]Of them were some who believed, and of them were some who disbelieved. And if Allāh had *so* willed, they would not have fought with one another; but Allāh does what He desires.

الجزء ٣ تِلْكَ الرُّسُلُ فَضَّلْنَا بَعْضَهُمْ عَلٰى بَعْضٍ ۘ مِنْهُمْ
مَّنْ كَلَّمَ اللّٰهُ وَ رَفَعَ بَعْضَهُمْ دَرَجٰتٍ ؕ وَ اٰتَيْنَا
عِيْسَى ابْنَ مَرْيَمَ الْبَيِّنٰتِ وَ اَيَّدْنٰهُ بِرُوْحِ الْقُدُسِ ؕ
وَ لَوْ شَآءَ اللّٰهُ مَا اقْتَتَلَ الَّذِيْنَ مِنْۢ بَعْدِهِمْ مِّنْۢ
بَعْدِ مَا جَآءَتْهُمُ الْبَيِّنٰتُ وَ لٰكِنِ اخْتَلَفُوْا فَمِنْهُمْ مَّنْ
اٰمَنَ وَ مِنْهُمْ مَّنْ كَفَرَ ؕ وَ لَوْ شَآءَ اللّٰهُ مَا اقْتَتَلُوْا ۟
ع ٣٣ وَ لٰكِنَّ اللّٰهَ يَفْعَلُ مَا يُرِيْدُ ﴿۲۵۴﴾

[a]22 : 41. [b]17 : 56. [c]4 : 165. [d]4 : 159; 19 : 58. [e]2 : 88. [f]4 : 56; 10 : 41.

312. Ṭālūt or Gideon was able to defeat Jālūt or the Midianites but their overwhelming defeat to which the verse refers as the killing of Jālūt came in the time of David about two hundred years afterwards. The Bible speaks of the man defeated by David as Goliath (1. Sam. 17 : 4), which is similar to Jālūt. Probably, the attributive name given by the Qur'ān to the people was also borne by their leader in the time of David.

313. These words give in a nutshell the whole philosophy of all wars of truth and justice. War should be resorted to only as a means of checking disorder and restoring peace and not for creating disorder and breaking peace and depriving weak nations of freedom.

314. The expression does not mean that there are some Prophets to whom Allāh does not speak or that there are some who are not spiritually exalted. It only means

R. 34 255. O ye who believe! [a]spend out of what We have bestowed on you before the day comes wherein there shall be no buying and selling,[315] [b]nor friendship,[316] [c]nor intercession,[317] and it is those who disbelieve that do wrong to themselves.

يٰٓاَيُّهَا الَّذِيْنَ اٰمَنُوْٓا اَنْفِقُوْا مِمَّا رَزَقْنٰكُمْ مِّنْ قَبْلِ
اَنْ يَّاْتِيَ يَوْمٌ لَّا بَيْعٌ فِيْهِ وَلَا خُلَّةٌ وَّلَا شَفَاعَةٌ ؕ
وَالْكٰفِرُوْنَ هُمُ الظّٰلِمُوْنَ ﴿۲۵۵﴾

256. Allāh—there is no god save Him, [d]the Living, the Self-Subsisting and All-Sustaining. Slumber seizes Him not, nor sleep. To Him belongs whatsoever is in the heavens and whatsoever is in the earth. [e]Who is he that dare intercede with Him save by His permission? [f]He knows what is before them and what is behind them; and they encompass nothing of His knowledge except what He pleases. His knowledge[318] extends over the heavens and the earth; and the care of them wearies Him not; and He is the High, the Great.

اَللّٰهُ لَآ اِلٰهَ اِلَّا هُوَ ۚ اَلْحَيُّ الْقَيُّوْمُ ۚ لَا تَاْخُذُهٗ سِنَةٌ
وَّلَا نَوْمٌ ؕ لَهٗ مَا فِي السَّمٰوٰتِ وَمَا فِي الْاَرْضِ ؕ مَنْ
ذَا الَّذِيْ يَشْفَعُ عِنْدَهٗٓ اِلَّا بِاِذْنِهٖ ؕ يَعْلَمُ مَا بَيْنَ
اَيْدِيْهِمْ وَمَا خَلْفَهُمْ ۚ وَلَا يُحِيْطُوْنَ بِشَيْءٍ مِّنْ
عِلْمِهٖٓ اِلَّا بِمَا شَآءَ ۚ وَسِعَ كُرْسِيُّهُ السَّمٰوٰتِ وَالْاَرْضَ ۚ
وَلَا يَئُوْدُهٗ حِفْظُهُمَا ۚ وَهُوَ الْعَلِيُّ الْعَظِيْمُ ﴿۲۵۶﴾

[a]2 : 196; 14 : 32; 47 : 39; 57 : 11; 63 : 11. [b]14 : 32; 43 : 68. [c]See 2 : 49
[d]3 : 3; 20 : 112; 25 : 59. [e]See 2 : 49. [f]20 : 111.

that there are two kinds of Prophets : (a) Those who bring a new Law. They are called *Mukallam* Prophets. (b) Those whose Prophethood consists only in the loftiness of their spiritual ranks. They are *Ghair Mukallam* Prophets. The Holy Prophet is reported to have said that Adam was a *Mukallam* Prophet (Musnad).

315. On that day salvation will not be had for a price. It will depend only on one's good works coupled with God's grace.

316. There will be no occasion for forming new friendships on that day.

317. See 85.

318. *Kursiy* means, a throne, a chair, buttress of a wall; knowledge; dominion and power (Aqrab); *Karāsī* is plural, meaning, men of learning. The verse beautifully describes the Unity of God and His great attributes. The Holy Prophet is reported to have said that *'Āyat al-Kursiy* is the loftiest verse of the Qur'ān (Muslim).

257. [a]There is no compulsion[319] in religion. Surely, the right way has become distinct from error; so whosoever refuses to be led by those whc transgress,[320] and believes in Allāh, [b]has surely grasped a strong handle which knows no breaking. And Allāh is All-Hearing. All-Knowing.

لَآ اِكْرَاهَ فِي الدِّيْنِ ۙ قَدْ تَّبَيَّنَ الرُّشْدُ مِنَ الْغَيِّ ۚ
فَمَنْ يَّكْفُرْ بِالطَّاغُوْتِ وَيُؤْمِنْ بِاللّٰهِ فَقَدِ
اسْتَمْسَكَ بِالْعُرْوَةِ الْوُثْقٰى ۗ لَا انْفِصَامَ لَهَا ۭ
وَاللّٰهُ سَمِيْعٌ عَلِيْمٌ ۝٢٥٧

258. [c]Allāh is the Friend of those who believe; [d]He brings them out of all *kinds of* darkness into light. And those who disbelieve, [e]their friends are the transgressors who bring them out of light into manifold darknesses. These are the inmates of the Fire, therein shall they abide.

اَللّٰهُ وَلِيُّ الَّذِيْنَ اٰمَنُوْا ۙ يُخْرِجُهُمْ مِّنَ الظُّلُمٰتِ اِلَى
النُّوْرِ ۬ؕ وَالَّذِيْنَ كَفَرُوْٓا اَوْلِيٰٓـُٔهُمُ الطَّاغُوْتُ ۙ
يُخْرِجُوْنَهُمْ مِّنَ النُّوْرِ اِلَى الظُّلُمٰتِ ؕ اُولٰٓئِكَ اَصْحٰبُ
النَّارِ ۚ هُمْ فِيْهَا خٰلِدُوْنَ ۝٢٥٨ ع

R. 35 259. Hast thou not heard of him who disputed with Abraham about his Lord, because Allāh had given him kingdom? When Abraham said, [f]'My Lord is He Who gives life and causes death,' he said, 'I *also* give life and cause death.' Abraham said, 'Well, Allāh brings the sun from the East; bring it thou from the West.' Thereupon the infidel was confounded.[321] And Allāh guides not the unjust people.

اَلَمْ تَرَ اِلَى الَّذِيْ حَآجَّ اِبْرٰهٖمَ فِيْ رَبِّهٖٓ اَنْ اٰتٰهُ
اللّٰهُ الْمُلْكَ ۘ اِذْ قَالَ اِبْرٰهٖمُ رَبِّيَ الَّذِيْ يُحْيٖ وَيُمِيْتُ ۙ
قَالَ اَنَا اُحْيٖ وَاُمِيْتُ ؕ قَالَ اِبْرٰهٖمُ فَاِنَّ اللّٰهَ يَاْتِيْ
بِالشَّمْسِ مِنَ الْمَشْرِقِ فَاْتِ بِهَا مِنَ الْمَغْرِبِ
فَبُهِتَ الَّذِيْ كَفَرَ ؕ وَاللّٰهُ لَا يَهْدِي الْقَوْمَ الظّٰلِمِيْنَ ۝٢٥٩

[a]10 : 100; 11 : 119; 18 : 30; 76 : 4. [b]31 : 23. [c]45 : 20. [d]5 : 17; 65 : 12. [e]7 : 28; 16 : 101. [f]3 : 157; 9 : 116; 40 : 69; 57 : 3.

319. The injunction (embodied in the preceding verses) to make special sacrifices in the cause of religion and to fight the enemies of Islām was likely to give rise to the misunderstanding that Allāh desired Muslims to use force for propagating their religion. This verse removes that misunderstanding and not only forbids Muslims in most emphatic words to use force for converting non-Muslims to Islām, but also gives reasons why force should not be used for this purpose. It is because truth stands out distinct from error, so there has remained no justification for using force. Islām is manifest Truth.

320. *Ṭāghūt* is one who exceeds proper bounds; the Devil; such persons as turn others from the right path; all idols. The word is used both as singular and plural (2 : 258 & 4 : 61).

321. Abraham was a great iconoclast. His people worshipped the sun and the stars, their chief god being Merodach (Madruk), originally the god of the morning and the spring sun (Enc. Bib. & Enc. Rel. Eth, ii. 296). They believed that all life depended on

260. Or *hast thou not heard of* the like of him who passed by a town[322] which had fallen down upon its roofs *and* exclaimed, 'When will Allāh restore it to life after its destruction?' Then Allāh caused him to die for a hundred years,[323] then He raised him and said, 'How long hast thou remained *in this state*?' He answered, 'I have remained a day or part of a day.'[323A] *Allāh* said, '*It is so* but[323B] thou hast

أَوْ كَالَّذِي مَرَّ عَلَىٰ قَرْيَةٍ وَّهِيَ خَاوِيَةٌ عَلَىٰ
عُرُوشِهَا ۚ قَالَ أَنَّىٰ يُحْيِي هَٰذِهِ اللَّهُ بَعْدَ مَوْتِهَا ۚ
فَأَمَاتَهُ اللَّهُ مِائَةَ عَامٍ ثُمَّ بَعَثَهُ ۖ قَالَ كَمْ لَبِثْتَ ۖ
قَالَ لَبِثْتُ يَوْمًا أَوْ بَعْضَ يَوْمٍ ۖ قَالَ بَلْ لَّبِثْتَ

the sun. Abraham very wisely asked the infidel that if he, as he claimed, controlled life and death, then let him reverse the course of the sun on which all life depended. He was in a fix. He could not say that he could not accept Abraham's challenge to bring the sun from the West to the East, for that would have demolished his claim of being the controller of life and death, and if he had said that he could do so, it meant that he claimed to exercise control over the sun which would have been a great blasphemy in the eyes of his people who worshipped the sun. Thus he was completely confounded and did not know what to say.

322. The ruined town referred to in the verse is Jerusalem which was laid waste by Nebuchadnezzar, the King of Babylon in 599 B.C. Ezekiel, the Prophet, was among the Jews whom Nebuchadnezzar carried away into captivity to Babylon and who was made to pass by, and witness the ghastly sight of, the devastated town.

323. Ezekiel was naturally shocked at the sad sight and prayed to God in words full of extreme pathos as to when the ruined town would be restored to life. His prayer was heard and he was made to see a vision that the restoration prayed for would take place in a hundred years. The verse does not mean that Ezekiel remained actually dead for a hundred years. Only he saw a vision that he had died and had remained dead for a hundred years and then had come back to life. The Qur'ān sometimes mentions scenes seen in a vision as having actually taken place without stating that they were witnessed in a vision or dream (12 : 5). The vision signified, and Ezekiel understood the significance, that the Children of Israel would remain in the state of captivity and complete national degradation for about a hundred years after which they would receive a new life and would come back to their sacred city. And it actually came to pass as Ezekiel had dreamt. Jerusalem was taken by Nebuchadnezzar in 599 B.C. (2 Kings 24: 10). Ezekiel probably saw the vision in 586 B.C. The city was rebuilt about a century after its destruction. Its building started in 537 B.C. by the permission and help of Cyrus, the King of Persia and Midia, and was completed in 515 B.C. It took the Israelites another fifteen years to settle in it and thus virtually a century passed between the destruction of Jerusalem and its restoration to life. It is puerile to think that God actually caused Ezekiel to die and that he remained dead for a hundred years and was then brought back to life; for that would not have been an answer to his prayer, which did not pertain to the death and resurrection of any individual but to that of a town representing a whole people.

323A. The words are intended to express indefiniteness of time (18 : 20 & 23: 114) and mean, according to the Quranic usage, that Ezekiel did not know how long he had remained in that state. *Yaum* here does not mean a day of 24 hours but time absolutely (see 1:4). The words, *I have remained a day or part of a day*, may also refer to the time for which Ezekiel slept or the time he took in seeing the vision. Apparently Ezekiel thought that he was being asked about the duration of the time of the vision.

323B. *Bal* is a particle of digression signifying (*a*) the cancellation of what precedes as in 21 : 27, or (*b*) transition from one object of discourse to another as in 87: 17. Here *bal* has been used in the latter sense.

مائة عام فانظر إلى طعامك وشرابك لم يتسنه
وانظر إلى حمارك ولنجعلك آية للناس وانظر إلى
العظام كيف ننشزها ثم نكسوها لحما فلما تبين
له قال أعلم أن الله على كل شيء قدير ﴿٢٦٠﴾

also remained *in this state* for a hundred years.[324] Now look at thy food and thy drink; they have not rotted. And look at thy ass.[325] And *We have done this* that We may make thee a Sign unto men. And [a]'look at the bones, how We set them and then clothe them with flesh.' And when this became clear to him, he said, 'I know that Allāh has the power to do all that He wills.'[326]

وإذ قال إبراهيم رب أرني كيف تحيي الموتى قال
أولم تؤمن قال بلى ولكن ليطمئن قلبي قال
فخذ أربعة من الطير فصرهن إليك ثم اجعل

261. And *remember* when Abraham said, 'My Lord, show me how Thou givest life to the dead.' *God* said, 'Dost thou not believe?' *Abraham* said, 'Yes, but *I ask this* that my heart may be at ease.[327] *God* answered, 'Take four birds and make them attached[328] to thee.

[a]23 : 15

324. The clause, *It is so but thou hast also remained in this state for a hundred years,* points out that although in one sense Ezekiel had remained in that state for a hundred years (for he had dreamt that he had been dead for a hundred years), yet the statement that he had tarried for a day or part of a day was also correct, for the actual time spent in seeing the vision was naturally very short.

325. To bring home this fact to the mind of Ezekiel, God directed his attention to his food and drink and his ass. That his food and drink had not rotted and his ass was still alive showed that he had really tarried only for a day or part of it. The words, *look at thy ass,* also indicate that Ezekiel saw the vision while sleeping in the fields with his ass by his side, for while in captivity, the Israelites were made to work in the fields as farmers.

326. Ezekiel represented in his person the whole Jewish nation. His symbolic death for a hundred years represented their national degradation and sorrows in captivity, for that was the period after which they came to their own. This is how Ezekiel became a Sign. See also Ezekiel, chap. 37.

327. The difference between *Īmān* (belief) and *Iṭmi'nān* (the heart being at ease) is that in the former state one simply believes that God can do a thing, while in the latter one receives the assurance that the thing would be done in his case also. Abraham did indeed believe that God could bring the dead to life, but what he desired was his personal satisfaction of knowing that God would do so in the case of his own posterity as well. Referring to the verse under comment, the Holy Prophet is reported to have said, "We are more deserving of entertaining *Shak* (doubt) than Abraham" (Muslim), the word *Shak* signifying an intense hidden desire anxiously awaiting fulfilment; for the Holy Prophet never entertained any doubt about any of God's promises or doings. This shows that Abraham's question was not prompted by doubt but simply by an anxious desire.

328. *Surtu al-Ghusna Ilayya* means, I inclined the branch towards myself (Lane). The preposition *ilā* determines the significance of the word *Surhunna* in the sense of inclining or attaching and not cutting.

Then put each[329] of them on a hill; then call them; they will come to thee in haste. And know that Allāh is Mighty *and* Wise.

عَلٰى كُلِّ جَبَلٍ مِّنْهُنَّ جُزْءًا ثُمَّ ادْعُهُنَّ يَأْتِيْنَكَ
سَعْيًا ۗ وَاعْلَمْ اَنَّ اللّٰهَ عَزِيْزٌ حَكِيْمٌ ﴿۲۶۱﴾ ع ۳۵

R. 36 262. The [a]similitude of those who spend their wealth in the way of Allāh is like the similitude of a grain of corn which grows seven ears, in each ear a hundred grains. And Allāh multiplies *it* further for whomsoever He pleases and Allāh is Bountiful, All-Knowing.[330]

مَثَلُ الَّذِيْنَ يُنْفِقُوْنَ اَمْوَالَهُمْ فِيْ سَبِيْلِ اللّٰهِ كَمَثَلِ
حَبَّةٍ اَنْۢبَتَتْ سَبْعَ سَنَابِلَ فِيْ كُلِّ سُنْۢبُلَةٍ مِّائَةُ
حَبَّةٍ ۗ وَاللّٰهُ يُضٰعِفُ لِمَنْ يَّشَآءُ ۗ وَاللّٰهُ وَاسِعٌ عَلِيْمٌ ﴿۲۶۲﴾

263. They who spend their wealth in the way of Allāh, then [b]follow not up what they have spent with taunt or injury;[331] for them is their reward with their Lord, and they shall have no fear, nor shall they grieve.

اَلَّذِيْنَ يُنْفِقُوْنَ اَمْوَالَهُمْ فِيْ سَبِيْلِ اللّٰهِ ثُمَّ لَا
يُتْبِعُوْنَ مَآ اَنْفَقُوْا مَنًّا وَّلَآ اَذًى ۙ لَّهُمْ اَجْرُهُمْ
عِنْدَ رَبِّهِمْ ۚ وَلَا خَوْفٌ عَلَيْهِمْ وَلَا هُمْ يَحْزَنُوْنَ ﴿۲۶۳﴾

[a]2 : 266; 30 : 40. [b]2 : 265; 74 : 7.

329. *Juz'* means, a part or portion or division of a thing. Thus, if a thing consists of or comprises a group, the word "part" or "division" would signify each member of it.

This is a vision of Abraham. In "taking four birds" the implication was that his posterity would rise and fall four times, which phenomenon was to be witnessed twice among the Israelites, and to be repeated twice among the followers of the Holy Prophet of Islām who was descended from Abraham through Ishmael. The power of the Jews, the progeny of Abraham through Isaac, was crushed twice, first by Nebuchadnezzar and then by Titus (17 : 5-8. Enc. Brit. under Jews); and each time God raised them after their fall, the second revival having been brought about by Constantine, the Roman Emperor who accepted Christianity. Similarly, the power of Islām, was first rudely shaken when Baghdad fell to the Tartar hordes, but soon it recovered from the crushing blow. The victors became the vanquished and the grandson of Halaku, the despoiler of Baghdad, was converted to Islām. The second fall came later when there was a general and wholesale decline of Muslims both in the spiritual and the political field. The second renaissance of Islām is being brought about by the Promised Messiah.

330. In the foregoing verses, it was pointed out that it is a Divine law that God gives new life to deserving nations after they become dead, and the case of the Israelites was mentioned as an instance. It was further indicated that the progeny of Abraham would rise four times, the Israelites and the Ishmaelites each rising twice. In order to prepare Muslims for the promised rise, God reverts to the means of national progress and exhorts the Faithful to spend freely in the cause of God.

331. Every good act may be abused, and the abuse of spending in the cause of Allāh is to follow it with *Mann* (boastfully speaking of one's good act) and *Adhā* (following it up with injury). Those, who spend their wealth in the cause of Allāh, are prohibited from making unnecessary and misplaced mention of the money they spend and the services they render to the cause of Truth, for, doing so would amount to *Mann* (taunt). Similarly, they are enjoined not to demand anything in return for their contributions.

264. [a]A kind word and forgiveness[332] are better than charity followed by injury. And Allāh is Self-Sufficient, Forbearing.

قَوْلٌ مَّعْرُوفٌ وَّمَغْفِرَةٌ خَيْرٌ مِّنْ صَدَقَةٍ يَّتْبَعُهَآ
اَذًى ۗ وَاللّٰهُ غَنِيٌّ حَلِيْمٌ ﴿٢٦٤﴾

265. O ye who believe! [b]render not vain your alms by reproach and injury like him [c]who spends his wealth to be seen[333] of men, and *he* believes not in Allāh and the Last Day. His case is like the case of a smooth rock *covered* with earth, on which heavy rain falls, leaving it bare and hard. [d]They shall not secure aught of what they earn. And Allāh guides not the disbelieving people.

يٰٓاَيُّهَا الَّذِيْنَ اٰمَنُوْا لَا تُبْطِلُوْا صَدَقٰتِكُمْ بِالْمَنِّ
وَالْاَذٰى ۙ كَالَّذِيْ يُنْفِقُ مَالَهٗ رِئَآءَ النَّاسِ وَلَا
يُؤْمِنُ بِاللّٰهِ وَالْيَوْمِ الْاٰخِرِ ؕ فَمَثَلُهٗ كَمَثَلِ صَفْوَانٍ
عَلَيْهِ تُرَابٌ فَاَصَابَهٗ وَابِلٌ فَتَرَكَهٗ صَلْدًا ؕ لَا
يَقْدِرُوْنَ عَلٰى شَيْءٍ مِّمَّا كَسَبُوْا ؕ وَاللّٰهُ لَا يَهْدِي
الْقَوْمَ الْكٰفِرِيْنَ ﴿٢٦٥﴾

266. And the case of those who spend their wealth to seek the pleasure of Allāh and to strengthen[334] their souls is like the case of a garden on elevated[335] ground. Heavy rain falls on it so that it [e]brings forth its fruit twofold. And if heavy rain does not fall on it, then light rain *suffices*. And Allāh sees what you do.

وَمَثَلُ الَّذِيْنَ يُنْفِقُوْنَ اَمْوَالَهُمُ ابْتِغَآءَ مَرْضَاتِ
اللّٰهِ وَتَثْبِيْتًا مِّنْ اَنْفُسِهِمْ كَمَثَلِ جَنَّةٍ بِرَبْوَةٍ
اَصَابَهَا وَابِلٌ فَاٰتَتْ اُكُلَهَا ضِعْفَيْنِ ۚ فَاِنْ لَّمْ يُصِبْهَا
وَابِلٌ فَطَلٌّ ؕ وَاللّٰهُ بِمَا تَعْمَلُوْنَ بَصِيْرٌ ﴿٢٦٦﴾

[a]47 : 22. [b]See 2 : 263. [c]4 : 39; 8 : 48. [d]14 : 19. [e]See 2 : 262.

332. It is better that one should say a kind word of sympathy or of excuse to the person who asks for help than that he should first help him and then follow it up with injury; or that he should try to cover and conceal the want of the person who comes to him for help and refrain from talking about it to others so that he may not feel humbled and humiliated, that being the significance of *Maghfirat*.

333. Elsewhere, Muslims have also been enjoined to spend their wealth openly (2 : 275); the object underlying being that other Muslims may be induced to follow their good example. But he who has no faith in God expends his money openly solely to win public approbation. Such a one loses all title to any reward from God.

334. Spending money in the cause of Allāh strengthens the soul of a person because by spending his hard-earned wealth he voluntarily imposes a burden on himself which makes him firmer and more steadfast in faith.

335. The hearts of believers who spend freely in the cause of God are like an elevated piece of ground to which heavy rain, which sometimes proves harmful for low-lying tracts, can do no harm. On the other hand, it is benefited by rain, whether it is heavy or light.

267. Would any of you desire that there should be for him a garden of palm trees and vines with streams flowing beneath it, and with all kinds of fruit for him therein—while old age has stricken him and he has weak offspring—and that a fiery whirlwind should smite it and it be *all* burnt?[336] Thus does Allāh make His Signs clear to you that you may reflect.

أَيَوَدُّ أَحَدُكُمْ أَنْ تَكُوْنَ لَهُ جَنَّةٌ مِّنْ نَّخِيْلٍ وَّأَعْنَابٍ تَجْرِيْ مِنْ تَحْتِهَا الْأَنْهٰرُ لَهُ فِيْهَا مِنْ كُلِّ الثَّمَرٰتِ وَأَصَابَهُ الْكِبَرُ وَلَهُ ذُرِّيَّةٌ ضُعَفَآءُ فَأَصَابَهَآ إِعْصَارٌ فِيْهِ نَارٌ فَاحْتَرَقَتْ كَذٰلِكَ يُبَيِّنُ اللّٰهُ لَكُمُ الْاٰيٰتِ لَعَلَّكُمْ تَتَفَكَّرُوْنَ ﴿٢٦٧﴾ ع ٣٦

R. 37 268. O ye who believe! spend of the good things that you have earned, and of what We produce for you from the earth; and seek not what is bad that you may spend out of it when you would not take it yourselves except that you connive at it.[337] And know that Allāh is Self-Sufficient, Praiseworthy.

يٰٓأَيُّهَا الَّذِيْنَ اٰمَنُوْٓا أَنْفِقُوْا مِنْ طَيِّبٰتِ مَا كَسَبْتُمْ وَمِمَّآ أَخْرَجْنَا لَكُمْ مِّنَ الْأَرْضِ وَلَا تَيَمَّمُوا الْخَبِيْثَ مِنْهُ تُنْفِقُوْنَ وَلَسْتُمْ بِاٰخِذِيْهِ إِلَّآ أَنْ تُغْمِضُوْا فِيْهِ وَاعْلَمُوْٓا أَنَّ اللّٰهَ غَنِيٌّ حَمِيْدٌ ﴿٢٦٨﴾

269. [a]Satan threatens you with poverty[338] and enjoins upon you what is foul,[339] whereas Allāh promises you forgiveness from Himself and bounty. And Allāh is Bountiful, All-Knowing.

اَلشَّيْطٰنُ يَعِدُكُمُ الْفَقْرَ وَيَأْمُرُكُمْ بِالْفَحْشَآءِ وَاللّٰهُ يَعِدُكُمْ مَّغْفِرَةً مِّنْهُ وَفَضْلًا وَاللّٰهُ وَاسِعٌ عَلِيْمٌ ﴿٢٦٩﴾

[a]See 2 : 170; 24 : 22.

336. By means of this similitude the believer is warned that, if he spends his property for show, or follows up his charity with reproaches and injury, all that he has spent will be wasted.

337. The verse implies that believers should spend in the cause of God what is good and pure; for even a lawfully earned property might include things that are bad. Old and used things may be given to the poor, but worn out articles of use alone should not be singled out for that purpose.

338. *Faqara* means, he bored a hole into a pearl; *Faqura* means, he became poor and needy and *Faqira* means, he had a complaint of his vertebrae. Thus *Faqr* means, poverty; want or need which breaks the back of the poor man; care or anxiety or disquietude of mind (Lane).

339. The verse removes the satanic misgiving that spending liberally in the cause of God may render one poor; on the contrary it emphatically declares that if wealthy people do not spend freely in good causes, the result would be national *Faqr*, i.e., the country would suffer economically and decline morally because, if the economic needs of the less fortunate members of the community are not adequately met, they are tempted to resort to *Faḥshā'* (foul and immoral means) to earn their livelihood.

270. [a]He grants wisdom [340] to whom He pleases, and whoever is granted wisdom has indeed been granted abundant good; and none would take heed except those *endowed* with understanding.

يُؤْتِي الْحِكْمَةَ مَنْ يَشَاءُ ۚ وَمَنْ يُؤْتَ الْحِكْمَةَ فَقَدْ
أُوتِيَ خَيْرًا كَثِيرًا ۗ وَمَا يَذَّكَّرُ إِلَّا أُولُو الْأَلْبَابِ ﴿٢٧٠﴾

271. And whatsoever you spend or whatsoever you vow,[341] Allāh surely knows it; and for the wrong-doers there shall be no helpers.

وَمَا أَنْفَقْتُمْ مِنْ نَفَقَةٍ أَوْ نَذَرْتُمْ مِنْ نَذْرٍ فَإِنَّ
اللَّهَ يَعْلَمُهُ ۗ وَمَا لِلظَّالِمِينَ مِنْ أَنْصَارٍ ﴿٢٧١﴾

272. If you give [c]alms openly, it is well *and good*; but if you hide them and give them to the poor, it is better[342] for you, and [d]He will remit from you *many*[343] of your evil deeds. And Allāh is Aware of what you do.

إِنْ تُبْدُوا الصَّدَقَاتِ فَنِعِمَّا هِيَ ۖ وَإِنْ تُخْفُوهَا وَ
تُؤْتُوهَا الْفُقَرَاءَ فَهُوَ خَيْرٌ لَكُمْ ۚ وَيُكَفِّرُ عَنْكُمْ مِنْ
سَيِّئَاتِكُمْ ۗ وَاللَّهُ بِمَا تَعْمَلُونَ خَبِيرٌ ﴿٢٧٢﴾

273. [e]It is not thy responsibility to make them follow the right path; but Allāh guides whomsoever He pleases. And whatever of wealth[344] you spend, *the benefit* of it will be for yourselves, for, you spend not but

لَيْسَ عَلَيْكَ هُدَاهُمْ وَلَٰكِنَّ اللَّهَ يَهْدِي مَنْ يَشَاءُ ۗ
وَمَا تُنْفِقُوا مِنْ خَيْرٍ فَلِأَنْفُسِكُمْ ۚ وَمَا تُنْفِقُونَ إِلَّا

[a]17 : 40. [b]22 : 30; 76 : 8. [c]9 : 60,103, 104. [d]4 : 32; 8 : 30; 29 : 8; 64 : 10; 66 : 9. [e]28 : 57; 92 : 13.

340. The verse means that the injunction, regarding spending wealth in charity which is the secret of national progress and prosperity, is based on wisdom.

341. There is a tradition to the effect that the Holy Prophet did not approve of making conditional vows for the performance of non-obligatory acts of goodness; but if a man does so, fulfilment of the vow becomes obligatory.

342. Islām has most wisely recommended both forms of giving alms, open and secret. By giving alms openly a man sets a good example to others which they may imitate. Secret alms-giving in some cases is better, because then one refrains from exposing the poverty of his less fortunate brethren, and there is also little occasion for feeling proud in giving secretly.

343. The particle *min* either may have been used for the sake of emphasis, or in the sense of "many" or "some."

344. The use of the word *Khair*, which also means, anything and everything good (Lane), enlarges the scope of charity and does not confine it to the spending of money alone. The word includes the doing of good in anv shape or form.

to seek the favour of Allāh.[345] And whatever of wealth you spend, [a]it shall be paid back to you in full and you shall not be wronged.

ابْتِغَاءَ وَجْهِ اللّٰهِ ۚ وَمَا تُنْفِقُوا مِنْ خَيْرٍ يُوَفَّ إِلَيْكُمْ
وَأَنْتُمْ لَا تُظْلَمُونَ ﴿٢٧٣﴾

274. *Alms are* for the poor who are detained[346] in the way of Allāh and are unable to move about in the land. The ignorant man imagines them to be free from want because of *their* abstaining *from begging*. [b]Thou shalt know them by their appearance;[347] they do not beg of men with importunity.[348] And whatever of wealth[348A] you spend, surely, Allāh has perfect knowledge thereof.[349]

لِلْفُقَرَاءِ الَّذِينَ أُحْصِرُوا فِي سَبِيلِ اللّٰهِ لَا يَسْتَطِيعُونَ
ضَرْبًا فِي الْأَرْضِ يَحْسَبُهُمُ الْجَاهِلُ أَغْنِيَاءَ مِنَ
التَّعَفُّفِ ۚ تَعْرِفُهُمْ بِسِيمَاهُمْ ۚ لَا يَسْأَلُونَ النَّاسَ
إِلْحَافًا ۗ وَمَا تُنْفِقُوا مِنْ خَيْرٍ فَإِنَّ اللّٰهَ بِهِ عَلِيمٌ ﴿٢٧٤﴾

R. 38 275. [c]Those who spend their wealth by night and day, secretly and openly, have their reward with their Lord; on them *shall come* no fear, nor shall they grieve.

الَّذِينَ يُنْفِقُونَ أَمْوَالَهُمْ بِاللَّيْلِ وَالنَّهَارِ سِرًّا وَ
عَلَانِيَةً فَلَهُمْ أَجْرُهُمْ عِنْدَ رَبِّهِمْ ۚ وَلَا خَوْفٌ عَلَيْهِمْ
وَلَا هُمْ يَحْزَنُونَ ﴿٢٧٥﴾

[a]2 : 282; 4 : 174; 8 : 61; 39 : 11. [b]48 : 30. [c]13 : 23; 14 : 32; 16 : 76; 35 : 30.

345. These words constitute a great testimonial to the inherent goodness of the Companions of the Holy Prophet. It signifies that they needed no commandment to spend their wealth in Allāh's way. They were already doing it out of an instinctive desire to win His pleasure.

346. Circumstances sometimes compel people to remain confined to a place where they are unable to earn their living. Such persons particularly deserve help from the better-off members of the community. Two kinds of people particularly fall under this category : (a) Those who voluntarily remain attached to a Man of God, never quitting his company in order to benefit spiritually from it. (b) Those, who being confined to hostile environments, are deprived of necessities of life.

347. *Sīmā* means, a distinguishing sign or mark, or general appearance serving as such (Aqrab).

348. The verse incidentally praises those self-respecting persons who abstain from begging and implies the impropriety of begging, as the words, *Ta'affuf* (abstaining from an improper or unlawful thing) and *Ilḥāf* (with importunity), indicate. The Holy Prophet has condemned begging.

348A. *Khair* means, wealth; abundant wealth; wealth honestly earned (Mufradāt).

349. There are two categories of charity—obligatory *Zakāt* and supererogatory (*Ṣadaqah*). *Zakāt* is collected by the State from every Muslim possessing a certain amount of money or property and is spent by the State on the poor, the needy, and on orphans, widows and wayfarers, etc.; the recipients not knowing the real source of charity are beholden to no individual. *Zakāt* is a State cheque and not charity. *Ṣadaqah* is voluntary and is given to individuals out of a desire to help them. It engenders feelings of sympathy among the well-to-do towards their poor brethren and feelings of gratefulness among the poor for their benefactors.. It also serves to distinguish sincere believers from the insincere.

276. Those [a]who devour interest[350] do not rise except as rises one whom Satan has smitten with insanity.[351] That is because they say, 'Trade *also* is like interest;' whereas Allāh has made trade lawful and has made interest unlawful. So he to whom an admonition comes from his Lord and he desists, then will that *which he received* in the past be his; and his affair *rests* with Allāh. And those who revert *to it* they are the inmates of the Fire; therein shall they abide

اَلَّذِيْنَ يَاْكُلُوْنَ الرِّبٰوا لَا يَقُوْمُوْنَ اِلَّا كَمَا يَقُوْمُ الَّذِيْ
يَتَخَبَّطُهُ الشَّيْطٰنُ مِنَ الْمَسِّ ؕ ذٰلِكَ بِاَنَّهُمْ قَالُوْٓا اِنَّمَا
الْبَيْعُ مِثْلُ الرِّبٰوا ۘ وَاَحَلَّ اللّٰهُ الْبَيْعَ وَحَرَّمَ الرِّبٰوا ؕ
فَمَنْ جَآءَهٗ مَوْعِظَةٌ مِّنْ رَّبِّهٖ فَانْتَهٰى فَلَهٗ مَا سَلَفَ ؕ
وَاَمْرُهٗٓ اِلَى اللّٰهِ ؕ وَمَنْ عَادَ فَاُولٰٓئِكَ اَصْحٰبُ النَّارِ ۚ
هُمْ فِيْهَا خٰلِدُوْنَ ﴿٢٧٦﴾

277. Allāh will blot out[352] interest and [b]will cause charity to increase. And Allāh loves not anyone who is a confirmed disbeliever *and* an arch-sinner.

يَمْحَقُ اللّٰهُ الرِّبٰوا وَيُرْبِي الصَّدَقٰتِ ؕ وَاللّٰهُ لَا يُحِبُّ
كُلَّ كَفَّارٍ اَثِيْمٍ ﴿٢٧٧﴾

[a]3 : 131; 30 : 40. [b]30 : 40.

350. *Ribā* literally meaning, an excess or addition, signifies an addition over and above the principal sum (Lane). It covers both usury and interest. According to the Ḥadīth "every loan advanced to draw profits" comes under this definition. The connotation of *Ribā* is not strictly identical with "interest," as commonly understood. But for lack of a better word "interest" may be used as a rough equivalent. In fact, any sum stipulated to be received or given over and above what one advances or receives as a loan is "interest," whether the dealing is with an individual or a bank or a society or a post office or any other organisation. "Interest" is not confined to money. It extends to any commodity which is given as a loan with the condition that it will be returned with an agreed excess.

351. The words signify that just as a mad man is heedless of the consequences of his actions, so are the money-lenders heartlessly oblivious of the moral and economic injury they do to individuals, the society and even the world at large. *Ribā* also causes a touch of insanity in the money-lender in the sense that his entire engrossment in profit-making renders him insensible to all good causes. *Ribā* is prohibited in Islām because it tends to draw wealth into the hands of a small circle and thereby adversely affects its equitable distribution. It promotes idleness in the money-lenders and kills in him all incentive to help others and chokes all springs of sympathetic behaviour. The money-lender takes advantage of, and makes profit from, the need and distress of others. While on the one hand *Ribā* causes the lender to exploit other people's wants, it creates in the debtor a tendency to do things carelessly and in haste, incurring debt regardless of his capacity to pay back, thus doing irreparable moral injury to himself and the lender. *Ribā* also leads to war. No prolonged war is possible without the help of loans, interest on which eventually leads to the economic ruin of both the victors and the vanquished. The system of easy loans makes it possible for governments to carry on destructive struggles as they can obtain sinews of war without having resort to direct taxation. Islām has prohibited all kinds of interest. In modern times business has become so inseparably linked with interest that it appears well-nigh impossible to avoid it altogether. But if a change of system and of surroundings and circumstances were brought about, business without interest could be carried on as was the case in the days when Islām was in the ascendance.

352. This seems to be a prophecy that economics based on interest will eventually disappear or will be destroyed.

278. Surely, those, who believe and do good deeds, and [a]observe Prayer and pay the *Zakāt*, shall have their reward from their Lord, and no fear *shall come* on them, nor shall they grieve.

إِنَّ الَّذِيْنَ اٰمَنُوْا وَعَمِلُوا الصّٰلِحٰتِ وَاَقَامُوا الصَّلٰوةَ
وَاٰتَوُا الزَّكٰوةَ لَهُمْ اَجْرُهُمْ عِنْدَ رَبِّهِمْ ۚ وَلَا خَوْفٌ
عَلَيْهِمْ وَلَا هُمْ يَحْزَنُوْنَ ﴿٢٧٨﴾

279. O ye who believe! fear Allāh and give up what remains of interest, if you are *truly* believers.

يٰٓاَيُّهَا الَّذِيْنَ اٰمَنُوا اتَّقُوا اللّٰهَ وَذَرُوْا مَا بَقِيَ مِنَ
الرِّبٰوٓا اِنْ كُنْتُمْ مُّؤْمِنِيْنَ ﴿٢٧٩﴾

280. But if you do *it* not, then beware of war from Allāh and His Messenger; and if you repent, then you shall have your principal; *thus* you shall not wrong nor shall you be wronged.

فَاِنْ لَّمْ تَفْعَلُوْا فَاْذَنُوْا بِحَرْبٍ مِّنَ اللّٰهِ وَرَسُوْلِهٖ ۚ
وَاِنْ تُبْتُمْ فَلَكُمْ رُءُوْسُ اَمْوَالِكُمْ ۚ لَا تَظْلِمُوْنَ
وَلَا تُظْلَمُوْنَ ﴿٢٨٠﴾

281. And if *the debtor* be in straitened circumstances, then *grant him* respite till a time of ease.[353] And that you remit it as charity shall be better for you, if only you knew.

وَاِنْ كَانَ ذُوْ عُسْرَةٍ فَنَظِرَةٌ اِلٰى مَيْسَرَةٍ ۭ وَاَنْ
تَصَدَّقُوْا خَيْرٌ لَّكُمْ اِنْ كُنْتُمْ تَعْلَمُوْنَ ﴿٢٨١﴾

282. And guard *yourselves* against the day when you shall be made to return to Allāh; [b]then shall every soul be paid in full what it has earned; and they shall not be wronged.

وَاتَّقُوْا يَوْمًا تُرْجَعُوْنَ فِيْهِ اِلَى اللّٰهِ ۣ ثُمَّ تُوَفّٰى كُلُّ
نَفْسٍ مَّا كَسَبَتْ وَهُمْ لَا يُظْلَمُوْنَ ﴿٢٨٢﴾ ع ٣٨

R. 39 283. O ye who believe! when you borrow one from another for a fixed period, then write it down. And let a scribe write *it* in your presence faithfully; and no scribe should refuse to write, because [c]Allāh has taught him, so let him write and let him who incurs the liability dictate,[354] and he should fear

يٰٓاَيُّهَا الَّذِيْنَ اٰمَنُوْٓا اِذَا تَدَايَنْتُمْ بِدَيْنٍ اِلٰٓى اَجَلٍ
مُّسَمًّى فَاكْتُبُوْهُ ۭ وَلْيَكْتُبْ بَّيْنَكُمْ كَاتِبٌۢ بِالْعَدْلِ ۠ وَ
لَا يَاْبَ كَاتِبٌ اَنْ يَّكْتُبَ كَمَا عَلَّمَهُ اللّٰهُ فَلْيَكْتُبْ ۚ
وَلْيُمْلِلِ الَّذِيْ عَلَيْهِ الْحَقُّ وَلْيَتَّقِ اللّٰهَ رَبَّهٗ وَلَا

[a]See 2 : 4. [b]See 2 : 273. [c]96 : 5.

353. Islām urges the giving of loans but they should be beneficent loans, without interest. If the debtor finds himself in straitened circumstances when the time for the repayment of a loan arrives, he should be granted respite till he finds himself in easier circumstances.

354. The borrower, and not the lender, is to dictate because; (1) it is the borrower who incurs the liability; and justice demands that the words defining the liability should be

Allāh, his Lord, and not diminish anything therefrom. But if the person incurring the liability be of low understanding or be weak or be unable himself to dictate, then let someone who can guard his interest dictate with justice. And call two witnesses from among your men; and if two men be not *available*, then a man and two women, of such as you approve as witnesses, so that if either of the two *women* should forget, then one may remind the other. And the witnesses should not refuse when they are called. And be not averse to writing it down whether it be small or large, along with its appointed time *of payment*. This is more equitable in the sight of Allāh and makes testimony surer and is more likely to save you from doubt; *so write it down* [a]except that it be ready transaction which you make among yourselves on the spot in which case it shall be no sin for you that you write it not.[354A] And have witnesses when you sell one to another,[354B] and let no harm be done to the scribe or the witness. And if you do *that*, then certainly it shall be disobedience on your part. And fear Allāh. And Allāh teaches you and Allāh knows all things quite well.

يَبْخَسْ مِنْهُ شَيْـًٔا ۭ فَاِنْ كَانَ الَّذِيْ عَلَيْهِ الْحَقُّ سَفِيْهًا
اَوْ ضَعِيْفًا اَوْ لَا يَسْتَطِيْعُ اَنْ يُّمِلَّ هُوَ فَلْيُمْلِلْ
وَلِيُّهٗ بِالْعَدْلِ ۭ وَاسْتَشْهِدُوْا شَهِيْدَيْنِ مِنْ رِّجَالِكُمْ ۚ
فَاِنْ لَّمْ يَكُوْنَا رَجُلَيْنِ فَرَجُلٌ وَّامْرَاَتٰنِ مِمَّنْ تَرْضَوْنَ
مِنَ الشُّهَدَاۗءِ اَنْ تَضِلَّ اِحْدٰىهُمَا فَتُذَكِّرَ اِحْدٰىهُمَا
الْاُخْرٰى ۭ وَلَا يَاْبَ الشُّهَدَاۗءُ اِذَا مَا دُعُوْا ۭ وَلَا تَسْــَٔـمُوْٓا
اَنْ تَكْتُبُوْهُ صَغِيْرًا اَوْ كَبِيْرًا اِلٰٓى اَجَلِهٖ ۭ ذٰلِكُمْ اَقْسَطُ
عِنْدَ اللّٰهِ وَاَقْوَمُ لِلشَّهَادَةِ وَاَدْنٰٓى اَلَّا تَرْتَابُوْٓا اِلَّآ اَنْ
تَكُوْنَ تِجَارَةً حَاضِرَةً تُدِيْرُوْنَهَا بَيْنَكُمْ فَلَيْسَ عَلَيْكُمْ
جُنَاحٌ اَلَّا تَكْتُبُوْهَا ۭ وَاَشْهِدُوْٓا اِذَا تَبَايَعْتُمْ ۠ وَلَا
يُضَاۗرَّ كَاتِبٌ وَّلَا شَهِيْدٌ ڛ وَاِنْ تَفْعَلُوْا فَاِنَّهٗ فُسُوْقٌۢ
بِكُمْ ۭ وَاتَّقُوا اللّٰهَ ۭ وَيُعَلِّمُكُمُ اللّٰهُ ۭ وَاللّٰهُ بِكُلِّ شَيْءٍ
عَلِيْمٌ ۝٢٨٣

[a]4 : 30.

selected by him; (2) the document is to be deposited with the lender and not the borrower. So the borrower has been asked to dictate so that the fact of his having dictated may serve as a proof of the correctness of the amount and the conditions about payment, and he may have no cause or ground to deny it.

354A. The implication is that it would be better to have a writing even in such a case like cash memo or voucher.

354B. This refers to big transactions.

284. And if you be on a journey, and you find not a scribe, then let there be a pledge with possession.[355] And if one of you entrusts another with something, then let him who is entrusted surrender his trust and let him fear Allāh, his Lord. And [a]hide not testimony; and whoever hides it, his heart is certainly sinful. And Allāh is Well-Aware of what you do.

وَاِنْ كُنْتُمْ عَلٰى سَفَرٍ وَّلَمْ تَجِدُوْا كَاتِبًا فَرِهٰنٌ
مَّقْبُوْضَةٌ ۭ فَاِنْ اَمِنَ بَعْضُكُمْ بَعْضًا فَلْيُؤَدِّ الَّذِي
اؤْتُمِنَ اَمَانَتَهٗ وَلْيَتَّقِ اللّٰهَ رَبَّهٗ ۭ وَلَا تَكْتُمُوا الشَّهَادَةَ ۭ
وَمَنْ يَّكْتُمْهَا فَاِنَّهٗٓ اٰثِمٌ قَلْبُهٗ ۭ وَاللّٰهُ بِمَا تَعْمَلُوْنَ
عَلِيْمٌ ﴿٢٨٤﴾ ٣٩ ع ٧

R. 40 285. To Allāh belongs whatever is in the heavens and whatever is in the earth; and whether you disclose what is in your minds or keep it hidden, Allāh [b]will call you to account for[356] it, [c]then will He forgive whomsoever He pleases and punish whomsoever He pleases; and Allāh has the power to do all that He wills.[357]

لِلّٰهِ مَا فِي السَّمٰوٰتِ وَمَا فِي الْاَرْضِ ۭ وَاِنْ تُبْدُوْا
مَا فِيْٓ اَنْفُسِكُمْ اَوْ تُخْفُوْهُ يُحَاسِبْكُمْ بِهِ اللّٰهُ ۭ فَيَغْفِرُ
لِمَنْ يَّشَاۗءُ وَيُعَذِّبُ مَنْ يَّشَاۗءُ ۭ وَاللّٰهُ عَلٰى كُلِّ شَيْءٍ
قَدِيْرٌ ﴿٢٨٥﴾

286. This Messenger *of Ours* believes in that which has been revealed to him from his Lord, and *so do* the believers; all *of them* believe in Allāh, and in His angels, and in His Books, and in His Messengers,[358] *saying*, [d]"We make no distinction

اٰمَنَ الرَّسُوْلُ بِمَآ اُنْزِلَ اِلَيْهِ مِنْ رَّبِّهٖ وَالْمُؤْمِنُوْنَ ۭ
كُلٌّ اٰمَنَ بِاللّٰهِ وَمَلٰۗىِٕكَتِهٖ وَكُتُبِهٖ وَرُسُلِهٖ ۣ لَا نُفَرِّقُ

[a]2 : 141 ; 5 : 107. [b]21 : 48. [c]5 : 19,41 ; 48 : 15. [d]See 2: 137.

355. Loans may also be advanced in the form of pledges, one party receiving the loan of money and the other the thing pledged in lieu of it. This form of practical transaction will be in the nature of an *Amānah*, *i.e.*, a trust or deposit affecting both parties. By identifying a loan with a trust it is hinted that loans should be returned with the same care and honesty with which property deposited as a trust is returned on demand.

356. The word *bihī* signifies; (a) by means of or on the basis of; (*b*) for or because of; and the clause would mean, "Allāh will call you to account for it or because of it," *i.e.*, no human thought or action will go unaccounted for, however hidden it may be, and that it will be punished or pardoned as Allāh may will.

357. The expression, "the will or pleasure of God," rather denotes the existence of a natural law (7:157). But as in the case of Allāh it is His Will which stands for His Law, therefore the Qur'ān has used this expression to point out (1) that God is the final authority in the universe; and (2) that His Will is the Law, and (3) that His Will manifests itself in a just and benevolent manner, for He is the Possessor of perfect attributes (17 : 111).

358. Good deeds are indeed the principal means for the attainment of spiritual purification, but they have their origin in the purity of the heart, which can be attained only by holding right beliefs. Hence the verse details the fundamental beliefs which the Qur'ān has taught, *i.e.*, belief in God and His angels, His Books and His Messengers, in their natural order.

between any of His Messengers;' and they say, 'We have heard and we are obedient. Our Lord, [a]we *implore* Thy forgiveness, and to Thee is the returning.'

بَيْنَ اَحَدٍ مِّنْ رُّسُلِهٖ ۗ وَقَالُوْا سَمِعْنَا وَاَطَعْنَا ۗ غُفْرَانَكَ
رَبَّنَا وَاِلَيْكَ الْمَصِيْرُ ﴿٢٨٦﴾

287. [b]Allāh burdens not any soul beyond its capacity.[359] It shall have *the reward* it earns, and it shall get *the punishment* it incurs.[360] Our Lord, do not punish us, if we forget or fall into error,[361] and our Lord, lay not on us a responsibility[362] as Thou didst lay upon those before us. Our Lord, burden us not with what we have not the strength to bear; and efface our *sins* and grant us forgiveness and have mercy on us; Thou art our Master; [c]so help us against the disbelieving people.

لَا يُكَلِّفُ اللّٰهُ نَفْسًا اِلَّا وُسْعَهَا ۗ لَهَا مَا كَسَبَتْ وَعَلَيْهَا
مَا اكْتَسَبَتْ ۗ رَبَّنَا لَا تُؤَاخِذْنَآ اِنْ نَّسِيْنَآ اَوْ اَخْطَاْنَا ۚ
رَبَّنَا وَلَا تَحْمِلْ عَلَيْنَآ اِصْرًا كَمَا حَمَلْتَهٗ عَلَى الَّذِيْنَ
مِنْ قَبْلِنَا ۚ رَبَّنَا وَلَا تُحَمِّلْنَا مَا لَا طَاقَةَ لَنَا بِهٖ ۚ
وَاعْفُ عَنَّا ۗ وَاغْفِرْ لَنَا ۗ وَارْحَمْنَا ۗ اَنْتَ مَوْلٰىنَا
فَانْصُرْنَا عَلَى الْقَوْمِ الْكٰفِرِيْنَ ﴿٢٨٧﴾ ع

[a]3 : 148, 194; 60 : 6. [b]See 2 : 234. [c]3 : 148.

359. The clause constitutes a powerful refutation of the doctrine of Atonement. It embodies two important principles : (1) That the commandments of God are always given with due regard for man's capacities and his natural limitations. (2) That moral purification in this world does not necessarily signify complete freedom from all kinds of failings and short-comings. All that man is expected to do is sincerely to strive for good and avoid sin to the best of his power, and the rest will be forgiven him by the Merciful God. So no Atonement is needed.

360. The word *Kasaba* generally denotes the doing of good deeds and *Iktasaba* the doing of evil deeds. Both words are from the same root but the latter denotes greater exertion on the part of the doer. A man will be rewarded for good deeds even if they are done casually and without conscious effort, while he will be punished for his evil deeds only if they are committed deliberately and with conscious effort.

361. In ordinary circumstances, *Nisyān* and *Khaṭī'ah* are not punishable for they lack intention or motive which are necessary for awarding punishment. But here the words denote forgetfulness and error which can be avoided if due care is taken.

362. *Isr* means, (1) a burden which restrains one from motion; (2) a heavy responsibility the breaking of which renders one deserving of punishment; (3) a sin or an offence; and (4) grievous punishment of a sin. The expression 'lay not on us a responsibility as Thou didst lay upon those before us,' does not mean that the burden to be laid upon us should be lighter than that which was laid upon those before us. The meaning is that we may be safeguarded against breaking Thy covenant and thus may be saved from incurring a heavy responsibility for disobedience as was incurred by those before us. This is a collective prayer for the preservation and protection of Islām and the safeguarding of Muslims against incurring the displeasure of God.

CHAPTER 3

ĀL 'IMRĀN

(Revealed after Hijrah)

Connection with the Preceding Sūrah

There exists such a deep and far-reaching connection between this *Sūrah* and the preceding one, Al-Baqarah, that the two are called Al-Zahrāwān (The Two Bright Ones). Whereas Al-Baqarah deals with the wrong beliefs and evil practices of the Jews with whom began the Mosaic Dispensation, the present *Sūrah* deals mainly with the wrong doctrines and dogmas of Christianity which subject constitutes its culmination. The *Sūrah* is named Āl 'Imrān (The Family of 'Imrān). 'Imrān or 'Amrān was the father of Moses and Aaron, the progenitors of the family from which sprang Mary, the mother of Jesus, brief account of whose life and mission is given in this *Sūrah*. Being closely connected with Al-Baqarah, the *Sūrah* may be safely supposed to have been revealed immediately after it. A detailed mention of the Battle of Uḥud places its revelation in the third year of the Hijrah.

Āl 'Imrān has a twofold connection with Al-Baqarah. First, there subsists a strong and deep link between the subject-matter of the whole of this *Sūrah* and that of the whole of *Sūrah* Al-Baqarah, and another link equally strong between the concluding portion of Al-Baqarah and the opening verses of this *Sūrah*. In fact, the order in the Qur'ān is of two kinds. Either, the topic with which one Chapter is concluded is continued in the following Chapter, or the whole of the subject-matter of the preceding Chapter is referred to in the next. This twofold connection also exists between Al-Baqarah and Āl 'Imrān. The connection of the whole subject-matter of Āl 'Imrān with that of Al-Baqarah mainly consists in a description of the causes that led to the transfer of Prophethood from the Mosaic to the Islamic Dispensation. This was the main theme of Al-Baqarah, and in explanation of it the degenerate condition of the Jews was dealt with at some length in that *Sūrah*. But in Al-Baqarah very little light was shed on Christianity, in which culminated the Mosaic Dispensation. This omission could have given rise to the seemingly legitimate doubt that though Judaism which constituted the beginning of the Mosaic Dispensation had become corrupt, its culmination, the Christian Faith, was still pure; and hence, apparently there was no necessity of introducing and establishing a new religion—Islām. To remove this doubt, the hollowness of the Christian dogmas has been exposed in the present *Sūrah*.

Title

The *Sūrah* is known by several names in the Ḥadīth, *i.e.*, Al-Zahrā' (The Bright One), Al-Amān (The Peace), Al-Kanz (The Treasure), Al-Mu'īnah (The Helper), Al-Mujādalah (The Pleading), Al-Istighfār (The Seeking of Forgiveness) and Al-Ṭayyibah (The Pure).

As the falsity of Christian doctrines is sought to be established in this Chapter it rightly opens with the hint that as Christianity had become corrupt and degenerate, it could not prove a bar to the introduction of a new and better Dispensation. On the contrary, Christianity itself constituted a strong testimony to the need for the introduction of a new Law. Consequently, the Divine attributes—the Living, the Self-Subsisting and All-Sustaining have been placed in the very beginning of this *Sūrah* to repudiate the Christian basic doctrines. The other connection between the two *Sūrahs*, *viz.*, that of the concluding portion of Al-Baqarah with the opening words of this *Sūrah* is apparent from the fact that Al-Baqarah had concluded with a prayer for national regeneration and reformation of Muslims and the triumph of Islām over its enemies, and the Divine attributes—the Living, the Self-Subsisting and All-Sustaining have been placed in the beginning of the present *Sūrah* to assure Muslims that God will certainly come to their aid because He being the Living, the Self-Subsisting and All-Sustaining, His power knows no weakening or diminution.

Subject-Matter

The *Sūrah*, like the preceding one, opens with the abbreviated letters, *Alif Lām Mīm*, (I am Allāh, the All-Knowing), which are intended to draw attention to the Divine attribute of knowledge; and, mention of the attributes, the Living, the Self-Subsisting and All-Sustaining is meant to point out that in this *Sūrah* the Divine attribute of knowledge has been substantiated by God's attributes, the Living, the Self-Subsisting and All-Sustaining, *i.e.*, the fact that God is Living, Self-Subsisting and All-Sustaining constitutes proof of His being All-Knowing, because death and decay are the result of lack of knowledge. The *Sūrah* proceeds to say that, as Jews and Christians have strayed away from the right path, Divine punishment will overtake them, and their being the followers of Torah and the Gospels will not save them from God's punishment, because these Books have been abrogated and, therefore, are unable to satisfy human needs and requirements. After this it tells Muslims to banish all doubt or misgiving from their minds that, in view of the numerical superiority of Jews and Christians and the preponderance of the material means at their disposal, they would not prevail against the latter, because God had already granted them predominance over their more powerful enemies, the Quraish and other infidel tribes of Arabia. The same phenomenon will be repeated now. Moreover, national victories do not result solely from the preponderance of material means but primarily and very largely from the superiority of national morals. And final victory will come to Muslims because, though they lack material means, they are in possession of ample moral and spiritual means and because also they follow a true religion.

Next, the *Sūrah* proceeds to disabuse the minds of the enemies of Islām of the fondly-held illusion that their national usages and customs are superior to those of Muslims. Further, they are told that by holding wrong beliefs and resorting to evil practices they appear to ignore the law of cause and effect which cannot be flouted with impunity. The *Sūrah* then develops the subject that the path to progress and prosperity for Muslims does not lie in imitating other peoples' ways and manners but in strictly following Islām and the Holy Prophet. After this a clear and detailed exposition of the real subject is taken in hand with a brief reference to the beginnings of Christianity, refutation of which is one of its main themes. Then attention of the People of the Book is drawn to the fact that when Muslims also believe in the truth of the Divine origin and source of their Faith, why should they fritter away their energies and resources in fighting with them; instead both should combine to preach to infidels the doctrine of the Oneness of God, on which they agree, and should keep within proper bounds their respective doctrinal differences. The Christians, then, are particularly warned that they cannot hope to continue to be the "Chosen Ones" of God and retain His grace and love if they refuse to accept the new Faith; they are asked how, after having already subscribed to the doctrine that Truth has always been revealed by God from time to time, can they with justification defy this principle ? It is further stated that matters regarding which the People of the Book dispute and quarrel with Muslims are not of much weight, because originally some of them were regarded as permissible by their own forefathers. The subject is further developed that Muslims and Jews have a meeting-point in Abraham, and since it was Abraham who laid the foundations of the Ka'bah, why should the Israelites quarrel with Muslims on the basis of fancied and insubstantial differences? Then a note of warning is sounded to Muslims that the People of the Book have gone so far in opposition to them that, if the latter had their way, they would certainly lead them astray. But Muslims will not go astray because they are the recipients of God's favour. They will meet strong opposition and persecution from them which they should endure with steadfastness and should try to strengthen their connection with God and establish their mutual relations on a firmer basis because they will soon need to develop a united front when confronted with a severe attack from Christians. Before that time comes they should add to their numbers by conveying the Message of Islām to as many people as they possibly can. They are further warned against harbouring the delusion that, in the event of their fight with Christians, the Jews would help them. On the contrary, the latter would spare no pains to harass and oppress them. In spite of this warning against the Jews the *Sūrah* does not fail to recognize the good wherever it is found and says that all the People of the Book are not bad. There are also good people among them, but only those, who entertain bad designs against Islām, will come to grief. It is these with whom the Muslims should eschew all friendly contact to avoid being influenced by the latter's undesirable morals.

Then a brief reference is made to the Battle of Badr. The Muslims are told that, just as in extremely adverse circumstances God protected and helped them against very heavy odds in that encounter and vouchsafed to them a clear victory over the idolaters of Mecca, the same will happen with regard to the People of the Book; God's mercy and grace will accompany them in opposition to the latter. The People of the Book depend for their power and material might on transactions based on interest. But the taking and giving of interest runs counter to good morals. By taking interest they oppress God's servants and by subscribing to the doctrine of Atonement and the dogma of the non-acceptance of repentance they declare God to be cruel like themselves. The believers are further enjoined to do their duty, make suitable sacrifices and employ properly the material means at their disposal, leaving the rest to God for the success of their life's mission. The *Sūrah* then enunciates a very sound principle, *viz.*, that the Holy Prophet is but a Divine Messenger; if he should die or be killed in a battle (though in conformity with Divine promise this would never happen), Muslims should not lose heart and should entertain no doubt about the truth of Islām because Islām relies for its success and prosperity on no individual however exalted. Another rule of conduct to be observed in time of war is that the leaders of Muslims should behave with greater leniency than in ordinary times towards other Muslims and should have proper regard for their susceptibilities, so that the enemy may not get an opportunity to create discord and dissension among them. It is further enjoined that at such time all matters should be decided after mutual consultation. Then, Muslims are reminded of the great good God has done to them in that He has raised for them a great Messenger. They should follow him and eschew the path of the disturbers of peace. The *Sūrah* lays down the principle, *viz.*, that those, who die while fighting for the cause of Truth, are entitled to special respect. By their death they receive eternal life and inspire their community, as it were, with a new life. Again, reference is made to the People of the Book saying that morally they have become so depraved that, while, on the one hand, they claim to be God's "Own Chosen People," on the other, they hesitate to spend their money in His way. Muslims are enjoined to take a lesson from this. The moral depravity of these people is further contrasted with their claim that they are commanded to give their allegiance only to that Messenger who should demand the greatest sacrifice of them. The *Sūrah* says that such Messengers did appear among them, but they refused to accept them. Next, the theme of sacrifice is developed and believers are told that it would be foolish on their part to be afraid of making sacrifices for national cause. They are then warned that their faith will be put to a severe test. They should not think that they will achieve success without passing through fire and blood. In the next few verses some special qualities and characteristics of true believers are mentioned and they are taught certain prayers which are essential for national progress and prosperity. The *Sūrah* concludes with the rules of conduct by observing which Muslims can achieve success and predominance in this life and the pleasure of God in the next.

—:o:—

سُوْرَةُ اٰلِ عِمْرٰنَ مَدَنِيَّةٌ

1. In the name of Allāh, the Gracious, the Merciful.

بِسْمِ اللّٰهِ الرَّحْمٰنِ الرَّحِيْمِ ①

2. [a]Alif Lām Mīm.[362A]

الٓمّٓ ②

3. [b]Allāh is He beside Whom there is none worthy of worship, the Living, the Self-Subsisting and All-Sustaining.[363]

اللّٰهُ لَآ اِلٰهَ اِلَّا هُوَ الْحَيُّ الْقَيُّوْمُ ③

4. [c]He has sent down to thee the Book containing the truth[364] *and* fulfilling that which precedes it; and He sent down the Torah[365] and

نَزَّلَ عَلَيْكَ الْكِتٰبَ بِالْحَقِّ مُصَدِّقًا لِّمَا بَيْنَ يَدَيْهِ

[a]See 2 : 2. [b]See 2 : 256. [c]4 : 106; 5 : 49; 29 : 52; 39 : 3.

362A. See 16.

363. The verse contains a strong refutation of the false doctrine of the divinity of Jesus. This doctrine being one of the principal topics dealt with in this *Sūrah*, the opening verses thereof fittingly refer to such attributes of God as cut at the very root of this doctrine. These attributes, *i.e.*, the Ever-Living, the Self-Subsisting and All-Sustaining, prove, on the one hand, that God, the Possessor of these attributes, should need no partner or helper; and on the other that Jesus, who was subject to the law of birth and death, and therefore was neither ever-living, nor self-subsisting and all-sustaining, could not be God. These attributes also prove the hollowness of the doctrine of Atonement which is a corollary to the above doctrine. Jesus, it is claimed by Christians, suffered death to atone for the sins of mankind. If that is so, he could not be God, for God is Ever-Living and cannot suffer death, permanent or temporary. It is futile to say that the death of Jesus meant only the separation of the god-Jesus from his physical habitat. The connection between the god-Jesus and his physical body was, according to Christian belief, in its very nature a temporary one and was bound to break one day, even if Jesus had not died on the Cross. So the mere breaking up of this connection could serve no useful purpose. It must be some other death which brought redemption to his sinful followers. That death, according to the Christians themselves, came upon Jesus when after his crucifixion he descended into Hades or Hell (Acts 2 : 31). Thus, far from being immune from death, which is God's exclusive prerogative, Jesus suffered death both in its literal and figurative sense. Similarly, the attributes, the Self-Subsisting and All-Sustaining prove the falsity of the Christian doctrine. God, being Self-Subsisting and All-Sustaining, should not only live by Himself without the support of any other being but all other beings should receive support from Him. But Jesus did not possess these attributes. Like other mortals, he was born of a woman, lived on food and drink, suffered pain and distress, asked others to pray for the alleviation of his sufferings, and finally, as Christians say, died on the Cross. The New Testament bears ample testimony to all these facts. But God being Ever-Living, Self-Subsisting and All-Sustaining is above all these physical weaknesses.

364. *Ḥaqqa* means, it was or became just, proper, right, true, authentic, genuine, substantial or real; or it was or became an established or confirmed fact; or it was or became binding, incumbent or due (Lane). The expression *Bil-Ḥaqq* signifies, (1) that the Qur'ān comprises teachings which are based on eternal truths and are incapable of being successfully assailed; (2) that its first recipients are the people best suited to receive it; (3) that it has come in the fulness of time and fulfils all true human needs; (4) that it has come to stay and no effort on the part of its opponents can destroy or tamper with it.

365. The word, *Taurāt*, is derived from *Warā* which means, he burnt; he concealed (Aqrab). Taurāt is so called probably because in its pristine purity reading it and acting upon its teaching kindled in the heart of men the fire of Divine love. Possibly, the word also contains a hint that bright prophecies about the advent of the last Law-giving Prophet lie hidden in the Book. Taurāt is the name applied to the five books of Moses : Genesis,

the Gospel[366] before *this*, as a guidance to the people; and He has sent down [a]the Discrimination.[367]

وَاَنْزَلَ التَّوْرٰىةَ وَالْاِنْجِيْلَ ۝٣
مِنْ قَبْلُ هُدًى لِّلنَّاسِ وَاَنْزَلَ الْفُرْقَانَ ؕ

5. Surely, those who deny the Signs of Allāh shall have a severe punishment. And [b]Allāh is Mighty, Lord of retribution.

اِنَّ الَّذِيْنَ كَفَرُوْا بِاٰيٰتِ اللّٰهِ لَهُمْ عَذَابٌ شَدِيْدٌ ؕ
وَاللّٰهُ عَزِيْزٌ ذُو انْتِقَامٍ ۝٥

6. Surely, [c]nothing in the earth or in the heavens is hidden from Allāh.

اِنَّ اللّٰهَ لَا يَخْفٰى عَلَيْهِ شَيْءٌ فِي الْاَرْضِ وَلَا فِي
السَّمَآءِ ۝٦

7. [d]He it is Who fashions you in the wombs[368] as He wills; there is none worthy of worship but He, the Mighty, the Wise.

هُوَ الَّذِيْ يُصَوِّرُكُمْ فِي الْاَرْحَامِ كَيْفَ يَشَآءُ ؕ لَآ اِلٰهَ
اِلَّا هُوَ الْعَزِيْزُ الْحَكِيْمُ ۝٧

8. He it is Who has sent down to thee the Book; [e]in it there are verses that are *firm and* decisive in meaning[369] —they are the basis[370]

هُوَ الَّذِيْٓ اَنْزَلَ عَلَيْكَ الْكِتٰبَ مِنْهُ اٰيٰتٌ مُّحْكَمٰتٌ

[a]2 : 54, 186; 8 : 42; 21 : 49; 25 : 2. [b]5 : 96; 14 : 48; 39 : 38. [c]14: 39; 40: 17; 64: 5; 86: 6. [d]22:6; 23 : 12-15; 39: 7; 40: 65; 64 : 4. [e]11 : 2.

Exodus, Leviticus, Numbers and Deuteronomy. The name is also sometimes applied to the Ten Commandments.

366. *Injīl*, which means, good news, is, according to Aqrab, a Greek word (un-derived from any Arabic root) from which the English word "Evangel" is derived. The Gospels were so called because they contained not only "good news" for those who accepted Jesus but also because they contained prophecies about the advent of the greatest Prophet whose coming Jesus had described as the coming of the Lord Himself (Matt. 21 : 40). The word does not refer to the present four Gospels which were written by the followers of Jesus long after his crucifixion and which give merely an account of his life and teachings, but to the actual revelation received by Jesus.

367. *Al-Furqān* may refer to the Qur'ān or to the heavenly Signs vouchsafed to the Holy Prophet which establish his truth.

368. As development of the child takes place in the womb of the mother, the offspring naturally is affected by her physical and moral condition. So Jesus, whose body like that of all other human beings was formed in the womb of a woman, could not escape being affected by the limitations and failings inherent in woman. This is why, in his discussion with the Christians of Najrān, the Holy Prophet pointedly referred to the birth of Jesus as an argument to disprove his so-called divinity. He is reported to have said to them: "Do you not know that it was a woman who conceived Jesus, and then she was delivered of him just as a normal woman is delivered of a child" (Jarir, iii. 101)?

369. *Muhkam* means, (1) that which has been made secure from change or alteration; (2) that in which there is no ambiguity or possibility of doubt; (3) that which is clear in meaning and decisive in exposition and (4) a verse which embodies a teaching special to the Qur'ān (Mufradāt & Lane)?

370. *Umm* means, (1) mother; (2) source or origin or basis of a thing; (3) anything which is a means of sustenance and support or of reformation and correction for another; (4) anything to which other things around it are linked (Aqrab & Mufradāt).

of the Book—and there are [a]others that are susceptible of different interpretations.[371] But those in whose hearts is perversity pursue such thereof as are susceptible of different interpretations, seeking *to cause* discord and seeking *wrong* interpretation of it. And none knows [b]its *right* interpretation[372] except Allāh [c]and those who are firmly grounded in knowledge; they say, 'We believe in it; the whole is from our Lord.' —And none take heed except those gifted with understanding—[373]

هُنَّ أُمُّ الْكِتٰبِ وَأُخَرُ مُتَشٰبِهٰتٌ ۖ فَأَمَّا الَّذِيْنَ فِيْ
قُلُوْبِهِمْ زَيْغٌ فَيَتَّبِعُوْنَ مَا تَشَابَهَ مِنْهُ ابْتِغَآءَ
الْفِتْنَةِ وَابْتِغَآءَ تَأْوِيْلِهٖ ۚ وَمَا يَعْلَمُ تَأْوِيْلَهٗٓ
إِلَّا اللّٰهُ ۘ وَالرّٰسِخُوْنَ فِي الْعِلْمِ يَقُوْلُوْنَ اٰمَنَّا بِهٖ ۙ كُلٌّ
مِّنْ عِنْدِ رَبِّنَا ۚ وَمَا يَذَّكَّرُ إِلَّآ أُولُوا الْأَلْبَابِ ۝٨

[a]39 : 24. [b]7 : 54; 18 : 79. [c]4 : 163.

371. *Mutashābih* is used about (1) that phrase, sentence or verse which is susceptible of different, though concordant, interpretations; (2) that whose parts resemble or are concordant with one another; (3) that whose true significance bears a similarity to a sense which is not meant; (4) that of which the true meaning is known only by referring it to what is termed *Muḥkam*; (5) that which cannot be rightly understood without repeated consideration; (6) a verse which contains teaching corresponding to or resembling those contained in the previous revealed Scriptures (Mufradāt).

372. *Ta'wīl* means, (1) interpretation or explanation; (2) conjecture about the meaning of a speech or writing; (3) turning away a speech or writing from its right interpretation; (4) interpretation of a dream; (5) end, result or sequel of a thing (Lane). In this verse the word occurs twice; in the former place it gives the second or the third meaning, while in the latter it gives the first or the fifth meaning.

373. The verse lays down the golden rule that, in order to prove a controversial point, the decisive and clearly worded parts of a Scripture should be taken into consideration, and if these are found to contradict the construction put upon a certain ambiguous passage that passage should be so interpreted as to make it harmonize with the decisive and clearly worded parts of the text. According to the verse, the Qur'ān has two sets of verses. Some are *Muhkam* (firm and decisive in meaning) and others *Mutashābih* (capable of different interpretations). The right way to interpret a *Mutashābih* verse is that only such interpretation of it should be accepted as agrees with the verses that are *Muḥkam*. In 39 : 24 the whole of the Qur'ān is called *Mutashābih* and in 11 : 2 all the Quranic verses have been described as *Muḥkam*. This should not be taken as contradicting the verse under comment, according to which some verses of the Qur'ān are *Muḥkam* and others *Mutashābih*. So far as the real significance of the Quranic verses is concerned the whole of the Qur'ān is *Muhkam*, in that all its verses contain decisive and eternal truths. In another sense, however, the whole of the Qur'ān is *Mutashābih* inasmuch as the Quranic verses have been so worded as to give at one and the same time, several meanings equally true and good. The Qur'ān is also *Mutashābih* (mutually resembling) in the sense that there is no contradiction or inconsistency in it, its different verses supporting one another. But parts of it are certainly *Muḥkam* and others *Mutashābih* for different readers according to their knowledge, mental make up and natural capacities, as the present verse points out. As regards prophecies, those that are couched in plain and direct language, susceptible of only one meaning, would be regarded as *Muḥkam* and those that are described in figurative or metaphorical language, capable of more than one interpretation, would be regarded as *Mutashābih*. The prophecies described in metaphorical language should, therefore, be interpreted in the light of the prophecies that are clearly and literally fulfilled and also in the light of the basic and fundamental principles of Islām. For *Muḥkam* prophecies, the reader is referred to 58 : 22; whereas 28 : 86 contains a *Mutashābih* prophecy. The term *Muḥkam* may also be applied to such verses as embody full and complete commandments while *Mutashābih* verses are those which give only part of a certain commandment, and are required to be read in conjunction with other verses

9. 'Our Lord, let not our hearts become perverse after Thou hast guided us,[374] and bestow on us mercy from Thyself; surely, Thou art the Great Bestower;

رَبَّنَا لَا تُزِغْ قُلُوْبَنَا بَعْدَ اِذْ هَدَيْتَنَا وَهَبْ لَنَا مِنْ لَّدُنْكَ رَحْمَةً ۚ اِنَّكَ اَنْتَ الْوَهَّابُ ⑨

10. 'Our Lord, [a]Thou wilt certainly assemble mankind together on the Day about which there is no doubt; surely, Allāh never fails in *His* promise.'

رَبَّنَآ اِنَّكَ جَامِعُ النَّاسِ لِيَوْمٍ لَّا رَيْبَ فِيْهِ ؕ اِنَّ اللّٰهَ لَا يُخْلِفُ الْمِيْعَادَ ⑩ ع

R. 2 11. Those who disbelieve[375]—[b]their possessions and their children shall not avail them at all against Allāh; and it is they that are the fuel of the Fire.

اِنَّ الَّذِيْنَ كَفَرُوْا لَنْ تُغْنِيَ عَنْهُمْ اَمْوَالُهُمْ وَلَآ اَوْلَادُهُمْ مِّنَ اللّٰهِ شَيْـًٔا ؕ وَاُولٰٓئِكَ هُمْ وَقُوْدُ النَّارِ ⑪

12. [c]*Their case*[376] *is* like the case of the people of Pharaoh and those before them; they rejected Our Signs; so Allāh punished them for their sins, and Allāh is Severe in punishing.

كَدَاْبِ اٰلِ فِرْعَوْنَ ۙ وَالَّذِيْنَ مِنْ قَبْلِهِمْ ؕ كَذَّبُوْا بِاٰيٰتِنَا ۚ فَاَخَذَهُمُ اللّٰهُ بِذُنُوْبِهِمْ ؕ وَاللّٰهُ شَدِيْدُ الْعِقَابِ ⑫

13. Say to those who disbelieve, [d]'You shall be overcome and gathered unto Hell; and an evil place of rest *it is*.'

قُلْ لِّلَّذِيْنَ كَفَرُوْا سَتُغْلَبُوْنَ وَتُحْشَرُوْنَ اِلٰى جَهَنَّمَ ؕ وَبِئْسَ الْمِهَادُ ⑬

[a]3 : 26; 4 : 88; 45 : 27. [b]3 : 117; 58 : 18; 92 : 12; 111 : 3. [c]8 : 53, 55. [d]8 : 37; 54 : 46.

to make a complete injunction. *Muḥkamāt* (decisive verses) generally deal with the Law and the doctrines of Faith, while *Mutashābihāt* generally deal with topics of secondary importance or describe incidents in the lives of Prophets or the history of peoples and, while so doing, sometimes make use of idioms and phrases capable of different meanings. Such verses should not be so interpreted as to contradict the clearly worded tenets of the Faith It may be noted here that the use of metaphors, the main basis of *Mutashābih* verses in religious Scriptures, is necessary in order to assure vastness of meaning in the fewest of words, to add beauty and grace to the style, and to provide for the people a trial without which spiritual development and perfection are not possible.

374. The right knowledge of the Qur'ān is vouchsafed only to those who are pure of heart (56 : 80).

375. As all these verses have particular reference to Christians the word "disbelievers" occurring in the verse under comment may apply to them.

376. *Dā'b* means, habit, custom or manner; case, affair or condition (Aqrab).

14. Certainly there was for you a Sign[377] in *the two armies which encountered each other—one army fighting in the way of Allāh and the other disbelieving, whom they saw with *their* own eyes *to be* twice as many as themselves.[378] *Thus* [b]Allāh strengthens with His aid whomsoever He pleases. In that surely is a lesson for those who have eyes.

قَدْ كَانَ لَكُمْ اٰيَةٌ فِيْ فِئَتَيْنِ الْتَقَتَا ۖ فِئَةٌ تُقَاتِلُ فِيْ سَبِيْلِ اللّٰهِ وَاُخْرٰى كَافِرَةٌ يَّرَوْنَهُمْ مِّثْلَيْهِمْ رَأْيَ الْعَيْنِ ۖ وَاللّٰهُ يُؤَيِّدُ بِنَصْرِهٖ مَنْ يَّشَآءُ ۚ اِنَّ فِيْ ذٰلِكَ لَعِبْرَةً لِّاُولِي الْاَبْصَارِ ۝

15. 'Fair-seeming to men is made the love of desired things—women and children, and stored-up heaps of gold and silver, and horses of mark and cattle and crops. [d]That is the provision of the present life; [379] but it is Allāh with Whom is an excellent home.

زُيِّنَ لِلنَّاسِ حُبُّ الشَّهَوٰتِ مِنَ النِّسَآءِ وَالْبَنِيْنَ وَالْقَنَاطِيْرِ الْمُقَنْطَرَةِ مِنَ الذَّهَبِ وَالْفِضَّةِ وَالْخَيْلِ الْمُسَوَّمَةِ وَالْاَنْعَامِ وَالْحَرْثِ ۗ ذٰلِكَ مَتَاعُ الْحَيٰوةِ الدُّنْيَا ۚ وَاللّٰهُ عِنْدَهٗ حُسْنُ الْمَاٰبِ ۝

16. Say, 'Shall I inform you of [e]something better than that?' For those who fear God, there are gardens with their Lord, beneath which streams flow; therein shall they abide; and [f]pure mates and [g]Allāh's pleasure. And Allāh is Mindful of *His* servants.

قُلْ اَؤُنَبِّئُكُمْ بِخَيْرٍ مِّنْ ذٰلِكُمْ ۚ لِلَّذِيْنَ اتَّقَوْا عِنْدَ رَبِّهِمْ جَنّٰتٌ تَجْرِيْ مِنْ تَحْتِهَا الْاَنْهٰرُ خٰلِدِيْنَ فِيْهَا وَاَزْوَاجٌ مُّطَهَّرَةٌ وَّرِضْوَانٌ مِّنَ اللّٰهِ ۗ وَاللّٰهُ بَصِيْرٌ بِالْعِبَادِ ۝

---

[a]8 : 42,43. [b]8 : 27. [c]18 : 47; 57 : 21. [d]3 : 186; 9 : 38; 10 : 71.
[e]8 : 47; 19 : 77. [f]See 2 : 26. [g]3 : 163, 175; 5 : 3; 9 : 72; 48 : 30; 59 : 9.

377. The verse refers to the Battle of Badr in which 313 ill-equipped and ill-armed Muslims inflicted a crushing defeat on a fully equipped and fully armed Meccan force—1,000 strong. This fulfilled two prophecies—one contained in an earlier revelation of the Qur'ān (54 : 45-49), and the other in the Bible (Isa. 21 : 13-17). 'n accordance with the biblical prophecy, about a year after the flight of the Holy Prophet from Mecca, the power of Kedar (the progenitor of the Meccans) was broken at Badr and their glory departed. The defeat of the infidels was as unexpected and complete as was the victory of the Muslims. Truly has the Battle of Badr been reckoned among the greatest battles of history. It virtually decided the fate of Arabia and established Islām on a very firm footing.

378. The clause points out that the Meccan army appeared to the Muslims to be less than their actual strength, *i.e.*, only twice instead of thrice the number of the Muslims, as was actually the case. This was quite in harmony with Divine design that the few weak and ill-equipped Muslims, seeing the full strength of the enemy, might not lose heart (8 : 45). What actually happened was that one-third of the Meccan army was behind a mound and the Muslims could see only two-thirds of them, *i.e.*, 600 or twice as many as their own number.

379. Islām does not prohibit the use or seeking of the good things of this world; but it certainly condemns those who are wholly engrossed in them and make them the very object of their life.

17. Those who say, 'Our Lord, we do believe; [a]forgive us, therefore, our sins [380] and save us from the punishment of the Fire;

الَّذِيْنَ يَقُوْلُوْنَ رَبَّنَآ اِنَّنَآ اٰمَنَّا فَاغْفِرْ لَنَا ذُنُوْبَنَا وَقِنَا عَذَابَ النَّارِ ﴿١٧﴾

18. [b]The steadfast, and the truthful, and the humble, and those who spend *in the way of Allāh* and those [c]who pray for pardon in the latter part of the night.[381]

اَلصّٰبِرِيْنَ وَالصّٰدِقِيْنَ وَالْقٰنِتِيْنَ وَالْمُنْفِقِيْنَ وَالْمُسْتَغْفِرِيْنَ بِالْاَسْحَارِ ﴿١٨﴾

19. Allāh bears witness that there is no god but He—and *also do* the angels and those possessed of knowledge, [d]maintaining[381A] justice; there is no god but He, the Mighty, the Wise.[382]

شَهِدَ اللّٰهُ اَنَّهٗ لَآ اِلٰهَ اِلَّا هُوَ ۙ وَالْمَلٰٓئِكَةُ وَاُولُوا الْعِلْمِ قَآئِمًا ۢ بِالْقِسْطِ ؕ لَآ اِلٰهَ اِلَّا هُوَ الْعَزِيْزُ الْحَكِيْمُ ﴿١٩﴾

النصف

[a]3: 194; 7 : 156; 23 : 110; 60 : 6. [b]33 : 36. [c]51 : 18,19. [d]5 : 9 ; 7 : 30.

380. *Dhunūb* is the plural of *Dhanb* which means, a fault, a misdeed, an offence, a thing for which one is blameable, if one does it intentionally. It differs from *Ithm* in that *Dhanb* may be either intentional or committed through inadvertence, *Ithm* is peculiarly intentional. Or *Dhanb* means, such errors and mistakes as bring about a harmful result or make one liable to be called to account. Really, *Dhanb* signifies such failings or short-comings as adhere to human nature, just as *Dhanab* (tail, or in man, the corresponding part of the body) adheres to the body, *i.e.*, natural failings and short-comings in man (Lane & Mufradāt).

381. The special marks of a true believer mentioned in this verse represent four stages of spiritual progress: (1) When a person embraces the true Faith, he generally is subjected to persecution; therefore, the first stage through which he has to pass is that of "patience and steadfastness." (2) When persecution comes to an end and he is free to act as he pleases, he carries into practice the teachings which he was unable fully to act upon before. This second stage relates to "living truthfully," *i.e.*, living up to one's convictions. (3) When, as a result of faithfully carrying out the commandments of Faith, true believers attain power, even then humility does not take leave of them. They remain as "humble" in spirit as ever. (4) Nay, their sense of service increases all the more. They "spend" whatever Allāh has given them for the welfare of fellow men. But, as the concluding words of the verse point out, all this time they continue to pray to God in the stillness of the night to forgive any falling short, on their part, of the high ideal of service to humanity.

381A. The words also mean, in accordance with justice.

382. The one central and indisputable fact in nature and the basic principle of every true religion is Divine Unity. The whole creation and the consummate order pervading it bear undeniable testimony to this fundamental fact. The angels who are the bearers of the Message of truth to the Prophets, the Messengers of God, who propagate it in the world, and those good people who receive and imbibe true knowledge from God's Messengers, all add their testimony to the Divine testimony. Similarly, all are united in testifying to the falsehood of the idea of setting up gods with Allāh, be it in the form of plurality, trinity, or duality of gods.

20. Surely, [a]the *true* religion with Allāh is Islām.[383] And those who were given the Book did not disagree but, after knowledge had come to them, out of mutual envy. And whoso denies the Signs of Allāh, then surely, Allāh is Quick at reckoning.

إِنَّ الدِّيْنَ عِنْدَ اللّٰهِ الْإِسْلَامُ قف وَمَا اخْتَلَفَ الَّذِيْنَ
أُوْتُوا الْكِتٰبَ إِلَّا مِنْ بَعْدِ مَا جَآءَهُمُ الْعِلْمُ بَغْيًا
بَيْنَهُمْ ۭ وَمَنْ يَّكْفُرْ بِاٰيٰتِ اللّٰهِ فَإِنَّ اللّٰهَ سَرِيْعُ
الْحِسَابِ ﴿٢٠﴾

21. But if they dispute with thee, say, [b]'I have surrendered myself completely to Allāh, and *also* those who follow me.' And say to those, who have been given the Book[384] and to the Unlearned,[385] 'Have you *also* surrendered?' If they surrender, then they will surely be rightly guided,[386] but if they turn back, then [c]thy duty is only to convey *the Message*. And Allāh is Watchful of *His* servants.

فَإِنْ حَآجُّوْكَ فَقُلْ أَسْلَمْتُ وَجْهِيَ لِلّٰهِ وَمَنِ اتَّبَعَنِ ۭ
وَقُلْ لِّلَّذِيْنَ أُوْتُوا الْكِتٰبَ وَالْأُمِّيّٖنَ ءَأَسْلَمْتُمْ ۭ فَإِنْ
أَسْلَمُوْا فَقَدِ اهْتَدَوْا ۚ وَإِنْ تَوَلَّوْا فَإِنَّمَا عَلَيْكَ الْبَلٰغُ ۭ
وَاللّٰهُ بَصِيْرٌ ۢ بِالْعِبَادِ ﴿٢١﴾ ع

R. 3 22. Surely, those who deny the Signs of Allāh and [d]seek to slay the Prophets unjustly and seek to slay such men as enjoin equity—announce to them a painful punishment.[387]

إِنَّ الَّذِيْنَ يَكْفُرُوْنَ بِاٰيٰتِ اللّٰهِ وَيَقْتُلُوْنَ النَّبِيّٖنَ
بِغَيْرِ حَقٍّ ۙ وَّيَقْتُلُوْنَ الَّذِيْنَ يَأْمُرُوْنَ بِالْقِسْطِ مِنَ
النَّاسِ ۙ فَبَشِّرْهُمْ بِعَذَابٍ أَلِيْمٍ ﴿٢٢﴾

[a]3 : 86. [b]4 : 126. [c]5: 93,100; 13 : 41; 16 : 83. [d]See 2 : 62.

383. All religions inculcate belief in the Oneness of God and submission to His Will, yet it is only in Islām that the idea of submission to God's Will has found its consummation; for complete submission requires complete manifestation of God's attributes and it is in Islām alone that such manifestation has taken place. So of all religious systems Islām alone deserves to be called God's own religion in the real sense of the term. All true religions were indeed more or less *Islām* in their original form and their adherents *Muslims* in the literal sense of the term, but not till the time when religion became complete in all its different aspects was it given the name of Al-Islām, which was reserved for the final Dispensation perfected in the Qur'ān. The verse further explains 2 : 63.

384. People of the Book and *Ummiyyīn* (those who follow no revealed Book) comprise the whole of mankind.

385. See 113A and 1058.

386. If the People of the Book and those who follow no revealed Scripture were to surrender themselves to God, they would surely accept the Holy Prophet and be rightly guided, the former because clear prophecies are found in their Scriptures regarding him and the latter because of the combined testimony of nature, human conscience and common sense.

387. No Prophet of God, whatever circumstances faced him, ever failed in his mission. No amount of persecution or attempts to murder the Prophets ever succeeded in arresting or retarding the progress of their Faith. The history of Religion provides a standing testimony to this fact.

23. Those are they [a]whose deeds shall come to naught in this world and in the next, and they shall have no helpers.[388]

أُولَٰٓئِكَ الَّذِينَ حَبِطَتْ أَعْمَالُهُمْ فِي الدُّنْيَا وَالْآخِرَةِ
وَمَا لَهُم مِّن نَّاصِرِينَ ﴿٢٣﴾

24. Hast thou not seen those who have been given *their* portion of the Book?[389] [b]They are called to the Book of Allāh that it may judge between them, but a party of them turn away in aversion.

أَلَمْ تَرَ إِلَى الَّذِينَ أُوتُوا نَصِيبًا مِّنَ الْكِتَابِ يُدْعَوْنَ
إِلَىٰ كِتَابِ اللَّهِ لِيَحْكُمَ بَيْنَهُمْ ثُمَّ يَتَوَلَّىٰ فَرِيقٌ مِّنْهُمْ وَ
هُم مُّعْرِضُونَ ﴿٢٤﴾

25. That is because they say, [c]"The Fire shall not touch us, except for a limited number of days.'[390] And what they used to forge has deceived them regarding their religion.

ذَٰلِكَ بِأَنَّهُمْ قَالُوا لَن تَمَسَّنَا النَّارُ إِلَّا أَيَّامًا مَّعْدُودَاتٍ
وَغَرَّهُمْ فِي دِينِهِم مَّا كَانُوا يَفْتَرُونَ ﴿٢٥﴾

26. How *will it be with them* [d]when We will gather them together on the Day about which there is no doubt; and when every soul shall be paid in full what it has earned, and they shall not be wronged?[391]

فَكَيْفَ إِذَا جَمَعْنَاهُمْ لِيَوْمٍ لَّا رَيْبَ فِيهِ وَوُفِّيَتْ
كُلُّ نَفْسٍ مَّا كَسَبَتْ وَهُمْ لَا يُظْلَمُونَ ﴿٢٦﴾

[a]2 : 218; 7 : 148; 18: 106. [b]24 : 49. [c]2 : 81; 5 : 19. [d]3 : 10; 4 : 88; 45 : 27.

388. Disbelievers have no faith in retribution of the Hereafter; so, as a proof of the fact that their deeds will not avail them at all on the Day of Resurrection, they are told that in the present life also their efforts to destory Islām will prove futile and this will be evidence of the fact that in the life to come also their works will be of no use to them.

389. (1) Prophecies contained in the Bible concerning the Holy Prophet which formed a portion of the Book; or (2) the genuine portion of the Bible, because only a portion of it had remained safe from interpolation and this alone could be called a part of the true Book; or (3) the Bible is but a portion of the Book as compared with the Qur'ān which is the Book *par excellence*.

390. Both Jews and Christians persuaded themselves into believing that they would be safe against the punishment of the Hereafter, the Jews thinking themselves immune owing to their being the "Favoured Ones" of God and the Christians deluding themselves with the idea that Jesus, the so-called son of God, had washed away all their sins with his supposed death on the Cross.

391. The verse constitutes an emphatic contradiction of the doctrine that the blood of any person, and not one's own good works, can bring about salvation.

27. Say, ' O Allāh, Lord of sovereignty, Thou givest sovereignty to whomsoever Thou pleasest; and Thou takest away sovereignty from whomsoever Thou pleasest. Thou exaltest whomsoever Thou pleasest and Thou abasest whomsoever Thou pleasest. In Thy hand is *all* good. Thou surely hast power to do all things.[392]

قُلِ اللّٰهُمَّ مٰلِكَ الْمُلْكِ تُؤْتِي الْمُلْكَ مَنْ تَشَآءُ وَتَنْزِعُ
الْمُلْكَ مِمَّنْ تَشَآءُ وَتُعِزُّ مَنْ تَشَآءُ وَتُذِلُّ مَنْ
تَشَآءُ ط بِيَدِكَ الْخَيْرُ ط إِنَّكَ عَلٰى كُلِّ شَيْءٍ قَدِيْرٌ ﴿٢٧﴾

28. [b]'Thou makest the night pass into the day and makest the day pass into the night.[393] And [c]Thou bringest forth the living from the dead and bringest forth the dead from the living. And Thou givest to whomsoever Thou pleasest without measure.'[394]

تُوْلِجُ الَّيْلَ فِي النَّهَارِ وَتُوْلِجُ النَّهَارَ فِي الَّيْلِ ز
وَتُخْرِجُ الْحَيَّ مِنَ الْمَيِّتِ وَتُخْرِجُ الْمَيِّتَ مِنَ الْحَيِّ ز
وَتَرْزُقُ مَنْ تَشَآءُ بِغَيْرِ حِسَابٍ ﴿٢٨﴾

29. [d]Let not the believers take disbelievers for friends[395] in preference to believers—and whoever does that has no connection with Allāh—except that you guard yourselves fully against them.[396] And Allāh cautions you against His punishment;[397] and to Allāh is the returning.

لَا يَتَّخِذِ الْمُؤْمِنُوْنَ الْكٰفِرِيْنَ أَوْلِيَآءَ مِنْ دُوْنِ
الْمُؤْمِنِيْنَ ج وَمَنْ يَّفْعَلْ ذٰلِكَ فَلَيْسَ مِنَ اللّٰهِ
فِيْ شَيْءٍ إِلَّآ أَنْ تَتَّقُوْا مِنْهُمْ تُقٰىةً ط وَيُحَذِّرُكُمُ
اللّٰهُ نَفْسَهُ ط وَإِلَى اللّٰهِ الْمَصِيْرُ ﴿٢٩﴾

[a]2 : 285; 5: 19, 41; 35: 14; 40: 17; 48: 15. [b]7 : 55; 13 : 4; 22 : 62; 35 : 14; 39 : 6; 57 : 7. [c]6 : 96; 10 : 32; 30 : 20. [d]3 : 119; 4 : 140, 145.

392. See next verse for explanation of this verse.

393. "The day" may here represent the prosperity and power of a people and "the night" their decline and degradation.

394. This and the preceding verse point to the immutable Divine law that nations rise and fall as they conform to, or defy, the Will of God, Who is the Source of all power and glory.

395. With the accession of political power to Islām, as promised in the preceding verses, forging of political alliances became necessary for the Muslim State. The verse under comment embodies the guiding principle that no Muslim State should enter into treaty or alliance with a non-Muslim State which should in any way injure, or conflict with, the interests of other Muslim States. The interests of Islām should transcend all other interests.

396. Muslims are warned to be on their guard against the plots and machinations of disbelievers. The expression, *except that you guard yourselves fully against them*, refers not to the power of the enemy but to his cunning of which Muslims should always be on their guard.

397. *Nafs* means, a person's self; purpose; will or desire; punishment, etc. (Aqrab).

30. Say, [a]'Whether you hide what is in your breasts or reveal it, Allāh knows it; and He knows whatever is in the heavens and whatever is in the earth. And Allāh has power to do all things.'

قُلْ إِنْ تُخْفُوا مَا فِي صُدُورِكُمْ أَوْ تُبْدُوهُ يَعْلَمْهُ
اللّٰهُ ۗ وَيَعْلَمُ مَا فِي السَّمٰوٰتِ وَمَا فِي الْأَرْضِ ۗ وَ
اللّٰهُ عَلٰى كُلِّ شَيْءٍ قَدِيرٌ ﴿٣٠﴾

31. *Beware of* the Day [b]when every soul shall find itself confronted with *all* the good it has done and *all* the evil it has done. It will wish there were a great distance between it and that *evil*. And Allāh cautions you against His punishment. And Allāh is Most Compassionate to *His* servants.

يَوْمَ تَجِدُ كُلُّ نَفْسٍ مَّا عَمِلَتْ مِنْ خَيْرٍ مُّحْضَرًا ۚ
وَّمَا عَمِلَتْ مِنْ سُوْٓءٍ ۚ تَوَدُّ لَوْ أَنَّ بَيْنَهَا وَبَيْنَهٗٓ
أَمَدًا بَعِيدًا ۗ وَيُحَذِّرُكُمُ اللّٰهُ نَفْسَهٗ ۗ وَاللّٰهُ رَءُوفٌ
بِالْعِبَادِ ﴿٣١﴾ ع

R. 4 32. Say, [c]'If you love Allāh, follow[398] me; *then* will Allāh love you and forgive you your sins. And Allāh is Most Forgiving *and* Merciful.

قُلْ إِنْ كُنْتُمْ تُحِبُّونَ اللّٰهَ فَاتَّبِعُونِي يُحْبِبْكُمُ
اللّٰهُ وَيَغْفِرْ لَكُمْ ذُنُوبَكُمْ ۗ وَاللّٰهُ غَفُورٌ رَّحِيمٌ ﴿٣٢﴾

33. Say, [d]'Obey Allāh and His Messenger;' but if they turn away, then *remember that* Allāh loves not the disbelievers.

قُلْ أَطِيعُوا اللّٰهَ وَالرَّسُولَ ۚ فَإِنْ تَوَلَّوْا فَإِنَّ اللّٰهَ لَا يُحِبُّ
الْكٰفِرِينَ ﴿٣٣﴾

34. Allāh chose Adam and Noah and the family of Abraham and the family of 'Imrān[399] above all peoples *of the time.*

إِنَّ اللّٰهَ اصْطَفٰٓى اٰدَمَ وَنُوحًا وَّاٰلَ إِبْرٰهِيمَ وَاٰلَ
عِمْرٰنَ عَلَى الْعٰلَمِينَ ﴿٣٤﴾

[a]27 : 75; 28 : 70. [b]18 : 50. [c]4 : 70. [d]4 : 60; 5 : 93; 8 : 47; 24 : 55; 58 : 14.

398. The verse emphatically declares that the goal to attain Divine love is now impossible of achievement except by following the Holy Prophet. It further removes the misunderstanding that may possibly arise from 2 : 63 that belief in the existence of God and in the Hereafter is alone sufficient for salvation.

399. 'Imrān may possibly refer to two persons: (1) Amram of the Bible, who was a son of Kohath and a grandson of Levi. He was the father of Moses, Aaron and Miriam, Moses being the youngest of the three (Jew. Enc. under Amram; Exod. 6 : 18-20); (2) 'Imrān, the father of Mary, mother of Jesus. This 'Imrān was the son of Yoshhim or Yoshim (Jarīr & Kathīr). The Qur'ān has chosen this name with a towfold purpose: (1) To include, besides Moses, a reference to Aaron, the elder brother of Moses, and (2) to use it as a sort of preamble for introducing the story of Mary, the mother of Jesus, and, through it, that of Jesus himself. The repetition of the name 'Imrān in 3 : 36 also points to the same conclusion. It is significant that whereas the verse mentions the names of Adam and Noah singly and individually, it refers to Abraham and 'Imrān as heads of families. This has been done to point out that the latter names include references to certain individuals from among their progeny. Thus the expression "family of Abraham" not only refers to Abraham personally but also to his sons and grandsons—Ishmael, Isaac, Jacob and Joseph. It may also include

35. [a]*They were* descendants of one another and Allāh is All-Hearing, All-Knowing.

ذُرِّيَّةً بَعْضُهَا مِنْ بَعْضٍ وَاللّٰهُ سَمِيْعٌ عَلِيْمٌ ﴿٣٥﴾

36. *Remember* when a woman of 'Imrān[400] said, 'My Lord, I have vowed to Thee what is in my womb to be dedicated[401] *to Thy service*. So do Thou accept *it* of me; verily, Thou alone art All-Hearing, All-Knowing.'

إِذْ قَالَتِ امْرَاَتُ عِمْرٰنَ رَبِّ اِنِّيْ نَذَرْتُ لَكَ مَا فِيْ بَطْنِيْ مُحَرَّرًا فَتَقَبَّلْ مِنِّيْ ۚ اِنَّكَ اَنْتَ السَّمِيْعُ الْعَلِيْمُ ﴿٣٦﴾

[a]6 : 88; 19 : 59.

a reference to the Holy Prophet of Islām who was likewise descended from Abraham. Similarly, the words " family of 'Imrān " refer to Aaron, Moses and Jesus. 'Imrān himself is not included, as he was not a Prophet.

400. 'Imrān in the present verse is either the abbreviated form of Āl 'Imrān (the family of 'Imrān, father of Moses) just as in 2: 41 Isrā'īl is the abbreviated form of Banī Isrā'īl (the Children of Israel) or it refers to 'Imrān, the father of Mary.

401. *Muḥarrar* means, emancipated; a child divorced from all worldly affairs and dedicated by its parents to the service of the Church (Lane & Mufradāt). It was a custom among the Israelites that those persons who were dedicated to the service of the Church remained unmarried (Gospel of Mary, 5 : 6 & Bayān under 3 : 36). In this verse the mother of Mary whose name was Hanna (Enc. Bib.) has been spoken of as *Imra'at Imrān* (woman of 'Imrān) while in 19 : 29 Mary herself has been addressed as *Ukht Hārūn* (sister of Aaron). 'Imrān (Amrān) and Aaron were respectively the father and brother of Moses, while he had also a sister named Miriam. Being ignorant of Arabic idiom and Quranic style, Christian writers, who ascribe the authorship of the Qur'ān to the Holy Prophet, think that in his ignorance he confused Mary, mother of Jesus, with Mary or Miriam, the sister of Moses. Thus they pretend to have discovered a serious anachronism in the Qur'ān—an altogether absurd charge, inasmuch as quite a number of passages can be cited to show that the Qur'ān considers Moses and Jesus as two Prophets separated from each other by a long line of Prophets (2 : 88; 5 : 45). It is on record that when the Holy Prophet sent Mughīrah to Najrān, the Chrisitans of that place asked him: "Do you not read in the Qur'ān Mary (mother of Jesus) being mentioned as the sister of Aaron, while you know that Jesus was born long time after Moses?" "I did not know the answer," says Mughīrah, "and on my return to Medina I enquired about it of the Holy Prophet who answered, 'Why did you not tell them that the Israelites used to name their children after their deceased Prophets and saints (Tirmidhī). In fact, there is actually a tradition to the effect that the husband of Hanna and the father of Mary was known as 'Imrān whose father (Mary's grandfather) had the name Yoshhim or Yoshim (Jarīr & Kathīr). Thus this 'Imrān is different from the 'Imrān who was the father of Moses and whose own father was Kohath (Exod. 6 : 18-20). The fact that Hanna's husband, or for that matter Mary's father, has been named Joachim in the Christain Scriptures (Gospel of the Birth of Mary & Enc. Brit. under Mary) should perplex no one as Joachim is the same as Yoshim, mentioned by Ibn Jarīr as the father of 'Imrān. The Christain Scriptures give the name of the grandfather instead of the father, which is a common practice. Besides, there are instances in the Bible of one person being known by two names. Gideon, for instance, was also called Jerubbaal (Judg. 7 : 1). So it should occasion no surprise if the second name of Jochim happened to be 'Imrān. Moreover, like individuals, families, too, are sometimes known after the names of their distinguished ancestors. In the Bible the name 'Israel' sometimes stands for the Israelites (Deut. 6 : 3, 4) and Kedar for the Ishmaelites (Isa. 21 : 16; 42 : 11). Similarly, Jesus has been called the son of David (Matt. 1 : 1). So the words *Imra'at 'Imrān* may also mean *Imra'at Āl'Imrān*, *i.e.*, a woman from the family of 'Imrān. This explanation finds further support from the fact that the words *Āl 'Imrān* (family of 'Imrān) have been used by the Qur'ān only two verses before. The word *Āl* (family) was dropped here owing to the nearness of reference. And it is admitted that Hanna, mother of Mary, who was the cousin of Elisabeth (John's mother) belonged to the House of Aaron and through him to that of 'Imrān (Luke 1 : 5, 36). For this and the next verse see also 'The Larger Edition of the Commentary'.

37. But when she was delivered of it, she said, 'My Lord, I am delivered of a female,'[402]—and Allāh knew best of what she was delivered[402A] and the male *she desired to have* was not like the female *she was delivered of*—'and I have named her Mary,[402B] and I commit her and her offspring to Thy protection[402C] from Satan, the rejected.'[402D]

فَلَمَّا وَضَعَتْهَا قَالَتْ رَبِّ إِنِّي وَضَعْتُهَآ أُنْثٰى وَاللّٰهُ
أَعْلَمُ بِمَا وَضَعَتْ وَلَيْسَ الذَّكَرُ كَالْأُنْثٰى ۚ وَإِنِّي
سَمَّيْتُهَا مَرْيَمَ وَإِنِّيٓ أُعِيذُهَا بِكَ وَذُرِّيَّتَهَا
مِنَ الشَّيْطٰنِ الرَّجِيمِ ﴿٣٧﴾

The vow of Mary's mother seems to have been taken under the influence of the Essenes who were generally held in high esteem by the people of that time and who practised celibacy and excluded women from their membership, and dedicated their lives to the service of religion and their fellow beings (Enc. Bib.; Jew. Enc.). It is remarkable that the teachings of the Gospels have much in common with those of the Essenes. It is also clear from the meaning of the word *Muḥarrar* that Mary's mother had vowed the dedication of her child to the service of the Church, and as such she intended her never to marry, which shows that Mary was meant to belong to the priestly class. This is why, elsewhere in the Qur'ān, she is called the sister of Aaron and not of Moses (19 : 29), though both were real brothers; for whereas Moses was the founder of the Jewish Law, Aaron was the head of the Jewish priestly class (Enc. Bib.; Enc. Brit. under Aaron). Thus Mary, mother of Jesus, was the sister of Aaron not in the sense that she was his real sister but because, like Aaron, she belonged to the priestly order.

402. Mary's mother had made the vow in the hope that she would be blessed with a son whom she would dedicate to the service of God. Instead a daughter was born to her. So she was naturally perplexed.

402A. The words, *Allāh knew best of what she was delivered*, form a parenthetical clause spoken by God, whereas the following words, *the male she desired to have was not like the female she was delivered of*, may be taken to have been spoken either by God or by Mary's mother. Most probably they are God's words and mean, as rendered in the text, that the female child she had brought forth was superior to the male child she desired to have. If taken to have been spoken by Mary's mother, they would mean that the female child she had given birth to could not be like the male child she desired to have, inasmuch as a boy only was fitted to do the special service to which she desired to dedicate him. The clause, *I have named her Mary*, contains an implied prayer to God to make the girl as exalted and as good and virtuous as the name Mary (meaning exalted or a pious worshipper) signified.

402B. Maryam was the mother of Jesus. She was probably named after the sister of Moses and Aaron, known as Mariam (later pronunciation, Miriam). The word, which is probably a compound one in Hebrew means, star of the sea; mistress or lady; exalted; pious worshipper (Cruden's Concordance; Kashshāf & Enc. Bib).

402C. These words offer some difficulty. If Mary's mother intended her child to be dedicated to the service of God, she must have known that *the child* would remain unmarried for life. What is, then, the sense in offering prayer for the child's offspring? The most probable explanation is that God had told her in a vision that her daughter would grow up to womanhood and would have a child, whereupon she prayed that Mary and her child might both be granted God's protection. In spite of this, however, she appears to have left the future of Mary in God's hand and dedicated her, as she had originally intended, to the service of God (3 : 36; Gospel of the Birth of Mary). This must have been an exceptional case, for ordinarily only males were eligible for such dedication. The assumption that Mary's mother had a vision that her daughter would have a son finds mention in the Gospel of Mary (3 : 5) though perhaps in a somewhat different form. There was nothing unusual about the prayer of Hanna, Mary's mother, that Mary and her offspring might be protected from satanic influences. All pious parents are actuated by such a desire for their

402D. See next page.

38. So her Lord accepted her with a gracious acceptance and caused her to grow an excellent growth and made Zachariah[403] her guardian. Whenever Zachariah visited her in the chamber, he found with her provisions. He said, 'O Mary whence hast thou this?' She replied, 'It is from Allāh.'[404] Surely, Allāh gives to whomsoever He pleases without measure.

فَتَقَبَّلَهَا رَبُّهَا بِقَبُولٍ حَسَنٍ وَّ أَنْبَتَهَا نَبَاتًا حَسَنًا
وَّكَفَّلَهَا زَكَرِيَّا ۚ كُلَّمَا دَخَلَ عَلَيْهَا زَكَرِيَّا الْمِحْرَابَ
وَجَدَ عِنْدَهَا رِزْقًا ۚ قَالَ يٰمَرْيَمُ أَنّٰى لَكِ هٰذَا ۚ
قَالَتْ هُوَ مِنْ عِنْدِ اللّٰهِ ۚ إِنَّ اللّٰهَ يَرْزُقُ مَنْ يَّشَآءُ
بِغَيْرِ حِسَابٍ ﴿٣٨﴾

39. Then *and there* did Zachariah pray[405] to His Lord, saying, [a]"My Lord, grant me from Thyself pure offspring; surely, Thou art the Hearer of prayer.'

هُنَالِكَ دَعَا زَكَرِيَّا رَبَّهُ ۚ قَالَ رَبِّ هَبْ لِي مِنْ
لَّدُنْكَ ذُرِّيَّةً طَيِّبَةً ۚ إِنَّكَ سَمِيعُ الدُّعَآءِ ﴿٣٩﴾

40. And the angels called to him as [b]he stood praying in the chamber, [c]'Allāh gives thee glad tidings of Yaḥyā,[406] who shall testify to the

فَنَادَتْهُ الْمَلٰٓئِكَةُ وَهُوَ قَآئِمٌ يُّصَلِّي فِي الْمِحْرَابِ ۙ
أَنَّ اللّٰهَ يُبَشِّرُكَ بِيَحْيٰى مُصَدِّقًا بِكَلِمَةٍ مِّنَ اللّٰهِ

[a]19 : 6, 7; 21 : 90, 91. [b]19 : 12. [c]19 : 8; 21 : 91.

children and pray that they should grow up to lead good and virtuous lives. It is also to be noted that though Islām declares all Prophets of God to be safe from the influence of Satan, the Bible does not ascribe this protection to Jesus (Mark, 1 : 12, 13).

402D. *Rajīm*, derived from *Rajama*, means: (1) One driven away from God's presence and mercy or one cursed; (2) forsaken and abandoned; (3) pelted with stones; (4) deprived of all goodness and virtue (Lane).

403. Zachariah or Zacharias was the name of an Israelite holy person whom the Qur'ān presents as a Prophet (6 : 86) but of whom the Bible speaks only as a priest (Luke, 1 : 5). The person presented as a Prophet by the Bible is Zechariah (mark the difference in spelling) of whom the Qur'ān, however, makes no mention. Zachariah of the Qur'ān was the father of Yaḥyā, (John) who was a cousin of Jesus.

404. The gifts were evidently brought by worshippers visiting the place and there was nothing extraordinary in Mary's reply that the gifts were from Allāh, for every good thing that comes to man is really from God, He being the Final Giver. In fact, from a girl of Mary's religious upbringing any other reply would have been rather surprising.

405. The pious reply of the child made a deep impression on the mind of Zachariah and awakened in the depths of his soul the latent and natural desire of possessing a similarly virtuous child of his own. He prayed to God to be blessed with a child like Mary. The prayer was probably repeated over a length of period as it is mentioned in varying words in different parts of the Qur'ān (3 : 39; 19 : 4-7; 21 : 90).

406. Yaḥyā or John is the name of the Prophet who appeared before Jesus to serve as his harbinger in fulfilment of the biblical prophecy (Mal. 3 : 1 and 4 : 5). The Hebrew form is *Yuḥannā* which in that language means, God has been gracious (Enc. Brit.). The name Yaḥyā was given by God Himself.

truth of a [a]word from Allāh—noble and chaste and a Prophet,[407] from among the righteous.

وَسَيِّدًا وَّحَصُوْرًا وَّ نَبِيًّا مِّنَ الصّٰلِحِيْنَ ﴿۴۰﴾

41. He said, [b]'My Lord, how shall I have a son,[408] when old age has overtaken me *already*, and my wife is barren?' He answered, 'Such is *the way of* Allāh; He does what He pleases.'

قَالَ رَبِّ اَنّٰى يَكُوْنُ لِىْ غُلٰمٌ وَّ قَدْ بَلَغَنِىَ الْكِبَرُ وَامْرَاَتِىْ عَاقِرٌ ؕ قَالَ كَذٰلِكَ اللّٰهُ يَفْعَلُ مَا يَشَآءُ ﴿۴۱﴾

42. [c]He said, 'My Lord, give me a commandment.'[409] He replied, 'The commandment for thee is that thou shalt not speak to men for three days[410] [d]except by signs. And remember thy Lord much and glorify Him in the evening and in the early morning.'

قَالَ رَبِّ اجْعَلْ لِّىْٓ اٰيَةً ؕ قَالَ اٰيَتُكَ اَلَّا تُكَلِّمَ النَّاسَ ثَلٰثَةَ اَيَّامٍ اِلَّا رَمْزًا ؕ وَاذْكُرْ رَّبَّكَ كَثِيْرًا وَّ سَبِّحْ بِالْعَشِىِّ وَالْاِبْكَارِ ﴿۴۲﴾ ع

R. 5 43. And *remember* when the angels[411] said, 'O Mary, Allāh has chosen[412] thee and purified thee and [e]chosen thee above all women *of the time*.

وَاِذْ قَالَتِ الْمَلٰٓئِكَةُ يٰمَرْيَمُ اِنَّ اللّٰهَ اصْطَفٰكِ وَ طَهَّرَكِ وَاصْطَفٰكِ عَلٰى نِسَآءِ الْعٰلَمِيْنَ ﴿۴۳﴾

[a]3 : 46; 4 : 172. [b]19 : 9, 10. [c]19 : 11. [d]19 : 12. [e]3 : 34.

407. John came in fulfilment of Malachi's prophecy, "Behold I will send you Elijah, the Prophet, before the great and terrrible day of the Lord" (Mal. 4 : 5).

408. *Ghulām* means a youth (Lane). Zachariah's query was a spontaneous expression of innocent surprise at the Divine promise. It also contained a veiled prayer that he might live long enough to see the child born and grow up into a young man.

409. Zachariah was to abstain from speaking for three days, and, then, was the promise to be fulfilled. He was not deprived of his power of speech, as the Gospels seem to allege, as a punishment for his not believing the words of God (Luke, 1 : 20-22).

410. The commandment about keeping silent was intended to afford Zachariah a suitable opportunity for passing his time in meditation and prayer—a condition particularly helpful in attracting Divine mercy and grace. Refraining from speech has also been found helpful, in some cases, in making one regain one's lost vitality and physical strength. This practice seems to have been in vogue among the Jews of those times.

411. The use of the word "angels" in the plural number has its own significance. If the mere conveying of a message was intended, only one angel could have acted as a message-bearer. In the Quranic idiom the use of the plural number signifies that, as God intended to bring about, through Mary's son, a great change in the world, affecting various spheres of life, He ordered all the different angels connected with the relevant spheres to take part in conveying the message, thus calling upon all of them to help him in bringing about the desired change.

412. In this verse the word "chosen" has been used twice. In the first place it has been used in regard to Mary without reference to any other person, signifying her exalted

44. 'O Mary, be obedient to thy Lord and prostrate thyself and worship the *One God* with those who worship *Him*.'

يٰمَرْيَمُ اقْنُتِيْ لِرَبِّكِ وَاسْجُدِيْ وَارْكَعِيْ مَعَ الرّٰكِعِيْنَ ﴿۴۴﴾

45. [a]This is of the tidings of things unseen[413] which We reveal to thee. And thou wast not with them when they cast their arrows, [b]as to which of them should be the guardian of Mary, nor wast thou with them when they disputed with one another.

ذٰلِكَ مِنْ اَنْۢبَآءِ الْغَيْبِ نُوْحِيْهِ اِلَيْكَ ؕ وَمَا كُنْتَ لَدَيْهِمْ اِذْ يُلْقُوْنَ اَقْلَامَهُمْ اَيُّهُمْ يَكْفُلُ مَرْيَمَ ۪ وَمَا كُنْتَ لَدَيْهِمْ اِذْ يَخْتَصِمُوْنَ ﴿۴۵﴾

46. When the angels said, 'O Mary, [c]Allāh gives thee glad tidings *of a son* through [d]a Word[414]

اِذْ قَالَتِ الْمَلٰٓئِكَةُ يٰمَرْيَمُ اِنَّ اللّٰهَ يُبَشِّرُكِ بِكَلِمَةٍ

[a]11 : 50; 12 : 103. [b]3 : 38. [c]19 : 30. [d]3 : 10; 4 : 172.

position absolutely; while in the second place it has been used to express her high position in relation to other women of her time. According to the usage of the Qur'ān, the expression *Nisā' al-'Ālamīn* does not here refer to the women of all times and all ages, but only to the women of the specific time in which Mary lived.

413. Many of the facts which the Qur'ān has brought to light regarding Mary are not found in the previous Scriptures. Hence, they are here spoken of as "things unseen." As narrated in the verses that follow, Mary had become pregnant, while leading a life of dedication in the Temple. The priests grew anxious when they came to know of the startling fact. They feared scandal and disputed among themselves and cast lots to decide as to who should take charge of Mary and arrange her disposal in marriage. One Joseph, a carpenter, as mentioned in the Gospels, was hit upon as a suitable person to be her husband and was persuaded to accept the awkward situation. All this was naturally done in secret and so it was a *Ghaib* (a thing unseen) which the Qur'ān has brought to light.

414. *Kalimah* means, a word; a decree; a command (Mufradāt). This word along with the word, *Rūḥ*, occurring together in 4 : 172 makes it clear without a shadow of doubt that, far from establishing it, these words have been used to demolish and repudiate the doctrine of the so-called divinity and sonship of Jesus. In it Jesus has been called *Kalimat Allāh* because his words were helpful to the cause of Truth. Just as a person who helps the cause of Truth by his valour is called *Saif Allāh* (the Sword of God) or *Asad Allāh* (the Lion of God), so was Jesus called *Kalimat Allāh* because also his birth did not take place through the agency of a male parent but by the direct "command" of God (19 : 22). Besides the literal meanings given above the Qur'ān has used the word *Kalimah* in the following senses: (1) "a Sign" (66 : 13 & 8 : 8); (2) "punishment" (10:97); (3) "plan" or "design" (9:40); (4) "glad tidings" (7 : 138); (5) "creation of God" (18 : 110); (6) "a mere word of mouth" or "a mere assertion" (23 : 101). Taken in any of the above senses, the use of the word *Kalimah* about Jesus in no way gives to him a status higher than that of other Prophets. Moreover, if Jesus has been called *Kalimah* (word) in the Qur'ān, the Holy Prophet has been called *Dhikr*, *i.e.*, a book or a good speech (65 : 11,12), which evidently consists of many *Kalimāt* (words). In fact, if *Kalimat Allāh* is taken in the sense of "Word of God", the utmost we can say is that God expressed Himself through Jesus just as He expressed Himself through other Prophets. Words are nothing but a vehicle for the expression of thoughts. They do not form part of our being nor do they become incarnated.

from Him; his name *shall be* the Messiah,[415] Jesus,[416] son of Mary,[417] honoured in this world and in the next, and of those who are granted nearness *to God*;[418]

مِّنْهُ ۖ اسْمُهُ الْمَسِيحُ عِيسَى ابْنُ مَرْيَمَ وَجِيهًا فِي الدُّنْيَا وَالْآخِرَةِ وَمِنَ الْمُقَرَّبِينَ ﴿٤٦﴾

47. 'And [a]he shall speak to the people in the cradle[418A] and when of middle age,[418B] and he shall be of the righteous.

وَيُكَلِّمُ النَّاسَ فِي الْمَهْدِ وَكَهْلًا وَمِنَ الصَّالِحِينَ ﴿٤٧﴾

---

[a]5 : 111

---

415. *Al-Masīḥ* is derived from *Masaḥa* which means, he wiped off the dirt from the thing with his hand; he anointed it with oil; he journeyed through the land; God blessed him (Aqrab). *Masīḥ*, therefore, means (1) one anointed; (2) one who travels much; (3) one blessed. *Al-Masīḥ* is the Arabic form of Messiah which represents the Hebrew Mashiah, *i.e.*, Anointed One (Enc. Bib.; Enc. Rel. & Eth.). Jesus was given this name because he was to travel much. But if in pursuance of the Gospel narrative, his ministry be admitted to have been confined to only three years and his travels to only a few Palestinian or Syrian towns, the title of *Masīḥ* in no way befits him. Recent historical research, however, has established the fact that after having recovered from the shock and the wounds of crucifixion, Jesus travelled far and wide in the East and finally reached Kashmir to give his message to the Lost Tribes of Israel who lived in those parts. See also 2000 where Jesus is spoken of as having been afforded shelter in a hilly tract of land. *Masīḥ* as stated above also means "One Anointed." As the birth of Jesus was out of the ordinary and was liable to be looked upon as illegitimate, therefore, to remove this possible accusation, he was spoken of as "being anointed" with God's own anointment, even as all Prophets of God are anointed.

416. 'Isā seems to be the inverted form of the Hebrew word Yasū'. Jesus is the Greek form of Josua and Jesua (Enc. Bib).

417. Ibn Maryam is a surname of Jesus known in Arabic as *Kunyah*. Jesus has been called Ibn Maryam probably because, being born without the agency of a male parent, he could not but be known after his mother.

418. This expression also gives to Jesus no higher status than that of a righteous servant of God. All highly righteous people have been spoken of in the Qur'ān as being granted nearness to God (56 : 11,12).

418A. Primary meaning of the word *Mahd* is the state or period of preparation when one is, as it were, being prepared and made smooth for the duties of ripe age. The fact that the two periods of *Kuhūlah* and *Mahd* have been mentioned together shows that there is no intervening period between them. The entire period before *Kuhūlah* (middle age) is *Mahd*.

418B. *Kahl* means, one of middle age or of the age when one's hair becomes intermixed with hoariness; or it means, one who is between thirty or thirty-four and fifty-one years of age or between 40 and 51 (Lane & Tha'labī).

That Jesus spoke words of wisdom in his childhood has nothing miraculous or supernatural about it. Many intelligent and well brought up children speak like that. The whole sentence means that he would speak to people words full of extraordinary wisdom and spiritual knowledge, much beyond his years and experience, both in the period of preparation which is youth and in his middle age. The reference to the two distinct periods of Jesus's life may also be taken to hint that his speaking in the latter period would be of a different nature from that in the former. In the latter period he would speak to men as a Prophet of God. Thus the glad tidings given to Mary consisted in the fact that Jesus

48. She said, 'My Lord, [a]how shall I have a son, when no man has touched me?'[419] He said, "Such is *the way of* Allāh. He creates what He pleases. [b]When He decrees a thing, He says to it, 'Be,' and it is;

قَالَتْ رَبِّ أَنّٰى يَكُوْنُ لِيْ وَلَدٌ وَّلَمْ يَمْسَسْنِيْ بَشَرٌ ۭ
قَالَ كَذٰلِكِ اللّٰهُ يَخْلُقُ مَا يَشَآءُ ۭ اِذَا قَضٰٓى اَمْرًا فَاِنَّمَا
يَقُوْلُ لَهٗ كُنْ فَيَكُوْنُ ﴿۴۸﴾

49. "And [c]He will teach him the Book and the Wisdom and the Torah and the Gospel;

وَيُعَلِّمُهُ الْكِتٰبَ وَالْحِكْمَةَ وَالتَّوْرٰىةَ وَالْاِنْجِيْلَ ﴿۴۹﴾

50. [d]"And *will send him as* a Messenger to the Children of Israel[419A] *with the Message*, [e]'I come to you with a Sign from your Lord, *which is*, that I will fashion[420] out for you *a creation* out of clay[420A] after the manner[420B]

وَرَسُوْلًا اِلٰى بَنِيْٓ اِسْرَآءِيْلَ ۵ اَنِّيْ قَدْ جِئْتُكُمْ بِاٰيَةٍ
مِّنْ رَّبِّكُمْ ۙ اَنِّيْٓ اَخْلُقُ لَكُمْ مِّنَ الطِّيْنِ كَهَيْـَٔةِ الطَّيْرِ

[a]19 : 21. [b]See 2 : 118. [c]5;111. [d]43:60; 61:7. [e]5: 111.

was not only destined to be an intelligent young man but was also to live to a ripe old age as a righteous servant of God.

419. The news of a son, however happy, in ordinary circumstances, must have greatly perplexed Mary who was not only still unmarried but was also meant to remain so for life. The verse reflects her justified perplexity. It also shows that Jesus had no father, as hinted in Mary's words, *no man has touched me.* Having been dedicated to the service of the Temple, Mary could not, consistently with her vow of celibacy, marry. If she was to marry and have children in due course, there was no occasion for her to be surprised when the birth of a child was announced to her by the angel in a vision. No normal girl would be surprised, if she were told in a vision that a son would be born to her; for she would naturally infer that the promised child would be born to her after marriage. In the Gospel of Mary, the vow of celibacy is clearly referred to. We have it in chapter 5 of the said Gospel that when the high priest made a general order that all the virgins living in the Temple who had reached their fourteenth year should return home, all other virgins complied with the order but "Mary, the virgin of the Lord" alone answered that she could not comply with it; and for this refusal of her she assigned the reason that both she and her parents had dedicated her to the service of the Lord, and that she had vowed virginity to the Lord, which vow she was resolved never to break (Gospel of Mary, 5 : 4. 5, 6). Mary's subsequent marriage with Joseph was thus contrary to the vow and against her own wish. She was, however, compelled by circumstances to marry when found with child. The priests had to arrange her marriage to avoid scandal. It does not, however, appear from the Gospels how Joseph was prevailed upon to consent, for he was obviously in the dark about her being pregnant at the time of marriage (Matt. 1 : 18, 19). Presumably, some plausible excuse was found to justify the breaking of the vow. For a detailed account of the manner of the birth of Jesus see 1750—1755.

419A. The words "a Messenger to the Children of Israel" show that the mission of Jesus was confined to the House of Israel. He was not a World-Messenger (Matt. 10 : 5-6; 15 : 24; 19 : 28. Acts, 3 : 25, 26; 13 : 46. Luke, 19 : 10; 22 : 28-30).

420. *Khalaqa* means, he measured, designed, fashioned or planned; God produced or created or brought into existence a thing or being without there being any previously existing pattern or model or similitude, *i.e.*, he originated it (Lane & Lisān).

420A. *Ṭīn* means, clay; earth; mould; etc. Figuratively, *al-Ṭīn* may signify such persons as possess docile natures suitable for being moulded into any good shape like pliable clay.

420B. *Hai'ah* means, form; fashion; garb; state; manner; mode or quality (Lane).

of a bird;[420C] then I will breathe into it *a new spirit* and it will become a soaring being by the command of Allāh; and I will heal[420D] the night-blind[420E] and the leprous, and I will quicken the dead, by the command of Allāh;[420F] and I will announce to you what you will eat[420G] and what you will store up in your houses. Surely, therein is a Sign for you, if you are believers.

فَأَنْفُخُ فِيهِ فَيَكُونُ طَيْرًا بِإِذْنِ اللَّهِ ۚ وَأُبْرِئُ
الْأَكْمَهَ وَالْأَبْرَصَ وَأُحْيِ الْمَوْتَىٰ بِإِذْنِ اللَّهِ ۚ وَ
أُنَبِّئُكُمْ بِمَا تَأْكُلُونَ وَمَا تَدَّخِرُونَ فِي بُيُوتِكُمْ ۚ
إِنَّ فِي ذَٰلِكَ لَآيَةً لَكُمْ إِنْ كُنْتُمْ مُؤْمِنِينَ ﴿٥٠﴾

420C. *Tair* means, a bird. Metaphorically the word signifies a highly spiritual man who soars high into spiritual regions as *Asad* (literally a lion) is used for a brave man and *Dābbah* for a worthless person, a worm of the earth (34 : 15).

420D. *'Ubri'u* is derived from *Bari'a* which means, he was or became clear or free from a thing and signifies, I heal; I declare a person free from the defect attributed to him (Lane).

420E. *Akmah* means, one who cannot see at night; one born blind; one who becomes blind afterward; one deprived of reason and understanding (Mufradāt).

420F. There is no mention in the Bible of the miracle which is popularly believed to have been performed by Jesus that he created birds. If Jesus had really created birds, there is no reason why the Bible should have omitted to mention this, particularly when the creating of birds was a miracle the like of which had never been shown before by any Messenger of God. The mention of such a miracle would certainly have established his great superiority over all other Prophets and would have lent some support to the claim to Divinity which has been foisted upon him by his later followers. Of the different meanings of *Khalq*—(1) measuring; determining; designing, (2) fashioning; making and creating, etc., it is in the former sense that this word has been used in this verse. In the sense of "creating," the act of *Khalq* has not been attributed in the Qur'ān to any other being or thing except God (13 : 17; 16 : 21; 22 : 74; 25 : 4; 31 : 11, 12; 35 : 41 & 46 : 5.) In the light of the above explanation, and keeping in view the figurative sense of the word "clay," the whole clause, *I will fashion out for you a creation....become a soaring being*, would mean that if ordinary men of humble origin but possessing the inherent capacity for growth and development came into contact with him and accepted his Message, they would undergo a complete transformation in their lives. From men grovelling in the dust and not seeing beyond their material cares and mundane concerns, they would become converted into birds soaring high into the lofty regions of the spiritual firmament. And this is exactly what happened. The humble and despised fishermen of Galilee, under the impact of the ennobling precept and example of their Master, began soaring high like birds, preaching to the world of Israel the Word of God.

As for healing the blind and the leprous, it appears from the Bible that persons suffering from certain diseases (leprosy, etc.) were considered unclean by the Israelites and were not allowed to have social contact with other men. The word, "I declare to be free;" signify that the legal or social disabilities and disadvantages, under which persons suffering from such maladies laboured, were removed by Jesus. Or that Jesus used to heal persons suffering from these diseases. The Prophets of God are spiritual physicians; they give eyes to those that have lost spiritual sight, and hearing to those who are spiritually deaf, and they restore to life those who are spiritually dead (Matt. 13 : 15). In this case the word *Akmah* would mean such a person as possesses the light of faith but being weak of resolve cannot stand trials. He sees in daytime, *i.e.*, so long as there are no trials and the sun of faith shines forth

420G. See next page.

51. 'And *I come* [a]fulfilling[421] that which is before me, *namely*, the Torah; and to allow you some of that which was forbidden unto you,[421A] and I come to you with a Sign from your Lord; so fear Allāh and obey me;

وَمُصَدِّقًا لِّمَا بَيْنَ يَدَيَّ مِنَ التَّوْرٰىةِ وَلِاُحِلَّ لَكُمْ بَعْضَ الَّذِيْ حُرِّمَ عَلَيْكُمْ وَجِئْتُكُمْ بِاٰيَةٍ مِّنْ رَّبِّكُمْ فَاتَّقُوا اللّٰهَ وَاَطِيْعُوْنِ ﴿٥١﴾

52. 'Surely, [b]Allāh is my Lord and your Lord; so worship Him; this is the right path.' "

اِنَّ اللّٰهَ رَبِّيْ وَرَبُّكُمْ فَاعْبُدُوْهُ ؕ هٰذَا صِرَاطٌ مُّسْتَقِيْمٌ ﴿٥٢﴾

53. And when Jesus perceived their disbelief, he said, [c]"Who will be my helpers in the cause of Allāh?' The disciples answered, 'We are the helpers[422] of Allāh. We have believed in Allāh. And bear thou witness that we are obedient;

فَلَمَّاۤ اَحَسَّ عِيْسٰى مِنْهُمُ الْكُفْرَ قَالَ مَنْ اَنْصَارِيْۤ اِلَى اللّٰهِ ؕ قَالَ الْحَوَارِيُّوْنَ نَحْنُ اَنْصَارُ اللّٰهِ ۚ اٰمَنَّا بِاللّٰهِ ۚ وَاشْهَدْ بِاَنَّا مُسْلِمُوْنَ ﴿٥٣﴾

5 : 47; 61 : 7. [b]5 : 73, 118; 19 : 37; 43 : 65. [c]5 : 112; 61 : 15.

unclouded, but when the night comes, *i.e.*, when there are trials and sacrifices have to be made, he loses his spiritual vision and stands still (cf. 2 : 21). Similarly, the word *Abraṣ* (leprous) would, in the spiritual sense, mean one who is imperfect in faith, having patches of diseased skin among healthy ones.

The clause, *I will quicken the dead*, does not mean that Jesus actually brought the dead to life. Those actually dead are never restored to life in this world. Such a belief is diametrically opposed to the whole Quranic teaching (2: 29; 23 : 100, 101; 21: 96; 39 : 59, 60; 40 : 12; 45 : 27). The marvellous moral transformation that God's Messengers bring about in the lives of their followers is termed "raising the dead to life," in spiritual terminology.

420G. The entire clause may mean that Jesus told his disciples what they should eat, *i.e.*, what they should spend to meet their physical needs, and what they should store up *i.e.*, what they should lay up as spiritual treasure in Heaven. In other words he told them that their earnings should be honestly and lawfully acquired and that they should spend their savings in the way of God, having no thought for the morrow which should be left to God (Matt. 6 : 25, 26).

421. Jesus came in fulfilment of the prophecies of the previous Prophets contained in the Torah. But he brought no new Law, being a follower of Moses in this respect. He himself was conscious of this limitation of his authority (Matt. 5 : 17, 18).

421A. The expression does not refer to any change or modification in the Mosaic Law. The reference is only to those things which the Jews had themselves rendered unlawful for their use (4 : 161 ; 43 : 64). These two verses show that there were differences among the various sects of the Jews regarding the lawfulness or otherwise of certain things and that by their iniquities and transgressions they had deprived themselves of certain Divine blessings. Jesus thus came as a judge to decide in what matters the Jews had deviated from the right path and to tell them that the blessings of which they had been deprived would be restored to them, if they followed him (Kathīr, Fatḥ & Muḥīṭ).

422. *Ḥawāriyyūn* is the plural of *Ḥawāriyy* which means, (1) a washerman; (2) one tried and found to be free from vice or fault (3) a person of pure and unsullied character; (4) one who advises or counsels or acts honestly and faithfully; (5) a true and sincere friend or helper; (6) a select friend and helper of a Prophet (Lane & Mufradāt).

54. 'Our Lord, we believe in that which Thou hast sent down and we follow this Messenger. So write us down among those who bear witness.'

رَبَّنَآ اٰمَنَّا بِمَآ اَنْزَلْتَ وَاتَّبَعْنَا الرَّسُوْلَ فَاكْتُبْنَا مَعَ الشّٰهِدِيْنَ ﴿۵۴﴾

55. And [a]*Jesus's enemies* planned and Allāh *also* planned, and Allāh is the Best of Planners.[423]

وَمَكَرُوْا وَمَكَرَ اللّٰهُ ۭ وَاللّٰهُ خَيْرُ الْمٰكِرِيْنَ ﴿۵۵﴾

R. 6 56. *Remember the time* when Allāh said, 'O Jesus, [b]I will cause thee to die[424] *a natural death* and [c]will raise[424A] thee to Myself, and will clear thee *of the charges* of those who disbelieve, and will exalt[424B] those who follow thee above those who disbelieve, until the Day of Resurrection; [d]then to Me shall be your return, and I will judge between you concerning that wherein you differ.

اِذْ قَالَ اللّٰهُ يٰعِيْسٰٓى اِنِّىْ مُتَوَفِّيْكَ وَرَافِعُكَ اِلَيَّ وَمُطَهِّرُكَ مِنَ الَّذِيْنَ كَفَرُوْا وَجَاعِلُ الَّذِيْنَ اتَّبَعُوْكَ فَوْقَ الَّذِيْنَ كَفَرُوْٓا اِلٰى يَوْمِ الْقِيٰمَةِ ۚ ثُمَّ اِلَيَّ مَرْجِعُكُمْ فَاَحْكُمُ بَيْنَكُمْ فِيْمَا كُنْتُمْ فِيْهِ تَخْتَلِفُوْنَ ﴿۵۶﴾

---

[a]8 : 31; 27 : 51. [b]3 : 194; 4 : 16; 7 : 127; 8 : 51; 10 : 47,105; 12 : 102; 13 : 141; 16 : 29,33; 22 : 6; 39 : 43; 40 : 68,78; 47 : 28. [c]4 : 159; 7 : 177; 19 : 58. [d]5 : 49; 6 : 165; 11 : 24; 31 : 16; 39 : 8.

---

423. The Jews had planned that Jesus should die an accursed death on the Cross (Deut. 21 : 24), but God's plan was that he should be saved from that death. The plan of the Jews miscarried and God's plan was successful, because Jesus did not die on the Cross but came down from it alive, and died a natural death in Kashmir, full of years, and far away from the scene of his crucifixion.

424. *Mutawaffī* is derived from *Tawaffa.* They say *Tawaffa Allāhu Zaidan, i.e.,* God took away the soul of Zaid, namely He caused him to die. When God is the subject and a human being the object, *Tawaffa* has no other meaning than that of taking away the soul, whether in sleep or death. Ibn 'Abbās has translated *Mutawaffī-ka* as *Mumītu-ka, i.e.,* I will cause thee to die (Bukhārī). Similarly, Zamakhsharī, an Arab linguist of great repute, says : "*Mutawaffī-ka* means, I will protect thee from being killed by the people and will grant thee full lease of life ordained for thee, and will cause thee to die a natural death, not being killed" (Kashshāf). In fact, all Arabic lexicographers are agreed on the point that the word *Tawaffa* as used in the aforesaid manner, can bear no other interpretation. and not a single instance from the whole Arabic literature can be cited of this word having been used in any other sense. Outstanding scholars and Commentators like (1) Ibn 'Abbās, (2) *Imām* Mālik, (3) *Imām* Bukhārī, (4) *Imām* Ibn Ḥazm, (5) *Imām* Ibn Qayyim, (6) Qatādah, (7) Wahhāb and others are of the same view (Bukhārī, ch. on Tafsīr; Bukhārī, ch. on Bad' al-Khalq ; Biḥār ; Al-Muḥallā, Ma'ād, p. 19 ; Manthūr ii.; Kathīr). The word has been used in no less than 25 different places in the Qur'ān and in no less than 23 of them the meaning is to take away the soul at the time of death. Only in two places the meaning is to take away the soul at the time of sleep; but here the qualifying word "sleep" or "night" has been added (6 : 61 ; 39 : 43). The fact cannot be denied that Jesus is dead. The Holy Prophet is reported to have said, "Had Moses and Jesus now been alive, they would have found themselves forced to follow me" (Kathīr). He even fixed the age of Jesus

424A & 424B. See next page

57. 'Then as for those who disbelieve, I will punish them with a severe punishment in this world and in the next, and they shall have no helpers;'

فَأَمَّا الَّذِينَ كَفَرُوا فَأُعَذِّبُهُمْ عَذَابًا شَدِيدًا فِي الدُّنْيَا وَالْآخِرَةِ وَمَا لَهُمْ مِنْ نَاصِرِينَ ٥٧

58. 'And as for those who believe and do good works, [a]He will give them their full rewards. And Allāh loves not the wrongdoers.'

وَأَمَّا الَّذِينَ آمَنُوا وَعَمِلُوا الصَّالِحَاتِ فَيُوَفِّيهِمْ أُجُورَهُمْ ۗ وَاللَّهُ لَا يُحِبُّ الظَّالِمِينَ ٥٨

59. That is what We recite unto thee of the Signs and the Reminder, full of wisdom.

ذَٰلِكَ نَتْلُوهُ عَلَيْكَ مِنَ الْآيَاتِ وَالذِّكْرِ الْحَكِيمِ ٥٩

60. Surely, the case of Jesus with Allāh is like the case of Adam.[425] He created him out of dust,[425A] then He said to him, 'Be', and he was.

إِنَّ مَثَلَ عِيسَىٰ عِنْدَ اللَّهِ كَمَثَلِ آدَمَ ۖ خَلَقَهُ مِنْ تُرَابٍ ثُمَّ قَالَ لَهُ كُنْ فَيَكُونُ ٦٠

61. [b]*This is* the truth from thy Lord, so be thou not of those who doubt.

الْحَقُّ مِنْ رَبِّكَ فَلَا تَكُنْ مِنَ الْمُمْتَرِينَ ٦١

---

[a]4 : 174; 35 : 31; 39 : 11,70. [b]2: 148; 6 : 115; 10: 95.

---

at 120 year ('Ummāl). The Qur'ān, in as many as 30 verses, has completely demolished the absurd belief of the physical ascension of Jesus to, and his supposed life in, heaven.

424A. *Raf'* signifies raising the status and rank of a person and honouring him. When the *Raf'* of a man is spoken of as being towards God, the meaning is invariably his spiritual ascension, because God not being material or confined to any place, no physical ascension to Him is possible. The word has been used in the Qur'ān in this sense (24 : 37 & 35 : 11). The raising of Jesus is mentioned in the verse under comment in reply to the false claim of the Jews that he died an accursed death on the Cross.

424B. *Ja'ala* means, He made; he prepared or made; he appointed; he pronounced; he exalted (2 : 144); he held, etc. (Lane).

425. Adam primarily stands for man, *i.e.*, the sons of Adam generally. Jesus is thus declared to be like other mortals who have all been created from dust (40 : 68), and so there can be no Divinity about him. If, however, the word "Ādam" be taken to refer to the progenitor of the human race,then the verse would be taken to point to the resemblace between Jesus and Adam in being born without the agency of a male parent. In this case, the fact that Jesus had a mother would not affect the likeness which, as stated above, need not be complete in all respects.

425A. Elsewhere, man is stated to have been born out of clay (6 : 3). The difference sought to be indicated by the use of 'dust ' and 'clay' is that when the word 'dust' is used, the idea of revelation (heavenly water) is not implied, but where 'clay' is used the idea of revelation is also indicated.

62. Now whoso disputes with thee concerning him, after what has come to thee of knowledge, say *to him*, 'Come, let us call our sons and your sons, and our women and your women, and our people and your people; then let us pray[426] fervently and [a]invoke the curse of Allāh on those who lie.

فَمَنْ حَآجَّكَ فِيْهِ مِنْۢ بَعْدِ مَا جَآءَكَ مِنَ الْعِلْمِ
فَقُلْ تَعَالَوْا نَدْعُ اَبْنَآءَنَا وَاَبْنَآءَكُمْ وَنِسَآءَنَا وَ
نِسَآءَكُمْ وَاَنْفُسَنَا وَاَنْفُسَكُمْ ثُمَّ نَبْتَهِلْ فَنَجْعَلْ
لَّعْنَتَ اللّٰهِ عَلَى الْكٰذِبِيْنَ ﴿٦٢﴾

63. This certainly is the true account. There is none worthy of worship save Allāh; and surely, it is Allāh Who is the Mighty, the Wise.

اِنَّ هٰذَا لَهُوَ الْقَصَصُ الْحَقُّ ۚ وَمَا مِنْ اِلٰهٍ اِلَّا اللّٰهُ
وَاِنَّ اللّٰهَ لَهُوَ الْعَزِيْزُ الْحَكِيْمُ ﴿٦٣﴾

64. But if they turn away, then *remember that* Allāh fully knows the mischief-makers.

فَاِنْ تَوَلَّوْا فَاِنَّ اللّٰهَ عَلِيْمٌۢ بِالْمُفْسِدِيْنَ ﴿٦٤﴾ ع

R. 7 65. Say, 'O People of the Book! come to a word equal between us and you—that we worship none but Allāh, and that we associate no partner with Him, and that [b]some of us take not others for Lords beside Allāh.' But if they turn away, then say, 'Bear witness that we have submitted *to God*.'[426A]

قُلْ يٰۤاَهْلَ الْكِتٰبِ تَعَالَوْا اِلٰى كَلِمَةٍ سَوَآءٍۢ بَيْنَنَا وَبَيْنَكُمْ
اَلَّا نَعْبُدَ اِلَّا اللّٰهَ وَلَا نُشْرِكَ بِهٖ شَيْـًٔا وَّلَا يَتَّخِذَ بَعْضُنَا
بَعْضًا اَرْبَابًا مِّنْ دُوْنِ اللّٰهِ ۚ فَاِنْ تَوَلَّوْا فَقُوْلُوا اشْهَدُوْا
بِاَنَّا مُسْلِمُوْنَ ﴿٦٥﴾

[a]62 : 7, 8. [b]9 : 31.

426. The discussion on Christian doctrines with which this *Sūrah* deals has been brought to a close in this verse. The reference, as mentioned above, is to the Christian deputation from Najrān which consisted of sixty persons and was headed by their chief, 'Abd al-Masīḥ, known as Al-'Āqib. They met the Holy Prophet in his Mosque and the discussion on the doctrine of the so-called divinity of Jesus continued at some length. When the question had been fully discussed and the members of the deputation were found to be still insisting on their false doctrine, the Holy Prophet, in obedience to Divine command contained in the present verse, invited them, as a last resort, to join him in a sort of prayer-contest technically known as *Mubāhalah*, *i.e*, invoking the curse of God on the holders of false beliefs. As, however, the Christians did not appear to be sure of their ground, they declined to accept the challenge, thus indirectly admitting the falsity of their doctrine (Zurqānī). Incidentally, it may be mentioned that during the discussion with the Christian deputation from Najrān the Holy Prophet allowed them to pray in his Mosque in their own way, which they did facing the East—an act of religious toleration unparalleled in the history of all religions (Zurqānī).

426A. This verse is wrongly considered by some to provide a basis for a compromise between Islām on the one hand and Christianity and Judaism on the other. It is argued that if these religions also teach and inculcate the doctrine of Divine Unity, then other Islamic teachings supposed to be of comparatively little importance could safely be left alone. It is unthinkable that the idea of compromise in matters of faith could ever have been

66. O People of the Book! [a]Why do you dispute concerning Abraham, when the Torah and the Gospel were not revealed till after him? Will you not then understand?

يٰٓاَهۡلَ الۡكِتٰبِ لِمَ تُحَآجُّوۡنَ فِيۡٓ اِبۡرٰهِيۡمَ وَمَآ اُنۡزِلَتِ
التَّوۡرٰىةُ وَالۡاِنۡجِيۡلُ اِلَّا مِنۡۢ بَعۡدِهٖ ؕ اَفَلَا تَعۡقِلُوۡنَ ﴿۶۶﴾

67. Behold! you are those who disputed about that whereof you had *some* knowledge. Why then do you *now* dispute about that whereof you have no knowledge [427] *at all*? Allāh knows, and you know not.

هٰٓاَنۡتُمۡ هٰٓؤُلَآءِ حَاجَجۡتُمۡ فِيۡمَا لَكُمۡ بِهٖ عِلۡمٌ فَلِمَ
تُحَآجُّوۡنَ فِيۡمَا لَيۡسَ لَكُمۡ بِهٖ عِلۡمٌ ؕ وَاللّٰهُ يَعۡلَمُ وَ
اَنۡتُمۡ لَا تَعۡلَمُوۡنَ ﴿۶۷﴾

68. Abraham was neither a Jew [b]nor a Christian, but he was ever [c]inclined *to God* and obedient *to Him*, and he was not of those who associate gods *with Allāh*.

مَا كَانَ اِبۡرٰهِيۡمُ يَهُوۡدِيًّا وَّلَا نَصۡرَانِيًّا وَّلٰكِنۡ كَانَ
حَنِيۡفًا مُّسۡلِمًا ؕ وَمَا كَانَ مِنَ الۡمُشۡرِكِيۡنَ ﴿۶۸﴾

69. Surely, the nearest of men to Abraham are those who followed him and [d]this Prophet and those who believe *in him*, and Allāh is the Friend of believers.

اِنَّ اَوۡلَى النَّاسِ بِاِبۡرٰهِيۡمَ لَلَّذِيۡنَ اتَّبَعُوۡهُ وَهٰذَا
النَّبِيُّ وَالَّذِيۡنَ اٰمَنُوۡا ؕ وَاللّٰهُ وَلِيُّ الۡمُؤۡمِنِيۡنَ ﴿۶۹﴾

[a]2 : 140. [b]2: 141. [c]3 : 96; 4 : 126; 6 : 162; 16 : 121, 124. [d]16 : 124.

encouraged, with a people who, in the immediately preceding verses, have been severely condemned for their false beliefs and who are so forcefully challenged to a prayer-contest to invoke the curse of God upon the holders of false beliefs. The Holy Prophet, while writing his missionary epistle to Heraclius, used this very verse, yet he forcefully invited the latter to accept Islām and threatened him with Divine punishment if he refused to do so (Bukhārī). This shows beyond doubt that the mere fact of his believing in Divine Unity could not, according to the Holy Prophet, save Heraclius from God's punishment. In fact, the verse is intended to suggest an easy and simple method by which Jews and Christians can arrive at a right decision regarding the truth of Islām. The Christians, in spite of professing belief in the Unity of Godhead, believed in the divinity of Jesus; and the Jews, notwithstanding their claim to be strict monotheists, gave blind allegiance to their priests and divines, practically placing them in the position of God Himself. The verse exhorts both of them to come back to their original belief in the Oneness of God and give up the worship of false deities who stand in the way of their accepting Islām. Thus, instead of seeking a compromise with these Faiths, the verse virtually invites their followers to accept Islām by drawing their attention to the doctrine of the Oneness of God which being, at least in its outer form, the common fundamental doctrine of all, could serve as a meeting ground for further approach. Incidentally, it may be noted here that the letter, mentioned by Bukhārī and other Muslim Traditionists as having been addressed by the Holy Prophet to Heraclius and some other rulers—Muqauqis, the King of Egypt being one of them—couched in the words of this verse and inviting them to accept Islām, has recently been discovered and found to contain the exact words quoted by Bukhārī (R. Rel. vol. v. no. 8). This furnishes a strong proof of the essential authenticity of Bukhārī and, for that matter, of other accepted works of Ḥadīth.

427. The reference is either to the Quranic teaching or to the claim of the Jews and Christians about Abraham referred to in the preceding verse.

70. [a]A party of the People of the Book would fain lead you astray;[427A] but they lead astray none except themselves, only they perceive not.

وَدَّتْ طَّآئِفَةٌ مِّنْ اَهْلِ الْكِتٰبِ لَوْ يُضِلُّوْنَكُمْ ؕ وَمَا يُضِلُّوْنَ اِلَّآ اَنْفُسَهُمْ وَمَا يَشْعُرُوْنَ ﴿۷۰﴾

71. [b]O People of the Book! why do you deny the Signs of Allāh, while you are witnesses thereof?[427B]

يٰٓاَهْلَ الْكِتٰبِ لِمَ تَكْفُرُوْنَ بِاٰيٰتِ اللّٰهِ وَاَنْتُمْ تَشْهَدُوْنَ ﴿۷۱﴾

72. O People of the Book! [c]why do you confound truth with falsehood and [d]hide the truth knowingly?[427C]

يٰٓاَهْلَ الْكِتٰبِ لِمَ تَلْبِسُوْنَ الْحَقَّ بِالْبَاطِلِ وَتَكْتُمُوْنَ الْحَقَّ وَاَنْتُمْ تَعْلَمُوْنَ ﴿۷۲﴾ ع ۸ ۱۵

R. 8 73. And a party of the People of the Book say, 'Declare your belief *outwardly* in that which has been revealed unto the believers, in the early part of the day, and disbelieve in the latter part thereof; perchance they may return;[428]

وَقَالَتْ طَّآئِفَةٌ مِّنْ اَهْلِ الْكِتٰبِ اٰمِنُوْا بِالَّذِيْٓ اُنْزِلَ عَلَى الَّذِيْنَ اٰمَنُوْا وَجْهَ النَّهَارِ وَاكْفُرُوْٓا اٰخِرَهٗ لَعَلَّهُمْ يَرْجِعُوْنَ ﴿۷۳﴾

[a]4 : 90. [b]3 : 99. [c]2 : 43. [d]See 2 : 43.

427A. The simplicity, straightforwardness and perfection of the religion of Islām very often create such strong feelings of appreciation in the hearts of the People of the Book that they feel irresistibly drawn towards it but, being inimical and jealous, their appreciation often takes the queer, though not unpsychological, course that they begin to wish that Muslims may become like themselves.

Taking the word *Ḍalālah* in the sense of ruin (40 : 35) the expression *Yuḍillūnakum* (lead you astray) may also be rendered as "lead you to ruin" and the next clause, *but they lead astray none except themselves*, may in that case mean that by seeking to ruin the Muslims, they only ruin themselves, because the rise of one's enemy signifies one's own fall.

427B. Rejection of God's Signs is a heinous crime for anyone, but it becomes still more heinous for him who is a direct witness thereof.

427C. By means of the Signs, mentioned in their Scriptures about the Holy Prophet, the People of the Book could easily know that Muḥammad (peace and the blessings of God be on him) was indeed the Promised Prophet, yet because of enmity and jealousy they would not recognize him and would insist on mixing up truth with falsehood rather than accept the truth in its unalloyed purity.

428. The Jews were held in high esteem by the pagan Arabs for their religious learning. They took undue advantage of this and thought of a device to turn Muslims away from their Faith by outwardly embracing Islām in the early part of the day and giving it up in the latter part, seeking in this way to make the unlettered Arabs believe that something must have been seriously wrong with Islām, otherwise these learned men would not have so hurriedly given it up. But these foolish people made a completely wrong estimate of the invincible faith of the Companions of the Holy Prophet.

74. 'And [a]obey none but him who follows your religion.' Say, 'Surely, *true* guidance — the guidance of Allāh, — is, that one be given the like of that which has been given to you'—'or [b]they would argue[428A] with you before your Lord.' Say, '*All* grace[428B] is in the [c]hand of Allāh. He gives it to whomsoever He pleases. And Allāh is Bountiful, All-Knowing;[428C]

وَلَا تُؤْمِنُوٓا إِلَّا لِمَنْ تَبِعَ دِينَكُمْ قُلْ إِنَّ الْهُدٰى
هُدَى اللّٰهِ أَنْ يُّؤْتٰٓى أَحَدٌ مِّثْلَ مَآ أُوْتِيتُمْ أَوْ
يُحَآجُّوكُمْ عِنْدَ رَبِّكُمْ قُلْ إِنَّ الْفَضْلَ بِيَدِ اللّٰهِ
يُؤْتِيهِ مَنْ يَّشَآءُ وَاللّٰهُ وَاسِعٌ عَلِيمٌ ﴿٧٤﴾

75. 'He [d]selects for His mercy whomsoever He pleases. And Allāh is the Lord of mighty grace.'

يَّخْتَصُّ بِرَحْمَتِهٖ مَنْ يَّشَآءُ وَاللّٰهُ ذُو الْفَضْلِ
الْعَظِيمِ ﴿٧٥﴾

76. Among the People of the Book there is he who, if thou trust him with a treasure, will return it to thee; and among them there is he who, if thou trust him with a *dinār*, will not return it to thee, unless thou keep standing over him. That is because they say, 'We are not liable to be called to account in the matter of the Unlearned *people*;[429] and they utter a lie against Allāh knowingly.

وَمِنْ أَهْلِ الْكِتٰبِ مَنْ إِنْ تَأْمَنْهُ بِقِنْطَارٍ يُّؤَدِّهٖٓ
إِلَيْكَ وَمِنْهُمْ مَّنْ إِنْ تَأْمَنْهُ بِدِينَارٍ لَّا يُؤَدِّهٖٓ
إِلَيْكَ إِلَّا مَا دُمْتَ عَلَيْهِ قَآئِمًا ذٰلِكَ بِأَنَّهُمْ قَالُوا
لَيْسَ عَلَيْنَا فِي الْأُمِّيّٖنَ سَبِيلٌ وَيَقُولُونَ عَلَى اللّٰهِ
الْكَذِبَ وَهُمْ يَعْلَمُونَ ﴿٧٦﴾

[a]2 : 121. [b]2 : 77. [c]57 : 30. [d]2 : 106.

428A. If we are wrong in holding this view, then they should remove this misunderstanding by some Divine argument.

428B. 'Grace' here may signify Prophethood.

428C. (1) The clause, *And obey none but him who follows your religion*, constitutes a continuation of the concluding clause of the preceding verse. Thereafter comes the parenthetical clause beginning with the words, *Say, surely true guidance—the guidance of Allāh—is that one may be given the like of that which has been given to you.* Then comes again the speech of the Jews in the words, *or they would argue with you before your Lord*, the verse finally ending with the Divine commandment : *Say*, '*All bounty*, *etc*. This style is peculiar to the Qur'ān and is intended to produce a good psychological effect. (2) According to another interpretation, only the words which in this case would be translated as "Say, the true guidance is the guidance of Allāh," would be considered as being parenthetical and the following words, *i.e., that one be given the like of that which has been given to you,. . . . before your Lord*, would be taken to form part of the speech of the Jews. (3) Yet according to a third interpretation the speech of the Jews is taken to end with the words, *obey none but him who follows your religion*, the succeeding clauses being considered to be all Divine speech. See also 'The Larger Edition of this Commentary'.

429. In the time of the Holy Prophet the idea had gained ground among the Jews that it was no sin to rob a Gentile (non-Jew) Arab of his possession and property because the latter followed a false religion. Possibly, the idea had its origin in the Jewish law of usury,

77. Nay, but [a]whoso fulfils his pledge and fears Alālh—verily, Allāh loves those who fear *Him.*

بَلٰى مَنْ أَوْفٰى بِعَهْدِهٖ وَاتَّقٰى فَإِنَّ اللّٰهَ يُحِبُّ
الْمُتَّقِيْنَ ﴿٧٧﴾

78. *As for* those who take [b]a paltry price in exchange for *their* covenant with Allāh and their oaths, they shall have no portion in the life to come, and [c]Allāh will neither speak to them nor look upon them[430] on the Day of Resurrection, nor will He purify them; and for them shall be a grievous punishment.

إِنَّ الَّذِيْنَ يَشْتَرُوْنَ بِعَهْدِ اللّٰهِ وَأَيْمَانِهِمْ ثَمَنًا
قَلِيْلًا أُولٰٓئِكَ لَا خَلَاقَ لَهُمْ فِي الْآخِرَةِ وَلَا يُكَلِّمُهُمُ
اللّٰهُ وَلَا يَنْظُرُ إِلَيْهِمْ يَوْمَ الْقِيٰمَةِ وَلَا يُزَكِّيْهِمْ
وَلَهُمْ عَذَابٌ أَلِيْمٌ ﴿٧٨﴾

79. And, surely, among them is a party [d]who twist their tongues while reciting the Book[431] that you may think it *to be part* of the Book, while it is not *part* of the Book. And they say, 'It is from Allāh;' while it is not from Allāh; and they utter a lie against Allāh while they know.

وَإِنَّ مِنْهُمْ لَفَرِيْقًا يَّلْوٗنَ أَلْسِنَتَهُمْ بِالْكِتٰبِ
لِتَحْسَبُوْهُ مِنَ الْكِتٰبِ وَمَا هُوَ مِنَ الْكِتٰبِ وَيَقُوْلُوْنَ
هُوَ مِنْ عِنْدِ اللّٰهِ وَمَا هُوَ مِنْ عِنْدِ اللّٰهِ وَيَقُوْلُوْنَ
عَلَى اللّٰهِ الْكَذِبَ وَهُمْ يَعْلَمُوْنَ ﴿٧٩﴾

80. It does not befit[432] a truthful man that Allāh should give him the Book and Wisdom and Prophethood, *and* then [e]he should say to men, 'Be my worshippers instead of Allāh; but *he would say,* 'Be solely devoted[432A] to the Lord because

مَا كَانَ لِبَشَرٍ أَنْ يُّؤْتِيَهُ اللّٰهُ الْكِتٰبَ وَالْحُكْمَ وَ
النُّبُوَّةَ ثُمَّ يَقُوْلَ لِلنَّاسِ كُوْنُوْا عِبَادًا لِّيْ مِنْ دُوْنِ
اللّٰهِ وَلٰكِنْ كُوْنُوْا رَبّٰنِيّٖنَ بِمَا كُنْتُمْ تُعَلِّمُوْنَ الْكِتٰبَ

[a]5 : 2; 6 : 153; 13 : 21; 16 : 92; 17 : 35. [b]See 2 : 42. [c]2 : 175; 23 : 109.
[d]2 : 76; 4 : 47; 5 : 42. [e]5 : 117, 118.

which makes an invidious distinction between a Jew and a non-Jew regarding the giving and taking of interest (Exod. 22 : 25; Lev. 25 : 36, 37; Deut. 23 : 20).

430. God will not speak to them words of kindness nor will look upon them with mercy and compassion, nor will adjudge them as pure.

431. It is an allusion to an evil practice of some Jews in the time of the Holy Prophet. They would recite a passage in Hebrew in such a manner as would deceive the hearers into believing that it was the Torah that was being recited. The word "Book" used thrice in this verse means "a passage in Hebrew" in the first place and "the Torah" in the last two. The passage is spoken of as "the Book" because the Jews tried to make it appear as such.

432. The expression *mā Kāna la-hū* is used in three senses: (*a*) It does not become him to do so. (*b*) It is not possible for him to do so; or, it does not stand to reason that he should have done so; (*c*) he cannot possibly do so, *i.e.*, it is physically impossible for him to do so.

432A. See next page.

you teach the Book and because you study *it*.'[432B]

وَبِمَا كُنْتُمْ تَدْرُسُوْنَ ﴿٨٠﴾

81. Nor *does it befit him* that he should bid you take the angels and the Prophets for lords. What! would he enjoin you to disbelieve after you have submitted *to God*?

وَلَا يَأْمُرَكُمْ اَنْ تَتَّخِذُوا الْمَلٰٓئِكَةَ وَالنَّبِيّٖنَ اَرْبَابًا ؕ
ع اَيَأْمُرُكُمْ بِالْكُفْرِ بَعْدَ اِذْ اَنْتُمْ مُّسْلِمُوْنَ ﴿٨١﴾

R. 9 82. And *remember the time* [a]when Allāh took a covenant[433] from *the people through* the Prophets, *saying*, 'Whatever I give you of the Book and Wisdom *and* then there comes to you a Messenger, fulfilling[433A] that which is with you, you shall believe in him and help him.' *And* He said, 'Do you agree, and do you accept the responsibility which I *lay* upon you in this *matter*?' They said, 'We agree.' He said, 'Then bear witness and I am with you among the witnesses.'[433B]

وَاِذْ اَخَذَ اللّٰهُ مِيْثَاقَ النَّبِيّٖنَ لَمَآ اٰتَيْتُكُمْ مِّنْ
كِتٰبٍ وَّحِكْمَةٍ ثُمَّ جَآءَكُمْ رَسُوْلٌ مُّصَدِّقٌ لِّمَا
مَعَكُمْ لَتُؤْمِنُنَّ بِهٖ وَلَتَنْصُرُنَّهٗ ؕ قَالَ ءَاَقْرَرْتُمْ
وَاَخَذْتُمْ عَلٰى ذٰلِكُمْ اِصْرِيْ ؕ قَالُوْٓا اَقْرَرْنَا ؕ قَالَ
فَاشْهَدُوْا وَاَنَا مَعَكُمْ مِّنَ الشّٰهِدِيْنَ ﴿٨٢﴾

[a]5 : 13.

432A. *Rabbāniyyīn* is the plural of *Rabbāniy* which means, (1) one who devotes himself to religious service or applies himself to acts of devotion; (2) one who possesses knowledge of God; (3) one who is learned in religious lore, or a good or righteous man; (4) a teacher who begins to nourish people with the small matters of knowledge or science before taking the great ones; (5) a lord or master or a leader; (6) a reformer (Lane, Sībawaih & Mubarrad).

432B. The words, *because you teach the Book and because you study it*, show that it is the duty of all those who themselves have acquired spiritual knowledge that they should impart it to others and should not let men grope in the darkness of ignorance.

433. The expression *Mīthāq al-Nabīyyīn* may either signify the covenant of the Prophets with God or the covenant which God took from the people through their Prophets. The expression has been used here in the latter sense because another reading of the expression as supported by Ubayy bin Ka'b and 'Abd Allāh bin Mas'ūd is *Mīthāq Alladhīna 'ūtū al-Kitāb* meaning, the covenant of those who were given the Book (Muḥīṭ). This rendering is also supported by the words that follow, *i.e., and then there comes to you a Messenger fulfilling that which is with you*, because it was to the people and not to their Prophets that the Messengers of God came.

433A. The word *Muṣaddiq* has been used here to denote the criterion by which a true claimant is distinguished from a false one. The word has been rightly translated here as "fulfilling," for it is only by "fulfilling" in his person the prophecies contained in the previous revealed Scriptures that a claimant can prove his truth.

433B. See next page.

83. Now [a]whoso turns away after this, then, surely, those are the transgressors.

فَمَنْ تَوَلّٰى بَعْدَ ذٰلِكَ فَاُولٰٓئِكَ هُمُ الْفٰسِقُوْنَ ﴿۸۳﴾

84. Do they seek a religion other than Allāh's, while to Him submits whosoever is in the heavens and the earth, willingly or unwillingly,[434] and to Him shall they *all* be returned?

اَفَغَيْرَ دِيْنِ اللّٰهِ يَبْغُوْنَ وَلَهٗٓ اَسْلَمَ مَنْ فِي السَّمٰوٰتِ
وَالْاَرْضِ طَوْعًا وَّكَرْهًا وَّاِلَيْهِ يُرْجَعُوْنَ ﴿۸۴﴾

85. Say, [b]'We believe in Allāh and in that which has been revealed to us, and that which was revealed to Abraham and Ishmael and Isaac and Jacob and the tribes, and in that which was given to Moses and Jesus and other Prophets from their Lord.[435] We make no distinction between any of them[435A] and to Him we submit.'

قُلْ اٰمَنَّا بِاللّٰهِ وَمَآ اُنْزِلَ عَلَيْنَا وَمَآ اُنْزِلَ عَلٰٓى اِبْرٰهِيْمَ
وَاِسْمٰعِيْلَ وَاِسْحٰقَ وَيَعْقُوْبَ وَالْاَسْبَاطِ وَمَآ
اُوْتِيَ مُوْسٰى وَعِيْسٰى وَالنَّبِيُّوْنَ مِنْ رَّبِّهِمْ لَا نُفَرِّقُ
بَيْنَ اَحَدٍ مِّنْهُمْ وَنَحْنُ لَهٗ مُسْلِمُوْنَ ﴿۸۵﴾

[a]5 : 48; 24 : 56. [b]2 : 137, 286.

433B. This verse is also considered to apply to other Prophets in general and to the Holy Prophet in particular. Both applications are correct. The verse lays down a general rule. The advent of every Prophet takes place in fulfilment of certain prophecies made by a previous Prophet in which he enjoins his followers to accept the next Prophet when he makes his appearance. If the Prophet comes in fulfilment of the prophecies contained in the Scriptures of one people only, as was the case with Jesus and other Israelite Prophets, then only that people are bound to accept and help him: but if the Scriptures of all religions predict the coming of a Prophet, as in the case of the Holy Prophet, then all nations are bound to accept him. The Holy Prophet appeared in fulfilment of the prophecies not only of the Israelite Prophets (Isa. 21 : 13-15. Deut. 18 : 18; 33 : 2. John 14 : 25, 26; 16 : 7-13) but also of the Aryan seers and Buddhist and Zoroastrian sages (Shafrang Dasātīr, p. 188, Sirājī Press, Delhi Jāmāspī, published by Niẓām al-Mashā'ikh, Delhi, 1330 A.H.).

434. As in the physical world man must submit to the laws of nature—and he knows by experience that such submission is useful for him—it is only reasonable that, in spiritual matters also wherein he has been granted a certain amount of freedom, he should obey the laws and commands of Allāh and thus win His pleasure to his own benefit.

435. The Jews refused to believe in non-Israelite Prophets as the words, *obey none but him who follows your religion* (3 : 74) show. The charge has been pressed home to them that while they rejected all but the Israelite Prophets, Islām requires its followers to believe in all the Prophets of God, irrespective of the country or the race or the community to which they belonged or of the time in which they lived. This constitutes Islām's great superiority over all other religions.

435A. The words do not mean that there is no difference of rank or status between various Prophets which view is contrary to 2 : 254. What they really signify is that there can be no discrimination between them as Divine Messengers.

86. And [a]whoso seeks a religion other than Islām, it shall not be accepted of him, and, in the Hereafter he shall be among the losers.

وَمَنْ يَّبْتَغِ غَيْرَ الْاِسْلَامِ دِيْنًا فَلَنْ يُّقْبَلَ مِنْهُ ۚ وَهُوَ فِي الْاٰخِرَةِ مِنَ الْخٰسِرِيْنَ ﴿۸۶﴾

87. How shall Allāh guide a people who have disbelieved after believing and who had borne witness that the Messenger was true and to whom clear proofs had come?[436] And Allāh guides not the wrongdoing people.

كَيْفَ يَهْدِي اللّٰهُ قَوْمًا كَفَرُوْا بَعْدَ اِيْمَانِهِمْ وَشَهِدُوْٓا اَنَّ الرَّسُوْلَ حَقٌّ وَّجَآءَهُمُ الْبَيِّنٰتُ ۭ وَاللّٰهُ لَا يَهْدِي الْقَوْمَ الظّٰلِمِيْنَ ﴿۸۷﴾

88. As for such—their reward is that on them shall be the [b]curse of Allāh and of angels and of men, all together.

اُولٰٓئِكَ جَزَآؤُهُمْ اَنَّ عَلَيْهِمْ لَعْنَةَ اللّٰهِ وَالْمَلٰٓئِكَةِ وَالنَّاسِ اَجْمَعِيْنَ ﴿۸۸﴾

89. [c]They shall abide thereunder. Their punishment shall not be lightened nor shall they be reprieved;

خٰلِدِيْنَ فِيْهَا ۚ لَا يُخَفَّفُ عَنْهُمُ الْعَذَابُ وَلَا هُمْ يُنْظَرُوْنَ ﴿۸۹﴾

90. [d]Except those who repent thereafter and amend.[436A] And surely Allāh is Most Forgiving, Merciful.

اِلَّا الَّذِيْنَ تَابُوْا مِنْ بَعْدِ ذٰلِكَ وَاَصْلَحُوْا ۣ فَاِنَّ اللّٰهَ غَفُوْرٌ رَّحِيْمٌ ﴿۹۰﴾

91. [e]Surely, those who disbelieve after they have believed and then increase in disbelief, their repentance shall not be accepted,[437] and these are they who have gone astray.

اِنَّ الَّذِيْنَ كَفَرُوْا بَعْدَ اِيْمَانِهِمْ ثُمَّ ازْدَادُوْا كُفْرًا لَّنْ تُقْبَلَ تَوْبَتُهُمْ ۚ وَاُولٰٓئِكَ هُمُ الضَّآلُّوْنَ ﴿۹۱﴾

---

[a]3 : 20; 5 : 4. [b]2 : 162; 4 : 53; 5 : 79. [c]2 : 163. [d]2 : 161; 4 : 147; 5 : 40; 24 : 6. [e]4 : 138; 63 : 4.

---

436. Certainly a people, who at first believe in the truth of a Prophet and proclaim their belief openly in him and become witnesses of Heavenly Signs but afterwards reject him through fear of men or other worldly considerations, lose all title to be again guided to the right path. Or the verse may refer to those who believed in the former Prophets but rejected the Holy Prophet.

436A. Mere repentance and sorrow at past misdeeds is not sufficient to secure Divine forgiveness; an honest promise to eschew evil ways and a firm resolve to reform others also is needed for the purpose.

437. The verse does not mean that the repentance of apostates shall in no case be accepted because this inference runs counter to 3 : 90 according to which repentance is

92. *As for* [a]those who have disbelieved, and die while they are disbelievers, there shall not be accepted from anyone of them *even* the earthful of gold though he offer it as ransom. It is these for whom shall be a grievous punishment, and they shall have no helpers.

إِنَّ الَّذِيْنَ كَفَرُوْا وَمَاتُوْا وَهُمْ كُفَّارٌ فَلَنْ يُّقْبَلَ
مِنْ اَحَدِهِمْ مِّلْءُ الْاَرْضِ ذَهَبًا وَّلَوِ افْتَدٰى بِهٖ
اُولٰۤئِكَ لَهُمْ عَذَابٌ اَلِيْمٌ وَّمَا لَهُمْ مِّنْ نّٰصِرِيْنَ ﴿٩٢﴾

PART IV

R. 10 93. [b]You cannot attain to righteousness[438] unless you spend out of that which you love; and whatever you spend, Allāh surely knows it well.

لَنْ تَنَالُوا الْبِرَّ حَتّٰى تُنْفِقُوْا مِمَّا تُحِبُّوْنَ وَمَا
تُنْفِقُوْا مِنْ شَيْءٍ فَاِنَّ اللّٰهَ بِهٖ عَلِيْمٌ ﴿٩٣﴾

94. All food was lawful[439] to the Children of Israel,[440] except what Israel forbade himself before the Torah was sent down. Say, 'Bring, then, the Torah and read it, if you are truthful.'

كُلُّ الطَّعَامِ كَانَ حِلًّا لِّبَنِيْٓ اِسْرَآءِيْلَ اِلَّا مَا حَرَّمَ
اِسْرَآءِيْلُ عَلٰى نَفْسِهٖ مِنْ قَبْلِ اَنْ تُنَزَّلَ التَّوْرٰىةُ
قُلْ فَاْتُوْا بِالتَّوْرٰىةِ فَاتْلُوْهَآ اِنْ كُنْتُمْ صٰدِقِيْنَ ﴿٩٤﴾

95. Now, whoso forges a lie against Allāh after this,[441] then it is these that are the wrongdoers.

فَمَنِ افْتَرٰى عَلَى اللّٰهِ الْكَذِبَ مِنْ بَعْدِ ذٰلِكَ فَاُولٰۤئِكَ
هُمُ الظّٰلِمُوْنَ ﴿٩٥﴾

[a]2 : 162; 4 : 19; 47 : 35. [b]9 : 34, 111; 63 : 11.

acceptable at every stage. Reference here is to those persons only who make a profession of repentance and, instead of reinforcing their profession by bringing about a real and practical change in their lives, actually increase in disbelief.

438. In order to attain true faith, which is the essence of all righteousness and is the highest form of good, one must be prepared to sacrifice everything that one holds dear. The highest stage of righteousness can be attained only by spending in the way of God that which one loves best. High morals (***Birr***) cannot be attained without imbibing a true spirit of sacrifice.

439. Certain foods which the Jews abstained from were allowed by Islām. One such thing was the sciatic nerve, to which reference is made in Gen. 32 : 32. Jacob suffered from sciatica, and, for medical reasons he forbade himself the sciatic nerve as food. This was his personal matter but the Israelites made it a rule of conduct to abstain from eating the sinew.

440. The name Israel was bestowed upon Jacob in a vision (Gen. 32 : 28).

441. *Dhālika* refers to the statement made in the preceding verse. To say that such and such parts of food were disallowed by God whereas He had not forbidden them, amounted to forging a lie against God.

96. Say, 'Allāh has declared the truth; follow, therefore, the religion of Abraham [a]*who was* ever inclined to Allāh;[442] and he was not of those who associate gods *with Him*.'

قُلْ صَدَقَ اللّٰهُ ۫ فَاتَّبِعُوْا مِلَّةَ اِبْرٰهِيْمَ حَنِيْفًا ؕ وَمَا
كَانَ مِنَ الْمُشْرِكِيْنَ ﴿۹۶﴾

97. Surely, [b]the first House founded for *all* mankind is that at Becca,[443] abounding in blessings and guidance for *all* peoples.

اِنَّ اَوَّلَ بَيْتٍ وُّضِعَ لِلنَّاسِ لَلَّذِيْ بِبَكَّةَ مُبٰرَكًا
وَّهُدًى لِّلْعٰلَمِيْنَ ﴿۹۷﴾

98. In it are manifest Signs; [c]*it is* the place of Abraham; and [d]whoso enters it, is safe. And [e]pilgrimage to the House is *a duty* which men—those who can find a way[444] thither—owe to Allāh. And whoever disbelieves, *let him remember* that Allāh is surely Independent of all creatures.

فِيْهِ اٰيٰتٌۢ بَيِّنٰتٌ مَّقَامُ اِبْرٰهِيْمَ ۚ وَمَنْ دَخَلَهٗ كَانَ
اٰمِنًا ؕ وَلِلّٰهِ عَلَى النَّاسِ حِجُّ الْبَيْتِ مَنِ اسْتَطَاعَ
اِلَيْهِ سَبِيْلًا ؕ وَمَنْ كَفَرَ فَاِنَّ اللّٰهَ غَنِيٌّ عَنِ الْعٰلَمِيْنَ ﴿۹۸﴾

99. Say, [f]'O People of the Book! why deny ye the Signs of Allāh, while Allāh is Witness[445] of what you do?

قُلْ يٰۤاَهْلَ الْكِتٰبِ لِمَ تَكْفُرُوْنَ بِاٰيٰتِ اللّٰهِ ۖۗ وَاللّٰهُ
شَهِيْدٌ عَلٰى مَا تَعْمَلُوْنَ ﴿۹۹﴾

[a]See 3 : 68. [b]5 : 98; 27 : 92; 28 : 58; 29 : 68; 106 : 4, 5. [c]2 : 126. [d]14 : 36; 28 : 58; 29 : 68. [e]22 : 28. [f]3 : 71.

442. By saying that Abraham was ever obedient to God, the verse hints that he did not prohibit the eating of any particular food of his own accord, as the Israelites have done. It purports to say that by differing from the Israelites in this matter, Islām does not go against the way and the practice of the Prophets of God, particularly that of Abraham.

443. *Becca* is the name given to the Valley of Mecca, the *mīm* of Mecca being changed into *bā'*. These two letters are interchangeable as in *Lāzim* and *Lāzib*. The Qur'ān here draws the attention of the People of the Book to the remote antiquity of the Ka'bah in order to point out that it is the real and original centre of God's religion; those adopted by Jews and Christians being of later origin. See also 2 : 128.

444. After alluding to the historical evidence in favour of the Ka'bah, the Qur'ān proceeds to adduce three reasons to show that the Ka'bah is entitled to be adopted as the *Qiblah* or the Centre of God's religion for all times: (*a*) Abraham, the great Patriarch prayed here; (*b*) it gives peace and security; (*c*) it shall ever remain the Centre to which men from different countries and diverse nations will resort for Pilgrimage.

445. *Shahīd* means, one who gives information of what he witnesses; one possessing much knowledge; a person slain in the way of God. When used about God the word signifies, He from Whose knowledge nothing is hidden (Lane).

100. Say, 'O People of the Book! [a]why hinder ye the believers from the path of Allāh, seeking *to make* it crooked,[446] while you are witnesses *thereof*? And Allāh is not unmindful of what you do.'

قُلْ يٰٓاَهْلَ الْكِتٰبِ لِمَ تَصُدُّوْنَ عَنْ سَبِيْلِ اللّٰهِ
مَنْ اٰمَنَ تَبْغُوْنَهَا عِوَجًا وَّ اَنْتُمْ شُهَدَآءُ ؕ وَمَا اللّٰهُ
بِغَافِلٍ عَمَّا تَعْمَلُوْنَ ﴿۱۰۰﴾

101. [b]O ye who believe! if you obey any party of those who have been given the Book, they will turn you again into disebelievers after you have believed.

يٰٓاَيُّهَا الَّذِيْنَ اٰمَنُوْٓا اِنْ تُطِيْعُوْا فَرِيْقًا مِّنَ الَّذِيْنَ
اُوْتُوا الْكِتٰبَ يَرُدُّوْكُمْ بَعْدَ اِيْمَانِكُمْ كٰفِرِيْنَ ﴿۱۰۱﴾

102. How would you disbelieve, while to you are rehearsed the Signs of Allāh, and His Messenger is in your midst? [c]And he who holds fast[447] to Allāh is indeed guided to the right path.

وَكَيْفَ تَكْفُرُوْنَ وَاَنْتُمْ تُتْلٰى عَلَيْكُمْ اٰيٰتُ اللّٰهِ وَ
فِيْكُمْ رَسُوْلُهٗ ؕ وَمَنْ يَّعْتَصِمْ بِاللّٰهِ فَقَدْ هُدِيَ
اِلٰى صِرَاطٍ مُّسْتَقِيْمٍ ﴿۱۰۲﴾ ع

11 103. O ye who believe! fear Allāh as He should be feared; and [d]let not death overtake you except when you are in a state of submission.[448]

يٰٓاَيُّهَا الَّذِيْنَ اٰمَنُوا اتَّقُوا اللّٰهَ حَقَّ تُقٰتِهٖ وَلَا
تَمُوْتُنَّ اِلَّا وَاَنْتُمْ مُّسْلِمُوْنَ ﴿۱۰۳﴾

104. And [e]hold fast, all together, to the rope[449] of Allāh and be not divided; and [f]remember the favour of Allāh *which He bestowed* upon

وَاعْتَصِمُوْا بِحَبْلِ اللّٰهِ جَمِيْعًا وَّلَا تَفَرَّقُوْا ۠
وَاذْكُرُوْا نِعْمَتَ اللّٰهِ عَلَيْكُمْ اِذْ كُنْتُمْ اَعْدَآءً

[a]7 : 46, 87; 8 : 48; 9 : 34; 14 : 4; 22 : 26. [b]2 : 110; 3 : 150. [c]4 : 147, 176. [d]2 : 133. [e]3 : 106; 6 : 160; 8 : 47. [f]2 : 232.

446. The meaning is : 'You desire that there should appear crookedness in Islām;' or "you desire to pervert its tenets."

447. (1) Whoever preserves himself from sin by acting upon God's commandments; (2) whoever establishes a connection with Allāh and cleaves firmly to Him.

448. As the hour of death is not known, one can be sure of dying in a state of resignation to God only when one remains continually in that condition; hence the expression signifies that one should always remain obedient to God.

449. *Ḥabl* means, a rope or cord with which a thing is tied or made fast; a bond; a covenant or compact; an obligation by which one becomes responsible for the safety of a person or thing; alliance and protection (Lane). The Holy Prophet is reported to have said, 'The Book of God is the rope of Allāh which has been extended from the heavens to the earth' (Jarīr, iv. 30).

you when you were enemies and ^aHe united your hearts in love'⁴⁵⁰ so that by His grace you became *as* brothers; and you were on the brink of a pit of fire⁴⁵¹ and He saved you from it. Thus does Allāh explain to you His commandments that you may be guided.

فَاَلَّفَ بَيۡنَ قُلُوۡبِكُمۡ فَاَصۡبَحۡتُمۡ بِنِعۡمَتِهٖۤ اِخۡوَانًا ۚ وَكُنۡتُمۡ عَلٰى شَفَا حُفۡرَةٍ مِّنَ النَّارِ فَاَنۡقَذَكُمۡ مِّنۡهَا ؕ كَذٰلِكَ يُبَيِّنُ اللّٰهُ لَكُمۡ اٰيٰتِهٖ لَعَلَّكُمۡ تَهۡتَدُوۡنَ ﴿۱۰۴﴾

105. And let there *always* be among you a body of men ^bwho should invite to goodness,⁴⁵² and enjoin virtue and forbid evil.⁴⁵³ And it is they who shall prosper.

وَلۡتَكُنۡ مِّنۡكُمۡ اُمَّةٌ يَّدۡعُوۡنَ اِلَى الۡخَيۡرِ وَيَاۡمُرُوۡنَ بِالۡمَعۡرُوۡفِ وَيَنۡهَوۡنَ عَنِ الۡمُنۡكَرِ ؕ وَاُولٰٓئِكَ هُمُ الۡمُفۡلِحُوۡنَ ﴿۱۰۵﴾

106. And be not like those who became ^cdivided and who disagreed⁴⁵⁴ *among themselves* after clear proofs had come to them. And it is they for whom there shall be grievous punishment,

وَلَا تَكُوۡنُوۡا كَالَّذِيۡنَ تَفَرَّقُوۡا وَاخۡتَلَفُوۡا مِنۡۢ بَعۡدِ مَا جَآءَهُمُ الۡبَيِّنٰتُ ؕ وَاُولٰٓئِكَ لَهُمۡ عَذَابٌ عَظِيۡمٌ ﴿۱۰۶﴾

107. On the day ^dwhen *some* faces shall be white, and *some* faces shall be black.⁴⁵⁵ As for those whose faces will be black, *it will be said to*

يَّوۡمَ تَبۡيَضُّ وُجُوۡهٌ وَّتَسۡوَدُّ وُجُوۡهٌ ۚ فَاَمَّا الَّذِيۡنَ اسۡوَدَّتۡ وُجُوۡهُهُمۡ ؕ اَكَفَرۡتُمۡ بَعۡدَ اِيۡمَانِكُمۡ فَذُوۡقُوا

---

^a8 : 64.   ^b3 : 111, 115;   7 : 158;   9 : 71;   31 : 18.   ^c3 : 104;   6 : 160;   8 : 47.
^d10 : 27, 28;   39 : 61;   80 : 39-43.

---

450. It will be hard to find a more disunited people than the Arabs before the Holy Prophet appeared among them, but, at the same time, human history fails to provide any example of the bond of loving brotherhood into which the Arabs were united by the noble teaching and example of their great Master.

451. The words "on the brink of a pit of fire" signify the internecine warfare in which the Arabs were constantly engaged and which was consuming their man-power.

452. *Al-Khair* here signifies Islām, because goodness in general is included in the word *Ma'rūf* occurring immediately after it.

453. The Holy Prophet is reported to have said, 'If anyone of you sees anything evil, let him remove it with his hand. If he cannot do so with his hand, then let him forbid it with his tongue. If he cannot do even that, then let him at least hate it in his heart, and that is the weakest kind of faith' (Muslim).

454. The verse refers to disunity and dissensions among the People of the Book in order to bring home to Muslims the dangers of discord and disagreement.

455. The Qur'ān has explained "whiteness" and "blackness" as emblematic of "happiness" and "sorrow" respectively (3 : 107, 108; 75 : 23—25; 80 : 39—41). When a person does a deed for which he is praised, the Arabs say of him : *Ibyaḍḍa Wajhu-hū*, i.e., the face of such a one has become white. And when he does a deed for which he is reproached, it is said of him *Iswadda Wajhu-hū*, i.e., his face has become black.

them: 'Did you disbelieve after believing? Taste, then, the punishment because you disbelieved.'

الْعَذَابَ بِمَا كُنْتُمْ تَكْفُرُوْنَ ﴿١٠٧﴾

108. And [a]as for those whose faces will be white, they will be in the mercy of Allāh; therein will they abide.

وَ اَمَّا الَّذِيْنَ ابْيَضَّتْ وُجُوْهُهُمْ فَفِيْ رَحْمَةِ اللّٰهِ ؕ
هُمْ فِيْهَا خٰلِدُوْنَ ﴿١٠٨﴾

109. These are the Signs of Allāh, comprising the Truth.[456] We rehearse them to thee and Allāh desires not any injustice to *His* creatures.

تِلْكَ اٰيٰتُ اللّٰهِ نَتْلُوْهَا عَلَيْكَ بِالْحَقِّ ؕ وَ مَا اللّٰهُ يُرِيْدُ
ظُلْمًا لِّلْعٰلَمِيْنَ ﴿١٠٩﴾

110. And [b]to Allāh belongs whatever is in the heavens and whatever is in the earth, and to Allāh shall *all* affairs be returned *for decision*.

وَ لِلّٰهِ مَا فِي السَّمٰوٰتِ وَ مَا فِي الْاَرْضِ ؕ وَ اِلَى اللّٰهِ تُرْجَعُ
الْاُمُوْرُ ﴿١١٠﴾ ع ١٢/٢

R. 12 111. [c]You are the best people, raised for *the good of* mankind; [d]you enjoin good and forbid evil[457] and believe in Allāh. And if the People of the Book had believed, it would have, surely, been better for them. Some of them are believers, but most of them are transgressors.

كُنْتُمْ خَيْرَ اُمَّةٍ اُخْرِجَتْ لِلنَّاسِ تَاْمُرُوْنَ بِالْمَعْرُوْفِ
وَ تَنْهَوْنَ عَنِ الْمُنْكَرِ وَ تُؤْمِنُوْنَ بِاللّٰهِ ؕ وَ لَوْ اٰمَنَ
اَهْلُ الْكِتٰبِ لَكَانَ خَيْرًا لَّهُمْ ؕ مِنْهُمُ الْمُؤْمِنُوْنَ وَ
اَكْثَرُهُمُ الْفٰسِقُوْنَ ﴿١١١﴾

112. They cannot harm you save *that they may cause you* slight hurt; and [e]if they fight you, they will turn *their* backs to you. Then they shall not be helped.

لَنْ يَّضُرُّوْكُمْ اِلَّاۤ اَذًى ؕ وَ اِنْ يُّقَاتِلُوْكُمْ يُوَلُّوْكُمُ
الْاَدْبَارَ قف ثُمَّ لَا يُنْصَرُوْنَ ﴿١١٢﴾

[a]10 : 27. [b]3 : 130, 190; 4 : 132; 57 : 11. [c]2 : 144. [d]3 : 105, 115; 7 : 158; 9 : 71; 31 : 18. [e]59 : 13.

456. The expression *Bi'l-Ḥaqq* (lit. 'with truth' and translated as, comprising the truth) signifies, firstly, that these Signs or words of God are full of truth; secondly, they have come as a matter of right, *i.e.*, you had a right to receive them; thirdly, this was the proper time for their revelation. See also 364.

457. The verse not only claims that the Muslims are the best people—a big claim indeed—but also gives reasons for it: (1) They have been raised for the good of all mankind; and (2) it is their duty to enjoin good and forbid evil and believe in one God. The glory of the Muslims is subject to and governed by these two conditions.

113. They shall be [a]smitten with abasement wherever they are found[458] unless *they are protected* by a covenant with Allāh or *by* a covenant with men. They have incurred the wrath of Allāh, and have been smitten with wretchedness. [b]That is because they rejected the Signs of Allāh and sought to slay the Prophets unjustly. That is because they rebelled and used to transgress.

ضُرِبَتْ عَلَيْهِمُ الذِّلَّةُ أَيْنَ مَا ثُقِفُوٓا إِلَّا بِحَبْلٍ مِّنَ اللّٰهِ
وَحَبْلٍ مِّنَ النَّاسِ وَبَآءُوْ بِغَضَبٍ مِّنَ اللّٰهِ وَضُرِبَتْ
عَلَيْهِمُ الْمَسْكَنَةُ ذٰلِكَ بِأَنَّهُمْ كَانُوا يَكْفُرُوْنَ بِاٰيٰتِ اللّٰهِ وَيَقْتُلُوْنَ
الْأَنْبِيَآءَ بِغَيْرِ حَقٍّ ذٰلِكَ بِمَا عَصَوا وَّكَانُوا يَعْتَدُوْنَ ﴿١١٣﴾

114. [c]They are not *all* alike. Among the People of the Book there is a party who stand *by their covenant*;[459] *they* recite the Word of Allāh in the hours of night and prostrate themselves *before Him*.

لَيْسُوْا سَوَآءً مِنْ أَهْلِ الْكِتٰبِ أُمَّةٌ قَآئِمَةٌ يَّتْلُوْنَ
اٰيٰتِ اللّٰهِ اٰنَآءَ الَّيْلِ وَهُمْ يَسْجُدُوْنَ ﴿١١٤﴾

115. They believe in Allāh and the Last Day, and [d]enjoin good and forbid evil, and [e]hasten to vie with one another in good works. And these are among the righteous.

يُؤْمِنُوْنَ بِاللّٰهِ وَالْيَوْمِ الْاٰخِرِ وَيَأْمُرُوْنَ بِالْمَعْرُوْفِ
وَيَنْهَوْنَ عَنِ الْمُنْكَرِ وَيُسَارِعُوْنَ فِي الْخَيْرٰتِ
وَأُولٰٓئِكَ مِنَ الصّٰلِحِيْنَ ﴿١١٥﴾

116. And [f]whatever good they do, they shall not be denied its due reward,[460] and Allāh well knows those who guard against evil.

وَمَا يَفْعَلُوْا مِنْ خَيْرٍ فَلَنْ يُّكْفَرُوْهُ وَاللّٰهُ عَلِيْمٌ
بِالْمُتَّقِيْنَ ﴿١١٦﴾

[a]2 : 62, 91; 5 : 61; 7: 168. [b]2 : 62, 92; 3 : 22. [c]4 : 163. [d]3 : 105, 111; 9 : 71. [e]21 : 91; 23 : 62; 35 : 33. [f]28 : 85; 99 : 8.

458. The verse contains an important and far-reaching prophecy regarding the Jews, *viz.*, that they are for ever doomed to disgrace and humiliation and to live in subjection to others. The history of the Jewish people from the time of the Holy Prophet up to the present day bears eloquent testimony to the truth of this awful prophecy. In all countries and in all ages, the present age of enlightenment and toleration not excepted, the Jews have been the victim of bitter persecution and have been subjected to diverse kinds of disgrace and humiliation. The establishment of the State of Israel is but a temporary phase in the life of Jewry.

459. The words *Ummatun Qā'imatun* may also mean: (1) A party or people who perform fully and faithfully their duties; (2) a people who stand up for Prayer in the latter part of the night. The words refer only to those Jews who had embraced Islām.

460. Islām is not a national or tribal religion. Whoever joins it, no matter what community or creed he comes from, receives the same reward as any other follower of the Faith, provided, of course, he acts righteously. No prejudicial treatment is meted out to the members of any particular nationality. A Jew, and for that matter any other person, after embracing Islām is on par with an Arab Muslim.

117. [a]As for those who disbelieve, their possessions and their children shall not avail them aught against Allāh, and these are the inmates of the Fire; therein shall they abide.

إِنَّ الَّذِينَ كَفَرُوا لَنْ تُغْنِيَ عَنْهُمْ أَمْوَالُهُمْ وَلَا
أَوْلَادُهُمْ مِنَ اللَّهِ شَيْئًا ۖ وَأُولَٰئِكَ أَصْحَابُ النَّارِ ۚ
هُمْ فِيهَا خَالِدُونَ ﴿١١٧﴾

118. [b]The likeness of what they spend for the present life is as the likeness of a wind wherein there is intense cold. It smites the harvest of a people who have wronged themselves and destroys it.[461] And Allāh wronged them not but they wronged themselves.

مَثَلُ مَا يُنْفِقُونَ فِي هَٰذِهِ الْحَيَاةِ الدُّنْيَا كَمَثَلِ
رِيحٍ فِيهَا صِرٌّ أَصَابَتْ حَرْثَ قَوْمٍ ظَلَمُوا أَنْفُسَهُمْ
فَأَهْلَكَتْهُ ۚ وَمَا ظَلَمَهُمُ اللَّهُ وَلَٰكِنْ أَنْفُسَهُمْ
يَظْلِمُونَ ﴿١١٨﴾

119. O ye who believe! [c]take not *others* than your own *people* as intimate friends; [d]they will spare no pains to ruin[462] you. They love to see you in trouble.[463] Hatred has already shown itself through *the utterances of* their mouths and what their breasts hide is greater still. We have made clear to you Our commandments, if you will only use your understanding.

يَا أَيُّهَا الَّذِينَ آمَنُوا لَا تَتَّخِذُوا بِطَانَةً مِنْ دُونِكُمْ
لَا يَأْلُونَكُمْ خَبَالًا وَدُّوا مَا عَنِتُّمْ ۚ قَدْ بَدَتِ
الْبَغْضَاءُ مِنْ أَفْوَاهِهِمْ ۚ وَمَا تُخْفِي صُدُورُهُمْ
أَكْبَرُ ۚ قَدْ بَيَّنَّا لَكُمُ الْآيَاتِ ۖ إِنْ كُنْتُمْ
تَعْقِلُونَ ﴿١١٩﴾

120. Behold! you are those who love them, but they love you not. [e]And you believe in the Book,[464] all of it. When they meet you, they say,

هَا أَنْتُمْ أُولَاءِ تُحِبُّونَهُمْ وَلَا يُحِبُّونَكُمْ وَتُؤْمِنُونَ
بِالْكِتَابِ كُلِّهِ ۚ وَإِذَا لَقُوكُمْ قَالُوا آمَنَّا ۚ وَإِذَا خَلَوْا

[a]3 : 11; 58 : 18. [b]10 : 25; 68 : 18—21. [c]3 : 21; 4 : 140, 145. [d]9 : 47; [e]2 : 15, 77; 5 : 62.

461. The idea underlying this verse is that the efforts of the disbelievers against Islām will recoil on themselves. Whatever they do or spend with a view to injuring the cause of Islām will only injure themselves.

462. *Khabāl* means, corruption whether of body or reason or actions; loss or deterioration; ruin or destruction; fatal poison (Aqrab).

463. They love to see you fall into calamity or misfortune; to perish or to become weak and broken; or they love to see that you deviate from the path of righteousness and take to a life of sin.

464. As borne out by the context, the words "while they do not believe in the Book, all of it" or similar words should be taken to be understood after the words, *you believe in the Book, all of it*.

'We believe;' but when they are alone, they bite their finger-tips at you for rage. Say, 'Perish in your rage.[465] Surely, Allāh has full knowledge of what is *hidden* in *your* breasts.'

عَضُّوا عَلَيْكُمُ الْأَنَامِلَ مِنَ الْغَيْظِ ۚ قُلْ مُوتُوا
بِغَيْظِكُمْ ۗ إِنَّ اللَّهَ عَلِيمٌ بِذَاتِ الصُّدُورِ ﴿١٢٠﴾

121. [a]If anything good befalls you, it grieves them; and if an evil afflicts you, they rejoice thereat. But if you be steadfast and righteous, their designs will not harm you at all; surely, Allāh encompasses *all* that they do.[466]

إِنْ تَمْسَسْكُمْ حَسَنَةٌ تَسُؤْهُمْ وَإِنْ تُصِبْكُمْ
سَيِّئَةٌ يَفْرَحُوا بِهَا ۖ وَإِنْ تَصْبِرُوا وَتَتَّقُوا لَا
يَضُرُّكُمْ كَيْدُهُمْ شَيْئًا ۗ إِنَّ اللَّهَ بِمَا يَعْمَلُونَ
مُحِيطٌ ﴿١٢١﴾ ع ١٢

R. 13 122. And *remember* when thou didst go forth early in the morning from thy household, assigning to the believers their positions for battle.[467] And Allāh is All-Hearing, All-Knowing.

وَإِذْ غَدَوْتَ مِنْ أَهْلِكَ تُبَوِّئُ الْمُؤْمِنِينَ مَقَاعِدَ
لِلْقِتَالِ ۗ وَاللَّهُ سَمِيعٌ عَلِيمٌ ﴿١٢٢﴾

123. When two parties from among you,[468] thought of *showing* cowardice, although Allāh was their Friend. And upon Allāh should the believers rely.

إِذْ هَمَّتْ طَائِفَتَانِ مِنْكُمْ أَنْ تَفْشَلَا وَاللَّهُ وَلِيُّهُمَا ۗ
وَعَلَى اللَّهِ فَلْيَتَوَكَّلِ الْمُؤْمِنُونَ ﴿١٢٣﴾

[a]9 : 50.

465. The words, *Perish in your rage*, have been addressed to such Jews as are the enemies of Islām and seek to destroy it.

466. God will bring to naught all their doings and will destroy them. Muslims should not therefore fear them. All machinations of the enemies of Islām are known to God, and He will frustrate them.

467. The reference is to the Battle of Uḥud. In order to wipe out the humiliation of their defeat at Badr, the Quraish of Mecca, in the third year of the Hijrah marched against Medina with a well-equipped army of 3,000 seasoned warriors. Much against his own wish the Holy Prophet with a force of 1,000 including 300 followers of 'Abd Allāh b. Ubayy, the notorious Hypocrite who afterwards defected, marched out of Medina to meet the enemy. The encounter took place near Uḥud.

468. The two parties were the two tribes of Banū Salimah and Banū Ḥārithah, belonging respectively to Khazraj and Aus (Bukhārī, *kitāb al-Maghāzī*). The verse indicates that they did not actually show cowardice, but seeing that by the defection of 'Abd Allāh's 300 followers, the small Muslim army had been further greatly depleted, they *only thought* of deserting but in fact did not do so.

124. [a]And Allāh had *already* helped you at Badr[469] [b]when you were weak. So take Allāh for your Protector that you may be grateful.

وَلَقَدْ نَصَرَكُمُ اللّٰهُ بِبَدْرٍ وَّاَنْتُمْ اَذِلَّةٌ ۚ فَاتَّقُوا اللّٰهَ لَعَلَّكُمْ تَشْكُرُوْنَ ﴿۱۲۴﴾

125. When thou didst say to the believers, [c]"Will it not suffice you that your Lord should help you with three thousand[470] angels sent down *from on high?*"

اِذْ تَقُوْلُ لِلْمُؤْمِنِيْنَ اَلَنْ يَّكْفِيَكُمْ اَنْ يُّمِدَّكُمْ رَبُّكُمْ بِثَلٰثَةِ اٰلٰفٍ مِّنَ الْمَلٰٓئِكَةِ مُنْزَلِيْنَ ﴿۱۲۵﴾

126. Yea,[471] if you be steadfast and righteous and they come upon you immediately in hot haste, your Lord will help you with five thousand[472] angels, attacking vehemently.[473]

بَلٰٓى ۙ اِنْ تَصْبِرُوْا وَتَتَّقُوْا وَيَاْتُوْكُمْ مِّنْ فَوْرِهِمْ هٰذَا يُمْدِدْكُمْ رَبُّكُمْ بِخَمْسَةِ اٰلٰفٍ مِّنَ الْمَلٰٓئِكَةِ مُسَوِّمِيْنَ ﴿۱۲۶﴾

[a]8 : 8,11; 9 : 25. [b]2 : 250. [c]8 : 10.

469. Badr is the name of a place on the route between Mecca and Medina. It takes its name from a spring which belonged to a man named Badr. The Battle of Badr referred to here took place near this place.

470. As mistakenly understood these words do not refer to the Battle of Badr which has been mentioned in the preceding verse only incidentally in order to cite an illustration of how God helped the steadfast Muslims in time of danger. The number of angels sent at the Battle of Badr was, according to 8 : 10, one thousand as the number of the enemy was then one thousand. In the Battle of Uḥud the number of the enemy was 3,000, so the Muslims were also promised the help of 3,000 angels. The fulfilment of the present promise is referred to in 3 : 153.

471. The word *balā* also denotes a connection between the verses and supplies the answer to the question in 3 : 125, *viz., Will it not suffice you?* Thus the meaning would be : "Yes, it will suffice us, and so will suffice a force of 5,000 angels if the enemy were to return to the attack at this very moment."

472. The words signify that if the disbelievers returned to the attack at once, without giving the Muslims any time to recoup themselves, God would help them with 5,000 angels. The difference in the number of angels—in the preceding verse the number mentioned being 3,000—was due to the later greatly weakened condition of the Muslims. They were at that time exhausted and badly mauled and, therefore, needed greater help. After having gone to some distance towards Mecca the Quraish decided to return and attack the Muslims again. When the Holy Prophet came to know of this, on the day following the battle, he gave immediate orders to march and directed that only those of his followers who had taken part in the Battle of Uḥud should go with him. The Muslims went as far as Ḥamrā' al-Asad, a place about eight miles from Medina. The Meccans were, however, so overawed by this unexpectedly bold and prompt appearance of the Holy Prophet and his followers that they decided to retreat hastily to Mecca. This was due to the fear which the angels had cast into their hearts. Otherwise there was no reason for them to flee from Muslims upon whom they had inflicted so heavy a loss only a day before and who, besides being very much reduced in number, were greatly exhausted and were suffering from grievous wounds as a result of the previous day's fighting.

473. *Musawwimīn* is derived from *Sawwaṃa.* They say *Sawwama 'Alaihim, i.e.,* he suddenly and vehemently attacked them and wrought havoc among them (Aqrab).

127. And [a]Allāh has made it only as glad tidings for you and to put your hearts at rest[474] thereby; and help comes from Allāh alone, the Mighty, the Wise.

وَمَا جَعَلَهُ اللّٰهُ اِلَّا بُشْرٰى لَكُمْ وَلِتَطْمَئِنَّ قُلُوْبُكُمْ بِهٖ ۭ وَمَا النَّصْرُ اِلَّا مِنْ عِنْدِ اللّٰهِ الْعَزِيْزِ الْحَكِيْمِ ﴿۱۲۷﴾

128. *This will be*, that He might cut off a part of the disbelievers or abase[475] them so that they might go back frustrated.

لِيَقْطَعَ طَرَفًا مِّنَ الَّذِيْنَ كَفَرُوْٓا اَوْ يَكْبِتَهُمْ فَيَنْقَلِبُوْا خَآئِبِيْنَ ﴿۱۲۸﴾

129. It is none of thy concern whether He may turn to them in mercy or punish them, for they are wrongdoers.[476]

لَيْسَ لَكَ مِنَ الْاَمْرِ شَيْءٌ اَوْ يَتُوْبَ عَلَيْهِمْ اَوْ يُعَذِّبَهُمْ فَاِنَّهُمْ ظٰلِمُوْنَ ﴿۱۲۹﴾

130. [b]And to Allāh belongs whatever is in the heavens and whatever is in the earth. He forgives whomsoever He pleases and punishes whomsoever He pleases, and Allāh is Most Forgiving, Merciful.

وَلِلّٰهِ مَا فِي السَّمٰوٰتِ وَمَا فِي الْاَرْضِ ۭ يَغْفِرُ لِمَنْ يَّشَآءُ وَيُعَذِّبُ مَنْ يَّشَآءُ ۭ وَاللّٰهُ غَفُوْرٌ رَّحِيْمٌ ﴿۱۳۰﴾

[a]8 : 11. [b]3 : 110,190; 4 : 132; 56 : 11.

474. The angels helped Muslims, on the one hand, by strengthening their hearts, and, on the other, by filling the hearts of their enemies with awe and fear. If God had so willed, a single angel would have been enough to help the Muslims at Uḥud, but He promised to send as many as five thousand of them. This constituted a veiled hint that a large number of the hidden forces of nature would work in their favour. It may incidentally be noted that some believers, and even some disbelievers, are reported to have actually seen angels in the Battle of Badr (Jarīr, iv. 47). See also 8 : 10.

475. When the Holy Prophet learnt that the Meccans were contemplating an immediate attack on Medina, he marched against them. The Meccans fled in disgrace and abasement.

476. This verse is erroneously considered to contain an admonition to the Holy Prophet for his having prayed to God to destroy the Meccans. There is no mention of any such prayer here, nor was there any occasion for such a one. In fact, a Prophet never prays for the destruction of any people without the permission of God. The verse is meant only as an answer to those who attributed the reverse of Muslims at Uḥud to the alleged error of their leaving the city against the advice of experienced men. It says that the temporary reverse was brought about by the supreme wisdom of God and that the Holy Prophet had nothing to do with the matter. One good result of this reverse was that many disbelievers were guided to Islām, among them being the famous Khālid. They saw how God had helped the Holy Prophet in the hour of distress and how He had afforded him protection although, at one time, he was left all by himself in the battle.

R. 14 131. O ye who believe ! [a]devour not interest involving multiple additions,[477] and fear Allāh that you may prosper.

يٰٓاَيُّهَا الَّذِيْنَ اٰمَنُوْا لَا تَاْكُلُوا الرِّبٰوٓا اَضْعَافًا مُّضٰعَفَةً ۪ وَّاتَّقُوا اللّٰهَ لَعَلَّكُمْ تُفْلِحُوْنَ ۚ﴿۱۳۱﴾

132. And [b]fear the Fire[478] which has been prepared for the disbelievers.

وَاتَّقُوا النَّارَ الَّتِيْٓ اُعِدَّتْ لِلْكٰفِرِيْنَ ۚ﴿۱۳۲﴾

133. And [c]obey Allāh and the Messenger that you be shown mercy.

وَاَطِيْعُوا اللّٰهَ وَالرَّسُوْلَ لَعَلَّكُمْ تُرْحَمُوْنَ ۚ﴿۱۳۳﴾

134. [d]And hasten towards forgiveness from your Lord, and the Paradise whose value[479] is the heavens and the earth. *It is* prepared for the God-fearing—[479A]

وَسَارِعُوْٓا اِلٰى مَغْفِرَةٍ مِّنْ رَّبِّكُمْ وَجَنَّةٍ عَرْضُهَا السَّمٰوٰتُ وَالْاَرْضُ ۙ اُعِدَّتْ لِلْمُتَّقِيْنَ ۙ﴿۱۳۴﴾

[a]2 : 276; 30 : 40. [b]2 : 25; 66 : 7. [c]See 3 : 33. [d]57 : 22; See also 2 : 26.

477. The words *Aḍ'āfan Muḍā'afah* are not used here as a qualifying phrase to restrict the meaning of *Ribā* (interest) so as to confine it to a particular kind of interest. They are used as a descriptive clause to point to the inherent nature of *Ribā* (interest) which continually goes on increasing. The charging of interest, although now legalized by Christian nations, was prohibited by Moses. (Exod. 22 : 25; Lev. 25: 36,37; Deut. 23 : 19, 20). The verse does not mean that interest is permissible at a moderate rate, only a high rate having been disallowed. All interest is prohibited, whether moderate or excessive; and the words *Aḍ'āfan Muḍā'afah* rendered as, *involving multiple additions*, have been added only to point to the practice actually in vogue in the time of the Holy Prophet. Thus the extreme limit has been mentioned merely to bring out its heinousness, otherwise, all interest is prohibited, as clearly stated in 2: 276-281. Mention of the commandment about the prohibition of interest while dealing with the subject of war is significant. In 2 : 280 also prohibition of interest has been mentioned in connection with the subject of war. This shows that war and interest are closely related to each other—a fact amply borne out by the wars of modern times. As a matter of fact, interest is one of the causes of war, and also helps to prolong it.

478. In 2 : 276 also the prohibition of interest has been followed by a warning against fire. Evidently, it is the fire of war that is primarily meant here. The word "disbelievers," besides being general, may here mean those who disobey the Divine commandment about interest.

479. '*Arḍ* means, (1) price or value of a thing in a form other than money; (2) breadth or width; (3) vastness (Aqrab).

479A. This verse is an answer to those who, obsessed by their present environments, think that commerce and trade cannot be carried on without interest. It says that by following the teachings of Islām Muslims can and will enjoy all sorts of benefits. The verse constitutes an invitation to Muslims to follow the commandments of Islām. It also signifies that Paradise will comprise both heavens and earth, *i.e.*, the believers will be in Paradise both in this life and in the life to come. A well-known saying of the Holy Prophet throws interesting light on the nature of Paradise and Hell. When asked, "If Paradise encompasses both the heavens and the earth, where is Hell," the Prophet replied, "Where is night when the day comes" (Kathīr)? He is further reported to have said that the smallest reward of Paradise will be as great as the space between heaven and earth. This also shows that Paradise is a spiritual state and not a particular physical place.

135. Those, who spend in prosperity and adversity, and those who suppress anger, and pardon[480] men; and Allāh loves those who do good;[481]

الَّذِينَ يُنْفِقُونَ فِي السَّرَّاءِ وَالضَّرَّاءِ وَالْكٰظِمِينَ
الْغَيْظَ وَالْعَافِينَ عَنِ النَّاسِ ۗ وَاللّٰهُ يُحِبُّ الْمُحْسِنِينَ ﴿١٣٥﴾

136. And those who, [a]when they commit a foul deed or wrong themselves, remember Allāh and implore forgiveness for their sins—and [b]who can forgive sins except Allāh —and do not knowingly persist in what they do.[482]

وَالَّذِينَ إِذَا فَعَلُوا فَاحِشَةً أَوْ ظَلَمُوا أَنْفُسَهُمْ ذَكَرُوا اللّٰهَ فَاسْتَغْفَرُوا
لِذُنُوبِهِمْ ۗ وَمَنْ يَغْفِرُ الذُّنُوبَ إِلَّا اللّٰهُ ۗ وَلَمْ
يُصِرُّوا عَلٰى مَا فَعَلُوا وَهُمْ يَعْلَمُونَ ﴿١٣٦﴾

137. [c]It is these whose reward is forgiveness from their Lord, and gardens[483] beneath which rivers flow, wherein they shall abide; and excellent is the reward of good workers.

أُولٰٓئِكَ جَزَآؤُهُمْ مَغْفِرَةٌ مِنْ رَبِّهِمْ وَجَنّٰتٌ تَجْرِي
مِنْ تَحْتِهَا الْأَنْهٰرُ خٰلِدِينَ فِيهَا ۗ وَنِعْمَ أَجْرُ
الْعٰمِلِينَ ﴿١٣٧﴾

[a]7 : 202. [b]14 : 11; 39 : 54; 61 : 13. [c]39 : 75.

480. A man is said to exercise the quality of '*Afw* when he obliterates from his mind, or totally forgets, the sins or offences committed against him by others. When used with reference to God, it signifies not only obliteration of sins but also of all traces thereof.

481. The verse mentions three stages of '*Afw*. In the first stage a believer, when offended against, restrains or suppresses his anger. In the second stage, he goes a step further and grants forgiveness and free pardon to the offender. In the third stage, he not only grants the offender complete pardon, but also does an additional act of kindness to him and bestows some favour upon him. These three stages—suppression of anger, pardoning, and doing of good—are well illustrated by an incident in the life of Ḥasan, son of 'Alī and a grandson of the Holy Prophet. A slave of his once committed an offence and Ḥasan became very angry and was about to punish him when the slave recited the first part of the verse, *i.e., those who suppress anger*. Hearing these words, Ḥasan withheld his hand. Then the slave recited the words, *and pardon men*, upon which Ḥasan promptly pardoned him. The slave then recited, *and Allāh loves those who do good*. In obedience to this Divine command Ḥasan was so moved that he at once set him free (Bayān, i. 366).

482. When good men happen to be guilty of a moral lapse, they do not seek to justify their conduct but frankly confess their guilt, and try to reform.

483. When a man truly turns to God after having committed a sin, and sincerely repents of his misdeeds, he is not only forgiven by God, but God leads him to higher stages of spiritual progress and promises him Heaven.

138. Surely, [a]there have been *many* dispensations[484] before you; [b]so travel through the earth and see how *evil* was the end of those who treated *the Prophets* as liars.

قَدْ خَلَتْ مِنْ قَبْلِكُمْ سُنَنٌ فَسِيْرُوْا فِي الْأَرْضِ
فَانْظُرُوْا كَيْفَ كَانَ عَاقِبَةُ الْمُكَذِّبِيْنَ ﴿۱۳۸﴾

139. This[485] *Qur'ān*, is [c]a clear demonstration to men, and [d]a guidance and [e]an admonition to the God-fearing.

هٰذَا بَيَانٌ لِّلنَّاسِ وَهُدًى وَّمَوْعِظَةٌ لِّلْمُتَّقِيْنَ ﴿۱۳۹﴾

140. [f]Slacken not, nor grieve; and you shall certainly have the upper hand, if[486] you are *true* believers.[487]

وَلَا تَهِنُوْا وَلَا تَحْزَنُوْا وَأَنْتُمُ الْأَعْلَوْنَ إِنْ كُنْتُمْ
مُّؤْمِنِيْنَ ﴿۱۴۰﴾

141. [g]If you have received an injury, surely the *disbelieving* people have already received a similar injury.[488] And such days[488A] We cause to alternate among men *that they may be admonished*, and that Allāh

إِنْ يَّمْسَسْكُمْ قَرْحٌ فَقَدْ مَسَّ الْقَوْمَ قَرْحٌ مِّثْلُهٗ
وَتِلْكَ الْأَيَّامُ نُدَاوِلُهَا بَيْنَ النَّاسِ وَلِيَعْلَمَ اللّٰهُ

[a]7 : 39; 13 : 31; 41 : 26; 46 : 19. [b]6 : 12; 12 : 110; 27 : 70. [c]5 : 16; 36 : 70. [d]2 : 3,186; 31 : 4. [e]24 : 35. [f]4 : 105; 47 : 36. [g]4 : 105.

484. *Sunan* is the plural of *Sunnah* which means, (1) way, course or rule of conduct; (2) way of acting instituted or pursued by a people and followed by others after them; (4) character, conduct, nature or disposition; (5) religious law or dispensation (Tāj).

485. The pronoun *Hādhā* may refer to the Qur'ān, or the verse immediately preceding, or to the subject of repentance discussed in the foregoing verses.

486. *In* means, if ; not ; verily ; because ; when ; etc. (Lane).

487. The verse embodies a very important principle how a nation or an individual can become and remain strong, the words "slacken not" being related to future dangers and "grieve not" to past errors and misfortunes. Nations decline and fall only when, either through lack of true realization of their responsibilities they begin to slacken in their efforts, or through brooding over the past, they give way to despair. The verse warns against both these dangers.

488. Elsewhere (3 : 166), it is said that Muslims inflicted upon disbelievers an injury double of what they themselves had suffered. This refers to the Battle of Badr, when seventy Meccans were killed and seventy were taken prisoner, thus making a total of 140. In the Battle of Uḥud, on the other hand, seventy Muslims were killed, but not one of them was taken prisoner. Thus Muslims had inflicted on the disbelievers a double injury in the Battle of Badr compared with what they themselves suffered in the Battle of Uḥud. Taking into account, however, only those killed in the two battles, the loss of Muslims and disbelievers has been spoken of in the present verse as similar. Or the verse might be taken to refer to the nature or quality of the misfortune, which was alike in both cases. In that case verse 166 below might be taken to refer to the quantity and the present verse to the quality of the loss.

488A. "Days of prosperity" or "days of misfortune."

may cause to be distinguished[489] those who believe and may take witnesses[490] from among you; and Allāh loves not the unjust;

الَّذِينَ آمَنُوا وَيَتَّخِذَ مِنكُمْ شُهَدَاءَ ۗ وَاللّٰهُ لَا يُحِبُّ الظّٰلِمِينَ ﴿١٤١﴾

142. And that Allāh may purify those who believe, and destroy the disbelievers.[491]

وَلِيُمَحِّصَ اللّٰهُ الَّذِينَ آمَنُوا وَيَمْحَقَ الْكٰفِرِينَ ﴿١٤٢﴾

143. [a]Do you suppose that you will enter Heaven while Allāh has not yet caused to be distinguished those of you that strive in *the way of* Allāh and has not yet caused to be distinguished the steadfast.[492]

أَمْ حَسِبْتُمْ أَن تَدْخُلُوا الْجَنَّةَ وَلَمَّا يَعْلَمِ اللّٰهُ الَّذِينَ جٰهَدُوا مِنكُمْ وَيَعْلَمَ الصّٰبِرِينَ ﴿١٤٣﴾

144. And you used to wish for such a death[493] before you met it; now you have seen it *face to face, then why do some of you seek to avoid it.*

وَلَقَدْ كُنتُمْ تَمَنَّوْنَ الْمَوْتَ مِن قَبْلِ أَن تَلْقَوْهُ فَقَدْ رَأَيْتُمُوهُ وَأَنتُمْ تَنظُرُونَ ﴿١٤٤﴾ ع ١٤ ٥

[a]2 : 215; 9: 16.

489. God being Omniscient does not stand in need of adding to His knowledge. It is only the act of distinguishing between two things that is meant here. Knowledge (*'Ilm*) is of two kinds. One kind of knowledge consists in knowing a thing before it comes into existence; and the other in knowing when, and as, it actually comes into existence. Here it is the latter kind of knowledge that is meant.

490. The Faithful bear witness to the truth of Islām by their steadfastness and by the noble example they set in time of misfortune.

491. The reverse suffered by Muslims at Uḥud served as a sort of atonement for their lapse. Besides, the battle made some disbelievers realize that Islām was God's own religion. The very Meccans who took a leading part against the Muslims in that battle became converted to Islām not long after the battle. Islām had conquered their hearts, "destroying" their erstwhile disbelief.

492. It is trials and afflictions which test the mettle of a man; and there can be no spiritual advance or purification without them.

493. "Death" here stands for war, for the result of war is death. War, as it were, meant death for the Muslims, who were extremely weak, both in equipment and numbers compared with their powerful enemy. In the Battle of Uḥud the Holy Prophet proposed to fight the enemy from inside Medina, but some of his Companions, particularly those, who had not taken part in the Battle of Badr, said, "We had longed for this day. Let us go out to fight our enemies, lest they think we are cowards" (Zurqānī, i. 22). It is to this desire of the Muslims that reference is made in the words, *you used to wish for such a death*.

R. 15 145. And [a]Muhammad is but a Messenger. Verily, *all* Messengers have passed away before him. If then he dies or is slain, will you turn back on your heels? [b]And he who turns back on his heels shall not harm Allāh at all.[494] And Allāh will certainly reward the grateful.

وَمَا مُحَمَّدٌ إِلَّا رَسُولٌ ۚ قَدْ خَلَتْ مِنْ قَبْلِهِ الرُّسُلُ ۗ
أَفَإِنْ مَاتَ أَوْ قُتِلَ انْقَلَبْتُمْ عَلَىٰ أَعْقَابِكُمْ ۚ وَمَنْ
يَنْقَلِبْ عَلَىٰ عَقِبَيْهِ فَلَنْ يَضُرَّ اللَّهَ شَيْئًا ۗ وَسَيَجْزِي
اللَّهُ الشَّاكِرِينَ ﴿١٤٥﴾

146. And no soul can die except by Allāh's leave,—a decree with a fixed term. [c]And whoever desires the reward of the present world, We will give him thereof; and whoever desires the reward of the Hereafter, We will give him thereof; and We will surely reward the grateful.

وَمَا كَانَ لِنَفْسٍ أَنْ تَمُوتَ إِلَّا بِإِذْنِ اللَّهِ كِتَابًا
مُؤَجَّلًا ۗ وَمَنْ يُرِدْ ثَوَابَ الدُّنْيَا نُؤْتِهِ مِنْهَا ۚ
وَمَنْ يُرِدْ ثَوَابَ الْآخِرَةِ نُؤْتِهِ مِنْهَا ۚ وَسَنَجْزِي
الشَّاكِرِينَ ﴿١٤٦﴾

[a]5 : 76. [b]2 : 144, 218; 5 : 55; 47 : 39. [c]3 : 149; 4 : 135; 42 : 21.

494. A false report was spread at Uhud that the Holy Prophet had been killed. The verse refers to that incident and purports to say that although the report was untrue, yet even if it had been true and the Prophet had in fact been killed, that should not have made the Faithful waver in their faith. Muhammad was only a Prophet; and as other Prophets before him had died, so would he. But the God of Islām is Ever Living. It is on record that when the Holy Prophet died, 'Umar stood up in the Mosque at Medina with a drawn sword in his hand and said, "Whoever will say that the Prophet of God is dead, I will cut off his head. He is not dead, but has gone to his Lord (he has ascended to heaven), even as Moses had gone to his Lord, and he would come back and punish the Hypocrites." Abū Bakr coming on the scene firmly told 'Umar to sit down and addressing the Muslims who had gathered in the Mosque, recited this very verse which convinced them that the Prophet was really dead and so they were overwhelmed with grief. The verse incidentally establishes the fact that all the Prophets before the Holy Prophet, had died; for if any of them had been alive, the verse could not have been quoted as proof of the Holy Prophet's death. In fact, Islām does not depend for its life on any individual, however great. God is its Revealer and its Protector and Guardian. But the verse should not be understood to mean that the Holy Prophet could ever be killed in war or at the hand of an assassin. He was promised Divine protection from all harm to his life (5 : 68). The enemy had rejoiced when the false report went round that the Prophet was dead. But it proved a blessing in disguise for Muslims. It prepared them for the great strain which his actual death was to bring upon them later. But for this experience, it would have proved unbearable for them.

147. And many a Prophet there has been beside whom fought numerous companies[495] *of their followers*. [a]They slackened not for aught that befell them in the way of Allāh, nor did they weaken, nor did they humiliate themselves *before the enemy*. And Allāh loves the steadfast.

وَكَاَيِّنْ مِّنْ نَّبِيٍّ قٰتَلَ مَعَهٗ رِبِّيُّوْنَ كَثِيْرٌ فَمَا وَهَنُوْا لِمَآ اَصَابَهُمْ فِيْ سَبِيْلِ اللّٰهِ وَمَا ضَعُفُوْا وَمَا اسْتَكَانُوْا وَاللّٰهُ يُحِبُّ الصّٰبِرِيْنَ ﴿١٤٧﴾

148. And they uttered not a word except that they said, [b]"Our Lord, forgive us our sins and our excesses in our conduct, and make firm our steps and help us against the disbelieving people.

وَمَا كَانَ قَوْلَهُمْ اِلَّآ اَنْ قَالُوْا رَبَّنَا اغْفِرْ لَنَا ذُنُوْبَنَا وَاِسْرَافَنَا فِيْٓ اَمْرِنَا وَثَبِّتْ اَقْدَامَنَا وَانْصُرْنَا عَلَى الْقَوْمِ الْكٰفِرِيْنَ ﴿١٤٨﴾

149. [c]So Allāh gave them the reward of this world, as also an excellent[496] reward of the Hereafter; and Allāh loves those who do good.

فَاٰتٰىهُمُ اللّٰهُ ثَوَابَ الدُّنْيَا وَحُسْنَ ثَوَابِ الْاٰخِرَةِ وَاللّٰهُ يُحِبُّ الْمُحْسِنِيْنَ ﴿١٤٩﴾ ع

R. 16 150. [d]O ye who believe! if you obey[497] those who have disbelieved, they will cause you to turn back on your heels, and you will become losers.

يٰٓاَيُّهَا الَّذِيْنَ اٰمَنُوْٓا اِنْ تُطِيْعُوا الَّذِيْنَ كَفَرُوْا يَرُدُّوْكُمْ عَلٰٓى اَعْقَابِكُمْ فَتَنْقَلِبُوْا خٰسِرِيْنَ ﴿١٥٠﴾

151. Nay, [e]Allāh is your Protector, and He is the Best of helpers.

بَلِ اللّٰهُ مَوْلٰىكُمْ وَهُوَ خَيْرُ النّٰصِرِيْنَ ﴿١٥١﴾

[a]4 : 105. [b]2 : 251, 287. [c]3 : 146. [d]2 : 110; 3 : 101. [e]8 : 41; 9 : 51; 22 : 79.

495. *Ribbīyyūn* is the plural of *Ribbīyy* which is derived from *Rabba* for which see 1 : 2. *Ribbīyy* means, one related to *Ribbah*, *i.e.*, a company or a large company or a numerous company. Thus the word means, those forming a large company or a large body of persons. The word also signifies learned, pious and patient men (Lane).

496. The rewards of the next life are of various degrees, and such believers, as have been described above, will get the best of them. The word *Husnā* rendered as "excellent" does not necessarily indicate superlative degree but is also used to express an intensified sense absolutely.

497. Muslims are not enjoined to eschew dealings with all non-Muslims; they are warned against following only such disbelievers as are the active enemies of Islām.

152. ªWe shall cast terror into the hearts of those that have disbelieved because they associate partners with Allāh,[498] for which He has sent down no authority. Their abode is the Fire; and evil is the habitation of the wrongdoers.

سَنُلْقِىْ فِىْ قُلُوْبِ الَّذِيْنَ كَفَرُوا الرُّعْبَ بِمَآ اَشْرَكُوْا بِاللّٰهِ مَا لَمْ يُنَزِّلْ بِهٖ سُلْطٰنًا ۚ وَمَأْوٰىهُمُ النَّارُ ۚ وَبِئْسَ مَثْوَى الظّٰلِمِيْنَ ۞

153. And Allāh had surely made good to you His promise[499] when you were slaying and destroying them by His leave, until, when your courage failed you[500] and you disputed among yourselves concerning the order[501] and you disobeyed[502] after He had shown you that which you loved, *He withdrew His help*. Among you were those who desired the present world,[503] and among you were those who desired the Hereafter. Then He turned you away from them, that He might try you— and He has surely pardoned you, and Allāh is Gracious to the believers—

وَلَقَدْ صَدَقَكُمُ اللّٰهُ وَعْدَهٗٓ اِذْ تَحُسُّوْنَهُمْ بِاِذْنِهٖ ۚ حَتّٰىٓ اِذَا فَشِلْتُمْ وَتَنَازَعْتُمْ فِى الْاَمْرِ وَعَصَيْتُمْ مِّنْۢ بَعْدِ مَآ اَرٰىكُمْ مَّا تُحِبُّوْنَ ۚ مِنْكُمْ مَّنْ يُّرِيْدُ الدُّنْيَا وَمِنْكُمْ مَّنْ يُّرِيْدُ الْاٰخِرَةَ ۚ ثُمَّ صَرَفَكُمْ عَنْهُمْ لِيَبْتَلِيَكُمْ ۚ وَلَقَدْ عَفَا عَنْكُمْ ۚ وَاللّٰهُ ذُوْ فَضْلٍ عَلَى الْمُؤْمِنِيْنَ ۞

ª8 : 13; 59 : 3.

498. Idolatry springs from superstition and fear; and one possessed of superstition and fear can never be truly brave.

499. The "promise" refers to the general promise of victory and success repeatedly given to Muslims, particularly in 3 : 124—126.

500. The verse refers to the party of archers posted in the rear of the Muslim army at Uḥud, and points out that they could not resist the temptation of taking part in actual fighting and in sharing the booty, and their failure to control that desire was an act of cowardice on their part. It is indeed the heart which is the seat of true bravery and courage.

501. The "order" may refer either to the order of the Holy Prophet given to the party of archers on the hill not to leave their station without his permission, or to its import and significance, *i.e.*, whether the Holy Prophet had really meant them to stay there even after the battle had been won; some saying that he did mean it and others alleging that he did not.

502. Muslims stationed at the hill paid no heed to their leader, 'Abd Allāh b. Jubair, who, in compliance with the order of the Holy Prophet, told them not to quit the place, even if victory was within sight. They could not control themselves, and the result was that their act caused great suffering to Muslims.

503. The words refer to those archers who quitted the place at which they had been stationed. The Arabic clause may also signify that some members of the party desired the present world, *i.e.*, taking part in the fighting and collecting the booty, while others (*viz.*, 'Abd Allāh. b. Jubair and those of his comrades who did not quit their posts) desired the

154. When you were running away and looked not back at any-one[504] while the Messenger was calling you, in your rear, then He gave you one sorrow after *another* sorrow,[505] [a]that you might not grieve for what escaped you nor for what befell you.[505A] And Allāh is quite Aware of what you do.

إِذْ تُصْعِدُوْنَ وَلَا تَلْوٗنَ عَلٰٓى اَحَدٍ وَّالرَّسُوْلُ
يَدْعُوْكُمْ فِيْٓ اُخْرٰىكُمْ فَاَثَابَكُمْ غَمًّۢا بِغَمٍّ لِّكَيْلَا
تَحْزَنُوْا عَلٰى مَا فَاتَكُمْ وَلَا مَآ اَصَابَكُمْ ؕ وَاللّٰهُ خَبِيْرٌۢ
بِمَا تَعْمَلُوْنَ ﴿١٥٤﴾

155. Then after the sorrow, [b]He sent down peace on you—a slumber[506] that overcame a party of you—while the other party[506A] was

ثُمَّ اَنْزَلَ عَلَيْكُمْ مِّنْۢ بَعْدِ الْغَمِّ اَمَنَةً نُّعَاسًا يَّغْشٰى
طَآئِفَةً مِّنْكُمْ ۙ وَطَآئِفَةٌ قَدْ اَهَمَّتْهُمْ اَنْفُسُهُمْ

[a]57 : 24. [b]8 : 12.

Hereafter, *i.e.*, they thought of the ultimate consequence of disobeying the command of the Holy Prophet. Some were short-sighted, while others were far-sighted.

504. The words refer to the incident which happened when in the Battle of Uḥud the Muslims were attacked from both the rear and the front and their ranks were broken and many of them fled in confusion in different directions. At first, when they heard that the enemy was coming from behind, they turned back to attack him, but it so happened that at that time a large body of Muslims was also coming from that direction. In the confusion those Muslims were mistaken for the enemy and were attacked. So great was the confusion and the panic that even the voice of the Holy Prophet was not heeded.

505. The Holy Prophet had stationed a party of archers at the hill. They abandoned their positions prematurely, thinking that the battle had been won. Consequently, the victory which was almost within the grasp of the Muslims became converted into a near defeat. It naturally caused a sorrow to them. This was the first sorrow. The second or the later sorrow was that which they felt at the unfounded report of the death of the Holy Prophet. God so designed that the sorrow pertaining to the unfounded report of the Prophet's death (the later sorrow) should come after the sorrow of the reverse which the Muslims had suffered (the first sorrow), in order that the later sorrow should remove the effect of the former sorrow at seeing that the Holy Prophet was safe. The words *Ghamman bi-Ghammin* also mean, sorrow upon sorrow.

505A. The words "what escaped you" signify, the victory which was almost within the grasp of the Muslims and "what befell you" signify the reverse they suffered and the loss of Muslims killed.

506. The reference in the verse is again to the Battle of Uḥud. Abū Ṭalhah says, "I lifted my head on the day of Uḥud and began to look about, and saw that there was none among us on that day whose head had not bent down on account of slumber" (Kathīr, II. 303). As sleep or slumber is a sign of mental peace and tranquillity, the Qur'ān refers to the incident as a Divine favour. The incident evidently occurred when the battle was practically over and the Muslims had returned to the neighbouring hill.

506A. The reference is to the Hypocrites who had remained behind at Medina. They were more concerned about their own security than about the honour of Islām and the security of the Holy Prophet and the Muslims. The words, *we should not have been killed here*, occurring a few lines further, mean, "If we had any voice in the determination of affairs and if our advice had been accepted, we, *i.e.*, our brethern, would not have been killed in the battle, the insinuation being that the Muslims were foolish enough to march to the battle-field against heavy odds, while they (the Hypocrites) had wisely refrained from going with them. According to Quranic idiom the slaying of one's self sometimes signifies the slaying of one's brethren or companions (2: 55, 86).

anxious concerning their ownselves. They entertained about Allāh wrong thoughts *like unto* the thoughts of ignorance. They said, 'Have we any part in the affair? Say, verily, the affair wholly belongs to Allāh.' They hide in their minds what they disclose not to thee. They say, *a*"If we had any part in *the determination of* affairs, we should not have been killed here.' Say, 'If you had *remained* in your homes, surely those on whom fighting[506B] had been enjoined would have gone forth to their death-beds[506C] *that Allāh might fulfil His decree* and that He might test what was in your breasts and that He might purge what was in your hearts. And Allāh knows well what is in the breasts;

يَظُنُّوْنَ بِاللّٰهِ غَيْرَ الْحَقِّ ظَنَّ الْجَاهِلِيَّةِ ؕ يَقُوْلُوْنَ هَلْ لَّنَا مِنَ الْاَمْرِ مِنْ شَيْءٍ ؕ قُلْ اِنَّ الْاَمْرَ كُلَّهٗ لِلّٰهِ ؕ يُخْفُوْنَ فِيْ اَنْفُسِهِمْ مَّا لَا يُبْدُوْنَ لَكَ ؕ يَقُوْلُوْنَ لَوْ كَانَ لَنَا مِنَ الْاَمْرِ شَيْءٌ مَّا قُتِلْنَا هٰهُنَا ؕ قُلْ لَّوْ كُنْتُمْ فِيْ بُيُوْتِكُمْ لَبَرَزَ الَّذِيْنَ كُتِبَ عَلَيْهِمُ الْقَتْلُ اِلٰى مَضَاجِعِهِمْ ۚ وَلِيَبْتَلِيَ اللّٰهُ مَا فِيْ صُدُوْرِكُمْ وَلِيُمَحِّصَ مَا فِيْ قُلُوْبِكُمْ ؕ وَاللّٰهُ عَلِيْمٌۢ بِذَاتِ الصُّدُوْرِ ۝

156. Those of you who turned their backs on the day when the two hosts met,[507] surely it was Satan who sought to make them stumble[507A] because of certain[508] doings of theirs. But certainly Allāh has *already* pardoned them. Verily, Allāh is Most Forgiving, Forbearing.

اِنَّ الَّذِيْنَ تَوَلَّوْا مِنْكُمْ يَوْمَ الْتَقَى الْجَمْعٰنِ ۙ اِنَّمَا اسْتَزَلَّهُمُ الشَّيْطٰنُ بِبَعْضِ مَا كَسَبُوْا ۚ وَلَقَدْ عَفَا اللّٰهُ عَنْهُمْ ؕ اِنَّ اللّٰهَ غَفُوْرٌ حَلِيْمٌ ۝

---

*a*3 : 169.

506B. *Qatl* has been used here in the sense of, *Qitāl*, *i.e.*, fighting (Muḥīṭ & Kashshāf). See 2 : 192 and Jarīr under 3 : 155.

506C. The word "death-beds" has been used in order to point to the abject cowardice of the Hypocrites on the one hand, and the steadfast devotion of the believers on the other. It reminds the Hypocrites that while they had deserted and returned to Medina, thinking that fighting in the circumstances was sure death, such was the firm faith of the believers that even if they (the Hypocrites) had kept back from the very beginning they (the believers) would have cheerfully gone forth to the battle-field—or the place of death, as it was thought to be. All this happened that God might purify the Faithful.

507. The reference is again to the Battle of Uḥud.

507A. The word "stumble," mentioned in the verse, refers to the disobeying of the orders given to the party stationed at the hill or the running away of some Muslims from the battle-field.

508. The words seem to contain an implied praise for the archers at the hill who misinterpreting the Holy Prophet's orders left their post, meaning that only "certain" of their misdeeds had brought them this temporary disgrace, otherwise they were really loyal and obedient to the Holy Prophet.

R. 17 157. O ye who believe! be not like those who have disbelieved, and who say of their brethren when they travel in the land[509] or go forth to war: 'Had they been with us, they would not have died or been slain.' *They say this* that Allāh may make it a cause of regret in their hearts.[510] And Allāh gives life and causes death and Allāh is Mindful of what you do.

يَاَيُّهَا الَّذِيْنَ اٰمَنُوْا لَا تَكُوْنُوْا كَالَّذِيْنَ كَفَرُوْا وَقَالُوْا
لِاِخْوَانِهِمْ اِذَا ضَرَبُوْا فِي الْاَرْضِ اَوْ كَانُوْا غُزًّى لَّوْ
كَانُوْا عِنْدَنَا مَا مَاتُوْا وَمَا قُتِلُوْا لِيَجْعَلَ اللّٰهُ ذٰلِكَ
حَسْرَةً فِيْ قُلُوْبِهِمْ وَاللّٰهُ يُحْيٖ وَيُمِيْتُ وَاللّٰهُ بِمَا
تَعْمَلُوْنَ بَصِيْرٌ ﴿١٥٧﴾

158. And if you are slain in the cause of Allāh or you die,[511] [a]surely, forgiveness from Allāh and mercy are better than what they hoard.[512]

وَلَئِنْ قُتِلْتُمْ فِيْ سَبِيْلِ اللّٰهِ اَوْ مُتُّمْ لَمَغْفِرَةٌ مِّنَ
اللّٰهِ وَرَحْمَةٌ خَيْرٌ مِّمَّا يَجْمَعُوْنَ ﴿١٥٨﴾

159. And if you[513] die or be slain, [b]surely unto Allāh shall you all be gathered together.

وَلَئِنْ مُّتُّمْ اَوْ قُتِلْتُمْ لَاِلَى اللّٰهِ تُحْشَرُوْنَ ﴿١٥٩﴾

160. And it is by the *great* mercy of Allāh that thou art kind[514] towards them, and if thou hadst been rough

فَبِمَا رَحْمَةٍ مِّنَ اللّٰهِ لِنْتَ لَهُمْ وَلَوْ كُنْتَ فَظًّا

[a]10 : 59; 43 : 33. [b]5 : 97; 6 : 73; 8 : 25; 23 : 80.

509. When they travel in the land in the cause of God.

510. The object of disbelievers was to frighten the Muslims in order to make them keep away from fighting, but the Muslims, far from being discouraged by such warnings, became all the more firm in their resolve to fight the disbelievers. This filled the disbelievers with regret for having made the effort which produced a result opposite to that which they had desired.

511. He who fights and lays down his life in the cause of Truth should not be regarded as dead, because he gives his life for the sake of Him Who is the Controller of all life. He may be regarded as physically dead; spiritually he lives for ever (2 : 155).

512. Whereas, hypocrites are afraid of death because of the wealth and property which they have to leave behind, the believers, killed in the cause of Allāh, will get what is incomparably greater than what hypocrites are greedily hoarding up, or what Muslims themselves may have collected in the form of wealth and other worldly things.

513. The pronoun "you" includes both hypocrites and believers; for all will be gathered unto God for reward or punishment, as the case may be.

514. The words give an insight into the beautiful character of the Holy Prophet, of which the most effable and prominent trait was his all-comprehensive mercy. He was full of the milk of human kindness and was not only kind towards his Companions and followers but was also full of mercy and sympathy for his enemies who were always on the lookout to stab him in the back. It is on record that he took no action against those treacherous Hypocrites who had deserted him in the Battle of Uḥud. He even consulted them in affairs of State.

and hard-hearted, they would surely have dispersed from around thee. So pardon them and ask forgiveness for them, and ^aconsult⁵¹⁵ them in matters *of administration*; and when thou art resolved, then put thy trust in Allāh. Surely, Allāh loves those who put their trust *in Him.*

غَلِيْظَ الْقَلْبِ لَانْفَضُّوْا مِنْ حَوْلِكَ فَاعْفُ عَنْهُمْ وَاسْتَغْفِرْ لَهُمْ وَشَاوِرْهُمْ فِى الْاَمْرِ فَاِذَا عَزَمْتَ فَتَوَكَّلْ عَلَى اللّٰهِ اِنَّ اللّٰهَ يُحِبُّ الْمُتَوَكِّلِيْنَ ۝

161. If Allāh helps you, none can overcome you; but if He forsakes you, then who is there that can help you beside⁵¹⁶ Him? In Allāh, then, let the believers put their trust.

اِنْ يَّنْصُرْكُمُ اللّٰهُ فَلَا غَالِبَ لَكُمْ ۚ وَاِنْ يَّخْذُلْكُمْ فَمَنْ ذَا الَّذِىْ يَنْصُرُكُمْ مِّنْ بَعْدِهٖ ۗ وَعَلَى اللّٰهِ فَلْيَتَوَكَّلِ الْمُؤْمِنُوْنَ ۝

162. And it is not possible for a Prophet to act dishonestly,⁵¹⁷ and whoever acts dishonestly shall bring *with him* that, concerning which he has been dishonest, on the Day of Resurrection. ^bThen shall every soul be fully paid what it has earned; and they shall not be wronged.

وَمَا كَانَ لِنَبِىٍّ اَنْ يَّغُلَّ ۚ وَمَنْ يَّغْلُلْ يَأْتِ بِمَا غَلَّ يَوْمَ الْقِيٰمَةِ ۚ ثُمَّ تُوَفّٰى كُلُّ نَفْسٍ مَّا كَسَبَتْ وَهُمْ لَا يُظْلَمُوْنَ ۝

---

^a42 : 39.   ^b3 : 26; 14 : 52; 40 : 18.

---

515. Besides other things Islām is unique in this respect that it has included the institution of *Mushāwarah* (consultation) in its basic principles. It has made it binding upon the Head of the Muslim State that he should consult Muslims in all important affairs of the State. The Holy Prophet used to consult his followers in all important matters, as he did before the battles of Badr, Uḥud, and Aḥzāb, and also when a false accusation was brought against his noble wife, 'Ā'ishah. Abū Hurairah says : "The Holy Prophet was most solicitous in consulting others in all matters of importance" (Manthūr, ii. 90). 'Umar, the Second Successor of the Holy Prophet, is reported to have said : " There is no *Khilāfat* without consultation" (Izālat al-Khifā' 'an Khilāfat al-Khulafā'). Thus the holding of consultation in important matters is a basic injunction of Islām and is binding on both spiritual and temporal Muslim Chiefs. The Khalīfah or the Head of the Muslim State must seek the advice of representative Muslims though the final decision may rest with him. The Islamic *Shūrā* or *Mushāwarah* is not a parliament in the sense in which the word is understood in the West. The Head of the Muslim State enjoys a certain discretion in rejecting the advice tendered to him. But he should not lightly use this discretion and should respect the advice of the majority.

516. The expression, *Min Ba'dihī*, translated as, "beside Him," literally means, "after Him" and may be rendered as "in opposition to Him."

517. The archers stationed by the Holy Prophet at the hill of Uḥud to protect the rear of the Muslim army left their posts (not all of them) when they saw the Meccan army in full flight. They thought that by leaving the hill at that stage they were not contravening the spirit of the Prophet's orders, which were to the effect that they were not to leave their posts in any circumstances. They further thought that as, according to Arab custom a soldier was entitled to the possession of the booty he laid his hand on during the fight they might be deprived of their share of the spoils of war if they stuck to their posts. This

163. [a]Is he who follows the pleasure of Allāh like him who draws on himself the wrath of Allāh[518] and whose abode is Hell? And an evil retreat it is!

أَفَمَنِ اتَّبَعَ رِضْوَانَ اللّٰهِ كَمَنْ بَآءَ بِسَخَطٍ مِّنَ اللّٰهِ
وَمَأْوٰىهُ جَهَنَّمُ ۚ وَبِئْسَ الْمَصِيْرُ ﴿١٦٣﴾

164. They have *different* ranks[519] with Allāh; and Allāh sees what they do.

هُمْ دَرَجٰتٌ عِنْدَ اللّٰهِ ۗ وَاللّٰهُ بَصِيْرٌۢ بِمَا يَعْمَلُوْنَ ﴿١٦٤﴾

165. Verily, Allāh has conferred a favour on the believers by [b]raising among them a Messenger from among themselves[520] who recites to them His Signs, and purifies them and teaches them the Book and wisdom; and, before that, they were surely in manifest error.

لَقَدْ مَنَّ اللّٰهُ عَلَى الْمُؤْمِنِيْنَ إِذْ بَعَثَ فِيْهِمْ رَسُوْلًا
مِّنْ أَنْفُسِهِمْ يَتْلُوْا عَلَيْهِمْ اٰيٰتِهٖ وَيُزَكِّيْهِمْ وَ
يُعَلِّمُهُمُ الْكِتٰبَ وَالْحِكْمَةَ ۚ وَإِنْ كَانُوْا مِنْ قَبْلُ
لَفِيْ ضَلٰلٍ مُّبِيْنٍ ﴿١٦٥﴾

166. What! [c]when a misfortune befalls you—and you had already inflicted twice *as much*[521]—you say, whence is this? Say, 'It is from your own selves.'[522] Surely, Allāh has power over all things.

أَوَلَمَّآ أَصَابَتْكُمْ مُّصِيْبَةٌ قَدْ أَصَبْتُمْ مِّثْلَيْهَا ۙ
قُلْتُمْ أَنّٰى هٰذَا ۖ قُلْ هُوَ مِنْ عِنْدِ أَنْفُسِكُمْ ۗ إِنَّ
اللّٰهَ عَلٰى كُلِّ شَيْءٍ قَدِيْرٌ ﴿١٦٦﴾

[a]2 : 208, 266; 3 : 16; 5 : 3,17; 9 : 72. [b]2 : 130,152; 9 : 128; 63 : 3; 65 : 12. [c]4 : 80.

precipitate action of the archers implied an apprehension on their part that the Holy Prophet might ignore their right to the booty. It is this apprehension that is condemned here. But no imputation of actual faithlessness to the Holy Prophet is implied. The verse simply purports to say that it was far from the Holy Prophet to ignore the rights to the booty of those whom he himself had stationed at a certain place.

518. Undaunted by the defection of the Hypocrites at Uḥud, which considerably weakened the ranks of Muslims, the Holy Prophet proceeded to fight the enemies of Islām. The Hypocrites, on the other hand, by their act of desertion, drew upon themselves the wrath of God.

519. The words, *Hum Darajātun*, mean "they are possessors of ranks;" the word, *'ulū*, is understood before the word *Darajāt*.

520. The words are intended to awaken in the hearts of Muslims a desire to follow the example of the Holy Prophet, who was like them and was one of them.

521. The words refer to the Battle of Badr, when 70 Meccans were killed and 70 taken prisoner. At Uḥud, 70 Muslims were killed, none being taken prisoner. Thus the Muslims had already inflicted a double loss on the Meccans.

522. As for the real cause of man's actions, both the good and evil ones are said to emanate from him, because he is their author, but as it is God Who, as the final Judge, brings about the results of those actions, whether good or bad, they can equally be said to proceed from Him (4 : 79). In this sense, both the good and evil results of man's actions would be attributed to God.

167. And that which befell you, on the day when two hosts met, was by Allāh's command; and *this was so* that He might cause the believers to be distinguished;

وَمَآ اَصَابَكُمْ يَوْمَ الْتَقَى الْجَمْعٰنِ فَبِاِذْنِ اللّٰهِ
وَلِيَعْلَمَ الْمُؤْمِنِيْنَ ﴿١٦٧﴾

168. And that He might cause the hypocrites to be distinguished.[523] And it was said to them, 'Come ye, fight in the cause of Allāh and[524] repel *the attack of the enemy*;' they said, 'If we knew how to fight, we would surely follow you.[525] They were, that day, nearer to disbelief than to belief. [a]They say with their mouths what is not in their hearts. And Allāh knows quite well what they hide.

وَلِيَعْلَمَ الَّذِيْنَ نَافَقُوْا ۚۖ وَقِيْلَ لَهُمْ تَعَالَوْا
قَاتِلُوْا فِيْ سَبِيْلِ اللّٰهِ اَوِ ادْفَعُوْا ۗ قَالُوْا لَوْ نَعْلَمُ قِتَالًا
لَّاتَّبَعْنٰكُمْ ۗ هُمْ لِلْكُفْرِ يَوْمَئِذٍ اَقْرَبُ مِنْهُمْ لِلْاِيْمَانِ ۚ
يَقُوْلُوْنَ بِاَفْوَاهِهِمْ مَّا لَيْسَ فِيْ قُلُوْبِهِمْ ۗ وَاللّٰهُ
اَعْلَمُ بِمَا يَكْتُمُوْنَ ﴿١٦٨﴾

169. *It is these* who said of their brethren,[526] while they *themselves* remained behind, 'If they had obeyed us, [b]they would not have been slain.' Say, "Then avert death from yourselves, if you are truthful.'

اَلَّذِيْنَ قَالُوْا لِاِخْوَانِهِمْ وَقَعَدُوْا لَوْ اَطَاعُوْنَا مَا
قُتِلُوْا ۗ قُلْ فَادْرَءُوْا عَنْ اَنْفُسِكُمُ الْمَوْتَ اِنْ كُنْتُمْ
صٰدِقِيْنَ ﴿١٦٩﴾

[a]48 : 12 [b]3 : 155. [c]4 : 79.

523. Trials and tribulations are intended to distinguish true believers from those weak of faith. In this way, the sufferings of the Muslims at Uhud proved a blessing in disguise. They served to distinguish the true believers from the Hypocrites who had so far remained mixed up with true believers.

524. The particle *au* rendered as "and" literally means "or" and is equivalent to "in other words," or "what is the same thing as" etc.

525. The expression, *Lau Na'lamu Qitālan*, may mean: (1) If we knew that there would be fighting, *i.e.*, we knew that there would be no fighting and that the Muslims would at once run away before their very powerful enemy without giving fight. (2) If we knew it to be a fight, *i.e.*, it was no fight in which the Muslims were going to be engaged but rather their certain destruction in view of the appalling difference between the numbers and equipment of the opposing forces. (3) If we knew how to fight. In this case, the words may be taken to have been spoken ironically, signifying : "We are unaware of the art of war; if we had been acquainted with it, we would have fought along with you." The allusion in the verse is obviously to the defection at Uḥud of a party of 300 Hypocrites under their leader 'Abd Allāh b. Ubayy, who deserted the Muslims and went back to Medina.

526. The words "said of their brethren" may mean "said concerning their brethren," *i.e.*, Muslims; or "talked among themselves about the Muslims."

170. ᵃThink not of those, who have been slain⁵²⁷ in the cause of Allāh, as dead. Nay, they are living, in the presence of their Lord, *and* are granted gifts *from Him*;

وَلَا تَحْسَبَنَّ الَّذِيْنَ قُتِلُوْا فِيْ سَبِيْلِ اللّٰهِ اَمْوَاتًا ۚ بَلْ اَحْيَاءٌ عِنْدَ رَبِّهِمْ يُرْزَقُوْنَ ۙ ١٧٠

171. Jubilant⁵²⁸ because of that which Allāh has given them of His bounty; and rejoicing for the sake of those who have not yet joined them from behind them, because on ᵇthem *shall come* no fear, nor shall they grieve.

فَرِحِيْنَ بِمَاۤ اٰتٰىهُمُ اللّٰهُ مِنْ فَضْلِهٖ ۙ وَيَسْتَبْشِرُوْنَ بِالَّذِيْنَ لَمْ يَلْحَقُوْا بِهِمْ مِّنْ خَلْفِهِمْ ۙ اَلَّا خَوْفٌ عَلَيْهِمْ وَلَا هُمْ يَحْزَنُوْنَ ۚ ١٧١

172. They rejoice at the favour of Allāh and *His* bounty, and *at the fact* that ᶜAllāh suffers not the reward of the believers to be lost.

يَسْتَبْشِرُوْنَ بِنِعْمَةٍ مِّنَ اللّٰهِ وَفَضْلٍ ۙ وَّاَنَّ اللّٰهَ لَا يُضِيْعُ اَجْرَ الْمُؤْمِنِيْنَ ۚ ١٧٢

R. 18　173. Those who ᵈanswered the call of Allāh and the Messenger after they had received an injury⁵²⁹— such of them as do good and act righteously shall have a great reward;

اَلَّذِيْنَ اسْتَجَابُوْا لِلّٰهِ وَالرَّسُوْلِ مِنْۢ بَعْدِ مَاۤ اَصَابَهُمُ الْقَرْحُ ۛ لِلَّذِيْنَ اَحْسَنُوْا مِنْهُمْ وَاتَّقَوْا اَجْرٌ عَظِيْمٌ ۚ ١٧٣

ᵃ2 : 155. ᵇ2 : 63; 6 : 49; 7 : 50; 46 : 14. ᶜ7 : 171; 9 : 129; 11 : 116. ᵈ8 : 25.

527. *Amwāt* is the plural of *Mayyit* which, besides meaning a dead person, signifies, (1) one whose blood has not been avenged; (2) one who leaves behind no successors; (3) one stricken with sorrow and grief.

528. The martyrs are glad that their brethren, who are left behind in the world and will follow them later, will soon triumph over their enemies, *i.e.*, after death the veils are removed and the martyrs are given the knowledge of the victories in store for the Muslims. They receive good tidings concerning their brethren, *i.e.*, the angels of God keep them informed of the later successes and victories of Islām.

529. The reference here and in the next verse is to the two expeditions which the Holy Prophet led against the Meccans after the Battle of Uḥud. The first was undertaken on the day immediately following the battle. When the Meccans withdrew from Uḥud, they were taunted by some Arab tribes for having brought no booty and no prisoners of war from a battle in which they claimed to have won a victory. They, therefore, thought of returning to Medina with a view to re-attacking the Muslims and completing their victory. The Holy Prophet had anticipated their return; so he called upon those of his Companions who had taken part in the Battle of Uḥud to join him in the expedition against them and on the following day he left Medina with 250 men. When the Meccans heard of this, they lost heart and fled. The Holy Prophet went as far as Ḥamrā' al-Asad, a distance of about eight miles from Medina on the route to Mecca and seeing that the enemy had fled, returned to Medina. The second expedition came a year later. Before leaving the battlefield of Uḥud, Abū Sufyān, commander of the Meccan army, had promised the Muslims another engagement next year at Badr. But the ensuing year being a year of famine, he could not carry out his boast. But he sent Nu'aim b. Mas'ūd to Medina to intimidate the Muslims by spreading false rumours of great preparations having been made by the Meccans. This clumsy ruse, however, completely failed to frighten the Muslims, who came to Badr at the appointed time,

174. Those to whom men said, 'People have mustered against you, therefore fear them,'[530] but this *only* increased their faith and they said, 'Sufficient for us is Allāh, and an excellent Guardian is He.'

الَّذِيْنَ قَالَ لَهُمُ النَّاسُ اِنَّ النَّاسَ قَدْ جَمَعُوْا لَكُمْ فَاخْشَوْهُمْ فَزَادَهُمْ اِيْمَانًا ۖ وَّقَالُوْا حَسْبُنَا اللّٰهُ وَنِعْمَ الْوَكِيْلُ ۴

175. So they returned with a *mighty* favour from Allāh and a *great* bounty,[531] while no evil had touched them; and they followed ᵃthe pleasure of Allāh; and Allāh is the Lord of great bounty.

فَانْقَلَبُوْا بِنِعْمَةٍ مِّنَ اللّٰهِ وَفَضْلٍ لَّمْ يَمْسَسْهُمْ سُوْۤءٌ ۙ وَّاتَّبَعُوْا رِضْوَانَ اللّٰهِ ۗ وَاللّٰهُ ذُوْ فَضْلٍ عَظِيْمٍ ۵

176. It is Satan who only frightens ᵇhis friends,[532] so fear them not but fear Me, if you are believers.

اِنَّمَا ذٰلِكُمُ الشَّيْطٰنُ يُخَوِّفُ اَوْلِيَآءَهٗ ۖ فَلَا تَخَافُوْهُمْ وَخَافُوْنِ اِنْ كُنْتُمْ مُّؤْمِنِيْنَ ۶

177. ᶜAnd let not those who hasten *to fall* into disbelief grieve thee; surely, they cannot harm Allāh[533] in any way. Allāh desires not to assign them any portion in the life to come; and they shall have a severe punishment.

وَلَا يَحْزُنْكَ الَّذِيْنَ يُسَارِعُوْنَ فِى الْكُفْرِ ۚ اِنَّهُمْ لَنْ يَّضُرُّوا اللّٰهَ شَيْئًا ۗ يُرِيْدُ اللّٰهُ اَلَّا يَجْعَلَ لَهُمْ حَظًّا فِى الْاٰخِرَةِ ۖ وَلَهُمْ عَذَابٌ عَظِيْمٌ ۷

178. Surely, ᵈthose who have purchased disbelief at the price of faith cannot harm Allāh at all; and they shall have a grievous punishment.

اِنَّ الَّذِيْنَ اشْتَرَوُا الْكُفْرَ بِالْاِيْمَانِ لَنْ يَّضُرُّوا اللّٰهَ شَيْئًا ۚ وَلَهُمْ عَذَابٌ اَلِيْمٌ ۸

ᵃ2 : 208, 266;   3 : 16, 163;   5 : 3, 17;   9 : 72;   57 : 21, 28.   ᵇ7 : 28;   16 : 101;   35 : 7.   ᶜ5 : 42.   ᵈ2 : 17, 87;   14 : 29.

---

only to find that the Meccans had not come. This expedition is known as the expedition of Badr al-Ṣughrā (the Smaller Badr) to distinguish it from the great Battle of Badr which had taken place about two years earlier.

530. The reference is to the false rumours spread by Nu'aim b. Mas'ūd.

531. The Muslims returned from Badr al-Ṣughrā after making great profit by trading at the annual fair held there. This is hinted in the word "bounty."

532. The words mean : (1) Satan tries to make believers fear disbelievers who are his friends. (2) By his plans Satan succeeds in frightening only his friends, the disbelievers.

533. Those who try to harm Islām or the Holy Prophet and his followers, in reality, try to harm God Himself, because the cause of the Holy Prophet is God's own cause.

179. And let not the disbelievers think that "Our granting them respite is good for them; *in fact the result* of Our granting them respite will only be that[534] they will increase in sin; and they shall have an humiliating punishment.

وَلَا يَحْسَبَنَّ الَّذِينَ كَفَرُوٓا اَنَّمَا نُمۡلِي لَهُمۡ خَيۡرٌ لِّاَنۡفُسِهِمۡ اِنَّمَا نُمۡلِي لَهُمۡ لِيَزۡدَادُوٓا اِثۡمًا ۚ وَلَهُمۡ عَذَابٌ مُّهِيۡنٌ ۝

180. [b]Allāh would not leave the believers *in the state* in which you are,[535] until He separated the wicked from the good. Nor would Allāh [c]reveal to you the unseen. But Allāh chooses[536] of His Messengers whom He pleases. Believe, therefore, in Allāh and His Messengers. If you believe and be righteous, you shall have a great reward.

مَا كَانَ اللّٰهُ لِيَذَرَ الۡمُؤۡمِنِيۡنَ عَلٰى مَآ اَنۡتُمۡ عَلَيۡهِ حَتّٰى يَمِيۡزَ الۡخَبِيۡثَ مِنَ الطَّيِّبِ ۗ وَمَا كَانَ اللّٰهُ لِيُطۡلِعَكُمۡ عَلَى الۡغَيۡبِ وَلٰكِنَّ اللّٰهَ يَجۡتَبِيۡ مِنۡ رُّسُلِهٖ مَنۡ يَّشَآءُ ۖ فَاٰمِنُوۡا بِاللّٰهِ وَرُسُلِهٖ ۚ وَاِنۡ تُؤۡمِنُوۡا وَتَتَّقُوۡا فَلَكُمۡ اَجۡرٌ عَظِيۡمٌ ۝

181. And let not those, [d]who are niggardly in *spending* what Allāh has given them of His bounty, think that it is good for them; nay, it is bad for them. That with respect to which they were niggardly shall be put as a collar round their necks on the Day of Resurrection. And to Allāh belongs the heritage[537] of the heavens and the earth, and Allāh is fully Aware of what you do.

وَلَا يَحۡسَبَنَّ الَّذِينَ يَبۡخَلُوۡنَ بِمَآ اٰتٰهُمُ اللّٰهُ مِنۡ فَضۡلِهٖ هُوَ خَيۡرًا لَّهُمۡ ۚ بَلۡ هُوَ شَرٌّ لَّهُمۡ ۚ سَيُطَوَّقُوۡنَ مَا بَخِلُوۡا بِهٖ يَوۡمَ الۡقِيٰمَةِ ۗ وَلِلّٰهِ مِيۡرَاثُ السَّمٰوٰتِ وَالۡاَرۡضِ ۗ وَاللّٰهُ بِمَا تَعۡمَلُوۡنَ خَبِيۡرٌ ۝

---

[a]22 : 45.   [b]8 : 38; 29 : 3-4.   [c]72 : 27-28.   [d]4 : 38; 17 : 30; 25 : 68.

534. The particle *Lām* in the expression *Liyazdādū* is *Lām 'Āqibah* denoting result.

535. The verse signifies that the trials and tribulations through which Muslims have so far passed would not end soon. There are yet many more in store for them, and they will continue to come till true believers are completely distinguished from hypocrites and those weak of faith.

536. The words do not mean that some of the Messengers are chosen and others are not. They mean that of the persons whom God ordains as His Messengers, He chooses the one most suited for the particular age in which he is raised.

537. *Mīrāth* rendered as "heritage" here signifies "ownership." The word also means, portion allotted to one. See 23 : 12 where it is stated "those who shall inherit Paradise." Paradise is not inherited by anyone; it is only received as an allotted portion from God.

R. 19 182. And, surely, Allāh has heard the utterance of those who said, [a]"Allāh is poor and we are rich.'[538] We shall record what they have said, and [b]their *attempts to* slay the Prophets unjustly; and We shall say, 'Taste ye the punishment of burning;

لَقَدْ سَمِعَ اللّٰهُ قَوْلَ الَّذِيْنَ قَالُوْٓا اِنَّ اللّٰهَ فَقِيْرٌ وَّ
نَحْنُ اَغْنِيَآءُ ۘ سَنَكْتُبُ مَا قَالُوْا وَقَتْلَهُمُ الْاَنْۢبِيَآءَ
بِغَيْرِ حَقٍّ ۙ وَّنَقُوْلُ ذُوْقُوْا عَذَابَ الْحَرِيْقِ ﴿۱۸۲﴾

183. 'That is because of that which your hands have sent on before.' and [c]Allāh is not *at all* unjust to *His* servants.

ذٰلِكَ بِمَا قَدَّمَتْ اَيْدِيْكُمْ وَاَنَّ اللّٰهَ لَيْسَ بِظَلَّامٍ
لِّلْعَبِيْدِ ﴿۱۸۳﴾ ج

184. Those who say, 'Allāh has charged us not to believe in any Messenger until he brings us an offering which fire devours.'[539] Say, 'There have already come to you Messengers before me with [d]clear Signs and with that which you ask for. Why, then, did you seek to slay them, if you are truthful?'

اَلَّذِيْنَ قَالُوْٓا اِنَّ اللّٰهَ عَهِدَ اِلَيْنَآ اَلَّا نُؤْمِنَ لِرَسُوْلٍ
حَتّٰى يَاْتِيَنَا بِقُرْبَانٍ تَاْكُلُهُ النَّارُ ؕ قُلْ قَدْ جَآءَكُمْ
رُسُلٌ مِّنْ قَبْلِيْ بِالْبَيِّنٰتِ وَبِالَّذِيْ قُلْتُمْ فَلِمَ قَتَلْتُمُوْهُمْ
اِنْ كُنْتُمْ صٰدِقِيْنَ ﴿۱۸۴﴾

185. [e]And if they accuse thee of lying, even so were accused of lying Messengers before thee who came with clear Signs and Books of wisdom[540] and the illuminating Book.[541]

فَاِنْ كَذَّبُوْكَ فَقَدْ كُذِّبَ رُسُلٌ مِّنْ قَبْلِكَ جَآءُوْ
بِالْبَيِّنٰتِ وَالزُّبُرِ وَالْكِتٰبِ الْمُنِيْرِ ﴿۱۸۵﴾

[a]5 : 65. [b]4 : 156. [c]8 : 52; 41 : 47; 50 : 30. [d]5 : 33; 14 : 10; 40 : 84. [e]35 : 5,26.

538. When the Jews were called upon to spend their wealth in the cause of Allāh, (3 : 181), they taunted the Muslims by saying, 'Is Allāh poor and we rich?' These words also express the inward feelings of those niggardly persons who join a new movement but find it hard to comply with its ever growing monetary demands.

539. The verse answers the objection of the Jews about the burnt offerings by saying that the observance of the law regarding such offerings was no criterion to test the truth of a Prophet, because that could easily be done by an impostor. It was only "clear signs" that demonstrated and established the truth of a claimant. But even if observance of burnt offerings was the criterion of a true Prophet, the Jews had no right to raise an objection. The charge is driven home to them in the words, "Why did they reject those Prophets who strictly conformed to that law?"

540. *Zabūr* means, a writing or a book of wisdom and science, not containing legal statutes, ordinances or commandments, particularly the Book of David containing the Psalms (Lane).

541. The Torah which all the Israelite Prophets followed though they had also their separate revelations containing warnings and words of wisdom.

186. [a]Every soul shall taste of death. And you shall be paid in full your [b]rewards only on the Day of Resurrection. So whosoever is removed away from the Fire and is made to enter Heaven has indeed attained his goal. And the life of this world is nothing but an illusory enjoyment.[542]

كُلُّ نَفْسٍ ذَآئِقَةُ الْمَوْتِ ۗ وَإِنَّمَا تُوَفَّوْنَ أُجُورَكُمْ
يَوْمَ الْقِيٰمَةِ ۗ فَمَنْ زُحْزِحَ عَنِ النَّارِ وَأُدْخِلَ الْجَنَّةَ
فَقَدْ فَازَ ۗ وَمَا الْحَيٰوةُ الدُّنْيَآ إِلَّا مَتَاعُ الْغُرُورِ ﴿١٨٦﴾

187. [c]You shall surely be tried[543] in your possessions and in your persons and [d]you shall surely hear many *hurtful* things from those who were given the Book before you and from those who set up equals to Allāh. But if you show patience *and fortitude* and act righteously, that indeed is a matter of high resolve.

لَتُبْلَوُنَّ فِيٓ أَمْوَالِكُمْ وَأَنْفُسِكُمْ وَلَتَسْمَعُنَّ مِنَ الَّذِينَ
أُوتُوا الْكِتٰبَ مِنْ قَبْلِكُمْ وَمِنَ الَّذِينَ أَشْرَكُوٓا أَذًى
كَثِيرًا ۗ وَإِنْ تَصْبِرُوا وَتَتَّقُوا فَإِنَّ ذٰلِكَ مِنْ عَزْمِ
الْأُمُورِ ﴿١٨٧﴾

188. And *remember* when Allāh took a covenant[544] from those who were given the Book, *saying*, 'You shall expound it to the people and not hide it.' But [e]they threw it away behind their backs, and bartered it for a paltry price. Evil is that which they purchased.

وَإِذْ أَخَذَ اللّٰهُ مِيثَاقَ الَّذِينَ أُوتُوا الْكِتٰبَ لَتُبَيِّنُنَّهٗ
لِلنَّاسِ وَلَا تَكْتُمُونَهٗ فَنَبَذُوهُ وَرَآءَ ظُهُورِهِمْ
وَاشْتَرَوْا بِهٖ ثَمَنًا قَلِيلًا ۗ فَبِئْسَ مَا يَشْتَرُونَ ﴿١٨٨﴾

---

[a]21 : 36; 29 : 58. [b]4 : 174; 35 : 31; 39 : 36. [c]2 : 156; 8 : 29; 64 : 16. [d]5 : 83. [e]2 : 102.

---

542. Death is the most certain phenomenon in nature and yet man's attitude towards it is of complete disregard and indifference. Worldly life has been here called a vain and illusory thing, because, on the face of it, it appears to be a very attractive and sweet thing, but when one becomes engrossed in seeking its pleasures and profits, one finds it bitter and deceptive.

543. Tests and trials serve a fourfold purpose: (1) They distinguish the waverers and the weak of faith from the sincere and steadfast votaries. (2) They are a means of spiritual advancement for those sincere in faith. (3) Those going through a trial come to know the strength or weakness of their own faith and are thus enabled to shape their conduct accordingly. (4) Trials also establish the title to reward of those deserving it.

544. The reference here is to no particular covenant but to a general covenant taken from the followers of every Prophet that they would preach and promulgate the Divine Message and would try to live up to it.

189. Think not that those [a]who exult in what they have done, and love to be praised for what they have not done—think not that they are secure[545] from punishment. They shall suffer a grievous chastisement.

لَا تَحْسَبَنَّ الَّذِيْنَ يَفْرَحُوْنَ بِمَآ اَتَوْا وَّيُحِبُّوْنَ اَنْ
يُّحْمَدُوْا بِمَا لَمْ يَفْعَلُوْا فَلَا تَحْسَبَنَّهُمْ بِمَفَازَةٍ مِّنَ
الْعَذَابِ ۚ وَلَهُمْ عَذَابٌ اَلِيْمٌ ﴿۱۸۹﴾

190. [b]And to Allāh belongs the Kingdom of the heavens and the earth; and Allāh has power over all things.

وَلِلّٰهِ مُلْكُ السَّمٰوٰتِ وَالْاَرْضِ ۗ وَاللّٰهُ عَلٰى كُلِّ شَيْءٍ
قَدِيْرٌ ﴿۱۹۰﴾

R. 20 191. [c]In the creation of the heavens and the earth and in the alternation of the night and the day there are indeed Signs for men of understanding;[546]

اِنَّ فِيْ خَلْقِ السَّمٰوٰتِ وَالْاَرْضِ وَاخْتِلَافِ الَّيْلِ
وَالنَّهَارِ لَاٰيٰتٍ لِّاُولِي الْاَلْبَابِ ﴿۱۹۱﴾

192. [d]Those who remember Allāh standing, sitting, and *lying* on their sides, and ponder over the creation of the heavens and the earth; and say, "Our Lord, Thou hast not created this *universe* in [e]vain.[547] Holy art Thou; save us, then, from the punishment of the Fire;

الَّذِيْنَ يَذْكُرُوْنَ اللّٰهَ قِيٰمًا وَّقُعُوْدًا وَّعَلٰى جُنُوْبِهِمْ
وَيَتَفَكَّرُوْنَ فِيْ خَلْقِ السَّمٰوٰتِ وَالْاَرْضِ ۚ رَبَّنَا مَا
خَلَقْتَ هٰذَا بَاطِلًا ۚ سُبْحٰنَكَ فَقِنَا عَذَابَ النَّارِ ﴿۱۹۲﴾

[a]61 : 3-4. [b]5 : 18-19, 121; 24 : 43; 42 : 50. [c]2 : 165; 3 : 28; 45 : 4—6. [d]4 : 104; 10 : 13; 39 : 10; 62 : 11. [e]38 : 28.

545. *Mafāzah* means, a place or state of security or escape; a means of success and prosperity (Aqrab).

546. The lesson implied in the creation of the heavens and the earth and in the alternation of night and day is that man has been created both for spiritual and temporal progress, and that if he acts righteously, his period of darkness and affliction must needs be followed by one of sunshine and happiness.

547. The grand system to which an allusion has been made in the previous verse could certainly not have been brought into being without a definite purpose. The whole universe having been created to serve man, the creation of man himself must have a great purpose. When man ponders over the spiritual implication of the physical phenomenon of the creation of the universe and the consummate order that pervades it, he is deeply impressed by the great wisdom of the Creator, and from the inmost depths of his being rises the cry : *Our Lord, Thou hast not created this universe in vain.*

193. 'Our Lord, whomsoever Thou causest to enter the Fire, him Thou hast surely disgraced. And the wrongdoers shall have no helpers;

رَبَّنَآ إِنَّكَ مَنْ تُدْخِلِ النَّارَ فَقَدْ أَخْزَيْتَهٗ ۖ وَمَا لِلظّٰلِمِيْنَ مِنْ أَنْصَارٍ ﴿١٩٣﴾

194. 'Our Lord, we have heard a Crier calling *us* unto faith, *saying*, 'Believe ye in your Lord,' and we have believed. Our Lord, forgive us, therefore, our sins[548] and remit from us our evils and in death join us with the righteous;

رَبَّنَآ إِنَّنَا سَمِعْنَا مُنَادِيًا يُّنَادِيْ لِلْإِيْمَانِ أَنْ اٰمِنُوْا بِرَبِّكُمْ فَاٰمَنَّا ۖ رَبَّنَا فَاغْفِرْ لَنَا ذُنُوْبَنَا وَكَفِّرْ عَنَّا سَيِّاٰتِنَا وَتَوَفَّنَا مَعَ الْأَبْرَارِ ﴿١٩٤﴾

195. "Our Lord, give us what Thou hast promised to us through Thy Messengers; and disgrace us not on the Day of Resurrection. Surely, Thou breakest not Thy promise."

رَبَّنَا وَاٰتِنَا مَا وَعَدْتَّنَا عَلٰى رُسُلِكَ وَلَا تُخْزِنَا يَوْمَ الْقِيٰمَةِ ۗ إِنَّكَ لَا تُخْلِفُ الْمِيْعَادَ ﴿١٩٥﴾

196. So their Lord answered their *prayers*, *saying*, [a]I will suffer not the work of any worker from among you, whether male or female, to be lost. You are from one another.[549] [b]Those, therefore, who have emigrated, and have been driven out from their homes, and have been persecuted for My cause, and have fought and been slain, I will surely remit from them their evil deeds and [c]will cause them to enter gardens through which streams flow —a reward from Allāh, and with Allāh is the best of rewards.

فَاسْتَجَابَ لَهُمْ رَبُّهُمْ أَنِّيْ لَآ أُضِيْعُ عَمَلَ عَامِلٍ مِّنْكُمْ مِّنْ ذَكَرٍ أَوْ أُنْثٰى ۚ بَعْضُكُمْ مِّنْ بَعْضٍ ۚ فَالَّذِيْنَ هَاجَرُوْا وَأُخْرِجُوْا مِنْ دِيَارِهِمْ وَأُوْذُوْا فِيْ سَبِيْلِيْ وَقٰتَلُوْا وَقُتِلُوْا لَأُكَفِّرَنَّ عَنْهُمْ سَيِّاٰتِهِمْ وَلَأُدْخِلَنَّهُمْ جَنّٰتٍ تَجْرِيْ مِنْ تَحْتِهَا الْأَنْهٰرُ ۚ ثَوَابًا مِّنْ عِنْدِ اللّٰهِ ۗ وَاللّٰهُ عِنْدَهٗ حُسْنُ الثَّوَابِ ﴿١٩٦﴾

[a]4 : 125; 16 : 98; 20 : 113. [b]16 : 42; 22 : 59,60. [c]See 2 : 26.

548. *Dhunūb*, which generally refers to natural human weaknesses and ordinary mistakes and omissions, may represent those dark recesses of the heart where the heavenly light does not properly reach; while *Sayyi'āt*, which is a comparatively stronger word, may mean the clouds of dust which hide the light of the sun from our view. See also 2 : 82 & 3 : 17.

549. As this *Sūrah* mainly deals with Christian doctrines and ideals and with their way of life, and as Christianity, in spite of the claims of the Christian Church to the contrary, gives woman a status definitely inferior to that of man, the insistence on the equality of the status of woman with that of man in the spiritual sphere forms a befitting sequal to it. The words, *you are from one another*, are intended to emphasize this equality of status of both men and women.

197. [a]Let not the moving about of the disbelievers in the land deceive thee.[550]

لَا يَغُرَّنَّكَ تَقَلُّبُ الَّذِينَ كَفَرُوا فِي الْبِلَادِ ﴿١٩٧﴾

198. *It is* a small *and temporary* advantage,[551] then Hell shall be their abode. What an evil place of rest !

مَتَاعٌ قَلِيلٌ ثُمَّ مَأْوٰىهُمْ جَهَنَّمُ وَبِئْسَ الْمِهَادُ ﴿١٩٨﴾

199. But those who fear their Lord shall have gardens through which streams flow; therein shall they abide—an entertainment[552] from Allāh. And that which is with Allāh is *still* better for the righteous.

لٰكِنِ الَّذِينَ اتَّقَوْا رَبَّهُمْ لَهُمْ جَنّٰتٌ تَجْرِي مِنْ تَحْتِهَا
الْأَنْهٰرُ خٰلِدِينَ فِيهَا نُزُلًا مِّنْ عِنْدِ اللّٰهِ وَمَا عِنْدَ
اللّٰهِ خَيْرٌ لِّلْأَبْرَارِ ﴿١٩٩﴾

200. And, surely, [b]among the People of the Book there are some who believe in Allāh and in what has been sent down to you and in what was sent down to them, humbling themselves before Allāh. They barter not the Signs of Allāh for a paltry price. It is these who shall have their reward with their Lord. Surely, Allāh is Swift in *settling* account.[553]

وَإِنَّ مِنْ أَهْلِ الْكِتٰبِ لَمَنْ يُّؤْمِنُ بِاللّٰهِ وَمَآ أُنْزِلَ
إِلَيْكُمْ وَمَآ أُنْزِلَ إِلَيْهِمْ خٰشِعِينَ لِلّٰهِ لَا يَشْتَرُونَ
بِاٰيٰتِ اللّٰهِ ثَمَنًا قَلِيلًا أُولٰٓئِكَ لَهُمْ أَجْرُهُمْ عِنْدَ
رَبِّهِمْ إِنَّ اللّٰهَ سَرِيعُ الْحِسَابِ ﴿٢٠٠﴾

[a]40 : 5. [b]3 : 111.

550. The verse, apart from its relevance to the time of the Holy Prophet, is appropriately applicable also to the present dazzling material progress of Christian nations in all departments of life, and warns Muslims against being deceived or overawed by the glamour of this transitory and fleeting progress.

551. The prosperity of Christian nations is only temporary, and the verse hints at the dreadful punishment which is in store for them and which has now actually begun to overtake them.

552. *Nuzul*, a noun-infinitive from *Nazala* which means, he alighted; he lodged or settled in a place; signifies (1) a place where guests are lodged; (2) food prepared for guests (Lane).

553. The words, *Allāh is Swift in settling account*, when used in regard to disbelievers, mean that God is Swift in taking account and dealing out punishment; but when used about believers they mean that God is quick in settling accounts and giving rewards.

201. O ye who believe ! be steadfast and strive to excel in steadfastness and *a*be on *your* guard[554] and fear Allāh that you may prosper.[555]	يٰۤاَيُّهَا الَّذِيْنَ اٰمَنُوا اصْبِرُوْا وَصَابِرُوْا وَرَابِطُوْا قف وَاتَّقُوا اللّٰهَ لَعَلَّكُمْ تُفْلِحُوْنَ ﴿۲۰۱﴾

*a*8 : 61.

554. *Rābiṭū* means, persevere in fighting against your enemy or tie your horses in readiness at the frontiers; or apply yourselves constantly and assiduously to the obligations of your religion; or be mindful of the times of Prayer (Lane).

555. The five requisites of success mentioned in the verse are : (1) Exercise of patience and steadfastness ; (2) showing greater patience and greater steadfastness than the enemy; (3) applying oneself constantly and assiduously to the service of one's religion and community; (4) keeping vigilant watch at the frontiers both for the purpose of defence and attack; and (5) leading a life of righteousness. *Ribāṭ* also signifies the human heart. Thus believers are enjoined to be always in a state of readiness to fight internal and external enemies.

——: *o* :——

CHAPTER 4

AL-NISĀ'

(*Revealed after Hijrah*)

Date of Revelation and Context

This *Sūrah* is appropriately entitled Al-Nisā', (The Women) because it deals chiefly with the rights and responsibilities of women and also with their status and position in society. It was revealed at Medina between the third and fifth year of the Hijrah after the Battle of Uḥud and it mainly deals with the subject of widows and orphans who were left behind in large numbers after that battle. Muslims and European scholars are all agreed on this point. Noldeke, the great German Orientalist, however, is inclined to place some of its verses among the Meccan revelations, because, according to him in those verses "the Jews are referred to in a friendly spirit," as they had not yet come into conflict with Muslims. Wherry thinks that the words "O people" in verse 134 show that at least this verse was revealed at Mecca because this form of address has been exclusively used in the Meccan *Sūrahs*. But to say that because a certain verse uses the expression "O people" it must, in spite of all evidence to the contrary, belong to the Meccan period is a mere assertion. The fact is that because at Mecca the number of the believers was very small and they had not yet been welded into a distinct and separate community and very few commandments of the *Sharī'ah* had been revealed, the Meccans—believers and disbelievers—were all addressed together by the words "O People." But as after the Emigration of the Holy Prophet to Medina the commandments of the *Sharī'ah* came thick and fast and an organised community of believers, quite distinct and separate from the disbelievers, had come into existence, they were addressed as "O ye who believe." But where the address is general, applying both to believers and non-believers, the expression "O people" has been used.

The connection of the *Sūrah* with the previous Chapter consists in the fact that in the former *Sūrah* one of the principal subjects dealt with was the Battle of Uḥud while this *Sūrah* deals with the various problems to which that battle gave rise. The *Sūrah* also sheds a flood of light on the evil designs and machinations of the Jews and the Hypocrites of Medina who, after the Battle of Uḥud, seeing that Islâm was gaining great power in the land, mustered all their resources to make a last effort to destroy it root and branch. In a way also the *Sūrah* constitutes an extension of the subject matter of the preceding *Sūrah* in that it demolishes the basic Christian doctrine of Atonement, and establishes that Jesus did not die on the Cross.

Summary of Subject-Matter

As in Āl 'Imrān, the Christian basic doctrines constitute one of the main themes of this *Sūrah* also. But in this *Sūrah* greater space has been assigned to a comparison of the detailed teachings of the two religions—Islām and Christianity—with special reference to the progress and domination of Christianity in the Latter Days. As in the Latter Days, Christian writers and speakers were to profess and proclaim loudly that Islām had degraded woman by giving her a much lower status than man, this *Sūrah* largely deals with the problems concerning females, and a cursory glance over the Quranic teaching about women establishes the fact that even in this respect Islamic teachings are far superior to those of Christianity. And as the subject of orphans is intimately connected with that of women, it has also received special mention in this *Sūrah* which is the first revelation to safeguard their rights and those of women. Women have not only been given all the rights to which they are legitimately entitled, particularly the right of inheritance, but have also been declared to be the sole masters and arbiters of their property. The second main topic dealt with in this *Sūrah* is that of hypocrisy. As in the Latter Days Christianity was to gain world-wide predominance and a large number of Muslims were to live under Christian Governments and, as a result of their subjugation by Christian rulers and their fear of Christian criticism of Islām they were to adopt hypocritical attitude towards their own Faith, the subject of hypocrisy has also been treated in this *Sūrah* along with that of women, and light is thrown on the depths to which a hypocrite can sink morally and spiritually. The hypocrites are warned that shame and abasement would seize them because they fear men more than their Creator. Towards its end the *Sūrah* sheds some light on the subject of Jesus's crucifixion and it is emphatically stated and convincingly established that the belief that Jesus died on the Cross is utterly false and unfounded. Like other human beings he died a natural death, and this false doctrine is belied by proven facts of history, and even the Gospels lend no support to it. The *Sūrah* closes with a brief reversion to the subject of *Kalālah* in order to draw attention to the spiritual heirlessness of Jesus who in a sense was a *Kalālah* inasmuch as he left no spiritual successor, Prophethood having been transferred from the House of Israel to that of Ishmael.

——: *o* :——

سُوْرَةُ النِّسَآءِ مَدَنِيَّةٌ (٤)

1. In the name of Allāh, the Gracious, the Merciful.

بِسْمِ اللّٰهِ الرَّحْمٰنِ الرَّحِيْمِ ①

2. O ye people! [a]fear your Lord [b]Who created you from a single soul[556] and of its *kind* created its mate,[557] and from them twain spread many men and women; and fear Allāh, in Whose name you appeal to one another, and *fear Him particularly respecting* ties of kinship.[558] Verily, Allāh watches over you.

يٰٓاَيُّهَا النَّاسُ اتَّقُوْا رَبَّكُمُ الَّذِيْ خَلَقَكُمْ مِّنْ نَّفْسٍ
وَّاحِدَةٍ وَّخَلَقَ مِنْهَا زَوْجَهَا وَبَثَّ مِنْهُمَا رِجَالًا كَثِيْرًا
وَّنِسَآءً ۚ وَاتَّقُوا اللّٰهَ الَّذِيْ تَسَآءَلُوْنَ بِهٖ وَالْاَرْحَامَ ۗ
اِنَّ اللّٰهَ كَانَ عَلَيْكُمْ رَقِيْبًا ②

3. And [c]give to the orphans their property and exchange not the bad for the good, and devour not their property *by mixing it* with your own. Surely, it is a great sin.[559]

وَاٰتُوا الْيَتٰمٰٓى اَمْوَالَهُمْ وَلَا تَتَبَدَّلُوا الْخَبِيْثَ بِالطَّيِّبِ ۪
وَلَا تَاْكُلُوْٓا اَمْوَالَهُمْ اِلٰٓى اَمْوَالِكُمْ ۗ اِنَّهٗ كَانَ حُوْبًا
كَبِيْرًا ③

[a]33:71; 59:19. [b]7:190; 16:73; 30:22; 39:7. [c]4:11, 128; 6:153; 17:35.

556. "Single soul" may signify: (1) Adam; (2) man and woman taken together, because when two things jointly perform one function, they may be spoken of as one; (3) man and woman taken separately, because mankind may be said to have been created from one "single soul" in the sense that each and every individual is created from the seed of man who is "one soul" and is also born of woman who is likewise "one soul."

557. The words do not mean that woman was created out of the body of man but that she belonged to the same species as man, possessing identical aptitudes and propensities. The idea that Eve had been created out of the rib of Adam seems to have arisen from a saying of the Holy Prophet, *viz.*, "Women have been created from a rib, and surely, the most crooked part of a rib is the highest part thereof. If you set yourself to straighten it, you will break it" (Bukhārī, ch. on *Nikāḥ*). This saying, if anything, constitutes an argument against the above view rather than being in its favour, for it makes no mention of Eve, but only speaks of all women, and it is clear that every woman has not been created from a rib. The word *Ḍil'* used in the above saying of the Prophet signifies a certain crookedness of manners, the word itself meaning crookedness (Bihār & Muḥīṭ). In fact, it refers to a certain peculiarity of woman, *viz.*, her affectation of displeasure and coquetry. This "crookedness" has been spoken of in this saying as the highest or the best trait in her character, and those who take affectation of anger on woman's part as an expression of her real anger and begin to deal harshly with her for that reason, in fact, destroy the most attractive and winning aspect of her personality.

558. The verse places "the fear of God," side by side with "respect for the ties of kinship," thus emphasizing the importance of good treatment of relatives, on which the Qur'ān has laid so much stress. The Holy Prophet used to recite this verse when delivering a marriage sermon in order to remind both the parties of their duties to each other.

559. After mentioning the two favours of God in the previous verse, *viz.*, the multiplication of many men and women from a "single soul," and their preservation from destruction by instituting ties of relationship, the Qur'ān proceeds to emphasize the need of protecting posterity by safeguarding the rights and interests of orphans.

4. And if you fear that you will not be just *in dealing* with the orphans, then marry of *other* women as may be agreeable to you, two, or three, or four;[560] and [a]if you fear you will not be able to do justice,

وَإِنْ خِفْتُمْ أَلَّا تُقْسِطُوا فِي الْيَتٰمٰى فَانْكِحُوا مَا طَابَ لَكُمْ مِّنَ النِّسَآءِ مَثْنٰى وَثُلٰثَ وَرُبٰعَ فَإِنْ خِفْتُمْ

[a]4 : 130.

560. The verse is important inasmuch as it permits polygamy under certain circumstances. Islām allows (though it certainly does not enjoin or encourage) a man to have more than one wife up to four at a time. As this permission has been given in connection with the subject of orphans, it should be taken primarily to be based on the question of the care of that much-neglected class of society. There are cases when the interests of orphans can only be protected by marrying one or more wives from among the female wards or from other women as the exigencies of circumstances may require. Though the verse mentions polygamy in connection with the subject of orphans, yet other situations may arise when it may become a necessary remedy for some social or moral evils. If only the objects of marriage itself are considered, the permission appears to be not only justifiable but in some cases desirable and even necessary; nay, in such cases it may become positively injurious to the best interests of individuals and of the community not to take advantage of this permission. According to the Qur'ān the objects of marriage are four, *viz.*, (1) protection against physical, moral and spiritual maladies (2 : 188; 4 : 25); (2) peace of mind and the availability of a loving companion (30 : 22); (3) procreation of children; and (4) widening of the circle of relationship (4 : 2). Now one or all of the above-mentioned four objects of marriage are sometimes not realized in the case of one wife; for instance, if the wife of a person becomes a permanent invalid or suffers from a contagious disease, the object of marriage is certainly defeated if such a person does not marry another wife. Indeed, no course is left to him but either to contract another lawful marriage or failing successfully to resist the attacks of carnal passions, to lead an immoral life. And an ailing wife cannot make a good companion either, because however worthy of regard and compassion she may be, her company cannot give peace of mind to her husband in all respects. Similarly, if she happens to be barren, the natural and perfectly legitimate desire of the husband to have an issue to succeed him and perpetuate his name remains unfulfilled in the absence of a polygamous marriage. It is to meet such exigencies that Islām has allowed the contraction of plural matrimonial connections. If, however, in any of the above cases a husband divorces his first wife, it would be a shame and disgrace for him. In fact, the objects of a polygamous marriage are, to a certain extent, the same as those of a monogamous marriage. When one or all of these objects are not realized by a monogamous marriage, a polygamous marriage becomes a necessity. There are, however, other reasons also which may sometimes render it necessary for a person to have one or more wives in addition to the one whom he dearly loves and who also fulfils the objects of marriage. Those reasons are: (*a*) to protect orphans; (*b*) to provide husbands for marriageable widows and (*c*) to supplement the depleted manhood of a family or community. It is clear from the verse under comment that polygamy is resorted to particularly with a view to taking under one's protection orphans left unprotected. The verse implies that the mother of such orphans as are left in the guardianship of a person should preferably be married by him so that he should become directly related to, and more intimately connected with, them and thus may become more interested in their welfare than he otherwise would be. To provide husbands for widows (24 : 33) is another object which the institution of polygamy fulfils. Muslims were perpetually engaged in fighting in the time of the Holy Prophet. Many fell in wars and left behind widows and orphans without near relatives to look after them. The preponderance of women over men and an exceptionally large number of orphans with no one to look after them, which is the inevitable result of wars, necessitated that in order to save Muslim society from moral degeneration, polygamous marriages should have been encouraged. The last two World Wars have vindicated this useful institution of Islām. They have left an abnormally large number of young women without husbands. Indeed, the great preponderance of females over males in the West, due to the appalling loss of manhood caused by these Wars, is responsible for the present laxity of morals which is eating into the vitals of Western society. Besides this contingency of providing husbands for young widows the institution of polygamy is also intended to meet the serious

then *marry only* one or *marry* what your right hands possess.[561] Thus it | اَلَّا تَعۡدِلُوۡا فَوَاحِدَةً اَوۡ مَا مَلَكَتۡ اَيۡمَانُكُمۡ ؕ ذٰلِكَ

situation that follows in the wake of a war, when, besides other aspects of decline, the manhood of a nation becomes so depleted as to threaten national destruction. The fall of birth-rate, which is a potent cause of the decay of a people can be effectively remedied only by resorting to polygamy. Polygamous marriages, instead of being an outlet for the gratification of sexual passions as is mistakenly understood, constitute a sacrifice demanded of men and women alike—a sacrifice in which personal and passing sentiments are required to be subordinated to the wider communal or national interests.

561. The expression, *Mā Malakat Aimānukum*, generally signifies, women prisoners of war who are not ransomed and who are in the custody and control of their Muslim captors because they had taken part in a war which was waged to destory Islām and thus had legitimately deprived themselves of their freedom. The term has been used in the Qur'ān in preference to '*Ibād* and *Imā*' (slaves and bondwomen) to point to a just and rightful possession, the expression *Milk Yamīn* signifying full and rightful possession (Lisān). It includes both slaves and bondwomen, and it is only the context which determines what the expression signifies in a particular place. Much misunderstanding prevails as to what the expression "their right hands possess" signifies, and what are the rights and status of the persons to whom it applies. Islām has condemned slavery in unequivocal terms. According to it, it is a mortal sin to deprive a person of his or her liberty, unless, of course, he or she renders himself or herself liable to deprivation of it by taking part in a war waged to destroy Islām or an Islamic State. It is also a grievous sin to buy or sell slaves. Islamic teaching on this point is quite clear, unequivocal and emphatic. According to it a person who makes another person his slave commits a grave sin against God and man (Bukhārī, *Kitāb al-Bai*' & Dawūd as quoted by Fatḥ al-Bārī). It is worthy of note that when Islām came into the world, slavery was an integral part of the human social system and there existed a large number of slaves in every country. It was, therefore, not feasible, nor even wise, to abolish with a stroke of the pen, an institution which had become so inextricably interwoven into the whole texture of human society, without doing serious injury to its moral tone. Islām, therefore, sought to abolish it gradually but effectively and surely. The Qur'ān has laid down the following very sound rules for the speedy and complete abolition of slavery : (1) Prisoners can only be taken after a regular battle. (2) They cannot be retained after the war is over, but (3) are to be set free either as a mark of favour or by exchange of prisoners (47 : 5). Those unfortunate persons, however, who, may fail to gain their freedom through any of these means, or should choose to remain with their Muslim masters, can purchase their emancipation by entering into a contract called *Mukātabah* with them (24 : 34). Now, if a woman is taken prisoner in a war of the nature mentioned above and thus loses her liberty and becomes *Milk Yamīn*, and she fails to get her release by the exchange of prisoners of war, and the exigencies of government also do not justify her immediate release as a mark of favour, nor do her own people or government get her ransomed and she does not even seek to buy her freedom by entering into *Mukātabah*, and her master, in the interest of morality, marries her without her prior consent, in what way can this arrangement be regarded as objectionable?

As regards establishing sexual relations with a female prisoner of war or a slave-wife without marrying her, neither this nor any other verse of the Qur'ān lends any support to it whatever. Not only does the Qur'ān not give any sanction for the treatment of female prisoners of war as wives without taking them into proper wedlock but there are clear and positive injunctions to the effect that these prisoners of war, like free women, should be married if they are to be treated as wives, the only difference between the two being a temporary difference of social status, inasmuch as prior consent of prisoners of war to their marriage which they forfeit by taking part in a war against Islām is not considered necessary as in the case of free women. Thus the expression *Mā Malakat Aimānukum*, signifying female prisoners, according to the Qur'ān, lends no support whatsoever to the view that Islām has upheld concubinage. Besides the present verse, at least in as many as four other verses, the injunction has been laid down in clear and unambiguous terms that female prisoners of war should not remain unmarried (2 : 222; 4 : 4; 4 : 26; 24 : 33). The Holy Prophet is also very explicit on this point. He is reported to have said, "He who has a slave girl, and gives her proper education and brings her up in a becoming manner and then frees and marries her, for him is double reward."

is more likely that you will not do injustice.[562]

أَدْنٰٓى أَلَّا تَعُوْلُوْا ﴿٤﴾

5. And [a]give the women their dowries[563] willingly.[564] But if they, of their own pleasure, remit to you a part thereof, then enjoy it *as something* pleasant and wholesome.

وَاٰتُوا النِّسَآءَ صَدُقٰتِهِنَّ نِحْلَةً ۚ فَاِنْ طِبْنَ لَكُمْ عَنْ شَیْءٍ مِّنْهُ نَفْسًا فَكُلُوْهُ هَنِیْٓـًٔا مَّرِیْٓـًٔا ﴿٥﴾

[a]4 : 25-26 ; 60 : 11.

Bukhārī, *Kitāb al-'Ilm*). This saying of the Holy Prophet implies that if a Muslim wishes to have a slave girl as wife, he should first set her free and then marry her. The Holy Prophet's own practice was quite in harmony with his precept. Two of the Holy Prophet's wives, Juwairiyah and Ṣafiyyah, came to him as prisoners of war. They were his *Milk Yamīn.* But he married them according to Islamic Law. He also married Māriyah who was sent to him by the King of Egypt, and she enjoyed the status of a free wife like the Prophet's other wives. She observed Purdah and was included among "The Mothers of the Faithful." The Qur'ān makes it clear that the commandment regarding marriage applies to "whom your right hands possess" as much as it does to"the daughters of the Holy Prophet's paternal and maternal uncles and aunts." Both are to be wedded before they are treated as wives. All the three categories mentioned above were made lawful to the Holy Prophet through marriage (33:51). Further, the verse "And forbidden to you are married women, except such as your right hands possess" (4:25) along with its preceding one deals with women whom it is unlawful for a man to marry and among these are included married women. But it makes one exception, which is that those married women who are taken prisoner in a religious war and then choose to remain with Muslims, can be married to their masters. The fact that they choose not to go to their former husbands is considered to be tantamount to the annulment of their former marriage.

It may also be noted in passing that it is not permitted to take in marriage such female relations of a bondwoman as correspond to the relations of a free woman within the prohibited degree. For instance, the mothers, sisters, daughters, etc., of a slave wife cannot be taken in marriage. It may further be stated that in view of the circumstances obtaining at the time of its revelation the Qur'ān had to make a distinction between the social status of two classes of women. That distinction was expressed by the word *Zauj* (a free woman taken in marriage) and *Milk Yamīn* (bondwoman taken in marriage). The former word connotes a sense of equality between husband and wife while the latter implies a somewhat inferior status of the wife. That was, however, a temporary phase. The Qur'ān and the Holy Prophet had strongly recommended that bondwomen should first be given full freedom and full status and then married as the Holy Prophet himself had done. Besides, Islām does not allow women taken prisoner in *ordinary* wars to be treated as bondwomen. The permission about marrying a bondwoman without her prior consent comes into operation only when a hostile nation first wages a religious war against Islām in order to extirpate it and to compel Muslims to abandon their religion at the point of the sword and then treats their prisoners—men and women—as slaves, as was done in the time of the Holy Prophet. At that time the enemy took away Muslim women as prisoners and treated them as bondwomen. The Islamic injunction was only a retaliatory measure and was in its very nature temporary. It also served the additional purpose of protecting the morals of captive women. Those conditions have ceased to exist now. There are no religious wars now and hence no prisoners of war to be treated as slaves or bondwomen.

562. *Ta'ūlū* (do injustice) is derived from *'Āla* which means; (1) he had a large family; (2) he supported the family; (3) he was or became poor; (4) he acted wrongfully; or deviated from the right course (Lane).

563. *Ṣaduqāt* is the plural of *Ṣaduqah* which means, dowry or a gift which is given to or for a bride (Lane).

564. The verse may be taken to be addressed to both the husband and the relations of the wife. In the latter case, it would mean that the relations of a woman should not spend

6. And give not to *those who are* weak of understanding[565] your property[566] which Allāh has made for you *a means* of support; but feed them therewith and clothe them and speak to them words of kind advice.

وَلَا تُؤْتُوا السُّفَهَآءَ اَمْوَالَكُمُ الَّتِيْ جَعَلَ اللّٰهُ لَكُمْ
قِيٰمًا وَّارْزُقُوْهُمْ فِيْهَا وَاكْسُوْهُمْ وَقُوْلُوْا لَهُمْ
قَوْلًا مَّعْرُوْفًا ۝٦

7. And test *the understanding of* the orphans until they attain *the age of* marriage, then, if you perceive in them mature judgment,[567] deliver to them their property; and devour it not in extravagance and haste against their growing up.[568] And whoso is rich, let him abstain; and whoso is poor, let him eat *thereof* with equity. And when you deliver to them their property, then call witnesses in their presence.[569] And Allāh is sufficient as a Reckoner.

وَابْتَلُوا الْيَتٰمٰى حَتّٰٓى اِذَا بَلَغُوا النِّكَاحَ ۚ فَاِنْ اٰنَسْتُمْ
مِّنْهُمْ رُشْدًا فَادْفَعُوْٓا اِلَيْهِمْ اَمْوَالَهُمْ ۚ وَلَا تَاْكُلُوْهَآ
اِسْرَافًا وَّبِدَارًا اَنْ يَّكْبَرُوْا ۗ وَمَنْ كَانَ غَنِيًّا فَلْيَسْتَعْفِفْ ۚ
وَمَنْ كَانَ فَقِيْرًا فَلْيَاْكُلْ بِالْمَعْرُوْفِ ۗ فَاِذَا دَفَعْتُمْ
اِلَيْهِمْ اَمْوَالَهُمْ فَاَشْهِدُوْا عَلَيْهِمْ ۗ وَكَفٰى بِاللّٰهِ حَسِيْبًا ۝٧

---

her dowry to meet their own needs, but should faithfully hand it over to her. Primarily, however, the verse is addressed to the husband whom it requires to pay the agreed dowry to his wife willingly, cheerfully and without demur. The words "giving the dowry willingly and cheerfully" also imply that the amount of the dowry should be well within the means of the husband so that its payment may not be a burden to him. He should be in a position to pay it willingly and cheerfully.

565. The words, "who are weak of understanding" have been substituted for "orphans" in the present verse to supply the required reason for the injunction, as well as to make it one of general application, including in its scope all such persons as are unable to take care of their property. In the case of grown-up imbeciles, the verse would be taken to be addressed to the State which should take effective steps to set up institutions like Courts of Wards to look after the property of persons who cannot manage it themselves.

566. The verse speaks of the property of oprhans as "your property," hinting thereby that the guardians of orphans should be very careful about spending their property and should treat it as their own. The expression "your property" may also signify "the property of the orphans which are in your custody." It is also possible that the expression has been used here to include all property whether belonging to the orphans or to their guardians.

567. Under no circumstances should the property of the orphans be made over to them before they attain puberty and are so mature of intellect as to take care of and properly manage it.

568. The verse also warns guardians not to squander away in haste the money of their wards before they are old enough to take charge of it. The guardian, if he is poor, is, however, allowed a reasonable wage, which should be in proportion to the amount of work he does and to the value of the ward's property.

569. The property should be handed over to the wards in the presence of reliable witnesses as the word "presence" hints.

8. [a]For men is a share of that which parents and near relations leave ; and for women is a share of that which parents and near relations leave, whether it be little or much—a determined share.[570]

لِلرِّجَالِ نَصِيبٌ مِّمَّا تَرَكَ الْوَالِدٰنِ وَالْأَقْرَبُونَ وَلِلنِّسَآءِ نَصِيبٌ مِّمَّا
تَرَكَ الْوَالِدٰنِ وَالْأَقْرَبُونَ مِمَّا قَلَّ مِنْهُ أَوْ كَثُرَ نَصِيبًا مَّفْرُوضًا ﴿٨﴾

9. And when *other* relations and orphans and the poor[571] are present at the division *of the heritage*, give them *something* therefrom and speak to[571A] them words of kindness.

وَإِذَا حَضَرَ الْقِسْمَةَ أُولُوا الْقُرْبٰى وَالْيَتٰمٰى وَالْمَسٰكِينُ
فَارْزُقُوهُم مِّنْهُ وَقُولُوا لَهُمْ قَوْلًا مَّعْرُوفًا ﴿٩﴾

10. And let those fear *Allāh* who, if they should leave behind them weak offspring, would be afraid on their account. Let them, therefore, fear Allāh and let them say the right word.[572]

وَلْيَخْشَ الَّذِينَ لَوْ تَرَكُوا مِنْ خَلْفِهِمْ ذُرِّيَّةً ضِعٰفًا
خَافُوا عَلَيْهِمْ فَلْيَتَّقُوا اللّٰهَ وَلْيَقُولُوا قَوْلًا سَدِيدًا ﴿١٠﴾

11. Surely, [b]they who devour the property of orphans unjustly, only swallow fire into their bellies, and they shall burn in a blazing fire.

إِنَّ الَّذِينَ يَأْكُلُونَ أَمْوٰلَ الْيَتٰمٰى ظُلْمًا إِنَّمَا يَأْكُلُونَ
فِي بُطُونِهِمْ نَارًا وَسَيَصْلَوْنَ سَعِيرًا ﴿١١﴾ ع

R. 2 12. Allāh commands you concerning your children ; a [c]male shall have as much as the share of two females; but if there be females *only*, *numbering* more than two, then they shall have two-thirds of what the *deceased* leave; and if there be one, she shall have the half. And his parents[573] each of them a sixth of the inheritance, if he have a

يُوصِيكُمُ اللّٰهُ فِي أَوْلٰدِكُمْ لِلذَّكَرِ مِثْلُ حَظِّ الْأُنْثَيَيْنِ
فَإِنْ كُنَّ نِسَآءً فَوْقَ اثْنَتَيْنِ فَلَهُنَّ ثُلُثَا مَا تَرَكَ
وَإِنْ كَانَتْ وٰحِدَةً فَلَهَا النِّصْفُ وَلِأَبَوَيْهِ لِكُلِّ
وٰحِدٍ مِّنْهُمَا السُّدُسُ مِمَّا تَرَكَ إِنْ كَانَ لَهُ وَلَدٌ

[a]4 : 34. [b]See 4 : 3. [c]4 : 177.

570. This verse forms the basis of the Islamic Law of Inheritance. It lays down the general principle of the social equality of man and woman. Both are entitled to a suitable share in the property. Detailed rules are given in the verses that follow.

571. By the words, *other relations and orphans and the poor*, are here meant those distant relatives and orphans and poor persons, who, being not included among the deceased's legal heirs, are not entitled to receive any part of his property as of right. The verse, though not giving a legal right of inheritance to them, exhorts Muslims, while making a will about the division of their property, to set apart a portion of it for them.

571A. *La-hum*, may also mean, in their favour.

572. The verse contains a strong and highly forceful appeal in favour of the orphans.

573. Father and mother both (Lane).

child,[574] but if he have no child and his parents be his heirs, then his mother shall have a third; and if he have brothers and sisters, then his mother shall have a sixth, after *the payment of* any bequests he may have bequeathed or of debts. Your fathers and your children; you know not which of them is more beneficent to you. *This* fixing *of portions*[574A] is from Allāh. Surely, Allāh is All-Knowing, Wise.

فَاِنْ لَّمْ يَكُنْ لَّهٗ وَلَدٌ وَّوَرِثَهٗٓ اَبَوٰهُ فَلِاُمِّهِ الثُّلُثُ ۚ
فَاِنْ كَانَ لَهٗٓ اِخْوَةٌ فَلِاُمِّهِ السُّدُسُ مِنْۢ بَعْدِ وَصِيَّةٍ
يُّوْصِيْ بِهَآ اَوْ دَيْنٍ ؕ اٰبَآؤُكُمْ وَاَبْنَآؤُكُمْ لَا تَدْرُوْنَ
اَيُّهُمْ اَقْرَبُ لَكُمْ نَفْعًا ؕ فَرِيْضَةً مِّنَ اللّٰهِ ؕ اِنَّ اللّٰهَ كَانَ
عَلِيْمًا حَكِيْمًا ﴿۱۲﴾

574. *Walad* means, (1) a child, son, daughter or a young one; (2) children, sons, daughters, offspring or young ones. The word is used both as singular and plural, feminine and masculine (Lane).

574A. The verse prescribes suitable shares for all near relatives in the property of a deceased person without distinction of sex or order of birth. Children, parents, husbands and wives are the principal heirs who, if alive, get suitable shares in all circumstances, other relations having a title only in special cases. A male has been given double the share of a female because he has been made responsible for the maintenance of his family (Ma'ānī, ii. p. 32). The verse begins by laying down a general rule as to the proportion of shares between sons and daughters. A son is to have as much as two daughters. So, wherever there are both sons and daughters, this rule will come in force. When, however, there are only daughters and no son, the verse allots two-thirds of the legacy to the daughters, if there are more than two of them; and one-half if there is only one. The share of daughters in case there are two is not expressly stated. But the use of the conjunction *fā'* (but) in the clause, *but if there be females only, numbering more than two*, clearly points to the fact that the share of two females has been referred to in the preceding words "two females." Moreover, the share of two females can be gathered from what has already been said in the beginning of the verse about the ratio between the shares of the males and the females. According to that ratio, a son is to have as much as two daughters. Thus, if there be one son and one daughter, the son will have two-third. But as the share of one son has been made equal to that of "two daughters," the latter, in case there is no son, will have two-thirds, *viz.*, the same share as has been expressly fixed for three daughters. Thus, the very construction of the verse shows that if there be two daughters and no son, they, too, as in the case of three daughters, will get two-thirds. If it had not been the object of the Qur'ān to point to the share of two daughters in the clause, the words would have been something like this, "a male shall have twice as much as a female," and not as it is now. The verse speaks of three cases as regards the share of the parents: (1) If a person dies leaving one or more children, then each of his parents shall have one-sixth. (2) If a person dies issueless and his parents are the sole heirs (there being no wife or husband of the deceased person). then the mother will have one-third of the property and the remaining two-thirds will go to the father. (3) There is a third case, which is really an exception to the second case. A man dies without issue and his parents are his sole heirs, but he has brothers or sisters. Then, although his brothers or sisters will not inherit from him, yet their presence will affect the share of the parents, for, in this case, the mother will have one-sixth (instead of one-third, as in the second case) and the remaining five-sixths will go to the father. The reason why the father is awarded a larger share in this case is that the father has also to support the brothers or sisters of the deceased. The subject of inheritance is continued in the succeeding verse.

13. And you shall have half of that which your wives leave, if they have no child; but if they have a child, then you shall have a fourth of that which they leave, after *the payment of* any bequests they may have bequeathed or of debts. And they shall have a fourth of that which you leave, if you have no child; but if you have a child, then they shall have an eighth of that which you leave, after *the payment of* any bequests you may have bequeathed or of debt. [a]And if there be a man or a woman whose heritage is to be divided and he *or she* has neither parent nor child,[575] and he *or she* has a brother and a sister, then each one of them shall have a sixth. But if they be more than that, then they shall be *equal* sharers in one-third, after *the payment of* any bequests which may have been bequeathed or of debt. *And all this shall be* without *intent to cause* injury to any one.[575A] *This is* an injunction from Allāh and Allāh is Wise, Forbearing.

وَلَكُمْ نِصْفُ مَا تَرَكَ اَزْوَاجُكُمْ اِنْ لَّمْ يَكُنْ لَّهُنَّ
وَلَدٌ ۚ فَاِنْ كَانَ لَهُنَّ وَلَدٌ فَلَكُمُ الرُّبُعُ مِمَّا تَرَكْنَ
مِنْۢ بَعْدِ وَصِيَّةٍ يُّوْصِيْنَ بِهَآ اَوْ دَيْنٍ ۗ وَلَهُنَّ الرُّبُعُ
مِمَّا تَرَكْتُمْ اِنْ لَّمْ يَكُنْ لَّكُمْ وَلَدٌ ۚ فَاِنْ كَانَ لَكُمْ وَلَدٌ
فَلَهُنَّ الثُّمُنُ مِمَّا تَرَكْتُمْ مِّنْۢ بَعْدِ وَصِيَّةٍ تُوْصُوْنَ
بِهَآ اَوْ دَيْنٍ ۗ وَاِنْ كَانَ رَجُلٌ يُّوْرَثُ كَلٰلَةً اَوِ امْرَاَةٌ
وَّلَهٗٓ اَخٌ اَوْ اُخْتٌ فَلِكُلِّ وَاحِدٍ مِّنْهُمَا السُّدُسُ ۚ فَاِنْ
كَانُوْٓا اَكْثَرَ مِنْ ذٰلِكَ فَهُمْ شُرَكَآءُ فِي الثُّلُثِ مِنْۢ
بَعْدِ وَصِيَّةٍ يُّوْصٰى بِهَآ اَوْ دَيْنٍ ۙ غَيْرَ مُضَآرٍّ ۚ وَصِيَّةً
مِّنَ اللّٰهِ ۗ وَاللّٰهُ عَلِيْمٌ حَلِيْمٌ ﴿١٣﴾

[a]4 : 177.

575. *Kalālah* is (1) a person who leaves behind neither parent nor child, male or female; (2) a person who leaves behind neither father nor son. According to Ibn 'Abbās he is a person who leaves no son irrespective of the fact whether his father is living or not. This would thus be the third meaning of the word (Lane & Mufradāt). The brothers and sisters of a *Kalālah* fall under three heads: first, real brothers or sisters—offspring of the same parents (such brothers or sisters are technically known as *A'yānī*); secondly, brothers and sisters on the side of the father only (these are technically known as *'Allātī*); thirdly, brothers and sisters on the side of the mother only, their father being not the same as that of the deceased (such brothers and sisters are technically called *Akhyāfī*). It is to the last-mentioned class that the commandment given in the present verse pertains; the law with regard to the first two classes of brothers and sisters having been given in the last verse of this *Sūrah*. The shares allotted to the brothers and sisters of the last-mentioned class are smaller than those allotted to the brothers and sisters of the first two classes, the reason being that the brothers and sisters of this class are on the side of the mother only, while the brothers and the sisters of the other two classes are the children of the same father as the deceased. In the property of a person who died as a *Kalālah* both brothers and sisters have equal shares, the usual ratio of two to one being not observed in their case.

575A. The words, "without intent to cause injury to any one" are important. They mean that the payment of debts should not suffer by the payment of bequests. In other words, debts are to be paid prior to the payment of bequests.

14. These are the limits *set* by Allāh; and [a]whoso obeys Allāh and His Messenger, [b]He will make him enter Gardens through which streams flow; therein shall they abide; and that is a great triumph.

تِلْكَ حُدُوْدُ اللّٰهِ ۚ وَمَنْ يُّطِعِ اللّٰهَ وَرَسُوْلَهٗ يُدْخِلْهُ
جَنّٰتٍ تَجْرِيْ مِنْ تَحْتِهَا الْاَنْهٰرُ خٰلِدِيْنَ فِيْهَا ۚ وَ
ذٰلِكَ الْفَوْزُ الْعَظِيْمُ ﴿۱۴﴾

15. [c]And whoso disobeys Allāh and His Messenger and transgresses His limits, He will make him enter into the Fire; therein he shall abide; and he shall have an humiliating punishment.

وَمَنْ يَّعْصِ اللّٰهَ وَرَسُوْلَهٗ وَيَتَعَدَّ حُدُوْدَهٗ يُدْخِلْهُ
نَارًا خَالِدًا فِيْهَا ۪ وَلَهٗ عَذَابٌ مُّهِيْنٌ ﴿۱۵﴾

R. 3 16. [d]And such of your women as are guilty of *any* flagrant impropriety[576]— call to witness four of you against them; and if they bear witness, then confine them to the houses until death overtakes them or Allāh opens for them some other way.

وَالّٰتِيْ يَاْتِيْنَ الْفَاحِشَةَ مِنْ نِّسَآئِكُمْ فَاسْتَشْهِدُوْا
عَلَيْهِنَّ اَرْبَعَةً مِّنْكُمْ ۚ فَاِنْ شَهِدُوْا فَاَمْسِكُوْهُنَّ
فِي الْبُيُوْتِ حَتّٰى يَتَوَفّٰىهُنَّ الْمَوْتُ اَوْ يَجْعَلَ اللّٰهُ
لَهُنَّ سَبِيْلًا ﴿۱۶﴾

17. And if two[577] from among you are guilty of it, punish them both. And if they repent and amend, then leave them alone; surely, Allāh is Oft-Returning *with compassion and is ever* Merciful.

وَالَّذٰنِ يَاْتِيٰنِهَا مِنْكُمْ فَاٰذُوْهُمَا ۚ فَاِنْ تَابَا وَاَصْلَحَا
فَاَعْرِضُوْا عَنْهُمَا ۗ اِنَّ اللّٰهَ كَانَ تَوَّابًا رَّحِيْمًا ﴿۱۷﴾

---

[a]3 : 133; 8 : 21; 33 : 72. [b]See 2 : 26. [c]72 : 24. [d]4 : 20,26; 24 : 20.

---

576. *Fāḥishah* as used in the Qur'ān (7 : 29; 33 : 31; 65 : 2) does not necessarily mean fornication or adultery for which punishment is prescribed in 24 : 3. The word refers to any glaringly improper conduct which may disturb social relations and may lead to breaches of the peace. The women referred to in this verse, as the men in the next in which similar offence with an undefined punishment is mentioned, are those guilty of foul or immoral conduct short of fornication or adultery. This is the view also of Abū Muslim and Mujāhid. Such women should be prevented from mixing with other women until they reform themselves or get married, marriage being the way opened for them by Allāh. As the offence mentioned is a serious one, four witnesses are considered necessary lest injustice be done to women reported against.

577. The word *Alladhāni* does not necessarily imply two males. What particular form the punishment mentioned here should take is left to the discretion of the authorities concerned. Both this and the preceding verse refer to offences for which no punishment has been fixed by the Law, the matter having been left to the discretion of the authorities to be decided according to the circumstances then obtaining. The verse may also refer to two males being guilty of an unnatural offence or something approaching it.

18. Verily, [a]Allāh accepts the repentance of only those who do evil in ignorance[578] and then repent soon after.[579] These are they to whom Allāh turns with mercy; and Allāh is All-Knowing, Wise.

إِنَّمَا التَّوْبَةُ عَلَى اللّٰهِ لِلَّذِيْنَ يَعْمَلُوْنَ السُّوْٓءَ بِجَهَالَةٍ
ثُمَّ يَتُوْبُوْنَ مِنْ قَرِيْبٍ فَاُولٰٓئِكَ يَتُوْبُ اللّٰهُ عَلَيْهِمْ ۭ
وَكَانَ اللّٰهُ عَلِيْمًا حَكِيْمًا ﴿۱۸﴾

19. There is no *acceptance of* repentance for those who continue to do evil until, when death faces one of them, he says, 'I do *indeed* repent now;' [b]nor for those who die disbelievers. It is these for whom We have prepared a painful punishment.

وَلَيْسَتِ التَّوْبَةُ لِلَّذِيْنَ يَعْمَلُوْنَ السَّيِّاٰتِ ۚ حَتّٰٓى اِذَا
حَضَرَ اَحَدَهُمُ الْمَوْتُ قَالَ اِنِّيْ تُبْتُ الْـٰٔنَ وَلَا
الَّذِيْنَ يَمُوْتُوْنَ وَهُمْ كُفَّارٌ ۭ اُولٰٓئِكَ اَعْتَدْنَا
لَهُمْ عَذَابًا اَلِيْمًا ﴿۱۹﴾

20. O ye who believe, it is not lawful for you to inherit women against their will; nor should you detain them *wrongfully* that you may take away part of that which you have given them, except that [c]they be guilty of a flagrant impropriety,[580] and consort with them in kindness,[581] and [d]if you dislike them, it may be that you dislike a thing wherein Allāh has placed much good.

يٰٓاَيُّهَا الَّذِيْنَ اٰمَنُوْا لَا يَحِلُّ لَكُمْ اَنْ تَرِثُوا النِّسَآءَ كَرْهًا ۭ
وَلَا تَعْضُلُوْهُنَّ لِتَذْهَبُوْا بِبَعْضِ مَآ اٰتَيْتُمُوْهُنَّ
اِلَّآ اَنْ يَّاْتِيْنَ بِفَاحِشَةٍ مُّبَيِّنَةٍ ۚ وَعَاشِرُوْهُنَّ بِالْمَعْرُوْفِ ۚ
فَاِنْ كَرِهْتُمُوْهُنَّ فَعَسٰٓى اَنْ تَكْرَهُوْا شَيْـًٔا وَّيَجْعَلَ اللّٰهُ
فِيْهِ خَيْرًا كَثِيْرًا ﴿۲۰﴾

[a]6 : 55; 16 : 120; 24 : 6. [b]2 :62; 3 : 92; 47 : 43. [c]See 4 : 16. [d]2 : 217.

578. The words "in ignorance" do not mean that the offenders do evil without knowing that it is evil. In fact, every evil deed which a man does is an act done in ignorance, born of lack of proper and adequate knowledge. The Holy Prophet is reported to have said, "There are some kinds of knowledge which are really ignorance," *i.e.*, the learning of which is injurious to man (Biḥār). So the words "in ignorance" have been added to point to the nature and philosophy of sin and to exhort people to acquire useful knowledge with a view to avoiding sin.

579. The words "soon after" here mean "before death." The next verse which says "who continue to do evil until when death faces one of them," supports this meaning.

580. The deceased person's relatives cannot prevent his widow from contracting a new marriage so that they may get hold of her property; but they can prevent her from doing so if she intends to marry a person of manifestly objectionable character. If the address is to the husbands, the verse would mean that if the wives do not want to live with their husbands and seek separation from them, which they can do by means of *Khul'*, the husbands should not prevent them from doing so out of greed for their money. But they can do so, if the wives are going to be guilty of a manifestly foul act.

581. The Holy Prophet is reported to have said, 'The best among you is he who treats his wife best' (Bukhārī). The expression *'Āshirūhunna* being of the measure *Mufā'alah* denotes reciprocity; husbands and wives are both enjoined to live amicably with each other and reciprocate each other's love.

21. And if you desire to take one wife in place of another and you have given one of them a treasure,[582] take not aught therefrom. Will you take it by false accusation and manifest sinfulness?

وَاِنْ اَرَدْتُّمُ اسْتِبْدَالَ زَوْجٍ مَّكَانَ زَوْجٍ ۙ وَّ
اٰتَيْتُمْ اِحْدٰىهُنَّ قِنْطَارًا فَلَا تَاْخُذُوْا مِنْهُ شَيْـًٔا ؕ
اَتَاْخُذُوْنَهٗ بُهْتَانًا وَّاِثْمًا مُّبِيْنًا ﴿۲۱﴾

22. And how can you take it when one of you may have consorted with the other,[583] and they (the women) have taken from you a strong covenant?[584]

وَكَيْفَ تَاْخُذُوْنَهٗ وَقَدْ اَفْضٰى بَعْضُكُمْ اِلٰى بَعْضٍ
وَّاَخَذْنَ مِنْكُمْ مِّيْثَاقًا غَلِيْظًا ﴿۲۲﴾

23. And marry not those women whom your fathers married, except what has already passed.[585] It is a thing foul and hateful and an evil way.

وَلَا تَنْكِحُوْا مَا نَكَحَ اٰبَآؤُكُمْ مِّنَ النِّسَآءِ اِلَّا مَا قَدْ
سَلَفَ ؕ اِنَّهٗ كَانَ فَاحِشَةً وَّمَقْتًا ؕ وَسَآءَ سَبِيْلًا ﴿۲۳﴾

R. 4 24. Forbidden to you are your mothers,[586] and your daughters, and your sisters, and your fathers' sisters, and your mothers' sisters, and brother's daughters, and sister's daughters, and your *foster-mothers* that have given you suck,[587] and your foster-sisters, and the

حُرِّمَتْ عَلَيْكُمْ اُمَّهٰتُكُمْ وَبَنٰتُكُمْ وَاَخَوٰتُكُمْ وَعَمّٰتُكُمْ
وَخٰلٰتُكُمْ وَبَنٰتُ الْاَخِ وَبَنٰتُ الْاُخْتِ وَاُمَّهٰتُكُمُ
الّٰتِيْٓ اَرْضَعْنَكُمْ وَاَخَوٰتُكُمْ مِّنَ الرَّضَاعَةِ وَاُمَّهٰتُ

---

582. If for some special reason a man wishes to divorce one wife and marry another, he is not allowed to take back from the former what he has already given her, no matter how big the sum may be.

583. These words do not necessarily imply sexual intercourse. They mean living with each other and meeting each other in private on terms of extreme intimacy. According to this verse, a man cannot take back from his wife any property or money he may have given her, even though he may not have gone in unto her.

584. Women are not slaves of the whims or caprices of men. Both are bound by a sacred contract and men owe to their wives obligations which they must respect because, as regards their social rights, both are on much the same level. Men are warned here not to treat light-heartedly the covenant—the tie of marriage—they have made with their wives.

585. The words do not mean that step-mothers taken as wives or two sisters taken in marriage together before this verse was revealed could be retained. What they mean is simply this that if such men repent and make amends, no harm will come to them for what unlawful acts they might have committed in the past. The past will be forgiven but the women whom it is unlawful to marry are to be divorced at once.

586. The Holy Prophet is reported to have said that the relatives of foster-mothers are as forbidden as those within the prohibited degrees of relationship of real mothers. It is not lawful to marry foster-sisters and foster daughters and so on.

587. Theologians differ as to what number of sucks makes the marriage of foster-mothers and foster-sisters and their relations (within prohibited degrees of marriage) unlawful.

mothers of your wives, and your step-daughters, who are your wards being *born* of your wives to whom you have gone in—but if you have not gone in unto them, there is no blame on you—and the wives of your sons that are from your loins; and *it is forbidden to you* to have two sisters together *in marriage*, except what has already passed; surely, Allāh is Most Forgiving, Ever Merciful.

نِسَآئِكُمْ وَرَبَآئِبُكُمُ الّٰتِيْ فِيْ حُجُوْرِكُمْ مِّنْ نِّسَآئِكُمُ
الّٰتِيْ دَخَلْتُمْ بِهِنَّ فَاِنْ لَّمْ تَكُوْنُوْا دَخَلْتُمْ بِهِنَّ فَلَا
جُنَاحَ عَلَيْكُمْ وَحَلَآئِلُ اَبْنَآئِكُمُ الَّذِيْنَ مِنْ
اَصْلَابِكُمْ وَاَنْ تَجْمَعُوْا بَيْنَ الْاُخْتَيْنِ اِلَّا مَا قَدْ
سَلَفَ اِنَّ اللّٰهَ كَانَ غَفُوْرًا رَّحِيْمًا ﴿٢٤﴾

PART V.

25. And *forbidden to you are* married women,[588] except such as your right hands possess.[589] This has Allāh enjoined on you. And allowed to you are those beyond that, that you seek *them* by means of your property, [a]marrying them properly and not committing fornication. And for the benefit you receive from them,[590] [b]give them their dowries, as fixed, and there is no blame on you what you do by mutual agreement after the fixing *of the dowry*. Surely, Allāh is All-Knowing, Wise.

الجزء ٥
وَّالْمُحْصَنٰتُ مِنَ النِّسَآءِ اِلَّا مَا مَلَكَتْ اَيْمَانُكُمْ
كِتٰبَ اللّٰهِ عَلَيْكُمْ وَاُحِلَّ لَكُمْ مَّا وَرَآءَ ذٰلِكُمْ اَنْ
تَبْتَغُوْا بِاَمْوَالِكُمْ مُّحْصِنِيْنَ غَيْرَ مُسٰفِحِيْنَ فَمَا
اسْتَمْتَعْتُمْ بِهٖ مِنْهُنَّ فَاٰتُوْهُنَّ اُجُوْرَهُنَّ فَرِيْضَةً
وَلَا جُنَاحَ عَلَيْكُمْ فِيْمَا تَرٰضَيْتُمْ بِهٖ مِنْ بَعْدِ الْفَرِيْضَةِ
اِنَّ اللّٰهَ كَانَ عَلِيْمًا حَكِيْمًا ﴿٢٥﴾

---

[a]4 : 26; 5 : 6. [b]4 : 5; 560 : 11.

---

588. *Muḥṣanāt* is the plural of *Muḥṣanah* which means, a married woman; a free woman; a chaste woman (Lane).

589. This means that whereas a woman who is already married to a man cannot be taken in marriage by another person, an exception is made here in case of women who are taken prisoner in a war waged by a non-Muslim State against an Islamic State. This is the significance of the words *Mā Malakat Aimānukum*. Such married women, if they become converted to Islām and therefore could not be sent back to their non-Muslim husbands, may be married to Muslim husbands. For a detailed note on "What your right hands possess" see 561.

590. *Tamatta'a bi'l Mar'ati* means, he benefited by the woman temporarily. *Istamta'a bi Kadhā* means, he benefited by it for a long time. The Arabic idiom does not countenance the use of *Istimtā'* with regard to a woman in the sense of temporary connection (Lisān). It may also be noted that whenever the noun *Tamattu'* is used to denote temporary connection with a woman, it is followed by the preposition *bā'* put before the word standing for the woman, as in the above example. An Arab poet says, *Tamatta' bihā mā Sā'afatka wa la Takun 'alaika Shajan fi'l Ḥalqi hīna Tabīnū* (Ḥamasah), *i.e.*, be benefited by her as long as she is agreeable to you, but when she gets separated from you, do not let her be a source of

26. And whoso of you cannot afford to marry free believing women, *let him marry* what your right hands possess, *namely*, your believing hand-maids.[591] And Allāh knows your faith best; you are *all* one from another; so marry them with the leave of their masters and give them their dowries according to what is fair, they being chaste, not committing fornication, nor taking secret paramours.[591A] And if, after they are married, [a]they are guilty of lewdness, they shall have half the punishment prescribed for free married women.[592] This is for him among you who fears lest he should commit sin. And that you restrain yourselves is better for you; and Allāh is Most Forgiving, Merciful.

وَمَنْ لَّمْ يَسْتَطِعْ مِنْكُمْ طَوْلًا اَنْ يَّنْكِحَ الْمُحْصَنٰتِ
الْمُؤْمِنٰتِ فَمِنْ مَّا مَلَكَتْ اَيْمَانُكُمْ مِّنْ فَتَيٰتِكُمُ
الْمُؤْمِنٰتِ ؕ وَاللّٰهُ اَعْلَمُ بِاِيْمَانِكُمْ ؕ بَعْضُكُمْ مِّنْۢ
بَعْضٍ ۚ فَانْكِحُوْهُنَّ بِاِذْنِ اَهْلِهِنَّ وَاٰتُوْهُنَّ
اُجُوْرَهُنَّ بِالْمَعْرُوْفِ مُحْصَنٰتٍ غَيْرَ مُسٰفِحٰتٍ
وَّلَا مُتَّخِذٰتِ اَخْدَانٍ ۚ فَاِذَاۤ اُحْصِنَّ فَاِنْ اَتَيْنَ
بِفَاحِشَةٍ فَعَلَيْهِنَّ نِصْفُ مَا عَلَى الْمُحْصَنٰتِ مِنَ
الْعَذَابِ ؕ ذٰلِكَ لِمَنْ خَشِيَ الْعَنَتَ مِنْكُمْ ؕ وَاَنْ
تَصْبِرُوْا خَيْرٌ لَّكُمْ ؕ وَاللّٰهُ غَفُوْرٌ رَّحِيْمٌ ﴿٢٦﴾ ع ٤

[a]4 : 16, 20; 24 : 20.

constant trouble for you like a piece of bone which remains stuck in the throat. But in this verse the pronoun *Hunna* referring to women is preceded by the preposition *min*. Misunderstanding about *Mut'ah* seems to have arisen from the failure to understand the difference between the words *Tamattu'* and *Istimtā'*. The author of Lisān quotes Zajjāj as saying: "Owing to their ignorance of the Arabic language. some persons have inferred from this verse the legality of *Mut'ah* which, by the consensus of opinion among Muslim theologians, has been declared to be unlawful, the words *Fa-mastamta'tum bihī Minhunna* simply meaning marriage, performed in accordance with the conditions mentioned above." If there had been any reference to *Mut'ah* here, the preposition used ought to have been *bā'* and not *min*. Moreover, the word used is *Istamta'a* and not *Ṭamatta'a* which possesses a sense different from that of the former word. Nor can any inference in favour of *Mut'ah* be drawn from the word *Ujūrahunna* which means "their dowries," the sense in which it has also been used in the Qur'ān (33 : 51). Thus the Qur'ān positively forbids *Mut'ah* and regards all sexual relations outside proper wedlock (*Iḥṣān*) as adultery.

591. In Islām no stigma attaches to the status of a handmaid as such; but owing to her relationships and associations she may not prove such a perfect companion as a free believing woman.

591A. This means that only such of them may be married as are chaste and virtuous. Once they are married their dowries must be paid just as in the case of free women.

592. The verse has laid down three vital principles: (*a*) Bondwomen should be properly married before conjugal relations are had with them. This is also clear from 2 : 222; 4 : 4; and 24 : 33. Thus Islām has cut at the root of concubinage which was so prevalent in Arab society before its advent. (*b*) If they commit adultery, bondwomen are to have half the punishment which is 100 stripes for free women for the same offence which shows that stoning to death is not the punishment for adultery, as mistakenly understood, because stoning to death cannot be halved. (*c*) Incidentally, the verse seems to indicate that a bondwoman taken in marriage had a lower social status in Arab society than a free woman taken in marriage, perhaps because of her having taken part in a war waged to destroy an Islamic State.

R. 5

27. ᵃAllāh desires to make clear to you, and guide you to, the paths of those before you and to turn to you in mercy. And Allāh is All-Knowing, Wise.

يُرِيْدُ اللّٰهُ لِيُبَيِّنَ لَكُمْ وَيَهْدِيَكُمْ سُنَنَ الَّذِيْنَ مِنْ قَبْلِكُمْ وَيَتُوْبَ عَلَيْكُمْ ۚ وَاللّٰهُ عَلِيْمٌ حَكِيْمٌ ۝

28. ᵇAnd Allāh wishes to turn to you in mercy, but those who follow *their low* desires wish that you should incline wholly *towards* evil.

وَاللّٰهُ يُرِيْدُ اَنْ يَّتُوْبَ عَلَيْكُمْ ۗ وَيُرِيْدُ الَّذِيْنَ يَتَّبِعُوْنَ الشَّهَوٰتِ اَنْ تَمِيْلُوْا مَيْلًا عَظِيْمًا ۝

29. Allāh desires to lighten your burden, for man has been created weak.⁵⁹³

يُرِيْدُ اللّٰهُ اَنْ يُّخَفِّفَ عَنْكُمْ ۚ وَخُلِقَ الْاِنْسَانُ ضَعِيْفًا ۝

30. O ye who believe! ᶜdevour not your property among yourselves by unlawful means, except that *you earn* by trade with mutual consent. And kill not your people. Surely, Allāh is Merciful towards you.

يٰٓاَيُّهَا الَّذِيْنَ اٰمَنُوْا لَا تَأْكُلُوْٓا اَمْوَالَكُمْ بَيْنَكُمْ بِالْبَاطِلِ اِلَّآ اَنْ تَكُوْنَ تِجَارَةً عَنْ تَرَاضٍ مِّنْكُمْ ۚ وَلَا تَقْتُلُوْٓا اَنْفُسَكُمْ ۗ اِنَّ اللّٰهَ كَانَ بِكُمْ رَحِيْمًا ۝

31. And whosoever does that by way of transgression and injustice, We shall cast him into Fire; and that is easy for Allāh.

وَمَنْ يَّفْعَلْ ذٰلِكَ عُدْوَانًا وَّظُلْمًا فَسَوْفَ نُصْلِيْهِ نَارًا ۚ وَكَانَ ذٰلِكَ عَلَى اللّٰهِ يَسِيْرًا ۝

32. If you ᵈkeep away from the more grievous⁵⁹⁴ of the things which are forbidden you, We will remove from you your *minor* evils and admit you to a place of great honour.

اِنْ تَجْتَنِبُوْا كَبَآئِرَ مَا تُنْهَوْنَ عَنْهُ نُكَفِّرْ عَنْكُمْ سَيِّاٰتِكُمْ وَنُدْخِلْكُمْ مُّدْخَلًا كَرِيْمًا ۝

ᵃ4 : 177.   ᵇ9 : 104;   33 : 74;   42 : 26.   ᶜ2 : 189.   ᵈ42 : 38;   53 : 33.

---

593. The reason why God has revealed the Law is that man is by nature weak and cannot himself find out the ways of spiritual advancement. God has taken away this burden from him. The verse also constitutes a refutation of the Christian doctrine of Atonement which rejects the Law (Sharī'ah) on the ground of human weakness. As a matter of fact, Islām declares human weakness to be the very reason for the revelation of the Law, so that it may help man to fulfil his high destiny. The Law, therefore, is not a curse but a help and a blessing.

594. There is no classification of less or more grievous sins in the Qur'ān. The term is rather a relative one. The commission of anything forbidden by God is a sin and the commission of all sins which one finds difficult to avoid is grievous. The meaning of the verse seems to be that if a person avoids doing those things the giving up of which seems difficult and burdensome to him, he will be enabled to get rid of other sins as well. Some scholars interpret the word Kabā'ir (grievous sins) as signifying the last stage of each act of sin. If one restrains oneself from committing the final act, the preliminary ones will be forgiven him.

33. And covet not that whereby [a]Allāh has made some of you excel others. Men shall have a share of that which they have earned, and women a share of that which they have earned.[595] And ask Allāh of His bounty. Surely, Allāh has perfect knowledge of all things.

وَلَا تَتَمَنَّوْا مَا فَضَّلَ اللّٰهُ بِهٖ بَعْضَكُمْ عَلٰى بَعْضٍ ؕ
لِلرِّجَالِ نَصِيْبٌ مِّمَّا اكْتَسَبُوْا ؕ وَلِلنِّسَآءِ نَصِيْبٌ مِّمَّا
اكْتَسَبْنَ ؕ وَسْـَٔلُوا اللّٰهَ مِنْ فَضْلِهٖ ؕ اِنَّ اللّٰهَ كَانَ
بِكُلِّ شَيْءٍ عَلِيْمًا ﴿۳۳﴾

34. And [b]to every one We have appointed heirs[596] to what the parents and the relations leave,[597] and *also* those with whom your oaths have ratified a contract. So give them their portion. Surely, Allāh watches over all things.

وَلِكُلٍّ جَعَلْنَا مَوَالِيَ مِمَّا تَرَكَ الْوَالِدٰنِ وَالْاَقْرَبُوْنَ ؕ
وَالَّذِيْنَ عَقَدَتْ اَيْمَانُكُمْ فَاٰتُوْهُمْ نَصِيْبَهُمْ ؕ اِنَّ
اللّٰهَ كَانَ عَلٰى كُلِّ شَيْءٍ شَهِيْدًا ﴿۳۴﴾ ع

R. 6 35. [c]Men are guardians[598] over women because [d]Allāh has made some of them excel others, and because *men* spend *on them* of their wealth. So virtuous women are obedient, and guard the secrets *of their husbands* with Allāh's protection. And *as for* those on whose part you fear disobedience,[599]

اَلرِّجَالُ قَوّٰمُوْنَ عَلَى النِّسَآءِ بِمَا فَضَّلَ اللّٰهُ بَعْضَهُمْ
عَلٰى بَعْضٍ وَّبِمَآ اَنْفَقُوْا مِنْ اَمْوَالِهِمْ ؕ فَالصّٰلِحٰتُ
قٰنِتٰتٌ حٰفِظٰتٌ لِّلْغَيْبِ بِمَا حَفِظَ اللّٰهُ ؕ وَالّٰتِيْ تَخَافُوْنَ

[a]4 : 35. [b]4 : 8. [c]2 : 229. [d]2 : 238; 4 : 33.

595. The verse establishes the equality of men and women so far as their works and rewards are concerned.

596. *Mawālī* is the plural of *Maulā* which among other things means, an heir.

597. Besides the meaning given in the text the words may mean: " To every one We have appointed heirs to what he leaves, they are the parents, the relations and those with whom your oaths have ratified contracts. So give them their portion." The words may also be rendered as, "to everything which parents and relations leave We have appointed heirs, etc."

598. *Qawwāmūn* is derived from *Qāma* and *Qāma* '*Alal-Mar'ati* means, he undertook the maintenance of the woman; he protected her. *Qawwāmūn*, therefore, means, maintainers, managers of affairs; protectors (Lisān). The verse gives two reasons why man has been made the head of the family, (*a*) his superior mental and physical faculties; and (*b*) his being the bread-earner and maintainer of the family. It is, therefore, natural and fair that he, who earns and supplies the money for the maintenance of the family, should enjoy a supervisory status in the disposal of its affairs.

599. *Nashazat al-Mar'atu 'alā Zauji-hā* means, the woman rose against her husband; resisted him; deserted him (Lane & Tāj).

admonish them and keep away from them in their beds[600] and chastise[601] them. Then if they obey you, seek not a way against them. Surely, Allāh is High *and* Great.

نُشُوْزَهُنَّ فَعِظُوْهُنَّ وَاهْجُرُوْهُنَّ فِي الْمَضَاجِعِ
وَاضْرِبُوْهُنَّ ۚ فَإِنْ أَطَعْنَكُمْ فَلَا تَبْغُوْا عَلَيْهِنَّ
سَبِيْلًا ۗ إِنَّ اللّٰهَ كَانَ عَلِيًّا كَبِيْرًا ﴿٣٥﴾

36. And [a]if you[602] fear a breach between them, then appoint an arbiter from his folk and an arbiter from her folk.[603] If they (the arbiters) desire reconciliation, Allāh will effect it between them. Surely, Allāh is All-Knowing, All-Aware.

وَإِنْ خِفْتُمْ شِقَاقَ بَيْنِهِمَا فَابْعَثُوْا حَكَمًا مِّنْ
أَهْلِهٖ وَحَكَمًا مِّنْ أَهْلِهَا ۚ إِنْ يُّرِيْدَآ إِصْلَاحًا يُّوَفِّقِ
اللّٰهُ بَيْنَهُمَا ۗ إِنَّ اللّٰهَ كَانَ عَلِيْمًا خَبِيْرًا ﴿٣٦﴾

37. And [b]worship Allāh and associate naught with Him, and *show* kindness to parents, and to kindred, and orphans, and the needy, and to the neighbour who is a kinsman and the neighbour who is a stranger,[604] and the companion by *your* side, and the wayfarer, and those whom your right hands possess.[605] Surely, Allāh loves not the arrogant *and* the boastful;

وَاعْبُدُوا اللّٰهَ وَلَا تُشْرِكُوْا بِهٖ شَيْـًٔا وَّبِالْوَالِدَيْنِ
إِحْسَانًا وَّبِذِي الْقُرْبٰى وَالْيَتٰمٰى وَالْمَسٰكِيْنِ وَالْجَارِ
ذِي الْقُرْبٰى وَالْجَارِ الْجُنُبِ وَالصَّاحِبِ بِالْجَنْۢبِ
وَابْنِ السَّبِيْلِ ۙ وَمَا مَلَكَتْ أَيْمَانُكُمْ ۗ إِنَّ اللّٰهَ لَا يُحِبُّ
مَنْ كَانَ مُخْتَالًا فَخُوْرَا ۙ﴿٣٧﴾

[a]4 : 129. [b]6 : 152; 7 : 34; 17 : 24, 25; 23 : 60.

600. The clause may signify, (*a*) abstention from conjugal relations; (*b*) sleeping in separate beds; (*c*) ceasing to talk to them. These measures are not to remain in force for an indefinite period, for wives are not to be left *like a thing suspended* (4 : 130). Four months, according to the Qur'ān, is the maximum limit for abstention from conjugal relations, *i.e.*, practical separation (2 : 227). If the husband deems the affair to be sufficiently grave, he will have to observe the conditions mentioned in 4 : 16.

601. The Holy Prophet is reported to have said that if at all a Muslim has to beat his wife, the beating should not be such as to leave any mark on her body (Tirmidhī & Muslim) but the husbands who beat their wives are not the best among men (Kathīr, iii).

602. The pronoun, "you" in the expression, "if you fear" refers to the Muslim State or to the whole community collectively or the people generally.

603. The arbiters should preferably be chosen from the relations of the contending parties, because they are expected to be acquainted with the real causes of differences and because also it is easier for both parties to put their differences before them.

604. After having enjoined in the preceding verses that one should be kind to one's wife, in the present verse the Qur'ān directs a Muslim to make his kindness so comprehensive as to include in its scope the whole of mankind, from parents, who are the nearest, to strangers who are the farthest removed.

605. Slaves, bondwomen, servants, subordinates.

38. [a]Who are niggardly and *also* enjoin people to be niggardly, and hide that which Allāh has given them of His bounty. And We have prepared for the disbelievers an humiliating punishment;

الَّذِينَ يَبْخَلُونَ وَيَأْمُرُونَ النَّاسَ بِالْبُخْلِ وَيَكْتُمُونَ
مَآ اٰتٰهُمُ اللّٰهُ مِنْ فَضْلِهٖ ۗ وَاَعْتَدْنَا لِلْكٰفِرِيْنَ عَذَابًا
مُّهِيْنًا ﴿٣٨﴾

39. And *as for* [b]those who spend their wealth in order to be seen of men, and believe not in Allāh nor the Last Day, *they are the companions of Satan*. And [c]whoso has Satan for a companion, an evil companion is he.

وَالَّذِيْنَ يُنْفِقُوْنَ اَمْوَالَهُمْ رِئَآءَ النَّاسِ وَلَا يُؤْمِنُوْنَ
بِاللّٰهِ وَلَا بِالْيَوْمِ الْاٰخِرِ ۗ وَمَنْ يَّكُنِ الشَّيْطٰنُ لَهٗ قَرِيْنًا
فَسَآءَ قَرِيْنًا ﴿٣٩﴾

40. And what *harm* would have befallen them if they had believed in Allāh and the Last Day and spent out of what Allāh has given them? And Allāh knows them well.

وَمَاذَا عَلَيْهِمْ لَوْ اٰمَنُوْا بِاللّٰهِ وَالْيَوْمِ الْاٰخِرِ وَاَنْفَقُوْا
مِمَّا رَزَقَهُمُ اللّٰهُ ۗ وَكَانَ اللّٰهُ بِهِمْ عَلِيْمًا ﴿٤٠﴾

41. Surely, [d]Allāh wrongs not *any one even so much* as the weight of an atom.[606] And if there be a good deed, He multiplies it and gives from Himself a great reward.

اِنَّ اللّٰهَ لَا يَظْلِمُ مِثْقَالَ ذَرَّةٍ ۚ وَاِنْ تَكُ حَسَنَةً
يُّضٰعِفْهَا وَيُؤْتِ مِنْ لَّدُنْهُ اَجْرًا عَظِيْمًا ﴿٤١﴾

42. And how *will it fare with them* [e]when We shall bring a witness from every people, and shall bring thee as a witness against these![607]

فَكَيْفَ اِذَا جِئْنَا مِنْ كُلِّ اُمَّةٍۢ بِشَهِيْدٍ وَّجِئْنَا بِكَ
عَلٰى هٰٓؤُلَآءِ شَهِيْدًا ﴿٤٢﴾

43. On that day [f]those who disbelieved and disobeyed the Messenger will wish that the earth were made level with them, and they will not *be able to* hide anything[608] from Allāh.

يَوْمَئِذٍ يَّوَدُّ الَّذِيْنَ كَفَرُوْا وَعَصَوُا الرَّسُوْلَ لَوْ تُسَوّٰى
بِهِمُ الْاَرْضُ ۗ وَلَا يَكْتُمُوْنَ اللّٰهَ حَدِيْثًا ﴿٤٣﴾

[a]3 : 181; 17 : 30; 25 : 68. [b]2 : 265. [c]43 : 37, 39. [d]10 : 45; 18 : 50; 28 : 85. [e]16 : 90. [f]78 : 41.

606. No action of man goes unrequited. Wherever the Qur'ān says that the deeds of disbelievers will not avail them, it only means that they will not succeed in their designs and efforts against Islām.

607. Every Prophet will bear witness on the Day of Judgment concerning those to whom he was sent as a Messenger. The word "these" includes both believers and disbelievers, the nature of evidence being different in different cases.

608. *Ḥadīth* means, a piece of information; an announcement; news or tidings (Lane).

R. 7 44. O ye who believe! go not near Prayer when you are not in *full* possession of your senses,[609] until you know what you are saying, nor when you are unclean,[610] except when you are travelling along a way,[611] until you have bathed. And if you are ill or *you are* on a journey *while unclean*, or *if* one of you comes from the privy or you have touched women[612] and you find no water, then betake yourselves to pure dust and wipe therewith your faces and your hands. Surely, Allāh is Effacer of sins, Forgiving.

يٰۤاَيُّهَا الَّذِيۡنَ اٰمَنُوۡا لَا تَقۡرَبُوا الصَّلٰوةَ وَ اَنۡتُمۡ سُكٰرٰى
حَتّٰى تَعۡلَمُوۡا مَا تَقُوۡلُوۡنَ وَ لَا جُنُبًا اِلَّا عَابِرِىۡ سَبِيۡلٍ
حَتّٰى تَغۡتَسِلُوۡا ؕ وَ اِنۡ كُنۡتُمۡ مَّرۡضٰۤى اَوۡ عَلٰى سَفَرٍ اَوۡ جَآءَ
اَحَدٌ مِّنۡكُمۡ مِّنَ الۡغَآئِطِ اَوۡ لٰمَسۡتُمُ النِّسَآءَ فَلَمۡ تَجِدُوۡا
مَآءً فَتَيَمَّمُوۡا صَعِيۡدًا طَيِّبًا فَامۡسَحُوۡا بِوُجُوۡهِكُمۡ وَ
اَيۡدِيۡكُمۡ ؕ اِنَّ اللّٰهَ كَانَ عَفُوًّا غَفُوۡرًا ﴿۴۴﴾

45. Hast thou not seen those who were given a portion of the Book? [a]They buy error and desire that you *too* may lose the way.

اَلَمۡ تَرَ اِلَى الَّذِيۡنَ اُوۡتُوۡا نَصِيۡبًا مِّنَ الۡكِتٰبِ يَشۡتَرُوۡنَ
الضَّلٰلَةَ وَ يُرِيۡدُوۡنَ اَنۡ تَضِلُّوا السَّبِيۡلَ ﴿ؕ۴۵﴾

46. And Allāh knows your enemies well. And sufficient is Allāh as a [b]Friend, and sufficient is Allāh as a Helper.

وَ اللّٰهُ اَعۡلَمُ بِاَعۡدَآئِكُمۡ ؕ وَ كَفٰى بِاللّٰهِ وَلِيًّا ٝ وَّ كَفٰى
بِاللّٰهِ نَصِيۡرًا ﴿۴۶﴾

[a]4 : 90. [b]4 : 174; 33 : 18.

609. *Sukārā* is the plural of *Sakarān* which means, a person who is drunk; or is in a fit of anger; in raptures of love; is stricken with fear; or is overpowered by sleep or some other disturbing element which may distract his attention or obscure his reason, ect. (Lane).

610. The expression, "nor when you are unclean," means that just as a man cannot perform Prayers when he is not in full possession of his senses, similarly he cannot perform Prayers when he is unclean until he performs total ablution by bathing. Sexual intercourse creates a sort of uncleanness in the body which must be removed by bathing in order to ensure proper state of purity, cheerfulness, and vivacity necessary for worship.

611. The clause, *except when you are travelling along a way*, means that though ordinarily a person who is in a state of "uncleanness" cannot perform his Prayers except after proper bathing, yet if he becomes "unclean" when he is actually travelling on the way, bathing is not obligatory for him. He can in this case perform *Tayammum* as ordered in the concluding part of the verse.

612. Of the four classes, *viz.*, the sick; those on a journey; those coming from the privy; and those having gone in unto their wives, only the last two, being in a state of uncleanness, need ablution or washing as the case may be, and if they do not find water, they can perform *Tayammum*. For the former two classes no condition as to water is necessary. They may resort to *Tayammum* even if they find water: This is why the words "while unclean" have been added after the words *if you are ill or you are on a journey*. It must be noted that the expression "on a journey" is the same as the expression "travelling along a way," both signifying the state of actual travelling when one is, as it were, on the wing. Dust has been chosen as a substitute for water because, just as water reminds a person of his origin (77 : 21), thus creating in him a sense of humility; similarly dust calls to his mind the other humble substance from which he is created (30 : 21).

مِنَ الَّذِيْنَ هَادُوْا يُحَرِّفُوْنَ الْكَلِمَ عَنْ مَّوَاضِعِهٖ
وَيَقُوْلُوْنَ سَمِعْنَا وَعَصَيْنَا وَاسْمَعْ غَيْرَ مُسْمَعٍ وَّ
رَاعِنَا لَيًّا بِاَلْسِنَتِهِمْ وَطَعْنًا فِي الدِّيْنِ ؕ وَلَوْ اَنَّهُمْ
قَالُوْا سَمِعْنَا وَاَطَعْنَا وَاسْمَعْ وَانْظُرْنَا لَكَانَ خَيْرًا
لَّهُمْ وَاَقْوَمَ ۙ وَلٰكِنْ لَّعَنَهُمُ اللّٰهُ بِكُفْرِهِمْ فَلَا
يُؤْمِنُوْنَ اِلَّا قَلِيْلًا ﴿۴۷﴾

47. There are some among the Jews who [a]pervert words from their *proper* places. And they say, 'We hear and we disobey' and 'hear *us* and *may God's Word* never be heard[613] *by you*,' and *they say*, [b]'Rā'inā'. *They say all this* twisting with their tongues and *seeking* to injure the Faith. And if they had said, 'We hear and we obey,' and 'hear *thou*,' and 'Unẓurnā,' it would have been better for them and more upright. But Allāh has cursed them for their disbelief; so they believe but little.

يٰۤاَيُّهَا الَّذِيْنَ اُوْتُوا الْكِتٰبَ اٰمِنُوْا بِمَا نَزَّلْنَا مُصَدِّقًا
لِّمَا مَعَكُمْ مِّنْ قَبْلِ اَنْ نَّطْمِسَ وُجُوْهًا فَنَرُدَّهَا عَلٰۤى
اَدْبَارِهَاۤ اَوْ نَلْعَنَهُمْ كَمَا لَعَنَّاۤ اَصْحٰبَ السَّبْتِ ؕ وَكَانَ
اَمْرُ اللّٰهِ مَفْعُوْلًا ﴿۴۸﴾

48. O ye People of the Book! believe in what We have *now* sent down, fulfilling that which is with you, [c]before We destroy *some of* your leaders and turn them on their backs or curse them[614] as [d]We cursed the people of the Sabbath. And the decree of Allāh is *bound* to be fulfilled.

اِنَّ اللّٰهَ لَا يَغْفِرُ اَنْ يُّشْرَكَ بِهٖ وَيَغْفِرُ مَا دُوْنَ
ذٰلِكَ لِمَنْ يَّشَآءُ ۚ وَمَنْ يُّشْرِكْ بِاللّٰهِ فَقَدِ افْتَرٰۤى
اِثْمًا عَظِيْمًا ﴿۴۹﴾

49. Surely, [e]Allāh will not forgive that a partner be associated[615] with Him; but He will forgive whatever is short of that to whomsoever He pleases. And whoso associates partners with Allāh has indeed devised a very great sin.

[a]2 : 76; 3 : 79; 5 ; 42. [b]2 : 105. [c]10 : 89. [d]2 : 66; 4 : 155; 7 : 164; 16 : 125. [e]4 : 117.

613. The expression *Ghaira Musma'in* means; (1) mayest thou not hear by reason of deafness; (2) mayest thou not hear what may please thee; (3) mayest thou not be obeyed.

614. The words signify that (1) either of the two punishments would befall the Jews; (2) some of them would be visited with one kind of punishment and others with the other.

615. *Shirk* which is tantamount to treason in spiritual terminology extends to loving or trusting a thing or a being as one should love or trust God. The verse only relates to the time after death, *i.e.*, one who dies in a state of *Shirk* will not be forgiven.

50. Hast thou not seen those who hold themselves to be pure? Nay, it is Allāh who purifies whomsoever He pleases, and [a]they will not be wronged a whit.

أَلَمْ تَرَ إِلَى الَّذِينَ يُزَكُّونَ أَنْفُسَهُمْ بَلِ اللّٰهُ يُزَكِّي
مَنْ يَشَآءُ وَلَا يُظْلَمُوْنَ فَتِيْلًا ﴿٥٠﴾

51. See how they [b]forge a lie against Allāh ![616] And sufficient is that as a manifest sin.

اُنْظُرْ كَيْفَ يَفْتَرُوْنَ عَلَى اللّٰهِ الْكَذِبَ وَكَفٰى بِهٖٓ
إِثْمًا مُّبِيْنًا ﴿٥١﴾ ع

R. 8 52. Hast thou not seen those who were given a portion of the Book? They believe in evil objects[617] and *follow* those who transgress, and they say of the disbelievers, 'These are better guided in religion than those who believe.'[618]

أَلَمْ تَرَ إِلَى الَّذِيْنَ أُوْتُوْا نَصِيْبًا مِّنَ الْكِتٰبِ يُؤْمِنُوْنَ
بِالْجِبْتِ وَالطَّاغُوْتِ وَيَقُوْلُوْنَ لِلَّذِيْنَ كَفَرُوْا هٰٓؤُلَآءِ
أَهْدٰى مِنَ الَّذِيْنَ اٰمَنُوْا سَبِيْلًا ﴿٥٢﴾

53. Those are they whom Allāh has cursed, and he whom Allāh curses, thou shalt not find for him a helper

أُولٰٓئِكَ الَّذِيْنَ لَعَنَهُمُ اللّٰهُ وَمَنْ يَّلْعَنِ اللّٰهُ فَلَنْ
تَجِدَ لَهٗ نَصِيْرًا ﴿٥٣﴾

54. Have they a share in the kingdom? Then they would not give men *even so much as* the little hollow in the back of a date-stone.

أَمْ لَهُمْ نَصِيْبٌ مِّنَ الْمُلْكِ فَإِذًا لَّا يُؤْتُوْنَ النَّاسَ
نَقِيْرًا ﴿٥٤﴾

55. Or do they envy men for what Allāh has given them out of His bounty? *If that is so*, surely, We gave to the children of Abraham the Book and wisdom and We gave them a great kingdom.

أَمْ يَحْسُدُوْنَ النَّاسَ عَلٰى مَآ اٰتٰهُمُ اللّٰهُ مِنْ فَضْلِهٖ
فَقَدْ اٰتَيْنَآ اٰلَ إِبْرٰهِيْمَ الْكِتٰبَ وَالْحِكْمَةَ وَاٰتَيْنٰهُمْ
مُّلْكًا عَظِيْمًا ﴿٥٥﴾

[a]4 : 78, 125; 17 : 72. [b]5 : 104; 10 : 70; 16 : 117. [c]2 : 160; 3 : 87, 88.

616. It was tantamount to forging a lie on the part of the Jews to say that God would raise no more Prophets because they needed none. If the people had become corrupt, a Prophet was sure to appear and he did appear in the person of the Holy Prophet of Islām.

617. *Al-jibt* means, an idol or idols; that wherein there is no good; a diviner; the Devil (Lane).

618. The Muslims believed in all the Prophets mentioned in the Bible and also in the Divine origin of the Law that was given to Moses, yet so great was the hatred of the Jews for them that they declared the idol-worshippers of Arabia, who rejected their Prophets as well as their Scriptures, to be better guided than the Muslims.

56. [a]And of them were some who believed in him; and of them were others who turned away from him. And sufficient *for them as punishment* is the blazing fire of Hell.

فَمِنْهُمْ مَّنْ اٰمَنَ بِهٖ وَ مِنْهُمْ مَّنْ صَدَّ عَنْهُ ؕ وَ
كَفٰى بِجَهَنَّمَ سَعِيْرًا ﴿۵۶﴾

57. Those who disbelieve in Our Signs, We shall soon cause them to enter Fire. As often as their skins are burnt up, We shall give them in exchange other skins[619] that they may continue to taste the punishment. Surely, Allāh is Mighty *and* Wise.

اِنَّ الَّذِيْنَ كَفَرُوْا بِاٰيٰتِنَا سَوْفَ نُصْلِيْهِمْ نَارًا ؕ كُلَّمَا
نَضِجَتْ جُلُوْدُهُمْ بَدَّلْنٰهُمْ جُلُوْدًا غَيْرَهَا لِيَذُوْقُوا
الْعَذَابَ ؕ اِنَّ اللّٰهَ كَانَ عَزِيْزًا حَكِيْمًا ﴿۵۷﴾

58. And [b]those who believe and do good works, We shall make them enter Gardens through which streams flow, to abide therein for ever; therein shall they have pure spouses, and We shall admit them to *a place of* [c]plenteous shade.[620]

وَ الَّذِيْنَ اٰمَنُوْا وَ عَمِلُوا الصّٰلِحٰتِ سَنُدْخِلُهُمْ جَنّٰتٍ
تَجْرِيْ مِنْ تَحْتِهَا الْاَنْهٰرُ خٰلِدِيْنَ فِيْهَاۤ اَبَدًا ؕ لَهُمْ
فِيْهَاۤ اَزْوَاجٌ مُّطَهَّرَةٌ ۫ وَّ نُدْخِلُهُمْ ظِلًّا ظَلِيْلًا ﴿۵۸﴾

59. Verily, Allāh commands you to [d]give over the trusts[621] to those entitled to them, and that, when you judge between men, you judge with justice.[622] And surely excellent is that with which Allāh admonishes you. Allāh is All-Hearing, All-Seeing.

اِنَّ اللّٰهَ يَاْمُرُكُمْ اَنْ تُؤَدُّوا الْاَمٰنٰتِ اِلٰۤى اَهْلِهَا ۙ وَ
اِذَا حَكَمْتُمْ بَيْنَ النَّاسِ اَنْ تَحْكُمُوْا بِالْعَدْلِ ؕ اِنَّ اللّٰهَ
نِعِمَّا يَعِظُكُمْ بِهٖ ؕ اِنَّ اللّٰهَ كَانَ سَمِيْعًۢا بَصِيْرًا ﴿۵۹﴾

[a]2 : 254; 10 : 41; 61 : 15. [b]4 : 123; 13 : 30; 14 : 24; 22 : 24; See also 2 : 26. [c]13 : 36; 56 : 31. [d]8 : 28.

619. Medical science has now established the fact that the skin is much more sensitive to pain than the flesh, there being a larger number of nerves in the former. The Qur'ān revealed this great truth about fourteen hundered years ago by saying that the skin and not the flesh of the inmates of Hell will be renewed after being burnt up.

620. The expression, *plenteous shade,* signifies an atmoshpere of peace and calm, free from all pain-giving elements.

621. Authority or power to rule has been here described as a "trust" of the people in order to point out that it belongs to the people and is not the birth-right of any individual or dynasty. The Qur'ān disapproves of dynastic or hereditary rule and institutes instead a representative form of government. The Chief is to be elected; and in electing him the people are bidden to vote for one best fitted for the office.

622. The Head of the Muslim State and all those persons who are entrusted with the duty of administration are enjoined to use their authority equitably and well.

60. O ye who believe! obey[623] Allāh, and obey *His* Messenger and [a]those who are in authority among you. And [b]if you differ in anything refer it to Allāh and *His* Messenger, if you are believers in Allāh and the Last Day. That is best and most commendable in the end.

يٰۤاَيُّهَا الَّذِيْنَ اٰمَنُوْۤا اَطِيْعُوا اللّٰهَ وَاَطِيْعُوا الرَّسُوْلَ وَ
اُولِي الْاَمْرِ مِنْكُمْ ۚ فَاِنْ تَنَازَعْتُمْ فِيْ شَيْءٍ فَرُدُّوْهُ
اِلَى اللّٰهِ وَالرَّسُوْلِ اِنْ كُنْتُمْ تُؤْمِنُوْنَ بِاللّٰهِ وَالْيَوْمِ
الْاٰخِرِ ؕ ذٰلِكَ خَيْرٌ وَّاَحْسَنُ تَاْوِيْلًا ﴿۶۰﴾

R. 9 61. Hast thou not seen those who assert that they believe in what has been revealed to thee and what has been revealed before thee? They desire to seek judgment from the Evil One, although they were commanded not to obey him. And Satan desires to lead them far astray.

اَلَمْ تَرَ اِلَى الَّذِيْنَ يَزْعُمُوْنَ اَنَّهُمْ اٰمَنُوْا بِمَاۤ اُنْزِلَ
اِلَيْكَ وَمَاۤ اُنْزِلَ مِنْ قَبْلِكَ يُرِيْدُوْنَ اَنْ يَّتَحَاكَمُوْۤا
اِلَى الطَّاغُوْتِ وَقَدْ اُمِرُوْۤا اَنْ يَّكْفُرُوْا بِهٖ ؕ وَيُرِيْدُ
الشَّيْطٰنُ اَنْ يُّضِلَّهُمْ ضَلٰلًا ۢ بَعِيْدًا ﴿۶۱﴾

62. And [c]when it is said to them, 'Come ye to what Allāh has sent down and to *His* Messenger,' thou seest the hypocrites turn away from thee with aversion.

وَاِذَا قِيْلَ لَهُمْ تَعَالَوْا اِلٰى مَاۤ اَنْزَلَ اللّٰهُ وَاِلَى الرَّسُوْلِ
رَاَيْتَ الْمُنٰفِقِيْنَ يَصُدُّوْنَ عَنْكَ صُدُوْدًا ﴿۶۲﴾

63. Then how is it that when an affliction befalls them because of what their hands have sent on before, they come to thee swearing by Allāh, *saying*, 'We meant nothing but *the doing of* good and conciliation.'

فَكَيْفَ اِذَاۤ اَصَابَتْهُمْ مُّصِيْبَةٌ ۢ بِمَا قَدَّمَتْ اَيْدِيْهِمْ
ثُمَّ جَآءُوْكَ يَحْلِفُوْنَ ۖ بِاللّٰهِ اِنْ اَرَدْنَاۤ اِلَّاۤ اِحْسَانًا
وَّتَوْفِيْقًا ﴿۶۳﴾

[a]4 : 84. [b]4 : 66. [c]63 : 6.

623. The word "obey" which has been repeated before the words "Allāh" and "Messenger" has been omitted before the words, *those who are in authority*, in order to point out that obedience to the authority properly constituted by Law amounts to obedience to God and His Messenger. The injunction embodied in the words, "refer it to Allāh and His Messenger" may either relate to differences between the rulers and the ruled or to those among the ruled themselves. In the former case the significance is that if there is a matter on which disagreement arises between the rulers and the ruled, it should be decided in the light of the Quranic teaching, or failing that, in that of the *Sunnah* and the Ḥadīth. If, however, the Qur'ān, the *Sunnah* and the Ḥadīth are silent on the question, it should be left to those in whom is vested the authority to manage the affairs of Muslims. The verse seems to refer to matters concerning particularly the affairs of the State. The basic commandment in this respect is that all obedience to authority is subject to the obedience to God and His Messenger. In case, however, of differences and disputes regarding social matters, etc., to which the words *if you differ* seem to refer, the Muslims should be guided by Islamic Law and not by any other law.

64. These are they, the secrets of whose hearts Allāh knows *well*. So turn away from them and admonish them and speak to them an effective word concerning themselves.[624]

أُولٰٓئِكَ الَّذِيْنَ يَعْلَمُ اللّٰهُ مَا فِيْ قُلُوْبِهِمْ ۗ فَأَعْرِضْ
عَنْهُمْ وَعِظْهُمْ وَقُلْ لَّهُمْ فِيْٓ أَنْفُسِهِمْ قَوْلًا بَلِيْغًا ﴿٦٤﴾

65. And We have sent no Messenger but that he should be obeyed[625] by the command of Allāh. And if they had come to thee, when they had wronged their [a]souls, and asked forgiveness of Allāh, and the Messenger *also* had asked forgiveness for them, they would have surely found Allāh Oft-Returning *with compassion*, *and* Merciful.

وَمَآ أَرْسَلْنَا مِنْ رَّسُوْلٍ إِلَّا لِيُطَاعَ بِإِذْنِ اللّٰهِ ۭ وَلَوْ
أَنَّهُمْ إِذْ ظَّلَمُوْٓا أَنْفُسَهُمْ جَآءُوْكَ فَاسْتَغْفَرُوا اللّٰهَ
وَاسْتَغْفَرَ لَهُمُ الرَّسُوْلُ لَوَجَدُوا اللّٰهَ تَوَّابًا رَّحِيْمًا ﴿٦٥﴾

66. But no, by thy Lord, [b]they will not be *true* believers until they make thee judge in all that is in dispute between them and then find not in their hearts any demur concerning that which thou decidest and submit with full submission.[626]

فَلَا وَرَبِّكَ لَا يُؤْمِنُوْنَ حَتّٰى يُحَكِّمُوْكَ فِيْمَا شَجَرَ
بَيْنَهُمْ ثُمَّ لَا يَجِدُوْا فِيْٓ أَنْفُسِهِمْ حَرَجًا مِّمَّا قَضَيْتَ
وَيُسَلِّمُوْا تَسْلِيْمًا ﴿٦٦﴾

67. And if We had commanded them: [c]'Slay your people[627] or leave your homes,' they would not have done it except a few of them; and if they had done what they are exhorted to do, it would surely have been

وَلَوْ أَنَّا كَتَبْنَا عَلَيْهِمْ أَنِ اقْتُلُوْٓا أَنْفُسَكُمْ أَوِ اخْرُجُوْا
مِنْ دِيَارِكُمْ مَّا فَعَلُوْهُ إِلَّا قَلِيْلٌ مِّنْهُمْ ۭ وَلَوْ أَنَّهُمْ
فَعَلُوْا مَا يُوْعَظُوْنَ بِهٖ لَكَانَ خَيْرًا لَّهُمْ وَأَشَدَّ

[a]4 : 111. [b]4 : 60. [c]6 : 78.

624. The Prophet was enjoined to deal kindly with the Hypocrites. They were not yet beyond redemption. It was possible that they might one day see the error of their ways and become sincere and true Muslims. War was never waged against them.

625. It is sometimes sought to be inferred from these words that though a Prophet is to be always obeyed by the people to whom he preaches his Message, yet he himself does not give allegiance to any other Prophet. This is evidently a wrong inference. The fact that a Prophet is the object of other people's obedience does not preclude the possibility of his being himself subordinate to, and a follower of, another Prophet. Aaron was a subordinate Prophet to Moses (20 : 94).

626. The commandment pertains to the Holy Prophet as Head of the Muslim State and may, therefore, apply also to his Rightly-guided Successors.

627. The words, *Uqtulū Anfusakum*, do not mean "slay yourselves" but "slay your people" (2 : 55), or "lay down your lives in the cause of God."

better for them and conducive to greater strength;

تَثْبِيْتًا ﴿٦٧﴾

68. And then We would have surely, given them a great reward from Ourselves;

وَّاِذًا لَّاٰتَيْنٰهُمْ مِّنْ لَّدُنَّآ اَجْرًا عَظِيْمًا ﴿٦٨﴾

69. And [a]We would surely have guided them in the right path.

وَّلَهَدَيْنٰهُمْ صِرَاطًا مُّسْتَقِيْمًا ﴿٦٩﴾

70. And [b]Whoso obeys Allāh and *this* Messenger shall be among[628] those [c]on whom Allāh has bestowed His blessings—the Prophets, the Truthful, the Martyrs, and the Righteous. And an excellent company are they.[629]

وَمَنْ يُّطِعِ اللّٰهَ وَالرَّسُوْلَ فَاُولٰٓئِكَ مَعَ الَّذِيْنَ اَنْعَمَ
اللّٰهُ عَلَيْهِمْ مِّنَ النَّبِيّٖنَ وَالصِّدِّيْقِيْنَ وَالشُّهَدَآءِ
وَالصّٰلِحِيْنَ ۚ وَحَسُنَ اُولٰٓئِكَ رَفِيْقًا ﴿٧٠﴾

71. This grace is from Allāh, and Allāh suffices as One Who is All-Knowing.

ع ذٰلِكَ الْفَضْلُ مِنَ اللّٰهِ ؕ وَكَفٰى بِاللّٰهِ عَلِيْمًا ﴿٧١﴾

R. 10 72. O ye who believe! take your precautions[630] *for security*, then go

يٰٓاَيُّهَا الَّذِيْنَ اٰمَنُوْا خُذُوْا حِذْرَكُمْ فَانْفِرُوْا ثُبَاتٍ

[a]19 : 37; 36 : 62; 42 : 53-54. [b]4 : 14; 8 : 25. [c]1 : 7; 5 : 21; 19 : 59; 57 : 20.

628. The particle *ma'* denotes concomitance of two or more persons in one place or at one time; or in position, rank or status. It also implies the sense of assistance as in 9 : 40 (Mufradāt). The particle has been used at several places in the Qur'ān in the sense of *fī* meaning "among" (3 : 194 & 4 : 147).

629. The verse is important as it describes all the avenues of spiritual progress open to Muslims. All the four spiritual ranks—the Prophets; the Truthful; the Martyrs and the Righteous—can now be attained only by following the Holy Prophet. This is an honour reserved for the Holy Prophet alone. No other Prophet shares it with him. The inference is further supported by the verse which speaks of Prophets generally and says : *And those who believe in Allāh and His Messengers, they are the Truthful and the Martyrs in the presence of their Lord* (57 : 20). When read together these two verses signify that, whereas the followers of other Prophets could only attain the rank of the Truthful, the Martyrs, and the Righteous and no higher, the followers of the Holy Prophet can rise to the rank of a Prophet also. The Baḥr al-Muḥīṭ (vol. iii, p. 287) quotes Al-Rāghib as saying: "God has divided the believers into four classes in this verse, and has appointed for them four stages, some of which are lower than the others, and He has exhorted true believers not to remain behind any of these stages." And adds that "Prophethood is of two kinds, general, and special. The *special* Prophethood, *viz.*, the Law-bearing Prophethood, is now unattainable; but the general Prophethood continues to be attained."

630. *Hidhr* means, caution or precaution; vigilance; guard; state of preparation; or of fear (Lane). The word extends to all kinds of precautions and preparations necessary for defence, and has been understood to include the putting on of weapons of defence.

forth in separate parties[631] or go forth all together.

اَوِ انْفِرُوْا جَمِيْعًا ﴿٧٢﴾

73. And among you there is he who tarries behind, and if a misfortune befalls you, he says, 'Surely, Allāh has been gracious to me, since I was not present with them.'[632]

وَاِنَّ مِنْكُمْ لَمَنْ لَّيُبَطِّئَنَّ ۚ فَاِنْ اَصَابَتْكُمْ مُّصِيْبَةٌ
قَالَ قَدْ اَنْعَمَ اللّٰهُ عَلَيَّ اِذْ لَمْ اَكُنْ مَّعَهُمْ شَهِيْدًا ﴿٧٣﴾

74. But if there comes to you some good fortune from Allāh, he says, as if there were no love between you and him, 'Would that I had been with them, then should I have *indeed* achieved a great success!'

وَلَئِنْ اَصَابَكُمْ فَضْلٌ مِّنَ اللّٰهِ لَيَقُوْلَنَّ كَاَنْ لَّمْ
تَكُنْ بَيْنَكُمْ وَبَيْنَهٗ مَوَدَّةٌ يّٰلَيْتَنِيْ كُنْتُ مَعَهُمْ
فَاَفُوْزَ فَوْزًا عَظِيْمًا ﴿٧٤﴾

75. Let those then fight in the cause of Allāh [a]who would sell the present life for the Hereafter. And whoso fights in the cause of Allāh, [b]be he slain or be he victorious, We shall soon give him a great reward.

فَلْيُقَاتِلْ فِيْ سَبِيْلِ اللّٰهِ الَّذِيْنَ يَشْرُوْنَ الْحَيٰوةَ الدُّنْيَا
بِالْاٰخِرَةِ ۭ وَمَنْ يُّقَاتِلْ فِيْ سَبِيْلِ اللّٰهِ فَيُقْتَلْ اَوْ
يَغْلِبْ فَسَوْفَ نُؤْتِيْهِ اَجْرًا عَظِيْمًا ﴿٧٥﴾

76. And why should you not fight[632A] in the cause of Allāh and *for the rescue of* [c]the weak[633] men, women and children—*who* say, 'Our Lord, take us out of this town whose people are oppressors, and give us a friend from Thyself and give us from Thyself a helper.'

وَمَا لَكُمْ لَا تُقَاتِلُوْنَ فِيْ سَبِيْلِ اللّٰهِ وَالْمُسْتَضْعَفِيْنَ
مِنَ الرِّجَالِ وَالنِّسَاۗءِ وَالْوِلْدَانِ الَّذِيْنَ يَقُوْلُوْنَ
رَبَّنَآ اَخْرِجْنَا مِنْ هٰذِهِ الْقَرْيَةِ الظَّالِمِ اَهْلُهَا ۚ
وَاجْعَلْ لَّنَا مِنْ لَّدُنْكَ وَلِيًّا ۚ وَّاجْعَلْ لَّنَا مِنْ
لَّدُنْكَ نَصِيْرًا ﴿٧٦﴾

77. Those who believe fight in the cause of Allāh, and those who disbelieve fight in the cause of the Evil One. Fight ye, therefore, against the friends of Satan; surely, Satan's strategy is weak.

اَلَّذِيْنَ اٰمَنُوْا يُقَاتِلُوْنَ فِيْ سَبِيْلِ اللّٰهِ ۚ وَالَّذِيْنَ كَفَرُوْا
يُقَاتِلُوْنَ فِيْ سَبِيْلِ الطَّاغُوْتِ فَقَاتِلُوْٓا اَوْلِيَاۗءَ الشَّيْطٰنِ ۚ
ع اِنَّ كَيْدَ الشَّيْطٰنِ كَانَ ضَعِيْفًا ﴿٧٧﴾

[a]9 : 111. [b]9 : 52. [c]4 : 99.

631. *Al-Thubah* means a company or body of men; a distinct body or company of men; a troop of horsemen (Lane).

632. The verse refers to Hypocrites or the internal enemies of Islām and mentions their two prominent traits.

632A. The words also mean, what is the matter with you that you fight not.

633. The verse is a clear proof of the fact that Muslims never started hostilities. They only fought in self-defence in order to protect their religion and save their weaker co-religionists.

R. 11 78. Hast thou not seen those to whom it was said : 'Restrain your hands, observe Prayer and pay the Zakāt.' And [a]when fighting is prescribed for them, behold ! a section of them fear men as they should fear Allāh, or with still greater fear; and they say, 'Our Lord, why hast Thou prescribed fighting for us? [b]Wouldst Thou not grant us respite yet a while?'[634] Say, [c]'The benefit of this world is little and the Hereafter will be better for him who fears *Allāh*; and [d]you shall not be wronged a whit.'

أَلَمْ تَرَ إِلَى الَّذِيْنَ قِيْلَ لَهُمْ كُفُّوْٓا أَيْدِيَكُمْ وَأَقِيْمُوا
الصَّلٰوةَ وَاٰتُوا الزَّكٰوةَ فَلَمَّا كُتِبَ عَلَيْهِمُ الْقِتَالُ
إِذَا فَرِيْقٌ مِّنْهُمْ يَخْشَوْنَ النَّاسَ كَخَشْيَةِ اللّٰهِ
أَوْ أَشَدَّ خَشْيَةً وَقَالُوْا رَبَّنَا لِمَ كَتَبْتَ عَلَيْنَا
الْقِتَالَ لَوْلَآ أَخَّرْتَنَآ إِلٰٓى أَجَلٍ قَرِيْبٍ قُلْ مَتَاعُ
الدُّنْيَا قَلِيْلٌ وَالْاٰخِرَةُ خَيْرٌ لِّمَنِ اتَّقٰى وَلَا
تُظْلَمُوْنَ فَتِيْلًا ﴿٧٨﴾

79. Wheresoever you may be, [e]death will overtake you, even if you be in strongly built towers.[635] And if some good befalls them, they say, 'This is from Allāh;' and if evil befalls them, they say, 'This is from thee.' Say, 'All is from Allāh.'[636] What has happened to these people that they would not try to understand anything?

أَيْنَ مَا تَكُوْنُوْا يُدْرِكْكُّمُ الْمَوْتُ وَلَوْ كُنْتُمْ فِيْ بُرُوْجٍ
مُّشَيَّدَةٍ وَإِنْ تُصِبْهُمْ حَسَنَةٌ يَّقُوْلُوْا هٰذِهٖ مِنْ
عِنْدِ اللّٰهِ وَإِنْ تُصِبْهُمْ سَيِّئَةٌ يَّقُوْلُوْا هٰذِهٖ مِنْ
عِنْدِكَ قُلْ كُلٌّ مِّنْ عِنْدِ اللّٰهِ فَمَالِ هٰٓؤُلَآءِ الْقَوْمِ
لَا يَكَادُوْنَ يَفْقَهُوْنَ حَدِيْثًا ﴿٧٩﴾

80. Whatever of good comes to thee is from Allāh; and whatever of evil befalls thee is from thyself.[637] And We have sent thee as a

مَآ أَصَابَكَ مِنْ حَسَنَةٍ فَمِنَ اللّٰهِ وَمَآ أَصَابَكَ مِنْ
سَيِّئَةٍ فَمِنْ نَّفْسِكَ وَأَرْسَلْنٰكَ لِلنَّاسِ رَسُوْلًا

[a]2 : 247 ; 4 : 67. [b]14 : 45 ; 63 : 11. [c]9 : 38 ; 57 : 21. [d]See 4 : 50. [e]62 : 9.

634. The verse refers to a class of men who show eagerness to fight when they are told not to fight, but when the actual time for fighting arrives, they refuse to fight or try to avoid it by various pretexts, thus showing that their former eagerness for fighting was either insincere or was due to temporary excitement.

635. The words either refer to the general physical law about the inevitability of death, or they may be taken as particularly addressed to the Hypocrites, who disobeyed the Divine command to fight, thinking that in this way they could avoid death.

636. The expression, *All is from Allāh*, is true in this sense that God is the Final Controlling Power in the universe and whatever good or evil befalls man is attributable either to a general law of nature or to one or other of His special decrees.

637. God has endowed man with natural powers and faculties by making right use of which he can achieve success in life and by making wrong use of them involves himself in trouble. Thus all good is here attributed to God and all evil to man.

Messenger to *all* mankind. And sufficient is Allāh as a Witness.

وَكَفَىٰ بِاللَّهِ شَهِيدًا ﴿٨٠﴾

81. Whoso obeys the Messenger obeys Allāh *indeed*; and whoso turns away, then We have not sent thee to be a keeper over them.

مَّن يُطِعِ الرَّسُولَ فَقَدْ أَطَاعَ اللَّهَ ۖ وَمَن تَوَلَّىٰ فَمَا
أَرْسَلْنَاكَ عَلَيْهِمْ حَفِيظًا ﴿٨١﴾

82. And they say : 'Obedience *is our guiding principle*;' but when they go forth from thy presence, a section of them [a]spends the night scheming[638] against what thou hast said. Allāh records whatever they scheme by night. So turn away from them, and put thy trust in Allāh. And sufficient is Allāh as a Disposer of affairs.

وَيَقُولُونَ طَاعَةٌ فَإِذَا بَرَزُوا مِنْ عِندِكَ بَيَّتَ طَائِفَةٌ
مِّنْهُمْ غَيْرَ الَّذِي تَقُولُ ۖ وَاللَّهُ يَكْتُبُ مَا يُبَيِّتُونَ ۖ
فَأَعْرِضْ عَنْهُمْ وَتَوَكَّلْ عَلَى اللَّهِ ۚ وَكَفَىٰ بِاللَّهِ
وَكِيلًا ﴿٨٢﴾

83. [b]Will they not, then, meditate upon the Qur'ān ? Had it been from anyone other than Allāh, they would surely have found therein much discrepancy.[639]

أَفَلَا يَتَدَبَّرُونَ الْقُرْآنَ ۚ وَلَوْ كَانَ مِنْ عِندِ غَيْرِ اللَّهِ
لَوَجَدُوا فِيهِ اخْتِلَافًا كَثِيرًا ﴿٨٣﴾

84. And when there comes to them any tidings *whether* of peace or of fear they spread it about,[640] whereas if they had referred it to the Messenger and to [c]those in authority among them, surely those of them, who can elicit *the truth from* it, would have understood it.

وَإِذَا جَاءَهُمْ أَمْرٌ مِّنَ الْأَمْنِ أَوِ الْخَوْفِ أَذَاعُوا
بِهِ ۖ وَلَوْ رَدُّوهُ إِلَى الرَّسُولِ وَإِلَىٰ أُولِي الْأَمْرِ مِنْهُمْ
لَعَلِمَهُ الَّذِينَ يَسْتَنبِطُونَهُ مِنْهُمْ ۗ وَلَوْلَا فَضْلُ اللَّهِ

[a]4 : 109. [b]47 : 25. [c]4 : 60.

638. The reference is to secret plotting, whether by night or during the day. As generally secret plotting is done at night, the word *Bayyata* has been used here, the night time affording a sort of cover and secrecy.

639. "Discrepancy" may either refer to contradictions in the text of the Qur'ān and the teachings contained therein; or to lack of agreement between the Quranic announcements in the form of prophecies and their result or fulfilment.

640. The reason why tidings relating to peace have been mentioned before those relating to fear is that the Qur'ān is here speaking of war, and during war it is sometimes more dangerous to give publicity to matters likely to lead to happy results than to matters of fear. Under normal conditions, too, the injunction mentioned is very important, exercising direct influence on the discipline and well-being of society. The words, *those in authority*, refer to the Holy Prophet or his Successors or to the Chiefs appointed by them.

عَلَيْكُمْ وَرَحْمَتُهٗ لَاتَّبَعْتُمُ الشَّيْطٰنَ اِلَّا قَلِيْلًا ﴿٨٤﴾

And had it not been for the grace of Allāh upon you and His mercy, you would have followed Satan, save a few.

فَقَاتِلْ فِيْ سَبِيْلِ اللّٰهِ ۚ لَا تُكَلَّفُ اِلَّا نَفْسَكَ وَ
حَرِّضِ الْمُؤْمِنِيْنَ ۚ عَسَى اللّٰهُ اَنْ يَّكُفَّ بَاْسَ الَّذِيْنَ
كَفَرُوْا ؕ وَ اللّٰهُ اَشَدُّ بَاْسًا وَّ اَشَدُّ تَنْكِيْلًا ﴿٨٥﴾

85. Fight, therefore, in the way of Allāh—thou art not made responsible except for thyself[641] —and [a]urge on the believers *to fight*. It may be that Allāh will restrain the might of those that disbelieve; and Allāh is stronger in might and stronger in inflicting punishment.

مَنْ يَّشْفَعْ شَفَاعَةً حَسَنَةً يَّكُنْ لَّهٗ نَصِيْبٌ مِّنْهَا ۚ
وَمَنْ يَّشْفَعْ شَفَاعَةً سَيِّئَةً يَّكُنْ لَّهٗ كِفْلٌ مِّنْهَا ؕ
وَكَانَ اللّٰهُ عَلٰى كُلِّ شَيْءٍ مُّقِيْتًا ﴿٨٦﴾

86. Whoso makes a righteous intercession shall have a share thereof, and whoso makes an evil intercession, shall have a like portion thereof,[642] and Allāh is Powerful over everything.

وَاِذَا حُيِّيْتُمْ بِتَحِيَّةٍ فَحَيُّوْا بِاَحْسَنَ مِنْهَاۤ اَوْ رُدُّوْهَا ؕ
اِنَّ اللّٰهَ كَانَ عَلٰى كُلِّ شَيْءٍ حَسِيْبًا ﴿٨٧﴾ نصف

87. And when you are greeted with a greeting, greet ye with a better greeting or *at least* return it.[643] Surely, Allāh takes account of all things.

اَللّٰهُ لَاۤ اِلٰهَ اِلَّا هُوَ ؕ لَيَجْمَعَنَّكُمْ اِلٰى يَوْمِ الْقِيٰمَةِ لَا

88. Allāh is He besides Whom there is none worthy of worship. He will certainly *continue to* assemble

[a]8 : 66.

641. The command to fight does not relate to the Holy Prophet alone. If that had been the case, the second clause in the verse would have read as *Illā Nafsuka, i.e.*, none is made responsible except thyself, and not as *Illā Nafsaka, i.e.*, thou art not made responsible except for thyself, as in the verse. What the verse means is that every Muslim, not excluding the Holy Prophet, was individually answerable to God. But the duty of the Holy Prophet was twofold, (1) to fight himself, and (2) to urge his followers to fight, though he was not responsible for them.

642. The verse signifies that the act of intercession or recommendation should not be treated lightly; for the person who intercedes on behalf of another is answerable for his act. If the intercession or recommendation is right and just, he will have a suitable reward; otherwise he will be held responsible for the evil consequences thereof. It is further noteworthy that in connection with "righteous intercession" the word used is *Naṣīb* (share or fixed share) whereas in connection with "evil intercession" the word is *Kifl* (like portion). This is to point out that whereas the punishment of an evil intercession will only be the like thereof, the good reward of a righteous intercession will have no such restriction but will be as large as God has fixed it, *i.e.*, ten times greater.

643. The verse points to a social duty.

you till the Day of Resurrection about which there is no doubt. And who is more truthful in his word than Allāh?

رَيْبَ فِيهِ وَمَنْ أَصْدَقُ مِنَ اللَّهِ حَدِيثًا ۝٨٨ ع ٨

R. 12 89. What is the matter with you that you are *divided into* two parties regarding the Hypocrites?[644] And Allāh has overthrown them because of what they earned. Desire ye to guide him whom Allāh has caused to perish? And for him whom Allāh causes to perish thou shalt not find a way.

فَمَا لَكُمْ فِي الْمُنٰفِقِيْنَ فِئَتَيْنِ وَاللّٰهُ أَرْكَسَهُمْ
بِمَا كَسَبُوْا أَتُرِيْدُوْنَ أَنْ تَهْدُوْا مَنْ أَضَلَّ اللّٰهُ
وَمَنْ يُّضْلِلِ اللّٰهُ فَلَنْ تَجِدَ لَهٗ سَبِيْلًا ۝٨٩

90. [a]They wish that you should disbelieve as they have disbelieved, so that you may become alike. Take not, therefore, friends from among them,[645] until they emigrate in the way of Allāh. And if they turn away, then seize them and kill[646] them wherever you find them; and take no friend nor helper from among them;

وَدُّوْا لَوْ تَكْفُرُوْنَ كَمَا كَفَرُوْا فَتَكُوْنُوْنَ سَوَآءً فَلَا
تَتَّخِذُوْا مِنْهُمْ أَوْلِيَآءَ حَتّٰى يُهَاجِرُوْا فِيْ سَبِيْلِ اللّٰهِ
فَإِنْ تَوَلَّوْا فَخُذُوْهُمْ وَاقْتُلُوْهُمْ حَيْثُ وَجَدْتُّمُوْهُمْ
وَلَا تَتَّخِذُوْا مِنْهُمْ وَلِيًّا وَّلَا نَصِيْرًا ۝٩٠

91. Except those who are connected with a people between whom and you there is a pact, or those who come to you, while their hearts shrink from fighting you or fighting their own people. And if Allāh had *so* pleased, He could have given them power against you, then

إِلَّا الَّذِيْنَ يَصِلُوْنَ إِلٰى قَوْمٍ بَيْنَكُمْ وَبَيْنَهُمْ مِّيْثَاقٌ
أَوْ جَآءُوْكُمْ حَصِرَتْ صُدُوْرُهُمْ أَنْ يُّقَاتِلُوْكُمْ أَوْ
يُقَاتِلُوْا قَوْمَهُمْ وَلَوْ شَآءَ اللّٰهُ لَسَلَّطَهُمْ عَلَيْكُمْ

[a]2 : 110 ; 4 : 45 ; 14 : 14.

644. Believers disagreed among themselves as to how the Hypocrites living in the suburbs of Medina, *i.e.*, the Bedouin tribes of the countryside, should be treated. Some sympathized with them and recommended leniency towards them, hoping that in this way they might gradually reform themselves,. while others looked upon them as a serious menace to Islām and advocated strict measures. Muslims are here told that these Hypocrites are the enemies of God and that they should not allow themselves to be divided on their account.

645. The reference is to the Bedouin tribes of the desert. The Qur'ān forbids Muslims to have anything to do with them, or make friends with them or seek their help.

646. As *Qatl* is also used in the sense of severing all social contacts (2 : 62), the expression *Uqtulūhum* may also mean, "have nothing to do with them." This meaning of the expression finds support from the words, *take no friend nor helper from among them.*

they would have surely fought you. So, if they keep aloof from you and fight you not, and make you an offer of peace, then Allāh has allowed you no way *of aggression* against them.

فَلَقٰتَلُوْكُمْ ۚ فَاِنِ اعْتَزَلُوْكُمْ فَلَمْ يُقَاتِلُوْكُمْ وَاَلْقَوْا
اِلَيْكُمُ السَّلَمَ ۙ فَمَا جَعَلَ اللّٰهُ لَكُمْ عَلَيْهِمْ سَبِيْلًا ﴿۹۱﴾

92. You will find others who desire to be secure from you and to be secure from their own people.[647] Whenever they are made to revert to hostility,[648] [a]they fall headlong into it. Therefore, if they do not keep aloof from you nor offer you peace nor restrain their hands, [b]then seize them and kill them, wherever you find them. Against these We have given you clear authority.

سَتَجِدُوْنَ اٰخَرِيْنَ يُرِيْدُوْنَ اَنْ يَّاْمَنُوْكُمْ وَيَاْمَنُوْا
قَوْمَهُمْ ۭ كُلَّمَا رُدُّوْٓا اِلَى الْفِتْنَةِ اُرْكِسُوْا فِيْهَا ۚ فَاِنْ لَّمْ
يَعْتَزِلُوْكُمْ وَيُلْقُوْٓا اِلَيْكُمُ السَّلَمَ وَيَكُفُّوْٓا اَيْدِيَهُمْ
فَخُذُوْهُمْ وَاقْتُلُوْهُمْ حَيْثُ ثَقِفْتُمُوْهُمْ ۭ وَاُولٰۗىِٕكُمْ
جَعَلْنَا لَكُمْ عَلَيْهِمْ سُلْطٰنًا مُّبِيْنًا ﴿۹۲﴾ ع

R. 13 93. It does not behove a believer to slay a believer unless it be by mistake.[649] And he who slays a believer by mistake shall free a believing slave, and *pay* blood-money to be handed over to his heirs, unless they remit it as charity. But if *the person slain* be of a people hostile to you, and *he is* a believer, then *the penalty is only* [b]the freeing of a believing slave, and if he[650] be

وَمَا كَانَ لِمُؤْمِنٍ اَنْ يَّقْتُلَ مُؤْمِنًا اِلَّا خَطَـًٔا ۚ وَمَنْ
قَتَلَ مُؤْمِنًا خَطَـًٔا فَتَحْرِيْرُ رَقَبَةٍ مُّؤْمِنَةٍ وَّدِيَةٌ
مُّسَلَّمَةٌ اِلٰٓى اَهْلِهٖٓ اِلَّآ اَنْ يَّصَّدَّقُوْا ۭ فَاِنْ كَانَ مِنْ
قَوْمٍ عَدُوٍّ لَّكُمْ وَهُوَ مُؤْمِنٌ فَتَحْرِيْرُ رَقَبَةٍ مُّؤْمِنَةٍ ۭ

[a]33 : 15. [b]9 : 5.

647. The reference seems to be to the two tribes, Asad and Ghaṭfān who had no treaty of alliance with the Muslims. They played a double game and awaited their opportunity. When invited by their people to join them in fighting against the Muslims, they readily accepted the invitation. The directions contained in these verses come into operation when a virtual state of war exists and danger stalks along the land.

648. By *Fitnah* is here meant, war with the Muslims.

649. As when actual or virtual state of war exists there is the likelihood that a Muslim may be killed by another Muslim by mistake, the present verse gives a timely warning to Muslims to be always on their guard against such an eventuality.

650. In case the slain person is a believer but happens to belong to a hostile people, then the offender shall only free a believing slave and no blood-money shall be levied on him, because money paid to a hostile people would go to strengthen their military power against Islām. In the expression, *and if he be of a people between whom and you is a pact*, the words, *and he be a believer*, have not been repeated, in order to point out that the law with regard to the *Dhimmīs* (disbelievers under the protection of Muslims), or *Mu'āhids* (disbelievers belonging to a people in alliance with Muslims) is the same as for the Muslims.

وَإِنْ كَانَ مِنْ قَوْمٍ بَيْنَكُمْ وَبَيْنَهُمْ مِّيْثَاقٌ فَدِيَةٌ
مُّسَلَّمَةٌ إِلٰٓى أَهْلِهٖ وَتَحْرِيْرُ رَقَبَةٍ مُّؤْمِنَةٍ فَمَنْ
لَّمْ يَجِدْ فَصِيَامُ شَهْرَيْنِ مُتَتَابِعَيْنِ تَوْبَةً مِّنَ
اللّٰهِ وَكَانَ اللّٰهُ عَلِيْمًا حَكِيْمًا ﴿٩٣﴾

of a people between whom and you is a pact, then *the penalty is* blood-money to be handed over to his heirs, and the freeing of a believing slave.[651] But whoso finds not *one*, then [a]he shall fast for two consecutive months—a mercy from Allāh. And Allāh is All-Knowing, Wise.

وَمَنْ يَّقْتُلْ مُؤْمِنًا مُّتَعَمِّدًا فَجَزَآؤُهٗ جَهَنَّمُ خٰلِدًا
فِيْهَا وَغَضِبَ اللّٰهُ عَلَيْهِ وَلَعَنَهٗ وَأَعَدَّ لَهٗ عَذَابًا
عَظِيْمًا ﴿٩٤﴾

94. And [b]whoso slays a believer intentionally, his reward shall be Hell wherein he shall abide. And Allāh shall be wroth with him and shall curse him and shall prepare for him a great punishment.

يٰٓأَيُّهَا الَّذِيْنَ اٰمَنُوْٓا إِذَا ضَرَبْتُمْ فِيْ سَبِيْلِ اللّٰهِ فَتَبَيَّنُوْا
وَلَا تَقُوْلُوْا لِمَنْ أَلْقٰٓى إِلَيْكُمُ السَّلٰمَ لَسْتَ مُؤْمِنًا
تَبْتَغُوْنَ عَرَضَ الْحَيٰوةِ الدُّنْيَا فَعِنْدَ اللّٰهِ مَغَانِمُ
كَثِيْرَةٌ كَذٰلِكَ كُنْتُمْ مِّنْ قَبْلُ فَمَنَّ اللّٰهُ عَلَيْكُمْ
فَتَبَيَّنُوْا إِنَّ اللّٰهَ كَانَ بِمَا تَعْمَلُوْنَ خَبِيْرًا ﴿٩٥﴾

95. O ye who believe! when you go forth *to fight* in the cause of Allāh, [c]make proper investigation and say not to any one who greets you with the greeting of peace, 'Thou art not a believer.'[652] You seek the goods of this life,[653] but with Allāh are good things in plenty. Such were you before this, but Allāh conferred *His special* favour on you; so *do* make proper investigation. Surely, Allāh is Aware of what you do.

[a]58 : 5. [b]25 : 69-70. [c]49 : 7.

651. It is worthy of note that disbelievers who are in alliance with Muslims have not only been placed on a par with the latter, but even a distinction has been made in their favour. In case a Muslim is slain, the command relating to the payment of penalty has been placed after the injunction to free a slave; while in case one belonging to a people in alliance with Muslims is slain, the order has been reversed; the injunction to pay the penalty to his heirs having been put before the injunction to free a slave. This has been done to impress upon Muslims the need of showing special regard for treaties and pacts. The payment of penalty was an obligation which Muslims owed to disbelievers with whom they had made a pact, and it is in order to bring home to them the lesson that they should have particular regard for their pacts and treaties, that the injunction to pay the penalty has in their case been placed before the injunction to free a slave.

652. When a people offers peace or shows a peaceful attitude towards Muslims, the latter are enjoined to respect that attitude and refrain from hostilities. Moreover, as the Muslim Community at Medina was surrounded by hostile tribes, they were enjoined to presume a person, who greeted them with Islamic salutation, to be a Muslim unless proved otherwise by investigation.

653. That is to say, if you hold such a person to be a disbeliever without proper investigation, this would mean that you desire to kill him and take possession of his goods. Such conduct would show that you prefer worldly goods to God's pleasure.

96. [a]Those of the believers who sit *at home*, excepting the disabled ones, and those who strive in the cause of Allāh with their wealth and their persons, are not equal. Allāh has exalted in rank those who strive with their wealth and their persons above those who sit *at home*. And to each Allāh has promised good. And Allāh has exalted those, who strive above those who sit *at home*, by a great reward[654]—

لَا يَسْتَوِي الْقٰعِدُونَ مِنَ الْمُؤْمِنِينَ غَيْرُ أُولِي الضَّرَرِ
وَالْمُجٰهِدُونَ فِي سَبِيلِ اللّٰهِ بِأَمْوَالِهِمْ وَأَنْفُسِهِمْ ؕ
فَضَّلَ اللّٰهُ الْمُجٰهِدِينَ بِأَمْوَالِهِمْ وَأَنْفُسِهِمْ عَلَى
الْقٰعِدِينَ دَرَجَةً ؕ وَكُلًّا وَّعَدَ اللّٰهُ الْحُسْنٰى ؕ وَفَضَّلَ
اللّٰهُ الْمُجٰهِدِينَ عَلَى الْقٰعِدِينَ أَجْرًا عَظِيمًا ﴿٩٦﴾

97. *By* degrees of excellence *bestowed* by Him, and *by special* forgiveness and mercy. And Allāh is Most Forgiving, Merciful.

دَرَجٰتٍ مِّنْهُ وَمَغْفِرَةً وَّرَحْمَةً ؕ وَكَانَ اللّٰهُ غَفُورًا
رَّحِيمًا ﴿٩٧﴾ ع ١٣ ٥

R. 14 98. Verily, [b]those whom the angels cause to die while they are wronging their own souls, *the angels* will say *to them* : 'What were you after?' They will say : 'We were treated as weak in the land.' *The angels* will say, 'Was not Allāh's earth spacious enough so that you could have emigrated therein?'[655] It is these whose abode shall be Hell, and an evil destination it is;

إِنَّ الَّذِينَ تَوَفّٰهُمُ الْمَلٰٓئِكَةُ ظَالِمِي أَنْفُسِهِمْ قَالُوا
فِيمَ كُنْتُمْ ؕ قَالُوا كُنَّا مُسْتَضْعَفِينَ فِي الْأَرْضِ ؕ قَالُوا
أَلَمْ تَكُنْ أَرْضُ اللّٰهِ وَاسِعَةً فَتُهَاجِرُوا فِيهَا ؕ فَأُولٰٓئِكَ
مَأْوٰىهُمْ جَهَنَّمُ ؕ وَسَآءَتْ مَصِيرًا ﴿٩٨﴾

[a]9 : 19-20 ; 57 : 11. [b]16 : 29.

654. The verse speaks of two classes of believers : (1) Those who sincerely accept Islām and then try to live up to its teachings but take no part in the struggle to defend and propagate the Faith. These are, as it were, passive believers—"sitters" as the verse calls them. (2) Those who not only live up to the teachings of Islām but also vigorously participate in the work of its propagation. These are active believers—the "strivers" or *Mujāhids* as they are called. There is, however, a third class of believers who, even though they do not join their brethren in actually fighting disbelievers get an equal reward with those who take part in the actual struggle. They are heart and soul with the Muslims who are *Mujāhids*, wherever the latter go to fight in the cause of God; but their particular circumstances—disease, poverty, etc., do not allow them to join the expeditions in person.

655. Islām would not be satisfied with a weak or passive belief. If the environments of a believer are not congenial to the Faith he must shift to a more congenial place and if he does not do so he will not be regarded as sincere in his Faith.

99. Except [a]such weak ones among men, women and children, as are incapable of adopting any plan or of finding any way *to escape*.[656]

إِلَّا الْمُسْتَضْعَفِينَ مِنَ الرِّجَالِ وَالنِّسَآءِ وَالْوِلْدَانِ لَا
يَسْتَطِيعُونَ حِيلَةً وَّلَا يَهْتَدُونَ سَبِيلًا ﴿٩٩﴾

100. As to these, may be [657] Allāh will efface their sins; for Allāh is the Effacer of sins, the Most Forgiving.

فَأُولٰٓئِكَ عَسَى اللّٰهُ أَنْ يَّعْفُوَ عَنْهُمْ ۚ وَكَانَ اللّٰهُ عَفُوًّا
غَفُورًا ﴿١٠٠﴾

101. And whoso emigrates from his country in the way of Allāh will find in the earth an abundant place of refuge and plentifulness.[658] And whoso goes forth from his home, emigrating in *the cause of* Allāh and His Messenger, and death overakes him, his reward *lies* on Allāh, and Allāh is Most Forgiving, Merciful.

وَمَنْ يُّهَاجِرْ فِي سَبِيلِ اللّٰهِ يَجِدْ فِي الْأَرْضِ مُرٰغَمًا
كَثِيرًا وَّسَعَةً ۚ وَمَنْ يَّخْرُجْ مِنْ بَيْتِهٖ مُهَاجِرًا إِلَى
اللّٰهِ وَرَسُولِهٖ ثُمَّ يُدْرِكْهُ الْمَوْتُ فَقَدْ وَقَعَ أَجْرُهٗ
عَلَى اللّٰهِ ۗ وَكَانَ اللّٰهُ غَفُورًا رَّحِيمًا ﴿١٠١﴾ ع

R. 15 102. And when you journey in the land, [b]it shall be no blame on you if you shorten the Prayer, if you fear that those who disbelieve will cause you trouble.[659] Verily, the disbelievers are an open enemy to you.

وَإِذَا ضَرَبْتُمْ فِي الْأَرْضِ فَلَيْسَ عَلَيْكُمْ جُنَاحٌ أَنْ
تَقْصُرُوا مِنَ الصَّلٰوةِ ۖ إِنْ خِفْتُمْ أَنْ يَّفْتِنَكُمُ
الَّذِينَ كَفَرُوا ۚ إِنَّ الْكٰفِرِينَ كَانُوا لَكُمْ عَدُوًّا مُّبِينًا ﴿١٠٢﴾

[a]4 : 76. [b]2 : 240.

656. Those believers, who are unable to emigrate, are excepted from the class mentioned in the preceding verse.

657. The particle *'asā* does not indicate doubt on the part of God but is used to keep the believers referred to here in a state of suspense—between hope and fear—so that they may not become lax in Prayer and good deeds. The expression is designed to hold out hope without creating a false sense of security or a state of complacency.

658. Islām accepts no excuse from believers to stay in environments hostile to their Faith if they can afford to leave such localities.

659. The subject of Prayers in time of fear has been dealt with in the Qur'ān in three separate verses, *viz.*, (1) in 2 : 240 which deals with Prayers performed in time of extreme fear when no formal Prayer is possible; (2) in the present verse which deals with Prayers performed individually in time of ordinary fear; and (3) in the following verse which deals with Prayers performed in congregation in time of fear. The "shortening of Prayer" as mentioned in the present verse, which relates to the saying of Prayers individually, does not here signify the lessening of the number of *Rak'ats* which has from the very beginning been fixed at two in a state of journey. It only signifies the saying of the prescribed Prayers quickly when there is danger of an attack from the enemy. The number of *Rak'ats* to

103. And when thou art among them, and leadest the Prayer for them, let a party of them stand with thee and let them take their arms. And when they have performed their prostrations, let them go to your rear, and let another party, who have not yet prayed, come forward and pray with thee,[660] and let them take their means of defence and their arms.[661] The disbelievers wish that you were neglectful of your arms and your baggage that they may fall upon you at once. And it shall be no sin for you, because of the inconvenience *caused* by rain or because you are sick, that you lay aside your arms. But you should *always* take your precautions. Surely, Allāh has prepared an humiliating punishment for the disbelievers.

وَإِذَا كُنْتَ فِيْهِمْ فَأَقَمْتَ لَهُمُ الصَّلٰوةَ فَلْتَقُمْ طَآئِفَةٌ مِّنْهُمْ مَّعَكَ وَلْيَأْخُذُوْا أَسْلِحَتَهُمْ فَإِذَا سَجَدُوْا فَلْيَكُوْنُوْا مِنْ وَّرَآئِكُمْ وَلْتَأْتِ طَآئِفَةٌ أُخْرٰى لَمْ يُصَلُّوْا فَلْيُصَلُّوْا مَعَكَ وَلْيَأْخُذُوْا حِذْرَهُمْ وَأَسْلِحَتَهُمْ وَدَّ الَّذِيْنَ كَفَرُوْا لَوْ تَغْفُلُوْنَ عَنْ أَسْلِحَتِكُمْ وَأَمْتِعَتِكُمْ فَيَمِيْلُوْنَ عَلَيْكُمْ مَّيْلَةً وَّاحِدَةً ۚ وَلَا جُنَاحَ عَلَيْكُمْ إِنْ كَانَ بِكُمْ أَذًى مِّنْ مَّطَرٍ أَوْ كُنْتُمْ مَّرْضٰى أَنْ تَضَعُوْا أَسْلِحَتَكُمْ ۚ وَخُذُوْا حِذْرَكُمْ ۗ إِنَّ اللّٰهَ أَعَدَّ لِلْكٰفِرِيْنَ عَذَابًا مُّهِيْنًا ۝

---

be said when a man is on a journey has ever been two; but in time of danger when one has to say one's Prayers individually, even these two *Rak'ats* may be gone through quickly (Kathīr). This view is endorsed by Mujāhid, Ḍaḥḥāk, and Bukhārī (ch. on *Ṣalāt al-Khauf*). 'Ā'ishah is reported to have said, 'At first the number of *Rak'ats* enjoined was two, whether one was on a journey or at home. Later on, however, it was increased to four for those staying at home, but for those on journey it continued to be the same as before' (Bukhārī, ch. on *Ṣalāt*). 'Umar said, 'The Prayer to be said on a journey is two *Rak'ats*; the Prayer of the two 'Īds is also two *Rak'ats* each; the Friday Prayer is also two *Rak'ats*; this is the full number of *Rak'ats* without having undergone any curtailment. We learnt this from the very lips of the Holy Prophet' (Musnad, Nasa'ī, & Mājah). Khālid bin Sa'īd once asked Ibn 'Umar where was Prayer for the wayfarer mentioned in the Qur'ān which prescribes only the Prayer in time of fear. To this Ibn 'Umar replied that they did what they saw the Holy Prophet doing, *i.e.*, saying two *Rak'ats* of Prayer while on a journey (Jarīr, v. 144 ; Nasa'ī, ch. on *Ṣalāt*).

660. Whereas the preceding verse spoke of Prayer in time of fear in the case of individuals, the present one gives the details of the manner of its performance when the Faithful are in the form of a company or group and the Prayer is to be performed in congregation. As many as eleven different forms in which the Prayer was said on different occasions are described in the Ḥadīth (Muḥīṭ).

661. The verse observes a difference between *Asliḥah* (arms) and *Ḥidhr* (precautions). Whereas the former may be put aside in moments of comparative security, the latter should never be neglected. See also 4 : 72.

104. And when you have finished the Prayer, [a]remember Allāh, standing and sitting, and lying on your sides.[662] And [b]when you are secure *from danger*, then observe Prayer *in the prescribed form*; verily Prayer is enjoined on the believers *to be performed* at fixed hours.

فَإِذَا قَضَيْتُمُ الصَّلٰوةَ فَاذْكُرُوا اللّٰهَ قِيٰمًا وَّقُعُوْدًا وَّعَلٰى
جُنُوْبِكُمْ ۚ فَإِذَا اطْمَأْنَنْتُمْ فَأَقِيْمُوا الصَّلٰوةَ ۚ إِنَّ
الصَّلٰوةَ كَانَتْ عَلَى الْمُؤْمِنِيْنَ كِتٰبًا مَّوْقُوْتًا ﴿١٠٤﴾

105. And [c]slacken not in seeking these people. If you suffer, they too suffer even as you suffer. But you hope from Allāh what they hope not. And Allāh is All-Knowing, Wise.

وَلَا تَهِنُوْا فِي ابْتِغَآءِ الْقَوْمِ ۭ إِنْ تَكُوْنُوْا تَأْلَمُوْنَ
فَإِنَّهُمْ يَأْلَمُوْنَ كَمَا تَأْلَمُوْنَ ۚ وَتَرْجُوْنَ مِنَ اللّٰهِ مَا
لَا يَرْجُوْنَ ۭ وَكَانَ اللّٰهُ عَلِيْمًا حَكِيْمًا ﴿١٠٥﴾ ع ١٥ ١٢

R. 16 106. We have surely sent down to thee the Book comprising the truth, [d]that thou mayest judge between men by what Allāh has taught thee. And be not thou a disputer on behalf of the faithless;[663]

إِنَّآ أَنْزَلْنَآ إِلَيْكَ الْكِتٰبَ بِالْحَقِّ لِتَحْكُمَ بَيْنَ النَّاسِ
بِمَآ أَرٰىكَ اللّٰهُ ۭ وَلَا تَكُنْ لِّلْخَآئِنِيْنَ خَصِيْمًا ﴿١٠٦﴾

107. And ask forgiveness[664] of Allāh. Surely, Allāh is Most Forgiving, Merciful.

وَّاسْتَغْفِرِ اللّٰهَ ۭ إِنَّ اللّٰهَ كَانَ غَفُوْرًا رَّحِيْمًا ﴿١٠٧﴾

108. And plead not on behalf of those who are dishonest to themselves.[665] Surely, Allāh loves not one who is perfidious *and* a great sinner.

وَلَا تُجَادِلْ عَنِ الَّذِيْنَ يَخْتَانُوْنَ أَنْفُسَهُمْ ۭ إِنَّ اللّٰهَ
لَا يُحِبُّ مَنْ كَانَ خَوَّانًا أَثِيْمًا ﴿١٠٨﴾

[a]3 : 192. [b]2 : 240. [c]3 : 147. [d]5 : 49.

662. As in the midst of a battle formal Prayers are either said in haste, or performed in the form of one *Rak'at*, Muslims are enjoined in this verse, that in order to make up the deficiency, they should remember God and pray to Him in an informal manner after the obligatory service is over. This is to compensate for the shortening of Prayer.

663. The address is to every Muslim.

664. *Istighfār* constitutes the keystone of all spiritual progress. It does not merely mean verbal asking for forgiveness but extends to such acts as lead to the covering up of one's sins and shortcomings.

665. The word *Anfusahum* may also mean "their brethren" (2 : 85,86; 4 : 67). The address is general as in the preceding verses.

109. They seek to hide *their designs* from men, but they cannot hide them from Allāh; and [a]He is *present* with them when they plot at night about matters which He does not approve. And Allāh encompasses what they do.

يَسْتَخْفُونَ مِنَ النَّاسِ وَلَا يَسْتَخْفُونَ مِنَ اللَّهِ
وَهُوَ مَعَهُمْ إِذْ يُبَيِّتُونَ مَا لَا يَرْضَىٰ مِنَ الْقَوْلِ ۚ
وَكَانَ اللَّهُ بِمَا يَعْمَلُونَ مُحِيطًا ﴿١٠٩﴾

110. Behold! you[666] are those who pleaded for them in the present life. But who will plead with Allāh for them on the Day of Resurrection, or who will be a guardian over them?

هَٰأَنتُمْ هَٰؤُلَاءِ جَٰدَلْتُمْ عَنْهُمْ فِي الْحَيَوٰةِ الدُّنْيَا
فَمَن يُجَٰدِلُ اللَّهَ عَنْهُمْ يَوْمَ الْقِيَٰمَةِ أَم مَّن يَكُونُ
عَلَيْهِمْ وَكِيلًا ﴿١١٠﴾

111. And whoso does evil or wrongs his soul, and then [b]asks forgiveness of Allāh, will find Allāh Most Forgiving, Merciful.

وَمَن يَعْمَلْ سُوٓءًا أَوْ يَظْلِمْ نَفْسَهُۥ ثُمَّ يَسْتَغْفِرِ اللَّهَ
يَجِدِ اللَّهَ غَفُورًا رَّحِيمًا ﴿١١١﴾

112. And [c]whoso commits a sin, commits it only against his own soul. And Allāh is All-Knowing, Wise.

وَمَن يَكْسِبْ إِثْمًا فَإِنَّمَا يَكْسِبُهُۥ عَلَىٰ نَفْسِهِۦ ۚ وَكَانَ
اللَّهُ عَلِيمًا حَكِيمًا ﴿١١٢﴾

113. And whoso commits a fault or a sin,[667] then [d]throws *the blame* thereof on an innocent person, certainly bears *the burden of* calumny and a manifest sin.

وَمَن يَكْسِبْ خَطِيٓـَٔةً أَوْ إِثْمًا ثُمَّ يَرْمِ بِهِۦ بَرِيٓـًٔا
فَقَدِ احْتَمَلَ بُهْتَٰنًا وَإِثْمًا مُّبِينًا ﴿١١٣﴾ ع ١٦ ١٤

[a]4 82. [b]4 65. [c]2 : 287 ; 99 : 9. [d]24 : 2,24; 33 : 59.

666. The word *Antum* (you) shows that in the previous verses it was not the Holy Prophet but Muslims in general who were addressed. The Holy Prophet could not be expected to dispute on behalf of dishonest people. The Qur'ān addresses him because he was the recipient of Divine commandment for the believers.

667. The difference between *Khaṭī'ah* (fault) and *Ithm* (sin) mentioned side by side in this verse is that the former can be both intentional and unintentional and is often confined to the doer, while the latter is intentional and its scope may extend to other people as well. Moreover, the former may signify a dereliction of duty due to God, but the latter is often an offence against both God and man and is, therefore, more serious and is deserving of greater punishment than the former. See also 2 : 82 and 2 : 174. The commission of a fault or a sin makes it doubly grave, if the offender tries to shift the blame to an innocent person. This is why such an attempt has been termed not only as *Buhtān* (calumny) but also as *Ithm Mubīn* (manifest sin).

R. 17 114. And but for the grace[668] of Allāh upon thee and His mercy, [a]a party of them had resolved to bring about thy ruin.[669] And they ruin none but themselves and they cannot harm thee at all. And Allāh has sent down to thee the Book and wisdom and [b]has taught thee what thou knewest not, and great is Allāh's grace on thee.

وَلَوْلَا فَضْلُ اللّٰهِ عَلَيْكَ وَرَحْمَتُهٗ لَهَمَّتْ طَّآئِفَةٌ
مِّنْهُمْ اَنْ يُّضِلُّوْكَ ؕ وَمَا يُضِلُّوْنَ اِلَّاۤ اَنْفُسَهُمْ وَمَا
يَضُرُّوْنَكَ مِنْ شَيْءٍ ؕ وَاَنْزَلَ اللّٰهُ عَلَيْكَ الْكِتٰبَ وَ
الْحِكْمَةَ وَعَلَّمَكَ مَا لَمْ تَكُنْ تَعْلَمُ ؕ وَكَانَ فَضْلُ اللّٰهِ
عَلَيْكَ عَظِيْمًا ﴿۱۱۴﴾

115. There is no good in many of their conferences[670] except the *conferences of* such as enjoin charity, or goodness or [c]the making of peace among men. And whoso does that, seeking the pleasure of Allāh, We shall soon bestow on him a great reward.

لَا خَيْرَ فِيْ كَثِيْرٍ مِّنْ نَّجْوٰىهُمْ اِلَّا مَنْ اَمَرَ بِصَدَقَةٍ
اَوْ مَعْرُوْفٍ اَوْ اِصْلَاحٍۭ بَيْنَ النَّاسِ ؕ وَمَنْ يَّفْعَلْ
ذٰلِكَ ابْتِغَآءَ مَرْضَاتِ اللّٰهِ فَسَوْفَ نُؤْتِيْهِ اَجْرًا
عَظِيْمًا ﴿۱۱۵﴾

116. And Whoso opposes the Messenger after guidance has become manifest to him, and [d]follows a way other than that of the believers, We shall let him pursue the way he is pursuing and shall cast him into Hell, and an evil destination it is.

وَمَنْ يُّشَاقِقِ الرَّسُوْلَ مِنْۢ بَعْدِ مَا تَبَيَّنَ لَهُ الْهُدٰى
وَيَتَّبِعْ غَيْرَ سَبِيْلِ الْمُؤْمِنِيْنَ نُوَلِّهٖ مَا تَوَلّٰى وَنُصْلِهٖ
جَهَنَّمَ ؕ وَسَآءَتْ مَصِيْرًا ﴿۱۱۶﴾ ع ۱۴

[a]17 : 74. [b]42 : 52; 96 : 6. [c]2 : 225. [d]7 : 4.

668. The words *Faḍl* (grace) and *Raḥmah* (mercy), though general in their significance, sometimes denote, "worldly goods" and "spiritual blessings" respectively (2 : 65). Thus the verse would mean that the Holy Prophet enjoyed God's protection in temporal as well as in spiritual matters.

669. The Hypocrites adopted various ways to bring the Holy Prophet to grief. They would try to mislead him into coming to a wrong decision in matters of vital importance. But their evil designs were always frustrated because he was invariably led by God to the right course concerning matters affecting the future of Islām.

670. *Najwā* means, a secret talk between two or more persons or telling secrets to another person or holding secret conferences. The word is not restricted to secret conferences but applies to all sorts of conferences whether secret or otherwise in which specially invited people meet to discuss vital matters (Lisān & Muḥīṭ).

R. 18 117. [a]Allāh shall not forgive that anything be associated with Him as partner, but He will forgive what is short of that to whomsoever He pleases. And [b]whoso associates anything with Allāh has indeed strayed far away.

إِنَّ اللّٰهَ لَا يَغْفِرُ أَنْ يُّشْرَكَ بِهٖ وَيَغْفِرُ مَا دُوْنَ ذٰلِكَ لِمَنْ يَّشَآءُ ۚ وَمَنْ يُّشْرِكْ بِاللّٰهِ فَقَدْ ضَلَّ ضَلٰلًا ۢ بَعِيْدًا ﴿۱۱۷﴾

118. They invoke besides Him none but lifeless objects,[671] and they invoke none but Satan the rebellious,

إِنْ يَّدْعُوْنَ مِنْ دُوْنِهٖٓ إِلَّآ إِنٰثًا ۚ وَإِنْ يَّدْعُوْنَ إِلَّا شَيْطٰنًا مَّرِيْدًا ﴿۱۱۸﴾

119. Whom Allāh has cursed. He said, [c]"I will assuredly take a fixed portion from Thy servants;

لَّعَنَهُ اللّٰهُ ۘ وَقَالَ لَأَتَّخِذَنَّ مِنْ عِبَادِكَ نَصِيْبًا مَّفْرُوْضًا ﴿۱۱۹﴾

120. 'And assuredly I will lead them astray and assuredly I will arouse in them vain desires, and assuredly I will incite them and they will cut the ears[672] of cattle; and assuredly I will incite them and they will alter[673] Allāh's creation.' And whoever takes Satan for a friend instead of Allāh, he certainly suffers a manifest loss.

وَّلَأُضِلَّنَّهُمْ وَلَأُمَنِّيَنَّهُمْ وَلَاٰمُرَنَّهُمْ فَلَيُبَتِّكُنَّ اٰذَانَ الْأَنْعَامِ وَلَاٰمُرَنَّهُمْ فَلَيُغَيِّرُنَّ خَلْقَ اللّٰهِ ۚ وَمَنْ يَّتَّخِذِ الشَّيْطٰنَ وَلِيًّا مِّنْ دُوْنِ اللّٰهِ فَقَدْ خَسِرَ خُسْرَانًا مُّبِيْنًا ﴿۱۲۰﴾

121. [d]He holds out promises to them and excites vain desires in them, and Satan promises them nothing but vain things.

يَعِدُهُمْ وَيُمَنِّيْهِمْ ۚ وَمَا يَعِدُهُمُ الشَّيْطٰنُ إِلَّا غُرُوْرًا ﴿۱۲۱﴾

122. For such, their abode shall be Hell, and [e]they shall find no way of escape from it.

أُولٰٓئِكَ مَأْوٰىهُمْ جَهَنَّمُ ۫ وَلَا يَجِدُوْنَ عَنْهَا مَحِيْصًا ﴿۱۲۲﴾

---

[a]4 : 49. [b]4 : 137. [c]14 : 23; 17 : 65. [d]14 : 23; 17 : 75. [e]14 : 22.

---

671. The word *Ināth* includes all false deities, whether living or dead. The word has been used to point to the utter weakness and helplessness of false deities.

672. As a mark of their devotion to false deities, the Arabs used to cut the ears of dedicated animals in order to distinguish them from other animals. This foolish practice persists even to this day in some countries.

673. The 'alteration of Allāh's creation' is done by (1) deifying God's creation; (2) by changing and corrupting the religion of God; (3) by deforming or disfiguring the body of a new-born child; and (4) by turning to evil use that which Allāh has created for good use.

123. But *as for* [a]those who believe and do good works, We will admit them into Gardens, beneath which streams flow, wherein they will abide for ever. *It is* Allāh's unfailing promise; and who can be more truthful than Allāh in word ?

وَالَّذِيْنَ اٰمَنُوْا وَعَمِلُوا الصّٰلِحٰتِ سَنُدْخِلُهُمْ جَنّٰتٍ
تَجْرِيْ مِنْ تَحْتِهَا الْاَنْهٰرُ خٰلِدِيْنَ فِيْهَآ اَبَدًا ؕ
وَعْدَ اللّٰهِ حَقًّا ؕ وَمَنْ اَصْدَقُ مِنَ اللّٰهِ قِيْلًا ﴿۱۲۳﴾

124. It shall not be according to your desires, nor according to the desires of the People of the Book. Whoso does evil shall be requited for it; and [b]he shall find for himself no friend or helper besides Allāh.

لَيْسَ بِاَمَانِيِّكُمْ وَلَآ اَمَانِيِّ اَهْلِ الْكِتٰبِ ؕ مَنْ يَّعْمَلْ
سُوْٓءًا يُّجْزَ بِهٖ ۙ وَلَا يَجِدْ لَهٗ مِنْ دُوْنِ اللّٰهِ وَلِيًّا
وَّلَا نَصِيْرًا ﴿۱۲۴﴾

125. But whoso does good works, whether male or female,[674] and he *or she* is a believer, such shall enter heaven, and shall not be wronged even *as much as* the little hollow in the back of a date-stone.

وَمَنْ يَّعْمَلْ مِنَ الصّٰلِحٰتِ مِنْ ذَكَرٍ اَوْ اُنْثٰى وَهُوَ
مُؤْمِنٌ فَاُولٰٓئِكَ يَدْخُلُوْنَ الْجَنَّةَ وَلَا يُظْلَمُوْنَ
نَقِيْرًا ﴿۱۲۵﴾

126. And who is better in faith than [d]he who submits himself entirely to Allāh, and he is a doer of good and follows the religion of Abraham, the upright? And Allāh took Abraham for a special friend.[675]

وَمَنْ اَحْسَنُ دِيْنًا مِّمَّنْ اَسْلَمَ وَجْهَهٗ لِلّٰهِ وَهُوَ
مُحْسِنٌ وَّاتَّبَعَ مِلَّةَ اِبْرٰهِيْمَ حَنِيْفًا ؕ وَاتَّخَذَ
اللّٰهُ اِبْرٰهِيْمَ خَلِيْلًا ﴿۱۲۶﴾

127. And [e]to Allāh belongs *all* that is in the heavens and that is in the earth; and [f]Allāh encompasses all things.

وَلِلّٰهِ مَا فِي السَّمٰوٰتِ وَمَا فِي الْاَرْضِ ؕ وَكَانَ اللّٰهُ
بِكُلِّ شَيْءٍ مُّحِيْطًا ﴿۱۲۷﴾ ع ۱۵

[a]See 2 : 26. [b]4 : 46; 33 : 18,66. [c]40 : 41. [d]2 : 132. [e]2 : 285; 4 : 132; 10 : 56; 16 : 53; 24 : 65. [f]41 : 55; 85 : 21.

674. The verse places men and women on the same level so far as their works and rewards are concerned. Both are equally entitled to good reward if they do good works.

675. This verse gives the essence of Islām which is complete submission to the will of God and the complete devotion of all one's faculties and powers to His service and holds out Abraham as true model for a Muslim to imitate and follow.

R. 19 128. And they seek of thee the decision[676] *of the Law* concerning *marriage with more* women *than one*. Say, Allāh gives you *His* decision concerning them. And [a]that which is recited to you *elsewhere* in the Book[677] concerns the orphan girls whom you give not what is prescribed for them and whom you desire to marry, and *also concerns* the weak among children.[677A] And *He enjoins you* to deal equitably with the orphans. And whatever good you do, surely Allāh knows it well.

وَيَسْتَفْتُونَكَ فِي النِّسَآءِ ۖ قُلِ اللّٰهُ يُفْتِيكُمْ فِيهِنَّ ۙ وَ
مَا يُتْلٰى عَلَيْكُمْ فِي الْكِتٰبِ فِي يَتٰمَى النِّسَآءِ الّٰتِي لَا
تُؤْتُونَهُنَّ مَا كُتِبَ لَهُنَّ وَتَرْغَبُونَ اَنْ تَنْكِحُوهُنَّ
وَالْمُسْتَضْعَفِيْنَ مِنَ الْوِلْدَانِ ۙ وَاَنْ تَقُومُوا لِلْيَتٰمٰى
بِالْقِسْطِ ۗ وَمَا تَفْعَلُوا مِنْ خَيْرٍ فَاِنَّ اللّٰهَ كَانَ بِهٖ
عَلِيمًا ﴿۱۲۸﴾

129. And [b]if a woman fears ill-treatment or indifference from her husband, it shall be no sin[678] for them that they be suitably reconciled to each other; and reconciliation is best. And people are prone to covetousness.[679] And if you do good and are righteous, surely Allāh is Aware of what you do.

وَاِنِ امْرَاَةٌ خَافَتْ مِنْ بَعْلِهَا نُشُوزًا اَوْ اِعْرَاضًا
فَلَا جُنَاحَ عَلَيْهِمَا اَنْ يُّصْلِحَا بَيْنَهُمَا صُلْحًا ۗ وَالصُّلْحُ
خَيْرٌ ۗ وَاُحْضِرَتِ الْاَنْفُسُ الشُّحَّ ۗ وَاِنْ تُحْسِنُوا
وَتَتَّقُوا فَاِنَّ اللّٰهَ كَانَ بِمَا تَعْمَلُونَ خَبِيرًا ﴿۱۲۹﴾

[a]4 : 4. [b]4 : 35.

676. The "decision" is referred to in the following three verses.

677. The allusion in the words, *that which is recited to you in the Book*, is to the 4th verse of the present *Sūrah*. It was prohibited to Muslims to marry those orphan girls whose rights they could not adequately safeguard. 'Umar, the Second Caliph would not allow the guardians of wealthy and handsome orphan girls to marry them and would insist on other and better husbands being found for them. The verse signifies that some instructions about women have already been given in the Qur'ān and that other instructions follow.

677A. *Walad* which is singular of *Wildān* is used both for a boy and a girl, but here *Wildān* signifies girls, marriage with whom is mentioned here.

678. The words, *it shall be no sin for them that they be suitably reconciled to each other*, constitute a peculiar Quranic expression denoting both exhortation and rebuke. They may be interpreted as something like this: "Do the contending parties think that they would be committing a sin if they became reconciled to each other ? It is no sin to do so. On the contrary, it is a commendable thing."

679. These words give the real cause that often leads to estrangement between husband and wife. It is niggardliness on the part of the husband and covetousness on the part of the wife.

130. And [a]you cannot keep *perfect* balance[680] between wives, however much you may desire it. But incline not wholly *to one* so [b]that you leave *the other* like *a thing* suspended. And if you are reconciled and act righteously, surely Allāh is Most Forgiving *and* Merciful.

وَلَنْ تَسْتَطِيعُوا أَنْ تَعْدِلُوا بَيْنَ النِّسَاءِ وَلَوْ حَرَصْتُمْ
فَلَا تَمِيلُوا كُلَّ الْمَيْلِ فَتَذَرُوهَا كَالْمُعَلَّقَةِ ۚ وَإِنْ
تُصْلِحُوا وَتَتَّقُوا فَإِنَّ اللَّهَ كَانَ غَفُورًا رَّحِيمًا ﴿١٣٠﴾

131. And if they separate, Allāh will make both independent[681] out of His abundance, and Allāh is Bountiful, Wise.

وَإِنْ يَتَفَرَّقَا يُغْنِ اللَّهُ كُلًّا مِّنْ سَعَتِهِ ۚ وَكَانَ اللَّهُ
وَاسِعًا حَكِيمًا ﴿١٣١﴾

132. And [c]to Allāh belongs whatever is in the heavens and whatever is in the earth. And [d]We have assuredly commanded those who were given the Book before you and *commanded* you also to fear Allāh. But if you disbelieve, then *remember that* to Allāh belongs whatever is in the heavens and whatever is in the earth, and Allāh is Self-Sufficient, Praiseworthy.

وَلِلَّهِ مَا فِي السَّمٰوٰتِ وَمَا فِي الْأَرْضِ ۗ وَلَقَدْ وَصَّيْنَا
الَّذِينَ أُوتُوا الْكِتٰبَ مِنْ قَبْلِكُمْ وَإِيَّاكُمْ أَنِ اتَّقُوا اللَّهَ ۚ
وَإِنْ تَكْفُرُوا فَإِنَّ لِلَّهِ مَا فِي السَّمٰوٰتِ وَمَا فِي الْأَرْضِ
وَكَانَ اللَّهُ غَنِيًّا حَمِيدًا ﴿١٣٢﴾

133. And [e]to Allāh belongs whatever is in the heavens and whatever is in the earth, and sufficient is Allāh as a Guardian.

وَلِلَّهِ مَا فِي السَّمٰوٰتِ وَمَا فِي الْأَرْضِ ۗ وَكَفٰى بِاللَّهِ
وَكِيلًا ﴿١٣٣﴾

134. If He please, He can take you away, O people, and bring others *in your stead*; and Allāh has full power to do that.

إِنْ يَّشَأْ يُذْهِبْكُمْ أَيُّهَا النَّاسُ وَيَأْتِ بِآخَرِينَ ۚ
وَكَانَ اللَّهُ عَلٰى ذٰلِكَ قَدِيرًا ﴿١٣٤﴾

[a]4 : 4. [b]2 : 232. [c]See 4 : 127. [d]42 : 14. [e]See 4 : 127.

680. It is humanly impossible for a man to keep perfect balance between his wives in all respects; for instance love being an affair of the heart over which man has no control, a husband cannot be expected to have equal love for all his wives. But he can certainly deal by them with equity in other respects, and this he must do. So acting equitably between one's wives pertains only to such acts over which one has control. This is the interpretation the Holy Prophet himself put upon this verse.

681. If, in spite of the husband and the wife having done their utmost to live amicably, they find that they cannot pull on together, and separation takes place, then God promises to provide for both parties more suitable matches. But according to Islām divorce is "Of all permissible things most hateful in the eyes of God" (Dawūd, ch. on *Ṭalāq*).

135. *Whoso desires the reward of this world, then *let him know that* with Allāh is the reward of this world and of the Hereafter; and Allāh is All-Hearing, All-Seeing.

مَنْ كَانَ يُرِيْدُ ثَوَابَ الدُّنْيَا فَعِنْدَ اللّٰهِ ثَوَابُ الدُّنْيَا وَالْاٰخِرَةِ ۚ وَكَانَ اللّٰهُ سَمِيْعًا بَصِيْرًا ۞

R. 20 136. O ye who believe! *be strict in observing justice, *and be* witnesses for Allāh, even though it be against yourselves[682] or *against your* parents or kindred. Whether he, *against whom witness is borne,* be rich or poor, Allāh is more regardful of them both *than you are.* Therefore follow not *your* low desires that you may *be able to* act equitably.[682A] And if you hide *the truth* or evade *it,* then *know that* Allāh is Well-Aware of what you do.

يٰٓاَيُّهَا الَّذِيْنَ اٰمَنُوْا كُوْنُوْا قَوّٰمِيْنَ بِالْقِسْطِ شُهَدَآءَ لِلّٰهِ وَلَوْ عَلٰٓى اَنْفُسِكُمْ اَوِ الْوَالِدَيْنِ وَالْاَقْرَبِيْنَ ۚ اِنْ يَّكُنْ غَنِيًّا اَوْ فَقِيْرًا فَاللّٰهُ اَوْلٰى بِهِمَا ۗ فَلَا تَتَّبِعُوا الْهَوٰٓى اَنْ تَعْدِلُوْا ۚ وَاِنْ تَلْوٗٓا اَوْ تُعْرِضُوْا فَاِنَّ اللّٰهَ كَانَ بِمَا تَعْمَلُوْنَ خَبِيْرًا ۞

137. O ye who believe![683] believe in Allāh and His Messenger, and in the Book which He has revealed to His Messenger, and *the Book which He revealed before *it.* And *whoso disbelieves in Allāh and His angels and His Books and His Messengers and the Last Day, *has surely strayed far away.

يٰٓاَيُّهَا الَّذِيْنَ اٰمَنُوْٓا اٰمِنُوْا بِاللّٰهِ وَرَسُوْلِهٖ وَالْكِتٰبِ الَّذِيْ نَزَّلَ عَلٰى رَسُوْلِهٖ وَالْكِتٰبِ الَّذِيْٓ اَنْزَلَ مِنْ قَبْلُ ۚ وَمَنْ يَّكْفُرْ بِاللّٰهِ وَمَلٰٓئِكَتِهٖ وَكُتُبِهٖ وَرُسُلِهٖ وَالْيَوْمِ الْاٰخِرِ فَقَدْ ضَلَّ ضَلٰلًۢا بَعِيْدًا ۞

138. *Those who believe, then disbelieve, then *again* believe, then disbelieve *and then increase in disbelief,*[684] Allāh will never forgive them nor will He guide them to the *right* way.

اِنَّ الَّذِيْنَ اٰمَنُوْا ثُمَّ كَفَرُوْا ثُمَّ اٰمَنُوْا ثُمَّ كَفَرُوْا ثُمَّ ازْدَادُوْا كُفْرًا لَّمْ يَكُنِ اللّٰهُ لِيَغْفِرَ لَهُمْ وَلَا لِيَهْدِيَهُمْ سَبِيْلًا ۞

---

*a*2 : 201, 202; 42 : 21. *b*5 : 9. *c*2 : 5, 137; 4 : 163; 5 : 60. *d*4 : 151. *e*4 : 117. *f*3 : 91; 63 : 4.

---

682. The expression, "against yourselves" may also signify "against your people or kith and kin." The words "parents and kindred" have been added to emphasize the force of the injunction.

682A. The words also mean, lest you deviate.

683. O ye who *profess* to be believers show by your deeds and actions that your faith is genuine and firmly founded.

684. The verse incidentally refutes the baseless allegation that apostasy in Islām is punishable with death.

139. [a]Give to the hypocrites the tidings that for them is a grievous punishment;

بَشِّرِ الْمُنٰفِقِيْنَ بِاَنَّ لَهُمْ عَذَابًا اَلِيْمًا ﴿١٣٩﴾

140. [b]Those who take disbelievers for friends rather than believers. Do they seek honour at their hands? Surely, [c]all honour belongs to Allāh.

اِلَّذِيْنَ يَتَّخِذُوْنَ الْكٰفِرِيْنَ اَوْلِيَآءَ مِنْ دُوْنِ
الْمُؤْمِنِيْنَ ۭ اَيَبْتَغُوْنَ عِنْدَهُمُ الْعِزَّةَ فَاِنَّ الْعِزَّةَ
لِلّٰهِ جَمِيْعًا ﴿١٤٠﴾

141. And He has already revealed to you in the Book[685] that, when you hear the Signs of God being denied and mocked at, sit not with those *who indulge in such talk* [d]until they engage in some other talk; for in that case you would be like them.[686] Surely, Allāh will assemble the hypocrites and the disbelievers in Hell, all together;

وَقَدْ نَزَّلَ عَلَيْكُمْ فِي الْكِتٰبِ اَنْ اِذَا سَمِعْتُمْ اٰيٰتِ
اللّٰهِ يُكْفَرُ بِهَا وَيُسْتَهْزَاُ بِهَا فَلَا تَقْعُدُوْا مَعَهُمْ
حَتّٰى يَخُوْضُوْا فِيْ حَدِيْثٍ غَيْرِهٖٓ ۖ اِنَّكُمْ اِذًا مِّثْلُهُمْ ۭ
اِنَّ اللّٰهَ جَامِعُ الْمُنٰفِقِيْنَ وَالْكٰفِرِيْنَ فِيْ جَهَنَّمَ
جَمِيْعَا ﴿١٤١﴾

142. [e]Those who await your ruin. If you have a victory from Allāh, they say, 'Were we not with you?' And if the disbelievers have a share *of it*, they say *to them*, 'Did we not *on a previous occasion* get the better of you and save you from the believers?' Allāh will judge between you on the Day of Resurrection; and Allāh will not grant the disbelievers a way *to prevail* against the believers.

اِلَّذِيْنَ يَتَرَبَّصُوْنَ بِكُمْ ۚ فَاِنْ كَانَ لَكُمْ فَتْحٌ مِّنَ اللّٰهِ
قَالُوْٓا اَلَمْ نَكُنْ مَّعَكُمْ ۖ وَاِنْ كَانَ لِلْكٰفِرِيْنَ نَصِيْبٌ ۙ
قَالُوْٓا اَلَمْ نَسْتَحْوِذْ عَلَيْكُمْ وَنَمْنَعْكُمْ مِّنَ الْمُؤْمِنِيْنَ ۭ
فَاللّٰهُ يَحْكُمُ بَيْنَكُمْ يَوْمَ الْقِيٰمَةِ ۭ وَلَنْ يَّجْعَلَ اللّٰهُ
لِلْكٰفِرِيْنَ عَلَى الْمُؤْمِنِيْنَ سَبِيْلًا ﴿١٤٢﴾ ع

[a]9 : 3. [b]3 : 29, 119; 4 : 145. [c]10 : 66; 35 : 11. [d]6 : 69. [e]9 : 98; 57 : 15.

685. The reference in the words, *He has already revealed to you in the Book*, is to 6 : 69 which was revealed at Mecca prior to the verse under comment; yet 6 : 69 has been placed after it in the existing arrangement of the Qur'ān which shows that the present arrangement of the Quranic verses is not the same in which they were revealed.

686. The underlying principle in the injunction contained in the present verse is threefold : (1) To emphasize the seriousness and importance of religious matters; (2) to protect the believers against the demoralizing influences of the disbelievers' company and (3) to engender and promote feelings of pious jealousy for religion in the hearts of Muslims.

R. 21 143. [a]The hypocrites seek to deceive Allāh, but He will punish them for their deception.[687] And when they stand up for Prayer, [b]they stand up lazily *and* to be seen of men, and they remember Allāh but little.

إِنَّ الْمُنٰفِقِيْنَ يُخٰدِعُوْنَ اللّٰهَ وَهُوَ خَادِعُهُمْ ۚ وَإِذَا
قَامُوْٓا إِلَى الصَّلٰوةِ قَامُوْا كُسَالٰى ۙ يُرَآءُوْنَ النَّاسَ
وَلَا يَذْكُرُوْنَ اللّٰهَ إِلَّا قَلِيْلًا ﴿١٤٣﴾

144. Wavering between *this and* that,[688] *belonging* neither to these nor to those. And he whom Allāh causes to perish, for him thou shalt not find a way *of escape*.

مُّذَبْذَبِيْنَ بَيْنَ ذٰلِكَ ۖ لَآ إِلٰى هٰٓؤُلَآءِ وَلَآ إِلٰى هٰٓؤُلَآءِ ۚ
وَمَنْ يُّضْلِلِ اللّٰهُ فَلَنْ تَجِدَ لَهٗ سَبِيْلًا ﴿١٤٤﴾

145. O ye who believe, [c]take not disbelievers for friends, in preference to believers. Do you mean to give Allāh a manifest proof against yourselves ?

يٰٓأَيُّهَا الَّذِيْنَ اٰمَنُوْا لَا تَتَّخِذُوا الْكٰفِرِيْنَ أَوْلِيَآءَ مِنْ
دُوْنِ الْمُؤْمِنِيْنَ ۚ أَتُرِيْدُوْنَ أَنْ تَجْعَلُوْا لِلّٰهِ عَلَيْكُمْ
سُلْطٰنًا مُّبِيْنًا ﴿١٤٥﴾

146. The hypocrites shall surely be in the lowest depths[689] of the Fire; and thou shalt find no helper for them,

إِنَّ الْمُنٰفِقِيْنَ فِي الدَّرْكِ الْأَسْفَلِ مِنَ النَّارِ ۚ وَلَنْ
تَجِدَ لَهُمْ نَصِيْرًا ﴿١٤٦﴾

147. [d]Except those who repent and amend and [e]hold fast to Allāh and are sincere in their obedience to Allāh—these are among the believers. And Allāh will soon bestow a great reward upon the believers.

إِلَّا الَّذِيْنَ تَابُوْا وَأَصْلَحُوْا وَاعْتَصَمُوْا بِاللّٰهِ وَأَخْلَصُوْا
دِيْنَهُمْ لِلّٰهِ فَأُولٰٓئِكَ مَعَ الْمُؤْمِنِيْنَ ۚ وَسَوْفَ يُؤْتِ
اللّٰهُ الْمُؤْمِنِيْنَ أَجْرًا عَظِيْمًا ﴿١٤٧﴾

---

[a]2 : 10. [b]9 : 54. [c]3 : 29, 119 ; 4 : 140. [d]See 2:161. [e]3: 102.

---

687. It is not God but the Holy Prophet whom, in reality, the hypocrites seek to deceive because the Prophet is an agent of God and all plots hatched against him are really so many plots hatched to frustrate the purpose of God. Therefore God Himself will punish them for their deceitful conduct. See also 2 : 16.

688. The expression means, "between belief and disbelief" or "between believers and disbelievers."

689. The Qur'ān's strong denunciation of the hypocrites is a clear refutation of the charge that it exhorts its followers to spread Islām by means of the sword. If a man is forced to accept Islām against his will, he will never make a sincere believer.

148. Why should Allāh punish you, if you are thankful and *if* you believe? And [a]Allāh is Appreciating,[690] All-Knowing.

مَا يَفْعَلُ اللّٰهُ بِعَذَابِكُمْ اِنْ شَكَرْتُمْ وَ اٰمَنْتُمْ ؕ وَ
كَانَ اللّٰهُ شَاكِرًا عَلِيْمًا ﴿١٤٨﴾

PART VI

149. Allāh likes not the uttering of unseemly speech in public,[691] except *on the part of* one who is *being* wronged. Verily, Allāh is All-Hearing, All-Knowing.

الجزء ٦ لَا يُحِبُّ اللّٰهُ الْجَهْرَ بِالسُّوْٓءِ مِنَ الْقَوْلِ اِلَّا
مَنْ ظُلِمَ ؕ وَ كَانَ اللّٰهُ سَمِيْعًا عَلِيْمًا ﴿١٤٩﴾

150. Whether you make public a good deed or keep it secret or pardon an evil, Allāh is certainly the Effacer of sins, All-Powerful.

اِنْ تُبْدُوْا خَيْرًا اَوْ تُخْفُوْهُ اَوْ تَعْفُوْا عَنْ سُوْٓءٍ
فَاِنَّ اللّٰهَ كَانَ عَفُوًّا قَدِيْرًا ﴿١٥٠﴾

151. Surely, [b]those who disbelieve in Allāh and His Messengers and seek to make a distinction between Allāh and His Messengers, and say, 'We believe in some and disbelieve in others,' and seek to take a way in between;[692]

اِنَّ الَّذِيْنَ يَكْفُرُوْنَ بِاللّٰهِ وَ رُسُلِهٖ وَ يُرِيْدُوْنَ اَنْ
يُّفَرِّقُوْا بَيْنَ اللّٰهِ وَ رُسُلِهٖ وَ يَقُوْلُوْنَ نُؤْمِنُ بِبَعْضٍ
وَّ نَكْفُرُ بِبَعْضٍ ۙ وَّ يُرِيْدُوْنَ اَنْ يَّتَّخِذُوْا بَيْنَ
ذٰلِكَ سَبِيْلًا ۙ ﴿١٥١﴾

152. These really are the disbelievers, and We have prepared for the disbelievers an humiliating punishment.

اُولٰٓئِكَ هُمُ الْكٰفِرُوْنَ حَقًّا ۚ وَ اَعْتَدْنَا لِلْكٰفِرِيْنَ
عَذَابًا مُّهِيْنًا ﴿١٥٢﴾

153. And [c]those who believe in Allāh and *in all* His Messengers and make no distinction between any of them, to such He will soon give their rewards. And Allāh is Most Forgiving, Merciful.

وَ الَّذِيْنَ اٰمَنُوْا بِاللّٰهِ وَ رُسُلِهٖ وَ لَمْ يُفَرِّقُوْا بَيْنَ
اَحَدٍ مِّنْهُمْ اُولٰٓئِكَ سَوْفَ يُؤْتِيْهِمْ اُجُوْرَهُمْ ؕ وَ
كَانَ اللّٰهُ غَفُوْرًا رَّحِيْمًا ﴿١٥٣﴾ ع

---

[a]2 : 159. [b]4 : 137. [c]2 : 137; 2: 286; 3 : 85.

---

690. *Shukr* on the part of God consists in forgiving a person or commending him or regarding him with satisfaction, goodwill or favour and hence necessarily recompensing him or rewarding him (Lane).

691. Islām does not allow Muslims to speak ill of other people in public, but he who is wronged may cry aloud when he is actually being transgressed against, so that other men may come to his help. He may as well seek redress in a law-court, but should not go about complaining to all and sundry.

692. The verse means that they accept God and reject His Prophets; or accept some Prophets and reject others; or accept some claims of a Prophet and reject other claims. True faith lies in total submission, accepting God and all His Messengers with all their claims. No middle course is permissible.

R. 22

154. The People of the Book ask thee to bring down upon them a Book from Heaven. [a]They asked Moses a greater thing than this. They said, [b]'Show us Allāh openly.'[693] Thereupon a destructive punishment overtook them because of their transgression. Then [c]they took the calf *for worship* after clear Signs had come to them, but We pardoned *even* that. And We gave Moses manifest authority.

155. And [d]We raised high above them the Mount while making a covenant with them, and We said to them, [e]'Enter the gate submissively' and We said to them, [f]'Transgress not in *the matter of* the Sabbath.[694] And We took from them a firm covenant.

156. So, for their breaking their covenant, and [g]their denial of the Signs of Allāh, and [h]their seeking to slay the Prophets unjustly, and their saying: "Our hearts are wrapped up in covers,'—nay, but [i]Allāh has sealed[695] them because of their disbelief, so they believe not but little—

157. And for their disbelief and *for* their uttering against Mary a grievous calumny;[696]

يَسْـَٔلُكَ أَهْلُ الْكِتٰبِ أَنْ تُنَزِّلَ عَلَيْهِمْ كِتٰبًا مِّنَ السَّمَآءِ فَقَدْ سَأَلُوْا مُوْسٰۤى أَكْبَرَ مِنْ ذٰلِكَ فَقَالُوْۤا أَرِنَا اللّٰهَ جَهْرَةً فَأَخَذَتْهُمُ الصّٰعِقَةُ بِظُلْمِهِمْ ثُمَّ اتَّخَذُوا الْعِجْلَ مِنْۢ بَعْدِ مَا جَآءَتْهُمُ الْبَيِّنٰتُ فَعَفَوْنَا عَنْ ذٰلِكَ ۚ وَاٰتَيْنَا مُوْسٰى سُلْطٰنًا مُّبِيْنًا ۞

وَرَفَعْنَا فَوْقَهُمُ الطُّوْرَ بِمِيْثَاقِهِمْ وَقُلْنَا لَهُمُ ادْخُلُوا الْبَابَ سُجَّدًا وَّقُلْنَا لَهُمْ لَا تَعْدُوْا فِى السَّبْتِ وَأَخَذْنَا مِنْهُمْ مِّيْثَاقًا غَلِيْظًا ۞

فَبِمَا نَقْضِهِمْ مِّيْثَاقَهُمْ وَكُفْرِهِمْ بِاٰيٰتِ اللّٰهِ وَقَتْلِهِمُ الْاَنْۢبِيَآءَ بِغَيْرِ حَقٍّ وَّقَوْلِهِمْ قُلُوْبُنَا غُلْفٌ ۚ بَلْ طَبَعَ اللّٰهُ عَلَيْهَا بِكُفْرِهِمْ فَلَا يُؤْمِنُوْنَ إِلَّا قَلِيْلًا ۞

وَّبِكُفْرِهِمْ وَقَوْلِهِمْ عَلٰى مَرْيَمَ بُهْتَانًا عَظِيْمًا ۙ ۞

---

[a]2 : 109. [b]2 : 56. [c]2 : 52, 93; 7 : 149, 153. [d]2 : 64, 94. [e]2 : 59; 7 : 162. [f]2 : 66; 4 : 48; 7 : 164; 16 : 125. [g]5 : 14. [h]3 : 182. [i]2 : 89. [j]2 : 89; 16 : 109; 83 : 15.

---

693. See 96.

694. See 4 : 48.

695. See 27.

696. The Jews accused Mary of fornication ("Jewish Life of Jesus" by Panther). The fact that the Jews uttered "a calumny" against Mary constitutes clear evidence of the fatherless birth of Jesus. For, if Jesus had a father, what "calumny" was it that the Jews uttered against Mary? Merely taunting her for the claims made by Jesus could in no sense be called a calumny. Elsewhere, the Qur'ān refutes this charge by saying that the mother of Jesus was a righteous woman (3 : 43 ; 5 : 76).

158. And *for* their saying, 'We did slay the Messiah, Jesus, son of Mary, the Messenger of Allāh;' whereas they slew him not, nor did they bring about his death on the cross,[697] but he was made to appear[698] to them like *one crucified*; and those who differ therein are certainly in a *state of* doubt about it; [a]they have no *certain* knowledge thereof, but only pursue a conjecture; and they did not arrive at a certainty concerning it.[699]

وَّ قَوۡلِهِمۡ اِنَّا قَتَلۡنَا الۡمَسِیۡحَ عِیۡسَی ابۡنَ مَرۡیَمَ
رَسُوۡلَ اللّٰهِ ۚ وَ مَا قَتَلُوۡهُ وَ مَا صَلَبُوۡهُ وَ لٰکِنۡ شُبِّهَ
لَهُمۡ ؕ وَ اِنَّ الَّذِیۡنَ اخۡتَلَفُوۡا فِیۡهِ لَفِیۡ شَکٍّ مِّنۡهُ ؕ
مَا لَهُمۡ بِهٖ مِنۡ عِلۡمٍ اِلَّا اتِّبَاعَ الظَّنِّ ۚ وَ مَا قَتَلُوۡهُ
یَقِیۡنًۢا ﴿۱۵۸﴾

[a]10 : 37; 53 : 29.

697. *Mā Ṣalabū-hu* means, they did not cause his death on the cross. *Ṣalab* being a well-known manner of killing. They say *Ṣalaba al-Lissa, i.e.*, he put the thief to death by putting him on the cross. The verse does not deny the fact of Jesus's being nailed to the cross but denies his having died on it.

698. The words *Shubbiha La-hum* mean, Jesus was made to appear to the Jews like one crucified; or the matter of the death of Jesus became obscure or dubious to them. *Shubbiha 'Alaihi al-Amru* means, the matter was rendered confused, obscure or dubious to him (Lane).

699. The expression, *Mā Qatalū-hu Yaqīnan*, means, (1) they did not kill him for certain; (2) they did not convert it (their conjecture) into certainty, *i.e.*, their knowledge about the death of Jesus on the cross was not so certain as to have left no doubt in their minds that they had really killed him. In this case the pronoun *hu* in *Qatalū-hu* would refer to the noun *Ẓann* (conjecture). The Arabs say *Qatala al-Shai'a Khubran, i.e.*, he acquired full and certain knowledge of the thing so as to dispel all possibility of doubt about it (Lane, Lisān & Mufradāt). That Jesus did not die on the cross but died a natural death is clear from the Qur'ān. The following facts, as narrated in the Gospels themselves lend powerful support to the Quranic version :—

1. Being a Divine Prophet Jesus could not have died on the cross because according to the Bible "he that is hanged is accursed of God" (Deut. 21 : 23). 2. He had prayed to God in great agony to "take away this cup (of death on the cross) from me" (Mark, 14 : 36; Matt. 26 : 29; Luke, 22 : 42); and his prayer was heard (Heb. 5 : 7). 3. He had predicted that like Jonah who had gone into the belly of the whale alive and had come out of it alive (Matt. 12 : 40) he would remain in an excavated sepulchre for three days and would come out of it alive. 4. He had also prophesied that he would go to seek out the Lost Ten Tribes of Israel (John 10 : 16). Even Jews in Jesus's time believed that the Lost Tribes of Israel had become dispersed in different lands (John, 7 : 34.35). 5. Jesus had remained hung on the cross only for about three hours (John, 19 : 14) and being a person of normal constitution he could not have died in such a short time. 6. Immediately after he had been taken down from the cross his side was pierced and blood and water flowed out of it which was a certain sign of life (John, 19 : 34). 7. The Jews themselves were not sure of Jesus's death because they had asked Pilate to have a guard posted at his sepulchre "lest his disciples come by night and steal him away and say unto the people, 'He is risen from the dead' (Matt. 27 : 64). 8. There is not to be found in all the Gospels a single recorded statement of an eye-witness to the effect that Jesus was dead when he was taken down from the cross or when he was placed in the tomb. Moreover, none of the disciples was present at the scene of Crucifixion, all having fled when Jesus was taken to Calvary. The fact of the case seems to be that, presumably due to the dream of his wife "to have nothing to do with that just man," Pilate had believed Jesus to be innocent and had, therefore, conspired with Joseph of Arimaethia, a respected member of the Essene Order to which Jesus himself belonged before he was commissioned as a Prophet,

159. [a]On the contrary, Allāh exalted him to Himself.[700] And Allāh is Mighty, Wise.

بَلْ رَّفَعَهُ اللّٰهُ اِلَيْهِ ۭ وَكَانَ اللّٰهُ عَزِيْزًا حَكِيْمًا ۝١٥٩

160. And there is none among the People of the Book but will *continue to* believe in it before his[701] death; and on the Day of Resurrection, [b]he (Jesus) shall be a witness against them

وَاِنْ مِّنْ اَهْلِ الْكِتٰبِ اِلَّا لَيُؤْمِنَنَّ بِهٖ قَبْلَ مَوْتِهٖ ۚ وَيَوْمَ الْقِيٰمَةِ يَكُوْنُ عَلَيْهِمْ شَهِيْدًا ۝١٦٠ۚ

[a]2 : 254 ; 3 : 56 ; 7 : 177 ; 58 : 12. [b]5 : 118.

to save his life. The trial of Jesus took place on Friday, Pilate having purposely prolonged it, knowing that the next day being the Sabbath Day the condemned persons could not be left on the cross after sunset. When at last he found himself compelled to condemn Jesus, Pilate gave his judgment only three hours before sunset, thus making himself sure that no person of normal health could die in such a short time by remaining on the cross. He took additional care to see that Jesus was given wine or vinegar mingled with myrrh to render him less sensitive to pain. When after three hours' suspension he was taken down from the cross in an unconscious state (probably under the influence of vinegar which was administered to him), Pilate readily granted Joseph of Arimaethia's request and handed over his body to him. Unlike those of the two malefactors who were hung along with Jesus, his bones were not broken and Joseph had him placed in a spacious room hewn in the side of a rock. There was no medical autopsy, no strethoscopic test, no inquest with the aid of the evidence of those who were last with him ("Mystical life of Jesus" by H. Spencer Lewis). 9. An ointment, the famous *Marham 'Īsā*, (Ointment of Jesus) was prepared and applied to Jesus's wounds and he was tended and looked after by Joseph of Arimaethia and Nicodemus, also a very learned and highly respected member of the Essene Brotherhood. 10. After his wounds had been sufficiently healed, Jesus left the tomb and met some of his disciples and had his food with them and walked the whole distance from Jerusalem to Galilee on foot (Luke, 24 : 50). 11. "The Crucifixion by an Eye Witness," a book, which was at first published in 1873 in U.S.A. and which is an English translation of an ancient Latin copy of a letter written seven years after the Crucifixion by an Essene Brother in Jerusalem to a member of this Brotherhood in Alexandria, lends powerful support to the view that Jesus had been taken down from the cross alive. The book narrates in detail all the events leading to the Crucifixion, the scenes at the Calvary and also the incidents that took place afterwards. See also 'The Larger Edition of the Commentary.'

Two different views prevail among the Jews regarding Jesus's alleged death by Crucifixion. Some of them hold that he was first killed and then his dead body was hung on the cross, while others are of the view that he was put to death by being fixed to the cross. The former view is reflected in The Acts 5 : 30 where we read "which ye slew and hanged on a tree." The Qur'ān refutes both these views by saying, *they slew him not, nor did they bring about his death on the cross*. The Qur'ān first rejects the slaying of Jesus in any form, and then proceeds to deny the particular way of killing by hanging on the cross. It does not deny that Jesus was hung on the cross; it only denies his death on it.

700. The Jews exultingly claimed to have killed Jesus on the cross and thus to have proved that his claim to be a Divine Prophet was not true. The verse along with the preceding one contains a strong refutation of the charge and clears him of the insinuated blemish and speaks of his spiritual elevation and of his having been honoured in the presence of God. There is absolutely no reference in the verse to his physical ascension to heavens. It only says that God exalted him towards Himself which clearly signifies a spiritual exaltation, because no fixed abode can be assigned to God.

701. The pronoun "his" in the expression "before his death" stands for the noun "none," meaning every one among the People of the Book before his own death. . . . .This meaning is supported by the second reading of *Mautihī* which is *Mautihim* (their death) as

161. So, because of the transgression of the Jews, [a]We forbade[702] them pure things which had been allowed to them, and *also* because of their hindering many *men* from Allah's way,

فَبِظُلْمٍ مِّنَ الَّذِيْنَ هَادُوْا حَرَّمْنَا عَلَيْهِمْ طَيِّبٰتٍ أُحِلَّتْ لَهُمْ وَبِصَدِّهِمْ عَنْ سَبِيْلِ اللّٰهِ كَثِيْرًا ﴿١٦١﴾

162. And *because of* [b]their taking interest although they had been forbidden it, and *because of* [c]their devouring people's wealth wrongfully. And We have prepared for those of them, who disbelieve, a painful punishment.[703]

وَّأَخْذِهِمُ الرِّبٰوا وَقَدْ نُهُوْا عَنْهُ وَأَكْلِهِمْ أَمْوَالَ النَّاسِ بِالْبَاطِلِ ۚ وَأَعْتَدْنَا لِلْكٰفِرِيْنَ مِنْهُمْ عَذَابًا أَلِيْمًا ﴿١٦٢﴾

163. But [d]those among them who are firmly grounded in knowledge,[704] and [e]the believers, believe in what has been sent down to thee and what was sent down before thee, and *especially* those who observe[705] Prayer and those who pay

لٰكِنِ الرّٰسِخُوْنَ فِي الْعِلْمِ مِنْهُمْ وَالْمُؤْمِنُوْنَ يُؤْمِنُوْنَ بِمَآ أُنْزِلَ إِلَيْكَ وَمَآ أُنْزِلَ مِنْ قَبْلِكَ وَالْمُقِيْمِيْنَ

[a]6 : 147. [b]2: 276,277; 3: 131; 30: 40. [c]9: 34. [d]3: 8. [e]2 : 5, 137; 3 : 200; 4 : 137; 5: 60.

reported by Ubayy (Jarır, vi. 13). The Jews believe that they killed Jesus on the cross because they seek to prove that he was not a true Prophet. The Christians believe that he had died on the cross, and this is because they have adopted the doctrine of Atonement.

702. The verse does not refer to any material thing which was forbidden to the Jews after having been allowed before, because no Law-giving Prophet had appeared among them after Moses to forbid them things that had been allowed to them by the Torah. It refers to the spiritual Divine favours of which they had become deprived. It was also to the spiritual blessings the Jews had lost that Jesus referred when he said, *I come to allow you some of that which had been farbidden to you* (3 : 51), *i.e.*, I come to restore to you some of the Divine blessings of which you have been deprived on account of your misdeeds.

703. The Jews were forbidden to lend money on interest to other Jews, but they were permitted to take interest from non-Jews (Exod. 22 : 25; Lev. 25 : 36,37; Deut. 23 : 19,20). But they broke the Law and began to take interest even from Jews (Neh. 5 : 7). Later they promised Nehemiah to give up this evil practice (Neh. 5 : 12). But they again broke their word; and so, in accordance with the prophecy of Ezekiel (Ezek. 18 : 13), they, as a nation, suffered death and were scattered over the earth to be persecuted at the hands of their enemies.

704. This means those learned men among the Jews who embraced Islām. The word "believers" has been added to indicate that only those Jews are meant here who became Muslims.

705. The variation in the vowel-points of *Muqīmīn* is permissible according to rules of Arabic grammar. It is resorted to for the purpose of emphasis (Kashshāf, i. 336).

the *Zakāt* and those who believe in Allāh and the Last Day. To these We will surely give a mighty reward.

الصَّلٰوةَ وَالْمُؤْتُوْنَ الزَّكٰوةَ وَالْمُؤْمِنُوْنَ بِاللّٰهِ وَ
الْيَوْمِ الْاٰخِرِ اُولٰٓئِكَ سَنُؤْتِيْهِمْ اَجْرًا عَظِيْمًا ﴿١٦٣﴾ ع ٢٢ ع ٢

R. 23 164. Surely, [a]We have sent revelation to thee, as We sent revelation to Noah and the Prophets after him; and We sent revelation to Abraham and Ishmael and Isaac and Jacob and *his* children and to Jesus and Job and Jonah and Aaron and Solomon, and [b]We gave David a Book.[706]

اِنَّآ اَوْحَيْنَآ اِلَيْكَ كَمَآ اَوْحَيْنَآ اِلٰى نُوْحٍ وَّالنَّبِيّٖنَ
مِنْ بَعْدِهٖ ۚ وَاَوْحَيْنَآ اِلٰٓى اِبْرٰهِيْمَ وَاِسْمٰعِيْلَ وَ
اِسْحٰقَ وَيَعْقُوْبَ وَالْاَسْبَاطِ وَعِيْسٰى وَاَيُّوْبَ
وَيُوْنُسَ وَهٰرُوْنَ وَسُلَيْمٰنَ ۚ وَاٰتَيْنَا دَاوٗدَ
زَبُوْرًا ۚ ﴿١٦٤﴾

165. *And We sent some* [c]Messengers whom We have already mentioned to thee and *some* Messengers whom We have not mentioned to thee[707]—and to Moses Allāh spoke at great length[707A]—

وَرُسُلًا قَدْ قَصَصْنٰهُمْ عَلَيْكَ مِنْ قَبْلُ وَرُسُلًا
لَّمْ نَقْصُصْهُمْ عَلَيْكَ ۗ وَكَلَّمَ اللّٰهُ مُوْسٰى تَكْلِيْمًا ﴿١٦٥﴾

166. Messengers, [d]bearers of glad tidings and Warners,[708] so that people may have no plea against Allāh after *the coming of* the Messengers.[709] And Allāh is Mighty, Wise.

رُسُلًا مُّبَشِّرِيْنَ وَمُنْذِرِيْنَ لِئَلَّا يَكُوْنَ لِلنَّاسِ
عَلَى اللّٰهِ حُجَّةٌۢ بَعْدَ الرُّسُلِ ۗ وَكَانَ اللّٰهُ عَزِيْزًا
حَكِيْمًا ﴿١٦٦﴾

[a]2 : 137; 3 : 85; 6 : 85-88. [b]17 : 56. [c]40 : 79. [d]2 : 214; 6 ; 49; 17 : 106; 18 : 57.

706. Some Prophets have been mentioned here, and in the succeeding verse, to point out that the mission of the Prophet of Islām was not a new thing. The specific mention of Zabūr, the Book of Wisdom given to David in the present verse and of the Law-bearing revelation vouchsafed to Moses in the succeeding one, is made to hint that the Qur'ān combines in itself both "Law and wisdom."

707. The Qur'ān mentions by name only 24 Prophets whereas according to a saying of the Holy Prophet as many as 1,24,000 Prophets appeared in the world (Musnad, v. 266). Elsewhere, the Qur'ān says: *There is not a people to whom a Warner has not been sent* (35 : 25).

707A. Besides the translation given in the text, the clause also means, "to Moses Allāh spoke particularly or directly."

708. The words, *bearers of glad tidings and Warners*, point to two essential functions of God's Messengers. They are bearers of glad tidings for those who accept them, promising them prosperity in this world and blissful felicity in the life to come, and are warners of impending misery and afflictions for those who reject them.

709. God sends His Messengers so that the people, on being punished, should have no excuse to say that no Warner was sent to them to point to their evil deeds and to warn them (20 : 135).

167. But [a]Allāh bears witness by means of *the revelation* which He has sent down to thee that He has sent it down *full* of His knowledge,[710] and the angels *also* bear witness; and sufficient is Allāh as a Witness.

لٰكِنِ اللّٰهُ يَشْهَدُ بِمَآ اَنْزَلَ اِلَيْكَ اَنْزَلَهٗ بِعِلْمِهٖ ۚ
وَالْمَلٰٓئِكَةُ يَشْهَدُوْنَ ۗ وَكَفٰى بِاللّٰهِ شَهِيْدًا ﴿١٦٧﴾

168. [b]Those who disbelieve and hinder *others* from the way of Allāh, have certainly strayed far away.

اِنَّ الَّذِيْنَ كَفَرُوْا وَصَدُّوْا عَنْ سَبِيْلِ اللّٰهِ قَدْ ضَلُّوْا
ضَلٰلًا بَعِيْدًا ﴿١٦٨﴾

169. Surely, [c]those who have disbelieved and have acted unjustly, Allāh will not forgive them, nor will He show them any way;

اِنَّ الَّذِيْنَ كَفَرُوْا وَظَلَمُوْا لَمْ يَكُنِ اللّٰهُ لِيَغْفِرَ لَهُمْ
وَلَا لِيَهْدِيَهُمْ طَرِيْقًا ﴿١٦٩﴾

170. Except the way of Hell, wherein they shall abide for a long, long period. And [d]that is easy for Allāh.

اِلَّا طَرِيْقَ جَهَنَّمَ خٰلِدِيْنَ فِيْهَآ اَبَدًا ۗ وَكَانَ ذٰلِكَ
عَلَى اللّٰهِ يَسِيْرًا ﴿١٧٠﴾

171. O mankind ! the Messenger has indeed come to you with truth from your Lord; believe therefore, *it will be* better for you. But if you disbelieve, verily, to Allāh belongs whatever is in the heavens and in the earth. And Allāh is All-Knowing, Wise.

يٰٓاَيُّهَا النَّاسُ قَدْ جَآءَكُمُ الرَّسُوْلُ بِالْحَقِّ مِنْ
رَّبِّكُمْ فَاٰمِنُوْا خَيْرًا لَّكُمْ ۗ وَاِنْ تَكْفُرُوْا فَاِنَّ لِلّٰهِ مَا
فِي السَّمٰوٰتِ وَالْاَرْضِ ۗ وَكَانَ اللّٰهُ عَلِيْمًا حَكِيْمًا ﴿١٧١﴾

172. [e]O People of the Book! exceed not the limits in your religion, and say not of Allāh anything but the truth. Verily, the Messiah, Jesus, son of Mary, was only a Messenger of Allāh, and *a fulfilment of* His Word[711] which He sent down to Mary, and [f]a mercy[712] from Him.

يٰٓاَهْلَ الْكِتٰبِ لَا تَغْلُوْا فِيْ دِيْنِكُمْ وَلَا تَقُوْلُوْا عَلَى
اللّٰهِ اِلَّا الْحَقَّ ۗ اِنَّمَا الْمَسِيْحُ عِيْسَى ابْنُ مَرْيَمَ
رَسُوْلُ اللّٰهِ وَكَلِمَتُهٗ ۚ اَلْقٰهَآ اِلٰى مَرْيَمَ وَرُوْحٌ مِّنْهُ

[a]3 : 19; 11 : 15. [b]4 : 138. [c]4 : 138. [d]33 : 31; 64 : 8. [e]5 : 78. [f]58 : 23.

710. God has placed in the Qur'ān vast treasures of eternal truth and spiritual knowledge that bear witness to its being the Word of God. The manifold qualities of the Qur'ān furnish irrefutable evidence of its Divine origin for those who ponder over it.

711. See 414.

712. *Rūḥ* means, soul or spirit; the breath which pervades the whole body after the exit of which man dies; Divine revelation or inspiration; the Qur'ān; angel; joy and

So believe in Allāh and His Messengers, and [a]say not '*They are* three.' Desist, *it will be* better for you. Verily, Allāh is the only One God. [b]Holy is He, far above having a [c]son. To Him belongs whatever is in the heavens and whatever is in the earth. And sufficient is Allāh as a Guardian.

فَاٰمِنُوْا بِاللّٰهِ وَرُسُلِهٖ ۚ وَلَا تَقُوْلُوْا ثَلٰثَةٌ ؕ اِنْتَهُوْا
خَيْرًا لَّكُمْ ؕ اِنَّمَا اللّٰهُ اِلٰهٌ وَّاحِدٌ ؕ سُبْحٰنَهٗۤ اَنْ يَّكُوْنَ
لَهٗ وَلَدٌ ۘ لَهٗ مَا فِي السَّمٰوٰتِ وَمَا فِي الْاَرْضِ ؕ وَكَفٰى
بِاللّٰهِ وَكِيْلًا ﴿۱۷۲﴾ ع ٢٣ ٣

R. 24 173. Surely, [d]the Messiah disdains not to be a servant of Allāh, nor do the angels *who are* near *to Him*, and whoso disdains to worship Him and is proud, He will gather them all to Himself.

لَنْ يَّسْتَنْكِفَ الْمَسِيْحُ اَنْ يَّكُوْنَ عَبْدًا لِّلّٰهِ وَلَا
الْمَلٰٓئِكَةُ الْمُقَرَّبُوْنَ ؕ وَمَنْ يَّسْتَنْكِفْ عَنْ عِبَادَتِهٖ وَ
يَسْتَكْبِرْ فَسَيَحْشُرُهُمْ اِلَيْهِ جَمِيْعًا ﴿۱۷۳﴾

174. Then as for those who believe and do good works, [e]He will give them their rewards in full and will give them more out of His grace; but as for those who disdain and are proud, He will punish them with a painful punishment. And they shall find for themselves beside Allāh no friend, nor helper.

فَاَمَّا الَّذِيْنَ اٰمَنُوْا وَعَمِلُوا الصّٰلِحٰتِ فَيُوَفِّيْهِمْ اُجُوْرَهُمْ
وَيَزِيْدُهُمْ مِّنْ فَضْلِهٖ ۚ وَاَمَّا الَّذِيْنَ اسْتَنْكَفُوْا وَ
اسْتَكْبَرُوْا فَيُعَذِّبُهُمْ عَذَابًا اَلِيْمًا ۙ وَّلَا يَجِدُوْنَ
لَهُمْ مِّنْ دُوْنِ اللّٰهِ وَلِيًّا وَّلَا نَصِيْرًا ﴿۱۷۴﴾

175. O ye people, manifest proof[713] has indeed come to you from your Lord, and We have sent down to you a clear [f]Light.[714]

يٰۤاَيُّهَا النَّاسُ قَدْ جَآءَكُمْ بُرْهَانٌ مِّنْ رَّبِّكُمْ وَ
اَنْزَلْنَاۤ اِلَيْكُمْ نُوْرًا مُّبِيْنًا ﴿۱۷۵﴾

---

[a]5 : 74. [b]2 : 117; 10 : 69. [c]17 : 112; 18 : 5; 112 : 4,5. [d]5 : 117, 118. [e]3 : 58; 16 : 97: 39 : 11. [f]4 : 46; 33 : 18,66. [g]7 : 158; 64 : 9.

---

happiness; mercy (Lane). From the above-mentioned different meanings of ***Rūḥ*** and ***Kalimah*** it becomes clear that no special spiritual status attaches to Jesus. These and similar expressions have been used in the Qur'ān about other Prophets and also about other righteous persons such as Mary (15 : 30; 32 : 10; 58 : 23). They have been used to clear Jesus and Mary of the foul charges that were brought against them by the Jews and not to assign to them any special spiritual status.

713. "Manifest proof" may either refer to the Qur'ān which contains great and manifest Signs and proofs; or to the Holy Prophet who, by his personal example, demonstrated that the Quranic teachings are a great blessing for mankind.

714. "A clear Light" may also either refer to the Holy Prophet or to the Qur'ān.

176. Then, as for those who believe in Allāh and ^ahold fast to Him, He will surely admit them to His mercy and grace and will guide them along a straight path *leading* to Himself.

فَاَمَّا الَّذِيْنَ اٰمَنُوْا بِاللّٰهِ وَاعْتَصَمُوْا بِهٖ فَسَيُدْخِلُهُمْ فِيْ رَحْمَةٍ مِّنْهُ وَفَضْلٍ ۙ وَّيَهْدِيْهِمْ اِلَيْهِ صِرَاطًا مُّسْتَقِيْمًا ۞

177. They ask thee for a decision. ^bSay, 'Allāh gives His decision concerning '*Kalālah*.⁷¹⁵ If a man dies leaving no child and he has a sister, then she shall have half of what he leaves; and he shall inherit her if she has no child. But if there be two sisters, then they shall have two-thirds of what he leaves. And if *the heirs* be brethren—*both* men and women—^cthen the male shall have as much as the portion of two females. ^dAllāh explains *this* to you lest you go astray and Allāh knows all things well.'

يَسْتَفْتُوْنَكَ ۚ قُلِ اللّٰهُ يُفْتِيْكُمْ فِى الْكَلَالَةِ ۚ اِنِ امْرُؤٌا هَلَكَ لَيْسَ لَهٗ وَلَدٌ وَّلَهٗٓ اُخْتٌ فَلَهَا نِصْفُ مَا تَرَكَ ۚ وَهُوَ يَرِثُهَآ اِنْ لَّمْ يَكُنْ لَّهَا وَلَدٌ ۚ فَاِنْ كَانَتَا اثْنَتَيْنِ فَلَهُمَا الثُّلُثٰنِ مِمَّا تَرَكَ ۚ وَاِنْ كَانُوْٓا اِخْوَةً رِّجَالًا وَّنِسَآءً فَلِلذَّكَرِ مِثْلُ حَظِّ الْاُنْثَيَيْنِ ۚ يُبَيِّنُ اللّٰهُ لَكُمْ اَنْ تَضِلُّوْا ۚ وَاللّٰهُ بِكُلِّ شَىْءٍ عَلِيْمٌ ۞

---

^a3 : 102; 4 : 147.   ^b4 : 13.   ^c4 : 12.   ^d4 : 27.

---

715. In 4 : 13 mention was made of one kind of *Kalālah* who leaves behind neither a parent nor an offspring and who has brothers and sisters from the side of mother only. The present verse refers to a *Kalālah* who has brothers and sisters from both his parents, or from the side of his father only. By comparing the verse under comment with 4 : 13 it becomes clear that for obvious reasons the share allotted to the former class of brothers and sisters is less than that allotted to those of the latter class.

This part of the law of inheritance has been purposely treated separately from the law dealt with in 4 : 12,13. After dealing at some length with the charges levelled against Jesus by the Jews, the Qur'ān reverts to the subject of *Kalālah* at the end of the *Sūrah*, thus seeking (beside completing the law relating to *Kalālah*) to draw attention to the spiritual heirlessness of Jesus who in a sense was also a *Kalālah*. Jesus was born without the agency of a father, and he left behind no spiritual successor. Ibn 'Abbās defines a *Kalālah* as one who leaves no child and Jesus was spiritually a *Kalālah* since he left behind him no spiritual successor.

---o---

CHAPTER 5

AL-MĀ'IDAH

(Revealed after Hijrah)

Date of Revelation

According to Commentators of the Qur'ān this *Sūrah* belongs to the Medinite period. 'Ā'ishah is reported by Ḥākim and Imām Aḥmad to have said that this is the last *Sūrah* which was revealed to the Holy Prophet. Taking into consideration all the relevant data one is inevitably led to the conclusion that the *Sūrah* was revealed in the last years of the Holy Prophet's ministry and some of its verses were actually among the last to be revealed. Though Imām Ahmad says on the authority of 'Asmā', daughter of Yazīd, that the whole of this *Sūrah* was revealed together, it seems that because a major portion of it was revealed at one time, the whole of it came to be regarded as having been revealed at the same time. This is why perhaps Rodwell has assigned the *Sūrah* the last place in order of revelation.

Subject-Matter

The *Sūrah*, like *Sūrahs* Āl 'Imrān and Al-Nisā', deals mainly with Christian doctrines and particularly denounces the doctrine that the Law is a curse. It opens with the injunction that all covenants must be fulfilled and that it was necessary to lay down laws as to what is lawful and what is unlawful. It further claims that the Qur'ān has laid down ordinances bearing upon man's complete moral and spiritual development, and it is in this respect that the Qur'ān constitutes the final and irrevocable Divine Law for all mankind. This claim of the Qur'ān is embodied in the fourth verse of the *Sūrah*, which also implies that because the Law is most essential for the spiritual guidance of man and his moral development, it is wrong to regard it as a curse. The verse further hints that when the eating of meat offered to idols and of blood and of strangled animals was forbidden to Christians and this commandment constituted an ordinance of the Law (The Acts, 15:20, 29), they could not take exception to the Law and condemn it as a curse. The *Sūrah* proceeds to lay down Islamic commandments with regard to eatables and enjoins that they should be *Ḥalāl*, *i.e.*, allowed by the Law and *Ṭayyib* (pure), *i.e.*, their use should in no way contravene or offend against medical or hygienic regulations. Islām, alone of all religions, while laying down ordinances regarding lawful and unlawful things, has pointed out the nice distinction between what is only lawful and what is both lawful and pure. Next, it is stated that the Jews and the Christians broke God's covenants and disregarded and defied Divine commandments which led to their moral and spiritual ruin and brought disgrace and humiliation on them. But they could now rehabilitate themselves into Divine favour by accepting the Holy Prophet. Christians are further warned that at first by deifying Jesus they caused the wrath of God to come down upon them and that now they have become jealous of the Holy Prophet because God has chosen him for His favours. This jealous attitude of theirs towards the Holy Prophet resembles that of Cain towards Abel. The *Sūrah* proceeds to state that while Jews and Christians lose no opportunity to oppose Islām, they themselves have become so depraved as to have ceased to act upon their own religious Scriptures and are increasingly becoming ignorant of the teachings of their own religions. They are told that if they do not see their way to accepting Islām they should at least follow their own Scriptures and abide by their own Law. But if, owing to the political supremacy of Islām, they have sometimes to seek the judgment of the Islamic Government, that judgment will and must inevitably be according to the Quranic Law. Then attention of the Muslims is drawn to the great change that has come over their political position and they are told that as the power of the infidels has been finally broken and Christians now are to be their principal enemies, and Jews, in spite of their enmity towards Christianity, are to side with Christians, they (Muslims) should be on their guard against both of them. Some light is then shed on the strategems and machinations employed by the enemies of Islām to turn Muslims away from their Faith and to lower it in their estimation. After this, importance of the preaching of Islām is impressed upon Muslims. They are told that the one real method effectively to defeat the activities of Jews and Christians is to preach the Message of Islām to them and to bring home to them its truth from their own Scriptures. It should also be made clear to them that now their salvation lies in Islām and that their idolatrous beliefs are false, particularly the doctrine that

Jesus was son of God. Similarly, mention is made of Jews who, by opposing and persecuting the two great Prophets—David and Jesus—incurred God's displeasure. Their attention is drawn to their past faults and failings, and Christians being more amenable to accepting the truth than Jews, commandments have been laid down which particularly concern them, *viz.*, commandments about what is lawful and what is unlawful; commandments about oaths; about the use of wine and games of chance and about hunting; and also commandments regarding criticism of religion and ordinances about religious rites and ceremonies and about evidence. Last of all a somewhat detailed mention is made of the particular circumstances of Jesus's ministry, and it is shown that they closely resemble those of other Prophets of God and that therefore there was nothing of Godhead or Divinity about him and that all material progress of Christian people was due to a prayer of his. But they have made improper use of their material progress and prosperity and have succumbed to polytheistic beliefs and practices. God will, on the Day of Judgment, establish their guilt and put them to shame from the mouth of Jesus himself. The *Sūrah* ends with the declaration that to God belongs the Kingdom of the heavens and the earth and He has power over all things, which implies the hint that the belief that the Kingdom of God is only in heaven as the Christians say, has no foundation.

———o———

ركوعاتها ١٦ سُورَةُ الْمَائِدَةِ مَدَنِيَّةٌ (٥) اٰياتها ١٢١

1. [a]In the name of Allāh, the Gracious, the Merciful.

بِسْمِ اللّٰهِ الرَّحْمٰنِ الرَّحِيْمِ ①

2. O ye who believe ! fulfil *your* compacts. Lawful are made to you quadrupeds *of the class* of cattle[716] other than [b]those which are being announced to you,[717] except that you should not hold game to be lawful while you are in a state of pilgrimage; verily, Allāh decrees what He wills.

المنزل ٢

يٰۤاَيُّهَا الَّذِيْنَ اٰمَنُوْۤا اَوْفُوْا بِالْعُقُوْدِ ۭ اُحِلَّتْ لَكُمْ
بَهِيْمَةُ الْاَنْعَامِ اِلَّا مَا يُتْلٰى عَلَيْكُمْ غَيْرَ مُحِلِّي الصَّيْدِ
وَاَنْتُمْ حُرُمٌ ۭ اِنَّ اللّٰهَ يَحْكُمُ مَا يُرِيْدُ ②

3. O ye who believe ! profane not the Signs of Allāh,[718] nor the Sacred Month,[719] nor the animals brought as an offering, nor the *animals of sacrifice wearing* collars[720] nor those repairing to the Sacred House, [c]seeking grace from their Lord and His pleasure. And when you put off the pilgrims' garb[720A] *and are clear of the Sacred Territory,*

يٰۤاَيُّهَا الَّذِيْنَ اٰمَنُوْا لَا تُحِلُّوْا شَعَاۗىِٕرَ اللّٰهِ وَلَا الشَّهْرَ
الْحَرَامَ وَلَا الْهَدْيَ وَلَا الْقَلَاۗىِٕدَ وَلَاۤ اٰۗمِّيْنَ الْبَيْتَ
الْحَرَامَ يَبْتَغُوْنَ فَضْلًا مِّنْ رَّبِّهِمْ وَرِضْوَانًا ۭ وَاِذَا

---

[a]See 1 : 1. [b]2 : 174; 5 : 4; 6 : 146 [c]59 : 9.

---

716. The expression *Bahīmat al-An'ām* does not mean the quadrupeds from among cattle for the obvious reason that quadrupeds form a class wider than cattle. It means the quadrupeds which belong to the class of cattle or which resemble cattle. This peculiar construction has been used to signify that whereas all quadrupeds do not make lawful food, those of them that form the counterparts of cattle are allowed. Thus the expression is intended to comprise not only cattle but also such beasts of the forest as correspond to cattle, *i.e.*, wild goat, wild cow, wild buffalo, etc.

717. The words, *other than those which are being announced to you*, refer to the animals mentioned in the verse below. The words, however, do not refer to *the flesh of an animal which dies of itself, and blood and the flesh of swine*, because "swine" is not included among cattle and the exception here made is from among the cattle only and not from among all animals and also because this portion had already been revealed in 2 : 174.

718. "Signs of Allāh" signifies anything that leads to the knowledge and realization of God (2 : 159).

719. Abstaining from profaning the Sacred Month may also mean, paying due respect to the works performed therein.

720. *Hady* and *Qalā'id* both signify animals that are taken to Mecca for sacrifice during the Pilgrimage, *Qalā'id* meaning particularly such animals as have collars round their necks (Muḥīṭ); and *Hady* meaning all animals without distinction that are brought to Mecca for sacrifice.

720A. Hunting is lawful for a pilgrim after he has finally put off the pilgrim's garb on completion of the Pilgrimage and he has gone out of the Sacred Territory.

you may hunt. And [a]let not the enmity of a people, that they hindered you from the Sacred Mosque, incite you to transgress. And help one another in righteousness and piety; but help not one another in sin and transgression.[720B] And fear Allāh; surely, Allāh is Severe in punishment.

حَلَلْتُمْ فَاصْطَادُوْا ۗ وَلَا يَجْرِمَنَّكُمْ شَنَاٰنُ قَوْمٍ اَنْ
صَدُّوْكُمْ عَنِ الْمَسْجِدِ الْحَرَامِ اَنْ تَعْتَدُوْا ۘ وَتَعَاوَنُوْا
عَلَى الْبِرِّ وَالتَّقْوٰى ۪ وَلَا تَعَاوَنُوْا عَلَى الْاِثْمِ وَالْعُدْوَانِ ۪
وَاتَّقُوا اللّٰهَ ۗ اِنَّ اللّٰهَ شَدِيْدُ الْعِقَابِ ﴿۳﴾

4. [b]Forbidden to you is *the flesh of an animal* which dies of itself, and blood and the flesh of swine; and that on which is invoked the name of any other than Allāh; and that which has been strangled; and that which has been beaten to death; and that which has been killed by a fall; and that which has been gored to death; and that of which a wild animal has eaten, except that which you have properly slaughtered; and that which has been slaughtered at an altar *as an offering to idols. And* [c]*forbidden is also this* that you seek to know your lot by the divining arrows. That is *an act of* disobedience. This day have those who disbelieve despaired of *harming* your religion. So fear them not, but fear Me. This day have I perfected your religion for you and completed[721] My favour upon you and [d]have chosen for

حُرِّمَتْ عَلَيْكُمُ الْمَيْتَةُ وَالدَّمُ وَلَحْمُ الْخِنْزِيْرِ وَ
مَآ اُهِلَّ لِغَيْرِ اللّٰهِ بِهٖ وَالْمُنْخَنِقَةُ وَالْمَوْقُوْذَةُ وَالْمُتَرَدِّيَةُ
وَالنَّطِيْحَةُ وَمَآ اَكَلَ السَّبُعُ اِلَّا مَا ذَكَّيْتُمْ ۣ وَمَا ذُبِحَ
عَلَى النُّصُبِ وَاَنْ تَسْتَقْسِمُوْا بِالْاَزْلَامِ ۗ ذٰلِكُمْ فِسْقٌ ۗ
اَلْيَوْمَ يَئِسَ الَّذِيْنَ كَفَرُوْا مِنْ دِيْنِكُمْ فَلَا تَخْشَوْهُمْ
وَاخْشَوْنِ ۗ اَلْيَوْمَ اَكْمَلْتُ لَكُمْ دِيْنَكُمْ وَاَتْمَمْتُ عَلَيْكُمْ

[a]5 : 9; 11 : 90. [b]2 : 174; 6 : 146. [c]5 : 91. [d]3 : 20, 86.

720B. What a beautiful principle of individual and international conduct. If this principle were carried into effect, all rancour, hatred and mutual animosity would disappear.

721. *Ikmāl* (perfecting) and *Itmām* (completing) are noun-infinitives, the first relating to quality and the second to quantity. The first word shows that doctrines and commandments affecting the physical, moral and spiritual development of man have been embodied in the Qur'ān in their most perfect form; while the second signifies that nothing which was needed by man has been left out. Again, the former word pertains to commandments relating to the physical side of man or his external self, while the latter relates to his spiritual side or his inner self. The perfection and completion of God's religion and favour have been mentioned side by side with the law relating to eatables in order to point out that the use of lawful and good food forms one of the very important bases of good morals which in turn provide a pedestal for spiritual progress. Incidentally, the verse was the last to be revealed, the Holy Prophet having died only 82 days after its revelation.

you Islām as religion. But [a]whoso is forced by hunger, without being wilfully inclined to sin, then, surely, Allāh is Most Forgiving *and is* Merciful.	نِعۡمَتِیۡ وَ رَضِیۡتُ لَکُمُ الۡاِسۡلَامَ دِیۡنًا ؕ فَمَنِ اضۡطُرَّ فِیۡ مَخۡمَصَۃٍ غَیۡرَ مُتَجَانِفٍ لِّاِثۡمٍ ۙ فَاِنَّ اللّٰہَ غَفُوۡرٌ رَّحِیۡمٌ ﴿۴﴾
5. They ask thee what is made lawful[722] for them. Say, 'All good things have been made lawful for you, and what you have taught the beasts and birds of prey *to catch for you,*[722A] training *them* for hunting *and* teaching them of what Allāh has taught you. So eat of that which they catch for you, and [b]pronounce thereon the name of Allāh. And fear Allāh, surely Allāh is Quick in reckoning.'	یَسۡـَٔلُوۡنَکَ مَاذَاۤ اُحِلَّ لَہُمۡ ؕ قُلۡ اُحِلَّ لَکُمُ الطَّیِّبٰتُ ۙ وَ مَا عَلَّمۡتُمۡ مِّنَ الۡجَوَارِحِ مُکَلِّبِیۡنَ تُعَلِّمُوۡنَہُنَّ مِمَّا عَلَّمَکُمُ اللّٰہُ ۫ فَکُلُوۡا مِمَّاۤ اَمۡسَکۡنَ عَلَیۡکُمۡ وَ اذۡکُرُوا اسۡمَ اللّٰہِ عَلَیۡہِ ۪ وَ اتَّقُوا اللّٰہَ ؕ اِنَّ اللّٰہَ سَرِیۡعُ الۡحِسَابِ ﴿۵﴾
6. This day all good things have been made lawful for you. And the food[723] of the People of the Book is lawful for you. And your food is lawful for them. And *lawful for you are* chaste believing women and chaste women from among those who were given the	اَلۡیَوۡمَ اُحِلَّ لَکُمُ الطَّیِّبٰتُ ؕ وَ طَعَامُ الَّذِیۡنَ اُوۡتُوا الۡکِتٰبَ حِلٌّ لَّکُمۡ ۪ وَ طَعَامُکُمۡ حِلٌّ لَّہُمۡ ۫ وَ الۡمُحۡصَنٰتُ مِنَ الۡمُؤۡمِنٰتِ وَ الۡمُحۡصَنٰتُ مِنَ الَّذِیۡنَ اُوۡتُوا الۡکِتٰبَ

[a]2 : 174; 6 : 146; 16 : 116. [b]6 : 119.

722. The forbidden things having been mentioned in the preceding verse, the rest are here declared lawful, provided they are *Ṭayyib* (good and pure) and are not harmful to one's health or morals, it being left to each individual to decide what is good for him and what is not, in view of his particular circumstances and the condition of his health. The Holy Prophet has definitely excluded beasts of prey and birds having claws from the category of lawful food.

722A. That which is caught by a trained beast or bird of prey is equated with that which is properly slaughtered, inasmuch as it has been killed through an agency trained by man. It is necessary, however, to pronounce the name of God over it to make its eating lawful.

723. This means that the meat of animals slaughtered in accordance with the Law of Torah is lawful for the Muslims inasmuch as all food permissible under the Law of Torah is lawful under the Law of Islām. As a precautionary measure, however, the name of Allāh may be invoked over such food. According to Ibn 'Abbās "food" here means, "lawful food" (*Dhabīḥah*) or the meat of an animal properly slaughtered (Bukhārī ; ch. *Dhabīḥah Ahl al-kitāb*).

Book[724] before you, when you give them their dowries, contracting valid marriage and not committing fornication, nor taking secret paramours. And whoever rejects the faith, his work indeed is vain, and in the Hereafter he will be among the losers.

مِنْ قَبْلِكُمْ إِذَآ اٰتَيْتُمُوْهُنَّ اُجُوْرَهُنَّ مُحْصِنِيْنَ
غَيْرَ مُسٰفِحِيْنَ وَلَا مُتَّخِذِيْٓ اَخْدَانٍ ۭ وَمَنْ يَّكْفُرْ
بِالْاِيْمَانِ فَقَدْ حَبِطَ عَمَلُهٗ ۡ وَهُوَ فِي الْاٰخِرَةِ مِنَ
الْخٰسِرِيْنَ ۝٦ ع ٥

R. 2 7. O ye who believe! when you stand up for Prayer, wash your faces, and your hands up to the elbows, and pass your *wet* hands over your heads, and *wash* your feet[725] to the ankles. And if you be unclean, purify yourselves by bathing. And if you are ill or *you are* on a journey *while unclean*, or one of you comes from the privy or you have touched women, and you find not water, betake yourselves to pure dust and wipe therewith your faces and your hands.[725A] Allāh desires not that He should place you in a [a]difficulty but He desires to purify you and to complete His favour upon you, so that you may be grateful.

يٰٓاَيُّهَا الَّذِيْنَ اٰمَنُوْٓا اِذَا قُمْتُمْ اِلَى الصَّلٰوةِ فَاغْسِلُوْا
وُجُوْهَكُمْ وَاَيْدِيَكُمْ اِلَى الْمَرَافِقِ وَامْسَحُوْا بِرُءُوْسِكُمْ
وَاَرْجُلَكُمْ اِلَى الْكَعْبَيْنِ ۭ وَاِنْ كُنْتُمْ جُنُبًا فَاطَّهَّرُوْا ۭ
وَاِنْ كُنْتُمْ مَّرْضٰٓى اَوْ عَلٰي سَفَرٍ اَوْ جَاۗءَ اَحَدٌ مِّنْكُمْ مِّنَ
الْغَاۗىِٕطِ اَوْ لٰمَسْتُمُ النِّسَاۗءَ فَلَمْ تَجِدُوْا مَاۗءً فَتَيَمَّمُوْا
صَعِيْدًا طَيِّبًا فَامْسَحُوْا بِوُجُوْهِكُمْ وَاَيْدِيْكُمْ مِّنْهُ ۭ
مَا يُرِيْدُ اللّٰهُ لِيَجْعَلَ عَلَيْكُمْ مِّنْ حَرَجٍ وَّلٰكِنْ يُّرِيْدُ
لِيُطَهِّرَكُمْ وَلِيُتِمَّ نِعْمَتَهٗ عَلَيْكُمْ لَعَلَّكُمْ تَشْكُرُوْنَ ۝٧

8. And remember Allāh's favour upon you and the covenant[726] which He made with you, when you

وَاذْكُرُوْا نِعْمَةَ اللّٰهِ عَلَيْكُمْ وَمِيْثَاقَهُ الَّذِيْ وَاثَقَكُمْ

[a]2 : 186; 2 : 287.

724. Whereas Islām permits marriage of Muslim men with non-Muslim women from among the People of the Book, it certainly prefers that Muslim men should ordinarily marry only Muslim women.

725. The feet are here mentioned after the head, not because they are intended to be only wiped like the head, but because they come last in the process of ablution. This is apparent from the fact that the word *Arjula* (feet) has been put in the accusative case in the standard text, like the words *Wujūha* (faces) and *Aidiya* (hands), thus showing that, like the latter, the word "feet" is also governed in the accusative case by the verb "wash" and not by the particle *bā'* (over) which governs the word *Ru'ūs* (heads) only.

725A. See 610—612.

726. It is the Muslims, and not the People of the Book, that are addressed here. As, however, no special covenant is known to have ever been made with Muslims, the "covenant" mentioned here must be taken to refer to the process of *Bai'ah* (oath of allegiance) taken from every new convert to Islām, or the word may refer to the Law revealed in the Qur'ān and accepted by Muslims.

said, [a]'We hear and we obey.' And fear Allāh. Surely, Allāh knows well what is in *your* minds.

بِهٖۤ اِذۡ قُلۡتُمۡ سَمِعۡنَا وَ اَطَعۡنَا ۫ وَ اتَّقُوا اللّٰہَ ؕ اِنَّ اللّٰہَ
عَلِیۡمٌۢ بِذَاتِ الصُّدُوۡرِ ﴿۸﴾

9. O ye who believe ! [b]be steadfast in the cause of Allāh, bearing witness in equity; and [c]let not a people's enmity incite you to act otherwise than with justice. Be *always* just, that is nearer to righteousness. And fear Allāh. Surely, Allāh is Aware of what you do.

یٰۤاَیُّہَا الَّذِیۡنَ اٰمَنُوۡا کُوۡنُوۡا قَوّٰمِیۡنَ لِلّٰہِ شُہَدَآءَ بِالۡقِسۡطِ ۫
وَ لَا یَجۡرِمَنَّکُمۡ شَنَاٰنُ قَوۡمٍ عَلٰۤی اَلَّا تَعۡدِلُوۡا ؕ اِعۡدِلُوۡا ۟
ہُوَ اَقۡرَبُ لِلتَّقۡوٰی ۫ وَ اتَّقُوا اللّٰہَ ؕ اِنَّ اللّٰہَ خَبِیۡرٌۢ بِمَا
تَعۡمَلُوۡنَ ﴿۹﴾

10. [d]Allāh has promised those who believe and do good deeds that they shall have forgiveness and a great reward.

وَعَدَ اللّٰہُ الَّذِیۡنَ اٰمَنُوۡا وَ عَمِلُوا الصّٰلِحٰتِ ۙ لَہُمۡ
مَّغۡفِرَۃٌ وَّ اَجۡرٌ عَظِیۡمٌ ﴿۱۰﴾

11. And *as for* [e]those who disbelieve and reject Our Signs, they are the people of Hell.

وَ الَّذِیۡنَ کَفَرُوۡا وَ کَذَّبُوۡا بِاٰیٰتِنَاۤ اُولٰٓئِکَ اَصۡحٰبُ الۡجَحِیۡمِ ﴿۱۱﴾

12. O ye who believe ! remember Allāh's favour upon you when a people intended to stretch out their hands against you, but [f]He withheld their hands[727] from you; and fear Allāh. And in Allāh should the believers put their trust.

یٰۤاَیُّہَا الَّذِیۡنَ اٰمَنُوا اذۡکُرُوۡا نِعۡمَتَ اللّٰہِ عَلَیۡکُمۡ اِذۡ ہَمَّ
قَوۡمٌ اَنۡ یَّبۡسُطُوۡۤا اِلَیۡکُمۡ اَیۡدِیَہُمۡ فَکَفَّ اَیۡدِیَہُمۡ
عَنۡکُمۡ ۚ وَ اتَّقُوا اللّٰہَ ؕ وَ عَلَی اللّٰہِ فَلۡیَتَوَکَّلِ الۡمُؤۡمِنُوۡنَ ﴿۱۲﴾ ع

R. 3 13. And indeed [g]Allāh did take a covenant from the Children of Israel; and [h]We raised among them twelve leaders.[727A] And Allāh said, 'Surely, I am with you. If you observe Prayer, and pay the *Zakāt*, and

وَ لَقَدۡ اَخَذَ اللّٰہُ مِیۡثَاقَ بَنِیۡۤ اِسۡرَآءِیۡلَ ۚ وَ بَعَثۡنَا مِنۡہُمُ
اثۡنَیۡ عَشَرَ نَقِیۡبًا ؕ وَ قَالَ اللّٰہُ اِنِّیۡ مَعَکُمۡ ؕ لَئِنۡ اَقَمۡتُمُ

[a]2 : 286. [b]4 : 136. [c]5 : 3; 11: 90. [d]24 : 56; 48 : 30. [e]5 : 87; 6 : 50; 7 : 37, 41; 22 : 58. [f]5 : 111. [g]2 : 41,84. [h]2 : 61; 7 : 161.

727. The verse may not necessarily be applied to any particular incident and may be taken to refer generally to the protection which God vouchsafed to Muslims from the aggressive attacks of their enemies. By the words "a people" are here primarily meant the disbelievers of Mecca who spared no pains to extirpate Islām and the Muslims.

727A. By "twelve leaders" are meant the twelve Prophets of Israel who came after Moses. According to some authorities, these were the twelve "princes" said to have been appointed by Moses (Num. 1 : 5-16; 43 : 3-15). See also 2 : 61.

believe in My Messengers and support them, and lend to Allāh a goodly loan, I will remove your evils from you and [a]admit you into Gardens beneath which streams flow. But [b]whoso from among you disbelieves thereafter does indeed stray away from the right path.'

الصَّلٰوةَ وَاٰتَيْتُمُ الزَّكٰوةَ وَاٰمَنْتُمْ بِرُسُلِيْ وَعَزَّرْتُمُوْهُمْ
وَاَقْرَضْتُمُ اللّٰهَ قَرْضًا حَسَنًا لَّاُكَفِّرَنَّ عَنْكُمْ سَيِّاٰتِكُمْ
وَلَاُدْخِلَنَّكُمْ جَنّٰتٍ تَجْرِيْ مِنْ تَحْتِهَا الْاَنْهٰرُ ۚ فَمَنْ
كَفَرَ بَعْدَ ذٰلِكَ مِنْكُمْ فَقَدْ ضَلَّ سَوَآءَ السَّبِيْلِ ﴿١٣﴾

14. So, because of their breaking their covenant, We have cursed them and have hardened their hearts. They pervert the words from their *proper* places and have forgotten a *good* part of that with which they were exhorted. And thou wilt not cease to discover treachery on their part, except a few of them. So pardon them and show forbearance. Surely, Allāh loves those who do good *to others*.[727B]

فَبِمَا نَقْضِهِمْ مِّيْثَاقَهُمْ لَعَنّٰهُمْ وَجَعَلْنَا قُلُوْبَهُمْ
قٰسِيَةً ۚ يُحَرِّفُوْنَ الْكَلِمَ عَنْ مَّوَاضِعِهٖ ۙ وَنَسُوْا حَظًّا
مِّمَّا ذُكِّرُوْا بِهٖ ۚ وَلَا تَزَالُ تَطَّلِعُ عَلٰى خَآئِنَةٍ مِّنْهُمْ
اِلَّا قَلِيْلًا مِّنْهُمْ فَاعْفُ عَنْهُمْ وَاصْفَحْ ۗ اِنَّ اللّٰهَ يُحِبُّ
الْمُحْسِنِيْنَ ﴿١٤﴾

15. And from those *also* who say, 'We are Christians,' We took a covenant,[727C] but they *too* have forgotten a *good* part of that with which they were exhorted. So We have caused enmity and hatred among them till the Day of Resurrection. And Allāh will soon let them know what they have been doing.

وَمِنَ الَّذِيْنَ قَالُوْٓا اِنَّا نَصٰرٰٓى اَخَذْنَا مِيْثَاقَهُمْ فَنَسُوْا
حَظًّا مِّمَّا ذُكِّرُوْا بِهٖ ۠ فَاَغْرَيْنَا بَيْنَهُمُ الْعَدَاوَةَ وَالْبَغْضَآءَ
اِلٰى يَوْمِ الْقِيٰمَةِ ۭ وَسَوْفَ يُنَبِّئُهُمُ اللّٰهُ بِمَا كَانُوْا
يَصْنَعُوْنَ ﴿١٥﴾

16. O People of the Book ! there has come to you Our Messenger who makes clear to you much of what you have kept hidden of the Book and forgives many *of your faults*. There has come to you indeed from Allāh a Light[727D] and a clear Book.

يٰٓاَهْلَ الْكِتٰبِ قَدْ جَآءَكُمْ رَسُوْلُنَا يُبَيِّنُ لَكُمْ كَثِيْرًا
مِّمَّا كُنْتُمْ تُخْفُوْنَ مِنَ الْكِتٰبِ وَيَعْفُوْا عَنْ كَثِيْرٍ ۬ۥ
قَدْ جَآءَكُمْ مِّنَ اللّٰهِ نُوْرٌ وَّكِتٰبٌ مُّبِيْنٌ ۙ ﴿١٦﴾

[a]See 2 : 26; [b]2 : 169.

727B. The verse contains a very apt description of the Jewish people.

727C. This seems to be a reference to Jesus's prophecy about the advent of the Holy Prophet (John, 16 : 12-13) which his followers deliberately ignored or upon which they vainly sought to put a wrong interpretation.

727D. The Holy Prophet (33 : 46, 47).

17. Thereby does Allāh guide those who seek His pleasure on the paths of peace, and [a]leads them out of *every kind of* darkness into light by His Will and guides them to the right path.

يَهْدِي بِهِ اللّٰهُ مَنِ اتَّبَعَ رِضْوَانَهٗ سُبُلَ السَّلٰمِ
وَيُخْرِجُهُمْ مِّنَ الظُّلُمٰتِ اِلَى النُّوْرِ بِاِذْنِهٖ وَيَهْدِيْهِمْ
اِلٰى صِرَاطٍ مُّسْتَقِيْمٍ ﴿١٧﴾

18. [b]They indeed have disbelieved who say, 'Surely Allāh—He is the Messiah, son of Mary.' Say, 'Who then has any power against Allāh, if He desired to destroy the Messiah, son of Mary,[728] and his mother and all those that are in the earth?' And [c]to Allāh belongs the Kingdom of the heavens and the earth and what is between them. He creates what He pleases and Allāh has power over all things.

لَقَدْ كَفَرَ الَّذِيْنَ قَالُوْٓا اِنَّ اللّٰهَ هُوَ الْمَسِيْحُ ابْنُ مَرْيَمَ ؕ
قُلْ فَمَنْ يَّمْلِكُ مِنَ اللّٰهِ شَيْـًٔا اِنْ اَرَادَ اَنْ يُّهْلِكَ
الْمَسِيْحَ ابْنَ مَرْيَمَ وَاُمَّهٗ وَمَنْ فِي الْاَرْضِ جَمِيْعًا ؕ
وَلِلّٰهِ مُلْكُ السَّمٰوٰتِ وَالْاَرْضِ وَمَا بَيْنَهُمَا ؕ يَخْلُقُ
مَا يَشَآءُ ؕ وَاللّٰهُ عَلٰى كُلِّ شَيْءٍ قَدِيْرٌ ﴿١٨﴾

19. The Jews and the Christians say, [d]'We are sons of Allāh and His beloved ones.' Say, 'Why then does He punish you for your sins? Nay, you are mortals from among those He has created.' [e]He forgives whom He pleases and punishes whom He pleases. And to Allāh belongs the Kingdom of the heavens and the earth and what is between them, and to Him shall be the *final* return.

وَقَالَتِ الْيَهُوْدُ وَالنَّصٰرٰى نَحْنُ اَبْنٰٓؤُا اللّٰهِ وَاَحِبَّآؤُهٗ ؕ
قُلْ فَلِمَ يُعَذِّبُكُمْ بِذُنُوْبِكُمْ ؕ بَلْ اَنْتُمْ بَشَرٌ مِّمَّنْ
خَلَقَ ؕ يَغْفِرُ لِمَنْ يَّشَآءُ وَيُعَذِّبُ مَنْ يَّشَآءُ ؕ وَلِلّٰهِ مُلْكُ
السَّمٰوٰتِ وَالْاَرْضِ وَمَا بَيْنَهُمَا ؗ وَاِلَيْهِ الْمَصِيْرُ ﴿١٩﴾

20. O People of the Book! there indeed has come to you Our Messenger, after a break in *the series* of Messengers, [f]who makes *things* clear to you lest you should say, 'There has come to us no bearer of glad tidings and no Warner.'[729]

يٰٓاَهْلَ الْكِتٰبِ قَدْ جَآءَكُمْ رَسُوْلُنَا يُبَيِّنُ لَكُمْ عَلٰى
فَتْرَةٍ مِّنَ الرُّسُلِ اَنْ تَقُوْلُوْا مَا جَآءَنَا مِنْ بَشِيْرٍ وَّ

[a]2 : 258; 14 : 2; 33 : 44; 57 : 10; 65 : 12. [b]5 : 73, 74; [c]See 3 : 190. [d]62 : 7. [e]2 : 285; 3 : 130; 5 : 41. [f]5 : 16.

728. The very strong language used here is intended to expose and condemn the monstrous doctrine that Jesus is son of God. Similarly, strong language is used in 19 : 89-92.

729. History is silent whether any Prophet had appeared in any country between the Holy Prophet and Jesus, at least not among the People of the Book. The world was, in fact, expecting and preparing for the advent of humanity's greatest Deliverer. Some statements of doubtful authenticity (Kalbī) mention that Jesus was followed by some

So a bearer of glad tidings and a Warner has indeed come to you. And Allāh has power over all things.

لَا نَذِيْرٍ فَقَدْ جَآءَكُمْ بَشِيْرٌ وَّ نَذِيْرٌ ۭ وَاللّٰهُ عَلٰى
كُلِّ شَيْءٍ قَدِيْرٌ ﴿٢٠﴾ ع

R. 4 21. And *remember* when Moses said to his people, 'O my people, call to mind [a]Allāh's favour upon you when He raised Prophets among you and made you kings,[730] and gave you what He gave not to any other among the peoples;

وَاِذْ قَالَ مُوْسٰى لِقَوْمِهٖ يٰقَوْمِ اذْكُرُوْا نِعْمَةَ اللّٰهِ
عَلَيْكُمْ اِذْ جَعَلَ فِيْكُمْ اَنْۢبِيَآءَ وَجَعَلَكُمْ مُّلُوْكًا ۖۗ
وَّاٰتٰىكُمْ مَّا لَمْ يُؤْتِ اَحَدًا مِّنَ الْعٰلَمِيْنَ ﴿٢١﴾

22. 'O my people, enter the Holy Land which Allāh has ordained[731] for you and do not turn back, for then you will return as losers.'

يٰقَوْمِ ادْخُلُوا الْاَرْضَ الْمُقَدَّسَةَ الَّتِيْ كَتَبَ اللّٰهُ لَكُمْ
وَلَا تَرْتَدُّوْا عَلٰٓى اَدْبَارِكُمْ فَتَنْقَلِبُوْا خٰسِرِيْنَ ﴿٢٢﴾

23. They said, 'O Moses, there is in that *land* an unruly and powerful people,[732] and we shall not enter it until they go forth from it. But if they go forth from it, then we will enter it.'[733]

قَالُوْا يٰمُوْسٰٓى اِنَّ فِيْهَا قَوْمًا جَبَّارِيْنَ ۖۗ وَاِنَّا لَنْ
نَّدْخُلَهَا حَتّٰى يَخْرُجُوْا مِنْهَا ۚ فَاِنْ يَّخْرُجُوْا مِنْهَا
فَاِنَّا دٰخِلُوْنَ ﴿٢٣﴾

[a]1 : 7; 4 : 70; 19 : 59.

Prophets, Khālid bin Salām, being one of them. But the Holy Prophet himself is reported to have said that there was no Prophet between him and Jesus (Bukhārī).

730. The substitution of the word *kum* (you) instead of *Fī-kum* implies the hint that whereas each and every member of a nation to which a ruling monarch belongs possesses, as it were, dominion and sovereignty, the followers of a Prophet are not sharers in his Prophethood.

731. The expression, *ordained for you*, contains an implied promise that God would help them and make them victorious, if only the Israelites had the courage to enter the Holy Land.

732. This means that the annals of these people were known to the Israelites. The Amalekites and other unruly Arab tribes lived in the Holy Land at that time. The Israelites were very much afraid of them.

733. Compare this insolent and cowardly attitude of the companions of Moses to the willing and almost unbelievable sacrifices of the Companions of the Holy Prophet, who were ever eager to jump into the very jaws of death at the slightest bidding of their Master. When the Holy Prophet, with a handful of his ill-equipped Companions, intended to go forth to meet the vastly superior and much better-equipped Meccan force at Badr, he consulted them about it. Thereupon one of the Companions stood up and addressed the Holy Prophet in the memorable words: "We would not say to thee, O Prophet of God, as was said by the companions of Moses, 'go thou and thy Lord and fight and here we sit.' On the contrary, O Prophet of the Lord! we are ever with thee and we will go with thee whither thou goest. We will fight the enemy on thy right and on thy left and in thy front and behind thy back; and we trust God that thou wilt see from us what will comfort thine eyes" (Bukhārī).

24. Thereupon two men[734] from among those who feared *their Lord*, on whom Allāh had conferred His special favour, said, "Enter the gate *advancing* against them; when *once* you have entered it, then surely you will be victorious. And [a]put your trust in Allāh, if you are believers.'

قَالَ رَجُلٰنِ مِنَ الَّذِيْنَ يَخَافُوْنَ اَنْعَمَ اللّٰهُ عَلَيْهِمَا
ادْخُلُوْا عَلَيْهِمُ الْبَابَ ۚ فَاِذَا دَخَلْتُمُوْهُ فَاِنَّكُمْ غٰلِبُوْنَ ۚ
وَعَلَى اللّٰهِ فَتَوَكَّلُوْٓا اِنْ كُنْتُمْ مُّؤْمِنِيْنَ ﴿٢٤﴾

25. They said, 'O Moses, we will never enter it, so long as they are in it. So go thou and thy Lord and fight, *and* here we sit.'

قَالُوْا يٰمُوْسٰٓى اِنَّا لَنْ نَّدْخُلَهَآ اَبَدًا مَّا دَامُوْا فِيْهَا
فَاذْهَبْ اَنْتَ وَرَبُّكَ فَقَاتِلَآ اِنَّا هٰهُنَا قٰعِدُوْنَ ﴿٢٥﴾

26. He said, 'My Lord, I have control only over myself and my brother, therefore distinguish Thou between us and the rebellious people.'

قَالَ رَبِّ اِنِّيْ لَآ اَمْلِكُ اِلَّا نَفْسِيْ وَاَخِيْ فَافْرُقْ بَيْنَنَا
وَبَيْنَ الْقَوْمِ الْفٰسِقِيْنَ ﴿٢٦﴾

27. *God* said: [b]Verily' it shall be forbidden them for forty years; in distraction shall they wander through the land.[735] So grieve not over the rebellious people.'

قَالَ فَاِنَّهَا مُحَرَّمَةٌ عَلَيْهِمْ اَرْبَعِيْنَ سَنَةً ۛ يَتِيْهُوْنَ
ع ٨ فِي الْاَرْضِ ۗ فَلَا تَاْسَ عَلَى الْقَوْمِ الْفٰسِقِيْنَ ﴿٢٧﴾

R. 5 28. And relate to them with truth the story of the two sons of Adam,[736] when they *each* offered an offering, and it was accepted from one of

وقف لازم وَاتْلُ عَلَيْهِمْ نَبَاَ ابْنَيْ اٰدَمَ بِالْحَقِّ ۘ اِذْ قَرَّبَا قُرْبَانًا
فَتُقُبِّلَ مِنْ اَحَدِهِمَا وَلَمْ يُتَقَبَّلْ مِنَ الْاٰخَرِ ۗ قَالَ

[a]3 : 161; 5 : 12; 9 : 51. [b]2 : 244.

734. The "two men" spoken of here are generally supposed to be Joshua, the son of Nun; and Caleb, the son of Jephunneh (Nun. 14 : 6). But from the context Moses and Aaron appear more likely to be the "two men" here referred to. The word *Rajul* (man) is expressive of manliness and courage. That these two brave men were Moses and Aaron themselves may also be inferred from the fact that Moses prayed for himself and his brother, Aaron (5 : 26). God does not name these two men but simply speaks of them as "two brave men" in order to praise their manliness and courage and also to condemn by implication the cowardice of the other Israelites who were with them.

735. When the Israelites behaved in a cowardly manner, God decreed that they should continue to wander in the wilderness for 40 years in order that the life of the desert should invigorate them and infuse in them a new life and should strengthen their morals. In the meantime, the old generation had become practically extinct and the younger generation grew brave and strong enough to conquer the Promised Land.

736. "The two sons of Adam" figuratively signify any two individuals from among mankind. The parable also illustrates the inimical attitude of the Israelites towards the descendants of Ishmael because Prophethood had become transferred from them to the Ishmaelites in the person of the Holy Prophet.

النصف

them and was not accepted from the other. *The latter* said, 'I will surely kill thee.' *The former* replied, 'Allāh accepts only from the righteous;

لَاَقْتُلَنَّكَ ۭ قَالَ اِنَّمَا يَتَقَبَّلُ اللّٰهُ مِنَ الْمُتَّقِيْنَ ﴿۲۸﴾

29. 'If thou stretch out thy hand against me to kill me, I shall not stretch out my hand against thee to kill thee. I do fear Allāh, the Lord of the Universe;

لَئِنْۢ بَسَطْتَّ اِلَيَّ يَدَكَ لِتَقْتُلَنِيْ مَآ اَنَا بِبَاسِطٍ يَّدِيَ
اِلَيْكَ لِاَقْتُلَكَ ۚ اِنِّيْٓ اَخَافُ اللّٰهَ رَبَّ الْعٰلَمِيْنَ ﴿۲۹﴾

30. 'I wish[737] that thou shouldst bear *the punishment of* the sin against me[738] as well as of thine own sin, and thus be among the inmates of the Fire, and that is the recompense of those who do wrong.'

اِنِّيْٓ اُرِيْدُ اَنْ تَبُوْۗاَ بِاِثْمِيْ وَاِثْمِكَ فَتَكُوْنَ مِنْ
اَصْحٰبِ النَّارِ ۚ وَذٰلِكَ جَزٰۗؤُا الظّٰلِمِيْنَ ﴿۳۰﴾

31. But his *evil* self induced him to kill his brother, so he killed him and became *one* of the losers.

فَطَوَّعَتْ لَهٗ نَفْسُهٗ قَتْلَ اَخِيْهِ فَقَتَلَهٗ فَاَصْبَحَ
مِنَ الْخٰسِرِيْنَ ﴿۳۱﴾

32. Then Allāh sent a raven which scratched in the ground,[739] that He might show him how to hide the corpse of his brother. He said, 'Woe is me ! Am I not able to be even like this raven so that I may hide the corpse of my brother?' And then he became remorseful.

فَبَعَثَ اللّٰهُ غُرَابًا يَّبْحَثُ فِي الْاَرْضِ لِيُرِيَهٗ كَيْفَ
يُوَارِيْ سَوْءَةَ اَخِيْهِ ۭ قَالَ يٰوَيْلَتٰٓى اَعَجَزْتُ اَنْ اَكُوْنَ
مِثْلَ هٰذَا الْغُرَابِ فَاُوَارِيَ سَوْءَةَ اَخِيْ ۚ فَاَصْبَحَ
مِنَ النّٰدِمِيْنَ ﴿۳۲﴾

737. *Urīdu* is derived from *Rāda* which sometimes does not express an actual wish but simply a practical state or condition likely to develop in a certain manner (18 : 78). The verse does not mean that Abel desired his brother Cain to be cast into Hell. What he meant was simply that the natural and inevitable result of his own non-aggressive attitude would be that his brother would go to Hell.

738. *Ithmī* means, "the sin committed against me." The would-be victim is only describing the consequences of his brother's intended action.

739. Commentators differ as to whether the incident of the raven did actually happen or it is only a parable. It is not improbable that an incident of this nature might have actually occurred. Study of the ways and habits of birds has led to many useful discoveries. See Gen. 4 : 1-15; and 'The Jerusalem Targum.'

33. On account of this, We prescribed for the Children of Israel that whosoever killed a person—unless it be for *killing* a person or for creating disorder in the land—it shall be as if he had killed all mankind; and whoso saved a life, it shall be as if he had saved the life of all mankind.[740] And [a]Our Messengers came to them with clear Signs, yet even after that, many of them commit excesses in the land.

مِنْ أَجْلِ ذٰلِكَ ۚ كَتَبْنَا عَلٰى بَنِيْٓ إِسْرَآءِيْلَ أَنَّهٗ مَنْ
قَتَلَ نَفْسًا بِغَيْرِ نَفْسٍ أَوْ فَسَادٍ فِي الْأَرْضِ فَكَأَنَّمَا
قَتَلَ النَّاسَ جَمِيْعًا ۖ وَمَنْ أَحْيَاهَا فَكَأَنَّمَآ أَحْيَا النَّاسَ
جَمِيْعًا ۖ وَلَقَدْ جَآءَتْهُمْ رُسُلُنَا بِالْبَيِّنٰتِ ثُمَّ إِنَّ
كَثِيْرًا مِّنْهُمْ بَعْدَ ذٰلِكَ فِي الْأَرْضِ لَمُسْرِفُوْنَ ﴿٣٣﴾

34. The *only* reward of those, [b]who wage war against Allāh and His Messenger and strive to create disorder in the land, is that they be slain or crucified or their hands and feet be cut off on account of *their* enmity, or they be expelled from the land.[741] That shall be a disgrace for them in this world, and in the Hereafter they shall have a great punishment;

إِنَّمَا جَزٰٓؤُا الَّذِيْنَ يُحَارِبُوْنَ اللّٰهَ وَرَسُوْلَهٗ وَيَسْعَوْنَ
فِي الْأَرْضِ فَسَادًا أَنْ يُّقَتَّلُوْٓا أَوْ يُصَلَّبُوْٓا أَوْ تُقَطَّعَ
أَيْدِيْهِمْ وَأَرْجُلُهُمْ مِّنْ خِلَافٍ أَوْ يُنْفَوْا مِنَ الْأَرْضِ ؕ
ذٰلِكَ لَهُمْ خِزْيٌ فِي الدُّنْيَا وَلَهُمْ فِي الْاٰخِرَةِ عَذَابٌ
عَظِيْمٌ ﴿٣٤﴾

35. Except those [c]who repent before you have them in your power. So know that Allāh is Most Forgiving, Merciful.[742]

إِلَّا الَّذِيْنَ تَابُوْا مِنْ قَبْلِ أَنْ تَقْدِرُوْا عَلَيْهِمْ ۚ فَاعْلَمُوْٓا
أَنَّ اللّٰهَ غَفُوْرٌ رَّحِيْمٌ ﴿٣٥﴾

[a]7 : 102; 9 : 70; 14 : 10; 40 : 23. [b]9 : 107. [c]4 : 18.

740. What is hinted at in the verse is that an incident similar to that of the two sons of Adam mentioned here but of much greater import was to take place later. There was to appear among the brethren of the Israelites a Prophet. This fact was to enrage the Israelites against that Prophet and they were to become thirsty for his blood on account of envy, even as Cain had become thirsty for the blood of his brother Abel. The Prophet was to be no ordinary soul. He was to be a World-Reformer, ordained to bring the eternal Law for all mankind whose entire future depended on him, and therefore slaying him was equivalent to slaying the whole of mankind, and the preservation of his life was, as it were, the preservation of the whole of mankind.

741. Islām does not hesitate to take extreme measures when the interests of the State or society at large so demand to uproot a dangerous evil. It refuses to pander to the false sentiments of emotional visionaries but follows the dictates of reason and sound judgment while prescribing punishment for public offences. The punishment prescribed here is of four categories, the form of the punishment to be inflicted in a particular case would depend upon the attending circumstances. Awarding or imposition of punishment is the concern of Government and not that of any individual. The words "expelled from the land" according to Imām Abū Ḥanīfah signify imprisonment.

742. This and the preceding verse refer not to ordinary dacoits and robbers but to rebels and those miscreants who make aggressive war upon the Muslim State, as is clear from the words, *who wage war against Allāh and His Messenger*. The inference finds further support from the fact that the present verse promises amnesty to offenders if they repent. But obviously those who commit heinous offences against individuals or society, such as dacoits, robbers and thieves, cannot, in ordinary circumstances, be pardoned by the State even if

R. 6 36. O ye who believe! fear Allāh and [a]seek the means of approach[743] unto Him and [b]strive in His way that you may prosper.

يٰٓاَيُّهَا الَّذِيْنَ اٰمَنُوا اتَّقُوا اللّٰهَ وَابْتَغُوْٓا اِلَيْهِ الْوَسِيْلَةَ وَجَاهِدُوْا فِيْ سَبِيْلِهٖ لَعَلَّكُمْ تُفْلِحُوْنَ ﴿٣٦﴾

37. Surely, if [c]those who disbelieve had all that is in the earth and as much over again to [c]ransom themselves therewith from the punishment of the Day of Resurrection, it would not be accepted from them; and they shall have a painful punishment.

اِنَّ الَّذِيْنَ كَفَرُوْا لَوْ اَنَّ لَهُمْ مَّا فِي الْاَرْضِ جَمِيْعًا وَّمِثْلَهٗ مَعَهٗ لِيَفْتَدُوْا بِهٖ مِنْ عَذَابِ يَوْمِ الْقِيٰمَةِ مَا تُقُبِّلَ مِنْهُمْ ۚ وَلَهُمْ عَذَابٌ اَلِيْمٌ ﴿٣٧﴾

38. They would wish to come out of the Fire, but they will not be able to come out of it and they shall have a lasting punishment.

يُرِيْدُوْنَ اَنْ يَّخْرُجُوْا مِنَ النَّارِ وَمَا هُمْ بِخٰرِجِيْنَ مِنْهَا ۫ وَلَهُمْ عَذَابٌ مُّقِيْمٌ ﴿٣٨﴾

39. And *as for* the man who steals and the woman who steals, cut off their hands in retribution of their offence as an exemplary punishment[744] from Allāh. And Allāh is Mighty, Wise.

وَالسَّارِقُ وَالسَّارِقَةُ فَاقْطَعُوْٓا اَيْدِيَهُمَا جَزَآءًۢ بِمَا كَسَبَا نَكَالًا مِّنَ اللّٰهِ ؕ وَاللّٰهُ عَزِيْزٌ حَكِيْمٌ ﴿٣٩﴾

[a]17 : 58. [b]9 : 41; 22 : 79. [c]13 : 19; 39 : 48.

they repent. They must suffer the penalty of their evil deeds as prescribed by the Law. Surely, repentance may secure for them pardon from God, but the powers of the State are limited in this respect. Political offenders, however, may be forgiven if they repent and desist from further acts of rebellion and other offences against the State.

743. *Wasīlah* signifies, a means of access to a thing; honourable rank with a king; degree; affinity, a tie or connection (Lane). The word does not mean "an intermediary between God and man." This latter meaning is not only unsupported by the usage of the Arabic language, but is also opposed to the Qur'ān and the sayings of the Holy Prophet. The prayer after the usual 'Call to Prayer' includes the words, "O God! give Muḥammad *Wasīlah*," meaning that God may vouchsafe to the Prophet increasing nearness to Himself, and not that the Prophet may have someone to act as intermediary between him and God.

744. Whereas in this verse the words *the man who steals* have been put before the words *the woman who steals* because stealing is more common among men than among women, in 24 : 3 the word *fornicatress* precedes the word *fornicator* because the guilt of fornication can more easily be proved against women than against men. This arrangement of words shows that there exists not only an intelligent order in the verses of the Qur'ān, as shown elsewhere, but also an intelligent order in its words. The punishment prescribed for stealing may appear to be too severe. But human experience shows that punishment, if it is to be deterrent, should be exemplary. It is better to be severe to one and save a thousand than to be indulgent to all and ruin many. He certainly is a good surgeon who does not hesitate to amputate a rotten limb to save the whole body. In the hay-day of Islām there were extremely rare cases of the cutting of hands of thieves because the punishment prescribed was deterrent and was put in force. Even today incidents of theft are very rare in Arabia where punishment for theft prescribed by the Qur'ān is in force.

40. But [a]whoso repents after his transgression and amends, then will Allāh surely turn to him in mercy; verily, Allāh is Most Forgiving *and* Merciful.

فَمَنْ تَابَ مِنْ بَعْدِ ظُلْمِهٖ وَاَصْلَحَ فَاِنَّ اللّٰهَ يَتُوْبُ
عَلَيْهِ ؕ اِنَّ اللّٰهَ غَفُوْرٌ رَّحِيْمٌ ۝٤٠

41. Dost thou not know that Allāh is He to Whom belongs the [b]Kingdom of the heavens and the earth? He punishes whom He pleases and forgives whom He pleases, and Allāh has power over all things.[745]

اَلَمْ تَعْلَمْ اَنَّ اللّٰهَ لَهٗ مُلْكُ السَّمٰوٰتِ وَالْاَرْضِ ؕ يُعَذِّبُ
مَنْ يَّشَآءُ وَيَغْفِرُ لِمَنْ يَّشَآءُ ؕ وَاللّٰهُ عَلٰى كُلِّ شَيْءٍ
قَدِيْرٌ ۝٤١

42. O Messenger! let not those grieve thee who hasten to fall into disbelief — those who say with their mouths, 'We believe,' but their hearts believe not. And among the Jews *too* are those who would *fondly* [c]listen to any lie[746]——who listen for *conveying it to* other

يٰۤاَيُّهَا الرَّسُوْلُ لَا يَحْزُنْكَ الَّذِيْنَ يُسَارِعُوْنَ فِي
الْكُفْرِ مِنَ الَّذِيْنَ قَالُوْۤا اٰمَنَّا بِاَفْوَاهِهِمْ وَلَمْ تُؤْمِنْ
قُلُوْبُهُمْ ۛۚ وَمِنَ الَّذِيْنَ هَادُوْا ۛۚ سَمّٰعُوْنَ لِلْكَذِبِ

[a]6 : 55; 20 : 83; 25 : 72. [b]5 : 19; 48 : 15. [c]9 : 47.

In order to arrive at a right understanding of the nature of this punishment, it is necessary to know both the literal and metaphorical use of the two words used here, *viz.*, *Qaṭ'* and *Yad*. The Arabic expression *Qaṭa'a-hū bi'l-Ḥujjati*, means, he silenced him with argument (Lane). And *Yad* among other things means, the power and capacity to do a certain thing. Thus the phrase. *Qaṭa'a Yada-hū*, metaphorically means, he deprived him of the power to do the thing; or he restrained him from doing it. See also 12 : 32. In view of this signification of the two words the Arabic expression used in the verse may mean, "deprive them of the power to commit theft or employ any practical means calculated to restrain them from committing theft." Taking the verse literally the punishment prescribed in the verse is maximum punishment, and maximum punishment is awarded in extreme cases only, the lesser punishment being the adoption of any practical means by which the offender is deprived of the capacity of, or restrained from, committing the offence. In awarding the punishment the nature and scope of all the attending circumstances are also to be taken into consideration. Moreover, the use of the word *al-Sāriq* which is a noun (instead of the verb *Saraqa*—he stole) implying the sense of intensiveness signifies an habitual thief or one addicted to theft, is worthy of special consideration. Scholars differ as to the amount of money or property stolen for which the prescribed punishment is to be imposed. Whereas according to some traditions it is three *dirhams* or a quarter of a *dīnār*, according to others the hand is not to be cut off for stealing fruit on a tree or when theft is committed in the course of journey (Dāwūd). Imām Abū Ḥanīfah holds it to be ten *dirhams*, while Imām Mālik and Imām Shāf'ī consider three *dirhams* to be the least amount. This disagreement among theologians shows that much discretion is left to the judge who awards the punishment regarding its form and scope.

745. Expressions like these do not mean that the Divine Government of the universe is arbitrary and is based on no system or law. They are intended to point out that God being the Final Authority in the universe, His Word is the law, there being no appeal or redress against His decrees.

746. The expression may also mean, they listen in order to lie; (2) they accept as true the lies which others utter about the Holy Prophet.

people who have not come to thee. They [a]pervert words after their being put in their *right* places; and say, 'If you are given this, then accept it, but if you are not given this, then keep away *from it.*' And as for him whom Allāh desires to try, thou shalt not avail him aught against Allāh. These are they whose hearts Allāh has not been pleased to purify; they shall have disgrace in this world, and in the Hereafter they shall have a severe punishment.

سَمّٰعُوْنَ لِقَوْمٍ اٰخَرِيْنَ لَمْ يَاْتُوْكَ ؕ يُحَرِّفُوْنَ الْكَلِمَ
مِنْۢ بَعْدِ مَوَاضِعِهٖ ۚ يَقُوْلُوْنَ اِنْ اُوْتِيْتُمْ هٰذَا فَخُذُوْهُ
وَاِنْ لَّمْ تُؤْتَوْهُ فَاحْذَرُوْا ؕ وَمَنْ يُّرِدِ اللّٰهُ فِتْنَتَهٗ
فَلَنْ تَمْلِكَ لَهٗ مِنَ اللّٰهِ شَيْـًٔا ؕ اُولٰٓئِكَ الَّذِيْنَ لَمْ يُرِدِ
اللّٰهُ اَنْ يُّطَهِّرَ قُلُوْبَهُمْ ؕ لَهُمْ فِى الدُّنْيَا خِزْيٌ ۚۖ وَّ
لَهُمْ فِى الْاٰخِرَةِ عَذَابٌ عَظِيْمٌ ﴿۴۲﴾

43. They are eager listeners to falsehood, [b]devourers of things forbidden.[747] If, then, they come to thee *for judgment*, judge between them or turn aside from them. And if thou turn aside from them, they cannot harm thee at all. And if thou judge, judge between them with justice. Surely, Allāh loves those who are just.

سَمّٰعُوْنَ لِلْكَذِبِ اَكّٰلُوْنَ لِلسُّحْتِ ؕ فَاِنْ جَآءُوْكَ
فَاحْكُمْ بَيْنَهُمْ اَوْ اَعْرِضْ عَنْهُمْ ۚ وَاِنْ تُعْرِضْ
عَنْهُمْ فَلَنْ يَّضُرُّوْكَ شَيْـًٔا ؕ وَاِنْ حَكَمْتَ فَاحْكُمْ
بَيْنَهُمْ بِالْقِسْطِ ؕ اِنَّ اللّٰهَ يُحِبُّ الْمُقْسِطِيْنَ ﴿۴۳﴾

44. And how will they make thee *their* judge when they have with them the Torah, wherein is Allāh's judgment?[748] Yet, in spite of that they turn their backs; and certainly they will not believe.

وَكَيْفَ يُحَكِّمُوْنَكَ وَعِنْدَهُمُ التَّوْرٰىةُ فِيْهَا حُكْمُ
اللّٰهِ ثُمَّ يَتَوَلَّوْنَ مِنْۢ بَعْدِ ذٰلِكَ ؕ وَمَآ اُولٰٓئِكَ
بِالْمُؤْمِنِيْنَ ﴿۴۴﴾ ع ٦/١٠

[a]2: 76; 3 : 79; 4 : 47. [b]5 : 63, 64.

747. *Suht* means, a thing which is forbidden or unlawful; that which is foul and of bad repute; a bribe that is given to a judge or the like; or anything paltry, mean and inconsiderable (Lane).

748. The verse does not mean that the Qur'ān regarded the Torah as it existed at the time of the Holy Prophet as containing God's judgment on matters of dispute. It only expresses the attitude of the Jews towards the Torah. But at the same time the Qur'ān does not regard it even in its present form as devoid of all truth. According to it the Torah did contain certain truths in their original, pure form, though it also believes that it has been tampered with (2 : 79). The verse further shows that the Torah in its pristine purity was meant only for the Israelites for a limited period while the Message of the Qur'ān is meant for all peoples for all times.

R. 7 45. Surely, We sent down [a]the Torah wherein was guidance and light. By it did the Prophets, who were obedient *to Us*, judge for the Jews, *as did* the godly people[749] and those learned *in the Law;*[750] because they were required to preserve the Book of Allāh, and *because* they were guardians over it. Therefore fear not men but fear Me; and [b]barter not My Signs for a paltry price. And [c]whoso judges not by that which Allāh has sent down, these it is who are the disbelievers.

إِنَّآ أَنْزَلْنَا التَّوْرٰىةَ فِيهَا هُدًى وَّنُورٌ ۚ يَحْكُمُ
بِهَا النَّبِيُّونَ الَّذِينَ أَسْلَمُوا لِلَّذِينَ هَادُوا وَالرَّبّٰنِيُّونَ
وَالْأَحْبَارُ بِمَا اسْتُحْفِظُوا مِنْ كِتٰبِ اللّٰهِ وَكَانُوا
عَلَيْهِ شُهَدَآءَ ۚ فَلَا تَخْشَوُا النَّاسَ وَاخْشَوْنِ وَ
لَا تَشْتَرُوا بِاٰيٰتِي ثَمَنًا قَلِيلًا ۗ وَمَنْ لَّمْ يَحْكُمْ بِمَآ
أَنْزَلَ اللّٰهُ فَأُولٰٓئِكَ هُمُ الْكٰفِرُونَ ﴿٤٥﴾

46. And therein We prescribed for them: Life for life, and eye for eye, nose for nose, ear for ear, and tooth for tooth, and for *other* injuries equitable retaliation.[751] And whoso waives the right thereto, it shall be an expiation for his *own* sins; and [d]whoso judges not by what Allāh has sent down, these it is who are wrongdoers.

وَكَتَبْنَا عَلَيْهِمْ فِيهَآ أَنَّ النَّفْسَ بِالنَّفْسِ ۙ وَالْعَيْنَ
بِالْعَيْنِ وَالْأَنْفَ بِالْأَنْفِ وَالْأُذُنَ بِالْأُذُنِ وَالسِّنَّ
بِالسِّنِّ ۙ وَالْجُرُوحَ قِصَاصٌ ۗ فَمَنْ تَصَدَّقَ بِهٖ فَهُوَ
كَفَّارَةٌ لَّهٗ ۗ وَمَنْ لَّمْ يَحْكُمْ بِمَآ أَنْزَلَ اللّٰهُ فَأُولٰٓئِكَ
هُمُ الظّٰلِمُونَ ﴿٤٦﴾

47. And We [e]caused Jesus, son of Mary, to follow in their footsteps, [f]fulfilling that which was *revealed* before him in the Torah; and We gave him the Gospel which *contained* guidance and light, fulfilling that which was *revealed* before him in the Torah; and a guidance and an admonition for the God-fearing.

وَقَفَّيْنَا عَلٰٓى اٰثَارِهِمْ بِعِيسَى ابْنِ مَرْيَمَ مُصَدِّقًا
لِّمَا بَيْنَ يَدَيْهِ مِنَ التَّوْرٰىةِ ۖ وَاٰتَيْنٰهُ الْإِنْجِيلَ فِيهِ
هُدًى وَّنُورٌ ۙ وَّمُصَدِّقًا لِّمَا بَيْنَ يَدَيْهِ مِنَ التَّوْرٰىةِ
وَهُدًى وَّمَوْعِظَةً لِّلْمُتَّقِينَ ﴿٤٧﴾

[a]6 : 92; 7 : 155. [b]2 : 42. [c]5 : 46, 48. [d]5 : 45,48. [e]2 : 88; 57 : 28. [f]3 : 51; 61 : 7.

749. See 432A.

750. *Aḥbār* is the plural of *Ḥibr* which means, a learned man of the Jews; or any learned man; a good or righteous man (Lane). In this verse the Qur'ān brings home to the Jews the charge mentioned in the previous verse, *viz.*, when even the Prophets of God who followed Moses were required to judge according to the Torah, who else can refuse to refer his disputes to it?

751. See Exod : 21: 23-25 and Leviticus 24: 19-21. The words, *and whoso waives the right thereto*, constitute evidence of the fact that teaching about forgiveness of which

48. And let the People of the Gospel judge according to what Allāh has revealed therein, and [a]whoso judges not by what Allāh has revealed, these it is who are the transgressors.

وَلْيَحْكُمْ أَهْلُ الْإِنْجِيلِ بِمَآ أَنْزَلَ اللّٰهُ فِيهِ ۚ وَمَنْ لَّمْ
يَحْكُمْ بِمَآ أَنْزَلَ اللّٰهُ فَأُولٰٓئِكَ هُمُ الْفٰسِقُونَ ﴿٤٨﴾

49. And We have [b]revealed unto thee the Book comprising the truth *and* fulfilling that which was *revealed* before it in the Book, and as a guardian[752] over it. [c]Judge, therefore, between them by what Allāh has revealed, and follow not their evil desires, *turning away* from the truth which has come to thee. For each of you We prescribed a *clear spiritual* Law[753] and a *manifest* way *in secular matters*. And [d]if Allāh had *enforced His* Will, He would have made you *all* one people, but *He wishes* to try you by that which He has given you. [e]Vie, then, with one another in *doing* good works. To Allāh shall you all return; then will He inform you of that wherein you differed;

وَأَنْزَلْنَآ إِلَيْكَ الْكِتٰبَ بِالْحَقِّ مُصَدِّقًا لِّمَا بَيْنَ يَدَيْهِ
مِنَ الْكِتٰبِ وَمُهَيْمِنًا عَلَيْهِ فَاحْكُمْ بَيْنَهُمْ بِمَآ أَنْزَلَ
اللّٰهُ وَلَا تَتَّبِعْ أَهْوَآءَهُمْ عَمَّا جَآءَكَ مِنَ الْحَقِّ ۚ لِكُلٍّ
جَعَلْنَا مِنْكُمْ شِرْعَةً وَّمِنْهَاجًا ۚ وَلَوْ شَآءَ اللّٰهُ لَجَعَلَكُمْ
أُمَّةً وَّاحِدَةً وَّلٰكِنْ لِّيَبْلُوَكُمْ فِي مَآ اٰتٰكُمْ فَاسْتَبِقُوا
الْخَيْرٰتِ ۚ إِلَى اللّٰهِ مَرْجِعُكُمْ جَمِيعًا فَيُنَبِّئُكُمْ بِمَا
كُنْتُمْ فِيهِ تَخْتَلِفُونَ ﴿٤٩﴾

[a]5 : 45-46. [b]6 : 106; 39 : 3. [c]5 : 50. [d]10 : 100; 11 : 119; 16 : 10. [e]3 : 134; 35 : 33; 57 : 22.

Christians boast so much was no monopoly of the Gospels. It also formed part of the teaching of Moses though Moses's teaching lays stress on retaliation, as does that of Jesus on forgiveness and non-resistance.

752. *Muhaimin* means, witness; afforder of security and peace; controller and superintendent of the affairs of men ; guardian and protector (Lisān). The Qur'ān is here spoken of as a guardian over the previous Scriptures in the sense that it has preserved all that was imperishable and of permanent worth and value in them, and has left out that which lacked the element of permanence and failed to meet the needs of mankind. Again, it is called a guardian over the previous Scriptures because it enjoys Divine protection against being tampered with, a blessing denied to them.

753. *Shir'ah* signifies the religious Law of God consisting of such ordinances as those about Fasting, Prayer and Pilgrimage and other acts of piety; a way of belief and conduct which is manifest and right (Lane). *Minhāj* means, manifest, plainly apparent and open road or way (Lane). Al-Mubarrad says that the former word signifies the beginning of a way and the latter the well-trodden body of it (Qadīr). Thus *Shir'ah* is the law that mostly relates to spiritual matters and *Minhāj* is the law that relates to secular matters. *Shir'ah* also means, a way leading to water. The meaning is that God has equipped all His creatures, according to the capacity of each, with the means to find the way to the spring of spiritual water, *i. e.*, Divine revelation.

50. And that thou shouldst [a]judge between them by that which Allāh has revealed and follow not their evil desires and be on thy guard against them, [b]lest they involve thee in trouble on account of a part of what Allāh has revealed to thee. But if they turn away, then know that Allāh intends to punish them for some of their sins. And indeed a large number of men are disobedient.

وَأَنِ احْكُمْ بَيْنَهُمْ بِمَآ أَنْزَلَ اللّٰهُ وَلَا تَتَّبِعْ أَهْوَآءَهُمْ
وَاحْذَرْهُمْ أَنْ يَّفْتِنُوْكَ عَنْ بَعْضِ مَآ أَنْزَلَ اللّٰهُ إِلَيْكَ ۖ
فَإِنْ تَوَلَّوْا فَاعْلَمْ أَنَّمَا يُرِيْدُ اللّٰهُ أَنْ يُّصِيْبَهُمْ بِبَعْضِ
ذُنُوْبِهِمْ ۗ وَإِنَّ كَثِيْرًا مِّنَ النَّاسِ لَفٰسِقُوْنَ ﴿٥٠﴾

51. Do they then seek the judgment[754] of *the days of* Ignorance.[755] And who is better than Allāh as a judge for a people who have firm faith?

أَفَحُكْمَ الْجَاهِلِيَّةِ يَبْغُوْنَ ۚ وَمَنْ أَحْسَنُ مِنَ اللّٰهِ
حُكْمًا لِّقَوْمٍ يُّوْقِنُوْنَ ﴿٥١﴾ ع

R. 8 52. O ye who believe! [c]take not the Jews and the Christians for friends.[756] They are friends of each other.[757] And whoso among you takes them for friends is indeed one of them. Verily, Allāh guides not the unjust people.

يٰٓأَيُّهَا الَّذِيْنَ اٰمَنُوْا لَا تَتَّخِذُوا الْيَهُوْدَ وَالنَّصٰرٰٓى أَوْلِيَآءَ ۘ
بَعْضُهُمْ أَوْلِيَآءُ بَعْضٍ ۚ وَمَنْ يَّتَوَلَّهُمْ مِّنْكُمْ فَإِنَّهٗ
مِنْهُمْ ۗ إِنَّ اللّٰهَ لَا يَهْدِي الْقَوْمَ الظّٰلِمِيْنَ ﴿٥٢﴾

53. And thou wilt see those in whose hearts is a disease, hastening towards them saying, 'We fear lest a misfortune[758] befall us.' Maybe,

فَتَرَى الَّذِيْنَ فِيْ قُلُوْبِهِمْ مَّرَضٌ يُّسَارِعُوْنَ فِيْهِمْ
يَقُوْلُوْنَ نَخْشٰٓى أَنْ تُصِيْبَنَا دَآئِرَةٌ ۚ فَعَسَى اللّٰهُ أَنْ يَّأْتِيَ

[a]5 : 49. [b]17 : 74. [c]3 : 29, 119; 4 : 145; 5 : 58; 60 : 10.

754. *Ḥukm* means, judgment, rule, jurisdiction, dominion, government, ordinance, decree, law; predicament (Lane).

755. The pre-Islamic period.

756. The verse should not be construed to prohibit or discourage just or benevolent treatment of Jews, Christians and other disbelievers (60 : 9). It refers only to those Jews or Christians who are at war with Muslims and who are always hatching plots against them.

757. Jews and Christians forget their own differences and become united in their opposition to Islām. Truly, has the Holy Prophet said, "All disbelief forms one community," *viz.*, all disbelievers, however inimical to one another, behave like one people when opposed to Muslims.

758. *Dā'irah* means, a turn of fortune, specially an evil accident, a misfortune; a calamity; defeat or rout; slaughter or death (Lane).

Allāh will bring about [a]victory[759] or some *other* event from Himself. Then they will regret what they hid in their minds.

بِالْفَتْحِ أَوْ أَمْرٍ مِّنْ عِنْدِهٖ فَيُصْبِحُوْا عَلٰى مَآ أَسَرُّوْا فِيْ
أَنْفُسِهِمْ نٰدِمِيْنَ ﴿٥٣﴾

54. And those who believe will say, 'Are these they who swore by Allāh their most solemn oaths that they were surely with you?' Their works are vain and they have become the losers.

وَيَقُوْلُ الَّذِيْنَ اٰمَنُوْآ أَهٰٓؤُلَآءِ الَّذِيْنَ أَقْسَمُوْا بِاللّٰهِ جَهْدَ
أَيْمَانِهِمْ إِنَّهُمْ لَمَعَكُمْ حَبِطَتْ أَعْمَالُهُمْ فَأَصْبَحُوْا
خٰسِرِيْنَ ﴿٥٤﴾

55. O ye who believe! whoso among you [b]turns back from his religion, then *let him know that* Allāh will soon bring *in his stead* a people whom He will love and who will love him[760] *and who will be* kind and humble towards believers, *and* hard *and firm* against disbelievers. They will strive in the cause of Allāh and will not fear the reproach of a fault-finder. That is Allāh's grace; He bestows it upon whomsoever He pleases and Allāh is Bountiful, All-Knowing.

يٰٓأَيُّهَا الَّذِيْنَ اٰمَنُوْا مَنْ يَّرْتَدَّ مِنْكُمْ عَنْ دِيْنِهٖ فَسَوْفَ
يَأْتِي اللّٰهُ بِقَوْمٍ يُّحِبُّهُمْ وَيُحِبُّوْنَهٗٓ أَذِلَّةٍ عَلَى الْمُؤْمِنِيْنَ
أَعِزَّةٍ عَلَى الْكٰفِرِيْنَ يُجَاهِدُوْنَ فِيْ سَبِيْلِ اللّٰهِ وَلَا
يَخَافُوْنَ لَوْمَةَ لَآئِمٍ ذٰلِكَ فَضْلُ اللّٰهِ يُؤْتِيْهِ مَنْ يَّشَآءُ
وَاللّٰهُ وَاسِعٌ عَلِيْمٌ ﴿٥٥﴾

56. Your [c]friend is Allāh and His Messenger and the believers who observe Prayer and pay the *Zakāt* and worship God alone.

إِنَّمَا وَلِيُّكُمُ اللّٰهُ وَرَسُوْلُهٗ وَالَّذِيْنَ اٰمَنُوا الَّذِيْنَ يُقِيْمُوْنَ
الصَّلٰوةَ وَيُؤْتُوْنَ الزَّكٰوةَ وَهُمْ رٰكِعُوْنَ ﴿٥٦﴾

57. And those who take Allāh and His Messenger and the believers for friends *should rest assured* that it is the [d]party of Allāh that must triumph.

وَمَنْ يَّتَوَلَّ اللّٰهَ وَرَسُوْلَهٗ وَالَّذِيْنَ اٰمَنُوْا فَإِنَّ حِزْبَ
اللّٰهِ هُمُ الْغٰلِبُوْنَ ﴿٥٧﴾

[a]32 : 30. [b]3 : 145. [c]2 : 258; 3 : 69. [d]58 : 23.

759. "Victory" mentioned in the verse may either refer to the Fall of Mecca or to victory in general. The word "event" coming after victory evidently refers to something greater than victory. It seems to refer to the entry into the fold of Islām of the whole of the Arabian peninsula and its establishment in it.

760. If the followers of a religion are found to be steadily and perpetually decreasing with no prospects for recovery, that religion must be considered as dead.

R. 9 58. O ye who believe! [a]take not those for friends[761] [b]who make a jest and sport of your religion from among those who were given the Book before you, and the disbelievers. And fear Allāh if you are believers;

يَا أَيُّهَا الَّذِينَ آمَنُوا لَا تَتَّخِذُوا الَّذِينَ اتَّخَذُوا دِينَكُمْ هُزُوًا وَلَعِبًا مِنَ الَّذِينَ أُوتُوا الْكِتَابَ مِنْ قَبْلِكُمْ وَالْكُفَّارَ أَوْلِيَاءَ ۚ وَاتَّقُوا اللَّهَ إِنْ كُنْتُمْ مُؤْمِنِينَ ﴿٥٨﴾

59. And *who,* when you call *people* to Prayer, take it for jest and sport. This is because they are a people who do not understand.

وَإِذَا نَادَيْتُمْ إِلَى الصَّلَاةِ اتَّخَذُوهَا هُزُوًا وَلَعِبًا ۚ ذَٰلِكَ بِأَنَّهُمْ قَوْمٌ لَا يَعْقِلُونَ ﴿٥٩﴾

60. Say, 'O People of the Book! do you [c]find fault with us because we believe in Allāh and what has been sent down to us and what was sent down previously?[762] Or *is it* because most of you are disobedient *to Allāh*?'

قُلْ يَا أَهْلَ الْكِتَابِ هَلْ تَنْقِمُونَ مِنَّا إِلَّا أَنْ آمَنَّا بِاللَّهِ وَمَا أُنْزِلَ إِلَيْنَا وَمَا أُنْزِلَ مِنْ قَبْلُ وَأَنَّ أَكْثَرَكُمْ فَاسِقُونَ ﴿٦٠﴾

61. Say, 'Shall I inform you of those[763] whose reward with Allāh is worse than that? *They are* those whom Allāh has cursed and on whom [d]His wrath *has fallen* and of whom He has made apes and swine[764] and *who* worship the [e]Evil One. [f]These indeed are in a worse plight, and farther astray from the right path.

قُلْ هَلْ أُنَبِّئُكُمْ بِشَرٍّ مِنْ ذَٰلِكَ مَثُوبَةً عِنْدَ اللَّهِ ۚ مَنْ لَعَنَهُ اللَّهُ وَغَضِبَ عَلَيْهِ وَجَعَلَ مِنْهُمُ الْقِرَدَةَ وَالْخَنَازِيرَ وَعَبَدَ الطَّاغُوتَ ۚ أُولَٰئِكَ شَرٌّ مَكَانًا وَأَضَلُّ عَنْ سَوَاءِ السَّبِيلِ ﴿٦١﴾

---

[a]3 : 29, 119 ; 4 : 145 ; 5 : 52 ; 60 : 10. [b]6 : 71 ; 7 : 52. [c]7 : 127 ; 60 : 2. [d]2 : 66 ; 7 : 167. [e]2 : 258 ; 4 : 52. [f]12 : 78 ; 25 : 35.

---

761. In 5 : 52 Muslims were forbidden to make friends with disbelievers because of the latter's hostile and belligerent attitude towards them. The present verse gives the reason for that commandment, but does not mean that Muslims are prevented from having friendly dealings of any kind with all disbelievers or from doing good to them and treating them kindly.

762. *Hal* is an interrogative particle which, when followed by *illā*, may signify, as in the present verse, a negative statement. The words besides the meaning given in the text may also mean, "you do not find fault with us but because we believe." Sometimes it is used to express a positive statement as in 76 : 2.

763. *Dhālika* may either refer to the persecution of the Muslims or to their persecutors.

764. The words "apes" and "swine" have been used here in a figurative sense. Certain traits are peculiar to particular animals, and these cannot be fully described unless

62. And when they come to you, they say, 'We believe,'[765] while they enter with disbelief and go out therewith; and Allāh best knows what they hide.

وَإِذَا جَآءُوكُمْ قَالُوٓا۟ ءَامَنَّا وَقَد دَّخَلُوا۟ بِٱلْكُفْرِ وَهُمْ قَدْ خَرَجُوا۟ بِهِۦ ۚ وَٱللَّهُ أَعْلَمُ بِمَا كَانُوا۟ يَكْتُمُونَ ﴿٦٢﴾

63. And thou seest many of them hastening towards sin and transgression and [a]the eating of things forbidden. Evil indeed is that which they practise.

وَتَرَىٰ كَثِيرًا مِّنْهُمْ يُسَٰرِعُونَ فِى ٱلْإِثْمِ وَٱلْعُدْوَٰنِ وَأَكْلِهِمُ ٱلسُّحْتَ ۚ لَبِئْسَ مَا كَانُوا۟ يَعْمَلُونَ ﴿٦٣﴾

64. Why do not the divines and those learned in the Law prohibit them from uttering sin[766] and eating things forbidden? [b]Evil indeed is that which they do.

لَوْلَا يَنْهَىٰهُمُ ٱلرَّبَّٰنِيُّونَ وَٱلْأَحْبَارُ عَن قَوْلِهِمُ ٱلْإِثْمَ وَأَكْلِهِمُ ٱلسُّحْتَ ۚ لَبِئْسَ مَا كَانُوا۟ يَصْنَعُونَ ﴿٦٤﴾

65. And [c]the Jews say, 'Allāh's hand is tied up.' Their *own* hands shall be tied up[767] and they shall be cursed for what they say. Nay, both His hands[768] are wide open. He spends as He pleases. And [d]what has been sent down to thee from thy Lord will most surely increase many of them in rebellion

وَقَالَتِ ٱلْيَهُودُ يَدُ ٱللَّهِ مَغْلُولَةٌ ۚ غُلَّتْ أَيْدِيهِمْ وَلُعِنُوا۟ بِمَا قَالُوا۟ ۘ بَلْ يَدَاهُ مَبْسُوطَتَانِ يُنفِقُ كَيْفَ يَشَآءُ ۚ وَلَيَزِيدَنَّ كَثِيرًا مِّنْهُم مَّآ أُنزِلَ إِلَيْكَ مِن

[a]5 : 43. [b]5 : 80. [c]3 : 182 ; 36 : 48. [d]5 : 69.

the animal to which they are known to belong is expressly named. The ape is noted for its mimicry and the swine is characterized by filthy and shameless habits and also by its stupidity. The expression, "who worship the Evil One," shows that the words "apes" and "swine" have been used here figuratively. See 107.

765. By hypocritically uttering the words, *we believe*, the Jews merely copied the believers' mode of expressing their belief without understanding and realizing their real import; thus they displayed (as hinted in the foregoing verse) the mimicking characteristic of the ape. See also the next verse.

766. As *Ithm* (sin) is generally committed and not uttered, some Commentators have suggested that the word *Qaul* (uttering) has been used here in the sense of "doing." But more probably it has been joined to the word *Ithm* (sin) in order to express the combined idea of both "uttering" and "doing," signifying both sinful words and evil deeds.

767. The expression signifies that the Jews shall be punished for their insolence in saying that the hand of Allāh is tied up. They shall become a miserly and stingy nation.

768. The hand is used both as an instrument for bestowing a favour or bounty and as a symbol of power and dominion for seizing and punishing an offender. God's both hands are wide open—the one to bestow plenty on the believers and the other to punish the Jews for their insolence.

and disbelief. And [a]We have cast among them enmity and hatred till the Day of Resurrection. Whenever they [b]kindle a fire for war,[769] Allāh extinguishes it. And they strive to create disorder in the earth, and Allāh loves not those who create disorder.

رَبِّكَ طُغْيَانًا وَّكُفْرًا ۚ وَأَلْقَيْنَا بَيْنَهُمُ الْعَدَاوَةَ
وَالْبَغْضَاءَ إِلَىٰ يَوْمِ الْقِيٰمَةِ ۚ كُلَّمَا أَوْقَدُوا نَارًا
لِّلْحَرْبِ أَطْفَأَهَا اللّٰهُ ۙ وَيَسْعَوْنَ فِي الْأَرْضِ فَسَادًا ۚ
وَاللّٰهُ لَا يُحِبُّ الْمُفْسِدِينَ ﴿٦٥﴾

66. And [c]if the People of the Book had believed and been righteous, We would surely have removed from them their evils and We would surely have admitted them into Gardens of bliss.[770]

وَلَوْ أَنَّ أَهْلَ الْكِتٰبِ اٰمَنُوا وَاتَّقَوْا لَكَفَّرْنَا عَنْهُمْ
سَيِّاٰتِهِمْ وَلَأَدْخَلْنٰهُمْ جَنّٰتِ النَّعِيمِ ﴿٦٦﴾

67. And if [d]they had observed the Torah and the Gospel and what has been *now* sent down to them from their Lord, they would, surely, have eaten *of good things* from above them and from under their feet.[771] Among them are a people who are moderate; but many of them *are such that* evil is what they do.

وَلَوْ أَنَّهُمْ أَقَامُوا التَّوْرٰىةَ وَالْإِنْجِيلَ وَمَا أُنْزِلَ
إِلَيْهِمْ مِّنْ رَّبِّهِمْ لَأَكَلُوا مِنْ فَوْقِهِمْ وَمِنْ تَحْتِ
أَرْجُلِهِمْ ۚ مِنْهُمْ أُمَّةٌ مُّقْتَصِدَةٌ ۖ وَكَثِيرٌ مِّنْهُمْ سَاءَ
مَا يَعْمَلُونَ ﴿٦٧﴾ ع ٩ ١٣

[a]3 : 56; 5 : 15. [b]2 : 18. [c]7: 97. [d]5 : 48 .

769. The words refer to the attempts of Jews to incite the idolaters of Arabia to wage war against Muslims as well as to their own hostile activities against Islām.

770. The expression, *Gardens of bliss*, denotes a perfect state of spiritual joy as well as an abode of bliss. While qualifying the words "Garden" and "Heaven" the Qur'ān has used four distinct expressions : (1) "Gardens of bliss" as in the present verse; (2) "Gardens of Refuge" (32 : 20); (3) "Gardens of Eternity" (9 : 72) and (4) "Gardens of Paradise" (18 : 108). These expressions represent different aspects as well as different grades of Heaven.

771. (1) They would have received heavenly blessings, such as Divine revelation and communion with God, as well as worldly prosperity. (2) They would have had not only timely and abundant rains from above but the earth would also have yielded its produce for them in abundance. (3) God would have provided them with both heavenly and earthly means of progress.

R. 10 68. O Messenger ! [a] convey *to the people* what has been revealed to thee from thy Lord; and if thou do it not, thou hast not conveyed His Message.[772] And Allāh will protect[773] thee from men. Surely, Allāh guides not the disbelieving people.

يٰٓاَيُّهَا الرَّسُوْلُ بَلِّغْ مَآ اُنْزِلَ اِلَيْكَ مِنْ رَّبِّكَ ؕ وَاِنْ لَّمْ
تَفْعَلْ فَمَا بَلَّغْتَ رِسَالَتَهٗ ؕ وَاللّٰهُ يَعْصِمُكَ مِنَ النَّاسِ ؕ
اِنَّ اللّٰهَ لَا يَهْدِي الْقَوْمَ الْكٰفِرِيْنَ ﴿۶۸﴾

69. Say, 'O People of the Book, you *stand* on nothing [774] until you observe the Torah and the Gospel and what has *now* been sent down to you from your Lord.' And surely what has been sent down to thee from thy Lord will increase many of them in [b]rebellion and disbelief; so grieve not for the disbelieving people.

قُلْ يٰٓاَهْلَ الْكِتٰبِ لَسْتُمْ عَلٰى شَيْءٍ حَتّٰى تُقِيْمُوا التَّوْرٰىةَ
وَالْاِنْجِيْلَ وَمَآ اُنْزِلَ اِلَيْكُمْ مِّنْ رَّبِّكُمْ ؕ وَلَيَزِيْدَنَّ
كَثِيْرًا مِّنْهُمْ مَّآ اُنْزِلَ اِلَيْكَ مِنْ رَّبِّكَ طُغْيَانًا وَّكُفْرًا ۚ
فَلَا تَاْسَ عَلَى الْقَوْمِ الْكٰفِرِيْنَ ﴿۶۹﴾

70. Surely, [c]those who have believed, and the Jews, and the Sabians,[775] and the Christians—whoso believes in Allāh and the Last Day and does good deeds, on them *shall come* [d]no fear, nor shall they grieve.

اِنَّ الَّذِيْنَ اٰمَنُوْا وَالَّذِيْنَ هَادُوْا وَالصّٰبِئُوْنَ وَالنَّصٰرٰى
مَنْ اٰمَنَ بِاللّٰهِ وَالْيَوْمِ الْاٰخِرِ وَعَمِلَ صَالِحًا فَلَا خَوْفٌ
عَلَيْهِمْ وَلَا هُمْ يَحْزَنُوْنَ ﴿۷۰﴾

[a]6 : 20. [b]5 : 65. [c]2 : 63; 22 : 18. [d]See 2 : 63.

772. The words do not indicate any remissness on the part of the Holy Prophet to convey the Divine Message. They only state a general principle that anyone who fails to convey a part of the message he is entrusted with, in fact, fails to deliver it at all.

773. The expression means that God will not suffer the disbelievers to take the life of the Holy Prophet or disable him permanently so as to render him unfit to discharge his duty.

774. In 2 : 114 Jews and Christians were rebuked for saying about one another that they stood on nothing, and in the present verse the Qur'ān itself uses an identical expression about the People of the Book. But there is an obvious difference between the two statements. Whereas the statement referred to in 2 : 114 was unqualified, that in the present verse is qualified by the clause, 'unless you observe the Torah......'

775. See 104.

71. Surely, We took a covenant from the Children of Israel, and We sent Messengers to[776] them. But [a]every time there came to them a Messenger with what their hearts desired not, they treated some as liars, and some they sought to kill.

لَقَدْ أَخَذْنَا مِيثَاقَ بَنِيٓ إِسْرَآءِيلَ وَأَرْسَلْنَآ إِلَيْهِمْ
رُسُلًا ۖ كُلَّمَا جَآءَهُمْ رَسُولٌۢ بِمَا لَا تَهْوَىٰٓ أَنفُسُهُمْ
فَرِيقًا كَذَّبُوا۟ وَفَرِيقًا يَقْتُلُونَ ﴿٧١﴾

72. And they imagined that no punishment *would result from their conduct*, so they became blind and deaf. But Allāh turned to them in mercy; yet again many of them became blind and deaf; and Allāh is Watchful of what they do.

وَحَسِبُوٓا۟ أَلَّا تَكُونَ فِتْنَةٌ فَعَمُوا۟ وَصَمُّوا۟ ثُمَّ تَابَ ٱللَّهُ
عَلَيْهِمْ ثُمَّ عَمُوا۟ وَصَمُّوا۟ كَثِيرٌ مِّنْهُمْ ۚ وَٱللَّهُ بَصِيرٌۢ بِمَا
يَعْمَلُونَ ﴿٧٢﴾

73. Indeed, [b]they are disbelievers who say, 'Allāh, He is the Messiah, son of Mary,' whereas the Messiah *himself* said, 'O Children of Israel, [c]worship Allāh Who is my Lord and your Lord.'[777] Surely, whoso associates partners with Allāh, him has Allāh forbidden Heaven, and the Fire will be his resort. And the wrongdoers shall have no helpers.

لَقَدْ كَفَرَ ٱلَّذِينَ قَالُوٓا۟ إِنَّ ٱللَّهَ هُوَ ٱلْمَسِيحُ ٱبْنُ مَرْيَمَ ۖ
وَقَالَ ٱلْمَسِيحُ يَٰبَنِيٓ إِسْرَآءِيلَ ٱعْبُدُوا۟ ٱللَّهَ رَبِّى
وَرَبَّكُمْ ۖ إِنَّهُۥ مَن يُشْرِكْ بِٱللَّهِ فَقَدْ حَرَّمَ ٱللَّهُ عَلَيْهِ
ٱلْجَنَّةَ وَمَأْوَىٰهُ ٱلنَّارُ ۖ وَمَا لِلظَّٰلِمِينَ مِنْ أَنصَارٍ ﴿٧٣﴾

74. [d]They surely disbelieve who say, 'Allāh is the third of three;'[778] there is no god but the One God. And if they do not desist from what they say, a grievous punishment shall surely befall those of them that disbelieve.

لَقَدْ كَفَرَ ٱلَّذِينَ قَالُوٓا۟ إِنَّ ٱللَّهَ ثَالِثُ ثَلَٰثَةٍ ۘ وَمَا مِنْ
إِلَٰهٍ إِلَّآ إِلَٰهٌ وَٰحِدٌ ۚ وَإِن لَّمْ يَنتَهُوا۟ عَمَّا يَقُولُونَ
لَيَمَسَّنَّ ٱلَّذِينَ كَفَرُوا۟ مِنْهُمْ عَذَابٌ أَلِيمٌ ﴿٧٤﴾

[a]2 : 88. [b]4 : 172; 5 : 18; 9 : 30. [c]5 : 118; 19 : 37. [d]4 : 172.

776. By comparing this verse with 5: 13, it appears that "the leaders" mentioned in the latter verse are the "Messengers" mentioned in the present verse.

777. That Jesus taught that God alone is to be worshipped is apparent from the Gospels even in their present distorted form (Matt. 4 : 10; Luke 4 : 8).

778. The reference in this verse is to the doctrine of Trinity, that mysterious and abstruse dogma of the three persons of Godhead—the Father, the Son and the Holy Ghost—co-existing and co-equal in all respects, combining to make one God and yet remaining three. It was the Nicene Council and especially the Athenasian Creed that first gave the dogma its definite shape. The doctrine forms the basic article of the Christian Faith.

75. Will they not then turn to Allāh and ask His forgiveness, while Allāh is Most Forgiving *and* Merciful?[779]

أَفَلَا يَتُوبُونَ إِلَى اللّٰهِ وَيَسْتَغْفِرُونَهُ ۚ وَاللّٰهُ غَفُورٌ
رَّحِيمٌ ﴿٧٥﴾

76. The Messiah, son of Mary, was only a Messenger; surely Messengers *like unto him* had passed away before him. And his mother was a truthful woman. [a]They both used to eat food.[780] See how We explain the Signs for their *good*, and see how they are turned away.

مَا الْمَسِيحُ ابْنُ مَرْيَمَ إِلَّا رَسُولٌ ۚ قَدْ خَلَتْ مِنْ
قَبْلِهِ الرُّسُلُ ۚ وَأُمُّهُ صِدِّيقَةٌ ۖ كَانَا يَأْكُلَانِ الطَّعَامَ ۗ
انْظُرْ كَيْفَ نُبَيِّنُ لَهُمُ الْآيٰتِ ثُمَّ انْظُرْ أَنّٰى يُؤْفَكُونَ ﴿٧٦﴾

77. Say, [b]"Will you worship beside Allāh that which has no power to do you harm or good?"[781] And Allāh—He is All-Hearing, All-Knowing.

قُلْ أَتَعْبُدُونَ مِنْ دُونِ اللّٰهِ مَا لَا يَمْلِكُ لَكُمْ ضَرًّا
وَّلَا نَفْعًا ۚ وَاللّٰهُ هُوَ السَّمِيعُ الْعَلِيمُ ﴿٧٧﴾

78. Say, [c]"O People of the Book, exceed not the limits in *the matter of* your religion unjustly, nor follow the low desires of a people who went astray before and caused many to go astray, and *who* have strayed away from the right path.'

قُلْ يٰٓأَهْلَ الْكِتٰبِ لَا تَغْلُوا فِي دِينِكُمْ غَيْرَ الْحَقِّ وَلَا تَتَّبِعُوٓا
أَهْوَآءَ قَوْمٍ قَدْ ضَلُّوا مِنْ قَبْلُ وَأَضَلُّوا كَثِيرًا وَّضَلُّوا
عَنْ سَوَآءِ السَّبِيلِ ﴿٧٨﴾ ع

[a]21 : 9. [b]6 : 72; 10 : 107; 21 : 67; 22 : 13. [c]4 : 172.

779. No vicarious sacrifice is needed for the salvation of man. God Himself can forgive all sins. Only a truly penitent and contrite heart is required to attract His forgiveness.

780. The verse advances a number of arguments against the alleged divinity of Jesus; (a) Jesus was no better than other Messengers of God in any way; (b) he was born of a woman; (c) like other human beings he was subject to the natural laws of hunger and thirst and was subject also to the natural ensuing phenomena.

781. Jesus possessed no power to do good or harm to any person. He could not hear prayer, nor was he conversant with the needs of men that he could satisfy them. These are all Divine prerogatives.

R. 11 79. Those amongst the Israel who disbelieved were [a]cursed by the tongue of David, and of Jesus, son of Mary.[782] That was because they disobeyed and used to transgress.

لُعِنَ الَّذِيْنَ كَفَرُوْا مِنْ بَنِيْٓ اِسْرَآءِيْلَ عَلٰى لِسَانِ
دَاوٗدَ وَعِيْسَى ابْنِ مَرْيَمَ ؕ ذٰلِكَ بِمَا عَصَوْا وَّكَانُوْا
يَعْتَدُوْنَ ﴿۷۹﴾

80. They did not [b]restrain one another from the iniquity which they committed.[783] Evil indeed was what they used to do.

كَانُوْا لَا يَتَنَاهَوْنَ عَنْ مُّنْكَرٍ فَعَلُوْهُ ؕ لَبِئْسَ مَا كَانُوْا
يَفْعَلُوْنَ ﴿۸۰﴾

81. Thou shalt see many of them making friends with those who disbelieve. Surely, evil is that which their souls have sent on before for themselves so that Allāh is [c]displeased with them; and in *this* punishment they shall abide.

تَرٰى كَثِيْرًا مِّنْهُمْ يَتَوَلَّوْنَ الَّذِيْنَ كَفَرُوْا ؕ لَبِئْسَ مَا
قَدَّمَتْ لَهُمْ اَنْفُسُهُمْ اَنْ سَخِطَ اللّٰهُ عَلَيْهِمْ وَفِي
الْعَذَابِ هُمْ خٰلِدُوْنَ ﴿۸۱﴾

82. And if they had believed in Allāh and *this* Prophet,[784] and *in* that which has been revealed to him, they would not have taken them for *their* friends, but many of them are transgressors.

وَلَوْ كَانُوْا يُؤْمِنُوْنَ بِاللّٰهِ وَالنَّبِيِّ وَمَآ اُنْزِلَ اِلَيْهِ
مَا اتَّخَذُوْهُمْ اَوْلِيَآءَ وَلٰكِنَّ كَثِيْرًا مِّنْهُمْ فٰسِقُوْنَ ﴿۸۲﴾

83. Thou shalt certainly find the Jews and those who associate partners with Allāh to be the most

لَتَجِدَنَّ اَشَدَّ النَّاسِ عَدَاوَةً لِّلَّذِيْنَ اٰمَنُوا الْيَهُوْدَ

[a]3 : 88; 4 : 48. [b]5 : 64, 4. [c]3 : 163.

782. Of all the Israelite Prophets, David and Jesus suffered most at the hands of the Jews. Jewish persecution of Jesus culminated in his being hung on the cross, and the hardships and privations to which David was subjected by these ungrateful people are reflected in the deep pathos of his Psalms. From the agony of their hearts did David and Jesus curse them. The curse of David resulted in the Israelites being punished by Nebuchadnezzar, who destroyed Jerusalem and carried the Israelites into captivity in 556 B.C.; and as a result of the curse of Jesus, they were visited by terrible afflictions by Titus, who captured Jerusalem in about 70 A.D., devastated the city and profaned the Temple by causing swine—an animal most hated and abhorred by Jews—to be slaughtered therein.

783. One of the great sins which drew the wrath of God upon the Jewish people was that they did not prohibit one another from the evil practices which were so rife among them.

784. The Prophet referred to in this verse is the Holy Prophet, for wherever in the Qur'ān the word *al-Nabī* (the Prophet) is used, it invariably refers to the Holy Prophet. Even the Gospels referred to him as "that Prophet" (John, 1 : 21,25), *i.e.*, the Prophet whose advent was foretold in Deut. 18 : 18.

vehement of men in enmity against the believers. And thou shalt assuredly find those who say, 'We are Christians,' to be the nearest of them in friendship to the believers. That is because amongst them are savants[785] and monks[786] and because they are not arrogant.[787]

وَالَّذِينَ أَشْرَكُوا ۚ وَلَتَجِدَنَّ أَقْرَبَهُمْ مَوَدَّةً لِلَّذِينَ
آمَنُوا الَّذِينَ قَالُوا إِنَّا نَصَارَىٰ ۚ ذَٰلِكَ بِأَنَّ مِنْهُمْ قِسِّيسِينَ
وَرُهْبَانًا وَأَنَّهُمْ لَا يَسْتَكْبِرُونَ ﴿٨٣﴾

PART VII

84. And when they hear what has been revealed to *this* Messenger, thou seest their eyes overflow with tears,[788] because of the truth which they have recognized. They say, [a]"Our Lord, we believe, so write us down among the witnesses;

وَإِذَا سَمِعُوا مَا أُنْزِلَ إِلَى الرَّسُولِ تَرَىٰ أَعْيُنَهُمْ
تَفِيضُ مِنَ الدَّمْعِ مِمَّا عَرَفُوا مِنَ الْحَقِّ ۖ يَقُولُونَ
رَبَّنَا آمَنَّا فَاكْتُبْنَا مَعَ الشَّاهِدِينَ ﴿٨٤﴾

85. 'And why should we not believe in Allāh and in the truth which has come to us, while we earnestly [b]wish that our Lord should include us among the righteous people?'

وَمَا لَنَا لَا نُؤْمِنُ بِاللَّهِ وَمَا جَاءَنَا مِنَ الْحَقِّ وَ
نَطْمَعُ أَنْ يُدْخِلَنَا رَبُّنَا مَعَ الْقَوْمِ الصَّالِحِينَ ﴿٨٥﴾

[a]3 : 54, 194. [b]26 : 52.

785. *Qissis* means, the head or chief of the Christians in knowledge or science; a learned man of the Christians who has sought after and acquired great knowledge; an intelligent and learned man (Lane).

786. *Ruhbān* is the plural of *Rāhib* which means an ascetic, a Christian monk; a religious recluse; one who devotes himself to religious services or exercises in a cell or monastery (Lane).

787. This state of affairs, however, was not to last for ever. The Qur'ān elsewhere warns Muslims that they were destined to suffer most grievously at the hands of Christians who would attack them from all sides (21 : 97). In the Ḥadīth also there are prophecies to this effect. The verse applies only to the Christians of the Holy Prophet's time. History bears out this inference. Najashī, the Christian King of Abyssinia, gave shelter to Muslim refugees; and Muqauqas, the Christian ruler of Egypt, sent presents to the Holy Prophet. Humility seemed to be one of the chief characteristics of the early Christians. This is evident from the different ways in which the epistles of the Holy Prophet were treated by the King of Persia, who was a heathen, and by Heraclius, Emperor of the Eastern Roman Empire, who was a Christian. The former tore the letter to pieces, while the latter received it with respect and even evinced some inclination towards Islām.

788. The verse has also been applied to the Najashī in particular. When Ja'far, a cousin of the Holy Prophet and spokesman of Muslim refugees in Abyssinia read to him the opening verses of the *Sūrah* Maryam, the Najashī was visibly moved and tears rolled down his cheeks and he said in a voice full of pathos that that exactly was his belief about Jesus, and that he did not look upon him by even a twig more than that (Hishām).

86. So 'Allāh [a]rewarded them for what they said with Gardens beneath which streams flow. Therein shall they abide; and that is the reward of those who do good.

فَأَثَابَهُمُ اللّٰهُ بِمَا قَالُوا جَنّٰتٍ تَجْرِي مِنْ تَحْتِهَا الْأَنْهٰرُ
خٰلِدِينَ فِيهَا ۚ وَذٰلِكَ جَزَاءُ الْمُحْسِنِينَ ﴿٨٦﴾

87. And [b]those who have disbelieved and rejected Our Signs, these are they who are inmates of Hell.

وَالَّذِينَ كَفَرُوا وَكَذَّبُوا بِاٰيٰتِنَا أُولٰئِكَ أَصْحٰبُ الْجَحِيمِ ﴿٨٧﴾ ع

R. 12 88. O ye who believe! [c]make not unlawful the good things which Allāh has made lawful for you, and do not transgress. Surely, Allāh loves not the transgressors.

يٰأَيُّهَا الَّذِينَ اٰمَنُوا لَا تُحَرِّمُوا طَيِّبٰتِ مَا أَحَلَّ اللّٰهُ لَكُمْ
وَلَا تَعْتَدُوا ۚ إِنَّ اللّٰهَ لَا يُحِبُّ الْمُعْتَدِينَ ﴿٨٨﴾

89. And [d]eat of that which Allāh has provided for you of what is lawful and good. And fear Allāh in Whom you believe.

وَكُلُوا مِمَّا رَزَقَكُمُ اللّٰهُ حَلٰلًا طَيِّبًا ۖ وَاتَّقُوا اللّٰهَ الَّذِي
أَنْتُمْ بِهِ مُؤْمِنُونَ ﴿٨٩﴾

90. [e]Allāh will not take you to task for such of your oaths as are vain,[789] but He will take you to task for *breaking* the oaths which you take in earnest. The expiation, thereof, then, is the feeding of ten poor persons with *such* average[790] *food* as you feed your families with, or the clothing of them or the freeing of a slave. But whoso finds not *the means* shall fast for three days. That is the expiation of your oaths when you have sworn. And keep your oaths. Thus does Allāh explain to you His Signs that you may be grateful.

لَا يُؤَاخِذُكُمُ اللّٰهُ بِاللَّغْوِ فِي أَيْمٰنِكُمْ وَلٰكِنْ يُؤَاخِذُكُمْ
بِمَا عَقَّدْتُّمُ الْأَيْمٰنَ ۚ فَكَفَّارَتُهُ إِطْعَامُ عَشَرَةِ مَسٰكِينَ
مِنْ أَوْسَطِ مَا تُطْعِمُونَ أَهْلِيكُمْ أَوْ كِسْوَتُهُمْ أَوْ تَحْرِيرُ
رَقَبَةٍ ۖ فَمَنْ لَمْ يَجِدْ فَصِيَامُ ثَلٰثَةِ أَيَّامٍ ۚ ذٰلِكَ كَفَّارَةُ
أَيْمٰنِكُمْ إِذَا حَلَفْتُمْ ۚ وَاحْفَظُوا أَيْمٰنَكُمْ ۚ كَذٰلِكَ
يُبَيِّنُ اللّٰهُ لَكُمْ اٰيٰتِهِ لَعَلَّكُمْ تَشْكُرُونَ ﴿٩٠﴾

[a]See 2 : 26. [b]5 : 87; 6 : 50; 7 : 37; 22 : 58. [c]10 : 60. [d]2 : 169; 8 : 70; 16 : 115. [e]2 : 226.

789. Oaths which are contrary to Islamic Law are mere wasted breath.

790. *Ausaṭ* means both "middle" (average) and "the best."

91. O ye who believe ! [a]wine and the game of chance and idols and [b]divining arrows are only an abomination of Satan's handiwork. So shun each one of them that you may prosper.

يٰۤاَيُّهَا الَّذِيْنَ اٰمَنُوْۤا اِنَّمَا الْخَمْرُ وَالْمَيْسِرُ وَالْاَنْصَابُ وَالْاَزْلَامُ رِجْسٌ مِّنْ عَمَلِ الشَّيْطٰنِ فَاجْتَنِبُوْهُ لَعَلَّكُمْ تُفْلِحُوْنَ ﴿٩١﴾

92. Satan seeks only to create enmity and hatred among you by means of wine and the game of chance, and to keep you back from the remembrance of Allāh and from Prayer.[790A] Then will you keep back ?

اِنَّمَا يُرِيْدُ الشَّيْطٰنُ اَنْ يُّوْقِعَ بَيْنَكُمُ الْعَدَاوَةَ وَالْبَغْضَآءَ فِي الْخَمْرِ وَالْمَيْسِرِ وَيَصُدَّكُمْ عَنْ ذِكْرِ اللّٰهِ وَعَنِ الصَّلٰوةِ ۚ فَهَلْ اَنْتُمْ مُّنْتَهُوْنَ ﴿٩٢﴾

93. And [c]obey Allāh and obey the Messenger, and be on *your* guard. But if you turn away, then know that [d]on Our Messenger *lies* only the clear conveyance of the Message.

وَاَطِيْعُوا اللّٰهَ وَاَطِيْعُوا الرَّسُوْلَ وَاحْذَرُوْا ۚ فَاِنْ تَوَلَّيْتُمْ فَاعْلَمُوْۤا اَنَّمَا عَلٰى رَسُوْلِنَا الْبَلٰغُ الْمُبِيْنُ ﴿٩٣﴾

94. On those who believe and do good works there shall be no sin for what they eat, provided they fear Allāh and believe and do good works, *and* again fear Allāh and believe, *yet* again fear Allāh and do good.[791] And Allāh loves those who do good.

لَيْسَ عَلَى الَّذِيْنَ اٰمَنُوْا وَعَمِلُوا الصّٰلِحٰتِ جُنَاحٌ فِيْمَا طَعِمُوْۤا اِذَا مَا اتَّقَوْا وَّاٰمَنُوْا وَعَمِلُوا الصّٰلِحٰتِ ثُمَّ اتَّقَوْا وَّاٰمَنُوْا ثُمَّ اتَّقَوْا وَّاَحْسَنُوْا ۗ وَاللّٰهُ يُحِبُّ الْمُحْسِنِيْنَ ﴿٩٤﴾ ع ١٢/٢

[a]2 : 220; 5 : 92. [b]5 : 4. [c]3 : 133; 4 : 70; 64 : 13. [d]5 : 100; 16 : 83; 36 : 18; 64 : 13.

790A. After stating that the four things mentioned in the previous verse are all abomination in one sense or another, the present verse is confined to two of them—wine and games of chance—and gives additional reasons against them. These reasons rest on political, social, spiritual and socio-religious grounds, these being implied in the words "enmity and hatred and keeping back from the remembrance of Allāh and from Prayer."

791. Two important principles emerge from this verse: (a) That the things of this world having been made for the use and benefit of man are, as a rule, pure and clean; the forbidden things being only exceptions. (b) That clean and pure food exercises a beneficial influence on man's moral development, while unclean and impure food produces an adverse effect. The verse lays down three stages of spiritual progress. In the first stage, believers fear God and believe and do good works; in the second stage they fear God and believe, their belief at this stage being so strong that the doing of good works becomes, as it were, a part and parcel of their belief. In the third stage they fear God and do good to their fellow beings as if they are actually seeing God.

R. 13   95. O ye who believe ! Allāh will surely try you in a *little* matter: the game which your hands and your lances can reach, so that Allāh may *a*cause to be known those who fear Him in secret.[792] Whoso, therefore, will transgress after this shall have a grievous punishment.

يَآيُّهَا الَّذِيْنَ اٰمَنُوْا لَيَبْلُوَنَّكُمُ اللهُ بِشَيْءٍ مِّنَ الصَّيْدِ تَنَالُهٗٓ اَيْدِيْكُمْ وَرِمَاحُكُمْ لِيَعْلَمَ اللهُ مَنْ يَّخَافُهٗ بِالْغَيْبِ فَمَنِ اعْتَدٰى بَعْدَ ذٰلِكَ فَلَهٗ عَذَابٌ اَلِيْمٌ ۞

96. O ye who believe ! *b*kill not game while you are in a state of Pilgrimage. And whoso amongst you kills it intentionally, *its* compensation is a quadruped like unto that which he has killed, as determined by two just men from among you, *the same* to be brought as an offering to the Ka'bah; or as an expiation he shall feed *a number of* poor persons, or fast an equivalent number *of days*, so that he may taste the penalty of his deed. *c*As for the past, Allāh forgives *it*; but whoso reverts to it, Allāh will punish him *for his offence*. And Allāh is Mighty, Lord of retribution.

يَآيُّهَا الَّذِيْنَ اٰمَنُوْا لَا تَقْتُلُوا الصَّيْدَ وَاَنْتُمْ حُرُمٌ وَمَنْ قَتَلَهٗ مِنْكُمْ مُّتَعَمِّدًا فَجَزَآءٌ مِّثْلُ مَا قَتَلَ مِنَ النَّعَمِ يَحْكُمُ بِهٖ ذَوَا عَدْلٍ مِّنْكُمْ هَدْيًۢا بٰلِغَ الْكَعْبَةِ اَوْ كَفَّارَةٌ طَعَامُ مَسٰكِيْنَ اَوْ عَدْلُ ذٰلِكَ صِيَامًا لِّيَذُوْقَ وَبَالَ اَمْرِهٖ عَفَا اللهُ عَمَّا سَلَفَ وَمَنْ عَادَ فَيَنْتَقِمُ اللهُ مِنْهُ وَاللهُ عَزِيْزٌ ذُو انْتِقَامٍ ۞

97. The game of the[793] sea and the eating thereof is made lawful for you as a provision for you and the travellers; but *d*forbidden to you is the game of the land as long as you are in a state of Pilgrimage. And fear Allāh to Whom you shall be gathered.

اُحِلَّ لَكُمْ صَيْدُ الْبَحْرِ وَطَعَامُهٗ مَتَاعًا لَّكُمْ وَلِلسَّيَّارَةِ وَحُرِّمَ عَلَيْكُمْ صَيْدُ الْبَرِّ مَا دُمْتُمْ حُرُمًا وَاتَّقُوا اللهَ الَّذِيْٓ اِلَيْهِ تُحْشَرُوْنَ ۞

---

*a*57 : 26.   *b*5 : 2, 97.   *c*2 : 276.   *d*5 : 2, 96.

792. As hunting is ordinarily done in a jungle where one is generally alone and where there is none beside God to observe one breaking the Divine commandments, the verse fittingly mentions hunting to illustrate God-fearingness. It also serves as an introduction to the commandment that follows in the next verse.

793. The word "sea" includes rivers, streams, lakes, ponds, etc. See 7 : 139.

98. Allāh has made the Ka'bah, [a]the Sacred House, a means of support and uplift for mankind,[794] as also the Sacred Month and the offerings and the [b]*animals with* collars. That is so that you may know that Allāh knows what is in the heavens and what is in the earth, and that Allāh knows all things well.

جَعَلَ اللّٰهُ الْكَعْبَةَ الْبَيْتَ الْحَرَامَ قِيٰمًا لِّلنَّاسِ وَ
الشَّهْرَ الْحَرَامَ وَالْهَدْيَ وَالْقَلَآئِدَ ذٰلِكَ لِتَعْلَمُوْٓا
اَنَّ اللّٰهَ يَعْلَمُ مَا فِي السَّمٰوٰتِ وَمَا فِي الْاَرْضِ وَاَنَّ
اللّٰهَ بِكُلِّ شَيْءٍ عَلِيْمٌ ﴿٩٨﴾

99. [c]Know that Allāh is Severe in punishment and that Allāh is *also* Most Forgiving *and* ever Merciful.

اِعْلَمُوْٓا اَنَّ اللّٰهَ شَدِيْدُ الْعِقَابِ وَاَنَّ اللّٰهَ غَفُوْرٌ
رَّحِيْمٌ ﴿٩٩﴾

100. On the Messenger *lies* only the [d]conveying of the Message. And Allāh knows what you [e]disclose and what you hide.

مَا عَلَى الرَّسُوْلِ اِلَّا الْبَلٰغُ وَاللّٰهُ يَعْلَمُ مَا تُبْدُوْنَ
وَمَا تَكْتُمُوْنَ ﴿١٠٠﴾

101. Say, [f]'The bad and the good are not alike,' even though the abundance of the bad may please thee.[795] So be mindful of your duty to Allāh, O men of understanding, that you may prosper.

قُلْ لَّا يَسْتَوِي الْخَبِيْثُ وَالطَّيِّبُ وَلَوْ اَعْجَبَكَ كَثْرَةُ
الْخَبِيْثِ فَاتَّقُوا اللّٰهَ يٰٓاُولِي الْاَلْبَابِ لَعَلَّكُمْ
تُفْلِحُوْنَ ﴿١٠١﴾ ع

[a]2 : 126; 3 : 97-98. [b]5 : 3. [c]15 : 50-51. [d]16 : 83; 36 : 18; 64 : 13.
[e]2 : 78; 6 : 4; 11 : 6; 16 : 20. [f]2 : 268.

794. God has made Pilgrimage to the Ka'bah a sign for the progress and prosperity of Muslims. So long as they will continue to perform Pilgrimage, God's grace will continue to attend them. Pilgrimage is a means of support for men in a material sense also. Muslims from all parts of the world visit the Ka'bah in hundreds of thousands every year and this serves as a potent means of support for the Meccans. But the promise is not confined to the people of Mecca but encompasses in its purview all mankind. *Qiyām* also signifies a teaching which is permanent and not subject to abrogation.

795. Being naturally influenced by his environment man is prone to follow and imitate others, particularly when they happen to be in the majority. The verse, contains a warning against unthinking and blind following of the majority.

R. 14 102. O ye who believe! [a]ask not about things which, if revealed to you, would cause you trouble,[796] though if you ask about them while the Qur'ān is being sent down they will be revealed to you. Allāh has left them out *on purpose*. And Allāh is Most Forgiving *and* Forbearing.

يٰۤاَيُّهَا الَّذِيۡنَ اٰمَنُوۡا لَا تَسۡـَٔلُوۡا عَنۡ اَشۡيَآءَ اِنۡ تُبۡدَ لَكُمۡ
تَسُؤۡكُمۡ ۚ وَاِنۡ تَسۡـَٔلُوۡا عَنۡهَا حِيۡنَ يُنَزَّلُ الۡقُرۡاٰنُ
تُبۡدَ لَكُمۡ ؕ عَفَا اللّٰهُ عَنۡهَا ؕ وَاللّٰهُ غَفُوۡرٌ حَلِيۡمٌ ﴿۱۰۲﴾

103. A people before you [b]asked about such *things, but* then they became disbelievers therein.[797]

قَدۡ سَاَلَهَا قَوۡمٌ مِّنۡ قَبۡلِكُمۡ ثُمَّ اَصۡبَحُوۡا بِهَا
كٰفِرِيۡنَ ﴿۱۰۳﴾

104. Allāh has [c]not ordained any 'Baḥīrah'[798] or 'Sā'ibah'[798A] or 'Waṣīlah'[798B] or 'Ḥāmī',[798C] but those who disbelieve forge a lie against Allāh, and most of them do not make use of their understanding.[798D]

مَا جَعَلَ اللّٰهُ مِنۡۢ بَحِيۡرَةٍ وَّلَا سَآئِبَةٍ وَّلَا وَصِيۡلَةٍ
وَّلَا حَامٍ ۙ وَّلٰـكِنَّ الَّذِيۡنَ كَفَرُوۡا يَفۡتَرُوۡنَ عَلَى اللّٰهِ
الۡـكَذِبَ ؕ وَاَكۡثَرُهُمۡ لَا يَعۡقِلُوۡنَ ﴿۱۰۴﴾

105. And when it is said to them, 'Come to what Allāh has revealed, and to the Messenger,' they say, 'Sufficient for us is that wherein we found our fathers.' What! even though their fathers had no knowledge and had no guidance.

وَاِذَا قِيۡلَ لَهُمۡ تَعَالَوۡا اِلٰى مَاۤ اَنۡزَلَ اللّٰهُ وَاِلَى
الرَّسُوۡلِ قَالُوۡا حَسۡبُنَا مَا وَجَدۡنَا عَلَيۡهِ اٰبَآءَنَا ؕ اَوَلَوۡ
كَانَ اٰبَآؤُهُمۡ لَا يَعۡلَمُوۡنَ شَيۡـًٔا وَّلَا يَهۡتَدُوۡنَ ﴿۱۰۵﴾

[a]2 : 109. [b]2 : 109. [c]6 : 137.

796. The basis of the Islamic *Sharī'ah* is threefold : (1) The Law as embodied in the Qur'ān, (2) the *Sunnah* or the practice of the Holy Prophet, and (3) injunctions and precepts contained in his authentic sayings. These three sources of Islamic Law deal with all the fundamental problems of man, but minor details are left to his discretion to solve them in the light of the above three torch-bearers of guidance, aided and assisted by his own God-given intellectual powers and faculties. It is to matters relating to minor details that the present verse refers.

797. Unnecessary questioning about minor details or seeking legislation on them is generally to the detriment of the questioner himself. It limits his discretion and fetters his judgment, besides binding him to unnecessary and irksome legislation. The Israelites put unnecessary questions to Moses in regard to minor details with the result that they created difficulties for themselves and ended by breaking the commandments of God (2 : 109).

798. *Baḥīrah* : A name given by pagan Arabs to a she-camel which had given birth to seven young ones and was then let loose to feed freely after its ears were slit. It was dedicated to some god and its milk was not used nor its back.

798A. *Sā'ibah* : A she-camel let loose to water and pasture after giving birth to five young ones.

798B, 798C, 798D—See next page.

106. O ye who believe! take care of your own selves. He who goes *astray cannot harm you when you yourselves* are rightly guided.[799] To Allāh will you all return; then He will inform you of what you used to do.

يَٰٓأَيُّهَا الَّذِينَ ءَامَنُوا۟ عَلَيۡكُمۡ أَنفُسَكُمۡ لَا يَضُرُّكُم مَّن ضَلَّ إِذَا اهۡتَدَيۡتُمۡ إِلَى اللهِ مَرۡجِعُكُمۡ جَمِيعًا فَيُنَبِّئُكُم بِمَا كُنتُمۡ تَعۡمَلُونَ ۞

107. O ye who believe! the *right* evidence among you, when death comes to one of you, at the time of making a will, is of two just men from among you; or of two others not from among you, in case you be journeying in the land and the calamity of death befalls[800] you.

يَٰٓأَيُّهَا الَّذِينَ ءَامَنُوا۟ شَهَٰدَةُ بَيۡنِكُمۡ إِذَا حَضَرَ أَحَدَكُمُ الۡمَوۡتُ حِينَ الۡوَصِيَّةِ اثۡنَانِ ذَوَا عَدۡلٍ مِّنكُمۡ أَوۡ ءَاخَرَانِ مِنۡ غَيۡرِكُمۡ إِنۡ أَنتُمۡ ضَرَبۡتُمۡ فِى الۡأَرۡضِ فَأَصَٰبَتۡكُم مُّصِيبَةُ الۡمَوۡتِ تَحۡبِسُونَهُمَا مِنۢ بَعۡدِ

---

*a*2 : 138.

798B. *Wasīlah* : A she-camel (or an ewe or she-goat) let loose in the name of a god after she had given birth to seven female young ones consecutively. If at the seventh birth she bore a pair, male and female, these were also let loose.

798C. *Hāmī* : A camel which had fathered seven young ones. It was let loose and was not used for riding or carrying. It was free to pasture and water.

798D. After having stated that minor matters and details have been left to man to legislate as he thinks proper, the verse fittingly draws attention to the fact that such freedom and discretion are not allowed in fundamentals, because in fundamentals unanimity is essential and divergence of opinion may prove immensely harmful. The verse gives an illustration to show that human intellect cannot be trusted with the making of the laws on fundamental matters. The Arabs used to let loose the animals mentioned in the verse in honour of their idols. Besides being based on disbelief and superstition, the practice was also highly foolish. The animals thus let loose wrought great havoc wherever they went. The Qur'ān refers to this evil practice as an example of man-made laws and warns Christians who question the wisdom of a revealed Law to learn a lesson from the morally degrading practices to which the pagan Arabs had resorted because they had no revealed Law to guide them.

799. Our duty only is to preach the truth to others. If they accept it, well and good, but if in spite of our best efforts they refuse to be weaned from their evil course, their rejection of truth will do us no harm. In no case should we compromise our principles in order to win others over to our way of thinking. That would be ruining our own souls to save the souls of others and that indeed would be a bad bargain.

800. An incident is reported to have occurred in the time of the Holy Prophet which throws some light on this and the following two verses. A Muslim who died far from home entrusted his goods to two Christian brothers—Tamīm Dārīy and 'Adī—before his death and asked them to deliver the same to his heirs at Medina. On receiving the goods the heirs found that a silver bowl was missing. The two men were thereupon called upon to explain the loss of the bowl, but they denied all knowledge of it on oath. Later, the heirs of the deceased person happened to see the bowl with some persons at Mecca who told them that it had been sold to them by the two men to whom the deceased had entrusted his belongings. Thereupon the two men were again summoned, and in their presence the heirs of the belongings stated on oath that the bowl was theirs, whereupon it was handed over to them (Manthūr).

You shall detain them both after Prayer[801] for *giving evidence*; and, if you have doubt *concerning their evidence*, they shall both swear by Allāh, *saying*, 'We will not take for this any price, even though *the person affected thereby* be a near relation, nor will we [a]hide the testimony enjoined by Allāh; surely, in that case, we shall be among the sinners.'

الصَّلٰوةِ فَيُقْسِمٰنِ بِاللّٰهِ اِنِ ارْتَبْتُمْ لَا نَشْتَرِيْ بِهٖ
ثَمَنًا وَّلَوْ كَانَ ذَا قُرْبٰى ۙ وَلَا نَكْتُمُ شَهَادَةَ اللّٰهِ
اِنَّآ اِذًا لَّمِنَ الْاٰثِمِيْنَ ﴿١٠٧﴾

108. But if it be discovered that the two *witnesses* are guilty of sin, then two others shall take their place from amongst those against whom the *former* two *witnesses*[802]—who were in a better position *to give true evidence*—had deposed, and the two *latter witnesses* shall swear by Allāh, *saying*, 'Surely, our testimony is truer than the testimony of the *former* two, and we have not been unfair *in any way*; for then, indeed, we should be of the unjust.'

فَاِنْ عُثِرَ عَلٰٓى اَنَّهُمَا اسْتَحَقَّآ اِثْمًا فَاٰخَرٰنِ يَقُوْمٰنِ
مَقَامَهُمَا مِنَ الَّذِيْنَ اسْتَحَقَّ عَلَيْهِمُ الْاَوْلَيٰنِ فَيُقْسِمٰنِ
بِاللّٰهِ لَشَهَادَتُنَآ اَحَقُّ مِنْ شَهَادَتِهِمَا وَمَا اعْتَدَيْنَآ ۖ
اِنَّآ اِذًا لَّمِنَ الظّٰلِمِيْنَ ﴿١٠٨﴾

109. Thus it is more likely that they will give evidence according to facts or that they will fear that other oaths will be taken after their oaths. And fear Allāh and hearken. And Allāh guides not the disobedient people.

ذٰلِكَ اَدْنٰٓى اَنْ يَّاْتُوْا بِالشَّهَادَةِ عَلٰى وَجْهِهَآ اَوْ يَخَافُوْٓا
اَنْ تُرَدَّ اَيْمَانٌۢ بَعْدَ اَيْمَانِهِمْ ۗ وَاتَّقُوا اللّٰهَ وَاسْمَعُوْا ۗ
وَاللّٰهُ لَا يَهْدِي الْقَوْمَ الْفٰسِقِيْنَ ﴿١٠٩﴾ ع

[a]2 : 141, 284.

801. The Prayer should preferably be the *'Asr* (Late Afternoon) Prayer, because it was after this Prayer that the Holy Prophet summoned the two witnesses to whom reference has been made above and who were believed to have stolen the silver bowl. The time after Prayer has been chosen with a view to inspiring the witnesses with God-fearingness and inclining their minds to truthfulness. If the witnesses be non-Muslims, then they may be called upon to swear after the time of their own worship, so that the solemnity of the hour may incline them to make true statement.

802. The word *Aulayān* refers to the first two witnesses and signifies that these two were in a better position to give true evidence, being the persons who were with the deceased at the time of his death and in whose presence the will was made and to whom the property was entrusted to be handed over to the heirs of the deceased. The "other" two witnesses should be from among the deceased person's heirs.

R. 15 110. *Think of* the day when Allāh will assemble the Messengers and say, [a]'What reply was made to you?' They will say, 'We have no knowledge, it is only Thou Who art the Knower of hidden things.[803]

يَوْمَ يَجْمَعُ اللّٰهُ الرُّسُلَ فَيَقُوْلُ مَاذَآ اُجِبْتُمْ ؕ قَالُوْا
لَا عِلْمَ لَنَا ؕ اِنَّكَ اَنْتَ عَلَّامُ الْغُيُوْبِ ﴿۱۱۰﴾

111. When Allāh will say, "O Jesus, son of Mary, remember My favour upon thee and upon thy mother; when [b]I strengthened thee with the Spirit of holiness *so that* [c]thou didst speak to the people in the cradle and when of middle age;[804] and when [d]I taught thee the Book and wisdom and the Torah and the Gospel; and when thou didst [e]fashion *a creation* out of clay, in the likeness of a bird, by My command; then thou didst breathe into it *a new spirit* and it became a soaring being by My command; and thou didst heal the night-blind and the leprous by My command;[805] and when thou didst raise the dead by My command; and when I [f]restrained the Children of Israel from *putting* thee *to death*[806] when thou didst come to them with clear Signs; and those who disbelieved from among them said, 'This is nothing but clear deception."

اِذْ قَالَ اللّٰهُ يٰعِيْسَى ابْنَ مَرْيَمَ اذْكُرْ نِعْمَتِيْ عَلَيْكَ
وَعَلٰى وَالِدَتِكَ ۘ اِذْ اَيَّدْتُّكَ بِرُوْحِ الْقُدُسِ ۟ تُكَلِّمُ
النَّاسَ فِي الْمَهْدِ وَكَهْلًا ۚ وَاِذْ عَلَّمْتُكَ الْكِتٰبَ وَ
الْحِكْمَةَ وَالتَّوْرٰىةَ وَالْاِنْجِيْلَ ۚ وَاِذْ تَخْلُقُ مِنَ الطِّيْنِ
كَهَيْـَٔةِ الطَّيْرِ بِاِذْنِيْ فَتَنْفُخُ فِيْهَا فَتَكُوْنُ طَيْرًا ۢ بِاِذْنِيْ
وَتُبْرِئُ الْاَكْمَهَ وَالْاَبْرَصَ بِاِذْنِيْ ۚ وَاِذْ تُخْرِجُ الْمَوْتٰى
بِاِذْنِيْ ۚ وَاِذْ كَفَفْتُ بَنِيْٓ اِسْرَآءِيْلَ عَنْكَ اِذْ جِئْتَهُمْ
بِالْبَيِّنٰتِ فَقَالَ الَّذِيْنَ كَفَرُوْا مِنْهُمْ اِنْ هٰذَآ اِلَّا
سِحْرٌ مُّبِيْنٌ ﴿۱۱۱﴾

[a]7 : 7; 28 : 66. [b]2 : 88; 2 : 254. [c]3 : 47. [d]3 : 49. [e]3 : 50. [f]5 : 12.

803. The answer of the Prophets implies that the object of God's questioning would not be to elicit information from them or to supplement His own knowledge, but that they should give testimony against the disbelievers, as is also clear from 4 : 42.

804. The act of speaking in the cradle signifies speaking words of wisdom and piety in childhood. This sort of speaking by Jesus reflected great credit on his mother, who, herself being a wise and pious lady, brought him up as a wise and pious child. And the speaking of good words in middle age shows that not only was Mary a pious woman, but Jesus too was a righteous man so that even when he was of middle age and was no longer under the direct influence of his mother, he spoke words of piety and wisdom. See also 418.

805. See 420D and 420E.

806. The reference is to the attempts of Jews to kill Jesus on the cross from which God delivered him.

112. And *remember my favour* when ª"I inspired the disciples *saying*, 'Believe in Me and in My Messenger, they said, 'We believe and bear Thou witness that we have submitted.'

وَإِذْ أَوْحَيْتُ إِلَى الْحَوَارِيِّيْنَ أَنْ اٰمِنُوْا بِيْ وَبِرَسُوْلِيْ قَالُوْا اٰمَنَّا وَاشْهَدْ بِأَنَّنَا مُسْلِمُوْنَ ۝

113. When the disciples said, 'O Jesus, son of Mary, is thy Lord able to send down to us a table spread with food[807] from heaven?[808] He said, 'Fear Allāh, if you are believers.'

إِذْ قَالَ الْحَوَارِيُّوْنَ يٰعِيْسَى ابْنَ مَرْيَمَ هَلْ يَسْتَطِيْعُ رَبُّكَ أَنْ يُّنَزِّلَ عَلَيْنَا مَآئِدَةً مِّنَ السَّمَآءِ قَالَ اتَّقُوا اللّٰهَ إِنْ كُنْتُمْ مُّؤْمِنِيْنَ ۝

114. They said, 'We desire that we may eat of it, and that our hearts may be at rest and that we may know that thou hast spoken the truth to us, and that we may be witnesses thereto.'

قَالُوْا نُرِيْدُ أَنْ نَّأْكُلَ مِنْهَا وَتَطْمَئِنَّ قُلُوْبُنَا وَنَعْلَمَ أَنْ قَدْ صَدَقْتَنَا وَنَكُوْنَ عَلَيْهَا مِنَ الشَّاهِدِيْنَ ۝

115. Said Jesus, son of Mary, 'O Allāh, our Lord, send down to us a table from heaven spread with food that it may be to us a festival, to the first of us and to the last [808A] of us, and a Sign from Thee; and provide sustenance for us, for Thou art the Best of sustainers.'[809]

قَالَ عِيْسَى ابْنُ مَرْيَمَ اللّٰهُمَّ رَبَّنَا أَنْزِلْ عَلَيْنَا مَآئِدَةً مِّنَ السَّمَآءِ تَكُوْنُ لَنَا عِيْدًا لِّأَوَّلِنَا وَاٰخِرِنَا وَاٰيَةً مِّنْكَ وَارْزُقْنَا وَأَنْتَ خَيْرُ الرَّازِقِيْنَ ۝

ª3 : 53-54; 61 : 15.

---

807. It was not a single meal that the disciples of Jesus asked for, but a permanent provision of sustenance which might be had without any trouble or hardship.

808. The words "from heaven" denote a thing that is obtained without much trouble and is sure and lasting.

808A. The Christians were granted temporal power in the beginning as under the Romans and they hold sway now over vast areas of the earth.

809. There were to be two periods of prosperity and progress for the Christian peoples, as the word 'Īd literally meaning "a day which returns," shows. Christian peoples were granted worldly goods in abundance in the early ages after Constantine and then in the 18th and 19th centuries they had material prosperity and political grandeur in such measure as has no parallel in the history of any other people.

116. Allāh said, 'Surely, I will send it down to you; but whosoever of you disbelieves afterwards—I will surely punish them with a punishment wherewith I will not punish any other of the peoples.'[810]

قَالَ اللّٰهُ إِنِّيْ مُنَزِّلُهَا عَلَيْكُمْ ۚ فَمَنْ يَّكْفُرْ بَعْدُ مِنْكُمْ
فَإِنِّيْٓ أُعَذِّبُهٗ عَذَابًا لَّآ أُعَذِّبُهٗٓ أَحَدًا مِّنَ الْعٰلَمِيْنَ ﴿١١٦﴾ ع

R. 16 117. And when Allāh will say, "O Jesus, son of Mary, didst thou say to men, 'Take me and my mother for two gods[811] beside Allāh?'" he will answer, "Holy art Thou, I could never say[812] that to which I had no right. If I had said it, Thou wouldst have surely known it. Thou knowest what is in my mind, and I know not what is in Thy mind. [a]It is Thou alone Who art the Knower of *all* hidden things;

وَإِذْ قَالَ اللّٰهُ يٰعِيْسَى ابْنَ مَرْيَمَ ءَأَنْتَ قُلْتَ لِلنَّاسِ
اتَّخِذُوْنِيْ وَأُمِّيَ إِلٰهَيْنِ مِنْ دُوْنِ اللّٰهِ ۗ قَالَ سُبْحٰنَكَ
مَا يَكُوْنُ لِيْٓ أَنْ أَقُوْلَ مَا لَيْسَ لِيْ ۗ بِحَقٍّ ۗ إِنْ كُنْتُ
قُلْتُهٗ فَقَدْ عَلِمْتَهٗ ۗ تَعْلَمُ مَا فِيْ نَفْسِيْ وَلَآ أَعْلَمُ
مَا فِيْ نَفْسِكَ ۗ إِنَّكَ أَنْتَ عَلَّامُ الْغُيُوْبِ ﴿١١٧﴾

118. "I said nothing to them except that which Thou didst command me—[b]'Worship Allāh, my Lord[813] and your Lord.' And I was a witness over them as long as I remained among them,[814] but since

مَا قُلْتُ لَهُمْ إِلَّا مَآ أَمَرْتَنِيْ بِهٖٓ أَنِ اعْبُدُوا اللّٰهَ رَبِّيْ
وَرَبَّكُمْ ۚ وَكُنْتُ عَلَيْهِمْ شَهِيْدًا مَّا دُمْتُ فِيْهِمْ ۚ فَلَمَّا

[a]5 : 110; 9 : 78; 34 : 49. [b]5 : 73; 19 : 37.

810. The punishment referred to in the verse is the same as mentioned in 19 : 91. The last two World Wars along with their repercussions may constitute one phase of the fulfilment of this prophecy and God alone knows what dire punishments are yet in store for the Christian nations of the West.

811. The verse refers to the practice of the Christian Church to ascribe Divine powers to Mary. Mary's help is invoked in Litany, and in Catechism of the Roman Church the doctrine that she is the mother of God is inculcated. Church Fathers in the past have regarded her as Divine and only a few years ago Pope Pius XII incorporated the bodily ascension of Mary in the doctrine of the Church. All this amounts to raising her to the pedestal of Divinity and this is what Protestants denounce as Mariolatry.

812. The Arabic expression in the text which is translated as "I could never" may also be interpreted as : It did not behove me ; or it was impossible for me ; or I had no right; to do so, etc.

813. Jesus taught the worship of one God alone (Matt. 4 : 10 & Luke, 4 : 8).

814. As long as Jesus was alive, he kept a careful watch over his followers and saw to it that they did not deviate from the right path, but he did not know how they behaved and what false doctrines they held after his death. Now, as his followers have gone astray, it conclusively follows that Jesus is dead, for, as the verse points out, it was after his death that he was to be worshipped as God. Similarly, the fact that this verse speaks of Jesus

[a]Thou didst cause me to die,[815] Thou hast been the Watcher over them, and Thou art Witness over all things;

تَوَفَّيْتَنِيْ كُنْتَ اَنْتَ الرَّقِيْبَ عَلَيْهِمْ ۭ وَاَنْتَ عَلٰى كُلِّ
شَيْءٍ شَهِيْدٌ ﴿١١٨﴾

119. "If Thou punish them, they are Thy servants; and if Thou forgive them, Thou surely art the Mighty, the Wise."

اِنْ تُعَذِّبْهُمْ فَاِنَّهُمْ عِبَادُكَ ۚ وَاِنْ تَغْفِرْ لَهُمْ فَاِنَّكَ
اَنْتَ الْعَزِيْزُ الْحَكِيْمُ ﴿١١٩﴾

120. Allāh will say, 'This is a day when *only* the truthful shall profit by their truthfulness. For them are Gardens beneath which streams flow; therein shall they abide for ever. Allāh is [b]well pleased with them, and they are well pleased with Him; that indeed is the supreme achievement.'

قَالَ اللّٰهُ هٰذَا يَوْمُ يَنْفَعُ الصّٰدِقِيْنَ صِدْقُهُمْ ۭ
لَهُمْ جَنّٰتٌ تَجْرِيْ مِنْ تَحْتِهَا الْاَنْهٰرُ خٰلِدِيْنَ
فِيْهَآ اَبَدًا ۭ رَضِيَ اللّٰهُ عَنْهُمْ وَرَضُوْا عَنْهُ ۭ ذٰلِكَ
الْفَوْزُ الْعَظِيْمُ ﴿١٢٠﴾

121. [c]To Allāh belongs the Kingdom of the heavens and the earth and whatever is in them; and He has power over all things.[816]

لِلّٰهِ مُلْكُ السَّمٰوٰتِ وَالْاَرْضِ وَمَا فِيْهِنَّ ۭ وَهُوَ عَلٰى
كُلِّ شَيْءٍ قَدِيْرٌ ﴿١٢١﴾

[a]3 : 57. [b]9 : 100; 58 : 23; 98 : 9. [c]5 : 18,41; 42 : 50; 48 : 15.

as expressing ignorance that his followers took him and his mother for two gods after he had left them, proves that he is not to come back to this world. For, if he were to come back and see with his own eyes that his followers had become corrupt and had deified him he could not plead ignorance of his deification by them. If he would do so, his answer pleading his ignorance would amount to a veritable lie. The verse thus positively proves that Jesus is dead and that he will never come back to this world. Moreover, according to a well-known saying of his, the Holy Prophet will use the same words on the Day of Resurrection as are put here in the mouth of Jesus, when he will see some of his followers being led to Hell. This lends further support to the fact that Jesus is dead like the Holy Prophet.

815. See 424.

816. The verse forms a befitting sequel to this *Sūrah* in which the errors of the Christian people are effectively exposed and demolished, containing a veiled declaration that their glory will not last and God will finally transfer His Kingdom to those who are more deserving of it.

CHAPTER 6

AL-AN'ĀM

(*Revealed before Hijrah*)

Date of Revelation and Context

This *Sūrah* belongs to the Meccan period. According to most accounts, the whole of it was revealed in one portion; and as reported by some traditionists, as many as 70,000 angels stood guard when it was being revealed, which points to the special protection which was afforded to its subject-matter. The *Sūrah* probably derives its title from vv. 137-139 where the *An'ām* have been condemned as one of the causes of idolatry.

Subject-Matter

In this *Sūrah* there is a change in the treatment of the subject matter from that adopted in the previous *Sūrahs*. It contains a refutation of non-Israelite religions and starts with the refutation of the Zoroastrian Faith, which believes in the duality of Godhead—in two separate gods of good and evil. The Qur'ān exposes this doctrine by declaring that both the powers of doing good and evil are, in reality, two links of the same chain, one remaining incomplete without the other ; so they cannot be said to have been created by two different gods. Light and darkness are indeed divine creation of the same God, and instead of pointing to the duality of the Godhead, they really constitute a strong argument in favour of Oneness of God and possess a peculiar affinity with the creation of man and his natural powers and faculties. The *Sūrah* proceeds to discuss the important subject that evil is born of the wrong use of God-given faculties, and that whenever men cease to make right use of them God raises a Prophet to teach them their right use. After this it is stated that the delay in Divine punishment overtaking disbelievers often emboldens them all the more, though the delay is always due to God's mercy. They persecute their Prophet and his followers, entertaining a false hope that in this way they would succeed in weakening the faith of the believers, but the faith of believers remains unflinching and steadfast under severest trials and tribulations, while disbelievers at once disown their own idolatrous beliefs whenever they are overtaken by misfortunes. Further, light is shed on the subject that irreligiousness is born of lack of faith in Life after death or in the failure of disbelievers to establish real connection with God. This dual lack of faith makes them bold in the rejection of truth. Opposition to the Prophets by the disbelievers appears to be not quite un-natural, since only those people seek God who possess some natural kinship with spiritual matters, for the spiritually-deaf cannot hear the Voice of God. They see Sign after Sign and yet continue to repeat parrot-like that no Sign has been shown to them. The opponents of the Holy Prophet have seen many Signs but have not profited by them. They are, therefore, warned that now they will see only the Sign of punishment. But God is not quick to punish. It is when disbelievers wilfully and persistently shut the door of repentance upon themselves and scornfully reject the Divine Message that they are punished. Next, it is stated that only those who have fear of God in their hearts accept the truth, and the Holy Prophet is told to address his appeal only to the God-fearing. For the others, it is necessary that fear of God should first be created in their hearts, then will arguments and reasons benefit them. Further, it is stated that it is essential for the progress of Islām that special attention be paid to the spiritual training of believers, because the Prophet is mortal and must die one day and only the community of believers will remain behind to preach and propagate the Divine Message. Next, the disbelievers are told that they are foolish to find fault with the Holy Prophet merely because the promised punishment has not already overtaken them. They are told that to punish the haughty and boastful rejectors of truth rests entirely in the hand of God Who punishes them as He thinks fit or opportune. It may be that a person, who is today the enemy of truth and seems to deserve Divine punishment, may bring about true reformation in himself tomorrow and deserve Divine mercy. So the infliction of punishment, or deferring thereof, is God's own work. The *Sūrah* then exposes the falsity of polytheistic doctrines by means of an argument which the Patriarch Abraham had with his people; and then mention is made of the favours and blessings which God bestowed upon him and his descendants because they strove hard to establish truth in the world. The *Sūrah* proceeds to state that the mission of God's

Messengers never fails. Like rain-water it gives fertility and freshness to a soil spiritually bleak and barren, and as it is not possible to attain true realization of God unless He reveals Himself to men, it is necessary that Divine Messengers should appear time after time as it is through them that God reveals Himself to the world. Then it is stated that for the attainment of true faith a corresponding wholesome change of heart is a *sine qua non*. Without such a change, even Signs and miracles prove of no avail. Next, a contrast is instituted between Islamic Teaching which answers and satisfies the demands of reason and justice and the doctrines and practices of idolaters, which are based neither on reason nor on argument. Towards the end of the *Sūrah* we are told that the Qur'ān has been revealed to raise and honour even those nations to whom no revelation has so far been sent in order that they may not suffer from a feeling of inferiority before the People of the Book. The Message of the Qur'ān, unlike that of former revealed Scriptures, is for the whole of mankind, and it seeks to establish real and permanent peace between different sections of humanity as well as between man and his Creator.

سُورَةُ الْأَنْعَامِ مَكِّيَّةٌ (٦)

اٰياتها ١٦٦ — رکوعاتها ٢٠

1. [a]In the name of Allāh, the Gracious, the Merciful.

بِسْمِ اللّٰهِ الرَّحْمٰنِ الرَّحِيْمِ ①

2. All praise belongs to Allāh Who created the heavens and the earth and brought into being darkness and[817] light; yet [b]those who disbelieve set up equals to their Lord.

اَلْحَمْدُ لِلّٰهِ الَّذِيْ خَلَقَ السَّمٰوٰتِ وَ الْاَرْضَ وَجَعَلَ الظُّلُمٰتِ وَ النُّوْرَ ۬ ثُمَّ الَّذِيْنَ كَفَرُوْا بِرَبِّهِمْ يَعْدِلُوْنَ ②

3. He it is [c]who created you from clay, and then He decreed a term.[818] And there is [d]another term fixed with Him.[819] Yet you doubt.

هُوَ الَّذِيْ خَلَقَكُمْ مِّنْ طِيْنٍ ثُمَّ قَضٰۤى اَجَلًا ؕ وَ اَجَلٌ مُّسَمًّى عِنْدَهٗ ثُمَّ اَنْتُمْ تَمْتَرُوْنَ ③

4. And [e]He is Allāh, *the God, both* in the heavens and in the earth.[820] He knows what you disclose and your secrets. And He knows what you earn.

وَهُوَ اللّٰهُ فِي السَّمٰوٰتِ وَ فِي الْاَرْضِ ؕ يَعْلَمُ سِرَّكُمْ وَ جَهْرَكُمْ وَ يَعْلَمُ مَا تَكْسِبُوْنَ ④

5. And [f]there comes not to them any Sign of the Signs[821] of their Lord, but they turn away from it.

وَ مَا تَاْتِيْهِمْ مِّنْ اٰيَةٍ مِّنْ اٰيٰتِ رَبِّهِمْ اِلَّا كَانُوْا عَنْهَا مُعْرِضِيْنَ ⑤

---

[a]See 1 : 1. [b]6 : 151; 27 : 61. [c]15 : 27; 23 : 13; 32 : 8; 37 : 12; 38 : 72. [d]71 : 5. [e]43 : 85. [f]21 : 3; 26 : 6; 36 : 47.

---

817. The word *Ja'ala* is sometimes used synonymously with *Khalaqa* (He created); but whereas the latter word gives the sense of creating a thing after measuring and designing it, the former word signifies the making of a thing in a particular state or condition, or constituting or appointing it for a definite purpose (Lane). Idolatry seems to be based on two theories. The Hindus are the chief protagonists of the theory that God has delegated His powers to certain beings. The Zoroastrians believe in two gods—Ormuzd—the god of light, and Ahriman—the god of darkness. The present verse refutes both these theories and says that God is the Creator of heavens and earth and that He is also the Creator of light and darkness; and since all power and praise belong to Him, what need is there for Him to delegate His powers and entrust part of His work to others?

818. Both the creation of man and his death (decreeing of a term) have been mentioned as acts of Divine mercy.

819. The first "term" refers to the span of individual life and the second "term" has reference to the life of the universe.

820. The verse does not mean that God's Person pervades the heavens and the earth. What is meant is that His knowledge comprehends the entire universe.

821. An important evidence of the knowledge and power of God are the prophecies that He reveals to His Messengers and the support and assistance that He vouchsafes to them against overwhelming odds. These are called Signs.

6. So [a]they rejected the truth when it came to them; but soon shall come to them the tidings[822] of that at which they mocked.

فَقَدْ كَذَّبُوْا بِالْحَقِّ لَمَّا جَآءَهُمْ ۚ فَسَوْفَ يَاْتِيْهِمْ
اَنْۢبٰٓؤُا مَا كَانُوْا بِهٖ يَسْتَهْزِءُوْنَ ۝٦

7. See they not how many a generation[823] We have destroyed before them? [b]We had established them in the earth as We have not established you[824] and [c]We sent the clouds over them, pouring down abundant rain; and We caused streams to flow beneath them; then did We destroy them because of their sins and raised up after them another generation.

اَلَمْ يَرَوْا كَمْ اَهْلَكْنَا مِنْ قَبْلِهِمْ مِّنْ قَرْنٍ مَّكَّنّٰهُمْ
فِي الْاَرْضِ مَا لَمْ نُمَكِّنْ لَّكُمْ وَاَرْسَلْنَا السَّمَآءَ عَلَيْهِمْ
مِّدْرَارًا ۪ وَّجَعَلْنَا الْاَنْهٰرَ تَجْرِيْ مِنْ تَحْتِهِمْ فَاَهْلَكْنٰهُمْ
بِذُنُوْبِهِمْ وَاَنْشَاْنَا مِنْۢ بَعْدِهِمْ قَرْنًا اٰخَرِيْنَ ۝٧

8. And if We had sent down to thee a writing upon the parchment and they had felt it with their hands[825] *even then* the disbelievers would have surely said, 'This is nothing but manifest sorcery.'

وَلَوْ نَزَّلْنَا عَلَيْكَ كِتٰبًا فِيْ قِرْطَاسٍ فَلَمَسُوْهُ بِاَيْدِيْهِمْ
لَقَالَ الَّذِيْنَ كَفَرُوْٓا اِنْ هٰذَآ اِلَّا سِحْرٌ مُّبِيْنٌ ۝٨

9. And they say, [d]'Why has not an angel been sent down to him?' And if We had sent down an angel,[826] the matter would have been decided, *and* then they would have been granted no respite.

وَقَالُوْا لَوْلَآ اُنْزِلَ عَلَيْهِ مَلَكٌ ۚ وَلَوْ اَنْزَلْنَا مَلَكًا لَّقُضِيَ
الْاَمْرُ ثُمَّ لَا يُنْظَرُوْنَ ۝٩

[a]26 : 7. [b]46 : 27. [c]11 : 53; 71 : 12. [d]2 : 211; 25 : 8.

822. *Anbā'* is the plural of *Naba'* which is generally used in the Qur'ān about important news relating to some great event (Kulliyyāt).

823. *Qarn* means, a generation of men succeeding or preceding another generation, as if both were conjoined; people of one time (Lane).

824. The words do not mean that the world is retrogressing. It is no doubt progressing as a whole, but some of the older nations which rose to heights of civilization in the past were so advanced in certain branches of art and science that in those specific branches they were not equalled by the generations that followed. For instance, the modern age, in spite of the marvels it has wrought in the domain of science, still gazes with wonder at some of the works of ancient Egyptian civilization.

825. They had made sure that it was a heavenly and not an earthly thing.

826. "The coming of angels" signifies the imminent approach of heavenly punishment.

10. And if We had appointed *as Messenger* an angel, We would have made him *appear as* a man; and *thus* We would have caused to be confused to them that which they are *themselves* confusing.[827]

وَلَوْ جَعَلْنٰهُ مَلَكًا لَّجَعَلْنٰهُ رَجُلًا وَّ لَلَبَسْنَا عَلَيْهِمْ
مَّا يَلْبِسُوْنَ ﴿۱۰﴾

11. And surely [a]the Messengers have been mocked at before thee, but that which they mocked at encompassed those of them who scoffed *at it*.

وَلَقَدِ اسْتُهْزِئَ بِرُسُلٍ مِّنْ قَبْلِكَ فَحَاقَ بِالَّذِيْنَ
سَخِرُوْا مِنْهُمْ مَّا كَانُوْا بِهٖ يَسْتَهْزِءُوْنَ ﴿۱۱﴾ ع

R. 2 12. Say, [b]'Go about in the earth, and see what was the end of those who treated *the Prophets* as liars.'

قُلْ سِيْرُوْا فِي الْاَرْضِ ثُمَّ انْظُرُوْا كَيْفَ كَانَ عَاقِبَةُ
الْمُكَذِّبِيْنَ ﴿۱۲﴾

13. Say, 'To whom belongs what is in the heavens and the earth?' Say, 'To Allāh.' [c]He has taken upon Himself *to show* mercy.[828] [d]He will certainly *continue to* assemble you till the Day of Resurrection. There is no doubt in it. Those who have ruined their souls will not believe.

قُلْ لِّمَنْ مَّا فِي السَّمٰوٰتِ وَالْاَرْضِ ؕ قُلْ لِّلّٰهِ ؕ كَتَبَ عَلٰى
نَفْسِهِ الرَّحْمَةَ ؕ لَيَجْمَعَنَّكُمْ اِلٰى يَوْمِ الْقِيٰمَةِ لَا رَيْبَ
فِيْهِ ؕ اَلَّذِيْنَ خَسِرُوْٓا اَنْفُسَهُمْ فَهُمْ لَا يُؤْمِنُوْنَ ﴿۱۳﴾

14. To Him belongs whatever exists in *the darkness of* the night and *the light of* the day. And He is the All-Hearing, the All-Knowing.

وَلَهٗ مَا سَكَنَ فِي الَّيْلِ وَالنَّهَارِ ؕ وَهُوَ السَّمِيْعُ الْعَلِيْمُ ﴿۱۴﴾

15. Say, 'Shall I take any protector other than Allāh, [e]the Maker[829] of the heavens and the earth, Who [f]feeds and is not fed?'

قُلْ اَغَيْرَ اللّٰهِ اَتَّخِذُ وَلِيًّا فَاطِرِ السَّمٰوٰتِ وَ الْاَرْضِ

[a]21 : 42. [b]3 : 138; 22 : 47; 27 : 70. [c]6 : 55; 7 : 157. [d]3 : 10; 4 : 88; 45 : 27. [e]12 : 102; 14 : 11; 35 : 2; 39 : 47. [f]20 : 133; 51 : 48-59.

827. The verse exposes the folly of the disbelievers' demand that an angel should have come to guide them.

828. As all things in the heavens and the earth belong to Allāh, the enemies of Faith also belong to Him. No one would like to destroy his own handiwork, much less would God do so. He is Merciful and grants respite to disbelievers in order that they may repent and be shown mercy.

829. The word *Fāṭir* when used about God means, the Originator or the Creator, or the Maker.

Say, [a]'I have been commanded to be the first of those who submit.' And be thou not of those who associate partners *with Allāh*.

وَهُوَ يُطْعِمُ وَلَا يُطْعَمُ ۗ قُلْ إِنِّىٓ أُمِرْتُ أَنْ أَكُونَ
أَوَّلَ مَنْ أَسْلَمَ وَلَا تَكُونَنَّ مِنَ الْمُشْرِكِينَ ﴿١٥﴾

16. Say, 'Indeed, [b]I fear, if I disobey[830] my Lord, the punishment of an awful day.'

قُلْ إِنِّىٓ أَخَافُ إِنْ عَصَيْتُ رَبِّى عَذَابَ يَوْمٍ عَظِيمٍ ﴿١٦﴾

17. He from whom it is averted on that day, *Allāh* indeed has had mercy on him. And that[831] indeed is a manifest achievement.

مَنْ يُصْرَفْ عَنْهُ يَوْمَئِذٍ فَقَدْ رَحِمَهُ ۚ وَذٰلِكَ الْفَوْزُ
الْمُبِينُ ﴿١٧﴾

18. And [c]if Allāh touch thee with affliction, there is none to remove it but He; and if He touch thee with happiness, then He has power to do all that He wills.

وَإِنْ يَمْسَسْكَ اللّٰهُ بِضُرٍّ فَلَا كَاشِفَ لَهُ إِلَّا هُوَ ۖ
وَإِنْ يَمْسَسْكَ بِخَيْرٍ فَهُوَ عَلٰى كُلِّ شَيْءٍ قَدِيرٌ ﴿١٨﴾

19. And [d]He is Supreme[832] over His servants; and He is the Wise, the All-Aware.

وَهُوَ الْقَاهِرُ فَوْقَ عِبَادِهِ ۚ وَهُوَ الْحَكِيمُ الْخَبِيرُ ﴿١٩﴾

20. Say, 'What thing is the weightiest in testimony.' Say, [e]"Allāh is a Witness[833] between me and you. And this Qur'ān has been revealed to me so that with it I may warn you, as well as whomsoever it reaches, of the impending punishment. What ! do you really bear witness that there are other gods besides Allāh ?' Say, 'I bear not witness *thereto*.' Say, 'He is the One God,

قُلْ أَيُّ شَيْءٍ أَكْبَرُ شَهَادَةً ۖ قُلِ اللّٰهُ ۖ شَهِيدٌ بَيْنِى
وَبَيْنَكُمْ ۚ وَأُوحِىَ إِلَيَّ هٰذَا الْقُرْاٰنُ لِأُنْذِرَكُمْ بِهِ
وَمَنْ بَلَغَ ۚ أَئِنَّكُمْ لَتَشْهَدُونَ أَنَّ مَعَ اللّٰهِ اٰلِهَةً
أُخْرٰى ۚ قُلْ لَّآ أَشْهَدُ ۚ قُلْ إِنَّمَا هُوَ إِلٰهٌ وَّاحِدٌ وَّ

[a]6 : 164; 39 : 13. [b]10 : 16; 39 : 14. [c]10 : 108. [d]6 : 62. [e]4 : 167; 13 : 44; 29 : 53.

830. The verse constitutes an emphatic exhortation to men to be on their guard against being disobedient to God, not that the Holy Prophet could ever disobey Him.

831. *Dhālika* may either refer to "the averting of punishment" or to "mercy."

832. The Divine attribute *Al-Qāhir* refutes the theory that matter and soul are co-existent with God and have not been created by Him. If they were not created by Him then He had no right or power to subdue or overrule them.

833. God bears witness in three different ways,—by the revelation of the Qur'ān. This is the first witness. The second and the third witnesses are mentioned in the following verses.

and certainly I am innocent of that which you associate *with Him.*'

إِنَّنِي بَرِيٓءٌ مِّمَّا تُشْرِكُونَ ﴿٢٠﴾

21. [a]Those to whom We gave the Book recognize him as they recognize[834] their sons. But those who ruin their souls—they will not believe.

ٱلَّذِينَ ءَاتَيْنَٰهُمُ ٱلْكِتَٰبَ يَعْرِفُونَهُۥ كَمَا يَعْرِفُونَ
ع أَبْنَآءَهُمُ ٱلَّذِينَ خَسِرُوٓا أَنفُسَهُمْ فَهُمْ لَا يُؤْمِنُونَ ﴿٢١﴾

R. 3 22. And [b]who is more unjust than he who forges a lie against Allāh or treats His Signs as lies? Surely, the unjust shall not prosper.[835]

وَمَنْ أَظْلَمُ مِمَّنِ ٱفْتَرَىٰ عَلَى ٱللَّهِ كَذِبًا أَوْ كَذَّبَ
بِـَٔايَٰتِهِۦٓ إِنَّهُۥ لَا يُفْلِحُ ٱلظَّٰلِمُونَ ﴿٢٢﴾

23. And [c]*think of* the day when We shall gather them all together; then shall We say to those who associated partners *with Allāh*, 'Where are the partners *you spoke of*—those whom you asserted?'[836]

وَيَوْمَ نَحْشُرُهُمْ جَمِيعًا ثُمَّ نَقُولُ لِلَّذِينَ أَشْرَكُوٓا
أَيْنَ شُرَكَآؤُكُمُ ٱلَّذِينَ كُنتُمْ تَزْعُمُونَ ﴿٢٣﴾

24. Then they will have no excuse save that they shall say, 'By Allāh, our Lord, we were not idolaters.'[837]

ثُمَّ لَمْ تَكُن فِتْنَتُهُمْ إِلَّآ أَن قَالُوا وَٱللَّهِ رَبِّنَا مَا
كُنَّا مُشْرِكِينَ ﴿٢٤﴾

25. See how they shall lie against themselves. And [d]that which they fabricated shall fail them.

ٱنظُرْ كَيْفَ كَذَبُوا عَلَىٰٓ أَنفُسِهِمْ وَضَلَّ عَنْهُم مَّا كَانُوا
يَفْتَرُونَ ﴿٢٥﴾

26. And among them are some [e]who give ear to thee; but [f]We have put veils on their hearts, that they should not understand, and deafness in their ears. And *even* if they see every Sign, they would not believe therein, so much so that

وَمِنْهُم مَّن يَسْتَمِعُ إِلَيْكَ وَجَعَلْنَا عَلَىٰ قُلُوبِهِمْ
أَكِنَّةً أَن يَفْقَهُوهُ وَفِىٓ ءَاذَانِهِمْ وَقْرًا وَإِن يَرَوْا

[a]2 : 147. [b]6 : 94; 7 : 38; 10 : 18; 11 : 19; 61 : 8. [c]10 : 39. [d]7 : 54; 11 : 22. [e]10 : 43; 17 : 48. [f]17 : 47; 41 : 6.

834. A Prophet (or for that matter anything pertaining to faith) is not recognized in the beginning. He is recognized only as a father recognizes his son, more as a matter of probability than of dead certainty. Faith must always begin in the region of the unseen.

835. The third kind of testimony is based on human reason. Every sane man will admit that if a person claims to speak in the name of God and forges lies against Him, he would but end his life in utter failure and destruction. On the other hand, those who oppose a Divine Messenger are never allowed to prosper and their efforts to arrest or retard the progress of the new Faith end in complete frustration.

836. You asserted, claimed, or spoke of.

837. This denial on the part of idolaters will really be a confession of their helplessness and a form of petition for Divine mercy.

كُلَّ آيَةٍ لَّا يُؤْمِنُوا بِهَا حَتَّىٰ إِذَا جَاءُوكَ يُجَادِلُونَكَ
يَقُولُ الَّذِينَ كَفَرُوا إِنْ هَٰذَا إِلَّا أَسَاطِيرُ الْأَوَّلِينَ ﴿٢٦﴾

when they come to thee, disputing with thee, those who disbelieve say, 'This is nothing but fables of the ancients.'

وَهُمْ يَنْهَوْنَ عَنْهُ وَيَنْأَوْنَ عَنْهُ وَإِن يُهْلِكُونَ
إِلَّا أَنفُسَهُمْ وَمَا يَشْعُرُونَ ﴿٢٧﴾

27. And they forbid *others* to *believe* in it and *themselves too* they keep away from it.[838] And they ruin none but their ownselves; only they perceive not.

وَلَوْ تَرَىٰ إِذْ وُقِفُوا عَلَى النَّارِ فَقَالُوا يَا لَيْتَنَا نُرَدُّ وَ
لَا نُكَذِّبَ بِآيَاتِ رَبِّنَا وَنَكُونَ مِنَ الْمُؤْمِنِينَ ﴿٢٨﴾

28. And if thou couldst only see [a]when they are made to stand before the Fire! [b]They will say, 'Oh, would that we might be sent back! And *then* we would not treat the Signs of our Lord as lies and we would be of the believers.'

بَلْ بَدَا لَهُم مَّا كَانُوا يُخْفُونَ مِن قَبْلُ وَلَوْ رُدُّوا
لَعَادُوا لِمَا نُهُوا عَنْهُ وَإِنَّهُمْ لَكَاذِبُونَ ﴿٢٩﴾

29. Nay, that which they used to hide before has *now* become clear to them.[839] And if they were sent back, they would surely return to that which they are forbidden. And they are certainly liars.

وَقَالُوا إِنْ هِيَ إِلَّا حَيَاتُنَا الدُّنْيَا وَمَا نَحْنُ بِمَبْعُوثِينَ ﴿٣٠﴾

30. And they say, [c]'There is nothing except *this* our present life, and we shall not be raised again.'

وَلَوْ تَرَىٰ إِذْ وُقِفُوا عَلَىٰ رَبِّهِمْ قَالَ أَلَيْسَ هَٰذَا بِالْحَقِّ
قَالُوا بَلَىٰ وَرَبِّنَا قَالَ فَذُوقُوا الْعَذَابَ بِمَا كُنتُمْ
تَكْفُرُونَ ﴿٣١﴾ ع

31. And if thou couldst only see when they are made to stand before their Lord, [d]He will say, 'Is not this *second life* the truth?' They will say, 'Yea, by our Lord.' He will say, 'Then taste the punishment because you disbelieved.'

[a]46 : 35. [b]2 : 168; 23 : 100-101; 26 : 103; 39 : 59. [c]23 : 38; 44 : 36; 45 : 25. [d]46 : 35.

838. The verse constitutes an eloquent commentary on the captivating power of the Qur'ān.

839. The words, *has now become clear to them*, signify that even the enemies of God's Prophets have in their minds a certain consciousness of the truth of Divine Messengers; but owing to their bigotry and waywardness they try to suppress such thoughts. On the Day of Judgment, however, these latent thoughts of theirs, which they tried to hide in this life, would become apparent, and the truthfulness of the Prophets of which they had dim consciousness would become manifest.

R. 4 32. [a]Those indeed are the losers who deny the meeting with Allāh, so much so, that when the Hour shall come on them unawares, they will say, [b]'O our grief for our neglecting this *Hour*!' And they shall bear their burdens on their backs.[840] Surely, evil is that which they bear.

قَدْ خَسِرَ الَّذِيْنَ كَذَّبُوْا بِلِقَآءِ اللّٰهِ ۗ حَتّٰٓى اِذَا جَآءَتْهُمُ
السَّاعَةُ بَغْتَةً قَالُوْا يٰحَسْرَتَنَا عَلٰى مَا فَرَّطْنَا فِيْهَا ۙ
وَهُمْ يَحْمِلُوْنَ اَوْزَارَهُمْ عَلٰى ظُهُوْرِهِمْ ۗ اَلَا سَآءَ مَا
يَزِرُوْنَ ﴿٣٢﴾

33. And the [c]life of the world is nothing but a sport and a pastime. And surely [d]the abode of the Hereafter is better for those who are righteous. Will you not then understand?

وَمَا الْحَيٰوةُ الدُّنْيَآ اِلَّا لَعِبٌ وَّلَهْوٌ ۗ وَلَلدَّارُ الْاٰخِرَةُ
خَيْرٌ لِّلَّذِيْنَ يَتَّقُوْنَ ۗ اَفَلَا تَعْقِلُوْنَ ﴿٣٣﴾

34. We know indeed that [e]what they say grieves thee; for surely it is not thee that they charge with falsehood but it is the Signs of Allāh that the evil-doers reject.[841]

قَدْ نَعْلَمُ اِنَّهٗ لَيَحْزُنُكَ الَّذِيْ يَقُوْلُوْنَ فَاِنَّهُمْ لَا
يُكَذِّبُوْنَكَ وَلٰكِنَّ الظّٰلِمِيْنَ بِاٰيٰتِ اللّٰهِ يَجْحَدُوْنَ ﴿٣٤﴾

35. And Messengers indeed have been rejected before thee,[842] but *notwithstanding their rejection and persecution* they remained patient until [f]Our help came to them. [g]There is none to change the words of Allāh.[843] And there have already come to thee *some of the* tidings of *past* Messengers.

وَلَقَدْ كُذِّبَتْ رُسُلٌ مِّنْ قَبْلِكَ فَصَبَرُوْا عَلٰى مَا كُذِّبُوْا
وَاُوْذُوْا حَتّٰٓى اَتٰىهُمْ نَصْرُنَا ۚ وَلَا مُبَدِّلَ لِكَلِمٰتِ اللّٰهِ ۚ
وَلَقَدْ جَآءَكَ مِنْ نَّبَاِی الْمُرْسَلِيْنَ ﴿٣٥﴾

[a]10 : 46. [b]2 : 168. [c]29 : 65; 47 : 37; 57 : 21. [d]7 : 170; 12 : 110.
[e]15 : 98; 16 : 104. [f]2 : 215; 40 : 52. [g]6 : 116.

840. The verse means that their burdens would be exceedingly heavy.

841. The Holy Prophet was full of the milk of human kindness. He was not upset by what the disbelievers said concerning him. He was grieved not because the disbelievers accused him of falsehood but because by rejecting Allāh's Signs they had shut on themselves the door of Divine mercy.

842. God lovingly addresses the Holy Prophet with these words of comfort and solace. He is told that Prophets before him were also rejected, scoffed at and ridiculed.

843. The Divine law that Divine help comes to the Prophets of God and their enemies come to grief is unalterable.

36. And if their turning away is hard on thee, then, if thou art able to seek a passage into the earth[844] or a ladder unto heaven and bring them a Sign, *thou canst do so*. And [a]had Allāh *enforced* His Will, He could surely have brought them all together to the guidance. So be thou not of those who lack knowledge.

وَإِنْ كَانَ كَبُرَ عَلَيْكَ إِعْرَاضُهُمْ فَإِنِ اسْتَطَعْتَ أَنْ
تَبْتَغِيَ نَفَقًا فِي الْأَرْضِ أَوْ سُلَّمًا فِي السَّمَآءِ فَتَأْتِيَهُمْ
بِآيَةٍ ۚ وَلَوْ شَآءَ اللّٰهُ لَجَمَعَهُمْ عَلَى الْهُدٰى فَلَا
تَكُونَنَّ مِنَ الْجٰهِلِينَ ﴿٣٦﴾ النصف

37. Only those can accept *the truth* who listen. And *as for* the dead,[844A] Allāh will raise them *to life*,[845] then to Him shall they *all* be brought back.

إِنَّمَا يَسْتَجِيبُ الَّذِينَ يَسْمَعُونَ ۘ وَالْمَوْتٰى يَبْعَثُهُمُ
اللّٰهُ ثُمَّ إِلَيْهِ يُرْجَعُونَ ﴿٣٧﴾

38. And they say, [b]"Why has not a Sign been sent down to him from his Lord?' Say, 'Surely, Allāh has power to send down a Sign, but most of them do not know.'

وَقَالُوا لَوْلَا نُزِّلَ عَلَيْهِ آيَةٌ مِّنْ رَّبِّهِ ۗ قُلْ إِنَّ اللّٰهَ
قَادِرٌ عَلٰى أَنْ يُّنَزِّلَ آيَةً وَّلٰكِنَّ أَكْثَرَهُمْ لَا
يَعْلَمُونَ ﴿٣٨﴾

[a]5 : 49; 6 : 150; 11 : 119; 13 : 32; 16 : 10. [b]10 : 21; 29 : 51.

844. The words, *to seek a passage into the earth*, signify 'using worldly means,' *i.e.* preaching and propagating the truth; and the words, *a ladder unto heaven*, imply 'using spiritual means,' *i.e.*, offering prayers to God for the guidance of disbelievers, etc. Prayer is indeed the ladder by which a man can spiritually mount to heaven. The Holy Prophet is told to employ both these means. The word *Jāhil* as in 2 : 274 means "one not knowing" or "unacquainted." The Holy Prophet is exhorted not to remain unacquainted with the law of God in this respect. The verse also sheds light on the Holy Prophet's great solicitude and concern for the spiritual well-being of his people. He was prepared to go to any length to bring them a Sign, even if he had "to seek a passage in the earth or a ladder unto heaven."

844A. This shows that the word *Mautā* has also been used in the Qur'ān about those deprived of truth.

845. The verse mentions two classes of men: (a) Those who are good at heart and listen to, and readily accept, the truth; and (b) those who are potentially dead but are fit for spiritual regeneration. God will quicken them with a Sign and then they will also listen and embrace Islām.

39. [a]There is not an animal *that crawls* in the earth, nor a bird that flies on its two wings, but *they are* communities[846] like you. [b]We have left out nothing in the Book. Then to their Lord shall they *all* be gathered together.

وَمَا مِنْ دَآبَّةٍ فِي الْاَرْضِ وَلَا طٰٓئِرٍ يَّطِيْرُ بِجَنَاحَيْهِ
اِلَّآ اُمَمٌ اَمْثَالُكُمْ مَا فَرَّطْنَا فِي الْكِتٰبِ مِنْ شَيْءٍ ثُمَّ
اِلٰى رَبِّهِمْ يُحْشَرُوْنَ ﴿٣٩﴾

40. [c]Those who have rejected Our Signs are deaf and dumb, in utter darkness. Whom Allāh wills He lets go astray and whom He wills He places on the right path.

وَالَّذِيْنَ كَذَّبُوْا بِاٰيٰتِنَا صُمٌّ وَّبُكْمٌ فِي الظُّلُمٰتِ
مَنْ يَّشَاِ اللّٰهُ يُضْلِلْهُ وَمَنْ يَّشَاْ يَجْعَلْهُ عَلٰى صِرَاطٍ
مُّسْتَقِيْمٍ ﴿٤٠﴾

41. Say, [d]"Will you tell me if the punishment of Allāh come or there come upon you the Hour,[847] will you call upon any other than Allāh, if you are truthful ?

قُلْ اَرَءَيْتَكُمْ اِنْ اَتٰىكُمْ عَذَابُ اللّٰهِ اَوْ اَتَتْكُمُ السَّاعَةُ
اَغَيْرَ اللّٰهِ تَدْعُوْنَ اِنْ كُنْتُمْ صٰدِقِيْنَ ﴿٤١﴾

42. Nay, [e]but on Him alone will you call; then will He remove, if He please, that which you call on Him *to remove*, and you will forget what you associate *with Him*."[848]

بَلْ اِيَّاهُ تَدْعُوْنَ فَيَكْشِفُ مَا تَدْعُوْنَ اِلَيْهِ اِنْ شَآءَ
ع وَتَنْسَوْنَ مَا تُشْرِكُوْنَ ﴿٤٢﴾

[a]11 : 7, 57. [b]16 : 90. [c]2 : 19, 172; 27 : 81-82; 30 : 53-54. [d]6 : 48; 12 : 108; 43 : 67. [e]10 : 23-24.

846. The verse points out that even birds and insects, like ants, can understand from atmospheric change that a storm is imminent, and animals like dogs understand the orders of their masters but the foolish disbelievers do not see the writing on the wall and do not realize that by rejecting the Holy Prophet they are incurring the displeasure of God. They are warned that all their actions have been recorded and they will have to answer for them. The verse further seems to point to two classes of men : (a) Those who like the beasts are wholly bent upon the earth and their entire life is confined to satisfying their physical desires. (b) Those who like birds soar high into spiritual regions—highly spiritual persons having been likened to birds in the Qur'ān (3 : 50).

847. "Hour" refers to the hour of the decisive victory of Islām, or, to the Fall of Mecca.

848. The words, *you will forget what you associate with Him*, were literally fulfilled on the day of the Fall of Mecca. On that day the Meccans lost all faith in their gods, as Abū Sufyān and his wife, Hindah and others had frankly admitted in the presence of the Holy Prophet. Ultimately, idolatry completely disappeared from Arabia.

R. 5 43. And indeed We sent *Messengers* to peoples before thee; then [a]We afflicted them with poverty and adversity[849] that they might humble themselves.

وَلَقَدْ أَرْسَلْنَآ إِلَىٰٓ أُمَمٍ مِّن قَبْلِكَ فَأَخَذْنٰهُم بِالْبَأْسَآءِ وَالضَّرَّآءِ لَعَلَّهُمْ يَتَضَرَّعُونَ ﴿٤٣﴾

44. Why, then,[850] when Our punishment came upon them, did they not humble themselves? But [b]their hearts were hardened *all the more* and [c]Satan made all that they did seem fair to them.

فَلَوْلَآ إِذْ جَآءَهُم بَأْسُنَا تَضَرَّعُوا وَلٰكِن قَسَتْ قُلُوبُهُمْ وَزَيَّنَ لَهُمُ الشَّيْطٰنُ مَا كَانُوا يَعْمَلُونَ ﴿٤٤﴾

45. When [d]they forgot that with which they had been admonished, and We opened unto them the gates of all things, till, even as they were rejoicing in what they were given, [e]We seized them suddenly, and lo! they were in utter despair.

فَلَمَّا نَسُوا مَا ذُكِّرُوا بِهِۦ فَتَحْنَا عَلَيْهِمْ أَبْوٰبَ كُلِّ شَيْءٍ حَتّٰىٓ إِذَا فَرِحُوا بِمَآ أُوتُوٓا أَخَذْنٰهُم بَغْتَةً فَإِذَا هُم مُّبْلِسُونَ ﴿٤٥﴾

46. [f]So the last remnant[851] of the people who did wrong was cut off; and all praise belongs to Allāh, the Lord of all the worlds.

فَقُطِعَ دَابِرُ الْقَوْمِ الَّذِينَ ظَلَمُوا ۚ وَالْحَمْدُ لِلّٰهِ رَبِّ الْعٰلَمِينَ ﴿٤٦﴾

47. Say, 'Will you tell me, [g]if Allāh should take away your hearing and your sight, and seal up your hearts who is the god other than Allāh who could bring it *back* to you?' See how We expound the Signs in various ways, yet they turn away.

قُلْ أَرَءَيْتُمْ إِنْ أَخَذَ اللّٰهُ سَمْعَكُمْ وَأَبْصٰرَكُمْ وَخَتَمَ عَلٰى قُلُوبِكُم مَّنْ إِلٰهٌ غَيْرُ اللّٰهِ يَأْتِيكُم بِهِ ۗ انظُرْ كَيْفَ نُصَرِّفُ الْاٰيٰتِ ثُمَّ هُمْ يَصْدِفُونَ ﴿٤٧﴾

---

[a]7 : 95. [b]2 : 75; 57 : 17. [c]6 : 123; 8 : 49; 16 : 64; 29 : 39. [d]5 : 14; 7 : 166. [e]7: 96; 39 : 56. [f]7 : 73; 15 : 67. [g]2 : 8; 16 : 109; 45 : 24.

---

849. The preceding verses referred to Divine punishment in general. In this verse its various forms have been mentioned.

850. The words *lau lā* are not here used to express mere interrogation but also a feeling of pity. Thus the verse signifies: "They ought to have humbled themselves before God; but it is a pity that they did not."

851. *Dābir* means, last remains of a people; the roots, stock, race, or the like. The words *Quṭi'a Dābir al-Qaum* mean : (1) The people were cut off to the last man. (2) The leaders of the people were cut off just as a tree is cut down to its roots. (3) The leaders' followers were cut off, *i.e.*, the leaders were deprived of their political power, for it is on the strength of their followers that the political power of their leaders depends.

48. Say, 'Will you tell me, [a]if the punishment of Allāh come upon you suddenly or openly, will any be destroyed save the wrongdoing people?'

قُلْ اَرَءَيْتَكُمْ اِنْ اَتٰىكُمْ عَذَابُ اللّٰهِ بَغْتَةً اَوْ
جَهْرَةً هَلْ يُهْلَكُ اِلَّا الْقَوْمُ الظّٰلِمُوْنَ ﴿٤٨﴾

49. And [b]We send not the Messengers but as bearers of glad tidings and as Warners. So [c]those who believe and reform *themselves*, on them *shall come* no fear nor shall they grieve.

وَمَا نُرْسِلُ الْمُرْسَلِيْنَ اِلَّا مُبَشِّرِيْنَ وَمُنْذِرِيْنَ ۚ
فَمَنْ اٰمَنَ وَاَصْلَحَ فَلَا خَوْفٌ عَلَيْهِمْ وَلَا هُمْ
يَحْزَنُوْنَ ﴿٤٩﴾

50. And [d]those who reject Our Signs, punishment will touch them, because they disobeyed.

وَالَّذِيْنَ كَذَّبُوْا بِاٰيٰتِنَا يَمَسُّهُمُ الْعَذَابُ بِمَا كَانُوْا
يَفْسُقُوْنَ ﴿٥٠﴾

51. Say, [e]"I do not say to you: 'I possess the treasures of Allāh, nor do I know the unseen; nor do I say to you: 'I am an angel, [f]I follow only that which is revealed to me.' Say, 'Can a blind man and one who sees be alike?' Will you not then reflect?

قُلْ لَّاۤ اَقُوْلُ لَكُمْ عِنْدِيْ خَزَآئِنُ اللّٰهِ وَلَاۤ اَعْلَمُ
الْغَيْبَ وَلَاۤ اَقُوْلُ لَكُمْ اِنِّيْ مَلَكٌ ۚ اِنْ اَتَّبِعُ اِلَّا مَا
يُوْحٰۤى اِلَيَّ ؕ قُلْ هَلْ يَسْتَوِى الْاَعْمٰى وَالْبَصِيْرُ ؕ اَفَلَا
تَتَفَكَّرُوْنَ ﴿٥١﴾ ع

R. 6 52. And warn thereby those who fear that they shall be gathered to their Lord that they shall have no friend nor intercessor besides Him, so that they may become righteous.

وَاَنْذِرْ بِهِ الَّذِيْنَ يَخَافُوْنَ اَنْ يُّحْشَرُوْۤا اِلٰى رَبِّهِمْ
لَيْسَ لَهُمْ مِّنْ دُوْنِهٖ وَلِيٌّ وَّلَا شَفِيْعٌ لَّعَلَّهُمْ
يَتَّقُوْنَ ﴿٥٢﴾

53. And [g]drive not away those who call upon their Lord morning and evening, [h]seeking His pleasure.[852] Thou art not at all accountable for them nor are they at all accountable for thee. So if thou shouldst drive them away thou wilt be of the unjust.

وَلَا تَطْرُدِ الَّذِيْنَ يَدْعُوْنَ رَبَّهُمْ بِالْغَدٰوةِ وَالْعَشِيِّ
يُرِيْدُوْنَ وَجْهَهٗ ؕ مَا عَلَيْكَ مِنْ حِسَابِهِمْ مِّنْ شَيْءٍ
وَّمَا مِنْ حِسَابِكَ عَلَيْهِمْ مِّنْ شَيْءٍ فَتَطْرُدَهُمْ فَتَكُوْنَ
مِنَ الظّٰلِمِيْنَ ﴿٥٣﴾

[a]6 : 41; 10 : 51; 12 : 108; 43 : 67. [b]4 : 166; 5 : 20; 18 : 57. [c]5 : 70; 7 : 36. [d]3 : 12; 5 : 11; 7 : 37, 73; 10 : 74; 22 : 58. [e]11 : 32. [f]10 : 16; 46 : 10. [g]11 : 30. [h]18 : 29.

852. *Wajh* means, pleasure; countenance; the thing itself (2 : 113).

54. And in like manner have We tried some of them by others, that they may say, [a]'Is it these[853] whom Allāh has favoured from among us?' Does not Allāh know best those who are grateful?

وَكَذٰلِكَ فَتَنَّا بَعْضَهُمْ بِبَعْضٍ لِّيَقُوْلُوْٓا اَهٰٓؤُلَآءِ مَنَّ اللّٰهُ عَلَيْهِمْ مِّنْۢ بَيْنِنَا ۭ اَلَيْسَ اللّٰهُ بِاَعْلَمَ بِالشّٰكِرِيْنَ ﴿٥٤﴾

55. And when those, who believe in Our Signs come to thee, say: 'Peace be unto you! [b]Your Lord has taken it upon Himself to show mercy, so that [c]whoso among you does evil in ignorance and repents thereafter and reforms, then He is Most Forgiving *and* Merciful.'

وَاِذَا جَآءَكَ الَّذِيْنَ يُؤْمِنُوْنَ بِاٰيٰتِنَا فَقُلْ سَلٰمٌ عَلَيْكُمْ كَتَبَ رَبُّكُمْ عَلٰى نَفْسِهِ الرَّحْمَةَ ۙ اَنَّهٗ مَنْ عَمِلَ مِنْكُمْ سُوْٓءًۢا بِجَهَالَةٍ ثُمَّ تَابَ مِنْۢ بَعْدِهٖ وَاَصْلَحَ فَاَنَّهٗ غَفُوْرٌ رَّحِيْمٌ ﴿٥٥﴾

56. And thus do We expound the Signs *that the truth may become manifest* and that the way of the sinners may become clear.

وَكَذٰلِكَ نُفَصِّلُ الْاٰيٰتِ وَلِتَسْتَبِيْنَ سَبِيْلُ الْمُجْرِمِيْنَ ﴿٥٦﴾ ع ٦ ١٣

R. 7 57. Say, 'I am forbidden to worship those on whom you call besides Allāh.' Say, [d]'I will not follow your low desires. In that case, I shall have gone astray and I shall not be of the rightly guided.'

قُلْ اِنِّيْ نُهِيْتُ اَنْ اَعْبُدَ الَّذِيْنَ تَدْعُوْنَ مِنْ دُوْنِ اللّٰهِ ۭ قُلْ لَّآ اَتَّبِعُ اَهْوَآءَكُمْ ۙ قَدْ ضَلَلْتُ اِذًا وَّمَآ اَنَا مِنَ الْمُهْتَدِيْنَ ﴿٥٧﴾

58. Say, [e]'I *take my stand* on a clear evidence from my Lord and you reject it. That which you desire to be hastened is not in my *power*. [f]The decision rests with Allāh *alone*. He explains the truth, and He is the Best of judges.'

قُلْ اِنِّيْ عَلٰى بَيِّنَةٍ مِّنْ رَّبِّيْ وَكَذَّبْتُمْ بِهٖ ۭ مَا عِنْدِيْ مَا تَسْتَعْجِلُوْنَ بِهٖ ۭ اِنِ الْحُكْمُ اِلَّا لِلّٰهِ ۭ يَقُصُّ الْحَقَّ وَهُوَ خَيْرُ الْفٰصِلِيْنَ ﴿٥٨﴾

59. Say, [g]'If that which you desire to be hastened were in my *power*, surely the matter would have been decided between me and you. And Allāh knows best the unjust.'

قُلْ لَّوْ اَنَّ عِنْدِيْ مَا تَسْتَعْجِلُوْنَ بِهٖ لَقُضِيَ الْاَمْرُ بَيْنِيْ وَبَيْنَكُمْ ۭ وَاللّٰهُ اَعْلَمُ بِالظّٰلِمِيْنَ ﴿٥٩﴾

---

[a]11 : 28. [b]6 : 13; 7 : 157. [c]4 : 18; 16 : 120.
[d]5 : 50; 42 : 16. [e]11 : 64; 12 : 109. [f]12 : 41,68. [g]6 : 9; 10 : 12.

---

853. Generally, presence of the poor in the community of believers proves a stumbling-block in the way of the rich to accept the new Message.

60. And with Him are the keys of the unseen; none knows them but He. And He knows whatsoever is in the land and *in* the sea. And there falls not a leaf but He knows it; nor is there a grain in the deep darkness of the earth, nor anything green or dry, but is *recorded* in a clear book.[854]

وَعِندَهُۥ مَفَاتِحُ ٱلۡغَيۡبِ لَا يَعۡلَمُهَآ إِلَّا هُوَۚ وَيَعۡلَمُ
مَا فِي ٱلۡبَرِّ وَٱلۡبَحۡرِۚ وَمَا تَسۡقُطُ مِن وَرَقَةٍ إِلَّا يَعۡلَمُهَا
وَلَا حَبَّةٖ فِي ظُلُمَٰتِ ٱلۡأَرۡضِ وَلَا رَطۡبٖ وَلَا يَابِسٍ
إِلَّا فِي كِتَٰبٖ مُّبِينٖ ٦٠

61. And [a]He it is Who takes your souls by night and knows what you do by day,[855] then He raises you up again therein, that the appointed term[856] may be completed. Then to Him is your return. Then will He inform you of what you used to do.

وَهُوَ ٱلَّذِي يَتَوَفَّىٰكُم بِٱلَّيۡلِ وَيَعۡلَمُ مَا جَرَحۡتُم
بِٱلنَّهَارِ ثُمَّ يَبۡعَثُكُمۡ فِيهِ لِيُقۡضَىٰٓ أَجَلٞ مُّسَمّٗىۖ ثُمَّ
إِلَيۡهِ مَرۡجِعُكُمۡ ثُمَّ يُنَبِّئُكُم بِمَا كُنتُمۡ تَعۡمَلُونَ ٦١ ع

[a]39 : 43.

854. This and the next verse lay down the guiding principle that it has not been left in the hands of the Holy Prophet to bring down punishment on disbelievers as demanded by them. If this had been the case, they would have since long met their deserved end, and then perhaps many erstwhile enemies of Islām like 'Umar and Khālid who later on were destined to play a leading role in extending and consolidating the power of Islām, would have died in disbelief. But God being All-Powerful is slow to punish and, being fully conversant with the inner working of the human heart, knows when and whom to punish. He alone knows how far hardships or ease can influence the actions of a man and whether or not good works done by a man are rendered null and void through the operation of other causes. He alone has knowledge of the grains of virtue that lie embedded in the heart of man and knows whether or not these grains will sprout forth and grow and thrive and bring forth fruit. He alone can tell whether a person who, to all appearances, is "dry" and "devoid of all spiritual life," will turn "green" when supplied with heavenly water or whether he is "dead" and beyond revival. In short, God alone has full knowledge of all things and of all conditions and all possibilities and potentialities and therefore He alone can say who is to be punished and who not.

855. God alone knows the condition of man by night and his actions by day, and all times are subject to His control, and therefore it is He alone Who knows the true character of the pious and the wicked, and consequently He alone is in a position to punish.

856. The "term" spoken of here is determined by the faculties and powers with which man is endowed from the time of his birth, and is liable to be extended or curtailed according as right or wrong use is made of it. There is no reference here to the eternal knowledge of God.

R. 8 62. And [a]He is Supreme[857] over His servants, and [b]He sends guardians *to watch* over you, until, when death comes to anyone of you, Our messengers take his soul, and they fail not.

وَهُوَ الْقَاهِرُ فَوْقَ عِبَادِهٖ وَيُرْسِلُ عَلَيْكُمْ حَفَظَةً ۭ حَتّٰٓى اِذَا جَآءَ اَحَدَكُمُ الْمَوْتُ تَوَفَّتْهُ رُسُلُنَا وَهُمْ لَا يُفَرِّطُوْنَ ﴿٦٢﴾

63. Then are they returned to Allāh, their true Lord. Surely, His is the judgment. And He is the Swiftest of reckoners.

ثُمَّ رُدُّوْٓا اِلَى اللّٰهِ مَوْلٰىهُمُ الْحَقِّ ۭ اَلَا لَهُ الْحُكْمُ ۣ وَهُوَ اَسْرَعُ الْحٰسِبِيْنَ ﴿٦٣﴾

64. Say, [c]"Who delivers you from the calamities[858] of the land and the sea, *when* you call upon Him in humility and in secret, *saying*, 'If He deliver us from this, we will surely be of those who are grateful."

قُلْ مَنْ يُّنَجِّيْكُمْ مِّنْ ظُلُمٰتِ الْبَرِّ وَالْبَحْرِ تَدْعُوْنَهٗ تَضَرُّعًا وَّخُفْيَةً ۚ لَئِنْ اَنْجٰىنَا مِنْ هٰذِهٖ لَنَكُوْنَنَّ مِنَ الشّٰكِرِيْنَ ﴿٦٤﴾

65. Say, 'Allāh delivers you from them and from every distress, yet you associate partners *with Him*.'

قُلِ اللّٰهُ يُنَجِّيْكُمْ مِّنْهَا وَمِنْ كُلِّ كَرْبٍ ثُمَّ اَنْتُمْ تُشْرِكُوْنَ ﴿٦٥﴾

66. Say, 'He has power to send punishment upon you from above you or from beneath your feet, or to confound you by *splitting you into* sects and make you taste the violence of one another.[859] See how We expound the Signs in various ways that they may understand !

قُلْ هُوَ الْقَادِرُ عَلٰٓى اَنْ يَّبْعَثَ عَلَيْكُمْ عَذَابًا مِّنْ فَوْقِكُمْ اَوْ مِنْ تَحْتِ اَرْجُلِكُمْ اَوْ يَلْبِسَكُمْ شِيَعًا وَّيُذِيْقَ بَعْضَكُمْ بَاْسَ بَعْضٍ ۭ اُنْظُرْ كَيْفَ نُصَرِّفُ الْاٰيٰتِ لَعَلَّهُمْ يَفْقَهُوْنَ ﴿٦٦﴾

[a]6 : 19; 13 : 17. [b]13 : 12; 82 : 11. [c]10 : 23; 17 : 68; 29 : 66; 31 : 33.

857. This verse provides another reason why God alone is entitled to punish. He is *Qāhir, i.e.*, Powerful and Mighty over all, therefore He can punish any of His creatures in His infallible knowledge whenever He thinks proper. The powerful are never in a hurry to punish.

858. *Zulumāt* literally meaning "darknesses," here signifies afflictions, calamities and misfortunes; for, with the Arabs, darkness is a symbol of misfortune.

859. "Punishments from above" signifies famines, earthquakes, floods, hurricanes, the oppression of the weak by the powerful, mental agony, etc., and "punishments from beneath" signifies diseases, pestilences, revolt by subject peoples, etc. Then there is the punishment of discord, disunity and dissension which sometimes end in civil war. This is hinted in the words *make you taste the violence of one another.*

67. And [a]thy people have rejected it[860] though it is the truth. Say, [b]'I am not a guardian over you.'

وَكَذَّبَ بِهٖ قَوْمُكَ وَهُوَ الْحَقُّ ۚ قُلْ لَّسْتُ عَلَيْكُمْ بِوَكِيْلٍ ﴿٦٧﴾

68. For every prophecy there is a fixed time;[861] and soon will you come to know.

لِكُلِّ نَبَاٍ مُّسْتَقَرٌّ ۚ وَّسَوْفَ تَعْلَمُوْنَ ﴿٦٨﴾

69. And [c]when thou seest those who engage in *vain discourse concerning* Our Signs, then turn thou away from them until they engage in a discourse other than that. And if Satan should cause thee to forget, then sit not, after recollection, with the unjust people.

وَاِذَا رَاَيْتَ الَّذِيْنَ يَخُوْضُوْنَ فِيْٓ اٰيٰتِنَا فَاَعْرِضْ عَنْهُمْ حَتّٰى يَخُوْضُوْا فِيْ حَدِيْثٍ غَيْرِهٖ ۚ وَاِمَّا يُنْسِيَنَّكَ الشَّيْطٰنُ فَلَا تَقْعُدْ بَعْدَ الذِّكْرٰى مَعَ الْقَوْمِ الظّٰلِمِيْنَ ﴿٦٩﴾

70. And [d]those who are righteous are not at all accountable for them, but *their duty is* to admonish them that they may fear *Allāh*

وَمَا عَلَى الَّذِيْنَ يَتَّقُوْنَ مِنْ حِسَابِهِمْ مِّنْ شَيْءٍ وَّلٰكِنْ ذِكْرٰى لَعَلَّهُمْ يَتَّقُوْنَ ﴿٧٠﴾

71. And leave alone [e]those who take their religion to be a sport and a pastime, and whom worldly life has beguiled. And admonish *people* thereby lest a soul be consigned to perdition for what it has earned. It shall have no helper nor intercessor beside Allāh; and even if it offer every ransom it shall not be accepted from it. These are they who have been delivered over to destruction for their own acts. [f]They will have a drink of boiling water and a grievous punishment, because they disbelieved.

وَذَرِ الَّذِيْنَ اتَّخَذُوْا دِيْنَهُمْ لَعِبًا وَّلَهْوًا وَّغَرَّتْهُمُ الْحَيٰوةُ الدُّنْيَا وَذَكِّرْ بِهٖٓ اَنْ تُبْسَلَ نَفْسٌ بِمَا كَسَبَتْ ۖ لَيْسَ لَهَا مِنْ دُوْنِ اللّٰهِ وَلِيٌّ وَّلَا شَفِيْعٌ ۚ وَاِنْ تَعْدِلْ كُلَّ عَدْلٍ لَّا يُؤْخَذْ مِنْهَا ۗ اُولٰٓئِكَ الَّذِيْنَ اُبْسِلُوْا بِمَا كَسَبُوْا ۚ لَهُمْ شَرَابٌ مِّنْ حَمِيْمٍ وَّعَذَابٌ اَلِيْمٌۢ بِمَا كَانُوْا يَكْفُرُوْنَ ﴿٧١﴾

[a]6 : 6. [b]39 : 42; 42 : 7. [c]4 : 141. [d]6 : 53. [e]58 : 5; 7 : 52; 8 : 36. [f]10 : 5.

860. The pronoun "it" refers to (1) the matter under discussion; (2) the Qur'ān; (3) Divine punishment. Taking the last meaning, the words "it is the truth" would mean that the promised punishment is sure to come.

861. The verse signifies that God, in His infallible wisdom, has fixed a time for the fulfilment of every prophecy. So the punishment that has been promised to the rejectors of truth will also come to pass in due time.

R. 9

قُلْ أَنَدْعُوا مِنْ دُونِ اللَّهِ مَا لَا يَنْفَعُنَا وَلَا يَضُرُّنَا
وَنُرَدُّ عَلَىٰ أَعْقَابِنَا بَعْدَ إِذْ هَدَانَا اللَّهُ كَالَّذِي
اسْتَهْوَتْهُ الشَّيَاطِينُ فِي الْأَرْضِ حَيْرَانَ لَهُ أَصْحَابٌ
يَدْعُونَهُ إِلَى الْهُدَى ائْتِنَا ۗ قُلْ إِنَّ هُدَى اللَّهِ
هُوَ الْهُدَىٰ ۖ وَأُمِرْنَا لِنُسْلِمَ لِرَبِّ الْعَالَمِينَ ﴿٧٢﴾

72. Say, "Shall we call, beside Allāh, upon that which can neither profit us nor harm us, and shall we be turned back on our heels after Allāh has guided us?—Like one whom the evil ones entice away, *leaving him* bewildered in the land,[862] *and* who has companions who call him to guidance, *saying*, 'Come to us.'" Say: 'Surely, the guidance of Allāh is the only *true* guidance and we have been commanded to submit to the Lord of all the worlds.

وَأَنْ أَقِيمُوا الصَّلَاةَ وَاتَّقُوهُ ۚ وَهُوَ الَّذِي إِلَيْهِ
تُحْشَرُونَ ﴿٧٣﴾

73. "And *we have been given the command*: [a]'Observe Prayers and fear Him;' and He it is to Whom you shall *all* be gathered."

وَهُوَ الَّذِي خَلَقَ السَّمَاوَاتِ وَالْأَرْضَ بِالْحَقِّ ۖ وَيَوْمَ
يَقُولُ كُنْ فَيَكُونُ ۚ قَوْلُهُ الْحَقُّ ۚ وَلَهُ الْمُلْكُ يَوْمَ
يُنْفَخُ فِي الصُّورِ ۚ عَالِمُ الْغَيْبِ وَالشَّهَادَةِ ۚ وَهُوَ
الْحَكِيمُ الْخَبِيرُ ﴿٧٤﴾

74. And [b]He it is Who created the heavens and the earth in accordance with the requirements of wisdom; and on the day when He will say, 'Be', it will be. His Word is the truth, and His will be the Kingdom on the day [c]when the trumpet[863] will be blown. *He is* [d]the Knower of the unseen and the seen. And He is the Wise, the All-Aware.

[a]21 : 67; 22 : 74. [b]4 : 78; 22 : 79; 24 : 57. [c]14 : 20; 16 : 4; 29 : 45.
[d]27 : 88; 39 : 69. [e]9 : 94; 13 : 10; 23 : 93; 39 : 47; 59 : 23.

862. The verse likens the case of an idol-worshipper to that of a distracted person who has no fixed course to pursue. But a true believer has a fixed purpose and a fixed goal in life. He always prays to the One God with a deep-rooted conviction and does not wander about distracted like an idolater.

863. A Divine Prophet is indeed a trumpet through whom the Voice of God is heard, and the sounding of it is a symbol for the wide dissemination of his teachings and the great revolution to be brought about by him in the lives of his people. The verse means that when the teachings of the Holy Prophet are widely published and accepted in the world and when Islām triumphs and predominates, then the Kingdom of God will become demonstrably established in the earth and on that day will idols be broken to pieces.

75. And *remember the time* [a]when Abraham said to his father, Āzar,[864] 'Dost thou take idols for gods? Surely, I see thee and thy people in manifest error.'

وَإِذْ قَالَ إِبْرٰهِيمُ لِأَبِيهِ اٰزَرَ أَتَتَّخِذُ أَصْنَامًا اٰلِهَةً
إِنِّيٓ أَرٰىكَ وَقَوْمَكَ فِي ضَلٰلٍ مُّبِينٍ ﴿٧٥﴾

76. And *thus* did We show Abraham the Kingdom of the heavens and the earth[865] *that he should have full knowledge* and that he might be of those who possess certainty of faith.

وَكَذٰلِكَ نُرِيٓ إِبْرٰهِيمَ مَلَكُوتَ السَّمٰوٰتِ
وَالْأَرْضِ وَلِيَكُونَ مِنَ الْمُوقِنِينَ ﴿٧٦﴾

77. And when the night darkened upon him, he saw a star. He said, 'Can this be my Lord?' But when it set, he said, 'I like not those that set.'

فَلَمَّا جَنَّ عَلَيْهِ الَّيْلُ رَاٰ كَوْكَبًا ۚ قَالَ هٰذَا رَبِّي ۚ
فَلَمَّآ أَفَلَ قَالَ لَآ أُحِبُّ الْاٰفِلِينَ ﴿٧٧﴾

[a]19 : 43.

864. In the Old Testament the name of Abraham's father is given as Terah (Gen. 11 : 26) and in the New Testament (Luke, 3 : 34) it is Tharah. The Talmud agrees with Luke. Eusebius, the father of ecclesiatical history, gives Āthar as the name of Abraham's father (Sale). This shows that even among the Jews there existed no unanimity of opinion about the name of Abraham's father. Eusebius must have strong reasons for differing from Genesis and Luke. The correct form appears to be Āthar, which later became changed into Tharah or Terah. Āthar closely resembles the name given in the Qur'ān (Āzar), only there is a slight difference of pronunciation, the two forms being almost identical. Christian writers, therefore, have no reason to quarrel with the Qur'ān for calling Abraham's father by the name Āzar. Moreover, Abraham's father is also called Zarah in the Talmud (Sale), and Zarah is approximately the same as Āzar. This shows that the Quranic version is much more reliable. Besides, Āzar has been called Abraham's *Ab* (26 : 87), a word applied both to father, uncle and grandfather, etc. In 2 : 133 Ishmael who was Jacob's uncle has been called his *Ab*. It, however, appears from the Qur'ān that Āzar, though called the *Ab* of Abraham, was not really his father. Abraham had made a promise to Āzar, his *Ab*, to pray to God to forgive him but when he came to know that he was an enemy of God, he abstained from praying for him; he was even actually forbidden to do so (9 : 114). But in 14 : 42 Abraham prays for his *Wālid* which word is applied only to father. This shows that Āzar who has been called the *Ab* of Abraham was a person different from his *Wālid*. Most probably he was his uncle. Some passages of the Bible also support this inference. Abraham married Sarah the daughter of Terah (Gen. 20 : 12) which shows that Terah was not his father, because he could not marry his own sister. It appears that his father being dead, Abraham was brought up by his uncle, Āzar or Āthar, who gave him his daughter, Sarah, in marriage. As Āzar brought up Abraham and was like a father to him, the latter seemed to have been called his son, and this led to the error of Āzar or Āthar being taken as the real father of Abraham. It also appears from the Talmud that Āzar prosecuted Abraham and took him to the King for the offence of breaking the idols. If Āzar had been the father of Abraham, he would not have taken such a drastic step against his own son.

865. The verse means that God granted Abraham the knowledge of, and an insight into, the natural laws that work in the universe, and of the all-pervading Divine power and control.

78. And when he saw the moon rise with spreading light, he said, 'Can this be my Lord?' But when it set, he said, 'If my Lord guide me not, I shall surely be of the people who go astray.'

فَلَمَّا رَاَ الْقَمَرَ بَازِغًا قَالَ هٰذَا رَبِّيْ ۚ فَلَمَّاۤ اَفَلَ
قَالَ لَئِنْ لَّمْ يَهْدِنِيْ رَبِّيْ لَاَكُوْنَنَّ مِنَ الْقَوْمِ
الضَّآلِّيْنَ ﴿۷۸﴾

79. And when he saw the sun rise with spreading light, he said, 'Can this be my Lord? This is the greatest.' But when it *also* set, he said, 'O my people! surely I am quit of that which you associate *with God*;[866]

فَلَمَّا رَاَ الشَّمْسَ بَازِغَةً قَالَ هٰذَا رَبِّيْ هٰذَاۤ اَكْبَرُ ۚ
فَلَمَّاۤ اَفَلَتْ قَالَ يٰقَوْمِ اِنِّيْ بَرِيْٓءٌ مِّمَّا تُشْرِكُوْنَ ﴿۷۹﴾

80. [a]'I have turned my face toward Him Who created the heavens and the earth, being ever inclined *to Allāh*, and I am not of those who associate gods *with Him*.'

اِنِّيْ وَجَّهْتُ وَجْهِيَ لِلَّذِيْ فَطَرَ السَّمٰوٰتِ وَالْاَرْضَ
حَنِيْفًا وَّمَاۤ اَنَا مِنَ الْمُشْرِكِيْنَ ﴿۸۰﴾

81. And his people argued with him. He said, 'Do you argue with me concerning Allāh when He has guided me aright? And I fear not that which you associate with Him except *that I* fear what my Lord wills. [b]My Lord comprehends all things in His knowledge. Will you not then be admonished?

وَحَآجَّهٗ قَوْمُهٗ ۗ قَالَ اَتُحَآجُّوْٓنِّيْ فِي اللّٰهِ وَقَدْ
هَدٰىنِ ۗ وَلَاۤ اَخَافُ مَا تُشْرِكُوْنَ بِهٖۤ اِلَّاۤ اَنْ يَّشَآءَ
رَبِّيْ شَيْئًا ۗ وَسِعَ رَبِّيْ كُلَّ شَيْءٍ عِلْمًا ۗ اَفَلَا تَتَذَكَّرُوْنَ ﴿۸۱﴾

---

[a]3 : 21. [b]7 : 90.

---

866. Verses 77 to 79 contain an argument which Abraham employed to bring home to his idolatrous people the absurdity of their belief that the sun, the moon and the stars were so many gods which they worshipped (Jew. Enc.). It is wrong to infer from these verses that Abraham was himself groping in the dark and did not know Who his God was, and that he took the evening star, the moon, and the sun for God one after the other and, when each of them set in its turn, he gave up his belief in their divinity and turned to the One God, the Creator of heavens and earth. In fact, the passage contains several arguments to show that Abraham, far from taking these heavenly bodies for gods, sought to demonstrate to his people the vanity of their beliefs step by step. Verses 75-76 show that Abraham was a firm believer in One God. He could not, therefore, be considered as groping in the dark and wandering from one deity to another. The words, 'can this be my Lord' constituted an argument against star-worship. He said these words to expose his people's belief that the star was their Lord. Moreover, he already knew that the star must set. So his argument contained in the words, "I like not those that set" must have been already present in his mind. In reality, he wanted to use his argument in a most effective manner. So he first assumed the star to be his Lord and, when it disappeared, he hastened to declare, *I like not those that set*. Similar was the case with the setting of the moon and the sun. Of the sun he used the word "greater" or "greatest" ironically in order to taunt his people for their folly. This

82. 'And why should I fear that which you associate *with Allāh*, when you fear not [a]to associate with Allāh that for which He has sent down to you no authority?' Which, then, of the two parties has better title to security,[867] if indeed you know?

وَكَيْفَ أَخَافُ مَآ أَشْرَكْتُمْ وَلَا تَخَافُونَ أَنَّكُمْ
أَشْرَكْتُم بِاللّٰهِ مَا لَمْ يُنَزِّلْ بِهٖ عَلَيْكُمْ سُلْطٰنًا ۚ
فَأَيُّ الْفَرِيقَيْنِ أَحَقُّ بِالْأَمْنِ ۚ إِنْ كُنْتُمْ تَعْلَمُونَ ﴿٨٢﴾

83. Those who believe and [b]mix not up their belief with injustice—it is they who shall have peace, and who are rightly guided.

اَلَّذِينَ اٰمَنُوا وَلَمْ يَلْبِسُوٓا إِيمَانَهُمْ بِظُلْمٍ أُولٰٓئِكَ
لَهُمُ الْأَمْنُ وَهُمْ مُّهْتَدُونَ ﴿٨٣﴾ ع ٩ ١٥

R. 10 84. And that is Our argument which We gave to Abraham against his people.[868] [c]We exalt in degrees of rank whomso We please. Thy Lord is indeed Wise, All-Knowing.

وَتِلْكَ حُجَّتُنَآ اٰتَيْنٰهَآ إِبْرٰهِيمَ عَلٰى قَوْمِهٖ ۚ نَرْفَعُ
دَرَجٰتٍ مَّنْ نَّشَآءُ ۗ إِنَّ رَبَّكَ حَكِيمٌ عَلِيمٌ ﴿٨٤﴾

85. And [d]We gave him Isaac and Jacob; each did We guide aright, and Noah did We guide aright aforetime, and of his progeny, David and Solomon and Job[869] and Joseph and Moses and Aaron. Thus do We reward those who do good.

وَوَهَبْنَا لَهٗٓ إِسْحٰقَ وَيَعْقُوبَ ۚ كُلًّا هَدَيْنَا ۚ وَنُوحًا
هَدَيْنَا مِنْ قَبْلُ وَمِنْ ذُرِّيَّتِهٖ دَاوٗدَ وَسُلَيْمٰنَ
وَأَيُّوبَ وَيُوسُفَ وَمُوسٰى وَهٰرُونَ ۚ وَكَذٰلِكَ
نَجْزِي الْمُحْسِنِينَ ﴿٨٥﴾

[a]7 : 34; 22 : 72. [b]31 : 14. [c]12: 77. [d]29 : 28.

clearly shows that by the line of arguments he adopted Abraham intended gradually to draw his people to God. A simple glance over vv. 80-82 makes it crystal clear that Abraham not only possessed firm faith in God but also had a deep knowledge of Divine attributes.

867. This and the preceding two verses definitely show that the incident related in vv. 77-79 was deliberately used by Abraham by way of argument; otherwise he himself was a staunch monotheist and had drunk deep at the fount of Divine love and knowledge.

868. This verse definitely settles the question whether Abraham gradually came to have faith in God by taking one heavenly body after another for his Lord or whether it was a skilfully graduated argument by means of which he sought to demonstrate the error of his people in worshipping these heavenly bodies as gods. The verse shows that Abraham had, from the beginning, been clear and firm in his faith in the Unity of God and that what he said concerning the sun and the moon, etc. was part of the argument which God had taught him.

869. Ayyūb or Job is the hero of the Book of Job. He is mentioned in the Bible as living in the land of Uz. Some authorities say that this is Idumea or Arabia Deserta; others fix Mesopotamia as his native place. It appears that Uz was somewhere in the north of Arabia. It is said that Job lived there before the departure of the Israelites from Egypt. He thus lived before Moses or, as some say, he was a compatriot of Moses, having received his prophetic mission about 20 years before him. He was not an Israelite, having descended

86. And *We guided* Zachariah and John and Jesus and Elias; each *one of them* was of the righteous.

وَزَكَرِيَّا وَيَحْيٰى وَعِيْسٰى وَإِلْيَاسَ ۖ كُلٌّ مِّنَ الصّٰلِحِيْنَ ﴿٨٦﴾

87. And *We also guided* Ishmael and Elisha and Jonah and Lot ! and [a]each *one of them* did We exalt above the people.[870]

وَإِسْمٰعِيْلَ وَالْيَسَعَ وَيُوْنُسَ وَلُوْطًا ۚ وَكُلًّا فَضَّلْنَا عَلَى الْعٰلَمِيْنَ ﴿٨٧﴾

88. And *We exalted* some of their fathers and their children and their brethren, and We chose them and We guided them in the straight path.

وَمِنْ اٰبَآئِهِمْ وَذُرِّيّٰتِهِمْ وَإِخْوَانِهِمْ ۚ وَاجْتَبَيْنٰهُمْ وَهَدَيْنٰهُمْ إِلٰى صِرَاطٍ مُّسْتَقِيْمٍ ﴿٨٨﴾

89. That is the guidance of Allāh. He guides thereby those of His servants whom He pleases. And [b]if they had worshipped aught beside Him, surely all they did would have been of no avail to them.

ذٰلِكَ هُدَى اللّٰهِ يَهْدِيْ بِهٖ مَنْ يَّشَآءُ مِنْ عِبَادِهٖ ۚ وَلَوْ أَشْرَكُوْا لَحَبِطَ عَنْهُمْ مَّا كَانُوْا يَعْمَلُوْنَ ﴿٨٩﴾

[a]2 : 49; 3 :34-35; 45 : 17. [b]39 : 66.

from Esau, the elder brother of Israel. He had a very chequered career, being "tried" by God in diverse ways; but he proved most faithful and righteous and was patient and steadfast in extreme adversity. He still lives in the memory of mankind as a paragon of patience (Jewish Enc. & Enc. of Islām).

870. The prophets descending from Noah have been divided in the present and the preceding two verses into three different groups and to each group has been added a distinctive adjective. The first group comprises David, Solomon, Job, Joseph, Moses and Aaron—Prophets who were given power and prosperity, and who consequently were able to do good to their fellow human beings. Hence members of this group have been designated as "doers of good," for, through their temporal power and prosperity they were able to do material good to their people. David and Solomon were kings; Joseph and Job were blessed with prosperity after they had been tried with afflictions which they both bore with extra-ordinary patience. Moses and Aaron enjoyed supreme authority over their people. The second group includes Zachariah, John, Jesus and Elias. None of these Prophets possessed temporal power or worldly goods; each lived a humble and lowly life, so much so that of Elias it is said that he was rarely seen and generally lived in the woods. The Prophets of this group have been described as "righteous." The third group consists of Ishmael, Elisha, Jonah and Lot. They had no worldly power, but God granted them grace and excellence. They were alleged to have coveted power and riches. Of Ishmael, we read in the Bible: "He will be a wild man; his hand will be against every man, and every man's hand against him" (Gen. 16:12). Of Elisha it is said that he caused a king who did not obey him to be slain so that he might thus gain political power. Jonah is supposed to have become displeased with God, because, as he thought, he was disgraced by the non-fulfilment of his prophecy, which, it is alleged, showed that he sought power for himself. Of Lot it is alleged that he coveted fertile pasture-lands and was always quarrelling with his kinsman, Abraham. Thus all these Prophets have been accused of coveting wealth and power. But Qur'ān declares all these charges to be false. They were a group of heavenly people whom God had exalted.

90. It is these to [a]whom We gave the Book[871] and dominion and Prophethood. But if they are ungrateful for these *favours it matters not*, for We have *now* entrusted them to a people who are not ungrateful for them.

أُولٰٓئِكَ الَّذِيْنَ اٰتَيْنٰهُمُ الْكِتٰبَ وَالْحُكْمَ وَالنُّبُوَّةَ
فَاِنْ يَّكْفُرْ بِهَا هٰٓؤُلَآءِ فَقَدْ وَكَّلْنَا بِهَا قَوْمًا لَّيْسُوْا
بِهَا بِكٰفِرِيْنَ ﴿٩٠﴾

91. These it is whom Allāh guided aright, so follow thou their guidance.[872] Say, 'I ask not of you any reward for it. This is naught but an admonition for all mankind.'

أُولٰٓئِكَ الَّذِيْنَ هَدَى اللّٰهُ فَبِهُدٰىهُمُ اقْتَدِهْ قُلْ لَّآ
اَسْـَٔلُكُمْ عَلَيْهِ اَجْرًا اِنْ هُوَ اِلَّا ذِكْرٰى لِلْعٰلَمِيْنَ ﴿٩١﴾ ع

R.11 92. And [b]they do not make a just estimate *of the attributes* of Allāh, when [c]they say, 'Allāh has not revealed anything to any man.'[873] Say, 'Who revealed the Book which Moses brought, a light and guidance for the people—though you treat it as scraps of paper, *some of* which you show while you hide

وَمَا قَدَرُوا اللّٰهَ حَقَّ قَدْرِهٖٓ اِذْ قَالُوْا مَآ اَنْزَلَ اللّٰهُ
عَلٰى بَشَرٍ مِّنْ شَيْءٍ قُلْ مَنْ اَنْزَلَ الْكِتٰبَ الَّذِيْ جَآءَ
بِهٖ مُوْسٰى نُوْرًا وَّهُدًى لِّلنَّاسِ تَجْعَلُوْنَهٗ قَرَاطِيْسَ

[a]45 : 17. [b]22 : 75; 39 : 68. [c]36 : 16; 67 : 10.

871. The verse does not mean that every Prophet was given a separate Book. "Giving of the Book" is an expression used in the Qur'ān generally in the sense of giving it through a Law-bearing Prophet. Elsewhere in the Qur'ān (45 : 17) it is stated that three things, *viz*., Book, dominion and Prophethood were given to all the Children of Israel. In 5:45 we read that a galaxy of Prophets appeared after Moses who were given no new Law but followed the Law as given in the Torah and judged by it. In fact, Prophets are of two categories—Law-bearing Prophets to whom a Book (Law or the *Sharī'ah*) is given and Prophets, who are given no Book or *Sharī'ah*, and who follow the *Sharī'ah* of the Law-bearing Prophet. In their case the expression "We gave them the Book" means that they were given the knowledge of the Book or they inherited the Book or the *Sharī'ah* from their Law-bearing predecessor.

872. The words may be taken to have been addressed either to the Holy Prophet or to every Muslim, because the fundamental teaching of all Prophets is the same. Or they may signify that the spiritual self or nature of the Holy Prophet was such that it was, as if, commanded to combine in itself all the excellent qualities that were to be found individually in all other Divine Prophets. The command expressed by the words "follow them" is in spiritual terminology called *Amr Kaunī* or *Khalqī* signifying a wish or quality inherent in a thing or person. For instances of such a command see 3 : 60 and 21 : 70.

873. The words mean, " If this Book (the Qur'ān) has not been revealed by God, then who embodied in it such wise and comprehensive teachings as were known neither to you nor to your forefathers—teachings which it was beyond your power to produce. Only God could give such teachings."

much *thereof*[874] and you have been taught that which neither you nor your fathers knew?' Say, 'Allāh.' Then leave them to amuse themselves with their idle talk.

تُبْدُونَهَا وَتُخْفُونَ كَثِيرًا ۚ وَعُلِّمْتُم مَّا لَمْ تَعْلَمُوٓا أَنتُمْ وَلَآ ءَابَآؤُكُمْ ۖ قُلِ ٱللَّهُ ۖ ثُمَّ ذَرْهُمْ فِى خَوْضِهِمْ يَلْعَبُونَ ﴿٩٢﴾

93. And [a]this is a Book which We have revealed, full of blessings, to fulfil that which preceded it, and to enable thee [b]to warn the Mother of towns[875] and those around her. And those, who believe in the Hereafter believe therein[876] and [c]they strictly observe their Prayers.

وَهَٰذَا كِتَٰبٌ أَنزَلْنَٰهُ مُبَارَكٌ مُّصَدِّقُ ٱلَّذِى بَيْنَ يَدَيْهِ وَلِتُنذِرَ أُمَّ ٱلْقُرَىٰ وَمَنْ حَوْلَهَا ۚ وَٱلَّذِينَ يُؤْمِنُونَ بِٱلْءَاخِرَةِ يُؤْمِنُونَ بِهِۦ ۖ وَهُمْ عَلَىٰ صَلَاتِهِمْ يُحَافِظُونَ ﴿٩٣﴾

94. And [d]who is more unjust than he who forges a lie against Allāh, or says, 'It has been revealed to me,' while nothing has been revealed to him; and who says, 'I will send down the like of that which Allāh has sent down?' And if thou couldst only see, when the wrongdoers are in the agonies of death,[877] and the angels stretch forth their hands, *saying*, 'Yield up your souls. [e]This day shall you be awarded the punishment of disgrace because of that which you spoke against Allāh falsely and *because* you turned away from His Signs with disdain.'

وَمَنْ أَظْلَمُ مِمَّنِ ٱفْتَرَىٰ عَلَى ٱللَّهِ كَذِبًا أَوْ قَالَ أُوحِىَ إِلَىَّ وَلَمْ يُوحَ إِلَيْهِ شَىْءٌ وَمَن قَالَ سَأُنزِلُ مِثْلَ مَآ أَنزَلَ ٱللَّهُ ۗ وَلَوْ تَرَىٰٓ إِذِ ٱلظَّٰلِمُونَ فِى غَمَرَٰتِ ٱلْمَوْتِ وَٱلْمَلَٰٓئِكَةُ بَاسِطُوٓا أَيْدِيهِمْ أَخْرِجُوٓا أَنفُسَكُمُ ۖ ٱلْيَوْمَ تُجْزَوْنَ عَذَابَ ٱلْهُونِ بِمَا كُنتُمْ تَقُولُونَ عَلَى ٱللَّهِ غَيْرَ ٱلْحَقِّ وَكُنتُمْ عَنْ ءَايَٰتِهِۦ تَسْتَكْبِرُونَ ﴿٩٤﴾

[a]6 : 156; 21 : 51; 38 : 30. [b]42 : 8. [c]23 : 10; 70 : 24. [d]6 : 22; 7 : 38; 10 : 18; 11 : 19; 61 : 8. [e]46 : 21.

874. The Jews have been condemned here for disclosing one part of the Torah and hiding the other part which contains prophecies and Signs about the advent of the Holy Prophet.

875. The place where a Prophet of God appears is called "The Mother of towns," for it is there that men drink spiritual milk, even as a child sucks milk from the breast of its mother. The words, *those around her*, may signify the whole world as the Message of the Holy Prophet was meant for the whole of mankind.

876. These words show that a believer in the life to come must believe in the Qur'ān also. Thus belief in the Qur'ān and belief in the Hereafter are inseparably linked together; the one is meaningless without the other.

877. This torment is not to be identified with the ordinary agonies of death, which are shared, under the general law of nature, by righteous and unrighteous alike, but to the specific punishment that clings to the rejectors of Prophets from the very moment of their death.

95. And *now* [a]you come to Us one by one even as We created you at first, and you have left behind your[878] backs that which we bestowed upon you, and We do not see with you your intercessors of whom you asserted that they were partners *with Allāh in* your affairs. Now you have been cut off from one another and that which you asserted has failed you.

وَلَقَدْ جِئْتُمُونَا فُرَادٰى كَمَا خَلَقْنٰكُمْ اَوَّلَ مَرَّةٍ
وَّتَرَكْتُمْ مَّا خَوَّلْنٰكُمْ وَرَآءَ ظُهُوْرِكُمْ ۚ وَمَا نَرٰى مَعَكُمْ
شُفَعَآءَكُمُ الَّذِيْنَ زَعَمْتُمْ اَنَّهُمْ فِيْكُمْ شُرَكٰٓؤُا ۭ
ع لَقَدْ تَّقَطَّعَ بَيْنَكُمْ وَضَلَّ عَنْكُمْ مَّا كُنْتُمْ تَزْعُمُوْنَ ﴿٩٥﴾

R. 12 96. Verily, it is Allāh Who causes the grain and the date-stones to sprout.[879] [b]He brings forth the living from the dead, and *He is* the Bringer forth of the dead from the living. That is Allāh; wherefore, then, are you turned back?

اِنَّ اللّٰهَ فَالِقُ الْحَبِّ وَالنَّوٰى ۭ يُخْرِجُ الْحَيَّ مِنَ
الْمَيِّتِ وَمُخْرِجُ الْمَيِّتِ مِنَ الْحَيِّ ۭ ذٰلِكُمُ اللّٰهُ فَاَنّٰى
تُؤْفَكُوْنَ ﴿٩٦﴾

97. [c]He causes the break of day and [d]He made the night for rest[880] and the sun and the moon for the reckoning *of time*.[881] That is the measuring of the Mighty, the Wise.

فَالِقُ الْاِصْبَاحِ ۚ وَجَعَلَ الَّيْلَ سَكَنًا وَّالشَّمْسَ وَالْقَمَرَ
حُسْبَانًا ۭ ذٰلِكَ تَقْدِيْرُ الْعَزِيْزِ الْعَلِيْمِ ﴿٩٧﴾

[a]18 : 49. [b]3 : 28; 10 : 32; 30 : 20. [c]113 : 2. [d]25 : 48; 78 : 11; [e]36 : 39-40; 55 : 6.

878. The words mean, "We gave you certain things so that you might thereby improve your spiritual condition, but you have left them behind your backs, *i.e.*, you made no use of them, and now the time for their use has passed away."

879. Attention is drawn to the seed from which a plant sprouts. How insignificant it is but how it grows and develops into a big tree. Similarly, like a seed, man is capable of growing into the recipient of Divine revelation and of being the reflector of God's great attributes.

880. Just as by working during the day, a man gets tired and he goes to sleep at night and is refreshed similarly, the people among whom the Holy Prophet made his appearance had a long night of rest, and their faculties having been re-invigorated they were full of spiritual energy and were eminently fitted to ascend the heights of spiritual development under his lead.

881. Just as in the physical world the sun and the moon are indispensable for measuring time and as sources of light, so are the Prophets of God indispensable in the spiritual world.

98. And He it is [a]Who has made the stars[882] for you that you may follow the right direction with their help amid the darkness of the land and the sea. We have explained the Signs in detail for a people who possess knowledge.

وَهُوَ الَّذِي جَعَلَ لَكُمُ النُّجُومَ لِتَهْتَدُوا بِهَا فِي
ظُلُمٰتِ الْبَرِّ وَالْبَحْرِ قَدْ فَصَّلْنَا الْاٰيٰتِ لِقَوْمٍ
يَّعْلَمُوْنَ ﴿٩٨﴾

99. And He it is [b]Who has produced you from a single soul and *there is for you* a temporary [c]resort and a permanent abode.[883] We have explained the Signs in detail for a people who understand.

وَهُوَ الَّذِيْٓ اَنْشَاَكُمْ مِّنْ نَّفْسٍ وَّاحِدَةٍ فَمُسْتَقَرٌّ
وَّمُسْتَوْدَعٌ قَدْ فَصَّلْنَا الْاٰيٰتِ لِقَوْمٍ يَّفْقَهُوْنَ ﴿٩٩﴾

100. And [d]He it is Who sends down water from the cloud; and We bring forth therewith every kind of growth; then We bring forth with that green foliage wherefrom We produce clustered grain. And from the date-palm, out of its sheaths *come forth* bunches hanging low. And *We produce therewith* [e]gardens of grapes, and the olive and the pomegranate—like and unlike. Look at the fruit thereof when it bears fruit, and the ripening thereof. Surely, in this are Signs for a people who believe.[884]

وَهُوَ الَّذِيْٓ اَنْزَلَ مِنَ السَّمَآءِ مَآءً فَاَخْرَجْنَا بِهٖ
نَبَاتَ كُلِّ شَيْءٍ فَاَخْرَجْنَا مِنْهُ خَضِرًا نُّخْرِجُ مِنْهُ
حَبًّا مُّتَرَاكِبًا وَمِنَ النَّخْلِ مِنْ طَلْعِهَا قِنْوَانٌ دَانِيَةٌ
وَّجَنّٰتٍ مِّنْ اَعْنَابٍ وَّالزَّيْتُوْنَ وَالرُّمَّانَ مُشْتَبِهًا
وَّغَيْرَ مُتَشَابِهٍ اُنْظُرُوْٓا اِلٰى ثَمَرِهٖٓ اِذَآ اَثْمَرَ وَيَنْعِهٖ
اِنَّ فِيْ ذٰلِكُمْ لَاٰيٰتٍ لِّقَوْمٍ يُّؤْمِنُوْنَ ﴿١٠٠﴾

[a]16 : 17. [b]4 : 3; 7 : 190; 39 : 7. [c]11 : 7. [d]14 : 33; 16 : 11; 22 : 64; 35 : 28. [e]6 : 142; 13 : 5.

882. Like the stars which guide the wayfarers in the night, the Divine and spiritual savants give guidance to the erring people groping in spiritual darkness.

883. *Mustaqarr* signifies the life of this world and *Mustauda'* the life after death, or the former word signifies the span between death and Resurrection and the latter the life after Resurrection. The verse signifies that when God has multiplied humanity out of "a single soul," it could not have been without a purpose. The great object for which He has created and multiplied human beings is that He has appointed for them not only a period of residence on this earth but also an everlasting life beyond the grave where the righteous will meet their Lord—a lofty goal indeed to which they can only rise under the guidance of Divine Messengers.

884. Revelation is likened here to rain-water, and the verse answers the question, why, if revelation is indeed a blessing, is there discord and strife whenever a Prophet is raised? It says that just as after rainfall all kinds of vegetation grow up, both bad and good, according to the seeds lying concealed in the earth, similarly, at the advent of a Divine Messenger, men, who so far had remained mixed up, become divided into good and bad. The words "like and unlike" imply that whereas some fruits resemble, and some differ from, each other.

101. And [a]they hold the jinn[885] to be partners with Allāh, although He created them; and they falsely ascribe to Him sons and daughters without any knowledge. Holy is He and exalted *far* above what they attribute *to Him*,

وَجَعَلُوْا لِلّٰهِ شُرَكَآءَ الْجِنَّ وَخَلَقَهُمْ وَخَرَقُوْا لَهٗ
بَنِيْنَ وَبَنٰتٍۢ بِغَيْرِ عِلْمٍ ؕ سُبْحٰنَهٗ وَتَعٰلٰى عَمَّا
يَصِفُوْنَ ﴿۱۰۱﴾

R. 13 102. [b]The Originator of the heavens and the earth. How can He have a son[886] when He has no consort, and *when* He has created everything and has knowledge of all things?

بَدِيْعُ السَّمٰوٰتِ وَالْاَرْضِ ؕ اَنّٰى يَكُوْنُ لَهٗ وَلَدٌ وَّ
لَمْ تَكُنْ لَّهٗ صَاحِبَةٌ ؕ وَخَلَقَ كُلَّ شَيْءٍ ۚ وَهُوَ بِكُلِّ
شَيْءٍ عَلِيْمٌ ﴿۱۰۲﴾

103. [c]Such is Allāh, your Lord. There is no god but He, [d]the Creator of all things; so worship Him. And He is Guardian over everything.

ذٰلِكُمُ اللّٰهُ رَبُّكُمْ ۚ لَآ اِلٰهَ اِلَّا هُوَ ۚ خَالِقُ كُلِّ شَيْءٍ
فَاعْبُدُوْهُ ۚ وَهُوَ عَلٰى كُلِّ شَيْءٍ وَّكِيْلٌ ﴿۱۰۳﴾

104. Eyes cannot reach Him but He reaches the eyes.[887] And [e]He is the Incomprehensible, the All-Aware.

لَا تُدْرِكُهُ الْاَبْصَارُ ۫ وَهُوَ يُدْرِكُ الْاَبْصَارَ ۚ وَهُوَ
اللَّطِيْفُ الْخَبِيْرُ ﴿۱۰۴﴾

---

[a]2 : 117; 9 : 31; 10 : 19. [b]2 : 118. [c]40 : 63. [d]13 : 17; 39 : 63. [e]22 : 64; 67 : 15.

This may apply either to fruits of different kinds, which resemble one another in certain respects and differ in others, or to fruits of the same kind which, although resembling one another in the main points, differ from one another in minor details, some tasting sweeter than others and some varying in colour or size. The same is the case with those persons who accept a Prophet and follow Divine guidance. Whereas they bear great resemblance to each other in one respect, they differ in another. Some are morally and spiritually more advanced than others. Again, some are more advanced in one phase of spiritual growth, others are more advanced in another. They attain to different stages of spiritual perfection and develop different characteristics according to their respective natural capacities and dispositions. The words "the ripening thereof" refer to the analogy of the ripening of fruit. Just as it is unfair to judge a fruit by an unripe specimen, similarly it is unfair to find fault with the fruits of revelation because some believers are as yet in the process of spiritual development and have not attained perfection.

885. Jinn are such beings as remain hidden or aloof from the common people. The verse signifies that man stumbles when he rejects Divine revelation and follows his own judgment and reason and associates the jinn and the angels as co-partners with God and attributes sons and daughters to Him.

886. The word *Waladun*, *Wuldun* or *Waldun* means, a child, a son, a daughter, or any young one; children; sons, daughters; or young ones; also offspring (Lane). One can have a son only when one has a wife. God has no spouse, so He cannot have a son. Moreover, as God is the Creator of everything and possesses perfect knowledge, He does not need a son to help Him or succeed Him.

887. *Abṣār* being the plural of *Baṣar* which means, sight or understanding, and *Laṭīf* meaning, incomprehensible; subtle (Lane & Tāj), the verse means that human reason alone, unaided by Divine revelation, is incapable of comprehending God. He cannot be seem

105. [a]Proofs[888] have indeed come to you from your Lord; so whoever sees,[889] it is for his own good; and whoever becomes blind,[890] it is to his own loss. And I am not a guardian[891] over you.

قَدْ جَآءَكُمْ بَصَآئِرُ مِنْ رَّبِّكُمْ ۚ فَمَنْ اَبْصَرَ فَلِنَفْسِهٖ ۚ وَمَنْ عَمِيَ فَعَلَيْهَا ۗ وَمَآ اَنَا عَلَيْكُمْ بِحَفِيْظٍ ﴿١٠٥﴾

106. And [b]thus do We explain the Signs in various ways *that the truth may become established* and that they may say, 'Thou hast read out *what thou hast learnt*' and that We may explain it to a people who have knowledge.

وَكَذٰلِكَ نُصَرِّفُ الْاٰيٰتِ وَلِيَقُوْلُوْا دَرَسْتَ وَلِنُبَيِّنَهٗ لِقَوْمٍ يَّعْلَمُوْنَ ﴿١٠٦﴾

107. [c]Follow that which has been revealed to thee from thy Lord; there is no god but He; and turn aside from the idolaters.

اِتَّبِعْ مَآ اُوْحِيَ اِلَيْكَ مِنْ رَّبِّكَ ۚ لَآ اِلٰهَ اِلَّا هُوَ ۚ وَاَعْرِضْ عَنِ الْمُشْرِكِيْنَ ﴿١٠٧﴾

108. And if Allāh had *enforced* His Will,[892] they would not have set up gods *with Him*. And [d]We have not made thee a keeper over them, nor art thou over them a guardian.[893]

وَلَوْ شَآءَ اللّٰهُ مَآ اَشْرَكُوْا ۗ وَمَا جَعَلْنٰكَ عَلَيْهِمْ حَفِيْظًا ۚ وَمَآ اَنْتَ عَلَيْهِمْ بِوَكِيْلٍ ﴿١٠٨﴾

---

[a]7 : 204. [b]7 : 59. [c]10 : 110; 33 : 3. [d]39 : 42; 42: 7; 88 : 23.

---

with physical eyes but reveals Himself to man through His Prophets or through the working of His attributes. He is also perceived by spiritual eyes.

888. *Baṣā'ir* (plural of *Baṣīrah*) means, proofs, arguments, signs, evidences (Lane).

889. Makes use of reason.

890. Shuts his eyes to truth and virtually becomes blind.

891. The duty of a Divine Prophet is confined to conveying what is revealed to him by God. It is not his business to compel people to accept it. Incidentally, the verse constitutes a refutation of the charge that Islām encourages or countenances the use of force for the propagation of its teaching.

892. In His infinite wisdom God has made man a free agent. If at all He should have compelled the people He would certainly have compelled them to follow the truth; but in the interest of man himself it has not pleased God to use compulsion.

893. The words "guardian," "keeper" or "disposer of affairs" used for the Holy Prophet in the Qur'ān are intended to signify that he is not responsible for the actions of other people.

109. And abuse[894] not those whom they call upon besides Allāh, lest they, out of spite, abuse Allāh in their ignorance. Thus [a]unto every people have We caused their doings *to seem* fair.[895] Then unto their Lord is their return; and He will inform them of what they used to do.

وَلَا تَسُبُّوا الَّذِينَ يَدْعُونَ مِنْ دُونِ اللّٰهِ فَيَسُبُّوا
اللّٰهَ عَدْوًا بِغَيْرِ عِلْمٍ كَذٰلِكَ زَيَّنَّا لِكُلِّ أُمَّةٍ
عَمَلَهُمْ ثُمَّ إِلٰى رَبِّهِمْ مَرْجِعُهُمْ فَيُنَبِّئُهُمْ بِمَا
كَانُوا يَعْمَلُونَ ﴿١٠٩﴾

110. And they swear by Allāh their strongest oaths that if there came to them a Sign, they would surely believe therein. Say, 'Surely, Signs are with Allāh. And what should make you know that when *the Signs* come, they will not believe?[896]

وَأَقْسَمُوا بِاللّٰهِ جَهْدَ أَيْمَانِهِمْ لَئِنْ جَاءَتْهُمْ آيَةٌ
لَيُؤْمِنُنَّ بِهَا قُلْ إِنَّمَا الْآيٰتُ عِنْدَ اللّٰهِ وَمَا يُشْعِرُكُمْ
أَنَّهَا إِذَا جَاءَتْ لَا يُؤْمِنُونَ ﴿١١٠﴾

111. And We shall confound their hearts and their eyes, for they believed not therein the first time, and [b]We shall leave them in their transgression to wander in distraction.[897]

وَنُقَلِّبُ أَفْئِدَتَهُمْ وَأَبْصَارَهُمْ كَمَا لَمْ يُؤْمِنُوا بِهِ أَوَّلَ
مَرَّةٍ وَنَذَرُهُمْ فِي طُغْيَانِهِمْ يَعْمَهُونَ ﴿١١١﴾ ع

الجزء ٨

PART VIII

R. 14 112. And even if We send down unto them angels, and [c]the dead[898]

وَلَوْ أَنَّنَا نَزَّلْنَا إِلَيْهِمُ الْمَلٰئِكَةَ وَكَلَّمَهُمُ الْمَوْتٰى

[a]6 : 123; 9 : 37; 10 : 13; 27 : 5; 40 : 38; 49 : 8. [b]2 :16. [c]13 : 32.

894. The verse not only inculcates respect for the susceptibilities of even the idol-worshippers but also seeks to create amity among different nations and communities.

895. *Zayyannā* does not mean that God Himself causes the evil actions of man to look fair. It only signifies that He has so created human nature (and in this law of God lies the secret of man's all-round progress) that when he persists in doing a certain action he acquires a liking for it, and his action begins to appear good in his sight. In accordance with this general Divine law, the idolaters come to like their worship of idols, which appears to them to be good and meritorious.

896. Besides the meaning given in the text the latter part of the verse may be rendered as: "Surely, Signs are with Allāh, and also that is with Allāh which will make you know that when the Signs come, they will not believe.

897. The past evil deeds of disbelievers, which are preserved with God, stand in the way of their accepting the truth even after Signs come to them, unless they give up their idolatrous practices.

898. One of the functions of the angels is to suggest good ideas to men and to invite them to truth (41:32, 33). Sometimes they perform this function through dreams and visions. The righteous, who are dead, appear to men in dreams to testify to the claim of the Prophets. There is another way in which the dead speak to men. When a people who are spiritually

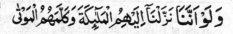

speak to them, and We gather to them all things face to face,[899] they would not believe, unless God *enforced* His Will. But most of them are ignorant.

وَ حَشَرْنَا عَلَيْهِمْ كُلَّ شَىْءٍ قُبُلًا مَّا كَانُوْا لِيُؤْمِنُوْۤا اِلَّاۤ اَنْ يَّشَآءَ اللّٰهُ وَ لٰكِنَّ اَكْثَرَهُمْ يَجْهَلُوْنَ ۞

113. And ^ain like manner have We made for every Prophet an enemy, the evil ones from among men and jinn.[900] They suggest one to another gilded speech in order to deceive. And if thy Lord had *enforced* His Will, they would not have done it; so leave them alone with that which they fabricate.

وَ كَذٰلِكَ جَعَلْنَا لِكُلِّ نَبِيٍّ عَدُوًّا شَيٰطِيْنَ الْاِنْسِ وَ الْجِنِّ يُوْحِىْ بَعْضُهُمْ اِلٰى بَعْضٍ زُخْرُفَ الْقَوْلِ غُرُوْرًا ؕ وَ لَوْ شَآءَ رَبُّكَ مَا فَعَلُوْهُ فَذَرْهُمْ وَ مَا يَفْتَرُوْنَ ۞

114. And *Allāh does this* in order that the hearts of those who believe not in the Hereafter may incline thereto and that they may be pleased therewith and that they may *continue to* earn what they are earning.[900A]

وَ لِتَصْغٰۤى اِلَيْهِ اَفْـِٕدَةُ الَّذِيْنَ لَا يُؤْمِنُوْنَ بِالْاٰخِرَةِ وَ لِيَرْضَوْهُ وَ لِيَقْتَرِفُوْا مَا هُمْ مُّقْتَرِفُوْنَ ۞

115. Shall I seek for a judge other than Allāh, when ^bHe it is Who has sent down to you the Book, fully explained? And those to whom We gave the Book[901] know that it has been sent down from thy Lord with truth; so be thou not of those who doubt.

اَفَغَيْرَ اللّٰهِ اَبْتَغِىْ حَكَمًا وَّ هُوَ الَّذِىْۤ اَنْزَلَ اِلَيْكُمُ الْكِتٰبَ مُفَصَّلًا ؕ وَ الَّذِيْنَ اٰتَيْنٰهُمُ الْكِتٰبَ يَعْلَمُوْنَ اَنَّهٗ مُنَزَّلٌ مِّنْ رَّبِّكَ بِالْحَقِّ فَلَا تَكُوْنَنَّ مِنَ الْمُمْتَرِيْنَ ۞

---

^a25 : 32.   ^b7 : 53;   12 : 112;   16 : 90.   ^c2 : 147;   6 : 21.

---

dead are quickened to a new spiritual life by the teaching of their Prophet, their spiritual regeneration, as it were, speaks to the disbelievers and testifies to the truth of his claim.

899. The words refer to the testimony of the different objects of nature which bear testimony to the truth of a Prophet in the form of earthquakes, pestilences, famines, wars and other visitations. Thus nature itself appears to be angry with disbelievers; the very elements are up in arms against them.

900. The words, *men and jinn*, which occur in many verses of the Qur'ān do not signify two different species of God's creatures, but two classes of human beings; "men" denoting the masses or the common folk, and "jinn" standing for the big people who often remain aloof from the common people and do not mix with them, practically remaining hidden from public gaze.

900A. That they may persist in their evil course. The words also mean that they experience the consequences of what they earn.

901. The "Book" may also refer to the Qur'ān; for not only the previous Divine Scriptures but also the Qur'ān itself bears testimony to the truth of the Holy Prophet. It

116. And the word of thy Lord has been fulfilled in truth and justice.[901A] None can change [a]His words,[902] and He is the All-Hearing, the All-Knowing.

وَتَمَّتْ كَلِمَتُ رَبِّكَ صِدْقًا وَّعَدْلًا ۭ لَا مُبَدِّلَ لِكَلِمٰتِهٖ ۚ وَهُوَ السَّمِيْعُ الْعَلِيْمُ ﴿۱۱۶﴾

117. And if thou obey most of those on earth, they will lead thee astray from Allāh's way. [b]They follow nothing but *mere* conjecture, and they do nothing but lie.

وَاِنْ تُطِعْ اَكْثَرَ مَنْ فِي الْاَرْضِ يُضِلُّوْكَ عَنْ سَبِيْلِ اللّٰهِ ۭ اِنْ يَّتَّبِعُوْنَ اِلَّا الظَّنَّ وَاِنْ هُمْ اِلَّا يَخْرُصُوْنَ ﴿۱۱۷﴾

118. Surely, [c]thy Lord knows best those who go astray from His way; and He knows best those who are rightly guided.[903]

اِنَّ رَبَّكَ هُوَ اَعْلَمُ مَنْ يَّضِلُّ عَنْ سَبِيْلِهٖ ۚ وَهُوَ اَعْلَمُ بِالْمُهْتَدِيْنَ ﴿۱۱۸﴾

119. [d]Eat, then, of that over which the name of Allāh has been pronounced, if you are believers in His Signs.[904]

فَكُلُوْا مِمَّا ذُكِرَ اسْمُ اللّٰهِ عَلَيْهِ اِنْ كُنْتُمْ بِاٰيٰتِهٖ مُؤْمِنِيْنَ ﴿۱۱۹﴾

120. And what reason have you that you should not eat of that over which the name of Allāh has been pronounced when [e]He has already explained to you that which He has forbidden unto you,—save that which you are forced to. And surely

وَمَا لَكُمْ اَلَّا تَاْكُلُوْا مِمَّا ذُكِرَ اسْمُ اللّٰهِ عَلَيْهِ وَقَدْ فَصَّلَ لَكُمْ مَّا حَرَّمَ عَلَيْكُمْ اِلَّا مَا اضْطُرِرْتُمْ

[a]6 : 35. [b]10 : 37; 53 : 29. [c]16 : 126. [d]5 : 5. [e]2 : 174; 5 : 4-5; 6 : 146; 16 : 116.

contains teachings which, though they run counter to current views and beliefs, yet fair-minded people to whom these teachings are rehearsed and explained feel constrained to acknowledge their reasonableness.

901A. It is reported that when Mecca fell and the Holy Prophet entered the Ka'bah which was at that time full of idols, and struck the idols one after the other with his stick, he recited the very words of this prophecy: *The word of thy Lord has been fulfilled in truth and justice*, thus alluding to the fact that with the Fall of Mecca the word of God had indeed been fulfilled (Manthūr).

902. The Divine prophecies or the way and manner in which God's laws work in favour of Divine Prophets.

903. In matters of faith it is neither the majority nor the minority that can be accepted as judge of what is right or wrong. God alone is the Infallible Judge. He gives His judgment by showing heavenly Signs and by helping the party which pursues the path of truth.

904. Vv. 2 : 173 and 23 : 52 show that the eating of good and pure food has a direct bearing on the actions of man. So believers are here enjoined to partake of pure and wholesome food to strengthen their faith and cleanse their hearts of impurity.

many mislead *others* by their evil desires through lack of knowledge. Assuredly, thy Lord knows best the transgressors.

إِلَيْهِ ۗ وَإِنَّ كَثِيرًا لَّيُضِلُّونَ بِأَهْوَآئِهِم بِغَيْرِ عِلْمٍ ۗ
إِنَّ رَبَّكَ هُوَ أَعْلَمُ بِالْمُعْتَدِينَ ﴿١٢٠﴾

121. And [a]eschew open sins as well as secret ones. Surely, those who earn sin will be rewarded for that which they have earned.

وَذَرُوا ظَاهِرَ الْإِثْمِ وَبَاطِنَهُ ۗ إِنَّ الَّذِينَ يَكْسِبُونَ
الْإِثْمَ سَيُجْزَوْنَ بِمَا كَانُوا يَقْتَرِفُونَ ﴿١٢١﴾

122. And [b]eat not of that on which the name of Allāh has not been pronounced,[905] for surely that is abomination. And certainly the evil ones inspire their friends *with such thoughts* that they may dispute with you. And if you obey them, you will indeed be of those who set up gods *with Allāh*.

وَلَا تَأْكُلُوا مِمَّا لَمْ يُذْكَرِ اسْمُ اللَّهِ عَلَيْهِ وَإِنَّهُ
لَفِسْقٌ ۗ وَإِنَّ الشَّيَاطِينَ لَيُوحُونَ إِلَىٰ أَوْلِيَائِهِمْ
لِيُجَادِلُوكُمْ ۖ وَإِنْ أَطَعْتُمُوهُمْ إِنَّكُمْ لَمُشْرِكُونَ ﴿١٢٢﴾ ع

R. 15 123. Can [c]he, who was dead, then We gave him life and made for him a light whereby he walks among men, be like him whose condition is *that he is* in utter darkness whence he cannot come forth?[906] [d]Thus have the doings of the disbelievers been made *to seem* fair to them.

أَوَمَن كَانَ مَيْتًا فَأَحْيَيْنَاهُ وَجَعَلْنَا لَهُ نُورًا
يَمْشِي بِهِ فِي النَّاسِ كَمَن مَّثَلُهُ فِي الظُّلُمَاتِ لَيْسَ
بِخَارِجٍ مِّنْهَا ۚ كَذَٰلِكَ زُيِّنَ لِلْكَافِرِينَ مَا كَانُوا
يَعْمَلُونَ ﴿١٢٣﴾

124. And thus [e]have We made in every town the leaders of its wicked ones *that their doings seem fair to them* with the result that they plot therein *against the Messengers of Allāh* and they plot not except against their own souls; but they perceive not.

وَكَذَٰلِكَ جَعَلْنَا فِي كُلِّ قَرْيَةٍ أَكَابِرَ مُجْرِمِيهَا لِيَمْكُرُوا
فِيهَا ۖ وَمَا يَمْكُرُونَ إِلَّا بِأَنفُسِهِمْ وَمَا يَشْعُرُونَ ﴿١٢٤﴾

---

[a]6 : 152; 7 : 34. [b]5 : 4; 6 : 146. [c]8 : 25. [d]6 : 109; 10: 13; 27 : 5. [e]17 : 17.

---

905. The verse explains why it is forbidden to eat such animals as die of themselves or such as are not duly slaughtered with an invocation of the name of God. The pronouncement of the name of God produces sanctifying effect on man's heart which nullifies the hardening effect which the killing of the animal is likely to produce.

906. In the foregoing verses it was pointed out that man-made laws are always defective. Now it is mentioned in the present verse that man-made teachings cannot stand against Divine teachings. The case of those who devise laws, with the aid of human reason alone, is like one who gropes in darkness from which he will never come out.

125. And when there comes to them a Sign, they say, "We will not believe until we are given the like of that which Allāh's Messengers have been given.' Allāh knows best where to place His Message.906A Surely, humiliation before Allāh and a severe punishment shall afflict the offenders because of their plotting.

وَ اِذَا جَآءَتْهُمْ اٰيَةٌ قَالُوْا لَنْ نُّؤْمِنَ حَتّٰى نُؤْتٰى مِثْلَ مَآ اُوْتِيَ رُسُلُ اللّٰهِ ؕ اَللّٰهُ اَعْلَمُ حَيْثُ يَجْعَلُ رِسَالَتَهٗ ؕ سَيُصِيْبُ الَّذِيْنَ اَجْرَمُوْا صَغَارٌ عِنْدَ اللّٰهِ وَ عَذَابٌ شَدِيْدٌ بِمَا كَانُوْا يَمْكُرُوْنَ ۝

126. So, whomsoever Allāh intends to guide, He expands his bosom for *the acceptance of* Islām; and whomsoever He intends that he should go astray, He makes his bosom narrow *and* close, as though he were mounting up into the skies.907 Thus does bAllāh inflict punishment on those who do not believe.

فَمَنْ يُّرِدِ اللّٰهُ اَنْ يَّهْدِيَهٗ يَشْرَحْ صَدْرَهٗ لِلْاِسْلَامِ ۚ وَ مَنْ يُّرِدْ اَنْ يُّضِلَّهٗ يَجْعَلْ صَدْرَهٗ ضَيِّقًا حَرَجًا كَاَنَّمَا يَصَّعَّدُ فِى السَّمَآءِ ؕ كَذٰلِكَ يَجْعَلُ اللّٰهُ الرِّجْسَ عَلَى الَّذِيْنَ لَا يُؤْمِنُوْنَ ۝

127. And 'this is the path of thy Lord *leading* straight *to Him*. We have, indeed, explained the Signs in detail for a people who would be admonished.

وَ هٰذَا صِرَاطُ رَبِّكَ مُسْتَقِيْمًا ؕ قَدْ فَصَّلْنَا الْاٰيٰتِ لِقَوْمٍ يَّذَّكَّرُوْنَ ۝

128. For them is dthe abode of peace with their Lord, and He is their Friend because of their works.

لَهُمْ دَارُ السَّلٰمِ عِنْدَ رَبِّهِمْ وَ هُوَ وَلِيُّهُمْ بِمَا كَانُوْا يَعْمَلُوْنَ ۝

129. And eon the day when He will gather them all together, *He will say*, 'O company908 of jinn! you won

وَ يَوْمَ يَحْشُرُهُمْ جَمِيْعًا ۚ يٰمَعْشَرَ الْجِنِّ قَدِ

---

a28 : 49.   b10 : 101.   c6 : 154.   d10 : 26.   e7 : 39-40; 10 : 29; 34 : 32.

906A. Allāh knows best who is fit to be His Messenger and who is not.

907. He regards Divine commandments as a burden and finds physical difficulty and mental trouble in carrying them out. His bosom, as it were, becomes narrow like one who is climbing up a steep height.

908. *Ma'shar* means, a company of men whose affair is the same (Lane). In this verse the word *jinn* clearly signifies great and powerful men as opposed to *Ins*, *i.e.*, the weak and poor classes.

over *to yourselves*[909] a great many from among men.' And their friends from among men will say, 'Our Lord! we profited from one another, but *now* we have reached our term which Thou didst appoint for us.' He will say, 'The Fire is your abode, wherein you shall abide, save what Allāh may will.' Surely, thy Lord is Wise, All-Knowing.[910]

اسْتَكْثَرْتُمْ مِّنَ الْإِنْسِ وَقَالَ أَوْلِيَـٰٓؤُهُمْ مِّنَ الْإِنْسِ رَبَّنَا اسْتَمْتَعَ بَعْضُنَا بِبَعْضٍ وَّبَلَغْنَآ أَجَلَنَا الَّذِيٓ أَجَّلْتَ لَنَا قَالَ النَّارُ مَثْوٰىكُمْ خٰلِدِيْنَ فِيْهَآ إِلَّا مَا شَآءَ اللّٰهُ إِنَّ رَبَّكَ حَكِيْمٌ عَلِيْمٌ ﴿١٢٩﴾

130. And thus do We make some of the wrongdoers friends[910A] of each other because of what they earn.

وَكَذٰلِكَ نُوَلِّيْ بَعْضَ الظّٰلِمِيْنَ بَعْضًا بِمَا كَانُوْا يَكْسِبُوْنَ ﴿١٣٠﴾ ع ١٥

R. 16 131. [a]'O company of jinn and men! did not Messengers come to you from among yourselves who related to you My Signs and who warned you of the meeting of this your day?' They will say, 'We bear witness against ourselves.' And the worldly life deceived them. And [b]they will bear witness against themselves that they were disbelievers.

يٰمَعْشَرَ الْجِنِّ وَالْإِنْسِ أَلَمْ يَأْتِكُمْ رُسُلٌ مِّنْكُمْ يَقُصُّوْنَ عَلَيْكُمْ اٰيٰتِيْ وَيُنْذِرُوْنَكُمْ لِقَآءَ يَوْمِكُمْ هٰذَا قَالُوْا شَهِدْنَا عَلٰٓى أَنْفُسِنَا وَغَرَّتْهُمُ الْحَيٰوةُ الدُّنْيَا وَشَهِدُوْا عَلٰٓى أَنْفُسِهِمْ أَنَّهُمْ كَانُوْا كٰفِرِيْنَ ﴿١٣١﴾

132. *The Messengers are sent* because [c]thy Lord would not destroy the towns[911] unjustly while their people were unwarned.[912]

ذٰلِكَ أَنْ لَّمْ يَكُنْ رَّبُّكَ مُهْلِكَ الْقُرٰى بِظُلْمٍ وَّأَهْلُهَا غٰفِلُوْنَ ﴿١٣٢﴾

[a]39 : 72; 40 : 51; 67:9-10. [b]7 : 38. [c]11 : 118; 20 : 135; 26 : 209; 28 : 60.

909. The Arabic words may mean: (1) You have won over many from among the common masses to your side and have made them follow you; (2) you have exploited them; (3) you have attached great importance to the masses, *i.e.*, you did not accept the Truth out of fear lest the masses should cease to follow you. Just as weak people do not accept the Truth out of fear of the great, similarly the great ones are sometimes afraid of their followers and do not accept the Truth out of fear lest they should desert them.

910. The verse provides another proof of the fact that by the word "jinn" is here meant only a class of human beings, *viz.*, the great and the powerful, for it is only one class of men that exploits another class, jinn as beings different from men have never been found to exploit men, neither are Divine Messengers known to have ever been raised among them.

910A. The words may also mean, 'And thus do We set some of the evil doers over others.'

911. As the Holy Prophet was raised for all mankind, the word *al-Qurā* would in his case apply to the whole world.

912. See next page.

133. And for all are degrees *of rank* according to what they do, and thy Lord is not unmindful of what they do.

وَلِكُلٍّ دَرَجٰتٌ مِّمَّا عَمِلُوْا ۭ وَمَا رَبُّكَ بِغَافِلٍ عَمَّا
يَعْمَلُوْنَ ﴿١٣٣﴾

134. And thy Lord is Self-Sufficient, [a]Lord of mercy. If He please, [b]He can do away with you and cause to succeed you whom He pleases, even as He raised you from the posterity of other people.

وَرَبُّكَ الْغَنِيُّ ذُو الرَّحْمَةِ ۭ اِنْ يَّشَاْ يُذْهِبْكُمْ
وَيَسْتَخْلِفْ مِنْ بَعْدِكُمْ مَّا يَشَاۗءُ كَمَآ اَنْشَاَكُمْ
مِّنْ ذُرِّيَّةِ قَوْمٍ اٰخَرِيْنَ ﴿١٣٤﴾

135. Surely, [c]that which you are promised shall come to pass and you cannot frustrate it.

اِنَّ مَا تُوْعَدُوْنَ لَاٰتٍ ۙ وَّمَآ اَنْتُمْ بِمُعْجِزِيْنَ ﴿١٣٥﴾

136. Say, [d]'O my people, act according to your power.[913] I, too, am acting. Soon will you know whose will be the ultimate reward of the abode.' Surely, the wrong-doers shall not prosper.

قُلْ يٰقَوْمِ اعْمَلُوْا عَلٰی مَكَانَتِكُمْ اِنِّیْ عَامِلٌ ۚ فَسَوْفَ
تَعْلَمُوْنَ ۙ مَنْ تَكُوْنُ لَهٗ عَاقِبَةُ الدَّارِ ۭ اِنَّهٗ لَا يُفْلِحُ
الظّٰلِمُوْنَ ﴿١٣٦﴾

137. And [e]they have assigned Allāh a portion of the crops and cattle which He has produced, and they say, 'This is for Allāh,'—so they assert—'and this is for our associate-gods.' But that which is for their associate-gods reaches not Allāh while that which is for Allāh reaches their associate-gods. Evil is what they judge.[914]

وَجَعَلُوْا لِلّٰهِ مِمَّا ذَرَاَ مِنَ الْحَرْثِ وَالْاَنْعَامِ نَصِيْبًا
فَقَالُوْا هٰذَا لِلّٰهِ بِزَعْمِهِمْ وَهٰذَا لِشُرَكَاۗىِٕنَا ۚ فَمَا
كَانَ لِشُرَكَاۗىِٕهِمْ فَلَا يَصِلُ اِلَى اللّٰهِ ۚ وَمَا كَانَ
لِلّٰهِ فَهُوَ يَصِلُ اِلٰی شُرَكَاۗىِٕهِمْ ۭ سَاۗءَ مَا يَحْكُمُوْنَ ﴿١٣٧﴾

[a]6 : 148; 18 : 59. [b]4 : 134; 14 : 20; 35 : 17. [c]11 : 34; 42 : 32. [d]11 : 94, 122; 39 : 40-41. [e]16 : 57.

912. God never sends down general calamities unless He first warns people of the impending visitation by raising a Warner. Calamities referred to here are general calamities such as earthquakes, devastating wars, epidemics, etc. which smite a whole people.

913. The words also mean, (1) act according to your way; (2) do your worst. The verse holds out a challenge to the idolatrous Meccans to do their worst and exert themselves to the utmost of their power and resources to extirpate Islām and destroy the small Muslim Community, but they will utterly fail in their nefarious designs and endeavours.

914. The reference is to an idolatrous custom of the Arabs. They would divide the produce of their lands between God and their deities. If the portion which they set apart for their deities was spent for other purposes, then the portion which they had reserved for God was given away as charity in the name of their deities, but if the portion set apart for God was spent for other ends, then the portion set aside for the deities was not transferred to God.

138. And in like manner have their associate-gods[915] made the slaying of their children[916] *seem* fair to many of the idolaters that they may ruin them and cause confusion in their religion. And if Allāh had *enforced* His Will, they would not have done this; so leave them alone with that which they invent.

وَكَذَٰلِكَ زَيَّنَ لِكَثِيرٍ مِّنَ الْمُشْرِكِينَ قَتْلَ أَوْلَادِهِمْ شُرَكَآؤُهُمْ لِيُرْدُوهُمْ وَلِيَلْبِسُوا عَلَيْهِمْ دِينَهُمْ ۖ وَلَوْ شَآءَ اللَّهُ مَا فَعَلُوهُ ۖ فَذَرْهُمْ وَمَا يَفْتَرُونَ ۝

139. And they say, 'Such and such cattle and crops are forbidden.[917] None shall eat thereof save whom we please—so they assert—and there are cattle whose backs are forbidden,[918] and there are cattle over which they pronounce not the name of Allāh,[919] forging a lie against Him. Soon will He requite them for that which they have fabricated.

وَقَالُوا هَٰذِهِ أَنْعَامٌ وَحَرْثٌ حِجْرٌ لَّا يَطْعَمُهَا إِلَّا مَن نَّشَآءُ بِزَعْمِهِمْ وَأَنْعَامٌ حُرِّمَتْ ظُهُورُهَا وَأَنْعَامٌ لَّا يَذْكُرُونَ اسْمَ اللَّهِ عَلَيْهَا افْتِرَآءً عَلَيْهِ ۚ سَيَجْزِيهِم بِمَا كَانُوا يَفْتَرُونَ ۝

140. And they say, 'That which is in the wombs of such and such cattle is reserved for our males and is forbidden to our wives;[920] but if it be *born* dead, then they are *all* partakers thereof. He will reward them for their assertion. Surely, He is Wise, All-Knowing.

وَقَالُوا مَا فِي بُطُونِ هَٰذِهِ الْأَنْعَامِ خَالِصَةٌ لِّذُكُورِنَا وَمُحَرَّمٌ عَلَىٰ أَزْوَاجِنَا ۖ وَإِن يَكُن مَّيْتَةً فَهُمْ فِيهِ شُرَكَآءُ ۚ سَيَجْزِيهِمْ وَصْفَهُمْ ۚ إِنَّهُ حَكِيمٌ عَلِيمٌ ۝

---

915. The "associate-gods" here referred to are divines, soothsayers and astrologers, etc.

916. The reference is to the most atrocious practice among some Arab tribes of slaying or burying alive their female children or offering them as sacrifice at the altar of their deities to avert natural calamities. Or it may be to their superstitious vow that if they had a certain number of children they would offer one of them as sacrifice.

917. By "forbidden crops" are meant such cultivated fields as were dedicated to the idols. These could be used only by the priests that attended upon them.

918. The cattle mentioned in 5 : 104. They were not used for riding or as beasts of burden.

919. Cattle dedicated to the associate-gods of Meccan idolaters. There is no reference here to the mentioning of God's name at the time of slaughtering.

920. Another absurd custom of the Arabs.

141. Losers indeed are they who slay their children foolishly for lack of knowledge, and make unlawful what Allāh has provided for them, forging a lie against Allāh. They have indeed gone astray and are not rightly guided.

قَدْ خَسِرَ الَّذِيْنَ قَتَلُوْٓا اَوْلَادَهُمْ سَفَهًاۢ بِغَيْرِ عِلْمٍ
وَّحَرَّمُوْا مَا رَزَقَهُمُ اللّٰهُ افْتِرَآءً عَلَى اللّٰهِ ؕ قَدْ ضَلُّوْا
وَمَا كَانُوْا مُهْتَدِيْنَ ﴿١٤١﴾

R. 17 142. And [a]He it is Who produces gardens, trellised and untrellised, and the date-palm and corn-fields whose fruits vary in taste, and the olive and the pomegranate, similar and dissimilar. Eat of the fruit thereof when they bear fruit, and pay His due[921] on the day of harvest and exceed not the bounds. Surely, Allāh loves not those who exceed the bounds.

وَهُوَ الَّذِيْٓ اَنْشَاَ جَنّٰتٍ مَّعْرُوْشٰتٍ وَّغَيْرَ مَعْرُوْشٰتٍ
وَّالنَّخْلَ وَالزَّرْعَ مُخْتَلِفًا اُكُلُهٗ وَالزَّيْتُوْنَ وَالرُّمَّانَ
مُتَشَابِهًا وَّغَيْرَ مُتَشَابِهٍ ؕ كُلُوْا مِنْ ثَمَرِهٖٓ اِذَآ اَثْمَرَ
وَاٰتُوْا حَقَّهٗ يَوْمَ حَصَادِهٖ ۖ وَلَا تُسْرِفُوْا ؕ اِنَّهٗ لَا يُحِبُّ
الْمُسْرِفِيْنَ ﴿١٤٢﴾

143. And of the cattle *He has created some* for burden and *some* for slaughter. Eat of that which Allāh has provided for you, and [b]follow not in the footsteps of Satan. Surely, he is to you an open foe.[922]

وَمِنَ الْاَنْعَامِ حَمُوْلَةً وَّفَرْشًا ؕ كُلُوْا مِمَّا رَزَقَكُمُ اللّٰهُ
وَلَا تَتَّبِعُوْا خُطُوٰتِ الشَّيْطٰنِ ؕ اِنَّهٗ لَكُمْ عَدُوٌّ
مُّبِيْنٌ ﴿١٤٣﴾

144. *And [c]of the cattle He has created* eight mates—of the sheep two, and of the goats two. Say, 'Is it the two males that He has forbidden or the two females or that which the wombs of the two females contain? Inform me with knowledge if you are truthful.'

ثَمٰنِيَةَ اَزْوَاجٍ ۚ مِنَ الضَّاْنِ اثْنَيْنِ وَمِنَ الْمَعْزِ
اثْنَيْنِ ؕ قُلْ ءٰٓالذَّكَرَيْنِ حَرَّمَ اَمِ الْاُنْثَيَيْنِ اَمَّا
اشْتَمَلَتْ عَلَيْهِ اَرْحَامُ الْاُنْثَيَيْنِ ؕ نَبِّـُٔوْنِيْ بِعِلْمٍ
اِنْ كُنْتُمْ صٰدِقِيْنَ ﴿١٤٤﴾

[a]6 : 100; 13 : 5; 16 : 12; 35 : 28; 36 : 35-36. [b]See 2 : 209. [c]39 : 7.

921. In the foregoing verses reference was made to some of the idolatrous customs or foolish practices and laws which the pagan Arabs had devised for themselves. With this verse the *Sūrah* proceeds to give some of the Divine laws.

922. Apart from its primary meaning the verse also hints that the eating of lawful things is a means of safeguarding one against the attacks of Satan.

145. And of the camels two, and of the oxen two. Say, 'Is it the two males that He has forbidden[923] or the two females or that which the wombs of the two females contain? Were you present when Allāh enjoined this on you?' [a]Who is then more unjust than he who forges a lie against Allāh that he may lead men astray without knowledge? Surely, Allāh guides not the unjust people.

وَمِنَ الْإِبِلِ اثْنَيْنِ وَمِنَ الْبَقَرِ اثْنَيْنِ قُلْ آلذَّكَرَيْنِ
حَرَّمَ أَمِ الْأُنْثَيَيْنِ أَمَّا اشْتَمَلَتْ عَلَيْهِ أَرْحَامُ
الْأُنْثَيَيْنِ أَمْ كُنْتُمْ شُهَدَاءَ إِذْ وَصّٰكُمُ اللَّهُ بِهٰذَا
فَمَنْ أَظْلَمُ مِمَّنِ افْتَرٰى عَلَى اللَّهِ كَذِبًا لِيُضِلَّ النَّاسَ
ع بِغَيْرِ عِلْمٍ إِنَّ اللَّهَ لَا يَهْدِي الْقَوْمَ الظّٰلِمِينَ ﴿١٤٥﴾

R. 18 146. Say, [b]'I find not in what has been revealed to me aught forbidden to an eater *who desires* to eat it, except it be that which dies of itself or blood poured forth, or the flesh of swine—for *all* that is unclean—or [c]what is profane, on which is invoked the name of other than Allāh.[924] But whoso is driven by necessity, being neither disobedient nor exceeding the limit, then, surely, thy Lord is Most Forgiving, Merciful.'

قُلْ لَا أَجِدُ فِي مَا أُوحِيَ إِلَيَّ مُحَرَّمًا عَلٰى طَاعِمٍ يَطْعَمُهُ
إِلَّا أَنْ يَكُونَ مَيْتَةً أَوْ دَمًا مَسْفُوحًا أَوْ لَحْمَ خِنْزِيرٍ
فَإِنَّهُ رِجْسٌ أَوْ فِسْقًا أُهِلَّ لِغَيْرِ اللَّهِ بِهِ فَمَنِ اضْطُرَّ
غَيْرَ بَاغٍ وَلَا عَادٍ فَإِنَّ رَبَّكَ غَفُورٌ رَحِيمٌ ﴿١٤٦﴾

[a]6 : 22; 7 : 38; 11 : 19. [b]2 : 174; 5 : 4; 16 : 116 [c]6 : 122.

923. The idolaters are asked whether they were present when Allāh forbade the eating of oxen and camels. They are called upon to produce a Divine authority showing that the cow and the camel were really forbidden. This is so because eating of the flesh of cows and the camel is regarded as forbidden by some people on Scriptural authority—the cow by the Hindus and the camel by some Jews.

924. The verse points out that the laws made by pagan Arabs with regard to permissible and forbidden foods were arbitrary, without any wisdom underlying them; while the food-laws prescribed by Islām are based on reason and wisdom. Basically speaking, Islām forbids four things—three on the basis of their being *Rijs*, *i.e.*, unclean and impure; and one on the basis of its being *Fisq*, *i.e.*, profane and irreligious. The first-mentioned three things are carrion, the blood which pours out when an animal is slaughtered or wounded and the flesh of swine. All these are, as the verse says, *Rijs* (unclean and impure), *i.e.*, they are harmful both to the physical and moral health of man. The word *Rijs*, it must be noted, is to be read with each of the three first-mentioned forbidden things. The fourth thing forbidden is that on which the name of anything other than Allāh, is pronounced. It is *Fisq* (profane), *i.e.*, a source of disobedience or rebellion against God. The eating of such food is calculated to injure the spiritual health of man and to kill his feelings of love and jealousy for Him.

147. And [a]to those who are Jews We forbade all animals having claws; and of the oxen and the sheep and goats did We forbid them their fats, save that which their backs bear or the entrails or that which is mixed with the bones.[925] With that did We recompense them for their rebellion.[926] And most surely We are truthful.

وَعَلَى الَّذِينَ هَادُوا حَرَّمْنَا كُلَّ ذِي ظُفُرٍ ۚ وَمِنَ
الْبَقَرِ وَالْغَنَمِ حَرَّمْنَا عَلَيْهِمْ شُحُومَهُمَا إِلَّا مَا
حَمَلَتْ ظُهُورُهُمَا أَوِ الْحَوَايَا أَوْ مَا اخْتَلَطَ بِعَظْمٍ ۚ ذَٰلِكَ
جَزَيْنَاهُمْ بِبَغْيِهِمْ ۖ وَإِنَّا لَصَادِقُونَ ﴿١٤٧﴾

148. But if they accuse thee of falsehood, say, [b]'Your Lord is the Lord of all-embracing mercy, and His wrath shall not be turned back from the guilty people.'

فَإِنْ كَذَّبُوكَ فَقُلْ رَبُّكُمْ ذُو رَحْمَةٍ وَاسِعَةٍ ۚ وَلَا
يُرَدُّ بَأْسُهُ عَنِ الْقَوْمِ الْمُجْرِمِينَ ﴿١٤٨﴾

149. [c]Those who associate gods with Allāh will say, 'If Allāh had pleased, we would not have associated gods with Him, nor would our fathers, nor would we have made anything unlawful.' In like manner did those who were before them accuse *God's Messengers* of falsehood, until they tasted of Our wrath. Say, 'Have you any knowledge? Then produce it for us. You only follow *mere* conjecture. And you only tell lies.'

سَيَقُولُ الَّذِينَ أَشْرَكُوا لَوْ شَاءَ اللَّهُ مَا أَشْرَكْنَا وَ
لَا آبَاؤُنَا وَلَا حَرَّمْنَا مِنْ شَيْءٍ ۚ كَذَٰلِكَ كَذَّبَ الَّذِينَ
مِنْ قَبْلِهِمْ حَتَّىٰ ذَاقُوا بَأْسَنَا ۗ قُلْ هَلْ عِنْدَكُمْ
مِنْ عِلْمٍ فَتُخْرِجُوهُ لَنَا ۖ إِنْ تَتَّبِعُونَ إِلَّا الظَّنَّ وَ
إِنْ أَنْتُمْ إِلَّا تَخْرُصُونَ ﴿١٤٩﴾

150. Say, 'Allāh's is the argument that reaches *home*. [d]If He had *enforced* His Will, He would have surely guided you all.'[927]

قُلْ فَلِلَّهِ الْحُجَّةُ الْبَالِغَةُ ۚ فَلَوْ شَاءَ لَهَدَاكُمْ
أَجْمَعِينَ ﴿١٥٠﴾

[a]16 : 119. [b]6 : 134; 7 : 157. [c]16 : 36; 43 : 21. [d]5 : 49; 11 : 119; 13 : 32; 16 : 10.

925. See Lev. 3 : 17 and 7 : 23. In the Talmud, exception is made of the fat that sticks to the ribs.

926. These things were forbidden to the Jews as a punishment for their transgression.

927. If God had decided to force men to do His Will, He would certainly have made them do things which are right and not the things which are wrong. But in His infinite wisdom He has made man a free agent. He has explained to him what is right and what is wrong, and then has left him free to follow whichever course he may like to choose.

151. Say, 'Produce your witnesses who testify that Allāh has forbidden this.' If they bear witness, bear thou not witness with them, [a]nor follow thou the evil desires of those who treat Our Signs as lies and those who believe not in the Hereafter and [b]who set up equals to their Lord.

قُلْ هَلُمَّ شُهَدَآءَكُمُ الَّذِيْنَ يَشْهَدُوْنَ اَنَّ اللّٰهَ
حَرَّمَ هٰذَا ۚ فَاِنْ شَهِدُوْا فَلَا تَشْهَدْ مَعَهُمْ ۚ وَلَا
تَتَّبِعْ اَهْوَآءَ الَّذِيْنَ كَذَّبُوْا بِاٰيٰتِنَا وَالَّذِيْنَ لَا يُؤْمِنُوْنَ
بِالْاٰخِرَةِ وَهُمْ بِرَبِّهِمْ يَعْدِلُوْنَ ﴿١٥١﴾ ع

R. 19 152. Say, 'Come, I will recite to you what your Lord has forbidden,[928] that you associate not anything as partner with Him; and *that you do* good to parents, and [d]that you slay not your children for *fear of* poverty—it is We Who provide for you and for them—and [e]that you approach not foul deeds, whether open or secret; and that you slay not the soul *the slaying of* which Allāh has forbidden, save in accordance *with the demands of* justice. That is what He has enjoined upon you, that you may understand.

قُلْ تَعَالَوْا اَتْلُ مَا حَرَّمَ رَبُّكُمْ عَلَيْكُمْ اَلَّا تُشْرِكُوْا
بِهٖ شَيْـًٔا وَّبِالْوَالِدَيْنِ اِحْسَانًا ۚ وَلَا تَقْتُلُوْٓا اَوْلَادَكُمْ
مِّنْ اِمْلَاقٍ ؕ نَحْنُ نَرْزُقُكُمْ وَاِيَّاهُمْ ۚ وَلَا تَقْرَبُوا
الْفَوَاحِشَ مَا ظَهَرَ مِنْهَا وَمَا بَطَنَ ۚ وَلَا تَقْتُلُوا
النَّفْسَ الَّتِيْ حَرَّمَ اللّٰهُ اِلَّا بِالْحَقِّ ؕ ذٰلِكُمْ وَصّٰىكُمْ
بِهٖ لَعَلَّكُمْ تَعْقِلُوْنَ ﴿١٥٢﴾

153. 'And [f]approach not the property of the orphan, except in *a way* which is best, till he attains his maturity. And [g]give full measure and weight with equity.[929] [h]We charge not any soul except according

وَلَا تَقْرَبُوْا مَالَ الْيَتِيْمِ اِلَّا بِالَّتِيْ هِيَ اَحْسَنُ حَتّٰى يَبْلُغَ
اَشُدَّهٗ ۚ وَاَوْفُوا الْكَيْلَ وَالْمِيْزَانَ بِالْقِسْطِ ۚ لَا نُكَلِّفُ

[a]5 : 49; 45 : 19. [b]6 : 2; 27 : 61. [c]4 : 37 ; 17 : 24. [d]17 : 32. [e]6 : 121; 7 : 34. [f]4 : 11; 17 : 35. [g]17 : 36; 26 : 182-183; 55 : 10. [h]2 : 287; 7 : 43.

928. The injunctions which follow the word 'forbidden' are what God commands us to carry out. The injunctions are expressly mentioned but the converse of them which is forbidden is implied. Thus, on the one hand, by using the word "forbidden" and, on the other, by following it up with positive commandments, the verse combines in itself both the direct injunctions and their converse. The verse may be construed in another way also. The first sentence should be taken as having ended with the words *what your Lord has forbidden*, and the next sentence as beginning with the word '*Alaikum* which would in this case mean, "it is enjoined on you." The verse will then read as follows: "Come, I will rehearse to you what your Lord has forbidden. It is enjoined on you that you associate not anything as partner with Him. . . . ."

929. Next to the injunctions about the protection of life is mentioned the commandment to protect property.

to its capacity. And when you speak, observe justice, even if *the person concerned* be a relative, and [a]fulfil the covenant of Allāh.[930] That is what He enjoins upon you, that you may take care.'

نَفْسًا إِلَّا وُسْعَهَا ۚ وَإِذَا قُلْتُمْ فَاعْدِلُوا وَلَوْ كَانَ ذَا
قُرْبَىٰ ۖ وَبِعَهْدِ اللَّهِ أَوْفُوا ۚ ذَٰلِكُمْ وَصَّاكُمْ بِهِ لَعَلَّكُمْ
تَذَكَّرُونَ ﴿١٥٣﴾

154. And *say*, [b]'This is My straight path. So follow it; and follow not *other* ways, lest they lead you away from His way. That is what He enjoins upon you, that you may *be able to* guard *against evils*.'

وَأَنَّ هَٰذَا صِرَاطِي مُسْتَقِيمًا فَاتَّبِعُوهُ ۖ وَلَا تَتَّبِعُوا
السُّبُلَ فَتَفَرَّقَ بِكُمْ عَنْ سَبِيلِهِ ۚ ذَٰلِكُمْ وَصَّاكُمْ بِهِ
لَعَلَّكُمْ تَتَّقُونَ ﴿١٥٤﴾

155. Moreover, [c]We gave Moses the Book—completing the favour upon him who did good, and [d]an explanation of all *necessary* things,[931] and a guidance and a mercy—that they might believe in the meeting with their Lord.

ثُمَّ آتَيْنَا مُوسَى الْكِتَابَ تَمَامًا عَلَى الَّذِي أَحْسَنَ وَ
تَفْصِيلًا لِكُلِّ شَيْءٍ وَهُدًى وَرَحْمَةً لَعَلَّهُمْ بِلِقَاءِ
رَبِّهِمْ يُؤْمِنُونَ ﴿١٥٥﴾ ع ١٩ ٦

R. 20 156. And [e]this is a Book which We have sent down; full of blessings. So follow[932] it, and guard against *evils* that you may be shown mercy,

وَهَٰذَا كِتَابٌ أَنْزَلْنَاهُ مُبَارَكٌ فَاتَّبِعُوهُ وَاتَّقُوا لَعَلَّكُمْ
تُرْحَمُونَ ﴿١٥٦﴾

157. Lest you should say, 'The Book was sent down only to two peoples[933] before us, and we were indeed unaware of what they read;'

أَنْ تَقُولُوا إِنَّمَا أُنْزِلَ الْكِتَابُ عَلَىٰ طَائِفَتَيْنِ مِنْ
قَبْلِنَا وَإِنْ كُنَّا عَنْ دِرَاسَتِهِمْ لَغَافِلِينَ ﴿١٥٧﴾

[a]5 : 2; 16 : 92; 17 : 35. [b]6 : 127.. [c]2 : 54; 5 : 45. [d]7 : 146. [e]6 : 93; 21 : 51.

930. After the injunction to guard the tongue comes the injunction to guard the heart, implied in the words *and fulfil the covenant of Allāh*; for whereas the previous injunctions pertained to the covenant with men, the present one relates to the covenant with God.

931. The words "all things" signify all those things which satisfied the moral and spiritual needs of the Jews. The Torah fulfilled all those needs.

932. The verse signifies that the Qur'ān is a revealed Book which contains all the imperishable teachings and eternal truths which were contained in the former Scriptures, this being the meaning of the word *Mubārak* (Lane). Thus by following the Qur'ān Muslims are relieved of the necessity of seeking guidance from them.

933. The "two peoples" mentioned in the verse may be the Jews to whom was given the Torah and whose religion originated in the region in the north of Arabia, and the Zoroastrians to whom was given the Zend-Avesta and who lived on the east side of Arabia. Or the words may refer to Jews and Christians, the two peoples who lived in Arabia and with whom the Arabs had come into contact.

158. [a]Or lest you should say, 'Had the Book been sent down to us, we should surely have been better guided than they.' There has *now* come to you a clear evidence from your Lord, and a guidance and a mercy. [b]Who, then, is more unjust than he who rejects the Signs of Allāh and turns away from them? We will requite those who turn away from Our Signs with an evil punishment because of their turning away.

اَوْ تَقُوْلُوْا لَوْ اَنَّآ اُنْزِلَ عَلَيْنَا الْكِتٰبُ لَكُنَّآ اَهْدٰى
مِنْهُمْ ۚ فَقَدْ جَآءَكُمْ بَيِّنَةٌ مِّنْ رَّبِّكُمْ وَهُدًى وَّ
رَحْمَةٌ ۚ فَمَنْ اَظْلَمُ مِمَّنْ كَذَّبَ بِاٰيٰتِ اللّٰهِ وَصَدَفَ
عَنْهَا ۗ سَنَجْزِي الَّذِيْنَ يَصْدِفُوْنَ عَنْ اٰيٰتِنَا سُوْٓءَ
الْعَذَابِ بِمَا كَانُوْا يَصْدِفُوْنَ ﴿١٥٨﴾

159. [c]They are but waiting that angels should come[934] to them or that thy Lord should come[935] or there should come some of the Signs[936] of thy Lord. The day when some of the Signs of thy Lord shall come, it shall not profit a soul to believe, which had not believed before, nor earned any good by its faith. Say, 'Wait ye, we *too* are waiting.'

هَلْ يَنْظُرُوْنَ اِلَّآ اَنْ تَاْتِيَهُمُ الْمَلٰٓئِكَةُ اَوْ يَاْتِيَ
رَبُّكَ اَوْ يَاْتِيَ بَعْضُ اٰيٰتِ رَبِّكَ ۗ يَوْمَ يَاْتِيْ بَعْضُ
اٰيٰتِ رَبِّكَ لَا يَنْفَعُ نَفْسًا اِيْمَانُهَا لَمْ تَكُنْ اٰمَنَتْ
مِنْ قَبْلُ اَوْ كَسَبَتْ فِيْٓ اِيْمَانِهَا خَيْرًا ۗ قُلِ انْتَظِرُوْٓا
اِنَّا مُنْتَظِرُوْنَ ﴿١٥٩﴾

160. *As for* [d]those who split up their religion[937] and became *divided into* sects, thou hast no concern at all with them. Surely, their affair is with Allāh, then shall He inform them of what they used to do.

اِنَّ الَّذِيْنَ فَرَّقُوْا دِيْنَهُمْ وَكَانُوْا شِيَعًا لَّسْتَ مِنْهُمْ
فِيْ شَيْءٍ ۗ اِنَّمَآ اَمْرُهُمْ اِلَى اللّٰهِ ثُمَّ يُنَبِّئُهُمْ بِمَا كَانُوْا
يَفْعَلُوْنَ ﴿١٦٠﴾

[a]35 : 43. [b]6 : 22; 7 : 38; 10 : 18. [c]2 : 211; 16 : 34. [d]30 : 33.

934. The "coming of angels" here refers to the punishment of the people through wars; because the coming of angels has been mentioned in connection with the battles that took place between Muslims and their enemies (3 : 125, 126 & 8 : 10).

935. The term "coming of the Lord" expresses complete destruction of the enemies of truth (2 : 211).

936. "The coming of the Signs" refers to earthly punishments such as famines, pestilences, calamities, etc.

937. The words, "split up their religion" signify that when people begin to follow their own caprices and fancies, differences arise among them and unanimity of views disappears.

161. [a]Whoso does a good deed shall have ten times[938] as much; but he who does an evil deed, shall be requited only with the like of it; and they shall not be wronged.

مَنْ جَآءَ بِالْحَسَنَةِ فَلَهٗ عَشْرُ اَمْثَالِهَا ۚ وَمَنْ جَآءَ
بِالسَّيِّئَةِ فَلَا يُجْزٰٓى اِلَّا مِثْلَهَا وَهُمْ لَا يُظْلَمُوْنَ ﴿۱۶۱﴾

162. Say, 'My Lord has guided me unto a straight path—the right religion, [b]the religion of Abraham, the upright. And he was not of those who associate gods *with Allāh*.'

قُلْ اِنَّنِيْ هَدٰىنِيْ رَبِّيْٓ اِلٰى صِرَاطٍ مُّسْتَقِيْمٍ ۚ دِيْنًا
قِيَمًا مِّلَّةَ اِبْرٰهِيْمَ حَنِيْفًا ۚ وَمَا كَانَ مِنَ الْمُشْرِكِيْنَ ﴿۱۶۲﴾

163. Say, 'My Prayer and my sacrifice and my life and my death are *all* for Allāh, the Lord of the worlds;[939]

قُلْ اِنَّ صَلَاتِيْ وَنُسُكِيْ وَمَحْيَايَ وَمَمَاتِيْ لِلّٰهِ رَبِّ
الْعٰلَمِيْنَ ﴿۱۶۳﴾

164. [c]"He has no partner. And so am I commanded, and I am the first of those who submit.'

لَا شَرِيْكَ لَهٗ ۚ وَبِذٰلِكَ اُمِرْتُ وَاَنَا اَوَّلُ الْمُسْلِمِيْنَ ﴿۱۶۴﴾

165. Say, [d]"Shall I seek a Lord other than Allāh while He is the Lord of all things?' And no soul earns *evil* but only against itself; [e]nor does any bearer of burden bear the burden of another.[940] Then to your Lord will be your return, and He will inform you of that wherein you used to differ.

قُلْ اَغَيْرَ اللّٰهِ اَبْغِيْ رَبًّا وَّهُوَ رَبُّ كُلِّ شَيْءٍ ۚ وَلَا تَكْسِبُ
كُلُّ نَفْسٍ اِلَّا عَلَيْهَا ۚ وَلَا تَزِرُ وَازِرَةٌ وِّزْرَ اُخْرٰى ۚ
ثُمَّ اِلٰى رَبِّكُمْ مَّرْجِعُكُمْ فَيُنَبِّئُكُمْ بِمَا كُنْتُمْ فِيْهِ
تَخْتَلِفُوْنَ ﴿۱۶۵﴾

[a]4 : 41; 27 : 90; 28 : 85. [b]3 : 96; 16 : 124. [c]6 : 15; 39 : 12-13. [d]7 : 141. [e]17 : 16; 35 : 19; 53 : 39

938. A good deed is like a good seed that multiplies tenfold and even more" (2 : 262; 4 : 41; 10 : 27, 28; also Tirmidhī, ch. on *Fasting*) whereas an evil deed is counted as only one.

939. Prayer, sacrifice, life and death, cover the entire field of man's actions, and the Holy Prophet had been asked to declare that all phases of this life were devoted to God alone. All his prayers were offered to God; all his sacrifices were made to Him; all his life was devoted to His service; and if in the cause of religion he sought death, that was also to win His pleasure.

940. This verse contains, as do vv. 17 : 16; 53 : 40-41, a forceful repudiation of the doctrine of Atonement and emphatically draws attention to the fact that everyone has to carry his own cross and to account for his own actions. Nobody's vicarious sacrifice can do one any good.

166. And He it is Who has made you successors *of others* on the earth and has exalted some of you over others in degrees *of rank*, [a]that He may try you by that which He has given you.[941] Surely, thy Lord is Quick in punishment; and surely, He is Most Forgiving, Merciful.

وَهُوَ الَّذِي جَعَلَكُمْ خَلَٰٓئِفَ الْأَرْضِ وَرَفَعَ بَعْضَكُمْ
فَوْقَ بَعْضٍ دَرَجَٰتٍ لِّيَبْلُوَكُمْ فِي مَآ ءَاتَىٰكُمْ إِنَّ رَبَّكَ
سَرِيعُ الْعِقَابِ وَإِنَّهُۥ لَغَفُورٌ رَّحِيمٌ ﴿١٦٦﴾

[a]5 : 49; 11 : 8; 67 : 3.

941. The verse constitutes at once an exhortation and a warning to the Muslims. They are told that they are going to be granted power and authority, and the duty of regulating the affairs of nations is about to devolve on them. They should discharge their responsibilities with equity and justice as they shall have to give account of their charge to their Creator.

CHAPTER 7

AL-A'RĀF

(*Revealed before Hijrah*)

Title and Date of Revelation

According to Ibn 'Abbās, Ibn Zubair, Ḥasan, Mujāhid, 'Ikrimah, 'Aṭā' and Jābir bin Zaid, this *Sūrah* belongs to the Meccan period with the exception of vv. 165-172. Qatādah however, is of the opinion that v. 165 was revealed at Medina. The *Sūrah* takes its title from v. 47. Commentators have not succeeded in finding out any real connection between the word *A'rāf* and the subject-matter of the *Sūrah*. This is because they have assigned a wrong meaning to the word. They think that *A'rāf* is the name of an intervening spiritual stage between Paradise and Hell and that the Fellows of *A'rāf* will appear distinct from the inmates of Hell but will not as yet have entered Paradise. The Qur'ān rejects this meaning of the word because it has mentioned only two groups of people—the dwellers of Paradise and the inmates of Hell. There is no mention in it of any third group or class of people. It lends no support to the interpretation of the word *A'rāf* as the place of persons of a middling spiritual status, nor can any internal evidence be adduced in support of this interpretation. The Qur'ān depicts the Fellows of *Al-A'rāf* as at one time addressing the dwellers of Paradise and at another time talking to the inmates of Hell; and their spiritual knowledge has been declared to be so great that they can recognize the dwellers of Paradise by their special marks and also the inmates of Hell by the latter's particular signs. They rebuke and upbraid the inmates of Hell and pray for the inmates of Paradise (7 : 47, 49, 50). Can a person, who himself is hanging, as it were, in a state of uncertainty between Paradise and Hell, be so presumptuous as to assume an air of superiority as the Fellows of *Al-A'rāf* have been shown to do? The fact is that the Fellows of *Al-A'rāf* are the Prophets of God, who will enjoy a special spiritual status on the Day of Judgment and will pray for the dwellers of Paradise and rebuke and reprimand the inmates of Hell. And because the *Sūrah* is the first among the Quranic Chapters in which the life stories of several Prophets have been dealt with at some length, it has rightly been given the name Al-A'rāf. Moreover, the very construction of the word supports this inference. *A'rāf* is the plural of '*Urf* which means a high and elevated place and means also that spiritual realization which a man acquires by the help of God-given intellect and the testimony of his inner self. So *A'rāf* may signify those teachings of which the truth is established by rational arguments and the testimony of human nature; and, as the teachings of Prophets possess all these qualities, they alone deserve this spiritually exalted position and so they can legitimately be called the Fellows of *Al-A'rāf* (Elevated Places). In short, the *Sūrah* Al-A'rāf is so called because in it illustrations have been given from the lives of those eminent men of very high spiritual position who in the past taught mankind eternal truths in accordance with the demands of human nature and human reason, and whom the men of this world resisted and sought to bring low, but whom the jealous God raised to a very exalted position.

Subject-Matter and Context

Spiritually speaking the *Sūrah* serves as a kind of *Barzakh* (intervening link) between the *Sūrahs* that precede it and those that follow it, which signifies that the subject-matter of the preceding *Sūrahs* has been developed into a new theme in this *Sūrah*. In the preceding *Sūrahs* the main theme consisted of refutation of Judaism and Christianity and that of other Faiths which profess to derive their authority mainly from Philosophy and Reason. In this *Sūrah* both these themes have been jointly treated and the falsity of the positions of both these sets of creeds is demonstrated and the truth of Islām established. First of all, it is stated that because the Qur'ān is the revealed Word of God, there is no possibility that it will ever meet with destruction or will fail to achieve its object. Then Muslims are warned that they should not, in a fit of despondency, come to a hasty compromise with the followers of other religions, because the opponents of a true religion have always suffered disgrace and humiliation in the end. Next, it is stated that God has created man for the attainment of a most sublime object, but most men forget this noble purpose of their lives. The paradisiacal life of Adam and his expulsion from it have been cited as an illustration of this subject, and it is added that in the very beginning after having created man God provided for him the means to attain a high spiritual status; but man gave no heed to God's plans for him, and followed Satan. Further, it is mentioned that, unlike former Faiths which aimed at individual development, Islām seeks to bring about reformation of whole communities. Whereas former Prophets sought to make individuals enter Paradise, Islām's aim is that whole communities and nations should attain bliss. But, as every effort at reformation has to encounter obstacles and vicissitudes before it attains its consummation, so whenever the Muslim community deviates from Islamic principles and teachings God raises for their reformation divinely-inspired Reformers from among the followers of the Holy Prophet so that man may not lose his newly-gained Paradise by deviating from the path of national progress and development. The *Sūrah* then proceeds to lay down standards and criteria for the recognition of these promised Reformers and light is also shed on the ultimate doom of their opponents. Next, it is said that all Divine plans work gradually. As in the material world, so in the realm of the spirit, all progress is subject to the law of evolution and it is by a process of progressive evolution that the spiritual development of man has taken place from the time of Adam to that of the Holy Prophet, and in his teaching greater attention has been devoted to the betterment and organization of the whole community. The believers, therefore, should always keep in mind that from small seeds grow big trees and that even great objects seem very insignificant in the beginning and remain hidden. So it behoves believers to keep their eyes open and let not the grand object of their creation remain hidden from their sight because, if once it was allowed to become hidden, it would remain hidden for ever.

With v. 60 begins a brief account of the life-history of some Prophets of antiquity whose mission it was to take man back to the blissful heavenly existence from which he was expelled. After that it is stated that good is ingrained in human nature of which it constitutes an integral part and that evil only comes later and is the result of external influences; and that, in spite of his instinctive goodness, man cannot attain perfection without the help of Divine revelation. By rejecting Divine guidance hé deprives himself of his instinctive goodness and is spiritually ruined. Again, reference is made to the mission of the Holy Prophet, and his opponents are warned not to ignore the patent fact that his intellect is sound and motives pure, that his teachings are in perfect harmony with human nature and natural law and that the testimony of the time also is in his favour. Then some misgivings and doubts of disbelievers have been removed and it is stated that they will put up a very strong opposition to the Holy Prophet, but God will protect him from all harm. Muslims, however, are admonished not only to endure patiently the opposition of disbelievers but also to pray for them. Further, the *Sūrah* observes that like the opponents of former Prophets, the opponents of the Holy Prophet will continue to demand Signs, but it lies entirely with God to show Signs. He shows them when in His infallible wisdom He thinks opportune. But does not, the disbelievers are asked, the Qur'ān which fulfils the real object and purpose of Prophethood, constitute a sufficient Sign? Muslims, therefore, are exhorted to give to the miracle of the Qur'ān that great measure of true appreciation which it richly deserves, because the more the Heavenly light is vouchsafed to man, the truer should be his appreciation of it.

سُوْرَةُ الْاَعْرَافِ مَكِّيَّةٌ (٧)

1. In the name of Allāh, the Gracious, the Merciful.

بِسْمِ اللّٰهِ الرَّحْمٰنِ الرَّحِيْمِ ﴿١﴾

2. [a]Alif Lām Mīm Ṣād.[942]

الٓمّٓصٓ ﴿٢﴾

3. [b]*This is* a Book revealed unto thee[943]—so let there be no straitness in thy bosom concerning it—that thou mayest warn thereby and *that it be* an exhortation to the believers.

كِتٰبٌ اُنْزِلَ اِلَيْكَ فَلَا يَكُنْ فِيْ صَدْرِكَ حَرَجٌ مِّنْهُ لِتُنْذِرَ بِهٖ وَ ذِكْرٰى لِلْمُؤْمِنِيْنَ ﴿٣﴾

4. [c]Follow that which has been sent down to you from your Lord, and follow no protectors other than Him. But you seldom take warning.

اِتَّبِعُوْا مَاۤ اُنْزِلَ اِلَيْكُمْ مِّنْ رَّبِّكُمْ وَلَا تَتَّبِعُوْا مِنْ دُوْنِهٖۤ اَوْلِيَآءَ ؕ قَلِيْلًا مَّا تَذَكَّرُوْنَ ﴿٤﴾

5. [d]How many a town have We destroyed! And Our punishment came upon it by night or while they slept at noon.[944]

وَكَمْ مِّنْ قَرْيَةٍ اَهْلَكْنٰهَا فَجَآءَهَا بَاْسُنَا بَيَاتًا اَوْ هُمْ قَآئِلُوْنَ ﴿٥﴾

6. So when Our punishment came upon them, their cry was nothing but that they said, [e]'We were indeed wrongdoers!'[945]

فَمَا كَانَ دَعْوٰىهُمْ اِذْ جَآءَهُمْ بَاْسُنَاۤ اِلَّاۤ اَنْ قَالُوْۤا اِنَّا كُنَّا ظٰلِمِيْنَ ﴿٦﴾

7. And [f]We will certainly question those to whom *the Messengers* were sent and [g]We will certainly question the Messengers.[946]

فَلَنَسْـَٔلَنَّ الَّذِيْنَ اُرْسِلَ اِلَيْهِمْ وَلَنَسْـَٔلَنَّ الْمُرْسَلِيْنَ ﴿٧﴾

---

[a]2 : 2; 3 : 2; 29 : 2; 30 ; 2: 31 : 2; 32 : 2. [b]6 : 52; 19 : 98; 25 : 2. [c]33 : 3; 39 : 56; [d]7: 98; 21 : 12; 28 : 59. [e]21 : 15. [f]28 : 66. [g]5 : 110.

---

942. According to Ibn 'Abbās, the combined four letters *Alif Lām Mīm Ṣād* signify "I am Allāh, the All-Knowing and I explain." For the first three letters see note 16, and the letter *Ṣād* stands for *Ufaṣṣilu, i.e.,* I explain. The contents of this *Sūrah* justify this interpretation, because the *Sūrah* not only embodies Divine knowledge of, but explains at greater length and with a greater wealth of illustrations, the subject dealt with in the preceding *Sūrah*. The letter *Ṣād* has also been understood to mean, "Most Truthful."

943. This verse is addressed to every believer, and not particularly to the Holy Prophet.

944. Latter part of the night ahd also mid-day are here mentioned as particularly the two times when Divine visitations generally come upon a people. These are the hours when they are often asleep or are in a state of negligence.

945. The reason, why even confirmed atheists have sometimes been found to cry to God for help when punishment overtakes them, is that at such a dreadful time realization comes to man not only of his own utter helplessness but also of the might and power of a Higher Being.

946. The verse embodies the important principle that in one form or another all are responsible to God. All people will be questioned how they received God's Messengers,

8. Then will We certainly relate to them *their deeds* with knowledge, for We are never absent.

فَلَنَقُصَّنَّ عَلَيْهِمْ بِعِلْمٍ وَّمَا كُنَّا غَآئِبِينَ ۝

9. And *a*the weighing[947] on that day will be true. Then as for those whose scales are heavy, it is they who shall prosper.

وَالْوَزْنُ يَوْمَئِذٍ الْحَقُّ فَمَنْ ثَقُلَتْ مَوَازِينُهُ فَأُولَٰئِكَ هُمُ الْمُفْلِحُونَ ۝

10. And as for those *b*whose scales are light, it is they who shall have ruined their souls because of their being unjust[948] concerning Our Signs.

وَمَنْ خَفَّتْ مَوَازِينُهُ فَأُولَٰئِكَ الَّذِينَ خَسِرُوا أَنْفُسَهُمْ بِمَا كَانُوا بِآيَاتِنَا يَظْلِمُونَ ۝

11. And *c*We have established you in the earth and provided for you therein the means of subsistence. But little thanks do you give.

وَلَقَدْ مَكَّنَّاكُمْ فِي الْأَرْضِ وَجَعَلْنَا لَكُمْ فِيهَا مَعَايِشَ ۗ قَلِيلًا مَّا تَشْكُرُونَ ۝

R. 2　12. And We indeed created you *and* then *d*We gave you shape;[949] then said We to the angels, "Submit to Adam;"[950] and they *all* submitted. But Iblīs[951] *did not*; he will not be of those who submit.

وَلَقَدْ خَلَقْنَاكُمْ ثُمَّ صَوَّرْنَاكُمْ ثُمَّ قُلْنَا لِلْمَلَائِكَةِ اسْجُدُوا لِآدَمَ فَسَجَدُوا إِلَّا إِبْلِيسَ لَمْ يَكُنْ مِّنَ السَّاجِدِينَ ۝

---

*a*21 : 48; 23 : 103; 101 : 9-10.　*b*23 : 104; 101 : 9-10.　*c*15 : 21; 46 : 27.
*d*23 : 15; 39 : 7; 40 : 65.　*e*2 : 35; 15 : 30-31; 17 : 62; 18 : 51; 20 : 117; 38 : 73—75.

---

and the Messengers will be questioned how they delivered the Divine Message and what response was made by the people to it.

947. The language used here is figurative. Material things are weighed in scales made of metal or wood, but the weighing of things which are not material signifies determining their real value, worth or importance.

948. The word *Zulm*, literally meaning 'to put a thing in the wrong place' (Lane), is here used to signify that the disbelievers did not treat the Signs of God in the manner in which they should have been treated. The Signs were meant to instil fear of God and humility into their minds, but instead they became all the more arrogant and insolent and rejected them with mockery and derision.

949. Man can mould his moral being into various shapes, as clay can be moulded.

950. Whereas the command to submit to Adam was addressed to the angels, it applied to all creation, as angels are Divine agents to give effect to God's commands.

951. Iblīs was not an angel (18 : 51). He is the chief of the evil spirits as Gabriel is the chief of angels. The incident mentioned here is in no way connected with the first progenitor of the human race, who may be called the first Adam. It is only with the latter Adam (who dwelt in this earth about six thousand years ago and from whom Noah and Abraham and their posterity were directly descended) that the present account deals.

13. [a]*God* said,[952] 'What prevented thee from submitting when I commanded thee?' He said, 'I am better than he. Thou hast created me of fire while him hast Thou created of clay.'[953]

قَالَ مَا مَنَعَكَ أَلَّا تَسْجُدَ إِذْ أَمَرْتُكَ ۖ قَالَ أَنَا خَيْرٌ مِّنْهُ
خَلَقْتَنِي مِن نَّارٍ وَخَلَقْتَهُ مِن طِينٍ ﴿١٣﴾

14. *God* said, [b]'Then go down hence;[954] it is not for thee to be arrogant here. Get out; thou art certainly of those who are abased.'

قَالَ فَاهْبِطْ مِنْهَا فَمَا يَكُونُ لَكَ أَن تَتَكَبَّرَ فِيهَا فَاخْرُجْ
إِنَّكَ مِنَ الصَّاغِرِينَ ﴿١٤﴾

15. [c]He said, 'Respite me till the day when they will be raised up.'[954A]

قَالَ أَنظِرْنِي إِلَىٰ يَوْمِ يُبْعَثُونَ ﴿١٥﴾

16. *God* said, 'Thou art of those who are respited.'

قَالَ إِنَّكَ مِنَ الْمُنظَرِينَ ﴿١٦﴾

17. [d]He said, 'Now, since Thou hast adjudged me to be erring, I will assuredly lie in wait for them on Thy straight path;

قَالَ فَبِمَا أَغْوَيْتَنِي لَأَقْعُدَنَّ لَهُمْ صِرَاطَكَ
الْمُسْتَقِيمَ ﴿١٧﴾

18. 'Then will I surely come upon them from before them and from behind them and from their right and from their left,[955] and Thou wilt not find most of them to be grateful.'

ثُمَّ لَآتِيَنَّهُم مِّن بَيْنِ أَيْدِيهِمْ وَمِنْ خَلْفِهِمْ
وَعَنْ أَيْمَانِهِمْ وَعَن شَمَائِلِهِمْ ۖ وَلَا تَجِدُ أَكْثَرَهُمْ
شَاكِرِينَ ﴿١٨﴾

[a]15 : 33-34; 38 : 76-77. [b]15 : 35; 38 : 78. [c]15 : 37; 38 : 80. [d]15 : 40; 38 : 83.

952. What is represented in the present verse as a dialogue between God and Iblis does not necessarily mean that an exchange of words did actually take place. The words may only depict a state of things, a picture of the conditions that came into existence as a result of the refusal of Iblīs to submit to Adam. See also 61.

953. For an explanation of the word "clay" see 420A

954. There being no noun mentioned in the verse to which the pronoun *hā* (it) implied in the expression *Minhā* (hence) refers, it may be taken to denote the condition or state in which Iblīs was, before he refused to submit to Adam.

954A. The resurrection referred to in this verse is not the great Resurrection of mankind decreed for the Hereafter, but the spiritual resurrection of man, or the state when his spiritual consciousness becomes fully developed. Iblīs can lead him astray only so long as he is not spiritually resurrected. But once he attains that high spiritual stage which is known by the term *Baqā'* (rebirth), Iblīs can do him no harm (17 : 66).

955. Note the network of seductions threatented by Satan.

19. *God* said, 'Get out hence, despised and banished. [a]Whosoever of them shall follow thee, I will surely fill Hell with you all;'

قَالَ اخْرُجْ مِنْهَا مَذْءُومًا مَّدْحُورًا لَّمَن تَبِعَكَ
مِنْهُمْ لَأَمْلَأَنَّ جَهَنَّمَ مِنكُمْ أَجْمَعِينَ ﴿١٩﴾

20. 'And [b]O Adam ! dwell thou and thy wife in the Garden[955A] and eat therefrom wherever you will,[956] but approach not this tree[957] lest you be among the wrongdoers.'

وَيَا آدَمُ اسْكُنْ أَنتَ وَزَوْجُكَ الْجَنَّةَ فَكُلَا مِنْ حَيْثُ
شِئْتُمَا وَلَا تَقْرَبَا هَٰذِهِ الشَّجَرَةَ فَتَكُونَا مِنَ
الظَّالِمِينَ ﴿٢٠﴾

21. But [c]Satan made evil suggestions to them so that he might make known to them what was hidden from them of their shame[957A] and said, 'Your Lord has only forbidden you this tree, lest you become angels or lest you become of the immortals.'

فَوَسْوَسَ لَهُمَا الشَّيْطَانُ لِيُبْدِيَ لَهُمَا مَا وُورِيَ
عَنْهُمَا مِن سَوْآتِهِمَا وَقَالَ مَا نَهَاكُمَا رَبُّكُمَا عَنْ
هَٰذِهِ الشَّجَرَةِ إِلَّا أَن تَكُونَا مَلَكَيْنِ أَوْ تَكُونَا مِنَ
الْخَالِدِينَ ﴿٢١﴾

22. And He swore to them, *saying*, 'Surely I am a sincere counsellor unto you.'

وَقَاسَمَهُمَا إِنِّي لَكُمَا لَمِنَ النَّاصِحِينَ ﴿٢٢﴾

23. So he caused them to fall *into disobedience* by deceit. And when they [d]tasted of the tree, their shame[958] became manifest to them

فَدَلَّاهُمَا بِغُرُورٍ فَلَمَّا ذَاقَا الشَّجَرَةَ بَدَتْ لَهُمَا

[a]11 : 20; 15 : 43-44; 32 : 14; 38 : 86. [b]2 : 38; 20 : 118. [c]2 : 37; 20 : 121. [d]2 : 37; 20 : 122.

955A. See 68.

956. This shows that every thing is lawful, except what may be forbidden as being harmful physically or spiritually.

957. "Forbidden tree" may also signify commandments whereby certain things were forbidden to Adam and his wife. "Good word" has been likened to "good tree" in the Qur'ān (14 : 25) and evil word to "evil tree" (14 : 27).

957A. While evil thoughts ultimately lead a person to his ruin, they also make manifest to him his weaknesses.

As the place where Adam was made to reside has been metaphorically described in the Qur'ān as a "Garden", therefore in the description that follows the metaphor is continued and Adam is represented as having been forbidden to approach a certain 'tree' which was not a tree in its literal and physical sense, but a certain family or tribe from which he was bidden to keep aloof, because the members of that family were his enemies and they would have spared no pains to do him harm.

958. The word *Sayy'ah* which means, any evil, foul, unseemly or abominable saying or habit or action which one would like to hide; shame; nakedness (Lane), is used here in the

and they both began to cover themselves with the leaves[959] of the Garden. And their Lord called them, *saying*, 'Did I not forbid you that tree and tell you, [a]verily Satan is to you an open enemy?'-

سَوْاٰتُهُمَا وَطَفِقَا يَخْصِفٰنِ عَلَيْهِمَا مِنْ وَّرَقِ
الْجَنَّةِ ؕ وَنَادٰىهُمَا رَبُّهُمَآ اَلَمْ اَنْهَكُمَا عَنْ تِلْكُمَا
الشَّجَرَةِ وَاَقُلْ لَّكُمَآ اِنَّ الشَّيْطٰنَ لَكُمَا عَدُوٌّ
مُّبِيْنٌ ﴿٢٣﴾

24. They said, [b]'Our Lord, we have wronged ourselves[960] and if Thou forgive us not and have not mercy on us, we shall surely be of the losers.'

قَالَا رَبَّنَا ظَلَمْنَآ اَنْفُسَنَا ٚ وَاِنْ لَّمْ تَغْفِرْ لَنَا وَ
تَرْحَمْنَا لَنَكُوْنَنَّ مِنَ الْخٰسِرِيْنَ ﴿٢٤﴾

25. *God* said, [c]'Go forth,[961] some of you will be enemies of others. And for you there is an abode on the earth and a provision for a time.'

قَالَ اهْبِطُوْا بَعْضُكُمْ لِبَعْضٍ عَدُوٌّ ۚ وَلَكُمْ فِي الْاَرْضِ
مُسْتَقَرٌّ وَّمَتَاعٌ اِلٰى حِيْنٍ ﴿٢٥﴾

---

[a]2 : 169, 209; 6 : 143; 12 : 6; 20 : 118; 28 : 16; 35 : 7; 36 : 61. [b]2 : 38.
[c]2 : 37,39; 20 : 124.

---

sense of "object of shame" or "weakness," because no man's nakedness is hidden from him. Some of Adam's weaknesses were indeed hidden from him and he came to realize them when his enemy lured him away from his position of security. Every person has certain weaknesses which are hidden even from himself, but which become exposed at time of strain and stress, or when he is tempted and tried. So it was when Adam was tempted and deceived by Satan that he became aware of some of his natural weaknesses. The Qur'ān does not say that the weaknesses of Adam and his wife became known to other people, but that they only themselves became conscious of them.

959. *Waraq*, meaning, the prime and freshness of a thing; the young lads of a community (Lisān), signifies that when Satan succeeded in causing a split in Adam's community and some of its weaker members had gone out of its fold, he gathered together the *Aurāq* (leaves) of the Garden, *i.e.*, the youth of the community, and began to re-unite and re-organize his people with their help. It is generally the youth who, being mostly free from preconceived ideas and prejudices, follow and help the Prophets of God (10 : 84). The being whom the Qur'ān has represented as having refused to submit to Adam is called Iblīs, while the person who tempted him is called Satan. This distinction is observed not only in the verse under comment, but in all the relevant verses throughout the Qur'ān. This shows that, so far as this narrative is concerned, Satan and Iblīs were two different persons. In fact, the word *Shaiṭān* (Satan) is applied not only to evil spirits but also to those human beings who, on account of their evil nature and wicked deeds, become, as it were, Satan incarnate. The *Shaiṭān* who tempted Adam and caused him to slip was not an invisible evil spirit but a wicked man of flesh and blood, a devil from among human beings, a manifestation of Satan and an agent of Iblīs. He was a member of the family which Adam had been bidden to avoid. The Holy Prophet is reported to have said that his name was Ḥārith, (Tirmidhī, ch. on *Tafsīr*) which is further evidence of his being a human being and not an evil spirit.

960. Adam soon realized his error and hastened to turn to God in repentance. In fact, Adam's error lay in taking this man-devil for a well-wisher, although God had warned him against having anything to do with him.

961. The verse shows that Adam was commanded to emigrate from the land of his birth because enmity and hatred had sprung up between different members of his community. This constitutes a further evidence of the fact that the "Garden" which Adam was commanded to leave was not Paradise. It appears that Adam emigrated from Mesopotamia, the land of his birth, to a neighbouring land. The emigration was perhaps a temporary one and he may have returned to his native land not long after. Indeed, the words, ***a provision for a***

26. He said, [a]'Therein shall you live and therein shall you die and therefrom shall you be brought forth.'[962]

قَالَ فِيهَا تَحْيَوْنَ وَفِيهَا تَمُوتُونَ وَمِنْهَا تُخْرَجُونَ ﴿٢٦﴾ ع ٢ ١٥ ٩

R. 3 27. O children of Adam, We have indeed sent down to you raiment to cover your nakedness and *to be a means of* adornment; but the raiment of righteousness[963]—that is the best. That is of the commandments of Allāh, that they may remember.

يٰبَنِيٓ اٰدَمَ قَدْ اَنْزَلْنَا عَلَيْكُمْ لِبَاسًا يُّوَارِيْ سَوْاٰتِكُمْ وَرِيْشًا ۗ وَلِبَاسُ التَّقْوٰى ۙ ذٰلِكَ خَيْرٌ ۗ ذٰلِكَ مِنْ اٰيٰتِ اللّٰهِ لَعَلَّهُمْ يَذَّكَّرُوْنَ ﴿٢٧﴾

28. O children of Adam, let not Satan seduce you, even as he turned your parents out of the Garden, stripping them of their raiment that he might show them their nakedness. Truly, he sees you, he and his tribe, from where you see them not.[964] Surely, [b]We have made Satans friends of those who believe not.

يٰبَنِيٓ اٰدَمَ لَا يَفْتِنَنَّكُمُ الشَّيْطٰنُ كَمَآ اَخْرَجَ اَبَوَيْكُمْ مِّنَ الْجَنَّةِ يَنْزِعُ عَنْهُمَا لِبَاسَهُمَا لِيُرِيَهُمَا سَوْاٰتِهِمَا ۗ اِنَّهٗ يَرٰىكُمْ هُوَ وَقَبِيْلُهٗ مِنْ حَيْثُ لَا تَرَوْنَهُمْ ۗ اِنَّا جَعَلْنَا الشَّيٰطِيْنَ اَوْلِيَآءَ لِلَّذِيْنَ لَا يُؤْمِنُوْنَ ﴿٢٨﴾

29. And when they commit an indecency, they say, 'We found our fathers doing it and Allāh has enjoined it upon us.' Say, 'Allāh never enjoins [c]indecencies. Do you say of Allāh that which you know not?'

وَاِذَا فَعَلُوْا فَاحِشَةً قَالُوْا وَجَدْنَا عَلَيْهَآ اٰبَآءَنَا وَاللّٰهُ اَمَرَنَا بِهَا ۗ قُلْ اِنَّ اللّٰهَ لَا يَاْمُرُ بِالْفَحْشَآءِ ۗ اَتَقُوْلُوْنَ عَلَى اللّٰهِ مَا لَا تَعْلَمُوْنَ ﴿٢٩﴾

[a]20 : 56; 71 : 18-19. [b]2: 258; 3 : 176; 16 : 101. [c]16 : 91.

time, contain a veiled hint at the emigration being a temporary one. Adam is warned in this verse to be careful in future; for it was in his native land that he was now to live for ever.

962. Taken in a general sense the verse hints that no human being can ascend to the heavens with his physical body. Man must live and die on this earth.

963. It was with the apparel of piety that Adam covered his "nakedness" in the "Garden."

964. The Evil Spirit, called *Shaiṭān*, and those of his kind are generally invisible to the eye. They exercise their influence imperceptibly and search for the hidden weaknesses of man in order to confirm him in his evil ways. God has created Satan only as a trial for men—Satan serves the purpose of a hurdle in the spiritual race in which man is engaged. Hurdles are meant not to block but to make the competitors in the race more vigilant and to redouble their efforts. The careless and the negligent, who stumble over hurdles and thus lose the race, have themselves to blame and not the person or persons who put them in their way in order to try and prove their mettle.

30. Say, 'My Lord has enjoined ^ajustice. And fix⁹⁶⁵ your attention aright at every *time and* place of worship and call upon Him, making yourselves sincere towards Him in religion. As He brought you into being, so shall you return *to Him*.'⁹⁶⁶

قُلْ اَمَرَ رَبِّيْ بِالْقِسْطِ وَاَقِيْمُوْا وُجُوْهَكُمْ عِنْدَ كُلِّ مَسْجِدٍ وَّادْعُوْهُ مُخْلِصِيْنَ لَهُ الدِّيْنَ ڛ كَمَا بَدَاَكُمْ تَعُوْدُوْنَ ۝

31. ^bSome has He guided and for some error has become their desert. They have taken evil ones for friends instead of Allāh and they think that they are rightly guided.

فَرِيْقًا هَدٰى وَفَرِيْقًا حَقَّ عَلَيْهِمُ الضَّلٰلَةُ ؕ اِنَّهُمُ اتَّخَذُوا الشَّيٰطِيْنَ اَوْلِيَآءَ مِنْ دُوْنِ اللّٰهِ وَيَحْسَبُوْنَ اَنَّهُمْ مُّهْتَدُوْنَ ۝

32. O children of Adam! take your adornment⁹⁶⁷ at every *time and* place of worship, and eat and drink, but ^cbe not immoderate; surely, He does not love those who are immoderate.

يٰبَنِيْٓ اٰدَمَ خُذُوْا زِيْنَتَكُمْ عِنْدَ كُلِّ مَسْجِدٍ وَّ كُلُوْا وَاشْرَبُوْا وَلَا تُسْرِفُوْا ؕ اِنَّهٗ لَا يُحِبُّ الْمُسْرِفِيْنَ ۧ۝

R. 4

33. Say, 'Who has forbidden the adornment of Allāh which He has produced⁹⁶⁸ for His servants and ^dthe good things of *His* providing?' Say, 'They are for the believers in the present life *and will be* exclusively *for them* on the Day of Resurrection.' Thus do We explain the Signs for a people who have knowledge.

قُلْ مَنْ حَرَّمَ زِيْنَةَ اللّٰهِ الَّتِيْٓ اَخْرَجَ لِعِبَادِهٖ وَالطَّيِّبٰتِ مِنَ الرِّزْقِ ؕ قُلْ هِيَ لِلَّذِيْنَ اٰمَنُوْا فِي الْحَيٰوةِ الدُّنْيَا خَالِصَةً يَّوْمَ الْقِيٰمَةِ ؕ كَذٰلِكَ نُفَصِّلُ الْاٰيٰتِ لِقَوْمٍ يَّعْلَمُوْنَ ۝

---

^a4 : 59; 16 : 91; 57 : 26.   ^b16 : 37; 22 : 19.   ^c17 : 28; 25 : 68.   ^d2 : 169, 173; 23 : 52.

---

965. When the time of Prayer approaches and Muslims are about to go to a mosque, they should concentrate all their attention on God, taking their mind away from the cares of the world. The ablution performed before every Prayer serves the useful purpose of turning the believer's thoughts towards God and putting him in the right state for Prayer.

966. The words, *As He brought you into being, so shall you return,* mean that just as our bodies gradually develop in the wombs of our mothers, so will our souls pass through a similar process of development after death.

967. The adornment should either be physical or spiritual. In the physical sense believers are enjoined to go to a place of worship, as far as possible, in a clean and decent dress.

968. The good and pure things provided by God are really meant for believers though they are also shared by disbelievers in this life; but in the life to come they will be enjoyed by believers to the exclusion of disbelievers.

34. Say, ⁿ"My Lord has only forbidden indecencies, open or secret and sin and wrongful transgression and that ᵇyou associate with Allāh that for which He has sent down no authority, and that you say of Allāh what you know not.'

قُلْ اِنَّمَا حَرَّمَ رَبِّيَ الْفَوَاحِشَ مَا ظَهَرَ مِنْهَا وَمَا بَطَنَ وَالْاِثْمَ وَالْبَغْيَ بِغَيْرِ الْحَقِّ وَاَنْ تُشْرِكُوْا بِاللّٰهِ مَا لَمْ يُنَزِّلْ بِهٖ سُلْطٰنًا وَّاَنْ تَقُوْلُوْا عَلَى اللّٰهِ مَا لَا تَعْلَمُوْنَ ۝

35. And for ᶜevery people there is a term, and when their term is come, they cannot remain behind a single moment, nor can they get ahead⁹⁶⁹ *of it.*

وَلِكُلِّ اُمَّةٍ اَجَلٌ ۚ فَاِذَا جَاءَ اَجَلُهُمْ لَا يَسْتَاْخِرُوْنَ سَاعَةً وَّلَا يَسْتَقْدِمُوْنَ ۝

36. O children of Adam,⁹⁷⁰ if ᵈMessengers come to you from among yourselves, rehearsing My Signs unto you, then whoso shall fear God and do good deeds, on them *shall come* no fear nor shall they grieve.

يٰبَنِيْٓ اٰدَمَ اِمَّا يَاْتِيَنَّكُمْ رُسُلٌ مِّنْكُمْ يَقُصُّوْنَ عَلَيْكُمْ اٰيٰتِيْ ۙ فَمَنِ اتَّقٰى وَاَصْلَحَ فَلَا خَوْفٌ عَلَيْهِمْ وَلَا هُمْ يَحْزَنُوْنَ ۝

37. But ᵉthose who reject Our Signs and turn away from them with disdain,—these are the inmates of the Fire; they shall abide therein.

وَالَّذِيْنَ كَذَّبُوْا بِاٰيٰتِنَا وَاسْتَكْبَرُوْا عَنْهَآ اُولٰٓئِكَ اَصْحٰبُ النَّارِ ۚ هُمْ فِيْهَا خٰلِدُوْنَ ۝

38. ᶠWho is, then, more unjust than he who forges a lie against Allāh or gives the lie to His Signs? It is these who shall have their lot as ordained⁹⁷¹ till when Our messengers shall visit them to take away their souls, they shall say,

فَمَنْ اَظْلَمُ مِمَّنِ افْتَرٰى عَلَى اللّٰهِ كَذِبًا اَوْ كَذَّبَ بِاٰيٰتِهٖ ؕ اُولٰٓئِكَ يَنَالُهُمْ نَصِيْبُهُمْ مِّنَ الْكِتٰبِ ؕ حَتّٰى اِذَا جَاءَتْهُمْ رُسُلُنَا يَتَوَفَّوْنَهُمْ ۙ قَالُوْٓا اَيْنَ مَا كُنْتُمْ

ⁿ6 : 152. ᵇ3 : 152; 7 : 72; 22 : 72. ᶜ10 : 50; 15 : 6; 16 : 62; 35 : 46.
ᵈ2 : 39; 20 : 124. ᵉ2 : 40; 5 : 11, 87; 6 : 50; 7 : 41; 22 : 58.
ᶠ6 : 22; 10 : 18; 11 : 19; 61 : 8.

---

969. When the time fixed for the punishment of a people arrives, it cannot be averted, delayed or postponed.

970. The point is worthy of special note that, like some preceding verses (*e.g.*, 7 : 27, 28 & 32), the address in the words, *O children of Adam*, is to the people of the Holy Prophet's time and to the generations that are yet to be born and not to the people who lived in the distant past and came immediately after Adam.

971. The words mean that the rejectors of God's Messengers will see with their own eyes the fulfilment of the prophecies foretelling their defeat and discomfiture and shall taste the punishment promised to them for opposing God's Messengers.

[a]'Where is that which you used to call upon besides Allāh?' They will answer, 'We cannot find them;' and they will [b]bear witness against themselves that they were disbelievers.

تَدْعُوْنَ مِنْ دُوْنِ اللّٰهِ ۗ قَالُوْا ضَلُّوْا عَنَّا وَشَهِدُوْا
عَلٰٓى اَنْفُسِهِمْ اَنَّهُمْ كَانُوْا كٰفِرِيْنَ ﴿۳۸﴾

39. He will say, 'Enter ye into the Fire among the nations of jinn and men who passed away before you.' Every time a nation enters, it shall curse its sister *nation* until, when they have all successively arrived therein, the last of them[972] will say with regard to the first of them, 'Our Lord, these led us astray, so give them a [c]double punishment of the Fire.' He will say, 'For each there is double *punishment*,[973] but you do not know.'

قَالَ ادْخُلُوْا فِيْٓ اُمَمٍ قَدْ خَلَتْ مِنْ قَبْلِكُمْ مِّنَ الْجِنِّ
وَالْاِنْسِ فِي النَّارِ ۗ كُلَّمَا دَخَلَتْ اُمَّةٌ لَّعَنَتْ اُخْتَهَا ۗ
حَتّٰٓى اِذَا ادَّارَكُوْا فِيْهَا جَمِيْعًا ۙ قَالَتْ اُخْرٰىهُمْ لِاُوْلٰىهُمْ
رَبَّنَا هٰٓؤُلَآءِ اَضَلُّوْنَا فَاٰتِهِمْ عَذَابًا ضِعْفًا مِّنَ النَّارِ ۬ۗ
قَالَ لِكُلٍّ ضِعْفٌ وَّلٰكِنْ لَّا تَعْلَمُوْنَ ﴿۳۹﴾

40. And the first of them will say to the last of them, 'You have then no superiority over us; taste, therefore, the punishment for all that you did.'

وَقَالَتْ اُوْلٰىهُمْ لِاُخْرٰىهُمْ فَمَا كَانَ لَكُمْ عَلَيْنَا مِنْ
فَضْلٍ فَذُوْقُوا الْعَذَابَ بِمَا كُنْتُمْ تَكْسِبُوْنَ ﴿۴۰﴾

R. 5 41. [d]Those who reject Our Signs and turn away from them with disdain, the gates of *spiritual* firmament will not be opened for them, nor will they enter Heaven until a camel goes through the eye of a needle.[974] And thus do We requite the offenders.

اِنَّ الَّذِيْنَ كَذَّبُوْا بِاٰيٰتِنَا وَاسْتَكْبَرُوْا عَنْهَا لَا تُفَتَّحُ
لَهُمْ اَبْوَابُ السَّمَآءِ وَلَا يَدْخُلُوْنَ الْجَنَّةَ حَتّٰى يَلِجَ
الْجَمَلُ فِيْ سَمِّ الْخِيَاطِ ۗ وَكَذٰلِكَ نَجْزِي الْمُجْرِمِيْنَ ﴿۴۱﴾

---

[a]6 : 23; 40 : 74-75. [b]6 : 131. [c]38 : 62. [d]See 7 : 37.

---

972. The leaders and their followers.

973. Pain and torment appear heavy while they last. God's torment will be unbearable.

974. *Jamal* may also mean a rope, for a rope bears a better resemblance to the thread which is passed through the eye of a needle. It will not be possible for rejectors of God's Signs to enter Heaven. See Matt. 19 : 24.

42. [a]They shall have a bed of Hell and over them coverings *of the same*. And thus do We requite the unjust.

لَهُم مِّن جَهَنَّمَ مِهَادٌ وَمِن فَوْقِهِمْ غَوَاشٍ ۚ وَكَذَٰلِكَ نَجْزِي الظَّالِمِينَ ﴿٤٢﴾

43. But *as to* those who believe and do good works—*and* [b]We charge not any soul beyond its capacity[975]—these are the inmates of Heaven; they shall abide therein.

وَالَّذِينَ آمَنُوا وَعَمِلُوا الصَّالِحَاتِ لَا نُكَلِّفُ نَفْسًا إِلَّا وُسْعَهَا أُولَٰئِكَ أَصْحَابُ الْجَنَّةِ ۖ هُمْ فِيهَا خَالِدُونَ ﴿٤٣﴾

44. And We shall [c]remove whatever rancour[976] may be in their hearts. [d]Beneath them shall flow rivers. And they shall say, [e]'All praise belongs to Allāh Who has guided us to this *Paradise*. And we could not have found guidance, if Allāh had not guided us. The Messengers of our Lord did indeed bring the Truth.' And it shall be proclaimed unto them, 'This is the Heaven to which you have been made heirs *as a reward* for what you did.'

وَنَزَعْنَا مَا فِي صُدُورِهِم مِّنْ غِلٍّ تَجْرِي مِن تَحْتِهِمُ الْأَنْهَارُ ۖ وَقَالُوا الْحَمْدُ لِلَّهِ الَّذِي هَدَانَا لِهَٰذَا وَمَا كُنَّا لِنَهْتَدِيَ لَوْلَا أَنْ هَدَانَا اللَّهُ ۖ لَقَدْ جَاءَتْ رُسُلُ رَبِّنَا بِالْحَقِّ ۖ وَنُودُوا أَن تِلْكُمُ الْجَنَّةُ أُورِثْتُمُوهَا بِمَا كُنتُمْ تَعْمَلُونَ ﴿٤٤﴾

45. And the inmates of Heaven will call out to the inmates of Hell, *saying*, 'We have indeed found what our Lord promised us to be true. Have you also found what your Lord promised you to be true?' They shall say, 'Yea!' Then a proclaimer shall proclaim between them, *saying*, 'The curse of Allāh is on the wrongdoers—

وَنَادَىٰ أَصْحَابُ الْجَنَّةِ أَصْحَابَ النَّارِ أَن قَدْ وَجَدْنَا مَا وَعَدَنَا رَبُّنَا حَقًّا فَهَلْ وَجَدتُّم مَّا وَعَدَ رَبُّكُمْ حَقًّا ۖ قَالُوا نَعَمْ ۚ فَأَذَّنَ مُؤَذِّنٌ بَيْنَهُمْ أَن لَّعْنَةُ اللَّهِ عَلَى الظَّالِمِينَ ﴿٤٥﴾

[a]39 : 17. [b]2 : 234, 287; 6 : 153; 7 : 43; 23 : 63. [c]15 : 48. [d]See 2 : 26. [e]10 : 11; 39 : 75.

975. The parenthetical clause, ***We charge not any soul beyond its capacity***, contradicts the Christian dogma that sin being ingrained in human nature, it is beyond the power of man to get rid of it.

976. In fact, heavenly life begins in this very world (55 : 47) and he is said to be enjoying it whose heart is free from enmity, jealousy, rancour and mental disquiet.

46. [a]'Who hinder *men* from the path of Allāh and seek to make it crooked[977] and who are disbelievers in the Hereafter.'

الَّذِيْنَ يَصُدُّوْنَ عَنْ سَبِيْلِ اللّٰهِ وَيَبْغُوْنَهَا عِوَجًا ۚ
وَهُمْ بِالْاٰخِرَةِ كٰفِرُوْنَ ۝٤٦

47. And between the two there shall be a partition, and on the Elevated Places[978] *in heaven* there shall be men who will know all by their marks. And they will call out to the people of Heaven, 'Peace be on you.' These will not have *yet* entered it[979] although they will be hoping *to do so*.

وَبَيْنَهُمَا حِجَابٌ ۚ وَعَلَى الْاَعْرَافِ رِجَالٌ يَّعْرِفُوْنَ كُلًّا ۢ
بِسِيْمٰىهُمْ ۚ وَنَادَوْا اَصْحٰبَ الْجَنَّةِ اَنْ سَلٰمٌ عَلَيْكُمْ ۣ
لَمْ يَدْخُلُوْهَا وَهُمْ يَطْمَعُوْنَ ۝٤٧

48. And when their eyes are turned towards the companions of the Fire, they will say, 'Our Lord, [b]place us not with the wrongdoing people.'

وَاِذَا صُرِفَتْ اَبْصَارُهُمْ تِلْقَآءَ اَصْحٰبِ النَّارِ ۙ قَالُوْا رَبَّنَا
لَا تَجْعَلْنَا مَعَ الْقَوْمِ الظّٰلِمِيْنَ ۝٤٨

R. 6 49. And the occupants of the Elevated Places will call out to men, whom they will know by their marks,[980] *and* say, 'Your numbers availed you not, nor your arrogance.

وَنَادٰٓى اَصْحٰبُ الْاَعْرَافِ رِجَالًا يَّعْرِفُوْنَهُمْ بِسِيْمٰىهُمْ
قَالُوْا مَآ اَغْنٰى عَنْكُمْ جَمْعُكُمْ وَمَا كُنْتُمْ تَسْتَكْبِرُوْنَ ۝٤٩

[a]7 : 87; 11 : 20; 14 : 4; 16 : 89. [b]23 : 95.

977. The expression signifies that the wrongdoers desire to corrupt true religion. They are not only themselves wicked but also try to make others like themselves and even seek to distort and tamper with religious teaching.

978. *A'rāf* is the plural of '*Urf* which means 'an elevated place.' They say '*Arafa 'alā al-Qaum*, *i.e.*, he was or became manager or superintendent of the affairs of the people, being acquainted with them. It is generally men of high dignity and distinguished position that are seated on elevated places. According to Ḥasan and Mujāhid the men on the Elevated Places will be the *elite* among the believers or the most learned among them; according to Kirmānī, they will be the Martyrs. Some others think that they will be the Prophets and this appears to be the most correct view. The men seated on the Elevated Places not only will command a better view, but, on account of their high rank and position, will also be better informed. They will know the rank and station of every person from his very appearance. It is evidently a wrong view that the men on the *A'rāf* (Elevated Places) will be those persons of middling ranks whose case will not have yet been decided, it beihg, as it were, still under consideration. There is no sense in placing such persons on elevated places while Martyrs and Prophets will be occupying lower positions.

979. The words refer to would-be dwellers of Heaven who will not have yet entered it, but will be hoping to do so soon. The people on the Elevated Places will recognize them as would-be dwellers of Heaven, even though they will not have yet entered it.

980. The occupants of the Elevated Places, *i.e.*, the Prophets, will call out to certain persons from among the people to whom they had been sent and whom they will recognize by their special marks and will say to them that they must have realized now the sorry end of their opposition to them.

50. [a]'Are these[981] the men about whom you swore that Allāh would not extend mercy to them?' *To them God* will say, 'Enter Paradise; no fear *shall come* upon you, nor shall you grieve.'

أَهٰؤُلَاءِ الَّذِينَ أَقْسَمْتُمْ لَا يَنَالُهُمُ اللّٰهُ بِرَحْمَةٍ
ادْخُلُوا الْجَنَّةَ لَا خَوْفٌ عَلَيْكُمْ وَلَا أَنْتُمْ تَحْزَنُونَ ﴿٥٠﴾

51. And the inmates of the Fire will call out to the inmates of Heaven, 'Pour out on us some water or some of that which Allāh has provided for you.' They will say, 'Verily, Allāh has forbidden them both to disbelievers,

وَنَادٰى أَصْحٰبُ النَّارِ أَصْحٰبَ الْجَنَّةِ أَنْ أَفِيضُوا عَلَيْنَا
مِنَ الْمَاءِ أَوْ مِمَّا رَزَقَكُمُ اللّٰهُ قَالُوا إِنَّ اللّٰهَ حَرَّمَهُمَا
عَلَى الْكٰفِرِينَ ﴿٥١﴾

52. [b]Those who took their religion for a pastime and a sport,[982] and whom the life of the world beguiled.' This day, then, shall [c]We forget them as they forgot the meeting of this day of theirs, and as they persisted in denying Our Signs.

الَّذِينَ اتَّخَذُوا دِينَهُمْ لَهْوًا وَلَعِبًا وَغَرَّتْهُمُ الْحَيٰوةُ
الدُّنْيَا فَالْيَوْمَ نَنْسٰهُمْ كَمَا نَسُوا لِقَاءَ يَوْمِهِمْ هٰذَا
وَمَا كَانُوا بِاٰيٰتِنَا يَجْحَدُونَ ﴿٥٢﴾

53. And surely [d]We have brought them a Book which We have expounded with knowledge, a guidance and a mercy for a people who believe.

وَلَقَدْ جِئْنٰهُمْ بِكِتٰبٍ فَصَّلْنٰهُ عَلٰى عِلْمٍ هُدًى وَّ
رَحْمَةً لِّقَوْمٍ يُّؤْمِنُونَ ﴿٥٣﴾

54. [e]Do they wait only for the fulfilment[983] *of warnings* thereof? On the day when the fulfilment thereof shall come, those who had

هَلْ يَنْظُرُونَ إِلَّا تَأْوِيلَهُ يَوْمَ يَأْتِي تَأْوِيلُهُ يَقُولُ

[a]23 : 111. [b]5 : 58; 6 : 71. [c]45 : 35. [d]6 : 115; 10 : 58; 12 : 112; 16 : 90; 29 : 52. [e]2 : 211; 6 : 159.

981. The reference in the word "these" is to the would-be inmates of Heaven. The Prophets will address the inmates of Hell and tell them to look at the would-be inmates of Heaven— the poor believers whom they ridiculed and looked down upon—and then will ask them, "Are these the men about whom you swore that Allāh would not extend mercy to them?"

982. The disbelievers were convinced in their heart of hearts of the truth of Islām but, as they took their religion for a pastime, they refused to listen to the dictates of reason and to the voice of their conscience. So God will ignore them as they refused to believe that they will ever meet their Creator and they will have to render account of their deeds to Him.

983. For the sake of convenience the word *Ta'wīl* has been rendered here as fulfilment of warning. See also 372.

forgotten it before shall say, 'The Messengers of our Lord did indeed bring the Truth. Have we then any intercessors to intercede for us? Or [a]could we be sent back so that we might do *good deeds* other than that which we used to do?' They have indeed ruined their souls and that which they used to fabricate has failed them.

الَّذِينَ نَسُوهُ مِن قَبْلُ قَدْ جَآءَتْ رُسُلُ رَبِّنَا بِالْحَقِّ
فَهَل لَّنَا مِن شُفَعَآءَ فَيَشْفَعُوا لَنَآ أَوْ نُرَدُّ فَنَعْمَلَ
غَيْرَ الَّذِي كُنَّا نَعْمَلُ قَدْ خَسِرُوٓا أَنفُسَهُمْ وَضَلَّ
عَنْهُم مَّا كَانُوا يَفْتَرُونَ ﴿٥٤﴾ ع ٦ ١٣

R. 7 55. Surely, your Lord is Allāh, Who [b]created the heavens and the earth in six periods,[984] then He settled[985] Himself firmly on the Throne.[986] He makes the night [c]cover the day, which it pursues swiftly. *And He created* the sun and the moon and the stars—*all* made

إِنَّ رَبَّكُمُ اللَّهُ الَّذِي خَلَقَ السَّمٰوٰتِ وَالْأَرْضَ فِي
سِتَّةِ أَيَّامٍ ثُمَّ اسْتَوَىٰ عَلَى الْعَرْشِ يُغْشِي الَّيْلَ النَّهَارَ
يَطْلُبُهُ حَثِيثًا وَالشَّمْسَ وَالْقَمَرَ وَالنُّجُومَ مُسَخَّرٰتٍ

[a]26 : 103; 35 : 38; 39 : 59. [b]10 : 4; 11 : 8; 25 : 60; 32 : 5; 41 : 10-13; 50 : 39; 57 : 5; [c]13 : 4; 36 : 38.

984. *Ayyām* is the plural of *Yaum* which denotes time absolutely (1 : 4); or it may signify an indefinite period, or a stage in the development of a thing. It is not possible to surmise and define the length of this period. It may be "a thousand years" (22 : 48), or "fifty thousand years" (70 : 5). But the word *Yaum* definitely does not refer here or in any other verse of the Qur'ān as the period of time determined by the rotation of the earth on its axis. God has not disclosed to us the extent of all His days. If some of God's days extend over a thousand years and others over fifty thousand years, there may be still others which extend over millions or billions of years. Science has disclosed the fact that it took the heavens and the earth millions of years to be evolved into their present shape. A vision of the eminent Muslim scholar, Muhyī al-Dīn Ibn 'Arabī, leads one to a similar conclusion. Thus we cannot definitely determine the length of the" six days" during which the creation of the heavens and the earth was completed. God brings about different changes in different periods, some taking a thousand years, others fifty thousand years and yet others even a longer period. All that we can say is that the creation of the heavens and the earth took six long cycles to become perfect and complete.

985. See 54.

986. '*Arsh* (Throne) represents God's transcendent attributes (*Ṣifāt Tanzīhiyyah*), *i.e.*, such attributes as are not found in any other being. The four attributes of God mentioned in *Sūrah* Ikhlāṣ are His transcendent attributes. These attributes are eternal and un-changeable and are manifested through God's attributes of similitude (*Ṣifāt Tashbīhiyyah*), *i.e.*, such attributes as are found more or less in other beings also. These latter attributes are said to be the bearers of the '*Arsh*. They are *Rabb Al-'Ālamīn*, *Al-Rahmān*, *Al-Raḥīm* and *Mālik Yaum al-Dīn*. That '*Arsh* represents the transcendent attributes of God is also clear from 23 : 117 which shows that the "Unity of God" and His '*Arsh* are intimately connected, for it is the transcendent attributes which constitute the real proof of Divine Unity, other attributes of God being shared by man in different degrees. The words, "Settled Himself on the Throne" signify that after the creation of the physical universe the transcendent attributes of God and His attributes of similitude came into operation and all the affairs of the world began to be conducted through the set laws of nature and became in perfect working order. See also 'The Larger Edition of the Commentary," pp. 973—976.

subservient by His command.[987] Verily, His is the creation and the command. Blessed is Allāh, the Lord of the worlds.

بِاَمْرِهٖ ؕ اَلَا لَهُ الْخَلْقُ وَالْاَمْرُ ؕ تَبٰرَكَ اللّٰهُ رَبُّ
الْعٰلَمِيْنَ ﴿۵۵﴾

56. [a]Call upon your Lord humbly and in secret. Surely, He does not love the transgressors.

اُدْعُوْا رَبَّكُمْ تَضَرُّعًا وَّخُفْيَةً ؕ اِنَّهٗ لَا يُحِبُّ
الْمُعْتَدِيْنَ ﴿۵۶﴾

57. And create not disorder in the earth after it has been set in order,[988] and [b]call upon Him in fear and hope. Surely, the mercy of Allāh is nigh unto those who do good.[989]

وَلَا تُفْسِدُوْا فِي الْاَرْضِ بَعْدَ اِصْلَاحِهَا وَادْعُوْهُ
خَوْفًا وَّطَمَعًا ؕ اِنَّ رَحْمَتَ اللّٰهِ قَرِيْبٌ مِّنَ الْمُحْسِنِيْنَ ﴿۵۷﴾

58. And [c]He it is Who sends the winds as glad tidings before His mercy[990] till, when they bear a heavy cloud, We drive it to a dead land; then We send down water therefrom and We bring forth therewith fruits of every kind. In like manner do We bring forth the dead that you may remember.

وَهُوَ الَّذِيْ يُرْسِلُ الرِّيٰحَ بُشْرًا بَيْنَ يَدَيْ رَحْمَتِهٖ ؕ
حَتّٰۤى اِذَاۤ اَقَلَّتْ سَحَابًا ثِقَالًا سُقْنٰهُ لِبَلَدٍ مَّيِّتٍ فَاَنْزَلْنَا
بِهِ الْمَآءَ فَاَخْرَجْنَا بِهٖ مِنْ كُلِّ الثَّمَرٰتِ ؕ كَذٰلِكَ نُخْرِجُ
الْمَوْتٰى لَعَلَّكُمْ تَذَكَّرُوْنَ ﴿۵۸﴾

[a]6 : 64; 7 : 206. [b]21 : 91; 32 : 17. [c]15 : 23; 24 : 44; 25 : 49; 27 : 64; 30 : 47; 35 : 10.

987. The distinction between *Khalq* (creation) and *'Amr* (command) is that while the former word generally means, the measuring out or evolving of a thing out of pre-existing matter, the latter means, bringing into being without matter by uttering the simple command word "be." The clause, ***His is the creation and the command***, may also mean that God has not only created the universe but He also exercises authority and command over it. *'Amr* also means, the making of laws.

988. The expression means that before the revelation of the Qur'ān the disbelievers had some excuse for leading unrighteous lives; but now that a perfect guidance has come to them, they will not be allowed to go on making mischief and grovelling in sin and iniquity and leading unrighteous lives with impunity. The word *Islāh* (order) refers to the good and ordered life that came into being with the revelation of the Qur'ān and the advent of the Holy Prophet

989. *Muhsin* signifies "one who strives to be perfect in good deeds." A famous saying of the Holy Prophet describes the *Muhsin* as one who does a good deed as if he is actually seeing God or that at least God is seeing him (Bukhārī & Muslim).

990. The word *Rahmah* here refers to rain. Just as in the physical world rain is preceded by cool breeze which serves as its harbinger, similarly before a Prophet of God makes his appearance, there is a sort of general religious awakening among men. The verse signifies that just as rain-water gives new life to a dead land and causes fruits, vegetables and corn to grow from it, similarly, the heavenly water of revelation breathes a new life into a people devoid of spiritual life. The verse thus holds out a promise that the bleak, arid and barren land of Arabia would soon blossom into a garden full of trees laden with fruits, and of plants bearing fragrant flowers, in consequence of the heavenly water that

59. And the good land — its vegetation comes forth *plentifully* by the command of its Lord; and that which is bad, *its vegetation* does not come forth but scantily.[991] In like manner do We expound the Signs in various forms for a people who are grateful.

وَالْبَلَدُ الطَّيِّبُ يَخْرُجُ نَبَاتُهُ بِإِذْنِ رَبِّهِ ۚ وَالَّذِي خَبُثَ لَا يَخْرُجُ إِلَّا نَكِدًا ۚ كَذَٰلِكَ نُصَرِّفُ الْآيَاتِ لِقَوْمٍ يَشْكُرُونَ ﴿٥٩﴾ ع ٥ ١٤

R. 8 60. We sent Noah[992] to his people and he said, 'O my people, worship Allāh, you have no other god but Him. Indeed, I fear for you the punishment of the great day.'

لَقَدْ أَرْسَلْنَا نُوحًا إِلَىٰ قَوْمِهِ فَقَالَ يَا قَوْمِ اعْبُدُوا اللَّهَ مَا لَكُمْ مِنْ إِلَٰهٍ غَيْرُهُ ۖ إِنِّي أَخَافُ عَلَيْكُمْ عَذَابَ يَوْمٍ عَظِيمٍ ﴿٦٠﴾

61. [b]The chiefs of his people said, 'Surely, we see thee to be in manifest error.'

قَالَ الْمَلَأُ مِنْ قَوْمِهِ إِنَّا لَنَرَاكَ فِي ضَلَالٍ مُبِينٍ ﴿٦١﴾

62. He said, 'O my people, [c]there is no error in me, but I am a Messenger from the Lord of the worlds;[993]

قَالَ يَا قَوْمِ لَيْسَ بِي ضَلَالَةٌ وَلَٰكِنِّي رَسُولٌ مِنْ رَبِّ الْعَالَمِينَ ﴿٦٢﴾

[a]11 : 26-27; 23 : 24. [b]11 : 28; 23 : 25-26. [c]7 : 68.

has descended on it in the form of the Qur'ān. No wonder that the Arabs, who had hitherto been regarded as the dregs and scum of humanity, suddenly emerged as teachers and leaders thereof.

991. Just as rain produces different effects upon different plots of land according to their nature and quality; so does Divine revelation affect different men in different ways. The Holy Prophet is reported to have said that there are three kinds of land: (*a*) The good, level land which, when watered by rain, absorbs the rain-water and yields good vegetation and brings forth abundant fruit. (*b*) The land which, being low-lying and rocky, only collects rain-water but does not absorb it and so brings forth no vegetation but provides drinking water for men and beasts. (*c*) The high stony ground which neither collects the water of rain nor absorbs it and is quite useless both for the purpose of vegetation and as a storage of rain-water. Similarly, men are of three kinds: (1) Those who not only themselves profit by Divine revelation but prove a source of spiritual guidance for others. (2) Those who do not themselves profit by the Divine revelation, but receive it and keep it stored up for others to benefit thereby. (3) Those who neither derive any benefit from the Divine revelation themselves nor keep it stored up for the use of others. They are like that piece of land which neither yields any produce nor collects water so that men and beasts may drink of it.

992. After having briefly described the great moral reformation that the appearance of a Divine Prophet brings about among his people and the evil consequences to which opposition to him leads, the *Sūrah* with this verse proceeds to give illustrations of some of the nations of antiquity, beginning with the people of Noah.

993. Noah refutes the charge of his being in error. He, in effect, says that a person who is proceeding to a place may indeed be said to be unacquainted with the way leading to it or to have lost the same owing to his having never trodden it before, but how can a person who is returning from a certain place be said not to know the way to that place and how

63. [a]'I deliver to you the messages of my Lord and give you sincere advice and I know from Allāh what you do not know;

أُبَلِّغُكُمْ رِسٰلٰتِ رَبِّيْ وَاَنْصَحُ لَكُمْ وَاَعْلَمُ مِنَ اللّٰهِ مَا لَا تَعْلَمُوْنَ ﴿۶۳﴾

64. [b]'Do you wonder that an exhortation has come to you from your Lord through a man from among yourselves, that he may warn you and that you may become righteous and that you may be shown mercy?'

اَوَعَجِبْتُمْ اَنْ جَآءَكُمْ ذِكْرٌ مِّنْ رَّبِّكُمْ عَلٰى رَجُلٍ مِّنْكُمْ لِيُنْذِرَكُمْ وَلِتَتَّقُوْا وَلَعَلَّكُمْ تُرْحَمُوْنَ ﴿۶۴﴾

65. But [c]they called him a liar, so We saved him and those with him in the Ark and We drowned those who rejected Our Signs. They were indeed a blind[994] people.

فَكَذَّبُوْهُ فَاَنْجَيْنٰهُ وَالَّذِيْنَ مَعَهٗ فِي الْفُلْكِ وَاَغْرَقْنَا الَّذِيْنَ كَذَّبُوْا بِاٰيٰتِنَا ۗ اِنَّهُمْ كَانُوْا قَوْمًا عَمِيْنَ ﴿۶۵﴾ ع ۸ ۱۵

R. 9 66. And [d]unto 'Ād[995] *We sent* their brother Hūd.[996] He said, 'O my people, worship Allāh; you have no other deity but Him. Will you not then fear *Him*?'

وَاِلٰى عَادٍ اَخَاهُمْ هُوْدًا ۗ قَالَ يٰقَوْمِ اعْبُدُوا اللّٰهَ مَا لَكُمْ مِّنْ اِلٰهٍ غَيْرُهٗ ۗ اَفَلَا تَتَّقُوْنَ ﴿۶۶﴾

67. The disbelieving chiefs of his people said, [e]"We surely see thee *lost* in foolishness and we surely think thee to be *one* of the liars.'

قَالَ الْمَلَاُ الَّذِيْنَ كَفَرُوْا مِنْ قَوْمِهٖٓ اِنَّا لَنَرٰىكَ فِيْ سَفَاهَةٍ وَّاِنَّا لَنَظُنُّكَ مِنَ الْكٰذِبِيْنَ ﴿۶۷﴾

68. He replied, [f]'O my people, there is no foolishness in me, but I am a Messenger from the Lord of the worlds;

قَالَ يٰقَوْمِ لَيْسَ بِيْ سَفَاهَةٌ وَّلٰكِنِّيْ رَسُوْلٌ مِّنْ رَّبِّ الْعٰلَمِيْنَ ﴿۶۸﴾

---

[a]7 : 69, 80; 46 : 24. [b]7 : 70; 10 : 3; 38 : 5; 50 : 3. [c]7 : 73; 26 : 120-121. [d]11 : 51; 46 : 22. [e]41 : 16. [f]7 : 62.

---

possibly can he lose it? Noah said that he could not be in error, for he had come from God and, therefore, there was no possibility of his wandering away from the path that leads to Him.

994. '*Amīn* is the plural of *A'mā* which means, blind in both eyes; blind in respect of the mind; erring (Lane).

995. '*Ād* was the name of a tribe who lived in the remote past in Arabia. At one time they ruled over most of the fertile parts of greater Arabia, particularly Yemen, Syria and Mesopotamia. They were the first people to exercise dominion over practically the whole of Arabia. They are known as '*Ād al-Ūlā* or the first '*Ād*. See also 1323.

996. *Hūd* was seventh in descent from Noah.

69. [a]'I deliver to you the messages of my Lord and I am to you a sincere and faithful counsellor.

أُبَلِّغُكُمْ رِسٰلٰتِ رَبِّيْ وَاَنَا لَكُمْ نَاصِحٌ اَمِيْنٌ ﴿٦٩﴾

70. [b]'Do you wonder that an exhortation has come to you from your Lord through a man from among yourselves that he may warn you? And remember *the time* when [c]He made you heirs to *His favours*[997] after the people of Noah and increasingly endowed you with great physical strength.[997A] Remember, then, the favours of Allāh, that you may prosper.'

اَوَعَجِبْتُمْ اَنْ جَآءَكُمْ ذِكْرٌ مِّنْ رَّبِّكُمْ عَلٰى رَجُلٍ
مِّنْكُمْ لِيُنْذِرَكُمْ ۗ وَاذْكُرُوْٓا اِذْ جَعَلَكُمْ خُلَفَآءَ مِنْۢ
بَعْدِ قَوْمِ نُوْحٍ وَّزَادَكُمْ فِي الْخَلْقِ بَصْۜطَةً ۚ فَاذْكُرُوْٓا
اٰلَآءَ اللّٰهِ لَعَلَّكُمْ تُفْلِحُوْنَ ﴿٧٠﴾

71. They said, [d]'Hast thou come to us that we may worship Allāh alone and forsake what our fathers used to worship? Bring us, then, that which thou threatenest us with, if thou art of the truthful.'

قَالُوْٓا اَجِئْتَنَا لِنَعْبُدَ اللّٰهَ وَحْدَهٗ وَنَذَرَ مَا كَانَ
يَعْبُدُ اٰبَآؤُنَا ۚ فَاْتِنَا بِمَا تَعِدُنَآ اِنْ كُنْتَ مِنَ
الصّٰدِقِيْنَ ﴿٧١﴾

72. He replied, 'Indeed there have *already* fallen on you punishment and wrath from your Lord. [e]Do you dispute with me about names which you have named—you and your fathers—for which Allāh has sent down no authority? Wait then, [f]I am with you among those who wait.'

قَالَ قَدْ وَقَعَ عَلَيْكُمْ مِّنْ رَّبِّكُمْ رِجْسٌ وَّغَضَبٌ ۗ
اَتُجَادِلُوْنَنِيْ فِيْٓ اَسْمَآءٍ سَمَّيْتُمُوْهَآ اَنْتُمْ وَاٰبَآؤُكُمْ
مَّا نَزَّلَ اللّٰهُ بِهَا مِنْ سُلْطٰنٍ ۗ فَانْتَظِرُوْٓا اِنِّيْ مَعَكُمْ
مِّنَ الْمُنْتَظِرِيْنَ ﴿٧٢﴾

73. And [g]We saved him and those who were with him by Our mercy and We cut off the last remnants of those who rejected Our Signs and had not believed.

فَاَنْجَيْنٰهُ وَالَّذِيْنَ مَعَهٗ بِرَحْمَةٍ مِّنَّا وَقَطَعْنَا دَابِرَ
الَّذِيْنَ كَذَّبُوْا بِاٰيٰتِنَا وَمَا كَانُوْا مُؤْمِنِيْنَ ﴿٧٣﴾ ع ٩ ١٦

[a]7 : 63,80; 46 : 24. [b]7 : 64; 10 : 3; 38 : 5; 50 : 3. [c]6 : 166; 7 : 75, 130; 10 : 15. [d]10 : 79; 11 : 63, 88. [e]3 : 152; 7 : 34; 22 : 72; 53: 24. [f]10 : 21, 103; 11 : 123. [g]7 : 165; 26 : 120-121.

997. The Adites were a very prosperous and powerful people

997A. The words also mean that He increased your posterity.

R. 10 74. And to [a]Thamūd[998] *We sent* their brother Ṣāliḥ.[999] He said, ‘O my people, worship Allāh; you have no god other than Him. Verily, there has come to you a clear evidence from your Lord—[b]this she-camel[1000] of Allāh, a Sign for you. So leave her that she may feed in Allāh’s earth[1001] and do her no harm, lest a painful punishment seize you;

وَإِلَىٰ ثَمُودَ أَخَاهُمْ صَٰلِحًا ۗ قَالَ يَٰقَوْمِ ٱعْبُدُوا۟ ٱللَّهَ مَا
لَكُم مِّنْ إِلَٰهٍ غَيْرُهُۥ ۖ قَدْ جَآءَتْكُم بَيِّنَةٌ مِّن رَّبِّكُمْ ۖ
هَٰذِهِۦ نَاقَةُ ٱللَّهِ لَكُمْ ءَايَةً ۖ فَذَرُوهَا تَأْكُلْ فِىٓ أَرْضِ
ٱللَّهِ ۖ وَلَا تَمَسُّوهَا بِسُوٓءٍ فَيَأْخُذَكُمْ عَذَابٌ أَلِيمٌ ﴿٧٤﴾

75. ‘And remember *the time* [c]when He made you heirs *to His favours* after ‘Ād and settled you in the land so *that* you build palaces in its plains and [d]you hew[1002] the mountains into dwellings. Remember, therefore, the favours of Allāh and commit not iniquity in the earth causing disorder.’

وَٱذْكُرُوٓا۟ إِذْ جَعَلَكُمْ خُلَفَآءَ مِنۢ بَعْدِ عَادٍ وَبَوَّأَكُمْ
فِى ٱلْأَرْضِ تَتَّخِذُونَ مِن سُهُولِهَا قُصُورًا وَتَنْحِتُونَ
ٱلْجِبَالَ بُيُوتًا ۖ فَٱذْكُرُوٓا۟ ءَالَآءَ ٱللَّهِ وَلَا تَعْثَوْا۟ فِى
ٱلْأَرْضِ مُفْسِدِينَ ﴿٧٥﴾

[a]11 : 62; 27 : 46. [b]7 : 78; 11 : 65; 17 : 60; 26 : 156; 24 : 28; 91 : 14. [c]6 : 166; 7 : 70, 130; 10 : 15. [d]15 : 83; 26 : 150.

998. The Thamūd tribe lived in the western parts of Arabia, having spread from Aden northward to Syria. They lived shortly before the time of Ishmael. Their territory was adjacent to that of ‘Ād, but they lived mostly in the hills.

999. The Prophet Ṣāliḥ lived after Hūd and was probably a contemporary of Abraham.

1000. The camel formed the chief means of conveyance in those parts and it was on his she-camel that the Prophet Ṣāliḥ used to travel from place to place to preach his Message. Placing obstruction in the way of the free movements of the she-camel or doing it harm was tantamount to obstructing the work with which God had entrusted Ṣāliḥ. There was nothing unusual about the she-camel itself. It was an ordinary animal. The sanctity that attached to it was that God had declared it to be a Sign and a symbol of the sanctity and inviolability of the person of the Prophet Ṣāliḥ, and so doing an injury to it was tantamount to doing an injury to Ṣāliḥ himself and to hampering his work.

1001. The words do not mean that she was to be allowed to graze in any field she entered. The meaning is that no obstruction was to be put in her way and that she was to be permitted to proceed to any place to which Ṣāliḥ might choose to go. The declaration by Ṣāliḥ about the free movements of his she-camel was in harmony with a time-honoured Arab custom.

1002. The words, *you build palaces in its plains*, refer to the winter residences of the tribe, while the expression, *and you hew the mountains into dwellings*, allude to their summer resorts in the hills. The tribe of Thamūd were a cultured people—industrious, wealthy and resourceful. Judged by the standards of their time, they led a luxurious and comfortable life, going up to the hills in the hot season and spending their winter in the plains.

76. The chief[1003] men of his people who were arrogant said to those who were considered weak—those among them who believed—'Do you know *for certain* that Ṣāliḥ is one sent by his Lord?' They answered, 'Surely, we believe in that with which he has been sent.'

قَالَ الْمَلَاُ الَّذِيْنَ اسْتَكْبَرُوْا مِنْ قَوْمِهٖ لِلَّذِيْنَ
اسْتُضْعِفُوْا لِمَنْ اٰمَنَ مِنْهُمْ اَتَعْلَمُوْنَ اَنَّ صٰلِحًا
مُّرْسَلٌ مِّنْ رَّبِّهٖ ؕ قَالُوْۤا اِنَّا بِمَاۤ اُرْسِلَ بِهٖ مُؤْمِنُوْنَ ﴿۷۶﴾

77. Those who were arrogant said, 'Verily, we do disbelieve in that in which you believe.'

قَالَ الَّذِيْنَ اسْتَكْبَرُوْۤا اِنَّا بِالَّذِيْۤ اٰمَنْتُمْ بِهٖ كٰفِرُوْنَ ﴿۷۷﴾

78. Then [a]they hamstrung the she-camel and revolted against the command of their Lord and said, 'O Ṣāliḥ, bring us that which thou threatenest us with, if thou art *indeed one* of the Messengers.'

فَعَقَرُوا النَّاقَةَ وَعَتَوْا عَنْ اَمْرِ رَبِّهِمْ وَقَالُوْا يٰصٰلِحُ
ائْتِنَا بِمَا تَعِدُنَاۤ اِنْ كُنْتَ مِنَ الْمُرْسَلِيْنَ ﴿۷۸﴾

79. So [b]the earthquake seized them and in their homes they lay prostrate upon the ground.

فَاَخَذَتْهُمُ الرَّجْفَةُ فَاَصْبَحُوْا فِيْ دَارِهِمْ جٰثِمِيْنَ ﴿۷۹﴾

80. Then *Ṣāliḥ* turned away from them and said, [c]'O my people, I delivered the Message of my Lord unto you and offered you sincere counsel, but you love not sincere counsellors.'[1004]

فَتَوَلّٰى عَنْهُمْ وَقَالَ يٰقَوْمِ لَقَدْ اَبْلَغْتُكُمْ رِسَالَةَ
رَبِّيْ وَنَصَحْتُ لَكُمْ وَلٰكِنْ لَّا تُحِبُّوْنَ النّٰصِحِيْنَ ﴿۸۰﴾

81. And [d]*We sent* Lot,[1005] when he said to his people, 'Do you commit an abomination such as no one in the world ever did before you?[1006]

وَلُوْطًا اِذْ قَالَ لِقَوْمِهٖۤ اَتَاْتُوْنَ الْفَاحِشَةَ مَا سَبَقَكُمْ
بِهَا مِنْ اَحَدٍ مِّنَ الْعٰلَمِيْنَ ﴿۸۱﴾

[a]See 7 : 74. [b]7 : 92; 11 : 68; 15 : 84; 26 : 159.
[c]7 : 63, 69; 46 : 24. [d]27 : 55; 29 : 29.

1003. *Mala'ā-hū* means, he filled it. *Mala'a al-Qaum* means, the leaders of the people; its wealthy members (Aqrab). They are so called because with their presence in an assembly it seems to be full.

1004. Ṣāliḥ left the stricken city in grief, as he could no longer bear to see the appalling sight, uttering the pathetic words mentioned in the verse with a sad and sorrowful heart, as did the Holy Prophet of Islām at Badr.

1005. Lot was a nephew and contemporary of Abraham (Gen. 11 : 27, 31).

1006. The words imply that it was a new kind of evil which was unknown before, or that its great extent at that time had no parallel before.

82. [a]'You approach men with lust instead of women. Nay, you are a people who exceed *all bounds*.'

إِنَّكُمْ لَتَأْتُونَ الرِّجَالَ شَهْوَةً مِّن دُونِ النِّسَاءِ ۚ
بَلْ أَنتُمْ قَوْمٌ مُّسْرِفُونَ ﴿٨٢﴾

83. And [b]the only answer of his people was that they said, 'Turn them out of your town, for they are men who take pride in their purity.'[1007]

وَمَا كَانَ جَوَابَ قَوْمِهِ إِلَّا أَن قَالُوا أَخْرِجُوهُم
مِّن قَرْيَتِكُمْ ۖ إِنَّهُمْ أُنَاسٌ يَتَطَهَّرُونَ ﴿٨٣﴾

84. And [c]We saved him and his family except his wife; she was of those who stayed behind.

فَأَنجَيْنَاهُ وَأَهْلَهُ إِلَّا امْرَأَتَهُ كَانَتْ مِنَ الْغَابِرِينَ ﴿٨٤﴾

85. And [d]We rained upon them a rain.[1008] Now see, what was the end of the sinners.[1009]

وَأَمْطَرْنَا عَلَيْهِم مَّطَرًا ۖ فَانظُرْ كَيْفَ كَانَ عَاقِبَةُ
الْمُجْرِمِينَ ﴿٨٥﴾

R. 11 86. [e]And to Midian[1010] *We sent* their brother Shu'aib.[1011] He said, 'O my people, worship Allāh; you have no god other than Him. A clear Sign has indeed come to you from your Lord. So [f]give full measure and full weight and diminish

وَإِلَىٰ مَدْيَنَ أَخَاهُمْ شُعَيْبًا ۗ قَالَ يَا قَوْمِ اعْبُدُوا اللَّهَ
مَا لَكُم مِّنْ إِلَٰهٍ غَيْرُهُ ۖ قَدْ جَاءَتْكُم بَيِّنَةٌ مِّن رَّبِّكُمْ
فَأَوْفُوا الْكَيْلَ وَالْمِيزَانَ وَلَا تَبْخَسُوا النَّاسَ أَشْيَاءَهُمْ

---

[a]26 : 166; 27 : 56; 29 : 30. [b]27 : 57. [c]26 : 171-172; 27 : 58; 29 : 34; 37 : 135-136. [d]26 : 174; 27 : 59. [e]11 : 85; 29 : 37. [f]6 : 153; 11 : 86.

1007. The opponents of Lot taunted his followers that they posed and paraded as extra righteous and holy persons.

1008. It often happens in a severe earthquake that rocks and rubble erupt and are carried to a height and then fall back on the earth. This happened at Pompeii; and at Kangra (India) in 1905.

1009. According to some the country round the Dead Sea is the site of the ruined cities. The Qur'ān, however, appears to place it on the route from Medina to Syria (15 : 80).

1010. Midian was Abraham's son from Keturah (Gen. 25 : 1, 2). His descendants settled in the north of Ḥijāz. Midian was also the name of a town on the Red Sea, opposite to Sinai on the Arabian shore. The town was so called because it was inhabited by the descendants of Midian. Some have referred to it as a seaport on account of its proximity to the sea, being situated only at a distance of about eight miles from the Gulf of 'Aqabah; others have spoken of it as an inland town. Midian had a large population of the descendants of Ishmael. Shu'aib had some resemblance with the Holy Prophet in that both had to leave their original home for another town, Midian in the case of Shu'aib and Medina in the case of the Holy Prophet.

1011. Shu'aib was the name of a non-Israelite Prophet who lived before Moses. He is generally looked upon as the father-in-law of Moses, though the Bible makes no mention of the name. According to the Bible, the name of the father-in-law of Moses was Jethro, who is not spoken of as a Prophet. The Qur'ān speaks of Moses as having been raised after Shu'aib, so he could not be his contemporary (7 : 104). As Shu'aib has been mentioned in this verse as the " brother " of Midian, the inference is inevitable that he was a descendant of Abraham, Midian being a son of the Patriarch from his bondmaid, Keturah.

not unto people their things and create not disorder in the earth after it has been set in order. This is better for you, if you are believers;

87. 'And sit not on every path, threatening and ^aturning away from the path of Allāh those who believe in Him and seeking to make it crooked. And ^bremember when you were few and He multiplied¹⁰¹² you. And behold, what was the end of those who created disorder!

88. 'And if there is a party among you, who believes in that with which I have been sent, and a party who does not believe, then have patience until Allāh judges between us. And He is the Best of judges.'

PART IX

89. ^cThe chief men of his people who were arrogant said, 'Assuredly, we will drive thee out, O Shu'aib, and the believers *that are* with thee from our town, or you shall return to our religion.' He said, 'Even though we be unwilling?¹⁰¹³

90. 'If we returned to your religion after Allāh has saved us therefrom, *we would indeed admit that* we had been forging a lie against Allāh. And it behoves us not to return thereto except that Allāh, our Lord, should *so* will. ^dOur Lord comprehends all things in His knowledge. In Allāh have we put our trust. So, O our Lord, decide Thou

وَلَا تُفۡسِدُوۡا فِى الۡاَرۡضِ بَعۡدَ اِصۡلَاحِهَا ذٰلِكُمۡ خَيۡرٌ لَّكُمۡ اِنۡ كُنۡتُمۡ مُّؤۡمِنِيۡنَ ۞

وَلَا تَقۡعُدُوۡا بِكُلِّ صِرَاطٍ تُوۡعِدُوۡنَ وَتَصُدُّوۡنَ عَنۡ سَبِيۡلِ اللّٰهِ مَنۡ اٰمَنَ بِهٖ وَتَبۡغُوۡنَهَا عِوَجًا ۚ وَاذۡكُرُوۡۤا اِذۡ كُنۡتُمۡ قَلِيۡلًا فَكَثَّرَكُمۡ وَانۡظُرُوۡا كَيۡفَ كَانَ عَاقِبَةُ الۡمُفۡسِدِيۡنَ ۞

وَاِنۡ كَانَ طَآئِفَةٌ مِّنۡكُمۡ اٰمَنُوۡا بِالَّذِىۡۤ اُرۡسِلۡتُ بِهٖ وَطَآئِفَةٌ لَّمۡ يُؤۡمِنُوۡا فَاصۡبِرُوۡا حَتّٰى يَحۡكُمَ اللّٰهُ بَيۡنَنَا ۚ وَهُوَ خَيۡرُ الۡحٰكِمِيۡنَ ۞

قَالَ الۡمَلَاُ الَّذِيۡنَ اسۡتَكۡبَرُوۡا مِنۡ قَوۡمِهٖ لَنُخۡرِجَنَّكَ يٰشُعَيۡبُ وَالَّذِيۡنَ اٰمَنُوۡا مَعَكَ مِنۡ قَرۡيَتِنَاۤ اَوۡ لَتَعُوۡدُنَّ فِىۡ مِلَّتِنَا ۚ قَالَ اَوَلَوۡ كُنَّا كٰرِهِيۡنَ ۞

قَدِ افۡتَرَيۡنَا عَلَى اللّٰهِ كَذِبًا اِنۡ عُدۡنَا فِىۡ مِلَّتِكُمۡ بَعۡدَ اِذۡ نَجّٰنَا اللّٰهُ مِنۡهَا ۚ وَمَا يَكُوۡنُ لَنَاۤ اَنۡ نَّعُوۡدَ فِيۡهَاۤ اِلَّاۤ اَنۡ يَّشَآءَ اللّٰهُ رَبُّنَا ۚ وَسِعَ رَبُّنَا كُلَّ شَىۡءٍ عِلۡمًا ۚ عَلَى اللّٰهِ تَوَكَّلۡنَا ۚ رَبَّنَا افۡتَحۡ بَيۡنَنَا وَبَيۡنَ قَوۡمِنَا

---

^a7 : 46; 11 : 20; 14 : 4; 16 : 89   ^b3 : 124; 8 : 27.   ^c14 : 14.   ^d2 : 256; 40 : 8.

1012. The children of Abraham from Keturah, who was a bondwoman, were despised by both the Israelites and the Ishmaelites. They were looked down upon as weak and despicable, but God increased their numbers and gave them wealth and power.

1013. The words show. that throughout the ages the good and intelligent men have believed that force should not be used in matters concerning conscience.

بِالْحَقِّ وَاَنْتَ خَيْرُ الْفٰتِحِيْنَ ﴿٩٠﴾

between us and between our people with truth and Thou art the Best of those who decide.'

وَقَالَ الْمَلَاُ الَّذِيْنَ كَفَرُوْا مِنْ قَوْمِهٖ لَىِٕنِ اتَّبَعْتُمْ
شُعَيْبًا اِنَّكُمْ اِذًا لَّخٰسِرُوْنَ ﴿٩١﴾

91. And the chief men of his people, who disbelieved, said, 'If you follow Shu'aib, you shall then certainly be the losers.'

فَاَخَذَتْهُمُ الرَّجْفَةُ فَاَصْبَحُوْا فِيْ دَارِهِمْ جٰثِمِيْنَ ﴿٩٢﴾

92. So [a]the earthquake seized them and in their homes they lay prostrate upon the ground;

الَّذِيْنَ كَذَّبُوْا شُعَيْبًا كَاَنْ لَّمْ يَغْنَوْا فِيْهَا ۚ اَلَّذِيْنَ كَذَّبُوْا
شُعَيْبًا كَانُوْا هُمُ الْخٰسِرِيْنَ ﴿٩٣﴾

93. Those who accused Shu'aib of lying became as if they had never dwelt therein. Those, who accused Shu'aib of lying—it was they who were the losers.

فَتَوَلّٰى عَنْهُمْ وَقَالَ يٰقَوْمِ لَقَدْ اَبْلَغْتُكُمْ رِسٰلٰتِ رَبِّيْ
وَنَصَحْتُ لَكُمْ ۚ فَكَيْفَ اٰسٰى عَلٰى قَوْمٍ كٰفِرِيْنَ ﴿٩٤﴾ ع

94. Then he turned away from them and said, [b]'O my people, indeed, I delivered to you the messages of my Lord and gave you sincere counsel. How then should I sorrow for a disbelieving people.'[1014]

وَمَاۤ اَرْسَلْنَا فِيْ قَرْيَةٍ مِّنْ نَّبِيٍّ اِلَّاۤ اَخَذْنَاۤ اَهْلَهَا
بِالْبَاْسَاۤءِ وَالضَّرَّاۤءِ لَعَلَّهُمْ يَضَّرَّعُوْنَ ﴿٩٥﴾

R. 12 95. And never did we send a Prophet to any town but [c]We did seize its people with adversity and suffering, that they might humble[1015] themselves.

ثُمَّ بَدَّلْنَا مَكَانَ السَّيِّئَةِ الْحَسَنَةَ حَتّٰى عَفَوْا وَّقَالُوْا
قَدْ مَسَّ اٰبَآءَنَا الضَّرَّاۤءُ وَالسَّرَّاۤءُ فَاَخَذْنٰهُمْ بَغْتَةً
وَّهُمْ لَا يَشْعُرُوْنَ ﴿٩٦﴾

96. Then We changed *their* evil *condition* into good until they grew *in affluence and numbers* and said, 'Suffering and happiness betided our fathers *also, what if they befell us.'* Then We seized them suddenly, while they perceived not.

[a]7 : 79; 11 : 68; 15 : 84; 26 : 159. [b]7 : 69, 80; 46 : 24. [c]6 : 43.

1014. The words are full of extreme pathos. Shu'aib, like every true Prophet, felt deep grief and distress for his people.

1015. This is a general law of God which invariably comes into operation whenever a Prophet of God makes his appearance. The advent of every Prophet is attended in an extraordinary degree with calamities and miseries of diverse kinds which are intended to serve as an eye-opener for the people.

97. And [a]if the people of *those* towns had believed and been righteous, We would have surely opened for them blessings from heaven and earth; but they disbelieved, so We seized them because of that which they earned.

وَلَوْ أَنَّ أَهْلَ الْقُرَىٰ آمَنُوا وَاتَّقَوْا لَفَتَحْنَا عَلَيْهِم
بَرَكَاتٍ مِّنَ السَّمَاءِ وَالْأَرْضِ وَلَٰكِن كَذَّبُوا فَأَخَذْنَاهُم
بِمَا كَانُوا يَكْسِبُونَ ﴿٩٧﴾

98. Are the people of *these* towns then secure from [b]the coming of Our punishment upon them by night while they are asleep?

أَفَأَمِنَ أَهْلُ الْقُرَىٰ أَن يَأْتِيَهُم بَأْسُنَا بَيَاتًا وَهُمْ نَائِمُونَ ﴿٩٨﴾

99. And are the people of *these* towns[1016] secure from [c]the coming of our punishment upon them in the early part of the forenoon while they play?

أَوَأَمِنَ أَهْلُ الْقُرَىٰ أَن يَأْتِيَهُم بَأْسُنَا ضُحًى وَهُمْ يَلْعَبُونَ ﴿٩٩﴾

100. Are they then secure from the design of Allāh? And none feels secure from the design of Allāh save the people who *are destined to* perish.

أَفَأَمِنُوا مَكْرَ اللَّهِ ۚ فَلَا يَأْمَنُ مَكْرَ اللَّهِ إِلَّا الْقَوْمُ
الْخَاسِرُونَ ﴿١٠٠﴾ ع ٢

R. 13 101. [d]Does it not lead those, who have inherited the earth in succession to its *former* inhabitants, to realize that if We please, We can smite them *also* for their sins and [e]seal up their hearts, so that they would not listen *to words of guidance*.

أَوَلَمْ يَهْدِ لِلَّذِينَ يَرِثُونَ الْأَرْضَ مِن بَعْدِ أَهْلِهَا
أَن لَّوْ نَشَاءُ أَصَبْنَاهُم بِذُنُوبِهِمْ ۚ وَنَطْبَعُ عَلَىٰ قُلُوبِهِمْ
فَهُمْ لَا يَسْمَعُونَ ﴿١٠١﴾

102. Such were the towns some of whose news We have related[1017] to thee. And verily [f]their Messengers

تِلْكَ الْقُرَىٰ نَقُصُّ عَلَيْكَ مِنْ أَنبَائِهَا ۚ وَلَقَدْ

---

[a]2 : 104; 5: 66. [b]7 : 5. [c]7 : 5 [d]20 : 129 ; 32 : 27. [e]10 : 75 ; 16 : 109 ; 45 : 24. [f]3 : 185 ; 5 : 33.

1016. The words "these towns" refer to Mecca and its sister towns of Ḥijāz. The meaning is "Do not the people of Mecca, etc., take a lesson from the fate of 'Ād, Thamūd, the people of Lot and from that of the people of Shu'aib?

1017. The Qur'ān does not give the entire history of by-gone peoples but only the relevant parts of it. Nevertheless, no book of history contains more reliable information about the tribes of 'Ād and Thamūd than does the Qur'ān, and students of history have admitted that what the Qur'ān tells us is the only authentic and reliable information that we possess about these ancient peoples and all other stories current about them are so many myths.

came to them with clear Signs. But they would not believe what they had rejected before. Thus does Allāh seal[1018] up the hearts of the disbelievers.

جَآءَتْهُمْ رُسُلُهُمْ بِالْبَيِّنٰتِ فَمَا كَانُوْا لِيُؤْمِنُوْا بِمَا كَذَّبُوْا مِنْ قَبْلُ ۚ كَذٰلِكَ يَطْبَعُ اللّٰهُ عَلٰى قُلُوْبِ الْكٰفِرِيْنَ ﴿١٠٢﴾

103. And We found not in most of them any *observance of* covenant and, surely, We found most of them to be evil-doers.

وَمَا وَجَدْنَا لِاَكْثَرِهِمْ مِّنْ عَهْدٍ ۚ وَاِنْ وَّجَدْنَآ اَكْثَرَهُمْ لَفٰسِقِيْنَ ﴿١٠٣﴾

104. Then, after them,[1019] [a]We sent Moses with Our Signs to Pharaoh and his chiefs, but they unjustly[1020] *rejected* them. Behold, then, what was the end of those who created disorder!

ثُمَّ بَعَثْنَا مِنْۢ بَعْدِهِمْ مُّوْسٰى بِاٰيٰتِنَآ اِلٰى فِرْعَوْنَ وَمَلَا۟ئِهٖ فَظَلَمُوْا بِهَا ۚ فَانْظُرْ كَيْفَ كَانَ عَاقِبَةُ الْمُفْسِدِيْنَ ﴿١٠٤﴾

105. And [b]Moses said, 'O Pharaoh, surely, I am a Messenger from the Lord of the worlds;

وَقَالَ مُوْسٰى يٰفِرْعَوْنُ اِنِّيْ رَسُوْلٌ مِّنْ رَّبِّ الْعٰلَمِيْنَ ﴿١٠٥﴾

106. 'It is not right[1021] that I should say anything of God except the truth. I have come to you with a clear Sign from your Lord; therefore, [c]let the Children of Israel go with me.'[1022]

حَقِيْقٌ عَلٰٓى اَنْ لَّآ اَقُوْلَ عَلَى اللّٰهِ اِلَّا الْحَقَّ ۗ قَدْ جِئْتُكُمْ بِبَيِّنَةٍ مِّنْ رَّبِّكُمْ فَاَرْسِلْ مَعِيَ بَنِيْٓ اِسْرَآءِيْلَ ﴿١٠٦﴾

[a]17 : 102 ; 28 : 37 ; 43 : 47. [b]26 : 17 ; 20 : 48 ; 43 : 47. [c]20 : 48 ; 26 : 18.

1018. The hearts of disbelievers are sealed up when they refuse to make use of their God-given power of reasoning and understanding.

1019. The words "after them," contradict the popular view that Shu'aib was a contemporary and father-in-law of Moses.

1020. *Ẓulm* meaning to put a thing in the wrong place or to make a wrong use of it (Lane), the clause signifies that Pharaoh and his chiefs made wrong use of the Signs. The Signs were meant to engender fear of God in their hearts but instead they jeered and mocked at them.

1021. *Ḥaqīq* means, adapted, disposed, apt, meet, right, fit or worthy (Lane).

1022. When Moses went to Pharaoh his object was not so much to preach his Message to him as to call upon him to let the Israelites go with him, though ordinarily he would have preached to him also. As a matter of fact the Message of Moses was meant primarily for the Israelites, but as long as the Israelites remained mixed up with the natives of Egypt, Moses had to preach to them both. When the Israelites left the land, he had no concern with the Egyptians and confined his attention to his own kith and kin to whom he was sent.

107. *Pharaoh* replied, [a]"If thou hast indeed come with a Sign, then produce it, if thou art truthful.'

قَالَ اِنْ كُنْتَ جِئْتَ بِاٰيَةٍ فَاْتِ بِهَآ اِنْ كُنْتَ مِنَ الصّٰدِقِيْنَ ۝۱۰۷

108. So [b]he flung down his rod and behold! it was a serpent plainly visible.[1023]

فَاَلْقٰى عَصَاهُ فَاِذَا هِيَ ثُعْبَانٌ مُّبِيْنٌ ۝۱۰۸

[a]26 : 32. [b]20 : 21 ; 26 : 33 ; 27 : 11 ; 28 : 32.

1023. The Qur'ān has used three different words to describe the turning of the rod of Moses into a serpent, *viz.*, *Ḥayyah* as in 20:21, *Jānn* as in 27 : 11 and 28 : 32 and *Thu'bān* as in 26 : 33 and in the present verse. The first word is of general application and is used for serpents of all categories. The second word means a small serpent. The third word (*Thu'bān*) means a bulky and long serpent. Thus the use of three different words at three different places in the Qur'ān is significant and evidently is intended to serve a definite purpose. The word *Jānn* has been used from the point of view of the serpent's quick movements and *Thu'bān* from the point of view of its large size. When the mere fact of the turning of the rod into a serpent is mentioned the word *Ḥayyah* is used, but when the rod is mentioned as turning into a serpent in the presence of Moses alone the word *Jānn* (a small serpent) is used. But when the miracle of the rod turning into a serpent is shown before Pharaoh, the magicians and the general public, the word *Thu'bān* is used. The significance of these different words on different occasions is different. The word *Ḥayyah* signifies that a dead people ('*Aṣā* signifies a community), as to all intents and purposes the Israelites were, would receive a new and vigorous life through Moses (this being the significance of the root word *Ḥayyah*), and the word *Jānn* (a small, fast moving serpent) signifies that from a small and decadent community, they would make rapid progress and would become *Thu'bān* (a large and bulky serpent) for Pharaoh and his people,*i.e.*, they would become the means and instrument of their destruction. It may be noted here that this miracle like other miracles shown by God's Prophets contradicted no law of nature. If a thing is proved to have actually taken place, it must be taken to be true even if it is not explicable or understandable in the light of the laws of nature as we understand them. Our knowledge of the laws of nature is, at best, very limited; so we must not deny an actual fact on the basis of our limited and imperfect knowledge. Moreover, the miracle shown by Moses did not take place in the manner in which it is popularly understood to have occurred. Miracles shown by God's Prophets are not like hand-tricks of jugglers. They are meant to serve some great moral or spiritual purpose—to bring about certainty of faith and engender feelings of piety and fear of God in the minds of those who witness them. If the rod had actually turned into a serpent, the whole performance must have looked more like the trick of a juggler than the miracle of a Prophet. In spite of what the Bible might say about this miracle, the Qur'ān lends no support to the view that the rod actually had turned into a real and living serpent. No such thing seems to have taken place. The rod only *looked* like a rapidly moving serpent. The miracle was a sort of vision in which God either exercised special control over the sight of onlookers in order to make them see the rod in the form of a serpent or the rod itself was made to look like a serpent; and this vision was shared by Pharaoh and his courtiers and the magicians along with Moses. The rod remained a rod, only it *appeared* to Moses and others as a serpent. It is a common spiritual phenomenon that in a vision when man rises above the encumbrances of the flesh and becomes temporarily transported to a spiritual sphere, he can see things taking place which are beyond his ken and are quite invisible to his physical eyes. The miracle of the rod turning into a serpent was one such spiritual experience. A similar spiritual phenomenon took place in the time of the Holy Prophet when the moon was seen not only by the Holy Prophet but by some of his followers and opponents, as if it had been rent asunder (Bukhārī, ch. on *Tafsīr*). Tradition tells us that Gabriel whom the Holy Prophet often saw in his visions, on one occasion was also seen by his Companions, who were sitting with him (Bukhārī, ch. on *Īmān*). Similarly, some angels were seen even by some of the disbelievers at the Battle of Badr (Jarīr, vi. p. 47). Another instance of this kind occurred when a Muslim army under the well-known Muslim general, Sāriyah, was fighting against the enemy in Iraq. 'Umar, the Second Caliph, while delivering his Friday sermon at Medina, in a vision saw that the Muslim

109. And [a]He drew forth his hand, and lo ! it *appeared* white to the beholders.[1024]

وَّنَزَعَ يَدَهٗ فَاِذَا هِىَ بَيۡضَآءُ لِلنّٰظِرِيۡنَ ﴿۱۰۹﴾ ع ۱۳/۳

R. 14 110. [b]The chiefs of Pharaoh's people said, 'This is most surely a skilful sorcerer;[1025]

قَالَ الۡمَلَاُ مِنۡ قَوۡمِ فِرۡعَوۡنَ اِنَّ هٰذَا لَسٰحِرٌ عَلِيۡمٌ ﴿۱۱۰﴾

111. [c]'He desires to turn you out from your land.[1026] Now what do you advise ?'

يُّرِيۡدُ اَنۡ يُّخۡرِجَكُمۡ مِّنۡ اَرۡضِكُمۡ‌ۚ فَمَاذَا تَاۡمُرُوۡنَ ﴿۱۱۱﴾

112. [d]They said, 'Put him off and his brother *awhile*, and send into the cities summoners,

قَالُوۡۤا اَرۡجِهۡ وَاَخَاهُ وَاَرۡسِلۡ فِى الۡمَدَآئِنِ حٰشِرِيۡنَ ﴿۱۱۲﴾

113. [e]'Who should bring to thee every skilful sorcerer.'

يَاۡتُوۡكَ بِكُلِّ سٰحِرٍ عَلِيۡمٍ ﴿۱۱۳﴾

[a]26 : 34; 27 : 13; 28 : 33. [b]20 : 64; 26 : 35. [c]20 : 64; 26 : 36. [d]26 : 37. [e]26 : 38.

army was being overwhelmed by the superior numbers of the enemy and that a disastrous defeat was imminent. Thereupon he suddenly discontinued his sermon and cried out from the pulpit, saying, 'O Sāriyah, take to the mountain, take to the mountain.' Sāriyah, who was hundreds of miles away, heard the voice of 'Umar amid the deafening noise of the battle-field, and obeyed the Caliph's instructions and the Muslim army was saved from sure destruction (Khamīs, ii. p. 370).

The miracle of Moses possessed a special significance. It may be interpreted something like this. God told Moses to throw down his rod which then *appeared* to him like a serpent; and when on God's bidding he took it up, it was only a piece of wood. Now the serpent, in the language of visions and dreams, symbolises an enemy, while a rod is emblematic of a community (Ta'ṭīr al-Anām). Thus, by means of this vision God let Moses know that if He cast away his people from him, they would become veritable serpents. But if he kept them under his fostering care, they would grow into a strong and well-knit community of righteous and God-fearing men.

1024. The bodies of highly spiritual men are known to emit rays of various colours according to the degree or nature of their spiritual development. The rays that are emitted by the bodies of Prophets are of pure white colour. Similarly, rays that issued from the hand of Moses must have been of that colour and, when they were made visible, his hand naturally appeared white to the beholders. Men are known to have had such spiritual experiences in the times of other Prophets of God as well. God said to Moses: *Thrust thy hand into thy bosom; it will come forth white without disease* (28 : 33). This constituted, in symbolic language, a clear hint to Moses that if he kept his followers close to him and under his fostering care, they would not only become men of light themselves but would also impart light to others, otherwise they would become not only black but also morally diseased. The miracle was not, therefore, the performance of a sorcerer but a Sign full of deep spiritual significance.

1025. The word *Sāḥir* does not necessarily mean, a magician. It also means, a fascinator; one skilful and intelligent; one able to make a thing look other than what it is: a deceiver, deluder or beguiler, etc. (Lane). See also 128.

1026. These words are intended to work up the feelings of the Egyptians against Moses, whereas the truth was that Moses had no desire to turn them out. His mission was confined to taking away his own people from Egypt.

114. And [a]the sorcerers came to Pharaoh *and* said: 'We shall, of course, have a reward, if we prevail.'

وَجَآءَ السَّحَرَةُ فِرْعَوْنَ قَالُوْٓا اِنَّ لَنَا لَاَجْرًا اِنْ كُنَّا نَحْنُ الْغٰلِبِيْنَ ﴿١١٤﴾

115. [b]He said, 'Yes, and you shall *also* be of those who are placed near *me*.'

قَالَ نَعَمْ وَاِنَّكُمْ لَمِنَ الْمُقَرَّبِيْنَ ﴿١١٥﴾

116. [c]They said, 'O Moses, wilt thou throw *first* or shall we be the *first* throwers?'[1027]

قَالُوْا يٰمُوْسٰٓى اِمَّآ اَنْ تُلْقِيَ وَاِمَّآ اَنْ نَّكُوْنَ نَحْنُ الْمُلْقِيْنَ ﴿١١٦﴾

117. He replied, 'Throw ye.'[1028] And when they [d]threw, they bewitched the eyes of the people and struck them with awe and produced a mighty magic.

قَالَ اَلْقُوْا ۚ فَلَمَّآ اَلْقَوْا سَحَرُوْٓا اَعْيُنَ النَّاسِ وَاسْتَرْهَبُوْهُمْ وَجَآءُوْ بِسِحْرٍ عَظِيْمٍ ﴿١١٧﴾

118. And We revealed to Moses: [e]'Throw thy rod,' and lo! it swallowed up whatever they feigned.[1029]

وَاَوْحَيْنَآ اِلٰى مُوْسٰٓى اَنْ اَلْقِ عَصَاكَ ۚ فَاِذَا هِيَ تَلْقَفُ مَا يَاْفِكُوْنَ ﴿١١٨﴾

119. So was the truth established and whatever they did, proved vain.

فَوَقَعَ الْحَقُّ وَبَطَلَ مَا كَانُوْا يَعْمَلُوْنَ ﴿١١٩﴾

120. Thus were they vanquished there and they retired humiliated.[1030]

فَغُلِبُوْا هُنَالِكَ وَانْقَلَبُوْا صٰغِرِيْنَ ﴿١٢٠﴾

[a]26 : 42. [b]26 : 43. [c]20 : 66. [d]20 : 67; 26 : 45. [e]20 : 70; 26 : 46.

1027. Mark the intensity of the scene—both parties arrayed against each other ready to come to grips in a decisive trial.

1028. Prophets of God never attack first. They wait for an attack on the part of their opponents, for they prefer to defend and look to God for succour.

1029. It was not the "serpent" made out of the rod, but the rod itself which undid the magic of the magicians. The rod of Moses wielded with the spiritual force of a great Prophet and thrown at the command of God exposed the deception they had wrought on the spectators and broke to pieces the things which, by their magic, they had made them take for real serpents. The words, "It swallowed up whatever they feigned" signify that the rod quickly exposed the deception wrought by the magicians, "swallowed up" signifying "destroyed the effect of, or the impression created by."

1030. The verse seems to refer to Pharaoh's party and not to the sorcerers. The latter have been spoken of in the next verse. The word "humiliated" could not have been used about men who had evinced such regard for truth as to have accepted it without even waiting to see what Pharaoh had to say about it. The meaning is that those, (Pharaoh and his party), who a few moments before had come to the scene of combat with a proud and arrogant attitude and were confident of success, now retired humbled and crest-fallen.

121. And [a]the sorcerers were impelled to fall down prostrate.[1031]

وَأُلْقِيَ السَّحَرَةُ سٰجِدِيْنَ ﴿۱۲۱﴾

122. *And* [b]they said, 'We believe in the Lord of the worlds,

قَالُوْٓا اٰمَنَّا بِرَبِّ الْعٰلَمِيْنَ ﴿۱۲۲﴾

123. [c]'The Lord of Moses and Aaron.

رَبِّ مُوْسٰى وَهٰرُوْنَ ﴿۱۲۳﴾

124. [d]Pharaoh said, 'You have believed in him before I gave you leave. Surely, this is a plot which you have plotted in the city, that you may turn out therefrom its inhabitants,[1032] but you shall soon know *the consequences*;

قَالَ فِرْعَوْنُ اٰمَنْتُمْ بِهٖ قَبْلَ اَنْ اٰذَنَ لَكُمْ ۚ اِنَّ هٰذَا لَمَكْرٌ مَّكَرْتُمُوْهُ فِى الْمَدِيْنَةِ لِتُخْرِجُوْا مِنْهَآ اَهْلَهَا ۚ فَسَوْفَ تَعْلَمُوْنَ ﴿۱۲۴﴾

125. [e]'Most surely will I cut off your hands and your feet on account of *your* disobedience. Then will I surely crucify you all together.'[1033]

لَاُقَطِّعَنَّ اَيْدِيَكُمْ وَاَرْجُلَكُمْ مِّنْ خِلَافٍ ثُمَّ لَاُصَلِّبَنَّكُمْ اَجْمَعِيْنَ ﴿۱۲۵﴾

126. [f]They answered, 'To our Lord *then* shall we return;

قَالُوْٓا اِنَّآ اِلٰى رَبِّنَا مُنْقَلِبُوْنَ ﴿۱۲۶﴾

127. 'And [g]thou dost not wreak vengeance on us but because we have believed in the Signs of our Lord, when they came to us. Our Lord, pour forth upon us steadfastness and cause us to die resigned *unto Thee*.'

وَمَا تَنْقِمُ مِنَّآ اِلَّآ اَنْ اٰمَنَّا بِاٰيٰتِ رَبِّنَا لَمَّا جَآءَتْنَا ۗ رَبَّنَآ اَفْرِغْ عَلَيْنَا صَبْرًا وَّتَوَفَّنَا مُسْلِمِيْنَ ﴿۱۲۷﴾ ع

[a]20 : 71; 26 : 47. [b]20 : 71; 26 : 48. [c]20 : 71; 26 : 49. [d]20 : 72; 26 : 50. [e]20 : 72; 26 : 50. [f]20 : 73; 26 : 51. [g]20 : 74.

1031. The discomfiture of the sorcerers was so complete that it appeared that some hidden power had taken the ground from under their feet. They were made to fall down prostrate on the ground in an attitude of prayer and humility before God.

1032. The words "its inhabitants" here signify Pharaoh's own people, who, however, were not the real inhabitants of Egypt, having wrested the country from the sons of the soil.

1033. Although crucifixion meant painful death, the punishment of cutting off the hands and feet was added to make the infliction all the more exemplary and death all the more painful. Incidentally, the verse shows that even as early as in the time of Moses the punishment of death by crucifixion was in vogue.

R. 15 128. And the chiefs of Pharaoh's people said, 'Wilt thou leave Moses and his people to create disorder in the land[1034] and forsake thee and thy gods?'[1035] He answered, [a]'We will *ruthlessly* slay[1036] their sons and let their women live. And surely we are dominant over them.'

وَقَالَ الْمَلَأُ مِنْ قَوْمِ فِرْعَوْنَ أَتَذَرُ مُوسَىٰ وَقَوْمَهُ
لِيُفْسِدُوا فِي الْأَرْضِ وَيَذَرَكَ وَآلِهَتَكَ ۚ قَالَ
سَنُقَتِّلُ أَبْنَاءَهُمْ وَنَسْتَحْيِي نِسَاءَهُمْ وَإِنَّا فَوْقَهُمْ
قَاهِرُونَ ﴿١٢٨﴾

129. [b]Moses said to his people, 'Seek help from Allāh and be steadfast. Verily the earth is Allāh's; He gives it as a heritage to whomsoever He pleases of His servants and the *good* end is for the God-fearing.'

قَالَ مُوسَىٰ لِقَوْمِهِ اسْتَعِينُوا بِاللَّهِ وَاصْبِرُوا ۖ إِنَّ
الْأَرْضَ لِلَّهِ يُورِثُهَا مَنْ يَشَاءُ مِنْ عِبَادِهِ ۖ وَ
الْعَاقِبَةُ لِلْمُتَّقِينَ ﴿١٢٩﴾

130. They replied, 'We were persecuted before thou camest to us and *even* after thou camest to us.' He said, [c]'Your Lord is about to destroy your enemy and make you rulers in the land, that He may see how you act.'[1037]

قَالُوا أُوذِينَا مِنْ قَبْلِ أَنْ تَأْتِيَنَا وَمِنْ بَعْدِ مَا
جِئْتَنَا ۚ قَالَ عَسَىٰ رَبُّكُمْ أَنْ يُهْلِكَ عَدُوَّكُمْ وَ
يَسْتَخْلِفَكُمْ فِي الْأَرْضِ فَيَنْظُرَ كَيْفَ تَعْمَلُونَ ﴿١٣٠﴾ ع ١٥ ٥

[a]2 : 50; 7 : 142; 14 : 7; 28 : 5. [b]2: 46, 154. [c]10 : 14,15.

1034. It were the chiefs themselves who had counselled Pharaoh to give respite to Moses and his brother (7 : 112); but now the same chiefs blame him for the time he had given to Moses and Aaron in accordance with their own advice. This is how those who meet with disgrace and humiliation become morally degraded.

1035. Pharaoh himself was worshipped as a god by his people (28 : 39) and he in turn worshipped other deities. Hence the chiefs accused Moses and Aaron of having denounced the worship of Pharaoh and his gods.

1036. The word *Nuqattilu* is in the intensified form and expresses the sense of ruthlessness and a slow and gradual process of killing.

1037. The verse does not necessarily mean that the Israelites were to be made to inherit Egypt after the destruction of Pharaoh. It only means that Pharaoh's power was to be broken and others were to take possession of his kingdom. We know that after the destruction of Pharaoh and the break-up of his kingdom, another dynasty, friendly to the Israelites, took possession of the land. "Land" mentioned in the verse refers not to Egypt but to the Holy Land which had been promised to the Israelites and which they inherited in accordance with that promise.

R. 16 131. And [a]We afflicted Pharaoh's people with *years of* drought[1038] and scarcity of fruits, that they might take heed.

وَلَقَدْ أَخَذْنَآ ءَالَ فِرْعَوْنَ بِالسِّنِينَ وَنَقْصٍ مِّنَ
الثَّمَرٰتِ لَعَلَّهُمْ يَذَّكَّرُونَ ﴿١٣١﴾

132. But whenever good befell them, they said, 'This is for us.' And [b]if evil afflicted them, they ascribed the evil fortune to Moses and those with him. Now, surely, *the cause of* their evil fortune[1039] was with Allāh. But most of them knew not.

فَإِذَا جَآءَتْهُمُ الْحَسَنَةُ قَالُوْا لَنَا هٰذِهٖ ۚ وَإِن تُصِبْهُمْ
سَيِّئَةٌ يَطَّيَّرُوْا بِمُوسٰى وَمَن مَّعَهٗ ۗ أَلَآ إِنَّمَا
طٰٓئِرُهُمْ عِندَ اللّٰهِ وَلٰكِنَّ أَكْثَرَهُمْ لَا يَعْلَمُونَ ﴿١٣٢﴾

133. And they said, 'Whatever Sign thou mayest bring us to bewitch us with, [c]we will not submit to thee.'

وَقَالُوْا مَهْمَا تَأْتِنَا بِهٖ مِنْ ءَايَةٍ لِّتَسْحَرَنَا بِهَا ۙ
فَمَا نَحْنُ لَكَ بِمُؤْمِنِينَ ﴿١٣٣﴾

134. Then We [d]sent upon them the storm and the locusts and the lice and the frogs and the blood—[1040] clear Signs; but they behaved proudly and were a sinful people.

فَأَرْسَلْنَا عَلَيْهِمُ الطُّوفَانَ وَالْجَرَادَ وَالْقُمَّلَ
وَالضَّفَادِعَ وَالدَّمَ ءَايٰتٍ مُّفَصَّلٰتٍ ۛ فَاسْتَكْبَرُوْا
وَكَانُوْا قَوْمًا مُّجْرِمِينَ ﴿١٣٤﴾

135. And [e]when there fell upon them the punishment, they said, 'O Moses, pray for us to thy Lord according to that which He has promised to thee. If thou remove from us the punishment, we will surely believe thee and we will surely send with thee the Children of Israel.'

وَلَمَّا وَقَعَ عَلَيْهِمُ الرِّجْزُ قَالُوْا يٰمُوسَى ادْعُ لَنَا رَبَّكَ
بِمَا عَهِدَ عِندَكَ ۚ لَئِن كَشَفْتَ عَنَّا الرِّجْزَ لَنُؤْمِنَنَّ
لَكَ وَلَنُرْسِلَنَّ مَعَكَ بَنِىٓ إِسْرَآءِيلَ ۚ ﴿١٣٥﴾

[a]17 : 102. [b]27 : 48; 36 : 19. [c]10 : 79. [d]17 : 102; 43 : 49. [e]43 : 50.

1038. *Sanah* which is the singular of *Sinīn* signifies a simple revolution of the earth round the sun. It is synonymous with *'Ām* (and also with *Ḥaul*) but whereas every *Sanah* is an *'Ām*, every *'Ām* is not a *Sanah*. It is also said to be longer than the *'Ām* which is applied to the twelve Arabian months collectively; but *Sanah* is also applied to twelve revolutions of the moon. According to Imām Rāghib *Sanah* is used as denoting a year in which there is difficulty, or drought or barrenness or dearth; and *'Ām* as denoting a year which brings ampleness of the means or circumstances of life and abundance of herbage or the like. *Sanah* also means, drought. The verse speaks of loss of life and property.

1039. *Ṭāi'r* means, an omen, a bodement of good or of evil; an evil fortune or ill-luck (Lane).

1040. The Bible mentions 10 Signs besides the Signs of the rod and the white hand (Exod chaps. 7-11). The biblical account seems to have greatly exaggerated the Signs.

136. But [a]when We removed from them the punishment for a term[1041] which they were to reach, lo ! they broke their promise.

فَلَمَّا كَشَفْنَا عَنْهُمُ الرِّجْزَ إِلَىٰ أَجَلٍ هُمْ بَالِغُوهُ
إِذَا هُمْ يَنْكُثُونَ ﴿١٣٦﴾

137. So We [b]took vengeance upon them and drowned them in the sea, because they treated Our Signs as lies and were heedless of them.

فَانْتَقَمْنَا مِنْهُمْ فَأَغْرَقْنَاهُمْ فِي الْيَمِّ بِأَنَّهُمْ كَذَّبُوا
بِآيَاتِنَا وَكَانُوا عَنْهَا غَافِلِينَ ﴿١٣٧﴾

138. And [c]We caused the people who were considered weak to inherit the eastern parts of the land and the western parts thereof,[1042] which we blessed.[1043] And the [d]gracious word of thy Lord was fulfilled for the Children of Israel because they were steadfast; and We utterly destroyed all that Pharaoh and his people had built and all that they had erected.

وَأَوْرَثْنَا الْقَوْمَ الَّذِينَ كَانُوا يُسْتَضْعَفُونَ مَشَارِقَ
الْأَرْضِ وَمَغَارِبَهَا الَّتِي بَارَكْنَا فِيهَا ۖ وَتَمَّتْ
كَلِمَتُ رَبِّكَ الْحُسْنَىٰ عَلَىٰ بَنِي إِسْرَائِيلَ بِمَا صَبَرُوا ۖ
وَدَمَّرْنَا مَا كَانَ يَصْنَعُ فِرْعَوْنُ وَقَوْمُهُ وَمَا كَانُوا
يَعْرِشُونَ ﴿١٣٨﴾

139. And We brought the Children of Israel across the sea and they came to a people who were devoted to their idols. They said, ‘O Moses, make for us a god just as they have gods.’ He said, ‘Surely, you are an ignorant people;

وَجَاوَزْنَا بِبَنِي إِسْرَائِيلَ الْبَحْرَ فَأَتَوْا عَلَىٰ قَوْمٍ
يَعْكُفُونَ عَلَىٰ أَصْنَامٍ لَهُمْ ۚ قَالُوا يَا مُوسَى اجْعَلْ
لَنَا إِلَٰهًا كَمَا لَهُمْ آلِهَةٌ ۚ قَالَ إِنَّكُمْ قَوْمٌ تَجْهَلُونَ ﴿١٣٩﴾

140. ‘Surely, all that these *people* are engaged in shall be destroyed, and vain shall be all that they do.’

إِنَّ هَٰؤُلَاءِ مُتَبَّرٌ مَا هُمْ فِيهِ وَبَاطِلٌ مَا كَانُوا
يَعْمَلُونَ ﴿١٤٠﴾

[a]43 : 5. [b]43 : 56. [c]28 : 6. [d]32 : 25.

1041. *Ajal* means both “term” and “end of term” (2 : 232). The punishment was removed only for a time to grant Pharaoh an opportunity to repent and comply with the demand of Moses.

1042. The words, *the eastern parts of the land and the western parts thereof*, signify, according to Arabic idiom, the entire country.

1043. The Holy Land which had been promised to the descendants of Abraham and Jacob (5 : 22). It was blessed because it was the land where the Israelites were to thrive and prosper and grow into a great nation.

141. [a]He said, 'Shall I seek for you a god other than Allāh, while He has [b]exalted you above all peoples?'

قَالَ اَغَيْرَ اللّٰهِ اَبْغِيْكُمْ اِلٰهًا وَّهُوَ فَضَّلَكُمْ عَلَى
الْعٰلَمِيْنَ ﴿۱۴۱﴾

142. And [c]*remember the time* when We delivered you from Pharaoh's people who afflicted you with grievous torment, slaughtering your sons and sparing your women. And therein was a great trial for you from your Lord.

وَاِذْ اَنْجَيْنٰكُمْ مِّنْ اٰلِ فِرْعَوْنَ يَسُوْمُوْنَكُمْ سُوْٓءَ
الْعَذَابِ ۚ يُقَتِّلُوْنَ اَبْنَآءَكُمْ وَيَسْتَحْيُوْنَ نِسَآءَكُمْ ۭ
وَفِيْ ذٰلِكُمْ بَلَآءٌ مِّنْ رَّبِّكُمْ عَظِيْمٌ ﴿۱۴۲﴾ ع

R. 17 143. And [d]We made Moses a promise of thirty nights and supplemented them with ten.[1044] Thus the period appointed by his Lord was completed—forty nights. And Moses said to his brother, Aaron, 'Take my place amongst my people in my absence,[1045] and manage *them* well and follow not the way of mischief-makers.

وَوٰعَدْنَا مُوْسٰى ثَلٰثِيْنَ لَيْلَةً وَّاَتْمَمْنٰهَا بِعَشْرٍ
فَتَمَّ مِيْقَاتُ رَبِّهٖٓ اَرْبَعِيْنَ لَيْلَةً ۚ وَقَالَ مُوْسٰى
لِاَخِيْهِ هٰرُوْنَ اخْلُفْنِيْ فِيْ قَوْمِيْ وَاَصْلِحْ وَلَا تَتَّبِعْ
سَبِيْلَ الْمُفْسِدِيْنَ ﴿۱۴۳﴾

144. And [e]when Moses came at Our appointed time and his Lord spoke to him, he said, 'My Lord, show *Thyself* to me that I may look at Thee.' *Allāh* replied, 'Thou shalt not see Me.[1046] But look at the mountain; and if it remains

وَلَمَّا جَآءَ مُوْسٰى لِمِيْقَاتِنَا وَكَلَّمَهٗ رَبُّهٗ ۙ قَالَ رَبِّ
اَرِنِيْٓ اَنْظُرْ اِلَيْكَ ۭ قَالَ لَنْ تَرٰىنِيْ وَلٰكِنِ انْظُرْ
اِلَى الْجَبَلِ فَاِنِ اسْتَقَرَّ مَكَانَهٗ فَسَوْفَ تَرٰىنِيْ ۚ فَلَمَّا

---

[a]6 : 15, 165. [b]2 : 48; 3 : 34. [c]2 : 50; 7 : 128; 14 : 7; 28 : 5. [d]2 : 52. [e]2 : 254; 4 : 165.

1044. God's communion with Moses was completed in the promised thirty nights. The prolongation of the period by ten nights did not form part of the promise but was an additional favour.

1045. The words show that Aaron's position was that of a subordinate to Moses. Moses called the Israelites "my people" and directed Aaron to act for him, *i.e.*, officiate in his place during his absence.

1046. This verse sheds some light on one of the most important religious subjects—whether it is possible for one to see God with the physical eyes. The verse lends no support to the view that God is visible to the physical eyes (6 : 104). Not to say of seeing God with the physical eyes, man cannot even see angels; we can see only a manifestation of them. Similarly, only a manifestation of God can be seen and not God Himself. It is, therefore, inconceivable that a great Prophet of God like Moses, with all his knowledge of the attributes of God, should have desired an impossibility. Moses knew that he could see only a mani-

in its place, then shalt thou see Me.' And when his Lord manifested Himself on the mountain, He broke it into pieces[1047] and Moses fell down unconscious. And when he recovered, he said, 'Holy art Thou, I turn to Thee and I am the first to believe.'

تَجَلّٰى رَبُّهٗ لِلْجَبَلِ جَعَلَهٗ دَكًّا وَّخَرَّ مُوْسٰى صَعِقًا ۚ
فَلَمَّآ اَفَاقَ قَالَ سُبْحٰنَكَ تُبْتُ اِلَيْكَ وَاَنَا اَوَّلُ
الْمُؤْمِنِيْنَ ﴿۱۴۴﴾

145. *Allāh* said, 'O Moses, I have chosen thee above the people *of thy time* by My Messages and by My Word. So take firm hold of that which I have given thee and be of the grateful.'[1048]

قَالَ يٰمُوْسٰٓى اِنِّى اصْطَفَيْتُكَ عَلَى النَّاسِ بِرِسٰلٰتِىْ
وَبِكَلَامِىْ ۖ فَخُذْ مَآ اٰتَيْتُكَ وَكُنْ مِّنَ الشّٰكِرِيْنَ ﴿۱۴۵﴾

---

festation of God and not God Himself. But he had already seen a manifestation of God in "the Fire" when travelling from Midian to Egypt (28 :30). What then did Moses mean by his request to see God, contained in the words, *My Lord, show Thyself to me that I may look at Thee.* The request seems to refer to the perfect manifestation of God which was to take place in the person of the Holy Prophet of Islām in some later time. Moses had already been given the promise that there would appear, from among the brethren of the Israelites a Prophet in whose mouth God would put His Word (Deut. 18 : 18-22). This prophecy implied a greater manifestation of God than had been vouchsafed to Moses. So he was naturally anxious to see what sort of God's Glory and Majesty the Promised Manifestation would be. He wished that something of that Glory and Majesty might be shown to him. He was told that the manifestation of that Glory was beyond his capacity to bear; it could not take place upon his heart and that God had chosen the mountain for its physical manifestation. The mountain shook violently and it appeared as if it had crumbled down and Moses, being overwhelmed with the impact of the shaking fell down unconscious. In this way he was made to realize that he had not attained to that high stage of spiritual eminence which should have made him the object of that Divine Manifestation which he had requested to witness. That unique privilege was reserved for one much greater than him—the Crown of God's creation—the Holy Prophet Muḥammad. Moses's request may also be taken as having been prompted by the demand of the Elders of the Israelites to see God with the naked eye (2 : 56). This very unusual experience of his made Moses realize that his request was inopportune. So he cried spontaneously, "I turn towards Thee, and I am the first to believe," which meant that he had realized that he was not endowed with the capacity to see that perfect manifestation of Divine Glory which was to take place on the heart of the Promised Prophet and that he was the first believer in the great spiritual eminence which that great Prophet was destined to attain. This belief of Moses in the Holy Prophet has also been referred to in 46 : 11.

1047. The mountain was not actually broken into pieces. The words have been used figuratively to express the great severity of the earthquake. See Exod. 24 : 18.

1048. The verse seems to be addressed to Moses by way of consolation after God had made him realize that he could not attain to that high spiritual rank to which the Great Prophet of the House of Ishmael was destined to attain. He was asked not to covet the high dignity which was reserved for "that Prophet" but to remain content with, and be grateful for, the rank that God had already bestowed upon him.

146. And [a]We wrote[1049] for him, upon the Tablets about everything[1050] an admonition and an explanation of all things. 'So hold them fast and bid thy people follow the best[1051] thereof. Soon shall I show you the abode [1052] of the transgressors.'

وَكَتَبْنَا لَهُ فِي الْأَلْوَاحِ مِنْ كُلِّ شَيْءٍ مَوْعِظَةً وَتَفْصِيلًا
لِكُلِّ شَيْءٍ فَخُذْهَا بِقُوَّةٍ وَأْمُرْ قَوْمَكَ يَأْخُذُوا بِأَحْسَنِهَا
سَأُورِيكُمْ دَارَ الْفٰسِقِينَ ﴿١٤٦﴾

147. I shall soon turn away from My Signs those who behave proudly in the land in an unjust manner; and even [b]if they see all the Signs, they will not believe therein; and if they see the way of righteousness, they will not adopt it as *their* way; but if they see the way of error, they will adopt it as *their* way. That is because they treated Our Signs as lies and were heedless of them.

سَأَصْرِفُ عَنْ آيٰتِيَ الَّذِينَ يَتَكَبَّرُونَ فِي الْأَرْضِ
بِغَيْرِ الْحَقِّ وَإِنْ يَرَوْا كُلَّ آيَةٍ لَا يُؤْمِنُوا بِهَا وَإِنْ
يَرَوْا سَبِيلَ الرُّشْدِ لَا يَتَّخِذُوهُ سَبِيلًا وَإِنْ يَرَوْا
سَبِيلَ الْغَيِّ يَتَّخِذُوهُ سَبِيلًا ذٰلِكَ بِأَنَّهُمْ كَذَّبُوا
بِآيٰتِنَا وَكَانُوا عَنْهَا غٰفِلِينَ ﴿١٤٧﴾

148. And [c]those who reject Our Signs and the meeting of the Hereafter—their works are vain. Can they *expect to* be rewarded *for anything* except for what they do ?

وَالَّذِينَ كَذَّبُوا بِآيٰتِنَا وَلِقَاءِ الْآخِرَةِ حَبِطَتْ أَعْمَالُهُمْ
ع هَلْ يُجْزَوْنَ إِلَّا مَا كَانُوا يَعْمَلُونَ ﴿١٤٨﴾

R. 18 149. And [d]the people of Moses made, in his absence, out of their ornaments, a calf—a *lifeless* body, producing a lowing sound. [e]Did they not see that it spoke[1053] not to

وَاتَّخَذَ قَوْمُ مُوسٰى مِنْ بَعْدِهِ مِنْ حُلِيِّهِمْ عِجْلًا
جَسَدًا لَهُ خُوَارٌ أَلَمْ يَرَوْا أَنَّهُ لَا يُكَلِّمُهُمْ وَلَا

[a]6 : 155. [b]6 : 26. [c]3 : 12; 5 : 11; 7 : 37; 21 : 78. [d]2 : 52,93; 4 : 154; 7 : 153; 20: 89. [e]20 : 90.

1049. *Katabnā* means, We prescribed, appointed, ordained or made binding (Lane).

1050. Everything that was required to be explained to the Israelites.

1051. Moses is asked here to exhort his people to try to practise higher forms of virtue and not to remain content with merely acting upon the injunctions that are meant for the weak of faith.

1052. *Dār* here signifies "station" or "position;" and the words, *Soon shall I show you the abode of the transgressors*, mean that soon the obedient shall be distinguished and separated from the disobedient.

1053. God can be proved to be a Living God only if He speaks to His servants. It does not stand to reason that God should have ceased to speak now when He spoke to His chosen servants in the past. No attribute of God can be supposed to have ceased to function. The gift of Divine revelation is attainable even now as it was attained in the past. Revelation necessarily does not contain a new Law. It is also meant to give freshness of spiritual life and bring man near unto his Lord and Master.

them, nor guided them to any way? They took it *for worship* and they were transgressors.

يَهْدِيهِمْ سَبِيلًا ۘ اِتَّخَذُوهُ وَكَانُوا ظٰلِمِينَ ﴿١٤٩﴾

150. And when they were smitten with remorse[1054] and saw that they had indeed gone astray, they said, 'If our Lord have not mercy on us and forgive us, we shall surely be of the losers.'

وَلَمَّا سُقِطَ فِيٓ اَيْدِيهِمْ وَرَاَوْا اَنَّهُمْ قَدْ ضَلُّوا ۙ
قَالُوا لَئِنْ لَّمْ يَرْحَمْنَا رَبُّنَا وَيَغْفِرْ لَنَا لَنَكُوْنَنَّ مِنَ
الْخٰسِرِيْنَ ﴿١٥٠﴾

151. And when Moses [a]returned to his people, indignant and grieved, he said, 'Evil is that which you did in my place in my absence. Did you hasten *to devise a way for yourselves without waiting for* the command of your Lord?' And he put down the Tablets and [b]seized his brother by the head, dragging him towards himself.[1055] *Aaron* said, 'Son of my mother,[1056] the people indeed deemed me weak, and were about to kill me. Therefore make not the enemies rejoice over my *misfortune* and place me not with the unjust people.'

وَلَمَّا رَجَعَ مُوْسٰٓى اِلٰى قَوْمِهٖ غَضْبَانَ اَسِفًا ۙ قَالَ
بِئْسَمَا خَلَفْتُمُوْنِيْ مِنْ بَعْدِيْ ۚ اَعَجِلْتُمْ اَمْرَ رَبِّكُمْ ۚ
وَاَلْقَى الْاَلْوَاحَ وَاَخَذَ بِرَاْسِ اَخِيْهِ يَجُرُّهٗٓ اِلَيْهِ ۭ
قَالَ ابْنَ اُمَّ اِنَّ الْقَوْمَ اسْتَضْعَفُوْنِيْ وَكَادُوْا
يَقْتُلُوْنَنِيْ ۡ ۖ فَلَا تُشْمِتْ بِيَ الْاَعْدَآءَ وَلَا تَجْعَلْنِيْ
مَعَ الْقَوْمِ الظّٰلِمِيْنَ ﴿١٥١﴾

152. *Moses* said, 'My Lord, forgive me and my brother, and admit us to Thy mercy and Thou art the Most Merciful of those who show mercy.'

قَالَ رَبِّ اغْفِرْ لِيْ وَلِاَخِيْ وَاَدْخِلْنَا فِيْ رَحْمَتِكَ ۡ ۖ
ع ١٨/٨ وَاَنْتَ اَرْحَمُ الرّٰحِمِيْنَ ﴿١٥٢﴾

[a]20 : 87. [b]20 : 95.

1054. The Arabic phrase in the text means, they repented; they wrung their hands by reason of repentance. The Arabs say of a man who repents, *Suqiṭa fī Yadihī* (Lane).

1055. Moses seized Aaron by the head, not because the latter had countenanced or supported calf-worship, as he is represented to have done in the Bible (Exod. 32 : 2—4), but because he did not successfully prevent the people from worshipping the calf. Display of anger on the part of Moses was due, not to any religious or legal offence committed by Aaron, but to his failure to manage affairs properly in his absence. The anger was justified because a great sacrilege had been committed and the whole work of Moses's life was put in jeopardy.

1056. Aaron appealed to Moses's feelings of tenderness and brotherly affection.

R. 19 153. *As to* [a]those, who took the calf [1057] *for worship*, wrath from their Lord shall overtake them and abasement in the present life. And thus do We reward those who invent lies.

إِنَّ الَّذِينَ اتَّخَذُوا الْعِجْلَ سَيَنَالُهُمْ غَضَبٌ مِّن رَّبِّهِمْ
وَذِلَّةٌ فِي الْحَيَاةِ الدُّنْيَا ۚ وَكَذَٰلِكَ نَجْزِي الْمُفْتَرِينَ ﴿١٥٣﴾

154. But [b]those who do evil deeds and repent and believe, surely thy Lord after that is Most Forgiving, Merciful.

وَالَّذِينَ عَمِلُوا السَّيِّئَاتِ ثُمَّ تَابُوا مِن بَعْدِهَا وَ
آمَنُوا إِنَّ رَبَّكَ مِن بَعْدِهَا لَغَفُورٌ رَّحِيمٌ ﴿١٥٤﴾

155. And when the anger of Moses subsided, he took the Tablets and [c]in their writing there was guidance and mercy for those who fear their Lord.

وَلَمَّا سَكَتَ عَن مُّوسَى الْغَضَبُ أَخَذَ الْأَلْوَاحَ ۖ وَفِي
نُسْخَتِهَا هُدًى وَرَحْمَةٌ لِّلَّذِينَ هُمْ لِرَبِّهِمْ يَرْهَبُونَ ﴿١٥٥﴾

156. And Moses chose *of* his people seventy men for Our appointment. But when the earthquake overtook[1057A] them, he said, 'My Lord, if Thou hadst pleased, [d]Thou couldst have destroyed them before *this*, and me *too*. Wilt Thou destroy us for that which the foolish among us have done ? This is nothing but a trial from Thee. Thou causest to perish thereby whom Thou pleasest and Thou guidest whom Thou pleasest. Thou art our Protector; forgive us then and have mercy on us and Thou art the Best of those who forgive ;

وَاخْتَارَ مُوسَىٰ قَوْمَهُ سَبْعِينَ رَجُلًا لِّمِيقَاتِنَا ۖ فَلَمَّا
أَخَذَتْهُمُ الرَّجْفَةُ قَالَ رَبِّ لَوْ شِئْتَ أَهْلَكْتَهُم مِّن
قَبْلُ وَإِيَّايَ ۖ أَتُهْلِكُنَا بِمَا فَعَلَ السُّفَهَاءُ مِنَّا ۖ
إِنْ هِيَ إِلَّا فِتْنَتُكَ تُضِلُّ بِهَا مَن تَشَاءُ وَتَهْدِي
مَن تَشَاءُ ۖ أَنتَ وَلِيُّنَا فَاغْفِرْ لَنَا وَارْحَمْنَا ۖ وَأَنتَ
خَيْرُ الْغَافِرِينَ ﴿١٥٦﴾

157. 'And [e]ordain for us good in this world, as well as in the next; we have turned to Thee with repentance.' *Allāh* replied, [f]I will inflict My punishment on whom I will; but [g]my mercy encompasses all

وَاكْتُبْ لَنَا فِي هَٰذِهِ الدُّنْيَا حَسَنَةً وَفِي الْآخِرَةِ
إِنَّا هُدْنَا إِلَيْكَ ۚ قَالَ عَذَابِي أُصِيبُ بِهِ مَنْ أَشَاءُ ۖ

[a]2 : 52, 93; 4 : 154 ; 7 : 149 ; 20 : 89. [b]5 : 40 ; 16 : 120. [c]5 : 45 ; 6 : 92. [d]13 : 28. [e]2 : 202. [f]2 : 285 ; 5 : 41. [g]40 : 8.

1057. The account of the Bible accusing Aaron of complicity in calf-worship is certainly misleading (Enc. Bib. vol. 1, col. 2).

1057A. The earthquake was a natural phenomenon. Moses feared that it was a Divine punishment for the sins of his people.

things ; so I will ordain it for those who act righteously and pay the *Zakāt* and those who believe in Our Signs—

وَ رَحْمَتِیْ وَسِعَتْ کُلَّ شَیْءٍ ۚ فَسَاَکْتُبُہَا لِلَّذِیْنَ یَتَّقُوْنَ وَیُؤْتُوْنَ الزَّکٰوۃَ وَالَّذِیْنَ ہُمْ بِاٰیٰتِنَا یُؤْمِنُوْنَ ۟ۙ

158. 'Those who follow the Messenger, *^a*the Prophet, the *Ummī*¹⁰⁵⁸ *^b*whom they find mentioned

الَّذِیْنَ یَتَّبِعُوْنَ الرَّسُوْلَ النَّبِیَّ الْاُمِّیَّ الَّذِیْ یَجِدُوْنَہٗ

---

*^a*29 : 49; 42 : 53; 62 : 3.   *^b*48 : 30.

1058. *Ummī* means, belonging to or pertaining to the mother, *i.e.*, as innocent as a child at the breast of its mother; one not having a revealed Scripture, particularly an Arab; one who does not know how to read or write; one belonging to Mecca which was known as *Umm al-Qurā, i.e.*, the mother of towns. If the word *Ummī* be taken in the sense of "unlettered," the verse would signify that although the Holy Prophet had received no education whatever and was quite unread, yet God vouchsafed to him such knowledge as would impart light and guidance even to those who are considered to be most advanced in learning and enlightenment. Some Christian writers have pretended to doubt the fact that the Holy Prophet could not read or write. Says Reverend Wherry in his 'Commentary of the Qur'ān— "Is it likely that he should have been trained in the same household with 'Alī, who knew both how to read and write and not have received similar instruction ? Could he have conducted an important mercantile business for years without some knowledge of letters ? That he could read and write in later years is certain. Tradition tells us, that he said to Mu'āwiyah, one of his secretaries: 'Draw the *bā* straight, divide the *sīn* properly', etc., and that in his last moments he called for writing material. His use of amanuenses does not militate against his knowledge of the art of writing, for such use of amanuenses was common in that age, even among the most learned." It is a poor argument that because the Prophet "had been trained in the same house with 'Alī who knew both how to read and write," therefore he should also have learnt reading and writing. It only betrays ignorance of elementary facts of the Holy Prophet's life on the part of the reverend gentleman. 'Alī and the Holy Prophet could not have been trained and brought up together, there being difference of many years between their ages. The Prophet was as much as twenty nine years older than 'Alī. Let alone the Prophet and 'Alī being educated and trained together which the great disparity in their ages evidently obviated, it was 'Alī who got his training in the house and under the fostering care and training of the Holy Prophet himself (Hishām). Abū Ṭālib, in whose house the Holy Prophet was brought up, was a man of very meagre means. He did not appreciate the value of learning and knowledge, nor was their possession regarded as an asset and acquisition in his time. The Holy Prophet, therefore, remained illiterate in his house. But 'Alī was brought up in the house of the Holy Prophet himself, whose marriage with Khadījah, a wealthy lady of great repute, had placed ample means at his disposal. He also fully realized how priceless a thing good education was. So under his benign care and ennobling influence 'Alī, judged by the standards of that time, naturally grew up to be a young man of good education.

Wherry's second objection that if the Holy Prophet had been illiterate and did not know how to read and write, he could not have proved such a successful businessman as he actually was, is born of the mistaken concept of a good and successful Arab business man of the Holy Prophet's time. Wherry would not have made this objection if he had known that in Asia, even in the present twentieth century, there are highly successful business men who have not received even elementary education. In Mecca, in the Holy Prophet's time, education was not much in favour. There were very few persons who could read and write, but many carried on most successful and flourishing business. Education was not at that time regarded in Arabia as the *sine qua non* of a good businessman. Moreover, the fact that Khadījah had given the Prophet a slave named Maisarah who knew reading and writing and who always accompanied him on his trade journeys, knocks the bottom out of Wherry's objection.

in the Torah and the Gospel[1059] *which are* with them. [a]He enjoins on them good and forbids them evil and makes lawful for them the good things and forbids them the bad things and removes from them their burden and the shackles that were upon them. So those who shall believe in him and honour and support him and help him and follow the light that has been sent down with him—these shall prosper.'

مَكْتُوبًا عِنْدَهُمْ فِي التَّوْرٰىةِ وَالْإِنْجِيلِ يَأْمُرُهُمْ
بِالْمَعْرُوفِ وَيَنْهٰىهُمْ عَنِ الْمُنْكَرِ وَيُحِلُّ لَهُمُ الطَّيِّبٰتِ
وَيُحَرِّمُ عَلَيْهِمُ الْخَبٰٓئِثَ وَيَضَعُ عَنْهُمْ إِصْرَهُمْ
وَالْأَغْلٰلَ الَّتِي كَانَتْ عَلَيْهِمْ ۚ فَالَّذِينَ اٰمَنُوا بِهٖ وَ
عَزَّرُوهُ وَنَصَرُوهُ وَاتَّبَعُوا النُّورَ الَّذِيٓ أُنْزِلَ مَعَهٗٓ ۙ
ع ١٩ ٩ أُولٰٓئِكَ هُمُ الْمُفْلِحُونَ ﴿١٥٨﴾

[a]See 3 : 105.

The tradition which says that the Holy Prophet had once asked Mu'āwiyah to write correctly the letters *bā'* and *sīn* does not seem to be quite reliable. In the 'Abbaside period many traditions derogatory to the Umayyads were forged. This tradition seeks to show off Mu'āwiyah, a prominent member of the distinguished House of Umayyah, as a man of very poor education who could not even write properly such simple letters as *bā'* and *sīn*. Even, however, if this tradition is proved to be reliable, it does not show that the Holy Prophet was literate because he had become so used to dictating the Qur'ān that it was not impossible for him to have become familiar with the general form of letters and to have given instruction regarding an improperly written word.

The fact that the Holy Prophet sent for pen and paper in the last moments of his life also lends no support to Wherry's assumption. It is an established fact of history that whenever any verse was revealed, the Holy Prophet used to send for pen and paper and dictate to one of his scribes what had been revealed to him. The mere fact of sending for pen and paper does not, therefore, prove that the Holy Prophet himself knew how to read and write. Nor do the words referred to by Wherry in support of his contention, *viz.*, "read in the name of thy Lord," prove anything. The Arabic word *Iqra'* (read) used in 96 : 2 not only means the reading of a written thing but also repeating and rehearsing what one hears from another person. Moreover, the Ḥadith establishes the fact that when at the time of the first revelation the angel, Gabriel uttered the word *Iqra'* no writing was actually placed before the Prophet to read. He was simply asked to repeat orally what the angel was reciting to him. Further, the claim of some Christian writers that the idea that the Holy Prophet could not read or write originated with a misunderstanding of his repeated claim that he was the "unlettered Prophet," is as strange as it is ill-based. It is surprising that those with whom he had lived day and night for years and who daily saw him reading and writing could not find out whether or not he was illiterate and were misled into this belief simply by his own repeated claim that he was illiterate. The contention that his (the Holy Prophet's) use of amanuenses does not militate against his knowledge of the art of writing, for such use of amanuenses was common in that age, even among the most learned, betrays Wherry's ignorance of Arab and Islamic history. The fact is that there were no *'Ulamā'* or learned men among the Arabs in the time of the Holy Prophet in the sense in which this word is understood now, nor were they used to keeping amanuenses and scribes. There is no instance on record of an amanuensis having been kept by an Arab. There obtains complete unanimity of opinion among scholars that the Holy Prophet could neither read nor write before revelation began to come to him. The Qur'ān is quite explicit on the point that the Prophet was not literate at least till he claimed to be a Divine Messenger (29 : 49). However, he had learnt to decipher a few words towards the later part of his life.

1059. For some of the prophecies of the Bible about the Holy Prophet see Matt. 23 : 39; John, 14 : 16, 26; 16 : 7-14; Deut. 18 : 18 and 33 : 2; Isa. 21 : 13—17 and 20 : 62; Song of Solomon, 1 :5—6; Habakkuk 3—7.

R. 20 159. Say, ‘O mankind, [a]truly I am a Messenger to you all[1060] from Allāh to Whom belongs the Kingdom of the heavens and the earth. There is no god but He. [b]He gives life and He causes death. So believe in Allāh and His Messenger, the *Ummī* Prophet, who believes in Allāh and His words; and follow him that you may be rightly guided.’

قُلْ يٰۤاَيُّهَا النَّاسُ اِنِّيْ رَسُوْلُ اللّٰهِ اِلَيْكُمْ جَمِيْعًا الَّذِيْ
لَهٗ مُلْكُ السَّمٰوٰتِ وَالْاَرْضِ لَاۤ اِلٰهَ اِلَّا هُوَ يُحْيٖ وَ
يُمِيْتُ فَاٰمِنُوْا بِاللّٰهِ وَرَسُوْلِهِ النَّبِيِّ الْاُمِّيِّ الَّذِيْ
يُؤْمِنُ بِاللّٰهِ وَكَلِمٰتِهٖ وَاتَّبِعُوْهُ لَعَلَّكُمْ تَهْتَدُوْنَ ﴿١٥٩﴾

160. And [c]of the people of Moses there is a party who guide with truth and do justice therewith.[1061]

وَمِنْ قَوْمِ مُوْسٰۤى اُمَّةٌ يَّهْدُوْنَ بِالْحَقِّ وَبِهٖ يَعْدِلُوْنَ ﴿١٦٠﴾

161. And [d]We divided them into twelve tribes, *distinct* peoples. And, We revealed to Moses, when his people [e]asked of him for water, *saying*, ‘Strike the rock[1061A] with thy rod;’ and from it there gushed forth twelve springs; every tribe knew their drinking place. And [f]We caused the clouds to overshadow them and We sent down for them Manna and Salwā *and We said*, ‘Eat of the good things We have provided for you.’ And they wronged[1062] Us

وَقَطَّعْنٰهُمُ اثْنَتَيْ عَشْرَةَ اَسْبَاطًا اُمَمًا ۗ وَاَوْحَيْنَاۤ
اِلٰى مُوْسٰۤى اِذِ اسْتَسْقٰىهُ قَوْمُهٗۤ اَنِ اضْرِبْ بِّعَصَاكَ
الْحَجَرَ ۚ فَانْۢبَجَسَتْ مِنْهُ اثْنَتَا عَشْرَةَ عَيْنًا ۗ قَدْ
عَلِمَ كُلُّ اُنَاسٍ مَّشْرَبَهُمْ ۗ وَظَلَّلْنَا عَلَيْهِمُ الْغَمَامَ
وَاَنْزَلْنَا عَلَيْهِمُ الْمَنَّ وَالسَّلْوٰى ۗ كُلُوْا مِنْ طَيِّبٰتِ مَا
رَزَقْنٰكُمْ ۗ وَمَا ظَلَمُوْنَا وَلٰكِنْ كَانُوْۤا اَنْفُسَهُمْ

[a]21 : 108; 25 : 2; 34 : 29. [b]2 : 259; 23 : 81; 44 : 9; 57 : 3. [c]7 : 82. [d]5 : 13. [e]2 : 61. [f]2 : 58; 20 : 81.

1060. Whereas all the Divine Messengers who appeared before the Prophet of Islām were national Prophets whose teachings were meant for the peoples to whom they were sent and for the particular periods in which they were raised, the Holy Prophet was raised for the whole of mankind till the end of time. His advent was a unique event in human history. It sought to weld all the different nations and communities into one brotherhood—the Brotherhood of Man in which all the distinctions of colour, clime and creed were completely obliterated.

1061. All the followers of Moses were not corrupt. Some among them were not only good themselves but also guided others to truth and acted justly. The Qur’ān never condemns a people wholesale and indiscriminately.

1061A. See 101.

1062. They only wronged themselves and could not harm the cause of truth.

not, but it was themselves that they wronged.

يَظْلِمُونَ ﴿١٦١﴾

162. And *remember the time* [a]when it was said to them, "Dwell in this town and eat therefrom wherever you will, and say, '*God* ! lighten *our* burden,' and enter the gate in humility, We shall forgive you your sins, *and* surely We shall give increase to those who do good."

وَإِذْ قِيلَ لَهُمُ اسْكُنُوا هَٰذِهِ الْقَرْيَةَ وَكُلُوا مِنْهَا
حَيْثُ شِئْتُمْ وَقُولُوا حِطَّةٌ وَادْخُلُوا الْبَابَ سُجَّدًا
تَغْفِرْ لَكُمْ خَطِيئَاتِكُمْ ۚ سَنَزِيدُ الْمُحْسِنِينَ ﴿١٦٢﴾

163. But the [b]transgressors among them changed *it* for a word other than that which was said to them. So We sent upon them a punishment from heaven, because of their wrongdoing.

فَبَدَّلَ الَّذِينَ ظَلَمُوا مِنْهُمْ قَوْلًا غَيْرَ الَّذِي قِيلَ
لَهُمْ فَأَرْسَلْنَا عَلَيْهِمْ رِجْزًا مِنَ السَّمَاءِ بِمَا كَانُوا
ع يَظْلِمُونَ ﴿١٦٣﴾

R. 21 164. And ask them concerning the town[1063] which stood by the sea. When they profaned the [c]Sabbath; when their fish came to them on their Sabbath day appearing on the surface *of the water*,[1064] but on the day when they did not keep Sabbath, they came not to them. Thus [d]did We try them because they were rebellious.

وَسْئَلْهُمْ عَنِ الْقَرْيَةِ الَّتِي كَانَتْ حَاضِرَةَ الْبَحْرِ
إِذْ يَعْدُونَ فِي السَّبْتِ إِذْ تَأْتِيهِمْ حِيتَانُهُمْ يَوْمَ
سَبْتِهِمْ شُرَّعًا وَيَوْمَ لَا يَسْبِتُونَ ۙ لَا تَأْتِيهِمْ ۚ كَذَٰلِكَ
النصف نَبْلُوهُمْ بِمَا كَانُوا يَفْسُقُونَ ﴿١٦٤﴾

165. And when a party among them said *to another party*, 'Why do you admonish a people whom

وَإِذْ قَالَتْ أُمَّةٌ مِنْهُمْ لِمَ تَعِظُونَ قَوْمًا ۙ اللَّهُ

[a]2 : 59. [b]2 : 60. [c]2 : 66; 4 : 155. [d]7 : 169.

1063. The *Qaryah* referred to in this verse is said to be Aila (Elath) on the Red Sea. It was situated on the N.E. arm of the Red Sea, in the Aelanitic Gulf (which has derived its name from the place itself) and is mentioned as one of the last stages of the Israelites during their wanderings (1 Kings, 9 : 26 & 2 Chron. 8 : 17). In Solomon's time the town came into the possession of the Israelites but afterwards it was probably taken from them. Later Uzziah reconquered it, but under Ahaz it was again lost (Enc. Bib. & Jew. Enc.).

1064. *Shurra'an* also means, they came in shoals.

1064A. As no fish were caught on the Sabbath day, they had instinctively come to know the time when they were safe and therefore this instinctive feeling of security made them appear on the surface or approach near the coast in large numbers on the Sabbath day. This fact proved too strong a temptation for the Jews and they made arrangements to catch them on the Sabbath day and thus profaned it.

Allāh is going to destroy or punish with a severe punishment?' They said, 'In order to be absolved *from blame* before your Lord and that they may turn to righteousness.'

مُهْلِكُهُمْ اَوْ مُعَذِّبُهُمْ عَذَابًا شَدِيدًا ۖ قَالُوْا مَعْذِرَةً اِلٰى رَبِّكُمْ وَلَعَلَّهُمْ يَتَّقُوْنَ ۝

166. And "when they forgot all that with which they had been admonished, We saved those who forbade evil and We seized the transgressors with a severe punishment because they were rebellious.

فَلَمَّا نَسُوْا مَا ذُكِّرُوْا بِهٖۤ اَنْجَيْنَا الَّذِيْنَ يَنْهَوْنَ عَنِ السُّوْٓءِ وَاَخَذْنَا الَّذِيْنَ ظَلَمُوْا بِعَذَابٍۭ بَئِيْسٍۭ بِمَا كَانُوْا يَفْسُقُوْنَ ۝

167. And when they insolently rebelled against that which they had been forbidden, We said to them, "Be ye apes despised.'[1065]

فَلَمَّا عَتَوْا عَنْ مَّا نُهُوْا عَنْهُ قُلْنَا لَهُمْ كُوْنُوْا قِرَدَةً خٰسِئِيْنَ ۝

168. And *remember the time* when thy Lord proclaimed that 'He would surely raise[1066] against them, till the Day of Resurrection, those who would afflict them with grievous torment. Surely, thy Lord is Quick in retribution[1066A] and surely He is *also* Most Forgiving, Merciful.

وَاِذْ تَاَذَّنَ رَبُّكَ لَيَبْعَثَنَّ عَلَيْهِمْ اِلٰى يَوْمِ الْقِيٰمَةِ مَنْ يَّسُوْمُهُمْ سُوْٓءَ الْعَذَابِ ۗ اِنَّ رَبَّكَ لَسَرِيْعُ الْعِقَابِ ۖ وَاِنَّهٗ لَغَفُوْرٌ رَّحِيْمٌ ۝

169. And We broke them up into *separate* peoples in the earth. Among them are those that are righteous and among them are those that are otherwise. And *d*We tried them with good things and bad things that they might return *to good*.

وَقَطَّعْنٰهُمْ فِى الْاَرْضِ اُمَمًا ۚ مِنْهُمُ الصّٰلِحُوْنَ وَمِنْهُمْ دُوْنَ ذٰلِكَ وَبَلَوْنٰهُمْ بِالْحَسَنٰتِ وَالسَّيِّاٰتِ لَعَلَّهُمْ يَرْجِعُوْنَ ۝

---

a6 : 45.   b2 : 66 ; 5 : 61.   c2 : 62 ; 3 : 113.   d7 : 164.

1065. See 107.

1066. This and the following several verses also show that the people who are spoken of as "apes despised" in the preceding verse were not actually transformed into apes but continued as human beings, though they led a miserable existence and were looked down upon by others.

1066A. It is clear from several verses of the Qur'ān that God is very slow in punishing the sinners. He grants them respite again and again. The words mean that when punishment is finally decreed to overtake a people, it is swift in coming and nothing can retard its coming.

170. [a]Then there came after them an *evil* generation who inherited the Book. They take the paltry[1067] goods of this low *world* and say, 'It will be forgiven us.' But if there came to them similar goods *again*, they would take them. Was not the covenant of the Book taken from them, that they would not say of Allāh *anything* but the truth ? And they have studied[1068] what is therein. And [b]the abode of the Hereafter is better for those who are righteous. Will you not then understand ?

فَخَلَفَ مِنْ بَعْدِهِمْ خَلْفٌ وَّرِثُوا الْكِتٰبَ يَأْخُذُوْنَ
عَرَضَ هٰذَا الْاَدْنٰى وَيَقُوْلُوْنَ سَيُغْفَرُ لَنَا ۚ وَاِنْ
يَّاْتِهِمْ عَرَضٌ مِّثْلُهٗ يَاْخُذُوْهُ ؕ اَلَمْ يُؤْخَذْ عَلَيْهِمْ مِّيْثَاقُ
الْكِتٰبِ اَنْ لَّا يَقُوْلُوْا عَلَى اللّٰهِ اِلَّا الْحَقَّ وَدَرَسُوْا مَا
فِيْهِ ؕ وَالدَّارُ الْاٰخِرَةُ خَيْرٌ لِّلَّذِيْنَ يَتَّقُوْنَ ؕ اَفَلَا
تَعْقِلُوْنَ ﴿۱۷۰﴾

171. And *as for* those [c]who hold fast by the Book and observe Prayer, surely We suffer not the reward of the righteous to perish.

وَالَّذِيْنَ يُمَسِّكُوْنَ بِالْكِتٰبِ وَاَقَامُوا الصَّلٰوةَ ؕ اِنَّا
لَا نُضِيْعُ اَجْرَ الْمُصْلِحِيْنَ ﴿۱۷۱﴾

172. And when We [d]shook the mountain over them as though it were a covering and they thought it was going to fall on them,[1069] *We said*, 'Hold fast that which We have given you and remember what is therein that you may guard against evil.

وَاِذْ نَتَقْنَا الْجَبَلَ فَوْقَهُمْ كَاَنَّهٗ ظُلَّةٌ وَّظَنُّوْٓا اَنَّهٗ
وَاقِعٌۢ بِهِمْ ۚ خُذُوْا مَآ اٰتَيْنٰكُمْ بِقُوَّةٍ وَّاذْكُرُوْا مَا
فِيْهِ لَعَلَّكُمْ تَتَّقُوْنَ ﴿۱۷۲﴾ ع ٢١ ١١

R. 22 173. And *remember* when thy Lord brought forth from Adam's children—out of their loins—their offspring and made them bear

وَاِذْ اَخَذَ رَبُّكَ مِنْ بَنِيْٓ اٰدَمَ مِنْ ظُهُوْرِهِمْ ذُرِّيَّتَهُمْ

[a]19 : 60. [b]6 : 33 ; 12 : 110. [c]31 : 23. [d]2 : 64.

1067. '*Araḍ* means, a thing that is not permanent; the paltry goods of the present world; worldly goods or commodities; an object of desire ; (Lane).

1068. *Darasa* means, (1) he read or studied a book; (2) he effaced, erased or obliterated something (Lane).

1069. The leading men of Israel were brought to the foot of the mountain (Exod. 19 : 17). It seemed to them to tower above them like a canopy which might at any time fall upon them.

witness against their ownselves[1070] *saying*, "'Am I not your Lord?' they said, 'Yea, we do bear witness.' *This He did* lest you should say on the Day of Resurrection, 'We were surely unaware of this.'

وَاَشْهَدَهُمْ عَلٰٓى اَنْفُسِهِمْ اَلَسْتُ بِرَبِّكُمْ قَالُوْا بَلٰى شَهِدْنَا اَنْ تَقُوْلُوْا يَوْمَ الْقِيٰمَةِ اِنَّا كُنَّا عَنْ هٰذَا غٰفِلِيْنَ ۟

174. Or *lest* you should say, [b]"*It was* only our fathers *who* associated co-partners *with Allāh* in the past and we were *merely* a generation after them. Wilt Thou then destroy us for what those, who lied, did ?

اَوْ تَقُوْلُوْا اِنَّمَآ اَشْرَكَ اٰبَآؤُنَا مِنْ قَبْلُ وَكُنَّا ذُرِّيَّةً مِّنْ بَعْدِهِمْ ۚ اَفَتُهْلِكُنَا بِمَا فَعَلَ الْمُبْطِلُوْنَ ۟

175. And thus do We make clear the Signs, *that they may be admonished*[1071] and that they may return *to good*.

وَكَذٰلِكَ نُفَصِّلُ الْاٰيٰتِ وَلَعَلَّهُمْ يَرْجِعُوْنَ ۟

176. And relate to them the story of him to whom We gave Our Signs, but he stepped away from them; so Satan followed him up and he became *one* of those who go astray.[1072]

وَاتْلُ عَلَيْهِمْ نَبَاَ الَّذِيْۤ اٰتَيْنٰهُ اٰيٰتِنَا فَانْسَلَخَ مِنْهَا فَاَتْبَعَهُ الشَّيْطٰنُ فَكَانَ مِنَ الْغٰوِيْنَ ۟

---

[a]43 : 38.   [b]7 : 39.

1070. The verse may refer to the evidence embedded in the very nature of man about the existence of the Supreme Being Who has created the universe and controls it (30 : 31). Or it may refer to the appearance of Divine Prophets who show the way to God, the expression 'offspring from the children of Adam,' signifying the people of every age to whom a Messenger of God is sent. It is, in fact, the advent of every new Messenger which prompts the Divine query, *Am I not your Lord* ? The query signifies that when God has made provision for the physical sustenance of man as well as for his moral and spiritual development, how can he deny His lordship. It is indeed by rejecting their Prophet that men bear witness against themselves; for in that case they cannot take shelter behind the excuse that they did not know God or His Law or the Day of Judgment.

1071. The appearance of a Prophet also debars the people of his time from urging the plea mentioned in v. 173 above, for then the truth is made manifest from falsehood and idolatry stands publicly condemned.

1072. The reference here is not to any particular individual but to all persons to whom God shows Signs through a Prophet and who reject them. Similar expressions occur elsewhere in the Qur'ān (*e.g.*, 2 : 18). The verse has been particularly applied to one Bal'am bin Ba'ūra who, it is related, lived in the time of Moses and who is reported to have been a virtuous man. Pride turned his head and he ended his life in disgrace. The verse may apply also to Abū-Jahl or 'Abd Allāh bin Ubayy bin Salūl or for that matter to every prominent leader of disbelief.

177. And if We had pleased, We would have exalted him thereby; but he inclined to the earth[1073] and followed his evil desires. His case, therefore, is like the case of a *thirsty* dog; if thou drive him away, he hangs out his tongue and if thou leave him, he hangs out his tongue.[1074] Such is the case of the people who disbelieve in Our Signs. So relate to them *this* narrative that they may reflect.

وَلَوْ شِئْنَا لَرَفَعْنٰهُ بِهَا وَلٰكِنَّهٗٓ اَخْلَدَ اِلَى الْاَرْضِ وَاتَّبَعَ هَوٰىهُ ۚ فَمَثَلُهٗ كَمَثَلِ الْكَلْبِ ۚ اِنْ تَحْمِلْ عَلَيْهِ يَلْهَثْ اَوْ تَتْرُكْهُ يَلْهَثْ ۗ ذٰلِكَ مَثَلُ الْقَوْمِ الَّذِيْنَ كَذَّبُوْا بِاٰيٰتِنَا ۚ فَاقْصُصِ الْقَصَصَ لَعَلَّهُمْ يَتَفَكَّرُوْنَ ﴿١٧٧﴾

178. Evil is the case of [a]the people who treat Our Signs as lies. And it was their ownselves that they wronged.

سَآءَ مَثَلًا ۨالْقَوْمُ الَّذِيْنَ كَذَّبُوْا بِاٰيٰتِنَا وَاَنْفُسَهُمْ كَانُوْا يَظْلِمُوْنَ ﴿١٧٨﴾

179. [b]He whom Allāh guides is on the right path. And they whom He leaves in error, these it is who shall be the losers.

مَنْ يَّهْدِ اللّٰهُ فَهُوَ الْمُهْتَدِيْ ۚ وَمَنْ يُّضْلِلْ فَاُولٰٓئِكَ هُمُ الْخٰسِرُوْنَ ﴿١٧٩﴾

180. Verily, We have created many of the jinn and the men whose end shall be Hell.[1075] [c]They have hearts wherewith they understand not and they have eyes wherewith they see not and they have ears wherewith they hear not. [d]They are like cattle; nay, they are *even* more astray. They are indeed *altogether* heedless.

وَلَقَدْ ذَرَاْنَا لِجَهَنَّمَ كَثِيْرًا مِّنَ الْجِنِّ وَالْاِنْسِ ۖ لَهُمْ قُلُوْبٌ لَّا يَفْقَهُوْنَ بِهَا وَلَهُمْ اَعْيُنٌ لَّا يُبْصِرُوْنَ بِهَا ۫ وَلَهُمْ اٰذَانٌ لَّا يَسْمَعُوْنَ بِهَا ۗ اُولٰٓئِكَ كَالْاَنْعَامِ بَلْ هُمْ اَضَلُّ ۗ اُولٰٓئِكَ هُمُ الْغٰفِلُوْنَ ﴿١٨٠﴾

[a]3 : 12; 7 : 183; 8 : 55. [b]17 : 98; 18 : 18. [c]2 : 8; 22 : 47; 45 : 24. [d]25 : 45.

1073. Material things, specially love of money.

1074. *Yalhath*, (from *Lahatha* which means, his breath rose on account of fatigue or weariness), signifies that whether or not such a one is asked to make sacrifices in the cause of religion, he seems to be always panting like a thirsty dog, as if the ever-increasing burden of sacrifices is leaving him completely exhausted.

1075. *Lām* is *lām 'Āqibat* denoting end or result. The verse has thus nothing to do with the object of man's creation but only makes mention of the regrettable end of the life of many a man and jinn, (the latter word also meaning a special class of men, *i.e.*, rulers or chiefs or great men). From the way in which they pass their days in sin and iniquity it seems as if they have been created for Hell.

181. And [a]to Allāh *alone* belong *all* perfect attributes. So call on Him by these *attributes*.[1076] And leave alone those who deviate from the right way with respect to His attributes.[1077] They shall be requited for what they do.

وَلِلّٰهِ الْاَسْمَآءُ الْحُسْنٰى فَادْعُوْهُ بِهَا ۪ وَذَرُوا الَّذِيْنَ يُلْحِدُوْنَ فِيْٓ اَسْمَآئِهٖ ؕ سَيُجْزَوْنَ مَا كَانُوْا يَعْمَلُوْنَ ﴿۱۸۱﴾

182. And [b]of those We have created, there are a people that guide *men* with truth and do justice therewith.

وَمِمَّنْ خَلَقْنَآ اُمَّةٌ يَّهْدُوْنَ بِالْحَقِّ وَبِهٖ يَعْدِلُوْنَ ﴿۱۸۲﴾ ع ۲۲ ۱۲

R. 23 183. And [c]those who reject Our Signs, We will draw them *towards destruction* step by step in a manner which they do not know.

وَالَّذِيْنَ كَذَّبُوْا بِاٰيٰتِنَا سَنَسْتَدْرِجُهُمْ مِّنْ حَيْثُ لَا يَعْلَمُوْنَ ﴿۱۸۳﴾

184. And [d]I give them respite, surely My plan is mighty.

وَاُمْلِيْ لَهُمْ ؕ اِنَّ كَيْدِيْ مَتِيْنٌ ﴿۱۸۴﴾

185. Do they not consider *that* [e]there is nothing of insanity about their companion?[1078] He is only a plain warner.

اَوَلَمْ يَتَفَكَّرُوْا ٚ مَا بِصَاحِبِهِمْ مِّنْ جِنَّةٍ ؕ اِنْ هُوَ اِلَّا نَذِيْرٌ مُّبِيْنٌ ﴿۱۸۵﴾

186. [f]And do they not look into the Kingdom of the heavens and the earth and all things[1079] that

اَوَلَمْ يَنْظُرُوْا فِيْ مَلَكُوْتِ السَّمٰوٰتِ وَالْاَرْضِ وَمَا

[a]17 : 111. [b]7 : 160. [c]3 : 12; 7 : 183; 8 : 55. [d]3 : 179; 68 : 46. [e]23 : 26; 34 : 47; 52 : 30; 81 : 23. [f]6 : 76; 10 : 102.

1076. The proper name of God is Allāh; all the rest strictly speaking are His attributes. While praying one should invoke such Divine attributes as are directly related to the object of one's prayer.

1077. Deviating from the right way with respect to God's attributes may signify that God being the Possessor of all the best attributes mentioned in the Qur'ān or the Ḥadīth, there is no need to devise other attributes for Him, which are inconsistent with His Majesty, Dignity and all-comprehensive Mercy.

1078. *Ṣāḥib* (companion) implies a refutation of the charge of insanity brought against the Holy Prophet, as well as a veiled rebuke to the Meccans. They are told that the Holy Prophet is their companion. He has lived and moved among them and they have known him for years; so they could easily see, and indeed in their heart of hearts they are convinced, that there is nothing of insanity about him.

1079. Do not the Meccans see the great and numerous changes that are taking place around them, which point to the approach of a new era? All signs point to the fact that idolatry is going to disappear from the country, giving place to Islām. The word "Kingdom" refers to the control which God exercises over heaven and earth.

Allāh has created? And *do they not see* that, it may be, their *own* term has already drawn near? [a]Then in what thing after this will they believe?[1080]

خَلَقَ اللّٰهُ مِنْ شَيْءٍ ۙ وَّ اَنْ عَسٰۤى اَنْ يَّكُوْنَ قَدِ اقْتَرَبَ
اَجَلُهُمْ ۚ فَبِاَيِّ حَدِيْثٍۭ بَعْدَهٗ يُؤْمِنُوْنَ ﴿۱۸۶﴾

187. [b]Whomsoever Allāh adjudges astray, there can be no guide for him. And [c]He leaves such in their transgression, wandering in distraction.

مَنْ يُّضْلِلِ اللّٰهُ فَلَا هَادِيَ لَهٗ ؕ وَيَذَرُهُمْ فِيْ طُغْيَانِهِمْ
يَعْمَهُوْنَ ﴿۱۸۷﴾

188. [d]They ask thee about the Hour: 'When will it come to pass?'[1081] Say, [e]'The knowledge thereof is only with my Lord. None can manifest it at its time but He. It *lies* heavy[1082] on the heavens and the earth. [f]It shall not come upon you but of a sudden.' They ask thee as if thou wert well-acquainted[1083] therewith. Say, 'The knowledge thereof is only with Allāh; but most men do not know.'

يَسْـَٔلُوْنَكَ عَنِ السَّاعَةِ اَيَّانَ مُرْسٰهَا ؕ قُلْ اِنَّمَا عِلْمُهَا
عِنْدَ رَبِّيْ ۚ لَا يُجَلِّيْهَا لِوَقْتِهَاۤ اِلَّا هُوَ ؕ ثَقُلَتْ فِي
السَّمٰوٰتِ وَالْاَرْضِ ؕ لَا تَاْتِيْكُمْ اِلَّا بَغْتَةً ؕ يَسْـَٔلُوْنَكَ
كَاَنَّكَ حَفِيٌّ عَنْهَا ؕ قُلْ اِنَّمَا عِلْمُهَا عِنْدَ اللّٰهِ وَلٰكِنَّ
اَكْثَرَ النَّاسِ لَا يَعْلَمُوْنَ ﴿۱۸۸﴾

189. [g]Say, 'I have no power to do good or harm to myself save as Allāh please. And if I had knowledge of the unseen, I should have secured abundance of good; and evil would not have touched me. [h]I am only a Warner and a bearer

قُلْ لَّاۤ اَمْلِكُ لِنَفْسِيْ نَفْعًا وَّلَا ضَرًّا اِلَّا مَا شَآءَ اللّٰهُ ؕ
وَلَوْ كُنْتُ اَعْلَمُ الْغَيْبَ لَاسْتَكْثَرْتُ مِنَ الْخَيْرِ ۛۚ
وَمَا مَسَّنِيَ السُّوْٓءُ ۛۚ اِنْ اَنَا اِلَّا نَذِيْرٌ وَّبَشِيْرٌ لِّقَوْمٍ

[a]45 : 7 ; 77 : 51. [b]7 : 179 ; 17 : 98 ; 18 : 18. [c]2 : 16 ; 6 : 111. [d]33 : 64 ; 78 : 2 ; 79 : 43. [e]31 : 35 ; 43 : 86. [f]16 : 78 ; 54 : 51. [g]10 : 50 ; 72 : 22. [h]2 : 120 ; 5 : 20 ; 11 : 3.

1080. When disbelievers are rejecting the Qur'ān which is such a perfect and complete Law, what else is there for them to believe in?

1081. *Mursā* is noun-infinitive or noun of time or noun of place (Lane).

1082. The awarding of punishment is as painful to God as the receiving of it is to men and this is the meaning of the words, *It lies heavy on the heavens and the earth*; "heavens" representing God and angels, and "earth" representing human beings.

1083. *Hafīyy* means, showing much solicitude and manifesting joy or pleasure at meeting another; going to the utmost limit in asking or inquiring; or knowing in the utmost degree (Lane).

of good tidings to a people who believe.'

يُؤْمِنُونَ ﴿١٨٩﴾ ع

٢٣ ع ١٣

R. 24 190. [a]He it is Who has created you from a single soul and made therefrom its mate, [b]that he might find comfort[1084] in her. And when he knows her, she bears a light burden and goes about with it. And when she grows heavy, they both pray to Allāh, their Lord, *saying*, 'If Thou give us a good *child*, we will surely be of the thankful.'

هُوَ الَّذِي خَلَقَكُم مِّن نَّفْسٍ وَّاحِدَةٍ وَّجَعَلَ مِنْهَا زَوْجَهَا لِيَسْكُنَ إِلَيْهَا ۚ فَلَمَّا تَغَشَّاهَا حَمَلَتْ حَمْلًا خَفِيفًا فَمَرَّتْ بِهِ ۚ فَلَمَّا أَثْقَلَت دَّعَوَا اللَّهَ رَبَّهُمَا لَئِنْ آتَيْتَنَا صَالِحًا لَّنَكُونَنَّ مِنَ الشَّاكِرِينَ ﴿١٩٠﴾

191. But when He gives them a good *child*, they associate with Him partners in respect of that which He has given them. But exalted is Allāh *far* above what they associate *with Him*.

فَلَمَّا آتَاهُمَا صَالِحًا جَعَلَا لَهُ شُرَكَاءَ فِيمَا آتَاهُمَا ۚ فَتَعَالَى اللَّهُ عَمَّا يُشْرِكُونَ ﴿١٩١﴾

192. Do [c]they associate *with Him* as partners those who create nothing, and are themselves created?

أَيُشْرِكُونَ مَا لَا يَخْلُقُ شَيْئًا وَّهُمْ يُخْلَقُونَ ﴿١٩٢﴾

193. And [d]they can give them no help, nor can they help themselves.

وَلَا يَسْتَطِيعُونَ لَهُمْ نَصْرًا وَّلَا أَنفُسَهُمْ يَنصُرُونَ ﴿١٩٣﴾

194. And if you [e]call them to guidance, they will not follow you. It is the same to you whether you call them or you remain silent.

وَإِن تَدْعُوهُمْ إِلَى الْهُدَىٰ لَا يَتَّبِعُوكُمْ ۚ سَوَاءٌ عَلَيْكُمْ أَدَعَوْتُمُوهُمْ أَمْ أَنتُمْ صَامِتُونَ ﴿١٩٤﴾

195. Surely, those whom you call on beside Allāh are creatures like you. Then [f]call on them and

إِنَّ الَّذِينَ تَدْعُونَ مِن دُونِ اللَّهِ عِبَادٌ أَمْثَالُكُمْ

[a]4 : 2; 16 : 73; 39 : 7. [b]30 : 22. [c]16 : 21; 25 : 4. [d]7 : 198; 21 : 44; 36 : 76. [e]7 : 199. [f]35 : 15.

1084. One of the primary objects of marriage is that man and woman should be a source of comfort and solace to each other. Man is social by nature and it is his natural craving for a close companion which is supplied by marriage.

let them answer you, if you are truthful.[1085]

فَادْعُوهُمْ فَلْيَسْتَجِيبُوا لَكُمْ إِنْ كُنْتُمْ صٰدِقِينَ ﴿١٩٥﴾

196. [a]Have they feet wherewith they walk, or have they hands wherewith they hold, or have they eyes wherewith they see, or have they ears wherewith they hear? Say, 'Call upon the partners you associate *with Allāh*, then [b]contrive you all against me and give me no respite.[1086]

أَلَهُمْ أَرْجُلٌ يَمْشُونَ بِهَآ أَمْ لَهُمْ أَيْدٍ يَبْطِشُونَ بِهَآ أَمْ لَهُمْ أَعْيُنٌ يُبْصِرُونَ بِهَآ أَمْ لَهُمْ آذَانٌ يَسْمَعُونَ بِهَا قُلِ ادْعُوا شُرَكَآءَكُمْ ثُمَّ كِيدُونِ فَلَا تُنْظِرُونِ ﴿١٩٦﴾

197. 'Truly, [c]my Protector is Allāh Who has revealed this Book. And He protects the righteous.

إِنَّ وَلِيِّيَ اللّٰهُ الَّذِي نَزَّلَ الْكِتٰبَ وَهُوَ يَتَوَلَّى الصّٰلِحِينَ ﴿١٩٧﴾

198. 'And [d]they whom you call on besides Him have no power to help you, nor can they help themselves;'

وَالَّذِينَ تَدْعُونَ مِنْ دُونِهِ لَا يَسْتَطِيعُونَ نَصْرَكُمْ وَلَآ أَنْفُسَهُمْ يَنْصُرُونَ ﴿١٩٨﴾

199. [e]And if you invite them to guidance, they hear not. And [f]thou seest them looking towards thee, but they see not.[1087]

وَإِنْ تَدْعُوهُمْ إِلَى الْهُدٰى لَا يَسْمَعُوا وَتَرٰىهُمْ يَنْظُرُونَ إِلَيْكَ وَهُمْ لَا يُبْصِرُونَ ﴿١٩٩﴾

200. [g]Do thou *ever* forbear, *O Prophet!* and enjoin kindness,[1087A] and turn away from the ignorant.

خُذِ الْعَفْوَ وَأْمُرْ بِالْعُرْفِ وَأَعْرِضْ عَنِ الْجٰهِلِينَ ﴿٢٠٠﴾

---

[a]2 : 8 ; 22 : 47 ; 45 : 24. [b]10 : 72 ; 11 : 56. [c]45 : 20. [d]7 : 193 ; 21 : 44 ; 36 : 76. [e]7 : 194. [f]10 : 44. [g]3 : 160 ; 31 : 18.

1085. The verse constitutes an open challenge to idol-worshippers to the effect that all animate and inanimate things that they call on besides Allāh can never answer their prayers, because the idols do not possess the power to do so. But the Living God answers the prayers of His devotees.

1086. This and the next verse constitute an amplification of the challenge held out to disbelievers in the previous verse. They are challenged to call upon their gods to help them in their campaign against Islām, to make use of their entire resources and to muster all their forces to attack it, leaving no stone unturned to bring it to naught and to lose no time in attacking the Holy Prophet and then see what harm their combined and determined efforts do to him. God has promised to help His Prophet and to make his cause prosper and triumph (5 : 68 & 58 : 22).

1087. A person steeped in error refuses to accept the truth, however clear and unmistakable may be the Signs shown to him to establish the untenability of his position. The disbelievers see the cause of Islām advancing by rapid strides before their very eyes, yet they pretend not to see it and refuse to acknowledge it.

1087A. '*Urf* means, such actions as are in harmony with unsullied human nature.

201. And "if an evil suggestion from Satan assail thee, then seek refuge in Allāh; surely, He is All-Hearing, All-Knowing.

وَإِمَّا يَنْزَغَنَّكَ مِنَ الشَّيْطٰنِ نَزْغٌ فَاسْتَعِذْ بِاللّٰهِ ۚ إِنَّهٗ سَمِيْعٌ عَلِيْمٌ ۞

202. *As to* ^bthose who are righteous, when an evil suggestion from Satan assails them,[1088] they remember *Allāh* and behold ! they begin to see *aright*.

إِنَّ الَّذِيْنَ اتَّقَوْا إِذَا مَسَّهُمْ طٰٓئِفٌ مِّنَ الشَّيْطٰنِ تَذَكَّرُوْا فَإِذَا هُمْ مُّبْصِرُوْنَ ۞

203. And the brethren *of disbelievers* draw them into error and then they relax not *their efforts*.

وَإِخْوَانُهُمْ يَمُدُّوْنَهُمْ فِى الْغَىِّ ثُمَّ لَا يُقْصِرُوْنَ ۞

204. And when thou bringest not to them a *fresh* Sign, they say, 'Why hast thou not forged one ?' Say, ^c"I follow only that which is revealed to me· from my Lord. ^dThese are clear proofs[1089] from your Lord and guidance and mercy for a people who believe.'

وَإِذَا لَمْ تَأْتِهِمْ بِاٰيَةٍ قَالُوْا لَوْلَا اجْتَبَيْتَهَا ۚ قُلْ إِنَّمَآ أَتَّبِعُ مَا يُوْحٰۤى إِلَيَّ مِنْ رَّبِّيْ ۚ هٰذَا بَصَآئِرُ مِنْ رَّبِّكُمْ وَهُدًى وَّرَحْمَةٌ لِّقَوْمٍ يُّؤْمِنُوْنَ ۞

205. And ^ewhen the Qur'ān is recited, give ear to it[1090] and keep silence, that you may be shown mercy.

وَإِذَا قُرِئَ الْقُرْاٰنُ فَاسْتَمِعُوْا لَهٗ وَأَنْصِتُوْا لَعَلَّكُمْ تُرْحَمُوْنَ ۞

---

^a41 : 37.   ^b3 : 136.   ^c6 : 51.   ^d6 : 105;   17 : 103.   ^e17 : 107.

1088. These words signify that when righteous people are incited to anger by Satan; or when some mischief is stirred up against them by wicked men, they remember Allāh.

1089. *Basā'ir* is the plural of *Basīrah* which means, perceptive faculty of the mind; understanding; firm belief of the heart; constancy or firmness in religion; a testimony; argument; a witness; an example by which one is admonished; a shield (Lane).

1090. In answer to their demand for fresh Signs disbelievers are here told to listen to the Qur'ān carefully, because it contains Signs and proofs enough and to spare.

206. And [a]remember thy Lord in thy mind humbly and fearing *Him*, and in a low voice in the mornings and evenings; and be not of the heedless.

وَاذْكُرْ رَّبَّكَ فِيْ نَفْسِكَ تَضَرُّعًا وَّخِيْفَةً وَّدُوْنَ الْجَهْرِ
مِنَ الْقَوْلِ بِالْغُدُوِّ وَالْاٰصَالِ وَلَا تَكُنْ مِّنَ الْغٰفِلِيْنَ ﴿٢٠٦﴾

207. Truly, [b]those, who are near to thy Lord, turn not away with pride from His worship, but they glorify Him and prostrate[1091] themselves before Him.

اِنَّ الَّذِيْنَ عِنْدَ رَبِّكَ لَا يَسْتَكْبِرُوْنَ عَنْ عِبَادَتِهٖ
وَيُسَبِّحُوْنَهٗ وَلَهٗ يَسْجُدُوْنَ ﴿٢٠٧﴾ السجدة ع ٢٤ / ١٤

[a]6 : 64; 7 : 56. [b]21 : 20-21; 41 : 39.

1091 *Āṣāl* (which is the plural of *Aṣīl* means, the evening time) may refer to the four daily Prayers, *viz.*, *Zuhr* (After-noon Prayer), *'Aṣr* (Late After-noon Prayer), *Maghrib* (Sun-set Prayer), and *'Ishā'* (Night Prayer), while *Ghuduww* may refer to the *Fajr* (Morning Prayer). This verse embodies the first *Sajdah* of the Qur'ān.

CHAPTERS 8 & 9

AL-ANFĀL & AL-TAUBAH

(Revealed after Hijrah)

Title, Date of Revelation and Connection Between the Two Sūrahs

Though, as commonly known, it is only the first of these two Chapters which is known by the name Anfāl, yet truly speaking this Chapter comprises both the parts—the one which is known as Anfāl and the other which is known as Taubah. This means that Taubah or Barā'at is really not a separate *Sūrah* but only a part of Anfāl. This is a solitary instance in the Qur'ān where a *Sūrah* has been split into parts, all the other *Sūrahs* being compact wholes. The proof of the fact that Taubah is not a separate *Sūrah* but is a part of Anfāl is that unlike all other Chapters Taubah is not pre-fixed by ***Bismillāh,*** which under Divine direction was placed at the head of every *Sūrah* and formed its integral part, and because also there obtains such a striking similarity between the subject-matter of these two Chapters that they both form but one *Sūrah*. Both Anfāl and Taubah were revealed at Medina; Anfāl was revealed about the time of the Battle of Badr, in the first or second year after *Hijrah,* and Taubah or Barā'at, according to Bukhārī, was among the last portions of the Qur'ān to be revealed in the ninth year after the *Hijrah.*

A Collective Note on Both Sūrahs

In Anfāl the prophecy was made that God would give to Muslims a great victory, and that the property and possessions of their enemies would fall into their hands. This prophecy continued to prove for disbelievers a constant source of mockery at the cost of the Faithful, because God, out of His infallible wisdom, and in conformity with His eternal law had delayed its fulfilment along with the revelation of that portion of Chapter Anfāl which contained a mention of it. When Mecca fell and the aforesaid prophecy was fulfilled, the remaining portion of the *Sūrah* was revealed. It began with *A declaration of complete vindication on the part of Allāh and His Messenger to the idolaters to whom you had announced a commitment that Islām would triumph in Arabia. So go about in the land for four months, and know that you cannot frustrate the plan of Allāh and that Allāh will humiliate the disbelievers.* Incidentally, it may be noted here that some Commentators have taken the above Declaration to mean that a period of four months was granted to those idolaters with whom Muslims had treaty engagements and that this period was intended as a notice, after which all treaties and agreements with them were to be considered as having terminated. This interpretation of the Declaration is evidently wrong; because if it was meant as only a notice of the denunciation of the treaties there was no sense in combining the Declaration with the injunction that they should go about the land and see for themselves that God's purpose had prevailed. He who is granted a limited respite naturally makes hasty preparations to depart for a place of safety and does not go about in the land sight-seeing. Again, if the verse be understood to give notice of termination of existing treaties and to grant a limited respite to those idolatrous tribes who had treaties of alliance with Muslims, how would the very next verse be explained which says that such people as have entered into treaties with Muslims are not to be expelled till the termination of their treaties. It is thus clear that the Quranic words *Alladhīna 'Āhadtum* used in the first verse of Chapter Taubah allude to no political treaty or agreement but only to such declarations as Muslims and disbelievers had made against each other about the ultimate triumph of their respective causes. On the side of Islām it was declared in Chapter Anfāl that the property and possessions of disbelievers would fall into the hands of Muslims, and the disbelievers, on their side, had declared that Islām would be exterminated and they would capture the belongings of the Muslims. It is these contradictory declarations that have been metaphorically termed as '*Ahd* or agreement in the verse referred to above, and the idolaters are told to go about in the country and see for themselves whether or not the declaration which was made in Chapter Anfāl about their eventual destruction had proved true. So, truly speaking, *Sūrah* Barā'at constitutes only a declaration of the fulfilment of the great prophecy made in *Sūrah* Anfāl and is thus not a separate *Sūrah.* In short, there exists a very real connection between these two Chapters which really constitute one Chapter, for, as stated above, *Sūrah* Anfāl was revealed at the time of the Battle of Badr and in it a clear prophecy was made about the ultimate destruction of disbelievers. Then after the last encounter with the idolaters of Mecca, *Sūrah* Barā'ah was revealed to announce the fulfilment of that prophecy and the ushering in of a new era.

Subject-Matter of the Sūrahs

Chapter Anfāl opens with a description of the Battle of Badr and at the outset Muslims are told that they will win a great victory over the disbelievers whose property and possessions will fall into their hands. These wars are the Signs of God and should not be made the means of seeking worldly gains. Next, they are told that they should fight courageously in the cause of God and should not be proud of their strength or organization, neither should they be afraid of the numbers and military prowess of their enemies. Further, obedience to authority is emphasized and it is stated that obedience to God's commands will open for the Muslims the avenues to success and prosperity and will protect them from the machinations and intrigues of their enemies, even as God had protected the Holy Prophet against the secret plots of the Meccans. The *Sūrah* proceeds to say that the enemy is proud of his numbers and military prowess and believes himself to be in the right, and even invokes the wrath of God upon the liar. Such a determined enemy would not easily admit defeat. The *Sūrah* exposes their false pretensions. It further says that the discrepancy between the words and deeds of disbelievers shows that their faith is a mere slave of their intellect and has no firm roots in their hearts. The Muslims are buoyed up with the Divine promise that the war in which they are engaged will end in a victory for them and success also will continue to attend their endeavours in future engagements. To achieve this, obedience to authority and endurance of hardships and unity of action are enjoined upon them.

The *Sūrah* further deals with the sanctity of treaty obligations and Muslims are told that disbelievers will repeatedly violate their agreements but this should not incite them to a breach of their own obligations. They should disabuse their minds of the misconception that their cause would suffer in any way if they did not avenge a breach of agreements on the disbelievers' part by a corresponding violation of an obligation by themselves. On the contrary, they should continue scrupulously to observe treaties; but agreements they have made should cause no mitigation of suitable preparations for war on their part. They are, however, enjoined that if during hostilities disbelievers sue for peace, such an offer should not be rejected, because if disbelievers violate terms of peace and restart hostilities, Muslims will not suffer on account of this fresh breach of trust by them. This injunction implied a reference to the treaty of Ḥudaibiyah when a breach of treaty obligations by the disbelievers led to the Fall of Mecca. Muslims are further told that captives will fall into their hands and they should treat them with kindness.

The promise of victory given to Muslims in Anfāl is declared to have been fulfilled in the opening verses of Barā'ah where it is stated that Muslims have become masters of the whole of Arabia, so the idolaters should go about in the land and see for themselves whether or not the whole country has come under Muslim domination. In verses that follow disbelievers are reprimanded for their repeated breach of solemn treaties and covenants and Muslims are warned not to enter into any fresh agreement with them and should not fear that the severance of ties with them would, in any way, adversely affect the prosperity of Mecca, because God Himself would provide for them. Next, they are told that they should not think that after they have conquered Arabia war would come to an end and they would have peace. On account of the intrigues and secret plots of Christians a new series of wars would start, and because they are idolatrous people they would not bear to see perfect Unity of God established in the earth. Moreover, they have become morally depraved while Islām seeks to establish true equality and freedom. How could then a Christian government view with equanimity the establishment by its side of another government based on equality and freedom, whose proximity would incline its subjects to rebellion ? So having proper regard for the things which God has declared sacred, Muslims are told to make suitable preparations for the impending war with them.

As there was an interval between the revelation of the first 37 verses of the *Sūrah* Barā'ah and those that follow, mention has been made in the latter verses about the fulfilment of the prophecy made in the former. In this connection a brief description is given of the expedition to Tabūk and of the circumstances in which the prophecy referred to above was fulfilled. The Hypocrites and those weak of faith who were seized with the fear of the powerful Kingdom of the Kaiser are reprimanded. Their moral weakness is exposed and believers are bidden not to accept their help, for even without their help God will grant victory to them over the Kaiser (this subject has been dealt with in fuller detail in Chapters Rūm and Fatḥ). In this connection, mention is made of the intrigues of the Hypocrites to injure the cause of Islām. Towards the close of *Sūrah* Taubah it is emphasized that in spite of the intrigues and plots of the Hypocrites and the great power and material resources of disbelievers the Holy Prophet will succeed in his mission through the help of God, "the Lord of the Mighty Throne."

سُوْرَةُ الْاَنْفَالِ مَدَنِيَّةٌ (٨)

1. [a]In the name of Allāh, the Gracious, the Merciful.

بِسْمِ اللّٰهِ الرَّحْمٰنِ الرَّحِيْمِ ①

2. They ask thee concerning the spoils.[1092] Say, 'The spoils *of war* are for Allāh and the Messenger. So fear Allāh, and set *things* right among yourselves, and [b]obey Allāh and His Messenger, if you are believers.'

يَسْـَٔلُوْنَكَ عَنِ الْاَنْفَالِ ؕ قُلِ الْاَنْفَالُ لِلّٰهِ وَالرَّسُوْلِ ۚ
فَاتَّقُوا اللّٰهَ وَاَصْلِحُوْا ذَاتَ بَيْنِكُمْ ۪ وَاَطِيْعُوا اللّٰهَ وَ
رَسُوْلَهٗۤ اِنْ كُنْتُمْ مُّؤْمِنِيْنَ ②

3. [c]They only are the *true* believers whose hearts tremble when *the name of* Allāh is mentioned, and [d]when His Signs are recited to them they increase their faith, and who put their trust in their Lord,

اِنَّمَا الْمُؤْمِنُوْنَ الَّذِيْنَ اِذَا ذُكِرَ اللّٰهُ وَجِلَتْ قُلُوْبُهُمْ
وَاِذَا تُلِيَتْ عَلَيْهِمْ اٰيٰتُهٗ زَادَتْهُمْ اِيْمَانًا وَّعَلٰى
رَبِّهِمْ يَتَوَكَّلُوْنَ ③

4. [e]Who observe Prayer and [f]spend out of that which We have provided for them.

الَّذِيْنَ يُقِيْمُوْنَ الصَّلٰوةَ وَمِمَّا رَزَقْنٰهُمْ يُنْفِقُوْنَ ④

5. [g]These it is who are true believers. They have exalted grades *of rank* with their Lord, as well as forgiveness and an honourable provision.

اُولٰٓئِكَ هُمُ الْمُؤْمِنُوْنَ حَقًّا ؕ لَهُمْ دَرَجٰتٌ عِنْدَ رَبِّهِمْ
وَمَغْفِرَةٌ وَّرِزْقٌ كَرِيْمٌ ⑤

6. *This is* because[1093] thy Lord has brought thee forth from thy house for a righteous purpose[1094]

كَمَاۤ اَخْرَجَكَ رَبُّكَ مِنْۢ بَيْتِكَ بِالْحَقِّ ۪ وَاِنَّ فَرِيْقًا

---

[a]See 1 : 1. [b]3 : 33; 4 : 60; 8 : 47; 9 : 71; 24 : 55. [c]22 : 36. [d]9 : 124. [e]5 : 56; 9 : 71; 27 : 4; 31 : 5; 73 : 21. [f]See 2 : 4. [g]8 : 75.

1092. *Anfāl* are such spoils and gains as come as a Divine gift without the Muslims having laboured for them (Mufradāt). The verse does not relate to the division of spoils for which see 8 : 42. It relates only to the attainment of gains and spoils which fell into the hands of Muslims after the victory at Badr.

1093. The particle *kamā* ordinarily meaning "just as" or "like unto" is also sometimes used in the sense of "as" or "since" or "because" (Muḥīṭ). If, the particle is taken in its ordinary sense of "just as," then the verse could be rendered as: "God grants victories and spoils to His servants and bestows on them honourable provision just as He did when He brought thee forth from thy house, etc."

1094. *Bi'l Ḥaqqi* means, for a righteous purpose. The verse relates to the Battle of Badr.

while a party of the believers were quite averse *to it*.[1095]

مِّنَ الْمُؤْمِنِيْنَ لَكٰرِهُوْنَ ۝۶

7. They[1096] (the disbelievers) dispute with thee concerning the truth after it has become manifest, as though they are being driven to death while they actually see *it*.

يُجَادِلُوْنَكَ فِي الْحَقِّ بَعْدَ مَا تَبَيَّنَ كَاَنَّمَا يُسَاقُوْنَ اِلَى الْمَوْتِ وَهُمْ يَنْظُرُوْنَ ۝۷

8. And *remember* when Allāh [a]promised you one of the two parties[1097] that it should be yours, and you wished that the one unarmed[1098] should be yours, but Allāh desired to establish the Truth by His words and to cut off the root of the disbelievers,

وَاِذْ يَعِدُكُمُ اللّٰهُ اِحْدَى الطَّآئِفَتَيْنِ اَنَّهَا لَكُمْ وَتَوَدُّوْنَ اَنَّ غَيْرَ ذَاتِ الشَّوْكَةِ تَكُوْنُ لَكُمْ وَيُرِيْدُ اللّٰهُ اَنْ يُّحِقَّ الْحَقَّ بِكَلِمٰتِهٖ وَيَقْطَعَ دَابِرَ الْكٰفِرِيْنَ ۝۸

9. [b]That He might establish the Truth and bring to naught that which is false, although the guilty might dislike it.

لِيُحِقَّ الْحَقَّ وَيُبْطِلَ الْبَاطِلَ وَلَوْ كَرِهَ الْمُجْرِمُوْنَ ۝۹

[a]8 : 43. [b]10 : 83.

1095. When Muslims marched out from Medina, as they did not know that they would have to fight a well-equipped Meccan army, they did not come fully prepared for fighting. So when on the way they learnt that they would have to fight the Meccan army they anxiously asked the Holy Prophet why he had not informed them of the real state of affairs so that they should have come fully prepared to meet the enemy. Thus their anxiety was not for their own sake but for the safety of the Holy Prophet. In their unpreparedness they were averse to exposing him to danger. This is clear from the verse "brought thee forth" and not "brought you forth," which signifies that God, in pursuance of Whose command the Holy Prophet had not informed the believers of the encounter with the Meccan army, would not leave him unprotected. The Muslims were not afraid of fighting. They were averse to it because they did not like to shed human blood and because also the person of the Holy Prophet had become exposed to danger.

1096. The verse does not refer to Muslims as wrongly understood by some Commentators, but to disbelievers. There is absolutely no evidence in history to show that the Holy Prophet's Companions ever disputed with him with regard to fighting the enemy. On the contrary, it is related that when before the Battle of Badr he consulted them, they all expressed their complete readiness and even eagerness to accompany him and fight the enemy wherever he might take them (Hishām). Even the disbelievers who came out to fight the Muslims admitted that the latter looked like so many "seekers after death" on the field of battle (Ṭabarī). The verse only signifies that as the enemies of Islām abhorred the truth as one abhors death, so, as a result of this, they were going to be punished with death.

1097. The "two parties" refer to (1) the well-equipped Meccan army that had come fully prepared to fight the Muslims, and (2) the Meccan caravan which was returning from the north and proceeding to Mecca and was lightly armed.

1098. The Muslims naturally wanted to meet the caravan which was lightly armed but God's design was to bring about an encounter with the fully equipped Meccan army. His object in doing so was *to establish the Truth by His words and to cut off the root of the disbelievers*. See also 3 : 14 and 8 : 42-45.

10. [a]When you implored the help of your Lord, and He answered your prayer *saying*, 'I will surely help you with a thousand[1099] of the angels, rank on rank.'[1099A]

إِذْ تَسْتَغِيثُونَ رَبَّكُمْ فَاسْتَجَابَ لَكُمْ أَنِّي مُمِدُّكُمْ
بِأَلْفٍ مِّنَ الْمَلٰٓئِكَةِ مُرْدِفِينَ ﴿١٠﴾

11. And Allāh [b]made it only as glad tidings so that your hearts might thereby be set at rest.[1100] But help comes from Allāh alone; surely Allāh is Mighty, Wise.

وَمَا جَعَلَهُ اللّٰهُ إِلَّا بُشْرٰى وَلِتَطْمَئِنَّ بِهِ قُلُوبُكُمْ ۚ
وَمَا النَّصْرُ إِلَّا مِنْ عِنْدِ اللّٰهِ ۚ إِنَّ اللّٰهَ عَزِيزٌ حَكِيمٌ ﴿١١﴾ ع

R. 2 12. [c]When He caused sleep[1101] to come upon you *as a sign of* security from Him, and He sent down water upon you from the clouds, that thereby He might purify you, and remove from you the uncleanness of Satan,[1102] and that He might strengthen your hearts and make *your* steps firm[1103] therewith.

إِذْ يُغَشِّيكُمُ النُّعَاسَ أَمَنَةً مِّنْهُ وَيُنَزِّلُ عَلَيْكُمْ مِّنَ
السَّمَآءِ مَآءً لِّيُطَهِّرَكُمْ بِهِ وَيُذْهِبَ عَنْكُمْ رِجْزَ الشَّيْطٰنِ
وَلِيَرْبِطَ عَلٰى قُلُوبِكُمْ وَيُثَبِّتَ بِهِ الْأَقْدَامَ ﴿١٢﴾

13. When thy Lord revealed to the angels, *saying*, 'I am with you; so make firm those who believe. I will cast terror into the hearts of those who disbelieve. Smite them above the necks,[1104] and smite off all finger-tips.'

إِذْ يُوحِي رَبُّكَ إِلَى الْمَلٰٓئِكَةِ أَنِّي مَعَكُمْ فَثَبِّتُوا الَّذِينَ
اٰمَنُوا ۚ سَأُلْقِي فِي قُلُوبِ الَّذِينَ كَفَرُوا الرُّعْبَ فَاضْرِبُوا
فَوْقَ الْأَعْنَاقِ وَاضْرِبُوا مِنْهُمْ كُلَّ بَنَانٍ ﴿١٣﴾

[a]3 : 124. [b]3 : 127. [c]3 : 155.

1099. See 934.

1099A. Following one another.

1100. See 474.

1101. The reference in the verse is to the Battle of Badr.

1102. The word *Shaiṭān* may also signify pangs of thirst and is called *Shaiṭān al-Falāt*, *i.e.*, devil of the desert. See 2535. The enemy had taken possession of water and the Muslims naturally feared that lack of it might prove a source of great hardship for them. The word may also signify the friends and associates of Satan.

1103. The Muslims had encamped at a sandy place and the Meccan army on hard ground. Timely rain made the former place firm and the latter slippery.

1104. The upper part of the neck which is just below the head and is considered to be most vulnerable for dealing an effective blow with the sword.

14. [a]That is because they have opposed Allāh and His Messenger. And whoso opposes Allāh and His Messenger, then Allāh is surely Severe in retribution.

ذٰلِكَ بِاَنَّهُمْ شَآقُّوا اللّٰهَ وَرَسُوْلَهٗ ۚ وَمَنْ يُّشَاقِقِ
اللّٰهَ وَرَسُوْلَهٗ فَاِنَّ اللّٰهَ شَدِيْدُ الْعِقَابِ ﴿١٤﴾

15. [b]That *is your punishment*, taste it then; and *remember* that for disbelievers there is the punishment of the Fire.

ذٰلِكُمْ فَذُوْقُوْهُ وَاَنَّ لِلْكٰفِرِيْنَ عَذَابَ النَّارِ ﴿١٥﴾

16. O ye who believe ! [c]when you meet those who disbelieve, advancing in force, turn not *your* backs to them.[1105]

يٰٓاَيُّهَا الَّذِيْنَ اٰمَنُوْٓا اِذَا لَقِيْتُمُ الَّذِيْنَ كَفَرُوْا زَحْفًا
فَلَا تُوَلُّوْهُمُ الْاَدْبَارَ ﴿١٦﴾

17. And whoso turns his back to them on such a day, unless manoeuvring for battle or turning to *join another* company,[1106] he indeed draws upon himself the wrath of Allāh, and Hell shall be his abode. And an evil resort it is.

وَمَنْ يُّوَلِّهِمْ يَوْمَئِذٍ دُبُرَهٗٓ اِلَّا مُتَحَرِّفًا لِّقِتَالٍ اَوْ
مُتَحَيِّزًا اِلٰى فِئَةٍ فَقَدْ بَآءَ بِغَضَبٍ مِّنَ اللّٰهِ وَمَاْوٰىهُ
جَهَنَّمُ ۗ وَبِئْسَ الْمَصِيْرُ ﴿١٧﴾

18. So you slew them not; but it was Allāh Who slew them. And thou threwest not when thou didst throw, but it was Allāh Who threw,[1107] *that* [d]*He might overthrow the disbelievers* and that He might confer on the believers a great favour from Himself. Surely, Allāh is All-Hearing, All-Knowing.

فَلَمْ تَقْتُلُوْهُمْ وَلٰكِنَّ اللّٰهَ قَتَلَهُمْ ۠ وَمَا رَمَيْتَ اِذْ
رَمَيْتَ وَلٰكِنَّ اللّٰهَ رَمٰى ۚ وَلِيُبْلِيَ الْمُؤْمِنِيْنَ مِنْهُ
بَلَآءً حَسَنًا ۗ اِنَّ اللّٰهَ سَمِيْعٌ عَلِيْمٌ ﴿١٨﴾

[a]6 : 116; 47 : 33; 59 : 5. [b]22 : 23; 34 : 43. [c]8 : 46; 47 : 5. [d]33 : 12.

1105. The Muslims must fight to the bitter end. They must win or die; there is no third course open to them.

1106. The verse defines and describes the circumstances in which an apparent retreat or withdrawal of a Muslim force against the enemy is permitted : (*a*) As war strategy or battle manoeuvre when a fighting force shifts its position to beguile the enemy or to occupy a better position; (*b*) when a part of the army decides to fall back to join the main body or another Muslim force before giving battle to the enemy.

1107. The victory at Badr really was not due to any skill or prowess on the part of the Muslims. They were too few, too weak and too ill-equipped to win a victory against a numerically vastly superior and much better equipped and trained army. The throwing of a handful of pebbles and sand by the Holy Prophet bears a remarkable resemblance to the striking of the waters of the sea by Moses with the rod. Just as in the latter case the act of Moses was, as it were, a signal for the wind to blow and the tide to return which led to the drowning of Pharaoh and his hosts in the sea, so was the throwing of a handful of pebbles

19. That *is what happened;* and *know* that Allāh will weaken the design of the disbelievers.

ذٰلِكُمْ وَاَنَّ اللّٰهَ مُوْهِنُ كَيْدِ الْكٰفِرِيْنَ ﴿١٩﴾

20. [a]If you, *O disbelievers*, sought a judgment, then judgment[1108] has indeed come to you. And if you desist, it will be better for you; but if you return *to mischief*, We *too* will return *to punishment*. And your party shall be of no avail to you, however numerous it be, and *know* that Allāh is with the believers.

اِنْ تَسْتَفْتِحُوْا فَقَدْ جَآءَكُمُ الْفَتْحُ ۚ وَاِنْ تَنْتَهُوْا فَهُوَ
خَيْرٌ لَّكُمْ ۚ وَاِنْ تَعُوْدُوْا نَعُدْ ۚ وَلَنْ تُغْنِيَ عَنْكُمْ فِئَتُكُمْ
شَيْـًٔا وَّلَوْ كَثُرَتْ ۙ وَاَنَّ اللّٰهَ مَعَ الْمُؤْمِنِيْنَ ﴿٢٠﴾

R. 3 21. O ye who believe! [b]obey Allāh and His Messenger, and do not turn away from him while you hear *his commands*.

يٰۤاَيُّهَا الَّذِيْنَ اٰمَنُوْۤا اَطِيْعُوا اللّٰهَ وَرَسُوْلَهٗ وَلَا تَوَلَّوْا
عَنْهُ وَاَنْتُمْ تَسْمَعُوْنَ ﴿٢١﴾

22. And be not like those [c]who say, 'We hear,' but they hear not.

وَلَا تَكُوْنُوْا كَالَّذِيْنَ قَالُوْا سَمِعْنَا وَهُمْ لَا يَسْمَعُوْنَ ﴿٢٢﴾

23. Surely, [d]the worst of beasts in the sight of Allāh are the deaf *and* the dumb, who have no sense.

اِنَّ شَرَّ الدَّوَآبِّ عِنْدَ اللّٰهِ الصُّمُّ الْبُكْمُ الَّذِيْنَ
لَا يَعْقِلُوْنَ ﴿٢٣﴾

24. And if Allāh had known any good in them, He would certainly have made them hear. And if He *now* makes[1109] them hear, they will turn away in aversion.

وَلَوْ عَلِمَ اللّٰهُ فِيْهِمْ خَيْرًا لَّاَسْمَعَهُمْ ۚ وَلَوْ اَسْمَعَهُمْ
لَتَوَلَّوْا وَّهُمْ مُّعْرِضُوْنَ ﴿٢٤﴾

[a]32 : 29. [b]3 : 33; 4 : 60; 8 : 47; 24 : 55. [c]2 : 94; 4 : 47. [d]8 : 56; 98 : 7.

by the Holy Prophet a signal for a strong wind to blow, which led to the destruction of Abū Jahl (to whom the Holy Prophet had referred as the Pharaoh of his people) and his host in the desert. In both cases the operation of the forces of nature coincided with the acts of the two Prophets under special Divine decree.

1108. The disbelievers demanded from the Holy Prophet Divine judgment in the form of victory. They are told that Divine judgment has indeed come in the form they had demanded.

1109. The expression "makes them hear" means that if in their present condition God should force them to accept the truth, they would in their heart of hearts remain unconverted and would never become true Muslims.

25. O ye who believe ! [a]respond to Allāh, and the Messenger when he calls you that he[1109A] may give you life,[1110] and know that Allāh comes in between a man and his heart,[1110A] and that He it is unto Whom you will be gathered.

يٰٓاَيُّهَا الَّذِيْنَ اٰمَنُوا اسْتَجِيْبُوْا لِلّٰهِ وَلِلرَّسُوْلِ اِذَا دَعَاكُمْ لِمَا يُحْيِيْكُمْ ۚ وَاعْلَمُوْٓا اَنَّ اللّٰهَ يَحُوْلُ بَيْنَ الْمَرْءِ وَقَلْبِهٖ وَاَنَّهٗٓ اِلَيْهِ تُحْشَرُوْنَ ﴿۲۵﴾

26. And [b]beware of an affliction which will surely not smite exclusively those among you who have done wrong.[1111] And know that Allāh is Severe in requiting.

وَاتَّقُوْا فِتْنَةً لَّا تُصِيْبَنَّ الَّذِيْنَ ظَلَمُوْا مِنْكُمْ خَآصَّةً ۚ وَاعْلَمُوْٓا اَنَّ اللّٰهَ شَدِيْدُ الْعِقَابِ ﴿۲۶﴾

27. And remember when you were few *and* deemed weak in the land, *and* were in fear lest people should snatch you away, but He sheltered you and strengthened you with His help, and provided you with good things that you might be thankful.[1112]

وَاذْكُرُوْٓا اِذْ اَنْتُمْ قَلِيْلٌ مُّسْتَضْعَفُوْنَ فِي الْاَرْضِ تَخَافُوْنَ اَنْ يَّتَخَطَّفَكُمُ النَّاسُ فَاٰوٰىكُمْ وَاَيَّدَكُمْ بِنَصْرِهٖ وَرَزَقَكُمْ مِّنَ الطَّيِّبٰتِ لَعَلَّكُمْ تَشْكُرُوْنَ ﴿۲۷﴾

28. O ye who believe ! prove not false to Allāh and the Messenger, nor betray your trusts knowingly.[1113]

يٰٓاَيُّهَا الَّذِيْنَ اٰمَنُوْا لَا تَخُوْنُوا اللّٰهَ وَالرَّسُوْلَ وَتَخُوْنُوْٓا اَمٰنٰتِكُمْ وَاَنْتُمْ تَعْلَمُوْنَ ﴿۲۸﴾

[a]4 : 60; 8 : 47; 24 : 55. [b]11 : 114.

1109A. The pronoun "he" refers to the Messenger, for it is the Messenger who actually calls. Calling by God is also through His Messenger. Or, "he" may be taken to refer to both Allāh and the Messenger separately, *i.e.*, when Allāh calls you or when the Messenger calls you.

1110. The giving of life to the dead when ascribed to a Prophet of God should be taken in its metaphorical or spiritual sense.

1110A. The words "Allāh comes in between a man and his heart" signify that man (or his ego) has no control over his heart, so he cannot make it obey his dictates. The words may also mean that one should hasten to listen and respond to Divine Call because if one delays doing so, unforeseen circumstances may intervene to make one's heart hard or rusty and then one may refuse to listen to it.

1111. It is not enough to make ourselves good. We are not safe unless we also reform our environment. A house surrounded by a raging fire is likely to fall a victim to it any moment.

1112. Muslims are here told that as God had saved them when they were weak in the land and were surrounded by strong and mischievous people, so they should strive to protect the weak when they are in power. The verse implies a prophecy that Muslims will soon attain political power.

1113. The verse speaks of man's two loyalties—his loyalty to God (and his Messenger) which is absolute and eternal because God is our Creator and Nourisher; and his loyalty to his fellow-beings which springs from the obligations he owes to them.

29. And know that [a]your possessions and your children are but a trial and that it is Allāh with Whom is a great reward.

وَاعْلَمُوْٓا اَنَّمَآ اَمْوَالُكُمْ وَاَوْلَادُكُمْ فِتْنَةٌ ۙ وَّ اَنَّ
اللّٰهَ عِنْدَهٗٓ اَجْرٌ عَظِيْمٌ ﴿۲۹﴾ ع

R. 4 30. O ye who believe ! [b]if you do your duty to Allāh, He will grant you a distinction[1114] and will remove your evils from you and will forgive you; and Allāh is *Lord* of great bounty.

يٰٓاَيُّهَا الَّذِيْنَ اٰمَنُوْٓا اِنْ تَتَّقُوا اللّٰهَ يَجْعَلْ لَّكُمْ
فُرْقَانًا وَّ يُكَفِّرْ عَنْكُمْ سَيِّاٰتِكُمْ وَ يَغْفِرْ لَكُمْ ؕ وَ اللّٰهُ
ذُو الْفَضْلِ الْعَظِيْمِ ﴿۳۰﴾

31. And *remember* when the disbelievers devised plans against thee that they might put thee in confinement or slay thee or expel thee. And [c]they planned and Allāh *also* planned,[1115] and Allāh is the Best of planners.

وَ اِذْ يَمْكُرُ بِكَ الَّذِيْنَ كَفَرُوْا لِيُثْبِتُوْكَ اَوْ يَقْتُلُوْكَ اَوْ
يُخْرِجُوْكَ ؕ وَ يَمْكُرُوْنَ وَ يَمْكُرُ اللّٰهُ ؕ وَ اللّٰهُ خَيْرُ
الْمٰكِرِيْنَ ﴿۳۱﴾

32. And [d]when Our verses are recited to them, they say, 'We have heard. If we wished we could certainly say the like of it.[1116] This is nothing but *mere* tales of the ancients.'

وَ اِذَا تُتْلٰى عَلَيْهِمْ اٰيٰتُنَا قَالُوْا قَدْ سَمِعْنَا لَوْ نَشَآءُ
لَقُلْنَا مِثْلَ هٰذَآ ۙ اِنْ هٰذَآ اِلَّآ اَسَاطِيْرُ الْاَوَّلِيْنَ ﴿۳۲﴾

[a]7 : 87; 3 : 124; 64 : 16. [b]18 : 6; 64 : 10; 66 : 9. [c]3 : 55; 27 : 51. [d]6 : 26; 68 : 16; 83 : 41.

1114. *Furqān* means, (1) that which distinguishes between right and wrong; (2) proof or evidence or argument; (3) aid or victory, and (4) dawn (Lane).

1115. Reference in the verse is to the secret conference which was held in *Dār al-Nadwah* (House of Consultation) in Mecca. Seeing that all their efforts to arrest the progress of the new Faith had failed and that most of those Muslims who could afford to leave Mecca had emigrated to Medina and were out of harm's way, the Elders of the town assembled in *Dār al-Nadwah* to devise plans to make a last attempt to finish Islām. After deep deliberation they hit upon a plan that a number of young men from various Quraish tribes should, in a joint attack, swoop down upon the Holy Prophet and kill him. The Holy Prophet left the house unnoticed at dead of night, when the watchers were over-powered by sleep, and took refuge in Cave Thaur along with Abū Bakr, his ever faithful Companion, and finally reached Medina in safety.

1116. The disbelievers boasted that they could produce a composition like that of the Qur'ān. It was, however, an empty boast, which they dared not translate into fact. The challenge that they would never be able to produce even a short chapter like unto a Chapter of the Qur'ān, has ever remained unaccepted.

33. And *remember the time* when they said, 'O Allāh, if this be indeed the truth from Thee, then rain down upon us stones from heaven or bring down upon us a grievous punishment.'[1117]

وَإِذْ قَالُوا اللّٰهُمَّ إِنْ كَانَ هٰذَا هُوَ الْحَقَّ مِنْ عِنْدِكَ
فَأَمْطِرْ عَلَيْنَا حِجَارَةً مِّنَ السَّمَآءِ أَوِ ائْتِنَا بِعَذَابٍ
أَلِيمٍ ﴿٣٣﴾

34. But Allāh would not punish them while thou wast among them,[1118] and [a]Allāh would not punish them while they sought forgiveness.

وَمَا كَانَ اللّٰهُ لِيُعَذِّبَهُمْ وَأَنْتَ فِيهِمْ ۚ وَمَا كَانَ
اللّٰهُ مُعَذِّبَهُمْ وَهُمْ يَسْتَغْفِرُونَ ﴿٣٤﴾

35. And [b]what excuse have they *now* that Allāh should not punish them, when they hinder *men* from the Sacred Mosque, and they are not its *true* guardians? [c]Its *true* guardians are only those who are righteous, but most of them know not.

وَمَا لَهُمْ أَلَّا يُعَذِّبَهُمُ اللّٰهُ وَهُمْ يَصُدُّونَ عَنِ
الْمَسْجِدِ الْحَرَامِ وَمَا كَانُوٓا أَوْلِيَآءَهُ ۚ إِنْ أَوْلِيَآؤُهُ
إِلَّا الْمُتَّقُونَ وَلٰكِنَّ أَكْثَرَهُمْ لَا يَعْلَمُونَ ﴿٣٥﴾

36. And their prayer at the *Sacred* House is nothing but whistling and clapping of hands. 'Taste then the punishment because you disbelieved.'

وَمَا كَانَ صَلَاتُهُمْ عِنْدَ الْبَيْتِ إِلَّا مُكَآءً وَّتَصْدِيَةً ۚ
فَذُوقُوا الْعَذَابَ بِمَا كُنْتُمْ تَكْفُرُونَ ﴿٣٦﴾

37. Surely, those who disbelieve, spend their wealth to turn *people* away from the way of Allāh. They will surely continue to spend it; *but* then shall it become a *source of* regret[1119] for them, *and* [d]then shall they be overcome. And the disbelievers shall be gathered unto Hell;

إِنَّ الَّذِينَ كَفَرُوا يُنْفِقُونَ أَمْوَالَهُمْ لِيَصُدُّوا عَنْ
سَبِيلِ اللّٰهِ ۚ فَسَيُنْفِقُونَهَا ثُمَّ تَكُونُ عَلَيْهِمْ حَسْرَةً
ثُمَّ يُغْلَبُونَ ۗ وَالَّذِينَ كَفَرُوٓا إِلٰى جَهَنَّمَ يُحْشَرُونَ ﴿٣٧﴾

[a]11 : 4. [b]22 : 26. [c]10 : 63; 64. [d]3 : 13.

1117. It was almost in these words that Abū-Jahl prayed in the battlefield of Badr (Bukhārī, ch. on *Tafsīr*). The prayer was literally fulfilled. Abū-Jahl along with many other leaders of the Quraish was killed and their bodies were thrown into a pit.

1118. The Meccans were punished after the Holy Prophet left Mecca. The Divine Messengers serve as a kind of shield against heavenly visitations.

1119. These words embody a prophecy that the wealth which the disbelievers were spending in wars against Islām would prove a source of great sorrow and grief for them in that their efforts to destroy it would come to naught and their sons by accepting Islām would spend it to further its cause.

38. [a]That Allāh may separate the bad from the good, and put the bad, one upon another, and heap them up all together, *and* then cast them into Hell. These indeed are the losers.

لِيَمِيزَ اللّٰهُ الْخَبِيْثَ مِنَ الطَّيِّبِ وَيَجْعَلَ الْخَبِيْثَ
بَعْضَهٗ عَلٰى بَعْضٍ فَيَرْكُمَهٗ جَمِيْعًا فَيَجْعَلَهٗ فِيْ جَهَنَّمَ ۗ
اُولٰٓئِكَ هُمُ الْخٰسِرُوْنَ ﴿٣٨﴾ ع ٤ ١٨

R. 5 39. Say to those who disbelieve, if they desist, that which is past will be forgiven them; and if they return *to their misdeeds*, then verily the example of the former peoples has *already* gone *before them*.

قُلْ لِّلَّذِيْنَ كَفَرُوْٓا اِنْ يَّنْتَهُوْا يُغْفَرْ لَهُمْ مَّا قَدْ
سَلَفَ ۚ وَاِنْ يَّعُوْدُوْا فَقَدْ مَضَتْ سُنَّتُ الْاَوَّلِيْنَ ﴿٣٩﴾

40. And [b]fight them until there is no persecution and religion is wholly for Allāh.[1120] But if they desist, then surely Allāh is Watchful of what they do.

وَقَاتِلُوْهُمْ حَتّٰى لَا تَكُوْنَ فِتْنَةٌ وَّيَكُوْنَ الدِّيْنُ
كُلُّهٗ لِلّٰهِ ۚ فَاِنِ انْتَهَوْا فَاِنَّ اللّٰهَ بِمَا يَعْمَلُوْنَ بَصِيْرٌ ﴿٤٠﴾

41. [c]And if they turn back,[1121] then know that Allāh is your Protector—an excellent Protector and an excellent Helper!

وَاِنْ تَوَلَّوْا فَاعْلَمُوْٓا اَنَّ اللّٰهَ مَوْلٰىكُمْ ۗ نِعْمَ الْمَوْلٰى
وَنِعْمَ النَّصِيْرُ ﴿٤١﴾

PART X

42. And know that [d]whatever you take as spoils *in war*, a fifth thereof is for Allāh and for the Messenger and the kindred and the orphans and the needy and the wayfarer,[1122] if you believe in Allāh

الجزء ١٠ وَاعْلَمُوْٓا اَنَّمَا غَنِمْتُمْ مِّنْ شَيْءٍ فَاَنَّ لِلّٰهِ خُمُسَهٗ
وَلِلرَّسُوْلِ وَلِذِي الْقُرْبٰى وَالْيَتٰمٰى وَالْمَسٰكِيْنِ
وَابْنِ السَّبِيْلِ ۙ اِنْ كُنْتُمْ اٰمَنْتُمْ بِاللّٰهِ وَمَآ اَنْزَلْنَا

[a]3 : 180. [b]2 : 194. [c]3 : 151; 22 : 79; 47 : 12. [d]8 : 70.

1120. Muslims were enjoined to fight till religious persecution had ceased and men were free to practise the religion of their choice. Islām undoubtedly is the greatest upholder of freedom of conscience (2 : 194).

1121. The words mean, "If they refuse to accept the offer of peace made to them and start hostilities again."

1122. The verse relates to the division of the spoils (see also 8 : 2), one-fifth of which is to be placed at the disposal of the Imām or the *Khalīfah*, as the case may be, to be divided as he deems fit among the five parties mentioned. The Holy Prophet's share was spent for the benefit of the poor Muslims, he himself having lived a life of austere simplicity. According to Imām Mālik, the division need not necessarily be made into equal portions, but is to be left to the discretion of the Imām, who is to divide it as circumstances and need of the hour demand. Such was also the practice of the Holy Prophet and his four Rightly-Guided Successors. The remaining four-fifths were divided among the soldiers who were paid no salaries and generally had even to incur the expenses of wars themselves. This was an exigency measure adopted to meet the conditions then obtaining, as there was then no regular army and no State treasury. "The kindred" included all the descendants of Hāshim and 'Abd al-Muṭṭalib who could not benefit from the *Zakāt*.

عَلَىٰ عَبْدِنَا يَوْمَ الْفُرْقَانِ يَوْمَ الْتَقَى الْجَمْعَانِ ۗ وَاللَّهُ
عَلَىٰ كُلِّ شَيْءٍ قَدِيرٌ ﴿٤٢﴾

and in what We sent down to Our servant on the Day of Distinction,[1123] —[a]the day when the two armies met—and Allāh has power to do all that He wills.

إِذْ أَنتُم بِالْعُدْوَةِ الدُّنْيَا وَهُم بِالْعُدْوَةِ الْقُصْوَىٰ
وَالرَّكْبُ أَسْفَلَ مِنكُمْ ۚ وَلَوْ تَوَاعَدتُّمْ لَاخْتَلَفْتُمْ فِي
الْمِيعَادِ ۙ وَلَٰكِن لِّيَقْضِيَ اللَّهُ أَمْرًا كَانَ مَفْعُولًا لِّيَهْلِكَ
مَنْ هَلَكَ عَن بَيِّنَةٍ وَيَحْيَىٰ مَنْ حَيَّ عَن بَيِّنَةٍ ۗ وَإِنَّ
اللَّهَ لَسَمِيعٌ عَلِيمٌ ﴿٤٣﴾

43. When you were on the nearer bank *of the Valley*, and they were on the farther bank, and the caravan was below you. And if you had to make an appointment between you, you would have certainly differed with regard to the *time of the* appointment.[1124] But *the encounter was brought about without appointment* that Allāh might accomplish the thing that was decreed,[1125] so that he, who had *already* perished by a clear proof, should perish, and he, who had *already* come to life by a clear proof, should live. And certainly Allāh is All-Hearing, All-Knowing.

إِذْ يُرِيكَهُمُ اللَّهُ فِي مَنَامِكَ قَلِيلًا ۖ وَلَوْ أَرَاكَهُمْ
كَثِيرًا لَّفَشِلْتُمْ وَلَتَنَازَعْتُمْ فِي الْأَمْرِ وَلَٰكِنَّ اللَّهَ سَلَّمَ ۗ
إِنَّهُ عَلِيمٌ بِذَاتِ الصُّدُورِ ﴿٤٤﴾

44. When Allāh showed them to thee in thy dream as few[1126] and if He had shown them to thee as many, you would certainly have faltered and would have disagreed with one another about the matter; but Allāh saved *you*. Surely, He has full knowledge of what is in *your* breasts.

[a]3 : 14,167. [b]3 : 14.

1123. The Day of Badr.

1124. The verse gives a graphic picture of the position of the three parties at Badr. The Muslims were on the side nearer to Medina, the Meccan army was in a place farther away from the town and the Meccan caravan which was coming from Syria was towards the sea-coast. The verse says that if it had been left to the Muslims to appoint the time of the encounter, they would certainly have differed with regard to it and would have preferred to postpone the date of the first clash, for at that time they did not feel strong enough to meet their much more powerful and far better equipped enemy in the field of battle. But God's object being to show a powerful Sign, He brought about the encounter.

1125. God had decreed that the Meccans should suffer defeat.

1126. On his way to Badr the Holy Prophet in a vision saw the Meccan army to be less in number than they actually were (Jarīr, x. 9). This meant that in spite of their superior numbers and equipment they would be defeated.

45. And *remember* [a]when at the time of your encounter, He made them appear to you as few in your eyes, and made you *appear* as few in their eyes,[1127] that Allāh might bring about the thing that was decreed. And [b]to Allāh are all affairs referred *for final decision.*

وَإِذْ يُرِيكُمُوهُمْ إِذِ الْتَقَيْتُمْ فِي أَعْيُنِكُمْ قَلِيلًا وَّ
يُقَلِّلُكُمْ فِي أَعْيُنِهِمْ لِيَقْضِيَ اللّٰهُ أَمْرًا كَانَ مَفْعُولًا ۗ
ع وَإِلَى اللّٰهِ تُرْجَعُ الْأُمُورُ ﴿٤٥﴾

R. 6 46. [c]O ye who believe! when you encounter an army, be firm, and [d]remember Allāh much that you may prosper.

يَا أَيُّهَا الَّذِينَ آمَنُوا إِذَا لَقِيتُمْ فِئَةً فَاثْبُتُوا وَاذْكُرُوا
اللّٰهَ كَثِيرًا لَّعَلَّكُمْ تُفْلِحُونَ ﴿٤٦﴾

47. And [e]obey Allāh and His Messenger and dispute not with one another, lest you falter and your strength[1128] depart *from you.* And be steadfast; surely, Allāh is with those who are steadfast.

وَأَطِيعُوا اللّٰهَ وَرَسُولَهُ وَلَا تَنَازَعُوا فَتَفْشَلُوا وَتَذْهَبَ
رِيحُكُمْ وَاصْبِرُوا ۚ إِنَّ اللّٰهَ مَعَ الصَّابِرِينَ ﴿٤٧﴾

48. And be not like those who came forth from their homes boastfully, and to be seen of men, and who turn *men* away from the path of Allāh, and Allāh encompasses all that they do.

وَلَا تَكُونُوا كَالَّذِينَ خَرَجُوا مِن دِيَارِهِم بَطَرًا وَّ
رِئَاءَ النَّاسِ وَيَصُدُّونَ عَن سَبِيلِ اللّٰهِ ۚ وَاللّٰهُ
بِمَا يَعْمَلُونَ مُحِيطٌ ﴿٤٨﴾

49. And when [f]Satan[1129] made their deeds seem fair to them and said, [g]"None from among men shall prevail against you this day, and

وَإِذْ زَيَّنَ لَهُمُ الشَّيْطَانُ أَعْمَالَهُمْ وَقَالَ لَا غَالِبَ
لَكُمُ الْيَوْمَ مِنَ النَّاسِ وَإِنِّي جَارٌ لَّكُمْ ۚ فَلَمَّا تَرَاءَتِ

[a]3 : 14. [b]2 : 211; 3 : 110; 35 : 5. [c]8 : 16; 47 : 5. [d]33 : 42; 62 : 11. [e]3 : 33; 4 : 60; 8 : 21; 24 : 55. [f]6 : 44; 16 : 64; 27 : 25; 29 : 49. [g]14 : 23; 59 : 17.

1127. Whereas the preceding verse referred to the appearance of the enemy in a vision to the Holy Prophet, the present verse refers to its actual disposition on the battlefield. The enemy had kept one-third of their number hidden behind the mounds so that, when both parties came face to face, the Muslims saw only two-thirds of their actual number. This naturally gave heart to them. The enemy on their part did so, as they thought, lest the Muslims being overawed might flee from battlefield and refuse to give battle. Both these impressions helped to encourage either party to come to grips with their opponents with the result that "the thing decreed" was brought about, *i.e.*, the Meccans suffered an ignominious and crushing defeat.

1128. *Rīḥ* among other things means, predominance, strength, victory (Lane).

1129. The person referred to in the verse is reported to be Surāqah bin Mālik bin Ju'sham who incited the Meccans against the Muslims, but who afterwards embraced Islām. The Meccan army was still at Mecca when some of the Quraishite leaders gave expression to the fear that Banū Bakr, a branch of Banū Kanānah, who were hostile to the Quraish, might surprise Mecca during their absence or attack the Meccan army from the rear. Their fears were allayed by Surāqah, a chief of Banū Kanānah, who assured them that his tribesmen would do them no harm (Jarīr, x.13).

I am your protector.' But when the two armies came in sight of each other, he turned on his heels, and said, 'Surely, I have nothing to do with you; surely, I see what you see not. Surely, I fear Allāh;[1130] and Allāh's punishment is severe.

الْفِئَتٰنِ نَكَصَ عَلٰى عَقِبَيْهِ وَقَالَ اِنِّيْ بَرِيْٓءٌ مِّنْكُمْ
اِنِّيْٓ اَرٰى مَا لَا تَرَوْنَ اِنِّيْٓ اَخَافُ اللّٰهَ ۗ وَاللّٰهُ شَدِيْدُ
الْعِقَابِ ﴿٤٩﴾

R. 7 50. [a]When the Hypocrites and those in whose hearts is a disease said, 'Their religion has deluded these *men.*' And [b]whoso puts his trust in Allāh, then surely, Allāh is Mighty, Wise.

اِذْ يَقُوْلُ الْمُنٰفِقُوْنَ وَالَّذِيْنَ فِيْ قُلُوْبِهِمْ مَّرَضٌ غَرَّ
هٰٓؤُلَآءِ دِيْنُهُمْ ۗ وَمَنْ يَّتَوَكَّلْ عَلَى اللّٰهِ فَاِنَّ اللّٰهَ عَزِيْزٌ
حَكِيْمٌ ﴿٥٠﴾

51. And if thou couldst see [c]when the angels take away the souls of those who disbelieve, smiting their faces and their backs and *saying :* [d]'Taste ye the punishment of burning.

وَلَوْ تَرٰٓى اِذْ يَتَوَفَّى الَّذِيْنَ كَفَرُوا ۙ الْمَلٰٓئِكَةُ يَضْرِبُوْنَ
وُجُوْهَهُمْ وَاَدْبَارَهُمْ ۚ وَذُوْقُوْا عَذَابَ الْحَرِيْقِ ﴿٥١﴾

52. 'This[1131] *torment* is because of that which your hands have sent on before and *know* that [e]Allāh is not at all unjust to *His* servants.'

ذٰلِكَ بِمَا قَدَّمَتْ اَيْدِيْكُمْ وَاَنَّ اللّٰهَ لَيْسَ بِظَلَّامٍ
لِّلْعَبِيْدِ ﴿٥٢﴾

53. [f]*Your* condition[1131A] *will be* like that of the people of Pharaoh and those before them, they disbelieved in the Signs of Allāh; so Allāh punished them for their sins. Surely, Allāh is Powerful *and* Severe in punishing.

كَدَاْبِ اٰلِ فِرْعَوْنَ ۙ وَالَّذِيْنَ مِنْ قَبْلِهِمْ ۗ كَفَرُوْا
بِاٰيٰتِ اللّٰهِ فَاَخَذَهُمُ اللّٰهُ بِذُنُوْبِهِمْ ۗ اِنَّ اللّٰهَ
قَوِيٌّ شَدِيْدُ الْعِقَابِ ﴿٥٣﴾

[a]33 : 13. [b]9 : 51; 12 : 68; 14 : 12; 33 : 4; 65 : 4. [c]47 : 28. [d]3 : 182; 22 : 10. [e]3 : 183; 22 : 11; 41 : 47. [f]3 : 12; 8: 55.

1130. When Surāqah saw the grim determination of the Muslims, fear took hold of him; for on seeing them he was convinced that they would win or die. This was exactly how 'Utbah and 'Umair felt on the day of Badr and told the Meccans that the Muslims looked like so many "seekers after death" (Ṭabarī)

1131. *Dhālika* refers to the punishment spoken of in the preceding verse.

1131A. See 376.

54. This is because [a]Allāh would never change a favour that He has conferred upon a people until they change their own condition,[1132] and *know* that Allāh is All-Hearing, All-Knowing.

ذٰلِكَ بِاَنَّ اللّٰهَ لَمْ يَكُ مُغَيِّرًا نِّعْمَةً اَنْعَمَهَا عَلٰى قَوْمٍ
حَتّٰى يُغَيِّرُوْا مَا بِاَنْفُسِهِمْ ۙ وَاَنَّ اللّٰهَ سَمِيْعٌ عَلِيْمٌ ﴿٥٤﴾

55. [b]*O disbelievers! your condition will also be* like that of the people of Pharaoh and those before them; they rejected the Signs[1133] of their Lord, so We destroyed them for their sins. And We drowned the people of Pharaoh, for they were all wrongdoers.

كَدَاْبِ اٰلِ فِرْعَوْنَ ۙ وَالَّذِيْنَ مِنْ قَبْلِهِمْ ؕ كَذَّبُوْا
بِاٰيٰتِ رَبِّهِمْ فَاَهْلَكْنٰهُمْ بِذُنُوْبِهِمْ وَاَغْرَقْنَاۤ اٰلَ
فِرْعَوْنَ ۚ وَكُلٌّ كَانُوْا ظٰلِمِيْنَ ﴿٥٥﴾

56. Surely, [c]the worst of beasts in the sight of Allāh are the disbelievers, who will not believe,

اِنَّ شَرَّ الدَّوَآبِّ عِنْدَ اللّٰهِ الَّذِيْنَ كَفَرُوْا فَهُمْ لَا
يُؤْمِنُوْنَ ﴿٥٦﴾

57. Those with whom thou hast made a covenant,—then [d]they break their covenant[1134] every time, and they do not fear *Allāh*.

اَلَّذِيْنَ عٰهَدْتَّ مِنْهُمْ ثُمَّ يَنْقُضُوْنَ عَهْدَهُمْ
فِيْ كُلِّ مَرَّةٍ وَّهُمْ لَا يَتَّقُوْنَ ﴿٥٧﴾

58. So, if thou overcomest them in war, then thereby strike fear[1135] in those that are behind them, that they may be mindful.

فَاِمَّا تَثْقَفَنَّهُمْ فِي الْحَرْبِ فَشَرِّدْ بِهِمْ مَّنْ خَلْفَهُمْ
لَعَلَّهُمْ يَذَّكَّرُوْنَ ﴿٥٨﴾

59. And if thou fearest treachery from a people, throw back to them *their covenant* with equity. Surely, [e]Allāh loves not the treacherous.[1136]

وَاِمَّا تَخَافَنَّ مِنْ قَوْمٍ خِيَانَةً فَانْۢبِذْ اِلَيْهِمْ عَلٰى
سَوَآءٍ ؕ اِنَّ اللّٰهَ لَا يُحِبُّ الْخَآئِنِيْنَ ﴿٥٩﴾ ع

[a]13 : 12. [b]3 : 12; 8 : 53. [c]8 : 23; 98 : 7. [d]2 : 28. [e]4 : 108.

1132. The verse states a general Divine law that God never deprives a people of a favour which He had conferred upon them until there is first a change for the worse in their own condition.

1133. *Āyah* means, a message; a commandment; a Sign, a verse of the Qur'ān (Lane).

1134. They repeatedly break their plighted word and dishonour agreements solemnly entered into.

1135. The believers are enjoined never to take up arms without a valid cause. But once they do, they should fight so valiantly and deal such deadly blows as should strike terror in the hearts of their enemies. A feebly pursued and lingering war is never a wise policy. If there is to be fighting it should be swift and deadly.

1136. If a people with whom Muslims have entered into a covenant dishonour it, they should be plainly told that the covenant has come to an end and Muslims, if attacked, would fight back with all the force at their command. But under no circumstances are Muslims permitted to make a surprise attack, without giving a prior notice. *'Alā Sawā'in* means, on terms of equality, *i.e.*, in such a manner that each party should know that it is free of its obligations.

R. 8   60. And *let not those who disbelieve think that they can outstrip *Us*. Surely, they cannot frustrate *Our purpose*

وَلَا يَحْسَبَنَّ الَّذِيْنَ كَفَرُوْا سَبَقُوْا ۗ اِنَّهُمْ لَا يُعْجِزُوْنَ ۝

61. And *make ready for them *who fight you* whatever you can of *armed* force[1137] and of mounted pickets[1138] at the frontier, whereby you may frighten the enemy of Allāh and your enemy and others besides them whom you know not, but Allāh knows them.[1139] And *whatever you spend in the way of Allāh, it shall be paid back to you in full and you shall not be wronged.

وَاَعِدُّوْا لَهُمْ مَّا اسْتَطَعْتُمْ مِّنْ قُوَّةٍ وَّمِنْ رِّبَاطِ الْخَيْلِ تُرْهِبُوْنَ بِهٖ عَدُوَّ اللّٰهِ وَعَدُوَّكُمْ وَاٰخَرِيْنَ مِنْ دُوْنِهِمْ ۚ لَا تَعْلَمُوْنَهُمْ ۚ اَللّٰهُ يَعْلَمُهُمْ ۗ وَمَا تُنْفِقُوْا مِنْ شَيْءٍ فِيْ سَبِيْلِ اللّٰهِ يُوَفَّ اِلَيْكُمْ وَاَنْتُمْ لَا تُظْلَمُوْنَ ۝

62. And if they incline towards peace, incline thou also towards it,[1140] and put thy trust in Allāh. Surely, it is He Who is All-Hearing, All-Knowing.

وَاِنْ جَنَحُوْا لِلسَّلْمِ فَاجْنَحْ لَهَا وَتَوَكَّلْ عَلَى اللّٰهِ ۗ اِنَّهٗ هُوَ السَّمِيْعُ الْعَلِيْمُ ۝

63. And if they seek to deceive thee, then surely *Allāh is Sufficient for thee. He it is Who has strengthened thee with His help and with the believers;

وَاِنْ يُّرِيْدُوْا اَنْ يَّخْدَعُوْكَ فَاِنَّ حَسْبَكَ اللّٰهُ ۗ هُوَ الَّذِيْٓ اَيَّدَكَ بِنَصْرِهٖ وَبِالْمُؤْمِنِيْنَ ۝

---

*3 : 179.   *3 : 201.   *2 : 273;   9 : 121;   64 : 18;   65 : 8.   *8 : 65.

1137. *Quwwah* signifies all the forces at the command of Muslims, including all sorts of implements of war, etc.

1138. For *Ribāṭ* see 554-555.

1139. The verse tells Muslims that efficient preparation is the best means of preventing war and enjoins them that they should not only keep sufficient force inside the country but should also station adequate troops on the frontiers and should conduct themselves with such wisdom, faith and energy that the enemy in areas far away from the site of fighting should be so impressed as to give up all idea of fighting them. The verse also points to the necessity of spending freely in war. It seems to contain also a warning and a prophecy for believers. The prophecy is that the pagan Arabs are not their only enemies. There are other people who would attack them in the near future. The prophecy referred to the Byzantine and the Persian Empires with whom Muslims had to fight soon after the death of the Holy Prophet.

1140. The verse, besides embodying an important principle about making of peace-treaties, throws interesting light on the character of the wars undertaken by Islām. Muslims did not resort to war to force men to embrace Islām but to establish and maintain peace. If any people after having made war upon Muslims sued for peace the latter were enjoined not to reject the offer, even if the enemy might be suing for peace only to deceive them and gain time. This shows to what lengths Islām goes to establish peace among nations.

64. And ^aHe has put affection between their hearts. If thou hadst expended all that is in the earth, thou couldst not have put affection between their hearts, but Allāh has put affection between them. Surely, He is Mighty, Wise.

وَاَلَّفَ بَيْنَ قُلُوْبِهِمْ لَوْاَنْفَقْتَ مَا فِى الْاَرْضِ جَمِيْعًا مَّآ اَلَّفْتَ بَيْنَ قُلُوْبِهِمْ وَلٰكِنَّ اللّٰهَ اَلَّفَ بَيْنَهُمْ اِنَّهٗ عَزِيْزٌ حَكِيْمٌ ۝

65. O Prophet, ^bAllāh is Sufficient for thee and those who follow thee of the believers.

يٰٓاَيُّهَا النَّبِيُّ حَسْبُكَ اللّٰهُ وَمَنِ اتَّبَعَكَ مِنَ الْمُؤْمِنِيْنَ ۝

R. 9

66. O Prophet, ^curge the believers to fight. If there be of you twenty[1141] who are steadfast, they shall overcome two hundred; and if there be a hundred of you, they shall overcome a thousand of those who disbelieve because they are a people who do not understand.[1142]

يٰٓاَيُّهَا النَّبِيُّ حَرِّضِ الْمُؤْمِنِيْنَ عَلَى الْقِتَالِ اِنْ يَّكُنْ مِّنْكُمْ عِشْرُوْنَ صَابِرُوْنَ يَغْلِبُوْا مِائَتَيْنِ وَاِنْ يَّكُنْ مِّنْكُمْ مِّائَةٌ يَّغْلِبُوْٓا اَلْفًا مِّنَ الَّذِيْنَ كَفَرُوْا بِاَنَّهُمْ قَوْمٌ لَّا يَفْقَهُوْنَ ۝

67. For the present Allāh has lightened your burden, for He knows that there is weakness in you. So, if there be a hundred of you who are steadfast, they shall overcome two hundred; and if there be a thousand of you, they shall overcome two thousand[1143] by the command of Allāh. And Allāh is with those who are steadfast.

اَلْـٰٔنَ خَفَّفَ اللّٰهُ عَنْكُمْ وَعَلِمَ اَنَّ فِيْكُمْ ضَعْفًا فَاِنْ يَّكُنْ مِّنْكُمْ مِّائَةٌ صَابِرَةٌ يَّغْلِبُوْا مِائَتَيْنِ وَاِنْ يَّكُنْ مِّنْكُمْ اَلْفٌ يَّغْلِبُوْٓا اَلْفَيْنِ بِاِذْنِ اللّٰهِ وَاللّٰهُ مَعَ الصّٰبِرِيْنَ ۝

---

^a3 : 104.   ^b8 : 63.   ^c4 : 85.

1141. The verse seems to give 20 as the minimum number that makes a fighting party.

1142. Because they are mercenaries, and do not realize the righteousness of the cause they fight for, they feel no real interest for it. Or the meaning may be that they have no higher ideals which they seek to pursue and serve.

1143. The verse should not be understood to abrogate the preceding one. The two verses refer to two different states of the Muslim Community. In the beginning they were weak, ill-equipped and ill-trained in the art of war. In that state of weakness they could successfully fight against only their double number. But as with the passage of time their all-round condition, fighting experience and military resources had very much improved they could defeat an enemy ten times their number. In the battles of Badr, Uḥud and of the Trench, the disparity between the number of forces of both sides progressively increased, yet the Muslims quite successfully held their own, till at the Battle of Yarmūk, mere 60,000 Muslims defeated an army of more than a million strong.

68. ^aIt does not behove a Prophet that he should have captives until he engages in a regular fighting[1144] in the land. ^b*If you take captives except in regular fighting* you will be *regarded as* desiring the goods of the world, while Allāh desires *for you* the Hereafter. And Allāh is Mighty, Wise.

مَا كَانَ لِنَبِيٍّ اَنْ يَّكُوْنَ لَهٗۤ اَسْرٰى حَتّٰى يُثْخِنَ فِى الْاَرْضِ ۚ تُرِيْدُوْنَ عَرَضَ الدُّنْيَا ۖ وَاللّٰهُ يُرِيْدُ الْاٰخِرَةَ ۚ وَاللّٰهُ عَزِيْزٌ حَكِيْمٌ ۝

69. Had there not been a decree from Allāh which had gone before,[1145] great distress would have surely overtaken you in *consequence of* what you took.[1145A]

لَوْلَا كِتٰبٌ مِّنَ اللّٰهِ سَبَقَ لَمَسَّكُمْ فِيْمَاۤ اَخَذْتُمْ عَذَابٌ عَظِيْمٌ ۝

70. So ^ceat, of that which you have won *in war as* lawful and good, and fear Allāh. Surely, Allāh is Most Forgiving, Merciful.

فَكُلُوْا مِمَّا غَنِمْتُمْ حَلٰلًا طَيِّبًا ۚ وَّاتَّقُوا اللّٰهَ ؕ اِنَّ اللّٰهَ غَفُوْرٌ رَّحِيْمٌ ۝

R. 10

71. O Prophet, say to the captives *who are* in your hands, 'If Allāh knows any good in your hearts, He will give you better than that which has been taken from you[1146] *as* ransom and will forgive you. And Allāh is Most Forgiving, Merciful.'

يٰۤاَيُّهَا النَّبِيُّ قُلْ لِّمَنْ فِيْۤ اَيْدِيْكُمْ مِّنَ الْاَسْرٰۤى ۙ اِنْ يَّعْلَمِ اللّٰهُ فِيْ قُلُوْبِكُمْ خَيْرًا يُّؤْتِكُمْ خَيْرًا مِّمَّاۤ اُخِذَ مِنْكُمْ وَيَغْفِرْ لَكُمْ ؕ وَاللّٰهُ غَفُوْرٌ رَّحِيْمٌ ۝

72. And if they intend to deal treacherously with thee, they have indeed been treacherous to Allāh before, but He gave *thee* power over them. And Allāh is All-Knowing, Wise.

وَاِنْ يُّرِيْدُوْا خِيَانَتَكَ فَقَدْ خَانُوا اللّٰهَ مِنْ قَبْلُ فَاَمْكَنَ مِنْهُمْ ؕ وَاللّٰهُ عَلِيْمٌ حَكِيْمٌ ۝

---

^a47 : 5. ^b4 : 95. ^c8 : 42.

1144. The verse lays down the general rule that captives should not be taken unless there is regular fighting and the enemy is completely overpowered. It cuts at the root of slavery. Only those, who take part in war in order to destroy Islām and are defeated, can be made prisoner. See also 2739.

1145. The words refer to the Divine promise of help (8 : 8—10).

1145A. Ransoming of captives was already in vogue. What is emphasised here is that prisoners could only be taken in regular fighting in the course of war.

1146. 'Abbās, the Prophet's uncle was taken prisoner at Badr. When subsequently he embraced Islām and came over to the Holy Prophet, he requested, on the authority of the verse under comment, that as God had promised to give the prisoners more than was taken from them as ransom, the promise may be fulfilled in his case. The Holy Prophet granted his request (Jarîr, x. 31).

73. Surely, [a]those who believed and left their homes and strove with their wealth and their lives for the cause of Allāh, and those who gave *them* shelter and help—these are friends one of another. But as for those who believed but did not leave their homes, you are not at all responsible for their protection until they leave their homes. But if they seek your help in *the matter of* religion, then it is your duty to help them, except against a people between whom and yourselves there is a treaty.[1147] And Allāh sees what you do.

إِنَّ الَّذِينَ آمَنُوا وَهَاجَرُوا وَجَاهَدُوا بِأَمْوَالِهِمْ
وَأَنفُسِهِمْ فِي سَبِيلِ اللَّهِ وَالَّذِينَ آوَوا وَّنَصَرُوا
أُولَٰئِكَ بَعْضُهُمْ أَوْلِيَاءُ بَعْضٍ ۚ وَالَّذِينَ آمَنُوا وَ
لَمْ يُهَاجِرُوا مَا لَكُم مِّن وَلَايَتِهِم مِّن شَيْءٍ حَتَّىٰ
يُهَاجِرُوا ۚ وَإِنِ اسْتَنصَرُوكُمْ فِي الدِّينِ فَعَلَيْكُمُ
النَّصْرُ إِلَّا عَلَىٰ قَوْمٍ بَيْنَكُمْ وَبَيْنَهُم مِّيثَاقٌ ۗ وَاللَّهُ
بِمَا تَعْمَلُونَ بَصِيرٌ ﴿٧٣﴾

74. And those who disbelieve—they are friends one of another. If you do not[1148] *what you are commanded*, there will be mischief in the land and great disorder.

وَالَّذِينَ كَفَرُوا بَعْضُهُمْ أَوْلِيَاءُ بَعْضٍ ۚ إِلَّا تَفْعَلُوهُ
تَكُن فِتْنَةٌ فِي الْأَرْضِ وَفَسَادٌ كَبِيرٌ ﴿٧٤﴾

75. And [b]those who believed and left their homes and strove for the cause of Allāh, and those who gave *them* shelter and help—these indeed are true believers. For them is forgiveness and an honourable provision.

وَالَّذِينَ آمَنُوا وَهَاجَرُوا وَجَاهَدُوا فِي سَبِيلِ اللَّهِ
وَالَّذِينَ آوَوا وَّنَصَرُوا أُولَٰئِكَ هُمُ الْمُؤْمِنُونَ حَقًّا ۚ
لَّهُم مَّغْفِرَةٌ وَرِزْقٌ كَرِيمٌ ﴿٧٥﴾

[a]2 : 219; 9 : 20; 61 : 12. [b]2 : 219; 9 : 20; 61 : 12.

1147. The verse lays down the principle that those Muslims who live in the same country and under the same administration. whether as immigrants or as original citizens, are bound to help one another in the hour of each other's need. But those Muslims who do not emigrate to a Muslim country have no claim on the help of the former in worldly matters. But if they are persecuted for the sake of their religion, then they must be helped. If, however, they are living under a non-Muslim government, with whom Muslims have entered into a treaty of peace, then no help should be rendered them even in matters of religion; and in this case the only way open to Muslims is to emigrate from the non-Muslim country.

1148. If this principle is not observed by Muslims, there will be oppression, tyranny and disturbance in the land.

76. And those who believe after this and leave their homes and strive *for the cause of Allāh* along with you—these are of you; and [a]*as to* blood relations,[1149] they are nearer one to another in the Book of Allāh. Surely, Allāh knows all things well.

وَالَّذِيْنَ اٰمَنُوْا مِنْۢ بَعْدُ وَهَاجَرُوْا وَجٰهَدُوْا مَعَكُمْ
فَاُولٰٓئِكَ مِنْكُمْ ؕ وَاُولُوا الْاَرْحَامِ بَعْضُهُمْ اَوْلٰى بِبَعْضٍ
فِىْ كِتٰبِ اللّٰهِ ؕ اِنَّ اللّٰهَ بِكُلِّ شَىْءٍ عَلِيْمٌ ﴿۷۶﴾ ع

[a]33 : 7.

1149. As all Muslims are declared to be brothers, one to another, in verse 73 and the Holy Prophet had established at Medina a sort of brotherhood between the Refugees and the Helpers, the misunderstanding might have arisen that they could inherit one another's property; so it is enjoined here that blood relations alone are entitled to inheritance and other Muslims are only brothers in Faith and not heirs.

سُوْرَةُ التَّوْبَةِ مَدَنِيَّةٌ

ركوعاتها ١٦ — (٩) — آياتها ١٢٩

1. *This is* a declaration of *complete* vindication[1150] on the part of Allāh and His Messenger to the idolaters to whom you had announced a commitment[1151] *that Islām would triumph in Arabia.*

بَرَآءَةٌ مِّنَ اللّٰهِ وَرَسُوْلِهٖٓ اِلَى الَّذِيْنَ عٰهَدْتُّمْ مِّنَ الْمُشْرِكِيْنَ ۝١

2. So go about in the land for four months, and [a]know that you cannot frustrate *the plan of* Allāh[1152] and that Allāh will humiliate the disbelievers.

فَسِيْحُوْا فِى الْاَرْضِ اَرْبَعَةَ اَشْهُرٍ وَّاعْلَمُوْٓا اَنَّكُمْ غَيْرُ مُعْجِزِى اللّٰهِ ۙ وَاَنَّ اللّٰهَ مُخْزِى الْكٰفِرِيْنَ ۝٢

3. And *this is* a proclamation[1153] from Allāh and His Messenger to the people on the day of the Greater Pilgrimage,[1153A] that Allāh is clear[1154] of the idolaters, and so is His

وَاَذَانٌ مِّنَ اللّٰهِ وَرَسُوْلِهٖٓ اِلَى النَّاسِ يَوْمَ الْحَجِّ الْاَكْبَرِ اَنَّ اللّٰهَ بَرِىْٓءٌ مِّنَ الْمُشْرِكِيْنَ ۙ وَرَسُوْلُهٗ

---

[a]6 : 135; 11 : 21.

1150. *Barā'ah* signifies a declaration of vindication; exemption, absolution from a fault or responsibility; exemption or absolution from a demand, etc. (Tāj).

1151. *'Āhada* is here used not in the sense of entering into a treaty or a compact but making a commitment or a solemn promise by which one binds oneself (Lisān). The verse makes a solemn declaration that Islām and the Holy Prophet have been completely vindicated by the Fall of Mecca. While the Prophet was being driven from Mecca as a friendless fugitive with a price on his head, it was then declared in unmistakable terms that he would come back to it in triumph and glory (28 : 86). That prophecy was fulfilled with the Fall of Mecca and the establishment of the rule of Islām throughout Arabia. Thus the Holy Prophet stood fully vindicated and absolved from the demand of the Meccans that in fulfilment of his repeated declaration Mecca should have fallen into his hands. See also Introduction to *Sūrah* Anfāl.

1152. With the Fall of Mecca and the defeat of Hawāzin in the Battle of Ḥunain, the rule and authority of Islām had been established throughout the Ḥijāz. Certain tribes had made treaties with the Muslims and had laid down arms. These treaties were to be fully observed. But there were other tribes who had not made formal submission, had not laid down their arms and also had not made any treaty with the Muslims, ensuring the maintenance of peace and the observance of law and order. They had commenced hostilities against the Muslims, and though they had in effect been vanquished, they had not yet acknowledged defeat nor had agreed to live in peace with the Muslims. These tribes were given a four-month period of respite during which operations against them would remain suspended. They could go about freely in the land and satisfy themselves that further resistance was useless. They could then make their submission and make treaties. It is to these tribes that this verse refers.

1153. *Adhān* means, notification, proclamation or call (Lane).

1153A. Greater Pilgrimage was so called because it was the first pilgrimage performed under the controi of the Muslims.

1154. Whereas in the preceding verse *Barā'ah* signifies a declaration of vindication

Messenger. So if you repent, it will be better for you; but if you turn away, then [a]know that you cannot frustrate *the plan* of Allāh. And [b]give tidings of a painful punishment to those who disbelieve,

فَإِنْ تُبْتُمْ فَهُوَ خَيْرٌ لَّكُمْ ۚ وَإِنْ تَوَلَّيْتُمْ فَاعْلَمُوٓا أَنَّكُمْ غَيْرُ مُعْجِزِي اللّٰهِ ۗ وَبَشِّرِ الَّذِينَ كَفَرُوا بِعَذَابٍ أَلِيمٍ ﴿٣﴾

4. [c]Except those of the disbelievers with whom you have entered into a treaty and who have not *subsequently* failed you in anything nor aided anyone against you.[1155] So fulfil to these the treaty *you have* made with them till their term. Surely, Allāh loves those who are righteous.

إِلَّا الَّذِينَ عَاهَدْتُّمْ مِّنَ الْمُشْرِكِينَ ثُمَّ لَمْ يَنْقُصُوكُمْ شَيْئًا وَّلَمْ يُظَاهِرُوا عَلَيْكُمْ أَحَدًا فَأَتِمُّوٓا إِلَيْهِمْ عَهْدَهُمْ إِلٰى مُدَّتِهِمْ ۚ إِنَّ اللّٰهَ يُحِبُّ الْمُتَّقِينَ ﴿٤﴾

5. And when the forbidden months[1155A] have passed, slay the

فَإِذَا انْسَلَخَ الْأَشْهُرُ الْحُرُمُ فَاقْتُلُوا الْمُشْرِكِينَ

[a]See 9 : 2. [b]4 : 139. [c]9 : 7.

that the promises about the complete triumpth of Islām had been fulfilled, in the present verse the word signifies "being clear of a person or a thing," *i.e.*, having nothing to do with him or it (Lane). The declaration, contained in this verse and the one that follows is different from that embodied in vv. 9 : 1—2; for whereas vv. 9 :1—2 relate to vindication that the promises made to the idolaters by the Holy Prophet had been fulfilled, the present verse pertains to the severance of all connections with them. This severance of relations should not be taken to mean that the verse declares that Muslims were free from all treaty obligations; for, as the following verse makes it quite clear, treaties are to be respected in all cases and must not be violated.

On his return from Tabūk in the ninth year of the Hijrah, the Holy Prophet sent 'Alı to Mecca, who, on the occasion of the Greater Pilgrimage, made, as his representative, a proclamation containing the announcement: (1) "No idolater shall approach the House of God after this year. (2) Treaties and engagements made by the Holy Prophet with idolatrous tribes who had not made their submission shall stand and shall be faithfully respected till the end of their terms. But henceforth no idolater could stay in the Ḥijāz except those with whom he had entered into a treaty or who had sought protection from him. The order was amply justified, not only by the persistently treacherous conduct of the idolatrous tribes and by repudiation on their part of solemn agreements, resorted to on a large scale when the Holy Prophet was absent from Medina on the Tabūk expedition (8 : 57), but also by other political and cultural considerations which demanded its promulgation. The Ḥijāz had now become the religious as well as the political centre of Islām, and its interests demanded that it should be purged of all foreign and harmful elements likely to endanger its integrity and prove dangerous to the nascent Muslim Community.

1155. These tribes were Banū Khuzā'ah, Banū Mudlij, Banū Bakr, Banū Ḍamrah and some of the Banū Sulaim tribes. The verse incidentally throws interesting light on the sanctity that Islām attaches to treaties and agreements.

1155A. "The forbidden months" are the four months of *Dhu'l-Qa'dah*, *Dhu'l-Hijjah*, *Muḥarram* and *Rajab*, the first three being the months of the Greater Pilgrimage, while in the last the Arabs generally performed the Lesser Pilgrimage or '*Umrah* (2 : 195 & 2 : 218). The term *Ashhur al-Ḥurum* does not signify "sacred months" but "forbidden months" and refers to the four months mentioned in 9 : 2 above. In these months the above-mentioned idolaters were granted protection to travel through the land and see for themselves whether Islām had not triumphed and whether the word of God had not been fulfilled. At the end of this period, during which all hostilities were to remain suspended, war was to be

idolaters[1156] wherever you find them and take them *captive*, and beleaguer them, and lie in wait for them at every place of ambush. But [a]if they repent and observe Prayer and pay the *Zakāt*, then leave their way *free*.[1157] Surely, Allāh is Most Forgiving, Merciful.

حَيْثُ وَجَدْتُّمُوْهُمْ وَخُذُوْهُمْ وَاحْصُرُوْهُمْ وَاقْعُدُوْا
لَهُمْ كُلَّ مَرْصَدٍ ۚ فَاِنْ تَابُوْا وَاَقَامُوا الصَّلٰوةَ وَاٰتَوُا
الزَّكٰوةَ فَخَلُّوْا سَبِيْلَهُمْ ؕ اِنَّ اللّٰهَ غَفُوْرٌ رَّحِيْمٌ ۝۵

6. And if any one of the idolaters seeks protection of thee, grant him protection so that he may hear the Word of Allāh; then convey him to his place of security.[1158] That is because they are a people who have no knowledge.

وَاِنْ اَحَدٌ مِّنَ الْمُشْرِكِيْنَ اسْتَجَارَكَ فَاَجِرْهُ حَتّٰى يَسْمَعَ
كَلٰمَ اللّٰهِ ثُمَّ اَبْلِغْهُ مَاْمَنَهٗ ؕ ذٰلِكَ بِاَنَّهُمْ قَوْمٌ لَّا
غ يَعْلَمُوْنَ ۝۶ ع

R. 2 7. How can there be a treaty for *these* idolaters with Allāh and His Messenger, [b]except those with whom you entered into a treaty at the Sacred Mosque? So, as long as they are true to you, be true to them.[1159] Surely, Allāh loves those who fulfil their obligations.

كَيْفَ يَكُوْنُ لِلْمُشْرِكِيْنَ عَهْدٌ عِنْدَ اللّٰهِ وَعِنْدَ رَسُوْلِهٖٓ
اِلَّا الَّذِيْنَ عٰهَدْتُّمْ عِنْدَ الْمَسْجِدِ الْحَرَامِ ۚ فَمَا
اسْتَقَامُوْا لَكُمْ فَاسْتَقِيْمُوْا لَهُمْ ؕ اِنَّ اللّٰهَ يُحِبُّ
الْمُتَّقِيْنَ ۝۷

[a]7 : 157; 9 : 11. [b]9 : 4.

resumed against such avowed enemies of Islām as had themselves started hostilities and had repeatedly broken their plighted word. The reason for this ultimatum is given in vv. 9: 8-13. As for those idolaters who had not been guilty of faithlessness and treachery, they were to be protected (9 : 4, 7).

1156. Those idolaters who had fought with the Muslims and had not yet asked for a fresh treaty with them.

1157. Even those enemies of Islām at whose hands Muslims had suffered very grievous losses were to be forgiven if they repented and accepted Islām of their own free will. In fact, there was a large number of men among the idolaters who, in their heart of hearts, had been convinced of the truth of Islām, but who, either through pride or for fear of persecution or other considerations, had refrained from making open confession of faith. This verse assured such people that if anyone of them declared his faith in Islām even during the war, his confession would not be taken as hypocritical or as having been made to save his skin.

1158. The verse clearly establishes the fact that war with idolaters was not undertaken in order to force them to embrace Islām, because, according to it, even when a state of war existed, idolaters were to be permitted to come to the Muslims' camp or Headquarters if they desired to investigate the truth. Then, after the truth had been preached to them and they had been acquainted with the teachings of Islām, they were to be safely conducted to their place of security, if they did not feel inclined to embrace the new Faith. In the face of such clear teachings, it is the height of injustice to accuse Islām of intolerance or of using or conniving at force; for its propagation.

1159. The verse shows that war was permissible only against such non-Muslims as had repeatedly violated most solemn covenants and had attacked Muslims treacherously. As for the rest, Muslims had been bidden to observe their engagements with them strictly and

8. How *can it be* when, if they prevail against you, [a]they would not observe any tie of kinship[1160] or covenant[1161] in respect of you. They would please you with their mouths, while their hearts repudiate *what they say* and most of them are perfidious.

كَيْفَ وَاِنْ يَّظْهَرُوْا عَلَيْكُمْ لَا يَرْقُبُوْا فِيْكُمْ اِلًّا
وَّلَا ذِمَّةً ۭ يُرْضُوْنَكُمْ بِاَفْوَاهِهِمْ وَتَاْبٰى قُلُوْبُهُمْ ۚ
وَاَكْثَرُهُمْ فٰسِقُوْنَ ﴿۸﴾

9. [b]They have bartered the Signs of Allāh for a paltry price and have turned *men* away from His way. Evil indeed is that which they do.

اِشْتَرَوْا بِاٰيٰتِ اللّٰهِ ثَمَنًا قَلِيْلًا فَصَدُّوْا عَنْ سَبِيْلِهٖ ۭ
اِنَّهُمْ سَآءَ مَا كَانُوْا يَعْمَلُوْنَ ﴿۹﴾

10. [c]They observe not any tie of kinship or covenant in respect of any believer.[1162] And it is they who are transgressors.

لَا يَرْقُبُوْنَ فِيْ مُؤْمِنٍ اِلًّا وَّلَا ذِمَّةً ۭ وَاُولٰٓئِكَ هُمُ
الْمُعْتَدُوْنَ ﴿۱۰﴾

11. [d]But if they repent, and observe Prayer and pay the *Zakāt*, then they are your brethren in Faith. And We explain the Signs for a people who have knowledge.

فَاِنْ تَابُوْا وَاَقَامُوا الصَّلٰوةَ وَاٰتَوُا الزَّكٰوةَ فَاِخْوَانُكُمْ
فِي الدِّيْنِ ۭ وَنُفَصِّلُ الْاٰيٰتِ لِقَوْمٍ يَّعْلَمُوْنَ ﴿۱۱﴾

[a]9 : 10. [b]2 : 175; 3 : 78, 188; 16 : 96. [c]9 : 8. [d]7 : 154; 9 : 5.

faithfully. Like 9 : 4, this verse describes the observance of covenants and treaties as an act of piety and righteousness which is pleasing to God. The Qur'ān repeatedly and most emphatically exhorts Muslims to be faithful to their treaties.

1160. *Ill* means, relationship or nearness with respect to kindred; good origin; a compact or covenant; a promise or an assurance of safety or security (Lane & Mufradāt).

1161. *Dhimmah* means, a compact; covenant; treaty; engagement, obligation or responsibility; a right or due for the neglect of which one is to be blamed (Lane). The expression *Ahl al-Dhimmah* is used for those non-Muslim people with whom the Muslim State has made a compact and who pay poll-tax to the State, in return for which the State is responsible for their security and freedom (Lane). The verse makes it further clear that the command to wage war applies only to such disbelievers as had not only been the first to open hostilities against Islām but were also perfidious and treacherous, paying no respect either to ties of relationship or to compacts and covenants.

1162. This and the preceding two verses give the reasons why Muslims were commanded to wage war against such idolaters (9 : 5). The reasons are : (1) They were treacherous and perfidious; they professed to be friendly to Muslims, but as soon as they found an opportunity to injure them, they broke their plighted word and this in spite of the fact that Muslims had trusted them. (2) They even disregarded the ties of relationship and slew their own kinsmen merely because the latter had embraced Islām (9 : 8). (3) Their object in making war was to prevent men from embracing Islām (9 : 9). (4) They were the first to attack Muslims (9 : 13).

12. And if they break their oaths after their covenant, and attack[1163] your religion, then ª"fight *these* leaders of disbelief[1164]—surely, they have no regard for their oaths—that they may desist.

وَإِنۡ نَّكَثُوۡۤا أَيۡمَانَهُمۡ مِّنۡۢ بَعۡدِ عَهۡدِهِمۡ وَطَعَنُوۡا فِىۡ دِيۡنِكُمۡ فَقَاتِلُوۡۤا أَئِمَّةَ الۡكُفۡرِ ۙ إِنَّهُمۡ لَاۤ أَيۡمَانَ لَهُمۡ لَعَلَّهُمۡ يَنۡتَهُوۡنَ ۝

13. Will you not fight a people who have broken their oaths, and who plotted to turn out the Messenger,[1165] and they were the first to commence *hostilities* against you?[1166] Do you fear them? Nay, Allāh is most worthy that you should fear Him, if you are believers.

أَلَا تُقَاتِلُوۡنَ قَوۡمًا نَّكَثُوۡۤا أَيۡمَانَهُمۡ وَهَمُّوۡا بِإِخۡرَاجِ الرَّسُوۡلِ وَهُمۡ بَدَءُوۡكُمۡ أَوَّلَ مَرَّةٍ ۚ أَتَخۡشَوۡنَهُمۡ ۚ فَاللّٰهُ أَحَقُّ أَنۡ تَخۡشَوۡهُ إِنۡ كُنۡتُمۡ مُّؤۡمِنِيۡنَ ۝

14. Fight them, that Allāh may punish them at your hands, and humiliate them, and help you *to victory* over them, and relieve the minds of a people who believe;

قَاتِلُوۡهُمۡ يُعَذِّبۡهُمُ اللّٰهُ بِأَيۡدِيۡكُمۡ وَيُخۡزِهِمۡ وَيَنۡصُرۡكُمۡ عَلَيۡهِمۡ وَيَشۡفِ صُدُوۡرَ قَوۡمٍ مُّؤۡمِنِيۡنَ ۝

15. And that He may remove the anger of their hearts. And Allāh turns *with mercy* to whomsoever He pleases. And Allāh is All-Knowing, Wise.

وَيُذۡهِبۡ غَيۡظَ قُلُوۡبِهِمۡ ۚ وَيَتُوۡبُ اللّٰهُ عَلَىٰ مَنۡ يَّشَاءُ ۚ وَاللّٰهُ عَلِيۡمٌ حَكِيۡمٌ ۝

ª2 : 191; 4 : 92.

1163. The words "attack your religion" do not refer to mere verbal taunts and reproaches but to actual attacks meant to injure the vital interests of Islām ; the word *Ṭa'ana* literally meaning "to pierce with a spear."

1164. The words, *these leaders of disbelief* are here applied not to a few leading individuals but to the whole people to whom this commandment to fight referred. They are called "leaders" because they were among the first to clash with Muslims and their example encouraged others; and because also their hostility towards Islām was so inveterate and implacable that they served, as it were, as evil models in this respect.

1165. The tribes in or about Medina who, when the Holy Prophet went on an expedition to Tabūk, plotted to bring about his downfall by inciting the various tribes of Arabia to stand up against him.

1166. These words also do not refer to the pagan Meccans but to those infidels, whether open or secret, who lived in and around Medina. They provided ample proof of the fact that, far from being the transgressor, Islām was transgressed against rather than being the aggressor.

16. [a]Do you think that you would be left *in peace*, while Allāh has not yet known those of you who strive *in the cause of Allāh* and [b]do not take *anyone* for an intimate friend besides Allāh and His Messenger and the believers.[1167] And Allāh is Well-Aware of what you do.

اَمْ حَسِبْتُمْ اَنْ تُتْرَكُوْا وَلَمَّا يَعْلَمِ اللّٰهُ الَّذِيْنَ جٰهَدُوْا
مِنْكُمْ وَلَمْ يَتَّخِذُوْا مِنْ دُوْنِ اللّٰهِ وَلَا رَسُوْلِهٖ وَ
ع لَا الْمُؤْمِنِيْنَ وَلِيْجَةً ۗ وَاللّٰهُ خَبِيْرٌۢ بِمَا تَعْمَلُوْنَ ﴿١٦﴾

R. 3 17. It is not for the idolaters to maintain the Mosques of Allāh while they bear witness against themselves to disbelief.[1168] It is they whose works shall be vain, and in the Fire shall they abide for ever.

مَا كَانَ لِلْمُشْرِكِيْنَ اَنْ يَّعْمُرُوْا مَسٰجِدَ اللّٰهِ شٰهِدِيْنَ
عَلٰٓى اَنْفُسِهِمْ بِالْكُفْرِ ۗ اُولٰٓئِكَ حَبِطَتْ اَعْمَالُهُمْ ۚۖ وَ
فِي النَّارِ هُمْ خٰلِدُوْنَ ﴿١٧﴾

18. He alone can maintain the Mosques of Allāh[1169] who believes in Allāh, and the Last Day, and observes Prayer, and pays the *Zakāt* and fears none but Allāh; so these it is who may be rightly guided.

اِنَّمَا يَعْمُرُ مَسٰجِدَ اللّٰهِ مَنْ اٰمَنَ بِاللّٰهِ وَالْيَوْمِ الْاٰخِرِ
وَاَقَامَ الصَّلٰوةَ وَاٰتَى الزَّكٰوةَ وَلَمْ يَخْشَ اِلَّا اللّٰهَ فَعَسٰٓى
اُولٰٓئِكَ اَنْ يَّكُوْنُوْا مِنَ الْمُهْتَدِيْنَ ﴿١٨﴾

19. Do you consider the giving of drink to the pilgrims, and the maintenance of the Sacred Mosque as *equal to the works* of him who believes in Allāh and the Last Day and strives in the path of Allāh? They are not *at all* equal in the sight of Allāh[1170] and Allāh guides not the unjust people.

اَجَعَلْتُمْ سِقَايَةَ الْحَآجِّ وَعِمَارَةَ الْمَسْجِدِ الْحَرَامِ
كَمَنْ اٰمَنَ بِاللّٰهِ وَالْيَوْمِ الْاٰخِرِ وَجٰهَدَ فِيْ سَبِيْلِ
اللّٰهِ ۗ لَا يَسْتَوٗنَ عِنْدَ اللّٰهِ ۗ وَاللّٰهُ لَا يَهْدِي الْقَوْمَ
الظّٰلِمِيْنَ ﴿١٩﴾

[a]3 : 143, 180; 20 : 3-4. [b]3 : 29; 4 : 140, 145; 9 : 23.

1167. The verse hints that the trials of Muslims were not yet over. They had still to face more grievous dangers.

1168. The verse relates to idolatrous pilgrims and serves as an introduction to the announcement contained in 9 : 28 below. No idolater was, henceforth, to be allowed to approach the Ka'bah, as announced by 'Alī to the pilgrims assembled at Mecca on the occasion of the Greater Pilgrimage in the year 9 A.H. The verse gives the reason for that prohibition. The Ka'bah being the Temple dedicated to the worship of the One God, idolaters had nothing to do with it. They were declared enemies of God's Unity and stood condemned by their own confession.

1169. The words "Mosques of Allāh" refer to the Sacred Mosque in v. 19 because the Sacred Mosque or the Ka'bah being the Central Mosque of Islām stands for all the mosques in the world.

1170. The outward and physical service of the Ka'bah, though in itself a meritorious act, is as nothing compared with the spiritual service thereof, which only a true

20. [a]Those who believed and left their homes *for the sake of God* and strove in the cause of Allāh with their wealth and their lives have the highest rank in the sight of Allāh. And it is they who shall triumph.

الَّذِينَ آمَنُوا وَهَاجَرُوا وَجَاهَدُوا فِي سَبِيلِ اللَّهِ
بِأَمْوَالِهِمْ وَأَنْفُسِهِمْ أَعْظَمُ دَرَجَةً عِنْدَ اللَّهِ ۚ وَ
أُولَٰئِكَ هُمُ الْفَائِزُونَ ﴿٢٠﴾

21. [b]Their Lord gives them glad tidings of mercy from Him, and of *His* pleasure, and Gardens wherein there shall be lasting bliss for them;

يُبَشِّرُهُمْ رَبُّهُمْ بِرَحْمَةٍ مِنْهُ وَرِضْوَانٍ وَجَنَّاتٍ لَهُمْ
فِيهَا نَعِيمٌ مُقِيمٌ ﴿٢١﴾

22. They will abide therein for ever. Verily, with Allāh there is a great reward.

خَالِدِينَ فِيهَا أَبَدًا ۚ إِنَّ اللَّهَ عِنْدَهُ أَجْرٌ عَظِيمٌ ﴿٢٢﴾

23. O ye who believe! [c]take not your fathers and your brothers for friends if they prefer disbelief to faith.[1171] And whoso of you takes them for friends, such are the wrongdoers.

يَا أَيُّهَا الَّذِينَ آمَنُوا لَا تَتَّخِذُوا آبَاءَكُمْ وَإِخْوَانَكُمْ
أَوْلِيَاءَ إِنِ اسْتَحَبُّوا الْكُفْرَ عَلَى الْإِيمَانِ ۚ وَمَنْ يَتَوَلَّهُمْ
مِنْكُمْ فَأُولَٰئِكَ هُمُ الظَّالِمُونَ ﴿٢٣﴾

24 Say, if your fathers and your sons and your brethren and your wives and your kinsfolk and the wealth you have acquired and the trade whose dullness you fear and the dwellings which you love are dearer to you than Allāh and His Messenger and striving in His cause,[1172] then wait until Allāh brings about His judgment; and Allāh guides not the disobedient people.

قُلْ إِنْ كَانَ آبَاؤُكُمْ وَأَبْنَاؤُكُمْ وَإِخْوَانُكُمْ وَأَزْوَاجُكُمْ
وَعَشِيرَتُكُمْ وَأَمْوَالٌ اقْتَرَفْتُمُوهَا وَتِجَارَةٌ تَخْشَوْنَ
كَسَادَهَا وَمَسَاكِنُ تَرْضَوْنَهَا أَحَبَّ إِلَيْكُمْ مِنَ اللَّهِ
وَرَسُولِهِ وَجِهَادٍ فِي سَبِيلِهِ فَتَرَبَّصُوا حَتَّىٰ يَأْتِيَ
اللَّهُ بِأَمْرِهِ ۗ وَاللَّهُ لَا يَهْدِي الْقَوْمَ الْفَاسِقِينَ ﴿٢٤﴾ ع ٣

[a]4 : 96; 57 : 11. [b]3 : 16; 5 : 13; 9 : 72; 10 : 10; 57 : 21. [c]3 : 29; 4 : 140, 145; 9 : 16; 58 : 23.

Muslim can perform. The verse implies that Islām attaches greater importance to the spirit underlying its ordinances than to their outward form. The Holy Prophet is reported to have said that the life of a believer possesses much greater sanctity than the Ka'bah (Mājah).

1171. The verse refers to that class of disbelievers who were actively hostile to Islām and strove hard to exterminate it.

1172. Ties of relationship and the love of kith and kin and other worldly considerations, of wealth, trade and property, should not be allowed to stand in the way when a dearer relationship and a nobler cause and more vital considerations demand their sacrifice.

R. 4 25. Surely, [a]Allāh has helped you on many a battlefield, and on the Day of Hunain, when your great numbers made you proud, but they availed you naught; and the earth, with *all* its vastness, became straitened for you, *and* then you turned back retreating.[1173]

لَقَدْ نَصَرَكُمُ اللّٰهُ فِيْ مَوَاطِنَ كَثِيْرَةٍ ۙ وَّيَوْمَ حُنَيْنٍ ۙ
اِذْ اَعْجَبَتْكُمْ كَثْرَتُكُمْ فَلَمْ تُغْنِ عَنْكُمْ شَيْـًٔا وَّ
ضَاقَتْ عَلَيْكُمُ الْاَرْضُ بِمَا رَحُبَتْ ثُمَّ وَلَّيْتُمْ
مُّدْبِرِيْنَ ﴿۲۵﴾

26. Then [b]Allāh sent down His peace upon His Messenger and upon the believers, and He sent down hosts which you did not see, and He punished those who disbelieved. And this is the reward of the disbelievers.

ثُمَّ اَنْزَلَ اللّٰهُ سَكِيْنَتَهٗ عَلٰى رَسُوْلِهٖ وَعَلَى الْمُؤْمِنِيْنَ
وَاَنْزَلَ جُنُوْدًا لَّمْ تَرَوْهَا وَعَذَّبَ الَّذِيْنَ كَفَرُوْا
وَذٰلِكَ جَزَآءُ الْكٰفِرِيْنَ ﴿۲۶﴾

27. Then after *such punishment* Allāh turns *with compassion* to whomsoever He pleases; and Allāh is Most Forgiving.

ثُمَّ يَتُوْبُ اللّٰهُ مِنْۢ بَعْدِ ذٰلِكَ عَلٰى مَنْ يَّشَآءُ ؕ وَاللّٰهُ
غَفُوْرٌ رَّحِيْمٌ ﴿۲۷﴾

28. O ye who believe! surely, the idolaters are unclean. So they shall not approach the Sacred Mosque after this year of theirs. And if you fear poverty, Allāh will enrich you out of His bounty,[1174] if He pleases. Surely, Allāh is All-Knowing, Wise.

يٰۤاَيُّهَا الَّذِيْنَ اٰمَنُوْۤا اِنَّمَا الْمُشْرِكُوْنَ نَجَسٌ فَلَا يَقْرَبُوا
الْمَسْجِدَ الْحَرَامَ بَعْدَ عَامِهِمْ هٰذَا ۚ وَاِنْ خِفْتُمْ
عَيْلَةً فَسَوْفَ يُغْنِيْكُمُ اللّٰهُ مِنْ فَضْلِهٖۤ اِنْ شَآءَ ؕ
اِنَّ اللّٰهَ عَلِيْمٌ حَكِيْمٌ ﴿۲۸﴾

[a]3 : 124. [b]9 : 40; 48 : 27.

1173. After the Fall of Mecca, Hawāzin and Thaqīf tribes joined forces and advanced to attack the Muslims. The Holy Prophet met them at Ḥunain, about 15 miles to the south-west of Mecca. He was accompanied by 12,000 men, among whom were 2,000 new converts who had joined the Muslim army at Mecca. Contrary to the practice of the Holy Prophet these men hastened to attack the enemy, but were quickly repulsed and fled from the battlefield in great confusion, throwing into disorder the advancing Muslim force which was passing through a narrow gorge. In the stampede that followed the Holy Prophet was left on the battlefield with only 100 men around him. Arrows from the archers of the enemy fell thick and fast all round him. It was a moment of extreme danger but the Holy Prophet, urging on his mule towards the enemy, advanced undaunted, shouting at the top of his voice : "I am indeed the Prophet of God. This is no lie. I am the son of 'Abd Al-Muṭṭalib." 'Abbās, uncle of the Holy Prophet, who possessed a stentorian voice, called out to the fleeing Muslims to stop and return to their Master who wanted them. This clarion call thrilled the Muslims like the trumpet call of the Day of Judgment, and rallying with great effort they rushed back to their beloved Master and attacked the enemy with a vehemence that put terror into the heart of the enemy and made him flee in utter confusion. The scales were turned and the day ended in a signal victory for the Muslims, and no less than 6,000 disbelievers were taken prisoner (Ṭabarī & Hishām).

1174. Mecca was a great commercial centre and the pilgrimage season was an occasion of great commercial activity and a source of great income for the Meccans.

29. [a]Fight those from among the People of the Book, who believe not in Allāh, nor in the Last Day, nor hold as unlawful what Allāh and His Messenger have declared to be unlawful, nor follow the true religion, until they pay the tax considering it a favour and acknowledge their subjection.[1175]

قَاتِلُوا الَّذِيْنَ لَا يُؤْمِنُوْنَ بِاللّٰهِ وَلَا بِالْيَوْمِ الْاٰخِرِ
وَلَا يُحَرِّمُوْنَ مَا حَرَّمَ اللّٰهُ وَرَسُوْلُهٗ وَلَا يَدِيْنُوْنَ
دِيْنَ الْحَقِّ مِنَ الَّذِيْنَ اُوْتُوا الْكِتٰبَ حَتّٰى يُعْطُوا الْجِزْيَةَ
عَنْ يَّدٍ وَّهُمْ صٰغِرُوْنَ ۝٢٩

R. 5 30. And [b]the Jews say, 'Ezra[1176] is the son of Allāh,' and the Christians say, 'the Messiah is the son of Allāh;' that is what they say with their mouths. They only imitate the saying of those who disbelieved before them. Allāh's curse be on them! How they are turned awav

وَقَالَتِ الْيَهُوْدُ عُزَيْرُ ابْنُ اللّٰهِ وَقَالَتِ النَّصٰرَى الْمَسِيْحُ
ابْنُ اللّٰهِ ۗ ذٰلِكَ قَوْلُهُمْ بِاَفْوَاهِهِمْ ۚ يُضَاهِـُٔوْنَ قَوْلَ
الَّذِيْنَ كَفَرُوْا مِنْ قَبْلُ ۗ قٰتَلَهُمُ اللّٰهُ ۚ اَنّٰى يُؤْفَكُوْنَ ۝٣٠

[a]2 : 191. [b]2 : 117; 5 : 18; 10 : 69.

The prohibition might have given rise to apprehension that it might adversely affect their income.

1175. The expression '*An Yadin*' means : (1) Willingly and in acknowledgment of the superior power of Muslims. (2) In ready money and not in the form of deferred payment. (3) Considering it as a favour from Muslims; the particle '*an* meaning, on account of, and *Yad* denoting power and favour (Lane). The verse refers to those People of the Book who lived in Arabia. Like the idolaters they too had been actively hostile to Islām and had planned and plotted to exterminate it. Muslims were, therefore, ordered to fight them unless they agreed to live as loyal and peaceful subjects The *Jizyah* was a tax which these non-Muslims had to pay as free subjects of the Muslim State in return for the protection they enjoyed under it. It may be noted that as against *Jizyah* which was imposed on non-Muslims, a much heavier tax—*Zakāt* was levied on the Muslims, and in addition to *Zakāt* they had to perform military service from which non-Muslims were exempt. Thus the latter in a way fared better, for they had to pay a lighter tax and were also free from military duty. The word *Ṣāghirūn* expresses their subordinate political status; otherwise they enjoyed all social rights equally with Muslims. The idolaters of Arabia and Jews and Christians who lived in their neighbourhood were the principal adversaries of Islām. After having dealt with the believers' relations with the idolaters, the *Sūrah* with this verse proceeds to deal with their relations with the People of the Book, especially with their religious beliefs and doctrines.

1176. 'Uzair or Ezra lived in the fifth century B.C. He was a descendant of Seraiah, the high priest, and, being himself a member of the priestly order, was known as Ezra, the Priest. He was one of the most important personages of his day and exercised a far-reaching influence on the development of Judaism. He was especially honoured among the Prophets of Israel. The Jews of Medina and a Jewish sect in Ḥadramaut believed him to be the son of God. The Rabbis associate his name with several important institutions. Renan has remarked in the preface to his *History of the People of Israel* that the definite constitution of Judaism may be dated only from the time of Ezra. In Rabbinical literature he was considered worthy of being the vehicle of the Law, had it not been already given through Moses. He worked in collaboration with Nehemiah and died at the age of 120 in Babylonia (Jew. Enc. & Enc. Bib).

31. They have taken their priests and their monks[1177] for lords besides Allāh. And *so have they taken* the Messiah, son of Mary. And [a]they were not commanded but to worship the One God. There is no god but He. Holy is He *far above* what they associate *with Him !*

اِتَّخَذُوْٓا اَحْبَارَهُمْ وَرُهْبَانَهُمْ اَرْبَابًا مِّنْ دُوْنِ
اللّٰهِ وَالْمَسِيْحَ ابْنَ مَرْيَمَ ۚ وَمَآ اُمِرُوْٓا اِلَّا لِيَعْبُدُوْٓا
اِلٰهًا وَّاحِدًا ۚ لَآ اِلٰهَ اِلَّا هُوَ ۗ سُبْحٰنَهٗ عَمَّا يُشْرِكُوْنَ ﴿۳۱﴾

32. [b]They seek to extinguish the light, of Allāh with their mouths; but Allāh refuses but to perfect His light, though the disbelievers may resent *it*.[1178]

يُرِيْدُوْنَ اَنْ يُّطْفِـُٔوْا نُوْرَ اللّٰهِ بِاَفْوَاهِهِمْ وَيَاْبَى اللّٰهُ
اِلَّآ اَنْ يُّتِمَّ نُوْرَهٗ وَلَوْ كَرِهَ الْكٰفِرُوْنَ ﴿۳۲﴾

33. [c]He it is Who sent His Messenger with guidance and the religion of truth, that He may make it prevail over every *other* religion, even though the idolaters may resent *it*.[1179]

هُوَ الَّذِيْٓ اَرْسَلَ رَسُوْلَهٗ بِالْهُدٰى وَدِيْنِ الْحَقِّ لِيُظْهِرَهٗ
عَلَى الدِّيْنِ كُلِّهٖ ۙ وَلَوْ كَرِهَ الْمُشْرِكُوْنَ ﴿۳۳﴾

34. O ye who believe ! surely, [d]many of the priests and monks devour the wealth of men by false means and [e]turn *men* away from the way of Allāh. And those who hoard gold and silver and spend it not in the way of Allāh—give to them the tidings of a painful punishment.

يٰٓاَيُّهَا الَّذِيْنَ اٰمَنُوْٓا اِنَّ كَثِيْرًا مِّنَ الْاَحْبَارِ وَالرُّهْبَانِ
لَيَاْكُلُوْنَ اَمْوَالَ النَّاسِ بِالْبَاطِلِ وَيَصُدُّوْنَ عَنْ
سَبِيْلِ اللّٰهِ ۗ وَالَّذِيْنَ يَكْنِزُوْنَ الذَّهَبَ وَالْفِضَّةَ
وَلَا يُنْفِقُوْنَهَا فِيْ سَبِيْلِ اللّٰهِ ۙ فَبَشِّرْهُمْ بِعَذَابٍ
اَلِيْمٍ ﴿۳۴﴾

[a]12 : 41; 17 : 24; 98 : 6. [b]61 : 9. [c]48 : 29; 61 ; 10. [d]4 : 162. [e]4 : 161.

1177. *Aḥbār* are Jewish savants and *Ruhbān* Christian monks.

1178. Christians living in Arabia had incited their powerful co-religionists in Syria, and, by their help, had sought to extinguish the light of Islām that God had kindled in Arabia. The Jews also had made a similar attempt by inciting the Persians against the Holy Prophet.

1179. Commentators of the Qur'ān agree that, as stated in a saying of the Holy Prophet, the ultimate triumph of Islām will take place in the time of the Promised Messiah (Jarīr) when all the various religions will have appeared and will make their utmost endeavours to propagate their own teachings. The excellence of the ideals and principles of Islām have already begun to be increasingly recognised, and the day is not far off when Islām will triumph over all other Faiths and their followers will enter its fold in large numbers.

35. On the day when it shall be made hot in the fire of Hell, and their foreheads and their sides and their backs shall be branded[1180] therewith *and it shall be said to them*: 'This is what you hoarded for yourselves; so *now* taste what you used to hoard.'

يَوْمَ يُحْمٰى عَلَيْهَا فِيْ نَارِ جَهَنَّمَ فَتُكْوٰى بِهَا جِبَاهُهُمْ
وَجُنُوْبُهُمْ وَظُهُوْرُهُمْ ۗ هٰذَا مَا كَنَزْتُمْ لِاَنْفُسِكُمْ
فَذُوْقُوْا مَا كُنْتُمْ تَكْنِزُوْنَ ﴿۳۵﴾

36. The number of months with Allāh is twelve months[1181] by Allāh's ordinance since the day when He created the heavens and the earth. Of these four are sacred.[1182] That is the right religion. So wrong not yourselves therein. And fight the idolaters all together as they fight you all together; and know that Allāh is with those who fear *Him*.

اِنَّ عِدَّةَ الشُّهُوْرِ عِنْدَ اللّٰهِ اثْنَا عَشَرَ شَهْرًا فِيْ كِتٰبِ
اللّٰهِ يَوْمَ خَلَقَ السَّمٰوٰتِ وَالْاَرْضَ مِنْهَآ اَرْبَعَةٌ حُرُمٌ ۗ
ذٰلِكَ الدِّيْنُ الْقَيِّمُ ۙ فَلَا تَظْلِمُوْا فِيْهِنَّ اَنْفُسَكُمْ
وَقَاتِلُوا الْمُشْرِكِيْنَ كَآفَّةً كَمَا يُقَاتِلُوْنَكُمْ كَآفَّةً ۗ
وَاعْلَمُوْٓا اَنَّ اللّٰهَ مَعَ الْمُتَّقِيْنَ ﴿۳۶﴾

37. Surely, the postponement[1183] *of a Sacred Month* is an addition to disbelief. Those who disbelieve are led astray thereby. They allow it one year and forbid it another year, that they may agree in the number of *the months* which Allāh has made sacred, and thus may make lawful what Allāh has forbidden. [a] The evil of their deeds is made *to seem* fair to them. And Allāh guides not the disbelieving people.

اِنَّمَا النَّسِيْٓءُ زِيَادَةٌ فِي الْكُفْرِ يُضَلُّ بِهِ الَّذِيْنَ كَفَرُوْا
يُحِلُّوْنَهٗ عَامًا وَّيُحَرِّمُوْنَهٗ عَامًا لِّيُوَاطِـُٔوْا عِدَّةَ مَا
حَرَّمَ اللّٰهُ فَيُحِلُّوْا مَا حَرَّمَ اللّٰهُ ۗ زُيِّنَ لَهُمْ سُوْٓءُ
اَعْمَالِهِمْ ۗ وَاللّٰهُ لَا يَهْدِي الْقَوْمَ الْكٰفِرِيْنَ ﴿۳۷﴾ ع

[a] 6 : 44; 13 : 34; 16 : 64; 27 : 25; 29 : 49; 35 : 9.

1180. The expression seems to be figurative. When a rich man, out of miserliness or pride, refuses to help a needy person, his forehead becomes contracted into a frown. Then he turns aside and finally disdainfully shows his back to the man seeking his help. Quite appropriately, it is mentioned that the foreheads, the sides and the backs will be branded.

1181. Both the lunar and the solar years comprise 12 months.

1182. The four Sacred Months are *Dhu'l-Qa'dah*, *Dhu'l-Ḥijjah*, *Muḥarram* and *Rajab*.

1183. The reference in this verse is to a long-standing Arab custom. The three successive Sacred Months—*Dhu'l-Qa'dah*, *Dhu'l-Ḥijjah* and *Muḥarram* sometimes seemed to them too long a time to refrain from their predatory expeditions. In order, therefore, to free themselves from the restrictions of the Sacred Months, they sometimes would treat a Sacred Month like an ordinary month and an ordinary month like a Sacred One.

R. 6 38. O ye who believe; what is the matter with you that, when it is said to you, go forth in the way of Allāh, you sink down heavily towards the earth?[1184] [a]Are you contented with the present life in preference to the Hereafter? But [b]the enjoyment of the present life is but little as compared with the Hereafter.

يٰٓاَيُّهَا الَّذِيْنَ اٰمَنُوْا مَا لَكُمْ اِذَا قِيْلَ لَكُمُ انْفِرُوْا
فِيْ سَبِيْلِ اللّٰهِ اثَّاقَلْتُمْ اِلَى الْاَرْضِ ؕ اَرَضِيْتُمْ بِالْحَيٰوةِ
الدُّنْيَا مِنَ الْاٰخِرَةِ ۚ فَمَا مَتَاعُ الْحَيٰوةِ الدُّنْيَا فِي
الْاٰخِرَةِ اِلَّا قَلِيْلٌ ﴿۳۸﴾

39. If you will not go forth *to fight, in the cause of Allāh*, He will punish you with a painful punishment, and will choose in your stead a people other than you, and you shall do Him no harm at all. And Allāh has full power over all things.

اِلَّا تَنْفِرُوْا يُعَذِّبْكُمْ عَذَابًا اَلِيْمًا ۙ وَّيَسْتَبْدِلْ قَوْمًا
غَيْرَكُمْ وَلَا تَضُرُّوْهُ شَيْـًٔا ؕ وَاللّٰهُ عَلٰى كُلِّ شَيْءٍ قَدِيْرٌ ﴿۳۹﴾

40. If you help him not, then *know that* Allāh helped him *even* when the disbelievers drove him forth while he was one of the two, when they were both in the Cave, when he said to his Companion, 'Grieve not, for Allāh is with us.' Then [c]Allāh sent down His peace on him,[1185] and succoured him with hosts which you did not see, and humbled the word of those who disbelieved, and it is the word of Allāh alone which is supreme. And Allāh is Mighty, Wise.[1186]

اِلَّا تَنْصُرُوْهُ فَقَدْ نَصَرَهُ اللّٰهُ اِذْ اَخْرَجَهُ الَّذِيْنَ كَفَرُوْا
ثَانِيَ اثْنَيْنِ اِذْ هُمَا فِي الْغَارِ اِذْ يَقُوْلُ لِصَاحِبِهٖ
لَا تَحْزَنْ اِنَّ اللّٰهَ مَعَنَا ۚ فَاَنْزَلَ اللّٰهُ سَكِيْنَتَهٗ عَلَيْهِ
وَاَيَّدَهٗ بِجُنُوْدٍ لَّمْ تَرَوْهَا وَجَعَلَ كَلِمَةَ الَّذِيْنَ
كَفَرُوا السُّفْلٰى ؕ وَكَلِمَةُ اللّٰهِ هِيَ الْعُلْيَا ؕ وَاللّٰهُ عَزِيْزٌ
حَكِيْمٌ ﴿۴۰﴾

[a]13 : 27. [b]See 3 : 15. [c]9 : 26 ; 48 : 27.

1184. The reference is to the expedition to Tabūk, a town situated about half-way between Medina and Damascus. News was brought to the Holy Prophet that the Greeks of the Eastern Roman Empire, popularly known as the Romans, had amassed on the Syrian frontier. At the head of an army about 30,000 strong the Holy Prophet left Medina in the 9th year of the Hijrah. On account of great hardships the Muslim army had to suffer in the long and difficult journey, it came to be known as *Jaish al-'Usrah*, *i.e.*, the distressed army.

1185. The pronoun "him" in the clause "His peace on him" may refer to Abū Bakr since the Holy Prophet had all along been perfectly calm and quiet and the pronoun "him" in the clause "succoured him," however, refers to the Holy Prophet. This divergence in the use of pronouns known as *Intishār al-Ḍamā'ir* is of common use in Arabic. See 48 : 10.

1186. The reference in this verse is to the emigration of the Holy Prophet from Mecca to Medina when, accompanied by Abū Bakr, he took shelter in a cave called Thaur.

41. Go forth, light or heavy,[1187] and *strive with your wealth and your lives in the cause of Allāh. That is best for you, if only you knew.

اِنْفِرُوْا خِفَافًا وَّثِقَالًا وَّجَاهِدُوْا بِاَمْوَالِكُمْ وَاَنْفُسِكُمْ فِيْ سَبِيْلِ اللّٰهِ ؕ ذٰلِكُمْ خَيْرٌ لَّكُمْ اِنْ كُنْتُمْ تَعْلَمُوْنَ ۝

42. If it had been an immediate gain and a short journey, they would certainly have followed thee, but the hard journey seemed too long[1188] to them. Yet they will swear by Allāh, *saying,* 'If we had been able, we would surely have gone forth with you.' They but ruin their souls; and Allāh knows that they are liars

لَوْ كَانَ عَرَضًا قَرِيْبًا وَّسَفَرًا قَاصِدًا لَّاتَّبَعُوْكَ وَ لٰكِنْۢ بَعُدَتْ عَلَيْهِمُ الشُّقَّةُ ؕ وَسَيَحْلِفُوْنَ بِاللّٰهِ لَوِ اسْتَطَعْنَا لَخَرَجْنَا مَعَكُمْ ۚ يُهْلِكُوْنَ اَنْفُسَهُمْ ۚ وَاللّٰهُ يَعْلَمُ اِنَّهُمْ لَكٰذِبُوْنَ ۝

R. 7   43. Allāh remove[1189] *the ill consequences of* thy mistake. Why didst thou permit them *to stay behind* till it had become clear to thee and thou hadst *also* known the liars ?

عَفَا اللّٰهُ عَنْكَ ۚ لِمَ اَذِنْتَ لَهُمْ حَتّٰى يَتَبَيَّنَ لَكَ الَّذِيْنَ صَدَقُوْا وَتَعْلَمَ الْكٰذِبِيْنَ ۝

44. Those who believe in Allāh and the Last Day will not ask leave of thee *to be exempted* from striving with their wealth and their persons. And Allāh well knows those who keep their duty *to Him.*

لَا يَسْتَأْذِنُكَ الَّذِيْنَ يُؤْمِنُوْنَ بِاللّٰهِ وَالْيَوْمِ الْاٰخِرِ اَنْ يُّجَاهِدُوْا بِاَمْوَالِهِمْ وَاَنْفُسِهِمْ ؕ وَاللّٰهُ عَلِيْمٌۢ بِالْمُتَّقِيْنَ ۝

---

*8 : 75; 9 : 88, 111; 61 : 12.

The verse sheds some light on the very high spiritual status of Abū Bakr who is referred to as "one of the two" with whom was God and whose fear God Himself allayed. It is on record that, while in the Cave, Abū Bakr began to weep, and when asked by the Holy Prophet why he was weeping he replied, "I do not weep for my life, O Prophet of God, because if I die, it is only the question of a single life. But if you die, it will be the death of Islām and of the entire Muslim community" (Zurqānī).

1187. The words "light or heavy" may mean, young or old; alone or in parties ; on foot or on horseback; with sufficient arms and provisions or with insufficient equipment and scanty provisions, etc.

1188. The journey was very hard and arduous. . The Muslim army had to travel in an extremely hot weather about 200 miles to the border of Syria to meet a very powerful army. It was also the harvesting season and the trees were laden with ripe fruit.

1189. The Arabic expression '*Afā Allāh 'Anka* signifies no forgiveness of any sin having been committed by the Holy Prophet, rather it expresses Divine love and solicitude for him.

إِنَّمَا يَسْتَأْذِنُكَ الَّذِينَ لَا يُؤْمِنُونَ بِاللّٰهِ وَالْيَوْمِ
الْآخِرِ وَارْتَابَتْ قُلُوبُهُمْ فَهُمْ فِي رَيْبِهِمْ يَتَرَدَّدُونَ ﴿٤٥﴾

45. Only those will ask leave of thee *to be exempted* who do not believe in Allāh and the Last Day, and whose hearts are full of doubt and in their doubt they waver.

وَلَوْ أَرَادُوا الْخُرُوجَ لَأَعَدُّوا لَهُ عُدَّةً وَلٰكِنْ كَرِهَ
اللّٰهُ انْبِعَاثَهُمْ فَثَبَّطَهُمْ وَقِيلَ اقْعُدُوا مَعَ
الْقٰعِدِينَ ﴿٤٦﴾

46. And if they had *really* intended to go forth, they would have made *some* preparation for it; but Allāh was averse to their marching forth. So He kept them back, and it was said *to them*: 'keep sitting *at home* with those who have kept sitting.'

لَوْ خَرَجُوا فِيكُمْ مَا زَادُوكُمْ إِلَّا خَبَالًا وَلَأَوْضَعُوا
خِلٰلَكُمْ يَبْغُونَكُمُ الْفِتْنَةَ ۚ وَفِيكُمْ سَمّٰعُونَ لَهُمْ ۗ
وَاللّٰهُ عَلِيمٌ بِالظّٰلِمِينَ ﴿٤٧﴾

47. Had they gone forth with you, [a]they would have added to you naught but trouble, and would have hurried to and fro in your midst, seeking *to sow* discord among you. And there are among you those who would listen *to you so as to convey information* to them. And Allāh well knows the wrong-doers.

لَقَدِ ابْتَغَوُا الْفِتْنَةَ مِنْ قَبْلُ وَقَلَّبُوا لَكَ الْأُمُورَ
حَتّٰى جَآءَ الْحَقُّ وَظَهَرَ أَمْرُ اللّٰهِ وَهُمْ كٰرِهُونَ ﴿٤٨﴾

48. They sought *to stir up* sedition even before *this*, and they devised plots against thee till the truth came and the purpose of Allāh prevailed, though they did not like *it*.

وَمِنْهُمْ مَنْ يَقُولُ ائْذَنْ لِي وَلَا تَفْتِنِّي ۚ أَلَا فِي
الْفِتْنَةِ سَقَطُوا ۗ وَإِنَّ جَهَنَّمَ لَمُحِيطَةٌ بِالْكٰفِرِينَ ﴿٤٩﴾

49. And among them is he who says, 'Permit me *to stay behind* and put me not to trial.' Surely, they have already fallen into trial. And surely, Hell shall encompass the disbelievers.

إِنْ تُصِبْكَ حَسَنَةٌ تَسُؤْهُمْ ۚ وَإِنْ تُصِبْكَ مُصِيبَةٌ
يَقُولُوا قَدْ أَخَذْنَا أَمْرَنَا مِنْ قَبْلُ وَيَتَوَلَّوْا وَهُمْ
فَرِحُونَ ﴿٥٠﴾

50. If good befalls thee, it grieves them, but if a misfortune befalls thee, they say, 'We had indeed taken our precaution beforehand.' And they turn away rejoicing.

[a] 3 : 119.

51. Say, 'Nothing shall befall us save that which Allāh has ordained for us. He is our Protector. And in Allāh then should the believers put their trust.'

قُلْ لَّنْ يُّصِيْبَنَآ اِلَّا مَا كَتَبَ اللّٰهُ لَنَا ۚ هُوَ مَوْلٰىنَا ۚ
وَعَلَى اللّٰهِ فَلْيَتَوَكَّلِ الْمُؤْمِنُوْنَ ﴿۵۱﴾

52. Say, 'You do not await for us *aught* save one of the two good things,[1190] while we await that Allāh will afflict you with a punishment either from Himself or at our hands. Wait then; we *also* are waiting with you.'

قُلْ هَلْ تَرَبَّصُوْنَ بِنَآ اِلَّآ اِحْدَى الْحُسْنَيَيْنِ ؕ
وَنَحْنُ نَتَرَبَّصُ بِكُمْ اَنْ يُّصِيْبَكُمُ اللّٰهُ بِعَذَابٍ
مِّنْ عِنْدِهٖٓ اَوْ بِاَيْدِيْنَا ۖ فَتَرَبَّصُوْٓا اِنَّا مَعَكُمْ
مُّتَرَبِّصُوْنَ ﴿۵۲﴾

53. Say, 'Spend willingly or unwillingly, it shall not be accepted[1191] from you. You are indeed a disobedient people.'

قُلْ اَنْفِقُوْا طَوْعًا اَوْ كَرْهًا لَّنْ يُّتَقَبَّلَ مِنْكُمْ ؕ اِنَّكُمْ
كُنْتُمْ قَوْمًا فٰسِقِيْنَ ﴿۵۳﴾

54. And nothing prevents that their contributions should be accepted from them save that they disbelieve in Allāh and His Messenger. And [a]they come not to Prayer except lazily and they spend not *in the way of Allāh* but reluctantly.

وَمَا مَنَعَهُمْ اَنْ تُقْبَلَ مِنْهُمْ نَفَقٰتُهُمْ اِلَّآ اَنَّهُمْ
كَفَرُوْا بِاللّٰهِ وَبِرَسُوْلِهٖ وَلَا يَاْتُوْنَ الصَّلٰوةَ اِلَّا وَهُمْ
كُسَالٰى وَلَا يُنْفِقُوْنَ اِلَّا وَهُمْ كٰرِهُوْنَ ﴿۵۴﴾

55. So [b]let not their wealth nor their children excite thy wonder. Allāh only intends to punish them therewith[1192] in the present life and that their souls may depart while they are disbelievers.

فَلَا تُعْجِبْكَ اَمْوَالُهُمْ وَلَآ اَوْلَادُهُمْ ؕ اِنَّمَا يُرِيْدُ
اللّٰهُ لِيُعَذِّبَهُمْ بِهَا فِي الْحَيٰوةِ الدُّنْيَا وَتَزْهَقَ
اَنْفُسُهُمْ وَهُمْ كٰفِرُوْنَ ﴿۵۵﴾

[a]4 : 143. [b]9 : 85.

1190. A true Muslim either dies fighting or wins victory. There is no other alternative left to him.

1191. Nature of the punishment meted out to the Hypocrites is worthy of special note. No fine was imposed on them, nor were they imprisoned nor subjected to punishment generally inflicted for offences of this nature. They were simply told that *Zakāt*, which was a means of purifying their souls would not be accepted from them. This shows that the dealings of the Holy Prophet with the Hypocrites were not dictated by any monetary or mundane considerations.

1192. Hypocrites are warned that their wealth and their children, for whose sake they had refrained from going to battle, would become a source of extreme mental torture for them. Their children would embrace the Faith they hate and would spend their wealth to further and strengthen its cause.

56. And they swear by Allāh that they are indeed of you, while they are not of you, but they are a cowardly people.

وَيَحْلِفُونَ بِاللّٰهِ إِنَّهُمْ لَمِنْكُمْ ۚ وَمَا هُمْ مِّنْكُمْ وَ
لٰكِنَّهُمْ قَوْمٌ يَّفْرَقُونَ ﴿٥٦﴾

57. If they could find a place of refuge, or caves, or *even* a hole to enter, they would surely turn thereto, rushing in uncontrollable haste.

لَوْ يَجِدُونَ مَلْجَأً أَوْ مَغٰرٰتٍ أَوْ مُدَّخَلًا لَّوَلَّوْا
إِلَيْهِ وَهُمْ يَجْمَحُونَ ﴿٥٧﴾

58. And among them are those [a]who find fault with thee with respect to *the division of* alms. If they are given thereof, they are pleased; but if they are not given thereof, behold ! they are indignant.

وَمِنْهُمْ مَّنْ يَّلْمِزُكَ فِي الصَّدَقٰتِ ۚ فَإِنْ أُعْطُوا
مِنْهَا رَضُوا وَإِنْ لَّمْ يُعْطَوْا مِنْهَا إِذَا هُمْ يَسْخَطُونَ ﴿٥٨﴾

59. And if they had been content with what Allāh and His Messenger had given them and had said, 'Sufficient for us is Allāh; Allāh will give us of His bounty, and so will His Messenger; to Allāh do we turn in supplication,' *it would have been better for them.*

وَلَوْ أَنَّهُمْ رَضُوا مَا آتٰهُمُ اللّٰهُ وَرَسُولُهُ ۙ وَقَالُوا
حَسْبُنَا اللّٰهُ سَيُؤْتِينَا اللّٰهُ مِنْ فَضْلِهِ وَرَسُولُهُ ۙ
إِنَّا إِلَى اللّٰهِ رٰغِبُونَ ﴿٥٩﴾ ع

R. 8 60. The alms[1193] are only for the poor and the needy, and for those employed in connection therewith, and for those whose hearts are to be reconciled, and for the *freeing of* slaves, and for those in debt, and for the cause of Allāh, and for the wayfarer—an ordinance from Allāh. And Allāh is All-Knowing, Wise.

إِنَّمَا الصَّدَقٰتُ لِلْفُقَرَاءِ وَالْمَسٰكِينِ وَالْعٰمِلِينَ
عَلَيْهَا وَالْمُؤَلَّفَةِ قُلُوبُهُمْ وَفِي الرِّقَابِ وَالْغٰرِمِينَ
وَفِي سَبِيلِ اللّٰهِ وَابْنِ السَّبِيلِ ۖ فَرِيضَةً مِّنَ اللّٰهِ ۗ
وَاللّٰهُ عَلِيمٌ حَكِيمٌ ﴿٦٠﴾

---

[a]9 : 79.

1193. *Ṣadaqāt* here means, obligatory alms, *i.e., Zakāt*. The verse defines the objects and persons on whom *Zakāt* is to be spent : (a) *Fuqarā'* (from the root *Faqara* which means, it broke the vertebrae of his back—Lane) *i.e.,* those broken with poverty or disease. (b) *Masākīn, i.e.,* those possessing the ability to work but lacking the means thereof. (c) Those employed in collecting the *Zakāt* or in keeping an account thereof or in the performance of any other duty connected with it. (d) New converts to Islām in need of monetary help. (e) Slaves, captives and such other persons as are called upon to pay blood-money to secure their freedom. (f) Those unable to pay their debts or have suffered extraordinary loss in business, etc. (g) Any noble cause. (h) Those stranded on a journey for lack of money or those who travel in search of knowledge or for promoting social relations.

61. And among them are those who annoy the Prophet and say, 'He is *all* ear.'[1194] Say, 'His *giving* ear *to all* is for your good; he believes in Allāh and believes the Faithful, and is [a]a mercy for those of you who believe.' And those who annoy the Messenger of Allāh shall have a grievous punishment.

وَمِنْهُمُ الَّذِينَ يُؤْذُونَ النَّبِيَّ وَيَقُولُونَ هُوَ أُذُنٌ
قُلْ أُذُنُ خَيْرٍ لَّكُمْ يُؤْمِنُ بِاللّٰهِ وَيُؤْمِنُ لِلْمُؤْمِنِينَ
وَرَحْمَةٌ لِّلَّذِينَ اٰمَنُوا مِنْكُمْ وَالَّذِينَ يُؤْذُونَ رَسُولَ
اللّٰهِ لَهُمْ عَذَابٌ أَلِيمٌ ﴿٦١﴾

62. [b]They swear by Allāh to you to please you; but Allāh with His Messenger has greater right that they should please Him if they are believers.

يَحْلِفُونَ بِاللّٰهِ لَكُمْ لِيُرْضُوكُمْ وَاللّٰهُ وَرَسُولُهٗٓ أَحَقُّ
أَنْ يُّرْضُوهُ إِنْ كَانُوا مُؤْمِنِينَ ﴿٦٢﴾

63. Do they not know that [c]whoso opposes Allāh and His Messenger, for him is the fire of Hell, wherein he shall abide? That is the great humiliation.

أَلَمْ يَعْلَمُوٓا أَنَّهٗ مَنْ يُّحَادِدِ اللّٰهَ وَرَسُولَهٗ فَأَنَّ
لَهٗ نَارَ جَهَنَّمَ خَالِدًا فِيهَا ذٰلِكَ الْخِزْيُ الْعَظِيمُ ﴿٦٣﴾

64. The Hypocrites *pretend they* fear[1195] lest a *Sūrah* should be revealed concerning them, informing them of what is in their hearts. Say, 'Mock on; surely, Allāh will bring to light that of which you *pretended you* were afraid *lest it might be disclosed.*

يَحْذَرُ الْمُنٰفِقُونَ أَنْ تُنَزَّلَ عَلَيْهِمْ سُورَةٌ تُنَبِّئُهُمْ
بِمَا فِي قُلُوبِهِمْ قُلِ اسْتَهْزِءُوا إِنَّ اللّٰهَ مُخْرِجٌ
مَّا تَحْذَرُونَ ﴿٦٤﴾

65. And if thou question them, [d]they will most surely say, 'We were only talking idly and jesting.' Say, 'Was it Allāh and His Signs and His Messenger that you mocked at?'

وَلَئِنْ سَأَلْتَهُمْ لَيَقُولُنَّ إِنَّمَا كُنَّا نَخُوضُ وَنَلْعَبُ
قُلْ أَبِاللّٰهِ وَاٰيٰتِهٖ وَرَسُولِهٖ كُنْتُمْ تَسْتَهْزِءُونَ ﴿٦٥﴾

[a]9 : 128 ; 21 : 108. [b]9 : 96. [c]58 : 6, 21. [d]2 : 45.

1194. *Udhun* (lit. meaning an ear) signifies, one who listens to and believes in everything that is said to him. Of the many contemptuous and disparaging remarks that the Holy Prophet's traducers made about him one was that he listened to and readily believed as true all reports that were conveyed to him so that he had become, as it were, the very organ of hearing.

1195. The Hypocrites did not actually entertain any such fear because they did not believe the Holy Prophet to be the recipient of Divine revelation. The verse alludes only to the ironical nature of their jokes and jeers.

66. [a]'Make ye no excuses. You certainly disbelieved after your believing. If We forgive a party from among you, a party shall We punish, for they are guilty.

لَا تَعْتَذِرُوْا قَدْ كَفَرْتُمْ بَعْدَ اِيْمَانِكُمْ ۚ اِنْ نَّعْفُ عَنْ
طَآئِفَةٍ مِّنْكُمْ نُعَذِّبْ طَآئِفَةً بِاَنَّهُمْ كَانُوْا مُجْرِمِيْنَ ۝٦٦

R. 9 67. The hypocrites,[1196] men and women, are *all as* one with another. They enjoin evil and forbid good, and withhold their hands *from spending for the cause of Allāh.* [b]They forgot Allāh, so He has forgotten[1197] them. Surely, the hypocrites are the transgressors.

اَلْمُنٰفِقُوْنَ وَالْمُنٰفِقٰتُ بَعْضُهُمْ مِّنْ بَعْضٍ ۘ يَاْمُرُوْنَ
بِالْمُنْكَرِ وَيَنْهَوْنَ عَنِ الْمَعْرُوْفِ وَيَقْبِضُوْنَ اَيْدِيَهُمْ ۚ
نَسُوا اللّٰهَ فَنَسِيَهُمْ ۗ اِنَّ الْمُنٰفِقِيْنَ هُمُ الْفٰسِقُوْنَ ۝٦٧

68. [c]Allāh promises the hypocrites, men and women, and the disbelievers the fire of Hell, wherein they shall abide. It will suffice them. And Allāh has cursed them. And they shall have a lasting punishment.

وَعَدَ اللّٰهُ الْمُنٰفِقِيْنَ وَالْمُنٰفِقٰتِ وَالْكُفَّارَ نَارَ جَهَنَّمَ
خٰلِدِيْنَ فِيْهَا ۗ هِيَ حَسْبُهُمْ ۚ وَلَعَنَهُمُ اللّٰهُ ۚ وَلَهُمْ
عَذَابٌ مُّقِيْمٌ ۝٦٨

69. Even as those before you—they were mightier than you in power and had more wealth and children. They enjoyed their lot for a time, so have you enjoyed your lot as those before you enjoyed their lot. And you indulged in idle talk as they indulged in idle talk. [d]It is they whose works shall be of no avail in this world and the Hereafter. And it is they who are the losers.

كَالَّذِيْنَ مِنْ قَبْلِكُمْ كَانُوْٓا اَشَدَّ مِنْكُمْ قُوَّةً وَّاَكْثَرَ
اَمْوَالًا وَّاَوْلَادًا ۗ فَاسْتَمْتَعُوْا بِخَلَاقِهِمْ فَاسْتَمْتَعْتُمْ
بِخَلَاقِكُمْ كَمَا اسْتَمْتَعَ الَّذِيْنَ مِنْ قَبْلِكُمْ بِخَلَاقِهِمْ
وَخُضْتُمْ كَالَّذِيْ خَاضُوْا ۗ اُولٰٓئِكَ حَبِطَتْ اَعْمَالُهُمْ
فِي الدُّنْيَا وَالْاٰخِرَةِ ۚ وَاُولٰٓئِكَ هُمُ الْخٰسِرُوْنَ ۝٦٩

[a]56 : 8. [b]59 : 20. [c]4 : 146. [d]15 : 106.

1196. *Munāfiq* is from *al-Nafaq* which means, a hole or passage in the earth leading up to some place through an opening at the other end, and *al-Nifāq* means, entering faith through one door and leaving it through another (Aqrab).

1197. *Nisyān* generally meaning "forgetfulness" really means, one's ceasing to think of a person or a thing either owing to loss of memory or negligence or doing it deliberately. When used about God the word means severing of His connection with a person by way of punishment or ceasing to think of him with feelings of love and affection (Mufradāt).

70. ^aHas not the news reached them of those before them—the people of Noah, and 'Ād, and Thamūd, and the people of Abraham, and the dwellers of Midian, and the cities which were overthrown?¹¹⁹⁸ Their Messengers came to them with clear Signs. So ^bAllāh wronged them not but they wronged themselves.

71. And the believers, men and women, are friends one of another. ^cThey enjoin good and forbid evil and ^dobserve Prayer and ^epay the Zakāt and ^fobey Allāh and His Messenger. It is these on whom Allāh will have mercy. Surely, Allāh is Mighty *and* Wise.

72. ^gAllāh has promised to believers, men and women, Gardens underneath which rivers flow, wherein they will abide, and delightful dwelling-places in Gardens of Eternity. And ^hthe pleasure of Allāh is the greatest of all. That is the supreme triumph.

R. 10   73. ⁱO Prophet ! strive hard against¹¹⁹⁹ the disbelievers and the Hypocrites. And be firm against them. Their abode is Hell, and an evil destination it is.

اَلَمْ يَاْتِهِمْ نَبَاُ الَّذِيْنَ مِنْ قَبْلِهِمْ قَوْمِ نُوْحٍ وَّعَادٍ وَّثَمُوْدَ وَقَوْمِ اِبْرٰهِيْمَ وَاَصْحٰبِ مَدْيَنَ وَالْمُؤْتَفِكٰتِ اَتَتْهُمْ رُسُلُهُمْ بِالْبَيِّنٰتِ فَمَا كَانَ اللّٰهُ لِيَظْلِمَهُمْ وَلٰكِنْ كَانُوْٓا اَنْفُسَهُمْ يَظْلِمُوْنَ ۞

وَالْمُؤْمِنُوْنَ وَالْمُؤْمِنٰتُ بَعْضُهُمْ اَوْلِيَآءُ بَعْضٍ يَاْمُرُوْنَ بِالْمَعْرُوْفِ وَيَنْهَوْنَ عَنِ الْمُنْكَرِ وَيُقِيْمُوْنَ الصَّلٰوةَ وَيُؤْتُوْنَ الزَّكٰوةَ وَيُطِيْعُوْنَ اللّٰهَ وَرَسُوْلَهٗ اُولٰٓئِكَ سَيَرْحَمُهُمُ اللّٰهُ اِنَّ اللّٰهَ عَزِيْزٌ حَكِيْمٌ ۞

وَعَدَ اللّٰهُ الْمُؤْمِنِيْنَ وَالْمُؤْمِنٰتِ جَنّٰتٍ تَجْرِيْ مِنْ تَحْتِهَا الْاَنْهٰرُ خٰلِدِيْنَ فِيْهَا وَمَسٰكِنَ طَيِّبَةً فِيْ جَنّٰتِ عَدْنٍ وَرِضْوَانٌ مِّنَ اللّٰهِ اَكْبَرُ ذٰلِكَ هُوَ الْفَوْزُ الْعَظِيْمُ ۞

يٰٓاَيُّهَا النَّبِيُّ جَاهِدِ الْكُفَّارَ وَالْمُنٰفِقِيْنَ وَاغْلُظْ عَلَيْهِمْ وَمَأْوٰىهُمْ جَهَنَّمُ وَبِئْسَ الْمَصِيْرُ ۞

---

^a14 : 10;   50 : 13-15.   ^b10 : 45;   29 : 41;   30 : 10.   ^c3 : 105, 111;   7 : 158;   9 : 112;   31 : 18.   ^dSee 2 : 4.   ^eSee 2 : 44.   ^fSee 8 : 2.   ^gSee 2 : 26.   ^h3 : 16;   5 : 3;   9 : 22;   57 : 21.   ⁱ66 : 10.

1198. Sodom and Gomorrah (Gen. 19 : 24 & 25). The site is believed to be the Dead Sea (Jew. Enc., under Sodom). The Qur'ān speaks of the place as being situated on or near a "permanent way" (15 : 75-77).

1199. *Jihād* (infinitive noun from *Jahada* meaning, he strove hard or with the utmost of his power with an object) has been generally used in this sense in the Qur'ān. How the Prophet should strive against the Hypocrites is not mentioned. But there is nothing to indicate the sense of fighting with the sword. In fact, the Holy Prophet never waged war against the Hypocrites.

74. They swear by Allāh that they said nothing, but they did certainly utter the word of disbelief, and disbelieved after they *had embraced* Islām. And they designed what they could not attian. And they cherished enmity *against believers* only because Allāh and His Messenger had enriched[1200] them out of His bounty. So if they repent, it will be better for them; but if they turn away, Allāh will punish them with a grievous punishment in this world and the Hereafter, and they shall have neither friend nor helper in the earth.

يَحْلِفُوْنَ بِاللّٰهِ مَا قَالُوْا ۭ وَلَقَدْ قَالُوْا كَلِمَةَ الْكُفْرِ وَ
كَفَرُوْا بَعْدَ اِسْلَامِهِمْ وَهَمُّوْا بِمَا لَمْ يَنَالُوْا ۚ وَمَا
نَقَمُوْٓا اِلَّآ اَنْ اَغْنٰىهُمُ اللّٰهُ وَرَسُوْلُهٗ مِنْ فَضْلِهٖ ۚ
فَاِنْ يَّتُوْبُوْا يَكُ خَيْرًا لَّهُمْ ۚ وَاِنْ يَّتَوَلَّوْا يُعَذِّبْهُمُ اللّٰهُ
عَذَابًا اَلِيْمًا ۙ فِي الدُّنْيَا وَالْاٰخِرَةِ ۚ وَمَا لَهُمْ فِي الْاَرْضِ
مِنْ وَّلِيٍّ وَّلَا نَصِيْرٍ ﴿٧٤﴾

75. And among them are those who made a covenant with Allāh, *saying*, 'If He give us of His bounty, we would most surely give alms and be of the virtuous.'

وَمِنْهُمْ مَّنْ عٰهَدَ اللّٰهَ لَئِنْ اٰتٰىنَا مِنْ فَضْلِهٖ لَنَصَّدَّقَنَّ
وَلَنَكُوْنَنَّ مِنَ الصّٰلِحِيْنَ ﴿٧٥﴾

76. But when He gave them of His bounty, they became niggardly of it, and they turned away in aversion.

فَلَمَّآ اٰتٰىهُمْ مِّنْ فَضْلِهٖ بَخِلُوْا بِهٖ وَتَوَلَّوْا وَّهُمْ مُّعْرِضُوْنَ ﴿٧٦﴾

77. So He requited them with hypocrisy *which shall last* in their hearts until the day when they shall meet Him, because they broke their promise to Allāh, and because they lied.

فَاَعْقَبَهُمْ نِفَاقًا فِيْ قُلُوْبِهِمْ اِلٰى يَوْمِ يَلْقَوْنَهٗ بِمَآ اَخْلَفُوا
اللّٰهَ مَا وَعَدُوْهُ وَبِمَا كَانُوْا يَكْذِبُوْنَ ﴿٧٧﴾

78. Know they not that [a]Allāh knows their hidden *thoughts* as well as their secret counsels and that Allāh knows full well all unseen things ?

اَلَمْ يَعْلَمُوْٓا اَنَّ اللّٰهَ يَعْلَمُ سِرَّهُمْ وَنَجْوٰىهُمْ وَاَنَّ
اللّٰهَ عَلَّامُ الْغُيُوْبِ ﴿٧٨﴾

[a]6 : 4; 11 : 6; 25 : 7; 28 : 70.

1200. With the arrival of the Holy Prophet in Medina, prosperity of the town very much increased, its trade throve and its inhabitants grew rich.

79. *These Hypocrites are* ^athose who find fault with such of the believers as give freely in charity and with such as find nothing *to give* save *the earnings of* their toil.[1201] So they deride them. Allāh shall punish them for their derision, and for them is a grievous punishment.

الَّذِيْنَ يَلْمِزُوْنَ الْمُطَّوِّعِيْنَ مِنَ الْمُؤْمِنِيْنَ فِى الصَّدَقٰتِ وَالَّذِيْنَ لَا يَجِدُوْنَ اِلَّا جُهْدَهُمْ فَيَسْخَرُوْنَ مِنْهُمْ سَخِرَ اللّٰهُ مِنْهُمْ وَلَهُمْ عَذَابٌ اَلِيْمٌ ۝

80. ^bAsk thou forgiveness for them, or ask thou not forgiveness for them; even if thou ask forgiveness for them seventy times, Allāh will never forgive them.[1202] That is because they disbelieved in Allāh and His Messenger. And Allāh guides not the perfidious people.

اِسْتَغْفِرْ لَهُمْ اَوْ لَا تَسْتَغْفِرْ لَهُمْ اِنْ تَسْتَغْفِرْ لَهُمْ سَبْعِيْنَ مَرَّةً فَلَنْ يَّغْفِرَ اللّٰهُ لَهُمْ ذٰلِكَ بِاَنَّهُمْ كَفَرُوْا بِاللّٰهِ وَرَسُوْلِهٖ وَاللّٰهُ لَا يَهْدِى الْقَوْمَ الْفٰسِقِيْنَ ۝

R. 11   81. ^cThose who *contrived to be left behind* rejoiced in their sitting *at home* behind the Messenger of Allāh, and were averse to striving with their wealth and their persons in the cause of Allāh. And they said, 'Go not forth in the heat.' Say, 'The fire of Hell is more intense in heat.' If only they could understand !

فَرِحَ الْمُخَلَّفُوْنَ بِمَقْعَدِهِمْ خِلٰفَ رَسُوْلِ اللّٰهِ وَكَرِهُوْا اَنْ يُّجَاهِدُوْا بِاَمْوَالِهِمْ وَاَنْفُسِهِمْ فِىْ سَبِيْلِ اللّٰهِ وَقَالُوْا لَا تَنْفِرُوْا فِى الْحَرِّ قُلْ نَارُ جَهَنَّمَ اَشَدُّ حَرًّا لَّوْ كَانُوْا يَفْقَهُوْنَ ۝

82. They should laugh little and weep much[1203] as a reward for that which they used to earn.

فَلْيَضْحَكُوْا قَلِيْلًا وَّلْيَبْكُوْا كَثِيْرًا جَزَآءً بِمَا كَانُوْا يَكْسِبُوْنَ ۝

---

^a9 : 58.   ^b63 : 7.   ^c9 : 87, 93.

1201. A poor Muslim, Abū ʿAqīl, who gave only a small quantity of dates, his whole day's earnings as his contribution, was scoffed at by the Hypocrites for his scanty offering.

1202. The word "seventy" does not denote a specific number but is used here to intensify the point that such Hypocrites as are doomed to perish will never be forgiven however much the Holy Prophet might ask forgiveness for them.

1203. The verse obviously does not contain a commandment. It only embodies a prophecy that the time was soon coming when the Hypocrites will *laugh little and weep much*.

83. And if Allāh bring thee back to a party of them, and they ask of thee leave to go forth *to fight*, say then, 'You shall never go forth with me, and shall never fight an enemy with me. You chose to sit *at home* the first time, so sit now with those who remain behind.'

فَإِنْ رَّجَعَكَ اللّٰهُ إِلٰى طَآئِفَةٍ مِّنْهُمْ فَاسْتَأْذَنُوْكَ
لِلْخُرُوْجِ فَقُلْ لَّنْ تَخْرُجُوْا مَعِيَ أَبَدًا وَّلَنْ تُقَاتِلُوْا
مَعِيَ عَدُوًّا ۖ إِنَّكُمْ رَضِيْتُمْ بِالْقُعُوْدِ أَوَّلَ مَرَّةٍ
فَاقْعُدُوْا مَعَ الْخٰلِفِيْنَ ﴿٨٣﴾

84. And never pray thou for any of them that dies, nor stand by his grave; for they disbelieved in Allāh and His Messenger and died while they were disobedient.

وَلَا تُصَلِّ عَلٰٓى أَحَدٍ مِّنْهُمْ مَّاتَ أَبَدًا وَّلَا تَقُمْ
عَلٰى قَبْرِهٖ ۖ إِنَّهُمْ كَفَرُوْا بِاللّٰهِ وَرَسُوْلِهٖ وَمَاتُوْا وَ
هُمْ فٰسِقُوْنَ ﴿٨٤﴾

85. [a]And let not their riches and their children excite thy wonder; Allāh only intends to punish them therewith in this world and that their souls may depart while they are disbelievers.

وَلَا تُعْجِبْكَ أَمْوَالُهُمْ وَأَوْلَادُهُمْ ۖ إِنَّمَا يُرِيْدُ
اللّٰهُ أَنْ يُّعَذِّبَهُمْ بِهَا فِي الدُّنْيَا وَتَزْهَقَ أَنْفُسُهُمْ
وَهُمْ كٰفِرُوْنَ ﴿٨٥﴾

86. And when a *Sūrah* is revealed, *enjoining*, 'Believe in Allāh and strive *in His cause* in company with His Messenger,' men of wealth and affluence among them ask leave of thee and say, 'Leave us that we be with those who sit *at home*.'[1204]

وَإِذَآ أُنْزِلَتْ سُوْرَةٌ أَنْ اٰمِنُوْا بِاللّٰهِ وَجَاهِدُوْا مَعَ
رَسُوْلِهِ اسْتَأْذَنَكَ أُولُوا الطَّوْلِ مِنْهُمْ وَقَالُوْا ذَرْنَا
نَكُنْ مَّعَ الْقٰعِدِيْنَ ﴿٨٦﴾

87. [b]They prefer to be with *the womenfolk*,[1205] who remain behind *at home* and [c]their hearts are sealed[1206] so that they understand not.

رَضُوْا بِأَنْ يَّكُوْنُوْا مَعَ الْخَوَالِفِ وَطُبِعَ عَلٰى قُلُوْبِهِمْ
فَهُمْ لَا يَفْقَهُوْنَ ﴿٨٧﴾

[a]9 : 55. [b]9 : 81,93. [c]6 : 26 ; 63 : 4.

1204. The words need not be taken to have been actually uttered by the Hypocrites. They simply express a state of affairs implying that they came to the Holy Prophet with various excuses for staying behind.

1205. *Khawālif* means, those who remain behind during war ; or the women (or children) remaining behind in houses or tents. The word also signifies, bad or corrupt persons (Lane).

1206. See 27.

88. [a]But the Messenger and those who believe with him strive *in the cause of Allāh* with their wealth and their persons, and it is they who shall have good things, and it is they who shall prosper.

لٰكِنِ الرَّسُوْلُ وَالَّذِيْنَ اٰمَنُوْا مَعَهٗ جٰهَدُوْا بِاَمْوَالِهِمْ
وَاَنْفُسِهِمْؕ وَاُولٰٓئِكَ لَهُمُ الْخَيْرٰتُ وَاُولٰٓئِكَ هُمُ
الْمُفْلِحُوْنَ ﴿۸۸﴾

89. [b]Allāh has prepared for them Gardens under which streams flow; therein they shall abide. That is the supreme triumph.

اَعَدَّ اللّٰهُ لَهُمْ جَنّٰتٍ تَجْرِيْ مِنْ تَحْتِهَا الْاَنْهٰرُ
خٰلِدِيْنَ فِيْهَاؕ ذٰلِكَ الْفَوْزُ الْعَظِيْمُ ﴿۸۹﴾ ع

R. 12 90. And those, who make excuses[1207] from among the desert Arabs, came *with the request* that exemption might be granted them. And those who lied to Allāh and His Messenger stayed *at home*. A grievous punishment shall befall those of them who disbelieve.

وَجَآءَ الْمُعَذِّرُوْنَ مِنَ الْاَعْرَابِ لِيُؤْذَنَ لَهُمْ
وَقَعَدَ الَّذِيْنَ كَذَبُوا اللّٰهَ وَرَسُوْلَهٗؕ سَيُصِيْبُ الَّذِيْنَ
كَفَرُوْا مِنْهُمْ عَذَابٌ اَلِيْمٌ ﴿۹۰﴾

91. [c]No blame lies on the weak, nor on the sick, nor on those who find naught to spend, if they are sincere to Allāh and His Messenger. There is no *cause of* reproach against those who do good deeds; and Allāh is Most Forgiving, Merciful,

لَيْسَ عَلَى الضُّعَفَآءِ وَلَا عَلَى الْمَرْضٰى وَلَا عَلَى
الَّذِيْنَ لَا يَجِدُوْنَ مَا يُنْفِقُوْنَ حَرَجٌ اِذَا نَصَحُوْا
لِلّٰهِ وَرَسُوْلِهٖؕ مَا عَلَى الْمُحْسِنِيْنَ مِنْ سَبِيْلٍؕ وَ
اللّٰهُ غَفُوْرٌ رَّحِيْمٌ ﴿۹۱﴾

92. Nor against those to whom, when they came to thee that thou shouldst furnish them with mounts thou didst say, 'I cannot find whereon I can mount you;' they turned back, their eyes overflowing with tears, out of grief that they could not find what they might spend.[1208]

وَّلَا عَلَى الَّذِيْنَ اِذَا مَآ اَتَوْكَ لِتَحْمِلَهُمْ قُلْتَ لَآ
اَجِدُ مَآ اَحْمِلُكُمْ عَلَيْهِ تَوَلَّوْا وَّاَعْيُنُهُمْ تَفِيْضُ مِنَ
الدَّمْعِ حَزَنًا اَلَّا يَجِدُوْا مَا يُنْفِقُوْنَؕ ﴿۹۲﴾

[a]8 : 75 ; 9 : 41,111; 61 : 12. [b]See 2 : 26. [c]48 : 18.

1207. *Mu'adhdhir* is derived from '*Adhdhara* which means, he excused or affected to excuse himself but did not adduce a valid excuse for doing so; he was remiss or wanting or deficient in an affair, setting up an excuse for being so. Thus the word means, one who falls short of his duty and then excuses himself without having any real excuse (Lane).

1208. The verse is general in its application but the persons particularly referred to were seven poor Muslims who were extremely desirous of going to *Jihād* but did not possess the means and wherewithal to fulfil the wish of their hearts.

93. The *cause of* reproach is only against those who ask leave of thee, while they are rich. [a]They are content to be with *the women-folk* who remain behind *at home.* And [b]Allāh has set a seal upon their hearts so that they know not.

إِنَّمَا السَّبِيلُ عَلَى الَّذِينَ يَسْتَأْذِنُونَكَ وَهُمْ
أَغْنِيَاءُ ۚ رَضُوا بِأَنْ يَكُونُوا مَعَ الْخَوَالِفِ وَطَبَعَ
اللَّهُ عَلَىٰ قُلُوبِهِمْ فَهُمْ لَا يَعْلَمُونَ ﴿٩٣﴾

PART XI

94. They will make excuses to you when you return to them. Say, 'Make no excuses; we shall not believe you. Allāh has already informed us of the *true* facts about you. And Allāh will observe your conduct, and *also* His Messenger ; then you will be brought back to Him Who knows the unseen and the seen, and He will tell you all that you used to do.'[1209]

يَعْتَذِرُونَ إِلَيْكُمْ إِذَا رَجَعْتُمْ إِلَيْهِمْ ۚ قُلْ
لَا تَعْتَذِرُوا لَنْ نُؤْمِنَ لَكُمْ قَدْ نَبَّأَنَا اللَّهُ مِنْ
أَخْبَارِكُمْ ۚ وَسَيَرَى اللَّهُ عَمَلَكُمْ وَرَسُولُهُ ثُمَّ تُرَدُّونَ
إِلَىٰ عَالِمِ الْغَيْبِ وَالشَّهَادَةِ فَيُنَبِّئُكُمْ بِمَا كُنْتُمْ
تَعْمَلُونَ ﴿٩٤﴾

95. They will swear to you by Allāh, when you return to them, that you may leave them alone. So leave them alone. Surely, they are an abomination, and their abode is Hell—a *fit* recompense for that which they used to earn.[1210]

سَيَحْلِفُونَ بِاللَّهِ لَكُمْ إِذَا انْقَلَبْتُمْ إِلَيْهِمْ لِتُعْرِضُوا
عَنْهُمْ ۖ فَأَعْرِضُوا عَنْهُمْ ۖ إِنَّهُمْ رِجْسٌ ۖ وَمَأْوَاهُمْ
جَهَنَّمُ جَزَاءً بِمَا كَانُوا يَكْسِبُونَ ﴿٩٥﴾

96. [c]They will swear to you that you may be pleased with them. But *even* if you be pleased with them, Allāh will not be pleased with the rebellious people.

يَحْلِفُونَ لَكُمْ لِتَرْضَوْا عَنْهُمْ ۖ فَإِنْ تَرْضَوْا عَنْهُمْ
فَإِنَّ اللَّهَ لَا يَرْضَىٰ عَنِ الْقَوْمِ الْفَاسِقِينَ ﴿٩٦﴾

97. The Arabs of the desert are the worst in disbelief and hypocrisy, and most apt not to know the ordinances of *the Revelation* which Allāh has sent down to His

الْأَعْرَابُ أَشَدُّ كُفْرًا وَنِفَاقًا وَأَجْدَرُ أَلَّا يَعْلَمُوا

[a]9 : 79, 87. [b]6 : 26; 9 : 87; 63 : 4. [c]9 : 62.

1209. The verse was revealed when the Holy Prophet had not yet returned to Medina from his expedition to Tabūk.

1210. As these 'stayers-behind' belonged to different categories, therefore they were treated differently.

Messenger. And Allāh is All-Knowing, Wise.

حُدُوْدَ مَآ اَنْزَلَ اللّٰهُ عَلٰى رَسُوْلِهٖ ۭ وَاللّٰهُ عَلِيْمٌ حَكِيْمٌ ﴿٩٧﴾

98. And among the Arabs of the desert are those who regard that which they spend *in the cause of Allāh* as a compulsory fine and they wait for calamities to *befall* you. [a]On themselves *shall fall* an evil calamity. And Allāh is All-Hearing, All-Knowing.

وَمِنَ الْاَعْرَابِ مَنْ يَّتَّخِذُ مَا يُنْفِقُ مَغْرَمًا وَّيَتَرَبَّصُ
بِكُمُ الدَّوَاۗىِٕرَ ۭ عَلَيْهِمْ دَاۗىِٕرَةُ السَّوْءِ ۭ وَاللّٰهُ سَمِيْعٌ
عَلِيْمٌ ﴿٩٨﴾

99. And among the Arabs of the desert are those who believe in Allāh and the Last Day,[1211] and regard that which they spend as means of bringing them near to Allāh and *of receiving* the prayers of the Prophet. Aye! it is for them certainly a means of bringing them near *to Allāh*. Allāh will soon admit them to His mercy. Surely, Allāh is Most Forgiving, Merciful.

وَمِنَ الْاَعْرَابِ مَنْ يُّؤْمِنُ بِاللّٰهِ وَالْيَوْمِ الْاٰخِرِ
وَيَتَّخِذُ مَا يُنْفِقُ قُرُبٰتٍ عِنْدَ اللّٰهِ وَصَلَوٰتِ الرَّسُوْلِ ۭ
اَلَآ اِنَّهَا قُرْبَةٌ لَّهُمْ ۭ سَيُدْخِلُهُمُ اللّٰهُ فِيْ رَحْمَتِهٖ ۭ
ع ١٣ اِنَّ اللّٰهَ غَفُوْرٌ رَّحِيْمٌ ﴿٩٩﴾

R. 13 100. And *as for* the foremost *among the believers*, the first of the Emigrants and the Helpers, and those who followed them in the best possible manner, [b]Allāh is well-pleased with them[1212] and they are well-pleased with Him, and He has prepared for them Gardens underneath which streams flow. They will abide therein for ever. That is the supreme triumph.

وَالسّٰبِقُوْنَ الْاَوَّلُوْنَ مِنَ الْمُهٰجِرِيْنَ وَالْاَنْصَارِ
وَالَّذِيْنَ اتَّبَعُوْهُمْ بِاِحْسَانٍ ۙ رَّضِيَ اللّٰهُ عَنْهُمْ
وَرَضُوْا عَنْهُ وَاَعَدَّ لَهُمْ جَنّٰتٍ تَجْرِيْ تَحْتَهَا
الْاَنْهٰرُ خٰلِدِيْنَ فِيْهَآ اَبَدًا ۭ ذٰلِكَ الْفَوْزُ الْعَظِيْمُ ﴿١٠٠﴾

---

[a]48 : 7. [b]58 : 23 ; 98 : 9.

1211. The Qur'ān never indiscriminately condemns a whole people. The verse seeks to remove a possible misunderstanding that all Arabs of the desert were bad.

1212. Incidentally, the verse constitutes a forcible refutation of the Shiah accusations against the first three Successors of the Holy Prophet and his other prominent Companions.

101. And of the desert Arabs around you *some* are hypocrites; and of the people of Medina *also*. They persist in hypocrisy.[1213] Thou knowest them not; We know them. We will punish them twice;[1214] then shall they be given over to a great punishment.

وَمِمَّنْ حَوْلَكُمْ مِّنَ الْاَعْرَابِ مُنٰفِقُوْنَ ۛؕ وَمِنْ
اَهْلِ الْمَدِيْنَةِ ۛ مَرَدُوْا عَلَى النِّفَاقِ ۟ لَا تَعْلَمُهُمْ ؕ
نَحْنُ نَعْلَمُهُمْ ؕ سَنُعَذِّبُهُمْ مَّرَّتَيْنِ ثُمَّ يُرَدُّوْنَ اِلٰى
عَذَابٍ عَظِيْمٍ ۚ﴿۱۰۱﴾

102. And there are others who have confessed their faults. They mixed good works with others *that are* evil.[1215] It may be that Allāh will turn to them with compassion. Surely, Allāh is Most Forgiving, Merciful.

وَاٰخَرُوْنَ اعْتَرَفُوْا بِذُنُوْبِهِمْ خَلَطُوْا عَمَلًا صَالِحًا
وَّاٰخَرَ سَيِّئًا ؕ عَسَى اللّٰهُ اَنْ يَّتُوْبَ عَلَيْهِمْ ؕ اِنَّ اللّٰهَ
غَفُوْرٌ رَّحِيْمٌ ﴿۱۰۲﴾

103. Take alms out of their wealth, so that thou mayest cleanse them and purify them thereby. And pray for them; thy prayer indeed is *a source of* tranquillity for them. And Allāh is All-Hearing, All-Knowing.

خُذْ مِنْ اَمْوَالِهِمْ صَدَقَةً تُطَهِّرُهُمْ وَتُزَكِّيْهِمْ
بِهَا وَصَلِّ عَلَيْهِمْ ؕ اِنَّ صَلٰوتَكَ سَكَنٌ لَّهُمْ ؕ وَاللّٰهُ
سَمِيْعٌ عَلِيْمٌ ﴿۱۰۳﴾

104. Know they not that [a]Allāh is He Who accepts repentance from His servants and takes alms, and that Allāh is He Who is Oft-Returning *with compassion*, *and* is Merciful ?

اَلَمْ يَعْلَمُوْۤا اَنَّ اللّٰهَ هُوَ يَقْبَلُ التَّوْبَةَ عَنْ عِبَادِهٖ وَ
يَاْخُذُ الصَّدَقٰتِ وَاَنَّ اللّٰهَ هُوَ التَّوَّابُ الرَّحِيْمُ ﴿۱۰۴﴾

[a]42 : 26.

1213. The reference particularly is to the five tribes of the desert living near Medina —Juhainah, Muzainah, Ashja', Aslam and Ghifār (Ma'ānī. iii. 361). After the death of the Holy Prophet the Hypocrites from among these tribes gathered togeher and made a raid on Medina (Khaldūn, ii. 66).

1214. "Twice" may not refer to the form of punishment but to the period thereof which is explained in 9 : 126. The word may signify that the Hypocrites would be punished in a period ranging from one to two years, *i.e.*, if the punishment comes twice a year, they will have it in one year; if it comes once, they will have it in two years.

1215. The verse may refer to those Muslims who did possess an excuse, but it was not strong enough to justify their staying behind. Their number, according to different reports, varied from seven to ten. As a self-inflicted punishment for their offence, these men bound themselves to the pillars of the Mosque at Medina, and when the Holy Prophet entered it to offer Prayers, they begged him to pardon them to which he replied that he could not do so unless so commanded by God. When this verse was revealed, they were ordered to be released.

105. And say, 'Go on working and [a]Allāh will surely watch your conduct and *also* His Messenger and the believers. And you shall be brought back to Him Who knows the unseen and the seen; then He will inform you of what you did.'

وَقُلِ اعْمَلُوْا فَسَيَرَى اللّٰهُ عَمَلَكُمْ وَرَسُوْلُهٗ وَالْمُؤْمِنُوْنَ
وَسَتُرَدُّوْنَ اِلٰى عٰلِمِ الْغَيْبِ وَالشَّهَادَةِ فَيُنَبِّئُكُمْ بِمَا
كُنْتُمْ تَعْمَلُوْنَ ﴿١٠٥﴾

106. And [b]*there are* others *whose case* has been postponed[1216] *pending* the decree of Allāh. He may punish them or He may turn to them with compassion. And Allāh is All-Knowing, Wise.

وَاٰخَرُوْنَ مُرْجَوْنَ لِاَمْرِ اللّٰهِ اِمَّا يُعَذِّبُهُمْ وَاِمَّا يَتُوْبُ
عَلَيْهِمْ ۗ وَاللّٰهُ عَلِيْمٌ حَكِيْمٌ ﴿١٠٦﴾

107. And *among the Hypocrites are*[1217] those who have built a mosque in order to injure *Islām* and *help* disbelief and to cause a division among the believers, and to prepare an ambush for him who warred against Allāh and His Messenger before *this*. And they will surely swear; 'We meant nothing but good'; but [c]Allāh bears witness that they are certainly liars.

وَالَّذِيْنَ اتَّخَذُوْا مَسْجِدًا ضِرَارًا وَّكُفْرًا وَّتَفْرِيْقًا
بَيْنَ الْمُؤْمِنِيْنَ وَاِرْصَادًا لِّمَنْ حَارَبَ اللّٰهَ وَرَسُوْلَهٗ
مِنْ قَبْلُ ۗ وَلَيَحْلِفُنَّ اِنْ اَرَدْنَآ اِلَّا الْحُسْنٰى ۗ وَاللّٰهُ يَشْهَدُ
اِنَّهُمْ لَكٰذِبُوْنَ ﴿١٠٧﴾

[a]9 : 94. [b]9 : 118. [c]63 : 2.

1216. They were Hilāl Ibn Umayyah, Murārah Ibn Rabī'ah and Ka'b Ibn Mālik. The Holy Prophet deferred pronouncing his decision regarding them in obedience to Divine command (Bukhārī).

1217. The verse may refer to a plot hatched by one Abū 'Āmir, a Christian monk, an arch-enemy of Islām. After having utterly failed in his evil designs against Islām and seeing that it had become firmly established in Arabia after the Battle of Ḥunain, he fled to Syria, designing and hoping to enlist the help of the Byzantines against the Holy Prophet. From there he sent word to the Hypocrites of Medina that they should build a mosque in the suburb of Medina which should serve as a place of hiding for him and in which they should concoct schemes and hatch plots. But Abū 'Āmir did not live long enough to see his scheme materialise and died at Kunnisrīn, a broken-hearted wretch. His accomplices built a mosque as designed by him and invited the Holy Prophet to bless it by saying his Prayers in it. The Holy Prophet was forbidden by Divine revelation to do so. He ordered the mosque which came to be known as Masjid Ḍirār to be set on fire and razed to the ground.

108. Never stand *to pray* therein. A Mosque founded upon piety from the *very* first[1218] day is surely more worthy that thou shouldst stand *to pray* therein. In it are men who love to become purified, and Allāh loves those who purify themselves.

لَا تَقُمْ فِيْهِ اَبَدًا ؕ لَمَسْجِدٌ اُسِّسَ عَلَى التَّقْوٰى مِنْ اَوَّلِ
يَوْمٍ اَحَقُّ اَنْ تَقُوْمَ فِيْهِ ؕ فِيْهِ رِجَالٌ يُّحِبُّوْنَ اَنْ يَّتَطَهَّرُوْا ؕ
وَاللّٰهُ يُحِبُّ الْمُطَّهِّرِيْنَ ﴿۱۰۸﴾

109. Is he, then, who founded his building on fear of Allāh and *His* pleasure better or he who has founded his building on the brink of a tottering water-worn bank which tumbled down with him into the fire of Hell? And Allāh guides not the wrongdoing people.

اَفَمَنْ اَسَّسَ بُنْيَانَهٗ عَلٰى تَقْوٰى مِنَ اللّٰهِ وَرِضْوَانٍ
خَيْرٌ اَمْ مَّنْ اَسَّسَ بُنْيَانَهٗ عَلٰى شَفَا جُرُفٍ هَارٍ
فَانْهَارَ بِهٖ فِيْ نَارِ جَهَنَّمَ ؕ وَاللّٰهُ لَا يَهْدِي الْقَوْمَ
الظّٰلِمِيْنَ ﴿۱۰۹﴾

110. *This* building of theirs, which they have built, will ever continue to be *a source of* disquiet in their hearts, unless their hearts be cut into pieces. And Allāh is All-Knowing, Wise.

لَا يَزَالُ بُنْيَانُهُمُ الَّذِيْ بَنَوْا رِيْبَةً فِيْ قُلُوْبِهِمْ
اِلَّآ اَنْ تَقَطَّعَ قُلُوْبُهُمْ ؕ وَاللّٰهُ عَلِيْمٌ حَكِيْمٌ ﴿۱۱۰﴾ ع

R. 14 111. Surely, [a]Allāh has purchased of the believers their persons and their property *in return* for the *heavenly* Garden they shall have; [b]they fight in the cause of Allāh, and they slay and are slain—an unfailing promise *that He has made* binding on Himself in the Torah, and the Gospel,[1219] and the Qur'ān. And who is more faithful to his promise than Allāh? Rejoice, then, in your bargain which you have made with Him; and that is the mighty triumph.

اِنَّ اللّٰهَ اشْتَرٰى مِنَ الْمُؤْمِنِيْنَ اَنْفُسَهُمْ وَاَمْوَالَهُمْ
بِاَنَّ لَهُمُ الْجَنَّةَ ؕ يُقَاتِلُوْنَ فِيْ سَبِيْلِ اللّٰهِ فَيَقْتُلُوْنَ
وَيُقْتَلُوْنَ وَعْدًا عَلَيْهِ حَقًّا فِي التَّوْرٰىةِ وَالْاِنْجِيْلِ
وَالْقُرْاٰنِ ؕ وَمَنْ اَوْفٰى بِعَهْدِهٖ مِنَ اللّٰهِ فَاسْتَبْشِرُوْا
بِبَيْعِكُمُ الَّذِيْ بَايَعْتُمْ بِهٖ ؕ وَذٰلِكَ هُوَ الْفَوْزُ الْعَظِيْمُ ﴿۱۱۱﴾

[a]4 : 75; 61 : 11-12. [b]3 : 196; 61 : 5.

1218. The reference is said to be to the Mosque at Qubā which was built on the site where the Holy Prophet had alighted before entering Medina on the day of his arrival from Mecca. According to some authorities, however, the reference is to the mosque which the Holy Prophet himself built at Medina and which later came to be known as "the Mosque of the Prophet."

1219. Torah (Deut. 6 : 3-5) and Gospel (Matt. 19 : 21 & 27-29).

112. Those who turn *to Allāh in repentance*, *a*who worship *Him*, who praise *Him*, who go about in the land *serving Him*, who bow down *to Him*, who prostrate themselves *in Prayer*, *b*who enjoin good and forbid evil, and who observe the limits *set* by Allāh. And give glad tidings to those who believe.

اَلتَّاۤئِبُوۡنَ الۡعٰبِدُوۡنَ الۡحٰمِدُوۡنَ السَّاۤئِحُوۡنَ الرّٰكِعُوۡنَ السّٰجِدُوۡنَ الۡاٰمِرُوۡنَ بِالۡمَعۡرُوۡفِ وَ النَّاهُوۡنَ عَنِ الۡمُنۡکَرِ وَ الۡحٰفِظُوۡنَ لِحُدُوۡدِ اللّٰهِ وَ بَشِّرِ الۡمُؤۡمِنِیۡنَ ۝

113. It does not behove the Prophet and those who believe that they should ask *of Allāh* forgiveness for the idolaters, even though they may be their kinsmen, after it has become plain to them that they are the companions of Hell.

مَا کَانَ لِلنَّبِیِّ وَ الَّذِیۡنَ اٰمَنُوۡۤا اَنۡ یَّسۡتَغۡفِرُوۡا لِلۡمُشۡرِکِیۡنَ وَ لَوۡ کَانُوۡۤا اُولِیۡ قُرۡبٰی مِنۡۢ بَعۡدِ مَا تَبَیَّنَ لَهُمۡ اَنَّهُمۡ اَصۡحٰبُ الۡجَحِیۡمِ ۝

114. And Abraham's asking forgiveness for his father was only because of a promise he had made to him,[1220] but when it became clear to him that he was an enemy of Allāh, he dissociated himself from him. *c*Surely, Abraham was most tender-hearted *and* forbearing.

وَ مَا کَانَ اسۡتِغۡفَارُ اِبۡرٰهِیۡمَ لِاَبِیۡهِ اِلَّا عَنۡ مَّوۡعِدَةٍ وَّعَدَهَاۤ اِیَّاهُ ۚ فَلَمَّا تَبَیَّنَ لَهٗۤ اَنَّهٗ عَدُوٌّ لِّلّٰهِ تَبَرَّاَ مِنۡهُ ؕ اِنَّ اِبۡرٰهِیۡمَ لَاَوَّاهٌ حَلِیۡمٌ ۝

115. And Allāh would not cause a people to go astray after He has guided them until He makes clear to them that which they ought to guard against. Surely, Allāh knows all things well.

وَ مَا کَانَ اللّٰهُ لِیُضِلَّ قَوۡمًۢا بَعۡدَ اِذۡ هَدٰىهُمۡ حَتّٰی یُبَیِّنَ لَهُمۡ مَّا یَتَّقُوۡنَ ؕ اِنَّ اللّٰهَ بِکُلِّ شَیۡءٍ عَلِیۡمٌ ۝

116. Surely, *d*it is Allāh to Whom belongs the Kingdom of the heavens and the earth. He gives life and causes death. And you have no friend nor helper besides Allāh.

اِنَّ اللّٰهَ لَهٗ مُلۡکُ السَّمٰوٰتِ وَ الۡاَرۡضِ ؕ یُحۡیٖ وَ یُمِیۡتُ ؕ وَ مَا لَکُمۡ مِّنۡ دُوۡنِ اللّٰهِ مِنۡ وَّلِیٍّ وَّ لَا نَصِیۡرٍ ۝

---

*a*33 : 36. *b*3 : 105, 111, 115; 7 : 158; 9 : 71; 31 : 18.
*c*19 : 48; 26 : 87; 60 : 5. *d*11 : 76. 39 : 45 ; 57 : 3.

1220. See 19 : 48.

117. Allāh has certainly turned with mercy[1221] to the Prophet and *to* the Emigrants and the Helpers who followed him in the hour of distress[1222] after the hearts of a party of them had almost swerved *from duty*. He again turned to them with mercy. Surely, He is to them Compassionate, Merciful.

لَقَدْ تَابَ اللّٰهُ عَلَى النَّبِيِّ وَالْمُهٰجِرِيْنَ وَالْاَنْصَارِ
الَّذِيْنَ اتَّبَعُوْهُ فِيْ سَاعَةِ الْعُسْرَةِ مِنْۢ بَعْدِ مَا
كَادَ يَزِيْغُ قُلُوْبُ فَرِيْقٍ مِّنْهُمْ ثُمَّ تَابَ عَلَيْهِمْ
اِنَّهٗ بِهِمْ رَءُوْفٌ رَّحِيْمٌ ﴿١١٧﴾

118. And *He has turned with mercy* to the three[1223] who *happened to be* left [a]behind until when the earth became too strait for them with *all* its vastness, and their souls were *also* straitened for them, and they became convinced that there was no refuge from Allāh save unto Himself, then He turned to them with mercy that they might turn *to him*. Surely, it is Allāh Who is Oft-Returning *with compassion and is* Merciful.

وَّعَلَى الثَّلٰثَةِ الَّذِيْنَ خُلِّفُوْا حَتّٰۤى اِذَا ضَاقَتْ عَلَيْهِمُ الْاَرْضُ بِمَا
رَحُبَتْ وَضَاقَتْ عَلَيْهِمْ اَنْفُسُهُمْ وَظَنُّوْۤا اَنْ لَّا مَلْجَاَ
مِنَ اللّٰهِ اِلَّاۤ اِلَيْهِ ثُمَّ تَابَ عَلَيْهِمْ لِيَتُوْبُوْا اِنَّ اللّٰهَ
هُوَ التَّوَّابُ الرَّحِيْمُ ﴿١١٨﴾ ع

R.15 119. O ye who believe! [b]fear Allāh and be with the truthful.

يٰۤاَيُّهَا الَّذِيْنَ اٰمَنُوا اتَّقُوا اللّٰهَ وَكُوْنُوْا مَعَ الصّٰدِقِيْنَ ﴿١١٩﴾

[a]9 : 106. [b]3 : 103; 5 : 36; 39 : 11; 57 : 29.

1221. The word *Tāba* also signifies "bestowing favour upon a person or being gracious to him," for in the case of the Holy Prophet and his faithful followers it was no occasion for granting forgiveness but for bestowing reward.

1222. As it was an " hour of distress" for the Muslims, the expedition to Tabūk is rightly known as *Ghazwat al-'Usrah*, *i.e.*, the expedition of distress.

1223. Ka'b bin Mālik, Hilāl bin Umayyah and Murārah bin Rabī'ah (9 : 106). They were sincere Muslims but failed to join the expedition to Tabūk, and therefore on his return to Medina, the Holy Prophet ordered their complete social ostracism so that they were even separated from their wives. They continued under this interdiction for no less than fifty days, when on their sincere repentance, they were granted pardon. They unreservedly confessed their guilt and offered no excuse. Being sincere and honest believers they severely took to heart the Divine punishment. They grieved and pined, *till the earth for all its vastness became too strait for them* (Bukhārī, ch. on Maghāzī).

120. It was not *proper* for the people of Medina and those around them from among the Arabs of the desert that they should have remained behind the Messenger of Allāh or that they should have preferred their own lives to his. That is because there afflicts them neither thirst nor fatigue nor hunger in the way of Allāh, nor do they tread a track which enrages the disbelievers, nor do they gain an advantage over the enemy but there is written down for them a good work on account of it. Surely, Allāh suffers not the reward of those who do good, to be lost.

مَا كَانَ لِاَهْلِ الْمَدِيْنَةِ وَمَنْ حَوْلَهُمْ مِّنَ الْاَعْرَابِ
اَنْ يَّتَخَلَّفُوْا عَنْ رَّسُوْلِ اللّٰهِ وَلَا يَرْغَبُوْا بِاَنْفُسِهِمْ عَنْ
نَّفْسِهٖ ذٰلِكَ بِاَنَّهُمْ لَا يُصِيْبُهُمْ ظَمَاٌ وَّلَا نَصَبٌ وَّلَا
مَخْمَصَةٌ فِيْ سَبِيْلِ اللّٰهِ وَلَا يَطَئُوْنَ مَوْطِئًا يَّغِيْظُ
الْكُفَّارَ وَلَا يَنَالُوْنَ مِنْ عَدُوٍّ نَّيْلًا اِلَّا كُتِبَ لَهُمْ بِهٖ
عَمَلٌ صَالِحٌ اِنَّ اللّٰهَ لَا يُضِيْعُ اَجْرَ الْمُحْسِنِيْنَ ﴿١٢٠﴾

121. And they spend not any sum, small or great, nor do they traverse a valley, but it is written down for them, *among their good works*, that [a]Allāh may give them the best reward for what they did.

وَلَا يُنْفِقُوْنَ نَفَقَةً صَغِيْرَةً وَّلَا كَبِيْرَةً وَّلَا يَقْطَعُوْنَ
وَادِيًا اِلَّا كُتِبَ لَهُمْ لِيَجْزِيَهُمُ اللّٰهُ اَحْسَنَ مَا كَانُوْا
يَعْمَلُوْنَ ﴿١٢١﴾

122. [b]It is not possible for the believers to go forth all together. Why, then, does not a party from every section of them go forth that they may become well-versed in religion,[1224] and that they may warn their people when they return to them, so that they may guard *against evil?*

وَمَا كَانَ الْمُؤْمِنُوْنَ لِيَنْفِرُوْا كَآفَّةً فَلَوْلَا نَفَرَ مِنْ
كُلِّ فِرْقَةٍ مِّنْهُمْ طَآئِفَةٌ لِّيَتَفَقَّهُوْا فِي الدِّيْنِ
وَلِيُنْذِرُوْا قَوْمَهُمْ اِذَا رَجَعُوْا اِلَيْهِمْ لَعَلَّهُمْ
يَحْذَرُوْنَ ﴿١٢٢﴾ ع ١٥

R.16 123. O ye who believe! [c]fight such of the disbelievers as are near[1225] to you and [d]let them find hardness in you; and know that Allāh is with the righteous.

يٰۤاَيُّهَا الَّذِيْنَ اٰمَنُوْا قَاتِلُوا الَّذِيْنَ يَلُوْنَكُمْ مِّنَ الْكُفَّارِ
وَلْيَجِدُوْا فِيْكُمْ غِلْظَةً وَاعْلَمُوْا اَنَّ اللّٰهَ مَعَ الْمُتَّقِيْنَ ﴿١٢٣﴾

[a]16 : 97-98 ; 24 : 39 ; 39 : 36. [b]3 : 105. [c]2 : 191. [d]48 : 30.

1224. As weakness in faith and in doing good works results from lack of true knowledge and training, the verse speaks of the way in which such weakness could be removed. The Arabs of the desert were quite ignorant of the teachings of Islām (9 : 97). The verse suggests a practical method of instructing them in the tenets and principles of the Faith.

1225. Refers to those Hypocrites who lived among Muslims and mixed with them. Muslims were enjoined to fight them as a class and not each and every one of them individually, and to fight them by exposing their malpractices and hypocritical deeds by bringing these to the notice of the Holy Prophet.

124. And whenever a *Sūrah* is sent down, there are some of them who say: 'Which of you has this *Sūrah* increased in faith?' But as to [a]those who believe, it increases their faith and they rejoice.

وَإِذَا مَآ أُنْزِلَتْ سُوْرَةٌ فَمِنْهُمْ مَّنْ يَّقُوْلُ أَيُّكُمْ زَادَتْهُ
هٰذِهٖٓ إِيْمَانًا ۚ فَأَمَّا الَّذِيْنَ اٰمَنُوْا فَزَادَتْهُمْ إِيْمَانًا
وَّهُمْ يَسْتَبْشِرُوْنَ ﴿١٢٤﴾

125. But *as for* [b]those in whose hearts is a disease, it adds *further* uncleanness to their *present* uncleanness and they die while they are disbelievers.

وَأَمَّا الَّذِيْنَ فِيْ قُلُوْبِهِمْ مَّرَضٌ فَزَادَتْهُمْ رِجْسًا
إِلٰى رِجْسِهِمْ وَمَاتُوْا وَهُمْ كٰفِرُوْنَ ﴿١٢٥﴾

126. Do they not see that they are tried every year once or twice?[1226] Yet they do not repent, nor do they take heed.

أَوَلَا يَرَوْنَ أَنَّهُمْ يُفْتَنُوْنَ فِيْ كُلِّ عَامٍ مَّرَّةً أَوْ
مَرَّتَيْنِ ثُمَّ لَا يَتُوْبُوْنَ وَلَا هُمْ يَذَّكَّرُوْنَ ﴿١٢٦﴾

127. And whenever a *Sūrah* is sent down, [c]they look at one another, *saying*, 'Does anyone see you?' Then they turn away. [d]Allāh has turned away their hearts because they are a people who would not understand.

وَإِذَا مَآ أُنْزِلَتْ سُوْرَةٌ نَّظَرَ بَعْضُهُمْ إِلٰى بَعْضٍ ۭ هَلْ
يَرٰىكُمْ مِّنْ أَحَدٍ ثُمَّ انْصَرَفُوْا ۭ صَرَفَ اللّٰهُ قُلُوْبَهُمْ
بِأَنَّهُمْ قَوْمٌ لَّا يَفْقَهُوْنَ ﴿١٢٧﴾

128. Surely, a Messenger has come unto you from among yourselves; grievous to him is it that you should fall into trouble; *he is* ardently desirous of your *welfare*; *and* [e]to the believers *he is specially* compassionate *and* merciful.[1227]

لَقَدْ جَآءَكُمْ رَسُوْلٌ مِّنْ أَنْفُسِكُمْ عَزِيْزٌ عَلَيْهِ مَا
عَنِتُّمْ حَرِيْصٌ عَلَيْكُمْ بِالْمُؤْمِنِيْنَ رَءُوْفٌ
رَّحِيْمٌ ﴿١٢٨﴾

129. But if they turn away, say, [f]'Allāh is sufficient for me. There is no god but He. In Him do I put my trust, and He is the Lord of the mighty Throne?

فَإِنْ تَوَلَّوْا فَقُلْ حَسْبِيَ اللّٰهُ ۖ لَآ إِلٰهَ إِلَّا هُوَ ۭ
عَلَيْهِ تَوَكَّلْتُ وَهُوَ رَبُّ الْعَرْشِ الْعَظِيْمِ ﴿١٢٩﴾ ع ١٦ ٥

[a]8 : 3. [b]2 : 11. [c]24 : 64. [d]61 : 6. [e]9 : 61. [f]39 : 39; 21 : 23; 23 : 117; 27 : 27; 40 : 16.

1226. The verse helps to explain 9 : 101.

1227. This verse may apply to both believers and disbelievers—preferably to the former—the opening part of it applying to disbelievers and the closing part to believers. To disbelievers it seems to say: "It grieves the Prophet to see you fall into trouble, *i.e.*, although you subject him to all manner of persecution and privation, yet his heart is so full of the milk of human kindness that no amount of persecution on your part can make him bitter against you and make him wish you ill. He is so kind and sympathetic to you that he cannot bear to see you turn away from the path of righteousness and thus put yourselves in trouble." To believers it says: 'The Prophet is full of love, compassion and mercy for you, *i.e.*, he cheerfully shares with you your sorrows and afflictions. Moreover, like an affectionate father he treats you with extreme kindness and mercy.'

CHAPTER 10

YŪNUS

(Revealed before Hijrah)

Date and Place of Revelation

This *Sūrah* was revealed at Mecca in the late Meccan period, *i.e.*, in the last four or five years of the Prophet's stay there. Some Commentators have ascribed some of its verses to the Medinite period, but their opinion is not based on historical data. They seem to have drawn the inference merely from the subject-matter of those verses. The *Sūrah* derives its name from v. 99.

Subject-Matter

On pondering over the contents of the Qur'ān we notice that not only its verses are inter-related but also that every *Sūrah* possesses a subtle connection with the one preceding it and the one following it. Moreover, certain groups of Quranic Chapters are linked with other groups. Thus a perfect order runs throughout the whole of the Qur'ān. Its different Chapters are related to one another in more ways than one; and when their order and arrangement are considered, no doubt is left that the Qur'ān is indeed a great miracle of diction. The present *Sūrah* possesses a threefold connection with the preceding Chapter. First, it constitutes a continuation of the preceding Chapter. Two subjects were mentioned in its concluding portions: (*a*) The revelation of the Book and its denial (9 : 127); (*b*) the coming of a Messenger of God and the benefits derived from following his teaching (9 : 128). The same subject is continued in the present *Sūrah*. It mentions the importance of the Book (10 : 2) and it refers to the Divine Messenger (10 : 3). Secondly, the *Sūrah* completes the subject-matter of the preceding one. In that Chapter (which is not really a separate Chapter but is a part of Chapter 8) reference was made to the fact that the time of the prosperity and predominance of Islām had come and that God's promises were going to be fulfilled in all their glory and grandeur. So the believers were exhorted to attend to the purification of their hearts in order that their repentance might be accepted. As doubts might have arisen in the hearts of some people that on account of the enormity of their sins their repentance will not be accepted, the present Chapter removes that doubt and stresses the fact that God's mercy encompasses and transcends all things, though it requires the highest form of repentance to attract it. Thirdly, all the Chapters of the Qur'ān from Chapter 2 to Chapter 9 (which are really seven in number; for, as stated above, Chapter 9 is not a separate Chapter but forms part of Chapter 8 and was written separately only on account of the special importance of its subject-matter) deal with one group of subjects, while with this Chapter begins a new group of *Sūrahs*, ending with Chapter 18. This second group deals with a distinct and separate theme, yet its subject-matter is closely connected with that of the first group. In the first group the truth of Islām is established by reference to the Holy Prophet and his work, and an appeal is made for the acceptance of Islām in view of the superiority of its principles, the excellence of its teachings, the vastness of the spiritual knowledge which it holds out to seekers after truth, the wisdom underlying its teachings and its extraordinary influence. In the second group, comprising Chapters 10—18, emphasis is laid on the need of Prophethood, the importance of religion and on the object of the Holy Prophet's advent, by referring particularly to the criteria and characteristics of Prophethood, the claims and history of previous Prophets and to the arguments based on, and supported by, human reason and commonsense.

Thus the subject-matter of the two groups is very closely linked and related to each other, the only difference being that whereas in the first group reference is made to the prophecies which were made at the advent of the Holy Prophet or which had been made by previous Prophets and were fulfilled in due time, thus bearing witness to the truth of the Holy Prophet; in the second group the truth of Islām has been explained on its own merits and on the basis of the canons of Prophethood.

سُوْرَةُ يُوْنُسَ مَكِّيَّةٌ

1. [a]In the name of Allāh, the Gracious, the Merciful.

بِسْمِ اللّٰهِ الرَّحْمٰنِ الرَّحِيْمِ ﴿۱﴾

2. [b]Alif Lām Rā.[1228] [c]These[1229] are the verses of the Book, full of wisdom.[1230]

الٓرٰ تِلْكَ اٰيٰتُ الْكِتٰبِ الْحَكِيْمِ ﴿۲﴾

3. [d]Is it *a matter of* wonder for men that We have sent down revelation to a man from among them, *saying*, 'Warn mankind and give glad tidings to those who believe that they have a true rank[1231] *of honour* with their Lord?' The disbelievers say, 'Surely, this is a manifest sorcerer.'[1231A]

اَكَانَ لِلنَّاسِ عَجَبًا اَنْ اَوْحَيْنَآ اِلٰى رَجُلٍ مِّنْهُمْ اَنْ اَنْذِرِ النَّاسَ وَ بَشِّرِ الَّذِيْنَ اٰمَنُوْٓا اَنَّ لَهُمْ قَدَمَ صِدْقٍ عِنْدَ رَبِّهِمْ ۘؔ قَالَ الْكٰفِرُوْنَ اِنَّ هٰذَا لَسٰحِرٌ مُّبِيْنٌ ﴿۳﴾

[a]See 1:1. [b]11:2; 12:2; 13:2; 14:2; 15:2. [c]26:3; 27:2; 31:3. [d]7:64,70; 50:3.

1228. See 16.

1229. *Tilka* is a demonstrative pronoun used to indicate something distant. The word is said to have been used in reference to those verses of the previous Scriptures which contained prophecies about the Qur'ān and which saw their fulfilment in the Quranic verses. While according to some Commentators God had with Him the complete Book written beforehand and it was out of that Heavenly Book that He revealed verses from time to time and the reference is to that original Book with God, according to others the pronoun denotes the remoteness of the Qur'ān in respect of its high rank and is meant to express the great eminence of the verses of the Qur'ān.

1230. The words 'full of wisdom' point to three distinctive qualities of the Qur'ān: (*a*) It is full of wisdom, inasmuch as it comprises the basis of all spiritual knowledge and inculcates all truths; (*b*) it embodies teachings suited to all occasions and circumstances; and (*c*) it gives right judgment in all religious differences.

1231. *Qadam* means, preference; rank; footing. They say *la-hū 'indī Qadamun*, *i.e.*, there is strength or rank for him with me (Lane).

1231A. The verse brings to light the important fact that those, who become morally depraved, lose all sense of self-respect as well as all confidence in themselves, for here the disbelievers are represented as so degenerate that they could not imagine that anyone from among themselves could come and rescue them from the morass of degradation into which they had fallen, and that only someone from outside could improve their condition.

4. Verily, your Lord is Allāh Who created [a]the heavens and the earth in six periods,[1232] then [b]He settled[1232A] Himself *firmly* on the Throne;[1233] [c]He governs everything.[1234] There is no [d]intercessor *with Him* save after His permission. This is Allāh, your Lord, so worship Him. Will you not, then, mind?

إِنَّ رَبَّكُمُ اللّٰهُ الَّذِيْ خَلَقَ السَّمٰوٰتِ وَالْاَرْضَ فِيْ
سِتَّةِ اَيَّامٍ ثُمَّ اسْتَوٰى عَلَى الْعَرْشِ يُدَبِّرُ الْاَمْرَ ؕ مَا
مِنْ شَفِيْعٍ اِلَّا مِنْۢ بَعْدِ اِذْنِهٖ ؕ ذٰلِكُمُ اللّٰهُ رَبُّكُمْ
فَاعْبُدُوْهُ ؕ اَفَلَا تَذَكَّرُوْنَ ۝٤

5. [e]To Him shall you all return. The promise of Allāh is true. Surely, [f]He originates the creation; then He reproduces[1235] it, that He may reward those, who believe and do good works, with equity; and *as for* those who disbelieve, they shall have boiling water to drink and a painful punishment, because they disbelieved.

اِلَيْهِ مَرْجِعُكُمْ جَمِيْعًا ؕ وَعْدَ اللّٰهِ حَقًّا ؕ اِنَّهٗ يَبْدَؤُا
الْخَلْقَ ثُمَّ يُعِيْدُهٗ لِيَجْزِيَ الَّذِيْنَ اٰمَنُوْا وَعَمِلُوا
الصّٰلِحٰتِ بِالْقِسْطِ ؕ وَالَّذِيْنَ كَفَرُوْا لَهُمْ شَرَابٌ مِّنْ
حَمِيْمٍ وَّعَذَابٌ اَلِيْمٌۢ بِمَا كَانُوْا يَكْفُرُوْنَ ۝٥

[a]7:55; 11 : 8 ; 25 : 60 ; 32 : 5. [b]13 : 3 ; 20 : 6; 32 : 5. [c]32 : 6. [d]2 : 256; 32 : 5.
[e]6 : 165 ; 11: 5 ; 39 : 8. [f]10 : 35 ; 27: 65 ; 29 : 20 ; 30: 12,28.

1232. See 984.

1232A. See 54.

1233. The word *'Arsh* represents God's transcendant attributes which are His exclusive prerogatives. These attributes are manifested through God's attributes of similitude which have been described in 69 : 18 as 'the bearers of God's Throne.' See 986.

1234. The words, *He governs everything*, point to the working of the universe and to the means which God uses to fulfil His decree and manifest His Will.

1235. Not only after death will man be given a new life in which his actions in this worldly life will be judged and requited; but in the present life also one generation of men is succeeded by another so that the good works of the former may not be wasted and may benefit the latter. *Ṣāliḥāt*, besides meaning good and righteous works, means works done in conformity with the exigencies of specific occasions and circumstances.

6. [a]He it is Who made the sun *radiate* a brilliant light[1236] and the moon *reflect* a lustre, and ordained for it *proper* stages, that [b]you might know the count of years and the reckoning[1237] *of time*. Allāh has not created this *system* but in accordance with the requirements of truth. He details the Signs for a people who possess knowledge.

هُوَ الَّذِيْ جَعَلَ الشَّمْسَ ضِيَآءً وَّالْقَمَرَ نُوْرًا وَّ
قَدَّرَهٗ مَنَازِلَ لِتَعْلَمُوْا عَدَدَ السِّنِيْنَ وَالْحِسَابَ ۭ مَا
خَلَقَ اللّٰهُ ذٰلِكَ اِلَّا بِالْحَقِّ ۚ يُفَصِّلُ الْاٰيٰتِ لِقَوْمٍ
يَّعْلَمُوْنَ ۞

7. Verily, [c]in the alternation of night and day, and in all that Allāh has created in the heavens and the earth there are Signs for a God-fearing people.[1238]

اِنَّ فِي اخْتِلَافِ الَّيْلِ وَالنَّهَارِ وَمَا خَلَقَ اللّٰهُ فِي
السَّمٰوٰتِ وَالْاَرْضِ لَاٰيٰتٍ لِّقَوْمٍ يَّتَّقُوْنَ ۞

[a]25 : 62; 71 : 17. [b]17 : 13. [c]2 : 165; 3 : 191; 23 : 81.

1236. *Diyā'* means, light; bright or brilliant light. The word is synonymous with *Nūr* though, according to some, it has a more intensive signification than *Nūr*. Some lexicologists consider *Diyā'* as signifying the rays that are diffused by what is termed *Nūr*. According to others *Diyā'* signifies that light which subsists by itself as that of the sun or of fire, and *Nūr* that which subsists by some other thing as the light of the moon, *i.e.*, reflected light (Lane & Aqrab). The fact appears to be that whereas *Diyā'* signifies strong light, *Nūr* is a more general term denoting light as opposed to darkness. This is why *Nūr* is one of the names of God.. It is also more extensive and more penetrating as well as more lasting in its significance (Muḥīṭ).

1237. The verse points to a very wise natural law. We can judge the size of space traversed by a body only by the change of its position relative to other bodies. God has appointed stages for the sun and the moon that we may be able to make a reckoning of time. In other words, He has caused these heavenly bodies to move and has appointed stages for their motion so that by observing the motion we may be able to know that a certain amount of time has passed and that we have moved on from our original position. All reckoning and all calendars depend on the movements of the sun and the moon. The moon moves round the earth and thereby we are able to know the measures of months. The earth moves round the sun and also rotates on its own axis, thus enabling us to measure our years as well as our days.

1238. In the present verse the words, *for a God-fearing people*, have been substituted for the expression, *for a people who possess knowledge*, in the preceding verse. This is because though the natural phenomenon of the alternation of day and night is known even to an ignorant person, it is only the God-fearing that derive real spiritual benefit from a reverential study of it. Also, the ordaining of various stages for the moon and the sun, to which the preceding verse referred was not so easy a thing as to be perceived and understood by each and every person and therefore only those endowed with knowledge could benefit by it. Moreover, the phenomenon of the alternation of day and night resembles the rise and fall of nations. The days of their glory and prosperity are followed by the nights of their decline and degradation. No nation has ever enjoyed perpetual glory, nor has any people for ever floundered and groped in the darkness of degradation and decline. A people may make their day of prosperity long and shorten their night of decline. It is also within their power to delay the coming of their night.

8. "Those who hope[1239] not for the meeting with Us and are pleased and satisfied with the life of this world and those who are heedless of Our Signs—

اِنَّ الَّذِيْنَ لَا يَرْجُوْنَ لِقَآءَنَا وَرَضُوْا بِالْحَيٰوةِ الدُّنْيَا وَاطْمَاَنُّوْا بِهَا وَالَّذِيْنَ هُمْ عَنْ اٰيٰتِنَا غٰفِلُوْنَ ۞

9. It is these whose abode is Fire, because of what they earned.

اُولٰٓئِكَ مَأْوٰىهُمُ النَّارُ بِمَا كَانُوْا يَكْسِبُوْنَ ۞

10. *As for* those ᵇwho believe, and do good works—their Lord shall guide them *along the path of success* because of their faith. Streams shall flow beneath[1240] them in the Gardens of Bliss.

اِنَّ الَّذِيْنَ اٰمَنُوْا وَعَمِلُوا الصّٰلِحٰتِ يَهْدِيْهِمْ رَبُّهُمْ بِاِيْمَانِهِمْ ۚ تَجْرِىْ مِنْ تَحْتِهِمُ الْاَنْهٰرُ فِىْ جَنّٰتِ النَّعِيْمِ ۞

11. Their prayer therein shall be, 'Glory be to Thee, O Allāh!'[1241] and ᶜtheir greeting therein *to each other* shall be, 'Peace!' And the end of their prayer shall be, 'All praise be to Allāh, the Lord of the worlds.'

دَعْوٰىهُمْ فِيْهَا سُبْحٰنَكَ اللّٰهُمَّ وَتَحِيَّتُهُمْ فِيْهَا سَلٰمٌ ۚ وَاٰخِرُ دَعْوٰىهُمْ اَنِ الْحَمْدُ لِلّٰهِ رَبِّ الْعٰلَمِيْنَ ۞

---

10 : 12, 46; 25 : 22. ᵇ2 : 278; 4 : 176; 13 : 30; 14 : 24; 22 : 15,24. ᶜ14 : 24; 36 : 59.

1239. The study of human nature reveals the important fact that all human progress is bound up with the instincts of hope and fear. Our best efforts are inspired by one or other of these two instincts. Some persons labour and sweat, actuated by hope of acquisition and aggrandizement; others work out of fear. The present verse makes an appeal to both these classes of men by using the word *Rajā* which means, he hoped; he feared (Lane).

1240. The word, *taht* (beneath), is used here figuratively denoting subordination. In this sense of the word the expression, *beneath them*, would signify that the inmates of Heaven will be the masters and owners of its streams and not merely their users as tenants or occupiers.

1241. The glorification of God will be spontaneous and instinctive, because in Heaven the reality of things will become manifest to men and they will realize that every work of God was based on deep wisdom. This realization will make them exclaim instinctively and spontaneously, *Glory be to Thee, O Allāh*. The verse also indicates that the ultimate end of the believers is always happy. They give expression to their joy by proclaiming the glory of God.

R. 2 12. And [a]if Allāh were to hasten for men the ill *consequences of their actions* as they would seek to hasten on the good,[1242] *the end of* their term *of life* would have been already brought upon them. But [b]We leave those who look not for the meeting with Us to wander distractedly in their transgression.

وَلَوْ يُعَجِّلُ اللّٰهُ لِلنَّاسِ الشَّرَّ اسْتِعْجَالَهُمْ بِالْخَيْرِ
لَقُضِيَ إِلَيْهِمْ أَجَلُهُمْ ۖ فَنَذَرُ الَّذِينَ لَا يَرْجُونَ لِقَاءَنَا
فِي طُغْيَانِهِمْ يَعْمَهُونَ ﴿١٢﴾

13. And [c]when trouble befalls a man, he calls on Us, *lying* on his side, or sitting or standing, but when We have removed his trouble from him, he goes his way as though he had never called on Us for *the removal* of the trouble that befell him. Thus it is that the doings of the extravagant are made to seem fair in their eyes.

وَإِذَا مَسَّ الْإِنْسَانَ الضُّرُّ دَعَانَا لِجَنْبِهِ أَوْ قَاعِدًا
أَوْ قَائِمًا ۚ فَلَمَّا كَشَفْنَا عَنْهُ ضُرَّهُ مَرَّ كَأَنْ لَمْ يَدْعُنَا
إِلَىٰ ضُرٍّ مَسَّهُ ۚ كَذَٰلِكَ زُيِّنَ لِلْمُسْرِفِينَ مَا كَانُوا
يَعْمَلُونَ ﴿١٣﴾

14. And [d]We destroyed many generations[1243] before you when they did wrong; and there came to them their Messengers with clear Signs, but they would not believe. Thus do We requite the guilty people.

وَلَقَدْ أَهْلَكْنَا الْقُرُونَ مِنْ قَبْلِكُمْ لَمَّا ظَلَمُوا ۙ
وَجَاءَتْهُمْ رُسُلُهُمْ بِالْبَيِّنَاتِ وَمَا كَانُوا لِيُؤْمِنُوا ۚ
كَذَٰلِكَ نَجْزِي الْقَوْمَ الْمُجْرِمِينَ ﴿١٤﴾

15. Then, [e]We made you *their* successors in the earth after them that We might see how you would act.

ثُمَّ جَعَلْنَاكُمْ خَلَائِفَ فِي الْأَرْضِ مِنْ بَعْدِهِمْ لِنَنْظُرَ
كَيْفَ تَعْمَلُونَ ﴿١٥﴾

[a]17 : 12. [b]See 10 : 8. [c]30 : 34; 39 : 9, 50. [d]6: 7; 20: 129; 32: 27. [e]2: 31 ; 7: 130.

1242. The word *Khair* also meaning wealth (Lane), the verse means that disbelievers direct all their energies to the earning of wealth, and neglect God altogether. Their conduct demands that evil should overtake them. But God is slow to punish. If He had been as quick in punishing them as their conduct deserves, they would have been destroyed long ago. If the word *Khair* be taken in the sense of 'good' as in the text, the verse would mean that if God were as quick to inflict punishment on disbelievers for their evil deeds as He is to bestow good, then they would already have been destroyed.

1243. Punishments are of two kinds: (1) Those that are the result of the contravention of the laws of nature, and (2) those that come when the law of the *Shari'ah* is flouted. The latter class of punishments overtake a people when they lead wicked lives, or when a Prophet appears among them and they reject him and put all sorts of obstacles in his way. Punishments of this kind are known by certain characteristics. Other class of punishments, such as the rise and fall of nations, come as the result of the contravention of the ordinary laws of nature.

16. And When Our clear Signs are recited unto them, [a]those who hope not for the meeting with Us say, [b]'Bring a Qur'ān other than this or change it.' Say, 'It is not for me to change it of my own accord. I only [c]follow what is revealed to me. Indeed, I fear, if I disobey my Lord, the punishment of an awful day.'[1244]

وَإِذَا تُتْلَىٰ عَلَيْهِمْ آيَاتُنَا بَيِّنَاتٍ ۙ قَالَ الَّذِينَ لَا يَرْجُونَ
لِقَاءَنَا ائْتِ بِقُرْآنٍ غَيْرِ هَٰذَا أَوْ بَدِّلْهُ ۚ قُلْ مَا يَكُونُ
لِي أَنْ أُبَدِّلَهُ مِنْ تِلْقَاءِ نَفْسِي ۖ إِنْ أَتَّبِعُ إِلَّا مَا يُوحَىٰ
إِلَيَّ ۖ إِنِّي أَخَافُ إِنْ عَصَيْتُ رَبِّي عَذَابَ يَوْمٍ عَظِيمٍ ﴿١٦﴾

17. Say, 'If Allāh had *so* willed, I should not have recited it to you, nor would He have made it known to you. I have indeed lived among you a *whole* lifetime before this. Will you not then understand?[1245]

قُلْ لَوْ شَاءَ اللَّهُ مَا تَلَوْتُهُ عَلَيْكُمْ وَلَا أَدْرَاكُمْ بِهِ ۖ
فَقَدْ لَبِثْتُ فِيكُمْ عُمُرًا مِنْ قَبْلِهِ ۚ أَفَلَا تَعْقِلُونَ ﴿١٧﴾

18. [d]Who is then more unjust than he who forges a lie against Allāh or he who treats His Signs as lies? Surely, the guilty shall never prosper.[1246]

فَمَنْ أَظْلَمُ مِمَّنِ افْتَرَىٰ عَلَى اللَّهِ كَذِبًا أَوْ كَذَّبَ بِآيَاتِهِ ۚ
إِنَّهُ لَا يُفْلِحُ الْمُجْرِمُونَ ﴿١٨﴾

[a]See 10 : 8. [b]17: 74. [c]6 : 51 ; 7: 204; 46 : 10. [d]6: 22 ; 11: 19 ; 61: 8.

1244. 'Punishment of an awful day' signifies a national disaster.

1245. The verse embodies an infallible criterion to test the truth of a claimant to Prophethood. If the life of a Prophet before he lays claim to Prophethood presents an extraordinarily high standard of truthfulness and integrity and between that period and his claim to Prophethood there is no interval during which it might be supposed that he has fallen from that high standard of moral excellence, then his claim to Prophethood must be accepted as that of a highly moral and truthful man. Naturally, a person confirmed in a certain course of conduct through habit or temperament takes a long time to develop in himself a major change for either good or evil. How then could the Prophet of Islām suddenly turn into an impostor when all his lifetime before his claim to Prophethood he had been a singularly upright man?

1246. The verse brings to light two eternal truths : (*a*) Those persons who invent lies about God and those who reject and oppose His Messengers can never escape God's punishment. (*b*) Impostors and false prophets cannot succeed in their mission.

19. And [a]they worship, instead of Allāh, that which neither harms them nor profits them; and they say, 'These are our intercessors with Allāh.'[1247] Say, [b]'Do you *presume to* inform Allāh of what He knows not in the heavens or in the earth? Glory be to Him! High be He exalted above *all* that which they associate *with Him*.

وَيَعْبُدُونَ مِنْ دُونِ اللّٰهِ مَا لَا يَضُرُّهُمْ وَلَا يَنْفَعُهُمْ وَيَقُولُونَ هٰٓؤُلَآءِ شُفَعَآؤُنَا عِنْدَ اللّٰهِ ۚ قُلْ أَتُنَبِّـُٔونَ اللّٰهَ بِمَا لَا يَعْلَمُ فِي السَّمٰوٰتِ وَلَا فِي الْأَرْضِ ۚ سُبْحٰنَهٗ وَتَعٰلٰى عَمَّا يُشْرِكُونَ ﴿١٩﴾

20. And [c]mankind were but one community,[1247A] then they differed[1248] *among themselves*; [d]and had it not been for a word[1248A] that had gone before from thy Lord, it would have *already* been decided between them concerning that in which they differed.

وَمَا كَانَ النَّاسُ إِلَّآ أُمَّةً وَّاحِدَةً فَاخْتَلَفُوْا ۚ وَلَوْلَا كَلِمَةٌ سَبَقَتْ مِنْ رَّبِّكَ لَقُضِيَ بَيْنَهُمْ فِيمَا فِيهِ يَخْتَلِفُونَ ﴿٢٠﴾

21. And they say, [e]'Why has not a Sign been sent down to him from his Lord? Say, 'The *knowledge of* the unseen belongs only to Allāh. So wait. I am with you among those who wait?'[1249]

وَيَقُولُونَ لَوْلَآ أُنْزِلَ عَلَيْهِ اٰيَةٌ مِّنْ رَّبِّهٖ ۚ فَقُلْ إِنَّمَا الْغَيْبُ لِلّٰهِ فَانْتَظِرُوْٓا ۚ إِنِّي مَعَكُمْ مِّنَ الْمُنْتَظِرِينَ ﴿٢١﴾ ع ٢

[a]16:74; 22:72; 29:18. [b]49:17. [c]2:214. [d]11:111; 20:130; 41:46 [e]6:38.

1247. The real cause of *Shirk* (idolatry) lies in failure on the part of idolaters to understand the object and purpose of their creation. A *Mushrik* (idolater) has a false conception of the person and attributes of God and also of his own great inborn God-given capacities and capabilities. He entertains the foolish belief that he cannot have access to God without the aid of an intermediary, and also that God cannot condescend to come to him except through the medium of those who have already attained His nearness. Islām is emphatically opposed to both these views.

1247A. They were united in wickedness and opposition to Divine Prophets. See also 254.

1248. The words may have one and all of the following meanings: (*a*) God endowed men with the capacity to find the right path and also directed them to it through revealed guidance, but they forsook that path and fell into error. (*b*) They are always shown the right path through Divine Messengers, but they continue to differ among themselves. (*c*) In their opposition to the Divine Messengers the disbelievers always take the same course and thus form one community. All through the ages they have opposed the Divine Prophets and differed with them. See 255.

1248A. The reference is to 'My Mercy encompasses all things' (7 : 157).

1249. The verse contains an effective reply to the disbelievers' demand for the coming of a speedy punishment. The Holy Prophet is told to say to them that it is he and not they who should have been impatient at the delay in the coming of the threatened punishment; for it is he who is being subjected to mocking for this delay; and when he is patiently waiting for God's decree, why should not they ?

R. 3 22. And [a]when We make people taste of mercy after adversity has touched them, behold! [b]they begin *to devise* plans against Our Signs.[1250] Say, 'Allāh is *far* swifter in planning.' Surely, Our messengers write down all that you plan.

وَإِذَآ أَذَقْنَا النَّاسَ رَحْمَةً مِّنْ بَعْدِ ضَرَّآءَ مَسَّتْهُمْ
إِذَا لَهُمْ مَّكْرٌ فِيْٓ اٰيَاتِنَا ۭ قُلِ اللّٰهُ اَسْرَعُ مَكْرًا ۭ اِنَّ
رُسُلَنَا يَكْتُبُوْنَ مَا تَمْكُرُوْنَ ﴿٢٢﴾

23. He it is Who enables you to journey through land and sea until [c]when you are on *board* the ships and they sail with them with a fair breeze and they rejoice in it, there overtakes them (the ships) a violent wind and the waves come on them from every side and they think that they are encompassed, then they call upon Allāh, in sincere submission to Him, *saying*, 'If Thou deliver us from this, we will surely be of the thankful.'[1251]

هُوَ الَّذِيْ يُسَيِّرُكُمْ فِي الْبَرِّ وَالْبَحْرِ ۭ حَتّٰٓى اِذَا كُنْتُمْ
فِي الْفُلْكِ ۚ وَجَرَيْنَ بِهِمْ بِرِيْحٍ طَيِّبَةٍ وَّفَرِحُوْا بِهَا
جَآءَتْهَا رِيْحٌ عَاصِفٌ وَّجَآءَهُمُ الْمَوْجُ مِنْ كُلِّ
مَكَانٍ وَّظَنُّوْٓا اَنَّهُمْ اُحِيْطَ بِهِمْ ۙ دَعَوُا اللّٰهَ مُخْلِصِيْنَ
لَهُ الدِّيْنَ ۥ لَئِنْ اَنْجَيْتَنَا مِنْ هٰذِهٖ لَنَكُوْنَنَّ مِنَ
الشّٰكِرِيْنَ ﴿٢٣﴾

24. But [d]when He has delivered them, lo! they begin to commit excesses in the earth wrongfully. O ye people, [e]your excesses *in seeking* the enjoyment of the present life are only against your own selves. Then to Us shall be your return; and We will inform you of what you used to do.

فَلَمَّآ اَنْجٰىهُمْ اِذَا هُمْ يَبْغُوْنَ فِي الْاَرْضِ بِغَيْرِ الْحَقِّ ۭ
يٰٓاَيُّهَا النَّاسُ اِنَّمَا بَغْيُكُمْ عَلٰٓى اَنْفُسِكُمْ ۙ مَّتَاعَ الْحَيٰوةِ
الدُّنْيَا ۡ ثُمَّ اِلَيْنَا مَرْجِعُكُمْ فَنُنَبِّئُكُمْ بِمَا كُنْتُمْ
تَعْمَلُوْنَ ﴿٢٤﴾

[a]30 : 37; 41 : 51, 52; 42 : 49. [b]8 : 31; 35 : 44. [c]17 : 67; 29 : 66; 31 : 33. [d]17 : 68; 31 : 33. [e]35 : 44.

1250. Mercy comes from God, but adversity is the result of man's own evil deeds.

1251. As a pleasant breeze sometimes develops into a violent gale and causes widespread destruction, similarly, the respite that is granted to disbelievers may prove the prelude to their destruction. To bring home to disbelievers this patent truth, their attention is drawn to the comforts and perils of a sea-voyage.

25. [a]"The likeness of the present life is only as water which We send down from the clouds, then there mingles with it the produce of the earth, of which men and cattle eat till when the earth takes on its ornament and looks beautiful and its owners think that they have *full* power over it, [b]there comes to it Our command by night or by day and We render it like a mown down field, as if [c]nothing had existed there the day before.[1252] Thus do We expound the Signs for a people who reflect.

إِنَّمَا مَثَلُ الْحَيٰوةِ الدُّنْيَا كَمَآءٍ أَنْزَلْنٰهُ مِنَ السَّمَآءِ
فَاخْتَلَطَ بِهٖ نَبَاتُ الْاَرْضِ مِمَّا يَأْكُلُ النَّاسُ وَ
الْاَنْعَامُ حَتّٰىٓ إِذَآ اَخَذَتِ الْاَرْضُ زُخْرُفَهَا وَ
ازَّيَّنَتْ وَظَنَّ اَهْلُهَآ اَنَّهُمْ قٰدِرُوْنَ عَلَيْهَآ اَتٰهَآ
اَمْرُنَا لَيْلًا اَوْ نَهَارًا فَجَعَلْنٰهَا حَصِيْدًا كَاَنْ لَّمْ تَغْنَ
بِالْاَمْسِ كَذٰلِكَ نُفَصِّلُ الْاٰيٰتِ لِقَوْمٍ يَّتَفَكَّرُوْنَ ﴿٢٥﴾

26. And [d]Allāh calls to the abode of peace,[1253] and guides whom He pleases to the straight path.

وَاللّٰهُ يَدْعُوْٓا اِلٰى دَارِ السَّلٰمِ وَيَهْدِيْ مَنْ يَّشَآءُ
اِلٰى صِرَاطٍ مُّسْتَقِيْمٍ ﴿٢٦﴾

27. [e]For those who do good deeds, there shall be the best[1254] *reward* and *yet* more *blessings*.[1255] And [f]neither darkness nor ignominy shall cover their faces. It is these who are the inmates of Heaven; therein shall they abide.

لِلَّذِيْنَ اَحْسَنُوا الْحُسْنٰى وَ زِيَادَةٌ وَلَا يَرْهَقُ وُجُوْهَهُمْ
قَتَرٌ وَّلَا ذِلَّةٌ اُولٰٓئِكَ اَصْحٰبُ الْجَنَّةِ هُمْ فِيْهَا
خٰلِدُوْنَ ﴿٢٧﴾

[a]18 : 46. [b]3 : 118. [c]11 : 69. [d]6 : 128. [e]50 : 36. [f]75 : 23, 24.

1252. The moral of the parable is that when nations become proud and vain and take life lightly, their decline sets in and they come to grief.

1253. *Salām* means, safety, security; immunity or freedom from faults or defects, imperfections, blemishes or vice ; or it means peace ; obedience ; Heaven. *Salām* is also one of the names of God (Lane).

1254. *Al-Husnā* meaning, a happy end; victory; keenness and activeness, the clause would signify, (1) that believers will come to a happy end ; (2) that they will attain success, and (3) that God will make them keen and active.

1255. The word *Ziyādah* (yet more) signifies that believers will have God Himself as their reward, and the word *al-Husnā* (also meaning the sight of God) confirms this inference.

28. And *as for* those who do evil deeds, [a]the punishment of an evil shall be the like thereof, and [b]ignominy shall cover them. They shall have none to protect them from Allāh. *And they shall look* as if their faces had been covered with dark patches of night.[1256] It is these who are the inmates of Fire; therein shall they abide.

وَالَّذِينَ كَسَبُوا السَّيِّاٰتِ جَزَآءُ سَيِّئَةٍۭ بِمِثْلِهَا وَ
تَرْهَقُهُمْ ذِلَّةٌ ؕ مَا لَهُمْ مِّنَ اللّٰهِ مِنْ عَاصِمٍ ۚ كَاَنَّمَآ
اُغْشِيَتْ وُجُوْهُهُمْ قِطَعًا مِّنَ الَّيْلِ مُظْلِمًا ؕ اُولٰٓئِكَ
اَصْحٰبُ النَّارِ ۚ هُمْ فِيْهَا خٰلِدُوْنَ ﴿٢٨﴾

29. And *remember* the day [c]when We shall gather them all together, then shall We say to those who associated other gods *with Us*, '*Stand back in* your places, you and your associate-gods.' Then We shall separate them widely one from another, and their associate-gods will say, [d]'Surely, it was not us that you worshipped;

وَيَوْمَ نَحْشُرُهُمْ جَمِيْعًا ثُمَّ نَقُوْلُ لِلَّذِيْنَ اَشْرَكُوْا
مَكَانَكُمْ اَنْتُمْ وَشُرَكَآؤُكُمْ ۚ فَزَيَّلْنَا بَيْنَهُمْ وَ قَالَ
شُرَكَآؤُهُمْ مَّا كُنْتُمْ اِيَّانَا تَعْبُدُوْنَ ﴿٢٩﴾

30. 'So Allāh is *now* sufficient as a Witness between us and you. [e]We were certainly unaware of your worship.'

فَكَفٰى بِاللّٰهِ شَهِيْدًۢا بَيْنَنَا وَ بَيْنَكُمْ اِنْ كُنَّا عَنْ
عِبَادَتِكُمْ لَغٰفِلِيْنَ ﴿٣٠﴾

[a]42 : 41. [b]68 : 44; 75 : 25; 80 : 41, 42; 88 : 3, 4.
[c]6 : 23; 46 : 7. [d]16 : 87; 28 : 64. [e]46 : 6.

1256. The verse embodies several important truths: (*a*) Whereas the reward of good is manifold (see preceding verse), the reward of evil is only the like thereof. (*b*) Those who break the laws of God cease to be inspired by high ideals and noble ambitions and become mere imitators of others, losing all initiative and never aspiring to be the leaders of men. (*c*) Having thus fallen and incurred the displeasure of God, they forfeit His succour. (*d*) The iniquities and transgressions of evil-doers cannot long remain hidden and sooner or later become exposed.

31. ªThere shall every soul realize[1257] what it shall have sent on before. And they shall be brought back to Allāh, their True Master, and all that they used to forge shall be lost to them.

هُنَالِكَ تَبْلُوْا كُلُّ نَفْسٍ مَّآ اَسْلَفَتْ وَرُدُّوْٓا اِلَى اللّٰهِ مَوْلٰهُمُ الْحَقِّ وَضَلَّ عَنْهُمْ مَّا كَانُوْا يَفْتَرُوْنَ ۝

R. 4   32. Say, ᵇ"Who provides sustenance for you from the heaven and the earth? Or who is it that has power over the ears and the eyes? And ᶜwho brings forth the living from the dead and brings forth the dead from the living? And ᵈwho regulates[1258] all affairs?' They will say, 'Allāh.' Then say, 'Will you not then seek His protection?'

قُلْ مَنْ يَّرْزُقُكُمْ مِّنَ السَّمَآءِ وَالْاَرْضِ اَمَّنْ يَّمْلِكُ السَّمْعَ وَالْاَبْصَارَ وَمَنْ يُّخْرِجُ الْحَيَّ مِنَ الْمَيِّتِ وَيُخْرِجُ الْمَيِّتَ مِنَ الْحَيِّ وَمَنْ يُّدَبِّرُ الْاَمْرَ فَسَيَقُوْلُوْنَ اللّٰهُ ۚ فَقُلْ اَفَلَا تَتَّقُوْنَ ۝

33. Such is Allāh, your True Lord. So what is there other than the truth but error? How then are you being turned away from the truth?

فَذٰلِكُمُ اللّٰهُ رَبُّكُمُ الْحَقُّ ۚ فَمَاذَا بَعْدَ الْحَقِّ اِلَّا الضَّلٰلُ ۚ فَاَنّٰى تُصْرَفُوْنَ ۝

34. ᵉThus is the word of thy Lord proved true against those who rebel, that they believe not.

كَذٰلِكَ حَقَّتْ كَلِمَتُ رَبِّكَ عَلَى الَّذِيْنَ فَسَقُوْٓا اَنَّهُمْ لَا يُؤْمِنُوْنَ ۝

ª86 : 10.   ᵇ27 : 65;   34 : 25;   35 : 4.   ᶜ3 : 28;   6 : 96.   ᵈ10 : 4.
ᵉ10 : 97;   40 : 7

1257. It is not given to man fully to comprehend and realize the reality of things in this world. It is only in the next world that the veil shall be completely lifted from all things and their real nature will come to light.

1258. There exists a beautiful and intelligent order in this verse. It begins with a reference to sustenance, which is the means of the preservation of physical life. Then it speaks of the organs of sight and hearing, which are the means of acquiring wisdom and knowledge. After that it speaks of the system of life and death, pointing to man's incentive to action which naturally comes into operation after the acquirement of wisdom and understanding. Last of all, it speaks of the government or management of affairs which is needed when one begins to exercise his power of action, *Tadbīr*, meaning conducting an affair in an ordered and regulated manner and maintaining proper balance between different acts. In short, all the four means which are needed for the achievement of the purpose of man's life have been mentioned here in their natural order.

35. Say, 'Is there any of your associate-gods [a]who originates creation and then reproduces it?' Say, 'It is Allāh *alone* Who originates creation and then reproduces it.[1259] Whither then are you turned away?'

قُلْ هَلْ مِنْ شُرَكَآئِكُمْ مَّنْ يَّبْدَؤُا الْخَلْقَ ثُمَّ
يُعِيْدُهٗ ؕ قُلِ اللّٰهُ يَبْدَؤُا الْخَلْقَ ثُمَّ يُعِيْدُهٗ فَاَنّٰى
تُؤْفَكُوْنَ ﴿۳۵﴾

36. Say, 'Is there any of your associate-gods who guides to the truth?' Say, 'It is Allāh *alone* Who guides to the truth. Is then He Who guides to the truth more worthy to be followed, or he who finds not the way *himself* unless he be guided? What, then, is the matter with you? How judge ye?'

قُلْ هَلْ مِنْ شُرَكَآئِكُمْ مَّنْ يَّهْدِيْۤ اِلَى الْحَقِّ ؕ قُلِ
اللّٰهُ يَهْدِيْ لِلْحَقِّ ؕ اَفَمَنْ يَّهْدِيْۤ اِلَى الْحَقِّ اَحَقُّ
اَنْ يُّتَّبَعَ اَمَّنْ لَّا يَهِدِّيْۤ اِلَّاۤ اَنْ يُّهْدٰى ۚ فَمَا لَكُمْ ۟
كَيْفَ تَحْكُمُوْنَ ﴿۳۶﴾

37. [b]And most of them follow only conjecture. Surely, conjecture avails naught against truth.[1260] Verily, Allāh is Well-Aware of what they do.

وَمَا يَتَّبِعُ اَكْثَرُهُمْ اِلَّا ظَنًّا ؕ اِنَّ الظَّنَّ لَا يُغْنِيْ
مِنَ الْحَقِّ شَيْـًٔا ؕ اِنَّ اللّٰهَ عَلِيْمٌۢ بِمَا يَفْعَلُوْنَ ﴿۳۷﴾

38. And this Qur'ān is not such as could have been produced by anyone other than Allāh. *On the contrary*, [c]it fulfils that *revelation* which is before it and is an exposition of the *perfect* Law. There is no doubt about it that *it is* from the Lord of all the worlds.[1261]

وَمَا كَانَ هٰذَا الْقُرْاٰنُ اَنْ يُّفْتَرٰى مِنْ دُوْنِ اللّٰهِ
وَلٰكِنْ تَصْدِيْقَ الَّذِيْ بَيْنَ يَدَيْهِ وَتَفْصِيْلَ الْكِتٰبِ
لَا رَيْبَ فِيْهِ مِنْ رَّبِّ الْعٰلَمِيْنَ ﴿۳۸﴾

[a]10 : 5. [b]6 : 117; 10 : 67; 53 : 29. [c]12 : 112; 16 : 90.

1259. The real test of a creator is his ability to reproduce what he has already created; otherwise the claim is open to serious objection and can be made by any impostor. After having laid down this test of Divinity, the verse asks idol-worshippers, who among their so-called deities is the author of this system of creation and reproduction which has been working from the beginning of the world?

1260. The beliefs and views held by those who set up associates with God are born of mere fancies and surmises, because their so-called deities have never revealed guidance to them.

1261. The verse gives five very cogent reasons to show that the Qur'ān is the revealed Word of God: (*a*) It deals with such themes as are beyond the power of man to know and as can be revealed by God alone. (*b*) The prophecies of the previous Prophets establish its Divine origin. (*c*) It explains and expounds the teachings of previous Scriptures, in such a clear and comprehensive manner as no other Scripture has done. (*d*) It contains all the reasons and arguments needed to prove its Divine origin and does not require the help or support of any outside person or book for this purpose. (*e*) Unlike former Scriptures it satisfies the moral needs and requirements of all mankind under all circumstances.

39. Do they say, 'He has forged it?' Say, [a]'Bring then a *Sūrah* like unto it,[1262] and call for help on all you can, apart from Allāh, if you are truthful.'

أَمْ يَقُولُونَ افْتَرٰىهُ ۚ قُلْ فَأْتُوْا بِسُوْرَةٍ مِّثْلِهٖ وَادْعُوْا مَنِ اسْتَطَعْتُمْ مِّنْ دُوْنِ اللّٰهِ اِنْ كُنْتُمْ صٰدِقِيْنَ ﴿۳۹﴾

40. Nay, [b]but they have rejected that, *full* knowledge of which they did not compass nor has the *true* significance thereof yet come to them. In like manner did those before them reject *the truth*. But see what was the end of the wrongdoers.

بَلْ كَذَّبُوْا بِمَا لَمْ يُحِيْطُوْا بِعِلْمِهٖ وَلَمَّا يَأْتِهِمْ تَاْوِيْلُهٗ ۚ كَذٰلِكَ كَذَّبَ الَّذِيْنَ مِنْ قَبْلِهِمْ فَانْظُرْ كَيْفَ كَانَ عَاقِبَةُ الظّٰلِمِيْنَ ﴿۴۰﴾

41. And of them [c]there are *some* who believe therein, and of them there are *others* who do not believe therein, and thy Lord knows the mischief-makers very well.

وَمِنْهُمْ مَّنْ يُّؤْمِنُ بِهٖ وَمِنْهُمْ مَّنْ لَّا يُؤْمِنُ بِهٖ ۚ وَرَبُّكَ اَعْلَمُ بِالْمُفْسِدِيْنَ ﴿۴۱﴾ ع

R. 5 42. And if they charge thee with lying, say, [d]'For me is my work and for you is your work. You are not accountable for what I do and I am not accountable for what you do.'

وَاِنْ كَذَّبُوْكَ فَقُلْ لِّيْ عَمَلِيْ وَلَكُمْ عَمَلُكُمْ ۚ اَنْتُمْ بَرِيْٓـُٔوْنَ مِمَّآ اَعْمَلُ وَاَنَا بَرِيْٓءٌ مِّمَّا تَعْمَلُوْنَ ﴿۴۲﴾

43. And among them are [e]*some* who give ear to thee. [f]But canst thou make the deaf hear, even though they understand not ?

وَمِنْهُمْ مَّنْ يَّسْتَمِعُوْنَ اِلَيْكَ ۗ اَفَاَنْتَ تُسْمِعُ الصُّمَّ وَلَوْ كَانُوْا لَا يَعْقِلُوْنَ ﴿۴۳﴾

44. And [g]among them are *some* who look towards thee. But canst thou guide the blind, even though they will not see ?[1263]

وَمِنْهُمْ مَّنْ يَّنْظُرُ اِلَيْكَ ۗ اَفَاَنْتَ تَهْدِي الْعُمْيَ وَلَوْ كَانُوْا لَا يُبْصِرُوْنَ ﴿۴۴﴾

---

[a]2 : 24; 11 : 14; 17 : 89; 52 : 34-35. [b]27 : 85. [c]2 : 254; 4 : 56. [d]2 : 140; 109 : 7. [e]6 : 26; 17 : 48. [f]27 : 81. [g]7 : 199.

1262. The verse challenges disbelievers that if a book with such excellences as the Qur'ān possesses could be a human forgery, then why do they not produce a similar one themselves? This challenge stands for all time. See also 44.

1263. The disbelievers do not possess the perceptive understanding and intelligence. In the preceding verse, they were spoken of as devoid of 'understanding' in addition to their being devoid of 'the faculty of hearing,' and in the present verse they are spoken of as destitute of the 'perceptive faculty of the mind,' in addition to their being blind.

45. Certainly, [a]Allāh wrongs not men at all; it is they who wrong their own souls.

إِنَّ اللّٰهَ لَا يَظْلِمُ النَّاسَ شَيْـًٔا وَّلٰكِنَّ النَّاسَ
أَنْفُسَهُمْ يَظْلِمُوْنَ ﴿٤٥﴾

46. And on the day when He will gather them together, [b]*it will appear to them* as though they had not tarried in the world save for an hour[1264] of a day. They will recognize one another. [c]Losers indeed are those who deny the meeting with Allāh and would not follow guidance.

وَيَوْمَ يَحْشُرُهُمْ كَأَنْ لَّمْ يَلْبَثُوْٓا إِلَّا سَاعَةً مِّنَ
النَّهَارِ يَتَعَارَفُوْنَ بَيْنَهُمْ ۭ قَدْ خَسِرَ الَّذِيْنَ كَذَّبُوْا
بِلِقَآءِ اللّٰهِ وَمَا كَانُوْا مُهْتَدِيْنَ ﴿٤٦﴾

47. And [d]if We show thee *in thy lifetime the fulfilment of* some of the things with which We have threatened them, *thou wilt know it;* or if We cause thee to die *before that*, then to Us is their return, *and thou wilt have knowledge of it in the next world;*[1265] and Allāh is Witness to all that they do.

وَإِمَّا نُرِيَنَّكَ بَعْضَ الَّذِيْ نَعِدُهُمْ أَوْ نَتَوَفَّيَنَّكَ فَإِلَيْنَا
مَرْجِعُهُمْ ثُمَّ اللّٰهُ شَهِيْدٌ عَلٰى مَا يَفْعَلُوْنَ ﴿٤٧﴾

48. And [e]for every people there is a Messenger.[1266] So when their Messenger comes, it is judged between them with equity, and they are not wronged.

وَلِكُلِّ أُمَّةٍ رَّسُوْلٌ ۚ فَإِذَا جَآءَ رَسُوْلُهُمْ قُضِيَ بَيْنَهُمْ
بِالْقِسْطِ وَهُمْ لَا يُظْلَمُوْنَ ﴿٤٨﴾

[a]4 : 41; 9 : 70; 18 : 50; 30 : 10. [b]30 : 56; 46 : 36. [c]6 : 32; 30 : 9; 32 : 11. [d]13 : 41; 40 : 78. [e]16 : 37; 35 : 25.

1264. Several times disbelievers have been spoken of in the Qur'ān as having stayed in the world only for an hour of a day. In all such verses it is not the actual time of their staying in the world that is meant, but their being engrossed in worldly affairs and idle pursuits that is condemned by implication. As they wasted their lives in idle pursuits they may rightly be said to have lived in the world only for a day, even though they may have actually lived for many years.

1265. The verse lays down an important principle that the prophecies comprising threats and warnings about an impending punishment are liable to be cancelled, while those containing promises of a general character, not applying to a particular Prophet but embodying a general rule that applies to all the Prophets, are not cancelled or revoked. The verse further implies that it is not necessary that all prophecies should have a time-limit for their fulfilment.

1266. The verse seems to refer to a Law-giving Prophet, for all religious Dispensations are founded by Law-giving Prophets.

49. And [a]they say, 'When will this promise be *fulfilled*, if you are truthful?'

وَيَقُوْلُوْنَ مَتٰى هٰذَا الْوَعْدُ اِنْ كُنْتُمْ صٰدِقِيْنَ ۝٤٩

50. Say, [b]'I have no power over any harm or benefit[1267] for myself save that which Allāh wills. [c]For every people there is an *appointed* term. When their term is come, they cannot remain behind a single moment, nor can they get ahead of it.'

قُلْ لَّآ اَمْلِكُ لِنَفْسِيْ ضَرًّا وَّلَا نَفْعًا اِلَّا مَا شَآءَ اللّٰهُ ۭ لِكُلِّ اُمَّةٍ اَجَلٌ ۭ اِذَا جَآءَ اَجَلُهُمْ فَلَا يَسْتَاْخِرُوْنَ سَاعَةً وَّلَا يَسْتَقْدِمُوْنَ ۝٥٠

51. Say, 'Tell me, [d]if His punishment comes upon you by night or by day, how will the guilty run away[1268] from it?

قُلْ اَرَءَيْتُمْ اِنْ اَتٰىكُمْ عَذَابُهٗ بَيَاتًا اَوْ نَهَارًا مَّاذَا يَسْتَعْجِلُ مِنْهُ الْمُجْرِمُوْنَ ۝٥١

52. 'Is it then when it has overtaken you that you will believe in it? [e]'What! *you believe* now! And *before this* you used to demand its speedy coming'?

اَثُمَّ اِذَا مَا وَقَعَ اٰمَنْتُمْ بِهٖ ۭ اٰۗلْـٰٔنَ وَقَدْ كُنْتُمْ بِهٖ تَسْتَعْجِلُوْنَ ۝٥٢

53. [f]Then will it be said to those who did wrong, 'Taste ye the abiding punishment.[1269] You are not requited save for that which you earned.'

ثُمَّ قِيْلَ لِلَّذِيْنَ ظَلَمُوْا ذُوْقُوْا عَذَابَ الْخُلْدِ ۚ هَلْ تُجْزَوْنَ اِلَّا بِمَا كُنْتُمْ تَكْسِبُوْنَ ۝٥٣

54. And they ask thee *to tell them* whether it is true? [g]Say, 'Yea, by my Lord! it is most surely true; and you cannot frustrate it.'[1269A]

وَيَسْتَنْۢبِـُٔوْنَكَ اَحَقٌّ هُوَ ۭ قُلْ اِيْ وَرَبِّيْٓ اِنَّهٗ لَحَقٌّ ۚ وَمَآ اَنْتُمْ بِمُعْجِزِيْنَ ۝٥٤ ع

[a]21 : 39; 27 : 72; 34 : 30; 36 : 49. [b]7 : 189. [c]7 : 35; 16 : 62; 35 : 46. [d]6 : 48; 7 : 98-99. [e]10 : 92. [f]34 : 43. [g]11 : 18.

1267. This verse embodies a reply to the disbelievers' demand for punishment (mentioned in the preceding verse). The Holy Prophet is bidden to ask them, how he could fulfil their demand for punishment when he possessed no power either to do good to, or avert evil from, himself.

1268. The verse may constitute a rebuke to disbelievers that they should not indulge in futile discussion as to the time and form of the promised punishment but should try to escape from it by effecting a wholesome change in their lives.

1269. *'Adhāb al-Khuld* means, a punishment that stays with disbelievers and not the punishment which knows no end and can in no circumstances be removed.

1269A. You cannot escape from it.

R. 6 55. And [a]if every soul that does wrong possessed all that is in the earth, it would surely offer to ransom itself therewith. [b]And they will conceal[1270] their remorse, when they see the punishment. And judgment shall be passed between them with equity and they shall not be wronged.

وَلَوْ أَنَّ لِكُلِّ نَفْسٍ ظَلَمَتْ مَا فِي الْأَرْضِ لَافْتَدَتْ
بِهِ ۗ وَأَسَرُّوا النَّدَامَةَ لَمَّا رَأَوُا الْعَذَابَ ۚ وَقُضِيَ
بَيْنَهُمْ بِالْقِسْطِ وَهُمْ لَا يُظْلَمُونَ ﴿٥٥﴾

56. Remember, [c]to Allāh surely belongs whatever is in the heavens and the earth. Remember, that Allāh's promise is surely true. But most of them understand not.

أَلَا إِنَّ لِلَّهِ مَا فِي السَّمٰوٰتِ وَالْأَرْضِ ۗ أَلَا إِنَّ وَعْدَ
اللّٰهِ حَقٌّ وَّلٰكِنَّ أَكْثَرَهُمْ لَا يَعْلَمُونَ ﴿٥٦﴾

57. [d]He it is Who gives life and causes death, and to Him shall you *all* be brought back.

هُوَ يُحْيٖ وَيُمِيْتُ وَإِلَيْهِ تُرْجَعُوْنَ ﴿٥٧﴾

58. O mankind! there indeed has come to you an Exhortation[1271] from your Lord and a healing for whatever *disease* there is in the hearts, and [e]a guidance and a mercy to the believers.

يٰٓأَيُّهَا النَّاسُ قَدْ جَآءَتْكُمْ مَّوْعِظَةٌ مِّنْ رَّبِّكُمْ
وَشِفَآءٌ لِّمَا فِي الصُّدُوْرِ ۙ وَهُدًى وَّرَحْمَةٌ
لِّلْمُؤْمِنِيْنَ ﴿٥٨﴾

59. Say, '*All this is* through the grace of Allāh and through His mercy; therein, therefore, let them rejoice. [f]That is better than what they hoard.'

قُلْ بِفَضْلِ اللّٰهِ وَبِرَحْمَتِهٖ فَبِذٰلِكَ فَلْيَفْرَحُوْا ۗ هُوَ
خَيْرٌ مِّمَّا يَجْمَعُوْنَ ﴿٥٩﴾

---

[a]39 : 48. [b]34 : 34. [c]2 : 285; 10 : 67; 31 : 27. [d]3 : 157; 7 : 159; 44 : 9; 57 : 3. [e]12 : 112; 27 : 3. [f]43 : 33.

1270. *Asarrū* may also mean, 'they will manifest or express their remorse.' The word has contrary meanings.

1271. The Qur'ān is *Mau'iẓah*, for, (*a*) it contains teachings which proceed from a genuine desire to impart good counsel. (*b*) Its teaching is calculated deeply to affect and touch the human heart; and (*c*) it has set forth in a beautiful manner all those principles and rules of conduct which lead to moral reformation and success in life.

60. Say, 'Have you *ever* considered that Allāh has sent down provision for you, [a]then you make *some* of it unlawful and *some* lawful?'[1272] Say, 'Has Allāh permitted you *that*, or do you invent lies against Allāh?'

قُلْ اَرَءَيْتُمْ مَّآ اَنْزَلَ اللّٰهُ لَكُمْ مِّنْ رِّزْقٍ فَجَعَلْتُمْ
مِّنْهُ حَرَامًا وَّحَلٰلًا ؕ قُلْ آٰللّٰهُ اَذِنَ لَكُمْ اَمْ عَلَى اللّٰهِ
تَفْتَرُوْنَ ﴿۶۰﴾

61. What think those who invent lies against Allāh of the Day of Resurrection? Surely, [b]Allāh is Gracious towards mankind, but most of them are not thankful.

وَمَا ظَنُّ الَّذِيْنَ يَفْتَرُوْنَ عَلَى اللّٰهِ الْكَذِبَ يَوْمَ
الْقِيٰمَةِ ؕ اِنَّ اللّٰهَ لَذُوْ فَضْلٍ عَلَى النَّاسِ وَلٰكِنَّ
اَكْثَرَهُمْ لَا يَشْكُرُوْنَ ﴿۶۱﴾ ع

R. 7 62. And thou art not *engaged* in anything, and thou recitest not from Him any portion of the Qur'ān, and [c]you do no work, but We are Witnesses of you when you are engrossed therein. And [d]there is not hidden from thy Lord even an atom's weight in the earth or in heaven. And there is nothing smaller[1273] than that or greater, but it is *recorded* in a clear Book.

وَمَا تَكُوْنُ فِيْ شَاْنٍ وَّمَا تَتْلُوْا مِنْهُ مِنْ قُرْاٰنٍ وَّ
لَا تَعْمَلُوْنَ مِنْ عَمَلٍ اِلَّا كُنَّا عَلَيْكُمْ شُهُوْدًا اِذْ تُفِيْضُوْنَ
فِيْهِ ؕ وَمَا يَعْزُبُ عَنْ رَّبِّكَ مِنْ مِّثْقَالِ ذَرَّةٍ فِي الْاَرْضِ
وَلَا فِي السَّمَآءِ وَلَآ اَصْغَرَ مِنْ ذٰلِكَ وَلَآ اَكْبَرَ اِلَّا
فِيْ كِتٰبٍ مُّبِيْنٍ ﴿۶۲﴾

63. [e]Behold! the friends of Allāh shall certainly have no fear, nor shall they grieve[1274]—

اَلَآ اِنَّ اَوْلِيَآءَ اللّٰهِ لَا خَوْفٌ عَلَيْهِمْ وَلَا هُمْ يَحْزَنُوْنَ ﴿۶۳﴾

64. Those who believed and were *ever* righteous—

الَّذِيْنَ اٰمَنُوْا وَكَانُوْا يَتَّقُوْنَ ﴿۶۴﴾

65. [f]For them are glad tidings in the present life and *also* in the Hereafter—there is no changing the words of Allāh—that indeed is the supreme achievement.

لَهُمُ الْبُشْرٰى فِي الْحَيٰوةِ الدُّنْيَا وَفِي الْاٰخِرَةِ ؕ لَا تَبْدِيْلَ
لِكَلِمٰتِ اللّٰهِ ؕ ذٰلِكَ هُوَ الْفَوْزُ الْعَظِيْمُ ﴿۶۵﴾

[a]5 : 104. [b]27 : 74; 40 : 62. [c]57 : 5; 58 : 8. [d]34 : 4. [e]2 : 63. [f]41 : 31.

1272. Eating and drinking are the primary needs of man and it is the first duty of a religion to guide him in this respect. It stands to reason, however, that there should be some medical, moral or religious grounds for declaring some things as lawful and others as unlawful. Islām has provided necessary teachings in this regard.

1273. While some things remain hidden on account of their smallness, there are others parts of which remain hidden owing to their largeness. God's vision is so sharp and penetrating that nothing, however small, can remain hidden from Him and it is so comprehensive that no part of a thing, however big, can escape His sight.

1274. 'Fear' pertains to the future actions of man and 'grief' to his past actions.

66. And [a]let not their words grieve[1275] thee. Surely, all power belongs to Allāh. He is the All-Hearing, the All-Knowing.

وَلَا يَحْزُنْكَ قَوْلُهُمْ إِنَّ الْعِزَّةَ لِلّٰهِ جَمِيعًا هُوَ السَّمِيعُ
الْعَلِيمُ ﴿٦٦﴾

67. Behold! [b]whoever is in the heavens and whoever is in the earth is Allāh's. Those who call on others than Allāh do not *really* follow *these associate-gods*; [c]they only follow conjecture, and they only make guesses.

أَلَآ إِنَّ لِلّٰهِ مَنْ فِي السَّمٰوٰتِ وَمَنْ فِي الْأَرْضِ وَمَا
يَتَّبِعُ الَّذِيْنَ يَدْعُوْنَ مِنْ دُوْنِ اللّٰهِ شُرَكَآءَ إِنْ
يَّتَّبِعُوْنَ إِلَّا الظَّنَّ وَإِنْ هُمْ إِلَّا يَخْرُصُوْنَ ﴿٦٧﴾

68. [d]He it is Who has made for you the night *dark* that you may rest therein, and the day full of light[1276] *that you may pursue your occupations*. Surely, therein are Signs for a people who listen *to the Divine Message*.

هُوَ الَّذِيْ جَعَلَ لَكُمُ الَّيْلَ لِتَسْكُنُوْا فِيْهِ وَالنَّهَارَ
مُبْصِرًا إِنَّ فِيْ ذٰلِكَ لَاٰيٰتٍ لِّقَوْمٍ يَّسْمَعُوْنَ ﴿٦٨﴾

69. [e]They say, 'Allāh has taken unto Him a son.' Holy is He! He is Self-Sufficient. To Him belongs whatever is in the heavens and whatever is in the earth. You have no authority for this. What! do you say concerning Allāh what you know not?[1277]

قَالُوا اتَّخَذَ اللّٰهُ وَلَدًا سُبْحٰنَهٗ هُوَ الْغَنِيُّ لَهٗ مَا فِي
السَّمٰوٰتِ وَمَا فِي الْأَرْضِ إِنْ عِنْدَكُمْ مِّنْ سُلْطٰنٍ
بِهٰذَا أَتَقُوْلُوْنَ عَلَى اللّٰهِ مَا لَا تَعْلَمُوْنَ ﴿٦٩﴾

[a]36 : 77. [b]10 : 56. [c]10 : 37. [d]17 : 13; 27 : 87; 28 : 74; 30 : 24.
[e]2 : 117; 4 : 172; 9 : 31; 17 : 112; 18 : 5,6.

1275. In v. 63 it was said that the friends of God never grieve, but here the Holy Prophet is bidden not to grieve In fact, the Prophet's grief was not for himself but for others. He cried and wept and grieved for mankind. See 1664.

1276. Just as night affords the fatigued and jaded physical limbs of man necessary time for recuperation, and fits him for the ensuing day's work, so do the intervals of inactivity and stagnation in the lives of nations serve as times of rest and recuperation for them and prepare them for their future work by refreshing their spirits and infusing a new vigour into them.

1277. (*a*) God is immune to the laws of decay and death and therefore requires no son to continue His work. (*b*) Being Self-Sufficient He needs no son to help Him in conducting the affairs of the universe. (*c*) The doctrine is based on no sound ground and does not go beyond mere idle philosophical surmises and conjectures. This is the significance of this verse.

70. Say, "Those who invent a lie against Allāh shall not prosper.'

قُلْ اِنَّ الَّذِيْنَ يَفْتَرُوْنَ عَلَى اللّٰهِ الْكَذِبَ لَا يُفْلِحُوْنَ ۞

71. ᵇ*They will have some* enjoyment in this world. Then to Us is their return. Then We shall make them taste a severe torment, because they continued to disbelieve.

مَتَاعٌ فِى الدُّنْيَا ثُمَّ اِلَيْنَا مَرْجِعُهُمْ ثُمَّ نُذِيقُهُمُ الْعَذَابَ الشَّدِيْدَ بِمَا كَانُوْا يَكْفُرُوْنَ ۞

R. 8   72. And recite unto them the story of Noah,[1278] when he said to his people, 'O my people, ᶜif my station *with God* and my reminding you *of your duty* through the Signs of Allāh offend you—and in Allāh do I put my trust—muster then *all* your designs, and your associate-gods; then let not your course of action remain obscure to you *in any respect*; then carry out *your designs* against me and give me no respite,

وَاتْلُ عَلَيْهِمْ نَبَاَ نُوْحٍ ۘ اِذْ قَالَ لِقَوْمِهٖٓ اِنْ كَانَ كَبُرَ عَلَيْكُمْ مَّقَامِىْ وَ تَذْكِيْرِىْ بِاٰيٰتِ اللّٰهِ فَعَلَى اللّٰهِ تَوَكَّلْتُ فَاَجْمِعُوْٓا اَمْرَكُمْ وَشُرَكَاۗءَكُمْ ثُمَّ لَا يَكُنْ اَمْرُكُمْ عَلَيْكُمْ غُمَّةً ثُمَّ اقْضُوْٓا اِلَىَّ وَلَا تُنْظِرُوْنِ ۞

73. 'But if you turn back, *then remember*, ᵈI have not asked of you any reward. [1279] My reward is with Allāh *alone*, and I have been commanded to be of those who are wholly resigned *to Him*.'

فَاِنْ تَوَلَّيْتُمْ فَمَا سَاَلْتُكُمْ مِّنْ اَجْرٍ ۗ اِنْ اَجْرِىَ اِلَّا عَلَى اللّٰهِ وَ اُمِرْتُ اَنْ اَكُوْنَ مِنَ الْمُسْلِمِيْنَ ۞

ᵃ4 : 51;   16 : 117.   ᵇ3 : 15,198;   9 : 38;   16 : 118;   28 : 61;   40 : 40.   ᶜ71 : 8.   ᵈ6 : 91;   11 : 30.

1278. A careful perusal of the accounts of the three Prophets—Noah, Moses and Jonah, mentioned in the following verses shows that their life story is epitomized in the life of the Holy Prophet. He played the part of Noah at Mecca, that of Moses at Medina and that of Jonah on his re-entry into Mecca. This is enough to show that the accounts of the Prophets given in the Qur'ān are not mere stories but constitute great prophecies about important events that were to occur in the life of the Holy Prophet.

1279. It is a common objection against the Prophets of God that they seek to gain ascendancy over their compatriots by raising the standard of revolt against the existing order of things with a view to establishing a new order under their own leadership. It is this baseless charge which is refuted in this verse. God's Prophets never seek self-aggrandizement. On the contrary, they choose the path of suffering and service.

74. But they rejected him, so [a]We saved him and those who were with him in the Ark. And We made them inheritors *of Our favours*, while We drowned those who rejected our Signs. See then, how *evil* was the end of those who had been warned.

فَكَذَّبُوْهُ فَنَجَّيْنٰهُ وَمَنْ مَّعَهٗ فِي الْفُلْكِ وَجَعَلْنٰهُمْ
خَلٰٓئِفَ وَاَغْرَقْنَا الَّذِيْنَ كَذَّبُوْا بِاٰيٰتِنَا ۚ فَانْظُرْ كَيْفَ
كَانَ عَاقِبَةُ الْمُنْذَرِيْنَ ﴿۷۴﴾

75. Then We sent, after him, *other* Messengers to their *respective* peoples, and [b]they brought them clear proofs. But they would not believe in them, because they had rejected them before. Thus do We seal[1280] the hearts of the transgressors.

ثُمَّ بَعَثْنَا مِنْۢ بَعْدِهٖ رُسُلًا اِلٰى قَوْمِهِمْ فَجَآءُوْهُمْ
بِالْبَيِّنٰتِ فَمَا كَانُوْا لِيُؤْمِنُوْا بِمَا كَذَّبُوْا بِهٖ مِنْ قَبْلُ ؕ
كَذٰلِكَ نَطْبَعُ عَلٰى قُلُوْبِ الْمُعْتَدِيْنَ ﴿۷۵﴾

76. [c]Then We sent after them Moses and Aaron to Pharaoh and his chiefs with Our Signs, but they behaved arrogantly. And they were a sinful people.

ثُمَّ بَعَثْنَا مِنْۢ بَعْدِهِمْ مُّوْسٰى وَهٰرُوْنَ اِلٰى فِرْعَوْنَ
وَمَلَا۟ئِهٖ بِاٰيٰتِنَا فَاسْتَكْبَرُوْا وَكَانُوْا قَوْمًا مُّجْرِمِيْنَ ﴿۷۶﴾

77. And [d]when there came to them the truth from Us, they said, 'This is surely a manifest enchantment.'[1281]

فَلَمَّا جَآءَهُمُ الْحَقُّ مِنْ عِنْدِنَا قَالُوْٓا اِنَّ هٰذَا لَسِحْرٌ
مُّبِيْنٌ ﴿۷۷﴾

78. Moses said, 'Do you say *this* of the truth when it has come to you? Can this be enchantment? And [e]the enchanters never prosper.

قَالَ مُوْسٰٓى اَتَقُوْلُوْنَ لِلْحَقِّ لَمَّا جَآءَكُمْ ؕ اَسِحْرٌ هٰذَا ؕ
وَلَا يُفْلِحُ السّٰحِرُوْنَ ﴿۷۸﴾

---

[a]29 : 16. [b]30 : 48; 40 : 24. [c]7 : 104. [d]40 : 26. [e]20 : 70.

1280. God does not arbitrarily seal up the hearts of disbelievers; it is the disbelievers who, by their own stubborn and unjustified refusal to listen to the Word of God, deprive themselves of the ability to see and accept the truth. They are themselves the architects of their evil destiny.

1281. In the two simple words *Siḥr* and *Mubīn* lie hidden almost all the stratagems and machinations that the enemies of the Prophets of God employ to defeat and discomfit them. People with a religious bent of mind are told by the enemies of Truth that the new teaching is nothing but *Siḥr* or fraud which would corrupt the religion of the land, whereas those nationalists, who profess to have the material good of their country at heart, are frightened away from it by being told that acceptance of the new teaching would create dissension and discord among the different communities in the land and would thus give a death-blow to the national unity; *Mubīn* meaning that which disunites or separates (Lane).

79. They said, 'Hast thou come to us that thou mayest turn us away from what we found our fathers following, and that you two may have greatness in the land? But [a]we will not believe in either of you.'

قَالُوْٓا اَجِئْتَنَا لِتَلْفِتَنَا عَمَّا وَجَدْنَا عَلَيْهِ اٰبَآءَنَا وَ
تَكُوْنَ لَكُمَا الْكِبْرِيَآءُ فِي الْاَرْضِ ؕ وَمَا نَحْنُ لَكُمَا
بِمُؤْمِنِيْنَ ﴿٧٩﴾

80. [b]And Pharaoh said, 'Bring to me every expert sorcerer.'

وَقَالَ فِرْعَوْنُ ائْتُوْنِيْ بِكُلِّ سٰحِرٍ عَلِيْمٍ ﴿٨٠﴾

81. And when the sorcerers came, Moses said to them, '[c]Cast ye what you would cast.'

فَلَمَّا جَآءَ السَّحَرَةُ قَالَ لَهُمْ مُّوْسٰٓى اَلْقُوْا مَآ اَنْتُمْ
مُّلْقُوْنَ ﴿٨١﴾

82. And when they had cast, [d]Moses said, 'What you have brought is *mere* sorcery. Surely, Allāh will bring it to naught. Verily, Allāh does not permit the work of mischief-makers to prosper.

فَلَمَّآ اَلْقَوْا قَالَ مُوْسٰى مَا جِئْتُمْ بِهِ ۙ السِّحْرُ ؕ اِنَّ اللّٰهَ
سَيُبْطِلُهٗ ؕ اِنَّ اللّٰهَ لَا يُصْلِحُ عَمَلَ الْمُفْسِدِيْنَ ﴿٨٢﴾

83. 'And [e]Allāh establishes the truth by His words,[1281A] even though the guilty be averse *to it*.'

وَ يُحِقُّ اللّٰهُ الْحَقَّ بِكَلِمٰتِهٖ وَلَوْ كَرِهَ الْمُجْرِمُوْنَ ﴿٨٣﴾ ع ١٢/٨

R. 9 84. And none obeyed Moses save some youths from among his people, because of the fear of Pharaoh and their chiefs, lest he should persecute them. And surely [f]Pharaoh was a tyrant in the land and surely he was of the transgressors.

فَمَآ اٰمَنَ لِمُوْسٰٓى اِلَّا ذُرِّيَّةٌ مِّنْ قَوْمِهٖ عَلٰى خَوْفٍ
مِّنْ فِرْعَوْنَ وَمَلَا۟ئِهِمْ اَنْ يَّفْتِنَهُمْ ؕ وَاِنَّ فِرْعَوْنَ
لَعَالٍ فِي الْاَرْضِ ۚ وَاِنَّهٗ لَمِنَ الْمُسْرِفِيْنَ ﴿٨٤﴾

85. And Moses said, 'O my people, if you have believed in Allāh, then in Him put your trust, if you have *truly* submitted[1282] *to His Will*.'

وَقَالَ مُوْسٰى يٰقَوْمِ اِنْ كُنْتُمْ اٰمَنْتُمْ بِاللّٰهِ فَعَلَيْهِ
تَوَكَّلُوْٓا اِنْ كُنْتُمْ مُّسْلِمِيْنَ ﴿٨٥﴾

[a]7 : 133. [b]7 : 113; 26 : 37,38. [c]7 : 117; 20 : 67; 26 : 44. [d]7 : 119; 20 : 70. [e]8 : 9. [f]28 : 5.

1281A. A righteous cause does not need the support of unrighteous means for its propagation. 'The end justifies the means' has never been the dictum of God's Prophets and their true followers. Truth spreads and triumphs by its own inherent strength and not by falsehood.

1282. *Īmān* signifies mental submission and *Islām* means outward obedience. Inner faith must be followed by real outward change in the conduct of a believer.

86. And they said, 'In Allāh do we put our trust. Our Lord, make us not a trial for the wrongdoing people;

فَقَالُوْا عَلَى اللّٰهِ تَوَكَّلْنَا ۚ رَبَّنَا لَا تَجْعَلْنَا فِتْنَةً لِّلْقَوْمِ
الظّٰلِمِيْنَ ﴿٨٦﴾

87. 'And deliver us by Thy mercy from the *tyranny of the* disbelieving people.'

وَنَجِّنَا بِرَحْمَتِكَ مِنَ الْقَوْمِ الْكٰفِرِيْنَ ﴿٨٧﴾

88. And We revealed to Moses and his brother, *saying*, 'Take for your people *some* houses in *the* town,[1283] and construct your houses so that they face[1284] each other and observe Prayer. And give glad tidings to the believers.'

وَاَوْحَيْنَآ اِلٰى مُوْسٰى وَاَخِيْهِ اَنْ تَبَوَّاٰ لِقَوْمِكُمَا
بِمِصْرَ بُيُوْتًا وَّاجْعَلُوْا بُيُوْتَكُمْ قِبْلَةً وَّاَقِيْمُوا الصَّلٰوةَ ۗ
وَبَشِّرِ الْمُؤْمِنِيْنَ ﴿٨٨﴾

89. And Moses said, 'Our Lord, Thou hast bestowed upon Pharaoh and his chiefs splendour and riches in the present life, with the result, our Lord, that they are leading *men* astray from Thy path. Our Lord! destroy[1284A] their riches and harden[1284B] their hearts so that [a]they believe not until they see the grievous punishment.'

وَقَالَ مُوْسٰى رَبَّنَآ اِنَّكَ اٰتَيْتَ فِرْعَوْنَ وَمَلَاَهٗ
زِيْنَةً وَّاَمْوَالًا فِى الْحَيٰوةِ الدُّنْيَا ۙ رَبَّنَا لِيُضِلُّوْا
عَنْ سَبِيْلِكَ ۚ رَبَّنَا اطْمِسْ عَلٰٓى اَمْوَالِهِمْ وَاشْدُدْ
عَلٰى قُلُوْبِهِمْ فَلَا يُؤْمِنُوْا حَتّٰى يَرَوُا الْعَذَابَ الْاَلِيْمَ ﴿٨٩﴾

[a]10 : 97-98.

1283. The injunction to live in a town does not mean that the Israelites lived in the wilderness before this. The verse only emphasizes the necessity and usefulness of a civilized and corporate life. There is a general tendency on the part of the members of weak minority communities to live together in big towns.

1284. The words, *so that they face each other*, signify that (1) the Israelites were instructed to live very close together so as to be able to help one another in time of need, because this object is only attainable when people build their houses near or facing each other. (2) They should have all their houses facing one direction, which figuratively means that they should have a common goal or ideal. (3) That all their houses should be of equal standing implying that there should obtain feelings of real brotherhood between the rich and the poor so that all should pull together as one team, because there can exist no real feeling of brotherhood when some members of a community live in palatial dwellings and others in wretched hovels.

1284A. *Ṭamasa 'alai-hi* means, he destroyed him or it; he obliterated its trace (Lane).

1284B. *Shadda al-Shai'a* means, he made the thing hard; *Shadda 'alai-hi* means, he attacked him (Lane).

90. *God* said, 'Your prayer is accepted. So be ye twain steadfast, and follow not the path of those who know not.'

قَالَ قَدْ اُجِيْبَتْ دَّعْوَتُكُمَا فَاسْتَقِيْمَا وَلَا تَتَّبِعٰنِّ
سَبِيْلَ الَّذِيْنَ لَا يَعْلَمُوْنَ ﴿٩٠﴾

91. And [a]We brought the Children of Israel across the sea; and [b]Pharaoh and his hosts pursued them wrongfully and aggressively, till when *the calamity of* drowning overtook him, he cried, 'I believe that there is no god but He in Whom the Children of Israel believe,[1285] and I am of those who submit *to Him*.'

وَجٰوَزْنَا بِبَنِيْٓ اِسْرَآءِيْلَ الْبَحْرَ فَاَتْبَعَهُمْ فِرْعَوْنُ
وَجُنُوْدُهٗ بَغْيًا وَّعَدْوًا حَتّٰٓى اِذَآ اَدْرَكَهُ الْغَرَقُ قَالَ
اٰمَنْتُ اَنَّهٗ لَآ اِلٰهَ اِلَّا الَّذِيْٓ اٰمَنَتْ بِهٖ بَنُوْٓا اِسْرَآءِيْلَ
وَاَنَا مِنَ الْمُسْلِمِيْنَ ﴿٩١﴾

92. [c]'What! Now! while thou wast disobedient before *this* and wast of the mischief-makers.

آٰلْـٰٔنَ وَقَدْ عَصَيْتَ قَبْلُ وَكُنْتَ مِنَ الْمُفْسِدِيْنَ ﴿٩٢﴾

93. So this day We will save thee in thy body *alone* that thou mayest be a Sign[1286] to those *who come* after thee. And surely many of mankind are heedless of Our Signs.

فَالْيَوْمَ نُنَجِّيْكَ بِبَدَنِكَ لِتَكُوْنَ لِمَنْ خَلْفَكَ اٰيَةً
وَاِنَّ كَثِيْرًا مِّنَ النَّاسِ عَنْ اٰيٰتِنَا لَغٰفِلُوْنَ ﴿٩٣﴾ ع ٩

R. 10 94. And We assigned to the Children of Israel an excellent abode and [d]We provided them with good things, and they differed not until there came to them the knowledge. Surely, thy Lord will [e]judge between them on the Day of Resurrection concerning that in which they *now* differ.

وَلَقَدْ بَوَّاْنَا بَنِيْٓ اِسْرَآءِيْلَ مُبَوَّاَ صِدْقٍ وَّرَزَقْنٰهُمْ
مِّنَ الطَّيِّبٰتِ فَمَا اخْتَلَفُوْا حَتّٰى جَآءَهُمُ الْعِلْمُ اِنَّ
رَبَّكَ يَقْضِيْ بَيْنَهُمْ يَوْمَ الْقِيٰمَةِ فِيْمَا كَانُوْا فِيْهِ
يَخْتَلِفُوْنَ ﴿٩٤﴾

[a]7 : 139; 20 : 78. [b]20 : 79; 26 : 61; 44 : 25. [c]10 : 52. [d]45 : 17. [e]45 : 18.

1285. These words express the depth of abasement to which the proud Pharaoh had sunk.

1286. It is remarkable that the Qur'ān alone of all religious Scriptures and books of history mentions this fact. The Bible makes no mention of it, nor does any book of history. But in what wonderful manner the Word of God has proved true ! After the lapse of more than 3,000 years the body of Pharaoh has been discovered and it now lies in a preserved state in the museum at Cairo. The body shows Pharaoh to have been a lean, short-bodied man, with a countenance expressive of anger and stupidity. Moses was born in the time of Rameses II and was brought up by him (Exod. 2 : 2—10), but it was in the reign of his son, Merneptah (Meneptah) that he was entrusted with the mission of a Prophet (Jew. Enc., vol. 9, p. 500 & Enc. Bib., under "Pharaoh" & under "Egypt").

95. And if thou art in doubt concerning that which We have sent down to thee, ask those who have been reading the Book before thee. Indeed the [a]truth has come to thee from thy Lord; be not, therefore, of those who doubt.[1287]

فَإِنْ كُنْتَ فِي شَكٍّ مِّمَّآ أَنْزَلْنَآ إِلَيْكَ فَسْئَلِ الَّذِيْنَ
يَقْرَءُوْنَ الْكِتٰبَ مِنْ قَبْلِكَ ۚ لَقَدْ جَآءَكَ الْحَقُّ مِنْ
رَّبِّكَ فَلَا تَكُوْنَنَّ مِنَ الْمُمْتَرِيْنَ ﴿٩٥﴾

96. And be not thou of those who reject the Signs of Allāh, or thou shalt be of the losers.

وَلَا تَكُوْنَنَّ مِنَ الَّذِيْنَ كَذَّبُوْا بِاٰيٰتِ اللّٰهِ فَتَكُوْنَ
مِنَ الْخٰسِرِيْنَ ﴿٩٦﴾

97. [b]Surely, those against whom the decree *of punishment* of thy Lord has taken effect will not believe,

إِنَّ الَّذِيْنَ حَقَّتْ عَلَيْهِمْ كَلِمَتُ رَبِّكَ لَا يُؤْمِنُوْنَ ﴿٩٧﴾

98. Even [c]if there come to them every Sign till they see the grievous punishment.

وَلَوْ جَآءَتْهُمْ كُلُّ اٰيَةٍ حَتّٰى يَرَوُا الْعَذَابَ الْأَلِيْمَ ﴿٩٨﴾

99. Why was there no town,[1287A] which believed so that their belief should have profited them, [d]save the people of Jonah?[1288] When they believed, We removed from them the punishment of disgrace in the present life, and We gave them provision for a while.

فَلَوْلَا كَانَتْ قَرْيَةٌ اٰمَنَتْ فَنَفَعَهَآ إِيْمَانُهَآ إِلَّا قَوْمَ
يُوْنُسَ ۚ لَمَّآ اٰمَنُوْا كَشَفْنَا عَنْهُمْ عَذَابَ الْخِزْيِ فِي
الْحَيٰوةِ الدُّنْيَا وَمَتَّعْنٰهُمْ إِلٰى حِيْنٍ ﴿٩٩﴾

[a]2 : 148; 10 : 95; 11 : 18. [b]10 : 34; 40 : 7. [c]10 : 89. [d]37 : 149.

1287. The address is not to the Holy Prophet but to every reader of the Qur'ān; nor, for that matter, do the words 'sent down to thee' show that the address is made to him, for at several places in the Qur'ān, it has been spoken of as being revealed to all the people (2:137; 21 : 11). The very next verse supports this view because the Holy Prophet could not possibly be one of those 'who reject the Signs of Allāh.'

1287A. People of the town.

1288. Jonah has been mentioned at six different places in the Qur'ān (4 : 164; 6 : 87; 21 : 88 ; 37 : 140 & 68 : 49). In the Bible he is spoken of as an Israelite Prophet (2 Kings, 14 : 25) who was bidden to go to Nineveh, the capital of Ashur and 'cry' against it. According to the Qur'ān, however, he was sent to his own people. He was either not an Israelite or he was sent not to Nineveh but to a section of his own people. Biblical scholars themselves are not agreed as to Jonah's being an Israelite.

100. And [a]if thy Lord had *enforced* His Will, surely, all who are in the earth would have believed together. [b]Wilt thou, then, force[1289] men to become believers?

وَلَوْ شَآءَ رَبُّكَ لَاٰمَنَ مَنْ فِي الْاَرْضِ كُلُّهُمْ جَمِيْعًا ۭ اَفَاَنْتَ تُكْرِهُ النَّاسَ حَتّٰى يَكُوْنُوْا مُؤْمِنِيْنَ ﴿١٠٠﴾

101. And no soul can believe except by the permission[1290] of Allāh. And [c]He causes *His* wrath *to descend* on those who would not use their judgment.

وَمَا كَانَ لِنَفْسٍ اَنْ تُؤْمِنَ اِلَّا بِاِذْنِ اللّٰهِ ۭ وَيَجْعَلُ الرِّجْسَ عَلَى الَّذِيْنَ لَا يَعْقِلُوْنَ ﴿١٠١﴾

102. Say, [d]'Ponder over what is *happening* in the heavens and the earth.'[1291] [e]But Signs and warnings avail not a people who will not believe.

قُلِ انْظُرُوْا مَاذَا فِي السَّمٰوٰتِ وَالْاَرْضِ ۭ وَمَا تُغْنِي الْاٰيٰتُ وَالنُّذُرُ عَنْ قَوْمٍ لَّا يُؤْمِنُوْنَ ﴿١٠٢﴾

103. [f]What, then, do they wait for, save the like of the days of *punishment suffered by* those who passed away before them? Say, [g]'Wait, then, *and* I am with you among those who wait.'

فَهَلْ يَنْتَظِرُوْنَ اِلَّا مِثْلَ اَيَّامِ الَّذِيْنَ خَلَوْا مِنْ قَبْلِهِمْ ۭ قُلْ فَانْتَظِرُوْٓا اِنِّيْ مَعَكُمْ مِّنَ الْمُنْتَظِرِيْنَ ﴿١٠٣﴾

104. Then shall We save Our Messengers and those who believe. [h]Thus have We made it incumbent on Us to save believers.

ثُمَّ نُنَجِّيْ رُسُلَنَا وَالَّذِيْنَ اٰمَنُوْا كَذٰلِكَ ۚ حَقًّا عَلَيْنَا نُنْجِ الْمُؤْمِنِيْنَ ﴿١٠٤﴾ ع ١٥

[a]6 : 150; 16 : 10. [b]2 : 257; 18 : 30. [c]6 : 126. [d]7 : 186. [e]54 : 6. [f]35 : 44. [g]11 : 123. [h]30 : 48; 40 : 52; 58 : 22.

1289. From this verse it is clear beyond any shadow of doubt that Islām does not allow or countenance the use of force for its propagation. See also 319.

1290. It is not possible to attain true belief by the mere profession of certain doctrines with the tongue. It is possible only by the permission of God, *i.e.*, by the observance of certain definite and fixed laws of God.

1291. The words, 'Ponder over what is happening in the heavevs and the earth,' mean that the factors which are destined to lead to the success and prosperity of the cause of the Holy Prophet are already apparent both in the heavens and the earth, and so no compulsion is needed to help a cause which prospers by the force of its own beautiful teachings.

R. 11 105. Say, 'O ye men, if you are in doubt concerning my religion, [a]then *know that* I worship not those whom you worship instead of Allāh, but I worship Allāh *alone* Who causes you to die and [b]I have been commanded to be of the believers;

قُلْ يٰٓاَيُّهَا النَّاسُ اِنْ كُنْتُمْ فِيْ شَكٍّ مِّنْ دِيْنِيْ
فَلَآ اَعْبُدُ الَّذِيْنَ تَعْبُدُوْنَ مِنْ دُوْنِ اللّٰهِ وَ لٰكِنْ
اَعْبُدُ اللّٰهَ الَّذِيْ يَتَوَفّٰىكُمْ ۚۖ وَ اُمِرْتُ اَنْ اَكُوْنَ
مِنَ الْمُؤْمِنِيْنَ ﴿۱۰۵﴾

106. "And [c]*I have also been commanded to convey to you God's command:* 'Set thy face toward religion *as one* ever inclined *to Allāh*, [d]and be not thou of those who ascribe partners *to Him;*

وَاَنْ اَقِمْ وَجْهَكَ لِلدِّيْنِ حَنِيْفًا ۚ وَلَا تَكُوْنَنَّ مِنَ
الْمُشْرِكِيْنَ ﴿۱۰۶﴾

107. [e]'And call not, besides Allāh, on any other that can neither profit thee nor harm thee. And if thou didst so, thou wouldst then certainly be of the wrongdoers.''

وَ لَا تَدْعُ مِنْ دُوْنِ اللّٰهِ مَا لَا يَنْفَعُكَ وَلَا يَضُرُّكَ ۚ
فَاِنْ فَعَلْتَ فَاِنَّكَ اِذًا مِّنَ الظّٰلِمِيْنَ ﴿۱۰۷﴾

108. [f]And if Allāh afflicts thee with harm, there is none who can remove it but He; and if He intends good for thee, there is none who can repel His grace.[1292] He causes it to reach whomsoever of His servants He wills. And He is the Most Forgiving, Merciful.

وَ اِنْ يَّمْسَسْكَ اللّٰهُ بِضُرٍّ فَلَا كَاشِفَ لَهٗٓ اِلَّا هُوَ ۚ وَ
اِنْ يُّرِدْكَ بِخَيْرٍ فَلَا رَآدَّ لِفَضْلِهٖ ؕ يُصِيْبُ بِهٖ مَنْ
يَّشَآءُ مِنْ عِبَادِهٖ ؕ وَهُوَ الْغَفُوْرُ الرَّحِيْمُ ﴿۱۰۸﴾

109. Say, 'O men, *now* has the Truth come to you from your Lord. So [g]whoever follows the guidance, follows it only for the good of his own soul, and whoever errs, errs only against it. And I am not a keeper over you.'

قُلْ يٰٓاَيُّهَا النَّاسُ قَدْ جَآءَكُمُ الْحَقُّ مِنْ رَّبِّكُمْ ۚ فَمَنِ
اهْتَدٰى فَاِنَّمَا يَهْتَدِيْ لِنَفْسِهٖ ۚ وَمَنْ ضَلَّ فَاِنَّمَا
يَضِلُّ عَلَيْهَا ۚ وَمَآ اَنَا عَلَيْكُمْ بِوَكِيْلٍ ؕ ﴿۱۰۹﴾

110. And [h]follow that which is revealed to thee and be steadfast until Allāh gives *His* judgment. And He is the Best of judges.

وَاتَّبِعْ مَا يُوْحٰٓى اِلَيْكَ وَاصْبِرْ حَتّٰى يَحْكُمَ اللّٰهُ ۚۖ وَهُوَ
خَيْرُ الْحٰكِمِيْنَ ﴿۱۱۰﴾ ع ۱۶

[a]109 : 3. [b]6 : 164. [c]30 : 31,44. [d]28 : 88. [e]28 : 89. [f]6 : 18; 39 : 39. [g]27 : 93; 39 : 42. [h]7 : 204.

1292. There is a kind of good which is subject to the laws of nature and can be achieved by man by his own efforts. But there is another kind of good which comes to man through God's special grace.

CHAPTER 11

HŪD

(*Revealed before Hijrah*)

Date of Revelation

According to Ibn 'Abbās, Al-Ḥasan, 'Ikrimah, Mujāhid, Qatādah and Jābir bin Zaid this *Sūrah* was revealed at Mecca and, according to Muqātil, the whole of it belongs to the Meccan period, with the exception of vv. 13,18 and 115, which are considered to have been revealed at Medina.

Subject-Matter

The preceding *Sūrah* had classified the enemies of God's Messengers under three categories : (*a*) Those who were completely destroyed; (*b*) others who were wholly spared ; ana (*c*) those who were partly destroyed and partly spared. In the present Chapter the Qur'ān discusses the first category and states that God destroyed the people of Hūd so completely that no trace of them was left behind, and that He raised in their place another people with whom started a new era in human activities. The *Sūrah* also points out that God watches men and deals with them according to their actions and makes provision for their guidance as circumstances demand. As this provision is made for their good, those who do not benefit by it suffer moral death. In this way the process goes on. And just as when one generation of men passes away it is succeeded by another generation, similarly, when one religious movement perishes, its place is taken by another. The *Sūrah* further tells us that while worldly progress may be possible for a time without observing Divine commandments, permanent success is granted to those people only—their memory being perpetuated and their name indelibly imprinted on world's history—who are honest and true to God and man. After this reasons are given, why believers triumph over disbelievers and the latter fail in their struggle against Truth. The *Sūrah* illustrates this Divine practice by citing examples of peoples who were once mighty in power and strong in numbers, but who met with destruction when they rose against the apparently humble followers of God's Messengers—the peoples of Noah, Hūd, Ṣāliḥ, Lot and Shu'aib. The great Patriarch Abraham is also mentioned but only incidentally in the course of the story of Lot. Reference to Abraham is followed by a brief account of Moses, in relation not to the Israelites but to Pharaoh, who along with his arrogant people was destroyed, because he rejected the Divine Message.

Next, believers are warned against associating with people for whom Divine punishment is decreed ; for association with such people is calculated naturally to involve them in punishment meant for the latter. Thereafter the Holy Prophet has been told not to worry about the threatened destruction of those of his people who will not believe, for the people of many a Prophet before him had met with a similar fate when they opposed and rejected the Truth. So many instances of Divine punishment have been cited in this *Sūrah* and such emphasis laid on the Holy Prophet's great responsibilites that he is reported to have said, '*Sūrah* Hūd has prematurely aged me' (Manthūr), meaning that the contents of the *Sūrah* weighed so heavily on his mind that he felt the impact of premature old age. Lastly, however, the Holy Prophet is cheered and comforted with the prophecy that great progress and prosperity await his followers.

سُوْرَةُ هُوْدٍ مَّكِّيَّةٌ (١١)

1. [a]In the name of Allāh, the Gracious, the Merciful.

بِسْمِ اللّٰهِ الرَّحْمٰنِ الرَّحِيْمِ ①

2. [b]Alif Lām Rā.[1293] [c]This is a Book, whose verses have been made firm[1293A] *and free from imperfection* and then they have been expounded in detail.[1294] It is from One Wise, and All-Aware.

الٓرٰ كِتٰبٌ اُحْكِمَتْ اٰيٰتُهٗ ثُمَّ فُصِّلَتْ مِنْ لَّدُنْ حَكِيْمٍ خَبِيْرٍ ②

3. *It teaches* that you should worship none but Allāh—[d]I am to you a Warner; and a bearer of glad tidings from Him—

اَلَّا تَعْبُدُوْٓا اِلَّا اللّٰهَ ؕ اِنَّنِيْ لَكُمْ مِّنْهُ نَذِيْرٌ وَّ بَشِيْرٌ ③

4. And that you [e]seek forgiveness of your Lord, and then turn[1295] to Him. He will provide for you a goodly provision until an appointed term. And He will grant His grace to everyone possessed of merit. And if you turn away, then surely I fear for you the punishment of a dreadful day.

وَّ اَنِ اسْتَغْفِرُوْا رَبَّكُمْ ثُمَّ تُوْبُوْٓا اِلَيْهِ يُمَتِّعْكُمْ مَّتَاعًا حَسَنًا اِلٰٓى اَجَلٍ مُّسَمًّى وَّ يُؤْتِ كُلَّ ذِيْ فَضْلٍ فَضْلَهٗ ؕ وَ اِنْ تَوَلَّوْا فَاِنِّيْٓ اَخَافُ عَلَيْكُمْ عَذَابَ يَوْمٍ كَبِيْرٍ ④

5. [f]To Allāh is your return; and He has *full* power over all things.

اِلَى اللّٰهِ مَرْجِعُكُمْ ۚ وَ هُوَ عَلٰى كُلِّ شَيْءٍ قَدِيْرٌ ⑤

---

[a]1 : 1. [b]10 : 2; 12 : 2; 13 : 2; 14 : 2; 15 : 2. [c]3 : 8; 10 : 2. [d]2 : 120; 5 : 20; 7 : 189; 25 : 57; 34 : 29; 35 : 25. [e]11 : 53, 62; 71 : 11. [f]10 : 5.

1293. I am Allāh, the All-Seeing. See 16.

1293A. *Aḥkama-hū* means, he made it solid, sound, firm or free from defect or imperfection. *Aḥkamat-hu al-Tajāribu* means, experiments rendered him wise or sound in judgment (Lane).

1294. The word *Fuṣṣilat* here has been substituted for *Mutashābihāt* in 3 : 8 which word signifies the details of the Quranic teaching. The fundamental teachings of Islām are so unassailable that it is difficult to take exception to them. But, in order to know the whole truth about Islām, a study of both its fundamental teachings and their details is necessary but the details are subordinated to the fundamentals.

1295. The verse shows that the stage of *Taubah* comes after, and is higher than, *Istighfār* in the spiritual development of man. *Taubah* is an act of sincere and whole-hearted turning to God after His protection has been sought against the evil effects of past sins. What better means than this can be imagined to attain God's nearness?

6. Now surely, they fold up their breasts that they may hide *their evil thoughts*[1296] from Him. Aye, *even* when they cover themselves up with their garments, [a]He knows what they hide and what they reveal. Surely, He knows full well what is in *their* breasts.

أَلَآ إِنَّهُمْ يَثْنُونَ صُدُورَهُمْ لِيَسْتَخْفُوا مِنْهُ ۚ أَلَا
حِينَ يَسْتَغْشُونَ ثِيَابَهُمْ يَعْلَمُ مَا يُسِرُّونَ وَمَا
يُعْلِنُونَ ۚ إِنَّهُ عَلِيمٌ بِذَاتِ الصُّدُورِ ﴿٦﴾

PART XII

7. And [b]there is no creature that moves on the earth but it is for Allāh to provide it with sustenance.[1297] And He knows its place of temporary sojourn and its permanent dwelling.[1298] All *this* is *recorded* in a clear Book.

وَمَا مِن دَآبَّةٍ فِي الْأَرْضِ إِلَّا عَلَى اللَّهِ رِزْقُهَا
وَيَعْلَمُ مُسْتَقَرَّهَا وَمُسْتَوْدَعَهَا ۚ كُلٌّ فِي كِتَابٍ
مُّبِينٍ ﴿٧﴾

[a]2 : 78; 16 : 24; 27 : 75; 28 : 70; 36 : 77. [b]11 : 57.

1296. The disbelievers keep their doubts and objections hidden in their minds and do not disclose them and have them removed. The reason why they are debarred from accepting the truth is their refusal to open their hearts and have their doubts satisfied.

1297. God has provided sustenance for all His creatures. He has even provided the means of subsistence for worms and reptiles that dwell in the bowels of the earth. Human reason is at a loss to know how and whence the worms and insects found in such unlimited numbers on and inside the earth get their food. Man who presumes to have solved the mysteries of the universe is not yet fully acquainted with all forms of life, to say nothing of the different kinds of food on which they subsist. But God has made ample provision for them all. The verse points out that God, having supplied the physical needs of the meanest of His creatures, certainly could not have neglected to make similar provision for the moral and spiritual needs of man who is the acme of His creation. The verse refers not only to the temporary and permanent abode of every living thing but also to the utmost limit to which its powers can develop.

1298. *Mustaqarr* and *Mustauda'* signify not only a place of temporary settlement and of permanent abode but also final or determined limit of a thing both as regards time or place; appointed term; end of one's course (Lane).

8. And [a]He it is Who created the heavens and the earth in six periods,[1299]—and His throne *rests* on water[1300]—[b]that He might try you which of you is best in conduct. And if thou sayest, 'You shall surely be raised after death,' those who disbelieve will certainly say, 'This is naught but clear deception.'

وَهُوَ الَّذِيْ خَلَقَ السَّمٰوٰتِ وَالْاَرْضَ فِيْ سِتَّةِ اَيَّامٍ وَّكَانَ عَرْشُهٗ عَلَى الْمَآءِ لِيَبْلُوَكُمْ اَيُّكُمْ اَحْسَنُ عَمَلًا ؕ وَلَئِنْ قُلْتَ اِنَّكُمْ مَّبْعُوْثُوْنَ مِنْۢ بَعْدِ الْمَوْتِ لَيَقُوْلَنَّ الَّذِيْنَ كَفَرُوْٓا اِنْ هٰذَآ اِلَّا سِحْرٌ مُّبِيْنٌ ﴿۸﴾

9. [c]And if We put off their punishment until a reckoned time, they would certainly say, 'What withholds it ?' Now, surely, on the day that it shall come unto them, it shall not be averted from them, and that which they used to mock at shall encompass them.

وَلَئِنْ اَخَّرْنَا عَنْهُمُ الْعَذَابَ اِلٰٓى اُمَّةٍ مَّعْدُوْدَةٍ لَّيَقُوْلُنَّ مَا يَحْبِسُهٗ ؕ اَلَا يَوْمَ يَاْتِيْهِمْ لَيْسَ مَصْرُوْفًا عَنْهُمْ وَحَاقَ بِهِمْ مَّا كَانُوْا بِهٖ يَسْتَهْزِءُوْنَ ﴿۹﴾ ع

R. 2 10. And [d]if We make man taste of mercy from Us, and then take it away from him, verily he is despairing, ungrateful.

وَلَئِنْ اَذَقْنَا الْاِنْسَانَ مِنَّا رَحْمَةً ثُمَّ نَزَعْنٰهَا مِنْهُ ۚ اِنَّهٗ لَيَئُوْسٌ كَفُوْرٌ ﴿۱۰﴾

11. And if, [e]after an adversity has touched him, We let him taste prosperity, he will assuredly say, 'Gone are the ills from me.' Lo ! he is exultant, boastful,

وَلَئِنْ اَذَقْنٰهُ نَعْمَآءَ بَعْدَ ضَرَّآءَ مَسَّتْهُ لَيَقُوْلَنَّ ذَهَبَ السَّيِّاٰتُ عَنِّيْ ؕ اِنَّهٗ لَفَرِحٌ فَخُوْرٌ ﴿۱۱﴾

12. [f]Save those who are steadfast and do good works. It is they who will have forgiveness and a great reward.

اِلَّا الَّذِيْنَ صَبَرُوْا وَعَمِلُوا الصّٰلِحٰتِ ؕ اُولٰٓئِكَ لَهُمْ مَّغْفِرَةٌ وَّاَجْرٌ كَبِيْرٌ ﴿۱۲﴾

[a]7 : 55; 10 : 4; 25 : 60. [b]5 : 49; 6 : 166; 67 : 3. [c]21 : 42; 46 : 27. [d]41 : 52. [e]41 : 51. [f]41 : 9; 84 : 26; 95 : 7.

1299. See 984.

1300. As water has been repeatedly described in the Qur'ān as the source of all life (21 : 31 ; 25 : 55 ; 77 : 21 & 86 : 7), the words, *His throne rests on water*, signify that the great Divine attributes find their manifestation through living creatures, above all through man, who is the culminating point of all creation. These words may also mean that the attributes of God depend for their manifestation on His Word which has been compared to water at several places in the Qur'ān. In the words, *you shall surely be raised after death*, it is pointed out that this system of creation itself shows that man should have a life after death, for the creation of such a vast universe in which a being with volition and independent will should live, makes it clear that the creation of that being is intended to serve a great purpose. But the life of this world is short-lived, a temporary existence of tests and trials so that, after this temporary abode of tests and trials man must pass on to his permanent or eternal abode of recompense.

13. [a]Perchance[1301] *the disbelievers vainly hope that* thou mayest *be persuaded to* abandon part of that which has been revealed to thee ; and thy bosom may become straitened thereby, because they say, [b]'Wherefore has not a treasure been sent down to him or an angel come with him ?'[1302] [c]Verily, thou art only a Warner, and Allāh is Guardian over all things.

فَلَعَلَّكَ تَارِكٌۢ بَعْضَ مَا يُوْحٰٓى اِلَيْكَ وَضَآئِقٌۢ بِهٖ
صَدْرُكَ اَنْ يَّقُوْلُوْا لَوْلَآ اُنْزِلَ عَلَيْهِ كَنْزٌ اَوْ جَآءَ
مَعَهٗ مَلَكٌ ؕ اِنَّمَآ اَنْتَ نَذِيْرٌ ؕ وَاللّٰهُ عَلٰى كُلِّ شَيْءٍ
وَّكِيْلٌ ؕ ﴿۱۳﴾

14. Do they say, [d]'He has forged it?' Say, 'Then bring ten *Sūrahs* like it forged, and call on whom you can apart from Allāh, if you are truthful.'

اَمْ يَقُوْلُوْنَ افْتَرٰىهُ ؕ قُلْ فَاْتُوْا بِعَشْرِ سُوَرٍ مِّثْلِهٖ
مُفْتَرَيٰتٍ وَّادْعُوْا مَنِ اسْتَطَعْتُمْ مِّنْ دُوْنِ اللّٰهِ اِنْ
كُنْتُمْ صٰدِقِيْنَ ﴿۱۴﴾

15. And if they do not accept your[1303] *challenge* [e]then know that it has been revealed comprising *that which is only within* Allāh's knowledge and that there is no god but He. Will you then submit ?

فَاِلَّمْ يَسْتَجِيْبُوْا لَكُمْ فَاعْلَمُوْٓا اَنَّمَآ اُنْزِلَ بِعِلْمِ اللّٰهِ
وَاَنْ لَّآ اِلٰهَ اِلَّا هُوَ ۚ فَهَلْ اَنْتُمْ مُّسْلِمُوْنَ ﴿۱۵﴾

16. [f]Whoso desires the present life and its adornment, We will fully repay them for their works in this *life* and they shall not be wronged therein.

مَنْ كَانَ يُرِيْدُ الْحَيٰوةَ الدُّنْيَا وَزِيْنَتَهَا نُوَفِّ
اِلَيْهِمْ اَعْمَالَهُمْ فِيْهَا وَهُمْ فِيْهَا لَا يُبْخَسُوْنَ ﴿۱۶﴾

[a]17 : 74. [b]17 : 94 ; 25 : 9. [c]13 : 8.
[d]2 : 24 ; 10 : 39 ; 17 : 89 ; 52 : 34-35. [e]4 : 167. [f]2 : 201 ; 17 : 19.

1301. The word, *la'alla*, is used to denote either a state of hope or of fear, whether that state pertains to the speaker or to the addressee or to someone else.

1302. It is a peculiarity of the Quranic diction that sometimes it omits the question and only gives the answer, the question being implied in the answer itself. The present verse is an example of this peculiarity. In the preceding verse believers were promised forgiveness and a great reward. Thereupon disbelievers mockingly asked the Holy Prophet, 'Where is the promised reward of which we do not see the slightest sign ? You do not have even the money which you need so badly, nor do the angels descend from heaven to help you.' The Qur'ān turns the tables upon them and answers their irony with an irony, saying, 'Ah ! how "weighty" is the objection of these people and perhaps, O Prophet, from fear of being unable to answer it, you would hide a part of Our revelation which contains prophecies regarding the prosperity and triumph of Islām ! This is only their wishful thinking, their vain and futile hope. Such a thing can never happen.'

1303. The use of plural pronoun 'your' instead of 'thy' shows that the challenge was not necessarily from the Holy Prophet alone, but Muslims in every age could deliver a challenge in these terms. The verse guarantees that the Qur'ān will ever stand unrivalled in its manifold excellent qualities.

17. "Those are they who shall have nothing in the Hereafter save the Fire, and that which they wrought in this *life* shall come to naught, and vain shall be that which they used to do.

اُولٰٓئِكَ الَّذِيْنَ لَيْسَ لَهُمْ فِي الْاٰخِرَةِ اِلَّا النَّارُ ۖ وَحَبِطَ مَا صَنَعُوْا فِيْهَا وَبٰطِلٌ مَّا كَانُوْا يَعْمَلُوْنَ ۞

18. *ᵇCan he, then, who *stands* upon a clear proof from his Lord, *ᶜand to testify to whose truth* a witness from ·Him shall follow him, and who was preceded by the Book of Moses, a guide and a mercy, *be an impostor?*[1304] Those *who are the true followers of Moses* believe therein, and whoever of the *opposing* parties disbelieve in it, the Fire shall be his promised place. *ᵈSo be not thou, O reader,* in doubt about it. Surely, it is the truth from thy Lord; but most men believe not.

اَفَمَنْ كَانَ عَلٰى بَيِّنَةٍ مِّنْ رَّبِّهٖ وَيَتْلُوْهُ شَاهِدٌ مِّنْهُ وَمِنْ قَبْلِهٖ كِتٰبُ مُوْسٰٓى اِمَامًا وَّرَحْمَةً ؕ اُولٰٓئِكَ يُؤْمِنُوْنَ بِهٖ ؕ وَمَنْ يَّكْفُرْ بِهٖ مِنَ الْاَحْزَابِ فَالنَّارُ مَوْعِدُهٗ ۚ فَلَا تَكُ فِيْ مِرْيَةٍ مِّنْهُ ۗ اِنَّهُ الْحَقُّ مِنْ رَّبِّكَ وَلٰكِنَّ اَكْثَرَ النَّاسِ لَا يُؤْمِنُوْنَ ۞

19. And *ᵉwho is more unjust than he who forges a lie against Allāh?* Such shall be presented before their Lord, and the witnesses[1305] will *all* say, *ᶠ'These are they who lied against their Lord.'* Now, surely, the curse of Allāh is on the wrongdoers,

وَمَنْ اَظْلَمُ مِمَّنِ افْتَرٰى عَلَى اللّٰهِ كَذِبًا ؕ اُولٰٓئِكَ يُعْرَضُوْنَ عَلٰى رَبِّهِمْ وَيَقُوْلُ الْاَشْهَادُ هٰٓؤُلَآءِ الَّذِيْنَ كَذَبُوْا عَلٰى رَبِّهِمْ ۚ اَلَا لَعْنَةُ اللّٰهِ عَلَى الظّٰلِمِيْنَ ۞

ᵃ17 : 19.   ᵇ47 : 15.   ᶜ46 : 11;   61 : 7.
ᵈ2 : 148 ;   10 : 95.   ᵉ6 : 22 ;   10 : 18 ;   61 : 8.   ᶠ39 : 61.

1304. Three arguments have been given in this verse in support of the Holy Prophet in the words : (a) 'Who *stands* upon a clear proof from his Lord,' (b) 'to testify to whose truth a witness from Him shall follow him,' and (c) ' who was preceded by the Book of Moses.' 'The clear proof from his Lord' was the great moral revolution which the Holy Prophet had brought about in the life of his corrupt and decadent people, and the witnesses who bore testimony to his truth were the Divine Teachers from among his followers who, by their precept and practice, established the truth of Islām and the Qur'ān in every age, the witness *par excellence* being the Promised Messiah, Founder of the Aḥmadiyya Movement ; and the words 'was preceded by the Book of Moses' point to the prophecies that are found in the Bible about the Holy Prophet. See 2135.

1305. The witnesses may be the Divine Prophets.

20. [a]Who turn *men* away from the path of Allāh and seek to make it crooked. And these it is who disbelieve in the Hereafter.

الَّذِينَ يَصُدُّونَ عَنْ سَبِيلِ اللّٰهِ وَيَبْغُونَهَا عِوَجًا
وَهُمْ بِالْآخِرَةِ هُمْ كٰفِرُونَ ﴿٢٠﴾

21. Such can never frustrate *God's plans* in the land nor have they any friends besides Allāh. Punishment will be doubled[1306] for them. [b]They can neither hear, nor can they see.

أُولٰٓئِكَ لَمْ يَكُونُوا مُعْجِزِينَ فِي الْأَرْضِ وَمَا كَانَ
لَهُمْ مِّنْ دُونِ اللّٰهِ مِنْ أَوْلِيَآءَ يُضٰعَفُ لَهُمُ
الْعَذَابُ مَا كَانُوا يَسْتَطِيعُونَ السَّمْعَ وَمَا كَانُوا
يُبْصِرُونَ ﴿٢١﴾

22. [c]It is these who have ruined their souls, and that which they fabricated shall fail them.

أُولٰٓئِكَ الَّذِينَ خَسِرُوٓا أَنْفُسَهُمْ وَضَلَّ عَنْهُمْ مَّا
كَانُوا يَفْتَرُونَ ﴿٢٢﴾

23. [d]Undoubtedly, it is they who shall be the greatest losers in the Hereafter.

لَا جَرَمَ أَنَّهُمْ فِي الْآخِرَةِ هُمُ الْأَخْسَرُونَ ﴿٢٣﴾

24. Verily, [e]those who believe and do good works, and humble themselves before their Lord[1307]—these are the dwellers of Heaven; therein shall they abide for ever.

إِنَّ الَّذِينَ آمَنُوا وَعَمِلُوا الصّٰلِحٰتِ وَأَخْبَتُوٓا إِلٰى
رَبِّهِمْ أُولٰٓئِكَ أَصْحٰبُ الْجَنَّةِ هُمْ فِيهَا خٰلِدُونَ ﴿٢٤﴾

25. [f]The case of the two parties is like *that of* the blind and the deaf, and the seeing and the hearing.[1308] Is *the case of* the two alike? Will you not then understand?

مَثَلُ الْفَرِيقَيْنِ كَالْأَعْمٰى وَالْأَصَمِّ وَالْبَصِيرِ وَ
السَّمِيعِ هَلْ يَسْتَوِيٰنِ مَثَلًا أَفَلَا تَذَكَّرُونَ ﴿٢٥﴾ ع ٢ ٣

R. 3 26. And [g]We sent Noah to his people, and he said, 'Truly, I am a plain Warner to you,

وَلَقَدْ أَرْسَلْنَا نُوحًا إِلٰى قَوْمِهٖٓ إِنِّي لَكُمْ نَذِيرٌ
مُّبِينٌ ﴿٢٦﴾

[a]3 : 100; 7 : 46; 14 : 4; 16 : 89. [b]26 : 213. [c]7 : 54; 10 : 31. [d]16 : 110. [e]2 : 83; 3 : 58; 4 : 58; 13 : 30; 22 : 57; 29 : 8; 30 : 16; 42 : 23. [f]13 : 17; 35 : 20-21. [g]7 : 60; 23 : 24; 71 : 3.

1306. The leaders of disbelief will be punished both for their own sins and for the sins of those whom they misled.

1307. In order to attain to the higher stages of spiritual progress, perfect conviction, complete submission to, and full trust in, God and sincere love for Him are essential in addition to right belief and good works.

1308. A beautiful contrast is instituted here between belief and disbelief. A believer is represented as one who is in perfect possession of the faculties of sight and hearing, while the disbeliever is likened to a blind and deaf person.

27. [a]'That you worship none but Allāh. Indeed, I fear for you the punishment of a grievous day.'[1309]

أَنْ لَّا تَعْبُدُوْٓا اِلَّا اللّٰهَ ؕ اِنِّیْٓ اَخَافُ عَلَیْكُمْ عَذَابَ
یَوْمٍ اَلِیْمٍ ﴿٢٧﴾

28. [b]The chiefs of his people, who disbelieved, replied, 'We see thee nothing but a mortal like ourselves, and [c]we see that none have followed thee but those who, to all outward appearance,[1310] are the meanest of us. And we do not see in you any superiority over us; nay, we believe you to be liars.'

فَقَالَ الْمَلَاُ الَّذِیْنَ كَفَرُوْا مِنْ قَوْمِهٖ مَا نَرٰىكَ اِلَّا
بَشَرًا مِّثْلَنَا وَ مَا نَرٰىكَ اتَّبَعَكَ اِلَّا الَّذِیْنَ هُمْ
اَرَاذِلُنَا بَادِیَ الرَّاْیِ ۚ وَ مَا نَرٰی لَكُمْ عَلَیْنَا مِنْ فَضْلٍۭ
بَلْ نَظُنُّكُمْ كٰذِبِیْنَ ﴿٢٨﴾

29. [d]He said, 'O my people, tell me if I *stand* on a clear proof from my Lord and He has bestowed upon me from Himself a *great* mercy which has remained obscure to you, *how will it fare with you?* Shall we force it upon you, while you are averse thereto?

قَالَ یٰقَوْمِ اَرَءَیْتُمْ اِنْ كُنْتُ عَلٰی بَیِّنَةٍ مِّنْ رَّبِّیْ
وَ اٰتٰىنِیْ رَحْمَةً مِّنْ عِنْدِهٖ فَعُمِّیَتْ عَلَیْكُمْ ؕ
اَنُلْزِمُكُمُوْهَا وَ اَنْتُمْ لَهَا كٰرِهُوْنَ ﴿٢٩﴾

30. [e]"And O my people, I do not ask of you any wealth in return for it. My reward is only with Allāh. And [f]I am not going to drive away those who believe. They shall certainly meet their Lord. But I see that you are an ignorant people;

وَ یٰقَوْمِ لَاۤ اَسْـَٔلُكُمْ عَلَیْهِ مَالًا ؕ اِنْ اَجْرِیَ اِلَّا
عَلَی اللّٰهِ وَ مَاۤ اَنَا بِطَارِدِ الَّذِیْنَ اٰمَنُوْا ؕ اِنَّهُمْ مُّلٰقُوْا
رَبِّهِمْ وَ لٰكِنِّیْۤ اَرٰىكُمْ قَوْمًا تَجْهَلُوْنَ ﴿٣٠﴾

[a]7 : 60; 71 : 4. [b]23 : 25. [c]26 : 112. [d]11 : 64; 47 : 15. [e]10 : 73; 26 : 110. [f]26 : 115.

1309. 'A grievous punishment' is different from 'the punishment of a grievous day.' The latter expression implies greater intensity. Certain punishments are very grievous, but there are 'certain days' the remembrance of which continues to haunt and cause pain even after the lapse of hundreds of years. Whereas the actual 'punishment' causes pain only to those on whom it falls, remembrance of the 'days of a grievous punishment' terrifies even those who come after.

1310. The expression *Bādi al-Ra'yi* meaning, at first thought; apparently; without proper consideration (Lane), the words *Ārāzilunā Bādi al-Ra'yi* signify that the followers of Noah (*a*) are mean to all outward appearance; (*b*) their faith is insincere; (*c*) it is the result of only superficial thinking. It is a pity that men test the claims of a Heavenly Messenger by their self-devised standards and, when he does not satisfy those standards, they deceive themselves with the idea that they had weighed his claims dispassionately and with an open mind and had found them to be false.

31. 'And O my people, who would help me against Allāh, if I were to drive them away? Will you not then take heed?

وَيٰقَوۡمِ مَنۡ يَّنۡصُرُنِىۡ مِنَ اللّٰهِ اِنۡ طَرَدْتُّهُمۡ ؕ اَفَلَا تَذَكَّرُوۡنَ ﴿۳۱﴾

32. 'And [a]I do not say to you, I possess the treasures of Allāh nor do I know the unseen,' nor do I say, 'I am an angel.' Nor do I say concerning those whom your eyes despise, 'Allāh will not bestow any good upon them'—Allāh knows best whatever is in their minds. Surely, in that case I should be of the unjust.'

وَلَاۤ اَقُوۡلُ لَـكُمۡ عِنۡدِىۡ خَزَآئِنُ اللّٰهِ وَلَاۤ اَعۡلَمُ الۡغَيۡبَ وَلَاۤ اَقُوۡلُ اِنِّىۡ مَلَكٌ وَّلَاۤ اَقُوۡلُ لِلَّذِيۡنَ تَزۡدَرِىۡۤ اَعۡيُنُكُمۡ لَنۡ يُّؤۡتِيَهُمُ اللّٰهُ خَيۡرًا ؕ اَللّٰهُ اَعۡلَمُ بِمَا فِىۡۤ اَنۡفُسِهِمۡ ۚۖ اِنِّىۡۤ اِذًا لَّمِنَ الظّٰلِمِيۡنَ ﴿۳۲﴾

33. They said, 'O Noah, [b]thou hast indeed disputed with us and disputed *long and* often; bring us now what thou threatenest us with, if thou art of the truthful.'

قَالُوۡا يٰنُوۡحُ قَدۡ جَادَلۡتَنَا فَاَكۡثَرۡتَ جِدَالَنَا فَاۡتِنَا بِمَا تَعِدُنَاۤ اِنۡ كُنۡتَ مِنَ الصّٰدِقِيۡنَ ﴿۳۳﴾

34. He said, "[c]Allāh alone will bring it to you, if He please, and you cannot frustrate *His purpose*;[1311]

قَالَ اِنَّمَا يَاۡتِيۡكُمۡ بِهِ اللّٰهُ اِنۡ شَآءَ وَمَاۤ اَنۡتُمۡ بِمُعۡجِزِيۡنَ ﴿۳۴﴾

35. 'And my advice will profit you not *even* if I seek to give you sincere advice if Allāh intends to destroy you.[1312] He is your Lord and to Him shall you be made to return.'

وَلَا يَنۡفَعُكُمۡ نُصۡحِىۡۤ اِنۡ اَرَدْتُّ اَنۡ اَنۡصَحَ لَـكُمۡ اِنۡ كَانَ اللّٰهُ يُرِيۡدُ اَنۡ يُّغۡوِيَكُمۡ ؕ هُوَ رَبُّكُمۡ وَاِلَيۡهِ تُرۡجَعُوۡنَ ﴿۳۵﴾

[a]6 : 51. [b]46 : 23. [c]46 : 24.

1311. The verse embodies three important rules about prophecies of punishment: (*a*) The time of their actual happening is generally not disclosed. (*b*) They are conditional and can be deferred or revoked as God may please. (*c*) Whatever changes may take place in regard to prophecies of punishment, God's immutable purpose never changes, because disbelievers 'cannot frustrate His purpose.'

1312. The verse removes the wrong notion commonly held that being very angry with his people because they did not believe, Noah paryed for their destruction (71 : 27, 28), for it shows that Noah had prayed for their destruction not of his own accord but God Himself had desired him to do so.

36. [a]Do they say, 'He has forged it ?' Say, 'If I have forged it, on me be my guilt and I am clear of *all* the crimes you commit.'

أَمْ يَقُولُونَ افْتَرَاهُ ۖ قُلْ إِنِ افْتَرَيْتُهُ فَعَلَيَّ إِجْرَامِي
وَأَنَا بَرِيءٌ مِّمَّا تُجْرِمُونَ ﴿٣٦﴾ ع

R. 4 37. And it was revealed to Noah: 'None of thy people will believe except those who have *already* believed ; grieve not, therefore, at what they have been doing.[1313]

وَأُوحِيَ إِلَىٰ نُوحٍ أَنَّهُ لَن يُؤْمِنَ مِن قَوْمِكَ إِلَّا
مَن قَدْ آمَنَ فَلَا تَبْتَئِسْ بِمَا كَانُوا يَفْعَلُونَ ﴿٣٧﴾

38. 'And [b]build thou the Ark under Our eyes[1314] and *as commanded by* Our revelation. And address Me not concerning the wrongdoers. They are surely going to be drowned.'

وَاصْنَعِ الْفُلْكَ بِأَعْيُنِنَا وَوَحْيِنَا وَلَا تُخَاطِبْنِي فِي
الَّذِينَ ظَلَمُوا ۚ إِنَّهُم مُّغْرَقُونَ ﴿٣٨﴾

39. And he started making the Ark; and every time the chiefs of his people passed by him, they mocked at him. He said, 'If *now* you mock at us, *the time is coming when* we shall mock at you even just as you mock *now*.

وَيَصْنَعُ الْفُلْكَ وَكُلَّمَا مَرَّ عَلَيْهِ مَلَأٌ مِّن قَوْمِهِ
سَخِرُوا مِنْهُ ۚ قَالَ إِن تَسْخَرُوا مِنَّا فَإِنَّا نَسْخَرُ مِنكُمْ
كَمَا تَسْخَرُونَ ﴿٣٩﴾

40. [c]"Then you shall know who it is on whom will come a punishment that will disgrace him ; and *on whom* will fall a lasting punishment.'

فَسَوْفَ تَعْلَمُونَ مَن يَأْتِيهِ عَذَابٌ يُخْزِيهِ وَ
يَحِلُّ عَلَيْهِ عَذَابٌ مُّقِيمٌ ﴿٤٠﴾

[a]46 : 9. [b]23 : 28. [c]11 : 94; 39 : 40-41.

1313. The prayer referred to in 71 : 27,28 seems to have been uttered after the verse under comment was revealed. According to the verse under comment Noah was informed of God's decision that no one from among his people would now believe in him. Hence his prayer (71 : 27,28) was nothing more than a submission to God's will and decree. All that the prayer meant was that God might carry out His decree about the destruction of his people.

1314. *A'yun* is the plural of *'Ain* which means, eye; look or view; inmates of a house ; protection (Lane).

41. Till—[a]when Our command came and the fountains *of the earth* gushed[1315] forth—We said, [b]'Embark therein two of every kind,[1316] male and female, and thy family, except those against whom the word has already gone forth, and those who believe.' And there had not believed in him except a few.

حَتّٰۤى اِذَا جَآءَ اَمۡرُنَا وَفَارَ التَّنُّوۡرُ ۙ قُلۡنَا احۡمِلۡ فِيۡهَا
مِنۡ كُلٍّ زَوۡجَيۡنِ اثۡنَيۡنِ وَاَهۡلَكَ اِلَّا مَنۡ سَبَقَ
عَلَيۡهِ الۡقَوۡلُ وَمَنۡ اٰمَنَ ؕ وَمَاۤ اٰمَنَ مَعَهٗۤ اِلَّا قَلِيۡلٌ ﴿۴۱﴾

42. And he said, 'Embark therein. In the name of Allāh, be its course and its mooring. My Lord is assuredly Most Forgiving, Merciful.'

وَقَالَ ارۡكَبُوۡا فِيۡهَا بِسۡمِ اللّٰهِ مَجۡرٖىهَا وَمُرۡسٰىهَا ؕ
اِنَّ رَبِّىۡ لَغَفُوۡرٌ رَّحِيۡمٌ ﴿۴۲﴾

43. And it moved along with them amid waves like mountains. And Noah cried unto his son, while he was *keeping* apart, 'O my son embark with us and be not with the disbelievers.'

وَهِىَ تَجۡرِىۡ بِهِمۡ فِىۡ مَوۡجٍ كَالۡجِبَالِ ۟ وَنَادٰى
نُوۡحُ اۨبۡنَهٗ وَكَانَ فِىۡ مَعۡزِلٍ يّٰبُنَىَّ ارۡكَبْ مَّعَنَا وَ
لَا تَكُنۡ مَّعَ الۡكٰفِرِيۡنَ ﴿۴۳﴾

44. He replied, 'I shall soon betake myself *for refuge* to a mountain[1317] which will shelter me from the water.' *Noah* said, 'There is no shelter *for anyone* this day from the decree of Allāh, except for him to whom He shows mercy.' And the wave came in between the two; so he was among the drowned.

قَالَ سَاٰوِىۡۤ اِلٰى جَبَلٍ يَّعۡصِمُنِىۡ مِنَ الۡمَآءِ ؕ قَالَ
لَا عَاصِمَ الۡيَوۡمَ مِنۡ اَمۡرِ اللّٰهِ اِلَّا مَنۡ رَّحِمَ ۚ وَحَالَ
بَيۡنَهُمَا الۡمَوۡجُ فَكَانَ مِنَ الۡمُغۡرَقِيۡنَ ﴿۴۴﴾

[a]23 : 28; 54 : 13. [b]23 : 28.

1315. The Deluge was not merely due to the gushing forth of the water from springs. But, as is clear from 54 : 12-13, its real cause was the bursting of the clouds. Rain fell in torrents and there was water everywhere and, as generally happens during heavy rain, water also began to gush forth from the depths of the earth, and springs and fountains began to sprout, and thus water, both from the heavens and the earth, flooded the whole land. Noah lived in a mountainous country where springs were found in large numbers.

1316. The words 'of every kind' do not here mean all the animals, but *all such* animals as were needed by Noah. Surely, the Ark was not big enough to carry a pair of all kinds of animals found in the world. The addition of the word 'two' also shows that as many animals were to be taken as were absolutely necessary.

1317. The verse shows that the place where Noah lived was surrounded by mountains. The word *Jabal* used as a common noun points to the fact that there was a chain of mountains on one of which Noah's son might have sought shelter. In fact, the place appears to have been a valley with mountains rising on all sides. That such a place should become quickly flooded with heavy rain is not extraordinary.

45. And it was said, 'O earth, swallow thy water, and O sky, cease *raining*.' And the water was made to subside and the matter was decided. And the Ark came to rest on Al-Jūdī.[1317A] And it was said, 'Cursed be the wrongdoing people.'

وَقِيْلَ يٰۤاَرْضُ ابْلَعِيْ مَآءَكِ وَيٰسَمَآءُ اَقْلِعِيْ
وَغِيْضَ الْمَآءُ وَقُضِيَ الْاَمْرُ وَاسْتَوَتْ عَلَى الْجُوْدِيِّ
وَقِيْلَ بُعْدًا لِّلْقَوْمِ الظّٰلِمِيْنَ ﴿۴۵﴾

46. And Noah cried unto his Lord and said, 'My Lord, verily, my son is of my family, and surely Thy promise is true, and Thou art the Most Just of judges.'

وَنَادٰى نُوْحٌ رَّبَّهٗ فَقَالَ رَبِّ اِنَّ ابْنِيْ مِنْ اَهْلِيْ
وَاِنَّ وَعْدَكَ الْحَقُّ وَاَنْتَ اَحْكَمُ الْحٰكِمِيْنَ ﴿۴۶﴾

47. *Allāh* said, 'O Noah, he is surely not of thy family; he[1318] is indeed *a man of* unrighteous conduct.[1319] So do not ask of Me that, of which thou hast no knowledge. I admonish thee lest thou be *one* of the ignorant.'

قَالَ يٰنُوْحُ اِنَّهٗ لَيْسَ مِنْ اَهْلِكَ ۚ اِنَّهٗ عَمَلٌ غَيْرُ
صَالِحٍ ۖ فَلَا تَسْـَٔلْنِ مَا لَيْسَ لَكَ بِهٖ عِلْمٌ ؕ اِنِّيْ
اَعِظُكَ اَنْ تَكُوْنَ مِنَ الْجٰهِلِيْنَ ﴿۴۷﴾

1317A. The mountain Al-Jūdī is, according to Yāqūt al-Ḥamwī, a long chain of mountains on the eastern side of the Tigris in the province of Moṣul (Mu'jam). According to Sale, "Al-Jūdī is one of those mountains which divide Armenia on the south from Mesopotamia and that part of Assyria which is inhabited by the Curds, from whom the mountain took the name of Cardu or Gardu, but the Greeks turned it into Gordyoei...... The tradition which affirms the Ark to have rested on these mountains must have been very ancient, since it is the tradition of the Chaldeans themselves (Berosus apud *Joseph. Antiq.....*). The relics of the Ark were also to be seen here in the time of Epiphanius...... and we are told, the Emperor Heraclius went from the town of Thamanin up to the mountain Al-Jūdī and saw the place of the Ark. There was also formerly a famous monastery, called the 'Monastery of the Ark.' Upon some of these mountains the Nestorians used to celebrate a feast-day on the spot where they supposed the Ark had rested; but in 776 A.D. that monastery was destroyed by lightning" (Sale, pp. 179, 180)....'Jūdī (Djudi) is a lofty mountain mass in the district of Bohtan, about 25 miles N.E. of Jazirah ibn 'Omar in 37°, 30′ N. Lat........It owes its fame to the Mesopotamian tradition, which identifies it, and not Mount Ararat, the mountain on which Noah's Ark rested....Older exegesis identified the mountain now called Judī, or according to Christian authorities the mountains of Gordyene, as the apobaterion of Noah' (Enc. of Islām, vol. I. P. 1059). Babylonian traditions also place the mount Al-Jûdī in Armenia (Jew. Enc. under "Ararat"), and the Bible admits that Babylon was the place where the descendants of Noah lived (Gen. 11 : 9).

1318. According to this verse only those persons were considered members of Noah's family who had established true relationship with God through him. The pronoun *hū* in *inna-hū* may also refer to Noah's prayer for his unrighteous son which act of his was *Ghair Ṣāliḥ, i.e.*, out of place.

1319. *'Amalun* (lit. a deed) here means *Dhū 'Amalin, i.e.*, the doer of a deed. The use of the infinitive as active participle when an intensified sense is intended is in harmony with Arabic idiom. See also 2 : 178, where *Birr* (lit. righteousness) means a righteous person. An Arab poet says of his she-camel : *Innamā hiya Iqbālun wa Idbārū, i.e.*, she is so restless that she has become the very act of moving forward and backward, meaning the embodiment thereof.

48. *Noah* said, 'My Lord, I beg Thee to protect me from asking Thee that whereof I have no knowledge. And [a]unless Thou forgive[1320] me and have mercy on me, I shall be among the losers.'

قَالَ رَبِّ اِنِّیۡۤ اَعُوۡذُ بِکَ اَنۡ اَسۡـَٔلَکَ مَا لَیۡسَ لِیۡ بِہٖ عِلۡمٌ ؕ وَ اِلَّا تَغۡفِرۡ لِیۡ وَ تَرۡحَمۡنِیۡۤ اَکُنۡ مِّنَ الۡخٰسِرِیۡنَ ﴿۴۸﴾

49. It was said, 'O Noah, descend then with peace from Us and blessings upon thee and upon peoples *to be born* of those with thee.[1321] And *there will be other* peoples whom We shall grant provision *for a time*, then shall a grievous punishment overtake them from Us.'

قِیۡلَ یٰنُوۡحُ اہۡبِطۡ بِسَلٰمٍ مِّنَّا وَ بَرَکٰتٍ عَلَیۡکَ وَ عَلٰۤی اُمَمٍ مِّمَّنۡ مَّعَکَ ؕ وَ اُمَمٌ سَنُمَتِّعُہُمۡ ثُمَّ یَمَسُّہُمۡ مِّنَّا عَذَابٌ اَلِیۡمٌ ﴿۴۹﴾

[a]7 : 24.

1320. Noah had committed no sin by saying that his son was included in his family. It was only an error of judgment which is human, yet he offered *Istighfār* which shows that the offering of *Istighfār* is not necessarily a proof of one's sinfulness. It may also be offered for protection against the evil consequences of human weaknesses or those of errors of judgment.

1321. The verse shows that apart from the progeny of Noah the progeny of those believers who were with him in the Ark also were saved from the Deluge and that they prospered and multiplied. Scholars now subscribe to the view that most of the inhabitants of the earth are descended from Noah.

The story of the Deluge with some variations is to be found in the traditions and literature of different countries (Enc. Rel. & Eth.; Enc.Bib. & Enc. Brit. under "Deluge"). The catastrophe seems to have taken place somewhere near the dawn of human civilization. It is a well-known historical fact that whenever a people, comparatively more advanced in culture and civilization, have come to settle in a country, they have either blotted out of existence the less civilized inhabitants of the land or have greatly weakened them. Thus it appears that when the descendants of Noah and those of his companions who were the founders of human civilization spread to other lands, because they were more powerful than the people already living there, they either exterminated them or absorbed them. Thus they must have introduced into all the countries they subjugated their own traditions and customs ; and consequently the tradition about the Deluge must also have come to be introduced into other lands. With the lapse of time however, the immigrants ceased to have any connection with their original home and the catastrophe consequently came to be regarded as a local occurrence, with the result that local names of persons and places came to be substituted for the original names. So the Deluge was not a universal visitation, nor should the traditions of different lands be taken to point to separate floods.

50. This is of the tidings of the unseen[1322] which We reveal to thee. Thou didst not know them, neither thou nor thy people, before this. So be thou patient; for the *good* end is for the God-fearing.

تِلْكَ مِنْ اَنْۢبَآءِ الْغَيْبِ نُوْحِيْهَآ اِلَيْكَ ۚ مَا كُنْتَ
تَعْلَمُهَآ اَنْتَ وَلَا قَوْمُكَ مِنْ قَبْلِ هٰذَا ۛ فَاصْبِرْ ۛ
اِنَّ الْعَاقِبَةَ لِلْمُتَّقِيْنَ ۝٥٠ ع

R. 5 51. And [a]to 'Ād[1323] *We sent* their brother, Hūd. He said, 'O my people worship Allāh *alone*. You have no god save Him. *In associating other gods with Him* you but forge lies;

وَاِلٰى عَادٍ اَخَاهُمْ هُوْدًا ۗ قَالَ يٰقَوْمِ اعْبُدُوا اللّٰهَ
مَا لَكُمْ مِّنْ اِلٰهٍ غَيْرُهٗ ۗ اِنْ اَنْتُمْ اِلَّا مُفْتَرُوْنَ ۝٥١

[a]7 : 66.

1322. The Quranic accounts of the various Prophets are not meant as mere stories. They are given in the Qur'ān because they contain a prophetic allusion to the analogous events that were to occur in the life of the Holy Prophet himself.

1323. Some European critics have denied the very existence of the Adites. They say that none of the inscriptions that have so far been discovered in Arabia mention 'Ād as the name of any people in that country, and therefore they allege that the Qur'ān has only quoted one of the popular legends that were current among the Arabs in the Holy Prophet's time. This objection is based on a misunderstanding. In fact, sections of the human race are generally known by two sets of names, one representing the whole race and the other some particular group thereof. 'Ād was not the name of a single tribe but of a group of tribes, whose different sections rose to power at different times. They left behind them inscriptions bearing the name of particular groups. But they all belonged to the main 'Ād family. The fact that this name is found in ancient books of geography also shows that a people of the name of 'Ād did indeed live. The geographical works compiled in Greece state that in the pre-Christian era, Yemen was ruled by a tribe called Adramitai who were none other than the 'Ād who have been called 'Ād Iram in the Qur'ān. The termination of the Greek name is a noun-suffix, the real name being 'Adram which is a corruption of 'Ād Iram (Al-'Arab Qabl al-Islām). The 'Ād tribe mentioned in the Qur'ān was called Iram. This Iram section of the Adites possessed a powerful kingdom which lasted up to 500 B.C. Their language was Aramaic, which is akin to Hebrew. The Aramaic Kingdom was established after the fall of the Semitic Kingdom and it included in its boundaries the whole of Mesopotamia, Palestine, Syria and Chaldea. Archaeological researches have discovered traces of this Kingdom. See also "The Larger Edition of the Commentary."

The 'Ād tribe lived immediately after the people of Noah (7 : 70). They built monuments on elevated places (26 : 129). There still exist ruins of big buildings in Arabia. The history of these people has now become wrapped in obscurity and only some remains of their buildings are to be seen (46 : 26). The territory in which these people lived is called Aḥqāf (46 : 22), which, literally meaning meandering and zig-zag sand-hills, is the name given to two parts of Arabia, one in the south, known as the Southern Aḥqāf, the other in the north, called the Northern Aḥqāf. These tracts are fertile, but as they lie near the desert, sand-hills are caused there by the sand of the desert being heaped up by the wind. These sand-hills may have been formed when 'Ād were punished by a sand-storm. Their destruction was caused by the blowing of a violent wind burying their chief cities under heaps of sand and dust (69 : 7, 8).

52. 'O my people, [a]I do not ask of you any reward therefor. My reward is only with Him Who created me. Will you not then understand ?

يٰقَوْمِ لَآ اَسْـَٔلُكُمْ عَلَيْهِ اَجْرًا ۭ اِنْ اَجْرِيَ اِلَّا عَلَى
الَّذِيْ فَطَرَنِيْ ۭ اَفَلَا تَعْقِلُوْنَ ﴿٥٢﴾

53. 'And O my people, [b]ask forgiveness of your Lord, then turn to Him, He will send over you clouds pouring down abundant[1324] rain, and will add strength to your strength. And turn not away *from Him, being* sinners.'

وَيٰقَوْمِ اسْتَغْفِرُوْا رَبَّكُمْ ثُمَّ تُوْبُوْٓا اِلَيْهِ يُرْسِلِ
السَّمَاۗءَ عَلَيْكُمْ مِّدْرَارًا وَّيَزِدْكُمْ قُوَّةً اِلٰى قُوَّتِكُمْ
وَلَا تَتَوَلَّوْا مُجْرِمِيْنَ ﴿٥٣﴾

54. They said, 'O Hūd, thou hast not brought us any clear proof, and [c]we are not going to forsake our gods *merely* because of thy saying, nor are we going to believe in thee;

قَالُوْا يٰهُوْدُ مَا جِئْتَنَا بِبَيِّنَةٍ وَّمَا نَحْنُ بِتَارِكِيْٓ
اٰلِهَتِنَا عَنْ قَوْلِكَ وَمَا نَحْنُ لَكَ بِمُؤْمِنِيْنَ ﴿٥٤﴾

55. 'We can only say that some of our gods have smitten thee with evil.' He replied, 'Surely, I call Allāh to witness, and do ye also bear witness that I am clear *of the sin* of your associating

اِنْ نَّقُوْلُ اِلَّا اعْتَرٰىكَ بَعْضُ اٰلِهَتِنَا بِسُوْۗءٍ ۭ قَالَ اِنِّيْٓ
اُشْهِدُ اللّٰهَ وَاشْهَدُوْٓا اَنِّيْ بَرِيْۗءٌ مِّمَّا تُشْرِكُوْنَ ﴿٥٥﴾

56. '*Other gods* with Him. [d]So devise plans against me, all *of you*, and give me no respite;

مِنْ دُوْنِهٖ فَكِيْدُوْنِيْ جَمِيْعًا ثُمَّ لَا تُنْظِرُوْنِ ﴿٥٦﴾

[a]26 : 128. [b]11 : 4, 62; 71 : 11. [c]71 : 24. [d]7 : 196; 10 : 72.

1324. It seems that the chief occupation of the people of 'Ād was agriculture and that they depended on rain-water for the cultivation of their land, there being no wells or canals to irrigate it.

57. 'I have indeed put my trust in Allāh, my Lord and your Lord. [a]There is no creature that moves on the earth but He holds it by the forelock.[1325] Surely, my Lord is on the straight path *to help those who put their trust in Him*;

إِنِّي تَوَكَّلْتُ عَلَى اللَّهِ رَبِّي وَرَبِّكُمْ ۚ مَا مِنْ دَابَّةٍ
إِلَّا هُوَ آخِذٌ بِنَاصِيَتِهَا ۚ إِنَّ رَبِّي عَلَىٰ صِرَاطٍ
مُسْتَقِيمٍ ﴿٥٧﴾

58. 'If, then, you turn away, [b]I have already conveyed to you that with which I have been sent to you, and [c]my Lord will make another people take your place. And you cannot harm Him at all. Surely, my Lord is Guardian over all things.'

فَإِنْ تَوَلَّوْا فَقَدْ أَبْلَغْتُكُمْ مَا أُرْسِلْتُ بِهِ إِلَيْكُمْ ۚ
وَيَسْتَخْلِفُ رَبِّي قَوْمًا غَيْرَكُمْ وَلَا تَضُرُّونَهُ شَيْئًا ۚ إِنَّ
رَبِّي عَلَىٰ كُلِّ شَيْءٍ حَفِيظٌ ﴿٥٨﴾

59. And when Our command came, We saved Hūd and those who believed with him, by Our *special* mercy. And [d]We saved them from a severe torment.

وَلَمَّا جَاءَ أَمْرُنَا نَجَّيْنَا هُودًا وَالَّذِينَ آمَنُوا مَعَهُ
بِرَحْمَةٍ مِنَّا وَنَجَّيْنَاهُمْ مِنْ عَذَابٍ غَلِيظٍ ﴿٥٩﴾

60. And such were 'Ād. They denied the Signs of their Lord and disobeyed His Messengers and followed the bidding of every haughty enemy *of truth*.

وَتِلْكَ عَادٌ ۖ جَحَدُوا بِآيَاتِ رَبِّهِمْ وَعَصَوْا رُسُلَهُ
وَاتَّبَعُوا أَمْرَ كُلِّ جَبَّارٍ عَنِيدٍ ﴿٦٠﴾

61. [e]And they were pursued by a curse in this world, and on the Day of Resurrection. Behold! the 'Ād were ungrateful to their Lord. Behold! destruction is decreed[1325A] for 'Ād, the people of Hūd.

وَأُتْبِعُوا فِي هَٰذِهِ الدُّنْيَا لَعْنَةً وَيَوْمَ الْقِيَامَةِ ۗ أَلَا
إِنَّ عَادًا كَفَرُوا رَبَّهُمْ ۗ أَلَا بُعْدًا لِعَادٍ قَوْمِ هُودٍ ﴿٦١﴾

[a]11 : 7. [b]7 : 69; 46 : 24. [c]4 : 134; 6 : 134. [d]7 : 73. [e]28 : 43.

1325. The words refer to an ancient custom of the Arabs. When a vanquished people were brought as captives before their victor, he would catch hold of their forelocks or got them shaved in token of victory.

1325A. *Bu'd* (which is derived from *Ba'uda* signifying, he was or became distant; he perished; he was cursed) means, remoteness; curse, malediction. They say *Bu'dan la-hū*, ***i.e.***, may he be cursed, may he perish (Lane).

R. 6 62. [a]And to *the tribe of* Thamūd[1326] We sent their brother Ṣāliḥ. He said, 'O my people, worship Allāh; you have no god other than Him. He raised you up from the earth and settled you therein. So ask forgiveness of Him, then turn to Him wholly. Verily, my Lord is nigh, *and* answers *prayers.*'

وَإِلَىٰ ثَمُودَ أَخَاهُمْ صَالِحًا قَالَ يَا قَوْمِ اعْبُدُوا اللَّهَ مَا لَكُمْ مِنْ إِلَٰهٍ غَيْرُهُ هُوَ أَنْشَأَكُمْ مِنَ الْأَرْضِ وَاسْتَعْمَرَكُمْ فِيهَا فَاسْتَغْفِرُوهُ ثُمَّ تُوبُوا إِلَيْهِ إِنَّ رَبِّي قَرِيبٌ مُجِيبٌ ﴿٦٢﴾

63. They said, 'O Ṣāliḥ, thou wast among us one in whom we placed our hopes. Dost thou forbid us to worship what our fathers worshipped? And we are surely in disquieting doubt concerning that to which thou callest us.'

قَالُوا يَا صَالِحُ قَدْ كُنْتَ فِينَا مَرْجُوًّا قَبْلَ هَٰذَا أَتَنْهَانَا أَنْ نَعْبُدَ مَا يَعْبُدُ آبَاؤُنَا وَإِنَّنَا لَفِي شَكٍّ مِمَّا تَدْعُونَا إِلَيْهِ مُرِيبٍ ﴿٦٣﴾

64. He said, [b]'O my people, tell me, if I *base my claim* on a clear proof from my Lord and He has granted me *a special* mercy from Himself, who then will help me against Allāh, if I disobey Him? So you will only add to my destruction;

قَالَ يَا قَوْمِ أَرَأَيْتُمْ إِنْ كُنْتُ عَلَىٰ بَيِّنَةٍ مِنْ رَبِّي وَآتَانِي مِنْهُ رَحْمَةً فَمَنْ يَنْصُرُنِي مِنَ اللَّهِ إِنْ عَصَيْتُهُ فَمَا تَزِيدُونَنِي غَيْرَ تَخْسِيرٍ ﴿٦٤﴾

[a]7 : 74. [b]11 : 29,89.

1326. Thamūd, being an Arabic word, shows that the tribe belonged to the Arab stock. It is futile to say that Ṣāliḥ may be the translation of a foreign name, for the Qur'ān has adopted all foreign names without translating them such as Mūsā (Moses), Hārūn (Aaron), Yūnus (Jonah) and Zakariyya (Zachariah). The Thamūd were successors to the 'Ād (7 : 75) which means that the 'Ād were also an Arab race. Again, the 'Ād, in their turn, were successors to the people of Noah. This shows that Noah was also an Arab. In fact, Noah was raised in Mesopotamia, which territory was in early times under Arab rule. Greek historians placed the Thamūd tribe in a period not long before the Christian era. Ḥijr or Agra, as they call it, is given as their home. They call them Thamudeni and mention a place near Ḥijr whlch, according to them, the Arabs called Fajj al-Nāqah. Ptolemy (140 B.C.) says that near Ḥijr is a place known as Badanata. Abū Ismā'īl, author of the 'Futūḥ al-Shām,' says, 'The tribe of Thamūd filled the land between Boṣra (in Syria) and Aden and ruled there. Perhaps they were migrating to the north.' Al-Ḥijr, (also known as Madā'in Ṣāliḥ) seems to have been the capital of these people. It lies between Medina and Tabūk, and the valley in which it is situated is called Wadī Qurā. It is worthy of note that accounts of the Prophets Hūd and Ṣāliḥ have been given at various places in the Qur'ān and everywhere the order observed is the same, *viz.*, the account of Hūd precedes that of Ṣāliḥ, which is the true chronological order. This shows that the Qur'ān gives accurately and in their true historical order the facts of history long consigned to oblivion and wrapped in obscurity. According to some, Thamūd is only another name of 'Ād Thāniyah or the second 'Ād, while according to others they came after the second 'Ād. The Thamūd ruled over plains and hills (7 : 75) and their country abounded in springs and gardens wherein grew date-palms of excellent quality. They also cultivated land and grew corn (26 : 148-149).

65. 'And O my people, [a]this is the she-camel of Allāh, a Sign for you, so leave her *free* that she may feed in Allāh's earth, and touch her not with harm lest a near punishment seize you.'

وَ يٰقَوْمِ هٰذِهٖ نَاقَةُ اللّٰهِ لَكُمْ اٰيَةً فَذَرُوْهَا تَاْكُلْ
فِيْٓ اَرْضِ اللّٰهِ وَلَا تَمَسُّوْهَا بِسُوْٓءٍ فَيَاْخُذَكُمْ عَذَابٌ
قَرِيْبٌ ﴿۶۵﴾

66. [b]But they hamstrung her; then he said, 'Enjoy yourselves in your houses for three[1327] days. This is a promise which will not be belied.'

فَعَقَرُوْهَا فَقَالَ تَمَتَّعُوْا فِيْ دَارِكُمْ ثَلٰثَةَ اَيَّامٍ ؕ
ذٰلِكَ وَعْدٌ غَيْرُ مَكْذُوْبٍ ﴿۶۶﴾

67. And when Our command came to pass, We saved Ṣāliḥ and those who believed with him by Our *special* mercy from the ignominy of that day. Surely, thy Lord is Powerful, Mighty.

فَلَمَّا جَآءَ اَمْرُنَا نَجَّيْنَا صٰلِحًا وَّالَّذِيْنَ اٰمَنُوْا مَعَهٗ
بِرَحْمَةٍ مِّنَّا وَمِنْ خِزْيِ يَوْمِئِذٍ ؕ اِنَّ رَبَّكَ هُوَ
الْقَوِيُّ الْعَزِيْزُ ﴿۶۷﴾

68. And [c]punishment[1328] overtook those who had done wrong, and they lay prostrate in their houses,

وَ اَخَذَ الَّذِيْنَ ظَلَمُوا الصَّيْحَةُ فَاَصْبَحُوْا فِيْ دِيَارِهِمْ
جٰثِمِيْنَ ﴿۶۸﴾

[a]7 : 74; 17 : 60; 26 : 156; 54 : 28; 91 : 14. [b]7 : 78; 26 : 158; 54 : 30; 91 : 15. [c]7 : 79; 26 : 159; 54 : 32.

This Quranic account is corroborated by the inscription said to have been read by some Muslims during the reign of Mu'āwiyah. Their decline seems to have begun soon after the time of Ṣāliḥ, for only a few centuries after his time their name fails to find mention among victorious nations. Arabia was invaded by an Assyrian king (722-705 B.C.) and the name Thamūd is found mentioned among the conquered tribes in an inscription which he caused to be engraved in memory of his victory. Of the Greek historians, Didorus (80 B.C.), Pliny (79 B.C.) and Ptolemy make mention of the Thamūd. When Justinian, the Roman Emperor, invaded Arabia, his army included 300 Thamūdi soldiers, but before the advent of Islām this tribe had become altogether extinct. See also "The Larger Edition of the Commentary."

1327. The respite of three days was probably meant as a last chance for repentance of which the unlucky people did not avail themselves.

1328. Seven different words and expressions have been used in the Qur'ān to describe the punishment which overtook the tribe of Thamūd. In the present verse and in 54 : 32, the word used is *Ṣaiḥah* (punishment) ; in 7 : 79, *Rajfah* (an earthquake) ; in 26 : 159 simply *'Adhāb* (chastisement) ; in 27 : 52, *Dammarnā-hum* (We utterly destroyed them) ; in 51 : 45, *Ṣā'iqah* (thunderbolt ; or any destructive punishment) ; in 69 : 6, *Ṭāghiyah* (an extraordinary punishment); and in 91:15, *Damdama 'Alaihim* (He destroyed them completely). Though the words and expressions employed to describe the visitation seem to be different in form, yet they possess no discrepancy in meaning. The words which, however, appear to be contradictory, are *Rajfah*, *Ṣaiḥah*, *Ṣā'iqah* and *Ṭāghiyah*. As the last three also mean punishment, therefore if the tribe of Thamūd were destroyed by means of an earthquake all the above words may be rightly used to describe that catastrophe.

69. [a]As though they had never dwelt therein. Remember! *The* Thamūd believed not in their Lord. So away with *the tribe of* Thamūd.[1329]

كَاَنْ لَّمْ يَغْنَوْا فِيْهَا ؕ اَلَاۤ اِنَّ ثَمُوْدَاۡ كَفَرُوْا رَبَّهُمْ ؕ
اَلَا بُعْدًا لِّثَمُوْدَ ﴿۶۹﴾ ع

R. 7 70. And [b]surely, Our messengers[1330] came to Abraham[1331] with glad tidings. [c]They said, '*We bid you* peace.' He answered, 'Peace *be on you*,' and he was not long in bringing a roasted calf.

وَلَقَدْ جَآءَتْ رُسُلُنَاۤ اِبْرٰهِيْمَ بِالْبُشْرٰى قَالُوْا سَلٰمًا ؕ
قَالَ سَلٰمٌ فَمَا لَبِثَ اَنْ جَآءَ بِعِجْلٍ حَنِيْذٍ ﴿۷۰﴾

71. But [d]when he saw their hands not reaching thereto, he considered this strange on their part and conceived fear of them. They said, 'Fear not, for we have been sent to the people of Lot.'[1332]

فَلَمَّا رَاٰۤ اَيْدِيَهُمْ لَا تَصِلُ اِلَيْهِ نَكِرَهُمْ وَاَوْجَسَ
مِنْهُمْ خِيْفَةً ؕ قَالُوْا لَا تَخَفْ اِنَّاۤ اُرْسِلْنَاۤ اِلٰى
قَوْمِ لُوْطٍ ﴿۷۱﴾

[a]10 : 25. [b]15 : 52 ; 51 : 25. [c]15 : 53 ; 51 : 26. [d]51 : 28-29.

1329. In v. 61 the words 'the people of Hūd' have been added to the word, 'Ād, for an historical reason, for 'Ād is, in fact, the name of two tribes, the first 'Ād and the second 'Ād, and the words 'the people of Hūd' have been added to show that it is the first and not the second 'Ād that is meant there. But as Thamūd was the name of one tribe only, the words 'the people of Ṣāliḥ' have been omitted, for their addition would have served no useful purpose.

1330. There exists much difference of opinion as to who the 'messengers' were. Some hold them to be human beings, others think that they were angels. The former view appears to be more akin to truth and reality. Both Abraham and Lot being strangers in the land, it is quite possible that God had enjoined some pious men of that locality to take Lot to a safe place before the visitation actually overtook his people. It should also be remembered that these 'messengers' had not come to give the first warning of the punishment. Lot's people had already been threatened with punishment (15:65). The 'messengers' came only to inform him that the appointed hour of the threatened punishment had arrived.

1331. Abraham's real name was Abram. After the birth of Ishmael, according to God's own command, he came to be called Abraham which means the 'Father of multitudes' or the 'Father of many nations.' One branch of his progeny, the Israelites, lived in Canaan and the other, the Ishmaelites, in Arabia.

1332. Abraham at first took the 'messengers' to be ordinary wayfarers, but when they refrained from eating of the roasted calf he realized that they were on some special mission which he had failed to understand. The words, *conceived fear of them*, do not mean that Abraham was afraid of the strangers but that, when they did not partake of the food, he feared that he might have done something against the etiquette of hospitality. The guests, it appears, read Abraham's perturbed state of mind from the uneasy expression of his face, so they at once removed his anxiety by telling him that they were in no way displeased and that the reason why they did not partake of food was that their dreadful mission had made them disinclined to eat. This answer of the visitors also shows that they were not angels ; for had they been angels, they would have said that being not human they could not partake of food.

72. And his wife was standing *by* and she *too* was frightened, whereupon *to assure her* [a]We gave her glad tidings of the birth of Isaac, and, after Isaac, of Jacob.

وَامْرَاَتُهٗ قَآئِمَةٌ فَضَحِكَتْ فَبَشَّرْنٰهَا بِاِسْحٰقَ ۙ وَ
مِنْ وَّرَآءِ اِسْحٰقَ يَعْقُوْبَ ﴿٧٢﴾

73. [b]She said, 'Oh, woe is me ! Shall I bear a child when I am an extremely old woman and this my husband *also* is a very old man ? This is indeed a strange thing !'

قَالَتْ يٰوَيْلَتٰۤى ءَاَلِدُ وَاَنَا عَجُوْزٌ وَّهٰذَا بَعْلِيْ شَيْخًا ؕ
اِنَّ هٰذَا لَشَيْءٌ عَجِيْبٌ ﴿٧٣﴾

74. [c]They said, 'Dost thou marvel at Allāh's decree ? The mercy of Allāh and His blessings are upon you, O people of the house.[1333] Surely, He is Praiseworthy, Glorious.'

قَالُوْۤا اَتَعْجَبِيْنَ مِنْ اَمْرِ اللّٰهِ رَحْمَتُ اللّٰهِ وَبَرَكٰتُهٗ
عَلَيْكُمْ اَهْلَ الْبَيْتِ ؕ اِنَّهٗ حَمِيْدٌ مَّجِيْدٌ ﴿٧٤﴾

75. And when fear departed from Abraham and the glad tidings came to him, he began to plead with Us[1334] for the people of Lot.

فَلَمَّا ذَهَبَ عَنْ اِبْرٰهِيْمَ الرَّوْعُ وَجَآءَتْهُ الْبُشْرٰى
يُجَادِلُنَا فِيْ قَوْمِ لُوْطٍ ؕ ﴿٧٥﴾

76. [d]Indeed, Abraham was clement, tender-hearted, *and* oft-returning *to Us*.

اِنَّ اِبْرٰهِيْمَ لَحَلِيْمٌ اَوَّاهٌ مُّنِيْبٌ ﴿٧٦﴾

77. 'O Abraham, desist from this. Surely, the decree of thy Lord has gone forth, and surely, there is coming to them a punishment that cannot be averted.'

يٰۤاِبْرٰهِيْمُ اَعْرِضْ عَنْ هٰذَا ۚ اِنَّهٗ قَدْ جَآءَ اَمْرُ
رَبِّكَ ۚ وَاِنَّهُمْ اٰتِيْهِمْ عَذَابٌ غَيْرُ مَرْدُوْدٍ ﴿٧٧﴾

---

[a]21 : 73; 51 : 29. [b]51 : 30. [c]51 : 31. [d]9 : 114.

Lot was the ancestor of the Palestinian peoples, Moab and Ammon, and as the son of Haran and the grandson of Terah, he was Abraham's nephew. He joined Abraham in Canaan.

1333. In this verse the words 'people of the house' are definitely applied to the wife of Abraham, because no child had yet been born to her. In fact, when the expression *Ahl al-Bait* is used in the Qur'ān in respect of a Prophet it generally applies to his wife or wives (28 : 13; 33 : 34).

1334. See Gen. 18 : 21-33

78. And [a]when Our messengers came to Lot, he was grieved on their account and felt helpless[1335] for them and he said, 'This is a distressful day.'

وَلَمَّا جَآءَتْ رُسُلُنَا لُوْطًا سِيْٓءَ بِهِمْ وَضَاقَ بِهِمْ ذَرْعًا وَّ قَالَ هٰذَا يَوْمٌ عَصِيْبٌ ﴿۷۸﴾

79. And his people came to him, running[1336] towards him, trembling *with rage*, and before this *too* [b]they used to do evils. He said, 'O my people, [c]these are my daughters; they are purer for you.[1337] So fear Allāh and do not disgrace me in *the presence* of my guests. Is there not among you one right-minded man?'

وَجَآءَهٗ قَوْمُهٗ يُهْرَعُوْنَ اِلَيْهِ ۭ وَمِنْ قَبْلُ كَانُوْا يَعْمَلُوْنَ السَّيِّاٰتِ ۭ قَالَ يٰقَوْمِ هٰٓؤُلَاۗءِ بَنَاتِيْ هُنَّ اَطْهَرُ لَكُمْ فَاتَّقُوا اللّٰهَ وَلَا تُخْزُوْنِ فِيْ ضَيْفِيْ ۭ اَلَيْسَ مِنْكُمْ رَجُلٌ رَّشِيْدٌ ﴿۷۹﴾

[a]29 : 34. [b]7 : 81 ; 29 : 29. [c]15 : 72.

1335. The expression, *Ḍāqabil-Amri Dhar'an*, means, he lacked ability, power or strength to do the thing, *Dhar'* meaning power or ability ; or the expression means, the thing or affair was rendered difficult or distressing to him (Lane). The words in the text mean, he found himself helpless or unable to protect them.

1336. The inhabitants of the two towns, Sodom and Gomorrah, had adopted the calling of the road and used to plunder wayfarers (Jew. Enc. under "Sodom"). Naturally they were constantly apprehensive of reprisals, particularly the inhabitants of Sodom who were practically in a state of war with their neighbours (Gen. 14). They would not welcome strangers into their town. Lot, like all Prophets of God, naturally would look after the comfort of the strangers and entertain them (15 : 71). His people, apprehensive as they were, had repeatedly warned him to give up that practice, so when he brought 'the messengers,' who were strangers, into his house they became infuriated and hastened to him with angry faces, because they thought they now had got a suitable opportunity to punish him for giving shelter to strangers in defiance of their repeated protests (15 : 68-71).

1337. The verse signifies that in view of their past mischievous behaviour Lot feared lest his people should do any mischief and thus disgrace him in the presence of his guests. There is no reference here to any particular mischief. They were wicked people, therefore, Lot was naturally apprehensive that they might do him some kind of harm. He therefore said to them that if they really entertained fear that he might do them harm in league with the strangers, they had his daughters in their custody and they could wreak vengeance on him by punishing them. That was a better and purer course for them to adopt, for in that way they would also avoid the disgraceful act of insulting his guests. Or the meaning may be that, being a venerable old man of the town, Lot referred to their own wives as his daughters who, he said, were purer for them.

80. They answered, 'Thou surely knowest that we have no claim against thy daughters, and thou surely knowest what we desire.'[1338]

قَالُوا لَقَدْ عَلِمْتَ مَا لَنَا فِي بَنٰتِكَ مِنْ حَقٍّ ۚ وَإِنَّكَ لَتَعْلَمُ مَا نُرِيدُ ﴿٨٠﴾

81. He said, 'Would that I had power to deal with you, or that I could betake myself to a mighty support *for shelter*.[1338A]

قَالَ لَوْ أَنَّ لِي بِكُمْ قُوَّةً أَوْ آوِي إِلَىٰ رُكْنٍ شَدِيدٍ ﴿٨١﴾

82. *The messengers* said, 'O Lot, we are the messengers of thy Lord.[1339] They shall by no means reach thee. So [a]depart with thy family [b]while yet a part of the night *remains* and let none of you look back, but thy wife. Surely, what is going to befall them shall befall her *also*. Verily, [c]their appointed time is the morning. Is not morning nigh?'

قَالُوا يٰلُوطُ إِنَّا رُسُلُ رَبِّكَ لَنْ يَصِلُوا إِلَيْكَ فَأَسْرِ بِأَهْلِكَ بِقِطْعٍ مِنَ اللَّيْلِ وَلَا يَلْتَفِتْ مِنْكُمْ أَحَدٌ إِلَّا امْرَأَتَكَ ۖ إِنَّهُ مُصِيبُهَا مَا أَصَابَهُمْ ۚ إِنَّ مَوْعِدَهُمُ الصُّبْحُ ۚ أَلَيْسَ الصُّبْحُ بِقَرِيبٍ ﴿٨٢﴾

83. [d]So when Our decree came *to pass*, [e]We turned that *town* upside down and We rained upon it stones of clay, layer upon layer,[1339A]

فَلَمَّا جَاءَ أَمْرُنَا جَعَلْنَا عَالِيَهَا سَافِلَهَا وَأَمْطَرْنَا عَلَيْهَا حِجَارَةً مِنْ سِجِّيلٍ ۙ مَنْضُودٍ ﴿٨٣﴾

[a]15 : 66. [b]7 : 84; 15 : 61; 29 : 34. [c]15 : 67. [d]15 : 75; [e]51 : 34.

1338. When Lot offered his daughters who were married in the town (Gen. 19:15) as hostages, his people refused to accept the offer, for that was against their custom to accept females as hostages (Enc. Brit.). The words, 'we have no claim against thy daughters,' show that they had not come with the motives which most Commentators ascribe to them, for a people who had become so depraved and corrupt in their morals as the people of Lot were, would raise no question of claim or no claim, right or no right with regard to the satisfaction of their carnal passions. The words, 'thou surely knowest what we desire' mean, 'you know that we want the strangers to be handed over to us.'

1338A. I shall pray to God to be saved from the humiliation you seek to inflict upon me by insisting that I should turn away my guests.

1339. The 'messengers' were righteous men of the neighbourhood who were commanded by God to warn Lot and to direct him where to go.

1339A. It appears that the people of Lot were destroyed by a terrible earthquake. Violent earthquakes often turn parts of the earth upside down and fragments of earth fly off into the air and then fall down.

84. [a]Marked *for them in the decree* of thy Lord. And such *punishment* is not far from the wrongdoers *of the present age.*

مُّسَوَّمَةً عِندَ رَبِّكَ ۖ وَمَا هِيَ مِنَ الظّٰلِمِيْنَ بِبَعِيْدٍ ﴿٨٤﴾

R. 8 85. [b]And to Midian [1340] *We sent* their brother Shu'aib. He said, 'O my people, worship Allāh. You have no god other than Him. And [c]give not short measure and short weight. I see you in *a state of* prosperity and I fear for you the punishment of a destructive day;

وَإِلٰى مَدْيَنَ اَخَاهُمْ شُعَيْبًا ۚ قَالَ يٰقَوْمِ اعْبُدُوا اللّٰهَ مَا لَكُمْ مِّنْ اِلٰهٍ غَيْرُهٗ ۖ وَلَا تَنْقُصُوا الْمِكْيَالَ وَالْمِيْزَانَ اِنِّيْٓ اَرٰىكُمْ بِخَيْرٍ وَّاِنِّيْٓ اَخَافُ عَلَيْكُمْ عَذَابَ يَوْمٍ مُّحِيْطٍ ﴿٨٥﴾

86. [d]'And O my people, give full measure and full weight with equity and defraud not people of their things and commit not iniquity in the land, causing disorder;

وَيٰقَوْمِ اَوْفُوا الْمِكْيَالَ وَالْمِيْزَانَ بِالْقِسْطِ وَلَا تَبْخَسُوا النَّاسَ اَشْيَآءَهُمْ وَلَا تَعْثَوْا فِي الْاَرْضِ مُفْسِدِيْنَ ﴿٨٦﴾

87. 'That which is left [1341] *with you* by Allāh is better for you, if you are believers. And I am not *appointed* a keeper over you.'

بَقِيَّتُ اللّٰهِ خَيْرٌ لَّكُمْ اِنْ كُنْتُمْ مُّؤْمِنِيْنَ ۚ وَمَآ اَنَا عَلَيْكُمْ بِحَفِيْظٍ ﴿٨٧﴾

88. They replied, 'O Shu'aib, does thy Prayer bid thee that we should leave what our fathers worshipped, or that we cease to do with our property what we please? Surely, thou *dost consider thyself* very intelligent *and* right-minded.'

قَالُوْا يٰشُعَيْبُ اَصَلٰوتُكَ تَاْمُرُكَ اَنْ نَّتْرُكَ مَا يَعْبُدُ اٰبَآؤُنَآ اَوْ اَنْ نَّفْعَلَ فِيْٓ اَمْوَالِنَا مَا نَشٰٓؤُا ۖ اِنَّكَ لَاَنْتَ الْحَلِيْمُ الرَّشِيْدُ ﴿٨٨﴾

---

[a]51 : 35. [b]7 : 86; 29 : 37. [c]26 : 182, 183. [d]7 : 86; 26 : 184.

1340. Midian was a son of Abraham from his third wife, Keturah (Gen. 25 : 1,2). His descendants were all called Midian. Their metropolis was also called Midian. This town was situated on the Gulf of 'Aqabah, on the Arabian coast, at a distance of some six or seven miles from the sea. The descendants of Midian lived in the north of the Ḥijāz and it is they who built this town. It was there that Moses fled for refuge from Pharaoh and it was in the neighbourhood of Midian that he stayed with the Israelites after crossing the Red Sea. See also 1010.

1341. *Baqiyyah* here signifies, wealth earned by fair and honest means and in accordance with the laws of God. It may also mean, God-given powers and capabilities. See also 309.

89. He said, [a]'O my people, tell me if I *stand* on a clear evidence from my Lord, and He has provided me from Himself with a handsome provision,[1342] *what answer will you give Him*? And I do not desire to do against you the *very* thing which I ask you not to do. I only desire to set *things* right as far as I [b]can. I have no power *to accomplish anything* save through Allāh. In Him do I trust and to Him do I turn;

قَالَ يٰقَوْمِ اَرَءَيْتُمْ اِنْ كُنْتُ عَلٰى بَيِّنَةٍ مِّنْ
رَّبِّيْ وَرَزَقَنِيْ مِنْهُ رِزْقًا حَسَنًا ؕ وَمَآ اُرِيْدُ اَنْ
اُخَالِفَكُمْ اِلٰى مَآ اَنْهٰكُمْ عَنْهُ ؕ اِنْ اُرِيْدُ اِلَّا
الْاِصْلَاحَ مَا اسْتَطَعْتُ ؕ وَمَا تَوْفِيْقِيْٓ اِلَّا بِاللّٰهِ ؕ
عَلَيْهِ تَوَكَّلْتُ وَاِلَيْهِ اُنِيْبُ ﴿۸۹﴾

90. 'And O my people, let not *your* hostility towards me lead you *to this* that there should befall you the like of that which befell the people of Noah or the people of Hūd or the people of Ṣāliḥ; and the people of Lot are not far from you;[1343]

وَيٰقَوْمِ لَا يَجْرِمَنَّكُمْ شِقَاقِيْٓ اَنْ يُّصِيْبَكُمْ مِّثْلُ
مَآ اَصَابَ قَوْمَ نُوْحٍ اَوْ قَوْمَ هُوْدٍ اَوْ قَوْمَ صٰلِحٍ ؕ
وَمَا قَوْمُ لُوْطٍ مِّنْكُمْ بِبَعِيْدٍ ﴿۹۰﴾

91. 'And [c]seek forgiveness of your Lord; then turn *wholly* to Him. Verily, my Lord is Merciful, Most Loving.'

وَاسْتَغْفِرُوْا رَبَّكُمْ ثُمَّ تُوْبُوْٓا اِلَيْهِ ؕ اِنَّ رَبِّيْ رَحِيْمٌ
وَّدُوْدٌ ﴿۹۱﴾

92. They replied, 'O Shu'aib, we do not understand much of what thou sayest, and [d]surely we see that thou art weak among us. And were it not for thy tribe, we would surely stone thee. And thou holdest no strong position among us.'

قَالُوْا يٰشُعَيْبُ مَا نَفْقَهُ كَثِيْرًا مِّمَّا تَقُوْلُ وَاِنَّا
لَنَرٰىكَ فِيْنَا ضَعِيْفًا ۚ وَلَوْلَا رَهْطُكَ لَرَجَمْنٰكَ ۫ وَ
مَآ اَنْتَ عَلَيْنَا بِعَزِيْزٍ ﴿۹۲﴾

93. He said, 'O my people, is my tribe mightier with you than Allāh? And you have cast Him behind your backs *as a thing neglected*. Surely, my Lord encompasses all that you do;

قَالَ يٰقَوْمِ اَرَهْطِيْٓ اَعَزُّ عَلَيْكُمْ مِّنَ اللّٰهِ ؕ وَاتَّخَذْتُمُوْهُ
وَرَآءَكُمْ ظِهْرِيًّا ؕ اِنَّ رَبِّيْ بِمَا تَعْمَلُوْنَ مُحِيْطٌ ﴿۹۳﴾

[a]11 : 64. [b]7 : 94. [c]11 : 4. [d]7 : 89.

1342. Shu'aib's opponents suspected that by restraining them from their fraudulent practices, he sought to foster his own business. Shu'aib removed their apprehension by these words.

1343. This verse shows that Shu'aib came after Noah, Hūd, Ṣāliḥ and Lot (and for that matter after Abraham also), but lived before the time of Moses, for he does not here speak of the people of Moses, although Moses and his people lived in the very territory of the people of Shu'aib.

94. 'And [a]O my people, act according to your power.[1343A] I, too, am acting. You will soon know on whom descends a punishment that will disgrace him, and who it is that is a liar. And wait ; surely, I *too* wait with you.'

وَيٰقَوْمِ اعْمَلُوْا عَلٰى مَكَانَتِكُمْ اِنِّيْ عَامِلٌ ۭ سَوْفَ
تَعْلَمُوْنَ ۙ مَنْ يَّاْتِيْهِ عَذَابٌ يُّخْزِيْهِ وَمَنْ هُوَ كَاذِبٌ ۭ
وَارْتَقِبُوْٓا اِنِّيْ مَعَكُمْ رَقِيْبٌ ﴿٩٤﴾

95. And when Our decree came *to pass* We saved Shu'aib, and those who had believed with him by Our *special* mercy; and [b]chastisement seized those who had done wrong, so that they lay prostrate in their houses,

وَلَمَّا جَاۗءَ اَمْرُنَا نَجَّيْنَا شُعَيْبًا وَّالَّذِيْنَ اٰمَنُوْا مَعَهٗ
بِرَحْمَةٍ مِّنَّا وَاَخَذَتِ الَّذِيْنَ ظَلَمُوا الصَّيْحَةُ فَاَصْبَحُوْا
فِيْ دِيَارِهِمْ جٰثِمِيْنَ ﴿٩٥﴾

96. As [c]though they had never dwelt therein. So perished Midian even as Thamūd had perished.

كَاَنْ لَّمْ يَغْنَوْا فِيْهَا ۭ اَلَا بُعْدًا لِّمَدْيَنَ كَمَا بَعِدَتْ
ثَمُوْدُ ﴿٩٦﴾

R. 9 97. And, surely, [d]We sent Moses with Our Signs and manifest authority,

وَلَقَدْ اَرْسَلْنَا مُوْسٰى بِاٰيٰتِنَا وَسُلْطٰنٍ مُّبِيْنٍ ﴿٩٧﴾

98. [e]To Pharaoh and his chiefs; but they followed the command of Pharaoh, and the command of Pharaoh was not at all rightful.

اِلٰى فِرْعَوْنَ وَمَلَا۟ىِٕهٖ فَاتَّبَعُوْٓا اَمْرَ فِرْعَوْنَ ۚ وَمَآ
اَمْرُ فِرْعَوْنَ بِرَشِيْدٍ ﴿٩٨﴾

99. He will go before his people on the Day of Resurrection and will lead them into the Fire. And evil indeed will be the watering-place[1343B] arrived at.

يَقْدُمُ قَوْمَهٗ يَوْمَ الْقِيٰمَةِ فَاَوْرَدَهُمُ النَّارَ ۭ وَبِئْسَ
الْوِرْدُ الْمَوْرُوْدُ ﴿٩٩﴾

---

[a]39 : 40. [b]7 : 92; 26 : 190; 29 : 38. [c]7 : 93. [d]14 : 6; 40 : 24. [e]23 : 47; 40 : 25.

1343A. The verse may also signify that they should go on working according to their own lights and plans, and he would work as guided by his Faith. The results would show who was working in accordance with God's Will and who was seeking to defy and frustrate His purpose.

1343B. *Wird* is derived from *Warada* and means, time; place and turn of watering; people or cattle coming to a watering place (Aqrab).

100. And [a]they are pursued by a curse in this life and on the Day of Resurrection. Evil is the gift[1344] which will be given *them*.

وَأُتْبِعُوا فِي هَٰذِهِ لَعْنَةً وَيَوْمَ الْقِيَامَةِ ۚ بِئْسَ الرِّفْدُ
الْمَرْفُودُ ﴿١٠٠﴾

101. [b]That is *part* of the tidings of the *ruined* cities, We relate it to thee. Of them *some* are standing and *some* have been mown down *like the harvest*.

ذَٰلِكَ مِنْ أَنْبَاءِ الْقُرَىٰ نَقُصُّهُ عَلَيْكَ ۖ مِنْهَا قَائِمٌ
وَحَصِيدٌ ﴿١٠١﴾

102. And [c]We did not wrong them, but they wronged themselves,[1345] and their gods on whom they called instead of Allāh were of no avail to them at all when the decree *of punishment* of thy Lord came *to pass*; and they added to them naught but perdition.

وَمَا ظَلَمْنَاهُمْ وَلَٰكِنْ ظَلَمُوا أَنْفُسَهُمْ ۖ فَمَا أَغْنَتْ
عَنْهُمْ آلِهَتُهُمُ الَّتِي يَدْعُونَ مِنْ دُونِ اللَّهِ مِنْ
شَيْءٍ لَمَّا جَاءَ أَمْرُ رَبِّكَ ۖ وَمَا زَادُوهُمْ غَيْرَ تَتْبِيبٍ ﴿١٠٢﴾

103. [d]Such is the seizure of thy Lord when He seizes the cities while they are doing wrong. Surely, His seizure is grievous and severe.

وَكَذَٰلِكَ أَخْذُ رَبِّكَ إِذَا أَخَذَ الْقُرَىٰ وَهِيَ ظَالِمَةٌ ۚ
إِنَّ أَخْذَهُ أَلِيمٌ شَدِيدٌ ﴿١٠٣﴾

104. [e]In that surely is a Sign[1346] for him who fears the punishment of the Hereafter. That is a day on which all mankind shall be gathered together[1347] and that is a day which shall be witnessed *by all*.

إِنَّ فِي ذَٰلِكَ لَآيَةً لِمَنْ خَافَ عَذَابَ الْآخِرَةِ ۚ ذَٰلِكَ
يَوْمٌ مَجْمُوعٌ لَهُ النَّاسُ وَذَٰلِكَ يَوْمٌ مَشْهُودٌ ﴿١٠٤﴾

[a]28 : 43. [b]20 : 100. [c]3 : 118; 16 : 34. [d]54 : 43; 85 : 13. [e]14 : 15.

1344. *Rifd* meaning a gift or support or aid (Lane), the verse may signify that Pharaoh, whom his people regarded as their support against God will prove an evil support for them on the Day of Resurrection, for he not only will land them into Hell, but himself will go into it with them.

1345. The Qur'ān repeatedly emphasizes the fact that God never punishes a people unjustly and that it is their own misdeeds that bring down punishment upon them. It denies the theory of predestination or of man's being the victim of a blind fate. It also contradicts the view that God makes nations rise and fall arbitrarily, without a just or real cause. This is why, wherever it speaks of punishment, it does not fail to add that punishment or reward is the result of man's own doings.

1346. 'Sign' means, 'a lesson.'

1347. Man is not wholly independent. He is influenced by his environment, education and heredity ; so in order to judge rightly a particular action of his it is necessary to take into consideration all the conditions and circumstances which lead to and influence it. Hence, for the full realization of the true nature of man's actions and to show that the seemingly

105. And We delay it not save for a computed term.[1348]

وَمَا نُؤَخِّرُهٗۤ اِلَّا لِاَجَلٍ مَّعْدُوْدٍؕ ﴿١٠٥﴾

106. [a]On the day it comes, no soul shall speak except by His permission; then *some* of them will be unfortunate and *others* fortunate.

يَوْمَ يَاْتِ لَا تَكَلَّمُ نَفْسٌ اِلَّا بِاِذْنِهٖ ۚ فَمِنْهُمْ شَقِيٌّ وَّسَعِيْدٌ ﴿١٠٦﴾

107. As for the unfortunate, [b]they shall be in the Fire, wherein there will be for them sighing and sobbing,[1349]

فَاَمَّا الَّذِيْنَ شَقُوْا فَفِي النَّارِ لَهُمْ فِيْهَا زَفِيْرٌ وَّشَهِيْقٌ ۙ ﴿١٠٧﴾

108. [c]Abiding therein, so long as the heavens and the earth endure,[1350] except as thy Lord may will. Surely, thy Lord does what He pleases.

خٰلِدِيْنَ فِيْهَا مَا دَامَتِ السَّمٰوٰتُ وَالْاَرْضُ اِلَّا مَا شَآءَ رَبُّكَ ؕ اِنَّ رَبَّكَ فَعَّالٌ لِّمَا يُرِيْدُ ﴿١٠٨﴾

109. [d]But as for the fortunate, they shall be in Heaven, abiding therein so long as the heavens and the earth endure save as thy Lord may wish—a gift that shall not be cut off.[1351]

وَاَمَّا الَّذِيْنَ سُعِدُوْا فَفِي الْجَنَّةِ خٰلِدِيْنَ فِيْهَا مَا دَامَتِ السَّمٰوٰتُ وَالْاَرْضُ اِلَّا مَا شَآءَ رَبُّكَ ؕ عَطَآءً غَيْرَ مَجْذُوْذٍ ﴿١٠٩﴾

[a]78 : 39. [b]21 : 101. [c]78 : 24. [d]15 : 49.

unfair and inexplicable determination in dealing out different punishments and rewards to different persons by God is not capricious or arbitrary but perfectly just and fair, being based on the extent to which the individual is independent or free in his actions, it was necessary that there should have been fixed a certain day when all men should assemble, attended by all conditions and circumstances under which they worked and the various causes and reasons that led to their actions, so that these circumstances and causes may be jointly considered while determining the nature of their rewards and punishments.

1348. *Ajal*, meaning both a period and the end of a period, is of two kinds, (*a*) that which is revocable or cancellable, and (*b*) that which is not revoked or cancelled. The revokable "term" moves within a known circle within which it is liable to change according to circumstances. For instance, the age of a man has certain limits; it can decrease or increase within those limits. But the "term" which cannot be abrogated and is irrevocable concerns the destruction of a whole people.

1349. *Zafīr* means, the beginning of the cry of an ass and *Shahīq* is the ending thereof (Lane). The disbelievers have been likened in the verse to an ass which is a timid and stupid animal, signifying that they have not the courage of their convictions and do not benefit by knowledge.

1350. The Quranic expression is an idiom signifying a very prolonged period. The Qur'ān teaches that the punishment of Hell is not eternal.

1351. According to the Hindu religion, both Heaven and Hell (*i.e.*, rewards and punishments) possess a limited duration; and man, after undergoing the punishment, or reaping the reward of his deeds is sent back to this world. Of the Semitic religions, Judaism

110. So be thou not in doubt, *O reader*, concerning that which these *people* worship. They only worship as their fathers worshipped before, and We shall surely pay them in full their portion undiminished.

فَلَا تَكُ فِي مِرْيَةٍ مِّمَّا يَعْبُدُ هٰٓؤُلَآءِ ۚ مَا يَعْبُدُوْنَ
إِلَّا كَمَا يَعْبُدُ اٰبَآؤُهُمْ مِّنْ قَبْلُ ۚ وَإِنَّا لَمُوَفُّوْهُمْ
نَصِيْبَهُمْ غَيْرَ مَنْقُوْصٍ ﴿١١٠﴾

R. 10 111. And [a]We certainly gave Moses the Book, but differences were created therein; and had it not been for a word already gone forth from thy Lord, surely the matter would have been decided between them *long before*;[1352] and *now* these people are in a disquieting doubt concerning it.

وَلَقَدْ اٰتَيْنَا مُوْسَى الْكِتٰبَ فَاخْتُلِفَ فِيْهِ ۚ وَلَوْلَا
كَلِمَةٌ سَبَقَتْ مِنْ رَّبِّكَ لَقُضِيَ بَيْنَهُمْ ۚ وَإِنَّهُمْ لَفِيْ
شَكٍّ مِّنْهُ مُرِيْبٍ ﴿١١١﴾

112. Thy Lord will certainly [b]repay them all in full, according to their works. He is surely Well-Aware of all that they do.

وَإِنَّ كُلًّا لَّمَّا لَيُوَفِّيَنَّهُمْ رَبُّكَ أَعْمَالَهُمْ ۚ إِنَّهُ بِمَا
يَعْمَلُوْنَ خَبِيْرٌ ﴿١١٢﴾

[a]41 : 46. [b]3 : 58; 16 : 97; 39 : 11.

denies Paradise to non-Jews while Jews are regarded as almost free from the torture of Hell. According to Christians, both Heaven and Hell are eternal, although some of their sects hold the belief that Heaven will at last come to an end (Tafsīr Kabīr). Islām fundamentally differs from all these religions in this respect. According to it Heaven is eternal and everlasting, while Hell is temporary and of limited duration. *Imām* Aḥmad bin Ḥanbal quotes a saying of the Holy Prophet, as reported by 'Abd Allāh bin 'Amr bin al-'Āṣ to the effect : 'There will come on Hell a day when its shutters will strike against each other and there will be none left in it. That will happen after the inmates of Hell will have lived in it for centuries' (Musnad). According to this tradition, the word *Khālidīn* (abiding) used with regard to Hell only means 'remaining for long centuries.' 'Abd Allāh bin 'Umar and Jābir agree with *Imām* Ḥanbal. Abū Sa'īd al-Khudrī also quotes an identical *ḥadīth* (Bukhārī). Some eminent religious authorities, among them Ibn Taimiyyah and Ibn Qayyim, however, hold that though wicked disbelievers will deserve to be kept in Hell for ever, Hell itself will one day cease to exist through God's mercy, and when there is no Hell, there will naturally be no inmates of Hell (Fath). The Qur'ān has used the words, *a reward that will never end* (41 : 9; 84 : 26; 95 : 7) about Heaven but no such expression has been used with regard to Hell. Moreover, in vv. 101 : 10—12, Hell is compared to a mother, and the embryo remains in the mother's womb until the child's body is formed and its different organs become complete. Similarly, those unfortunate persons who are cast into Hell will remain there till their faculties are fully developed so as to enable them to see the beautiful face of the Lord.

1352. So serious was the guilt of men that if there had not been a decree preordained that mankind had been created for spiritual progress and that eventually they would become the object of Divine mercy (7 : 157; 11 : 120; 51 : 57), they would have been destroyed long ago.

113. [a]So stand thou upright, as thou hast been commanded, and *also* those who have turned *to Allāh* with thee;[1353] and exceed ye not the bounds, *for* surely He sees what you do.

فَاسْتَقِمْ كَمَآ اُمِرْتَ وَمَنْ تَابَ مَعَكَ وَلَا تَطْغَوْا ؕ
اِنَّهٗ بِمَا تَعْمَلُوْنَ بَصِيْرٌ ﴿۱۱۳﴾

114. And incline not toward those who do wrong,[1354] lest the Fire touch you; and you will have no friends other than Allāh, nor shall you be helped.

وَلَا تَرْكَنُوْٓا اِلَى الَّذِيْنَ ظَلَمُوْا فَتَمَسَّكُمُ النَّارُ ۙ وَمَا
لَكُمْ مِّنْ دُوْنِ اللّٰهِ مِنْ اَوْلِيَآءَ ثُمَّ لَا تُنْصَرُوْنَ ﴿۱۱۴﴾

115. And [b]observe Prayer at the two ends of the day, and in some hours of the night. Surely, good works drive away the evil ones. This is a reminder for those who would remember.

وَاَقِمِ الصَّلٰوةَ طَرَفَيِ النَّهَارِ وَزُلَفًا مِّنَ الَّيْلِ ؕ اِنَّ
الْحَسَنٰتِ يُذْهِبْنَ السَّيِّاٰتِ ؕ ذٰلِكَ ذِكْرٰى
لِلذّٰكِرِيْنَ ﴿۱۱۵﴾ۚ

116. And [c]be thou steadfast; surely, Allāh suffers not the reward of the righteous to perish.

وَاصْبِرْ فَاِنَّ اللّٰهَ لَا يُضِيْعُ اَجْرَ الْمُحْسِنِيْنَ ﴿۱۱۶﴾

117. Why, then, were there not among the generations before you persons possessed of understanding, who would have forbidden corruption in the earth, except a few among them whom We saved? But [d]the wrongdoers pursued the enjoyment of the good things which they were given in plenty, and they became guilty.

فَلَوْلَا كَانَ مِنَ الْقُرُوْنِ مِنْ قَبْلِكُمْ اُولُوْا بَقِيَّةٍ
يَّنْهَوْنَ عَنِ الْفَسَادِ فِي الْاَرْضِ اِلَّا قَلِيْلًا مِّمَّنْ
اَنْجَيْنَا مِنْهُمْ ۚ وَاتَّبَعَ الَّذِيْنَ ظَلَمُوْا مَآ اُتْرِفُوْا فِيْهِ
وَكَانُوْا مُجْرِمِيْنَ ﴿۱۱۷﴾

[a]42 : 16. [b]17 : 79. [c]12 : 91. [d]13 : 34.

1353. The Holy Prophet alone was not required to mould his own life in accordance with Divine Will. He had to see that all those who believed in him also followed his example. It was the realization of this grave dual responsibility which weighed so heavily upon him as to have rendered him prematurely aged (Baihaqui).

1354. As man is influenced by his enviornments and, if his surroundings are corrupt, the corruption thereof is sure to affect him sooner or later, so, in the present verse the believers are enjoined to sever all connections with the wicked and the unjust even though they are their own kith and kin.

118. And [a]thy Lord would not destroy the cities unjustly while the people thereof were righteous.

وَمَا كَانَ رَبُّكَ لِيُهْلِكَ الْقُرٰى بِظُلْمٍ وَّأَهْلُهَا
مُصْلِحُوْنَ ﴿١١٨﴾

119. And [b]if thy Lord had *enforced* His Will, He would have surely made mankind one people; but they would not cease to differ;

وَلَوْ شَاءَ رَبُّكَ لَجَعَلَ النَّاسَ أُمَّةً وَّاحِدَةً وَّلَا
يَزَالُوْنَ مُخْتَلِفِيْنَ ﴿١١٩﴾

120. Save those on whom thy Lord has had mercy, and for this has He created them. [c]But the word of thy Lord shall be fulfilled: 'Verily, I will fill Hell with *the disobedient* jinn and men all together.'

إِلَّا مَنْ رَّحِمَ رَبُّكَ ۚ وَلِذٰلِكَ خَلَقَهُمْ ۚ وَتَمَّتْ كَلِمَةُ
رَبِّكَ لَأَمْلَئَنَّ جَهَنَّمَ مِنَ الْجِنَّةِ وَالنَّاسِ أَجْمَعِيْنَ ﴿١٢٠﴾

121. And We relate unto thee [d]all the *important* tidings of the Messengers, whereby We strengthen thy heart. And herein has come to thee the truth and an exhortation and a reminder for believers.

وَكُلًّا نَّقُصُّ عَلَيْكَ مِنْ أَنْبَاءِ الرُّسُلِ مَا نُثَبِّتُ بِهٖ
فُؤَادَكَ ۚ وَجَاءَكَ فِيْ هٰذِهِ الْحَقُّ وَمَوْعِظَةٌ وَّذِكْرٰى
لِلْمُؤْمِنِيْنَ ﴿١٢١﴾

122. And [e]say to those who believe not, 'Act as you can,[1355] we *too* are acting;'

وَقُلْ لِّلَّذِيْنَ لَا يُؤْمِنُوْنَ اعْمَلُوْا عَلٰى مَكَانَتِكُمْ ۖ إِنَّا عٰمِلُوْنَ ﴿١٢٢﴾

123. 'And [f]wait ye, we *too* are waiting.'

وَانْتَظِرُوْا ۚ إِنَّا مُنْتَظِرُوْنَ ﴿١٢٣﴾

124. And [g]to Allāh belongs the unseen in the heavens and the earth, and to Him shall the whole affair be referred. So worship Him and put thy trust in Him *alone*. And thy Lord is not unmindful of what you do.

وَلِلّٰهِ غَيْبُ السَّمٰوٰتِ وَالْأَرْضِ وَإِلَيْهِ يُرْجَعُ الْأَمْرُ كُلُّهٗ
فَاعْبُدْهُ وَتَوَكَّلْ عَلَيْهِ ۚ وَمَا رَبُّكَ بِغَافِلٍ عَمَّا تَعْمَلُوْنَ ﴿١٢٤﴾

---

[a]6 : 132; 20 : 135; 26 : 209; 28 : 60. [b]2 : 214; 10 : 20; 42 : 9. [c]15 : 44; 32 : 14; 38 : 85-86. [d]25 : 33. [e]6 : 136 ; 11 : 94 ; 39 : 40. [f]10 : 103 ; 32 : 31. [g]16 : 78; 27 : 66; 35 : 39.

1355. *Makānah* is derived from *Kana* or *Makana* and means, station or power (Aqrab). The verse means that though the great prophecies made in this *Sūrah* about the ultimate triumph of Islām and the defeat and discomfiture of disbelievers appear to be incredible and impossible of fulfilment at the present time, yet nothing is impossible with God and these prophecies will surely come to pass.

CHAPTER 12

YŪSUF

(Revealed before Hijrah)

Date of Revelation, Context and Subject-Matter

According to most Companions of the Holy Prophet, the whole of this *Sūrah* was revealed at Mecca; but, according to Ibn 'Abbās and Qatādah, verses 2—4 were revealed after *Hijrah*. As already pointed out, Chapter 10 (*Sūrah* Yūnus) deals with both aspects of God's dealings with man—His punishment and mercy. But whereas Chapter 11 (*Sūrah* Hūd) deals with the subject of Divine punishment, the present Chapter (Chapter 12) deals with that of God's mercy. The *Sūrah* which deals with God's punishment (Hūd) has been placed before the present *Sūrah* which deals with His mercy, because the enemies of the Holy Prophet were to be shown mercy after they had been punished for their misdeeds. The *Sūrah*, however, possesses one peculiarity. The whole of it deals with the life-story of only one Prophet—Joseph. In this it differs from all other *Sūrahs*. The reason for this peculiarity is that the life of the Prophet Joseph bears a very close resemblance to that of the Holy Prophet, even in minor details. The entire *Sūrah* has been devoted to a somewhat detailed account of the Prophet Joseph's life in order that it might serve as a fore-warning of the incidents that were to occur during the life-time of the Holy Prophet. In Chapter 10 the story of the Prophet Jonah was chosen as an illustration of Divine mercy, while in the detailed account given in the present Chapter the example of Joseph has been cited as an illustration for that purpose. Two reasons may be given for this: (1) The lives of Jonah and that of the Holy Prophet resemble each other only in their closing stages but Joseph's life resembles that of the Holy Prophet even in small details. (2) Although the case of Jonah resembles that of the Holy Prophet in that as the peoples of both Jonah and the Holy Prophet were ultimately pardoned through God's mercy, the resemblance between the two is only partial, but the resemblance between Joseph and the Holy Prophet, especially in the way in which God treated Joseph's brethren and the Holy Prophet's people is very close and is almost complete. The mercy shown to Jonah's people was the direct result of God's grace, Jonah having no hand in it, but the declaration of pardon for Joseph's brethren was made by Joseph himself, and so in the case of the Quraish of Mecca the announcement of their full and unqualified forgiveness came directly from the Holy Prophet's own mouth.

ركوعاتها ١٢ سُوْرَةُ يُوْسُفَ مَكِّيَّةٌ (١٢) اٰياتها ١١٢

1. [a]In the name of Allah, the Gracious, the Merciful.

بِسْمِ اللّٰهِ الرَّحْمٰنِ الرَّحِيْمِ ﴿١﴾

2. [b]Alif Lām Rā.[1355] [c]These are verses of the clear[1356] Book.

الٓرٰ تِلْكَ اٰيٰتُ الْكِتٰبِ الْمُبِيْنِ ﴿٢﴾

3. [d]We have revealed it—the Qur'ān in Arabic[1357] — that you may understand.

اِنَّآ اَنْزَلْنٰهُ قُرْءٰنًا عَرَبِيًّا لَّعَلَّكُمْ تَعْقِلُوْنَ ﴿٣﴾

---

[a]1 : 1. [b]10 : 2; 11 : 2; 13 :2; 14 : 2; 15 : 2. [c]15 : 2; 26 : 3; 27 : 2; 28 : 3. [d]42 : 8; 43 : 4; 46 : 13.

1355. See 16.

1356. *Mubīn* (clear) being active participle from *Abāna*, which is used both as transitive and intransitive, means, (1) that which itself is clear and manifest; (2) that which makes other things clear and (3) that which cuts off one thing from another and renders it distinct and separate from it (Lane). The word as its meanings show, points to three salient features of the Qur'ān, *viz*., (1) that it not only clearly states facts and makes prophecies and lays down laws and ordinances but also supports and substantiates what it says and claims by solid arguments and sound reasons; (2) that it is not only clear in itself but makes clear the obscurities and ambiguities that are to be found in previous revealed Scriptures; and (3) that all that is essential for the attainment of nearness to God and relates to the laws of the *Sharī'ah*, ethics and to matters of belief has been made quite clear in it. This is a quality which the Qur'ān possesses to the entire exclusion of all other revealed Books. Other Scriptures are only *Mustabīn* (clear in themselves) but the Qur'ān is not only *Mustabīn* but is also *Mubīn* (makes clear the obscurities that are to be found in other Books). What adds to the beauty of the Qur'ān as a "clear and perspicuous Book" is that all its teachings are in perfect harmony with human nature and also with the laws of nature.

1357. '*Arabiyy* is derived from '*Ariba* or '*Aruba*. '*Aribat al-B'iru* means, the well contained much water. '*Aruba al-Rajulu* means, the man spoke clearly, plainly or distinctly after being barbarous in speech; he was or became brisk or lively. The expression, *Qur'ānan 'Arabiyyan*, therefore would mean, (1) a Book which is most extensively and regularly read and (2) which can express its meanings in a clear, eloquent and comprehensive language (Lane). The word '*Arabiyy* conveys the sense of fulness, abundance and clearness, and the Arabic language is so called because its roots are innumerable and are full of meanings and because it is most expressive, eloquent and comprehensive. It possesses suitable words and phrases for the full expression of all sorts of ideas and shades of meaning. Any topic can be discussed in this language with a precision and thoroughness unmatched in any other. European scholars have had to admit that Arabic language is complete in respect of its roots. It consists of hundreds of thousands of roots which are pregnant with a vast variety of meanings. Ibn Jinnī, an eminent linguist has claimed, on the authority of another very eminent linguist, Abū 'Alī, that even the letters of the Arabic language possess clear and definite meanings. For instance, he declared that the letters *Mīm*, *Lām* and *Kāf*, in whatever combination they occur, express the idea of 'power,' which is more or less common to all the words that are formed with these letters or are derived from this root. In the preceding verse the Qur'ān was called 'the Book,' which implied a prophecy that it would always continue to be preserved in the form of a book. In the present verse it has been called 'the Qur'ān,' which constitutes a prophecy that it will be very widely read and studied. It is a fact which no opponent of Islām can justifiably deny that no other book is so widely and frequently read as the Qur'ān. Professor Noldeke says, 'Since the use of the Koran in public worship, in schools and otherwise, is much more extensive than, for example, the reading of the Bible in most Christian countries, it has been truly described as the most widely read book in existence' (Enc. Bri. 9th Edition).

4. We narrate unto thee the best of narrative in that We have revealed to thee this Qur'ān though thou wast, before this, among those unaware *of the truth*.[1358]

نَحْنُ نَقُصُّ عَلَيْكَ أَحْسَنَ الْقَصَصِ بِمَآ أَوْحَيْنَآ
إِلَيْكَ هٰذَا الْقُرْاٰنَ ۖ وَإِنْ كُنْتَ مِنْ قَبْلِهٖ لَمِنَ
الْغٰفِلِيْنَ ﴿٤﴾

5. *Remember the time* [a]when Joseph[1359] said to his father, 'O my father, I saw *in a dream* eleven stars and the sun and the moon—I saw them making obeisance to me.'[1360]

إِذْ قَالَ يُوسُفُ لِأَبِيْهِ يٰٓأَبَتِ إِنِّيْ رَأَيْتُ أَحَدَ عَشَرَ
كَوْكَبًا وَّالشَّمْسَ وَالْقَمَرَ رَأَيْتُهُمْ لِيْ سٰجِدِيْنَ ﴿٥﴾

6. He said, 'O my dear son, relate not thy dream to thy brothers, lest they contrive a plot against thee, [b]for Satan is to man an open enemy;

قَالَ يٰبُنَيَّ لَا تَقْصُصْ رُءْيَاكَ عَلٰٓى إِخْوَتِكَ فَيَكِيْدُوْا
لَكَ كَيْدًا ۖ إِنَّ الشَّيْطٰنَ لِلْإِنْسَانِ عَدُوٌّ مُّبِيْنٌ ﴿٦﴾

7. 'And thus, *as thou hast seen*, thy Lord shall choose thee and [c]teach thee the interpretation of things *Divine* and perfect His favour upon thee and upon the family of Jacob[1361] as He perfected it upon thy two forefathers—Abraham and Isaac. Verily, thy Lord is All-Knowing, Wise.'

وَكَذٰلِكَ يَجْتَبِيْكَ رَبُّكَ وَيُعَلِّمُكَ مِنْ تَأْوِيْلِ
الْأَحَادِيْثِ وَيُتِمُّ نِعْمَتَهٗ عَلَيْكَ وَعَلٰٓى اٰلِ يَعْقُوْبَ
كَمَآ أَتَمَّهَا عَلٰٓى أَبَوَيْكَ مِنْ قَبْلُ إِبْرٰهِيْمَ وَإِسْحٰقَ ۗ
ع إِنَّ رَبَّكَ عَلِيْمٌ حَكِيْمٌ ﴿٧﴾

[a]12:101. [b]2:169; 18:51; 35:7. [c]12:22, 102.

1358. The reason why the story of Joseph was revealed to the Holy Prophet in such detail is that it contains many prophetic allusions to his own life. The whole story was to be, as it were, re-enacted in the person of the Holy Prophet himself and his brethren, the Quraish.

1359. Joseph was the twelve son of Prophet Jacob, otherwise known as Israel. He was the elder of the two sons of Rachel. The meaning given to the name is 'shall add,' *i.e.*, 'The Lord shall add to me another son' (Gen. 30 : 24).

1360. The Bible mentions the sun and the moon first and the eleven stars afterwards, as making obeisance to Joseph (Gen. 37 : 9), but the Qur'ān reverses the order; and the actual facts of history support the order followed by the Qur'ān, for it was the brethren of Joseph (the eleven stars) who met him first and made obeisance to him, and his parents came afterwards. The verse signifies that the parents and brethren of Joseph would submit to his authority.

1361. The name is explained in the Bible as 'the supplanter' (Gen. 27 : 36). It is the prevalent critical opinion that Ya'ākob (Jacob) is really a shortened form of Ya'ākobel admitting several meanings such as 'God follows' or 'God rewards.' Jacob was the son of Isaac and Rebekah and the grandson of Abraham and the traditional ancestor of the people of Israel and known as the Third Patriarch (Enc. Bib. & Jew. Enc).

R. 2. 8. Surely, in Joseph and his brethren there are Signs for the inquirers;

لَقَدْ كَانَ فِي يُوسُفَ وَإِخْوَتِهٖٓ اٰيٰتٌ لِّلسَّآئِلِيْنَ ۝٨

9. When they said *to each other*, 'Verily, Joseph and his brother are dearer to our father than we *are*, although we are a strong party.[1362] [a]Surely, our father is in manifest error;

إِذْ قَالُوْا لَيُوْسُفُ وَأَخُوْهُ أَحَبُّ إِلٰٓى أَبِيْنَا مِنَّا وَ
نَحْنُ عُصْبَةٌ ؕ إِنَّ أَبَانَا لَفِيْ ضَلٰلٍ مُّبِيْنِ ۝٩

10. *So contrive to* kill Joseph[1363] or cast him out to some distant land, so that your father's favour may become exclusively yours, and you can thereafter *repent and* become a righteous people.'

اقْتُلُوْا يُوْسُفَ أَوِ اطْرَحُوْهُ أَرْضًا يَّخْلُ لَكُمْ وَجْهُ
أَبِيْكُمْ وَتَكُوْنُوْا مِنْ بَعْدِهٖ قَوْمًا صٰلِحِيْنَ ۝١٠

11. One[1364] of them said, 'Kill not Joseph, but if you must do *something*, cast him into the bottom of a deep well; some of the travellers will pick him up.'

قَالَ قَآئِلٌ مِّنْهُمْ لَا تَقْتُلُوْا يُوْسُفَ وَأَلْقُوْهُ فِيْ
غَيٰبَتِ الْجُبِّ يَلْتَقِطْهُ بَعْضُ السَّيَّارَةِ إِنْ كُنْتُمْ
فٰعِلِيْنَ ۝١١

12. They said, 'O our father, why dost thou not trust us with respect to Joseph, when we are certainly his sincere well-wishers?

قَالُوْا يٰٓأَبَانَا مَا لَكَ لَا تَأْمَنَّا عَلٰى يُوْسُفَ وَإِنَّا
لَهٗ لَنٰصِحُوْنَ ۝١٢

13. 'Send him with us tomorrow that he may enjoy himself and play, and we shall surely keep guard over him.'

أَرْسِلْهُ مَعَنَا غَدًا يَّرْتَعْ وَيَلْعَبْ وَإِنَّا لَهٗ لَحٰفِظُوْنَ ۝١٣

[a]12 : 96.

1362. Like Joseph's brothers who were angry that instead of themselves, who, as they imagined, were superior to him in every respect, he had won the affection of their father and had become the centre of his attention, the Quraish leaders said that the Qur'ān ought to have been revealed to one of the great men of Mecca or Ṭā'if (43 : 32). They looked upon the Holy Prophet as too small a person to be selected for the exalted office of a Prophet.

1363. Just as the brothers of Joseph plotted to kill him, the Quraish also conspired to put the Holy Prophet to death (8 : 31).

1364. Reuben (Gen. 37 : 22).

14. He said, 'It grieves me that you should take him away, and I fear lest the wolf should devour[1365] him while you are heedless of him.'

قَالَ إِنِّي لَيَحْزُنُنِيٓ أَنْ تَذْهَبُوا بِهٖ وَأَخَافُ أَنْ يَأْكُلَهُ الذِّئْبُ وَأَنْتُمْ عَنْهُ غٰفِلُوْنَ ﴿١٤﴾

15. They said, 'Surely, if the wolf should devour him while we are a strong party, then we shall indeed be *great* losers.'

قَالُوْا لَئِنْ أَكَلَهُ الذِّئْبُ وَنَحْنُ عُصْبَةٌ إِنَّآ إِذًا لَّخٰسِرُوْنَ ﴿١٥﴾

16. So, when they took him away, and agreed to put him into the bottom of a deep well, and *carried out their malicious design*, We sent revelation to him, *saying*, 'Thou shalt surely *one day* tell them of this affair of theirs, and they did not know.'

فَلَمَّا ذَهَبُوْا بِهٖ وَأَجْمَعُوْٓا أَنْ يَّجْعَلُوْهُ فِيْ غَيٰبَتِ الْجُبِّ وَأَوْحَيْنَآ إِلَيْهِ لَتُنَبِّئَنَّهُمْ بِأَمْرِهِمْ هٰذَا وَهُمْ لَا يَشْعُرُوْنَ ﴿١٦﴾

17. And they came to their father in the evening, weeping.

وَجَآءُوْٓ أَبَاهُمْ عِشَآءً يَّبْكُوْنَ ﴿١٧﴾

18. They said, 'O our father, we went forth racing with one another and left Joseph with our things, and the wolf devoured him, but thou wilt not believe us though we are telling the truth.'[1366]

قَالُوْا يٰٓأَبَانَآ إِنَّا ذَهَبْنَا نَسْتَبِقُ وَتَرَكْنَا يُوْسُفَ عِنْدَ مَتَاعِنَا فَأَكَلَهُ الذِّئْبُ وَمَآ أَنْتَ بِمُؤْمِنٍ لَّنَا وَلَوْ كُنَّا صٰدِقِيْنَ ﴿١٨﴾ الثلثة

19. And they came with false blood on his shirt. [a]He said, 'This *what you say* is not *true* but your souls have made a great thing appear light in your eyes.[1367] So comely patience *is now called for*. And it is Allāh alone Whose help is to be sought against what you assert.'

وَجَآءُوْ عَلٰى قَمِيْصِهٖ بِدَمٍ كَذِبٍ قَالَ بَلْ سَوَّلَتْ لَكُمْ أَنْفُسُكُمْ أَمْرًا فَصَبْرٌ جَمِيْلٌ وَاللّٰهُ الْمُسْتَعَانُ عَلٰى مَا تَصِفُوْنَ ﴿١٩﴾

[a]12 : 84

1365. It appears from this verse that Jacob had already been informed by God in a general way of the plot of Joseph's brothers to kill him. So, as if pre-arraigning them, he used the same words which they were to use later in extenuation of their heinous crime.

1366. The words be-spoke their nervousness and betrayed their guilty minds.

1367. These words indicate that Jacob regarded the report of his sons as a concocted story.

20. And there came a caravan of travellers and they sent their water-drawer. And he let down his bucket *into the well.* 'Oh, good news!' said he, 'Here is a youth!' And they hid him as a piece of merchandise,[1368] and Allāh well knew what they did.

وَجَآءَتْ سَيَّارَةٌ فَأَرْسَلُوْا وَارِدَهُمْ فَأَدْلٰى دَلْوَهٗ
قَالَ يٰبُشْرٰى هٰذَا غُلٰمٌ ۗ وَاَسَرُّوْهُ بِضَاعَةً ۗ وَاللّٰهُ
عَلِيْمٌۢ بِمَا يَعْمَلُوْنَ ﴿٢٠﴾

21. And they sold him for a paltry price, a few *dirhems*, and they were not at all keen on it.[1368A]

وَشَرَوْهُ بِثَمَنٍۢ بَخْسٍ دَرَاهِمَ مَعْدُوْدَةٍ ۚ وَكَانُوْا
فِيْهِ مِنَ الزّٰهِدِيْنَ ﴿٢١﴾ ع ۲/۱۲

R. 3 22. And *the man* from Egypt[1369] who bought him said to his wife, 'Make his stay among us honourable. Maybe we will benefit from him or we may adopt him as a son.' [a]And thus did We establish Joseph in the land, and *We did so* that We might *also* teach him the interpretation of things. And Allāh has full power over His decree, but most men know *it* not.

وَقَالَ الَّذِي اشْتَرٰىهُ مِنْ مِّصْرَ لِامْرَاَتِهٖٓ اَكْرِمِيْ
مَثْوٰىهُ عَسٰٓى اَنْ يَّنْفَعَنَآ اَوْ نَتَّخِذَهٗ وَلَدًا ۗ وَكَذٰلِكَ
مَكَّنَّا لِيُوْسُفَ فِي الْاَرْضِ ۡ وَلِنُعَلِّمَهٗ مِنْ تَاْوِيْلِ
الْاَحَادِيْثِ ۗ وَاللّٰهُ غَالِبٌ عَلٰٓى اَمْرِهٖ وَلٰكِنَّ اَكْثَرَ
النَّاسِ لَا يَعْلَمُوْنَ ﴿٢٢﴾

23. [b]And when he attained his *age of* full strength, We granted him judgment and knowledge. And thus do We reward those who do good.

وَلَمَّا بَلَغَ اَشُدَّهٗٓ اٰتَيْنٰهُ حُكْمًا وَّعِلْمًا ۗ وَكَذٰلِكَ
نَجْزِي الْمُحْسِنِيْنَ ﴿٢٣﴾

[a]12 : 57. [b]28 : 15.

1368. The members of the caravan looked upon Joseph as a precious asset.

1368A. The particle *hi* in the expression *fīhi* may mean either 'him' or 'it', standing either for Jospeh or price. See also "The Larger Edition of the Commentary."

1369. The Egyptian who bought Joseph is known as Potiphar in Jewish literature (Enc. Bib. & Gen. 39 : 1). He was captain of the royal guard, an officer of high rank in ancient times.

24. And she, in whose house he was, sought to seduce[1370] him against his will. And she bolted the doors, and said, 'Now come.'[1371] He said, 'I seek refuge with Allāh. He is my Lord.[1372] He has made my stay *with you* honourable. Verily, the wrongdoers never prosper.'

وَرَاوَدَتْهُ الَّتِي هُوَ فِي بَيْتِهَا عَنْ نَفْسِهِ وَغَلَّقَتِ
الْأَبْوَابَ وَقَالَتْ هَيْتَ لَكَ ۚ قَالَ مَعَاذَ اللَّهِ إِنَّهُ
رَبِّي أَحْسَنَ مَثْوَايَ ۖ إِنَّهُ لَا يُفْلِحُ الظَّالِمُونَ ﴿٢٤﴾

25. And she made up her mind with regard to him, *to seduce him* and he made up his mind with regard to her[1373] *to resist her*. If he had not seen manifest Sign of his Lord,[1374] *he could not have shown such determination. Thus did it come about* that We might turn away from him *all* evil and indecency. Surely, he was *one* of Our chosen servants.[1375]

وَلَقَدْ هَمَّتْ بِهِ ۖ وَهَمَّ بِهَا لَوْلَا أَنْ رَّأَىٰ بُرْهَانَ رَبِّهِ ۚ
كَذَٰلِكَ لِنَصْرِفَ عَنْهُ السُّوءَ وَالْفَحْشَاءَ ۚ إِنَّهُ مِنْ
عِبَادِنَا الْمُخْلَصِينَ ﴿٢٥﴾

1370. *Rāwada-hū* means, he endeavoured or sought to turn him to or from a thing by blandishments or deceitful arts (Lane).

1371. *Haita* meaning, 'come or come forward' or 'hasten,' and the expression *haita laka* means, 'come thou' or 'now come;' also, 'come I am ready for thee or I am ready to receive thee' (Lane & Mufradāt).

1372. The verse shows that the woman who sought to seduce Joseph failed in her efforts and that Joseph successfully resisted her evil suggestion. The words, 'He is my Lord," refer to God, and not to Joseph's Egyptian master, as some Commentators have wrongly supposed.

1373. The wife of Joseph's master intended a thing about Joseph (*i.e.*, copulation). Similarly, Joseph intended a thing about her, *i.e.*, resisting her evil intention. That Joseph did not intend anything evil is clear from the previous verse. His only object was to dissuade her from her evil purpose.

1374. By 'manifest Sign' are meant the heavenly Signs which Joseph had already witnessed, *e.g.*, the wonderful dream which foretold his future greatness (v. 5), the revelation he had received when cast into the well, which also pointed to his later eminence and glory (v. 16) and also his being taken out alive from the well.

1375. Just as an attempt was made to tempt Joseph away from the path of piety and rectitude, similarly, the idolaters of Mecca made an unsuccessful attempt to make the Holy Prophet give up preaching the Unity of God by offering to make him their king or to collect great wealth for him or to give him in marriage the most beautiful girl in Arabia. The offer was of course contemptuously rejected by the Holy Prophet with the historic words, 'If you place the sun on my right hand and the moon on my left hand, even then I will not give up preaching God's Unity (Hishām).

26. And they both raced to the door, and *in the struggle* she tore his shirt from behind, and they found her lord at the door. She said *to him*, 'What shall be the punishment of one who intended evil to thy wife, save imprisonment or a grievous chastisement?'

وَاسْتَبَقَا الْبَابَ وَقَدَّتْ قَمِيْصَهٗ مِنْ دُبُرٍ وَّ
اَلْفَيَا سَيِّدَهَا لَدَا الْبَابِ ؕ قَالَتْ مَا جَزَآءُ مَنْ اَرَادَ
بِاَهْلِكَ سُوْٓءًا اِلَّآ اَنْ يُّسْجَنَ اَوْ عَذَابٌ اَلِيْمٌ ﴿٢٦﴾

27. *Joseph* said, 'She it was who sought to seduce me against my will.' And a witness of her household bore witness *saying*, 'If his shirt is torn from the front, then she has spoken the truth and he is a liar;

قَالَ هِيَ رَاوَدَتْنِيْ عَنْ نَّفْسِيْ وَشَهِدَ شَاهِدٌ مِّنْ
اَهْلِهَا ۚ اِنْ كَانَ قَمِيْصُهٗ قُدَّ مِنْ قُبُلٍ فَصَدَقَتْ
وَهُوَ مِنَ الْكٰذِبِيْنَ ﴿٢٧﴾

28. 'But if his shirt is torn from behind, then she has lied and he is of the truthful.'

وَاِنْ كَانَ قَمِيْصُهٗ قُدَّ مِنْ دُبُرٍ فَكَذَبَتْ وَهُوَ
مِنَ الصّٰدِقِيْنَ ﴿٢٨﴾

29. So when he[1376] saw his shirt torn from behind, he said, 'Surely, this is a device of you women. Your device is indeed mighty;[1377]

فَلَمَّا رَاٰ قَمِيْصَهٗ قُدَّ مِنْ دُبُرٍ قَالَ اِنَّهٗ مِنْ كَيْدِكُنَّ ؕ
اِنَّ كَيْدَكُنَّ عَظِيْمٌ ﴿٢٩﴾

30. 'O Joseph, do thou overlook this *mischief* and thou, *O woman*, ask forgiveness for thy sin. Certainly thou art of the guilty.'

يُوْسُفُ اَعْرِضْ عَنْ هٰذَا ٜ وَاسْتَغْفِرِيْ لِذَنْۢبِكِ ۚۖ
اِنَّكِ كُنْتِ مِنَ الْخٰطِـِٕيْنَ ﴿٣٠﴾ ع ٣ ١٣

R. 4 31. And the women in the city said, 'The wife of the 'Azīz[1378] seeks to seduce her slave-boy against his will. He has infatuated her with love.[1379] Indeed we see her in manifest error.'

وَقَالَ نِسْوَةٌ فِي الْمَدِيْنَةِ امْرَاَتُ الْعَزِيْزِ تُرَاوِدُ
فَتٰىهَا عَنْ نَّفْسِهٖ ۚ قَدْ شَغَفَهَا حُبًّا ؕ اِنَّا لَنَرٰىهَا
فِيْ ضَلٰلٍ مُّبِيْنٍ ﴿٣١﴾

1376. The pronoun 'he' stands for the master of the house and not for the man who bore witness.

1377. In his endeavour to screen his wife so far as possible Potiphar seems to accuse the whole fair sex of cunning and guile.

1378. Al-'Azīz stands for Potiphar. He was the captain of the King's guard. It seems that at the time of the Holy Prophet the chiefs and dignitaries of Egypt were known by this title.

1379. The Arabic expression means that the woman's love of Joseph had entered beneath the pericardium of her heart; or, love of him had struck or smitten her or had rent the *Shighāf* (pericardium) of her heart (Lane).

32. And when she heard of their sly whisperings, she sent for them and prepared for them a repast, and gave everyone of them a knife and *then* said *to Joseph*, 'Come forth to them.' And when they saw him they found him *to be a person* of great dignity[1379A] and *in their amazement* [a]cut their hands,[1380] and [b]said, 'Allāh be glorified! This is not a human being; this is but a noble angel.'

فَلَمَّا سَمِعَتْ بِمَكْرِهِنَّ أَرْسَلَتْ إِلَيْهِنَّ وَأَعْتَدَتْ
لَهُنَّ مُتَّكَأً وَآتَتْ كُلَّ وَاحِدَةٍ مِّنْهُنَّ سِكِّينًا وَّ
قَالَتِ اخْرُجْ عَلَيْهِنَّ ۚ فَلَمَّا رَأَيْنَهُ أَكْبَرْنَهُ وَقَطَّعْنَ
أَيْدِيَهُنَّ وَقُلْنَ حَاشَ لِلّٰهِ مَا هٰذَا بَشَرًا ۖ إِنْ هٰذَا
إِلَّا مَلَكٌ كَرِيمٌ ﴿٣٢﴾

33. She said, 'And this is he about whom you blamed me. I did seek to seduce him against his will, but he preserved himself *from sin*. And now if he do not what I bid him, he shall certainly be imprisoned and become *one* of the humbled.'

قَالَتْ فَذٰلِكُنَّ الَّذِي لُمْتُنَّنِي فِيهِ ۖ وَلَقَدْ رَاوَدْتُّهُ
عَنْ نَّفْسِهِ فَاسْتَعْصَمَ ۖ وَلَئِنْ لَّمْ يَفْعَلْ مَا آمُرُهُ
لَيُسْجَنَنَّ وَلَيَكُونًا مِّنَ الصّٰغِرِينَ ﴿٣٣﴾

34. *Thereupon Joseph prayed:* 'O my Lord, prison is dearer to me than what they invite me to; and unless Thou turn away their guile from me I shall be inclined towards them and be of the ignorant.'

قَالَ رَبِّ السِّجْنُ أَحَبُّ إِلَيَّ مِمَّا يَدْعُونَنِي إِلَيْهِ ۚ
وَإِلَّا تَصْرِفْ عَنِّي كَيْدَهُنَّ أَصْبُ إِلَيْهِنَّ وَأَكُنْ
مِّنَ الْجٰهِلِينَ ﴿٣٤﴾

35. So his Lord heard his prayer, and turned away their guile from him. Verily, He is the All-Hearing, the All-Knowing.

فَاسْتَجَابَ لَهُ رَبُّهُ فَصَرَفَ عَنْهُ كَيْدَهُنَّ ۚ إِنَّهُ
هُوَ السَّمِيعُ الْعَلِيمُ ﴿٣٥﴾

[a]12 : 51. [b]12 : 52.

1379A. They thought very highly of him.

1380. The expression, *cut their hands*, may signify that when the women looked at Joseph, they were so struck with his saintly and handsome visage that in a state of forgetfulness some of them happened to cut their hands with the knives they were holding in their hands. Or the sentence may be taken as figuratively expressing their wonder and amazement. The Arabic expression, *'Addul Anāmili, i.e.*, biting the finger-ends is also used to express surprise, and because sometimes the whole of a thing is used for a part, the word 'hands' may be said to have been here used for 'finger-ends.' According to the Talmud, oranges were served to the guests and the women inadvertently cut their hands owing to their being engrossed in looking at Joseph (Jew. Enc. & Talmud).

36. Then it occurred to them (the chiefs) after they had seen the signs *of his innocence* that *to preserve their good name*, they should imprison him for a time.[1381]

ثُمَّ بَدَا لَهُمْ مِّنْ بَعْدِ مَا رَاَوُا الْاٰيٰتِ لَيَسْجُنُنَّهٗ
حَتّٰى حِيْنٍ ﴿۳۶﴾

R. 5 37. And with him there entered the prison two young men. One of them said, 'I see myself *in a dream* pressing wine.' And the other said, 'I see myself *in a dream* carrying upon my head bread of which the birds are eating.[1382] Inform us of the interpretation thereof; for we see thee to be of the righteous.'

وَدَخَلَ مَعَهُ السِّجْنَ فَتَيٰنِ ؕ قَالَ اَحَدُهُمَآ اِنِّيْٓ
اَرٰىنِيْٓ اَعْصِرُ خَمْرًا ۚ وَقَالَ الْاٰخَرُ اِنِّيْٓ اَرٰىنِيْٓ اَحْمِلُ
فَوْقَ رَاْسِيْ خُبْزًا تَاْكُلُ الطَّيْرُ مِنْهُ ؕ نَبِّئْنَا بِتَاْوِيْلِهٖ ۚ
اِنَّا نَرٰىكَ مِنَ الْمُحْسِنِيْنَ ﴿۳۷﴾

38. He replied, 'The food which you are given shall not come to you but I shall inform you of the interpretation thereof before it comes to you. This is on account of what my Lord has taught me. I have renounced the religion of the people who do not believe in Allāh and who are disbelievers in the Hereafter;

قَالَ لَا يَاْتِيْكُمَا طَعَامٌ تُرْزَقٰنِهٖٓ اِلَّا نَبَّاْتُكُمَا بِتَاْوِيْلِهٖ
قَبْلَ اَنْ يَّاْتِيَكُمَا ؕ ذٰلِكُمَا مِمَّا عَلَّمَنِيْ رَبِّيْ ؕ اِنِّيْ تَرَكْتُ
مِلَّةَ قَوْمٍ لَّا يُؤْمِنُوْنَ بِاللّٰهِ وَهُمْ بِالْاٰخِرَةِ هُمْ
كٰفِرُوْنَ ﴿۳۸﴾

39. [a]'And I have followed the religion of my fathers—Abraham and Iṣaac and Jacob. It behoves us not to associate anything as partner with Allāh. This is of Allāh's grace upon us and upon mankind, but most men are ungrateful;

وَاتَّبَعْتُ مِلَّةَ اٰبَآءِيْٓ اِبْرٰهِيْمَ وَاِسْحٰقَ وَيَعْقُوْبَ ؕ
مَا كَانَ لَنَآ اَنْ نُّشْرِكَ بِاللّٰهِ مِنْ شَيْءٍ ؕ ذٰلِكَ مِنْ
فَضْلِ اللّٰهِ عَلَيْنَا وَعَلَى النَّاسِ وَلٰكِنَّ اَكْثَرَ النَّاسِ
لَا يَشْكُرُوْنَ ﴿۳۹﴾

---

[a]2 : 134.

1381. It appears that as the ill-fame of Potiphar's wife spread, her people thought that the best way to put a stop to this scandal-mongering was to imprison Joseph. in order that public opinion might come to regard him as the offender and the blame might be shifted from that guilty woman to him.

1382. For the dreams of the butler and the baker see Gen. ch. 40.

40. 'O my two companions of the prison, are many lords differing among themselves better or Allāh, the One, the Most Supreme?

يٰصَاحِبَيِ السِّجْنِ ءَاَرْبَابٌ مُّتَفَرِّقُوْنَ خَيْرٌ اَمِ اللّٰهُ الْوَاحِدُ الْقَهَّارُ ۝٤٠

41. [a]'You worship nothing besides Allāh, but *mere* names that you have named, you and your fathers; Allāh has sent down no authority for that. [b]The decision *rests* with Allāh *alone*. [c]He has commanded that you shall not worship *anything*, save Him. [d]That is the right religion, but most men know not;

مَا تَعْبُدُوْنَ مِنْ دُوْنِهٖٓ اِلَّآ اَسْمَآءً سَمَّيْتُمُوْهَآ اَنْتُمْ وَاٰبَآؤُكُمْ مَّآ اَنْزَلَ اللّٰهُ بِهَا مِنْ سُلْطٰنٍ ۚ اِنِ الْحُكْمُ اِلَّا لِلّٰهِ ۚ اَمَرَ اَلَّا تَعْبُدُوْٓا اِلَّآ اِيَّاهُ ۚ ذٰلِكَ الدِّيْنُ الْقَيِّمُ وَلٰكِنَّ اَكْثَرَ النَّاسِ لَا يَعْلَمُوْنَ ۝٤١

42. 'O my two companions of the prison, as for one of you he will pour out wine for his lord to drink; and as for the other, he will be crucified so that the birds will eat from of his head. The matter about which you inquired has been decreed.'

يٰصَاحِبَيِ السِّجْنِ اَمَّآ اَحَدُكُمَا فَيَسْقِيْ رَبَّهٗ خَمْرًا ۚ وَاَمَّا الْاٰخَرُ فَيُصْلَبُ فَتَاْكُلُ الطَّيْرُ مِنْ رَّاْسِهٖ ۚ قُضِيَ الْاَمْرُ الَّذِيْ فِيْهِ تَسْتَفْتِيٰنِ ۝٤٢

43. And of the two he said to him whom he thought to be the one who would be released, 'Mention me to thy lord.' But Satan caused him to forget mentioning it to his lord, so he remained in prison for some years.[1383]

وَقَالَ لِلَّذِيْ ظَنَّ اَنَّهٗ نَاجٍ مِّنْهُمَا اذْكُرْنِيْ عِنْدَ رَبِّكَ ۫ فَاَنْسٰىهُ الشَّيْطٰنُ ذِكْرَ رَبِّهٖ فَلَبِثَ فِي السِّجْنِ بِضْعَ سِنِيْنَ ۝٤٣ ع

R. 6 44. And the King said *to his courtiers*, 'I see *in a dream* seven fat kine which seven lean ones were eating, and seven green ears of corn and seven others withered. O ye chiefs, explain to me the meaning of my dream if you can interpret dreams.'

وَقَالَ الْمَلِكُ اِنِّيْٓ اَرٰى سَبْعَ بَقَرٰتٍ سِمَانٍ يَّاْكُلُهُنَّ سَبْعٌ عِجَافٌ وَّسَبْعَ سُنْۢبُلٰتٍ خُضْرٍ وَّاُخَرَ يٰبِسٰتٍ ۗ يٰٓاَيُّهَا الْمَلَاُ اَفْتُوْنِيْ فِيْ رُءْيَايَ اِنْ كُنْتُمْ لِلرُّءْيَا تَعْبُرُوْنَ ۝٤٤

---

[a]7 : 72; 53 : 24. [b]6 : 58; 12 : 68. [c]2 : 84; 17 : 24; 41 : 15. [d]30 : 31; 98 : 6.

1383. *Biḍ'* denotes a variety of numbers but is generally understood to mean from three to nine (Lane).

45. They replied, '*These are* confused dreams and we do not know the interpretation of *confused* dreams.'

قَالُوْٓا اَضْغَاثُ اَحْلَامٍ ۚ وَمَا نَحْنُ بِتَاْوِيْلِ الْاَحْلَامِ
بِعٰلِمِيْنَ ﴿۴۵﴾

46. And he of the two who was released and who *now* remembered after a time, said, 'I will let you know its interpretation, therefore, send ye me.'

وَقَالَ الَّذِيْ نَجَا مِنْهُمَا وَادَّكَرَ بَعْدَ اُمَّةٍ اَنَا اُنَبِّئُكُمْ
بِتَاْوِيْلِهٖ فَاَرْسِلُوْنِ ﴿۴۶﴾

47. *And he came to Joseph and said*, 'Joseph! O thou man of truth, explain to us the meaning of *seeing in a dream* seven fat kine which seven lean ones devour, and of seven green ears of corn and seven others withered; that I may return to the people so that they may know *the interpretation*.'

يُوْسُفُ اَيُّهَا الصِّدِّيْقُ اَفْتِنَا فِيْ سَبْعِ بَقَرٰتٍ سِمَانٍ
يَّاْكُلُهُنَّ سَبْعٌ عِجَافٌ وَّسَبْعِ سُنْۢبُلٰتٍ خُضْرٍ وَّاُخَرَ
يٰبِسٰتٍ ۙ لَّعَلِّيْٓ اَرْجِعُ اِلَى النَّاسِ لَعَلَّهُمْ يَعْلَمُوْنَ ﴿۴۷﴾

48. *Joseph* replied, 'You shall sow for seven years, working diligently throughout; then leave, what you reap in its ear, except a little which you shall eat;

قَالَ تَزْرَعُوْنَ سَبْعَ سِنِيْنَ دَاَبًا ۚ فَمَا حَصَدْتُّمْ فَذَرُوْهُ
فِيْ سُنْۢبُلِهٖٓ اِلَّا قَلِيْلًا مِّمَّا تَاْكُلُوْنَ ﴿۴۸﴾

49. 'Then there shall come after that seven hard years,[1384] which shall consume all that you shall have laid by in advance for them except a little which you may preserve;

ثُمَّ يَاْتِيْ مِنْ بَعْدِ ذٰلِكَ سَبْعٌ شِدَادٌ يَّاْكُلْنَ مَا
قَدَّمْتُمْ لَهُنَّ اِلَّا قَلِيْلًا مِّمَّا تُحْصِنُوْنَ ﴿۴۹﴾

50. 'Then there shall come after that a year in which people shall be relieved[1385] and in which they shall give presents[1386] *to each other*.

ثُمَّ يَاْتِيْ مِنْ بَعْدِ ذٰلِكَ عَامٌ فِيْهِ يُغَاثُ النَّاسُ
ع ۱۶ وَفِيْهِ يَعْصِرُوْنَ ﴿۵۰﴾

1384. Arabia, in the Holy Prophet's time, was visited with a terrible famine which lasted for seven long years. It was so severe that people were forced to eat carrion (Bukhārī).

1385. In their ignorance of the meaning of the word *Yughāthu* which besides meaning, 'They will be rained upon' also means, 'They will be relieved of their distress' or 'They will be aided and helped,' some Christian writers have objected that as it very seldom rains in Egypt and that the fertility of its soil depends upon the flooding of the Nile, the Quranic statement is against the elementary facts of geography. Obviously, the latter two meanings quite agree with the text of the Qur'ān. But if the word be taken in the first-mentioned sense, even then there is no ground for any objection, for though the fertility of the soil of Egypt depends on the flooding of the Nile, the flooding of the Nile itself depends on rain on the mountains in which lies its source.

1386. See next page.

R. 7. 51. And the King said, 'Bring him to me.' But when the messenger came to him, he said, 'Go back to thy lord and [a]ask him how fare the women who cut their hands;[1387] for, my Lord well knows their *crafty* design.'

وَقَالَ الْمَلِكُ ائْتُونِي بِهِ ۚ فَلَمَّا جَاءَهُ الرَّسُولُ قَالَ
ارْجِعْ إِلَىٰ رَبِّكَ فَسْئَلْهُ مَا بَالُ النِّسْوَةِ الَّتِي قَطَّعْنَ
أَيْدِيَهُنَّ ۚ إِنَّ رَبِّي بِكَيْدِهِنَّ عَلِيمٌ ﴿٥١﴾

52. *The King* said *to the women*, 'What was *the truth of* that matter of yours when you sought to seduce Joseph against his will?' [b]They said 'He kept away *from sin* for fear of Allāh[1388]—we have known no evil against him.' The wife of the 'Azīz said, 'Now has the truth come to light. It was I who sought to seduce him against his will and surely, he is of the truthful.'

قَالَ مَا خَطْبُكُنَّ إِذْ رَاوَدْتُّنَّ يُوسُفَ عَنْ نَّفْسِهِ ۚ
قُلْنَ حَاشَ لِلّٰهِ مَا عَلِمْنَا عَلَيْهِ مِنْ سُوْٓءٍ ۚ قَالَتِ امْرَاَتُ
الْعَزِيْزِ الْـٰٔنَ حَصْحَصَ الْحَقُّ ۫ اَنَا رَاوَدْتُّهٗ عَنْ نَّفْسِهٖ
وَاِنَّهٗ لَمِنَ الصّٰدِقِيْنَ ﴿٥٢﴾

53. *Joseph said*, '*I asked for* this *enquiry to be made* so that *the* '*Azīz* might know that I was not unfaithful to him in *his* absence and that Allāh suffers not the device of the unfaithful to succeed;

ذٰلِكَ لِيَعْلَمَ اَنِّيْ لَمْ اَخُنْهُ بِالْغَيْبِ وَاَنَّ اللّٰهَ لَا يَهْدِيْ
كَيْدَ الْخَآئِنِيْنَ ﴿٥٣﴾

[a]12 : 32. [b]12 : 32.

1386. *Ya'ṣirūn* is derived from '*Aṣira* which means, (1) he pressed or squeezed the thing so as to force out its juice, etc.; (2) he aided or succoured or saved or preserved (him); (3) he gave something to someone or did some benefit to someone (Lane).

1387. Realizing that Joseph was no ordinary person the King wanted to release him from the prison forthwith. But Joseph refused to be released until a full inquiry was made into his case and he was proved to be innocent of the charge laid against him. His object in demanding an inquiry seems to be two-fold: First, that the King might know that he was innocent so that on no future occasion his mind might be poisoned against him by evilly-disposed persons on the basis of the alleged cause of his imprisonment. Secondly, that Potiphar, his benefactor, might not remain under the impression that Joseph had proved faithless to him.

1388. The words seem to show that the incident of the cutting of their hands by the women did actually take place; otherwise Joseph could not have referred to it. Either in amazement or being absorbed in conversation, some of them did inadvertently cut their hands. Or the words might mean that by bringing a false accusation against Joseph the women had cut their own hands, *i.e.*, they had landed themselves into a false position. But if nothing actual had happened, Joseph could not have referred to 'the cutting of the hands.' *Ḥāsha Lillāhi* also means, God forbid; or how far is Allāh from every imperfection (Lane).

PART XIII

54. 'And I do not hold my own self to be free from weakness—surely the soul is prone to enjoin evil—save that whereon my Lord has mercy.[1389] Surely, my Lord is Most Forgiving, Merciful.'

الجزء ١٣ وَمَآ اُبَرِّئُ نَفْسِيْ ۚ اِنَّ النَّفْسَ لَاَمَّارَةٌۢ بِالسُّوْٓءِ اِلَّا مَا رَحِمَ رَبِّيْ ۗ اِنَّ رَبِّيْ غَفُوْرٌ رَّحِيْمٌ ﴿۵۴﴾

55. And the King said, 'Bring him to me that I may take him specially for my own person. And when he had spoken to him, he said, 'Thou art this day *a person* of established position *and* trust with us.'

وَقَالَ الْمَلِكُ ائْتُوْنِيْ بِهٖٓ اَسْتَخْلِصْهُ لِنَفْسِيْ ۚ فَلَمَّا كَلَّمَهٗ قَالَ اِنَّكَ الْيَوْمَ لَدَيْنَا مَكِيْنٌ اَمِيْنٌ ﴿۵۵﴾

56. *Joseph* said, 'Appoint me over the treasures of the land, for I am a good keeper,[1390] *and* possessed of knowledge *of these matters.*'

قَالَ اجْعَلْنِيْ عَلٰى خَزَآئِنِ الْاَرْضِ ۚ اِنِّيْ حَفِيْظٌ عَلِيْمٌ ﴿۵۶﴾

57. [a]And thus did We establish Joseph in the land. He dwelt therein wherever he pleased. [b]We bestow Our mercy on whomsoever We please and We suffer not the reward of the righteous to be lost.

وَكَذٰلِكَ مَكَّنَّا لِيُوْسُفَ فِي الْاَرْضِ ۚ يَتَبَوَّاُ مِنْهَا حَيْثُ يَشَآءُ ۗ نُصِيْبُ بِرَحْمَتِنَا مَنْ نَّشَآءُ وَلَا نُضِيْعُ اَجْرَ الْمُحْسِنِيْنَ ﴿۵۷﴾

58. And surely the reward of the Hereafter, is better for those who believe and fear *God*.

ع وَلَاَجْرُ الْاٰخِرَةِ خَيْرٌ لِّلَّذِيْنَ اٰمَنُوْا وَكَانُوْا يَتَّقُوْنَ ﴿۵۸﴾

[a]12 : 22. [b]2 : 106; 3 : 75.

1389. The clause *Illā mā Rahima Rabbī* (save that whereon my Lord has mercy) may have three different interpretations : (*a*) Save the *Nafs* (soul) whereupon my Lord has mercy, the particle *mā* standing for *Nafs*. (*b*) Save him upon whom my Lord has mercy; *mā* here meaning, *man*. (*c*) Yes, but it is God's mercy which saves whom it chooses. These three meanings refer to the three stages in the spiritual development of man. The first meaning refers to the stage when man has attained the stage of spiritual perfection—the stage of *Nafs Muṭma'innah* (the soul at rest—89 : 28). The second meaning applies to man when he is yet in the stage of *Nafs Lawwāmah* (self-accusing soul—75 : 3) when man is struggling against sin and his evil propensities, sometimes overcoming them and at others being vanquished by them. The third meaning applies to man when the animal in him predominates. This stage is called *Nafs Ammārah* (the soul prone to evil).

1390. Joseph preferred charge of the finance department. His choice seems to have been dictated by the desire to give his single-minded attention to the successful running of the department which so deeply concerned the fulfilment of the King's dream.

R. 8 59. And Joseph's brethren came and presented themselves before him; and he knew them, [a]but they recognized him not.

وَجَآءَ اِخْوَةُ يُوْسُفَ فَدَخَلُوْا عَلَيْهِ فَعَرَفَهُمْ وَهُمْ
لَهٗ مُنْكِرُوْنَ ﴿٥٩﴾

60. And when he had provided them with their provision, he said, 'Bring me your brother on your father's *side*.[1390A] Do you not see that I give you full measure *of corn* and that I am the best of hosts?

وَلَمَّا جَهَّزَهُمْ بِجَهَازِهِمْ قَالَ ائْتُوْنِيْ بِاَخٍ لَّكُمْ
مِّنْ اَبِيْكُمْ اَلَا تَرَوْنَ اَنِّيْٓ اُوْفِي الْكَيْلَ وَاَنَا خَيْرُ
الْمُنْزِلِيْنَ ﴿٦٠﴾

61. 'But if you bring him not to me, then there shall be no measure *of corn* for you from me, nor shall you come near me.'

فَاِنْ لَّمْ تَاْتُوْنِيْ بِهٖ فَلَا كَيْلَ لَكُمْ عِنْدِيْ وَلَا
تَقْرَبُوْنِ ﴿٦١﴾

62. They replied, 'We will try to induce his father to part with him and we will certainly do *it*.'

قَالُوْا سَنُرَاوِدُ عَنْهُ اَبَاهُ وَاِنَّا لَفٰعِلُوْنَ ﴿٦٢﴾

63. And he said to his servants, 'Put their money back into their saddle-bags that they may recognize it when they return to their family; haply, they may come back.'

وَقَالَ لِفِتْيٰنِهِ اجْعَلُوْا بِضَاعَتَهُمْ فِيْ رِحَالِهِمْ
لَعَلَّهُمْ يَعْرِفُوْنَهَآ اِذَا انْقَلَبُوْٓا اِلٰٓى اَهْلِهِمْ لَعَلَّهُمْ
يَرْجِعُوْنَ ﴿٦٣﴾

64. And when they returned to their father, they said, 'O our father, *any further* measure *of corn* has been denied us, so send with us our brother that we may obtain our measure, and we will surely be able to take care of him.'

فَلَمَّا رَجَعُوْٓا اِلٰٓى اَبِيْهِمْ قَالُوْا يٰٓاَبَانَا مُنِعَ مِنَّا الْكَيْلُ
فَاَرْسِلْ مَعَنَآ اَخَانَا نَكْتَلْ وَاِنَّا لَهٗ لَحٰفِظُوْنَ ﴿٦٤﴾

65. He said, 'Can I trust you with him, except *with the same result* as *when* I trusted you with his brother before. But Allāh is the Best Protector, and He is the Most Merciful of those who show mercy.'

قَالَ هَلْ اٰمَنُكُمْ عَلَيْهِ اِلَّا كَمَآ اَمِنْتُكُمْ عَلٰٓى اَخِيْهِ
مِنْ قَبْلُ فَاللّٰهُ خَيْرٌ حٰفِظًا وَّهُوَ اَرْحَمُ الرّٰحِمِيْنَ ﴿٦٥﴾

[a]12 : 16.

1390A. Jacob had twelve sons, two sons — Joseph and Benjamin, from his wife, Rachel, and ten other sons from other wives.

66. And when they unpacked their goods, they found their money returned to them. They said, 'O our father, what *more* can we desire? Here is our money returned to us. We shall bring provision for our family, and guard our brother and we shall have an extra measure of a camel-load.[1391] That is a measure which is easy *to obtain*.'

وَلَمَّا فَتَحُوْا مَتَاعَهُمْ وَجَدُوْا بِضَاعَتَهُمْ رُدَّتْ
إِلَيْهِمْ ۖ قَالُوْا يَاَبَانَا مَا نَبْغِيْ ۖ هٰذِهٖ بِضَاعَتُنَا رُدَّتْ
إِلَيْنَا ۚ وَنَمِيْرُ اَهْلَنَا وَنَحْفَظُ اَخَانَا وَنَزْدَادُ كَيْلَ
بَعِيْرٍ ۖ ذٰلِكَ كَيْلٌ يَّسِيْرٌ ﴿٦٦﴾

67. He said, 'I will not send him with you until you give me a solemn promise in the name of Allāh that you will surely bring him to me, unless *it be that* you are encompassed.' And when they had given him their solemn promise, he said, 'Allāh watches over what we say.'

قَالَ لَنْ اُرْسِلَهٗ مَعَكُمْ حَتّٰى تُؤْتُوْنِ مَوْثِقًا مِّنَ
اللّٰهِ لَتَاْتُنَّنِيْ بِهٖٓ اِلَّآ اَنْ يُّحَاطَ بِكُمْ ۚ فَلَمَّآ اٰتَوْهُ مَوْثِقَهُمْ
قَالَ اللّٰهُ عَلٰى مَا نَقُوْلُ وَكِيْلٌ ﴿٦٧﴾

68. And he said, 'O my sons, enter not by one gate, but enter by different gates, and I can avail you naught against Allāh. The decision *rests* only with Allāh. [a]In Him do I put my trust and in Him let all who would trust put their trust.'

وَقَالَ يٰبَنِيَّ لَا تَدْخُلُوْا مِنْۢ بَابٍ وَّاحِدٍ وَّادْخُلُوْا
مِنْ اَبْوَابٍ مُّتَفَرِّقَةٍ ۗ وَمَآ اُغْنِيْ عَنْكُمْ مِّنَ اللّٰهِ
مِنْ شَيْءٍ ۗ اِنِ الْحُكْمُ اِلَّا لِلّٰهِ ۗ عَلَيْهِ تَوَكَّلْتُ ۚ وَعَلَيْهِ
فَلْيَتَوَكَّلِ الْمُتَوَكِّلُوْنَ ﴿٦٨﴾

69. And when they entered in the manner their father had commanded them, *Jacob's purpose was fulfilled* but it could not avail them anything against Allāh, except that there was a desire in Jacob's mind which he *thus* satisfied;[1392] and he was surely possessed of *great* knowledge We had taught him, but most men know not.

وَلَمَّا دَخَلُوْا مِنْ حَيْثُ اَمَرَهُمْ اَبُوْهُمْ ۗ مَا كَانَ يُغْنِيْ
عَنْهُمْ مِّنَ اللّٰهِ مِنْ شَيْءٍ اِلَّا حَاجَةً فِيْ نَفْسِ يَعْقُوْبَ
قَضٰىهَا ۗ وَاِنَّهٗ لَذُوْ عِلْمٍ لِّمَا عَلَّمْنٰهُ وَلٰكِنَّ اَكْثَرَ
ع النَّاسِ لَا يَعْلَمُوْنَ ﴿٦٩﴾

[a]11: 57, 89; 14: 12.

1391. A 'camel-load' may not necessarily mean a load put on a camel's back, but may denote also the load which a camel can ordinarily carry, though it may be loaded on an ass.

1392. Jacob seemed to have realized or he had possibly been informed by Divine revelation that the man in Egypt was Joseph and therefore he asked his sons to enter the town separately so that Joseph might have an opportunity to meet and talk to his brother, Benjamin, in private.

R. 9 70. And when they visited Joseph, he lodged his brother with himself. *And* he said, 'I am thy brother; so *now* grieve not at what they have been doing.'

وَلَمَّا دَخَلُوا عَلَىٰ يُوسُفَ آوَىٰ إِلَيْهِ أَخَاهُ قَالَ إِنِّي أَنَا أَخُوكَ فَلَا تَبْتَئِسْ بِمَا كَانُوا يَعْمَلُونَ ﴿٧٠﴾

71. And when he had given them their provision, he put[1393] the drinking-cup in his brother's saddle-bag. Then a crier cried, 'O ye *men of the* caravan, you are surely thieves.'[1394]

فَلَمَّا جَهَّزَهُم بِجَهَازِهِمْ جَعَلَ السِّقَايَةَ فِي رَحْلِ أَخِيهِ ثُمَّ أَذَّنَ مُؤَذِّنٌ أَيَّتُهَا الْعِيرُ إِنَّكُمْ لَسَارِقُونَ ﴿٧١﴾

72. They said, turning round towards them, 'What is it that you miss?'

قَالُوا وَأَقْبَلُوا عَلَيْهِم مَّاذَا تَفْقِدُونَ ﴿٧٢﴾

73. They replied, 'We miss the King's measuring-vessel and whoso brings it shall have a camel-load *of corn* and I am surety for it.'

قَالُوا نَفْقِدُ صُوَاعَ الْمَلِكِ وَلِمَن جَاءَ بِهِ حِمْلُ بَعِيرٍ وَأَنَا بِهِ زَعِيمٌ ﴿٧٣﴾

74. They answered, 'By Allāh, you know well that we came not to make mischief in the land, and we are not thieves.'

قَالُوا تَاللَّهِ لَقَدْ عَلِمْتُم مَّا جِئْنَا لِنُفْسِدَ فِي الْأَرْضِ وَمَا كُنَّا سَارِقِينَ ﴿٧٤﴾

75. They said, 'What then shall be the punishment for it, if you are *found to be* liars?'

قَالُوا فَمَا جَزَاؤُهُ إِن كُنتُمْ كَاذِبِينَ ﴿٧٥﴾

1393. The word *Ja'ala* (put) may either signify that Joseph himself ordered the cup to be put in his brother's sack so that he might use it on his way home; or that the cup happened to be placed among Benjamin's articles, Joseph not knowing that it was there.

1394. It is incorrect to say that Joseph himself first ordered the drinking-cup to be placed in his brother's sack, and then accused him of theft—an action much below his dignity. In fact, it was a *Siqāyah* (a drinking-cup) which Joseph had ordered to be placed in the sack of his brother while the vessel which was declared by the royal proclaimer to have been lost was a *Ṣuwā'* (a measuring-vessel). It seems that in the excitement of helping his brothers to prepare for their return journey and in view of the approaching separation from Benjamin, after only a brief meeting, Joseph felt thirst and called for water. It was brought to him in the royal measuring vessel. Such vessels were then used both as measuring-vessels and drinking-cups. After satisfying his thirst he inadvertently placed the vessel among Benjamin's things, and it thus became packed with the effects of his brother without having been noticed by any body. Joseph at once understood how the mistake had occurred, but, thinking that all this was God's own plan for detaining Benjamin, he judiciously kept silent until the caravan was gone.

76. They replied, 'The punishment for it—he in whose saddle-bag it is found shall himself be the penalty for[1395] it. Thus do we punish wrongdoers.'

قَالُوا جَزَاؤُهُ مَنْ وُجِدَ فِي رَحْلِهِ فَهُوَ جَزَاؤُهُ كَذَٰلِكَ
نَجْزِي الظَّالِمِينَ ﴿٧٦﴾

77. Then he[1396] began with *the search of* their sacks before the sack of *Joseph's* brother;[1396A] then he took it out of the sack of his brother. Thus did We plan for Joseph.[1397] He could not have taken his brother under the King's law unless Allāh had so willed. [a]We raise in degrees *of rank* whomsoever We please; and over every possessor of knowledge is One, Most-Knowing.

فَبَدَأَ بِأَوْعِيَتِهِمْ قَبْلَ وِعَاءِ أَخِيهِ ثُمَّ اسْتَخْرَجَهَا
مِنْ وِعَاءِ أَخِيهِ ۚ كَذَٰلِكَ كِدْنَا لِيُوسُفَ ۖ مَا كَانَ
لِيَأْخُذَ أَخَاهُ فِي دِينِ الْمَلِكِ إِلَّا أَنْ يَشَاءَ اللَّهُ ۚ
نَرْفَعُ دَرَجَاتٍ مَنْ نَشَاءُ ۗ وَفَوْقَ كُلِّ ذِي عِلْمٍ
عَلِيمٌ ﴿٧٧﴾

78. They said, 'If he has stolen, a brother of his had also committed theft before.'[1398] But Joseph kept it secret in his heart and did not disclose it to them. He simply said, 'You are in a worst condition; and Allāh knows best what you allege.'

قَالُوا إِنْ يَسْرِقْ فَقَدْ سَرَقَ أَخٌ لَهُ مِنْ قَبْلُ ۚ
فَأَسَرَّهَا يُوسُفُ فِي نَفْسِهِ وَلَمْ يُبْدِهَا لَهُمْ ۚ قَالَ
أَنْتُمْ شَرٌّ مَكَانًا ۖ وَاللَّهُ أَعْلَمُ بِمَا تَصِفُونَ ﴿٧٨﴾

---

[a]6 : 84.

1395. Joseph's brothers, in a fit of excitement, themselves suggested that he in whose sack the measuring-vessel might be found should be detained to explain his conduct. Thus Joseph was able to keep back his brother without the latter having been accused of theft.

1396. The pronoun 'he' refers to the man who announced the loss of the measuring-vessel and who naturally himself came forward to make the search.

1396A. This was due to the special consideration which Joseph had shown to Benjamin.

1397. The whole thing was planned by God—Joseph having no hand in it. Quite inadvertently Joseph happened to place the King's measuring-vessel, which he used as a drinking-cup on that occasion, in Benjamin's luggage and his brothers themselves made the suggestion which enabled Joseph to detain Benjamin. Thus a providential combination of circumstances enabled Joseph to satisfy his heart's desire.

1398. One sin leads to another. Joseph's brothers had first sought to put him to death. Now quite unashamedly they hastened to accuse him of theft.

79. They said, 'O noble chief, he has a very aged father,[1399] so take one of us in his place; for we see thee to be of those who are benevolent.'

قَالُوْا يٰٓاَيُّهَا الْعَزِيْزُ اِنَّ لَهٗٓ اَبًا شَيْخًا كَبِيْرًا فَخُذْ اَحَدَنَا مَكَانَهٗ ۚ اِنَّا نَرٰىكَ مِنَ الْمُحْسِنِيْنَ ﴿۷۹﴾

80. He replied, 'Allāh forbid that we should take *any* other but him with whom we have found our property; for then we should certainly be unjust.'

قَالَ مَعَاذَ اللّٰهِ اَنْ نَّاْخُذَ اِلَّا مَنْ وَّجَدْنَا مَتَاعَنَا عِنْدَهٗٓ ۙ اِنَّآ اِذًا لَّظٰلِمُوْنَ ﴿۸۰﴾

R. 10 81. And when they despaired of him, they retired, conferring together in private.[1399A] Then their leader[1400] said, 'Know ye not that your father has taken from you a solemn pledge in the name of Allāh and how, before this, you failed in your duty with respect to Joseph? I will not, therefore, leave the land until my father permits me or Allāh decides for me. And He is the Best of judges;

فَلَمَّا اسْتَيْـَٔسُوْا مِنْهُ خَلَصُوْا نَجِيًّا ؕ قَالَ كَبِيْرُهُمْ اَلَمْ تَعْلَمُوْٓا اَنَّ اَبَاكُمْ قَدْ اَخَذَ عَلَيْكُمْ مَّوْثِقًا مِّنَ اللّٰهِ وَمِنْ قَبْلُ مَا فَرَّطْتُّمْ فِيْ يُوْسُفَ ۚ فَلَنْ اَبْرَحَ الْاَرْضَ حَتّٰى يَاْذَنَ لِيْٓ اَبِيْٓ اَوْ يَحْكُمَ اللّٰهُ لِيْ ۚ وَهُوَ خَيْرُ الْحٰكِمِيْنَ ﴿۸۱﴾

82. "Go back to your father, and say, 'O our father, thy son committed theft and we have stated only what we know and we could not be guardians over the unseen;

اِرْجِعُوْٓا اِلٰٓى اَبِيْكُمْ فَقُوْلُوْا يٰٓاَبَانَآ اِنَّ ابْنَكَ سَرَقَ ۚ وَمَا شَهِدْنَآ اِلَّا بِمَا عَلِمْنَا وَمَا كُنَّا لِلْغَيْبِ حٰفِظِيْنَ ﴿۸۲﴾

1399. Not being satisfied with accusing Benjamin of theft, they proceed to disown him and even refuse to acknowledge him as their brother saying, 'he has a very aged father.'

1399A. *Najiyy* means, (1) a secret; (2) one to whom a secret is confided; (3) one who confers with another in private; (4) the act of conferring in private (Aqrab).

1400. According to the Bible it was Judah, the fourth among the brothers, and not Reuben, the eldest of them, who refused to go back to his father without Benjamin. The word which the Qur'ān has used is *Kabīr* which means, 'big' or 'elder' and not *Akbar* which means, 'the eldest.' Judah, being the fourth son of Jacob, was indeed one of the bigger or elder brothers of Joseph. Moreover, *Kabīr* does not only mean 'big' or 'elder' but also means 'leader' and 'great in estimation, rank or dignity,' and it is in this sense that the word has been used here and so applies to Judah and not to Reuben. Judah was more important than Reuben in the eyes of Jacob (Gen. 43 : 8-10).

83. 'And inquire *of the people* of the town[1401] wherein we were, and of the caravan with which we came, and certainly we are speaking the truth.''

وَسْـَٔلِ الْقَرْيَةَ الَّتِيْ كُنَّا فِيْهَا وَالْعِيْرَ الَّتِيْٓ اَقْبَلْنَا فِيْهَا ۭ وَاِنَّا لَصٰدِقُوْنَ ﴿۸۲﴾

84. [a]He replied, 'Nay, but your minds have embellished to you an *evil* thing. So *now there is nothing left for me but* goodly patience. May be Allāh will bring them all[1402] to me; for He is the All-Knowing, the Wise.'

قَالَ بَلْ سَوَّلَتْ لَكُمْ اَنْفُسُكُمْ اَمْرًا ۭ فَصَبْرٌ جَمِيْلٌ ۭ عَسَى اللّٰهُ اَنْ يَّاْتِيَنِيْ بِهِمْ جَمِيْعًا ۭ اِنَّهٗ هُوَ الْعَلِيْمُ الْحَكِيْمُ ﴿۸۳﴾

85. And he turned away from them and said, 'O my grief for Joseph!' And his eyes were filled with tears[1403] because of grief, and he was suppressing *his sorrow*.

وَتَوَلّٰى عَنْهُمْ وَقَالَ يٰٓاَسَفٰى عَلٰى يُوْسُفَ وَابْيَضَّتْ عَيْنٰهُ مِنَ الْحُزْنِ فَهُوَ كَظِيْمٌ ﴿۸۴﴾

86. They said, 'By Allāh, thou wilt not cease talking of Joseph until thou art wasted away or thou art of those who perish.'[1404]

قَالُوْا تَاللّٰهِ تَفْتَؤُا تَذْكُرُ يُوْسُفَ حَتّٰى تَكُوْنَ حَرَضًا اَوْ تَكُوْنَ مِنَ الْهٰلِكِيْنَ ﴿۸۵﴾

87. He replied, 'I only complain of my sorrow and my grief to Allāh, and I know from Allāh that which you know not,[1404A]

قَالَ اِنَّمَآ اَشْكُوْا بَثِّيْ وَحُزْنِيْٓ اِلَى اللّٰهِ وَاَعْلَمُ مِنَ اللّٰهِ مَا لَا تَعْلَمُوْنَ ﴿۸۶﴾

[a]12 : 19.

1401. In the verse *Qaryah* (town) is in reality *Ahl al-Qaryah* (people of the town) and *'Īr* (caravan) is *Aṣḥāb al-'Īr* (members of the caravan). The words *Ahl* and *Aṣḥāb* have been omitted to lend emphasis to the statement.

1402. Joseph, Benjamin and Judah.

1403. *Bayyaḍa al-Siqāa'* means, he filled the skin with water or milk. The expression *Ibyaḍḍat 'Ainā-hu* is used regarding a person who is stricken with grief and his eyes become filled with tears. The verse thus only signifies that the world became dark for Jacob and his eyes became filled with tears on account of grief (Lane, Rāzī & Biḥār).

1404. *Ḥaraḍ* means, a man corrupt in body and intellect; sick or diseased; suffering from protracted disquietude of mind and disease; weary or fatigued and at the point of death; emaciated or dissolved by excessive grief or love, etc. (Lane).

1404A. The verse implies that Jacob had been informed by God that Joseph, Benjamin and Judah were alive.

88. 'O my sons, go ye and enquire about Joseph and his brother[1405] and [a]despair not of the mercy of Allāh; for none despairs of Allāh's mercy save the disbelieving people.'

يٰبَنِيَّ اذْهَبُوْا فَتَحَسَّسُوْا مِنْ يُّوْسُفَ وَ اَخِيْهِ وَلَا تَايْـَٔسُوْا مِنْ رَّوْحِ اللّٰهِ ۭ اِنَّهٗ لَا يَايْـَٔسُ مِنْ رَّوْحِ اللّٰهِ اِلَّا الْقَوْمُ الْكٰفِرُوْنَ ﴿۸۸﴾

89. And, when they came before *Joseph again*, they said, 'O noble chief, poverty has smitten us and our family, and we have brought a paltry sum of money, but *nonetheless* give us full measure, and be charitable[1405A] to us. Surely, Allāh does reward the charitable.'

فَلَمَّا دَخَلُوْا عَلَيْهِ قَالُوْا يٰٓاَيُّهَا الْعَزِيْزُ مَسَّنَا وَاَهْلَنَا الضُّرُّ وَجِئْنَا بِبِضَاعَةٍ مُّزْجٰىةٍ فَاَوْفِ لَنَا الْكَيْلَ وَتَصَدَّقْ عَلَيْنَا ۭ اِنَّ اللّٰهَ يَجْزِي الْمُتَصَدِّقِيْنَ ﴿۸۹﴾

90. He said, 'Do you know what you did to Joseph and his brother in your ignorance?'[1406]

قَالَ هَلْ عَلِمْتُمْ مَّا فَعَلْتُمْ بِيُوْسُفَ وَاَخِيْهِ اِذْ اَنْتُمْ جٰهِلُوْنَ ﴿۹۰﴾

91. They replied, 'Art thou Joseph?' He said, 'Yes, I am Joseph and this is my brother. Allāh has indeed been gracious to us. Verily, whoso fears *Allāh* and is steadfast—[b]Allāh never suffers the reward of the good to be lost.'

قَالُوْٓا ءَاِنَّكَ لَاَنْتَ يُوْسُفُ ۭ قَالَ اَنَا يُوْسُفُ وَهٰذَآ اَخِيْ ۡ قَدْ مَنَّ اللّٰهُ عَلَيْنَا ۭ اِنَّهٗ مَنْ يَّتَّقِ وَيَصْبِرْ فَاِنَّ اللّٰهَ لَا يُضِيْعُ اَجْرَ الْمُحْسِنِيْنَ ﴿۹۱﴾

92. They replied, 'By Allāh; surely, Allāh has preferred thee above us and we have indeed been sinners.'

قَالُوْا تَاللّٰهِ لَقَدْ اٰثَرَكَ اللّٰهُ عَلَيْنَا وَاِنْ كُنَّا لَخٰطِــِٕيْنَ ﴿۹۲﴾

[a]15 : 57; 39 : 54. [b]12 : 57.

1405. This verse also shows that Jacob was convinced that Joseph, Benjamin and Judah were alive in Egypt.

1405A. The conduct of Joseph's brothers on this occasion seems to be inexplicable. They seemed to have morally sunk so low that, ignoring the real purpose of their present visit to Egypt, which was to make a search for Joseph, Benjamin and Judah, they began to beg for corn.

1406. Bearing no longer to see his brothers degrade themselves by thus begging for corn Joseph decided to reveal himself to them; but approached the subject indirectly.

93. He said, 'No blame shall lie on you this day;[1407] may Allāh forgive you! And He is the Most Merciful of those who show mercy;

قَالَ لَا تَثْرِيْبَ عَلَيْكُمُ الْيَوْمَ ۖ يَغْفِرُ اللّٰهُ لَكُمْ ۡ وَهُوَ اَرْحَمُ الرّٰحِمِيْنَ ﴿۹۳﴾

94. 'Go with this shirt of mine and lay it before my father; he will come to know everything. And bring to me the whole of your family.'

اِذْهَبُوْا بِقَمِيْصِيْ هٰذَا فَاَلْقُوْهُ عَلٰى وَجْهِ اَبِيْ يَاْتِ بَصِيْرًا ۚ وَاْتُوْنِيْ بِاَهْلِكُمْ اَجْمَعِيْنَ ﴿۹۴﴾ ع

R. 11 95. And when the caravan departed, their father said, 'Surely, I perceive the scent of Joseph, even though you take me to be a dotard.'[1408]

وَلَمَّا فَصَلَتِ الْعِيْرُ قَالَ اَبُوْهُمْ اِنِّيْ لَاَجِدُ رِيْحَ يُوْسُفَ لَوْلَآ اَنْ تُفَنِّدُوْنِ ﴿۹۵﴾

96. [a]They replied, 'By Allāh, thou art assuredly *still* in thy old error.'

قَالُوْا تَاللّٰهِ اِنَّكَ لَفِيْ ضَلٰلِكَ الْقَدِيْمِ ﴿۹۶﴾

97. And when the bearer of glad tidings came, he laid *the shirt* before him and he became enlightened.[1409] Then he said, "Did I not say to you, 'I know from Allāh what you know not?"

فَلَمَّآ اَنْ جَآءَ الْبَشِيْرُ اَلْقٰهُ عَلٰى وَجْهِهٖ فَارْتَدَّ بَصِيْرًا ۚ قَالَ اَلَمْ اَقُلْ لَّكُمْ ۚ اِنِّيْٓ اَعْلَمُ مِنَ اللّٰهِ مَا لَا تَعْلَمُوْنَ ﴿۹۷﴾

---

[a]12 : 9.

1407. Joseph did not keep his brothers in suspense and at once removed all their fears and apprehensions concerning the treatment he would extend to them, by telling them forthwith that his pardon was unreserved and unqualified. This large-hearted and generous forgiving of his brothers by Joseph constitutes his greatest and most outstanding resemblance to the Holy Prophet. Like Joseph, the Holy Prophet, too, gained honour and power in flight and banishment; and when after years of exile he entered his native town as a conqueror, at the head of ten thousand Companions, and Mecca lay prostrate at his feet, he asked his people what treatment did they expect from him. 'The treatment that Joseph accorded to his brethren,' they replied. 'Then no reproach shall lie on you this day,' promptly returned the Holy Prophet. This noble treatment by the Holy Prophet of his erstwhile blood-thirsty enemies, the Quraish of Mecca, who had left no stone unturned to compass his death and destroy Islām root and branch stands unparalleled in the whole annals of human history.

1408. Even before the caravan reached home, Jacob had told his people that, in spite of all appearances to the contrary, he hoped to meet Joseph soon; and in order to lend emphasis to his conviction, he added the words 'even though you take me to be a dotard' meaning thereby, 'you consider this meeting to be an impossibility, being not more than the illusion and wishful thinking of an old man, but I know it as a fact and a certainty.'

1409. When Joseph's shirt was laid before Jacob, the conviction that Joseph was alive which, being based on revelation was previously only a matter of faith, now became converted into factual knowledge. This is the meaning of the words, *he became enlightened*. The Qur'ān lends no support whatsoever to the view that Jacob had become blind. Not only was it inconsistent with his dignity as a great Prophet of God but several verses also contradict this view. It seems that it was the same shirt which Joseph had worn when he was thrown into the well.

98. They said, 'O our father, ask *of Allāh* forgiveness of our sins for us; we have indeed been sinners.'

قَالُوْا يٰٓاَبَانَا اسْتَغْفِرْ لَنَا ذُنُوْبَنَآ اِنَّا كُنَّا
خٰطِـِٕيْنَ ﴿۹۸﴾

99. He said, 'I will certainly ask forgiveness for you of my Lord. Surely, He is the Most Forgiving, the Merciful.'

قَالَ سَوْفَ اَسْتَغْفِرُ لَكُمْ رَبِّيْ ؕ اِنَّهٗ هُوَ الْغَفُوْرُ
الرَّحِيْمُ ﴿۹۹﴾

100. And when they came to Joseph, he put up his parents[1410] with himself and said, 'Enter Egypt in peace, if it please Allāh.'

فَلَمَّا دَخَلُوْا عَلٰى يُوْسُفَ اٰوٰٓى اِلَيْهِ اَبَوَيْهِ وَقَالَ
ادْخُلُوْا مِصْرَ اِنْ شَآءَ اللّٰهُ اٰمِنِيْنَ ﴿۱۰۰﴾

101. And he raised his parents upon the throne[1411] and they *all* fell down prostrate *before Allāh* for him.[1412] And he said, 'O my father, this is the fulfilment of my dream of old. My Lord has made it come true. And He bestowed a favour upon me when He took me out of the prison[1413] and brought you from the desert after Satan had stirred up discord between me and my brethren. Surely, my Lord is Benignant to whomsoever He pleases; for He is the All-Knowing, the Wise.

وَرَفَعَ اَبَوَيْهِ عَلَى الْعَرْشِ وَخَرُّوْا لَهٗ سُجَّدًا ۚ وَ
قَالَ يٰٓاَبَتِ هٰذَا تَاْوِيْلُ رُءْيَايَ مِنْ قَبْلُ ۫ قَدْ
جَعَلَهَا رَبِّيْ حَقًّا ؕ وَقَدْ اَحْسَنَ بِيْٓ اِذْ اَخْرَجَنِيْ مِنَ
السِّجْنِ وَجَآءَ بِكُمْ مِّنَ الْبَدْوِ مِنْۢ بَعْدِ اَنْ نَّزَغَ
الشَّيْطٰنُ بَيْنِيْ وَبَيْنَ اِخْوَتِيْ ؕ اِنَّ رَبِّيْ لَطِيْفٌ لِّمَا
يَشَآءُ ؕ اِنَّهٗ هُوَ الْعَلِيْمُ الْحَكِيْمُ ﴿۱۰۱﴾

1410. Joseph's own mother Rachel had already died, but the use of the word 'parents' in the verse implies that a step-mother is as much entitled to one's respect and affection as one's real mother.

1411. The words may mean that Joseph presented his parents to the King (Gen. 47 : 2,7) or that he made them sit on his own throne with King's permission. In olden times the ministers and deputies of kings also had their own thrones.

1412. Joseph's brothers and parents fell prostrate and thanked God for raising Joseph to such an eminent position. Thus Joseph was the cause, and not the object, of their prostration.

1413. While mentioning God's favours Joseph refers only to his being taken out of prison and makes no mention of being rescued from the well, lest his brothers should feel ashamed.

102. 'O my Lord, Thou hast bestowed *a portion of* sovereignty upon me and [a]taught me the interpretation of dreams. O [b]Maker of the heavens and the earth, Thou art my Protector in this world and the Hereafter. Let death come to me in *a state of* submission *to Thy Will* and join me to the righteous.'

رَبِّ قَدْ اٰتَيْتَنِيْ مِنَ الْمُلْكِ وَعَلَّمْتَنِيْ مِنْ تَاْوِيْلِ
الْاَحَادِيْثِ ۚ فَاطِرَ السَّمٰوٰتِ وَالْاَرْضِ ۟ اَنْتَ وَلِيّٖ فِي
الدُّنْيَا وَالْاٰخِرَةِ ۚ تَوَفَّنِيْ مُسْلِمًا وَّاَلْحِقْنِيْ بِالصّٰلِحِيْنَ ﴿١٠٢﴾

103. [c]That is of the tidings of the unseen,[1414] *which* We reveal to thee. And thou wast not with them when they[1415] agreed upon their plan while they were plotting.

ذٰلِكَ مِنْ اَنْۢبَآءِ الْغَيْبِ نُوْحِيْهِ اِلَيْكَ ۚ وَمَا كُنْتَ
لَدَيْهِمْ اِذْ اَجْمَعُوْۤا اَمْرَهُمْ وَهُمْ يَمْكُرُوْنَ ﴿١٠٣﴾

104. [d]And most men will not believe even though thou eagerly desire *it*.

وَمَاۤ اَكْثَرُ النَّاسِ وَلَوْ حَرَصْتَ بِمُؤْمِنِيْنَ ﴿١٠٤﴾

105. And thou dost not ask of them any reward for it. [e]It is but *a source of* honour for all mankind.

وَمَا تَسْـَٔلُهُمْ عَلَيْهِ مِنْ اَجْرٍ ۚ اِنْ هُوَ اِلَّا ذِكْرٌ لِّلْعٰلَمِيْنَ ﴿١٠٥﴾ ع

R. 12 106. [f]And how many a Sign is there in the heavens and the earth, which they pass by, turning away from it![1416]

وَكَاَيِّنْ مِّنْ اٰيَةٍ فِي السَّمٰوٰتِ وَالْاَرْضِ يَمُرُّوْنَ عَلَيْهَا
وَهُمْ عَنْهَا مُعْرِضُوْنَ ﴿١٠٦﴾

107. And most of them believe not in Allāh without *at the same time* associating partners *with Him*.

وَمَا يُؤْمِنُ اَكْثَرُهُمْ بِاللّٰهِ اِلَّا وَهُمْ مُّشْرِكُوْنَ ﴿١٠٧﴾

---

[a]12 : 7,22. [b]6 : 15; 14 : 11; 35 : 2; 39 : 47. [c]3 : 45; 11 : 50. [d]18 : 7. [e]38 : 88; 81 : 28. [f]21 : 33; 23 : 67.

1414. The verse means that this account of Joseph was not a mere story. It embodied mighty prophecies relating to the future of the Holy Prophet and Islām.

1415. The pronoun 'they' refers to the enemies of the Holy Prophet.

1416. The verse points to a fundamental difference between the attitude of a believer and a disbeliever. Whereas the believer goes about with his eyes open and is ready to grasp the slightest Divine hint, the disbeliever behaves like a blind man, refusing to benefit even from clear and manifest Signs.

108. Do they, then, feel secure from the coming on them of an overwhelming punishment from Allāh [a]or the sudden coming of the Hour upon them while they are unaware?

أَفَأَمِنُوٓا أَنْ تَأْتِيَهُمْ غَاشِيَةٌ مِّنْ عَذَابِ اللّٰهِ أَوْ
تَأْتِيَهُمُ السَّاعَةُ بَغْتَةً وَّهُمْ لَا يَشْعُرُونَ ﴿١٠٨﴾

109. Say, [b]"This is my way; I call unto Allāh *standing* on sure knowledge,[1417]—I and those who follow me. Holy is Allāh, and I am not of those who associate gods *with Allāh*.

قُلْ هٰذِهٖ سَبِيْلِيْٓ أَدْعُوْٓا إِلَى اللّٰهِ ۚ عَلٰى بَصِيْرَةٍ أَنَا وَمَنِ
اتَّبَعَنِيْ ۖ وَسُبْحٰنَ اللّٰهِ وَمَآ أَنَا مِنَ الْمُشْرِكِيْنَ ﴿١٠٩﴾

110. And [c]We sent not before thee *as Messengers* any but men to whom We sent revelation, from among the people of the towns. Have they not then travelled in the earth so that they should see what was the end of those before them? And surely, the abode of the Hereafter is better for those who fear *Allāh*. Will you not then use your understanding?'

وَمَآ أَرْسَلْنَا مِنْ قَبْلِكَ إِلَّا رِجَالًا نُّوْحِيْٓ إِلَيْهِمْ مِّنْ
أَهْلِ الْقُرٰى ۗ أَفَلَمْ يَسِيْرُوْا فِي الْأَرْضِ فَيَنْظُرُوْا كَيْفَ
كَانَ عَاقِبَةُ الَّذِيْنَ مِنْ قَبْلِهِمْ ۗ وَلَدَارُ الْاٰخِرَةِ خَيْرٌ
لِّلَّذِيْنَ اتَّقَوْا ۚ أَفَلَا تَعْقِلُوْنَ ﴿١١٠﴾

[a]10 : 51; 22 : 56; 43 : 67. [b]6 : 58. [c]16 : 44; 21 : 8.

1417. Blind and unthinking faith which is not based on sound reasons and firm conviction carries no weight in the sight of God.

111. And[1417A] [a]when the Messengers despaired *of the disbelievers* and *the disbelievers* were convinced that they had been told *only* lies,[1418] Our help came *to the Messengers, and* then were saved those whom We pleased. And Our chastisement cannot be averted from the sinful people.

حَتّٰۤى اِذَا اسْتَيْـَٔسَ الرُّسُلُ وَ ظَنُّوْۤا اَنَّهُمْ قَدْ كُذِبُوْا
جَآءَهُمْ نَصْرُنَا ۙ فَنُجِّيَ مَنْ نَّشَآءُ ؕ وَ لَا يُرَدُّ بَاْسُنَا
عَنِ الْقَوْمِ الْمُجْرِمِيْنَ ﴿۱۱۱﴾

112. Assuredly, in their narrative is a lesson for men of understanding. [b]It is not a thing that has been forged, but a fulfilment of that which is before it and a detailed exposition of all things, and [c]a guidance and a mercy to a people who believe.

لَقَدْ كَانَ فِيْ قَصَصِهِمْ عِبْرَةٌ لِّاُولِي الْاَلْبَابِ ؕ مَا
كَانَ حَدِيْثًا يُّفْتَرٰى وَ لٰكِنْ تَصْدِيْقَ الَّذِيْ بَيْنَ
يَدَيْهِ وَ تَفْصِيْلَ كُلِّ شَيْءٍ وَّ هُدًى وَّ رَحْمَةً
لِّقَوْمٍ يُّؤْمِنُوْنَ ﴿۱۱۲﴾ ع ١٢

[a]2 : 215. [b]10 : 38. [c]16 : 90.

1417A. The particle *ḥatta* is sometimes used as a conjunction like *wa* signifying 'and' or 'even' as in *Akaltu al-Samaka ḥatta Ra'sahā*, *i.e.*, I ate the fish and (even) its head (Lane).

1418. The enemies of Prophets of God continue to increase in wickedness and opposition to them till a stage is reached when the Prophets begin to feel that those who were destined to believe had already believed and as for the rest they despair of their believing in them. But God's Prophets never despair of God's mercy and help (15 : 57). Their opponents, on the other hand, owing to the delay in the coming of Divine punishment, begin to feel secure in the thought that they will never be visited with any punishment and that the prophecies about the Prophets' final success and about the discomfiture of their enemies were nothing but false utterances.

CHAPTER 13

AL-RA'D

(*Revealed before Hijrah*)

Date of Revelation and Context

Preponderance of scholarly opinion is in favour of the view that this *Sūrah* was revealed at Mecca. Its subject-matter also confirms this view. Some verses, however, were revealed at Medina. These verses are 44th (according to'Aṭā), 32nd (according to Qatādah), and 13-15th (according to certain other authorities). In Chapter 10 (*Sūrah* Yūnus) it was stated that whenever a Prophet appears in the world, people are made to accept the Divine Messenger either by being visited with Heavenly punishment or God showers his mercy upon them if they deserve it. Stress was laid in Chapter 11 (*Sūrah* Hūd) on Divine punishment and in Chapter 12 (*Sūrah* Yūsuf) on God's mercy. The present *Sūrah*, however, explains how the promises and prophecies about the rise and prosperity of the Holy Prophet, made in the three preceding Chapters, will be fulfilled and how Islām eventually will prevail over other religions.

Subject-Matter

The *Sūrah* opens with the theme that God works in inscrutable ways. The means by which His Messengers and Prophets rise to power remain hidden from human eyes till the results, towards the accomplishment of which they work, become apparent. It proceeds to draw attention to a well-known law of nature that different kinds of fruits and vegetations grow from a soil which is watered by the same water. Similarly, the Holy Prophet, born and brought up in the same environment with the pagan Meccans, rose to be God's great Messenger. The disbelievers are further told that they should not judge the Holy Prophet by his present weak state and by the paucity of his means and resources, nor should they wonder at the promises of his ultimate success. It is not his promised success that is to be wondered at; rather it would have been strange if he had not appeared at the time of humanity's crying need. The Holy Prophet is bound to succeed and his enemies must fail. The cause of Islām shall triumph and the children of the leaders of disbelief themselves shall join its fold. God will withdraw His help from disbelievers and their power and glory will depart. All the laws and elements of nature being under God's control, He will make them subservient to the Holy Prophet's cause. The false gods of the idolaters will be quite powerless to impede or arrest the progress of the new Faith. The *Sūrah* goes on to develop the theme that so great are the spiritual powers of the Holy Prophet that he could overcome his enemies single-handed, even as a man having eyes could overcome a host of blind men. Polytheism cannot stand against the doctrine of the Unity of God, nor can the votaries of false gods against the devotees of the True God. The enemies of truth shall melt away and vanish like foam or froth. Men of weak understanding see only the rising foam and froth and do not care or have the intelligence to see the pure water underneath. The foam and froth disappear but pure water and gold remain. Similarly, the superficial and trifling beliefs of the polytheists are bound to perish and the great and noble ideals preached by the Qur'ān will endure and its teachings, being in harmony with human nature, will find their way into the hearts of men, who will gradually come to realize on which side lies the truth when they compare the moral stature of believers with that of disbelievers. Mighty Signs will be shown and great miracles wrought by means of the Qur'ān and human hearts, the strongest of all earthly citadels shall fall. One of these Signs will be that his people will drive out the Holy Prophet from Mecca and will draw the sword against him. But Islām shall continue to make headway till Mecca, the centre of disbelief and opposition will fall to the victorious arms of the Holy Prophet. Idolatry shall disappear from Arabia for all time and Islām shall be firmly established there. The world shall witness all these Signs wrought not by human agency but by the hand of the Almighty God Himself. The *Sūrah* contains many prophecies about the discomfiture and destruction of the leaders of disbelief and foretells a bright future for Islām.

The Title

The above constitutes the main theme of the *Sūrah* and it is in conformity with this theme that it has been named Ra'd or Thunder. Rain brings with it lightning and thunder and it is in the fitness of things that heavenly rain—the Quranic revelation—should also be accompanied by thunder and lightning. Islām has brought with it thunderbolts. Those who draw the sword against Islām shall perish by the sword and those who owe allegiance to it shall sit on the thrones of power and glory.

سُوْرَةُ الرَّعْدِ مَكِّيَّةٌ (١٣)

1. [a]In the name of Allāh, the Gracious, the Merciful.

بِسْمِ اللّٰهِ الرَّحْمٰنِ الرَّحِيْمِ ①

2. [b]Alif Lām Mīm Rā.[1419] [c]These are verses of the *perfect* Book. That which has been revealed to thee from thy Lord is the Truth, but most men believe not.

الٓمّٓرٰ تِلْكَ اٰيٰتُ الْكِتٰبِ وَالَّذِيْٓ اُنْزِلَ اِلَيْكَ مِنْ
رَّبِّكَ الْحَقُّ وَلٰكِنَّ اَكْثَرَ النَّاسِ لَا يُؤْمِنُوْنَ ②

3. [d]Allāh is He Who raised up the heavens without any pillars that you can see.[1420] Then He settled Himself on the Throne.[1420A] [e]And He pressed the sun and the moon into *your* service ; each *planet* pursues its course until an appointed term. [f]He regulates all affairs *and* He clearly explains the Signs that you may have firm belief in the meeting with your Lord.

اَللّٰهُ الَّذِيْ رَفَعَ السَّمٰوٰتِ بِغَيْرِ عَمَدٍ تَرَوْنَهَا ثُمَّ اسْتَوٰى
عَلَى الْعَرْشِ وَسَخَّرَ الشَّمْسَ وَالْقَمَرَ كُلٌّ يَّجْرِيْ لِاَجَلٍ
مُّسَمًّى يُدَبِّرُ الْاَمْرَ يُفَصِّلُ الْاٰيٰتِ لَعَلَّكُمْ بِلِقَآءِ
رَبِّكُمْ تُوْقِنُوْنَ ③

---

[a]1 : 1. [b]2 : 2. [c]13 : 20; 32 : 3-4. [d]31 : 11. [e]7 : 55; 16 : 13; 29 : 62; 31 : 30; 35 : 14; 39 : 6. [f]32 : 6.

1419. Whereas Chapters 10,11 &12 begin with the letters *Alif Lām Rā*, the present *Sūrah* which is the 13th in number opens with the letters, *Alif Lām Mīm Rā*. This difference in the abbreviated letters shows that the subject-matter of this *Sūrah* varies a little from that of the three preceding Chapters. These four abbreviated letters mean, I am Allāh, the All-Knowing, the All-Seeing; the attribute, 'Knowing,' having been added to the attribute, 'Seeing,' referred to in the preceding Chapters.

1420. These words mean : (1) You see that the heavens stand without pillars ; (2) the heavens do not stand on pillars which you can see, *i.e.*, they have supports but you cannot see them. Taken literally the verse means that the heavens stand without the support of pillars. Figuratively, it means that the heavens or, for that matter, the heavenly bodies, do stand on supports but these supports are not visible to the human eye, *e.g.*, the force of gravity, or magnetic power or the special movements of planets or other means which science has discovered so far or which may be discovered in future.

1420A. The word *'Arsh* (Throne) has been used in the Qur'ān to express the bringing to perfection of spiritual or physical laws. The use of this expression is analogous to the practice of worldly monarchs. They make their important proclamations 'from the throne.'

4. And *a*He it is Who spread out the earth and made therein mountains and rivers, and of *b*fruits of every kind He made therein two sexes.[1421] *c*He causes the night to cover the day. Therein, verily, are Signs for a people who reflect.

وَهُوَ الَّذِي مَدَّ الْأَرْضَ وَجَعَلَ فِيهَا رَوَاسِيَ وَ
أَنْهٰرًا ۖ وَمِنْ كُلِّ الثَّمَرٰتِ جَعَلَ فِيهَا زَوْجَيْنِ اثْنَيْنِ
يُغْشِي الَّيْلَ النَّهَارَ ۚ إِنَّ فِي ذٰلِكَ لَاٰيٰتٍ لِّقَوْمٍ يَّتَفَكَّرُوْنَ ﴿٤﴾

5. *d*And in the earth are *diverse* tracts, adjoining one another, and gardens of vines, and corn-fields, and date-palms, growing together from one root and *others* not so growing; they are *all* watered with the same water, *e*yet We make some of them excel others in fruit.[1422] Therein are Signs for a people who use their understanding.

وَفِي الْأَرْضِ قِطَعٌ مُّتَجٰوِرٰتٌ وَّجَنّٰتٌ مِّنْ أَعْنَابٍ وَّ
زَرْعٌ وَّنَخِيْلٌ صِنْوَانٌ وَّغَيْرُ صِنْوَانٍ يُّسْقٰى بِمَآءٍ
وَّاحِدٍ ۟ وَنُفَضِّلُ بَعْضَهَا عَلٰى بَعْضٍ فِي الْأُكُلِ ۚ إِنَّ
فِي ذٰلِكَ لَاٰيٰتٍ لِّقَوْمٍ يَّعْقِلُوْنَ ﴿٥﴾

6. *f*And if thou shouldst wonder *at their saying*, 'What! when we have become dust, shall we then be in a *state of* new creation,' then wondrous indeed is what they say. These it is who disbelieve in their Lord; and *g*these it is who shall have shackles[1423] round their necks, and they shall be the inmates of the Fire, wherein they shall abide.

وَإِنْ تَعْجَبْ فَعَجَبٌ قَوْلُهُمْ ءَإِذَا كُنَّا تُرٰبًا ءَإِنَّا لَفِي
خَلْقٍ جَدِيْدٍ ۗ أُولٰٓئِكَ الَّذِيْنَ كَفَرُوْا بِرَبِّهِمْ ۚ وَأُولٰٓئِكَ
الْأَغْلٰلُ فِيٓ أَعْنَاقِهِمْ ۚ وَأُولٰٓئِكَ أَصْحٰبُ النَّارِ ۚ هُمْ فِيهَا
خٰلِدُوْنَ ﴿٦﴾

*a*15 : 20; 16 : 16: 21 : 32. *b*36 : 37; 51 : 50. *c*7 : 55; 39 : 6. *d*6 : 100; 16 : 12. *e*16 : 14; 39 : 22. *f*27 : 68; 37: 17; 50 : 4. *g*36 : 9; 76 : 5.

1421. Though the present verse refers only to fruits, elsewhere the Qur'ān speaks of God having made pairs—male and female—of all things (36 : 37; 51 : 50). This is a truth which of all religious Scriptures the Qur'ān was the first to propound. Scientists have begun to discover pairs even in inorganic matter. The verse draws attention to the fact that the law that everything has a pair applies to the human intellect also. Until heavenly light descends on it, man cannot have true knowledge, which is born of a combination of both Divine revelation and human reason.

1422. The expression signifies that when trees watered with the same water bear fruits vastly different in taste and colour, why cannot the Holy Prophet, even though he lives in the same town and among the same people, excel them, especially when he is nourished by the elixir of Divine revelation and his opponents are brought up under the fostering care of Satan?

1423. The shackles of false beliefs and evil practices.

7. [a]And they ask thee to hasten on the evil rather than the good, whereas exemplary punishments have *already* come to pass before them. And, verily, thy Lord is full of forgiveness for mankind despite their wrongdoing, and [b]verily, thy Lord is *also* Severe in retribution.

وَيَسْتَعْجِلُوْنَكَ بِالسَّيِّئَةِ قَبْلَ الْحَسَنَةِ وَقَدْ خَلَتْ
مِنْ قَبْلِهِمُ الْمَثُلٰتُ ۗ وَاِنَّ رَبَّكَ لَذُوْمَغْفِرَةٍ لِّلنَّاسِ
عَلٰى ظُلْمِهِمْ ۚ وَاِنَّ رَبَّكَ لَشَدِيْدُ الْعِقَابِ ﴿۷﴾

8. [c]And those who disbelieve say, 'Wherefore has not a Sign[1424] been sent down to him from his Lord?' [d]Thou art surely a Warner. And there is a Guide for every people.

وَيَقُوْلُ الَّذِيْنَ كَفَرُوْا لَوْلَآ اُنْزِلَ عَلَيْهِ اٰيَةٌ مِّنْ
رَّبِّهٖ ۗ اِنَّمَآ اَنْتَ مُنْذِرٌ وَّلِكُلِّ قَوْمٍ هَادٍ ﴿۸﴾ ع

R. 2 9. [e]Allāh knows what every female bears, and what the wombs render defective *and discard* and what they cause to grow.[1425] [f]And with Him everything has a *proper* measure.

اَللّٰهُ يَعْلَمُ مَا تَحْمِلُ كُلُّ اُنْثٰى وَمَا تَغِيْضُ الْاَرْحَامُ
وَمَا تَزْدَادُ ۗ وَكُلُّ شَيْءٍ عِنْدَهٗ بِمِقْدَارٍ ﴿۹﴾

10. [g]*He is the* Knower of the unseen and the seen, the Incomparably Great, the Most High.

عٰلِمُ الْغَيْبِ وَالشَّهَادَةِ الْكَبِيْرُ الْمُتَعَالِ ﴿۱۰﴾

[a]22 : 48; 29 : 54-55. [b]41 : 44; 53 : 33. [c]6 : 38; 10 : 21. [d]11 : 13; 35 : 24. [e]35: : 12; 41 : 48. [f]15 : 22. [g]6 : 74; 9 : 94; 59 : 23; 64 : 19.

1424. 'Sign' invariably means, the Sign of punishment unless the context points to some other meaning.

1425. In v. 4 we are told that all things in the universe have pairs and that in the spiritual world also some individuals act like males and others like females, the former exercising influence and the latter receiving it. The verse under comment points out that in the person of the Holy Prophet there has appeared one who is spiritually a male and that nobody can attain any spiritual rank without receiving his stamp. It further says that God knows well the natural capacities and aptitudes of the Holy Prophet's people, whether they will accept Divine or satanic influence, and which influence will grow and which will decline. Those who accept the Holy Prophet and receive his stamp will grow and increase in power, influence and numbers, while his opponents will decline and decrease.

11. He among you who utters *his* word secretly, and he who utters it openly are equal *in His knowledge;* and *also* he who hides by night, and he who goes forth *openly* by day.[1426]

سَوَآءٌ مِّنۡكُمۡ مَّنۡ اَسَرَّ الۡقَوۡلَ وَمَنۡ جَهَرَ بِهٖ وَمَنۡ هُوَ مُسۡتَخۡفٍۢ بِالَّيۡلِ وَسَارِبٌۢ بِالنَّهَارِ ﴿۱۱﴾

12. For him (the Messenger) is a succession *of angels*[1427] before him and behind him; they guard him by the command of Allāh. Surely, [a]Allāh changes not the condition of a people until they change that which is in their hearts. And when Allāh decides to punish a people, there is no repelling it, nor have they any helper besides Him.

لَهٗ مُعَقِّبٰتٌ مِّنۡۢ بَيۡنِ يَدَيۡهِ وَمِنۡ خَلۡفِهٖ يَحۡفَظُوۡنَهٗ مِنۡ اَمۡرِ اللّٰهِ ؕ اِنَّ اللّٰهَ لَا يُغَيِّرُ مَا بِقَوۡمٍ حَتّٰى يُغَيِّرُوۡا مَا بِاَنۡفُسِهِمۡ ؕ وَاِذَاۤ اَرَادَ اللّٰهُ بِقَوۡمٍ سُوۡۤءًا فَلَا مَرَدَّ لَهٗ ۚ وَمَا لَهُمۡ مِّنۡ دُوۡنِهٖ مِنۡ وَّالٍ ﴿۱۲﴾

13. [b]He it is Who shows you the lightning *to inspire* fear and hope,[1428] and He raises the heavy clouds.

هُوَ الَّذِىۡ يُرِيۡكُمُ الۡبَرۡقَ خَوۡفًا وَّطَمَعًا وَّيُنۡشِئُ السَّحَابَ الثِّقَالَ ﴿۱۳﴾ ۚ

14. And the thunder glorifies Him with His praise [c]and *likewise do* the angels for awe of Him; and [d]He sends the thunderbolts, and smites therewith whom He wills, yet they dispute concerning Allāh, while He is Severe in punishing.

وَيُسَبِّحُ الرَّعۡدُ بِحَمۡدِهٖ وَالۡمَلٰۤٮِٕكَةُ مِنۡ خِيۡفَتِهٖ ۚ وَ يُرۡسِلُ الصَّوَاعِقَ فَيُصِيۡبُ بِهَا مَنۡ يَّشَآءُ وَهُمۡ يُجَادِلُوۡنَ فِى اللّٰهِ ۚ وَهُوَ شَدِيۡدُ الۡمِحَالِ ﴿۱۴﴾

[a]8 : 54. [b]30 : 25. [c]16 : 51; 42 : 6. [d]24 : 44.

1426. The overt or covert plans of the Holy Prophet's enemies cannot succeed because God, Who knows them all, is his Helper and Protector.

1427. The word *Al-Mu'aqqibāt* signifies, the angels of the night and the day because they succeed each other by turns. The plural feminine form is used because of the frequency of their doing so, since in Arabic the feminine form is sometimes employed to impart emphasis and frequency. The word, rendered here as 'a succession of angels,' may refer to the celestial beings in Heaven; or to the devoted Companions of the Holy Prophet who guarded him risking their lives.

1428. Lightning inspires both fear and hope. It inspires fear because sometimes men die of it and embryos, and certain plants get adversely affected. It also brings hope to men, for it heralds fertilizing rain and also helps to destroy germs of different diseases and thus serves to put an end to epidemics.

15. Unto Him *alone* is *due* the true prayer.[1429] [a]And those on whom they call instead of Him answer them not at all. *Their case is but* like *the case of* him who stretches forth his two hands towards water that it may reach his mouth, but it reaches it not.[1430] [b]And the prayer of the disbelievers is but a thing wasted.

لَهٗ دَعْوَةُ الْحَقِّ ؕ وَالَّذِيْنَ يَدْعُوْنَ مِنْ دُوْنِهٖ لَا
يَسْتَجِيْبُوْنَ لَهُمْ بِشَيْءٍ اِلَّا كَبَاسِطِ كَفَّيْهِ اِلَى الْمَآءِ
لِيَبْلُغَ فَاهُ وَمَا هُوَ بِبَالِغِهٖ ؕ وَمَا دُعَآءُ الْكٰفِرِيْنَ
اِلَّا فِيْ ضَلٰلٍ ﴿۱۵﴾

16. And to Allāh submits whosoever is in the heavens and the earth willingly or unwillingly[1431] and *likewise* do their shadows in the mornings and the evenings.

وَلِلّٰهِ يَسْجُدُ مَنْ فِي السَّمٰوٰتِ وَالْاَرْضِ طَوْعًا وَّ
كَرْهًا وَّظِلٰلُهُمْ بِالْغُدُوِّ وَالْاٰصَالِ ﴿۱۶﴾

[a]35 : 14; 40 : 21. [b]40 : 51.

1429. The expression may be translated as: (1) God alone is worthy of worship; (2) it is praying to God alone that can be useful or beneficial for man; (3) the Voice of God alone rises in support of truth; and (4) the Voice of God alone must prevail.

1430. The right way to succeed in life is to place all things in their proper places—to give God the status which is His due and to created things the position which they rightly possess. That alone is the way to success and true happiness.

1431. The verse embodies a great truth, *viz.*, that all creation is bound to obey God-made laws of nature, willingly or unwillingly. The tongue must perform the function of tasting and the ear cannot help hearing. This obedience to the laws of nature may be called compulsory. But man is given a certain freedom of action where he can use his volition and discretion. But even in actions in which he appears to have been granted freedom, he is subject to certain amount of compulsion, and he must obey God's laws in whatever he does, whether he likes it or not. The words, *willingly or unwillingly*, may also refer to two classes of men, *viz.*, believers who give willing submission to God and disbelievers who obey His laws grudgingly.

17. [a]Say, 'Who is the Lord of the heavens and the earth?' Say, 'Allāh.' Say, 'Have you then taken instead of Him helpers [b]who have no power for good or harm *even* for themselves?' Say, [c]'Can the blind and the seeing be equal? Or, can darkness be equal to light? Or, do they assign to Allāh partners who have created the like of His creation so that the *two* creations appear similar to them?' Say, 'Allāh *alone* is the Creator of all things, and He is the One,[1432] the Most Supreme.'

قُلْ مَنْ رَّبُّ السَّمٰوٰتِ وَالْاَرْضِ قُلِ اللّٰهُ قُلْ
اَفَاتَّخَذْتُمْ مِّنْ دُوْنِهٖٓ اَوْلِيَآءَ لَا يَمْلِكُوْنَ لِاَنْفُسِهِمْ
نَفْعًا وَّلَا ضَرًّا قُلْ هَلْ يَسْتَوِي الْاَعْمٰى وَالْبَصِيْرُ
اَمْ هَلْ تَسْتَوِي الظُّلُمٰتُ وَالنُّوْرُ اَمْ جَعَلُوْا لِلّٰهِ
شُرَكَآءَ خَلَقُوْا كَخَلْقِهٖ فَتَشَابَهَ الْخَلْقُ عَلَيْهِمْ
قُلِ اللّٰهُ خَالِقُ كُلِّ شَيْءٍ وَّهُوَ الْوَاحِدُ الْقَهَّارُ ﴿١٧﴾

18. [d]He sends down water from the sky so that valleys flow according to their measure and the flood bears *on its surface* swelling foam. And from that which they heat in the fire, seeking *to make* ornaments or utensils, *comes out* a foam similar to it. Thus does Allāh illustrate truth and falsehood. Now, as to the foam, it goes away as rubbish *and perishes* but as to that which benefits men, it stays in the earth. Thus does Allāh set forth parables.[1433]

اَنْزَلَ مِنَ السَّمَآءِ مَآءً فَسَالَتْ اَوْدِيَةٌۢ بِقَدَرِهَا
فَاحْتَمَلَ السَّيْلُ زَبَدًا رَّابِيًا وَمِمَّا يُوْقِدُوْنَ
عَلَيْهِ فِي النَّارِ ابْتِغَآءَ حِلْيَةٍ اَوْ مَتَاعٍ زَبَدٌ مِّثْلُهٗ
كَذٰلِكَ يَضْرِبُ اللّٰهُ الْحَقَّ وَالْبَاطِلَ فَاَمَّا الزَّبَدُ
فَيَذْهَبُ جُفَآءً وَاَمَّا مَا يَنْفَعُ النَّاسَ فَيَمْكُثُ
فِي الْاَرْضِ كَذٰلِكَ يَضْرِبُ اللّٰهُ الْاَمْثَالَ ﴿١٨﴾

[a]23 : 87. [b]25 : 4. [c]11 : 25; 35 : 20. [d]39 : 22.

1432. The Qur'ān has used two different words to express Divine Unity: (1) *Aḥad* and (2) *Wāḥid*. Whereas the former word denotes the absolute Unity of God without relation to any other being, the latter means only 'the first' or 'the starting point,' and requires a second and a third to follow it. The Divine attribute, *Wāḥid* (One), shows that God is the real 'Source' from which all creation springs, and everything points to Him just as a second or a third thing necessarily points to the first. But where the Qur'ān seeks to refute the doctrine of the sonship of those who have been falsely given that status, it uses the word *Aḥad*, *i.e.*, He Who is and has ever been One and Alone and Who has begotten no child (112 : 2).

1433. The verse has used two very apt illustrations. In the first illustration, truth is compared to water and falsehood to foam. Falsehood in the beginning seems to prevail over truth, but in the end it is swept away by truth even as rubbish is swept away by a powerful current of water. In the second illustration, truth is likened to gold or silver which, when melted, throws off the dross leaving behind the unmixed metal, pure and bright.

19. For those who respond to their Lord is *eternal* good; and *as for* those who respond not to Him, [a]if they had all that is in the earth and the like of it added thereto, they would *readily* ransom themselves therewith. It is these that shall have an evil reckoning and their abode is Hell. What a wretched place of rest !

لِلَّذِيْنَ اسْتَجَابُوْا لِرَبِّهِمُ الْحُسْنٰى ؕ وَالَّذِيْنَ لَمْ يَسْتَجِيْبُوْا
لَهٗ لَوْ اَنَّ لَهُمْ مَّا فِى الْاَرْضِ جَمِيْعًا وَّمِثْلَهٗ مَعَهٗ
لَافْتَدَوْا بِهٖ ؕ اُولٰٓئِكَ لَهُمْ سُوْٓءُ الْحِسَابِ ۙ وَمَاْوٰىهُمْ
جَهَنَّمُ ؕ وَبِئْسَ الْمِهَادُ ﴿۱۹﴾ ع النصف

R. 3 20. Is he, then, who knows that what has been revealed to thee from thy Lord is the truth, like one who is blind? But only those gifted with understanding take heed;

اَفَمَنْ يَّعْلَمُ اَنَّمَآ اُنْزِلَ اِلَيْكَ مِنْ رَّبِّكَ الْحَقُّ كَمَنْ
هُوَ اَعْمٰى ؕ اِنَّمَا يَتَذَكَّرُ اُولُوا الْاَلْبَابِ ﴿۲۰﴾

21. [b]Those who fulfil Allāh's pact, and break not the covenant;

الَّذِيْنَ يُوْفُوْنَ بِعَهْدِ اللّٰهِ وَلَا يَنْقُضُوْنَ الْمِيْثَاقَ ﴿۲۱﴾

22. And those who join what Allāh has commanded to be joined, and fear their Lord,[1434] and dread the evil reckoning;

وَالَّذِيْنَ يَصِلُوْنَ مَآ اَمَرَ اللّٰهُ بِهٖٓ اَنْ يُّوْصَلَ وَ
يَخْشَوْنَ رَبَّهُمْ وَيَخَافُوْنَ سُوْٓءَ الْحِسَابِ ﴿۲۲﴾

23. And those who persevere in seeking the favour of their Lord, [c]and observe Prayer, and spend out of that with which We have provided them, secretly and openly, [d]and repel evil with good.[1435] It is these who shall have the *best* reward of the *final* Abode—

وَالَّذِيْنَ صَبَرُوا ابْتِغَآءَ وَجْهِ رَبِّهِمْ وَاَقَامُوا
الصَّلٰوةَ وَاَنْفَقُوْا مِمَّا رَزَقْنٰهُمْ سِرًّا وَّعَلَانِيَةً وَّ
يَدْرَءُوْنَ بِالْحَسَنَةِ السَّيِّئَةَ اُولٰٓئِكَ لَهُمْ عُقْبَى
الدَّارِ ﴿۲۳﴾

[a]5 : 37; 39 : 48. [b]6 : 152; 16 : 92; 17 : 35. [c]2 : 4; 8 : 4; 14 : 32; 27 : 4. [d]41 : 35.

1434. After faithfully discharging their duties to God, the believers fulfil the obligations they owe to His creatures. The observance of these two duties constitutes the basis on which the whole fabric of religion stands.

1435. The believers follow the course best suited for the eradication of evil. They resort to punishment where it serves a useful purpose and to forgiveness if forgiveness is calculated to bring about the desired result. In short, they cut at the very root of evil by whatever method is appropriate in the circumstances.

24. [a]Gardens of Eternity. They shall enter them and *also* those who are righteous from among their fathers, and their wives and their children.[1436] And angels shall enter unto them from every gate,[1437] *saying*,

جَنّٰتُ عَدْنٍ يَّدْخُلُوْنَهَا وَمَنْ صَلَحَ مِنْ اٰبَآئِهِمْ
وَاَزْوَاجِهِمْ وَذُرِّيّٰتِهِمْ وَالْمَلٰٓئِكَةُ يَدْخُلُوْنَ عَلَيْهِمْ
مِّنْ كُلِّ بَابٍ ﴿٢٤﴾

25. [b]'Peace be unto you, because you were steadfast; behold, how excellent is the reward of the *final* Abode !'

سَلٰمٌ عَلَيْكُمْ بِمَا صَبَرْتُمْ فَنِعْمَ عُقْبَى الدَّارِ ﴿٢٥﴾

26. And those who [c]break the covenant of Allāh, after having established it and cut asunder what Allāh has commanded to be joined, and act corruptly in the earth, on them is the curse *of Allāh* and they shall have a grievous abode.

وَالَّذِيْنَ يَنْقُضُوْنَ عَهْدَ اللّٰهِ مِنْۢ بَعْدِ مِيْثَاقِهٖ
وَيَقْطَعُوْنَ مَآ اَمَرَ اللّٰهُ بِهٖٓ اَنْ يُّوْصَلَ وَيُفْسِدُوْنَ
فِى الْاَرْضِ اُولٰٓئِكَ لَهُمُ اللَّعْنَةُ وَلَهُمْ سُوْٓءُ الدَّارِ ﴿٢٦﴾

27. [d]Allāh enlarges *His* provision and straitens *it* for whomsoever He pleases. And [e]they rejoice in the present life, while the present life is but a *temporary* enjoyment as compared[1438] with the Hereafter.

اَللّٰهُ يَبْسُطُ الرِّزْقَ لِمَنْ يَّشَآءُ وَيَقْدِرُ وَفَرِحُوْا
بِالْحَيٰوةِ الدُّنْيَا وَمَا الْحَيٰوةُ الدُّنْيَا فِى الْاٰخِرَةِ اِلَّا
٣ ع ٤ مَتَاعٌ ﴿٢٧﴾

R. 4 28. And those who disbelieve say, [f]'Why is not a Sign sent down to him from his Lord?' Say, 'Allāh leaves to go astray[1439] whom He wills and [g]guides to Himself those who turn *to Him;*

وَيَقُوْلُ الَّذِيْنَ كَفَرُوْا لَوْلَآ اُنْزِلَ عَلَيْهِ اٰيَةٌ مِّنْ
رَّبِّهٖ قُلْ اِنَّ اللّٰهَ يُضِلُّ مَنْ يَّشَآءُ وَيَهْدِيْٓ اِلَيْهِ
مَنْ اَنَابَ ﴿٢٨﴾

[a]40 : 9. [b]39 : 74. [c]2 : 28. [d]29 : 63; 30 : 38; 39 : 53. [e]10 : 8.
[f]6 : 38; 10 : 21; 29 : 51. [g]14 : 5; 74 : 32.

1436. This verse enunciates a great principle. Any good act that a man does, is done with the intentional or unintentional help or co-operation of his relatives and kinsmen. Therefore, they all are made to participate, proportionately to their share, in the reward he wins.

1437. The various categories of good deeds of believers will, in the next world, be represented as so many gates of Heaven.

1438. The particle *fī* is sometimes used to denote comparison (Lane).

1439. It is God's immutable law that He guides those who are desirous of turning to Him and leaves to go astray those who themselves turn away from Him and refuse to accept His guidance.

29. ‘Those who believe, and whose hearts find comfort in the remembrance of Allāh.[1440] Aye! It is in the remembrance of Allāh that hearts can find comfort;

الَّذِيْنَ اٰمَنُوْا وَتَطْمَئِنُّ قُلُوْبُهُمْ بِذِكْرِ اللّٰهِ ؕ اَلَا
بِذِكْرِ اللّٰهِ تَطْمَئِنُّ الْقُلُوْبُ ۝٢٩

30. [a]‘Those who believe and do good works—happiness is *decreed* for them, and an excellent place of return.’

اَلَّذِيْنَ اٰمَنُوْا وَعَمِلُوا الصّٰلِحٰتِ طُوْبٰى لَهُمْ
وَحُسْنُ مَاٰبٍ ۝٣٠

31. Thus have We sent thee to a people, before whom other peoples have passed away, that thou mayest recite to them what We have revealed to thee, for [b]they deny the Gracious *God*. Say, ‘He is my Lord; there is no god but He. In Him do I put my trust and towards Him is my return.’

كَذٰلِكَ اَرْسَلْنٰكَ فِيْٓ اُمَّةٍ قَدْ خَلَتْ مِنْ قَبْلِهَآ اُمَمٌ
لِّتَتْلُوَاْ عَلَيْهِمُ الَّذِيْٓ اَوْحَيْنَآ اِلَيْكَ وَهُمْ يَكْفُرُوْنَ
بِالرَّحْمٰنِ ؕ قُلْ هُوَ رَبِّيْ لَآ اِلٰهَ اِلَّا هُوَ ۚ عَلَيْهِ تَوَكَّلْتُ
وَاِلَيْهِ مَتَابِ ۝٣١

[a]3 : 16; 18 : 31, 108; 68 : 35; 98 : 8-9. [b]25 : 61.

1440. Search after God is the innermost yearning of the human soul and is the real object and goal of man’s life, and when that goal is attained man enjoys perfect peace of mind, for then he rests, as it were, in the very lap of God.

32. And if there were a Qur'ān by which mountains[1441] could be moved or by which the earth could be cut asunder[1442] or by which the dead could be spoken[1443] to, *they would still not believe in it*. [a]Nay, the matter *of their believing rests* entirely with Allāh. Have not the believers *yet* come to know that if Allāh had *enforced* His Will He could have surely guided all mankind? And *as for* those who disbelieve, [b]disaster shall not cease to befall them for what they have wrought or to alight near their home,[1444] until the promise of Allāh comes to pass. Surely, Allāh fails not in *His* promise.

وَلَوْ أَنَّ قُرْآنًا سُيِّرَتْ بِهِ الْجِبَالُ أَوْ قُطِّعَتْ بِهِ
الْأَرْضُ أَوْ كُلِّمَ بِهِ الْمَوْتٰى ۗ بَلْ لِّلّٰهِ الْأَمْرُ جَمِيعًا ۗ
أَفَلَمْ يَايْـَٔسِ الَّذِيْنَ اٰمَنُوْٓا أَنْ لَّوْ يَشَآءُ اللّٰهُ لَهَدَى
النَّاسَ جَمِيعًا ۗ وَلَا يَزَالُ الَّذِيْنَ كَفَرُوْا تُصِيْبُهُمْ بِمَا
صَنَعُوْا قَارِعَةٌ أَوْ تَحُلُّ قَرِيْبًا مِّنْ دَارِهِمْ حَتّٰى
ع يَأْتِيَ وَعْدُ اللّٰهِ ۗ إِنَّ اللّٰهَ لَا يُخْلِفُ الْمِيْعَادَ ﴿٣٢﴾

R. 5 33. And surely, Messengers were mocked at before thee; but [c]I granted respite to those who disbelieved. Then I seized them and how *terrible* was My punishment!

وَلَقَدِ اسْتُهْزِئَ بِرُسُلٍ مِّنْ قَبْلِكَ فَأَمْلَيْتُ لِلَّذِيْنَ
كَفَرُوْا ثُمَّ أَخَذْتُهُمْ ۗ فَكَيْفَ كَانَ عِقَابِ ﴿٣٣﴾

[a]3 : 155; 30 : 5. [b]22 : 56. [c]22 : 45.

1441. *Jibāl* is the plural of *Jabal* which figuratively means, (1) chief of a tribe or community; (2) a learned man towering above those around him; (3) great hardship or calamity (Aqrab). The clause may mean that the Qur'ān solves all the difficult problems that confront man, or it may mean that it has abrogated the old order of things and has inculcated a new approach to the various human problems.

1442. These words figuratively mean that the Qur'ān would speedily spread throughout the whole earth. Literally, it means that portions of land would be cut off from enemy territory and would pass into the possession of believers.

1443. By means of the Qur'ān those spiritually dead will not only be quickened into a new life, but will also be made to speak words of wisdom and will preach the Message of the Qur'ān to the world.

1444. Calamity after calamity shall continue to befall the disbelievers and they shall suffer reverses one after the other, till the prophecy relating to the utter destruction of their power will be fulfilled by the Fall of Mecca, their metropolis and chief citadel.

34. Will then He, Who stands over every soul *watching* what it earns, *let them go unpunished?* Yet [a]they ascribe partners to Allāh. Say, 'Do name them.'[1445] Would you inform Him of what He does not know in the earth? Or, is it a *mere* empty saying? Nay, but the design of the disbelievers has been made *to appear*[1446] beautiful in their eyes, and they have been kept back from the *right* way. And [b]he whom Allāh lets go astray shall have no guide.

أَفَمَنْ هُوَ قَآئِمٌ عَلٰى كُلِّ نَفْسٍ بِمَا كَسَبَتْ وَجَعَلُوْا لِلّٰهِ
شُرَكَآءَ ۭ قُلْ سَمُّوْهُمْ ۭ اَمْ تُنَبِّئُوْنَهٗ بِمَا لَا يَعْلَمُ فِى
الْاَرْضِ اَمْ بِظَاهِرٍ مِّنَ الْقَوْلِ ۭ بَلْ زُيِّنَ لِلَّذِيْنَ كَفَرُوْا
مَكْرُهُمْ وَصُدُّوْا عَنِ السَّبِيْلِ ۭ وَمَنْ يُّضْلِلِ اللّٰهُ فَمَا
لَهٗ مِنْ هَادٍ ﴿٣٤﴾

35. [c]For them is a punishment in the present life; and, surely, the punishment of the Hereafter is harder, and they will have no defender against Allāh.

لَهُمْ عَذَابٌ فِى الْحَيٰوةِ الدُّنْيَا وَلَعَذَابُ الْاٰخِرَةِ
اَشَقُّ ۚ وَمَا لَهُمْ مِّنَ اللّٰهِ مِنْ وَّاقٍ ﴿٣٥﴾

36. [d]The similitude of the *Garden* promised to the God-fearing is that through it flow streams; its fruit is everlasting,[1447] and *so* is its shade. That is the reward of those who are righteous; and the end of the disbelievers is Fire.

مَثَلُ الْجَنَّةِ الَّتِىْ وُعِدَ الْمُتَّقُوْنَ ۭ تَجْرِىْ مِنْ تَحْتِهَا
الْاَنْهٰرُ ۭ اُكُلُهَا دَآئِمٌ وَّظِلُّهَا ۭ تِلْكَ عُقْبَى الَّذِيْنَ اتَّقَوْا ۖ
وَّعُقْبَى الْكٰفِرِيْنَ النَّارُ ﴿٣٦﴾

[a]6 : 101; 10 : 67; 13 : 17. [b]17 : 98; 39 : 24, 37. [c]39 : 27; 68 : 34. [d]2 : 26; 4 : 58; 47 : 16.

1445. Idolaters are called upon to state what are the functions which their gods perform. The word 'name' in the verse does not mean personal name but attributive name, for the personal names of some of the gods have been given in the Qur'ān itself (71: 24); the words, *do name them*, may also be an expression of contempt, meaning that the gods of the disbelievers are so worthless that even the mention of their names would put them to shame.

1446. It often happens that when a man commits a fraud or imposture in order to gain worldly advantage, he himself gradually falls a victim to his own imposture which gradually appears attractive to him.

1447. The words, *its fruit is everlasting*, signify that the fruits of Heaven will see no autumn, no season of decay, nor even of dormancy. Thus, there will be no interruption in the boons and blessings of Paradise. "Fruit" and "shade" stand respectively for inward and outward blessings, and imply that believers will enjoy all kinds of blessings in Heaven, both external and internal.

37. And *a*those to whom We have given the Book rejoice in what has been revealed to thee. And *b*of the *different* parties[1448] there are *some* who deny a part thereof. Say, *c*'I am only commanded to worship Allāh and not to set up equals to Him. Unto Him do I call and unto Him is my return.

وَالَّذِيْنَ اٰتَيْنٰهُمُ الْكِتٰبَ يَفْرَحُوْنَ بِمَآ اُنْزِلَ اِلَيْكَ وَمِنَ الْاَحْزَابِ مَنْ يُّنْكِرُ بَعْضَهٗ ؕ قُلْ اِنَّمَآ اُمِرْتُ اَنْ اَعْبُدَ اللّٰهَ وَلَآ اُشْرِكَ بِهٖ ؕ اِلَيْهِ اَدْعُوْا وَاِلَيْهِ مَاٰبِ ﴿۳۷﴾

38. And thus *d*have We revealed it, a clear judgment in Arabic. And *e*if thou follow their evil desires after the knowledge that has come to thee, thou shalt have no friend nor defender against Allāh.

وَكَذٰلِكَ اَنْزَلْنٰهُ حُكْمًا عَرَبِيًّا ؕ وَلَئِنِ اتَّبَعْتَ اَهْوَآءَهُمْ بَعْدَ مَا جَآءَكَ مِنَ الْعِلْمِ ۙ مَا لَكَ مِنَ اللّٰهِ مِنْ وَّلِيٍّ وَّلَا وَاقٍ ﴿۳۸﴾ ع

R. 6 39. And, indeed, We sent Messengers before thee, and We gave them wives and children. And *f*it is not possible for a Messenger to bring a Sign save by the command of Allāh. For every term there is a Divine decree.

وَلَقَدْ اَرْسَلْنَا رُسُلًا مِّنْ قَبْلِكَ وَجَعَلْنَا لَهُمْ اَزْوَاجًا وَّذُرِّيَّةً ؕ وَمَا كَانَ لِرَسُوْلٍ اَنْ يَّاْتِيَ بِاٰيَةٍ اِلَّا بِاِذْنِ اللّٰهِ ؕ لِكُلِّ اَجَلٍ كِتَابٌ ﴿۳۹﴾

40. *g*Allāh effaces and establishes[1449] what He wills, and with Him is *h*the source of all commandments.[1450]

يَمْحُوا اللّٰهُ مَا يَشَآءُ وَيُثْبِتُ ۚ وَعِنْدَهٗٓ اُمُّ الْكِتٰبِ ﴿۴۰﴾

*a*28 : 53. *b*2 : 86. *c*18 : 111; 39 : 12; 72 : 21. *d*12 : 3; 20 : 114; 43 : 4. *e*2 : 121,146; 42 : 16. *f*14 : 12; 40 : 79. *g*42 : 25. *h*43 : 5.

1448. By the word, *Aḥzāb* (parties), is meant all those people to whom a Prophet is sent and who do not accept him.

1449. The verse lays down two laws relating to Divine punishment: (*a*) God either cancels the punishment wholly or partially; or (*b*) He lets it stand as decreed.

1450. (*a*) God alone knows the root cause of all commandments or the wisdom underlying them. (*b*) All the commandments of the *Sharī'ah* are based on Divine attributes, so the source of the Law lies with God; *Umm* means, source, basis, origin; stay or support (Lane).

41. And [a]whether We show thee *in thy life-time the fulfilment of* some of the things with which We threaten them or whether We cause thee to die, *it makes little difference,* for [b]on thee *lies* only the delivery of the Message, and on Us the reckoning.

وَإِنْ مَّا نُرِيَنَّكَ بَعْضَ الَّذِي نَعِدُهُمْ أَوْ نَتَوَفَّيَنَّكَ
فَإِنَّمَا عَلَيْكَ الْبَلٰغُ وَعَلَيْنَا الْحِسَابُ ﴿٤١﴾

42. Do they not see that [c]We are visiting the land, reducing it from its outlying borders?[1451] And Allāh judges; there is none to reverse His judgment. And He is Swift at reckoning.

أَوَلَمْ يَرَوْا أَنَّا نَأْتِي الْأَرْضَ نَنْقُصُهَا مِنْ أَطْرَافِهَا ط
وَاللّٰهُ يَحْكُمُ لَا مُعَقِّبَ لِحُكْمِهِ ط وَهُوَ سَرِيعُ الْحِسَابِ ﴿٤٢﴾

43. And those who were before them [d]did also devise plans but all *effective* devising of plans belongs to Allāh.[1451A] He knows what every soul earns; and the disbelievers shall soon know [e]whose will be the final reward of the Abode.

وَقَدْ مَكَرَ الَّذِينَ مِنْ قَبْلِهِمْ فَلِلّٰهِ الْمَكْرُ جَمِيعًا ط
يَعْلَمُ مَا تَكْسِبُ كُلُّ نَفْسٍ ط وَسَيَعْلَمُ الْكُفّٰرُ لِمَنْ
عُقْبَى الدَّارِ ﴿٤٣﴾

44. And those who disbelieve say, [f]‘Thou art not a Messenger.’ Say, [g]‘Sufficient is Allāh as a Witness between me and you and so *also is* he who possesses knowledge of the Book.[1451B]

وَيَقُولُ الَّذِينَ كَفَرُوا لَسْتَ مُرْسَلًا ط قُلْ كَفٰى بِاللّٰهِ
شَهِيدًا بَيْنِي وَبَيْنَكُمْ وَمَنْ عِنْدَهُ عِلْمُ الْكِتٰبِ ﴿٤٤﴾

[a]10 : 47; 40 : 78. [b]3 : 21; 5 : 93; 16 : 83. [c]21 : 45. [d]3 : 55; 8 : 31; 14 : 47; 27 : 51. [e]28 : 38; [f]25 : 42. [g]4 : 167; 6 : 20; 29 : 53; 48 : 29.

1451. *Aṭrāf* meaning good and generous, (and also) low and mean persons, the verse means: ‘Do they not see that God is gradually reducing and curtailing the land from its sides? *i.e.,* Islām is spreading through the length and breadth of Arabia and making inroads into every home and all sections and stations of society—the high and the low, the rich and the poor, the slave and the master.

1451A. All the secret designs of the enemies of Islām are known to God and so none of their plans or strategems can frustrate His purpose—the ultimate victory of Islām.

1451B. The words, *knowledge of the Book,* may mean, fresh Signs from Heaven and the prophecies of the previous Scriptures regarding the Holy Prophet.

CHAPTER 14

IBRĀHĪM

(Revealed before Hijrah)

Introduction

The subject-matter of the preceding *Sūrah* is continued and explained more fully and clearly in this *Sūrah*. The truth of the Quranic teaching is sought to be proved from observation, inferences to this effect having been drawn from facts of history. It is pointed out that in circumstances similar to those of the Holy Prophet, Messengers of God were successful in their own day against very powerful opposition. The Holy Prophet, therefore, is also bound to succeed in his mission, in spite of the meagreness of his means. Then the *Sūrah* proceeds to say that the real purpose of the Quranic revelation is to provide guidance for mankind which is groping in darkness, and the Holy Prophet has been raised to bring people out of this Cimmerian darkness into light. Prophets had also appeared before him, prominent among them being Moses. The *Sūrah* sheds light on the main reason for the triumph of Divine Messengers over their opponents which is that they worship God and preach the Truth. After dealing with this subject the *Sūrah* lays down some prominent marks and characteristics of the revealed Word of God and the criteria by which its truth can be tested. Judged by these criteria the Qur'ān is definitely proved to be God's own revealed Word. Muslims then are advised how best to profit by its noble ideals and teachings. Next, the *Sūrah* points out that the change which was about to take place in Arabia through the Message of the Qur'ān had been decreed ages ago by Almighty God. It had been God's plan and purpose since Abraham went to the wilderness of Paran and settled his son Ishmael and his wife Hagar there that that barren and bleak country would one day become the centre of the greatest religious Movement the world had ever seen. Mecca was founded to fulfil this Divine plan. This is why, in spite of the sterility and barrenness of its soil, God has ever provided for its inhabitants their means of livelihood in an ample measure. While Abraham was reconstructing the House of God with the help of his son, Ishmael, he prayed that God might raise up among the Meccans a Messenger, who should recite to them His Signs and teach them the Book and wisdom and should purify them (2 : 130). This prayer was fulfilled in the person of the Holy Prophet. The *Sūrah* reminds the Faithful that their duties and responsibilities had already been explained to them by Prophet Abraham and that they should never lose sight of them. It ends with a warning to disbelievers that since Mecca had been founded to become the centre and citadel for the preaching and propagation of the doctrine of the Divine Unity, they should give up idolatry. All efforts on their part to oppose the Divine purpose were bound to end in complete failure and frustration.

سُوْرَةُ اِبْرٰهِيْمَ مَكِّيَّةٌ (١٤)

آياتها ٥٣ — ركوعاتها ٧

1. [a]In the name of Allāh, the Gracious, the Merciful.

بِسْمِ اللّٰهِ الرَّحْمٰنِ الرَّحِيْمِ ﴿١﴾

2. [b]Alif Lām Rā.[1452] *This is* a Book which We have revealed to thee that [c]thou mayest bring mankind out of the depths of darkness into light, by the command of their Lord, to the path of the Mighty, the Praiseworthy—

الٓرٰ كِتٰبٌ اَنْزَلْنٰهُ اِلَيْكَ لِتُخْرِجَ النَّاسَ مِنَ الظُّلُمٰتِ
اِلَى النُّوْرِ ۙ بِاِذْنِ رَبِّهِمْ اِلٰى صِرَاطِ الْعَزِيْزِ الْحَمِيْدِ ۙ ﴿٢﴾

3. *The path of* Allāh to Whom belongs whatever is in the heavens and whatever is in the earth. And [d]woe to the disbelievers for a terrible punishment;

اللّٰهِ الَّذِيْ لَهٗ مَا فِي السَّمٰوٰتِ وَمَا فِي الْاَرْضِ ؕ وَوَيْلٌ
لِّلْكٰفِرِيْنَ مِنْ عَذَابٍ شَدِيْدِ ۙ ﴿٣﴾

4. [e]Those who prefer the present life to the Hereafter, and [f]hinder men from the way of Allāh and seek to make it crooked. It is these who have gone far off in error.

الَّذِيْنَ يَسْتَحِبُّوْنَ الْحَيٰوةَ الدُّنْيَا عَلَى الْاٰخِرَةِ
وَيَصُدُّوْنَ عَنْ سَبِيْلِ اللّٰهِ وَيَبْغُوْنَهَا عِوَجًا ؕ
اُولٰٓئِكَ فِيْ ضَلٰلٍۢ بَعِيْدٍ ﴿٤﴾

5. And We have not sent any Messenger except with *revelation in* the language of his people[1453] in order that he might make *things* clear to them. [g]Then Allāh leaves to go astray whom He wills and guides whom He wills. And He is the Mighty, the Wise.

وَمَاۤ اَرْسَلْنَا مِنْ رَّسُوْلٍ اِلَّا بِلِسَانِ قَوْمِهٖ لِيُبَيِّنَ
لَهُمْ ؕ فَيُضِلُّ اللّٰهُ مَنْ يَّشَآءُ وَيَهْدِيْ مَنْ يَّشَآءُ ؕ
وَهُوَ الْعَزِيْزُ الْحَكِيْمُ ﴿٥﴾

---

[a]1 : 1. [b]10 : 2 ; 11 : 2 ; 12 : 2 ; 13 : 2; 15 : 2. [c]2 : 258 ; 5 : 17 ; 14 : 6; 65 : 12.
[d]19 : 38 ; 38 : 28; 51 : 61 [e]16 : 108. [f]3 : 100 ; 7 : 46 ; 11 : 20. [g]13 : 28 ; 74 : 32.

1452. See 16.

1453. The verse does not mean that the Message of the Holy Prophet was confined to the Arabs alone. Such an assumption is belied by other verses of the Qur'ān in which he is clearly and unequivocally declared to be a Divine Messenger sent for the whole world (7 : 159 ; 34 : 29). Not only does the Qur'ān claim a universal mission for the Holy Prophet, but the Holy Prophet himself is reported to have said, 'I have been sent to the black and the red,' meaning the whole of mankind (Biḥār) ; and 'I have been raised for all mankind' (Bukhārī). The Qur'ān was revealed in the Arabic language because the Arabs were its first addressees (and also because Arabic, being the most expressive, eloquent and comprehensive language, was eminently suited to be the vehicle for the delivery of the Quranic Message) and through them its Message was to be preached to the world and not that the Message was meant for the Arabs only.

6. And We sent Moses with Our Signs, *saying*, [a]'Bring forth thy people from *the depths of* darkness into light and remind them of the days of Allāh.'[1454] Surely, therein are Signs for every patient *and* thankful person.

وَلَقَدْ أَرْسَلْنَا مُوسَىٰ بِآيَاتِنَا أَنْ أَخْرِجْ قَوْمَكَ مِنَ
الظُّلُمَاتِ إِلَى النُّورِ وَذَكِّرْهُمْ بِأَيَّامِ اللَّهِ ۚ إِنَّ فِي ذَٰلِكَ
لَآيَاتٍ لِكُلِّ صَبَّارٍ شَكُورٍ ﴿٦﴾

7. And *call to mind* when Moses said to his people, [b]'Remember Allāh's favour upon you when He delivered you from Pharaoh's people who afflicted you with grievous torment, slaying your sons and sparing your women; and in that there was a great trial for you from your Lord.'

وَإِذْ قَالَ مُوسَىٰ لِقَوْمِهِ اذْكُرُوا نِعْمَةَ اللَّهِ عَلَيْكُمْ
إِذْ أَنْجَاكُمْ مِنْ آلِ فِرْعَوْنَ يَسُومُونَكُمْ سُوءَ الْعَذَابِ
وَيُذَبِّحُونَ أَبْنَاءَكُمْ وَيَسْتَحْيُونَ نِسَاءَكُمْ ۚ وَفِي ذَٰلِكُمْ
بَلَاءٌ مِنْ رَبِّكُمْ عَظِيمٌ ﴿٧﴾ ع

R. 2 8. And when your Lord declared: [c]'If you are grateful,[1455] I will surely bestow more *favours* on you; but if you are ungrateful, *then know* that My punishment is severe indeed.'

وَإِذْ تَأَذَّنَ رَبُّكُمْ لَئِنْ شَكَرْتُمْ لَأَزِيدَنَّكُمْ ۖ وَلَئِنْ
كَفَرْتُمْ إِنَّ عَذَابِي لَشَدِيدٌ ﴿٨﴾

9. And Moses said, 'If [d]you disbelieve, you and those who are in the earth all together, *you can do no harm to Allāh*; verily, Allāh is Self-Sufficient, Praiseworthy.'

وَقَالَ مُوسَىٰ إِنْ تَكْفُرُوا أَنْتُمْ وَمَنْ فِي الْأَرْضِ
جَمِيعًا فَإِنَّ اللَّهَ لَغَنِيٌّ حَمِيدٌ ﴿٩﴾

[a]14 : 2. [b]2 : 50; 7 : 142; 28 : 5. [c]3 : 116; 4 : 148. [d]31 : 13.

1454. The expression *Ayyām Allāh* signifies the favours and punishments of Allāh (Tāj), like the well-known Arabic phrase *Ayyām al-'Arab* which means, the fights and conflicts of the Arabs.

1455. *Shukr* (gratefulness) is of three kinds: (1) With the heart or mind, which consists in forming an adequate idea of the benefit received; (2) with the tongue, which consists in praising, eulogizing or commending the benefactor; and (3) with the limbs, which consists in requiting the benefit received according to its desert. It rests upon five foundations, (*a*) humility of him who renders it towards him to whom it is rendered; (*b*) his love of him; (*c*) his acknowledgment of his benefit; (*d*) his eulogizing him for it; and (*e*) his not making use of the benefit in a manner which he (who has conferred it) may dislike. This is *Shukr* on the part of man. *Shukr* on the part of God consists in forgiving a person or commending him, or regarding him with satisfaction, goodwill or favour, and hence necessarily recompensing or rewarding him (Lane). One can only be truly grateful to God when one makes right use of His gifts.

10. [a]Have not the tidings come to you of those before you, the people of Noah and *the tribes of* ‘Ād and Thamūd and those after them ? None knows them *now* save Allāh.[1456] Their Messengers came to them with clear Signs, but they thrust their hands into their mouths[1457] and said, ‘We disbelieve in what you have been sent with and surely, we are in disquieting doubt concerning that to which you call us.’

اَلَمْ يَاْتِكُمْ نَبَؤُا الَّذِيْنَ مِنْ قَبْلِكُمْ قَوْمِ نُوْحٍ وَّعَادٍ
وَّثَمُوْدَ ۛ وَالَّذِيْنَ مِنْۢ بَعْدِهِمْ ۛ لَا يَعْلَمُهُمْ اِلَّا اللّٰهُ ؕ
جَآءَتْهُمْ رُسُلُهُمْ بِالْبَيِّنٰتِ فَرَدُّوْٓا اَيْدِيَهُمْ فِيْٓ اَفْوَاهِهِمْ
وَقَالُوْٓا اِنَّا كَفَرْنَا بِمَآ اُرْسِلْتُمْ بِهٖ وَاِنَّا لَفِيْ شَكٍّ مِّمَّا
تَدْعُوْنَنَآ اِلَيْهِ مُرِيْبٍ ﴿١٠﴾

11. Their Messengers said, ‘Are you in doubt concerning Allāh, [b]Maker of the heavens and the earth ?[1458] He calls you that He may forgive you your sins and grant you respite till an appointed term.’ They said, “[c]You are but mortals like us, you desire to turn us away from that which our fathers used to worship. Bring us, then, some clear proof.’

قَالَتْ رُسُلُهُمْ اَفِي اللّٰهِ شَكٌّ فَاطِرِ السَّمٰوٰتِ وَالْاَرْضِ ؕ
يَدْعُوْكُمْ لِيَغْفِرَ لَكُمْ مِّنْ ذُنُوْبِكُمْ وَيُؤَخِّرَكُمْ اِلٰٓى اَجَلٍ
مُّسَمًّى ؕ قَالُوْٓا اِنْ اَنْتُمْ اِلَّا بَشَرٌ مِّثْلُنَا ؕ تُرِيْدُوْنَ اَنْ
تَصُدُّوْنَا عَمَّا كَانَ يَعْبُدُ اٰبَآؤُنَا فَاْتُوْنَا بِسُلْطٰنٍ
مُّبِيْنٍ ﴿١١﴾

[a]9 : 70; 40 : 32; 50 : 13-15. [b]6 : 15; 12 : 102; 35 : 2; 39 : 47. [c]11 : 28; 23 : 25.

1456. These words indicate that Prophets were also raised among nations other than the progeny of Abraham, for, the tribes of ‘Ād and Thamūd were followed by some other peoples whom ‘none knows now save Allāh,’ whereas the Prophets that appeared among the progeny of Abraham have been mentioned both in the Qur’ān and the Bible.

1457. The words mean that disbelievers thrust their hands into their own mouths in amazement at the high-sounding claims of the Prophets. Or they bit their hands in rage at what the Prophets said. Or they put their hands on the mouths of the Prophets so as to silence them and make them cease talking about their claims.

1458. The creation of the heavens and the earth has been adduced to prove the Divine origin of the teachings given to the Prophets. God being the Creator of the heavens and the earth it would be unreasonable to suppose that, having created man, He had left him without guidance. It would be equally inconsistent with reason to think that, whereas God had made ample provision for the material welfare and advancement of man by creating the heavens and the earth, He had neglected to provide for his spiritual welfare.

12. Their Messengers said to them, [a]'We are indeed only mortals like you[1459] but [b]Allāh bestows *His* favours on whomsoever He wills from among His servants. And it is not for us to bring you a proof except by the permission of Allāh. And in Allāh *alone* should the believers put their trust;

قَالَتْ لَهُمْ رُسُلُهُمْ إِنْ نَحْنُ إِلَّا بَشَرٌ مِثْلُكُمْ وَلَٰكِنَّ اللّٰهَ يَمُنُّ عَلٰى مَنْ يَشَاءُ مِنْ عِبَادِهٖ ۖ وَمَا كَانَ لَنَا أَنْ نَأْتِيَكُمْ بِسُلْطٰنٍ إِلَّا بِإِذْنِ اللّٰهِ ۚ وَعَلَى اللّٰهِ فَلْيَتَوَكَّلِ الْمُؤْمِنُونَ ﴿١٢﴾

13. 'And [c]why should we not put our trust in Allāh when He has showed us our *appropriate* ways? And we will, surely, bear with patience all the harm you do us. So, in Allāh let those who trust put their trust.'

وَمَا لَنَا أَلَّا نَتَوَكَّلَ عَلَى اللّٰهِ وَقَدْ هَدٰنَا سُبُلَنَا ۚ وَلَنَصْبِرَنَّ عَلٰى مَا آذَيْتُمُونَا ۚ وَعَلَى اللّٰهِ فَلْيَتَوَكَّلِ الْمُتَوَكِّلُونَ ﴿١٣﴾ ع

R. 3 14. And [d]those who disbelieved said to their Messengers, 'We will, surely, expel you from our land unless you return to our religion.' Then their Lord sent unto them the revelation: 'We will, surely, destroy the wrongdoers,

وَقَالَ الَّذِينَ كَفَرُوا لِرُسُلِهِمْ لَنُخْرِجَنَّكُمْ مِنْ أَرْضِنَا أَوْ لَتَعُودُنَّ فِي مِلَّتِنَا ۖ فَأَوْحٰى إِلَيْهِمْ رَبُّهُمْ لَنُهْلِكَنَّ الظّٰلِمِينَ ﴿١٤﴾

15. 'And [e]We shall, surely, make you dwell in the land after them. This *promise* is for him who fears to stand before My Tribunal and fears My[1460] warning.'

وَلَنُسْكِنَنَّكُمُ الْأَرْضَ مِنْ بَعْدِهِمْ ۚ ذٰلِكَ لِمَنْ خَافَ مَقَامِي وَخَافَ وَعِيدِ ﴿١٥﴾

[a]18 : 111; 41 : 7. [b]3 : 165; 6 : 125. [c]11 : 57,89; 12 : 68. [d]7 : 89. [e]21 : 106.

1459. A Messenger of God who is sent for the guidance of men and to serve as a model or exemplar for them must be a man like themselves; for, without being a human being like themselves, he could not be a model for them.

1460. The Qur'ān has used both singular and plural numbers for the personal pronoun with reference to the Supreme Being. Where the Power and Majesty of God are meant to be expressed, the plural number is used ; and where His Self-Sufficiency and Independence are intended to be emphasized the singular number is used. Or, as some Muslim divines have stated, where God intends to bring about a result through the agency of angels, the plural number is used ; but where a work is to be performed through some special Divine decree, the singular number is resorted to. The present verse combines both.

16. And they prayed for victory, and every haughty enemy *of truth* came to naught:

وَاسْتَفْتَحُوْا وَخَابَ كُلُّ جَبَّارٍ عَنِيْدٍ ﴿١٦﴾

17. Before him is Hell; and he [a]shall be made to drink boiling water.

مِّنْ وَّرَآئِهٖ جَهَنَّمُ وَيُسْقٰى مِنْ مَّآءٍ صَدِيْدٍ ﴿١٧﴾

18. He shall sip it and shall not be able to swallow it easily. And [b]death shall come to him from every quarter,[1461] *yet* he shall not die. And besides that there shall be *for him* a severe chastisement.

يَّتَجَرَّعُهٗ وَلَا يَكَادُ يُسِيْغُهٗ وَيَأْتِيْهِ الْمَوْتُ مِنْ
كُلِّ مَكَانٍ وَّمَا هُوَ بِمَيِّتٍ ؕ وَمِنْ وَّرَآئِهٖ عَذَابٌ
غَلِيْظٌ ﴿١٨﴾

19. [c]The case of those who disbelieve in their Lord is that their works[1462] are like ashes, on which the wind blows violently on a stormy day. [d]They shall have no power over what they earned. That, indeed, is utter ruin.

مَثَلُ الَّذِيْنَ كَفَرُوْا بِرَبِّهِمْ اَعْمَالُهُمْ كَرَمَادِ
ٍ اشْتَدَّتْ بِهِ الرِّيْحُ فِيْ يَوْمٍ عَاصِفٍ ؕ لَا يَقْدِرُوْنَ
مِمَّا كَسَبُوْا عَلٰى شَيْءٍ ؕ ذٰلِكَ هُوَ الضَّلٰلُ الْبَعِيْدُ ﴿١٩﴾

20. Dost thou not see that [e]Allāh created the heavens and the earth in accordance with the requirements of wisdom? [f]If He please, He can do away with you, and bring a new creation.

اَلَمْ تَرَ اَنَّ اللّٰهَ خَلَقَ السَّمٰوٰتِ وَالْاَرْضَ بِالْحَقِّ ؕ
اِنْ يَّشَاْ يُذْهِبْكُمْ وَيَاْتِ بِخَلْقٍ جَدِيْدٍ ﴿٢٠﴾

21. And [g]that is not *at all* difficult for Allāh.

وَّمَا ذٰلِكَ عَلَى اللّٰهِ بِعَزِيْزٍ ﴿٢١﴾

22. They shall all appear before Allāh;[1463] [h]then shall those who were considered weak say to those

وَبَرَزُوْا لِلّٰهِ جَمِيْعًا فَقَالَ الضُّعَفٰٓؤُا لِلَّذِيْنَ اسْتَكْبَرُوْٓا

[a]69 : 37; 78 : 25, 26. [b]20 : 75; 87 : 14.
[c]24 : 40. [d]2 : 265. [e]6 : 74; 16 : 4; 29 : 45; 39 : 6. [f]4 : 134; 6 : 134; 35 : 17. [g]35 : 18.
[h]6 : 129; 7 : 39, 40; 28 : 64; 33 : 68, 69; 34 : 32, 33; 40 : 48, 49.

1461. The coming of death from every quarter means that the many sins and crimes of disbelievers will assume different forms of death for them.

1462. "Their works" may mean, the efforts which disbelievers made in opposition to the Prophets of God.

1463. It is not so much the actual misdeeds of a people that bring about their downfall as the exposure of their weaknesses. With their weaknesses having become exposed, their prestige and reputation which, more than their achievements, are the mainstay of their success, suffer a mortal blow, lowering them in the estimation of rival communities and bringing in their wake their decline and decadence. This is the significance of the verse, 'they shall appear before Allāh'.

who were arrogant, 'Surely, we were your followers can you not then avail us aught against Allāh's punishment?' They will say, 'If Allāh had guided us, we should have, surely, guided you. It is the same for us whether we show impatience or are patient, there is no way of escape for us.'[1464]

إِنَّا كُنَّا لَكُمْ تَبَعًا فَهَلْ أَنْتُمْ مُّغْنُونَ عَنَّا مِنْ
عَذَابِ اللّٰهِ مِنْ شَيْءٍ ۚ قَالُوْا لَوْ هَدٰىنَا اللّٰهُ لَهَدَيْنٰكُمْ ۖ
سَوَآءٌ عَلَيْنَآ أَجَزِعْنَآ أَمْ صَبَرْنَا مَا لَنَا مِنْ مَّحِيْصٍ ﴿٢٢﴾

R. 4 23. And when the matter is decided, Satan will say, 'Allāh promised you a promise of truth, but I promised you and failed you. [a]I had no power over you except that I called you and you obeyed me. So blame me not, but blame your ownselves. I cannot succour you nor can you succour me. I have already disclaimed your associating me *with Allāh*. For the wrongdoers there shall, surely, be a grievous punishment.'

وَقَالَ الشَّيْطٰنُ لَمَّا قُضِيَ الْأَمْرُ إِنَّ اللّٰهَ وَعَدَكُمْ
وَعْدَ الْحَقِّ وَوَعَدْتُّكُمْ فَأَخْلَفْتُكُمْ ۖ وَمَا كَانَ لِيَ
عَلَيْكُمْ مِّنْ سُلْطٰنٍ إِلَّآ أَنْ دَعَوْتُكُمْ فَاسْتَجَبْتُمْ لِيْ ۚ
فَلَا تَلُوْمُوْنِيْ وَلُوْمُوْآ أَنْفُسَكُمْ ۖ مَآ أَنَا بِمُصْرِخِكُمْ
وَمَآ أَنْتُمْ بِمُصْرِخِيَّ ۖ إِنِّيْ كَفَرْتُ بِمَآ أَشْرَكْتُمُوْنِ
مِنْ قَبْلُ ۗ إِنَّ الظّٰلِمِيْنَ لَهُمْ عَذَابٌ أَلِيْمٌ ﴿٢٣﴾

24. And [b]those who believe and act righteously will be admitted into Gardens through which streams flow, wherein they will abide by the command of their Lord. [c]Their greeting therein *for each other* will be, 'Peace *be on you*.'

وَأُدْخِلَ الَّذِيْنَ اٰمَنُوْا وَعَمِلُوا الصّٰلِحٰتِ جَنّٰتٍ تَجْرِيْ
مِنْ تَحْتِهَا الْأَنْهٰرُ خٰلِدِيْنَ فِيْهَا بِإِذْنِ رَبِّهِمْ ۖ تَحِيَّتُهُمْ
فِيْهَا سَلٰمٌ ﴿٢٤﴾

25. Dost thou not see how Allāh sets forth a parable of a good word? *It is* like a good tree, whose root is firm and whose branches *reach* into heaven?[1465]

أَلَمْ تَرَ كَيْفَ ضَرَبَ اللّٰهُ مَثَلًا كَلِمَةً طَيِّبَةً كَشَجَرَةٍ
طَيِّبَةٍ أَصْلُهَا ثَابِتٌ وَّفَرْعُهَا فِي السَّمَآءِ ﴿٢٥﴾

[a]15 : 43; 16 : 100; 17 : 66 [b]10 : 10; 22 : 24. [c]10 : 11; 15 : 47; 36 : 59; 50 : 35.

1464. A people who are destined to perish give way to despair and become readily resigned to their low state.

1465. The Word of God has been likened in these verses to a tree which possesses four essential qualities : (*a*) It is good, meaning it is free from all such teachings as may, in any way, offend against human reason and conscience or against human feelings and susceptibilities. (*b*) Like a good and deep-rooted fruitful tree it possesses a strong and stable foundation and receives fresh life and sustenance from its Source, and like a strong tree it does not bend before the blasts of objections and adverse criticism but stands firm against

26. It brings forth its fruit at all times by the command of its Lord. And [a]Allāh sets forth parables for men that they may be reminded.

تُؤْتِيْٓ اُكُلَهَا كُلَّ حِيْنٍۭ بِاِذْنِ رَبِّهَا ۭ وَيَضْرِبُ اللّٰهُ
الْاَمْثَالَ لِلنَّاسِ لَعَلَّهُمْ يَتَذَكَّرُوْنَ ﴿۲۶﴾

27. And the case of an evil word[1466] is like *that* of an evil tree, which is uprooted from above the earth and has no stability.

وَمَثَلُ كَلِمَةٍ خَبِيْثَةٍ كَشَجَرَةٍ خَبِيْثَةِۨ اجْتُثَّتْ
مِنْ فَوْقِ الْاَرْضِ مَا لَهَا مِنْ قَرَارٍ ﴿۲۷﴾

28. Allāh strengthens the believers with the word that is firmly established, both in the present life and in the Hereafter; and Allāh lets the wrongdoers go astray. And Allāh does what He wills.

يُثَبِّتُ اللّٰهُ الَّذِيْنَ اٰمَنُوْا بِالْقَوْلِ الثَّابِتِ فِي الْحَيٰوةِ
الدُّنْيَا وَفِي الْاٰخِرَةِ ۚ وَيُضِلُّ اللّٰهُ الظّٰلِمِيْنَ ۣ وَ
يَفْعَلُ اللّٰهُ مَا يَشَاۗءُ ﴿۲۸﴾ ع

R. 5 29. [b]Dost thou not see those who changed Allāh's favour for ingratitude and landed their people into the abode of ruin—

اَلَمْ تَرَ اِلَى الَّذِيْنَ بَدَّلُوْا نِعْمَتَ اللّٰهِ كُفْرًا وَّاَحَلُّوْا
قَوْمَهُمْ دَارَ الْبَوَارِ ﴿۲۹﴾

30. *Into* Hell. They shall burn therein; and an evil place of rest it is.

جَهَنَّمَ ۚ يَصْلَوْنَهَا ۭ وَبِئْسَ الْقَرَارُ ﴿۳۰﴾

31. And [c]they have set up rivals to Allāh to lead *people* astray from His way. Say, [d]'Enjoy yourselves a while, then, surely, your journey is toward the Fire.'

وَجَعَلُوْا لِلّٰهِ اَنْدَادًا لِّيُضِلُّوْا عَنْ سَبِيْلِهٖ ۭ قُلْ تَمَتَّعُوْا
فَاِنَّ مَصِيْرَكُمْ اِلَى النَّارِ ﴿۳۱﴾

[a]13 : 18; 29 : 44. [b]2 : 212. [c]2 : 23; 13 : 34. [d]47 : 13; 77 : 47.

all storms. It derives life and sustenance from only One Source and there is therefore no disharmony or discard in its principles and teachings. (c) Its branches reach into heaven, which means that by acting upon it a man can scale the highest summits of spiritual eminence. (d) It yields its fruits in abundance in all seasons which signifies that its blessings are witnessed at all times and it continues to produce in every age men who by acting upon its teaching attain communion with God and by their uprightness and the purity of their conduct tower high above their contemporaries. The Qur'ān possesses all these qualities in full measure.

1466. Unlike the good tree a book which is forged by a fabricator is like an evil tree. It does not possess permanence or stability. Its teachings are supported neither by reason nor by the laws of nature. It cannot stand criticism and its principles and ideals keep on changing with the change in human conditions and circumstances. It is a hotch-potch of teachings collected from doubtful sources. It fails to produce men who can claim to have established true and real connection with God. It does not receive fresh life from the Divine Source and is subject to decay and degeneration.

32. Say to My servants who believe that they should observe Prayer, and [a]spend out of what We have given them, secretly and openly, before [b]there comes a day where there will be neither bargaining nor friendship.

قُلْ لِّعِبَادِيَ الَّذِيْنَ اٰمَنُوْا يُقِيْمُوا الصَّلٰوةَ وَيُنْفِقُوْا
مِمَّا رَزَقْنٰهُمْ سِرًّا وَّعَلَانِيَةً مِّنْ قَبْلِ اَنْ يَّاْتِيَ
يَوْمٌ لَّا بَيْعٌ فِيْهِ وَلَا خِلٰلٌ ﴿۳۲﴾

33. Allāh is He Who created the heavens and the earth and [c]caused water to come down from the clouds, and brought forth therewith fruits for your sustenance, and [d]He has subjected to you the ships that they may sail through the sea by His command, and the rivers *too* has He subjected to you.

اَللّٰهُ الَّذِيْ خَلَقَ السَّمٰوٰتِ وَالْاَرْضَ وَاَنْزَلَ مِنَ
السَّمَآءِ مَآءً فَاَخْرَجَ بِهٖ مِنَ الثَّمَرٰتِ رِزْقًا لَّكُمْ
وَسَخَّرَ لَكُمُ الْفُلْكَ لِتَجْرِيَ فِي الْبَحْرِ بِاَمْرِهٖ
وَسَخَّرَ لَكُمُ الْاَنْهٰرَ ﴿۳۳﴾

34. And [e]He has *also* subjected to you the sun and the moon, both performing their functions constantly. And He has subjected to you the night as well as the day.

وَسَخَّرَ لَكُمُ الشَّمْسَ وَالْقَمَرَ دَآئِبَيْنِ وَسَخَّرَ
لَكُمُ الَّيْلَ وَالنَّهَارَ ﴿۳۴﴾

35. And He gives you all that you ask[1467] of Him, and [f]if you try to count the favours of Allāh, you will not be able to number them. Verily, man is very unjust, very ungrateful.

وَاٰتٰىكُمْ مِّنْ كُلِّ مَا سَاَلْتُمُوْهُ وَاِنْ تَعُدُّوْا نِعْمَتَ
اللّٰهِ لَا تُحْصُوْهَا اِنَّ الْاِنْسَانَ لَظَلُوْمٌ كَفَّارٌ ﴿۳۵﴾ ع

R. 6 36. And *call to mind* [g]when Abraham said, 'My Lord, make this city *a city of* peace, and [h]preserve me and my children from worshipping idols,[1468]

وَاِذْ قَالَ اِبْرٰهِيْمُ رَبِّ اجْعَلْ هٰذَا الْبَلَدَ اٰمِنًا
وَّاجْنُبْنِيْ وَبَنِيَّ اَنْ نَّعْبُدَ الْاَصْنَامَ ﴿۳۶﴾

[a]2 : 275; 13 : 23; 16 : 76. [b]2 : 255; 43 : 68. [c]2 : 23; 20 : 54; 22 : 64; 35 : 28. [d]22 : 66; 43 : 14; 45 : 13. [e]7 : 55; 13 : 3; 16 : 13; 39 : 6. [f]16 : 19. [g]2 : 127. [h]2 : 129

1467. The words, 'You ask of Him', refer to the demands of human nature which have all been fully met. God has made full provision for the satisfaction of all the cravings and demands of human nature.

1468. Abraham's prayer, referred to in the present verse, shows that he knew that idolatry would one day prevail in Mecca and the country around it. Hence his anxiety for the protection of his progeny against idol-worship when the prayer was offered many hundred years ago.

37. 'My Lord, [a]they have indeed led astray many among mankind. So whoever follows me, he is certainly of me; and whoever disobeys me Thou art, surely, Most Forgiving, Merciful,

رَبِّ إِنَّهُنَّ أَضْلَلْنَ كَثِيرًا مِّنَ النَّاسِ ۚ فَمَنْ تَبِعَنِي
فَإِنَّهُ مِنِّي ۚ وَمَنْ عَصَانِي فَإِنَّكَ غَفُورٌ رَّحِيمٌ ﴿٣٧﴾

38. [b]'Our Lord, I have settled *some* of my progeny in an uncultivable valley near Thy Sacred House.[1469]—Our Lord,—that they may observe Prayer.[1470] So make men's hearts incline[1471] towards them and [c]provide them with fruits that they may be thankful,

رَبَّنَا إِنِّي أَسْكَنتُ مِن ذُرِّيَّتِي بِوَادٍ غَيْرِ ذِي زَرْعٍ
عِندَ بَيْتِكَ الْمُحَرَّمِ ۙ رَبَّنَا لِيُقِيمُوا الصَّلٰوةَ فَاجْعَلْ
أَفْئِدَةً مِّنَ النَّاسِ تَهْوِي إِلَيْهِمْ وَارْزُقْهُم مِّنَ
الثَّمَرٰتِ لَعَلَّهُمْ يَشْكُرُونَ ﴿٣٨﴾

39. 'Our Lord, certainly, [d]Thou knowest what we keep secret and what we make known. And nothing whatever is hidden from Allāh, whether in the earth or in the heaven,

رَبَّنَا إِنَّكَ تَعْلَمُ مَا نُخْفِي وَمَا نُعْلِنُ ۗ وَمَا يَخْفٰى
عَلَى اللّٰهِ مِن شَيْءٍ فِي الْأَرْضِ وَلَا فِي السَّمَاءِ ﴿٣٩﴾

40. 'All praise belongs to Allāh Who has given me, despite *my* old age, Ishmael and Isaac. Surely, my Lord is the Hearer of Prayer,

الْحَمْدُ لِلّٰهِ الَّذِي وَهَبَ لِي عَلَى الْكِبَرِ إِسْمٰعِيلَ
وَإِسْحٰقَ ۚ إِنَّ رَبِّي لَسَمِيعُ الدُّعَاءِ ﴿٤٠﴾

[a]71 : 25 [b]22 : 27. [c]2 : 127; 28 : 58 [d]2 : 78; 3 : 6; 27 : 66.

1469. The reference is to the settling by Abraham of his son Ishmael and his wife Hagar in the wilderness of Arabia. Ishmael was yet a child when in obedience to Divine command and in fulfilment of Divine plan Abraham brought him and his mother Hagar in the bleak and barren tract where Mecca now stands. At that time there was no sign of life and no means of subsistence at the place (Bukhārī). But God had so designed that the place should become the scene of the activities of God's last Message for mankind. Ishmael was chosen as the vehicle for the implementation of the Divine plan.

1470. This prayer of Abraham found its complete fulfilment in the Holy Prophet; for before him it was only the Arabs who visited Mecca to offer their oblations but, after his advent, people from all over the world began to visit it.

1471. The prayer was made at a time when not a blade of grass was to be seen for many miles around Mecca. Yet the prophecy met with fulfilment in a marvellous manner, for the choicest fruits come to Mecca in plenty in all seasons.

41. "My Lord, make me *constant in* observing Prayer, and my children *too*. Our Lord ! [b]*bestow Thy grace on me and* accept *my* prayer,

رَبِّ اجْعَلْنِيْ مُقِيْمَ الصَّلٰوةِ وَمِنْ ذُرِّيَّتِيْ رَبَّنَا وَتَقَبَّلْ دُعَآءِ ۝

42. [c]'Our Lord, forgive[1472] me and my parents and the believers on the day when the reckoning will take place.'

رَبَّنَا اغْفِرْ لِيْ وَلِوَالِدَيَّ وَلِلْمُؤْمِنِيْنَ يَوْمَ يَقُوْمُ الْحِسَابُ ۝

R. 7   43. And think not that Allāh is unaware of what the wrongdoers do. He only gives them respite till the day on which *their* eyes will fixedly stare *in horror*;

وَلَا تَحْسَبَنَّ اللّٰهَ غَافِلًا عَمَّا يَعْمَلُ الظّٰلِمُوْنَ ۚ اِنَّمَا يُؤَخِّرُهُمْ لِيَوْمٍ تَشْخَصُ فِيْهِ الْاَبْصَارُ ۝

44. They will hurry along in fright, raising up their heads, their gaze not returning to them, and their hearts utterly void.[1473]

مُهْطِعِيْنَ مُقْنِعِيْ رُءُوْسِهِمْ لَا يَرْتَدُّ اِلَيْهِمْ طَرْفُهُمْ وَاَفْئِدَتُهُمْ هَوَآءٌ ۝

---

[a]2 : 129.   [b]2 : 128.   [c]71 : 29.

1472. The reason, why Divine Prophets pray to God for forgiveness not withstanding the fact that they enjoy protection against Satan, is their realization of the holiness and majesty of God and of their own weakness. It is this realization of human weakness which makes them humbly pray to God that He may "cover" them with His grace and mercy so that their very self may become completely obliterated and may merge completely in Him.

1473. This and the preceding verse give a graphic description of the bewilderment and consternation of the Meccans when they suddenly found the Holy Prophet at the gates of Mecca with an army ten thousand strong, without their having the least inkling of his coming.

45. And warn people of the day when *the promised* chastisement will come upon them, and [a]the wrong-doers will say, 'Our Lord, grant us respite for a short term, we will respond to Thy call and will follow the Messengers.' *He will say*, 'Did you not swear before this that you would never have a fall ?

وَأَنذِرِ النَّاسَ يَوْمَ يَأْتِيهِمُ الْعَذَابُ فَيَقُولُ
الَّذِينَ ظَلَمُوا رَبَّنَا أَخِّرْنَا إِلَىٰ أَجَلٍ قَرِيبٍ نُّجِبْ
دَعْوَتَكَ وَنَتَّبِعِ الرُّسُلَ أَوَلَمْ تَكُونُوا أَقْسَمْتُم
مِّن قَبْلُ مَا لَكُم مِّن زَوَالٍ ﴿٤٥﴾

46. 'And you dwell in the dwellings of those who wronged themselves and it has become plain to you how We dealt with them; and We set forth *clear* parables for you.'

وَسَكَنتُمْ فِي مَسَاكِنِ الَّذِينَ ظَلَمُوا أَنفُسَهُمْ وَتَبَيَّنَ
لَكُمْ كَيْفَ فَعَلْنَا بِهِمْ وَضَرَبْنَا لَكُمُ الْأَمْثَالَ ﴿٤٦﴾

47. And [b]they have tried *all* their designs; but their designs are with Allāh.[1474] And even though their designs be such as to make the mountains move, *they will not succeed.*

وَقَدْ مَكَرُوا مَكْرَهُمْ وَعِندَ اللَّهِ مَكْرُهُمْ وَإِن
كَانَ مَكْرُهُمْ لِتَزُولَ مِنْهُ الْجِبَالُ ﴿٤٧﴾

48. Think not then that [c]Allāh will *ever* fail to keep His promise to His Messengers. Surely, Allāh is Mighty, Lord of retribution,

فَلَا تَحْسَبَنَّ اللَّهَ مُخْلِفَ وَعْدِهِ رُسُلَهُ إِنَّ اللَّهَ
عَزِيزٌ ذُو انتِقَامٍ ﴿٤٨﴾

49. On the day when this earth will be changed into another earth, and the heavens *too*;[1475] and they will *all* appear before Allāh, the One, the Most Supreme.

يَوْمَ تُبَدَّلُ الْأَرْضُ غَيْرَ الْأَرْضِ وَالسَّمَاوَاتُ وَبَرَزُوا
لِلَّهِ الْوَاحِدِ الْقَهَّارِ ﴿٤٩﴾

50. And [d]thou wilt see the guilty on that day bound in chains.

وَتَرَى الْمُجْرِمِينَ يَوْمَئِذٍ مُّقَرَّنِينَ فِي الْأَصْفَادِ ﴿٥٠﴾

[a]63 : 11. [b]3 : 55; 8 : 31; 13 : 43; 27 : 51. [c]3 : 195; 10 : 104; 58 : 22. [d]38 : 39.

1474. God knows their evil designs full well and will frustrate them.

1475. With the Fall of Mecca and the establishment of Islām in Arabia as a mighty force, a new universe, as it were, came into being with a new heaven and a new earth. The old order was swept away, and a new one, completely different from the old one, took its place.

51. Their garments will be, *as if*, of pitch and [a]the fire shall envelop their faces.

سَرَابِيْلُهُمْ مِّنْ قَطِرَانٍ وَّ تَغْشٰى وُجُوْهَهُمُ النَّارُ ﴿۵۱﴾

52. [b]*This will be so* that Allāh may requite each soul for what it has wrought. Surely, Allāh is Swift at reckoning.

لِيَجْزِيَ اللّٰهُ كُلَّ نَفْسٍ مَّا كَسَبَتْ ۭ اِنَّ اللّٰهَ سَرِيْعُ الْحِسَابِ ﴿۵۲﴾

53. [c]This is a sufficient admonition for mankind *that they may benefit by it* and that they may be warned thereby, and that they may know that He is the only One God and that those possessed of understanding may take heed.

هٰذَا بَلٰغٌ لِّلنَّاسِ وَلِيُنْذَرُوْا بِهٖ وَلِيَعْلَمُوْٓا اَنَّمَا هُوَ
اِلٰهٌ وَّاحِدٌ وَّلِيَذَّكَّرَ اُولُوا الْاَلْبَابِ ﴿۵۳﴾ ع

[a]10 : 28; 23 : 105; 54 : 49. [b]40 : 18; 45 : 23; 74 : 39. [c]5 : 68; 6 : 20.

CHAPTER 15

AL-ḤIJR

(*Revealed before Hijrah*)

Date of Revelation and Context

According to consensus of scholarly opinion the *Sūrah* was revealed at Mecca. In the preceding *Sūrah* it was pointed out that though the former Prophets possessed no material means, yet their mission progressed and prospered because they had the Word of God to guide and help them. So will the Holy Prophet succeed in his mission. The Word of God, the present *Sūrah* emphatically declares, is a great force before which no worldly power can stand. Forging of lies against God is not a thing to be trifled with and impostors and forgers of lies against God soon meet their deserved end, and it is stated that the Qur'ān is the revealed Word of God and possesses irrefutable proofs to establish its Divine origin.

Subject-Matter

The basic theme of the *Sūrah* is that no heavenly Scripture can approach the Qur'ān in beauty of diction and style and in the grandeur of its contents. It is a revealed Scripture *par excellence*. It stands unequalled and unrivalled in every respect. Its beauties and good qualities are so many and so varied that even disbelievers on occasions are forced to confess that they possess nothing like it and wish that they too had possessed a Scripture like it. In spite of this confession on their part, they do not see their way to accept it and do not realize that by their refusal to accept the Qur'ān they would be deprived of truth and would draw upon themselves the displeasure and punishment of God. The Quranic Message is bound to succeed and nothing can stand in its way. Those who hesitate or refuse to accept it will themselves be the sufferers. The *Sūrah* then states that if the Quranic revelation is ridiculed and treated with contempt, it is nothing to be wondered at, for the revelations of previous Prophets also were held up to scorn. But the scoffers do not appreciate this patent fact that it is no easy thing to forge lies against God, because to do so is to invite sure destruction. The All-Powerful God sees to it that lies are not successfully forged against Him and that a forgery becomes easily distinguished from His revealed Word. He vouchsafes it a special distinction and eminence and creates a favourable atmosphere for its acceptance by right thinking men, and raises those who accept it from a low to a very high level of moral excellence.

سُوۡرَۃُ الۡحِجۡرِ مَکِّیَّۃٌ (١٥)

1. [a]In the name of Allāh, the Gracious, the Merciful.

بِسۡمِ اللّٰہِ الرَّحۡمٰنِ الرَّحِیۡمِ ①

2. [b]Alif Lām Rā. [c]These are verses of the *perfect* Book and of the illuminating Qur'ān.[1476]

الٓرٰ ۟ تِلۡکَ اٰیٰتُ الۡکِتٰبِ وَ قُرۡاٰنٍ مُّبِیۡنٍ ②

PART XIV

الجزء ١٤

3. Often do the disbelievers wish that they were Muslims.[1477]

رُبَمَا یَوَدُّ الَّذِیۡنَ کَفَرُوۡا لَوۡ کَانُوۡا مُسۡلِمِیۡنَ ③

4. [d]Leave them alone that they may eat and enjoy themselves and that vain hope[1478] may beguile them, but they will soon know.

ذَرۡہُمۡ یَاۡکُلُوۡا وَ یَتَمَتَّعُوۡا وَ یُلۡہِہِمُ الۡاَمَلُ فَسَوۡفَ یَعۡلَمُوۡنَ ④

5. And never a town[1479] have We destroyed but there was for it a known decree.[1479A]

وَ مَاۤ اَہۡلَکۡنَا مِنۡ قَرۡیَۃٍ اِلَّا وَ لَہَا کِتَابٌ مَّعۡلُوۡمٌ ⑤

6. [e]No people can *escape their doom by* outstripping their appointed term, nor can they remain behind.

مَا تَسۡبِقُ مِنۡ اُمَّۃٍ اَجَلَہَا وَ مَا یَسۡتَاۡخِرُوۡنَ ⑥

---

[a]1 : 1. [b]10 : 2; 11 : 2; 12 : 2; 13 : 2; 14 : 2. [c]27 : 2; 31 : 3. [d]47 : 13. [e]7 : 35; 10 : 50; 16 : 62.

1476. Only in 27 : 2 and in the verse under comment do the words, 'Book' and 'Qur'ān', occur together but, whereas in the present verse the word 'Book' precedes the word 'Qur'ān', in 27 : 2 the order has been reversed. While the word 'Book' implies a prophecy that the Holy Book of Islām will continue to be written, the word 'Qur'ān' points to the prophecy that it will continue to be increasingly read and recited. Moreover, whereas the words 'illuminating Qur'ān' have been used in the Qur'ān only twice, the words 'illuminating Book' have been used no less than twelve times. This is to hint that a record in writing is much more useful than mere oral transmission. Muslims should, therefore, give more attention to education and to the study of written knowledge.

1477. It is on record that such a desire was actually expressed by some disbelievers in the time of the Holy Prophet.

1478. The verse may mean that the wish of disbelievers mentioned in the last verse —that they had been Muslims—is simply a 'vain hope,' *i.e.*, a mere passing wish; their real desire being the pursuit of worldly enjoyment and material gains.

1479. 'Town' stands for the people to whom a Prophet is sent. The 'town' of the Holy Prophet has been called 'Mother of towns' in the Qur'ān (6 : 93).

1479A. The words, 'known decree', here signifies the time appointed for the destruction of the opponents of a Prophet as predicted by him.

7. And they said, [a]'O thou to whom this exhortation has been sent down, thou art surely a madman,[1480]

وَقَالُوا يَا أَيُّهَا الَّذِي نُزِّلَ عَلَيْهِ الذِّكْرُ إِنَّكَ لَمَجْنُونٌ ۝٧

8. [b]'Why dost thou not bring angels to us, if thou art of the truthful?'

لَوْ مَا تَأْتِينَا بِالْمَلَائِكَةِ إِنْ كُنْتَ مِنَ الصَّادِقِينَ ۝٨

9. [c]We do not send down angels but with the requirements of justice, and *when We do send them, the disbelievers* are not respited.[1481]

مَا نُنَزِّلُ الْمَلَائِكَةَ إِلَّا بِالْحَقِّ وَمَا كَانُوا إِذًا مُنْظَرِينَ ۝٩

10. Verily, it is [d]We Who have sent down this Exhortation, and most surely We are its Guardian.[1482]

إِنَّا نَحْنُ نَزَّلْنَا الذِّكْرَ وَإِنَّا لَهُ لَحَافِظُونَ ۝١٠

11. And We sent *Messengers* before thee among parties of ancient peoples.

وَلَقَدْ أَرْسَلْنَا مِنْ قَبْلِكَ فِي شِيَعِ الْأَوَّلِينَ ۝١١

---

[a]37 : 37; 44 : 15; 68 : 52. [b]6 : 9; 11 : 13; 25 : 8. [c]6 : 9. [d]36 : 70; 65 : 11.

1480. *Majnūn* does not mean 'one possessed by a devil or a jinn' or simply 'possessed,' but 'a mad or insane person,' or 'one whose intellectual faculties have become very much impaired' (Lane).

1481. Disbelievers are here told that when in accordance with the requirements of truth, justice and wisdom (*Bi'lḥaqq*) they will become deserving of Divine punishment, angels will descend upon them and they will be granted no respite.

1482. The promise about the protection and preservation of the Qur'ān made in this verse has been so remarkably fulfilled that even if there had been no other proof, this fact alone would have sufficed to establish its Divine origin. This *Sūrah* was revealed at Mecca (Noldeke) when the life of the Holy Prophet and his followers was extremely precarious and the enemy could easily crush the new Faith. It was then that disbelievers were challenged to do their worst to destroy it and were warned that God would frustrate all their designs because He Himself was its Guardian. The challenge was open and unequivocal and the enemy strong and ruthless, and yet the Qur'ān remained safe against corruption and interpolation and tampering with and has ever continued to enjoy perfect security. This distinction of the Qur'ān is not shared by any other revealed Book. Sir William Muir, the notoriously hostile critic of Islām, says: 'We may, upon the strongest presumption, affirm that every verse in the Qur'ān is the genuine and unaltered composition of Moḥammad himself.........There is otherwise every security, internal and external, that we possess the text which Moḥammad himself gave forth and used.....To compare their pure text with the various readings of our Scriptures, is to compare things between which there is no analogy' (Introduction to 'The Life of Moḥammad'). Prof. Noldeke, the great German Orientalist writes as follows: 'Efforts of European scholars to prove the existence of later interpolations in the Qur'ān have failed' (Enc. Brit.). The utter failure of Dr. Mingana, a few years ago, to find fault with the purity of the Quranic text, on the contrary, set the seal on the truth of its claim that among all revealed Scriptures the Qur'ān alone has remained completely immune from all interpolation or tampering with it. See "The Larger Edition of the Commentary," pp.1263-1266.

12. And [a]there never came to them a Messenger but they mocked at him.

وَمَا يَأْتِيْهِمْ مِّنْ رَّسُوْلٍ إِلَّا كَانُوْا بِهٖ يَسْتَهْزِءُوْنَ ⑫

13. [b]Thus do We cause this[1483] *habit of mocking* to enter into the hearts of the sinful people;

كَذٰلِكَ نَسْلُكُهٗ فِيْ قُلُوْبِ الْمُجْرِمِيْنَ ⑬

14. [c]They believe not in this *Qur'ān*, though the example of the former peoples has gone *before them*.

لَا يُؤْمِنُوْنَ بِهٖ وَقَدْ خَلَتْ سُنَّةُ الْأَوَّلِيْنَ ⑭

15. And even if We opened to them a gate in heaven, and they kept ascending[1484] through it,

وَلَوْ فَتَحْنَا عَلَيْهِمْ بَابًا مِّنَ السَّمَآءِ فَظَلُّوْا فِيْهِ يَعْرُجُوْنَ ⑮

16. They would surely say, 'Only our eyes are dazed; rather we are a bewitched[1485] people.'

لَقَالُوْٓا إِنَّمَا سُكِّرَتْ أَبْصَارُنَا بَلْ نَحْنُ قَوْمٌ مَّسْحُوْرُوْنَ ⑯ ع

R. 2 17. And [d]We have, indeed, made mansions *of stars* in the heaven and have adorned[1486] it for beholders.

وَلَقَدْ جَعَلْنَا فِي السَّمَآءِ بُرُوْجًا وَّزَيَّنّٰهَا لِلنّٰظِرِيْنَ ⑰

18. And [e]We have guarded it against *the intrusion of* every rejected Satan.[1487]

وَحَفِظْنٰهَا مِنْ كُلِّ شَيْطٰنٍ رَّجِيْمٍ ⑱

[a]36: 31; 43 : 8. [b]26 : 201. [c]26 : 202 [d]37 : 7; 41 : 13; 67 : 6. [e]37 : 8; 41 : 13.

1483. The pronoun 'this' refers to the disbelievers' practice of ridiculing the Divine Prophets mentioned in the preceding verse.

1484. The verse may mean that if God were to open the gates of His mercy and avert punishment, then instead of turning to Him, the disbelievers would become engaged in the acquisition of material prosperity and comforts.

1485. Disbelievers have become such strangers to spiritual matters that even if they were to enjoy some of the spiritual experiences which the Holy Prophet had gone through and were to have some of the visions of the spiritual heights to which he had arisen, they would not believe and would only say that they had become victims of magic or witchcraft.

1486. It is not merely the beautiful appearance of the planets and the stars at night that is meant here. The great purpose which their creation serves is mentioned in the following verses as well as in 16 : 17 and 67 : 6, and it is in the fulfilment of that great purpose that their real beauty lies.

1487. The verse points out that just as in the physical world evilly disposed persons exercise some sort of power or influence and can cause a certain amount of injury to other men but cannot completely deprive them of heavenly blessings, *e.g.*, the wholesome influence of stars, etc., similarly, in the spiritual world, satans too have no control over the Prophets and their true followers (v. 43). "Satan" in the verse under comment refers to such disbelievers as desire to attain union with God independently of the Prophets (vv. 14-16). Against such persons the spiritual heavens have indeed been guarded and their gates barred.

19. But [a]if anyone hears stealthily *something of revelation and distorts it*,[1488] there pursues him a bright flame.[1488A]

إِلَّا مَنِ اسْتَرَقَ السَّمْعَ فَأَتْبَعَهُ شِهَابٌ مُّبِينٌ ﴿١٩﴾

20. [b]And the earth have We spread out,[1489] and [c]set therein firm mountains[1489A] and caused every thing to grow therein in proper proportion.

وَالْأَرْضَ مَدَدْنٰهَا وَأَلْقَيْنَا فِيهَا رَوَاسِيَ وَأَنْبَتْنَا
فِيهَا مِنْ كُلِّ شَيْءٍ مَّوْزُونٍ ﴿٢٠﴾

[a]37 : 11; 67 : 6. [b]13 : 4. [c]16 : 16; 21 : 32.

1488. 'Stealing the Word of God' may signify the deceitful action of such people as pretend to represent the teachings of the Prophets as their own. They seek to deceive people into believing that the Prophets bring no new teaching and that they too have access to that knowledge which the Prophets claim to possess. Or the verse may mean that they tear out a passage from its context and try to mislead simple-minded folk by putting a wrong interpretation upon it and distorting its meaning. The words, *if anyone hears stealthily*, make it clear that in verse 17 the words, 'the heaven' represent the spiritual system and not the physical firmament, for the stealing away of the Word of God has nothing to do with the physical. heavens.

1488A. The word 'mansions of stars' in v. 17 represents Divine Messengers in general, while the words 'bright flame' in the present verse or 'penetrating flame' occurring in 37 : 11 stand for the Prophet of the day, or the Master-Prophet (the Holy Prophet). The pursuit of satans by *Shihāb* signifies that so long as a religious teaching remains based on Divine revelation (*al-Dhikr*—v. 10) and gives light and guidance, Divine Reformers also continue to appear to guard it. One of the signs of the appearance of Divine Reformers in the world is the frequent occurrence of meteoric phenomenon, called the falling of stars in large numbers. In the time of the Holy Prophet meteors fell in such large numbers that disbelievers thought that both heaven and earth were going to fall asunder (Kathīr). It was from these extraordinary happenings that Heraclius who, it appears, had some knowledge of astronomy, inferred that the Prophet-King of the Arabs must have appeared (Bukhārī. ch. *Bad' al-Waḥy*). In the time of Jesus also meteors fell in unusually large numbers (Biḥār). This celestial phenomenon was also witnessed in our own time—in 1885. Thus both history and *Ḥadīth* bear testimony to the fact that the falling of meteors in unusually large numbers is a sure sign of the appearance of a Divine Reformer. See also "The Larger Edition of the Commentary,' pp. 1272—1276.

'Satan' in v. 18 may be taken to refer to diviners and soothsayers. In that case 'the pelting of the satans' (67 : 6) would mean that during the time when there is no Divine Reformer in the world, astrologers and soothsayers succeed, to some extent, in their nefarious trade of hoodwinking simple-minded people but, with the appearance of a Divine Reformer, their false knowledge becomes exposed and people can easily distinguish between the true prophecies of heavenly Messengers and the conjectures of astrologers and soothsayers. The verse may also signify that when some mischievous people, after tearing out a passage from the text of the heavenly revelation, seek to spread it in a distorted form, a fresh Sign comes like a brilliant flash and destroys the machinations of the satanic people.

1489. The words, *Wa'l Arḍa Madadnā-hā* mean, 'We have spread out the earth or, 'We have enriched it.' Both meanings are applicable here. The verse signifies that God has made the earth so large that in spite of its being round, man feels no discomfort on account of its roundness; or it means that God has enriched the earth with fertilizers. Astronomical researches have disclosed the fact that the earth continues to acquire new strength and fertility from the stars from which particles of matter fall on it in the form of meteors or meteoric dust which serves to increase its fertility.

1489A. The earth needs a good supply of water to grow food. For this purpose God has created mountains which serve as reservoirs of water, storing it in the form of snow and distributing it over the earth by means of rivers.

21. And [a]We have made for you therein means of livelihood and *also* for *all* those for whom you do not provide.

وَجَعَلْنَا لَكُمْ فِيْهَا مَعَايِشَ وَمَنْ لَّسْتُمْ لَهٗ بِرٰزِقِيْنَ ﴿٢١﴾

22. And [b]there is not a thing but are *limitless* treasures thereof with Us and We send it not down except in a known measure.[1490]

وَاِنْ مِّنْ شَيْءٍ اِلَّا عِنْدَنَا خَزَآئِنُهٗ وَمَا نُنَزِّلُهٗٓ اِلَّا بِقَدَرٍ مَّعْلُوْمٍ ﴿٢٢﴾

23. And [c]We send fecundating[1491] winds, then We send down water from the clouds, then We give it to you to drink, and you could not yourselves store it.

وَاَرْسَلْنَا الرِّيٰحَ لَوَاقِحَ فَاَنْزَلْنَا مِنَ السَّمَآءِ مَآءً فَاَسْقَيْنٰكُمُوْهُ وَمَآ اَنْتُمْ لَهٗ بِخٰزِنِيْنَ ﴿٢٣﴾

24. And verily, [d]it is We Who give life, and We Who cause death; and [e]it is We Who are the *sole* Inheritors *of all*.[1492]

وَاِنَّا لَنَحْنُ نُحْيٖ وَنُمِيْتُ وَنَحْنُ الْوٰرِثُوْنَ ﴿٢٤﴾

25. And We do know those who go ahead among you and We *also* do know those who lag behind.

وَلَقَدْ عَلِمْنَا الْمُسْتَقْدِمِيْنَ مِنْكُمْ وَلَقَدْ عَلِمْنَا الْمُسْتَاْخِرِيْنَ ﴿٢٥﴾

26. And, surely, [f]it is thy Lord Who will gather them together. Surely, He is Wise, All-Knowing.

وَاِنَّ رَبَّكَ هُوَ يَحْشُرُهُمْ اِنَّهٗ حَكِيْمٌ عَلِيْمٌ ﴿٢٦﴾ ع

[a]7 : 11. [b]40 : 14. [c]7 : 58; 24 : 44; 25 : 49. [d]50 : 44. [e]19 : 41. [f]6 : 129; 25 : 18; 34 : 41.

1490. God possesses an unlimited stock of everything. But in His infinite mercy He directs the minds of men to a particular thing only when a real and genuine need for it arises. Like the material universe, the Qur'ān is a spiritual universe in which lie hidden treasures of spiritual knowledge which are revealed to man according to the needs of the time.

1491. *Lawāqiḥ* are such winds as carry pollen from the male to the female trees in order to fecundate them. The word also means such winds as carry vapours rising from the earth to the upper regions where they assume the form of clouds.

1492. A great revolution will take place through the teachings of the Qur'ān, causing the old order to die, and true believers will inherit the earth.

R. 3 27. And, surely, [a]We created man of dry ringing clay, of black mud wrought into shape.[1493]

وَلَقَدْ خَلَقْنَا الْإِنسَانَ مِن صَلْصَالٍ مِّنْ حَمَإٍ مَّسْنُونٍ ﴿٢٧﴾

28. And [b]the jinn We had created before of the fire of hot wind.[1494]

وَالْجَانَّ خَلَقْنَاهُ مِن قَبْلُ مِن نَّارِ السَّمُومِ ﴿٢٨﴾

29. And *remember* when thy Lord said to the angels, [c]"I am about to create man of dry ringing clay, of black mud wrought into shape;

وَإِذْ قَالَ رَبُّكَ لِلْمَلَائِكَةِ إِنِّي خَالِقٌ بَشَرًا مِّن صَلْصَالٍ مِّنْ حَمَإٍ مَّسْنُونٍ ﴿٢٩﴾

[a]6 : 3; 15 : 29, 34; 55 : 15. [b]7 : 13; 38 : 77; 55 : 16. [c]7 : 13; 38 : 77; 55 : 15.

1493. The creation of man from *Ṣalṣāl* (dry ringing clay) signifies that he has been created from a matter in which the faculty and attribute of speech lay latent. This shows that man has been endowed with the power to respond to the heavenly voice. But as *Ṣalṣāl* (dry ringing clay) emits a sound only when struck with something extraneous, the word is intended to hint that man's power to respond is subject to his receiving the Divine Call. This faculty establishes his superiority over the whole creation. The word *Hama'* signifies that man has been created from black mud, *i.e.*, earth and water; earth being the source of the body and water of the soul. Elsewhere, the Qur'ān speaks of 'earth' and 'water' separately as things of which man has been created (3 : 60; 21 : 31). By joining the word *Ṣalṣāl* (dry ringing clay) to the word *Ḥama'* (black mud), the Qur'ān means to point out that while other living creatures are created of *Ḥama'* (black mud) only, *viz.*, of earth and water, for they too possess a certain kind of undeveloped soul, man is created of *Ḥama'* (black mud) combined with *Ṣalṣāl* (dry ringing clay), *i.e.*, the attribute of speech. He is also *Masnūn*, *i.e.*, wrought into perfect shape (95 : 5). The verse does not mean that clay became at once moulded into a living being when God breathed life into it. The Qur'ān repeatedly states that the creation of the universe was gradual. The present verse speaks of only the first stage of man's creation. Other stages of his creation have been mentioned in 30 : 21; 35 : 12; 22 : 6; 23 : 15 and 40 : 68. The Quranic statement that man was created out of "earth" (which, incidentally, means that the long process of his creation started with it) finds corroboration from the fact that even now man's food is derived from the earth, certain parts of it being derived directly and others indirectly. This shows that the matter contained in the earth forms the origin of man; for if such had not been the case, he could not have derived his nutrition from it, because only that thing of which a being is made can supply it with nutrition, a foreign element being unable to replenish the wastage. See also "The Larger Edition of the Commentary" under this verse.

1494. A similar Quranic expression, *man is made of haste* (21 : 38)—shows that the verse under comment means that the jinn possessed a fiery nature and not that they were actually made of fire. Thus creation from clay or from fire are metaphors signifying a pliant and submissive nature or a fiery and inflammable temperament.

30. 'So [a]when I have fashioned him *in perfection* and have breathed into him of My Spirit, [b]fall ye down in submission to him.'[1495]

فَإِذَا سَوَّيْتُهُ وَنَفَخْتُ فِيهِ مِن رُّوحِي فَقَعُوا لَهُ سٰجِدِينَ ۝٣٠

31. [c]So the angels submitted, all of them together.

فَسَجَدَ الْمَلٰٓئِكَةُ كُلُّهُمْ أَجْمَعُونَ ۝٣١

32. [d]But Iblīs *did not;* he refused to be among those who submit.[1496]

إِلَّآ إِبْلِيسَ أَبٰىٓ أَن يَّكُونَ مَعَ السّٰجِدِينَ ۝٣٢

33. [e]*God* said, 'O Iblīs, what has happened to thee[1496A] that thou wouldst not be among those who submit?'

قَالَ يٰٓإِبْلِيسُ مَا لَكَ أَلَّا تَكُونَ مَعَ السّٰجِدِينَ ۝٣٣

34. [f]He answered, 'I am not going to submit to a mortal whom Thou hast created of dry ringing clay, of black mud wrought into shape.'

قَالَ لَمْ أَكُن لِّأَسْجُدَ لِبَشَرٍ خَلَقْتَهُ مِن صَلْصٰلٍ مِّنْ حَمَإٍ مَّسْنُونٍ ۝٣٤

35. [g]*God* said, 'Then get out hence,[1497] for, surely, thou art rejected.

قَالَ فَاخْرُجْ مِنْهَا فَإِنَّكَ رَجِيمٌ ۝٣٥

[a]32 : 10; 38 : 73. [b]2 : 35; 7 : 12; 17 : 62; 18 : 51; 20 : 117. [c]2 : 35; 7 : 12; 17 : 62; 18 : 51; 20 : 117. [d]2 : 35; 7 : 12; 17 : 62; 18 : 51; 20 : 117. [e]7 : 13; 38 : 76. [f]7 : 13; 17 : 62; 18 : 51. [g]7 : 14, 19; 38 : 78.

1495. By the word "angels" is meant the whole of creation, because angels constitute the first link of all creation and, as such, a command given to them really applies to the whole of creation. It is significant that whereas elsewhere the Qur'ān speaks of the command of God to the angels to submit to "Adam," in the present and the following verses the word used is "man." Thus both these words have been used synonymously in the Qur'ān. The command given to angels with regard to Adam applies to every man. Into every man God breathes His Spirit and angels are commanded to serve him. Man is God's vicegerent on earth and in his person he reflects Divine attributes.

1496. God punished Satan (vv. 35,36) for his failure to carry out a command which was addressed only to angels (vv. 29,30), because a command given to angels automatically applied to all those creatures which were subject to the authority of the angels. Elsewhere, the Qur'ān itself makes the point clear that the command to angels applied to Iblīs also (7 : 12,13).

1496A. The Arabic expression also means, what ails thee ; what is your reason ; what is the matter with thee?

1497. The pronoun *hā* in the expression *min-hā* does not refer to the post-mortal Heaven because Heaven is a place where Satan could not possibly enter and tempt Adam and from where no one is ever turned out (15 : 49). It refers to that state of apparent bliss in this world in which men happen to be before the advent of a Prophet when, though they might be victim to wrong beliefs, yet, not having rejected a Prophet, they are not altogether deprived of Divine favours which are represented as *Jannah* (garden) in the Qur'ān.

36. 'And, [a]surely, on thee shall be *My* curse till the Day of Judgement.'

وَإِنَّ عَلَيْكَ اللَّعْنَةَ إِلَىٰ يَوْمِ الدِّينِ ﴿٣٦﴾

37. [b]He said, 'My Lord, then grant me respite till the day when they shall be raised.'[1498]

قَالَ رَبِّ فَأَنظِرْنِي إِلَىٰ يَوْمِ يُبْعَثُونَ ﴿٣٧﴾

38. [c]*God* said, 'Thou art of those who are respited

قَالَ فَإِنَّكَ مِنَ الْمُنظَرِينَ ﴿٣٨﴾

39. [d]'Till the day of the appointed time.'[1499]

إِلَىٰ يَوْمِ الْوَقْتِ الْمَعْلُومِ ﴿٣٩﴾

40. [e]He answered, 'My Lord, since Thou hast adjudged me as gone astray, I will surely make *straying from the right path appear* beautiful to them on the earth and I will surely lead them all astray,

قَالَ رَبِّ بِمَا أَغْوَيْتَنِي لَأُزَيِّنَنَّ لَهُمْ فِي الْأَرْضِ وَلَأُغْوِيَنَّهُمْ أَجْمَعِينَ ﴿٤٠﴾

41. [f]'Except Thy chosen servants from among them.'

إِلَّا عِبَادَكَ مِنْهُمُ الْمُخْلَصِينَ ﴿٤١﴾

42. *God* said, 'This is a path *leading* straight to Me;

قَالَ هَٰذَا صِرَاطٌ عَلَيَّ مُسْتَقِيمٌ ﴿٤٢﴾

43. 'Surely, [g]thou shalt have no power over My servants, except such of the [h]erring ones as *choose to* follow thee.'[1500]

إِنَّ عِبَادِي لَيْسَ لَكَ عَلَيْهِمْ سُلْطَانٌ إِلَّا مَنِ اتَّبَعَكَ مِنَ الْغَاوِينَ ﴿٤٣﴾

[a]38 : 79. [b]7 : 15; 17 : 63; 38 : 80. [c]7 : 16; 38 : 81. [d]38 : 82.
[e]7 : 17,18; 38 : 83. [f]38 : 84. [g]17 : 66; 34 : 22. [h]7 : 19; 17 : 64; 38 : 86.

1498. The words 'when they shall be raised' signify the spiritual rebirth of man when having attained the stage of *Nafs Muṭma'innah* (the soul at peace with God) he becomes immune to satanic seduction and spiritual fall. This dialogue between God and Satan is, as hinted here, only an allegory or a metaphor.

1499. The words 'appointed time' mean, as explained in v. 37, the day when the Prophets and their followers achieve final victory over their adversaries, and falsehood and its votaries are finally crushed.

1500. The verse seems to suggest that human nature is intrinsically pure. Only those lose the right path who defile their own nature and choose to follow Satan. This idea has been further explained in 91 : 11.

44. And, surely, [a]Hell is the promised place for them all.

وَإِنَّ جَهَنَّمَ لَمَوْعِدُهُمْ أَجْمَعِينَ ﴿٤٤﴾

45. It has seven[1501] gates, *and* each gate has a portion of them allotted *to it*.

لَهَا سَبْعَةُ أَبْوَابٍ لِكُلِّ بَابٍ مِنْهُمْ جُزْءٌ مَقْسُومٌ ﴿٤٥﴾ ع

R. 4 46. Verily, the [b]righteous will be *placed* amid gardens and fountains.

إِنَّ الْمُتَّقِينَ فِي جَنَّاتٍ وَعُيُونٍ ﴿٤٦﴾

47. 'Enter therein with peace, in security.'[1502]

ادْخُلُوهَا بِسَلَامٍ آمِنِينَ ﴿٤٧﴾

48. And [c]We shall remove whatever of rancour[1503] may be in their breasts *so that they will be as* brothers *seated* on thrones, facing one another;

وَنَزَعْنَا مَا فِي صُدُورِهِمْ مِنْ غِلٍّ إِخْوَانًا عَلَىٰ سُرُرٍ مُتَقَابِلِينَ ﴿٤٨﴾

49. [d]Fatigue shall not touch them there,[1504] [e]nor shall they *ever* be ejected therefrom.

لَا يَمَسُّهُمْ فِيهَا نَصَبٌ وَمَا هُمْ مِنْهَا بِمُخْرَجِينَ ﴿٤٩﴾

50. [f]Tell My servants, *O Prophet*, that I am surely the All-Forgiving, All-Merciful;

نَبِّئْ عِبَادِي أَنِّي أَنَا الْغَفُورُ الرَّحِيمُ ﴿٥٠﴾

51. And [g]*also* that My punishment is the most grievous punishment.

وَأَنَّ عَذَابِي هُوَ الْعَذَابُ الْأَلِيمُ ﴿٥١﴾

[a]17 : 64; 38 : 86. [b]51 : 16; 52 : 18; 68 : 35; 77 : 42; 78 : 33. [c]7 : 44. [d]35 : 36. [e]11 : 109; 18 : 109. [f]5 : 99. [g]5 : 99.

1501. In Arabic the number "seven," as also "seventy," are often used to express not a specific numeral but the idea either of perfection and completeness or of profusion. The verse signifies that Hell will have the number of gates corresponding to the number and variety of sins committed by the guilty persons. The number "seven" may also refer to the seven exteroceptive senses, *viz*., the senses of vision, hearing, smell, taste, touch, pain and temperature, by which man receives impressions from the outer world.

1502. The words "peace" and "security" signify, respectively, freedom from internal anxieties that eat into the heart of a person and from external pain and punishment.

1503. Only those persons can be said to be enjoying a truly heavenly life whose hearts are free from all feelings of rancour and spite against their brethren.

1504. The verse implies that Heaven will be a place of constant and continuous work. In spite of this, however, believers will feel none of the fatigue which is the inevitable result of hard work and there will also be no waste or decay which are the result of fatigue.

52. And [a]tell them about Abraham's guests.

وَ نَبِّئْهُمْ عَنْ ضَيْفِ اِبْرٰهِيْمَ ﴿۵۲﴾

53. [b]When they came to him and said, 'Peace *be upon you*,' he answered, 'Verily, [c]we are afraid of you.'[1505]

اِذْ دَخَلُوْا عَلَيْهِ فَقَالُوْا سَلٰمًا ۗ قَالَ اِنَّا مِنْكُمْ وَجِلُوْنَ ﴿۵۳﴾

54. [d]They said, 'Be not afraid; we give thee glad tidings of a son *who shall be* endowed with great knowledge.'

قَالُوْا لَا تَوْجَلْ اِنَّا نُبَشِّرُكَ بِغُلٰمٍ عَلِيْمٍ ﴿۵۴﴾

55. [e]He said, 'Do you give me *this* glad tidings despite the fact that old age has overtaken me? On what *basis*, then, do you give me this glad tidings?'

قَالَ اَبَشَّرْتُمُوْنِيْ عَلٰۤى اَنْ مَّسَّنِيَ الْكِبَرُ فَبِمَ تُبَشِّرُوْنَ ﴿۵۵﴾

56. They said, 'We have indeed given thee true glad tidings, be not, therefore, of those who despair.'

قَالُوْا بَشَّرْنٰكَ بِالْحَقِّ فَلَا تَكُنْ مِّنَ الْقٰنِطِيْنَ ﴿۵۶﴾

57. He said, 'And [f]who despairs of the mercy of his Lord but *such* as go astray?'

قَالَ وَمَنْ يَّقْنَطُ مِنْ رَّحْمَةِ رَبِّهٖۤ اِلَّا الضَّآلُّوْنَ ﴿۵۷﴾

58. He said, [g]'What *now* is your *real* business, O ye messengers?'[1506]

قَالَ فَمَا خَطْبُكُمْ اَيُّهَا الْمُرْسَلُوْنَ ﴿۵۸﴾

59. They said, [h]'We have been sent unto a guilty people,

قَالُوْۤا اِنَّاۤ اُرْسِلْنَاۤ اِلٰى قَوْمٍ مُّجْرِمِيْنَ ۙ ﴿۵۹﴾

60. [i]'Except the followers of Lot. Them shall we save all,

اِلَّاۤ اٰلَ لُوْطٍ ۗ اِنَّا لَمُنَجُّوْهُمْ اَجْمَعِيْنَ ۙ ﴿۶۰﴾

61. [j]'Except his wife. We have decreed that she shall be of those who remain behind.'

اِلَّا امْرَاَتَهٗ قَدَّرْنَاۤ ۙ اِنَّهَا لَمِنَ الْغٰبِرِيْنَ ﴿۶۱﴾ ع

[a]51 : 25. [b]11 : 70; 51 : 26. [c]11 : 71; 51 : 29. [d]11 : 71; 51 : 29. [e]11 : 73. [f]12 : 88. [g]51 : 32. [h]51 : 33. [i]29 : 33; 51 : 36. [j]7 : 84; 11 : 82; 26 : 172; 27 : 58.

1505. Probably signs of grief and sorrow were apparent on the faces of the messengers because they had brought the news of an impending catastrophe. Abraham understood it either from the troubled expression of their faces or from their refusal to partake of the food offered to them (11 : 71).

1506. By using the word *al-Mursalūn* (messengers), the Qur'ān hints that the bearers of the message were humans. The Bible, however, sometimes mentions them as men (Gen. 18 : 2, 16,22) and sometimes as angels (Gen : 19 : 11, 15).

R. 5 62. And [a]when the messengers came unto Lot *and his* followers;

فَلَمَّا جَآءَ اٰلَ لُوۡطِ ۣالۡمُرۡسَلُوۡنَ ۙ﴿۶۲﴾

63. He said, [b]'Verily, you are a party of strangers.'[1507]

قَالَ اِنَّکُمۡ قَوۡمٌ مُّنۡکَرُوۡنَ ﴿۶۳﴾

64. They said, 'Yea; but we have brought thee that *news of the punishment* concerning which they have been in doubt;

قَالُوۡا بَلۡ جِئۡنٰکَ بِمَا کَانُوۡا فِیۡہِ یَمۡتَرُوۡنَ ﴿۶۴﴾

65. 'And we have brought thee sure news, and certainly we are truthful;

وَ اَتَیۡنٰکَ بِالۡحَقِّ وَ اِنَّا لَصٰدِقُوۡنَ ﴿۶۵﴾

66. [c]'So go forth with thy family in the *latter* part of the night, and follow thou in their[1508] rear. And let none of you look back,[1509] and *now* proceed to where you are commanded.'

فَاَسۡرِ بِاَہۡلِکَ بِقِطۡعٍ مِّنَ الَّیۡلِ وَ اتَّبِعۡ اَدۡبَارَہُمۡ وَ لَا یَلۡتَفِتۡ مِنۡکُمۡ اَحَدٌ وَّ امۡضُوۡا حَیۡثُ تُؤۡمَرُوۡنَ ﴿۶۶﴾

67. And [d]We communicated to him clearly this decree that the roots of these *people* would be cut off by the morning.

وَ قَضَیۡنَاۤ اِلَیۡہِ ذٰلِکَ الۡاَمۡرَ اَنَّ دَابِرَ ہٰۤؤُلَآءِ مَقۡطُوۡعٌ مُّصۡبِحِیۡنَ ﴿۶۷﴾

68. And [e]the people of the city came rejoicing.[1510]

وَ جَآءَ اَہۡلُ الۡمَدِیۡنَۃِ یَسۡتَبۡشِرُوۡنَ ﴿۶۸﴾

69. He said, [f]'These are my guests, so put me not to shame.

قَالَ اِنَّ ہٰۤؤُلَآءِ ضَیۡفِیۡ فَلَا تَفۡضَحُوۡنِ ۙ﴿۶۹﴾

[a]11 : 78; 29 : 34. [b]51 : 26. [c]11 : 82. [d]6 : 46; 7 : 73,85. [e]11 : 79. [f]11 : 79.

1507. Lot thought these men to be mere wayfarers whose visit to the place was only casual.

1508. The pronoun *hum* (their) in the expression *Adbāra-hum* (their rear) used in this verse shows that the party who left the city with Lot did not consist of his two daughters only, as stated in the Bible (Gen. chap. 19), but of other believers as well, some of whom must have been males, as the plural masculine pronoun indicates. This view is supported by another passage in the Bible (Gen. 18 : 32).

1509. The words may have been used figuratively, meaning 'let none of you give thought to,' or 'feel anxious for,' those left behind.

1510. Lot had been told by his people not to bring strangers into the city and so when the guests came to him they were glad that he would be taken to task for having defied their warnings.

70. 'And fear Allāh and do not humiliate me.'[1511]

وَاتَّقُوا اللّٰهَ وَلَا تُخْزُوْنِ ۝٧٠

71. They said, 'Did we not forbid thee *to entertain* any people?'[1512]

قَالُوْٓا اَوَلَمْ نَنْهَكَ عَنِ الْعٰلَمِيْنَ ۝٧١

72. [a]He said, 'These are my daughters[1513] *who are guarantee enough* if you must do *something*.'

قَالَ هٰٓؤُلَآءِ بَنٰتِيْٓ اِنْ كُنْتُمْ فٰعِلِيْنَ ۝٧٢

73. By thy life, they, *too*, in their mad intoxication are wandering in distraction.

لَعَمْرُكَ اِنَّهُمْ لَفِيْ سَكْرَتِهِمْ يَعْمَهُوْنَ ۝٧٣

74. [b]Then the punishment seized them at sunrise.

فَاَخَذَتْهُمُ الصَّيْحَةُ مُشْرِقِيْنَ ۝٧٤

75. [c]We turned *their town* upside down and We rained upon them stones of clay.

فَجَعَلْنَا عَالِيَهَا سَافِلَهَا وَاَمْطَرْنَا عَلَيْهِمْ حِجَارَةً مِّنْ سِجِّيْلٍ ۝٧٥

76. [d]Surely, in this are *many* Signs for those who use their understanding.[1514]

اِنَّ فِيْ ذٰلِكَ لَاٰيٰتٍ لِّلْمُتَوَسِّمِيْنَ ۝٧٦

77. And that *town* [e]lies on a road that *still* exists.[1515]

وَاِنَّهَا لَبِسَبِيْلٍ مُّقِيْمٍ ۝٧٧

[a]11 : 79. [b]11 : 82. [c]11 : 83. [d]29 : 36; 51 : 38. [e]37 : 138.

1511. Lot begged his people not to disgrace him for offering hospitality to the strangers.

1512. As relations between Lot's people and the neighbouring tribes were strained, his people had warned him not to bring strangers into the city. But as travel was neither safe nor comfortable in those parts of the country, Prophet Lot would entertain lonely and stranded wayfarers in his house. This was resented by his people, who were looking for a pretext to expel him from the city, being already tired of his teaching and preaching. But they could not do so without a valid excuse. Now they found a seemingly good excuse for venting their wrath on him because he had given shelter to strangers in his house against their warnings. From this it is clear that Lot's people did not come to him with the wicked intention of committing sodomy with his guests, but to convey to him the warning that they had found a valid excuse to expel him from the town. This seemed to be the reason of their rejoicing.

1513. See 11 : 79.

1514. *Mutawassimīn* is plural of *Mutawassim* which is derived from *Twassama* and means, one who deliberates over a thing and examines it or does so repeatedly to obtain a clear knowledge of it (Aqrab).

1515. A way is said to be *Muqīm* when it continues to be used by wayfarers. The way referred to here, *i.e.*, the one connecting Arabia with Syria, is still in use, thus fulfilling the prophecy implied in the adjective used for it in this verse. The way passes along the Dead Sea which is locally known as the Sea of Lot.

78. Surely, [a]in this is a Sign for believers.

إِنَّ فِي ذَٰلِكَ لَآيَةً لِّلْمُؤْمِنِينَ ﴿٧٨﴾

79. And [b]the People of the Wood,[1516] *too*, were surely wrong-doers.

وَإِن كَانَ أَصْحَابُ الْأَيْكَةِ لَظَالِمِينَ ﴿٧٩﴾

80. So [c]We chastised them *also*. And they both *lie* on an open highway.[1517]

ع فَانتَقَمْنَا مِنْهُمْ وَإِنَّهُمَا لَبِإِمَامٍ مُّبِينٍ ﴿٨٠﴾

R. 6 81. And the People of the Ḥijr[1518] *also* treated the Messengers as liars.

وَلَقَدْ كَذَّبَ أَصْحَابُ الْحِجْرِ الْمُرْسَلِينَ ﴿٨١﴾

82. And We gave them[1519] Our Signs, but they turned away from them.

وَآتَيْنَاهُمْ آيَاتِنَا فَكَانُوا عَنْهَا مُعْرِضِينَ ﴿٨٢﴾

[a]26 : 9. [b]26 : 177; 38 : 14; 50 : 15. [c]26 : 190; 38 : 15; 50 : 15.

1516. The fact that, according to the Qur'ān, the Prophet Shu'aib was sent both to *Aṣḥāb al-Aikah, i.e.*, People of the Wood (26 : 177,178) and *Ahl Madyan*, People of Midian (11 : 85) shows that both are the names of the same people or, rather of two sections of the same people who had adopted two different means of livelihood, one living on commerce and the other keeping herds of camels and sheep. Evidence of the close relationship of the "People of the Wood" with the "People of Midian" is furnished by the fact that identical faults have been ascribed to both in the Qur'ān (7 : 86 & 26 : 182-184). Midian seems to be both the name of the tribe and the town in which these people lived at the head of the Gulf of Aqabah, near which was situated the wilderness of Aikah, abounding in dwarf trees of the species of wild plums and affording shelter to camels, sheep and goats ("The Gold Mines of Midian" by Sir Richard Francis Burton).

1517. In the case of the city of Lot the highway has been called 'the way that still exists' (v. 77) which implies a prophecy that it will continue to exist in the future. In the case of the habitation of 'the People of the Wood,' the road has been called 'an open highway.' The old road which connected Asia with Egypt has now ceased to be used by caravans, though as the word "open" hints, the track still remains.

1518. Ḥijr lay between Tabūk and Medina. Here lived the tribe of Thamūd to whom Ṣālih was sent as a Warner. The city appears to have been largely built of stones and was surrounded by a stone wall and ramparts. Hence this name.

1519. In the foregoing verses three different peoples have been mentioned— (*a*) the people of Lot; (*b*) the people of Shu'aib and (*c*) the people of Ṣāliḥ. They have not been mentioned in their chronological order but in the order of the distance of their towns from Mecca. The town of the people of Lot was the most distant of the three. Next in order of distance lived the people of Aikah. Ḥijr being situated between Tabūk and Medina, the tribe of Thamūd were the nearest of the three and it has consequently been mentioned last of all. This unusual order has been adopted in preference to the more natural one with a view to making the statement effective from the point of view of the persons addressed, the tribe that was least known to the Arabs being mentioned first and the tribe which the Arabs knew most being mentioned last.

83. And [a]they used to hew out houses in the mountains, in security.[1520]

وَكَانُوْا يَنْحِتُوْنَ مِنَ الْجِبَالِ بُيُوْتًا اٰمِنِيْنَ ﴿٨٣﴾

84. [b]But the punishment seized them in the morning,[1521]

فَاَخَذَتْهُمُ الصَّيْحَةُ مُصْبِحِيْنَ ﴿٨٤﴾

85. And all that they had earned availed them not.

فَمَآ اَغْنٰى عَنْهُمْ مَّا كَانُوْا يَكْسِبُوْنَ ﴿٨٥﴾

86. And [c]We have not created the heavens and the earth and all that is between the two but in accordance with the requirements of wisdom;[1521A] and [d]the Hour is sure to come. So do thou forbear with goodly forbearance.

وَمَا خَلَقْنَا السَّمٰوٰتِ وَالْاَرْضَ وَمَا بَيْنَهُمَآ اِلَّا بِالْحَقِّ ۭ
وَاِنَّ السَّاعَةَ لَاٰتِيَةٌ فَاصْفَحِ الصَّفْحَ الْجَمِيْلَ ﴿٨٦﴾

87. Verily, it is thy Lord Who is the Great Creator, the All-Knowing.

اِنَّ رَبَّكَ هُوَ الْخَلّٰقُ الْعَلِيْمُ ﴿٨٧﴾

88. And [e]We have, indeed, given thee the seven oft-repeated *verses*,[1522] and the Great Qur'ān.

وَلَقَدْ اٰتَيْنٰكَ سَبْعًا مِّنَ الْمَثَانِيْ وَالْقُرْاٰنَ الْعَظِيْمَ ﴿٨٨﴾

---

[a]7 : 75; 26 : 150. [b]7 : 79; 11 : 68. [c]3 : 192; 16 : 4; 38 : 28. [d]20 : 16; 40 : 60. [e]39 : 24.

1520. This verse shows that the Thamūd were a civilized, powerful and rich people. They had separate summer and winter resorts and led secure and comfortable lives. Even when they went to the hills in summer for recreation and change of climate and left their winter habitations, they felt free from attacks from any quarter. The verse also hints at the highly developed state of their architecture.

1521. It appears from 7 : 79 that the calamity referred to in this verse was an earthquake.

1521A. The creation of the universe and the wonderful design and order that pervade it surely lead to the one inescapable inference that human life is not limited to the temporary and short existence on this earth, and that a great purpose underlies it and man has not been created just to eat, drink and be merry for a while and then die an eternal death.

1522. According to such eminent authorities as 'Umar, 'Alī, Ibn 'Abbās and Ibn Mas'ūd, these words refer to the Opening Chapter of the Qur'ān, *i.e.*, Al-Fātiḥah, because it is repeated and recited in every *Rak'at* of the Prayer. The Holy Prophet is reported to have said that *Al-Sab'al-Mathānī* is the Opening Chapter of the Qur'ān (Bukhārī). This Chapter is also called 'Mother of the Qur'ān' (*Umm al-Qur'ān*) and 'the Opening Chapter of the Book' (*Fātiḥat Al-Kitāb*). According to Zajjāj and Abū Ḥayyān, the Opening Chapter is given this name because it contains the praises of God. The rest of the Qur'ān which follows the Opening Chapter has been called 'the Great Qur'ān' (*Al-Qur'ān al-'Aẓīm*). This name, however, equally applies to the First Chapter also inasmuch as a portion of the Book may rightly be called the Book itself. There is a saying of the Holy

89. [a]Stretch not thine eyes towards what We have bestowed on some classes of them for temporary enjoyment and grieve[1523] not for them; and lower thy wing *of mercy* for the believers.

لَا تَمُدَّنَّ عَيْنَيْكَ إِلَىٰ مَا مَتَّعْنَا بِهِۦٓ أَزْوَٰجًا مِّنْهُمْ وَ
لَا تَحْزَنْ عَلَيْهِمْ وَٱخْفِضْ جَنَاحَكَ لِلْمُؤْمِنِينَ ﴿٨٩﴾

90. And say, [b]'I am, indeed, a plain Warner.'

وَقُلْ إِنِّيٓ أَنَا ٱلنَّذِيرُ ٱلْمُبِينُ ﴿٩٠﴾

91. Because We *have decided to* send down *punishment* on those who have formed themselves into groups[1524] *against thee;*

كَمَآ أَنزَلْنَا عَلَى ٱلْمُقْتَسِمِينَ ﴿٩١﴾

92. Who have pronounced the Qur'ān to be *so many* lies.[1525]

ٱلَّذِينَ جَعَلُوا۟ ٱلْقُرْءَانَ عِضِينَ ﴿٩٢﴾

93. So by thy Lord, We will, surely, question them all

فَوَرَبِّكَ لَنَسْـَٔلَنَّهُمْ أَجْمَعِينَ ﴿٩٣﴾

94. Concerning that which they used to do.

عَمَّا كَانُوا۟ يَعْمَلُونَ ﴿٩٤﴾

95. So [c]declare openly that which thou art commanded *to convey* and turn aside from those who ascribe partners *to Allāh.*

فَٱصْدَعْ بِمَا تُؤْمَرُ وَأَعْرِضْ عَنِ ٱلْمُشْرِكِينَ ﴿٩٥﴾

96. [d]We will, certainly, suffice thee against those who mock—

إِنَّا كَفَيْنَٰكَ ٱلْمُسْتَهْزِءِينَ ﴿٩٦﴾

---

[a]20 : 132. [b]22 : 50; 29 : 51; 51 51,52; 67: 27. [c]5 : 68. [d]2 : 138.

Prophet to the effect that the Opening Chapter of the Qur'ān is also 'the Great Qur'ān' (Musnad v. 2, p. 448). In fact, this Chapter constitutes an abridgement of the whole of the Qur'ān or, as it is said, it is the Qur'ān in miniature; the Book as a whole having been summarised and epitomised in it. *Mathānī* being also the plural of *Mathnā*, which means praise, the verse would mean that *Sūrah* Al-Fātiḥah gives a comprehensive description of Divine attributes. *Mathānī* also meaning a bend of the valley, the verse would mean that Al-Fātiḥah fully explains the relationship of God to man.

1523. The real significance of the verse is that the Holy Prophet has been told not to grieve over the fact that disbelievers were about to be punished and all their riches, prosperity and glory of which they are so proud would be of no avail to them.

1524. The Meccans had formed themselves into several groups and had taken upon themselves different duties to put obstacles in the way of the Holy Prophet, or these different groups had assigned to themselves different roles when they had resolved to kill him; *Muqtasimīn* also signifying, 'those who allotted different duties to one another.'

1525. *'Iḍīn* is the plural of *'Iḍah* which means, a lie or falsehood; a calumny; an enchantment; a piece, part or portion of a thing; a party, sect or class of people (Lane).

الَّذِيْنَ يَجْعَلُوْنَ مَعَ اللّٰهِ اِلٰهًا اٰخَرَ ۚ فَسَوْفَ يَعْلَمُوْنَ ﴿٩٧﴾

97. Who set up another god with Allāh, but soon shall they come to know.

وَلَقَدْ نَعْلَمُ اَنَّكَ يَضِيْقُ صَدْرُكَ بِمَا يَقُوْلُوْنَ ﴿٩٨﴾

98. And, indeed, [a]We know that thy bosom becomes straitened[1526] because of what they say.

فَسَبِّحْ بِحَمْدِ رَبِّكَ وَكُنْ مِّنَ السّٰجِدِيْنَ ﴿٩٩﴾

99. But [b]glorify thy Lord praising Him, and be of those who prostrate themselves *before Him.*

وَاعْبُدْ رَبَّكَ حَتّٰى يَاْتِيَكَ الْيَقِيْنُ ﴿١٠٠﴾

100. And continue worshipping thy Lord till death comes to thee.[1527]

---

[a]6 : 34; 11 : 13. [b]20 : 131; 50 : 40; 110 : 4.

1526. The Holy Prophet was not grieved because the disbelievers mocked at him but because they associated other gods with Allāh. His grief was due to his jealous love for God on the one hand and to his sincere solicitude for his people on the other.

1527. The verse purports to say that inasmuch as the main purpose of the Holy Prophet's mission, *viz.*, the establishment of the Unity of God, was now going to be fulfilled, he should in joyous thanks-giving extol the praises of God and bow down to Him in devoted prostration.

CHAPTER 16

AL-NAḤL

(*Revealed before Hijrah*)

Date of Revelation and Context

This *Sūrah* was revealed at Mecca. Ibn 'Abbās makes an exception of vv. 96, 97 and 98, which according to him were revealed at Medina. Professor Noldeke, however, thinks that the *Sūrah* was revealed at Mecca with the exception of vv. 44,112, 120, 121 and 126. It is prefaced with no abbreviated letters. As the subject-matter of a *Sūrah* is an amplification and expansion of the abbreviated letters placed at its head and is governed by them, the subject-matter of a *Sūrah* which has no abbreviated letters constitutes, in fact, a continuation of the subject-matter of the preceding *Sūrah* which has abbreviated letters in its beginning; and is subject to, and governed by, those abbreviated letters. Thus the subject-matter of this *Sūrah* should be considered as a continuation of the subject-matter of the preceding *Sūrah* Al-Ḥijr, and should be taken as governed by the letters *Alif Lām Rā*, placed in the beginning of that *Sūrah* ; only the method of approach and treatment of the subject is different.

Subject-Matter

Quite appropriately the *Sūrah* has been given the title of Al-Naḥl (lit. the Bee), because by a reference to the natural instinct of the bee which has been termed *Waḥy* in the Qur'ān (16 : 69) attention is drawn to the fact that the entire universe depends for its smooth and successful working on *Waḥy*, whether manifest or hidden, direct or indirect. This subject constitutes the pivot or basic theme of the *Sūrah*. Moreover, the subject of *Jihād* has been introduced here as an important subject. As *Jihād* was to become the target of attacks from all quarters, it is hinted that, like honey which is protected by the bee from undue interference by its God-given sting, the Qur'ān which is a store-house of spiritual honey shall be protected by the use of force which Muslims will have to employ to protect it. Believers are then told that if they wish their kith and kin to accept the Qur'ān they should see that their own hearts are cleansed because without purity of heart it is impossible to know God. God does not compel anyone to accept the truth, because by using force the very purpose of religion is defeated.

Next, the *Sūrah* enters into a discussion of the Life after death and it is stated that even in this world nations are resurrected and given a new life, and it is with their *Hijrah* (Emigration) that their resurrection begins. Accordingly, the Holy Prophet also would have to leave his native place and emigrate to Medina because it was essential for the spiritual development of his followers that they should be separated from disbelievers and be educated and trained in the teaching of their religion in congenial environments From this the conclusion is drawn that if it is so necessary for the spiritual progress of believers to undergo *Hijrah* in this world, how far more is it necessary for the permanent spiritual advancement of man that he should undergo a spiritual *Hijrah* which is another name for death. After this *Hijrah* the Faithful and the disbelievers begin to travel on separate paths ; the disbelievers go to Hell and the Faithful bask in the sunshine of Divine Grace and scale the heights of at-one-ment with God. The subject that great and wholesome results will flow from the Holy Prophet's *Hijrah* (Emigration) is continued. The *Sūrah* proceeds briefly to deal with the question, why respite is granted to disbelievers and why they are not forced to accept the Truth. This leads to the treatment of the objection that if the Holy Prophet is a true Messenger of God, why is his teaching at variance with that of earlier Prophets. In answer to this objection it is stated that the real teaching which former Prophets gave to their peoples greatly differed from the current, adulterated and corrupt teachings attributed to them. In fact, a new Prophet comes only when former Teachings become corrupt and lose their title to Divine protection. By citing the example of the bee, the *Sūrah* draws attention to the fact that just as, guided by Divine inspiration, the bee collects its food from fruits and flowers and converts it into delicious and wholesome honey, it is in the fitness of things that for his moral regeneration and spiritual development man should be guided by revelation, and proceeds to say that just as honey varies in quality, so are all men not of equal spiritual development. Like the different colours and flavours of honey, revelations of various Prophets also are of different patterns. Then one more argument is given to establish the need of Divine revelation. When with the passage of time people become separated from the era of a Prophet and vested interests grow up and become entrenched and privileges flow from father to son and all natural avenues of progress and advancement are closed upon the common man, God raises a new Prophet who wages a relentless war against this tyranny of man against man, and the so-called leaders who erstwhile enjoyed monopoly of power and benefit are dethroned from seats of authority and the common men who follow the new Prophet take their place. The chains of bondage of men are broken and they begin to breathe in an atmosphere of true freedom. Next, disbelievers are warned that great changes which are decreed to be brought about by means of the Qur'ān would take place very soon. The time cries for a change and the new Message possesses all the essential qualities and ingredients of a perfect Teaching. The followers of this new Teaching will succeed and all power and dominion will pass into their hands. A veritable war will be waged against disbelief and its leaders will be destroyed. Towards the end of the *Sūrah* the Holy Prophet is told that the sphere and scope of his preaching should now widen and embrace in its orbit Christians and Jews. This would excite a new opposition and Muslims would suffer persecution from all quarters; but the Divine cause of Islām would continue to grow and prosper amid opposition and persecution, and its enemies would meet with their deserved fate.

سُوْرَةُ النَّحْلِ مَكِّيَّةٌ (١٦)

1. [a]In the name of Allāh, the Gracious, the Merciful.

بِسْمِ اللّٰهِ الرَّحْمٰنِ الرَّحِيْمِ ①

2. [b]The decree of Allāh is at hand,[1528] so seek ye not to hasten it. Holy is He and Exalted far above all that which they associate *with Him*.

اَتٰۤى اَمْرُ اللّٰهِ فَلَا تَسْتَعْجِلُوْهُ ؕ سُبْحٰنَهٗ وَتَعٰلٰى عَمَّا يُشْرِكُوْنَ ②

3. He sends down the angels with revelation[1529] by His command on whomsoever of His servants He pleases, *saying*, 'Warn *people* that there is no god but I, so take Me *alone* for your Protector.'

يُنَزِّلُ الْمَلٰٓئِكَةَ بِالرُّوْحِ مِنْ اَمْرِهٖ عَلٰى مَنْ يَّشَآءُ مِنْ عِبَادِهٖۤ اَنْ اَنْذِرُوْۤا اَنَّهٗ لَاۤ اِلٰهَ اِلَّاۤ اَنَا فَاتَّقُوْنِ ③

4. [c]He has created the heavens and the earth in accordance with the requirements of wisdom.[1530] Exalted is He far above all that they associate *with Him*.

خَلَقَ السَّمٰوٰتِ وَالْاَرْضَ بِالْحَقِّ ؕ تَعٰلٰى عَمَّا يُشْرِكُوْنَ ④

5. [d]He has created man from a *mere* drop of fluid, but lo ! he is an open disputer.[1531]

خَلَقَ الْاِنْسَانَ مِنْ نُّطْفَةٍ فَاِذَا هُوَ خَصِيْمٌ مُّبِيْنٌ ⑤

---

[a]1 : 1. [b]5 : 53. [c]3: 192 ; 14 : 20 ; 15 : 86 ; 29 : 45 ; 39 : 6 ; 64 : 4.
[d]18 : 38 ; 22 : 6 ; 23 : 13-14 ; 35 : 12 ; 36 : 78 ; 40 : 68.

1528. The words mean that the time of punishment for disbelievers, or the time of the ushering in of the new order has already arrived.

1529. By ***Rūḥ***, (which signifies soul or spirit; Divine revelation; the Qur'ān; etc.—Lane), is here meant the life-giving Word of God. The word also denotes a Prophet's Divine Message because of its life-giving qualities.

1530. The expression 'with the requirements of wisdom' may mean that heavens and earth have their allotted tasks in the spiritual regeneration of man so that both jointly produce the desired result. Or it may mean that God has created the heavens and the earth so that they may serve to turn man's attention to God, and man may see that nothing is perfect by itself except Him. The heavens stand in need of earth for the performance of their work and likewise the earth is dependent on heavens and both are subject to the Will of God. So the purpose of the creation of the heavens and the earth is to demonstrate to man the fact that nothing is perfect in itself except God.

1531. After God had created the heavens and the earth according to a definite system of laws, He created man and sent down His revelation for his guidance. But notwithstanding the fact that after having created man from an apparently contemptible seed God endowed him with the highest faculties, he, instead of acting upon the guidance vouchsafed to him by God, starts questioning His powers and prerogatives.

6. And [a]the cattle too He has created; you find in them warmth and *other* uses; and of *the flesh of some of* them you eat.

وَالْاَنْعَامَ خَلَقَهَا ۚ لَكُمْ فِيْهَا دِفْءٌ وَّمَنَافِعُ وَمِنْهَا
تَاْكُلُوْنَ ﴿٦﴾

7. And in them there is ornament *and dignity* for you when you bring *them* home in the evening and when you drive *them* forth to pasture in the morning.

وَلَكُمْ فِيْهَا جَمَالٌ حِيْنَ تُرِيْحُوْنَ وَحِيْنَ تَسْرَحُوْنَ ﴿٧﴾

8. And [b]they carry your loads to a land which you could not reach except with great hardship to yourselves. Surely, your Lord is Compassionate, Merciful.

وَتَحْمِلُ اَثْقَالَكُمْ اِلٰى بَلَدٍ لَّمْ تَكُوْنُوْا بٰلِغِيْهِ اِلَّا بِشِقِّ
الْاَنْفُسِ ۚ اِنَّ رَبَّكُمْ لَرَءُوْفٌ رَّحِيْمٌ ﴿٨﴾

9. And [c]*He has created* horses and mules and asses that you may ride them, and *as a source of* beauty.[1532] And He will create what you do not *yet* know.[1532A]

وَّالْخَيْلَ وَالْبِغَالَ وَالْحَمِيْرَ لِتَرْكَبُوْهَا وَزِيْنَةً ۚ وَّيَخْلُقُ
مَا لَا تَعْلَمُوْنَ ﴿٩﴾

10. And upon Allāh rests *the showing of* the right way, and there are ways which deviate *from the right course*. And [d]if He had *enforced* His Will, He would have guided you all.

وَعَلَى اللّٰهِ قَصْدُ السَّبِيْلِ وَمِنْهَا جَآئِرٌ ۚ وَلَوْ شَآءَ
لَهَدٰىكُمْ اَجْمَعِيْنَ ﴿١٠﴾ ع

R. 2 11. [e]He it is Who sends down water for you from the clouds; out of it you have your drink, and *there grow* from it trees on which you pasture *your cattle*.

هُوَ الَّذِيْٓ اَنْزَلَ مِنَ السَّمَآءِ مَآءً لَّكُمْ مِّنْهُ شَرَابٌ
وَّمِنْهُ شَجَرٌ فِيْهِ تُسِيْمُوْنَ ﴿١١﴾

[a]6 : 143; 23 : 22; 36 : 72-74; 40 : 80-81. [b]6 : 143; 36 : 73; 40 : 81. [c]36 : 73; 40 : 81; 43 : 13. [d]6 : 150 ; 10 : 100 ; 11 : 119. [e]2 : 23 ; 6 : 100 ; 13 : 18 ; 16 : 66 ; 22 : 64.

1532. When God has taken so much care to provide for the physical and material needs of man, the idea cannot be entertained for a single moment that He should have neglected to make a similar provision for his spiritual needs.

1532A. The words may mean that God will bring into existence new means of transport which were yet unknown to man. The prophecy has been wonderfully fulfilled in the form of railway trains, steamships, motor-cars, aeroplanes, etc. God alone knows what new means of transport are yet to be invented.

12. [a]Therewith He grows corn for you and the olive and the date-palm and the grapes and all manner of fruit. Surely, in that is a Sign for a people who reflect.[1533]

يُنْبِتُ لَكُمْ بِهِ الزَّرْعَ وَالزَّيْتُوْنَ وَالنَّخِيْلَ وَالْاَعْنَابَ وَمِنْ كُلِّ الثَّمَرٰتِ ؕ اِنَّ فِيْ ذٰلِكَ لَاٰيَةً لِّقَوْمٍ يَّتَفَكَّرُوْنَ ﴿۱۲﴾

13. And [b]He has pressed into service for you the night and the day and the sun and the moon; and the stars *too* have been pressed into service by His command. Surely, in that are Signs for a people who use their understanding.

وَسَخَّرَ لَكُمُ الَّيْلَ وَالنَّهَارَ ۙ وَالشَّمْسَ وَالْقَمَرَ ؕ وَالنُّجُوْمُ مُسَخَّرٰتٌۢ بِاَمْرِهٖ ؕ اِنَّ فِيْ ذٰلِكَ لَاٰيٰتٍ لِّقَوْمٍ يَّعْقِلُوْنَ ﴿۱۳﴾

14. And the things of diverse hues that He has created for you in the [c]earth *also serve your purpose*.[1534] Surely, in that is a Sign for a people who take heed.[1535]

وَمَا ذَرَاَ لَكُمْ فِي الْاَرْضِ مُخْتَلِفًا اَلْوَانُهٗ ؕ اِنَّ فِيْ ذٰلِكَ لَاٰيَةً لِّقَوْمٍ يَّذَّكَّرُوْنَ ﴿۱۴﴾

15. And [d]He it is Who has subjected to you the sea that you may eat therefrom fresh flesh and may take forth therefrom *articles* which you wear as ornaments.

وَهُوَ الَّذِيْ سَخَّرَ الْبَحْرَ لِتَاْكُلُوْا مِنْهُ لَحْمًا طَرِيًّا وَّتَسْتَخْرِجُوْا مِنْهُ حِلْيَةً تَلْبَسُوْنَهَا ۚ وَتَرَى

[a]6 : 100; 13 : 5. [b]7 : 55; 13 : 3; 14 : 34; 35 14; 39 : 6. [c]13 : 5; 39 : 22. [d]35 : 13 ; 45 : 13.

1533. The energy, which makes plants grow, might be latent in the soil, but it does not come into play unless the soil receives water from heaven. Even so man may possess most excellent inherent faculties, but he cannot develop them without the help of Divine revelation. To base man's spiritual development upon his intellect alone is like saying that the earth can grow plants without the help of water.

1534. One of the most wonderful features of God's creation is that no two things or persons are exactly alike. But for this diversity there would have been indescribable confusion and chaos in the world. It would have been difficult to distinguish one thing from another or one person from another person. Similarly, there is such diversity in the dispositions and temperaments of men that it is beyond human power to devise a teaching which may equally suit all natures. No man has full knowledge of the diversity that exists in nature. God alone knows these differences and diversities and, therefore, He alone can give a Teaching which can equally suit and benefit all.

1535. Each of the three words, *viz.*, *Yatafakkarūn*, *Ya'qilūn* and *Yadhdhakkarūn* which have been placed at the end of vv. 12th, 13th and 14th respectively may be understood not only as especially appropriate to the theme of the particular verse in which it is used, but also as applicable to the general theme dealt with collectively in the three verses, their use in their particular places being determined by the degree of their importance. The word "reflection" has been used first because it constitutes the first means for, and of all moral qualities it is the first to be awakened in, the process of the moral reformation of man. From the habit of reflection grows understanding or 'making use of reason.' At this second stage man accomplishes his moral reformation. After this comes the third stage when temptations have been completely overcome and moral struggle ceases and man 'takes heed' and is self-admonished and the doing of good works becomes a part of his nature.

And thou seest the ships ploughing through it, *that you may journey*[1536] *thereby* and that you may seek of His bounty *in other ways* and that you may be grateful.

الْفُلْكَ مَوَاخِرَ فِيهِ وَلِتَبْتَغُوا مِنْ فَضْلِهِ وَلَعَلَّكُمْ
تَشْكُرُونَ ﴿١٥﴾

16. And [a]He has placed in the earth firm mountains lest it quake[1537] with you and rivers and routes[1538] that you may find the way *to your destination*.

وَأَلْقَىٰ فِي الْأَرْضِ رَوَاسِيَ أَنْ تَمِيدَ بِكُمْ وَأَنْهَارًا
وَسُبُلًا لَعَلَّكُمْ تَهْتَدُونَ ﴿١٦﴾

17. And, *He has set up other* marks; *by them* and by the stars they follow the right direction.[1539]

وَعَلَامَاتٍ ۚ وَبِالنَّجْمِ هُمْ يَهْتَدُونَ ﴿١٧﴾

18. Is He, then, Who creates like one who creates not? Will you not then take heed?

أَفَمَنْ يَخْلُقُ كَمَنْ لَا يَخْلُقُ ۗ أَفَلَا تَذَكَّرُونَ ﴿١٨﴾

19. And [b]if you try to count the favours of Allāh, you will not be able to number them. Surely, Allāh is Most Forgiving, Merciful.

وَإِنْ تَعُدُّوا نِعْمَةَ اللَّهِ لَا تُحْصُوهَا ۗ إِنَّ اللَّهَ
لَغَفُورٌ رَحِيمٌ ﴿١٩﴾

20. And [c]Allāh knows what you keep hidden and what you disclose.

وَاللَّهُ يَعْلَمُ مَا تُسِرُّونَ وَمَا تُعْلِنُونَ ﴿٢٠﴾

21. And [d]those on whom they call beside Allāh create not anything, but they are themselves created.

وَالَّذِينَ يَدْعُونَ مِنْ دُونِ اللَّهِ لَا يَخْلُقُونَ شَيْئًا
وَهُمْ يُخْلَقُونَ ﴿٢١﴾

[a]13 : 4 ; 21 : 32. [b]14 : 35. [c]2: 78 ; 27 : 26; 64 : 5. [d]7 : 192; 25 : 4.

1536. The sea is a most important source of material benefits to man. It is the great repository of water from which the sun supplies us with rain. It is also a great highway for travel and commerce and an important source of food for man.

1537. Geology has established the fact that mountains have, to a great extent, made secure the earth against earthquakes.

1538. The word *Subul* (routes) here does not mean the artificial roads constructed by human hands but natural pathways formed by mountain-passes, rivers and valleys which have served as highways throughout the ages.

1539. The verse signifies that had the earth been of uniform surface and there had been no ups and downs, no valleys, mountains or rivers, it would have been almost impossible for men to find their way from one place to another. The distinctive physical features of the earth's surface help men to know their way. Today these landmarks have proved to be of great help in air navigation. The stars also help wayfarers to find their way on land and sea.

22. *They are* dead, not living; and they know not when they will be raised.

ع ٢ أَمْوَاتٌ غَيْرُ أَحْيَاءٍ ۖ وَمَا يَشْعُرُونَ أَيَّانَ يُبْعَثُونَ ﴿٢٢﴾

R. 3 23. [a]Your God is One God. And as to those who believe not in the Hereafter, their hearts are strangers *to truth* and they are full of pride.

إِلَٰهُكُمْ إِلَٰهٌ وَاحِدٌ ۚ فَالَّذِينَ لَا يُؤْمِنُونَ بِالْآخِرَةِ
قُلُوبُهُمْ مُنْكِرَةٌ وَهُمْ مُسْتَكْبِرُونَ ﴿٢٣﴾

24. Undoubtedly, [b]Allāh knows what they keep secret and what they disclose. Surely, He loves not the proud.

لَا جَرَمَ أَنَّ اللَّهَ يَعْلَمُ مَا يُسِرُّونَ وَمَا يُعْلِنُونَ ۚ
إِنَّهُ لَا يُحِبُّ الْمُسْتَكْبِرِينَ ﴿٢٤﴾

25. And When it is said to them, 'What *think ye* of that which your Lord has sent down?' [c]they say, 'They are mere stories of the ancients.'

وَإِذَا قِيلَ لَهُمْ مَاذَا أَنْزَلَ رَبُّكُمْ ۙ قَالُوا أَسَاطِيرُ
الْأَوَّلِينَ ﴿٢٥﴾

26. *The consequences will be* [d]that they shall bear their burdens in full on the Day of Resurrection, and *also a portion* of the burdens of those whom they lead astray without knowledge. Behold ! evil is that which they bear.

لِيَحْمِلُوا أَوْزَارَهُمْ كَامِلَةً يَوْمَ الْقِيَامَةِ ۙ وَمِنْ أَوْزَارِ
ع ٩ الَّذِينَ يُضِلُّونَهُمْ بِغَيْرِ عِلْمٍ ۗ أَلَا سَاءَ مَا يَزِرُونَ ﴿٢٦﴾

R. 4 27. Those who were before them *also* devised plans, but [e]Allāh came upon their structure from the *very* foundations, so that the roof fell down upon them from above them,[1540] and the punishment came upon them from where they knew not.

قَدْ مَكَرَ الَّذِينَ مِنْ قَبْلِهِمْ فَأَتَى اللَّهُ بُنْيَانَهُمْ مِنَ
الْقَوَاعِدِ فَخَرَّ عَلَيْهِمُ السَّقْفُ مِنْ فَوْقِهِمْ وَأَتَاهُمُ
الْعَذَابُ مِنْ حَيْثُ لَا يَشْعُرُونَ ﴿٢٧﴾

[a]2 : 164; 5 : 74; 22 : 35 ; 37 : 5. [b]16 : 20. [c]8 : 32; 68 : 16; 83 : 14. [d]29 : 14.
[e]39 : 26; 59 : 3.

1540. It was no ordinary destruction which overtook the opponents of past Prophets. They were destroyed root and branch. The very foundations of the edifices they had erected and the walls and the roofs thereof tumbled down upon them, that is to say, neither the leaders nor their followers were spared.

28. Then on the Day of Resurrection He will humiliate them and will say, [a]'Where are My partners for whose sake you used to oppose *My Prophets*?' Those endowed with knowledge will say, 'This day humiliation and affliction will surely *befall* the disbelievers.'

ثُمَّ يَوْمَ الْقِيٰمَةِ يُخْزِيْهِمْ وَيَقُوْلُ اَيْنَ شُرَكَآءِيَ
الَّذِيْنَ كُنْتُمْ تُشَآقُّوْنَ فِيْهِمْ ۭ قَالَ الَّذِيْنَ اُوْتُوا
الْعِلْمَ اِنَّ الْخِزْيَ الْيَوْمَ وَالسُّوْٓءَ عَلَى الْكٰفِرِيْنَ ﴿۲۸﴾

29. [b]Those whom the angels cause to die while they are wronging their souls, [c]will offer submission, *pleading*, 'We used not to do any evil.' *It will be said to them*, 'Nay, surely, Allāh knows well what you used to do,[1541]

الَّذِيْنَ تَتَوَفّٰىهُمُ الْمَلٰٓئِكَةُ ظَالِمِيْٓ اَنْفُسِهِمْ فَاَلْقَوُا
السَّلَمَ مَا كُنَّا نَعْمَلُ مِنْ سُوْٓءٍ ۭ بَلٰٓى اِنَّ اللّٰهَ عَلِيْمٌۢ
بِمَا كُنْتُمْ تَعْمَلُوْنَ ﴿۲۹﴾

30. [d]'So enter the gates of Hell, to abide therein. Evil indeed is the abode of the arrogant.'

فَادْخُلُوْٓا اَبْوَابَ جَهَنَّمَ خٰلِدِيْنَ فِيْهَا ۭ فَلَبِئْسَ مَثْوَى
الْمُتَكَبِّرِيْنَ ﴿۳۰﴾

31. And *when* it is said to the righteous, 'What *think ye of* that which your Lord has revealed?' they say, 'The best.' [e]For those who do good there is good in this world, and [f]the home of the Hereafter is *even* better. Excellent indeed is the abode of the righteous—

وَقِيْلَ لِلَّذِيْنَ اتَّقَوْا مَاذَآ اَنْزَلَ رَبُّكُمْ ۭ قَالُوْا خَيْرًا ۭ
لِلَّذِيْنَ اَحْسَنُوْا فِيْ هٰذِهِ الدُّنْيَا حَسَنَةٌ ۭ وَلَدَارُ
الْاٰخِرَةِ خَيْرٌ ۭ وَلَنِعْمَ دَارُ الْمُتَّقِيْنَ ﴿۳۱﴾

32. [g]Gardens of Eternity, which they will enter; through them flow streams. They will have therein what they wish for.[1542] Thus does Allāh reward the righteous,

جَنّٰتُ عَدْنٍ يَّدْخُلُوْنَهَا تَجْرِيْ مِنْ تَحْتِهَا الْاَنْهٰرُ
لَهُمْ فِيْهَا مَا يَشَآءُوْنَ ۭ كَذٰلِكَ يَجْزِي اللّٰهُ
الْمُتَّقِيْنَ ﴿۳۲﴾

---

[a]28 : 63, 75. [b]4 : 98; 8 : 51; 47 : 28. [c]16 : 88. [d]39 : 73; 40 : 77.
[e]39 : 11. [f]6 : 33; 12 : 110. [g]9 : 72; 13 : 24; 35 : 34; 61 : 13; 98 : 9.

1541. The disbelievers would protest that what they did was actuated by good intentions and pure motives and that they worshipped their false gods only as an aid to concentration on Divine attributes. The verse gives the lie to this sense of injured innocence of disbelievers.

1542. The desires of the righteous will become identified with God's Will, so they will desire only those things which it will be the Will of God to give them.

33. Those whom the angels cause to die while they are pure, [a]they say *to them*, 'Peace be unto you. Enter Heaven because of what you used to do.'

الَّذِيْنَ تَتَوَفّٰىهُمُ الْمَلٰٓئِكَةُ طَيِّبِيْنَ ۙ يَقُوْلُوْنَ سَلٰمٌ
عَلَيْكُمُ ۙ ادْخُلُوا الْجَنَّةَ بِمَا كُنْتُمْ تَعْمَلُوْنَ ﴿٣٣﴾

34. [b]What do *these disbelievers* wait for except that the angels should come upon them or that the decree of thy Lord[1543] should come to pass? So did those who were before them. [c]Allāh did not wrong them, but they used to wrong themselves.

هَلْ يَنْظُرُوْنَ اِلَّآ اَنْ تَاْتِيَهُمُ الْمَلٰٓئِكَةُ اَوْ يَاْتِيَ
اَمْرُ رَبِّكَ ۗ كَذٰلِكَ فَعَلَ الَّذِيْنَ مِنْ قَبْلِهِمْ ۗ وَمَا ظَلَمَهُمُ
اللّٰهُ وَلٰكِنْ كَانُوْٓا اَنْفُسَهُمْ يَظْلِمُوْنَ ﴿٣٤﴾

35. So the evil *consequences* of what they did overtook them and [d]that which they used to mock at encompassed them.[1544]

فَاَصَابَهُمْ سَيِّاٰتُ مَا عَمِلُوْا وَحَاقَ بِهِمْ مَّا كَانُوْا
بِهٖ يَسْتَهْزِءُوْنَ ﴿٣٥﴾ ع ١٠

R. 5 36. [e]And the idolaters say, 'If Allāh had *so* willed, we should not have worshipped anything beside Him, neither we nor our fathers, nor should we have forbidden anything without *command from* Him.' So did those who *opposed the Truth* before them. [f]Are the Messengers responsible for anything except the plain delivery of the Message?

وَقَالَ الَّذِيْنَ اَشْرَكُوْا لَوْ شَآءَ اللّٰهُ مَا عَبَدْنَا مِنْ
دُوْنِهٖ مِنْ شَيْءٍ نَّحْنُ وَلَآ اٰبَآؤُنَا وَلَا حَرَّمْنَا مِنْ
دُوْنِهٖ مِنْ شَيْءٍ ۗ كَذٰلِكَ فَعَلَ الَّذِيْنَ مِنْ قَبْلِهِمْ ۚ
فَهَلْ عَلَى الرُّسُلِ اِلَّا الْبَلٰغُ الْمُبِيْنُ ﴿٣٦﴾

37. And [g]We did raise among every people a Messenger *with the teaching*, 'Worship Allāh and shun the Evil One.' [h]Then among them were *some* whom Allāh guided and among them were *some* who became deserving of ruin. [i]So travel through the earth and see what was the end of those who treated *the Prophets* as liars!

وَلَقَدْ بَعَثْنَا فِيْ كُلِّ اُمَّةٍ رَّسُوْلًا اَنِ اعْبُدُوا اللّٰهَ
وَاجْتَنِبُوا الطَّاغُوْتَ ۚ فَمِنْهُمْ مَّنْ هَدَى اللّٰهُ
وَمِنْهُمْ مَّنْ حَقَّتْ عَلَيْهِ الضَّلٰلَةُ ۗ فَسِيْرُوْا فِي الْاَرْضِ
فَانْظُرُوْا كَيْفَ كَانَ عَاقِبَةُ الْمُكَذِّبِيْنَ ﴿٣٧﴾

---

[a]10 : 11; 13 : 25; 36 : 59; 39 : 74. [b]2 : 211; 6 : 159; 7 : 54. [c]9 : 70; 16 : 119; 29; 41; 30 : 10. [d]6 : 11; 21 : 42; 39 : 49; 45 : 34. [e]6 : 149; 43 : 21. [f]5 : 93,100; 24 : 55; 29 : 19; 36 : 18. [g]10 : 48; 13 : 8; 35 : 25. [h]7 : 31. [i]3 : 138; 6 : 12.

1543. 'The coming of angels' signifies the destruction of individual disbelievers, and 'the coming of God or of His decree' signifies their national ruin.

1544. The punishment of an evil deed is not an extraneous thing, but is the natural consequence of the deed itself and is also proportionate to it.

38. [a]If thou art solicitous of their guidance, then *know that* Allāh surely guides not those who lead *others* astray. And for such there are no helpers.

إِن تَحْرِصْ عَلَىٰ هُدَاهُمْ فَإِنَّ اللَّهَ لَا يَهْدِي مَن يُضِلُّ وَمَا لَهُم مِّن نَّاصِرِينَ ٣٨

39. And they swear by Allāh their strongest oaths, [b]that Allāh will not raise up those who die. [c]Nay, *He will certainly raise them up*. *This is* a true promise *the fulfilment of which is* binding on Him but most men know not.

وَأَقْسَمُوا بِاللَّهِ جَهْدَ أَيْمَانِهِمْ لَا يَبْعَثُ اللَّهُ مَن يَمُوتُ بَلَىٰ وَعْدًا عَلَيْهِ حَقًّا وَلَٰكِنَّ أَكْثَرَ النَّاسِ لَا يَعْلَمُونَ ٣٩

40. *He will surely raise them up* that He may make clear to them that wherein they differed, and that those who disbelieved may realize that they were liars.[1545]

لِيُبَيِّنَ لَهُمُ الَّذِي يَخْتَلِفُونَ فِيهِ وَلِيَعْلَمَ الَّذِينَ كَفَرُوا أَنَّهُمْ كَانُوا كَاذِبِينَ ٤٠

41. [d]Our word concerning a thing, when We will it, is only that We say to it, 'Be,'[1546] and it is.

إِنَّمَا قَوْلُنَا لِشَيْءٍ إِذَا أَرَدْنَاهُ أَن نَّقُولَ لَهُ كُن فَيَكُونُ ٤١

R. 6 42. And [e]*as to* those who leave their homes for the sake[1547] of Allāh after they are wronged, We will surely give them a goodly abode in this world; and truly the reward of the Hereafter is greater; if they but knew—

وَالَّذِينَ هَاجَرُوا فِي اللَّهِ مِن بَعْدِ مَا ظُلِمُوا لَنُبَوِّئَنَّهُمْ فِي الدُّنْيَا حَسَنَةً وَلَأَجْرُ الْآخِرَةِ أَكْبَرُ لَوْ كَانُوا يَعْلَمُونَ ٤٢

43. [f]Those who are steadfast and put their trust in their Lord.

الَّذِينَ صَبَرُوا وَعَلَىٰ رَبِّهِمْ يَتَوَكَّلُونَ ٤٣

---

[a]12 : 104; 28 : 57. [b]23 : 38; 45 : 25. [c]10 : 5; 21 : 105. [d]2 : 118; 3 : 48; 36 : 83; 40 : 69. [e]2 : 219; 4 : 101; 22 : 59. [f]29 : 60.

1545. Realization of truth on the Day of Resurrection will be so complete that disbelievers will admit that they were foolish to deny Resurrection. Indeed, it would be a full and complete realization.

1546. The word *kun* (be) does not mean that God gives the command to something already existing. It merely gives expression to a wish, and means that when God so expresses a wish, it finds immediate objective fulfilment.

1547. The expression, *fi-Allāh*, may mean: (*a*) For the sake of Allāh; (*b*) for the sake of God's religion, *i.e.*, for the sake of free and unfettered exercise of religion; (*c*) "in Allāh" which signifies that they had become completely lost in Allāh.

44. [a]And We sent not *as Messengers* before thee but men to whom We sent revelation—so ask those who possess the Reminder, if you know not—

وَمَآ اَرْسَلْنَا مِنْ قَبْلِكَ اِلَّا رِجَالًا نُّوْحِيْٓ اِلَيْهِمْ فَسْـَٔلُوْٓا اَهْلَ الذِّكْرِ اِنْ كُنْتُمْ لَا تَعْلَمُوْنَ ﴿٤٤﴾

45. [b]With clear Signs and Scriptures. And [c]We have sent down to thee the Reminder that thou mayest explain to mankind that which has been sent down to them, and that they may reflect.

بِالْبَيِّنٰتِ وَالزُّبُرِ ؕ وَاَنْزَلْنَآ اِلَيْكَ الذِّكْرَ لِتُبَيِّنَ لِلنَّاسِ مَا نُزِّلَ اِلَيْهِمْ وَلَعَلَّهُمْ يَتَفَكَّرُوْنَ ﴿٤٥﴾

النصف

46. [d]Do, then, those, who devise evil plans, feel secure that Allāh will not humiliate them in *their own* land, or that the punishment will not come upon them whence they do not know?

اَفَاَمِنَ الَّذِيْنَ مَكَرُوا السَّيِّاٰتِ اَنْ يَّخْسِفَ اللّٰهُ بِهِمُ الْاَرْضَ اَوْ يَاْتِيَهُمُ الْعَذَابُ مِنْ حَيْثُ لَا يَشْعُرُوْنَ ﴿٤٦﴾

47. Or that He will not seize them in their going to and fro[1548] so that they shall not be able to frustrate *His plans?*

اَوْ يَاْخُذَهُمْ فِيْ تَقَلُّبِهِمْ فَمَا هُمْ بِمُعْجِزِيْنَ ﴿٤٧﴾

48. Or that He will not destroy *them* through *a process of* gradual attrition?[1549] Your Lord is indeed Compassionate, Merciful.

اَوْ يَاْخُذَهُمْ عَلٰى تَخَوُّفٍ ؕ فَاِنَّ رَبَّكُمْ لَرَءُوْفٌ رَّحِيْمٌ ﴿٤٨﴾

49. Have they not observed, bowing in humility before Allāh, that the shadows of everything which Allāh has created shift from

اَوَلَمْ يَرَوْا اِلٰى مَا خَلَقَ اللّٰهُ مِنْ شَيْءٍ يَّتَفَيَّؤُا ظِلٰلُهٗ

[a]12 : 110; 21 : 8. [b]35 :26. [c]3 : 59 ; 15 : 7, 10; 20 : 100. [d]6 : 66 ; 17 : 69; 34 : 10; 67 : 17-18.

1548. The frequent journeying of disbelievers and their free and unrestricted movements in the land should not lead believers to think that their might is invincible and that their glory will never depart. Soon these movements will result in the destruction of their political power.

1549. *Takhawwuf* meaning "to take little by little" (Lane), the verse signifies that the power of disbelievers will gradually decline, or that before their final overthrow they would be seized with a consuming fear of the growing power of Islām and its ultimate triumph.

the right and *from* the left,[1550] and they are being humbled?

عَنِ الْيَمِيْنِ وَالشَّمَآئِلِ سُجَّدًا لِّلّٰهِ وَهُمْ دٰخِرُوْنَ ﴿٤٩﴾

50. And [a]whatever is in the heavens and whatever creature is in the earth submits humbly to Allāh, and the angels *too*, and they are not proud.

وَلِلّٰهِ يَسْجُدُ مَا فِي السَّمٰوٰتِ وَمَا فِي الْأَرْضِ مِنْ
دَآبَّةٍ وَّالْمَلٰٓئِكَةُ وَهُمْ لَا يَسْتَكْبِرُوْنَ ﴿٥٠﴾

51. They fear their Lord above them, and [b]do what they are commanded.

يَخَافُوْنَ رَبَّهُمْ مِّنْ فَوْقِهِمْ وَيَفْعَلُوْنَ مَا
ع يُؤْمَرُوْنَ ﴿٥١﴾ السجدة

R. 7 52. Allāh has said, 'Take not *for worship* two gods. [c]There is only One[1551] God. So fear Me alone.'

وَقَالَ اللّٰهُ لَا تَتَّخِذُوْٓا إِلٰهَيْنِ اثْنَيْنِ إِنَّمَا هُوَ إِلٰهٌ
وَّاحِدٌ فَإِيَّايَ فَارْهَبُوْنِ ﴿٥٢﴾

53. And to Him belongs whatever is in the heavens and the earth and [d]to Him is obedience due for ever. Will you then take any other than Allāh as your Protector?

وَلَهُ مَا فِي السَّمٰوٰتِ وَالْأَرْضِ وَلَهُ الدِّيْنُ وَاصِبًا
أَفَغَيْرَ اللّٰهِ تَتَّقُوْنَ ﴿٥٣﴾

54. And [e]whatever blessing you have, it is from Allāh. And when affliction befalls you, it is unto Him that you cry *for help*;

وَمَا بِكُمْ مِّنْ نِّعْمَةٍ فَمِنَ اللّٰهِ ثُمَّ إِذَا مَسَّكُمُ الضُّرُّ
فَإِلَيْهِ تَجْـَٔرُوْنَ ﴿٥٤﴾

55. [f]Then, when He removes the affliction from you, behold! a party among you begins to ascribe associates to their Lord,

ثُمَّ إِذَا كَشَفَ الضُّرَّ عَنْكُمْ إِذَا فَرِيْقٌ مِّنْكُمْ بِرَبِّهِمْ
يُشْرِكُوْنَ ﴿٥٥﴾

[a]13 : 16; 22 : 19. [b]66 : 7. [c]16 : 23. [d]39 : 4. [e]4 : 80; 10 : 13; 23; 23 : 65; 30 : 34; 39 : 9. [f]10 : 13, 24; 29 : 66; 30 : 34; 39 : 9.

1550. It is a natural phenomenon that the shadow of everything after reaching a certain stage becomes contracted, signifying that its power, influence and glory are about to depart and that it is about to be reduced to a mere shadow of its former self. Thus disbelievers are warned that Divine punishment will result in the complete obliteration of their shadows while the shadow of the Holy Prophet will continue to expand and lengthen, because things have long shadows when the sun is at their backs, and the sun of the grace of God is at the back of the Holy Prophet.

1551. A study of the working of the universe reveals a wonderful uniformity of the system running through it. If there had been more gods than one, this uniformity would have disappeared. Moreover, if there had been two gods, one would have to be subordinate to the other to carry out his orders. In that case the existence of one of the two would be superfluous. But if both of them had been of an equal status, then each of them would have his own separate sphere of influence and control. In such an event differences certainly would have arisen between them. But both these suppositions are absurd. Hence there must be One God, the Only Creator of the entire universe.

56. [a]So as to deny that which We have bestowed upon them. Well, then, enjoy yourselves a while, but soon will you know.

لِيَكْفُرُوْا بِمَآ اٰتَيْنٰهُمْ ۚ فَتَمَتَّعُوْا ۗ فَسَوْفَ تَعْلَمُوْنَ ﴿۵۶﴾

57. And [b]they set apart *for their false gods* of which they know nothing, a portion of that which We have bestowed on them. By Allāh, you shall certainly be called to account for all that you have forged.

وَ يَجْعَلُوْنَ لِمَا لَا يَعْلَمُوْنَ نَصِيْبًا مِّمَّا رَزَقْنٰهُمْ ۗ
تَاللّٰهِ لَتُسْـَٔلُنَّ عَمَّا كُنْتُمْ تَفْتَرُوْنَ ﴿۵۷﴾

58. And [c]they ascribe daughters to Allāh—Holy is He—while they *themselves* have what they desire.[1552]

وَ يَجْعَلُوْنَ لِلّٰهِ الْبَنٰتِ سُبْحٰنَهٗ ۙ وَلَهُمْ مَّا يَشْتَهُوْنَ ﴿۵۸﴾

59. And [d]when to one of them is conveyed the tidings of *the birth of* a female, his face darkens[1552A] with *inward* suppressed grief;

وَ اِذَا بُشِّرَ اَحَدُهُمْ بِالْاُنْثٰى ظَلَّ وَجْهُهٗ مُسْوَدًّا
وَّ هُوَ كَظِيْمٌ ﴿۵۹﴾

60. He hides himself from the people because of the bad news he has had. Shall he keep it in spite of disgrace or shall he bury it in the dust?[1553] Verily, evil is that which they judge.

يَتَوَارٰى مِنَ الْقَوْمِ مِنْ سُوْٓءِ مَا بُشِّرَ بِهٖ ۗ اَيُمْسِكُهٗ
عَلٰى هُوْنٍ اَمْ يَدُسُّهٗ فِى التُّرَابِ ۗ اَلَا سَآءَ مَا
يَحْكُمُوْنَ ﴿۶۰﴾

61. The state of those who do not believe in the Hereafter is evil, [e]while all sublime attributes belong to Allāh and He is the Mighty, the Wise.

لِلَّذِيْنَ لَا يُؤْمِنُوْنَ بِالْاٰخِرَةِ مَثَلُ السَّوْءِ ۚ وَ لِلّٰهِ
الْمَثَلُ الْاَعْلٰى ۗ وَ هُوَ الْعَزِيْزُ الْحَكِيْمُ ﴿۶۱﴾ ع ۱۴

[a]29 : 67; 30 : 35. [b]6 : 137. [c]6 : 101; 37 : 153, 154; 43 : 17; 52 : 40; 53 : 22. [d]43 : 18. [e]30 : 28.

1552. The verse does not imply that the offence of disbelievers lies in attributing to God daughters and not sons though the Qur'ān has also strongly denounced the attribution of a son to God (19 : 91, 92). The verse only points to the folly of the disbelievers that they attribute daughters to God while they themselves feel humiliated at daughters being attributed to them.

1552A. *Iswadda Wajhu-hū* means, his face became black, *i.e*, his face became expressive of grief or overcast with gloom; he became grieved, sorrowful or confounded; he became disgraced (Lane).

1553. The reference is to the barbarous custom of burying alive of female children which was in vogue among certain Arab tribes. They had a very low conception of their womenfolk and accorded them an extremely degraded position in their society. The Qur'ān has strongly upheld the honour of women and has recognized all their legitimate rights, and in this respect it stands unique among all the Scriptures of the world.

R. 8 62. And *a*if Allāh were to punish men for their wrongdoing, He would not leave on *the earth* a living creature,[1554] but He gives them respite till an appointed term; and *b*when their term is come, they cannot remain behind a single hour, nor can they go ahead *of it*.

وَلَوْ يُؤَاخِذُ اللّٰهُ النَّاسَ بِظُلْمِهِمْ مَّا تَرَكَ عَلَيْهَا
مِنْ دَآبَّةٍ وَّلٰكِنْ يُّؤَخِّرُهُمْ اِلٰٓى اَجَلٍ مُّسَمًّى ۚ فَاِذَا
جَآءَ اَجَلُهُمْ لَا يَسْتَاْخِرُوْنَ سَاعَةً وَّلَا يَسْتَقْدِمُوْنَ ﴿٦٢﴾

63. And they assign to Allāh what they dislike *for themselves* and their tongues utter the lie that they will have the best *of everything*. Undoubtedly, theirs shall be the Fire, and *therein* shall they be abandoned.

وَيَجْعَلُوْنَ لِلّٰهِ مَا يَكْرَهُوْنَ وَتَصِفُ اَلْسِنَتُهُمُ الْكَذِبَ
اَنَّ لَهُمُ الْحُسْنٰى ۗ لَا جَرَمَ اَنَّ لَهُمُ النَّارَ وَاَنَّهُمْ
مُّفْرَطُوْنَ ﴿٦٣﴾

64. By Allāh, *c*We verily sent *Messengers* to *all* the peoples before thee; *d*but Satan made their works *appear* beautiful to them. So he is their patron this day, and they shall have a grievous punishment.

تَاللّٰهِ لَقَدْ اَرْسَلْنَآ اِلٰٓى اُمَمٍ مِّنْ قَبْلِكَ فَزَيَّنَ لَهُمُ
الشَّيْطٰنُ اَعْمَالَهُمْ فَهُوَ وَلِيُّهُمُ الْيَوْمَ وَلَهُمْ عَذَابٌ
اَلِيْمٌ ﴿٦٤﴾

65. And We have not sent down to thee the Book except that thou mayest explain to them that concerning which they have *created* differences and *e*as a guidance, and a mercy for a people who believe.

وَمَآ اَنْزَلْنَا عَلَيْكَ الْكِتٰبَ اِلَّا لِتُبَيِّنَ لَهُمُ الَّذِى اخْتَلَفُوْا
فِيْهِ ۙ وَهُدًى وَّرَحْمَةً لِّقَوْمٍ يُّؤْمِنُوْنَ ﴿٦٥﴾

66. And *f*Allāh has sent down water from the sky and has quickened therewith the earth after its death. Surely, in that is a Sign for a people who would listen *to the truth*.

وَاللّٰهُ اَنْزَلَ مِنَ السَّمَآءِ مَآءً فَاَحْيَا بِهِ الْاَرْضَ بَعْدَ
مَوْتِهَا ۗ اِنَّ فِىْ ذٰلِكَ لَاٰيَةً لِّقَوْمٍ يَّسْمَعُوْنَ ﴿٦٦﴾ ع

*a*10 : 12 ; 18 : 59 ; 35 : 46. *b*7 : 35 ; 10 : 50. *c*6 : 43 ; 22 : 53. *d*6 : 44 ; 8 : 49.
*e*6 : 158 ; 12 : 112 ; 16 : 90. *f*2 : 165 ; 13 : 18.

1554. The reason why punishment is delayed is that if all sins had been at once punished by God, the world would have come to an end and all life on earth would have become extinct. Man would have perished as a result of his sins and there would have been left no purpose in the survival of beasts, animals and birds, etc., after his destruction. Being created for man's use and benefit they would have perished with him.

R. 9   67. And ^asurely in the cattle *too* there is a lesson[1555] for you. We provide for you drink out of that which is in their bellies—from betwixt the faeces and the blood—milk pure *and* pleasant for those who drink *it*.

وَإِنَّ لَكُمْ فِى الْأَنْعَامِ لَعِبْرَةً نُسْقِيْكُمْ مِّمَّا فِىْ بُطُوْنِهٖ مِنْۢ بَيْنِ فَرْثٍ وَّدَمٍ لَّبَنًا خَالِصًا سَآئِغًا لِّلشّٰرِبِيْنَ ۝

68. ^bAnd of the fruits of the date-palms and the grapes, whence you obtain intoxicating 'drink and wholesome food.[1555A] Verily, in that is a Sign for a people who use their understanding.

وَمِنْ ثَمَرٰتِ النَّخِيْلِ وَالْأَعْنَابِ تَتَّخِذُوْنَ مِنْهُ سَكَرًا وَّرِزْقًا حَسَنًا ۗ إِنَّ فِىْ ذٰلِكَ لَاٰيَةً لِّقَوْمٍ يَّعْقِلُوْنَ ۝

69. And thy Lord revealed[1556] to the bee: 'Make thou houses in the hills and in the trees and in the trellises which they build,

وَأَوْحٰى رَبُّكَ إِلَى النَّحْلِ أَنِ اتَّخِذِىْ مِنَ الْجِبَالِ بُيُوْتًا وَّمِنَ الشَّجَرِ وَمِمَّا يَعْرِشُوْنَ ۝

70. 'Then eat of all *manner of* fruits, and follow the ways *taught thee by* thy Lord and *which* have been made easy *for thee.*' There comes forth from their bellies a drink of varying hues. Therein is healing for mankind. Surely, in

ثُمَّ كُلِىْ مِنْ كُلِّ الثَّمَرٰتِ فَاسْلُكِىْ سُبُلَ رَبِّكِ ذُلُلًا ۗ يَخْرُجُ مِنْۢ بُطُوْنِهَا شَرَابٌ مُّخْتَلِفٌ أَلْوَانُهٗ فِيْهِ شِفَآءٌ

---

^a23 : 22.   ^b13 : 5; 16 : 12; 23 : 20; 36 : 35.

1555. '*Ibrah*, meaning 'an indication or evidence whereby one passes from ignorance to knowledge' (Lane), alludes to some subtle process taking place inside the bellies of the animals. A study of the process of conversion of grass or leaves of trees which the animals eat into milk in the bellies of the animals leads to the conclusion that the natural propensities and inclinations of man cannot lead him to the right path unless they are controlled and regulated by some heavenly agency which is Divine revelation.

1555A. When things created by God remain in their natural and unadulterated form they constitute pure, wholesome and invigorating food. But when man interferes with their natural use he corrupts them. Similarly, as long as Divine Teaching remains intact, it is a source of great spiritual benefit, but when it is interfered with, it loses all its usefulness.

1556. Revelation here signifies the natural instincts with which God has endowed all creatures. The verse contains a beautiful hint that the entire universe depends for its smooth and successful working on revelation (or inspiration), whether manifest or hidden. In other words, all things and creatures serve the purpose of their existence only by working according to their natural instincts and inborn faculties and aptitudes. The bee has been selected as a prominent example, because its wonderful organization and work impress even a casual observer and are discernible even by the naked eye.

that is a Sign for a people who reflect.[1557]

لِلنَّاسِ ۭ اِنَّ فِيْ ذٰلِكَ لَاٰيَةً لِّقَوْمٍ يَّتَفَكَّرُوْنَ ۝٧٠

71. And Allāh creates you, then He causes you to die; and [a]there are *some* among you who are driven to the worst *state of* life with the result that they know nothing after *having had* knowledge. Surely, Allāh is All-Knowing, Powerful.

وَاللّٰهُ خَلَقَكُمْ ثُمَّ يَتَوَفّٰىكُمْ ڐ وَمِنْكُمْ مَّنْ يُّرَدُّ اِلٰٓى
اَرْذَلِ الْعُمُرِ لِكَيْ لَا يَعْلَمَ بَعْدَ عِلْمٍ شَيْـًٔا ۭ اِنَّ اللّٰهَ عَلِيْمٌ
قَدِيْرٌ ۝٧١ ع ٩/١٥

R. 10 72. And [b]Allāh has favoured some of you above others in *worldly* gifts. But those more favoured will not restore *any part of* their *worldly* gifts[1558] to those whom their right hands possess,[1559] so that they may be equal *sharers* in them. *Knowing this*, will they still deny the favour of Allāh?

وَاللّٰهُ فَضَّلَ بَعْضَكُمْ عَلٰي بَعْضٍ فِي الرِّزْقِ ۚ فَمَا
الَّذِيْنَ فُضِّلُوْا بِرَاۗدِّيْ رِزْقِهِمْ عَلٰي مَا مَلَكَتْ اَيْمَانُهُمْ
فَهُمْ فِيْهِ سَوَاۗءٌ ۭ اَفَبِنِعْمَةِ اللّٰهِ يَجْحَدُوْنَ ۝٧٢

[a]22 : 6. [b]24 : 23; 30 : 29.

1557. The subject of the bee has been further elaborated in this verse. God inspires the bee to collect its food from different fruits and flowers and then by means of the mechanism provided in its body and by the methods revealed to it by God it converts the collected food into honey. Honey possesses different colours and flavours, but all its different varieties are highly useful for men. This suggests that revelation has continued to descend on Prophets at different times and that the teachings of one Prophet differed in some details from the teachings of others, nevertheless all were the means of moral and spiritual regeneration for the people for whom they were designed.

1558. In every age some individuals or nations, by their superior intellect and harder work, come to acquire ascendancy and control over other individuals or nations. This is neither unfair nor unjust so long as proper opportunities are not denied to the less fortunate peoples also to make proper use of their talents and intelligence to earn the good things of life. But the "haves" have always set their face against all attempts on the part of the "have-nots" to better their condition and to have a share in the power and privileges they enjoy. In order to save the world from the tyranny of those in possession of power and privileges and to open the doors of progress and advancement to real merit and talent and thereby to rehabilitate justice and equality among mankind, God raises Reformers. Their advent heralds a new era and the dispossessed and the "have-nots" have their rights restored to them. Briefly, but very beautifully, the verse has laid down the Islamic law with regard to private ownership. Whereas on the one hand Islām has recognized the right of private ownership by emphasizing the word "their" in the expression 'of their worldly gifts' it has, by using the words 'will restore', also laid down the principle of the collective ownership of all things by all human beings as such, because only that thing is "restored" to another person which belongs to him. In fact, the Qur'ān has accepted the principle of dual ownership of everything—the right to possess a property to be recognized in the person who earns it by the sweat of his brow and the right in that property of all human beings as human beings. Islām, in reality, neither believes in the right of unrestricted private ownership nor in complete and unreserved possession of wealth and the means of its production by the State. It adopts the middle course.

1559. The expression clearly includes all persons under one's control such as private servants, subordinates, labourers, ryots etc.

73. And [a]Allāh has made for you mates from among yourselves, and has made for you, from your mates, sons and grandsons, and has provided you with good things. [b]Will they then believe in that which perishes and deny the favour of Allāh?[1560]

وَاللّٰهُ جَعَلَ لَكُمْ مِّنْ اَنْفُسِكُمْ اَزْوَاجًا وَّجَعَلَ لَكُمْ
مِّنْ اَزْوَاجِكُمْ بَنِيْنَ وَحَفَدَةً وَّرَزَقَكُمْ مِّنَ الطَّيِّبٰتِ
اَفَبِالْبَاطِلِ يُؤْمِنُوْنَ وَبِنِعْمَتِ اللّٰهِ هُمْ يَكْفُرُوْنَ ﴿٧٣﴾

74. And [c]they worship beside Allāh such as have no power to bestow on them any gift from the heavens or the earth, nor can they *ever* have such power.

وَيَعْبُدُوْنَ مِنْ دُوْنِ اللّٰهِ مَا لَا يَمْلِكُ لَهُمْ رِزْقًا
مِّنَ السَّمٰوٰتِ وَالْاَرْضِ شَيْـًٔا وَّلَا يَسْتَطِيْعُوْنَ ﴿٧٤﴾

75. So coin not similitudes for Allāh. Surely, Allāh knows and you know not.[1561]

فَلَا تَضْرِبُوْا لِلّٰهِ الْاَمْثَالَ ۗ اِنَّ اللّٰهَ يَعْلَمُ وَاَنْتُمْ لَا
تَعْلَمُوْنَ ﴿٧٥﴾

76. Allāh sets forth for you the parable of a slave who is owned,[1562] having no power over anything; and *a free man* whom We have provided with a fair provision from Us and [d]he spends thereof secretly and openly.[1563] Are they equal? Praise be to Allāh. But most of them know not.

ضَرَبَ اللّٰهُ مَثَلًا عَبْدًا مَّمْلُوْكًا لَّا يَقْدِرُ عَلٰى شَيْءٍ
وَّمَنْ رَّزَقْنٰهُ مِنَّا رِزْقًا حَسَنًا فَهُوَ يُنْفِقُ مِنْهُ سِرًّا
وَّجَهْرًا ۗ هَلْ يَسْتَوٗنَ ۗ اَلْحَمْدُ لِلّٰهِ ۗ بَلْ اَكْثَرُهُمْ لَا
يَعْلَمُوْنَ ﴿٧٦﴾

[a]4 : 2; 7 : 190; 30 : 22; 39 : 7. [b]29 : 68. [c]10 : 19; 22 : 72; 29 : 18. [d]2 : 275; 13 : 23.

1560. The verse refers to the instinct of private possession as an argument in support of the Unity of God.

1561. It is highly presumptuous on the part of man to devise a law regarding God while he is quite ignorant of His great and unlimited powers.

1562. The disbelievers are like a person who has lost all freedom of will and action and is the slave of his own low desires and fancies.

1563. The implied reference may be to the Holy Prophet—God's servant *par excellence.* (1) He served mankind secretly (by praying for them at night) and openly (by tangible acts of service). (2) He served mankind at all hours of the day and night.

77. And Allāh sets forth *another* parable of two men—one of them is dumb, having no power over anything, and he is a burden on his master; withersoever he sends him, he brings no good. Can he be equal to him who enjoins justice and who is on the straight path?[1564]

وَضَرَبَ اللّٰهُ مَثَلًا رَّجُلَيْنِ اَحَدُهُمَآ اَبْكَمُ لَا يَقْدِرُ
عَلٰى شَيْءٍ وَّهُوَ كَلٌّ عَلٰى مَوْلٰىهُ اَيْنَمَا يُوَجِّهْهُّ لَا يَاْتِ
بِخَيْرٍ هَلْ يَسْتَوِيْ هُوَ وَمَنْ يَّاْمُرُ بِالْعَدْلِ وَهُوَ
عَلٰى صِرَاطٍ مُّسْتَقِيْمٍ ﴿٧٧﴾ ع

R. 11 78. [a]And to Allāh belongs the *knowledge of the* unseen[1565] in the heavens and the earth; and [b]the matter of the *coming of the promised* Hour is but as the twinkling of an eye, nay, it is nearer still. Surely, Allāh has full power over all things.

وَلِلّٰهِ غَيْبُ السَّمٰوٰتِ وَالْاَرْضِ وَمَآ اَمْرُ السَّاعَةِ
اِلَّا كَلَمْحِ الْبَصَرِ اَوْ هُوَ اَقْرَبُ اِنَّ اللّٰهَ عَلٰى كُلِّ شَيْءٍ
قَدِيْرٌ ﴿٧٨﴾

79. And [c]Allāh brought you forth from the wombs of your mothers while you knew nothing, and [d]gave you ears and eyes and hearts,[1566] that you might be grateful.

وَاللّٰهُ اَخْرَجَكُمْ مِّنْۢ بُطُوْنِ اُمَّهٰتِكُمْ لَا تَعْلَمُوْنَ شَيْئًا
وَّجَعَلَ لَكُمُ السَّمْعَ وَالْاَبْصَارَ وَالْاَفْـِٕدَةَ لَعَلَّكُمْ
تَشْكُرُوْنَ ﴿٧٩﴾

80. [e]Do they not observe the birds held under subjection in the vault of heaven? None keeps them back[1567] save Allāh. Verily, in that are Signs for a people who believe.

اَلَمْ يَرَوْا اِلَى الطَّيْرِ مُسَخَّرٰتٍ فِيْ جَوِّ السَّمَآءِ مَا
يُمْسِكُهُنَّ اِلَّا اللّٰهُ اِنَّ فِيْ ذٰلِكَ لَاٰيٰتٍ لِّقَوْمٍ يُّؤْمِنُوْنَ ﴿٨٠﴾

[a]11 : 124; 18 : 27; 35 : 39. [b]7 : 188; 54 : 51. [c]39 : 7. [d]23 : 79; 67 : 24. [e]67 : 20.

1564. This and the preceding verse refer to two different classes of disbelievers. The preceding verse refers to those disbelievers, who are slaves to superstitious beliefs and idolatrous practices and customs and, though possessing some means and the ability to do some useful work, are prevented from doing it because they are deprived of freedom of action. And the present verse refers to such disbelievers as are not only slaves to superstitious practices but are also totally lacking in the means and the ability to do any real good work.

1565. "The unseen," *i.e.*, the eventual defeat and discomfiture of disbelief and the victory of Islām.

1566. The faculties of hearing, seeing and understanding have been mentioned in the order in which they help man to acquire knowledge. First of all a new-born child makes use of the power of hearing. The faculty of seeing develops later and that of understanding is the last to mature.

1567. The verse only contains a reference to the punishment which was soon to overtake the disbelievers of Mecca. The keeping back of the birds signifies the withholding of the punishment that was in store for them. Arabic poetry abounds in verses where birds are spoken of as following in the rear of a victorious army to feed on the dead bodies of the enemy killed and left on the field of battle. And the hovering of birds, according to

81. And Allāh has made for you, in your houses, a place of rest and has *also* made for you, of the skins of cattle, abodes which you find light at the time when you travel and *useful* at the time when you halt; and of their wool and their furs and their hair *He has supplied you with* household goods and articles of use for a time.

وَاللّٰهُ جَعَلَ لَكُمْ مِّنْ بُيُوْتِكُمْ سَكَنًا وَّجَعَلَ لَكُمْ مِّنْ
جُلُوْدِ الْاَنْعَامِ بُيُوْتًا تَسْتَخِفُّوْنَهَا يَوْمَ ظَعْنِكُمْ وَيَوْمَ
اِقَامَتِكُمْ ۙ وَمِنْ اَصْوَافِهَا وَاَوْبَارِهَا وَاَشْعَارِهَاۤ
اَثَاثًا وَّمَتَاعًا اِلٰى حِيْنٍ ﴿۸۱﴾

82. And Allāh has made for you of that which He has created, *many things affording* shade; and He has made for you in the mountains places of shelter; and He has made for you garments which protect you from heat, and coats of mail which protect you in your wars. Thus does He complete His favours on you, that you may submit *wholly to Him*.

وَاللّٰهُ جَعَلَ لَكُمْ مِّمَّا خَلَقَ ظِلٰلًا وَّجَعَلَ لَكُمْ مِّنَ
الْجِبَالِ اَكْنَانًا وَّجَعَلَ لَكُمْ سَرَابِيْلَ تَقِيْكُمُ الْحَرَّ
وَسَرَابِيْلَ تَقِيْكُمْ بَاْسَكُمْ ؕ كَذٰلِكَ يُتِمُّ نِعْمَتَهٗ عَلَيْكُمْ
لَعَلَّكُمْ تُسْلِمُوْنَ ﴿۸۲﴾

83. [a]But if they turn away, then thou art responsible only for the plain delivery *of the Message*.

فَاِنْ تَوَلَّوْا فَاِنَّمَا عَلَيْكَ الْبَلٰغُ الْمُبِيْنُ ﴿۸۳﴾

84. They recognize the favour of Allāh, yet they deny it; and most of them are *confirmed* disbelievers.

يَعْرِفُوْنَ نِعْمَتَ اللّٰهِ ثُمَّ يُنْكِرُوْنَهَا وَاَكْثَرُهُمُ
ع الْكٰفِرُوْنَ ﴿۸۴﴾

R. 12 85. [b]And *remember* the day when We shall raise up a witness from every people,[1568] then those who disbelieve shall not be permitted *to make amends*, [c]nor shall their plea be accepted.

وَيَوْمَ نَبْعَثُ مِنْ كُلِّ اُمَّةٍ شَهِيْدًا ثُمَّ لَا يُؤْذَنُ
لِلَّذِيْنَ كَفَرُوْا وَلَا هُمْ يُسْتَعْتَبُوْنَ ﴿۸۵﴾

[a]3 : 21; 5 : 93. [b]4 : 42; 16 : 90. [c]30 : 58; 41 : 25.

Arabic idiom, is symbolic of the defeat and destruction of a people (see 67 : 20). The present verse declares that God has withheld Muslims from waging war against disbelievers. But once they were given permission to fight, the disbelievers will be defeated and destroyed and their dead bodies will be eaten by the birds which they see flying in the sky.

1568. The verse says that Messengers were sent to all peoples and nations of the world. This is a claim which has been put forth by the Qur'ān alone of all the revealed Scriptures. The truth of this claim, revealed to the world about fourteen hundred years ago by the Qur'ān, has now begun to dawn upon mankind.

86. ªAnd when those who did wrong *actually* see the punishment, it will not be lightened for them. nor will they be respited.

وَاِذَا رَاَ الَّذِيْنَ ظَلَمُوا الْعَذَابَ فَلَا يُخَفَّفُ عَنْهُمْ وَلَا هُمْ يُنْظَرُوْنَ ۝

87. And ᵇwhen those, who associate partners *with Allāh*, will see their associate-gods, they will say, 'Our Lord, these are our associate-gods whom we used to call upon instead of Thee.' Thereupon they will retort on them with the words, 'Surely, you are liars.'¹⁵⁶⁹

وَاِذَا رَاَ الَّذِيْنَ اَشْرَكُوْا شُرَكَآءَهُمْ قَالُوْا رَبَّنَا هٰؤُلَآءِ شُرَكَآؤُنَا الَّذِيْنَ كُنَّا نَدْعُوْا مِنْ دُوْنِكَ ۚ فَاَلْقَوْا اِلَيْهِمُ الْقَوْلَ اِنَّكُمْ لَكٰذِبُوْنَ ۝

88. And ᶜthey will offer submission to Allāh on that day, and all that they used to forge shall fail them.

وَاَلْقَوْا اِلَى اللّٰهِ يَوْمَئِذِ السَّلَمَ وَضَلَّ عَنْهُمْ مَّا كَانُوْا يَفْتَرُوْنَ ۝

89. ᵈ*As for* those who disbelieve and turn *men* away from the way of Allāh, We will add punishment to their punishment because they made mischief.

اَلَّذِيْنَ كَفَرُوْا وَصَدُّوْا عَنْ سَبِيْلِ اللّٰهِ زِدْنٰهُمْ عَذَابًا فَوْقَ الْعَذَابِ بِمَا كَانُوْا يُفْسِدُوْنَ ۝

90. ᵉAnd *remember* the day when We will raise up in every people a witness against them from amongst themselves, and We will bring thee as a witness against all of them. And ᶠWe have sent down to thee the Book to explain everything and a guidance and a mercy and glad tidings to those who submit *to Allāh.*

وَيَوْمَ نَبْعَثُ فِيْ كُلِّ اُمَّةٍ شَهِيْدًا عَلَيْهِمْ مِّنْ اَنْفُسِهِمْ وَجِئْنَا بِكَ شَهِيْدًا عَلٰى هٰؤُلَآءِ ۚ وَنَزَّلْنَا عَلَيْكَ الْكِتٰبَ تِبْيَانًا لِّكُلِّ شَيْءٍ وَّهُدًى وَّرَحْمَةً وَّبُشْرٰى لِلْمُسْلِمِيْنَ ۝

R. 13   91. Verily, Allāh enjoins justice, and the doing of good to others; and giving *like* kindred; and forbids indecency and manifest evil

اِنَّ اللّٰهَ يَأْمُرُ بِالْعَدْلِ وَالْاِحْسَانِ وَاِيْتَآئِ ذِي الْقُرْبٰى وَيَنْهٰى عَنِ الْفَحْشَآءِ وَالْمُنْكَرِ وَالْبَغْيِ ۚ

ª2 : 166.   ᵇ30 : 14.   ᶜ16 : 29.   ᵈ7 : 46; 11 : 20; 14 : 4.   ᵉ4 : 42; 16 : 85.   ᶠ10 : 38; 12 : 112.

1569. This altercation between false gods and their followers shows that friendships based on sin and denial of truth never endure.

and transgression.[1570] He admonishes you that you may take heed.

يَعِظُكُمْ لَعَلَّكُمْ تَذَكَّرُونَ ﴿٩١﴾

92. And [a]fulfil the covenant of Allāh when you have made *one*, and break not your oaths[1571] after making them firm, while you have made Allāh your surety. Certainly, Allāh knows what you do.

وَأَوْفُوا بِعَهْدِ اللّٰهِ إِذَا عٰهَدْتُّمْ وَلَا تَنْقُضُوا الْأَيْمَانَ
بَعْدَ تَوْكِيْدِهَا وَقَدْ جَعَلْتُمُ اللّٰهَ عَلَيْكُمْ كَفِيْلًا
إِنَّ اللّٰهَ يَعْلَمُ مَا تَفْعَلُوْنَ ﴿٩٢﴾

93. And be not like unto her who cuts up her yarn into pieces after having spun it strong by [b]making your oaths a means of deceit[1572] between you, *for fear* lest one people become more powerful than another people.[1573] Surely, Allāh tries you therewith, and on the Day of Resurrection He will make clear to you that wherein you differed.

وَلَا تَكُوْنُوْا كَالَّتِيْ نَقَضَتْ غَزْلَهَا مِنْ بَعْدِ قُوَّةٍ
أَنْكَاثًا تَتَّخِذُوْنَ أَيْمَانَكُمْ دَخَلًا بَيْنَكُمْ أَنْ تَكُوْنَ
أُمَّةٌ هِيَ أَرْبٰى مِنْ أُمَّةٍ إِنَّمَا يَبْلُوْكُمُ اللّٰهُ بِهٖ وَلَيُبَيِّنَنَّ
لَكُمْ يَوْمَ الْقِيٰمَةِ مَا كُنْتُمْ فِيْهِ تَخْتَلِفُوْنَ ﴿٩٣﴾

[a]6 : 153; 13 : 21; 17 : 35. [b]16 : 95.

1570. The verse contains three commandments and three prohibitions which briefly deal with all the various stages of the moral and spiritual development of man and with both its positive and negative sides. It enjoins justice, the doing of good to others and kindness as between kindred; and forbids indecency, manifest evil and transgression. Justice implies that a person should treat others as he is treated by them. He should return to others the good or evil to the extent or measure to which he receives it from them. Higher than *'Adl* (justice) is the stage of *Iḥsān* (goodness) when man should do good to others regardless of what sort of treatment he receives from them, or even if he is maltreated by them. His conduct should not be actuated by considerations of reciprocity. At the last and highest stage of moral development, *viz.*, *'Ītā'i Dhil Qurbā* (giving like kindred), a believer is expected to do good to others not in return for any good received from them, nor with the idea of doing more good than the good received, but to do good prompted by a natural impulse, as good is done to very near blood relations. His condition at this stage resembles that of a mother whose love for her children springs from natural impulse. After a believer has attained this stage his moral development becomes complete. These three stages of morals constitute the positive side of man's moral development. Its negative side is portrayed in the three words, *viz.*, *Faḥshā'* (indecency), *Munkar* (manifest evil) and *Baghy* (transgression). *Faḥshā'* signifies vice of which the knowledge is confined to the doer and *Munkar* signifies those evils which other men also see and condemn, though they may not suffer any loss or infringement of their own rights by them. *Baghy*, however, comprehends all those vices and evils which not only are seen, felt and denounced by other people but which do them positive harm also. These three simple words cover all conceivable vices.

1571. Obligations which the believers owe to God are covered by the words "covenant of Allāh" and the duties they owe to their fellowmen are implied in the words, "the oaths."

1572. This and the preceding verse lay the greatest stress on the inviolability of oaths which should be observed at all costs.

1573. The Arabic expression is capable of three interpretations :

94. And [a]if Allāh had *enforced* His Will, He would surely have made you *all* one people; but He lets go astray him who wishes *it*, and guides him who wishes *it*, and you shall surely be questioned concerning that which you have been doing.

وَلَوْ شَاءَ اللّٰهُ لَجَعَلَكُمْ أُمَّةً وَّاحِدَةً وَّلٰكِنْ يُّضِلُّ مَنْ يَّشَاءُ وَيَهْدِيْ مَنْ يَّشَاءُ ۚ وَلَتُسْـَٔلُنَّ عَمَّا كُنْتُمْ تَعْمَلُوْنَ ﴿٩٤﴾

95. And make not your oaths a means of deceit between you; or *your* foot will slip after it has been firmly established[1574] and you will taste evil because *by acting thus* you turned *people* away from the path of Allāh, and you will have a severe punishment.

وَلَا تَتَّخِذُوْٓا أَيْمَانَكُمْ دَخَلًا بَيْنَكُمْ فَتَزِلَّ قَدَمٌ بَعْدَ ثُبُوْتِهَا وَتَذُوْقُوا السُّوْٓءَ بِمَا صَدَدْتُّمْ عَنْ سَبِيْلِ اللّٰهِ ۚ وَلَكُمْ عَذَابٌ عَظِيْمٌ ﴿٩٥﴾

96. [b]And barter not the covenant of Allāh for a paltry price.[1575] Surely, that which is with Allāh is better for you if you knew.

وَلَا تَشْتَرُوْا بِعَهْدِ اللّٰهِ ثَمَنًا قَلِيْلًا ۚ إِنَّمَا عِنْدَ اللّٰهِ هُوَ خَيْرٌ لَّكُمْ إِنْ كُنْتُمْ تَعْلَمُوْنَ ﴿٩٦﴾

97. That which you have shall pass away, but that which is with Allāh is lasting. [c]And We will certainly give those, who are steadfast, their reward according to the best of their works.

مَا عِنْدَكُمْ يَنْفَدُ وَمَا عِنْدَ اللّٰهِ بَاقٍ ۗ وَلَنَجْزِيَنَّ الَّذِيْنَ صَبَرُوْٓا أَجْرَهُمْ بِأَحْسَنِ مَا كَانُوْا يَعْمَلُوْنَ ﴿٩٧﴾

[a]5 : 49; 11 : 119. [b]3 : 78. [c]11 : 12; 39 : 11.

(1) Because one people (non-Muslims) are stronger and wealthier than the other people (Muslims), *i.e.*, Muslims should not put other stronger people out of their guard by concluding with them a peace treaty, thus biding their time till a favourable opportunity arises and they are strong enough to dishonour it.

(2) For fear lest one people (non-Muslims) should become stronger and wealthier than the other people (Muslims).

(3) So that one people (Muslims) should become stronger than the other people (non-Muslims), *i.e.*, Muslims should not make a treaty with non-Muslims with this object in view that by taking advantage of it they should add to their own strength and break it when they find themselves stronger than non-Muslims.

1574. Such conduct will weaken your power.

1575. When people attain to power they generally fall victim to all sorts of temptations. Their enemies employ spies and informers among them and offer large bribes to know their State secrets. The Muslims are warned against succumbing to such temptations in the words : *And barter not the covenant of Allāh for a paltry price.*

98. [a]Whoso acts righteously, whether male or female[1576] and is a believer, We will surely grant him a pure life; and We will surely bestow on such their reward according to the best of their works.

مَنْ عَمِلَ صَالِحًا مِّنْ ذَكَرٍ اَوْ اُنْثٰى وَهُوَ مُؤْمِنٌ فَلَنُحْيِيَنَّهٗ حَيٰوةً طَيِّبَةً ۚ وَلَنَجْزِيَنَّهُمْ اَجْرَهُمْ بِاَحْسَنِ مَا كَانُوْا يَعْمَلُوْنَ ﴿۹۸﴾

99. And when thou recitest the Qur'ān, seek refuge with Allāh from Satan, the rejected.

فَاِذَا قَرَاْتَ الْقُرْاٰنَ فَاسْتَعِذْ بِاللّٰهِ مِنَ الشَّيْطٰنِ الرَّجِيْمِ ﴿۹۹﴾

100. Surely, [b]he has no power over those who believe and who put their trust in their Lord.

اِنَّهٗ لَيْسَ لَهٗ سُلْطٰنٌ عَلَى الَّذِيْنَ اٰمَنُوْا وَعَلٰى رَبِّهِمْ يَتَوَكَّلُوْنَ ﴿۱۰۰﴾

101. [c]His power is only over those who make friends with him and who associate partners with Him.

اِنَّمَا سُلْطٰنُهٗ عَلَى الَّذِيْنَ يَتَوَلَّوْنَهٗ وَالَّذِيْنَ هُمْ بِهٖ مُشْرِكُوْنَ ﴿۱۰۱﴾

R. 14 102. And [d]when We bring one Sign in place of another[1577]—and Allāh knows best *the object of* what He reveals—they say, 'Thou art but a fabricator.' Nay, but most of them know not.

وَاِذَا بَدَّلْنَاۤ اٰيَةً مَّكَانَ اٰيَةٍ ۙ وَّاللّٰهُ اَعْلَمُ بِمَا يُنَزِّلُ قَالُوْۤا اِنَّمَاۤ اَنْتَ مُفْتَرٍ ؕ بَلْ اَكْثَرُهُمْ لَا يَعْلَمُوْنَ ﴿۱۰۲﴾

103. Say, [e]'The Spirit of holiness has brought it down from thy Lord with truth, that He may strengthen *in their faith* those who believe and [f]as a guidance and glad tidings for Muslims.

قُلْ نَزَّلَهٗ رُوْحُ الْقُدُسِ مِنْ رَّبِّكَ بِالْحَقِّ لِيُثَبِّتَ الَّذِيْنَ اٰمَنُوْا وَهُدًى وَّبُشْرٰى لِلْمُسْلِمِيْنَ ﴿۱۰۳﴾

104. And indeed We know that they say that it is only a man who teaches[1578] him. *But* the tongue of

وَلَقَدْ نَعْلَمُ اَنَّهُمْ يَقُوْلُوْنَ اِنَّمَا يُعَلِّمُهٗ بَشَرٌ ؕ

[a]3 : 196; 4 : 125; 20 : 113. [b]15 : 43; 17 : 66; 34 : 22. [c]2 : 258; 3 : 176; 7 : 28. [d]2 : 107. [e]2 : 98; 26 : 194. [f]12 : 112.

1576. The verse recognizes the equality of the rights of men and women and promises both equal share in Divine favours.

1577. The meaning is : "When We avert or delay punishment on account of a change for the better on the part of those who are threatened with it." There is no reference here to the abrogation of any of the verses of the Qur'ān. There is no verse in the Qur'ān which clashes with any other verse of the Book and which may therefore have to be regarded as abrogated. All parts of the Qur'ān support and corroborate one another. There is nothing in the context either to suggest any reference to the idea of abrogation.

1578. Names of different persons have been mentioned in the traditions who, according to the allegations of the disbelievers, helped the Holy Prophet in composing

him towards whom *their minds* incline *in making this insinuation* is foreign while this is Arabic *tongue* plain and clear.

لِسَانُ الَّذِي يُلْحِدُونَ إِلَيْهِ أَعْجَمِيٌّ وَهَٰذَا لِسَانٌ عَرَبِيٌّ مُبِينٌ ﴿١٠٤﴾

105. *As for* those who do not believe in the Signs of Allāh, surely, Allāh will not guide them, and they shall have a grievous punishment.

إِنَّ الَّذِينَ لَا يُؤْمِنُونَ بِآيَاتِ اللَّهِ لَا يَهْدِيهِمُ اللَّهُ وَلَهُمْ عَذَابٌ أَلِيمٌ ﴿١٠٥﴾

106. It is only those who believe not in the Signs of Allāh, who forge falsehood, and they it is who are the liars.

إِنَّمَا يَفْتَرِي الْكَذِبَ الَّذِينَ لَا يُؤْمِنُونَ بِآيَاتِ اللَّهِ ۖ وَأُولَٰئِكَ هُمُ الْكَاذِبُونَ ﴿١٠٦﴾

107. [a]Whoso disbelieves in Allāh after he has believed—save him who is forced *to make a declaration of disbelief* while his heart finds peace in faith[1579]—but such as open their breasts to disbelief, on them is Allāh's wrath; and for them is *decreed* a severe punishment.

مَنْ كَفَرَ بِاللَّهِ مِنْ بَعْدِ إِيمَانِهِ إِلَّا مَنْ أُكْرِهَ وَقَلْبُهُ مُطْمَئِنٌّ بِالْإِيمَانِ وَلَٰكِنْ مَنْ شَرَحَ بِالْكُفْرِ صَدْرًا فَعَلَيْهِمْ غَضَبٌ مِنَ اللَّهِ وَلَهُمْ عَذَابٌ عَظِيمٌ ﴿١٠٧﴾

[a]3 : 91; 4 : 138; 63 : 4.

the Qur'ān—Jabar, a Christian slave, 'Aish or Ya'ish, a servant of Al-Ḥuwaiṭib Ibn 'Abd al-'Uzzā and Abū Fukaih who was known as Yasār and 'Adas or 'Addās, a slave of Aus bin Rabī' (Ma'ānī & Fatḥ). The names of 'Ammār, Ṣuhaib, Salmān, 'Abd Allāh bin Salām and of Sergius, a Nestorian monk, have also been mentioned in this connection. In fact, the Qur'ān here makes reference to two objections of disbelievers, one relating to certain slave converts from whom the Holy Prophet is alleged to have received help in composing the Qur'ān which is mentioned in 25 : 5-7, and the other relating to what he heard of the Gospels from a certain Christian slave convert to Islām, and which was incorporated in the Qur'ān to which this verse refers. Now with regard to the second objection, did the slave in question read the Arabic version of the Gospels or their Greek or Hebrew version? If he read the Arabic version then it will have to be proved that the new Testament had been translated into Arabic in the Holy Prophet's time and the translation was so common that even slaves read it while working at their shops. But upto the time of the Holy Prophet, translations of the Gospels had not been made in any language. The Jewish tribes of Medina had not even translated the Torah into Arabic by that time, and whenever he needed a reference to this Book, he consulted 'Abd Allāh bin Salām a great Hebrew scholar. Dr. Alexander Souter, M.A., LL.D., writes in his book, "The Test and Canon of the New Testament" (Second Edition, 1925, p. 74), under the caption, "Arabic Versions".... 'The oldest manuscript goes no further back than the 8th century. Two versions of the Arabic are reported to have taken place at Alexandria in the 13th century.' And if the Christian slave-convert read to the Holy Prophet Hebrew or Greek Gospels, how could he benefit by listening to a Book which he could not understand and how could the man from whom he was alleged to have received help for composing the Qur'ān being '*Ajamī* (foreign and defective in speech) explain to him in his defective Arabic those great eternal truths which the Qur'ān comprises and for explaining which a sound and deep knowledge of Arabic was essential? See also "The Larger Edition of the Commentary" under this verse.

1579. The verse is silent about the treatment which a person who, under the severest trial, utters words that may appear to express disbelief though inwardly he may be satisfied

108. [a]That is because they have preferred the present life to the Hereafter, and because Allāh guides not the disbelieving people.

ذٰلِكَ بِاَنَّهُمُ اسْتَحَبُّوا الْحَيٰوةَ الدُّنْيَا عَلَى الْاٰخِرَةِ وَ
اَنَّ اللّٰهَ لَا يَهْدِي الْقَوْمَ الْكٰفِرِيْنَ ﴿۱۰۸﴾

109. [b]It is they on whose hearts and ears and eyes Allāh has set a seal. And it is they who are the heedless.

اُولٰٓئِكَ الَّذِيْنَ طَبَعَ اللّٰهُ عَلٰى قُلُوْبِهِمْ وَ سَمْعِهِمْ وَ
اَبْصَارِهِمْ ۚ وَ اُولٰٓئِكَ هُمُ الْغٰفِلُوْنَ ﴿۱۰۹﴾

110. [c]Undoubtedly, it is they who will be the losers in the Hereafter.

لَا جَرَمَ اَنَّهُمْ فِي الْاٰخِرَةِ هُمُ الْخٰسِرُوْنَ ﴿۱۱۰﴾

111. [d]Then, surely thy Lord—to those who migrated after they had been persecuted and then strove[1580] hard *in the cause of Allāh* and remained steadfast—surely, after that, thy Lord is Most Forgiving, Merciful,

ثُمَّ اِنَّ رَبَّكَ لِلَّذِيْنَ هَاجَرُوْا مِنْۢ بَعْدِ مَا فُتِنُوْا
ثُمَّ جٰهَدُوْا وَ صَبَرُوْٓا ۙ اِنَّ رَبَّكَ مِنْۢ بَعْدِهَا لَغَفُوْرٌ
رَّحِيْمٌ ﴿۱۱۱﴾ ع

R. 15 112. On the day when every soul will come pleading for itself, and [e]every soul will be fully recompensed for what it did, and they will not be wronged.

يَوْمَ تَاْتِيْ كُلُّ نَفْسٍ تُجَادِلُ عَنْ نَّفْسِهَا وَ تُوَفّٰى
كُلُّ نَفْسٍ مَّا عَمِلَتْ وَ هُمْ لَا يُظْلَمُوْنَ ﴿۱۱۲﴾

113. [f]And Allāh sets forth the parable of a city[1581] which enjoyed security and peace; its provisions came to it in plenty from every quarter; but it was ungrateful for

وَ ضَرَبَ اللّٰهُ مَثَلًا قَرْيَةً كَانَتْ اٰمِنَةً مُّطْمَئِنَّةً
يَّاْتِيْهَا رِزْقُهَا رَغَدًا مِّنْ كُلِّ مَكَانٍ فَكَفَرَتْ

[a]10 : 8; 87 : 17. [b]2 : 8; 4 : 156; 7 : 180. [c]11 : 23. [d]2 : 219. [e]2 : 282. [f]34 : 16-17.

with Islām, will receive from God. It implies that final judgment in the case of such persons has been reserved and that their future behaviour will determine the nature of the treatment they will receive from God.

1580. Whereas vv. 109,110 referred to those persons who revert to disbelief and open up their hearts to it and join the ranks of the enemies of Islām, the verse under comment deals with such persons regarding whom judgment had been reserved (verse 107). The judgment given in their case is that if they migrate from their homes and strive in the cause of God and endure with patience all the hardships that may befall them in the way of Islām, then, and not till then, will God pardon their previous sins, for only then will it become established that they have made full amends for their past lapse. The *Sūrah* being of Meccan origin, *Jihād* mentioned in the verse is not fighting with the sword but is only "striving" to promote the cause of Islām.

1581. The "city" referred to in this verse is Mecca.

the favours of Allāh, so Allāh made it taste hunger[1582] and fear *which clothed it like* a garment[1583] because of what they used to do.

بِأَنْعُمِ اللّٰهِ فَأَذَاقَهَا اللّٰهُ لِبَاسَ الْجُوْعِ وَالْخَوْفِ
بِمَا كَانُوْا يَصْنَعُوْنَ ﴿١١٣﴾

114. And indeed there has come to them a Messenger from among themselves, but they treated him as a liar, so punishment overtook them while they were wrongdoers.

وَلَقَدْ جَآءَهُمْ رَسُوْلٌ مِّنْهُمْ فَكَذَّبُوْهُ فَأَخَذَهُمُ
الْعَذَابُ وَهُمْ ظٰلِمُوْنَ ﴿١١٤﴾

115. [a]So eat of the lawful *and* good[1584] things which Allāh has provided for you; and be grateful for the bounty of Allāh, if it is Him you worship.

فَكُلُوْا مِمَّا رَزَقَكُمُ اللّٰهُ حَلٰلًا طَيِّبًا وَّاشْكُرُوْا
نِعْمَتَ اللّٰهِ إِنْ كُنْتُمْ إِيَّاهُ تَعْبُدُوْنَ ﴿١١٥﴾

116. [b]He has made unlawful for you only that which dies of itself and blood and the flesh of swine and that on which the name of any other than Allāh has been invoked. But he who is driven by necessity *to eat any of these things*, being neither disobedient nor exceeding the limit, then, surely, Allāh is Most Forgiving, Merciful.

إِنَّمَا حَرَّمَ عَلَيْكُمُ الْمَيْتَةَ وَالدَّمَ وَلَحْمَ الْخِنْزِيْرِ
وَمَآ أُهِلَّ لِغَيْرِ اللّٰهِ بِهٖ فَمَنِ اضْطُرَّ غَيْرَ بَاغٍ وَّ
لَا عَادٍ فَإِنَّ اللّٰهَ غَفُوْرٌ رَّحِيْمٌ ﴿١١٦﴾

117. [c]And say not—because of the falsehood which your tongues utter—'This is lawful, and this is unlawful,' so as to *be of those who* forge lies against Allāh. Surely, those who forge lies against Allāh do not prosper.

وَلَا تَقُوْلُوْا لِمَا تَصِفُ أَلْسِنَتُكُمُ الْكَذِبَ هٰذَا
حَلٰلٌ وَّهٰذَا حَرَامٌ لِّتَفْتَرُوْا عَلَى اللّٰهِ الْكَذِبَ
إِنَّ الَّذِيْنَ يَفْتَرُوْنَ عَلَى اللّٰهِ الْكَذِبَ لَا يُفْلِحُوْنَ ﴿١١٧﴾

---

[a]2 : 169; 5 : 89; 8 : 70. [b]2 : 174; 5 : 4; 6 : 146. [c]6 : 145.

1582. The dreadful famine which held Mecca in its grip for seven long years. See 2694.

1583. Fear of war in which the Meccans were involved with Muslims and were defeated. They lived in a state of extreme fear as if fear of war had quite covered them. In Arabic idiom the word *Dhāqa* (tasting) sometimes is used for *Libās* (dress). There is a well-known Arabic verse :—*Qālū Iqtariḥ Shai'an Nujid Laka Ṭabkha-hū. Qultu Itbakhū Lī Jubbatan wa Qamīṣā, i.e.*, they said what would you desire us to cook for you. I said, 'Cook for me a long coat and a shirt.'

1584. See notes on vv. 2 : 169, 174 ; 5 : 4; 6 : 119, 120 & 146.

118. *ᵃThis life* is a brief enjoyment and then they shall have a grievous punishment.

مَتَاعٌ قَلِيلٌ وَّلَهُمْ عَذَابٌ اَلِيْمٌ ﴿۱۱۸﴾

119. And to those *also* who are Jews, We forbade before *this* all that We have related to thee. And ᵇWe wronged them not, but they used to wrong themselves.

وَعَلَى الَّذِيْنَ هَادُوْا حَرَّمْنَا مَا قَصَصْنَا عَلَيْكَ
مِنْ قَبْلُ ۚ وَمَا ظَلَمْنٰهُمْ وَلٰكِنْ كَانُوْٓا اَنْفُسَهُمْ
يَظْلِمُوْنَ ﴿۱۱۹﴾

120. Then surely, ᶜthy Lord—to those who do evil in ignorance[1585] and repent thereafter and make amends—surely, after that thy Lord is Most Forgiving, Merciful.

ثُمَّ اِنَّ رَبَّكَ لِلَّذِيْنَ عَمِلُوا السُّوْٓءَ بِجَهَالَةٍ ثُمَّ
تَابُوْا مِنْۢ بَعْدِ ذٰلِكَ وَاَصْلَحُوْٓا ۙ اِنَّ رَبَّكَ مِنْۢ بَعْدِهَا
لَغَفُوْرٌ رَّحِيْمٌ ﴿۱۲۰﴾ ع

R. 16 121. Abraham was indeed a paragon of virtue,[1586] ᵈobedient to Allāh, ever inclined to Him, and he was not of those who set up equals *to Allāh;*

اِنَّ اِبْرٰهِيْمَ كَانَ اُمَّةً قَانِتًا لِّلّٰهِ حَنِيْفًا ۭ وَلَمْ يَكُ
مِنَ الْمُشْرِكِيْنَ ﴿۱۲۱﴾

122. *Ever* grateful for His favours; ᵉHe chose him and guided him to a straight path.

شَاكِرًا لِّاَنْعُمِهٖ ۭ اِجْتَبٰىهُ وَهَدٰىهُ اِلٰى صِرَاطٍ
مُّسْتَقِيْمٍ ﴿۱۲۲﴾

123. And ᶠWe bestowed on him good in this world, and in the Hereafter he will surely be among the righteous.

وَاٰتَيْنٰهُ فِي الدُّنْيَا حَسَنَةً ۭ وَاِنَّهٗ فِي الْاٰخِرَةِ لَمِنَ
الصّٰلِحِيْنَ ﴿۱۲۳﴾

124. And *now* We have sent revelation to thee, *enjoining,* ᵍ'Follow the way of Abraham who was ever inclined *to Allāh* and was not of those who set up equals *to Him.*'

ثُمَّ اَوْحَيْنَآ اِلَيْكَ اَنِ اتَّبِعْ مِلَّةَ اِبْرٰهِيْمَ حَنِيْفًا ۭ
وَمَا كَانَ مِنَ الْمُشْرِكِيْنَ ﴿۱۲۴﴾

ᵃ3 : 198; 4 : 78. ᵇ11 : 102; 16 : 34. ᶜ4 : 18; 6 : 55. ᵈ2 : 136; 3 : 68; 6 : 80. ᵉ2 : 131. ᶠ2 : 131; 29 : 28. ᵍ2 : 136; 4 : 126; 22 : 79.

1585. *Jahālah* means, both lack of knowledge and lack of spiritual realization. Here it is used in the second sense because there is no justification for punishing a person who does not possess knowledge of a commandment for the non-observance of which he is being punished.

1586. *Ummah* among other things means a nation; a race; a righteous man who is an object of imitation; a man possessing all good qualities, a paragon of virtue (Lane).

125. *The punishment for profaning* the Sabbath[1587] was imposed only on those who had differed about it and *b*thy Lord will surely judge between them on the Day of Resurrection concerning that wherein they differed.

اِنَّمَا جُعِلَ السَّبْتُ عَلَى الَّذِيْنَ اخْتَلَفُوْا فِيْهِ ؕ وَ اِنَّ رَبَّكَ لَيَحْكُمُ بَيْنَهُمْ يَوْمَ الْقِيٰمَةِ فِيْمَا كَانُوْا فِيْهِ يَخْتَلِفُوْنَ ۝

126. Call unto the way of thy Lord with wisdom[1588] and goodly exhortation and *c*argue with them in a way that is best. Surely, *d*thy Lord knows best who has strayed from His way; and He *also* knows those who are rightly guided.

اُدْعُ اِلٰى سَبِيْلِ رَبِّكَ بِالْحِكْمَةِ وَ الْمَوْعِظَةِ الْحَسَنَةِ وَ جَادِلْهُمْ بِالَّتِيْ هِيَ اَحْسَنُ ؕ اِنَّ رَبَّكَ هُوَ اَعْلَمُ بِمَنْ ضَلَّ عَنْ سَبِيْلِهٖ وَ هُوَ اَعْلَمُ بِالْمُهْتَدِيْنَ ۝

127. *e*And if you *decide to* punish *the oppressors*, then punish *them* to the extent to which you have been wronged; *f*but if you show patience then, surely, that is best for those who are patient.

وَ اِنْ عَاقَبْتُمْ فَعَاقِبُوْا بِمِثْلِ مَا عُوْقِبْتُمْ بِهٖ ؕ وَ لَئِنْ صَبَرْتُمْ لَهُوَ خَيْرٌ لِّلصّٰبِرِيْنَ ۝

128. And, *O Prophet,* endure thou with patience; and verily thy patience is *possible* only with *the help* of Allāh. *g*And grieve not for them, nor feel distressed because of their *evil* designs.

وَ اصْبِرْ وَ مَا صَبْرُكَ اِلَّا بِاللّٰهِ وَ لَا تَحْزَنْ عَلَيْهِمْ وَ لَا تَكُ فِيْ ضَيْقٍ مِّمَّا يَمْكُرُوْنَ ۝

129. *h*Verily, Allāh is with those who are righteous and those who do good.[1589]

اِنَّ اللّٰهَ مَعَ الَّذِيْنَ اتَّقَوْا وَّ الَّذِيْنَ هُمْ مُّحْسِنُوْنَ ۝

---

*a*2 : 66; 4 : 48,155.   *b*3 : 56; 22 : 70.   *c*41 : 35.   *d*6 : 118.   *e*42 : 41.   *f*42 : 44.
*g*15 : 89, 98; 27 : 71.   *h*45 : 20.

1587. The Jews believed that their national degradation and misery were due to their profaning the Sabbath. They are told that now they could retrieve their departed glory by accepting Islām and not by observing the Sabbath.

1588. *Ḥikmah* means: (1) knowledge or science; (2) equity or justice; (3) forbearance or clemency; (4) firmness; (5) any saying or discourse which is conforming or agreeable to truth and is in accordance with the exigencies of the occasion; (6) gift of prophecy and (7) what prevents or restrains a person from foolish behaviour (Lane).

1589. A *Muttaqī* is one who establishes such a strong connection with God that God Himself becomes his Protector and shields him from every evil. A *Muḥsin* is he who, after he himself has come under the protection of God, tries to bring others also under His protection. Thus a *Muḥsin* possesses a higher spiritual stature than a *Muttaqī*.

CHAPTER 17

BANĪ ISRĀ'ĪL

(*Revealed before Hijrah*)

Date of Revelation and Context

This Chapter is known as Banī Isrā'īl because it deals with some important incidents in the history of the Israelites and with the experiences through which they had to pass. It also bears the title of Isrā' because it opens with the Holy Prophet's great Vision about his spiritual Night Journey to Jerusalem which forms one of the most outstanding topics of this Chapter. According to Ibn Mas'ūd, one of the earliest Companions of the Holy Prophet, the revelation of this *Sūrah* was completed between the 4th and 11th year of the Call. Christian writers assign this period between the 6th and the 12th year. Towards the end of the previous *Sūrah* Muslims were warned that very soon they would meet with opposition from 'the People of the Book' as severe as they had already experienced at the hands of Meccan idolaters, but that they should bear it with patience and fortitude till God should give them victory over their opponents. In the present *Sūrah* their attention is drawn to the fact that this opposition will start at Medina and will end in the total defeat and discomfiture of 'the People of the Book;' their sacred places falling into the hands of Muslims.

Subject-Matter

The *Sūrah*, as its title shows, deals with the history of the Jewish people, with a pointed reference to two outstanding occasions when they openly disobeyed and defied the two great Prophets of God—David and Jesus. As a result of this defiance they suffered the destruction of their national life, first at the hands of the Babylonian Nebuchadnezzar and then at those of the Roman Emperor Titus. This special reference to the twofold destruction of Jews implied a warning to Muslims that their wrongdoings and transgressions would also result in the double eclipse of their national life. The warning, however, was also accompanied with a word of hope and good cheer for them. It was to this effect that since the Holy Prophet was the last Law-giving Prophet, his Dispensation would not, like the Jewish Dispensation, suffer total extinction but after initial reverses would emerge triumphant with increased lustre and effulgence. Besides, some other subjects to which only an implied reference was made in the preceding *Sūrah* have also been dealt with at some length. The *Sūrah* opens with the subject of Isrā' (Spiritual Night Journey of the Holy Prophet) in order to show that as the successor and counterpart of Moses, his followers will conquer the lands which were promised to Moses, and that like Moses he will have to leave his native place. But his Emigration will lead to very rapid progress and advancement of his noble cause. Then it is briefly stated that the people of Moses acquired great power and prestige through their Prophet, though subsequently they came to grief by defying and ignoring Divine warning. But the Qur'ān, being a much more complete code of Laws, is capable of bringing about a greater and a completer change in the lives of its followers than was the Book of Moses. This brief reference to the rise and decline of Jews is attended with a warning to Muslims that God would bestow upon them His favours and like the Jews they would also rise to great heights of material greatness and glory, but that after they had acquired wealth, power and influence, they should not forget God. Then some rules of conduct are mentioned by acting upon which a people could rise to a very high spiritual stature. But, instead of benefiting by these rules, disbelievers arrogantly turn away from them and give no thought to the dreadful end to which their conceit and pride are likely to lead them. They are warned that rejection of truth never produces wholesome results and that they will be visited with severe Divine punishment, particularly in the Latter Days, when the world will witness a fight to the finish between the forces of Light and Darkness and finally the forces of Satan shall be completely routed. The *Sūrah* then administers a severe rebuke to disbelievers that they seek to annihilate the Holy Prophet, but God has decreed a great and noble purpose for him and a mighty destiny awaits him. His name shall be known unto the remotest corners of the earth and shall be honoured to the end of time. The world shall recognize him as humanity's greatest Guide and Leader and the Qur'ān as a store-house of limitless spiritual knowledge. The *Sūrah* closes with a brief description of the signs of the Latter Days and of the evils which will then prevail in the world and declares that it is prayer and true connection with God that can save man from sin.

رُكُوْعَاتُهَا ١٢ سُوْرَةُ بَنِيْٓ اِسْرَآءِيْلَ مَكِّيَّةٌ (١٧) اٰيَاتُهَا ١١٢

1. [a]In the name of Allāh, the Gracious, the Merciful.

بِسْمِ اللّٰهِ الرَّحْمٰنِ الرَّحِيْمِ ①

2. Glory be to Him Who carried[1590] His servant by night from the Sacred Mosque to the Distant Mosque,[1591] the [b]environs of which We have blessed, that We might show him *some of* Our Signs.[1591A] Surely, He alone is the All-Hearing, the All-Seeing.

سُبْحٰنَ الَّذِيْٓ اَسْرٰى بِعَبْدِهٖ لَيْلًا مِّنَ الْمَسْجِدِ
الْحَرَامِ اِلَى الْمَسْجِدِ الْاَقْصَا الَّذِيْ بٰرَكْنَا حَوْلَهٗ
لِنُرِيَهٗ مِنْ اٰيٰتِنَا ۭ اِنَّهٗ هُوَ السَّمِيْعُ الْبَصِيْرُ ②

المنزل ٤ الجزء ١٥

[a]1 : 1. [b]5 : 22; 7 : 138.

1590. The verse which seems to mention a vision of the Holy Prophet is supposed by most Commentators of the Qur'ān to refer to his *Mi'rāj* (Spiritual Ascension). Contrary to popular opinion we are inclined to the view that the verse deals with the *Isrā'* (Spiritual Night Journey) of the Holy Prophet in a vision from Mecca to Jerusalem, while his *Mi'rāj* (Spiritual Ascension) has been dealt with at some length in *Sūrah* Al-Najm. All the facts, mentioned in *Sūrah* Al-Najm (vv. 8-18) which was revealed immediately after the Emigration to Abyssinia which took place in the month of Rajab in the 5th year of the Call, are to be found narrated in detail in the traditions which deal with the *Mi'rāj* of the Holy Prophet. The *Isrā'* or the Spiritual Night Journey of the Holy Prophet from Mecca to Jerusalem, with which the present verse deals, took place in the eleventh year of the Call, according to Zurqānī, and in the 12th year according to Muir and some other Christian writers. According to Merdawaih and Ibn Sa'd, however, the *Isrā'* took place on the 17th of Rabī 'Al-Awwal, a year before *Hijrah* (Al-Khaṣāiṣ Al-Kubrā). Baihaquī also relates that the *Isrā'* took place a year or six months before the *Hijrah*. Thus all relevant traditions go to show that the *Isrā'* took place a year or six months prior to *Hijrah* about the 12th year of the Call when after the death of Khadījah which took place in the 10th year, the Holy Prophet was living with Umm Hānī', his cousin. But the *Mi'rāj*, according to overwhelming scholarly opinion, took place about the 5th year. Thus the two incidents are separated from each other by an interval of six or seven years and, therefore, cannot be identical; the one must be regarded as quite distinct and separate from the other. Moreover, the incidents which are mentioned in the Traditions to have taken place in the Prophet's *Mi'rāj*, are of quite a distinct nature from those which took place in his *Isrā*.' It may also be stated in passing that the two incidents were only spiritual phenomena and that the Holy Prophet did not physically go up to heaven or travelled to Jerusalem.

In addition to this strong historical evidence, other relevant circumstances lend support to the view that the two incidents were quite distinct and separate from each other: (*a*) The Qur'ān gives an account of the Holy Prophet's *Mi'rāj* (Spiritual Ascension) in Chapter, 53, but makes no reference to his *Isrā'* (Night Journey to Jerusalem), while in the present *Sūrah* it speaks of his *Isrā'* but omits all allusion to his *Mi'rāj*. (*b*) Umm Hānī' the Holy Prophet's cousin with whom he was staying on the night when the *Isrā'* (Spiritual Night Journey to Jerusalem) took place speaks only of his visit to Jerusalem and makes no mention of his journey to the heavens. She was the first person whom the Holy Prophet informed of his Night Journey to Jerusalem and at least seven collectors of Traditions have given her account of the incident on the authority of four different reporters who have reported the incident from her. All these four reporters concur in saying that the Holy Prophet went to Jerusalem and returned to Mecca the same night. If the Holy Prophet had spoken of his Ascension to the heavens also, Umm Hānī' could not have failed to refer to it in one or other of her reports. But she does not do so in any of her reports, which conclusively shows that during the night in question the Holy

1591, 1591A. See next page.

3. And [a]We gave Moses the Book and We made it a guidance for the Children of Israel, *commanding* [b]"Take ye no guardian beside Me,

وَاٰتَيْنَا مُوْسَى الْكِتٰبَ وَجَعَلْنٰهُ هُدًى لِّبَنِيْٓ اِسْرَآءِيْلَ اَلَّا تَتَّخِذُوْا مِنْ دُوْنِيْ وَكِيْلًا ۝٣

4. 'O ye, the progeny of those [c]whom We carried *in the Ark* with Noah.' He was indeed a grateful servant *of Ours*.

ذُرِّيَّةَ مَنْ حَمَلْنَا مَعَ نُوْحٍ اِنَّهٗ كَانَ عَبْدًا شَكُوْرًا ۝٤

5. And We had clearly conveyed to the Children of Israel in the Book: 'You will surely do *great* mischief in the land twice,[1592] and you will surely become excessively overbearing.'

وَقَضَيْنَآ اِلٰى بَنِيْٓ اِسْرَآءِيْلَ فِي الْكِتٰبِ لَتُفْسِدُنَّ فِي الْاَرْضِ مَرَّتَيْنِ وَلَتَعْلُنَّ عُلُوًّا كَبِيْرًا ۝٥

[a]2 : 54,88; 23 : 50; 32 : 24; 40 : 54. [b]17 : 69. [c]19 : 59; 23 : 28.

Prophet made the *Isrā'* or the Spiritual Night Journey to Jerusalem only and that the *Mi'rāj* did not take place on that occasion. It seems that some reporters of Traditions mixed up the two accounts of the *Isrā'* and the *Mi'rāj*. The confusion appears to have arisen from the word *Isrā'* (Night Journey) having been used both for the *Isrā'* and the *Mi'rāj;* and the resemblance that existed in some of the details in the descriptions of the *Isrā'* and the *Mi'rāj* heightened and confirmed it. (*c*) The Traditions which first give an account of the Holy Prophet's visit to Jerusalem and then of his transportation from Jerusalem to heaven also state that at Jerusalem he met the former Prophets, including Adam, Abraham, Moses and Jesus, and that in the heavens he met the same Prophets again but did not recognize them. How did these Prophets whom he had met at Jerusalem reach the heavens before him and why could he not recognize them while he had seen them only a short while ago in the course of the same journey. It is inconceivable that he should have failed to recognize them when he had met them only a short while ago in the course of the same journey. For a detailed discussion of this important subject see "The Larger Edition of the Commentary," pp. 1404-1409.

1591. "The Distant Mosque" refers to Prophet Solomon's Temple at Jerusalem.

1591A. The Vision of the Prophet referred to in the present verse implied a great prophecy. His journey to "The Distant Mosque" meant his Emigration to Medina where he was to build a Mosque which was destined to become later on the Central Mosque of Islām, and his seeing himself in the Vision that he was leading other Prophets of God in Prayers signified that the New Faith—Islām—was not to remain confined to the place of its birth but was to spread all over the world and the followers of all religions were to join its fold. His going to Jerusalem in the Vision may also be understood to mean that he was to be given dominion over the territory in which Jerusalem was situated. This prophecy was fulfilled during the Caliphate of 'Umar. The Vision may also be taken as referring to a spiritual journey of the Holy Prophet to a distant land in some future time. It meant that when spiritual darkness would envelop the entire world, the Holy Prophet would appear in a spiritual sense a second time in the person of one of his followers, in a land far away from the scene of his First Advent. A pointed reference to this Second Advent of the Holy Prophet is to be found in 62 : 3-4.

1592. The two transgressions of the Israelites mentioned in the Book of Moses (Deut. 28 : 15; 49-53, 63-64 & 30 : 15) are referred to in this verse. Those amongst the Children of Israel who disbelieved were cursed twice by David and Jesus, son of Mary (5 : 79) and consequently were punished twice.

6. So when the time for *the fulfilment of* the first[1593] of the two warnings came, We sent against you *some* servants of Ours, possessed of great might in war, and they penetrated into *your* houses and it was a warning that was bound to be fulfilled.

فَإِذَا جَآءَ وَعْدُ أُولٰىهُمَا بَعَثْنَا عَلَيْكُمْ عِبَادًا لَّنَآ
أُولِىْ بَأْسٍ شَدِيْدٍ فَجَاسُوْا خِلٰلَ الدِّيَارِ ۚ وَكَانَ وَعْدًا
مَّفْعُوْلًا ⑥

7. Then We gave you back the power against them and aided you with wealth and children and *also* made you larger in numbers[1594] *than before.*

ثُمَّ رَدَدْنَا لَكُمُ الْكَرَّةَ عَلَيْهِمْ وَأَمْدَدْنٰكُمْ بِأَمْوَالٍ
وَّبَنِيْنَ وَجَعَلْنٰكُمْ أَكْثَرَ نَفِيْرًا ⑦

1593. The first Divine punishment overtook the Israelites after David, and the second after Jesus. It appears from the Bible that the Jews had become a very powerful nation after Moses, and in the time of David they laid the foundations of a mighty kingdom which continued to flourish for sometime after his death in its old might and glory. Then it fell a prey to gradual decay and in about 733 B.C. Samaria was conquered by the Assyrians, who annexed the whole of Israel north of Jezreel. In 608 B.C. Palestine was ravaged by an Egyptian force under Pharaoh Necho and the Israelites came under Egyptian sway (Jew. Enc., vol. 6, p. 665). The loss of their temporal power and their destruction and desolation, however, did not induce them to mend their ways. They persisted in their old wicked practices. The Prophet Jeremiah warned them to give up their evil ways as the wrath of God was about to overtake them, but they paid no heed to Jeremiah's warnings. In the reign of Jehoiakim, Nebuchadnezzar of Babylon made his first invasion of Palestine and carried off some of the Temple vessels, but the city was spared the rigours of a siege. In 597 B.C. also the city was invested and fell victim to a severe famine. The rebellion of Zedekiah, however, caused a second invasion by **Nebuchadnezzar** in 587 B.C., and after a siege of a year and a half, the city was taken by storm. King Zedekiah fled from the city but was taken prisoner. His sons were slain and his eyes were put out, and bound in fetters he was carried off to Babylon. The Temple, the King's palace and all the great buildings in the city were burnt down, the chief priests and other leaders were put to death and many people were carried off in captivity (Jew. Enc. vol. 6, p. 665 & vol. 7, p. 122 under "Jerusalem").

1594. The Jews fared well in exile. Most of them were employed on public works in central Babylonia and many among them eventually gained their freedom and rose to influential positions. Their faith and religious devotion were renewed; the literature of the Kingdom was studied, re-edited, and adapted to the needs of the reviving Community, and the hope of restoration to Palestine was preached and cherished. About 545 B.C., this aspiration took a more definite form. The Jews made a secret agreement with Cyrus, King of Media and Persia and helped him to conquer Babylon. The city surrendered to his army without resistance in July, 539 B.C. As a reward for their services Cyrus permitted the Jews to return to Jerusalem and also helped them to rebuild the Temple (Historians' History of the World, vol. II, p. 126; Jew. Enc., vol. 7, under "Jerusalem;" Enc. Bib., under "Cyrus" and 2 Chronicles 36 : 22,23). The Judean, Sheshbazzar (a governor under Cyrus) brought back to the Temple vessels which Nebuchadnezzar had carried away and prepared to undertake the work at the expense of the royal purse. A large body of exiles returned to Jerusalem (Ezra 1 : 3-5). The work of rebuilding the Temple steadily progressed and was completed in 516 B.C. It is to these events and the subsequent prosperity of the Jews that the verse under comment refers. All this, however, was foretold by Moses long before it came to pass (Deut. 30 : 1-5).

8. *Now*, [a]if you do good, you will do good for your own souls; and if you do evil, it will be to your own loss. So when the time for *the fulfilment of* the latter warning came, *We raised a people against you* that they might cover your faces with grief,[1594A] and that they enter the Mosque, as they entered it the first time, and that they might destroy utterly all that they conquered.[1595]

إِنْ أَحْسَنتُمْ أَحْسَنتُمْ لِأَنفُسِكُمْ وَإِنْ أَسَأْتُمْ فَلَهَا
فَإِذَا جَآءَ وَعْدُ الْآخِرَةِ لِيَسُوٓءُوا وُجُوهَكُمْ وَلِيَدْخُلُوا
الْمَسْجِدَ كَمَا دَخَلُوهُ أَوَّلَ مَرَّةٍ وَلِيُتَبِّرُوا مَا عَلَوْا
تَتْبِيرًا ﴿٨﴾

9. It may be that your Lord will *now* have mercy on you; but if you return *to mischief*, We too will return *to punishment*, and *remember* We have made Hell a prison for the disbelievers.

عَسٰى رَبُّكُمْ أَن يَرْحَمَكُمْ وَإِنْ عُدتُّمْ عُدْنَا وَجَعَلْنَا
جَهَنَّمَ لِلْكٰفِرِينَ حَصِيرًا ﴿٩﴾

10. Surely, [b]this Qur'ān guides to what is most right; and gives to the believers who do good deeds the glad tidings that they shall have a great reward;[1596]

إِنَّ هٰذَا الْقُرْآنَ يَهْدِي لِلَّتِي هِيَ أَقْوَمُ وَيُبَشِّرُ
الْمُؤْمِنِينَ الَّذِينَ يَعْمَلُونَ الصّٰلِحٰتِ أَنَّ لَهُمْ
أَجْرًا كَبِيرًا ﴿١٠﴾

[a]4 : 124-125; 6 : 161; 28 : 85; 41 : 47; 99 : 8-9. [b]12 : 112; 16 : 103; 18 : 3.

1594A. The words also mean : 'They might humiliate your leaders,' *wujūh* meaning leaders (Lane).

1595. This verse speaks of the second relapse into iniquitous ways of the Jews and of the punishment which befell them in consequence. They persecuted Jesus and sought to kill him on the Cross and stamp out his Movement. So God afflicted them with a terrible punishment when in 70 A.D. the Roman forces under Titus swept the country and amid circumstances of unparalleled horror Jerusalem was destroyed and the Temple of Solomon was burnt down (Enc. Bib., under "Jerusalem"). This disaster took place when Jesus was yet living in Kashmir. This was also foretold by Moses (Deut. 32 : 18-26). It may be noted here that this prophecy about the second punishment is mentioned in the Bible after the prophecy which speaks of the first punishment (Deut. chap. 28). More than that, it is mentioned even after the prophecy which speaks of the return of the Jews to Jerusalem (Deut. 30 : 1-5). This shows that this prophecy (Deut. 32 : 18-26) refers to the second punishment, to which reference has been made in the Qur'ān, *viz.*, *You will surely do great mischief in the land twice* (17 : 5). The verse implied a warning for Muslims that, like the Jews, they too will be punished twice if they did not give up their evil ways. But they did not profit by the timely warning and did not give up their evil ways and were punished twice. The first punishment overtook them when Bagdad fell in 1258 A.D. The barbarous hordes of Halaku completely destroyed that great seat of learning and power and 18,00,000 Muslims are said to have been put to the sword. Islām, however, emerged triumphant from that dreadful catastrophe. The victors became the vanquished. The grandson of Halaku along with a large number of Mongols and the Tartars accepted Islām. The second punishment was decreed to overtake them in the Latter Days.

1596. The goal which the Qur'ān sets before its followers is nobler and more sublime than that of the former peoples, and promises its true followers both spiritual and temporal blessings. They should, therefore, make great efforts to attain them and be on their guard against a lax and undisciplined life and in every way prove themselves deserving of the promised Divine boons.

11. And *warns* that for [a]those who do not believe in the Hereafter We have prepared a grievous punishment.

وَّاَنَّ الَّذِيْنَ لَا يُؤْمِنُوْنَ بِالْاٰخِرَةِ اَعْتَدْنَا لَهُمْ عَذَابًا
اَلِيْمًا ﴿١١﴾ ع

R. 2 12. And [b]man prays for evil as he should pray for good;[1597] and man is very hasty.

وَيَدْعُ الْاِنْسَانُ بِالشَّرِّ دُعَآءَهٗ بِالْخَيْرِ ۭ وَكَانَ الْاِنْسَانُ
عَجُوْلًا ﴿١٢﴾

13. And [c]We have made the night and the day two Signs, and the Sign of night We have made dark, and the Sign of day We have made sight-giving, that you may seek bounty from your Lord, and [d]that you may know the computation of years and *the process of* reckoning.[1598] And everything We have explained with a detailed explanation.

وَجَعَلْنَا الَّيْلَ وَالنَّهَارَ اٰيَتَيْنِ فَمَحَوْنَآ اٰيَةَ الَّيْلِ
وَجَعَلْنَآ اٰيَةَ النَّهَارِ مُبْصِرَةً لِّتَبْتَغُوْا فَضْلًا مِّنْ
رَّبِّكُمْ وَلِتَعْلَمُوْا عَدَدَ السِّنِيْنَ وَالْحِسَابَ ۭ وَكُلَّ
شَيْءٍ فَصَّلْنٰهُ تَفْصِيْلًا ﴿١٣﴾

14. And every man's works have We [e]fastened to his neck;[1599] 'and on the Day of Resurrection We shall bring out for him a book which he will find wide open.

وَكُلَّ اِنْسَانٍ اَلْزَمْنٰهُ طٰٓئِرَهٗ فِيْ عُنُقِهٖ ۭ وَنُخْرِجُ
لَهٗ يَوْمَ الْقِيٰمَةِ كِتٰبًا يَّلْقٰىهُ مَنْشُوْرًا ﴿١٤﴾

[a]16 : 23; 27 : 5; 34 : 9. [b]10 : 12. [c]36 : 38; 40 : 62; 41 : 38. [d]10 : 6. [e]45 : 29; 83 : 7-10.

1597. The Arabic expression means that such is the condition of man that while by words of his mouth he prays to God to grant him good, by his actual evil deeds he invites the displeasure and punishment of God. Thus his actions belie his words. The expression may also be taken to mean that 'man calls for evil as he should have called for good.' According to both the renderings the verse signifies that when nations or individuals attain material wealth and rise to power and influence, they tend to neglect their duties and responsibilities and thus in the very hour of their power and glory they lay the foundations of their later decay and death. The verse may also mean that man invites evil to himself with the same zeal and vehemence as God invites him to good. In this case the act of inviting to good will be taken as referring to God.

1598. Both night and day have their benefits for man; but whereas the benefits of the night are subtle and hidden, those of the day are clear and manifest. The verse may also signify that the natural phenomenon of the alternation of night and day helps man to determine dates of the year and to prepare calendars. This phenomenon has also led to the development and progress of the science of mathematics.

1599. The fastening of the works to the neck of a man denotes that his actions and their effects stick to him permanently as long as he lives, *Ṭā'ir* (bird) signifying an habitual act (Aqrab). He is reminded that a deed once done cannot be undone and has far-reaching effects and, even if hidden from the human eye, it remains attached to the doer's neck, and it is impossible to obliterate it. The verse may also mean that man augurs good or evil from outside things while his good or bad augury is inseparably linked to his own neck.

15. *It will be said to him,* [a]'Read thy book. Sufficient is thy own soul as reckoner against thee this day.'

اِقْرَاْ كِتٰبَكَ ۭ كَفٰى بِنَفْسِكَ الْيَوْمَ عَلَيْكَ حَسِيْبًا ﴿١٥﴾

16. [b]He who follows the right way follows it only *for* the good of his *own* soul; and he who goes astray, goes astray only to his *own loss.*[1600] [c]And no bearer of burden shall bear the burden of another.[1601] And [d]We never punish until We have sent a Messenger.[1602]

مَنِ اهْتَدٰى فَاِنَّمَا يَهْتَدِيْ لِنَفْسِهٖ ۚ وَمَنْ ضَلَّ
فَاِنَّمَا يَضِلُّ عَلَيْهَا ۭ وَلَا تَزِرُ وَازِرَةٌ وِّزْرَ اُخْرٰى ۭ
وَمَا كُنَّا مُعَذِّبِيْنَ حَتّٰى نَبْعَثَ رَسُوْلًا ﴿١٦﴾

17. And [e]when We intend to destroy a township,[1603] We command its people who live in comfort *to adopt the way of righteousness* but they transgress therein, so the sentence *of punishment* becomes due against it, so We destroy it with utter destruction.

وَاِذَآ اَرَدْنَآ اَنْ نُّهْلِكَ قَرْيَةً اَمَرْنَا مُتْرَفِيْهَا
فَفَسَقُوْا فِيْهَا فَحَقَّ عَلَيْهَا الْقَوْلُ فَدَمَّرْنٰهَا تَدْمِيْرًا ﴿١٧﴾

18. [f]How many generations did We destroy after Noah! And thy Lord suffices as Knower and Seer of the sins of His servants.

وَكَمْ اَهْلَكْنَا مِنَ الْقُرُوْنِ مِنْۢ بَعْدِ نُوْحٍ ۭ وَكَفٰى
بِرَبِّكَ بِذُنُوْبِ عِبَادِهٖ خَبِيْرًۢا بَصِيْرًا ﴿١٨﴾

19. [g]Whoso desires the present life, We hasten for him therein *of its provision* what We will—for such

مَنْ كَانَ يُرِيْدُ الْعَاجِلَةَ عَجَّلْنَا لَهٗ فِيْهَا مَا نَشَآءُ لِمَنْ

[a]17 : 72; 45 : 30; 69 : 20,26,27. [b]10 : 109; 39 : 42. [c]6 : 165; 35 : 19; 39 : 8; 53 : 39. [d]28 : 60. [e]22 : 46; 28 : 59. [f]21 : 12; 65 : 9. [g]3 : 146; 42 : 21.

1600. Punishment is not something that comes from outside but it takes its birth within man himself. In fact, the punishments and rewards of Heaven and Hell will only be so many embodiments and representations of the deeds, good or bad, of man done by him in this life. Thus in this life man is the architect of his own destiny and in the next he will be, so to say, his own rewarder or punisher.

1601. Everyone has to bear his own cross. Nobody's vicarious sacrifice can do him any good. The verse strikes at the root of the doctrine of atonement.

1602. The world has, in our own generation, seen pestilences, famines, wars, earthquakes and other calamities of unprecedented severity and unparalleled magnitude in such rapid succession as to embitter human life. Before these calamities and catastrophes visited the earth, God must have raised a Warner.

1603. By *Qaryah* (township) is here meant the Mother-town, *i.e.,* a town which serves as a metropolis or centre of culture and politics for other towns.

of them as We please; then We appoint Hell for him; he shall burn therein condemned *and* rejected.

نُرِيْدُ ثُمَّ جَعَلْنَا لَهٗ جَهَنَّمَ يَصْلٰهَا مَذْمُوْمًا مَّدْحُوْرًا ﴿۱۹﴾

20. [a]And whoso desires the Hereafter and strives for it[1604] as it should be striven for and is a believer—these are the ones whose striving shall be duly appreciated.

وَمَنْ اَرَادَ الْاٰخِرَةَ وَسَعٰى لَهَا سَعْيَهَا وَهُوَ مُؤْمِنٌ فَاُولٰٓئِكَ كَانَ سَعْيُهُمْ مَّشْكُوْرًا ﴿۲۰﴾

21. To all We render aid—to those as well as to these—a gift from thy Lord. And the gift of thy Lord is not restricted.[1605]

كُلًّا نُّمِدُّ هٰٓؤُلَآءِ وَهٰٓؤُلَآءِ مِنْ عَطَآءِ رَبِّكَ ؕ وَمَا كَانَ عَطَآءُ رَبِّكَ مَحْظُوْرًا ﴿۲۱﴾

22. Behold, how We have exalted some of them over others *in the present life;* [b]and surely the Hereafter shall be greater in degrees *of rank* and greater in excellence.

اُنْظُرْ كَيْفَ فَضَّلْنَا بَعْضَهُمْ عَلٰى بَعْضٍ ؕ وَلَلْاٰخِرَةُ اَكْبَرُ دَرَجٰتٍ وَّاَكْبَرُ تَفْضِيْلًا ﴿۲۲﴾

23. So [c]set not up another god with Allāh[1606] lest thou sit down condemned *and* forsaken.

لَا تَجْعَلْ مَعَ اللّٰهِ اِلٰهًا اٰخَرَ فَتَقْعُدَ مَذْمُوْمًا مَّخْذُوْلًا ﴿۲۳﴾ ع٢

R. 3 24. [d]Thy Lord has commanded, *that ye* worship none but Him, [e]and *that ye* show kindness to parents.[1607] If one or both of them

وَقَضٰى رَبُّكَ اَلَّا تَعْبُدُوْٓا اِلَّآ اِيَّاهُ وَبِالْوَالِدَيْنِ اِحْسَانًا ؕ اِمَّا يَبْلُغَنَّ عِنْدَكَ الْكِبَرَ اَحَدُهُمَآ اَوْ

[a]3 : 146; 42: 21. [b]6 : 33; 12 : 58; 16 : 42. [c]17 : 40; 26 : 214; 28 : 89. [d]2 : 84; 4 : 37; 12 : 41; 41 : 15. [e]6 : 152; 29 : 9; 31 : 15; 46 : 16.

1604. The pronoun 'it' refers to the Hereafter and the meaning is that only such efforts, as are calculated to secure the good of the Hereafter, will be productive of really good results.

1605. Divine aid is of two kinds: (1) General aid, as a result of which good works and efforts of all sorts of peoples—Muslims, Christians, Jews, Hindus, etc., bear fruit according to their scope and magnitude; and (2) special grace and succour of God which is confined to spiritual matters and which is given to His true servants only and is denied to disbelievers.

1606. *Shirk* (associating false gods with Allāh) causes man to sink morally and spiritually. Never has a people, steeped in *Shirk*, been known to have made any real moral or material progress. In fact all evils spring from *Shirk*.

1607. With this verse begin those principles and rules of conduct by observing which a people can preserve the integrity of their organization and render it safe against disintegration and decline. Pride of place is given to belief in the Oneness of God and condemnation of *Shirk* (setting up equals with Allāh), because belief in Divine Unity is a seed out of which grow all virtues, and lack of which lies at the root of all sins. It constitutes the basis and the foundation for both the law of nature and the law of the *Sharī'ah*. That the whole law of the

attain old age with thee, never say to them as much as ugh[1608] nor reproach them, but always address them with kindly speech.

كِلٰهُمَا فَلَا تَقُلْ لَّهُمَآ اُفٍّ وَّلَا تَنْهَرْهُمَا وَقُلْ لَّهُمَا
قَوْلًا كَرِيْمًا ﴿٢٤﴾

25. And lower to them the wing of humility out of tenderness. And say, [a]'My Lord, have mercy on them[1609] even as they nourished me *when I was a* little *child.*'

وَاخْفِضْ لَهُمَا جَنَاحَ الذُّلِّ مِنَ الرَّحْمَةِ وَقُلْ
رَّبِّ ارْحَمْهُمَا كَمَا رَبَّيٰنِيْ صَغِيْرًا ﴿٢٥﴾

26. Your Lord knows best what is in your minds, if you are righteous, then surely, He is Most Forgiving to those who turn *to Him* again and again.

رَبُّكُمْ اَعْلَمُ بِمَا فِيْ نُفُوْسِكُمْ اِنْ تَكُوْنُوْا صٰلِحِيْنَ
فَاِنَّهٗ كَانَ لِلْاَوَّابِيْنَ غَفُوْرًا ﴿٢٦﴾

27. [b]And give to the kinsman his due, and to the poor and the wayfarer, and squander not *thy wealth* extravagantly.

وَاٰتِ ذَا الْقُرْبٰى حَقَّهٗ وَالْمِسْكِيْنَ وَابْنَ السَّبِيْلِ
وَلَا تُبَذِّرْ تَبْذِيْرًا ﴿٢٧﴾

28. [c]Verily, the squanderers are brothers of satans and Satan is ungrateful[1610] to his Lord.

اِنَّ الْمُبَذِّرِيْنَ كَانُوْٓا اِخْوَانَ الشَّيٰطِيْنِ وَكَانَ
الشَّيْطٰنُ لِرَبِّهٖ كَفُوْرًا ﴿٢٨﴾

---

[a]14 : 42; 46 : 16; 71 : 29. [b]16 : 91; 30 : 39. [c]6 : 142; 7 : 32; 25 : 68.

Sharī'ah is based on belief in the Unity of God is too patent a reality to need any explanation; but even the law of nature and all scientific progress are also based on it. For, if it be supposed that there are more gods than one, it necessarily follows that there are more than one law of nature. But in the absence of one fixed and uniform natural law all progress of science will come to an end, because all the discoveries and inventions made by science are due to the belief that an ordered, fixed and unchangeable system pervades the whole universe. The second important commandment laid down in the verse concerns man's moral conduct. His obligations towards his parents form the most important part of it, because it is his parents who first of all direct a man's attention to God and it is in the parental mirror that Divine attributes are reflected and on a minor human scale are given practical expression. But whereas the commandment in relation to God is negative, in the case of parents it is positive. Man is told that since it is not possible for him to make a return of God's favours, he should at least refrain from *Shirk*, but as in the case of parents he is in a position to return their love and kindness, though only very inadequately, he is given a positive commandment to be kind and generous to them.

1608. In Arabic the word *Uff* is used to express one's disgust by words of mouth and *Nahr* is used to express it by actual deed. By combining these two words the verse means that one should never speak harshly to one's parents, much less act unkindly towards them.

1609. By a beautiful simile the verse inculcates kindness to parents. As parental love is incapable of being adequately repaid, the deficiency in this respect is enjoined to be made up by prayer for them. The prayer shows that in old age parents need to be tended as carefully and affectionately as little children are looked after in their childhood by their parents.

1610. He who does not make right use of God-given gifts is guilty of ingratitude to Him, and he who, squanders away his wealth, in fact, seeks to shirk the responsibilities which lie upon him for its proper use.

29. And if thou hast to turn away from them while seeking thy Lord's mercy for which thou hopest, *even then* [a]speak to them a kind word.[1611]

وَإِمَّا تُعْرِضَنَّ عَنْهُمُ ابْتِغَاءَ رَحْمَةٍ مِّن رَّبِّكَ تَرْجُوهَا فَقُل لَّهُمْ قَوْلًا مَّيْسُورًا ﴿٢٩﴾

30. [b]And keep not thy hand chained to thy neck *out of miserliness*, nor stretch it forth to its utmost limit *out of extravagance*, lest thou sit down blamed, exhausted.[1612]

وَلَا تَجْعَلْ يَدَكَ مَغْلُولَةً إِلَىٰ عُنُقِكَ وَلَا تَبْسُطْهَا كُلَّ الْبَسْطِ فَتَقْعُدَ مَلُومًا مَّحْسُورًا ﴿٣٠﴾

31. Surely, [c]thy Lord enlarges *His* provision for whom He pleases, and straitens *it for whom He pleases*. Verily, He knows *and* sees His servants full well.

إِنَّ رَبَّكَ يَبْسُطُ الرِّزْقَ لِمَن يَشَاءُ وَيَقْدِرُ ۚ إِنَّهُ كَانَ بِعِبَادِهِ خَبِيرًا بَصِيرًا ﴿٣١﴾ ع

R. 4 32. And [d]slay not your children for fear of poverty.[1613] It is We Who provide for them and for you. Surely, the slaying of them is a grievous sin.[1614]

وَلَا تَقْتُلُوا أَوْلَادَكُمْ خَشْيَةَ إِمْلَاقٍ ۖ نَّحْنُ نَرْزُقُهُمْ وَإِيَّاكُمْ ۚ إِنَّ قَتْلَهُمْ كَانَ خِطْئًا كَبِيرًا ﴿٣٢﴾

[a]93 : 10-11. [b]9 : 34; 25 : 68. [c]13 : 27; 29 : 63; 30 : 38; 39 : 53. [d]6 : 152.

1611. Help may sometimes be denied to a seemingly needy person when it is feared that the giving of it would have an adverse effect upon him; for instance, he may be a professional beggar or may be addicted to some bad habit. In such a case a word of good cheer may be used to give comfort to the beggar.

1612. A believer should not be so miserly as not to spend his money even when there is a real and genuine need for it, nor should he squander away his money thoughtlessly and without purpose so that when money is required for a real national need he should find to his regret that he could not contribute to it.

1613. Those miserly parents who do not give proper education to, or provide proper food and clothing for, their children, in fact, contribute both to their physical and moral death. The verse strongly condemns such "slaying" of innocent children who, if given right kind of education and afforded proper opportunities to rise to their full stature, are likely to become very useful members of the society. The "slaying of children" may also signify the questionable practice of unnecessary birth control which is encouraged in modern society.

1614. The words *Khiṭ'* and *Khaṭa'* differ in their significance. Whereas the former is intentional, the latter may both be intentional and unintentional (Aqrab). The Qur'ān has used the former word to establish the fact that the slaying of children is a crime at which human nature revolts and recoils and only a person devoid of all human feelings is capable of doing it.

33. [a]And go not nigh unto adultery,[1615] surely, it is a manifest indecency and an evil way.

وَلَا تَقْرَبُوا الزِّنٰٓى اِنَّهٗ كَانَ فَاحِشَةً ۭ وَسَآءَ سَبِيْلًا ﴿٣٣﴾

34. [b]And slay not the soul, *the slaying of* which Allāh has forbidden, save for a just cause. And whoso is slain wrongfully, We have surely given his heir authority *to demand retribution* but let him not exceed the *prescribed* bounds in slaying; for *therein* he will be supported *by law*.[1616]

وَلَا تَقْتُلُوا النَّفْسَ الَّتِيْ حَرَّمَ اللّٰهُ اِلَّا بِالْحَقِّ ۭ وَمَنْ قُتِلَ مَظْلُوْمًا فَقَدْ جَعَلْنَا لِوَلِيِّهٖ سُلْطٰنًا فَلَا يُسْرِفْ فِّي الْقَتْلِ ۭ اِنَّهٗ كَانَ مَنْصُوْرًا ﴿٣٤﴾

35. [c]And come not near the property of the orphan, except, in the best way, until he attains his maturity and [d]fulfil the covenant;[1617] for the covenant shall be questioned about.

وَلَا تَقْرَبُوْا مَالَ الْيَتِيْمِ اِلَّا بِالَّتِيْ هِيَ اَحْسَنُ حَتّٰى يَبْلُغَ اَشُدَّهٗ ۠ وَاَوْفُوْا بِالْعَهْدِ ۚ اِنَّ الْعَهْدَ كَانَ مَسْـُٔوْلًا ﴿٣٥﴾

[a]25 : 69. [b]6 : 152; 25 : 69. [c]4 : 7,11; 6 : 153. [d]5 : 2; 16 : 92.

1615. The commandment forbidding 'the slaying of children' is followed by another equally weighty injunction about adultery because adultery also causes the death of innumerable children in different forms. Unlike the biblical commandment, 'Thou shalt not commit adultery,' the Qur'ān says, 'Go not nigh unto adultery,' which is clearly a more comprehensive and more effective and sensible commandment. The Qur'ān not only prohibits and condemns the actual act of adultery but seeks to close and shut all those avenues that lead to it.

1616. In the preceding two verses reference was made to the two indirect ways of slaying. The verse under comment speaks of direct murder. After the murderer is convicted by a properly constituted court, the heirs of the murdered person have the right either to have the murderer legally executed or accept blood-money in lieu of the death of the murdered person. If, however, it is against the interests of public peace or morality to allow blood-money to the heirs or if the demand of the heirs be found to be not *bona-fide*, the court may refuse to accept their option and order the murderer's execution. In fact, both the heirs and the State equally share the right to pardon or punish the guilty person. This right of the State in regard to the punishment of the guilty person covers all matters to which the injunction about retribution applies. Whereas in the earlier part of the verse the rights of the party offended against have been safeguarded, the words, *let him not exceed the prescribed bounds in slaying*, imply a recommendation in favour of the murderer. The words show that although 'life for life' is the general rule, the heirs of the murdered person should not always insist upon the literal execution of this commandment. The murderer is to suffer the extreme penalty of the law only when the dictates of equity, public peace and morality demand it. His life may be spared and blood-money accepted if this act of grace is calculated to lead to his moral reformation.

1617. After having laid down the law about the punishment for murder which leaves behind orphans in two families—in the family of the murderer and in that of the murdered person—the Qur'ān proceeds to give directions about the rights of orphans. One of the most important of these is with regard to their property. The word "covenant" (meaning an obligation) has been used here to emphasize the fact that taking proper care of the property of the orphans constitutes no favour to them but is a responsibility and a duty to be discharged fully and honestly.

36. [a]And give full measure when you measure and weigh with a right balance; that is best and most commendable in the end.[1618]

وَأَوْفُوا الْكَيْلَ إِذَا كِلْتُمْ وَزِنُوا بِالْقِسْطَاسِ الْمُسْتَقِيمِ ذَٰلِكَ خَيْرٌ وَأَحْسَنُ تَأْوِيلًا ﴿٣٦﴾

37. [b]And follow not that of which thou hast no knowledge. [c]Verily, the ear and the eye and the heart—all these shall be called to account.[1619]

وَلَا تَقْفُ مَا لَيْسَ لَكَ بِهِ عِلْمٌ إِنَّ السَّمْعَ وَالْبَصَرَ وَالْفُؤَادَ كُلُّ أُولَٰئِكَ كَانَ عَنْهُ مَسْئُولًا ﴿٣٧﴾

38. [d]And walk not in the earth haughtily, for thou canst not *thus* rend the earth, nor canst thou reach the mountains in height.[1620]

وَلَا تَمْشِ فِي الْأَرْضِ مَرَحًا إِنَّكَ لَنْ تَخْرِقَ الْأَرْضَ وَلَنْ تَبْلُغَ الْجِبَالَ طُولًا ﴿٣٨﴾

39. The evil of all these is hateful in the Sight of thy Lord.

كُلُّ ذَٰلِكَ كَانَ سَيِّئُهُ عِنْدَ رَبِّكَ مَكْرُوهًا ﴿٣٩﴾

40. These *injunctions* are *part* of that wisdom which thy Lord has revealed to thee. [e]And set not up with Allāh any other god, lest thou be cast into Hell, condemned *and* rejected.

ذَٰلِكَ مِمَّا أَوْحَىٰ إِلَيْكَ رَبُّكَ مِنَ الْحِكْمَةِ وَلَا تَجْعَلْ مَعَ اللَّهِ إِلَٰهًا آخَرَ فَتُلْقَىٰ فِي جَهَنَّمَ مَلُومًا مَدْحُورًا ﴿٤٠﴾

41. [f]What! has your Lord favoured you with sons and taken for Himself females from among the angels? Surely, you say a grievous saying.

أَفَأَصْفَاكُمْ رَبُّكُمْ بِالْبَنِينَ وَاتَّخَذَ مِنَ الْمَلَائِكَةِ إِنَاثًا إِنَّكُمْ لَتَقُولُونَ قَوْلًا عَظِيمًا ﴿٤١﴾

[a]7 : 86; 11 : 85-86; 26 : 182,183; 55 : 10. [b]11 : 47. [c]24 : 25; 36 : 66; 41 : 21-23. [d]31 : 19. [e]17 : 23; 26 : 214; 28 : 89. [f]37 : 151; 43 : 20; 52 40.

1618. The secret of the commercial progress and prosperity of a people lies in honest and fair dealing in commercial transactions.

1619. The verse cuts at the root of all sources of suspicion which in natural order are "the ear," "the eye" and "the heart." "The ear" is the first avenue through which most suspicions enter one's mind. Most suspicions are caused by ill-founded reports which one hears about another person. Next source is that of sight. A person sees another doing a certain act and interprets it wrongly and is led to suspect the latter's motives and intentions. The last and most degraded kind of suspicion is that which a person entertains about another person not as the result of a bad report which he might have heard about him, nor in consequence of a bad act or deed which he might have seen him committing but which is purely the figment of his own diseased mind. Thus it is not only human life and property (to which a reference has already been made in the preceding verse) which are sacred and inviolable, but human honour also is sacrosanct and an attack upon it also will have to be accounted for.

1620. To be proud of and exult over one's achievements not only smacks of frivolity, but does moral injury to the proud person, for such an attitude makes him content with what he has already achieved and is thus calculated to impede and arrest his moral progress.

R. 5 42. [a]We have explained *the truth* in this Qur'ān in various ways[1621] that they may be admonished, but it only increases them in aversion.

وَلَقَدْ صَرَّفْنَا فِي هٰذَا الْقُرْاٰنِ لِيَذَّكَّرُوْا ۭ وَمَا يَزِيْدُهُمْ
اِلَّا نُفُوْرًا ﴿٤٢﴾

43. Say, 'Had there been other gods with Him as they allege, then certainly *by their help the idolaters* would have sought out a way to the Owner of the Throne.'

قُلْ لَّوْ كَانَ مَعَهٗۤ اٰلِهَةٌ كَمَا يَقُوْلُوْنَ اِذًا لَّابْتَغَوْا اِلٰى
ذِي الْعَرْشِ سَبِيْلًا ﴿٤٣﴾

44. [b]Holy is He, and Exalted far above that which they say.

سُبْحٰنَهٗ وَتَعٰلٰى عَمَّا يَقُوْلُوْنَ عُلُوًّا كَبِيْرًا ﴿٤٤﴾

45. The seven heavens and the earth and those that are therein extol His glory; and there is not a thing but [c]glorifies Him with His praise;[1622] but you understand not their glorification. Verily, He is Forbearing, Most Forgiving.

تُسَبِّحُ لَهُ السَّمٰوٰتُ السَّبْعُ وَالْاَرْضُ وَمَنْ فِيْهِنَّ ۭ
وَاِنْ مِّنْ شَيْءٍ اِلَّا يُسَبِّحُ بِحَمْدِهٖ وَلٰكِنْ لَّا تَفْقَهُوْنَ
تَسْبِيْحَهُمْ ۭ اِنَّهٗ كَانَ حَلِيْمًا غَفُوْرًا ﴿٤٥﴾

46. And when thou recitest the Qur'ān, We put between thee and those who believe not in the Hereafter an invisible veil;

وَاِذَا قَرَاْتَ الْقُرْاٰنَ جَعَلْنَا بَيْنَكَ وَبَيْنَ الَّذِيْنَ
لَا يُؤْمِنُوْنَ بِالْاٰخِرَةِ حِجَابًا مَّسْتُوْرًا ﴿٤٦﴾

[a]17 : 90; 18 : 55. [b]6 : 101; 39 : 68. [c]24: 42; 59 : 25; 61 : 2; 62 : 2; 64 : 2.

1621. For a revealed Book which has to deal with all matters of importance it is but natural and even necessary that it should revert, time and again, to the relevant points which bear on the main theme. When repetition is intended to throw light upon a matter from a new angle or to refute a new objection, no sane and intelligent person can take objection to it.

1622. Whereas the words, *The seven heavens and the earth and those that are therein extol His glory*, refer to the collective evidence that the whole universe bears to the Unity of God, the words, *and there is not a thing but glorifies Him with His praise*, refer to the evidence which all things bear to Oneness of the Divine Being individually and separately. The former means that the beautiful arrangement and order existing in the universe unmistakably show that its Creator is One, and the latter mean that everything in this universe, within its own limited sphere and in its own inimitable way, demonstrates God's various attributes.

47. [a]And We put coverings[1623] over their hearts lest they should understand it, and in their ears a deafness. [b]And when thou makest mention in the Qur'ān of thy Lord alone, they turn their backs in aversion.

وَّجَعَلْنَا عَلٰى قُلُوْبِهِمْ اَكِنَّةً اَنْ يَّفْقَهُوْهُ وَفِيْٓ اٰذَانِهِمْ
وَقْرًا ۭ وَاِذَا ذَكَرْتَ رَبَّكَ فِي الْقُرْاٰنِ وَحْدَهٗ وَلَّوْا
عَلٰٓي اَدْبَارِهِمْ نُفُوْرًا ﴿٤٧﴾

48. We know best what they listen for, when they listen to thee, and when they confer in private, when the wrongdoers say, [c]'You follow none but a man who is a victim of deception.'

نَحْنُ اَعْلَمُ بِمَا يَسْتَمِعُوْنَ بِهٖٓ اِذْ يَسْتَمِعُوْنَ اِلَيْكَ وَاِذْ هُمْ نَجْوٰٓى
اِذْ يَقُوْلُ الظّٰلِمُوْنَ اِنْ تَتَّبِعُوْنَ اِلَّا رَجُلًا مَّسْحُوْرًا ﴿٤٨﴾

49. [d]See, how they coin similitudes for thee, and have *in consequence* gone astray so that they cannot find a way.

اُنْظُرْ كَيْفَ ضَرَبُوْا لَكَ الْاَمْثَالَ فَضَلُّوْا فَلَا يَسْتَطِيْعُوْنَ
سَبِيْلًا ﴿٤٩﴾

50. And they say, [e]'What! when we shall have become bones and broken particles, shall we be really raised up *again* as a new creation?'

وَقَالُوْٓا ءَاِذَا كُنَّا عِظَامًا وَّرُفَاتًا ءَاِنَّا لَمَبْعُوْثُوْنَ
خَلْقًا جَدِيْدًا ﴿٥٠﴾

51. Say, 'Be ye stones or iron,

قُلْ كُوْنُوْا حِجَارَةً اَوْ حَدِيْدًا ﴿٥١﴾

52. 'Or created matter of *any kind* which appears hardest[1624] in your minds, *even then shall you be raised up*.' [f]Then will they ask, 'Who shall restore us to life?' Say, 'He Who created you the first time.' Still they will shake their heads at thee and say, [g]'When will it be?' Say, 'May be, it is nigh,

اَوْ خَلْقًا مِّمَّا يَكْبُرُ فِيْ صُدُوْرِكُمْ ۚ فَسَيَقُوْلُوْنَ
مَنْ يُّعِيْدُنَا ۭ قُلِ الَّذِيْ فَطَرَكُمْ اَوَّلَ مَرَّةٍ ۚ
فَسَيُنْغِضُوْنَ اِلَيْكَ رُءُوْسَهُمْ وَيَقُوْلُوْنَ مَتٰى
هُوَ ۭ قُلْ عَسٰٓى اَنْ يَّكُوْنَ قَرِيْبًا ﴿٥٢﴾

[a]6 : 26; 18 : 58; 41 : 6. [b]17 : 49 [c]25 : 9. [d]25 : 10. [e]17 : 99; 23 : 83; 37 : 17; 56 : 48. [f]36 : 79-80. [g]34 : 30; 36 : 49; 67 : 26.

1623. It is the covering of malice and envy, or that of a false sense of dignity and racial pride or of the fear of loss of social position and income, or the covering of a long-standing custom and belief fondly and firmly held that stands in the way of the acceptance of truth by disbelievers. It is a subtle covering which disbelievers themselves do not properly perceive.

1624. The verse may either be taken as saying to disbelievers that even if their hearts should become hard like iron or stone or any other similar substance, God would bring about among them that wholesome change which He has decreed to bring about through the Holy Prophet. Or, it may be taken as answering their doubts about Resurrection mentioned in the previous verse, and says to them that they could not escape Divine punishment even if they became converted into iron or stone or any other hard substance.

53. 'It will be on the day when He will call you; then you will respond praising Him and you will think that [a]you have tarried *in the world* but a little while.'

يَوْمَ يَدْعُوكُمْ فَتَسْتَجِيبُونَ بِحَمْدِهِ وَتَظُنُّونَ إِن
لَّبِثْتُمْ إِلَّا قَلِيلًا ﴿٥٣﴾ ع ۵ ۱۲

R. 6 54. [b]And say to My servants that they should *always* speak that which is best. [c]Surely, Satan stirs up discord among them. Surely, Satan is an open enemy to man.

وَقُل لِّعِبَادِي يَقُولُوا الَّتِي هِيَ أَحْسَنُ ۚ إِنَّ الشَّيْطَٰنَ
يَنزَغُ بَيْنَهُمْ ۚ إِنَّ الشَّيْطَٰنَ كَانَ لِلْإِنسَٰنِ عَدُوًّا
مُّبِينًا ﴿٥٤﴾

55. Your Lord knows you best [d]If He please, He will have mercy on you; or if He please, He will punish you. [e]And We have not sent thee *to be* a keeper over them.

رَّبُّكُمْ أَعْلَمُ بِكُمْ ۖ إِن يَشَأْ يَرْحَمْكُمْ أَوْ إِن يَشَأْ
يُعَذِّبْكُمْ ۚ وَمَا أَرْسَلْنَٰكَ عَلَيْهِمْ وَكِيلًا ﴿٥٥﴾

56. And thy Lord knows best those that are in the heavens and the earth. And [f]We exalted some of the Prophets over the others and to David We gave a Book.

وَرَبُّكَ أَعْلَمُ بِمَن فِي السَّمَٰوَٰتِ وَالْأَرْضِ ۗ وَلَقَدْ
فَضَّلْنَا بَعْضَ النَّبِيِّينَ عَلَىٰ بَعْضٍ ۖ وَآتَيْنَا دَاوُودَ
زَبُورًا ﴿٥٦﴾

57. [g]Say, 'Call on those whom you assert *to be gods* beside Him; then *you will know that* they have no power to remove affliction from you nor to change *your condition*.'

قُلِ ادْعُوا الَّذِينَ زَعَمْتُم مِّن دُونِهِ فَلَا يَمْلِكُونَ
كَشْفَ الضُّرِّ عَنكُمْ وَلَا تَحْوِيلًا ﴿٥٧﴾

58. Those, whom they call on,[1625] *themselves* seek nearness to their Lord—*even* those of them who are nearest—and hope for His mercy, and fear His punishment. Surely, the punishment of thy Lord is a thing to be feared.

أُولَٰئِكَ الَّذِينَ يَدْعُونَ يَبْتَغُونَ إِلَىٰ رَبِّهِمُ الْوَسِيلَةَ
أَيُّهُمْ أَقْرَبُ وَيَرْجُونَ رَحْمَتَهُ وَيَخَافُونَ عَذَابَهُ ۚ
إِنَّ عَذَابَ رَبِّكَ كَانَ مَحْذُورًا ﴿٥٨﴾

---

[a]20 : 105; 23 : 114-115. [b]16 : 126; 23 : 97; 41 : 35. [c]7 : 201; 12 : 101; 41 : 37. [d]2 : 285; 3 : 129; 5 : 41; 29 : 22. [e]6 : 108; 39 : 42; 42 : 7. [f]2 : 254; 27 : 16. [g]22 : 74; 25 : 4; 34 : 23.

1625. The verse may refer to angels, Prophets and saints whom some people worship as gods.

59. [a]There is not a township but We shall destroy it before the Day of Resurrection, or punish it with a severe punishment.[1626] That is written down in the Book.

وَإِنْ مِّنْ قَرْيَةٍ إِلَّا نَحْنُ مُهْلِكُوهَا قَبْلَ يَوْمِ الْقِيٰمَةِ
أَوْ مُعَذِّبُوهَا عَذَابًا شَدِيدًا ۚ كَانَ ذٰلِكَ فِي الْكِتٰبِ
مَسْطُورًا ﴿٥٩﴾

60. [b]And nothing could hinder Us from sending Signs, except that the former people rejected[1627] them, but this *did not hinder Us*. And We gave Thamūd the she-camel as a clear Sign, but they unjustly rejected it. And We send not Signs but to warn.

وَمَا مَنَعَنَآ أَنْ نُّرْسِلَ بِالْاٰيٰتِ إِلَّآ أَنْ كَذَّبَ بِهَا
الْأَوَّلُونَ ۚ وَاٰتَيْنَا ثَمُودَ النَّاقَةَ مُبْصِرَةً فَظَلَمُوا
بِهَا ۚ وَمَا نُرْسِلُ بِالْاٰيٰتِ إِلَّا تَخْوِيفًا ﴿٦٠﴾

61. And *call to mind* when We said to thee, 'Surely, thy Lord has *decreed* the ruin of *this* people.' [c]And We made not the Vision[1627A] which We showed thee but as a trial for men, as also the tree cursed[1628] in the Qur'ān. And We *continue to* warn them, but it only increases them in great transgression.

وَإِذْ قُلْنَا لَكَ إِنَّ رَبَّكَ أَحَاطَ بِالنَّاسِ ۚ وَمَا جَعَلْنَا
الرُّءْيَا الَّتِيْٓ أَرَيْنٰكَ إِلَّا فِتْنَةً لِّلنَّاسِ وَالشَّجَرَةَ
الْمَلْعُونَةَ فِي الْقُرْاٰنِ ۚ وَنُخَوِّفُهُمْ فَمَا يَزِيدُهُمْ
إِلَّا طُغْيَانًا كَبِيرًا ﴿٦١﴾ ع

[a]21 : 12; 22 : 46; 28 : 59. [b]17 : 95; 18 : 56. [c]17 : 2.

1626. The reference is to the punishment which presages a universal calamity or series of calamities as foretold by God's Prophets and also in the Qur'ān.

1627. Or, the meaning may be: Could the fact that former people rejected the Prophets be the reason that further Signs should not be sent, *i.e.*, it could not be the reason for the withholding of heavenly Signs.

1627A. The reference here is to the Vision mentioned in v. 2 of this *Sūrah*. In this Vision the Holy Prophet saw himself leading all *other* Prophets in Prayers in the Temple at Jerusalem which was the *Qiblah* of the Jews. The Vision implied that in some future time the followers of those Prophets would join the fold of Islām. This is what is meant by the words, ***thy Lord has decreed the ruin of this people.*** The general spread of Islām would follow in the wake of the world-wide disasters of which mention has been made in v. 59.

1628. 'The cursed tree' seems to be the Jewish people who have been repeatedly mentioned in the Qur'ān as having been cursed by God (5:14,61,65,79). The curse of God has dogged the footsteps of these unfortunate people from the time of the Prophet David right down to our own time. This interpretation of the expression finds additional support from the fact that the present *Sūrah* particularly deals with the Israelites as its very name, Banī Isrā'īl, suggests. The fact that the verse begins with a mention of the Vision in which the Holy Prophet saw himself leading the Israelite Prophets in Prayers in Jerusalem, the centre of the Jewish Faith, lends further support to the assumption that by 'cursed tree' is meant the Jewish people, the word ***Shajarah*** signifying a tribe. The verse speaks both of the Vision and the Jewish people (the accursed tree) to whom this Vision specially refers as 'a trial for men.' The Jews have, throughout the ages, proved to be a source of much misery and distress for mankind, particularly for Muslims.

R. 7 62. [a]And *call to mind* when We said to the angels, 'Submit to[1629] Adam,' and they all submitted. But Iblīs *did not*. He said, 'Shall I submit to one whom Thou hast created of clay?'

وَاِذْ قُلْنَا لِلْمَلٰٓئِكَةِ اسْجُدُوْا لِاٰدَمَ فَسَجَدُوْٓا اِلَّاۤ
اِبْلِيْسَ قَالَ ءَاَسْجُدُ لِمَنْ خَلَقْتَ طِيْنًا ﴿٦٢﴾

63. *And* he said, 'What thinkest Thou? *Can* this [b]whom Thou hast honoured above me *be my superior?* If Thou wilt grant me respite till the Day of Resurrection,[1630] [c]I will most surely bring his descendants under my sway except a few.'[1631]

قَالَ اَرَءَيْتَكَ هٰذَا الَّذِيْ كَرَّمْتَ عَلَيَّ لَئِنْ اَخَّرْتَنِ
اِلٰى يَوْمِ الْقِيٰمَةِ لَاَحْتَنِكَنَّ ذُرِّيَّتَهٗۤ اِلَّا قَلِيْلًا ﴿٦٣﴾

64. [d]*Allāh* said, 'Begone! and whoso shall follow thee from among them, Hell shall surely be the recompense of you all—a full recompense;

قَالَ اذْهَبْ فَمَنْ تَبِعَكَ مِنْهُمْ فَاِنَّ جَهَنَّمَ جَزَآؤُكُمْ
جَزَآءً مَّوْفُوْرًا ﴿٦٤﴾

65. [e]'And entice whomsoever of them thou canst with thy voice, and urge against them thy horsemen and thy footmen and share with them in wealth, and *their* children, and make promises to them.'[1632] [f]And Satan promises them naught but deceit.

وَاسْتَفْزِزْ مَنِ اسْتَطَعْتَ مِنْهُمْ بِصَوْتِكَ وَاَجْلِبْ
عَلَيْهِمْ بِخَيْلِكَ وَرَجِلِكَ وَشَارِكْهُمْ فِي الْاَمْوَالِ
وَالْاَوْلَادِ وَعِدْهُمْ ؕ وَمَا يَعِدُهُمُ الشَّيْطٰنُ اِلَّا غُرُوْرًا ﴿٦٥﴾

---

[a]2 : 35; 7 : 12; 15 : 30-31; 18 : 51; 20 : 117; 38 : 73-75. [b]7 : 13; 15 : 34; 38 : 77. [c]7 : 17-18; 15 : 40. [d]7 : 19; 15 : 43-44; 38 : 86. [e]7 : 18. [f]4 : 121; 14 : 23.

1629. The particle *lām* among other things means, "with." The expression *li Ādama* may mean 'with Adam.'

1630. By "resurrection" is here meant the spiritual resurrection which is experienced by every believer when his faith becomes perfect and Satan ceases to exercise control over him.

1631. Whether or not Satan has succeeded in carrying out his threat in leading astray a vast majority of mankind is an important question which calls for an answer. A hurried and thoughtless glance over the state of good and evil in the world may lead one to the wrong conclusion that evil predominates over good in the world. But the truth is the other way about. If, for example, all the utterances of the greatest of liars were to be critically examined, the number of his truthful utterances will be found to be far exceeding his lies. Similarly, the number of the wicked people in the world is much smaller than that of the good and the virtuous people. The fact that wickedness attracts such wide notice in itself constitutes a proof of the fact that human nature is innately good and recoils at even a slight touch of evil. It is, therefore, wrong to suppose that Satan has succeeded in carrying his threat into actual fact.

1632. See next page.

66. [a]*As to* My servants, thou shalt certainly have no power[1633] over them, and sufficient is thy Lord as a Guardian.

إِنَّ عِبَادِي لَيْسَ لَكَ عَلَيْهِمْ سُلْطٰنٌ وَكَفٰى بِرَبِّكَ
وَكِيلًا ﴿٦٦﴾

67. [b]Your Lord is He Who drives for you the ships in the sea, that you may seek of His bounty. Surely, He is Ever-Merciful towards you.

رَبُّكُمُ الَّذِي يُزْجِي لَكُمُ الْفُلْكَ فِي الْبَحْرِ لِتَبْتَغُوا
مِنْ فَضْلِهٖ إِنَّهٗ كَانَ بِكُمْ رَحِيمًا ﴿٦٧﴾

68. [c]And when harm touches you on the sea, *all* those whom you call upon, except Him, are lost *to you*. But when He brings you safe to land, you turn aside; and man is very ungrateful.[1634]

وَإِذَا مَسَّكُمُ الضُّرُّ فِي الْبَحْرِ ضَلَّ مَنْ تَدْعُوْنَ إِلَّا
إِيَّاهُ فَلَمَّا نَجّٰىكُمْ إِلَى الْبَرِّ أَعْرَضْتُمْ وَكَانَ
الْإِنْسَانُ كَفُوْرًا ﴿٦٨﴾

69. [d]Do you then feel secure that He will not cause you to sink *in the earth* on the side of the shore or send against you a violent sandstorm and then you will find no guardian for yourselves?

أَفَأَمِنْتُمْ أَنْ يَّخْسِفَ بِكُمْ جَانِبَ الْبَرِّ أَوْ يُرْسِلَ
عَلَيْكُمْ حَاصِبًا ثُمَّ لَا تَجِدُوْا لَكُمْ وَكِيلًا ﴿٦٩﴾

70. Or, do you feel secure that He will not send you back therein a second time, and [e]then send against you a storm-blast, and drown you because of your disbelief? You will then find therein no helper for yourselves against Us.

أَمْ أَمِنْتُمْ أَنْ يُّعِيْدَكُمْ فِيْهِ تَارَةً أُخْرٰى فَيُرْسِلَ
عَلَيْكُمْ قَاصِفًا مِّنَ الرِّيْحِ فَيُغْرِقَكُمْ بِمَا كَفَرْتُمْ
ثُمَّ لَا تَجِدُوْا لَكُمْ عَلَيْنَا بِهٖ تَبِيْعًا ﴿٧٠﴾

[a]15 : 41; 38 : 84. [b]14 : 33; 22 : 66; 45 : 13. [c]10 : 13; 11 : 10-11; 23 : 65; 30 : 34; 39 : 9; 41 : 50-52; 70 : 21-22. [d]67 : 17-18. [e]67 : 18.

1632. The verse describes the three devices that are adopted by the sons of darkness to entice men away from the right way: (1) They try to intimidate the poor and the weak by holding out threats of violence to them. (2) They use more drastic measures against those who are not frightened by verbal threats of violence by forming alliances against them and making a concerted attack upon them and persecuting and oppressing them in every way. (3) They seek to entice away the powerful and the more influential by offering to make them their leaders if only they cease to support the cause of truth.

1633. Man is amenable to the enticements of Satan so long as he is not "resurrected," *i.e.*, so long as his faith does not attain its full stature.

1634. Such is the nature of man that when he is in distress he becomes humble and prays to God and promises and vows to lead a virtuous life. But once he is out of danger he is as arrogant and boastful as ever.

71. Indeed, We have honoured the children of Adam,[1635] and We carry them by land and sea,[1635A] and provide them with good things and have exalted them far above many of those whom We have created.[1635B]

وَلَقَدْ كَرَّمْنَا بَنِيٓ اٰدَمَ وَحَمَلْنٰهُمْ فِي الْبَرِّ وَالْبَحْرِ وَرَزَقْنٰهُمْ مِّنَ الطَّيِّبٰتِ وَفَضَّلْنٰهُمْ عَلٰى كَثِيْرٍ مِّمَّنْ خَلَقْنَا تَفْضِيْلًا ﴿۷۱﴾

R. 8 72. *Call to mind* the day when We shall summon every people with their Leader. [a]Then whoso shall be given his book in his right hand[1636]—such will read their book *eagerly* and they will not be wronged a whit.

يَوْمَ نَدْعُوْا كُلَّ اُنَاسٍۭ بِاِمَامِهِمْ ۚ فَمَنْ اُوْتِيَ كِتٰبَهٗ بِيَمِيْنِهٖ فَاُولٰٓئِكَ يَقْرَءُوْنَ كِتٰبَهُمْ وَلَا يُظْلَمُوْنَ فَتِيْلًا ﴿۷۲﴾

73. [b]But whoso is blind in this world shall be blind in the Hereafter,[1637] and even more astray from the way.

وَمَنْ كَانَ فِيْ هٰذِهٖٓ اَعْمٰى فَهُوَ فِي الْاٰخِرَةِ اَعْمٰى وَاَضَلُّ سَبِيْلًا ﴿۷۳﴾

[a]69 : 20; 84 : 8, 9. [b]20 : 125.

1635. God has equally honoured all the children of Adam and has not favoured any particular nation or tribe. The verse demolishes all foolish notions of superiority based on colour, creed, race or nationality. It further says that all avenues of progress and prosperity have been kept open equally for all men and these avenues lie as much in travel by land as by sea.

1635A. The laying of stress on travel by sea in the Qur'ān seems to be rather strange. The fact, that a Book revealed to an Arab, and of all Arabs the Holy Prophet, who throughout his life never experienced a sea-voyage, should have so much emphasized the importance of sea-voyaging, does indeed show that the Qur'ān could not have been his composition. He did not and could not know the great benefits of sea-voyaging.

1635B. As a class man, being God's vicegerent on earth, is superior to all other creation.

1636. The right hand is a symbol of blessing while the left is that of punishment. Also in the human body the right side enjoys a certain superiority over the left since the tissues of the right side generally are stronger than those of the left. Giving of the record of one's deeds in one's right hand as mentioned in this verse signifies that it will be a favourable and blessed record. Again, the right hand signifies strength and power (69 : 46). The holding by believers of their records in their right hands is meant to signify that they had taken hold of virtue with strength and resolution, while the holding by disbelievers of their records in their left hands would signify that they did not strive after virtue with requisite strength and zeal.

1637. Those, who do not make proper use of their spiritual eyes in this world, would remain deprived of spiritual sight in the life to come. The Qur'ān speaks of those who do not ponder over the Signs of God and do not benefit by them as "blind." Such men will remain spiritually blind in the next life also.

74. [a]And they had well-nigh caused thee *severest* affliction on account of what We have revealed to thee that thou mightest forge against Us something other than that;[1638] and then they would have certainly taken thee for a *special* friend.

وَإِنْ كَادُوْا لَيَفْتِنُوْنَكَ عَنِ الَّذِيْٓ أَوْحَيْنَآ إِلَيْكَ لِتَفْتَرِيَ عَلَيْنَا غَيْرَهٗ ۖ وَإِذًا لَّاتَّخَذُوْكَ خَلِيْلًا ﴿٧٤﴾

75. [b]And if We had not strengthened thee *with the Qur'an even then* thou wouldst have inclined to them but little.[1639]

وَلَوْلَآ أَنْ ثَبَّتْنٰكَ لَقَدْ كِدْتَّ تَرْكَنُ إِلَيْهِمْ شَيْـًٔا قَلِيْلًا ﴿٧٥﴾

76. *But if, as they imagine, thou hadst been one to forge a lie against Us*, then We would have made thee taste a heavy *punishment* in life and a heavy *punishment* in death, *and* then thou wouldst not have found for thyself any helper against Us.

إِذًا لَّأَذَقْنٰكَ ضِعْفَ الْحَيٰوةِ وَضِعْفَ الْمَمَاتِ ثُمَّ لَا تَجِدُ لَكَ عَلَيْنَا نَصِيْرًا ﴿٧٦﴾

77. And indeed they are near to scare thee to drive thee away from the land that [c]they might expel[1640] thee therefrom, but in that case they *themselves* would not have stayed after thee save a little.

وَإِنْ كَادُوْا لَيَسْتَفِزُّوْنَكَ مِنَ الْأَرْضِ لِيُخْرِجُوْكَ مِنْهَا وَإِذًا لَّا يَلْبَثُوْنَ خِلٰفَكَ إِلَّا قَلِيْلًا ﴿٧٧﴾

78. [d]*This has been Our* way with Our Messengers whom We sent before thee; and thou wilt not find any change in Our way.

سُنَّةَ مَنْ قَدْ أَرْسَلْنَا قَبْلَكَ مِنْ رُّسُلِنَا وَلَا تَجِدُ لِسُنَّتِنَا تَحْوِيْلًا ﴿٧٨﴾ ع ٨

[a]10 : 16; 68 : 10. [b]25 : 33. [c]8 : 31; 60 : 2. [d]33 : 63; 35 : 44; 48 : 24.

1638. Disbelievers were determined to put the Holy Prophet to great hardship on account of the Teaching which had been revealed to him so that they might compel him to alter it and devise other than the one embodied in the Qur'ān. It is to these evil designs of disbelievers and their complete failure in getting them carried out that reference has been made in this verse.

1639. The Prophet's nature was so pure that even if the Qur'ān had not been revealed to him and he had no knowledge of God's great intentions about him, he would hardly have stooped to practise *Shirk*.

1640. The enemies of the Holy Prophet wanted to brand him with the stigma of legal banishment so that he might lose all dignity with his people, but God Himself commanded him to leave Mecca and thus saved him from this stigma which involved for him the loss of citizenship of that town.

R. 9 79. [a]Observe Prayer from the declining and paling of the sun till the darkness of the night, and recite *the Qur'ān* at dawn. Verily, the recitation *of the Qur'ān* at dawn is *specially* acceptable *to Allāh.*[1641]

أَقِمِ الصَّلٰوةَ لِدُلُوْكِ الشَّمْسِ إِلٰى غَسَقِ الَّيْلِ وَ قُرْاٰنَ الْفَجْرِ ۖ إِنَّ قُرْاٰنَ الْفَجْرِ كَانَ مَشْهُوْدًا ﴿٧٩﴾

80. [b]And during *a part of* the night wake up for *its recitation*—a supererogatory[1642] service for thee. It may be that thy Lord will raise thee to an exalted station.[1643]

وَمِنَ الَّيْلِ فَتَهَجَّدْ بِهٖ نَافِلَةً لَّكَ ۖ عَسٰٓى أَنْ يَّبْعَثَكَ رَبُّكَ مَقَامًا مَّحْمُوْدًا ﴿٨٠﴾

81. And say, 'O my Lord, make my entry a good entry and make me go forth a good going forth.[1644] And grant me from Thyself a helping power.'

وَقُلْ رَّبِّ أَدْخِلْنِيْ مُدْخَلَ صِدْقٍ وَّأَخْرِجْنِيْ مُخْرَجَ صِدْقٍ وَّاجْعَلْ لِّيْ مِنْ لَّدُنْكَ سُلْطٰنًا نَّصِيْرًا ﴿٨١﴾

[a]11 : 115; 20 : 131; 30 : 18,19; 50 : 40. [b]50 : 41; 52 : 50; 73 : 3-5; 76 : 27.

1641. *Dalakat al-Shamsu* means, (1) the sun declined from the meridian; (2) it became yellow; (3) it set. *Ghasaq* means, the darkness of the night, or when redness in the horizon after sunset disappears (Lane). This verse seems to denote the hours of the five daily Prayers of Islām. The three meanings of *Dulūk* indicate the times of Afternoon Prayer, the Late Afternoon Prayer and the Sunset Prayer. The expression, *Ghasaqil-Lail,* includes the times of Sun-set Prayer but particularly refers to the Night Prayer, and the words *Qur'ān al-Fajr* indicate the hour of the Morning Prayer.

1642. In addition to the meaning given in the text *Nāfilah* means a special favour, and signifies that Prayers are not a burden to weary the flesh but a privilege and a special favour from God.

1643. Perhaps no other person has been so much maligned and abused as the Holy Prophet of Islām and certainly no other person has been the recipient of so much Divine praise and the object of the invocation of so many Divine blessings and favours upon him as he. The *Tahajjud* Prayer is best suited for the believer's spiritual exaltation as in the stillness of the night, being all alone with his Creator, he enjoys special Divine communion.

1644. In acceptance of his prayers and supplications, the Holy Prophet in this verse has been vouchsafed the glad tidings that in fulfilment of the prophecy made in the words, *Glory be to Him Who carried His servant by night from the Sacred Mosque to the Distant Mosque* (17 : 2), he would be taken to Medina. In anticipation of the fulfilment of this prophecy he is commanded to pray that his entry in Medina may be doubly blessed and so may his departure from the town—Mecca—in which he is now living.

82. And proclaim: [a]'Truth has come and falsehood has vanished.[1645] Verily, falsehood is bound to vanish.'

وَقُلْ جَآءَ الْحَقُّ وَزَهَقَ الْبَاطِلُ ۭ اِنَّ الْبَاطِلَ كَانَ
زَهُوْقًا ﴿٨٢﴾

83. And [b]We *gradually* reveal of the Qur'ān that which is a healing and a mercy to the believers; but it only adds to the loss of the wrongdoers.

وَنُنَزِّلُ مِنَ الْقُرْاٰنِ مَا هُوَ شِفَآءٌ وَّرَحْمَةٌ
لِّلْمُؤْمِنِيْنَ ۙ وَلَا يَزِيْدُ الظّٰلِمِيْنَ اِلَّا خَسَارًا ﴿٨٣﴾

84. [c]And when We bestow favour on man, he turns away and goes aside; and when evil touches him, he gives *himself* up to despair.

وَاِذَآ اَنْعَمْنَا عَلَى الْاِنْسَانِ اَعْرَضَ وَنَاٰ بِجَانِبِهٖ ۚ وَاِذَا
مَسَّهُ الشَّرُّ كَانَ يَـُٔوْسًا ﴿٨٤﴾

85. Say, 'Everyone acts according to his own way,[1646] [d]and your Lord knows well who is best guided.'

قُلْ كُلٌّ يَّعْمَلُ عَلٰى شَاكِلَتِهٖ ۭ فَرَبُّكُمْ اَعْلَمُ بِمَنْ هُوَ
اَهْدٰى سَبِيْلًا ﴿٨٥﴾ ع ٩

R. 10 86. And they ask thee concerning the soul.[1647] Say, 'The soul has been *created* by the command of my Lord; and of the knowledge *thereof* you have been given but a little.

وَيَسْـَٔلُوْنَكَ عَنِ الرُّوْحِ ۭ قُلِ الرُّوْحُ مِنْ اَمْرِ رَبِّيْ
وَمَآ اُوْتِيْتُمْ مِّنَ الْعِلْمِ اِلَّا قَلِيْلًا ﴿٨٦﴾

[a]21 : 19; 34 : 50. [b]10 : 58; 12 : 112; 16 : 90. [c]17 : 68. [d]28 : 86.

1645. It is among the marvels of Quranic diction that to convey a certain sense it selects that particular word which points to a long sequence of events. In this particular instance the sense of the vanishing of falsehood might as well have been expressed by some other word such as *Halaka* (perished) or *Baṭala* (became useless), but neither of these words would have conveyed the sense of gradual weakening and ultimate disappearance which is expressed by *Zahaqa.* The verse contains the hint that with the entry of the Holy Prophet into Medina, his power would continue to grow and that of his enemy decline till it would be finally broken. Again, it is a marvel of the style of the Qur'ān that, without being poetry, its verses possess poetic rhythm and cadence without which it is not possible to give full expression to feelings of extreme delight. The verse under comment furnishes one such example. After the conquest of Mecca as the Holy Prophet was clearing the Ka'bah of the idols which had desecrated it, he repeatedly recited this verse as he struck the idols (Bukhārī).

1646. The words, *'Alā Shākilati-hī*, mean, according to his own motives; way of thinking; aims and purposes.

1647. In the period of their spiritual decline and decadence the Jews seem to have come to dabble in occult practices like many modern Spiritualists, Theosophists and Hindu Yogis. Some of the Jews of Medina also seem to have resorted to these practices in the time of the Holy Prophet. This is why when the Meccan idolaters sought their help to confute the Holy Prophet, they suggested that they (the Meccan idolaters) should question him about the human soul. The Qur'ān answers them by the verse under comment by saying that the soul derives its powers from the command of God and anything else that is claimed to be acquired by the so called spiritual exercises and magical art is all humbug. The question

87. And if We pleased, We could certainly take away[1648] that which We have revealed to thee and then thou wouldst find no guardian for thyself against Us *in the matter*,

وَلَئِن شِئْنَا لَنَذْهَبَنَّ بِالَّذِي أَوْحَيْنَا إِلَيْكَ ثُمَّ لَا تَجِدُ لَكَ بِهِ عَلَيْنَا وَكِيلًا ﴿٨٧﴾

88. [a]Except *through the special* mercy of thy Lord. Surely, great is His grace on thee.

إِلَّا رَحْمَةً مِّن رَّبِّكَ إِنَّ فَضْلَهُ كَانَ عَلَيْكَ كَبِيرًا ﴿٨٨﴾

89. [b]Say, 'If men and jinn should gather together to produce the like of this Qur'ān, they could not produce the like thereof,[1649] even though they should help one another.'

قُل لَّئِنِ اجْتَمَعَتِ الْإِنسُ وَالْجِنُّ عَلَىٰ أَن يَأْتُوا بِمِثْلِ هَٰذَا الْقُرْآنِ لَا يَأْتُونَ بِمِثْلِهِ وَلَوْ كَانَ بَعْضُهُمْ لِبَعْضٍ ظَهِيرًا ﴿٨٩﴾

90. And surely [c]We have set forth for mankind in various ways[1650] all kinds of similitudes in this Qur'ān, but most men would reject everything *in respect of it* but disbelief.

وَلَقَدْ صَرَّفْنَا لِلنَّاسِ فِي هَٰذَا الْقُرْآنِ مِن كُلِّ مَثَلٍ فَأَبَىٰ أَكْثَرُ النَّاسِ إِلَّا كُفُورًا ﴿٩٠﴾

[a]28 : 87. [b]2 : 24; 10 : 39; 11 : 14; 52 : 35. [c]17 : 42; 18 : 55.

regarding the nature of the human soul is reported to have been first put to the Holy Prophet at Mecca by the Quraish and then, according to 'Abd Allāh bin Mas'ūd, by the Jews at Medina. The soul has been described here as something created by the direct command of God. According to the Qur'ān all creation falls under two categories: (1) Original creation which is brought about without the aid or help of any substance or matter previously created. (2) Subsequent creation which is brought about with the aid and help of the means and matter previously created. The former kind of creation falls under the category of *Amr* (lit. command) for which see 2 : 118, and the latter is known as *Khalq* (lit. creating). The human soul belongs to the first category.

The word *Rūḥ* also means, Divine revelation (Lane). The context seems to support this meaning.

1648. The verse seems to imply a prophecy that a time would come when Quranic knowledge would depart from the earth. A similar prophecy of the Holy Prophet has been reported by Merdawaih, Baihaquī and Ibn Mājah that there would come a time when the kernel and spirit of the Qur'ān would disappear from the earth, and not all the so-called mystics and *Sufīs* of the time claiming, like their Jewish prototypes, to possess supernatural powers, would be able to restore it with their concerted efforts.

1649. The challenge is held out in the first place to those people who indulge in occult practices that they should summon to their aid the hidden spirits from whom they claim to receive spiritual knowledge. The challenge also stands for all time to all people who deny the Divine origin of the Holy Qur'ān.

1650. Human faculties being limited man can, at best, deal with only a limited number of problems. But the Qur'ān has fully dealt with all those matters that concern his moral and spiritual development.

91. And they say, 'We will not believe in thee until thou cause a spring to gush forth for us from the earth;

وَقَالُوا لَنْ نُّؤْمِنَ لَكَ حَتّٰى تَفْجُرَ لَنَا مِنَ الْاَرْضِ
يَنْبُوْعًا ﴿٩١﴾

92. [a]"Or, thou have a garden of date-palms and vines and cause streams to gush forth in the midst thereof in abundance;[1651]

اَوْ تَكُوْنَ لَكَ جَنَّةٌ مِّنْ نَّخِيْلٍ وَّعِنَبٍ فَتُفَجِّرَ
الْاَنْهٰرَ خِلٰلَهَا تَفْجِيْرًا ﴿٩٢﴾

93. 'Or, thou cause the heaven to fall upon us in pieces, as thou hast claimed, or, thou bring Allāh and the angels before us face to face;

اَوْ تُسْقِطَ السَّمَآءَ كَمَا زَعَمْتَ عَلَيْنَا كِسَفًا اَوْ تَاْتِيَ
بِاللّٰهِ وَالْمَلٰٓئِكَةِ قَبِيْلًا ﴿٩٣﴾

94. 'Or, thou have a house of gold or thou ascend up into heaven; and we will not believe in thy ascension until thou send down to us a Book that we can read.' Say, 'Holy is my Lord! I am but a mortal *sent as* a Messenger.'[1652]

اَوْ يَكُوْنَ لَكَ بَيْتٌ مِّنْ زُخْرُفٍ اَوْ تَرْقٰى فِي السَّمَآءِ
وَلَنْ نُّؤْمِنَ لِرُقِيِّكَ حَتّٰى تُنَزِّلَ عَلَيْنَا كِتٰبًا نَّقْرَؤُهٗ
ع قُلْ سُبْحَانَ رَبِّيْ هَلْ كُنْتُ اِلَّا بَشَرًا رَّسُوْلًا ﴿٩٤﴾

R. 11 95. [b]And nothing prevents people from believing when the guidance comes to them save that they say, 'Has Allāh sent a man *like us as* a Messenger?'

وَمَا مَنَعَ النَّاسَ اَنْ يُّؤْمِنُوْٓا اِذْ جَآءَهُمُ الْهُدٰٓى
اِلَّآ اَنْ قَالُوْٓا اَبَعَثَ اللّٰهُ بَشَرًا رَّسُوْلًا ﴿٩٥﴾

---

[a]25 : 11. [b]17 : 60; 23 : 25; 34 : 44.

1651. When the Meccans were confounded by the answers of the Qur'ān to their questions and objections, they turned round and demanded of the Holy Prophet that if the Qur'ān comprehended every kind of knowledge then he should be able to work miracles —cause springs to gush forth from the earth, grow gardens and build houses of gold for himself, etc.

1652. In answer to their impudent demands the disbelievers are told that these demands pertain either to God or to the Prophet. The demands of the first category are frivolous in character and God is above such frivolities. As for their demands pertaining to the Holy Prophet, they are incompatible with his limited powers as a human being and his mission as a Prophet of God.

96. Say, 'Had there been in the earth angels walking about in peace and quiet, [a]We should have certainly sent down to them from heaven an angel *as a* Messenger.'[1653]

قُلْ لَّوْ كَانَ فِي الْاَرْضِ مَلٰٓئِكَةٌ يَّمْشُوْنَ مُطْمَئِنِّيْنَ
لَنَزَّلْنَا عَلَيْهِمْ مِّنَ السَّمَآءِ مَلَكًا رَّسُوْلًا ﴿٩٦﴾

97. Say, [b]'Sufficient is Allāh for a witness between me and you; surely, He knows and sees His servants full well.'

قُلْ كَفٰى بِاللّٰهِ شَهِيْدًاۢ بَيْنِيْ وَبَيْنَكُمْ ۭ اِنَّهٗ كَانَ
بِعِبَادِهٖ خَبِيْرًاۢ بَصِيْرًا ﴿٩٧﴾

98. [c]And he whom Allāh guides, is the *only* one rightly guided; but *as for* those whom He leaves to go astray, thou wilt find for them no helpers beside Him. And [d]on the Day of Resurrection We shall gather them together on their faces blind, dumb and deaf. Their abode shall be Hell; every time it abates, We shall increase[1654] for them the flame.

وَمَنْ يَّهْدِ اللّٰهُ فَهُوَ الْمُهْتَدِ ۚ وَمَنْ يُّضْلِلْ فَلَنْ
تَجِدَ لَهُمْ اَوْلِيَآءَ مِنْ دُوْنِهٖ ۭ وَنَحْشُرُهُمْ يَوْمَ
الْقِيٰمَةِ عَلٰى وُجُوْهِهِمْ عُمْيًا وَّبُكْمًا وَّصُمًّا ۭ مَاْوٰىهُمْ
جَهَنَّمُ ۭ كُلَّمَا خَبَتْ زِدْنٰهُمْ سَعِيْرًا ﴿٩٨﴾

99. [e]That is their recompense, because they rejected Our Signs and said, 'What! [f]when we *die and* are *reduced to* bones and broken particles, shall we really be raised up as a new creation?'[1655]

ذٰلِكَ جَزَآؤُهُمْ بِاَنَّهُمْ كَفَرُوْا بِاٰيٰتِنَا وَقَالُوْٓا ءَاِذَا
كُنَّا عِظَامًا وَّرُفَاتًا ءَاِنَّا لَمَبْعُوْثُوْنَ خَلْقًا جَدِيْدًا ﴿٩٩﴾

[a]23 : 25; 25 : 22; 43 : 61. [b]10 : 30; 13 : 44; 29 : 53; 46 : 9. [c]7 : 179; 18 : 18; 39 : 37-38. [d]6 : 129; 19 : 69. [e]18 : 107; 34 : 18. [f]17 : 50; 23 : 83; 36 : 79; 37 : 17; 56 : 48.

1653. The verse may have two meanings: (*a*) Angels descend upon angel-like men, and not upon their opposites, and if the disbelievers should also bring about an angelic change in their lives, angels would descend upon them. (*b*) Beings of the same species only can serve as exemplars or models for one another. Thus only a man could be the bearer of Divine Message for mankind, because only he alone could serve as a model for other men.

1654. When, by burning in the Fire for a long time, the disbelievers' feelings became dull, God would again sharpen them and they would once more begin to feel the torment of burning as keenly as before.

1655. All rejection of religion and truth is, in fact, the result of denial of the Hereafter. This is why the Qur'ān has laid so much stress on Life after death and reverts to this all important subject time and again.

100. Do they not see that [a]Allāh, Who created the heavens and the earth, has the power to create the like of them?[1656] And He has appointed for them a term; there is no doubt about it. But the wrongdoers would reject everything but disbelief.

أولم يروا أن الله الذي خلق السموت والأرض
قادر على أن يخلق مثلهم وجعل لهم أجلا لا
ريب فيه فأبى الظلمون إلا كفورا ﴿١٠٠﴾

101. Say, 'Even if you possessed the *limitless* treasures of the mercy of my Lord, you would surely hold them back for fear of exhausting *them*, for man is niggardly.'

قل لو أنتم تملكون خزائن رحمة ربي إذا لأمسكتم
خشية الإنفاق وكان الإنسان قتورا ﴿١٠١﴾ ع

R. 12 102. And certainly [b]We gave Moses nine manifest Signs.[1657] So ask then the Children of Israel. When he came to them, [c]Pharaoh said to him, 'I do think thee, O Moses, to be a victim of deception.'

ولقد آتينا موسى تسع آيت بينت فسئل بني إسرائيل
إذ جاءهم فقال له فرعون إني لأظنك يموسى
مسحورا ﴿١٠٢﴾

103. He said, 'Thou knowest well that none has sent down these Signs but the Lord of the heavens and the earth as *so many* evidences; and I certainly consider thee, O Pharaoh, to be doomed to perish.'

قال لقد علمت ما أنزل هؤلاء إلا رب السموت
والأرض بصائر وإني لأظنك يفرعون مثبورا ﴿١٠٣﴾

104. So he resolved to remove them from the land; [d]but We drowned him and those who were with him, all together.

فأراد أن يستفزهم من الأرض فأغرقنه ومن
معه جميعا ﴿١٠٤﴾

[a]36 : 82; 46 : 34; 86 : 9. [b]7 : 134; 27 : 13. [c]27 : 14; 28 : 37; 40 : 25.
[d]2 : 51; 7 : 137; 8 : 55; 20 : 79; 26 : 67; 28 : 41.

1656. The verse embodies an invincible argument to prove the existence of Life after death. It does not straightway say to disbelievers that they would be born again because God has the power to give them a new birth. Such a statement would have been an empty assertion. On the contrary, it says to them that if they would not believe that there is a life after death, they would as well disbelieve if they were told that they would lose their power and prestige to those very weak and poor Muslims whom they now looked down upon as of no worth and consequence. If this seemingly impossible prophecy about their own destruction and about that of the rise to power of the poor Muslims turned out to be true, the claim that there is a life after death would automatically become established.

1657. These nine Signs mentioned elsewhere in the Qur'ān are, (*a*) the rod (7 : 108); (*b*) the white hand (7 : 109); (*c*), (*d*) drought and scarcity of fruits (7 : 131); (*e*) the storm; (*f*) the locusts; (*g*) the lice; (*h*) the frogs; and (*i*) the punishment of the blood (7 : 134).

105. And after him We said to the Children of Israel, [a]'Dwell ye in the *promised* land; and when *the time of* the promise of the Latter Days comes,[1658] We shall bring you together *out of various peoples*.'

وَّقُلْنَا مِنْۢ بَعْدِهٖ لِبَنِيْٓ اِسْرَآءِيْلَ اسْكُنُوا الْاَرْضَ فَاِذَا جَآءَ وَعْدُ الْاٰخِرَةِ جِئْنَا بِكُمْ لَفِيْفًا ﴿١٠٥﴾

106. [b]And, in accordance with the requirements of truth and wisdom We have sent it down, and with truth and wisdom has it descended. And We have sent thee only as a bearer of good tidings and a Warner.

وَبِالْحَقِّ اَنْزَلْنٰهُ وَبِالْحَقِّ نَزَلَ ۭ وَمَآ اَرْسَلْنٰكَ اِلَّا مُبَشِّرًا وَّنَذِيْرًا ﴿١٠٦﴾

107. And [c]We have divided the Qur'ān in parts that thou mayest read it to mankind *slowly and* at intervals[1659] and We have sent it down piecemeal.

وَقُرْاٰنًا فَرَقْنٰهُ لِتَقْرَاَهٗ عَلَى النَّاسِ عَلٰى مُكْثٍ وَّنَزَّلْنٰهُ تَنْزِيْلًا ﴿١٠٧﴾

108. Say, 'Whether you believe therein or believe not, those to whom knowledge has been given before it, [d]do fall down prostrate on their faces when it is recited to them.'

قُلْ اٰمِنُوْا بِهٖٓ اَوْ لَا تُؤْمِنُوْا ۭ اِنَّ الَّذِيْنَ اُوْتُوا الْعِلْمَ مِنْ قَبْلِهٖٓ اِذَا يُتْلٰى عَلَيْهِمْ يَخِرُّوْنَ لِلْاَذْقَانِ سُجَّدًا ﴿١٠٨﴾

[a]7 : 138. [b]4 : 106; 5 : 49; 39 : 3. [c]25 : 33; 73 : 5. [d]19 : 59; 32 : 16; 38 : 25.

1658. The verse implies that like Jews, the Muslims would suffer national disaster twice. The first of these two disasters befell Muslims when Baghdad fell to the arms of the Tartars under Halaku Khan. They are here told that they would be visited with Divine punishment for the second time in the Latter Days—in the time of the Promised Messiah, just as the Jews were punished in that of the first Messiah—Jesus. The verse signifies that when Muslims are punished for the second time, which means the fulfilment of 'the promise of the Latter Days,' the Jews would be brought back to the Holy Land from all parts of the world. The prophecy has been remarkably fulfilled by the return of the Jews to Palestine under the Balfour Declaration and by the setting up of the so-called State of Israel. 'The promise of the Latter Days' applies to the time of the Promised Messiah (Bayān).

1659. The Qur'ān had to meet the needs of two classes of people: (*a*) It had to answer the temporary objections of its immediate addressees and to satisfy the immediate spiritual needs of the first converts to Islām; and (*b*) it had to lay down guidance for the multitudinous and multifarious problems of mankind for all time. The verses dealing with the objections of Meccan idolaters and the spiritual up-bringing of early Muslims naturally had to be revealed first and those which dealt with the lasting spiritual human needs were revealed afterwards. Thus the Quranic verses were revealed piecemeal and at intervals. Whenever a particular objection was raised by disbelievers, verses containing the answer to such an objection were revealed. Similarly, when the early Muslims were required to be provided with guidance at a particular occasion, necessary and relevant verses were revealed to meet the needs of that occasion. That was the order in which the Qur'ān was originally revealed. But since the temporary needs of the immediate addressees of the Qur'ān were different from the permanent requirements of mankind in general, the order in which the Qur'ān was later compiled in the form of a book had naturally to be different from that in which it was originally revealed.

109. And say, 'Holy is our Lord. [a]Surely, the promise of our Lord is bound to be fulfilled.'

وَّيَقُولُوْنَ سُبْحٰنَ رَبِّنَآ إِنْ كَانَ وَعْدُ رَبِّنَا لَمَفْعُوْلًا ﴿١٠٩﴾

110. They fall down on their faces weeping,[1660] and it increases humility in them.

السجدة
وَيَخِرُّوْنَ لِلْاَذْقَانِ يَبْكُوْنَ وَيَزِيْدُهُمْ خُشُوْعًا ﴿١١٠﴾

111. [b]Say, 'Call upon Allāh or call upon *Al-Raḥmān*, *by* whichever name you call *on Him*, His are the most beautiful names.'[1661] [c]And utter not thy prayer aloud, nor utter it *too* low, but seek a way between.

قُلِ ادْعُوا اللّٰهَ اَوِ ادْعُوا الرَّحْمٰنَ ۭ اَيًّا مَّا تَدْعُوْا فَلَهُ الْاَسْمَآءُ
الْحُسْنٰى ۚ وَلَا تَجْهَرْ بِصَلَاتِكَ وَلَا تُخَافِتْ بِهَا وَ
ابْتَغِ بَيْنَ ذٰلِكَ سَبِيْلًا ﴿١١١﴾

112. [d]And say, 'All praise belongs to Allāh Who has taken unto Himself no son, and Who has no partner in His Kingdom, nor has He anyone to help Him because of any weakness *of His*.' And proclaim His greatness, glorifying *Him*.

وَقُلِ الْحَمْدُ لِلّٰهِ الَّذِيْ لَمْ يَتَّخِذْ وَلَدًا وَّلَمْ يَكُنْ
لَّهٗ شَرِيْكٌ فِي الْمُلْكِ وَلَمْ يَكُنْ لَّهٗ وَلِيٌّ مِّنَ الذُّلِّ
وَكَبِّرْهُ تَكْبِيْرًا ﴿١١٢﴾ ع ١٢ ١٢

[a]18 : 99; 19 : 62; 46 : 17; 73 : 19. [b]7 : 181; 20 : 9; 59 : 25. [c]7 : 56; 206. [d]18 : 5; 19 : 36,93; 25 : 3; 72 : 4.

1660. The verse expresses a Muslim's state of mind when in the posture of prostration the realization of the greatness of God and of his own weakness humbles his spirit. The believers are required to prostrate themselves after reciting those verses in which the command to fall down in prostration is contained. The Holy Prophet used to prostrate himself after having recited any of those verses.

1661. God possesses innumerable attributes and a Muslim should invoke in his prayer that particular Divine attribute which has special bearing on the matter for which he seeks Divine guidance and help.

CHAPTER 18

AL-KAHF

(Revealed before Hijrah)

Date of Revelation and Context

According to Ibn 'Abbās and Ibn Zubair the whole of this *Sūrah* was revealed at Mecca (Manthūr). Almost all the Commentators of the Qur'ān appear to be agreed upon this point. Western scholars have assigned the *Sūrah* to the sixth year of the Call, but most probably it was revealed in the fourth or fifth year. Anas reports that the *Sūrah* was revealed in one whole and was guarded by seventy thousand angels (Manthūr,vol. 4,p, 210). In Chapter Al-Naḥl the prophecy that the Holy Prophet would meet with severe opposition from the Jews and the Christians had been dealt with at some length. This subject was further elaborated in *Sūrah* Banī Isrā'īl in which it was stated that he would be taken to regions where he would live among the Jews and would establish new contacts with them and later meet with opposition from both the Jews and the Christians and in the end would conquer them. The *Sūrah* Banī Isrā'īl mentioned a Vision of the Holy Prophet, which also embodied a prophecy that he would conquer the Holy Land of the Jews, and alluded to two revolts of the Jews foretold in the Book of Deuteronomy. The first revolt took place after the time of David as a consequence of which the Jews were expelled from their native land. They repented of their sins and their homeland was restored to them. But they again relapsed into iniquitous practices, defied God's commandments and revolted for the second time in the time of Jesus. This second defiance brought upon them severer punishment. Their holy places were destroyed and they were exiled from their beloved Land of Promise. These prophecies had also mentioned the conditions and circumstances under which the first part of the Israelites—the Jews—had to pass. A description of their condition, however, gave rise to two obvious questions : (*a*) If Christians, who form the second part of the Mosaic Dispensation, have been spared the punishment with which the Jews who were its first part were afflicted, does it not follow that Christians are heirs to the Divine blessings and favours promised to the Jews? (*b*) Why are Muslims warned to be on their guard lest they incur Divine displeasure by following in the footsteps of the Jews, and what does this warning portend and what has the future in store for them ?

Subject-Matter

Both these very natural and pertinent questions have been answered in the present Chapter and some light has also been shed on the vicissitudes through which Christianity—second branch of the Mosaic Dispensation—was to pass. Mention has also been made of how Muslims would behave and make themselves the object of Divine wrath by imitating the iniquitous ways of the Jews. An answer has also been supplied to yet another question, *viz.*, what connection is there between these matters and the story of the Dwellers of the Cave, and of Dhu'l Qarnain and Gog and Magog and the parable of "Two Gardens" and the *Isrā'* (Spiritual Journey) of Moses? The answer which this *Sūrah* gives to this question is that these parables describe in metaphorical language the rise and fall of Christian nations and also the hardships and tribulations which the Muslims were to suffer from them on account of their own iniquities.

In order to expand the subject and give it more clarity, the *Isrā'* (Spiritual Journey) of Moses has been mentioned after the parable of the "Two Gardens." This Spiritual Journey of Moses describes in metaphorical language the great material and moral progress which his followers were to make, just as the phenomenal progress of the followers of the Holy Prophet has been described in his own *Isrā'*, mentioned in Chapter Banī Isrā'īl. The *Isrā'* of Moses describes in detail when and how this great advancement would commence and where it would stop and when the Israelites would become deprived of Divine favours which would be transferred to the House of Ishmael. After this we are told that the Ishmaelites, after having inherited God's favours, would, in their turn, incur

His displeasure by defying His commandments and would be punished by Gog and Magog who would, at one time, spread over and dominate the entire world. Towards the end of the *Sūrah* mention is made of one—Dhu'l Qarnain, who stood in the way of the domination of the whole world by Gog and Magog. Thus light is thrown on the material and spiritual conditions of Christians both in the early stages of their Faith and in the Latter Days. The Dwellers of the Cave symbolize early Christians in the period of their weakness, and Gog and Magog represent them in the heyday of their glory in the Latter Days. The *Sūrah* closes with an assurance to the followers of Islām that God would break and shatter the forces of irreligiousness unleashed by Gog and Magog, and would bring about the deliverance of Muslims by means of a second Dhu'l Qarnain. This second Dhu'l Qarnain is the Holy Founder of the Aḥmadiyya Movement who is a follower of the Holy Prophet.

The *Sūrah* being very important, some additional details of its subject-matter may be mentioned. It states that God has revealed the Qur'ān in order to remove the errors that had crept into previous heavenly Scriptures. It warns those who ascribe a son to God that by so doing they incur Divine displeasure. These people hate Islām, and their beginning is not like their end. In the beginning they were very weak and were subjected to bitter persecution. God had mercy on them and delivered them from their trials and tribulations and put them on the road to progress and prosperity. But when they grew rich and prosperous, they resorted to idolatrous practices, and instead of turning to God they turned to the world and became entirely lost in it. Muslims are warned to take a lesson from their fate and in the day of their own power and glory to be on their guard, particularly against being remiss in Divine worship, against excessive love of wealth and worldly possessions, and against a life of ease and luxury. The glory and power of Christian nations as compared with the degradation and poverty of Muslims are then graphically depicted in 'the parable of two men,' one rich and the other poor. The rich man—Christian nations—would be proud of his riches while the poor man would turn to God. Pride and conceit would come to grief in the long run and circumstances beyond human control would bring about the rich man's decline and fall. The *Sūrah* proceeds to give some details of those great changes which were revealed to Moses in his Vision in which he was told that the development and progress of his Dispensation would fall far short of the great heights which another and a later Dispensation would attain. This later Dispensation—Islām—would bring to perfection and completion the teaching which the Mosaic Dispensation had left incomplete, and would emerge triumphant from the ashes of a declining and decadent Christendom. After having dealt with the decline and fall of Christian nations and with the rise of Islām, the *Sūrah* describes the conditions which would follow the triumph of Islām. It is stated that a time would come when Muslims would also turn their backs upon religion and would become entirely engrossed in the pursuit of material wealth and power. To punish them for their sins God would once again grant success and prosperity to Christian nations which for a time had been restrained from advancing into Southern and Eastern regions. Then would come great destruction upon the world and nations of the world would become divided into two hostile camps, wedded to two opposite ideologies. Sin and iniquity would prevail in the world and injustice and tyranny would become rampant. When things would come to such a pass God would create circumstances which would finally check the seemingly irresistible onrush of the flood threatening to engulf the entire world. While dealing with this subject the *Sūrah* clearly hints that the same people would play an important part in arresting and stopping this flood who had once before broken the political power of Gog and Magog—true followers of the Holy Prophet. See also "The Larger Edition of the Commentary," pp. 1474-1480.

سُوۡرَةُ الۡكَهۡفِ مَكِّيَّةٌ

آياتها ١١١ (١٨) ركوعاتها ١٢

1. [a]In the name of Allāh, the Gracious, the Merciful.

بِسۡمِ اللّٰهِ الرَّحۡمٰنِ الرَّحِيۡمِ ۝١

2. [b]All praise belongs to Allāh Who has sent down the Book to His servant, and has not placed therein any crookedness.

اَلۡحَمۡدُ لِلّٰهِ الَّذِىۡۤ اَنۡزَلَ عَلٰى عَبۡدِهِ الۡكِتٰبَ وَلَمۡ يَجۡعَلْ لَّهٗ عِوَجًا ۝٢

3. *He has made it* a guardian,[1662] that [c]it may give warning of a severe chastisement from Him, and that it may give the believers, who do good works, the glad tidings that they shall have a goodly reward,

قَيِّمًا لِّيُنۡذِرَ بَاۡسًا شَدِيۡدًا مِّنۡ لَّدُنۡهُ وَيُبَشِّرَ الۡمُؤۡمِنِيۡنَ الَّذِيۡنَ يَعۡمَلُوۡنَ الصّٰلِحٰتِ اَنَّ لَهُمۡ اَجۡرًا حَسَنًا ۝٣

4. Wherein they shall abide for ever;

مّٰكِثِيۡنَ فِيۡهِ اَبَدًا ۝٤

5. And that it may warn those [d]who say, 'Allāh has taken unto Himself a son.'[1663]

وَّيُنۡذِرَ الَّذِيۡنَ قَالُوا اتَّخَذَ اللّٰهُ وَلَدًا ۝٥

6. [e]No knowledge have they thereof, nor *had* their fathers. [f]Monstrous is the word that comes out of their mouths. They speak naught but a lie.

مَا لَهُمۡ بِهٖ مِنۡ عِلۡمٍ وَّلَا لِاٰبَآئِهِمۡ ؕ كَبُرَتۡ كَلِمَةً تَخۡرُجُ مِنۡ اَفۡوَاهِهِمۡ ؕ اِنۡ يَّقُوۡلُوۡنَ اِلَّا كَذِبًا ۝٦

---

[a]1 : 1. [b]25 : 2 ; 57 : 10. [c]17 : 10,11. [d]17 : 112; 19 : 36; 21 : 27; 25 : 3; 39 : 5; 72 : 4. [e]22 : 72; 40 : 43. [f]19 : 91-92.

1662. The Qur'ān as *Qayyim* (guardian) performs a double function. It is a guardian over the previous Scriptures in that it corrects and removes the errors that have found their way into them, and it is also a guardian over future generations because it takes upon itself their spiritual up-bringing and guides them to the paths which lead to the realization of the sublime object of human life.

1663. The Qur'ān is first spoken of as 'giving warning,' next as 'giving glad tidings' (v. 3), and then again as 'giving warning' as in the present verse. Disbelievers have been warned twice and in between these two warnings the believers have been given glad tidings. This double warning interspersed with glad tidings for Muslims implied three prophecies: (*a*) the discomfiture and destruction of the Holy Prophet's opponents in his own time, (*b*) the phenomenal rise of Muslims to power and glory, and, (*c*) after the departure of their glory, the punishment in store for the nations who say that 'Allāh has taken unto Himself a son'.

7. So it may be, thou wilt grieve thyself to [a]death[1664] sorrowing after them if they believe not in this Discourse.

فَلَعَلَّكَ بَاخِعٌ نَّفْسَكَ عَلٰٓى اٰثَارِهِمْ اِنْ لَّمْ يُؤْمِنُوْا بِهٰذَا الْحَدِيْثِ اَسَفًا ۝٧

8. Verily, We have made all that is on the earth an ornament[1665] for it, [b]that We may try them as to which of them is best in conduct.

اِنَّا جَعَلْنَا مَا عَلَى الْاَرْضِ زِيْنَةً لَّهَا لِنَبْلُوَهُمْ اَيُّهُمْ اَحْسَنُ عَمَلًا ۝٨

9. [c]And We shall *destroy* all that is thereon *and* make *it* a barren soil.[1666]

وَاِنَّا لَجٰعِلُوْنَ مَا عَلَيْهَا صَعِيْدًا جُرُزًا ۝٩

10. Dost thou think that the Companions of the Cave[1666A] and the Inscription were a wonder among Our Signs?[1667]

اَمْ حَسِبْتَ اَنَّ اَصْحٰبَ الْكَهْفِ وَالرَّقِيْمِ كَانُوْا مِنْ اٰيٰتِنَا عَجَبًا ۝١٠

[a]26 : 4. [b]5 : 49; 6 : 166; 11 : 8; 67 : 3. [c]18 : 41.

1664. *Bākhi'* being active participle from *Bakha'a* which means, he did a thing most effectively, the verse speaks volumes for the Holy Prophet's concern and solicitude for the spiritual well-being of his people. His grief over their rejection of the Divine Message and opposition to it had almost killed him. God's Messengers and His Prophets are full of the milk of human kindness. They cry and weep and grieve for mankind. But such is human ingratitude that those very people for whom they feel so deeply persecute them and seek to kill them.

1665. Of all the innumerable things that God has created there is not one which has not its particular use or which is devoid of all good. All of them add to the beauty of human life. Muslims were enjoined always to keep in view the great truth underlying these simple words and to devote their time and energy to delving in to the great secrets of nature and to exploring the unlimited properties of elements.

1666. The verse implies a prophecy that the Christian nations of the West, after acquiring wealth, power and dominion and making great discoveries and inventions, would make God's earth abound, as the Bible says, in sin and iniquity. Divine wrath would be excited and, as the prophecies uttered by the mouths of God's great Prophets in the Old and New Testaments and the Qur'ān and Ḥadīth, widespread calamities would descend upon the earth and all the progress that they will have made and all their handiworks, their lofty and stately buildings, the beauty of their land and all their pomp, glory and grandeur would be completely destroyed.

1666A. The expression, *Aṣḥāb al-Kahf*, has been variously interpreted as 'People of the Cave;' 'Men of the Cave;' 'Companions of the Cave;' 'Inmates of the Cave' and 'Dwellers of the Cave.'

1667. The verse declares that the Dwellers of the Cave were not strange things. There was nothing about them which might be considered as a departure from the ordinary laws of nature. Curiously enough many fantastic legends have been woven round them. The memorable story of the "Seven Sleepers," as told by Gibbon in his "Decline and Fall of the Roman Empire," provides an important clue to the solution of the mystery that surrounds the Dwellers of the Cave. 'When the Emperor Decius,' says Gibbon, 'persecuted the Christians, seven noble youths of Ephesus concealed themselves in a spacious cavern in the

11. When the young men betook themselves to the Cave for refuge they said, 'Our Lord, bestow on us mercy from Thyself, and furnish us with right guidance in our affair.'

إِذْ أَوَى الْفِتْيَةُ إِلَى الْكَهْفِ فَقَالُوا رَبَّنَآ آتِنَا مِن لَّدُنكَ رَحْمَةً وَهَيِّئْ لَنَا مِنْ أَمْرِنَا رَشَدًا ⑪

side of an adjacent mountain, where they were doomed to perish by the tyrant, who gave orders that the entrance of the cavern should be firmly secured with a pile of huge stones. Now it is a well-known historical fact that early Christians had to suffer untold persecution at the hands of the idolatrous Roman Emperors for their belief in Divine Unity. This persecution began as early as the time of the notorious Emperor Nero who is said to have set fire to Rome; he was fiddling while that great seat of learning and civilization burnt. It continued intermittently till after a brief respite of about forty years it began with renewed fury under Emperor Decius who wanted to restore the religion and institutions of ancient Rome, and with this object in view he began a systematic extermination of Christians. The edicts of Diocletian in 303 A.D., however, surpassed all anti-Christian measures. By these edicts Christian churches in all the provinces of the Empire were demolished, all their sacred books were publicly burnt and the property of the Church was confiscated and Christians were put out of the protection of the land' (Gibbon's Roman Empire, Enc. Brit. & Story of Rome). To save themselves from this cruel and inhuman persecution its helpless victims sought refuge in hiding in the catacombs at Rome. For this purpose these catacombs were admirably adapted both by the intricacy of their labyrinthine passages and the numerous small chambers and hiding places at different levels which might remain undetected in the dark by pursuers. From the inscriptions on the tomb-stones in the catacombs it appears that the early Christians were strict monotheists. Jesus has been mentioned only as a shepherd, or a Prophet of God and Mary, his mother, as nothing more than a pious woman. It also appears that Christians who took refuge in the catacombs kept dogs at their entrance which would announce the approach of strangers by their barking. The account of the Dwellers of the Cave thus, in fact, represents the history of early Christians and shows how they suffered untold persecution for their belief in the Unity of God. The position and description of the Cave, as given in v. 18, is of secondary importance. It applies more fully and in greater detail and exactness to the catacombs at Rome than to any other place.

The story of the Dwellers of the Cave may also be taken to apply to Joseph of Arimathaea and his companions. According to William of Malmesbury, Joseph was sent to Britain by St. Philip and having been given a small island in Somersetshire there constructed with twisted twigs the first Christian church in Britain, which afterwards became the Abbey of Glastonbury. According to another account Joseph is said to have wandered into Britain in the year 63 A.D.... According to legends the first Church of Glastonbury was a little wattled building erected by Joseph of Arimathaea as the leader of the twelve apostles sent over to Britain from Gaul by St. Philip (Enc. Brit., 10th edition & 13th edition, under "Joseph of Arimathaea" & under "Glastonbury"). The latest theory, which also finds powerful support from a study of "Dead Sea Scrolls," assigns the caves, in which the early Christians sought refuge and where they committed to writing their beliefs and teachings, to the valley near the Dead Sea.

"Cave" and "Inscription" represent two most prominent aspects of the Christian Faith, *viz.*, that it began as a religion of renunciation and withdrawal from the world and has ended by becoming a religion of entire engrossment in worldly affairs, a religion of business and trade in a world of writings and inscriptions. See also "The Larger Edition of the Commentary," pp. 1486-1490.

12. So We prevented them from hearing[1668] in the Cave for a number of years.

فَضَرَبْنَا عَلَىٰٓ اٰذَانِهِمْ فِي الْكَهْفِ سِنِيْنَ عَدَدًا ﴿١٢﴾

13. Then We raised them up that We might know which of the two parties[1669] would preserve a better reckoning of the time that they tarried.

ثُمَّ بَعَثْنٰهُمْ لِنَعْلَمَ اَيُّ الْحِزْبَيْنِ اَحْصٰى لِمَا
لَبِثُوْٓا اَمَدًا ﴿١٣﴾ ع

R. 2 14. We will relate to thee their story with truth. They were youngmen who believed in their Lord and [a]We increased them in guidance.[1670]

نَحْنُ نَقُصُّ عَلَيْكَ نَبَاَهُمْ بِالْحَقِّ ۚ اِنَّهُمْ فِتْيَةٌ
اٰمَنُوْا بِرَبِّهِمْ وَ زِدْنٰهُمْ هُدًى ﴿١٤﴾

15. And We strengthened their hearts[1671] when they stood up and said, 'Our Lord is the Lord of the heavens and the earth. Never shall we call upon any god beside Him; *for if we did so*, we would utter a preposterous thing;

وَّ رَبَطْنَا عَلٰى قُلُوْبِهِمْ اِذْ قَامُوْا فَقَالُوْا رَبُّنَا رَبُّ
السَّمٰوٰتِ وَ الْاَرْضِ لَنْ نَّدْعُوَاۡ مِنْ دُوْنِهٖٓ اِلٰهًا
لَّقَدْ قُلْنَآ اِذًا شَطَطًا ﴿١٥﴾

[a]8 : 3; 47 : 18.

1668. The Arabic expression *Daraba 'alā Udhnihī* means, he prevented him from hearing. The Quranic expression means, 'We prevented them from hearing.' It also means, 'We made them sleep by preventing any sound from penetrating into their ears in consequence of which they would have awakened' (Lane). Literally, the verse means, 'We prevented any sound from penetrating into their ears,' *i.e.*, for a number of years they remained wholly isolated from the affairs of the outside world and did not know what was happening there.

1669. There seemed to be two parties among the early Christians : (*a*) Those who did not like to dissemble or dissimulate and knowing no compromise with unbelief and idolatry suffered persecution for their faith with patience and fortitude. These people had to seek refuge in caves. (*b*) Those who thinking prudence to be the better part of valour concealed their faith and saved themselves from persecution. "Two parties" may also refer to the persecutors and the persecuted.

1670. The verse shows that many fantastic stories were current about the Dwellers of the Cave in the Holy Prophet's time. The truth about them, however, is that they were young men of noble conduct who had staked their all for the sake of their Lord and that their faith had steadily grown under persecution.

1671. Though their people were against them and mercilessly persecuted them, yet the Dwellers of the Cave could not be intimidated into giving up their religion. God had strengthened their hearts and had bestowed upon them firmness of faith.

16. [a]"These, our people, have taken *for worship* other gods beside Him.[1672] Wherefore do they not bring a clear authority regarding them ? And [b]who is more unjust than he who invents a lie concerning Allāh?

هٰٓؤُلَآءِ قَوْمُنَا اتَّخَذُوْا مِنْ دُوْنِهٖٓ اٰلِهَةً ؕ لَوْلَا
يَاْتُوْنَ عَلَيْهِمْ بِسُلْطٰنٍۭ بَيِّنٍ ؕ فَمَنْ اَظْلَمُ مِمَّنِ
افْتَرٰى عَلَى اللّٰهِ كَذِبًا ﴿١٦﴾

17. 'And *now* when you have withdrawn from them and from that which they worship beside Allāh, then seek refuge in the Cave;[1673] your Lord will unfold to you His mercy and will provide for you some easy and comfortable course in *this* affair of yours.'

وَاِذِ اعْتَزَلْتُمُوْهُمْ وَمَا يَعْبُدُوْنَ اِلَّا اللّٰهَ فَاْوٗٓا
اِلَى الْكَهْفِ يَنْشُرْ لَكُمْ رَبُّكُمْ مِّنْ رَّحْمَتِهٖ وَيُهَيِّئْ
لَكُمْ مِّنْ اَمْرِكُمْ مِّرْفَقًا ﴿١٧﴾

18. And thou couldst see the sun, as it rose, move away from their Cave on the right, and when it set, turn away from them on the left; and they were in a spacious hollow[1674] thereof. This is among the Signs of Allāh. [c]He whom Allāh guides is *alone* rightly guided; but he whom He leaves to go astray, for him thou wilt find no helper *or* guide.

وَتَرَى الشَّمْسَ اِذَا طَلَعَتْ تَّزٰوَرُ عَنْ كَهْفِهِمْ
ذَاتَ الْيَمِيْنِ وَاِذَا غَرَبَتْ تَّقْرِضُهُمْ ذَاتَ
الشِّمَالِ وَهُمْ فِيْ فَجْوَةٍ مِّنْهُ ؕ ذٰلِكَ مِنْ اٰيٰتِ
اللّٰهِ ؕ مَنْ يَّهْدِ اللّٰهُ فَهُوَ الْمُهْتَدِ ۚ وَمَنْ يُّضْلِلْ فَلَنْ
تَجِدَ لَهٗ وَلِيًّا مُّرْشِدًا ﴿١٨﴾ ع ٢ ١٤

[a]21 : 25; 25 : 4. [b]6 : 145; 7 : 38; 10 : 18; 11 : 19. [c]7 : 179; 17 : 98; 39 : 37-38.

1672. The people to whom the Dwellers of the Cave belonged were idol-worshippers. Such were the Romans.

1673. The verse brings to light the fact that those monotheistic young men were no scattered individuals but formed part of an organized and disciplined religious community whose members met frequently in private. The verse shows that when these young men talked of taking shelter in the Cave they had some specific Cave in mind. This Cave seems to have already been used as a place of refuge by Roman slaves when they fled from their cruel masters. The words, *And now when you have withdrawn from them*, signify that they had already been the victims of a severe social boycott and had lived apart from their people in a separate group of their own.

1674. It appears that the Cave was so situated that it faced north-west, for the sun passes a place, which has its face to the north, from right to left. It seemed to cover a vast area as the words '*spacious hollow*' show. The catacombs at Rome which still exist confirm this view. They enclose a vast area, which has been estimated variously as extending over as many as 870 miles (Enc. Brit). It also appears that the catacombs admitted very little light. The Cave was made in such a way as to serve as a hiding place. St. Jerome, who visited the catacombs in the 4th century, says, "It is all so dark that the language of the Prophet (Ps. 55:15) seems to be fulfilled, 'let them go down quick into Hell." Only occasionally is light let in to mitigate the horror of the gloom, and then not so much through a window as through a hole' (Enc. Brit., 11th edition).

R. 3 19. Thou mightest deem them awake, whilst they are asleep;[1675] and We shall cause them to turn over to the right and to the left;[1675A] their dog stretching out its forelegs on the threshold.[1676] If thou hadst had a look at them, thou wouldst surely turn away from them in fright, and wouldst surely be filled with awe of them.[1677]

وَتَحْسَبُهُمْ اَيْقَاظًا وَّهُمْ رُقُوْدٌ ۖ وَّنُقَلِّبُهُمْ ذَاتَ الْيَمِيْنِ وَذَاتَ الشِّمَالِ ۖ وَكَلْبُهُمْ بَاسِطٌ ذِرَاعَيْهِ بِالْوَصِيْدِ ۖ لَوِ اطَّلَعْتَ عَلَيْهِمْ لَوَلَّيْتَ مِنْهُمْ فِرَارًا وَّلَمُلِئْتَ مِنْهُمْ رُعْبًا ۝

20. And so We raised them up that they might question one another. One of them said, "How long have you tarried?" They said, "We have tarried a day or part of a day." *Others* said, 'Your Lord knows best *the time* you have

وَكَذٰلِكَ بَعَثْنٰهُمْ لِيَتَسَآءَلُوْا بَيْنَهُمْ ۖ قَالَ قَآئِلٌ مِّنْهُمْ كَمْ لَبِثْتُمْ ۖ قَالُوْا لَبِثْنَا يَوْمًا اَوْ بَعْضَ يَوْمٍ ۖ قَالُوْا رَبُّكُمْ اَعْلَمُ بِمَا لَبِثْتُمْ ۖ فَابْعَثُوْا اَحَدَكُمْ

---

*a*2 : 260;   23 : 113-114.

1675. The Muslims in the Holy Prophet's time were fore-warned that Christian nations in northern regions were lying in a state of dormancy but they would soon rise from their deep sleep of centuries and would spread all over the world and hold it under their sway.

1675A. The words, 'We shall cause them to turn over to the right and to the left' seem to refer to their going about in the world, spreading in all directions in search of new markets and making new conquests.

1676. The words, besides referring to the great fondness of Western Christian nations for dogs, may also be taken as referring to the Byzantine Empire which then kept guard over Europe on both sides of the Sea of Marmora, and which looks like a dog keeping watch with its forelegs stretched forth on both sides.

1677. These words refer to the time when Christian nations of the West were to acquire great political power. The Qur'ān foretold this fact hundreds of years ago when Christian nations were yet sunk in a deep sleep of centuries and the wildest stretch of imagination could not have foreseen the power and glory to which they subsequently rose. The verse contains a characteristic picture of the domination of Western nations over Eastern and Southern lands, their peculiar mode of life and the fear and awe they inspire among the peoples of these regions.

tarried.[1678] Now send one of you with these silver coins of yours to the city; and let him see which of its *inhabitants* has the purest food,[1679] and let him bring you provisions thereof. And let him be courteous[1680] but let him not inform[1681] anyone about you;

بِوَرِقِكُمْ هٰذِهٖۤ اِلَى الْمَدِيْنَةِ فَلْيَنْظُرْ اَيُّهَاۤ اَزْكٰى طَعَامًا فَلْيَاْتِكُمْ بِرِزْقٍ مِّنْهُ وَلْيَتَلَطَّفْ وَلَا يُشْعِرَنَّ بِكُمْ اَحَدًا ﴿٢٠﴾

21. 'For, if they should prevail against you, they would stone you or force you to return to their religion and then you will never prosper.'[1682]

اِنَّهُمْ اِنْ يَّظْهَرُوْا عَلَيْكُمْ يَرْجُمُوْكُمْ اَوْ يُعِيْدُوْكُمْ فِيْ مِلَّتِهِمْ وَلَنْ تُفْلِحُوْۤا اِذًا اَبَدًا ﴿٢١﴾

22. And thus did We disclose them *to the people* that they might know [a]that the promise of Allāh was true, and that, [b]as to the *promised* Hour, there was no doubt about it. *And call to mind the time*

وَكَذٰلِكَ اَعْثَرْنَا عَلَيْهِمْ لِيَعْلَمُوْۤا اَنَّ وَعْدَ اللّٰهِ حَقٌّ وَّاَنَّ السَّاعَةَ لَا رَيْبَ فِيْهَا ۚ اِذْ يَتَنَازَعُوْنَ

[a]31 : 34; 35 : 6. [b]15 : 86; 20 : 16; 22 : 8.

1678. The verse seems to refer to the Christian nations of the West after they had spread all over the world. The words, *We raised them up*, refer to the great progress which these nations were destined to make in the future. The words, *One of them said, 'How long have you tarried,'* signify that Christian nations would begin to feel that it was now time for them to bestir themselves and shake off their lethargy. This awakening took place in the time of the Crusades when the monarchs of England, France and Germany made common cause and the whole of Europe united to make a concerted attack upon Muslims to wrest the Holy Land from their hands. According to Arabic idiom the words 'a day or part of a day' denote an indefinite period. Elsewhere the Qur'ān (20 : 103-104) has specified as one thousand years the period during which Christian nations of the West remained in a state of sleep or inactivity. "Ten days" in 20 : 103-104 stand for ten centuries and the words "blue-eyed" in these verses refer to the peoples of the West who generally have blue eyes. It is a well-known historical fact that the foundations of British power in the East were laid in the beginning of the seventeenth century ("March of Man"). This period approximates to one thousand years after the Holy Prophet.

1679. When the Dwellers of the Cave saw that the wave of persecution against them had subsided, they sent one of their members to the city with some old coins to buy provisions and to find out how matters stood with regard to them. *Ṭa'ām* may signify such articles of food as wheat, barley, millet, dates, etc. (Lane). This refers to the commercial expeditions of the Western nations to all parts of the world.

1680. European business-men have a special knack for being gentle and courteous in their commercial dealings. To this characteristic of theirs the expression, *And let him be courteous*, seems to refer. It also means, 'Let him conduct himself with caution.'

1681. The words, *but let him not inform anyone about you*, refer to the quiet and unobtrusive penetration of the Western influence in the East.

1682. The words mean, 'If the people to whom you are sending trade parties became acquainted with your real intentions, or before your feet became firmly established in their country some political quarrel or commercial disagreement arose and you were overpowered, then you would either have to quit their country or embrace their religion. In either case you would fail to gain a permanent foothold and all your dreams of establishing a great empire in their country would come to naught.'

when people disputed among themselves concerning them, and said *to each other*, 'Build over them a building.' Their Lord knew them best. Those who won their point said, 'We will, surely, build a place of worship over them.'[1683]

بَيْنَهُمْ اَمْرَهُمْ فَقَالُوا ابْنُوْا عَلَيْهِمْ بُنْيَانًا رَبُّهُمْ
اَعْلَمُ بِهِمْ قَالَ الَّذِيْنَ غَلَبُوْا عَلٰٓى اَمْرِهِمْ لَنَتَّخِذَنَّ
عَلَيْهِمْ مَّسْجِدًا ﴿٢٢﴾

23. *Some* say, '*They were* three, the fourth of them *was* their dog;' and *others* say, '*They were* five, the sixth of them *was* their dog,' guessing at random. And *yet others* say, '*They were* seven, the eighth of them *was* their dog.'[1684] Say, 'My Lord knows best their correct number. None knows them except a few.' So argue not concerning them except with unanswerable arguments, nor seek information concerning them from anyone of them.

سَيَقُوْلُوْنَ ثَلٰثَةٌ رَّابِعُهُمْ كَلْبُهُمْ وَيَقُوْلُوْنَ
خَمْسَةٌ سَادِسُهُمْ كَلْبُهُمْ رَجْمًا بِالْغَيْبِ وَ
يَقُوْلُوْنَ سَبْعَةٌ وَّثَامِنُهُمْ كَلْبُهُمْ قُلْ رَّبِّيْٓ اَعْلَمُ
بِعِدَّتِهِمْ مَّا يَعْلَمُهُمْ اِلَّا قَلِيْلٌ فَلَا تُمَارِ
فِيْهِمْ اِلَّا مِرَآءً ظَاهِرًا وَّلَا تَسْتَفْتِ فِيْهِمْ
مِّنْهُمْ اَحَدًا ﴿٢٣﴾ ع ٣ ١٥

R. 4 24. And say not of anything, 'I shall do that tomorrow,'[1685]

وَلَا تَقُوْلَنَّ لِشَايْءٍ اِنِّيْ فَاعِلٌ ذٰلِكَ غَدًا ﴿٢٤﴾

1683. The words, *We will surely build a place of worship over them*, mention one of the distinctive marks of the Dwellers of the Cave which is that their successors, the Christian nations, will build churches in memory of their dead saints. It is further worthy of note that many such churches have been found in the catacombs.

1684. These guesses seem to be based on inscriptions on the walls of some of the chambers in the catacombs; but each inscription has reference only to a particular family, party or group. The total number of those who took refuge in the catacombs at any time is not known. A dog seems, from the inscriptions, to have always accompanied a party of refugees.

1685. The verse may mean that in the time of their decline and degradation Muslims will lose all initiative for any real and useful work and will indulge only in day-dreaming and all their activities will remain confined to talking about the future, and they will do nothing to improve their lot.

25. [a]Unless Allāh should will. And remember thy Lord when thou forgetest and say, 'I hope my Lord will guide me to what is *even* nearer than this to the right path.'

إِلَّآ أَن يَشَآءَ ٱللَّهُ ۚ وَٱذْكُر رَّبَّكَ إِذَا نَسِيتَ وَقُلْ
عَسَىٰٓ أَن يَهْدِيَنِ رَبِّى لِأَقْرَبَ مِنْ هَٰذَا رَشَدًا ﴿٢٥﴾

26. And they stayed in their Cave three hundred years and *to that* they added nine.[1686]

وَلَبِثُوا۟ فِى كَهْفِهِمْ ثَلَٰثَ مِا۟ئَةٍ سِنِينَ وَ
ٱزْدَادُوا۟ تِسْعًا ﴿٢٦﴾

27. Say, 'Allāh knows best how long they tarried.'[1687] [b]To Him belong the secrets of the heavens and the earth . [c]How Seeing is He, and how Hearing ![1687A] They have no helper beside Him, and He does not let anyone share in His judgment.

قُلِ ٱللَّهُ أَعْلَمُ بِمَا لَبِثُوا۟ ۖ لَهُۥ غَيْبُ ٱلسَّمَٰوَٰتِ وَٱلْأَرْضِ ۖ
أَبْصِرْ بِهِۦ وَأَسْمِعْ ۚ مَا لَهُم مِّن دُونِهِۦ مِن وَلِىٍّ
وَلَا يُشْرِكُ فِى حُكْمِهِۦٓ أَحَدًا ﴿٢٧﴾

28. 'And recite what has been revealed to thee of the Book of thy Lord. [d]There is none who can change His words, and thou wilt find no refuge beside Him.

وَٱتْلُ مَآ أُوحِىَ إِلَيْكَ مِن كِتَابِ رَبِّكَ ۖ لَا مُبَدِّلَ
لِكَلِمَٰتِهِۦ وَلَن تَجِدَ مِن دُونِهِۦ مُلْتَحَدًا ﴿٢٨﴾

[a]18 : 40; 74 : 57; 76 : 31; 81 : 30. [b]11 : 124; 16 : 78; 35 : 39. [c]19 : 39. 29 : 46. [d]6 : 35: 116; 10 : 65.

1686. The period in which early Christians were subjected to persecution and had, frequently to take refuge in caves and other places of hiding extends approximately over 309 years, and historical data have corroborated this calculation. As popularly believed the persecution of Christians began with Jesus's Crucifixion in 28 A.D., and ended with Emperor Constantine's conversion to Christianity in 337 A.D. (Enc. Brit), a period of about 309 years. And Constantine was not converted in 337 A.D., but in 309 A.D. The tragedy of the Crucifixion took place 28 years later than is generally believed (Chronology by Archbishop Ushers & Daily Bible Illustrations by Dr. Kitto).

1687. The early Christians were persecuted in many lands and at different times, *e.g.*, in Rome, Alexandria, etc. They were compelled to seek refuge in caves and catacombs at different times and for different periods. Their stay in the catacombs was not a single, uninterrupted episode. The exact length of the total period of such stay is known only to Allāh.

1687A. The words also mean : 'Clear is His Sight and keen His Hearing' or 'He sees all and hears all.'

29. [a]And keep thyself *attached* to those who call on their Lord morning and evening, seeking His pleasure; and let not thine eyes pass beyond them, seeking the adornment of the life of the world; and obey not him whose heart We have made heedless of Our remembrance and who follows his low desires, and his case exceeds all *legitimate* bounds.

وَاصْبِرْ نَفْسَكَ مَعَ الَّذِيْنَ يَدْعُوْنَ رَبَّهُمْ بِالْغَدٰوةِ
وَالْعَشِيِّ يُرِيْدُوْنَ وَجْهَهٗ وَلَا تَعْدُ عَيْنٰكَ عَنْهُمْ
تُرِيْدُ زِيْنَةَ الْحَيٰوةِ الدُّنْيَا وَلَا تُطِعْ مَنْ
اَغْفَلْنَا قَلْبَهٗ عَنْ ذِكْرِنَا وَاتَّبَعَ هَوٰىهُ
وَكَانَ اَمْرُهٗ فُرُطًا ﴿۲۹﴾ الثلثة

30. And say, [b]'*It is* the truth from your Lord; wherefore let him who will, believe, and let him, who will, disbelieve.' [c]Verily, We have prepared for the wrongdoers a fire whose *flaming* canopy shall enclose them. And if they cry for help, they will be helped with water like molten lead which would scald *their* faces. How dreadful the drink and how evil the resting place!

وَقُلِ الْحَقُّ مِنْ رَّبِّكُمْ فَمَنْ شَآءَ فَلْيُؤْمِنْ
وَّمَنْ شَآءَ فَلْيَكْفُرْ اِنَّآ اَعْتَدْنَا لِلظّٰلِمِيْنَ نَارًا
اَحَاطَ بِهِمْ سُرَادِقُهَا وَاِنْ يَّسْتَغِيْثُوْا يُغَاثُوْا بِمَآءٍ
كَالْمُهْلِ يَشْوِي الْوُجُوْهَ بِئْسَ الشَّرَابُ وَسَآءَتْ
مُرْتَفَقًا ﴿۳۰﴾

31. Verily, those who believe and do good works—surely [d]We suffer not the reward of those who do good works to be lost.

اِنَّ الَّذِيْنَ اٰمَنُوْا وَعَمِلُوا الصّٰلِحٰتِ اِنَّا لَا نُضِيْعُ
اَجْرَ مَنْ اَحْسَنَ عَمَلًا ﴿۳۱﴾

32. [e]It is these who will have Gardens of Eternity underneath which streams shall flow. They will be adorned therein with bracelets of gold and will wear green garments of fine silk and heavy brocade, [f]reclining therein upon raised couches.[1688] How good the reward and how excellent the place of rest!

اُولٰٓئِكَ لَهُمْ جَنّٰتُ عَدْنٍ تَجْرِيْ مِنْ تَحْتِهِمُ
الْاَنْهٰرُ يُحَلَّوْنَ فِيْهَا مِنْ اَسَاوِرَ مِنْ ذَهَبٍ
وَّيَلْبَسُوْنَ ثِيَابًا خُضْرًا مِّنْ سُنْدُسٍ وَّ
اِسْتَبْرَقٍ مُّتَّكِـِٕيْنَ فِيْهَا عَلَى الْاَرَآئِكِ نِعْمَ
الثَّوَابُ وَحَسُنَتْ مُرْتَفَقًا ﴿۳۲﴾ ع

[a]6 : 53; 7 : 206. [b]2 : 257; 10 : 100. [c]25 : 38; 42 : 46. [d]7 : 171; 9 : 120; 12 : 57. [e]9 : 72; 13 : 24; 19 : 62; 20 : 77; 35 : 34; 38 : 51; 61 : 13; 98 : 9. [f]15 : 48; 36 : 57; 83 : 24.

1688. Gold bracelets being symbols of royalty, the verse may signify that Muslims will become rulers of vast and mighty empires and will enjoy great power, honour and dignity and their womenfolk will wear garments of fine silk and heavy brocade interwoven with gold. This prophecy was fulfilled when the treasures of Persia and Rome were laid at the feet of the illiterate Arabs who used to wear clothes made of coarse skins and of the hair of animals.

R. 5 33. And set forth for them the parable of two men — one of them We provided with two gardens of grapes and surrounded them with date-palms, and between the two We placed corn-fields.[1689]

وَاضْرِبْ لَهُمْ مَّثَلًا رَّجُلَيْنِ جَعَلْنَا لِأَحَدِهِمَا
جَنَّتَيْنِ مِنْ أَعْنَابٍ وَّحَفَفْنٰهُمَا بِنَخْلٍ وَّجَعَلْنَا
بَيْنَهُمَا زَرْعًا ﴿٣٣﴾

34. Each of the gardens yielded its fruits *in abundance* and failed not the least therein. And in between the two We caused a stream[1690] to flow.

كِلْتَا الْجَنَّتَيْنِ اٰتَتْ اُكُلَهَا وَلَمْ تَظْلِمْ مِّنْهُ شَيْئًا ۙ
وَّفَجَّرْنَا خِلٰلَهُمَا نَهَرًا ﴿٣٤﴾

35. And he had fruit *in abundance*. And he said to his companion *boastfully*, arguing with him, 'I am richer than thou in wealth and stronger in respect of men.'[1690A]

وَّكَانَ لَهٗ ثَمَرٌ ۚ فَقَالَ لِصَاحِبِهٖ وَهُوَ يُحَاوِرُهٗۤ
اَنَا اَكْثَرُ مِنْكَ مَالًا وَّاَعَزُّ نَفَرًا ﴿٣٥﴾

36. And he entered his Garden while he was wronging his soul. He said, 'I do not think that this will ever perish;[1691]

وَدَخَلَ جَنَّتَهٗ وَهُوَ ظَالِمٌ لِّنَفْسِهٖ ۚ قَالَ مَاۤ
اَظُنُّ اَنْ تَبِيْدَ هٰذِهٖۤ اَبَدًا ﴿٣٦﴾

37. 'And I do not think the *promised* Hour will *ever* come. And even if I am ever brought back to my Lord, I shall, surely, find a better resort than this.'

وَّمَاۤ اَظُنُّ السَّاعَةَ قَآئِمَةً ۙ وَّلَئِنْ رُّدِدْتُّ اِلٰى
رَبِّيْ لَاَجِدَنَّ خَيْرًا مِّنْهَا مُنْقَلَبًا ﴿٣٧﴾

1689. With this verse begins, in the form of a parable, the conditions of the two peoples—Christians and Muslims, the "two men" representing these two peoples and "two gardens" the two periods of the rise of the Christian nations. The verse denotes that in their chequered history Christian nations would rise to great power twice. The first period preceded the advent of Islām while the second began with the dawn of the 17th century A.D., when Christian nations of Europe began to make great progress and acquire unprecedented power and prestige which reached its zenith in the nineteenth century.

1690. "The stream" represents the time of the Holy Prophet, through whom portions of the true teachings of Moses and Jesus were preserved.

1690A. The powerful and prosperous Christian nations would look down upon and taunt the poor and powerless Muslims for their poverty and lack of material resources.

1691. Being proud of their material progress Western Christian nations would give themselves up to a life of ease and luxury and in their conceit and arrogance misconceive that their power, progress and prosperity will last for ever, and being lulled into a false sense of security and complacency, they would be entirely lost in a life of sin and iniquity.

38. His companion said to him, while he was arguing with him, 'Dost thou disbelieve in Him [a]Who created thee *first* from dust, then from a sperm drop, then fashioned thee into a *perfect* man?

قَالَ لَهُ صَاحِبُهُ وَهُوَ يُحَاوِرُهُ أَكَفَرْتَ بِالَّذِي
خَلَقَكَ مِنْ تُرَابٍ ثُمَّ مِنْ نُطْفَةٍ ثُمَّ سَوّٰىكَ
رَجُلًا ﴿٣٨﴾

39. 'But *as for me, I believe that* [b]Allāh alone is my Lord, and I will not associate anyone with my Lord;

لٰكِنَّا هُوَ اللّٰهُ رَبِّي وَلَا أُشْرِكُ بِرَبِّي أَحَدًا ﴿٣٩﴾

40. 'And why didst thou not say when thou didst enter thy garden, '*Only* that which Allāh wills *comes to pass.* There is no power save in Allāh,' if thou seest me as less than thyself in riches and offspring;

وَلَوْلَا إِذْ دَخَلْتَ جَنَّتَكَ قُلْتَ مَا شَاءَ اللّٰهُ
لَا قُوَّةَ إِلَّا بِاللّٰهِ إِنْ تَرَنِ أَنَا أَقَلَّ مِنْكَ مَالًا
وَوَلَدًا ﴿٤٠﴾

41. [c]'It may be, my Lord will give me something better than thy garden,[1692] and will send on *thy garden* a thunderbolt from heaven[1693] so that it will become bare slippery ground;

فَعَسٰى رَبِّي أَنْ يُؤْتِيَنِ خَيْرًا مِنْ جَنَّتِكَ وَيُرْسِلَ
عَلَيْهَا حُسْبَانًا مِنَ السَّمَاءِ فَتُصْبِحَ صَعِيدًا
زَلَقًا ﴿٤١﴾

42. 'Or its water will dry up[1694] so that thou wilt not be able to find it.'

أَوْ يُصْبِحَ مَاؤُهَا غَوْرًا فَلَنْ تَسْتَطِيعَ لَهُ طَلَبًا ﴿٤٢﴾

---

[a]22 : 6; 23 : 13; 35 : 12; 36 : 78; 40 : 68. [b]13 : 37; 72 : 21. [c]68 : 33.

1692. This verse and vv. 36 and 40 speak of one garden only because of the two gardens (v. 33) one had practically perished before Islām. The "garden" which proved to be the greatest source of pride for Christians is the one which flourished after Islām—their present material great progress and power.

1693. The words 'from heaven' show that no earthly power will be able effectively to combat and resist the military might of Western Christian nations. God Himself will create circumstances which will bring about their destruction. It is to this irresistible might of Gog and Magog who represent the material glory of Christianity that the Holy Prophet referred when he is reported to have said, 'None will have the power to fight them' (Muslim, ch. on "Dajjāl").

1694. The springs of their great talents and intellectual attainments on which their material progress mainly depends or which, in the words of the Qur'ān, keep their garden fresh and green, will dry up, resulting in the complete desolation of their "garden." Their springs of spiritual freshness will also dry up.

43. [a]And his fruit was *totally* destroyed, and he began to wring his hands *bewailing all* that he had spent on it, and it had *all* fallen down on its trellises.[1695] And he said, [b]"Would that I had not associated anyone with my Lord!"

وَأُحِيطَ بِثَمَرِهٖ فَأَصْبَحَ يُقَلِّبُ كَفَّيْهِ عَلٰى مَآ أَنْفَقَ
فِيهَا وَهِيَ خَاوِيَةٌ عَلٰى عُرُوشِهَا وَيَقُولُ يٰلَيْتَنِي
لَمْ أُشْرِكْ بِرَبِّيٓ أَحَدًا ﴿٤٣﴾

44. [c]And he had no party to help him against Allāh, nor was he able to defend himself.

وَلَمْ تَكُنْ لَّهٗ فِئَةٌ يَّنْصُرُونَهٗ مِنْ دُونِ اللّٰهِ وَمَا
كَانَ مُنْتَصِرًا ﴿٤٤﴾

45. [d]In such a case protection *comes only* from Allāh, the True. He is Best in rewarding and Best in respect of the final outcome.

هُنَالِكَ الْوَلَايَةُ لِلّٰهِ الْحَقِّ هُوَ خَيْرٌ ثَوَابًا وَّ
خَيْرٌ عُقْبًا ﴿٤٥﴾ ع

R. 6 46. [e]And set forth for them the similitude of the life of this world. It is like the water which We send down from the sky, and the vegetation of the earth is mingled with it, and then it becomes dry grass broken into pieces which the winds scatter.[1696] And Allāh has full power over everything.

وَاضْرِبْ لَهُمْ مَّثَلَ الْحَيٰوةِ الدُّنْيَا كَمَآءٍ أَنْزَلْنٰهُ
مِنَ السَّمَآءِ فَاخْتَلَطَ بِهٖ نَبَاتُ الْأَرْضِ فَأَصْبَحَ
هَشِيمًا تَذْرُوهُ الرِّيٰحُ وَكَانَ اللّٰهُ عَلٰى كُلِّ
شَيْءٍ مُّقْتَدِرًا ﴿٤٦﴾

47. [f]Wealth and children are ornaments of the life of this world. But enduring good works are better in the sight of thy Lord in respect of *immediate* reward, and better in respect of *future* hope.

اَلْمَالُ وَالْبَنُونَ زِينَةُ الْحَيٰوةِ الدُّنْيَا وَالْبٰقِيٰتُ
الصّٰلِحٰتُ خَيْرٌ عِنْدَ رَبِّكَ ثَوَابًا وَّخَيْرٌ أَمَلًا ﴿٤٧﴾

[a]68 : 20. [b]68 : 32. [c]28. 82. [d]40 : 17; 82 : 20. [e]10 : 25; 57 : 21. [f]3 : 15; 57 : 21.

1695. All the efforts and endeavours of Christian peoples to maintain continuity of their material wealth will end in smoke and their power and prestige will speedily and unexpectedly decline. The verse incidentally shows that the word "garden" used in these verses has not been used in its literal sense because gardens do not fall upon their trellises.

1696. What an apt and forceful description of the transitoriness of worldly life !

48. And *bethink of* the day when *a*We shall remove the mountains and thou wilt see *the nations of* the earth march forth *against one another* and We shall gather them *all* together[1697] and shall not leave any one of them behind.

وَيَوْمَ نُسَيِّرُ الْجِبَالَ وَتَرَى الْأَرْضَ بَارِزَةً وَّحَشَرْنٰهُمْ فَلَمْ نُغَادِرْ مِنْهُمْ أَحَدًا ۞

49. *b*And they will be presented to thy Lord *standing* in rows; *and it will be said to them,* "Now have you come to Us as We created you at first.[1698] But you thought that We would not appoint a time *for the fulfilment of* Our promise to you.'

وَعُرِضُوْا عَلٰى رَبِّكَ صَفًّا لَقَدْ جِئْتُمُوْنَا كَمَا خَلَقْنٰكُمْ أَوَّلَ مَرَّةٍ بَلْ زَعَمْتُمْ أَلَّنْ نَّجْعَلَ لَكُمْ مَّوْعِدًا ۞

50. *d*And the Book of *their deeds* will be placed *before them,* and thou wilt see the guilty ones fearful at what is therein; and they will say, 'O woe to us! What kind of a Book is this! It leaves out nothing small or great but has recorded it.' *c*And they will find all that they did confronting *them,* and thy Lord does not wrong anyone.

وَوُضِعَ الْكِتٰبُ فَتَرَى الْمُجْرِمِيْنَ مُشْفِقِيْنَ مِمَّا فِيْهِ وَيَقُوْلُوْنَ يٰوَيْلَتَنَا مَالِ هٰذَا الْكِتٰبِ لَا يُغَادِرُ صَغِيْرَةً وَّلَا كَبِيْرَةً إِلَّا أَحْصٰهَا وَوَجَدُوْا مَا عَمِلُوْا حَاضِرًا وَلَا يَظْلِمُ رَبُّكَ أَحَدًا ۞

R. 7 51. *f*And *call to mind the time* when We said to the angels, 'Submit to Adam,' and they all submitted but Iblīs *did not.* He was *one of* the jinn; and he disobeyed the command of his Lord. Will you then take him and his offspring for friends instead of Me while they are your enemies? Evil is the exchange for the wrongdoers.

وَإِذْ قُلْنَا لِلْمَلٰئِكَةِ اسْجُدُوْا لِآدَمَ فَسَجَدُوْا إِلَّا إِبْلِيْسَ كَانَ مِنَ الْجِنِّ فَفَسَقَ عَنْ أَمْرِ رَبِّهِ أَفَتَتَّخِذُوْنَهُ وَذُرِّيَّتَهُ أَوْلِيَآءَ مِنْ دُوْنِيْ وَهُمْ لَكُمْ عَدُوٌّ بِئْسَ لِلظّٰلِمِيْنَ بَدَلًا ۞

---

*a*52 : 11; 78 : 21; 81 : 4. *b*78 : 39. *c*6 : 95. *d*39 : 70. *e*3 : 31; 99 : 8-9. *f*2 : 35; 7 : 12; 15 : 30-31; 17 : 62; 20 : 117; 38 : 73-75.

1697. *Jibāl* meaning "chiefs" (Lane), the verse may mean that the prophecy about the complete destruction of the forces of evil—Gog and Magog—mentioned in the few preceding verses will be fulfilled when in the words of the Bible 'nation shall rise against nation and kingdom against kingdom, and there shall be famines and pestilences and earthquakes in diverse places' (Matt. 24 : 7). The expression, *Hasharnā-hum,,* means that they will be gathered in battle array, facing each other, and will fight to the bitter end.

1698. The words signify that they will become divested of all power and authority and will be reduced to a state of subjection and disgrace as before.

52. I did not make them witness the creation of the heavens and the earth,[1699] nor their own creation; nor could I take as helpers those who lead *people* astray.

مَآ اَشْهَدْتُّهُمْ خَلْقَ السَّمٰوٰتِ وَالْاَرْضِ وَلَا خَلْقَ
اَنْفُسِهِمْ وَمَا كُنْتُ مُتَّخِذَ الْمُضِلِّيْنَ عَضُدًا ﴿۵۲﴾

53. And *remember* the day when He will say *to them*, [a]'Call those whom you deemed to be My partners.' Then they will call on them, but they will not answer them; and We shall place a barrier[1700] between them.

وَيَوْمَ يَقُوْلُ نَادُوْا شُرَكَآءِيَ الَّذِيْنَ زَعَمْتُمْ فَدَعَوْهُمْ
فَلَمْ يَسْتَجِيْبُوْا لَهُمْ وَجَعَلْنَا بَيْنَهُمْ مَّوْبِقًا ﴿۵۳﴾

54. And [b]the guilty shall see the fire and realize that they are going to fall therein; and they shall find no escape therefrom.[1701]

وَرَاَ الْمُجْرِمُوْنَ النَّارَ فَظَنُّوْٓا اَنَّهُمْ مُّوَاقِعُوْهَا وَ
لَمْ يَجِدُوْا عَنْهَا مَصْرِفًا ﴿۵۴﴾ ع ۱۹

R. 8 55. [c]And, surely, We have explained in various ways in this Qur'ān for *the good of* mankind all manner of similitudes, [d]but of all things man is most contentious.[1702]

وَلَقَدْ صَرَّفْنَا فِيْ هٰذَا الْقُرْاٰنِ لِلنَّاسِ مِنْ كُلِّ
مَثَلٍ ؕ وَكَانَ الْاِنْسَانُ اَكْثَرَ شَيْءٍ جَدَلًا ﴿۵۵﴾

[a]16 : 28; 28 : 63, 75; 41 : 48. [b]21 : 40; 38 : 60; 52 : 14. [c]17 : 42, 90. [d]16 : 5; 36 : 78.

1699. The verse seems to signify that at that time there will be general talk about a new world order which will herald an era of permanent peace and concord in the world and the so-called leaders of political and social thought will seek and claim to establish it, but they will not succeed in their efforts because God has reserved for Himself the consummation of this supreme task.

1700. The verse may mean that these nations will set up high tariff walls or iron curtains and impose economic boycott upon one another, or it may mean that they will become involved in deadly wars which will ruin them.

1701. The disbelieving nations of the West will see a most destruetive war approaching. They will try all possible means to avoid it but all their plans and efforts to this end will prove futile. The West has already passed through the ordeal of two most destructive wars which have almost destroyed its political domination and prestige in the world and have shaken Western civilization to its foundation. A third holocaust is staring it—perhaps the whole world—in the face.

1702. The verse may mean : (*a*) Of all God's creation man has been endowed with reason and intellectual faculties but regrettably he employs them to reject truth and for other evil purposes(*b*) Or, it may mean that he is a victim of chronic misgivings and doubts, which seldom find satisfaction, and being a confirmed sceptic seeks to discover loop-holes even in the most convincing arguments.

56. [a]And nothing hinders people from believing when the guidance comes to them, and from asking forgiveness of their Lord, but that *they wait for* the fate of the ancients to overtake them or that punishment should come upon them face to face.

وَمَا مَنَعَ النَّاسَ أَنْ يُّؤْمِنُوٓا إِذْ جَآءَهُمُ الْهُدٰى
وَيَسْتَغْفِرُوا رَبَّهُمْ إِلَّآ أَنْ تَأْتِيَهُمْ سُنَّةُ الْأَوَّلِينَ
أَوْ يَأْتِيَهُمُ الْعَذَابُ قُبُلًا ٥٦

57. [b]And We send not the Messengers but as bearers of glad tidings and as Warners. And those who disbelieve contend by means of falsehood that they may rebut the truth thereby. And they take My Signs and what they are warned of *only* as a jest.

وَمَا نُرْسِلُ الْمُرْسَلِينَ إِلَّا مُبَشِّرِينَ وَمُنْذِرِينَ
وَيُجَادِلُ الَّذِينَ كَفَرُوا بِالْبَاطِلِ لِيُدْحِضُوا بِهِ
الْحَقَّ وَاتَّخَذُوٓا اٰيٰتِي وَمَآ أُنْذِرُوا هُزُوًا ٥٧

58. And who is more unjust than he who is reminded of the Signs of his Lord, but turns away from them, and forgets what his hands have sent forward? [c]Verily, We have placed veils over their hearts that they understand it not and in their ears a deafness.[1703] And if thou call them to guidance, they will never accept it.

وَمَنْ أَظْلَمُ مِمَّنْ ذُكِّرَ بِاٰيٰتِ رَبِّهِ فَأَعْرَضَ عَنْهَا
وَنَسِيَ مَا قَدَّمَتْ يَدٰهُ إِنَّا جَعَلْنَا عَلٰى قُلُوبِهِمْ
أَكِنَّةً أَنْ يَّفْقَهُوهُ وَفِيٓ اٰذَانِهِمْ وَقْرًا وَإِنْ
تَدْعُهُمْ إِلَى الْهُدٰى فَلَنْ يَّهْتَدُوٓا إِذًا أَبَدًا ٥٨

59. [d]And thy Lord is Most Forgiving, Lord of Mercy. [e]If He were to seize them for what they have earned, then surely He would have hastened the punishment for them. But they have an appointed time from which they will find no refuge.

وَرَبُّكَ الْغَفُورُ ذُو الرَّحْمَةِ لَوْ يُؤَاخِذُهُمْ بِمَا
كَسَبُوا لَعَجَّلَ لَهُمُ الْعَذَابَ بَلْ لَّهُمْ مَّوْعِدٌ
لَّنْ يَّجِدُوا مِنْ دُونِهِ مَوْئِلًا ٥٩

60. [f]And these towns—We destroyed them when they committed iniquities. And We appointed a time for their destruction.

وَتِلْكَ الْقُرٰٓى أَهْلَكْنٰهُمْ لَمَّا ظَلَمُوا وَجَعَلْنَا
لِمَهْلِكِهِمْ مَّوْعِدًا ٦٠

[a]17 : 95. [b]2 : 214; 4 : 166; 6 : 49; 17 : 106. [c]2 : 8; 6 : 26; 17 : 47; 41 : 6; 47 : 17. [d]6 : 134,148. [e]10 : 12; 35 : 46. [f]11 : 101.

1703. The disbelievers persistently refuse to see reason and to make use of their God-given powers with the result that these powers and faculties become rusted and corroded and they are left floundering in sin and iniquity.

R. 9 61. And *remember the time* when Moses said to his young *companion*, 'I will not cease *pursuing my course* until I reach the junction of the two seas,[1704] though I may have to journey on for ages.'[1704A]

وَاِذْ قَالَ مُوْسٰى لِفَتٰىهُ لَآ اَبْرَحُ حَتّٰٓى اَبْلُغَ مَجْمَعَ الْبَحْرَيْنِ اَوْ اَمْضِيَ حُقُبًا ﴿٦١﴾

1704. With this verse begins the subject of the *Isrā'* (Spiritual Night Journey) of Moses. As stated above, the followers of Jesus Christ achieved great material power and prosperity, and in their chequered career left their indelible imprint twice on world's history. This double prosperity of Christian nations has been likened to "two gardens" in v. 33. The first of these two periods began with the conversion to Christianity of the Roman Emperor, Constantine, when it became the religion of the State, and continued till the birth of the Holy Prophet of Islām. The second and more important of these two periods is represented by the present age when Christian nations of the West have acquired so much power and prestige that the nations of Asia and Africa have to dance attendance upon them like serfs and slaves. Between these "two gardens" flowed a "stream" (v. 34). This "stream" denoted the birth and rise to power of Islām which left its deep mark on human history during the interval between these two periods. In order to provide an historical setting to the account and to make it look like a connected whole, a somewhat detailed description of the *Isrā'* or Spiritual Journey of Moses has been given in the present and following few verses. Moses had fore-told the advent of a Prophet like unto him (Deut. 18 : 18). This prophecy has been referred to in the Qur'ān in 73 : 16. By putting the account of Moses's Spiritual Journey between those of the Dwellers of the Cave and Gog and Magog—representing the two periods of the beginning of Christianity and its later progress and advance—the Qur'ān has pointed out to the fact that the Prophet referred to in Moses's prophecy, who was also to be his counterpart, was to appear during the interval between these two periods. Thus have these incidents been mentioned in their historical order.

1704A. *Ḥuqub* is plural of *Ḥuqbah* which means, long time, indefinite time; an age ; seventy years or more (Lane & Mufradāt).

The *Isrā'* of Moses was, like the *Isrā'* of the Holy Prophet (17 : 2), no physical journey but a spiritual experience by means of which Moses was transported from his body of flesh and blood to a spiritual tabernacle. The Bible and the Qur'ān both support this view. Some of the arguments advanced in its support are as follows :

(1) The Bible which is considered by Christians to be more or less a reliable record of Moses's life has omitted all mention of this most unusual and wonderful incident and has failed even to make a passing reference to it. (2) Before and after he was commissioned as a Divine Prophet, Moses is known to have undertaken only one journey and that was to Midian. The Bible and the Qur'ān have both referred to this journey. Both also agree that Moses undertook the journey to Midian alone, while in the journey referred to in the present and the following verses he is described as having been accompanied by 'his young companion.' (3) There is no place in the world which is known by the name, *Majma'a al-Baḥrain*. The expression can only mean 'the junction of two seas.' Such junctions nearest to the place where Moses lived, after he had left Egypt, are Bāb al-Mandab which unites the Red Sea and the Indian Ocean and the Straits of Dardanelles which joins the Mediterranean Sea with the Sea of Marmora and Al-Baḥrain where the waters of the Persian Gulf and the Indian Ocean meet. Of all these places the Straits of Dardanelles alone can possibly be the point where such a meeting could have taken place because on its way from Egypt lies Canaan which was the destination of Moses but which he could not reach in his life-time. All these three points were about one thousand miles distant from Moses's place of living, and considering the absence of good means of communication and transport in those days it would have taken him several months to cover such a long distance and Moses could not afford to remain absent from his people for such a long time without seriously jeopardising their spiritual well-being, specially after his bitter experience with them when he was absent from them on Mount Ṭūr only for forty days. The expression *Majma'al-Baḥrain*, seems to mean the junction of the two Dispensations—Mosaic and Islamic.

62. But when they reached the place where the two *seas* met, they forgot their fish,[1705] and it made its way into the sea *going away* quickly.

فَلَمَّا بَلَغَا مَجْمَعَ بَيْنِهِمَا نَسِيَا حُوتَهُمَا فَاتَّخَذَ سَبِيلَهُ فِي الْبَحْرِ سَرَبًا ﴿٦٢﴾

63. And when they had gone beyond *that place*, he said to his young *companion*, 'Bring us our morning meal.[1706] Surely, we have suffered much fatigue on account of this journey of ours.'

فَلَمَّا جَاوَزَا قَالَ لِفَتٰىهُ اٰتِنَا غَدَآءَنَا لَقَدْ لَقِيْنَا مِنْ سَفَرِنَا هٰذَا نَصَبًا ﴿٦٣﴾

Besides this external evidence there is much internal evidence in vv. 61—83 which shows that the journey was not a physical event but a spiritual experience of Moses :—

(*a*) The "Servant of God" made a big hole in the boat (v. 72) to save it from being forcibly seized by the king. But did the boat remain sea-worthy after it was damaged, or did it not? If it did, why did not the king seize it? If it did not, why did it not sink? In this physical world no boat is ever known to have remained floating after a big hole had been made in its bottom. In the world of visions, however, such things are possible. (*b*) In this world of flesh and bones no sensible person, much less a Prophet of God, would take the life of another person without a legitimate cause, as "the Servant of God" is stated to have done (v. 75). (*c*) How could a great Prophet of God and a most noble and broadminded person like Moses have found fault with the "Man of God" for not demanding payment from two poor orphan boys for repairing their broken wall because the people of their town had refused to entertain them? What had the two orphan boys done to deserve Moses's displeasure? It was the people of the town and not they who had refused to entertain them as guests. (*d*) It is inconceivable that a great Prophet of God like Moses should have undertaken a long arduous journey in search of a "Servant of God" to learn from him how to break a hole in a boat or to kill a young man or to repair a wall and demand no remuneration for it. Moreover, the 'Holy' Prophet is reported to have said, 'Would that Moses had kept silent, so that God would have revealed to us many more secrets of the unseen (Bukhārī, *Kitāb al-Tafsīr*). But there was nothing of the secrets of the unseen in the unusual acts which the "Servant of God" is stated to have done. According to Māwardī, the person whom Moses had gone to see was no human being but an angel of God (Kathīr). All these facts taken together constitute very solid and weighty evidence, that the journey of Moses was but a vision which needs to be interpreted and explained in order to understand its reality and significance. The words 'young companion' (v. 61) may refer to Joshua, the son of Nun, but they may more fittingly apply to Jesus. Jesus was the young companion of Moses who came not to destroy but to fulfil the Law and the Prophets (Matt. 5 : 17). The words, *I will not cease pursuing my course until I reach the junction of the two seas*, show that Moses's young companion had joined him towards the end of his journey. Moses did not seem to have taken the young man with him from the very outset of his journey. Jesus came fourteen hundred years after him. The words, *though I may have to journey on for ages*, signify that the Mosaic Dispensation would remain in force for many centuries. The period from the time of Moses to the advent of the Holy Prophet, when the Mosaic Dispensation came to an end, extends over 2000 years.

1705. *Ḥūt* when seen in a vision denotes houses of worship of the righteous people (Ta'ṭīr al-Anām). In this sense of the word the expression, *when they reached the place where the two seas met, they forgot their fish*, signifies that at the time when the Mosaic and the Islamic Dispensations would meet, *i.e.*, when Mosaic Dispensation would cease to function and the Islamic Dispensation would come into force, true righteousness would depart from among the followers of Moses and Jesus, and would henceforward become the special mark of the followers of the new Dispensation (48 : 30).

1706. 'Asking for morning meal or breakfast' in a vision denotes 'weariness' (Ta'ṭīr al-Anām), and the verse purports to say that after passing the 'junction of the two seas' and going on their separate journeys for a long time and being tired of vainly waiting for the Promised Prophet (Deut. 18 : 18), Moses and his young companion would begin to wonder that he may have already appeared but that they had failed to recognize him. In the verse Moses and his young companion (Jesus) may stand for Jews and Christians respectively.

64. He replied, 'Didst thou see, when we betook ourselves to the rock[1707] for rest and I forgot the fish—and none but Satan caused me to forget to mention it *to thee*—it took its way into the sea *in a marvellous manner*?'

قَالَ اَرَءَيْتَ اِذْ اَوَيْنَآ اِلَى الصَّخْرَةِ فَاِنِّيْ نَسِيْتُ الْحُوْتَ وَمَآ اَنْسٰنِيْهُ اِلَّا الشَّيْطٰنُ اَنْ اَذْكُرَهٗ وَاتَّخَذَ سَبِيْلَهٗ فِى الْبَحْرِ عَجَبًا ﴿٦٤﴾

65. He said, 'That is what we have been seeking.' So they both returned, retracing their footsteps.

قَالَ ذٰلِكَ مَا كُنَّا نَبْغِ فَارْتَدَّا عَلٰٓى اٰثَارِهِمَا قَصَصًا ﴿٦٥﴾

66. Then they found a servant of Ours,[1708] upon whom We had bestowed mercy from Us, and whom We had taught knowledge from Ourselves.

فَوَجَدَا عَبْدًا مِّنْ عِبَادِنَآ اٰتَيْنٰهُ رَحْمَةً مِّنْ عِنْدِنَا وَعَلَّمْنٰهُ مِنْ لَّدُنَّا عِلْمًا ﴿٦٦﴾

67. Moses said to him, 'May I follow thee *on condition* that thou teach me *some* of the guidance which thou hast been taught?'[1709]

قَالَ لَهٗ مُوْسٰى هَلْ اَتَّبِعُكَ عَلٰٓى اَنْ تُعَلِّمَنِ مِمَّا عُلِّمْتَ رُشْدًا ﴿٦٧﴾

1707. *Ṣakhrāh* in the language of dreams and visions denotes 'a life of vice and sin.' So the expression, *when we betook ourselves to the rock*, signifies that when the two seas would meet, *i.e.*, when the Mosaic Dispensation would come to an end and a new Prophet and a new Dispensation would appear, the Jews and Christians would be sunk into a life of sin and iniquity. The words, *it took its way into the sea in a marvellous manner* signify that true piety and worship of God would take leave of these peoples.

1708. Who is this "Servant of God" (*'Abd*) upon whom God had bestowed mercy and whom He had taught knowledge and in search of whom Moses, in pursuance of Divine command, had undertaken such a long and difficult journey and who is the central figure and the hero of the whole story? He is none other than the Holy Prophet Muḥammad—his soul having taken an embodied form in Moses's Vision. Reasons for this are: (*a*) He has been called '*Abd* servant of God, in the Qur'ān (2 : 24; 8 : 42; 17 : 2; 18 : 2; 25 : 2; 39 : 37; 53 : 11 & 72 : 20). In fact, he is '*Abd Allāh* (God's servant) *par excellence.* (*b*) He has been spoken of as 'a mercy to the whole world' (21 : 108), an epithet applied in the Qur'ān to none other than the Holy Prophet. (*c*) He was vouchsafed Divine knowledge in a very large measure (4 : 114 ; 20 : 115 & 27 : 7). (*d*) This "Servant of God" had told Moses that he (Moses) would not keep silent (v. 68 below), and the Holy Prophet is reported to have said, 'Would that Moses had kept silent ! If he had done so, we would have been vouchsafed more knowledge about the unseen' (Bukhārī, *Kitāb al-Tafsīr*). As a matter of fact, Moses had seen a manifestation of God 'in the fire' when travelling from Midian to Egypt (28 : 30). Later on, however, he was told that a Prophet would appear from among the brethren of the Israelites in whose mouth God would put His own Word (Deut. 18 : 18-22). The words of the prophecy signified that the Promised Prophet would be the object of a greater manifestation of God than Moses. Moses, therefore, naturally wished to see who 'that Prophet' could be. To satisfy his curiosity God made him see in his Vision 'that Prophet' of much higher spiritual powers. This learned "Servant of God" of Moses's Vision who has been popularly known by the name of *Khaḍir* was the spirit of our noble Master, the Holy Prophet Muḥammad, which had assumed a physical tabernacle. See also 7:144.

1709. Moses was denied the heights which the spiritual knowledge of the Holy Prophet had attained.

68. He replied, 'Thou canst not have patience with me;[1710]

قَالَ إِنَّكَ لَنْ تَسْتَطِيعَ مَعِيَ صَبْرًا ﴿٦٨﴾

69. 'And how canst thou have patience about things the knowledge of which thou comprehendest not?'

وَكَيْفَ تَصْبِرُ عَلَىٰ مَا لَمْ تُحِطْ بِهِ خُبْرًا ﴿٦٩﴾

70. He said, 'Thou wilt find me, if Allāh please, patient and I shall not disobey any command of thine.'

قَالَ سَتَجِدُنِي إِنْ شَاءَ اللَّهُ صَابِرًا وَلَا أَعْصِي لَكَ
أَمْرًا ﴿٧٠﴾

71. He said, 'Well, if thou wouldst follow me, then [a]ask me no questions about anything till I *myself* speak to thee about it.'

قَالَ فَإِنِ اتَّبَعْتَنِي فَلَا تَسْأَلْنِي عَنْ شَيْءٍ حَتَّىٰ أُحْدِثَ
لَكَ مِنْهُ ذِكْرًا ﴿٧١﴾ ع

R. 10 72. So they both set out till, when they embarked in a boat, he made a hole[1711] in it. *Moses* said, 'Hast thou made a hole in it to drown those who are in it? Surely, thou hast done a grievous thing.'

فَانْطَلَقَا حَتَّىٰ إِذَا رَكِبَا فِي السَّفِينَةِ خَرَقَهَا ۖ قَالَ
أَخَرَقْتَهَا لِتُغْرِقَ أَهْلَهَا لَقَدْ جِئْتَ شَيْئًا إِمْرًا ﴿٧٢﴾

73. He replied, 'Did I not tell *thee* that thou canst not have patience with me?'[1712]

قَالَ أَلَمْ أَقُلْ إِنَّكَ لَنْ تَسْتَطِيعَ مَعِيَ صَبْرًا ﴿٧٣﴾

---

[a]11 : 47; 17 : 37.

1710. The patience and steadfastness under severe trials and difficulties of the followers of Moses were not of the same high order and pattern as those of the Holy Prophet's followers (5 : 22-25 & Bukhārī, *Kitāb al-Maghāzī*). The verse also compares the natural dispositions of Moses and the Holy Prophet. Moses impatiently inquired the "Servant of God" about things which he did not understand, but the Holy Prophet waited patiently till Archangel Gabriel explained to him the meanings of the various things he saw in his own *Mi'rāj.* This difference in the temperaments of these two great Prophets was also reflected in the behaviour of their respective followers. While the Israelites continued to pester Moses with all sorts of unnecessary and foolish questions, the demeanour of the Holy Prophet's Companions was characterized by great dignity and restraint. They scrupulously avoided putting him questions on religious matters. Both the Holy Prophet and his Companions most faithfully observed the admonition contained in 20 : 115.

1711. The preceding several verses served only as an introduction to the subject of the *Isrā'* of Moses. With the present verse, however, begins an account of the actual incidents which Moses actually saw in his Vision. The words, *he made a hole in it,* when interpreted, signify that the Holy Prophet would lay down commandments which would, as it were, make a hole in the boat which in the language of dreams denotes worldly riches, *i.e.,* he would see to it that wealth did not accumulate in the hands of a few persons but was fairly distributed.

1712. The righteous "Servant of God" in Moses's Vision (the Holy Prophet) is here represented as saying to him that as there existed great difference between the teachings of the two, therefore he (Moses) could not accompany him, *i.e.,* Moses's people would not accept him (the Holy Prophet).

74. *Moses* said, 'Take me not to task for what I forgot and be not hard on me for this *lapse* of mine.'

قَالَ لَا تُؤَاخِذْنِي بِمَا نَسِيتُ وَلَا تُرْهِقْنِي مِنْ أَمْرِي عُسْرًا ﴿٧٤﴾

75. So they journeyed on[1713] till when they met a young boy;[1713A] he slew him. *Moses* said, [a]'What, hast thou slain an innocent person without *his having slain* anyone! Surely, thou hast done a hideous thing.'

فَانْطَلَقَا حَتَّىٰ إِذَا لَقِيَا غُلَامًا فَقَتَلَهُ قَالَ أَقَتَلْتَ نَفْسًا زَكِيَّةً بِغَيْرِ نَفْسٍ لَقَدْ جِئْتَ شَيْئًا نُكْرًا ﴿٧٥﴾

PART XVI

76. He replied, 'Did I not tell thee that thou couldst never bear with me patiently?'

الجزء ١٦ قَالَ أَلَمْ أَقُلْ لَكَ إِنَّكَ لَنْ تَسْتَطِيعَ مَعِيَ صَبْرًا ﴿٧٦﴾

77. *Moses* said, 'If I ask thee concerning anything after this, keep me not in thy company, for *then* thou shalt have got sufficient excuse from me.'

قَالَ إِنْ سَأَلْتُكَ عَنْ شَيْءٍ بَعْدَهَا فَلَا تُصَاحِبْنِي قَدْ بَلَغْتَ مِنْ لَدُنِّي عُذْرًا ﴿٧٧﴾

78. So they went on till, when they came to the people of a town, they asked its people for food, but they refused to receive them as their guests.[1714] And they found therein a wall which was about to fall and he repaired it. *Moses* said, 'If thou hadst so desired, thou couldst have taken payment for it.'

فَانْطَلَقَا حَتَّىٰ إِذَا أَتَيَا أَهْلَ قَرْيَةٍ اسْتَطْعَمَا أَهْلَهَا فَأَبَوْا أَنْ يُضَيِّفُوهُمَا فَوَجَدَا فِيهَا جِدَارًا يُرِيدُ أَنْ يَنْقَضَّ فَأَقَامَهُ قَالَ لَوْ شِئْتَ لَاتَّخَذْتَ عَلَيْهِ أَجْرًا ﴿٧٨﴾

---

[a]5 : 33.

1713. The word *Intalaqā* which has been used several times in these verses was exactly the one used by the Archangel Gabriel for the Holy Prophet in his *Mi'rāj* (Spiritual Ascension).

1713A. A youth in the language of visions, among other things, signifies ignorance, strength and wild impulses. The killing of the young boy by the righteous "Servant of God," in Moses's Vision meant that Islām would require its Followers to bring a veritable death over their carnal desires and passions.

1714. The verse seems to signify that Moses and the Holy Prophet would seek the co-operation of Jews and Christians in the cause of God but it would be denied to both of them.

79. He said, 'This is the parting *of the ways* between me and thee. [a]I will now tell thee the meaning of that which thou wast not able to bear with patience;

قَالَ هٰذَا فِرَاقُ بَيْنِيْ وَبَيْنِكَ ۚ سَاُنَبِّئُكَ بِتَاْوِيْلِ مَا لَمْ تَسْتَطِعْ عَّلَيْهِ صَبْرًا ﴿٧٩﴾

80. 'As for the boat, it belonged to *certain* poor people[1715] who worked on the sea and I desired to damage it, for there was behind them a king who seized every boat by force;

اَمَّا السَّفِيْنَةُ فَكَانَتْ لِمَسٰكِيْنَ يَعْمَلُوْنَ فِي الْبَحْرِ فَاَرَدْتُّ اَنْ اَعِيْبَهَا وَكَانَ وَرَآءَهُمْ مَّلِكٌ يَّاْخُذُ كُلَّ سَفِيْنَةٍ غَصْبًا ﴿٨٠﴾

81. 'And as for the youth,[1716] his parents were believers, and we feared lest *on growing up* he should involve them into trouble through rebellion and disbelief;

وَاَمَّا الْغُلٰمُ فَكَانَ اَبَوٰهُ مُؤْمِنَيْنِ فَخَشِيْنَآ اَنْ يُّرْهِقَهُمَا طُغْيَانًا وَّكُفْرًا ﴿٨١﴾

82. 'So we desired that their Lord should give them in exchange *one* better than he in purity and closer in *filial* affection;

فَاَرَدْنَآ اَنْ يُّبْدِلَهُمَا رَبُّهُمَا خَيْرًا مِّنْهُ زَكٰوةً وَّاَقْرَبَ رُحْمًا ﴿٨٢﴾

[a]3 : 8; 12 : 22.

1715. The words, "poor people", here may represent "the Muslims". Making a hole in the boat meant that Islām would exhort Muslims to spend their money in the cause of Allāh, by way of *Zakāt* and charity. This would appear to be a source of economic weakness rather than of strength and true prosperity, which in fact it would not be. The tyrant king of the *Isrā'* were the Byzantine and Iranian Empires which would have swallowed up Arabia had it not seemed to them a poor and barren land, not worth the trouble of conquering. It was thus preserved intact for the Holy Prophet.

1716. *Ghulām* (a youth), as stated above, in a dream or vision signifies ignorance, strength and wild impulses. "His parents" in the verse are the human body and soul, because the source (or the parents) from which spring all moral qualities is the combination of the human body and soul which are represented here as "believers" because, as taught by Islām, man by nature is inclined to virtue. These "believers" may be dragged into vice by the impulses represented as "youth." Islām eradicates these impulses and leaves man—the human body and soul combined, to develop along beneficent lines and thus to achieve the high purpose of human life.

83. 'And as for the wall, it belonged to two orphan boys[1717] in the town, and beneath it was a treasure belonging to them, and their father had been *a* righteous *man*, so thy Lord desired that they should reach their *age of* full strength and take out their treasure, as a mercy from thy Lord and I did it not of my own accord.[1717A] This is the explanation of that which thou could not bear with patience.'[1718]

وَاَمَّا الْجِدَارُ فَكَانَ لِغُلٰمَيْنِ يَتِيْمَيْنِ فِي الْمَدِيْنَةِ
وَكَانَ تَحْتَهٗ كَنْزٌ لَّهُمَا وَكَانَ اَبُوْهُمَا صَالِحًا ۚ
فَاَرَادَ رَبُّكَ اَنْ يَّبْلُغَآ اَشُدَّهُمَا وَيَسْتَخْرِجَا كَنْزَهُمَا ۖ
رَحْمَةً مِّنْ رَّبِّكَ ۚ وَمَا فَعَلْتُهٗ عَنْ اَمْرِيْ ۭ ذٰلِكَ
تَاْوِيْلُ مَا لَمْ تَسْطِعْ عَّلَيْهِ صَبْرًا ﴿٨٣﴾ ع

R. 11 84. And they ask thee concerning Dhu'l Qarnain.[1719] Say, 'I will recite to you *something* of his account.'

وَيَسْـَٔلُوْنَكَ عَنْ ذِي الْقَرْنَيْنِ ۭ قُلْ سَاَتْلُوْا عَلَيْكُمْ
مِّنْهُ ذِكْرًا ﴿٨٤﴾

1717. The orphan boys are Moses and Jesus, and their righteous father is Abraham. Their treasure was the true teaching bequeathed by them to their peoples which was in danger of being lost through the latter's irreligiousness. This treasure was safeguarded in the Qur'ān in order that when they may awaken to a realization of truth of the Quranic teaching they may accept it.

1717A. It was done under Divine command.

1718. The Vision of Moses points to the fact that because Islamic teaching was based on laws and principles which differed fundamentally from some principles of the Mosaic Law, true and real co-operation between Jews and Muslims was impossible. For a detailed explanation of v. 61-83, see "The Larger Edition of the Commentary", (pp. 1517-1530).

1719. Before proceeding to know and establish the identity of Dhu'l Qarnain, it is necessary to state the reasons why at all his story has been related in the Qur'ān and why it has found such prominent mention in the present *Sūrah*. A pointed reference has already been made in this *Sūrah* to the two periods of the great material progress of Western Christian nations. Its opening verses give a somewhat detailed account of the Dwellers of the Cave. After an account of the early persecution of the Dwellers of the Cave and the later material progress and prosperity of their successors, the Western Christian nations, an account of the *Isrā'* or Spiritual Journey of Moses which represents the advent of the Holy Prophet of Islām has been given in some detail in order to show that with the Holy Prophet's appearance the first period of the material prosperity and progress of the Christian peoples would come to an end, and though it would still be possible for them to make some progress they would reach the zenith of their material glory and greatness for a second time long after his advent. This second period of material pomp and grandeur of the Christian people is represented in Divine Scriptures by the phenomenal rise to power of Gog and Magog which forms one of the central themes of the present *Sūrah*. Because politically Gog and Magog and Dhu'l Qarnain are inseparably linked with each other, as will appear from the following paragraphs, Dhu'l Qarnain's account also has been given at some length in this *Sūrah*. Dhu'l Qarnain seems to be the King who founded the Medo-Persian Empire which represented the two horns of the ram of Daniel's famous dream. "I saw the ram pushing westward and northward and southward, so that no beast might stand before him, neither was there any that could deliver out of his hand; but he did according to his will and became great" (Dan. 8 : 4, 20, 21). Quite in harmony with this part of Daniel's dream, the Qur'ān mentions three journeys of Dhu'l Qarnain (vv. 87, 91, 94). This fact lends powerful support to the inference that Dhu'l Qarnain was the descriptive name of a king of Media and Persia. And of all kings of Media and Persia, the description given in the Qur'ān most fitly applies to Cyrus. The Qur'ān has mentioned four distinctive marks of Dhu'l Qarnain : (*a*) He was a powerful monarch and a

85. [a]"We established him in the earth and gave him the means to *achieve* everything.[1720]

إِنَّا مَكَّنَّا لَهُ فِي الْأَرْضِ وَآتَيْنَاهُ مِنْ كُلِّ شَيْءٍ سَبَبًا ﴿٨٥﴾

86. Then he followed a *certain* way.

فَأَتْبَعَ سَبَبًا ﴿٨٦﴾

87. Until when he reached the setting-place of the sun,[1721] he found it setting *as if* in a pool of murky water, and near it he found a people. We said, 'O Dhu'l Qarnain, you may punish them, or treat them with kindness.'

حَتَّىٰ إِذَا بَلَغَ مَغْرِبَ الشَّمْسِ وَجَدَهَا تَغْرُبُ فِي عَيْنٍ حَمِئَةٍ وَوَجَدَ عِنْدَهَا قَوْمًا ۗ قُلْنَا يَا ذَا الْقَرْنَيْنِ إِمَّا أَنْ تُعَذِّبَ وَإِمَّا أَنْ تَتَّخِذَ فِيهِمْ حُسْنًا ﴿٨٧﴾

88. He said, [b]"As for him who does wrong, we shall certainly punish him; then shall he be brought back to his Lord,[1722] Who will punish him with a dreadful punishment;

قَالَ أَمَّا مَنْ ظَلَمَ فَسَوْفَ نُعَذِّبُهُ ثُمَّ يُرَدُّ إِلَىٰ رَبِّهِ فَيُعَذِّبُهُ عَذَابًا نُكْرًا ﴿٨٨﴾

89. [c]"But as for him who believes and acts righteously, he will have a good reward *with his Lord,* and We too shall speak to him easy *words* of Our command.'[1723]

وَأَمَّا مَنْ آمَنَ وَعَمِلَ صَالِحًا فَلَهُ جَزَاءً الْحُسْنَىٰ ۖ وَسَنَقُولُ لَهُ مِنْ أَمْرِنَا يُسْرًا ﴿٨٩﴾

[a]12 ; 22, 57. [b]7 : 166. [c]2 : 26; 3 : 58; 6 : 49; 19 : 61; 25 : 71; 34 : 38

kind and just ruler (vv. 85, 89). (*b*) He was a righteous servant of God and was blessed with Divine revelation (vv. 92, 99). (*c*) He marched to the West and made great conquests till he came to a place where he found the sun setting, as it were, in a pool of murky water and then he turned to the East and conquered and subdued vast territories (vv. 87, 88). (*d*) He went to a midway region where a savage people lived and where Gog and Magog made great inroads; and he built a wall there to stop these inroads (vv. 94-98). Of the great rulers and famous military captains of ancient times Cyrus possesses, in the greatest measure, the four above-mentioned qualities. He, therefore, rightly deserves to be considered the Dhu'l Qarnain of the Qur'ān, (Isaiah, ch. 45; Ezra, ch. 1 & 2; II Chron., ch. 36 : 22, 23; Historians' History of the World, under "Cyrus").

1720. See Ezra, 1 : 1-2; Isa., 45 : 1-3 & Historians' History of the World.

1721. The words, *the setting-place of the sun*, signify the westernmost parts of Cyrus's Empire or the north-western boundary of Asia Minor and refer to the Black Sea, because it formed the north-western boundary of his Empire. The verse refers to the expedition which Cyrus undertook against his enemies in the West (Enc. Brit & Historians' History of the World, under "Cyrus").

1722. Cyrus believed in Life after death. He was a follower of Zoroaster and of all religions, second only to Islām, Zoroastrianism has laid the greatest stress on Life after death. 'There can be no doubt that Cyrus and his Persian followers were faithful believers in the pure doctrine of Zoroaster, and disdainfully regarded foreign cults' (Jew. Enc., vol. 4, p. 404).

1723. See Isa., 45 : 1-3 & 2 Chron.36 : 22-23.

90. Then *indeed* he followed *another* way.

ثُمَّ اَتْبَعَ سَبَبًا ﴿٩٠﴾

91. Until when he reached the rising-place of the sun,[1724] he found it rising on a people for whom We had made no shelter against it.

حَتّٰۤى اِذَا بَلَغَ مَطْلِعَ الشَّمْسِ وَجَدَهَا تَطْلُعُ عَلٰى قَوْمٍ لَّمْ نَجْعَلْ لَّهُمْ مِّنْ دُوْنِهَا سِتْرًا ﴿٩١﴾

92. Thus *indeed it was*. Verily, We had full knowledge of all that he had with him.

كَذٰلِكَ ؕ وَقَدْ اَحَطْنَا بِمَا لَدَيْهِ خُبْرًا ﴿٩٢﴾

93. Then he followed *another* way.[1725]

ثُمَّ اَتْبَعَ سَبَبًا ﴿٩٣﴾

94. Until when he reached the *open* place between the two mountains,[1726] he found, beneath them a people who could scarcely understand a word *of*[1727] *what he said*.

حَتّٰۤى اِذَا بَلَغَ بَيْنَ السَّدَّيْنِ وَجَدَ مِنْ دُوْنِهِمَا قَوْمًا ۙ لَّا يَكَادُوْنَ يَفْقَهُوْنَ قَوْلًا ﴿٩٤﴾

1724. This verse refers to Cyrus's expedition to the East—to Afghanistan and Baluchistan which were treeless barren tracts on which the sun beat down fiercely. It may also apply to the people who lived in the plains which extended for hundreds of miles to the east of Seistan and Herat and to the north of Duzdab up to Meshed.

1725. The verse refers to Cyrus's third expedition to the north of Persia—to the territory between the Caspian Sea and the Caucasian mountains.

1726. "The two mountains" signify two barriers. The pass of Derbent in which the Wall was built was bounded on one side by the Caspian Sea and on the other by the Caucasian mountains. These two served as two barriers for it.

1727. The people of these regions spoke a language different from that of Cyrus but living in the immediate neighbourhood of Persia and, having constant contact with the Persians and the Medians, they had learnt to understand and speak their language, though very imperfectly and with very great difficulty. The region in which the Wall was built was adjacent to Persia and later formed a part of it. Now, however, it is included in the Russian territories. For a fuller note on Dhu'l Qarnain see "The Larger Edition of the Commentary," pp. 1531—1540.

95. They said, 'O Dhu'l Qarnain, verily, Gog and Magog are[1728] creating disorder in the earth; shall we then pay thee tribute on condition that thou set up a barrier[1729] between us and them?'

قَالُوْا يٰذَا الْقَرْنَيْنِ اِنَّ يَاْجُوْجَ وَمَاْجُوْجَ مُفْسِدُوْنَ فِي الْاَرْضِ فَهَلْ نَجْعَلُ لَكَ خَرْجًا عَلٰٓى اَنْ تَجْعَلَ بَيْنَنَا وَبَيْنَهُمْ سَدًّا ﴿٩٥﴾

1728. The words, *Ya'jūj and Ma'jūj* (Gog and Magog), are both derived from the root-word *Ajja* which means, he was quick in his pace; he or it became the flaming fire (Lane), and refer to the Scythians of the farthest East. Or, as some say, all nations inhabiting the north of Asia and Europe (Enc. Brit. & Jewish Ency, under "Gog" and "Magog", and Historians' History of the World, vol. 2, p. 582 & Ezekiel, 38 : 2-6 & 39 : 6). The words may also apply to Christian nations of the West as they have made much use of burning fire and boiling water and because all their material progress and great discoveries and inventions are due to the right and very extensive use of these things. Or, the words may imply the restless behaviour of these nations as they are always on the lookout restlessly and impatiently to make new conquests.

The description of Gog and Magog as given in the Bible leaves no doubt that it applies to some Christian Powers of the West : First, because they are represented as very numerous, powerful and mighty:— 'Thou shalt ascend, and come like a storm, Thou shalt be like a cloud to cover the land, Thou and all thy bands and many people with thee (Ezekiel, 38 : 9). 'Gog and Magog..the number of whom is as the sand of the sea' (Rev. 20 : 8). 'Every feathered fowl, and every beast of the field is thus addressed, ye shall eat the flesh of the mighty, and drink the blood of the princes of the earth" (Ezekiel 39 : 18, 19). Secondly, they are shown coming forth from the northern parts of the earth, and from the isles:— 'And thou (O Gog) shalt come from thy place out of the north, thou and many people with thee' (Ezekiel 38 : 15). Thirdly, they will spread all over the world:— 'They went up on the breadth of the earth' (Rev. 20 : 9). Fourthly, from their home in the north, they will migrate to other lands and settle in all the four corners of the earth and in time of war they will gather together from their distant colonies: ' Satan....shall go out to deceive the nations which are in the four quarters of the earth, Gog and Magog, to gather them together to battle' (Rev. 20 : 8). The Book of Ezekiel mentions Gog as 'Prince of Rosh, Meshech and Tubal,' evidently Rosh standing for Russia, Meshech for Moscow and Tubal for Tobolsk. Gog is also spoken of as 'of the land of Magog' (Ezekiel, 38 : 2), and Magog, according to the commentators of the Bible, represents the regions which of old went by the name of Scythia (including Russia and Tartary), from which in the past issued many hordes of barbarians. As Russia was included in the land of Magog; Rosh, Meshech and Tubal may be taken as standing for Russia, Moscow and Tobolsk. Magog has also been spoken of as the name of a people in Ezekiel, 39 : 6 and in Rev., 20 : 8. In the former, Magog has been mentioned along with those 'that dwell carelessly in the isles.' According to these passages Gog and Magog represent some of the great Powers of Europe, including Russia. In the Qur'ān (18:95) they have been spoken of as making raids into territories on the northern border of Iran, which signifies that they were the tribes generally known as Scythians. It is a known historical fact that in olden times the Scythians continued to move in large bodies from Asia into Europe, their route lying north of the Caucasus (Enc. Brit. vol. 12, p. 263, 14th Edit.). As one horde settled down in Europe, new hordes came forth from the East, pushing their predecessors further and further West. Thus the nations of Europe have been legitimately called Gog and Magog in the biblical prophecy. It is curious that the memory of two heroes named Gog and Magog is preserved to this day in Guild Hall (London) in the form of two statues. Again from Ezekiel and Revelation it appears that Gog and Magog were to make their appearance in the Latter Days, *i.e.*, in the time just before the Second Coming of the Messiah: 'After many years thou shalt be visited in the latter years, thou shalt come into the land that is brought back from the sword' (Ezekiel, 38 : 16. See also Rev., 20 : 7-10). These verses show that this prophecy refers to a people who were to appear in the distant future. The age in which Gog and Magog were to make their appearance was to be marked by wars, earthquakes, pestilences and terrible catastrophes. (See also "The Larger Edition of the Commentary," pp. 1718—1720.)

1729. See next page.

96. He replied, 'The power with which my Lord has endowed me about this is better *than the resources of my enemies* but you may help me with strength *of labourers*,[1730] I will set up a rampart between you and them;

قَالَ مَا مَكَّنِّي فِيهِ رَبِّي خَيْرٌ فَأَعِينُونِي بِقُوَّةٍ أَجْعَلْ بَيْنَكُمْ وَبَيْنَهُمْ رَدْمًا ﴿٩٦﴾

1729. The Scythians or Gog and Magog occupied territories to the north and north-east of the Black Sea and they came from these regions through the pass of Darband and invaded and conquered and ruled over the Persians. Cyrus defeated them and delivered the Persians from their clutches (Historians' History of the World). Exactly, at the place which, according to Herodotus, was the pass through which the Scythians made raids upon Persia stood a wall, the famous Wall of Derbent.

> Derbent or Darband, a town of Persia, Caucasia, in the province of Deghestan, on the western shore of the Caspian....And to the south lies the seaward extremity of the Caucasian wall, 50 miles long otherwise known as Alexander's Wall, blocking the narrow pass of the Iron Gate or the Caspian Gate. This, when entire, had a height of 29 feet and a thickness of about 10 feet, and with its iron gates and numerous watch-towers formed a veritable defence of the Persian Frontier (Enc. Brit. under "Derbent").

Against established historical data it is popularly believed that the Wall was built ay Alexander the Great. But Alexander's military expeditions were like a whirlwind amidst which he could not attend to any vast project as the building of such a huge wall, nor did his death at a very early age leave him time for such a grand undertaking. The popular notion seems to have arisen from the fact that Muslim Commentators of the Qur'ān mistook Dhu'l Qarnain for Alexander. The following circumstantial evidence shows that Cyrus built it ;

(*a*) In order to break the power of the Scythians, Darius, who ascended the throne after the death of the son of Cyrus, passed through Greece and attacked them from across Europe. It is inconceivable that he should have undertaken such a long, arduous and round-about journey to attack these people from across south-east Europe when they lived very near him in the north. The inevitable conclusion is that the existence of a huge wall which only Cyrus could have built before him had made it impossible for him to cross over to the other side with a large force, leaving his own country exposed to their attacks from across north, if there was no wall to bar their way.

(*b*) The fact, that before the time of Cyrus the Scythians made constant and uninterrupted raids upon Persia but after his conquests these raids completely ceased, leads to the very probable conclusion that he must have set up a barrier which effectively checked these attacks and that the barrier must be the famous wall at Derbent, mistakenly known as Alexander's Wall.

1730. Cyrus told the inhabitants of the place to provide him with human labour, *Quwwah* meaning physical strength, *i.e.*, human labour.

97. 'Bring me blocks of iron.'[1731] *They did so* till, when he had filled up[1731A] the space between the two mountain sides, he said, '*Now* blow *with your bellows*.' *They blew* till, when he had made *it red as* fire, he said, 'Bring me molten copper that I may pour it thereon.'

آتُونِي زُبَرَ الْحَدِيدِ ۖ حَتَّىٰ إِذَا سَاوَىٰ بَيْنَ الصَّدَفَيْنِ
قَالَ انفُخُوا ۖ حَتَّىٰ إِذَا جَعَلَهُ نَارًا قَالَ آتُونِي أُفْرِغْ
عَلَيْهِ قِطْرًا ﴿٩٧﴾

98. So they (Gog and Magog) were not able to scale it, nor were they able to dig through it.[1732]

فَمَا اسْطَاعُوا أَن يَظْهَرُوهُ وَمَا اسْتَطَاعُوا لَهُ
نَقْبًا ﴿٩٨﴾

99. *Thereupon* he said, 'This is a mercy from my Lord. But when the promise of my Lord shall come to pass, He will break[1733] it into pieces. [a]And the promise of my Lord is *certainly* true.'

قَالَ هَٰذَا رَحْمَةٌ مِّن رَّبِّي ۖ فَإِذَا جَاءَ وَعْدُ رَبِّي
جَعَلَهُ دَكَّاءَ ۖ وَكَانَ وَعْدُ رَبِّي حَقًّا ﴿٩٩﴾

100. And on that day We shall leave some of them to surge against others, [b]and the trumpet will be blown. Then shall We gather them all together.[1734]

وَتَرَكْنَا بَعْضَهُمْ يَوْمَئِذٍ يَمُوجُ فِي بَعْضٍ ۖ وَنُفِخَ
فِي الصُّورِ فَجَمَعْنَاهُمْ جَمْعًا ﴿١٠٠﴾

---

[a]19 : 62; 46 : 17; 73 : 19. [b]23 : 102; 36 : 52; 39 : 69; 50 : 21; 69 : 14.

1731. In addition to human labour Cyrus demanded iron and molten copper from the local people. Copper, unlike iron, does not rust and when it is mixed with iron the mixture becomes harder still and defies rusting and corrosion. The engineering and technical skill were supplied by the technicians of Cyrus.

1731A. The rampart was built between the Caspian Sea and the Caucasus range.

1732. When the building of the wall was completed, the raids of Gog and Magog from the north ceased. The wall was too thick to be broken through and too high to be scaled. It was 29 feet high and 10 feet thick (Enc. Brit.) and had iron gates and watch-towers. It most effectively defended the Persian frontier.

1733. Cyrus must have been informed by revelation that sometime in future Gog and Magog would again spread to the south-east and this wall would then fail to retard or check their progress. This may be the significance of the words, 'He will break it.' In 21 : 97 we are told that Gog and Magog would spread their tentacles all over the world. Metaphorically, the 'breaking of the wall' may mean the decline of the political power of Islām, particularly of the Turks in Europe. With the weakening of the Turkish power the way for Christian nations of Europe to conquer the East was made clear.

1734. At the time of the rise to power of Gog and Magog all the peoples of the world will come together and the whole world will become united like one country. And according to the Bible, nation shall fight against nation and kingdom against kingdom and malice, hatred and iniquity will abound. The reference seems to be to the present age. A veritable hell was let loose upon the world in the last two World Wars and human imagination shudders at the destruction that the Third World War will cause. According to Ezekiel (chaps. 38 & 39) the U.S.S.R. is Gog and the Western nations are Magog. Even now they are preparing for Armageddon.

101. And on that day We shall present Hell, face to face, to the disbelievers[1734A]

وَّعَرَضْنَا جَهَنَّمَ يَوْمَئِذٍ لِّلْكٰفِرِيْنَ عَرْضَا ﴿١٠١﴾

102. [a]Whose eyes were under a veil, *not heeding* My Reminder,[1734B] and they could not even afford to hear.

الَّذِيْنَ كَانَتْ اَعْيُنُهُمْ فِيْ غِطَآءٍ عَنْ ذِكْرِيْ وَكَانُوْا
لَا يَسْتَطِيْعُوْنَ سَمْعًا ﴿١٠٢﴾ ع

R. 12 103. Do the disbelievers think that they can take My servants as protectors instead of Me? Surely, [b]We have prepared Hell as an entertainment for the disbelievers.

اَفَحَسِبَ الَّذِيْنَ كَفَرُوْٓا اَنْ يَّتَّخِذُوْا عِبَادِيْ مِنْ
دُوْنِيْٓ اَوْلِيَآءَ ؕ اِنَّآ اَعْتَدْنَا جَهَنَّمَ لِلْكٰفِرِيْنَ
نُزُلًا ﴿١٠٣﴾

104. Say, 'Shall We tell you of those who are the greatest losers in respect of their works?—

قُلْ هَلْ نُنَبِّئُكُمْ بِالْاَخْسَرِيْنَ اَعْمَالًا ﴿١٠٤﴾

105. 'Those whose labour is *all* lost in *pursuit of* the life of this world,[1735] and *yet* they imagine that they are doing good works.'

اَلَّذِيْنَ ضَلَّ سَعْيُهُمْ فِي الْحَيٰوةِ الدُّنْيَا وَهُمْ
يَحْسَبُوْنَ اَنَّهُمْ يُحْسِنُوْنَ صُنْعًا ﴿١٠٥﴾

106. Those are they who deny the Signs of their Lord and the meeting with Him. [c]So their works are vain, and on the Day of Resurrection We shall give them no weight.

اُولٰٓئِكَ الَّذِيْنَ كَفَرُوْا بِاٰيٰتِ رَبِّهِمْ وَلِقَآئِهٖ
فَحَبِطَتْ اَعْمَالُهُمْ فَلَا نُقِيْمُ لَهُمْ يَوْمَ الْقِيٰمَةِ
وَزْنًا ﴿١٠٦﴾

107. That is their reward—Hell; because they disbelieved, and made a jest of My Signs and My Messengers.

ذٰلِكَ جَزَآؤُهُمْ جَهَنَّمُ بِمَا كَفَرُوْا وَاتَّخَذُوْٓا اٰيٰتِيْ
وَرُسُلِيْ هُزُوًا ﴿١٠٧﴾

108. Surely, those who believe and act righteously, will have Gardens of Paradise for an abode,

اِنَّ الَّذِيْنَ اٰمَنُوْا وَعَمِلُوا الصّٰلِحٰتِ كَانَتْ لَهُمْ
جَنّٰتُ الْفِرْدَوْسِ نُزُلًا ﴿١٠٨﴾

[a]21 : 43; 39 : 46. [b]29 : 69; 33 : 9; 48 : 14; 76 : 5.
[c]2 : 218; 3 : 23; 7 : 148; 9 : 69.

1734A. For the dreadful and devastating Divine punishment that shall descend upon Gog and Magog see *Sūrah* Al-Raḥmān.

1734B. The Qur'ān.

1735. These people look upon the acquisition of physical comforts and worldly gains as the sole aim and object of their life. They have no place for God in their hearts.

109. [a]Wherein they will abide; having no desire to be removed therefrom.

خٰلِدِيْنَ فِيْهَا لَا يَبْغُوْنَ عَنْهَا حِوَلًا ﴿۱۰۹﴾

110. Say, [b]'If *every* ocean became ink for the words of my Lord, surely, the ocean would be exhausted before the words of my Lord were exhausted, even though We brought the like thereof as *further* help.'[1736]

قُلْ لَّوْ كَانَ الْبَحْرُ مِدَادًا لِّكَلِمٰتِ رَبِّيْ لَنَفِدَ
الْبَحْرُ قَبْلَ اَنْ تَنْفَدَ كَلِمٰتُ رَبِّيْ وَلَوْ جِئْنَا
بِمِثْلِهٖ مَدَدًا ﴿۱۱۰﴾

111. Say [c]'I am but a man like yourselves; *but* it is revealed to me that your God is only One God. [d]So let him, who hopes to meet his Lord, do good deeds, and let him join no one in the worship of his Lord.'[1737]

قُلْ اِنَّمَآ اَنَا بَشَرٌ مِّثْلُكُمْ يُوْحٰۤى اِلَيَّ اَنَّمَآ اِلٰهُكُمْ اِلٰهٌ
وَّاحِدٌ ۚ فَمَنْ كَانَ يَرْجُوْا لِقَآءَ رَبِّهٖ فَلْيَعْمَلْ عَمَلًا
صَالِحًا وَّلَا يُشْرِكْ بِعِبَادَةِ رَبِّهٖۤ اَحَدًا ﴿۱۱۱﴾

[a]11 : 109; 15 : 49. [b]31 : 28. [c]14 : 12; 41 : 7. [d]2 : 47,224; 11 : 30; 29 : 6; 84 : 7.

1736. Christian nations of the West boast of their great inventions and scientific discoveries and seem to labour under the misconception that they have succeeded in fathoming the secrets of creation itself. This is but a vain boast. God's secrets are so inexhaustible and unfathomable that what these people have discovered and what they will discover hereafter by all their strivings will not be even like a drop in the ocean.

1737. The Holy Prophet is reported to have said that the recitation of the first and last ten verses of this *Sūrah* makes one secure against the spiritual onslaughts of the *Dajjāl*. This shows that the *Dajjāl* and Gog and Magog are one and the same people—Christian nations of the West—the *Dajjāl* representing their pernicious religious propaganda against Islām, and Gog and Magog their material and political power and predominance.

CHAPTER 19

MARYAM

(*Revealed before Hijrah*)

Date of Revelation and Context

Consensus of opinion among the Companions of the Holy Prophet is that the *Sūrah* was revealed very early at Mecca, probably towards the end of the fourth year of the Call, before the Emigration to Abyssinia which took place in the month of Rajab in the fifth year. Its connection with Chapters Banī Isrā'īl and Al-Kahf consists in the fact that some account of the rise and progress of the Jews and Christians was given in these two Chapters. In Banī Isrā'īl it was particularly stated that the Jews would suffer national eclipse twice and twice they would rise to power and glory, and that the followers of Islām would, like the Jews, also rise to power twice and twice like them they would decline and fall. In *Sūrah* Al-Kahf the same subject was dealt with at greater length, specially the part dealing with Christians. After it had been explained in that *Sūrah* that Muslims would sustain national disaster at the hands of the followers of the Messiah of the Mosaic Dispensation and would regain their lost glory under the lead and guidance of the Messiah of the Islamic Dispensation, a brief history of the Christian Faith is given in the present *Sūrah*. The *Sūrah* thus constitutes a third link in the chain in which Chapters Banī Isrā'īl and Al-Kahf respectively form the first and second link. In fact, the three Chapters deal with the same subject and follow the same pattern in dealing with that subject.

Subject-Matter

In the abbreviated letters at the head of the *Sūrah* a comparison has been instituted between Christian and Islamic doctrines and attention has been drawn to the fact that while originally Christianity was a Divine Dispensation, subsequently some false doctrines and dogmas found their way into its teaching. As these doctrines run counter to Divine attributes, a brief account of Jesus's birth has been given to refute them. This account is preceded by a brief mention of Prophet Zachariah, because according to biblical prophecies Prophet Elijah was to have descended from heaven 'before the coming of the great and dreadful day of the Lord' (Mal. 4 : 5); and Jesus on being asked by the Jews about Elijah, who was to have appeared before him, answered that he was John who had come in his power and spirit (Matt. 11 : 14,15; 17 : 12; Mark 9 : 13). He also told them that Elijah was not to have come from heaven but like all mortals was to have been born of an earthly mother in the form of another man and that he was John (Matt. 11 : 11; Luke 7 : 28).

While giving an account of Jesus, the *Sūrah* refers to the unusual manner of his birth without the agency of a human father. The procedure adopted to bring about this most extraordinary consummation implied that Prophethood was now going to be transferred from the House of Isaac to that of Ishmael, since there had remained among the Israelites no male from whose loins a Prophet of God should have been born. After this the *Sūrah* reinforces the argument against the godhead of Jesus by stating that if all the Prophets from Adam down to the last Israelite Prophet before Jesus, to whom a brief reference is made in the *Sūrah*, were mere human beings, why should Jesus, who was also only a Prophet of God, be invested with Divine attributes and be regarded as God or Son of God. As Resurrection and Life after death were to be widely denied in the Latter Days by Christians, with whom the *Sūrah* particularly deals, much stress has also been laid on the Hereafter, and stale and hackneyed arguments of disbelievers against it exposed and refuted. The disbelievers, the *Sūrah* says, seem to derive false comfort from their wealth, material means and large numbers and adduce these things as an argument in support of their denial of the Life after death and of their belief that what really matters is the present life. They are warned that they should not be deceived by the apparent material weakness of believers and of their own power, wealth and vast resources since Truth always progresses gradually and in stages but most surely it does triumph in the end. The *Sūrah* ends with an answer to an implied question, *viz.*, why Arabic has been adopted as a vehicle for the revelation of the Quranic teaching. The answer given is: Since the Arabs are the first addressees of the Qur'ān, and it is natural and also sensible that a Message should be addressed to a people in their own tongue in order that they should easily understand it and having understood it should convey it to others; therefore the Qur'ān has been revealed in Arabic.

سُوۡرَۃُ مَرۡیَمَ مَکِّیَّۃٌ

1. [a]In the name of Allāh, the Gracious, the Merciful.

بِسۡمِ اللّٰہِ الرَّحۡمٰنِ الرَّحِیۡمِ ①

2. Kāf Hā Yā 'Ain Ṣād.[1738]

کٓہٰیٰعٓصٓ ②

3. *This is* an account of the mercy of thy Lord *shown* to His servant, Zachariah,[1739]

ذِکۡرُ رَحۡمَتِ رَبِّکَ عَبۡدَہٗ زَکَرِیَّا ③

4. [b]When he called upon his Lord in a low voice.[1740]

اِذۡ نَادٰی رَبَّہٗ نِدَآءً خَفِیًّا ④

---

[a]1 : 1. [b]3 : 39; 21 : 90.

1738. According to Umm Hāni', the Holy Prophet said that in the combined letters *Kāf Hā Yā 'Ain Ṣād, Kāf* stands for *Kāfin* (All-Sufficient), *Hā* for *Hādī* (True Guide), *'Ain* for *'Alīm* (All-Knowing) and *Ṣād* for *Ṣādiq* (Truthful), and thus the combined abbreviated letters would read something like this: *Anta Kāfin Anta Hādin Yā 'Alīm Yā Ṣādiq, i.e.*, Thou art Sufficient for all and Thou art the True Guide, O All-Knowing, Truthful God. The four Divine attributes as represented by these combined letters expose and repudiate the basic Christian doctrine of atonement; and if this doctrine is proved to be false, the whole structure of the doctrines of the trinity and godhead of Jesus would automatically fall to the ground. Of these four attributes *'Alīm* and *Ṣādiq* are the principal and basic attributes and *Kāfin* and *Hādin* are subordinate ones and flow from the former two attributes and are their inevitable manifestations and result. . If God is *'Alīm* (All-Knowing), then there is no place for the dogma of atonement, because this dogma pre-supposes that God had designed to carry on the business of the world according to a certain plan, but His knowledge being defective that plan had miscarried and, therefore, He was compelled to offer His own son as sacrifice to save the world. The failure of God's plan contradicts His attribute 'All-Knowing,' and when God's knowledge is shown to be defective, He cannot claim to be *Kāfin* (All-Sufficient), because the Being Who is *'Alīm* (All-Knowing) must necessarily be *Kāfin* (All-Sufficient). In the same way the attribute *Ṣādiq* (Truthful) and its subordinate attribute *Hādī* (Guide) demolish this dogma. If God is not the true Guide and salvation without belief in the vicarious sacrifice of Jesus is impossible, then all Divine Messengers will have to be accepted as so many liars and cheats because, contrary to Christian belief, they preached and taught that salvation was possible only through right beliefs and righteous actions; and a reflection on the truthfulness of God's Messengers constitutes a reflection on the truthfulness of God Himself and consequently on His being *Hādī, i.e.*, the True Guide. Thus in this combination of abbreviated letters a hint is given that in dealing with the beliefs and doctrines of Christians the best way to drive home to them the untenability of these doctrines is to dwell and lay emphasis upon Divine attributes, particularly on these four attributes. For a detailed discussion on *Muqaṭṭa'āt* see 16.

1739. The account of Zachariah precedes that of Jesus, because Yaḥyā, (John the Baptist), the son of Zachariah, was the harbinger of Jesus. He heralded Jesus's advent to give to the Jews the glad tidings that their deliverer was about to make his appearance (Mal. 4 : 5). As according to Malachi's prophecy Elias should have come before the coming of Jesus, it was in the fitness of things that while giving an account of Jesus, the Qur'ān should have made a mention of Yaḥyā (John) who came in the spirit and power of Elijah.

1740. Zachariah had understood from biblical prophecies and heavenly warnings that were administered to the Jews because of their repeated rejection of God's Prophets that Prophethood was soon to be transferred from the House of Isaac to that of Ishmael. So he gave vent to his feelings in the form of a prayer for the birth of a righteous son.

5. He said, 'My Lord, my [a]bones have indeed become feeble and *my* head is *all* aflame with hoariness but never, my Lord, have I been unblessed in my prayer to Thee;

قَالَ رَبِّ إِنِّي وَهَنَ الْعَظْمُ مِنِّي وَاشْتَعَلَ الرَّأْسُ شَيْبًا وَلَمْ أَكُنْ بِدُعَائِكَ رَبِّ شَقِيًّا ⑤

6. 'And I fear my relations after me, and [b]my wife is barren. So [c]grant me from Thyself a successor,[1741]

وَإِنِّي خِفْتُ الْمَوَالِيَ مِنْ وَرَائِي وَكَانَتِ امْرَأَتِي عَاقِرًا فَهَبْ لِي مِنْ لَدُنْكَ وَلِيًّا ⑥

7. 'To be my heir and the heir of *the blessings of* the House of Jacob. And [d]make him, my Lord, well-pleasing *to Thee*.'

يَرِثُنِي وَيَرِثُ مِنْ آلِ يَعْقُوبَ وَاجْعَلْهُ رَبِّ رَضِيًّا ⑦

8. *God said*, 'O Zachariah, [e]We give thee glad tidings of a son whose name shall be Yaḥyā. We have not called any one before him [f]by that name.'[1742]

يَا زَكَرِيَّا إِنَّا نُبَشِّرُكَ بِغُلَامٍ اسْمُهُ يَحْيَى لَمْ نَجْعَلْ لَهُ مِنْ قَبْلُ سَمِيًّا ⑧

9. He said, 'My Lord, how shall I have a son when [g]my wife is barren, and I have reached the extreme *limit of* old age?'[1743]

قَالَ رَبِّ أَنَّى يَكُونُ لِي غُلَامٌ وَكَانَتِ امْرَأَتِي عَاقِرًا وَقَدْ بَلَغْتُ مِنَ الْكِبَرِ عِتِيًّا ⑨

[a]3 : 41. [b]3 : 41; 21 : 91. [c]3 : 39; 21 : 90. [d]3 : 39. [e]3 : 40; 21 : 91. [f]19 : 66. [g]3 : 41; 21 : 91.

1741. The prayer of Zachariah possesses all the ingredients of a complete and successful prayer. A successful prayer should be offered with fervour and in humility. The supplicant should confess his own weakness and helplessness. He should have firm faith in the power of God to accept his prayers. Zachariah's prayer fulfils all these conditions.

1742. *Samiyy* means, competitor or contender for superiority in eminence or glory or excellence; a like or an equal; a namesake of another (Lane). The verse does not mean that there had lived before Yaḥyā (John) no man who was his namesake. From the Bible itself it appears that there had been several persons before him who were called John (II Kings, 25:23; I Chronicles, 3:15; Ezra, 8 : 12). Nor does it mean that John was peerless and unequalled in every respect. He himself confesses that 'there cometh one mightier than I after me, the latchet of whose shoes I am not worthy to stoop down and unloose' (Mark, 1 : 7). The verse only signifies that Yaḥyā or John was peerless in this respect that he was the first Prophet to come as a precursor to another Prophet—Jesus. And he was peerless in this respect also that he was the first Prophet who came with the power and spirit of another Prophet—Elijah.

1743. The verse expresses Zachariah's innocent and spontaneous surprise at the greatness of the favour which God was about to bestow upon him. Every person, situated as Zachariah was, would be naturally surprised at the unusual glad tidings that he had received.

10. *The angel bearing the revelation* said, [a]'So *it shall be*.' But thy Lord says, 'It is easy for Me, and indeed I created thee before, when thou wast nothing.'

قَالَ كَذٰلِكَ ۚ قَالَ رَبُّكَ هُوَ عَلَيَّ هَيِّنٌ وَّقَدْ
خَلَقْتُكَ مِنْ قَبْلُ وَلَمْ تَكُ شَيْـًٔا ﴿١٠﴾

11. *Zachariah* said, 'My Lord appoint for me a commandment.' *God* said, 'The commandment for thee is that thou shalt not speak to the people for [b]three successive days and nights.'[1744]

قَالَ رَبِّ اجْعَلْ لِّيْٓ اٰيَةً ۭ قَالَ اٰيَتُكَ اَلَّا تُكَلِّمَ
النَّاسَ ثَلٰثَ لَيَالٍ سَوِيًّا ﴿١١﴾

12. Then he came forth unto his people from the chamber and asked them in a low voice[1745] [c]to glorify *God* morning and evening.

فَخَرَجَ عَلٰى قَوْمِهٖ مِنَ الْمِحْرَابِ فَاَوْحٰٓى اِلَيْهِمْ
اَنْ سَبِّحُوْا بُكْرَةً وَّعَشِيًّا ﴿١٢﴾

13. *God said*, 'O Yaḥyā, hold fast the Book.' And We gave him wisdom while *yet* a child,

يٰيَحْيٰى خُذِ الْكِتٰبَ بِقُوَّةٍ ۭ وَاٰتَيْنٰهُ الْحُكْمَ
صَبِيًّا ﴿١٣﴾

14. And tenderness *of heart* from Us and purity, and he was pious,

وَّحَنَانًا مِّنْ لَّدُنَّا وَزَكٰوةً ۭ وَكَانَ تَقِيًّا ﴿١٤﴾

15. [d]And dutiful toward his parents. And he was not haughty and rebellious.

وَّبَرًّۢا بِوَالِدَيْهِ وَلَمْ يَكُنْ جَبَّارًا عَصِيًّا ﴿١٥﴾

16. [e]And peace was on him the day he was born, and the day he died, and *peace will be on him* the day he will be raised up to life *again*.[1746]

وَسَلٰمٌ عَلَيْهِ يَوْمَ وُلِدَ وَيَوْمَ يَمُوْتُ وَيَوْمَ يُبْعَثُ
حَيًّا ﴿١٦﴾ ع

[a]3 : 41,48: 19 : 22; 51 : 31. [b]3 : 42. [c]3 : 42; 33 : 43. [d]6 : 152; 19 : 33; 29 : 9; 31 : 15; 46 : 16. [e]19 : 34.

1744. The commandment enjoining upon Zachariah to abstain from talking and to devote himself fully to the remembrance and glorification of God was a spiritual measure calculated to recuperate his exhausted physical powers. He had not become deprived of his power of speech, as the Gospels seem to suggest, as a punishment for his not believing in the words of God (Luke 1 : 20-22).

1745. *Auḥā ilā fulānin* means, he communicated to such a one or gave order or made a request by gesture or sign, or he talked to him in such a way that others could not hear him (Aqrab). In 3 : 42 the word *Ramz*, which means to communicate by means of movements of the lips and not by using one's throat, has been used to express the same sense.

1746. During the first few centuries of its life Islām made very rapid progress. Large numbers of people from every religion—especially from Christianity—entered its fold.

R. 2 17. And relate *the story of* Mary *as mentioned* in the Book, when she withdrew from her people to an eastern place;[1747]

وَاذْكُرْ فِي الْكِتٰبِ مَرْيَمَ إِذِ انْتَبَذَتْ مِنْ أَهْلِهَا مَكَانًا شَرْقِيًّا ﴿١٧﴾

18. And screened herself off from them. Then We sent Our [a]angel[1748] to her and he appeared to her in the form of a well-proportioned man.[1749]

فَاتَّخَذَتْ مِنْ دُوْنِهِمْ حِجَابًا فَأَرْسَلْنَا إِلَيْهَا رُوْحَنَا فَتَمَثَّلَ لَهَا بَشَرًا سَوِيًّا ﴿١٨﴾

---

[a]3 : 43.

They brought with them their erroneous beliefs about Jesus. As they had not imbibed fully the true spirit of Islamic teachings, their false ideas and beliefs subsequently found their way into Muslim religious literature with the result that subsequently they came to form part of Muslim beliefs. All these beliefs had been invented to invest Jesus with an extraordinary personality—a personality much above human level. It is these foolish beliefs about Jesus that the Qur'ān seeks to demolish in the present *Sūrah*. By instituting a comparison between Yaḥyā and Jesus, this *Sūrah* and the *Sūrah* Āl-'Imrān mean to suggest that there was nothing in Jesus which distinguished him from other Divine Messengers. See "The Larger Edition of the Commentary," pp. 1565.

1747. It seems relevant and necessary to mention, as a prelude to the somewhat detailed account of Jesus's fatherless birth as given in the next several verses, some facts related about Mary in the Qur'ān and the New Testament. The New Testament sheds practically no light on the life of Mary before she became pregnant. The Gospels of Matthew and Luke give an extremely brief and discursive description of her circumstances before the above important event took place while Mark and John are completely silent over it. According to Matthew, Mary, on being married to Joseph, was found to be with child. Joseph intended secretly to put her away but was refrained from taking this extreme step by an angel saying to him in a dream, 'Joseph, thou son of David, fear not to take unto thee Mary thy wife' (Matt. 1 : 19, 20). The Qur'ān, however, gives a much more detailed account of Mary's family, the circumstances that attended her birth, the vow of her mother, of her being dedicated to the service of the Church and lastly of her having conceived Jesus (3: 36,37,48). The present *Sūrah*, however, gives a still more detailed account of Mary having conceived Jesus and of what happened to her and to Jesus after his birth and after he was commissioned with Divine mission, thus providing all necessary details about Mary that have any bearing on the important subject of Prophethood which was about to be transferred from the House of Israel to that of Ishmael and which forms the principal thesis of the present *Sūrah*. Special mention has been made here of 'an eastern place' in the verse, in order, perhaps to point to the time-honoured customs of the Jews to hold the East sacred. Both the Jews and the Christians hold the East in special respect. They build their places of worship facing the East.

1748. For the different meanings of *Rūh* see 712.

1749. The expression signifies that the Divine glad tidings about the birth of a great son was not conveyed to Mary in the form of spoken words which she could hear ; it took the form of a dream or vision. In a vision an angel came to her in the form of a healthy man and conveyed to her the Divine Message about the birth of a son. So it was no spirit that had entered Mary's body, but only an angel appeared to her in a vision in the form of a man.

19. She said, 'I seek refuge with the Gracious *God* from thee if indeed thou dost fear *Him*.'[1750]

قَالَتْ إِنِّيٓ أَعُوذُ بِالرَّحْمٰنِ مِنكَ إِن كُنتَ تَقِيًّا ﴿١٩﴾

20. *The angel* said, 'I am only a messenger[1751] of thy Lord, that [a]I may give thee *glad tidings of* a righteous son.'

قَالَ إِنَّمَآ أَنَا۠ رَسُولُ رَبِّكِ ۖ لِأَهَبَ لَكِ غُلٰمًا زَكِيًّا ﴿٢٠﴾

21. She said, [b]'How can I have a son when no man has touched me, neither have I been unchaste?'[1752]

قَالَتْ أَنّٰى يَكُونُ لِي غُلٰمٌ وَلَمْ يَمْسَسْنِي بَشَرٌ وَلَمْ أَكُ بَغِيًّا ﴿٢١﴾

[a]3 : 46. [b]3 : 48; 19 : 9.

1750. As is apparent from the previous verse it was a mere vision which Mary had seen; and it generally happens that when a person sees a thing in a vision which he does not like in his waking state, he does not like it either when he sees it in a vision. When Mary saw the angel standing before her in the form of a man she, being a virtuous young woman, was naturally frightened and perplexed as she would have been frightened and perplexed if she had seen him near her in her state of wakefulness, and it is, therefore, quite natural that she sought Divine protection from him.

1751. The word 'messenger' shows that the angel was only the bearer of a Divine message and that he had not come to give Mary a son but only the glad tidings about the birth of a son. Who does not know that it is God Who can bestow a son and not an angel? An angel's mission is confined only to conveying the wish and decree of God.

1752. The incident referred to in this and the preceding verses took place in a vision, and in a vision or dream a person experiences different kinds of sensations on different occasions. Sometimes his feelings and talk in the dream are subject to and under the effect of the dream while at another time they are not and he feels and talks as he would feel and talk if he were awake. For example, if in a dream a person is glad over the death of his son, his feelings will be regarded as under the effect of the dream because in his state of wakefulness no normal person would be glad over the death of his son. So if the words spoken by Mary when she saw the angel in her vision were under the effect of the vision, then they would signify that when the glad tidings was given to her she had a pleasant surprise whether God would work such a miracle as to give her—a virgin—a son. But if the words be regarded as a natural expression on her part when the tidings of the birth of a son was given to her, then they would signify that she was completely perplexed and horror-struck at the thought that a son should be born to her—a virgin. In the former case hers would be a very pleasant surprise at the great favour that God was going to do her, and in the latter case it would be an expression of bewilderment indicating the horrified state of her mind.

Whereas the words, *no man has touched me*, show that Mary thought that the glad tidings meant that she would have a child without contracting a legal marriage, otherwise there was no sense in her denial to have known any man in a married state, the words, *neither have I been unchaste*, refer to her denial to have known any man outside legal wedlock. In her reply to the angel she seemed to be thinking of her vow of celibacy which obviated the possibility of her having any offspring. If she thought that the promise made in the preceding verse referred to the birth of a son as a result of her conjugal relations in some future time, as some Commentators of the Qur'ān think, then there was no occasion for her to express any surprise.

22. [a]*The angel* said, 'Thus *it shall be.*' But says thy Lord, 'It is easy for Me; and *We shall do so* that We may make him a Sign[1753] unto men, and a mercy from Us, and it is a [c]thing decreed.'[1754]

قَالَ كَذٰلِكِ ۚ قَالَ رَبُّكِ هُوَ عَلَيَّ هَيِّنٌ ۚ وَلِنَجْعَلَهُ آيَةً لِّلنَّاسِ وَرَحْمَةً مِّنَّا ۚ وَكَانَ أَمْرًا مَّقْضِيًّا ﴿٢٢﴾

23. So she conceived[1755] him, and withdrew with him to a remote place.[1756]

فَحَمَلَتْهُ فَانتَبَذَتْ بِهِ مَكَانًا قَصِيًّا ﴿٢٣﴾

[a]3 : 41, 48; 19 : 22; 51 : 31.

1753. The expression, *that We may make him a Sign unto men*, implies the fatherless birth of Jesus which was indeed a great Sign for the Israelites. It pointed to the impending transition of Prophethood from the House of Israel to that of Ishmael and constituted a warning to the Israelites that they had become spiritually so corrupt and morally so degenerate that no male among them was fit enough to become the father of a Prophet of God. It is in this sense that Jesus has also been spoken of as 'a Sign of the Hour' in the Qur'ān (43 : 62), *i.e.*, a Sign of the time when Prophethood was to have passed from the Israelites to the Ishmaelites.

1754. The expression, *and it is a thing decreed*, means that God had decreed that a fatherless son would be born to Mary and that this Divine decree was irrevocable. The Qur'ān has used two words *Qadar* and *Qaḍā'* to express the sense of Divine decree. The former word means designing or determining, while the latter means decreeing. When a scheme or plan is only designed to be put into execution, it is called *Qadar*, and when it is decreed by God that it should be carried into effect, it is named *Qaḍā'*. The fatherless birth of Jesus was a *Qaḍā'* (decree) of God.

1755. How Mary came to conceive Jesus without the agency of a husband is one of those Divine secrets which at present may be considered beyond human intellect to fathom. It may be regarded as above the ordinary natural law as we *now* know it. But the knowledge of man, at best, is limited. He has not been able to comprehend all Divine secrets. There are mysteries in nature which man has not been able to solve as yet; perhaps he may never be able to solve them. Among them may be included the fatherless birth of Jesus. God's ways are inscrutable and His powers limitless. He Who could create the whole universe by the word, *Kun* (be), surely can bring about such changes in matter as should make this apparently insoluble mystery yield to a solution. Moreover, medical science has not altogether ruled out the possibility, from a purely biological standpoint, under certain conditions of natural parthenogenesis or the production of a child by a female without any relation to a male. Medical men call attention to this possibility as a result of a certain type of tumours, which are occasionally found in the female pelvis or lower body. These tumours which are known as arrhenoblastoma are capable of generating male sperm-cells. If living male sperm-cells are produced in a female body by arrhenoblastoma the possibility of self-fertilization of a woman, even though virgin, cannot be denied. That is to say, her own body would produce the same result as though sperm-cells from a male's body had been transferred to hers in the usual way, or by a physician's aid. Recently a group of gynaecologists in Europe have published data to prove instances of child-birth where the mother had had no contact with a male (Lancet). Jesus's birth is perhaps not altogether unique in this respect that he was born without the agency of a father. Cases are on record of children having been born without fathers (Enc. Brit. under "Virgin Birth" and "Anomalies and Curiosities of Medicine," published by W.B. Saunders & Co., London). If we dismiss all these possibilities, then Jesus's birth will have to be regarded, God forbid, as illegitimate. Christians and Jews are both agreed that the birth of Jesus was something out of the ordinary—the Christians holding it as supernatural and the Jews as illegitimate (Jew. Enc.). Even in the family birth register the birth of Jesus was recorded as such (Talmud). This fact alone should constitute a valid proof of Jesus's birth being out of the ordinary. Joseph, Mary's husband, according to the Gospels, had not established conjugal relations with her till after the birth of Jesus (Matt. 1 : 25). So the words, 'she conceived him', refer to this extraordinary conception of Mary without the agency of a male.

1756. See next page.

24. And the pains of child-birth drove her unto the trunk of a palm-tree.[1757] She said, 'O, would that I had died before this and had become a thing quite forgotten !'	فَاَجَآءَهَا الْمَخَاضُ اِلٰی جِذْعِ النَّخْلَةِ ۚ قَالَتْ يٰلَيْتَنِيْ مِتُّ قَبْلَ هٰذَا وَكُنْتُ نَسْيًا مَّنْسِيًّا ﴿۲۴﴾
25. Then *the angel* called her from beneath[1758] her, *saying*, 'Grieve not. Thy Lord has placed a rivulet below thee;	فَنَادٰىهَا مِنْ تَحْتِهَآ اَلَّا تَحْزَنِيْ قَدْ جَعَلَ رَبُّكِ تَحْتَكِ سَرِيًّا ﴿۲۵﴾
26. 'And shake towards thyself the trunk of the palm-tree; it will drop upon thee fresh ripe dates;[1759]	وَهُزِّيْٓ اِلَيْكِ بِجِذْعِ النَّخْلَةِ تُسٰقِطْ عَلَيْكِ رُطَبًا جَنِيًّا ﴿۲۶﴾

1756. 'A remote place,' refers to Bethlehem which is about seventy miles from Nazareth to the south. There Joseph took Mary sometime before Jesus's birth which took place in that town.

1757. As it appears from the Gospels, there was no room in the inn in which Jesus was born in Bethlehem. Joseph and Mary must have stayed in the open field and Mary might have betaken herself to the trunk of a palm-tree in order to take rest under its shade and possibly also to find some support in her throes of child-birth.

1758. The word *taḥt* also meaning the slope and declivity of a mountain (Lane), the verse signifies that the voice came to Mary from the side of the slope of the mountain. As a matter of fact Bethlehem is situated on a rock 2350 ft. above sea-level and is surrounded by very fertile valleys. There are fountains in this rock, one of which is known as the "Fountain of Solomon." Another fountain is situated at a distance of about 800 yards to the south-east of the town. From these fountains water is supplied to the town of Bethlehem.

1759. According to this verse the birth of Jesus took place at a time when fresh dates are found on palm-trees in Judaea. That season evidently is in the months of August-September, but, according to the view generally held by Christians, Jesus was born on 25th December which day is celebrated all over the Christian world every year with great fervour. Now this Christian view is contradicted not only by the Qur'ān but also by history and even by the New Testament itself. Writing about the time of Jesus's birth Luke says : 'And there were shepherds in the same country (Judaea) abiding in the field, and keeping watch by night over their flocks' (Luke 2 : 7,8). Commenting on this statement of Luke, Bishop Barns in his famous book, "The Rise of Christianity," on page 79 says : "There is, moreover, no authority for the belief that December 25 was the actual birthday of Jesus. If we can give any credence to the birth-story of Luke, with the shepherds keeping watch by night in the fields near Bethlehem, the birth of Jesus did not take place in winter when the night temperature is so low in the hill country of Judaea that snow is not uncommon. After much argument our Christmas day seems to have been accepted about A.D. 300.' This view of Bishop Barns is supported by Encyclopaedia Britannica and Chambers Encyclopaedia (under "Christmas") :—

> The exact day and year of Christ's birth have never been satisfactorily settled; but when the fathers of the Church in A.D. 340 decided upon a date to celebrate the event, they wisely chose the day of the winter solstice which was firmly fixed in the minds of the people and which was their most important festival. Owing to changes in man-made calendars, the time of the solstice and the date of Christmas day vary by a few days (Enc. Brit. 15th edition, vol. 5, pp. 642 & 642A).......In the second place the winter solstice was regarded as the birthday of the sun, and at Rome 25th December was observed as a pagan festival of the nativity of Sol-invictus. The Church, unable to stamp out this popular festival, spiritualized it as the feast of the Nativity of the Sun of Righteousness (Ch. Enc.).

27. "So, eat and drink and cool *thine* eye. And if thou seest any man, say, 'I have vowed a fast to the Gracious *God;* I will, therefore, not speak this day to any human being."[1760]

فَكُلِيْ وَاشْرَبِيْ وَقَرِّيْ عَيْنًا ۚ فَإِمَّا تَرَيِنَّ مِنَ الْبَشَرِ أَحَدًا ۙ فَقُوْلِيْٓ إِنِّيْ نَذَرْتُ لِلرَّحْمٰنِ صَوْمًا فَلَنْ أُكَلِّمَ الْيَوْمَ إِنْسِيًّا ﴿٢٧﴾

28. Then she brought him to her people, mounted.[1761] They said,

فَأَتَتْ بِهٖ قَوْمَهَا تَحْمِلُهٗ ۖ قَالُوْا يٰمَرْيَمُ لَقَدْ جِئْتِ

These statements of the two Encyclopaedias are further supported by Peake's "Commentary on the Bible." In this book on page 727, Peake says : 'The season (of Jesus's birth) would not be December ; our Christmas day is a comparatively late tradition found first in the West.' Thus recent historical research into the origins of Christianity has established the fact beyond any reasonable doubt that Jesus was not born in December. In his "Dictionary of the Bible" Dr. John D. Davis, under the word "Year" writes that dates become ripe in the Jewish month of Elul; and in Peake's "Commentary on the Bible" (page, 117) we have that the month of Elul corresponds to the months of August—September. Furthermore, Dr. Peake says, "J. Stewart in his book 'When did our Lord actually live?' arguing from an Angora temple inscription and a quotation in an old Chinese classic which speaks of the Gospel story reaching China, A.D. 25-28, puts the birth of Jesus in 8 B.C. (Sept. or Oct.) and the Crucifixion on Wednesday in A.D. 24." From the above statements of the two Encyclopaedias supported by quotations from the "Commentary on the Bible" by Dr. Arthur S. Peake, M.A., D.D., the fact becomes quite clear that Jesus was born in the Jewish month of Elul which corresponds to the months of August-September when dates ripen in Judaea, and not on 25th December as the Christian Church would have us believe. And that is the view which is expressed by the Qur'ān. In fact, the whole trouble of fixing the date of Jesus's birth seems to have arisen from a confusion of the date of Mary's conception. The pregnancy of Mary seemed to have taken place sometime in November or December and not in March or April as the Church historians believe. When after four or five months' conception pregnancy became too obvious to be concealed any longer, Joseph was prevailed upon to take Mary to his house in the month of March or April of the next year. Thus Christian historians mistake the date when Joseph took Mary to his house—in the month of March or April—for the date of her conception which had taken place four or five months earlier.

It also appears from the present verse that Mary was lying in a sheltered place in the upper part of the hill and the date-palm was standing on the slope, and therefore she could easily reach to its trunk and shake it. That the territory of Bethlehem abounded in date-palms is clear from the Bible (Judges, 1 : 16) and from "A Dictionary of the Bible" by Dr. John D. Davis, D.D. Moreover, the fact of Mary having been guided to a fountain, as mentioned in the preceding verse, in order to drink of its water and wash herself, points to Jesus's birth having taken place in the month of August-September because in the icy cold weather of Judaea in December Mary could not have washed herself in the open. See also "The Larger Edition of the Commentary," pp. 1573—1576.

1760. The command to abstain from useless talk was meant, on the one hand, to conserve her physical strength and, on the other, to give her more time to devote to remembrance of God.

1761. For this meaning of the word see 9 : 92. It appears from the Gospels that after Jesus's birth at Bethlehem, in pursuance of a Divine command Joseph had taken him and Mary to Egypt where they lived for some years and it was after the death of Herod that the family came back to Nazareth and dwelt there (Matt. 2 : 13-23). There was also a biblical prophecy to the effect that Jesus would come to his people along with his mother riding on an ass (Matt. 21 : 4-7). Jesus and Mary were actually riding on asses when they entered Jerusalem. The expression, *Taḥmilu-hū*, may possibly refer to that prophecy of the Bible. The verse refers to the time when Jesus had already attained Prophethood as is clear from vv. 31—34.

'O Mary, surely, thou hast committed a monstrous thing ![1762]

شَيْـًٔا فَرِيًّا ﴿٢٨﴾

29. 'O sister of Aaron,[1763] thy father was not a wicked man, nor was thy mother an unchaste woman !'

يٰٓاُخْتَ هٰرُوْنَ مَا كَانَ اَبُوْكِ امْرَاَ سَوْءٍ وَّمَا كَانَتْ اُمُّكِ بَغِيًّا ﴿٢٩﴾

30. Thereupon she pointed to him.[1764] They said, 'How can we talk to one who is a child in the cradle ?'[1765]

فَاَشَارَتْ اِلَيْهِ ۗ قَالُوْا كَيْفَ نُكَلِّمُ مَنْ كَانَ فِي الْمَهْدِ صَبِيًّا ﴿٣٠﴾

31. *Jesus* said, 'I am a servant of Allāh. He has given me the Book, and has made me a Prophet;

قَالَ اِنِّيْ عَبْدُ اللّٰهِ ۗ اٰتٰنِيَ الْكِتٰبَ وَجَعَلَنِيْ نَبِيًّا ﴿٣١﴾

1762. *Fariyy* also means, a forger of lies (Lane). By using this word the elders of the Jews insinuated that Mary was a bad woman and Jesus a forger of lies and a false prophet.

1763. The question of Mary having been called the sister of Aaron in the Qur'ān was put before the Holy Prophet himself and he asked the questioner if he did not know that the Israelites used to name their children after their Prophets and saints (Bayān, vol. 6, p. 16 ; Jarīr, vol. 16, p. 52). Mary has been here called the sister of Aaron and not that of Moses though both were brothers, for, whereas Moses was the founder of the Jewish Law, Aaron was the head of the Jewish priestly class (Enc. Bib. & Enc. Brit. under "Aaron"), and Mary also belonged to the priestly order. Ṭabarī has related an incident from the life of the Holy Prophet which gives an insight into the meanings of such Arabic words as *ab*, *'am*, *ukht*, etc. When Ṣafiyyah, the Holy Prophet's wife, and incidentally a Jewess by descent, once complained to the Holy Prophet that some of his other wives had called her a Jewess in contempt, the Holy Prophet told her to return the taunt by saying that Aaron was her father, Moses her uncle and Muḥammad her husband. Now, the Holy Prophet certainly knew that Aaron was not Ṣafiyyah's father nor Moses her uncle. A reference to this accusation is also to be found in the Qur'ān in 33 : 70. The elders of the Jews, by calling Jesus's mother "sister of Aaron" might have meant that as Mary, the sister of Aaron, had, by accusing Moses of unlawfully marrying a woman, committed a heinous crime (a reference to this accusation is to be found in 33 : 70), so did she, like her namesake, commit a heinous act of giving birth to an illegitimate child. See also 401.

1764. The words 'she pointed to him' indicate that Mary knew what answer Jesus would give if the elders of the Jews addressed their question to him. These words may also indicate that Mary knew that if she declared herself innocent nobody would believe her. The only evidence of her innocence was her son. She meant that such a holy and righteous son whom God had endowed with such noble qualities could not be the result of an immoral union and that his virtues and good qualities by themselves constituted a sufficient vindication of her innocence. So she pointed to him.

1765. The verse presents no difficulty. When Mary, on being taunted by the elders of the Jews, directed their attention to Jesus, they disdained to talk to him and contemptuously said, how could they talk to 'a child in the cradle' meaning a mere boy, who was born and brought up before their very eyes? Elderly people are wont to talk like that when invited to learn wisdom from one who is much younger to them in age. The words merely constitute an expression of contempt and disdain for Jesus. See also 3 : 47.

32. 'And He has made me blessed wheresoever I may be, and has enjoined upon me Prayer and alms-giving so long as I live;

وَّجَعَلَنِيْ مُبٰرَكًا اَيْنَ مَا كُنْتُ وَاَوْصٰنِيْ بِالصَّلٰوةِ وَالزَّكٰوةِ مَا دُمْتُ حَيًّا ﴿٣٢﴾

33. 'And *He has made me* [a]dutiful towards my mother, and has not made me arrogant *and* graceless;[1766]

وَّبَرًّا بِوَالِدَتِيْ وَلَمْ يَجْعَلْنِيْ جَبَّارًا شَقِيًّا ﴿٣٣﴾

34. 'And peace was on me [b]the day I was born, and peace *will be on me* the day I shall die, and the day I shall be raised up to life *again*.'

وَالسَّلٰمُ عَلَيَّ يَوْمَ وُلِدْتُّ وَيَوْمَ اَمُوْتُ وَيَوْمَ اُبْعَثُ حَيًّا ﴿٣٤﴾

35. That was Jesus, son of Mary.[1767] *This is* a statement of the truth concerning which they entertain doubt.[1768]

ذٰلِكَ عِيْسَى ابْنُ مَرْيَمَ قَوْلَ الْحَقِّ الَّذِيْ فِيْهِ يَمْتَرُوْنَ ﴿٣٥﴾

[a]19 : 15 [b]19 : 16.

1766. The talk which Jesus gave to the elders of the Jews and which is contained in these verses (31-34) could not possibly be the talk of a child. All these affirmations from the lips of a child sound like so many lies; and who would call these lies a miracle? Jesus was neither a Prophet at that time, nor did he say Prayer or give *Zakāt* or was given a Book. Moreover, in 3 : 47 this miracle is mentioned as Jesus having spoken to the people in the cradle and when of middle age. But talk by a man in middle age is no miracle; and by joining the word 'cradle' with the words 'of middle age,' the Qur'ān implies that the talk of Jesus in 'the cradle' and when he was 'of middle age' was no miracle in the sense in which it is popularly understood, but that it was a miracle in the sense that he spoke words of exceptional wisdom and intelligence in childhood as well as in middle age. The joining of these two sets of words also implied a prophecy that Jesus would not die young but would live up to a ripe old age. The prophecy did constitute a real miracle. But if the word *Mahd* is taken in the sense of 'period of preparation' which is also one of the meanings of this word, then verse (3 : 47) would mean that Jesus would speak to people words full of extraordinary wisdom and spiritual knowledge much beyond his years and experience, both in the period of preparation which is youth and in his middle age.

1767. The expression "Ibn Maryam" is Jesus's distinctive name. Whereas, on the one hand, it seems to imply his fatherless birth, on the other it confers on him a name which is incapable of being confused with that of anybody else. The Gospels have used for Jesus the epithet "Ibn Adam" (son of man) also but this latter epithet has been used in the Bible for other persons as well. "Son of Mary" is at once a distinctive and descriptive name of Jesus.

1768. Perhaps there is no other individual in religious history concerning whom so many and so far-reaching differences exist as about Jesus, son of Mary. The Jews, the Christians and the Muslims all hold widely different views about Jesus's birth, the manner of his death and about some prominent incidents in his life.

36. [a]It does not befit *the majesty of* Allāh to take unto Himself a son.[1769] Holy is He. When He decrees a thing, He says to it, 'Be,'[1770] and it comes into being.

مَا كَانَ لِلّٰهِ اَنْ يَّتَّخِذَ مِنْ وَّلَدٍ ۙ سُبْحٰنَهٗ ؕ اِذَا قَضٰۤى اَمْرًا فَاِنَّمَا يَقُوْلُ لَهٗ كُنْ فَيَكُوْنُ ؕ ﴿۳۶﴾

37. *Said Jesus*, 'Surely, [b]Allāh is my Lord and your Lord, so worship Him *alone*, this is the right path.'

وَاِنَّ اللّٰهَ رَبِّىْ وَرَبُّكُمْ فَاعْبُدُوْهُ ؕ هٰذَا صِرَاطٌ مُّسْتَقِيْمٌ ﴿۳۷﴾

38. But the parties differed among themselves; so [c]woe to those who disbelieve, because of the meeting of a grievous day.

فَاخْتَلَفَ الْاَحْزَابُ مِنْۢ بَيْنِهِمْ ۚ فَوَيْلٌ لِّلَّذِيْنَ كَفَرُوْا مِنْ مَّشْهَدِ يَوْمٍ عَظِيْمٍ ﴿۳۸﴾

39. How well they will hear and see[1771] on the day when they will come to Us ! But today the wrong-doers are in manifest error.

اَسْمِعْ بِهِمْ وَاَبْصِرْ ۙ يَوْمَ يَاْتُوْنَنَا لٰكِنِ الظّٰلِمُوْنَ الْيَوْمَ فِىْ ضَلٰلٍ مُّبِيْنٍ ﴿۳۹﴾

40. And warn them of [d]the day of sorrow when the matter will be decided. But *now* they are in *a state of* heedlessness, so they do not believe.

وَاَنْذِرْهُمْ يَوْمَ الْحَسْرَةِ اِذْ قُضِىَ الْاَمْرُ ۘ وَهُمْ فِىْ غَفْلَةٍ وَّهُمْ لَا يُؤْمِنُوْنَ ﴿۴۰﴾

---

[a]10 : 69; 17 : 112; 18 : 5; 19 : 89 ; 21: 27; 25 : 3; 39 : 5. [b]3 : 52; 5 : 73; 43 : 65. [c]14 : 3; 38 : 28; 51 : 61. [d]2 : 168; 6 : 32; 39 : 57.

1769. Christians believe that Jesus was God's son. They base this belief on the assumption that the Bible calls him "son of God." But in the Bible other persons have also been called or addressed as "sons of God." Jesus enjoys no special distinction in this respect and he is, therefore, no more a son of God than those persons who have also been addressed as such (Luke, 20 : 36; Jer., 31 : 9; Matt., 6 : 9; John, 8 : 41 & Ephes, 4 : 6).

1770. In the Arabic language the word *Kun*, besides being addressed to a thing, is also used to express a greatly felt desire. In an expedition the Holy Prophet's very brave and loyal Companion, Abū Khaithamah happened to be absent. The Holy Prophet keenly felt his absence. When in the midst of the battle he saw from a great distance a rider coming to him at full speed, he exclaimed *Kun Abā Khaithamah, i.e.*, would that it were Abū Khaithamah; and lo ! it was really Abū Khaithamah (Ḥalbiyyah). So the word *Kun* would signify that when God desires or intends a thing to come into being, it comes into being ; or when God expresses such a desire it takes a concrete form. The word lends no support to the view that soul and matter are primaeval or co-eternal with God.

1771. The verse means to say that the disbelievers' faculties of seeing and hearing will become much keener and sharper on the Day of Judgment, because the veil will then be lifted from their eyes and ears and they will realize that they were in the wrong; but that realization being too late will prove to be of no avail to them.

41. [a]It is We Who shall inherit[1772] the earth and all who are thereon, and to Us will they *all* be returned.

إِنَّا نَحْنُ نَرِثُ الْأَرْضَ وَمَنْ عَلَيْهَا وَإِلَيْنَا يُرْجَعُونَ ﴿٤١﴾

R. 3 42. [b]And relate *the story of* Abraham *as mentioned* in the Book.[1773] He was *a* truthful *man and* a Prophet.

وَاذْكُرْ فِي الْكِتٰبِ إِبْرٰهِيمَ إِنَّهُ كَانَ صِدِّيقًا نَّبِيًّا ﴿٤٢﴾

43. When he said to his father, [c]'O my father, why dost thou worship that which neither hears nor sees, nor can avail thee aught ?

إِذْ قَالَ لِأَبِيهِ يٰٓأَبَتِ لِمَ تَعْبُدُ مَا لَا يَسْمَعُ وَلَا يُبْصِرُ وَلَا يُغْنِي عَنْكَ شَيْئًا ﴿٤٣﴾

44. 'O my father, there has indeed come to me knowledge such as has not come to thee; so follow me, I will guide thee to a straight path;

يٰٓأَبَتِ إِنِّي قَدْ جَآءَنِي مِنَ الْعِلْمِ مَا لَمْ يَأْتِكَ فَاتَّبِعْنِيٓ أَهْدِكَ صِرَاطًا سَوِيًّا ﴿٤٤﴾

45. 'O my father, [d]worship[1774] not Satan; surely Satan is a rebel against the Gracious *God*;[1775]

يٰٓأَبَتِ لَا تَعْبُدِ الشَّيْطٰنَ إِنَّ الشَّيْطٰنَ كَانَ لِلرَّحْمٰنِ عَصِيًّا ﴿٤٥﴾

46. 'O my father, indeed I fear lest a punishment from the Gracious *God* seize thee and thou become a friend of Satan.'

يٰٓأَبَتِ إِنِّيٓ أَخَافُ أَنْ يَمَسَّكَ عَذَابٌ مِّنَ الرَّحْمٰنِ فَتَكُونَ لِلشَّيْطٰنِ وَلِيًّا ﴿٤٦﴾

[a]15 : 24; 28 : 59. [b]38 : 46; 53 : 38. [c]6 : 75; 21 : 53; 26 : 71; 37 : 86-87. [d]6 : 143; 24 : 22 ; 36 : 61.

1772. The verse embodies two prophecies : (*a*) The Christian people will first come to rule over almost the whole of the earth, and will be dominating it by their large numbers; and (*b*) as a result of their disbelief they will then be deprived of their dominion which will ultimately be given to the followers of Islām.

1773. "The Book" means the Qur'ān. The Holy Prophet is here directed to relate the story of Abraham as it is given in the Qur'ān and not as it is related in the Bible. Whereas the Qur'ān depicts Abraham as a truthful man, the Bible accuses him of telling lies (Gen. 20 : 13). The Qur'ān has laid great stress on the truthfulness of Abraham, perhaps because sometime in future, lies were to be attributed to him by some Commentators of the Qur'ān.

1774. '*Ibādah* which is noun-infinitive from the verb '*Abada* does not consist only in prostrating before God or an idol, but also signifies blindly or unthinkingly following a person or accepting an idea or belief without subjecting it to sane and searching criticism. This latter significance of the word is clear from the verse itself, because nobody has ever been seen to worship Satan in the sense that he prostrates before him and prays to him.

1775. In this verse, in fact, in the whole *Sūrah*, *Shirk* (idolatry) has been repeatedly denounced and condemned in the strongest and most scathing terms and the Divine attribute *Al-Raḥmān* (The Gracious) has also been mentioned again and again, because *Shirk* (idolatry) in every shape and form is the direct result of the denial of *Raḥmāniyyah* (Divine Grace).

47. He replied, 'Dost thou turn away from my gods, O Abraham? [a]If thou desist not, I shall surely cut off[1776] all relations with thee. *Now*, leave me alone for a while.'

قَالَ أَرَاغِبٌ أَنْتَ عَنْ آلِهَتِي يَا إِبْرَاهِيمُ ۚ لَئِنْ لَمْ
تَنْتَهِ لَأَرْجُمَنَّكَ ۖ وَاهْجُرْنِي مَلِيًّا ﴿٤٧﴾

48. *Abraham* said, 'Peace be upon thee. [b]I will ask forgiveness of my Lord for thee. He is indeed gracious to me;

قَالَ سَلَامٌ عَلَيْكَ ۖ سَأَسْتَغْفِرُ لَكَ رَبِّي ۖ إِنَّهُ كَانَ بِي
حَفِيًّا ﴿٤٨﴾

49. 'And [c]I shall keep away[1777] from you and from that which you call upon beside Allāh; and I will pray unto my Lord. Maybe that in praying to my Lord I shall not be disappointed.'

وَأَعْتَزِلُكُمْ وَمَا تَدْعُونَ مِنْ دُونِ اللَّهِ وَأَدْعُو
رَبِّي عَسَىٰ أَلَّا أَكُونَ بِدُعَاءِ رَبِّي شَقِيًّا ﴿٤٩﴾

50. So when he had separated himself from them and from that which they worshipped beside Allāh, [d]We bestowed upon him Isaac and Jacob[1778] and each of them We made a Prophet.

فَلَمَّا اعْتَزَلَهُمْ وَمَا يَعْبُدُونَ مِنْ دُونِ اللَّهِ ۙ
وَهَبْنَا لَهُ إِسْحَاقَ وَيَعْقُوبَ ۖ وَكُلًّا جَعَلْنَا
نَبِيًّا ﴿٥٠﴾

51. And We granted them *abundantly* of Our mercy; and [e]We bestowed upon them true *and lasting* renown.[1779]

وَوَهَبْنَا لَهُمْ مِنْ رَحْمَتِنَا وَجَعَلْنَا لَهُمْ لِسَانَ
صِدْقٍ عَلِيًّا ﴿٥١﴾ ع ٣

[a]21 : 69; 29 : 25; 37 : 98. [b]9 : 114; 26 : 87; 60 : 5. [c]29 : 27. [d]14 : 40; 21 : 73. [e]26 : 85.

1776. *Rajama-hū* means, he stoned him to death; he accused or slandered him; cursed him or abused him; he drove him away; he cut off all relations with him (Lane).

1777. In this verse Abraham seems to be referring to his emigration to Canaan. He went from Iraq to Canaan and from there to Egypt. He left his father and people behind him in Iraq.

1778. Ishmael has not been mentioned here, though he was the eldest son of Abraham. Isaac and Jacob have been mentioned by the way only as subordinate Prophets while Ishmael has found a separate and independent mention in v. 55. This shows that Ishmael possessed a higher spiritual status than both Isaac and Jacob.

1779. The words, *Ja'alnā Lahum Lisāna Ṣidqin 'Aliyyā* (*We bestowed upon them true and lasting renown*), mean: (1) They acquired good reputation and were remembered with respect, affection and love by their contemporaries and future generations. (2) Their talk was full of wisdom and intelligence and was free from all sorts of bitterness, obscenity, falsehood and hatred. (3) They were fearless in expressing their beliefs and were hard upon disbelievers and untruthful persons. (4) Their good works constituted and continued as so many monuments and memorials to their good name.

R. 4 52. And relate *the story of* Moses *as mentioned* in the Book. [a]He was, indeed, a chosen one; and he was a Messenger, a Prophet.[1780]

وَاذْكُرْ فِي الْكِتٰبِ مُوْسٰٓى اِنَّهٗ كَانَ مُخْلَصًا وَّكَانَ رَسُوْلًا نَّبِيًّا ﴿٥٢﴾

53. And We called him from [b]the right side of the Mount[1781] and We made him draw near *to Us* for *special* communion.

وَنَادَيْنٰهُ مِنْ جَانِبِ الطُّوْرِ الْاَيْمَنِ وَقَرَّبْنٰهُ نَجِيًّا ﴿٥٣﴾

54. And We bestowed upon him, out of Our mercy, [c]his brother Aaron *whom We made* a Prophet.

وَوَهَبْنَا لَهٗ مِنْ رَّحْمَتِنَآ اَخَاهُ هٰرُوْنَ نَبِيًّا ﴿٥٤﴾

55. And relate *the story of* Ishmael[1782] *as mentioned* in the Book. He was indeed true to his promises. And he was a Messenger, a Prophet.

وَاذْكُرْ فِي الْكِتٰبِ اِسْمٰعِيْلَ اِنَّهٗ كَانَ صَادِقَ الْوَعْدِ وَكَانَ رَسُوْلًا نَّبِيًّا ﴿٥٥﴾

56. [d]He used to enjoin Prayer and alms-giving on his people, and he was well-pleasing to his Lord.

وَكَانَ يَاْمُرُ اَهْلَهٗ بِالصَّلٰوةِ وَالزَّكٰوةِ وَكَانَ عِنْدَ رَبِّهٖ مَرْضِيًّا ﴿٥٦﴾

[a]33 : 70. [b]20 : 81; 28 : 31. [c]20 : 30, 31; 25 : 36; 28 : 36. [d]20 : 133; 33 : 34.

1780. The words, *he was a Messenger a Prophet*, explain and remove a popular misconception, *viz.*, that a *Rasūl* (Messenger) is one who brings a new Law and a new Book and a *Nabī* (Prophet) is one who is commissioned by God only for the reformation of his people, and though, like a *Rasūl*, a *Nabī* receives Divine revelations, yet he brings no Law or Book containing new commandments and ordinances. According to this popular notion every *Rasūl* (Messenger) is necessarily a *Nabī* (Prophet) but not every *Nabī* a *Rasūl*. The verse under comment demolishes this wrong notion because if a *Rasūl* (Messenger) is one who brings a new Book and a new Law and as such is necessarily a *Nabī* (Prophet), then the addition of the word *Nabī* to the word *Rasūl* in this and other verses is superfluous and redundant. The fact is that every *Rasūl* is a *Nabī* and every *Nabī* a *Rasūl*. These two words are interchangeable and represent two aspects of the same office and two functions of the same person. A Divine Reformer is a *Rasūl* inasmuch as he receives Messages from God (*Risālah* meaning a message), and he is a *Nabī* in the sense that he conveys those Messages to the people to whom he is sent (*Nubuwwah* meaning the conveying of a message). Thus every *Rasūl* (Messenger) is a *Nabī* (Prophet) because after receiving Divine Messages he conveys them to his people and every *Nabī* is a *Rasūl* because he conveys to his people those Messages which he receives from God. Only the functions of *Nabī* follow those of *Rasūl*. In his capacity as *Rasūl* he first receives Messages from God and then in his capacity as *Nabī* he conveys them to his people. This is why here and everywhere in the Qur'ān when these two words *Rasūl* and *Nabī* occur together, invariably the word *Nabī* follows the word *Rasūl* because that is the natural order.

1781. The words in the text mean : (*a*) from the right side of the Mount; (*b*) from the blessed side of the Mount ; (*c*) from the side of the blessed Mount.

1782. After Moses, mention has been made of Ishmael. His account is introduced with the words 'and relate' which shows that one chapter of religious history—that of the House of Israel, is closed and a new one, that of the House of Ishmael, has begun.

57. And relate *the story of* Idrīs[1783] *as mentioned* in the Book. He was *a* truthful *man, and* a Prophet.

وَاذْكُرْ فِي الْكِتٰبِ اِدْرِيْسَ اِنَّهٗ كَانَ صِدِّيْقًا نَّبِيًّا ﴿٥٧﴾

58. And [a]We exalted him to a lofty station.

وَّرَفَعْنٰهُ مَكَانًا عَلِيًّا ﴿٥٨﴾

59. These are the people [b]upon whom Allāh bestowed His blessings from among the Prophets of the posterity of Adam, and of *the posterity* of those whom We carried *in the Ark* with Noah, and of the posterity of Abraham and Israel;[1784] and *they are* of those whom We guided and chose. [c]When the Signs of the Gracious *God* were recited unto them, they fell down, prostrating themselves *before Allāh* and weeping.

اُولٰٓئِكَ الَّذِيْنَ اَنْعَمَ اللّٰهُ عَلَيْهِمْ مِّنَ النَّبِيّٖنَ مِنْ
ذُرِّيَّةِ اٰدَمَ وَمِمَّنْ حَمَلْنَا مَعَ نُوْحٍ وَّمِنْ ذُرِّيَّةِ
اِبْرٰهِيْمَ وَاِسْرَآءِيْلَ وَمِمَّنْ هَدَيْنَا وَاجْتَبَيْنَا
اِذَا تُتْلٰى عَلَيْهِمْ اٰيٰتُ الرَّحْمٰنِ خَرُّوْا سُجَّدًا وَّبُكِيًّا ﴿٥٩﴾

60. Then there came after them [d]an evil generation who neglected Prayer,[1785] and followed their evil desires. So they will meet destruction,

فَخَلَفَ مِنْ بَعْدِهِمْ خَلْفٌ اَضَاعُوا الصَّلٰوةَ وَاتَّبَعُوا
الشَّهَوٰتِ فَسَوْفَ يَلْقَوْنَ غَيًّا ﴿٦٠﴾

[a]2 : 254; 4 : 159. [b]1 : 7; 4 : 70; 5 : 21; 57 : 20. [c]17 : 108, 110; 32 : 16. [d]7 : 170.

1783. Most Commentators of the Qur'ān are of the opinion that Idrīs is Enoch of the Bible. The words *Ḥanūk* (Enoch) and *Idrīs* closely resemble each other in their meanings and significations. Whereas *Idrīs* means one who reads much or instructs much, *Hanūk* means instruction or dedication (Enc. Bib.). Moreover, the account of Enoch as given in the Bible and in Jewish religious literature closely resembles that of Idrīs as given in the Qur'ān. See also "The Larger Edition of the Commentary," pp. 1597-98.

1784. Some Commentators of the Qur'ān think that the words, *of the posterity of Adam*, refer to Idrīs, and, *whom We carried in the Ark with Noah*, refer to Abraham, and the words, *of the posterity of Abraham*, refer to Ishmael, Isaac and Jacob ; and the words, *of the posterity of*, are understood before the word Israel and refer to Moses, Aaron, Zachariah, Yaḥyā and Jesus, all of whom have been mentioned in the preceding verses of the present *Sūrah*.

1785. In fact, negligence and remissness in observing Prayers make a person ignorant of Divine attributes and kill in him the desire to establish his connection with his Creator which in turn throws him into the clutches of the Devil. And whereas negligence in invoking Divine mercy and in praying to God leads to failure, the pursuit of evil desires results in apathy towards true knowledge and indulgence in obscenities and idle pursuits; and all these things combined together bring about complete moral and spiritual ruin of a person.

61. Except those [a]who repent and believe and do good deeds.[1786] These will enter Heaven and they will not be wronged in the least—

إِلَّا مَنْ تَابَ وَآمَنَ وَعَمِلَ صَالِحًا فَأُولَٰئِكَ يَدْخُلُونَ
الْجَنَّةَ وَلَا يُظْلَمُونَ شَيْئًا ﴿٦١﴾

62. [b]Gardens of Eternity, which the Gracious *God* has promised to His servants while *they are yet* hidden *from their sight*.[1787] Surely, His promise must come to pass.

جَنَّاتِ عَدْنٍ الَّتِي وَعَدَ الرَّحْمَٰنُ عِبَادَهُ بِالْغَيْبِ ۚ
إِنَّهُ كَانَ وَعْدُهُ مَأْتِيًّا ﴿٦٢﴾

63. [c]They will not hear therein anything vain but only *greetings of* peace; they will have their sustenance therein, morning and evening.

لَا يَسْمَعُونَ فِيهَا لَغْوًا إِلَّا سَلَامًا ۖ وَلَهُمْ رِزْقُهُمْ فِيهَا
بُكْرَةً وَعَشِيًّا ﴿٦٣﴾

64. [d]Such is the Heaven which We shall give for an inheritance to those of Our servants who are righteous.

تِلْكَ الْجَنَّةُ الَّتِي نُورِثُ مِنْ عِبَادِنَا مَنْ كَانَ
تَقِيًّا ﴿٦٤﴾

65. And *the angels will say to them*, 'We do not come down save by the command of thy Lord. To Him belongs all that is before us and all that is behind us and all that is between; and thy Lord is not forgetful;'

وَمَا نَتَنَزَّلُ إِلَّا بِأَمْرِ رَبِّكَ ۖ لَهُ مَا بَيْنَ أَيْدِينَا وَمَا
خَلْفَنَا وَمَا بَيْنَ ذَٰلِكَ ۚ وَمَا كَانَ رَبُّكَ نَسِيًّا ﴿٦٥﴾

66. *He is* [e]the Lord of the heavens and the earth and of all that is between the two. Serve Him, therefore, and be steadfast in His service. Dost thou know anyone equal to Him?

رَبُّ السَّمَاوَاتِ وَالْأَرْضِ وَمَا بَيْنَهُمَا فَاعْبُدْهُ وَاصْطَبِرْ
لِعِبَادَتِهِ ۚ هَلْ تَعْلَمُ لَهُ سَمِيًّا ﴿٦٦﴾

[a]6 : 49; 18 : 89; 25 : 71; 34 : 38. [b]9 : 72; 13 : 24; 61 : 13. [c]52 : 24; 56 : 26; 78 : 36. [d]7 : 44; 43 : 73; 52 : 18. [e]37 : 6; 38 : 67; 44 : 8; 78 : 38.

1786. **The epithet "good deeds" is more applicable to such acts as are done at the proper occasion and suit the exigencies of time than to mere devotional acts, as is generally understood.**

1787. **The expression, *Bi'l Ghaib*, may also signify that the Faithful will get "Gardens of Eternity" because they believed in things which they did not see—God, angels, Hereafter, etc.**

R. 5 67. And says man,[1788] [a]'What! when I am dead, shall I be brought forth alive?'

وَيَقُولُ الْإِنسَانُ ءَإِذَا مَا مِتُّ لَسَوْفَ أُخْرَجُ حَيًّا ﴿٦٧﴾

68. Does not man remember that [b]We created him before, when he was nothing?[1789]

أَوَلَا يَذْكُرُ الْإِنسَانُ أَنَّا خَلَقْنَٰهُ مِن قَبْلُ وَلَمْ يَكُ شَيْـًٔا ﴿٦٨﴾

69. And, by thy Lord, [c]We shall assuredly gather them together, and the satans *too;* then shall We bring them on their knees around Hell.[1790]

فَوَرَبِّكَ لَنَحْشُرَنَّهُمْ وَالشَّيَٰطِينَ ثُمَّ لَنُحْضِرَنَّهُمْ حَوْلَ جَهَنَّمَ جِثِيًّا ﴿٦٩﴾

70. Then[1791] shall We certainly pick out, from every group, those of them who were most stubborn in rebellion against the Gracious *God.*

ثُمَّ لَنَنزِعَنَّ مِن كُلِّ شِيعَةٍ أَيُّهُمْ أَشَدُّ عَلَى الرَّحْمَٰنِ عِتِيًّا ﴿٧٠﴾

71. And[1792] surely, We know best those deserving[1793] to be burnt therein.

ثُمَّ لَنَحْنُ أَعْلَمُ بِالَّذِينَ هُمْ أَوْلَىٰ بِهَا صِلِيًّا ﴿٧١﴾

---

[a]23 : 38; 36 : 79. [b]19 : 10; 76 : 2. [c]10 : 29; 17 : 98; 34 : 41.

1788. *Al-Insān* (man) does not here mean man in general but a particular class of men, *viz.*, those unfortunate disbelievers who doubt the existence of the Life after death. In fact, there are very few people in the world who totally deny the existence of the Hereafter. It is not by words of mouth but by their actual actions and deeds—their entire engrossment in material pursuits—that they express their doubt or denial of the Life beyond the grave.

1789. Anything worth mentioning or having any significance or importance.. This meaning is supported by 76 : 2.

1790. In Hebrew, *Jahannam* is used as Gehenna which in Aramaic originally was 'Hinnom,' but later on came to be changed into "Ge-Hinnom" (Enc. Bib.) which means, 'The valley of death or destruction.' The word may also have been a combination of *Jahana* which means, he went near, and *Jahuma* which means, his face became contracted. So *Jahannam* may also mean a thing or place which a person at first likes but when he goes near it, he comes to dislike it and contracts his face to show his dislike for it. Thus the very construction of the word explains the nature and character of Hell.

1791. *Thumma* meaning, then, *i.e.*, afterwards, is a particle or conjunction denoting order and delay. Sometimes it is used to denote the order of enunciation, not the virtual order. It also has the meaning of 'and' and 'so' (Lane).

1792. In this verse, *thumma* is a conjunction denoting order of enunciation and not proper order, meaning 'and.' The word would signify, *'and We tell you another thing that......*

1793. The words may mean : (*a*) Those who are more fitted to burn in the fire than to be left out of it; (*b*) those who are more deserving than others to burn in the fire; (*c*) those who deserve to be punished more by being thrown into the fire than by any other means

72. And [a]there is not one of you[1793A] but will come to it. This is an absolute decree of thy Lord.

وَإِنْ مِّنكُمْ إِلَّا وَارِدُهَا ۚ كَانَ عَلَىٰ رَبِّكَ حَتْمًا مَّقْضِيًّا ﴿٧٢﴾

73. [b]And We shall save the righteous and shall leave the wrongdoers therein, on their knees.

ثُمَّ نُنَجِّي الَّذِينَ اتَّقَوا وَّنَذَرُ الظَّالِمِينَ فِيهَا جِثِيًّا ﴿٧٣﴾

74. And when Our manifest Signs[1794] are recited unto them, the disbelievers say to the believers, '*Tell us*, which of the two parties is better in *respect of* position and is more impressive in *respect of* companions?'

وَإِذَا تُتْلَىٰ عَلَيْهِمْ آيَاتُنَا بَيِّنَاتٍ قَالَ الَّذِينَ كَفَرُوا لِلَّذِينَ آمَنُوا أَيُّ الْفَرِيقَيْنِ خَيْرٌ مَّقَامًا وَأَحْسَنُ نَدِيًّا ﴿٧٤﴾

75. And [c]how many a generation have We destroyed before them, who were better off *than these* in wealth and *better* in outward show.

وَكَمْ أَهْلَكْنَا قَبْلَهُم مِّن قَرْنٍ هُمْ أَحْسَنُ أَثَاثًا وَرِئْيًا ﴿٧٥﴾

[a]21 : 99. [b]21 : 102; 39 : 62. [c]6 : 7; 17 : 18; 19 : 99; 21 : 12; 36 : 32; 50 : 37.

1793A. The pronoun *kum* (you) in *Minkum* is not of general application. It applies, as the context shows, only to the disbelievers and to those who doubt the existence of the Life after death. All these categories of men have been mentioned in the preceding verses. According to Ibn 'Abbās and 'Ikrimah, another reading of *Minkum* (of you) is *Minhum* (of them) and Ibn 'Abbās used to say that the expression *Minkum* is addressed to disbelievers (Qurṭubī). So it is to disbelievers mentioned in vv. 67-71 that the pronoun *kum* (you) clearly refers. On the other hand the Qur'ān quite clearly and emphatically supports the view that the righteous believers will never go to Hell; they will ever bask in the sunshine of God's love and mercy (27 : 90; 39 : 62; 43 : 69; etc.) and will remain far removed from the fire of Hell and will not hear even its faintest sound (21 : 102-103). But if the pronoun *kum* (you) be taken to include both the believers and the disbelievers, then in the case of disbelievers the verse would mean that all of them will go to Hell and in the case of believers the fire of Hell referred to in the verse would signify the fire of trials and tribulations through which they have to pass in the present life and which they endure with patience and fortitude and out of which eventually they are taken to be brought into the heaven of Divine bliss and peace as the next verse shows. The Holy Prophet himself has explained the meaning of this verse. His wife Ḥafṣah is reported to have said: 'On one occasion when the Holy Prophet said that none of those of his Companions who had taken part in the Battle of Badr or Uḥud will go to Hell, I drew his attention to the present verse, upon which he slightly reprimanded me for having misunderstood its meaning and directed me to read the next verse' (Muslim, as quoted by Jāmi' al-Bayān). The fact that the Holy Prophet referred Ḥafṣah to the next verse (v. 73) shows that he also had understood the particle *thumma* occurring in that verse to mean 'and,' and had taken the next verse as an independent and separate clause, otherwise he could not have reprimanded Ḥafṣah for having misunderstood the meaning of the verse under comment.

1794. Mere 'Signs' are those proofs and arguments based on reason, intellect and experience which point to the existence of a thing, its aim and purpose, and establish it. But 'manifest Signs' are those Signs and arguments or reasons which not only point to the existence of a thing and prove it, but are quite suited to the occasion and to the problem they are intended to prove and which also have a very noble and sublime purpose to serve, that they eminently do.

76. Say, 'The Gracious *God* grants those, who are in error, respite for a time [a]until, when they will see that with which they are threatened — whether it be punishment or the *final* Hour[1795]— they will realize who is worse in *respect of* position and weaker in forces.'

قُلْ مَنْ كَانَ فِي الضَّلٰلَةِ فَلْيَمْدُدْ لَهُ الرَّحْمٰنُ مَدًّا ۚ
حَتّٰٓى إِذَا رَاَوْا مَا يُوْعَدُوْنَ إِمَّا الْعَذَابَ وَإِمَّا السَّاعَةَ ؕ
فَسَيَعْلَمُوْنَ مَنْ هُوَ شَرٌّ مَّكَانًا وَّاَضْعَفُ جُنْدًا ﴿٧٦﴾

77. [b]And Allāh increases in guidance those who follow guidance. [c]And the good works that endure are best in the Sight of thy Lord in *respect of* reward and *in respect of* the ultimate end.'

وَيَزِيْدُ اللّٰهُ الَّذِيْنَ اهْتَدَوْا هُدًى ؕ وَالْبٰقِيٰتُ الصّٰلِحٰتُ
خَيْرٌ عِنْدَ رَبِّكَ ثَوَابًا وَّ خَيْرٌ مَّرَدًّا ﴿٧٧﴾

78. Hast thou not seen him who disbelieves in Our Signs, and says, [d]'I shall certainly be given *great* wealth and children?'[1796]

اَفَرَءَيْتَ الَّذِيْ كَفَرَ بِاٰيٰتِنَا وَقَالَ لَاُوْتَيَنَّ مَالًا
وَّوَلَدًا ﴿٧٨﴾ؕ

79. Has he got knowledge of the unseen or has taken a promise from the Gracious *God*?

اَطَّلَعَ الْغَيْبَ اَمِ اتَّخَذَ عِنْدَ الرَّحْمٰنِ عَهْدًا ﴿٧٩﴾ۙ

80. Indeed not![1797] We shall note down what he says and shall prolong for him the punishment.

كَلَّا ؕ سَنَكْتُبُ مَا يَقُوْلُ وَنَمُدُّ لَهُ مِنَ الْعَذَابِ مَدًّا ﴿٨٠﴾ۙ

81. And We shall inherit[1798] from him all that he talks of and [e]he shall come to Us all alone.

وَّ نَرِثُهُ مَا يَقُوْلُ وَيَاْتِيْنَا فَرْدًا ﴿٨١﴾

[a]72 : 25. [b]9 : 124; 47: 18; 48 : 5; [c]87 : 18. [d]18 : 35; 74 : 13-14. [e]6 : 95; 18 : 49.

1795. 'Punishment' here may signify the intervening punishment which will overtake disbelievers in stages before their final destruction, and "final Hour" may signify their complete and final destruction.

1796. The disbeliever sets great store by his wealth and children and takes great pride in them and so do the disbelieving proud nations of the West, with whom the *Sūrah* particularly deals.

1797. The particle *kallā* (indeed not) signifies rejection, rebuke; and reprimanding a person for what he has said being untrue. It also signifies that what has been said before is wrong and what follows is right (Lane). The words, 'what he says,' refer to the proud talk in which the disbelievers indulge because of their great wealth, power, influence and children.

1798. The words, *We shall inherit from him all that he talks of and he shall come to Us all alone*, may mean: he shall have to leave all his wealth and children behind; (*a*) We shall preserve his insolent talk and will remind him of it when he comes to Us and will punish him for it; and (*b*) his inheritors will enter the fold of Islām and all his wealth and resources will be used in Our cause.

82. [a]And they have taken *other* gods than Allāh that they may be *a source of* honour *and power* for them.

وَاتَّخَذُوْا مِنْ دُوْنِ اللّٰهِ اٰلِهَةً لِّيَكُوْنُوْا لَهُمْ عِزًّا ﴿٨٢﴾

83. Not at all! [b]They will deny[1799] their worship, and will be their opponents.

كَلَّا ۭ سَيَكْفُرُوْنَ بِعِبَادَتِهِمْ وَيَكُوْنُوْنَ عَلَيْهِمْ ضِدًّا ﴿٨٣﴾ ع

R 6 84. Seest thou not that [c]We send satans against the disbelievers, inciting them *to acts of disobedience?*

اَلَمْ تَرَ اَنَّآ اَرْسَلْنَا الشَّيٰطِيْنَ عَلَى الْكٰفِرِيْنَ تَؤُزُّهُمْ اَزًّا ﴿٨٤﴾

85. So be not thou in haste against them; We are keeping full account[1800] *of their doings.*

فَلَا تَعْجَلْ عَلَيْهِمْ ۭ اِنَّمَا نَعُدُّ لَهُمْ عَدًّا ﴿٨٥﴾

86. *Remember* the day when [d]We shall gather the righteous before the Gracious *God* as *honoured* guests;

يَوْمَ نَحْشُرُ الْمُتَّقِيْنَ اِلَى الرَّحْمٰنِ وَفْدًا ﴿٨٦﴾

87. And [e]We shall drive the guilty to Hell *like* a herd of thirsty camels.[1801]

وَّنَسُوْقُ الْمُجْرِمِيْنَ اِلٰى جَهَنَّمَ وِرْدًا ﴿٨٧﴾

88. [f]None will have the power of intercession save he who has received a promise from the Gracious *God.*

لَا يَمْلِكُوْنَ الشَّفَاعَةَ اِلَّا مَنِ اتَّخَذَ عِنْدَ الرَّحْمٰنِ عَهْدًا ﴿٨٨﴾

89. [g]And they say, 'The Gracious *God* has taken unto Himself a son.'

وَقَالُوا اتَّخَذَ الرَّحْمٰنُ وَلَدًا ﴿٨٩﴾

90. Assuredly, you have indeed uttered a most hideous thing.

لَقَدْ جِئْتُمْ شَيْـًٔا اِدًّا ﴿٩٠﴾

---

[a]21 : 25; 36 : 7; 5. [b]6 : 24; 10 : 29. [c]8 : 49; 47 : 26; 59 : 17. [d]39 : 74. [e]39 : 72. [f]2 : 49; 20 : 100; 21 : 29; 34 : 24; 39 : 45; 43 : 87; 53 : 27; 74 : 49. [g]2 : 117; 4 : 172; 6 : 101-102; 10 : 69; 17 : 112; 18 : 5; 19 : 36; 21 : 27; 25 : 3; 39 : 5; 43 : 82.

1799. The words may mean: (*a*) The false deities will deny that the idolaters ever worshipped them; (*b*) the idolaters will deny that they ever worshipped false deities. For (*a*) see 2 : 167 ; 10 : 29 ; 16 : 87 ; 28 : 64; and for (*b*) see 6 : 24 ; 30 : 14.

1800. The verse means: (*a*) We are keeping full account of their wicked deeds; and (*b*) We are keeping account of the time when their punishment will be due.

1801. *Al-Wird* means, (*a*) coming to or arriving at water; (*b*) water to which one comes to drink; (*c*) the turn of coming to water; (*d*) the number of camels or the herd of thirsty camels (Aqrab). See also 11 : 99.

91. The heavens might well-nigh burst thereat, and the earth cleave asunder, and the mountains fall down in pieces.[1802]

تَكَادُ السَّمٰوٰتُ يَتَفَطَّرْنَ مِنْهُ وَ تَنْشَقُّ الْاَرْضُ وَ تَخِرُّ الْجِبَالُ هَدًّا ۙ﴿۹۱﴾

92. Because they ascribe a son to the Gracious *God*.

اَنْ دَعَوْا لِلرَّحْمٰنِ وَلَدًا ﴿۹۲﴾

93. [a]It becomes not the Gracious *God* that He should take unto Himself a son.[1803]

وَ مَا يَنْۢبَغِيْ لِلرَّحْمٰنِ اَنْ يَّتَّخِذَ وَلَدًا ﴿۹۳﴾

94. [b]There is none in the heavens and the earth but he shall come to the Gracious *God* as a bondman.[1804]

اِنْ كُلُّ مَنْ فِي السَّمٰوٰتِ وَ الْاَرْضِ اِلَّاۤ اٰتِي الرَّحْمٰنِ عَبْدًا ﴿۹۴﴾

95. Verily, He comprehends them *by His knowledge* and has numbered them *all* fully.

لَقَدْ اَحْصٰىهُمْ وَ عَدَّهُمْ عَدًّا ﴿۹۵﴾

96. And each of them shall come to Him on the Day of Resurrection, all alone.

وَ كُلُّهُمْ اٰتِيْهِ يَوْمَ الْقِيٰمَةِ فَرْدًا ﴿۹۶﴾

[a]2 : 117; 4 : 172; 10 : 69; 37 : 152-155. [b]20 : 109.

1802. The dogma that Jesus is the son of God is so hideous that the heavens, the earth and the mountains might well break into pieces and fall asunder at its enormity. The belief is repugnant to heavenly beings (*al-Samāwāt*) because it is against Divine attributes and against all that they stand for. It is revolting for human beings living on the earth (*al-Arḍ*), because it offends against the dictates of human nature and man's intellect and reason recoil in sheer disgust from it. Men of high and noble ideals such as Divine Prophets and God's Elect (*al-Jibāl*) also deny and denounce it because the idea that man should stand in need of the vicarious sacrifice of anybody for the attainment of salvation and a high moral status runs counter to their own spiritual experience.

1803. The *Sūrah* contains most emphatic and clear denunciation of Christian dogmas, particularly their basic doctrine that Jesus is son of God, from which all other dogmas flow. In the present and preceding four verses special stress has been laid on the refutation and condemnation of this doctrine. It is worthy of special note that the Divine attribute *al-Raḥmān* has been repeatedly referred to in this *Sūrah*—it has been mentioned as many as sixteen times. As the fundamental dogma of the sonship of Jesus and its corollary, the dogma of atonement involve a denial of the Divine attribute *Al-Rahmān* and as the central theme of this *Sūrah* is the refutation of this dogma, this attribute inevitably has been repeatedly referred to. The dogma of atonement implies that God cannot forgive the sins of men whereas the Divine attribute '*Al-Raḥmān*' implies that He can and actually does often forgive them, hence its repetition in this *Sūrah*.

1804. The Gracious God needs no son to help Him or succeed Him, because He is the Lord of the heavens and the earth and His Kingdom extends over the whole universe, and because all men are His servants and Jesus is one of them.

97. Those who believe and do good deeds—the Gracious *God* will create *deep* love for them.[1805]

اِنَّ الَّذِیْنَ اٰمَنُوْا وَ عَمِلُوا الصّٰلِحٰتِ سَیَجْعَلُ لَهُمُ الرَّحْمٰنُ وُدًّا ۝

98. So [a]We have made *the* Qur'ān easy in thy tongue that thou mayest give thereby glad tidings to the righteous, and warn thereby a contentious people.

فَاِنَّمَا یَسَّرْنٰهُ بِلِسَانِکَ لِتُبَشِّرَ بِهِ الْمُتَّقِیْنَ وَ تُنْذِرَ بِهٖ قَوْمًا لُّدًّا ۝

99. [b]And how many a generation have We destroyed before them! Canst thou perceive a single one of them, or hear *even* a whisper of them?[1806]

وَ کَمْ اَهْلَکْنَا قَبْلَهُمْ مِّنْ قَرْنٍ هَلْ تُحِسُّ مِنْهُمْ مِّنْ اَحَدٍ اَوْ تَسْمَعُ لَهُمْ رِکْزًا ۝

---

[a]44 : 59; 54 : 18.   [b]17 : 18; 19 : 75; 21 : 12; 36 : 32; 50 : 37.

1805. The verse may have one of the following meanings: (a) God will put His own love in the hearts of the righteous; (b) He will have deep love for the righteous; (c) He will put deep love for mankind in the hearts of the righteous ; and (d) He will create deep love for the righteous in the hearts of men.

1806. The verse embodies for the Western Christian nations a grim warning about the dreadful fate that is in store for them if they did not accept the Truth and give up their evil ways. They are proud of their material power and resources and their worldly prosperity and progress, but have ignored the patent fact that wrong beliefs and a life of sin lead only to destruction.

CHAPTER 20

ṬĀ HĀ

(*Revealed before Hijrah*)

Date of Revelation and Context

The *Sūrah* was revealed very early at Mecca. This is the opinion of 'Abd Allāh bin Mas'ūd, one of the earliest Companions of the Holy Prophet. The *Sūrah* continues to deal with Christian beliefs and doctrines which formed the primary theme of the preceding Chapter. One of the basic doctrines of Christianity is that the Law is a curse. The *Sūrah* opens with an emphatic repudiation of this Christian doctrine. The Law, it says, is not only not a curse but is positively a great Divine boon and mercy, and instead of being a burden and an encumbrance, its object is to afford solace and spiritual contentment to man. This is one of the principal objects of the Qur'ān which it fulfils most adequately. The Holy Prophet is comforted with the message that God has revealed the Qur'ān to lighten man's burdens and not to add to his difficulties. It meets all human major needs and requirements.

Subject-Matter

The *Sūrah* proceeds to tell Christians that in order to understand and realize the truths embodied in the Qur'ān, they should ponder over the circumstances and conditions through which Moses had to pass. It is stated that after his spiritual upbringing had become complete and he was found fit to be entrusted with the great responsibilities of a Prophet, Moses was commanded to go to Pharaoh and convey to him the Divine Message. Pharaoh refused to accept it, behaved arrogantly and sought to kill Moses. Thereupon Moses was commanded by God to take the Israelites out of Egypt to Canaan. Pharaoh pursued them with his mighty hosts but Divine punishment overtook him and he was drowned in the sea before the very eyes of the Israelites. Moses then went up to the "Mount" where the Law was revealed to him. The *Sūrah* then administers a subtle rebuke to Christians. They are told that when before the advent of Jesus the Israelites believed in the doctrine that God was One and later great stress had also been laid in the Qur'ān upon Divine Unity and upon the importance and significance of the Law or the *Sharī'ah*, how could a teaching which regarded the Law as a curse and entertained and preached polytheistic doctrines intervene between these two strictly monotheistic creeds? Next, mention is made of Divine punishment that would overtake Christian nations for their sins and iniquities after they had enjoyed material prosperity for a thousand years. Of these the last three centuries would be marked by uniform progress and prosperity of a very high order. This would make them disdainfully ignore the Divine warning that a dreadful fate was in store for them. The *Sūrah* emphatically declares that this event will certainly come to pass and Christian nations of the West will be seized with a terrible visitation; lofty mountains shall crumble and become like scattered dust (vv. 106, 107). Then the subject with which the *Sūrah* has opened is rehearsed, *viz*., that the Qur'ān easily yields to understanding and comprehension because it has been revealed in the national tongue of the people who are its first addressees. Like the Christian Scriptures it usually does not talk in parables and metaphors, thus leaving the subject confused and lacking in clarity, but explains its teaching in an easily comprehensible language. The importance of the Law is driven home by strong and forceful arguments and it is shown to be not an unmitigated curse but a great Divine blessing. Then mention is made of the expulsion of Adam from "the garden." This incident on which the whole fabric of the Christian doctrine of atonement stands is either misunderstood or deliberately misinterpreted and misrepresented by Christians. The truth is that the birth of Adam took place according to a fixed Divine plan, and Divine plans never miscarry or fail in their object. While according to the Bible, God created Adam in His own image (Gen. 1 : 27) and then, beguiled by Eve, Adam fell into sin, the Qur'ān declares that having been created in God's own image and likeness, Adam could not possibly have been guilty of any such fall. It describes him as only having slipped into an inadvertent lapse (v. 116). The *Sūrah* ends with a stern warning to disbelievers that Signs and miracles of their own devising will never be shown to them and that if, in spite of having seen many heavenly Signs, they still persisted in denying the Divine Message, they will be punished as were punished the disbelievers of the former Messengers of God.

سُوْرَةُ طٰهٰ مَكِّيَّةٌ (٢٠)

1. [a]In the name of Allāh, the Gracious, the Merciful.

بِسْمِ اللّٰهِ الرَّحْمٰنِ الرَّحِيْمِ ۝١

2. Ṭā Hā.[1807]

طٰهٰ ۝٢

3. We have not sent down the Qur'ān to thee that thou shouldst be distressed;[1808]

مَآ اَنْزَلْنَا عَلَيْكَ الْقُرْاٰنَ لِتَشْقٰۤى ۝٣

4. But as a [b]reminder to him who fears *God;*

اِلَّا تَذْكِرَةً لِّمَنْ يَّخْشٰى ۝٤

5. *And* a revelation from Him Who created the earth and the high heavens.

تَنْزِيْلًا مِّمَّنْ خَلَقَ الْاَرْضَ وَالسَّمٰوٰتِ الْعُلٰى ۝٥

6. *He is* [c]the Gracious *God Who* has settled Himself firmly on the Throne.[1809]

اَلرَّحْمٰنُ عَلَى الْعَرْشِ اسْتَوٰى ۝٦

7. [d]To Him belongs whatsoever is in the heavens and whatsoever is in the earth, and whatsoever is between them, and whatsoever is beneath the moist sub-soil.

لَهٗ مَا فِى السَّمٰوٰتِ وَمَا فِى الْاَرْضِ وَمَا بَيْنَهُمَا وَمَا تَحْتَ الثَّرٰى ۝٧

[a]1 : 1. [b]73 : 20 ; 74 : 55; 76 : 30; 80 : 12. [c]7 : 55; 10 : 4. [d]2 : 285; 3 : 130; 5 : 19.

1807. *Ṭā Hā* is a combination of *ṭā* and *hā.* In the dialect of 'Akk, an Arab tribe, it means, 'O my beloved,' or 'O perfect man.' The author of Kashshāf interprets it as 'O you.' By some, the expression is interpreted as, 'Be thou at rest' (Bayān & Lisān). The expression points to the fact that the Holy Prophet was gifted, in the fullest measure, with all those natural faculties, qualities and attributes which contribute to the building up of a man's full moral stature. The Holy Prophet was indeed a complete and perfect man, a perfect human specimen, in the fullest sense of the word. See also 2343 and 3091.

1808. The verse contains a message of comfort and hope for the Holy Prophet and Muslims. It purports to say that it is incompatible with the perfect and unerring Quranic revelation that its bearer should fail in his mission. The cause of the Holy Prophet, therefore, must triumph. The verse also refutes the Christian dogma that the Law or the *Sharī'ah* is a curse. There is nothing in the Qur'ān which is repugnant to human nature and which, if acted upon, should put man into trouble.

1809. Briefly, "The Throne" represents the transcendent attributes of God, *i.e.,* the attributes which are technically known as *Ṣifāt Tanzīhiyyah.* These attributes, which are eternal and unchangeable and are God's exclusive prerogatives, are manifested through His other attributes which are known as *Ṣifāt Tashbīhiyyah, i.e.,* such attributes as are found more or less in human beings also. The former attributes, *i.e.,* transcendent attributes, are said to constitute God's Throne and the latter attributes are the bearers of His Throne. See also 986 & 1233.

8. [a]And if thou speakest aloud, *He hears it and also if thou speakest in a low voice*, for He knows the secret *thoughts of man* and what is *yet* more hidden.[1810]

وَإِنْ تَجْهَرْ بِالْقَوْلِ فَإِنَّهُ يَعْلَمُ السِّرَّ وَأَخْفَى ﴿٨﴾

9. Allāh—there is no god but He. [b]His are the most beautiful names.[1811]

اللّٰهُ لَآ إِلٰهَ إِلَّا هُوَ لَهُ الْأَسْمَآءُ الْحُسْنٰى ﴿٩﴾

10. [c]And has the story of Moses come to thee ?[1812]

وَهَلْ أَتٰكَ حَدِيْثُ مُوْسٰى ﴿١٠﴾

[a]2 : 78; 6 : 4; 11 : 6; 67 : 14. [b]7 : 181; 59 : 25. [c]19 : 52; 79 : 16.

1810. The word *Sirr* (secret thoughts) signifies the thoughts that lie hidden in man's breast which he alone knows, and *Akhfā* (more hidden) comprises all those ideals, ideas and ambitions of a person which lie hidden in the womb of futurity and have never crossed his mind.

1811. The verse contains the quintessence and kernel of the Quranic revelation referred to in v. 3, above. It is that God exists. He is One. He possesses all perfect attributes and is completely free from all conceivable defects and imperfections and, therefore, He alone is entitled to our worship and adoration.

1812. Against all accepted canons of history Freud in his "Moses and Monotheism" has adumbrated quite a novel theory that Moses was not an Israelite and that he did not belong to the Hebrew stock and also that the Israelites never settled in Egypt. He has advanced the following arguments in support of this strange claim : (1) That Moses is an Egyptian name. (2) That the idea of the Oneness of God was originally Egyptian, having been first conceived and adopted by an ancient Egyptian king, named Ikhnaten (or Akhenaten). (3) That Moses, himself being an Egyptian, borrowed it from the Egyptians and preached it among the Israelites. (4) That because Moses was an Egyptian he could not properly express himself in Hebrew.

All these arguments possess no basis in fact. Moses is certainly a Hebrew word, having derivation both in Hebrew and Arabic. But even if the name Moses was of Egyptian origin, it does not follow that the man Moses also was an Egyptian. As the Israelites were a subject race in Egypt, living under the rule of the Pharaohs, it seems quite plausible that they had adopted Egyptian names. The members of a subject race generally feel a particular delight in adopting the names and imitating the customs, modes of living and dress etc., of their rulers. The argument that the idea of the Oneness of God was originally Egyptian, having been first conceived and adopted by Akhenaten, an ancient Egyptian king, and preached by him among the Israelites, is equally wrong. It is unreasonable to suppose that a certain concept is the monopoly of one people. Different peoples may independently form similar ideas without having borrowed them from one another. But even supposing that the idea of God's Unity is of Egyptian origin, the inference cannot be justified that Moses was an Egyptian. If an American or a German can borrow an idea from an Englishman and *vice versa*, why cannot an Israelite borrow an idea from an Egyptian ? The truth is that the idea of God's Oneness was neither conceived by Egyptians nor by Syrians or any other people. It has its origin in Divine revelation. Further, Freud bases his claim that Moses was an Egyptian on Exod. 4:10 where it is stated that he was slow of speech and could not adequately express himself, and arbitrarily draws the conclusion that Moses was slow of speech in Hebrew. On the contrary, the fact is, and both the Qur'ān and the Bible lend support to it, that when commanded by God to go to Pharaoh and preach his mission to him, Moses requested to be excused on the plea of his inability to express himself adequately. This, if any thing, shows that Moses could not freely express himself in the tongue which Pharaoh spoke and understood, *i.e.*, the Egyptian tongue, and therefore he was not an Egyptian. In fact, the linguistic evidence of Hebrew and Arabic, combined with the evidence of Jewish history and tradition and added to the account of Moses as given in the Bible and the Qur'ān—all go to substantiate and support the contention that Moses was not an Egyptian nor was his name of Egyptian origin. See also "The Larger Edition of the Commentary," pp. 1621—1623.

11. [a]When he saw a fire, and he said to his family, 'Tarry ye, I perceive a fire; perhaps I may bring you a brand therefrom or find guidance at the fire.[1813]

إِذْ رَاٰ نَارًا فَقَالَ لِاَهْلِهِ امْكُثُوْٓا اِنِّيْٓ اٰنَسْتُ نَارًا لَّعَلِّيْٓ اٰتِيْكُمْ مِّنْهَا بِقَبَسٍ اَوْ اَجِدُ عَلَى النَّارِ هُدًى ⑪

12. [b]And when he came to it, he was called *by a voice*, 'O Moses,

فَلَمَّآ اَتٰىهَا نُوْدِيَ يٰمُوْسٰى ⑫

13. 'Verily, I am thy Lord. So take off thy shoes;[1814] [c]for thou art in the sacred Valley of Ṭuwā;

اِنِّيْٓ اَنَا رَبُّكَ فَاخْلَعْ نَعْلَيْكَ اِنَّكَ بِالْوَادِ الْمُقَدَّسِ طُوًى ⑬

14. [d]'And I Myself have chosen thee; so hearken to what is revealed *to thee;*

وَاَنَا اخْتَرْتُكَ فَاسْتَمِعْ لِمَا يُوْحٰى ⑭

15. [e]'Verily, I am Allāh; there is no god but I, so worship Me *alone* and observe Prayer for My remembrance;

اِنَّنِيْٓ اَنَا اللّٰهُ لَآ اِلٰهَ اِلَّآ اَنَا فَاعْبُدْنِيْ وَاَقِمِ الصَّلٰوةَ لِذِكْرِيْ ⑮

16. [f]'Surely, the Hour is coming and I am going to manifest[1815] it, that every soul may be recompensed for its labours;

اِنَّ السَّاعَةَ اٰتِيَةٌ اَكَادُ اُخْفِيْهَا لِتُجْزٰى كُلُّ نَفْسٍ بِمَا تَسْعٰى ⑯

17. 'So let not him, who believes not therein and follows his own low desires, turn thee away therefrom, lest thou perish;

فَلَا يَصُدَّنَّكَ عَنْهَا مَنْ لَّا يُؤْمِنُ بِهَا وَاتَّبَعَ هَوٰىهُ فَتَرْدٰى ⑰

[a]27 : 8; 28 : 30. [b]27 : 9; 28 : 31; 79 : 17. [c]20 : 13; 28 : 31; 79 : 17. [d]20 : 42. [e]27 : 10; 28 : 31. [f]5 : 86; 40 : 60.

1813. The verse refers to a vision of Moses, and visions are of two kinds: (*a*) The visions that concern only the Prophet who sees such a one. In such visions the Divine manifestation remains confined to the Prophet concerned. (*b*) The visions in which Divine manifestation extends also to the Prophet's people. Moses meant to say that if the vision that he had seen was the manifestation of the latter class, then he would be given a new *Sharī'ah* for his people, but if it were of the former kind, he would receive some guidance for his own spiritual advancement.

1814. As stated above it was a vision that Moses had seen, and "shoes" in the language of visions signify worldly relations such as wife, children, friends, etc. The words 'Thy two shoes' signify 'thy relations with thy family and those with thy community.' Thus at the time of close communion with God Moses was commanded to banish from his mind all thoughts of wife and children and of other worldly connections. Taken literally, the verse would mean that because Moses was in a sacred place he was bidden to take off his shoes.

1815. *Akhfa al-Shaia'* means, he concealed the thing; he removed its covering or manifested it (Lane).

18. ‘And what is that in thy right hand, O Moses?’	وَمَا تِلْكَ بِيَمِيْنِكَ يٰمُوْسٰى ﴿١٨﴾
19. *Moses* said, ‘This is my rod, I lean on it and beat down therewith leaves for my sheep and other uses[1816] *also* I find in it.’	قَالَ هِيَ عَصَايَ اَتَوَكَّؤُا عَلَيْهَا وَاَهُشُّ بِهَا عَلٰى غَنَمِيْ وَلِيَ فِيْهَا مَاٰرِبُ اُخْرٰى ﴿١٩﴾
20. *God* said, [a]‘Cast it down, O Moses.’	قَالَ اَلْقِهَا يٰمُوْسٰى ﴿٢٠﴾
21. So he cast it down, and behold! it was a serpent running.[1816A]	فَاَلْقٰىهَا فَاِذَا هِيَ حَيَّةٌ تَسْعٰى ﴿٢١﴾
22. *God* said, ‘Take hold of it, and fear not. We shall restore it to its former state.	قَالَ خُذْهَا وَلَا تَخَفْ سَنُعِيْدُهَا سِيْرَتَهَا الْاُوْلٰى ﴿٢٢﴾
23. [b]‘And draw thy hand[1817] closer under thy arm-pit,[1818] it shall come forth white, without any disease—another Sign;	وَاضْمُمْ يَدَكَ اِلٰى جَنَاحِكَ تَخْرُجْ بَيْضَآءَ مِنْ غَيْرِ سُوْٓءٍ اٰيَةً اُخْرٰى ﴿٢٣﴾
24. ‘That We may show thee some of Our greater Signs;[1819]	لِنُرِيَكَ مِنْ اٰيٰتِنَا الْكُبْرٰى ﴿٢٤﴾

[a]7 : 118; 26 : 33; 27 : 11; 28 : 32. [b]7 : 109; 27 : 13; 28 : 33.

1816. *Ma'āṛib* (uses) is the plural of *Mā'ribah* which is derived from *ariba.* They say *ariba Ilaihi*, *i.e.*, he wanted it and sought it; and *Ma'ārib* means, wants, uses, needs, requirements, purposes (Lane).

1816A. The rod did not actually turn into a serpent but was merely made to appear like one. It, therefore, contradicted or contravened no law of nature. The miracle was intended, besides providing a very powerful proof in support of Moses, to comfort him that his people would not remain permanently wedded to idolatry and other evil practices but, the instant they came under his fostering care, they would again become his good and God-fearing companion, *‘Aṣā* signifying a community (Lane). See also 1023.

1817. *Yad* means, hand or arm and figuratively signifies favour, beneficence; power, authority; help, protection; community, party (Aqrab).

1818. One of the meanings of *Yad* (hand) being a community or people, the expression in the text contains an injunction for Moses that he should always keep his people close to him and under his fostering care. If he did so they would become highly righteous men, radiating spiritual light and would be free from all moral evils. *Yad Baiḍā'* may also signify clear and strong arguments. Moses was endowed with strong and solid arguments to prove his case. See also 7 : 109; and 26 : 34.

1819. Sign of the rod was one of the greatest heavenly Signs given to Moses. When Moses was entrusted with Prophethood, the Sign of the rod appeared (20 : 19). When he went to preach his Message to Pharaoh it was again the miracle of the rod that was shown to him and the sorcerers (20 : 70-74). When the Israelites wanted water, he was ordered to strike the rock with his rod (2 : 61), and when he had to cross the sea, God commanded him to strike it with his rod (26 : 64).

25. 'Go thou to Pharaoh; he has indeed exceeded *all* bounds.'

اِذْهَبْ اِلٰى فِرْعَوْنَ اِنَّهٗ طَغٰى ﴿٢٥﴾ ع

R. 2 26. *Moses* said, 'My Lord, expand for me my breast;

قَالَ رَبِّ اشْرَحْ لِيْ صَدْرِيْ ﴿٢٦﴾

27. 'And make my task easy for me;

وَيَسِّرْ لِيْٓ اَمْرِيْ ﴿٢٧﴾

28. [a]'And loose the knot from my tongue,

وَاحْلُلْ عُقْدَةً مِّنْ لِّسَانِيْ ﴿٢٨﴾

29. 'That they may understand my speech;

يَفْقَهُوْا قَوْلِيْ ﴿٢٩﴾

30. 'And grant me an assistant[1820] from my family—

وَاجْعَلْ لِّيْ وَزِيْرًا مِّنْ اَهْلِيْ ﴿٣٠﴾

31. [b]'Aaron, my brother;

هٰرُوْنَ اَخِي ﴿٣١﴾

32. 'Increase my strength by him;

اشْدُدْ بِهٖٓ اَزْرِيْ ﴿٣٢﴾

33. [c]'And make him share my task;

وَاَشْرِكْهُ فِيْٓ اَمْرِيْ ﴿٣٣﴾

34. 'That we may glorify Thee much;

كَيْ نُسَبِّحَكَ كَثِيْرًا ﴿٣٤﴾

35. 'And remember Thee much;

وَّنَذْكُرَكَ كَثِيْرًا ﴿٣٥﴾

36. Thou art, surely, Ever-Watching over us.'

اِنَّكَ كُنْتَ بِنَا بَصِيْرًا ﴿٣٦﴾

37. *God* said, 'Granted is thy prayer, O Moses,

قَالَ قَدْ اُوْتِيْتَ سُؤْلَكَ يٰمُوْسٰى ﴿٣٧﴾

38. 'And We did indeed confer a favour upon thee at another time *also*;

وَلَقَدْ مَنَنَّا عَلَيْكَ مَرَّةً اُخْرٰٓى ﴿٣٨﴾

[a]26 : 14. [b]28 : 35. [c]26 : 16.

1820. Moses did not feel himself equal to the great task entrusted to him. He asked for an helper to assist him. The Holy Prophet to whom an infinitely heavier and more onerous task was entrusted never prayed to be given an assistant. He alone, unassisted and unhelped, discharged fully and completely the responsibility of raising a people, sunk deep into the depths of moral turpitude, to the highest pinnacle of spiritual glory.

39. 'When [a]We revealed to thy mother what [1821] was an *important* revelation, *to wit :*

إِذْ أَوْحَيْنَآ إِلَىٰٓ أُمِّكَ مَا يُوحَىٰٓ ﴿٣٩﴾

40. 'Put him in the ark, and place it into the river, then the river will cast it on to the shore, and there [b]*one who is* an enemy to Me and *also* an enemy to him will take him up.' And I wrapped thee with love from Me; and *this I did* that thou mightest be reared before My eye ;[1822]

أَنِ ٱقْذِفِيهِ فِى ٱلتَّابُوتِ فَٱقْذِفِيهِ فِى ٱلْيَمِّ فَلْيُلْقِهِ ٱلْيَمُّ بِٱلسَّاحِلِ يَأْخُذْهُ عَدُوٌّ لِّى وَعَدُوٌّ لَّهُۥ ۚ وَأَلْقَيْتُ عَلَيْكَ مَحَبَّةً مِّنِّى ۚ وَلِتُصْنَعَ عَلَىٰ عَيْنِىٓ ﴿٤٠﴾

41. [c]'When thy sister walked along and said, 'Shall I direct you to one who will take charge of him?' So [d]We restored thee to thy mother that her eye might be cooled and she might not grieve. And [e]thou didst slay a man, but We delivered thee from sorrow. Then We tried thee with various trials. And thou didst tarry several years among the people of Midian. Then thou camest up to the *required* standard,[1823] O Moses;

إِذْ تَمْشِىٓ أُخْتُكَ فَتَقُولُ هَلْ أَدُلُّكُمْ عَلَىٰ مَن يَكْفُلُهُۥ ۖ فَرَجَعْنَٰكَ إِلَىٰٓ أُمِّكَ كَىْ تَقَرَّ عَيْنُهَا وَلَا تَحْزَنَ ۚ وَقَتَلْتَ نَفْسًا فَنَجَّيْنَٰكَ مِنَ ٱلْغَمِّ وَفَتَنَّٰكَ فُتُونًا ۚ فَلَبِثْتَ سِنِينَ فِىٓ أَهْلِ مَدْيَنَ ۚ ثُمَّ جِئْتَ عَلَىٰ قَدَرٍ يَٰمُوسَىٰ ﴿٤١﴾

42. 'And [f]I have chosen thee for Myself;

وَٱصْطَنَعْتُكَ لِنَفْسِى ﴿٤٢﴾

43. [g]'Go, thou and thy brother, with My Signs, and slacken not in remembering Me;

ٱذْهَبْ أَنتَ وَأَخُوكَ بِـَٔايَٰتِى وَلَا تَنِيَا فِى ذِكْرِى ﴿٤٣﴾

---

[a]28 : 8-9. [b]28 : 9. [c]28 : 12-13. [d]28 : 14. 28 : 16,34. 12 : 55. [g]28 : 36.

1821. *Mā* being *Māṣdariyyah*, the verb following it imparts to it an intensiveness of meaning. The expression *Mā Yūḥā* thus means, an important revelation; or what was necessary to be revealed at that time.

1822. *'Ain* means (1) the eye; (2) inmates of a house; (3) protection (Lane). As Moses was to have been entrusted with the great and difficult task of delivering a people, held in bondage for long by a cruel and powerful monarch, it was necessary that he should have received the requisite training for the great mission under royal tutors and teachers. So it was in fulfilment of this Divine plan that Moses found his way into Pharaoh's own house.

1823. The sojourn of Moses among the people of Midian fulfilled yet another Divine plan. As he was destined to live with the Israelites in the deserts and forests of the Valley of Sinai, he was made to become used to a hard life by living for several years in Midian.

44. [a]"Go, both of you, to Pharaoh, for he has transgressed *all* bounds ;

اِذْهَبَآ اِلٰى فِرْعَوْنَ اِنَّهٗ طَغٰى ﴿٤٤﴾

45. 'But speak to him a gentle word,[1824] haply he might take heed or fear.'

فَقُوْلَا لَهٗ قَوْلًا لَّيِّنًا لَّعَلَّهٗ يَتَذَكَّرُ اَوْ يَخْشٰى ﴿٤٥﴾

46. They replied, [b]"Our Lord, we fear lest he commit some excess against us, or exceed *all* bounds *in persecuting us*.'

قَالَا رَبَّنَآ اِنَّنَا نَخَافُ اَنْ يَّفْرُطَ عَلَيْنَآ اَوْ اَنْ
يَّطْغٰى ﴿٤٦﴾

47. *God* said, 'Fear not ; for I am with you both. I hear and I see.'

قَالَ لَا تَخَافَآ اِنَّنِيْ مَعَكُمَآ اَسْمَعُ وَاَرٰى ﴿٤٧﴾

48. "So go ye both to him and say, 'We are the Messengers of thy Lord; so let the Children of Israel go with us; and torment them not. We have, indeed, brought thee a great Sign from thy Lord; and peace shall be on him who follows the guidance ;

فَاْتِيٰهُ فَقُوْلَآ اِنَّا رَسُوْلَا رَبِّكَ فَاَرْسِلْ مَعَنَا بَنِيْٓ
اِسْرَآءِيْلَ ۙ۬ وَلَا تُعَذِّبْهُمْ ؕ قَدْ جِئْنٰكَ بِاٰيَةٍ مِّنْ
رَّبِّكَ ؕ وَالسَّلٰمُ عَلٰى مَنِ اتَّبَعَ الْهُدٰى ﴿٤٨﴾

49. 'It has, indeed, been revealed to us that punishment shall come upon him who rejects *the Message of God* and turns away."

اِنَّا قَدْ اُوْحِيَ اِلَيْنَآ اَنَّ الْعَذَابَ عَلٰى مَنْ كَذَّبَ
وَتَوَلّٰى ﴿٤٩﴾

50. *Pharaoh* said, "Who then is the Lord of you two, O Moses?'

قَالَ فَمَنْ رَّبُّكُمَا يٰمُوْسٰى ﴿٥٠﴾

51. *Moses* said, 'Our Lord is He [d]Who gave unto everything its proper form *and* then guided[1825] it *to its proper function*.'

قَالَ رَبُّنَا الَّذِيْٓ اَعْطٰى كُلَّ شَيْءٍ خَلْقَهٗ ثُمَّ هَدٰى ﴿٥١﴾

[a]79 : 18. [b]26 : 13 [c]26 : 24. [d]87 : 3-4.

1824. The verse teaches a two-fold lesson to a religious teacher or preacher. He should use gentle language when preaching. He should also show due respect to those whom God has endowed with worldly honour or has placed in the seat of authority.

1825. The verse means that there exists perfect order in the world and that God has endowed everything with properties which are best suited to its particular requirements and needs, and by making proper use of which it can attain its fullest development.

52. *Pharaoh* said, 'What will be the fate of the former generations?'[1826]

قَالَ فَمَا بَالُ الْقُرُوْنِ الْاُوْلٰى ﴿۵۲﴾

53. *Moses* said, 'The knowledge thereof is with my Lord *preserved* in a Book. My Lord neither errs [a]nor forgets;[1827]

قَالَ عِلْمُهَا عِنْدَ رَبِّيْ فِيْ كِتٰبٍ ۚ لَا يَضِلُّ رَبِّيْ وَ لَا يَنْسَى ﴿۵۳﴾

54. [b]'*It is He* Who has made the earth for you a bed and has caused pathways for you to run through it; and Who sends down rain from the sky and thereby We bring forth various kinds of vegetation in pairs;

الَّذِيْ جَعَلَ لَكُمُ الْاَرْضَ مَهْدًا وَّ سَلَكَ لَكُمْ فِيْهَا سُبُلًا وَّ اَنْزَلَ مِنَ السَّمَآءِ مَآءً ۚ فَاَخْرَجْنَا بِهٖۤ اَزْوَاجًا مِّنْ نَّبَاتٍ شَتّٰى ﴿۵۴﴾

55. [c]'Eat ye and pasture your cattle. Verily, in this are Signs for those endowed with reason.'

كُلُوْا وَ ارْعَوْا اَنْعَامَكُمْ ۚ اِنَّ فِيْ ذٰلِكَ لَاٰيٰتٍ لِّاُولِي النُّهٰى ﴿۵۵﴾ ع

R. 3 56. [d]From this *earth* have We created you, and into it shall We cause you to return, and from it shall We bring you forth a second time.

مِنْهَا خَلَقْنٰكُمْ وَ فِيْهَا نُعِيْدُكُمْ وَ مِنْهَا نُخْرِجُكُمْ تَارَةً اُخْرٰى ﴿۵۶﴾

57. And [e]We did show *Pharaoh* Our Signs, all of them; but he rejected *them* and refused *to believe*.

وَ لَقَدْ اَرَيْنٰهُ اٰيٰتِنَا كُلَّهَا فَكَذَّبَ وَ اَبٰى ﴿۵۷﴾

---

[a]19 : 65. [b]43 : 11. [c]10 : 25; 25 : 50; 32 : 28. [d]7 : 26; 71 : 18-19. [e]27 : 13-15; 43 : 48-49; 79 : 21-22.

1826. Moses's reply to Pharaoh's query contained in the previous verse seemed to have entirely confounded the latter, so he adroitly turned away from the subject which he himself had started and put Moses a new question, asking him whether his God knew anything about the former generations who were dead and gone, meaning how they would fare when they had not had the benefit of receiving guidance from him (Moses). Thus in a subtle manner Pharaoh sought to incite his people against Moses by making an oblique hint that he (Moses) had insinuated that their forefathers were bereft of Heavenly guidance and, therefore, were deserving of Divine punishment.

1827. Moses gives a crushing reply to Pharaoh's evasive tactics. He tells Pharaoh that he should not bother about the former generations. God knew all about them and every detail concerning them was well-preserved in His knowledge and on the Day of Resurrection He would requite them all according to their deeds and actions, taking into consideration their particular conditions and circumstances.

58. He said, [a]"Hast thou come to us, O Moses, to drive us out of our land by thy magic?[1828]

قَالَ أَجِئْتَنَا لِتُخْرِجَنَا مِنْ أَرْضِنَا بِسِحْرِكَ يٰمُوسٰى ﴿٥٨﴾

59. [b]'But we shall assuredly bring thee magic the like thereof; so make an appointment between us and thyself which we shall not fail to keep—neither we nor thou—at a place alike *for us both.*'

فَلَنَأْتِيَنَّكَ بِسِحْرٍ مِّثْلِهِ فَاجْعَلْ بَيْنَنَا وَبَيْنَكَ مَوْعِدًا لَّا نُخْلِفُهُ نَحْنُ وَلَآ أَنْتَ مَكَانًا سُوًى ﴿٥٩﴾

60. *Moses* said, [c]'Your appointment shall be the day of the festival and let the people be assembled when the sun is risen high.'[1829]

قَالَ مَوْعِدُكُمْ يَوْمُ الزِّينَةِ وَأَنْ يُّحْشَرَ النَّاسُ ضُحًى ﴿٦٠﴾

61. Then Pharaoh withdrew and concerted his plan[1830] and then came *to the place of appointment.*

فَتَوَلّٰى فِرْعَوْنُ فَجَمَعَ كَيْدَهٗ ثُمَّ أَتٰى ﴿٦١﴾

62. . Moses said to them, 'Woe to you, forge not a lie against Allāh, lest He destroy you utterly by some punishment and, surely, he who forges a lie shall perish.'[1831]

قَالَ لَهُمْ مُّوسٰى وَيْلَكُمْ لَا تَفْتَرُوْا عَلَى اللّٰهِ كَذِبًا فَيُسْحِتَكُمْ بِعَذَابٍ ۚ وَقَدْ خَابَ مَنِ افْتَرٰى ﴿٦٢﴾

63. Then they argued their affair among themselves and conferred in secret.

فَتَنَازَعُوْٓا أَمْرَهُمْ بَيْنَهُمْ وَأَسَرُّوا النَّجْوٰى ﴿٦٣﴾

[a]26 : 36. [b]7 : 112,113; 26 : 37. [c]26 : 39.

1828. This verse seems to refer to an insidious device of Pharaoh. He told his people that Moses who was a foreigner in Egypt was seeking to turn the ruling dynasty out of Egypt by his clever manoeuvres.

1829. There seems a curious analogy here between Moses and the Holy Prophet, *viz.*, that whereas the contest between Moses and the magicians in which they were fully and finally routed took place at the time of *Ḍuḥā*, the Holy Prophet also entered Mecca as conqueror at the time of *Ḍuḥā* which marked the final defeat of disbelief and idolatry in Arabia.

1830. The expression, *Jama'a Kaida-hū*, besides the meaning given in the text, may also mean : He mustered all his designs ; he contrived all sorts of plans ; he did all that he could do.

1831. The verse lays down an infallible criterion to test the truth of a claimant to Divine revelation, *viz.*, that a forger of lies against God, though he may appear to progress and prosper for a short while, ultimately perishes and comes to a miserable and ignoble end. This is a truth writ large on the pages of all religious history.

64. They said, 'Certainly [a]these two are magicians who seek to drive you out from your land by their magic and to destroy your best way of life ;[1831A]

قالوا إن هذان لساحران يريدان أن يخرجاكم من أرضكم بسحرهما ويذهبا بطريقتكم المثلى ﴿٦٤﴾

65. 'Concert, therefore, your plan; and then come forward in a body. And, surely, he who gains ascendancy this day shall prosper.'

فأجمعوا كيدكم ثم ائتوا صفا وقد أفلح اليوم من استعلى ﴿٦٥﴾

66. [b]They said, 'O Moses, either do thou cast first, or we shall be the first to cast.'

قالوا يا موسى إما أن تلقي وإما أن نكون أول من ألقى ﴿٦٦﴾

67. [c]*Moses* said, 'Nay, cast[1832] ye.' Then lo! their cords and their staves [d]appeared[1833] to him, by their magic, as though they ran about.

قال بل ألقوا فإذا حبالهم وعصيهم يخيل إليه من سحرهم أنها تسعى ﴿٦٧﴾

68. And Moses conceived a fear in his mind.[1834]

فأوجس في نفسه خيفة موسى ﴿٦٨﴾

69. We said, 'Fear not, for thou wilt have the upper hand;

قلنا لا تخف إنك أنت الأعلى ﴿٦٩﴾

---

[a]7 : 110-111; 26 : 35-36. [b]7 : 116. [c]7 : 117; 26 : 44. [d]7 : 117.

1831A. *Ṭarīqah* means, way of life ; ideal ; institution, tradition (Lane).

1832. God's Prophets never take the offensive. They wait till they are attacked and then they defend themselves.

1833. The cords and staves of the magicians appeared to Moses only as though they ran about. Actually they did nothing of the kind. The forces of evil at first appear to carry the day for a short while, but they soon come to grief.

1834. Moses was not afraid of the cords and staves of the magicians. The Prophets of God stand on a rock of certainty and are never afraid of anything. Moses only feared lest the people should be led astray by the antics of the magicians.

70. 'And cast that which is in thy right hand; [a]it will swallow that which they have wrought,[1835] for that which they have wrought is only a sorcerer's trick. And a sorcerer shall not thrive, contrive[1835A] what he may:

وَأَلْقِ مَا فِي يَمِينِكَ تَلْقَفْ مَا صَنَعُوا ۖ إِنَّمَا صَنَعُوا
كَيْدُ سَاحِرٍ ۖ وَلَا يُفْلِحُ السَّاحِرُ حَيْثُ أَتَىٰ ﴿٧٠﴾

71. Then [b]*the realization of the truth* made the sorcerers fall down prostrate. They said, [c]"We believe in the Lord of Aaron and Moses.'

فَأُلْقِيَ السَّحَرَةُ سُجَّدًا قَالُوا آمَنَّا بِرَبِّ هَارُونَ
وَمُوسَىٰ ﴿٧١﴾

72. *Pharaoh* said, [d]"Do you believe in him before I give you leave? He must be your chief who has taught you magic. [e]I will, therefore, surely cut off your hands and your feet on alternate sides[1835B], and I will surely crucify you on the trunks of palm trees; and you shall know which of us can impose severer and more abiding punishment.'

قَالَ آمَنتُمْ لَهُ قَبْلَ أَنْ آذَنَ لَكُمْ ۖ إِنَّهُ لَكَبِيرُكُمُ
الَّذِي عَلَّمَكُمُ السِّحْرَ ۖ فَلَأُقَطِّعَنَّ أَيْدِيَكُمْ وَ
أَرْجُلَكُم مِّنْ خِلَافٍ وَلَأُصَلِّبَنَّكُمْ فِي جُذُوعِ
النَّخْلِ وَلَتَعْلَمُنَّ أَيُّنَا أَشَدُّ عَذَابًا وَأَبْقَىٰ ﴿٧٢﴾

73. They said, 'We shall not prefer thee to the manifest Signs that have come to us, nor *shall we prefer thee* to Him Who has created us. [f]So decree what thou wilt decree; thou canst only decree concerning this present life;[1836]

قَالُوا لَن نُّؤْثِرَكَ عَلَىٰ مَا جَاءَنَا مِنَ الْبَيِّنَاتِ وَ
الَّذِي فَطَرَنَا ۖ فَاقْضِ مَا أَنتَ قَاضٍ ۖ إِنَّمَا تَقْضِي
هَٰذِهِ الْحَيَاةَ الدُّنْيَا ﴿٧٣﴾

[a]7 : 118; 26 : 46. [b]7 : 121; 26 : 47. [c]7 : 122-123; 26 : 48-49. [d]7 : 124; 26 : 50. [e]7 : 125; 26 : 50. [f]26 : 51.

1835. The verse makes it clear that it was the rod of Moses and not anything else which "swallowed" that which the sorcerers had wrought, and which undid their sorcery. The rod of Moses wielded with the spiritual force of a great Divine Prophet and thrown at the command of Almighty God exposed the deception that the sorcerers had wrought on the spectators by their tricks. Elsewhere in the Qur'ān, the staves and cords of the sorcerers have been described as their lies (7 : 118).

1835A. *Atā al-Shai'a* means, he did the thing (Lane).

1835B. The particle *min* also means, on account of, or because of and *Khilāf* means, opposition (Lane)

1836. Mark the wonderful change that true faith works in man. The greedy and materialistic sorcerers who only a short while ago were asking for reward from Pharaoh, in the form of money, position or honour (7 : 114), became quite indifferent even to the most horrible form of death with which he threatened them when they had found and accepted the truth.

74. 'Surely, [a]we have believed in our Lord that He may forgive us our sins and *forgive us* the magic which thou didst force us *to practise*. And Allāh is the Best and the Most Abiding.'

اِنَّآ اٰمَنَّا بِرَبِّنَا لِيَغْفِرَ لَنَا خَطٰيٰنَا وَمَآ اَكْرَهْتَنَا عَلَيْهِ مِنَ السِّحْرِ ؕ وَاللّٰهُ خَيْرٌ وَّاَبْقٰى ﴿۷۴﴾ النصف

75. Verily, he who comes to his Lord a sinner—for him is Hell; he shall neither die therein nor live.[1837]

اِنَّهٗ مَنْ يَّاْتِ رَبَّهٗ مُجْرِمًا فَاِنَّ لَهٗ جَهَنَّمَ ؕ لَا يَمُوْتُ فِيْهَا وَلَا يَحْيٰى ﴿۷۵﴾

76. But he who comes to Him a believer, having done good deeds, [b]for such are the highest ranks—

وَمَنْ يَّاْتِهٖ مُؤْمِنًا قَدْ عَمِلَ الصّٰلِحٰتِ فَاُولٰٓئِكَ لَهُمُ الدَّرَجٰتُ الْعُلٰى ۙ﴿۷۶﴾

77. [c]Gardens of Eternity, beneath which streams flow; they will abide therein *for ever*. And that is the recompense of those who keep themselves pure.

جَنّٰتُ عَدْنٍ تَجْرِيْ مِنْ تَحْتِهَا الْاَنْهٰرُ خٰلِدِيْنَ فِيْهَا ؕ وَذٰلِكَ جَزٰٓؤُا مَنْ تَزَكّٰى ﴿۷۷﴾ ع

R. 4 78. And [d]We directed Moses by revelation: 'Take away My servants by night, and [e]strike for them a dry path through the sea, fearing not to be overtaken, nor having *any other* fear.'[1838]

وَلَقَدْ اَوْحَيْنَآ اِلٰى مُوْسٰٓى ۙ اَنْ اَسْرِ بِعِبَادِيْ فَاضْرِبْ لَهُمْ طَرِيْقًا فِي الْبَحْرِ يَبَسًا ۙ لَّا تَخٰفُ دَرَكًا وَّلَا تَخْشٰى ﴿۷۸﴾

---

[a]7 : 127; 26 : 52. [b]4 : 96-97; 8 : 5. [c]9 : 72; 18 : 32; 19 : 62; 61 : 13. [d]26 : 53. [e]26 : 64.

1837. Death delivers man from pain. So the sinners will not die in Hell and will continue to suffer its torment. Neither will they live therein, because real life consists in the enjoyment of Divine love, and they will be deprived of it. Or, the verse may mean that the sinners will be completely deprived of all comfort and happiness and this condition is described here as worse than death.

1838. Against all unimpeachable historical data, most extraordinary theories have been propounded about the Israelites, *viz.*, (*a*) they never lived in Egypt; because no reference to them is to be found in the old Egyptian historical records. (*b*) In the fifth year of the reign of Pharaoh Meneptah (or Merenptah) when Moses is said to have taken the Israelites out of Egypt, some Israelite tribes were actually living in Canaan, therefore the theory that Moses had taken the Israelites out of Egypt to Canaan during his reign and that they settled there some fifty years later is all wrong.

The propounders of these strange theories seem to forget that the Israelites were foreigners in Egypt and were a subject race and had lived the miserable life of serfs and slaves under their cruel rulers. How could such people be considered worthy of any notice being taken

79. [a]Then Pharaoh pursued them with his hosts, and *the waters* of the sea completely covered them.

فَأَتْبَعَهُمْ فِرْعَوْنُ بِجُنُودِهِ فَغَشِيَهُم مِّنَ الْيَمِّ
مَا غَشِيَهُمْ ﴿٧٩﴾

80. And Pharaoh led his people astray and did not guide them aright.

وَأَضَلَّ فِرْعَوْنُ قَوْمَهُ وَمَا هَدَىٰ ﴿٨٠﴾

81. O Children of Israel, [b]We delivered you from your enemy, and We made a covenant with you on [c]the right side of the Mount, and sent down on you Manna and Salwā.[1839]

يَٰبَنِيٓ إِسْرَٰٓءِيلَ قَدْ أَنجَيْنَٰكُم مِّنْ عَدُوِّكُمْ وَ
وَٰعَدْنَٰكُمْ جَانِبَ الطُّورِ الْأَيْمَنَ وَنَزَّلْنَا عَلَيْكُمُ
الْمَنَّ وَالسَّلْوَىٰ ﴿٨١﴾

[a]10 : 91; 26 : 61. [b]2 : 51; 14 : 7; 44 : 31-32. [c]19 : 53; 20 : 13; 28 : 31; 79 : 17.

of them by historians ? When even in this 20th century historians cannot find it easy to prepare a well-connected and harmonious narrative about a people from the remnants of its ruined civilization, it was much more difficult for historians in the remote past to reconstruct a consistent record from the fragmentary accounts of a people who lived in the hoary past and who were treated like beasts of burden by their rulers. As to the doubtful theory that certain Israelite tribes were found to be living in Canaan in the 5th year of the reign of Pharaoh Meneptah, it cannot disprove the fact that other Israelite tribes had remained behind in Egypt. Is it not possible that some of these tribes might have left Egypt for Canaan sometime before all of them were taken out of it by Moses ? It is strange that on the one hand these very writers say that Moses is an Egyptian name and that some of the Israelites also had Egyptian names, and on the other that they never went to Egypt. Moreover, the Bible gives a detailed and well-connected story of the Israelites having lived in Egypt. There was no compelling reason for the writers of the Bible to have done so, especially when the Israelites had lived there only as slaves and worse than beasts of burden. No people would feel any urge or pride in forging and falsely inventing such a miserable record of shame and sorrow of themselves. The biblical details with regard to the customs, culture and mode of life of the Pharaohs of that time is another proof of the fact that the Israelites had lived there. The Bible had no interest in the Pharaoh dynasty of Egypt apart from the fact that they were rulers of the Israelites. Besides, as stated by ancient Greek historians, the Egyptians themselves had admitted that the Israelites had lived in Egypt for a long time and later on had left this country. The present Egypt, however, should not be confused with the territory which in ancient times was also known as Egypt, but which formed a part of northern Syria or northern Arabia.

The date of the Exodus has also been much contested and there seems to be considerable difficulty in determining its exact date from the biblical records alone. The theory, largely prevalent, which receives much support from historical data, archaeological research and Hebrew tradition is that the Exodus occurred in the Nineteenth Dynasty (1328-1202 B.C.), in the reign of Merenptah II or Meneptah II (1234-1214 B.C.) and still seems to be the most probable one. The Exodus appears to have taken place about 1230 B.C. According to this view the Pharaoh of the Oppression was Rameses II, and his successor Merenptah II, the Pharaoh of the Exodus ("Peake's Commentary on the Bible" pp. 119, 955, 956). See also "The Larger Edition of the Commentary" pp. 1646—1647.

1839. The Israelites had lived long in bondage under the heartless tyranny of the Pharaohs and consequently had come to lose all those manly qualities that go to make a people hardy, brave and courageous. According to the Divine scheme of things, they were destined to conquer and rule over Canaan. Therefore, after Moses had taken them out of Egypt, they were made to live in the arid and barren region of Sinai in order that they might

82. *And admonished you:* [a]'Eat of the good things that We have provided for you, and transgress not therein, lest My wrath descend upon you; and he, on whom My wrath descends, shall perish;[1840]

كُلُوا مِنْ طَيِّبٰتِ مَا رَزَقْنٰكُمْ وَلَا تَطْغَوْا فِيْهِ فَيَحِلَّ عَلَيْكُمْ غَضَبِيْ ۚ وَمَنْ يَّحْلِلْ عَلَيْهِ غَضَبِيْ فَقَدْ هَوٰى ﴿٨٢﴾

83. 'But, [b]surely, I am All-Forgiving to him who repents and believes and does righteous deeds, then sticks to guidance.'

وَاِنِّيْ لَغَفَّارٌ لِّمَنْ تَابَ وَاٰمَنَ وَعَمِلَ صَالِحًا ثُمَّ اهْتَدٰى ﴿٨٣﴾

84. *When Moses arrived for his tryst with his Lord He said,* 'And what has made thee hasten away from thy people, O Moses ?'

وَمَآ اَعْجَلَكَ عَنْ قَوْمِكَ يٰمُوْسٰى ﴿٨٤﴾

85. He said, 'They are *closely following* in my footsteps and I have hastened to Thee, my Lord, that Thou mightest be pleased.'

قَالَ هُمْ اُولَآءِ عَلٰٓى اَثَرِيْ وَعَجِلْتُ اِلَيْكَ رَبِّ لِتَرْضٰى ﴿٨٥﴾

86. *God* said, [c]'We have tried thy people in thy absence, and the Sāmirī[1841] has led them astray.'

قَالَ فَاِنَّا قَدْ فَتَنَّا قَوْمَكَ مِنْ بَعْدِكَ وَاَضَلَّهُمُ السَّامِرِيُّ ﴿٨٦﴾

[a]2 : 58; 7 : 161. [b]3 : 136; 39 : 54. [c]7 : 149.

become used to an open and hard life and thus acquire and develop those qualities which were so essential for a great future that lay in store for them. But having lived in bondage for a long time, they had lost all initiative and had become used to a life of lethargy and lassitude. So when they saw that they would have to live in the wilderness where no amenities of life were to be found and even food was lacking, they were utterly dismayed and fretted and fumed and quarrelled with Moses saying, 'Would to God, we had died by the hand of the Lord in the land of Egypt when we sat by the flesh pots, and when we did eat bread to the full; for ye have brought us forth into this wilderness to kill this whole assembly with hunger' (Exod. 16 : 3). God heard their murmurings and commanded Moses to tell those ungrateful people, 'As even ye shall eat flesh, and in the morning ye shall be filled with bread; and ye shall know that I am the Lord, your God.' And how this Divine promise was fulfilled has been fully described in the Bible (Exod. 16 : 12-15). See also 98 & 99.

1840. See 1839.

1841. *Sāmirī* may be a relative noun from *Sāmirah* (the Samaritans), a people said to be one of the tribes of the Children of Israel ; or a sect of the Jews, differing from them in many of their institutions. Properly speaking, they were inhabitants of Samaria. The name is now restricted to a small tribe of people living in Nablus and calling themselves "Bene Yisrael." Their history as a distinct community began with the taking of Samaria by the Assyrians in 722 B.C. (Lane & Jew. Enc.).

87. So [a]Moses returned to his people, angry and sad, *and* he said, 'O my people, did not your Lord promise you a gracious promise? Did, then, the time *of its fulfilment* appear too long to you, or did you desire that wrath should descend upon you from your Lord, that you broke *your* promise to me?'

فَرَجَعَ مُوسَىٰٓ إِلَىٰ قَوْمِهِۦ غَضْبَٰنَ أَسِفًا ۚ قَالَ يَٰقَوْمِ أَلَمْ يَعِدْكُمْ رَبُّكُمْ وَعْدًا حَسَنًا ۚ أَفَطَالَ عَلَيْكُمُ ٱلْعَهْدُ أَمْ أَرَدتُّمْ أَن يَحِلَّ عَلَيْكُمْ غَضَبٌ مِّن رَّبِّكُمْ فَأَخْلَفْتُم مَّوْعِدِى ﴿٨٧﴾

88. They said, 'We did not break *our* promise to thee of our own accord; but we were laden with loads of people's ornaments[1842] and we cast them away, and likewise did the Sāmirī cast *away*.'

قَالُوا۟ مَآ أَخْلَفْنَا مَوْعِدَكَ بِمَلْكِنَا وَلَٰكِنَّا حُمِّلْنَآ أَوْزَارًا مِّن زِينَةِ ٱلْقَوْمِ فَقَذَفْنَٰهَا فَكَذَٰلِكَ أَلْقَى ٱلسَّامِرِىُّ ﴿٨٨﴾

89. Then he produced for them [b]a calf—a mere body which emitted a lowing sound. Then *he and his companions* said, 'This is your god, and the god of Moses[1843] but he has forgotten it *and left it behind*.'

فَأَخْرَجَ لَهُمْ عِجْلًا جَسَدًا لَّهُۥ خُوَارٌ فَقَالُوا۟ هَٰذَآ إِلَٰهُكُمْ وَإِلَٰهُ مُوسَىٰ فَنَسِىَ ﴿٨٩﴾

90. Could they not see that it returned to them no answer,[1844] and had no power to do them either harm or good?

أَفَلَا يَرَوْنَ أَلَّا يَرْجِعُ إِلَيْهِمْ قَوْلًا وَلَا يَمْلِكُ لَهُمْ
ضَرًّا وَلَا نَفْعًا ﴿٩٠﴾ ع ٤ ١٣

[a]7 : 151. [b]2 : 52,93; 4 : 154; 7 : 149.

1842. Whereas the Qur'ān in this verse says that the Egyptians gave the Israelites jewels of gold and silver of their own accord, the Bible accuses them of having despoiled the Egyptians of their ornaments (Exod. 12 : 36). But, as generally is the case, in this respect also, the Bible has contradicted itself. At another place (Exod. 12 : 33) it says that the Egyptians themselves gave the ornaments to the Israelites and insisted that they should leave Egypt forthwith. Reason and common sense support the Quranic statement.

1843. The Israelites had lived in Egypt under bondage for a long time and during their bondage they had adopted many of the customs, ways of life and religious rites of their rulers, the Egyptians, who worshipped the cow (Enc. Rel. & Ethics, vol. 1, p. 507). In this way they had developed a great liking for the cow, and taking advantage of Moses's absence the Sāmirī led them into cow-worship.

1844. The calf is denounced and condemned as a deity because it does not speak to its votaries. Of what use is that god who does not answer the prayer of his worshippers (21 : 66-67)? He is as dead as a log of wood. The difference between a living and a lifeless god is that the One speaks to His votaries and hears their supplications, while the other does not. The God of Islām has not ceased to speak to His true worshippers. He still speaks to them as He spoke to Adam, Abraham, Moses, Jesus and the Holy Prophet Muḥammad (peace be upon them all) and will continue to do so till the end of time.

R. 5 91. And Aaron had said to them before *the return of Moses*, 'O my people, you have only been tried by means of *the calf*. And, surely, the Gracious *God* is your Lord, so follow me and obey my command.'[1845]

وَلَقَدْ قَالَ لَهُمْ هٰرُوْنُ مِنْ قَبْلُ يٰقَوْمِ اِنَّمَا
فُتِنْتُمْ بِهٖ ۚ وَاِنَّ رَبَّكُمُ الرَّحْمٰنُ فَاتَّبِعُوْنِيْ وَاَطِيْعُوْٓا
اَمْرِيْ ﴿٩١﴾

92. They replied, 'We shall not cease to worship it until Moses return to us.'

قَالُوْا لَنْ نَّبْرَحَ عَلَيْهِ عٰكِفِيْنَ حَتّٰى يَرْجِعَ اِلَيْنَا
مُوْسٰى ﴿٩٢﴾

93. *Moses* said, 'O Aaron, what prevented thee, when thou didst see them gone astray

قَالَ يٰهٰرُوْنُ مَا مَنَعَكَ اِذْ رَاَيْتَهُمْ ضَلُّوْٓا ۙ﴿٩٣﴾

94. 'From following me? Didst thou then disobey my command?'

اَلَّا تَتَّبِعَنِ ۭ اَفَعَصَيْتَ اَمْرِيْ ﴿٩٤﴾

95. *Aaron* answered, [a]'Son of my mother, seize *me* not by my beard, nor by *the hair of* my head. I feared lest thou shouldst say: 'Thou hast caused a division among the Children of Israel, and didst not wait for my word.'

قَالَ يَبْنَؤُمَّ لَا تَاْخُذْ بِلِحْيَتِيْ وَلَا بِرَاْسِيْ ۚ اِنِّيْ
خَشِيْتُ اَنْ تَقُوْلَ فَرَّقْتَ بَيْنَ بَنِيْٓ اِسْرَآءِيْلَ
وَلَمْ تَرْقُبْ قَوْلِيْ ﴿٩٥﴾

96. *Moses* said, 'And what then is thy plea,[1846] O Sāmirī?'

قَالَ فَمَا خَطْبُكَ يٰسَامِرِيُّ ﴿٩٦﴾

97. He said, 'I perceived what they perceived not.[1847] I had *only* adopted part of what the Messenger (Moses) inculcated, but I threw *even that* away. Thus it is that my mind commended to me.'

قَالَ بَصُرْتُ بِمَا لَمْ يَبْصُرُوْا بِهٖ فَقَبَضْتُ قَبْضَةً
مِّنْ اَثَرِ الرَّسُوْلِ فَنَبَذْتُهَا وَكَذٰلِكَ سَوَّلَتْ لِيْ نَفْسِيْ ﴿٩٧﴾

[a]7 : 151.

1845. The Qur'ān here contradicts the Bible and clears Aaron of the charge of having made a molten calf for the Israelites to worship (Exod. 32 : 4). It says that not only did Aaron not fashion the calf for them, on the other hand he prohibited them from worshipping the one which the Sāmirī had made for them. The charge has been dismissed as unfounded by Christian writers themselves (Enc. Brit. under "The Golden Calf").

1846. *Khaṭb* means, object; design; case or plea; business; affair; etc. (Lane). The whole sentence also means, what thou hast to say (Lane).

1847. The words may also mean, 'My mental perception was clearer than that of the Israelites.' The Sāmirī means to say that he had followed Moses and had accepted his teachings intelligently and not blindly like them. But when Moses went to the Mount, he

98. *Moses* said, "Begone then! It shall be thine all this life to say *to everyone*, 'Touch *me* not,'[1848] and there is a promise *of punishment* for thee which shall not fail to be fulfilled about thee. Now, look at thy god of which thou hast become a devoted worshipper. We will certainly burn it and then We will scatter its *ashes* into the sea;

قَالَ فَاذْهَبْ فَإِنَّ لَكَ فِي الْحَيٰوةِ أَنْ تَقُولَ لَا
مِسَاسَ وَإِنَّ لَكَ مَوْعِدًا لَّنْ تُخْلَفَهُ وَانْظُرْ
إِلٰٓى إِلٰهِكَ الَّذِي ظَلْتَ عَلَيْهِ عَاكِفًا لَّنُحَرِّقَنَّهُ ثُمَّ
لَنَنْسِفَنَّهُ فِي الْيَمِّ نَسْفًا ﴿٩٨﴾

99. 'Your God is only Allāh, there is no god but He. He comprehends all things in *His* knowledge.'

إِنَّمَآ إِلٰهُكُمُ اللّٰهُ الَّذِي لَآ إِلٰهَ إِلَّا هُوَ وَسِعَ كُلَّ
شَيْءٍ عِلْمًا ﴿٩٩﴾

100. Thus do We relate to thee the tidings of what has happened before. And We have given thee from Us a Reminder.

كَذٰلِكَ نَقُصُّ عَلَيْكَ مِنْ أَنْبَآءِ مَا قَدْ سَبَقَ
وَقَدْ اٰتَيْنٰكَ مِنْ لَّدُنَّا ذِكْرًا ﴿١٠٠﴾

101. Whoso [a]turns away from it, he will surely bear a heavy burden on the Day of Resurrection,

مَنْ أَعْرَضَ عَنْهُ فَإِنَّهُ يَحْمِلُ يَوْمَ الْقِيٰمَةِ وِزْرًا ﴿١٠١﴾

102. Abiding thereunder, and evil will the burden be to them on the Day of Resurrection;

خٰلِدِينَ فِيهِ وَسَآءَ لَهُمْ يَوْمَ الْقِيٰمَةِ حِمْلًا ﴿١٠٢﴾

103. The day when [b]the trumpet will be blown. And on that day We shall gather the sinful together, blue-eyed.[1849]

يَوْمَ يُنْفَخُ فِي الصُّورِ وَنَحْشُرُ الْمُجْرِمِينَ يَوْمَئِذٍ
زُرْقًا ﴿١٠٣﴾

---

[a]18 : 102; 43 : 37. 72 : 18. [b]18 : 100; 27 : 88; 36 : 52; 78: 19.

---

threw away the cloak of expediency and discarded what little of his teachings (*athar*, meaning remains or relics of knowledge transmitted or handed down from the former generations, *i.e.*, teachings) he had accepted and that was what his mind suggested to him.

1848. The words 'Touch me not' may signify : (*a*) That the Sāmirī was punished with a rigorous social boycott for having misled the Israelites into calf-worship. (*b*) That he was afflicted with some contagious skin disease so that people avoided contact with him. (*c*) That he suffered from hypochondriasis and consequently shunned the company of men.

1849. The allusion in this verse primarily seems to be to the Western Christian nations who have blue eyes and are spiritually blind and possess an undying hatred for Islām.

104. They will talk to one another in a low tone *saying*, 'You tarried only ten *days*.'[1850]

يَتَخَافَتُونَ بَيْنَهُمْ إِن لَّبِثْتُمْ إِلَّا عَشْرًا ﴿١٠٤﴾

105. We know best what they will say—when the one most upright in conduct among them will say, [1850A] 'You have tarried only a day.'

نَحْنُ أَعْلَمُ بِمَا يَقُولُونَ إِذْ يَقُولُ أَمْثَلُهُمْ طَرِيقَةً إِن لَّبِثْتُمْ إِلَّا يَوْمًا ﴿١٠٥﴾

R. 6 106. And [a]they ask thee concerning the mountains.[1851] Say, 'My Lord will break them into pieces and scatter them as dust;

وَيَسْأَلُونَكَ عَنِ الْجِبَالِ فَقُلْ يَنسِفُهَا رَبِّي نَسْفًا ﴿١٠٦﴾

107. 'And He will leave them a barren, level plain;

فَيَذَرُهَا قَاعًا صَفْصَفًا ﴿١٠٧﴾

108. 'Wherein thou wilt see no depression or elevation.'[1852]

لَّا تَرَىٰ فِيهَا عِوَجًا وَلَا أَمْتًا ﴿١٠٨﴾

109. On that day they will follow the Caller[1853] *in* whose *teaching* is no crookedness; and *all* voices shall be hushed before the Gracious *God* and thou shalt not hear but a subdued murmur.

يَوْمَئِذٍ يَتَّبِعُونَ الدَّاعِيَ لَا عِوَجَ لَهُ وَخَشَعَتِ الْأَصْوَاتُ لِلرَّحْمَٰنِ فَلَا تَسْمَعُ إِلَّا هَمْسًا ﴿١٠٩﴾

[a]56 : 6; 70 : 10; 101 : 6.

1850. "Ten days" here signifies ten centuries. The reference is to the ten centuries after the *Hijrah* during which the European nations remained almost in a state of dormancy. It was in the beginning of the 17th century, about one thousand years after the Holy Prophet began to preach his mission in the beginning of the 7th century A.D., that the nations of Europe came out of their hibernation and began to spread over the world and conquer it.

1850A. *Ṭarīqat al-Qaum* means, best or most upright of the people (Aqrab). *Yaum* here signifies one thousand years referred to in 22 : 48 and corresponds to 'ten days' of the preceding verse, *i.e.*, ten centuries or a thousand years. *Yaum* also means time absolutely. In this sense of the word the disbelievers, when they are seized with Divine punishment, are depicted as saying that the time of their prosperity and progress was but a day, *i.e.*, very short.

1851. The reference in the word *al-Jibāl* (mountains) here is to the powerful Christian nations of the West. The prophecy in this verse is in regard to their complete destruction. The decline of the West has already begun. The last two World Wars have greatly weakened it (Spengler's "Decline of the West" & Toynbee's "A Study of History"). See also 1666.

1852. The allusion seems to be to the rise of Socialism and Democracy when great and powerful empires will be swept away and there will be a general levelling up of the social and economic conditions of different sections of human society.

1853. The Holy Prophet.

110. On that day [a]intercession shall not avail save *the intercession of* him whom the Gracious *God* grants permission and with whose word *of faith* He is pleased.

يَوْمَئِذٍ لَّا تَنفَعُ الشَّفَاعَةُ إِلَّا مَنْ أَذِنَ لَهُ الرَّحْمٰنُ وَرَضِيَ لَهُ قَوْلًا ﴿١١٠﴾

111. [b]He knows *all* that is before them and *all* that is behind them,[1854] but they cannot compass it with *their* knowledge.

يَعْلَمُ مَا بَيْنَ أَيْدِيهِمْ وَمَا خَلْفَهُمْ وَلَا يُحِيطُونَ بِهِ عِلْمًا ﴿١١١﴾

112. And *all* great leaders[1854A] shall humble themselves before the Living, the Self-Subsisting and All-Sustaining *God*. And he indeed is undone who bears *the burden of* iniquity.

وَعَنَتِ الْوُجُوهُ لِلْحَيِّ الْقَيُّومِ ۖ وَقَدْ خَابَ مَنْ حَمَلَ ظُلْمًا ﴿١١٢﴾

113. But he [c]who does good works, being a believer, shall apprehend neither injustice nor loss.

وَمَن يَعْمَلْ مِنَ الصّٰلِحٰتِ وَهُوَ مُؤْمِنٌ فَلَا يَخٰفُ ظُلْمًا وَلَا هَضْمًا ﴿١١٣﴾

114. And thus have [d]We sent it down—the Qur'ān in Arabic—and We have explained therein every kind of warning, that they may fear *God* or that it may cause them to remember *Him*.

وَكَذٰلِكَ أَنزَلْنٰهُ قُرْاٰنًا عَرَبِيًّا وَصَرَّفْنَا فِيهِ مِنَ الْوَعِيدِ لَعَلَّهُمْ يَتَّقُونَ أَوْ يُحْدِثُ لَهُمْ ذِكْرًا ﴿١١٤﴾

115. [e]Exalted then is Allāh, the True King. And make no haste to recite the Qur'ān ere its revelation is completed unto thee, but only say; Lord, bestow on me increase of knowledge.'[1855]

فَتَعٰلَى اللّٰهُ الْمَلِكُ الْحَقُّ ۚ وَلَا تَعْجَلْ بِالْقُرْاٰنِ مِن قَبْلِ أَن يُقْضٰى إِلَيْكَ وَحْيُهُ ۖ وَقُل رَّبِّ زِدْنِي عِلْمًا ﴿١١٥﴾

[a]21 : 29; 78 : 39. [b]2 : 256; 21 : 29. [c]10: 10 ; 16 : 98; 21 : 95. [d]42 : 8; 43 : 4; 46 : 13. [e]23 : 117.

1854. The words '*all that is behind them*' refer to great accomplishments they will have already made, and the words '*that is before them*' refer to the great achievements they will aspire to make in the future.

1854 A. *Wujūh* means, great leaders (Aqrab).

1855. The Holy Prophet is reported to have said, 'Seek knowledge though it may be found in a country as far away as China' (Ṣaghīr, vol. 1). Elsewhere in the Qur'ān, knowledge has been styled as 'God's great grace' (2 : 270 & 4 : 114). Knowledge is of two kinds : (*a*) That which is vouchsafed to man through revelation and which has found its perfect manifestation in the Qur'ān. (*b*) That which man acquires by his own effort and labour.

116. And verily, We had made a covenant with Adam beforehand, but he forgot, and We found in him no resolve[1856] *to disobey Us.*

وَلَقَدْ عَهِدْنَآ إِلَىٰٓ آدَمَ مِن قَبْلُ فَنَسِيَ وَلَمْ نَجِدْ لَهُۥ عَزْمًا ﴿١١٦﴾

R. 7 117. And *remember* [a]when We said to the angels, 'Submit to Adam,' and they all submitted. But Iblīs *did not.* He refused *to submit.*

وَإِذْ قُلْنَا لِلْمَلَٰٓئِكَةِ ٱسْجُدُوا۟ لِآدَمَ فَسَجَدُوٓا۟ إِلَّآ إِبْلِيسَ أَبَىٰ ﴿١١٧﴾

118. Then We said, 'O Adam, [b]this is an enemy to thee and to thy wife; so let him not drive you both out of the garden,[1857] lest thou come to grief;

فَقُلْنَا يَٰٓآدَمُ إِنَّ هَٰذَا عَدُوٌّ لَّكَ وَلِزَوْجِكَ فَلَا يُخْرِجَنَّكُمَا مِنَ ٱلْجَنَّةِ فَتَشْقَىٰٓ ﴿١١٨﴾

119. 'It is *decreed* for thee that thou shalt not hunger therein nor shalt thou be naked;

إِنَّ لَكَ أَلَّا تَجُوعَ فِيهَا وَلَا تَعْرَىٰ ﴿١١٩﴾

120. 'And that thou shalt not thirst therein, nor shalt thou be exposed to the sun.'[1858]

وَأَنَّكَ لَا تَظْمَؤُا۟ فِيهَا وَلَا تَضْحَىٰ ﴿١٢٠﴾

[a]2 : 35; 7 : 12-13; 15 : 27-34; 17 : 62; 18 : 51; 38 : 72-75.
[b]7 : 23; 18 : 51.

1856. The verse shows that Adam's lapse was only an error of judgment. It was inadvertent and involuntary and not at all intentional or deliberate. To err is human.

1857. Adam is warned that if he succumbed to the blandishments held out to him by Iblīs and accepted his advice, he would become deprived of *Jannah, i.e.,* life of bliss and spiritual contentment which he formerly enjoyed.

1858. Reference in this and the preceding verse seems to be to the amenities and comforts which are the concomitants of civilized life. These two verses point to the fact that to provide food, clothing and shelter to its people—their primary necessities of life—is the first duty of a civilized government and that a society can only be called civilized when all its members are adequately provided with these necessities. Mankind will continue to suffer from social upheavals, and the moral tone of human society will never really improve unless economic inequalities of such a serious nature, that some sections of society roll in wealth and others die of starvation, are done away with. Adam is told here that he will live in a place where amenities and necessities of life will be adequately available to all its inhabitants. This state of affairs has been described elsewhere in the Qur'ān in the words, *and eat therefrom plentifully wherever you will* (2 : 36). The verse under comment also shows that with Adam began a new social order and that he laid the foundations of a kingdom which ushered in the era of social progress of man.

121. But [a]Satan whispered evil suggestions to him. He said, 'O Adam, shall I direct thee to the tree of eternity,[1859] and to a kingdom that never decays?'

فَوَسْوَسَ إِلَيْهِ الشَّيْطٰنُ قَالَ يٰٓاٰدَمُ هَلْ أَدُلُّكَ عَلٰى شَجَرَةِ الْخُلْدِ وَمُلْكٍ لَّا يَبْلٰى ﴿۱۲۱﴾

122. Then [b]they both ate thereof, so that their nakedness became manifest[1860] to them, and they began to cover themselves with the leaves[1861] of the garden. And Adam observed not the commandment of his Lord, so his life became miserable.

فَأَكَلَا مِنْهَا فَبَدَتْ لَهُمَا سَوْاٰتُهُمَا وَطَفِقَا يَخْصِفٰنِ عَلَيْهِمَا مِنْ وَّرَقِ الْجَنَّةِ وَعَصٰٓى اٰدَمُ رَبَّهٗ فَغَوٰى ﴿۱۲۲﴾

123 Then his Lord chose him *for His grace*,[1862] and [c]turned to him with mercy and guided *him*.

ثُمَّ اجْتَبٰهُ رَبُّهٗ فَتَابَ عَلَيْهِ وَهَدٰى ﴿۱۲۳﴾

[a]2 : 37; 7 : 21 [b]7 : 23; 20 : 122. [c]2 : 38.

1859. There exists in the world no such tree as 'the tree of eternity.' The 'tree,' as mentioned here and elsewhere in the Qur'ān, was a certain family or tribe from which Adam was bidden to keep aloof because its members were his enemies.

1860. As a result of acceptance by Adam of Satan's suggestions a split occurred among his people which caused him much distress and mental anguish. Adam and Eve discovered that by acting upon the evil suggestions of Satan, they had made a grievous mistake and had involved themselves in great trouble. The verse does not mean that their weakness became known to other people but that only Adam and Eve themselves became conscious of it.

1861. *Waraq* also meaning young lads of a community (Lane), the verse purports to say that as Satan had succeeded in causing a split in Adam's community and some of the morally weak members had gone out of its fold, Adam gathered together the youth and other righteous and good members of the community and with their help began to reorganize his people. According to the Bible, Adam used fig leaves (Gen. 3 : 6-7) which in the language of visions signify young righteous and pious people.

1862. The verse shows that Adam's act of disobedience was inadvertent and accidental, for an act of deliberate disobedience could not have been followed by the great honour of his being selected by God for His special favour.

124. *God* said, [a]'Go forth, both[1863] of you from here; some of you will be enemies of others. And if there comes to you guidance from Me, then whoso will follow My guidance, will not go astray, nor will he come to grief;

قَالَ اهْبِطَا مِنْهَا جَمِيعًا بَعْضُكُمْ لِبَعْضٍ عَدُوٌّ ۚ فَإِمَّا
يَأْتِيَنَّكُمْ مِنِّي هُدًى ۙ فَمَنِ اتَّبَعَ هُدَايَ فَلَا
يَضِلُّ وَلَا يَشْقَىٰ ﴿١٢٤﴾

125. 'But [b]whosoever will turn away from My remembrance, his will be a straitened life, and on the Day of Resurrection We shall raise him up blind.'[1864]

وَمَنْ أَعْرَضَ عَنْ ذِكْرِي فَإِنَّ لَهُ مَعِيشَةً ضَنْكًا
وَنَحْشُرُهُ يَوْمَ الْقِيَامَةِ أَعْمَىٰ ﴿١٢٥﴾

126. He will say, 'My Lord, why hast Thou raised me up blind, while I possessed sight *before?*'

قَالَ رَبِّ لِمَ حَشَرْتَنِي أَعْمَىٰ وَقَدْ كُنْتُ بَصِيرًا ﴿١٢٦﴾

127. *God* will say, 'Thus did Our Signs come to thee and thou didst ignore them[1865] and in like manner wilt thou be ignored this day.'

قَالَ كَذَٰلِكَ أَتَتْكَ آيَاتُنَا فَنَسِيتَهَا ۖ وَكَذَٰلِكَ الْيَوْمَ
تُنْسَىٰ ﴿١٢٧﴾

---

[a]2 : 37-39; 7 : 25. [b]18 : 102.

1863. The words, 'both of you,' signify two groups of people, *i.e.*, the followers of Adam and the followers of Satan. The words, *kum* (you) and *Jamī'* (all of you), also show that the verse refers not to two persons but to two groups of persons or to two parties. This is also clear from 7 : 25 where the plural number *Ihbiṭū* (go forth all of you) has been used instead of *Ihbiṭā* (go forth both of you). It appears that Adam emigrated from Iraq, the land of his birth, to a neighbouring country. The emigration was perhaps a temporary one, and he must have returned to his native land not long after. The words, *a provision for a time* (7 : 25), contain a hint about the emigration being a temporary one.

1864. A person, who consigns God to oblivion in this life and leads a life which obstructs or impedes his spiritual development and thus deprives himself of heavenly light, will be born blind at the time of his second birth in the life after. This will be because his soul in this life which will serve as a body for the more spiritually developed soul in the next world had become blind, because he had led a life of sin in this world.

1865. In answer to the disbeliever's protestation as to why he was raised up blind while he was possessed of sight in the former life, God would say that he had become spiritually blind in his worldly life on account of his having led a life of sin; and as his soul was to serve as a body for another much more spiritually developed soul in the life after, therefore he was born blind in the Hereafter. The verse may also mean that as a disbeliever does not develop in him Divine attributes and remains a stranger to them, so when on the Day of Resurrection those attributes will be manifested in all their splendour and glory, he, being a stranger to them, will not be able to recognize them, and thus will stand like a blind man, having no recollection or remembrance of them.

128. And thus do We recompense him who transgresses *the limits of Divine Law* and believes not in the Signs of his Lord; and the punishment of the Hereafter is even severer and more lasting.

وَكَذٰلِكَ نَجْزِيْ مَنْ اَسْرَفَ وَلَمْ يُؤْمِنْ بِاٰيٰتِ رَبِّهٖ
وَلَعَذَابُ الْاٰخِرَةِ اَشَدُّ وَاَبْقٰى ﴿۱۲۸﴾

129. Does it not furnish guidance to them, [a]how many a generation We destroyed before them, amid whose dwellings they *now* walk? Therein, verily, are Signs for those who possess understanding.

اَفَلَمْ يَهْدِ لَهُمْ كَمْ اَهْلَكْنَا قَبْلَهُمْ مِّنَ الْقُرُوْنِ
يَمْشُوْنَ فِيْ مَسٰكِنِهِمْ ۭ اِنَّ فِيْ ذٰلِكَ لَاٰيٰتٍ لِّاُولِي
النُّهٰى ﴿۱۲۹﴾

R. 8 130. And [b]had it not been for a word[1866] already gone forth from thy Lord, and a term *already* fixed, *their punishment* would have been abiding.

وَلَوْلَا كَلِمَةٌ سَبَقَتْ مِنْ رَّبِّكَ لَكَانَ لِزَامًا وَّاَجَلٌ
مُّسَمًّى ﴿۱۳۰﴾

131. Bear patiently then what they say, and [c]glorify thy Lord with His praise before the rising of the sun and before its setting; and glorify *Him* in the hours of the night and *all* parts[1867] of the day, that thou mayest find *true* happiness.

فَاصْبِرْ عَلٰى مَا يَقُوْلُوْنَ وَسَبِّحْ بِحَمْدِ رَبِّكَ قَبْلَ
طُلُوْعِ الشَّمْسِ وَقَبْلَ غُرُوْبِهَا ۚ وَمِنْ اٰنَآئِ الَّيْلِ
فَسَبِّحْ وَاَطْرَافَ النَّهَارِ لَعَلَّكَ تَرْضٰى ﴿۱۳۱﴾

[a]17 : 18; 36 : 32. [b]8 : 69; 10 : 20. [c]17 : 79-80; 30 : 18-19; 50 : 40-41.

1866. The reference is to the Divine declaration contained in the verse, 'My mercy encompasses all things' (7 : 157). God in His infallible wisdom has decreed that His mercy will continue to transcend all His other attributes.

1867. The glorification of God at the hours mentioned in the verse may signify the hours of the five daily Prayers; the words, *before the rising of the sun*, signifying the Morning (*Fajr*) Prayer; and the words, *before its setting*, the Late-afternoon ('*Asr*) Prayer; and the expression, *and glorify Him in the hours of the night*, signifying the Evening Prayer (*Maghrib*) and Night Prayer ('*Ishā*'), while the words, *parts of the day*, signifying the Afternoon (*Ẓuhr*) Prayer.

132. And [a]strain[1868] not thine eyes after what We have bestowed on some classes of them of the splendour of the present world that We may try them thereby. And the provision of thy Lord is better and more lasting.

وَلَا تَمُدَّنَّ عَيْنَيْكَ إِلَىٰ مَا مَتَّعْنَا بِهِۦٓ أَزْوَٰجًا مِّنْهُمْ
زَهْرَةَ ٱلْحَيَوٰةِ ٱلدُّنْيَا ۙ لِنَفْتِنَهُمْ فِيهِ ۚ وَرِزْقُ رَبِّكَ
خَيْرٌ وَأَبْقَىٰ ﴿١٣٢﴾

133. And [b]enjoin Prayer on thy people and be constant therein. We ask thee not for provision; it is We who provide for thee. And the *good* end is for those who guard against evil.

وَأْمُرْ أَهْلَكَ بِٱلصَّلَوٰةِ وَٱصْطَبِرْ عَلَيْهَا ۖ لَا نَسْـَٔلُكَ
رِزْقًا ۖ نَّحْنُ نَرْزُقُكَ ۗ وَٱلْعَٰقِبَةُ لِلتَّقْوَىٰ ﴿١٣٣﴾

134. And they say, 'Why does he not bring us a Sign from his Lord ?' Has there not come to them clear evidence of what is *contained* in the former Books ?

وَقَالُوا۟ لَوْلَا يَأْتِينَا بِـَٔايَةٍ مِّن رَّبِّهِۦٓ ۚ أَوَلَمْ تَأْتِهِم
بَيِّنَةُ مَا فِى ٱلصُّحُفِ ٱلْأُولَىٰ ﴿١٣٤﴾

135. And if We had destroyed them with a punishment before *the coming of* this *Messenger*, they would have surely said, "Our Lord, wherefore didst Thou not send to us a Messenger that we might have followed Thy commandments before we were humbled and disgraced ?'

وَلَوْ أَنَّآ أَهْلَكْنَٰهُم بِعَذَابٍ مِّن قَبْلِهِۦ لَقَالُوا۟ رَبَّنَا
لَوْلَآ أَرْسَلْتَ إِلَيْنَا رَسُولًا فَنَتَّبِعَ ءَايَٰتِكَ مِن قَبْلِ
أَن نَّذِلَّ وَنَخْزَىٰ ﴿١٣٥﴾

136. Say, 'Each one is waiting; wait ye, therefore, and you will soon know who are the people of the right path and who follow *true* guidance, *and who do not*.

قُلْ كُلٌّ مُّتَرَبِّصٌ فَتَرَبَّصُوا۟ ۖ فَسَتَعْلَمُونَ مَنْ أَصْحَٰبُ
ع ٱلصِّرَٰطِ ٱلسَّوِىِّ وَمَنِ ٱهْتَدَىٰ ﴿١٣٦﴾

[a]15 : 89; 26 : 206-208; 28 : 61-62. [b]19 : 56; 33 : 34.

1868. All international jealousies and rivalries which result in wars and consequently in much human misery and bloodshed are the result, direct or indirect, of mad hunger for material wealth and physical comforts. Muslims are warned not to cast covetous looks on the wealth of other people.

CHAPTER 21

AL-ANBIYĀ'

(*Revealed before Hijrah*)

Date of Revelation and Context

The *Sūrah*, like the three preceding ones, was revealed at Mecca, very early in the Holy Prophet's ministry. Ibn Mas'ūd says that it was revealed before the 5th year of the Call, along with Chapters Ṭā Hā, Al-Kahf and Maryam. The opening verses of *Sūrah* Maryam were recited by Ja'far before the Negus during the Emigration to Abyssinia which took place in that year. The immediate connection of the *Sūrah* with *Sūrah* Ṭā Hā consists in the fact that towards the end of that *Sūrah* it was stated that Divine punishment would overtake disbelievers at its appointed time, and the Holy Prophet was enjoined to bear their opposition and persecution patiently and with fortitude. The present *Sūrah* opens with a warning to disbelievers that the time of their punishment has already arrived and that though they will now have to render an account of their actions, they will continue to wander in the wilderness of heedlessness and disbelief. This is the immediate connection of the *Sūrah* with the preceding one. But it is its subject-matter as a whole which, in fact, constitutes the real connecting link between the present *Sūrah* and some of the preceding Chapters. In *Sūrah* Maryam some of the false Christian doctrines were repudiated and rebutted, *viz*., that Jesus possessed Divine attributes, that he had abrogated the Law and had declared it to be a curse and that salvation depended not on good works but upon atonement. In *Sūrah* Ṭā Ḥā a detailed account of Moses was given in order to refute again these false doctrines. The Christians were told that Christianity was but a link in the Mosaic Dispensation, and that Moses's circumstances constituted a flat repudiation of their doctrines. His whole pride lay in the fact that he was a Law-giving Prophet. If the Law was a curse, then, according to Christian belief, Moses, instead of having been regarded as an object of respect and pride, should have been condemned and denounced. After this, the *Sūrah* Ṭā Ḥā gave a brief account of the lapse suffered by Adam and thus traced the Christian theory of the original sin to its very root and then refuted it. It was made clear in that *Sūrah* that sin formed no part of the heritage of man and that he is punished only for his own trespasses and offences Next, it was stated that if it was not possible for man to get rid of sin, then the very purpose of Divine punishment is defeated and God's Prophets and His Messengers, instead of holding out warnings to sinners, should have given them the comforting message that being mere creatures of circumstances and possessing no volition or discretion they will not be called to account for their actions. The same subject has been enlarged and expanded in the present *Sūrah* and the lesson is driven home that the enemies not only of this or that Prophet but those of all Messengers of God—from Adam to Jesus and then to the Holy Prophet Muḥammad—were punished for their wicked deeds and the righteous rewarded for their good actions. If man had inherited sin and if he could not shed it, then there was no sense or justification in punishing the sinners and rewarding the righteous. So the dogma of inherited sin is a baseless invention.

Subject-Matter

The *Sūrah* opens with a warning to disbelievers that Divine punishment is fast approaching, but they are deluding themselves into a false sense of security. There never came in the world a Divine Messenger who was not jeered and scoffed at. But out of sympathy with and solicitude for the spiritual well-being of their peoples the Prophets of God invited them to accept Truth and be saved. If sin formed a part of man's heritage, then of what avail was this invitation? The *Sūrah* then proceeds to state some objections of disbelievers which are effectively answered. After this disbelievers are asked to consider, what new burden the Qur'ān imposes upon them that they should be bent upon rejecting its Message. The primary object of that Message is to exalt and raise them to moral eminence. As it is God's own revealed Word, its rejectors will not escape punishment. The *Sūrah* then asks disbelievers whether they have ever given the idea serious consideration that an All-Knowing and Wise God could not have created the universe without a great and grim purpose, and that those who stand in the way of its fulfilment are bound to fail. Next, the *Sūrah* deals with the all-important subject of Divine Unity which forms the basic and fundamental belief of all religions. When one uniform law pervades and governs the whole universe, it says, how can the polytheists justify *Shirk* (belief in the plurality of gods)? Belief in the plurality of gods implies disagreement on the part of these gods in regard to the management and control of the universe. And as evidently there exists perfect order in it, there should be only One Creator and One Controller of the whole universe. And why God should have a son, for a son is needed only when the father is likely to fall a victim to decay or death or when he cannot perform his work single-handed and unassisted. But all such notions about God are blasphemous and unfounded. After this the *Sūrah* points to another Divine law, *viz.*, that whenever darkness enshrouds the entire face of the earth and the world suffers from a dearth of righteous men, God opens the gates of His mercy upon mankind and heavenly water, in the form of Divine revelation, descends upon earth and gives new life to a world steeped in sin and iniquity. The phenomenon of the alternation of light and darkness in the spiritual realm corresponds to a similar phenomenon in the physical world where day and night follow each other. Then the *Sūrah* drives home the argument that it is foolish on the part of disbelievers to reject the Holy Prophet on the plea that he is but an ordinary mortal. It is not the status and the position of the bearer of the Quranic Message so much that matters. What really matters is, who has sent him. In order to show that the Holy Prophet's cause will prevail, the *Sūrah* cites the cases of some former Prophets—Noah, Abraham, David, Solomon, Idrīs, and others, who in the teeth of bitter, persistent and organized opposition succeeded in their missions. All these chosen servants of God like Jesus were models of noble and righteous conduct and like him they suffered great hardships and privations in the way of God. Then why of all of them Jesus alone should be regarded as son of God and not they ? After the account of these Prophets, special mention is made of Jesus and his mother whose circumstances were in no way different from theirs. Even the unusual manner of Jesus's birth entitles him to no particular spiritual status. The birth of Yaḥyā had also taken place in very exceptional circumstances. If Jesus was born without the agency of a father, Yaḥyā's birth took place when his father had reached an extreme old age and his mother had become barren and was quite unfit to give birth to a child. Similarly, Jesus's suffering in the cause of Truth was nothing novel. Though he was hung on the Cross he was taken down alive, but Yaḥyā suffered actual death for the sake of God. Then why should Jesus's death alone atone for the sins of man and not that of Yaḥyā? Towards the end the *Sūrah* points to the phenomenal rise and great material might and dazzling prosperity, progress and power of Gog and Magog—Christian nations of the West. When these nations, the *Sūrah* proceeds to say, will spread all over the world and will occupy every position of power and eminence, and when other nations of the world will bow down to them in submission and pay homage to them, then will the promise about their ultimate destruction be fulfilled. Divine punishment will come down upon them so sudden and swift that they will be taken completely by surprise. All their handiworks, the source and cause of their pride, and all their pomp, glory and grandeur will be destroyed and reduced to ashes and dust.

سُوْرَةُ الْاَنْبِيَاۤءِ مَكِّيَّةٌ (٢١) اٰيَاتُهَا ١١٣ رُكُوْعَاتُهَا ٧

الجزء ١٧

1. [a]In the name of Allāh, the Gracious, the Merciful.

بِسْمِ اللّٰهِ الرَّحْمٰنِ الرَّحِيْمِ ﴿١﴾

2. [b]Nigh unto men has drawn their reckoning, yet they turn away in heedlessness.

اِقْتَرَبَ لِلنَّاسِ حِسَابُهُمْ وَهُمْ فِيْ غَفْلَةٍ مُّعْرِضُوْنَ ﴿٢﴾

3. [c]There comes not to them any new admonition[1869] from their Lord, but they listen to it while they make sport *of it*.

مَا يَأْتِيْهِمْ مِّنْ ذِكْرٍ مِّنْ رَّبِّهِمْ مُّحْدَثٍ اِلَّا اسْتَمَعُوْهُ وَهُمْ يَلْعَبُوْنَ ﴿٣﴾

4. *And* their hearts are forgetful. And they—the wrongdoers—confer together in secret *and say*, 'Is this *man* aught but a mortal like yourselves? Will you then yield to *his* sorcery[1870] with your eyes open?'

لَاهِيَةً قُلُوْبُهُمْ وَاَسَرُّوا النَّجْوَى الَّذِيْنَ ظَلَمُوْا هَلْ هٰذَآ اِلَّا بَشَرٌ مِّثْلُكُمْ اَفَتَأْتُوْنَ السِّحْرَ وَاَنْتُمْ تُبْصِرُوْنَ ﴿٤﴾

5. *In reply to this the Prophet* said, 'My Lord knows what is said in the heaven and the earth. And He is the All-Hearing, the All-Knowing.'[1871]

قٰلَ رَبِّيْ يَعْلَمُ الْقَوْلَ فِي السَّمَآءِ وَالْاَرْضِ وَهُوَ السَّمِيْعُ الْعَلِيْمُ ﴿٥﴾

6. Nay, they say, '*These are but* confused dreams; nay, he has forged it *himself*: nay, [d]he is but a

بَلْ قَالُوْٓا اَضْغَاثُ اَحْلَامٍ بَلِ افْتَرٰىهُ بَلْ هُوَ شَاعِرٌ

[a]1 : 1. [b]54 : 2-3. [c]21 : 43; 26 : 6. [d]52 : 31.

1869. In form every Message which a Prophet brings is a new one, but in substance and essence it is the same old Message. 'I am not a new Messenger,' the Qur'ān depicts the Holy Prophet as saying with regard to himself (46 : 10).

1870. The main objection of disbelievers against every Prophet has always been that he is an ordinary mortal like themselves (14 : 11; 23 : 25,34; 26 : 155; 36 : 16 & 64 : 7). This objection has been answered in 12 : 110; 14 : 12; 16 : 44-45 & 17 : 96. Here it is answered in v. 8. The answer is this that while on the one hand the disbelievers say that there is nothing in the Holy Prophet different from an ordinary man, on the other they concede that he is a sorcerer, *i.e.*, he possesses superior intellect. Divine Prophets are called sorcerers because their teachings produce a magical effect on the listeners. The verse implies an admission on the part of disbelievers that the Qur'ān does possess a fascinating power and that it is really difficult for an unprejudiced and fair-minded person to reject its teaching.

1871. God knows all the secret and open plots and machinations of disbelievers against Islām and He hears the prayers of the Holy Prophet and His chosen servants and will frustrate all the evil designs of disbelievers.

poet.[1872] Let him then bring us a Sign just as the former *Prophets* were sent *with Signs*.'

فَلْيَأْتِنَا بِآيَةٍ كَمَا أُرْسِلَ الْأَوَّلُونَ ﴿٦﴾

7. No township, before them, which We destroyed, ever believed. Would they then believe?

مَا آمَنَتْ قَبْلَهُمْ مِنْ قَرْيَةٍ أَهْلَكْنَاهَا أَفَهُمْ يُؤْمِنُونَ ﴿٧﴾

8. [a]And We sent none *as Messengers* before thee but men to whom We sent revelations. So ask the people of the Reminder, if you know not;

وَمَا أَرْسَلْنَا قَبْلَكَ إِلَّا رِجَالًا نُوحِي إِلَيْهِمْ فَاسْأَلُوا أَهْلَ الذِّكْرِ إِنْ كُنْتُمْ لَا تَعْلَمُونَ ﴿٨﴾

9. [b]Nor did We give them bodies that ate not food, neither were they to live for ever.[1873]

وَمَا جَعَلْنَاهُمْ جَسَدًا لَا يَأْكُلُونَ الطَّعَامَ وَمَا كَانُوا خَالِدِينَ ﴿٩﴾

10. Then We fulfilled to them *Our* promise; and We saved them and those whom We pleased; and We destroyed the transgressors.

ثُمَّ صَدَقْنَاهُمُ الْوَعْدَ فَأَنْجَيْنَاهُمْ وَمَنْ نَشَاءُ وَأَهْلَكْنَا الْمُسْرِفِينَ ﴿١٠﴾

11. We have *now* sent down to you a Book *which makes provision* for your eminence; will you not then understand?[1874]

لَقَدْ أَنْزَلْنَا إِلَيْكُمْ كِتَابًا فِيهِ ذِكْرُكُمْ أَفَلَا تَعْقِلُونَ ﴿١١﴾ ع

[a]12 : 110; 16 : 44. [b]25 : 21.

1872. In this verse three different objections of disbelievers with regard to the Qur'ān have been mentioned. The first is that the Qur'ān is a mixture of confused dreams. But realizing the untenability of their position, since there exists a beautiful arrangement and order in it and since it forms a connected whole and contains excellent teachings, the disbelievers shift their ground and say that the Holy Prophet has forged it himself. But again realizing that throughout his life he was, by common consent, known and looked upon as 'the Trusty' and 'the Truthful,' they give up this objection also and proceed to accuse him of being a poet and a sorcerer. These objections have been mentioned in an ascending order and the continuous shifting of the ground by disbelievers implies an admission on their part that the objections cannot stand examination or scrutiny and are foolish and self-contradictory. The Qur'ān, therefore, has refused to entertain them here.

1873. Though disbelievers regarded all the Divine Messengers as ordinary mortals, yet the objection was invariably repeated to every one of them that like ordinary mortals 'he eats and drinks and walks about in the streets and is subject to all human needs and demands of the body'(25 : 8), and on the basis of this very plea they rejected him. An implied reference is made here to this inconsistent attitude of disbelievers. They do not want to understand this simple fact, the verse purports to say, that Prophets are raised as 'models' for men, and, how could they serve as models if they were not men like them and were not like them subject to the demands of the physical body? As human beings they were not and could not be immune from the demands of the flesh or from decay or death.

1874. The verse means to say that not only will the deniers of the Qur'ān come to grief and its followers achieve progress and prosperity and rise from the lowest rung of the ladder to the highest pinnacle of material and spiritual glory, but this fact will also constitute an infallible proof that the Qur'ān is neither forgery, nor poetry, nor a collection of confused dreams but the true Word of the Almighty God, the Creator of heavens and earth.

R. 2 12. [a]And how many a township that acted wrongfully have We utterly destroyed, and raised up after it another people.

وَكَمْ قَصَمْنَا مِنْ قَرْيَةٍ كَانَتْ ظَالِمَةً وَّأَنْشَأْنَا بَعْدَهَا قَوْمًا اٰخَرِيْنَ ﴿١٢﴾

13. And when they perceived Our punishment, lo! they began to flee from it.

فَلَمَّآ اَحَسُّوْا بَأْسَنَآ اِذَا هُمْ مِّنْهَا يَرْكُضُوْنَ ﴿١٣﴾

14. *Thereupon We said*, 'Flee not, but return to the luxuries in which you exulted, and to your dwellings that you might be questioned *about your conduct*.'

لَا تَرْكُضُوْا وَارْجِعُوْٓا اِلٰى مَآ اُتْرِفْتُمْ فِيْهِ وَمَسٰكِنِكُمْ لَعَلَّكُمْ تُسْـَٔلُوْنَ ﴿١٤﴾

15. They said, 'Alas for us, we were indeed wrongdoers!'

قَالُوْا يٰوَيْلَنَآ اِنَّا كُنَّا ظٰلِمِيْنَ ﴿١٥﴾

16. And this ceased not to be their cry till We made them *like* a mown down field, extinct.[1875]

فَمَا زَالَتْ تِّلْكَ دَعْوٰىهُمْ حَتّٰى جَعَلْنٰهُمْ حَصِيْدًا خٰمِدِيْنَ ﴿١٦﴾

17. [b]And We created not the heaven and the earth and all that is between the two in sport.[1875A]

وَمَا خَلَقْنَا السَّمَآءَ وَالْاَرْضَ وَمَا بَيْنَهُمَا لٰعِبِيْنَ ﴿١٧﴾

18. Had We wished to find a pastime, We would, surely, have found it in what is with Us, if at all We were to do *such a thing*.[1876]

لَوْ اَرَدْنَآ اَنْ نَّتَّخِذَ لَهْوًا لَّاتَّخَذْنٰهُ مِنْ لَّدُنَّآ ۖ اِنْ كُنَّا فٰعِلِيْنَ ﴿١٨﴾

19. Nay, [c]We hurl the truth at falsehood, and it breaks its head,[1876A] and lo! it perishes. And woe to you for that which you ascribe *to Allāh*.

بَلْ نَقْذِفُ بِالْحَقِّ عَلَى الْبَاطِلِ فَيَدْمَغُهٗ فَاِذَا هُوَ زَاهِقٌ ۗ وَلَكُمُ الْوَيْلُ مِمَّا تَصِفُوْنَ ﴿١٩﴾

---

[a]7 : 5; 22 : 46; 28 : 59; 50 : 37; 65 : 9. [b]15 : 86; 38 : 28; 44 : 39. [c]17 : 82; 34 : 49, 50.

1875. The verse gives a graphic description of the people upon whom descends Divine punishment. They are completely ruined, and all their ambitions and aspirations become extinguished. The very will to live dies in them and they despair of their future and lose all initiative and thus to all intents and purposes they become defunct and dead.

1875A. When the universe has not been created as a mere pastime and sport and a little reflection over its creation reveals the great wisdom underlying its creation, the creation of man, who is its axis and centre, must also have been designed to serve a grand and sublime object. The verse implies that man is God's vicegerent on earth and that he has been created to serve as a mirror to reflect in his person the beautiful image of his Creator (2 : 31).

1876. It is inconsistent with the dignity, majesty and wisdom of God that He should have created this universe without a great object and thus should have done a purposeless thing.

1876A. *Damagha-hū* means, he broke his head so that the wound reached his brain; he overcame him (Lane).

20. To Him belongs whosoever is in the heavens and the earth. [a]And those who are in His presence do not disdain to worship Him, nor do they weary *of it;*

وَلَهٗ مَنْ فِي السَّمٰوٰتِ وَالْاَرْضِ ۭ وَمَنْ عِنْدَهٗ لَا يَسْتَكْبِرُوْنَ عَنْ عِبَادَتِهٖ وَلَا يَسْتَحْسِرُوْنَ ۝۲۰

21. They glorify *Him* night and day; and they flag not.[1877]

يُسَبِّحُوْنَ الَّيْلَ وَالنَّهَارَ لَا يَفْتُرُوْنَ ۝۲۱

22. Have they taken gods from the earth who raise *the dead*?[1878]

اَمِ اتَّخَذُوْٓا اٰلِهَةً مِّنَ الْاَرْضِ هُمْ يُنْشِرُوْنَ ۝۲۲

23. If there had been in *the heavens and the earth* other gods beside Allāh, then surely both would have gone to ruin.[1879] Glorified then be Allāh, the Lord of the Throne, far above what they attribute *to Him.*

لَوْ كَانَ فِيْهِمَآ اٰلِهَةٌ اِلَّا اللّٰهُ لَفَسَدَتَا ۚ فَسُبْحٰنَ اللّٰهِ رَبِّ الْعَرْشِ عَمَّا يَصِفُوْنَ ۝۲۳

24. He cannot be questioned as to what He does, but they will be questioned.[1880]

لَا يُسْـَٔلُ عَمَّا يَفْعَلُ وَهُمْ يُسْـَٔلُوْنَ ۝۲۴

[a]7 : 207; 41 : 39 ; 21 : 20.

1877. The verse gives some marks of the true servants of God. They are not tired of serving God and humanity. They do not accept a Divine Prophet under a momentary impulse and then under the stress of hardships and privations lose heart. Once they accept the truth, they stick to it through thick and thin. Their zeal and enthusiasm for the service of truth never flag or fail. Worship of God is a source of delight to them and a means of relief from worries and anxieties (13 :29). 'The cheer of my eyes is in Prayer,' the Holy Prophet is reported to have said (Nasa'ī).

1878. Creating or raising the dead to life is the exclusive attribute and prerogative of God. Neither Jesus nor any other person can share this attribute with Him. The reference to this attribute is intended to smash the divinity of Jesus which, in particular, forms the subject-matter of these verses.

1879. The verse constitutes an effective and conclusive argument against polytheism. Even atheists cannot deny that perfect order pervades and permeates the entire universe. This order points to the fact that one uniform law governs it; and the uniformity of laws proves the Unity of the Maker and Controller of the universe. If there had been more than one God, then more than one law would have governed the universe—because for a god it is necessary to create the universe with his own special laws—and thus disorder and confusion would have been the inevitable result and the whole universe would have gone to pieces. It is, therefore, manifestly absurd to say that three gods, equally perfect in all respects are jointly the creators and controllers of the universe.

1880. The verse points to the perfection and completeness of the order in the universe and, therefore, to the perfection of its Author and Controller and hence to His Unity. It also signifies that God's authority is supreme while all other beings and things are subject to His authority. This constitutes another argument against polytheism.

25. [a]Have they taken gods beside Him? Say, 'Bring forth your proof. This *Qur'ān* is a *source of* honour for those with me, and *a source of* honour for those before me.'[1880A] Nay, most of them know not the truth, and so they turn away.

أَمِ اتَّخَذُوا مِنْ دُونِهٖٓ اٰلِهَةً قُلْ هَاتُوا بُرْهَانَكُمْ
هٰذَا ذِكْرُ مَنْ مَّعِيَ وَذِكْرُ مَنْ قَبْلِيْ بَلْ اَكْثَرُهُمْ
لَا يَعْلَمُوْنَ الْحَقَّ فَهُمْ مُّعْرِضُوْنَ ﴿٢٥﴾

26. And We sent no Messenger before thee but We revealed to him: 'There is no god but I; so worship Me *alone*.'

وَمَآ اَرْسَلْنَا مِنْ قَبْلِكَ مِنْ رَّسُوْلٍ اِلَّا نُوْحِيْٓ اِلَيْهِ
اَنَّهٗ لَآ اِلٰهَ اِلَّآ اَنَا فَاعْبُدُوْنِ ﴿٢٦﴾

27. [b]And they say, 'The Gracious *God* has taken to Himself a son.' Holy is He. Nay, those *whom they so designate* are *only His* honoured servants;

وَقَالُوا اتَّخَذَ الرَّحْمٰنُ وَلَدًا سُبْحٰنَهٗ بَلْ عِبَادٌ
مُّكْرَمُوْنَ ﴿٢٧﴾

28. They[1881] speak not before He speaks, and they *only* carry out His commands.

لَا يَسْبِقُوْنَهٗ بِالْقَوْلِ وَهُمْ بِاَمْرِهٖ يَعْمَلُوْنَ ﴿٢٨﴾

29. [c]He knows what is before them and what is behind them,[1882] and they intercede not except for him whom He approves *it* and they tremble in awe of Him.

يَعْلَمُ مَا بَيْنَ اَيْدِيْهِمْ وَمَا خَلْفَهُمْ وَلَا يَشْفَعُوْنَ
اِلَّا لِمَنِ ارْتَضٰى وَهُمْ مِّنْ خَشْيَتِهٖ مُشْفِقُوْنَ ﴿٢٩﴾

30. And whosoever of them should say, 'I am a god beside Him,' him shall We requite with Hell. Thus do We requite the wrongdoers.[1883]

وَمَنْ يَّقُلْ مِنْهُمْ اِنِّيْٓ اِلٰهٌ مِّنْ دُوْنِهٖ فَذٰلِكَ نَجْزِيْهِ
جَهَنَّمَ كَذٰلِكَ نَجْزِي الظّٰلِمِيْنَ ﴿٣٠﴾

[a]18 : 16; 23 : 118; 27 : 65. [b]2 : 117; 4: 172; 10 : 69; 19 : 89-90. [c]2 : 256; 20 : 111.

1880A. The Qur'ān is a source of honour and dignity for previous Prophets also, because it clears them of the charges of which their people falsely accused them.

1881. The pronoun 'they' as the context shows refers to Prophets. Divine Messengers are incapable of disobeying God or committing a moral offence or sin. The verse establishes the sinlessness of the Prophets.

1882. The words may mean, 'what they did and what they did not or could not do;' or they may refer to the influences to which they were subject or the changes which they brought about.

1883. It is significant that whereas claimants to God-head will only be punished in the Hereafter for their false claims, those pretenders and mountebanks who falsely lay claim to Prophethood are punished in this very world. They meet with death and destruction and all their organizations come to naught in this very life (69 : 45-48). This difference in the treatment of these two kinds of pretenders is due to the fact that the absurdity of a claim to Godhead is self-evident, therefore such a claimant need not be punished here. But a

R. 3 31. Do not the disbelievers see that the heavens and the earth were *a* closed-up *mass*,[1884] then We opened them out ? And we made of water every living thing. Will they not then believe ?

أَوَلَمْ يَرَ الَّذِينَ كَفَرُوٓا أَنَّ السَّمٰوٰتِ وَالْأَرْضَ كَانَتَا رَتْقًا فَفَتَقْنٰهُمَا ۖ وَجَعَلْنَا مِنَ الْمَآءِ كُلَّ شَيْءٍ حَيٍّ ۖ أَفَلَا يُؤْمِنُونَ ﴿٣١﴾

32. [a]And We have placed in the earth firm mountains lest it should quake[1885] with them; and We have made therein wide pathways, that they may be rightly guided.

وَجَعَلْنَا فِي الْأَرْضِ رَوَاسِيَ أَنْ تَمِيدَ بِهِمْ وَجَعَلْنَا فِيهَا فِجَاجًا سُبُلًا لَّعَلَّهُمْ يَهْتَدُونَ ﴿٣٢﴾

33. And We have made the heaven a roof, well-protected,[1886] yet they turn away from its Signs.

وَجَعَلْنَا السَّمَآءَ سَقْفًا مَّحْفُوظًا ۖ وَّهُمْ عَنْ اٰيٰتِهَا مُعْرِضُونَ ﴿٣٣﴾

[a]13 : 4; 15 : 20; 16 : 16; 31 : 11; 77 : 28.

false claimant to Prophethood, if allowed to go scot-free, may succeed in deceiving innocent people into accepting his false claim; therefore he ultimately is made to suffer defeat, discomfiture and destruction in this very life and is not allowed to live long, and his mission is not allowed to prosper.

1884. The verse points to a great scientific truth. It seems to refer to the prematerial stage of the universe and purports to say that the whole universe, particularly the solar system, has developed out of an amorphous or nebular mass. God, in accordance with the laws which He had set in motion, split the mass of matter, and its scattered bits became the units of the solar system ("The Universe Surveyed" by Harold Richards, & "The Nature of the Universe" by Fred Hoyle). God then created all life out of water. The verse seems to imply that like the material universe a spiritual universe also develops out of an amorphous mass of confused ideas and foolish beliefs. Just as God in His infallible wisdom and in pursuance of a supreme design split the mass of matter and its scattered bits became the units of the solar system, in the same way He brings about a new spiritual order in a world weltering in the morass of confused ideas. When mankind sink into an impenetrable gloom of moral turpitude, and spiritual atmosphere becomes dense and oppressive, God causes a light to appear in the form of a Heavenly Messenger who shakes up the overspreading spiritual gloom, and out of this confused and lifeless mass of moral depravity and spiritual degeneration, a spiritual universe is born which begins to reach out from its centre and eventually embraces the whole earth, receiving life and direction from the impetus behind it.

1885. The expression, *an Tamīda Bihim*, means, lest it should quake with them; go round with them; be a source of benefit to them; *Māda* also meaning, he bestowed a benefit (Aqrab). The verse throws light on yet another scientific truth. Geology has established the fact that mountains have, to a great extent, secured the earth against earthquakes. In the beginning the earth was very hot from inside. When as the result of the intense heat gases were formed in the bowels of the earth, they forced a way out, thus causing violent agitations and eruptions in the form of volcanoes, which having cooled down took the shape of mountains ("Marvels & Mysteries of Science" by Allison Hox; & Enc. Brit. under "Geology"). The verse may also signify that the mountains are a great help to the earth in moving steadily on its axis. The Qur'ān spoke of the earth as 'moving round' long before it was discovered that it was not stationary and moved on its axis and round the sun.

1886. The solar system with its sun, moon, planets and stars is a well-ordered and well-regulated system which has existed for millions of years, never having once suffered the slightest disorder or deviation in the movements of these bodies. These heavenly bodies exercise a very wholesome influence on the terrestrial globe and its inhabitants. Just as a roof is a means of protection from rain, cold and heat for the residents of a house, similarly the heaven serves as a protection for the earth below and heavenly bodies exert their beneficial influence upon mankind.

34. And He it is Who created the night and the day, and the sun and the moon,[1886A] [a]each gliding along smoothly in *its* orbit.

وَهُوَ الَّذِي خَلَقَ اللَّيْلَ وَالنَّهَارَ وَالشَّمْسَ وَالْقَمَرَ ۖ كُلٌّ فِي فَلَكٍ يَسْبَحُونَ ﴿٣٤﴾

35. We granted not everlasting life to any mortal before thee. If thou shouldst die, shall they live *here* for ever?[1887]

وَمَا جَعَلْنَا لِبَشَرٍ مِنْ قَبْلِكَ الْخُلْدَ ۖ أَفَإِنْ مِتَّ فَهُمُ الْخَالِدُونَ ﴿٣٥﴾

36. Every soul shall taste of death; and We test you with evil and good by way of trial. And to Us shall you be returned.

كُلُّ نَفْسٍ ذَائِقَةُ الْمَوْتِ ۗ وَنَبْلُوكُمْ بِالشَّرِّ وَالْخَيْرِ فِتْنَةً ۖ وَإِلَيْنَا تُرْجَعُونَ ﴿٣٦﴾

37. [b]And when the disbelievers see thee, they only make a jest of thee, *and say*, 'Is this the one who speaks ill[1887A] of your gods?' Yet it is they themselves [c]who deny all mention of the Gracious *God*.

وَإِذَا رَآكَ الَّذِينَ كَفَرُوا إِنْ يَتَّخِذُونَكَ إِلَّا هُزُوًا ۚ أَهَٰذَا الَّذِي يَذْكُرُ آلِهَتَكُمْ وَهُمْ بِذِكْرِ الرَّحْمَٰنِ هُمْ كَافِرُونَ ﴿٣٧﴾

38. Man is created of haste.[1888] I will *certainly* show you My Signs, but ask Me not to hasten.

خُلِقَ الْإِنْسَانُ مِنْ عَجَلٍ ۚ سَأُرِيكُمْ آيَاتِي فَلَا تَسْتَعْجِلُونِ ﴿٣٨﴾

39. [d]And they say, 'When will this promise be *fulfilled*, if you are truthful?'

وَيَقُولُونَ مَتَىٰ هَٰذَا الْوَعْدُ إِنْ كُنْتُمْ صَادِقِينَ ﴿٣٩﴾

[a]36 : 41. [b]25 : 42. [c]13 : 31. [d]34 : 30; 36 : 49; 67 : 26.

1886A. The night and the day, the sun and the moon have all been created by God and they all fulfil human needs and are indispensable for man's existence on earth.

1887. All the different Dispensations and religious systems before the Holy Prophet were decreed and destined to suffer spiritual decay and death, and it was only the Dispensation of the Holy Prophet—the Islamic Dispensation—which was to live and continue till the end of time. The implication of the verse may also be that no human being is immune from decay or death, not even the Holy Prophet. Eternity and everlastingness are God's own exclusive attributes.

1887A. An Arab would say: *La'in dhakartanī la-tandamanna*, *i. e.*, if thou speak ill of me, thou wilt assuredly repent (Lane).

1888. The expression, *Khuliqal Insānu min 'Ajal*, signifies that haste forms a part of man's being, and that it is so prominent a trait of his character that he can be said to have been created, as it were, out of haste, *i.e.*, he is hasty by nature. When the Arabs have to express a prominent natural characteristic of a person they say, *Khuliqa Minhu*, *i.e*, he has been created of it. Similar expressions have been used in the Qur'ān elsewhere (7: 13 ; 30 : 55).

40. If only the disbelievers knew the time when they will not be able to ward off the fire[1889] from their faces, nor from their backs, and they will not be helped.

لَوْ يَعْلَمُ الَّذِيْنَ كَفَرُوْا حِيْنَ لَا يَكُفُّوْنَ عَنْ وُّجُوْهِهِمُ
النَّارَ وَلَا عَنْ ظُهُوْرِهِمْ وَلَا هُمْ يُنْصَرُوْنَ ۝٤٠

41. Nay, [a]it will come upon them unawares so that it will utterly confound[1890] them; and they will not be able to repel it, nor will they be granted respite.

بَلْ تَأْتِيْهِمْ بَغْتَةً فَتَبْهَتُهُمْ فَلَا يَسْتَطِيْعُوْنَ رَدَّهَا
وَلَا هُمْ يُنْظَرُوْنَ ۝٤١

42. [b]And Messengers have indeed been mocked at before thee, but [c]whereat they mocked encompassed those of them who scoffed.

وَلَقَدِ اسْتُهْزِئَ بِرُسُلٍ مِّنْ قَبْلِكَ فَحَاقَ بِالَّذِيْنَ
سَخِرُوْا مِنْهُمْ مَّا كَانُوْا بِهٖ يَسْتَهْزِءُوْنَ ۝٤٢ ع

R. 4 43. Say, 'Who can protect you by night and by day from[1891] the Gracious *God?*' Yet[d] they turn away from the remembrance of their Lord.

قُلْ مَنْ يَّكْلَؤُكُمْ بِالَّيْلِ وَالنَّهَارِ مِنَ الرَّحْمٰنِ ۭ
بَلْ هُمْ عَنْ ذِكْرِ رَبِّهِمْ مُّعْرِضُوْنَ ۝٤٣

44. Have they any gods that can protect them against Us? They cannot help themselves, nor can they be befriended *by anyone* against Us.

اَمْ لَهُمْ اٰلِهَةٌ تَمْنَعُهُمْ مِّنْ دُوْنِنَا ۭ لَا يَسْتَطِيْعُوْنَ
نَصْرَ اَنْفُسِهِمْ وَلَا هُمْ مِّنَّا يُصْحَبُوْنَ ۝٤٤

45. Nay, We provided those and their fathers *with the good things of this world* till [e]life grew long for them.

بَلْ مَتَّعْنَا هٰٓؤُلَآءِ وَاٰبَآءَهُمْ حَتّٰى طَالَ عَلَيْهِمُ

[a]36 : 50; 67 : 28. [b]6 : 11; 13 : 33. [c]11 : 9; 46 : 27. [d]18 : 102; 21 : 3; 26 : 6. [e]57 : 17.

1889. "Fire" here means "the fire of war." The disbelievers ignited that fire and then were themselves consumed in it. They drew the sword against Islām and by the sword they perished. The words, *from their faces*, signify the punishment they will see in front of them, *i.e.*, its signs will be apparent and manifest; and the words, *nor from their backs*, signify that the punishment will overtake them suddenly and unawares. Moreover, the punishment will overwhelm all of them—their leaders and the ordinary men (*Wujūh* also meaning leaders—Lane).

1890. The reference in the verse may be to the Fall of Mecca when the Quraish were taken completely by surprise and were utterly confounded.

1891. *Min* means, against; from; instead of (Aqrab).

[a]Do they not see that We are visiting the land, reducing it from its outlying borders?[1892] Can they even then be the victors?

الْعُمُرُ ۗ أَفَلَا يَرَوْنَ أَنَّا نَأْتِي الْأَرْضَ نَنْقُصُهَا مِنْ أَطْرَافِهَا ۚ أَفَهُمُ الْغٰلِبُوْنَ ﴿٤٥﴾

46. Say, 'I warn you only according to *Divine* revelation.' But [b]the deaf cannot hear the call when they are warned.

قُلْ إِنَّمَآ أُنْذِرُكُمْ بِالْوَحْيِ ۖ وَلَا يَسْمَعُ الصُّمُّ الدُّعَآءَ إِذَا مَا يُنْذَرُوْنَ ﴿٤٦﴾

47. [c]And if even a breath of thy Lord's punishment touch them, they will surely cry out, 'Woe to us! we were indeed wrongdoers.'

وَلَئِنْ مَّسَّتْهُمْ نَفْحَةٌ مِّنْ عَذَابِ رَبِّكَ لَيَقُوْلُنَّ يٰوَيْلَنَآ إِنَّا كُنَّا ظٰلِمِيْنَ ﴿٤٧﴾

48. And We shall set up just balances on the Day of Resurrection, so that [d]no soul will be wronged in the least.[1893] And even if it be the weight of a grain of mustard seed, We would bring it forth. And sufficient are We as reckoners.

وَنَضَعُ الْمَوَازِيْنَ الْقِسْطَ لِيَوْمِ الْقِيٰمَةِ فَلَا تُظْلَمُ نَفْسٌ شَيْـًٔا ۗ وَإِنْ كَانَ مِثْقَالَ حَبَّةٍ مِّنْ خَرْدَلٍ أَتَيْنَا بِهَا ۗ وَكَفٰى بِنَا حٰسِبِيْنَ ﴿٤٨﴾

49. [e]And We gave Moses and Aaron the Discrimination and a Light and a Reminder for the righteous,

وَلَقَدْ اٰتَيْنَا مُوْسٰى وَهٰرُوْنَ الْفُرْقَانَ وَضِيَآءً وَّذِكْرًا لِّلْمُتَّقِيْنَ ﴿٤٩﴾

50. [f]Those who fear their Lord in secret, and who dread the Hour *of Judgment*.

الَّذِيْنَ يَخْشَوْنَ رَبَّهُمْ بِالْغَيْبِ وَهُمْ مِّنَ السَّاعَةِ مُشْفِقُوْنَ ﴿٥٠﴾

[a]13 : 42. [b]30 : 53. [c]7 : 6. [d]4 : 41; 18 : 50. [e]2 : 54. [f]67 : 13.

1892. When the time of the national prosperity of a people becomes prolonged, they come to labour under the misconception that their prosperity and progress will never see decline and consequently they become arrogant and their hearts are hardened. Thus prolongation of the period of their prosperity becomes the cause of their downfall. The verse warns disbelievers against the wishful thinking and false complacency that their progress and prosperity will continue indefinitely and tells them not to shut their eyes to the patent fact that God is gradually but surely reducing and curtailing the land from all its sides, *i.e.*, Islām is making inroads into every home and all sections and strata of their society.

1893. The verse makes it clear that Hell is not everlasting. If even the slightest good work done by a man is to be rewarded, then a time must come when punishment should come to an end and the reward of good works should begin. Contrary to the teachings of other religions the Qur'ān teaches that it is Heaven and not Hell that is everlasting. See also 1351.

51. And this *Qur'ān* which We have sent down is a blessed[1894] Reminder; will you then reject it?

وَهٰذَا ذِكْرٌ مُّبٰرَكٌ اَنْزَلْنٰهُ ؕ اَفَاَنْتُمْ لَهٗ مُنْكِرُوْنَ ﴿٥١﴾

R. 5 52. And before this We gave Abraham his guidance and We knew him well.

وَلَقَدْ اٰتَيْنَاۤ اِبْرٰهِيْمَ رُشْدَهٗ مِنْ قَبْلُ وَكُنَّا بِهٖ عٰلِمِيْنَ ﴿٥٢﴾

53. [a]When he said to his father and his people, 'What[1895] are these images to which you are so devoted?'

اِذْ قَالَ لِاَبِيْهِ وَقَوْمِهٖ مَا هٰذِهِ التَّمَاثِيْلُ الَّتِيْۤ اَنْتُمْ لَهَا عٰكِفُوْنَ ﴿٥٣﴾

54. [b]They replied, 'We found our fathers worshipping them.'

قَالُوْا وَجَدْنَاۤ اٰبَآءَنَا لَهَا عٰبِدِيْنَ ﴿٥٤﴾

55. [c]He said, 'Then, you, as well as your fathers, have indeed been in manifest error.'

قَالَ لَقَدْ كُنْتُمْ اَنْتُمْ وَاٰبَآؤُكُمْ فِيْ ضَلٰلٍ مُّبِيْنٍ ﴿٥٥﴾

56. They said, 'Is it *really* the truth that thou hast brought us, or art thou jesting?'

قَالُوْۤا اَجِئْتَنَا بِالْحَقِّ اَمْ اَنْتَ مِنَ اللّٰعِبِيْنَ ﴿٥٦﴾

57. He replied, 'Nay, your Lord is the Lord of the heavens and the earth Who created them; and I am of those who bear witness[1896] to this;

قَالَ بَلْ رَّبُّكُمْ رَبُّ السَّمٰوٰتِ وَالْاَرْضِ الَّذِيْ فَطَرَهُنَّ ۖ وَاَنَا عَلٰى ذٰلِكُمْ مِّنَ الشّٰهِدِيْنَ ﴿٥٧﴾

58. 'And, by Allāh, I will certainly plan against your idols after you have gone away *and* turned your backs.'

وَتَاللّٰهِ لَاَكِيْدَنَّ اَصْنَامَكُمْ بَعْدَ اَنْ تُوَلُّوْا مُدْبِرِيْنَ ﴿٥٨﴾

[a]6 : 75; 19 : 43; 26 : 71. [b]26 : 75; 43 : 24. [c]60 : 5.

1894. The word *Mubārak* possesses the sense of firmness; steadiness; continuity; abundance of good; exaltation and collection, etc. (Lane). It is an epithet exclusively reserved for the Qur'ān (6 : 93), and in this title lies its outstanding distinction. Being *Mubārak* the Qur'ān combines in itself all good qualities that a heavenly Scripture should possess. There is no good which it does not possess in abundance and in which it does not excel all other Scriptures.

1895. The particle *mā* here denotes contempt and not a question. While talking to idol-worshippers Abraham generally made use of irony. See 6 : 77, 78,79. He seems to say to his people, 'how useless and futile are these images which you worship!' While Abraham used to talk in ironical language, Jesus talked in metaphors.

1896. The verse points to the supreme truth that Divine Messengers, when they talk about God, speak from personal experience. They do not invite people to God merely because human reason demands belief in His existence, but they do so with full conviction and firm faith (12 : 109).

59. [a]So he broke them into pieces, *all* except the chief of them, that they might return to it.[1897]

فَجَعَلَهُمْ جُذٰذًا اِلَّا كَبِيْرًا لَّهُمْ لَعَلَّهُمْ اِلَيْهِ يَرْجِعُوْنَ ﴿٥٩﴾

60. They said, 'Who has done this to our gods? Surely, he is a wrongdoer.'

قَالُوْا مَنْ فَعَلَ هٰذَا بِاٰلِهَتِنَآ اِنَّهٗ لَمِنَ الظّٰلِمِيْنَ ﴿٦٠﴾

61. Some *others* said, 'We heard a young man speak *ill*[1898] of them; he is called Abraham.'

قَالُوْا سَمِعْنَا فَتًى يَّذْكُرُهُمْ يُقَالُ لَهٗٓ اِبْرٰهِيْمُ ﴿٦١﴾

62. They said, 'Then bring him before the eyes of the people, that they may bear witness *against him*.'[1899]

قَالُوْا فَاْتُوْا بِهٖ عَلٰٓى اَعْيُنِ النَّاسِ لَعَلَّهُمْ يَشْهَدُوْنَ ﴿٦٢﴾

63. *Then* they said to Abraham, 'Is it thou who hast done this to our gods, O Abraham?'

قَالُوْٓا ءَاَنْتَ فَعَلْتَ هٰذَا بِاٰلِهَتِنَا يٰٓاِبْرٰهِيْمُ ﴿٦٣﴾

64. He replied, 'Well, *someone* has surely done this. Here is the chief of them. So ask them if they can speak.'[1900]

قَالَ بَلْ فَعَلَهٗ ۖ كَبِيْرُهُمْ هٰذَا فَسْـَٔلُوْهُمْ اِنْ كَانُوْا يَنْطِقُوْنَ ﴿٦٤﴾

65. Then they turned towards one another and said, 'You yourselves are surely in the wrong.'

فَرَجَعُوْٓا اِلٰٓى اَنْفُسِهِمْ فَقَالُوْٓا اِنَّكُمْ اَنْتُمُ الظّٰلِمُوْنَ ﴿٦٥﴾

[a]37 : 94.

1897. The pronoun *hi* in the expression, *Ilaihi*, may refer either to God, or to the chief idol or to Abraham himself.

1898. *Dhakara-hū* means, he spoke well or ill of him ; mentioned his faults (Lane).

1899. The reason why Abraham was summoned before the public was either that those, who had heard him speak ill of the idols, should bear witness against him, or that having listened to the evidence against him might decide what punishment should be meted out to him and that they should witness the punishment that was to be inflicted on him.

1900. Besides the meaning given in the text, the Arabic expression may have been spoken ironically by Abraham as was his wont while talking to his idolatrous people. In this case the sense of the words would be something like this : 'Why should I have done this, their chief may have done this,' meaning thereby that the fact is too evident to warrant any questioning or need any explanation that I have done this. If I had not done this, could this lifeless block of stone have done this ? Abraham seems to have rebuked his people and to have brought home to them the futility of their idolatrous practices, first by breaking the idols and then by challenging their votaries to ask those idols, if they could speak, to tell them who had broken them.

66. And they were made to hang down their heads[1901] *for shame and said to Abraham*, 'Certainly thou knowest well that these do not speak.'

ثُمَّ نُكِسُوا عَلٰى رُءُوْسِهِمْ لَقَدْ عَلِمْتَ مَا هٰٓؤُلَآءِ يَنْطِقُوْنَ ﴿٦٦﴾

67. He said, [a]'Do you then worship, instead of Allāh, that which cannot profit you at all, nor harm you?

قَالَ اَفَتَعْبُدُوْنَ مِنْ دُوْنِ اللّٰهِ مَا لَا يَنْفَعُكُمْ شَيْـًٔا وَّلَا يَضُرُّكُمْ ﴿٦٧﴾

68. 'Fie on you and on that which you worship instead of Allāh! Can you not understand?'

اُفٍّ لَّكُمْ وَلِمَا تَعْبُدُوْنَ مِنْ دُوْنِ اللّٰهِ ۭ اَفَلَا تَعْقِلُوْنَ ﴿٦٨﴾

69. [b]They said, 'Burn him and help your gods if *at all* you mean to do *something*.'

قَالُوْا حَرِّقُوْهُ وَانْصُرُوْٓا اٰلِهَتَكُمْ اِنْ كُنْتُمْ فٰعِلِيْنَ ﴿٦٩﴾

70. We said, 'O fire, be thou *a means of* coolness and safety[1902] for Abraham!'

قُلْنَا يٰنَارُ كُوْنِيْ بَرْدًا وَّسَلٰمًا عَلٰٓى اِبْرٰهِيْمَ ﴿٧٠﴾

71. [c]And they had intended an *evil* plan against him, but We made them the worst losers.

وَاَرَادُوْا بِهٖ كَيْدًا فَجَعَلْنٰهُمُ الْاَخْسَرِيْنَ ﴿٧١﴾

72. And We delivered him and Lot *and brought them* to the Land which We had blessed[1903] for the peoples.

وَنَجَّيْنٰهُ وَلُوْطًا اِلَى الْاَرْضِ الَّتِيْ بٰرَكْنَا فِيْهَا لِلْعٰلَمِيْنَ ﴿٧٢﴾

[a]29 : 18; 37 : 96. [b]29 : 25; 37 : 98. [c]37 : 99.

1901. The Arabic expression may mean: (*a*) They returned to their former state of disbelief, or wicked behaviour; (*b*) they reverted to disputation after they had taken the right course; (*c*) they hung down their heads for shame and were completely dumb-founded (Lane & Ma'ānī).

1902. How the fire became cool we are not told. Timely rain or a stormy hurricane might have extinguished it. In any event God did bring about circumstances which led to Abraham's deliverance. There is always an element of mystery in heavenly miracles; and the manner of Abraham being saved from the fire was indeed a great miracle. That Abraham had been cast into the fire is credited not only by the Jews, but also by the eastern Christians—25th of the second Canun, or January being set apart in the Syrian Calendar for the commemoration of the event (Hyde, De Rel. Vet Pers., p. 73). See also Mdr. Rabbah on Gen. Par. 17; Schalacheleth Hakabala, 2; Maimon de Idol. Ch. 1; and Jad Hachazakah, Vet, 6).

1903. Abraham journeyed from Ur (Mesopotamia) to Harran and from there, by God's command, to Canaan, which God had decreed to give to his posterity. This journey had a precise objective and aim. In pursuance of Divine plan and design all the great Prophets or their followers, at one time or another, have to emigrate from their homes.

73. [a]And We bestowed upon him Isaac, and a grandson, Jacob, and We made all *of them* righteous.

وَوَهَبْنَا لَهُ إِسْحٰقَ ۖ وَيَعْقُوبَ نَافِلَةً ۖ وَكُلًّا
جَعَلْنَا صٰلِحِينَ ﴿٧٣﴾

74. [b]And We made them leaders who guided *people* by Our command, and We sent revelation to them *enjoining* the doing of good works, and the observance of Prayer, and the giving of alms. And Us *alone* they worshipped.

وَجَعَلْنٰهُمْ أَئِمَّةً يَهْدُونَ بِأَمْرِنَا وَأَوْحَيْنَا
إِلَيْهِمْ فِعْلَ الْخَيْرٰتِ وَإِقَامَ الصَّلٰوةِ وَإِيتَاءَ
الزَّكٰوةِ ۚ وَكَانُوا لَنَا عٰبِدِينَ ﴿٧٤﴾

75. And to Lot We gave wisdom and knowledge. [c]And We saved him from the city which practised abominations. They were indeed a wicked *and* rebellious people.

وَلُوطًا اٰتَيْنٰهُ حُكْمًا وَعِلْمًا وَنَجَّيْنٰهُ مِنَ الْقَرْيَةِ
الَّتِي كَانَتْ تَعْمَلُ الْخَبٰٓئِثَ ۗ إِنَّهُمْ كَانُوا قَوْمَ سَوْءٍ
فٰسِقِينَ ﴿٧٥﴾

76. And We admitted him to Our mercy; surely he was *one* of the righteous.

ع ٥ وَأَدْخَلْنٰهُ فِي رَحْمَتِنَا ۖ إِنَّهُ مِنَ الصّٰلِحِينَ ﴿٧٦﴾

R. 6 77. [d]And *remember* Noah when he cried *to Us* aforetime, and We heard his prayer and delivered him and his family from the great distress,[1904]

وَنُوحًا إِذْ نَادٰى مِنْ قَبْلُ فَاسْتَجَبْنَا لَهُ فَنَجَّيْنٰهُ
وَأَهْلَهُ مِنَ الْكَرْبِ الْعَظِيمِ ﴿٧٧﴾

78. And We helped him against the people who rejected Our Signs. They were surely a wicked people; so [e]We drowned them all.

وَنَصَرْنٰهُ مِنَ الْقَوْمِ الَّذِينَ كَذَّبُوا بِاٰيٰتِنَا ۚ
إِنَّهُمْ كَانُوا قَوْمَ سَوْءٍ فَأَغْرَقْنٰهُمْ أَجْمَعِينَ ﴿٧٨﴾

[a]11 : 72; 19 : 50; 29 : 28; 37 : 113; 51 : 29. [b]2 : 125; 32 : 25. [c]7 : 84; 27 : 58; 29 : 34. [d]26 : 118-120; 37 : 76-77; 54 : 11. [e]26 : 121; 37 : 83; 54 : 12-13; 71 : 26.

1904. It is worthy of note that this *Sūrah* makes a special mention of the trials and tribulations through which almost all the Prophets of God had to pass in their times and also of the way in which God helped them and delivered them from their afflictions, the implication being that like those Prophets the Holy Prophet of Islām too will have to suffer hardships and privations and like them he too will come out of his ordeal with success.

79. And *remember* David and Solomon when they exercised their *respective* judgments concerning the crop,[1905] when the sheep *of certain people* strayed therein by night, and We were bearers of witness to their judgment.

وَدَاوُدَ وَسُلَيْمٰنَ إِذْ يَحْكُمٰنِ فِي الْحَرْثِ إِذْ
نَفَشَتْ فِيهِ غَنَمُ الْقَوْمِ ۚ وَكُنَّا لِحُكْمِهِمْ شٰهِدِينَ ﴿٧٩﴾

80. We gave Solomon the *right* understanding[1906] of *the matter* and to each of them We gave wisdom and knowledge. [a]And We subjected the mountains and the birds to David to celebrate *God's* praises with him.[1907] And *it was* We *Who* did *all these things*.

فَفَهَّمْنٰهَا سُلَيْمٰنَ ۚ وَكُلًّا اٰتَيْنَا حُكْمًا وَّعِلْمًا ۚ وَّ
سَخَّرْنَا مَعَ دَاوُدَ الْجِبَالَ يُسَبِّحْنَ وَالطَّيْرَ ۚ وَكُنَّا
فٰعِلِينَ ﴿٨٠﴾

81. And We taught him the making of coats of mail[1908] for you, that they might protect you from each other's violence *in your battles*. Will you then be grateful ?

وَعَلَّمْنٰهُ صَنْعَةَ لَبُوسٍ لَّكُمْ لِتُحْصِنَكُمْ مِّنْ
بَأْسِكُمْ ۚ فَهَلْ أَنْتُمْ شٰكِرُونَ ﴿٨١﴾

[a]34 : 11; 38 : 19-20.

1905. In order to add to the beauty of expression, use has been made of metaphorical language in this and the following few verses. *Al-Ḥarth* may signify Solomon's country and the words *Ghanam al-Qaum* may represent those wild and predatory neighbouring tribes who raided Solomon's country. The reference is to the policy which David and Solomon adopted to repel and defeat the depradations of those savage tribes. David was a great warrior and as such was in favour of adopting a strong policy. Solomon, however, wished to pursue a milder policy and to win over those tribes by entering into treaties of friendship with them.

1906. The words signify that Solomon's policy of moderation and conciliation was right in the then obtaining circumstances, and that the charge levelled against him by some Jewish writers of having pursued a weak policy which brought about the downfall of his dynasty is ill-founded. But the defence of Solomon should not be taken to mean that the strong policy adopted by David in his own time was wrong. Any misunderstanding leading to this inference has been dispelled by the clause, *and to each of them We gave wisdom and knowledge*, which makes it clear that the policies of both David and Solomon were best in the circumstances and quite suited to the particular occasions.

1907. The words, *We subjected the mountains and the birds to David to celebrate God's praises with* him, have been taken literally to mean that the mountains and birds were under David's control and when he sang the praises of God they actually joined with him in that pious act. The words merely mean that big men (*al-Jibāl*) and highly spiritual men (*al-Ṭair*) glorified God and sang Divine praises along with David. At several places in the Qur'ān not only mountains and birds but all other things in the heavens and the earth—the sun, the moon, the stars, the day and the night, the animals, the birds, the rivers, the seas, the winds, the clouds, etc., are stated to have been subjected to man (2 : 165; 7 : 55; 22 : 38 &

1908. See next page.

82. [a]And *We subjected* to Solomon the violent wind. It blew, at his bidding, toward the land which We had blessed.[1909] And We have knowledge of all things.

وَلِسُلَيْمٰنَ الرِّيْحَ عَاصِفَةً تَجْرِيْ بِاَمْرِهٖۤ اِلَى
الْاَرْضِ الَّتِيْ بٰرَكْنَا فِيْهَا ۗ وَكُنَّا بِكُلِّ شَيْءٍ
عٰلِمِيْنَ ﴿٨٢﴾

83. And *We subjected to him* [b]deep divers[1910] who dived for him, and did other works besides that; and it was We Who guarded them.

وَمِنَ الشَّيٰطِيْنِ مَنْ يَّغُوْصُوْنَ لَهٗ وَيَعْمَلُوْنَ
عَمَلًا دُوْنَ ذٰلِكَ ۚ وَكُنَّا لَهُمْ حٰفِظِيْنَ ﴿٨٣﴾

84. [c]And *call to mind* Job[1911] when he cried to his Lord, 'Distress has afflicted me, and Thou art the Most Merciful of all who show mercy.'

وَاَيُّوْبَ اِذْ نَادٰى رَبَّهٗۤ اَنِّيْ مَسَّنِيَ الضُّرُّ وَاَنْتَ
اَرْحَمُ الرّٰحِمِيْنَ ﴿٨٤﴾

[a]34 : 13. [b]34 : 13; 38 : 37 ; 38 : 38-39. [c]38 : 42.

45 : 13-14). The word *Jibāl* may also signify 'people living in the mountains' as the name of a place sometimes stands for its people (12 : 83). Thus the subjection of "the mountains" to David may signify that he conquered and subjugated wild and savage mountain tribes. He was a great conqueror and subduer of wild mountain tribes. The Bible also refers to the subjugation of mountain tribes by David (II Sam., chapter 5). Similarly, celebration by birds of God's praises should occasion no surprise. Elsewhere in the Qur'ān, we read that all things, animate or inanimate, the angels, animals, birds, the heavens and the earth even the forces of nature, sing the praises of God, only man cannot understand their glorification (13 : 14; 17 : 45; 21 : 20-21; 24 : 42; 59 : 2; 61 : 2; & 64 : 2) which is that they carry out the duties assigned to them by God and thus demonstrate that God is perfect and completely free from all flaws, failings and frailties and so is His handiwork. The word "birds" may also signify actual birds. In this sense the meaning would be that David made use of birds which had been especially trained for this purpose to carry messages in time of war. It may also signify flocks of birds which followed David's victorious armies and feasted on the dead bodies of his fallen foes.

1908. The reference in the verse is again to the military might of David and to his great skill in making implements of war and coats of mail. David invented and developed various kinds of armours by means of which he made great conquests. In his reign the Israelite Kingdom had attained the zenith of its power. It was the golden period in Israelite history.

1909. It appears that the vessels of Solomon plied in the Persian Gulf, the Red and the Mediterranean Seas and regular trade was carried on between Palestine and the countries lying round the Persian Gulf and these two seas (1 Kings, 10 : 27-29). 'In partnership with Hiram of Tyre he maintained a fleet of ocean-going ships trading at regular intervals to Mediterranean ports, bringing gold, silver, ivory, apes and peacocks' (1 Kings, 10: 22 ; 10 : 27-29; II Chron. 8: 18 ; Enc. Brit. under "Solomon)". Here the adjective used about the wind is '*Āsifah* (violent) while in 38 : 37 it is *Rukhā'* (gentle) which shows that though the wind blew fast, it was gentle and did no damage to Solomon's ships.

1910. *Shaiṭān* meaning a rebel and recalcitrant person and also one who is expert in anything (2 : 15), the verse purports to say that the non-Israelite people whom Solomon subjugated were employed on various arduous works by his orders. They worked as carpenters, iron-smiths, divers etc., professions which members of a subject race generally adopt (see I Kings, 9 : 21-22). The words, *who dived for him*, may refer to the divers of Baḥrain and Masqaṭ who dived in the Persian Gulf for taking out pearls. They were employed for that purpose by Solomon.

1911. See next page.

85. So We heard his prayer and removed the distress from which *he suffered*, [a]and We restored to him his family and the like thereof with them, as a mercy from Us. and as an admonition to the worshippers.

فَاسْتَجَبْنَا لَهٗ فَكَشَفْنَا مَا بِهٖ مِنْ ضُرٍّ وَّاٰتَيْنٰهُ اَهْلَهٗ
وَمِثْلَهُمْ مَّعَهُمْ رَحْمَةً مِّنْ عِنْدِنَا وَذِكْرٰى
لِلْعٰبِدِيْنَ ﴿٨٥﴾

86. And *call to mind* [b]Ishmael and Idrīs and [c]Dhu'l-Kifl.[1912] All were men of patience.

وَاِسْمٰعِيْلَ وَاِدْرِيْسَ وَذَا الْكِفْلِ كُلٌّ مِّنَ
الصّٰبِرِيْنَ ﴿٨٦﴾

87. And We admitted them to Our mercy. Surely, they were of the righteous ones.

وَاَدْخَلْنٰهُمْ فِيْ رَحْمَتِنَا اِنَّهُمْ مِّنَ الصّٰلِحِيْنَ ﴿٨٧﴾

[a]38 : 44. [b]6 : 87; 38 : 49. [c]38 : 49.

1911. Job is mentioned in the Bible as having lived in the land of 'Uz which appeared to have been situated somewhere in the north of Arabia, between Syria and the Gulf of 'Aqbah. It is said that Job lived there before the departure of the Israelites from Egypt. According to some Jewish writers he lived about 200 years before Moses. According to some other authorities, however, he was a compatriot of Moses, but was not an Israelite Prophet, having descended from Esau, the elder brother of Israel. Of all the Books of the Old Testament, the Book of Job is unique in this respect that with the exception of the word, Jehovah, which is a Jewish name for God, the whole history of the Mosaic Law and that of the Jews is conspicuous by its absence in it. The Qur'ān has confined itself to mentioning a few relevant facts about Job in the present and the next verse. It is stated that he was a holy man of God and that he had to suffer great hardships and privations as a result of which he became separated from his family, and followers, who subsequently were made to join him, having increased manifold in the meantime. Job has also been mentioned in vv. 4: 164; 6 : 85 & 38 : 42 along with David and Solomon. This shows that like these two great Prophets, he was a man of influence and affluence and like them he had to pass through trials and tribulations which he bore with exemplary patience and fortitude. The courage and fortitude displayed by Job under very severe affliction and distress has become proverbial. See also Jew. Enc., under "Job" and Enc. of Islām under "Aiyūb."

1912. The identity of Dhu'l-Kifl is wrapped in uncertainty. Muslim Commentators of the Qur'ān identify him with several persons, chiefly with some biblical Prophets. But the Prophet known by this name appears to be Ezekiel who is called Dhu'l-Kifl by the Arabs. There seems to exist a close resemblance between the words *Dhu'l-Kifl* (*Ḥizqīl*) and Ezekiel, both in form and meaning, the former word meaning 'possessed of an abundant portion' and the latter 'God gives strength.' Rodwell says that Ezekiel is called Dhu'l-Kifl by the Arabs. According to Karsten Niebuhr, a little town called Kefil which is situated midway between Najaf and Ḥilla (Babylon) contains the shrine of Ezekiel which is still visited by Jewish pilgrims. He is further of the view that *Dhu'l Kifl* is the Arabic form of Ezekiel. The Jews too regard Ezekiel as Dhu'l Kifl (Enc. of Islām under "Dhu'l-Kifl" & Niebuhr's "Travels" ii, 265). Born probably about 622 B.C. in a priestly family Dhu'l-Kifl had spent the first twenty-five years of his life in Judah. In 592 B.C. at the age of thirty he received the Call and began to preach against idol-worship and the injustice and immorality of his people. In the meantime Babylon had taken the place of Assyria as the dominant Power in Western Asia and Judah had acknowledged its overlordship. But Jehoiakim, the King of Judah under the influence of his evil councillors revolted against the authority of Babylon, thus drawing upon himself the vengeance of Nebuchadnezzar who successfully besieged Jerusalem in 597 and carried into exile many of her leading citizens, including Ezekiel and Jehoiachim, a king of three months' standing—his father Jehoiakim having

88. [a]And *remember* Dhu'l-Nūn, when he went away in anger, and he was sure *in his mind* that We would not cause him distress[1913] and [b]he cried out in the midst of *his* afflictions: 'There is no god but Thou, Holy art Thou. I have indeed been of the wrongdoers.'

وَذَا النُّوْنِ اِذْ ذَّهَبَ مُغَاضِبًا فَظَنَّ اَنْ لَّنْ نَّقْدِرَ
عَلَيْهِ فَنَادٰى فِى الظُّلُمٰتِ اَنْ لَّآ اِلٰهَ اِلَّآ اَنْتَ
سُبْحٰنَكَ اِنِّىْ كُنْتُ مِنَ الظّٰلِمِيْنَ ﴿۸۸﴾

89. [c]So We heard his prayer and delivered him from *his* distress. And thus do We deliver *true* believers.

فَاسْتَجَبْنَا لَهٗ وَنَجَّيْنٰهُ مِنَ الْغَمِّ وَكَذٰلِكَ
نُـْۨجِى الْمُؤْمِنِيْنَ ﴿۸۹﴾

90. [d]And *remember* Zachariah also when he cried to his Lord: 'My Lord, leave me not alone and Thou art the Best of inheritors.'

وَزَكَرِيَّآ اِذْ نَادٰى رَبَّهٗ رَبِّ لَا تَذَرْنِىْ فَرْدًا
وَّاَنْتَ خَيْرُ الْوٰرِثِيْنَ ﴿۹۰﴾

91. So We heard his prayer and bestowed upon him John and cured his wife *of sterility* for him. They used to vie with one another in good works and [e]they called on Us in hope and in fear, and they humbled themselves before Us.

فَاسْتَجَبْنَا لَهٗ وَوَهَبْنَا لَهٗ يَحْيٰى وَاَصْلَحْنَا لَهٗ
زَوْجَهٗ اِنَّهُمْ كَانُوْا يُسٰرِعُوْنَ فِى الْخَيْرٰتِ وَ
يَدْعُوْنَنَا رَغَبًا وَّرَهَبًا وَكَانُوْا لَنَا خٰشِعِيْنَ ﴿۹۱﴾

[a]37 : 140-141; 68 : 49. [b]37 : 144. [c]68 : 50-51. [d]3: 39; 19 : 3-7. [e]32 : 17.

meanwhile died. Jehoiachim was succeeded by his uncle, Zedekiah, who for a time remained faithful to Babylon, but foolishly depending upon the support of Egypt renounced his allegiance to Babylon, an act which Ezekiel bitterly resented and denounced as treachery to Yahweh himself. The result was that Jerusalem was invested by Nebuchadnezzar, and after a siege of eighteen months it was destroyed amid horrors untold. The Temple on which such a passion of love had been lavished was reduced to ashes and the people deported to Babylon (586 B.C.). Such was the situation which confronted Ezekiel. In 592 B.C. five years before the downfall he had foreseen it and with some detail had predicted it and had warned the Jews of the impending disaster. The first terrific blow by Babylon in 597 B.C. had left the Jews unconvinced of the probability of their imminent political extinction—a probability which to Ezekiel was a certainty as clear as noonday. But as Ezekiel foretold the destruction of the Jews, so did he predict their restoration. The picture drawn by him of the salvation in store for his people is as gracious and brilliant as his forecast of their downfall had been stern. His prophecy about the restoration and return to Jerusalem was based upon a vision which he had seen (Ezekiel, ch. 37) and to which a reference is to be found in the Qur'ān also (2 : 260). But he did not live long to see the fulfilment of his prophecy because he died in captivity in 570 B.C. at the age of 52. Ezekiel and Daniel are called the Prophets of the Exile ("The Holy Bible," edited by Rev. Sc.I. Cofield & Peake's "Commentary of the Bible").

1913. The verse does not specify the cause of Jonah's anger. Apparently he did not and could not have become angry with God. It must have been the obstinate refusal of his people to accept his Message which enraged him, because for a Prophet to become angry with God is inconceivable. The Elect of God do not even speak, nor do they act until God commands them to do so (21 : 28). The words, *Lan Naqdira 'Alaihi*, mean, 'We will not straiten him' or 'We will not decree against him any distress' (Lisān & Aqrab).

92. [a]And *remember* her who guarded her chastity, so We breathed[1914] into her of Our Word and We made her and her son a Sign for *all* peoples.

وَالَّتِيْٓ اَحْصَنَتْ فَرْجَهَا فَنَفَخْنَا فِيْهَا مِنْ رُّوْحِنَا وَجَعَلْنٰهَا وَابْنَهَآ اٰيَةً لِّلْعٰلَمِيْنَ ﴿۹۲﴾

93. [b]Verily, this community of yours is one community[1915] and I am your Lord, so worship Me.

اِنَّ هٰذِهٖٓ اُمَّتُكُمْ اُمَّةً وَّاحِدَةً ۖ وَّاَنَا رَبُّكُمْ فَاعْبُدُوْنِ ﴿۹۳﴾

94. [c]And they split up their affair among themselves[1916] and all will return to Us.

وَتَقَطَّعُوْٓا اَمْرَهُمْ بَيْنَهُمْ ؕ كُلٌّ اِلَيْنَا رٰجِعُوْنَ ﴿۹۴﴾ ع

R. 7 95. [d]So whoever does good works and is a believer, his endeavour will not be rejected and We shall surely record it.

فَمَنْ يَّعْمَلْ مِنَ الصّٰلِحٰتِ وَهُوَ مُؤْمِنٌ فَلَا كُفْرَانَ لِسَعْيِهٖ ۚ وَاِنَّا لَهٗ كٰتِبُوْنَ ﴿۹۵﴾

96. [e]And it is an inviolable law for a township which We have destroyed that they shall not return.[1917]

وَحَرٰمٌ عَلٰى قَرْيَةٍ اَهْلَكْنٰهَآ اَنَّهُمْ لَا يَرْجِعُوْنَ ﴿۹۶﴾

97. *It shall be so* even when [f]Gog and Magog[1918] are let loose and they shall hasten forth from every height *and from the top of every wave.*[1919]

حَتّٰٓى اِذَا فُتِحَتْ يَاْجُوْجُ وَمَاْجُوْجُ وَهُمْ مِّنْ كُلِّ حَدَبٍ يَّنْسِلُوْنَ ﴿۹۷﴾

[a]66 : 13. [b]23 : 53. [c]23 : 54. [d]4 : 125; 10 : 10; 16 : 98; 20 : 113. [e]23 : 100 : 101 ; 36 : 32. [f]18 : 95.

1914. The verse refutes the calumnious charges that the Jews had levelled against Mary. It may also apply to any person who leads a righteous and upright life. In 66 : 13 a certain class of righteous believers are likened to Mary. Everyone of such righteous believers, so to say, is Mary, and when God breathes into him of His spirit he becomes a "son of Mary," *i.e.*, he acquires the Divine attributes possessed by Jesus.

1915. In the preceding few verses some Prophets of God and some other righteous persons have been mentioned together. This is no mere coincidence. The mentioning together of these Prophets serves a definite purpose. All of them had one thing in common. They all suffered great hardships and distress in one form or another and displayed the highest and noblest form of patience and endurance under severest trials. They also taught the one basic principle of all religions—Divine Unity.

1916. One class of people—the righteous servants of God has been mentioned in the preceding few verses. The present verse refers to another class—those who reject God's Prophets with the result that they fall victim to differences and disagreements among themselves and come to hold mutually antagonistic beliefs and doctrines.

1917. It is an inviolable Divine law that the dead are never sent back to this world. Those, who pass away from this world, pass away for ever (23 : 100, 101).

1918 & 1919. See next page.

98. And *the fulfilment of God's* promise draws nigh;[1920] then behold, [a]the eyes of those who disbelieve will fixedly stare[1920A] *and they will exclaim* 'Alas for us! we were indeed heedless of this; nay, we were wrongdoers.'

وَاقْتَرَبَ الْوَعْدُ الْحَقُّ فَإِذَا هِيَ شَاخِصَةٌ أَبْصَارُ الَّذِينَ كَفَرُوا يَا وَيْلَنَا قَدْ كُنَّا فِي غَفْلَةٍ مِنْ هَٰذَا بَلْ كُنَّا ظَالِمِينَ ﴿٩٨﴾

99. *It will be said to them*, 'Surely, you and that which you worship beside Allāh are the fuel of Hell. [b]To it you will all come.'

إِنَّكُمْ وَمَا تَعْبُدُونَ مِنْ دُونِ اللَّهِ حَصَبُ جَهَنَّمَ أَنْتُمْ لَهَا وَارِدُونَ ﴿٩٩﴾

100. If these, *as you allege*, had been gods, they would not have entered it; and all will abide therein.

لَوْ كَانَ هَٰؤُلَاءِ آلِهَةً مَا وَرَدُوهَا وَكُلٌّ فِيهَا خَالِدُونَ ﴿١٠٠﴾

101. [c]Therein groaning will be their *lot* and they will not hear therein *anything else*.[1921]

لَهُمْ فِيهَا زَفِيرٌ وَهُمْ فِيهَا لَا يَسْمَعُونَ ﴿١٠١﴾

102. [d]But *as for those* for whom *the promise of* a good reward has already gone forth from Us, these will be removed far from it.

إِنَّ الَّذِينَ سَبَقَتْ لَهُمْ مِنَّا الْحُسْنَىٰ أُولَٰئِكَ عَنْهَا مُبْعَدُونَ ﴿١٠٢﴾

[a]14 : 43. [b]19 : 72. [c]11 : 107; 25 :14; 67 : 8. [d]19 : 73.

1918. See 1728.

1919. When read in conjunction with the preceding one, this verse purports to say that the law of nature works in this way that once a people, after the hey-day of their grandeur and glory, fall a victim to death and destruction they never regain their lost glory. Even Gog and Magog, notwithstanding their great material grandeur and glory, will fall a victim to the same law. They will fall, never to rise again. Gog and Magog, or the Christian nations of the West, have already scaled all the heights of political power and have spread over the whole world. The Quranic expression means, they will occupy every point of vantage and will dominate the whole world.

1920. The domination of Gog and Magog will be followed by catastrophic occurrences in the world which eventually will result in the triumph of Islām (61 : 10) and the vanquishment of the forces of falsehood and materialism as represented by Gog and Magog.

1920A. When after the complete destruction of Gog and Magog Islām will regain its former greatness and glory those, who had lost all hope of its regeneration, will scarcely believe their eyes.

1921. They will not hear anything that will give them solace and comfort; or there will be so much crying and shrieking and wailing in Hell that its inmates will not hear each other's voice.

103. They will not hear the slightest sound thereof,[1922] [a]and they shall abide in the *state* which their souls desire.

لَا يَسْمَعُوْنَ حَسِيْسَهَا ۚ وَهُمْ فِيْ مَا اشْتَهَتْ
اَنْفُسُهُمْ خٰلِدُوْنَ ﴿١٠٣﴾

104. The Great Terror will not grieve them, and [b]the angels will meet them, *saying*, 'This is your day which you were promised;

لَا يَحْزُنُهُمُ الْفَزَعُ الْاَكْبَرُ وَتَتَلَقّٰىهُمُ الْمَلٰٓئِكَةُ
هٰذَا يَوْمُكُمُ الَّذِيْ كُنْتُمْ تُوْعَدُوْنَ ﴿١٠٤﴾

105. [c]'The day when We shall roll up the heavens[1923] like the rolling up of written scrolls *by a scribe*.' [d]As We began the first creation, so shall We repeat[1924] it—a promise *binding* upon Us; We shall certainly fulfil it.

يَوْمَ نَطْوِي السَّمَآءَ كَطَيِّ السِّجِلِّ لِلْكُتُبِ ۭ كَمَا
بَدَاْنَآ اَوَّلَ خَلْقٍ نُّعِيْدُهٗ ۭ وَعْدًا عَلَيْنَا ۭ اِنَّا كُنَّا
فٰعِلِيْنَ ﴿١٠٥﴾

106. And We have *already* written in the Book *of David*, after the Reminder, that My righteous servants shall inherit the land.[1925]

وَلَقَدْ كَتَبْنَا فِي الزَّبُوْرِ مِنْۢ بَعْدِ الذِّكْرِ
اَنَّ الْاَرْضَ يَرِثُهَا عِبَادِيَ الصّٰلِحُوْنَ ﴿١٠٦﴾

[a]41 : 32. [b]41 : 31. [c]39 : 68. [d]20 : 56; 29 : 20; 30 : 12.

1922. This and the next verse show that the righteous servants of God will be kept far away from Hell, and will not even hear its slightest sound, much less enter it as is generally misunderstood from 19 : 72.

1923. 'The rolling up of the heavens' may mean that great empires will be swept away and powerful nations will be destroyed and other peoples will rise to power in their place. Or, the meaning may be that through the Holy Prophet a great transformation will come about and the old heaven will be rolled up and in its place a new heaven and a new earth will be created. The old order will die and in its place a new and better order will come into being. Never had the world witnessed such a complete transformation in the lives of a people as it did in the Holy Prophet's time.

1924. The expression, *so shall We repeat it,* implies that the order brought into being by the Holy Prophet will receive a set-back through the material outlook on life of Muslims, created by the godless and mechanistic Western civilization. But this set-back will be temporary and Islām will experience a new spiritual awakening and will again emerge triumphant.

1925. By "the land" is meant Palestine. Christian writers have also interpreted the words 'inherit the land' or 'inherit the earth' in the Psalms as meaning, inherit Canaan, 'the pledge of God's covenant.' The reference in the words, 'in the Book of David' is to Psalms, 37 : 9, 11, 22 & 29. There is also a prophecy in Deuteronomy (28 : 11 & 34 : 4) that Palestine will be given to the Israelites. Palestine remained in the hands of Christians till Muslims conquered it in the Caliphate of 'Umar, the Second Successor of the Holy Prophet. It is to this conquest of Palestine by Muslim arms that the prophecy embodied in the verse under comment may refer. It remained under Muslim possession for about 1350 years with the exception of a brief space of 92 years, when during the Crusades it changed hands, till in our own time through the evil designs of some so-called democratic

107. Herein, surely, is a message for a people who worship *God*.

إِنَّ فِي هٰذَا لَبَلٰغًا لِّقَوْمٍ عٰبِدِيْنَ ۝١٠٧

108. [a]And We have not sent thee but as a mercy for *all* peoples.[1926]

وَمَآ أَرْسَلْنٰكَ إِلَّا رَحْمَةً لِّلْعٰلَمِيْنَ ۝١٠٨

109. [b]Say, 'Surely it has been revealed to me that your God is but One God. Will you then submit?'

قُلْ إِنَّمَا يُوْحٰٓى إِلَيَّ أَنَّمَآ إِلٰهُكُمْ إِلٰهٌ وَّاحِدٌ ۚ
فَهَلْ أَنْتُمْ مُّسْلِمُوْنَ ۝١٠٩

110. But if they turn back, say, 'I have warned you all alike and [c]I know not whether that which you are promised is near or far;[1927]

فَإِنْ تَوَلَّوْا فَقُلْ اٰذَنْتُكُمْ عَلٰى سَوَآءٍ ۖ وَإِنْ أَدْرِيْٓ
أَقَرِيْبٌ أَمْ بَعِيْدٌ مَّا تُوْعَدُوْنَ ۝١١٠

111. [d]'Verily, He knows what is open in speech, and He knows that which you hide;

إِنَّهٗ يَعْلَمُ الْجَهْرَ مِنَ الْقَوْلِ وَيَعْلَمُ مَا تَكْتُمُوْنَ ۝١١١

112. 'And I know not but that it may be a trial for you, and only an enjoyment for a while.'

وَإِنْ أَدْرِيْ لَعَلَّهٗ فِتْنَةٌ لَّكُمْ وَمَتَاعٌ إِلٰى
حِيْنٍ ۝١١٢

113. [e]*And the Prophet* said, 'My Lord, judge Thou with truth.[1928] Our Lord is the Gracious *God* Whose help is sought against that which you assert.'

قٰلَ رَبِّ احْكُمْ بِالْحَقِّ ۗ وَرَبُّنَا الرَّحْمٰنُ الْمُسْتَعَانُ
عَلٰى مَا تَصِفُوْنَ ۝١١٣ ع

[a]34 : 29. [b]18 : 111; 41 : 7. [c]72 : 26. [d]2 : 34; 20 : 8; 87 : 8. [e]7 : 90.

Christian Powers, the country of the name of Palestine has altogether ceased to exist and on its ruins the State of Israel has been built. The Jews have come to their own after wandering in wilderness for about 2000 years. But this great historical event, too, has taken place in fulfilment of a Quranic prophecy (17 : 105). This, however, is only a temporary phase. The Muslims are destined to win it back. Sooner or later—sooner rather than later—Palestine will revert to Muslim possession. This is a Divine decree and nobody can alter the decree of God.

1926. The Holy Prophet was a mercy for the whole of mankind as his Message is not confined to any particular country or people. Through him the nations of the world have been blessed as they were never blessed before.

1927. God is not bound by days and hours for the fulfilment of His promises. He knows best if and when a certain prophecy is to be fulfilled.

1928. The Holy Prophet is commanded to offer the prayer contained in this verse as a protection against the powers of evil that were to be let loose upon the world in the Latter Days in the form of Gog and Magog. It is clear from the Bible that in the time of Gog and Magog physical force will not be the only danger to Islām. There will be other factors which will constitute a far greater source of danger to it. The Holy Prophet may also be represented as praying in this verse that the duration of the possession of Palestine by the Jews may be the shortest possible and that it may revert to its legitimate heirs—the Muslims.

CHAPTER 22

AL-ḤAJJ

(Revealed partly before and partly after Hijrah)

Date of Revelation and Context

According to scholarly opinion a part of the *Sūrah* was revealed before the *Hijrah* and a part after it. Ḍaḥḥāk, however, holds that the whole of it was revealed after the *Hijrah*. In *Sūrah* Al-Anbiyā' it was stated that Divine punishment continues to dog the footsteps of disbelievers because they reject the truth. In its last verse the Holy Prophet was enjoined to invoke Divine punishment upon disbelievers because of their persistently hostile attitude. The opening verse of the present *Sūrah* constitutes an answer to his prayer. This is the immediate connection of the *Sūrah* with Al-Anbiyā'. But there exists a broader connection and deeper relationship between the subject-matter of some preceding Chapters and this *Sūrah*. The subject which began in *Sūrah* Maryam and was later developed and elaborated in *Sūrahs* Ṭā Hā and Al-Anbiyā' is brought to completion in the present *Sūrah*. In *Sūrah* Maryam the basic principles of the Christian Faith were explained and effectively refuted, as without their refutation there could have been no justification for a new Message. The Holy Prophet had claimed to have brought a new Message and a new Law for the whole of mankind. If Christianity could be shown to have existed in the world in its pristine purity and if there was extant in the world a Faith which claimed to be true, practical and practicable, then the need of a new Faith could not arise. So the basic principles of Christianity had to be proved to be false and unfounded. This was done in *Sūrah* Maryam where by shedding light on the incidents attending his birth Jesus was shown to have been in no way different from, or superior to, other Messengers of God. In Chapter Ṭā Hā, the Christian doctrine that Law is a curse was fully and completely repudiated, while in *Sūrah* Al-Anbiyā' the same subject was treated in a different manner, and the doctrine of original sin was shown to be quite untenable. It was made clear that if man suffered from the legacy of original sin and being devoid of free will he could not get rid of it, then the very object of the advent of Divine Messengers was defeated and man could not have been regarded as accountable for his actions and deeds. In the present *Sūrah*, however, we are told that if Jesus had attained the highest stage of spiritual perfection, then there was no need of a new *Sharī'ah* (Law) and a new Messenger. But the fact that the Holy Prophet had claimed to be a new Messenger and to have brought a new Law, in itself constitutes a challenge to this Christian belief.

Subject-Matter

The subject-matter of the *Sūrah* is split into five main parts : (1) The disbelievers are threatened with Divine punishment because they reject the claim of the Holy Prophet which rests on the following very sound hypotheses : (*a*) His teachings are indispensable for mankind and are based on truth and wisdom and have sound and solid arguments to establish their abiding utility and the emptiness of the objections of disbelievers. (*b*) Heavenly Signs uphold the Prophet's cause—his followers are prospering both materially and spiritually and his enemies like those of the former Prophets are suffering defeat at his hands. (*c*) He will be blessed with Divine boons and blessings in an unusual measure. (*d*) His teachings are designed to bring about peace, harmony and goodwill among nations of the world. (*e*) All false Faiths and religious systems including Christianity will retreat before the invincible onrush of Islām and will eventually be completely routed. (2) All Divine Messengers were opposed and satanic people placed all sorts of obstacles and impediments in their way. But God removed all those obstacles and the cause of Truth ultimately prevailed. (3) The advent of the Holy Prophet has fulfilled that Divine purpose for which Patriarch Abraham had prayed to God in the barren and arid Valley of Mecca when he left his son Ishmael and his wife Hagar there. (4) The Holy Prophet has met with long and hard opposition and has endured untold hardships with great patience and fortitude, and the time has now arrived that he be granted permission to fight his opponents in self-defence.

Defensive warfare is not only permissible but is commendable when the cause of Truth is at stake; and Divine succour comes to those who fight in its defence. If fighting in defence of Truth had not been allowed, man would have become deprived of freedom of conscience which is his most precious heritage, and God would have ceased to be worshipped and sin and iniquity would have reigned supreme in the world. (5) Divine Teaching like fresh rain gives new life and vigour to a spiritually dead world and is, therefore, bound to succeed. The cycle of a new Revelation taking the place of an old one continues. When a particular Teaching completes its allotted span of life and serves its intended purpose, a new Teaching replaces it and becomes the vehicle of Divine Will and Purpose. The *Sūrah* ends with the Divine promise that Heavenly help will come to the Holy Prophet because he is the Promised Teacher. His followers should, therefore, give him full and unconditional allegiance. This is the way to victory and success.

سُوۡرَۃُ الۡحَجِّ مَدَنِیَّۃٌ (۲۲)

1. [a]In the name of Allāh, the Gracious, the Merciful.

بِسۡمِ اللّٰہِ الرَّحۡمٰنِ الرَّحِیۡمِ ﴿۱﴾

2. O people, fear your Lord; verily the earthquake of the Hour[1929] is a tremendous thing—

یٰۤاَیُّہَا النَّاسُ اتَّقُوۡا رَبَّکُمۡ ۚ اِنَّ زَلۡزَلَۃَ السَّاعَۃِ شَیۡءٌ عَظِیۡمٌ ﴿۲﴾

3. On the day when you see it, every woman giving suck shall forget her suckling and every pregnant woman shall cast her burden; and thou shalt see men *as they were* drunken while they will not be drunken,[1930] but severe will indeed be the chastisement of Allāh.

یَوۡمَ تَرَوۡنَہَا تَذۡہَلُ کُلُّ مُرۡضِعَۃٍ عَمَّاۤ اَرۡضَعَتۡ وَ تَضَعُ کُلُّ ذَاتِ حَمۡلٍ حَمۡلَہَا وَ تَرَی النَّاسَ سُکٰرٰی وَ مَا ہُمۡ بِسُکٰرٰی وَ لٰکِنَّ عَذَابَ اللّٰہِ شَدِیۡدٌ ﴿۳﴾

4. [b]And among men there are some who dispute about Allāh without knowledge and follow every rebellious satan—

وَ مِنَ النَّاسِ مَنۡ یُّجَادِلُ فِی اللّٰہِ بِغَیۡرِ عِلۡمٍ وَّ یَتَّبِعُ کُلَّ شَیۡطٰنٍ مَّرِیۡدٍ ﴿۴﴾

5. Concerning whom it is decreed that [c]whosoever makes friends with him,[1931] him he will lead astray and will guide to the torment of the Fire.

کُتِبَ عَلَیۡہِ اَنَّہٗ مَنۡ تَوَلَّاہُ فَاَنَّہٗ یُضِلُّہٗ وَ یَہۡدِیۡہِ اِلٰی عَذَابِ السَّعِیۡرِ ﴿۵﴾

---

[a]1 : 1. [b]13 : 14; 22 : 9; 31 : 21; 40 : 70. [c]4 : 39, 120.

1929. *Al-Sā'ah* (Hour), or *al-Qiyāmah*, is used in three senses: (*a*) Death of a great and famous person (*al-Sā'at al-Ṣughrā*); (*b*) a national calamity (*al-Sā'at al-Wusṭā*); (*c*) the Day of Judgment (*al-Sā'at al-Kubrā*). The word has been used in the Qur'ān in the last two senses. The context shows that here it has been used in the sense of a national calamity that shakes the very foundations of a people. It may have particular reference to the impending doom of the Arabs when Mecca, the citadel of their political power, was to fall and their political power and their social system were to break and crumble; or it may refer to a terrible calamity that would overtake mankind in the form of a global war and would bring calamitous changes in its wake. The present verse, read along with 2 : 213, lends further support to the inference that the words "the Hour" or "the Day of Judgment" used in the Qur'ān generally signify a great national calamity that overtakes a whole people.

1930. The verse has used three metaphors or similes to express the extreme severity of *the earthquake of the Hour*, referred to in the preceding verse. Nothing is dearer to a mother than the baby to which she gives suck, and there could be no terror more dreadful in its effects than the one that makes a woman cast down her burden and which drives men to frenzy and yet the verse says that the suddenness and severity of the terror inspired by the dreadful event would be such that mothers would abandon the babes at their breasts and pregnant women would cast down their burdens and people would go mad with fright and, like drunken men, would lose all control over their actions.

1931. Only those are led astray by Satan who make friends with him and follow him. At another place the Qur'ān says that Satan has no power over righteous servants of God. It is only those who accept his evil suggestions that are led astray (16 : 100-101; 17 : 66).

6. O people, if you are in doubt concerning the Resurrection, *then consider* that We have indeed created you from dust, then from a sperm-drop, then from clotted blood, then from a lump of flesh, partly formed and partly unformed, in order that We make *Our power* manifest to you. [a]And We cause what We will to remain in the wombs for an appointed term; then We bring you forth as babes; then *We rear you* that you may attain to your *age of* full strength. And there are some of you who are caused to die *in the normal course*, [b]and there are others among you who are kept back till the worst part of life *with the result* that they know nothing after *having had* knowledge. And thou seest the earth lifeless, [c]but when We send down water thereon it stirs and swells and grows every kind of beauteous vegetation.[1932]

يَٰٓأَيُّهَا ٱلنَّاسُ إِن كُنتُمْ فِى رَيْبٍ مِّنَ ٱلْبَعْثِ فَإِنَّا
خَلَقْنَٰكُم مِّن تُرَابٍ ثُمَّ مِن نُّطْفَةٍ ثُمَّ مِنْ عَلَقَةٍ
ثُمَّ مِن مُّضْغَةٍ مُّخَلَّقَةٍ وَغَيْرِ مُخَلَّقَةٍ لِّنُبَيِّنَ
لَكُمْ وَنُقِرُّ فِى ٱلْأَرْحَامِ مَا نَشَآءُ إِلَىٰٓ أَجَلٍ مُّسَمًّى
ثُمَّ نُخْرِجُكُمْ طِفْلًا ثُمَّ لِتَبْلُغُوٓا أَشُدَّكُمْ وَمِنكُم
مَّن يُتَوَفَّىٰ وَمِنكُم مَّن يُرَدُّ إِلَىٰٓ أَرْذَلِ ٱلْعُمُرِ لِكَيْلَا
يَعْلَمَ مِنۢ بَعْدِ عِلْمٍ شَيْـًٔا ۚ وَتَرَى ٱلْأَرْضَ هَامِدَةً
فَإِذَآ أَنزَلْنَا عَلَيْهَا ٱلْمَآءَ ٱهْتَزَّتْ وَرَبَتْ وَأَنۢبَتَتْ
مِن كُلِّ زَوْجٍۭ بَهِيجٍ ﴿٦﴾

7. That is because Allāh is Self-Subsisting and All-Sustaining, and that [d]it is He Who brings the dead to life, and that He has power over all things;

ذَٰلِكَ بِأَنَّ ٱللَّهَ هُوَ ٱلْحَقُّ وَأَنَّهُۥ يُحْىِ ٱلْمَوْتَىٰ وَ
أَنَّهُۥ عَلَىٰ كُلِّ شَىْءٍ قَدِيرٌ ﴿٧﴾

[a]13 : 9; 35 : 12; 41 : 48. [b]16 : 71; 36 : 69. [c]16 : 66; 27 : 61; 30 : 49-51; 35 : 28; 45 : 6. [d]2 : 74; 30 : 51; 35 : 10; 41 : 40; 42 : 10; 57 : 18.

1932. Man's creation and physical development constitutes a strong argument in favour of Life after death. This creation is a process of evolution, a gradual unfolding, a development from one stage to another, from lifeless matter to a seed, then to a fertilized ovum, then to a foetus and then it culminates in the birth of a perfectly formed human being. This process of evolution, however, does not stop with man's birth. It continues. The wonderful physical growth of man from lifeless matter to a fully developed human being constitutes an irrefutable proof that the Creator of man and the Author of all these stages of his development possesses the power to give him a new life after he is dead. The inference also seems to be that just as the creation and physical development of man is a process of evolution and gradual growth, so is his spiritual development. Another argument is taken from nature, *viz.*, that the barren, bleak or dead earth vibrates with new life when rain falls upon it. This phenomenon also leads to the same conclusion that God, Who has the power to make the dead and barren earth vibrate with new life, has the power to bring man to life after his death.

8. [a]And because the Hour will *certainly* come, there is no doubt about it, and because Allāh will raise up those who are in the graves.

وَّاَنَّ السَّاعَةَ اٰتِيَةٌ لَّا رَيْبَ فِيْهَا ۙ وَ اَنَّ اللّٰهَ يَبْعَثُ مَنْ فِي الْقُبُوْرِ ﴿۸﴾

9. [b]And among men is he who disputes concerning Allāh without knowledge and without guidance and without an illuminating Book,[1933]

وَ مِنَ النَّاسِ مَنْ يُّجَادِلُ فِي اللّٰهِ بِغَيْرِ عِلْمٍ وَّ لَا هُدًى وَّ لَا كِتٰبٍ مُّنِيْرٍ ۙ ﴿۹﴾

10. Turning his side *disdainfully*, that he may lead *men* astray from the way of Allāh. For him is disgrace in this world; and on the Day of Resurrection We shall make him taste the punishment of burning.[1934]

ثَانِيَ عِطْفِهٖ لِيُضِلَّ عَنْ سَبِيْلِ اللّٰهِ ؕ لَهٗ فِي الدُّنْيَا خِزْيٌ وَّ نُذِيْقُهٗ يَوْمَ الْقِيٰمَةِ عَذَابَ الْحَرِيْقِ ﴿۱۰﴾

11. [c]This is because of what thy hands have sent on before, and Allāh is not unjust to His servants.

ذٰلِكَ بِمَا قَدَّمَتْ يَدٰكَ وَ اَنَّ اللّٰهَ لَيْسَ بِظَلَّامٍ لِّلْعَبِيْدِ ﴿۱۱﴾ ع

R. 2 12. And among men is he who serves Allāh, *standing, as it were*, on the verge.[1935] Then if [d]good befalls him, he is content therewith; and if there befalls him a trial, he returns to his *former* way. He loses *both* this world as well as the Hereafter. That indeed is a manifest loss.

وَ مِنَ النَّاسِ مَنْ يَّعْبُدُ اللّٰهَ عَلٰى حَرْفٍ ۚ فَاِنْ اَصَابَهٗ خَيْرُ اِطْمَاَنَّ بِهٖ ۚ وَ اِنْ اَصَابَتْهُ فِتْنَةُ اِنْقَلَبَ عَلٰى وَجْهِهٖ ۚ۫ خَسِرَ الدُّنْيَا وَ الْاٰخِرَةَ ؕ ذٰلِكَ هُوَ الْخُسْرَانُ الْمُبِيْنُ ﴿۱۲﴾

[a]15 : 86; 18 : 22; 20 : 16; 40 : 60; 45 : 33. [b]22 : 4. [c]3 : 183; 8 : 52; 41 : 47. [d]70 : 21-22.

1933. *'Ilm* (knowledge) signifies, intellectual proofs and arguments, ***Hudā*** Divine guidance and *Kitāb Munīr* scriptural evidence.

1934. Two kinds of punishment are in store for the deniers of truth, *viz.*, defeat and discomfiture in the present life and disgrace and ignominy in the life to come. The punishment in this life constitutes a proof of punishment in the life to come.

1935. The Arabs say, *Fulānun 'Alā Ḥarfin min Amrihī*, *i.e.*, such a one is in a vacillating condition, looking to the result of an affair he turns to it if he sees what he likes and turns away from it if he sees what does not please him (Lane). The Quranic expression means, one who serves Allāh stanoing aloof with respect to religion, in a fluctuating state, like the person who is in the outskirts of the army, so that if he is sure of victory and spoil, he stands firm, otherwise he flees away. The sense of the expression 'on the verge' is explained in the very next sentence, *viz.*, "if good befalls him, he is content therewith; and if there befalls him a trial, he returns to his former way." Or, the expression may signify that people of weak

13. [a]He calls beside Allāh on that which can neither harm him nor benefit him. That is indeed straying far away.

يَدْعُوْا مِنْ دُوْنِ اللّٰهِ مَا لَا يَضُرُّهٗ وَمَا لَا
يَنْفَعُهٗ ذٰلِكَ هُوَ الضَّلٰلُ الْبَعِيْدُ ﴿١٣﴾

14. He calls on him whose harm is much more likely than his benefit.[1936] Evil indeed is the patron, and evil indeed the associate.

يَدْعُوْا لَمَنْ ضَرُّهٗٓ اَقْرَبُ مِنْ نَّفْعِهٖ لَبِئْسَ
الْمَوْلٰى وَلَبِئْسَ الْعَشِيْرُ ﴿١٤﴾

15. [b]Verily, Allāh will cause those who believe and do good deeds to enter Gardens beneath which streams flow; surely, Allāh does what He pleases.

اِنَّ اللّٰهَ يُدْخِلُ الَّذِيْنَ اٰمَنُوْا وَعَمِلُوا الصّٰلِحٰتِ
جَنّٰتٍ تَجْرِيْ مِنْ تَحْتِهَا الْاَنْهٰرُ اِنَّ اللّٰهَ يَفْعَلُ
مَا يُرِيْدُ ﴿١٥﴾

16. Whoso thinks that Allāh will not help him in this world and the Hereafter, let him stretch a rope to heaven, and let him cut *it* off. Then let him see if his device can remove that which enrages *him*.[1937]

مَنْ كَانَ يَظُنُّ اَنْ لَّنْ يَّنْصُرَهُ اللّٰهُ فِي الدُّنْيَا وَ
الْاٰخِرَةِ فَلْيَمْدُدْ بِسَبَبٍ اِلَى السَّمَآءِ ثُمَّ لْيَقْطَعْ
فَلْيَنْظُرْ هَلْ يُذْهِبَنَّ كَيْدُهٗ مَا يَغِيْظُ ﴿١٦﴾

17. And thus have We sent down *the Qur'ān* as manifest Signs, and surely Allāh guides whom He desires.

وَكَذٰلِكَ اَنْزَلْنٰهُ اٰيٰتٍ بَيِّنٰتٍ وَّاَنَّ اللّٰهَ يَهْدِيْ مَنْ
يُّرِيْدُ ﴿١٧﴾

---

[a]6 : 72; 10 : 107; 21 : 67; 25 : 56. [b]2 : 278; 4 : 176; 10 : 10; 13 : 30; 14 : 24.

---

faith are always in a state of doubt and suspense. If, by accepting the truth, they hope to get some material benefit they remain and behave as believers, but if belief is attended with trials and tribulations, they turn back on their heels.

1936. The moral injury which the worship of false gods does to their votaries is immediate and patent inasmuch as they degrade themselves before lifeless things and thus do a great injury to their own dignity and self-respect, but any benefit that they hope to get from it is only illusory and far-fetched.

1937. The verse seems to hold out a challenge to disbelievers to do their worst against the Holy Prophet and then see if they can stop Divine help which he is constantly receiving and will continue to receive from On High. It is decreed in the heavens that Islām shall make steady and uninterrupted progress and that no one can alter the Divine decree; and that only death will save disbelievers from the humiliating and painful sight of seeing Islām making rapid progress. If the word *Samā'* be interpreted as "roof" or "ceiling" (Lane), the verse would signify, 'If the opponents of the Holy Prophet are enraged at the success of his mission, then let them hang themselves by fixing a rope to the ceiling and cutting it off, even then Divine assistance will not stop coming.' This meaning is supported by 3 : 120 where disbelievers are reproved and reprimanded in the words, *Perish in your rage. Surely, Allāh has full knowledge of what is hidden in your breasts.*

18. As to those who believe, and the Jews and the Sabians,[1938] and the Christians, and the Magians and the idolaters; verily, Allāh will judge between them on the Day of Resurrection.[1939] Surely, Allāh watches over all things.

اِنَّ الَّذِيْنَ اٰمَنُوْا وَالَّذِيْنَ هَادُوْا وَالصّٰبِـِٕيْنَ وَ
النَّصٰرٰى وَالْمَجُوْسَ وَالَّذِيْنَ اَشْرَكُوْاۤ ۖ اِنَّ اللّٰهَ
يَفْصِلُ بَيْنَهُمْ يَوْمَ الْقِيٰمَةِ ۭ اِنَّ اللّٰهَ عَلٰى كُلِّ
شَيْءٍ شَهِيْدٌ ﴿١٨﴾

19. Hast thou not seen that [a]to Allāh submits whosoever is in the heavens and whosoever is in the earth, and the sun, and the moon, and the stars, and the mountains, and the trees, and the beasts, and many of mankind?[1940] But there are many who become deserving of punishment. And whomsoever Allāh disgraces, none can raise him to honour. Verily, Allāh does what He pleases.

اَلَمْ تَرَ اَنَّ اللّٰهَ يَسْجُدُ لَهٗ مَنْ فِي السَّمٰوٰتِ وَمَنْ
فِي الْاَرْضِ وَالشَّمْسُ وَالْقَمَرُ وَالنُّجُوْمُ وَالْجِبَالُ
وَالشَّجَرُ وَالدَّوَآبُّ وَكَثِيْرٌ مِّنَ النَّاسِ ۭ وَكَثِيْرٌ
حَقَّ عَلَيْهِ الْعَذَابُ ۭ وَمَنْ يُّهِنِ اللّٰهُ فَمَا لَهٗ مِنْ
مُّكْرِمٍ ۭ اِنَّ اللّٰهَ يَفْعَلُ مَا يَشَآءُ ۩ ﴿١٩﴾ السجدة

20. These are two[1941] *groups of* disputants who dispute concerning their Lord. As for those who disbelieve, garments of fire will be

هٰذٰنِ خَصْمٰنِ اخْتَصَمُوْا فِيْ رَبِّهِمْ ۡ فَالَّذِيْنَ كَفَرُوْا
قُطِّعَتْ لَهُمْ ثِيَابٌ مِّنْ نَّارٍ ۭ يُصَبُّ مِنْ فَوْقِ

[a]13 : 16; 16 : 49-50; 55 : 7.

1938. In later Arabic literature, the word has been also used to denote the people of northern Europe (Enc. of Islām).

1939. This verse and vv. 2 : 63 and 5 : 70 do not signify that Chritsians, Jews and Sabians are equally eligible to salvation along with true believers. The Qur'ān does not support any such belief. According to it the only religion acceptable to God is Islām (3 : 20, 86). The present verse only lays down a criterion to test the truth of all the different religions and not that it regards all of them as true. The implied criterion is, that of all religions the true one will prevail over others in the "Hour of Decision." Or, the verse may mean that false beliefs of a person constitute no reason that he should be punished in this life. That matter will be decided on the Day of Judgment.

1940. God has fixed certain laws—natural laws, which all created things, animate or inanimate, have to obey. There is no escape from submission to these laws. There are, however, certain other laws — the laws of the *Sharī'ah* which God has revealed for the guidance of man. Man may obey or disobey and defy these laws and may suffer the consequences of his defiance. The verse further brings home to idolaters the folly and futility of their taking the objects of nature for worship beside Allāh. It says that all these things depend upon Him for their very existence. They submit to the laws He has fixed for them and cannot live independently of God for a moment. It is sheer folly, therefore, to adore and worship things and beings which are themselves subject to God-made laws.

1941. The reference in the words "These are two" is to two classes of men—the believers and disbelievers.

cut out for them; *and* [a]boiling water will be poured down over their heads,

رُءُوْسِهِمُ الْحَمِيْمُ ﴿٢٠﴾

21. [b]Whereby that which is in their bellies, and *their* skins too, will be melted;

يُصْهَرُ بِهٖ مَا فِيْ بُطُوْنِهِمْ وَالْجُلُوْدُ ﴿٢١﴾

22. And *for their further punishment* there will be maces of iron.

وَلَهُمْ مَّقَامِعُ مِنْ حَدِيْدٍ ﴿٢٢﴾

23. [c]Whenever in *their* anguish they will seek to get out of it, they will be driven back into it; and *it will be said to them*, [d]'Taste ye the torment of burning!'

كُلَّمَآ اَرَادُوْٓا اَنْ يَّخْرُجُوْا مِنْهَا مِنْ غَمٍّ اُعِيْدُوْا
فِيْهَا وَذُوْقُوْا عَذَابَ الْحَرِيْقِ ﴿٢٣﴾

R. 3 24. But Allāh will cause those who believe and do righteous deeds to enter gardens beneath which rivers flow. [e]They will be adorned therein with bracelets of gold and with pearls; and [f]their raiment therein will be of silk.[1942]

اِنَّ اللّٰهَ يُدْخِلُ الَّذِيْنَ اٰمَنُوْا وَعَمِلُوا الصّٰلِحٰتِ
جَنّٰتٍ تَجْرِيْ مِنْ تَحْتِهَا الْاَنْهٰرُ يُحَلَّوْنَ فِيْهَا
مِنْ اَسَاوِرَ مِنْ ذَهَبٍ وَّلُؤْلُؤًا ۗ وَلِبَاسُهُمْ فِيْهَا
حَرِيْرٌ ﴿٢٤﴾

25. And they will be guided to pure speech, and they will be guided to the path of the Praiseworthy *God*.

وَهُدُوْٓا اِلَى الطَّيِّبِ مِنَ الْقَوْلِ ۚ وَهُدُوْٓا اِلٰى
صِرَاطِ الْحَمِيْدِ ﴿٢٥﴾

26. *As to* those who disbelieve, and hinder *men* from the way of Allāh and *from* [g]the Sacred Mosque, which We have appointed equally for *the benefit of* all men, be they dwellers therein or visitors from the desert, and whoso seeks wrongfully to deviate therein *from the right path*—We shall cause him to taste of a grievous punishment.

اِنَّ الَّذِيْنَ كَفَرُوْا وَيَصُدُّوْنَ عَنْ سَبِيْلِ اللّٰهِ
وَالْمَسْجِدِ الْحَرَامِ الَّذِيْ جَعَلْنٰهُ لِلنَّاسِ سَوَآءَ
ۨالْعَاكِفُ فِيْهِ وَالْبَادِ ۗ وَمَنْ يُّرِدْ فِيْهِ بِاِلْحَادٍۢ
بِظُلْمٍ نُّذِقْهُ مِنْ عَذَابٍ اَلِيْمٍ ﴿٢٦﴾

[a]44 : 49; 55 : 45; 56 : 43-54. [b]44 : 46. [c]5 : 38; 32 : 21. [d]8 : 15; 34 : 43. [e]18 : 32; 35 : 34; 76 : 22. [f]76 : 13. [g]8 : 35; 16 : 89; 43 : 38; 48 : 26.

1942. The Holy Prophet is reported to have said, 'The Nile and the Euphrates are two of the streams of Paradise' (Muslim, ch. *al-Jannah*). The Holy Prophet and his Companions knew that they were promised "gardens" not only in the next life but in this world also and they also knew that by "gardens" in this world were meant rich and fertile lands once ruled by the Kings of Persia and the Emperors of the Eastern Roman Empire. During the Caliphate of 'Umar, Muslim armies fought on two fronts, in Mesopotamia and Syria, and when some Arab chiefs presented themselves before him and offered their services, he asked them to which of "the two promised lands" (Mesopotamia or Syria) they would like to go. The prophecy was literally fulfilled when 'Umar asked Sūrāqah bin Mālik to wear the bracelets of gold which the Kings of Iran used to wear on special State ceremonies.

R. 4 27. And *call to mind* when We assigned[1943] to Abraham the site of the House[1943A] *and said*, 'Associate not anything with Me and [a]keep My house clean[1944] for those who perform the circuits,[1945] and those who stand up and those who bow *and* prostrate themselves *in Prayer*;

وَإِذْ بَوَّأْنَا لِإِبْرٰهِيْمَ مَكَانَ الْبَيْتِ أَنْ لَّا تُشْرِكْ بِيْ شَيْـًٔا وَّطَهِّرْ بَيْتِيَ لِلطَّآئِفِيْنَ وَالْقَآئِمِيْنَ وَالرُّكَّعِ السُّجُوْدِ ﴿٢٧﴾

28. [b]'And proclaim[1946] unto men the Pilgrimage. They will come to thee on foot, and on every lean camel, coming by every distant, deep track,

وَأَذِّنْ فِي النَّاسِ بِالْحَجِّ يَأْتُوْكَ رِجَالًا وَّعَلٰى كُلِّ ضَامِرٍ يَّأْتِيْنَ مِنْ كُلِّ فَجٍّ عَمِيْقٍ ﴿٢٨﴾

---

[a]2 : 126. [b]2 : 198; 3 : 98.

1943. The verse shows that the site of the Ka'bah had existed long before Abraham's time. In fact, the Ka'bah was built by Adam. It was the first House of worship built in the world (3 : 97). By the time of Abraham it had fallen into ruins and its site having been disclosed to him by revelation, he and his son Ishmael, the Holy Prophet's great progenitor, rebuilt it. See also 146.

1943A. The Ka'bah is variously mentioned in the Qur'ān as "My House" (2 : 126 & 22 : 27), "The Sacred House" (14 : 38), "The Sacred Mosque" (2 : 151), "The House" (2 : 128, 159; 3 : 98; 8 : 36; 22 : 27), "The Ancient House" (22 : 30, 34), and "The Frequented House" (52 : 5). All these different appellations point to the eminence of the Ka'bah as the greatest centre of worship for mankind.

1944. The words, *keep My house clean*, embodied both a commandment and a prophecy. The commandment was that the Ka'bah was not to be polluted with idol-worship as it had been built for the worship of the One True God, and the prophecy lay in the fact that this commandment would be defied and the House of God would become a house of idols but would eventually be completely cleared of them.

1945. This verse serves as an introduction to the subject of Pilgrimage which is the central theme of this *Sūrah*. Circumambulation of the Sacred Mosque is the most important ceremony of the Pilgrimage, so a brief reference to the sanctity and importance of the Ka'bah forms a befitting introduction to the subject of Ḥajj.

1946. The Pilgrimage as an institution began with the Patriarch Abraham as the words, *And proclaim unto men the Pilgrimage*, show. It was not an idolatrous institution incorporated into Islām by the Holy Prophet to conciliate the idol-worshipping Arabs as some Christian writers have been led to think. From the time of Abraham Pilgrimage has continued without break to this day. The gathering in Mecca every year of many hundreds of thousands of Muslims from very distant lands bears an irrefutable testimony to the fulfilment of this prophecy.

29. 'That [a]they may witness the benefits[1947] *provided* for them and may mention the name of Allāh, [b]during the appointed days, over the quadrupeds of *the class of* cattle that He has provided for them. So eat thereof and feed the distressed *and* the needy.

لِّيَشْهَدُوا مَنَافِعَ لَهُمْ وَيَذْكُرُوا اسْمَ اللَّهِ فِي أَيَّامٍ مَّعْلُومَاتٍ عَلَىٰ مَا رَزَقَهُم مِّن بَهِيمَةِ الْأَنْعَامِ ۖ فَكُلُوا مِنْهَا وَأَطْعِمُوا الْبَائِسَ الْفَقِيرَ ﴿٢٩﴾

30. 'Then let them accomplish their needful acts of cleansing, and fulfil their vows, and go round the Ancient House.'[1948]

ثُمَّ لْيَقْضُوا تَفَثَهُمْ وَلْيُوفُوا نُذُورَهُمْ وَلْيَطَّوَّفُوا بِالْبَيْتِ الْعَتِيقِ ﴿٣٠﴾

31. That is *Allāh's commandment.* [c]And whoso honours the things declared sacred by Allāh, it will be good for him with his Lord. [d]And *the eating of the flesh of* all cattle is made lawful to you except that which has *already* been announced to you *in the Qur'ān*. Shun, therefore, the abomination of idols, and shun all words of untruth,

ذَٰلِكَ وَمَن يُعَظِّمْ حُرُمَاتِ اللَّهِ فَهُوَ خَيْرٌ لَّهُ عِندَ رَبِّهِ ۗ وَأُحِلَّتْ لَكُمُ الْأَنْعَامُ إِلَّا مَا يُتْلَىٰ عَلَيْكُمْ ۖ فَاجْتَنِبُوا الرِّجْسَ مِنَ الْأَوْثَانِ وَاجْتَنِبُوا قَوْلَ الزُّورِ ﴿٣١﴾

[a]2 : 199; 5 : 3. [b]2 : 204. [c]5 : 3. [d]5 : 2; 6 : 146.

1947. Apart from the spiritual good that the Pilgrimage does to a Muslim, it possesses great social and political significance. It also possesses great potentialities to weld Muslims of different nationalities into one strong international brotherhood of Islām. Muslims from all parts of the world who meet at Mecca once a year can exchange views on matters of international importance, renew old and, establish new contacts. They have opportunities to acquaint themselves with problems that confront their brethren in Faith in other countries, to profit by one another's experience and to co-operate with one another in many other ways. Mecca being God's appointed Centre of Islām, the Pilgrimage can serve as a sort of a United Nations Organization for the whole of the Muslim world.

1948. *Al-Bait al-'Atīq* means, free, excellent and very old House (Lane). The epithet 'free' implies a prophecy that no hostile power will ever be able to conquer it. It shall always remain free. The epithet, 'excellent' signifies that the Ka'bah shall always occupy a position of honour in the world. The fact that the Ka'bah is a very ancient House of worship in the world finds corroboration in another verse of the Qur'ān (3 : 97). It was in existence long before Abraham brought his wife Hagar and his son Ishmael to settle in the barren, bleak and arid valley of Mecca (14 : 38). Noah is believed by some to have performed the circuit of the Ka'bah (Ṭabarī as quoted by Enc. of Islām). Historians of established repute and authority, including even some very hostile critics of Islām, have admitted that the Ka'bah had been held sacred from time immemorial. Diodorus Siculus writing about the region now known as the Ḥijāz says : 'There is in this country a temple greatly revered by all the Arabs to which the neighbouring peoples throng from all sides.' 'These words,' says Sir William Muir, 'must refer to the Holy House of Mecca, for we know of no other which ever commanded the universal homage of Arabia..............Tradition represents the Ka'bah as from time immemorial the scene of pilgrimage from all quarters of Arabia ....

32. Devoting *all your worship and obedience* to Allāh, not associating anything with Him. And whoso associates anything with Allāh, falls, as it were, from a height, and the birds snatch him away or the wind blows him away to a far-off place.[1949]

حُنَفَآءَ لِلّٰهِ غَيْرَ مُشْرِكِيْنَ بِهٖ ۗ وَمَنْ يُّشْرِكْ
بِاللّٰهِ فَكَاَنَّمَا خَرَّ مِنَ السَّمَآءِ فَتَخْطَفُهُ الطَّيْرُ
اَوْ تَهْوِيْ بِهِ الرِّيْحُ فِيْ مَكَانٍ سَحِيْقٍ ۝٣٢

33. *The truth* is that [a]whoso honours the sacred Signs of Allāh—that, indeed, *proceeds* from the righteousness of hearts.[1950]

ذٰلِكَ ۗ وَمَنْ يُّعَظِّمْ شَعَآئِرَ اللّٰهِ فَاِنَّهَا مِنْ تَقْوَى
الْقُلُوْبِ ۝٣٣

34. In these *offerings* are benefits[1951] for you for an appointed term, then [b]their place of sacrifice is at the Ancient House.

لَكُمْ فِيْهَا مَنَافِعُ اِلٰٓى اَجَلٍ مُّسَمًّى ثُمَّ مَحِلُّهَآ
اِلَى الْبَيْتِ الْعَتِيْقِ ۝٣٤ ع

R. 5 35. And for every people We appointed rites[1952] of Sacrifice, that [c]they might mention the name of Allāh over the quadrupeds *of the*

وَلِكُلِّ اُمَّةٍ جَعَلْنَا مَنْسَكًا لِّيَذْكُرُوا اسْمَ اللّٰهِ
عَلٰى مَا رَزَقَهُمْ مِّنْ بَهِيْمَةِ الْاَنْعَامِ ۗ فَاِلٰهُكُمْ

[a]2 : 159. [b]2 : 197; 48 : 26. [c]5 : 5; 6 : 119.

so extensive an homage must have had its beginning in an extremely remote age' (Muir,p. ciii). It seems that the Ka'bah was first built by Adam and, after it was washed away by the great Deluge in the time of Noah, was later rebuilt by Abraham, assisted by his son, Ishmael.

1949. Man is the noblest creation of God. The whole universe—the sun, the moon, the stars, the earth, the oceans, the mountains, etc., have been made to serve him. He can rise morally and spiritually so high as to reflect in his person Divine attributes. So if he degrades himself so low as to worship lifeless objects, he falls, as it were, from the heights of spiritual eminence to the depths of moral and intellectual degradation.

1950. The verse implies that the object underlying all the commandments and ordinances of Islām is to inculcate righteousness and purity of heart. All Islamic rites and acts of worship are only means that lead to this supreme goal.

1951. The animals that are brought to Mecca for sacrifice may be used for riding and carrying burdens or their milk may be used before they are sacrificed. They can serve many other useful purposes.

1952. *Nasaka Lillāhi* means, he sacrificed and did good deeds willingly and spontaneously to win nearness to God. *Mansak*, therefore, means, rites of sacrifice; place where such rites are performed (Aqrab). With this verse begins the subject of Sacrifice, one of the three main themes with which this *Sūrah* deals, the other two being *Ḥajj* and *Jihād*. The verse further shows that the commandment relating to Sacrifice is not confined to Islām. It is common to all religions because they have proceeded from the same Divine Source. The verse also shows that it was the sacrifice of animals that was originally enjoined on the followers of all religions and that the cruel practice of offering human beings as sacrifice was a later innovation. In view of the different meanings of the root-word *Nasaka* (Lane), true sacrifice possesses three essential characteristics : (*a*): It should be voluntary and spontaneous. (*b*) It should be offered with the purest of motives. (*c*) It should not be offered from material considerations.

class of cattle that He has provided for them. So [a]your God is One God,[1953] therefore, submit ye all to Him. And give thou glad tidings to the humble,

إِلٰهٌ وَّاحِدٌ فَلَهٗٓ اَسْلِمُوْا ۗ وَبَشِّرِ الْمُخْبِتِيْنَ ﴿٣٥﴾

36. [b]Whose hearts are filled with awe when the name of Allāh is mentioned, and who patiently endure whatever befalls them, and who observe Prayer and spend out of what We have bestowed upon them.

الَّذِيْنَ اِذَا ذُكِرَ اللّٰهُ وَجِلَتْ قُلُوْبُهُمْ وَالصّٰبِرِيْنَ
عَلٰى مَآ اَصَابَهُمْ وَالْمُقِيْمِي الصَّلٰوةِ ۙ وَمِمَّا رَزَقْنٰهُمْ
يُنْفِقُوْنَ ﴿٣٦﴾

37. And among the sacred Signs of Allāh We have appointed for you the sacrificial camels. In them there is much good for you. So mention the name of Allāh over them as they stand *tied up* in rows. And when they fall down *dead* on their sides, eat thereof and feed him who is *needy but* contented and him *also* who supplicates.[1954] Thus have We subjected them to you, that you may be grateful.

وَالْبُدْنَ جَعَلْنٰهَا لَكُمْ مِّنْ شَعَآئِرِ اللّٰهِ لَكُمْ
فِيْهَا خَيْرٌ ۖ فَاذْكُرُوا اسْمَ اللّٰهِ عَلَيْهَا صَوَآفَّ ۚ فَاِذَا
وَجَبَتْ جُنُوْبُهَا فَكُلُوْا مِنْهَا وَاَطْعِمُوا الْقَانِعَ وَ
الْمُعْتَرَّ ۗ كَذٰلِكَ سَخَّرْنٰهَا لَكُمْ لَعَلَّكُمْ تَشْكُرُوْنَ ﴿٣٧﴾

38. Their flesh reaches not Allāh, nor does their blood, but it is your righteousness that reaches Him.[1955]

لَنْ يَّنَالَ اللّٰهَ لُحُوْمُهَا وَلَا دِمَآؤُهَا وَلٰكِنْ يَّنَالُهُ

[a]5 : 74; 16 : 23; 37 : 5. [b]23 : 61.

1953. The verse has twofold significance : (1) The fact that the rite of Sacrifice is common to all religions, although they are so widely separated from one another as regards the time and place of their origin, shows that originally they all emanated from the same Supreme Source and that the God of all nations is One God. (2) That the object underlying Sacrifice is to realize and proclaim the Oneness of God by sacrificing our ambitions and aspirations, all our ideas and ideals and even life and honour for His sake. The concept of Sacrifice according to Islām does not consist in appeasing an offended deity or in atoning for one's sins but in sacrificing one's all for the sake of God and in the way of God.

1954. The slaughtering of camels which are brought to Mecca for sacrifice is but a symbol of man's readiness to lay down his life for the sake of his Creator and Master just as camels lay down their lives for their own masters. This is the supreme object and purpose of Sacrifice, other objects mentioned in the verse being of secondary importance. The pilgrim is reminded of the significance of Sacrifice when he slaughters an animal which serves as a Sign of God. The verse also shows that the flesh of the slaughtered animal should be properly distributed and not wasted.

1955. The verse throws a flood of light on the essence, inwardness and real object and purpose of Sacrifice. It teaches the supreme lesson that it is not the outward act of sacrifice which pleases God but the spirit underlying it and the motive behind it. The flesh

Thus has He subjected them to you, that you may glorify Allāh for His guiding you. And give glad tidings to those who do good.

التَّقْوٰى مِنْكُمْ كَذٰلِكَ سَخَّرَهَا لَكُمْ لِتُكَبِّرُوا اللّٰهَ
عَلٰى مَا هَدٰىكُمْ وَبَشِّرِ الْمُحْسِنِيْنَ ۝۳۸

39. Surely, Allāh defends those who believe.[1956] Surely, Allāh loves not anyone who is perfidious, ungrateful.

اِنَّ اللّٰهَ يُدٰفِعُ عَنِ الَّذِيْنَ اٰمَنُوْا اِنَّ اللّٰهَ لَا يُحِبُّ
كُلَّ خَوَّانٍ كَفُوْرٍ ۝۳۹

R. 6 40. Permission *to take up arms* is given to those against whom war is made, because they have been wronged[1957] and Allāh, indeed, has power to help them.—

اُذِنَ لِلَّذِيْنَ يُقٰتَلُوْنَ بِاَنَّهُمْ ظُلِمُوْا وَاِنَّ اللّٰهَ عَلٰى
نَصْرِهِمْ لَقَدِيْرُ ۝۴۰

---

or blood of the slaughtered animal does not reach God; it is righteousness of the heart which is acceptable to Him. God demands and accepts total sacrifice of all that is near and dear to us—our material possessions, the ideals that are dear to us, our honour and life itself. In reality, God wants and demands no offering from us in the form of flesh and blood of animals but demands the offering of our hearts. It is, however, a mistake to think that because it is not the outward act of sacrifice but the motive behind it that really matters, the outward act is of no importance. True, the outward act of sacrifice is the shell, and the spirit underlying it is the kernel and essence, yet the shell or the body of a thing, like its spirit or kernel, is of very great importance because no soul can exist without a body and no kernel without a shell.

1956. With this verse is introduced the subject of *Jihād*. The theme of Sacrifice has formed a befitting prelude to this all-important subject. Before the permission to fight in self-defence was given to Muslims, they were apprised of the importance of Sacrifice. The verse throws a flood of light on the Islamic conception of *Jihād*. *Jihād*, as the verse shows, is fighting in defence of Truth. But whereas Islām allows no aggressive war, it regards the waging of it to defend one's honour, country or Faith as an act of the highest virtue. Man is God's noblest handiwork. He is the acme of His creation, its aim and end. He is God's vicegerent on earth and the king of His whole creation (2 : 31). This is the Islamic conception of man's high place in the universe. It is, therefore, only natural that the religion which has raised man to such a high pedestal should also have attached very great importance and sanctity to human life. Of all things man's life, according to the Qur'ān, is most sacred and inviolable. It is a sacrilege to take it except under very rare circumstances which the Qur'ān has specifically mentioned (5 : 33; 17 : 34). But no less important, according to Islām, is freedom of conscience. It is man's most precious heritage—perhaps more precious than life itself. The Qur'ān, which has attached the greatest sanctity to man's life, could not have failed to acknowledge and declare the sacredness and inviolability of this, his most precious possession. It is in defence of this most precious of their possessions that the Muslims were allowed to take up arms.

1957. According to consensus of scholarly opinion this is the first verse which gave Muslims the permisson to take up arms in self-defence. It lays down principles according to which Muslims can wage a defensive war, and sets forth along with the following verses the reasons which led a handful of Muslims, without arms and other material means, to fight in self-defence after they had suffered at Mecca ceaseless persecution for years and had been pursued with relentless hatred to Medina and were harassed and harried there too. The first reason given in this verse is that they have been wronged.

41. Those who have been driven out from their homes unjustly, only because they said, 'Our Lord is Allāh.'[1958] [a]And if Allāh had not repelled some people by means of others, cloisters and churches and synagogues and mosques, wherein the name of Allāh is oft remembered,[1959] would surely have been destroyed. [b]And Allāh will, surely, help him who helps Him. Allāh is, indeed, Powerful, Mighty—

الَّذِيْنَ اُخْرِجُوْا مِنْ دِيَارِهِمْ بِغَيْرِ حَقٍّ اِلَّآ اَنْ
يَّقُوْلُوْا رَبُّنَا اللّٰهُ ۭ وَلَوْلَا دَفْعُ اللّٰهِ النَّاسَ بَعْضَهُمْ
بِبَعْضٍ لَّهُدِّمَتْ صَوَامِعُ وَبِيَعٌ وَّصَلَوٰتٌ وَّ
مَسٰجِدُ يُذْكَرُ فِيْهَا اسْمُ اللّٰهِ كَثِيْرًا ۭ وَلَيَنْصُرَنَّ
اللّٰهُ مَنْ يَّنْصُرُهٗ ۭ اِنَّ اللّٰهَ لَقَوِيٌّ عَزِيْزٌ ﴿۴۱﴾

42. Those who, if We establish them in the earth, will observe Prayer and pay the *Zakāt* and enjoin good and forbid evil.[1960] And with Allāh *rests* the final issue of all affairs.

اَلَّذِيْنَ اِنْ مَّكَّنّٰهُمْ فِي الْاَرْضِ اَقَامُوا الصَّلٰوةَ
وَاٰتَوُا الزَّكٰوةَ وَاَمَرُوْا بِالْمَعْرُوْفِ وَنَهَوْا عَنِ
الْمُنْكَرِ ۭ وَلِلّٰهِ عَاقِبَةُ الْاُمُوْرِ ﴿۴۲﴾

[a]2 : 252. [b]47 : 8.

1958. This verse gives the second reason. It is that Muslims were driven out from their hearths and homes without a just and legitimate cause; their only offence being that they believed in One God. For years the Muslims were persecuted at Mecca, then they were driven out from it and were not left in peace even in their exile at Medina. Islām was threatened with complete extirpation by a combined attack by the Arabian tribes around Medina, among whom the influence of the Quraish, on account of their being the custodians of the Ka'bah, was very great. Medina itself was honey-combed with sedition and treachery. The Jews, compact and united, were opposed to the Holy Prophet whose difficulties instead of lessening had greatly increased by Emigration. It was under these highly unfavourable circumstances that Muslims had to take up arms to save themselves, their Faith and the Holy Prophet from extermination. If ever a people had a legitimate cause to fight, it were the Holy Prophet Muhammad and his Companions, and yet the unconscionable critics of Islām have accused him of waging aggressive wars to impose his Faith on an unwilling people.

1959. After giving reasons why the Muslims were obliged to take up arms, the verse mentions the object and purpose of the wars of Islām. The object was never to deprive other people of their homes and possessions or to deprive them of national freedom and compel them to submit to foreign yoke, or to explore new markets and get new colonies as the Western Powers do. It was to fight in self-defence and to save Islām from extermination and to establish freedom of conscience and liberty of thought. It was also to defend places of worship belonging to other religions—the churches, the synagogues, the temples, the cloisters, etc. (2 : 194; 2 : 257; 8 : 40 & 8 : 73). Thus the first and foremost object of the wars of Islām was, and will always be, to establish freedom of belief and worship and to fight in defence of country, honour and freedom against an unprovoked attack. Could there be a better cause to fight for than this ?

1960. The verse implies a commandment for the Muslims that when they get power, they should not use it for the furtherance of their own selfish ends but should employ it to ameliorate the lot of the poor and the down trodden people and to establish peace and security in their dominions, and that they should respect and protect places of worship.

43. [a]And if they accuse thee of falsehood, even so, before them, the people of Noah and the tribes of 'Ād and Thamud *also* accused *their Prophets* of falsehood;

وَإِنْ يُكَذِّبُوكَ فَقَدْ كَذَّبَتْ قَبْلَهُمْ قَوْمُ نُوحٍ
وَّعَادٌ وَّثَمُودُ ﴿٤٣﴾

44. And *so did* the people of Abraham and the people of Lot;

وَقَوْمُ إِبْرٰهِيمَ وَقَوْمُ لُوطٍ ﴿٤٤﴾

45. And the inhabitants of Midian. And Moses *too* was accused of falsehood. But I gave respite to the disbelievers; then I seized them, and how *terrible* were *the consequences of* denying Me!

وَّأَصْحٰبُ مَدْيَنَ وَكُذِّبَ مُوسٰى فَأَمْلَيْتُ لِلْكٰفِرِيْنَ
ثُمَّ أَخَذْتُهُمْ فَكَيْفَ كَانَ نَكِيرِ ﴿٤٥﴾

46. [b]And how many a city have We destroyed, which was given to wrongdoing, so that it is fallen down on its roofs; and *how many a* well is deserted and *how many a* lofty castle *lies in ruins!*

فَكَأَيِّنْ مِّنْ قَرْيَةٍ أَهْلَكْنٰهَا وَهِيَ ظَالِمَةٌ فَهِيَ
خَاوِيَةٌ عَلٰى عُرُوشِهَا وَبِئْرٍ مُّعَطَّلَةٍ وَّقَصْرٍ
مَّشِيدٍ ﴿٤٦﴾

47. [c]Have they not travelled in the land, so that they may have hearts wherewith to understand, or ears wherewith to hear? For, surely, it is not the eyes that are blind, but blind are the hearts which are in the breasts.[1961]

أَفَلَمْ يَسِيرُوا فِي الْأَرْضِ فَتَكُونَ لَهُمْ قُلُوبٌ
يَّعْقِلُونَ بِهَا أَوْ أٰذَانٌ يَّسْمَعُونَ بِهَا فَإِنَّهَا لَا
تَعْمَى الْأَبْصَارُ وَلٰكِنْ تَعْمَى الْقُلُوبُ الَّتِي فِي
الصُّدُورِ ﴿٤٧﴾

48. [d]And they demand of thee to hasten on the punishment, but Allāh will never break His promise. And, verily, a day with thy Lord is *sometimes* as a thousand years of your reckoning.[1961A]

وَيَسْتَعْجِلُونَكَ بِالْعَذَابِ وَلَنْ يُّخْلِفَ اللّٰهُ وَعْدَهُ
وَإِنَّ يَوْمًا عِنْدَ رَبِّكَ كَأَلْفِ سَنَةٍ مِّمَّا تَعُدُّونَ ﴿٤٨﴾

---

[a]6 : 35; 35 : 26; 40 : 6; 54 : 10. [b]7 : 5; 21 : 12; 28 : 59; 65 : 9-10. [c]12 : 110; 30 : 10; 35 : 45; 40 : 22; 47 : 11. [d]26 : 205; 27 : 72; 29 : 54-55; 37 : 177; 51 : 15.

1961. It is clear from this verse that the dead, the blind and the deaf spoken of here and elsewhere in the Qur'ān are the spiritually dead, blind and deaf.

1961A. The Holy Prophet is reported to have said that the first three centuries of Islām would be its best period after which falsehood would spread and a period of darkness would set in which would extend to over a thousand years (Tirmidhī). This period of thousand years is likened to one day (32 : 6). In this period a people, having blue eyes, would arise and spread all over the earth (20 : 103-104). It is these people having blue eyes who in their conceit and arrogance, born of their material glory and political power, are depicted as challenging the Holy Prophet to hasten on the punishment which, he said, would overtake them at the appointed and promised time.

49. And how many a city I have respited, while it was given to wrongdoing. Then I seized it, and unto Me is the return.

وَكَأَيِّنْ مِّنْ قَرْيَةٍ أَمْلَيْتُ لَهَا وَهِيَ ظَالِمَةٌ ثُمَّ أَخَذْتُهَا وَإِلَيَّ الْمَصِيرُ ﴿٤٩﴾

R. 7 50. Say, 'O mankind, [a]I am but a plain Warner to you;

قُلْ يَا أَيُّهَا النَّاسُ إِنَّمَا أَنَا لَكُمْ نَذِيرٌ مُّبِينٌ ﴿٥٠﴾

51. 'Those who believe and do good works, [b]for them is forgiveness and an honourable provision;

فَالَّذِينَ آمَنُوا وَعَمِلُوا الصَّالِحَاتِ لَهُم مَّغْفِرَةٌ وَرِزْقٌ كَرِيمٌ ﴿٥١﴾

52. 'But [c]those who strive against Our Signs, seeking to frustrate *Our purpose*—these shall be the inmates of the Fire.'

وَالَّذِينَ سَعَوْا فِي آيَاتِنَا مُعَاجِزِينَ أُولَٰئِكَ أَصْحَابُ الْجَحِيمِ ﴿٥٢﴾

53. Never did We send a Messenger or a Prophet before thee, but when he sought *to attain his object*, Satan put *obstacles in the way of* what he sought after. But Allāh removes *the obstacles* that are placed by Satan.[1962] Then Allāh firmly establishes His Signs. And Allāh is All-Knowing, Wise.

وَمَا أَرْسَلْنَا مِن قَبْلِكَ مِن رَّسُولٍ وَلَا نَبِيٍّ إِلَّا إِذَا تَمَنَّىٰ أَلْقَى الشَّيْطَانُ فِي أُمْنِيَّتِهِ فَيَنسَخُ اللَّهُ مَا يُلْقِي الشَّيْطَانُ ثُمَّ يُحْكِمُ اللَّهُ آيَاتِهِ وَاللَّهُ عَلِيمٌ حَكِيمٌ ﴿٥٣﴾

[a]26 : 116; 29 : 51; 51 : 51; 67 : 27. [b]8 : 75; 24 : 27; 34 : 5. [c]34 : 6; 39.

1962. This verse has been deliberately misinterpreted and its meaning purposely distorted by prejudiced Christian writers. They say that one day at Mecca when the Holy Prophet recited the 20th and 21st verses of *Sūrah* Al-Najm: *Now tell me about Lāt and 'Uzzā, and Manāt, the third one, another goddess,* Satan put in his mouth the words *Tilkal-Gharānīq al-'Ulā, wa Inna Shafā'atahunna Laturtajā, i.e.*, these are exalted goddesses and their intercession is hoped for. They call it the 'Lapse of Muḥammad' or his 'Compromise with idolatry.' The Holy Prophet never made any compromise with idolatry nor was there any lapse on his part. The charge is a case of wish being father to the thought. These critics are always on the look-out to discover a lapse in the Holy Prophet and when they can find none, they invent one and impute it to him. They say that the verse refers to the above incident. We shall deal at length with the whole episode when we come to the relevant verses (53 : 20, 21). Suffice it to say here that the whole story is belied by the fact that 53rd Chapter was, according to consensus of scholarly opinion, revealed in the 5th year of the Call at Mecca while the present *Sūrah* was revealed at Medina or on the eve of the Holy Prophet's departure from Mecca in the 13th year of the Call. It is inconceivable that God should have waited for eight long years to refer to that incident in this verse. Moreover, the story has been rejected as totally unfounded by all learned Commentators of the Qur'ān. Besides, there is nothing in the words of the verse itself to warrant the forging of such a blatant lie. The meaning of the verse is quite clear. It purports to say that whenever a Prophet desires to attain his object, *i.e.*, whenever he preaches the message of truth and desires that Divine Unity may be established in the earth, satanic persons seek to retard the progress of truth by putting all sorts of obstacles in his way. They wish to see his mission fail. But they cannot frustrate the Divine plan and God removes all those impediments and makes the cause of Truth prevail and triumph. The verse is of general import. There is no warrant for the suggestion that it applies exclusively to the Holy Prophet. Moreover, it is not possible for Satan to interfere with the purity of the Quranic revelation. God has taken upon Himself to protect and safeguard it against all interference and interpolation (15 : 10 ; 72 : 27-29), and even Christian scholarly opinion has confirmed the truth of this Quranic claim.

54. *This happens* that He may make *the obstacles* which Satan puts *in the way of the Prophet* a trial for those in whose hearts is a disease[1963] and, those whose hearts are hardened and surely, the wrong-doers are *gone* far *in opposition*—

لِّيَجْعَلَ مَا يُلْقِي الشَّيْطٰنُ فِتْنَةً لِّلَّذِيْنَ فِيْ
قُلُوْبِهِمْ مَّرَضٌ وَّالْقَاسِيَةِ قُلُوْبُهُمْ ۭ وَاِنَّ الظّٰلِمِيْنَ
لَفِيْ شِقَاقٍۭ بَعِيْدٍ ﴿٥٤﴾

55. And that [a]those to whom knowledge is given may know that it is the truth from thy Lord, so that they may believe therein and their hearts may be humble unto Him. And, surely, Allāh guides those who believe to the right path;

وَّلِيَعْلَمَ الَّذِيْنَ اُوْتُوا الْعِلْمَ اَنَّهُ الْحَقُّ مِنْ رَّبِّكَ
فَيُؤْمِنُوْا بِهٖ فَتُخْبِتَ لَهٗ قُلُوْبُهُمْ ۭ وَاِنَّ اللّٰهَ
لَهَادِ الَّذِيْنَ اٰمَنُوْٓا اِلٰى صِرَاطٍ مُّسْتَقِيْمٍ ﴿٥٥﴾

56. And those who disbelieve will not cease [b]to be in doubt about it until the Hour[1964] comes suddenly upon them, or there comes to them the punishment of a destructive day.[1965]

وَلَا يَزَالُ الَّذِيْنَ كَفَرُوْا فِيْ مِرْيَةٍ مِّنْهُ حَتّٰى
تَاْتِيَهُمُ السَّاعَةُ بَغْتَةً اَوْ يَاْتِيَهُمْ عَذَابُ يَوْمٍ
عَقِيْمٍ ﴿٥٦﴾

57. [c]The Kingdom on that day[1966] shall be Allāh's. He will judge between them. So [d]those who believe and do righteous deeds will be in Gardens of Bliss;

اَلْمُلْكُ يَوْمَئِذٍ لِّلّٰهِ ۭ يَحْكُمُ بَيْنَهُمْ ۭ فَالَّذِيْنَ اٰمَنُوْا
وَعَمِلُوا الصّٰلِحٰتِ فِيْ جَنّٰتِ النَّعِيْمِ ﴿٥٧﴾

[a]13 : 20; 34 : 7; 35 : 32; 47 : 3; 56 96. [b]11 : 18. [c]25 : 27. [d]13 : 30; 14 : 24; 18 : 31; 30 : 16; 68 : 35; 78 : 32-37.

1963. This verse also supports the interpretation we have placed on the preceding verse. There is no warrant for the baseless story which some ignorant Commentators have taken into their heads to forge in connection with that verse. The verse purports to say that satanic people seek to place all sorts of obstacles in the way of the propagation of the mission of a Prophet in order that its progress may be retarded and 'those in whose hearts is a disease' may be misled. But God removes all such obstacles and after initial and temporary set-backs Truth marches on its course of uniform progress.

1964. "The Hour" signifies the final triumph of Islām. It may also refer to the Fall of Mecca, when the power of the disbelieving Quraish was finally and completely crushed. The Fall took place quite suddenly. The Quraish did not have the least inkling about the Muslim army till it had reached the very gates of Mecca.

1965. *'Imra'atun 'Aqīmun* means, a barren woman. *Yaumun 'Aqīmun* means, a destructive day, a day of hard fighting, so called because many women having lost their sons in the fighting become *'Aqīm* (Lane).

1966. Besides being of general application the verse may particularly refer to the Fall of Mecca. On that day the Kingdom of God was established in Arabia and idolatry departed from its stronghold never to return, and Divine Judgment was pronounced in the words, 'Truth has come and falsehood has vanished away. Falsehood does indeed vanish away fast' (17 : 82).

58. But ᵃthose, who disbelieve and reject Our Signs, will have an humiliating punishment.

وَالَّذِيْنَ كَفَرُوْا وَكَذَّبُوْا بِاٰيٰتِنَا فَاُولٰٓئِكَ لَهُمْ عَذَابٌ مُّهِيْنٌ ۝

R. 8   59. ᵇAnd those who leave their homes for the cause of Allāh, and are then slain or die,¹⁹⁶⁷ Allāh will, surely, provide for them a goodly provision. And, surely, Allāh is the Best of providers.

وَالَّذِيْنَ هَاجَرُوْا فِيْ سَبِيْلِ اللّٰهِ ثُمَّ قُتِلُوْٓا اَوْ مَاتُوْا لَيَرْزُقَنَّهُمُ اللّٰهُ رِزْقًا حَسَنًا ۚ وَاِنَّ اللّٰهَ لَهُوَ خَيْرُ الرّٰزِقِيْنَ ۝

60. He will, surely, admit them to a place with which they will be well-pleased. And Allāh is indeed All-Knowing, Forbearing.

لَيُدْخِلَنَّهُمْ مُّدْخَلًا يَّرْضَوْنَهٗ ؕ وَاِنَّ اللّٰهَ لَعَلِيْمٌ حَلِيْمٌ ۝

61. That indeed is so. And whoso retaliates with the like of that with which he is afflicted and is then transgressed against, Allāh will surely help him.¹⁹⁶⁸ Allāh is indeed the Effacer of sins and is Most Forgiving.

ذٰلِكَ ۚ وَمَنْ عَاقَبَ بِمِثْلِ مَا عُوْقِبَ بِهٖ ثُمَّ بُغِيَ عَلَيْهِ لَيَنْصُرَنَّهُ اللّٰهُ ؕ اِنَّ اللّٰهَ لَعَفُوٌّ غَفُوْرٌ ۝

62. That system of punishment operates to show that it is ᶜAllāh Who causes the night to enter into the day and causes the day to enter into the night,¹⁹⁶⁹ and that Allāh is All-Hearing, All-Seeing,

ذٰلِكَ بِاَنَّ اللّٰهَ يُوْلِجُ الَّيْلَ فِى النَّهَارِ وَيُوْلِجُ النَّهَارَ فِى الَّيْلِ وَاَنَّ اللّٰهَ سَمِيْعٌ بَصِيْرٌ ۝

ᵃ2 : 40; 7 : 37; 30 : 17; 57 : 20; 64 : 11; 78 : 22-27.   ᵇ3 : 196; 8 : 75; 9 : 20-22; 16 : 42.   ᶜ3 : 28; 31 : 30; 35 : 14; 57 : 7.

1967. Those, who leave their hearths and homes and all that is dear to them for the sake of God and spend their lives in serving His cause and then die in harness, deserve to be classed with those who are actually slain fighting in the cause of God, for their sacrifice is as great as that of the actual martyrs; only, God in His infallible wisdom spares their lives. This is the significance of the words, 'or die.'

1968. The verse has twofold significance. It holds out a promise of help to Muslims and also implies a prophecy about their eventual success. In the former sense it purports to say that the Muslims have been oppressed and transgressed against. They may retaliate but their retaliation should not exceed legitimate bounds. The injury they should inflict on the enemy should be proportionate to the injury they receive. According to the second meaning, Muslims are told that they are going to have their enemies in their power and that they will be perfectly justified in inflicting as much injury on them as they had received from them, but it would be far better if in the hour of victory and success, by copying the Divine attributes of mercy and forgiveness, they pardoned and forgave them.

1969. Nahār (day) in the verse represents power and prosperity and Lail (night) signifies the loss of power combined with national decline and decadence. The verse uses this metaphor to point to the fact hinted at in the preceding verse that the night of misery

63. And that is because [a]it is Allāh Who is the Truth, and that which they call on beside Him is falsehood and because Allāh is the High, the Great.

ذٰلِكَ بِاَنَّ اللّٰهَ هُوَ الْحَقُّ وَاَنَّ مَا يَدْعُوْنَ مِنْ دُوْنِهٖ هُوَ الْبَاطِلُ وَاَنَّ اللّٰهَ هُوَ الْعَلِيُّ الْكَبِيْرُ ﴿٦٣﴾

64. Seest thou not that [b]Allāh sends down water from the sky and the earth becomes green?[1970] Allāh is indeed the Knower of subtleties, the All-Aware.

اَلَمْ تَرَ اَنَّ اللّٰهَ اَنْزَلَ مِنَ السَّمَآءِ مَآءً فَتُصْبِحُ الْاَرْضُ مُخْضَرَّةً ۚ اِنَّ اللّٰهَ لَطِيْفٌ خَبِيْرٌ ﴿٦٤﴾

65. [c]To Him belongs *all* that is in the heavens and *all* that is in the earth. And, surely, Allāh is Self-Sufficient, Praiseworthy.

لَهٗ مَا فِي السَّمٰوٰتِ وَمَا فِي الْاَرْضِ ۚ وَاِنَّ اللّٰهَ لَهُوَ الْغَنِيُّ الْحَمِيْدُ ﴿٦٥﴾ ع

R. 9 66. Seest thou not that [d]Allāh has subjected to you whatever is in the earth, and the ships that sail through the sea by His command? And He holds back the heaven lest it should fall on the earth save by His leave. Surely, Allāh is Compassionate and Merciful to people.

اَلَمْ تَرَ اَنَّ اللّٰهَ سَخَّرَ لَكُمْ مَّا فِي الْاَرْضِ وَالْفُلْكَ تَجْرِيْ فِي الْبَحْرِ بِاَمْرِهٖ ۚ وَيُمْسِكُ السَّمَآءَ اَنْ تَقَعَ عَلَى الْاَرْضِ اِلَّا بِاِذْنِهٖ ۚ اِنَّ اللّٰهَ بِالنَّاسِ لَرَءُوْفٌ رَّحِيْمٌ ﴿٦٦﴾

67. [e]And He it is Who gave you life, then He will cause you to die, then He will give you life *again*.[1971] Surely, man is most ungrateful.

وَهُوَ الَّذِيْٓ اَحْيَاكُمْ ثُمَّ يُمِيْتُكُمْ ثُمَّ يُحْيِيْكُمْ ۚ اِنَّ الْاِنْسَانَ لَكَفُوْرٌ ﴿٦٧﴾

[a]20 : 115; 23 : 117; 24 : 26. [b]22 : 6; 30 : 51; 35 : 28; 39 : 22; 45 : 6. [c]2 : 256; 10 : 56; 31 : 27. [d]16 : 15; [e]2 : 29; 16 : 71; 30 : 41; 40 : 69.

and oppression to which Muslims were subjected for so long was about to pass away and the day of their glory and might was about to dawn.

1970. The verse draws the attention of disbelievers to the natural phenomenon that is unfolding itself before their very eyes. Do they not see, it purports to say, that Divine rain has fallen on the bleak, barren and spiritually dead land of Arabia and that it has begun to vibrate with new life and there is verdure and greenness all over, *i.e.*, there is spiritual awakening all over the country and Islām has taken deep roots ?

1971. The phenomenon of life and death operates simultaneously. Every death is followed by, and brings the hope of, a new life. A few Muslims killed on the battle-fields of Badr, Uḥud, etc., brought about the spiritual resurrection of the whole of Arabia.

68. For every people We have appointed ways of worship[1972] which they observe; so let them not dispute with thee in the matter *of the Islamic way of worship;* and call thou *the people* to thy Lord, for, surely, thou art on the right guidance.

لِكُلِّ أُمَّةٍ جَعَلْنَا مَنْسَكًا هُمْ نَاسِكُوْهُ فَلَا يُنَازِعُنَّكَ
فِي الْأَمْرِ وَادْعُ إِلٰى رَبِّكَ ۖ إِنَّكَ لَعَلٰى هُدًى
مُّسْتَقِيمٍ ﴿٦٨﴾

69. And if they contend with thee, say, 'Allāh knows best what you do;

وَإِنْ جٰدَلُوْكَ فَقُلِ اللّٰهُ أَعْلَمُ بِمَا تَعْمَلُوْنَ ﴿٦٩﴾

70. [a]'Allāh will judge between you *and me* on the Day of Resurrection concerning that about which you differ.'

اَللّٰهُ يَحْكُمُ بَيْنَكُمْ يَوْمَ الْقِيٰمَةِ فِيْمَا كُنْتُمْ فِيْهِ
تَخْتَلِفُوْنَ ﴿٧٠﴾

71. Knowest thou not that [b]Allāh knows whatsoever is in the heavens and the earth? Surely, it is *all preserved* in a Book, *and* that is easy for Allāh.

أَلَمْ تَعْلَمْ أَنَّ اللّٰهَ يَعْلَمُ مَا فِي السَّمَآءِ وَالْأَرْضِ ۗ
إِنَّ ذٰلِكَ فِي كِتٰبٍ ۗ إِنَّ ذٰلِكَ عَلَى اللّٰهِ يَسِيْرٌ ﴿٧١﴾

72. [c]And they worship instead of Allāh that for which He has sent down no authority, and that of which they have no knowledge.[1973] And for the wrongdoers there is no helper.

وَيَعْبُدُوْنَ مِنْ دُوْنِ اللّٰهِ مَا لَمْ يُنَزِّلْ بِهٖ سُلْطٰنًا وَّ
مَا لَيْسَ لَهُمْ بِهٖ عِلْمٌ ۗ وَمَا لِلظّٰلِمِيْنَ مِنْ نَّصِيْرٍ ﴿٧٢﴾

73. [d]And when Our clear Signs are recited unto them, thou seest on the faces of those, who disbelieve, manifest *signs of* displeasure. They would well-nigh attack those who recite Our Signs to them. Say,

وَإِذَا تُتْلٰى عَلَيْهِمْ اٰيٰتُنَا بَيِّنٰتٍ تَعْرِفُ فِيْ وُجُوْهِ
الَّذِيْنَ كَفَرُوا الْمُنْكَرَ ۖ يَكَادُوْنَ يَسْطُوْنَ بِالَّذِيْنَ
يَتْلُوْنَ عَلَيْهِمْ اٰيٰتِنَا ۗ قُلْ أَفَأُنَبِّئُكُمْ بِشَرٍّ مِّنْ

[a]2 : 114; 4 : 142. [b]20 : 8; 27 : 66; 49 : 17. [c]7 : 72; 12 : 41; 53 : 24. [d]17 : 47; 23 : 67-68; 39 : 46.

1972. Divine worship is found in one form or another among all nations and peoples. This fact leads to the great truth which Islām, among all religions, was the first to proclaim that Divine Messengers appeared among all peoples to teach them the different forms and ways of worship.

1973. Three arguments have been given in this verse against idolatry : (*a*) There is found no authority in any revealed Book for idol-worship; (*b*) human reason and conscience are against it and idolaters can give no sound argument based on their personal experience and observation in support of it; and (*c*) during the ages in the struggle between idolaters and believers, the latter have invariably come off triumphant. Thus Divine revelation, human reason and the verdict of history are all against idolatry.

[a]"Shall I tell you of something worse than that? *It is* the Fire! Allāh has promised it to those who disbelieve. And an evil destination it is!'

ذٰلِكُمُ النَّارُ وَعَدَهَا اللّٰهُ الَّذِيْنَ كَفَرُوْا وَبِئْسَ
الْمَصِيْرُ ٧٣ ع ٩ ١٦

R. 10 74. O men, a similitude is set forth, so listen to it. [b]Surely, those on whom you call upon instead of Allāh cannot create even a fly, though they should all combine together for *the purpose*. And if the fly should snatch away anything from them, they cannot recover it therefrom. Weak, indeed, are *both* the seeker and the sought.[1974]

يٰٓاَيُّهَا النَّاسُ ضُرِبَ مَثَلٌ فَاسْتَمِعُوْا لَهٗ اِنَّ
الَّذِيْنَ تَدْعُوْنَ مِنْ دُوْنِ اللّٰهِ لَنْ يَّخْلُقُوْا ذُبَابًا
وَّلَوِ اجْتَمَعُوْا لَهٗ وَاِنْ يَّسْلُبْهُمُ الذُّبَابُ شَيْـًٔا
لَّا يَسْتَنْقِذُوْهُ مِنْهُ ضَعُفَ الطَّالِبُ وَالْمَطْلُوْبُ ٧٤

75. [c]They have not formed a true concept of *the attributes of* Allāh.[1975] Surely, Allāh is Powerful, Mighty.

مَا قَدَرُوا اللّٰهَ حَقَّ قَدْرِهٖ اِنَّ اللّٰهَ لَقَوِيٌّ عَزِيْزٌ ٧٥

76. Allāh chooses *His* Messengers from among angels and from among men. Surely, Allāh is All-Hearing, All-Seeing.

اَللّٰهُ يَصْطَفِيْ مِنَ الْمَلٰٓئِكَةِ رُسُلًا وَّمِنَ النَّاسِ
اِنَّ اللّٰهَ سَمِيْعٌۢ بَصِيْرٌ ٧٦

77. [d]He knows what is before them and what is behind them, and to Allāh are *all* affairs returned *for decision*.

يَعْلَمُ مَا بَيْنَ اَيْدِيْهِمْ وَمَا خَلْفَهُمْ وَاِلَى اللّٰهِ تُرْجَعُ
الْاُمُوْرُ ٧٧

78. O ye who believe! [e]bow you down and prostrate yourselves *in Prayer*, and worship your Lord, and do good deeds that you may prosper.

يٰٓاَيُّهَا الَّذِيْنَ اٰمَنُوا ارْكَعُوْا وَاسْجُدُوْا وَاعْبُدُوْا
رَبَّكُمْ وَافْعَلُوا الْخَيْرَ لَعَلَّكُمْ تُفْلِحُوْنَ ٧٨ السجدة

[a]5:61. [b]16:21. [c]6:92; 39:68. [d]2:256; 27:66; 49:17. [e]3:44; 41:38; 96:20.

1974. The verse brings home to disbelievers the utter powerlessness and helplessness of their gods and their own folly in worshipping them.

1975. The fact that idolaters degrade themselves so low as to worship idols—gods made of wood and stone, shows that they have a very poor concept of the powers and attributes of the Almighty God, the Great Creator. In fact, all polytheistic beliefs and idolatrous ideas spring from this poor concept that God's powers and attributes are limited and defective like those of man.

79. [a]And strive in *the cause of* Allāh[1976] as it behoves *you* to strive for it. He has chosen you and has laid no hardship upon you in *the matter of* religion; [b]*so follow* the faith of your father Abraham; *He* has named you Muslims[1977] *both* before and in this *Book*,[1977A] [c]so that the Messenger may be a witness over you, and you may be witnesses over mankind. Therefore, observe Prayer and pay the *Zakāt*, and hold fast to Allāh. He is your Protector. An excellent Protector and an Excellent Helper!

وَجَاهِدُوْا فِي اللّٰهِ حَقَّ جِهَادِهٖ هُوَ اجْتَبٰكُمْ
وَمَا جَعَلَ عَلَيْكُمْ فِي الدِّيْنِ مِنْ حَرَجٍ مِلَّةَ
اَبِيْكُمْ اِبْرٰهِيْمَ هُوَ سَمّٰكُمُ الْمُسْلِمِيْنَ ۥ مِنْ
قَبْلُ وَفِيْ هٰذَا لِيَكُوْنَ الرَّسُوْلُ شَهِيْدًا عَلَيْكُمْ
وَتَكُوْنُوْا شُهَدَآءَ عَلَى النَّاسِ ۚ فَاَقِيْمُوا الصَّلٰوةَ
وَاٰتُوا الزَّكٰوةَ وَاعْتَصِمُوْا بِاللّٰهِ هُوَ مَوْلٰىكُمْ فَنِعْمَ
ع الْمَوْلٰى وَنِعْمَ النَّصِيْرُ ﴿٧٩﴾

[a]9 : 41. [b]2 : 136; 16 : 124. [c]2 : 144; 16 : 90.

1976. *Jihād* is of two kinds : (*a*) *Jihād* against one's evil desires and propensities ; and (*b*) *Jihād* against the enemies of truth which includes fighting in self-defence. The first kind of *Jihād* may be termed '*Jihād* in Allāh' and the latter kind of *Jihād*, '*Jihād* in the way of Allāh.' The Holy Prophet has termed the first kind of *Jihād* as *the greater Jihād* and the latter kind of *Jihād* as *the smaller Jihād.*

1977. The words, ' He has named you Muslims both before, and in this Book,' refer to Isaiah's prophecy : 'And thou shalt be called by a new name which the mouth of the Lord shall name...... (Isa. 62 : 2 & 65 : 15).

1977A. The allusion in the words 'and in this Book' is to Abraham's prayer quoted in the Qur'ān, *viz.*, 'Our Lord make us 'Muslims' to Thee and make our offspring a people submissive to Thee' (2 : 129).

CHAPTER 23

AL-MU'MINŪN

(*Revealed before Hijrah*)

Date of Revelation and Context

There is sufficient internal evidence to show that the *Sūrah* was revealed towards the end of the Holy Prophet's stay at Mecca. Sayūṭī regards it as the last *Sūrah* to have been revealed at Mecca just before the Holy Prophet's departure for Medina. Though it may not have been actually the last, it was certainly one of the last *Sūrahs* to be revealed at Mecca. In the closing verses of the previous *Sūrah* believers were told to turn to God and obey His commandments as in this lay the secret of their future progress and prosperity. They were also enjoined to wage war with the sword so that those who had drawn the sword against Islām should themselves perish by the sword. They were further enjoined to strive in the way of the Lord with the Qur'ān and the promise was held out to them that if they did so, God would help them and vouchsafe to them success and prosperity. The promise was conditional. A sure guarantee, however, is given here that a community of believers will certainly be born who, because they will fulfil the above-mentioned conditions, will achieve success. Thus a thing, which was presumed in the preceding *Sūrah* to have existed, is claimed in this *Sūrah* to have come into being as an actual fact.

Subject-Matter

The *Sūrah* opens with the glad tidings to the true believers that the time of their success and prosperity has already arrived, and proceeds to give a brief description of their characteristics and special marks which is indicative of the process of their spiritual growth and development. This description is followed by a brief but beautiful account of the growth of the human foetus and defines the different stages through which the child passes—from the stage of a drop of sperm to that of a fully developed human being, and then explains that just as every physical birth is followed by death and Resurrection, similarly nations or communities among whom at one time a spiritual renaissance takes place, are at another time subject to decay and decadence and in due course are succeeded by another people. In fact, spiritual and physical developments bear close resemblance. Both of them have to pass through seven stages of development. Next, the *Sūrah* develops the theme that all things are sent down into the world according to a determined measure and each one of them continues to exist and is afforded protection till an appointed time. When, however, it has served its utility it decays and dies. In the same way Divine Teachings, sent down before the Qur'ān, became defunct when they had served their intended purpose. Thus, the mere fact that a Teaching is Divine does not entitle it to immunity from decay. It is only the Qur'ān which has been granted continuity of life and which will, therefore, continue to provide spiritual food to all humanity for all time. The *Sūrah* then recounts some of the favours which God has bestowed upon man and which are necessary for his physical sustenance, and then draws the moral lesson that when God has taken so much care to provide for man's physical needs, He must have taken equal, even greater, care to provide for his spiritual requirements. Next, it is stated that the most essential prerequisite to ensure spiritual progress is belief in the Unity of God which since the inception of the world the Prophets of God have taught and preached. Noah preached and propagated the Oneness of God. After him came a galaxy of Prophets, all of whom taught that God was One, and those Divine Teachers who came after them also emphasized and stressed it. The devotees of darkness, however, always opposed and persecuted these Prophets. The result of the struggle between Truth and falsehood invariably was that the believers were successful and those, who disbelieved and rejected the Divine Messengers, suffered defeat and came to grief. The righteous servants of God fear their Lord and believe in His Signs and have firm faith in His Unity and do good deeds to the best of their power, and yet consider that they have not fully discharged their duties and responsibilities. They strive to vie with one another in doing good deeds. After this, disbelievers are warned that they will be punished if they persisted in their rejection of the Divine Message. But they do not desist from their evil course and continue to indulge in iniquitous deeds till when the hour of punishment arrives they beg and beseech that they might be granted one last opportunity to reform themselves. But then it is too late, and they are made to realize that pain and punishment even for a brief period after a whole life of ease and comfort are doubly mortifying. The *Sūrah* ends by stating the great spiritual truth that man is not created without purpose. His life has a noble aim. He should not, therefore, doubt or dispute the truth of Divine Law and of God's Messengers and should realize that he will have to render account of his deeds before his Lord.

سُوْرَةُ الْمُؤْمِنُوْنَ مَكِّيَّةٌ

(٢٣) آياتها ١١٩ ركوعاتها ٦

الجزء ١٨

1. [a]In the name of Allāh, the Gracious, the Merciful.	بِسْمِ اللّٰهِ الرَّحْمٰنِ الرَّحِيْمِ ﴿١﴾
2. Successful indeed are the believers,[1978]	قَدْ اَفْلَحَ الْمُؤْمِنُوْنَ ﴿٢﴾
3. Who are humble[1979] in their Prayers,	الَّذِيْنَ هُمْ فِيْ صَلَاتِهِمْ خٰشِعُوْنَ ﴿٣﴾
4. And [b]who shun all that which is vain,[1980]	وَالَّذِيْنَ هُمْ عَنِ اللَّغْوِ مُعْرِضُوْنَ ﴿٤﴾
5. And [c]who are prompt *and regular* in paying the *Zakāt*,[1981]	وَالَّذِيْنَ هُمْ لِلزَّكٰوةِ فٰعِلُوْنَ ﴿٥﴾
6. And [d]who guard their chastity—	وَالَّذِيْنَ هُمْ لِفُرُوْجِهِمْ حٰفِظُوْنَ ﴿٦﴾
7. [e]Except from their wives or what their right hands possess,[1981A] for then they are not to be blamed ;	اِلَّا عَلٰٓى اَزْوَاجِهِمْ اَوْ مَا مَلَكَتْ اَيْمَانُهُمْ فَاِنَّهُمْ غَيْرُ مَلُوْمِيْنَ ﴿٧﴾
8. [f]But those, who seek *anything* beyond that are the transgressors—	فَمَنِ ابْتَغٰى وَرَآءَ ذٰلِكَ فَاُولٰٓئِكَ هُمُ الْعٰدُوْنَ ﴿٨﴾

[a]1 : 1. [b]25 : 73. [c]5 : 56; 9 : 71. [d]70 : 30. [e]70 : 31. [f]70 : 32.

1978. The verse refers to believers of a very high spiritual calibre whose characteristics and special marks have been mentioned in the verses that follow. Such believers will achieve *Falāḥ* (success) and not only *Najāh* (salvation), because the achievement of *Falāḥ* is a much higher spiritual stage than the attainment of *Najāh*.

1979. With this verse begins a description of the conditions or prerequisites which a believer must fulfil before he should aspire to attain success in life and achieve the supreme object for which God has created him. These conditions may be regarded as so many stages in the spiritual development of man. The first stage or milestone in this journey of the human soul is that a believer turns to God in all humility, overawed by Divine Majesty, and with a penitent heart and humbled soul.

1980. The second stage consists in the avoidance of all vain talk and thoughts and also of idle, vain and futile actions. Life is a grim and serious fact and a believer must take it as such. He must employ every moment of it usefully and shun all vain and useless pursuits.

1981. The object of *Zakāt* is not only to provide means for the relief of the distressed, or for the promotion of the welfare of the economically less favoured sections of the community, but also to discourage the hoarding of money and commodities and thus to ensure a brisk circulation of both, resulting in healthy economic adjustments.

1981A. See 561.

9. [a]And who are watchful of their trusts and their covenants,

وَالَّذِيْنَ هُمْ لِاَمٰنٰتِهِمْ وَعَهْدِهِمْ رٰعُوْنَ ۝٩

10. [b]And who are strict in the observance of their Prayers.[1982]

وَالَّذِيْنَ هُمْ عَلٰى صَلَوٰتِهِمْ يُحَافِظُوْنَ ۝١٠

11. These are the heirs,

اُولٰٓئِكَ هُمُ الْوٰرِثُوْنَ ۝١١

12. [c]Who will inherit Paradise.[1983] They will abide therein *for ever*.

الَّذِيْنَ يَرِثُوْنَ الْفِرْدَوْسَ هُمْ فِيْهَا خٰلِدُوْنَ ۝١٢

13. Verily, [d]We created man from an extract of clay;[1984]

وَلَقَدْ خَلَقْنَا الْاِنْسَانَ مِنْ سُلٰلَةٍ مِّنْ طِيْنٍ ۝١٣

14. Then [e]We placed him as a drop of sperm in a safe depository;

ثُمَّ جَعَلْنٰهُ نُطْفَةً فِيْ قَرَارٍ مَّكِيْنٍ ۝١٤

15. Then We fashioned the sperm into a clot; then We fashioned the clot into a *shapeless* lump; then We fashioned bones out of this *shapeless* lump; then We clothed the bones with flesh; then We developed it into another creation.[1985] So blessed be Allāh, the Best of creators.

ثُمَّ خَلَقْنَا النُّطْفَةَ عَلَقَةً فَخَلَقْنَا الْعَلَقَةَ مُضْغَةً فَخَلَقْنَا الْمُضْغَةَ عِظٰمًا فَكَسَوْنَا الْعِظٰمَ لَحْمًا ثُمَّ اَنْشَاْنٰهُ خَلْقًا اٰخَرَ فَتَبٰرَكَ اللّٰهُ اَحْسَنُ الْخٰلِقِيْنَ ۝١٥

---

[a]70 : 33. [b]6 : 93; 70 : 35. [c]18 : 108; 70 : 36. [d]32 : 8-9. [e]22 : 6.

1982. This verse marks the last and the highest stage of spiritual development, when remembrance of God becomes a second nature with the believer, a part and parcel of his being, the solace of his soul. At this stage he takes particular care about acts of collective worship which implies that the national instinct becomes very strong in him and he subordinates individual interests to communal and national good.

1983. As believers mentioned in the foregoing verses combine in themselves all kinds of virtues, therefore they will be made to reside in *Firdaus* which contains everything that is found in any garden (Lane). As they brought death over their desires, so in return God will give them ever-lasting life and they will have everything they desired (50 : 36).

1984. After having mentioned in the first ten verses of the *Sūrah* the different stages of spiritual evolution of man, the Qur'ān proceeds to describe in this and the next few verses the different stages of his physical development and thus establishes a remarkable parallelism between his physical and spiritual birth and growth. Leaving out biological technicalities, the *Sūrah* gives the description in a clear and easily understandable language. Biology has not discovered anything which even remotely contradicts the Quranic description. The words, *We created man from an extract of clay*, mention the process of man's creation from the earliest stage when he lies dormant in the form of dust, and the inorganic constituents of the earth through a subtle process of change become converted into the life-germ by way of food which a human being eats. At the stage, *then We clothed the bones with flesh*, (23 : 15), the physical growth of the embryo becomes complete.

1985. The words, *then We developed it into another creation*, show that the soul is not imported into the human body from outside but grows in the body as it develops in

16. Then after that [a]you, surely, must die.[1986]

ثُمَّ إِنَّكُمْ بَعْدَ ذٰلِكَ لَمَيِّتُونَ ﴿١٦﴾

17. [b]Then on the Day of Resurrection you shall, surely, be raised up.[1987]

ثُمَّ إِنَّكُمْ يَوْمَ الْقِيٰمَةِ تُبْعَثُونَ ﴿١٧﴾

18. [c]And We have created above you seven ways,[1988] and We are never neglectful of the creation.

وَلَقَدْ خَلَقْنَا فَوْقَكُمْ سَبْعَ طَرَآئِقَ ۖ وَمَا كُنَّا عَنِ الْخَلْقِ غٰفِلِينَ ﴿١٨﴾

19. [d]And We sent down water from the sky according to a measure,[1989] and We caused it to stay in the earth—and, surely, We have the power to take it away.

وَأَنْزَلْنَا مِنَ السَّمَآءِ مَآءً بِقَدَرٍ فَأَسْكَنّٰهُ فِي الْأَرْضِ ۖ وَإِنَّا عَلٰى ذَهَابٍ بِهٖ لَقٰدِرُونَ ﴿١٩﴾

20. [e]And We produced for you thereby gardens of date-palms and vines; for you therein are abundant fruits; and of them you eat;

فَأَنْشَأْنَا لَكُمْ بِهٖ جَنّٰتٍ مِّنْ نَّخِيلٍ وَّأَعْنَابٍ لَّكُمْ فِيهَا فَوَاكِهُ كَثِيرَةٌ وَّمِنْهَا تَأْكُلُونَ ﴿٢٠﴾

[a]39 : 31. [b]39 : 32. [c]78 : 13. [d]15 : 23. [e]16 : 12, 68; 36 : 35.

the womb. At first it has no separate existence from the body but the processes through which the body passes during its development in the womb distil from the body a delicate essence which is called the soul. As soon as the relationship between the soul and the body becomes completely adjusted, the heart begins to function. The soul then has a distinct existence of its own apart from the body which henceforth serves it as a shell. See also "The Larger Edition of the Commentary," pp. 1787—1790.

1986. After man has attained full development, there sets in a process of decay which ends in his death. It is an immutable law of nature that all life must end in decay, dissolution and death. God alone is Ever-Living.

1987. After death man again will be restored to life in order that he might continue to make spiritual progress in the life to come which knows no end. The progress he makes in the present life constitutes only a preparatory stage. Here he is like a child in his mother's womb. After death he is born into a new and fuller life which is the beginning of a never-ending progress.

1988. The six stages of spiritual progress described in the first ten verses of this *Sūrah* become seven if "Paradise" (v. 12) be counted as the last stage of spiritual development. Similarly, if the preparatory stage previous to the formation of the sperm (v. 13) be added to the six stages of the embryonic development, this number also becomes seven. Thus the 'seven ways in the spiritual heaven' to which reference has been made in this verse correspond to the seven stages of the physical development of man mentioned in vv. 13—15.

1989. This verse gives an illustration of how God supplies the physical and spiritual needs of man. All life, it says, depends on water which descends from heaven, in the form of rain, snow or hail. Similarly, spiritual water descends from heaven in the form of Divine revelation without which no spiritual life can exist.

21. And a tree which springs forth from Mount Sinai;[1990] it produces oil and sauce for those who eat.

وَشَجَرَةً تَخْرُجُ مِنْ طُوْرِ سَيْنَآءَ تَنْبُتُ بِالدُّهْنِ وَصِبْغٍ لِّلْاٰكِلِيْنَ ۞

22. ᵃAnd in the cattle also there is a lesson for you. We give you to drink of that which is in their bellies and you have in them many other benefits,[1991] and of *the flesh of some of* them you *also* eat;

وَاِنَّ لَكُمْ فِى الْاَنْعَامِ لَعِبْرَةً ۗ نُسْقِيْكُمْ مِّمَّا فِىْ بُطُوْنِهَا وَلَكُمْ فِيْهَا مَنَافِعُ كَثِيْرَةٌ وَّمِنْهَا تَأْكُلُوْنَ ۞

23. And ᵇon them and on ships you are borne.

وَعَلَيْهَا وَعَلَى الْفُلْكِ تُحْمَلُوْنَ ۞

R. 2   24. ᶜAnd We, certainly, sent Noah to his people, and he said, 'O my people, worship Allāh *alone*. You have no other god but Him. Will you not then seek *His* protection?'

وَلَقَدْ اَرْسَلْنَا نُوْحًا اِلٰى قَوْمِهٖ فَقَالَ يٰقَوْمِ اعْبُدُوا اللّٰهَ مَا لَكُمْ مِّنْ اِلٰهٍ غَيْرُهٗ ۗ اَفَلَا تَتَّقُوْنَ ۞

25. ᵈAnd the chiefs of his people, who disbelieved, said, 'He is only a mortal like yourselves;[1992] he seeks to gain superiority over you. And if Allāh had so willed, ᵉHe could have, surely, sent down angels *with him*. We have never heard of such a thing among our forefathers;

فَقَالَ الْمَلَؤُا الَّذِيْنَ كَفَرُوْا مِنْ قَوْمِهٖ مَا هٰذَآ اِلَّا بَشَرٌ مِّثْلُكُمْ ۙ يُرِيْدُ اَنْ يَّتَفَضَّلَ عَلَيْكُمْ ۗ وَلَوْ شَآءَ اللّٰهُ لَاَنْزَلَ مَلٰٓئِكَةً ۖ مَّا سَمِعْنَا بِهٰذَا فِىْٓ اٰبَآئِنَا الْاَوَّلِيْنَ ۞

ᵃ6 : 143; 16 : 6; 36 : 72-73; 40 : 80-81. ᵇ16 : 8-9; 36 : 42-43; 43 : 13. ᶜ7 : 60; 11 : 26; 71 : 2. ᵈ7 : 61; 11 : 28; 17 : 95; 34 : 44. ᵉ17 : 96.

1990. The words, "Mount Sinai," remind us of the great prophecy of the Bible: 'The Lord came from Sinai, and rose from Seir unto them ; He shined forth from Mount Paran and he came with ten thousands of saints ; from his right hand went a fiery law for them' (Deut. 33 : 2). See also "Once to Sinai" by H.F. Prescott.

1991. The word, 'Ibrah, which means an 'indication or evidence whereby one passes from ignorance to knowledge' (Lane), seems to allude to the subtle process which takes place in the bellies of the animals and which turns grass or herbage eaten by them into pure and wholesome milk, and by pondering over which one is led to acquire an insight into God's great power and into the subtle ways through which Divine laws work.

1992. The disbelievers suffer from superiority complex and therefore reject Divine Messengers on the plea that they cannot accept the lead of one who is 'only a mortal like themselves.' The verse incidentally implies that belief in the existence of angels was entertained from time immemorial. As far back as Noah's time his opponents wanted to see angels descending on them.

26. [a]"'He is but a man *stricken* with madness; wait, therefore, concerning him for a while.'

إِنْ هُوَ إِلَّا رَجُلٌۢ بِهِۦ جِنَّةٌ فَتَرَبَّصُوا۟ بِهِۦ حَتَّىٰ حِينٍ ٢٦

27. [b]*Noah* said, 'O my Lord, help me, for they treat me as a liar.'

قَالَ رَبِّ ٱنصُرْنِى بِمَا كَذَّبُونِ ٢٧

28. So We directed him by revelation: [c]"Make the Ark under Our eyes and *according to* Our revelation. [d]And when Our command comes, and the fountains *of the earth* gush forth, take thou into it two pairs of every species and thy family, except those of them against whom the word has already gone forth. And address Me not concerning those who have done wrong; they shall, surely, be drowned.[1993]

فَأَوْحَيْنَآ إِلَيْهِ أَنِ ٱصْنَعِ ٱلْفُلْكَ بِأَعْيُنِنَا وَوَحْيِنَا
فَإِذَا جَآءَ أَمْرُنَا وَفَارَ ٱلتَّنُّورُ فَٱسْلُكْ فِيهَا مِن
كُلٍّ زَوْجَيْنِ ٱثْنَيْنِ وَأَهْلَكَ إِلَّا مَن سَبَقَ عَلَيْهِ
ٱلْقَوْلُ مِنْهُمْ وَلَا تُخَٰطِبْنِى فِى ٱلَّذِينَ ظَلَمُوٓا۟ إِنَّهُم
مُّغْرَقُونَ ٢٨

29. [e]"'And when thou art settled in the Ark—thou and those that are with thee—say, 'All praise belongs to Allāh Who has saved **us** from the unjust people.'"

فَإِذَا ٱسْتَوَيْتَ أَنتَ وَمَن مَّعَكَ عَلَى ٱلْفُلْكِ فَقُلِ
ٱلْحَمْدُ لِلَّهِ ٱلَّذِى نَجَّىٰنَا مِنَ ٱلْقَوْمِ ٱلظَّٰلِمِينَ ٢٩

30. 'And *when thou dost disembark from the Ark* say, [f]'My Lord, cause me to land a blessed landing, for Thou art the Best of those who bring *people* to land.'

وَقُل رَّبِّ أَنزِلْنِى مُنزَلًا مُّبَارَكًا وَأَنتَ خَيْرُ
ٱلْمُنزِلِينَ ٣٠

31. [g]Verily, in this there are Signs. Surely, We do try *people*.

إِنَّ فِى ذَٰلِكَ لَءَايَٰتٍ وَإِن كُنَّا لَمُبْتَلِينَ ٣١

32. [h]Then We raised after them another generation.[1994]

ثُمَّ أَنشَأْنَا مِنۢ بَعْدِهِمْ قَرْنًا ءَاخَرِينَ ٣٢

[a]54 : 10. [b]26 : 118-119; 54 : 11. [c]11 : 38. [d]11 : 41; 54 : 13-14. [e]11 : 42; 43 : 14. [f]11 : 49. [g]29 : 16. [h]23 : 43; 25 : 39.

1993. See 1315 & 1316.

1994. The reference in the words, "another generation," is to the 'Ād tribe, the people of the Prophet Hūd, because the conditions and circumstances of "another generation" mentioned in the verse under comment and the following few verses closely resemble those of 'Ād mentioned in 7 : 66-70.

33. And We sent among them a Messenger from among themselves *with the Message*, 'Serve Allāh, you have no god other than Him. Will you not then make *Him* your shield *against all calamities?*

فَاَرْسَلْنَا فِيْهِمْ رَسُوْلًا مِّنْهُمْ اَنِ اعْبُدُوا اللّٰهَ مَا لَكُمْ مِّنْ اِلٰهٍ غَيْرُهٗ ؕ اَفَلَا تَتَّقُوْنَ ﴿۳۳﴾

R. 3 34. And the chiefs of his people, who disbelieved and denied the meeting of the Hereafter *with their Lord* and [a]whom We had afforded ease and comfort in this life, said, 'This is but a mortal like yourselves. [b]He eats of that of which you eat, and drinks of that of which you drink;

وَقَالَ الْمَلَاُ مِنْ قَوْمِهِ الَّذِيْنَ كَفَرُوْا وَكَذَّبُوْا بِلِقَآءِ الْاٰخِرَةِ وَاَتْرَفْنٰهُمْ فِي الْحَيٰوةِ الدُّنْيَا ۙ مَا هٰذَآ اِلَّا بَشَرٌ مِّثْلُكُمْ ۙ يَاْكُلُ مِمَّا تَاْكُلُوْنَ مِنْهُ وَيَشْرَبُ مِمَّا تَشْرَبُوْنَ ﴿۳۴﴾

35. [c]'And if you obey a mortal like yourselves, you will then be surely losers;

وَلَئِنْ اَطَعْتُمْ بَشَرًا مِّثْلَكُمْ اِنَّكُمْ اِذًا لَّخٰسِرُوْنَ ﴿۳۵﴾

36. [d]'Does he promise you that when you are dead and have become dust and bones, you will be brought forth *again?*

اَيَعِدُكُمْ اَنَّكُمْ اِذَا مِتُّمْ وَكُنْتُمْ تُرَابًا وَّعِظَامًا اَنَّكُمْ مُّخْرَجُوْنَ ﴿۳۶﴾

37. [e]'Far, very far *from truth*[1995] is that which you are promised;

هَيْهَاتَ هَيْهَاتَ لِمَا تُوْعَدُوْنَ ﴿۳۷﴾

38. [f]'There is no life other than our present life; we die and we live, and we shall not be raised up *again;*

اِنْ هِيَ اِلَّا حَيَاتُنَا الدُّنْيَا نَمُوْتُ وَنَحْيَا وَمَا نَحْنُ بِمَبْعُوْثِيْنَ ﴿۳۸﴾

39. 'He is only a man who has forged a lie against Allāh; and we are not going to believe in him.'

اِنْ هُوَ اِلَّا رَجُلُ ِافْتَرٰى عَلَى اللّٰهِ كَذِبًا وَّمَا نَحْنُ لَهٗ بِمُؤْمِنِيْنَ ﴿۳۹﴾

40. He said, 'My Lord, help me, for they treat me as a liar.'

قَالَ رَبِّ انْصُرْنِيْ بِمَا كَذَّبُوْنِ ﴿۴۰﴾

41. *Allāh* said, 'In a little while they will, surely, become repentant.'

قَالَ عَمَّا قَلِيْلٍ لَّيُصْبِحُنَّ نٰدِمِيْنَ ﴿۴۱﴾

[a]17 : 17. [b]21 : 9; 25 : 8. [c]23 : 48. [d]17 : 50; 36 : 79; 50 : 4.
[e]50 : 4. [f]6 : 30; 19 : 67; 36 : 79; 44 : 36; 45 : 25.

1995. *Haihāta* denotes one's deeming a thing remote or improbable and despairing of it, and means, *Ba'uda Jiddan* (he or it was or became very far off), or *Mā Ab'ada-hū* (how far it is), signifying the intensification of the sense of being very far (Lane).

42. [a]"Then punishment overtook them rightfully, and We made them *as* rubbish.[1996] Cursed,[1997] then, be the people who do wrong !

فَاَخَذَتْهُمُ الصَّيْحَةُ بِالْحَقِّ فَجَعَلْنٰهُمْ غُثَآءً ۚ
فَبُعْدًا لِّلْقَوْمِ الظّٰلِمِيْنَ ﴿٤٢﴾

43. [b]Then We raised after them other generations.

ثُمَّ اَنْشَاْنَا مِنْ بَعْدِهِمْ قُرُوْنًا اٰخَرِيْنَ ﴿٤٣﴾

44. [c]No people can go ahead of their appointed time, nor can they remain behind *it*.[1998]

مَا تَسْبِقُ مِنْ اُمَّةٍ اَجَلَهَا وَمَا يَسْتَاْخِرُوْنَ ﴿٤٤﴾

45. Then We sent Our Messengers one after the other. [d]Every time there came to a people their Messenger, they treated him as a liar. So We made them follow one another *to destruction* and We made them mere tales[1999] *of the past*. Cursed, then, be the people who believe not!

ثُمَّ اَرْسَلْنَا رُسُلَنَا تَتْرَا ؕ كُلَّمَا جَآءَ اُمَّةً رَّسُوْلُهَا
كَذَّبُوْهُ فَاَتْبَعْنَا بَعْضَهُمْ بَعْضًا وَّجَعَلْنٰهُمْ اَحَادِيْثَ ۚ
فَبُعْدًا لِّقَوْمٍ لَّا يُؤْمِنُوْنَ ﴿٤٥﴾

46. Then [e]We sent Moses and his brother Aaron with Our Signs and a clear authority,

ثُمَّ اَرْسَلْنَا مُوْسٰى وَاَخَاهُ هٰرُوْنَ ۙ بِاٰيٰتِنَا
وَسُلْطٰنٍ مُّبِيْنٍ ﴿٤٦﴾

47. To Pharaoh and his chiefs; but they behaved arrogantly and they were a haughty people.

اِلٰى فِرْعَوْنَ وَمَلَا۟ئِهٖ فَاسْتَكْبَرُوْا وَكَانُوْا قَوْمًا
عَالِيْنَ ۚ ﴿٤٧﴾

48. And they said, 'Shall we believe in two mortals like ourselves while their people are our slaves ?'

فَقَالُوْٓا اَنُؤْمِنُ لِبَشَرَيْنِ مِثْلِنَا وَقَوْمُهُمَا لَنَا
عٰبِدُوْنَ ۚ ﴿٤٨﴾

[a]7 : 92; 11 : 68. [b]23 : 32. [c]15 : 6. [d]2 : 88; 36 : 31. [e]20 : 30, 31 ; 43-44.

1996. *Ghuthā'* means, the rubbish or particles of things or refuse and scum and rotten leaves with the scum borne upon the surface of a torrent. *Ghuthā' al-Nās* means, the low and the vile and the refuse of mankind (Lane).

1997. *Bu'd* means, perdition or death ; curse or malediction, etc. (Lane).

1998. No people can thwart their decreed destiny, and rejection of Divine Prophets never goes unpunished, but it is for God to determine the form and the time of the punishment to be meted out to disbelievers.

1999. Their destruction was so complete that generations coming after them talked of them as of a people who once lived on this earth, as no trace of their existence was left.

49. So they called them liars, and became a ruined people.

فَكَذَّبُوهُمَا فَكَانُوا مِنَ الْمُهْلَكِينَ ﴿٤٩﴾

50. [a]And We gave Moses the Book, that they might be guided.

وَلَقَدْ آتَيْنَا مُوسَى الْكِتَابَ لَعَلَّهُمْ يَهْتَدُونَ ﴿٥٠﴾

51. And We made the son of Mary and his mother a Sign; and gave them shelter on an elevated land of *green* valleys and springs of running water.[2000]

وَجَعَلْنَا ابْنَ مَرْيَمَ وَأُمَّهُ آيَةً وَآوَيْنَاهُمَا إِلَى رَبْوَةٍ ذَاتِ قَرَارٍ وَمَعِينٍ ﴿٥١﴾

[a]2 : 88; 17 : 3; 32 : 24; 40 : 54.

2000. As Jesus's death, like his birth, has become a subject of great controversy, and some confusion and doubt still persist as to how and where he passed the last days of his crowded life, and as the question of the manner of his death also forms a vital question with the Christian Faith, a somewhat exhaustive note on this very important, *albeit* baffling religious question is called for. The Qur'ān and the Bible, reinforced by authenticated facts of history, lend powerful support to the view that Jesus did not die on the Cross. The following arguments substantiate and support this contention :

(1) In his book " The Unknown Life of Jesus " Nicholas Notovitch, a Russian traveller, who visited the Far East in about 1877 tells us that Jesus came to Kashmir and Afghanistan. Sir Francis Younghusband, who at the time when Nicholas Notovitch visited Kashmir, was British resident at the court of the Maharaja of Kashmir, met him near the Zojila Pass. Recent research about Jesus's travels in the East lends powerful support to Notovitch's book. 'In Srinagar,' says Professor Nicholus Roerich in his book "Heart of Asia," 'we first encountered the curious legend about Christ's visit to the place. Afterwards we saw how widely spread in India, in Laddakh and in Central Asia, was the legend of the visit of Christ to those parts........All over Central Asia, in Kashmir and Laddakh and Tibet and even further north, there still exists a strong belief that Jesus or Issa travelled about there' ("Glimpses of World History" by Jawahar Lal Nehru).

Some scholars have taken refuge behind some obscure passages in Notovitch's book to claim that Jesus came to East before and not after he was commissioned as a Divine Prophet. But a mere boy of 13 or 14 years of age as Jesus is stated to have been when he came to India, he could not have conceived of undertaking so long and arduous a journey to a far-off land, and thus of exposing himself to mortal danger on the way. After all, what attraction or motives Jesus had, at such an early age, in coming over to India? And if at all he came to India at that time, what interest the people of India and Kashmir had in keeping a record of the activities, doings and wanderings of a boy of 13 or 14? The fact based on historical data is that after he had been rejected by the Jews and his life had become unsafe in Palestine, Jesus forsook that country to search, in fulfilment of the old biblical prophecies, for 'The Lost Ten Tribes of Israel,' and undertook the long and dangerous journey to India and Kashmir and lived an eventful life to the very ripe age of 120 (Kanz al-'Ummāl, vol. 6). It is then that records came to be kept of his activities. These 'Lost Tribes of Israel' had, after their great dispersion by the Assyrians and the Babylonians, lived in Iraq and Iran; and later, when the Iranians under Darius and Cyrus extended their territories further East to Afghanistan and India, these tribes migrated with them to these countries.

(2) The Kashmiris and Afghans are the descendants of 'The Lost Tribes of Israel.' This fact is quite evident from the traditions, history and written records of these two peoples. The names of their towns and tribes, their customs, habits, mode and manner of living, their dress, their physical features, etc., all resemble those of the Jews. Their ancient monuments and old inscriptions also support this view. Their folk-lore is full of Jewish stories. The name Kashmir itself is in reality Kashir meaning "like Syria" (or it seems to have been named after Kash or Cush, a grandson of Noah). All these facts impart certainty to the view that the Afghans and Kashmiris are largely the descendants of "The Lost Ten Tribes of Israel."

R. 4 52. O ye Messengers, [a]eat of the pure things[2001] and do good works. Verily, I am Well-Aware of what you do.

يٰٓاَيُّهَا الرُّسُلُ كُلُوْا مِنَ الطَّيِّبٰتِ وَاعْمَلُوْا صَالِحًا ۭ اِنِّيْ بِمَا تَعْمَلُوْنَ عَلِيْمٌ ۝

53. And *know* [b]that this community of yours is one community,[2002] and I am your Lord. So take Me as *your* Protector.

وَاِنَّ هٰذِهٖٓ اُمَّتُكُمْ اُمَّةً وَّاحِدَةً وَّاَنَا رَبُّكُمْ فَاتَّقُوْنِ ۝

[a]7 : 33. [b]21 : 93.

(3) These proofs are evidence enough to establish the fact that Jesus did come to Kashmir and that the Kashmiris are the descendants of "The Lost Ten Tribes of Israel." But the greatest and best proof of his having come to Kashmir and of having lived and died there is the presence of his tomb in Khanyar Street, Srinagar, Kashmir. This tomb which is called Rauzabal is variously known as the tomb of Yūz Āsaf, of Nabī Ṣāḥib, of Shahzādah Nabī and even of 'Isā Ṣaḥib. According to well-established historical accounts this Yūz Āsaf came to Kashmir more than 1900 years ago and preached in parables and used many of the parables recorded in the Gospels. In certain books of history he is described as a *Nabī* (Prophet). Moreover, Yūz Āsaf is a biblical name meaning 'Yasū,' the gatherer,' which is one of the descriptive names of Jesus as his mission was to gather the lost tribes of Israel into the Master's fold as he himself says: 'And other sheep I have which are not of this fold, them also must I bring, and they shall hear my voice, and there shall be one fold and one shepherd' (John 10 : 16).

The following historical quotations also shed some light on this subject :

'The tomb is generally known as that of a Prophet. He was a Prince who came to Kashmir from a foreign land, and was engaged in preaching to the Kashmiris. His name was Yūz Āsaf (Tārīkh A'ẓamī, pp. 82-85)........'Yūz Āsaf wandered about in several lands till he reached a country called Kashmir. He travelled in it far and wide and lived and stayed there till death overtook him' (Ikmāl al-Dīn, pp. 358—359)........'Kashmir legend, I have been told, contains reference to a Prophet who lived here and taught as Jesus did by parables and little stories that are repeated in Kashmir to the present day' (John Noel's article in Asia, Oct. 1930).......'The flight of Jesus, therefore, to India and his death in Srinagar is not foreign to the truth rationally or historically (Tafsīr al-Manār, vol. 6).

For a better and fuller treatment, however, of this subject see "Masīḥ Hindustān Main" by Aḥmad, the Promised Messiah. See also the well-known book, 'Nazarene Gospel Restored,' whose authors maintain that though officially crucified in A.D. 30, Jesus was still alive some twenty years after the Resurrection.

There could be no better description of the place where after his deliverance from accursed death on the Cross, Jesus and his mother lived in peace and tranquillity and went to their eternal rest, than in the Quranic words, *viz.*, 'elevated land of green valleys and springs of running water,' which is quite an apt description of the beautiful Valley of Kashmir. Nicholas Notovitch calls Kashmir "the Valley of Eternal Bliss."

2001. The fact that there exists a deep and subtle connection between the food that a person eats and his actions, good or bad, has now begun to be increasingly recognized by medical science. But Islām laid down as far back as 1400 years directions relating to food which possess great moral significance. The basic principle laid down by Islām in this regard is that as man must develop all his natural instincts and faculties, therefore he should partake of all kinds of food, except those that are likely to do him physical, moral or spiritual harm. The use of pure and good food produces healthy mental condition which in turn produces good and righteous actions.

2002. All the Messengers of God formed one brotherhood, as they came from the same Divine Source and their basic teachings were more or less identical and the object and purpose of their advent was also one and the same—to establish upon earth Unity of God and oneness of humanity.

54. But *the people* have cut up their affair among themselves, *forming themselves into* parties, each group rejoicing in what is with them.[2003]

فَتَقَطَّعُوۡۤا اَمۡرَهُمۡ بَيۡنَهُمۡ زُبُرًا ۚ كُلُّ حِزۡبٍۭ بِمَا لَدَيۡهِمۡ فَرِحُوۡنَ ۞

55. So ^aleave them in their confusion for a time.

فَذَرۡهُمۡ فِىۡ غَمۡرَتِهِمۡ حَتّٰى حِيۡنٍ ۞

56. Do they imagine that because We bestow upon them wealth and children,

اَيَحۡسَبُوۡنَ اَنَّمَا نُمِدُّهُمۡ بِهٖ مِنۡ مَّالٍ وَّبَنِيۡنَ ۙ

57. We hasten to do them good? Nay, but they understand not.[2004]

نُسَارِعُ لَهُمۡ فِى الۡخَيۡرٰتِ ؕ بَلۡ لَّا يَشۡعُرُوۡنَ ۞

58. Verily, those ^bwho tremble with fear of their Lord,

اِنَّ الَّذِيۡنَ هُمۡ مِّنۡ خَشۡيَةِ رَبِّهِمۡ مُّشۡفِقُوۡنَ ۙ

59. And those who believe in the Signs of their Lord,

وَالَّذِيۡنَ هُمۡ بِاٰيٰتِ رَبِّهِمۡ يُؤۡمِنُوۡنَ ۙ

60. And those who ascribe not partners to their Lord,

وَالَّذِيۡنَ هُمۡ بِرَبِّهِمۡ لَا يُشۡرِكُوۡنَ ۙ

61. And those who give what they give while ^ctheir hearts are full of fear that to their Lord they will return—

وَالَّذِيۡنَ يُؤۡتُوۡنَ مَاۤ اٰتَوۡا وَّقُلُوۡبُهُمۡ وَجِلَةٌ اَنَّهُمۡ اِلٰى رَبِّهِمۡ رٰجِعُوۡنَ ۙ

62. These it is who hasten to do good works, and they are foremost in *doing* them.

اُولٰٓئِكَ يُسٰرِعُوۡنَ فِى الۡخَيۡرٰتِ وَهُمۡ لَهَا سٰبِقُوۡنَ ۞

---

*70 : 43; 73 : 12.   *79 : 41.   *22 : 36.

2003. After the death of a Prophet his followers generally begin to differ among themselves and split up into sects and sections, each sect regarding itself as his true followers and other sects as devoid of all truth.

2004. Man is so constituted that he regards abundance of wealth and the power and prestige of his party as the measure of success and even as the only criterion of being the recipient of God's favour. It is this common error that the present and the preceding verse seek to correct.

63. And [a]We burden not any soul beyond its capacity,[2005] [b]and with Us is a Book that speaks the truth,[2006] and they will not be wronged.

وَلَا نُكَلِّفُ نَفْسًا اِلَّا وُسْعَهَا وَلَدَيْنَا كِتٰبٌ يَّنْطِقُ
بِالْحَقِّ وَهُمْ لَا يُظْلَمُوْنَ ﴿٦٣﴾

64. But [c]their hearts are utterly heedless of this *Book*, and besides that, they have other *evil* deeds which they do;

بَلْ قُلُوْبُهُمْ فِيْ غَمْرَةٍ مِّنْ هٰذَا وَلَهُمْ اَعْمَالٌ
مِّنْ دُوْنِ ذٰلِكَ هُمْ لَهَا عٰمِلُوْنَ ﴿٦٤﴾

65. Until, [d]when We seize with punishment those of them who indulge in luxury, behold, they cry for help;

حَتّٰۤى اِذَاۤ اَخَذْنَا مُتْرَفِيْهِمْ بِالْعَذَابِ اِذَا هُمْ
يَجْـَٔرُوْنَ ﴿٦٥﴾

66. *Whereupon We say* [e]"Cry not for help this day, surely you shall not be helped by Us,

لَا تَجْـَٔرُوا الْيَوْمَ اِنَّكُمْ مِّنَّا لَا تُنْصَرُوْنَ ﴿٦٦﴾

67. 'Verily, [f]My Signs were recited unto you, but you used to turn back on your heels,

قَدْ كَانَتْ اٰيٰتِيْ تُتْلٰى عَلَيْكُمْ فَكُنْتُمْ عَلٰۤى اَعْقَابِكُمْ
تَنْكِصُوْنَ ﴿٦٧﴾

68. 'In arrogance,[2007] [g]talking nonsense by night about *the Qur'ān*.'

مُسْتَكْبِرِيْنَ بِهٖ سٰمِرًا تَهْجُرُوْنَ ﴿٦٨﴾

69. Have they not, then, pondered over the *Divine* Word, or has there come to them that which did not come to their fathers of old?

اَفَلَمْ يَدَّبَّرُوا الْقَوْلَ اَمْ جَآءَهُمْ مَّا لَمْ يَاْتِ
اٰبَآءَهُمُ الْاَوَّلِيْنَ ﴿٦٩﴾

---

[a]2 : 287; 7 : 43. [b]17 : 14-15; 45 : 30; 69 : 20. [c]21 : 4. [d]10 : 23; 16 : 54; 30 : 34; 39 : 9. [e]21 : 14. [f]22 : 73; 39 : 46. [g]83 : 14.

2005. The laws which God has laid down in the Qur'ān for the moral and spiritual development of man are such as are within his power and capacity to act upon. They are suited to all conditions, circumstances, temperaments and dispositions.

2006. These verses may also signify that the teaching embodied in the Qur'ān is based on wisdom and is suited to all conditions and circumstances, and to men of different temperaments and dispositions and is in agreement with the requirements of justice, equity and wisdom. This is the meaning of the words *Yanṭiqu bi'l Ḥaqqi*.

2007. The word, *Mustakbirīn*, may signify that disbelievers regard the revelation of the Qur'ān to be too big and important an affair to be entrusted to a weak human being. Or, it means that when disbelievers hear the Qur'ān being recited, they turn away from it in pride and arrogance.

70. Or, do they not recognize their Messenger,[2008] that they deny him? أَمْ لَمْ يَعْرِفُوْا رَسُوْلَهُمْ فَهُمْ لَهُ مُنْكِرُوْنَ ۝

71. Or, *do they say, 'There is madness in him?' Nay, he has brought them the truth, and most of them hate the truth. أَمْ يَقُوْلُوْنَ بِهِ جِنَّةٌ ۚ بَلْ جَآءَهُمْ بِالْحَقِّ وَاَكْثَرُهُمْ لِلْحَقِّ كٰرِهُوْنَ ۝

72. And if the Truth had followed their desires, verily the heavens and the earth and whosoever is therein would have been corrupted. Nay, *We have brought them their admonition, but from their own admonition they *now* turn aside. وَلَوِ اتَّبَعَ الْحَقُّ اَهْوَآءَهُمْ لَفَسَدَتِ السَّمٰوٰتُ وَالْاَرْضُ وَمَنْ فِيْهِنَّ ۚ بَلْ اَتَيْنٰهُمْ بِذِكْرِهِمْ فَهُمْ عَنْ ذِكْرِهِمْ مُّعْرِضُوْنَ ۝

73. *Or, dost thou ask of them any reward?[2009] But the reward of thy Lord is best; and He is the Best of providers. أَمْ تَسْـَٔلُهُمْ خَرْجًا فَخَرَاجُ رَبِّكَ خَيْرٌ ۖ وَّهُوَ خَيْرُ الرّٰزِقِيْنَ ۝

74. And, most surely, thou invitest them to a right path. وَاِنَّكَ لَتَدْعُوْهُمْ اِلٰى صِرَاطٍ مُّسْتَقِيْمٍ ۝

75. And those, who believe not in the Hereafter, are indeed deviating from that path. وَاِنَّ الَّذِيْنَ لَا يُؤْمِنُوْنَ بِالْاٰخِرَةِ عَنِ الصِّرَاطِ لَنٰكِبُوْنَ ۝

76. *And if We had mercy on them and relieved them of their affliction, they would persist in their transgression, wandering blindly. وَلَوْ رَحِمْنٰهُمْ وَكَشَفْنَا مَا بِهِمْ مِّنْ ضُرٍّ لَّلَجُّوْا فِيْ طُغْيَانِهِمْ يَعْمَهُوْنَ ۝

---

*7 : 185; 34 : 47. *21 : 3. *52 : 41; 68 : 47. *7 : 136; 43 : 51.

2008. An appeal to the good sense and reasonableness of the opponents of the Holy Prophet has been made in this verse. They are told that his life lies like an open book before them. They are quite familiar with all its different phases. It is spotless. For years they have known him as an honest man, a model of virtue and uprightness and yet they dare ascribe falsehood to him. See also 1245.

2009. Could there be any better evidence of the Holy Prophet's sincerity of motives and honesty of purpose and of his complete disregard for any recompense or reward for his selfless service than the answer he gave to his kind and loving uncle, Abū Ṭālib, when he asked him to make a compromise with the idolaters and give up preaching against idolworship? The never-to-be-forgotten answer was: "If they would place the sun on my right hand and the moon on my left and ask me to give up preaching against idolatry, I will never do so till my mission is fulfilled, or I perish in the attempt" (Ṭabarī, vol. 3).

77. *We had already seized them with punishment, but they humbled not themselves before their Lord, nor they would supplicate *in lowliness;*

وَلَقَدْ اَخَذْنٰهُمْ بِالْعَذَابِ فَمَا اسْتَكَانُوْا لِرَبِّهِمْ وَمَا يَتَضَرَّعُوْنَ ۝

78. *Until, when We open on them a door of severe punishment, lo! they are in despair thereat.[2010]

حَتّٰۤى اِذَا فَتَحْنَا عَلَيْهِمْ بَابًا ذَا عَذَابٍ شَدِيْدٍ اِذَا هُمْ فِيْهِ مُبْلِسُوْنَ ۝

R. 5   79. And He it is Who has ᶜcreated for you ears and eyes and hearts, *but* little thanks do you give.[2011]

وَهُوَ الَّذِىْۤ اَنْشَاَ لَكُمُ السَّمْعَ وَالْاَبْصَارَ وَالْاَفْـِٕدَةَ قَلِيْلًا مَّا تَشْكُرُوْنَ ۝

80. And He it is Who has multiplied you in the earth, and unto Him you shall be gathered.

وَهُوَ الَّذِىْ ذَرَاَكُمْ فِى الْاَرْضِ وَاِلَيْهِ تُحْشَرُوْنَ ۝

81. And He it is Who gives life and causes death, and ᵈin His *control* is the alternation of night and day. Will you not then understand?[2012]

وَهُوَ الَّذِىْ يُحْىِ وَيُمِيْتُ وَلَهُ اخْتِلَافُ الَّيْلِ وَالنَّهَارِ اَفَلَا تَعْقِلُوْنَ ۝

82. But they say *things* similar to what the former people said.

بَلْ قَالُوْا مِثْلَ مَا قَالَ الْاَوَّلُوْنَ ۝

83. They say, *"What! when we are dead and have become *mere* dust and bones, shall we, indeed, be raised up again?

قَالُوْۤا ءَاِذَا مِتْنَا وَكُنَّا تُرَابًا وَّعِظَامًا ءَاِنَّا لَمَبْعُوْثُوْنَ ۝

ᵃ6 : 44. ᵇ6 : 45. ᶜ16 : 79; 67 : 24. ᵈ2 : 165; 3 : 191; 10 : 7.
ᵉ17 : 99; 27 : 68; 37 : 17; 56 : 48.

2010. Man is so constituted that when he is in comfort and easy circumstances, he throws all caution to the winds and begins to indulge in unseemly conduct. But when his transgression and wicked pursuits produce evil results, he gives himself up to despair.

2011. One of the meanings of *Shukr* being to make proper use of a gift (14 : 8), the verse signifies that God has given us ears, eyes and hearts that we may make proper use of them and benefit thereby materially and spiritually, observe His Signs, listen to the Divine Message and ponder over it.

2012. The verse alludes to the phenomenon of the rise and fall of nations. At one time a people rise to power and eminence and the sun of progress and prosperity seems to shine upon them, at another time decadence and death overtake them as a consequence of their evil deeds.

84. [a]'This is what we have been promised before, we and our fathers. This is nothing but fables of the ancients.'

لَقَدْ وُعِدْنَا نَحْنُ وَاٰبَآؤُنَا هٰذَا مِنْ قَبْلُ اِنْ هٰذَآ اِلَّآ اَسَاطِيْرُ الْاَوَّلِيْنَ ﴿٨٤﴾

85. Say, 'To whom belongs the earth and whosoever is therein, if you know?'

قُلْ لِّمَنِ الْاَرْضُ وَمَنْ فِيْهَآ اِنْ كُنْتُمْ تَعْلَمُوْنَ ﴿٨٥﴾

86. 'To Allāh,' they will say. Say, 'Will you not then be admonished?'

سَيَقُوْلُوْنَ لِلّٰهِ قُلْ اَفَلَا تَذَكَّرُوْنَ ﴿٨٦﴾

87. Say, 'Who is the Lord of the seven heavens, and the Lord of the Great Throne?'

قُلْ مَنْ رَّبُّ السَّمٰوٰتِ السَّبْعِ وَرَبُّ الْعَرْشِ الْعَظِيْمِ ﴿٨٧﴾

88. They will say, '*They are* Allāh's.' Say, 'Will you not then take *Him* as *your* Protector?'

سَيَقُوْلُوْنَ لِلّٰهِ قُلْ اَفَلَا تَتَّقُوْنَ ﴿٨٨﴾

89. Say, [b]'In Whose hand is the dominion of all things and Who protects, but against Whom there is no protection, if you know?'

قُلْ مَنْ بِيَدِهٖ مَلَكُوْتُ كُلِّ شَيْءٍ وَّهُوَ يُجِيْرُ وَلَا يُجَارُ عَلَيْهِ اِنْ كُنْتُمْ تَعْلَمُوْنَ ﴿٨٩﴾

90. They will say, '*All this belongs* to Allāh.' Say, 'How then are you being deluded?'

سَيَقُوْلُوْنَ لِلّٰهِ قُلْ فَاَنّٰى تُسْحَرُوْنَ ﴿٩٠﴾

91. Yea, We have brought them the truth, and they are certainly liars.

بَلْ اَتَيْنٰهُمْ بِالْحَقِّ وَاِنَّهُمْ لَكٰذِبُوْنَ ﴿٩١﴾

92. [c]Allāh has not taken unto Himself any son, nor is there any other god along with Him; in that case [d]each god would have taken away what he had created, and some of them would, surely, have sought domination over others. Glorified be Allāh *far* above that which they allege;[2013]

مَا اتَّخَذَ اللّٰهُ مِنْ وَّلَدٍ وَّمَا كَانَ مَعَهٗ مِنْ اِلٰهٍ اِذًا لَّذَهَبَ كُلُّ اِلٰهٍۭ بِمَا خَلَقَ وَلَعَلَا بَعْضُهُمْ عَلٰى بَعْضٍ سُبْحٰنَ اللّٰهِ عَمَّا يَصِفُوْنَ ﴿٩٢﴾

[a]27 : 69. [b]36 : 84. [c]18 : 5; 19 : 36; 21 : 27; 25 : 3; 39 : 5; 43 : 82; 72 : 4. [d]21 : 23.

2013. The verse very effectively demonstrates the futility and falsity of the Christian dogma that Jesus is God's son. It purports to say that a son is needed by a person to help him

93. [a]Knower *alike* of the unseen and of the seen. Exalted is He above all that which they associate *with Him !*

ع عٰلِمِ الْغَيْبِ وَالشَّهَادَةِ فَتَعٰلٰى عَمَّا يُشْرِكُوْنَ ﴿۹۳﴾

R. 6 94. Say, 'My Lord, if Thou wilt show me that which they are promised;

قُلْ رَّبِّ اِمَّا تُرِيَنِّيْ مَا يُوْعَدُوْنَ ﴿۹۴﴾

95. 'My Lord, then place me not with the wrongdoing people.'[2014]

رَبِّ فَلَا تَجْعَلْنِيْ فِي الْقَوْمِ الظّٰلِمِيْنَ ﴿۹۵﴾

96. And certainly [b]We have the power to show thee that which We have promised them.

وَاِنَّا عَلٰٓى اَنْ نُّرِيَكَ مَا نَعِدُهُمْ لَقٰدِرُوْنَ ﴿۹۶﴾

97. [c]Repel evil with that which is best.[2015] We know very well what they allege.

اِدْفَعْ بِالَّتِيْ هِيَ اَحْسَنُ السَّيِّئَةَ ۭ نَحْنُ اَعْلَمُ بِمَا يَصِفُوْنَ ﴿۹۷﴾

98. And say, 'My Lord, I seek refuge in Thee from the incitements of the evil ones;[2016]

وَقُلْ رَّبِّ اَعُوْذُ بِكَ مِنْ هَمَزٰتِ الشَّيٰطِيْنِ ﴿۹۸﴾

99. 'And I seek refuge in Thee, my Lord, lest they should come near me.'

وَاَعُوْذُ بِكَ رَبِّ اَنْ يَّحْضُرُوْنِ ﴿۹۹﴾

---

[a]6 : 74; 32 : 7; 34 : 4; 59 : 23; 64 : 19. [b]40 : 78. [c]13 : 23; 16 : 126; 41 : 35.

---

to carry on his affairs, but as God is the Creator of the heavens and the earth and the sole Master and Controller of the whole universe, He does not need the help or assistance of any helper or son. Moreover, the whole universe appears to be subject to one uniform law, and the unity of the design, purpose and control points to the unity of the Designer and the Controller. The duality of control and authority implies confusion and disorder.

2014. The *Sūrah* was revealed towards the end of the Meccan period. The Holy Prophet was about to leave Mecca. His departure was a signal and a sign that as the result of his persistent denial, persecution and expulsion from Mecca by the Quraish, Divine punishment was about to overtake them. He is taught to pray to God that when the threatened punishment should seize them he might not be present with them in Mecca.

2015. The Holy Prophet is here enjoined that as long as he is with disbelievers in Mecca he should patiently bear up with all the abuse and persecution to which he is subjected and should return good for evil.

2016. The words, "evil ones" refer to the leading men among the Holy Prophet's enemies, and the word, "incitements" signifies the campaign of vilification and misrepresentation by which they sought to incite the people against him.

100. Until, when death comes to onc of them, [a]he says *entreating repeatedly*, 'My Lord, send me back,

حَتّٰىٓ اِذَا جَآءَ اَحَدَهُمُ الْمَوْتُ قَالَ رَبِّ ارْجِعُوْنِ ۝١٠٠

101. 'That I may do righteous deeds *in the life* that I have left *behind*.' That cannot be! It is only a word that he utters. [b]And behind them is a barrier[2017] until the day when they shall be raised again.

لَعَلِّيْٓ اَعْمَلُ صَالِحًا فِيْمَا تَرَكْتُ كَلَّا ؕ اِنَّهَا كَلِمَةٌ هُوَ قَآئِلُهَا ؕ وَمِنْ وَّرَآئِهِمْ بَرْزَخٌ اِلٰى يَوْمِ يُبْعَثُوْنَ ۝١٠١

102. And when [c]the trumpet is blown, there will be no ties of relationship[2018] any more between them on that day, nor will they ask after one another.

فَاِذَا نُفِخَ فِي الصُّوْرِ فَلَآ اَنْسَابَ بَيْنَهُمْ يَوْمَئِذٍ وَّلَا يَتَسَآءَلُوْنَ ۝١٠٢

103. Then those [d]whose scales are heavy—these will be prosperous;

فَمَنْ ثَقُلَتْ مَوَازِيْنُهٗ فَاُولٰٓئِكَ هُمُ الْمُفْلِحُوْنَ ۝١٠٣

104. But those [e]whose scales are light—these are they who will have ruined their souls; in Hell will they abide.

وَمَنْ خَفَّتْ مَوَازِيْنُهٗ فَاُولٰٓئِكَ الَّذِيْنَ خَسِرُوْٓا اَنْفُسَهُمْ فِيْ جَهَنَّمَ خٰلِدُوْنَ ۝١٠٤

105. [f]The Fire will scorch their faces and they will grin *with fear* therein.

تَلْفَحُ وُجُوْهَهُمُ النَّارُ وَهُمْ فِيْهَا كٰلِحُوْنَ ۝١٠٥

106. *It will be said to them*, [g]'Were not My Signs recited unto you, and you treated them as lies?'

اَلَمْ تَكُنْ اٰيٰتِيْ تُتْلٰى عَلَيْكُمْ فَكُنْتُمْ بِهَا تُكَذِّبُوْنَ ۝١٠٦

107. They will say, 'Our Lord, our ill fortune overwhelmed us, and we were an erring people,

قَالُوْا رَبَّنَا غَلَبَتْ عَلَيْنَا شِقْوَتُنَا وَكُنَّا قَوْمًا ضَآلِّيْنَ ۝١٠٧

[a]39 : 59. [b]21 : 96; 36 : 32. [c]18 : 100; 36 : 52; 50 : 21; 69 : 14. [d]7 : 9; 101 : 7-8. [e]7 : 10; 101 : 9-10. [f]10 : 28; 14 : 51; 54 : 49; 80 : 42. [g]40 : 51; 45 : 32; 67 : 9.

2017. *Barzakh* means, a barrier; or a thing that intervenes between any two things. The word is technically applied to the period or state from the day of death to the day of Resurrection (Lane). It is an intermediate state of incomplete realization of the punishments and rewards of Hell and Heaven. The Qur'ān has compared it to the embryonic state and the Resurrection to the birth of the fully developed soul.

2018. When punishment overtakes a people, pedigree, descent and relationship prove of no avail. On the Judgment Day good works alone will be of any use or benefit to man and not his blood relations or friendships.

108. 'Our Lord, [a]take us out of this, then if we revert *to disobedience*, we shall, indeed, be wrongdoers.'

رَبَّنَآ أَخْرِجْنَا مِنْهَا فَإِنْ عُدْنَا فَإِنَّا ظٰلِمُوْنَ ﴿١٠٨﴾

109. *Allāh* will say, 'Away with you, despised[2019] therein, and speak not unto Me;

قَالَ اخْسَـُٔوْا فِيْهَا وَلَا تُكَلِّمُوْنِ ﴿١٠٩﴾

110. 'There was a party of My servants who said, [b]"Our Lord, we believe; forgive us therefore our sins, and have mercy on us; for Thou art the Best of those who show mercy;

إِنَّهٗ كَانَ فَرِيْقٌ مِّنْ عِبَادِيْ يَقُوْلُوْنَ رَبَّنَآ اٰمَنَّا
فَاغْفِرْ لَنَا وَارْحَمْنَا وَأَنْتَ خَيْرُ الرّٰحِمِيْنَ ﴿١١٠﴾

111. 'But you ridiculed[2020] them so much so that *ridicule of* them caused you to forget My remembrance while you *continued to* laugh at them;

فَاتَّخَذْتُمُوْهُمْ سِخْرِيًّا حَتّٰٓى أَنْسَوْكُمْ ذِكْرِيْ وَكُنْتُمْ
مِّنْهُمْ تَضْحَكُوْنَ ﴿١١١﴾

112. 'I have rewarded them this day for their patient endurance; they are, indeed, the ones who have achieved bliss.'

إِنِّيْ جَزَيْتُهُمُ الْيَوْمَ بِمَا صَبَرُوْٓا أَنَّهُمْ هُمُ الْفَآئِزُوْنَ ﴿١١٢﴾

113. *Allāh* will *then* say, 'What number of years did you tarry in the earth?'

قٰلَ كَمْ لَبِثْتُمْ فِي الْأَرْضِ عَدَدَ سِنِيْنَ ﴿١١٣﴾

114. They will say, 'We tarried for a day or part of a day,[2021] but ask those who keep count.'

قَالُوْا لَبِثْنَا يَوْمًا أَوْ بَعْضَ يَوْمٍ فَسْـَٔلِ الْعَآدِّيْنَ ﴿١١٤﴾

115. He will say, 'You tarried but a little, if only you knew!'

قٰلَ إِنْ لَّبِثْتُمْ إِلَّا قَلِيْلًا لَّوْ أَنَّكُمْ كُنْتُمْ تَعْلَمُوْنَ ﴿١١٥﴾

[a]6 : 28. [b]3 : 17,194.

2019. On the Judgment Day the despisers and deniers of God's Messengers will be dragged into Hell, hated and despised. They will not be allowed to offer an explanation of the wicked deeds they would have committed in their lives, God being fully conversant with their doings.

2020. *Sakhkhara-hū* means, he compelled him to do what he did not like or to work without recompense (Lane). The verse, therefore, may also mean that believers being poor and weak, the disbelievers employed them against their will or desire, exploited them and exacted compulsory service from them without paying them any wages or compensation for the work they did.

2021. A whole life spent in ease and comfort, when followed by pain and punishment, appears very short and even becomes a source of regret and mortification. The reply of the disbelievers shows how vain and short-lived are the comforts of this life.

116. What! Did you then think that We had created you without purpose, and that you would not be brought back to Us?[2022]

أَفَحَسِبْتُمْ أَنَّمَا خَلَقْنٰكُمْ عَبَثًا وَّأَنَّكُمْ إِلَيْنَا لَا تُرْجَعُوْنَ ﴿١١٦﴾

117. [a]Exalted be Allāh, the True King. There is no god but He, the Lord of the Glorious Throne.

فَتَعٰلَى اللّٰهُ الْمَلِكُ الْحَقُّ ۚ لَآ إِلٰهَ إِلَّا هُوَ ۚ رَبُّ الْعَرْشِ الْكَرِيْمِ ﴿١١٧﴾

118. And he, who calls on another god along with Allāh, for which he has no proof, shall have to render an account to his Lord. Certainly, the disbelievers do not prosper.

وَمَنْ يَّدْعُ مَعَ اللّٰهِ إِلٰهًا اٰخَرَ ۙ لَا بُرْهَانَ لَهٗ بِهٖ ۙ فَإِنَّمَا حِسَابُهٗ عِنْدَ رَبِّهٖ ۗ إِنَّهٗ لَا يُفْلِحُ الْكٰفِرُوْنَ ﴿١١٨﴾

119. And say, 'My Lord, forgive and have mercy, and Thou art the Best of those who show mercy.'

وَقُلْ رَّبِّ اغْفِرْ وَارْحَمْ وَأَنْتَ خَيْرُ الرّٰحِمِيْنَ ﴿١١٩﴾

[a]20 : 115; 22 : 63; 24 : 26.

2022. Man has been created to serve a great purpose—to develop and reflect in his person Divine attributes. He has been endowed with a Divine personality and is manifestly the central figure in the whole creation or at least that part of the creation which is related to our universe. Having a great purpose to fulfil, his life will not end with his departure from this world and with the soul's flight from its physcial habitat. The human soul will continue its never-ending journey in a new world, in a new form and a new body. The very idea that with the dissolution of its physical tabernacle the human soul suffers death militates against God's wisdom and His whole design and purpose in creating the universe.

CHAPTER 24

AL-NŪR

(*Revealed after Hijrah*)

Date of Revelation and Context

The consensus of scholarly opinion assigns this Chapter to the Medinite period. The regrettable incident relating to 'Ā'ishah, the Holy Prophet's noble wife, to which special reference has been made in it, took place in 5 A.H. after the Holy Prophet's return from the expedition against Banī Muṣṭaliq in the month of Ramaḍān of that year. Its connection with the preceding Chapter, *Sūrah* Al-Mu'minūn, consists in the fact that in that *Sūrah* it was stated that Islām would continue to produce men who would, by their righteousness and godly conduct, win God's pleasure and succour. The present *Sūrah* deals with the means and methods which help to draw Divine grace and succour and lays down as a principle that the adoption of the ways of virtue and righteousness and the protection and preservation of national morals, and the maintenance of discipline of a high order in the family and the community, are very essential for this purpose. This is why the *Sūrah* at the very outset lays great stress on the preservation of national morals with an added emphasis on the regulation and reformation of relations between the sexes. The preceding *Sūrah* had stated that one of the essential characteristics of believers who were decreed to meet with Divine succour was that they guarded their chastity. This *Sūrah* is an extension and amplification of the subject-matter of the preceding one. The achievement and maintenance of success, it says, demands that the intellect, ideals and morals of a people should be chaste and that there should exist perfect harmony and appreciative understanding between the relations of the individual and those of the community, and that great emphasis ought to be laid on national discipline and organization, and precedence should be accorded to national requirements over the needs of the individual.

Subject-Matter

The *Sūrah* deals with certain special subjects and has laid particular stress on the problems which constitute the foundation on which the whole social and moral structure of society stands and which cannot be defied without doing mortal injury to the moral well-being of a people. As sexual immorality is calculated to break the discipline and organization of a community and as the evils associated with it are likely to affect severely its morals, great emphasis has been laid in the *Sūrah* on the avoidance of suspicion in matters of sex; and believers are told not to become panicky on account of a few individuals having strayed away from the path of moral rectitude, as such cases of moral lapse may cause the whole community to become alert and careful ; and thus eventually may prove conducive to good results. The subject is further developed, and slander-mongering receives a severe reprimand. Because, if, on the basis of mere suspicion or the testimony of witnesses of doubtful integrity, haphazard aspersions are permitted to be cast on one another's chastity, sexual immorality is likely to become widespread in the community and young people become prone to run away with the notion that there is no harm in indulging freely in sex. Next, believers are strongly enjoined to guard and preserve national morals and it is considered very essential for Muslims to develop watchfulness and extreme awareness about their protection and preservation. If vigilance is allowed to relax, deterioration in national morals is sure to ensue. But whereas it is true that sexual immorality, if permitted to spread unchecked, brings about the degradation and disintegration of a whole community, individuals suspected of stray acts of immorality should not be hunted down and crushed. As in every community there are to be found some persons of lax morals, such individuals may be treated with a certain indulgence. But at the same time a warning is held out to those who seek, by their continued pernicious activities, to create discord among Muslims and to indulge in abusive language and calumny that they will be punished in this world and in the next. God will expose their iniquities and sins and will bring upon them disgrace and humiliation. The *Sūrah* then proceeds to observe that it is his careless acts that subject a man to suspicion and calumny and that most careless of all such acts is promiscuous intermingling between the sexes. In order to put a stop to such occasions as cause suspicion and lead to slander-mongering, the *Sūrah* directs Muslims not to enter a house without having obtained prior permission. Further, it enjoins on Muslim men and women that if they happen to confront each other, they should restrain their looks and guard all avenues of sin and vice. As an additional safeguard, Muslim women are further enjoined not to display their beauty, natural as well as artificial, to those males as are outside the prohibited degrees of marriage (v. 32), except such parts of the body as it is not possible for them to cover; for instance, the build of the body or their stature. For this purpose they should wear their head-coverings in such a manner as to cover their breasts. (For a detailed note on "Pardah" see v. 32). Another safeguard enjoined for the improvement and preservation of national morals is that widows should not be allowed to remain unmarried. It is further stated that steps should be taken to set free prisoners of war at the earliest occasion and a captive, who does not find it possible to earn his or her freedom immediately, may be allowed to pay the indemnity money in easy instalments.

Towards its close the *Sūrah* strongly urges Muslims to set right their family and national affairs and to be on their guard against promiscuous intermingling of the sexes. A special direction to be observed in this respect is that even prisoners of war serving as house servants and also minor children should not enter the private apartments of their masters or parents before dawn, at noon and after nightfall. At other times all members of the household are at liberty to move about the house freely. When, however, children reach their puberty, they should observe the regulations in regard to "Pardah." Old women, however, who have no desire or need for marriage can, if they so choose, relax the rules about "Pardah," but even they are not allowed to display their adornments to strangers. Next to family organization, and even more important than this, is the social organization of the whole people, and the *Sūrah* has not neglected to lay down requisite rules for the smooth and successful conduct of national affairs. The *Sūrah* then holds out a promise to Muslims that if they carried out the programme of life which God has laid down for them, they will become the leaders of the world both in spiritual and temporal spheres and their religion will become firmly established in the world. But when their rule is established and their cause triumphs and prevails they should worship God, help the poor and the needy and obey the commandments of their Prophet.

ركوعاتها ٩ سُوۡرَةُ النُّوۡرِ مَدَنِيَّةٌ (٢٤) آياتها ٦٥

1. [a]In the name of Allāh, the Gracious, the Merciful.

بِسۡمِ اللّٰهِ الرَّحۡمٰنِ الرَّحِيۡمِ ﴿۱﴾

2. This is a *Sūrah*[2023] which We have revealed and *the ordinances of* which We have made obligatory;[2024] and We have revealed therein clear commandments that you may take heed.[2025]

سُوۡرَةٌ اَنۡزَلۡنٰهَا وَ فَرَضۡنٰهَا وَ اَنۡزَلۡنَا فِيۡهَاۤ اٰيٰتٍۭ بَيِّنٰتٍ
لَّعَلَّكُمۡ تَذَكَّرُوۡنَ ﴿۲﴾

3. The adulteress and the adulterer[2025A]—flog each one of them *with* a hundred stripes.[2026] And let not pity for the twain take hold of you in *executing* the judgment of Allāh, if you believe in Allāh and the Last Day. And let a party of the believers witness their punishment.

اَلزَّانِيَةُ وَ الزَّانِيۡ فَاجۡلِدُوۡا كُلَّ وَاحِدٍ مِّنۡهُمَا مِائَةَ
جَلۡدَةٍ ۪ وَّ لَا تَاۡخُذۡكُمۡ بِهِمَا رَاۡفَةٌ فِيۡ دِيۡنِ اللّٰهِ اِنۡ
كُنۡتُمۡ تُؤۡمِنُوۡنَ بِاللّٰهِ وَ الۡيَوۡمِ الۡاٰخِرِ ۚ وَ لۡيَشۡهَدۡ عَذَابَهُمَا
طَآئِفَةٌ مِّنَ الۡمُؤۡمِنِيۡنَ ﴿۳﴾

[a]1 : 1.

2023. Of all the Quranic Chapters, the present one has been specifically called 'a *Sūrah*,' the significance being that as the word, "*Sūrah*," means rank or dignity, the Muslims by acting upon the commandments and ordinances embodied in this *Sūrah* can and will rise to great honour and dignity.

2024. The emphasis on the words, *which We have revealed and the ordinances of which We have made obligatory*, points to the great importance of the commandments of this *Sūrah* inasmuch as all other Quranic Chapters also have been revealed by God and their commandments have also been made obligatory.

2025. It is to be regretted that in slavish imitation of the customs and manners of other nations the Muslims have infringed and violated the commandments of this *Sūrah* more than the ordinances embodied in other *Sūrahs* of the Qur'ān.

2025A. The words, *al-Zānī* and *al-Zāniyah*, signify respectively both an adulterer and a fornicator; and an adulteress and a fornicatress.

2026. Chastity as a moral virtue holds a very high place in the code of Islamic laws that govern relations between the sexes. The present *Sūrah* has laid down comprehensive commandments to safeguard and protect it. Islām views with extreme disapprobation the slightest breach of these laws. It is Islām's very great sensitiveness about chastity that is reflected in the punishment prescribed for adultery or fornication in the verse under comment. The punishment prescribed is hundred stripes, no distinction having been made whether the guilty persons are married or unmarried or one of the party is married and the other unmarried. Flogging and not stoning to death, according to this verse, is the prescribed punishment. Nowhere in the Qur'ān stoning to death has been laid down as punishment for adultery and, for that matter, for any other crime, however serious. Islām has not prescribed killing as a necessary and unqualified punishment even for crimes much more heinous than adultery such as unprovoked murder, dacoity, treason against the State and disturbing the peace of the land. Though extreme penalty for these crimes is death, yet the payment of blood money in the case of the first offence (2:179) and imprisonment or banishment for the other crimes (5 : 33-34) have been laid down as alternative punishments. Elsewhere in the Qur'ān, where punishment for adultery for a married slave-girl is mentioned it is stated that she will get half the punishment prescribed for that of a free, married woman (4 : 26), and evidently the punishment of stoning to death cannot be halved.

In spite of the fact that the Qur'ān has quite clearly and unequivocally laid down flogging as the punishment for adultery and has made no discrimination whatever between a married or an unmarried culprit in the matter of awarding punishment (because *Zānī* means, both a fornicator and an adulterer) and that the present and other relevant verses were revealed in connection with slander-mongering about 'Ā'ishah, the Holy Prophet's noble consort, who herself was a married lady, it is curious that the misconception has persisted without any justification or linguistic authority among certain schools of Muslim religious thought that the verse under comment deals with punishment for unmarried persons only and that the punishment for a married adulterer and adulteress is stoning to death. The misconception seems to be due to a few cases recorded in the Ḥadīth when married persons guilty of adultery were stoned to death by the order of the Holy Prophet. One of these few cases was that of a Jew and a Jewess who were stoned to death in accordance with the Mosaic Law (Bukhārī). It was invariably the Holy Prophet's practice that he abided by the Law of the Torah in deciding cases till a new commandment was revealed to him. In one or two other cases on record in which the punishment accorded was stoning to death, it has not been established whether the crime was committed before or after the verse under comment had been revealed. It seems that in such cases the crime was committed before the revelation of this verse, but by some miscalculation on the part of some chronicler it was believed to have taken place after it. There are to be found such historical anachronisms in the books of Ḥadīth. Or, there might have been some other aggravating circumstances besides the crime of adultery which made the Holy Prophet award the guilty person or persons the extreme punishment of death and which the chronicler of the incident failed to take into account. Otherwise, it is inconceivable that the Holy Prophet should have contravened the quite clear and unequivocal Divine commandment in this respect.

Another possible cause of misunderstanding about the form of punishment for adultery may be some sayings attributed to Caliphs 'Umar and 'Alī. 'Umar is reported to have said 'There was a verse in the Book of God about *Rajm* (stoning). We read it, we understood it and we remembered it. The Holy Prophet stoned adulterers to death and we also stoned after him. Were it not that people might say that 'Umar had added in the Book of God what was not in it, I would have written it down' (Kashf al-Ghummah, vol. 2, p. 111). The whole *ḥadīth* seems to be pure fabrication or at best the result of misunderstanding of what 'Umar might actually have said. How by writing down in the Qur'ān what was part of it could be called an addition to it, and how of all men, 'Umar could have been afraid of any body for doing the right thing, least of all for restoring to the Qur'ān a lost text. And 'Alī after flogging a woman, who had committed adultery, and then stoning her to death, is reported to have said : 'I have flogged her in obedience to the commandment of the Book of God and have stoned her to death in accordance with the practice of the Holy Prophet' (Bukhārī). From these sayings two inferences manifestly emerge : (1) In the matter of punishing an adulterer the practice of the Holy Prophet was at variance with the commandment of God as laid down in the Qur'ān, which is impossible. (2) Whereas according to 'Umar there was a commandment in the Book of God about stoning to death of an adulterer, according to 'Alī there was no such commandment, but it was only the practice of the Holy Prophet according to which he ('Alī) stoned to death persons guilty of adultery. These sayings are not only mutually contradictory but demonstrably conflict with the express Divine commandment and therefore must be rejected as pure fabrications or at best distorted versions of what they said. See also "The Larger Edition of the Commentary," pp. 1836-1838.

4. The adulterer cannot have sexual intercourse but with an adulteress or an idolatrous woman, and an adulteress—none can have sexual intercourse with her but an adulterer or an idolatrous[2026A] man. That[2027] indeed is forbidden to the believers.

الزَّانِي لَا يَنْكِحُ إِلَّا زَانِيَةً أَوْ مُشْرِكَةً وَّالزَّانِيَةُ
لَا يَنْكِحُهَا إِلَّا زَانٍ أَوْ مُشْرِكٌ وَحُرِّمَ ذٰلِكَ عَلَى
الْمُؤْمِنِينَ ④

5. And [a]those who calumniate chaste women but bring not four witnesses—flog them *with* eighty stripes, and do not admit their evidence *ever after*, for it is they that are the transgressors,[2028]

وَالَّذِينَ يَرْمُونَ الْمُحْصَنٰتِ ثُمَّ لَمْ يَأْتُوا بِأَرْبَعَةِ
شُهَدَآءَ فَاجْلِدُوهُمْ ثَمٰنِينَ جَلْدَةً وَّلَا تَقْبَلُوا
لَهُمْ شَهَادَةً أَبَدًا وَأُولٰٓئِكَ هُمُ الْفٰسِقُونَ ⑤

[a]24 : 24.

2026A. *Nikāḥ* signifying coitus with or without marriage and marriage without coitus (Lane), the meaning of the verse is quite clear, *viz.*, that when a man is having sexual intercourse with a woman who is not his wife, he is evidently an adulterer and the woman an adulteress ; *Nikāḥ* here signifying sexual intercourse and not marriage. But if *Nikāḥ* here be taken to signify marriage, as some have done, then the meaning would be that *Al-Zānī*, *i.e.*, a wicked man, who is not ashamed of freely indulging in adultery, can never prevail upon a chaste believing woman to marry him. Only a bad woman of low moral character or an idolatrous woman whose standard of morality like him is very low can be persuaded to marry him.

2027. The pronoun 'that' signifies the committing of adultery. Islām regards adultery as one of the most heinous of all social crimes and seeks to close all those avenues through which this disease finds its way among a people and severely punishes it and condemns the guilty parties as social pariahs. While the preceding verse has laid down the punishment which is to be meted out to adulterers or fornicators the present one stigmatizes them as social lepers with whom all social relationship should be avoided.

2028. The other social evil, second to adultery in heinousness, which eats into the vitals of human society, is the slandering of innocent persons. Islām also views with extreme disfavour this social evil which has become so common in the so-called civilized modern society, and severely punishes the accusers of innocent people. The verse mentions three forms of punishment in an ascending order which are to be meted out to a slanderer: (*a*) the physical punishment of scourging ; (*b*) the disgrace of being branded as a perjurer and a liar which invalidates his evidence and (*c*) the spiritual stigma of being adjudged as a transgressor. It may be noted that no mention is made here of the accusation being true or false. So long as the accuser cannot produce the necessary evidence in support of his charge, the charge would be considered as false and the accuser would render himself liable to the prescribed punishment. Whatever the facts of the case, the woman with whom adultery is alleged to have been committed will be held innocent so long as the required evidence is not produced. The law, in fact, is intended to suppress with a strong hand the offence of slandering and scandal-mongering. The commandment contained in this verse covers both men and women although the word used is *Muḥsanāt* which means 'chaste women.' In the Arabic language when something has to be said which relates equally to both men and women the gender used is masculine. But when something is said regarding a matter which concerns women more than men, then feminine gender is used. The commandment here relates to punishment for slandering whether the victim of the slander is a man or a woman but as women generally are more often the victims of such slanders, the verse speaks of 'chaste women.' Similarly, the word *Allāhdhīna* (those), though in masculine gender, applies to both men and women slanderers.

6. Except those who repent thereafter and make amends, for truly Allāh is Most Forgiving,[2029] Merciful.

إِلَّا الَّذِينَ تَابُوا مِنْ بَعْدِ ذٰلِكَ وَأَصْلَحُوا فَإِنَّ اللّٰهَ غَفُورٌ رَّحِيمٌ ۝٦

7. And *as for* those who charge their wives with adultery[2030] and have no witnesses except themselves—the evidence of anyone of such people *shall suffice if he* bears witness four times in the name of Allāh *solemnly affirming* that he is of those who speak the truth;

وَالَّذِينَ يَرْمُونَ أَزْوَاجَهُمْ وَلَمْ يَكُنْ لَّهُمْ شُهَدَاءُ إِلَّا أَنْفُسُهُمْ فَشَهَادَةُ أَحَدِهِمْ أَرْبَعُ شَهٰدٰتٍ بِاللّٰهِ إِنَّهُ لَمِنَ الصّٰدِقِينَ ۝٧

8. And the fifth *time* that Allāh's curse be upon him if he be of the liars.

وَالْخَامِسَةُ أَنَّ لَعْنَتَ اللّٰهِ عَلَيْهِ إِنْ كَانَ مِنَ الْكٰذِبِينَ ۝٨

9. But it shall avert the punishment from her if she bears witness four times in the name of Allāh that he is of the liars;

وَيَدْرَؤُا عَنْهَا الْعَذَابَ أَنْ تَشْهَدَ أَرْبَعَ شَهٰدٰتٍ بِاللّٰهِ إِنَّهُ لَمِنَ الْكٰذِبِينَ ۝٩

10. And the fifth *time* that the wrath of Allāh be upon her if he has spoken the truth.[2031]

وَالْخَامِسَةَ أَنَّ غَضَبَ اللّٰهِ عَلَيْهَا إِنْ كَانَ مِنَ الصّٰدِقِينَ ۝١٠

11. And were it not for Allāh's grace and His mercy upon you, and that Allāh is Compassionate and Wise, *you would have come to grief*.

وَلَوْلَا فَضْلُ اللّٰهِ عَلَيْكُمْ وَرَحْمَتُهُ وَأَنَّ اللّٰهَ تَوَّابٌ حَكِيمٌ ۝١١ ع

a4 : 18.

2029. Opinions differ as to which of the punishments prescribed for slandering is to be remitted after a slanderer repents and makes amends. The question of the first punishment does not arise because the corporal punishment is administered as soon as the offence of the guilty person is proved. The last two punishments only can be remitted after a real and true repentance is proved.

2030. As suspicion between husband and wife is likely to cast a severe strain on the whole family relations, a special regulation has been laid down in the verse under comment to meet such an unhappy situation if it ever happens to arise.

2031. After the accused woman has established her innocence by taking four oaths that her husband had falsely accused her and the fifth oath invoking God's curse upon herself if her husband's accusation was true, no punishment is awarded to her and the husband is also not held punishable for accusing her. But after such a serious breach the couple will cease to live as husband and wife, because no chance will then be left of the restoration of amicable relations between them.

R. 2 12. Verily, those who invented the great lie are a party from among you.[2032] Think not that this *incident* is an evil for you; nay, it is good for you. Every one of them shall have *his share of* what he has earned of the sin; and he among them who took the principal part[2033] therein shall have a grievous punishment.

إِنَّ الَّذِينَ جَاءُوا بِالْإِفْكِ عُصْبَةٌ مِّنكُمْ ۚ لَا تَحْسَبُوهُ
شَرًّا لَّكُم ۖ بَلْ هُوَ خَيْرٌ لَّكُمْ ۚ لِكُلِّ امْرِئٍ مِّنْهُم مَّا اكْتَسَبَ
مِنَ الْإِثْمِ ۚ وَالَّذِي تَوَلَّىٰ كِبْرَهُ مِنْهُمْ لَهُ عَذَابٌ
عَظِيمٌ ﴿١٢﴾

13. When you heard of it, why did not the believing men and believing women think well of their own people and say, 'This is a manifest lie?'

لَّوْلَا إِذْ سَمِعْتُمُوهُ ظَنَّ الْمُؤْمِنُونَ وَالْمُؤْمِنَاتُ
بِأَنفُسِهِمْ خَيْرًا وَقَالُوا هَٰذَا إِفْكٌ مُّبِينٌ ﴿١٣﴾

14. Why did not those, *who gave currency to this charge*, bring four witnesses to *prove* it? Since they have not brought the *required* witnesses, they are indeed liars in the sight of Allāh.[2034]

لَّوْلَا جَاءُوا عَلَيْهِ بِأَرْبَعَةِ شُهَدَاءَ ۚ فَإِذْ لَمْ يَأْتُوا
بِالشُّهَدَاءِ فَأُولَٰئِكَ عِندَ اللَّهِ هُمُ الْكَاذِبُونَ ﴿١٤﴾

2032. The extremely painful incident referred to in this verse took place when on the Holy Prophet's return from the expedition against Banī Muṣṭaliq in 5 A.D., the Muslim army had to halt for the night at a place, a short distance from Medina. In this expedition the Holy Prophet was accompanied by his noble and talented wife, 'Ā'ishah. As it so happened, 'Ā'ishah went out some distance from the camp to attend to the call of nature. When she returned, she discovered that she had dropped her necklace somewhere. The necklace itself was of no great value, but as it was a loan from a friend 'Ā'ishah went out again to search for it. On her return, to her great grief and mortification, the army had already marched away with the camel she was riding, her attendants thinking that she was in the litter as she was then very young and light of weight. In her helplessness she sat down and cried till sleep overpowered her. Ṣafwān, a Refugee who was coming in the rear recognized her as he had seen her before the verse enjoining "Pardah" was revealed, and brought her on his camel to Medina, himself walking behind the animal (Bukhārī, *Kitāb al-Nikāḥ*). The Hypocrites of Medina, led by 'Abd Allāh bin Ubayy bin Salūl, sought to make capital out of this incident and spread a malicious scandal against 'Ā'ishah and unfortunately some of the Muslims also became involved in it. 'Ā'ishah's innocence was established by Divine revelation. Those who had taken part in fabricating and spreading the accusation were punished and injunctions were revealed to deal effectively with scandal-mongers and their evil designs and activities.

2033. The words, 'who took the principal part,' are understood to refer to 'Abd Allāh bin Ubayy, the leader of the Hypocrites of Medina, who had invented the lie and gave it wide publicity. He died an ignominious death, frustrated in all his designs against Islām and in his ambition and aspiration to become the crowned king of Medina.

2034. He, who accuses a Muslim man or woman of adultery and does not produce four witnesses to prove his allegation, shall be held to be a liar and treated as such by the Islamic Law if he can produce only one, two or even three persons as eye-witnesses to the act. The fact of one person seeing another person committing this immoral act does not entitle him to go about spreading the evil report.

15. [a]Were it not for the grace of Allāh and His mercy upon you, in this world and the Hereafter, a great punishment would have befallen you on account of *the slander* you plunged in;

وَلَوْلَا فَضْلُ اللّٰهِ عَلَيْكُمْ وَرَحْمَتُهٗ فِي الدُّنْيَا وَ
الْاٰخِرَةِ لَمَسَّكُمْ فِيْ مَآ اَفَضْتُمْ فِيْهِ عَذَابٌ عَظِيْمٌ ﴿۱۵﴾

16. For, you began to learn it from each other's tongue and *then* you uttered with your mouths that of which you had no knowledge, and you thought it to be a light *matter*, while in the sight of Allāh it was a grievous *thing*.

اِذْ تَلَقَّوْنَهٗ بِاَلْسِنَتِكُمْ وَتَقُوْلُوْنَ بِاَفْوَاهِكُمْ مَّا لَيْسَ
لَكُمْ بِهٖ عِلْمٌ وَّتَحْسَبُوْنَهٗ هَيِّنًا ۖ وَّهُوَ عِنْدَ اللّٰهِ
عَظِيْمٌ ﴿۱۶﴾

17. And wherefore did you not say, when you heard of it, 'It is not proper for us to talk about it. Holy art Thou, *O God*, this is a grievous calumny.'

وَلَوْلَآ اِذْ سَمِعْتُمُوْهُ قُلْتُمْ مَّا يَكُوْنُ لَنَآ اَنْ نَّتَكَلَّمَ
بِهٰذَا ۖ سُبْحٰنَكَ هٰذَا بُهْتَانٌ عَظِيْمٌ ﴿۱۷﴾

18. Allāh admonishes you that you never repeat the like thereof, if you are believers.

يَعِظُكُمُ اللّٰهُ اَنْ تَعُوْدُوْا لِمِثْلِهٖٓ اَبَدًا اِنْ كُنْتُمْ
مُّؤْمِنِيْنَ ﴿۱۸﴾

19. And Allāh explains to you the commandments; and Allāh is All-Knowing, Wise.

وَيُبَيِّنُ اللّٰهُ لَكُمُ الْاٰيٰتِ ۭ وَاللّٰهُ عَلِيْمٌ حَكِيْمٌ ﴿۱۹﴾

20. Those, who love that indecency should spread among the believers, will have a painful punishment in this world and the Hereafter.[2035] And Allāh knows, and you know not.

اِنَّ الَّذِيْنَ يُحِبُّوْنَ اَنْ تَشِيْعَ الْفَاحِشَةُ فِي الَّذِيْنَ
اٰمَنُوْا لَهُمْ عَذَابٌ اَلِيْمٌ ۙ فِي الدُّنْيَا وَالْاٰخِرَةِ ۭ وَاللّٰهُ
يَعْلَمُ وَاَنْتُمْ لَا تَعْلَمُوْنَ ﴿۲۰﴾

[a]2 : 65; 4 : 84.

2035. Islām has taken as serious a view of the spreading and circulation of false accusations as that of crimes against chastity. It has condemned and prescribed punishment for both the crimes—for scandal-mongering even a severer punishment since it is calculated to produce more grievous consequences as far as the prevalence of sexual immorality in a community is concerned than the stray acts of sexual misconduct. If scandal-mongering is allowed to be indulged in unchecked in a community, it will come to lose all sense of horror and abhorrence at the commission of immoral acts with the result that immorality will become rampant and a sense of pessimism with regard to its future will begin to prevail in the community, thus shaking its whole moral foundation.

21. And but for the grace of Allāh and His mercy upon you and that Allāh is Compassionate and Merciful, *you would have been ruined.*

وَلَوْلَا فَضْلُ اللّٰهِ عَلَيْكُمْ وَرَحْمَتُهٗ وَاَنَّ اللّٰهَ رَءُوْفٌ رَّحِيْمٌ ﴿٢١﴾ ع النصف

R. 3 22. O ye who believe! [a]follow not the footsteps of Satan,[2036] and whoso follows the footsteps of Satan *should know that* he, surely, enjoins indecency and manifest evil. And, but for the grace of Allāh and His mercy upon you, not one of you would ever be pure; but Allāh purifies whom He pleases. And Allāh is All-Hearing, All-Knowing.

يٰۤاَيُّهَا الَّذِيْنَ اٰمَنُوْا لَا تَتَّبِعُوْا خُطُوٰتِ الشَّيْطٰنِ وَمَنْ يَّتَّبِعْ خُطُوٰتِ الشَّيْطٰنِ فَاِنَّهٗ يَاْمُرُ بِالْفَحْشَآءِ وَالْمُنْكَرِ وَلَوْلَا فَضْلُ اللّٰهِ عَلَيْكُمْ وَرَحْمَتُهٗ مَا زَكٰى مِنْكُمْ مِّنْ اَحَدٍ اَبَدًا وَّلٰكِنَّ اللّٰهَ يُزَكِّيْ مَنْ يَّشَآءُ وَاللّٰهُ سَمِيْعٌ عَلِيْمٌ ﴿٢٢﴾

23. And let not persons of wealth and means among you swear that they will not give *aught* to the kindred and to the needy[2037] and to those who have left their homes in the cause of Allāh. Let them forgive and forbear. Do you not desire that Allāh should forgive you? And Allāh is Most Forgiving, Merciful.

وَلَا يَاْتَلِ اُولُوا الْفَضْلِ مِنْكُمْ وَالسَّعَةِ اَنْ يُّؤْتُوْۤا اُولِي الْقُرْبٰى وَالْمَسٰكِيْنَ وَالْمُهٰجِرِيْنَ فِيْ سَبِيْلِ اللّٰهِ وَلْيَعْفُوْا وَلْيَصْفَحُوْا اَلَا تُحِبُّوْنَ اَنْ يَّغْفِرَ اللّٰهُ لَكُمْ وَاللّٰهُ غَفُوْرٌ رَّحِيْمٌ ﴿٢٣﴾

24. Verily, those, who calumniate chaste, unwary,[2038] believing women, are cursed in this world and the Hereafter. And for them is a grievous chastisement,

اِنَّ الَّذِيْنَ يَرْمُوْنَ الْمُحْصَنٰتِ الْغٰفِلٰتِ الْمُؤْمِنٰتِ لُعِنُوْا فِي الدُّنْيَا وَالْاٰخِرَةِ وَلَهُمْ عَذَابٌ عَظِيْمٌ ﴿٢٤﴾

[a]6 : 143; 19 : 45; 36 : 61.

2036. As there is implanted in human nature an inherent sense of hesitancy and horror at committing what is clearly and manifestly an evil act, to begin with, Satan avoids tempting his victim to commit a manifestly immoral act. He leads him to his moral ruin gradually and in stages, beginning with what apparently seems to be quite a harmless act. Beginning with slander-mongering a man ends by committing the very offence he had begun by foisting it upon others.

2037. The reference may be to Abū Bakr who stopped the allowance he used to give to Misṭaḥ, a poor relative who had unfortunately become involved in the calumny against 'Ā'ishah.

2038. The use of the word *Ghāfilāt* in connection with the calumny about 'Ā'ishah establishes her complete innocence, implying that that paragon of virtue and righteousness had no idea or consciousness of having done any wrongful act.

25. [a]On the day when their tongues and their hands and their feet will bear witness[2039] against them as to what they used to do ;

يَوْمَ تَشْهَدُ عَلَيْهِمْ أَلْسِنَتُهُمْ وَأَيْدِيهِمْ وَأَرْجُلُهُمْ
بِمَا كَانُوا يَعْمَلُونَ ﴿٢٥﴾

26. On that day will Allāh pay them in full their just due, and they will know that [b]Allāh alone is the Manifest Truth.[2040]

يَوْمَئِذٍ يُوَفِّيهِمُ اللَّهُ دِينَهُمُ الْحَقَّ وَيَعْلَمُونَ أَنَّ
اللَّهَ هُوَ الْحَقُّ الْمُبِينُ ﴿٢٦﴾

27. Evil things are *a characteristic of* bad men, and bad men are *inclined towards* bad things. And good things are *a characteristic of* good men, and good men are *inclined towards* good things,[2041] these are innocent of all that *the calumniators* allege. [c]For them is forgiveness and an honourable provision.

الْخَبِيثَاتُ لِلْخَبِيثِينَ وَالْخَبِيثُونَ لِلْخَبِيثَاتِ ۖ وَ
الطَّيِّبَاتُ لِلطَّيِّبِينَ وَالطَّيِّبُونَ لِلطَّيِّبَاتِ ۚ أُولَٰئِكَ
مُبَرَّءُونَ مِمَّا يَقُولُونَ ۖ لَهُمْ مَغْفِرَةٌ وَرِزْقٌ
كَرِيمٌ ﴿٢٧﴾ ع

R. 4 28. O ye who believe! [d]enter not houses other than your own until you have asked leave and saluted[2042] the inmates thereof. That is better for you that you may be heedful.

يَا أَيُّهَا الَّذِينَ آمَنُوا لَا تَدْخُلُوا بُيُوتًا غَيْرَ بُيُوتِكُمْ
حَتَّىٰ تَسْتَأْنِسُوا وَتُسَلِّمُوا عَلَىٰ أَهْلِهَا ۚ ذَٰلِكُمْ خَيْرٌ لَكُمْ
لَعَلَّكُمْ تَذَكَّرُونَ ﴿٢٨﴾

---

[a]17 : 37; 36 : 66; 41 : 21-23. [b]20 : 115; 22 : 63; 23 : 117. [c]8 : 75; 22 : 51. [d]24 ; 62.

2039. Recent scientific researches have established the truth of this verse. Scientific instruments have been invented which, if placed in a place, can preserve the talk of a person and even the sound of the movements of his hands, feet or other organs of his body. These instruments have greatly helped the police in apprehending thieves and other culprits and in bringing them to book. Thus with the help of these instruments the tongue, hands and feet of a guilty person, as it were, are made to bear witness against him. Science has also established the fact that every spoken word and movement or action leaves its impress in the atmosphere. According to the Qur'ān these impresses will be given an embodied form in the next life, and thus the limbs of the author of deeds, good or bad, will bear witness against or in favour of him.

2040. All truth is relative. A thing may be true from one angle or one point of view, but false from another angle. It is God alone Who is Absolute Truth.

2041. The word, *al-Khabīthāt*, meaning evil deeds or obscene words, the verse purports to say that evil persons do evil deeds or indulge in obscene and foul talk and scandal-mongering, while nothing comes out of good and virtuous persons but righteous deeds and pure and noble words.

2042. The practice of sending in a name-slip or introduction card to a person with whom interview is sought in his office or home is a correct way of finding out whether or not he agrees to seeing the visitor, and is in conformity with the above-mentioned Quranic injunction.

29. And if you find no one therein, do not enter them until you are given permission. And if it be said to you, 'Go back,' then go back; that is purer for you. And Allāh knows well what you do.

فَإِن لَّمْ تَجِدُوا فِيهَا أَحَدًا فَلَا تَدْخُلُوهَا حَتَّىٰ يُؤْذَنَ
لَكُمْ ۚ وَإِن قِيلَ لَكُمُ ارْجِعُوا فَارْجِعُوا هُوَ أَزْكَىٰ لَكُمْ ۚ
وَاللَّهُ بِمَا تَعْمَلُونَ عَلِيمٌ ﴿٢٩﴾

30. It is not wrong on your part to enter uninhabited houses wherein are your goods. And [a]Allāh knows what you do openly and what you hide.

لَيْسَ عَلَيْكُمْ جُنَاحٌ أَن تَدْخُلُوا بُيُوتًا غَيْرَ مَسْكُونَةٍ
فِيهَا مَتَاعٌ لَّكُمْ ۗ وَاللَّهُ يَعْلَمُ مَا تُبْدُونَ وَمَا تَكْتُمُونَ ﴿٣٠﴾

31. Say to the believing men that they restrain their looks[2043] and guard their private parts.[2043A] That is purer for them. Surely, Allāh is Well-Aware of what they do.

قُل لِّلْمُؤْمِنِينَ يَغُضُّوا مِنْ أَبْصَارِهِمْ وَيَحْفَظُوا فُرُوجَهُمْ ۚ
ذَٰلِكَ أَزْكَىٰ لَهُمْ ۗ إِنَّ اللَّهَ خَبِيرٌ بِمَا يَصْنَعُونَ ﴿٣١﴾

32. And say to the believing women that they restrain their looks and guard their private parts, and that they display not their beauty *or their embellishment* except that which is apparent thereof, and that they draw their head-coverings over their bosoms, and that they display not their beauty *or their embellishment* save to their husbands, or to their fathers, or the fathers of their husbands, or their sons, or the sons of their husbands, or their brothers, or the sons of their brothers, or the sons of their sisters, or women *who are their companions*,[2043B] or those that their right hands possess, or such of male

وَقُل لِّلْمُؤْمِنَاتِ يَغْضُضْنَ مِنْ أَبْصَارِهِنَّ وَيَحْفَظْنَ
فُرُوجَهُنَّ وَلَا يُبْدِينَ زِينَتَهُنَّ إِلَّا مَا ظَهَرَ مِنْهَا
وَلْيَضْرِبْنَ بِخُمُرِهِنَّ عَلَىٰ جُيُوبِهِنَّ ۖ وَلَا يُبْدِينَ
زِينَتَهُنَّ إِلَّا لِبُعُولَتِهِنَّ أَوْ آبَائِهِنَّ أَوْ آبَاءِ بُعُولَتِهِنَّ
أَوْ أَبْنَائِهِنَّ أَوْ أَبْنَاءِ بُعُولَتِهِنَّ أَوْ إِخْوَانِهِنَّ أَوْ
بَنِي إِخْوَانِهِنَّ أَوْ بَنِي أَخَوَاتِهِنَّ أَوْ نِسَائِهِنَّ أَوْ مَا
مَلَكَتْ أَيْمَانُهُنَّ أَوِ التَّابِعِينَ غَيْرِ أُولِي الْإِرْبَةِ

[a]2 : 34; 21 : 111; 87 : 8.

2043. As stated above the Qur'ān is not content with merely taking a superficial view of things but goes to their very root. According to it, every good or bad quality springs from a certain root. In the case of a good quality, the Qur'ān enjoins that the root should be mastered and fully kept under control and, in the case of an evil, it aims at its complete eradication and extermination and thus bolts and bars all the avenues to it. As it is the eyes through which most evil thoughts enter the mind, so in the verse under comment believing men and women have been commanded to restrain their looks when they happen to meet one another.

2043A. *Furūj* may also signify "senses."

2043B. Decent women.

attendants as have no desire for women, or young children who have not *yet* attained knowledge of the hidden parts of women. And that they strike not their feet so that what they hide of their ornaments may become known. And turn ye to Allāh all together, O believers, that you may prosper.[2044]

مِنَ الرِّجَالِ اَوِ الطِّفْلِ الَّذِيْنَ لَمْ يَظْهَرُوْا عَلٰى عَوْرٰتِ
النِّسَآءِ وَلَا يَضْرِبْنَ بِاَرْجُلِهِنَّ لِيُعْلَمَ مَا يُخْفِيْنَ
مِنْ زِيْنَتِهِنَّ وَتُوْبُوْٓا اِلَى اللّٰهِ جَمِيْعًا اَيُّهَ الْمُؤْمِنُوْنَ
لَعَلَّكُمْ تُفْلِحُوْنَ ٣٢

2044. As a good deal of misunderstanding and lack of proper knowledge as to what constitutes Islamic "Pardah" prevails even among Muslims, a somewhat detailed note on this much-vexed question is called for. The following verses deal with every aspect of "Pardah" :—

(i) And say to the believing women that they restrain their looks and guard their private parts, and that they display not their beauty or their embellishment except that which is apparent thereof, and that they draw their head-coverings over their bosoms, and that they display not their beauty ....(24 : 32, *i.e.*, the verse under comment).

(ii) O Prophet, tell thy wives and thy daughters and the women of the believers that they should let down over them their loose outer garments. That is more likely that they will *thus* be recognized and not molested (33 : 60).

The Arabic word used in this verse (33: 60) is *Jalābīb* of which the singular is *Jilbāb* which means an outer or wrapping garment (Lane).

(iii) O wives of the Prophet! you are not like any *other* women if you are righteous. So be not soft in speech, lest he, in whose heart is a disease, should feel tempted; and speak decent words. And stay in your houses with dignity and do not show off yourselves in the manner of the showing off *of the women* of the former days of ignorance....(33 : 33-34).

(iv) O ye who believe! let those whom your right hands possess, and those of you who have not attained to puberty, ask leave of you at three times *before coming into your private apartments*, before the Morning Prayer and when you lay aside your clothes at noon *in summer* and after the Night Prayer....(24 : 59).

The following inferences emerge from these four verses :

(*a*) When they go out, Muslim women are required to wear *Jilbāb, i.e.*, an outer and wrapping garment, which should cover their heads and bosoms in such a manner that the garment should come down from the head to the bosom covering the whole body. This is the significance of the Quranic words *Yudnīna 'Alaihinna min Jalābībihinna* (33 : 60). The wearing of an outer garment is intended to save a Muslim woman, when she goes about her business, from the mental anguish of being stared at or molested or in any other way inconvenienced by persons of questionable character.

(*b*) Muslim men and women are to restrain their looks when they happen to face each other.

(*c*) The third commandment, though apparently applying to the wives of the Holy Prophet, includes, as is the practice of the Qur'ān, other Muslim women. The words, 'And stay in your houses' (33 : 34) imply that whereas women may go out when necessary, the principal and primary sphere of their activities is inside the house.

(*d*) At three stated hours, even children are not allowed to enter the private apartments of their parents, nor are domestic servants or female slaves allowed to enter the sleeping rooms of their masters.

The first commandment applies to women when they go out. Then they are to use an outer garment which should cover their whole body. The second commandment relates to "Pardah": primarily inside the four walls of the house when near male relatives frequently come and go. In that case men and women are required only to restrain their looks and as an additional precaution women are to take care that their *Zīnah, i.e.*, beauty of person, dress and ornaments, is not displayed. They are not required to use *Jilbāb* (outer garment) at that time because that would be very irksome and even impracticable in view of the free and frequent visits of very near blood relations. The context shows that this commandment relates to "Pardah" inside the four walls of the house, because all the persons mentioned in the verse under comment are very near relations who generally visit the houses of their relatives. The special mention in it of four categories of persons besides near relatives, *viz.*, decent women, old servants, female slaves and minor boys, lends additional weight to the inference that the commandment in this verse relates to "Pardah" within the four walls of the house. The fact that the first commandment refers to "Pardah" outside the house and the second commandment basically refers to "Pardah" within the four walls of the house is also apparent from the different words that have been used to express the two forms of "Pardah" in the relevant verses, *i.e.*, 33 : 60, and the verse under comment. Whereas in 33 : 60 the garment which a woman is to use when she goes out is *Jilbāb* (an outer garment), the garment which she has to use inside the house when relatives visit is *Khimār* (a head-covering). Moreover, whereas in 33 : 60 the words used are *Yudnīna 'Alaihinna min Jalābībihinna, i.e.*, they should let down over them their outer garments (for a detailed discussion of *Jilbāb* and *Yudnīna* see 33 : 60); in the verse under comment the words used are *Yaḍribna Bikhumurihinna 'Alā Juyūbihinna, i.e.*, they should cast their head-coverings across their bosoms. It is clear that in the former case the garment will cover the head, the face and the bosom while in the latter case only the head and the bosom will become covered and the face may remain uncovered.

It may be noted in passing that the shape and form of the outer-garment which, as mentioned above, a woman must wear when she goes out and which covers her whole body will vary according to the customs, habits, social status, family traditions and usages of various classes of the Muslim Community. The commandment with regard to "Pardah" within the four walls of the house will also apply to shops, fields, etc., where women of certain sections of Muslim society have to work to earn their living. There a woman will not be required to veil her face. She will have only to restrain her looks and to cover her *Zīnah, i.e.*, her ornaments and other embellishments, as women within the four walls of the house have to do when their near male relatives visit them.

The third commandment requires women to behave with dignity bordering on austerity when talking to stranger men; and they are also required to give their full attention to the discharge of their serious and important duties in regard to the affairs connected with the well-being of their own sex and the management of the household affairs and to looking after and bringing up of children and kindred matters. The fourth commandment enjoins husband and wife to have, as far as possible, sleeping apartments separate from those of other members of the family which even minor boys are not allowed to enter at hours stated in v. 59.

The word, *Zīnah*, used in the verse under comment includes both natural and artificial beauty—beauty of person, dress and ornaments. The expression, 'except that which is apparent thereof,' contains all those things which it is not possible for a woman to cover such as her voice, gait or stature, and also certain parts of her body which have to remain uncovered according to her social status, her family traditions, her avocation and the custom of the society. The permission to keep certain parts of the body uncovered will be subject to certain variations. Thus the words, 'they display not their beauty' will have different connotations with regard to women belonging to different sections and grades of society and

33. And arrange marriages for widows[2045] from among you, and for your male slaves and female slaves who are fit *for marriage*. If they be poor, Allāh will grant them means out of His bounty; and Allāh is Bountiful, All-Knowing.

وَاَنْكِحُوا الْاَيَامٰى مِنْكُمْ وَالصّٰلِحِيْنَ مِنْ عِبَادِكُمْ
وَاِمَآئِكُمْ اِنْ يَّكُوْنُوْا فُقَرَآءَ يُغْنِهِمُ اللّٰهُ مِنْ فَضْلِهٖ
وَاللّٰهُ وَاسِعٌ عَلِيْمٌ ﴿٣٣﴾

34. And let those who find no *means of* marriage keep themselves chaste, until Allāh grants them means out of His bounty. And such as desire *a deed of manumission*[2046] *in* writing from among those whom your right hands possess, write it for them if you know any good in them; and give them out of the wealth of Allāh which He has bestowed upon you. And force not your maids into unchaste life *by keeping them unmarried* if they desire to keep chaste, in order that you may seek the gain of the present life. But if anyone forces them, then after their compulsion Allāh will be Forgiving *and* Merciful *to them*.

وَلْيَسْتَعْفِفِ الَّذِيْنَ لَا يَجِدُوْنَ نِكَاحًا حَتّٰى يُغْنِيَهُمُ
اللّٰهُ مِنْ فَضْلِهٖ وَالَّذِيْنَ يَبْتَغُوْنَ الْكِتٰبَ مِمَّا مَلَكَتْ
اَيْمَانُكُمْ فَكَاتِبُوْهُمْ اِنْ عَلِمْتُمْ فِيْهِمْ خَيْرًا وَّاٰتُوْهُمْ
مِّنْ مَّالِ اللّٰهِ الَّذِيْٓ اٰتٰىكُمْ وَلَا تُكْرِهُوْا فَتَيٰتِكُمْ
عَلَى الْبِغَآءِ اِنْ اَرَدْنَ تَحَصُّنًا لِّتَبْتَغُوْا عَرَضَ الْحَيٰوةِ
الدُّنْيَا وَمَنْ يُّكْرِهْهُّنَّ فَاِنَّ اللّٰهَ مِنْ بَعْدِ اِكْرَاهِهِنَّ
غَفُوْرٌ رَّحِيْمٌ ﴿٣٤﴾

---

the connotation will change with the change in the customs and modes of living and professions of a people. The words, 'And that they strike not their feet so that what they hide of their ornaments may become known' (24 : 32), show that public dancing which is so much in vogue in certain countries is definitely not allowed by Islām.

This is the Islamic conception of "Pardah." According to it Muslim women may go out as often as it is legitimately necessary for them to do so, but their primary and principal functions are confined to their homes which are as important and serious, if not more, as the avocations of men are. If women take to men's avocations they seek to defy nature and nature does not allow its laws to be defied with impunity.

2045. *Ayāmā* is the plural of *Ayyim* which means, a woman having no husband, whether she be a virgin or not, or whether she had married before or not ; a free woman (Lane) ; also a man having no wife (Mufradāt). The marriage of widows and virgins, is strongly urged. In fact, Islām views with extreme disfavour the unmarried state and regards the married state as the normal and natural one. The Holy Prophet is reported to have said : 'Marriage is my *Sunnah* (usage or practice) and whoso disapproves and forsakes my *Sunnah* is not of me' (Muslim, *Kitāb al-Nikāḥ*).

2046. *Mukātabah* (deed of manumission) is a written contract by means of which a slave could earn his or her emancipation, independently and irrespective of the fact whether his or her master likes it or not. According to this contract a definite amount of money or labour is fixed as the price of the freedom of the slave.

35. [a]And We have sent down to you manifest Signs, and *have related to you* the example of those who have passed away before you, and an admonition to the God-fearing.

وَلَقَدْ أَنْزَلْنَا إِلَيْكُمْ آيٰتٍ مُّبَيِّنٰتٍ وَّمَثَلًا مِّنَ الَّذِيْنَ
خَلَوْا مِنْ قَبْلِكُمْ وَمَوْعِظَةً لِّلْمُتَّقِيْنَ ﴿٣٥﴾

R. 5

36. Allāh is the Light[2046A] of the heavens and the earth. His light is as if there were a *lustrous* niche,[2046B] wherein is a lamp. The lamp is inside a glass-globe.[2046C] The globe is, as it were, a glittering star. *The lamp* is lit from *the oil of* a blessed tree—an olive—neither of the East nor of the West, whose oil well-nigh would shine forth even though fire touched it not. Light upon light! Allāh guides to His light whomsoever He pleases. And Allāh sets forth parables for men, and Allāh knows all things full well.[2047]

اَللّٰهُ نُوْرُ السَّمٰوٰتِ وَالْاَرْضِ مَثَلُ نُوْرِهٖ كَمِشْكٰوةٍ فِيْهَا
مِصْبَاحٌ اَلْمِصْبَاحُ فِيْ زُجَاجَةٍ اَلزُّجَاجَةُ كَاَنَّهَا كَوْكَبٌ
دُرِّيٌّ يُّوْقَدُ مِنْ شَجَرَةٍ مُّبٰرَكَةٍ زَيْتُوْنَةٍ لَّا شَرْقِيَّةٍ
وَّلَا غَرْبِيَّةٍ يَّكَادُ زَيْتُهَا يُضِيْٓءُ وَلَوْ لَمْ تَمْسَسْهُ
نَارٌ نُوْرٌ عَلٰى نُوْرٍ يَهْدِي اللّٰهُ لِنُوْرِهٖ مَنْ يَّشَآءُ
وَيَضْرِبُ اللّٰهُ الْاَمْثَالَ لِلنَّاسِ وَاللّٰهُ بِكُلِّ شَيْءٍ
عَلِيْمٌ ﴿٣٦﴾

[a]22 : 17; 57 : 10; 58 : 6.

2046A. *Nūr* means, light as opposed to darkness. It is more extensive and more penetrating as well as more lasting in its significance than *Ḍiyā*' (Lane).

2046B. *Mishkāt* means, a niche in a wall, *i.e.*, a hole or hollow in a wall, not extending through, in which a lamp placed gives more light than it gives elsewhere; a pillar on the top of which the lamp is put (Lane).

2046C. *Zujājah* means a glass ; a globe of glass (Lane).

2047. The verse is a beautiful metaphor. It speaks of three things—a lamp, a glass-globe and a niche. The Divine Light is stated to have been confined to these three things which combined together make its brightness and effulgence complete and perfect. 'The lamp' is the very source of the light; the 'glass-globe' which is over the lamp protects its light from being extinguished by the puffs of wind and increases its brightness; and 'the niche' preserves the light. The simile may aptly apply to an electric torch of which the constituent parts are the electric wires which give light, the bulb which protects the light and the reflector which spreads and diffuses the light and gives it direction. In spiritual terminology the three things—'the lamp,' 'the glass-globe' and 'the niche'—may respectively stand for Divine Light, God's Prophets who protect that light from being extinguished and add to its effulgence and brightness, and the *Khalīfahs* or Successors of the Prophets who diffuse and disseminate the Divine Light and give it a direction and purpose for the guidance and illumination of the world. The verse further states that the oil used to light the lamp is of the highest possible purity and is inflammable to a degree which makes it (the oil) burst out into a flame even without being ignited. It is extracted from a tree which belongs neither to the East nor to the West, *i.e.*, which does not discriminate in favour of or against any particular people.

The verse may have another interpretation. The light mentioned in the verse may be taken to refer to the Holy Prophet because he has been spoken of as 'light' in the Qur'ān (5 : 16) ; 'the niche' in that case would signify the heart of the Holy Prophet, and 'the lamp' his most pure and unsullied nature which is endowed with the best and noblest attributes

37. *This light illumines* houses with regard to which Allāh has ordained that they be exalted and that His name be remembered in them. Therein do glorify Him in the mornings and the evenings[2047A]

فِيْ بُيُوْتٍ اَذِنَ اللّٰهُ اَنْ تُرْفَعَ وَيُذْكَرَ فِيْهَا اسْمُهٗ ۙ يُسَبِّحُ لَهٗ فِيْهَا بِالْغُدُوِّ وَالْاٰصَالِ ﴿٣٧﴾

38. [a]Men, whom neither merchandise nor traffic diverts from the remembrance of Allāh and the observance of Prayer, and the giving of the *Zakāt*.[2048] They fear a day in which hearts and eyes will be in *a state of* agitation *and anguish;*

رِجَالٌ ۙ لَّا تُلْهِيْهِمْ تِجَارَةٌ وَّلَا بَيْعٌ عَنْ ذِكْرِ اللّٰهِ وَاِقَامِ الصَّلٰوةِ وَاِيْتَآءِ الزَّكٰوةِ ۙ يَخَافُوْنَ يَوْمًا تَتَقَلَّبُ فِيْهِ الْقُلُوْبُ وَالْاَبْصَارُ ﴿٣٨﴾

39. So [b]Allāh will give them the best reward of their deeds, and give them increase out of His bounty. And Allāh does provide for whomsoever He pleases without measure.

لِيَجْزِيَهُمُ اللّٰهُ اَحْسَنَ مَا عَمِلُوْا وَيَزِيْدَهُمْ مِّنْ فَضْلِهٖ ؕ وَاللّٰهُ يَرْزُقُ مَنْ يَّشَآءُ بِغَيْرِ حِسَابٍ ﴿٣٩﴾

[a]63 : 10. [b]9 : 121; 16 : 98.

and qualities, and 'the glass' would signify that the Divine Light with which his nature has been invested is as clear and bright as crystal. When the light of heavenly revelation descended upon the light of the Holy Prophet's nature, it shone with a twofold effulgence which in the words of the Qur'ān has been described as 'light upon light.' This light of the Prophet was sustained by an oil which emanated from a blessed tree, which means that the Holy Prophet's light was not only bright and brilliant but abundant and stable and perpetual (as the word *Mubārakah* signifies), and was meant to illumine both the East and the West. Further, the Holy Prophet's heart was so pure and his nature gifted with such noble qualities that he was almost fit to discharge the duties of his great mission even before the light of Divine revelation had descended upon him. This is the significance of the words, ***whose oil well-nigh would shine forth even though fire touched it not.***

The metaphor may have yet another explanation. The niche in the verse is the human body. The human body contains the spirit which makes itself manifest through the organs of the body. Like the niche the human body protects the light, namely, the spirit ; and guides its expression, *i.e.*, the human body contains *Misbāh* or the lamp of the soul which illumines the human mind and brings it into touch with God. The lamp is contained in a '*Zujājah*' (globe of glass) which protects it from harm or injury and enhances and reflects its light. This *Zujājah* which is the human brain of which the mechanism is so perfect as to have led some philosophers to think that it is the ultimate source of the Divine Light. The light is sustained by the oil from a blessed tree, namely from those basic and eternal truths which are not the exclusive possession of any people of the East or of the West. These eternal truths are implanted in the very nature of man and would almost make themselves manifest even without the help of Divine revelation.

2047A. The verse contains both a proof and a prophecy. It predicts that houses illumined by the light contained in the Qur'ān will be exalted and their inmates will always celebrate the praises of God. This will be a proof that they are illumined by Allāh's light.

2048. The verse constitutes a great testimonial to the righteousness and goodness of the Holy Prophet's Companions and to their love for God. They are men, says the verse, of flesh and bones. They have their worldly ambitions and aspirations, their professions

40. And *as to* those who disbelieve, *a*their deeds are like a mirage in a desert. The thirsty one imagines it to be water until, when he comes up to it, he finds it to be nothing. And he finds Allāh near him, Who then pays him his account in full; and Allāh is Swift at reckoning.

وَالَّذِيْنَ كَفَرُوْٓا اَعْمَالُهُمْ كَسَرَابٍۭ بِقِيْعَةٍ يَّحْسَبُهُ الظَّمْاٰنُ مَآءً ۚ حَتّٰٓى اِذَا جَآءَهٗ لَمْ يَجِدْهُ شَيْئًا وَّوَجَدَ اللّٰهَ عِنْدَهٗ فَوَفّٰٮهُ حِسَابَهٗ ۚ وَاللّٰهُ سَرِيْعُ الْحِسَابِ ۙ ۞

41. Or, *their deeds are* like thick layers of darkness *spread* over a vast and deep sea, on whose surface *rise* waves above waves, above which are clouds—layers upon layers of darkness. When he holds out his hands, he can hardly see it; and he whom Allāh gives no light—for him there is no light at all.2049

اَوْ كَظُلُمٰتٍ فِىْ بَحْرٍ لُّجِّيٍّ يَّغْشٰٮهُ مَوْجٌ مِّنْ فَوْقِهٖ مَوْجٌ مِّنْ فَوْقِهٖ سَحَابٌ ۚ ظُلُمٰتٌۢ بَعْضُهَا فَوْقَ بَعْضٍ ۗ اِذَآ اَخْرَجَ يَدَهٗ لَمْ يَكَدْ يَرٰٮهَا ۗ وَمَنْ لَّمْ يَجْعَلِ اللّٰهُ لَهٗ نُوْرًا فَمَا لَهٗ مِنْ نُّوْرٍ ۞

R. 6　42. Seest thou not that *b*it is Allāh Whose praises, all who are in the heavens2050 and the earth2050A celebrate, and *so do* the birds with their wings outspread?2050B Each one knows his own *mode of* prayer and praise.2051 And Allāh knows well what they do.

اَلَمْ تَرَ اَنَّ اللّٰهَ يُسَبِّحُ لَهٗ مَنْ فِى السَّمٰوٰتِ وَالْاَرْضِ وَالطَّيْرُ صٰٓفّٰتٍ ۗ كُلٌّ قَدْ عَلِمَ صَلَاتَهٗ وَتَسْبِيْحَهٗ ۗ وَاللّٰهُ عَلِيْمٌۢ بِمَا يَفْعَلُوْنَ ۞

---

*a*14 : 19.　*b*17 : 45;　59 : 25;　61 : 2;　62 : 2.

and avocations. They are not monks and hermits, cut apart from the world. Yet amidst all their mundane pursuits and engagements they do not neglect to discharge their duties to God and man.

2049. In vv. 37-39 above an appreciative reference is made to a class of men—the lovers of Divine light and the righteous servants of God. The present and the immediately preceding verse speak of another class of people—the sons of darkness. People of one class accept the Divine Light and walk in it. Their enviable condition is described in the simile, 'light upon light.' The other class of people reject the Divine Light, choose to grope in the darkness of doubts. All their works prove futile and deceptive like a mirage. They love darkness, follow darkness and live in darkness, so their unenviable condition has been very aptly and graphically described in the words, *their deeds are like thick layers of darkness spread over a vast and deep sea on whose surface rise waves over waves, above which are clouds—layers upon layers of darkness.*

2050. Angels of the Heavens.

2050A. Animate and inanimate things which are upon the earth such as men, animals, vegetables, and minerals.

2050B. The birds which fly in the air. In a spiritual sense, the three expressions respectively signify : (*a*) persons of very high spiritual status; (*b*) worldly-minded men whose whole attention and efforts are devoted to the acquirement of material pursuits and who have no thought or time for spiritual things and (*c*) people whose spiritual condition is midway between that of the two above-mentioned categories.

2051. See next page.

43. [a]And to Allāh belongs the Kingdom of the heavens and the earth, and to Allāh shall be the return.

وَلِلّٰهِ مُلْكُ السَّمٰوٰتِ وَالْاَرْضِ ۚ وَاِلَى اللّٰهِ الْمَصِيْرُ ﴿۴۳﴾

44. Seest thou not that [b]Allāh drives the clouds slowly, then joins them together, then piles them up so that thou seest rain issue forth from the midst thereof? And He sends down from the sky *clouds like* mountains wherein is hail, [c]and He smites therewith whom He pleases, and turns it away from whom He pleases. The flash of its lightning may well-nigh take away the sight.[2052]

اَلَمْ تَرَ اَنَّ اللّٰهَ يُزْجِيْ سَحَابًا ثُمَّ يُؤَلِّفُ بَيْنَهٗ ثُمَّ يَجْعَلُهٗ رُكَامًا فَتَرَى الْوَدْقَ يَخْرُجُ مِنْ خِلٰلِهٖ ۚ وَيُنَزِّلُ مِنَ السَّمَآءِ مِنْ جِبَالٍ فِيْهَا مِنْۢ بَرَدٍ فَيُصِيْبُ بِهٖ مَنْ يَّشَآءُ وَيَصْرِفُهٗ عَنْ مَّنْ يَّشَآءُ ۗ يَكَادُ سَنَا بَرْقِهٖ يَذْهَبُ بِالْاَبْصَارِ ﴿۴۴﴾

45. Allāh alternates the night and the day.[2053] Therein, surely, is a lesson for those who have eyes.

يُقَلِّبُ اللّٰهُ الَّيْلَ وَالنَّهَارَ ۗ اِنَّ فِيْ ذٰلِكَ لَعِبْرَةً لِّاُولِى الْاَبْصَارِ ﴿۴۵﴾

46. [d]And Allāh has created every animal from water. Of them are *some* that go upon their bellies, and of them are *some* that go upon two feet, and among them are *some* that go upon four.[2054] Allāh creates what He pleases. Surely, Allāh has the power to do all that He pleases.

وَاللّٰهُ خَلَقَ كُلَّ دَآبَّةٍ مِّنْ مَّآءٍ ۚ فَمِنْهُمْ مَّنْ يَّمْشِيْ عَلٰى بَطْنِهٖ ۚ وَمِنْهُمْ مَّنْ يَّمْشِيْ عَلٰى رِجْلَيْنِ ۚ وَمِنْهُمْ مَّنْ يَّمْشِيْ عَلٰۤى اَرْبَعٍ ۗ يَخْلُقُ اللّٰهُ مَا يَشَآءُ ۗ اِنَّ اللّٰهَ عَلٰى كُلِّ شَيْءٍ قَدِيْرٌ ﴿۴۶﴾

[a]3 : 190; 5 : 121. [b]30 : 49. [c]13 : 14. [d]25 : 55.

2051. Whereas the clause, *Whose praises all who are in the heavens and the earth celebrate*, refers to the collective testimony that the whole universe bears to the Unity and Holiness of God, the words, *Each one knows his own mode of prayer and praise*, refer to the evidence which everything bears to Divine Unity and Holiness individually and separately by carrying out faithfully the task allotted to it by God. *Ṣalāt* has different meanings with reference to different objects. Used about God it means Divine mercy; used about angels it means their asking forgiveness of God for men and used about man it means the prescribed form of Prayer (Lane).

2052. The verse may signify that for some the revealed Law serves as timely rain which proves highly beneficial and for others it takes the form of hail and storm which brings in its wake destruction and ruin.

2053. The verse purports to say that the spiritual development of man referred to in the preceding verse is not always uniform and uninterrupted. Sometimes it is very rapid, at another time it is slow and yet at some other time it comes to a dead stop. This ebb and flow in the spiritual development of man is called *Qabḍ* (contraction) and *Basṭ* (expansion), or the alternation of night and day in spiritual terminology. Everything in the world is subject to the law of acceleration and retardation and so is the spiritual evolution of man.

2054. The verse describes the nature and form of the progress of spiritual pilgrims to their destined goal. The progress of some of them is extremely slow. They creep and

47. We have indeed sent down manifest Signs. And Allāh guides whom He pleases to the right path.

لَقَدْ اَنْزَلْنَآ اٰيٰتٍ مُّبَيِّنٰتٍ ؕ وَاللّٰهُ يَهْدِيْ مَنْ يَّشَآءُ اِلٰى صِرَاطٍ مُّسْتَقِيْمٍ ﴿۴۷﴾

48. And they say, 'We believe in Allāh and in the Messenger, and we obey;' then *after that* some of them turn away. Such are not believers *at all*.

وَيَقُوْلُوْنَ اٰمَنَّا بِاللّٰهِ وَبِالرَّسُوْلِ وَاَطَعْنَا ثُمَّ يَتَوَلّٰى فَرِيْقٌ مِّنْهُمْ مِّنْۢ بَعْدِ ذٰلِكَ ؕ وَمَآ اُولٰٓئِكَ بِالْمُؤْمِنِيْنَ ﴿۴۸﴾

49. *And when they are called to Allāh and His Messenger that he may judge between them, lo! a party of them turn away.

وَاِذَا دُعُوْٓا اِلَى اللّٰهِ وَرَسُوْلِهٖ لِيَحْكُمَ بَيْنَهُمْ اِذَا فَرِيْقٌ مِّنْهُمْ مُّعْرِضُوْنَ ﴿۴۹﴾

50. And if *they consider* the right *to be* on their side, they come to him running in submission.

وَاِنْ يَّكُنْ لَّهُمُ الْحَقُّ يَاْتُوْٓا اِلَيْهِ مُذْعِنِيْنَ ؕ ﴿۵۰﴾

51. Is it that there is a disease in their hearts? Or, do they doubt, or, do they fear[2055] that Allāh and His Messenger will be unjust to them? Nay, it is they themselves who are the wrongdoers.

اَفِيْ قُلُوْبِهِمْ مَّرَضٌ اَمِ ارْتَابُوْٓا اَمْ يَخَافُوْنَ اَنْ يَّحِيْفَ اللّٰهُ عَلَيْهِمْ وَرَسُوْلُهٗ ؕ بَلْ اُولٰٓئِكَ هُمُ الظّٰلِمُوْنَ ﴿۵۱﴾ ع

R. 7 52. All that the believers say, when they are called to Allāh and His Messenger in order that he may judge between them, is that they say, 'We hear and we obey.'[2056] And it is they who will prosper.

اِنَّمَا كَانَ قَوْلَ الْمُؤْمِنِيْنَ اِذَا دُعُوْٓا اِلَى اللّٰهِ وَرَسُوْلِهٖ لِيَحْكُمَ بَيْنَهُمْ اَنْ يَّقُوْلُوْا سَمِعْنَا وَاَطَعْنَا ؕ وَاُولٰٓئِكَ هُمُ الْمُفْلِحُوْنَ ﴿۵۲﴾

*3 : 24.

crawl to their destination. Others go quicker like animals that move on two legs, yet others go faster like four-legged animals. What is hinted at here is speed and not the method of locomotion. The four-legged animals are, as a rule, speedier of movement than the bipeds or the crawlers. The same is the case with the spiritual travellers.

2055. The verse signifies that disbelievers suffer from one or all of the three spiritual diseases, or that some of them suffer from one disease and others from other diseases. In fact, the three main things that stand in the way of a man's spiritual progress and retard and arrest it, are doubt, fear and envy.

2056. The present and adjacent verses point to a basic and most fundamental Islamic principle, *viz.*, that Islām is a perfect code of laws and its injunctions and commandments cover all the different aspects of human life and that the Holy Prophet is the final authority on all matters that concern the national life of Muslims.

53. [a]And whoso obeys Allāh and His Messenger, and fears Allāh, and takes Him as a shield *for protection*, it is they who will be successful.

وَمَنْ يُّطِعِ اللّٰهَ وَرَسُوْلَهٗ وَيَخْشَ اللّٰهَ وَيَتَّقْهِ فَاُولٰٓئِكَ هُمُ الْفَآئِزُوْنَ ﴿۵۳﴾

54. And they swear by Allāh their strongest oaths that, if thou command them, they will surely go forth. Say, 'Swear not; *what is required of you* is [b]obedience *to what is right*. Surely, Allāh is Aware of what you do.'

وَاَقْسَمُوْا بِاللّٰهِ جَهْدَ اَيْمَانِهِمْ لَئِنْ اَمَرْتَهُمْ لَيَخْرُجُنَّ ۭ قُلْ لَّا تُقْسِمُوْا ۚ طَاعَةٌ مَّعْرُوْفَةٌ ۭ اِنَّ اللّٰهَ خَبِيْرٌۢ بِمَا تَعْمَلُوْنَ ﴿۵۴﴾

55. Say, [c]'Obey Allāh, and obey the Messenger.' But if you turn away, he is responsible for what he is charged with and you are responsible for what you are charged with. And if you obey him, you will be rightly guided. [d]And the Messenger is only responsible for the plain delivery of the Message.

قُلْ اَطِيْعُوا اللّٰهَ وَاَطِيْعُوا الرَّسُوْلَ ۚ فَاِنْ تَوَلَّوْا فَاِنَّمَا عَلَيْهِ مَا حُمِّلَ وَعَلَيْكُمْ مَّا حُمِّلْتُمْ ۭ وَاِنْ تُطِيْعُوْهُ تَهْتَدُوْا ۭ وَمَا عَلَى الرَّسُوْلِ اِلَّا الْبَلٰغُ الْمُبِيْنُ ﴿۵۵﴾

56. Allāh has promised to those among you who believe and do good works that He will, surely, make them Successors in the earth, as He made Successors *from among* those who were before them; and that He will, surely, establish for them their religion which He has chosen for them; and that He will, surely, give them in exchange security *and peace* after their fear; They will worship Me, *and* they will not associate anything with Me. Then whoso disbelieves after that, they will be the rebellious.[2057]

وَعَدَ اللّٰهُ الَّذِيْنَ اٰمَنُوْا مِنْكُمْ وَعَمِلُوا الصّٰلِحٰتِ لَيَسْتَخْلِفَنَّهُمْ فِي الْاَرْضِ كَمَا اسْتَخْلَفَ الَّذِيْنَ مِنْ قَبْلِهِمْ ۠ وَلَيُمَكِّنَنَّ لَهُمْ دِيْنَهُمُ الَّذِي ارْتَضٰى لَهُمْ وَلَيُبَدِّلَنَّهُمْ مِّنْ بَعْدِ خَوْفِهِمْ اَمْنًا ۭ يَعْبُدُوْنَنِيْ لَا يُشْرِكُوْنَ بِيْ شَيْـًٔا ۭ وَمَنْ كَفَرَ بَعْدَ ذٰلِكَ فَاُولٰٓئِكَ هُمُ الْفٰسِقُوْنَ ﴿۵۶﴾

[a]4 : 14. [b]5 : 93; 64 : 13. [c]4 : 14; 33 : 72; 48 : 18. [d]16 : 36; 29 : 19; 36 : 18.

2057. Because it serves as a prelude to the introduction of the subject of *Khilāfat* emphasis is repeatedly laid in vv. 52—55 on obedience to Allāh and His Messenger. This emphasis implies a hint to the status and position of a ***Khalīfāh*** in Islām. The verse embodies a promise that Muslims will be vouchsafed both spiritual and temporal leadership. The promise is made to the whole Muslim nation but the institution of *Khilāfat* will take a palpable form in the person of certain individuals who will be the Holy Prophet's Successors and the representatives of the whole nation. The promise of the establishment of *Khilāfat* is clear and unmistakable. As the Holy Prophet is now humanity's sole guide

57. [a]And observe Prayer and give the *Zakāt* and obey the Messenger, that you may be shown mercy.

وَاَقِيْمُوا الصَّلٰوةَ وَاٰتُوا الزَّكٰوةَ وَاَطِيْعُوا الرَّسُوْلَ
لَعَلَّكُمْ تُرْحَمُوْنَ ﴿٥٧﴾

58. Think not that those who disbelieve can frustrate Our design in the earth; their abode is Hell; and it is indeed an evil resort.

لَا تَحْسَبَنَّ الَّذِيْنَ كَفَرُوْا مُعْجِزِيْنَ فِي الْاَرْضِ ۚ
وَمَاْوٰىهُمُ النَّارُ ۖ وَلَبِئْسَ الْمَصِيْرُ ﴿٥٨﴾ ع

R. 8 59. O ye who believe! let those whom your right hands possess, and those of you, who have not reached puberty, ask leave of you at three times *before coming into your private apartments*—before the Morning Prayer, and when you lay aside your clothes at noon *in summer* and after the Night Prayer.[2058] *These are* three times of privacy for you. At other *times* there is no blame on you nor on them, *for* some of you have to attend upon others and to move about *freely according to need.* Thus does Allāh make plain to you the Signs; for Allāh is All-Knowing, Wise.

يٰۤاَيُّهَا الَّذِيْنَ اٰمَنُوْا لِيَسْتَاْذِنْكُمُ الَّذِيْنَ مَلَكَتْ
اَيْمَانُكُمْ وَالَّذِيْنَ لَمْ يَبْلُغُوا الْحُلُمَ مِنْكُمْ ثَلٰثَ
مَرّٰتٍ ۚ مِنْ قَبْلِ صَلٰوةِ الْفَجْرِ وَحِيْنَ تَضَعُوْنَ ثِيَابَكُمْ
مِّنَ الظَّهِيْرَةِ وَمِنْۢ بَعْدِ صَلٰوةِ الْعِشَآءِ ۚ ثَلٰثُ عَوْرٰتٍ
لَّكُمْ ۚ لَيْسَ عَلَيْكُمْ وَلَا عَلَيْهِمْ جُنَاحٌۢ بَعْدَهُنَّ ۚ
طَوّٰفُوْنَ عَلَيْكُمْ بَعْضُكُمْ عَلٰى بَعْضٍ ۚ كَذٰلِكَ يُبَيِّنُ
اللّٰهُ لَكُمُ الْاٰيٰتِ ۚ وَاللّٰهُ عَلِيْمٌ حَكِيْمٌ ﴿٥٩﴾

60. And when the children among you reach puberty, they *too* should ask leave, even as their *elders* before them asked leave. Thus does Allāh make plain to you His commandments; and Allāh is All-Knowing, Wise.

وَاِذَا بَلَغَ الْاَطْفَالُ مِنْكُمُ الْحُلُمَ فَلْيَسْتَاْذِنُوْا كَمَا
اسْتَاْذَنَ الَّذِيْنَ مِنْ قَبْلِهِمْ ۚ كَذٰلِكَ يُبَيِّنُ اللّٰهُ لَكُمْ
اٰيٰتِهٖ ۚ وَاللّٰهُ عَلِيْمٌ حَكِيْمٌ ﴿٦٠﴾

[a]22 : 78.

for all time, his *Khilāfat* will continue to exist in one form or another in the world till the end of time, all other *Khilāfats* having ceased to exist. This is, among many others, the Holy Prophet's distinctive superiority over all other Prophets and Messengers of God. Our age has witnessed his greatest spiritual *Khalīfah* in the person of the Founder of the Aḥmadiyya Movement. See also "The Larger Edition of the Commentary," pp. 1869—1870.

2058. The subject of "Pardah," as stated under v. 32 above, has been referred to at four different places in the Qur'ān. Whereas 24 : 32 deals with "Pardah" primarily within four walls of the house, v. 33 : 60 discusses "Pardah" outside the house and on thoroughfares, while vv. 33 : 33-34 speak of a restricted kind of "Pardah," particularly enjoined on the Holy Prophet's wives and by implication on all Muslim women, and by inference point to the fact that the principal centre of a woman's activities is her home. The present verse, however, refers to another kind of "Pardah," *viz*., that domestic servants and minor children too should not enter the private apartments of their masters or parents at three particular hours mentioned here without getting prior permission. *Ẓahīrah* means, vehement heat of the midday ; the period from a little before *to* a little after midday in summer (Lane).

61. Such elderly women as are past the age of marriage[2058A]—there is no blame on them if they lay aside their *outer* clothing without displaying their beauty. But to abstain *even from that* is better for them. And Allāh is All-Hearing, All-Knowing.

وَالْقَوَاعِدُ مِنَ النِّسَآءِ الّٰتِيْ لَا يَرْجُوْنَ نِكَاحًا
فَلَيْسَ عَلَيْهِنَّ جُنَاحٌ اَنْ يَّضَعْنَ ثِيَابَهُنَّ غَيْرَ
مُتَبَرِّجٰتٍۭ بِزِيْنَةٍ ؕ وَاَنْ يَّسْتَعْفِفْنَ خَيْرٌ لَّهُنَّ ؕ
وَاللّٰهُ سَمِيْعٌ عَلِيْمٌ ﴿٦١﴾

62. There is no harm for the blind, and there is no harm for the lame, and there is no harm for the sick and none for yourselves, that you eat from your own houses, or the houses of your fathers, or the houses of your mothers, or the houses of your brothers, or the houses of your sisters, or the houses of your fathers' brothers, or the houses of your fathers' sisters, or the houses of your mothers' brothers, or the houses of your mothers' sisters, or the houses of which the keys are in your possession, or *from the house of* a friend of yours. Nor is there any harm whether you eat together or separately.[2059] But [a]when you enter houses, salute your people with the greeting of peace—a greeting from your Lord, *full* of blessing and purity. Thus does Allāh expound to you the commandments, that you may understand.

لَيْسَ عَلَى الْاَعْمٰى حَرَجٌ وَّلَا عَلَى الْاَعْرَجِ حَرَجٌ وَّلَا
عَلَى الْمَرِيْضِ حَرَجٌ وَّلَا عَلٰۤى اَنْفُسِكُمْ اَنْ تَاْكُلُوْا مِنْ
بُيُوْتِكُمْ اَوْ بُيُوْتِ اٰبَآئِكُمْ اَوْ بُيُوْتِ اُمَّهٰتِكُمْ اَوْ
بُيُوْتِ اِخْوَانِكُمْ اَوْ بُيُوْتِ اَخَوٰتِكُمْ اَوْ بُيُوْتِ اَعْمَامِكُمْ
اَوْ بُيُوْتِ عَمّٰتِكُمْ اَوْ بُيُوْتِ اَخْوَالِكُمْ اَوْ بُيُوْتِ خٰلٰتِكُمْ
اَوْ مَا مَلَكْتُمْ مَّفَاتِحَهٗۤ اَوْ صَدِيْقِكُمْ ؕ لَيْسَ عَلَيْكُمْ
جُنَاحٌ اَنْ تَاْكُلُوْا جَمِيْعًا اَوْ اَشْتَاتًا ؕ فَاِذَا دَخَلْتُمْ
بُيُوْتًا فَسَلِّمُوْا عَلٰۤى اَنْفُسِكُمْ تَحِيَّةً مِّنْ عِنْدِ اللّٰهِ
مُبٰرَكَةً طَيِّبَةً ؕ كَذٰلِكَ يُبَيِّنُ اللّٰهُ لَكُمُ الْاٰيٰتِ لَعَلَّكُمْ
تَعْقِلُوْنَ ﴿٦٢﴾ ع ١٤

[a]24 : 28.

2058A. *Qawā'id* is the plural of *Qā'id* which signifies a woman who has ceased to bear children and to have the menstrual discharge or who has no husband, or an old woman, much advanced in years (Lane).

2059. The verse deals with some rules of social conduct which dispose of those foolish prejudices which prevail among certain sections of human society and which tend to restrict free intercourse between the rich and the poor. Islām enjoins complete social equality and is the avowed enemy of division of people within water-tight compartments. Here it has stressed the importance and usefulness of free social intercourse and collective dining among all classes of society, and has encouraged and preferred eating together to promote familiarity and remove those bars that keep apart people of different social standing, though it has not disallowed eating separately. The Arabs and the Jews had scruples to eat with the blind or with persons suffering from certain social disabilities, as the Hindus of India even to this day do not eat or sit with the "untouchables." Islām looks askance at all such practices and encourages inter-dining and free intercourse among all classes and sections of people. *Ḥaraj* means, a sin; an objection ; harm; blame or crime (Lane).

R. 9 63. Those alone are *true* believers who believe in Allāh and His Messenger, and who, when they are with him for *the consideration of* some matter *of common concern* which has brought them together,[2059A] go not away until they have asked leave of him.[2060] Surely, those who ask leave of thee, it is they *alone* who truly believe in Allāh and His Messenger. So, when they ask leave of thee for some *urgent* affair of theirs, give leave to those of them whom thou pleasest and ask forgiveness for them of Allāh. Surely, Allāh is Most Forgiving, Merciful.

إِنَّمَا الْمُؤْمِنُونَ الَّذِينَ آمَنُوا بِاللَّهِ وَرَسُولِهِ وَإِذَا
كَانُوا مَعَهُ عَلَىٰ أَمْرٍ جَامِعٍ لَّمْ يَذْهَبُوا حَتَّىٰ يَسْتَأْذِنُوهُ ۚ
إِنَّ الَّذِينَ يَسْتَأْذِنُونَكَ أُولَٰئِكَ الَّذِينَ يُؤْمِنُونَ
بِاللَّهِ وَرَسُولِهِ ۚ فَإِذَا اسْتَأْذَنُوكَ لِبَعْضِ شَأْنِهِمْ
فَأْذَن لِّمَن شِئْتَ مِنْهُمْ وَاسْتَغْفِرْ لَهُمُ اللَّهَ ۚ إِنَّ
اللَّهَ غَفُورٌ رَّحِيمٌ ﴿٦٣﴾

64. Treat not the calling of the Messenger among you like the calling of one of you to another.[2061] Allāh indeed knows [a]those of you who steal away covertly. So let those who go against His command beware lest a trial afflict them or a grievous punishment overtake them.

لَا تَجْعَلُوا دُعَاءَ الرَّسُولِ بَيْنَكُمْ كَدُعَاءِ بَعْضِكُم بَعْضًا ۚ
قَدْ يَعْلَمُ اللَّهُ الَّذِينَ يَتَسَلَّلُونَ مِنكُمْ لِوَاذًا ۚ فَلْيَحْذَرِ
الَّذِينَ يُخَالِفُونَ عَنْ أَمْرِهِ أَن تُصِيبَهُمْ فِتْنَةٌ أَوْ
يُصِيبَهُمْ عَذَابٌ أَلِيمٌ ﴿٦٤﴾

65. Hearken! [b]To Allāh belongs whatsoever is in the heavens and the earth. He knows in what *condition* you are. And on the day when they will be returned unto Him, He will inform them of what they did. And Allāh knows everything full well.

أَلَا إِنَّ لِلَّهِ مَا فِي السَّمَاوَاتِ وَالْأَرْضِ ۖ قَدْ يَعْلَمُ مَا أَنتُمْ
عَلَيْهِ وَيَوْمَ يُرْجَعُونَ إِلَيْهِ فَيُنَبِّئُهُم بِمَا عَمِلُوا ۗ وَاللَّهُ
بِكُلِّ شَيْءٍ عَلِيمٌ ﴿٦٥﴾

[a]9 : 127. [b]2 : 285; 10 : 56; 31 : 27.

2059A. *Amr Jāmi'* means, a momentous affair on account of which people gather together as though the affair itself gathers them (Lane).

2060. The several preceding verses contained directions for Muslims as how to conduct themselves in affairs of social importance. The present verse, however, deals with affairs of national importance. The Muslims are enjoined that when they are with the Holy Prophet, engaged in transacting a business of national importance, they should not leave the assembly without his permission. It may also be inferred from this verse that in affairs concerning a whole nation or community, the individual loses his independence of action. He must abide by the decision arrived at by the assembly of Muslims, presided over by the Holy Prophet, his Successor or their accepted and elected Leader.

2061. The Prophet's or the Leader's call is not to be treated lightly. It must be accorded the respect it deserves, as it always concerns highly important affairs. The verse may also mean that the privacy of the Holy Prophet or the *Khalīfah* should not be intruded upon, and unnecessary demands should not be made upon his very precious time, and when addressed he should be treated with the respect due to his very exalted position.

CHAPTER 25

AL-FURQĀN

(*Revealed before Hijrah*)

Date of Revelation and Context

Preponderance of scholarly opinion regards this *Sūrah* as of Meccan origin and assigns it to the last Meccan period. Certain Western writers are of the view that it was revealed very early in the Holy Prophet's ministry. They attribute this inference to the absence of any reference to persecution of Muslims on the part of the Quraish which, they say, began some years later. This assumption is too flimsy to merit serious consideration. This is like saying that because some Medinite Chapters are almost devoid of any mention of disbelievers, therefore, no fighting had taken place between Muslims and disbelievers in the Medinite period.

Sūrah Al-Nūr had ended on a note about the very great importance and usefulness of the Islamic organization. It had also stated that certain Musiims were unacquainted with its great potentialities; on the other hand, they were afraid of the organization of disbelievers which was rotten to the core. The present *Sūrah* gives the reasons why the fear of the people of weak of faith is but an illusion and a figment of their own distraught imagination and does not exist in fact.

Subject-Matter

The *Sūrah* opens with the categorical statement that the Quranic Message is meant for the whole of mankind. It further says that the Almighty God Who has revealed the Qur'ān is the sole and undisputed Master of the heavens and the earth, and the sole Creator of every atom of the universe. His Word, therefore, is and must be in perfect harmony with the laws of nature, hence its acceptance or rejection does not merely mean the acceptance or rejection of a revealed Law but amounts to submission to or violation of the laws of nature itself. Next, it is stated that because disbelievers find it difficult to deny the excellence and superiority of the teachings of the Qur'ān, they take refuge behind the subterfuge that it is not the work of a single individual but is the result of the combined efforts of many persons. They further allege that its teaching has been plagiarized from old Scriptures. But these pleas possess no substance because if the Qur'ān had been the work of human effort, it could not have possessed a teaching which it is beyond the power of man to produce. And if it had been merely a copy of the ancient Scriptures, those Scriptures should also have possessed the excellences and beauties possessed by it, but that is not the case. Next, it answers some worn-out and hackneyed objections of disbelievers such as the Holy Prophet is a mere mortal and is subject to the demands of the flesh. Then, a brief reference is made to the law of the rise and fall of nations and disbelievers are warned that the time of their decadence and downfall and that of the rise, progress and prosperity of Muslims has already arrived. Further, attention of disbelievers is drawn to the phenomenon that God has made two waters, one bitter and the other sweet, both flowing side by side. They continue their parallel course and do not mix with each other. Similarly, the teachings of the Qur'ān and those of other Scriptures will continue to exist side by side in order that by comparing them people might distinguish the true from the false and the sweet from the bitter. Towards its end the *Sūrah* mentions a few special signs and marks of those righteous servants of God who by acting upon the teachings of the Qur'ān attain to the highest pinnacle of spiritual eminence, and closes with a pointed reference to the great truth that God has created man to serve a very sublime and noble object and whosoever fails to fulfil this object will forfeit God's mercy and grace.

سُوۡرَةُ الۡفُرۡقَانِ مَکِّیَّةٌ (٢٥)

1. [a]In the name of Allāh, the Gracious, the Merciful.

بِسۡمِ اللّٰہِ الرَّحۡمٰنِ الرَّحِیۡمِ ①

2. Blessed[2062] is He Who has sent down Al-Furqān[2063] to His servant, that he may be a Warner to *all* the worlds—

تَبٰرَکَ الَّذِیۡ نَزَّلَ الۡفُرۡقَانَ عَلٰی عَبۡدِہٖ لِیَکُوۡنَ لِلۡعٰلَمِیۡنَ نَذِیۡرَا ②

3. He to Whom belongs the Kingdom of the heavens and the earth. [b]And He has taken unto Himself no son, and has no partner in the Kingdom, and He has created everything, and has determined its *proper* measure.[2064]

الَّذِیۡ لَہٗ مُلۡکُ السَّمٰوٰتِ وَ الۡاَرۡضِ وَ لَمۡ یَتَّخِذۡ وَلَدًا وَّ لَمۡ یَکُنۡ لَّہٗ شَرِیۡکٌ فِی الۡمُلۡکِ وَ خَلَقَ کُلَّ شَیۡءٍ فَقَدَّرَہٗ تَقۡدِیۡرًا ③

4. Yet [c]they have taken beside Him gods, [d]who create nothing but are themselves created, and who have no power to harm or benefit themselves, nor have they any power over death or life or Resurrection.[2065]

وَ اتَّخَذُوۡا مِنۡ دُوۡنِہٖۤ اٰلِہَۃً لَّا یَخۡلُقُوۡنَ شَیۡئًا وَّ ہُمۡ یُخۡلَقُوۡنَ وَ لَا یَمۡلِکُوۡنَ لِاَنۡفُسِہِمۡ ضَرًّا وَّ لَا نَفۡعًا وَّ لَا یَمۡلِکُوۡنَ مَوۡتًا وَّ لَا حَیٰوۃً وَّ لَا نُشُوۡرًا ④

---

[a]1 : 1. [b]2 : 117; 10 : 69; 17 : 112; 18 : 5; 19 : 89; 21 : 27; 39 : 5; 43 : 82. [c]17 : 57; 18 : 16; 21 : 25. [d]7 : 192; 16 : 21.

2062. The word *Tabāraka* means, highly exalted; far removed from every defect, impurity, imperfection, and everything derogatory; possessing abundant good (6:156 & 21:51). The Qur'ān possesses all the qualities and attributes implicit in this word. It is not only completely free from every defect and imperfection but possesses all the conceivably excellent qualities that the last Divine Law for the whole of mankind should possess, and it possesses them in full measure.

2063. *Furqān* means something which differentiates between what is true and what is false; an argument, a proof or evidence, because an argument or a proof serves to discriminate between right and wrong. It also signifies morning or dawn, because dawn distinguishes the day from the night. The Qur'ān is *Furqān par excellence*. Among the multifarious and multitudinous beauties and excellences that distinguish it from other revealed Books and which establish its superiority over them all, two stand out most marked, *viz.*, (*i*) it makes no statement or claim in support of which it does not give sound and solid proofs and arguments, and (*ii*) it makes truth so distinguishable from falsehood as day is from night.

2064. The clause, 'and has determined its proper measure,' signifies that there is a limit to the powers and functions or development of everything which it cannot defy or go beyond. These limitations point to one law that operates in the whole universe and hence to one Designer, Creator and Controller—a Creator Whose powers are limitless but Who has imposed limits on all things.

2065. Everything has to pass through three stages of development: (*a*) The stage of lifelessness; (*b*) of potential life, when a thing is endowed with the attributes and powers of growth; and (*c*) of actual life. God, the Creator of all life, possesses complete and undisputed control over all these stages.

5. And those who disbelieve say, 'It is naught but a lie which he has forged, [a]and other people have helped him with it.' Indeed,[2066] they have perpetrated a *great* injustice and a *great* falsehood.

وَقَالَ الَّذِينَ كَفَرُوا إِنْ هٰذَا إِلَّا إِفْكٌ افْتَرٰىهُ وَأَعَانَهُ عَلَيْهِ قَوْمٌ اٰخَرُونَ ۚ فَقَدْ جَاءُوا ظُلْمًا وَزُورًا ۝٥

6. And they say, [b]'*These are* fables of the ancient; *and* he has got them written down, and they are read out to him morning and evening.'

وَقَالُوا أَسَاطِيرُ الْأَوَّلِينَ اكْتَتَبَهَا فَهِيَ تُمْلٰى عَلَيْهِ بُكْرَةً وَأَصِيلًا ۝٦

7. Say, [c]'He, Who knows every secret of the heavens and the earth, has revealed it. Verily, He is Most Forgiving, Merciful.'

قُلْ أَنْزَلَهُ الَّذِي يَعْلَمُ السِّرَّ فِي السَّمٰوٰتِ وَالْأَرْضِ ۗ إِنَّهُ كَانَ غَفُورًا رَحِيمًا ۝٧

8. And they say, 'What *sort of* a Messenger[2066A] is this that he eats food, and walks in the streets? [d]Why has not an angel been sent down to him that he might be a warner with him?

وَقَالُوا مَالِ هٰذَا الرَّسُولِ يَأْكُلُ الطَّعَامَ وَيَمْشِي فِي الْأَسْوَاقِ ۗ لَوْلَا أُنْزِلَ إِلَيْهِ مَلَكٌ فَيَكُونَ مَعَهُ نَذِيرًا ۝٨

9. 'Or [e]a treasure should have been sent down to him, or he should have had a garden to eat therefrom.' And the wrongdoers say, [f]'You follow but a man bewitched.'

أَوْ يُلْقٰى إِلَيْهِ كَنْزٌ أَوْ تَكُونُ لَهُ جَنَّةٌ يَأْكُلُ مِنْهَا ۗ وَقَالَ الظّٰلِمُونَ إِنْ تَتَّبِعُونَ إِلَّا رَجُلًا مَسْحُورًا ۝٩

[a]16 : 104. [b]8 : 32 ; 16 : 25 ; 68 : 16 ; 83 : 14. [c]6 : 4 ; 11 : 6 ; 67 : 14. [d]11 : 13; 15 : 8; 17 : 93. [e]11 : 13; 17 : 94. [f]17 : 48.

2066. This and the next verse refer to two charges of disbelievers against the Holy Prophet and answer them. The answer to the first charge that the Holy Prophet has forged a lie is that it was unjust on their part to prefer such a charge. The Holy Prophet had lived among them a life-time before and they themselves had borne unanimous testimony to his integrity and truthfulness. How could they now charge him with forgery? The answer to the second charge is that whosoever the Holy Prophet's so-called helpers were, they must have held some beliefs and doctrines, but the Qur'ān refutes and demolishes all false beliefs and abrogates and improves upon others. How could any people be supposed to help him to produce a Book which had laid the axe at the root of those very beliefs and doctrines which they held so dear?

2066A. What is the matter with this Messenger?

10. "See how they coin similitudes for thee![2067] Thus they have gone astray and cannot find a way.

انْظُرْ كَيْفَ ضَرَبُوْا لَكَ الْاَمْثَالَ فَضَلُّوْا فَلَا يَسْتَطِيْعُوْنَ سَبِيْلًا ۝

R. 2.   11. Blessed is He Who, if He please, will assign to thee better than all that—[b]gardens through which streams flow—and will *also* assign to thee palaces.[2068]

تَبٰرَكَ الَّذِيْٓ اِنْ شَاءَ جَعَلَ لَكَ خَيْرًا مِّنْ ذٰلِكَ جَنّٰتٍ تَجْرِيْ مِنْ تَحْتِهَا الْاَنْهٰرُ ۙ وَيَجْعَلْ لَّكَ قُصُوْرًا ۝

12. Nay, they deny the Hour, and for those who deny the Hour, We have prepared a blazing fire.[2069]

بَلْ كَذَّبُوْا بِالسَّاعَةِ ۫ وَاَعْتَدْنَا لِمَنْ كَذَّبَ بِالسَّاعَةِ سَعِيْرًا ۝

13. When it sees them from a place far-off, [c]they will hear its raging and roaring.[2070]

اِذَا رَاَتْهُمْ مِّنْ مَّكَانٍۭ بَعِيْدٍ سَمِعُوْا لَهَا تَغَيُّظًا وَّزَفِيْرًا ۝

14. And when they are thrown into a narrow place thereof, [d]chained together, they will pray there for destruction.

وَاِذَآ اُلْقُوْا مِنْهَا مَكَانًا ضَيِّقًا مُّقَرَّنِيْنَ دَعَوْا هُنَالِكَ ثُبُوْرًا ۝

15. 'Pray not this day for one destruction, but pray for many destructions.'

لَا تَدْعُوا الْيَوْمَ ثُبُوْرًا وَّاحِدًا وَّادْعُوْا ثُبُوْرًا كَثِيْرًا ۝

---

[a]17 : 49.   [b]17 : 92.   [c]11 : 107;   21 : 101;   67 : 8.   [d]14 : 50.

2067. The disbelievers have a very poor concept of the real values of life. They have set up criteria of their own devising to test the truth of Divine Messengers, with the result that instead of finding the right path they continue to grope in the darkness of doubt and disbelief.

2068. The verse signifies that the disbelievers' idea of what a Divine Prophet should be like is far removed from reality and betrays their ignorance of the very object and purpose for which Prophets are raised. Prophets are raised, it purports to say, to lead men out of the darkness of doubt and disbelief into the light of certainty and spiritual bliss and not to amass, and roll and revel in, wealth. But although the self-devised criterion of disbelievers, namely, that the Holy Prophet must possess wealth, rank, gardens and palaces, has no weight or substance, yet in order to bring home to them the falsity of their position God will give him and his followers greater wealth and bigger and better gardens and palaces than those of the disbelievers' demand. And He really gave the Holy Prophet's followers the palaces and gardens of the Iranian and Byzantine Emperors.

2069. Whereas believers are decreed to achieve eminence and glory, a dreadful punishment (*al-Sā'ah*) is in store for disbelievers. Their punishment is impending; nay it is at their very doors; but they do not see it and therefore refuse to believe it.

2070. This and the next verse mean that the punishment will be overwhelming and all-embracing and in order to add to the bitterness of the disbelievers' pain and sense of humiliation and to make it complete and thorough, all their organs will be made to feel it— the organs of sight and hearing—and being in great distress they would wish that death should make a speedy end of them.

16. Say, 'Is that better or the Garden of Eternity, which is [a]promised to the righteous? It will be their reward and *ultimate* resort.'

قُلْ أَذٰلِكَ خَيْرٌ أَمْ جَنَّةُ الْخُلْدِ الَّتِي وُعِدَ الْمُتَّقُونَ ۚ كَانَتْ لَهُمْ جَزَآءً وَّمَصِيرًا ﴿١٦﴾

17. [b]They will have therein whatsoever they desire,[2071] abiding *therein* for ever. It is a promise binding upon thy Lord, *and* to be *always* prayed for *from Him*.

لَهُمْ فِيهَا مَا يَشَآءُونَ خٰلِدِينَ ۚ كَانَ عَلٰى رَبِّكَ وَعْدًا مَّسْئُولًا ﴿١٧﴾

18. [c]On the day when He will assemble them and those whom they worship instead of Allāh, He will ask *the latter*, 'Was it you that led astray these My servants, or did they *themselves* stray away from the path?'

وَيَوْمَ يَحْشُرُهُمْ وَمَا يَعْبُدُونَ مِنْ دُونِ اللّٰهِ فَيَقُولُ ءَأَنْتُمْ أَضْلَلْتُمْ عِبَادِي هٰٓؤُلَآءِ أَمْ هُمْ ضَلُّوا السَّبِيلَ ﴿١٨﴾

19. [d]They will say, 'Holy art Thou! It was not *right* for us to take protectors other than Thee; but Thou didst bestow on them and their fathers the good things *of this life* until they forgot *Thy* admonition and became a ruined people.'

قَالُوا سُبْحٰنَكَ مَا كَانَ يَنْبَغِي لَنَآ أَنْ نَّتَّخِذَ مِنْ دُونِكَ مِنْ أَوْلِيَآءَ وَلٰكِنْ مَّتَّعْتَهُمْ وَاٰبَآءَهُمْ حَتّٰى نَسُوا الذِّكْرَ ۚ وَكَانُوا قَوْمًا بُورًا ﴿١٩﴾

20. *Then We shall say to their worshippers*, 'They have given you the lie regarding what you said, so you cannot avert *the punishment*, neither can you *get* help. And whosoever among you does wrong, We shall make him taste a grievous punishment.

فَقَدْ كَذَّبُوكُمْ بِمَا تَقُولُونَ ۙ فَمَا تَسْتَطِيعُونَ صَرْفًا وَّلَا نَصْرًا ۚ وَمَنْ يَّظْلِمْ مِّنْكُمْ نُذِقْهُ عَذَابًا كَبِيرًا ﴿٢٠﴾

21. And We did not send any Messengers before thee but surely [e]they ate food and walked in the streets. And We make some of you a trial for others *to see* whether you are steadfast. And thy Lord is All-Seeing.

وَمَآ أَرْسَلْنَا قَبْلَكَ مِنَ الْمُرْسَلِينَ إِلَّآ إِنَّهُمْ لَيَأْكُلُونَ الطَّعَامَ وَيَمْشُونَ فِي الْأَسْوَاقِ ۗ وَجَعَلْنَا بَعْضَكُمْ لِبَعْضٍ فِتْنَةً ۗ أَتَصْبِرُونَ ۚ وَكَانَ رَبُّكَ بَصِيرًا ﴿٢١﴾ ع

[a]21 : 104; 41 : 31. [b]41 : 32. [c]10 : 29; 15 : 26; 34 : 41. [d]34 : 42. [e]21 : 9.

2071. The desires of believers in the next life will become identified with the will of God. So naturally all their desires will be satisfied.

PART XIX

الجزء ١٩

R.3. 22. [a]And those, who do not expect a meeting with Us, say, 'Why are not angels sent down to us?[2071A] Or, why do we not see our Lord?' Surely, they are too proud of themselves and have gone far in rebellion.

وَقَالَ الَّذِيْنَ لَا يَرْجُوْنَ لِقَآءَنَا لَوْلَآ أُنْزِلَ عَلَيْنَا الْمَلٰٓئِكَةُ أَوْ نَرٰى رَبَّنَا ۗ لَقَدِ اسْتَكْبَرُوْا فِيْٓ أَنْفُسِهِمْ وَعَتَوْ عُتُوًّا كَبِيْرًا ﴿٢٢﴾

23. On the day [b]when they see the angels—there will be no good tidings on that day for the guilty; and they will cry *in distress*, 'Would that there were a strong barrier!'[2072]

يَوْمَ يَرَوْنَ الْمَلٰٓئِكَةَ لَا بُشْرٰى يَوْمَئِذٍ لِّلْمُجْرِمِيْنَ وَيَقُوْلُوْنَ حِجْرًا مَّحْجُوْرًا ﴿٢٣﴾

24. And We shall turn to the work they did and We shall scatter it into particles of dust.[2073]

وَقَدِمْنَآ إِلٰى مَا عَمِلُوْا مِنْ عَمَلٍ فَجَعَلْنٰهُ هَبَآءً مَّنْثُوْرًا ﴿٢٤﴾

25. The inmates of Heaven on that day will be better off as regards *their* abode, and better off in respect of *their* place of repose.

أَصْحٰبُ الْجَنَّةِ يَوْمَئِذٍ خَيْرٌ مُّسْتَقَرًّا وَّأَحْسَنُ مَقِيْلًا ﴿٢٥﴾

26. And on that day [c]when the heaven shall burst asunder with the clouds *overhanging it*, and the angels shall be sent down in large numbers—

وَيَوْمَ تَشَقَّقُ السَّمَآءُ بِالْغَمَامِ وَنُزِّلَ الْمَلٰٓئِكَةُ تَنْزِيْلًا ﴿٢٦﴾

27. [d]The true Kingdom on that day[2074] shall belong to the Gracious *God;* and it shall be a hard day for the disbelievers.

اَلْمُلْكُ يَوْمَئِذِنِ الْحَقُّ لِلرَّحْمٰنِ ۗ وَكَانَ يَوْمًا عَلَى الْكٰفِرِيْنَ عَسِيْرًا ﴿٢٧﴾

[a]10 : 8,12. [b]6 : 9, 159. [c]2 : 211. [d]6 : 74; 22 : 57.

2071A. See 252.

2072. An Arab would use the words *Hijran Maḥjūran* when he is faced with a thing he does not like, meaning 'let it remain away from me so that I should not suffer from it' (Lane & Mufradāt). In reply to their first insolent demand mentioned in the preceding verse, disbelievers are told that angels will certainly descend, but they will be angels of punishment and when they come, the disbelievers will hate the very sight of them and will pray that a strong barrier might be set up between them and the angels.

2073. And their second demand will be met by all their works being totally rendered null and void and by their being destroyed and scattered into thin air like particles of dust.

2074. The day of Badr was indeed a most distressful day for disbelievers. It was on that day that the foundations of Islām were firmly laid and the Quraish had realized to their bitter mortification and discomfiture that it had come to stay.

28. On that day the wrongdoer will bite his hands *and* will say, [a]'O, would that I had taken a way along with the Messenger !

وَيَوْمَ يَعَضُّ الظَّالِمُ عَلٰى يَدَيْهِ يَقُوْلُ يٰلَيْتَنِي اتَّخَذْتُ مَعَ الرَّسُوْلِ سَبِيْلًا ﴿٢٨﴾

29. 'O, woe is me ! would that I had never taken such a one for a friend !

يٰوَيْلَتٰى لَيْتَنِيْ لَمْ اَتَّخِذْ فُلَانًا خَلِيْلًا ﴿٢٩﴾

30. 'He led me astray from the Reminder after it had come to me.' And Satan always deserts man *in the hour of need.*

لَقَدْ اَضَلَّنِيْ عَنِ الذِّكْرِ بَعْدَ اِذْ جَآءَنِيْ ؕ وَكَانَ الشَّيْطٰنُ لِلْاِنْسَانِ خَذُوْلًا ﴿٣٠﴾

31. And the Messenger will say, 'O my Lord, my people indeed treated this Qur'ān *as a thing* to be discarded.'[2075]

وَقَالَ الرَّسُوْلُ يٰرَبِّ اِنَّ قَوْمِي اتَّخَذُوْا هٰذَا الْقُرْاٰنَ مَهْجُوْرًا ﴿٣١﴾

32. [b]Thus did We make for every Prophet an enemy from among the sinners; and sufficient is thy Lord as a Guide and a Helper.

وَكَذٰلِكَ جَعَلْنَا لِكُلِّ نَبِيٍّ عَدُوًّا مِّنَ الْمُجْرِمِيْنَ ؕ وَكَفٰى بِرَبِّكَ هَادِيًا وَّنَصِيْرًا ﴿٣٢﴾

33. [c]And those who disbelieve say, 'Why was not the Qur'ān revealed to him all at once?' *We have revealed it* in this manner [d]that We may strengthen thy heart therewith. And We have arranged it in the best form.[2076]

وَقَالَ الَّذِيْنَ كَفَرُوْا لَوْلَا نُزِّلَ عَلَيْهِ الْقُرْاٰنُ جُمْلَةً وَّاحِدَةً ۚ كَذٰلِكَ ۚ لِنُثَبِّتَ بِهٖ فُؤَادَكَ وَرَتَّلْنٰهُ تَرْتِيْلًا ﴿٣٣﴾

[a]33 : 67; 67 : 11. [b]6 : 113. [c]17 : 107; 73 : 5. [d]11 : 121.

2075. Quite appropriately the verse may apply to those so-called Muslims who have discarded the Qur'ān and have thrown it behind their backs. Perhaps never during the last 14 centuries the Qur'ān was so much neglected and ignored by the Muslims as it is today. There is a saying of the Holy Prophet to the effect : 'A time will come upon my people when there will remain nothing of Islām but its name and of the Qur'ān but its words' (Baihaquī, *Shu'ab al-Īmān*). The present indeed is that time.

2076. The Qur'ān was revealed piecemeal and at intervals. This was intended to serve some very useful purposes : (i) The interval between the revelation of different passages afforded the believers an opportunity to witness fulfilment of some of the prophecies contained in the passages already revealed and thus their faith became strengthened and fortified. Further, it was intended to answer the objections raised by disbelievers during the interval. (ii) When Muslims needed guidance on a particular occasion to meet a particular need, necessary and relevant verses were revealed. The revelation of the Qur'ān was spread over a period of 23 years in order to enable the Companions of the Holy Prophet to remember, learn and assimilate it. If it had been revealed all at once and in the form of one complete book, the disbelievers could have said that the Holy Prophet had got it prepared from

34. And they do not come to thee with an objection but We provide thee with the truth and an excellent explanation.[2077]

وَلَا يَأْتُونَكَ بِمَثَلٍ إِلَّا جِئْنَٰكَ بِالْحَقِّ وَأَحْسَنَ تَفْسِيرًا ﴿٣٤﴾

35. [a]Those who will be gathered unto Hell on their faces[2077A]—[b]they will be the worst in plight and most astray from the *right* path.

الَّذِينَ يُحْشَرُونَ عَلَىٰ وُجُوهِهِمْ إِلَىٰ جَهَنَّمَ أُولَٰٓئِكَ شَرٌّ مَّكَانًا وَأَضَلُّ سَبِيلًا ﴿٣٥﴾

R. 4 36. We gave Moses the Book, and [c]appointed with him his brother Aaron as *his* assistant.

وَلَقَدْ ءَاتَيْنَا مُوسَى الْكِتَٰبَ وَجَعَلْنَا مَعَهُۥٓ أَخَاهُ هَٰرُونَ وَزِيرًا ﴿٣٦﴾

37. And We said *to them*, [d]'Go both of you to the people who have rejected Our Signs;' then We destroyed them utterly.

فَقُلْنَا اذْهَبَآ إِلَى الْقَوْمِ الَّذِينَ كَذَّبُوا بِـَٔايَٰتِنَا فَدَمَّرْنَٰهُمْ تَدْمِيرًا ﴿٣٧﴾

38. And the people of Noah, when they rejected the Messengers, We drowned them, and We made them a Sign for mankind. [e]And We have prepared a painful punishment for the wrongdoers.

وَقَوْمَ نُوحٍ لَّمَّا كَذَّبُوا الرُّسُلَ أَغْرَقْنَٰهُمْ وَجَعَلْنَٰهُمْ لِلنَّاسِ ءَايَةً ۖ وَأَعْتَدْنَا لِلظَّٰلِمِينَ عَذَابًا أَلِيمًا ﴿٣٨﴾

[a]17 : 98. [b]5 : 61. [c]20 : 30-33; 26 : 14; 28 : 35. [d]20 : 44; 28 : 35-36. [e]18 : 30;

somebody. Thus its gradual revelation at different times, on different occasions and under vastly different conditions and circumstances, answered this possible objection. The Qur'ān was revealed in parts in order that it could be easily committed to memory. The piecemeal revelation of the Qur'ān also fulfilled the following biblical prophecy :

> Whom shall he teach knowledge and whom shall he make to understand the message ? Them that are weaned from the milk; and drawn from the breast? For it is precept upon precept, precept upon precept, line upon line, line upon line ; here a little and there a little for, with strange lips and another tongue will he speak to this people (Isa. 28 : 9-10).

2077. It is one of the distinctive features of the Qur'ān in which it stands unique among all revealed Books that whenever it makes a claim about the existence of God, the truth of Islām, or about its own Divine origin, or any other related religious subject, it gives the required arguments to prove and substantiate the claim and looks to no other agency for aid or assistance.

2077A. Will be dragged into Hell along with their leaders; the word *Wujūh* also means, "leaders."

39. And *We destroyed* ^a'Ād *and* Thamūd, and the People of the Well,²⁰⁷⁸ and many a generation between them,

وَعَادًا وَّثَمُوْدَا۟ وَاَصْحٰبَ الرَّسِّ وَقُرُوْنًا بَيْنَ ذٰلِكَ كَثِيْرًا ۝

40. And to each one We set forth examples; and each one We utterly destroyed.

وَكُلًّا ضَرَبْنَا لَهُ الْاَمْثَالَ وَكُلًّا تَبَّرْنَا تَتْبِيْرًا ۝

41. And these *Meccans* must have visited ^bthe town²⁰⁷⁹ whereon was rained an evil rain. Have they not seen it? Nay, they expect not to be raised *after death*.

وَلَقَدْ اَتَوْا عَلَى الْقَرْيَةِ الَّتِيْ اُمْطِرَتْ مَطَرَ السَّوْءِ ۖ اَفَلَمْ يَكُوْنُوْا يَرَوْنَهَا ۚ بَلْ كَانُوْا لَا يَرْجُوْنَ نُشُوْرًا ۝

42. ^cAnd when they see thee, they only make a jest of thee, *and say*, 'What! is this he whom Allāh has sent as a Messenger?

وَاِذَا رَاَوْكَ اِنْ يَّتَّخِذُوْنَكَ اِلَّا هُزُوًا ۭ اَهٰذَا الَّذِيْ بَعَثَ اللّٰهُ رَسُوْلًا ۝

43. 'He indeed had well-nigh led us astray from our gods, had we not steadily adhered to them.' And they shall know, when they see the punishment, who is most astray from the *right* path.

اِنْ كَادَ لَيُضِلُّنَا عَنْ اٰلِهَتِنَا لَوْلَا اَنْ صَبَرْنَا عَلَيْهَا ۭ وَسَوْفَ يَعْلَمُوْنَ حِيْنَ يَرَوْنَ الْعَذَابَ مَنْ اَضَلُّ سَبِيْلًا ۝

44. ^dHast thou seen him who takes his own evil desire for his god? Canst thou be a guardian over him?

اَرَءَيْتَ مَنِ اتَّخَذَ اِلٰهَهٗ هَوٰىهُ ۭ اَفَاَنْتَ تَكُوْنُ عَلَيْهِ وَكِيْلًا ۝

45. Dost thou think that most of them hear or understand? ^eThey are like cattle²⁰⁸⁰—nay, they are worse *than cattle* in *their* behaviour.

اَمْ تَحْسَبُ اَنَّ اَكْثَرَهُمْ يَسْمَعُوْنَ اَوْ يَعْقِلُوْنَ ۭ اِنْ هُمْ اِلَّا كَالْاَنْعَامِ بَلْ هُمْ اَضَلُّ سَبِيْلًا ۝

---

^a9 : 70; 38 : 13; 50 : 13-15.   ^b7 : 85; 27 : 59.   ^c21 : 37.   ^d45 : 24.   ^e7 : 180.

2078. Some Commentators are of the view that *Rass* was a town in Yamāmah where one of the tribes of Thamūd resided. According to others, these people were so called because they threw their Prophet into a well. They were the remnants of Thamūd.

2079. Sodom, the town of Lot, which was situated on the way from Arabia to Syria.

2080. It is his own desires, fancies and pre-conceived ideas, more than anything else, that man generally adores and it is these that stand in the way of his accepting the truth. Intellectually man may have advanced far enough so as not to bow before stones and stars, but he has not outgrown the worship of his false ideals, prejudices and pre-conceived ideas. It is these idols that lie enthroned in his heart whose worship is condemned here. When instead of making use of his God-given faculties of intellect and hearing, which should help man to recognize and realize truth, he chooses to grope in darkness, he comes down to the level of cattle, even lower than that, because cattle are not given the gift of discretion and discrimination while man is.

R. 5. 46. Dost thou not see [a]how thy Lord lengthens the shade?[2081] And if He had pleased, He could have made it stationary. Then We make *the position of* the sun an indicator thereof.[2082]

أَلَمْ تَرَ إِلَىٰ رَبِّكَ كَيْفَ مَدَّ الظِّلَّ ۚ وَلَوْ شَاءَ لَجَعَلَهُ
سَاكِنًا ۚ ثُمَّ جَعَلْنَا الشَّمْسَ عَلَيْهِ دَلِيلًا ﴿٤٦﴾

47. Then We draw it in towards Ourselves, drawing in little by little.[2082A]

ثُمَّ قَبَضْنَاهُ إِلَيْنَا قَبْضًا يَسِيرًا ﴿٤٧﴾

48. [b]And He it is Who has made the night[2083] a covering for you, and *Who has made sleep* for rest, and *He* has made the day to rise up *and work.*

وَهُوَ الَّذِي جَعَلَ لَكُمُ اللَّيْلَ لِبَاسًا وَالنَّوْمَ سُبَاتًا
وَجَعَلَ النَّهَارَ نُشُورًا ﴿٤٨﴾

49. [c]And He it is Who sends the winds as glad tidings before His mercy, and We send down pure water from the clouds,

وَهُوَ الَّذِي أَرْسَلَ الرِّيَاحَ بُشْرًا بَيْنَ يَدَيْ رَحْمَتِهِ ۚ
وَأَنْزَلْنَا مِنَ السَّمَاءِ مَاءً طَهُورًا ﴿٤٩﴾

50. That We may thereby give life to a dead land, and give it for drink to Our creation—cattle and men in large numbers.

لِنُحْيِيَ بِهِ بَلْدَةً مَيْتًا وَنُسْقِيَهُ مِمَّا خَلَقْنَا أَنْعَامًا
وَأَنَاسِيَّ كَثِيرًا ﴿٥٠﴾

[a]16 : 49. [b]6 : 97; 78 : 11. [c]7 : 58; 15 : 23.

2081. The verse alludes in figurative language to the rise, progress and power of Islām and illustrates this fact by drawing attention to a phenomenon of nature. When the sun is behind an object, its shadow lengthens. Similarly, when God is at the back of a people, their power and influence increase. The verse implies that God is at the back of Islām and therefore its shadow would continue to expand and extend till it would reach the ends of the earth, and nations of the world will seek and find solace and comfort under it. "The sun," in the verse symbolises Islām or the Holy Prophet.

2082. The position of the sun determines the size of the shade.

2082A. The verse refers to the decline of Islām after it had reached its zenith. While 'shade' in the preceding verse symbolized power and influence, its 'drawing in' in the present verse signifies decline and decay.

2083. 'Night' in the verse represents the period of spiritual darkness before the advent of a Divine Reformer; and 'day' symbolizes spiritual dawn when a Divine Reformer has already made his appearance.

51. And We have expounded the *Qur'ān* to them in diverse ways that they may take heed, but most men would reject everything but disbelief.

وَلَقَدْ صَرَّفْنٰهُ بَيْنَهُمْ لِيَذَّكَّرُوْا ۖ فَاَبٰۤى اَكْثَرُ النَّاسِ اِلَّا كُفُوْرًا ﴿۵۱﴾

52. If We had pleased, We could have surely raised a Warner in every city;

وَلَوْ شِئْنَا لَبَعَثْنَا فِيْ كُلِّ قَرْيَةٍ نَّذِيْرًا ۖ ﴿۵۲﴾

53. So obey not the disbelievers and strive against them by means of *the Qur'ān with* a mighty striving.[2084]

فَلَا تُطِعِ الْكٰفِرِيْنَ وَجَاهِدْهُمْ بِهٖ جِهَادًا كَبِيْرًا ﴿۵۳﴾

54. [a]And He it is Who has caused the two seas to flow, this palatable *and* sweet, and that salt *and* bitter; and between them He has placed a barrier and an insurmountable partition.[2085]

وَهُوَ الَّذِيْ مَرَجَ الْبَحْرَيْنِ هٰذَا عَذْبٌ فُرَاتٌ وَّ هٰذَا مِلْحٌ اُجَاجٌ ۚ وَجَعَلَ بَيْنَهُمَا بَرْزَخًا وَّحِجْرًا مَّحْجُوْرًا ﴿۵۴﴾

55. [b]And He it is Who has created man from water, and has made for him kindred by descent and kindred by marriage; and thy Lord is All-Powerful.

وَهُوَ الَّذِيْ خَلَقَ مِنَ الْمَآءِ بَشَرًا فَجَعَلَهٗ نَسَبًا وَّصِهْرًا ۭ وَكَانَ رَبُّكَ قَدِيْرًا ﴿۵۵﴾

[a]35 : 13; 55 : 20,21. [b]32 : 9.

2084. The great and real *Jihād*, according to this verse, is to preach the Message of the Qur'ān. Thus to strive for the propagation of Islām and the dissemination and diffusion of its teachings is the *Jihād* which the Muslims are enjoined always to carry on with unabated zeal. It is this *Jihād* to which the Holy Prophet referred when, on returning from an expedition, he is reported to have said: "We have returned from the smaller *Jihād* to the greater *Jihād* (Radd al-Muḥtār). See also 1957 and 1958.

2085. Taking 'two waters' in the verse to represent the true religion and the false, the verse signifies that both Islām, the true religion, and other corrupted Faiths will continue to exist side by side, the former yielding sweet fruit and slaking the thirst of the spiritual wayfarers and the latter barren and bitter, incapable of producing any good result. The 'two waters' may also signify the water of the sea and that of the river. The former is saltish and bitter to taste while the latter is drinkable and sweet. When the sweet water of the river flows into the sea and becomes mixed with its saltish water, it also becomes bitter. As long as these two waters keep themselves separate, they have different tastes. Similarly, when the teaching of a true religion becomes mixed up with the teachings of false religions, it loses its sweetness and usefulness. But God has so ordained that in spite of its close proximity to false religions, Islām will never lose its sweet taste as God has taken upon Himself to protect and guard it (15 : 10). There lies an unbridgeable barrier between the two which keeps them apart.

56. [a]And they worship beside Allāh that which can neither benefit them nor harm them. And the disbeliever is ever opposed to *the designs of* his Lord.

وَيَعْبُدُوْنَ مِنْ دُوْنِ اللّٰهِ مَا لَا يَنْفَعُهُمْ وَلَا
يَضُرُّهُمْ ۗ وَكَانَ الْكَافِرُ عَلٰى رَبِّهٖ ظَهِيْرًا ﴿٥٦﴾

57. [b]And We have not sent thee but as a bearer of glad tidings and a Warner.

وَمَآ اَرْسَلْنٰكَ اِلَّا مُبَشِّرًا وَّنَذِيْرًا ﴿٥٧﴾

58. [c]Say, 'I ask of you no recompense for it, save that whoso chooses may take a way *that leads* to his Lord.'[2086]

قُلْ مَآ اَسْـَٔلُكُمْ عَلَيْهِ مِنْ اَجْرٍ اِلَّا مَنْ شَآءَ اَنْ
يَّتَّخِذَ اِلٰى رَبِّهٖ سَبِيْلًا ﴿٥٨﴾

59. [d]And trust thou in the *One, Who is* Ever-Living *and is the Source of all life, and* Who dies not, and glorify *Him* with His praise. And sufficient is He as the Knower of the sins of his servants,

وَتَوَكَّلْ عَلَى الْحَيِّ الَّذِيْ لَا يَمُوْتُ وَسَبِّحْ بِحَمْدِهٖ ۗ
وَكَفٰى بِهٖ بِذُنُوْبِ عِبَادِهٖ خَبِيْرًا ﴿٥٩﴾

60. [e]He Who created the heavens and the earth and all that is between them in six periods, then He settled Himself firmly on the Throne.—The Gracious *God!* Ask thou then concerning Him one who knows.[2087]

اِلَّذِيْ خَلَقَ السَّمٰوٰتِ وَالْاَرْضَ وَمَا بَيْنَهُمَا فِيْ سِتَّةِ
اَيَّامٍ ثُمَّ اسْتَوٰى عَلَى الْعَرْشِ ۚ اَلرَّحْمٰنُ فَسْـَٔلْ بِهٖ
خَبِيْرًا ﴿٦٠﴾

61. And when it is said to them, 'Submit to the Gracious *God*,' they say, 'And who is the Gracious *God?* Shall we submit to whatever thou biddest us ?' And it increases their aversion.

وَاِذَا قِيْلَ لَهُمُ اسْجُدُوْا لِلرَّحْمٰنِ قَالُوْا وَمَا الرَّحْمٰنُ ۗ
اَنَسْجُدُ لِمَا تَاْمُرُنَا وَزَادَهُمْ نُفُوْرًا ﴿٦١﴾ السجدة ع

[a]6 : 72; 10 : 107; 21 : 67; 22 : 13. [b]2 : 120; 5 : 20; 11 : 3; 35 : 25. [c]38 : 87; 42 : 24. [d]26 : 218; 27 : 80; 33 : 49. [e]7 : 55; 11 : 8; 32 : 5; 57 : 5.

2086. According to this verse Islām clearly forbids the use of force for the propagation of its teaching.

2087. (1) God; (2) The Holy Prophet.

R. 6 62. Blessed is He [a]Who has made in the heaven mansions *of the stars* and has placed therein a Lamp *producing light* and a moon that reflects light.[2087A]

تَبٰرَكَ الَّذِيْ جَعَلَ فِي السَّمَآءِ بُرُوْجًا وَّجَعَلَ فِيْهَا سِرٰجًا وَّقَمَرًا مُّنِيْرًا ﴿۶۲﴾

63. [b]And He it is Who has made the night and the day,[2088] each following the other, for *the benefit of* him who desires to remember, or desires to be grateful.

وَهُوَ الَّذِيْ جَعَلَ الَّيْلَ وَالنَّهَارَ خِلْفَةً لِّمَنْ اَرَادَ اَنْ يَّذَّكَّرَ اَوْ اَرَادَ شُكُوْرًا ﴿۶۳﴾

64. And the *true* servants of the Gracious *God* are [c]those who walk on the earth humbly and [d]when the ignorant address them, they *avoid them gracefully by* saying, 'Peace!'[2089]

وَعِبَادُ الرَّحْمٰنِ الَّذِيْنَ يَمْشُوْنَ عَلَى الْاَرْضِ هَوْنًا وَّاِذَا خَاطَبَهُمُ الْجٰهِلُوْنَ قَالُوْا سَلٰمًا ﴿۶۴﴾

65. [e]And who spend the night in prostration and standing before their Lord,

وَالَّذِيْنَ يَبِيْتُوْنَ لِرَبِّهِمْ سُجَّدًا وَّقِيَامًا ﴿۶۵﴾

66. And who say, 'Our Lord, avert from us the punishment of Hell; for the punishment thereof is a most vehement torment,

وَالَّذِيْنَ يَقُوْلُوْنَ رَبَّنَا اصْرِفْ عَنَّا عَذَابَ جَهَنَّمَ اِنَّ عَذَابَهَا كَانَ غَرَامًا ﴿۶۶﴾

67. 'It is indeed evil as a place of rest and as an abode.'

اِنَّهَا سَآءَتْ مُسْتَقَرًّا وَّمُقَامًا ﴿۶۷﴾

68. And those who, when they spend, [f]are neither extravagant nor niggardly but *adopt* a moderate *position* in the middle;

وَالَّذِيْنَ اِذَآ اَنْفَقُوْا لَمْ يُسْرِفُوْا وَلَمْ يَقْتُرُوْا وَكَانَ بَيْنَ ذٰلِكَ قَوَامًا ﴿۶۸﴾

[a]15 : 17; 85 : 2. [b]36 : 38-41. [c]17 : 38; 31 : 19. [d]28 : 56. [e]41 : 39; 73 : 21. [f]7 : 32; 17 : 28.

2087A. By alluding to the creation of the heavens, and the sun, the moon and the stars that embellish and beautify them, the verse draws attention to the spiritual heaven which has its own sun, moon and stars—the Holy Prophet, the Promised Messiah and the Companions of the Holy Prophet about whom he is reported to have said: 'My Companions are like so many stars, whomsoever of them you will follow, you will get right guidance' (Razīn).

2088. Just as in the physical world day follows night, similarly in the spiritual realm when darkness enshrouds the world, God raises a Reformer to give light to it.

2089. With this verse begins a brief description of the great moral revolution which that Sun of the spiritual firmament—the Holy Prophet—brought about among his people.

69. And those who call not on any other god along with Allāh, [a]nor slay a person whose slaying Allāh has forbidden except for a just cause, nor commit adultery[2090]—and he who does that shall meet the punishment of *his* sin;

وَالَّذِيْنَ لَا يَدْعُوْنَ مَعَ اللّٰهِ اِلٰهًا اٰخَرَ وَلَا يَقْتُلُوْنَ النَّفْسَ الَّتِيْ حَرَّمَ اللّٰهُ اِلَّا بِالْحَقِّ وَلَا يَزْنُوْنَ ۚ وَمَنْ يَّفْعَلْ ذٰلِكَ يَلْقَ اَثَامًا ﴿۶۹﴾

70. [b]Doubled for him shall be the punishment on the Day of Resurrection, and he will abide therein disgraced—

يُّضٰعَفْ لَهُ الْعَذَابُ يَوْمَ الْقِيٰمَةِ وَيَخْلُدْ فِيْهٖ مُهَانًا ﴿۷۰﴾

71. Except those who repent,[2091] and [c]believe and do righteous deeds; for as to these, Allāh will convert their evil deeds into good ones, and Allāh is Most Forgiving, Merciful.

اِلَّا مَنْ تَابَ وَاٰمَنَ وَعَمِلَ عَمَلًا صَالِحًا فَاُولٰٓئِكَ يُبَدِّلُ اللّٰهُ سَيِّاٰتِهِمْ حَسَنٰتٍ ۚ وَكَانَ اللّٰهُ غَفُوْرًا رَّحِيْمًا ﴿۷۱﴾

72. [d]And those who repent and do righteous deeds, indeed turn to Allāh with *true* repentance;

وَمَنْ تَابَ وَعَمِلَ صَالِحًا فَاِنَّهٗ يَتُوْبُ اِلَى اللّٰهِ مَتَابًا ﴿۷۲﴾

73. And those who bear not false witness,[2092] and [e]when they pass by anything vain, they pass by with dignity;

وَالَّذِيْنَ لَا يَشْهَدُوْنَ الزُّوْرَ ۙ وَاِذَا مَرُّوْا بِاللَّغْوِ مَرُّوْا كِرَامًا ﴿۷۳﴾

---

[a]6 : 152; 17 : 33,34. [b]4 : 15. [c]3 : 58; 6 : 49; 18 : 89; 19 : 61; 34 : 38. [d]5 : 40; 20 : 83; 28 : 68. [e]23 : 4; 28 : 56.

From being the sons of darkness they became the servants of the Gracious and Beneficent God. The various qualities of the righteous servants of the Gracious God, referred to in this and the following verses, are the opposites of the vices from which the people of the Holy Prophet particularly suffered.

2090. Idolatry, murder and adultery are the three basic sins and the fountain-heads of individual depravity and social and sexual immorality. The Qur'ān has reverted to these sins again and again.

2091. *Taubah* (repentance) signifies repenting sincerely, truly and honestly of past moral lapses with a firm resolve completely to shun all evil and to do good deeds, and making amends for all wrongs done to people. It consists in bringing about a complete change in one's life, turning one's back completely and thoroughly on one's past.

2092. *Zūr* means a lie; false witness; association of false gods with Allāh; a place where lies are told and people entertain themselves with vain or frivolous diversion ; the assemblies of polytheists, etc. (Lane).

74. And those who, when they are reminded of the Signs of their Lord, fall not down thereat deaf and blind;[2092A]

وَالَّذِيْنَ اِذَا ذُكِّرُوْا بِاٰيٰتِ رَبِّهِمْ لَمْ يَخِرُّوْا عَلَيْهَا
صُمًّا وَّعُمْيَانًا ﴿٧٤﴾

75. And those who say, 'Our Lord, grant us of our wives and children the delight of our eyes, and make us a model for the righteous.'

وَالَّذِيْنَ يَقُوْلُوْنَ رَبَّنَا هَبْ لَنَا مِنْ اَزْوَاجِنَا وَ
ذُرِّيّٰتِنَا قُرَّةَ اَعْيُنٍ وَّاجْعَلْنَا لِلْمُتَّقِيْنَ اِمَامًا ﴿٧٥﴾

76. It is such as will be rewarded with lofty [a]chambers *in Paradise*, because they were steadfast, and they will be received therein with greeting and peace,

اُولٰٓئِكَ يُجْزَوْنَ الْغُرْفَةَ بِمَا صَبَرُوْا وَيُلَقَّوْنَ فِيْهَا
تَحِيَّةً وَّسَلٰمًا ﴿٧٦﴾

77. Abiding therein. Excellent it is as a place of rest and as an abode.

خٰلِدِيْنَ فِيْهَا حَسُنَتْ مُسْتَقَرًّا وَّمُقَامًا ﴿٧٧﴾

78. Say *to the disbelievers*, 'But for your prayer *to Him* my Lord would not care for you[2093] *at all*. But *now that* you have rejected *His Message*, *His punishment* will cleave *to you*.'

قُلْ مَا يَعْبَؤُا بِكُمْ رَبِّيْ لَوْلَا دُعَآؤُكُمْ فَقَدْ
كَذَّبْتُمْ فَسَوْفَ يَكُوْنُ لِزَامًا ﴿٧٨﴾ ع

[a]34 : 38.

2092A. They listen to the Signs of God attentively and with their eyes open. Their belief is based on conviction and certainty and not on mere hearsay.

2093. *Mā A'ba'ubihi* means, I do not care for, mind, heed or regard, him or I do not hold him to be of any weight or worth; or I do not esteem him (Lane & Mufradāt).

CHAPTER 26

AL-SHU'ARĀ'

(*Revealed before Hijrah*)

Date of Revelation, Title and Context

A large majority of Muslim scholars regards this *Sūrah* as of Meccan origin. It is entitled Al-Shu'arā' (poets) in order to drive home to Muslims the supreme lesson that success comes to a people only when their profession and practice go together and that empty talk like that of the poets leads nowhere. From this *Sūrah* a departure has been made in the subject-matter of the preceding sixteen Chapters. From *Sūrah* Yūnus the Qur'ān had directed its address principally to the Jews and the Christians. With this Chapter the believers take their place; and the form, nature and scope of the address have been changed; therefore a change has also taken place in the *Muqaṭṭa'āt* placed at the head of the *Sūrah*. The preceding *Sūrah* had ended on the note that it would be a great mistake to suppose that God would allow the time-honoured system that had come into being through the great religions of the world to be destroyed. On the contrary, He had created man to demonstrate in his person His great attributes and in order also that he should respond to the Divine Call. If man does not fulfil the object of his creation, then there is no need or justification for him to exist and no need for God to feel any hesitancy in destroying him. In this *Sūrah* we are told that in his love and solicitude for humanity, the Holy Prophet felt grieved at this apprehended possibility and desired that man may be saved. The destruction of man also clearly does not seem to be in harmony with the Divine design which is that he should be vouchsafed the opportunity to discover, with his own will and endeavour, the way of nearness to God and then should try to attain it. But if he refuses to do so, he should suffer the consequences of his refusal. The *Sūrah* further says that if man had not been endowed with the discretion and the ability to make a choice, he would have become a mere machine and an automaton and would not have been the image of his Creator as he is considered to be. So he must act and conduct himself in harmony with Divine scheme without which he cannot attain true and real salvation.

Subject-Matter

At the outset the *Sūrah* makes the claim that the Qur'ān gives its own proofs and arguments and needs no extraneous help or support to substantiate and establish the truth of its claims and teachings and proceeds to say that when, for the fulfilment of human requirements and needs God has created pairs in all things in the physical world, it stands to reason that in the spiritual realm also He should have created their counterparts. Then quite appropriately the *Sūrah* gives the account of some Divine Messengers and opens this account with the story of Moses, who in pursuance of Divine command succeeded in taking the Israelites out of Egypt. To illustrate further that truth always triumphs in the long run and opposition to it comes to grief, the *Sūrah*, gives a brief account of Prophets Abraham, Noah, Hūd, Ṣāliḥ, Lot and Shu'aib. Abraham demonstrated to his people the folly and futility of idol-worship. His account is followed by that of Noah whose people rejected him on the ground that he sought to remove all social distinctions. He was followed by Hūd and Ṣāliḥ. Both these Divine Prophets tried hard to make their people realize that it was not material pomp and power but good morals and spiritual strength upon which really depended their life and prosperity but their peoples threw their preaching and warnings to the wind. The peoples of Lot and Shu'aib fared no better. The former indulged in an unnatural vice and the latter were dishonest in their commercial dealings. Towards the end the *Sūrah* reverts to the subject with which it had commenced, *viz.*, that the Qur'ān is the revealed Word of God and that it gives sound and solid arguments to prove this claim; and adds that the Prophets of yore had testified to its truth and that the learned men of Israel also are convinced in their heart of hearts that it is God's own revealed Word because it fulfils the prophecies which are contained in their Scriptures. The *Sūrah* invites disbelievers to ponder over the teachings of the Qur'ān and to see that if they could have been the work of satans or could the Holy Prophet himself have produced them. It further says that the teachings of the Qur'ān bear close resemblance to those of the earlier Scriptures, and satanic people evidently could have no access to their Divine Source. Satans descend only upon liars and sinners and upon those who forge lies and coin and copy falsehood. The poets derive inspiration from these votaries of falsehood and are in turn followed by men of low morals and of no fixed principles. They and their followers take delight in tall, meaningless talk, but do not act upon what they profess and preach. The *Sūrah* closes with enjoining the Holy Prophet to continue to preach the Unity and Oneness of God to his people and educate and train them for the promotion of the cause of Islām. He is further enjoined to trust in the Almighty and Merciful God under Whose protection and fostering care he passes his days, and Who will very soon end the state of dispersion of Muslims and will bring them together in a place where they will live in peace and prosperity and will worship the One True God in perfect safety and security.

سُوۡرَۃُ الشُّعَرَآءِ مَکِّیَّۃٌ

آیاتها ۲۲۸ (۲۶) رکوعاتها ۱۱

1. [a]In the name of Allāh, the Gracious, the Merciful.

بِسۡمِ اللّٰہِ الرَّحۡمٰنِ الرَّحِیۡمِ ﴿۱﴾

2. Ṭā Sīn Mīm.[2094]

طٰسٓمّٓ ﴿۲﴾

3. [b]These are verses of the Book that makes *things* clear.[2094A]

تِلۡکَ اٰیٰتُ الۡکِتٰبِ الۡمُبِیۡنِ ﴿۳﴾

4. [c]Haply thou wilt grieve thyself to death[2094B] because they believe not.

لَعَلَّکَ بَاخِعٌ نَّفۡسَکَ اَلَّا یَکُوۡنُوۡا مُؤۡمِنِیۡنَ ﴿۴﴾

5. If We please, We can send down to them a Sign from the heaven, so that their necks[2095] will bow down before it.

اِنۡ نَّشَاۡ نُنَزِّلۡ عَلَیۡہِمۡ مِّنَ السَّمَآءِ اٰیَۃً فَظَلَّتۡ اَعۡنَاقُہُمۡ لَہَا خٰضِعِیۡنَ ﴿۵﴾

6. [d]And there comes not to them a new[2096] Reminder from the Gracious *God*, but they turn away from it.

وَ مَا یَاۡتِیۡہِمۡ مِّنۡ ذِکۡرٍ مِّنَ الرَّحۡمٰنِ مُحۡدَثٍ اِلَّا کَانُوۡا عَنۡہُ مُعۡرِضِیۡنَ ﴿۶﴾

7. [e]They have, indeed, treated it as a lie but soon there will come to them the tidings of that at which they mocked.

فَقَدۡ کَذَّبُوۡا فَسَیَاۡتِیۡہِمۡ اَنۡۢبٰٓؤُا مَا کَانُوۡا بِہٖ یَسۡتَہۡزِءُوۡنَ ﴿۷﴾

---

[a]1 : 1. [b]12 : 2; 15 : 2; 27 : 2; 28 : 3. [c]18 : 7. [d]21 : 3, 43.
[e]6 : 35; 22 : 43; 35 : 26; 40 : 6.

2094. In the *Muqaṭṭa'āt* (abbreviated letters) *Ṭā Sīn Mīm*, *Ṭā* stands for *Ṭāhir* (Lord of Purity); *Sīn* for *Samī'* (All-Hearing) and *Mīm* for *Majīd* (Lord of Dignity), thus indicating that the *Sūrah* deals with the means to achieve purity of heart, acceptance of prayer and dignity. This and the next two Chapters form a special group known as the *Ṭā Sīn Mīm* group and all of them bear a very close resemblance to each other in their subject-matter. They were revealed about the same time at Mecca. As these *Sūrahs* deal particularly with the life-story of Moses in some detail, some Commentators have taken these abbreviated letters as standing for Mount Sinai and Moses—*Ṭā Sīn* standing for Ṭūr Sīnīn (Mount Sinai) and *Mīm* for Mūsā (Moses).

2094A. See 1356.

2094B. See 1664.

2095. The Holy Prophet's grief will not be in vain. If his people do not cease opposing him, they will be visited with the Sign of punishment which will humiliate and debase their leaders, *A'nāq* meaning leaders (Lane).

2096. The word, 'new' means, 'in a new form,' or 'with new details.' In fact, all Divine Laws are similar in their fundamentals and basic teachings. It is only in details that they differ. Or a new Law is revealed in a changed and improved form in order that it may suit the ideas, needs and requirements of the particular time in which it is revealed. Some Prophets come with a new Law, while others only serve the existing Law.

8. [a]See they not the earth, how many of every noble species have We caused to grow therein?

أَوَلَمْ يَرَوْا إِلَى الْأَرْضِ كَمْ أَنْبَتْنَا فِيهَا مِنْ كُلِّ زَوْجٍ كَرِيمٍ ﴿٨﴾

9. In that there is a Sign indeed; but most of these would not believe.

إِنَّ فِي ذَٰلِكَ لَآيَةً ۖ وَمَا كَانَ أَكْثَرُهُمْ مُؤْمِنِينَ ﴿٩﴾

10. And verily thy Lord—He is the Mighty, the Merciful.[2097]

وَإِنَّ رَبَّكَ لَهُوَ الْعَزِيزُ الرَّحِيمُ ﴿١٠﴾ ع

R. 2 11. [b]And *call to mind* when thy Lord called Moses, *and directed him:* 'Go to the wrongdoing people—

وَإِذْ نَادَىٰ رَبُّكَ مُوسَىٰ أَنِ ائْتِ الْقَوْمَ الظَّالِمِينَ ﴿١١﴾

12. 'The people of Pharaoh. Will they not fear *God?*'

قَوْمَ فِرْعَوْنَ ۚ أَلَا يَتَّقُونَ ﴿١٢﴾

13. He said, 'My Lord, [c]I fear that they will reject me;

قَالَ رَبِّ إِنِّي أَخَافُ أَنْ يُكَذِّبُونِ ﴿١٣﴾

14. 'And my breast is straitened[2098] [d]and my tongue is not fluent; so [e]send *word* to Aaron *also;*

وَيَضِيقُ صَدْرِي وَلَا يَنْطَلِقُ لِسَانِي فَأَرْسِلْ إِلَىٰ هَارُونَ ﴿١٤﴾

15. [f]'And they have a charge[2099] against me, so I fear that they will kill me.'

وَلَهُمْ عَلَيَّ ذَنْبٌ فَأَخَافُ أَنْ يَقْتُلُونِ ﴿١٥﴾

16. [g]*God* said, 'That shall not be, go both of you with Our Signs; We are with you hearing *your prayers.*'

قَالَ كَلَّا ۖ فَاذْهَبَا بِآيَاتِنَا ۖ إِنَّا مَعَكُمْ مُسْتَمِعُونَ ﴿١٦﴾

---

[a]36 : 34-37. [b]20 : 25; 79 : 17-18. [c]20 : 46; 28 : 35. [d]20 : 28. [e]26 : 14. [f]28 : 34. [g]28 : 36.

2097. The words, 'verily thy Lord—He is the Mighty, the Merciful,' imply that the circumstances of the Holy Prophet will resemble those of the Prophets mentioned in this *Sūrah*, but whereas the Mighty God had seized and destroyed the enemies of those Prophets, in the case of the Holy Prophet the Mighty God will not only manifest His might and power in giving victory to the Holy Prophet and in making his cause triumph and prosper, but will also show mercy to his people, inasmuch as only a small fraction of them will be destroyed while a great majority will receive Divine forgiveness and mercy and in the end will accept his Message.

2098. Moses seemed to feel that he was not quite equal to the great task with which he was being entrusted. The responsibilities of Prophethood are indeed very heavy. At the time of the first revelation the Holy Prophet himself felt overwhelmed with anxiety.

2099. The words show that the people of Pharaoh had charged Moses with the murder of an Egyptian. This incident is mentioned in Exod. 2 : 11-15 and also in the Qur'ān in 28 : 16-21, where it is stated that it was not intentional or deliberate murder. Moses was defending an Israelite whom an Egyptian was beating and in the scuffle the latter happened to be killed.

17. 'So go to Pharaoh and say, "We are the Messengers[2100] of the Lord of the worlds

فَأْتِيَا فِرْعَوْنَ فَقُوْلَآ إِنَّا رَسُوْلُ رَبِّ الْعٰلَمِيْنَ ﴿۱۷﴾

18. '*To tell thee* to send the Children of Israel with us."

أَنْ أَرْسِلْ مَعَنَا بَنِيْٓ إِسْرَآءِيْلَ ﴿۱۸﴾

19. *Pharaoh* said, '*O Moses*, did we not bring thee up among us as a child? And thou didst stay among us *many* years of thy life;

قَالَ أَلَمْ نُرَبِّكَ فِيْنَا وَلِيْدًا وَّلَبِثْتَ فِيْنَا مِنْ
عُمُرِكَ سِنِيْنَ ﴿۱۹﴾

20. 'And thou didst do that deed which thou didst, and thou art *one* of the ungrateful.'[2101]

وَفَعَلْتَ فَعْلَتَكَ الَّتِيْ فَعَلْتَ وَأَنْتَ مِنَ الْكٰفِرِيْنَ ﴿۲۰﴾

21. *Moses* said, 'I did it then *inadvertently*, and I was in a perplexed state of mind;[2102]

قَالَ فَعَلْتُهَآ إِذًا وَّأَنَا مِنَ الضَّآلِّيْنَ ﴿۲۱﴾

22. [a]'So I fled from you when I feared you; then my Lord granted me *right* judgment and made me *one* of the Messengers.[2103]

فَفَرَرْتُ مِنْكُمْ لَمَّا خِفْتُكُمْ فَوَهَبَ لِيْ رَبِّيْ حُكْمًا
وَّجَعَلَنِيْ مِنَ الْمُرْسَلِيْنَ ﴿۲۲﴾

23. 'And this favour *of bringing me up as a child* with which thou *now* tauntest me, *dost thou put forward*

وَتِلْكَ نِعْمَةٌ تَمُنُّهَا عَلَيَّ

---

[a]28 : 22.

2100. The word *Rasūl* in the verse is in the singular while the subject *innā* and the verbs used are in the dual number. In Arabic it is permissible sometimes to use singular predicate for a subject in the dual or plural number (Bayān). See also 26 : 78.

2101. The reference in the verse seems to be to an Egyptian having been killed by Moses. Pharaoh regards himself and his people, the Egyptians, as the great benefactors of the Israelites and accuses Moses of gross ingratitude for having killed an Egyptian.

2102. *Dāll* is derived from *Dalla* which means, he did not know what to do; he was in a perplexed state of mind; he was lost in love (Lane). When the Israelite called him for help against the Egyptian, Moses did not know what to do, and being anxious to help the poor, helpless Israelite (28 : 16-21) gave the Egyptian a blow with his closed fist which caused his death. The death was accidental because ordinarily a blow with the fist does not cause the death of a person. Or the verse may mean that on account of his great love for his oppressed people he came to the help of the Israelite and gave a blow to the Egyptian, which resulted in his death. Or it means that he did it being unaware of the consequences.

2103. The fact that after he had killed the Egyptian and fled, God made him a Prophet —a great Divine favour indeed—is proof positive of the fact that what Moses did was an inadvertent act done on the spur of the moment.

against thy having enslaved the Children of Israel?'[2104]

أَنْ عَبَّدْتَّ بَنِيْٓ إِسْرَآءِيْلَ ﴿٢٣﴾

24. Pharaoh said, [a]'And what is the Lord of the worlds?'[2105]

قَالَ فِرْعَوْنُ وَمَا رَبُّ الْعٰلَمِيْنَ ﴿٢٤﴾

25. *Moses* said, [b]"The Lord of the heavens and the earth[2106] and of all that is between the two, if you would believe.'

قَالَ رَبُّ السَّمٰوٰتِ وَالْأَرْضِ وَمَا بَيْنَهُمَا ۭ إِنْ كُنْتُمْ مُّوْقِنِيْنَ ﴿٢٥﴾

26. *Pharaoh* said to those around him, 'Do you not hear?'[2107]

قَالَ لِمَنْ حَوْلَهٗٓ أَلَا تَسْتَمِعُوْنَ ﴿٢٦﴾

27. *Moses* said, 'Your Lord, and the Lord of your fathers of yore.'[2108]

قَالَ رَبُّكُمْ وَرَبُّ اٰبَآئِكُمُ الْأَوَّلِيْنَ ﴿٢٧﴾

28. *Pharoah* said, [c]"Most surely, this Messenger of yours who has been sent to you is a madman.'[2109]

قَالَ إِنَّ رَسُوْلَكُمُ الَّذِيْٓ أُرْسِلَ إِلَيْكُمْ لَمَجْنُوْنٌ ﴿٢٨﴾

29. *Moses* said, [d]'The Lord of the East and of the West,[2110] and of all that is between the two, if only you have sense.'

قَالَ رَبُّ الْمَشْرِقِ وَالْمَغْرِبِ وَمَا بَيْنَهُمَا ۭ إِنْ كُنْتُمْ تَعْقِلُوْنَ ﴿٢٩﴾

30. [e]*Pharaoh* said, 'If thou takest a god other than me, I will certainly put thee in prison.'

قَالَ لَئِنِ اتَّخَذْتَ إِلٰهًا غَيْرِيْ لَأَجْعَلَنَّكَ مِنَ الْمَسْجُوْنِيْنَ ﴿٣٠﴾

[a]20 : 50. [b]44 : 8. [c]44 : 15. [d]2 : 116; 55 : 18. [e]28 : 39.

2104. To Pharaoh's impudent remark Moses is described as saying to him that he himself should be ashamed of referring to any good that he thinks he had done to his (Moses's) people as he (Pharaoh) had kept them for generations under the most debasing and degrading form of bondage which had killed in them all sense of dignity, initiative and ambition to rise to their full stature.

2105. Moses's reply to Pharaoh, as mentioned in the preceding verse, seemed to have utterly confounded him and he at once changed the subject, seeking to involve Moses in a metaphysical discussion about the existence and person of the Divine Being and the nature of His attributes.

2106. The words 'Lord of the heavens and the earth' refer to the vastness of God's dominion in respect of space.

2107. The verse depicts Pharaoh as trying to incite his people against Moses by hinting that he was insulting their gods by ascribing the Kingdom of the heavens and earth to Allāh because it were their own gods who held sway over all the universe.

2108. In the 25th verse Moses had referred to the vastness of God's dominion and control in respect of space; in this verse he refers to God's dominion in respect of time.

2109. Pharaoh thought that like a madman Moses would listen to nobody but would go on harping on his own tune; and he said so in so many words.

2110. The verse refers to the vastness of God's Kingdom in respect of directions and sides.

31. *Moses* said, 'What, even though I bring thee something that is manifest !'

قَالَ أَوَلَوْ جِئْتُكَ بِشَيْءٍ مُّبِينٍ ﴿٣١﴾

32. [a]*Pharaoh* said, 'Bring it then, if thou speakest the truth.'

قَالَ فَأْتِ بِهِ إِن كُنتَ مِنَ الصَّادِقِينَ ﴿٣٢﴾

33. So *Moses* threw down his rod, and behold! [b]it was a serpent plainly visible.

فَأَلْقَىٰ عَصَاهُ فَإِذَا هِيَ ثُعْبَانٌ مُّبِينٌ ﴿٣٣﴾

34. [c]And he drew out his hand, and lo! it was white for the beholders.[2111]

وَنَزَعَ يَدَهُ فَإِذَا هِيَ بَيْضَاءُ لِلنَّاظِرِينَ ﴿٣٤﴾ ع

R. 3 35. [d]*Pharaoh* said to the chiefs around him, 'This is surely a skilful sorcerer;

قَالَ لِلْمَلَإِ حَوْلَهُ إِنَّ هَٰذَا لَسَاحِرٌ عَلِيمٌ ﴿٣٥﴾

36. [e]'He seeks to turn you out of your land by his sorcery. Now, what do you advise ?'

يُرِيدُ أَن يُخْرِجَكُم مِّنْ أَرْضِكُم بِسِحْرِهِ فَمَاذَا تَأْمُرُونَ ﴿٣٦﴾

37. [f]They said, 'Put him off and his brother *awhile* and send into the cities summoners,

قَالُوا أَرْجِهْ وَأَخَاهُ وَابْعَثْ فِي الْمَدَائِنِ حَاشِرِينَ ﴿٣٧﴾

38. [g]'Who should bring thee every skilful and cunning sorcerer.'

يَأْتُوكَ بِكُلِّ سَحَّارٍ عَلِيمٍ ﴿٣٨﴾

39. [h]So the sorcerers were assembled together at the appointed time on a fixed day,

فَجُمِعَ السَّحَرَةُ لِمِيقَاتِ يَوْمٍ مَّعْلُومٍ ﴿٣٩﴾

40. [i]And it was said to the people, 'Will you also gather together?

وَقِيلَ لِلنَّاسِ هَلْ أَنتُم مُّجْتَمِعُونَ ﴿٤٠﴾

41. 'So that we may follow the sorcerers if they are the winners ?'

لَعَلَّنَا نَتَّبِعُ السَّحَرَةَ إِن كَانُوا هُمُ الْغَالِبِينَ ﴿٤١﴾

---

[a]7 : 107. [b]7 : 108. [c]7 : 109; 20 : 23. [d]7 : 110. [e]7 : 111; 20 : 58,64. [f]7 : 112; 10 : 80. [g]7 : 113. [h]7 : 114; 20 : 59. [i]20 : 60.

2111. See 1024.

42. And, when the sorcerers came, they said to Pharaoh, 'Shall we have a reward[2112] if we are the winners?'

فَلَمَّا جَآءَ السَّحَرَةُ قَالُوْا لِفِرْعَوْنَ اَئِنَّ لَنَا لَاَجْرًا اِنْ كُنَّا نَحْنُ الْغٰلِبِيْنَ ﴿۴۲﴾

43. [a]He said, 'Yes, and surely then you will be among my favourites.'

قَالَ نَعَمْ وَاِنَّكُمْ اِذًا لَّمِنَ الْمُقَرَّبِيْنَ ﴿۴۳﴾

44. [b]Moses said to them, '*Now* throw you what you have to throw.'

قَالَ لَهُمْ مُّوْسٰۤى اَلْقُوْا مَاۤ اَنْتُمْ مُّلْقُوْنَ ﴿۴۴﴾

45. So they threw down their ropes and their rods and said, 'By Pharaoh's honour, it is we who will surely win.'

فَاَلْقَوْا حِبَالَهُمْ وَعِصِيَّهُمْ وَقَالُوْا بِعِزَّةِ فِرْعَوْنَ اِنَّا لَنَحْنُ الْغٰلِبُوْنَ ﴿۴۵﴾

46. [c]Then Moses threw down his rod, and lo! it swallowed[2113] up all that which they had fabricated.

فَاَلْقٰى مُوْسٰى عَصَاهُ فَاِذَا هِیَ تَلْقَفُ مَا يَاْفِكُوْنَ ﴿۴۶﴾

47. [d]Thereupon the sorcerers were impelled to fall down prostrate;

فَاُلْقِیَ السَّحَرَةُ سٰجِدِيْنَ ﴿۴۷﴾

48. They said, 'We believe in the Lord of the worlds,

قَالُوْۤا اٰمَنَّا بِرَبِّ الْعٰلَمِيْنَ ﴿۴۸﴾

49. [e]"The Lord of Moses and Aaron.'

رَبِّ مُوْسٰى وَهٰرُوْنَ ﴿۴۹﴾

50. [f]*Pharaoh* said, 'You have believed in him before I gave you leave? He is surely your chief who has taught you sorcery. But you shall know *the consequences thereof*. I will most surely cut off your hands and your feet on account[2113A] of *your* disobedience and I will most surely crucify you all.'

قَالَ اٰمَنْتُمْ لَهٗ قَبْلَ اَنْ اٰذَنَ لَكُمْ اِنَّهٗ لَكَبِيْرُكُمُ الَّذِیْ عَلَّمَكُمُ السِّحْرَ فَلَسَوْفَ تَعْلَمُوْنَ لَاُقَطِّعَنَّ اَيْدِيَكُمْ وَاَرْجُلَكُمْ مِّنْ خِلَافٍ وَّلَاُصَلِّبَنَّكُمْ اَجْمَعِيْنَ ﴿۵۰﴾

[a]7 : 115. [b]7 : 117; 10 : 81; 20 : 67. [c]7 : 118; 20 : 70. [d]7 : 121; 20 : 71. [e]7 : 123; 20 : 71. [f]7 : 124-125; 20 : 72.

2112. The sorcerers seemed to be professional traders in sorcery whose standard of morality was very low.

2113. The verse makes it quite clear that the rod of Moses did not swallow the rods and ropes of the sorcerers but swallowed up all that which they had fabricated, *i.e.*, it utterly destroyed their imposture, forgery and deception. Moreover, it was the rod itself and not the serpent which exposed the deception the sorcerers had wrought on the spectators by breaking to pieces the things which under the influence of their sorcery the spectators had taken for real serpents.

2113A. '*An* means, on account of (Lane).

51. [a]They said, '*It can do us* no harm; to our Lord shall We return;[2114]

قَالُوْا لَا ضَيْرَ ۡ اِنَّاۤ اِلٰى رَبِّنَا مُنْقَلِبُوْنَ ﴿٥١﴾ ۚ

52. [b]'We do hope that our Lord will forgive us our sins, since [b]we are the first among the believers.'

اِنَّا نَطْمَعُ اَنْ يَّغْفِرَ لَنَا رَبُّنَا خَطٰيٰنَاۤ اَنْ كُنَّاۤ اَوَّلَ
الْمُؤْمِنِيْنَ ﴿٥٢﴾ ؑ ع

R. 4 53. [c]And We revealed to Moses, *directing him*, 'Take away My servants by night, you will surely be pursued.'

وَاَوْحَيْنَاۤ اِلٰى مُوْسٰۤى اَنْ اَسْرِ بِعِبَادِيْۤ اِنَّكُمْ مُّتَّبَعُوْنَ ﴿٥٣﴾

54. And Pharaoh sent summoners into the cities, *announcing*,

فَاَرْسَلَ فِرْعَوْنُ فِى الْمَدَآئِنِ حٰشِرِيْنَ ﴿٥٤﴾ ۚ

55. 'These are a small party,

اِنَّ هٰۤؤُلَآءِ لَشِرْذِمَةٌ قَلِيْلُوْنَ ﴿٥٥﴾ ۙ

56. 'Yet they have offended us;[2115]

وَاِنَّهُمْ لَنَا لَغَآئِظُوْنَ ﴿٥٦﴾ ۙ

57. 'And we are a multitude *fully prepared and* vigilant.'

وَاِنَّا لَجَمِيْعٌ حٰذِرُوْنَ ﴿٥٧﴾ ؕ

58. [d]So We turned them out of gardens and springs,

فَاَخْرَجْنٰهُمْ مِّنْ جَنّٰتٍ وَّعُيُوْنٍ ﴿٥٨﴾ ۙ

59. And treasures and an abode of honour.

وَّكُنُوْزٍ وَّمَقَامٍ كَرِيْمٍ ﴿٥٩﴾ ۙ

60. [e]Thus *it was*; and We gave them as heritage[2116] to the Children of Israel.

كَذٰلِكَ ؕ وَاَوْرَثْنٰهَا بَنِيْۤ اِسْرَآءِيْلَ ﴿٦٠﴾ ؕ

61. [f]And *the hosts of Pharaoh* pursued and overtook them at sunrise.

فَاَتْبَعُوْهُمْ مُّشْرِقِيْنَ ﴿٦١﴾

62. And when the two hosts came in sight of each other the companions of Moses said, 'We are surely caught.'[2117]

فَلَمَّا تَرَآءَ الْجَمْعٰنِ قَالَ اَصْحٰبُ مُوْسٰۤى اِنَّا لَمُدْرَكُوْنَ ﴿٦٢﴾ ۚ

[a]7 : 126; 20 : 73. [b]5 : 85. [c]20 : 74. [d]44 : 26, 27. [e]44 : 29. [f]10 : 91; 20 : 79; 44 : 24.

2114. The erstwhile professional sorcerers, who, only a few minutes ago, were prepared to resort to any trick and subterfuge for the sake of filthy lucre, had come to acquire a faith that would defy death.

2115. The appearance of a Divine Prophet among a people is a sure guarantee of their great and bright future if only they accept his Message and follow his lead. The Prophet gives them a new life and creates in them a new hope and confidence which change their whole outlook on life. After the advent of Moses Pharaoh must have felt a great change in the Israelites and this must have cut him to the quick.

2116. The verse does not mean that the springs and gardens and treasures of Pharaoh and the Egyptians were given over to the Israelites. The latter had left Egypt for Canaan, the land of promise which "flowed with milk and honey." It is there that they were given these things. In fact, Palestine resembles Egypt in the abundance of its gardens and springs.

2117. See next page.

63. 'Never!' said he, 'My Lord is with me; He will guide me *to safety*.'

قَالَ كَلَّا ۚ إِنَّ مَعِيَ رَبِّي سَيَهْدِينِ ﴿٦٣﴾

64. [a]Then We revealed to Moses: 'Strike the sea with thy rod.'[2117A] Thereupon it parted and every part looked like a huge mound.

فَأَوْحَيْنَا إِلَىٰ مُوسَىٰ أَنِ اضْرِب بِّعَصَاكَ الْبَحْرَ ۖ فَانفَلَقَ فَكَانَ كُلُّ فِرْقٍ كَالطَّوْدِ الْعَظِيمِ ﴿٦٤﴾

65. And We made the others approach nearer.

وَأَزْلَفْنَا ثَمَّ الْآخَرِينَ ﴿٦٥﴾

66. [b]And We saved Moses and those who were with him.

وَأَنجَيْنَا مُوسَىٰ وَمَن مَّعَهُ أَجْمَعِينَ ﴿٦٦﴾

67. [c]Then We drowned the others.

ثُمَّ أَغْرَقْنَا الْآخَرِينَ ﴿٦٧﴾

68. In this, verily, there is a Sign; but most of these would not believe.

إِنَّ فِي ذَٰلِكَ لَآيَةً ۖ وَمَا كَانَ أَكْثَرُهُم مُّؤْمِنِينَ ﴿٦٨﴾

69. And surely thy Lord—He is the Mighty, the Merciful.

وَإِنَّ رَبَّكَ لَهُوَ الْعَزِيزُ الرَّحِيمُ ﴿٦٩﴾

R. 5 70. And recite unto them the story of Abraham.

وَاتْلُ عَلَيْهِمْ نَبَأَ إِبْرَاهِيمَ ﴿٧٠﴾

71. [d]When he said to his father and his people, 'What do you worship?'[2118]

إِذْ قَالَ لِأَبِيهِ وَقَوْمِهِ مَا تَعْبُدُونَ ﴿٧١﴾

72. [e]They said, 'We worship idols, and we shall continue to be devoted to them.'

قَالُوا نَعْبُدُ أَصْنَامًا فَنَظَلُّ لَهَا عَاكِفِينَ ﴿٧٢﴾

73. He said, 'Do they hear you when you call *on them?*

قَالَ هَلْ يَسْمَعُونَكُمْ إِذْ تَدْعُونَ ﴿٧٣﴾

74. 'Or, do you good or harm *you*?'

أَوْ يَنفَعُونَكُمْ أَوْ يَضُرُّونَ ﴿٧٤﴾

[a]20 : 78. [b]20 : 81 ; 44 : 31-32. [c]2 : 51 ; 7 : 137 ; 17 : 104 ; 20 : 79. [d]6 : 75; 19 : 43; 21 : 53; 37 : 86-87. [e]21 : 54; 26 : 72.

2117. The companions of Moses seemed to possess very weak faith. This is also clear from 5 : 22-23; 7 : 149; 20 : 87-92.

2117A. The words also mean, 'take thy people to the sea,' '*Aṣā* meaning people or community (Lane).

2118. Throughout the Qur'ān, Abraham has been associated with a vigorous campaign against idolat ry. He seems to be the first uncompromising iconoclast of whose activities history has kept a record.

75. [a]They said, '*Not so*, but we found our fathers doing likewise.'

قَالُوْا بَلْ وَجَدْنَآ اٰبَآءَنَا كَذٰلِكَ يَفْعَلُوْنَ ﴿٧٥﴾

76. [b]*Abraham* said, 'Do you know that those you have been worshipping—

قَالَ اَفَرَءَيْتُمْ مَّا كُنْتُمْ تَعْبُدُوْنَ ﴿٧٦﴾

77. 'You and your fathers before *you*,

اَنْتُمْ وَاٰبَآؤُكُمُ الْاَقْدَمُوْنَ ﴿٧٧﴾

78. 'They are all enemies to me but *it is* the Lord of the worlds,

فَاِنَّهُمْ عَدُوٌّ لِّيْٓ اِلَّا رَبَّ الْعٰلَمِيْنَ ﴿٧٨﴾

79. 'Who has created me, and it is He Who guides me;

الَّذِيْ خَلَقَنِيْ فَهُوَ يَهْدِيْنِ ﴿٧٩﴾

80. 'And Who gives me food and gives me drink;

وَالَّذِيْ هُوَ يُطْعِمُنِيْ وَيَسْقِيْنِ ﴿٨٠﴾

81. 'And when I fall ill, it is He Who restores me to health;2119

وَاِذَا مَرِضْتُ فَهُوَ يَشْفِيْنِ ﴿٨١﴾

82. 'And Who will cause me to die,2120 and then bring me to life *again;*

وَالَّذِيْ يُمِيْتُنِيْ ثُمَّ يُحْيِيْنِ ﴿٨٢﴾

83. 'And Who, I hope, will forgive me my faults on the Day of Judgment;

وَالَّذِيْٓ اَطْمَعُ اَنْ يَّغْفِرَ لِيْ خَطِيْٓـَٔتِيْ يَوْمَ الدِّيْنِ ﴿٨٣﴾

84. 'My Lord, bestow wisdom on me and join me with the righteous;

رَبِّ هَبْ لِيْ حُكْمًا وَّاَلْحِقْنِيْ بِالصّٰلِحِيْنَ ﴿٨٤﴾

85. [c]'And grant me true *and lasting* reputation among posterity;2121

وَاجْعَلْ لِّيْ لِسَانَ صِدْقٍ فِي الْاٰخِرِيْنَ ﴿٨٥﴾

---

[a]21 : 54; 43 : 24. [b]21 : 67; 37 : 86-87. [c]19 : 51.

2119. In this verse Abraham attributes all malady and ailment to himself and all remedy and cure to God. In fact, every misfortune that befalls a man is the result of the contravention by him of a particular law of nature, so he himself is responsible for it. See also 4 : 80.

2120. While Abraham ascribes disease and ailment to himself, he attributes death to God which shows that according to him death was not, and really is not, an evil thing to be dreaded or shunned. In fact, death is the natural and necessary end of all life and like life it is a great Divine boon.

2121. Abraham left behind him such a good name that the followers of the three great Faiths of the world—Judaism, Christianity and Islām, look upon him as their great progenitor and spiritual ancestor whose memory they revere.

86. 'And make me *one* of the heirs of the Garden of Bliss;

وَاجْعَلْنِيْ مِنْ وَّرَثَةِ جَنَّةِ النَّعِيْمِ ۙ﴿۸۶﴾

87. [a]'And forgive my father, for he is of the erring ones;

وَاغْفِرْ لِاَبِيْٓ اِنَّهٗ كَانَ مِنَ الضَّآلِّيْنَ ۙ﴿۸۷﴾

88. 'And disgrace me not on the day when they will be raised up,[2122]

وَلَا تُخْزِنِيْ يَوْمَ يُبْعَثُوْنَ ۙ﴿۸۸﴾

89. 'The day when wealth and sons shall not avail;

يَوْمَ لَا يَنْفَعُ مَالٌ وَّلَا بَنُوْنَ ۙ﴿۸۹﴾

90. [b]'Save him who comes to Allāh with a sound heart.'

اِلَّا مَنْ اَتَى اللّٰهَ بِقَلْبٍ سَلِيْمٍ ؕ﴿۹۰﴾

91. And Heaven shall be brought near[2123] to the righteous.

وَاُزْلِفَتِ الْجَنَّةُ لِلْمُتَّقِيْنَ ۙ﴿۹۱﴾

92. And Hell shall be placed in full view to those who have gone astray.

وَبُرِّزَتِ الْجَحِيْمُ لِلْغٰوِيْنَ ۙ﴿۹۲﴾

93. And it will be said to them, 'Where are those that you worshipped

وَقِيْلَ لَهُمْ اَيْنَمَا كُنْتُمْ تَعْبُدُوْنَ ۙ﴿۹۳﴾

94. 'Beside Allāh? Can they help you or help *themselves?*'

مِنْ دُوْنِ اللّٰهِ ؕ هَلْ يَنْصُرُوْنَكُمْ اَوْ يَنْتَصِرُوْنَ ؕ﴿۹۴﴾

95. [c]Then will they be thrown headlong therein, they and those who have gone astray,

فَكُبْكِبُوْا فِيْهَا هُمْ وَالْغَاوٗنَ ۙ﴿۹۵﴾

96. [d]And the hosts of Iblīs, all together.

وَجُنُوْدُ اِبْلِيْسَ اَجْمَعُوْنَ ؕ﴿۹۶﴾

97. They will say, whilst they dispute between themselves therein,

قَالُوْا وَهُمْ فِيْهَا يَخْتَصِمُوْنَ ۙ﴿۹۷﴾

98. 'By Allāh, we were in manifest error,

تَاللّٰهِ اِنْ كُنَّا لَفِيْ ضَلٰلٍ مُّبِيْنٍ ۙ﴿۹۸﴾

99. 'When we held you *as* equal with the Lord of the worlds,

اِذْ نُسَوِّيْكُمْ بِرَبِّ الْعٰلَمِيْنَ ﴿۹۹﴾

[a]9 : 114; 19 : 48; 60 : 5. [b]37 : 85. [c]27 : 91. [d]7 : 19; 38 : 86.

2122. Resurrection is called *Ba'th* because after death man will be endowed with new and better faculties and new avenues for spiritual advancement will be opened to him.

2123. The words mean that the righteous will be given new and better faculties to enjoy the bliss of Paradise.

100. 'And none led us astray but the guilty ones,

وَمَآ اَضَلَّنَآ اِلَّا الْمُجْرِمُوْنَ ﴿۱۰۰﴾

101. 'And *now* we have no intercessors,

فَمَا لَنَا مِنْ شَافِعِيْنَ ﴿۱۰۱﴾

102. 'Nor any warm friend;

وَلَا صَدِيْقٍ حَمِيْمٍ ﴿۱۰۲﴾

103. [a]"Could we but return *to the world*, we would be among the believers !'

فَلَوْ اَنَّ لَنَا كَرَّةً فَنَكُوْنَ مِنَ الْمُؤْمِنِيْنَ ﴿۱۰۳﴾

104. In this verily there is a Sign, but most of these would not believe.

اِنَّ فِيْ ذٰلِكَ لَاٰيَةً ۚ وَمَا كَانَ اَكْثَرُهُمْ مُّؤْمِنِيْنَ ﴿۱۰۴﴾

105. And verily thy Lord—He is the Mighty, the Merciful.

وَاِنَّ رَبَّكَ لَهُوَ الْعَزِيْزُ الرَّحِيْمُ ﴿۱۰۵﴾ ع

R. 6 106. The people of Noah treated the Messengers as liars,

كَذَّبَتْ قَوْمُ نُوْحِ ۣالْمُرْسَلِيْنَ ﴿۱۰۶﴾

107. When their brother Noah said to them, 'Will you not be God-fearing?

اِذْ قَالَ لَهُمْ اَخُوْهُمْ نُوْحٌ اَلَا تَتَّقُوْنَ ﴿۱۰۷﴾

108. 'Surely, I am unto you a Messenger, faithful to *my* trust

اِنِّيْ لَكُمْ رَسُوْلٌ اَمِيْنٌ ﴿۱۰۸﴾

109. 'So fear Allāh, and obey me;[2124]

فَاتَّقُوا اللّٰهَ وَاَطِيْعُوْنِ ﴿۱۰۹﴾

110. [b]'And I ask of you no reward for it. My reward is only with the Lord of the worlds;

وَمَآ اَسْـَٔلُكُمْ عَلَيْهِ مِنْ اَجْرٍ ۚ اِنْ اَجْرِيَ اِلَّا عَلٰى رَبِّ الْعٰلَمِيْنَ ﴿۱۱۰﴾

111. 'So fear Allāh, and obey me.'

فَاتَّقُوا اللّٰهَ وَاَطِيْعُوْنِ ﴿۱۱۱﴾

112. They said, 'Shall we believe in thee, when [c]it is the meanest *of us* who follow thee?'

قَالُوْٓا اَنُؤْمِنُ لَكَ وَاتَّبَعَكَ الْاَرْذَلُوْنَ ﴿۱۱۲﴾

---

[a]2 : 168; 6 : 28; 23 : 100; 39 : 59. [b]10 : 73; 11 ; 30. [c]11 : 28.

2124. The words, *So fear Allāh and obey me*, which have been addressed to his people from the mouth of every Prophet in this *Sūrah*, show that apart from the general commandments embodied in Divine revelation, the believers are enjoined to obey the commands and instructions issued from time to time by their own Prophets.

113. He said, 'And what knowledge have I as to what they have been doing?

قَالَ وَمَا عِلْمِیْ بِمَا كَانُوْا يَعْمَلُوْنَ ﴿١١٣﴾

114. 'Their account is only with my Lord, if you only knew;[2125]

اِنْ حِسَابُهُمْ اِلَّا عَلٰى رَبِّيْ لَوْ تَشْعُرُوْنَ ﴿١١٤﴾

115. [a]'And I am not going to drive away the believers;[2125A]

وَمَآ اَنَا بِطَارِدِ الْمُؤْمِنِيْنَ ﴿١١٥﴾

116. 'I am only a plain Warner.'

اِنْ اَنَا اِلَّا نَذِيْرٌ مُّبِيْنٌ ﴿١١٦﴾

117. They said, 'If thou desist not, O Noah, thou shalt surely be stoned to death.'

قَالُوْا لَئِنْ لَّمْ تَنْتَهِ يٰنُوْحُ لَتَكُوْنَنَّ مِنَ الْمَرْجُوْمِيْنَ ﴿١١٧﴾

118. He said, 'My Lord, my people have treated me as a liar;

قَالَ رَبِّ اِنَّ قَوْمِيْ كَذَّبُوْنِ ﴿١١٨﴾

119. 'Therefore judge Thou decisively between me and them; and save me and the believers that are with me.'

فَافْتَحْ بَيْنِيْ وَبَيْنَهُمْ فَتْحًا وَّنَجِّنِيْ وَمَنْ مَّعِيَ مِنَ الْمُؤْمِنِيْنَ ﴿١١٩﴾

120. [b]So We saved him and those who were with him in the fully laden Ark.

فَاَنْجَيْنٰهُ وَمَنْ مَّعَهٗ فِي الْفُلْكِ الْمَشْحُوْنِ ﴿١٢٠﴾

121. [c]Then We drowned thereafter those who remained behind.

ثُمَّ اَغْرَقْنَا بَعْدُ الْبٰقِيْنَ ﴿١٢١﴾

122. In this, verily, there is a Sign, but most of them would not believe.

اِنَّ فِيْ ذٰلِكَ لَاٰيَةً وَمَا كَانَ اَكْثَرُهُمْ مُّؤْمِنِيْنَ ﴿١٢٢﴾

123. And verily thy Lord—He is the Mighty, the Merciful.

وَاِنَّ رَبَّكَ لَهُوَ الْعَزِيْزُ الرَّحِيْمُ ﴿١٢٣﴾

---

[a]11 : 30. [b]21 : 77; 37:77. [c]37 : 83; 54 : 12-13; 71 : 26.

2125. The Qur'ān has used five different words at different places and in different contexts to suit the particular occasion and to explain fully the meaning. In a general sense they are all alike but as regards their finer shades of meaning they are different. The words are *Shu'ūr, i.e.,* perceiving a thing by means of any of the senses to know its minute particulars (2 : 155); *'Aql, i.e.,* withholding or restraining a person from adopting an evil course (12:3); *Fikr, i.e.,* reflecting upon and calculating a thing (6:51); *Tafaqquh, i.e.,* applying oneself to the acquisition of knowledge and becoming well-versed in it (9:122)); and *Tadabbur, i.e.,* considering, examining or studying a thing repeatedly in order to know it (4 : 83).

2125A. God's Prophets and worldly men have different standards to judge the values of life. Whereas the former judge the worth and value of a man by his actions and deeds, the latter judge it by his material means and his social status.

R. 7 124. [a]*The tribe of* 'Ād rejected the Messengers,

كَذَّبَتْ عَادُ ٱلْمُرْسَلِينَ ﴿١٢٤﴾

125. When their brother Hūd said to them, 'Will you not fear God?

إِذْ قَالَ لَهُمْ أَخُوهُمْ هُودٌ أَلَا تَتَّقُونَ ﴿١٢٥﴾

126. 'Surely, I am unto you a Messenger, faithful to *my* trust;

إِنِّي لَكُمْ رَسُولٌ أَمِينٌ ﴿١٢٦﴾

127. 'So fear Allāh, and obey me;

فَاتَّقُوا اللّٰهَ وَأَطِيعُونِ ﴿١٢٧﴾

128. [b]'And I ask of you no reward for it. My reward is only with the Lord of the worlds;

وَمَآ أَسْئَلُكُمْ عَلَيْهِ مِنْ أَجْرٍ إِنْ أَجْرِيَ إِلَّا عَلٰى رَبِّ الْعٰلَمِينَ ﴿١٢٨﴾

129. 'Do you build monuments on every high place, seeking vain glory?

أَتَبْنُونَ بِكُلِّ رِيعٍ آيَةً تَعْبَثُونَ ﴿١٢٩﴾

130. 'And do you erect palaces as if you will live for ever?[2126]

وَتَتَّخِذُونَ مَصَانِعَ لَعَلَّكُمْ تَخْلُدُونَ ﴿١٣٠﴾

131. 'And when you lay hands *upon any one*, you lay hands as tyrants.

وَإِذَا بَطَشْتُمْ بَطَشْتُمْ جَبَّارِينَ ﴿١٣١﴾

132. 'So fear Allāh, and obey me;

فَاتَّقُوا اللّٰهَ وَأَطِيعُونِ ﴿١٣٢﴾

133. 'And fear Him Who has helped you with all that you know;

وَاتَّقُوا الَّذِيٓ أَمَدَّكُمْ بِمَا تَعْلَمُونَ ﴿١٣٣﴾

134. 'He has helped you with cattle and sons,

أَمَدَّكُمْ بِأَنْعَامٍ وَّبَنِينَ ﴿١٣٤﴾

[a]7 : 66-67. [b]11 : 52.

2126. This, the preceding and the following verse show that the Adites were a powerful and cultured people. They had made great progress in science in their time. They built fortresses, palatial buildings and great reservoirs. They had their summer residences, their factories and mechanical works. They were specially advanced in architecture. They invented new weapons and implements of war and erected great monuments. In short, like the present-day nations of the West, they possessed all the complicated paraphernalia of a highly advanced civilization. They made great strides in knowledge but they consigned to oblivion the one supreme lesson of history, *viz.*, that nations derive their real strength not from material things but from high ideals and good morals. As they became morally corrupt and spiritually depraved and turned a deaf ear to the warnings of their Prophet to mend their ways, they fell a victim to that terrible doom which is the inevitable lot of those who ignore Divine warning. See 1323.

135. 'And gardens and springs; وَجَنّٰتٍ وَّعُيُوْنٍ ﴿١٣٥﴾

136. 'Indeed, I fear for you the punishment of an awful day.' اِنِّيْٓ اَخَافُ عَلَيْكُمْ عَذَابَ يَوْمٍ عَظِيْمٍ ﴿١٣٦﴾

137. They said, 'It is the same to us whether thou admonish *us* or whether thou be not of those who admonish; قَالُوْا سَوَآءٌ عَلَيْنَآ اَوَعَظْتَ اَمْ لَمْ تَكُنْ مِّنَ الْوٰعِظِيْنَ ﴿١٣٧﴾

138. 'This is nothing but the habit[2127] of the ancients, اِنْ هٰذَآ اِلَّا خُلُقُ الْاَوَّلِيْنَ ﴿١٣٨﴾

139. 'And We shall not be punished.' وَمَا نَحْنُ بِمُعَذَّبِيْنَ ﴿١٣٩﴾

140. [a]So they rejected him, and We destroyed them. In that indeed there is a Sign, but most of these would not believe. فَكَذَّبُوْهُ فَاَهْلَكْنٰهُمْ ؕ اِنَّ فِيْ ذٰلِكَ لَاٰيَةً ؕ وَمَا كَانَ اَكْثَرُهُمْ مُّؤْمِنِيْنَ ﴿١٤٠﴾

141. And verily thy Lord—He is the Mighty, the Merciful. وَاِنَّ رَبَّكَ لَهُوَ الْعَزِيْزُ الرَّحِيْمُ ﴿١٤١﴾

R. 8 142. [b]*The tribe of* Thamūd[2128] *also* rejected the Messengers, كَذَّبَتْ ثَمُوْدُ الْمُرْسَلِيْنَ ﴿١٤٢﴾

143. When their brother Ṣāliḥ said to them, 'Will you not guard against *evil?*' اِذْ قَالَ لَهُمْ اَخُوْهُمْ صٰلِحٌ اَلَا تَتَّقُوْنَ ﴿١٤٣﴾

---

[a]7 : 73; 50 : 15. [b]7 : 74; 11 : 62-63; 27 : 46.

2127. *Khuluq* means, habit or second nature; custom or manner; religion; a lie (Lane).

2128. This and the following several verses deal with the tribe of Thamūd. According to Futūḥ al-Shām, they were a very powerful people. Their rule and dominion had extended from Buṣrā, a town in Syria, to Aden. They had made great progress in agriculture and architecture and were a highly civilized and cultured people. The tribe has been mentioned by Greek historians. They place it in a period not long before the Christian era. Ḥijr or Agra, as they call it, is given as their home. Al-Ḥijr which has also been known as Madā'ini Ṣāliḥ (the Cities of Ṣāliḥ) and which seems to have been the capital of these people lies between Medina and Tabūk, and the valley in which it is situated is called Wādī Qurā. The Qur'ān represents them as the immediate successors of 'Ād (7 : 75). It is worthy of note that the accounts of the Prophets Noah, Hūd and Ṣāliḥ have been given at various places in the Qur'ān and everywhere the order observed is the same, *viz.*, the account of Noah precedes that of Hūd and the account of Hūd precedes that of Ṣāliḥ, which is the true chronological order. This shows that the Qur'ān gives accurately and in their historical order the facts of history long consigned to oblivion and quite wrapped in obscurity. See also 1326.

144. 'Surely, I am unto you a Messenger, faithful to *my* trust;

إِنِّي لَكُمْ رَسُولٌ أَمِينٌ ﴿١٤٤﴾

145. 'So fear Allāh, and obey me;

فَاتَّقُوا اللَّهَ وَأَطِيعُونِ ﴿١٤٥﴾

146. [a]'And I ask of you no reward for it. My reward is only with the Lord of the worlds;

وَمَا أَسْأَلُكُمْ عَلَيْهِ مِنْ أَجْرٍ إِنْ أَجْرِيَ إِلَّا عَلَىٰ رَبِّ الْعَالَمِينَ ﴿١٤٦﴾

147. '*Do you think that* you will be left secure amid the things *that you have* here,

أَتُتْرَكُونَ فِي مَا هَاهُنَا آمِنِينَ ﴿١٤٧﴾

148. 'Amid gardens and springs,

فِي جَنَّاتٍ وَعُيُونٍ ﴿١٤٨﴾

149. 'And cornfields, and date-palms with *heavy* spathes near breaking?

وَزُرُوعٍ وَنَخْلٍ طَلْعُهَا هَضِيمٌ ﴿١٤٩﴾

150. [b]'And you hew out houses in the mountains, elated *with your greatness*;[2128A]

وَتَنْحِتُونَ مِنَ الْجِبَالِ بُيُوتًا فٰرِهِينَ ﴿١٥٠﴾

151. 'So fear Allāh, and obey me;

فَاتَّقُوا اللَّهَ وَأَطِيعُونِ ﴿١٥١﴾

152. 'And obey not the bidding of those who exceed the bounds,

وَلَا تُطِيعُوا أَمْرَ الْمُسْرِفِينَ ﴿١٥٢﴾

153. [c]'Who create disorder in the earth, and do not promote order *and security*.'

الَّذِينَ يُفْسِدُونَ فِي الْأَرْضِ وَلَا يُصْلِحُونَ ﴿١٥٣﴾

154. They said, 'Thou art but *one* of the bewitched;[2129]

قَالُوا إِنَّمَا أَنْتَ مِنَ الْمُسَحَّرِينَ ﴿١٥٤﴾

155. 'Thou art only a mortal like us. So bring a Sign, if thou art of the truthful.'

مَا أَنْتَ إِلَّا بَشَرٌ مِثْلُنَا فَأْتِ بِآيَةٍ إِنْ كُنْتَ مِنَ الصَّادِقِينَ ﴿١٥٥﴾

---

[a]11 : 52. [b]7 : 75; 15 : 83. [c]27 : 49.

2128A. *Fārihīn* also means, with great skill (Lane).

2129. Whereas the peoples of Noah and Hūd accused their Prophets of forging lies, Prophet Ṣāliḥ, to whose uprightness and unimpeachable character his people had themselves borne testimony (11 : 63), has been declared here as *Musaḥḥar, i.e.*, one who is deceived, deluded, beguiled, bewitched, circumvented or outwitted (Lane). Consistently with their admission of Ṣāliḥ's sincerity, honesty of purpose and uprightness, his people could not accuse him of forgery. The words *Musaḥḥar* and *Masḥūr* also mean, one fed by others.

156. [a]He said, 'Here is a she-camel; she has *her* turn of drinking, and you have *your* turn of drinking on an appointed day;

قَالَ هٰذِهٖ نَاقَةٌ لَّهَا شِرْبٌ وَّلَكُمْ شِرْبُ يَوْمٍ
مَّعْلُوْمٍ ﴿۱۵۶﴾

157. [b]'And touch her not with evil lest there overtake you the punishment of an awful day.'

وَلَا تَمَسُّوْهَا بِسُوْٓءٍ فَيَاْخُذَكُمْ عَذَابُ يَوْمٍ عَظِيْمٍ ﴿۱۵۷﴾

158. [c]But they hamstrung her; and then they became remorseful.

فَعَقَرُوْهَا فَاَصْبَحُوْا نٰدِمِيْنَ ﴿۱۵۸﴾

159. [d]So the punishment overtook them. In that verily there is a Sign, but most of these would not believe.

فَاَخَذَهُمُ الْعَذَابُ ۭ اِنَّ فِيْ ذٰلِكَ لَاٰيَةً ۭ وَمَا كَانَ
اَكْثَرُهُمْ مُّؤْمِنِيْنَ ﴿۱۵۹﴾

160. And surely thy Lord—He is the Mighty, the Merciful.

وَاِنَّ رَبَّكَ لَهُوَ الْعَزِيْزُ الرَّحِيْمُ ﴿۱۶۰﴾

R. 9 161. [e]The people of Lot rejected the Messengers,

كَذَّبَتْ قَوْمُ لُوْطِ ِۨالْمُرْسَلِيْنَ ﴿۱۶۱﴾

162. When their brother Lot said to them, 'Will you not fear *God* ?

اِذْ قَالَ لَهُمْ اَخُوْهُمْ لُوْطٌ اَلَا تَتَّقُوْنَ ﴿۱۶۲﴾

163. 'Surely, I am unto you a Messenger, faithful to *my* trust;

اِنِّيْ لَكُمْ رَسُوْلٌ اَمِيْنٌ ﴿۱۶۳﴾

164. 'So fear Allāh, and obey me.

فَاتَّقُوا اللّٰهَ وَاَطِيْعُوْنِ ﴿۱۶۴﴾

165. 'And I ask of you no reward for it. My reward is only with the Lord of the worlds ;

وَمَآ اَسْـَٔلُكُمْ عَلَيْهِ مِنْ اَجْرٍ ۚ اِنْ اَجْرِيَ اِلَّا عَلٰى
رَبِّ الْعٰلَمِيْنَ ﴿۱۶۵﴾

166. [f]'Do you, of all creatures, come to males ?

اَتَاْتُوْنَ الذُّكْرَانَ مِنَ الْعٰلَمِيْنَ ﴿۱۶۶﴾

167. 'And leave your wives whom your Lord has created for you? Nay, you are a people who transgress *all limits*.'

وَتَذَرُوْنَ مَا خَلَقَ لَكُمْ رَبُّكُمْ مِّنْ اَزْوَاجِكُمْ ۭ
بَلْ اَنْتُمْ قَوْمٌ عٰدُوْنَ ﴿۱۶۷﴾

168. [g]They said, 'If thou desist not, O Lot, thou wilt surely be banished.'[2129A]

قَالُوْا لَئِنْ لَّمْ تَنْتَهِ يٰلُوْطُ لَتَكُوْنَنَّ مِنَ الْمُخْرَجِيْنَ ﴿۱۶۸﴾

---

[a]7 : 74; 11 : 65; 17 : 60; 54 : 28; 91 : 14. [b]26 : 156.
[c]7 : 78; 11 : 66; 54 : 30 ; 91 : 15. [d]7 : 79; 11 : 68; 54 : 32.
[e]7 : 81-83; 54 : 34. [f]7 : 82; 27 : 56; 29 : 29-30. [g]7 : 83; 27 : 57.

2129A. *Rajama-hū* means, he stoned him, he banished him; excommunicated him, cut off all connections with him (Lane)

169. He said, 'Certainly I hate your conduct.'

قَالَ إِنِّى لِعَمَلِكُمْ مِّنَ الْقَالِيْنَ ۩

170. 'My Lord, save me and my family from what they do.'

رَبِّ نَجِّنِىْ وَأَهْلِىْ مِمَّا يَعْمَلُوْنَ ۞

171. "So We saved him and his family, all *of them*,

فَنَجَّيْنٰهُ وَأَهْلَهٗ أَجْمَعِيْنَ ۞

172. ᵇSave an old woman, among those who stayed behind.

إِلَّا عَجُوْزًا فِى الْغٰبِرِيْنَ ۞

173. ᶜThen We destroyed the others.

ثُمَّ دَمَّرْنَا الْاٰخَرِيْنَ ۞

174. ᵈAnd We rained upon them a rain; and evil was the rain *that descended* upon those who were warned.

وَأَمْطَرْنَا عَلَيْهِمْ مَّطَرًا ۚ فَسَآءَ مَطَرُ الْمُنْذَرِيْنَ ۞

175. In that verily there is a Sign, but most of these would not believe.

إِنَّ فِى ذٰلِكَ لَاٰيَةً ۚ وَمَا كَانَ أَكْثَرُهُمْ مُّؤْمِنِيْنَ ۞

176. And surely thy Lord—He is the Mighty, the Merciful.

وَإِنَّ رَبَّكَ لَهُوَ الْعَزِيْزُ الرَّحِيْمُ ۞

R. 10   177. ᵉThe People of the Wood rejected the Messengers,

كَذَّبَ أَصْحٰبُ لْـَٔيْكَةِ الْمُرْسَلِيْنَ ۞

178. ᶠWhen Shu'aib said to them, 'Will you not fear God?

إِذْ قَالَ لَهُمْ شُعَيْبٌ أَلَا تَتَّقُوْنَ ۞

179. 'Surely, I am unto you a Messenger, faithful to *my* trust.

إِنِّىْ لَكُمْ رَسُوْلٌ أَمِيْنٌ ۞

180. 'So fear Allāh, and obey me.

فَاتَّقُوا اللّٰهَ وَأَطِيْعُوْنِ ۞

181. 'And I ask of you no reward for it. My reward is with the Lord of the worlds;

وَمَآ أَسْـَٔلُكُمْ عَلَيْهِ مِنْ أَجْرٍ ۚ إِنْ أَجْرِىَ إِلَّا عَلٰى رَبِّ الْعٰلَمِيْنَ ۞

182. ᵍGive full measure, and be not of those who give less,²¹³⁰

أَوْفُوا الْكَيْلَ وَلَا تَكُوْنُوْا مِنَ الْمُخْسِرِيْنَ ۞

ᵃ15:60; 29:33; 37:135; 51:36.   ᵇ7:84; 11:82; 15:61; 27:58; 37:136.
ᶜ37:137.   ᵈ7:85; 25:41; 27:59.   ᵉ15:79; 38:14; 50:15.
ᶠ7:86; 11:85.   ᵍ11:85; 17:36; 55:10; 83:2-4.

2130. As at several places in the Qur'ān (Chapters 7th & 11th) and in the present *Sūrah* also the five Prophets—Noah, Hūd, Ṣāliḥ, Lot and Shu'aib have been mentioned

183. [a]'And weigh with a true balance,

وَزِنُوْا بِالْقِسْطَاسِ الْمُسْتَقِيْمِ ﴿١٨٣﴾

184. [b]'And diminish not unto people their things, nor go about the earth, creating disorder;

وَلَا تَبْخَسُوا النَّاسَ اَشْيَآءَهُمْ وَلَا تَعْثَوْا فِي الْاَرْضِ مُفْسِدِيْنَ ﴿١٨٤﴾

185. 'And fear Him Who created you and the earlier peoples.'

وَاتَّقُوا الَّذِيْ خَلَقَكُمْ وَالْجِبِلَّةَ الْاَوَّلِيْنَ ﴿١٨٥﴾

186. They said, 'Thou art but a bewitched person,

قَالُوْۤا اِنَّمَاۤ اَنْتَ مِنَ الْمُسَحَّرِيْنَ ﴿١٨٦﴾

187. 'And thou art only a mortal like us, and we believe thee to be a liar;

وَمَاۤ اَنْتَ اِلَّا بَشَرٌ مِّثْلُنَا وَاِنْ نَّظُنُّكَ لَمِنَ الْكٰذِبِيْنَ ﴿١٨٧﴾

188. 'So cause fragments of the sky to fall on us, if thou art truthful.'

فَاَسْقِطْ عَلَيْنَا كِسَفًا مِّنَ السَّمَآءِ اِنْ كُنْتَ مِنَ الصّٰدِقِيْنَ ﴿١٨٨﴾

189. He said, 'My Lord knows best what you do.'[2131]

قَالَ رَبِّيْۤ اَعْلَمُ بِمَا تَعْمَلُوْنَ ﴿١٨٩﴾

190. So they rejected him. [c]Then the punishment of the day of overshadowing gloom overtook them. That was indeed the punishment of a dreadful day.

فَكَذَّبُوْهُ فَاَخَذَهُمْ عَذَابُ يَوْمِ الظُّلَّةِ اِنَّهٗ كَانَ عَذَابَ يَوْمٍ عَظِيْمٍ ﴿١٩٠﴾

191. In that verily there is a Sign, but most of these would not believe.

اِنَّ فِيْ ذٰلِكَ لَاٰيَةً وَمَا كَانَ اَكْثَرُهُمْ مُّؤْمِنِيْنَ ﴿١٩١﴾

[a]11 : 85. [b]7 : 86; 11 : 86. [c]7 : 92; 11 : 95; 29 : 38.

together and in the same order, and identical words have been put in their mouths. In addition to the two fundamental teachings of all religions, *viz.*, Unity of God and obedience to the Prophet of the time, great emphasis has been laid in the case of each Prophet on the vice from which his people particularly suffered. Noah's people seemed to have been divided into water-tight compartments and the socially well-to-do among them suffered from an exaggerated notion of false superiority. The wealthy among them would not mix with the poorer sections of the society. The tribe of Hūd took great pride in their military exploits, architectural achievements and in their factories and chemical works. The people of Ṣāliḥ gloried in their power, prestige and wealth. Lot's people shamelessly indulged in a most unnatural and depraved sexual vice, while those of Shu'aib were dishonest in their commercial dealings. Each one of these vices has been separately dealt with in the account of the Prophet whose people particularly suffered from it. This is the way of Divine Prophets that, besides stressing the basic principles of religion, they lay special emphasis on the particular vice from which their people are found to suffer.

2131. To the insolent challenge of his people to bring down punishment upon them, (*Kisaf* meaning, Divine punishment), Shu'aib replied that his knowledge being imperfect it was not for him to decide if and when the punishment should and would overtake them and that it was God, their Lord and Creator, Who being fully acquainted with the nature of their deeds, knew whether or not they had rendered themselves deserving of the punishment they demanded.

192. And surely thy Lord—He is the Mighty, the Merciful. وَاِنَّ رَبَّكَ لَهُوَ الْعَزِيْزُ الرَّحِيْمُ ﴿١٩٢﴾

R. 11 193. [a]And verily this *Qur'ān* is a revelation from the Lord of all the worlds.[2132] وَاِنَّهٗ لَتَنْزِيْلُ رَبِّ الْعٰلَمِيْنَ ﴿١٩٣﴾

194. [b]The Spirit, faithful to the trust,[2133] has descended with it نَزَلَ بِهِ الرُّوْحُ الْاَمِيْنُ ﴿١٩٤﴾

195. On thy heart,[2134] that thou mayest be a Warner, عَلٰى قَلْبِكَ لِتَكُوْنَ مِنَ الْمُنْذِرِيْنَ ﴿١٩٥﴾

196. [c]In plain and clear Arabic tongue. بِلِسَانٍ عَرَبِيٍّ مُّبِيْنٍ ﴿١٩٦﴾

197. And it is surely *mentioned* in the Scriptures[2135] of the former peoples. وَاِنَّهٗ لَفِيْ زُبُرِ الْاَوَّلِيْنَ ﴿١٩٧﴾

198. And is it not a *sufficient* Sign for them that the learned among the Children of Israel know it? اَوَلَمْ يَكُنْ لَّهُمْ اٰيَةً اَنْ يَّعْلَمَهٗ عُلَمٰٓؤُا بَنِيْٓ اِسْرَآءِيْلَ ﴿١٩٨﴾

199. And if We had sent it down to one of the non-Arabs, وَلَوْ نَزَّلْنٰهُ عَلٰى بَعْضِ الْاَعْجَمِيْنَ ﴿١٩٩﴾

---

[a]20 : 5; 56 : 81. [b]2 : 98; 16 : 103. [c]16 : 104; 41 : 45; 46 : 13.

2132. The verse purports to say that the revelation of the Qur'ān is no new phenomenon. Like the Messages of the Prophets mentioned above the Quranic Message has also been revealed by God, but with this difference that whereas the former Prophets were sent to their respective peoples, the Qur'ān has been revealed for all the nations of the world, because *it is a revelation from the Lord of all the worlds.*

2133. In this verse the angel who brought the Quranic revelation has been called *Rūḥ al-Amīn*, *i.e.*, the Spirit faithful to the trust. Elsewhere, he is called *Rūḥ al-Qudus* (16 : 103), *i.e.*, the Spirit of holiness. The latter epithet has been used to point to the eternal and complete freedom from every error or blemish in the Qur'ān and the use of the former epithet (*Rūḥ al-Amīn*) implies that it shall continue to enjoy Divine protection against all attempts to tamper with its text. This epithet has been used exclusively with regard to the revelation of the Qur'ān because the promise of everlasting Divine protection was held out to no other Divine Scripture ; and their texts, in course of time, came to be interfered and tampered with. Strangely enough, the Holy Prophet himself was known as *Al-Amīn* (the Trusty) at Mecca. What a great Divine tribute to, and evidence of, the trustworthiness of the Qur'ān that its revelation was brought by an *Amīn* to an *Amīn* !

2134. The words 'on thy heart' have been added to indicate that the Quranic revelations were not merely inspired ideas which the Holy Prophet expressed in his own words but were the actual words of God Himself which descended upon the Prophet's heart through the medium of Gabriel.

2135. The advent of the Holy Prophet and the revelation of the Qur'ān both have been foretold in the previous Divine Scriptures. Prophecies to this effect are to be found in

200. And he had read it to them, they would never have believed in it.

فَقَرَاَهٗ عَلَيْهِمْ مَّا كَانُوْا بِهٖ مُؤْمِنِيْنَ ﴿٢٠٠﴾

201. Thus have We caused *disbelief* to enter into the hearts[2136] of the sinful.

كَذٰلِكَ سَلَكْنٰهُ فِيْ قُلُوْبِ الْمُجْرِمِيْنَ ﴿٢٠١﴾

202. They will not believe in it until they see the grievous punishment,

لَا يُؤْمِنُوْنَ بِهٖ حَتّٰى يَرَوُا الْعَذَابَ الْاَلِيْمَ ﴿٢٠٢﴾

203. Which will come upon them suddenly, while they are not aware *of it*.

فَيَاْتِيَهُمْ بَغْتَةً وَّهُمْ لَا يَشْعُرُوْنَ ﴿٢٠٣﴾

204. And they will say, 'Shall we be respited?'

فَيَقُوْلُوْا هَلْ نَحْنُ مُنْظَرُوْنَ ﴿٢٠٤﴾

205. [a]What! do they seek to hasten Our punishment?

اَفَبِعَذَابِنَا يَسْتَعْجِلُوْنَ ﴿٢٠٥﴾

206. [b]What thinkest thou that if We let them enjoy the good things *of this world* for years;

اَفَرَءَيْتَ اِنْ مَّتَّعْنٰهُمْ سِنِيْنَ ﴿٢٠٦﴾

207. Then there comes to them *the punishment* that they are promised,

ثُمَّ جَآءَهُمْ مَّا كَانُوْا يُوْعَدُوْنَ ﴿٢٠٧﴾

208. Of what avail will be to them that which they were *allowed* to enjoy?

مَآ اَغْنٰى عَنْهُمْ مَّا كَانُوْا يُمَتَّعُوْنَ ﴿٢٠٨﴾

209. [c]And never did We destroy any township but it had *its* Warners.[2137]

وَمَآ اَهْلَكْنَا مِنْ قَرْيَةٍ اِلَّا لَهَا مُنْذِرُوْنَ ﴿٢٠٩﴾

[a]22 : 48; 27 : 72-73; 51 : 15. [b]20 : 132; 28 : 62. [c]6: 132; 11 : 118; 20 : 135; 28 : 60.

the religious Scriptures of almost every Faith but the Bible, being the best known and most widely read of all revealed Books before the Qur'ān and also being its fore-runner and in its pristine purity being its counterpart as a Book of Divine laws, contains the largest number of such prophecies. See Deut. 18 : 18 & 33 : 2; Isaiah 21 : 13-17; Song of Solomon 1 : 5-6 Habakkuk3 : 3-5 Matt. 21 : 42-45 & John 16 : 12-14.

2136. This bad habit of disbelievers has its roots in their own hearts and is born of their indulgence in sin and vice and does not come from outside. The verse, in fact, states a general truth that when a man indulges in sin, his consciousness of it becomes blunted and in course of time he even comes to develop a liking for it. It is in this way that sin corrodes and vitiates 'the hearts of the sinful.'

2137. The verse refers to a Divine law that punishment does not overtake a people unless a Prophet is first sent to them and by rejecting and opposing him they render themselves deserving of it. See also 17 : 16; 28 : 60; 35 : 38.

210. *So that* they may be admonished; and We are not unjust.

ذِكْرٰى ۛ وَ مَا كُنَّا ظٰلِمِيْنَ ﴿۲۱۰﴾

211. And the evil ones have not brought it down;

وَ مَا تَنَزَّلَتْ بِهِ الشَّيٰطِيْنُ ﴿۲۱۱﴾

212. It does neither suit them nor have they the power *to produce it.*[2138]

وَ مَا يَنْۢبَغِيْ لَهُمْ وَ مَا يَسْتَطِيْعُوْنَ ﴿۲۱۲﴾

213. [a]Surely, they are debarred from listening *to the Divine Word.*

اِنَّهُمْ عَنِ السَّمْعِ لَمَعْزُوْلُوْنَ ﴿۲۱۳﴾

214. [b]Call not, therefore, on any other god beside Allāh,[2139] lest thou become *one* of those who are punished,

فَلَا تَدْعُ مَعَ اللّٰهِ اِلٰهًا اٰخَرَ فَتَكُوْنَ مِنَ الْمُعَذَّبِيْنَ ﴿۲۱۴﴾

215. And warn thy nearest kinsmen,[2140]

وَ اَنْذِرْ عَشِيْرَتَكَ الْاَقْرَبِيْنَ ﴿۲۱۵﴾

216. [c]And lower thy wing *of mercy* to the believers who follow thee.

وَ اخْفِضْ جَنَاحَكَ لِمَنِ اتَّبَعَكَ مِنَ الْمُؤْمِنِيْنَ ﴿۲۱۶﴾

217. Then if they disobey thee, say, 'I repudiate all connection with what you do.'[2140A]

فَاِنْ عَصَوْكَ فَقُلْ اِنِّيْ بَرِيْٓءٌ مِّمَّا تَعْمَلُوْنَ ﴿۲۱۷﴾

218. [d]And put thy trust in the Mighty, the Merciful,

وَ تَوَكَّلْ عَلَى الْعَزِيْزِ الرَّحِيْمِ ﴿۲۱۸﴾

[a]11 : 21. [b]17 : 23, 40; 28 : 89. [c]15 : 89. [d]25 : 59; 33 : 49.

2138. The verse contains three arguments in support of the claim that satans could have no hand in the production of the Qur'ān : (*a*) Its teaching constitutes a most effective and uncompromising condemnation of all that satans stand for. (*b*) It is of such exalted character and contains such sublime truths that it is beyond the power of satans to produce the like of them (17 : 89). (*c*) The Qur'ān contains mighty prophecies about the ultimate triumph of Islām. The satans could not make them as they have no knowledge of the future.

2139. The Qur'ān could not have been the Devil's work. A satanic production could not have laid so much stress on Divine Unity as has been laid in the Qur'ān.

2140. It is on record that when this verse was revealed the Holy Prophet stood on mount Ṣafā and called every Quraish tribe by name and warned them of the Divine punishment that would overtake them if they did not accept his Message and give up their evil ways (Bukhārī).

2140A. I am quit of you ; I dissociate myself completely from what you do ; I disclaim all responsibility for your actions.

219. [a]Who sees thee when thou standest *in Prayer*,

الَّذِىْ يَرٰىكَ حِيْنَ تَقُوْمُ ﴿٢١٩﴾

220. And *Who sees* thy movements among those who prostrate[2141] themselves *before Allāh*.

وَتَقَلُّبَكَ فِى السّٰجِدِيْنَ ﴿٢٢٠﴾

221. He is indeed the All-Hearing, the All-Knowing.

اِنَّهٗ هُوَ السَّمِيْعُ الْعَلِيْمُ ﴿٢٢١﴾

222. Shall I inform you on whom the evil ones descend?

هَلْ اُنَبِّئُكُمْ عَلٰى مَنْ تَنَزَّلُ الشَّيٰطِيْنُ ﴿٢٢٢﴾

223. They descend on every lying sinner.

تَنَزَّلُ عَلٰى كُلِّ اَفَّاكٍ اَثِيْمٍ ﴿٢٢٣﴾

224. They strain their ears *towards heaven*, and most of them are liars.

يُّلْقُوْنَ السَّمْعَ وَاَكْثَرُهُمْ كٰذِبُوْنَ ﴿٢٢٤﴾

225. And *as for* the poets—it is the erring ones who follow them.

وَالشُّعَرَآءُ يَتَّبِعُهُمُ الْغَاوٗنَ ﴿٢٢٥﴾

226. Dost thou not see how they wander aimlessly in every valley,

اَلَمْ تَرَ اَنَّهُمْ فِىْ كُلِّ وَادٍ يَّهِيْمُوْنَ ﴿٢٢٦﴾

227. And that they say what they do not?[2142]

وَاَنَّهُمْ يَقُوْلُوْنَ مَا لَا يَفْعَلُوْنَ ﴿٢٢٧﴾

228. Save those who believe and do righteous deeds, and remember Allāh much, and defend themselves after they are wronged. And the wrongdoers shall soon know to what place of return they shall return.

اِلَّا الَّذِيْنَ اٰمَنُوْا وَعَمِلُوا الصّٰلِحٰتِ وَذَكَرُوا اللّٰهَ كَثِيْرًا وَّانْتَصَرُوْا مِنْۢ بَعْدِ مَا ظُلِمُوْا ۗ وَسَيَعْلَمُ الَّذِيْنَ ظَلَمُوْٓا اَىَّ مُنْقَلَبٍ يَّنْقَلِبُوْنَ ﴿٢٢٨﴾

[a]73 : 21.

2141. This verse pays a glowing tribute to the righteousness and nobility of the Holy Prophet's Companions. The word *Sājidīn* refers to them. Blessed was the Holy Prophet who was surrounded by such godly men. Human history has failed to produce another example of such a noble Master, loved and followed by such devoted and righteous disciples.

2142. In these verses the imputation that the Holy Prophet is a poet (21 : 6) is rebutted. Three reasons given for this rebuttal are: (1) Those who follow and associate with the poets are not men of high moral character, but the Holy Prophet's followers were possessed of very noble ideals and of very high moral character. (2) The poets have no fixed ideal or programme in life. They, as it were, wander about aimlessly in every valley. But the Holy Prophet had a very great and sublime mission in life. (3) The poets do not practise what they preach, but the Holy Prophet was not only the noblest preceptor but the greatest man of action and a model exemplar.

CHAPTER 27

AL-NAML

(*Revealed before Hijrah*)

Date of Revelation and Context

Towards the close of the preceding *Sūrah* the disbelievers' charge that the Holy Prophet was a poet and that satans descended upon him was most effectively refuted and it was stated that satans descended only upon sinful liars and forgers who mixed falsehood with truth, and that hotchpotch of much falsehood mixed with a little truth could never produce any good results. The *Sūrah* further said that the poets had no great aim or fixed programme in life, and wandered, as it were, distractedly in every valley and did not practise what they preached. To continue and elaborate the subject the present *Sūrah* opens with a firm declaration that the Qur'ān is God's own revealed Word. It explains fully and completely all matters that concern man's spiritual life and supports its principles and ideals with sound and cogent arguments. According to Ibn 'Abbās and Ibn Zubair the *Sūrah* was revealed at Mecca. Other Muslim scholars also support this view.

Subject-Matter

Whereas the preceding *Sūrah* opened with the abbreviated letters *Ṭā Sīn Mīm*, this *Sūrah* begins with the letters *Ṭā Sīn*, the letter *Mīm* having been omitted. This shows that the subject-matter of this *Sūrah* constitutes a continuation of the subject-matter of the preceding *Sūrah* though in a little different form. It begins with a brief reference to a vision in which Moses saw a manifestation of Divine Majesty and proceeds to give a somewhat detailed account of David and Solomon in whose reigns the Israelite conquests, power and material glory had attained their zenith. After this, the *Sūrah* deals at some length with the two most fundamental and basic religious beliefs—existence of God and Life after death. To support and substantiate the first belief the *Sūrah* adduces arguments from nature, man's inner self and from his collective life. After alluding to the fact that God's great powers are manifested in the marvellous working of the laws of nature, the *Sūrah* advances the acceptance of prayer by God as an invincible argument in support of His existence. Another unanswerable argument given by the *Sūrah* is that God reveals Himself to His Messengers and righteous servants and vouchsafes to them the knowledge of the unknown, instances of which are to be witnessed in every age. Next, the *Sūrah* deals with Life after death. After briefly pointing to other arguments it advances as one unassailable proof in support of Life after death the great moral and spiritual revolution which the Holy Prophet brought about among his people, and then proceeds to expatiate upon it. The argument begins and develops in this way. The Arabs had completely despaired of their future. They heedlessly wallowed in the quagmire of immoral ways and practices and rejected the Holy Prophet's Message and refused to believe that they will have to render an account of their deeds in an after life. Morally and spiritually they were virtually a dead people. But they received a new life through the Qur'ān. The water of Divine revelation descended upon the bleak and barren soil of Arabia and it bloomed and blossomed and pulsated with a new vigorous life, and by acting upon its teachings the Arabs, erstwhile the scum and dregs of humanity, became its leaders and teachers. This marvellous revolution constituted a proof positive of the fact that God, Who could raise a spiritually dead people to a new life, had the power to raise also the physically dead to life again. The *Sūrah* closes on the note that God has chosen Mecca to be the Centre for His last Message and that from this town shall emanate a Divine Light which will illumine the whole world.

سُوْرَةُ النَّمْلِ مَكِّيَّةٌ

(٢٧) اٰياتها ٩٤ — ركوعاتها ٧

1. [a]In the name of Allāh, the Gracious, the Merciful.

بِسْمِ اللّٰهِ الرَّحْمٰنِ الرَّحِيْمِ ①

2. [b]Ṭā Sīn.[2143] [c]These are verses of the Qur'ān, and of an illuminating Book,[2144]

طٰسٓ تِلْكَ اٰيٰتُ الْقُرْاٰنِ وَكِتَابٍ مُّبِيْنٍ ②

3. [d]A guidance and good tidings to those who would believe,

هُدًى وَّبُشْرٰى لِلْمُؤْمِنِيْنَ ③

4. [e]Who observe Prayer and pay the *Zakāt*, and have firm faith in the Hereafter.

الَّذِيْنَ يُقِيْمُوْنَ الصَّلٰوةَ وَيُؤْتُوْنَ الزَّكٰوةَ وَهُمْ بِالْاٰخِرَةِ هُمْ يُوْقِنُوْنَ ④

5. [f]*As to* those who believe not in the Hereafter, We have made their deeds *appear* beautiful[2145] to them, so they wander blindly.

اِنَّ الَّذِيْنَ لَا يُؤْمِنُوْنَ بِالْاٰخِرَةِ زَيَّنَّا لَهُمْ اَعْمَالَهُمْ فَهُمْ يَعْمَهُوْنَ ⑤

6. It is they who shall have a grievous torment, and they *alone* it is who shall be the greatest losers in the Hereafter.

اُولٰٓئِكَ الَّذِيْنَ لَهُمْ سُوْٓءُ الْعَذَابِ وَهُمْ فِي الْاٰخِرَةِ هُمُ الْاَخْسَرُوْنَ ⑥

---

[a]1 : 1. [b]26 : 2; 27 : 2; 28 : 2. [c]15 : 2; 26 : 3; 28 : 3. [d]2 : 3; 10 : 58; 12 : 112; 31 : 4. [e]2 : 4; 8 : 4; 14 : 32; 31 : 5. [f]16 : 23; 17 : 11; 34 : 9.

2143. For a general discussion of the abbreviated letters see 16 and 1738 and about *Ṭā Sīn*, see 2094. It is significant that whereas 26th and 28th Chapters which have the abbreviated letters *Ṭā Sīn Mīm* in their beginning open with the verse, *These are verses of the Book that makes things clear*, the present *Sūrah* which is prefixed with the letters *Ṭā Sīn* begins with the verse, *These are verses of the Qur'ān, and of an illuminating Book*. This shows that while in the former two Chapters the Qur'ān is alluded to only with reference to Moses's Book, in the present *Sūrah* it has been mentioned by name, in its own right as in the verse under comment as well as in vv. 7 and 93.

2144. The use of 'Al-Qur'ān' and 'the Book' as qualifying words implies a mighty prophecy that the Holy Book of Islām will continue to be preserved in the form of a book till the end of time and that it will be widely studied and read, the word Qur'ān meaning a book that is read. 'Since the use of the Koran in public worship, in schools and otherwise, is much more extensive than, for example, the reading of the Bible in most Christian countries, it has been truly described as the most widely read book in existence' (Enc. Bri. 9th edit. vol. 16, p. 597).

2145. From vv. 6 : 44 and 8 : 49 it is clear that it is Satan who makes evil and mischievous deeds of evil-doers look beautiful in their eyes. But in the verse under comment it is stated that God makes the deeds of disbelievers appear beautiful to them. It is a natural law that when a person pursues an evil course, thinking that he is not accountable for what he does, he begins to justify his conduct as good and proper, and thus it begins to appear to him in that light. This, in fact, is the consequence of his own conduct but inasmuch as it comes about in accordance with a Divine Law, it is here attributed to God.

7. Verily, thou receivest the Qur'ān from the One Wise, All-Knowing.[2146]

وَإِنَّكَ لَتُلَقَّى الْقُرْاٰنَ مِنْ لَّدُنْ حَكِيْمٍ عَلِيْمٍ ﴿٧﴾

8. [a]*Call to mind* when Moses said to his family, 'I perceive a fire.[2147] I will bring you from there some news *of great import*, or I will bring you a flaming brand that you may warm yourselves.'

إِذْ قَالَ مُوْسٰى لِأَهْلِهٖٓ إِنِّيْٓ اٰنَسْتُ نَارًا ۭ سَاٰتِيْكُمْ
مِّنْهَا بِخَبَرٍ أَوْ اٰتِيْكُمْ بِشِهَابٍ قَبَسٍ لَّعَلَّكُمْ
تَصْطَلُوْنَ ﴿٨﴾

9. So when he came to it, he was called *by a voice*, 'Blessed is he who is in the fire and also those around[2148] it, and glorified be Allāh, the Lord of the worlds;

فَلَمَّا جَآءَهَا نُوْدِيَ أَنْ بُوْرِكَ مَنْ فِي النَّارِ وَ
مَنْ حَوْلَهَا ۭ وَسُبْحٰنَ اللّٰهِ رَبِّ الْعٰلَمِيْنَ ﴿٩﴾

10. 'O Moses, [b]verily, I am Allāh, the Mighty, the Wise;

يٰمُوْسٰٓى إِنَّهٗٓ أَنَا اللّٰهُ الْعَزِيْزُ الْحَكِيْمُ ﴿١٠﴾

11. [c]'Throw down thy rod.' And when he saw it move as though it were a serpent,[2148A] he turned back retreating and did not look back, *whereupon We said,* 'O Moses, fear, not. Verily, I am the One in Whose presence the Messengers need have no fear;

وَأَلْقِ عَصَاكَ ۭ فَلَمَّا رَاٰهَا تَهْتَزُّ كَأَنَّهَا جَآنٌّ وَّلّٰى
مُدْبِرًا وَّلَمْ يُعَقِّبْ ۭ يٰمُوْسٰى لَا تَخَفْ ۣ إِنِّيْ لَا يَخَافُ
لَدَيَّ الْمُرْسَلُوْنَ ﴿١١﴾

[a]20 : 11; 28 : 30. [b]20 : 12-13; 28 : 31; [c]7 : 118; 20 : 20; 28 : 32.

2146. The verse constitutes a clear denial of the charge that the Holy Prophet had his own ideas written down and collected in the form of a book and called it 'The Qur'ān,' and is an unequivocal declaration that he received the Qur'ān direct from the Wise and All-Knowing God.

2147. It was not actual fire that Moses had seen. Had it been so he would have used the expression 'I have perceived *the* fire,' instead of 'I have perceived *a* fire.' In fact, it was a vision that Moses had seen, 'fire' symbolizing love of God. It is worthy of note that most of the major incidents, connected with Moses that have been mentioned in the Qur'ān, were not incidents which actually took place in the physical world but only visions symbolizing great landmarks in the course of his spiritual development and prophetic mission. Besides the vision about the rod there are mentioned other important instances of such visions in the Qur'ān (7 : 144), the verse under comment affording one such instance.

2148. The expression may mean, (*a*) who is in search of the fire, and who is near it; (*b*) who is actually in the fire and who is about to enter it, 'fire' symbolizing the fire of God's love or the fire of trials and tribulations. The fire was not God, nor was God in the fire. It was only a Divine manifestation which cast its glow upon all that was near.

2148A. See 1023.

12. 'As to those who do wrong and then adopt good instead of evil; *to them* I am indeed Most Forgiving, Merciful;

إِلَّا مَنْ ظَلَمَ ثُمَّ بَدَّلَ حُسْنًا بَعْدَ سُوٓءٍ فَإِنِّي غَفُورٌ رَّحِيمٌ ⑫

13. [a]'And put thy hand into thy bosom; it will come forth white without evil. This is among the nine Signs[2149] unto Pharaoh and his people, for they are a rebellious people.'

وَأَدْخِلْ يَدَكَ فِي جَيْبِكَ تَخْرُجْ بَيْضَآءَ مِنْ غَيْرِ سُوٓءٍ فِي تِسْعِ آيَاتٍ إِلَىٰ فِرْعَوْنَ وَقَوْمِهِۦٓ إِنَّهُمْ كَانُوا قَوْمًا فَاسِقِينَ ⑬

14. But when Our sight-giving[2150] Signs came to them, they said, [b]'This is manifest magic.'

فَلَمَّا جَآءَتْهُمْ آيَاتُنَا مُبْصِرَةً قَالُوا هَٰذَا سِحْرٌ مُّبِينٌ ⑭

15. [c]And they rejected them wrongfully and arrogantly, while their souls were convinced of their *truth*. See then, how *evil* was the end of those who acted corruptly!

وَجَحَدُوا بِهَا وَاسْتَيْقَنَتْهَآ أَنفُسُهُمْ ظُلْمًا وَعُلُوًّا فَانظُرْ كَيْفَ كَانَ عَاقِبَةُ الْمُفْسِدِينَ ⑮ ع

R. 2 16. And We gave knowledge to David and Solomon,[2151] and they said, 'All praise belongs to Allāh, Who has exalted us above many of His believing servants.'

وَلَقَدْ آتَيْنَا دَاوُودَ وَسُلَيْمَانَ عِلْمًا وَقَالَا الْحَمْدُ لِلَّهِ الَّذِي فَضَّلَنَا عَلَىٰ كَثِيرٍ مِّنْ عِبَادِهِ الْمُؤْمِنِينَ ⑯

[a]20 : 23, 24. 17 : 102; 20 : 24. [b]43 : 31; 61 : 7. [c]2 : 88.

2149. For 'nine Signs' see 17 : 102. Briefly, they were the Signs (1) of the rod and (2) of the white hand (7: 108-109); (3) of lice; (4) of frogs which implied unusual, incessant rains; and (5) of locusts; (6) of blood, *i.e.*, a plague which caused bleeding from the nose; (7) and of storm which caused the sea-water to overwhelm Pharaoh and his hosts when they were crossing the sea after the Israelites had crossed it safely (7 : 134); (8) of drought and (9) of destruction of fruits (7 : 131).

2150. *Mubṣirah* means, clear, manifest; illumining; sight-giving, causing to have mental perception or knowledge (Lane).

2151. David was a great warrior and a mighty and sagacious statesman. He was the founder of the Judean dynasty and the real builder of the Hebrew Kingdom. Through him all the tribes of Israel from Dan to Beersheba became united and organized into a powerful nation whose Kingdom extended from the Euphrates to the Nile. Solomon consolidated the Kingdom he had inherited from his father. He too was a great and good monarch. He greatly extended and developed the trade and commerce of his country. He was the master-builder among the Israelite Kings and is best known for the building of the famous Temple at Jerusalem, which became the *Qiblah* of the Israelites.

17. And Solomon was heir to David. And he said, 'O ye people, we have been taught the language[2152] of birds, and we have had all *necessary* things bestowed upon us. This indeed is *God's* manifest grace.'

وَوَرِثَ سُلَيْمٰنُ دَاوٗدَ وَقَالَ يٰۤاَيُّهَا النَّاسُ عُلِّمْنَا مَنْطِقَ الطَّيْرِ وَاُوْتِيْنَا مِنْ كُلِّ شَيْءٍ ؕ اِنَّ هٰذَا لَهُوَ الْفَضْلُ الْمُبِيْنُ ﴿۱۷﴾

18. [a]And there were gathered together unto Solomon his hosts of jinn[2153] and men and birds,[2154] and they were formed into *separate*[2155] divisions,

وَحُشِرَ لِسُلَيْمٰنَ جُنُوْدُهٗ مِنَ الْجِنِّ وَالْاِنْسِ وَالطَّيْرِ فَهُمْ يُوْزَعُوْنَ ﴿۱۸﴾

[a]38 : 19-20.

2152. *Manṭiq* (language) is derived from *Naṭaqa* which means, he spoke with sound and letters which made clear his meaning. Thus *Nuṭq* applies to both articulate and inarticulate speech and also to the condition of a thing which is as significant as articulate speech. It is external, *viz.*, spoken words; and internal, *viz.*, understanding. The word is also used with regard to animals and birds when the use is metaphorical (Mufradāt). Birds and insects have their own means of communication. Migratory birds fly from one region to another with the change in weather. They fly in flocks and their flight is orderly. Similarly, ants live in communities and the bees have a well-regulated system of government. This could not be possible without there being some means of communication between them. This means of communication may be called their language. Prophets David and Solomon are here stated to have been taught the language of birds which may be taken as signifying that they had learnt how to make use of birds. The art of using birds for carrying messages from one place to another was very much developed by Solomon and frequent use of it was made in the management of the far-flung empire over which he ruled.

2153. 'Jinn' here may signify mountain or wild tribes. The verse under comment should be read along with vv. 21 : 83; 34 : 13 and 38 : 38. It seems to refer to the military personnel of Solomon's army. The three words—*Jinn, Ins* (men) and *Ṭair* (birds)—may represent three departments of his army. In the present verse and in 34 : 13, the word *Jinn* has been used to represent a particular section of the army while in 21 : 83 and 38:38, the word *Shayāṭīn,* has been used to represent the same class. It seems that Solomon had subdued and subjugated some wild tribes, this approximately being the sense of both the words, *Jinn* and *Shayāṭīn* who formed an integral part of his army and did sundry other hard tasks for him. The word *Ṭair* denoting swift-footed horses may represent Solomon's cavalry. This meaning of the word finds corroboration in 38 : 32-34 where Solomon has been stated to possess great love for horses. Thus whereas *Jinn* and *Ins* (men) represented two sections of Solomon's infantry, *Ṭair* (birds) stood for his cavalry. But if *Ṭair* may be taken to mean actual birds then the word would signify birds which Solomon employed for carrying messages. Thus they also formed a very useful and necessary adjunct to his army. But these three words used in a metaphorical sense may signify respectively 'big men,' 'ordinary men' and 'highly spiritual men.'

2154. *Ṭair*, besides meaning 'birds', may also apply to swift-footed animals such as horses, etc. *Ṭayyār* which is an intensive form of *Ṭāir* signifies a sharp-spirited and quick-footed horse which runs so fast that it seems to be flying (Lane & Lisān).

2155. *Waza'a* means, he stopped the first part of the army so that their last part may join them. *Huwa Yaza'u al-Jaisha* means, he was arranging the soldiers in proper order and placing them in rows (Aqrab). The Quranic expression means : They were formed into separate groups. (2) They marched like an ordered and disciplined army. (3) Their first part was stopped so that their last part might join them. These words show that Solomon had a well-trained and disciplined army which had several separate and distinct departments.

19. Until when they came to the Valley of Al-Naml,[2156] a Namlite said, 'O ye Naml, enter your habitations, lest Solomon and his hosts crush you, while they know not.'[2157]

حَتّٰٓى اِذَآ اَتَوْا عَلٰى وَادِ النَّمْلِ قَالَتْ نَمْلَةٌ يّٰٓاَيُّهَا
النَّمْلُ ادْخُلُوْا مَسٰكِنَكُمْ لَا يَحْطِمَنَّكُمْ سُلَيْمٰنُ
وَجُنُوْدُهٗ وَهُمْ لَا يَشْعُرُوْنَ ﴿١٩﴾

20. Thereupon he smiled, wondering[2158] at her words and said, 'My Lord, grant me that I may be grateful *to Thee* for Thy favour which Thou hast bestowed upon me and upon my parents, and that I may do such good works as would please Thee, and admit me, by Thy mercy, among Thy righteous servants.'

فَتَبَسَّمَ ضَاحِكًا مِّنْ قَوْلِهَا وَقَالَ رَبِّ اَوْزِعْنِيْٓ
اَنْ اَشْكُرَ نِعْمَتَكَ الَّتِيْٓ اَنْعَمْتَ عَلَيَّ وَعَلٰى وَالِدَيَّ
وَاَنْ اَعْمَلَ صَالِحًا تَرْضٰىهُ وَاَدْخِلْنِيْ بِرَحْمَتِكَ
فِيْ عِبَادِكَ الصّٰلِحِيْنَ ﴿٢٠﴾

21. And he reviewed[2159] the birds and said, 'How is it that I do not see Hudhud? Is he *deliberately* absent?

وَتَفَقَّدَ الطَّيْرَ فَقَالَ مَا لِيَ لَآ اَرَى الْهُدْهُدَ ۖ
اَمْ كَانَ مِنَ الْغَآئِبِيْنَ ﴿٢١﴾

2156. Naml being a proper noun, "the Valley of Al-Naml" does not mean the valley of ants as is generally misunderstood but the valley where a tribe named Naml lived. In Qāmūs we have, *al-Abriqatu min Miyāhil Namlati, i.e.*, Abriqah is one of the springs of Namlah. So Naml was the name of a tribe just as Māzin (Ḥamāsah), which means the eggs of ants, was the name of an Arab. In Arabia it was not an uncommon practice that tribes were named after animals and beasts such as Banū Asad, Banū Kalb, Banū Naml, etc. Moreover, the use of the words *Udkhulū* (enter) and *Masākinakum* (your habitations) in the verse lends powerful support to the view that Naml was a tribe, since the former verb is used only for rational beings and the latter expression (your habitations) also has been used in the Qur'ān exclusively for human habitations (29 : 39 ; 32 : 27). Thus *Namlah* means a person of the tribe of *Al-Naml*—a Namlite. The said Namlite was possibly their leader and had ordered the people to get out of the way of the army of Solomon and enter their houses. According to some authorities this valley is situated between Jibrīn and 'Asqalān which is a town on the sea-coast, twelve miles to the north of Gaz, near Sinai (Taqwīm al-Buldān). Jibrīn is a town in the north, situated in the *Vilāyah* of Damascus. This shows that the Valley of Naml is situated near the sea-coast, opposite to or near Jerusalem, lying on the route from Damascus to Ḥijāz, at a distance of about a hundred miles from it. This part of the country was, up to the time of Solomon, inhabited by the Arabs and the Midianites. (See ancient and modern maps of Syria and Palestine). According to other authorities, however, it is situated in Yemen. This latter view seems to be more akin to reality. In view of this historical fact, legends woven round this valley are mere conjectures. The simple fact seems to be that while on a military expedition to Saba', Solomon might have passed by the valley where the tribe called Naml lived.

2157. It appears that the piety and godliness of Solomon's soldiers was famed far and wide. They would not knowingly harm or injure any people. This seems to be the implication of the words, *while they knew not*, and this is what pleased Solomon as is clear from the next verse.

2158. *Daḥika* meaning, he wondered or he was pleased (Lane), the verse signifies that Solomon wondered and was pleased with the good opinion the Namlite expressed about his own and that of his army's power and piety.

2159. *Tafaqqada* (he reviewed) is derived from *Faqada, i.e.*, he lost it, it was or became absent from him. *Tafaqqada-hū* means, he sought for or after it leisurely or repeatedly, it being absent from him, or he sought to obtain knowledge of it (Mufradāt). Solomon seemed to have reviewed his army and Hudhud, an important officer of the State, possibly a general, was absent at the important occasion.

22. 'I will surely punish[2160] him with a severe punishment or I will slay him, unless he brings me a clear reason *for his absence*.

لَاُعَذِّبَنَّهٗ عَذَابًا شَدِيْدًا اَوْ لَاَاذْبَحَنَّهٗٓ اَوْ
لَيَاْتِيَنِّيْ بِسُلْطٰنٍ مُّبِيْنٍ ﴿٢٢﴾

23. And he did not tarry long *before Hudhud came* and said, 'I have acquired knowledge of that of which thou hast no knowledge; and I have come to thee from Saba' with sure tidings;[2161]

فَمَكَثَ غَيْرَ بَعِيْدٍ فَقَالَ اَحَطْتُّ بِمَا لَمْ تُحِطْ بِهٖ
وَجِئْتُكَ مِنْ سَبَاٍۭ بِنَبَاٍ يَّقِيْنٍ ﴿٢٣﴾

24. 'I found a woman ruling over them, and she has been given every *necessary* thing[2162] and she has a mighty throne;

اِنِّيْ وَجَدْتُّ امْرَاَةً تَمْلِكُهُمْ وَاُوْتِيَتْ مِنْ كُلِّ
شَيْءٍ وَّلَهَا عَرْشٌ عَظِيْمٌ ﴿٢٤﴾

25. 'I found her and her people worshipping the sun[2163] instead of

وَجَدْتُّهَا وَقَوْمَهَا يَسْجُدُوْنَ لِلشَّمْسِ مِنْ دُوْنِ

2160. Contrary to popular belief, based on fable and fiction, Hudhud was not a bird employed by Solomon as his message-bearer since (*a*) it was inconsistent with Solomon's dignity as a great monarch and a Divine Prophet to be so angry with a small bird as to be prepared to inflict severe punishment upon it or even to kill it. (*b*) Hudhud seems to be well-acquainted with the rules and requirements of States and also well-versed in the knowledge about Divine Unity (vv. 25-26) which birds are not. (*c*) Hudhud, being not a migratory bird, cannot fly long distances and therefore could not have been selected for the journey to Sheba and back (v. 23). It follows from these facts that Hudhud was not a bird but a man, even a very responsible officer of State or a general who had been entrusted with an important political mission by Solomon to the Queen of Sheba. The practice of exchange of envoys seems to have been quite popular in Solomon's time. Moreover, it is a known fact that men are named after birds and animals. Hudhud was a popular name among Solomon's people. The word seems to be the Arabicised form of Hudad, a biblical name. It appears to have been the name of several Edomite kings. A son of Ishmael, too, bore this name. Similarly, an Edomite prince who fled to Egypt for fear of Jacob's massacre was known by this name (1. Kings 11 : 14). The name appeared to be so popular and is so frequently used in the Old Testament that when used without a qualifying word it means, 'a man of the Edomite family' (Jew.Enc.). Hudhud is also said to be the name of the father of Bilqīs, the Queen of Sheba (Muntaha al-Irab).

2161. It appears from this verse that Hudhud was sent on an important State mission and he brought for Solomon an important piece of news. Saba' may be identified with Sheba of the Bible (1 Kings, ch. 10). It was a city in Yemen, situated at about three days' journey from the city of Ṣan'ā' and was the seat of Government of Queen of Sheba. Moreover, Saba' is a well-known branch of the Qaḥṭānī tribes.

2162. The verse shows that Queen of Sheba ruled over a very prosperous people who had attained a very high degree of civilization and that she possessed all those things which had made her a powerful monarch.

2163. The Sabaeans worshipped the sun and the stars, a creed which in all likelihood had been imported into Yemen from Iraq with which the people of Yemen were in close contact by way of the sea and the Persian Gulf. The Sabaeans should not be confounded with Sabians who have been mentioned in 2 : 63; 5 : 70 and 22 : 18, and have been variously described as (1) a star-worshipping people living in Iraq ; (2) a people believing in a Faith which was a sort of a patchwork of Judaism, Christianity and Zoroastrianism; (3) a people who lived near Mosul in Iraq and believed in the Unity of God, but possessed no known

Allāh, [a]and Satan has made their works look beautiful to them, and has thus hindered them from the *right* way, so that they are not rightly guided—

اللّٰهِ وَزَيَّنَ لَهُمُ الشَّيْطٰنُ اَعْمَالَهُمْ فَصَدَّهُمْ عَنِ السَّبِيْلِ فَهُمْ لَا يَهْتَدُوْنَ ۝٢٥

26. '*And they insist that* they will not worship Allāh, *while Allāh is He* Who brings to light that which is hidden in the heavens and the earth, and [b]Who knows what you conceal and what you disclose *of your design;*

اَلَّا يَسْجُدُوْا لِلّٰهِ الَّذِيْ يُخْرِجُ الْخَبْءَ فِي السَّمٰوٰتِ وَالْاَرْضِ وَيَعْلَمُ مَا تُخْفُوْنَ وَمَا تُعْلِنُوْنَ ۝٢٦

27. 'Allāh! there is no god but He, the Lord of the Mighty Throne.'

اَللّٰهُ لَآ اِلٰهَ اِلَّا هُوَ رَبُّ الْعَرْشِ الْعَظِيْمِ ۝٢٧ السجدة

28. *Thereupon Solomon* said, 'We shall see whether thou hast spoken the truth or whether thou art a liar;[2164]

قَالَ سَنَنْظُرُ اَصَدَقْتَ اَمْ كُنْتَ مِنَ الْكٰذِبِيْنَ ۝٢٨

29. 'Go thou, with this letter of mine, and lay it before them; then withdraw from them and see what *answer* they return.'[2165]

اِذْهَبْ بِّكِتٰبِيْ هٰذَا فَاَلْقِهْ اِلَيْهِمْ ثُمَّ تَوَلَّ عَنْهُمْ فَانْظُرْ مَاذَا يَرْجِعُوْنَ ۝٢٩

30. *The Queen* said, 'Ye chiefs, there has been delivered to me a noble letter;

قَالَتْ يٰٓاَيُّهَا الْمَلَؤُا اِنِّيْٓ اُلْقِيَ اِلَيَّ كِتٰبٌ كَرِيْمٌ ۝٣٠

31. "It is from Solomon, and it is: 'In the name of Allāh, the Gracious, the Merciful;[2166]

اِنَّهٗ مِنْ سُلَيْمٰنَ وَاِنَّهٗ بِسْمِ اللّٰهِ الرَّحْمٰنِ الرَّحِيْمِ ۝٣١

[a]8 : 49; 16 : 64; 35 : 9. [b]2 : 78; 16 : 20; 64 : 5.

Sharī'ah, and (4) a people who lived round about Iraq and professed belief in all Divine Prophets.

2164. Birds are never known to speak the truth or tell lies. The verse affords yet one more proof of Hudhud being not a bird but an important official in Solomon's government.

2165. Even if it be conceded that David and Solomon could understand the language of birds, there is nothing in the Qur'ān to show that the Queen of Sheba also could understand their language and yet Hudhud was entrusted with the mission to take Solomon's letter to her and to have a talk with her on Solomon's behalf and as his representative.

2166. Some Christian Orientalists, as is their wont, have vainly sought to impugn the Divine origin of the Qur'ān by trying to show that the expression *Bismillāh* has been borrowed from earlier Scriptures. Wherry in his "Commentary" says that it has been borrowed from Zend-Avesta. Sale has expressed an identical view, while Rodwell is of the opinion that pre-Islamic Arabs borrowed it from Jews and subsequently it was incorporated

32. 'Behave not arrogantly towards me, but come to me in submission.'[2167]

اَلَّا تَعْلُوْا عَلَيَّ وَأْتُوْنِيْ مُسْلِمِيْنَ ۞

R. 3   33. She said, 'Ye chiefs, advise me concerning my affair. I never decide any affair until you are present *to advise me*.'

قَالَتْ يٰٓاَيُّهَا الْمَلَؤُا اَفْتُوْنِيْ فِيْٓ اَمْرِيْ مَا كُنْتُ قَاطِعَةً اَمْرًا حَتّٰى تَشْهَدُوْنِ ۞

34. They replied, 'We possess power and we possess great prowess in war, but it is for thee to command; so consider what thou wilt command.'[2168]

قَالُوْا نَحْنُ اُولُوْا قُوَّةٍ وَّ اُولُوْا بَأْسٍ شَدِيْدٍ ەۙ وَّ الْاَمْرُ اِلَيْكِ فَانْظُرِيْ مَا ذَا تَأْمُرِيْنَ ۞

35. She said, 'Surely, the kings, when they enter a country, despoil it, and turn the highest of its people into the lowest. And thus they always do;

قَالَتْ اِنَّ الْمُلُوْكَ اِذَا دَخَلُوْا قَرْيَةً اَفْسَدُوْهَا وَ جَعَلُوْٓا اَعِزَّةَ اَهْلِهَآ اَذِلَّةً ۚ وَكَذٰلِكَ يَفْعَلُوْنَ ۞

36. 'But I am going to send them a present and wait to see what *answer* the envoys bring back.'

وَاِنِّيْ مُرْسِلَةٌ اِلَيْهِمْ بِهَدِيَّةٍ فَنٰظِرَةٌۢ بِمَ يَرْجِعُ الْمُرْسَلُوْنَ ۞

37. So when *the Queen's envoy* came to Solomon, he said, 'Do you presume *to* help me with *your*

فَلَمَّا جَآءَ سُلَيْمٰنَ قَالَ اَتُمِدُّوْنَنِ بِمَالٍ فَمَآ اٰتٰىنَ

---

in the Qur'ān by the Holy Prophet. To say that because this expression is found in some former Scriptures, therefore it must have necessarily been borrowed from one of them by the Qur'ān is evidently a flimsy inference. If anything, it only proves that the Qur'ān has originated from the same Source from which those Scriptures had originated. Moreover, no other Scripture has used this expression in the form and manner in which the Qur'ān has done. Also, the pre-Islamic Arabs had never used it before it was revealed in the Qur'ān. On the contrary, they had a special aversion for the use of the Divine attribute *Al-Raḥmān* (25 : 61) which forms an integral part of *Bismillāh*. See also 1 : 1.

2167. Solomon's letter constitutes a beautiful specimen of how great and comprehensive meaning can be condensed in a few brief words, devoid of all useless bombast and verbosity. The letter was at once a warning against the futility of revolt which seemed to be then raising its head in some parts of the country and an invitation to the Queen to submit to Solomon to avoid unnecessary bloodshed and also to give up idolatry and accept the true Faith.

2168. The verse shows that the Queen of Sheba was a very powerful monarch and possessed great material resources and also commanded the affection, co-operation and willing obedience of her subjects and was the arbiter of their destinies. The power and glory of Saba' was at its height in about 1100 B.C. The period of the Queen's rule continued up to 950 B.C., when she is believed to have submitted to Solomon. With her submission was fulfilled the biblical prophecy, *viz.*, 'the Kings of Sheba and Saba' shall offer gifts' (Psalms 72 : 10).

اللّٰهُ خَيْرٌ مِّمَّآ اٰتٰىكُمْ ۚ بَلْ اَنْتُمْ بِهَدِيَّتِكُمْ تَفْرَحُوْنَ ﴿۳۷﴾

wealth? But that which Allāh has given me is better than that which He has given you. Nay, you take pride in your gift;[2169]

اِرْجِعْ اِلَيْهِمْ فَلَنَاْتِيَنَّهُمْ بِجُنُوْدٍ لَّا قِبَلَ لَهُمْ بِهَا
وَلَنُخْرِجَنَّهُمْ مِّنْهَآ اَذِلَّةً وَّهُمْ صٰغِرُوْنَ ﴿۳۸﴾

38. 'Go back to them, for we shall surely come to them with hosts against which they will have no power *of resistance*,[2170] and we shall drive them out *of their land* disgraced, and they will be humbled.'

قَالَ يٰٓاَيُّهَا الْمَلَؤُا اَيُّكُمْ يَاْتِيْنِيْ بِعَرْشِهَا قَبْلَ اَنْ
يَّاْتُوْنِيْ مُسْلِمِيْنَ ﴿۳۹﴾

39. He said, 'O nobles, which of you will bring me her throne[2171] before they come to me submitting?'

قَالَ عِفْرِيْتٌ مِّنَ الْجِنِّ اَنَا اٰتِيْكَ بِهٖ قَبْلَ اَنْ
تَقُوْمَ مِنْ مَّقَامِكَ ۚ وَاِنِّيْ عَلَيْهِ لَقَوِيٌّ اَمِيْنٌ ﴿۴۰﴾

40. A powerful chieftain[2172] from among the jinn said, 'I will bring it to thee before thou strikest thy camp; and indeed I possess power therefor *and I am* trustworthy.'[2173]

2169. Solomon seems evidently to have become greatly offended with the Queen's behaviour in sending him presents. He took it as an insult. He had demanded her surrender and instead was presented with paltry presents. The Sabaeans first had either attacked Solomon's territory or had sought to create unrest in it. This is why the sending of presents by the Queen offended and annoyed him. In ordinary circumstances he would have been pleased with the presents.

2170. *Qibal* means, power, strength, authority. They say *mālī bihī Qibalun, i.e.*, I have no power against him (Aqrab).

2171. The expression, *bi-'Arshihā*, seems to signify the throne which Solomon had ordered to be built for the Queen. It seemed to be a practice in vogue at that time that when the ruler of a State paid a visit to another ruler, a throne was built for the reception of the royal guest. Solomon also ordered a throne to be built for the reception of the Queen. It is called 'her throne' because it was specially built for her use. The expression may also mean, 'the like of her throne,' and *Ya'tīnī*, may mean, 'will prepare for me.'

2172. '*Ifrīt*, derived from '*Afara* which means, he threw him on the ground or humbled him, is a word used both for men and jinn and means, (1) one strong and powerful; (2) sharp, vigorous and effective in an affair, exceeding ordinary bounds therein with intelligence and sagacity; (3) a chief, etc. (Lane).

2173. These words indicate that the said '*Ifrīt* was a very high official who wielded great authority and was, therefore, quite confident of carrying out the orders of his master to his entire satisfaction within the time allotted to him. *Maqāmika* signifies the place where Solomon had encamped on his way to Saba' and was waiting for his envoy to come back with the reply to his letter to the Queen of Sheba.

41. Said one who had knowledge of the book, 'I will bring it to thee before thy noble *envoy*[2174] returns to thee.' And when he saw it set before him, he said, 'This is of the grace of my Lord, that He may try me whether I am grateful or ungrateful. And whosoever is grateful is grateful for *the good of* his own soul; but whosoever is ungrateful, truly my Lord is Self-Sufficient, Gracious.'

قَالَ الَّذِیۡ عِنۡدَهٗ عِلۡمٌ مِّنَ الۡكِتٰبِ اَنَا اٰتِیۡكَ بِهٖ
قَبۡلَ اَنۡ یَّرۡتَدَّ اِلَیۡكَ طَرۡفُكَ ؕ فَلَمَّا رَاٰهُ مُسۡتَقِرًّا عِنۡدَهٗ
قَالَ هٰذَا مِنۡ فَضۡلِ رَبِّیۡ ۟ۖ لِیَبۡلُوَنِیۡۤ ءَاَشۡكُرُ اَمۡ
اَكۡفُرُ ؕ وَ مَنۡ شَكَرَ فَاِنَّمَا یَشۡكُرُ لِنَفۡسِهٖ ۚ وَ مَنۡ كَفَرَ
فَاِنَّ رَبِّیۡ غَنِیٌّ كَرِیۡمٌ ﴿۴۱﴾

42. He said, 'Make *the throne so beautiful as to make* her own throne appear quite ordinary[2175] to her, *and* let us see whether she follows the right way or whether she is *one* of those who follow not the right way.'

قَالَ نَكِّرُوۡا لَهَا عَرۡشَهَا نَنۡظُرۡ اَتَهۡتَدِیۡۤ اَمۡ تَكُوۡنُ
مِنَ الَّذِیۡنَ لَا یَهۡتَدُوۡنَ ﴿۴۲﴾

43. And when she came, it was said *to her*, 'Is thy throne like this?'

فَلَمَّا جَآءَتۡ قِیۡلَ اَهٰكَذَا عَرۡشُكِ ؕ قَالَتۡ كَاَنَّهٗ هُوَ

2174. *Ṭarf* meaning, a glance; a noble man; government revenue; a messenger from Yemen (Lane). The expression may mean: (1) Before thy envoy from Yemen returns to thee; (2) in the twinkling of an eye; (3) before the government revenue is deposited in the treasury. In the last-mentioned meaning the expression would signify, 'I would need no more money; the money already in the government treasury would be quite enough to meet the expenses of constructing a throne for the queen.' The expression, 'who had knowledge of the book,' seems to refer to one who knew the intricacies of finance. Possibly, he was Solomon's finance minister.

In this and the previous verse two offers to make the throne for Solomon have been mentioned, one by the *'Ifrīt* who offered to prepare the throne before Solomon should strike camp and start back, and the other by 'the man who had knowledge.' The latter made a still better offer of finishing the throne before Solomon's envoy came back with the reply to his letter from the Queen. The context shows that Solomon accepted the second offer because he wanted to have the throne finished before the Queen came to pay her respects to him as he was to stay at that place till she should come and the whole ceremony was over. The verse also implies that all sorts of men were employed by Solomon—men of knowledge and experience, skilled and unskilled labourers, craftsmen and technicians.

2175. *Nakkara-hū* means, he changed or altered it so as not to be recognized; he made it look quite ordinary (Lane). The expression in the text may, therefore, mean, 'make this throne better than her throne so that her throne should appear quite ordinary.' The verse purports to say that Solomon had ordered the official who was entrusted with the task of preparing the throne for the Queen to make it so beautiful that she might realize the superiority of its workmanship and come to dislike her own throne and thus should understand that Solomon's power and resources were much greater and superior to those of her. This seems to be the significance of the sentence, '*whether she follows the right way*.' Solomon sought to bring home to the Queen the futility of any opposition or resistance to him. She and her ministers and courtiers seemed to be proud of their power and resources (27:34) and Solomon wanted to disabuse their minds of this misconception (27:37). If the words 'her throne' be taken to mean the throne which, it is said, the Queen may have sent as a present to Solomon, the word *Nakkirū* would mean that the throne should be so embellished and made beautiful and the figures of idols on it, if any, so completely wiped off that she might not recognize it.

She replied, 'It is 'as though it were the same. And we had been given knowledge before this, and we have already submitted.'²¹⁷⁶

وَاُوۡتِیۡنَا الۡعِلۡمَ مِنۡ قَبۡلِهَا وَکُنَّا مُسۡلِمِیۡنَ ۝

44. And that which she used to worship beside Allāh prevented her *from believing;* for she came of a disbelieving people.

وَصَدَّهَا مَا کَانَتۡ تَّعۡبُدُ مِنۡ دُوۡنِ اللّٰهِ ؕ اِنَّهَا کَانَتۡ مِنۡ قَوۡمٍ کٰفِرِیۡنَ ۝

45. It was said to her, 'Enter the palace.' And when she saw it, she thought it to be a great expanse of water, and she bared her shanks.²¹⁷⁷ *Solomon* said, 'It is a palace paved smooth with slabs of glass.' She said, 'My Lord, indeed I have wronged my soul; and I submit myself with Solomon to Allāh, the Lord of the worlds.'

قِیۡلَ لَهَا ادۡخُلِی الصَّرۡحَ ۚ فَلَمَّا رَاَتۡهُ حَسِبَتۡهُ لُجَّةً وَّکَشَفَتۡ عَنۡ سَاقَیۡهَا ؕ قَالَ اِنَّهٗ صَرۡحٌ مُّمَرَّدٌ مِّنۡ قَوَارِیۡرَ ؕ قَالَتۡ رَبِّ اِنِّیۡ ظَلَمۡتُ نَفۡسِیۡ وَاَسۡلَمۡتُ مَعَ سُلَیۡمٰنَ لِلّٰهِ رَبِّ الۡعٰلَمِیۡنَ ۝

R. 4   46. ªAnd 'We sent to Thamūd their brother Ṣāliḥ *who said,* 'Worship Allāh.' And at once they became two parties contending with each other.

وَلَقَدۡ اَرۡسَلۡنَاۤ اِلٰی ثَمُوۡدَ اَخَاهُمۡ صٰلِحًا اَنِ اعۡبُدُوا اللّٰهَ فَاِذَا هُمۡ فَرِیۡقٰنِ یَخۡتَصِمُوۡنَ ۝

ª7 : 74;   11 : 62;   26 : 142;   54 : 24.

2176. The words, *we had been given knowledge before this,* signify that the Queen had already become conversant with the great power and resources of Solomon and had made up her mind to give her allegiance to him.

2177. *Kashafa 'an Sāqihī* is a well-known Arabic idiom meaning, to become prepared to meet the difficulty or to become perturbed or perplexed. *Kashafat 'an Sāqaihā* means: (1) she uncovered her shanks; (2) she got ready to meet the situation; (3) she became perturbed or perplexed or was taken aback (Lane & Lisān). Solomon wanted the Queen to give up idol-worship and accept the true Faith. For this purpose he wisely adopted such means as should have led the noble and sagacious lady to see the error of her ways. The throne which Solomon had caused to be prepared for her was prepared with this end in view. It was made much more beautiful and in every respect superior to her own throne of which she was very proud. Solomon did so in order that she might realize that he was God's favourite and had been endowed with material and spiritual gifts in far greater abundance than those given to her. The palace referred to in the verse was also constructed with the same object in view. As the verse shows, the entrance to the palace was paved with slabs of glass, below which ran a stream of crystal clear water. When the Queen entered the palace she mistook the transparent glass for water and bared her shanks, and the sight of the water perplexed her and she did not know what to do. By this device Solomon directed her attention to the fact that just as she had mistaken the slabs of glass for water, similarly the sun and other celestial bodies which she worshipped were not the real source of light. They only emitted light but were lifeless things. It was Almighty God Who had bestowed upon them the light which they emitted. In this way Solomon succeeded in the object he had in view. The noble lady made a confession of her error and from a worshipper of idols of wood and stone she became a devoted votary of the One True God.

47. He said, 'O, my people, why do you seek to hasten on evil rather than good? [a]Wherefore do you not ask forgiveness of Allāh that you may be shown mercy?'

قَالَ يٰقَوْمِ لِمَ تَسْتَعْجِلُوْنَ بِالسَّيِّئَةِ قَبْلَ الْحَسَنَةِ ۚ لَوْلَا تَسْتَغْفِرُوْنَ اللّٰهَ لَعَلَّكُمْ تُرْحَمُوْنَ ﴿٤٧﴾

48. They said, 'We augur[2177A] ill of thee and of those that are with thee.' He said, '*The true cause of* your ill-fortune is with Allāh, but you are a people who are on trial.'

قَالُوا اطَّيَّرْنَا بِكَ وَبِمَنْ مَّعَكَ ۚ قَالَ طٰٓئِرُكُمْ عِنْدَ اللّٰهِ بَلْ اَنْتُمْ قَوْمٌ تُفْتَنُوْنَ ﴿٤٨﴾

49. And there were in the city a party of nine *persons*[2178] [b]who made mischief in the land, and would not reform.

وَكَانَ فِي الْمَدِيْنَةِ تِسْعَةُ رَهْطٍ يُّفْسِدُوْنَ فِي الْاَرْضِ وَلَا يُصْلِحُوْنَ ﴿٤٩﴾

50. They said, 'Swear one to another by Allāh that we will surely attack him and his family by night, and then we will say to his heir,[2178A] 'We witnessed not the destruction of his family, and most surely we are truthful.'

قَالُوْا تَقَاسَمُوْا بِاللّٰهِ لَنُبَيِّتَنَّهٗ وَاَهْلَهٗ ثُمَّ لَنَقُوْلَنَّ لِوَلِيِّهٖ مَا شَهِدْنَا مَهْلِكَ اَهْلِهٖ وَاِنَّا لَصٰدِقُوْنَ ﴿٥٠﴾

51. [c]And they planned a plan, and We *also* planned a plan, but they perceived[2179] *it* not.

وَمَكَرُوْا مَكْرًا وَّمَكَرْنَا مَكْرًا وَّهُمْ لَا يَشْعُرُوْنَ ﴿٥١﴾

52. [d]Then see how *evil* was the end of their plan! Verily, We utterly destroyed them and their people all together.

فَانْظُرْ كَيْفَ كَانَ عَاقِبَةُ مَكْرِهِمْ ۙ اَنَّا دَمَّرْنٰهُمْ وَقَوْمَهُمْ اَجْمَعِيْنَ ﴿٥٢﴾

[a]27 : 47. [b]26 : 153. [c]3 : 55; 8 : 31; 13 : 43; 14 : 47. [d]7 : 79; 26 : 173, 37 : 137.

2177A. *Taṭayyara bihī* means, he augured ill of it or him; he regarded him or it as ill-omened (Lane).

2178. By implication the reference in the verse is to the nine prominent enemies of the Holy Prophet. Eight of them were killed in the Battle of Badr and the ninth, the notorious Abū Lahab, died at Mecca on hearing the news of the defeat at Badr. These eight were: Abū Jahl, Muṭ'im bin 'Adiyy, Shaibah bin Rabī'ah, 'Utbah bin Rabī'ah, Walīd bin 'Utbah, Umayyah bin Khalf, Naḍr bin Ḥarth and 'Aqbah bin Abī Mu'aiṭ. They conspired to murder the Holy Prophet. The actual plan was to select one man from every tribe of the Quraish and then make a concerted murderous attack upon him so that no particular tribe might be held responsible for his murder. The plan came from Abū Jahl, the leader of this wicked junta

2178A. *Waliyy* means, an heir; one who demands retribution for murder; an avenger of blood (Lane).

2179. The Holy Prophet had to flee from Mecca but the flight eventually resulted in the destruction of the power of the Quraish, who did not realize that by compelling the Holy Prophet to flee from Mecca they were laying the foundation of their own destruction.

53. And yonder are their houses fallen down because of their wrongdoing. In that verily is a Sign for a people who have knowledge.

فَتِلْكَ بُيُوتُهُمْ خَاوِيَةً بِمَا ظَلَمُوا ۗ إِنَّ فِي ذَٰلِكَ لَآيَةً لِّقَوْمٍ يَعْلَمُونَ ﴿٥٣﴾

54. And We saved those who believed and feared *God*.

وَأَنجَيْنَا الَّذِينَ آمَنُوا وَكَانُوا يَتَّقُونَ ﴿٥٤﴾

55. [a]And *We sent* Lot *as a Messenger*, when he said to his people, 'Do you commit abomination while you see?[2179A]

وَلُوطًا إِذْ قَالَ لِقَوْمِهِ أَتَأْتُونَ الْفَاحِشَةَ وَأَنتُمْ تُبْصِرُونَ ﴿٥٥﴾

56. [b]'What! do you approach men lustfully rather than women? Nay, you are indeed an ignorant people.'

أَئِنَّكُمْ لَتَأْتُونَ الرِّجَالَ شَهْوَةً مِّن دُونِ النِّسَاءِ ۚ بَلْ أَنتُمْ قَوْمٌ تَجْهَلُونَ ﴿٥٦﴾

57. But the only answer of his people was that they said, [c]'Drive out Lot's family from your city. They are a people who would keep pure.[2180]

فَمَا كَانَ جَوَابَ قَوْمِهِ إِلَّا أَن قَالُوا أَخْرِجُوا آلَ لُوطٍ مِّن قَرْيَتِكُمْ ۖ إِنَّهُمْ أُنَاسٌ يَتَطَهَّرُونَ ﴿٥٧﴾

58. [d]So We saved him and his family, except his wife; her We decreed to be of those who stayed behind.

فَأَنجَيْنَاهُ وَأَهْلَهُ إِلَّا امْرَأَتَهُ قَدَّرْنَاهَا مِنَ الْغَابِرِينَ ﴿٥٨﴾

59. [e]And We rained upon them a rain; and evil was the rain *that descended* upon those who had been warned.

وَأَمْطَرْنَا عَلَيْهِم مَّطَرًا ۖ فَسَاءَ مَطَرُ الْمُنذَرِينَ ﴿٥٩﴾

R. 5 60. Say, [f]'All praise belongs to Allāh, and peace be upon those servants of His whom He has chosen. Is Allāh better or that which they associate *with Him*?[2181]

قُلِ الْحَمْدُ لِلَّهِ وَسَلَامٌ عَلَىٰ عِبَادِهِ الَّذِينَ اصْطَفَىٰ ۗ آللَّهُ خَيْرٌ أَمَّا يُشْرِكُونَ ﴿٦٠﴾

[a]7 : 81; 29 : 29. [b]7 : 82; 26 : 166-167; 29 : 30. [c]7 : 83; 26 : 168. [d]7 : 84; 29 : 34. [e]7 : 85; 25 : 41; 26 : 174. [f]37 : 182-183.

2179A. The words may also mean, with your eyes open.

2180. *Yataṭahharūn* means, they pose and parade as extra pure and righteous; they take pride in their righteousness and purity (Lane).

2181. With this verse is closed the discourse about Moses, David, Solomon, Ṣāliḥ and Lot with an invocation of Divine peace and blessings on God's Messengers and His Elect to whom humanity is indebted for all that is good and virtuous in the world; and then the *Sūrah* proceeds to give arguments in support of the existence of God and of His great power and Unity.

PART XX

الجزء ٢٠

61. Or, Who created the heavens and the earth, and [a]Who sent down water for you from the sky wherewith We cause to grow beautiful orchards?[2182] You could not cause their trees to grow. Is there a god with Allāh? Nay, [b]they are a people who deviate *from the right path.*

أَمَّنْ خَلَقَ السَّمٰوٰتِ وَالْأَرْضَ وَأَنْزَلَ لَكُمْ مِّنَ
السَّمَآءِ مَآءً فَأَنْبَتْنَا بِهٖ حَدَآئِقَ ذَاتَ بَهْجَةٍ
مَا كَانَ لَكُمْ أَنْ تُنْبِتُوْا شَجَرَهَا ءَاِلٰهٌ مَّعَ اللّٰهِ
بَلْ هُمْ قَوْمٌ يَّعْدِلُوْنَ ٦١

62. Or, [c]Who made the earth a place of rest, and placed rivers in its midst, and placed upon it firm mountains, and [d]put a barrier between the two waters?[2183] Is there a god with Allāh? Nay, most of them know not.

أَمَّنْ جَعَلَ الْأَرْضَ قَرَارًا وَّجَعَلَ خِلٰلَهَآ أَنْهٰرًا
وَّجَعَلَ لَهَا رَوَاسِيَ وَجَعَلَ بَيْنَ الْبَحْرَيْنِ حَاجِزًا
ءَاِلٰهٌ مَّعَ اللّٰهِ بَلْ أَكْثَرُهُمْ لَا يَعْلَمُوْنَ ٦٢

63. Or, [e]Who answers *the cry of* the distressed person when he calls upon Him,[2184] and removes the evil, [f]and makes you successors in the earth? Is there a god with Allāh? Little is it that you reflect.

أَمَّنْ يُّجِيْبُ الْمُضْطَرَّ إِذَا دَعَاهُ وَيَكْشِفُ السُّوْٓءَ
وَيَجْعَلُكُمْ خُلَفَآءَ الْأَرْضِ ءَاِلٰهٌ مَّعَ اللّٰهِ قَلِيْلًا
مَّا تَذَكَّرُوْنَ ٦٣

64. Or, Who guides you in the *depths of* darkness on land and sea, and Who sends the winds[2185] as glad tidings before His mercy? Is there a god with Allāh? Exalted is Allāh above what they associate *with Him.*

أَمَّنْ يَّهْدِيْكُمْ فِيْ ظُلُمٰتِ الْبَرِّ وَالْبَحْرِ وَمَنْ يُّرْسِلُ
الرِّيٰحَ بُشْرًا بَيْنَ يَدَيْ رَحْمَتِهٖ ءَاِلٰهٌ مَّعَ اللّٰهِ
تَعٰلَى اللّٰهُ عَمَّا يُشْرِكُوْنَ ٦٤

[a]31 : 11; 50 : 10. [b]6 : 2. [c]20 : 54; 78 : 7. [d]25 : 54; 55 : 20-21. [e]2 : 187; 7 : 56. [f]10 : 15.

2182. The first argument in favour of the subject introduced in the preceding verse is taken from nature—from the creation of heavens and earth, from the coming down of rain and the life it gives to the dead earth, and from mountains and rivers.

2183. The argument, begun in the preceding verse, is here further developed and expanded.

2184. As God's great powers are manifested in the marvellous working of the laws of nature (preceding verse), so are they manifested in man's inner conscience when he cries to God in the agony of his soul and God listens to his cry.

2185. When *Rīḥ* (wind) is used in the singular number, it generally signifies Divine punishment (17 : 70; 54 : 20; 69 : 7, etc.), but when it is used in the plural number it generally signifies Divine blessings.

65. Or, Who [a]originates creation, *and* then repeats[2186] it and [b]Who provides for you from the heaven *and* the earth? Is there a god with Allāh? Say, 'Bring forward your proof if you are truthful.'

اَمَّنْ يَّبْدَؤُا الْخَلْقَ ثُمَّ يُعِيْدُهٗ وَمَنْ يَّرْزُقُكُمْ
مِّنَ السَّمَآءِ وَالْاَرْضِ ؕ ءَاِلٰهٌ مَّعَ اللّٰهِ ؕ قُلْ هَاتُوْا بُرْهَانَكُمْ
اِنْ كُنْتُمْ صٰدِقِيْنَ ﴿٦٥﴾

66. Say, [c]'None in the heavens and the earth knows the unseen save Allāh; and they do not know when they will be raised up.'

قُلْ لَّا يَعْلَمُ مَنْ فِي السَّمٰوٰتِ وَالْاَرْضِ الْغَيْبَ
اِلَّا اللّٰهُ ؕ وَمَا يَشْعُرُوْنَ اَيَّانَ يُبْعَثُوْنَ ﴿٦٦﴾

67. Nay, their knowledge respecting the Hereafter has reached its limit, rather they are in doubt about it; rather they are blind to it.[2187]

بَلِ ادّٰرَكَ عِلْمُهُمْ فِي الْاٰخِرَةِ ۚ بَلْ هُمْ فِيْ شَكٍّ
مِّنْهَا ۚ بَلْ هُمْ مِّنْهَا عَمُوْنَ ﴿٦٧﴾ ع

R. 6 68. [d]And those who disbelieve say, 'What! when we and our fathers have become dust, shall we indeed be brought forth *again?*

وَقَالَ الَّذِيْنَ كَفَرُوْٓا ءَاِذَا كُنَّا تُرٰبًا وَّاٰبَآؤُنَآ اَئِنَّا
لَمُخْرَجُوْنَ ﴿٦٨﴾

69. [e]'We were surely promised this before—we and our fathers; this is nothing but tales of the ancients.'

لَقَدْ وُعِدْنَا هٰذَا نَحْنُ وَاٰبَآؤُنَا مِنْ قَبْلُ ۙ اِنْ
هٰذَآ اِلَّآ اَسَاطِيْرُ الْاَوَّلِيْنَ ﴿٦٩﴾

70. Say, [f]'Travel in the earth and see how *evil* was the end of the sinful.'

قُلْ سِيْرُوْا فِي الْاَرْضِ فَانْظُرُوْا كَيْفَ كَانَ عَاقِبَةُ
الْمُجْرِمِيْنَ ﴿٧٠﴾

71. [g]And grieve thou not for them, nor be thou in distress because of what they devise.

وَلَا تَحْزَنْ عَلَيْهِمْ وَلَا تَكُنْ فِيْ ضَيْقٍ مِّمَّا يَمْكُرُوْنَ ﴿٧١﴾

72. [h]And they say, 'When will this promise be *fulfilled*, if you are truthful?'

وَيَقُوْلُوْنَ مَتٰى هٰذَا الْوَعْدُ اِنْ كُنْتُمْ صٰدِقِيْنَ ﴿٧٢﴾

[a]10 : 35; 29 : 20; 30 : 12, 28. [b]10 : 32; 34 : 25; 35 : 4. [c]11 : 124; 16 : 78; 35 : 39. [d]13 : 6; 37 : 17; 50 : 4. [e]23 : 84. [f]16 : 37; 30 : 43; 40 : 83. [g]15 : 89; 16 : 128. [h]10 : 49; 21 : 39; 34 : 30; 36 : 49.

2186. The words, *originates creation and then repeats it*, signify creation and procreation.

2187. No amount of human knowledge and intelligence alone can satisfy the cravings of the human soul, nor can it prove beyond doubt the existence of God and of Life after death, the two basic religious beliefs, because their full comprehension is beyond human ken. It is Divine knowledge acquired through Divine revelation that can and does actually engender certainty in human mind about them. Man's knowledge can, at best, lead to the conclusion that there must be a Divine Being and a Life after death, but it is Divine revelation alone that can change this *must be* into the certain *is*.

73. Say, 'May be that [a]a part of that which you would hasten on is close behind you.'

قُلْ عَسٰۤى اَنْ يَّكُوْنَ رَدِفَ لَكُمْ بَعْضُ الَّذِيْ تَسْتَعْجِلُوْنَ ﴿٧٣﴾

74. And, truly, [b]thy Lord is gracious to mankind, but most of them are not grateful.

وَاِنَّ رَبَّكَ لَذُوْ فَضْلٍ عَلَى النَّاسِ وَلٰكِنَّ اَكْثَرَهُمْ لَا يَشْكُرُوْنَ ﴿٧٤﴾

75. [c]And, surely, thy Lord knows what their bosoms conceal and what they disclose.

وَاِنَّ رَبَّكَ لَيَعْلَمُ مَا تُكِنُّ صُدُوْرُهُمْ وَمَا يُعْلِنُوْنَ ﴿٧٥﴾

76. And there is nothing hidden in the heaven and the earth, but it is *recorded* in a clear Book.

وَمَا مِنْ غَآئِبَةٍ فِي السَّمَآءِ وَالْاَرْضِ اِلَّا فِيْ كِتٰبٍ مُّبِيْنٍ ﴿٧٦﴾

77. Verily, this Qur'ān explains to the Children of Israel most of that concerning which they differ.[2188]

اِنَّ هٰذَا الْقُرْاٰنَ يَقُصُّ عَلٰى بَنِيْۤ اِسْرَآءِيْلَ اَكْثَرَ الَّذِيْ هُمْ فِيْهِ يَخْتَلِفُوْنَ ﴿٧٧﴾

78. And verily, it is a guidance and a mercy for the believers.

وَاِنَّهٗ لَهُدًى وَّرَحْمَةٌ لِّلْمُؤْمِنِيْنَ ﴿٧٨﴾

79. Verily, thy Lord will decide between them by His judgment, and He is the Mighty, the All-Knowing.

اِنَّ رَبَّكَ يَقْضِيْ بَيْنَهُمْ بِحُكْمِهٖ ۚ وَهُوَ الْعَزِيْزُ الْعَلِيْمُ ﴿٧٩﴾

80. [d]So put thy trust in Allāh; surely, thou art on manifest truth.

فَتَوَكَّلْ عَلَى اللّٰهِ ؕ اِنَّكَ عَلَى الْحَقِّ الْمُبِيْنِ ﴿٨٠﴾

81. Verily, thou canst not make the dead to hear, [e]nor canst thou make the deaf to hear the call, when they retreat turning *their* backs.[2189]

اِنَّكَ لَا تُسْمِعُ الْمَوْتٰى وَلَا تُسْمِعُ الصُّمَّ الدُّعَآءَ اِذَا وَلَّوْا مُدْبِرِيْنَ ﴿٨١﴾

82. [f]And thou canst not guide the blind out of their error. Thou canst make only those to hear who believe in Our Signs, so they submit.

وَمَاۤ اَنْتَ بِهٰدِي الْعُمْيِ عَنْ ضَلٰلَتِهِمْ ؕ اِنْ تُسْمِعُ اِلَّا مَنْ يُّؤْمِنُ بِاٰيٰتِنَا فَهُمْ مُّسْلِمُوْنَ ﴿٨٢﴾

[a]22 : 48; 26 : 205; 29 : 55. [b]10 : 61; 40 : 62. [c]2 : 78; 16 : 24; 28 : 70; 36 : 77. [d]11 : 124; 25 : 59; 33 : 49. [e]10 : 43; 30 : 53. [f]10 : 44; 30 : 54.

2188. The implied reference in this verse may be to Solomon whom the Jews accused of resorting to *Shirk* (idolatry) in order to win the affection of the Queen of Sheba. As there had existed difference of opinion among the Jews about Solomon's behaviour towards the Queen, the Qur'ān has lifted the veil from this obscure fact.

2189. The words, *when they retreat turning their backs*, make it clear that 'the dead' mentioned here are 'the spiritually dead' just as 'the blind' in the next verse are 'the spiritually blind.'

83. And when the sentence is passed against[2190] them, We shall bring forth for them an insect[2191] out of the earth which shall wound them because people did not believe in Our Signs.

وَإِذَا وَقَعَ الْقَوْلُ عَلَيْهِمْ أَخْرَجْنَا لَهُمْ دَابَّةً مِّنَ الْأَرْضِ تُكَلِّمُهُمْ أَنَّ النَّاسَ كَانُوا بِآيَاتِنَا لَا يُوقِنُونَ ﴿٨٣﴾ ع

R. 7 84. And *remind them of* the day [a]when We shall gather together from every people a party from among those who rejected Our Signs, and they shall be formed into *separate* groups.

وَيَوْمَ نَحْشُرُ مِن كُلِّ أُمَّةٍ فَوْجًا مِّمَّن يُكَذِّبُ بِآيَاتِنَا فَهُمْ يُوزَعُونَ ﴿٨٤﴾

85. Till, when they come, He will say, [b]'Did you reject My Signs, while you had not full knowledge concerning them? Or, what was it that you were doing *about them?*

حَتَّىٰ إِذَا جَاءُوا قَالَ أَكَذَّبْتُم بِآيَاتِي وَلَمْ تُحِيطُوا بِهَا عِلْمًا أَمَّاذَا كُنتُمْ تَعْمَلُونَ ﴿٨٥﴾

86. And the sentence shall come to pass against them because they did wrong, and they will be speechless.[2192]

وَوَقَعَ الْقَوْلُ عَلَيْهِم بِمَا ظَلَمُوا فَهُمْ لَا يَنطِقُونَ ﴿٨٦﴾

87. [c]See they not that We have made the night that they may rest therein, and the day sight-giving? In that verily are Signs for a people who believe.

أَلَمْ يَرَوْا أَنَّا جَعَلْنَا اللَّيْلَ لِيَسْكُنُوا فِيهِ وَالنَّهَارَ مُبْصِرًا إِنَّ فِي ذَٰلِكَ لَآيَاتٍ لِّقَوْمٍ يُؤْمِنُونَ ﴿٨٧﴾

---

[a]25 : 18; 67 : 9. [b]10 : 40. [c]10 : 68; 17 : 13; 28 : 74; 30 : 24.

2190. The words, *Waqa'a al-Qaulu 'Alaihim*, mean, the sentence or the decree became due against them or came to pass; they made themselves deserving of the Divine sentence or the Divine decree (Aqrab).

2191. This is a prophecy concerning the appearance of plague in the Latter Days. The verse was so construed by the Holy Prophet himself. But if *Dābbah* is taken in the sense of a grossly materialistic person all whose endeavours are wholly directed to the acquisition of worldly riches and material comforts (34 : 15), the reference in the verse seems to be to the materialistic Western nations 'whose labour is all lost in search after things pertaining to the life of this world' (18 : 105) and who have fallen on this world with all their might and main.

2192. They will not be able to put in defence of their misdeeds. The charge against them being quite true and manifest will be incapable of being defended, and so the sentence of punishment will be passed against them.

88. [a]And *call to mind* the day when the trumpet will be blown[2193] and whoever is in the heavens and whoever is in the earth will be struck with terror, save him whom Allāh pleases. And all shall come unto Him humbled.

وَيَوْمَ يُنْفَخُ فِي الصُّوْرِ فَفَزِعَ مَنْ فِي السَّمٰوٰتِ وَ
مَنْ فِي الْاَرْضِ اِلَّا مَنْ شَآءَ اللّٰهُ ۗ وَكُلٌّ اَتَوْهُ دٰخِرِيْنَ ﴿۸۸﴾

89. And thou seest the mountains, which thou thinkest to be firmly fixed, pass away as the clouds pass away[2194]—the handiwork of Allāh Who has made everything perfect. Verily, He is fully Aware of what you do.

وَتَرَى الْجِبَالَ تَحْسَبُهَا جَامِدَةً وَّهِيَ تَمُرُّ مَرَّ
السَّحَابِ ۗ صُنْعَ اللّٰهِ الَّذِيْٓ اَتْقَنَ كُلَّ شَيْءٍ ۗ اِنَّهٗ خَبِيْرٌ
بِمَا تَفْعَلُوْنَ ﴿۸۹﴾

90. [b]Whoever does a good deed shall have a better *reward* than that, and such will be secure from terror that day.

مَنْ جَآءَ بِالْحَسَنَةِ فَلَهٗ خَيْرٌ مِّنْهَا ۚ وَهُمْ مِّنْ فَزَعٍ
يَّوْمَئِذٍ اٰمِنُوْنَ ﴿۹۰﴾

91. And those who do evil, [c]shall be thrown down on their faces into the Fire; *and it will be said to them*, 'Are you not rewarded for what you have been doing?'

وَمَنْ جَآءَ بِالسَّيِّئَةِ فَكُبَّتْ وُجُوْهُهُمْ فِي النَّارِ ۗ هَلْ
تُجْزَوْنَ اِلَّا مَا كُنْتُمْ تَعْمَلُوْنَ ﴿۹۱﴾

92. *Say*, 'I am commanded only to serve the Lord of this City[2195] which He has made sacred, and to Him belong all things; and I am commanded to be of those who submit *to God*,

اِنَّمَآ اُمِرْتُ اَنْ اَعْبُدَ رَبَّ هٰذِهِ الْبَلْدَةِ الَّذِيْ
حَرَّمَهَا وَلَهٗ كُلُّ شَيْءٍ ۫ وَّاُمِرْتُ اَنْ اَكُوْنَ مِنَ الْمُسْلِمِيْنَ ﴿۹۲﴾

---

[a]18 : 100; 20 : 103; 36 : 52; 78 : 19. [b]4 : 41; 6 : 161; 28 : 85. [c]26 : 95.

2193. The words, *when the trumpet will be blown*, besides referring to the Day of Resurrection, refer to the new order that was ushered in by the Holy Prophet as if by the blowing of a trumpet.

2194. At the advent of the Holy Prophet old ideas and institutions which seemed to have been firmly rooted like mountains, melted and vanished away like the passing of clouds. 'Mountains' may here equally refer to the great and firmly established Roman and Persian Empires which were scattered like chaff before the irresistible victorious Muslim armies.

2195. The Meccans feared that if idol-worship disappeared from Arabia, the Ka'bah, being the repository of all their well-known idols, will lose its importance and with it they will lose their prestige and influence as its custodians. The verse disabuses their minds of this

93. 'And to recite the Qur'ān.' So [a]whoever follows guidance, follows it only for *the good of* his own soul; and *as to him* who goes astray, say, 'I am only a Warner.'

وَاَنْ اَتْلُوَا الْقُرْاٰنَ ۚ فَمَنِ اهْتَدٰى فَاِنَّمَا يَهْتَدِيْ لِنَفْسِهٖ ۚ وَمَنْ ضَلَّ فَقُلْ اِنَّمَآ اَنَا مِنَ الْمُنْذِرِيْنَ ﴿٩٣﴾

94. And say, 'All praise belongs to Allāh; He will soon show you His Signs, and you will know them.' And thy Lord is not unaware of what you do.

وَقُلِ الْحَمْدُ لِلّٰهِ سَيُرِيْكُمْ اٰيٰتِهٖ فَتَعْرِفُوْنَهَا ۗ وَمَا رَبُّكَ بِغَافِلٍ عَمَّا تَعْمَلُوْنَ ﴿٩٤﴾

---

[a]10 : 109; 39 : 42.

---

false notion and purports to say that being the Centre of a World Movement and of the Message for all mankind, Mecca, far from losing its importance, will, on the contrary, add to its prestige and will continue to be respected and revered till the end of time.

CHAPTER 28

AL-QAṢAṢ

(Revealed before Hijrah)

Date of Revelation and Context

By common agreement the *Sūrah* was revealed at Mecca. According to 'Umar bin Muḥammad it was revealed while the Holy Prophet, during the *Hijrah*, was on his way to Medina. The verse, *He Who has made the teaching of the Qur'ān binding on thee will most surely bring thee back to thy ordained place of return* (v. 86), clearly shows that the Holy Prophet was yet in Mecca when he was told that at first he would have to leave Mecca as a fugitive and then would come back to it as a conqueror. The preceding *Sūrah* had ended with the verse, *So whoever follows guidance, follows it only for the good of his own soul*; *and as to him who goes astray, say, I am only a Warner*, which meant that no force would be allowed to be used in the propagation of the teachings of the Qur'ān. It was to establish truth of this Quranic claim that the present *Sūrah* was revealed.

Subject-Matter

The present is the third and last of the Chapters which belong to the *Ṭā Sīn Mīm* group. These three Chapters open with the same abbreviated letters and, therefore, possess a striking similarity in the subject-matter. They all begin with the important subject of the revelation of the Qur'ān and end with the same subject. In Chapter 26th much space is devoted to the presentation by Moses of his Message to Pharaoh. In Chapter 27th pride of place is given to the manifestation that Moses saw of the Divine Glory and Majesty and to the spiritual experience which he had in the blessed Valley of Ṭuwā. In the present *Sūrah*, however, the different phases of Moses's life have been treated in greater detail than perhaps in any other *Sūrah*—his being taken out of the sea in a miraculous manner, his infancy and childhood, his youth, his *Hijrah* and his Call—the implication being that the Holy Prophet, who was the like of Moses, would also have to go through similar experiences, though under different conditions and in different circumstances. The *Sūrah* opens with an account of the pitiable condition of the Israelites under Pharaoh—how by his policy of ruthless exploitation and suppression he sought to kill in them all manly qualities and how when their humiliation had reached its nadir, God raised Moses and through him brought about their emancipation by drowning Pharaoh and his mighty hosts in the sea before their very eyes. After the account of Moses's life-story, the *Sūrah* refers to the prophecies that are found in the Bible about the Holy Prophet and proceeds to tell the Quraish that if they accepted him, they would enjoy all those spiritual and material blessings and benefits of which Mecca, as the Centre and Citadel of the new Faith, was destined to receive. But if they rejected him, they would incur the displeasure of God. The *Sūrah* then proceeds to say that when disbelievers, on account of their persistent rejection of truth are seized with punishment, they start condemning and denouncing their leaders who, they say, lead them astray and are the cause of their ruin. The leaders, on their part, disown them and even curse them for having blindly followed them. The real cause, however, of the rejection of the Divine Message, the *Sūrah* says, is that puffed up with material wealth and thereby lulled into a false sense of security, men of wealth and influence make light of God's Prophets, mock at them and persecute them, ignoring the supreme moral lesson which is writ large on the pages of history that the rejection of Truth has never been allowed to go unpunished and disbelief has always landed its protagonists into ruin. Towards its close the *Sūrah* makes a pointed reference to a mighty prophecy which was implied in Moses's flight from Egypt to Midian, in his sojourn there for ten years and his subsequent return to Egypt and in delivering the Israelites from Pharaoh. The prophecy was to the effect that like Moses the Holy Prophet of Islām also would leave his native place and go to live in a strange place for ten years and then would come back to the cradle of his Faith and conquer Mecca and establish Islām on a firm footing. The last few verses of the *Sūrah* sum up its subject-matter, and the Holy Prophet is told that he never had the remotest idea that he will ever be made the bearer of the Divine Message, but now that he has actually been entrusted with his great mission, he should call all mankind to the ways of the Lord, and trusting in Him and refusing to be discouraged or dismayed, should fight his way to success like the great and valiant votary of Truth he is.

سُوۡرَۃُ الۡقَصَصِ مَکِّیَّۃٌ

(٢٨) اٰیاتہا ٨٩ رکوعاتہا ٩

1. [a]In the name of Allāh, the Gracious, the Merciful.

بِسۡمِ اللّٰہِ الرَّحۡمٰنِ الرَّحِیۡمِ ﴿۱﴾

2. [b]Ṭā Sīn Mīm.[2195A]

طٰسٓمّٓ ﴿۲﴾

3. [c]These are verses of the perspicuous Book.

تِلۡکَ اٰیٰتُ الۡکِتٰبِ الۡمُبِیۡنِ ﴿۳﴾

4. We rehearse unto thee a true account of Moses and Pharaoh for *the benefit of* a people who would believe.

نَتۡلُوۡا عَلَیۡکَ مِنۡ نَّبَاِ مُوۡسٰی وَ فِرۡعَوۡنَ بِالۡحَقِّ
لِقَوۡمٍ یُّؤۡمِنُوۡنَ ﴿۴﴾

5. [d]Verily, Pharaoh behaved arrogantly in the earth, and divided[2196] the people thereof into sections; he sought to weaken one section of them, [e]slaughtering their sons and sparing their women. Certainly, he was *one* of the mischief-makers.

اِنَّ فِرۡعَوۡنَ عَلَا فِی الۡاَرۡضِ وَ جَعَلَ اَہۡلَہَا شِیَعًا
یَّسۡتَضۡعِفُ طَآئِفَۃً مِّنۡہُمۡ یُذَبِّحُ اَبۡنَآءَہُمۡ وَ یَسۡتَحۡیٖ
نِسَآءَہُمۡ ؕ اِنَّہٗ کَانَ مِنَ الۡمُفۡسِدِیۡنَ ﴿۵﴾

6. And We desired to show favour unto those who were considered weak in the earth, and to make them leaders and to make them inheritors *of Our favours,*

وَ نُرِیۡدُ اَنۡ نَّمُنَّ عَلَی الَّذِیۡنَ اسۡتُضۡعِفُوۡا فِی الۡاَرۡضِ
وَ نَجۡعَلَہُمۡ اَئِمَّۃً وَّ نَجۡعَلَہُمُ الۡوٰرِثِیۡنَ ﴿۶﴾

---

[a]1 : 1. [b]26 : 2; 27 : 2. [c]12 : 2; 15 : 2; 26 : 3; 27 : 2. [d]10 : 84. [e]2 : 50; 7 : 142; 14 : 7.

2195A. See 2143.

2196. The policy of "divide and rule" which has been practised with such deadly effect by the Western colonial Powers in this twentieth century seemed also to have been followed by Pharaoh with great success. He had split the people of Egypt into parties and sections and had made invidious distinctions between them. Some of them he favoured and others he exploited and suppressed. Moses's people belonged to the latter unfortunate class. The words, *slaughtering their sons and sparing their women*, besides bearing the apparent sense that in order to keep the Israelites under permanent subjection Pharaoh destroyed their men and kept alive their women, may also signify that by his policy of exploitation and heartless suppression, he sought to kill all their manly qualities and thus made them timid like women.

7. [a]And to establish them in the earth,[2197] and to make Pharaoh and Hāmān[2198] and their hosts see from them that which they feared.[2199]

وَنُمَكِّنَ لَهُمْ فِي الْأَرْضِ وَنُرِيَ فِرْعَوْنَ وَهَامٰنَ وَجُنُوْدَهُمَا مِنْهُمْ مَّا كَانُوْا يَحْذَرُوْنَ ﴿٧﴾

8. [b]And We *directed* the mother of Moses by revelation, 'Suckle him; and when thou fearest for him, then cast him into the river and fear not, nor grieve; *for* We shall restore him to thee, and shall make him *one* of the Messengers.'

وَاَوْحَيْنَآ اِلٰٓى اُمِّ مُوْسٰٓى اَنْ اَرْضِعِيْهِ ۚ فَاِذَا خِفْتِ عَلَيْهِ فَاَلْقِيْهِ فِي الْيَمِّ وَلَا تَخَافِيْ وَلَا تَحْزَنِيْ ۚ اِنَّا رَآدُّوْهُ اِلَيْكِ وَجَاعِلُوْهُ مِنَ الْمُرْسَلِيْنَ ﴿٨﴾

9. *She did accordingly* [c]and *one of* the family of Pharaoh picked him up so that[2200] he became for them an enemy and *a source of* sorrow. Verily, Pharaoh and Hāmān and their hosts were wrongdoers.

فَالْتَقَطَهٗٓ اٰلُ فِرْعَوْنَ لِيَكُوْنَ لَهُمْ عَدُوًّا وَّحَزَنًا ؕ اِنَّ فِرْعَوْنَ وَهَامٰنَ وَجُنُوْدَهُمَا كَانُوْا خٰطِـِٕيْنَ ﴿٩﴾

[a]7 : 138; 26 : 60; 44 : 29. [b]20 : 39. [c]20 : 40.

2197. When degradation of the Israelites in Egypt reached its nadir and the cup of iniquities of Pharaoh and his people became full to the brim and God in His infallible wisdom decreed that the oppressors should be punished and those held in bondage be emancipated, He raised Moses. This phenomenon which took place in the time of every Divine Messenger witnessed its fullest and finest manifestation during the ministry of the Holy Prophet of Islām.

2198. Hāmān was the title of the high priest of the god Amon; 'hām', in Egyptian language meaning, high priest. The god Amon dominated all other Egyptian gods. 'Hāmān was the director of both the treasury and the granary and director also of the soldiers and all the craftsmen of Thebes. His name was Nebunnef and he was high priest under Rameses II and his son Merneptah. Being the head of the extremely rich sacerdotal organization, embracing all the priesthoods of the country, his power and prestige had increased so much that he controlled a most influential political faction and even kept his own private army' ("A Story of Egypt" by James Henry Breasted, Ph.D.). Hāmān is also said to be the name of a minister of Ahasuerus, a king of Persia who lived many ages after Moses's time. There is nothing strange or objectionable in two persons living in two different periods bearing the same name.

2199. Exploitation and tyranny produce their own Nemesis and the exploiters and oppressors never feel secure from the standard of revolt being raised against them by those whom they exploit, suppress or oppress. The greater the oppression of the tyrant, the greater his fear of revolt from those who are oppressed. Pharaoh, too, was seized with this fear.

2200. The particle *lām* in *Liyakūna* (so that he became) is called *Lām al 'Āqibah* and denotes result and consequence.

10. And Pharaoh's wife said, '*He will be* a joy of the eye for me and for thee. Slay him not. Haply he may prove to be useful for us, or we may adopt him as a son.' And they knew not *Our purpose*.[2201]

وَقَالَتِ امْرَاَتُ فِرْعَوْنَ قُرَّتُ عَيْنٍ لِّيْ وَلَكَ ۖ لَا
تَقْتُلُوْهُ ۖ عَسٰۤى اَنْ يَّنْفَعَنَاۤ اَوْ نَتَّخِذَهٗ وَلَدًا وَّهُمْ
لَا يَشْعُرُوْنَ ۝١٠

11. And the heart of the mother of Moses became free *from anxiety*. She had almost disclosed *his identity*,[2202] were it not that We had strengthened her heart so that she might be of the *firm* believers.

وَاَصْبَحَ فُؤَادُ اُمِّ مُوْسٰى فٰرِغًا ۖ اِنْ كَادَتْ لَتُبْدِيْ
بِهٖ لَوْلَاۤ اَنْ رَّبَطْنَا عَلٰى قَلْبِهَا لِتَكُوْنَ مِنَ الْمُؤْمِنِيْنَ ۝١١

12. And she said to his sister, 'Follow him up.' So she observed him from afar; and they were unaware *of this*.

وَقَالَتْ لِاُخْتِهٖ قُصِّيْهِ ۫ فَبَصُرَتْ بِهٖ عَنْ جُنُبٍ وَّهُمْ
لَا يَشْعُرُوْنَ ۝١٢

13. And We had already decreed that he shall refuse the wet-nurses; so she said, [a]'Shall I direct you to *the people of* a household who will bring him up for you and will be his sincere well-wishers?'

وَحَرَّمْنَا عَلَيْهِ الْمَرَاضِعَ مِنْ قَبْلُ فَقَالَتْ هَلْ اَدُلُّكُمْ
عَلٰۤى اَهْلِ بَيْتٍ يَّكْفُلُوْنَهٗ لَكُمْ وَهُمْ لَهٗ نٰصِحُوْنَ ۝١٣

14. Thus We restored him to his mother that her eye might be gladdened and that she might not grieve, and that she might know that the promise of Allāh is true. But most of people know not.

فَرَدَدْنٰهُ اِلٰۤى اُمِّهٖ كَيْ تَقَرَّ عَيْنُهَا وَلَا تَحْزَنَ وَلِتَعْلَمَ
اَنَّ وَعْدَ اللّٰهِ حَقٌّ وَّلٰكِنَّ اَكْثَرَهُمْ لَا يَعْلَمُوْنَ ۝١٤

[a]20 : 41.

2201. God's ways indeed are inscrutable. Pharaoh did not know that the very child, upon whom he was lavishing so much care and love, would one day prove an instrument of punishment for him in the hands of Destiny because he had flouted and defied Divine commandments and had held the Israelites in bondage and tyrannized over them for a long time.

2202. Moses's mother was so much pleased with Moses having been restored to her that out of extreme joy she was on the point of declaring that the child belonged to her. If God had not restrained her, she almost had told people about the whole affair—how she had received a Divine revelation and how in pursuance of it she had put the child into the river and so on.

R. 2 15. ªAnd when he reached his *age of* full strength and attained maturity, We bestowed wisdom and knowledge upon him; and thus do We reward those who do good.²²⁰³

وَلَمَّا بَلَغَ أَشُدَّهُ وَاسْتَوَى اٰتَيْنٰهُ حُكْمًا وَّعِلْمًا ۚ وَكَذٰلِكَ نَجْزِى الْمُحْسِنِيْنَ ۝

16. And *one day* he entered the city at a time when its inhabitants were in *a state of* heedlessness; and he found therein two men fighting—one of his own party and the other of his enemies. And he who was of his party sought his help²²⁰⁴ against him who was of his enemies. ᵇSo Moses struck *the latter* with his fist ; and *thereby* caused his death. *Then* Moses said, 'This is of Satan's doing,²²⁰⁵ he is indeed an enemy, a manifest misleader.'

وَدَخَلَ الْمَدِيْنَةَ عَلٰى حِيْنِ غَفْلَةٍ مِّنْ أَهْلِهَا فَوَجَدَ فِيْهَا رَجُلَيْنِ يَقْتَتِلٰنِ ۖ هٰذَا مِنْ شِيْعَتِهٖ وَهٰذَا مِنْ عَدُوِّهٖ ۚ فَاسْتَغَاثَهُ الَّذِيْ مِنْ شِيْعَتِهٖ عَلَى الَّذِيْ مِنْ عَدُوِّهٖ ۙ فَوَكَزَهٗ مُوْسٰى فَقَضٰى عَلَيْهِ ۖ قَالَ هٰذَا مِنْ عَمَلِ الشَّيْطٰنِ ۖ إِنَّهٗ عَدُوٌّ مُّضِلٌّ مُّبِيْنٌ ۝

17. He said, 'My Lord, I have wronged my soul,²²⁰⁶ so do Thou forgive me.' So He forgave him; He is Most Forgiving, *ever* Merciful.

قَالَ رَبِّ إِنِّيْ ظَلَمْتُ نَفْسِيْ فَاغْفِرْ لِيْ فَغَفَرَ لَهٗ ۚ إِنَّهٗ هُوَ الْغَفُوْرُ الرَّحِيْمُ ۝

ª12 : 23; 46 : 16. ᵇ20 : 41; 26 : 20.

2203. Moses was fully equipped with temporal as well as Divine knowledge. Having been brought up in the house of a great monarch of the time he must have had the best tutors to teach him the current sciences. His physical development was also perfect as is apparent from the next verse, and he was inspired by noble ideals. As God had marked him out for a great destiny, he was endowed with wisdom and spiritual knowledge in a very large measure. By the time Moses had attained maturity he was a *Muḥsin*, *i.e.*, a constant doer of good deeds.

2204. Being of a very noble nature and having been inspired by very high ideals, Moses was always ready to help weak and oppressed people; so when a poor Israelite sought his help against an arrogant and cruel Egyptian, he at once went to his rescue.

2205. The expression, *This is of Satan's doing*, according to Arabic idiom means that some evil thing has happened, *i.e.*, 'Satan had caused an Egyptian and an Israelite to fight and I had to come to the assistance of the oppressed Israelite which resulted in an evil thing' *i.e.*, the death of a person. Or the words might have been addressed to the dead Egyptian meaning, 'This is the outcome of your satanic deed,' *i.e.*, 'Your death is the result of your own wickedness and transgression.' The fact that Moses used no lethal weapon and only repelled the Egyptian or struck him with his fist shows that the latter's death was accidental. Evidently, there was no intention on Moses's part to kill him. The Qur'ān has not mentioned the wicked deed of the Egyptian to which Moses refers in this verse. The Egyptian is reported to have forced an Israelite woman to commit adultery with him. It apparently led to the quarrel referred to in the verse and ultimately to Moses's interference and the death of the Egyptian (Jew. Enc. under "Moses").

2206. *Ẓalama-hū* means, he imposed upon him a burden which was beyond his power or ability to bear; he exposed himself to danger (Lane & Mufradāt). Moses realized that in

18. He said, 'My Lord, because of the favour Thou hast bestowed upon me, I will never be a helper of the guilty.'[2207]

قَالَ رَبِّ بِمَآ اَنۡعَمۡتَ عَلَیَّ فَلَنۡ اَکُوۡنَ ظَهِیۡرًا
لِّلۡمُجۡرِمِیۡنَ ﴿۱۸﴾

19. And morning found him in the city, apprehensive, watchful; and lo! he who had sought his help the day before cried out to him *again* for help. Moses said to him, 'Verily, thou art manifestly a misguided fellow.'[2208]

فَاَصۡبَحَ فِی الۡمَدِیۡنَةِ خَآئِفًا یَّتَرَقَّبُ فَاِذَا الَّذِی
اسۡتَنۡصَرَهٗ بِالۡاَمۡسِ یَسۡتَصۡرِخُهٗ ؕ قَالَ لَهٗ مُوۡسٰۤی
اِنَّکَ لَغَوِیٌّ مُّبِیۡنٌ ﴿۱۹﴾

20. And when he made up his mind to lay hold of the man who was an enemy[2209] to both of them, he said, 'O Moses, dost thou intend to kill me even as thou didst kill a person yesterday? Thou only desirest to be a tyrant in the land, and thou desirest not to be a peace-maker.'

فَلَمَّاۤ اَنۡ اَرَادَ اَنۡ یَّبۡطِشَ بِالَّذِیۡ هُوَ عَدُوٌّ لَّهُمَا ۙ
قَالَ یٰمُوۡسٰۤی اَتُرِیۡدُ اَنۡ تَقۡتُلَنِیۡ کَمَا قَتَلۡتَ نَفۡسًۢا
بِالۡاَمۡسِ ٭ۖ اِنۡ تُرِیۡدُ اِلَّاۤ اَنۡ تَکُوۡنَ جَبَّارًا فِی الۡاَرۡضِ
وَمَا تُرِیۡدُ اَنۡ تَکُوۡنَ مِنَ الۡمُصۡلِحِیۡنَ ﴿۲۰﴾

21. And there came a man from the far side of the city, running. He said, 'O Moses, of a truth, the chiefs are taking counsel together against thee to kill thee. Therefore get thee away; surely, I am thy well-wisher.'

وَجَآءَ رَجُلٌ مِّنۡ اَقۡصَا الۡمَدِیۡنَةِ یَسۡعٰی ۫ قَالَ یٰمُوۡسٰۤی
اِنَّ الۡمَلَاَ یَاۡتَمِرُوۡنَ بِکَ لِیَقۡتُلُوۡکَ فَاخۡرُجۡ اِنِّیۡ لَکَ
مِنَ النّٰصِحِیۡنَ ﴿۲۱﴾

---

trying to help the poor Israelite he had happened to kill the Egyptian and thus had exposed himself to a great danger and had taken upon himself a burden which apparently he could not bear. So he prayed to God to protect him from the evil consequences that might flow from his accidentally killing a member of the ruling race.

2207. The verse shows Moses as saying, 'My Lord! Thou hast always been gracious to me, so in my gratitude to Thee for Thy favour, I promise that I will always help the oppressed as I did on the last occasion, and will never take sides with the oppressor.' Or it may mean, 'My Lord, since Thou hast been always kind and gracious to me, how can I be a helper and supporter of the oppressors?'

2208. Moses seems to reproach the Israelite who called him for help by saying to him, 'You are a foolish fellow and not being able to realize the consequences of your actions you readily become involved in trouble.' The words do not mean, as is generally misunderstood, that Moses regarded the man as an offender.

2209. The words, *who was an enemy to both of them*, show that the man referred to was an Egyptian. But if he was an Israelite, as the Bible says, then he must have been in league with the Egyptians and must have reported the previous day's incident to the authorities and thus was an enemy both to Moses and the Israelite who called Moses for help.

22. [a]So he went forth therefrom, fearful *and* watchful. He said, 'My Lord, deliver me from the unjust people.'

فَخَرَجَ مِنْهَا خَآئِفًا يَّتَرَقَّبُ ۫ قَالَ رَبِّ نَجِّنِىْ مِنَ
الْقَوْمِ الظّٰلِمِيْنَ ﴿٢٢﴾

R. 3 23. And when he turned his face towards Midian, he said, 'I hope, my Lord will guide me to the right way.'

وَلَمَّا تَوَجَّهَ تِلْقَآءَ مَدْيَنَ قَالَ عَسٰى رَبِّىْٓ اَنْ
يَّهْدِيَنِىْ سَوَآءَ السَّبِيْلِ ﴿٢٣﴾

24. And when he arrived at the water of Midian, he found there a party of men, watering their flocks. And he found beside them two women holding back *their flocks*. He said, 'What is your problem?'[2209A] They replied, 'We cannot water our flocks until the shepherds depart *with their flocks*, and our father is a very old man.'

وَلَمَّا وَرَدَ مَآءَ مَدْيَنَ وَجَدَ عَلَيْهِ اُمَّةً مِّنَ
النَّاسِ يَسْقُوْنَ ۬ۖ وَوَجَدَ مِنْ دُوْنِهِمُ امْرَاَتَيْنِ
تَذُوْدٰنِ ۚ قَالَ مَا خَطْبُكُمَا ؕ قَالَتَا لَا نَسْقِىْ حَتّٰى
يُصْدِرَ الرِّعَآءُ ٜ وَاَبُوْنَا شَيْخٌ كَبِيْرٌ ﴿٢٤﴾

25. So he watered *their flocks* for them. Then he turned aside into the shade and said, 'My Lord, I stand in need of whatever good Thou mayest send down to me.'

فَسَقٰى لَهُمَا ثُمَّ تَوَلّٰٓى اِلَى الظِّلِّ فَقَالَ رَبِّ اِنِّىْ لِمَآ
اَنْزَلْتَ اِلَىَّ مِنْ خَيْرٍ فَقِيْرٌ ﴿٢٥﴾

26. And one of the two *women* came to him, walking bashfully. She said, 'My father calls thee that he may reward thee for thy having watered *our flocks* for us.' So when he came to him and told him the story, he said, 'Fear not; thou hast escaped from the unjust people.'[2210]

فَجَآءَتْهُ اِحْدٰىهُمَا تَمْشِىْ عَلَى اسْتِحْيَآءٍ ۫ قَالَتْ اِنَّ
اَبِىْ يَدْعُوْكَ لِيَجْزِيَكَ اَجْرَ مَا سَقَيْتَ لَنَا ؕ فَلَمَّا
جَآءَهٗ وَقَصَّ عَلَيْهِ الْقَصَصَ ۙ قَالَ لَا تَخَفْ ٙ نَجَوْتَ
مِنَ الْقَوْمِ الظّٰلِمِيْنَ ﴿٢٦﴾

27. One of the two *women* said, 'O my father, take him into thy service; for the best man that thou canst employ is the *one who is* strong *and* trustworthy.'

قَالَتْ اِحْدٰىهُمَا يٰۤاَبَتِ اسْتَاْجِرْهُ ۫ اِنَّ خَيْرَ مَنِ
اسْتَاْجَرْتَ الْقَوِىُّ الْاَمِيْنُ ﴿٢٧﴾

---

[a]26 : 22.

2209A. What is your trouble; or what is the matter with you ?

2210. The words, *thou hast escaped from the unjust people*, show that on hearing Moses's story the old and righteous man was convinced that Moses had committed no murder and that the death of the Egyptian was only accidental. On the other hand he dubbed and denounced the Egyptians as a wicked people.

28. *Their father* said *to Moses* 'I intend to marry to thee one of these two daughters of mine on condition that thou stay in my service for eight years. But if thou complete ten *years*, it will be of thine own accord.[2211] And I would not lay any hardship upon thee; thou wilt find me, if Allāh wills, of the righteous.'

قَالَ إِنِّيٓ أُرِيدُ أَنْ أُنكِحَكَ إِحْدَى ٱبْنَتَيَّ هَٰتَيْنِ
عَلَىٰٓ أَن تَأْجُرَنِي ثَمَٰنِيَ حِجَجٍ ۖ فَإِنْ أَتْمَمْتَ عَشْرًا
فَمِنْ عِندِكَ ۖ وَمَآ أُرِيدُ أَنْ أَشُقَّ عَلَيْكَ ۚ سَتَجِدُنِيٓ
إِن شَآءَ ٱللَّهُ مِنَ ٱلصَّٰلِحِينَ ﴿٢٨﴾

29. *Moses* said, 'That is *settled* between me and thee. Whichever of the two terms I fulfil, there shall be no injustice to me; and Allāh watches over what we say.'

قَالَ ذَٰلِكَ بَيْنِي وَبَيْنَكَ ۖ أَيَّمَا ٱلْأَجَلَيْنِ قَضَيْتُ فَلَا
عُدْوَٰنَ عَلَيَّ ۖ وَٱللَّهُ عَلَىٰ مَا نَقُولُ وَكِيلٌ ﴿٢٩﴾ ع

R. 4 30. And when Moses had fulfilled the term, and set forth with his family, he perceived a fire in the direction of the Mount. He said to his family, 'Wait,[2212] [a]I perceive a fire; haply I may bring you some *useful* information therefrom, or a burning brand from the fire that you may warm yourselves.'

فَلَمَّا قَضَىٰ مُوسَى ٱلْأَجَلَ وَسَارَ بِأَهْلِهِۦٓ ءَانَسَ مِن
جَانِبِ ٱلطُّورِ نَارًا ۖ قَالَ لِأَهْلِهِ ٱمْكُثُوٓا۟ إِنِّيٓ ءَانَسْتُ
نَارًا لَّعَلِّيٓ ءَاتِيكُم مِّنْهَا بِخَبَرٍ أَوْ جَذْوَةٍ مِّنَ ٱلنَّارِ
لَعَلَّكُمْ تَصْطَلُونَ ﴿٣٠﴾

[a]20 : 11; 27 : 8.

2211. The construction of the verse does not seem to lend countenance to the conclusion generally considered derivable from it, *viz.*, that Shu'aib or Jethro agreed to marry one of his daughters to Moses in lieu of eight or ten years of service The fact of the matter appears to be that Shu'aib having grown very old needed an honest man to look after his flocks and Moses having been found by him to be possessed of the required qualifications was taken in service by him at the instance of one of his daughters. Eight or ten years were agreed upon as the tenure of service. Shu'aib, however, being a godly person either himself realized, or was informed by God by revelation, that a great future lay before Moses. He, therefore, offered to marry one of his daughters to him and, desiring that his son-in-law should live with him for some time and benefit by his noble company, laid it down as one of the conditions of marriage that Moses should stay with him for eight or ten years. Thus it is not correct to say that Shu'aib offered to marry his daughter to Moses in lieu of the latter serving him for eight or ten years. Whatever remuneration Moses might have received from Shu'aib had nothing to do with the marriage proposal.

2212. Seclusion and solitude are very essential for meditation and communion with the Divine Being. Moses sought separation from his family, in fact from all worldly contacts and connections, in order that he might be blessed with Divine communion.

31. And when he came to it, [a]he was called *by a voice* from the right side[2213] of the Valley, in the blessed spot, out of the tree: 'O Moses, verily I am Allāh, the Lord of the worlds;

فَلَمَّآ أَتٰىهَا نُوْدِيَ مِنْ شَاطِئِ الْوَادِ الْاَيْمَنِ فِي الْبُقْعَةِ
الْمُبٰرَكَةِ مِنَ الشَّجَرَةِ اَنْ يّٰمُوْسٰٓى اِنِّيْٓ اَنَا اللّٰهُ رَبُّ
الْعٰلَمِيْنَ ﴿٣١﴾

32. [b]'Cast down thy rod.' And when he saw it move as though it were a serpent, he turned back retreating and did not look back. 'O Moses,' *said the voice*, 'Come forward and fear not; surely, thou art of those who are safe,

وَاَنْ اَلْقِ عَصَاكَ ۚ فَلَمَّا رَاٰهَا تَهْتَزُّ كَاَنَّهَا جَآنٌّ وَّلّٰى
مُدْبِرًا وَّلَمْ يُعَقِّبْ ۚ يٰمُوْسٰٓى اَقْبِلْ وَلَا تَخَفْ ۟ اِنَّكَ
مِنَ الْاٰمِنِيْنَ ﴿٣٢﴾

33. [c]'Insert thy hand into thy bosom; it will come forth white without evil *effect*, and draw back thy arm toward thyself *in order to still thy* fear. So these *shall be* two proofs from thy Lord to Pharaoh and his chiefs. Surely, they are a rebellious people.

اُسْلُكْ يَدَكَ فِيْ جَيْبِكَ تَخْرُجْ بَيْضَآءَ مِنْ غَيْرِ سُوْٓءٍ ۫
وَّاضْمُمْ اِلَيْكَ جَنَاحَكَ مِنَ الرَّهْبِ فَذٰنِكَ بُرْهَانٰنِ
مِنْ رَّبِّكَ اِلٰى فِرْعَوْنَ وَمَلَا۟ئِهٖ ۚ اِنَّهُمْ كَانُوْا قَوْمًا
فٰسِقِيْنَ ﴿٣٣﴾

34. [d]*Moses* said, 'My Lord, I killed[2214] a person from among them, and I fear that they will kill me;

قَالَ رَبِّ اِنِّيْ قَتَلْتُ مِنْهُمْ نَفْسًا فَاَخَافُ اَنْ
يَّقْتُلُوْنِ ﴿٣٤﴾

35. 'And my brother Aaron—he is more eloquent in speech than I; [e]send him, therefore, with me as a helper[2215] that he may bear witness to my truth. I fear that they will charge me with falsehood.'

وَاَخِيْ هٰرُوْنُ هُوَ اَفْصَحُ مِنِّيْ لِسَانًا فَاَرْسِلْهُ مَعِيَ
رِدْاً يُّصَدِّقُنِيْٓ ۡ اِنِّيْٓ اَخَافُ اَنْ يُّكَذِّبُوْنِ ﴿٣٥﴾

[a]19 : 53; 20 : 81; 79 : 17. [b]7 : 118; 20 : 20; 26 : 46. [c]7 : 109; 20 : 23; 27 : 13. [d]20 : 41; 26 : 15. [e]20 : 30-33; 26 : 14.

2213. Whereas Moses was only on the side of the blessed spiritual valley, the Holy Prophet Muḥammad had actually entered it (53 : 14, 15). Moses could not attain that high stage of nearness to God which was reserved for the Holy Prophet.

2214. Moses alludes to the mere fact of a man having been accidentally killed by him and not that he pleads guilty to the charge of deliberately killing him.

2215. *Rid'* means, a buttress or the like by means of which a wall is strengthened and supported; a thing by means of which one is helped, aided or assisted; an aider or helper. They say, *Fulānun Rid'u Fulānin, i.e.*, such a one is an aider to such a one (Lane).

36. [a]*God* said, 'We will strengthen thine arm[2216] with thy brother, and We will give power to you both so that they shall not reach you. So *go* with Our Signs. You two and those who follow you will prevail.'

قَالَ سَنَشُدُّ عَضُدَكَ بِأَخِيكَ وَنَجْعَلُ لَكُمَا سُلْطٰنًا
فَلَا يَصِلُونَ إِلَيْكُمَا ۚ بِاٰيٰتِنَآ ۚ أَنْتُمَا وَمَنِ اتَّبَعَكُمَا
الْغٰلِبُونَ ﴿٣٦﴾

37. [b]And when Moses came to them with Our clear Signs, they said, 'This is nothing but a forged sorcery, and we never heard *the like* of this among our forefathers.'

فَلَمَّا جَآءَهُمْ مُّوسٰى بِاٰيٰتِنَا بَيِّنٰتٍ قَالُوا مَا هٰذَآ
إِلَّا سِحْرٌ مُّفْتَرًى وَّمَا سَمِعْنَا بِهٰذَا فِيٓ اٰبَآئِنَا
الْأَوَّلِينَ ﴿٣٧﴾

38. Moses said, 'My Lord knows best who it is that has brought guidance from Him, and whose will be the reward of the *final* abode. Verily, the wrongdoers never prosper.'

وَقَالَ مُوسٰى رَبِّيٓ أَعْلَمُ بِمَنْ جَآءَ بِالْهُدٰى مِنْ
عِنْدِهٖ وَمَنْ تَكُونُ لَهُ عَاقِبَةُ الدَّارِ ۚ إِنَّهُ لَا يُفْلِحُ
الظّٰلِمُونَ ﴿٣٨﴾

39. And Pharaoh said, 'O chiefs, [c]I know of no god for you other than myself; so burn me *bricks of* clay, [d]O Hāmān, and build me a tower, that I may, *by climbing it*, have a look at the God of Moses,[2217] for I think that he is a liar.'

وَقَالَ فِرْعَوْنُ يٰٓأَيُّهَا الْمَلَأُ مَا عَلِمْتُ لَكُمْ مِّنْ
إِلٰهٍ غَيْرِيْ ۚ فَأَوْقِدْ لِيْ يٰهَامٰنُ عَلَى الطِّيْنِ فَاجْعَلْ
لِّيْ صَرْحًا لَّعَلِّيٓ أَطَّلِعُ إِلٰٓى إِلٰهِ مُوسٰى وَإِنِّيْ لَأَظُنُّهُ
مِنَ الْكٰذِبِيْنَ ﴿٣٩﴾

40. [e]And he and his hosts behaved arrogantly in the land without justification. And they thought that they would never be brought back to Us.

وَاسْتَكْبَرَ هُوَ وَجُنُوْدُهٗ فِي الْأَرْضِ بِغَيْرِ الْحَقِّ وَ
ظَنُّوْٓا أَنَّهُمْ إِلَيْنَا لَا يُرْجَعُوْنَ ﴿٤٠﴾

[a]20 : 43. [b]29 : 40. [c]26 : 30. [d]40 : 37. [e]7 : 134.

2216. '*Aḍud* means, the upper arm or upper half of the arm; an aider or assistant (Lane).

2217. The verse is susceptible of two interpretations: (1) The Israelites were already working as labourers at the kilns. Pharaoh alludes to this ignoble condition of theirs and seems derisively to say to Hāmān, 'These people do not appear to have sufficient work to do. Having more than enough leisure they have begun to dream of Prophethood. They must be put to hard labour; then will they come to their senses and give up having false illusions about God and Prophethood.' (2) The Egyptians were well-versed in astronomy. They built high observatories for observing the movements of the stars. So Pharaoh jeeringly asked Hāmān to build for him a lofty observatory so that he might have a peep at the God of Moses.

41. [a]So We seized him and his hosts and cast them into the sea. See, then, how *evil* was the end of the wrongdoers !

فَأَخَذْنٰهُ وَجُنُوْدَهٗ فَنَبَذْنٰهُمْ فِي الْيَمِّ ۚ فَانْظُرْ كَيْفَ كَانَ عَاقِبَةُ الظّٰلِمِيْنَ ﴿٤١﴾

42. And We made them leaders [b]who called *people* unto the Fire; and on the Day of Resurrection they will not be helped.

وَجَعَلْنٰهُمْ أَئِمَّةً يَّدْعُوْنَ إِلَى النَّارِ ۚ وَيَوْمَ الْقِيٰمَةِ لَا يُنْصَرُوْنَ ﴿٤٢﴾

43. [c]And We caused them to be followed by a curse in this world; and on the Day of Resurrection they will be among those deprived of *all* good.[2217A]

وَأَتْبَعْنٰهُمْ فِيْ هٰذِهِ الدُّنْيَا لَعْنَةً ۚ وَيَوْمَ الْقِيٰمَةِ هُمْ مِّنَ الْمَقْبُوْحِيْنَ ﴿٤٣﴾ ع

R. 5 44. [d]And We gave Moses the Book, after We had destroyed the earlier generations, as *a source of* enlightenment for men, and a guidance and a mercy, that they might reflect.

وَلَقَدْ اٰتَيْنَا مُوْسَى الْكِتٰبَ مِنْۢ بَعْدِ مَا أَهْلَكْنَا الْقُرُوْنَ الْأُوْلٰى بَصَآئِرَ لِلنَّاسِ وَهُدًى وَّرَحْمَةً لَّعَلَّهُمْ يَتَذَكَّرُوْنَ ﴿٤٤﴾

45. And thou wast not on the western side *of the Mount* when We committed the matter *of Prophethood* to Moses nor wast thou among the witnesses.[2218]

وَمَا كُنْتَ بِجَانِبِ الْغَرْبِيِّ إِذْ قَضَيْنَآ إِلٰى مُوْسَى الْأَمْرَ وَمَا كُنْتَ مِنَ الشّٰهِدِيْنَ ﴿٤٥﴾

46. But We brought forth generations *after Moses,* and life became prolonged for them.[2219] And thou

وَلٰكِنَّآ أَنْشَأْنَا قُرُوْنًا فَتَطَاوَلَ عَلَيْهِمُ الْعُمُرُ ۚ وَمَا

[a]2 : 51; 7 : 137; 17 : 104; 20 : 79; 26 : 67; 79 : 26. [b]11 : 99. [c]11 : 61,100. [d]7 : 155; 46 : 13.

2217A. *Maqbūḥ* means, removed from or deprived of good ; driven from good like a dog; rendered abominable (Lane).

2218. The verse purports to say that the prophecy of Moses about the advent of the Holy Prophet (Deut. 18 : 18) has been fulfilled so clearly and in such detail as if he was present in person with Moses when the latter was making the prophecy.

2219. Ages passed and a long line of Prophets appeared after Moses and they preached their Messages, yet none of these Prophets ever claimed to be 'the Prophet like unto Moses' about whom Moses had made the prophecy mentioned in Deut. 18 : 18, till the Qur'ān was revealed and it claimed that the grand prophecy of Moses had been fulfilled in the person of the Holy Prophet of Islām (73 : 16). So the prophecy evidently was from God and could not have been put into his mouth by the Holy Prophet who came centuries after him. The people of Moses had almost forgotten this and other prophecies concerning the Holy Prophet on account of the lapse of time.

wast not a dweller among the people of Midian,²²¹⁹ᴬ rehearsing Our Signs unto them; but it is We Who send Messengers.

كُنْتَ ثَاوِيًا فِىٓ أَهْلِ مَدْيَنَ تَتْلُوْا عَلَيْهِمْ اٰيٰتِنَا ۙ وَلٰكِنَّا كُنَّا مُرْسِلِيْنَ ۞

47. And thou wast not on the side of the Mount *with Moses,* ᵃwhen We called *to him and revealed to him Our prophecy concerning thee.*²²²⁰ But *We have sent thee as a* mercy from thy Lord, ᵇthat thou mayest warn a people to whom no warner had come before thee, that they may be mindful.

وَمَا كُنْتَ بِجَانِبِ الطُّوْرِ إِذْ نَادَيْنَا وَلٰكِنْ رَّحْمَةً مِّنْ رَّبِّكَ لِتُنْذِرَ قَوْمًا مَّآ أَتٰهُمْ مِّنْ نَّذِيْرٍ مِّنْ قَبْلِكَ لَعَلَّهُمْ يَتَذَكَّرُوْنَ ۞

48. And were it not that if an affliction should befall them because of what their hands have sent before *them,* they would say, ᶜ'Our Lord, wherefore didst Thou not send a Messenger to us that we might have followed Thy commandments and been of the believers?' *We should not have sent thee as a Messenger.*

وَلَوْلَآ أَنْ تُصِيْبَهُمْ مُّصِيْبَةٌۢ بِمَا قَدَّمَتْ أَيْدِيْهِمْ فَيَقُوْلُوْا رَبَّنَا لَوْلَآ أَرْسَلْتَ إِلَيْنَا رَسُوْلًا فَنَتَّبِعَ اٰيٰتِكَ وَنَكُوْنَ مِنَ الْمُؤْمِنِيْنَ ۞

49. But *now* when the truth has come to them from Us, they say, ᵈ'Why has he not been given the like of what was given to Moses?' Did they not reject that which was given to Moses before? They said, 'Aaron and Moses are but two sorcerers who back up each other.' And they say, 'We reject *the claim of* both.'

فَلَمَّا جَآءَهُمُ الْحَقُّ مِنْ عِنْدِنَا قَالُوْا لَوْلَآ أُوْتِىَ مِثْلَ مَآ أُوْتِىَ مُوْسٰى ۚ أَوَلَمْ يَكْفُرُوْا بِمَآ أُوْتِىَ مُوْسٰى مِنْ قَبْلُ ۚ قَالُوْا سِحْرٰنِ تَظٰهَرَا ۫ وَقَالُوٓا إِنَّا بِكُلٍّ كٰفِرُوْنَ ۞

ᵃ20 : 12-13; 79 : 17. ᵇ32 : 4; 36 : 7. ᶜ20 : 135. ᵈ6 : 125.

2219A. These words refer to a striking resemblance of the Holy Prophet with Moses. Like Moses who lived in Midian for ten years among a strange people and then went back to Egypt to reclaim his oppressed people from the bondage of Pharaoh, the Holy Prophet lived in Medina for ten years and then came to Mecca to conquer it.

2220. The verse implies that it was not possible for the Holy Prophet first to have caused Moses to make a prophecy concerning him (Deut. 18 : 18) and then to have claimed to have come in fulfilment of that prophecy.

50. Say, 'Then bring a Book from Allāh which is a better guide than these two *Books*[2221]—*the Torah and the Qur'ān*—that I may follow it, if you are truthful'

قُلْ فَأْتُوْا بِكِتٰبٍ مِّنْ عِنْدِ اللّٰهِ هُوَ اَهْدٰى مِنْهُمَآ
اَتَّبِعْهُ اِنْ كُنْتُمْ صٰدِقِيْنَ ۝٥٠

51. [a]But if they answer thee not, then know that they only follow their own evil desires. And who is more erring than he who follows his evil desires without any guidance from Allāh. Verily, Allāh guides not the wrongdoing people.

فَاِنْ لَّمْ يَسْتَجِيْبُوْا لَكَ فَاعْلَمْ اَنَّمَا يَتَّبِعُوْنَ اَهْوَآءَهُمْ ۗ
وَمَنْ اَضَلُّ مِمَّنِ اتَّبَعَ هَوٰىهُ بِغَيْرِ هُدًى مِّنَ اللّٰهِ ۗ
اِنَّ اللّٰهَ لَا يَهْدِي الْقَوْمَ الظّٰلِمِيْنَ ۝٥١

R. 6 52. And We have, indeed, sent revelation to them continuously, that they may be admonished.

وَلَقَدْ وَصَّلْنَا لَهُمُ الْقَوْلَ لَعَلَّهُمْ يَتَذَكَّرُوْنَ ۝٥٢

53. Those to whom We gave the Book[2222] before *the Qur'ān*—they believe in it.

اَلَّذِيْنَ اٰتَيْنٰهُمُ الْكِتٰبَ مِنْ قَبْلِهٖ هُمْ بِهٖ يُؤْمِنُوْنَ ۝٥٣

54. And when it is recited unto them, they say, 'We believe in it. Verily, it is the truth from our Lord. Indeed, even before it we had submitted *to its teaching*.'

وَاِذَا يُتْلٰى عَلَيْهِمْ قَالُوْٓا اٰمَنَّا بِهٖٓ اِنَّهُ الْحَقُّ مِنْ رَّبِّنَآ
اِنَّا كُنَّا مِنْ قَبْلِهٖ مُسْلِمِيْنَ ۝٥٤

55. These will be given their reward twice, for they have been steadfast,[2223] and [b]they repel evil with good, and [c]spend out of what We have given them.

اُولٰٓئِكَ يُؤْتَوْنَ اَجْرَهُمْ مَّرَّتَيْنِ بِمَا صَبَرُوْا وَ
يَدْرَءُوْنَ بِالْحَسَنَةِ السَّيِّئَةَ وَمِمَّا رَزَقْنٰهُمْ يُنْفِقُوْنَ ۝٥٥

56. [d]'And when they hear idle talk, they turn away from it and say, 'For us are our works and for you your works. Peace be upon you. We have no concern with the ignorant.'

وَاِذَا سَمِعُوا اللَّغْوَ اَعْرَضُوْا عَنْهُ وَقَالُوْا لَنَآ اَعْمَالُنَا
وَلَكُمْ اَعْمَالُكُمْ سَلٰمٌ عَلَيْكُمْ لَا نَبْتَغِي الْجٰهِلِيْنَ ۝٥٦

[a]11 : 15. [b]13 : 23; 23 : 97; 41 : 35. [c]23 : 5; [d]25 : 64. 25 : 73.

2221. The verse alludes to the very high position which both the Qur'ān and the Torah hold among heavenly Scriptures, the Qur'ān being *par excellence* the best among the revealed Books and the Torah taking the second place.

2222. *Al-Kitāb* referring particularly to the Torah or to every revealed Book, the verse may either mean: (1) Those, who have been given a right understanding of the Book—the Torah, and ponder over it, are sure to believe in it—the Qur'ān. Or (2) from among the followers of every revealed Book a large section will believe in the Qur'ān and join the fold of Islām during the ages.

2223. Such persons from among the 'People of the Book' as believe in the Qur'ān will have double reward for the belief both in the Torah and the Qur'ān and also for suffering patiently for the cause of Truth.

57. ªSurely, thou canst not guide whomsoever thou lovest; but Allāh guides whomsoever He pleases; and He knows best those who would accept guidance.

اِنَّكَ لَا تَهۡدِیۡ مَنۡ اَحۡبَبۡتَ وَ لٰکِنَّ اللّٰهَ یَهۡدِیۡ مَنۡ یَّشَآءُ ۚ وَ هُوَ اَعۡلَمُ بِالۡمُهۡتَدِیۡنَ ۝

58. And they say, 'If we were to follow the guidance with thee, we should be snatched²²²⁴ away from our land.' *Say to them,* 'Have We not established for them a safe sanctuary, ᵇto which are brought the fruits of all things, *as* a provision from Us?' But most of them know not.

وَ قَالُوۡۤا اِنۡ نَّتَّبِعِ الۡهُدٰی مَعَکَ نُتَخَطَّفۡ مِنۡ اَرۡضِنَا ؕ اَوَ لَمۡ نُمَکِّنۡ لَّهُمۡ حَرَمًا اٰمِنًا یُّجۡبٰۤی اِلَیۡهِ ثَمَرٰتُ کُلِّ شَیۡءٍ رِّزۡقًا مِّنۡ لَّدُنَّا وَ لٰکِنَّ اَکۡثَرَهُمۡ لَا یَعۡلَمُوۡنَ ۝

59. 'And how many a town have We destroyed which exulted in its life *of ease and plenty*! And these are their dwellings which have been but little inhabited after them.²²²⁵ And it is We Who became the inheritors *thereof*.

وَ کَمۡ اَهۡلَکۡنَا مِنۡ قَرۡیَةٍۭ بَطِرَتۡ مَعِیۡشَتَهَا ۚ فَتِلۡکَ مَسٰکِنُهُمۡ لَمۡ تُسۡکَنۡ مِّنۡۢ بَعۡدِهِمۡ اِلَّا قَلِیۡلًا ؕ وَ کُنَّا نَحۡنُ الۡوٰرِثِیۡنَ ۝

60. ᵈAnd thy Lord would never destroy the towns until He has raised in the mother-town thereof a Messenger,²²²⁶ reciting unto them Our Signs; nor would We destroy the towns unless the people thereof were wrongdoers.

وَ مَا کَانَ رَبُّکَ مُهۡلِکَ الۡقُرٰی حَتّٰی یَبۡعَثَ فِیۡۤ اُمِّهَا رَسُوۡلًا یَّتۡلُوۡا عَلَیۡهِمۡ اٰیٰتِنَا ۚ وَ مَا کُنَّا مُهۡلِکِی الۡقُرٰۤی اِلَّا وَ اَهۡلُهَا ظٰلِمُوۡنَ ۝

ª12 : 104;   16 : 38.   ᵇ2 : 127;   14 : 38.   ᶜ7 : 5;   21 : 12;   22 : 46;   65 : 9.
ᵈ6 : 132;   11 : 118;   20 : 135;   26 : 209.

2224. The verse signifies that the fear is ill-founded that if the new Message were accepted, people will swoop down upon Mecca and deprive the Meccans of their possessions and freedom. It purports to say that from time immemorial Mecca (which is now going to be the Centre of the new Faith) has remained a safe sanctuary and those who ever sought to interfere with its sacred character themselves met with ruin and destruction.

2225. There had lived in the past peoples who were more powerful and wealthier and possessed superior civilizations than the people of whom the Meccans are afraid, and yet when they rejected the truth and behaved proudly they were so completely wiped out from the face of the earth as if they had never lived on it, and those who were considered weak were made to take their place.

2226. The unusual frequency and universality of natural calamities in the form of famines, wars, earthquakes and epidemics during the last five or six decades call for the appearance of a Divine Reformer in the present time.

61. [a]And whatever of anything you are given is only a temporary enjoyment of the present life and an adornment thereof; and that which is with Allāh is better and more lasting. Will you not then understand?

وَمَآ اُوْتِيْتُمْ مِّنْ شَيْءٍ فَمَتَاعُ الْحَيٰوةِ الدُّنْيَا وَ
زِيْنَتُهَا ۚ وَمَا عِنْدَ اللّٰهِ خَيْرٌ وَّ اَبْقٰى ۭ اَفَلَا تَعْقِلُوْنَ ﴿٦١﴾ ع

R. 7 62. Is he, then, to whom We have promised a goodly promise, *the fulfilment of* which he will meet, [b]like him whom We have provided with the good things of this life *only*, and then on the Day of Resurrection he will be among those who are brought *before God to give an account of their deeds?*

اَفَمَنْ وَّعَدْنٰهُ وَعْدًا حَسَنًا فَهُوَ لَاقِيْهِ كَمَنْ مَّتَّعْنٰهُ
مَتَاعَ الْحَيٰوةِ الدُّنْيَا ثُمَّ هُوَ يَوْمَ الْقِيٰمَةِ مِنَ الْمُحْضَرِيْنَ ﴿٦٢﴾

63. And on that day He will call to them, and say, [c]'Where are *those* whom you alleged to be My associates?'

وَيَوْمَ يُنَادِيْهِمْ فَيَقُوْلُ اَيْنَ شُرَكَآءِيَ الَّذِيْنَ
كُنْتُمْ تَزْعُمُوْنَ ﴿٦٣﴾

64. Then those, against whom the sentence *of punishment* will have become due, will say, [d]'Our Lord, these are those whom we led astray. We led them astray even as we had gone astray ourselves. We *now* dissociate ourselves *from them and turn* to Thee. [e]It was not us that they worshipped.'

قَالَ الَّذِيْنَ حَقَّ عَلَيْهِمُ الْقَوْلُ رَبَّنَا هٰٓؤُلَآءِ الَّذِيْنَ
اَغْوَيْنَا ۚ اَغْوَيْنٰهُمْ كَمَا غَوَيْنَا ۚ تَبَرَّاْنَآ اِلَيْكَ مَا
كَانُوْٓا اِيَّانَا يَعْبُدُوْنَ ﴿٦٤﴾

65. And it will be said *to the idolaters*, [f]'Now call upon your *so-called* partners.' And they will call upon them, but they will not answer them. And they will see the punishment and wish that they had followed the guidance.

وَقِيْلَ ادْعُوْا شُرَكَآءَكُمْ فَدَعَوْهُمْ فَلَمْ يَسْتَجِيْبُوْا
لَهُمْ وَرَاَوُا الْعَذَابَ ۚ لَوْ اَنَّهُمْ كَانُوْا يَهْتَدُوْنَ ﴿٦٥﴾

66. And on that day *Allāh* will call to them and say, [g]'What answer gave you to the Messengers?'

وَيَوْمَ يُنَادِيْهِمْ فَيَقُوْلُ مَاذَآ اَجَبْتُمُ الْمُرْسَلِيْنَ ﴿٦٦﴾

[a]3 : 15; 9 : 38; 10 : 71; 16 : 118; 40 : 40. [b]20 : 132; 26 : 206-208. [c]28 : 75; 41 : 48. [d]7 : 39, 40; 14 : 22; 33 : 68-69; 34 : 32-33; 40 : 48-49. [e]10 : 29; 16 : 87. [f]10 : 29-30; 16 : 87. [g]5 : 110; 7 : 7.

67. Then all excuses[2227] will become obscure[2228] to them on that day and they shall not *even* ask each other.

فَعَمِيَتْ عَلَيْهِمُ الْاَنْبَآءُ يَوْمَئِذٍ فَهُمْ لَا يَتَسَآءَلُوْنَ ﴿٦٧﴾

68. [a]But he who repents and believes and does righteous deeds, maybe, he will be among the prosperous.[2229]

فَاَمَّا مَنْ تَابَ وَاٰمَنَ وَعَمِلَ صَالِحًا فَعَسٰٓى اَنْ يَّكُوْنَ مِنَ الْمُفْلِحِيْنَ ﴿٦٨﴾

69. And thy Lord creates whatever He pleases, and chooses *whomsoever He pleases.* It is not for them to choose. Glorified be Allāh. He is far above all that they associate *with Him.*

وَرَبُّكَ يَخْلُقُ مَا يَشَآءُ وَيَخْتَارُ ۗ مَا كَانَ لَهُمُ الْخِيَرَةُ ۗ سُبْحٰنَ اللّٰهِ وَتَعٰلٰى عَمَّا يُشْرِكُوْنَ ﴿٦٩﴾

70. [b]And thy Lord knows what their breasts conceal, and what they disclose.

وَرَبُّكَ يَعْلَمُ مَا تُكِنُّ صُدُوْرُهُمْ وَمَا يُعْلِنُوْنَ ﴿٧٠﴾

71. And He is Allāh; there is no god but He. To Him belongs all praise in the beginning and the Hereafter. His is the dominion, and to Him shall you be brought back.

وَهُوَ اللّٰهُ لَآ اِلٰهَ اِلَّا هُوَ ۗ لَهُ الْحَمْدُ فِى الْاُوْلٰى وَالْاٰخِرَةِ ۫ وَلَهُ الْحُكْمُ وَاِلَيْهِ تُرْجَعُوْنَ ﴿٧١﴾

72. Say, 'Tell me, if Allāh should make the night to continue perpetually over you till the Day of Resurrection; what god is there other than Allāh who could bring you light? Will you not *then* hearken?'

قُلْ اَرَءَيْتُمْ اِنْ جَعَلَ اللّٰهُ عَلَيْكُمُ الَّيْلَ سَرْمَدًا اِلٰى يَوْمِ الْقِيٰمَةِ مَنْ اِلٰهٌ غَيْرُ اللّٰهِ يَاْتِيْكُمْ بِضِيَآءٍ ۗ اَفَلَا تَسْمَعُوْنَ ﴿٧٢﴾

[a]20 : 83; 25 : 72. [b]2 : 78; 11 : 6; 16 : 24; 36 : 77.

2227. *Anbā'* (excuses) is the plural of *Naba'* which means, important news; information; message; excuse (Lane & Kulliyyāt). At the time of Reckoning, the disbelievers will be in utter confusion and despair, and will be completely at a loss to defend themselves. The untenability of all false pleas and excuses becoming manifest they will not be allowed to consult each other to prepare their defence.

2228. *'Amiya 'Alaihi'l Amru* means, the affair became obscure or confused to him (Lane).

2229. According to Islām the door of repentance always remains open. The sinner can repent even with the last breath of life. He is never beyond redemption except when by persistent rejection of Truth he himself deliberately chooses to shut the door of repentance upon him.

73. Say, 'Tell me, if Allāh should make the day to continue perpetually over you till the Day of Resurrection, what god is there other than Allāh who could bring you night wherein you could rest?[2230] Will you not *then* see?'

قُلْ اَرَءَيْتُمْ اِنْ جَعَلَ اللّٰهُ عَلَيْكُمُ النَّهَارَ سَرْمَدًا اِلٰى يَوْمِ الْقِيٰمَةِ مَنْ اِلٰهٌ غَيْرُ اللّٰهِ يَاْتِيْكُمْ بِلَيْلٍ تَسْكُنُوْنَ فِيْهِ ۚ اَفَلَا تُبْصِرُوْنَ ﴿٧٣﴾

74. [a]And of His mercy He has made for you the night and the day, that you may rest therein and that you may seek of His bounty, and that you may be grateful.

وَمِنْ رَّحْمَتِهٖ جَعَلَ لَكُمُ الَّيْلَ وَالنَّهَارَ لِتَسْكُنُوْا فِيْهِ وَلِتَبْتَغُوْا مِنْ فَضْلِهٖ وَلَعَلَّكُمْ تَشْكُرُوْنَ ﴿٧٤﴾

75. And on that day He will call to them and say, [b]'Where are those whom you alleged to be My associates?'

وَيَوْمَ يُنَادِيْهِمْ فَيَقُوْلُ اَيْنَ شُرَكَآءِيَ الَّذِيْنَ كُنْتُمْ تَزْعُمُوْنَ ﴿٧٥﴾

76. [c]And We shall take out from every people a witness and We shall say, 'Bring your proof.' Then they will know that the truth belongs to Allāh *alone*. And that which they used to forge will *all* be lost unto them.

وَنَزَعْنَا مِنْ كُلِّ اُمَّةٍ شَهِيْدًا فَقُلْنَا هَاتُوْا بُرْهَانَكُمْ فَعَلِمُوْٓا اَنَّ الْحَقَّ لِلّٰهِ وَضَلَّ عَنْهُمْ مَّا كَانُوْا يَفْتَرُوْنَ ﴿٧٦﴾ ع

R. 8 77. [d]Verily, Korah[2231] was of the people of Moses, but he behaved

اِنَّ قَارُوْنَ كَانَ مِنْ قَوْمِ مُوْسٰى فَبَغٰى عَلَيْهِمْ ۪ وَاٰتَيْنٰهُ

[a]10 : 68; 17 : 13; 27 : 87; 30 : 24. [b]16 : 28; 18 : 53; 28 : 63; 41 : 48. [c]4 : 42; 16 : 85. [d]29 : 40; 40 ; 25.

2230. Whereas both perpetual work and perpetual rest are injurious to man's physical health, periodical rest in the form of night and periodical work in the shape of day are great boons of God. At night our jaded and tired limbs are rested and we are able with renewed vigour to do the next day's work, and in the day we work and earn our livelihood. Thus their alternation constitutes a great Divine blessing.

2231. *Qārūn* (Korah) was fabulously rich. He stood high in the favour of Pharaoh and was very likely his treasurer. It seems that he was officer in charge of the gold mines belonging to Pharaoh and was a specialist in the art of digging out gold from the mines. In Southern Egypt the territory of Karu was famed for gold mines. The suffix "An" or "On" meaning "pillar, or "light" the combined word "Kur-on" signifies, 'the pillar of Karu' and was the title of Pharaoh's Minister of Mineralogy. He is said to be an Israelite and a believer in Moses. In order to win favours from Pharaoh he seemed to have persecuted his own people and to have behaved arrogantly towards them. As a result Divine punishment descended upon him and he perished.

tyrannically towards them. And We had given him treasures[2232] *of hoarded wealth* so much that the keys thereof would have weighed down a party of strong men. When his people said to him, 'Exult not, surely Allāh loves not those who exult ;

مِنَ الۡكُنُوۡزِ مَاۤ اِنَّ مَفَاتِحَهٗ لَتَنُوۡٓاُ بِالۡعُصۡبَةِ اُولِی الۡقُوَّةِ ۪ اِذۡ قَالَ لَهٗ قَوۡمُهٗ لَا تَفۡرَحۡ اِنَّ اللّٰهَ لَا یُحِبُّ الۡفَرِحِیۡنَ ۞

78. 'And seek, in that which Allāh has given thee, the Home of the Hereafter; and neglect not thy lot in this world; and do good to *others* as Allāh has done good to thee; and seek not to create mischief in the land. Verily, Allāh loves not those who create mischief;'

وَابۡتَغِ فِیۡمَاۤ اٰتٰىكَ اللّٰهُ الدَّارَ الۡاٰخِرَةَ وَ لَا تَنۡسَ نَصِیۡبَكَ مِنَ الدُّنۡیَا وَ اَحۡسِنۡ كَمَاۤ اَحۡسَنَ اللّٰهُ اِلَیۡكَ وَ لَا تَبۡغِ الۡفَسَادَ فِی الۡاَرۡضِ ؕ اِنَّ اللّٰهَ لَا یُحِبُّ الۡمُفۡسِدِیۡنَ ۞

79. ᵃHe said, '*All* this has been given to me because of the knowledge I possess.' Did he not know that Allāh had destroyed before him generations that were mightier than he and greater in riches? And the guilty shall not be asked *to offer an explanation* of their sins.[2233]

قَالَ اِنَّمَاۤ اُوۡتِیۡتُهٗ عَلٰی عِلۡمٍ عِنۡدِیۡ ؕ اَوَ لَمۡ یَعۡلَمۡ اَنَّ اللّٰهَ قَدۡ اَهۡلَكَ مِنۡ قَبۡلِهٖ مِنَ الۡقُرُوۡنِ مَنۡ هُوَ اَشَدُّ مِنۡهُ قُوَّةً وَّ اَكۡثَرُ جَمۡعًا ؕ وَ لَا یُسۡـَٔلُ عَنۡ ذُنُوۡبِهِمُ الۡمُجۡرِمُوۡنَ ۞

80. So he went forth before his people in *all* his pomp. Those who were desirous of the life of this world said, 'Would that we had the like of what Korah has been given! Truly, he is the master of a great fortune.'

فَخَرَجَ عَلٰی قَوۡمِهٖ فِیۡ زِیۡنَتِهٖ ؕ قَالَ الَّذِیۡنَ یُرِیۡدُوۡنَ الۡحَیٰوةَ الدُّنۡیَا یٰلَیۡتَ لَنَا مِثۡلَ مَاۤ اُوۡتِیَ قَارُوۡنُ ۙ اِنَّهٗ لَذُوۡ حَظٍّ عَظِیۡمٍ ۞

ᵃ39 : 50.

2232. *Mafātiḥ* is the plural of both *Maftaḥ* and *Miftaḥ*, the former word meaning a hoard; a treasure; and the latter meaning a key (Lane).

2233. The guilt of the disbelievers will be so patent that no further investigation will be considered necessary to establish it; or the meaning is that the guilty will not be given an opportunity to defend themselves, their sins and crimes being all too patent.

81. But those who had been given knowledge said, 'Woe unto you, Allāh's reward is best for those who believe and do good works; and it shall be granted to no one except those who are steadfast.'

وَقَالَ الَّذِينَ أُوتُوا الْعِلْمَ وَيْلَكُمْ ثَوَابُ اللّٰهِ خَيْرٌ
لِّمَنْ اٰمَنَ وَعَمِلَ صَالِحًا ۚ وَلَا يُلَقّٰهَآ اِلَّا الصّٰبِرُوْنَ ﴿٨١﴾

82. [a]Then We caused the earth to swallow him up and his dwelling; and he had no party to help him against Allāh, nor was he of those who can defend themselves.

فَخَسَفْنَا بِهٖ وَبِدَارِهِ الْاَرْضَ ۫ فَمَا كَانَ لَهٗ مِنْ فِئَةٍ
يَّنْصُرُوْنَهٗ مِنْ دُوْنِ اللّٰهِ ۚ وَمَا كَانَ مِنَ الْمُنْتَصِرِيْنَ ﴿٨٢﴾

83. And those who had coveted his position the day before began to say, 'Ruin seize thee! [b]it is indeed Allāh Who enlarges the provision for such of His servants as He pleases and straitens *it for whom He pleases.* Had not Allāh been gracious to us, He would have caused it to swallow us up *also.* Ah! the ungrateful never prosper.'

وَاَصْبَحَ الَّذِيْنَ تَمَنَّوْا مَكَانَهٗ بِالْاَمْسِ يَقُوْلُوْنَ وَيْكَاَنَّ
اللّٰهَ يَبْسُطُ الرِّزْقَ لِمَنْ يَّشَآءُ مِنْ عِبَادِهٖ وَيَقْدِرُ ۚ
لَوْلَآ اَنْ مَّنَّ اللّٰهُ عَلَيْنَا لَخَسَفَ بِنَا ۖ وَيْكَاَنَّهٗ لَا يُفْلِحُ
الْكٰفِرُوْنَ ﴿٨٣﴾ ع

R. 9 84. [c]This is the Home of the Hereafter. We give it to those who seek not self-exaltation in the earth, nor corruption. And the *good* end is for the righteous.

تِلْكَ الدَّارُ الْاٰخِرَةُ نَجْعَلُهَا لِلَّذِيْنَ لَا يُرِيْدُوْنَ عُلُوًّا
فِي الْاَرْضِ وَلَا فَسَادًا ۚ وَالْعَاقِبَةُ لِلْمُتَّقِيْنَ ﴿٨٤﴾

85. [d]He who does a good deed shall have a reward better than that; and *as for him* who does an evil deed—those who do evil deeds shall not be rewarded but *according to* what they did.[2234]

مَنْ جَآءَ بِالْحَسَنَةِ فَلَهٗ خَيْرٌ مِّنْهَا ۚ وَمَنْ جَآءَ بِالسَّيِّئَةِ
فَلَا يُجْزَى الَّذِيْنَ عَمِلُوا السَّيِّاٰتِ اِلَّا مَا كَانُوْا يَعْمَلُوْنَ ﴿٨٥﴾

[a]29 : 41. [b]13 : 27; 29 : 63; 34 : 37. [c]7 : 170; 16 : 31.
[d]4 : 125; 6 : 161; 17 : 8; 41 : 47; 99 : 8-9.

2234. The Divine law of compensation works in this way that whereas for good works the reward is many times greater, the punishment for an evil deed is less than what the guilty person incurs, or at the most proportionate to it.

86. He Who has made *the teaching of* the Qur'ān binding on thee will most surely bring thee back to *thy ordained* place of return.[2235] Say, [a]'My Lord knows best him who has brought the guidance, and him who is in manifest error.'

إِنَّ الَّذِي فَرَضَ عَلَيْكَ الْقُرْآنَ لَرَادُّكَ إِلَىٰ مَعَادٍ ۚ قُلْ رَبِّي أَعْلَمُ مَنْ جَاءَ بِالْهُدَىٰ وَمَنْ هُوَ فِي ضَلَالٍ مُبِينٍ ﴿٨٦﴾

87. And thou didst never expect that the Book would be revealed to thee; [b]but *it is* a mercy from thy Lord; so never be a helper of disbelievers.

وَمَا كُنْتَ تَرْجُو أَنْ يُلْقَىٰ إِلَيْكَ الْكِتَابُ إِلَّا رَحْمَةً مِنْ رَبِّكَ ۖ فَلَا تَكُونَنَّ ظَهِيرًا لِلْكَافِرِينَ ﴿٨٧﴾

88. And let them not turn thee away from the Signs of Allāh, after they have been sent down to thee; and call *mankind* to thy Lord, and be not of those who associate partners *with Him*.

وَلَا يَصُدُّنَّكَ عَنْ آيَاتِ اللَّهِ بَعْدَ إِذْ أُنْزِلَتْ إِلَيْكَ ۖ وَادْعُ إِلَىٰ رَبِّكَ ۖ وَلَا تَكُونَنَّ مِنَ الْمُشْرِكِينَ ﴿٨٨﴾

89. [c]And call not on any other god beside Allāh. There is no god but He. Everything will perish but He.[2236] His is the judgment, and to Him will you *all* be brought back.

وَلَا تَدْعُ مَعَ اللَّهِ إِلَٰهًا آخَرَ ۘ لَا إِلَٰهَ إِلَّا هُوَ ۚ كُلُّ شَيْءٍ هَالِكٌ إِلَّا وَجْهَهُ ۚ لَهُ الْحُكْمُ وَإِلَيْهِ تُرْجَعُونَ ﴿٨٩﴾

[a]17 : 85. [b]17 : 88. [c]10 : 107; 17 : 40; 26 : 214.

2235. This verse is considered by some scholars to have been revealed while the Holy Prophet was on his way from Mecca to Medina. It embodied a great prophecy, *viz.*, that one day he will have to leave Mecca and then eventually he will come back to it as a victor and conqueror. The verse constitutes a befitting sequel to the *Sūrah* which gives a somewhat detailed life-story of Moses, the like of the Holy Prophet. Moses fled from Egypt and lived in Midian for ten years which were the years of preparation for the great task which lay ahead of him. Then he went back to Egypt with the Divine Message and succeeded in delivering the Israelites from the bondage of Pharaoh. Similarly, the Holy Prophet fled from Mecca and spent ten precious years of his life in Medina which were the years of preparation for the great object of conquering Mecca, the Centre and Citadel of his Faith. He returned to it as a conqueror and a victor and was fully successful in his life's mission.

2236. *Wajh* means, self; face; chief of a people; object or purpose which one is pursuing; place to which one goes or directs his attention; pleasure; favour; sake; etc. (Lane).

CHAPTER 29

AL-'ANKABŪT

(*Revealed before Hijrah*)

Date of Revelation and Context

A large majority of Muslim scholarly opinion is inclined to place the revelation of the *Sūrah* in the middle or the late middle Meccan period. The *Sūrah* seems to derive its title from v. 42 where the falsity and futility of polytheistic beliefs are illustrated by a beautiful simile that these beliefs, being frail and brittle like a spider's web, cannot stand intelligent criticism. The preceding *Sūrah* had ended on the note that the Holy Prophet will come back as a victor and conqueror to his native town, Mecca, from where he had been driven out as a friendless fugitive, a price being placed on his head. The present *Sūrah* opens with a warning to believers that long and hard work; and hardships and privations patiently borne, are the *sine qua non* of a successful life.

Subject-Matter

The *Sūrah* continues to develop the theme that great favours and blessings which are to be bestowed upon believers in this and the next life will not be conferred upon them unless their belief is put to a severe test. They will have to pass through the crucible of fire and blood to deserve them. It is only by true and sincere repentance and by turning to God with a humble and contrite heart and by bringing about real and abiding reformation in one's life that one can earn God's forgiveness and become entitled to Divine boons and bounties. Reverting to the subject of the persecution of believers the *Sūrah* proceeds to say that they should allow no amount of hardships and privations to stand in the way of their serving the cause of Truth, and are forcefully exhorted to place their loyalty to God above the loyalty to their parents when the two loyalties clash and conflict. Then brief references are made to the life-stories of the Prophets Noah, Abraham, Lot and some other Divine Messengers, to show that persecution can never arrest or retard the progress of the true Faith and that compulsion in matters of religion never pays, and a people cannot be compelled permanently to continue to subscribe to views forcibly imposed upon them. The *Sūrah* further says that polytheistic beliefs, being as frail as a spider's web, cannot stand intelligent and searching criticism. The disbelievers, therefore, have no reason or justification to continue to hold idolatrous beliefs when a book like the Qur'ān which fully meets all the moral needs and requirements of man and is eminently fitted to raise him to the highest moral summits has been revealed. The *Sūrah* further disposes of an oft-quoted objection of disbelievers that the Qur'ān has been composed by the Holy Prophet; on the contrary, it is presented as the greatest Divine miracle in answer to the disbelievers' demand for Signs and miracles. Towards its close believers are consoled and comforted with the assurance that if they remained steadfast under the persecution to which they are being subjected a great and bright future lies before them. The *Sūrah* ends on the note that believers will have to take up the sword in defence of Islām and to conduct vigorous *Jihād* against the forces of evil. But the real *Jihād*, it says, does not consist in killing and being killed, but in striving hard to win the pleasure of God and in preaching the Message of the Qur'ān.

سُورَةُ العَنكَبُوتِ مَكِّيَّةٌ (٢٩)

1. [a]In the name of Allāh, the Gracious, the Merciful.

بِسْمِ اللّٰهِ الرَّحْمٰنِ الرَّحِيْمِ ①

2. [b]Alif Lām Mīm.[2236A]

الٓمّٓ ②

3. [c]Do men think that they will be left alone because they say, 'We believe,' and that they will not be tried?

اَحَسِبَ النَّاسُ اَنْ يُّتْرَكُوْٓا اَنْ يَّقُوْلُوْٓا اٰمَنَّا وَهُمْ لَا يُفْتَنُوْنَ ③

4. And We did try those who were before them. So Allāh will, assuredly, know[2237] those who are truthful and He will, assuredly, know the liars.

وَلَقَدْ فَتَنَّا الَّذِيْنَ مِنْ قَبْلِهِمْ فَلَيَعْلَمَنَّ اللّٰهُ الَّذِيْنَ صَدَقُوْا وَلَيَعْلَمَنَّ الْكٰذِبِيْنَ ④

5. Or, do those who commit evil deeds imagine that they will escape Us? How ill they judge!

اَمْ حَسِبَ الَّذِيْنَ يَعْمَلُوْنَ السَّيِّاٰتِ اَنْ يَّسْبِقُوْنَا ۭ سَاۗءَ مَا يَحْكُمُوْنَ ⑤

6. [d]Whoso hopes[2238] to meet Allāh, *let him be prepared for it*, for Allāh's appointed time is certainly coming. And He is the All-Hearing, the All-Knowing.

مَنْ كَانَ يَرْجُوْا لِقَاۗءَ اللّٰهِ فَاِنَّ اَجَلَ اللّٰهِ لَاٰتٍ ۭ وَهُوَ السَّمِيْعُ الْعَلِيْمُ ⑥

---

[a]1 : 1. [b]2 : 2; 3 : 2; 13 : 2; 30 : 2; 31 : 2; 32 : 2. [c]3 : 180; 9 : 16. [d]11 : 30; 18 : 111; 84 : 7.

2236A. See 16.

2237. '*Ilm* (knowledge) is of two kinds: (*a*) That which consists in knowing a thing before it comes into existence. This kind of knowledge is not meant here because God is the Knower of the seen and the unseen (59 : 23). (*b*) The kind of knowledge which consists in knowing an event after it has actually taken place. It is this knowledge which is meant here. The verse signifies that the primeval knowledge of God will take the form of the matter-of-fact knowledge. Or, it means that God will distinguish the liars from the truthful as the word '*Ilm* also possesses the sense of distinguishing between two things, particularly when it is followed by the particle *min* (from). See also 2 : 144 and 3 : 141.

Believers are made to pass through great hardships and privations and their belief is put to a severe test, and it is after they come out of the ordeal successfully that the fact becomes established that they are true and sincere servants of God. It is in this way that they are distinguished from the hypocrites and from those who are false in their profession of faith.

2238. *Yarjū* (hopes) is derived from *Rajā*, *i.e.*, he hoped to get the thing or he feared it. In the sense of hoping, the word is used on those occasions when the thing hoped for is likely to afford satisfaction (Mufradāt).

7. And whoso strives, strives[2239] only for his own soul; verily, Allāh is Independent of all *His* creatures.

وَمَنْ جَاهَدَ فَإِنَّمَا يُجَاهِدُ لِنَفْسِهٖ ۭ اِنَّ اللّٰهَ لَغَنِيٌّ
عَنِ الْعٰلَمِيْنَ ۝٧

8. And *as to* [a]those who believe and do righteous deeds We shall, surely, remove from them their evils, and We shall, surely, give them the best reward of their works.

وَالَّذِيْنَ اٰمَنُوْا وَعَمِلُوا الصّٰلِحٰتِ لَنُكَفِّرَنَّ عَنْهُمْ
سَيِّاٰتِهِمْ وَلَنَجْزِيَنَّهُمْ اَحْسَنَ الَّذِيْ كَانُوْا يَعْمَلُوْنَ ۝٨

9. [b]And We have enjoined on man kindness to his parents; but if they contend with thee to make thee associate that with Me of which thou hast no knowledge,[2240] then obey them not. Unto Me is your return, and I shall inform you of what you did.

وَوَصَّيْنَا الْاِنْسَانَ بِوَالِدَيْهِ حُسْنًا ۭ وَاِنْ جَاهَدٰكَ
لِتُشْرِكَ بِيْ مَا لَيْسَ لَكَ بِهٖ عِلْمٌ فَلَا تُطِعْهُمَا ۭ اِلَيَّ
مَرْجِعُكُمْ فَاُنَبِّئُكُمْ بِمَا كُنْتُمْ تَعْمَلُوْنَ ۝٩

10. And those who believe and do righteous deeds—[c]them We shall, surely, admit into *the company of* the righteous.

وَالَّذِيْنَ اٰمَنُوْا وَعَمِلُوا الصّٰلِحٰتِ لَنُدْخِلَنَّهُمْ فِي
الصّٰلِحِيْنَ ۝١٠

11. And of men there are *some* who say, 'We believe in Allāh;' but when they are made to suffer in the cause of Allāh, they regard the persecution of men as if it were the punishment of Allāh. [d]And if help comes from thy Lord, they are sure to say, 'Certainly, we were with you.'[2241] Is not Allāh best aware of what is in the breasts of *His* creatures?

وَمِنَ النَّاسِ مَنْ يَّقُوْلُ اٰمَنَّا بِاللّٰهِ فَاِذَآ اُوْذِيَ فِي
اللّٰهِ جَعَلَ فِتْنَةَ النَّاسِ كَعَذَابِ اللّٰهِ ۭ وَلَئِنْ جَاۗءَ
نَصْرٌ مِّنْ رَّبِّكَ لَيَقُوْلُنَّ اِنَّا كُنَّا مَعَكُمْ ۭ اَوَلَيْسَ اللّٰهُ
بِاَعْلَمَ بِمَا فِيْ صُدُوْرِ الْعٰلَمِيْنَ ۝١١

[a]2 : 83; 3 : 58; 13 : 30; 22 : 57; 30 : 16; 35 : 8; 42 : 23; 47 : 13. [b]2 : 84; 4 : 37; 6 : 152; 17 : 24; 31 : 15; 46 : 16. [c]14 : 24. [d]4 : 142.

2239. The verse gives a brief but very apt description of a *Mujāhid*—true striver in the way of God. High and noble ideals and consistent and constant effort to carry them out into actual practice is what in Islamic terminology is called *Jihād*, and the person who possesses these noble ideals and lives up to them is a *Mujāhid* in the true sense of the word.

2240. The *alpha and omega* of all religious teachings is God's Unity. Man's loyalty, first and last, is to his Creator. All other loyalties proceed from, and are subject to, it. Even man's loyalty to his parents is not allowed to clash with it.

2241. In contrast to the unflinching faith which early Muslims exhibited under the severest trials and which true believers have demonstrated in every age, there are always to be found in the ranks of believers persons so weak of faith that they flinch under ordinary

12. [a]And Allāh will, certainly, make manifest those who believe and He will, surely, distinguish the hypocrites *from the believers*.

وَلَيَعْلَمَنَّ اللّٰهُ الَّذِيْنَ اٰمَنُوْا وَلَيَعْلَمَنَّ الْمُنٰفِقِيْنَ ﴿۱۲﴾

13. And those who disbelieve say to those who believe, 'Follow our way, [b]and we will, surely, bear *the burden of* your sins.' But they will bear none of *the burden of* their sins.[2242] They are, surely, liars.

وَقَالَ الَّذِيْنَ كَفَرُوْا لِلَّذِيْنَ اٰمَنُوا اتَّبِعُوْا سَبِيْلَنَا
وَلْنَحْمِلْ خَطٰيٰكُمْ ۭ وَمَا هُمْ بِحٰمِلِيْنَ مِنْ خَطٰيٰهُمْ
مِّنْ شَيْءٍ ۭ اِنَّهُمْ لَكٰذِبُوْنَ ﴿۱۳﴾

14. But they shall, surely, bear their own burdens, and *other* burdens along with their own burdens. And they will, surely, be questioned on the Day of Resurrection concerning that which they fabricated.

وَلَيَحْمِلُنَّ اَثْقَالَهُمْ وَاَثْقَالًا مَّعَ اَثْقَالِهِمْ ۡ وَلَيُسْـَٔلُنَّ
يَوْمَ الْقِيٰمَةِ عَمَّا كَانُوْا يَفْتَرُوْنَ ﴿۱۴﴾ ع

R. 2 15. And We, certainly, sent Noah to his people, and he remained among them a thousand years, short of fifty years.[2243] Then the Deluge overtook them, while they were wrongdoers.

وَلَقَدْ اَرْسَلْنَا نُوْحًا اِلٰى قَوْمِهٖ فَلَبِثَ فِيْهِمْ اَلْفَ
سَنَةٍ اِلَّا خَمْسِيْنَ عَامًا ۭ فَاَخَذَهُمُ الطُّوْفَانُ وَ
هُمْ ظٰلِمُوْنَ ﴿۱۵﴾

16. [c]But We saved him and those who were *with him* in the Ark; and We made it a Sign for all peoples.

فَاَنْجَيْنٰهُ وَاَصْحٰبَ السَّفِيْنَةِ وَجَعَلْنٰهَآ اٰيَةً لِّلْعٰلَمِيْنَ ﴿۱۶﴾

[a]3 : 142; 47 : 32. [b]14 : 22; 40 : 48. [c]10 : 74; 11 : 42.

privations and are ready rather to renounce their faith than suffer loss. On the other hand, they are always on the look-out to claim comradeship with believers when they see that Divine help is coming to them (believers) and the cause of Truth is gaining ground.

2242. Besides the hypocrites, there is another class of men, the aggressive leaders of disbelief, who, taking advantage of their own high social status, seek to mislead others who are not so highly placed in life, telling them that they will bear all the loss the latter will incur by accepting their lead and by refusing to accept the true new Faith.

2243. Here the age of Noah has been mentioned as 950 years. The Bible places it at 952. It is difficult to assign a definite date as to when the Prophets of antiquity, such as Noah, Hūd, Ṣāliḥ and others lived and how long they lived. 'None knows them save Allāh,' says the Qur'ān (14: 10). The period, nine hundred and fifty years, does not seem to be the span of Noah's personal physical life. It seems to be the period of his Dispensation. Thus it seemed first to extend to Abraham's ministry because Abraham 'was of his party' (37 : 84) and then to Joseph's and then down even to that of Moses. In fact, the age of a Prophet is the age of his Dispensation and teaching. In describing the limit of Noah's age, two words *Sanah* and *'Ām* have been used. Whereas the root meaning of the former word possesses a sense of badness, that of the latter has a sense of goodness. It seems that the first fifty years of Noah's Dispensation were years of all round spiritual progress and regeneration and that after that moral decadence and degeneration set in and his people gradually became degraded morally, till their degeneration became complete in nine hundred years.

17. And *We sent* Abraham when he said to his people, 'Worship Allāh and fear Him. That is better for you, if only you knew;

وَإِبْرٰهِيْمَ إِذْ قَالَ لِقَوْمِهِ اعْبُدُوا اللّٰهَ وَاتَّقُوْهُ ۖ
ذٰلِكُمْ خَيْرٌ لَّكُمْ إِنْ كُنْتُمْ تَعْلَمُوْنَ ﴿١٧﴾

18. [a]'You only worship idols beside Allāh, and you invent a lie. Those, whom you worship beside Allāh, have no power to provide sustenance for you. Then seek sustenance from Allāh, and worship Him, and be grateful to Him. Unto Him will you be brought back'.

إِنَّمَا تَعْبُدُوْنَ مِنْ دُوْنِ اللّٰهِ أَوْثَانًا وَّتَخْلُقُوْنَ
إِفْكًا ۚ إِنَّ الَّذِيْنَ تَعْبُدُوْنَ مِنْ دُوْنِ اللّٰهِ لَا يَمْلِكُوْنَ
لَكُمْ رِزْقًا فَابْتَغُوْا عِنْدَ اللّٰهِ الرِّزْقَ وَاعْبُدُوْهُ
وَاشْكُرُوْا لَهٗ ۖ إِلَيْهِ تُرْجَعُوْنَ ﴿١٨﴾

19. And if you reject *the truth*, then the generations before you *also* rejected *it*. And [b]the Messenger is only responsible for the clear delivery *of the Message*.

وَإِنْ تُكَذِّبُوْا فَقَدْ كَذَّبَ أُمَمٌ مِّنْ قَبْلِكُمْ ۖ وَمَا
عَلَى الرَّسُوْلِ إِلَّا الْبَلٰغُ الْمُبِيْنُ ﴿١٩﴾

20. [c]See they not how Allāh originates creation, then repeats it?[2244] That, surely, is easy for Allāh.

أَوَلَمْ يَرَوْا كَيْفَ يُبْدِئُ اللّٰهُ الْخَلْقَ ثُمَّ يُعِيْدُهٗ ۖ
إِنَّ ذٰلِكَ عَلَى اللّٰهِ يَسِيْرٌ ﴿٢٠﴾

21. Say, 'Travel in the earth,[2245] and see [d]how He originated the creation. Then will Allāh create the second creation. Surely, Allāh has power over all things;

قُلْ سِيْرُوْا فِي الْأَرْضِ فَانْظُرُوْا كَيْفَ بَدَأَ الْخَلْقَ
ثُمَّ اللّٰهُ يُنْشِئُ النَّشْأَةَ الْآخِرَةَ ۚ إِنَّ اللّٰهَ عَلٰى كُلِّ
شَيْءٍ قَدِيْرٌ ﴿٢١﴾

22. [e]He punishes whom He pleases and shows mercy unto whom He pleases;[2245A] and to Him will you be turned back;

يُعَذِّبُ مَنْ يَّشَآءُ وَيَرْحَمُ مَنْ يَّشَآءُ ۚ وَإِلَيْهِ تُقْلَبُوْنَ ﴿٢٢﴾

---

[a]22 : 72. [b]16 : 36; 24 : 55; 36 : 18. [c]10 : 35; 21 : 105; 27 : 65; 30 : 12, 28. [d]10 : 5; 30 : 28. [e]3 : 129; 5 : 41; 17 : 55.

2244. The verse signifies that the Divine law of creation and reproduction will work in this way that God would create through the Holy Prophet a new humanity and a new order on the ashes of the old one.

2245. The expression has been used at several places in the Qur'ān (6 : 12; 12 : 110; 30 : 10; 35 : 45; 40 : 83), and almost everywhere it has been followed by a sentence which points to the destruction of one people and the creation of another in their place. The verse does not refer to the Resurrection after death, but only to the phenomenon of the rise and fall of nations.

2245A. As stated at several places in the Qur'ān, God does not punish arbitrarily but only after punishment has been fully deserved. The verse only emphasizes this fact.

23. [a]And you cannot frustrate[2246] *the designs of Allāh* in the earth, nor in the heaven; nor have you any friend or helper beside Allāh.'

وَمَآ اَنۡتُمۡ بِمُعۡجِزِيۡنَ فِي الۡاَرۡضِ وَلَا فِي السَّمَآءِ ۡ وَ
مَا لَكُمۡ مِّنۡ دُوۡنِ اللّٰهِ مِنۡ وَّلِيٍّ وَّلَا نَصِيۡرٍ ﴿٢٣﴾ ع

R. 3 24. [b]Those who disbelieve in the Signs of Allāh and the meeting with Him—it is they who despair of My mercy. And they will have a grievous punishment.

وَالَّذِيۡنَ كَفَرُوۡا بِاٰيٰتِ اللّٰهِ وَلِقَآئِهٖۤ اُولٰٓئِكَ
يَئِسُوۡا مِنۡ رَّحۡمَتِيۡ وَاُولٰٓئِكَ لَهُمۡ عَذَابٌ
اَلِيۡمٌ ﴿٢٤﴾

25. And the only answer of his people was that they said, [c]'Slay him or burn him.' But Allāh delivered him from the fire. In that, surely, are, Signs for a people who would believe.[2247]

فَمَا كَانَ جَوَابَ قَوۡمِهٖۤ اِلَّاۤ اَنۡ قَالُوا اقۡتُلُوۡهُ اَوۡ حَرِّقُوۡهُ
فَاَنۡجٰىهُ اللّٰهُ مِنَ النَّارِ ؕ اِنَّ فِيۡ ذٰلِكَ لَاٰيٰتٍ لِّقَوۡمٍ
يُّؤۡمِنُوۡنَ ﴿٢٥﴾

26. And *Abraham* said, 'Verily, you have taken for yourselves idols beside Allāh, out of love for each other[2248] in the present life. Then on the Day of Resurrection [d]you will deny each other, and curse each other. And your abode will be the Fire; and you will have no helpers.'

وَقَالَ اِنَّمَا اتَّخَذۡتُمۡ مِّنۡ دُوۡنِ اللّٰهِ اَوۡثَانًا ۙ مَّوَدَّةَ
بَيۡنِكُمۡ فِي الۡحَيٰوةِ الدُّنۡيَا ۚ ثُمَّ يَوۡمَ الۡقِيٰمَةِ يَكۡفُرُ
بَعۡضُكُمۡ بِبَعۡضٍ وَّيَلۡعَنُ بَعۡضُكُمۡ بَعۡضًا ۫ وَّمَاۡوٰٮكُمُ
النَّارُ وَمَا لَكُمۡ مِّنۡ نّٰصِرِيۡنَ ﴿٢٦﴾

27. And Lot believed in him, and *Abraham* said, [e]'I flee unto my Lord; surely, He is the Mighty, the Wise.'

فَاٰمَنَ لَهٗ لُوۡطٌ ۘ وَقَالَ اِنِّيۡ مُهَاجِرٌ اِلٰى رَبِّيۡ ؕ اِنَّهٗ
هُوَ الۡعَزِيۡزُ الۡحَكِيۡمُ ﴿٢٧﴾

[a]10 : 54; 11 : 34; 42 : 32. [b]18 : 106; 30 : 17; 32 : 11. [c]21 : 69; 37 : 98. [d]16 : 87. [e]19 : 49.

2246. Disbelievers are most emphatically warned that they cannot frustrate God's plan and avert the terrible fate that is in store for them as the Divine decree has gone forth that Islām shall make progress and its cause shall triumph.

2247. Abraham's account began with the 17th verse and in the 18th verse he gave strong arguments in refutation of *Shirk*. From 19th to 24th verse, in consonance with the Quranic style and practice which adds to its elegance and beauty, a digression intervened and a great religious principle was briefly discussed in relation to the Holy Prophet. The principle discussed was that when one nation, as a result of its rejection of the Divine Message, falls a victim to decay and decadence another people takes its place. From this verse the thread is taken up of Abraham's story.

2248. The expression, *Mawaddata Bainikum*, may mean : (1) Social relations or the desire to win each other's love are the basis of your idolatrous ideals and practices. (2) You have made your idolatrous beliefs and practices the foundation of your love with each other, *i.e.*, you have made the identity of your idolatrous beliefs the means to preserve the homogeneity of your community.

28. [a]And We bestowed on him Isaac and Jacob, and We placed Prophethood and the Book among his descendants, and [b]We gave him his reward in this life, and in the Hereafter he will, surely, be among the righteous.

وَوَهَبْنَا لَهُ إِسْحٰقَ وَيَعْقُوبَ وَجَعَلْنَا فِي ذُرِّيَّتِهِ
النُّبُوَّةَ وَالْكِتٰبَ وَآتَيْنٰهُ أَجْرَهُ فِي الدُّنْيَا ۚ وَإِنَّهُ فِي
الْآخِرَةِ لَمِنَ الصّٰلِحِينَ ﴿٢٨﴾

29. And *call to mind* Lot when he said to his people, "You commit an abomination such as no one among mankind has ever committed before you;

وَلُوطًا إِذْ قَالَ لِقَوْمِهِ إِنَّكُمْ لَتَأْتُونَ الْفَاحِشَةَ مَا
سَبَقَكُمْ بِهَا مِنْ أَحَدٍ مِنَ الْعٰلَمِينَ ﴿٢٩﴾

30. [d]'What ! do you approach men *with lust* and commit robbery on the highway,[2249] and you commit abomination in your meetings?'[2250] But the only answer of his people was that they said, 'Bring upon us the punishment of Allāh if thou speakest the truth.'

أَئِنَّكُمْ لَتَأْتُونَ الرِّجَالَ وَتَقْطَعُونَ السَّبِيلَ ۙ وَ
تَأْتُونَ فِي نَادِيكُمُ الْمُنْكَرَ ۖ فَمَا كَانَ جَوَابَ قَوْمِهِ
إِلَّا أَنْ قَالُوا ائْتِنَا بِعَذَابِ اللّٰهِ إِنْ كُنْتَ مِنَ
الصّٰدِقِينَ ﴿٣٠﴾

31. He said, "Help me, my Lord, against the wicked people.'

قَالَ رَبِّ انْصُرْنِي عَلَى الْقَوْمِ الْمُفْسِدِينَ ﴿٣١﴾ ع ٣

R. 4 32. [f]And when Our messengers brought Abraham the tidings, they said, "*The tidings is*, 'We are about to destroy the people of this town; surely, its people are wrongdoers."

وَلَمَّا جَاءَتْ رُسُلُنَا إِبْرٰهِيمَ بِالْبُشْرٰى قَالُوا إِنَّا
مُهْلِكُوا أَهْلِ هٰذِهِ الْقَرْيَةِ ۚ إِنَّ أَهْلَهَا كَانُوا
ظٰلِمِينَ ﴿٣٢﴾

33. He said, 'But Lot is there !' They said, 'We know very well who is there. [g]We will, surely, save him and his family, [h]except his wife, who is of those who remain behind.'

قَالَ إِنَّ فِيهَا لُوطًا ۚ قَالُوا نَحْنُ أَعْلَمُ بِمَنْ فِيهَا ۖ
لَنُنَجِّيَنَّهُ وَأَهْلَهُ إِلَّا امْرَأَتَهُ ۖ كَانَتْ مِنَ
الْغٰبِرِينَ ﴿٣٣﴾

[a]19 : 50; 21 : 73; 37 : 113. [b]2 : 131; 16 : 123. [c]7 : 81; 11 : 79. [d]7 : 82; 11 : 79; 26 : 166. [e]26 : 170. [f]11 : 70-71. [g]15 : 60; 51 : 36. [h]7 : 84; 15 : 61; 26 : 172; 27 : 58.

2249. *Qaṭa'a al-Ṭarīqa* meaning, he made the way dangerous for wayfarers and forbade them to use it, the Quranic expression signifies : (*a*) You rob travellers on the highway (Lot's people had adopted the calling of the road). (*b*) You violate the Divinely appointed sex-laws and commit unnatural offences.

2250. Three vices have been ascribed to the people of Lot in this verse, (1) unnatural vice; (2) highway robbery; (3) committing crimes openly and unashamedly in their assemblies.

34. And when Our messengers came to Lot, [a]he was distressed on their account and felt powerless[2251] with regard to them. And they said, "Fear not, nor grieve, *and we have been charged with the Divine Message:* [b]'We will, surely, save thee and thy family except thy wife, who is of those who remain behind,	وَلَمَّآ اَنْ جَآءَتْ رُسُلُنَا لُوْطًا سِيْٓءَ بِهِمْ وَضَاقَ بِهِمْ ذَرْعًا وَّقَالُوْا لَا تَخَفْ وَلَا تَحْزَنْ اِنَّا مُنَجُّوْكَ وَاَهْلَكَ اِلَّا امْرَاَتَكَ كَانَتْ مِنَ الْغٰبِرِيْنَ ﴿۳۴﴾
35. *And* [c]'We are, surely, going to bring down on the people of this town a punishment from heaven, for they have been rebellious."	اِنَّا مُنْزِلُوْنَ عَلٰٓى اَهْلِ هٰذِهِ الْقَرْيَةِ رِجْزًا مِّنَ السَّمَآءِ بِمَا كَانُوْا يَفْسُقُوْنَ ﴿۳۵﴾
36. [d]And We have left thereof a clear Sign for a people who would understand.	وَلَقَدْ تَّرَكْنَا مِنْهَآ اٰيَةًۢ بَيِّنَةً لِّقَوْمٍ يَّعْقِلُوْنَ ﴿۳۶﴾
37. [e]And to Midian *We sent* their brother Shu'aib who said, 'O my people, worship Allāh, and be mindful of the Last Day and commit not iniquity in the earth, creating disorder.'	وَاِلٰى مَدْيَنَ اَخَاهُمْ شُعَيْبًا فَقَالَ يٰقَوْمِ اعْبُدُوا اللّٰهَ وَارْجُوا الْيَوْمَ الْاٰخِرَ وَلَا تَعْثَوْا فِي الْاَرْضِ مُفْسِدِيْنَ ﴿۳۷﴾
38. But they called him a liar. [f]So a violent earthquake seized them, and in their homes they lay prostrate upon the ground.	فَكَذَّبُوْهُ فَاَخَذَتْهُمُ الرَّجْفَةُ فَاَصْبَحُوْا فِيْ دَارِهِمْ جٰثِمِيْنَ ﴿۳۸﴾
39. And *We destroyed* [g]'Ād and Thamūd; and it is evident to you from their dwelling places. And Satan made their deeds *appear* attractive to them, and thus turned them away from the *right* path, sagacious though they were.[2252]	وَعَادًا وَّثَمُوْدَا۟ وَقَدْ تَّبَيَّنَ لَكُمْ مِّنْ مَّسٰكِنِهِمْ وَزَيَّنَ لَهُمُ الشَّيْطٰنُ اَعْمَالَهُمْ فَصَدَّهُمْ عَنِ السَّبِيْلِ وَ كَانُوْا مُسْتَبْصِرِيْنَ ﴿۳۹﴾

[a]11 : 78. [b]7 : 84; 27 : 58. [c]27 : 59. [d]15 : 76; 51 : 38. [e]7 : 86; 11 : 85.
[f]7 : 92; 11 : 95; 26 : 190. [g]9 : 70.

2251. *Dāqa Bihī Dhar'an* means, he lacked strength or ability or power to do the thing (Lane). Who the messengers mentioned in the verse were and what their mission was has been explained in 11 : 70-71 and 15 : 68-72. Their visit distressed and grieved Prophet Lot because his people, having adopted the calling of the road, did not like strangers to visit their town and therefore they had forbidden Lot to receive outsiders. He feared that his people might humiliate him before his guests.

2252. The Quranic expression means: (1) They clearly saw that the course they had adopted was wrong. (2) They deliberately adopted a course knowing full well what the end would be.

40. And *We destroyed* Korah and Pharaoh and Hāmān. And [a]Moses did come to them with manifest Signs, but they behaved arrogantly in the land, yet they could not outstrip *Us*.

وَقَارُوْنَ وَفِرْعَوْنَ وَهَامٰنَ ۟ وَلَقَدْ جَآءَهُمْ مُّوْسٰى
بِالْبَيِّنٰتِ فَاسْتَكْبَرُوْا فِي الْاَرْضِ وَمَا كَانُوْا سٰبِقِيْنَ ﴿٤٠﴾

41. So each one *of them* We seized for his sin; of them were those against whom We sent a violent sandstorm, and of them were those whom a roaring blast overtook, and of them were [b]those whom We caused the earth to swallow up, and of them were those whom We drowned.[2253] [c]And Allāh did not wrong them, but they wronged themselves.

فَكُلًّا اَخَذْنَا بِذَنْۢبِهٖ ۚ فَمِنْهُمْ مَّنْ اَرْسَلْنَا عَلَيْهِ حَاصِبًا ۚ
وَمِنْهُمْ مَّنْ اَخَذَتْهُ الصَّيْحَةُ ۚ وَمِنْهُمْ مَّنْ خَسَفْنَا
بِهِ الْاَرْضَ ۚ وَمِنْهُمْ مَّنْ اَغْرَقْنَا ۚ وَمَا كَانَ اللّٰهُ
لِيَظْلِمَهُمْ وَلٰكِنْ كَانُوْۤا اَنْفُسَهُمْ يَظْلِمُوْنَ ﴿٤١﴾

42. The case of those who take helpers beside Allāh is like unto the case of the spider that takes to itself a house; and, surely, the frailest[2254] of all houses is the house of the spider, if they but knew.

مَثَلُ الَّذِيْنَ اتَّخَذُوْا مِنْ دُوْنِ اللّٰهِ اَوْلِيَآءَ كَمَثَلِ
الْعَنْكَبُوْتِ ۚ اِتَّخَذَتْ بَيْتًا ۚ وَاِنَّ اَوْهَنَ الْبُيُوْتِ لَبَيْتُ
الْعَنْكَبُوْتِ ۘ لَوْ كَانُوْا يَعْلَمُوْنَ ﴿٤٢﴾

43. Verily, Allāh knows whatever they call upon beside Him; and He is the Mighty, the Wise.

اِنَّ اللّٰهَ يَعْلَمُ مَا يَدْعُوْنَ مِنْ دُوْنِهٖ مِنْ شَيْءٍ ۚ وَهُوَ
الْعَزِيْزُ الْحَكِيْمُ ﴿٤٣﴾

[a]28 : 37. [b]28 : 82. [c]16 : 34; 30 : 10.

2253. The Qur'ān has used different words and expressions for the punishment which overtook the opponents of the various Prophets in their respective times. The punishment that came upon 'Ād is described as furious wind (41 : 17; 54 : 20 & 69 : 7); that which overtook Thamūd as earthquake (7 : 79), blast (11 : 68; 54 : 32), thunderbolt (41 : 18) and violent blast (69 : 6); that which destroyed the people of Lot as stones of clay (11 : 83; 15 : 75), storm of stones (54 : 35); and that which overtook Midian, the people of Shu'aib, as earthquake (7 : 92; 29 : 38), blast (11 : 95), and punishment of the day of overshadowing doom (26 : 190). Last of all the heavenly punishment which seized Pharaoh and his mighty hosts and courtiers, Hāmān and Korah and destroyed them root and branch, has been described by the expressions : *We .... drowned Pharaoh's people* (2 : 51; 7 : 137 & 17 : 104), and *We caused the earth to swallow him up* (28 : 82).

2254. The subject of the Unity of God with which the *Sūrah* primarily deals is brought to a close in this verse with a beautiful metaphor which drives home to polytheists the folly, futility and falsity of idolatrous beliefs and practices. They are as frail as the web of a spider and cannot stand intelligent criticism.

44. And [a]these are similitudes which We set forth for mankind, but only those understand them who have knowledge.

وَتِلْكَ الْاَمْثَالُ نَضْرِبُهَا لِلنَّاسِ ۚ وَمَا يَعْقِلُهَآ اِلَّا
الْعٰلِمُوْنَ ﴿٤٤﴾

45. [b]Allāh created the heavens and the earth in accordance with the requirements of wisdom.[2255] In that, surely, is a Sign for the believers.

خَلَقَ اللّٰهُ السَّمٰوٰتِ وَالْاَرْضَ بِالْحَقِّ ۭ اِنَّ فِيْ ذٰلِكَ
لَاٰيَةً لِّلْمُؤْمِنِيْنَ ﴿٤٥﴾

PART XXI

R. 5
46. [c]Recite[2256] that which has been revealed to thee of the Book, and observe Prayer. Surely, Prayer restrains *one* from indecency and manifest evil; and remembrance of Allāh, indeed, is the greatest *virtue*. And Allāh knows what you do.[2256A]

اُتْلُ مَآ اُوْحِيَ اِلَيْكَ مِنَ الْكِتٰبِ وَاَقِمِ الصَّلٰوةَ ۭ اِنَّ
الصَّلٰوةَ تَنْهٰى عَنِ الْفَحْشَآءِ وَالْمُنْكَرِ ۭ وَلَذِكْرُ اللّٰهِ
اَكْبَرُ ۭ وَاللّٰهُ يَعْلَمُ مَا تَصْنَعُوْنَ ﴿٤٦﴾

47. And argue not with the People of the Book except [d]with what is best *as an argument*, but *argue not at all* with such of them as are unjust. And say, 'We believe in that which has been revealed to us and that which has been revealed to you; and our God and your God is One,[2257] and to Him we submit.'

وَلَا تُجَادِلُوْٓا اَهْلَ الْكِتٰبِ اِلَّا بِالَّتِيْ هِيَ اَحْسَنُ ۖ اِلَّا الَّذِيْنَ
ظَلَمُوْا مِنْهُمْ وَقُوْلُوْٓا اٰمَنَّا بِالَّذِيْٓ اُنْزِلَ اِلَيْنَا وَاُنْزِلَ
اِلَيْكُمْ وَاِلٰهُنَا وَاِلٰهُكُمْ وَاحِدٌ وَّنَحْنُ لَهٗ مُسْلِمُوْنَ ﴿٤٧﴾

[a]13 : 18; 14 : 26. [b]6 : 74; 16 : 4; 39 : 6. [c]18 : 28. [d]16 : 126; 23 : 97; 41 : 35.

2255. The expression *Bilḥaqqi* signifies that there is clear evidence of an intelligent design and purpose in the creation of the heavens and the earth and that a profound and consummate plan works in all the celestial and terrestrial bodies.

2256. *Utlu* means, proclaim; preach; read, recite, rehearse, follow (Lane).

2256A. Three things have been mentioned in this verse, *viz.*, preaching and reading of the Qur'ān, observance of Prayer and the remembrance of Allāh. The purpose of all three is to deliver man from the bondage of sin and to help him to rise morally and spiritually. A living faith in a Supreme Being is the basic principle of all revealed religions because it is this faith that can serve as a potent and effective check on man's evil propensities and actions. This is why the Qur'ān reverts again and again to the subject of God's existence and speaks of His great power, glory and love and lays the greatest emphasis on Divine remembrance in the form of the Islamic Prayer, which, if performed with all its necessary conditions, purity of mind and actions is the inevitable result.

2257. The verse lays down a very sound principle to guide us when preaching our Faith to others. We should begin preaching by laying stress on those beliefs and religious principles which are common between us and our adversary. As an instance we are told that while talking to "the People of the Book" we should start with the two basic religious principles of the Unity of God and Divine revelation.

48. And in like manner have We sent down the Book to thee; [a]so those to whom We have given *true knowledge of* the Book (Torah) believe in it (the Qur'ān); and of these *Meccans also* there are some who believe in it. And none but the disbelievers persist in rejecting Our Signs.

وَكَذٰلِكَ اَنْزَلْنَاۤ اِلَيْكَ الْكِتٰبَ ؕ فَالَّذِيْنَ اٰتَيْنٰهُمُ الْكِتٰبَ
يُؤْمِنُوْنَ بِهٖ ۚ وَمِنْ هٰۤؤُلَآءِ مَنْ يُّؤْمِنُ بِهٖ ؕ وَمَا يَجْحَدُ
بِاٰيٰتِنَاۤ اِلَّا الْكٰفِرُوْنَ ﴿۴۸﴾

49. [b]And thou didst not recite any Book before *the Qur'ān*, nor didst thou write one with thy right hand; in that case the liars would have had *cause to* doubt.[2258]

وَمَا كُنْتَ تَتْلُوْا مِنْ قَبْلِهٖ مِنْ كِتٰبٍ وَّلَا تَخُطُّهٗ بِيَمِيْنِكَ
اِذًا لَّارْتَابَ الْمُبْطِلُوْنَ ﴿۴۹﴾

50. Nay, it is *a collection of* clear Signs in the hearts of those who are given knowledge.[2259] And none but the wrongdoers deny Our Signs.

بَلْ هُوَ اٰيٰتٌۢ بَيِّنٰتٌ فِيْ صُدُوْرِ الَّذِيْنَ اُوْتُوا الْعِلْمَ ؕ
وَمَا يَجْحَدُ بِاٰيٰتِنَاۤ اِلَّا الظّٰلِمُوْنَ ﴿۵۰﴾

51. And they say, [c]"Why are not Signs sent down to him from his Lord?' Say, 'The Signs are with Allāh, and I am but a [d]plain Warner.'

وَقَالُوْا لَوْلَاۤ اُنْزِلَ عَلَيْهِ اٰيٰتٌ مِّنْ رَّبِّهٖ ؕ قُلْ اِنَّمَا
الْاٰيٰتُ عِنْدَ اللّٰهِ ؕ وَاِنَّمَاۤ اَنَا نَذِيْرٌ مُّبِيْنٌ ﴿۵۱﴾

52. Is it not enough *for a Sign* for them that We have sent down to thee the *perfect* Book which is recited to them? Verily, in this there is *great* mercy and a reminder for a people who believe.[2260]

اَوَلَمْ يَكْفِهِمْ اَنَّاۤ اَنْزَلْنَا عَلَيْكَ الْكِتٰبَ يُتْلٰى عَلَيْهِمْ ؕ
اِنَّ فِيْ ذٰلِكَ لَرَحْمَةً وَّذِكْرٰى لِقَوْمٍ يُّؤْمِنُوْنَ ﴿۵۲﴾ ع

[a]11 : 18. [b]42 : 53. [c]6 : 38; 13 : 28. [d]22 : 50; 26 : 116; 51 : 51; 67 : 27.

2258. The fact that a man who could neither read nor write, and, who being born in a country, and having lived among a people, cut off from all contact with civilized humanity, could conceivably have no knowledge of the other revealed Scriptures, should have been able to produce a Book which not only contains all that is of permanent value in those Scriptures but is also a compendium of all the universal teachings that are calculated to satisfy the moral and spiritual needs and requirements of humanity for all time, does constitute an infallible proof of the Qur'ān being a revealed Book and the Holy Prophet being a Divine Teacher.

2259. While the preceding verse referred to external evidence in support of the Qur'ān being the revealed Word of God, the present one furnishes an internal evidence, which is that from the hearts of those who have been endowed with knowledge of the Qur'ān gush forth fountains of Divine light.

2260. To the demand of disbelievers for a Sign of punishment (see preceding verse), the present verse gives an answer full of pathos. It asks them, why do they demand a Sign of punishment when God has already given them a Sign of mercy in the form of the Qur'ān by acting upon which they can acquire eminence and become an honoured and respected people in the world.

R. 6 53. Say, [a]'Allāh is sufficient as a Witness between me and you. He knows what is in the heavens and the earth. And *as for* those who believe in falsehood and disbelieve in Allāh, they it is who are the losers.'

قُلْ كَفٰى بِاللّٰهِ بَيْنِيْ وَبَيْنَكُمْ شَهِيْدًا ۚ يَعْلَمُ مَا فِي السَّمٰوٰتِ وَالْاَرْضِ ۗ وَالَّذِيْنَ اٰمَنُوْا بِالْبَاطِلِ وَكَفَرُوْا بِاللّٰهِ ۙ اُولٰٓئِكَ هُمُ الْخٰسِرُوْنَ ﴿٥٣﴾

54. [b]They ask thee to hasten on the punishment; and had there not been an appointed term, the punishment would have come upon them. And it shall, surely, overtake them unexpectedly,[2261] while they perceive not.

وَيَسْتَعْجِلُوْنَكَ بِالْعَذَابِ ۭ وَلَوْلَآ اَجَلٌ مُّسَمًّى لَّجَآءَهُمُ الْعَذَابُ ۭ وَلَيَاْتِيَنَّهُمْ بَغْتَةً وَّهُمْ لَا يَشْعُرُوْنَ ﴿٥٤﴾

55. They ask thee to hasten on the punishment;[2261A] but [c]Hell will, certainly, encompass the disbelievers;

يَسْتَعْجِلُوْنَكَ بِالْعَذَابِ ۭ وَاِنَّ جَهَنَّمَ لَمُحِيْطَةٌۢ بِالْكٰفِرِيْنَ ﴿٥٥﴾

56. [d]On the day when the punishment will overwhelm them from above them and from underneath their feet,[2262] and He will say, 'Taste ye *the fruit of* your actions.'

يَوْمَ يَغْشٰىهُمُ الْعَذَابُ مِنْ فَوْقِهِمْ وَمِنْ تَحْتِ اَرْجُلِهِمْ وَيَقُوْلُ ذُوْقُوْا مَا كُنْتُمْ تَعْمَلُوْنَ ﴿٥٦﴾

57. O My servants who believe! verily, My earth is vast, so worship Me alone.

يٰعِبَادِيَ الَّذِيْنَ اٰمَنُوْٓا اِنَّ اَرْضِيْ وَاسِعَةٌ فَاِيَّايَ فَاعْبُدُوْنِ ﴿٥٧﴾

58. [e]Every soul shall taste of death; then to Us shall you *all* be brought back.

كُلُّ نَفْسٍ ذَآئِقَةُ الْمَوْتِ ۣ ثُمَّ اِلَيْنَا تُرْجَعُوْنَ ﴿٥٨﴾

[a]4 : 167; 6 : 20; 13 : 44; 48 : 29. [b]22 : 48; 26 : 205; 27 : 72-73; 37 : 177-178. [c]9 : 49; 13 : 36; 17 : 9. [d]6 : 9. [e]3 : 186; 21 : 36.

2261. The verse gives a direct answer to the disbelievers' demand for the Sign of punishment and says that instead of benefiting by the Sign of mercy which has been given to them in the form of the Qur'ān, these ill-fated people persist in their demand for punishment. So they will have this Sign and the punishment will come upon them all of a sudden and from quarters least expected. But they will have to wait for a fixed and appointed term.

2261A. The punishment referred to in the preceding verse is the punishment promised to the disbelievers in this life. The punishment mentioned in this verse is the punishment promised to them in the Hereafter.

2262. When Divine punishment comes, it is sudden and swift and like a cataract overwhelms disbelievers from every direction.

59. And those who believe and do righteous deeds—them shall We, surely, [a]house in lofty mansions of Paradise,[2263] beneath which streams flow. They will abide therein. Excellent is the reward of those who labour *for good*,

وَالَّذِيْنَ اٰمَنُوْا وَعَمِلُوا الصّٰلِحٰتِ لَنُبَوِّئَنَّهُمْ مِّنَ
الْجَنَّةِ غُرَفًا تَجْرِيْ مِنْ تَحْتِهَا الْاَنْهٰرُ خٰلِدِيْنَ فِيْهَا ۭ
نِعْمَ اَجْرُ الْعٰمِلِيْنَ ﴿٥٩﴾

60. [b]Those who are steadfast, and put their trust in their Lord.

الَّذِيْنَ صَبَرُوْا وَعَلٰى رَبِّهِمْ يَتَوَكَّلُوْنَ ﴿٦٠﴾

61. And how many an animal there is that carries not its sustenance! [c]Allāh provides for it and for you.[2264] And He is the All-Hearing, the All-Knowing.

وَكَاَيِّنْ مِّنْ دَاۗبَّةٍ لَّا تَحْمِلُ رِزْقَهَا ڰ اللّٰهُ يَرْزُقُهَا
وَاِيَّاكُمْ ڮ وَهُوَ السَّمِيْعُ الْعَلِيْمُ ﴿٦١﴾

62. And if thou ask them, 'Who has created the heavens and the earth and [d]pressed into service the sun and the moon?'[2265] they will, surely, say, 'Allāh.' How then are they being turned away *from the truth?*

وَلَىِٕنْ سَاَلْتَهُمْ مَّنْ خَلَقَ السَّمٰوٰتِ وَالْاَرْضَ وَسَخَّرَ
الشَّمْسَ وَالْقَمَرَ لَيَقُوْلُنَّ اللّٰهُ ۚ فَاَنّٰى يُؤْفَكُوْنَ ﴿٦٢﴾

63. [e]Allāh enlarges *the means of* sustenance for such of His servants as He pleases, and straitens *them* for whom *He pleases*. Surely, Allāh has full knowledge of all things.

اَللّٰهُ يَبْسُطُ الرِّزْقَ لِمَنْ يَّشَاۗءُ مِنْ عِبَادِهٖ وَيَقْدِرُ
لَهٗ ۭ اِنَّ اللّٰهَ بِكُلِّ شَيْءٍ عَلِيْمٌ ﴿٦٣﴾

64. And if thou ask them, 'Who sends down water from the sky and therewith gives life to the earth after its death?' they will, surely, say, 'Allāh.' Say, 'All praise belongs to Allāh.' But most of them understand not.

وَلَىِٕنْ سَاَلْتَهُمْ مَّنْ نَّزَّلَ مِنَ السَّمَاۗءِ مَاۗءً فَاَحْيَا بِهِ
الْاَرْضَ مِنْۢ بَعْدِ مَوْتِهَا لَيَقُوْلُنَّ اللّٰهُ ۭ قُلِ الْحَمْدُ
لِلّٰهِ ۭ بَلْ اَكْثَرُهُمْ لَا يَعْقِلُوْنَ ﴿٦٤﴾ ع

[a]25 : 76; 34 : 38. [b]16 : 43. [c]11 : 7. [d]7 : 55; 13 : 3; 31 : 30; 35 : 14; 39 : 6. [e]13 : 27; 30 : 38; 34 : 37; 39 : 53; 42 : 13.

2263. Believers are here promised in clear and unequivocal terms that those who leave their hearths and homes in the way of God, and then remain steadfast in their belief and do righteous deeds, the reward they get far exceeds all that they lose for God's sake.

2264. When even animals and birds do not go without food, it is inconceivable that man, who is God's noblest creation and its acme and apex, should starve.

2265. God is the Creator and Source of all life, and for its continuity He has pressed into the service of man all the forces of nature.

R. 7   65.   ^aAnd the life of this world is nothing but a pastime and a sport, and the Home of the Hereafter—that indeed is Life, if they but knew!²²⁶⁶

وَمَا هٰذِهِ الْحَيٰوةُ الدُّنْيَآ اِلَّا لَهْوٌ وَّلَعِبٌ وَاِنَّ الدَّارَ الْاٰخِرَةَ لَهِىَ الْحَيَوَانُ لَوْ كَانُوْا يَعْلَمُوْنَ ۝

66.   ^bAnd when they go on board a ship, they call on Allāh, with sincere and single-minded faith in Him. But when He brings them safe to land, behold! they associate partners *with Him again,*

فَاِذَا رَكِبُوْا فِى الْفُلْكِ دَعَوُا اللّٰهَ مُخْلِصِيْنَ لَهُ الدِّيْنَ ۚ فَلَمَّا نَجّٰىهُمْ اِلَى الْبَرِّ اِذَا هُمْ يُشْرِكُوْنَ ۝

67.   ^cBeing ungrateful for what We have bestowed on them, and enjoying themselves *for a time.* But they will soon come to know *the consequences of their conduct.*

لِيَكْفُرُوْا بِمَآ اٰتَيْنٰهُمْ ۙ وَلِيَتَمَتَّعُوْا ۣ فَسَوْفَ يَعْلَمُوْنَ ۝

68.   Do they not see that We have made the sanctuary *of Mecca* secure *for them,* while people are snatched away from all around them?²²⁶⁷ ^dWould they then believe in falsehood and deny the favour of Allāh?

اَوَلَمْ يَرَوْا اَنَّا جَعَلْنَا حَرَمًا اٰمِنًا وَّيُتَخَطَّفُ النَّاسُ مِنْ حَوْلِهِمْ ۖ اَفَبِالْبَاطِلِ يُؤْمِنُوْنَ وَبِنِعْمَةِ اللّٰهِ يَكْفُرُوْنَ ۝

69.   ^eAnd who is more unjust than he who invents a lie concerning Allāh, or rejects the truth when it comes to him? ^fIs there not an abode in Hell for disbelievers?

وَمَنْ اَظْلَمُ مِمَّنِ افْتَرٰى عَلَى اللّٰهِ كَذِبًا اَوْ كَذَّبَ بِالْحَقِّ لَمَّا جَآءَهٗ ؕ اَلَيْسَ فِىْ جَهَنَّمَ مَثْوًى لِّلْكٰفِرِيْنَ ۝

70.   And *as for* those who strive²²⁶⁸ *to meet* Us—We will, surely, guide them in Our ways. And, verily, Allāh is with those who do good.

وَالَّذِيْنَ جَاهَدُوْا فِيْنَا لَنَهْدِيَنَّهُمْ سُبُلَنَا ؕ وَاِنَّ اللّٰهَ لَمَعَ الْمُحْسِنِيْنَ ۝

---

^a6 : 33; 47 : 37; 57 : 21.   ^b10 : 23; 31 : 33.   ^c16 : 56; 30 : 35.   ^d16 : 73.   ^e6 : 22; 10 : 18; 39 : 33.   ^f18 : 103; 33 : 9; 48 : 14.

2266.   Life without hardships and privations borne for a noble cause, and without sacrifices undergone for the sake of God, is 'but a pastime and a sport,' a useless and purposeless existence. The purposeful life is that which is spent in the quest of a sublime and noble object and in preparation for everlasting life for which God has created man.

2267.   This verse constitutes a standing testimony to Ka'bah being God's own Sacred House. Ever since the advent of Islām when it was Divinely declared to be humanity's everlasting *Qiblah* and even in the Days of Ignorance when the Arabs had no respect for human life, the territory called the *Haram*—the precincts of the Ka'bah, remained a haven of safety. While there was no safety outside, complete security and peace reigned in it.

2268.   *Jihād* as ordained by Islām does not consist in killing and being killed, but in striving hard to win the pleasure of God, the word, *Finā* meaning 'to meet Us.'

CHAPTER 30

AL-RŪM

(Revealed before Hijrah)

Date of Revelation and Context

The *Sūrah* was revealed at Mecca, but it is difficult to assign an exact date to its revelation. The most reliable authorities, however, place it in the sixth or seventh year of the Call, as in that year the tide of the Persian conquest to which the *Sūrah* pointedly refers was at its height; the Persian armies were knocking at the very gates of Constantinople and the disgrace and degradation of the Romans had touched its nadir. Towards the close of the preceding *Sūrah* it was stated that 'the present life is but a pastime and a sport' if it is not spent in a noble cause, and that life, real and everlasting, is the one in which a spiritual wayfarer strives with might and main to win the pleasure of God. The present *Sūrah* opens with the prophetic words that the believers will successfully meet the ordeal of trials and tribulations through which they will be made to pass and as a reward of their sacrifice and suffering the gates of Divine grace and mercy will be opened to them.

Subject-Matter

The dominant theme of the *Sūrah* is the defeat and discomfiture of the forces of disbelief and darkness and the rise and triumph of Islām. It states with an emphasis and certainty which dispel all doubt that the old order is about to die and a new and better one will emerge from its ruins. The *Sūrah* opens with the declaration of a prophecy about the ultimate success of the Romans over the Persians. The prophecy was made at a time when the tide of the Persian conquest was sweeping away everything before its irresistible onrush and the degradation and humiliation of the Romans had sunk to its lowest depths. It was then beyond human knowledge and ingenuity to predict that within a period ranging from three to nine years, tables would be completely turned upon the Persians, and the vanquished would become the victors. The prophecy was literally fulfilled in most extraordinary and unforeseen circumstances. Its fulfilment implied another and a greater prophecy that the forces of disbelief which were then too powerful for the poor and the weak Muslims to withstand would also be put to complete rout, and Islām would march triumphantly from strength to strength. Next, the *Sūrah* refers to the great powers of God manifested in the creation of the heavens and the earth, the alternation of day and night, the perfect design and order that exist in the universe, and in the birth of man from a very insignificant beginning. All these things lead to the irresistible and inevitable conclusion that God Who possesses such vast and unlimited powers does also have the power to make Islām grow from a small seed into a mighty tree under whose shade the whole of humanity will some day take rest. Islām is bound to succeed because it is *Dīn al-Fiṭrah, i.e.*, it conforms to human nature and appeals to man's conscience, reason and commonsense. Its triumph will come about through a great and wonderful revolution which will take place in Arabia. A people, morally as good as dead, will be roused from their deep sleep of ages, and drinking deep at the spiritual fountain caused by the Holy Prophet to flow, will become the torch-bearers of spiritual light and will carry the Message of Islām to the ends of the earth. The *Sūrah* ends on the note that opposition to Islām cannot arrest or retard its progress. Truth in the long run triumphs and prospers and falsehood is defeated and humiliated. This phenomenon has taken place in the time of every Prophet of God and it will again take place in the time of the Holy Prophet. The Prophet is then asked to bear with patience and fortitude all the persecution and mockery to which he is being subjected, as success will soon come to him

سُورَةُ الرُّومِ مَكِّيَّةٌ

1. [a]In the name of Allāh, the Gracious, the Merciful.

بِسۡمِ اللّٰہِ الرَّحۡمٰنِ الرَّحِیۡمِ ①

2. [b]Alif Lām Mīm.[2669]

الٓمّٓ ②

3. The Romans have been defeated

غُلِبَتِ الرُّوۡمُ ③

4. In the land nearby,[2269A] and they, after their defeat, will be victorious

فِیۡۤ اَدۡنَی الۡاَرۡضِ وَ ہُمۡ مِّنۡۢ بَعۡدِ غَلَبِہِمۡ سَیَغۡلِبُوۡنَ ④

5. In a few years[2270]—[c]Allāh's is the dominion before and after *that*—and on that day the believers will rejoice[2271]

فِیۡ بِضۡعِ سِنِیۡنَ ۬ؕ لِلّٰہِ الۡاَمۡرُ مِنۡ قَبۡلُ وَ مِنۡۢ بَعۡدُ ؕ وَ یَوۡمَئِذٍ یَّفۡرَحُ الۡمُؤۡمِنُوۡنَ ⑤

[a]1 : 1. [b]29 : 2. [c]3 : 155; 13 : 32.

2269. See 16.

2269A. Palestine.

2270. *Biḍ'* denotes a variety of numbers such as five, seven, ten, etc., but is generally understood to signify from three to nine (Lane).

2271. In order fully to appreciate the significance of this and the preceding two verses it is necessary to cast a cursory glance over the political conditions that obtained in the two great Empires that lay on the borders of Arabia—the Persian and the Roman Empires—shortly before the advent of the Holy Prophet of Islām. They were at war with each other. The first round had gone in favour of the Persians whose tide of conquest began in 602 A.D., when in order to avenge the death of Maurice, his patron and benefactor, at the hands of Phocas, Chosroes II, started the war with Rome. For twenty years the Roman Empire was overrun by Persian armies as it had never been before. The Persians plundered Syria and Asia Minor and in 608 A.D. advanced to Chalcedon. Damascus was taken in 613. The surrounding country on which no Persian had ever set foot since the founding of the Empire was utterly and completely laid waste. In June 614 Jerusalem was also captured. The whole of Christendom was horrified by the news that together with the Patriarch the Persians had carried off the Cross of Christ. Christianity had been humbled in the dust. The flood of Persian conquest did not stop with the capture of Jerusalem. Egypt was next conquered, Asia Minor again overrun, and the Persian armies were knocking at the very gates of Constantinople. The Romans could offer but little resistance as they were torn by internal dissensions. The humiliation of Heraclius was so complete that 'Chosroes wanted to see him brought in chains to the foot of his throne and was not prepared to give him peace till he had abjured his crucified god and embraced the worship of the sun' (Historians' History of the World, vol. 7, p. 159; vol. 8, pp. 94-95 & Enc. Brit. under "Chosroes" II & "Heraclius"). This state of affairs very much grieved the Muslims as they had much in common with the Romans who were the 'People of the Book.' But the Quraish of Mecca who, like the Persians, were idolaters, were glad to see in this discomfiture of Christian armies a happy augury for the overthrow and destruction of Islām. It was shortly after this complete *debacle* of Roman forces that in 616 A.D. came the revelation to the Holy Prophet which forms the subject-matter of the verse under comment and the two preceding verses. These verses possessed a twofold significance They foretold, in circumstances then quite inconceivable, that the whole position would be completely reversed within the short space of eight or nine years (*Biḍ'* meaning from three

6. In Allāh's help. He helps whom He pleases; and He is the Mighty, the Merciful.

بِنَصۡرِ اللّٰهِ ؕ يَنۡصُرُ مَنۡ يَّشَآءُ ؕ وَ هُوَ الۡعَزِيۡزُ الرَّحِيۡمُ ۙ﴿۶﴾

7. Allāh *has made* this promise.[2272] [a]Allāh breaks not His promise, but most men know not.

وَعۡدَ اللّٰهِ ؕ لَا يُخۡلِفُ اللّٰهُ وَعۡدَهٗ وَ لٰكِنَّ اَكۡثَرَ النَّاسِ
لَا يَعۡلَمُوۡنَ ﴿۷﴾

8. They know *only* the outer part of the life[2273] of this world, and of the Hereafter they are utterly unmindful.

يَعۡلَمُوۡنَ ظَاهِرًا مِّنَ الۡحَيٰوةِ الدُّنۡيَا ۚۖ وَ هُمۡ عَنِ
الۡاٰخِرَةِ هُمۡ غٰفِلُوۡنَ ﴿۸﴾

---

[a]3 : 195 ; 39 : 21.

---

to nine years—Lane) and the erstwhile victorious Persian armies would suffer a crushing defeat at the hands of the utterly defeated, prostrated and humbled Romans. The significance of the prophecy lay in the fact that, within this short period, the foundations of the ultimate triumph of Islām and that of the defeat and discomfiture of the forces of disbelief and darkness would also be firmly laid. The prophecy was fulfilled in circumstances beyond human calculation and comprehension. 'In the midst of the Persian triumphs he (the Holy Prophet) ventured to foretell that before many years should elapse, victory would return to the banners of the Romans......At the time when this prediction is said to have been delivered, no prophecy could be more distant from its accomplishment, since the first twelve years of Heraclius announced the approaching dissolution of the Empire' (Rise, Decline & Fall of the Roman Empire by Gibbon, vol. 5. p. 74).

After licking his wounds for several years, Heraclius was at last able to take the field against the Persians in 622, the year of the Holy Prophet's *Hijrah* to Medina. In 624 he advanced into northern Media, where he destroyed the great fire-temple of Goudzak (Gazaca) and thus avenged the destruction of Jerusalem. This happened exactly within nine years, the period foretold in the verse; and to add to its importance and significance it happened in the year when the power of the Quraish also suffered a very serious reverse in the Battle of Badr, which recalled a biblical prophecy foretelling the fading of the glory of Kedar (Isa. 21:16-17). In 627 Heraclius defeated the Persian army at Nineveh and advanced towards Ctesiphon. Chosroes fled from his favourite residence Dastgerd (near Baghdad) and, after dragging on an inglorious existence, was murdered by his own son, Siroes, on 19th February, 628, A.D.; and thus the Persian Empire, from the apparent greatness which it had reached a few years earlier sank into hopeless anarchy (Enc. Brit.). The fulfilment of the prophecy was so remarkable and unforeseen that prejudiced Christian writers have been hard put to it to explain it away. Rodwell says that the vowel points of the Arabic expression used in the verse were left undecided so that it would read either way, *i.e.*, *Sayaghlibūn* meaning, "they will be victorious," or *Sayughlabūn* meaning, "they will be defeated." He even adds that the ambiguity was intentional. The Rev. gentleman pretends not to understand this simple fact that the vowels of an expression which had been recited hundreds of times in daily Prayers and otherwise could hardly be left undecided. Mr. Wherry goes a step further. He says : 'Our daily newspapers constantly forecast political events of this kind.' To this futile attempt of Mr. Wherry to explain away and belittle the importance of the prophecy Gibbon's quotation given above provides a crushing reply.

2272. The promise is referred to in 8 : 43.

2273. The knowledge of disbelievers is limited to an understanding of the physical causes of the incidents, but the causes of the defeat of the Persians and that of the Quraish lay deeper and were more spiritual than material or physical.

9. [a]Do they not reflect within themselves *that* Allāh has not created the heavens and the earth and all that is between the two but in accordance with the requirements of wisdom[2274] and for a fixed term? [b]But many among men believe not in the meeting with their Lord.

أَوَلَمْ يَتَفَكَّرُوا فِيٓ أَنْفُسِهِمْ ۗ مَا خَلَقَ اللّٰهُ السَّمٰوٰتِ
وَالْأَرْضَ وَمَا بَيْنَهُمَآ إِلَّا بِالْحَقِّ وَأَجَلٍ مُّسَمًّى ۗ
وَإِنَّ كَثِيرًا مِّنَ النَّاسِ بِلِقَآئِ رَبِّهِمْ لَكٰفِرُونَ (9)

10. [c]Have they not travelled in the earth so that they might see how *evil* was the end of those who were before them? They were stronger than these in power, and they tilled the soil and populated it more *and better* than these have populated it. And their Messengers came to them with manifest Signs. [d]And Allāh would not wrong them, but they wronged their own souls.

أَوَلَمْ يَسِيرُوا فِي الْأَرْضِ فَيَنْظُرُوا كَيْفَ كَانَ عَاقِبَةُ
الَّذِينَ مِنْ قَبْلِهِمْ ۚ كَانُوٓا أَشَدَّ مِنْهُمْ قُوَّةً وَّأَثَارُوا
الْأَرْضَ وَعَمَرُوهَآ أَكْثَرَ مِمَّا عَمَرُوهَا وَجَآءَتْهُمْ
رُسُلُهُمْ بِالْبَيِّنٰتِ ۖ فَمَا كَانَ اللّٰهُ لِيَظْلِمَهُمْ وَلٰكِنْ
كَانُوٓا أَنْفُسَهُمْ يَظْلِمُونَ (10)

11. Then evil was the end of those who did evil, because, they rejected the Signs of Allāh and scoffed at them.

ثُمَّ كَانَ عَاقِبَةَ الَّذِينَ أَسَآءُوا السُّوٓأٰى أَنْ كَذَّبُوا
ع بِاٰيٰتِ اللّٰهِ وَكَانُوا بِهَا يَسْتَهْزِءُونَ (11)

R. 2 12. [e]Allāh originates creation; then He keeps repeating it; then to Him shall you be brought back.

اللّٰهُ يَبْدَؤُا الْخَلْقَ ثُمَّ يُعِيدُهُ ثُمَّ إِلَيْهِ تُرْجَعُونَ (12)

13. And on the day when the Hour will arrive [f]the guilty shall be *seized* with despair.

وَيَوْمَ تَقُومُ السَّاعَةُ يُبْلِسُ الْمُجْرِمُونَ (13)

14. And they shall have no intercessors from *among those* whom they associate *with Allāh;* and [g]they will deny those whom they associate *with Him.*

وَلَمْ يَكُنْ لَّهُمْ مِّنْ شُرَكَآئِهِمْ شُفَعٰٓؤُا وَكَانُوا
بِشُرَكَآئِهِمْ كٰفِرِينَ (14)

[a]7 : 186. [b]10 : 46; 29 : 24; 32 : 11. [c]12 : 110; 22 : 47; 35 : 45; 47 : 11. [d]4 : 41; 10 : 45. [e]29 : 20. [f]6 : 45. [g]10 : 29.

2274. If disbelievers had reflected over the great powers and faculties with which man has been endowed and had reflected also over the very limited duration of their worldly existence, they would have realized that man's life on this earth is not the be-all and end-all of his creation and that there is a fuller and better life beyond the grave where man's spiritual progress will know no end and would have realized that the present life is only a preparation for the life hereafter.

15. And on the day when the Hour will arrive—on that day they will become separated *from one another*.

وَيَوْمَ تَقُوْمُ السَّاعَةُ يَوْمَئِذٍ يَّتَفَرَّقُوْنَ ﴿۱۵﴾

16. Then those [a]who believed and acted righteously will be honoured *and made happy* in *stately* gardens.[2275]

فَاَمَّا الَّذِيْنَ اٰمَنُوْا وَعَمِلُوا الصّٰلِحٰتِ فَهُمْ فِيْ رَوْضَةٍ
يُّحْبَرُوْنَ ﴿۱۶﴾

17. But as for those [b]who disbelieved and rejected Our Signs and the meeting of the Hereafter, these shall be confronted with punishment.

وَاَمَّا الَّذِيْنَ كَفَرُوْا وَكَذَّبُوْا بِاٰيٰتِنَا وَلِقَآئِ الْاٰخِرَةِ
فَاُولٰٓئِكَ فِي الْعَذَابِ مُحْضَرُوْنَ ﴿۱۷﴾

18. [c]So glorify Allāh when you enter the evening and when you enter the morning—

فَسُبْحٰنَ اللّٰهِ حِيْنَ تُمْسُوْنَ وَحِيْنَ تُصْبِحُوْنَ ﴿۱۸﴾

19. And to Him belongs all praise in the heavens and the earth[2276]—and *glorify Him* in the afternoon and when you enter upon the time of the decline of the sun.

وَلَهُ الْحَمْدُ فِي السَّمٰوٰتِ وَالْاَرْضِ وَعَشِيًّا وَّحِيْنَ
تُظْهِرُوْنَ ﴿۱۹﴾

20. [d]He brings forth the living from the dead, and He brings forth the dead from the living; and He gives life to the earth after its death. And in like manner shall you be brought forth.

يُخْرِجُ الْحَيَّ مِنَ الْمَيِّتِ وَيُخْرِجُ الْمَيِّتَ مِنَ
الْحَيِّ وَيُحْيِ الْاَرْضَ بَعْدَ مَوْتِهَا ۗ وَكَذٰلِكَ
تُخْرَجُوْنَ ﴿۲۰﴾ ع

R. 3 21. And of His Signs is that He created you from dust; then, behold, you are men spreading[2277] *over the earth*.

وَمِنْ اٰيٰتِهٖۤ اَنْ خَلَقَكُمْ مِّنْ تُرَابٍ ثُمَّ اِذَآ اَنْتُمْ
بَشَرٌ تَنْتَشِرُوْنَ ﴿۲۱﴾

---

[a]4 : 176; 13 : 30; 14 : 24; 22 : 57; 42 : 23; 68 : 35. [b]2 : 40; 7 : 37; 57 : 20; 64 : 11; 78 : 22-29. [c]17 : 79; 20 : 131; 50 : 40. [d]10 : 32.

2275. How through Islām the Arabs rose from the lowest depths of degradation to the highest pinnacle of spiritual and material glory and eminence is writ large on the face of history.

2276. When one reflects over the sublime purpose of man's creation and on how a people sunk deep in moral bankruptcy rose to the heights of spiritual glory, as did the Arabs by following the Holy Prophet, one is bound spontaneously to exclaim 'Glory be to Allāh, the great Creator of heavens and earth and all that is between them.'

2277. Whereas in the present verse we have, 'He created you from dust' (*Turāb*), elsewhere man is stated to have been created from *Ṭīn*, *i.e.*, clay (6 : 3; 17: 62; 23 : 13; 32 : 8; 37 : 12; 38 : 72). Man's creation from dust or dry earth refers to that stage of

22. And of His Signs is that [a]He has created wives for you from among yourselves that you may find peace of mind in them, and He has put love and tenderness[2278] between you. In that, surely, are Signs for a people who reflect.

وَمِنْ اٰيٰتِهٖٓ اَنْ خَلَقَ لَكُمْ مِّنْ اَنْفُسِكُمْ اَزْوَاجًا
لِّتَسْكُنُوْٓا اِلَيْهَا وَجَعَلَ بَيْنَكُمْ مَّوَدَّةً وَّرَحْمَةً ؕ
اِنَّ فِيْ ذٰلِكَ لَاٰيٰتٍ لِّقَوْمٍ يَّتَفَكَّرُوْنَ ﴿۲۲﴾

23. [b]And of His Signs is the creation of the heavens and the earth and the diversity of your tongues and colours. In that, surely, are Signs for those who possess knowledge.[2279]

وَمِنْ اٰيٰتِهٖ خَلْقُ السَّمٰوٰتِ وَالْاَرْضِ وَاخْتِلَافُ
اَلْسِنَتِكُمْ وَاَلْوَانِكُمْ ؕ اِنَّ فِيْ ذٰلِكَ لَاٰيٰتٍ لِّلْعٰلِمِيْنَ ﴿۲۳﴾

24. [c]And of His Signs is your sleep by night and day, and your seeking of His bounty. In that, surely, are Signs for a people who would listen.

وَمِنْ اٰيٰتِهٖ مَنَامُكُمْ بِالَّيْلِ وَالنَّهَارِ وَابْتِغَآؤُكُمْ
مِّنْ فَضْلِهٖ ؕ اِنَّ فِيْ ذٰلِكَ لَاٰيٰتٍ لِّقَوْمٍ يَّسْمَعُوْنَ ﴿۲۴﴾

25. And of His Signs is that [d]He shows you the lightning for fear and hope,[2280] [e]and He sends down water from the sky, and quickens therewith the earth after its death. In that, surely, are Signs for a people who understand.

وَمِنْ اٰيٰتِهٖ يُرِيْكُمُ الْبَرْقَ خَوْفًا وَّطَمَعًا وَّيُنَزِّلُ
مِنَ السَّمَآءِ مَآءً فَيُحْيٖ بِهِ الْاَرْضَ بَعْدَ مَوْتِهَا ؕ
اِنَّ فِيْ ذٰلِكَ لَاٰيٰتٍ لِّقَوْمٍ يَّعْقِلُوْنَ ﴿۲۵﴾

[a]4 : 2; 7 : 190; 16 : 73; 39 : 7. [b]42 : 30. [c]10 : 68; 27: 87; 28 : 74. [d]13 : 13. [e]40 : 14; 42 : 29.

his creation which preceded his formation from clay—to man's food which is derived from earth and from which human body derives its sustenance. The verse gives three arguments to prove God's existence : (*a*) God has created man from dust which apparently has no relation to life and does not possess the attribute to produce it. (*b*) He has endowed him with very subtle emotions and has implanted in his nature a yearning and craving to make progress and has bestowed upon him aptitude and capabilities to achieve the object of his desire. (*c*) He has placed in man the desire to spread about and dominate the world and has given him the necessary powers for the achievement of this great object.

2278. Love between man and woman leads to procreation and continuity of human life on earth. This shows a design and a purpose behind it and the existence of a designer and also of a better and fuller life after the life on this earth.

2279. Human progress is closely linked with the diversity of tongues and colours. This diversity again points to a design and a designer. That designer is the Creator of heavens and earth. Underneath the diversity of tongues and colours which has resulted in diversity of civilizations and cultures there lies a unity—the unity of mankind. This oneness of humanity leads to the inevitable conclusion of the Oneness of its Creator.

2280. Apart from heralding rain which brings fertility and prosperity in its wake, lightning kills germs of various diseases and eliminates worms that destroy crops. Thus, besides causing fear, it is a source of manifold benefits to man. Every element of nature plays its allotted part in the Divine scheme of things, thus bearing testimony to God's existence, and to His great wisdom and power.

26. [a]And of His Signs is that the heaven and the earth stand *firm* by His command.[2281] Then when He calls you by a single call *to come forth* from the earth, behold, you will come forth.

وَمِنْ اٰيٰتِهٖٓ اَنْ تَقُوْمَ السَّمَآءُ وَالْاَرْضُ بِاَمْرِهٖ ؕ ثُمَّ
اِذَا دَعَاكُمْ دَعْوَةً ٭ۖ مِّنَ الْاَرْضِ ٭ۖ اِذَآ اَنْتُمْ
تَخْرُجُوْنَ ﴿۲۶﴾

27. [b]And to Him belongs whosoever is in the heavens and the earth. All are obedient to Him.[2282]

وَلَهٗ مَنْ فِي السَّمٰوٰتِ وَالْاَرْضِ ؕ كُلٌّ لَّهٗ قٰنِتُوْنَ ﴿۲۷﴾

28. [c]And He it is Who originates the creation, then keeps repeating it, and it is most easy for Him. His is the most exalted state in the heavens and the earth; and He is the Mighty, the Wise.

وَهُوَ الَّذِيْ يَبْدَؤُا الْخَلْقَ ثُمَّ يُعِيْدُهٗ وَهُوَ اَهْوَنُ
عَلَيْهِ ؕ وَلَهُ الْمَثَلُ الْاَعْلٰى فِي السَّمٰوٰتِ وَالْاَرْضِ ۚ
وَهُوَ الْعَزِيْزُ الْحَكِيْمُ ﴿۲۸﴾ ع

R. 4 29. He sets forth for you a parable concerning yourselves. Have you, among those whom your right hands possess, partners in what We have provided for you *so that* you become equal *sharers* therein,[2283] *and* you fear them as you fear each other? Thus do We explain the Signs to a people who understand.

ضَرَبَ لَكُمْ مَّثَلًا مِّنْ اَنْفُسِكُمْ ؕ هَلْ لَّكُمْ مِّنْ مَّا
مَلَكَتْ اَيْمَانُكُمْ مِّنْ شُرَكَآءَ فِيْ مَا رَزَقْنٰكُمْ فَاَنْتُمْ
فِيْهِ سَوَآءٌ تَخَافُوْنَهُمْ كَخِيْفَتِكُمْ اَنْفُسَكُمْ ؕ كَذٰلِكَ
نُفَصِّلُ الْاٰيٰتِ لِقَوْمٍ يَّعْقِلُوْنَ ﴿۲۹﴾

30. Nay, but those, who are unjust, follow their own low desires without knowledge. Then [d]who can guide him whom Allāh lets go astray? There will be no helpers for them.

بَلِ اتَّبَعَ الَّذِيْنَ ظَلَمُوْٓا اَهْوَآءَهُمْ بِغَيْرِ عِلْمٍ ۚ فَمَنْ
يَّهْدِيْ مَنْ اَضَلَّ اللّٰهُ ؕ وَمَا لَهُمْ مِّنْ نّٰصِرِيْنَ ﴿۳۰﴾

[a]35 : 42. [b]16 : 53; 20 : 7; 21 : 20; 22 : 65. [c]10 : 35; 27 : 65; 29 : 20. [d]7 : 187; 13 : 34; 39 : 37; 40 : 34.

2281. Long ages have passed since the solar system came into being, yet nothing has gone wrong with it. Such is God's handiwork that planets keep their orbits without any visible support.

2282. It is beyond human ken or comprehension to guess when this great universe came into being. From an unknown and untraced past the sun with all the planets and heavenly bodies has travelled on its appointed course with a regularity and uniformity that have known no flaw or fault. There are millions of these satellites and yet they never come into collision; so perfect and consummate is the law and order that pervade the universe. This is the meaning of the words, 'All are obedient to Him.'

2283. The verse purports to say that when a master and a slave are not equal though they are both human beings, and when the master would not share his wealth and property with his slave, how then could God, the sole Creator and Controller ofall things, be regarded as sharing the control of the universe with anybody?

31. [a]So set thy face to *the service of* religion with single-minded devotion. *And follow* the nature made by Allāh,[2284] the nature according to which He has fashioned mankind. There is no altering the creation of Allāh. [b]That is the right religion—but most men know not—

فَأَقِمْ وَجْهَكَ لِلدِّينِ حَنِيفًا ۚ فِطْرَتَ اللّٰهِ الَّتِي فَطَرَ
النَّاسَ عَلَيْهَا ۚ لَا تَبْدِيلَ لِخَلْقِ اللّٰهِ ۚ ذٰلِكَ الدِّينُ
الْقَيِّمُ ۙ وَلٰكِنَّ أَكْثَرَ النَّاسِ لَا يَعْلَمُونَ ﴿٣١﴾

32. *So you all* turn to Him, *in repentance*, and seek His protection and observe Prayer,[2285] and be not of those who associate partners *with Allāh*—

مُنِيبِينَ إِلَيْهِ وَاتَّقُوهُ وَأَقِيمُوا الصَّلٰوةَ وَلَا تَكُونُوا
مِنَ الْمُشْرِكِينَ ﴿٣٢﴾

33. [c]Of those who split up their religion and have become divided into sects;[2286] every party rejoicing in what they have.

مِنَ الَّذِينَ فَرَّقُوا دِينَهُمْ وَكَانُوا شِيَعًا ۖ كُلُّ حِزْبٍ
بِمَا لَدَيْهِمْ فَرِحُونَ ﴿٣٣﴾

34. [d]And when an affliction befalls people, they cry unto their Lord, turning sincerely to Him; then, when He has made them taste of mercy from Him, lo! a section of them associate partners with their Lord,

وَإِذَا مَسَّ النَّاسَ ضُرٌّ دَعَوْا رَبَّهُمْ مُنِيبِينَ إِلَيْهِ
ثُمَّ إِذَا أَذَاقَهُمْ مِنْهُ رَحْمَةً إِذَا فَرِيقٌ مِنْهُمْ بِرَبِّهِمْ
يُشْرِكُونَ ﴿٣٤﴾

35. [e]So that they *begin to* deny that which We have bestowed upon them. So enjoy yourselves *awhile* but soon you will come to know.

لِيَكْفُرُوا بِمَا آتَيْنٰهُمْ ۚ فَتَمَتَّعُوا فَسَوْفَ تَعْلَمُونَ ﴿٣٥﴾

[a]10 : 106; 30 : 44. [b]98 : 6. [c]6 : 160. [d]10 : 13; 39 : 9, 50. [e]16 : 56; 29 : 67.

2284. God is One and humanity is one. This is *Fiṭrat Allāh* or *Dīn al-Fiṭrah*—the religion which is rooted in the nature of man and to which he conforms and instinctively reacts. It is in this religion that a child is born, but his environments, the ideas and beliefs of his parents and the training he receives from them subsequently make him a Jew, a Magian or a Christian (Bukhārī).

2285. Mere belief in the Almightiness and Oneness of God, though it forms the basic principle of true religion, is not enough. A true religion must possess certain ordinances and commandments. Of these the top priority goes to Prayer.

2286. Deviation from true religion led people in the past to be split up into warring sections and caused differences among them.

36. Have We sent down to them any authority[2287] which speaks *in favour* of what they associate with Him?

أَمْ أَنْزَلْنَا عَلَيْهِمْ سُلْطٰنًا فَهُوَ يَتَكَلَّمُ بِمَا كَانُوْا بِهٖ
يُشْرِكُوْنَ ﴿٣٦﴾

37. [a]And when We make people taste of mercy, they rejoice therein; but if some evil befalls them because of that which their own hands have sent on, behold! they are in despair.

وَإِذَآ أَذَقْنَا النَّاسَ رَحْمَةً فَرِحُوْا بِهَا ۭ وَإِنْ تُصِبْهُمْ
سَيِّئَةٌ بِمَا قَدَّمَتْ أَيْدِيْهِمْ إِذَا هُمْ يَقْنَطُوْنَ ﴿٣٧﴾

38. See they not that [b]Allāh enlarges the provision to whomsoever He pleases and straitens *it to whomsoever He pleases?* In that, truly, are Signs for a people who believe.

أَوَلَمْ يَرَوْا أَنَّ اللّٰهَ يَبْسُطُ الرِّزْقَ لِمَنْ يَّشَآءُ وَ
يَقْدِرُ ۭ إِنَّ فِيْ ذٰلِكَ لَاٰيٰتٍ لِّقَوْمٍ يُّؤْمِنُوْنَ ﴿٣٨﴾

39. [c]So give to the kinsman his due[2288] and to the needy and to the wayfarer. That is best for those who seek the favour of Allāh, and it is they who will prosper.

فَاٰتِ ذَا الْقُرْبٰى حَقَّهٗ وَالْمِسْكِيْنَ وَابْنَ السَّبِيْلِ ۭ
ذٰلِكَ خَيْرٌ لِّلَّذِيْنَ يُرِيْدُوْنَ وَجْهَ اللّٰهِ ۡ وَأُولٰٓئِكَ
هُمُ الْمُفْلِحُوْنَ ﴿٣٩﴾

40. [d]Whatever you lay out at interest that it may increase the wealth of the people, it does not increase in the sight of Allāh; but whatever you give in *Zakāt*, seeking the pleasure of Allāh—it is these who will increase *their wealth* manifold.[2289]

وَمَآ اٰتَيْتُمْ مِّنْ رِّبًا لِّيَرْبُوَا۟ فِيْٓ أَمْوَالِ النَّاسِ فَلَا
يَرْبُوْا عِنْدَ اللّٰهِ ۚ وَمَآ اٰتَيْتُمْ مِّنْ زَكٰوةٍ تُرِيْدُوْنَ
وَجْهَ اللّٰهِ فَأُولٰٓئِكَ هُمُ الْمُضْعِفُوْنَ ﴿٤٠﴾

---

[a]10 : 22; 41 : 51-52; 42 : 49. [b]29 : 63. [c]16 : 91; 17 : 27. [d]2 : 276-277.

2287. Having referred in the previous few verses to the Unity of God as the basic principle of all religions, this and the next three verses deal with *Shirk*, *i.e.*, associating false gods with Allāh. Polytheists possess no argument whatsoever in support of their false beliefs. Human nature, reason and commonsense all revolt against idolatry.

2288. The words 'his due,' embody a fine principle, *viz.*, that the monetary help which the wealthy people give to their poorer brethren in the form of *Zakāt*, charity or gift, are the latter's right and due, because they make a substantial contribution to the production of wealth of the rich by their labour (51 : 20). Wherever the Qur'ān commands the believers to give monetary help to the needy and the poor, it invariably uses the word *Āti* instead of *I'ṭi*. By so doing it seeks to safeguard the self-respect of the poor person who receives charity, because, whereas the latter word expresses the sense of giving, the former expresses that of presenting (Kashshāf).

2289. The verse institutes a contrast between *Zakāt* and interest. Whereas by means of *Zakāt* Islām seeks to improve the miserable lot of the poor, at the same time safeguarding their dignity and self-respect, the institution of interest not only does not better the economic

41. It is Allāh Who has created you, *and* then He has provided for you; then [a]He will cause you to die, *and* then He will bring you to life.[2290] Is there any of your *so-called* associate-gods, who can do any of these *things?* Glorified be He and exalted far above that which they associate *with Him.*

اَللّٰهُ الَّذِيْ خَلَقَكُمْ ثُمَّ رَزَقَكُمْ ثُمَّ يُمِيْتُكُمْ ثُمَّ يُحْيِيْكُمْ ۭ هَلْ مِنْ شُرَكَاۗىِٕكُمْ مَّنْ يَّفْعَلُ مِنْ ذٰلِكُمْ مِّنْ شَيْءٍ ۭ سُبْحٰنَهٗ وَتَعٰلٰى عَمَّا يُشْرِكُوْنَ ﴿۴۱﴾

R. 5 42. Corruption has spread on land and sea because of what men's hands have wrought,[2291] that He may make them taste *the fruit* of some of their doings, so that they may turn back *from evil.*

ظَهَرَ الْفَسَادُ فِي الْبَرِّ وَالْبَحْرِ بِمَا كَسَبَتْ اَيْدِي النَّاسِ لِيُذِيْقَهُمْ بَعْضَ الَّذِيْ عَمِلُوْا لَعَلَّهُمْ يَرْجِعُوْنَ ﴿۴۲﴾

[a]2 : 29; 22 : 67; 40 : 69; 45 : 27.

condition of the poor, but actually tends to make the rich richer and the poor poorer. The vast disparity of wealth between different sections of human society, as a result of which a large majority grovels in grinding indigence and penury and a tiny section rolls in unmeasured wealth, is inevitably due to the institution of interest. This verse particularly prohibits taking of interest on money loaned to banks or companies, etc.

2290. God is our Creator. He is our Sustainer and Provider; and He possesses complete control over life and death—the three very essential attributes that the Supreme Being Who commands and demands our worship must and does possess.

2291. The main theme of the foregoing verses consisted in engendering and instilling in man belief in an Almighty and All-Powerful God Who creates, regulates and guides all life. In the present verse we are told that when darkness enshrouds the face of the earth and man consigns God to oblivion and gives himself up to the worship of the gods of his own conception and creation, God raises a Prophet to 'bring back the erring flock into the Master's fold.'

The beginning of the seventh century was an epoch of disintegration—national and social—and religion had become extinct as a moral force and had become reduced to mere ritual and ceremony and the great Faiths of the world had ceased to exert any healthy influence on the lives of their followers. The Holy flames kindled by Zoroaster, Moses and Jesus had been quenched in the blood of man......In the fifth and sixth centuries the civilized world stood on the verge of chaos. It seemed that the great civilization that it had taken four thousand years to construct was on the verge of disintegration...... ......Civilization like a gigantic tree whose foliage had over-arched the world and whose branches had borne the golden fruits of art and science and literature, stood tottering, its trunk no longer alive with the flowing sap of devotion and reverence, but rotten to the core ("Emotion as the Basis of Civilization" & "Spirit of Islām").

Such was the condition of mankind when the Holy Prophet Muhammad, humanity's greatest Teacher appeared on the world's stage and the most perfect and last Divine Law in the form of the Qur'ān was revealed, because a perfect Law could only be revealed when all or most of the evils, particularly those known as root evils, had made their appearance and had become established.

The words 'land and sea,' may signify: (*a*) Nations whose cultures and civilizations were based purely on reason and collective human experience, and those whose cultures and civilizations were based on Divine revelation; (*b*) peoples living on the continents and those living in the islands. The verse means that all the nations of the world had become corrupt to the very core politically, socially and morally.

43. Say, [a]"Travel in the earth and see how *evil* was the end of those before *you*. Most of them were idolaters.'

قُلْ سِيرُوا فِي الْأَرْضِ فَانْظُرُوا كَيْفَ كَانَ عَاقِبَةُ
الَّذِينَ مِنْ قَبْلُ ۚ كَانَ أَكْثَرُهُمْ مُشْرِكِينَ ﴿٤٣﴾

44. [b]So set thy face to *the service of* the right religion, before there comes the day from Allāh for which there will be no averting. On that day *believers and disbelievers* will be separated *from each other*.

فَأَقِمْ وَجْهَكَ لِلدِّينِ الْقَيِّمِ مِنْ قَبْلِ أَنْ يَأْتِيَ
يَوْمٌ لَا مَرَدَّ لَهُ مِنَ اللَّهِ ۖ يَوْمَئِذٍ يَصَّدَّعُونَ ﴿٤٤﴾

45. Those who disbelieve will bear *the consequences of* their disbelief; and those who do righteous deeds prepare *good* for their own souls,

مَنْ كَفَرَ فَعَلَيْهِ كُفْرُهُ ۖ وَمَنْ عَمِلَ صَالِحًا فَلِأَنْفُسِهِمْ
يَمْهَدُونَ ﴿٤٥﴾

46. [c]That He, out of His bounty, may reward those who believe and act righteously. Surely, He loves not the disbelievers.

لِيَجْزِيَ الَّذِينَ آمَنُوا وَعَمِلُوا الصَّالِحَاتِ مِنْ فَضْلِهِ ۚ
إِنَّهُ لَا يُحِبُّ الْكَافِرِينَ ﴿٤٦﴾

47. And of His Signs is that He sends the winds as bearers of glad tidings[2292] and that He may make you taste of His mercy, and that [d]the ships may sail at His command, and that you may seek of His bounty, and that you may be grateful.

وَمِنْ آيَاتِهِ أَنْ يُرْسِلَ الرِّيَاحَ مُبَشِّرَاتٍ وَلِيُذِيقَكُمْ
مِنْ رَحْمَتِهِ وَلِتَجْرِيَ الْفُلْكُ بِأَمْرِهِ وَلِتَبْتَغُوا مِنْ
فَضْلِهِ وَلَعَلَّكُمْ تَشْكُرُونَ ﴿٤٧﴾

48. And, surely, We sent Messengers before thee to their own people, and they brought them clear Signs. Then We punished those who were guilty. [e]And it was certainly incumbent upon Us to help the believers.

وَلَقَدْ أَرْسَلْنَا مِنْ قَبْلِكَ رُسُلًا إِلَىٰ قَوْمِهِمْ فَجَاءُوهُمْ
بِالْبَيِّنَاتِ فَانْتَقَمْنَا مِنَ الَّذِينَ أَجْرَمُوا ۖ وَكَانَ حَقًّا
عَلَيْنَا نَصْرُ الْمُؤْمِنِينَ ﴿٤٨﴾

---

[a]16 : 37; 27 : 70; 40 : 83. [b]10 : 106; 30 : 31. [c]10 : 5; 34 : 5.
[d]17 : 67; 31 : 32; 45 : 13. [e]10 : 104; 40 : 52; 58 : 22.

2292. These words point to a Divine law which works with as much effect in the physical universe as it does in the spiritual world. Just as winds precede rain, heralding its advent, similarly before the advent of a Divine Reformer there come into existence conditions which are favourable to the spread of his teachings and there appear good and righteous men who prepare the ground and "make the paths straight for him."

49. [a]*It is* Allāh Who sends the winds so that they raise *the vapours in the form of* a cloud. Then He spreads it in the sky as He pleases, and then He spreads it into fragments, and thou seest the rain issuing forth from its midst. And when He causes it to fall on whom He pleases of His servants, behold! they rejoice;

اَللّٰهُ الَّذِيْ يُرْسِلُ الرِّيٰحَ فَتُثِيْرُ سَحَابًا فَيَبْسُطُهٗ فِي السَّمَآءِ كَيْفَ يَشَآءُ وَيَجْعَلُهٗ كِسَفًا فَتَرَى الْوَدْقَ يَخْرُجُ مِنْ خِلٰلِهٖ ۚ فَاِذَآ اَصَابَ بِهٖ مَنْ يَّشَآءُ مِنْ عِبَادِهٖٓ اِذَا هُمْ يَسْتَبْشِرُوْنَ ﴿٤٩﴾

50. Though before that—before it was sent down upon them—they were in despair.

وَاِنْ كَانُوْا مِنْ قَبْلِ اَنْ يُّنَزَّلَ عَلَيْهِمْ مِّنْ قَبْلِهٖ لَمُبْلِسِيْنَ ﴿٥٠﴾

51. Observe, then, the marks of Allāh's mercy; how [b]He quickens the earth after its death. Verily, it is He Who quickens the dead;[2293] for He has power over all things.

فَانْظُرْ اِلٰٓى اَثَرِ رَحْمَتِ اللّٰهِ كَيْفَ يُحْيِ الْاَرْضَ بَعْدَ مَوْتِهَا ؕ اِنَّ ذٰلِكَ لَمُحْيِ الْمَوْتٰى ۚ وَهُوَ عَلٰى كُلِّ شَيْءٍ قَدِيْرٌ ﴿٥١﴾

52. And if We sent a wind and [c]they saw *their harvest* turn yellow, they would, certainly thereafter, *begin to* deny *Our favours*.

وَلَئِنْ اَرْسَلْنَا رِيْحًا فَرَاَوْهُ مُصْفَرًّا لَّظَلُّوْا مِنْۢ بَعْدِهٖ يَكْفُرُوْنَ ﴿٥٢﴾

53. And thou canst not make the dead to hear, [d]nor canst thou make the deaf to hear the call, when they retreat turning their backs;

فَاِنَّكَ لَا تُسْمِعُ الْمَوْتٰى وَلَا تُسْمِعُ الصُّمَّ الدُّعَآءَ اِذَا وَلَّوْا مُدْبِرِيْنَ ﴿٥٣﴾

54. [e]Nor canst thou guide the blind out of their error. Thou canst make only those to hear who would believe in Our Signs and submit.[2294]

وَمَآ اَنْتَ بِهٰدِ الْعُمْيِ عَنْ ضَلٰلَتِهِمْ ؕ اِنْ تُسْمِعُ اِلَّا مَنْ يُّؤْمِنُ بِاٰيٰتِنَا فَهُمْ مُّسْلِمُوْنَ ﴿٥٤﴾ ع

[a]24 : 44. [b]16 : 66; 22 : 6; 39 : 22; 45 : 6. [c]56 : 66; 57 : 21. [d]10 : 43; 21 : 46; 27 : 81. [e]10 : 44; 27 : 82.

2293. After attention has been drawn in the preceding two verses to the natural phenomenon that when, after severe drought, welcome rain comes, and the parched and dry earth gets a new life, in the present verse we are told that a similar formula operates in the spiritual renaissance of a morally corrupt people. A people virtually as good as dead receive a new life through a Divine Prophet.

2294. Man himself makes or mars his destiny. No Prophet or Divine revelation can lead him to God unless he has the will to listen to truth. The initiative first must come from man himself, the result then follows from God.

R 6 55. [a]Allāh is He Who created you in *a state of* weakness,[2295] and after weakness gave *you* strength; then, after strength, caused weakness and old age. He creates what He pleases. He is the All-Knowing, the All-Powerful.

اَللّٰهُ الَّذِيْ خَلَقَكُمْ مِّنْ ضُعْفٍ ثُمَّ جَعَلَ مِنْ بَعْدِ
ضُعْفٍ قُوَّةً ثُمَّ جَعَلَ مِنْ بَعْدِ قُوَّةٍ ضُعْفًا وَّشَيْبَةً
يَخْلُقُ مَا يَشَآءُ وَهُوَ الْعَلِيْمُ الْقَدِيْرُ ﴿٥٥﴾

56. And on the day when the *appointed* Hour[2296] shall arrive, the guilty will swear that [b]they tarried not save a brief period—thus are they turned away *from the right path.*

وَيَوْمَ تَقُوْمُ السَّاعَةُ يُقْسِمُ الْمُجْرِمُوْنَ مَا لَبِثُوْا
غَيْرَ سَاعَةٍ كَذٰلِكَ كَانُوْا يُؤْفَكُوْنَ ﴿٥٦﴾

57. But those, who are given knowledge and faith, will say, 'You have indeed tarried according to the Book of Allāh, till the Day of Resurrection. And this indeed is the Day of Resurrection,[2297] but you did not *care to* know.

وَقَالَ الَّذِيْنَ اُوْتُوا الْعِلْمَ وَالْاِيْمَانَ لَقَدْ لَبِثْتُمْ
فِيْ كِتٰبِ اللّٰهِ اِلٰى يَوْمِ الْبَعْثِ فَهٰذَا يَوْمُ الْبَعْثِ وَ
لٰكِنَّكُمْ كُنْتُمْ لَا تَعْلَمُوْنَ ﴿٥٧﴾

58. So [c]on that day their excuses will not avail the wrongdoers; nor will they be allowed to make amends.[2298]

فَيَوْمَئِذٍ لَّا يَنْفَعُ الَّذِيْنَ ظَلَمُوْا مَعْذِرَتُهُمْ وَلَا هُمْ
يُسْتَعْتَبُوْنَ ﴿٥٨﴾

59. And, truly, [d]We have set forth for men in this Qur'ān every type of parable,[2299] and indeed, if thou bring them a Sign, those who disbelieve will, surely, say, 'You are but liars.'

وَلَقَدْ ضَرَبْنَا لِلنَّاسِ فِيْ هٰذَا الْقُرْاٰنِ مِنْ كُلِّ
مَثَلٍ وَلَئِنْ جِئْتَهُمْ بِاٰيَةٍ لَّيَقُوْلَنَّ الَّذِيْنَ كَفَرُوْا
اِنْ اَنْتُمْ اِلَّا مُبْطِلُوْنَ ﴿٥٩﴾

---

[a]40 : 68. [b]10 : 46; 46 : 36. [c]16 : 85; 41 : 25; 45 : 36. [d]17 : 90; 39 : 28.

2295. The word *Du'f* (weakness) has been mentioned thrice in this verse and describes three states of human weakness—the state of embryo, of childhood and that of old age.

2296. The hour of the triumph of Islām.

2297. The expression, 'Day of Resurrection,' here does not refer to Resurrection after death but to the advent of a new Divine Reformer when people are raised to a renewed spiritual life.

2298. The Arabic expression in the text means : (*a*) They will not be allowed to approach the Divine threshold; (*b*) they will not be permitted to make amends for the sins they would have committed; (*c*) no excuse in their defence will be accepted from them; and (*d*) they will not be taken into God's favour (Lane). All these meanings are implicit in the root word '*Ataba*.

2299. *Mathal* means, a description; argument; discourse; lesson; proverb; sign; parable or similitude (Lane).

60. [a]Thus does Allāh seal the hearts of those who have no knowledge.[2300]

كَذٰلِكَ يَطْبَعُ اللّٰهُ عَلٰى قُلُوْبِ الَّذِيْنَ لَا يَعْلَمُوْنَ ﴿٦٠﴾

61. So be thou patient. Surely, the promise of Allāh is true; and let not those who have no certainty *of faith* hold thee in light estimation *so as to move thee from* the stand thou hast taken.

فَاصْبِرْ اِنَّ وَعْدَ اللّٰهِ حَقٌّ وَّلَا يَسْتَخِفَّنَّكَ الَّذِيْنَ
لَا يُوْقِنُوْنَ ﴿٦١﴾ ع

---

[a]9 : 93; 16 : 109; 47 : 17.

2300. The hearts of only those people are 'sealed' who reject Divine knowledge that comes to them through a Divine Reformer. The 'sealing' of the hearts of disbelievers is the inevitable result of their own refusal to accept Divine knowledge.

CHAPTER 31

LUQMĀN

(*Revealed before Hijrah*)

Date of Revelation, Title and Context

By common consent the *Sūrah* is considered to have been revealed at Mecca, towards the middle of the Meccan period, or, as some say, in the sixth or seventh year of the Call. The preceding *Sūrah*, Al-Rūm, had ended on the note that the Qur'ān explains fully all those teachings that deal with the spiritual development and progress of man. But the disbelievers have not the eyes to see the truth, their hearts being sealed. They see Sign after Sign and yet go on harping on the tune that the Holy Prophet is a liar and a forger. The present *Sūrah* opens with the solemn affirmation that the Holy Prophet is not a forger or a liar and that this Book, the Qur'ān, has been revealed to him by the Wise and All-Knowing God. It is full of wisdom and leads an honest seeker-after truth to the right path. It was further mentioned in the preceding *Sūrah* that the cause of Islām will continue to prosper and triumph and disbelievers will meet with defeat, disgrace and humiliation. In the present *Sūrah* some light is shed on those noble moral principles by acting upon which nations and individuals can achieve success and prosperity and can rise to greatness and eminence.

Subject-Matter

The *Sūrah* in its very beginning refers to the *sine qua non* of success—correct belief and right action—and proceeds to discuss some universal moral principles from the mouth of a non-Arab sage, Luqmān, the basic principle being that God is One and that all other noble ideals flow from this belief. The principle, second in importance to Divine Unity, concerns man's obligations to man, the most essential of which are his obligations to his parents. In between these two basic commandments a Muslim is taught to subordinate all his loyalties to God and to allow no other loyalty, not even loyalty to parents, to conflict or clash with his loyalty to His Creator. But under no circumstances should he cease to be kind and considerate and respectful to them. Next, it is stated that man's duty to God takes practical shape in the observance of Prayers and his obligations to mankind in doing good and abstaining from evil. The *Sūrah* says that when a true believer enters upon the noble and arduous task of preaching the truth and calling upon people to live righteously, difficulties and impediments bar his way and he has to put up with opposition, abuse, and persecution. He is told to bear all this opposition and persecution with patience and fortitude. When he is not discouraged or dismayed by the opposition and persecution he has to face in the discharge of his great and noble task, success comes his way and large crowds of people give their allegiance to him. In the hour of public applause and acclamation he should not lose his mental poise and should particularly be on his guard against conceit and arrogance. The *Sūrah* then refers to the laws of nature implying that these laws are working in favour of Islām. It ends on a note of warning to disbelievers that the day of their reckoning when their wealth and their influence, power and prestige, would prove of no avail, is fast approaching. Even their children will accept Islām and spend their wealth to promote its cause.

سُوۡرَۃُ لُقۡمٰنَ مَکِّیَّۃٌ (۳۱)

آیاتها — رکوعاتها

1. [a]In the name of Allāh, the Gracious, the Merciful.	بِسۡمِ اللّٰہِ الرَّحۡمٰنِ الرَّحِیۡمِ ﴿۱﴾
2. [b]Alif Lām Mīm.	الٓمّٓ ﴿۲﴾
3. [c]These are verses of the Book, *full* of wisdom,[2301]	تِلۡکَ اٰیٰتُ الۡکِتٰبِ الۡحَکِیۡمِ ﴿۳﴾
4. [d]A guidance and a mercy for those who do good,	ہُدًی وَّ رَحۡمَۃً لِّلۡمُحۡسِنِیۡنَ ﴿۴﴾
5. [e]Those who observe Prayer and pay the *Zakāt* and who have firm faith in the Hereafter.	الَّذِیۡنَ یُقِیۡمُوۡنَ الصَّلٰوۃَ وَ یُؤۡتُوۡنَ الزَّکٰوۃَ وَ ہُمۡ بِالۡاٰخِرَۃِ ہُمۡ یُوۡقِنُوۡنَ ﴿۵﴾
6. [f]It is they who follow guidance from their Lord, and it is they who shall prosper.	اُولٰٓئِکَ عَلٰی ہُدًی مِّنۡ رَّبِّہِمۡ وَ اُولٰٓئِکَ ہُمُ الۡمُفۡلِحُوۡنَ ﴿۶﴾
7. And of men is he who takes idle tales in exchange *for guidance*[2302] to lead *men* astray from the path of Allāh, without knowledge, and to make a fun of it. For such there will be humiliating punishment.	وَ مِنَ النَّاسِ مَنۡ یَّشۡتَرِیۡ لَہۡوَ الۡحَدِیۡثِ لِیُضِلَّ عَنۡ سَبِیۡلِ اللّٰہِ بِغَیۡرِ عِلۡمٍ ٭ۖ وَّ یَتَّخِذَہَا ہُزُوًا ؕ اُولٰٓئِکَ لَہُمۡ عَذَابٌ مُّہِیۡنٌ ﴿۷﴾
8. And when Our Signs are recited to him, he turns away disdainfully, as though he heard them not, as if there were a heaviness in his ears. So announce to him a painful punishment.	وَ اِذَا تُتۡلٰی عَلَیۡہِ اٰیٰتُنَا وَلّٰی مُسۡتَکۡبِرًا کَاَنۡ لَّمۡ یَسۡمَعۡہَا کَاَنَّ فِیۡۤ اُذُنَیۡہِ وَقۡرًا ۚ فَبَشِّرۡہُ بِعَذَابٍ اَلِیۡمٍ ﴿۸﴾
9. Surely, those who believe and do good works—they will have Gardens of Delight,	اِنَّ الَّذِیۡنَ اٰمَنُوۡا وَ عَمِلُوا الصّٰلِحٰتِ لَہُمۡ جَنّٰتُ النَّعِیۡمِ ﴿۹﴾

[a]1 : 1. [b]30 : 2. [c]10 : 2. [d]16 : 90; 27 : 3. [e]2 : 4; 5 : 56; 9 : 71; 27 : 4, [f]2 : 6.

2301. The Qur'ān is indeed such a wonderful Book that not a single one of the great truths, principles and ideals, enumerated and proclaimed by it, has been contradicted or falsified by ancient learning or science, or by modern discoveries and inventions. It has eminently held its own and proved equal to the exigencies of time in every age and period.

2302. Life is a very serious thing. Man has been created to serve a very noble and grand purpose. But men of frivolous turn of mind fritter away their precious time and energy in vain pursuits and foolish diversions (23 : 116).

10. Wherein they will abide. Allāh has *made* a true promise; and He is the Mighty, the Wise.

خٰلِدِيْنَ فِيْهَا ۭ وَعْدَ اللّٰهِ حَقًّا ۭ وَهُوَ الْعَزِيْزُ الْحَكِيْمُ ﴿١٠﴾

11. [a]He has created the heavens without any pillars that you can see, and [b]He has placed[2303] in the earth firm mountains that it may not quake with you, and He has spread therein all kinds of creatures; and We have sent down water from the clouds, and have [c]caused to grow therein of every fine species.

خَلَقَ السَّمٰوٰتِ بِغَيْرِ عَمَدٍ تَرَوْنَهَا وَاَلْقٰى فِي الْاَرْضِ
رَوَاسِيَ اَنْ تَمِيْدَ بِكُمْ وَبَثَّ فِيْهَا مِنْ كُلِّ دَاۗبَّةٍ ۭ
وَاَنْزَلْنَا مِنَ السَّمَاۗءِ مَاۗءً فَاَنْۢبَتْنَا فِيْهَا مِنْ كُلِّ زَوْجٍ
كَرِيْمٍ ﴿١١﴾

12. This is the creation of Allāh. Now show me what others beside Him have created. Nay, but the wrongdoers are in manifest error.

هٰذَا خَلْقُ اللّٰهِ فَاَرُوْنِيْ مَاذَا خَلَقَ الَّذِيْنَ مِنْ دُوْنِهٖ ۭ
بَلِ الظّٰلِمُوْنَ فِيْ ضَلٰلٍ مُّبِيْنٍ ﴿١٢﴾ ع

R. 2 13. And We bestowed wisdom on Luqmān *and said*, 'Be grateful to Allāh,' for, whoso is grateful, is grateful for *the good of* his own soul. And whoso is ungrateful, then, surely, Allāh is Self-Sufficient, Praiseworthy.

وَلَقَدْ اٰتَيْنَا لُقْمٰنَ الْحِكْمَةَ اَنِ اشْكُرْ لِلّٰهِ ۭ وَمَنْ
يَّشْكُرْ فَاِنَّمَا يَشْكُرُ لِنَفْسِهٖ ۚ وَمَنْ كَفَرَ فَاِنَّ اللّٰهَ غَنِيٌّ
حَمِيْدٌ ﴿١٣﴾

14. And *call to mind* when Luqmān[2304] said to his son while he admonished him, 'O my dear son! associate not partners with Allāh. Surely, associating partners *with Allāh* is a grievous wrong.[2305]

وَاِذْ قَالَ لُقْمٰنُ لِابْنِهٖ وَهُوَ يَعِظُهٗ يٰبُنَيَّ لَا تُشْرِكْ
بِاللّٰهِ ۭ اِنَّ الشِّرْكَ لَظُلْمٌ عَظِيْمٌ ﴿١٤﴾

[a]13 : 3. [b]13 : 4; 15 : 20; 16 : 16; 77 : 28. [c]27 : 61; 50 : 8.

2303. Elsewhere (13 : 4) the Qur'ān has used the word *Ja'ala* (He has made) to express the sense of *Alqā* (He has placed) which shows that mountains formed a part of the earth and were not placed on it from outside.

2304. Luqmān seems to be a non-Arab, very probably an Ethiopian. He is said to belong to Egypt or Nubia. By some he has also been identified with the Greek "Aesop." From the beautiful moral precepts he gave to his son and which are embodied in the present and the next few verses, Luqmān appears to be a Prophet of God.

2305. The first and basic principle of all religious teaching is that God is One. All noble ideals and principles flow from this doctrine. By worshipping any other thing or being beside Allāh man degrades himself and stunts, stifles and stultifies his personality.

15. [a]And We have enjoined on man *to be good to* his parents[2306]—his mother bears him in weakness upon weakness, and his weaning takes two years[2306A]—*and said*, 'Give thanks to Me and to thy parents. Unto Me is the *final* return ;

وَوَصَّيْنَا الْإِنْسَانَ بِوَالِدَيْهِ ۚ حَمَلَتْهُ أُمُّهُ وَهْنًا
عَلٰى وَهْنٍ وَّفِصٰلُهُ فِيْ عَامَيْنِ اَنِ اشْكُرْ لِيْ وَلِوَالِدَيْكَ ؕ
اِلَيَّ الْمَصِيْرُ ﴿١٥﴾

16. 'And if they contend with thee to make thee set up equals with Me concerning which thou hast no knowledge, obey them not, but be a kind companion to them in worldly affairs,[2307] and *in spiritual matters* follow the way of him who turns to Me. Then unto Me will be your return and I shall inform you of what you used to do ;

وَاِنْ جَاهَدٰكَ عَلٰٓى اَنْ تُشْرِكَ بِيْ مَا لَيْسَ لَكَ بِهٖ
عِلْمٌ ۙ فَلَا تُطِعْهُمَا وَصَاحِبْهُمَا فِي الدُّنْيَا مَعْرُوْفًا ؗ
وَّاتَّبِعْ سَبِيْلَ مَنْ اَنَابَ اِلَيَّ ۚ ثُمَّ اِلَيَّ مَرْجِعُكُمْ
فَاُنَبِّئُكُمْ بِمَا كُنْتُمْ تَعْمَلُوْنَ ﴿١٦﴾

17. 'O my dear son, even though it be the weight of a grain of mustard seed, and even though it be in a rock, or in the heavens, or in the earth, Allāh will, surely, bring it out.[2308] Verily, Allāh is the Knower of the most hidden secrets, *and is* All-Aware ;

يٰبُنَيَّ اِنَّهَآ اِنْ تَكُ مِثْقَالَ حَبَّةٍ مِّنْ خَرْدَلٍ فَتَكُنْ فِيْ
صَخْرَةٍ اَوْ فِي السَّمٰوٰتِ اَوْ فِي الْاَرْضِ يَاْتِ بِهَا اللّٰهُ ؕ
اِنَّ اللّٰهَ لَطِيْفٌ خَبِيْرٌ ﴿١٧﴾

18. 'O my dear son, observe Prayer and enjoin good and forbid evil and endure patiently whatever may befall thee. Surely, this is of those matters *which require* high resolve ;

يٰبُنَيَّ اَقِمِ الصَّلٰوةَ وَاْمُرْ بِالْمَعْرُوْفِ وَانْهَ عَنِ الْمُنْكَرِ
وَاصْبِرْ عَلٰى مَآ اَصَابَكَ ؕ اِنَّ ذٰلِكَ مِنْ عَزْمِ الْاُمُوْرِ ﴿١٨﴾

[a]6 : 152; 29 : 9; 46 : 16.

2306. This and the next verse form a parenthetical clause and refer to the second most important duty of man after his duty to God—his obligations to his fellow-beings which begin with his obligations to his parents.

2306A. The apparent contradiction between this and 46 : 16 seems to be that some children are born earlier than others and, therefore, being weaker in constitution, take longer time to be weaned.

2307. If man's duty to parents appears to clash and conflict with his duty to God, his first loyalty is to his Creator. But in disregarding any of the wishes or commands of his parents which clash with his loyalty to God he must not be arrogant or insolent to them; but should continue to show uniform courtesy, love and kindness to them.

2308. No action, good or bad, goes vain. It leaves its permanent imprint. It is to this great truth that reference has also been made in 50 : 19.

19. 'And turn not thy cheek away from men in scorn,[2309] [a]nor walk in the earth haughtily; surely, Allāh loves not any arrogant boaster;

وَلَا تُصَعِّرْ خَدَّكَ لِلنَّاسِ وَلَا تَمْشِ فِي الْأَرْضِ مَرَحًا ۖ
إِنَّ اللَّهَ لَا يُحِبُّ كُلَّ مُخْتَالٍ فَخُورٍ ﴿١٩﴾

20. 'And walk thou at a moderate pace, and lower thy voice; verily, the most hateful of voices is the braying of the ass.'

وَاقْصِدْ فِي مَشْيِكَ وَاغْضُضْ مِنْ صَوْتِكَ ۚ إِنَّ
أَنكَرَ الْأَصْوَاتِ لَصَوْتُ الْحَمِيرِ ﴿٢٠﴾

R. 3 21. Do you not see that Allāh has pressed for you into service whatever is in the heavens and whatever is in the earth, and has completed His favours on you, *both* visible and invisible?[2310] And among men there are some who [b]dispute concerning Allāh, without knowledge or guidance or an illuminating Book.[2311]

أَلَمْ تَرَوْا أَنَّ اللَّهَ سَخَّرَ لَكُم مَّا فِي السَّمَاوَاتِ وَمَا فِي
الْأَرْضِ وَأَسْبَغَ عَلَيْكُمْ نِعَمَهُ ظَاهِرَةً وَبَاطِنَةً ۗ وَ
مِنَ النَّاسِ مَن يُجَادِلُ فِي اللَّهِ بِغَيْرِ عِلْمٍ وَلَا هُدًى
وَلَا كِتَابٍ مُّنِيرٍ ﴿٢١﴾

22. And when it is said to them, 'Follow that which Allāh has revealed', [c]they say, 'Nay, we shall follow that which we found our fathers following.'[2312] What! even though Satan was inviting them to the punishment of the burning fire?

وَإِذَا قِيلَ لَهُمُ اتَّبِعُوا مَا أَنزَلَ اللَّهُ قَالُوا بَلْ نَتَّبِعُ
مَا وَجَدْنَا عَلَيْهِ آبَاءَنَا ۚ أَوَلَوْ كَانَ الشَّيْطَانُ
يَدْعُوهُمْ إِلَىٰ عَذَابِ السَّعِيرِ ﴿٢٢﴾

23. [d]And he who submits himself *wholly* to Allāh, and is a doer of good, he has, surely, grasped a firm handle. With Allāh *rests* the end of all affairs.[2313]

وَمَن يُسْلِمْ وَجْهَهُ إِلَى اللَّهِ وَهُوَ مُحْسِنٌ فَقَدِ
اسْتَمْسَكَ بِالْعُرْوَةِ الْوُثْقَىٰ ۗ وَإِلَى اللَّهِ عَاقِبَةُ
الْأُمُورِ ﴿٢٣﴾

[a]17 : 38; 25 : 64. [b]13 : 14; 22 : 4, 9. [c]5 : 105; 10 : 79; 21 : 54. [d]2 : 113.

2309. *Ṣa'aara Khadda-hū* means, he turned away his cheek from the people on account of pride or contempt (Lane).

2310. The words may signify all needs of man—physical and spiritual; material and intellectual; known and unknown.

2311. The combined testimony of human reason and commonsense, of observation and experience and of Divine revelation, goes to show that belief in plurality of gods is a false and foolish belief. This is the significance of the words, *without knowledge or guidance or an illuminating Book*.

2312. Man is so constituted that he is not easily persuaded to give up his old ideas and beliefs. The one constant obstacle that the Prophets of God have had to meet from disbelievers is that the latter would not give up their old ancestral ways and beliefs. Old superstitions indeed die hard.

2313. God alone causes all actions to produce their results.

24. And *as for* him [a]who disbelieves, let not his disbelief grieve thee. Unto Us is their return and We shall tell them that which they did. Surely, Allāh knows full well what is in the breasts.

وَمَنْ كَفَرَ فَلَا يَحْزُنْكَ كُفْرُهُ ۚ إِلَيْنَا مَرْجِعُهُمْ فَنُنَبِّئُهُمْ
بِمَا عَمِلُوا ۚ إِنَّ اللّٰهَ عَلِيمٌ بِذَاتِ الصُّدُورِ ﴿٢٤﴾

25. We shall let them enjoy themselves for a while; then shall We drive them to a severe torment.

نُمَتِّعُهُمْ قَلِيلًا ثُمَّ نَضْطَرُّهُمْ إِلَىٰ عَذَابٍ غَلِيظٍ ﴿٢٥﴾

26. [b]And if thou ask them, 'Who created the heavens and the earth?' they will, surely, answer, 'Allāh.'[2314] Say, 'All praise belongs to Allāh.' But most of them have no knowledge.

وَلَئِنْ سَأَلْتَهُمْ مَنْ خَلَقَ السَّمٰوٰتِ وَالْأَرْضَ لَيَقُولُنَّ
اللّٰهُ ۚ قُلِ الْحَمْدُ لِلّٰهِ ۚ بَلْ أَكْثَرُهُمْ لَا يَعْلَمُونَ ﴿٢٦﴾

27. [c]To Allāh belongs whatever is in the heavens and the earth. Verily, Allāh is Self-Sufficient, Praiseworthy.

لِلّٰهِ مَا فِي السَّمٰوٰتِ وَالْأَرْضِ ۚ إِنَّ اللّٰهَ هُوَ الْغَنِيُّ
الْحَمِيدُ ﴿٢٧﴾

28. [d]And if all the trees that are in the earth were pens, and the ocean—seven[2315] more oceans to replenish it—*were ink*, the words of Allāh would not be exhausted. Surely, Allāh is Mighty, Wise.

وَلَوْ أَنَّ مَا فِي الْأَرْضِ مِنْ شَجَرَةٍ أَقْلَامٌ وَالْبَحْرُ
يَمُدُّهُ مِنْ بَعْدِهِ سَبْعَةُ أَبْحُرٍ مَا نَفِدَتْ كَلِمٰتُ
اللّٰهِ ۗ إِنَّ اللّٰهَ عَزِيزٌ حَكِيمٌ ﴿٢٨﴾

29. Your creation and your resurrection are only like *the creation and resurrection of* a single soul.[2315A] Verily, Allāh is All-Hearing, All Seeing.

مَا خَلْقُكُمْ وَلَا بَعْثُكُمْ إِلَّا كَنَفْسٍ وَاحِدَةٍ ۗ إِنَّ اللّٰهَ
سَمِيعٌ بَصِيرٌ ﴿٢٩﴾

[a]3 : 177. [b]29 : 62; 39 : 39 [c]2 : 285; 10 : 56; 24 : 65. [d]18 : 110.

2314. An intelligent study of the creation of the universe and of the perfect design and order that pervade and permeate it, leads to the one inescapable inference that there must be a Creator of this universe. The expression *la-Yaqūlunna* signifies that disbelievers will have no option but to admit that it is Allāh Who has brought the universe into being.

2315. Numbers "7" and "70" are used in Arabic to denote a large number, and not exactly "seven" and "seventy" as ordinary numerals.

2315A. The verse signifies that all human beings are subject to the same laws of nature. It also points to the fact that the rise or fall of nations and communities is subject to the same laws of nature as is the progress or degradation of individuals.

30. Seest thou not that [a]Allāh makes the night pass into[2316] the day and makes the day pass into the night, and [b]He has pressed the sun and the moon into service; each pursuing its course till an appointed term, and that Allāh is Well-Aware of what you do?

اَلَمْ تَرَ اَنَّ اللّٰهَ يُوْلِجُ الَّيْلَ فِي النَّهَارِ وَيُوْلِجُ النَّهَارَ
فِي الَّيْلِ وَسَخَّرَ الشَّمْسَ وَالْقَمَرَ ۡ كُلٌّ يَّجْرِيْٓ اِلٰٓى اَجَلٍ
مُّسَمًّى وَّاَنَّ اللّٰهَ بِمَا تَعْمَلُوْنَ خَبِيْرٌ ۝٣١

31. That is because it is Allāh alone Who is the True *God*, and whatever they call upon beside Him is false, and because it is Allāh alone Who is the Most High, the Incomparably Great.

ذٰلِكَ بِاَنَّ اللّٰهَ هُوَ الْحَقُّ وَاَنَّ مَا يَدْعُوْنَ مِنْ دُوْنِهِ
الْبَاطِلُ ۙ وَاَنَّ اللّٰهَ هُوَ الْعَلِيُّ الْكَبِيْرُ ۝٣٢ ع

R. 4 32. Dost thou not see that [c]the ships sail on the sea by the favour of Allāh,[2317] that He may show you of His Signs? Therein, surely, are Signs for every patient and grateful person.

اَلَمْ تَرَ اَنَّ الْفُلْكَ تَجْرِيْ فِي الْبَحْرِ بِنِعْمَتِ اللّٰهِ لِيُرِيَكُمْ
مِّنْ اٰيٰتِهٖ ۭ اِنَّ فِيْ ذٰلِكَ لَاٰيٰتٍ لِّكُلِّ صَبَّارٍ شَكُوْرٍ ۝٣٣

33. And when waves engulf them like *so many* coverings, [d]they call upon Allāh, in full sincerity of faith; but when [e]He brings them safe to land, then some of them keep to the right course.[2318] And none denies Our Signs save every perfidious, ungrateful *person*.

وَاِذَا غَشِيَهُمْ مَّوْجٌ كَالظُّلَلِ دَعَوُا اللّٰهَ مُخْلِصِيْنَ
لَهُ الدِّيْنَ ۥ فَلَمَّا نَجّٰىهُمْ اِلَى الْبَرِّ فَمِنْهُمْ مُّقْتَصِدٌ ۭ
وَمَا يَجْحَدُ بِاٰيٰتِنَآ اِلَّا كُلُّ خَتَّارٍ كَفُوْرٍ ۝٣٤

[a]22 : 62; 35 : 14; 57 : 7. [b]7 : 55; 13 : 3; 35 : 14; 39 : 6. [c]17 : 67; 30 : 47; 45 : 13. [d]10 : 23; 17 : 68; 29 : 66. [e]10 : 24; 17 : 68.

2316. The natural law of the day following the night, and *vice versa*, operates with equal force in regard to the fate of nations as well as individuals.

2317. The sailing of ships is indeed a great Divine boon. Much of the prosperity of mankind depends on it. The greatest sea-power is generally the richest and the most powerful country in the world.

2318. The verse refers to a very common characteristic of a *Mushrik* (polytheist). He is weak of faith and is very superstitious. Even a small misfortune is sufficient to frighten and upset him because his faith is only a jumble of make-beliefs and hearsays and superstitions.

34. O men, seek protection with your Lord and fear [a]the day when the father will not be of any avail to his child, nor will the child at all be of any avail to his father. Allāh's promise is, surely, true. So let not worldly life beguile you, nor let the Deceiver deceive you concerning Allāh.

يٰۤاَيُّهَا النَّاسُ اتَّقُوْا رَبَّكُمْ وَاخْشَوْا يَوْمًا لَّا يَجْزِيْ
وَالِدٌ عَنْ وَّلَدِهٖ ۘ وَلَا مَوْلُوْدٌ هُوَ جَازٍ عَنْ وَّالِدِهٖ
شَيْـًٔا ؕ اِنَّ وَعْدَ اللّٰهِ حَقٌّ فَلَا تَغُرَّنَّكُمُ الْحَيٰوةُ الدُّنْيَا ٝ
وَلَا يَغُرَّنَّكُمْ بِاللّٰهِ الْغَرُوْرُ ﴿٣٤﴾

35. Verily, with Allāh alone is the knowledge of the Hour. [b]And He sends down the rain, and He knows what is in the wombs. And no soul knows what it will earn tomorrow, and no soul knows in what land it will die. Surely, Allāh is All-Knowing, All-Aware.[2319]

اِنَّ اللّٰهَ عِنْدَهٗ عِلْمُ السَّاعَةِ ۚ وَيُنَزِّلُ الْغَيْثَ ۚ وَيَعْلَمُ
مَا فِي الْاَرْحَامِ ؕ وَمَا تَدْرِيْ نَفْسٌ مَّاذَا تَكْسِبُ غَدًا ؕ
وَمَا تَدْرِيْ نَفْسٌ بِاَيِّ اَرْضٍ تَمُوْتُ ؕ اِنَّ اللّٰهَ عَلِيْمٌ
خَبِيْرٌ ﴿٣٥﴾ ع

[a]2 : 124; 82 : 20. [b]30 : 25; 42 : 29.

2319. The *Sūrah* ends by reverting to its basic theme—the ultimate triumph of Islām; and mentions some important facts concerning it : (1) With God alone rests the knowledge of the hour of the final overthrow of disbelief and the triumph of Islām. (2) He alone knows when the condition of a people demands the sending down of Divine revelation and so He has revealed the Qur'ān in the fulness of time. (3) To Him alone belongs the knowledge whether the generations yet unborn will accept Islām or stick to disbelief, *i.e.*, whether the sons and grandsons of the leaders of disbelief, who are now fighting Islām tooth and nail, will enter its fold and will willingly give their lives to safeguard it and further its cause. (4) The disbelievers do not know that all their efforts against Islām will prove futile and abortive. (5) The leaders of disbelief, who have turned the Holy Prophet and Muslims out of their hearths and homes, will themselves meet death away from their homes.

CHAPTER 32

AL-SAJDAH

(Revealed before Hijrah)

Date of Revelation and Context

This *Sūrah* was also revealed at Mecca. The preceding *Sūrah* had ended with the statement that God alone knows when a particular people are to rise or fall and that He alone provides for the physical needs of man and for his moral and spiritual requirements. The present *Sūrah* opens with the declaration that God being the Lord of all the worlds, in His hands lie all those means upon which the progress and prosperity of nations and individuals depend and He alone controls those causes that lead to their decline and downfall.

Subject-Matter

The main theme of the *Sūrah* is the ultimate triumph of Islām. It opens with a strong repudiation of the disbelievers' charge that the Qur'ān is a forgery and the Holy Prophet an impostor. The Prophet, it says, is not an impostor because impostors never succeed in their missions, but the cause of the Holy Prophet is daily advancing by leaps and bounds; neither is the Qur'ān a forgery because it has been revealed in the fulness of time and in accordance with the demands of truth and justice and fulfils all the moral and spiritual needs and requirements of man and because also the whole universe seems to be working in support and furtherance of its Message. The *Sūrah* then makes a little digression and makes a prophecy that after its initial phenomenal progress Islām will receive a temporary set-back; a comparative eclipse of a thousand years which will be followed by a second renaissance, as a result of which it will regain its pristine glory and will march on its course of uniform success. Next, the *Sūrah* gives a beautiful illustration how from a very insignificant beginning Islām will grow in strength, expand and spread and will become a mighty force. The illustration is taken from the insignificant birth of man from mere clay. Towards its close the *Sūrah* sums up its central theme and adds that the advent of the Holy Prophet is not anything novel. Just as in the physical world when the earth becomes parched and scorched God sends down rain and it begins to vibrate with a new life, in the same way in the spiritual realm, when mankind gropes and flounders in spiritual darkness, a Divine Messenger is raised and the spiritually dead receive a new life through him.

سُوۡرَةُ السَّجۡدَةِ مَكِّيَّةٌ (٣٢)

1. [a]In the name of Allāh, the Gracious, the Merciful.

بِسۡمِ اللّٰهِ الرَّحۡمٰنِ الرَّحِيۡمِ ۝١

2. [b]Alif Lām Mīm.

الٓمّٓ ۝٢

3. [c]The revelation of the Book—there is no doubt about it—is from the Lord of the worlds.

تَنۡزِيۡلُ الۡكِتٰبِ لَا رَيۡبَ فِيۡهِ مِنۡ رَّبِّ الۡعٰلَمِيۡنَ ؕ ۝٣

4. Do they say, 'He has forged it?' Nay, it is the truth from thy Lord, [d]that thou mayest warn a people to whom no Warner has come before thee, that they may be guided.[2320]

اَمۡ يَقُوۡلُوۡنَ افۡتَرٰٮهُ ۚ بَلۡ هُوَ الۡحَـقُّ مِنۡ رَّبِّكَ لِتُنۡذِرَ
قَوۡمًا مَّاۤ اَتٰٮهُمۡ مِّنۡ نَّذِيۡرٍ مِّنۡ قَبۡلِكَ لَعَلَّهُمۡ يَهۡتَدُوۡنَ ۝٤

5. [e]Allāh is He Who created the heavens and the earth, and that which is between them, in six periods,[2321] then He settled *Himself* on the Throne.[2322] You have no helper or intercessor beside Him. Will you not then reflect?

اَللّٰهُ الَّذِىۡ خَلَقَ السَّمٰوٰتِ وَالۡاَرۡضَ وَمَا بَيۡنَهُمَا فِىۡ
سِتَّةِ اَيَّامٍ ثُمَّ اسۡتَوٰى عَلَى الۡعَرۡشِ ؕ مَا لَـكُمۡ مِّنۡ دُوۡنِهٖ
مِنۡ وَّلِىٍّ وَّلَا شَفِيۡعٍ ؕ اَفَلَا تَتَذَكَّرُوۡنَ ۝٥

6. He will plan *His* Ordinance from the heaven unto the earth, then will it go up to Him in a day the duration of which is a thousand years according as you reckon.[2323]

يُدَبِّرُ الۡاَمۡرَ مِنَ السَّمَآءِ اِلَى الۡاَرۡضِ ثُمَّ يَعۡرُجُ اِلَيۡهِ فِىۡ يَوۡمٍ
كَانَ مِقۡدَارُهٗۤ اَلۡفَ سَنَةٍ مِّمَّا تَعُدُّوۡنَ ۝٦

---

[a]1 : 1. [b]30 : 2. [c]20 : 5; 40 : 3; 46 : 3. [d]28 : 47; 36 : 7. [e]7 : 55; 11 : 8; 25 : 60.

2320. The *Sūrah* is the last of the *Alif Lām Mīm* group. The central theme of these four Chapters (29-32) is the regeneration of a people who had sunk deep in the morass of moral turpitude and who were now going to be raised to the apex of spiritual glory through the Holy Prophet Muḥammad. This awakening to new life of a morally dead people has been adduced as an argument in support of Resurrection and the Hereafter. In all these Chapters this subject has been introduced with reference to the creation of the universe.

2321. See 894.

2322. See 54.

2323. The verse refers to a very serious crisis that was destined to come over Islām in its chequered career. Islām was to pass through a period of sustained progress and prosperity during the first three centuries of its life. The Holy Prophet is reported to have pointedly alluded to this fact in his saying: 'The best century is the one in which I live, then the next century, then the century after that (Tirmidhī & Bukhārī, *Kitāb al-Shahādāt*). Islām began to decline after the first three centuries of uninterrupted conquests. The process

7. [a]Such is the Knower of the unseen and the seen, the Mighty, the Merciful;

ذٰلِكَ عٰلِمُ الْغَيْبِ وَالشَّهَادَةِ الْعَزِيْزُ الرَّحِيْمُ ⑦

8. Who has made perfect everything He has created. [b]And He began the creation of man from clay;

الَّذِيْٓ اَحْسَنَ كُلَّ شَيْءٍ خَلَقَهٗ وَبَدَاَ خَلْقَ الْاِنْسَانِ مِنْ طِيْنٍ ⑧

9. Then He made his progeny from an extract of [c]an insignificant fluid ;

ثُمَّ جَعَلَ نَسْلَهٗ مِنْ سُلٰلَةٍ مِّنْ مَّآءٍ مَّهِيْنٍ ⑨

10. [d]Then He endowed him with perfect faculties and breathed into him of His spirit.[2324] And He has given you ears, and eyes, and hearts. *But* little thanks do you give !

ثُمَّ سَوّٰىهُ وَنَفَخَ فِيْهِ مِنْ رُّوْحِهٖ وَجَعَلَ لَكُمُ السَّمْعَ وَالْاَبْصَارَ وَالْاَفْـِٕدَةَ ۭ قَلِيْلًا مَّا تَشْكُرُوْنَ ⑩

11. And they say, 'What ! when we are lost in the earth, shall we then be *raised up in the form of* a new creation?' Nay, [e]but they disbelieve in the meeting with their Lord.

وَقَالُوْٓا ءَاِذَا ضَلَلْنَا فِي الْاَرْضِ ءَاِنَّا لَفِيْ خَلْقٍ جَدِيْدٍ ۬ بَلْ هُمْ بِلِقَآئِ رَبِّهِمْ كٰفِرُوْنَ ⑪

12. Say, 'The angel of death that has been put in charge of you will cause you to die; then to your Lord will you be brought back.'

قُلْ يَتَوَفّٰىكُمْ مَّلَكُ الْمَوْتِ الَّذِيْ وُكِّلَ بِكُمْ ثُمَّ اِلٰى رَبِّكُمْ تُرْجَعُوْنَ ⑫

R. 2 13. If only thou couldst see when the guilty ones will hang down their heads before their Lord, *and say*, 'Our Lord, we have seen and we have heard, so [f]send us back that we may do good works; for *now* we are convinced *of the truth of what we were told*'

وَلَوْ تَرٰٓى اِذِ الْمُجْرِمُوْنَ نَاكِسُوْا رُءُوْسِهِمْ عِنْدَ رَبِّهِمْ ۭ رَبَّنَآ اَبْصَرْنَا وَسَمِعْنَا فَارْجِعْنَا نَعْمَلْ صَالِحًا اِنَّا مُوْقِنُوْنَ ⑬

[a]34 : 4; 59 : 23. [b]6 : 3; 15 : 27; 37 : 12. [c]77 : 21. [d]15 : 30; 38 : 73. [e]18 : 106; 29 : 24; 30 : 17. [f]23 : 100, 101; 35 : 38; 39 : 59.

of decline and decay continued in the next thousand years. It is to this period of a thousand years that reference has been made in the words, *then will it go up to Him in a day the duration of which is a thousand years*. In another of his sayings the Holy Prophet is reported to have said that Faith will ascend to the Pleiades and a man of Persian descent will bring it back to the earth (Bukhārī, *Kitab al-Tafsīr*). With the appearance of the Promised Messiah in the 14th century A.H., the process of decay has been arrested and renaissance of Islām has begun to take place.

2324. *Rūḥ* meaning, human soul and Divine revelation (Lane), the verse signifies that after the physical development of the embryo becomes complete in the womb, it develops a soul; or the meaning may be that after the spiritual development of man becomes complete he receives Divine revelation.

14. And if We had *enforced* Our will, We could have given every soul its *appropriate* guidance, but the word from Me has come true that [a]'I will fill Hell with jinn and men all together.[2325]

وَلَوْ شِئْنَا لَآتَيْنَا كُلَّ نَفْسٍ هُدٰىهَا وَلٰكِنْ حَقَّ الْقَوْلُ مِنِّيْ لَأَمْلَئَنَّ جَهَنَّمَ مِنَ الْجِنَّةِ وَالنَّاسِ أَجْمَعِيْنَ ﴿١٤﴾

15. So taste ye *the punishment of your evil deeds*, for you forgot the meeting of this day of yours. We, *too*, have forgotten you. Taste ye then the lasting punishment because of that which you used to do.

فَذُوْقُوْا بِمَا نَسِيْتُمْ لِقَآءَ يَوْمِكُمْ هٰذَا إِنَّا نَسِيْنٰكُمْ وَذُوْقُوْا عَذَابَ الْخُلْدِ بِمَا كُنْتُمْ تَعْمَلُوْنَ ﴿١٥﴾

16. Only those *really* believe in Our Signs who, when they are reminded of them, [b]fall down prostrate and celebrate the praises of their Lord, and they are not proud.

إِنَّمَا يُؤْمِنُ بِاٰيٰتِنَا الَّذِيْنَ إِذَا ذُكِّرُوْا بِهَا خَرُّوْا سُجَّدًا وَّسَبَّحُوْا بِحَمْدِ رَبِّهِمْ وَهُمْ لَا يَسْتَكْبِرُوْنَ ﴿١٦﴾ السجدة

17. Their sides keep away from their beds; *and* [c]they call on their Lord in fear and hope, and spend out of what We have bestowed on them.

تَتَجَافٰى جُنُوْبُهُمْ عَنِ الْمَضَاجِعِ يَدْعُوْنَ رَبَّهُمْ خَوْفًا وَّطَمَعًا وَّمِمَّا رَزَقْنٰهُمْ يُنْفِقُوْنَ ﴿١٧﴾

18. And no soul knows what joy of the eyes is kept hidden for them, as a reward for *the good* they used to do.[2326]

فَلَا تَعْلَمُ نَفْسٌ مَّآ أُخْفِيَ لَهُمْ مِّنْ قُرَّةِ أَعْيُنٍ جَزَآءً بِمَا كَانُوْا يَعْمَلُوْنَ ﴿١٨﴾

19. [d]Is he, then, who is a believer like one who is disobedient? They are not equal.

أَفَمَنْ كَانَ مُؤْمِنًا كَمَنْ كَانَ فَاسِقًا لَا يَسْتَوٗنَ ﴿١٩﴾

[a]11 : 120; 15 : 44; 38 : 86. [b]17 : 108, 110; 19 : 59. [c]21 : 91. [d]40 : 59.

2325. The reference in these words is to 15 : 43-44 where it is stated, 'Such of the erring ones as choose to follow thee, surely, Hell is the promised place for them,' meaning thereby that only the 'erring ones,' will be cast into Hell.

2326. Describing the form and nature of the blessings and comforts of Paradise the Holy Prophet is reported to have said : 'No eye has yet seen them (the blessings of Paradise), nor has any ear heard of them, nor can human mind conceive of them' (Bukhārī, *Kitāb Bad'al-Khalq*). The *hadīth* shows that the blessings of the life to come will not be material. They will be the spiritual representations of good deeds and actions the righteous believers might have done in the present life. The words used to describe them in the Qur'ān have been used only in a metaphorical sense. The present verse may also mean that Divine boons and blessings that will be bestowed upon the righteous believers in the next world are far too good and too plentiful, even to be imagined or conceived of. They will be far beyond the widest stretch of human imagination.

20. As for those [a]who believe and do good works, they will have Gardens of Eternal Abode as an entertainment *in return* for what they used to do.

أَمَّا الَّذِينَ آمَنُوا وَعَمِلُوا الصّٰلِحٰتِ فَلَهُمْ جَنّٰتُ الْمَأْوٰى نُزُلًا بِمَا كَانُوا يَعْمَلُونَ ﴿٢٠﴾

21. And as for those who are disobedient, their abode will be the Fire. [b]Every time they desire to come out of it, they will be turned back into it, and it will be said to them, 'Taste ye the punishment of the Fire which you used to deny.'

وَأَمَّا الَّذِينَ فَسَقُوا فَمَأْوٰىهُمُ النَّارُ ۖ كُلَّمَا أَرَادُوا أَنْ يَخْرُجُوا مِنْهَا أُعِيدُوا فِيهَا وَقِيلَ لَهُمْ ذُوقُوا عَذَابَ النَّارِ الَّذِي كُنْتُمْ بِهِ تُكَذِّبُونَ ﴿٢١﴾

22. And most surely [c]We will make them taste of the lesser punishment before the greater punishment,[2327] that they may return *to Us with repentance.*

وَلَنُذِيقَنَّهُمْ مِنَ الْعَذَابِ الْأَدْنٰى دُونَ الْعَذَابِ الْأَكْبَرِ لَعَلَّهُمْ يَرْجِعُونَ ﴿٢٢﴾

23. And who is more unjust than he who is reminded of the Signs of his Lord and then turns away from them? We will, surely, exact retribution from the guilty.

وَمَنْ أَظْلَمُ مِمَّنْ ذُكِّرَ بِاٰيٰتِ رَبِّهِ ثُمَّ أَعْرَضَ عَنْهَا ۚ إِنَّا مِنَ الْمُجْرِمِينَ مُنْتَقِمُونَ ﴿٢٣﴾

R. 3 24. [d]And We indeed gave Moses the Book—be not, therefore, in doubt about receiving *a perfect Book thyself*—and We made it a guidance for the Children of Israel.

وَلَقَدْ اٰتَيْنَا مُوسَى الْكِتٰبَ فَلَا تَكُنْ فِي مِرْيَةٍ مِنْ لِقَائِهِ وَجَعَلْنٰهُ هُدًى لِبَنِي إِسْرَاءِيلَ ﴿٢٤﴾

25. [e]And We appointed from among them leaders, who guided *the people* by Our command, because they were steadfast and had firm faith in Our Signs.

وَجَعَلْنَا مِنْهُمْ أَئِمَّةً يَهْدُونَ بِأَمْرِنَا لَمَّا صَبَرُوا ۗ وَكَانُوا بِاٰيٰتِنَا يُوقِنُونَ ﴿٢٥﴾

[a]30 : 16; 35 : 8; 42 : 23; 45 : 31. [b]5 : 38; 22 : 23. [c]52 : 48.
[d]2 : 88; 17 : 3; 23 : 50. [e]21 : 74.

2327. 'The lesser punishment' and 'the greater punishment' may respectively signify, (1) afflictions of the present life and those of the Hereafter; (2) defeat of the Quraish in the Battle of Badr and Fall of Mecca; (3) smaller miseries and misfortunes which befall a disbelieving people by way of warning before their final destruction.

26. Verily, thy Lord—He will [a]judge between them on the Day of Resurrection concerning that in which they used to disagree.

إِنَّ رَبَّكَ هُوَ يَفْصِلُ بَيْنَهُمْ يَوْمَ الْقِيٰمَةِ فِيْمَا كَانُوْا فِيْهِ يَخْتَلِفُوْنَ ﴿٢٦﴾

27. Does it not furnish guidance to them how many a generation have We destroyed before them, amid whose dwellings they *now* walk about? In that, surely, are Signs. Will they not then listen?

أَوَلَمْ يَهْدِ لَهُمْ كَمْ أَهْلَكْنَا مِنْ قَبْلِهِمْ مِّنَ الْقُرُوْنِ يَمْشُوْنَ فِيْ مَسٰكِنِهِمْ ۭ إِنَّ فِيْ ذٰلِكَ لَاٰيٰتٍ ۭ أَفَلَا يَسْمَعُوْنَ ﴿٢٧﴾

28. Do they not see that We drive the water to the dry land and produce thereby [b]crops of which their cattle eat, and they themselves *also*? Will they not then see?

أَوَلَمْ يَرَوْا أَنَّا نَسُوْقُ الْمَآءَ إِلَى الْأَرْضِ الْجُرُزِ فَنُخْرِجُ بِهٖ زَرْعًا تَأْكُلُ مِنْهُ أَنْعَامُهُمْ وَأَنْفُسُهُمْ ۭ أَفَلَا يُبْصِرُوْنَ ﴿٢٨﴾

29. And they say, 'When will this victory come, if you are truthful?'

وَيَقُوْلُوْنَ مَتٰى هٰذَا الْفَتْحُ إِنْ كُنْتُمْ صٰدِقِيْنَ ﴿٢٩﴾

30. Say, 'On the day of victory[2328] the faith of the disbelievers shall not avail them, nor will they be respited.'

قُلْ يَوْمَ الْفَتْحِ لَا يَنْفَعُ الَّذِيْنَ كَفَرُوْٓا إِيْمَانُهُمْ وَلَا هُمْ يُنْظَرُوْنَ ﴿٣٠﴾

31. So turn away from them, and wait. They are also waiting.

فَأَعْرِضْ عَنْهُمْ وَانْتَظِرْ إِنَّهُمْ مُّنْتَظِرُوْنَ ﴿٣١﴾

[a]4 : 142; 22 : 70; 39 : 4. [b]10 : 25; 20 : 55; 25 : 50.

2328. **The day of the Battle of Badr which has also been called the Day of Decision (8 : 42).**

CHAPTER 33

AL-AḤZĀB

(*Revealed after Hijrah*)

Date of Revelation and Context

The *Sūrah* was revealed at Medina. It was revealed between the 5th and the 7th year of the *Hijrah*, possibly up to the 8th and the 9th year. There is sufficient internal evidence to establish this fact. In the preceding few Chapters the prophecy was repeatedly and emphatically made that Islām would continue to make progress and gather strength, till the whole of Arabia would accept its Message, and idolatry would disappear from the country, never to return. In the immediately preceding *Sūrah*—Al-Sajdah—it was stated that Muslims would be favoured with all sorts of physical comforts and material prosperity. Towards its end the disbelievers had tauntingly asked when the prophecy about the victory of Islām and its great spread and expansion would be fulfilled. That question has received an emphatic answer in the present *Sūrah*. It is stated that prophecy about the rise and progress of Islām has already been fulfilled and Islām has become a great power.

Subject-Matter

With the accession to Islām of great political power and prestige and with its emergence as a full-fledged State, the ordinances of the *Sharī'ah* began to be revealed in quick succession to guide Muslims in political and social matters. This *Sūrah* embodies several such ordinances. At the outset it abolishes a deep-rooted custom of the Arabs—the adoption of another person's son as one's own. Then it refers to a very deep and real spiritual relationship that subsists between the Holy Prophet and Muslims. In his capacity as their spiritual father he stands closer to them than even their own selves and his wives are their spiritual mothers. Next, the *Sūrah* gives a somewhat detailed description of the Battle of the Trench which was the fiercest encounter in which the Muslims had so far been engaged. The whole of Arabia had risen like one man against Islām and a well-equipped army, numbering from 10,000 to 20,000 strong, had marched on Medina. The Muslims were a paltry 1200, though according to some writers the total number of those employed in digging the Trench including women and children was in the neighbourhood of 3000. The combat was quite unequal. The Muslims were in sore straits. But God sent His hosts and the powerful enemy was routed and scattered. In the next few verses the *Sūrah* states that while in a religious community there is no dearth of sincere and devoted followers, there are also to be found in its ranks hypocrites and the weak of faith. These hypocrites loudly profess to be true followers but when in the Prophet's time Medina was attacked by a mighty force, they asked to be excused from fighting on the side of Muslims on very lame excuses. They broke their plighted word. The Banū Quraiẓah were the first to dishonour their pledge and to leave Muslims in the lurch when the latter were hemmed in on all sides and the very fate of Islām hung in the balance. After the Confederates dispersed, the Holy Prophet marched against them and they received deserved punishment.

As a result of the Battle of the Trench and of the subsequent banishment of the Banū Quraiẓah large booty fell into the hands of Muslims. From a persecuted and economically very poor minority they had grown into a rich, powerful and prosperous State. Material wealth brings in its train worldly-mindedness, a desire for ease and comfort and apathy towards service and sacrifice. This is a state of affairs which a Reformer has specially to guard against. Love of ease and comfort generally makes appearance first in the domestic circle, and as the members of the Holy Prophet's household were to serve as a model in social behaviour, it was in the fitness of things that they should have been required to set an example in self-denial. The Holy Prophet's wives were asked to make a choice between a life of comfort and ease and his simple and even austere companionship and they lost no time in making their choice. They preferred the Prophet's company. The wives of the Holy Prophet were particularly enjoined to set an example in piety and righteous conduct, as befitted the wives of the greatest of God's Prophets and in preserving the dignity and decorum of their exalted position, and by teaching Muslims the precepts and commandments of their religion. The *Sūrah*, then, makes a reference to Zainab's marriage with Zaid. The failure of this marriage and Zainab's subsequent marriage with the Holy Prophet served a double purpose. By giving in marriage Zainab, his own cousin and a full-blooded Arab lady, intensely proud of her ancestry and exalted social position, to a freed slave, the Holy Prophet had sought to level to the ground all those invidious class distinctions and divisions from which the Arabian society had suffered, as according to Islām all men were free and equal in the sight of God. Next, the *Sūrah* removes a possible misgiving to which the abolition of the custom of adoption might have given rise, *viz*., that in the absence of real sons the Holy Prophet will die issueless and his Movement will wither and die out for want of an heir. It says that it was God's own plan that the Prophet should have no male issue; but this did not mean that he would be issueless since he was the spiritual father of the whole of mankind. As practical proof of this claim he would bring into being a community of righteous and most loyal spiritual sons. The *Sūrah* further says that since the Holy Prophet is the spiritual father of the Faithful, his wives are their spiritual mothers, and therefore marriage with them, after the death of the Holy Prophet, is a grievous sin. The Holy Prophet himself is told that he is not to divorce anyone of his existing wives, nor to add to their number, and his wives are enjoined that, consistently with their dignity as "Mothers of the Faithful," they should observe certain rules regarding dress, etc. when going out. This injunction enjoining privacy and decorum applies equally to all Muslim women. Towards its close the *Sūrah* points to the very high destiny of man and to his great responsibilities as the crown of God's whole creation. He has been endowed with great powers and capabilities denied to other beings and, therefore, he alone among all creation can, by acting upon the laws of the *Sharī'ah*, imbibe and reflect in his person Divine attributes.

سُوْرَةُ الْاَحْزَابِ مَدَنِيَّةٌ (٣٣)

1. [a]In the name of Allāh the Gracious, the Merciful.

بِسْمِ اللّٰهِ الرَّحْمٰنِ الرَّحِيْمِ ۝١

2. O thou Prophet,[2329] seek protection in Allāh, and follow not *the wishes of* the disbelievers and the hypocrites. Verily, Allāh is All-Knowing, Wise.

يٰۤاَيُّهَا النَّبِيُّ اتَّقِ اللّٰهَ وَلَا تُطِعِ الْكٰفِرِيْنَ وَالْمُنٰفِقِيْنَ ؕ اِنَّ اللّٰهَ كَانَ عَلِيْمًا حَكِيْمًا ۝٢

3. [b]And follow that which is revealed to thee from thy Lord. Verily, Allāh is Well-Aware of what you do.

وَّاتَّبِعْ مَا يُوْحٰۤى اِلَيْكَ مِنْ رَّبِّكَ ؕ اِنَّ اللّٰهَ كَانَ بِمَا تَعْمَلُوْنَ خَبِيْرًا ۝٣

4. [c]And put thy trust in Allāh, and Allāh is sufficient as a Guardian.

وَّتَوَكَّلْ عَلَى اللّٰهِ ؕ وَكَفٰى بِاللّٰهِ وَكِيْلًا ۝٤

5. Allāh has not made for any man two hearts in his breast; nor has He made those of your wives from whom you keep away by calling them mothers,[2330] your mothers *in fact*, nor has He made those whom you[2331] adopt as sons, your sons *in fact*. These are *merely* the words of your mouths; but Allāh declares the truth, and He guides to the *right* path.

مَا جَعَلَ اللّٰهُ لِرَجُلٍ مِّنْ قَلْبَيْنِ فِيْ جَوْفِهٖ ۚ وَمَا جَعَلَ اَزْوَاجَكُمُ الّٰٓـِٔيْ تُظٰهِرُوْنَ مِنْهُنَّ اُمَّهٰتِكُمْ ۚ وَمَا جَعَلَ اَدْعِيَآءَكُمْ اَبْنَآءَكُمْ ؕ ذٰلِكُمْ قَوْلُكُمْ بِاَفْوَاهِكُمْ ؕ وَاللّٰهُ يَقُوْلُ الْحَقَّ وَهُوَ يَهْدِى السَّبِيْلَ ۝٥

---

[a]1 : 1. [b]10 : 110. [c]3 : 160; 26 : 218.

2329. The Holy Prophet has been addressed as *Al-Nabī* (The Prophet) in this verse and at several other places in the Qur'ān. No other Prophet in any revealed Scripture, or in the Qur'ān, has been addressed as such. All other Prophets have been addressed by their proper names. This peculiarity of address shows that the Holy Prophet is *Al-Nabī*, *i.e.*, the Prophet *par excellence*. Or, the reference in this form of address may be to a biblical Prophecy in which the advent of "that Prophet" has been foretold (John, 1 : 21, 25).

2330. *Ẓihār or Muẓāharah* means, separating oneself from one's wife, calling her mother (Lane).

2331. *Ad'iyā'* is plural of *da'iyy* which means, one who is claimed as a son by a person who is not his father; adopted son; one whose origin or lineage or parentage is doubted; one who attributes his descent to other than his father (Lane). The verse sought to abolish two very deep-rooted and widespread customs of the Arabs in the Holy Prophet's time. The more obnoxious of these two was that of *Ẓihār*. A husband, in a fit of anger, would call his wife his mother. The poor woman was deprived of her conjugal rights and yet remained tied to him without the right of marrying another man. Islām, a great champion of women's rights, could not tolerate such a savage custom. The other custom was that of adopting the son of another man as one's own. This custom, apart from being calculated to cause

6. Call them after their fathers. That is more equitable in the sight of Allāh. But if you know not their fathers, then they are your brothers in Faith and your friends. And there is no blame on you *in respect of* any mistake you may unintentionally make *in this matter;* but *you will be called to account for* that which your hearts purpose. And Allāh is Most Forgiving, Ever Merciful.

ادْعُوهُمْ لِآبَائِهِمْ هُوَ أَقْسَطُ عِنْدَ اللّٰهِ ۚ فَإِنْ لَّمْ
تَعْلَمُوْٓا اٰبَآءَهُمْ فَإِخْوَانُكُمْ فِي الدِّيْنِ وَمَوَالِيْكُمْ ۭ
وَلَيْسَ عَلَيْكُمْ جُنَاحٌ فِيْمَآ أَخْطَأْتُمْ بِهٖ ۙ وَلٰكِنْ مَّا
تَعَمَّدَتْ قُلُوْبُكُمْ ۭ وَكَانَ اللّٰهُ غَفُوْرًا رَّحِيْمًا ٦

7. The Prophet is nearer to the believers than their own selves, and his wives are *as* mothers[2332] to them [a]And blood-relations are nearer to one another, according to the Book of Allāh, than *other* believers *from among the Helpers* and the Emigrants except that you show kindness to your friends.[2333] This *also* is written down in the Book.

اَلنَّبِيُّ أَوْلٰى بِالْمُؤْمِنِيْنَ مِنْ أَنْفُسِهِمْ وَأَزْوَاجُهٗٓ
أُمَّهٰتُهُمْ ۭ وَأُولُوا الْأَرْحَامِ بَعْضُهُمْ أَوْلٰى بِبَعْضٍ
فِيْ كِتٰبِ اللّٰهِ مِنَ الْمُؤْمِنِيْنَ وَالْمُهٰجِرِيْنَ إِلَّآ أَنْ
تَفْعَلُوْٓا إِلٰٓى أَوْلِيٰٓئِكُمْ مَّعْرُوْفًا ۭ كَانَ ذٰلِكَ فِي الْكِتٰبِ
مَسْطُوْرًا ٧

[a]8 : 76.

complications in blood relationships was puerile and foolish. The reason for the abolition of these customs is implied in the words, *Allāh has not made for any man two hearts in his breast*. Human heart is understood to be the seat of emotions and feelings. It can entertain only one kind of emotion at one time. Contradictory emotions cannot possibly be entertained by it at the same time. Moreover, different human relations evoke different emotions. Merely calling one's wife one's mother or calling a stranger one's son cannot evoke the corresponding emotions in one's heart. A wife can never become a mother nor a stranger a real son. Mere words of mouth cannot change the state of mind of the utterer of those words, nor can they alter hard facts of physical relationship.

2332. The verse clears a possible ambiguity that might have arisen from misunderstanding the injunction contained in v.6 above. While in that verse the believers were enjoined to *call them after their fathers,* in the present verse the Holy Prophet, by implication, has been called the father of the Faithful. The preceding verse speaks of blood-relationship but the verse under comment speaks of the spiritual relationship that subsists between the Holy Prophet and the Faithful.

2333. The Islamic Brotherhood which had come into being through the spiritual fatherhood of the Holy Prophet might have led to the misconception that Muslims could inherit each other's property. The verse seeks to remove this misconception by laying down that only blood-relations can inherit each other and that from among the blood-relations only the believers can inherit, the disbelievers having been debarred from inheriting their believing relatives. The verse also abolishes that form of brotherhood which was established between the Emigrants of Mecca and the Helpers of Medina on the former's arrival in Medina, according to which an "Emigrant" would even inherit the property left by an "Helper." That brotherhood, which was but a temporary measure and was adopted to rehabilitate the Emigrants from Mecca, ceased to exist, and blood-relationship, and not faith alone, became the decisive factor in determining inheritance and other kindred matters. But the wider Brotherhood of Islām continued and Muslims were expected to treat one another like brothers.

8. And *call to mind* [a]when We took from the Prophets their covenant, and from thee, and from Noah and Abraham, and Moses and Jesus, son of Mary, and We, *indeed*, took from them a solemn covenant;[2334]

وَإِذْ أَخَذْنَا مِنَ النَّبِيّٖنَ مِيْثَاقَهُمْ وَمِنْكَ وَمِنْ نُوْحٍ وَّإِبْرٰهِيْمَ وَمُوْسٰى وَعِيْسَى ابْنِ مَرْيَمَ وَأَخَذْنَا مِنْهُمْ مِّيْثَاقًا غَلِيْظًا ۝٨

9. That *Allāh* may question the truthful about their truthfulness. [b]And for the disbelievers He has prepared a painful punishment.

لِّيَسْـَٔلَ الصّٰدِقِيْنَ عَنْ صِدْقِهِمْ وَأَعَدَّ لِلْكٰفِرِيْنَ عَذَابًا أَلِيْمًا ۝٩

R. 2 10. O ye who believe, remember the favour of Allāh to you when there came against you hosts,[2335] and We sent against them a wind and hosts[2336] that you saw not. And Allāh sees what you do.

يٰٓأَيُّهَا الَّذِيْنَ اٰمَنُوا اذْكُرُوْا نِعْمَةَ اللّٰهِ عَلَيْكُمْ إِذْ جَآءَتْكُمْ جُنُوْدٌ فَأَرْسَلْنَا عَلَيْهِمْ رِيْحًا وَّجُنُوْدًا لَّمْ تَرَوْهَا وَكَانَ اللّٰهُ بِمَا تَعْمَلُوْنَ بَصِيْرًا ۝١٠

---

[a]3 : 82. [b]18 : 103; 48 : 14; 76 : 5.

2334. The four Prophets—Noah, Abraham, Moses and Jesus, have found special mention in this verse inasmuch as they occupy a unique position among the hierarchy of pre-Islamic Divine Prophets. Noah was the first Law-bearing Prophet in the real sense of the word and in Abraham converged both the Mosaic and Islamic Dispensations, and Moses was the Holy Prophet's counterpart while Jesus was the last of the Israelite Prophets and the Holy Prophet's harbinger. The words "their covenant" mean the covenant which was taken from them or which befitted their dignity and exalted position and was in harmony with their high duties and responsibilities. See also 433.

2335. With this verse begins an account of the Battle of the Trench which took place in the 5th year of the *Hijrah* and was the fiercest encounter in which the Muslims had so far been engaged. The whole of Arabia rose like one man against Islām. The Quraish of Mecca, their allies, the Ghaṭfān, the Ashja' and Murrah, the Fararah, the Sulaim and the Banū Sa'd and Banū Asad, the desert tribes of Central Arabia, aided and abetted by the perfidious Jews and treacherous Hypocrites of Medina, formed themselves into a grand confederacy against the Holy Prophet. A mighty force numbering from ten to twenty thousand strong was pitched against 1200 (according to some writers 3000 Muslims including women and children were employed in digging the Trench) ill-prepared and ill-provisioned Muslims. The siege of Medina lasted from fifteen days to four weeks. Islām emerged stronger from this severe ordeal and the disbelieving Quraish were never again able to march against Muslims in force.

2336. Forces of nature—wind, rain and cold which wearied the disbelievers and damped their spirits. The words may also refer to the hosts of angels which cast fear in the hearts of disbelievers and heartened and encouraged the Muslims. Says William Muir : 'Forage was obtained with the utmost difficulty; provisions were running short, and the camels and horses dying daily in great numbers ; wearied and damped in spirit the night set in upon them, cold and tempestuous wind and rain beat mercilessly on the unprotected camp. The storm rose to a hurricane. Fires were extinguished, tents blown down, cooking vessels and other equippage overthrown' ("Life of Moḥammad").

11. When they came upon you from above you, and from below you,[2337] and when *your* eyes became distracted, and *your* hearts reached up to *your* throats, and you thought *diverse* thoughts about Allāh.

إِذْ جَآءُوكُم مِّن فَوْقِكُمْ وَمِنْ أَسْفَلَ مِنكُمْ وَإِذْ
زَاغَتِ الْأَبْصَارُ وَبَلَغَتِ الْقُلُوبُ الْحَنَاجِرَ وَتَظُنُّونَ
بِاللَّهِ الظُّنُونَا ﴿١١﴾

12. Then were the believers sorely tried, [a]and they were shaken with a violent shaking.

هُنَالِكَ ابْتُلِيَ الْمُؤْمِنُونَ وَزُلْزِلُوا زِلْزَالًا شَدِيدًا ﴿١٢﴾

13. [b]And *call to mind* when the Hypocrites and those in whose hearts was a disease said, 'Allāh and His Messenger promised us only delusion;'

وَإِذْ يَقُولُ الْمُنَافِقُونَ وَالَّذِينَ فِي قُلُوبِهِم مَّرَضٌ
مَّا وَعَدَنَا اللَّهُ وَرَسُولُهُ إِلَّا غُرُورًا ﴿١٣﴾

14. And when a party of them said, 'O people of Yathrib,[2337A] you can *possibly* make no stand *against the enemy*, therefore turn back.[2338] And a section of them *even* asked leave of the Prophet, saying, 'Our houses are exposed,' whereas they were not exposed. They only sought to flee.

وَإِذْ قَالَت طَّآئِفَةٌ مِّنْهُمْ يَٰٓأَهْلَ يَثْرِبَ لَا مُقَامَ
لَكُمْ فَارْجِعُوا ۚ وَيَسْتَأْذِنُ فَرِيقٌ مِّنْهُمُ النَّبِيَّ يَقُولُونَ
إِنَّ بُيُوتَنَا عَوْرَةٌ ۛ وَمَا هِيَ بِعَوْرَةٍ ۛ إِن يُرِيدُونَ
إِلَّا فِرَارًا ﴿١٤﴾

15. If the enemy were to enter *the Town* from its environs, and then they were asked *to join in* the disturbance *against the Muslims*, they would certainly have done so, and would not have tarried *in their houses* save a little.[2339]

وَلَوْ دُخِلَتْ عَلَيْهِم مِّنْ أَقْطَارِهَا ثُمَّ سُئِلُوا الْفِتْنَةَ
لَآتَوْهَا وَمَا تَلَبَّثُوا بِهَآ إِلَّا يَسِيرًا ﴿١٥﴾

[a]8 : 18. [b]8 : 50.

2337. The disbelievers burst upon Muslims from every direction—from the heights of Medina as well as from the plains. The reference in the words 'and you thought *diverse* thoughts about Allāh,' is to the 'Hypocrites' and not to sincere and steadfast Muslims (v.13).

2337A. This was the name of Medina before the *Hijrah*.

2338. The words mean, 'Return to your old faith, or go back to your homes.'

2339. The verse purports to say that if an enemy had entered into Medina from another direction and the Hypocrites were invited to make common cause with him against the Muslims, they would have willingly and readily done so.

16. And truly they had already covenanted with Allāh[2340] that they would not turn their backs. And a covenant with Allāh will have to be answered for.

وَلَقَدْ كَانُوْا عَاهَدُوا اللّٰهَ مِنْ قَبْلُ لَا يُوَلُّوْنَ
الْاَدْبَارَ ۗ وَكَانَ عَهْدُ اللّٰهِ مَسْـُٔوْلًا ﴿١٦﴾

17. Say, [a]'Flight shall not avail you if you flee from death or slaughter; and *even* then you will *not be allowed to* enjoy yourselves but little.'

قُلْ لَّنْ يَّنْفَعَكُمُ الْفِرَارُ اِنْ فَرَرْتُمْ مِّنَ الْمَوْتِ اَوِ
الْقَتْلِ وَاِذًا لَّا تُمَتَّعُوْنَ اِلَّا قَلِيْلًا ﴿١٧﴾

18. Say, [b]'Who is it that can save you from Allāh if it be His wish to do you harm, or *can deprive you of it,* if it be His wish to show you mercy?' And they will not find for themselves any friend nor helper other than Allāh.

قُلْ مَنْ ذَا الَّذِيْ يَعْصِمُكُمْ مِّنَ اللّٰهِ اِنْ اَرَادَ بِكُمْ
سُوْٓءًا اَوْ اَرَادَ بِكُمْ رَحْمَةً ۗ وَلَا يَجِدُوْنَ لَهُمْ
مِّنْ دُوْنِ اللّٰهِ وَلِيًّا وَّلَا نَصِيْرًا ﴿١٨﴾

19. Verily, Allāh knows *well* those among you who hinder *others from fighting* and those who say to their brethren, 'Come *and be with* us;' and they *themselves* come not to the fight but little,

قَدْ يَعْلَمُ اللّٰهُ الْمُعَوِّقِيْنَ مِنْكُمْ وَالْقَآئِلِيْنَ لِاِخْوَانِهِمْ
هَلُمَّ اِلَيْنَا ۚ وَلَا يَاْتُوْنَ الْبَاْسَ اِلَّا قَلِيْلًا ﴿١٩﴾

20. Being niggardly *of their help* to you. But when danger comes, thou seest them looking towards thee, their eyes rolling like one who is fainting at *the approach of* death. But when the fear has passed away, they assail you with sharp tongues, being niggardly of *any* good *coming to your way.*[2341] These have never believed; so Allāh has rendered their works null and void. And that is easy for Allāh.

اَشِحَّةً عَلَيْكُمْ ۚ فَاِذَا جَآءَ الْخَوْفُ رَاَيْتَهُمْ
يَنْظُرُوْنَ اِلَيْكَ تَدُوْرُ اَعْيُنُهُمْ كَالَّذِيْ يُغْشٰى
عَلَيْهِ مِنَ الْمَوْتِ ۚ فَاِذَا ذَهَبَ الْخَوْفُ سَلَقُوْكُمْ
بِاَلْسِنَةٍ حِدَادٍ اَشِحَّةً عَلَى الْخَيْرِ ۗ اُولٰٓئِكَ لَمْ
يُؤْمِنُوْا فَاَحْبَطَ اللّٰهُ اَعْمَالَهُمْ ۗ وَكَانَ ذٰلِكَ عَلَى
اللّٰهِ يَسِيْرًا ﴿٢٠﴾

---

[a]4 : 79; 62 : 9. [b]39 : 39.

2340. The words refer to the treaty which the Jews of Medina had made with the Holy Prophet that they would fight on his side against any enemy who invaded Medina.

2341. *Shuh* meaning both niggardliness and greed,the expression means, (*a*) that the Hypocrites are very niggardly in giving help to the Muslims; (*b*) that they are very greedy of getting money, and taunt the Muslims if their greed is not satisfied.

21. They *still* hope that the Confederates may not have gone away; and if the Confederates should come *again*, they would wish to be among the nomad Arabs in the desert, asking for news about you. And if they were among you, they would fight but little.[2342]

يَحْسَبُونَ الْأَحْزَابَ لَمْ يَذْهَبُوا ۚ وَإِنْ يَأْتِ الْأَحْزَابُ
يَوَدُّوا لَوْ أَنَّهُمْ بَادُونَ فِي الْأَعْرَابِ يَسْأَلُونَ عَنْ
أَنْبَائِكُمْ ۖ وَلَوْ كَانُوا فِيكُمْ مَا قَاتَلُوا إِلَّا قَلِيلًا ﴿٢١﴾ ع ٢ ١٨

R. 3 22. Verily, you have in the Prophet of Allāh [a]an excellent model,[2343] for him who hopes *to meet* Allāh and the Last Day and who remembers Allāh much.

لَقَدْ كَانَ لَكُمْ فِي رَسُولِ اللَّهِ أُسْوَةٌ حَسَنَةٌ لِمَنْ كَانَ
يَرْجُو اللَّهَ وَالْيَوْمَ الْآخِرَ وَذَكَرَ اللَّهَ كَثِيرًا ﴿٢٢﴾

[a]3 : 32.

2342. With the 13th verse the description had begun of an hypocrite's state of mind, particularly when he is face to face with danger. The picture has become complete with the present verse. The hypocrite is a coward and a defeatist. He is a liar and has no regard for pledges solemnly made. He is treacherous, disloyal and perfidious. He is niggardly and greedy. In short, he is the complete antithesis of a true believer.

2343. The Battle of the Trench perhaps constituted the hardest ordeal in the Holy Prophet's whole career and from that supreme test he emerged with enhanced moral stature and prestige. In fact, it is in time of danger, when all around is dark, or in the hour of success and victory when a person's enemy lies prostrate at his feet, that his real mettle is tested; and history bears eloquent testimony to the fact that the Holy Prophet was as great and noble in time of distress as he was in the hour of success. The battles of the Trench, Uḥud and Ḥunain shed a flood of light on the one beautiful facet of his character, and the Fall of Mecca on the other. Peril and danger did not discourage or dismay him nor could victory and success spoil him. When left almost alone on the day of Ḥunain with the fate of Islām hanging in the balance, he fearlessly and single-handed advanced into the enemy's ranks with the memorable words on his lips : 'I am the Prophet of God and I am telling no lie. I am the son of 'Abd al-Muṭṭalib.' And when Mecca fell and the whole of Arabia lay prostrate at his feet, absolute and undisputed power failed to corrupt him. He showed unparalleled magnanimity to his enemies.

What greater testimony there could possibly be to the Holy Prophet's nobility of character than the fact that those who were nearest to him and knew him most loved him most and were the first to believe in his mission—his dear wife Khadījah, his life-long friend Abū Bakr, his cousin and son-in-law 'Alī, his freed slave Zaid. The Prophet was humanity's noblest specimen and a perfect model in beauty and beneficence. In all the various facets of his variegated life and character he stands unrivalled and an excellent exemplar for men to copy and follow. His whole life lies before the flood-light of history. He started life as an orphaned child and ended it by being the arbiter of the destinies of a whole nation. As a boy he was sedate and dignified and at the threshold of youth he was a perfect example of moral virtue, righteousness and sobriety. In middle age he won the title of *Al-Amīn*, (The Trusty and Truthful) and as a businessman he proved himself to be most honest and scrupulous. He married ladies both much older and much younger than himself and all of them swore by his faithfulness, love and godliness. As a father he was most affectionate, and as a friend most loyal and considerate. When entrusted with the great and difficult task of reforming a corrupt society and subjected to persecution and exile, he bore it all with dignity and decorum. He fought as a soldier and commanded armies. He faced defeat and won victories. He legislated and decided cases. He was a statesman, a teacher and a leader of men. 'Head of the state as well as of the Church he was Caesar and Pope in one; but he was Pope without the Pope's pretentions, and Caesar without the legions of Caesar. Without a standing army, without a bodyguard, without a palace, without a

23. And when the believers saw the Confederates, they said, 'This is what Allāh and His Messenger promised us;[2344] and Allāh and His Messenger spoke the truth.' And it only added to their faith and submission.

وَلَمَّا رَاَ الْمُؤْمِنُوْنَ الْاَحْزَابَ قَالُوْا هٰذَا مَا وَعَدَنَا
اللّٰهُ وَرَسُوْلُهٗ وَصَدَقَ اللّٰهُ وَرَسُوْلُهٗ وَمَا زَادَهُمْ
اِلَّآ اِيْمَانًا وَّتَسْلِيْمًا ﴿٢٣﴾

24. Among the believers are men who have been true to the covenant they had made with Allāh.[2345] Some of them have fulfilled their vow, and there are others who wait, and they have not changed in the least.

مِنَ الْمُؤْمِنِيْنَ رِجَالٌ صَدَقُوْا مَا عَاهَدُوا اللّٰهَ عَلَيْهِ
فَمِنْهُمْ مَّنْ قَضٰى نَحْبَهٗ وَمِنْهُمْ مَّنْ يَّنْتَظِرُ وَمَا
بَدَّلُوْا تَبْدِيْلًا ﴿٢٤﴾

25. [a]That Allāh may reward the truthful for their truth, and punish the hypocrites if He so please, or turn to them in mercy. Verily, Allāh is Most Forgiving, Merciful.

لِّيَجْزِيَ اللّٰهُ الصّٰدِقِيْنَ بِصِدْقِهِمْ وَيُعَذِّبَ الْمُنٰفِقِيْنَ
اِنْ شَآءَ اَوْ يَتُوْبَ عَلَيْهِمْ اِنَّ اللّٰهَ كَانَ غَفُوْرًا
رَّحِيْمًا ﴿٢٥﴾

26. And Allāh turned back the disbelievers in their rage;[2346] they gained no good. And Allāh sufficed the believers in their fight. Allāh is Powerful, Mighty.

وَرَدَّ اللّٰهُ الَّذِيْنَ كَفَرُوْا بِغَيْظِهِمْ لَمْ يَنَالُوْا خَيْرًا
وَكَفَى اللّٰهُ الْمُؤْمِنِيْنَ الْقِتَالَ وَكَانَ اللّٰهُ قَوِيًّا
عَزِيْزًا ﴿٢٦﴾

[a]48 : 6, 7.

fixed revenue, if ever any man had the right to say that he ruled by a right Divine, it was Muḥammad, for he had all the power without its instruments and without its supports. He would do his household work with his own hands, would sleep upon a leathern mat, and his menu consisted of dates and water or barley-bread, and after having done a full day of multifarious duties, he would spend the hours of night in prayer and supplication till his feet got swollen. No man under so vastly changed circumstances and conditions had changed so little' ("Muḥammad and Muḥammadanism" by Bosworth Smith).

2344. The reference is to the prophecy about the defeat and discomfiture of the hosts of disbelief and the victory of Islām (38 : 12 & 54 : 46).

2345. The verse constitutes a great memorial to the fidelity, sincerity and steadfastness in faith of the Holy Prophet's disciples. Never did the followers of any Prophet receive from God such certificate of good conduct and faithfulness. Just as the Master was unique among all Divine Messengers in discharging his prophetic duties, so were his Companions matchless in fulfilling the role assigned to them.

2346. Allāh repelled the attack of the Confederates. They had to raise the siege and, consumed with anger and rage at having completely failed in their unholy and nefarious undertaking, they went back to their homes, never being in a position again to attack Medina. Henceforward the initiative passed into the hands of Muslims. The Battle of the Trench marked a turning point in the history of Islām. From a weak and continuously harassed and harried minority Islām became a mighty force in Arabia.

27. And He brought those of the People of the Book who had aided them down [a]from their fortresses, and cast terror into their hearts. Some you slew, and some you took captive.[2347]

وَاَنْزَلَ الَّذِيْنَ ظَاهَرُوْهُمْ مِّنْ اَهْلِ الْكِتٰبِ مِنْ
صَيَاصِيْهِمْ وَقَذَفَ فِيْ قُلُوْبِهِمُ الرُّعْبَ فَرِيْقًا
تَقْتُلُوْنَ وَتَاْسِرُوْنَ فَرِيْقًا ﴿٢٧﴾

28. And He made you inherit their land and their houses and their wealth, and *also* a land on which you have not *yet* set foot.[2348] And Allāh has power over all things.

وَاَوْرَثَكُمْ اَرْضَهُمْ وَدِيَارَهُمْ وَاَمْوَالَهُمْ وَاَرْضًا
لَّمْ تَطَئُوْهَا ۚ وَكَانَ اللّٰهُ عَلٰى كُلِّ شَيْءٍ قَدِيْرًا ﴿٢٨﴾ ع ١٩

R. 4 29. O Prophet! say to thy wives, 'If you desire the life of this world and its adornment, come then, I will provide for you and send you away in a handsome manner;[2349]

يٰٓاَيُّهَا النَّبِيُّ قُلْ لِّاَزْوَاجِكَ اِنْ كُنْتُنَّ تُرِدْنَ الْحَيٰوةَ
الدُّنْيَا وَزِيْنَتَهَا فَتَعَالَيْنَ اُمَتِّعْكُنَّ وَاُسَرِّحْكُنَّ
سَرَاحًا جَمِيْلًا ﴿٢٩﴾

30. 'But if you desire Allāh and His Messenger and the Home of the Hereafter, then, truly, Allāh has prepared for those of you, who do good, a great reward.'

وَاِنْ كُنْتُنَّ تُرِدْنَ اللّٰهَ وَرَسُوْلَهٗ وَالدَّارَ الْاٰخِرَةَ
فَاِنَّ اللّٰهَ اَعَدَّ لِلْمُحْسِنٰتِ مِنْكُنَّ اَجْرًا عَظِيْمًا ﴿٣٠﴾

[a]59 : 3.

2347. The perfidious Banū Quraiẓah had entered into a solemn treaty with the Holy Prophet that they would help Muslims if an enemy attacked Medina. But at the time of the Battle of the Trench they were prevailed upon by Ḥuyayy, the leader of the Banū Naḍīr to break their plighted word and join the grand confederacy against Islām. When the attack fizzled out, the Holy Prophet marched against them, and besieged them in their strongholds. The siege continued for about 25 days after which they agreed to lay down their arms and preferred to submit to the award of Sa'd bin Ma'ādh, the chief of the tribe of Aus, rather than to that of the Holy Prophet. Sa'd decided the case according to the Mosaic Law (Deut: 20 : 10-15).

2348. The allusion here seems to be either to the lands of Khaibar or to the eventual conquest of Persian and Roman Empires and of the countries beyond, upon which Muslims had not so far set their feet.

2349. As the Holy Prophet's wives were to serve as a model in social behaviour, it was in the fitness of things that they should have been required to set an example in self-denial. Not that the use of money and the amenities of life were completely forbidden to them, but they were certainly expected to set a very high standard of self-abnegation. It is to this high standard of the sacrifice of material benefits and of an affluent and easy living to which the present and the following few verses refer. The companionship of the Holy Prophet demanded this sacrifice, and his wives were told to make a choice between comfortable life and his companionship.

31. O wives of the Prophet! if any of you be guilty of manifestly dishonourable conduct,[2349A] the punishment will be doubled[2350] for her. And that is easy for Allāh.

يٰنِسَآءَ النَّبِيِّ مَنْ يَّأْتِ مِنْكُنَّ بِفَاحِشَةٍ مُّبَيِّنَةٍ
يُّضٰعَفْ لَهَا الْعَذَابُ ضِعْفَيْنِ ۚ وَكَانَ ذٰلِكَ عَلَى
اللّٰهِ يَسِيْرًا ﴿۳۱﴾

PART XXII

الجزء ۲۲

32. But whoever[2351] of you is obedient to Allāh and His Messenger and does good works, We shall give her her reward twice over; and We have prepared for her an honourable provision.

وَمَنْ يَّقْنُتْ مِنْكُنَّ لِلّٰهِ وَرَسُوْلِهٖ وَتَعْمَلْ صَالِحًا
نُّؤْتِهَآ اَجْرَهَا مَرَّتَيْنِ ۙ وَاَعْتَدْنَا لَهَا رِزْقًا كَرِيْمًا ﴿۳۲﴾

33. O wives of the Prophet! you are not like any *other* women if you are righteous. So be not soft in speech,[2352] lest he, in whose heart is a disease, should feel tempted; and speak decent words.

يٰنِسَآءَ النَّبِيِّ لَسْتُنَّ كَاَحَدٍ مِّنَ النِّسَآءِ اِنِ اتَّقَيْتُنَّ
فَلَا تَخْضَعْنَ بِالْقَوْلِ فَيَطْمَعَ الَّذِيْ فِيْ قَلْبِهٖ مَرَضٌ
وَّقُلْنَ قَوْلًا مَّعْرُوْفًا ﴿۳۳﴾

34. And stay[2353] in your houses *with dignity*, and display not your beauty like the displaying of the former days of ignorance, and [a]observe Prayer, and pay the *Zakāt*, and obey Allāh and His Messenger. Surely, Allāh desires to remove from you all uncleanness, O Members of the Household, and purify you completely.

وَقَرْنَ فِيْ بُيُوْتِكُنَّ وَلَا تَبَرَّجْنَ تَبَرُّجَ الْجَاهِلِيَّةِ
الْاُوْلٰى وَاَقِمْنَ الصَّلٰوةَ وَاٰتِيْنَ الزَّكٰوةَ وَاَطِعْنَ
اللّٰهَ وَرَسُوْلَهٗ ۗ اِنَّمَا يُرِيْدُ اللّٰهُ لِيُذْهِبَ عَنْكُمُ
الرِّجْسَ اَهْلَ الْبَيْتِ وَيُطَهِّرَكُمْ تَطْهِيْرًا ﴿۳۴﴾

[a]19 : 56; 20 : 133.

2349A. Conduct falling short of the highest standards of faith.

2350. If they prefer physical comforts, which is the significance of the word *Fāhishah* (Lane) used in the verse, they would be setting a very bad example, and as wives of the Holy Prophet whose example was bound to be followed by other women they would be incurring a grave responsibility and would, therefore, deserve double punishment. On the other hand, if they were devoted to God and His Messenger and had set a noble example of self-denial for others to copy, their reward would also be double.

2351. The masculine gender for the verb *Yaqnut* is used because of the subject *man* which is invariably followed by a verb in the masculine gender.

2352. The wives of the Holy Prophet are here enjoined to maintain the dignity of their very exalted position and to conduct themselves with due propriety and decorum while talking to members of the opposite sex. All Muslim women are included in this injunction.

2353. The words show that the principal sphere of the activities of a woman is her house—not that she is not allowed to leave its four walls. She may go out as many times

35. And remember what is rehearsed in your houses of the Signs of Allāh and wisdom.[2354] Verily, Allāh is Subtle, All-Aware.

وَاذْكُرْنَ مَا يُتْلٰى فِيْ بُيُوْتِكُنَّ مِنْ اٰيٰتِ اللّٰهِ وَالْحِكْمَةِ ۚ اِنَّ اللّٰهَ كَانَ لَطِيْفًا خَبِيْرًا ۝

R. 5 36. "Surely, men who submit themselves *to God* and women who submit themselves *to Him*, and believing men and believing women, and obedient men and obedient women, and truthful men and truthful women, and men steadfast *in their faith* and steadfast women, and men who are humble and women who are humble, and men who give alms and women who give alms, and men who fast and women who fast, and men who guard their chastity and women who guard *their chastity* and men who remember Allāh much and women who remember *Him*—Allāh has prepared for *all of* them forgiveness and a great reward.[2355]

اِنَّ الْمُسْلِمِيْنَ وَالْمُسْلِمٰتِ وَالْمُؤْمِنِيْنَ وَالْمُؤْمِنٰتِ وَالْقٰنِتِيْنَ وَالْقٰنِتٰتِ وَالصّٰدِقِيْنَ وَالصّٰدِقٰتِ وَ الصّٰبِرِيْنَ وَالصّٰبِرٰتِ وَالْخٰشِعِيْنَ وَالْخٰشِعٰتِ وَالْمُتَصَدِّقِيْنَ وَالْمُتَصَدِّقٰتِ وَالصَّآئِمِيْنَ وَالصّٰٓئِمٰتِ وَالْحٰفِظِيْنَ فُرُوْجَهُمْ وَالْحٰفِظٰتِ وَالذّٰكِرِيْنَ اللّٰهَ كَثِيْرًا وَّ الذّٰكِرٰتِ ۙ اَعَدَّ اللّٰهُ لَهُمْ مَّغْفِرَةً وَّ اَجْرًا عَظِيْمًا ۝

---

a 9 : 112.

as she may require for the performance of a legitimate errand or the satisfaction of a legitimate need. But to move about in mixed society and take part in all sorts of avocations and professions, shoulder to shoulder with man, and to do so to the neglect and detriment of her special domestic duties as the mistress of the house is not the Islamic conception of ideal womanhood. The Holy Prophet's wives were particularly required to 'stay in their houses' because the dignity of their exalted position as ''Mothers of the Faithful' demanded this and also because Muslims often visited them to pay their respects and sought necessary guidance from them on important religious matters. The commandment equally applies to all Muslim women. It is the Quranic way of address that while it appears to be particularly addressing the Holy Prophet, the address is meant equally for all Muslims. Similarly, a commandment addressed to the wives of the Holy Prophet applies also to all Muslim women.

The expression *Ahl al-Bait* applies principally and primarily to the Holy Prophet's wives. This is quite clear from the context and also from vv. 11 : 74 and 28 : 13. In its wider sense, however, it includes all members of a family who form one's household, even one's children and children's children. The expression had also been used by the Holy Prophet for some of his select Companions. 'Salmān is a member of our household' is a well-known saying of the Holy Prophet (Ṣaghīr).

2354. The Holy Prophet's noble consorts were required not only to serve as model of virtue, piety and righteousness for the Faithful but to teach them the principles and precepts of Islām which they had learnt direct from the Holy Prophet.

2355. This verse embodies a most effective repudiation of the charge that Islām accords a lower status to women. According to the Qur'ān women stand on the same level with men, and they can attain to all those spiritual heights to which men can attain and enjoy all those political and social rights which men enjoy. Only their spheres of activities being different, their duties are different. It is this difference in duties of both the sexes that has mistakenly, or perhaps deliberately, been misunderstood by hostile critics of Islām as implying a lower status for women.

37. And it behoves not a believing man or a believing woman, [a]when Allāh and His Messenger have decided a matter, that they should exercise *their* own choice in the matter concerning them.[2356] And whoso disobeys Allāh and His Messenger, surely, strays away in manifest error.

وَمَا كَانَ لِمُؤْمِنٍ وَّلَا مُؤْمِنَةٍ اِذَا قَضَى اللّٰهُ وَرَسُوْلُهٗۤ
اَمْرًا اَنْ يَّكُوْنَ لَهُمُ الْخِيَرَةُ مِنْ اَمْرِهِمْ ؕ وَمَنْ يَّعْصِ
اللّٰهَ وَرَسُوْلَهٗ فَقَدْ ضَلَّ ضَلٰلًا مُّبِيْنًا ﴿۳۷﴾

38. And *call to mind* when thou didst say to him on whom Allāh had bestowed favours and on whom thou *also* hadst bestowed favours:[2357] 'Keep thy wife to thyself, and fear Allāh,' and thou didst conceal in thy heart what Allāh was going to bring to light, and thou didst fear the people, whereas Allāh has better right that thou shouldst fear Him. Then, when Zaid had accomplished his want concerning her,[2357A] We joined her in marriage to thee, so that *there* may be no difficulty for the believers with regard to *marriage with* the wives of their adopted sons, when they have accomplished their wants concerning them. And Allāh's decree was bound to be fulfilled.[2357B]

وَاِذْ تَقُوْلُ لِلَّذِيْۤ اَنْعَمَ اللّٰهُ عَلَيْهِ وَاَنْعَمْتَ عَلَيْهِ
اَمْسِكْ عَلَيْكَ زَوْجَكَ وَاتَّقِ اللّٰهَ وَتُخْفِيْ فِيْ نَفْسِكَ
مَا اللّٰهُ مُبْدِيْهِ وَتَخْشَى النَّاسَ ۚ وَاللّٰهُ اَحَقُّ اَنْ
تَخْشٰىهُ ؕ فَلَمَّا قَضٰى زَيْدٌ مِّنْهَا وَطَرًا زَوَّجْنٰكَهَا لِكَيْ
لَا يَكُوْنَ عَلَى الْمُؤْمِنِيْنَ حَرَجٌ فِيْۤ اَزْوَاجِ اَدْعِيَآئِهِمْ
اِذَا قَضَوْا مِنْهُنَّ وَطَرًا ؕ وَكَانَ اَمْرُ اللّٰهِ مَفْعُوْلًا ﴿۳۸﴾

---

[a]4 : 66.

2356. The immediate occasion for the revelation of this verse may have been Zainab's hesitation to comply with the Holy Prophet's greatly cherished wish that she should marry Zaid, his freed slave. It goes to Zainab's credit that in deference to the Prophet's wish she agreed to her marriage with Zaid, much against her personal inclination. The Holy Prophet did not press her to accept Zaid as her husband. She only deferred to the wish of the Holy Prophet.

2357. Zaid ibn Ḥārith, a young freed man of the Holy Prophet whom he had adopted as his son before adoption was declared unlawful in Islām.

2357A. Had divorced her ; *Waṭar* means, need ; want ; an object of want (Lane).

2357B. Zainab was the daughter of the Holy Prophet's aunt, hence a full-blooded Arab lady, intensely proud of her ancestry and exalted social status. Islām had envisaged and given to the world a civilization and culture in which there were no class divisions, no hereditary nobility, no vested interests. All men were free and equal in the sight of God. The Holy Prophet wanted to start with his own family to carry into actual effect this noble ideal of Islām. He wished to marry Zainab to Zaid, who in spite of having been freed by the Prophet, unfortunately still carried the stigma of slavery in the minds of some people. It was exactly this stigma of slavery, this invidious distinction between 'free' and 'slave' which the Holy Prophet sought to remove by Zainab's marriage with Zaid.

39. No blame can attach to the Prophet with respect to that which Allāh has made incumbent[2358] upon him. *Such, indeed, was* the way of Allāh with those who have passed before—and the command of Allāh is a decree ordained—

مَا كَانَ عَلَى النَّبِيِّ مِنْ حَرَجٍ فِيمَا فَرَضَ اللّٰهُ لَهٗ ۚ سُنَّةَ اللّٰهِ فِي الَّذِينَ خَلَوْا مِنْ قَبْلُ ۚ وَكَانَ أَمْرُ اللّٰهِ قَدَرًا مَّقْدُورًا ﴿٣٩﴾

40. Those who delivered the Messages of Allāh [a]and feared Him, and feared none but Allāh. And sufficient is Allāh as a Reckoner.

الَّذِينَ يُبَلِّغُونَ رِسٰلٰتِ اللّٰهِ وَيَخْشَوْنَهٗ وَلَا يَخْشَوْنَ أَحَدًا إِلَّا اللّٰهَ ۗ وَكَفٰى بِاللّٰهِ حَسِيبًا ﴿٤٠﴾

[a]67 : 13.

In deference to the Holy Prophet's wish Zainab agreed to the proposal. The purpose of the Holy Prophet was achieved. The marriage levelled to the ground class distinctions and divisions. It was a practical demonstration of Islām's noble ideal. But the marriage unfortunately ended in failure, not so much due to a difference in the social status of Zainab and Zaid as to the incompatibility of their dispositions and temperaments and also due to a feeling of inferiority from which Zaid himself suffered. The failure of the marriage naturally grieved the Holy Prophet. But it also served a very useful purpose. In pursuance of a Divine command, as mentioned in the latter part of the verse, the Holy Prophet himself married Zainab, thus cutting at the very root of the obnoxious and deep-seated Arab custom that it was a sacrilege to marry the wife of one's adopted son. The custom of adoption was abolished and with it went also this foolish notion. Thus Zainab's marriage with Zaid served one very noble object and its failure another.

The words 'fear Allah' signify that Zaid wanted to divorce Zainab, and as divorce according to Islām is very hateful in the sight of God, the Holy Prophet exhorted him not to do so. The clause *and......thou shouldst fear Him*, may apply to both Zaid and the Holy Prophet. Applying to Zaid it would mean that Zaid did not like that the cause of his separation from Zainab should come to light, perhaps because as the words 'fear Allāh' indicate the fault lay more with him than with Zainab. As, however, applying to the Holy Prophet, it would signify that as the marriage between Zaid and Zainab was arranged at his instance and wish, he naturally did not like its breach. The clause also shows that the Prophet feared that the break-down of the marriage which resulted in an ostensible failure of the experiment in Islamic brotherhood, would cause some mental confusion and uneasiness among people whose faith was weak. This was the anxiety that lay heavy on the Prophet's heart. The words, 'thou didst fear the people,' seem to point to this fear of his.

Some Christian critics of Islām pretend to find in the Holy Prophet's marriage with Zainab a basis for mean attacks on him. It is stated that the Prophet, having by chance seen Zainab, became enamoured of her beauty and Zaid, having come to know of his desire to marry her, sought divorce from her. The fact that the Holy Prophet's most inveterate enemies, before whose eyes the whole affair had actually taken place, dared not attribute the base motives ascribed to him by these critics after so many centuries, completely knocks the bottom from under this base and totally unfounded charge. Zainab was the Prophet's own cousin and, being so closely related to him, he must have seen her many times before "Pardah" was enjoined. Besides, it was in deference to his own persistently expressed wish that Zainab had reluctantly agreed to marry Zaid. It is on record that she and her brother had desired before her marriage with Zaid that she should be taken into marriage by the Holy Prophet himself. What was it that prevented the Holy Prophet from marrying her when she was a virgin and when she herself desired to get married to him? The whole story evidently seems to be a figment of the "fertile" imagination of the Holy Prophet's hostile critics and it is an insult to human intellect to give credence to it.

2358. The reference in the words is to the Holy Prophet's marriage with Zainab. The words show that his marriage took place in obedience to express Divine command.

41. Muḥammad is not the father of any of your men, but *he is* the Messenger of Allāh, and the Seal of the Prophets[2359] and Allāh has full knowledge of all things.

مَا كَانَ مُحَمَّدٌ اَبَآ اَحَدٍ مِّنْ رِّجَالِكُمْ وَلٰكِنْ رَّسُوْلَ اللّٰهِ وَخَاتَمَ النَّبِيّٖنَ ؕ وَكَانَ اللّٰهُ بِكُلِّ شَيْءٍ عَلِيْمًا ﴿٤١﴾

2359. *Khātam* is derived from *Khatama* which means, he sealed, stamped, impressed or imprinted the thing. This is the primary signification of this word. The secondary meaning is he reached the end of the thing; or covered the thing; or protected what is in a writing by marking or stamping a piece of clay upon it, or by means of a seal of any kind. *Khātam* means, a signet-ring; a seal or stamp and a mark; the end or last part or portion and result or issue of a thing. The word also signifies embellishment or ornament; the best and most perfect. The words *Khātim* and *Khatm* and *Khātam* are almost synonymous (Lane, Mufradāt, Fatḥ & Zurqānī). So the expression *Khātam al-Nabiyyīn* would mean, the Seal of the Prophets ; the best and most perfect of the Prophets ; the embellishment and ornament of the Prophets. Secondarily it means, the last of the Prophets.

At Mecca when all the Holy Prophet's male children had died in their childhood, his enemies taunted him with being *Abtar* (one who has no male issue), meaning that in the absence of male heirs to succeed him his Movement would sooner or later come to an end (Muḥīṭ). In answer to this taunt of disbelievers it was emphatically declared in *Sūrah* Kausar that not the Prophet but his enemies would remain issueless. After the revelation of *Sūrah* Kausar the idea naturally found favour with early Muslims that the Prophet would be blessed with sons who would live to an adult age. The verse under comment removed that misconception inasmuch as it declared that the Prophet is not, never was, nor will ever be the father of any grown-up young men (*Rijāl* meaning grown-up young men). The verse while appearing to be in conflict with *Sūrah* Kausar in which not the Holy Prophet but his enemies were threatened with being issueless, in reality seeks to set at rest doubts and misgivings to which this seeming contradiction gives rise. It says that the Holy Prophet is *Rasūl Allāh*, signifying that he is the spiritual father of a whole *Ummah*' and he is also *Khātam al-Nabiyyīn*, signifying that he is the spiritual father of all the Prophets. So when he is the spiritual father of all believers and of all Prophets, how can he be said to be *Abtar* (issueless). If the expression be taken to mean that he is the last of the Prophets and that no Prophet will come after him, then the verse would appear to be out of tune and to possess no relevance with the context, and instead of refuting the taunt of disbelievers that the Holy Prophet was issueless, would support and reinforce it. Briefly, according to the meaning of the word *Khātam*, given above, the expression *Khātam al-Nabiyyīn* can have four possible meanings : (1) The Holy Prophet was the Seal of the Prophets, *i.e.*, no Prophet can be regarded as true unless his Prophethood bears the seal of the Holy Prophet. The Prophethood of every past Prophet must be confirmed and testified to by the Holy Prophet, and also nobody can attain to Prophethood after him except by being his follower. (2) The Holy Prophet was the best, the noblest and the most perfect of all the Prophets and he was also a source of embellishment for them (Zurqānī, Sharaḥ Mawāhib al-Ladunniyyah). (3) The Holy Prophet was the last of the law-bearing Prophets. This interpretation has been accepted by eminent Muslim theologians, saints and savants such as Ibn 'Arabī, Shāh Walī-Allāh, Imām 'Alī Qārī, Mujaddid Alf Thānī, and others. According to these great scholars and saints no Prophet can come after the Holy Prophet who could abrogate his *Millah* or who should be from outside his *Ummah* (Futūḥāt, Tafhīmāt, Maktūbāt & Yawāqīt wa'l Jawāhir). 'Ā'ishah, the talented spouse of the Holy Prophet, is reported to have said, 'Say that he (the Holy Prophet) is *Khātam al-Nabiyyīn*, but do not say that there will be no Prophet after him' (Manthūr). (4) The Holy Prophet was the last of the Prophets only in this sense that all the qualities and attributes of Prophethood found their most perfect and complete consummation and expression in him; *Khātam* in the sense of being the last word in excellence and perfection is of common use. Moreover the Qur'ān clearly speaks of the advent of Prophets after the Holy Prophet (7 : 36). The Holy Prophet himself was clear in his mind as to the continuity of Prophethood after him. He is reported to have said: 'If Ibrāhīm (his son) had remained alive, he would have been a Prophet' (Mājah, *Kitāb al-Janā'iz*), and, 'Abū Bakr is best of men after me, except that a Prophet should appear' (Kanz).

R. 6

42. O ye who believe! [a]remember Allāh much;

يَٰٓأَيُّهَا ٱلَّذِينَ ءَامَنُوا ٱذْكُرُوا ٱللَّهَ ذِكْرًا كَثِيرًا ﴿٤٢﴾

43. [b]And glorify Him morning and evening.

وَسَبِّحُوهُ بُكْرَةً وَأَصِيلًا ﴿٤٣﴾

44. He it is Who sends down *His* blessings on you, and His angels *pray for you*,[2359A] that He may bring you forth from all *kinds of* darkness into [c]light. And He is Merciful to the believers.

هُوَ ٱلَّذِى يُصَلِّى عَلَيْكُمْ وَمَلَٰٓئِكَتُهُۥ لِيُخْرِجَكُم مِّنَ ٱلظُّلُمَٰتِ إِلَى ٱلنُّورِ ۚ وَكَانَ بِٱلْمُؤْمِنِينَ رَحِيمًا ﴿٤٤﴾

45. [d]Their greeting on the day, when they meet Him, will be 'peace.' And He has prepared for them an honourable reward.

تَحِيَّتُهُمْ يَوْمَ يَلْقَوْنَهُۥ سَلَٰمٌ ۚ وَأَعَدَّ لَهُمْ أَجْرًا كَرِيمًا ﴿٤٥﴾

46. O Prophet! truly We have sent thee as a Witness, and a Bearer of glad tidings, and a Warner,

يَٰٓأَيُّهَا ٱلنَّبِىُّ إِنَّآ أَرْسَلْنَٰكَ شَٰهِدًا وَمُبَشِّرًا وَنَذِيرًا ﴿٤٦﴾

47. [e]And as a Summoner unto Allāh by His command, and as a light-giving Lamp.[2360]

وَدَاعِيًا إِلَى ٱللَّهِ بِإِذْنِهِۦ وَسِرَاجًا مُّنِيرًا ﴿٤٧﴾

48. And announce to the believers the glad tidings that they will have great bounty from Allāh.

وَبَشِّرِ ٱلْمُؤْمِنِينَ بِأَنَّ لَهُم مِّنَ ٱللَّهِ فَضْلًا كَبِيرًا ﴿٤٨﴾

49. [f]And follow not the disbelievers and the hypocrites, and overlook their annoying talk and put thy trust in Allāh; for Allāh is sufficient as a Guardian.

وَلَا تُطِعِ ٱلْكَٰفِرِينَ وَٱلْمُنَٰفِقِينَ وَدَعْ أَذَىٰهُمْ وَتَوَكَّلْ عَلَى ٱللَّهِ ۚ وَكَفَىٰ بِٱللَّهِ وَكِيلًا ﴿٤٩﴾

[a]4 : 104; 8 : 46; 62 : 11. [b]3 : 42; 19 : 12. [c]2 : 258; 14 : 6; 57 : 10; 65 : 12. [d]10 : 11; 36 : 59. [e]25 : 57; 35 : 25; 48 : 9. [f]18 : 29; 25 : 53.

2359A. The word *Yuṣallī* signifies both sending down blessings and praying.

2360. As the sun is the central point in the physical universe, so is the Holy Prophet the central point in the spiritual realm. He is the sun in the firmament of Prophets and Heavenly Reformers who like so many stars and moons revolve round him and borrow light from him. He is reported to have said: 'My Companions are like so many stars; whomsoever of them you follow you will be rightly guided' (Ṣaghīr).

50. O ye who believe! when you marry believing women and then divorce them [a]before you have touched them, then you have no right *to reckon* the period of waiting with regard to them. So make *some* provision for them and send them away in a handsome manner.[2361]

يٰٓاَيُّهَا الَّذِيْنَ اٰمَنُوْٓا اِذَا نَكَحْتُمُ الْمُؤْمِنٰتِ ثُمَّ طَلَّقْتُمُوْهُنَّ
مِنْ قَبْلِ اَنْ تَمَسُّوْهُنَّ فَمَا لَكُمْ عَلَيْهِنَّ مِنْ عِدَّةٍ
تَعْتَدُّوْنَهَا ۚ فَمَتِّعُوْهُنَّ وَسَرِّحُوْهُنَّ سَرَاحًا جَمِيْلًا ﴿٥٠﴾

51. O Prophet! We have made lawful to thee thy wives whom thou hast paid their dowries, and those whom thy right hand possesses from among those whom Allāh has given thee as gains of war, and the daughters of thy paternal uncle, and the daughters of thy paternal aunts, and the daughters of thy maternal uncle, and the daughters of thy maternal aunts who have emigrated with thee and any *other* believing woman if she offers herself *for marriage* to the Prophet provided the Prophet desires to marry her; *this provision is* only for thee, and not for *other* believers—We have *already* made known what We have enjoined on them concerning their wives and those whom their right hands possess—in order that there may be no difficulty for thee *in explaining the Law to them.* And Allāh is Most Forgiving, Merciful.[2362]

يٰٓاَيُّهَا النَّبِيُّ اِنَّآ اَحْلَلْنَا لَكَ اَزْوَاجَكَ الّٰتِيْٓ اٰتَيْتَ
اُجُوْرَهُنَّ وَمَا مَلَكَتْ يَمِيْنُكَ مِمَّآ اَفَآءَ اللّٰهُ عَلَيْكَ
وَبَنٰتِ عَمِّكَ وَبَنٰتِ عَمّٰتِكَ وَبَنٰتِ خَالِكَ وَبَنٰتِ
خٰلٰتِكَ الّٰتِيْ هَاجَرْنَ مَعَكَ ۫ وَامْرَاَةً مُّؤْمِنَةً اِنْ
وَّهَبَتْ نَفْسَهَا لِلنَّبِيِّ اِنْ اَرَادَ النَّبِيُّ اَنْ يَّسْتَنْكِحَهَا ۗ
خَالِصَةً لَّكَ مِنْ دُوْنِ الْمُؤْمِنِيْنَ ؕ قَدْ عَلِمْنَا مَا
فَرَضْنَا عَلَيْهِمْ فِيْٓ اَزْوَاجِهِمْ وَمَا مَلَكَتْ اَيْمَانُهُمْ
لِكَيْلَا يَكُوْنَ عَلَيْكَ حَرَجٌ ۭ وَكَانَ اللّٰهُ غَفُوْرًا رَّحِيْمًا ﴿٥١﴾

---

[a]2 : 237.

2361. The words, *and send them away in a handsome manner*, signify (1) that no reproach or disgrace should be considered to attach to the divorced woman; (2) that the divorced woman should ordinarily be paid more than her part of the stipulated dower, and (3) that after divorce her freedom to act as she likes with regard to herself should not be interfered with.

2362. This verse should be read along with vv.29 and 30 above, in which the wives of the Holy Prophet were offered a choice between his companionship and the material benefits and comforts of life, and they preferred the Prophet's company. The present verse, by implication, refers to that reply of the Prophet's consorts which is recorded in the books of history but expressly nowhere in the Qur'ān. Till they gave their reply, the physical relations between them and the Holy Prophet remained, as it were, in a state of suspension. While the wives of the Holy Prophet preferred his company to material goods and amenities of life, he too had great consideration for their feelings, and though he was given the choice to retain such of them as he liked (v. 52), he did not exercise the choice and retained all of them.

52. Thou mayest put aside any of them that thou pleasest, and keep with thyself whom thou pleasest; and if thou desirest *to take back* any of those whom thou hast put aside, there is no blame on thee. That is more likely that their eyes may be cooled, and that they may not grieve, and that they may all be pleased with that which thou hast

تُرْجِيْ مَنْ تَشَآءُ مِنْهُنَّ وَتُؤْوِيْٓ اِلَيْكَ مَنْ تَشَآءُ ۭ
وَمَنِ ابْتَغَيْتَ مِمَّنْ عَزَلْتَ فَلَاجُنَاحَ عَلَيْكَ ۭ ذٰلِكَ
اَدْنٰٓى اَنْ تَقَرَّ اَعْيُنُهُنَّ وَلَا يَحْزَنَّ وَيَرْضَيْنَ بِمَآ

The Holy Prophet's marriages were motivated by highly noble considerations and not by those imputed to him by his ignorant and ignoble critics. With the solitary exception of his marriage with 'Ā'ishah, which later circumstances fully justified, he married only widows or divorced women. He married Ḥafṣah whose husband was killed in the battle of Badr; Zainab bint Khuzaimah whose husband was killed in the battle of Uḥud; Umm Salmah whose husband died in 4.A.H.; and Umm Ḥabībah, daughter of Abū Sufyān, who became a widow in 5 or 6 A.H. (in exile in Abyssinia). He married Juwairiyah and Ṣafiyyah, both widows, in 5 A.H. and 7 A.H. respectively, seeking a union with and pacification of their tribes. It is worthy of note that a hundred families of the Banī Muṣṭaliq were liberated by Muslims when the Holy Prophet married Juwairiyah. Maimūnah, another widow, it is said, offered herself to be taken in marriage by the Holy Prophet which offer he condescended to accept in the interest of the education and training of Muslim women. He married Zainab, the divorced wife of Zaid in 5 A.H., in order to put a stop to a foolish custom prevailing among the Arabs and in order also to assuage her wounded feelings as the respected lady had felt deeply humiliated at being divorced by Zaid. He married Māriah in 7 A.H. and thus by raising a freed slave girl to the highly eminent spiritual status of the "Mother of the Faithful" he gave a death blow to slavery. Such were the pious and righteous motives of our noble Master in marrying widows and divorced women, by no means noted for their youth or beauty. His critics deliberately ignore the patent fact that up to the age of 25 he lived the spotless life of a celibate. Then in the prime of his youth he married a lady many years his senior and lived with her a most happy life till he was an old man of fifty and she about sixty-five. After her death he married Saudah, another lady of very advanced age. He married all his other wives, to which exception has been taken by evil-minded carpers, between 2 A.H. and 7 A.H., a period when he was constantly engaged in active fighting and his life was perpetually in danger and the fate of Islām itself hung in the balance. Could any sane person in such situation of danger and uncertainty conceive of contracting marriage after marriage from bad motives such as are attributed to the Holy Prophet by his evil-minded critics? After this he lived for about three years as virtual ruler of the whole of Arabia when all the comforts and amenities of life were at his disposal, and yet he entered into no further marriage. Does not this fact alone establish the honesty and sincerity of the Holy Prophet's motives in contracting his marriages?

The words 'if she offers herself *for marriage* to the Prophet' have been taken as specially referring to Maimūnah who is reported to have offered herself to be taken into marriage by the Holy Prophet. The clause, *this provision is only for thee and not for other believers*, means that it was a special privilege of the Holy Prophet and was due to the special nature of his duties as a Divine Prophet. The clause may also refer to the special permission granted to the Holy Prophet, to retain all his wives, after the commandment contained in 4 : 4 was revealed limiting to four the number of wives allowed to Muslims at one time. The words, *We have already made known what We have enjoined on them concerning their wives*, refer to the commandment contained in 4 : 4, according to which only four wives at the most at a time are allowed to a Muslim. But in view of the Holy Prophet's own and of his wives' very high spiritual status and other spiritual and moral considerations, exception was made in the case of the Holy Prophet in the opening words of this verse.

given[2363] them. And Allāh knows what is in your hearts; and Allāh is All-Knowing, Forbearing.

اٰتَيْتَهُنَّ كُلُّهُنَّ ۚ وَاللّٰهُ يَعْلَمُ مَا فِيْ قُلُوْبِكُمْ ۚ وَكَانَ
اللّٰهُ عَلِيْمًا حَلِيْمًا ﴿۵۲﴾

53. It is not allowed to thee *to marry* women after that, nor to change them for *other* wives[2364] even, though their goodness please thee, except any that thy right hand possesses. And Allāh is Watchful over all things.

لَا يَحِلُّ لَكَ النِّسَآءُ مِنْۢ بَعْدُ وَلَآ اَنْ تَبَدَّلَ بِهِنَّ
مِنْ اَزْوَاجٍ وَّلَوْ اَعْجَبَكَ حُسْنُهُنَّ اِلَّا مَا مَلَكَتْ
يَمِيْنُكَ ۚ وَكَانَ اللّٰهُ عَلٰى كُلِّ شَيْءٍ رَّقِيْبًا ﴿۵۳﴾ ع

R. 7 54. O ye who believe! enter not the houses of the Prophet unless leave is granted to you for a meal, not waiting till it is cooked.[2364A] But enter when you are invited, and when you have had your meal, disperse, without seeking to engage in talk.[2365] That causes inconvenience to the Prophet, and he feels shy of *asking* you *to leave*, but Allāh is not shy of *saying* what is true. And when you ask them—*the wives of the Prophet*—for anything, ask them[2366] from behind a curtain. That is purer for your hearts and their hearts.

يٰۤاَيُّهَا الَّذِيْنَ اٰمَنُوْا لَا تَدْخُلُوْا بُيُوْتَ النَّبِيِّ اِلَّاۤ اَنْ
يُّؤْذَنَ لَكُمْ اِلٰى طَعَامٍ غَيْرَ نٰظِرِيْنَ اِنٰىهُ ۙ وَلٰكِنْ
اِذَا دُعِيْتُمْ فَادْخُلُوْا فَاِذَا طَعِمْتُمْ فَانْتَشِرُوْا وَ
لَا مُسْتَاْنِسِيْنَ لِحَدِيْثٍ ۭ اِنَّ ذٰلِكُمْ كَانَ يُؤْذِي
النَّبِيَّ فَيَسْتَحْيٖ مِنْكُمْ ۡ وَاللّٰهُ لَا يَسْتَحْيٖ مِنَ الْحَقِّ ۭ
وَاِذَا سَاَلْتُمُوْهُنَّ مَتَاعًا فَسْـَٔلُوْهُنَّ مِنْ وَّرَآءِ حِجَابٍ ۭ
ذٰلِكُمْ اَطْهَرُ لِقُلُوْبِكُمْ وَقُلُوْبِهِنَّ ۭ وَمَا كَانَ لَكُمْ

2363. Whereas, on the one hand, the wives of the Holy Prophet were given the option to choose between his companionship and the material comforts of life and worldly goods (33 : 29-30), on the other, the Holy Prophet was also given the choice to retain or part with any of his wives. All his wives lost no time in indicating their preference. They chose to cast in their lot with him. The Holy Prophet, on his part, was equally considerate. He signified his intention to retain all of them. This decision of the Prophet greatly pleased them. This is the meaning of the words : *that they may all be pleased with that which thou hast given them*.

2364. This verse was revealed in 7 A.H. after which the Holy Prophet contracted no further marriage. He was also not allowed to divorce any of the existing wives, possibly in deference to their dignity as "Mothers of the Faithful" and perhaps also because they had preferred the rigour and austerity of the Holy Prophet's domestic life to worldly comforts. God appreciated their sacrifice and forbade the Holy Prophet to marry any more wife or to divorce any of the existing wives.

2364A. For the food to get ready.

2365. One should not enter a house uninvited, and when invited he should be punctual. It is as bad to be before time as to be behind time. After meals one should depart, not wasting one's own and other peoples' time in the usual post-prandial idle talk.

2366. The commandment is intended to discourage too much familiarity between the sexes, the pronoun *hunna* (them) by implication applying to all women.

And it behoves you not to cause inconvenience to the Messenger of Allāh, nor that you should ever marry his wives after him. That, indeed, is a monstrous thing in the sight of Allāh.[2367]

أَنْ تُؤْذُوا رَسُولَ اللَّهِ وَلَا أَنْ تَنْكِحُوا أَزْوَاجَهُ مِنْ
بَعْدِهِ أَبَدًا ۚ إِنَّ ذَٰلِكُمْ كَانَ عِنْدَ اللَّهِ عَظِيمًا ﴿٥٤﴾

55. [a]Whether you disclose a thing or conceal it, Allāh knows all things well.

إِنْ تُبْدُوا شَيْئًا أَوْ تُخْفُوهُ فَإِنَّ اللَّهَ كَانَ بِكُلِّ شَيْءٍ
عَلِيمًا ﴿٥٥﴾

56. There is no blame on them *in this respect* with regard to their fathers or their sons or their brothers, or the sons of their brothers or the sons of their sisters, or their womenfolk or those whom their right hands possess. And fear Allāh, *O wives of the Prophet*. Verily, Allāh is Witness over all things.

لَا جُنَاحَ عَلَيْهِنَّ فِي آبَائِهِنَّ وَلَا أَبْنَائِهِنَّ وَلَا
إِخْوَانِهِنَّ وَلَا أَبْنَاءِ إِخْوَانِهِنَّ وَلَا أَبْنَاءِ أَخَوَاتِهِنَّ
وَلَا نِسَائِهِنَّ وَلَا مَا مَلَكَتْ أَيْمَانُهُنَّ ۗ وَاتَّقِينَ
اللَّهَ ۚ إِنَّ اللَّهَ كَانَ عَلَىٰ كُلِّ شَيْءٍ شَهِيدًا ﴿٥٦﴾

57. Allāh sends down *His* blessings on the Prophet and His angels pray for him. O ye who believe, you *too* should invoke *His* blessings on him and salute him with the salutation of peace.

إِنَّ اللَّهَ وَمَلَائِكَتَهُ يُصَلُّونَ عَلَى النَّبِيِّ ۚ يَا أَيُّهَا الَّذِينَ
آمَنُوا صَلُّوا عَلَيْهِ وَسَلِّمُوا تَسْلِيمًا ﴿٥٧﴾

58. Verily, [b]those who malign Allāh and His Messenger[2368]—Allāh has cursed them in this world and in the Hereafter, and has prepared for them an abasing punishment.

إِنَّ الَّذِينَ يُؤْذُونَ اللَّهَ وَرَسُولَهُ لَعَنَهُمُ اللَّهُ فِي
الدُّنْيَا وَالْآخِرَةِ وَأَعَدَّ لَهُمْ عَذَابًا مُهِينًا ﴿٥٨﴾

59. [c]And those, who malign believing men and believing women for what they have not earned, shall bear *the guilt of* a calumny and a manifest sin.

وَالَّذِينَ يُؤْذُونَ الْمُؤْمِنِينَ وَالْمُؤْمِنَاتِ بِغَيْرِ مَا
اكْتَسَبُوا فَقَدِ احْتَمَلُوا بُهْتَانًا وَإِثْمًا مُبِينًا ﴿٥٩﴾

---

[a]3 : 30; 4 : 150. [b]9 : 61. [c]4 : 113; 24 : 24.

2367. Marriage with the widows of the Holy Prophet has been declared a grievous sin in this verse. Being the "Mothers of the Faithful" it was inconsistent with their spiritual dignity that any of their "spiritual sons" should marry any of them.

2368. By 'maligning Allāh' is meant 'seeking to put obstacles in the way of the cause of truth' and by 'maligning His Messenger,' is meant 'seeking to slander and defame him.'

R. 8 60. O Prophet ! tell thy wives and thy daughters, and the women of the believers, that they should pull down upon them of their outer cloaks *from their heads over their faces.*[2369] That is more likely that they may *thus* be recognized and not molested. And Allāh is Most Forgiving, Merciful.

يٰٓاَيُّهَا النَّبِيُّ قُلْ لِّاَزْوَاجِكَ وَ بَنٰتِكَ وَنِسَآءِ الْمُؤْمِنِيْنَ
يُدْنِيْنَ عَلَيْهِنَّ مِنْ جَلَابِيْبِهِنَّ ؕ ذٰلِكَ اَدْنٰٓى اَنْ
يُّعْرَفْنَ فَلَا يُؤْذَيْنَ ؕ وَكَانَ اللّٰهُ غَفُوْرًا رَّحِيْمًا ﴿٦٠﴾

61. If the Hypocrites and those in whose hearts is a disease and those who cause agitation in the City *by spreading false rumours,* desist not, We shall, surely, urge thee on against[2370] them ; then they will not dwell therein as thy neighbours save for a little while.

لَئِنْ لَّمْ يَنْتَهِ الْمُنٰفِقُوْنَ وَالَّذِيْنَ فِيْ قُلُوْبِهِمْ مَّرَضٌ
وَّالْمُرْجِفُوْنَ فِي الْمَدِيْنَةِ لَنُغْرِيَنَّكَ بِهِمْ ثُمَّ لَا
يُجَاوِرُوْنَكَ فِيْهَآ اِلَّا قَلِيْلًا ﴿٦١﴾

62. *They are* accursed. Wherever they are found they will be seized, and cut into pieces.[2371]

مَّلْعُوْنِيْنَ ۚ اَيْنَمَا ثُقِفُوْٓا اُخِذُوْا وَقُتِّلُوْا تَقْتِيْلًا ﴿٦٢﴾

63. "[a]*Such has been* the way of Allāh with those who passed away before, and never thou wilt find a change in the way of Allāh.

سُنَّةَ اللّٰهِ فِي الَّذِيْنَ خَلَوْا مِنْ قَبْلُ ۚ وَلَنْ تَجِدَ لِسُنَّةِ
اللّٰهِ تَبْدِيْلًا ﴿٦٣﴾

[a]17 : 78; 35 : 44; 48 : 24.

2369. *Jalābīb* (outer cloaks) is the plural of *Jilbāb* which means, (*a*) a woman's outer wrapping garment; (*b*) a garment that envelops the whole body; (*c*) a garment worn by a woman that entirely envelops the body so that not even a hand is left uncovered (Lane). Islamic "Pardah" serves a double purpose. It enjoins privacy and recommends decorum and dignified behaviour. Women are not allowed to meet men promiscuously, and they are also expected to observe certain rules regarding dress when going out of their houses. For a detailed discussion of the subject of "Pardah" see 2044.

2370. The Hypocrites and Jews of Medina sought to put all sorts of obstacles in the way of Islām, the main weapon in their armoury against it being the spreading of false news. This capacity to create mischief received a severe set-back when the defeat and dispersion of the confederated armies added vastly to its political power and prestige. The expression, *Lanughriyannaka bi-him,* also means 'We shall surely make thee take action against them', or give thee authority over them.'

2371. Ignominy and humiliation have dogged the footsteps of the ill-fated Jewish people throughout the ages. Their return to Palestine and the establishment of the State of Israel seems to be only a temporary phase.

64. [a]People ask thee concerning the Hour. Say, 'The knowledge of it is with Allāh *alone*.' And what will make thee know that the Hour may be nigh?

يَسْـَٔلُكَ النَّاسُ عَنِ السَّاعَةِ ۚ قُلْ اِنَّمَا عِلْمُهَا عِنْدَ
اللّٰهِ ؕ وَ مَا يُدْرِيْكَ لَعَلَّ السَّاعَةَ تَكُوْنُ قَرِيْبًا ﴿۶۴﴾

65. [b]Allāh has, surely, cursed the disbelievers, and has prepared for them a blazing fire,

اِنَّ اللّٰهَ لَعَنَ الْكٰفِرِيْنَ وَ اَعَدَّ لَهُمْ سَعِيْرًا ﴿۶۵﴾

66. Wherein they will abide for ever. They will find *therein* no friend, nor helper.

خٰلِدِيْنَ فِيْهَاۤ اَبَدًا ۚ لَا يَجِدُوْنَ وَلِيًّا وَّ لَا نَصِيْرًا ﴿۶۶﴾

67. On the day when their faces are turned over into the fire, they will say, [c]'O, would that we had obeyed Allāh and obeyed the Messenger!'

يَوْمَ تُقَلَّبُ وُجُوْهُهُمْ فِي النَّارِ يَقُوْلُوْنَ يٰلَيْتَنَاۤ
اَطَعْنَا اللّٰهَ وَ اَطَعْنَا الرَّسُوْلَا ﴿۶۷﴾

68. [d]And they will say, 'Our Lord, we obeyed our chiefs and our great ones and they led us astray from the way,[2372]

وَ قَالُوْا رَبَّنَاۤ اِنَّاۤ اَطَعْنَا سَادَتَنَا وَ كُبَرَآءَنَا فَاَضَلُّوْنَا
السَّبِيْلَا ﴿۶۸﴾

69. 'Our Lord, give them double punishment and curse them with a mighty curse.'

رَبَّنَاۤ اٰتِهِمْ ضِعْفَيْنِ مِنَ الْعَذَابِ وَ الْعَنْهُمْ لَعْنًا
كَبِيْرًا ﴿۶۹﴾ ع

R. 9 70. O ye who believe! be not like those who maligned[2373] Moses;[2373A] but Allāh cleared him of what they said *about him*. [e]And he had a great position in the sight of Allāh.

يٰۤاَيُّهَا الَّذِيْنَ اٰمَنُوْا لَا تَكُوْنُوْا كَالَّذِيْنَ اٰذَوْا مُوْسٰى
فَبَرَّاَهُ اللّٰهُ مِمَّا قَالُوْا ؕ وَ كَانَ عِنْدَ اللّٰهِ وَجِيْهًا ﴿۷۰﴾

71. O ye who believe! fear Allāh and say the straightforward word.

يٰۤاَيُّهَا الَّذِيْنَ اٰمَنُوا اتَّقُوا اللّٰهَ وَ قُوْلُوْا قَوْلًا سَدِيْدًا ﴿۷۱﴾

[a]7 : 188; 78 : 3. [b]7 : 45. [c]25 : 28. [d]7 : 39; 14 : 22; 28 : 64; 34 : 32-33; 40 : 48-49. [e]19 : 52, 53.

2372. In the preceding verse reference was made to the leaders of disbelief, *Wujūh* also meaning leaders. Here the rank and file are mentioned. It is human nature to seek to shift the blame for one's own evil deeds to others.

2373. *Ādhāhu* means, he did or said what was disagreeable or hateful to him; maligned or annoyed or hurt him.

2373A. Moses was made the butt of serious calumnies, some of which were: (1) Korah induced a woman to bring against him a charge of illicit connection with her. (2) Having become jealous of Aaron's increasing influence with his people, Moses sought to kill him. (3) He was a victim of leprosy and syphilis; and (4) Sāmirī charged him with idolatry. (5) His own sister brought false accusations against him.

72. He will set right your actions for you and forgive you your sins. *And whoso obeys Allāh and His Messenger shall, surely, attain a supreme triumph.

يُصْلِحْ لَكُمْ اَعْمَالَكُمْ وَ يَغْفِرْ لَكُمْ ذُنُوْبَكُمْ وَمَنْ يُّطِعِ اللّٰهَ وَ رَسُوْلَهُ فَقَدْ فَازَ فَوْزًا عَظِيْمًا ۞

73. Verily, We offered the trust *of the Divine Law* to the heavens and the earth and the mountains, but they refused to bear it and were afraid of it. But man bore it. Indeed, he is *capable of being* unjust *to, and* neglectful *of, himself.*[2374]

اِنَّا عَرَضْنَا الْاَمَانَةَ عَلَى السَّمٰوٰتِ وَ الْاَرْضِ وَ الْجِبَالِ فَاَبَيْنَ اَنْ يَّحْمِلْنَهَا وَ اَشْفَقْنَ مِنْهَا وَ حَمَلَهَا الْاِنْسَانُ اِنَّهُ كَانَ ظَلُوْمًا جَهُوْلًا ۞

74. *The consequence is that* Allāh will punish hypocritical men and hypocritical women, and idolatrous men and idolatrous women; *and Allāh turns in mercy to believing men and believing women; and Allāh is Most Forgiving, Merciful.

لِيُعَذِّبَ اللّٰهُ الْمُنٰفِقِيْنَ وَ الْمُنٰفِقٰتِ وَ الْمُشْرِكِيْنَ وَ الْمُشْرِكٰتِ وَ يَتُوْبَ اللّٰهُ عَلَى الْمُؤْمِنِيْنَ وَ الْمُؤْمِنٰتِ ۞ وَ كَانَ اللّٰهُ غَفُوْرًا رَّحِيْمًا ۞

---

*4 : 14;   24 : 53;   48 : 18.   *4 : 28;   9 : 104.

2374. *Hamala al-Amānata* means, he took upon himself or accepted the trust; he betrayed it. *Zalūm* is the intensive form of *Zālim* which is active participle from *Zalama,* which means, he put the thing in a wrong place; and *Zalama-hū* means, he imposed upon himself a burden which it was beyond his power or ability to bear. *Jahūl* is the intensive form of *Jāhil* which means, neglectful; foolish: heedless (Lane).

Man is gifted with great natural capacities and powers to assimilate and manifest in his person Divine attributes and to become the image of his Creator (2 : 31). This is, indeed, a great trust which man, alone of all the universe, was found capable of discharging; other beings and things—the angels, the heavens, the earth and the mountains being quite unequal to it. They refused, as it were, to bear it. Man accepted this responsibility because he alone could discharge it. He is capable of being *Zalūm* (unjust to himself) and *Jahūl* (neglectful of himself) *i.e.,* he could be unjust to himself in the sense that he could bear any hardship and undergo any sacrifice for the sake of his Creator, and he is capable of being neglectful or heedless in the sense that in the discharge of his great and sacred trust he could be neglectful of his own interest and desire for a life of ease and comfort. (2) Taking *al-Amānat* (trust) in the sense of the Law of the Qur'ān and *al-Insān* signifying the perfect man, *i.e.,* the Holy Prophet, the verse would mean that of all the denizens of the heavens and the earth, the Holy Prophet alone was found to be capable of being entrusted with the revelation of the most perfect and final Law—the Qur'ān, because no other man or being was endowed with those great qualities which were indispensable for the full and adequate discharge of this great responsibility. (3) Taking *Hamala* in the sense of betraying or proving false to a trust, the verse would mean that the trust of the Divine Law was imposed upon man and other terrestrial and celestial beings. All of them with the exception of man refused to betray this trust, *i.e.,* they carried out fully and faithfully all the laws to which they were made subject. The whole nature was true to its laws and the angels also carried out their duties loyally and faithfully (16 : 50, 51). It is man alone who having been endowed with discretion and volition, defies and violates Divine commandments because he is unjust and neglects and ignores his duties and responsibilities. This meaning of the verse is supported by 41 : 12.

CHAPTER 34

AL-SABA'

(*Revealed before Hijrah*)

Date of Revelation, Title and Context

The *Sūrah* was revealed at Mecca. It is difficult to assign it a definite date. Some scholars place it in the Middle Meccan Period; some others like Rodwell and Noldeke give it a later date. The preceding several Chapters embodied prophecies about the rise, progress and the ultimate victory of Islām over other Faiths, while in the immediately preceding Chapter, Al-Aḥzāb, the subject was dealt with at some length; how the combined forces of darkness utterly failed in their nefarious designs to destroy Islām and how Islām emerged from one of the severest ordeals with flying colours; its power and prestige having been considerably enhanced. In the present *Sūrah*, however, Muslims have been warned that they should be on their guard against falling into bad ways because when wealth and prosperity come to a people they are prone to give themselves up to a life of ease and luxury. Since God has no particular relation with any community for all time, if Muslims in the heyday of their glory and material prosperity led a life of sin—as did the Sabaeans or the Israelites after Solomon—they too would suffer the same fate.

Subject-Matter

The *Sūrah* opens with the celebration of the praises of Allāh 'to Whom belongs whatever is in the heavens and whatever is in the earth, ' implying that as God is Great and Almighty a people who seek to defy His authority are sure to meet with failure and frustration. It proceeds to say that disbelievers delude themselves into the belief that their rejection of the Message of Islām will go unpunished and that 'the Hour will never come upon them.' They are warned that their power will break and their glory depart and that this fact will constitute a proof of the truth of the Holy Prophet's mission. Next, the *Sūrah* makes a somewhat detailed reference to Prophets David and Solomon, who made vast conquests and subdued rebellious tribes and in whose reigns the Israelite power and glory rose to its zenith. But in the pride of their power and prosperity the Israelites fell into evil ways and began to lead a life of sin. This reference to the Israelites is followed by a reference to the Sabaeans who were a highly prosperous and cultured people, but who like the Israelites defied and disobeyed Divine commandments and like them incurred the displeasure of God and were destroyed by a mighty flood. By referring to the might, glory and prosperity of the Israelites under David and Solomon, and to that of the Sabaeans, and to the subsequent destruction of both, the *Sūrah* gives a warning to Muslims that wealth, power and prosperity will also be bestowed on them, but if in the heyday of their glory they, like the Israelites and the Sabaeans, gave themselves up to a life of luxury and ease, they will be punished like them. Next, the *Sūrah* deals with its main theme, *viz.*, the progressive rise of the cause of Islām and the sad fate that is in store for idol-worshippers and their false deities. The disbelievers are challenged to call upon their deities to obstruct the progress of Islām, and to arrest the decline and downfall of their own false ideals and institutions. They are told that no power on earth could stop this from happening. In order to make them realize that their cause was destined to perish and Islām to sweep away everything before it, they are further told to study the operation of the laws of nature, which were all working in its favour. In answer to the disbelievers' demand as to when the prophecy about the rise and progress of Islām will be fulfilled, the *Sūrah* goes so far as to fix a definite date for it. Its signs, it says, will begin to appear about a year after the Flight of the Holy Prophet from Mecca when the Quraishites, by expelling him from his native town, will render themselves deserving of Divine punishment. After this the *Sūrah* observes that whenever a Divine Reformer makes his appearance it is the vested interests and privileged classes that stand in his way. They feel and apprehend that the rise of the new Movement will weaken their hold on the poor people who, by accepting the new Message, will refuse to be exploited or suppressed any more. So they fight it tooth and nail and try to nip it in the bud and the suppressed and exploited classes are, by threats and intimidation, dragooned into accepting their lead and opposing the Divine Reformer. Towards its close the *Sūrah* refers to a simple criterion by which it could be easily found out that the Holy Prophet is neither an impostor nor a maniac but a true Prophet of God. An impostor, it says, is never allowed to prosper and eventually comes to a sad end but the cause of the Prophet is progressing, and a madman cannot bring about such a wonderful revolution in the life of a whole people as the Holy Prophet has done.

سُورَةُ سَبَإٍ مَكِّيَّةٌ

(٣٤) آياتها ٥٥ ركوعاتها ٦

1. [a]In the name of Allāh, the Gracious, the Merciful.

بِسْمِ اللّٰهِ الرَّحْمٰنِ الرَّحِيْمِ ۝١

2. All praise is due to Allāh, to Whom belongs whatever is in the heavens and whatever is in the earth.[2375] And His is all praise in the Hereafter; and He is the Wise, the All-Aware.

اَلْحَمْدُ لِلّٰهِ الَّذِيْ لَهٗ مَا فِي السَّمٰوٰتِ وَمَا فِي الْاَرْضِ وَلَهُ الْحَمْدُ فِي الْاٰخِرَةِ ۭ وَهُوَ الْحَكِيْمُ الْخَبِيْرُ ۝٢

3. [b]He knows whatever goes into the earth and whatever comes forth from it, and whatever descends from the heaven and whatever ascends into it;[2376] and He is Merciful, Most Forgiving.

يَعْلَمُ مَا يَلِجُ فِي الْاَرْضِ وَمَا يَخْرُجُ مِنْهَا وَمَا يَنْزِلُ مِنَ السَّمَاۗءِ وَمَا يَعْرُجُ فِيْهَا ۭ وَهُوَ الرَّحِيْمُ الْغَفُوْرُ ۝٣

4. And those who disbelieve say, 'The Hour will never come upon us.' Say, 'Yea, by my Lord Who knows the unseen, it will, surely, come upon you. [c]Not an atom's weight in the heavens or in the earth or anything less than that or greater escapes Him, but *all is recorded* in a perspicuous Book,[2377]

وَقَالَ الَّذِيْنَ كَفَرُوْا لَا تَاْتِيْنَا السَّاعَةُ ۭ قُلْ بَلٰى وَرَبِّيْ لَتَاْتِيَنَّكُمْ ۙ عٰلِمِ الْغَيْبِ ۚ لَا يَعْزُبُ عَنْهُ مِثْقَالُ ذَرَّةٍ فِي السَّمٰوٰتِ وَلَا فِي الْاَرْضِ وَلَآ اَصْغَرُ مِنْ ذٰلِكَ وَلَآ اَكْبَرُ اِلَّا فِيْ كِتٰبٍ مُّبِيْنٍ ۝٤

---

[a]1 : 1. [b]57 : 5. [c]10 : 62.

2375. Five Chapters of the Qur'ān, *i.e.*, 1st, 6th, 18th, 35th and the present one, begin with the words 'All praise is due to Allāh.' All these Chapters, expressly or by implication, deal with the subject of the Lordship, Almightiness and Majesty of God.

2376. The words, 'His is all praise in the Hereafter' refer to the time when Islām again will become triumphant after its temporary decline. The allusion in this verse is to the subject dealt with in 32 : 6. It signifies that it is God alone Who knows what kind of teaching is needed in a particular age. Similarly, it is He who knows when to take back to heaven the teaching which had descended from it, after it has been corrupted by the people, just as He takes water back to heaven in the form of vapours after it becomes corrupt, and sends it down in a purified form in the shape of rain. The words, 'whatever goes into the earth and whatever comes forth from it,' may also signify that whatever man shall sow, so shall he reap. Good actions produce good results and bad deeds lead to evil consequences. The verse may also be taken as signifying that God is aware of every phenomenon and every event, including the rise and fall of nations.

2377. The subject of the preceding verse is further elaborated and developed in the present one, *viz.*, that no action good or bad goes unrequited. The disbelievers are thus warned that their opposition to Islām and their persecution of Muslims will not go unpunished.

5. [a]"That He may reward those who believe and do righteous deeds. It is these who will have forgiveness and an honourable provision.'

لِيَجْزِيَ الَّذِينَ آمَنُوا وَعَمِلُوا الصَّالِحَاتِ ۚ أُولَٰئِكَ لَهُمْ مَغْفِرَةٌ وَرِزْقٌ كَرِيمٌ ٥

6. [b]But *as to* those who strive against Our Signs, seeking to frustrate *Our plans*, it is they for whom there will be the torment of a painful punishment.

وَالَّذِينَ سَعَوْ فِي آيَاتِنَا مُعَاجِزِينَ أُولَٰئِكَ لَهُمْ عَذَابٌ مِنْ رِجْزٍ أَلِيمٌ ٦

7. [c]And those who are given knowledge see that whatever has been revealed to thee from thy Lord is the truth, and *that it* guides unto the path of the Mighty, the Praiseworthy.

وَيَرَى الَّذِينَ أُوتُوا الْعِلْمَ الَّذِي أُنْزِلَ إِلَيْكَ مِنْ رَبِّكَ هُوَ الْحَقَّ وَيَهْدِي إِلَىٰ صِرَاطِ الْعَزِيزِ الْحَمِيدِ ٧

8. And those who disbelieve say, 'Shall we show you a man who will tell you *that* when you are broken up into pieces, you shall be *raised as* a new creation?

وَقَالَ الَّذِينَ كَفَرُوا هَلْ نَدُلُّكُمْ عَلَىٰ رَجُلٍ يُنَبِّئُكُمْ إِذَا مُزِّقْتُمْ كُلَّ مُمَزَّقٍ إِنَّكُمْ لَفِي خَلْقٍ جَدِيدٍ ٨

9. 'Has he forged a lie against Allāh or is he afflicted with madness?' Nay, [d]but those who believe not in the Hereafter are *already* suffering the punishment and are too far gone in error.

أَفْتَرَىٰ عَلَى اللَّهِ كَذِبًا أَمْ بِهِ جِنَّةٌ ۗ بَلِ الَّذِينَ لَا يُؤْمِنُونَ بِالْآخِرَةِ فِي الْعَذَابِ وَالضَّلَالِ الْبَعِيدِ ٩

10. Do they not see *how they are encompassed by* that which is before them and that which is behind them of the heaven and the earth? [e]If We please, We could cause the earth to sink with them, or cause pieces of the sky to fall upon[2378] them. In that verily is a Sign for every repentant servant *of Allāh*.

أَفَلَمْ يَرَوْا إِلَىٰ مَا بَيْنَ أَيْدِيهِمْ وَمَا خَلْفَهُمْ مِنَ السَّمَاءِ وَالْأَرْضِ ۚ إِنْ نَشَأْ نَخْسِفْ بِهِمُ الْأَرْضَ أَوْ نُسْقِطْ عَلَيْهِمْ كِسَفًا مِنَ السَّمَاءِ ۚ إِنَّ فِي ذَٰلِكَ لَآيَةً لِكُلِّ عَبْدٍ مُنِيبٍ ١٠

[a]10 : 5; 30 : 46. [b]22 : 52; 34 : 39. [c]13 : 20; 22 : 55; 35 : 32; 56 : 96. [d]17 : 11; 27 : 5. [e]6 : 66; 17 : 69; 67 : 17-18.

2378. The words, 'We could cause the earth to sink with them,' refer to the Signs of the earth; and the words 'or cause pieces of the sky to fall upon them' allude to heavenly Signs.

R. 2 11. And certainly, We bestowed grace upon David from Us *and said*, [a]'O ye mountains,[2378A] celebrate *the praises of Allāh* with him,[2378B] and O birds, *ye also*.' And We made the iron soft for him,[2379]

وَلَقَدْ اٰتَيْنَا دَاوٗدَ مِنَّا فَضْلًا ۖ يٰجِبَالُ اَوِّبِيْ مَعَهٗ وَ
الطَّيْرَ ۚ وَاَلَنَّا لَهُ الْحَدِيْدَ ﴿۱۱﴾

12. *And We said*, 'Make thou full-length coats of mail, and make the rings of a proper measure. And act righteously, surely I see all that you do.'

اَنِ اعْمَلْ سٰبِغٰتٍ وَّقَدِّرْ فِي السَّرْدِ وَاعْمَلُوْا صَالِحًا ۖ
اِنِّيْ بِمَا تَعْمَلُوْنَ بَصِيْرٌ ﴿۱۲﴾

13. [b]And to Solomon *We subjected* the wind; its morning course was a month's *journey*, and its evening course was a month's *journey too*. And We caused a fount of molten copper to flow for him. And of the jinn were *some* who worked under him by the command of his Lord.[2380] And *We said* that whoever of them turned away from Our command, We would make him taste the punishment of the burning fire.

وَلِسُلَيْمٰنَ الرِّيْحَ غُدُوُّهَا شَهْرٌ وَّرَوَاحُهَا شَهْرٌ ۚ وَ
اَسَلْنَا لَهٗ عَيْنَ الْقِطْرِ ۖ وَمِنَ الْجِنِّ مَنْ يَّعْمَلُ بَيْنَ
يَدَيْهِ بِاِذْنِ رَبِّهٖ ۖ وَمَنْ يَّزِغْ مِنْهُمْ عَنْ اَمْرِنَا نُذِقْهُ
مِنْ عَذَابِ السَّعِيْرِ ﴿۱۳﴾

[a]21 : 80; 38 : 19-20. [b]21 : 82 ; 38 : 37.

2378A. Mountain tribes. For a similar expression see 12 : 83.

2378B. See 1907.

2379. The expression, 'And We made the iron soft for him,' shows that the art of making implements of war from iron was very much developed by David and he freely made use of it for making coats of mail as the next verse shows.

2380. Solomon's dominions extended from northern Syria along the coast of the eastern Mediterranean down to the Red Sea, along the Arabian Sea and up to the Persian Gulf. In fact, in Solomon's time, the Israelite Empire had reached its zenith in wealth, power and prestige as the word *Rīḥ* which, among other things, means power and conquests, (Lane), used in the verse, shows. The verse also shows that Solomon possessed a large mercantile navy (1 Kings, 9 : 26-28 & Jew. Enc. vol. XI. p. 437) and that industry and craftsmanship had greatly developed under him and that he had also conquered and pressed into service wild and rebellious mountain tribes (11 Chron. 4 : 1-2 & 2 : 18).

14. They made for him what he desired—places of worship and statues, and basins like reservoirs,[2381] and large cooking vessels fixed in their places. *And We said*, [a]'Act gratefully, O House of David,' but few of My servants are grateful.

يَعْمَلُوْنَ لَهٗ مَا يَشَآءُ مِنْ مَّحَارِيْبَ وَتَمَاثِيْلَ وَجِفَانٍ كَالْجَوَابِ وَقُدُوْرٍ رّٰسِيٰتٍ ۭ اِعْمَلُوْٓا اٰلَ دَاوٗدَ شُكْرًا ۭ وَقَلِيْلٌ مِّنْ عِبَادِيَ الشَّكُوْرُ ﴿١٤﴾

15. And when We decreed his (Solomon's) death, nothing indicated to them that he was dead save a worm of the earth[2382] that ate away his staff. So when it fell down, the jinn plainly realized that if they had known the unseen, they would not have remained in a state of degrading torment.[2383]

فَلَمَّا قَضَيْنَا عَلَيْهِ الْمَوْتَ مَا دَلَّهُمْ عَلٰى مَوْتِهٖٓ اِلَّا دَآبَّةُ الْاَرْضِ تَاْكُلُ مِنْسَاَتَهٗ ۚ فَلَمَّا خَرَّ تَبَيَّنَتِ الْجِنُّ اَنْ لَّوْ كَانُوْا يَعْلَمُوْنَ الْغَيْبَ مَا لَبِثُوْا فِي الْعَذَابِ الْمُهِيْنِ ۭ ﴿١٥﴾

16. There was, indeed, a Sign for Saba'[2383A] in their homeland—two gardens, *one* on the right hand and *one* on the left; *and We said to them*, 'Eat of the provision of your Lord and give thanks to Him. *Your town is* a beautiful town and *your* Lord Most Forgiving.'

لَقَدْ كَانَ لِسَبَاٍ فِيْ مَسْكَنِهِمْ اٰيَةٌ ۚ جَنَّتٰنِ عَنْ يَّمِيْنٍ وَّشِمَالٍ ۥ كُلُوْا مِنْ رِّزْقِ رَبِّكُمْ وَاشْكُرُوْا لَهٗ ۭ بَلْدَةٌ طَيِّبَةٌ وَّرَبٌّ غَفُوْرٌ ﴿١٦﴾

[a]21 : 81.

2381. Besides being a highly prosperous, powerful and civilized monarch, Solomon was the prince of builders among Israelite rulers. He had a special taste for architecture which had greatly developed under him. The Temple of Jerusalem bears an eloquent testimony to his fine architectural taste.

2382. Solomon's worthless son and successor, Rehoboam, under whose weak rule Solomon's great and mighty Kingdom fell to pieces (1 Kings, chaps. 12, 13, 14 & Jewish. Enc. under "Rehoboam").

2383. Disruption and disintegration of Solomon's Kingdom set in in Rehoboam's time.

2383A. Saba', as is mentioned under 27 : 23, was a city of Yemen situated about three days' journey from Ṣan'ā', also called Ma'ārib. This town finds frequent references in the Old Testament and in Greek, Roman and Arabic literatures, especially in the south Arabian inscriptions. The Sabaeans were a highly prosperous and cultured people whom God had blessed in great abundance with all the comforts and amenities of life. The whole country was made very fertile by dams and other irrigation works and was full of gardens and streams. Of public works built to assist agriculture like barriers and dams the most celebrated was the dam of Ma'ārib (Enc. of Islām, vol. 4, p. 16). Tirmidhī quotes a tradition on the authority of Farwah bin Mālik that when asked whether Saba' was the name of a land or of a woman, the Holy Prophet is reported to have said, 'It is neither the name of a land nor that of a woman, but the name of a man in Yemen who had ten sons. Six of them remained back in Yemen while four of them went to Syria and made it their home' (Tāj).

17. But they turned away; so We sent against them a devastating flood.[2384] And We gave them, in place of their two *excellent* gardens, two gardens bearing bitter fruit and *containing* tamarisk and a few lote-trees.

فَأَعْرَضُوا فَأَرْسَلْنَا عَلَيْهِمْ سَيْلَ الْعَرِمِ وَبَدَّلْنٰهُمْ
بِجَنَّتَيْهِمْ جَنَّتَيْنِ ذَوَاتَيْ أُكُلٍ خَمْطٍ وَّأَثْلٍ وَّشَيْءٍ
مِّنْ سِدْرٍ قَلِيلٍ ﴿١٧﴾

18. Thus We requited them because of their ingratitude; and it is only the ungrateful that We requite *in this manner*.

ذٰلِكَ جَزَيْنٰهُمْ بِمَا كَفَرُوا وَهَلْ نُجْزِي إِلَّا الْكَفُورَ ﴿١٨﴾

19. And We placed, between them and the towns which We had blessed, *other* towns that were prominently visible, and We fixed *easy* stages[2385] between them *and said*: 'Travel in them by night and day in security.'

وَجَعَلْنَا بَيْنَهُمْ وَبَيْنَ الْقُرَى الَّتِي بٰرَكْنَا فِيهَا
قُرًى ظَاهِرَةً وَّقَدَّرْنَا فِيهَا السَّيْرَ سِيرُوا فِيهَا
لَيَالِيَ وَأَيَّامًا آمِنِينَ ﴿١٩﴾

20. But *instead of giving thanks to God* they said, 'Our Lord, place longer distances between *the stages of* our journeys.' And they wronged themselves; so We made them bywords and We broke them into pieces, an utter breaking up.[2386] In that, verily, are Signs for every steadfast *and* grateful *person*.

فَقَالُوا رَبَّنَا بَعِّدْ بَيْنَ أَسْفَارِنَا وَظَلَمُوا أَنْفُسَهُمْ
فَجَعَلْنٰهُمْ أَحَادِيثَ وَمَزَّقْنٰهُمْ كُلَّ مُمَزَّقٍ إِنَّ فِي
ذٰلِكَ لَآيٰتٍ لِّكُلِّ صَبَّارٍ شَكُورٍ ﴿٢٠﴾

2384. '*Arim* means, a dam or dams constructed in valleys or torrent-beds; or a torrent of which the rush is not to be withstood; or violent rain (Lane). A mighty flood caused the dam of Ma'ārib, to which the Sabaeans owed all their prosperity, to burst and inundate the whole area causing wide-spread ruin. A land full of beautiful gardens, streams and great works of art, was turned into a vast waste. The dam was about two miles long and 120 ft. high. It was destroyed about the first or second century A.D. (Palmer).

2385. The words, 'the towns which We had blessed,' refer to the towns of Palestine, the seat of Solomon's government with which the Sabaeans carried on prosperous trade. The words, 'towns that were prominently visible,' signify that the towns were situated so near each other as to be easily visible, or the words may mean, prominent towns and show that the route from Yemen to Palestine and Syria was very frequented, safe and well-populated. According to Muir there were 70 stages or stops from Ḥaḍarmaut to Ailāh on the road from Yemen to Syria. It was a very frequented and safe route, flanked on both sides by shady trees.

2386. The words put in the mouth of the Sabaeans, in fact, describe their actual condition when they defied and disobeyed Divine commandments and consequently fell on evil days. The prosperous and frequented route became deserted and desolate. The words, 'place longer distances between *the stages of* our journeys,' signify that because many towns on the route fell into ruin, the distance between one stage to the other became much longer and less safe. The Sabaeans were so utterly destroyed that no sign or mark was left of them. They became only a subject for story-tellers.

21. And Iblīs, indeed, found true his judgment concerning them,[2387] so ªthey followed him, all except a party of *true* believers.

وَلَقَدْ صَدَّقَ عَلَيْهِمْ اِبْلِيْسُ ظَنَّهٗ فَاتَّبَعُوْهُ اِلَّا فَرِيْقًا مِّنَ الْمُؤْمِنِيْنَ ۞

22. ᵇAnd he had no power over them,[2388] but *it was so* that We might distinguish those who believed in the Hereafter from those who were in doubt about it. And thy Lord is Watchful over all things.

وَمَا كَانَ لَهٗ عَلَيْهِمْ مِّنْ سُلْطٰنٍ اِلَّا لِنَعْلَمَ مَنْ يُّؤْمِنُ بِالْاٰخِرَةِ مِمَّنْ هُوَ مِنْهَا فِيْ شَكٍّ ۚ وَرَبُّكَ عَلٰى كُلِّ شَيْءٍ حَفِيْظٌ ۞

R. 3　23. Say, "Call upon those whom you assert *to be gods* beside Allāh. They control not *even* the weight of an atom in the heavens or in the earth, nor have they any share in either, nor has He any helper among them."[2389]

قُلِ ادْعُوا الَّذِيْنَ زَعَمْتُمْ مِّنْ دُوْنِ اللّٰهِ ۚ لَا يَمْلِكُوْنَ مِثْقَالَ ذَرَّةٍ فِي السَّمٰوٰتِ وَلَا فِي الْاَرْضِ وَمَا لَهُمْ فِيْهِمَا مِنْ شِرْكٍ وَّمَا لَهٗ مِنْهُمْ مِّنْ ظَهِيْرٍ ۞

24. ᶜNo intercession avails with Him, except of him whom He permits *it*,[2389A] until when the hearts[2390] of those *who are granted permission to intercede* are relieved of awe, others[2391] would say, 'What is it that your Lord said?' They[2392] will answer, 'The truth.' And He is the High, the Great.

وَلَا تَنْفَعُ الشَّفَاعَةُ عِنْدَهٗۤ اِلَّا لِمَنْ اَذِنَ لَهٗ ۚ حَتّٰۤى اِذَا فُزِّعَ عَنْ قُلُوْبِهِمْ قَالُوْا مَاذَا ۙ قَالَ رَبُّكُمْ ۫ قَالُوا الْحَقَّ ۚ وَهُوَ الْعَلِيُّ الْكَبِيْرُ ۞

ª15 : 43; 16 : 100.　ᵇ34 : 22.　ᶜ2 : 256; 20 : 110; 78 : 39.

2387. By their evil deeds the people of Saba' justified Satan's estimate that he would be successful in leading them astray. The reference to this estimate of Satan about the wicked people and their evil deeds may be found in 17 : 63 where he is mentioned as saying that he will cause his (Adam's) progeny to perish except a few of them.

2388. Satan has no authority over man. It is by his own wrong beliefs and evil deeds that man brings about his spiritual ruin.

2389. Disbelievers are challenged to call upon all their false gods to arrest or retard the progress and advance of Islām and are told that they cannot do so; in fact, no power on earth can stop truth from spreading.

2389A. The Holy Prophet. The words may also mean, 'About whom God permits that intercession may be made in his favour.'

2390. The hearts of the intercessors.

2391. The sinful people who will be punished.

2392. The intercessors or the Messengers of God.

25. Say, ᵃ'Who gives you sustenance from the heavens and the earth?' Say, 'Allah. Either We or you are on right guidance or in manifest error.'[2393]

قُلْ مَنْ يَّرْزُقُكُمْ مِّنَ السَّمٰوٰتِ وَالْاَرْضِ ۭ قُلِ اللّٰهُ ۙ
وَاِنَّآ اَوْ اِيَّاكُمْ لَعَلٰى هُدًى اَوْ فِيْ ضَلٰلٍ مُّبِيْنٍ ﴿٢٥﴾

26. Say, 'You will not be questioned as to our sins, nor shall we be questioned as to what you do.'

قُلْ لَّا تُسْـَٔلُوْنَ عَمَّآ اَجْرَمْنَا وَلَا نُسْـَٔلُ عَمَّا تَعْمَلُوْنَ ﴿٢٦﴾

27. Say, 'Our Lord will bring us all together;[2394] then He will judge between us with truth, and He is the Best Judge, the All-Knowing.'

قُلْ يَجْمَعُ بَيْنَنَا رَبُّنَا ثُمَّ يَفْتَحُ بَيْنَنَا بِالْحَقِّ ۭ وَهُوَ
الْفَتَّاحُ الْعَلِيْمُ ﴿٢٧﴾

28. Say, ᵇ'Show me those whom you have joined with Him as associates.' Nay! *that cannot be*, for He is Allāh, the Mighty, the Wise.

قُلْ اَرُوْنِيَ الَّذِيْنَ اَلْحَقْتُمْ بِهٖ شُرَكَاۗءَ كَلَّا ۭ بَلْ هُوَ
اللّٰهُ الْعَزِيْزُ الْحَكِيْمُ ﴿٢٨﴾

29. And We have not sent thee but as a ᶜbearer of glad tidings and a Warner for all mankind,[2395] but most men know not.

وَمَآ اَرْسَلْنٰكَ اِلَّا كَاۗفَّةً لِّلنَّاسِ بَشِيْرًا وَّنَذِيْرًا وَّ
لٰكِنَّ اَكْثَرَ النَّاسِ لَا يَعْلَمُوْنَ ﴿٢٩﴾

30. ᵈAnd they say, 'When will this promise *be fulfilled*, if you are truthful?'

وَيَقُوْلُوْنَ مَتٰى هٰذَا الْوَعْدُ اِنْ كُنْتُمْ صٰدِقِيْنَ ﴿٣٠﴾

31. Say, 'For you is the promise of a day[2396] from which ᵉyou cannot remain behind a single moment, nor can you get ahead *of it*.'

قُلْ لَّكُمْ مِّيْعَادُ يَوْمٍ لَّا تَسْتَاْخِرُوْنَ عَنْهُ سَاعَةً
وَّلَا تَسْتَقْدِمُوْنَ ﴿٣١﴾ ع النصف

ᵃ10 : 32; 27 : 65; 35 : 4. ᵇ35 : 41; 46 : 5. ᶜ21 : 108. ᵈ21 : 39; 36 : 49; 67 : 26. ᵉ7 : 35; 10 : 50.

2393. As surely, we (the believers) are on the right, so surely, you (the disbelievers) are in error.

2394. The verse generally is taken as referring to the Fall of Mecca when it was decided beyond a shadow of doubt as to which of the two parties—Muslims or disbelievers—was 'on right guidance' and which 'in manifest error.' It was after that great victory that a union of hearts was brought about between Muslims and their adversaries.

2395. The Holy Prophet has been repeatedly declared in the Qur'ān as having been sent as a Messenger to all mankind till the end of time. See also 21 : 108 and 25: 2. The Message of Islām is a universal Message and the Qur'ān is the last revealed Book which has laid claim to finality.

2396. The Day of the Battle of Badr or the day mentioned in 32 : 6 which is stated to be equal to one thousand years after the expiry of which the period of the recognition and acceptance of Islām as a universal Faith will begin.

R. 4   32. And those who disbelieve say, 'We will never believe in this Qur'ān nor in what is before it.' Couldst thou but see ᵃwhen the wrongdoers will be made to stand before their Lord, casting the blame on one another? Those who were deemed weak will say to those who were arrogant, 'Had it not been for you, we should, surely, have been believers.'²³⁹⁷

وَقَالَ الَّذِيْنَ كَفَرُوْا لَنْ نُّؤْمِنَ بِهٰذَا الْقُرْاٰنِ وَلَا بِالَّذِيْ بَيْنَ يَدَيْهِ ۖ وَلَوْ تَرٰۤى اِذِ الظّٰلِمُوْنَ مَوْقُوْفُوْنَ عِنْدَ رَبِّهِمْ ۖ يَرْجِعُ بَعْضُهُمْ اِلٰى بَعْضِۨ الْقَوْلَ ۚ يَقُوْلُ الَّذِيْنَ اسْتُضْعِفُوْا لِلَّذِيْنَ اسْتَكْبَرُوْا لَوْلَاۤ اَنْتُمْ لَكُنَّا مُؤْمِنِيْنَ ۝

33. ᵇThose who were big with pride will say to those who were considered weak, 'Was it we that kept you away from the guidance, after it had come to you? Nay, it was you *yourselves* who were guilty.'

قَالَ الَّذِيْنَ اسْتَكْبَرُوْا لِلَّذِيْنَ اسْتُضْعِفُوْۤا اَنَحْنُ صَدَدْنٰكُمْ عَنِ الْهُدٰى بَعْدَ اِذْ جَاۤءَكُمْ بَلْ كُنْتُمْ مُّجْرِمِيْنَ ۝

34. ᶜAnd those who were deemed weak will say to those who were proud, 'Nay, but it was *your* scheming night and day, when you bade us disbelieve in Allāh and set up equals with Him.' ᵈAnd they will conceal²³⁹⁸ *their* remorse when they see the punishment; and We shall put chains round the necks²³⁹⁸ᴬ of those who disbelieved. They will not be requited but for what they did.

وَقَالَ الَّذِيْنَ اسْتُضْعِفُوْا لِلَّذِيْنَ اسْتَكْبَرُوْا بَلْ مَكْرُ الَّيْلِ وَالنَّهَارِ اِذْ تَأْمُرُوْنَنَاۤ اَنْ نَّكْفُرَ بِاللّٰهِ وَنَجْعَلَ لَهٗۤ اَنْدَادًا ۚ وَاَسَرُّوا النَّدَامَةَ لَمَّا رَاَوُا الْعَذَابَ ۚ وَجَعَلْنَا الْاَغْلٰلَ فِيْۤ اَعْنَاقِ الَّذِيْنَ كَفَرُوْا ۚ هَلْ يُجْزَوْنَ اِلَّا مَا كَانُوْا يَعْمَلُوْنَ ۝

35. And We never sent a Warner to any city but ᵉthe wealthy ones thereof said, 'Surely, we disbelieve in what you have been sent with.'²³⁹⁹

وَمَاۤ اَرْسَلْنَا فِيْ قَرْيَةٍ مِّنْ نَّذِيْرٍ اِلَّا قَالَ مُتْرَفُوْهَاۤ ۙ اِنَّا بِمَاۤ اُرْسِلْتُمْ بِهٖ كٰفِرُوْنَ ۝

ᵃ7 : 39; 14 : 22; 28 : 64; 33 : 68; 40 : 48.   ᵇ14 : 22; 28 : 64; 40 : 48.
ᶜ14 : 22; 40 : 48.   ᵈ10 : 55.   ᵉ6 : 124; 17 : 17.

2397. It is human nature that when a guilty person is face to face with the punishment of his guilt, he tries to excuse himself by seeking to shift the responsibility for his misdeeds to another person. It is to this aspect of human nature that reference has been made in this and the next two verses.

2398. *Asarra-hū* means, he concealed it; he manifested it (Lane).

2398A. *A'nāq* also means, chiefs of men or great ones (Lane).

2399. The Prophets of God come to raise the depressed and suppressed humanity to their rightful place in society and to restore to them the rights which are denied to them by the vested interests. That is why in all ages it is the rich, the wealthy, the men of power and influence—the vested interests—who range themselves against the new Divine Message.

36. And they say, 'We have more wealth and children; and we shall not be punished.'

وَقَالُوْا نَحْنُ اَكْثَرُ اَمْوَالًا وَّاَوْلَادًا ۙ وَّمَا نَحْنُ بِمُعَذَّبِيْنَ ﴿۳۶﴾

37. Say, 'Verily, [a]my Lord enlarges the provision for whomsoever He pleases, and straitens *it for whomsoever He pleases;* but most men do not know.'

قُلْ اِنَّ رَبِّيْ يَبْسُطُ الرِّزْقَ لِمَنْ يَّشَآءُ وَيَقْدِرُ وَلٰكِنَّ
ع اَكْثَرَ النَّاسِ لَا يَعْلَمُوْنَ ﴿۳۷﴾

R. 5 38. And it is not your wealth nor your children that will bring you near Us in rank but [b]those, who believe and do good works,[2400] will have a double reward for what they did. [c]And in lofty mansions will they be secure.

وَمَآ اَمْوَالُكُمْ وَلَآ اَوْلَادُكُمْ بِالَّتِيْ تُقَرِّبُكُمْ عِنْدَنَا
زُلْفٰٓى اِلَّا مَنْ اٰمَنَ وَعَمِلَ صَالِحًا ۫ فَاُولٰٓئِكَ لَهُمْ
جَزَآءُ الضِّعْفِ بِمَا عَمِلُوْا وَهُمْ فِي الْغُرُفٰتِ اٰمِنُوْنَ ﴿۳۸﴾

39. [d]And *as to* those who strive to frustrate *the purpose of* Our Signs, it is they who will be brought to face[2401] punishment.

وَالَّذِيْنَ يَسْعَوْنَ فِيْٓ اٰيٰتِنَا مُعٰجِزِيْنَ اُولٰٓئِكَ فِي
الْعَذَابِ مُحْضَرُوْنَ ﴿۳۹﴾

40. Say, 'Surely, my Lord enlarges the provision for such of His servants as He pleases and straitens *it* for such of them *as He pleases.* And whatever you spend, He will replace it; and He is the Best of providers.'

قُلْ اِنَّ رَبِّيْ يَبْسُطُ الرِّزْقَ لِمَنْ يَّشَآءُ مِنْ عِبَادِهٖ وَ
يَقْدِرُ لَهٗ ۭ وَمَآ اَنْفَقْتُمْ مِّنْ شَيْءٍ فَهُوَ يُخْلِفُهٗ ۚ وَ
هُوَ خَيْرُ الرّٰزِقِيْنَ ﴿۴۰﴾

41. And *remember* the day, when [e]He will gather them all together; then He will say to the angels, 'Was it you that they worshipped?'

وَيَوْمَ يَحْشُرُهُمْ جَمِيْعًا ثُمَّ يَقُوْلُ لِلْمَلٰٓئِكَةِ اَهٰٓؤُلَآءِ
اِيَّاكُمْ كَانُوْا يَعْبُدُوْنَ ﴿۴۱﴾

42. They will say, [f]'Holy art Thou. Thou art our Protector against them. Nay, but they worshipped the jinn; it was in them that most of them believed.'

قَالُوْا سُبْحٰنَكَ اَنْتَ وَلِيُّنَا مِنْ دُوْنِهِمْ ۚ بَلْ كَانُوْا
يَعْبُدُوْنَ الْجِنَّ ۚ اَكْثَرُهُمْ بِهِمْ مُّؤْمِنُوْنَ ﴿۴۲﴾

[a]13 : 27; 29 : 63; 39 : 53; 42 : 13. [b]3 : 58; 6 : 49; 18 : 89; 19 : 61. [c]25 : 76. [d]22 : 52. [e]10 : 29; 17 : 98; 19 : 69. [f]25 : 19.

2400. Wealth, power and position are not the means of achieving nearness to God. On the contrary, they tend to keep men away from Him. It is right belief and good actions which are man's real wealth and which can bring him salvation and God's pleasure.

2401. All the efforts and machinations of disbelievers to retard or arrest the progress of the cause of Truth and frustrate God's purpose prove futile and recoil on their own heads.

43. *It will be said to disbelievers*, 'So, this day, you will have no power either to profit or harm one another.' And We shall say to those who did wrong: [a]'Taste ye the punishment of the Fire that you denied.'

فَالْيَوْمَ لَا يَمْلِكُ بَعْضُكُمْ لِبَعْضٍ نَّفْعًا وَّلَا ضَرًّا
وَنَقُوْلُ لِلَّذِيْنَ ظَلَمُوْا ذُوْقُوْا عَذَابَ النَّارِ الَّتِيْ كُنْتُمْ
بِهَا تُكَذِّبُوْنَ ﴿٤٣﴾

44. And when Our manifest Signs are recited to them, they say, [b]'This is but a man who seeks to turn you away from that which your fathers worshipped.' And they say, 'This *Qur'ān* is but a forged lie.' And those who disbelieve say about the truth when it comes to them, 'This is nothing but manifest sorcery.'

وَإِذَا تُتْلٰى عَلَيْهِمْ اٰيٰتُنَا بَيِّنٰتٍ قَالُوْا مَا هٰذَآ إِلَّا رَجُلٌ
يُّرِيْدُ أَنْ يَّصُدَّكُمْ عَمَّا كَانَ يَعْبُدُ اٰبَآؤُكُمْ ۚ وَ
قَالُوْا مَا هٰذَآ إِلَّآ إِفْكٌ مُّفْتَرًى ۚ وَقَالَ الَّذِيْنَ كَفَرُوْا
لِلْحَقِّ لَمَّا جَآءَهُمْ ۙ إِنْ هٰذَآ إِلَّا سِحْرٌ مُّبِيْنٌ ﴿٤٤﴾

45. And We gave them no Books which they studied, nor did We send to them any Warner before thee.

وَمَآ اٰتَيْنٰهُمْ مِّنْ كُتُبٍ يَّدْرُسُوْنَهَا وَمَآ أَرْسَلْنَآ إِلَيْهِمْ
قَبْلَكَ مِنْ نَّذِيْرٍ ﴿٤٥﴾

46. And those who were before them *also* rejected *the truth* and these have not attained *even* to a tenth[2402] of *the power* which We gave them, but they rejected My Messengers. So *they shall see* how *terrible* are *the consequences of* denying Me.

وَكَذَّبَ الَّذِيْنَ مِنْ قَبْلِهِمْ ۙ وَمَا بَلَغُوْا مِعْشَارَ
مَآ اٰتَيْنٰهُمْ فَكَذَّبُوْا رُسُلِيْ ۫ فَكَيْفَ كَانَ نَكِيْرِ ﴿٤٦﴾ ع

R. 6 47. Say, 'I only exhort you *to do only* one thing: that you stand up before Allāh in twos and singly and reflect. *You will then realize that* [c]there is no insanity in your companion;[2403] he is only a Warner to you of an impending severe punishment.'

قُلْ إِنَّمَآ أَعِظُكُمْ بِوَاحِدَةٍ ۚ أَنْ تَقُوْمُوْا لِلّٰهِ مَثْنٰى
وَفُرَادٰى ثُمَّ تَتَفَكَّرُوْا ۫ مَا بِصَاحِبِكُمْ مِّنْ جِنَّةٍ ۚ
إِنْ هُوَ إِلَّا نَذِيْرٌ لَّكُمْ بَيْنَ يَدَيْ عَذَابٍ شَدِيْدٍ ﴿٤٧﴾

[a]8 : 15; 10 : 53; 22 : 23. [b]17 : 95; 23 : 25. [c]7 : 185; 23 : 71.

2402. *Mi'shār* means, a tenth part; a hundredth part; according to some a thousandth part (Lane).

2403. The verse recommends an objective and detached examination of the Holy Prophet's claim. The disbelievers are urged to ponder dispassionately without prejudice and without being influenced by crowd mentality, whether the Holy Prophet suffers from insanity or unsoundness of mind.

48. Say, [a]'Whatever reward I might have asked of you—let it be yours. My reward is only with Allāh; and He is Witness over all things.'

قُلْ مَا سَاَلْتُكُمْ مِّنْ اَجْرٍ فَهُوَ لَكُمْ ۭ اِنْ اَجْرِيَ اِلَّا عَلَى اللّٰهِ ۚ وَهُوَ عَلٰى كُلِّ شَيْءٍ شَهِيْدٌ ﴿۴۸﴾

49. Say, 'Truly, My Lord hurls the Truth *at falsehood and breaks it into pieces*. He is [b]the Great Knower of the unseen.'

قُلْ اِنَّ رَبِّيْ يَقْذِفُ بِالْحَقِّ ۚ عَلَّامُ الْغُيُوْبِ ﴿۴۹﴾

50. Say, [c]'The Truth has come, and falsehood could neither originate *anything*, nor reproduce it'[2404]

قُلْ جَآءَ الْحَقُّ وَمَا يُبْدِئُ الْبَاطِلُ وَمَا يُعِيْدُ ﴿۵۰﴾

51. Say, 'If I err, I err only against myself; and if I am rightly guided, it is because of what my Lord revealed to me. [d]Verily, He is All-Hearing, Nigh.'

قُلْ اِنْ ضَلَلْتُ فَاِنَّمَآ اَضِلُّ عَلٰى نَفْسِيْ ۚ وَاِنِ اهْتَدَيْتُ فَبِمَا يُوْحِيْٓ اِلَيَّ رَبِّيْ ۭ اِنَّهٗ سَمِيْعٌ قَرِيْبٌ ﴿۵۱﴾

52. Couldst thou but see when they will be smitten with fear? Then *there will be* no escape, and they will be seized from a place nearby.

وَلَوْ تَرٰٓى اِذْ فَزِعُوْا فَلَا فَوْتَ وَاُخِذُوْا مِنْ مَّكَانٍ قَرِيْبٍ ﴿۵۲﴾

53. And they will say, 'We now believe therein.' But how can they attain *faith* from a position so far-off ?[2405]

وَّقَالُوْٓا اٰمَنَّا بِهٖ ۚ وَاَنّٰى لَهُمُ التَّنَاوُشُ مِنْ مَّكَانٍ بَعِيْدٍ ﴿۵۳﴾

54. They had disbelieved in it before, while they indulged in conjectures with regard to the unseen from a far-off place.

وَّقَدْ كَفَرُوْا بِهٖ مِنْ قَبْلُ ۚ وَيَقْذِفُوْنَ بِالْغَيْبِ مِنْ مَّكَانٍ بَعِيْدٍ ﴿۵۴﴾

55. And a barrier will be placed between them and that which they long for, as was done with the like of them before.[2406] They *too* were in disquieting doubt.

وَحِيْلَ بَيْنَهُمْ وَبَيْنَ مَا يَشْتَهُوْنَ كَمَا فُعِلَ بِاَشْيَاعِهِمْ مِّنْ قَبْلُ ۭ اِنَّهُمْ كَانُوْا فِيْ شَكٍّ مُّرِيْبٍ ﴿۵۵﴾

[a]38 : 87; 42 : 24; 52 : 41; 68 : 47. [b]5 : 117. [c]17 : 82; 21 : 19. [d]2 : 187; 11 : 62.

2404. The words, 'nor reproduce it,' embody a mighty prophecy that idolatry will never regain a foothold in Arabia. It will disappear from that country for ever.

2405. The words may mean "after death" and the verse may signify that disbelievers will surely, realize after death that they were in the wrong. Disbelievers make foolish conjectures about the failure of the Prophet's mission which, being far removed from the source of "the unseen" or from reality, reason and truth are foolish and baseless.

2406. The opponents of Islām are here told that like the rejectors of the Prophets of yore they will also utterly fail to realize their heart's desire—failure of the mission of the Holy Prophet.

CHAPTER 35

AL-FĀṬIR

(*Revealed before Hijrah*)

Date of Revelation and Context

The *Sūrah* was revealed at Mecca, probably at the time at which the preceding *Sūrah* was revealed. In that *Sūrah* Muslims were told that like the Israelites they will be given wealth, power, prosperity and prestige and that if in the heyday of their glory and greatness they consigned God to oblivion and abandoned themselves to a life of luxury and ease, they will draw upon their heads His wrath as did the Israelites before them. In the present *Sūrah* they are promised honour and eminence through the Qur'ān whose commandments they should not fail to observe.

Subject-Matter

The *Sūrah* opens with the declaration that all praise belongs to God Who is the Originator of the heavens and the earth. The declaration implies that being the Creator of the universe God has not only provided for the physical needs of man but also for his moral and spiritual needs, and that for this purpose He has created angels through whose instrumentality He controls the physical universe and conveys His Will to men. It further says that since the creation of man God has been sending Prophets and Messengers to convey His Will and that now He has decreed to bestow His mercy upon mankind in the form of the Qur'ān. After this announcement of the bestowal of Divine mercy upon man he has been warned not to reject it, as this will entail grave consequences. The *Sūrah* proceeds to draw a moral lesson from the quite insignificant beginning of man, that Islām will, from a humble start, grow into a mighty organization. It further compares it to a sea whose water is sweet which slakes the thirst of spiritual wayfarers. Next, it observes that Islām is no novel phenomenon. Alternate periods of spiritual light and darkness continue to come over the world as day follows night and *vice versa*. After a long period of darkness and cessation of revelation, the sun of Islām has risen to illumine the dark world and God has decreed to bring into being a new creation and a new order of things through its teachings. Through the Qur'ān God will give eyes to the blind and ears to the deaf and the dead will also receive a new life, but those who will deliberately shut the avenues of their hearts and refuse to listen to the Divine Call will incur spiritual death. The *Sūrah* then invites attention to the study of the physical phenomenon which bears a striking resemblance to a similar phenomenon in the spiritual realm. When rain falls on dry and parched land, it begins to bloom, blossom and vibrate with a new life, and crops, flowers and fruits of varying hues, tastes and forms, are brought forth. The water that comes down in the form of rain is the same but the crops and fruits are different. Similarly, the same water of Divine revelation produces different results among men of different natures and moral aptitudes. While on the one hand it produces highly righteous and God-fearing men, on the other, a community of vicious and wicked men also comes into being who carry on relentless fight against the cause of truth. This fight between the devotees of truth and the forces of darkness invariably ends in one inevitable result—the triumph of truth over falsehood. Towards its close the *Sūrah* brings home to idolaters the untenability of their position and warns them that if, in spite of the falsity and futility of their beliefs and practices, they continued to stick to them, Divine punishment will overtake them, though God is very slow in punishing and continues to grant respite to sinners till by persisting in their perverse attitude they shut upon themselves the doors of His mercy.

سُورَةُ فَاطِرٍ مَكِّيَّةٌ (٣٥)

1. [a]In the name of Allāh, the Gracious, the Merciful.

بِسْمِ اللّٰهِ الرَّحْمٰنِ الرَّحِيْمِ ۝١

2. All praise belongs to Allāh, [b]the Originator of the heavens and the earth, Who employs the angels as Messengers, having wings, two, three and four. He adds to *His* creation [2407] whatever He pleases; for Allāh has power over all things.

اَلْحَمْدُ لِلّٰهِ فَاطِرِ السَّمٰوٰتِ وَالْاَرْضِ جَاعِلِ الْمَلٰٓئِكَةِ رُسُلًا اُولِيْٓ اَجْنِحَةٍ مَّثْنٰى وَثُلٰثَ وَرُبٰعَ ۗ يَزِيْدُ فِي الْخَلْقِ مَا يَشَآءُ ۗ اِنَّ اللّٰهَ عَلٰى كُلِّ شَيْءٍ قَدِيْرٌ ۝٢

3. [c]Whatever *sources*[2408] of mercy Allāh lays open for mankind[2408]—there is none to withhold them; and whatever *of such sources* He withholds, there is none who can release them after that; and He is the Mighty, the Wise.

مَا يَفْتَحِ اللّٰهُ لِلنَّاسِ مِنْ رَّحْمَةٍ فَلَا مُمْسِكَ لَهَا ۚ وَمَا يُمْسِكْ ۙ فَلَا مُرْسِلَ لَهٗ مِنْ بَعْدِهٖ ۗ وَهُوَ الْعَزِيْزُ الْحَكِيْمُ ۝٣

4. O ye men, remember the favour of Allāh *that He has bestowed* upon you. [d]Is there any creator other than Allāh who provides for you from the heaven and the earth? There is none worthy of worship but He. Whither then are you turned away?

يٰٓاَيُّهَا النَّاسُ اذْكُرُوْا نِعْمَتَ اللّٰهِ عَلَيْكُمْ ۗ هَلْ مِنْ خَالِقٍ غَيْرُ اللّٰهِ يَرْزُقُكُمْ مِّنَ السَّمَآءِ وَالْاَرْضِ ۗ لَآ اِلٰهَ اِلَّا هُوَ ۖ فَاَنّٰى تُؤْفَكُوْنَ ۝٤

---

[a]1 : 1. [b]6 : 15; 12 : 102; 14 : 11; 42 : 12. [c]39 : 39. [d]10 : 32; 27 : 65; 34 : 25.

2407. To angels is entrusted the control, management and supervision of the affairs of the physical world (79 : 6). This is one duty and responsibility placed upon them. Their other and heavier duty is to carry God's commandments and will to His Messengers. The angels bearing revelation manifest two, three, or four Divine attributes at the same time, and there are others who manifest even a larger number of these attributes. *Ajniḥah* being a symbol of power and ability (Lane), the verse signifies that angels possess powers and qualities in varying degrees and in accordance with the importance of the work entrusted to each one of them. Some of the angels are endowed with powers and qualities greater than the others. The Arch-angel Gabriel is the chief of all the angels and, therefore, the most important work of carrying Divine revelation to God's Messengers is entrusted to him and is done under his care and supervision.

2408. After having mentioned in the previous verse that God has created the heavens and the earth and that He has made full provision for man's physical and spiritual needs the verse under comment signifies that God has now decreed to bestow His mercy upon mankind in the form of the revelation of the Qur'ān.

5. [a]And if they reject thee, verily, *God's* Messengers have been rejected before thee; and unto Allāh *all* matters are brought back *for decision*.

وَإِنْ يُكَذِّبُوكَ فَقَدْ كُذِّبَتْ رُسُلٌ مِّنْ قَبْلِكَ ۚ وَإِلَى اللّٰهِ تُرْجَعُ الْأُمُوْرُ ﴿٥﴾

6. O ye men, assuredly the promise of Allāh is true, so let not the present life deceive you, nor let the Deceiver deceive you with respect to Allāh.

يٰٓأَيُّهَا النَّاسُ إِنَّ وَعْدَ اللّٰهِ حَقٌّ فَلَا تَغُرَّنَّكُمُ الْحَيٰوةُ الدُّنْيَا ۖ وَلَا يَغُرَّنَّكُمْ بِاللّٰهِ الْغَرُوْرُ ﴿٦﴾

7. [b]Surely, Satan is an enemy to you; so treat him as an enemy. He calls his followers only that they may become inmates of the burning Fire.

إِنَّ الشَّيْطٰنَ لَكُمْ عَدُوٌّ فَاتَّخِذُوْهُ عَدُوًّا ۚ إِنَّمَا يَدْعُوْا حِزْبَهٗ لِيَكُوْنُوْا مِنْ أَصْحٰبِ السَّعِيْرِ ﴿٧﴾

8. For those who disbelieve there is a severe punishment. And for those who believe and do righteous deeds there is forgiveness and a great reward.

اَلَّذِيْنَ كَفَرُوْا لَهُمْ عَذَابٌ شَدِيْدٌ ۚ وَالَّذِيْنَ اٰمَنُوْا وَعَمِلُوا الصّٰلِحٰتِ لَهُمْ مَّغْفِرَةٌ وَّأَجْرٌ كَبِيْرٌ ﴿٨﴾ ع

R. 2 9. Can he, then, to whom the evil of his conduct is made *to appear* pleasing, so that he looks upon it as good, *be like him who believes and does good deeds?* Surely, Allāh lets go astray whom He wills and guides whom He wills. So let not thy soul waste away in sorrow[2409] for them. Surely, Allāh knows what they do.

أَفَمَنْ زُيِّنَ لَهٗ سُوْٓءُ عَمَلِهٖ فَرَاٰهُ حَسَنًا ۖ فَإِنَّ اللّٰهَ يُضِلُّ مَنْ يَّشَآءُ وَيَهْدِيْ مَنْ يَّشَآءُ ۖ فَلَا تَذْهَبْ نَفْسُكَ عَلَيْهِمْ حَسَرٰتٍ ۚ إِنَّ اللّٰهَ عَلِيْمٌ بِمَا يَصْنَعُوْنَ ﴿٩﴾

10. And Allāh is He Who sends the winds which raise the clouds; then do We drive them to a lifeless tract of land, [d]and quicken therewith the earth after its death. Likewise shall the Resurrection be.[2410]

وَاللّٰهُ الَّذِيْٓ أَرْسَلَ الرِّيٰحَ فَتُثِيْرُ سَحَابًا فَسُقْنٰهُ إِلٰى بَلَدٍ مَّيِّتٍ فَأَحْيَيْنَا بِهِ الْأَرْضَ بَعْدَ مَوْتِهَا ۚ كَذٰلِكَ النُّشُوْرُ ﴿١٠﴾

[a]6 : 35; 22 : 43; 40 : 6; 54 : 10. [b]2 : 169; 12 : 6; 18 : 51; 20 : 118. [c]16 : 64; 27 : 25; 29 : 39. [d]22 : 7; 57 : 18.

2409. The verse constitutes an eloquent commentary on the solicitude and concern of the Holy Prophet for the spiritual well-being of his people and on his deep grief for their opposition to truth. See also 18 : 7.

2410. Resurrection here signifying the resurrection of a people from a state of spiritual decline and degradation, the verse means that just as a dead and dry land blossoms into new life when rain falls upon it, so will a people, morally and spiritually dead and steeped in sin and wickedness, rise to a new life by means of the heavenly water of Divine revelation.

11. Whoso desires honour, *let him know that* all honour belongs to Allāh. Unto Him ascend pure words, and righteous deeds does He exalt, [a]and those who plan evils—for them is a severe punishment; and the planning of such will perish.

مَنْ كَانَ يُرِيْدُ الْعِزَّةَ فَلِلّٰهِ الْعِزَّةُ جَمِيْعًا ۭ اِلَيْهِ
يَصْعَدُ الْكَلِمُ الطَّيِّبُ وَالْعَمَلُ الصَّالِحُ يَرْفَعُهٗ ۭ
وَالَّذِيْنَ يَمْكُرُوْنَ السَّيِّاٰتِ لَهُمْ عَذَابٌ شَدِيْدٌ ۭ
وَمَكْرُ اُولٰۗىِٕكَ هُوَ يَبُوْرُ ﴿١١﴾

12. [b]And Allāh created you from dust, then from a sperm-drop, then He made you pairs. And no female conceives, nor does she bring forth *a child* save with His knowledge. And no one is granted long life who is granted long life, nor is anything diminished of his life, but *it is all recorded* in a Book.[2411] That, surely, is easy for Allāh.

وَاللّٰهُ خَلَقَكُمْ مِّنْ تُرَابٍ ثُمَّ مِنْ نُّطْفَةٍ ثُمَّ جَعَلَكُمْ
اَزْوَاجًا ۭ وَمَا تَحْمِلُ مِنْ اُنْثٰى وَلَا تَضَعُ اِلَّا بِعِلْمِهٖ ۭ
وَمَا يُعَمَّرُ مِنْ مُّعَمَّرٍ وَّلَا يُنْقَصُ مِنْ عُمُرِهٖٓ اِلَّا
فِيْ كِتٰبٍ ۭ اِنَّ ذٰلِكَ عَلَى اللّٰهِ يَسِيْرٌ ﴿١٢﴾

13. And the two seas[2412] are not alike: this one palatable, sweet *and* pleasant to drink and this other saltish, bitter. [c]And yet from each you eat fresh meat, and take forth ornaments which you wear. And thou seest the ships therein ploughing *the waves* that you may seek of His bounty, and that you may be grateful.

وَمَا يَسْتَوِي الْبَحْرٰنِ ڰ هٰذَا عَذْبٌ فُرَاتٌ سَاۗىِٕغٌ
شَرَابُهٗ وَهٰذَا مِلْحٌ اُجَاجٌ ۭ وَمِنْ كُلٍّ تَاْكُلُوْنَ
لَحْمًا طَرِيًّا وَّتَسْتَخْرِجُوْنَ حِلْيَةً تَلْبَسُوْنَهَا ۚ وَ
تَرَى الْفُلْكَ فِيْهِ مَوَاخِرَ لِتَبْتَغُوْا مِنْ فَضْلِهٖ وَ
لَعَلَّكُمْ تَشْكُرُوْنَ ﴿١٣﴾

---

[a]27 : 51, 52 ; 35 : 44. [b]18 : 38; 22 : 6 ; 23 : 13-14; 36 : 78 ; 40 : 68. [c]16 : 15; 45 : 13.

2411. The verse implies a prophecy that just as out of an insignificant sperm-drop there grows a well-proportioned and fully-developed human being, similarly the lowly and poor Muslims will one day grow into a mighty community. Reference to what a female conceives and what she gives birth to, and to the lengthening and diminishing of a man's life implies another prophecy that the progeny of opponents of the Holy Prophet will decrease and that of Muslims increase. The words in the text translated as, 'it is all recorded in a Book,' may also mean, 'it is in accordance with Divine law.'

2412. Metaphorically, the two seas spoken of are true and false religions. See 2085. The verse continuing the metaphor purports to say that though saltish water is not fit for drinking and irrigation, it has other uses. From it come out fresh meat and ornaments. Similarly, though the present opponents of Islām are, like saltish water, bitter and worthless, yet out of their loins there will be born those who will be zealous and devout bearers of its Message.

14. [a]He merges the night into the day, and He merges the day into the night.[2413] [b]And He has pressed into service the sun and the moon, each runs *its* course to an appointed term. Such is Allāh, your Lord; His is the Kingdom, [c]and those whom you call upon beside Allāh own not even a whit.[2413A]

يُولِجُ الَّيْلَ فِي النَّهَارِ وَيُولِجُ النَّهَارَ فِي الَّيْلِ
وَسَخَّرَ الشَّمْسَ وَالْقَمَرَ ۖ كُلٌّ يَجْرِي لِأَجَلٍ
مُّسَمًّى ۚ ذَٰلِكُمُ اللَّهُ رَبُّكُمْ لَهُ الْمُلْكُ ۚ وَالَّذِينَ تَدْعُونَ
مِن دُونِهِ مَا يَمْلِكُونَ مِن قِطْمِيرٍ ﴿١٤﴾

15. [d]If you call on them, they will not hear your call; and even if they heard it, they could not answer you. And on the Day of Resurrection they will deny your having associated *them with Allāh*. And none can inform thee like the One *Who is* All-Aware.

إِن تَدْعُوهُمْ لَا يَسْمَعُوا دُعَاءَكُمْ ۖ وَلَوْ سَمِعُوا مَا
اسْتَجَابُوا لَكُمْ ۖ وَيَوْمَ الْقِيَامَةِ يَكْفُرُونَ بِشِرْكِكُمْ ۚ
وَلَا يُنَبِّئُكَ مِثْلُ خَبِيرٍ ﴿١٥﴾

R. 3 16. O men, [e]it is you who are dependent upon Allāh, but Allāh is He Who is Self-Sufficient, the Praiseworthy.

يَا أَيُّهَا النَّاسُ أَنتُمُ الْفُقَرَاءُ إِلَى اللَّهِ ۖ وَاللَّهُ هُوَ
الْغَنِيُّ الْحَمِيدُ ﴿١٦﴾

17. [f]If He please, He could destroy you, and bring a new creation *instead*.

إِن يَشَأْ يُذْهِبْكُمْ وَيَأْتِ بِخَلْقٍ جَدِيدٍ ﴿١٧﴾

18. [g]And that is not *at all* difficult for Allāh.[2414]

وَمَا ذَٰلِكَ عَلَى اللَّهِ بِعَزِيزٍ ﴿١٨﴾

[a]22 : 62 ; 31 : 30 ; 57 : 7. [b]7 : 55 ; 13 : 3 ; 31 : 21. [c]13 : 15 ; 40 : 21.
[d]7 : 194. [e]47 : 39. [f]4 : 134 ; 6 : 134 ; 14 : 20. [g]14 : 21.

2413. The metaphor of the preceding verse is continued here. *Al-Nahār* (day) represents prosperity and power and *al-Lail* (night) signifies loss of these things combined with national decline and decadence.

2413A. *Qiṭmīr* means, the white point in the back of a date-stone, hence a mean, paltry or contemptible thing (Lane).

2414. God has decreed to bring into being a new creation, a new order, through the Holy Prophet and it is not at all difficult for Him to do so.

19. [a]And no burdened *soul* can bear the burden of another; and if a heavily laden *soul* call another to *bear* its load, naught of it shall be carried *by the other*, even though he be a kinsman. [b]Thou canst warn only those who fear their Lord in secret and observe Prayer. And whoso purifies himself, purifies himself only to his own good; and to Allāh shall be the return.

وَلَا تَزِرُ وَازِرَةٌ وِّزْرَ اُخْرٰى ۚ وَاِنْ تَدْعُ مُثْقَلَةٌ
اِلٰى حِمْلِهَا لَا يُحْمَلْ مِنْهُ شَيْءٌ وَّلَوْ كَانَ ذَا قُرْبٰى ۗ
اِنَّمَا تُنْذِرُ الَّذِيْنَ يَخْشَوْنَ رَبَّهُمْ بِالْغَيْبِ وَ
اَقَامُوا الصَّلٰوةَ ۗ وَمَنْ تَزَكّٰى فَاِنَّمَا يَتَزَكّٰى لِنَفْسِهٖ ۗ
وَاِلَى اللّٰهِ الْمَصِيْرُ (١٩)

20. [c]The blind and the seeing are not alike,

وَمَا يَسْتَوِي الْاَعْمٰى وَالْبَصِيْرُ (٢٠)

21. Nor the darkness and the light,

وَلَا الظُّلُمٰتُ وَلَا النُّوْرُ (٢١)

22. Nor the shade and the heat,

وَلَا الظِّلُّ وَلَا الْحَرُوْرُ (٢٢)

23. Nor alike are the living and the dead.[2415] Surely, Allāh causes him to hear whom He pleases; and thou canst not make those hear who are in the graves.[2416]

وَمَا يَسْتَوِي الْاَحْيَآءُ وَلَا الْاَمْوَاتُ ۗ اِنَّ اللّٰهَ يُسْمِعُ
مَنْ يَّشَآءُ ۚ وَمَآ اَنْتَ بِمُسْمِعٍ مَّنْ فِي الْقُبُوْرِ (٢٣)

24. [d]Thou art only a Warner.

اِنْ اَنْتَ اِلَّا نَذِيْرٌ (٢٤)

25. Verily, We have sent thee with the Truth, [e]as a bearer of glad tidings and as a Warner; and [f]there is no people to whom a Warner has not been sent.[2417]

اِنَّآ اَرْسَلْنٰكَ بِالْحَقِّ بَشِيْرًا وَّنَذِيْرًا ۗ وَاِنْ مِّنْ اُمَّةٍ
اِلَّا خَلَا فِيْهَا نَذِيْرٌ (٢٥)

[a]6 : 165; 39 : 8; 53 : 39. [b]36 : 12. [c]11 : 25; 13 : 17; 40 : 59. [d]11 : 13; 13 : 8. [e]2 : 120; 5 : 20; 11 : 3; 25 : 57; 48 : 9. [f]10 : 48; 13 : 8; 16 : 37.

2415. The believers have been called 'the living' because by accepting the truth they receive a new life, and the disbelievers are called 'the dead' because by rejecting the truth which is the elixir of life eternal they bring spiritual death upon themselves.

2416. It is not possible for a Prophet of God to make those who have deliberately shut their hearts and ears listen to and accept the Divine Message. Such people spiritually are as dead and defunct as those buried in the graves.

2417. The verse unfolds a great truth which had remained unknown to the world till the Qur'ān revealed it, *viz.*, that there had been sent to every people in the past a Heavenly Messenger who preached to them the same Message of truth and righteousness. This great and noble principle leads to the belief in the Divine origin of all religions, and in their Founders as Divine Messengers. It is an article of faith with a Muslim to believe in and equally respect and revere all of them. By giving to the world this sublime truth, Islām has sought to create an atmosphere of amity and goodwill among different creeds, and to remove and banish rancour and bitterness which has embittered relations between the followers of these creeds all over the world.

26. [a]And if they treat thee as a liar, those who were before them *also* treated *their Messengers* as liars. Their Messengers came to them with [b]clear Signs, and with the Scriptures, and with the illuminating Book.

وَإِنْ يُّكَذِّبُوْكَ فَقَدْ كَذَّبَ الَّذِيْنَ مِنْ قَبْلِهِمْ ۚ
جَآءَتْهُمْ رُسُلُهُمْ بِالْبَيِّنٰتِ وَبِالزُّبُرِ وَبِالْكِتٰبِ
الْمُنِيْرِ ﴿٢٦﴾

27. Then I seized those who disbelieved, and how *terrible* were *the consequences of* denying Me!

ثُمَّ اَخَذْتُ الَّذِيْنَ كَفَرُوْا فَكَيْفَ كَانَ نَكِيْرِ ﴿٢٧﴾ ع ٣ ١٥

R. 4 28. [c]Dost thou not see that Allāh sends down water from the sky, and We bring forth therewith fruits of different colours; and in the mountains are streaks white and red, of diverse hues, and others raven black?[2418]

اَلَمْ تَرَ اَنَّ اللّٰهَ اَنْزَلَ مِنَ السَّمَآءِ مَآءً ۚ فَاَخْرَجْنَا بِهٖ
ثَمَرٰتٍ مُّخْتَلِفًا اَلْوَانُهَا ۭ وَمِنَ الْجِبَالِ جُدَدٌۢ بِيْضٌ
وَّحُمْرٌ مُّخْتَلِفٌ اَلْوَانُهَا وَغَرَابِيْبُ سُوْدٌ ﴿٢٨﴾

29. And in like manner, there are men and beasts and cattle, of various colours. Only those of His servants who are endowed with knowledge fear Allāh.[2419] Verily, Allāh is Mighty, Most Forgiving.

وَمِنَ النَّاسِ وَالدَّوَآبِّ وَالْاَنْعَامِ مُخْتَلِفٌ اَلْوَانُهٗ
كَذٰلِكَ ۭ اِنَّمَا يَخْشَى اللّٰهَ مِنْ عِبَادِهِ الْعُلَمٰٓؤُا ۭ اِنَّ
اللّٰهَ عَزِيْزٌ غَفُوْرٌ ﴿٢٩﴾

[a]6 : 35; 22 : 43; 40 : 6; 54 : 10. [b]16 : 45. [c]14 : 33; 22 : 6; 45 : 6.

2418. The verse purports to say that when rain falls upon dry and parched land it gives rise to a vast variety of crops, flowers and fruits of different colours, tastes, forms and kinds. The rain-water is the same but the crops, flowers and fruits it produces are vastly different from one another. This difference is evidently due to the nature of the soil and the seed. Similarly, when Divine revelation, which at many places in the Qur'ān has been likened to water, comes to a people, it produces different effects upon different men according to the soil of their hearts and to the way in which they receive it.

2419. The kaleidoscopic variety in form, colour and kind to which reference has been made in the preceding verse does not only exist in flowers, fruits and rocks but in men, beasts and cattle as well. The words, *al-Nās* (men), *al-Dawābb* (beasts) and *al-An'ām* (cattle) may also represent men of different capabilities, dispositions and natural aptitudes. The expression, 'Only those of His servants, who are endowed with knowledge fear God,' lends weight to the view that these three words stand for three classes of men from among whom only those endowed with right knowledge fear God. Knowledge, here, however, does not necessarily mean spiritual knowledge but also knowledge of the laws of nature. A reverent study of nature and its laws inevitably leads one to realize the great powers of God and consequently makes him hold God in reverential awe.

30. Surely, *only* those who follow the Book of Allāh and observe Prayer [a]and spend out of what We have provided for them, secretly and in public,[2420] look for a bargain which will never fail;

إِنَّ الَّذِيْنَ يَتْلُوْنَ كِتٰبَ اللّٰهِ وَاَقَامُوا الصَّلٰوةَ وَ
اَنْفَقُوْا مِمَّا رَزَقْنٰهُمْ سِرًّا وَّعَلَانِيَةً يَّرْجُوْنَ تِجَارَةً
لَّنْ تَبُوْرَ ﴿۳۰﴾

31. [b]In order that He may give them their full rewards, and *even* increase them out of His bounty. He is, surely, Most Forgiving, Most Appreciating.

لِيُوَفِّيَهُمْ اُجُوْرَهُمْ وَيَزِيْدَهُمْ مِّنْ فَضْلِهٖ ۭ اِنَّهٗ
غَفُوْرٌ شَكُوْرٌ ﴿۳۱﴾

32. And the Book which We have revealed to thee is the [c]truth *itself*, fulfilling that which is before it. Surely, Allāh is All-Aware of His servants, All-Seeing *concerning His servants*.

وَالَّذِيْٓ اَوْحَيْنَآ اِلَيْكَ مِنَ الْكِتٰبِ هُوَ الْحَقُّ مُصَدِّقًا
لِّمَا بَيْنَ يَدَيْهِ ۭ اِنَّ اللّٰهَ بِعِبَادِهٖ لَخَبِيْرٌۢ بَصِيْرٌ ﴿۳۲﴾

33. Then We have *always* made inheritors of the Book those of Our servants whom We choose. Some of them are hard upon themselves and of them are some who take the middle course, and of them are some who excel *others* in deeds of goodness[2421] by Allāh's leave. And that *indeed* is the great grace *from Allāh*.

ثُمَّ اَوْرَثْنَا الْكِتٰبَ الَّذِيْنَ اصْطَفَيْنَا مِنْ عِبَادِنَا ۚ
فَمِنْهُمْ ظَالِمٌ لِّنَفْسِهٖ ۚ وَمِنْهُمْ مُّقْتَصِدٌ ۚ وَمِنْهُمْ
سَابِقٌۢ بِالْخَيْرٰتِ بِاِذْنِ اللّٰهِ ۭ ذٰلِكَ هُوَ الْفَضْلُ
الْكَبِيْرُ ﴿۳۳﴾

34. *Their reward will be* [d]Gardens of Eternity. [e]They will enter them *and* will be adorned therein with bracelets of gold and pearl; and their garments therein will be of silk.

جَنّٰتُ عَدْنٍ يَّدْخُلُوْنَهَا يُحَلَّوْنَ فِيْهَا مِنْ اَسَاوِرَ
مِنْ ذَهَبٍ وَّلُؤْلُؤًا ۚ وَلِبَاسُهُمْ فِيْهَا حَرِيْرٌ ﴿۳۴﴾

[a]14 : 32; 16 : 76. [b]3 : 58; 39 : 11. [c]22 : 55; 47 : 3; 56 : 96. [d]9 : 72; 13 : 24; 16 : 32; 61 : 13; 98 : 9. [e]18 : 32; 22 : 24; 76 : 22.

2420. This verse gives a description of '*Ulamā*' (those who are endowed with knowledge) mentioned in the preceding verse.

2421. A believer passes through various stages of rigorous spiritual discipline. At the first stage he wages a veritable war against his low desires and passions and practises strict self-denial. At the next stage his progress towards his goal is only gradual, and at the last stage he attains his full moral stature and his progress towards his great goal is very rapid and uniform.

وَقَالُوا الْحَمْدُ لِلّٰهِ الَّذِيْٓ اَذْهَبَ عَنَّا الْحَزَنَ ۭ اِنَّ
رَبَّنَا لَغَفُوْرٌ شَكُوْرُ ۙ ﴿٣٥﴾

35. And they will say, 'All praise belongs to Allāh Who has removed *all* grief from us. Surely, our Lord is Most Forgiving, Most Appreciating;

الَّذِيْٓ اَحَلَّنَا دَارَ الْمُقَامَةِ مِنْ فَضْلِهٖ ۚ لَا يَمَسُّنَا
فِيْهَا نَصَبٌ وَّلَا يَمَسُّنَا فِيْهَا لُغُوْبٌ ﴿٣٦﴾

36. 'Who has, out of His bounty, settled us in the Abode of Eternity, [a]where no toil will touch us, nor any *sense of* weariness affect[2422] us therein.'

وَالَّذِيْنَ كَفَرُوْا لَهُمْ نَارُ جَهَنَّمَ ۚ لَا يُقْضٰى عَلَيْهِمْ
فَيَمُوْتُوْا وَلَا يُخَفَّفُ عَنْهُمْ مِّنْ عَذَابِهَا ۭ كَذٰلِكَ
نَجْزِيْ كُلَّ كَفُوْرٍ ﴿٣٧﴾

37. But *as for* those who disbelieve, for them is the fire of Hell. [b]*Death* will not be decreed for them so that they may die; nor will the punishment thereof be lightened for them. Thus do We requite every ungrateful *person*.

وَهُمْ يَصْطَرِخُوْنَ فِيْهَا ۚ رَبَّنَآ اَخْرِجْنَا نَعْمَلْ صَالِحًا
غَيْرَ الَّذِيْ كُنَّا نَعْمَلُ ۭ اَوَلَمْ نُعَمِّرْكُمْ مَّا يَتَذَكَّرُ
فِيْهِ مَنْ تَذَكَّرَ وَجَاۗءَكُمُ النَّذِيْرُ ۭ فَذُوْقُوْا فَمَا
لِلظّٰلِمِيْنَ مِنْ نَّصِيْرٍ ﴿٣٨﴾

38. And they will cry for help therein: 'Our Lord, take us out, [c]we will do righteous deeds other than those we used to do.' *Allāh will say to them*, 'Did We not give you a life long enough so that he, who would take heed, could take heed therein? And there came unto you a Warner *too*. So taste ye *the punishment;* for wrongdoers have no helper.'

اِنَّ اللّٰهَ عٰلِمُ غَيْبِ السَّمٰوٰتِ وَالْاَرْضِ ۭ اِنَّهٗ عَلِيْمٌۢ
بِذَاتِ الصُّدُوْرِ ﴿٣٩﴾

R. 5 39. [d]Verily, Allāh knows all that is hidden in the heavens and the earth and He knows well what *passes* in the minds *of people*.

[a]15 : 49. [b]20 :75; 87 : 14. [c]7 : 54; 26 : 103; 32 : 13; 39 : 59. [d]11 : 124; 16 : 78; 27 : 66.

2422. Complete freedom from every kind of fear and anxiety and perfect peace of mind and satisfaction of heart coupled with the pleasure of God is the highest stage of Paradise that the Qur'ān, as the verse under comment and the preceding one show, has promised to believers in this and the next world.

40. He it is Who made you successors in the earth *of those who have passed away*. So he, who disbelieves, will himself suffer *the consequences of* his disbelief. Their disbelief will bring the disbelievers no increase in the sight of their Lord except *His* displeasure, and their disbelief will increase for the disbelievers nothing but loss.

هُوَ الَّذِيْ جَعَلَكُمْ خَلٰٓئِفَ فِي الْاَرْضِ ۭ فَمَنْ كَفَرَ
فَعَلَيْهِ كُفْرُهٗ ۭ وَلَا يَزِيْدُ الْكٰفِرِيْنَ كُفْرُهُمْ عِنْدَ
رَبِّهِمْ اِلَّا مَقْتًا ۚ وَلَا يَزِيْدُ الْكٰفِرِيْنَ كُفْرُهُمْ اِلَّا
خَسَارًا ﴿٤٠﴾

41. Say, [a]'Have you seen your associate-gods whom you call on beside Allāh? Show me, *then*, what they have created of the earth. Or, have they a share in *the creation of* the heavens? Or, have We given them a Book so that they have an evidence therefrom?' Nay, the wrongdoers promise one another nothing but delusion.

قُلْ اَرَءَيْتُمْ شُرَكَآءَكُمُ الَّذِيْنَ تَدْعُوْنَ مِنْ دُوْنِ
اللّٰهِ ۭ اَرُوْنِيْ مَاذَا خَلَقُوْا مِنَ الْاَرْضِ اَمْ لَهُمْ شِرْكٌ
فِي السَّمٰوٰتِ ۚ اَمْ اٰتَيْنٰهُمْ كِتٰبًا فَهُمْ عَلٰى بَيِّنَتٍ مِّنْهُ ۚ
بَلْ اِنْ يَّعِدُ الظّٰلِمُوْنَ بَعْضُهُمْ بَعْضًا اِلَّا غُرُوْرًا ﴿٤١﴾

42. [b]Surely, Allāh holds the heavens and the earth lest they deviate *from their positions*. And if they did deviate, none can hold them back but He.[2423] Verily, He is Forbearing, Most Forgiving.

اِنَّ اللّٰهَ يُمْسِكُ السَّمٰوٰتِ وَالْاَرْضَ اَنْ تَزُوْلَا ۥ وَ
لَئِنْ زَالَتَآ اِنْ اَمْسَكَهُمَا مِنْ اَحَدٍ مِّنْ بَعْدِهٖ ۭ اِنَّهٗ
كَانَ حَلِيْمًا غَفُوْرًا ﴿٤٢﴾

43. [c]And they swore by Allāh their strongest oaths, that if a Warner came to them, they would follow guidance better than any other people. But when a Warner did come to them, it only increased them in aversion,

وَاَقْسَمُوْا بِاللّٰهِ جَهْدَ اَيْمَانِهِمْ لَئِنْ جَآءَهُمْ نَذِيْرٌ
لَّيَكُوْنُنَّ اَهْدٰى مِنْ اِحْدَى الْاُمَمِ ۚ فَلَمَّا جَآءَهُمْ
نَذِيْرٌ مَّا زَادَهُمْ اِلَّا نُفُوْرًا ﴿٤٣﴾

[a]34 : 28; 46 : 5. [b]22 : 66. [c]6 : 158.

2423. Both the celestial and terrestrial systems continue to work in perfect harmony without deviating the least from their set courses. This harmony reveals the existence of an Intelligent and All-Powerful Being behind it. That Supreme and Intelligent Being is God Who deserves and demands our worship and adoration.

44. [a]For, they sought exaltation in the earth and *devised* evil schemes: But the evil schemes encompass none but the authors thereof. Do they, then, look for anything other than *Allāh's* way of *dealing with* the people of old? But thou wilt never find any [b]change in the way of Allāh; nor wilt thou ever find any alteration in the way of Allāh.

اِسْتِكْبَارًا فِي الْاَرْضِ وَمَكْرَ السَّيِّئِ ۚ وَلَا يَحِيْقُ
الْمَكْرُ السَّيِّئُ اِلَّا بِاَهْلِهٖ ۚ فَهَلْ يَنْظُرُوْنَ اِلَّا سُنَّتَ
الْاَوَّلِيْنَ ۚ فَلَنْ تَجِدَ لِسُنَّتِ اللّٰهِ تَبْدِيْلًا ۚ وَلَنْ تَجِدَ
لِسُنَّتِ اللّٰهِ تَحْوِيْلًا ﴿٤٤﴾

45. [c]Have they not travelled in the earth and seen how *evil* was the end of those who were before them? And they were stronger than these in power. And Allāh is not such that anything in the heavens or the earth can frustrate His *plans*;[2424] verily, He is All-Knowing, All-Powerful.

اَوَلَمْ يَسِيْرُوْا فِي الْاَرْضِ فَيَنْظُرُوْا كَيْفَ كَانَ عَاقِبَةُ
الَّذِيْنَ مِنْ قَبْلِهِمْ وَكَانُوْٓا اَشَدَّ مِنْهُمْ قُوَّةً ۚ وَمَا
كَانَ اللّٰهُ لِيُعْجِزَهٗ مِنْ شَيْءٍ فِي السَّمٰوٰتِ وَلَا فِي
الْاَرْضِ ۚ اِنَّهٗ كَانَ عَلِيْمًا قَدِيْرًا ﴿٤٥﴾

46. [d]And if Allāh were to punish people for what they do, He would not leave a living creature on the surface of *the earth;* but He gives them respite until an [e]appointed term;[2425] and when their appointed time comes *they find that* Allāh has *all* His servants well under His eyes.

وَلَوْ يُؤَاخِذُ اللّٰهُ النَّاسَ بِمَا كَسَبُوْا مَا تَرَكَ عَلٰى
ظَهْرِهَا مِنْ دَآبَّةٍ وَّلٰكِنْ يُّؤَخِّرُهُمْ اِلٰٓى اَجَلٍ
مُّسَمًّى ۚ فَاِذَا جَآءَ اَجَلُهُمْ فَاِنَّ اللّٰهَ كَانَ بِعِبَادِهٖ
بَصِيْرًا ﴿٤٦﴾

[a]27 : 51-52. [b]17 : 78; 33 : 63; 48 : 24. [c]12 : 110; 22 : 46, 47; 30 : 10; 40 : 22; 47 : 11. [d]10 : 12; 18 : 59. [e]7 : 35; 10 : 50; 16 : 62.

2424. It is God's unalterable decree that all the plans and plots of disbelievers to bring the Holy Prophet to naught will end in failure and the cause of Islām will triumph.

2425. The Merciful God is slow to punish. He grants respite and affords chances to the wicked and the rebellious in order that they may mend their ways. If God had meted out swift and quick punishment that the sinners deserved they would have been destroyed in no time, and the world would have come to an end, and all life on earth would have become extinct, because then there would be no purpose left in the beasts, animals, birds, etc., remaining alive after man's destruction. Or, the verse may mean that God will not hesitate to destroy these abominable worms of the earth, *i.e.*, disbelievers.

CHAPTER 36

YĀ SĪN

(*Revealed before Hijrah*)

Date of Revelation and Context

All scholarly opinion is agreed on this point that the *Sūrah* was revealed at Mecca. Its style and contents support this view. On account of the importance of its subject-matter, the Holy Prophet called it the heart of the Qur'ān. In the preceding *Sūrah* it was stated that God, being the Maker of the heavens and the earth, has made full provision not only for the physical needs of man but also for his moral and spiritual requirements. This He did by revealing Himself to His chosen servants whom He raised among every people. To the Holy Prophet whom the present *Sūrah* designates as "The Perfect Leader" or "The Leader *par excellence*," God revealed Himself in His completest manifestation and gave him the most perfect and infallible Book in the form of the Qur'ān.

Subject-Matter

The *Sūrah* opens with addressing the Holy Prophet as "The Perfect Leader," meaning that the system of Divine Messengers which began with Adam found its most perfect example in him. The Holy Prophet's path is now the only right and straight path that leads to God. All other paths that formerly led to the Supreme Being have now been closed and shall remain closed till the end of time. God will now reveal Himself to the world through the Holy Prophet's followers. In His infallible wisdom He has chosen the Arabs, among whom no Messenger had come for centuries, to preach to humanity the last Divine Message. The land of Arabia was dreary and dry. The water of Divine revelation descended upon it and it has now begun to blossom into a new and vigorous spiritual life. The *Sūrah* then proceeds to tell in metaphorical language how God had been revealing Himself to mankind through His Messengers. It tells of Moses and Jesus and of the Holy Prophet, who were raised in the fulness of time to call men to God. Then it tells of a "certain man" whom God will raise from among the followers of the Holy Prophet in a land far away from the centre of Islām (36 : 21) in the Latter Days, when religion would be at its lowest ebb and the very idea of Divine revelation would be doubted and denied. This Divine Reformer will call mankind to Islām. But like the Prophets of yore, his will be a voice in the wilderness. The forces of evil will hold the whole world in their firm grip. Man will worship false gods and Divine punishment will descend upon the world. Next, the *Sūrah* invites attention to a well-known law of nature, *viz.*, that when all the earth becomes dry and parched, God sends down rain and the dead soil begins to vibrate with a new life; and herbage, vegetables and flowers and fruits of various kinds and colours grow up. Similarly, when man's soul becomes corroded and contaminated God causes spiritual water to descend from heaven in the form of Divine revelation. The *Sūrah* then gives another simile to explain the same subject. It points to the law of the alternation of day and night. It further points to a revealed truth that God has created all things in pairs; there are pairs even in vegetables and in inorganic matter. This simile points out that all true knowledge is the result of the combination of Divine revelation and human reason. Towards its close the *Sūrah* draws attention to a great and bright future for Islām. It says that the Divine decree that a people, like the Arabs, who had remained very low in the scale of humanity for long centuries, would now rise to the height of material power and spiritual glory, is not an idle dream or poetic fancy. A Prophet of God, a Divine Messenger, has appeared among them and he will lead them to the highest pinnacle of spiritual and material grandeur and glory.

سُوْرَةُ يٰسٓ مَكِّيَّةٌ (٣٦) آياتها ركوعاتها

1. [a]In the name of Allāh, the Gracious, the Merciful.

بِسْمِ اللّٰهِ الرَّحْمٰنِ الرَّحِيْمِ ۝١

2. Yā Sīn.[2426]

يٰسٓ ۝٢

3. By the Qur'ān,[2427] full of wisdom,

وَالْقُرْاٰنِ الْحَكِيْمِ ۝٣

4. Thou art, indeed, *one* of the Messengers,

اِنَّكَ لَمِنَ الْمُرْسَلِيْنَ ۝٤

5. On the right path.[2427A]

عَلٰى صِرَاطٍ مُّسْتَقِيْمٍ ۝٥

6. [b]*This is* a revelation from the Mighty, the Merciful,

تَنْزِيْلَ الْعَزِيْزِ الرَّحِيْمِ ۝٦

7. [c]That thou mayst warn a people whose fathers were not warned, and so they are heedless.

لِتُنْذِرَ قَوْمًا مَّآ اُنْذِرَ اٰبَآؤُهُمْ فَهُمْ غٰفِلُوْنَ ۝٧

8. Surely, the word has proved true against most of them, for they believe not.

لَقَدْ حَقَّ الْقَوْلُ عَلٰٓى اَكْثَرِهِمْ فَهُمْ لَا يُؤْمِنُوْنَ ۝٨

---

[a]1 : 1. [b]20 : 5; 32 : 3; 40 : 3; 41 : 3; 45 : 3; 46 : 3.. [c]28 : 47; 32 : 4.

2426. In the combined abbreviated letters *Yā Sīn*, the letter *Sīn* according to Ibn 'Abbās stands for *al-Insān* meaning, man or perfect man; or for *Sayyid* (chief or leader). Thus the expression *Yā Sīn* would mean, 'O Perfect Man!' or 'O Perfect Leader!' According to consensus of scholarly opinion, the reference is to the Holy Prophet. He was 'the perfect man' because humanity found its best and most perfect specimen in him and he was 'the perfect leader,' because after his advent great religious Reformers and Divine Teachers were to rise only from among his followers, the door of revelation having been closed to the followers of all other Prophets.

2427. The most effective and convincing argument to prove the truth of the Holy Prophet's mission is the Qur'ān itself. There could be no greater testimony to his truth than the fact that being himself unlettered he gave to the world a Book which is full of wisdom and which far excels all other revealed Scriptures in its multifarious and multitudinous beauties and excellences and is a complete code of laws, meant for the moral uplift and spiritual regeneration of humanity for all time.

2427A. The Holy Prophet's path now is the only right and straight path that leads to God. The verse makes a fine distinction between a Prophet and a philosopher. A philosopher takes long time to find out truth and often gets lost in the quest, but a Prophet of God discovers it by the shortest route and in the shortest time. Unlike philosophers he is guided to it direct by Divine revelation without wandering in the labyrinth of abstract and abstruse ideas.

9. [a]We have put round their necks collars[2428] reaching unto their chins, so that their heads are raised up.[2428A]

إِنَّا جَعَلْنَا فِيٓ أَعْنَاقِهِمْ أَغْلَٰلًا فَهِيَ إِلَى الْأَذْقَانِ فَهُمْ مُّقْمَحُونَ ﴿٩﴾

10. And We have set a barrier before them and a barrier behind them, and have covered them over, so that they cannot see.[2429]

وَجَعَلْنَا مِنۢ بَيْنِ أَيْدِيهِمْ سَدًّا وَّمِنْ خَلْفِهِمْ سَدًّا فَأَغْشَيْنَٰهُمْ فَهُمْ لَا يُبْصِرُونَ ﴿١٠﴾

11. [b]Alike it is to them whether thou warn them or warn them not; they will not believe.[2430]

وَسَوَآءٌ عَلَيْهِمْ ءَأَنذَرْتَهُمْ أَمْ لَمْ تُنذِرْهُمْ لَا يُؤْمِنُونَ ﴿١١﴾

12. [c]Thou canst warn only him who would follow the Reminder and fear the Gracious *God* in secret. So give him the glad tidings of forgiveness and a noble reward.

إِنَّمَا تُنذِرُ مَنِ اتَّبَعَ الذِّكْرَ وَخَشِيَ الرَّحْمَٰنَ بِالْغَيْبِ ۖ فَبَشِّرْهُ بِمَغْفِرَةٍ وَّأَجْرٍ كَرِيمٍ ﴿١٢﴾

13. Surely, We *alone* give life to the dead, and We write down that which they send forward and that which they leave behind; [d]and all things We have recorded in a clear Book.[2431]

إِنَّا نَحْنُ نُحْيِ الْمَوْتَىٰ وَنَكْتُبُ مَا قَدَّمُوا وَءَاثَٰرَهُمْ ۚ
وَكُلَّ شَيْءٍ أَحْصَيْنَٰهُ فِيٓ إِمَامٍ مُّبِينٍ ﴿١٣﴾ ع ١٣ ١٨

R. 2 14. And set forth to them the parable of a people of the town,[2432] when the Messengers came to it.

وَاضْرِبْ لَهُم مَّثَلًا أَصْحَٰبَ الْقَرْيَةِ إِذْ جَآءَهَا الْمُرْسَلُونَ ﴿١٤﴾

[a]13 : 6; 76 : 5. [b]2 : 7. [c]35 : 19. [d]18 : 50; 72 : 29.

2428. Shackles of customs, usages and prejudices, by which disbelievers are fettered and which prevent them from accepting the truth and smother all efforts at reform.

2428A. Even when a person tries to use his intelligence and to get away from the stranglehold of customs, etc., he is under pressure from various quarters, and he can scarcely see aright.

2429. On account of the barriers of usages, prejudices and pride the disbelievers could not have looked forward to the great and bright future which lay before them if they accepted Islām, and they did not look back to the histories of past peoples who rejected the truth and were seized with Divine punishment.

2430. See 26.

2431. *Imām* means, a leader of a people or army; a model or an example; the religious Scripture of any people; a road or way, etc. (Lane).

2432. *Qaryah* may mean any town or place, or metaphorically speaking it may stand for the whole world. Thus *Aṣḥāb al-Qaryah* may signify humanity at large. Or, the word signifying a particular town may refer to Mecca, the Centre and Citadel of Islām. In this case the word 'the Messengers' will apply to the Holy Prophet who represented in his person all the Messengers and Prophets of God.

15. When We sent to them two *Messengers*[2433] they rejected them both; so We strengthened *them* by a third;[2434] and they said, 'Verily, we have been sent to you as Messengers.'

إِذْ أَرْسَلْنَا إِلَيْهِمُ اثْنَيْنِ فَكَذَّبُوهُمَا فَعَزَّزْنَا بِثَالِثٍ فَقَالُوا إِنَّا إِلَيْكُمْ مُرْسَلُونَ ﴿١٥﴾

16. They replied, [a]'You are only human beings like us and the Gracious *God* has not revealed anything. You are only lying.'

قَالُوا مَا أَنْتُمْ إِلَّا بَشَرٌ مِثْلُنَا وَمَا أَنْزَلَ الرَّحْمَٰنُ مِنْ شَيْءٍ إِنْ أَنْتُمْ إِلَّا تَكْذِبُونَ ﴿١٦﴾

17. They said, 'Our Lord knows that we are, indeed, *His* Messengers to you;

قَالُوا رَبُّنَا يَعْلَمُ إِنَّا إِلَيْكُمْ لَمُرْسَلُونَ ﴿١٧﴾

18. [b]'And our duty is only plain delivery of the Message.'

وَمَا عَلَيْنَا إِلَّا الْبَلَاغُ الْمُبِينُ ﴿١٨﴾

19. *The disbelievers* said, 'Surely, we augur evil fortune from you; if you desist not, we will, certainly, stone[2435] you, and a painful punishment will, surely, befall you at our hands.'

قَالُوا إِنَّا تَطَيَّرْنَا بِكُمْ لَئِنْ لَمْ تَنْتَهُوا لَنَرْجُمَنَّكُمْ وَلَيَمَسَّنَّكُمْ مِنَّا عَذَابٌ أَلِيمٌ ﴿١٩﴾

20. *The Messengers* replied, 'Your evil fortune is with your ownselves. *Do you say this* because you have been admonished? Nay, you are a people transgressing all bounds.'

قَالُوا طَائِرُكُمْ مَعَكُمْ أَئِنْ ذُكِّرْتُمْ بَلْ أَنْتُمْ قَوْمٌ مُسْرِفُونَ ﴿٢٠﴾

[a]14 : 11; 26 · 155. [b]13 : 41; 16 : 36; 24 : 55; 29 : 19.

2433. Moses and Jesus or Abraham and Ishmael.

2434. The Holy Prophet 'strengthened' Moses and Jesus by fulfilling in his person the prophecies they had made about his advent (Deut. 18 : 18 & Matt. 21 : 33-46). And he 'strengthened' Abraham and Ishmael because in his person was fulfilled their prayer referred to in 2 : 129—130.

2435. *Rajama-hū* means, he stoned him; he smote and killed him; he cursed him; he excommunicated him (Lane).

21. [a]And from the farthest part of the town[2436] there came a man[2437] running.[2438] He said, 'O my people, follow the Messengers,

وَجَآءَ مِنْ اَقْصَا الْمَدِيْنَةِ رَجُلٌ يَّسْعٰى قَالَ يٰقَوْمِ اتَّبِعُوا الْمُرْسَلِيْنَ ۝٢١

22. 'Follow those who ask of you no reward, and who are rightly guided;

اتَّبِعُوْا مَنْ لَّا يَسْـَٔلُكُمْ اَجْرًا وَّهُمْ مُّهْتَدُوْنَ ۝٢٢

PART XXIII

23. 'And why should I not worship Him Who has created me, and unto Whom you will be brought back?

الجزء ٢٣ وَمَا لِيَ لَآ اَعْبُدُ الَّذِيْ فَطَرَنِيْ وَاِلَيْهِ تُرْجَعُوْنَ ۝٢٣

24. 'Shall I take *others* beside Him as gods?[2439] [b]If the Gracious *God* should intend me any harm, their intercession will avail me naught, nor can they rescue me.

ءَاَتَّخِذُ مِنْ دُوْنِهٖٓ اٰلِهَةً اِنْ يُّرِدْنِ الرَّحْمٰنُ بِضُرٍّ لَّا تُغْنِ عَنِّيْ شَفَاعَتُهُمْ شَيْـًٔا وَّلَا يُنْقِذُوْنِ ۝٢٤

25. 'In that case I should, indeed, be in manifest error.

اِنِّيْٓ اِذًا لَّفِيْ ضَلٰلٍ مُّبِيْنٍ ۝٢٥

26. 'I believe in your Lord; so listen to me.'

اِنِّيْٓ اٰمَنْتُ بِرَبِّكُمْ فَاسْمَعُوْنِ ۝٢٦

27. It was said *to him*, 'Do thou enter Paradise.'[2440] He said, 'O, would that my people knew,

قِيْلَ ادْخُلِ الْجَنَّةَ قَالَ يٰلَيْتَ قَوْمِيْ يَعْلَمُوْنَ ۝٢٧

[a]28 : 21. [b]22 : 13-14; 39 : 39.

2436. The words 'farthest part of the town' may signify a place far away from the Centre of Islām.

2437. The implied reference in the word *Rajulun* may be to the Promised Messiah who has been referred to as such in a well-known saying of the Holy Prophet (Bukhārī, *Kitāb al-Tafsīr*).

2438. Words analogous in meaning and significance to the word *Yas'ā* (running) have also been used about the Promised Messiah by the Holy Prophet in some of his sayings which point to his tireless, quick and indefatigable work for the cause of Islām.

2439. People will worship various gods in the time of the Promised Messiah—Mammon, material power, false political philosophies and impracticable economic theories, etc.

2440. Special mention of Paradise in this verse in connection with *Rajulun Yas'ā* is very significant. When all true believers have been promised Paradise in the Qur'ān, this special mention seems to be superfluous and out of place. The establishment by the Promised Messiah, under a special Divine command, of a special graveyard at Qadian known as the *Bahishtī Maqbarah* (Paradise Graveyard) may be the physical fulfilment of the commandment embodied in the words 'Do thou enter Paradise.' There is a revelation

28. 'How *graciously* my Lord has granted me forgiveness and has made me of the honoured ones!'

بِمَا غَفَرَ لِي رَبِّي وَجَعَلَنِي مِنَ الْمُكْرَمِينَ ﴿٢٨﴾

29. And We sent not down against his people, after him, any host from heaven, nor do We send down *any such*.

وَمَآ أَنْزَلْنَا عَلٰى قَوْمِهٖ مِنْۢ بَعْدِهٖ مِنْ جُنْدٍ مِّنَ السَّمَآءِ وَمَا كُنَّا مُنْزِلِينَ ﴿٢٩﴾

30. [a]It was but a single blast and lo! they were extinct.[2441]

إِنْ كَانَتْ إِلَّا صَيْحَةً وَّاحِدَةً فَإِذَا هُمْ خٰمِدُونَ ﴿٣٠﴾

31. Alas for *My* servants! [b]there comes not a Messenger to them but they mock at him.[2442]

يٰحَسْرَةً عَلَى الْعِبَادِ ۚ مَا يَأْتِيهِمْ مِّنْ رَّسُولٍ إِلَّا كَانُوا بِهٖ يَسْتَهْزِءُونَ ﴿٣١﴾

32. [c]Do they not see how many generations We have destroyed before them, *and* that [d]they never come back to them?[2443]

أَلَمْ يَرَوْا كَمْ أَهْلَكْنَا قَبْلَهُمْ مِّنَ الْقُرُونِ أَنَّهُمْ إِلَيْهِمْ لَا يَرْجِعُونَ ﴿٣٢﴾

33. And all of them, gathered together, will certainly be brought before Us.

ع وَإِنْ كُلٌّ لَّمَّا جَمِيعٌ لَّدَيْنَا مُحْضَرُونَ ﴿٣٣﴾

R. 3 34. [e]And the dead earth is a Sign for them; We quicken it and bring forth therefrom grain, of which they eat.

وَآيَةٌ لَّهُمُ الْأَرْضُ الْمَيْتَةُ ۖ أَحْيَيْنٰهَا وَأَخْرَجْنَا مِنْهَا حَبًّا فَمِنْهُ يَأْكُلُونَ ﴿٣٤﴾

[a]21 : 41 ; 36 : 50; [b]15 : 12; 43 : 8. [c]17 : 18; 19 : 99; 20 : 129; 50 : 37. [d]21 : 96; 23 : 100, 101. [e]16 : 66.

of the Promised Messiah to the effect: *Innī Anzaltu Ma'aka al-Jannah*, *i.e.* I have caused the Paradise to descend with thee ("Tadhkirah"). The revelation also seems to support this interpretation of the words 'enter Paradise.'

2441. The description seems to apply to the falling of shells, incendiary and atom bombs, which come down with a crashing sound. The fire caused by the bombs destroys everything on which they fall and reduces it to rubble, and all life for miles around becomes extinct. Elsewhere, the Qur'ān describes this punishment in the words, *We shall make all that is thereon a barren soil* (18 : 9).

2442. The words of this verse are full of pathos. The Almighty Himself seems, as it were, to be full of grief over the rejection and mocking of His Prophets by men. While the Prophets grieved and pined for their peoples, the latter requited their grief with contempt and mockery.

2443. The reference seems to be to Divine punishment which will be universal in character.

35. [a]And We have placed in it gardens of date-palms and grapes, and We have caused springs to gush forth therein,[2444]

وَجَعَلْنَا فِيهَا جَنّٰتٍ مِّنْ نَّخِيلٍ وَّاَعْنَابٍ وَّفَجَّرْنَا
فِيهَا مِنَ الْعُيُونِ ﴿٣٥﴾

36. That they may eat of the fruit thereof, and it was not their hands that made them *grow up*. Will they not then be grateful?

لِيَاْكُلُوْا مِنْ ثَمَرِهٖ وَمَا عَمِلَتْهُ اَيْدِيْهِمْ اَفَلَا
يَشْكُرُوْنَ ﴿٣٦﴾

37. [b]Holy is He Who created all things in pairs,[2445] of what the earth grows and of themselves, and of what they know not.

سُبْحٰنَ الَّذِيْ خَلَقَ الْاَزْوَاجَ كُلَّهَا مِمَّا تُنْۢبِتُ
الْاَرْضُ وَمِنْ اَنْفُسِهِمْ وَمِمَّا لَا يَعْلَمُوْنَ ﴿٣٧﴾

38. [c]And a Sign for them is the night from which We strip off the day, and lo! they are *left* in darkness.

وَاٰيَةٌ لَّهُمُ الَّيْلُ ۚ نَسْلَخُ مِنْهُ النَّهَارَ فَاِذَا هُمْ
مُّظْلِمُوْنَ ﴿٣٨﴾

39. [d]And the sun is moving on to its determined goal. That is the decree of the Almighty, the All-Knowing *God*.

وَالشَّمْسُ تَجْرِيْ لِمُسْتَقَرٍّ لَّهَا ۭ ذٰلِكَ تَقْدِيْرُ
الْعَزِيْزِ الْعَلِيْمِ ﴿٣٩﴾

40. [e]And for the moon We have appointed stages, till it becomes again like an old dry twig of a palm-tree.

وَالْقَمَرَ قَدَّرْنٰهُ مَنَازِلَ حَتّٰى عَادَ كَالْعُرْجُوْنِ
الْقَدِيْمِ ﴿٤٠﴾

41. It is not for the sun to overtake the moon, [f]nor can the night outstrip the day. [g]All of them float smoothly in an orbit.[2446]

لَا الشَّمْسُ يَنْۢبَغِيْ لَهَآ اَنْ تُدْرِكَ الْقَمَرَ وَلَا
الَّيْلُ سَابِقُ النَّهَارِ ۭ وَكُلٌّ فِيْ فَلَكٍ يَّسْبَحُوْنَ ﴿٤١﴾

[a]13 : 5; 16 : 68; 23 : 20. [b]13 : 4; 51 : 50. [c]17 : 13; 40 : 62. [d]6 : 97; 55 : 6. [e]10 : 6. [f]25 : 63. [g]21 : 34.

2444. The metaphor used in the preceding verse is continued here. The verse means to say that from the dry land of Arabia will gush forth springs and fountains of spiritual knowledge, and trees laden with different kinds of spiritual fruit will grow up all over the land.

2445. Science has discovered the fact that pairs exist in all things—in vegetable kingdom, and even in inorganic matter. Even the so-called elements do not exist by themselves. They also depend upon other things for their sustenance. This scientific truth applies to human intellect also. Until heavenly light descends man cannot have true knowledge which is born of a combination of Divine revelation and human intelligence.

2446. The reference in this verse is to the floating of the heavenly bodies through space or ether. The Qur'ān contradicted the view held for a long time that the heavens were solid in their formation. It is characteristic of the Qur'ān that it uses expressions which not only contradict erroneous views and ideas but also anticipate new discoveries

42. And a Sign for them is that We carry their offspring in the laden ships.

وَآيَةٌ لَّهُمْ أَنَّا حَمَلْنَا ذُرِّيَّتَهُمْ فِي الْفُلْكِ الْمَشْحُونِ ﴿٤٢﴾

43. And We will create for them the like thereof [a]whereon they will ride.[2447]

وَخَلَقْنَا لَهُم مِّن مِّثْلِهِ مَا يَرْكَبُونَ ﴿٤٣﴾

44. And if We *so* willed, We could drown them; then they would have no one to succour *them*, nor would they be rescued,

وَإِن نَّشَأْ نُغْرِقْهُمْ فَلَا صَرِيخَ لَهُمْ وَلَا هُمْ يُنقَذُونَ ﴿٤٤﴾

45. Except through mercy from Us and as a provision for a time.

إِلَّا رَحْمَةً مِّنَّا وَمَتَاعًا إِلَىٰ حِينٍ ﴿٤٥﴾

46. And when it is said to them, 'Guard yourselves against that which is before[2448] you *through prayer*, and that which is behind[2449] you *through repentance*, that you may receive mercy,' *they turn away*.

وَإِذَا قِيلَ لَهُمُ اتَّقُوا مَا بَيْنَ أَيْدِيكُمْ وَمَا خَلْفَكُمْ لَعَلَّكُمْ تُرْحَمُونَ ﴿٤٦﴾

47. [b]And there comes not to them any Sign out of the Signs of their Lord, but they turn away from it.

وَمَا تَأْتِيهِم مِّنْ آيَةٍ مِّنْ آيَاتِ رَبِّهِمْ إِلَّا كَانُوا عَنْهَا مُعْرِضِينَ ﴿٤٧﴾

[a]16 : 9 ; 43 : 13. [b]6 : 5 ; 21 : 3; 26 : 6.

in the domain of science and philosophy. The verse also points to the excellent design and order that pervade the entire universe; all the celestial and terrestrial bodies performing their allotted tasks regularly, punctually and unerringly, without trespassing on one another's sphere of action. The solar system is but one of hundreds of millions of systems, some of which are incalculably larger than it. Yet the countless millions of suns and stars profusely scattered over the immense void are so arranged and distributed in relation to one another as to secure the safety of one and all and to produce everywhere harmony and beauty. Each orb is reflecting the orbit of every other, yet each proceeds safely on its destined way, and all united form a glorious harmony of structure and motion.

2447. The Qur'ān foretold long ago that God would bring into existence new means of conveyance. Steamers and big liners, airships and aeroplanes, etc., which are so much in use in these days, are a clear fulfilment of this Quranic prophecy.

2448. The evil consequences of your future evil deeds.

2449. The results of the wicked deeds you might have done in the past.

48. And when it is said to them, 'Spend out of that which Allāh has given you,' those who disbelieve say to those who believe, [a]'Shall we feed him whom Allāh would have fed, if He had *so* willed? You are but in manifest error.'

وَإِذَا قِيلَ لَهُمْ أَنفِقُوا مِمَّا رَزَقَكُمُ اللَّهُ ۙ قَالَ الَّذِينَ كَفَرُوا لِلَّذِينَ آمَنُوا أَنُطْعِمُ مَن لَّوْ يَشَاءُ اللَّهُ أَطْعَمَهُ ۖ إِنْ أَنتُمْ إِلَّا فِي ضَلَالٍ مُّبِينٍ ﴿٤٨﴾

49. [b]And they say, 'When will this promise *of punishment be fulfilled*, if you are truthful?'

وَيَقُولُونَ مَتَىٰ هَٰذَا الْوَعْدُ إِن كُنتُمْ صَادِقِينَ ﴿٤٩﴾

50. They are waiting only for a [c]single blast[2450] which will seize them while they are *still* disputing.

مَا يَنظُرُونَ إِلَّا صَيْحَةً وَاحِدَةً تَأْخُذُهُمْ وَهُمْ يَخِصِّمُونَ ﴿٥٠﴾

51. And they will not be able to make a will nor will they return to their families.

فَلَا يَسْتَطِيعُونَ تَوْصِيَةً وَلَا إِلَىٰ أَهْلِهِمْ يَرْجِعُونَ ﴿٥١﴾ ع

R. 4 52. [d]And the trumpet shall be blown,[2451] and lo! from the graves they will hasten on to their Lord.

وَنُفِخَ فِي الصُّورِ فَإِذَا هُم مِّنَ الْأَجْدَاثِ إِلَىٰ رَبِّهِمْ يَنسِلُونَ ﴿٥٢﴾

53. They will say *to one another*, 'O, woe to us! who has raised us from our place of sleep?[2452] This is what the Gracious *God* had promised, and the Messengers, indeed, spoke the truth.'

قَالُوا يَا وَيْلَنَا مَن بَعَثَنَا مِن مَّرْقَدِنَا ۜ سكتة هَٰذَا مَا وَعَدَ الرَّحْمَٰنُ وَصَدَقَ الْمُرْسَلُونَ ﴿٥٣﴾

---

[a]3 : 182; 5 : 65. [b]21 : 39; 34 : 30; 67 : 26. [c]21 : 41; 36 : 30; 38 : 16. [d]18 : 100; 39 : 69; 50 : 21; 69 : 14.

2450. The punishment mentioned here will be like a bolt from the blue. It will be so swift and sudden that, as mentioned in the next verse, the guilty people will not be able even to make a will.

2451. The words, 'the trumpet shall be blown,' may signify, besides the blowing of the trumpet on the Judgment Day, the appearance of a great Divine Reformer at whose clarion call those who are spiritually dead rise from their graves (their state of spiritual death) and hasten to listen to and accept the Divine Summons.

2452. When on the Judgment Day men will be raised and disbelievers confronted with their evil deeds, and punishment will stare them in the face, they will be seized with despair and will cry in consternation, 'Woe to us! who has raised us from our place of sleep?' To continue the metaphor of the preceding verse, however, this verse applies to those people who at the time of the appearance of a Prophet of God do not listen to the Divine Call and prefer to remain in their existing state of spiritual death. At hearing the Divine Call they exclaim, 'Why should anyone disturb the even tenor of our lives and cause commotion and excitement amongst us by inviting us to follow him and adopt a new way of life?'

54. It will be but one blast[2453] and lo! they will all be brought before Us.

اِنْ كَانَتْ اِلَّا صَيْحَةً وَّاحِدَةً فَاِذَا هُمْ جَمِيعٌ لَّدَيْنَا مُحْضَرُوْنَ ۝

55. "And on that day no soul will be wronged in aught; nor will you be requited but for what you used to do.

فَالْيَوْمَ لَا تُظْلَمُ نَفْسٌ شَيْئًا وَّلَا تُجْزَوْنَ اِلَّا مَا كُنْتُمْ تَعْمَلُوْنَ ۝

56. Verily, the inmates of Heaven will, on that day, be happy in *their* occupation.[2454]

اِنَّ اَصْحَابَ الْجَنَّةِ الْيَوْمَ فِيْ شُغُلٍ فٰكِهُوْنَ ۝

57. They and their wives will be in pleasant shades, *b*reclining on raised couches.[2455]

هُمْ وَاَزْوَاجُهُمْ فِيْ ظِلٰلٍ عَلَى الْاَرَآئِكِ مُتَّكِئُوْنَ ۝

58. *c*They will have fruits therein, and they will have whatever they call for.

لَهُمْ فِيْهَا فَاكِهَةٌ وَّلَهُمْ مَّا يَدَّعُوْنَ ۝

59. *They will be greeted with* *d*"Peace"[2456]—a word *of greeting* from the Merciful Lord.

سَلٰمٌ قَوْلًا مِّنْ رَّبٍّ رَّحِيْمٍ ۝

60. And *God will say,* 'Separate yourselves *from the righteous* this day, O ye guilty ones !

وَامْتَازُوا الْيَوْمَ اَيُّهَا الْمُجْرِمُوْنَ ۝

61. 'Did I not enjoin on you, O ye sons of Adam, that you worship not Satan—for he is to you an *e*open enemy—

اَلَمْ اَعْهَدْ اِلَيْكُمْ يٰبَنِيْۤ اٰدَمَ اَنْ لَّا تَعْبُدُوا الشَّيْطٰنَ اِنَّهٗ لَكُمْ عَدُوٌّ مُّبِيْنٌ ۝

---

*a*3 : 26 ; 40 : 18 ; 45 : 23.　*b*15 : 48 ; 18 : 32 ; 83 : 24.　*c*52 : 23 ; 55 : 53.
*d*10 : 11 ; 14 : 24 ; 33 : 45.　*e*6 : 143 ;

2453. The repeated mention of the word 'blast,' within the space of a few verses signifies that the *Sūrah* speaks of a time when Divine punishment will take the form of a blast. The reference may be to the attack of atom bombs which will destroy whole towns and cities within a few minutes.

2454. Life in the next world, as generally misunderstood, will not be a life of inaction and inertness but a life of constant work and progressive spiritual advance.

2455. All joy and happiness increases manifold if one shares it with another whom he loves.

2456. In a single word *Salām* meaning 'peace,' the verse sums up all the various blessings of Paradise—peace with God and peace with oneself. *i.e.,* peace of mind and soul. This is the highest stage of heavenly bliss.

62. 'And that you worship Me? This is the right path.

وَّاَنِ اعْبُدُوْنِيْ ۚ هٰذَا صِرَاطٌ مُّسْتَقِيْمٌ ﴿٦٢﴾

63. 'And he did lead astray a great multitude of you. Why did you not then understand?

وَلَقَدْ اَضَلَّ مِنْكُمْ جِبِلًّا كَثِيْرًا ۚ اَفَلَمْ تَكُوْنُوْا تَعْقِلُوْنَ ﴿٦٣﴾

64. [a]"This is the Hell which you were promised,

هٰذِهٖ جَهَنَّمُ الَّتِيْ كُنْتُمْ تُوْعَدُوْنَ ﴿٦٤﴾

65. 'Enter it this day, because you disbelieved.'

اِصْلَوْهَا الْيَوْمَ بِمَا كُنْتُمْ تَكْفُرُوْنَ ﴿٦٥﴾

66. This day We shall put a seal on their mouths, [b]and their hands will speak to Us, and their feet will bear witness to what they had earned.[2457]

اَلْيَوْمَ نَخْتِمُ عَلٰٓى اَفْوَاهِهِمْ وَتُكَلِّمُنَآ اَيْدِيْهِمْ وَتَشْهَدُ اَرْجُلُهُمْ بِمَا كَانُوْا يَكْسِبُوْنَ ﴿٦٦﴾

67. And if We had *so* willed, We could have put out their eyes,[2458] then they would have rushed *unseeing* to *find* the way. But, how could they see?

وَلَوْ نَشَآءُ لَطَمَسْنَا عَلٰٓى اَعْيُنِهِمْ فَاسْتَبَقُوا الصِّرَاطَ فَاَنّٰى يُبْصِرُوْنَ ﴿٦٧﴾

68. And if We had *so* willed, We could have transformed[2458A] them in their places, then they would not be able to move forward or turn back.

وَلَوْ نَشَآءُ لَمَسَخْنٰهُمْ عَلٰى مَكَانَتِهِمْ فَمَا اسْتَطَاعُوْا مُضِيًّا وَّلَا يَرْجِعُوْنَ ﴿٦٨﴾ ع

[a]52 : 15; 55 : 44. [b]17 : 37; 24 : 25; 41 : 21-23.

2457. When the guilt of disbelievers will be established and proved to the hilt they will be dumb-founded, their mouths will, as it were, become sealed and they will not be able to say anything in their defence and in extenuation of their guilt, and their hands and feet will also bear witness against them—these being the principal instruments of man's actions, good or bad. The speech and movements of a person can now be exactly reproduced by the tape-recorder and on the screen by television miles away. This is how the tongue and limbs of man even in this world have begun to bear witness for or against him.

2458. As man has been endowed with discretion and free will, he must bear the responsibility of his actions. The disbelievers persistently refuse to see the truth with the result that they become totally deprived of the power to see it. This is also the significance of the words, 'We shall put a seal on their mouths,' in the immediately preceding verse.

2458A. According to Ibn 'Abbās the expression means, 'We would have destroyed them in their houses;' and according to Ḥasan, it signifies that all their physical and mental faculties would become paralysed (Jarīr). Or, the expression may mean, 'We would have humiliated them.'

R.5 69. [a]And him whom We grant long life—We revert him to a weak *state* in creation.[2459] Will they not then understand?

وَمَنْ نُّعَمِّرْهُ نُنَكِّسْهُ فِي الْخَلْقِ ۚ أَفَلَا يَعْقِلُوْنَ ﴿٦٩﴾

70. And We have not taught him poetry, nor does it behove him *to be a poet*.[2460] [b]It is but a Reminder and a Qur'ān that expounds and makes *things* plain,

وَمَا عَلَّمْنٰهُ الشِّعْرَ وَمَا يَنْۢبَغِيْ لَهٗ ۚ إِنْ هُوَ إِلَّا ذِكْرٌ وَّقُرْاٰنٌ مُّبِيْنٌ ﴿٧٠﴾

71. That it may warn all who are alive,[2461] and that the decree *of Allāh* may be fulfilled concerning the disbelievers.

لِّيُنْذِرَ مَنْ كَانَ حَيًّا وَّيَحِقَّ الْقَوْلُ عَلَى الْكٰفِرِيْنَ ﴿٧١﴾

72. Do they not see that, among the things which Our hands have wrought, We have created for them cattle of which they are masters?[2462]

أَوَلَمْ يَرَوْا أَنَّا خَلَقْنَا لَهُمْ مِّمَّا عَمِلَتْ أَيْدِيْنَآ أَنْعَامًا فَهُمْ لَهَا مٰلِكُوْنَ ﴿٧٢﴾

73. [c]And We have subjected the same to them, so that some of them they use for riding, and of *the flesh of* some they eat.

وَذَلَّلْنٰهَا لَهُمْ فَمِنْهَا رَكُوْبُهُمْ وَمِنْهَا يَأْكُلُوْنَ ﴿٧٣﴾

74. [d]And in them they have *other* uses, and *also* drinks. Will they not, then, be grateful?

وَلَهُمْ فِيْهَا مَنَافِعُ وَمَشَارِبُ ۚ أَفَلَا يَشْكُرُوْنَ ﴿٧٤﴾

[a]16 : 71. [b]15 : 10; 65 : 11. [c]6 : 143; 16 : 6; 40 : 80-81. [d]16 : 6, 67.

2459. Everything that has life is subject to decay and deterioration. This law applies to nations as to individuals. Like individuals, nations also develop, grow and find their full stature, and then fall a victim to decay, decrepitude and death.

2460. It is inconsistent with the dignity of a Divine Prophet that he should be a poet, because poets are generally given to idle dreaming and making castles in the air. Prophets of God have before them very high and noble ideals and programmes. The verse, however, does not mean that all poetry is bad and that all poets are dreamers, but it does mean that a Divine Prophet is far too dignified and spiritually exalted to be a mere poet.

2461. The words, 'who are alive,' mean, who are not spiritually dead, *i.e.*, who are capable of receiving and accepting the Divine Message and have the aptitude to respond to the call of truth.

2462. When God has provided all the necessary things which man needs to meet his physical wants and requirements, it does not stand to reason that He should have neglected to make similar provision for his moral and spiritual needs. This and the next few verses refer to some of the things which man needs and uses most in daily life.

75. And they have taken *other* gods beside Allāh that they might be helped.

وَاتَّخَذُوْا مِنْ دُوْنِ اللّٰهِ اٰلِهَةً لَّعَلَّهُمْ يُنْصَرُوْنَ ۝٧٥

76. [a]*But* they are not able to help them. *On the contrary*, they will be brought *before God* in a body *to bear witness against them*.

لَا يَسْتَطِيْعُوْنَ نَصْرَهُمْ ۙ وَهُمْ لَهُمْ جُنْدٌ مُّحْضَرُوْنَ ۝٧٦

77. [b]So let not their speech grieve thee. Verily, [c]We know what they conceal and what they proclaim.

فَلَا يَحْزُنْكَ قَوْلُهُمْ ۘ اِنَّا نَعْلَمُ مَا يُسِرُّوْنَ وَمَا
يُعْلِنُوْنَ ۝٧٧

78. Does not man see that [d]We have created him from a mere sperm-drop? Then lo! he is an open quarreller!

اَوَلَمْ يَرَ الْاِنْسَانُ اَنَّا خَلَقْنٰهُ مِنْ نُّطْفَةٍ فَاِذَا هُوَ
خَصِيْمٌ مُّبِيْنٌ ۝٧٨

79. And he coins similitudes for Us and forgets his own creation. He says, [e]"Who can quicken the bones when they are decayed?"

وَضَرَبَ لَنَا مَثَلًا وَّنَسِيَ خَلْقَهٗ ۭ قَالَ مَنْ يُّحْيِ
الْعِظَامَ وَهِيَ رَمِيْمٌ ۝٧٩

80. [f]Say, 'He, Who created them the first time, will quicken them; and He knows well *the condition of* every created thing;

قُلْ يُحْيِيْهَا الَّذِيْٓ اَنْشَاَهَآ اَوَّلَ مَرَّةٍ ۭ وَهُوَ بِكُلِّ
خَلْقٍ عَلِيْمُۨ ۝٨٠

81. [g]'*He* Who produces for you fire out of the green[2463] tree, and behold, you kindle from it.

اِۨلَّذِيْ جَعَلَ لَكُمْ مِّنَ الشَّجَرِ الْاَخْضَرِ نَارًا فَاِذَآ
اَنْتُمْ مِّنْهُ تُوْقِدُوْنَ ۝٨١

82. [h]"Has not He Who created the heavens and the earth the power to create the like of them?' Yea, and He is, indeed, the Supreme Creator, the All-Knowing.

اَوَلَيْسَ الَّذِيْ خَلَقَ السَّمٰوٰتِ وَالْاَرْضَ بِقٰدِرٍ
عَلٰٓى اَنْ يَّخْلُقَ مِثْلَهُمْ ۭ بَلٰى ۤ وَهُوَ الْخَلّٰقُ الْعَلِيْمُ ۝٨٢

---

[a]7 : 193. [b]10 : 66. [c]11 : 6; 16 : 24; 27 : 75; 28 : 70. [d]18 : 38; 22 : 6; 23 : 14; 35 : 12; 40 : 68. [e]19 : 67; 23 : 38; 45 : 25. [f]17 : 52; 46 : 34; 75 : 41. [g]56 : 72, 73. [h]17 : 100; 46 : 34; 86 : 9.

2463. 'Green tree' seems to be the resinous tree whose branches get easily ignited and catch fire when friction is caused by the blowing of the wind, the implication being that just as fire is caused by friction between the branches of a tree, even so does new spiritual life result when spiritually weak people come in contact with a Prophet of God, or a Divine Reformer.

83. [a]Verily, His command, when He intends a thing, is *only* that He says concerning it, 'Be,' and it comes into being.[2464]

إِنَّمَآ أَمۡرُهُۥٓ إِذَآ أَرَادَ شَيۡـًٔا أَن يَقُولَ لَهُۥ كُن فَيَكُونُ ﴿٨٣﴾

84. So Holy is He, [b]in Whose hand is the dominion of all things. And to Him will you *all* be brought back.

فَسُبۡحَٰنَ ٱلَّذِي بِيَدِهِۦ مَلَكُوتُ كُلِّ شَيۡءٖ وَإِلَيۡهِ تُرۡجَعُونَ ﴿٨٤﴾

[a]2 : 118; 3 : 48; 40 : 69. [b]23 : 89.

2464. Wherever in the Qur'ān the expression, *when He intends a thing, He says concerning it, 'Be,' and it comes into being*, is used, the reference invariably seems to be to the occurrence of an event of exceptional importance, particularly to the coming into being of a great moral and spiritual revolution through a Divine Reformer. In the verse under comment also the reference is to the great change which was wrought by the Holy Prophet.

CHAPTER 37

AL-ṢĀFFĀT

(Revealed before Hijrah)

Place of Revelation and Context

Baihaquī and Ibn Mardawaih report Ibn 'Abbās as saying that the *Sūrah* was revealed at Mecca. According to Qurṭubī the consensus of scholarly opinion also regards the *Sūrah* as having been revealed very early in the Holy Prophet's ministry at Mecca. Its style and subject-matter also support this view. In the preceding *Sūrah* the Holy Prophet was called "The Perfect Leader" who was given the Qur'ān as an infallible guide for the whole of humanity till the end of time. In the beginning of the present *Sūrah* it is stated that this "Perfect Leader" will, with the help of the Qur'ān and by his own noble example, succeed in bringing into being a community of righteous men.

Subject-Matter

The *Sūrah* opens with a firm declaration that under the fostering care of the Holy Prophet—"The Perfect Leader"—a community of noble and righteous men will be born who not only themselves will glorify God and sing His praises—so much so that the sandy wilderness of Arabia will resound with them—but by precept and practice will prevent others from idol-worship and evil practices, till the Unity of God will become firmly established in Arabia and from there the light of Islām will spread to the ends of the earth. The *Sūrah*, then proceeds to say that whenever there appears a Prophet of God in the world, forces of darkness seek to obstruct the spread of his Message by misrepresenting and misinterpreting it, or by misquoting the Prophet and tearing a passage out of his revelation and mixing much falsehood with it. But they completely fail in their evil designs, and truth continues to make progress. It further says that when disbelievers are told that the teachings of the Qur'ān will bring about a great change in Arabia and the spiritually dead Arabs will not only receive a new life but, having received it themselves, will impart it to others, the disbelievers jeer and scoff at the idea and call it the ravings of a maniac and the phenomenon as outside the bounds of possibility like the coming into life of those who are physically dead. The *Sūrah* replies to the firm denial of the disbelievers of this phenomenon with a firmer affirmation that such a thing will certainly come to pass and they will suffer disgrace and humiliation. Next, the *Sūrah* gives a brief description of the heavenly blessings that will be bestowed upon the righteous and chosen servants of God. The account of heavenly blessings and bounties, to be bestowed on the believers is followed by an account of the punishment which will be meted out to the rejectors of truth and persecutors of God's Prophets. Further, the *Sūrah* gives a few illustrations from the lives of Divine Prophets to show that the cause of truth never fails and its rejection is never productive of good results. The illustrations given are from the lives of Noah, Abraham, Moses, Elias, Jonas and Lot. The *Sūrah*, then, repudiates and condemns idol-worship, particularly the worship of angels. The idol-worshippers are reprimanded that they are foolish enough not to understand this simple fact that the ascription of Divine powers and attributes to weak human beings or to forces of nature or even to angels who themselves are created beings, offends against human reason, commonsense and conscience. They are further told that the angels are only God's creatures who have specific duties to perform. The *Sūrah* ends on the note that it is an unalterable Divine decree that when forces of darkness are pitted against God's Prophets and His chosen servants, the latter receive Divine succour, while the votaries of Satan meet with defeat and discomfiture. This fact has been proved again and again in the lives of Divine Messengers and it leads to but one conclusion that 'all praise belongs to God, the Lord of all the worlds.'

ركوعاتها ٥ — سُوۡرَةُ الصّٰٓفّٰتِ مَكِّيَّةٌ (٣٧) — اٰياتها ١٨٣

1. [a]In the name of Allāh, the Gracious, the Merciful.

بِسۡمِ اللّٰهِ الرَّحۡمٰنِ الرَّحِيۡمِ ①

2. By[2465] those who range themselves in close ranks,[2466]

وَالصّٰٓفّٰتِ صَفًّا ②

3. And those who repel *evil* vigorously,[2467]

فَالزّٰجِرٰتِ زَجۡرًا ③

4. And those who recite the Reminder—*the Qur'ān*,[2468]

فَالتّٰلِيٰتِ ذِكۡرًا ④

5. [b]Surely, your God is One,[2469]

اِنَّ اِلٰهَكُمۡ لَوَاحِدٌ ⑤

---

[a]1 : 1. [b]5 : 74; 16 : 23; 22 : 35.

2465. The particle *wāw* means, also; then; while; during; at the same time, together; with; but; however. It is also synonymous with *rubba*, *i.e.*, frequently; sometimes, perhaps. It is also a particle of swearing meaning, 'by' or 'I swear', or 'I cite as witness' (Aqrab & Lane). *Wāw* has been used in the present and the next two verses in the sense of 'by', or 'I swear', or 'I cite as witness.' In the Qur'ān God has sworn by certain beings or things or has cited them as witnesses. Ordinarily, when a person takes an oath and swears by Allāh his object is to supply the deficiency of insufficient testimony or to add weight or conviction to his statement. By so doing he calls God to witness that he speaks the truth when there is no other person to bear witness to his statement. But such is not the case with the Quranic oaths. When the Qur'ān adopts such a form the truth of the statement it makes is not sought to be proved by a mere assertion but by a solid argument implied in the oath itself. Sometimes these oaths refer to the obvious laws of nature and by implication draw attention to what may be inferred, *i.e.*, spiritual laws, from what is obvious. Another object of a Quranic oath is to make a prophecy the fulfilment of which establishes its truth. This is the case here.

2466. Muslims standing in battle array facing the enemy or standing behind their *Imām* in the five daily Prayers.

2467. Waging a relentless war against the enemy of Islām and driving them away vigorously. The words may also signify the custodians of law and order.

2468. Reciters of the Qur'ān.

2469. These verses (2-5) embody both a prophecy and a statement of fact. As a statement of fact they signify that there live in all times and among every people a group of righteous and God-fearing men who, by word and deed and by precept and practice, bear testimony to the truth that God is One. As a prophecy, however, the verses signify that though at present the whole of Arabia is sunk deep in idol-worship and moral turpitude, yet a community of the Faithful will soon be born who not only will themselves glorify God and sing His praises and make the whole country resound with their hosannas but will also succeed in establishing Divine Unity in the land. Thus the Companions of the Holy Prophet, some of whose characteristics are mentioned in these verses, are cited as witnesses to the Unity of God. The verses may have yet another interpretation, *viz.*, that if a representative gathering of the learned men of various Faiths were held in a peaceful atmosphere and the basic religious principles were discussed and debated impartially and dispassionately in a calm atmosphere, under the supervision of the custodians of law and order, the inevitable outcome of the deliberations of such a gathering will be the affirmation of the doctrine that 'God is One'

6. [a]Lord of the heavens and the earth and all that is between them and the Lord of the places from which light spreads forth.[2470]

رَبُّ السَّمٰوٰتِ وَالْاَرْضِ وَمَا بَيْنَهُمَا وَرَبُّ الْمَشَارِقِ ۝٦

7. [b]We have adorned the lowest heaven with an adornment—the planets;[2471]

اِنَّا زَيَّنَّا السَّمَآءَ الدُّنْيَا بِزِيْنَةِ ۣالْكَوَاكِبِ ۝٧

8. [c]And have guarded *it* against all rebellious satans.[2472]

وَحِفْظًا مِّنْ كُلِّ شَيْطٰنٍ مَّارِدٍ ۝٨

9. They cannot listen to *anything* from the Exalted Assembly *of angels*—and they are pelted from every side,

لَا يَسَّمَّعُوْنَ اِلَى الْمَلَاِ الْاَعْلٰى وَيُقْذَفُوْنَ مِنْ كُلِّ جَانِبٍ ۝٩

10. Repulsed, and for them is a perpetual punishment—

دُحُوْرًا وَّلَهُمْ عَذَابٌ وَّاصِبٌ ۝١٠

11. [d]But if any of them snatches away *something* by stealth, he is pursued by a piercing flame.[2473]

اِلَّا مَنْ خَطِفَ الْخَطْفَةَ فَاَتْبَعَهٗ شِهَابٌ ثَاقِبٌ ۝١١

12. So ask them whether it is they who are harder to create, or those[2474] *others* whom We have created? Them We have created of cohesive [e]clay.

فَاسْتَفْتِهِمْ اَهُمْ اَشَدُّ خَلْقًا اَمْ مَّنْ خَلَقْنَا ؕ اِنَّا خَلَقْنٰهُمْ مِّنْ طِيْنٍ لَّازِبٍ ۝١٢

---

[a]19 : 66; 38 : 67; 44 : 8; 78 : 38. [b]15 : 17; 41 : 13; 67 : 6. [c]15 : 18; 41 : 13; 67 : 6. [d]15 : 19. [e]6 : 3; 23 : 13; 32 : 8; 38 : 72.

2470. The implication may be to the spread of Islām first in eastern countries, then from there to other parts of the world.

2471. The verse points to a parallelism between the physical and spiritual realms, *viz.*, that just as the physical heaven is sustained by physical planets and stars, so is the spiritual heaven sustained by their spiritual counterparts who are the Prophets and Divine Reformers. Each one of them serves as an ornament for the spiritual heaven, as the stars and planets beautify and embellish the physical heaven.

2472. Satans are of two categories : (*a*) Internal enemies of the Muslim Community such as the hypocrites, etc. They are called 'the rebellious satans' as in this verse : and (*b*) external enemies or disbelievers who are described as 'satans, the rejected' (15 : 18).

2473. As long as the Word of God is preserved in the heavens it is quite safe and secure against all interference, stealing or snatching, but after it is revealed to a Prophet, 'satans,' or the enemies of God's Prophets, seek to misrepresent or misinterpret it by misquoting the Prophet. or by tearing a passage out of his revelation and mixing much falsehood with it, or they even try to represent the Prophet's teaching as their own. But their falsehood becomes exposed by the true exposition of his revelation by the Divine Reformer.

2474. In the word *man* the allusion may be to those righteous Companions of the Holy Prophet to whom reference has been made in vv. 2-5. The reference may also be to the system of the universe.

13. Nay, thou dost wonder[2475] *at what they say*, and they ridicule *what thou sayest*.

بَلْ عَجِبْتَ وَيَسْخَرُونَ ﴿١٣﴾

14. And when they are admonished, they pay no heed.

وَإِذَا ذُكِّرُوا لَا يَذْكُرُونَ ﴿١٤﴾

15. And when they see a Sign, they mock *at it*.

وَإِذَا رَأَوْا آيَةً يَسْتَسْخِرُونَ ﴿١٥﴾

16. And they say, [a]'This is nothing but plain sorcery,

وَقَالُوا إِنْ هَٰذَا إِلَّا سِحْرٌ مُبِينٌ ﴿١٦﴾

17. [b]'What! when we are dead and have become dust and *broken* bones, shall we then be raised up *again?*

أَإِذَا مِتْنَا وَكُنَّا تُرَابًا وَعِظَامًا أَإِنَّا لَمَبْعُوثُونَ ﴿١٧﴾

18. 'And our forefathers of yore *also?*'

أَوَآبَاؤُنَا الْأَوَّلُونَ ﴿١٨﴾

19. Say, 'Yea; and you will, *then*, be abased.'

قُلْ نَعَمْ وَأَنْتُمْ دَاخِرُونَ ﴿١٩﴾

20. It will be but [c]one stern call, and lo ! they will be up *and* seeing;

فَإِنَّمَا هِيَ زَجْرَةٌ وَاحِدَةٌ فَإِذَا هُمْ يَنْظُرُونَ ﴿٢٠﴾

21. And they will say, 'Alas for us! this is the Day of Requital.'[2476]

وَقَالُوا يَا وَيْلَنَا هَٰذَا يَوْمُ الدِّينِ ﴿٢١﴾

22. *Allāh will say*, [d]'This is the day[2476] of the final Decision which you used to deny.'

هَٰذَا يَوْمُ الْفَصْلِ الَّذِي كُنْتُمْ بِهِ تُكَذِّبُونَ ﴿٢٢﴾

R. 2 23. [e]*The angels will be commanded:* 'Assemble those who acted wrongfully along with their companions and what they used to worship

احْشُرُوا الَّذِينَ ظَلَمُوا وَأَزْوَاجَهُمْ وَمَا كَانُوا يَعْبُدُونَ ﴿٢٣﴾

24. 'Beside Allāh; and lead them along the path of Hell;

مِنْ دُونِ اللَّهِ فَاهْدُوهُمْ إِلَىٰ صِرَاطِ الْجَحِيمِ ﴿٢٤﴾

[a]7 : 110. 61 : 7. [b]13 : 6 ; 27 : 68 ; 50 : 4. [c]79 : 14. [d]46 : 35; 52 : 14, 15. [e]6 : 23.

2475. The coming into being of a company of truly righteous and God-fearing men through the Holy Prophet and the establishment of Islām on a firm footing in Arabia is, indeed, a marvel to wonder at even by the Holy Prophet himself.

2476. May be the day on which Mecca fell.

25. 'And stop them, for they shall be questioned.'

وَقِفُوهُمْ اِنَّهُمْ مَّسْـُٔوْلُوْنَ ۝

26. *They will be asked,* 'What is the matter with you that you help not one another?'[2477]

مَا لَكُمْ لَا تَنَاصَرُوْنَ ۝

27. Nay, on that day they will surrender themselves completely.[2478]

بَلْ هُمُ الْيَوْمَ مُسْتَسْلِمُوْنَ ۝

28. And some of them will address others, [a]questioning one another.

وَاَقْبَلَ بَعْضُهُمْ عَلَى بَعْضٍ يَّتَسَآءَلُوْنَ ۝

29. They will say, 'Verily, you used to come to us from the right.'[2478A]

قَالُوْۤا اِنَّكُمْ كُنْتُمْ تَأْتُوْنَنَا عَنِ الْيَمِيْنِ ۝

30. *The others* will answer, [b]'Nay, you yourselves were not believers,

قَالُوْا بَلْ لَّمْ تَكُوْنُوْا مُؤْمِنِيْنَ ۝

31. [c]'And we had no power over you; but you yourselves were a transgressing people;

وَمَا كَانَ لَنَا عَلَيْكُمْ مِّنْ سُلْطٰنٍ بَلْ كُنْتُمْ قَوْمًا طٰغِيْنَ ۝

32. 'Now the word of our Lord has been fulfilled against us that we must taste *the punishment;*

فَحَقَّ عَلَيْنَا قَوْلُ رَبِّنَآ اِنَّا لَذَآئِقُوْنَ ۝

33. 'And we caused you to go astray for we ourselves had gone astray.'[2479]

فَاَغْوَيْنٰكُمْ اِنَّا كُنَّا غٰوِيْنَ ۝

34. Truly, on that day they will *all* be sharers in the punishment.

فَاِنَّهُمْ يَوْمَئِذٍ فِى الْعَذَابِ مُشْتَرِكُوْنَ ۝

---

[a]34 : 32.   [b]34 : 33.   [c]14 : 23; 15 : 43.

2477. The realization of utter helplessness of the guilty people to assist each other will be brought home to them.

2478. The guilty will offer no defence but will only indulge in mutual recrimination as the following verses show.

2478A. 'The right side' may signify religion and the verse may mean, 'You masqueraded under the cloak of religion to deceive us.' Or, the word, *Yamīn*, may signify power and force, and the verse may mean, 'You approached us with great power and force.' Or, it may mean, 'You came to us swearing that you were truthful.'

2479. The leaders of disbelief will say to their followers : 'You yourselves chose to follow us, and since we ourselves had gone astray, you could expect nothing better from us.' It was a case of blind leading the blind.

35. Surely, thus do We deal with the guilty.

إِنَّا كَذٰلِكَ نَفْعَلُ بِالْمُجْرِمِيْنَ ﴿٣٥﴾

36. For when it was said to them, 'There is no god but Allāh,' they behaved arrogantly,

إِنَّهُمْ كَانُوْٓا إِذَا قِيْلَ لَهُمْ لَآ إِلٰهَ إِلَّا اللّٰهُ يَسْتَكْبِرُوْنَ ﴿٣٦﴾

37. And said, 'Shall we give up our gods for a [a]mad poet?'

وَيَقُوْلُوْنَ أَئِنَّا لَتَارِكُوْٓا اٰلِهَتِنَا لِشَاعِرٍ مَّجْنُوْنٍ ﴿٣٧﴾

38. Nay, he has brought the truth and has testified to the truth of *all* the Messengers.

بَلْ جَآءَ بِالْحَقِّ وَصَدَّقَ الْمُرْسَلِيْنَ ﴿٣٨﴾

39. You shall, surely, taste the painful punishment;

إِنَّكُمْ لَذَآئِقُوا الْعَذَابِ الْأَلِيْمِ ﴿٣٩﴾

40. [b]And you will be requited only for what you have wrought—

وَمَا تُجْزَوْنَ إِلَّا مَا كُنْتُمْ تَعْمَلُوْنَ ﴿٤٠﴾

41. Save the chosen servants of Allāh;

إِلَّا عِبَادَ اللّٰهِ الْمُخْلَصِيْنَ ﴿٤١﴾

42. They will have a known provision :[2480]

أُولٰٓئِكَ لَهُمْ رِزْقٌ مَّعْلُوْمٌ ﴿٤٢﴾

43. [c]Fruits;[2481] and they shall be honoured,

فَوَاكِهُ ۚ وَهُمْ مُّكْرَمُوْنَ ﴿٤٣﴾

44. [d]In the Gardens of Bliss,

فِيْ جَنّٰتِ النَّعِيْمِ ﴿٤٤﴾

45. [e]*Seated* on thrones, facing one another;

عَلٰى سُرُرٍ مُّتَقٰبِلِيْنَ ﴿٤٥﴾

46. [f]They will be served round with a cup from a flowing fountain,

يُطَافُ عَلَيْهِمْ بِكَأْسٍ مِّنْ مَّعِيْنٍ ﴿٤٦﴾

47. *Sparkling* white, delicious to the drinkers;

بَيْضَآءَ لَذَّةٍ لِّلشّٰرِبِيْنَ ﴿٤٧﴾

48. [g]Wherein there will be no intoxication, nor will they be exhausted thereby.

لَا فِيْهَا غَوْلٌ وَّلَا هُمْ عَنْهَا يُنْزَفُوْنَ ﴿٤٨﴾

[a]15 : 7; 44 : 15; 68 : 52. [b]36 : 55; 45 : 29. [c]52 : 23; 55 : 53; 56 : 21. [d]44 : 53; 68 : 35; 78 : 32. [e]56 : 16-17. [f]56 : 18, 19 [g]56 : 20.

2480. The words, 'a known provision,' signify that Muslims knew beforehand that they would receive Divine favours mentioned in the following verses.

2481. The blessings which the believers would get would be the fruit of right beliefs and good deeds of the believers.

49. [a]And with them will be *chaste* women, with restrained looks *and* large beautiful eyes;[2482]

وَعِنْدَهُمْ قٰصِرٰتُ الطَّرْفِ عِيْنٌ ﴿٤٩﴾

50. [b]As though they were sheltered eggs.

كَاَنَّهُنَّ بَيْضٌ مَّكْنُوْنٌ ﴿٥٠﴾

51. Then some of them will address the others, questioning one another.

فَاَقْبَلَ بَعْضُهُمْ عَلٰى بَعْضٍ يَّتَسَآءَلُوْنَ ﴿٥١﴾

52. A speaker from among them will say, 'I had an intimate companion,

قَالَ قَآئِلٌ مِّنْهُمْ اِنِّيْ كَانَ لِيْ قَرِيْنٌ ﴿٥٢﴾

53. 'Who used to say, 'Art thou, indeed, among those who believe *the Resurrection* to be true?

يَّقُوْلُ اَئِنَّكَ لَمِنَ الْمُصَدِّقِيْنَ ﴿٥٣﴾

54. [c]"When we are dead, and have become dust and *broken* bones, shall we, indeed, be requited?'

ءَاِذَا مِتْنَا وَكُنَّا تُرَابًا وَّعِظَامًا ءَاِنَّا لَمَدِيْنُوْنَ ﴿٥٤﴾

55. *The speaker* will then ask *those around him*, 'Will you have a look *and find out about him*?'[2483]

قَالَ هَلْ اَنْتُمْ مُّطَّلِعُوْنَ ﴿٥٥﴾

56. Then he will look *himself* and see him in the midst of the Fire,

فَاطَّلَعَ فَرَاٰهُ فِيْ سَوَآءِ الْجَحِيْمِ ﴿٥٦﴾

57. And will say *to him*, 'By Allāh, thou hadst almost caused my ruin,

قَالَ تَاللّٰهِ اِنْ كِدْتَّ لَتُرْدِيْنِ ﴿٥٧﴾

58. 'But for the grace of my Lord, I should, surely, have been of those who are called up *before Hell*;

وَلَوْلَا نِعْمَةُ رَبِّيْ لَكُنْتُ مِنَ الْمُحْضَرِيْنَ ﴿٥٨﴾

---

[a]55 : 57. [b]55 : 59. [c]13 : 6; 50 : 4; 56 : 48.

2482. '*In* (women having large beautiful eyes) is the plural of '*Ainā*' which means, a woman having large beautiful eyes. The word also means a good or beautiful word or saying. *Arḍun 'Ainā'u* means, green or black earth (Lane). History bears testimony to the fact that Muslims were endowed with all the blessings mentioned in the foregoing verses. They had gardens of bliss; they sat on thrones and enjoyed power and dominion; they had all the innocent pleasures of life; they had beautiful chaste women as their spouses and, over and above all this, 'God was well-pleased with them and they were well-pleased with Him' (58 : 23). This was their greatest achievement.

2483. The speaker is the inmate of Paradise referred to in v. 52. He will ask other inmates of Paradise if they would like to have a look at his former disbelieving companion.

59. *'Tell me*, is it not so that we are not going to suffer death *again?*

أَفَمَا نَحْنُ بِمَيِّتِينَ ﴿٥٩﴾

60. [a]'Save our first death,[2484] and that we are not to be punished?

إِلَّا مَوْتَتَنَا الْأُولَىٰ وَمَا نَحْنُ بِمُعَذَّبِينَ ﴿٦٠﴾

61. [b]'Surely, this is the supreme triumph.'[2485]

إِنَّ هَٰذَا لَهُوَ الْفَوْزُ الْعَظِيمُ ﴿٦١﴾

62. For the like of this, then, let the workers work.

لِمِثْلِ هَٰذَا فَلْيَعْمَلِ الْعَامِلُونَ ﴿٦٢﴾

63. Is that better as an entertainment, or [c]the tree of *Zaqqūm?*[2486]

أَذَٰلِكَ خَيْرٌ نُّزُلًا أَمْ شَجَرَةُ الزَّقُّومِ ﴿٦٣﴾

64. Verily, We have made it a trial for the wrongdoers.[2487]

إِنَّا جَعَلْنَاهَا فِتْنَةً لِّلظَّالِمِينَ ﴿٦٤﴾

65. It is a tree that springs forth in the bottom of Hell;[2488]

إِنَّهَا شَجَرَةٌ تَخْرُجُ فِي أَصْلِ الْجَحِيمِ ﴿٦٥﴾

66. The fruit thereof is as though it were the heads of serpents.

طَلْعُهَا كَأَنَّهُ رُءُوسُ الشَّيَاطِينِ ﴿٦٦﴾

67. [d]And they shall eat of it and fill *their* bellies therewith.

فَإِنَّهُمْ لَآكِلُونَ مِنْهَا فَمَالِئُونَ مِنْهَا الْبُطُونَ ﴿٦٧﴾

68. Then will they have in addition to it a mixture of boiling water *to drink*.

ثُمَّ إِنَّ لَهُمْ عَلَيْهَا لَشَوْبًا مِّنْ حَمِيمٍ ﴿٦٨﴾

69. Then, surely, their return shall be to Hell.

ثُمَّ إِنَّ مَرْجِعَهُمْ لَإِلَى الْجَحِيمِ ﴿٦٩﴾

[a]23 : 38; 44 : 36. [b]44 : 58; 61 : 13. [c]44 : 44; 56 : 53. [d]56 : 54.

2484. The believer in Paradise is here mentioned as referring to the great destiny of man—his eternal life. He says that man will not suffer death after his departure from this world. His spiritual journey to Eternity will know no end or retreat.

2485. Man's greatest achievement and the fulfilment of his highest destiny lies in enjoying eternal life and making incessant and everlasting spiritual progress.

2486. *Zaqqūm* denotes the tree of disbelief. The Qur'ān has compared true belief to a good tree which brings forth its fruit at all times (14 : 25-26) and disbelief to an evil tree—*Zaqqūm* (14 : 27). Taking it in the sense of deadly food, the verse would mean that eating of the fruit of the accursed tree of disbelief brings about spiritual death.

2487. The evil tree of disbelief has always proved a great source of mischief for men.

2488. Eating of the tree of disbelief takes men to the bottom of Hell.

70. [a]They found their fathers erring.

إِنَّهُمْ أَلْفَوْا آبَاءَهُمْ ضَالِّينَ ﴿٧٠﴾

71. [b]And they hurried on in their footsteps.[2489]

فَهُمْ عَلَىٰ آثَارِهِمْ يُهْرَعُونَ ﴿٧١﴾

72. And most of the ancient peoples had erred before them.

وَلَقَدْ ضَلَّ قَبْلَهُمْ أَكْثَرُ الْأَوَّلِينَ ﴿٧٢﴾

73. And We had sent Warners among them.

وَلَقَدْ أَرْسَلْنَا فِيهِمْ مُنْذِرِينَ ﴿٧٣﴾

74. Behold, then, how *evil* was the end of those who were warned,

فَانْظُرْ كَيْفَ كَانَ عَاقِبَةُ الْمُنْذَرِينَ ﴿٧٤﴾

75. Save the chosen servants of Allāh.

إِلَّا عِبَادَ اللَّهِ الْمُخْلَصِينَ ﴿٧٥﴾

R. 3 76. And Noah, indeed, did cry unto Us, and how excellent Answerer *of prayers* are We !

وَلَقَدْ نَادَانَا نُوحٌ فَلَنِعْمَ الْمُجِيبُونَ ﴿٧٦﴾

77. [c]And We saved him and his family from the great distress;

وَنَجَّيْنَاهُ وَأَهْلَهُ مِنَ الْكَرْبِ الْعَظِيمِ ﴿٧٧﴾

78. And We made his offspring the only survivors.[2490]

وَجَعَلْنَا ذُرِّيَّتَهُ هُمُ الْبَاقِينَ ﴿٧٨﴾

79. And We left for him *a good name* among the later generations.

وَتَرَكْنَا عَلَيْهِ فِي الْآخِرِينَ ﴿٧٩﴾

80. Peace be upon Noah among the peoples !

سَلَامٌ عَلَىٰ نُوحٍ فِي الْعَالَمِينَ ﴿٨٠﴾

81. Thus, indeed, do We reward those who do good.

إِنَّا كَذَٰلِكَ نَجْزِي الْمُحْسِنِينَ ﴿٨١﴾

[a]7 : 174. [b]43 : 24. [c]21 : 77; 26 : 120; 54 : 14.

2489. Men are generally slaves to old usages, traditions and customs. Time-worn ideas and prejudices die hard. Perhaps the greatest obstacle in the way of acceptance of truth by the people, as repeatedly mentioned in the Qur'ān, is their strong disinclination to accept new ideas.

2490. Noah laid the foundations of human civilization and it is an established fact of history that with the progress of a people in civilization their numbers tend to increase and a corresponding decrease takes place in the numbers of less civilized communities living with them in the same or surrounding lands. The descendants of Noah being more civilized and having more material resources at their command seemed to have spread to other lands and subjugated less civilized peoples, who in course of time became absorbed in them and consequently became extinct.

82. He was, surely, *one* of Our believing servants.

إِنَّهُ مِنْ عِبَادِنَا الْمُؤْمِنِينَ ﴿٨٢﴾

83. Then We drowned the others.

ثُمَّ أَغْرَقْنَا الْآخَرِينَ ﴿٨٣﴾

84. And, verily, of his party was Abraham;

وَإِنَّ مِنْ شِيعَتِهِ لَإِبْرَاهِيمَ ﴿٨٤﴾

85. [a]When he came to his Lord with a pure heart;

إِذْ جَاءَ رَبَّهُ بِقَلْبٍ سَلِيمٍ ﴿٨٥﴾

86. [b]When he said to his father and to his people, 'What is it that you worship?

إِذْ قَالَ لِأَبِيهِ وَقَوْمِهِ مَاذَا تَعْبُدُونَ ﴿٨٦﴾

87. 'A lie—*false* gods[2491] beside Allāh do you desire?

أَئِفْكًا آلِهَةً دُونَ اللَّهِ تُرِيدُونَ ﴿٨٧﴾

88. 'What think ye of the Lord of the worlds?'

فَمَا ظَنُّكُمْ بِرَبِّ الْعَالَمِينَ ﴿٨٨﴾

89. [c]Then he cast a glance at the stars,[2492]

فَنَظَرَ نَظْرَةً فِي النُّجُومِ ﴿٨٩﴾

90. And said, 'I am feeling unwell.'[2493]

فَقَالَ إِنِّي سَقِيمٌ ﴿٩٠﴾

91. So they went away from him, turning their backs.

فَتَوَلَّوْا عَنْهُ مُدْبِرِينَ ﴿٩١﴾

92. Then he went quietly to their gods and *addressing them* said, 'Will you not eat?

فَرَاغَ إِلَىٰ آلِهَتِهِمْ فَقَالَ أَلَا تَأْكُلُونَ ﴿٩٢﴾

---

[a]26 : 90. [b]19 : 43; 26 : 71. [c]6 : 77.

2491. Man is prone to worship false gods in the form of human beings to whom he attributes Divine powers, or objects of nature such as the sun, the moon and the stars, or inanimate things such as gods hewed out of wood and stone, or his own time-worn customs, usages, prejudices and superstitions, his desires, passions, etc.

2492. It seems that the controversy between Abraham and his people about Divine attributes dragged on till late into the night, and seeing that the talk had served no useful purpose Abraham wanted to cut it short. So he cast a glance at the stars, suggesting thereby that the talk had dragged on long and far into the night and it should better stop.

2493. In view of the useless nature of the talk Abraham told his people that they had better leave him alone as he was not feeling well. Or, the words, ***Innī Saqīm***, may mean, 'I am sick of your worshipping false gods,' or, 'I am sorely distressed at heart because you worship false gods,' or, 'I hate your worship of false gods.'

93. 'What is the matter with you that you speak not?'[2494]

مَا لَكُمْ لَا تَنْطِقُوْنَ ۝

94. ᵃThen he turned upon them, striking *them* with the right hand.[2495]

فَرَاغَ عَلَيْهِمْ ضَرْبًۢا بِالْيَمِيْنِ ۝

95. Thereupon *the people* came towards him, hastening.

فَاَقْبَلُوْٓا اِلَيْهِ يَزِفُّوْنَ ۝

96. He said, ᵇ'Do you worship that which you yourselves carve out,

قَالَ اَتَعْبُدُوْنَ مَا تَنْحِتُوْنَ ۝

97. 'Whereas Allāh has created you and *also* your handiwork?'[2495A]

وَاللّٰهُ خَلَقَكُمْ وَمَا تَعْمَلُوْنَ ۝

98. They said, 'Build for him a structure and ᶜcast him into the fire.'

قَالُوا ابْنُوْا لَهٗ بُنْيَانًا فَاَلْقُوْهُ فِي الْجَحِيْمِ ۝

99. ᵈThus they designed an *evil* design against him, but We made them most humiliated.[2496]

فَاَرَادُوْا بِهٖ كَيْدًا فَجَعَلْنٰهُمُ الْاَسْفَلِيْنَ ۝

100. 'And he said, 'I am going to my Lord. He will, surely, guide me.'

وَقَالَ اِنِّيْ ذَاهِبٌ اِلٰى رَبِّيْ سَيَهْدِيْنِ ۝

101. *And he prayed,* 'My Lord, grant me a righteous *son.*'

رَبِّ هَبْ لِيْ مِنَ الصّٰلِحِيْنَ ۝

102. So We gave him the glad tidings of a forbearing son.

فَبَشَّرْنٰهُ بِغُلٰمٍ حَلِيْمٍ ۝

ᵃ21 : 59.   ᵇ21 : 67-68.   ᶜ21 : 69;   29 : 25.   ᵈ21 : 71.   ᵉ19 : 49;   29 : 27.

2494. The most distinctive attribute of a Living God is that He speaks to His chosen servants and listens to and answers their prayers. It is a dead and defunct deity that has not the power to speak or listen to and accept the prayers of his votaries.

2495. The right hand being the symbol of power and strength, the verse signifies that Abraham struck the idols with full force and broke them into pieces. *Yamīn* also meaning a vow, the verse may signify that Abraham broke the idols in fulfilment of his vow (21 : 58).

2495A. Your hands and feet with which you work.

2496. As the enemies of Abraham were frustrated in their plans against him, they had a deep feeling of humiliation.

103. And when he was old enough to run along with him, he said, 'O my dear son, I have seen in a dream that I offer thee in sacrifice.[2497] So consider what thou thinkest *of it!*' He replied, 'O my father, do as thou art commanded; thou wilt find me, if Allāh please, steadfast *in my faith.*'

فَلَمَّا بَلَغَ مَعَهُ السَّعْيَ قَالَ يٰبُنَيَّ إِنِّيٓ أَرٰى فِي
الْمَنَامِ أَنِّيٓ أَذْبَحُكَ فَانْظُرْ مَاذَا تَرٰى ۚ قَالَ
يٰٓأَبَتِ افْعَلْ مَا تُؤْمَرُ ۖ سَتَجِدُنِيٓ إِنْ شَآءَ اللّٰهُ
مِنَ الصّٰبِرِينَ ﴿١٠٣﴾

104. And when they both submitted *to the Will of God*, and *Abraham* had thrown him down on his forehead,

فَلَمَّآ أَسْلَمَا وَتَلَّهٗ لِلْجَبِينِ ﴿١٠٤﴾

105. We called to him, 'O Abraham,

وَنَادَيْنٰهُ أَنْ يّٰٓإِبْرٰهِيمُ ﴿١٠٥﴾

106. 'Thou hast, indeed, fulfilled the dream.' Thus, indeed, do We reward those who do good.

قَدْ صَدَّقْتَ الرُّءْيَا ۚ إِنَّا كَذٰلِكَ نَجْزِي الْمُحْسِنِينَ ﴿١٠٦﴾

2497. The Qur'ān and the Bible are at variance as to which of his two sons—Ishmael or Isaac—Abraham, in pursuance of God's command, offered for sacrifice. According to the Bible it was Isaac (Gen. 22 : 2). The Qur'ān, on the other hand, declares clearly and unequivocally that it was Ishmael. The Bible contradicts itself in this respect. According to it, Abraham was commanded to offer his *only son* for sacrifice, but Isaac was at no time his only son. Ishmael was senior to Isaac by 13 years and for these many years was Abraham's only son, and, being also his first born, was doubly dear to him. It stands to reason, therefore, that Abraham must have been required by God to offer for sacrifice his nearest and dearest thing which was his only and first born son who was Ishmael. Some Christian evangelists have vainly tried to show that, 'Ishmael being of the handmaid, was born after the flesh while Isaac being born of the free woman was by promise' (Galatians, 4 : 22, 23). Apart from the fact that Hagar, Ishmael's mother, belonged to the royal family of Egypt and was no handmaid, Ishmael has repeatedly been mentioned in the Bible as Abraham's son, exactly as Isaac has been mentioned as his son (Gen. 16 : 16; 17 : 23,25). Moreover, analogous promises were made to Abraham in regard to the future greatness of Ishmael as were made to him about Isaac (Gen., 16 : 10, 11 ; 17 : 20). Apart from the substitution in the Bible of Isaac for Ishmael which seems to be deliberate, and of Moriah for Marwah, an hillock which lies in the vicinity of Mecca near which Abraham left Ishmael with his mother Hagar while yet a child, there is nothing in the Bible to lend the slightest support to the view that Abraham offered Isaac for sacrifice and not Ishmael. But whereas no trace is to be found in the religious ceremonies of Jews and Christians of the supposed sacrifice of Isaac by Abraham, Muslims who are the spiritual descendants of Ishmael, commemorate with great fervour his intended sacrifice, by slaughtering every year rams and goats all over the world on the tenth day of Dhu'l-Ḥijjah. This universal sacrifice of rams and goats by Muslims establishes beyond dispute or doubt the fact that it was Ishmael whom Abraham offered for sacrifice and not Isaac. In reality Abraham was not required to fulfil his vision in actual fact. It was only a practical demonstration of his intention and preparedness to sacrifice his son which was desired of him. The vision had already symbolically been fulfilled in Hagar and Ishmael having been left by Abraham in the Valley of Mecca which was at that time an arid and barren waste. That brave act, had, in fact, symbolised the sacrifice of Ishmael. The Divine command to Abraham first to sacrifice his son and then to abstain from carrying it into actual fact showed also that it was intended to abolish human sacrifice, a most inhuman practice which was prevalent at that time among most nations.

107. That, surely, was a manifest trial.

إِنَّ هَٰذَا لَهُوَ الْبَلَٰٓؤُا الْمُبِينُ ﴿١٠٧﴾

108. And We ransomed him with a mighty sacrifice.[2498]

وَفَدَيْنَٰهُ بِذِبْحٍ عَظِيمٍ ﴿١٠٨﴾

109. And We left for him *a good name* among the succeeding generations.[2499]

وَتَرَكْنَا عَلَيْهِ فِي الْآخِرِينَ ﴿١٠٩﴾

110. Peace be upon Abraham!

سَلَٰمٌ عَلَىٰٓ إِبْرَٰهِيمَ ﴿١١٠﴾

111. Thus do We reward those who do good.

كَذَٰلِكَ نَجْزِي الْمُحْسِنِينَ ﴿١١١﴾

112. Surely, he was *one* of Our believing servants.

إِنَّهُۥ مِنْ عِبَادِنَا الْمُؤْمِنِينَ ﴿١١٢﴾

113. [a]And We gave him the glad tidings of Isaac, a Prophet, *and one* of the righteous.

وَبَشَّرْنَٰهُ بِإِسْحَٰقَ نَبِيًّا مِّنَ الصَّٰلِحِينَ ﴿١١٣﴾

114. And We bestowed blessings on him[2500] and on Isaac. [b]And among their progeny are *some* who do good and others who clearly wrong themselves.

وَبَٰرَكْنَا عَلَيْهِ وَعَلَىٰٓ إِسْحَٰقَ ۚ وَمِن ذُرِّيَّتِهِمَا
ع مُحْسِنٌ وَظَالِمٌ لِّنَفْسِهِۦ مُبِينٌ ﴿١١٤﴾

R. 4 115. [c]And, indeed, We bestowed favours on Moses and Aaron.

وَلَقَدْ مَنَنَّا عَلَىٰ مُوسَىٰ وَهَٰرُونَ ﴿١١٥﴾

116. [d]And We saved them both and their people from the great distress;

وَنَجَّيْنَٰهُمَا وَقَوْمَهُمَا مِنَ الْكَرْبِ الْعَظِيمِ ﴿١١٦﴾

117. And We helped them, and it was they who were victorious.

وَنَصَرْنَٰهُمْ فَكَانُوا هُمُ الْغَٰلِبِينَ ﴿١١٧﴾

[a]11 : 72; 19 : 50; 21 : 73; 29 : 28. [b]57 : 27. [c]20 : 31; 28 : 35. [d]20 : 81; 26 : 66.

2498. Abraham's preparedness to sacrifice Ishmael was perpetuated in the Islamic institution of 'Sacrifice' which forms an integral part of the ceremonies of *Hajj*. The implication in the verse may also be to the abolition of human sacrifice which seemed to be in vogue in Abraham's time and to the substitution for it of animal sacrifice.

2499. What greater testimony could there be to Abraham having left behind him a good name than that the followers of three great religions—Islām, Christianity and Judaism—take pride in ascribing their ancestry to the great Patriarch.

2500. The words, 'We bestowed blessings on him,' refer to the blessings that God bestowed upon Abraham's progeny through Ishmael, as Isaac has been mentioned separately by name.

118. And We gave them the Book that made *everything* clear;

وَاٰتَيْنٰهُمَا الْكِتٰبَ الْمُسْتَبِيْنَ ﴿۱۱۸﴾

119. And We guided them to the right path.

وَهَدَيْنٰهُمَا الصِّرَاطَ الْمُسْتَقِيْمَ ﴿۱۱۹﴾

120. And We left for them *a good name* among the succeeding generations—

وَتَرَكْنَا عَلَيْهِمَا فِي الْاٰخِرِيْنَ ﴿۱۲۰﴾

121. Peace be on Moses and Aaron !

سَلٰمٌ عَلٰى مُوْسٰى وَهٰرُوْنَ ﴿۱۲۱﴾

122. Thus, indeed, do We reward those who do good.

اِنَّا كَذٰلِكَ نَجْزِي الْمُحْسِنِيْنَ ﴿۱۲۲﴾

123. Surely, they were both among Our believing servants.

اِنَّهُمَا مِنْ عِبَادِنَا الْمُؤْمِنِيْنَ ﴿۱۲۳﴾

124. And, assuredly, Elias[2501] *also* was *one* of the Messengers,

وَاِنَّ اِلْيَاسَ لَمِنَ الْمُرْسَلِيْنَ ﴿۱۲۴﴾

125. When he said to his people, 'Will you not be God-fearing?

اِذْ قَالَ لِقَوْمِهٖٓ اَلَا تَتَّقُوْنَ ﴿۱۲۵﴾

126. 'Do you call on Ba'l,[2502] and forsake the Best of creators—

اَتَدْعُوْنَ بَعْلًا وَّتَذَرُوْنَ اَحْسَنَ الْخَالِقِيْنَ ﴿۱۲۶﴾

127. Allāh, your Lord and the Lord of your forefathers of old?'

اللّٰهَ رَبَّكُمْ وَرَبَّ اٰبَآئِكُمُ الْاَوَّلِيْنَ ﴿۱۲۷﴾

128. But they rejected him, and they will, surely, be brought *before God to render an account of their deeds ;*

فَكَذَّبُوْهُ فَاِنَّهُمْ لَمُحْضَرُوْنَ ﴿۱۲۸﴾

129. Except the chosen servants of Allāh.

اِلَّا عِبَادَ اللّٰهِ الْمُخْلَصِيْنَ ﴿۱۲۹﴾

130. And We left for him *a good name* among the later generations—

وَتَرَكْنَا عَلَيْهِ فِي الْاٰخِرِيْنَ ﴿۱۳۰﴾

2501. Elias or Elijah lived about 900 B.C. He was a native of Gilead, a place on the eastern bank of the Jordan. His mantle was taken by Elisha (Jew. Enc. & 1 Kings, 17 : 1).

2502. Ba'l was the name of an idol belonging to the people of the Prophet Elias. These people worshipped the sun. Ba'l may also stand for the sun-god which belonged to the people of a town in Syria now called Bal-Bekk (Lane).

131. Peace be on Elias and his people ![2503]

سَلٰمٌ عَلٰٓى اِلْ يَاسِيْنَ ﴿۱۳۱﴾

132. Thus, indeed, do We reward those who do good.

اِنَّا كَذٰلِكَ نَجْزِى الْمُحْسِنِيْنَ ﴿۱۳۲﴾

133. Surely, he was *one* of Our believing servants.

اِنَّهٗ مِنْ عِبَادِنَا الْمُؤْمِنِيْنَ ﴿۱۳۳﴾

134. [a]And, assuredly, Lot, *too*, was *one* of the Messengers,

وَاِنَّ لُوْطًا لَّمِنَ الْمُرْسَلِيْنَ ﴿۱۳۴﴾

135. When We delivered him and all his family,

اِذْ نَجَّيْنٰهُ وَاَهْلَهٗٓ اَجْمَعِيْنَ ﴿۱۳۵﴾

136. [c]Except an old woman *who was* among those who stayed behind.

اِلَّا عَجُوْزًا فِى الْغٰبِرِيْنَ ﴿۱۳۶﴾

137. [d]Then We utterly destroyed the others.

ثُمَّ دَمَّرْنَا الْاٰخَرِيْنَ ﴿۱۳۷﴾

138. [e]And, surely, you pass by them in the morning,

وَاِنَّكُمْ لَتَمُرُّوْنَ عَلَيْهِمْ مُّصْبِحِيْنَ ﴿۱۳۸﴾

139. And by night.[2504] Will you not understand?

وَبِالَّيْلِ ۭ اَفَلَا تَعْقِلُوْنَ ﴿۱۳۹﴾ ع

R. 5 140. [f]And, surely, Jonah[2505] *also* was *one* of the Messengers,

وَاِنَّ يُوْنُسَ لَمِنَ الْمُرْسَلِيْنَ ﴿۱۴۰﴾

141. When he fled[2506] to the laden ship;

اِذْ اَبَقَ اِلَى الْفُلْكِ الْمَشْحُوْنِ ﴿۱۴۱﴾

[a]7 : 81; 26 : 161; 29 : 29. [b]26 : 171; 29 : 33; 51 : 36. [c]7 : 84; 11 : 82; 15 : 61; 27 : 58. [d]26 : 173. [e]15 : 77. [f]21 : 88; 68 : 49.

2503. *Ilyāsīn* may be another form of *Ilyās* as *Sīnīn* (95 : 3) is that of *Sīnā*' (23 : 21); or being plural of *Ilyās* it may meah *Ilyās* and his people.

2504. Sodom and Gomorrah, the towns to which Lot preached his Message were situated on the highway from Arabia to Syria where the Arab caravans passed by day and night. At another place in the Qur'ān these towns are mentioned as having been situated 'on a road that still exists' (15 : 77).

2505. Jonah was an Israelite Prophet and lived in the 9th century in the reign of Jeroboam II or Jehoahaz. See also 6 : 87, 88.

2506. According to the Bible Jonah was commissioned by God to go to Nineveh and 'cry against' it, but instead he fled to Tarshish 'from the presence of the Lord' (Jonah, 1 : 3). The Qur'ān contradicts this biblical statement as it is calculated to impugn a Divine Prophet. In fact, being angry with his people, because they had rejected the Divine Message, Jonah fled from them.

142. And he cast lots with *the crew of the ship* and was of the losers.

فَسَاهَمَ فَكَانَ مِنَ الْمُدْحَضِينَ ﴿١٤٢﴾

143. And the fish swallowed him while he was reproaching *himself*.

فَالْتَقَمَهُ الْحُوتُ وَهُوَ مُلِيمٌ ﴿١٤٣﴾

144. And had he not been of those who glorify *God*,

فَلَوْلَا أَنَّهُ كَانَ مِنَ الْمُسَبِّحِينَ ﴿١٤٤﴾

145. He would, surely, have tarried in its belly till the Day of Resurrection.

لَلَبِثَ فِي بَطْنِهِ إِلَىٰ يَوْمِ يُبْعَثُونَ ﴿١٤٥﴾

146. Then We cast him on a bare tract of land, and he was sick;

فَنَبَذْنَاهُ بِالْعَرَاءِ وَهُوَ سَقِيمٌ ﴿١٤٦﴾

147. And We caused a gourd plant to grow over him.

وَأَنْبَتْنَا عَلَيْهِ شَجَرَةً مِنْ يَقْطِينٍ ﴿١٤٧﴾

148. And We sent him *as a Messenger* to a hundred thousand *people* or more,

وَأَرْسَلْنَاهُ إِلَىٰ مِائَةِ أَلْفٍ أَوْ يَزِيدُونَ ﴿١٤٨﴾

149. [a]And they *all* believed; so We permitted them to enjoy life for a *long* while.

فَآمَنُوا فَمَتَّعْنَاهُمْ إِلَىٰ حِينٍ ﴿١٤٩﴾

150. [b]Now ask *them*[2506A] whether thy Lord has daughters, whereas they have sons.[2507]

فَاسْتَفْتِهِمْ أَلِرَبِّكَ الْبَنَاتُ وَلَهُمُ الْبَنُونَ ﴿١٥٠﴾

151. [c]Did We create the angels females while they were witnesses?

أَمْ خَلَقْنَا الْمَلَائِكَةَ إِنَاثًا وَهُمْ شَاهِدُونَ ﴿١٥١﴾

152. Now, surely, it is of their fabrications that they say,

أَلَا إِنَّهُمْ مِنْ إِفْكِهِمْ لَيَقُولُونَ ﴿١٥٢﴾

153. 'Allāh has begotten *children*;' and they are certainly liars.

وَلَدَ اللَّهُ وَإِنَّهُمْ لَكَاذِبُونَ ﴿١٥٣﴾

154. [d]Has He chosen daughters in preference to sons?

أَصْطَفَى الْبَنَاتِ عَلَى الْبَنِينَ ﴿١٥٤﴾

[a]10 : 99. [b]6 : 101; 16 : 58; 43 : 17; 52 : 40; 53 : 22. [c]17 : 41; 37 : 151; 43 : 20. [d]43 : 17; 53 : 22.

2506A. The disbelieving Meccans.

2507. The Arabs ascribed Divine powers to angels, believing them to be God's daughters. It is this form of idolatry that has been condemned here.

155. What is the matter with you? How judge ye?

مَا لَكُمْ كَيْفَ تَحْكُمُونَ ﴿١٥٥﴾

156. Will you not take heed?

أَفَلَا تَذَكَّرُونَ ﴿١٥٦﴾

157. [a]Or, have you a clear authority?

أَمْ لَكُمْ سُلْطَٰنٌ مُّبِينٌ ﴿١٥٧﴾

158. Then produce your Book,[2508] if you are truthful.

فَأْتُوا بِكِتَٰبِكُمْ إِن كُنتُمْ صَٰدِقِينَ ﴿١٥٨﴾

159. [b]And they assert a kinship between Him and the jinn while the jinn *themselves* know *well* that they will be brought *before Allāh for judgment*.

وَجَعَلُوا بَيْنَهُ وَبَيْنَ الْجِنَّةِ نَسَبًا ۚ وَلَقَدْ عَلِمَتِ
الْجِنَّةُ إِنَّهُمْ لَمُحْضَرُونَ ﴿١٥٩﴾

160. Holy is Allāh *and free* from what they attribute *to Him !*

سُبْحَٰنَ اللَّهِ عَمَّا يَصِفُونَ ﴿١٦٠﴾

161. But the chosen servants of Allāh *do not attribute anything derogatory to Him.*

إِلَّا عِبَادَ اللَّهِ الْمُخْلَصِينَ ﴿١٦١﴾

162. Verily, you and what you worship—

فَإِنَّكُمْ وَمَا تَعْبُدُونَ ﴿١٦٢﴾

163. None of you can mislead *anyone*[2509] against Him,

مَا أَنتُمْ عَلَيْهِ بِفَٰتِنِينَ ﴿١٦٣﴾

164. Except *only* him who shall burn in Hell.

إِلَّا مَنْ هُوَ صَالِ الْجَحِيمِ ﴿١٦٤﴾

165. *They say*, 'There is not one of us but has a known station;[2510]

وَمَا مِنَّا إِلَّا لَهُ مَقَامٌ مَّعْلُومٌ ﴿١٦٥﴾

166. 'And, verily, we are those who stand ranged in rows,

وَإِنَّا لَنَحْنُ الصَّآفُّونَ ﴿١٦٦﴾

---

[a]52 : 39. [b]6 : 101.

2508. No Divine Book accords the slightest countenance to this most foolish and obnoxious doctrine.

2509. It is people of their own ilk that evil spirits can mislead. They have no control or influence over godly men.

2510. The reference may be, as some say, to the angels. According to others it is to the believers.

167. "And we, verily, are those who glorify *Allāh*.'

وَاِنَّا لَنَحْنُ الْمُسَبِّحُوْنَ ۝

168. And, surely, *the Meccan disbelievers* used to say,

وَاِنْ كَانُوْا لَيَقُوْلُوْنَ ۝

169. 'If we had with us a Reminder like that of the people of old,

لَوْ اَنَّ عِنْدَنَا ذِكْرًا مِّنَ الْاَوَّلِيْنَ ۝

170. 'We would, surely, have been Allāh's chosen servants.'

لَكُنَّا عِبَادَ اللّٰهِ الْمُخْلَصِيْنَ ۝

171. Yet *when it has come to them* they disbelieve therein, but they will soon come to know.

فَكَفَرُوْا بِهٖ فَسَوْفَ يَعْلَمُوْنَ ۝

172. And, surely, Our word has gone forth to Our servants, the Messengers,

وَلَقَدْ سَبَقَتْ كَلِمَتُنَا لِعِبَادِنَا الْمُرْسَلِيْنَ ۝

173. *b*That it is, certainly, they who will be helped;

اِنَّهُمْ لَهُمُ الْمَنْصُوْرُوْنَ ۝

174. And that it is Our host that will, certainly, be victorious.

وَاِنَّ جُنْدَنَا لَهُمُ الْغٰلِبُوْنَ ۝

175. So turn thou away from them for a while.

فَتَوَلَّ عَنْهُمْ حَتّٰى حِيْنٍ ۝

176. And watch them, for they will soon see *their own end.*

وَّاَبْصِرْهُمْ فَسَوْفَ يُبْصِرُوْنَ ۝

177. *c*Is it then Our punishment that they seek to hasten on?

اَفَبِعَذَابِنَا يَسْتَعْجِلُوْنَ ۝

178. But when it descends into their courtyard,[2511] it shall be an evil morning for those who were warned.

فَاِذَا نَزَلَ بِسَاحَتِهِمْ فَسَآءَ صَبَاحُ الْمُنْذَرِيْنَ ۝

---

*a*2 : 31; 21 : 21; 41 : 39. *b*40 : 52; 58 : 22. *c*22 : 48; 27 : 72; 29 : 54.

2511. The reference may be to the day of the Fall of Mecca which was indeed an evil day for the Meccans when a Muslim army ten thousand strong entered its suburbs. Then the cup of their mortification and humiliation became full to the brim, as all their evil designs against Islām had completely failed and it had won a glorious victory over disbelievers.

179. So turn thou away from them for a while,

وَتَوَلَّ عَنْهُمْ حَتّٰى حِيْنٍ ﴿۱۷۹﴾

180. And watch, for they will soon see *their own end.*

وَّاَبْصِرْ فَسَوْفَ يُبْصِرُوْنَ ﴿۱۸۰﴾

181. Holy is thy Lord, the Lord of power, far above that which they assert.

سُبْحٰنَ رَبِّكَ رَبِّ الْعِزَّةِ عَمَّا يَصِفُوْنَ ﴿۱۸۱﴾

182. [a]And peace is *ever* upon the Messengers![2512]

وَسَلٰمٌ عَلَى الْمُرْسَلِيْنَ ﴿۱۸۲﴾

183. [b]And all praise belongs to Allāh, the Lord of the worlds.

وَالْحَمْدُ لِلّٰهِ رَبِّ الْعٰلَمِيْنَ ﴿۱۸۳﴾

[a]27 : 60. [b]1 : 2; 6 : 46.

2512. The reference seems to be to the Holy Prophet who represents in his person all the Prophets and Messengers of God.

CHAPTER 38

ṢĀD

(Revealed before Hijrah)

Date of Revelation and Context

The *Sūrah* was revealed in the early years of the Holy Prophet's life at Mecca. Ibn 'Abbās, as reported by Baihaquī and Ibn Mardawaih, subscribes to this view, and other scholars, too, agree with him. From its contents and subject-matter the *Sūrah* bears a very close resemblance to Al-Ṣāffāt which had ended with the challenging Divine declaration : God's hosts shall be victorious and it shall be an evil day for the disbelievers when Divine punishment shall descend into their courtyard. The *Sūrah* opens with an equally emphatic declaration that it is an unalterable decree of the Truthful God that the believers shall attain wealth, power and eminence while the disbelievers shall meet with disgrace and destruction.

Subject-Matter

The *Sūrah* opens with a firm declaration—in fact God swears by the Qur'ān—that by acting upon its teachings and by making it a rule of their lives the believers will achieve glory and eminence and will come to occupy a most honoured place among the comity of mighty nations. It further says that the Meccan disbelievers repeat the parrot-like cry that they will not give up the worship of their gods at the behest of a man who is just one of them. In reply to this foolish plea they are told, 'Since when have they begun to arrogate to themselves the possession of the treasures of God's grace and mercy ? It is God's own prerogative that He chooses whom He deems fit for the conveyance of His Will to His creatures; and that now He has chosen the Prophet Muḥammad for this purpose.' After making an emphatic prediction that the forces of evil will suffer defeat and disgrace and the votaries of the One God will be given power, wealth and distinction, the *Sūrah*, by way of introduction, gives a somewhat detailed description of the great glory and prosperity which the Israelite nation had attained in the reigns of two of their Prophet-kings—David and Solomon. It also refers to the plots that were hatched in David's glorious reign to undermine his power and influence and to the seeds of decay and disintegration that had been sown during Solomon's reign when the Israelites rolled in wealth and were at the peak of material prosperity. The Holy Prophet, by implication, is told that, consumed with jealousy at his growing power, his enemies will also hatch plots to take his life and will seek to nip the tender plant of Islām in the bud but they will fail in their wicked designs and Islām will continue to gain power and strength. But if Muslims did not take proper care they would find, to their cost, that in the very heyday of their glory, forces of darkness would seek to undermine the solidarity and stability of Islām. After this a brief mention is made of Prophet Job who had to suffer great hardships, but the temporary phase of his tribulation quickly passed away and he came to his own and his loss was doubly made up. The reference to Job is followed by a fleeting allusion to Abraham, Isaac, Jacob and Prophets Ishmael, Elisha and Dhu'l Kifl, and it is added that those good people who copy their example and follow in their footsteps receive God's favours which know no decrease or diminution. The *Sūrah* closes on the note that whenever men stray away from the path of rectitude, and begin to worship false gods, a Divine Messenger is raised among them to bring them back to the worship of the One True God. The sons of darkness seek to put all sorts of obstacles and impediments in his way and deceive and beguile men away from God. But truth overcomes all hindrances, and triumphs and prevails in the long run.

سُوۡرَةُ صٓ مَكِّيَّةٌ (٣٨)

1. [a]In the name of Allāh, the Gracious, the Merciful.

بِسۡمِ اللّٰهِ الرَّحۡمٰنِ الرَّحِيۡمِ ١

2. Ṣād,[2513] [b]We cite *as proof* the Qur'ān, *which is* full of exhortation,[2514] *that it is Our revealed Word.*

صٓ وَالۡقُرۡاٰنِ ذِى الذِّكۡرِ ٢

3. But those who disbelieve are *steeped* in *false* pride and enmity.[2515]

بَلِ الَّذِيۡنَ كَفَرُوۡا فِىۡ عِزَّةٍ وَّشِقَاقٍ ٣

4. [c]How many a generation have We destroyed before them! They cried out *for help*, but it was no longer[2516] the time for escape.

كَمۡ اَهۡلَكۡنَا مِنۡ قَبۡلِهِمۡ مِّنۡ قَرۡنٍ فَنَادَوۡا وَّلَاتَ حِيۡنَ مَنَاصٍ ٤

5. [d]And they wonder that a Warner has come to them from among themselves; and the disbelievers say, 'This is a sorcerer, a great liar.

وَعَجِبُوۡۤا اَنۡ جَآءَهُمۡ مُّنۡذِرٌ مِّنۡهُمۡ وَقَالَ الۡكٰفِرُوۡنَ هٰذَا سٰحِرٌ كَذَّابٌ ٥

6. 'What! has he made *all* the gods into one God? This is, indeed, an astounding thing.'

اَجَعَلَ الۡاٰلِهَةَ اِلٰهًا وَّاحِدًا ۖۚ اِنَّ هٰذَا لَشَىۡءٌ عُجَابٌ ٦

---

[a]1 : 1. [b]43 : 45. [c]6 : 7; 19 : 75; 36 : 32; 50 : 37. [d]7 : 64.

2513. The letter *Ṣad* may signify 'the Truthful God,' or 'I am Allāh, the Truthful,' or 'God has spoken the truth.'

2514. The Truthful God swears by the Qur'ān that the followers of the Holy Prophet, by acting upon the teachings of the Qur'ān and making it a rule of their lives, shall achieve eminence and shall come to occupy a most honoured place among the comity of great nations, *Dhikr* also meaning eminence (Lane).

2515. The root-cause of all sin and disbelief are false pride, conceit and arrogance. The first recorded sin committed by Satan was that he refused to submit to Adam on the plea of his fancied superiority over him (Adam). 'I am better than he' (7: 13) has always been the boast of disbelievers which has prevented them from accepting the truth in the time of every Prophet.

2516. According to some scholars *Lāta* is originally *Laisa*; some others think that the feminine *ta* is added to the negative *lā* to render the negation more intensive. According to a third school it is an independent word, neither originally *Laisa* nor *lā*. The fourth school, however, is of the view that it is a word and also a part of a word, namely the negative *lā*, and *ta*, prefixed to *Ḥīna*. It is generally accompanied by *Ḥīna* or some other word synonymous with it.

7. And the leaders among them went about *saying* 'Go and [a]stick to your gods. This is a thing to be desired;

وَانْطَلَقَ الْمَلَأُ مِنْهُمْ أَنِ امْشُوا وَاصْبِرُوا عَلَىٰ
آلِهَتِكُمْ ۖ إِنَّ هَٰذَا لَشَيْءٌ يُرَادُ ﴿٧﴾

8. [b]"We have not heard of *anything like* this in any previous creed.[2517] This is nothing but a forgery;

مَا سَمِعْنَا بِهَٰذَا فِي الْمِلَّةِ الْآخِرَةِ ۖ إِنْ هَٰذَا إِلَّا
اخْتِلَاقٌ ﴿٨﴾

9. [c]"Has the Reminder been sent down to him alone out of us *all?*" Nay, they are in doubt concerning My Reminder. Nay, they have not yet tasted My punishment.

أَأُنْزِلَ عَلَيْهِ الذِّكْرُ مِنْ بَيْنِنَا ۚ بَلْ هُمْ فِي شَكٍّ
مِنْ ذِكْرِي ۖ بَلْ لَمَّا يَذُوقُوا عَذَابِ ﴿٩﴾

10. [d]Do they possess the treasures of the mercy of thy Lord, the Mighty, the Great Bestower?

أَمْ عِنْدَهُمْ خَزَائِنُ رَحْمَةِ رَبِّكَ الْعَزِيزِ الْوَهَّابِ ﴿١٠﴾

11. Or, is theirs the Kingdom of the heavens and the earth and all that is between them? Then let them ascend with the means *at their disposal.*[2518]

أَمْ لَهُمْ مُلْكُ السَّمَاوَاتِ وَالْأَرْضِ وَمَا بَيْنَهُمَا ۖ
فَلْيَرْتَقُوا فِي الْأَسْبَابِ ﴿١١﴾

12. [e]*They are* a host of the confederates which *shall be* routed here.[2519]

جُنْدٌ مَا هُنَالِكَ مَهْزُومٌ مِنَ الْأَحْزَابِ ﴿١٢﴾

13. [f]Before them *too* the people of Noah, and *the tribe of* 'Ād and Pharaoh, the Lord of stakes,[2520] rejected *the Messengers as* liars;

كَذَّبَتْ قَبْلَهُمْ قَوْمُ نُوحٍ وَعَادٌ وَفِرْعَوْنُ
ذُو الْأَوْتَادِ ﴿١٣﴾

---

[a]71 : 24. [b]23 : 25. [c]54 : 26. [d]17 : 101; 52 : 38. [e]54 : 46. [f]9 : 70; 40 : 32; 50 : 13.

2517. The 'previous creed' may refer to Christianity or the idolatrous faith of the pagans of Mecca, or it may refer to all religions preceding Islām, because in no religion before Islām had belief in the Unity of God remained pure and unadulterated.

2518. Let disbelievers collect all their means and resources against the Holy Prophet and multiply them as much as they can and use them against him.

2519. The verse at once contains a prophecy and a challenge. The challenge is to the forces of evil to muster all their resources and form themselves into a strong confederacy to stop the onward march of Islām. And the prophecy is to the effect that the combined forces of disbelief shall be put to an ignominious rout if they dared oppose Islām. This mighty prophecy was literally fulfilled in the Battle of the Trench.

2520. *Autād al-Arḍ* means, mountains; and *Autād al-Bilād* signifies, the chief men of the towns; and *Dhu'l Autād* signifies, lord of large armies or stakes (Aqrab).

14. And *the tribe of* Thamūd, and the people of Lot, and [a]the Dwellers of the Wood—these were the confederates *too*.

وَثَمُودُ وَقَوْمُ لُوطٍ وَّأَصْحٰبُ لْـَٔيْكَةِ ۚ أُولٰٓئِكَ الْأَحْزَابُ ﴿١٤﴾

15. Not one *of them* but treated *their* Messengers as liars, [b]so My punishment justly overtook *them*.

إِنْ كُلٌّ إِلَّا كَذَّبَ الرُّسُلَ فَحَقَّ عِقَابِ ﴿١٥﴾ (ع)

R. 2 16. And these *now* wait only for a single blast, and there shall be no delaying it.[2521]

وَمَا يَنْظُرُ هٰٓؤُلَآءِ إِلَّا صَيْحَةً وَّاحِدَةً مَّا لَهَا مِنْ فَوَاقٍ ﴿١٦﴾

17. They say, Our Lord, [c]hasten to us our portion *of the punishment* before the Day of Reckoning.'

وَقَالُوا رَبَّنَا عَجِّلْ لَّنَا قِطَّنَا قَبْلَ يَوْمِ الْحِسَابِ ﴿١٧﴾

18. Bear patiently what they say, and remember Our servant David, *the man* of might ;[2522] surely he was always turning *to God*.

اِصْبِرْ عَلٰى مَا يَقُولُونَ وَاذْكُرْ عَبْدَنَا دَاوٗدَ ذَا الْأَيْدِ ۚ إِنَّهٗٓ أَوَّابٌ ﴿١٨﴾

19. [d]We subjected *to him* the mountains—they celebrated God's praises with him at nightfall and sunrise.

إِنَّا سَخَّرْنَا الْجِبَالَ مَعَهٗ يُسَبِّحْنَ بِالْعَشِيِّ وَالْإِشْرَاقِ ﴿١٩﴾

20. And *We subjected to him* the birds gathered together; all constantly turned to him.

وَالطَّيْرَ مَحْشُورَةً ۚ كُلٌّ لَّهٗٓ أَوَّابٌ ﴿٢٠﴾

21. And We strengthened his kingdom, [e]and gave him wisdom and decisive judgment.

وَشَدَدْنَا مُلْكَهٗ وَآتَيْنٰهُ الْحِكْمَةَ وَفَصْلَ الْخِطَابِ ﴿٢١﴾

22. And has the story of the disputants reached thee when they climbed over the wall of *his* private chamber?—

وَهَلْ أَتٰىكَ نَبَؤُا الْخَصْمِ ۘ إِذْ تَسَوَّرُوا الْمِحْرَابَ ﴿٢٢﴾

---

[a]15 : 79; 26 : 177; 50 : 15. [b]15 : 80; 26 : 190; 50 : 15. [c]17 : 19. [d]21 : 80; 34 : 11. [e]2 : 252.

2521. *Fawāq* means, the time between two milkings; the time between two suckings; the returning of the milk into the udder of the she-camel after the milking; the time between the opening of one's hand and the grasping with it the udder of the she-camel; or when the milker grasps the udder and then lets it go in milking (Lane).

2522. Prophets David, Solomon and Job possessed great power, influence and wealth and that is why perhaps they have always been mentioned together in the Qur'ān (4 : 164, 6 : 85 & 21 : 80-84).

23. When they entered in upon David, and he was afraid of them. They said, 'Fear not. *We are* two disputants; one of us has transgressed against the other; so judge between us with justice, and deviate not from the right course and guide us to the right way.'[2523]

إِذْ دَخَلُوا عَلَىٰ دَاوُدَ فَفَزِعَ مِنْهُمْ قَالُوا لَا تَخَفْ
خَصْمٰنِ بَغٰى بَعْضُنَا عَلٰى بَعْضٍ فَاحْكُمْ بَيْنَنَا
بِالْحَقِّ وَلَا تُشْطِطْ وَاهْدِنَا إِلٰى سَوَاءِ الصِّرَاطِ ﴿٢٣﴾

24. "Now this my brother has ninety-nine ewes, and I have *only* one ewe. Yet he says, 'Give it to me,' and he has been overbearing to me in his address."[2524]

إِنَّ هٰذَا أَخِي لَهُ تِسْعٌ وَتِسْعُونَ نَعْجَةً وَلِيَ
نَعْجَةٌ وَاحِدَةٌ فَقَالَ أَكْفِلْنِيهَا وَعَزَّنِي
فِي الْخِطَابِ ﴿٢٤﴾

25. *David* said, 'Surely, he has wronged thee in asking for thy ewe *to add* to his own ewes. And certainly many partners transgress against one another, except those who believe *in Allāh* and act righteously; and these are but few.' And David thought that We had tried him; so he asked forgiveness of his Lord, and fell down bowing in worship and turned[2525] *to Him.*

قَالَ لَقَدْ ظَلَمَكَ بِسُؤَالِ نَعْجَتِكَ إِلٰى نِعَاجِهِ
وَإِنَّ كَثِيرًا مِّنَ الْخُلَطَاءِ لَيَبْغِي بَعْضُهُمْ عَلٰى بَعْضٍ
إِلَّا الَّذِينَ آمَنُوا وَعَمِلُوا الصّٰلِحٰتِ وَقَلِيلٌ مَّا هُمْ
وَظَنَّ دَاوُدُ أَنَّمَا فَتَنّٰهُ فَاسْتَغْفَرَ رَبَّهُ وَخَرَّ رَاكِعًا
وَأَنَابَ ﴿٢٥﴾ السجدة

2523. It appears from history that though Israelite power was at its zenith in the reigns of David and Solomon, yet mischief-mongers were busy stirring up discord and disaffection, and false charges were constantly raked up and spread against them and some evil-minded persons even sought to kill David. It is to one such attempt at David's life that reference has been made in the verse under comment. Two of his enemies scaled the wall of his private chamber with the intention of taking him unawares, but finding him on his guard and realizing that their plan had miscarried, they tried to put him at ease and pretended as if they were merely two litigants who had come to seek his decision in a dispute. David, however, rightly understood their evil intention, and so naturally he was afraid of them.

2524. This verse refers to the story which the two intending murderers of David, finding him quite vigilant, seemed to have invented, at the spur of the moment, in an endeavour to disabuse his mind of any misgiving he might have entertained about them, and to set his fear at rest.

2525. David was not taken in by the mask of ordinary litigants that the two intruders had put on; he saw through the game. Though he did not lose his presence of mind and gave his decision like a sane and sedate judge, yet he realized that his control over his people had weakened and that, despite the precautions he had taken, he was not quite safe from the schemes and plots of his enemies. He felt that the incident was a reminder from God. So he adopted the only course which the righteous and the God-fearing adopt in such circumstances. He prayed to God and sought His protection against the schemes and conspiracies of his enemies. The insinuation behind the tale of the litigants was that David was a tyrant who was extending his domination over small and weak neighbouring tribes.

26. So We forgave him *his default;* and, indeed, he had a position of nearness with Us and an excellent resort.[2526]

فَغَفَرْنَا لَهٗ ذٰلِكَ ۖ وَاِنَّ لَهٗ عِنْدَنَا لَزُلْفٰى وَحُسْنَ
مَاٰبٍ ﴿٢٦﴾

27. *Then We said to him,* 'O David, We have made thee a vicegerent in the earth; so judge between men with justice, and follow not vain desire, lest it should lead thee astray from the way of Allāh.' Surely, those, who go astray from the way of Allāh, will have a severe punishment, because they forgot the Day of Reckoning.

يٰدَاوٗدُ اِنَّا جَعَلْنٰكَ خَلِيْفَةً فِى الْاَرْضِ فَاحْكُمْ
بَيْنَ النَّاسِ بِالْحَقِّ وَلَا تَتَّبِعِ الْهَوٰى فَيُضِلَّكَ
عَنْ سَبِيْلِ اللّٰهِ ؕ اِنَّ الَّذِيْنَ يَضِلُّوْنَ عَنْ سَبِيْلِ
اللّٰهِ لَهُمْ عَذَابٌ شَدِيْدٌۢ بِمَا نَسُوْا يَوْمَ الْحِسَابِ ﴿٢٧﴾

R. 3 28. [a]And We have not created the heavens and the earth and all that is between them in vain. That is the view of those who disbelieve. [b]Woe, then, to the disbelievers because *of the punishment* of the Fire *that shall overtake them.*

وَمَا خَلَقْنَا السَّمَآءَ وَالْاَرْضَ وَمَا بَيْنَهُمَا بَاطِلًا ؕ
ذٰلِكَ ظَنُّ الَّذِيْنَ كَفَرُوْا ۚ فَوَيْلٌ لِّلَّذِيْنَ كَفَرُوْا
مِنَ النَّارِ ﴿٢٨﴾

29. [c]Shall We treat those who believe and do good works like those who act corruptly in the earth? Shall We treat the righteous like the wicked?

اَمْ نَجْعَلُ الَّذِيْنَ اٰمَنُوْا وَعَمِلُوا الصّٰلِحٰتِ كَالْمُفْسِدِيْنَ
فِى الْاَرْضِ ۫ اَمْ نَجْعَلُ الْمُتَّقِيْنَ كَالْفُجَّارِ ﴿٢٩﴾

30. *This is* a Book which We have revealed to thee, [d]full of excellences,[2527] that they may reflect over its verses, and that those *gifted* with understanding may take heed.

كِتٰبٌ اَنْزَلْنٰهُ اِلَيْكَ مُبٰرَكٌ لِّيَدَّبَّرُوْٓا اٰيٰتِهٖ وَ
لِيَتَذَكَّرَ اُولُوا الْاَلْبَابِ ﴿٣٠﴾

---

[a]21 : 17; 44 : 39. [b]14 : 3; 19 : 38; 51 : 61. [c]68 : 36. [d]6 : 93; 21 : 51.

2526. The expression *Ghafarnā la-hū* may mean, 'We gave him Our protection,' or, 'We set his affairs right' (Lane). The words, 'he had a position of nearness with Us and an excellent resort,' show that David did not suffer from any moral defect or spiritual weakness, and most effectively negative and demolish the wicked charge of David having committed adultery as imputed to him by the Bible (2 Sam. 11 : 4 & 5).

2527. The Qur'ān contains the basic and universal principles of all religions and their permanent and imperishable teachings along with much more that is indispensable for the growing needs and requirements of man. This is the meaning of the word *Mubārak*.

31. [a]And We bestowed on David. Solomon who was an excellent servant *of Ours*. He was *always* turning *to Us*.

وَوَهَبْنَا لِدَاوٗدَ سُلَيْمٰنَ ۭ نِعْمَ الْعَبْدُ ۭ اِنَّهٗٓ اَوَّابٌ ۝۳۱

32. When there were brought before him at eventide steeds of noblest breed[2528] and swift of foot,[2528A]

اِذْ عُرِضَ عَلَيْهِ بِالْعَشِيِّ الصّٰفِنٰتُ الْجِيَادُ ۝۳۲

33. He said, 'I love the love of good things because[2529] they remind *me of* my Lord.'[2530] And when they were hidden behind the veil,

فَقَالَ اِنِّيْٓ اَحْبَبْتُ حُبَّ الْخَيْرِ عَنْ ذِكْرِ رَبِّيْ ۚ حَتّٰى تَوَارَتْ بِالْحِجَابِ ۝۳۳

34. *He said*, 'Bring them back to me.' Then he started stroking *their* legs and *their* necks.[2531]

رُدُّوْهَا عَلَيَّ ۭ فَطَفِقَ مَسْحًۢا بِالسُّوْقِ وَالْاَعْنَاقِ ۝۳۴

35. Certainly, We tried Solomon and We placed on his throne a *mere* body.[2532] Then he turned *to God, seeking His mercy*.

وَلَقَدْ فَتَنَّا سُلَيْمٰنَ وَاَلْقَيْنَا عَلٰى كُرْسِيِّهٖ جَسَدًا ثُمَّ اَنَابَ ۝۳۵

---

[a]27 : 17.

2528. *Ṣāfināt* (steeds) is the plural of *Ṣāfinah* which is feminine of *Ṣāfin* which means, a horse standing upon three legs and the extremity of the hoof of the fourth leg. Standing in this posture is considered to be the peculiarity of Arabian breed which are regarded as the best bred horses.

2528A. *Jiyād* (swift-footed horses) is the plural of *Jawād*, and the expression, *Farasun Jawādun* means, a quick-footed horse (Lane).

2529. '*An* denotes transition; compensation (2 : 49); superiority (47 : 39). It also denotes a cause as in the present verse, and it has the same sense as *li* (53 : 4).

2530. God had bestowed upon Solomon power and wealth. He ruled over a vast kingdom and, therefore, he had to keep a strong army. Naturally, he had a great liking for horses of good breed because cavalry formed a strong wing of his army. Solomon's love for horses was not that of a race-goer or a professional breeder of horses. It only sprang from his love for his Creator as the horses were used for fighting in the cause of God.

2531. It seems that Solomon was seeing a horse parade and in order to show his admiration for his horses he stroked their necks and legs.

2532. In 34 : 15 the expression used is 'a worm of the earth'. The reference may either be to Solomon's son and heir, Rehoboam, a worthless fellow or to Jeroboam who raised the standard of revolt against the House of David (I Kings, 12 : 28). Solomon had realized that after his death his kingdom would not maintain its integrity under his incompetent and inefficient successors. So he turned to God and prayed to Him. The prayer is given in the next verse.

36. He said, 'O My Lord, grant me forgiveness and bestow on me a kingdom that may not be *inherited* by anyone after me;[2533] surely, Thou art the Great Bestower.'

قَالَ رَبِّ اغْفِرْ لِي وَهَبْ لِي مُلْكًا لَّا يَنْۢبَغِي لِأَحَدٍ مِّنْ بَعْدِي ۚ إِنَّكَ أَنْتَ الْوَهَّابُ ﴿٣٦﴾

37. So [a]We subjected to him the wind, blowing gently by his command withersoever he would go,

فَسَخَّرْنَا لَهُ الرِّيحَ تَجْرِي بِأَمْرِهِ رُخَاءً حَيْثُ أَصَابَ ﴿٣٧﴾

38. [b]And the giants, all *sorts of* architects *and builders*, and divers,

وَالشَّيٰطِيْنَ كُلَّ بَنَّاءٍ وَّغَوَّاصٍ ﴿٣٨﴾

39. [c]And others bound in fetters.[2534]

وَّاٰخَرِيْنَ مُقَرَّنِيْنَ فِي الْأَصْفَادِ ﴿٣٩﴾

40. 'This is Our gift—so give freely or withhold—without reckoning.'

هٰذَا عَطَاؤُنَا فَامْنُنْ أَوْ أَمْسِكْ بِغَيْرِ حِسَابٍ ﴿٤٠﴾

41. And certainly he had a position of nearness with Us and an excellent resort.

وَإِنَّ لَهُ عِنْدَنَا لَزُلْفٰى وَحُسْنَ مَاٰبٍ ﴿٤١﴾

R. 4 42. And remember Our servant [d]Job, when he cried unto his Lord: 'Satan has afflicted me with toil and torment.'[2535]

وَاذْكُرْ عَبْدَنَا أَيُّوبَ ۘ إِذْ نَادٰى رَبَّهُ أَنِّي مَسَّنِيَ الشَّيْطٰنُ بِنُصْبٍ وَّعَذَابٍ ﴿٤٢﴾

[a]21 : 82; 34 : 13. [b]21 : 83; 34 : 13-14. [c]14 : 50 [d]21 : 84.

2533. As it appears from the preceding verse Solomon had foreseen that his temporal kingdom would become disrupted after his death through the imbecility of his foolish and worthless son, so he prayed that the spiritual kingdom which God had bestowed upon his House might continue. If the words, 'a kingdom that may not be inherited by anyone after me,' are taken in their literal sense, then Solomon's prayer would be understood to have been accepted in the sense that after his death no king possessing the power and prestige that he possessed ever appeared among the Israelites.

2534. Solomon, as stated in 21 : 83 and 34 : 13, 14, had subdued and subjected to his rule savage and rebellious mountain tribes. He had forced them into his service and had compelled them to do sundry works for him. *Shayāṭīn* of the preceding verse and jinn of 34 : 13 are the same people, and the work on which they were employed by Solomon was also of the same nature (II Chron. 2 : 1-2).

2535. *Nuṣb* means, fatigue, toil; affliction, distress, disease; misfortune (Lane). In the present and the next three verses the language used is as fittingly metaphorical as that used in the preceding several verses. It seems that Prophet Job lived in a country of which the ruler was, as the word *Shaiṭān* (leader of mischief) shows, a cruel and tyrannical idol-worshipper, who opposed the monotheistic teaching of Job and severely persecuted him. Job had to leave his native land and take refuge in another country and as a result of this emigration he was separated from his family and followers. If the word *Shaiṭān*, as some

43. *We directed him*: 'Urge *thy riding beast* with thy foot *and depart swiftly*. Yonder is cool water to wash with, and a drink.'[2536]

ارْكُضْ بِرِجْلِكَ هٰذَا مُغْتَسَلٌ بَارِدٌ وَّشَرَابٌ ﴿٤٣﴾

44. [a]And We bestowed on him, his family and as many more with them,[2537] *by way of* mercy from Us, and as a reminder for *men* of understanding.

وَوَهَبْنَا لَهٗٓ اَهْلَهٗ وَمِثْلَهُمْ مَّعَهُمْ رَحْمَةً مِّنَّا وَذِكْرٰى لِاُولِي الْاَلْبَابِ ﴿٤٤﴾

45. And *We commanded him*: 'Take in thy hand a handful of dry twigs and strike therewith,[2538] and incline not towards falsehood.'[2539] Indeed, We found him steadfast. An excellent servant was he. Surely, he was constantly turning *to God*.

وَخُذْ بِيَدِكَ ضِغْثًا فَاضْرِبْ بِّهٖ وَلَا تَحْنَثْ اِنَّا وَجَدْنٰهُ صَابِرًا نِعْمَ الْعَبْدُ اِنَّهٗٓ اَوَّابٌ ﴿٤٥﴾

[a]21 : 85.

authorities hold, should signify *Shaiṭān al-Falāt* (satan of the desert), *i.e.*, thirst, the verse would mean that Job in his long and tiresome journey had suffered from extreme thirst and fatigue. According to some other authorities the reference in the words, 'Satan has afflicted me with toil and torment,' is to a skin disease from which Prophet Job is said to have temporarily suffered and which left him very much exhausted.

2536. Job was enjoined to strike and urge on his riding beast in order to reach a place of safety soon. And as in his long and tiresome journey he greatly suffered from thirst and fatigue, he was comforted with the information that there lay ahead of him a fountain of sweet, cool water where he could slake his thirst and wash himself. Or, the meaning may be that having been left alone at a place where there was no water, he was told by God to urge on his riding beast as there lay ahead a fountain of cool, sweet water where he could take rest, satisfy his thirst and take a bath. Or, the verse may signify that as Job suffered from a skin disease, he was directed by God to take bath in a particular fountain whose water contained such minerals as would cure his skin disease. It seems that the country through which Job had to travel abounded in springs and fountains.

2537. When, in obedience to Divine command, Job continued his journey, he not only found cool and refreshing water with which he washed himself and assuaged his thirst, he found also his family and the people from whom he had become separated. It is possible that on account of some skin disease from which he suffered, Job's people might have left him.

2538. While in v.43 Job was enjoined to urge his riding beast with his foot, in the present verse he is told to strike the beast with a bundle of twigs to make it run fast that he may be out of danger and reach a place of safety soon.

2539. The words, *lā Taḥnath* mean, do not incline to falsehood, *i.e.*, make no compromise with idol-worship or polytheistic beliefs and remain steadfast in your belief in the Unity of God. If the expression means, break not thy oath, the verse would signify that as Job had become separated from his people due to negligence on their part, he had vowed that he would punish the guilty for their negligence after he joined them. When, however, he was united with them he was told by God (as the verse shows) not to treat them severely in the hour of joy and thanks-giving and to fulfil his oath in a way which should cause them least distress.

46. And remember Our servants Abraham and Isaac and Jacob, *men* of might[2540] and vision.

وَاذْكُرْ عِبٰدَنَآ إِبْرٰهِيْمَ وَإِسْحٰقَ وَيَعْقُوْبَ أُولِي الْأَيْدِيْ وَالْأَبْصَارِ ﴿٤٦﴾

47. We chose them for a special *purpose*—to remind *people* of the abode *of the Hereafter*.

إِنَّآ أَخْلَصْنٰهُمْ بِخَالِصَةٍ ذِكْرَى الدَّارِ ﴿٤٧﴾

48. And truly, they are in Our sight among the elect *and* the best.

وَإِنَّهُمْ عِنْدَنَا لَمِنَ الْمُصْطَفَيْنَ الْأَخْيَارِ ﴿٤٨﴾

49. [a]And remember Ishmael and Elisha[2541] and Dhu'l-Kifl;[2542] they were all of the best.

وَاذْكُرْ إِسْمٰعِيْلَ وَالْيَسَعَ وَذَا الْكِفْلِ وَكُلٌّ مِّنَ الْأَخْيَارِ ﴿٤٩﴾

50. This is a reminder. And the righteous will, surely, have an excellent resort—

هٰذَا ذِكْرٌ وَإِنَّ لِلْمُتَّقِيْنَ لَحُسْنَ مَاٰبٍ ﴿٥٠﴾

51. Gardens of Eternity, with *their* gates thrown open to them,

جَنّٰتِ عَدْنٍ مُّفَتَّحَةً لَّهُمُ الْأَبْوَابُ ﴿٥١﴾

52. [b]Reclining therein *on cushions;* they will therein call *at pleasure* for plenteous fruit and drink;

مُتَّكِـِٕيْنَ فِيْهَا يَدْعُوْنَ فِيْهَا بِفَاكِهَةٍ كَثِيْرَةٍ وَّشَرَابٍ ﴿٥٢﴾

53. And with them will be [c]*chaste women* with their eyes downcast, *companions* of equal age.

وَعِنْدَهُمْ قٰصِرٰتُ الطَّرْفِ أَتْرَابٌ ﴿٥٣﴾

54. This is what you are promised for the Day of Reckoning.[2543]

هٰذَا مَا تُوْعَدُوْنَ لِيَوْمِ الْحِسَابِ ﴿٥٤﴾

55. Verily, this is Our provision which will never be exhausted.

إِنَّ هٰذَا لَرِزْقُنَا مَا لَهٗ مِنْ نَّفَادٍ ﴿٥٥﴾

[a]6 : 87; 21 : 86-87. [b]18 : 32; 36 : 57; 83 : 24. [c]55 : 57.

2540. *Yad* means, (1) benefit; (2) influence; (3) might; (4) army; (5) wealth; (6) promise; (7) submission (Aqrab).

2541. Elisha was the disciple and successor of Elijah. He lived from 938 B.C. to 828 B.C. See also 870.

2542. Dhu'l-Kifl. The Prophet known by this name appears to be the Prophet Ezekiel who is called Dhu'l-Kifl by the Arabs. See 1912.

2543. The day of national reckoning when a whole people become deserving of reward or punishment according to their deeds and actions. A day of reckoning comes to every individual, community and nation in this very life.

56. This *is for the believers.* [a]But for the rebellious there is an evil place of return—

هٰذَا ؕ وَاِنَّ لِلطّٰغِيْنَ لَشَرَّ مَاٰبٍ ﴿٥٦﴾

57. Hell, wherein they will burn. What an evil resting place !

جَهَنَّمَ ۚ يَصْلَوْنَهَا ۚ فَبِئْسَ الْمِهَادُ ﴿٥٧﴾

58. This *is what they will have.* So let them taste it—[b]a boiling fluid, and an intensely cold and stinking drink.[2544]

هٰذَا ۙ فَلْيَذُوْقُوْهُ حَمِيْمٌ وَّغَسَّاقٌ ﴿٥٨﴾

59. And *various kinds of* other torments of a similar nature.[2545]

وَّاٰخَرُ مِنْ شَكْلِهٖٓ اَزْوَاجٌ ؕ ﴿٥٩﴾

60. *It will be said to the leaders of disbelief:* 'This is an army [c]rushing headlong[2546] with you. No welcome for them. They shall burn in the Fire.

هٰذَا فَوْجٌ مُّقْتَحِمٌ مَّعَكُمْ ۚ لَا مَرْحَبًا بِهِمْ ؕ اِنَّهُمْ صَالُوا النَّارِ ﴿٦٠﴾

61. *The followers* will say, 'Nay, it is you. No welcome for you *either.* It is you who prepared this for us *by leading us astray.*'[2547] What an evil resting place it is !

قَالُوْا بَلْ اَنْتُمْ ۟ لَا مَرْحَبًا بِكُمْ ؕ اَنْتُمْ قَدَّمْتُمُوْهُ لَنَا ۚ فَبِئْسَ الْقَرَارُ ﴿٦١﴾

62. They will *also* say, 'Our Lord, whosoever prepared this for us, do Thou [d]multiply manifold his punishment in the Fire.'[2548]

قَالُوْا رَبَّنَا مَنْ قَدَّمَ لَنَا هٰذَا فَزِدْهُ عَذَابًا ضِعْفًا فِي النَّارِ ﴿٦٢﴾

[a]78 : 22-23. [b]78 : 26. [c]52 : 14. [d]7 : 39.

2544. The inmates of Hell will be made to drink intensely hot or intensely cold water. As they did not make proper use of their God-given faculties and went to extremes in using them and did not follow the golden mean, so they will be made to drink extremely hot or extremely cold water.

2545. Besides the meaning given in the text, the verse may also mean, 'And like them there will be other groups with similar records.'

2546. When the leaders of disbelief will see a party of their followers coming to Hell, they will be told that a host of their followers will also enter into fire along with them. As the latter rushed to follow their leaders blindly and unthinkingly rejected truth, so they will enter Hell rushing headlong.

2547. The followers of the leaders of disbelief will curse their leaders in these words. Both the leaders and the led will curse one another. It is human nature that when man is confronted with the evil consequences of his deeds, he tries to shift the blame to others. This is exactly what the guilty people generally do when they find themselves face to face with the dreadful results of their wicked deeds.

2548. The followers of the leaders of disbelief will invoke the curse of God upon the heads of their erstwhile leaders.

63. And *the inmates of Hell* will say, 'What is the matter with us that we see not the men[2549] whom we used to reckon among the wicked?

وَقَالُوا مَا لَنَا لَا نَرٰى رِجَالًا كُنَّا نَعُدُّهُمْ مِّنَ الْاَشْرَارِ ﴿٦٣﴾

64. 'Is it because we *unjustly* took them for a laughing-stock, or have the eyes missed[2550] them?'

اَتَّخَذْنٰهُمْ سِخْرِيًّا اَمْ زَاغَتْ عَنْهُمُ الْاَبْصَارُ ﴿٦٤﴾

65. Surely, this is the truth—[a]the disputing together of the dwellers in the Fire.

اِنَّ ذٰلِكَ لَحَقٌّ تَخَاصُمُ اَهْلِ النَّارِ ﴿٦٥﴾ ع

R. 5 66. Say, 'I am only a Warner; and there is no god but Allāh, the One, the Most Supreme;

قُلْ اِنَّمَآ اَنَا مُنْذِرٌ ۖ وَّمَا مِنْ اِلٰهٍ اِلَّا اللّٰهُ الْوَاحِدُ الْقَهَّارُ ﴿٦٦﴾

67. 'The Lord of the heavens and the earth, and *all* that is between the two, the Mighty, the Great Forgiver.'

رَبُّ السَّمٰوٰتِ وَالْاَرْضِ وَمَا بَيْنَهُمَا الْعَزِيْزُ الْغَفَّارُ ﴿٦٧﴾

68. Say, 'It is a big news,[2551]

قُلْ هُوَ نَبَؤٌا عَظِيْمٌ ﴿٦٨﴾

69. 'From which you are turning away;

اَنْتُمْ عَنْهُ مُعْرِضُوْنَ ﴿٦٩﴾

70. 'I had no knowledge of the Exalted Assembly[2552] when they discussed *the matter* among themselves,

مَا كَانَ لِيَ مِنْ عِلْمٍ بِالْمَلَاِ الْاَعْلٰٓى اِذْ يَخْتَصِمُوْنَ ﴿٧٠﴾

71. 'But *this* that it has been revealed to me, that I am a plain Warner.'

اِنْ يُّوْحٰٓى اِلَيَّ اِلَّآ اَنَّمَآ اَنَا نَذِيْرٌ مُّبِيْنٌ ﴿٧١﴾

[a]34 : 32; 40 : 48.

2549. The reference in the words, 'the men,' is to the believers.

2550. The inmates of Hell will say to one another, 'What is the matter with us that we do not see here those men whom we looked upon as of no consequence and ridiculed in the earthly life. Did they not deserve our ridicule and were really good and godly men, or are they in Hell but we do not see them?'

2551. *Naba'* means, a piece of information; an announcement of great importance; message; or news which fills the heart of a person with fear (Lane). The words, 'a big news' may refer to the great event of the revelation of the Qur'ān, or to the advent of the Holy Prophet.

2552. It appears from 2:31 and from the Ḥadīth that when God decrees to raise a Prophet in the world, He discloses His intention to those angels who are nearest to Him. They discuss this affair of the highest import among themselves. These angels are referred to as 'the Exalted Assembly.' The Holy Prophet is represented as saying that he had no knowledge of what was being discussed and debated in heavens about his being entrusted with the great Divine mission.

72. [a]*Call to mind* when thy Lord said to the angels, 'I am about to create man from clay ;

إِذْ قَالَ رَبُّكَ لِلْمَلَٰٓئِكَةِ إِنِّي خَالِقٌۢ بَشَرًا مِّن طِينٍ ۝٧٢

73. [b]'And so when I have fashioned him in perfection, and have breathed into him of My Spirit, fall ye down in submission to him.'[2553]

فَإِذَا سَوَّيْتُهُۥ وَنَفَخْتُ فِيهِ مِن رُّوحِي فَقَعُوا لَهُۥ سَٰجِدِينَ ۝٧٣

74. So the angels[2554] submitted, all of them together.

فَسَجَدَ ٱلْمَلَٰٓئِكَةُ كُلُّهُمْ أَجْمَعُونَ ۝٧٤

75. But Iblīs *did not.* He behaved proudly, and was of those who disbelieved.

إِلَّآ إِبْلِيسَ ۖ ٱسْتَكْبَرَ وَكَانَ مِنَ ٱلْكَٰفِرِينَ ۝٧٥

76. [c]*God* said, 'O Iblīs, what hindered thee from submitting to what I had created with My two hands?[2555] Is it that thou art too proud, or art thou *really* above *obeying my command ?*'

قَالَ يَٰٓإِبْلِيسُ مَا مَنَعَكَ أَن تَسْجُدَ لِمَا خَلَقْتُ بِيَدَيَّ ۖ أَسْتَكْبَرْتَ أَمْ كُنتَ مِنَ ٱلْعَالِينَ ۝٧٦

77. He said, 'I am better[2556] than he. [d]Thou hast created me of fire and him hast Thou created of clay.'

قَالَ أَنَا۠ خَيْرٌ مِّنْهُ ۖ خَلَقْتَنِي مِن نَّارٍ وَخَلَقْتَهُۥ مِن طِينٍ ۝٧٧

78. [e]*God* said, 'Then get out hence,[2557] for, surely, thou art rejected ;

قَالَ فَٱخْرُجْ مِنْهَا فَإِنَّكَ رَجِيمٌ ۝٧٨

[a]15 : 29-33; 17 : 62. [b]15 : 30; 32 : 10. [c]7 : 13; 15 : 33.
[d]7 : 13; 15 : 28; 55 : 16. [e]7 : 14; 15 : 35.

2553. When a Prophet is raised in the world, angels are commanded to assist him in the furtherance of his cause and to render null and void all the schemes and machinations of his enemies.

2554. Angels or men of angelic nature.

2555. The words, 'with my two hands,' signify, 'I have made him to manifest in himself all My attributes.'

2556. The opponents of a Prophet always regard themselves as superior to him in power, position and prestige. It hurts their sense of pride to give their allegiance to a man whom they consider to be like, or even inferior to, them.

2557. The pronoun *hā* in the expression, *min-hā*, does not refer to post-mortal Heaven because Heaven is a place where Satan could not possibly enter and from which no one who has once entered is turned out (15 : 49). It refers to that state of apparent bliss which men enjoy before the advent of a Prophet, and which is represented in the Qur'ān as *Jannah.*

79. [a]"And, surely, on thee shall be My curse till the Day of Judgment.'

وَّاِنَّ عَلَيۡكَ لَعۡنَتِيۡۤ اِلٰى يَوۡمِ الدِّيۡنِ ﴿۷۹﴾

80. He said, 'My Lord, [b]then grant me respite till the day when they shall be raised.'[2558]

قَالَ رَبِّ فَاَنۡظِرۡنِيۡۤ اِلٰى يَوۡمِ يُبۡعَثُوۡنَ ﴿۸۰﴾

81. *God* said, [c]"Certainly thou art of the respited ones,

قَالَ فَاِنَّكَ مِنَ الۡمُنۡظَرِيۡنَ ﴿۸۱﴾

82. [d]'Till the day of the known time.'[2559]

اِلٰى يَوۡمِ الۡوَقۡتِ الۡمَعۡلُوۡمِ ﴿۸۲﴾

83. He said, 'So by Thy glory, [e]I will, surely, lead them all astray,

قَالَ فَبِعِزَّتِكَ لَاُغۡوِيَنَّهُمۡ اَجۡمَعِيۡنَ ﴿۸۳﴾

84. 'Except Thy chosen servants from among them.'

اِلَّا عِبَادَكَ مِنۡهُمُ الۡمُخۡلَصِيۡنَ ﴿۸۴﴾

85. *God* said, 'The truth is, and the truth *alone* I speak,

قَالَ فَالۡحَقُّ ۫ وَالۡحَقَّ اَقُوۡلُ ﴿۸۵﴾

86. '*That* I will, certainly, fill Hell with thee and with those who follow thee, all together.'[2560]

لَاَمۡلَئَنَّ جَهَنَّمَ مِنۡكَ وَمِمَّنۡ تَبِعَكَ مِنۡهُمۡ اَجۡمَعِيۡنَ ﴿۸۶﴾

87. Say, 'I ask not of you any reward for it, nor am I of those who are given to affectation.

قُلۡ مَاۤ اَسۡـَٔلُكُمۡ عَلَيۡهِ مِنۡ اَجۡرٍ وَّمَاۤ اَنَا مِنَ الۡمُتَكَلِّفِيۡنَ ﴿۸۷﴾

88. "*The Qur'ān* is nothing but a Reminder for all peoples.

اِنۡ هُوَ اِلَّا ذِكۡرٌ لِّلۡعٰلَمِيۡنَ ﴿۸۸﴾

89. 'And you shall, surely, know *the truth of* it after a while.'[2561]

وَلَتَعۡلَمُنَّ نَبَاَهٗ بَعۡدَ حِيۡنٍ ﴿۸۹﴾

[a]15 : 36. [b]7 : 15; 15 : 37; 17 : 63. [c]7 : 16; 15 : 38. [d]15 : 39. [e]7 : 17-18; 15 : 40.

2558. Man's spiritual rebirth—when having attained to the stage of 'the soul at peace,' he becomes immune to spiritual fall. See also 1498.

2559. The time when truth finally triumphs over falsehood and the votaries of falsehood are completely crushed.

2560. The dialogue between God and Satan does not refer to any talk that actually took place but represents, in metaphorical language, the state of things as they exist at the time when a Prophet of God is raised. The "man" referred to in verse 72 stands particularly for the Prophet of the day, and Iblīs represents those wicked and evil-minded persons who oppose him and seek to impede and retard the progress of his mission.

2561. The Holy Prophet is here represented as saying to disbelievers that they will not have to wait for long to realize the truth of his mission.

CHAPTER 39

AL-ZUMAR

(Revealed before Hijrah)

Date of Revelation and Context

Like the preceding five Chapters with which it has great resemblance in style and subject-matter, this *Sūrah* was revealed early in the Holy Prophet's ministry. Some writers like Rodwell and Muir assign it to the late Meccan period. Predominance of scholarly opinion, however, is in favour of the *Sūrah* having been revealed early in the Holy Prophet's life at Mecca. The principal theme of the six Chapters, which begin with *Saba'*, is Divine revelation with special reference to the revelation of the Qur'ān and the doctrine of the Unity of God. The fact that there is one Designer and One Controller and Creator of the whole universe is inescapably inferable from the order, adaptation, proportion and co-ordination which pervade the whole universe and to which all the sciences bear undeniable testimony. The success of Divine Messengers with their extremely meagre resources against very heavy odds constitutes another argument to prove God's Existence and His Unity.

Subject-Matter

The *Sūrah* opens with the subject of Quranic revelation and proceeds to deal with the need, purpose and the supreme object of all revealed Books and Divine Prophets which is the establishment of Unity of God on earth. The greatest impediment that bars the way to the achievement of this great and noble object lies in the fact that man is prone to worship false gods—the idols of his own creation. Of all forms of idolatry, perhaps the most hideous and most prevalent, and which has done the greatest injury to the spiritual development of whole communities, is the belief that Jesus is son of God. The *Sūrah* cites the most beautiful and consummate design and order in the universe as an argument in support of the belief that there is only one Designing Mind behind all creation. The three stages, through which the embryo passes before it develops into a full-fledged human being, are adduced as an additional argument. After having briefly discussed the need and purpose of Divine revelation, the *Sūrah* gives two very strong and sound arguments in its support, *viz*., (1) those who invent lies against God, and those who reject truth, never succeed in life. Failure and ignominy dog their footsteps. (2) The Prophets of God and those who accept them and follow their lead always meet with success and their cause prospers. These two arguments constitute an infallible criterion to judge the truth of a claimant to Divine revelation. Judged by these standards, the claim of the Holy Prophet as a Divine Messenger, and of the Qur'ān as Heavenly revelation, stands unchallenged and proved beyond doubt. Next, the *Sūrah* gives sinners a message of hope and good cheer. It tells them that God is Most Merciful and Forgiving. His mercy encompasses all things. He only requires a change of heart on the part of the sinner. Man has to work out his own destiny and the vicarious sacrifice of nobody can save him. But he is vouchsafed many opportunities to repent and reform, but if he continues to walk in evil ways deliberately, he is severely punished. Towards the close the *Sūrah* devotes quite a few verses to the description of the Day of Resurrection.

سُوْرَةُ الزُّمَرِ مَكِّيَّةٌ (٣٩)

1. [a]In the name of Allāh, the Gracious, the Merciful.

بِسْمِ اللّٰهِ الرَّحْمٰنِ الرَّحِيْمِ ①

2. [b]The revelation of this Book is from Allāh, the Mighty, the Wise.

تَنْزِيْلُ الْكِتٰبِ مِنَ اللّٰهِ الْعَزِيْزِ الْحَكِيْمِ ②

3. [c]Surely, it is We Who have revealed the Book to thee comprising *the whole* truth, so worship Allāh, being sincere to Him in obedience.

إِنَّآ أَنْزَلْنَآ إِلَيْكَ الْكِتٰبَ بِالْحَقِّ فَاعْبُدِ اللّٰهَ مُخْلِصًا لَّهُ الدِّيْنَ ③

4. Remember, it is to Allāh *alone* that sincere obedience is due. And those who take as protectors others beside Him, *say*, 'We serve them only that they may bring us near to Allāh in station.'[2562] Surely, [d]Allāh will judge between them concerning that wherein they differ. Surely, Allāh guides not him who is an ungrateful liar.

أَلَا لِلّٰهِ الدِّيْنُ الْخَالِصُ ۭ وَالَّذِيْنَ اتَّخَذُوْا مِنْ دُوْنِهٖٓ أَوْلِيَآءَ ۘ مَا نَعْبُدُهُمْ إِلَّا لِيُقَرِّبُوْنَآ إِلَى اللّٰهِ زُلْفٰى ۭ إِنَّ اللّٰهَ يَحْكُمُ بَيْنَهُمْ فِيْ مَا هُمْ فِيْهِ يَخْتَلِفُوْنَ ۭ إِنَّ اللّٰهَ لَا يَهْدِيْ مَنْ هُوَ كٰذِبٌ كَفَّارٌ ④

5. [e]If Allāh had desired to take to Himself a son, He could have chosen whom He pleased out of what He creates. Holy is He! He is Allāh, the One, the Most Supreme.

لَوْ أَرَادَ اللّٰهُ أَنْ يَّتَّخِذَ وَلَدًا لَّاصْطَفٰى مِمَّا يَخْلُقُ مَا يَشَآءُ ۙ سُبْحٰنَهٗ ۭ هُوَ اللّٰهُ الْوَاحِدُ الْقَهَّارُ ⑤

6. [f]He created the heavens and the earth in accordance with the requirements of wisdom. He makes the night to cover the day, and He makes the day to cover the night; [g]and He has pressed the sun and the moon into service; each pursues *its* course until an appointed time. Remember, *it is* He *alone Who* is the Mighty, the Great Forgiver.

خَلَقَ السَّمٰوٰتِ وَالْأَرْضَ بِالْحَقِّ ۚ يُكَوِّرُ الَّيْلَ عَلَى النَّهَارِ وَيُكَوِّرُ النَّهَارَ عَلَى الَّيْلِ وَسَخَّرَ الشَّمْسَ وَالْقَمَرَ ۭ كُلٌّ يَّجْرِيْ لِأَجَلٍ مُّسَمًّى ۭ أَلَا هُوَ الْعَزِيْزُ الْغَفَّارُ ⑥

---

[a]1 : 1. [b]32 : 3; 36 : 6; 40 : 3; 41 : 3; 46 : 3. [c]5 : 49; 6 : 107. [d]4 : 142; 22 : 70; 32 : 26. [e]2 : 117; 10 : 69; 17 : 112; 19 : 89-93. [f]6 : 74; 14 : 20; 16 : 4; 29 : 45. [g]7 : 55; 13 : 3; 29 : 62; 31 : 30; 35 : 14.

2562. Man is prone to worship false gods, the idols of his own imagination, such as saints and holy men; wealth, power and passion; inherited beliefs and customs, etc., always pretending to believe that these can help him to understand and realize the Divine Being.

7. [a]He created you from a single being; then from that He made its mate; and He has sent[2563] down for you of the cattle eight pairs.[2564] He creates you in the wombs of your mothers, creation after creation, through three *stages of* darkness.[2565] This is Allāh, your Lord. His is the Kingdom. There is no god but He. Whither then are you being turned away?

خَلَقَكُم مِّن نَّفْسٍ وَّاحِدَةٍ ثُمَّ جَعَلَ مِنْهَا زَوْجَهَا
وَاَنْزَلَ لَكُم مِّنَ الْاَنْعَامِ ثَمٰنِيَةَ اَزْوَاجٍ ؕ يَخْلُقُكُمْ
فِيْ بُطُوْنِ اُمَّهٰتِكُمْ خَلْقًا مِّنْۢ بَعْدِ خَلْقٍ فِيْ
ظُلُمٰتٍ ثَلٰثٍ ؕ ذٰلِكُمُ اللّٰهُ رَبُّكُمْ لَهُ الْمُلْكُ ؕ لَاۤ اِلٰهَ
اِلَّا هُوَ ۚ فَاَنّٰى تُصْرَفُوْنَ ۝٧

8. If you are ungrateful, surely Allāh is Self-Sufficient, *being independent* of you. And He is not pleased with ingratitude in His servants. But if you are grateful,[2566] He likes it in you. [b]And no bearer of burden shall bear the burden of another. Then to your Lord is your return; and He will inform you of what you have been doing. Surely, He knows full well all that is *hidden* in the breasts.

اِنْ تَكْفُرُوْا فَاِنَّ اللّٰهَ غَنِيٌّ عَنْكُمْ ۟ وَلَا يَرْضٰى لِعِبَادِهِ
الْكُفْرَ ۚ وَاِنْ تَشْكُرُوْا يَرْضَهُ لَكُمْ ؕ وَلَا تَزِرُ وَازِرَةٌ
وِّزْرَ اُخْرٰى ؕ ثُمَّ اِلٰى رَبِّكُمْ مَّرْجِعُكُمْ فَيُنَبِّئُكُمْ
بِمَا كُنْتُمْ تَعْمَلُوْنَ ؕ اِنَّهٗ عَلِيْمٌۢ بِذَاتِ الصُّدُوْرِ ۝٨

[a]4 : 2; 7 : 190; 16 : 73. [b]6 : 165; 35 : 19; 53 : 39.

2563. The word, *Anzala*, when used in connection with the Word of God, means *Auḥā*, *i.e.*, He revealed; and when used about things of constant daily use, it means *A'ṭā*, *i.e.*, he gave or bestowed. The word has been used in the latter sense in the present verse and in vv. 7 : 27 and 57 : 26.

2564. Special reference in the words 'eight pairs of cattle' is to the pairs of goat, sheep, camel and the ox, mentioned in 6 : 144-145, perhaps because they are animals of daily use for man.

2565. The expression, 'three stages of darkness,' may refer to the three stages of development of the embryo, *Nutfah* (sperm drop), *'Alaqah* (clot) and *Mudghah* (lump of flesh) or to the three forms mentioned in 86 : 7-8; 3 : 7 and 16 : 79, or to the three critical periods of pregnancy : (*a*) from the second to the third month of pregnancy; (*b*) from the third to the fifth month and (*c*) the beginning of the eighth month. During pregnancy there is danger of miscarriage at these three stages.

2566. Whereas *Shukr* denotes the proper use of Divine favours in a manner intended by God (14 : 8), *Kufr* is the misuse of these favours.

9. [a]And when an affliction befalls man, he calls upon his Lord, turning *penitently* to Him. Then, when He confers upon him a favour from Himself, he forgets what he used to pray for before, and starts assigning rivals to Allāh, that he may lead *people* astray from His way. Say, 'Profit from thy disbelief a little; *while in the end* thou art, surely, of the inmates of the Fire.'

وَإِذَا مَسَّ الْإِنْسَانَ ضُرٌّ دَعَا رَبَّهُ مُنِيبًا إِلَيْهِ
ثُمَّ إِذَا خَوَّلَهُ نِعْمَةً مِّنْهُ نَسِيَ مَا كَانَ يَدْعُوٓا
إِلَيْهِ مِنْ قَبْلُ وَجَعَلَ لِلّٰهِ أَنْدَادًا لِّيُضِلَّ عَنْ
سَبِيلِهٖ ۚ قُلْ تَمَتَّعْ بِكُفْرِكَ قَلِيلًا ۖ إِنَّكَ مِنْ أَصْحٰبِ
النَّارِ ⑨

10. Is he who prays devoutly *to Allāh* in the hours of the night, prostrating himself and standing *in prayer and* fears the Hereafter and hopes for the mercy of his Lord, *like him who is disobedient?* Say, [b]"Are those who know equal to those who know not?' Verily, only those *endowed* with understanding will take heed.

أَمَّنْ هُوَ قَانِتٌ آنَاۤءَ الَّيْلِ سَاجِدًا وَّقَاۤئِمًا يَّحْذَرُ
الْاٰخِرَةَ وَيَرْجُوْا رَحْمَةَ رَبِّهٖ ۗ قُلْ هَلْ يَسْتَوِي
الَّذِيْنَ يَعْلَمُوْنَ وَالَّذِيْنَ لَا يَعْلَمُوْنَ ۗ إِنَّمَا يَتَذَكَّرُ
ع أُولُوا الْأَلْبَابِ ⑩

R. 2 11. Say, 'O ye My servants who believe, fear your Lord. [c]There is good for those who do good in this life. And Allāh's earth is spacious. Verily, [d]the steadfast will have their reward without measure'[2567]

قُلْ يٰعِبَادِ الَّذِيْنَ اٰمَنُوا اتَّقُوْا رَبَّكُمْ ۗ لِلَّذِيْنَ أَحْسَنُوْا
فِيْ هٰذِهِ الدُّنْيَا حَسَنَةٌ ۗ وَأَرْضُ اللّٰهِ وَاسِعَةٌ ۗ
إِنَّمَا يُوَفَّى الصّٰبِرُوْنَ أَجْرَهُمْ بِغَيْرِ حِسَابٍ ⑪

12. [e]Say, 'Verily, I am commanded to worship Allāh with sincere devotion,

قُلْ إِنِّيْۤ أُمِرْتُ أَنْ أَعْبُدَ اللّٰهَ مُخْلِصًا لَّهُ الدِّيْنَ ⑫

13. 'And I am commanded to be the foremost of those who submit *to Him*.'

وَأُمِرْتُ لِأَنْ أَكُوْنَ أَوَّلَ الْمُسْلِمِيْنَ ⑬

14. [f]Say, 'Indeed I fear, if I disobey my Lord, the punishment of a grievous day.'

قُلْ إِنِّيْۤ أَخَافُ إِنْ عَصَيْتُ رَبِّيْ عَذَابَ يَوْمٍ
عَظِيْمٍ ⑭

[a]17 : 68; 30 : 34; 39 : 50. [b]40 : 59. [c]16 : 31. [d]3 : 58; 11 : 112; 16 : 97. [e]13: 37; [f]6 : 16; 10 : 16.

2567. The verse warns believers that they will be made to pass through trials and tribulations and will have to leave even their hearths and homes for the sake of God. It is when they have met the ordeal successfully that they will find God's earth spacious for them and will have their full reward from God without measure.

15. [a]Say, 'It is Allāh I worship in sincerest obedience to Him.[2568]

قُلِ اللّٰهَ اَعْبُدُ مُخْلِصًا لَّهٗ دِيْنِيْ ﴿۱۵﴾

16. '*As to you*, worship what you like beside Him.' Say, 'Surely, the *real* losers are they who ruin their souls and their families on the Day of Resurrection.' Beware! that is, surely, the manifest loss.

فَاعْبُدُوْا مَا شِئْتُمْ مِّنْ دُوْنِهٖ ۭ قُلْ اِنَّ الْخٰسِرِيْنَ
الَّذِيْنَ خَسِرُوْٓا اَنْفُسَهُمْ وَاَهْلِيْهِمْ يَوْمَ الْقِيٰمَةِ ۭ
اَلَا ذٰلِكَ هُوَ الْخُسْرَانُ الْمُبِيْنُ ﴿۱۶﴾

17. [b]They will have over them coverings of fire, and beneath them *similar* coverings. It is this against which Allāh warns His servants. 'O My servants, take Me, then, for your Protector.'

لَهُمْ مِّنْ فَوْقِهِمْ ظُلَلٌ مِّنَ النَّارِ وَمِنْ تَحْتِهِمْ
ظُلَلٌ ۭ ذٰلِكَ يُخَوِّفُ اللّٰهُ بِهٖ عِبَادَهٗ ۭ يٰعِبَادِ فَاتَّقُوْنِ ﴿۱۷﴾

18. And those who eschew *the worship of* false gods and turn to Allāh—for them is glad tidings. So give good tidings to My servants,

وَالَّذِيْنَ اجْتَنَبُوا الطَّاغُوْتَ اَنْ يَّعْبُدُوْهَا وَاَنَابُوْٓا
اِلَى اللّٰهِ لَهُمُ الْبُشْرٰى ۚ فَبَشِّرْ عِبَادِ ﴿۱۸﴾

19. [c]Who listen to the Word and follow the best thereof.[2569] It is they whom Allāh has guided, and it is they who are *really* endowed with understanding.

الَّذِيْنَ يَسْتَمِعُوْنَ الْقَوْلَ فَيَتَّبِعُوْنَ اَحْسَنَهٗ ۭ اُولٰۗىِٕكَ
الَّذِيْنَ هَدٰىهُمُ اللّٰهُ وَاُولٰۗىِٕكَ هُمْ اُولُوا الْاَلْبَابِ ﴿۱۹﴾

20. Can he, then, against whom the sentence of punishment has become due, *be saved?* Canst thou rescue him who is in the Fire?

اَفَمَنْ حَقَّ عَلَيْهِ كَلِمَةُ الْعَذَابِ ۭ اَفَاَنْتَ تُنْقِذُ
مَنْ فِي النَّارِ ﴿۲۰﴾

21. But for them who fear their Lord [d]there are lofty mansions, built over lofty mansions,[2570] beneath which streams flow. Allāh has *made that* promise; *and* Allāh breaks not *His* promise.

لٰكِنِ الَّذِيْنَ اتَّقَوْا رَبَّهُمْ لَهُمْ غُرَفٌ مِّنْ فَوْقِهَا
غُرَفٌ مَّبْنِيَّةٌ ۙ تَجْرِيْ مِنْ تَحْتِهَا الْاَنْهٰرُ وَعْدَ
اللّٰهِ ۭ لَا يُخْلِفُ اللّٰهُ الْمِيْعَادَ ﴿۲۱﴾

[a]40 : 66; 98 : 6. [b]7 : 42; 18 : 30. [c]7 : 205. [d]25 : 76; 29 : 59; 34 : 38.

2568. In the brief space of four verses (3rd, 4th, 12th and 15th) the Holy Prophet has been enjoined to worship Allāh with sincere devotion. The verses seemed to prepare Muslims for the severe trials that lay ahead of them in Medina. The *Sūrah* was revealed in the later Meccan period, when Muslims were leaving for Medina singly or in small groups.

2569. When two equally permissible courses are open to a believer, he adopts the one which is productive of the best results.

2570. The difference in ranks of believers in Paradise shows that there will be a corresponding difference in their endeavour and labour which signifies that the next life will not be a life of inactivity and lassitude but of incessant work and continuous advance.

22. Hast thou not seen that [a]Allāh sends down water from the sky, and causes it to flow in springs in the earth and then brings forth thereby [b]herbage of diverse hues? Then it dries up and thou seest it turn yellow; then He reduces it to broken straw. In that, verily, is a reminder for men of understanding.

أَلَمْ تَرَ أَنَّ اللّٰهَ أَنْزَلَ مِنَ السَّمَآءِ مَآءً فَسَلَكَهٗ
يَنَابِيعَ فِي الْأَرْضِ ثُمَّ يُخْرِجُ بِهٖ زَرْعًا مُّخْتَلِفًا
أَلْوَانُهٗ ثُمَّ يَهِيجُ فَتَرٰىهُ مُصْفَرًّا ثُمَّ يَجْعَلُهٗ
حُطَامًا ۭ إِنَّ فِي ذٰلِكَ لَذِكْرٰى لِأُولِي الْأَلْبَابِ ﴿٢٢﴾ ع

R. 3 23. [c]Is he then whose bosom Allāh has opened for *the acceptance of* Islām, so that he possesses a light[2571] from his Lord, *like him who is groping in the darkness of disbelief?* Woe, then, to those whose hearts are hardened against the remembrance of Allāh! They are in manifest error.

أَفَمَنْ شَرَحَ اللّٰهُ صَدْرَهٗ لِلْإِسْلَامِ فَهُوَ عَلٰى نُوْرٍ
مِّنْ رَّبِّهٖ ۭ فَوَيْلٌ لِّلْقٰسِيَةِ قُلُوْبُهُمْ مِّنْ ذِكْرِ اللّٰهِ ۭ
أُولٰٓئِكَ فِي ضَلٰلٍ مُّبِيْنٍ ﴿٢٣﴾

24. Allāh has sent down the best Discourse—a Book, [d]*whose verses are* mutually supporting *and* repeated *in diverse forms.*[2572] The skins of those, who fear their Lord, do creep at *its recital*, then their skins and their hearts soften to the remembrance of Allāh. Such is the guidance of Allāh; He guides therewith whom He pleases. [e]And he whom Allāh adjudges astray—he shall have no guide.

اَللّٰهُ نَزَّلَ أَحْسَنَ الْحَدِيْثِ كِتٰبًا مُّتَشَابِهًا مَّثَانِيَ ۖ
تَقْشَعِرُّ مِنْهُ جُلُوْدُ الَّذِيْنَ يَخْشَوْنَ رَبَّهُمْ ۚ ثُمَّ تَلِيْنُ
جُلُوْدُهُمْ وَقُلُوْبُهُمْ إِلٰى ذِكْرِ اللّٰهِ ۭ ذٰلِكَ هُدَى
اللّٰهِ يَهْدِيْ بِهٖ مَنْ يَّشَآءُ ۭ وَمَنْ يُّضْلِلِ اللّٰهُ
فَمَا لَهٗ مِنْ هَادٍ ﴿٢٤﴾

[a]35 : 28. [b]13 : 5; 16 : 14. [c]6 : 126. [d]15 : 88. [e]17 : 98.

2571. The teaching of Islām has such depth and vastness that it makes the hearts of believers expand and overflow with Divine knowledge and love. It certainly opens up new and endless vistas of thought, knowledge and truth.

2572. Divine revelation has found the completest and most perfect expression in the Qur'ān. In the verse under comment the Qur'ān has been described as *Kitāban Mutashābihan* signifying that it is a Book which is susceptible of different interpretations which are consistent with and support each other. There is no contradiction or inconsistency anywhere in the Qur'ān. This constitutes one of its inimitable excellences. Another excellence of the Qur'ān lies in the fact that it has made use of metaphors, allegories and parables. This greatly adds to the beauty and grace of its style and assures vastness of meaning in the fewest possible words. Again, the Qur'ān is called *Mathānī* which signifies that it describes its basic beliefs and principles repeatedly and in different ways and forms, in order to emphasize their importance, necessity and purpose. The word also signifies that some of the teachings of the Qur'ān resemble those of other revealed Scriptures and some are new and inapproachable and incomparable in their excellences and beauties.

25. Is he, then, who has only his own face[2573] to shield him from the evil punishment on the Day of Resurrection, *like him who is secure?* And it will be said to the wrongdoers, 'Taste ye *the recompense of* what you used to earn.'

أَفَمَنْ يَتَّقِي بِوَجْهِهِ سُوْٓءَ الْعَذَابِ يَوْمَ الْقِيٰمَةِ ؕ
وَقِيْلَ لِلظّٰلِمِيْنَ ذُوْقُوْا مَا كُنْتُمْ تَكْسِبُوْنَ ﴿٢٥﴾

26. Those, who were before them, rejected *Our Messengers*, so [a]the punishment came upon them whence they knew not.

كَذَّبَ الَّذِيْنَ مِنْ قَبْلِهِمْ فَأَتٰىهُمُ الْعَذَابُ
مِنْ حَيْثُ لَا يَشْعُرُوْنَ ﴿٢٦﴾

27. So Allāh made them taste humiliation in the present life and [b]the punishment of the Hereafter will certainly be greater, if they but knew.

فَأَذَاقَهُمُ اللّٰهُ الْخِزْيَ فِي الْحَيٰوةِ الدُّنْيَا ۚ وَ
لَعَذَابُ الْاٰخِرَةِ أَكْبَرُ ۘ لَوْ كَانُوْا يَعْلَمُوْنَ ﴿٢٧﴾

28. [c]And, indeed, We have set forth for mankind all manner of parables in this Qur'ān that they may take heed.[2574]

وَلَقَدْ ضَرَبْنَا لِلنَّاسِ فِيْ هٰذَا الْقُرْاٰنِ مِنْ
كُلِّ مَثَلٍ لَّعَلَّهُمْ يَتَذَكَّرُوْنَ ﴿٢٨﴾

29. [d]*We have revealed* the Qur'ān in Arabic wherein there is no deviation from rectitude, that they may become righteous.

قُرْاٰنًا عَرَبِيًّا غَيْرَ ذِيْ عِوَجٍ لَّعَلَّهُمْ يَتَّقُوْنَ ﴿٢٩﴾

30. Allāh sets forth a parable—a man belonging to several partners, who disagree with one another, and a man belonging wholly to one man. Are the two equal in

ضَرَبَ اللّٰهُ مَثَلًا رَّجُلًا فِيْهِ شُرَكَآءُ مُتَشٰكِسُوْنَ
وَرَجُلًا سَلَمًا لِّرَجُلٍ ؕ هَلْ يَسْتَوِيٰنِ مَثَلًا ؕ اَلْحَمْدُ

[a]16 : 27; 59 : 3. [b]13 : 35; 68 : 34. [c]17 : 90; 30 : 59. [d]12 : 3; 42 : 8; 43 : 4.

2573. The words signify the severity of the punishment which disbelievers will receive on the Day of Reckoning. They will become so confused and confounded by the severe punishment that, instead of protecting their faces, which are the most sensitive part of the body, they will put them forward.

2574. The verse develops the argument given in v. 24, *viz.*, that the Qur'ān contains the best Message for mankind, in that it has comprehensively dealt with all those principles and teachings which have deep bearing on man's spiritual and moral development, and also with all those subjects which can make his life useful and pleasant. It has provided guidance in matters of belief and conduct.

لِلّٰهِ ۚ بَلْ أَكْثَرُهُمْ لَا يَعْلَمُونَ ﴿٣٠﴾

condition?[2575] All praise belongs to Allāh. But most of them know not.

إِنَّكَ مَيِّتٌ وَإِنَّهُمْ مَيِّتُونَ ﴿٣١﴾

31. [a]Surely, thou wilt die, and surely they, *too*, will die.

ثُمَّ إِنَّكُمْ يَوْمَ الْقِيَامَةِ عِنْدَ رَبِّكُمْ تَخْتَصِمُونَ ﴿٣٢﴾

32. [b]Then, surely, on the Day of Resurrection you will dispute with one another before your Lord.

PART XXIV

فَمَنْ أَظْلَمُ مِمَّنْ كَذَبَ عَلَى اللّٰهِ وَكَذَّبَ بِالصِّدْقِ إِذْ جَاءَهُ ۚ أَلَيْسَ فِي جَهَنَّمَ مَثْوًى لِلْكَافِرِينَ ﴿٣٣﴾

R. 4 33. [c]Who, then, is more unjust than he who lies against Allāh and he who rejects the truth when it comes to him? Is there not in Hell an abode for the disbelievers?

وَالَّذِي جَاءَ بِالصِّدْقِ وَصَدَّقَ بِهِ ۙ أُولٰئِكَ هُمُ الْمُتَّقُونَ ﴿٣٤﴾

34. But he who has brought the truth, and *he who* testifies to it as truth—these it is who are the righteous.

لَهُمْ مَا يَشَاءُونَ عِنْدَ رَبِّهِمْ ۚ ذٰلِكَ جَزَاءُ الْمُحْسِنِينَ ﴿٣٥﴾

35. [d]They will have with their Lord whatever they desire; that is the reward of those who do good.

لِيُكَفِّرَ اللّٰهُ عَنْهُمْ أَسْوَأَ الَّذِي عَمِلُوا وَيَجْزِيَهُمْ أَجْرَهُمْ بِأَحْسَنِ الَّذِي كَانُوا يَعْمَلُونَ ﴿٣٦﴾

36. [e]So that Allāh will remove from them the evil *consequences* of what they did, and will give them their reward according to the best of their actions.[2576]

أَلَيْسَ اللّٰهُ بِكَافٍ عَبْدَهُ ۖ وَيُخَوِّفُونَكَ بِالَّذِينَ مِنْ دُونِهِ ۚ وَمَنْ يُضْلِلِ اللّٰهُ فَمَا لَهُ مِنْ هَادٍ ﴿٣٧﴾

37. Is not Allāh sufficient for His servant? And yet they would frighten thee with those beside Him. [f]And he whom Allāh leaves in error—for him there is no guide.

---

[a]23 : 16. [b]23 : 17. [c]6 : 22; 10 : 18; 29 : 69. [d]16 : 32; 50 : 36. [e]16 : 98; 29 : 8. [f]39 : 24.

2575. A polytheist is like a person who has to serve several masters, having mutually antagonistic interests and who also are ill-tempered and quarrelsome. Pitiable indeed is the lot of such a person! Can he be like a true believer who has to serve and please only one Master—Allāh?

2576. God rewards the good actions of believers, of whatever degree and measure, as He would reward their best actions.

38. [a]And he whom Allāh guides—there is none to lead him astray. Is not Allāh the Mighty, the Lord of retribution?

وَمَنْ يَّهْدِ اللّٰهُ فَمَا لَهٗ مِنْ مُّضِلٍّ ؕ اَلَيْسَ
اللّٰهُ بِعَزِيْزٍ ذِي انْتِقَامٍ ﴿۳۸﴾

39. [b]And if thou ask them, 'Who created the heavens and the earth?' they will, surely, say, 'Allāh.'[2577] Say, 'What think ye, if Allāh intends to do me harm, will those whom you call upon beside Allāh be able to remove the harm *He may intend*? Or, if He wills to show me mercy, could they withhold His mercy?' [c]Say, 'Allāh is sufficient for me. In Him trust those who would trust.'

وَلَئِنْ سَاَلْتَهُمْ مَّنْ خَلَقَ السَّمٰوٰتِ وَالْاَرْضَ
لَيَقُوْلُنَّ اللّٰهُ ؕ قُلْ اَفَرَءَيْتُمْ مَّا تَدْعُوْنَ مِنْ دُوْنِ
اللّٰهِ اِنْ اَرَادَنِيَ اللّٰهُ بِضُرٍّ هَلْ هُنَّ كٰشِفٰتُ
ضُرِّهٖۤ اَوْ اَرَادَنِيْ بِرَحْمَةٍ هَلْ هُنَّ مُمْسِكٰتُ رَحْمَتِهٖ ؕ
قُلْ حَسْبِيَ اللّٰهُ ؕ عَلَيْهِ يَتَوَكَّلُ الْمُتَوَكِّلُوْنَ ﴿۳۹﴾

40. Say, 'O my people, [d]act as best as you can; I, *too*, am acting; soon shall you know,[2578]

قُلْ يٰقَوْمِ اعْمَلُوْا عَلٰى مَكَانَتِكُمْ اِنِّيْ عَامِلٌ ۚ فَسَوْفَ
تَعْلَمُوْنَ ۙ﴿۴۰﴾

41. [e]'Who it is unto whom comes a punishment that will disgrace him, and on whom there descends an abiding punishment?'

مَنْ يَّاْتِيْهِ عَذَابٌ يُّخْزِيْهِ وَيَحِلُّ عَلَيْهِ عَذَابٌ
مُّقِيْمٌ ﴿۴۱﴾

42. Verily, We have revealed to thee the Book comprising *all* truth for *the good of* mankind. [f]So whoever follows guidance, follows it for the benefit of his own soul; and whoever goes astray, goes astray only to its detriment.[2579] And thou art not a guardian over them.

اِنَّاۤ اَنْزَلْنَا عَلَيْكَ الْكِتٰبَ لِلنَّاسِ بِالْحَقِّ ۚ فَمَنِ
اهْتَدٰى فَلِنَفْسِهٖ ۚ وَمَنْ ضَلَّ فَاِنَّمَا يَضِلُّ عَلَيْهَا ۚ
وَمَاۤ اَنْتَ عَلَيْهِمْ بِوَكِيْلٍ ﴿۴۲﴾ ع

[a]18 : 18. [b]29 : 62; 31 : 26. [c]9 : 129. [d]6 : 136; 11 : 122. [e]11 : 40. [f]10 : 109; 17 : 16; 27 : 93.

2577. Though idolaters, out of superstition or traditional attachment, worship false gods, yet if the argument is driven home to them, they have to, and invariably do, confess that God is the Creator of the heavens and the earth and in Him alone resides all real power.

2578. The verse throws out an open challenge to disbelievers to do their worst and use all their power, resources and influence to destroy Islām, but they will never succeed in their evil designs. Islām is humanity's last hope and final destiny and, therefore, its cause is bound to triumph and prevail.

2579. Man himself is the architect of his destiny—good or bad.

R. 5 43. [a]Allāh takes away the souls of men at the time of their death; and of those *also* that are not *yet* dead, during their sleep. And then He withholds those against which He has decreed death, and sends *back* the others till an appointed term.[2580] In that, surely, are Signs for a people who reflect.

اَللّٰهُ يَتَوَفَّى الْاَنْفُسَ حِيْنَ مَوْتِهَا وَالَّتِيْ لَمْ تَمُتْ
فِيْ مَنَامِهَا ۚ فَيُمْسِكُ الَّتِيْ قَضٰى عَلَيْهَا الْمَوْتَ
وَيُرْسِلُ الْاُخْرٰٓى اِلٰٓى اَجَلٍ مُّسَمًّى ؕ اِنَّ فِيْ ذٰلِكَ
لَاٰيٰتٍ لِّقَوْمٍ يَّتَفَكَّرُوْنَ ﴿۴۳﴾

44. [b]Have they taken intercessors beside Allāh? Say, 'Even if they have no power over anything and no understanding?'[2581]

اَمِ اتَّخَذُوْا مِنْ دُوْنِ اللّٰهِ شُفَعَآءَ ؕ قُلْ اَوَلَوْ كَانُوْا
لَا يَمْلِكُوْنَ شَيْـًٔا وَّلَا يَعْقِلُوْنَ ﴿۴۴﴾

45. Say, 'All intercession rests with Allāh.[2582] To Him belongs the Kingdom of the heavens and the earth. And to Him, then, shall you be brought back.'

قُلْ لِّلّٰهِ الشَّفَاعَةُ جَمِيْعًا ؕ لَهٗ مُلْكُ السَّمٰوٰتِ وَ
الْاَرْضِ ؕ ثُمَّ اِلَيْهِ تُرْجَعُوْنَ ﴿۴۵﴾

46. [c]And when Allāh alone is mentioned, the hearts of those, who believe not in the Hereafter, shrink with aversion; but when those beside Him are mentioned, behold! they begin to rejoice.

وَاِذَا ذُكِرَ اللّٰهُ وَحْدَهُ اشْمَاَزَّتْ قُلُوْبُ الَّذِيْنَ
لَا يُؤْمِنُوْنَ بِالْاٰخِرَةِ ۚ وَاِذَا ذُكِرَ الَّذِيْنَ مِنْ دُوْنِهٖٓ
اِذَا هُمْ يَسْتَبْشِرُوْنَ ﴿۴۶﴾

47. [d]Say, 'O Allāh! Originator of the heavens and the earth; Knower of the unseen and the seen; Thou *alone* wilt judge between Thy servants concerning that in which they differed.'

قُلِ اللّٰهُمَّ فَاطِرَ السَّمٰوٰتِ وَالْاَرْضِ عٰلِمَ الْغَيْبِ
وَالشَّهَادَةِ اَنْتَ تَحْكُمُ بَيْنَ عِبَادِكَ فِيْ مَا كَانُوْا
فِيْهِ يَخْتَلِفُوْنَ ﴿۴۷﴾

[a]6 : 61. [b]17 : 57. [c]17 : 47; 22 : 73; 40 : 13. [d]6 : 15; 12 : 102; 14 : 11; 35 : 2.

2580. With his death man's soul does not die or disintegrate but is taken away from its mortal habitat and is kept in other regions to account for man's actions in due course.

2581. As the human soul is immortal, man is warned against committing deeds which might vitiate it. The most heinous of all evil deeds is the setting up of 'partners' with God.

2582. See 85.

48. ªAnd even if the wrongdoers possessed all that is in the earth, and the like thereof in addition to it, they would, surely, *seek to* ransom themselves with it *to escape* from the evil punishment on the Day of Resurrection, but there shall appear unto them from Allāh that which they had never thought of.

وَلَوْ أَنَّ لِلَّذِينَ ظَلَمُوا مَا فِي الْأَرْضِ جَمِيعًا وَّمِثْلَهُ مَعَهُ لَافْتَدَوْا بِهِ مِنْ سُوْءِ الْعَذَابِ يَوْمَ الْقِيَامَةِ وَبَدَا لَهُمْ مِّنَ اللّٰهِ مَا لَمْ يَكُوْنُوْا يَحْتَسِبُوْنَ ۞

49. ᵇAnd the evil *consequences* of what they had earned will become apparent to them and that which they used to mock at will encompass them.

وَبَدَا لَهُمْ سَيِّاتُ مَا كَسَبُوْا وَحَاقَ بِهِمْ مَّا كَانُوْا بِهِ يَسْتَهْزِءُوْنَ ۞

50. ᶜAnd when harm touches man, he cries unto Us. But when We bestow on him a favour from Us, he says, 'This has been given to me on account of *my own* knowledge.'²⁵⁸³ Nay, it is only a trial; but most of them know not.

فَإِذَا مَسَّ الْإِنْسَانَ ضُرٌّ دَعَانَا ثُمَّ إِذَا خَوَّلْنَاهُ نِعْمَةً مِّنَّا قَالَ إِنَّمَا أُوْتِيتُهُ عَلٰى عِلْمٍ بَلْ هِيَ فِتْنَةٌ وَّلٰكِنَّ أَكْثَرَهُمْ لَا يَعْلَمُوْنَ ۞

51. Those who were before them said the same thing, yet all that they had earned availed them not.

قَدْ قَالَهَا الَّذِينَ مِنْ قَبْلِهِمْ فَمَا أَغْنٰى عَنْهُمْ مَّا كَانُوْا يَكْسِبُوْنَ ۞

52. So the evil *consequences of* what they had earned overtook them; and those who do wrong from among these *disbelievers*—the evil *consequences* of what they earned shall overtake them *also* and they cannot escape.

فَأَصَابَهُمْ سَيِّاتُ مَا كَسَبُوْا وَالَّذِينَ ظَلَمُوْا مِنْ هٰؤُلَاءِ سَيُصِيبُهُمْ سَيِّاتُ مَا كَسَبُوْا وَمَا هُمْ بِمُعْجِزِيْنَ ۞

53. Know they not that ᵈAllāh enlarges the provision for whomsoever He pleases, and straitens *it for whomsoever* He pleases? Verily, in that are Signs for a people who believe.

أَوَلَمْ يَعْلَمُوْا أَنَّ اللّٰهَ يَبْسُطُ الرِّزْقَ لِمَنْ يَّشَاءُ وَيَقْدِرُ إِنَّ فِيْ ذٰلِكَ لَآيٰتٍ لِّقَوْمٍ يُّؤْمِنُوْنَ ۞

ª5 : 37; 10 : 55; 13 : 19.   ᵇ21 : 42; 45 : 34.   ᶜ11 : 10, 11; 17 : 68; 30 : 34; 39 : 9.   ᵈ13 : 27; 29 : 63; 30 : 38; 34 : 37; 42 : 13.

2583. It is human nature that when man is involved in trouble he prays to God, but when he is in affluent circumstances he consigns Him to oblivion and attributes all his success in life to his own ability and knowledge.

R. 6 54. Say, 'O My servants who have sinned against their souls, [a]despair not[2584] of the mercy of Allāh, surely, Allāh forgives all sins. Verily, He is Most Forgiving, Ever Merciful;

قُلْ يٰعِبَادِيَ الَّذِيْنَ اَسْرَفُوْا عَلٰٓى اَنْفُسِهِمْ لَا تَقْنَطُوْا
مِنْ رَّحْمَةِ اللّٰهِ ؕ اِنَّ اللّٰهَ يَغْفِرُ الذُّنُوْبَ جَمِيْعًا ؕ
اِنَّهٗ هُوَ الْغَفُوْرُ الرَّحِيْمُ ﴿۵۴﴾

55. 'And turn to your Lord, and submit[2585] yourselves to Him, before there comes unto you the punishment; *for* then you shall not be helped;

وَاَنِيْبُوْٓا اِلٰى رَبِّكُمْ وَاَسْلِمُوْا لَهٗ مِنْ قَبْلِ اَنْ يَّاْتِيَكُمُ
الْعَذَابُ ثُمَّ لَا تُنْصَرُوْنَ ﴿۵۵﴾

56. 'And follow the best *Teaching* that has been revealed to you from your Lord, before the punishment comes upon you suddenly, while you perceive not.'

وَاتَّبِعُوْٓا اَحْسَنَ مَآ اُنْزِلَ اِلَيْكُمْ مِّنْ رَّبِّكُمْ مِّنْ
قَبْلِ اَنْ يَّاْتِيَكُمُ الْعَذَابُ بَغْتَةً وَّاَنْتُمْ لَا تَشْعُرُوْنَ ﴿۵۶﴾

57. Lest a soul should say, [b]'O, woe is me in that I neglected *my duty* in respect of Allāh! Surely, I was among the scoffers.'

اَنْ تَقُوْلَ نَفْسٌ يّٰحَسْرَتٰى عَلٰى مَا فَرَّطْتُّ فِيْ جَنْۢبِ
اللّٰهِ وَاِنْ كُنْتُ لَمِنَ السّٰخِرِيْنَ ﴿۵۷﴾

58. Or, lest it should say, 'If Allāh had guided me, I should certainly have been among those who fully carry out their duties;

اَوْ تَقُوْلَ لَوْ اَنَّ اللّٰهَ هَدٰىنِيْ لَكُنْتُ مِنَ الْمُتَّقِيْنَ ﴿۵۸﴾

59. Or, lest it should say, when it sees the punishment, 'Would that there were for me a return *to the world*, I would then be among those who do good.'

اَوْ تَقُوْلَ حِيْنَ تَرَى الْعَذَابَ لَوْ اَنَّ لِيْ كَرَّةً فَاَكُوْنَ
مِنَ الْمُحْسِنِيْنَ ﴿۵۹﴾

[a]12 : 88; 15 : 57. [b]6 : 32; 23 : 100; 26 : 103; 35 : 38.

2584. The verse holds out a message of hope and good cheer to the sinners. It encourages optimism and kills despair and despondency. It denounces and condemns pessimism because pessimism lies at the root of most sins and failures in life. Again and again the Qur'ān gives a promise of Divine mercy and forgiveness (6 : 55; 7 : 157; 12 : 88; 15 : 57; 18 : 59) than which there could be no greater message of solace and comfort for the grieved and the heavy-laden.

2585. Whereas the preceding verse holds out to sinners the message of hope and good cheer, this verse warns them that they will have to work out their destiny themselves by submitting to Divine laws.

60. *He will be told:* 'Aye, there came to thee My Signs, but thou didst treat them as lies, and thou wast arrogant, and thou wast of the disbelievers.'[2586]

بَلٰى قَدْ جَآءَتْكَ اٰيٰتِيْ فَكَذَّبْتَ بِهَا وَاسْتَكْبَرْتَ وَكُنْتَ مِنَ الْكٰفِرِيْنَ ﴿٦٠﴾

61. And on the Day of Resurrection, thou wilt see those who lied against Allāh that their [a]faces shall be overcast with gloom. Is there not in Hell an abode for the proud?

وَيَوْمَ الْقِيٰمَةِ تَرَى الَّذِيْنَ كَذَبُوْا عَلَى اللّٰهِ وُجُوْهُهُمْ مُّسْوَدَّةٌ ؕ اَلَيْسَ فِيْ جَهَنَّمَ مَثْوًى لِّلْمُتَكَبِّرِيْنَ ﴿٦١﴾

62. [b]And Allāh will deliver the righteous *from all troubles* and *will confer* success upon them; evil shall not touch them, nor shall they grieve.

وَيُنَجِّي اللّٰهُ الَّذِيْنَ اتَّقَوْا بِمَفَازَتِهِمْ ۫ لَا يَمَسُّهُمُ السُّوْٓءُ وَلَا هُمْ يَحْزَنُوْنَ ﴿٦٢﴾

63. [c]Allāh is the Creator of all things, and He is Guardian over all things.

اَللّٰهُ خَالِقُ كُلِّ شَيْءٍ ۫ وَّهُوَ عَلٰى كُلِّ شَيْءٍ وَّكِيْلٌ ﴿٦٣﴾

64. [d]To Him belong the keys of the heavens and the earth; and as for those who disbelieve in the Signs of Allāh, these it is who are the losers.

لَهٗ مَقَالِيْدُ السَّمٰوٰتِ وَالْاَرْضِ ؕ وَالَّذِيْنَ كَفَرُوْا بِاٰيٰتِ اللّٰهِ اُولٰٓئِكَ هُمُ الْخٰسِرُوْنَ ﴿٦٤﴾

R. 7 65. [e]Say, 'Is it other *gods* than Allāh that ye bid me worship, O ignorant ones?'

قُلْ اَفَغَيْرَ اللّٰهِ تَاْمُرُوْٓنِّيْٓ اَعْبُدُ اَيُّهَا الْجٰهِلُوْنَ ﴿٦٥﴾

66. And, verily, it has been revealed to thee as unto those before thee, [f]'If thou associate *partners with Allāh*, thy work shall, surely, come to naught and thou shalt certainly be of the losers.'

وَلَقَدْ اُوْحِيَ اِلَيْكَ وَاِلَى الَّذِيْنَ مِنْ قَبْلِكَ ۚ لَئِنْ اَشْرَكْتَ لَيَحْبَطَنَّ عَمَلُكَ وَلَتَكُوْنَنَّ مِنَ الْخٰسِرِيْنَ ﴿٦٦﴾

67. Aye, worship Allāh and be thou among the grateful.

بَلِ اللّٰهَ فَاعْبُدْ وَكُنْ مِّنَ الشّٰكِرِيْنَ ﴿٦٧﴾

---

[a]3 : 107; 10 : 28. [b]19 : 73; 21 : 102. [c]6 : 103; 13 : 17. [d]42 : 13. [e]6 : 15. [f]6 : 89.

2586. Many chances are given to the man who is steeped in sin to repent and reform himself. It is when his rejection of Truth is deliberate and repeated, and when he exceeds all legitimate bounds in committing sin and transgression and when the day of reckoning is actually upon him that his sighs and regrets prove of no avail to him.

68. [a]And they have not formed a true concept *of the attributes* of Allāh. [b]And the *entire* earth will be under His *complete* control on the Day of Resurrection, and the heavens rolled up in His right hand.[2587] Glory be to Him and exalted is He above that which they associate *with Him*.

وَمَا قَدَرُوا اللّٰهَ حَقَّ قَدْرِهٖ ۖ وَالْاَرْضُ جَمِيْعًا قَبْضَتُهٗ يَوْمَ الْقِيٰمَةِ وَالسَّمٰوٰتُ مَطْوِيّٰتٌۢ بِيَمِيْنِهٖ ؕ سُبْحٰنَهٗ وَتَعٰلٰى عَمَّا يُشْرِكُوْنَ ﴿۶۸﴾

69. [c]And the trumpet will be blown, and all who are in the heavens and all who are in the earth will *fall down in a* swoon, except those whom Allāh will be pleased *to spare*. Then will it be blown a second *time*, and lo! they will be standing, awaiting[2588] *judgment*.

وَنُفِخَ فِي الصُّوْرِ فَصَعِقَ مَنْ فِي السَّمٰوٰتِ وَمَنْ فِي الْاَرْضِ اِلَّا مَنْ شَآءَ اللّٰهُ ؕ ثُمَّ نُفِخَ فِيْهِ اُخْرٰى فَاِذَا هُمْ قِيَامٌ يَّنْظُرُوْنَ ﴿۶۹﴾

70. And the earth will shine with the light of her Lord, [d]and the Book will be laid *open before them*, and the Prophets and the witnesses will be brought,[2589] and judgment will be given between them with justice, and they will not be wronged.

وَاَشْرَقَتِ الْاَرْضُ بِنُوْرِ رَبِّهَا وَوُضِعَ الْكِتٰبُ وَجِايْٓءَ بِالنَّبِيّٖنَ وَالشُّهَدَآءِ وَقُضِيَ بَيْنَهُمْ بِالْحَقِّ وَهُمْ لَا يُظْلَمُوْنَ ﴿۷۰﴾

71. [e]And every soul will be fully rewarded for what it did. And He knows well what they do.

وَوُفِّيَتْ كُلُّ نَفْسٍ مَّا عَمِلَتْ وَهُوَ اَعْلَمُ بِمَا يَفْعَلُوْنَ ﴿۷۱﴾ ع

[a]6 : 92; 22 : 75. [b]21 : 105. [c]18 : 100; 23 : 102; 36 : 52; 50 : 21; 69 : 14. [d]18 : 50. [e]2 : 282; 3 : 26.

2587. *Yamīn* signifying power and strength, the verse refers to the great Power and Majesty of God and purports to say that nothing is more derogatory to His great attributes than that idols made of wood and stone or weak human beings should be worshipped.

2588. The verse seems to apply to Resurrection in the next life. But it may also apply to the spiritual condition of people immediately before the appearance of a Divine Teacher in the world whose advent is here likened to the blowing of the trumpet. In view of this simile the words, 'will fall down into a swoon,' may signify spiritual torpor of the people immediately before the appearance of a Divine Reformer and the words, 'will be standing, awaiting', may signify their having seen and followed the right path after he has made his appearance.

2589. Applied to the next life, the words, 'And the earth will shine with the light of her Lord,' would mean that the veil will be lifted from the mysteries of life and the consequences of good and bad actions which man will have done in this life and which remain hidden here, will become manifest. With reference, however, to the appearance of a Divine Teacher in the world, particularly to that of the Holy Prophet, the words may signify that now that the Holy Prophet has appeared the whole earth will shine with Divine Light, and spiritual darkness will be completely dispelled. The words, ' The Prophets and witnesses will be brought, may signify the advent of the Holy Prophet who represents in his person all the Prophets and Divine Teachers; and 'witnesses' refers to his true followers who enjoy the proud privilege of having been appointed witnesses over all men (2 : 144).

R. 8 72. [a]And those who disbelieve will be driven to Hell in troops until, when they arrive there, its gates will be opened, [b]and its Keepers will say to them, 'Did not the Messengers from among yourselves come to you, reciting unto you the Signs of your Lord, and warning you of the meeting of this day of yours?' They will say, 'Yea, but the word of punishment was bound to be fulfilled in respect of the disbelievers.'

وَسِيقَ الَّذِينَ كَفَرُوا إِلَىٰ جَهَنَّمَ زُمَرًا ۖ حَتَّىٰ إِذَا
جَاءُوهَا فُتِحَتْ أَبْوَابُهَا وَقَالَ لَهُمْ خَزَنَتُهَا أَلَمْ
يَأْتِكُمْ رُسُلٌ مِّنكُمْ يَتْلُونَ عَلَيْكُمْ آيَاتِ رَبِّكُمْ
وَيُنذِرُونَكُمْ لِقَاءَ يَوْمِكُمْ هَٰذَا ۚ قَالُوا بَلَىٰ وَلَٰكِنْ
حَقَّتْ كَلِمَةُ الْعَذَابِ عَلَى الْكَافِرِينَ ﴿٧٢﴾

73. It will be said, [c]'Enter ye the gates of Hell, abiding therein. And evil is the abode of the arrogant.'

قِيلَ ادْخُلُوا أَبْوَابَ جَهَنَّمَ خَالِدِينَ فِيهَا ۖ فَبِئْسَ
مَثْوَى الْمُتَكَبِّرِينَ ﴿٧٣﴾

74. And those, who feared their Lord, will be conducted to Heaven in groups until when they arrive there, its gates will be opened and its Keepers will say to them, [d]'Peace be upon you! be ye happy,[2590] and enter it, abiding *therein*.'

وَسِيقَ الَّذِينَ اتَّقَوْا رَبَّهُمْ إِلَى الْجَنَّةِ زُمَرًا ۖ
حَتَّىٰ إِذَا جَاءُوهَا وَفُتِحَتْ أَبْوَابُهَا وَقَالَ لَهُمْ
خَزَنَتُهَا سَلَامٌ عَلَيْكُمْ طِبْتُمْ فَادْخُلُوهَا خَالِدِينَ ﴿٧٤﴾

75. And they will say, [e]"All praise belongs to Allāh Who has made good to us His promise, and has given us the earth to inherit, we shall make our abode in the Garden wherever we please.' How excellent is the reward of the *righteous* workers!

وَقَالُوا الْحَمْدُ لِلَّهِ الَّذِي صَدَقَنَا وَعْدَهُ وَأَوْرَثَنَا
الْأَرْضَ نَتَبَوَّأُ مِنَ الْجَنَّةِ حَيْثُ نَشَاءُ ۖ فَنِعْمَ
أَجْرُ الْعَامِلِينَ ﴿٧٥﴾

76. And thou wilt see the angels going round the Throne, glorifying their Lord with *His* praise,[2591] and judgment will be given between *the people* with justice. And it will be said, 'All praise belongs to Allāh, the Lord of the worlds.'

وَتَرَى الْمَلَائِكَةَ حَافِّينَ مِنْ حَوْلِ الْعَرْشِ يُسَبِّحُونَ
بِحَمْدِ رَبِّهِمْ ۖ وَقُضِيَ بَيْنَهُم بِالْحَقِّ وَقِيلَ
الْحَمْدُ لِلَّهِ رَبِّ الْعَالَمِينَ ﴿٧٦﴾ ع

[a]19 : 87. [b]40 : 51; 67 : 9-10. [c]16 : 30; 40 : 77. [d]13 : 25.
[e]1 : 2; 7 : 44; 37 : 183; 40 : 8.

2590. *Ṭibtum* may also mean, because you led good and pure lives.

2591. God's attributes will see their most complete manifestation on the Judgment Day and the cherubs will be on duty singing alleluias to the Divine Being. Or, the verse may mean that the Unity of God will become established in Arabia, and God's true servants in the world together with the angels in heavens will celebrate His praises.

CHAPTER 40

AL-MU'MIN

(*Revealed before Hijrah*)

Date of Revelation and Context

With this *Sūrah* begins a group of Chapters all of which have the same abbreviated letters, *Ḥā Mīm*, affixed to them and which open with the subject of the revelation of the Qur'ān, and belong to the same period. According to Ibn 'Abbās and 'Ikrimah, all these *Sūrahs* were revealed at Mecca at a time when opposition to Islām had become persistent, organized and bitter (vv. 56 & 78) and the Holy Prophet's enemies were even seeking to kill him (v. 29). Towards the close of the last *Sūrah* the Holy Prophet was comforted with the assurance that very soon Divine judgment will issue forth between him and his enemies. The forces of darkness will be routed; idolatry will disappear from Arabia, and the whole country will reverberate with the praises of God. The present *Sūrah* opens with the most welcome declaration that the Great and Mighty God has revealed the Qur'ān in order that Divine Majesty and Holiness be established in the world and disbelief obliterated from it.

Subject-Matter

As mentioned above, the *Sūrah* opens with a firm declaration that the time has come when truth will triumph over falsehood and righteousness over evil, and the praises of God will be sung in the land where idolatry had been rampant. This great consummation will be brought about by means of the Qur'ān. The enemies of truth will strain every nerve and use their influence and powerful resources to nip the tender plant of Islām in the bud. But they will fail in their evil designs and endeavours. The Holy Prophet is told not to be deceived and overawed by the glamour of power and great material resources of disbelievers, because they are destined to come to a sad end. He is further told that his opponents are not the only and the first people to oppose truth. There have been people before who also sought to kill their Prophets and exterminate their missions. But God's punishment overtook them. So will punishment seize his opponents. The *Sūrah* then refers to the case of Moses as an illustration of the sad end to which the opponents of the Holy Prophet are bound to come. While Pharaoh rejected Moses's invitation to truth, a 'believing man' from his own household gave a most pathetic but convincing speech, exhorting his people not to seek to kill a man (Moses) whose only fault was that he said that Allāh was his Lord, and who possessed sound and solid proofs to support and establish his case. He further warned them that they should not be misled by their wealth, power and material resources, for all these were transitory things. But instead of benefiting by his sincere advice Pharaoh mocked at him. Next, the *Sūrah* makes pointed reference to the invariable Divine law, *viz.*, that help and succour of God are always with His Messengers and with their followers and that failure and frustration continue to dog the footsteps of disbelievers till the end of time. This Divine law operated in the time of every Prophet and it will see its fullest manifestation in the time of the Holy Prophet. The disbelievers are then told that they have no reason to reject the Holy Prophet. His advent is not a novel phenomenon. Just as day follows night in the physical world, so does spiritual awakening follow a period of moral decadence in the spiritual realm. As the world had become spiritually dead, God raised the Holy Prophet to give it a new life. The *Sūrah* closes on the note that when God has made adequate provision for the physical needs of man, He could not have ignored to make a similar provision for his spiritual needs. He has been making this provision from time immemorial. He sent His Messengers and Prophets in the world who invited men to their Lord and Creator ; but out of ingratitude and folly the sons of darkness rejected the Divine Message in every age and earned God's displeasure.

سُوْرَةُ الْمُؤْمِنِ مَكِّيَّةٌ

ركوعاتها ٩ (٤٠) اٰياتها ٨٦

1. [a]In the name of Allāh, the Gracious, the Merciful.

بِسْمِ اللّٰهِ الرَّحْمٰنِ الرَّحِيْمِ ①

2. [b]Ḥā Mīm.[2592]

حٰمٓ ②

3. [c]The revelation of this Book is from Allāh, the Mighty, the All-Knowing,

تَنْزِيْلُ الْكِتٰبِ مِنَ اللّٰهِ الْعَزِيْزِ الْعَلِيْمِ ③

4. Forgiver of sin, Acceptor of repentance, Severe in punishment, the Lord of bounty.[2593] There is no god but He. Towards Him is the *final* return.

غَافِرِ الذَّنْۢبِ وَقَابِلِ التَّوْبِ شَدِيْدِ الْعِقَابِ ذِي الطَّوْلِ ۭ لَآ اِلٰهَ اِلَّا هُوَ ۭ اِلَيْهِ الْمَصِيْرُ ④

5. [d]None disputes concerning the Signs of Allāh except those who disbelieve. [e]Let not, then, their going about[2594] in the land deceive thee.

مَا يُجَادِلُ فِيْٓ اٰيٰتِ اللّٰهِ اِلَّا الَّذِيْنَ كَفَرُوْا فَلَا يَغْرُرْكَ تَقَلُّبُهُمْ فِي الْبِلَادِ ⑤

6. [f]Before them the people of Noah and *other* groups after them rejected Our Signs and every nation strove to seize their Messenger, and disputed by means of false *arguments* that they might rebut the truth thereby. Then I seized them, and how *terrible* was My retribution!

كَذَّبَتْ قَبْلَهُمْ قَوْمُ نُوْحٍ وَّالْاَحْزَابُ مِنْۢ بَعْدِهِمْ ۠ وَهَمَّتْ كُلُّ اُمَّةٍۢ بِرَسُوْلِهِمْ لِيَاْخُذُوْهُ وَجٰدَلُوْا بِالْبَاطِلِ لِيُدْحِضُوْا بِهِ الْحَقَّ فَاَخَذْتُهُمْ ۣ فَكَيْفَ كَانَ عِقَابِ ⑥

---

[a]1 : 1. [b]41 : 2; 42 : 2; 43 : 2; 44 : 2; 45 : 2; 46 : 2. [c]20 : 5; 32 : 3; 41 : 3; 45 : 3; 46 : 3. [d]22 : 4; 42 : 36. [e]3 : 197. [f]6 : 35; 22 : 43; 35 : 26; 54 : 10.

2592. The abbreviated letters *Ḥā Mīm* stand for the Divine attributes *Ḥamīd, Majīd* (Praiseworthy and Lord of Honour), or for *Ḥayy, Qayyūm* (Living, Self-Subsisting and All-Sustaining). Both these groups of Divine attributes have a strong bearing on the subject-matter of this *Sūrah*. The *Sūrah* makes repeated reference to the Glory, Majesty and Power of God as the word *'Arsh* which signifies these attributes and which has been twice mentioned in the first few verses, shows. The second main theme is the rise of a spiritually dead people to new life. Both the attributes *Ḥayy* (Living) and *Qayyūm* (Self-Subsisting and All-Sustaining) have an obvious connection with this subject. This fact explains why the abbreviated letters *Ḥā Mīm* have been placed in the beginning. It is worthy of particular note that the present and next six Chapters form a special group. Each of them opening with the same abbreviated letters, which indicates that a deep connection exists between their subject-matter.

2593. *Ṭaul* means, beneficence; bounty; excellence; superabundance; power; wealth; ampleness of circumstances; superiority, ascendancy (Lane).

2594. Believers are told not to be deceived by the glamour of the material power of disbelievers, as it is bound to fall into decay in the long run.

7. ^aAnd thus was the word of thy Lord fulfilled against the disbelievers, that they are the inmates of the Fire.

وَكَذَٰلِكَ حَقَّتْ كَلِمَتُ رَبِّكَ عَلَى الَّذِيْنَ كَفَرُوْۤا اَنَّهُمْ اَصْحٰبُ النَّارِ ۟

8. ^bThose who bear the Throne²⁵⁹⁵ and those who are around it, proclaim the praise of their Lord and believe in Him, and ask forgiveness for those who believe, *saying*, 'Our Lord, Thou dost comprehend all things in *Thy* mercy and knowledge. So forgive those who repent and follow Thy way, and protect them from the punishment of Hell ;

اَلَّذِيْنَ يَحْمِلُوْنَ الْعَرْشَ وَمَنْ حَوْلَهٗ يُسَبِّحُوْنَ بِحَمْدِ رَبِّهِمْ وَيُؤْمِنُوْنَ بِهٖ وَيَسْتَغْفِرُوْنَ لِلَّذِيْنَ اٰمَنُوْا ۚ رَبَّنَا وَسِعْتَ كُلَّ شَيْءٍ رَّحْمَةً وَّعِلْمًا فَاغْفِرْ لِلَّذِيْنَ تَابُوْا وَاتَّبَعُوْا سَبِيْلَكَ وَقِهِمْ عَذَابَ الْجَحِيْمِ ۟

9. 'Our Lord, make them enter the Gardens of Eternity which Thou hast promised them, as well as ^csuch of their fathers and their wives²⁵⁹⁶ and their children as are virtuous. Surely, Thou art the Mighty, the Wise;

رَبَّنَا وَاَدْخِلْهُمْ جَنّٰتِ عَدْنِ ِۨالَّتِيْ وَعَدْتَّهُمْ وَمَنْ صَلَحَ مِنْ اٰبَآئِهِمْ وَاَزْوَاجِهِمْ وَذُرِّيّٰتِهِمْ ۚ اِنَّكَ اَنْتَ الْعَزِيْزُ الْحَكِيْمُ ۟

10. 'And guard them against evils; ^dand he whom Thou dost guard against evils on that day—him hast Thou, surely, shown mercy. And that, *indeed*, is the mighty triumph.'

وَقِهِمُ السَّيِّاٰتِ ۚ وَمَنْ تَقِ السَّيِّاٰتِ يَوْمَئِذٍ فَقَدْ رَحِمْتَهٗ ۚ وَذٰلِكَ هُوَ الْفَوْزُ الْعَظِيْمُ ۟

---

^a10 : 34, 97. ^b39 : 76; 69 : 18. ^c13 : 24; 52 : 22. ^d6 : 17.

2595. As 'Arsh signifies Divine attributes (see 986 & 1233), the words, 'Those who bear the Throne,' would, therefore, mean, those beings or persons through whom those attributes are manifested. As the laws of nature work through the angels, and the Prophets are the instruments through whom God's Word is preached to mankind, the words, 'Those who bear the Throne,' may signify both the angels and the Divine Messengers, and the words, 'those who are around it,' may signify subordinate angels who assist the principal angels in executing the affairs of the world or the true followers of the Prophets who preach and disseminate the teachings of the Prophets. See also 986.

2596. The verse lays down a great principle. No work is accomplished and no success achieved by anyone in this world single-handed. Several other persons, consciously or unconsciously, make their contribution to it. These conscious or unconscious associates and helpers primarily are a person's parents, wife and children. So these near relatives will also be allowed to participate in the blessings which will be bestowed upon believers for his good works.

R. 2   11. It will be announced to those who disbelieve: 'Greater was the abhorrence of Allāh, when you were called to the faith and you disbelieved, than your own abhorrence of yourselves[2597] *today*.'

اِنَّ الَّذِیْنَ كَفَرُوْا یُنَادَوْنَ لَمَقْتُ اللهِ اَكْبَرُ مِنْ مَّقْتِكُمْ اَنْفُسَكُمْ اِذْ تُدْعَوْنَ اِلَی الْاِیْمَانِ فَتَكْفُرُوْنَ ۝

12. They will say, 'Our Lord, [a]Thou hast caused us to die twice,[2598] and Thou hast given us life twice and now we confess our sins. Is, then, there a way out?'

قَالُوْا رَبَّنَاۤ اَمَتَّنَا اثْنَتَیْنِ وَاَحْیَیْتَنَا اثْنَتَیْنِ فَاعْتَرَفْنَا بِذُنُوْبِنَا فَهَلْ اِلٰی خُرُوْجٍ مِّنْ سَبِیْلٍ ۝

13. *It will be said to them*, 'This is because, [b]when Allāh alone was called upon, you disbelieved, but when partners were associated with Him, you believed. The decision *now* rests only with Allāh, the High, the Incomparably Great.'

ذٰلِكُمْ بِاَنَّهٗۤ اِذَا دُعِیَ اللهُ وَحْدَهٗ كَفَرْتُمْ وَاِنْ یُّشْرَكْ بِهٖ تُؤْمِنُوْا فَالْحُكْمُ لِلّٰهِ الْعَلِیِّ الْكَبِیْرِ ۝

14. [c]He it is Who shows you His Signs and sends down provision[2599] for you from heaven; but none pays heed save he who turns *to Allāh*.

هُوَ الَّذِیْ یُرِیْكُمْ اٰیٰتِهٖ وَیُنَزِّلُ لَكُمْ مِّنَ السَّمَآءِ رِزْقًا ۚ وَمَا یَتَذَكَّرُ اِلَّا مَنْ یُّنِیْبُ ۝

15. Call ye, then, upon Allāh, [d]devoting your obedience wholly *and* sincerely to Him, though the disbelievers may be averse *to it*.

فَادْعُوا اللهَ مُخْلِصِیْنَ لَهُ الدِّیْنَ وَلَوْ كَرِهَ الْكٰفِرُوْنَ ۝

---

[a]30 : 41.   [b]39 : 46.   [c]30 : 25.   [d]29 : 66;   31 : 33;   98 : 6.

2597. It is human nature that when a person is confronted with the evil consequences of his bad deeds, he begins to curse himself. The disbelievers are told that when they are face to face with punishment they feel disgusted with themselves. But the Merciful and Gracious God was more disgusted with them when they rejected His Message and opposed and persecuted His Messengers.

2598. The state before birth is a sort of death and the end of this life is the second death. The birth and the Resurrection are the two lives.

2599. All sustenance, spiritual as well as physical, descends from heaven. Water, upon which all life depends (21 : 31), comes down from heaven and so does revelation upon which man's spiritual life depends.

16. *He is* of most exalted attributes, Lord of the Throne.[2600] [a]He sends His word by His command to whomsoever of His servants He pleases, that He may give warning of the Day of Meeting,

رَفِيعُ الدَّرَجٰتِ ذُو الْعَرْشِ يُلْقِي الرُّوحَ مِنْ
اَمْرِهٖ عَلٰى مَنْ يَّشَآءُ مِنْ عِبَادِهٖ لِيُنْذِرَ يَوْمَ
التَّلَاقِ ﴿١٦﴾

17. The day when they will *all* come forth; [b]nothing concerning them will be hidden from Allāh. [c]'Whose is the Kingdom this day!' *It is* Allāh's, the One, the Most Supreme.

يَوْمَ هُمْ بٰرِزُوْنَ ۚ لَا يَخْفٰى عَلَى اللّٰهِ مِنْهُمْ
شَيْءٌ ۗ لِمَنِ الْمُلْكُ الْيَوْمَ ۗ لِلّٰهِ الْوَاحِدِ الْقَهَّارِ ﴿١٧﴾

18. [d]This day will every soul be requited for that which it has earned. No injustice this day! Surely, Allāh is Swift at reckoning.

اَلْيَوْمَ تُجْزٰى كُلُّ نَفْسٍ بِمَا كَسَبَتْ ۗ لَا ظُلْمَ
الْيَوْمَ ۗ اِنَّ اللّٰهَ سَرِيْعُ الْحِسَابِ ﴿١٨﴾

19. [e]And warn them of the day *that is* fast approaching, when the hearts will reach up to the throats, full of suppressed grief. The wrong-doers will have no warm friend, nor any intercessor whose *intercession* would be accepted.

وَاَنْذِرْهُمْ يَوْمَ الْاٰزِفَةِ اِذِ الْقُلُوْبُ لَدَى
الْحَنَاجِرِ كٰظِمِيْنَ ۚ مَا لِلظّٰلِمِيْنَ مِنْ حَمِيْمٍ
وَّلَا شَفِيْعٍ يُّطَاعُ ﴿١٩﴾

20. [f]He knows the treachery[2600A] of the eyes and what the breasts conceal.

يَعْلَمُ خَآئِنَةَ الْاَعْيُنِ وَمَا تُخْفِي الصُّدُوْرُ ﴿٢٠﴾

21. And Allāh judges with truth, but those upon whom they call beside Him cannot judge at all. Surely, Allāh is the All-Hearing, the All-Seeing.

وَاللّٰهُ يَقْضِيْ بِالْحَقِّ ۗ وَالَّذِيْنَ يَدْعُوْنَ مِنْ
دُوْنِهٖ لَا يَقْضُوْنَ بِشَيْءٍ ۗ اِنَّ اللّٰهَ هُوَ السَّمِيْعُ
الْبَصِيْرُ ﴿٢١﴾ ع

[a]16 : 3; 97 : 5. [b]3 : 6; 14 : 39. [c]18 : 45; 48 : 15; 82 : 20. [d]14 : 52; 45 : 23; 74 : 39. [e]19 : 40. [f]27 : 75; 28 : 70.

2600. The expression, *Dhu'l 'Arsh* (Lord of the Throne), is like *Dhu'l Raḥmah* (Lord of Mercy) and refutes the popular wrong notion that *'Arsh* is something material.

2600A. Look of anger, contempt or lust.

R. 3 22. [a]Have they not travelled in the earth *that they could see* what was the end of those before them? They were mightier than these in power and *they left* firmer marks in the earth. But Allāh seized them for their sins, and they had no one to protect them from Allāh.

أَوَلَمْ يَسِيرُوا فِي الْأَرْضِ فَيَنْظُرُوا كَيْفَ
كَانَ عَاقِبَةُ الَّذِينَ كَانُوا مِنْ قَبْلِهِمْ كَانُوا هُمْ أَشَدَّ
مِنْهُمْ قُوَّةً وَآثَارًا فِي الْأَرْضِ فَأَخَذَهُمُ اللّٰهُ بِذُنُوبِهِمْ
وَمَا كَانَ لَهُمْ مِنَ اللّٰهِ مِنْ وَاقٍ ﴿٢٢﴾

23. That was because [b]their Messengers came to them with manifest Signs but they disbelieved; so Allāh seized them. Surely, He is Powerful, Severe in punishment.

ذٰلِكَ بِأَنَّهُمْ كَانَتْ تَأْتِيهِمْ رُسُلُهُمْ بِالْبَيِّنٰتِ فَكَفَرُوا
فَأَخَذَهُمُ اللّٰهُ إِنَّهُ قَوِيٌّ شَدِيدُ الْعِقَابِ ﴿٢٣﴾

24. [c]And, surely, We sent Moses with Our Signs and manifest authority,

وَلَقَدْ أَرْسَلْنَا مُوسٰى بِآيٰتِنَا وَسُلْطٰنٍ مُبِينٍ ﴿٢٤﴾

25. Unto Pharaoh and Hāmān and Korah;[2601] but they said, '*He is* a sorcerer *and* a great liar.'

إِلٰى فِرْعَوْنَ وَهَامٰنَ وَقَارُونَ فَقَالُوا سٰحِرٌ كَذَّابٌ ﴿٢٥﴾

26. [d]And when he came to them with truth from Us, they said, [e]'Slay the sons of those who have believed with him, and let their women live.' But the design of the disbelievers is *ever* bound to fail.

فَلَمَّا جَاءَهُمْ بِالْحَقِّ مِنْ عِنْدِنَا قَالُوا اقْتُلُوا أَبْنَاءَ
الَّذِينَ آمَنُوا مَعَهُ وَاسْتَحْيُوا نِسَاءَهُمْ وَمَا كَيْدُ
الْكٰفِرِينَ إِلَّا فِي ضَلٰلٍ ﴿٢٦﴾

27. Pharaoh said, 'Leave me alone that I may slay Moses, and let him call on his Lord. [f]I fear lest he should change your religion or cause disorder to appear in the land.'

وَقَالَ فِرْعَوْنُ ذَرُونِي أَقْتُلْ مُوسٰى وَلْيَدْعُ
رَبَّهُ إِنِّي أَخَافُ أَنْ يُبَدِّلَ دِينَكُمْ أَوْ أَنْ يُظْهِرَ
فِي الْأَرْضِ الْفَسَادَ ﴿٢٧﴾

[a]12 : 110; 22 : 47; 35 : 45; 47 : 11. [b]23 : 45; 41 : 15.
[c]23 : 46. [d]29 : 40. [e]7 : 128; [f]20 : 64; 26 : 36.

2601. For Korah and Hāmān see 2198 and 2231. Every Prophet of God had had his Pharaoh, Hāmān and Korah. These names respectively may symbolise power, priesthood and material wealth, as Hāmān was the head of priestly class, and Korah an extremely rich man among Pharaoh's nobles. Unlimited political power, servile priesthood and uncontrolled capitalism are the three evils which have ever retarded and arrested the political, economic, moral and spiritual growth of a people, and naturally it is against these enemies of man that Heavenly Reformers have waged relentless war in every age.

28. And Moses said, [a]"I take refuge[2602] with my Lord and your Lord from every arrogant person who believes not in the Day of Reckoning.'

وَقَالَ مُوسَىٰ إِنِّي عُذْتُ بِرَبِّي وَرَبِّكُم مِّن كُلِّ
مُتَكَبِّرٍ لَّا يُؤْمِنُ بِيَوْمِ الْحِسَابِ ﴿٢٨﴾ ع

R. 4 29. And a believing man from among the people of Pharaoh, who kept hidden his faith,[2603] said, "Will you slay a man because he says, 'My Lord is Allāh,' while he has *also* brought you clear proofs from your Lord? [b]And if he be a liar, on him will be *the sin of* his lie; but if he is truthful, then some of that which he threatens you with will, *surely*, befall you. Certainly, Allāh guides not one who exceeds the bounds *and* is a great liar;'

وَقَالَ رَجُلٌ مُّؤْمِنٌ مِّنْ آلِ فِرْعَوْنَ يَكْتُمُ إِيمَانَهُ
أَتَقْتُلُونَ رَجُلًا أَن يَقُولَ رَبِّيَ اللَّهُ وَقَدْ جَاءَكُم
بِالْبَيِّنَاتِ مِن رَّبِّكُمْ ۖ وَإِن يَكُ كَاذِبًا فَعَلَيْهِ
كَذِبُهُ ۖ وَإِن يَكُ صَادِقًا يُصِبْكُم بَعْضُ الَّذِي
يَعِدُكُمْ ۖ إِنَّ اللَّهَ لَا يَهْدِي مَنْ هُوَ مُسْرِفٌ
كَذَّابٌ ﴿٢٩﴾

30. 'O my people, yours is the sovereignty this day, you being dominant in the land. But who will help us *and protect* us from the punishment of Allāh if it comes upon us?" Pharaoh said, 'I only point out to you that which I see myself, and I guide you only to the path of rectitude.'

يَا قَوْمِ لَكُمُ الْمُلْكُ الْيَوْمَ ظَاهِرِينَ فِي الْأَرْضِ
فَمَن يَنصُرُنَا مِن بَأْسِ اللَّهِ إِن جَاءَنَا ۚ قَالَ
فِرْعَوْنُ مَا أُرِيكُمْ إِلَّا مَا أَرَىٰ وَمَا أَهْدِيكُمْ
إِلَّا سَبِيلَ الرَّشَادِ ﴿٣٠﴾

31. And he who believed said, 'O my people, I fear for you *something* like the day *of destruction* of the *great* peoples *of the past;*

وَقَالَ الَّذِي آمَنَ يَا قَوْمِ إِنِّي أَخَافُ عَلَيْكُم مِّثْلَ
يَوْمِ الْأَحْزَابِ ﴿٣١﴾

32. [c]'Like that *which happened to* the people of Noah, and *the tribes* of 'Ād and Thamūd and those after them. And Allāh intends no injustice to *His* servants:

مِثْلَ دَأْبِ قَوْمِ نُوحٍ وَعَادٍ وَثَمُودَ وَالَّذِينَ
مِن بَعْدِهِمْ ۚ وَمَا اللَّهُ يُرِيدُ ظُلْمًا لِّلْعِبَادِ ﴿٣٢﴾

[a]44 : 21. [b]69 : 45, 47. [c]9 : 70; 14 : 10; 50 : 13-15.

2602. God is the ultimate refuge of His Prophets and the Elect. They knock at His door when they see darkness all around them and when the powers of evil are determined to exterminate the truth preached by them.

2603. The believing man had kept hidden his faith in order to give expression to it on a suitable occasion. The bold manner in which he expressed his belief and spoke to the people of Pharaoh shows that the concealment was not due to fear.

33. 'And O my people, I fear for you the day when people will call one another *for help*,[2604]

وَيٰقَوْمِ اِنِّیْٓ اَخَافُ عَلَیْکُمْ یَوْمَ التَّنَادِ ﴿٣٣﴾

34. 'The day when you shall turn back fleeing; and there will be no one to save you from Allāh's *wrath*. And for him whom Allāh leaves to go astray, there shall be no guide.'

یَوْمَ تُوَلُّوْنَ مُدْبِرِیْنَ ۚ مَا لَکُمْ مِّنَ اللّٰہِ مِنْ
عَاصِمٍ ۚ وَمَنْ یُّضْلِلِ اللّٰہُ فَمَا لَہٗ مِنْ ہَادٍ ﴿٣٤﴾

35. And Joseph, indeed, came to you before with clear proofs, but you ceased not to be in doubt concerning that with which he came to you till, when he died, you said, 'Allāh will never raise a Messenger after him.'[2605] Thus does Allāh adjudge as having gone astray every transgressor, doubter—

وَلَقَدْ جَآءَکُمْ یُوْسُفُ مِنْ قَبْلُ بِالْبَیِّنٰتِ فَمَا
زِلْتُمْ فِیْ شَکٍّ مِّمَّا جَآءَکُمْ بِہٖ ؕ حَتّٰۤی اِذَا ہَلَکَ قُلْتُمْ
لَنْ یَّبْعَثَ اللّٰہُ مِنْۢ بَعْدِہٖ رَسُوْلًا ؕ کَذٰلِکَ یُضِلُّ
اللّٰہُ مَنْ ہُوَ مُسْرِفٌ مُّرْتَابُ ﴿٣٥﴾

36. Those who dispute concerning the Signs of Allāh without any authority having come to them *from Allāh*. Grievously hateful is this in the Sight of Allāh and in the sight of those who believe. Thus does Allāh set a seal upon the heart of every arrogant, haughty *person*.

الَّذِیْنَ یُجَادِلُوْنَ فِیْۤ اٰیٰتِ اللّٰہِ بِغَیْرِ سُلْطٰنٍ اَتٰىہُمْ ؕ
کَبُرَ مَقْتًا عِنْدَ اللّٰہِ وَعِنْدَ الَّذِیْنَ اٰمَنُوْا ؕ کَذٰلِکَ
یَطْبَعُ اللّٰہُ عَلٰی کُلِّ قَلْبِ مُتَکَبِّرٍ جَبَّارٍ ﴿٣٦﴾

37. And Pharaoh said, [a]'O Hāmān, build thou for me a lofty tower that I may attain to the means *of access*—

وَقَالَ فِرْعَوْنُ یٰہَامٰنُ ابْنِ لِیْ صَرْحًا لَّعَلِّیْۤ
اَبْلُغُ الْاَسْبَابَ ﴿٣٧﴾

[a]28 : 39.

2604. The day when people will take fright and disperse in different directions; or when they will hate and oppose each other and will become separated, or when they will call one another for help (Aqrab).

2605. Prophets have been coming in the world from time immemorial but so perverse is men's thinking that whenever there comes a new Prophet they reject and oppose him and when he dies those who had believed in him said that no more Prophets would come and that the door of revelation is shut for ever.

38. 'The means *of access* to the heavens, [a]so that I may have a look at the God of Moses,[2606] and I, surely, consider him to be a liar.' And thus the evil of his conduct was made *to look* fair in the eyes of Pharaoh, and he was barred from the *right* path; and the design of Pharaoh was *bound* to end in ruin.

أَسْبَابَ السَّمٰوٰتِ فَأَطَّلِعَ إِلَىٰ إِلٰهِ مُوسٰى وَإِنِّي
لَأَظُنُّهُ كَاذِبًا ۚ وَكَذٰلِكَ زُيِّنَ لِفِرْعَوْنَ سُوءُ عَمَلِهِ
وَصُدَّ عَنِ السَّبِيلِ ۚ وَمَا كَيْدُ فِرْعَوْنَ إِلَّا فِي
تَبَابٍ ﴿٣٨﴾ ع

R. 5 39. And he who believed said, 'O my people, follow me. I will guide you to the path of rectitude;

وَقَالَ الَّذِي آمَنَ يٰقَوْمِ اتَّبِعُونِ أَهْدِكُمْ سَبِيلَ
الرَّشَادِ ﴿٣٩﴾

40. 'O my people, [b]this life of the world is but a *temporary* provision; and the Hereafter is certainly the permanent abode;[2607]

يٰقَوْمِ إِنَّمَا هٰذِهِ الْحَيٰوةُ الدُّنْيَا مَتَاعٌ وَإِنَّ الْآخِرَةَ
هِيَ دَارُ الْقَرَارِ ﴿٤٠﴾

41. [c]'Whoso does evil will be requited only with the like of it; [d]but whoso does good, whether male or female, and is a believer—these will enter the Garden; they will be provided therein without measure;[2608]

مَنْ عَمِلَ سَيِّئَةً فَلَا يُجْزٰى إِلَّا مِثْلَهَا ۚ وَمَنْ
عَمِلَ صَالِحًا مِّنْ ذَكَرٍ أَوْ أُنْثٰى وَهُوَ مُؤْمِنٌ فَأُولٰئِكَ
يَدْخُلُونَ الْجَنَّةَ يُرْزَقُونَ فِيهَا بِغَيْرِ حِسَابٍ ﴿٤١﴾

42. 'And O my people, how *strange* it is that I call you to salvation, and you call me to Fire;

وَيٰقَوْمِ مَا لِي أَدْعُوكُمْ إِلَى النَّجٰوةِ وَتَدْعُونَنِي
إِلَى النَّارِ ﴿٤٢﴾ النصف

43. 'You invite me that I should disbelieve in Allāh and should associate with Him that of which I have no knoweldge, while I invite you to the Mighty, the Great Forgiver;

تَدْعُونَنِي لِأَكْفُرَ بِاللّٰهِ وَأُشْرِكَ بِهِ مَا لَيْسَ
لِي بِهِ عِلْمٌ وَأَنَا أَدْعُوكُمْ إِلَى الْعَزِيزِ الْغَفَّارِ ﴿٤٣﴾

[a]28 : 39. [b]3 : 15; 198, 199; 9 : 38; 16 : 118; 28 : 61. [c]10 : 28; 4 : 124. [d]4 : 125.

2606. Pharaoh sarcastically said that he wanted to go up to heavens to have a peep at Moses's God, but God made him see a manifestation of His power in the depths of the sea.

2607. The speech of 'the believing man' shows that true believers are fully convinced of the righteousness of their cause. It is this rock-like faith which enables them to suffer gladly all sorts of hardships and privations.

2608. Whereas the requital of the evil deeds of disbelievers will be proportionate to their deeds, the reward of the good deeds of believers will be without limit or measure. This is the Islamic conception of Heaven and Hell.

44. 'Surely, that to which you call me has no title[2608A] to be called upon in this world or in the Hereafter; and that our return is certainly to Allāh and that the transgressors will be the inmates of the Fire;

لَا جَرَمَ اَنَّمَا تَدْعُوْنَنِيْٓ اِلَيْهِ لَيْسَ لَهٗ دَعْوَةٌ فِي الدُّنْيَا وَلَا فِي الْاٰخِرَةِ وَاَنَّ مَرَدَّنَآ اِلَى اللّٰهِ وَاَنَّ الْمُسْرِفِيْنَ هُمْ اَصْحٰبُ النَّارِ ﴿٤٤﴾

45. 'So you will soon remember what I say to you. And I entrust my affair to Allāh. Verily, Allāh watches over *His* servants.'

فَسَتَذْكُرُوْنَ مَآ اَقُوْلُ لَكُمْ ۗ وَاُفَوِّضُ اَمْرِيْٓ اِلَى اللّٰهِ ۗ اِنَّ اللّٰهَ بَصِيْرٌۢ بِالْعِبَادِ ﴿٤٥﴾

46. So Allāh preserved him from the evils of whatever they plotted, and a grievous punishment encompassed the people of Pharaoh—

فَوَقٰىهُ اللّٰهُ سَيِّاٰتِ مَا مَكَرُوْا وَحَاقَ بِاٰلِ فِرْعَوْنَ سُوْٓءُ الْعَذَابِ ﴿٤٦﴾

47. The Fire. They are exposed to it morning and evening.[2609] And on the day when the *appointed* Hour is come, *it will be said to the angels*, 'Cast Pharaoh's people into the severest punishment.'

اَلنَّارُ يُعْرَضُوْنَ عَلَيْهَا غُدُوًّا وَّعَشِيًّا ۚ وَيَوْمَ تَقُوْمُ السَّاعَةُ ۗ اَدْخِلُوْٓا اٰلَ فِرْعَوْنَ اَشَدَّ الْعَذَابِ ﴿٤٧﴾

48. [a]And when they will dispute with one another in the Fire, the weak will say to those who were proud, 'Verily, we were your followers; [b]will you then relieve us of a portion *of the torment* of the Fire?'

وَاِذْ يَتَحَآجُّوْنَ فِي النَّارِ فَيَقُوْلُ الضُّعَفٰٓؤُا لِلَّذِيْنَ اسْتَكْبَرُوْٓا اِنَّا كُنَّا لَكُمْ تَبَعًا فَهَلْ اَنْتُمْ مُّغْنُوْنَ عَنَّا نَصِيْبًا مِّنَ النَّارِ ﴿٤٨﴾

49. [c]Those, who were proud, will say, '*Now*, we are all in it. Allāh has already judged between *His* servants.'

قَالَ الَّذِيْنَ اسْتَكْبَرُوْٓا اِنَّا كُلٌّ فِيْهَآ ۙ اِنَّ اللّٰهَ قَدْ حَكَمَ بَيْنَ الْعِبَادِ ﴿٤٩﴾

[a]7 : 39; 14 : 22; 34 : 32. [b]14 : 22. [c]7 : 40; 34 : 33.

2608A. Is not fit to be called upon; ought not to be called upon; has no title or claim to be called upon.

2609. The implied reference in the words, 'They are exposed to it morning and evening,' may be to the punishment the disbelievers are made to suffer in *Barzakh* which is an intervening stage and where the realization of pain or joy is incomplete. The complete and full manifestation of Heaven and Hell will take place on the Day of Judgment.

50. And those in the Fire will say to the Keepers of Hell, 'Pray to your Lord that He may lighten for us the punishment for a day.'

وَقَالَ الَّذِيْنَ فِي النَّارِ لِخَزَنَةِ جَهَنَّمَ ادْعُوْا
رَبَّكُمْ يُخَفِّفْ عَنَّا يَوْمًا مِّنَ الْعَذَابِ ﴿٥٠﴾

51. *The Keepers* will say, [a]"Did not your Messengers come to you with manifest Signs?' They will say, 'Yea.' *The Keepers* will say, 'Then pray on.' but the prayer of disbelievers is of no avail.[2610]

قَالُوْٓا اَوَلَمْ تَكُ تَاْتِيْكُمْ رُسُلُكُمْ بِالْبَيِّنٰتِ ۭ قَالُوْا
بَلٰى ۭ قَالُوْا فَادْعُوْا ۚ وَمَا دُعٰٓؤُا الْكٰفِرِيْنَ اِلَّا فِيْ
ضَلٰلٍ ﴿٥١﴾ ع

R. 6 52. [c]Most surely, We help Our Messengers and those who believe,[2611] *both* in the present life and on the day when the witnesses will stand forth,

اِنَّا لَنَنْصُرُ رُسُلَنَا وَالَّذِيْنَ اٰمَنُوْا فِي الْحَيٰوةِ الدُّنْيَا
وَيَوْمَ يَقُوْمُ الْاَشْهَادُ ﴿٥٢﴾

53. The day when their pleading will not profit the wrongdoers, and [d]for them will be the curse and for them will be the evil abode

يَوْمَ لَا يَنْفَعُ الظّٰلِمِيْنَ مَعْذِرَتُهُمْ وَلَهُمُ اللَّعْنَةُ
وَلَهُمْ سُوْٓءُ الدَّارِ ﴿٥٣﴾

54. [e]And, indeed, We gave Moses the guidance, and made the Children of Israel heirs to the Book—

وَلَقَدْ اٰتَيْنَا مُوْسَى الْهُدٰى وَاَوْرَثْنَا بَنِيْٓ
اِسْرَآءِيْلَ الْكِتٰبَ ﴿٥٤﴾

55. A guidance and a reminder for men of understanding.

هُدًى وَّذِكْرٰى لِاُولِي الْاَلْبَابِ ﴿٥٥﴾

56. [g]So have patience. Surely, the promise of Allāh is true. And ask forgiveness[2612] for *them for* the

فَاصْبِرْ اِنَّ وَعْدَ اللّٰهِ حَقٌّ وَّاسْتَغْفِرْ لِذَنْبِكَ وَ

[a]23 : 106; 39 : 72; 67 : 9-10. [b]13 : 15. [c]10 : 104; 30 : 48; 58 : 22. [d]13 : 26. [e]2 : 88; 17 : 3; 23 : 50; 32 : 24. [f]30 : 61.

2610. The efforts and prayers of disbelievers against God's Prophets prove abortive, not that all their prayers as such are not accepted. God does answer the prayers of a distressed person when he calls upon Him whether he be a believer or a disbeliever (27 : 63).

2611. The verse holds out an emphatic promise to Divine Messengers and their followers that God's help and succour will always be with them and that, try as they might, the evil designs of disbelievers against them are bound to fail.

2612. *Ghafar al-Matā'a* means, he put the goods in the bag and covered and protected them. *Ghufrān* and *Maghfirah* are both infinitive nouns from *Ghafara* and mean, protection and preservation. *Mighfar* means helmet, because it protects the head. *Dhanb* means, such natural failings or frailties as adhere to human nature or such errors as bring about harmful results. *Dhanaba-hū* means, he followed his trail, not quitting his track (Lane & Mufradāt). *Istighfār* is not only needed by ordinary believers but also by holy men of God, even by God's great Prophets. While the former offer *Istighfār* to seek protection against wrongs *they have done* thee[2612A] and glorify thy Lord with His praise in the evening and in the morning.

سَبِّحْ بِحَمْدِ رَبِّكَ بِالْعَشِيِّ وَالْإِبْكَارِ ﴿٥٦﴾

57. [a]Those who dispute concerning the Signs of Allāh without any authority having come to them *from Allāh*—there is nothing in their breasts but *an ambition* to become great[2613] which they will never attain. So seek refuge in Allāh. Surely, He is the All-Hearing, the All-Seeing.

إِنَّ الَّذِينَ يُجَادِلُونَ فِي آيَاتِ اللَّهِ بِغَيْرِ سُلْطَانٍ
أَتَاهُمْ إِنْ فِي صُدُورِهِمْ إِلَّا كِبْرٌ مَا هُمْ بِبَالِغِيهِ
فَاسْتَعِذْ بِاللَّهِ إِنَّهُ هُوَ السَّمِيعُ الْبَصِيرُ ﴿٥٧﴾

58. Certainly, the creation of the heavens and the earth is greater than the creation of mankind;[2614] but most men know not.

لَخَلْقُ السَّمَاوَاتِ وَالْأَرْضِ أَكْبَرُ مِنْ خَلْقِ النَّاسِ
وَلَٰكِنَّ أَكْثَرَ النَّاسِ لَا يَعْلَمُونَ ﴿٥٨﴾

59. [b]And the blind and the seeing are not equal; neither are those who believe and do good deeds *equal to* those who do evil. Little do you reflect.

وَمَا يَسْتَوِي الْأَعْمَىٰ وَالْبَصِيرُ وَالَّذِينَ آمَنُوا
وَعَمِلُوا الصَّالِحَاتِ وَلَا الْمُسِيءُ ۚ قَلِيلًا مَا
تَتَذَكَّرُونَ ﴿٥٩﴾

60. [c]The Hour *of punishment* will, surely, come; there is no doubt about it; yet most men believe not.

إِنَّ السَّاعَةَ لَآتِيَةٌ لَا رَيْبَ فِيهَا وَلَٰكِنَّ أَكْثَرَ
النَّاسِ لَا يُؤْمِنُونَ ﴿٦٠﴾

[a]40 : 36. [b]13 : 17; 35 : 20; 39 : 10. [c]15 : 86; 20 : 16.

future sins as well as from the evil consequences of past lapses, the latter seek protection from human shortcomings and weaknesses that may hinder the progress of their cause. The Prophets also are human and though they are immune to sin, yet they, too, are heirs to human failings and frailties; so they also need offering *Istighfār* to seek Divine help and protection. See also 2765.

2612A. *Dhanbaka*, means, sins committed against thee ; sins alleged by thy enemies to have been committed by thee ; thine human shortcomings and frailties. See 2765.

2613. *Kibr* signifies pride; desire or ambition to become great; great designs (Lane).

2614. According to learned scholars and Commentators, such as Baghvī, Ibn Ḥajr and others, the word *al-Nās* in the verse signifies the *Dajjāl*. This interpretation finds its confirmation in a well-known saying of the Holy Prophet, *viz.*, 'From the creation of Adam to the Day of Resurrection there has not been a greater creation than that of the *Dajjāl*' (**Bukhārī**). This *ḥadīth* points to the mightiness and all-powerfulness of the *Dajjāl*; and as he is a great deceiver and beguiler, the Faithful are warned to be on their guard against being deceived or intimidated by his glamour and material glory. In view of this *ḥadīth* the implication of the verse seems to be that the forces of darkness, of which the *Dajjāl* is the greatest representative, however, mighty and powerful they may be, will not be able to retard the progress of Islām, and that these forces will eventually be vanquished by it. The verse may also mean that quite insignificant as compared to the great universe created by God, man in his conceit and arrogance refuses to respond to the Divine Call.

61. [a]And your Lord says, 'Pray unto Me; I will answer your *prayer*. But those who are too proud to worship Me will, surely, enter Hell, despised.'

وقال ربكم ادعوني أستجب لكم إن الذين
يستكبرون عن عبادتي سيدخلون جهنم داخرين ٦١ ع

R. 7 62. [b]Allāh is He Who has made the night for you that you may rest therein, and the day *to enable you* to see. Verily, Allāh is Bountiful to mankind, yet most men are ungrateful.

الله الذي جعل لكم الليل لتسكنوا فيه والنهار
مبصرا إن الله لذو فضل على الناس ولكن
أكثر الناس لا يشكرون ٦٢

63. [c]Such is Allāh, your Lord, the Creator of all things. There is no god but He. How then, are, you turned away?

ذلكم الله ربكم خالق كل شيء لا إله إلا هو
فأنى تؤفكون ٦٣

64. Thus, indeed, are turned away those who deny the Signs of Allāh.

كذلك يؤفك الذين كانوا بآيات الله يجحدون ٦٤

65. Allāh is He Who has made for you the earth a resting-place, and the heaven a structure *for protection*, [d]and has given you shapes and made your shapes perfect, and has provided you with pure things. Such is Allāh, your Lord. So blessed is Allāh, the Lord of the worlds.

الله الذي جعل لكم الأرض قرارا والسماء
بناء وصوركم فأحسن صوركم ورزقكم
من الطيبات ذلكم الله ربكم فتبارك الله
رب العالمين ٦٥

66. He is the Living *God*. There is no god but He. [e]So pray unto Him, devoting your worship wholly and sincerely to Him. All praise belongs to Allāh, the Lord of the worlds.

هو الحي لا إله إلا هو فادعوه مخلصين له
الدين الحمد لله رب العالمين ٦٦

67. [f]Say, 'I have been forbidden to worship those whom you call upon beside Allāh since there have come clear proofs unto me from my Lord; and I have been commanded to submit myself *solely* to the Lord of the worlds.'

قل إني نهيت أن أعبد الذين تدعون من
دون الله لما جاءني البينات من ربي وأمرت
أن أسلم لرب العالمين ٦٧

[a]2 : 187; 6 : 42; 25 : 78; 27 : 63. [b]17 : 13; 41 : 38. [c]6 : 103. [d]7 : 12; 23 : 15; 64 : 4. [e]39 : 12; 98 : 6. [f]6 : 57; 39 : 65.

68. He it is [a]Who created you from dust,[2615] then from a sperm-drop, then from a clot; then He brings you forth as a child; then *He lets you grow*, so that you attain your full strength; and *afterward* become old—though some among you are caused to die before—and that you may reach a term appointed and that you may learn wisdom.

هُوَ الَّذِیۡ خَلَقَکُمۡ مِّنۡ تُرَابٍ ثُمَّ مِنۡ نُّطۡفَۃٍ
ثُمَّ مِنۡ عَلَقَۃٍ ثُمَّ یُخۡرِجُکُمۡ طِفۡلًا ثُمَّ لِتَبۡلُغُوۡۤا
اَشُدَّکُمۡ ثُمَّ لِتَکُوۡنُوۡا شُیُوۡخًا ۚ وَ مِنۡکُمۡ مَّنۡ یُّتَوَفّٰی
مِنۡ قَبۡلُ وَ لِتَبۡلُغُوۡۤا اَجَلًا مُّسَمًّی وَّ لَعَلَّکُمۡ
تَعۡقِلُوۡنَ ﴿۶۸﴾

69. [b]He it is Who gives life and causes death. [c]And when He decrees a thing, He says concerning it, 'Be !' and it comes into being.[2616]

هُوَ الَّذِیۡ یُحۡیٖ وَ یُمِیۡتُ ۚ فَاِذَا قَضٰۤی اَمۡرًا فَاِنَّمَا
یَقُوۡلُ لَہٗ کُنۡ فَیَکُوۡنُ ﴿۶۹﴾ ع

R. 8 70. [d]Seest thou not those who dispute concerning the Signs of Allāh? How they are being turned away *from the truth!*

اَلَمۡ تَرَ اِلَی الَّذِیۡنَ یُجَادِلُوۡنَ فِیۡۤ اٰیٰتِ اللّٰہِ ؕ اَنّٰی
یُصۡرَفُوۡنَ ﴿ۚۛ۷۰﴾

71. Those who reject the Book and that with which We sent Our Messengers. But soon will they come to know,

الَّذِیۡنَ کَذَّبُوۡا بِالۡکِتٰبِ وَ بِمَاۤ اَرۡسَلۡنَا بِہٖ رُسُلَنَا ۟ۛ
فَسَوۡفَ یَعۡلَمُوۡنَ ﴿ۙ۷۱﴾

72. [e]When the iron-collars will be round their necks, and chains *too. And* they will be dragged

اِذِ الۡاَغۡلٰلُ فِیۡۤ اَعۡنَاقِہِمۡ وَ السَّلٰسِلُ ؕ یُسۡحَبُوۡنَ ﴿ۙ۷۲﴾

73. [f]Into boiling water; then in the Fire will they be burnt.

فِی الۡحَمِیۡمِ ۬ۙ ثُمَّ فِی النَّارِ یُسۡجَرُوۡنَ ﴿ۚ۷۳﴾

74. Then it will be said to them, 'Where are those who were your associate gods

ثُمَّ قِیۡلَ لَہُمۡ اَیۡنَ مَا کُنۡتُمۡ تُشۡرِکُوۡنَ ﴿ۙ۷۴﴾

[a]22 : 6; 23 : 13—15; 35 : 12; [b]2 : 29; 22 : 67; 30 : 41.
[c]2 : 118; 3 : 48; 16 : 41; 36 : 83. [d]13 : 14; 22 : 9; 31 : 21. [e]36 : 9; 76 : 5.
[f]55 : 45; 78 : 26.

2615. See 1932.

2616. It is the will and decree of God, Who gives life and causes death that a people —the Arabs—who were morally and spiritually as good as dead, should now rise to a new life through the Holy Prophet; and none can thwart and frustrate Allāh's decree.

75. 'Beside Allāh?' They will say, [a]"They have vanished away from us. Nay, we never prayed to anything *beside Allāh* before.' Thus will Allāh confound the disbelievers.

مِنْ دُوْنِ اللّٰهِ ۭ قَالُوْا ضَلُّوْا عَنَّا بَلْ لَّمْ نَكُنْ
نَّدْعُوْا مِنْ قَبْلُ شَيْـًٔا ۭ كَذٰلِكَ يُضِلُّ اللّٰهُ
الْكٰفِرِيْنَ ﴿٧٥﴾

76. That is because you exulted in the earth without justification, and because you behaved insolently.

ذٰلِكُمْ بِمَا كُنْتُمْ تَفْرَحُوْنَ فِي الْاَرْضِ بِغَيْرِ
الْحَقِّ وَبِمَا كُنْتُمْ تَمْرَحُوْنَ ﴿٧٦﴾

77. [b]Enter ye the gates of Hell, to abide therein. And evil is the abode of the arrogant.

اُدْخُلُوْٓا اَبْوَابَ جَهَنَّمَ خٰلِدِيْنَ فِيْهَا ۚ فَبِئْسَ
مَثْوَى الْمُتَكَبِّرِيْنَ ﴿٧٧﴾

78. So be thou patient. Surely, the promise of Allāh is bound to be fulfilled. [c]And whether We show thee *in this life* part of what We have promised them or whether We cause thee to die *before the fulfilment of Our promise*, to Us will they be brought back.[2617]

فَاصْبِرْ اِنَّ وَعْدَ اللّٰهِ حَقٌّ ۚ فَاِمَّا نُرِيَنَّكَ بَعْضَ
الَّذِيْ نَعِدُهُمْ اَوْ نَتَوَفَّيَنَّكَ فَاِلَيْنَا يُرْجَعُوْنَ ﴿٧٨﴾

79. And We, indeed, sent Messengers before thee; [d]of them are some whom We have mentioned to thee; and of them are some whom We have not mentioned to thee, [e]and it is not possible for any Messenger to bring a Sign except by the leave of Allāh.[2618] But when Allāh's decree comes, the matter is decided with justice and then there perish those who utter falsehoods.

وَلَقَدْ اَرْسَلْنَا رُسُلًا مِّنْ قَبْلِكَ مِنْهُمْ مَّنْ قَصَصْنَا
عَلَيْكَ وَمِنْهُمْ مَّنْ لَّمْ نَقْصُصْ عَلَيْكَ ۭ وَمَا كَانَ
لِرَسُوْلٍ اَنْ يَّاْتِيَ بِاٰيَةٍ اِلَّا بِاِذْنِ اللّٰهِ ۚ فَاِذَا جَاۗءَ
اَمْرُ اللّٰهِ قُضِيَ بِالْحَقِّ وَخَسِرَ هُنَالِكَ الْمُبْطِلُوْنَ ﴿٧٩﴾ ع

[a]41 : 49. [b]16 : 30; 39 : 73. [c]10 : 47; 13 : 41; 43 : 43.
[d]4 : 165. [e]13 : 39; 14 : 12.

2617. The verse embodies two religious principles : (1) Truth must prevail in the long run, but before success comes to men of God they have to go through severe trials and tribulations and their faith has to be tested and proved up to the mark. (2) Prophecies containing warnings of punishment to disbelievers are conditional and subject to postponement, revocation or even cancellation. The word *Ba'd* signifies that not all prophecies containing threats are literally fulfilled. They change with the change in the attitude of disbelievers.

2618. Though the prophecies containing warnings and threats meant for disbelievers are subject to postponement, revocation or cancellation, yet if, by closing the door of repentance upon themselves, they make themselves deserving of Divine punishment, they are punished. But it is not for the Prophet to say when and how they will be punished.

R. 9 80. [a]Allāh is He Who has made cattle for you, that you may ride on some of them, and eat *of the flesh* of some of them—

اَللّٰهُ الَّذِیْ جَعَلَ لَكُمُ الْاَنْعَامَ لِتَرْكَبُوْا مِنْهَا وَ مِنْهَا تَاْكُلُوْنَ ﴿۸۰﴾

81. [b]And you derive *other* benefits from them—and that, by means of them you may satisfy any desire[2619] *that may be* in your breasts. And on them and on ships are you borne.

وَ لَكُمْ فِیْهَا مَنَافِعُ وَ لِتَبْلُغُوْا عَلَیْهَا حَاجَةً فِیْ صُدُوْرِكُمْ وَ عَلَیْهَا وَ عَلَی الْفُلْكِ تُحْمَلُوْنَ ﴿۸۱﴾

82. And He shows you His Signs; which, then, of the Signs of Allāh will you deny?

وَ یُرِیْكُمْ اٰیٰتِهٖ فَاَیَّ اٰیٰتِ اللّٰهِ تُنْكِرُوْنَ ﴿۸۲﴾

83. [c]Have they not travelled in the earth that they might see what was the end of those who were before them? They were more numerous than these, and mightier in power and *left firmer* traces in the earth. But all that which they earned was of no avail to them.

اَفَلَمْ یَسِیْرُوْا فِی الْاَرْضِ فَیَنْظُرُوْا كَیْفَ كَانَ عَاقِبَةُ الَّذِیْنَ مِنْ قَبْلِهِمْ كَانُوْۤا اَكْثَرَ مِنْهُمْ وَ اَشَدَّ قُوَّةً وَّ اٰثَارًا فِی الْاَرْضِ فَمَاۤ اَغْنٰی عَنْهُمْ مَّا كَانُوْا یَكْسِبُوْنَ ﴿۸۳﴾

84. And when their Messengers came to them with manifest Signs, they exulted in the *little* knowledge they had. And that at which they mocked encompassed them.

فَلَمَّا جَآءَتْهُمْ رُسُلُهُمْ بِالْبَیِّنٰتِ فَرِحُوْا بِمَا عِنْدَهُمْ مِّنَ الْعِلْمِ وَ حَاقَ بِهِمْ مَّا كَانُوْا بِهٖ یَسْتَهْزِءُوْنَ ﴿۸۴﴾

85. [d]And when they saw Our punishment they said, 'We believe in Allāh alone and we reject all that which we used to associate with Him.'

فَلَمَّا رَاَوْا بَاْسَنَا قَالُوْۤا اٰمَنَّا بِاللّٰهِ وَحْدَهٗ وَ كَفَرْنَا بِمَا كُنَّا بِهٖ مُشْرِكِیْنَ ﴿۸۵﴾

86. [e]But their faith could not profit them when they saw Our punishment.[2620] This is Allāh's law that has *ever* been in operation in respect of His servants. And thus perished those who disbelieved.

فَلَمْ یَكُ یَنْفَعُهُمْ اِیْمَانُهُمْ لَمَّا رَاَوْا بَاْسَنَا سُنَّتَ اللّٰهِ الَّتِیْ قَدْ خَلَتْ فِیْ عِبَادِهٖ وَ خَسِرَ هُنَالِكَ الْكٰفِرُوْنَ ﴿۸۶﴾ ع

[a]6 : 143; 16 : 6; 23 : 22; 36 : 72-74. [b]16 : 6-8; 23 : 22-23; 36 : 73-74. [c]16 : 37; 27 : 70; 30 : 43. [d]10 : 52, 91. [e]10 : 92.

2619. *Ḥājah* means, want; need; desire; object of want or need (Lane).

2620. When the cup of the iniquities of disbelievers becomes full, and the Divine decree that they should be punished comes into operation, no profession of faith on their part is of any avail, and repentance then is too late.

CHAPTER 41

ḤĀ MĪM AL-SAJDAH

(*Revealed before Hijrah*)

Date of Revelation and Context

The *Sūrah* bears the title of Ḥā Mīm Al-Sajdah. It is also known as Fuṣṣliat. Being the second of the seven Chapters of *Ḥā Mīm* group, it possesses a very close resemblance with the *Sūrah* that goes before it and those that follow it in style and subject-matter, and like them it was revealed at Mecca at a time when opposition to Islām had grown strong, determined and persistent. While towards the close of the preceding *Sūrah* the disbelievers were warned that when Divine punishment overtook them, belief and repentance would be of no avail, the present *Sūrah* opens with the statement that it is those people, who close the avenues of their hearts and persistently refuse to listen to the Qur'ān, that render themselves deserving of punishment. It further declares that the Qur'ān contains all that is necessary for the moral development of man and explains fully and completely all its tenets, teachings and principles in the most explicit, expressive and intelligible language and adduces as an argument the creation of the universe in six periods or stages to prove Divine Unity, and proceeds to say that all Prophets brought the self-same Message of Divine Unity. Even the Prophets of antiquity like Hūd and Ṣāliḥ preached the same doctrine. Next, it is stated that whenever a new Prophet comes in the world, the leaders of disbelief try to stifle the voice of Truth by raising a loud hue and cry against it and seek to confuse the minds of the people by using all sorts of guiles and subterfuges; but falsehood has never succeeded in drowning the voice of Truth. Likewise will the efforts of opponents of the Holy Prophet fail against him. The angels of God will descend upon those who believe in him and stand by him through thick and thin, consoling and comforting them, blessing their endeavours with success and telling them that they will inherit Divine blessings in this world and will be God's guests in the next. The *Sūrah* proceeds to say that night of sin and iniquity will pass away and the sun of righteousness and God's Unity will shine upon Arabia, and a people, who for centuries had groped in the darkness of ignorance, will receive a new life, and Islām, after having taken deep roots in Arabia, will spread and expand to the farthest ends of the earth. This marvellous change will come about through the noble teaching of this wonderful Book—the Qur'ān. God alone knows how and when the seed of truth that the Holy Prophet has sown in the soil of Arabia will develop and grow into a mighty tree, but grow it must, and under its cool and comfortable shade great nations will take rest.

ایاتها (٤١) سُوۡرَةُ حٰمٓ السَّجۡدَةِ مَكِّيَّةٌ ركوعاتها

1. [a]In the name of Allāh, the Gracious, the Merciful.

بِسۡمِ اللّٰهِ الرَّحۡمٰنِ الرَّحِیۡمِ ﴿١﴾

2. [b]Ḥā Mīm.[2620A]

حٰمٓ ﴿٢﴾

3. [c]*This Qur'ān is* a revelation from the Gracious, the Merciful *God*,

تَنۡزِیۡلٌ مِّنَ الرَّحۡمٰنِ الرَّحِیۡمِ ﴿٣﴾

4. [d]A Book, the verses of which have been expounded in detail *and* which will be repeatedly read, *couched* in clear, eloquent language, for a people who have knowledge,

کِتٰبٌ فُصِّلَتۡ اٰیٰتُهٗ قُرۡاٰنًا عَرَبِیًّا لِّقَوۡمٍ یَّعۡلَمُوۡنَ ﴿٤﴾

5. [e]A bringer of glad tidings and a warner. But most of them turn away and they hear not.

بَشِیۡرًا وَّ نَذِیۡرًا ۚ فَاَعۡرَضَ اَکۡثَرُهُمۡ فَهُمۡ لَا
یَسۡمَعُوۡنَ ﴿٥﴾

6. [f]And they say, 'Our hearts are *secure* under coverings against that to which thou callest us, and in our ears there is a heaviness,[2621] and between us and thee there is a veil. So carry on thy work; we, too, are working.'

وَ قَالُوۡا قُلُوۡبُنَا فِیۡۤ اَکِنَّةٍ مِّمَّا تَدۡعُوۡنَاۤ اِلَیۡهِ
وَ فِیۡۤ اٰذَانِنَا وَقۡرٌ وَّ مِنۡۢ بَیۡنِنَا وَ بَیۡنِکَ حِجَابٌ
فَاعۡمَلۡ اِنَّنَا عٰمِلُوۡنَ ﴿٦﴾

7. [g]Say, 'I am only a mortal like you. It is revealed to me that your God is One God; so go ye straight to Him *without deviating*, and ask forgiveness of Him.' And woe to the idolaters,

قُلۡ اِنَّمَاۤ اَنَا بَشَرٌ مِّثۡلُکُمۡ یُوۡحٰۤی اِلَیَّ اَنَّمَاۤ اِلٰـهُکُمۡ
اِلٰهٌ وَّاحِدٌ فَاسۡتَقِیۡمُوۡۤا اِلَیۡهِ وَ اسۡتَغۡفِرُوۡهُ ؕ وَ وَیۡلٌ
لِّلۡمُشۡرِکِیۡنَ ﴿٧﴾

[a]1:1. [b]40:2; 42:2; 43:2; 44:2; 45:2; 46:2. [c]32:3; 40:3; 45:3; 46:3. [d]11:2. [e]5:20; 25:57; 35:25; 48:9. [f]6:26; 17:47; 18:58. [g]14:12; 18:111; 21:109.

2620A. See 2592.

2621. The verse depicts disbelievers as saying sarcastically to the Holy Prophet, 'your teaching is too good for us sinners to accept and your ideals too sublime to be understood and realized by us.' If the words are taken to be spoken seriously they would mean, 'We are fully determined not to accept your teaching. We have closed all the avenues of our hearts, eyes and ears against it.'

8. Who give not the *Zakāt*, and they it is who disbelieve in the Hereafter.

الَّذِيْنَ لَا يُؤْتُوْنَ الزَّكٰوةَ وَهُمْ بِالْاٰخِرَةِ هُمْ كٰفِرُوْنَ ﴿٨﴾

9. [a]*As to* those who believe and do righteous deeds, for them, *surely*, is a reward that will never end.

اِنَّ الَّذِيْنَ اٰمَنُوْا وَعَمِلُوا الصّٰلِحٰتِ لَهُمْ اَجْرٌ غَيْرُ
ع ٩/١٥ مَمْنُوْنٍ ﴿٩﴾

R. 2 10. Say, 'Do you really disbelieve in Him Who created the earth in two days?[2622] And do you set up equals to Him?' That is the Lord of the worlds.

قُلْ اَئِنَّكُمْ لَتَكْفُرُوْنَ بِالَّذِيْ خَلَقَ الْاَرْضَ فِيْ
يَوْمَيْنِ وَتَجْعَلُوْنَ لَهٗۤ اَنْدَادًا ؕ ذٰلِكَ رَبُّ
الْعٰلَمِيْنَ ﴿١٠﴾

11. [b]He placed therein firm mountains rising above its *surface*, and blessed it *with abundance*, and provided therein its foods in proper measure in four days[2623]—alike for *all* seekers.[2624]

وَجَعَلَ فِيْهَا رَوَاسِيَ مِنْ فَوْقِهَا وَبٰرَكَ فِيْهَا
وَقَدَّرَ فِيْهَآ اَقْوَاتَهَا فِيْۤ اَرْبَعَةِ اَيَّامٍ ؕ سَوَآءً
لِّلسَّآئِلِيْنَ ﴿١١﴾

[a]11 : 12; 84 : 26; 95 : 7. [b]13 : 4; 15 : 20; 77 : 28.

2622. It is not possible to surmise as to the length of these 'two days.' They may have extended over thousands of years. Even in the Qur'ān *Yaum* (day) has been spoken of as equal to a thousand years (22 : 48), or even equal to fifty thousand years (70 : 5). The making of the earth in two days may signify the two stages through which the earth passed from a formless matter into a gradually evolved form after it had cooled down and become condensed.

2623. The 'two days' or stages mentioned in the previous verse through which the earth had to pass before it assumed its present form are included among the 'four days' mentioned in the present verse, the additional 'two days' signifying the two stages of the placing on it of mountains, rivers, etc., and the growth on it of vegetable and animal life. See also v. 13. The words, 'provided therein its foods in proper measure,' signify that the earth is and will ever remain to be fully capable of providing food for *all* the creatures that live on it.

2624. The expression, 'alike for all seekers,' may signify that the foods which God has provided in the earth are equally accessible to all seekers who try to get them according to the laws of nature. It may also mean that all the physical needs and requirements of man have been adequately met in the foods that grow out of earth. So the fear that the earth may not some day be able to grow sufficient food for the fast increasing population of the world is groundless. 'The world can provide food, fibre and all other agricultural requirements for 28 billion people, ten times the world's present population' (Prof. Colin Clark, Director of the Agricultural Economics Research Institute of Oxford University). Only recently the United Nations Food and Agricultural Organization pointed out in its report, 'The State of Food and Agriculture, 1959,' that the world's food supply grows twice as fast as its population.

12. Then He turned to the heaven, while it was *something like* smoke, and said to it and to the earth; 'Come ye both of you *in obedience*, willingly or unwillingly.'[2625] They said, 'We come willingly.[2626]

ثُمَّ اسْتَوٰى إِلَى السَّمَاءِ وَهِيَ دُخَانٌ فَقَالَ لَهَا
وَلِلْأَرْضِ ائْتِيَا طَوْعًا أَوْ كَرْهًا قَالَتَا أَتَيْنَا
طَائِعِينَ ﴿١٢﴾

13. So He completed them *in the form of* seven heavens in two days,[2627] and He revealed to each heaven its function. [a]And We adorned the lowest heaven with lamps *for light* and *provided it with the means of* protection. That is the decree of the Mighty, the All-Knowing.

فَقَضٰهُنَّ سَبْعَ سَمٰوٰتٍ فِي يَوْمَيْنِ وَأَوْحٰى
فِي كُلِّ سَمَاءٍ أَمْرَهَا ۚ وَزَيَّنَّا السَّمَاءَ الدُّنْيَا
بِمَصَابِيحَ ۖ وَحِفْظًا ۚ ذٰلِكَ تَقْدِيرُ الْعَزِيزِ
الْعَلِيمِ ﴿١٣﴾

14. But if they turn away, then say, [b]'I warn you of a destructive punishment like the punishment which *overtook* 'Ād and Thamūd.'

فَإِنْ أَعْرَضُوا فَقُلْ أَنْذَرْتُكُمْ صٰعِقَةً مِّثْلَ
صٰعِقَةِ عَادٍ وَّثَمُودَ ﴿١٤﴾

15. When their Messengers came to them from before them and from behind them,[2627A] *admonishing them*, 'Worship none but Allāh,' they said, 'If our Lord had *so* willed, He would, certainly; have sent down angels. So we do disbelieve in that with which you have been sent.'

إِذْ جَاءَتْهُمُ الرُّسُلُ مِنْ بَيْنِ أَيْدِيهِمْ وَمِنْ
خَلْفِهِمْ أَلَّا تَعْبُدُوا إِلَّا اللّٰهَ ۖ قَالُوا لَوْ شَاءَ رَبُّنَا
لَأَنْزَلَ مَلٰئِكَةً فَإِنَّا بِمَا أُرْسِلْتُمْ بِهِ كٰفِرُونَ ﴿١٥﴾

[a]15 : 17; 37 : 7; 67 : 6. [b]40 : 31-32.

2625. *Kurhan* or *Karhan* in both forms is infinitive-noun from *Kariha* (he disliked), the former (*Kurhan*) meaning, what you yourself do not like and the latter (*Karhan*) meaning, what you are compelled to do against your will by someone else. *Fa'ala-hū Karhan* means, he did it unwillingly (Lane).

2626. The verse signifies that everything in the universe is subject to certain laws which it obeys and according to which it works. It has no discretion. It is man alone who has been endowed with volition or discretion to obey or defy the Divine laws and it is not unoften that he uses his discretion to his detriment. This is also the meaning and significance of 33 : 73.

2627. In vv. 10 and 11 it is stated that the making of the earth took two days and the placing on it of the mountains, rivers, etc., and of vegetable and animal life, another two days. In the present verse, however, it is mentioned that like the earth the solar system with its planets and satellites took two days to become complete. Thus the whole universe came into existence in six days or periods which is quite in harmony with vv. 7 : 55 and 50 : 39. Taking the word *Yaum* in the sense of 'stage,' the three vv. 10, 11 and 13 taken together would mean that the whole physical universe was completed in six stages. After the creation of the universe, man came into existence and his creation also was completed in six stages (23 : 13-15).

2627A. Divine Messengers continued to appear during the whole span of their national life.

16. As for 'Ād, they behaved arrogantly in the earth without any justification and sāid, 'Who is mightier than we in power?' Do they not see that Allāh, Who created them, is mightier than they in power? Still they continued to deny Our Signs.

فَأَمَّا عَادٌ فَاسْتَكْبَرُوا فِي الْأَرْضِ بِغَيْرِ الْحَقِّ وَ
قَالُوا مَنْ أَشَدُّ مِنَّا قُوَّةً ۖ أَوَلَمْ يَرَوْا أَنَّ اللَّهَ
الَّذِي خَلَقَهُمْ هُوَ أَشَدُّ مِنْهُمْ قُوَّةً ۖ وَكَانُوا
بِآيَاتِنَا يَجْحَدُونَ ﴿١٦﴾

17. So We sent upon them a furious wind for several ominous days, that We might make them taste the punishment of humiliation in this life. And the punishment of the Hereafter will, surely, be more humiliating, and they will not be helped.

فَأَرْسَلْنَا عَلَيْهِمْ رِيحًا صَرْصَرًا فِي أَيَّامٍ نَحِسَاتٍ
لِنُذِيقَهُمْ عَذَابَ الْخِزْيِ فِي الْحَيَاةِ الدُّنْيَا ۖ
وَلَعَذَابُ الْآخِرَةِ أَخْزَىٰ ۖ وَهُمْ لَا يُنْصَرُونَ ﴿١٧﴾

18. And as for Thamūd, We guided them, but they preferred blindness to guidance, so the calamity of a humiliating punishment seized them, on account of what they had earned.

وَأَمَّا ثَمُودُ فَهَدَيْنَاهُمْ فَاسْتَحَبُّوا الْعَمَىٰ عَلَى
الْهُدَىٰ فَأَخَذَتْهُمْ صَاعِقَةُ الْعَذَابِ الْهُونِ
بِمَا كَانُوا يَكْسِبُونَ ﴿١٨﴾

19. And We saved those who believed and acted righteously.

وَنَجَّيْنَا الَّذِينَ آمَنُوا وَكَانُوا يَتَّقُونَ ﴿١٩﴾ ع

R. 3 20. And *warn them of* the day when [a]the enemies of Allāh will be gathered together *and driven* to the Fire, and they will be divided into groups;

وَيَوْمَ يُحْشَرُ أَعْدَاءُ اللَّهِ إِلَى النَّارِ فَهُمْ
يُوزَعُونَ ﴿٢٠﴾

21. Till, when they reach it, [b]their ears and their eyes and their skins will bear witness against them as to what they had been doing.[2628]

حَتَّىٰ إِذَا مَا جَاءُوهَا شَهِدَ عَلَيْهِمْ سَمْعُهُمْ وَ
أَبْصَارُهُمْ وَجُلُودُهُمْ بِمَا كَانُوا يَعْمَلُونَ ﴿٢١﴾

[a]27 : 84. [b]24 : 25; 36 : 66.

2628. The ears and eyes of the guilty will bear witness against disbelievers in three ways : (1) The evil consequences of their actions will take a physical form. (2) The very organs of their bodies having been vitiated by misuse, their vitiated condition will bear witness against them; and (3) all the movements of the organs of their bodies, having been preserved, will be reproduced on the Last Day.

22. And they will say to their skins,[2629] 'Why have you borne witness against us?' They will say, 'Allāh has made us speak as He has made everything *else* speak. And He it is Who created you the first time, and unto Him have you been brought back.

وَقَالُوا لِجُلُودِهِمْ لِمَ شَهِدْتُّمْ عَلَيْنَا ۖ قَالُوٓا
أَنطَقَنَا اللّٰهُ الَّذِىٓ أَنطَقَ كُلَّ شَىْءٍ وَّهُوَ خَلَقَكُمْ
أَوَّلَ مَرَّةٍ وَّإِلَيْهِ تُرْجَعُونَ ۝٢٢

23. 'And you did not apprehend, *while committing sins*, that your ears and your eyes and your skins would bear witness against you; nay, you thought that *even* Allāh did not know much of what you used to do.

وَمَا كُنتُمْ تَسْتَتِرُونَ أَن يَّشْهَدَ عَلَيْكُمْ سَمْعُكُمْ
وَلَآ أَبْصَارُكُمْ وَلَا جُلُودُكُمْ وَلٰكِن ظَنَنتُمْ أَنَّ
اللّٰهَ لَا يَعْلَمُ كَثِيرًا مِّمَّا تَعْمَلُونَ ۝٢٣

24. 'And that thought of yours, which you entertained concerning your Lord,[2630] has ruined you. So *now* you have become of those who are lost.'

وَذٰلِكُمْ ظَنُّكُمُ الَّذِى ظَنَنتُم بِرَبِّكُمْ أَرْدٰكُمْ
فَأَصْبَحْتُم مِّنَ الْخٰسِرِينَ ۝٢٤

25. [a]Now if they can endure, the Fire is their abode; and if they ask for favour, they are not of those [b]whom favour will be shown.[2631]

فَإِن يَّصْبِرُوا فَالنَّارُ مَثْوًى لَّهُمْ ۖ وَإِن يَّسْتَعْتِبُوا
فَمَا هُم مِّنَ الْمُعْتَبِينَ ۝٢٥

26. And We had assigned to them companions who made *to appear* attractive[2632] to them what was before them and what was

وَقَيَّضْنَا لَهُمْ قُرَنَآءَ فَزَيَّنُوا لَهُم مَّا بَيْنَ
أَيْدِيهِمْ وَمَا خَلْفَهُمْ وَحَقَّ عَلَيْهِمُ الْقَوْلُ

[a]14 : 22; [b]16 : 85; 30 : 58

2629. The skin plays the most important part in man's actions. It includes not only the sense of touch but also all the other senses. While the sins of the eyes and the ears are confined to seeing and hearing, the sins of 'the skin' extend to all organs or limbs of the body.

2630. In fact, all sins are the result of lack of a living faith in God.

2631. The crimes of disbelievers are so heinous and hideous that they will not be granted, or taken back into God's favour, or the meaning is that the disbelievers will not be allowed even to approach the '*Atabah* (threshold) of the Throne of God to ask for His mercy.

2632. The evil companions of disbelievers admired and praised their evil acts so as to make those acts appear commendable to them. These evil associates will be made to share the punishment with those whom they beguiled and deceived. The words, 'what was before them and what was behind them,' may mean, the deeds which they did in consequence of association with their bad companions and those they did in imitation of the bad deeds of their forefathers.

behind them *of their deeds*, and the *same* sentence was proved true concerning them as had proved true concerning the communities of jinn and men [a]that had gone before them. Surely, they were the losers.

فِيْٓ اُمَمٍ قَدْ خَلَتْ مِنْ قَبْلِهِمْ مِّنَ الْجِنِّ وَالْاِنْسِ ۚ
اِنَّهُمْ كَانُوْا خٰسِرِيْنَ ﴿۲۶﴾

R. 4 27. And those who disbelieve say, 'Listen not to this Qur'ān, but make noise during its *recital*[2633] that you may have the upper hand.'

وَقَالَ الَّذِيْنَ كَفَرُوْا لَا تَسْمَعُوْا لِهٰذَا الْقُرْاٰنِ
وَالْغَوْا فِيْهِ لَعَلَّكُمْ تَغْلِبُوْنَ ﴿۲۷﴾

28. [b]And, most certainly, We will make those who disbelieve taste a severe punishment, and, most certainly, We will requite them for the worst of their deeds.

فَلَنُذِيْقَنَّ الَّذِيْنَ كَفَرُوْا عَذَابًا شَدِيْدًا ۙ وَّ
لَنَجْزِيَنَّهُمْ اَسْوَاَ الَّذِيْ كَانُوْا يَعْمَلُوْنَ ﴿۲۸﴾

29. That is the reward of the enemies of Allāh—the Fire. For them there will be an abiding home therein as a requital because they persisted in denying Our Signs.

ذٰلِكَ جَزَآءُ اَعْدَآءِ اللّٰهِ النَّارُ ۚ لَهُمْ فِيْهَا دَارُ
الْخُلْدِ ۭ جَزَآءًۢ بِمَا كَانُوْا بِاٰيٰتِنَا يَجْحَدُوْنَ ﴿۲۹﴾

30. And those who disbelieve will say, 'Our Lord, show us [c]those who led us astray from among both the jinn and men,[2634] that we may trample them under our feet so that they may be abased.'

وَقَالَ الَّذِيْنَ كَفَرُوْا رَبَّنَآ اَرِنَا الَّذَيْنِ اَضَلّٰنَا
مِنَ الْجِنِّ وَالْاِنْسِ نَجْعَلْهُمَا تَحْتَ اَقْدَامِنَا
لِيَكُوْنَا مِنَ الْاَسْفَلِيْنَ ﴿۳۰﴾

31. [d]*As for* those who say, 'Our Lord is Allāh,' and then remain steadfast, the angels descend on them, *reassuring them:* 'Fear not, nor grieve; and rejoice in the *glad tidings of the* Garden which you were promised;[2635]

اِنَّ الَّذِيْنَ قَالُوْا رَبُّنَا اللّٰهُ ثُمَّ اسْتَقَامُوْا تَتَنَزَّلُ
عَلَيْهِمُ الْمَلٰٓئِكَةُ اَلَّا تَخَافُوْا وَلَا تَحْزَنُوْا وَاَبْشِرُوْا
بِالْجَنَّةِ الَّتِيْ كُنْتُمْ تُوْعَدُوْنَ ﴿۳۱﴾

[a]3 : 138; 7 : 39; 13 : 31; 46 : 19. [b]27 : 91; 32 : 22; [c]33 : 69; 38 : 62. [d]21 : 104; 46 : 14.

2633. The votaries of darkness have always tried to stifle the voice of Truth by raising a hue and cry against it and have sought to confuse the minds of people by using all sorts of guiles and subterfuges.

2634. Two groups or sets of people, one from among the jinn and the other from among men.

2635. It is in this very life that angels descend upon the Faithful to give them consolation and comfort when they exhibit perseverance in the midst of severe trials and tribulations.

32. 'We are your friends in this life and in the Hereafter. Therein *a*you will have all that your souls will desire, and therein you will have all that you will ask for—

33. 'An entertainment from the Most Forgiving, Merciful *God*.'

R. 5   34. And Who is better in speech than he who invites *men* to Allāh and does righteous deeds and says, 'I am, surely, of those who submit?'

35. And good and evil are not alike. *b*Repel *evil* with that which is best.²⁶³⁶ And lo, he, between whom and thyself was enmity, will become as though he were a warm friend.

36. But none is granted it save those who are steadfast; and none is granted it save those who possess a large share of good.

37. *c*And if an incitement from Satan incite thee, then seek refuge in Allāh. Surely, He is the All-Hearing, the All-Knowing.

38. *d*And of His Signs are the night and the day and the sun and the moon. Prostrate not yourselves before the sun, nor before the moon, but prostrate yourselves before Allāh, Who created them, if it is Him Whom you *really* worship.

39. But if they turn away with disdain, *they do it to their own detriment*, while those who are with thy Lord glorify Him night and day, and they are never wearied.

نَحْنُ اَوْلِيَآؤُكُمْ فِى الْحَيٰوةِ الدُّنْيَا وَفِى الْاٰخِرَةِ وَلَكُمْ فِيْهَا مَا تَشْتَهِىٓ اَنْفُسُكُمْ وَلَكُمْ فِيْهَا مَا تَدَّعُوْنَ ۞

نُزُلًا مِّنْ غَفُوْرٍ رَّحِيْمٍ ۞

وَمَنْ اَحْسَنُ قَوْلًا مِّمَّنْ دَعَآ اِلَى اللّٰهِ وَعَمِلَ صَالِحًا وَّقَالَ اِنَّنِىْ مِنَ الْمُسْلِمِيْنَ ۞

وَلَا تَسْتَوِى الْحَسَنَةُ وَلَا السَّيِّئَةُ ۗ اِدْفَعْ بِالَّتِىْ هِىَ اَحْسَنُ فَاِذَا الَّذِىْ بَيْنَكَ وَبَيْنَهٗ عَدَاوَةٌ كَاَنَّهٗ وَلِىٌّ حَمِيْمٌ ۞

وَمَا يُلَقّٰىهَآ اِلَّا الَّذِيْنَ صَبَرُوْا ۚ وَمَا يُلَقّٰىهَآ اِلَّا ذُوْ حَظٍّ عَظِيْمٍ ۞

وَاِمَّا يَنْزَغَنَّكَ مِنَ الشَّيْطٰنِ نَزْغٌ فَاسْتَعِذْ بِاللّٰهِ ۗ اِنَّهٗ هُوَ السَّمِيْعُ الْعَلِيْمُ ۞

وَمِنْ اٰيٰتِهِ الَّيْلُ وَالنَّهَارُ وَالشَّمْسُ وَالْقَمَرُ ۗ لَا تَسْجُدُوْا لِلشَّمْسِ وَلَا لِلْقَمَرِ وَاسْجُدُوْا لِلّٰهِ الَّذِىْ خَلَقَهُنَّ اِنْ كُنْتُمْ اِيَّاهُ تَعْبُدُوْنَ ۞

فَاِنِ اسْتَكْبَرُوْا فَالَّذِيْنَ عِنْدَ رَبِّكَ يُسَبِّحُوْنَ لَهٗ بِالَّيْلِ وَالنَّهَارِ وَهُمْ لَا يَسْـَٔمُوْنَ ۩ ۞

---

*a*25 : 17.   *b*13 : 23;   28 : 55.   *c*12 : 101. *d*17 : 13;   40 : 62.

2636. As the preaching of truth inevitably brings in its wake hardships for the preacher, the verse enjoins upon him to bear them patiently and with fortitude, and even to return good for the evil he receives at the hands of his persecutors.

40. And of His Signs is that thou seest the earth *lying* withered, [a]but when We send down water on it, it stirs and swells *with verdure*. Surely, He, Who quickened it, can quicken the dead *also*. Verily, He has power over all things.

وَمِنْ آيَاتِهِ أَنَّكَ تَرَى الْأَرْضَ خَاشِعَةً فَإِذَا أَنْزَلْنَا
عَلَيْهَا الْمَاءَ اهْتَزَّتْ وَرَبَتْ ۚ إِنَّ الَّذِي أَحْيَاهَا
لَمُحْيِي الْمَوْتَىٰ ۚ إِنَّهُ عَلَىٰ كُلِّ شَيْءٍ قَدِيرٌ ﴿٤٠﴾

41. Surely, those, who distort Our Signs to seek deviation therein, are not hidden from Us. Is he, then, [b]who is cast into the Fire better, or he who comes *to Us* in security on the Day of Resurrection? Do what you will. Surely, He sees all that you do.

إِنَّ الَّذِينَ يُلْحِدُونَ فِي آيَاتِنَا لَا يَخْفَوْنَ عَلَيْنَا ۗ
أَفَمَنْ يُلْقَىٰ فِي النَّارِ خَيْرٌ أَمْ مَنْ يَأْتِي آمِنًا يَوْمَ
الْقِيَامَةِ ۚ اعْمَلُوا مَا شِئْتُمْ ۖ إِنَّهُ بِمَا تَعْمَلُونَ بَصِيرٌ ﴿٤١﴾

42. Those who disbelieve in the Reminder[2637]—*the Qur'ān*—when it has come to them *are the losers*. And, truly, it is a mighty Book,

إِنَّ الَّذِينَ كَفَرُوا بِالذِّكْرِ لَمَّا جَاءَهُمْ ۖ وَإِنَّهُ لَكِتَابٌ
عَزِيزٌ ﴿٤٢﴾

43. [c]Falsehood cannot approach it either from before it nor from behind it.[2638] *It is* a revelation from the Wise, the Praiseworthy.

لَا يَأْتِيهِ الْبَاطِلُ مِنْ بَيْنِ يَدَيْهِ وَلَا مِنْ خَلْفِهِ ۖ
تَنْزِيلٌ مِنْ حَكِيمٍ حَمِيدٍ ﴿٤٣﴾

44. Nothing is said *in opposition* to thee but what was said to the Messengers before thee. [d]Thy Lord is, indeed, the Master of *great* forgiveness; and *also* the Master of painful chastisement.

مَا يُقَالُ لَكَ إِلَّا مَا قَدْ قِيلَ لِلرُّسُلِ مِنْ قَبْلِكَ ۚ
إِنَّ رَبَّكَ لَذُو مَغْفِرَةٍ وَذُو عِقَابٍ أَلِيمٍ ﴿٤٤﴾

---

[a]22 : 6; 30 : 51; 35 : 28. [b]38 : 29. [c]15 : 11. [d]13 : 7; 53 : 33.

2637. The Qur'ān has been called *Dhikr* because (*a*) it presents and repeats its principles and themes in different forms, thus making men remember them; (*b*) it reminds men of the noble teachings that were revealed in former Scriptures; and (*c*) by acting upon its teachings men can rise to the heights of spiritual eminence (*Dhikr* also meaning, honour).

2638. The Qur'ān is such a wonderful Book that not one of the great truths, principles and ideals enunciated by it has ever been contravened or contradicted by ancient learning or modern science.

45. And if We had made it a [a]Qur'ān in a foreign tongue, they, surely, would have said, 'Why have not its verses been made clear? What! a foreign tongue and an Arab *Prophet?*' Say, 'It is a guidance and a healing for those who believe.' But *as to those* who believe not, there is a deafness in their ears and to them it is blindness.[2638A] They are, *as it were*, being called from a far-off place.[2639]

وَلَوْ جَعَلْنٰهُ قُرْاٰنًا اَعْجَمِيًّا لَّقَالُوْا لَوْلَا فُصِّلَتْ اٰيٰتُهٗ ؕ
ءَاَعْجَمِيٌّ وَّعَرَبِيٌّ ؕ قُلْ هُوَ لِلَّذِيْنَ اٰمَنُوْا هُدًى
وَّشِفَآءٌ ؕ وَالَّذِيْنَ لَا يُؤْمِنُوْنَ فِيْٓ اٰذَانِهِمْ وَقْرٌ
وَّهُوَ عَلَيْهِمْ عَمًى ؕ اُولٰٓئِكَ يُنَادَوْنَ مِنْ مَّكَانٍۭ
بَعِيْدٍ ﴿٤٥﴾ ع ١٩

R. 6 46. And, indeed, We gave Moses the Book, but differences were created concerning it; [b]and had it not been for a word[2639A] that had gone forth from thy Lord, *the matter* would have been decided between them, and certainly they are in a disquieting doubt about it.

وَلَقَدْ اٰتَيْنَا مُوْسَى الْكِتٰبَ فَاخْتُلِفَ فِيْهِ ؕ وَلَوْلَا
كَلِمَةٌ سَبَقَتْ مِنْ رَّبِّكَ لَقُضِيَ بَيْنَهُمْ ؕ وَاِنَّهُمْ
لَفِيْ شَكٍّ مِّنْهُ مُرِيْبٍ ﴿٤٦﴾

47 [c]Whoso does right, it is for *the benefit of* his own soul; and whoso does evil, *the burden thereof* will be on it. And thy Lord is not in the least unjust to *His* servants.

مَنْ عَمِلَ صَالِحًا فَلِنَفْسِهٖ وَمَنْ اَسَآءَ فَعَلَيْهَا ؕ
وَمَا رَبُّكَ بِظَلَّامٍ لِّلْعَبِيْدِ ﴿٤٧﴾

[a]16 : 104; 26 : 196; 46 : 13. [b]10 : 20; 11 : 111; 20 : 130; 42 : 15. [c]3 : 183; 8 : 52; 17 : 8; 22 : 11.

2638A. The meaning of the Qur'ān is obscure to them and the beauty and usefulness of its teaching are hidden from them.

2639. The expression, *They are being called from a far-off place*, signifies that on the Day of Judgment the disbelievers will not be allowed to approach the Throne of the Almighty, but will be called from a far-off place to render an account of their evil deeds. It may also mean that the disbelievers have shut their ears to the Qur'ān, and refuse to ponder over it, so it has become as unintelligible to them as an indistinct and confused voice that a person hears from a far-off place.

2639A. The reference is to the Divine words, "My mercy encompasses all things (7 : 157).

PART XXV

48. To Him *alone* is referred the knowledge of the Hour. And no fruits come forth from their spathes, [a]nor does any female bear *a child*, nor does she give birth *to it*, but with His knowledge.[2640] And on the day when He will call unto them, *saying*, [b]'Where are My partners?' they will say, 'We declare unto Thee, not one of us is a witness *thereto*.'

الجزء ٢٥

إِلَيْهِ يُرَدُّ عِلْمُ السَّاعَةِ ۚ وَمَا تَخْرُجُ مِنْ ثَمَرٰتٍ
مِّنْ أَكْمَامِهَا وَمَا تَحْمِلُ مِنْ أُنْثٰى وَلَا تَضَعُ
إِلَّا بِعِلْمِهٖ ۚ وَيَوْمَ يُنَادِيْهِمْ أَيْنَ شُرَكَآءِيْ ۙ قَالُوْٓا
اٰذَنّٰكَ ۙ مَا مِنَّا مِنْ شَهِيْدٍ ﴿٤٨﴾

49. [c]And all that they used to call upon before will be lost to them, and they will know for certain that they have no place of escape.

وَضَلَّ عَنْهُمْ مَّا كَانُوْا يَدْعُوْنَ مِنْ قَبْلُ وَظَنُّوْا
مَا لَهُمْ مِّنْ مَّحِيْصٍ ﴿٤٩﴾

50. [d]Man tires not of praying for good; but if evil touch him, he despairs, giving up *all* hope.

لَا يَسْـَٔمُ الْإِنْسَانُ مِنْ دُعَآءِ الْخَيْرِ ۫ وَإِنْ مَّسَّهُ الشَّرُّ
فَيَـُٔوْسٌ قَنُوْطٌ ﴿٥٠﴾

51. [e]And if We make him taste of mercy from Us after *some* affliction that has befallen him, he is sure to say, 'This is *but* my *due*[2641] and I do not think the Hour will *ever* come. But *even* if I am returned to my Lord, I will, surely, have with Him the very best.' Then We will, surely, inform the disbelievers of all that they did, and We will, certainly, make them taste a hard punishment.

وَلَئِنْ أَذَقْنٰهُ رَحْمَةً مِّنَّا مِنْۢ بَعْدِ ضَرَّآءَ مَسَّتْهُ
لَيَقُوْلَنَّ هٰذَا لِيْ ۙ وَمَآ أَظُنُّ السَّاعَةَ قَآئِمَةً ۙ وَّلَئِنْ
رُّجِعْتُ إِلٰى رَبِّيْٓ إِنَّ لِيْ عِنْدَهٗ لَلْحُسْنٰى ۚ فَلَنُنَبِّئَنَّ
الَّذِيْنَ كَفَرُوْا بِمَا عَمِلُوْا ۫ وَلَنُذِيْقَنَّهُمْ مِّنْ عَذَابٍ
غَلِيْظٍ ﴿٥١﴾

[a]13 : 9; 35 : 12. [b]18 : 53; 28 : 65. [c]40 : 75. [d]11 : 10-11; 17 : 84. [e]10 : 22; 11 : 11.

2640. God alone knows how the seed that the Holy Prophet has sown in the soil of Arabia would grow, and what kinds of fruit it would bear. If the fruits were rotten they would be destroyed, but if they were wholesome and delicious they would be preserved with care.

2641. It is human nature that when man is in trouble he is despondent and despairing, but when he is in affluent circumstances, he is the very embodiment of conceit and arrogance, and behaves as if no affliction had ever touched him, and in his conceit he begins to attribute all his success to his own effort and ability.

52. [a]And when We bestow a favour on man, he goes away, turning aside; but when evil touches him, lo! he *starts* offering long prayers.

وَإِذَآ أَنْعَمْنَا عَلَى الْإِنْسَانِ أَعْرَضَ وَنَا بِجَانِبِهٖ
وَإِذَا مَسَّهُ الشَّرُّ فَذُو دُعَآءٍ عَرِيضٍ ﴿۵۲﴾

53. Say, 'Tell me, if it is from Allāh, but you disbelieve in it—who is more astray than one who has drifted far away from *the truth?*

قُلْ أَرَءَيْتُمْ إِنْ كَانَ مِنْ عِنْدِ اللّٰهِ ثُمَّ كَفَرْتُمْ
بِهٖ مَنْ أَضَلُّ مِمَّنْ هُوَ فِي شِقَاقٍۭ بَعِيدٍ ﴿۵۳﴾

54. [b]Soon We will show them Our Signs in farthest regions[2642] *of the earth* and among their own people until it becomes manifest to them that it is the truth. Is it not enough that thy Lord is Witness over all things?

سَنُرِيهِمْ اٰيٰتِنَا فِي الْاٰفَاقِ وَفِيٓ أَنْفُسِهِمْ حَتّٰى
يَتَبَيَّنَ لَهُمْ أَنَّهُ الْحَقُّ أَوَلَمْ يَكْفِ بِرَبِّكَ أَنَّهٗ
عَلٰى كُلِّ شَيْءٍ شَهِيدٌ ﴿۵۴﴾

55. Aye, they are, surely, in doubt concerning the meeting with their Lord; aye, He, certainly, encompasses all things.

أَلَآ إِنَّهُمْ فِي مِرْيَةٍ مِّنْ لِّقَآءِ رَبِّهِمْ أَلَآ إِنَّهٗ
بِكُلِّ شَيْءٍ مُّحِيطٌ ﴿۵۵﴾

[a]11 : 10; 17 : 84. [b]51 : 21-22.

2642. The verse makes in most clear and emphatic terms the prophecy that Islām will spread not only nearer home among the Arabs but in the remotest parts of the earth, *Āfāq* meaning remote regions (Lane).

CHAPTER 42

AL-SHŪRĀ

(*Revealed before Hijrah*)

Date of Revelation and Context

This *Sūrah*, like the preceding one, was revealed at Mecca about the same time; but according to Noldeke a little later. Ibn 'Abbās, as reported by Mardawaih and Ibn Zubair, holds the view that it was revealed at Mecca when opposition to Islām was extremely severe and Muslims were in a tight corner. The preceding *Sūrah* had ended on the note that anyone who opposes and rejects Heavenly Teaching injures only his own soul and himself suffers the consequences of rejection. The present *Sūrah* opens with the declaration that the Qur'ān has been revealed by the High, Wise and Mighty God; if the Prophet's people rejected its Message they would be so doing at their own cost.

Subject-Matter

The *Sūrah* opens with the important subject of the Quranic revelation and proceeds to say that man's sins are many and great but God's forgiveness is greater and His grace unbounded. His mercy demanded that the Qur'ān should have been revealed to deliver man from the bondage of sin but he is so constituted that instead of benefiting from God's mercy he worships gods of his own creation. The Prophet, therefore, is told not to grieve over what the disbelievers do, as he is not appointed a guardian over them. His duty only is to convey the Divine Message, the rest is God's own affair. The *Sūrah* then refers to the invariable Divine practice that whenever differences arise among the followers of various Faiths on the basic principles of religion, God raises a Prophet to remove those differences and to lead them to the right path. But the basic principles of all religions being the same, all Divine Messengers followed the same religion—total submission to God. This "religion" found its best and completest exposition in the revelation of the Qur'ān and, therefore, it received a specific name—Al-Islām. The Holy Prophet is enjoined to invite the whole of mankind to this most perfect and last Divine Teaching, and to let no persecution or persuasion stand in his way. Compliance with the Quranic commandments or their defiance, the *Sūrah* continues, constitutes good or bad action. It is their deeds which determine the destiny of nations and individuals and make or mar their furture. In their lives there comes a day when their actions are weighed in the balance. If their good actions outweigh their bad actions, a life of bliss and happiness awaits them. If, on the other hand, their evil deeds exceed their good deeds, then they have a life of regrets and sighs. Next, the *Sūrah* says that the Holy Prophet has worked very hard and suffered much in the cause of truth, and this from no personal motives. Being full of the milk of human kindness his only concern and desire is that men should establish true and real relationship with God. Could such a sincere and honest well-wisher of mankind be capable of forging lies against God? Yet his people accuse him of this most heinous of sins. Why cannot they understand this simple fact that the forging of lies against God is a deadly poison which brings about the complete ruin of the forger? Instead of being ruined, however, the noble efforts of the Holy Prophet are producing excellent results and his cause is making uniform and rapid progress. The *Sūrah* then draws attention to the physical phenomenon that whenever dry earth needs water God sends down rain from the clouds. Similarly, when the spiritual earth had become dry, God had sent down heavenly rain in the form of the Qur'ān. Then after briefly referring to the fundamental principle that the affairs of the Islamic State and other matters of national importance should be transacted by mutual consultation, the *Sūrah* lays down the basis of the penal laws of Islām. According to it the real object underlying punishment is the moral reformation of the guilty person. There is no place in Islām for the monastic Christian teaching of turning the other cheek under all conditions, nor the Jewish doctrine of "an eye for an eye and a tooth for a tooth." Towards its close the *Sūrah* tells disbelievers that the Holy Prophet has done his duty. He is but a Warner and he has warned them. He has not been made a guardian over them. He is the Life and the Light and his is the way that leads to the realization of the object of man's creation. At the end, the *Sūrah* mentions three forms of Divine revelation.

سُوْرَةُ الشُّوْرٰى مَكِّيَّةٌ

1. [a]In the name of Allāh, the Gracious, the Merciful.

بِسْمِ اللّٰهِ الرَّحْمٰنِ الرَّحِيْمِ ﴿١﴾

2. [b]Ḥā Mīm.[2643]

حٰمٓ ﴿٢﴾

3. 'Ain Sīn Qāf.[2643A]

عٓسٓقٓ ﴿٣﴾

4. Thus does Allāh, the Mighty, the Wise, send revelation to thee as *He revealed* to those before thee.

كَذٰلِكَ يُوْحِيْٓ اِلَيْكَ وَاِلَى الَّذِيْنَ مِنْ قَبْلِكَ ۙ اللّٰهُ الْعَزِيْزُ الْحَكِيْمُ ﴿٤﴾

5. [c]To Him belongs whatever is in the heavens and whatever is in the earth, and He is the High, the Great.

لَهٗ مَا فِي السَّمٰوٰتِ وَمَا فِي الْاَرْضِ ۭ وَهُوَ الْعَلِيُّ الْعَظِيْمُ ﴿٥﴾

6. The heavens may well-nigh rend asunder from above them; [d]and the angels proclaim the praises of their Lord and ask forgiveness for those on earth.[2643B] Behold! it is, surely, Allāh Who is the Most Forgiving, the Merciful.

تَكَادُ السَّمٰوٰتُ يَتَفَطَّرْنَ مِنْ فَوْقِهِنَّ وَالْمَلٰٓئِكَةُ يُسَبِّحُوْنَ بِحَمْدِ رَبِّهِمْ وَيَسْتَغْفِرُوْنَ لِمَنْ فِي الْاَرْضِ ۭ اَلَآ اِنَّ اللّٰهَ هُوَ الْغَفُوْرُ الرَّحِيْمُ ﴿٦﴾

7. *And as for those* who take for themselves protectors beside Him—Allāh watches[2644] over them, [e]and thou art not a guardian over them.

وَالَّذِيْنَ اتَّخَذُوْا مِنْ دُوْنِهٖٓ اَوْلِيَاۗءَ اللّٰهُ حَفِيْظٌ عَلَيْهِمْ ۖ وَمَآ اَنْتَ عَلَيْهِمْ بِوَكِيْلٍ ﴿٧﴾

---

[a]1 : 1. [b]41 : 2; 43 : 2; 44 : 2; 45 : 2; 46 : 2. [c]16 : 53; 22 : 65; 31 : 27. [d]13 : 14. [e]6 : 108; 88 : 23.

2643. *Ḥā Mīm* may stand for *Ḥāfiẓ al-Kitāb* (Guardian of the Book) and *Munazzil al-Kitāb* (Revealer of the Book), because all the Chapters which open with these two abbreviated letters deal particularly with the subject of revelation of the Qur'ān and its protection and guardianship.

2643A. *'Ain* stands for *Al-'Aliyy* (the High); *Al-'Alīm* (the All-Knowing); *'Al-'Aẓīm* (the Great); *Al-'Azīz* (the Mighty). *Sīn* stands for *Al-Samī'* (the All-Hearing), and *Qāf* may represent *Al-Qadīr* (the Possessor of Power and Authority).

2643B. Man's sin is great but greater is God's mercy which transcends all His attributes. God's mercy and the asking for forgiveness by angels for man combine to save him from Divine punishment and he is granted respite to make amends.

2644. God is watching over the blasphemous beliefs of men and is keeping an account of them and will punish them if they did not repent.

8. Thus have [a]We revealed to thee the Qur'ān in Arabic, [b]that thou mayest warn the Mother of towns,[2645] and *all* those around it; and that thou mayest warn *them* of the Day of Gathering, whereof there is no doubt; *when a* party *will be* in the Garden and a party in the blazing Fire.

وَكَذٰلِكَ اَوْحَيْنَآ اِلَيْكَ قُرْاٰنًا عَرَبِيًّا لِّتُنْذِرَ اُمَّ
الْقُرٰى وَمَنْ حَوْلَهَا وَتُنْذِرَ يَوْمَ الْجَمْعِ لَا رَيْبَ
فِيْهِ فَرِيْقٌ فِي الْجَنَّةِ وَفَرِيْقٌ فِي السَّعِيْرِ ﴿٨﴾

9. [c]And if Allāh had *so* willed, He could have made them one people; but He admits into His mercy whomsoever He pleases. The wrongdoers will have no protector and no helper.

وَلَوْ شَآءَ اللّٰهُ لَجَعَلَهُمْ اُمَّةً وَّاحِدَةً وَّلٰكِنْ
يُّدْخِلُ مَنْ يَّشَآءُ فِيْ رَحْمَتِهٖ وَالظّٰلِمُوْنَ مَا لَهُمْ
مِّنْ وَّلِيٍّ وَّلَا نَصِيْرٍ ﴿٩﴾

10. [d]Have they taken *for themselves* protectors other than Him? But it is Allāh Who is the *real* Protector. And He quickens the dead, and He has power over all things.

اَمِ اتَّخَذُوْا مِنْ دُوْنِهٖٓ اَوْلِيَآءَ فَاللّٰهُ هُوَ الْوَلِيُّ
وَهُوَ يُحْيِ الْمَوْتٰى وَهُوَ عَلٰى كُلِّ شَيْءٍ قَدِيْرٌ ﴿١٠﴾

R. 2 11. And in whatsoever you differ, the *final* decision thereof *rests* with Allāh. *Say*, Such is Allāh, my Lord; in Him I put my trust, and to Him I *always* turn.'

وَمَا اخْتَلَفْتُمْ فِيْهِ مِنْ شَيْءٍ فَحُكْمُهٗٓ اِلَى اللّٰهِ
ذٰلِكُمُ اللّٰهُ رَبِّيْ عَلَيْهِ تَوَكَّلْتُ وَاِلَيْهِ اُنِيْبُ ﴿١١﴾

12. *He is* [e]the Originator of the heavens and the earth. He has made for you pairs of your own selves, and of the cattle *also He has made* pairs. He multiplies[2646]

فَاطِرُ السَّمٰوٰتِ وَالْاَرْضِ جَعَلَ لَكُمْ مِّنْ اَنْفُسِكُمْ
اَزْوَاجًا وَّمِنَ الْاَنْعَامِ اَزْوَاجًا يَذْرَؤُكُمْ فِيْهِ

[a]20 : 114; 39 : 29; 43 : 4; 46 : 13. [b]6 : 93. [c]11 : 119. [d]13 : 17; 39 : 44. [e]6 : 15; 14 : 11; 35 : 2.

2645. The reference may be to Mecca, because Mecca was not only the commercial and political metropolis of Arabia at the time when the Qur'ān was revealed but was destined for all time to be the spiritual centre of the whole world and from its breast the whole of humanity was to suck the milk of spiritual life. Geographically also Mecca is situated in the centre of the world. The Qur'ān has also been called *Umm al-Kitāb* (Mother of the Book) and Arabic in which it has been revealed *Umm al-Alsinah* (Mother of tongues) and Mecca has been called *Umm al-Qurā* (Mother of towns or Mother-town).

2646. God multiplies mankind by the relationship that exists between husband and wife.

لَيْسَ كَمِثْلِهٖ شَيْءٌ ۚ وَهُوَ السَّمِيْعُ الْبَصِيْرُ ﴿١٢﴾

you therein. There is nothing whatever like unto Him,[2647] and He is the All-Hearing, the All-Seeing.

لَهٗ مَقَالِيْدُ السَّمٰوٰتِ وَالْاَرْضِ ۚ يَبْسُطُ الرِّزْقَ
لِمَنْ يَّشَآءُ وَيَقْدِرُ ۚ اِنَّهٗ بِكُلِّ شَيْءٍ عَلِيْمٌ ﴿١٣﴾

13. [a]To Him belong the keys of the heavens and the earth. [b]He enlarges the provision for whomsoever He pleases and straitens *it for whomsoever He pleases.* Surely, He knows all things full well.

شَرَعَ لَكُمْ مِّنَ الدِّيْنِ مَا وَصّٰى بِهٖ نُوْحًا وَّالَّذِيْٓ
اَوْحَيْنَآ اِلَيْكَ وَمَا وَصَّيْنَا بِهٖٓ اِبْرٰهِيْمَ وَمُوْسٰى
وَعِيْسٰٓى اَنْ اَقِيْمُوا الدِّيْنَ وَلَا تَتَفَرَّقُوْا فِيْهِ ۚ كَبُرَ
عَلَى الْمُشْرِكِيْنَ مَا تَدْعُوْهُمْ اِلَيْهِ ۚ اَللّٰهُ يَجْتَبِيْٓ
اِلَيْهِ مَنْ يَّشَآءُ وَيَهْدِيْٓ اِلَيْهِ مَنْ يُّنِيْبُ ﴿١٤﴾

14. He has prescribed for you the religion which He enjoined on Noah, and which We have *now* revealed to thee, and which We enjoined on Abraham and Moses and Jesus, *viz.*, 'Establish obedience *to Allāh in the earth,* and be not divided therein. Hard upon the idolaters is that to which thou callest them. Allāh chooses for Himself whom He pleases, and guides to Himself him who turns *to Him.*'

وَمَا تَفَرَّقُوْٓا اِلَّا مِنْ بَعْدِ مَا جَآءَهُمُ الْعِلْمُ
بَغْيًا بَيْنَهُمْ ۚ وَلَوْلَا كَلِمَةٌ سَبَقَتْ مِنْ رَّبِّكَ
اِلٰٓى اَجَلٍ مُّسَمًّى لَّقُضِيَ بَيْنَهُمْ ۚ وَاِنَّ الَّذِيْنَ
اُوْرِثُوا الْكِتٰبَ مِنْ بَعْدِهِمْ لَفِيْ شَكٍّ مِّنْهُ مُرِيْبٍ ﴿١٥﴾

15. [c]And they did not become divided but, after knowledge had come to them, through jealousy among themselves. [d]And had it not been for a word that had already gone forth from thy Lord for an appointed term, *the matter* would, surely, have been decided between them. Surely, those who were made to inherit the Book after them are in a disquieting doubt concerning it.

[a]39 : 64. [b]13 : 27; 29 : 63; 34 : 37; 39 : 53. [c]45 : 18; 98 : 5. [d]10 : 20; 20 : 130; 41 : 46

2647. The words, 'There is nothing whatever like unto Him', remove a possible misunderstanding to which the sentence, 'God has made a pair of everything,' might have given rise, *viz.*, that God also needs a consort to make a pair. The words signify that it is impossible to conceive of anything like God. He is far above human perception and comprehension. It is, therefore, foolish to try to find likeness between Divine and human attributes, though the two may possess some remote and incomplete resemblance.

16. To this *religion*, then, do thou invite *mankind*. [a]And be thou steadfast *in it* as thou art commanded, [b]and follow not their evil inclinations, but say, 'I believe in whatever Book Allāh has sent down, and I am commanded to judge justly between you; Allāh is our Lord and your Lord. [c]For us *is the reward of* our works, and for you *the reward of* your works. There is no quarrel[2648] between us and you. Allāh will gather us together, and to Him is the return.'

فَلِذٰلِكَ فَادْعُ ۚ وَاسْتَقِمْ كَمَآ أُمِرْتَ ۚ وَلَا تَتَّبِعْ
أَهْوَآءَهُمْ ۚ وَقُلْ اٰمَنْتُ بِمَآ أَنْزَلَ اللّٰهُ مِنْ كِتٰبٍ ۚ
وَأُمِرْتُ لِأَعْدِلَ بَيْنَكُمْ ۖ اللّٰهُ رَبُّنَا وَرَبُّكُمْ ۖ
لَنَآ أَعْمَالُنَا وَلَكُمْ أَعْمَالُكُمْ ۖ لَا حُجَّةَ بَيْنَنَا وَ
بَيْنَكُمْ ۖ اللّٰهُ يَجْمَعُ بَيْنَنَا ۚ وَإِلَيْهِ الْمَصِيرُ ﴿١٦﴾

17. And those who dispute concerning Allāh after His *call* has been responded to—their contention is null and void[2649] in the sight of their Lord; and on them *will fall God's* wrath and for them will be a severe punishment.

وَالَّذِينَ يُحَآجُّونَ فِي اللّٰهِ مِنْ بَعْدِ مَا اسْتُجِيبَ
لَهٗ حُجَّتُهُمْ دَاحِضَةٌ عِنْدَ رَبِّهِمْ وَعَلَيْهِمْ
غَضَبٌ وَّلَهُمْ عَذَابٌ شَدِيدٌ ﴿١٧﴾

18. Allāh is He [d]Who has sent down the Book with truth and *also* the Balance.[2650] And what will make thee know that the Hour may be nigh?

اللّٰهُ الَّذِيٓ أَنْزَلَ الْكِتٰبَ بِالْحَقِّ وَالْمِيزَانَ ۗ وَمَا
يُدْرِيكَ لَعَلَّ السَّاعَةَ قَرِيبٌ ﴿١٨﴾

[a]11 : 113. [b]5 : 50. [c]2 : 140; 10 : 42. [d]55 : 8; 57 : 26.

2648. The Holy Prophet is here enjoined to tell the followers of earlier Prophets that he believes in all the revealed Scriptures that had come before him. There exists, therefore, no cause for them to quarrel with him.

2649. The truth of Islām has been established and people have begun to enter its fold in large numbers, so it is futile on the part of disbelievers to go on disputing and doubting its Divine origin.

2650. God has sent down two important things for man's guidance and benefit: (*a*) "The Book," *i.e.*, the laws of the *Sharī'ah*; (*b*) "The Balance," *i.e.*, standards by which human actions are appraised, judged, measured and weighed. Or, "The Balance" may signify the faculty by which man can distinguish between right and wrong. In fact, in this life (and more so in the next life) all human actions are weighed in Divine scales. "The Balance" may also refer to the Qur'ān itself, because it constitutes an infallible criterion (*Mīzān*) to judge what is right and what is wrong.

Elsewhere in the Qur'ān (57 : 26) the expression, 'He has sent down,' has also been used about "iron" which represents power that enforces Divine and human laws.

19. *Those who believe not therein seek to hasten it; but those who believe are fearful[2651] of it, and know that it is bound to come. Beware! those who dispute concerning the Hour are in error, far gone.

يَسْتَعْجِلُ بِهَا الَّذِيْنَ لَا يُؤْمِنُوْنَ بِهَا وَالَّذِيْنَ اٰمَنُوْا مُشْفِقُوْنَ مِنْهَا وَ يَعْلَمُوْنَ اَنَّهَا الْحَقُّ اَلَا اِنَّ الَّذِيْنَ يُمَارُوْنَ فِي السَّاعَةِ لَفِيْ ضَلٰلٍ بَعِيْدٍ ۝

20. ᵇAllāh is Benignant to His servants. He provides for whom He pleases. And He is the Powerful, the Mighty.

اَللّٰهُ لَطِيْفٌ بِعِبَادِهٖ يَرْزُقُ مَنْ يَّشَآءُ وَ هُوَ الْقَوِيُّ الْعَزِيْزُ ۝

R. 3 21. ᶜWhoso desires the harvest of the Hereafter, We give him increase in his harvest; and whoso desires the harvest of this world, We give him *his portion* thereof, but in the Herafter he will have no share.[2652]

مَنْ كَانَ يُرِيْدُ حَرْثَ الْاٰخِرَةِ نَزِدْ لَهٗ فِيْ حَرْثِهٖ وَ مَنْ كَانَ يُرِيْدُ حَرْثَ الدُّنْيَا نُؤْتِهٖ مِنْهَا وَ مَا لَهٗ فِي الْاٰخِرَةِ مِنْ نَّصِيْبٍ ۝

22. Have they *such associates of Allāh* as have made lawful for them in religion that which Allāh has not allowed? And but for *Our* word about the final judgment, *the matter* would have been decided *by now* between them. And, surely, the wrongdoers will have a grievous punishment.

اَمْ لَهُمْ شُرَكٰٓؤُا شَرَعُوْا لَهُمْ مِّنَ الدِّيْنِ مَا لَمْ يَأْذَنْ بِهِ اللّٰهُ وَ لَوْلَا كَلِمَةُ الْفَصْلِ لَقُضِيَ بَيْنَهُمْ وَ اِنَّ الظّٰلِمِيْنَ لَهُمْ عَذَابٌ اَلِيْمٌ ۝

---

*13 : 7.   ᵇ6 : 104;   22 : 64.   ᶜ3 : 146;   17 : 20;   3 : 146;   17 : 19.

2651. As disbelievers do not believe in the Day of Judgment, they have no fear of it, so they demand its speedy coming; but believers know that on that awful Day they will have to render an account of their actions and, therefore, while they make every preparation for it, they are at the same time afraid of facing it.

2652. Those whose efforts are wholly directed towards acquiring the vain and paltry things of this life will be deprived of the bliss and blessings of everlasting life of the Hereafter, but those who prepare for the next life will have Divine blessings bestowed upon them without measure and diminution.

23. Thou wilt see the wrongdoers in fear on account of that which they have earned, and it is sure to befall them. [a]But those who believe and do good works will be in meadows of the Gardens.[2653] They shall have with their Lord whatever they will desire. That is the great bounty *of Allāh*.

تَرَى الظّٰلِمِيْنَ مُشْفِقِيْنَ مِمَّا كَسَبُوْا وَهُوَ وَاقِعٌۢ
بِهِمْ ۗ وَالَّذِيْنَ اٰمَنُوْا وَعَمِلُوا الصّٰلِحٰتِ فِيْ رَوْضٰتِ
الْجَنّٰتِ ۚ لَهُمْ مَّا يَشَآءُوْنَ عِنْدَ رَبِّهِمْ ۗ ذٰلِكَ هُوَ
الْفَضْلُ الْكَبِيْرُ ﴿٢٣﴾

24. This it is whereof Allāh gives the glad tidings to His servants who believe and do good works. [b]Say, 'I ask of you no reward for *my service to you*, except *such* love *as subsists* between kindred.'[2654] And whoso earns a good deed, We give him increase of good therein. Surely, Allāh is Most Forgiving, Most Appreciating.

ذٰلِكَ الَّذِيْ يُبَشِّرُ اللّٰهُ عِبَادَهُ الَّذِيْنَ اٰمَنُوْا وَعَمِلُوا
الصّٰلِحٰتِ ۗ قُلْ لَّآ اَسْـَٔلُكُمْ عَلَيْهِ اَجْرًا اِلَّا الْمَوَدَّةَ
فِي الْقُرْبٰى ۗ وَمَنْ يَّقْتَرِفْ حَسَنَةً نَّزِدْ لَهٗ فِيْهَا
حُسْنًا ۗ اِنَّ اللّٰهَ غَفُوْرٌ شَكُوْرٌ ﴿٢٤﴾

25. Do they say, 'He has forged a lie against Allāh?' If Allāh had *so* willed, He could seal thy heart.[2655] [c]But Allāh blots out falsehood *through thee* and establishes the truth by His words. Surely, He knows quite well what is in the breasts.

اَمْ يَقُوْلُوْنَ افْتَرٰى عَلَى اللّٰهِ كَذِبًا ۚ فَاِنْ يَّشَاِ اللّٰهُ
يَخْتِمْ عَلٰى قَلْبِكَ ۗ وَيَمْحُ اللّٰهُ الْبَاطِلَ وَيُحِقُّ الْحَقَّ
بِكَلِمٰتِهٖ ۗ اِنَّهٗ عَلِيْمٌۢ بِذَاتِ الصُّدُوْرِ ﴿٢٥﴾

[a]2 : 83; 13 : 30; 22 : 57; 68 : 35. [b]25 : 58; 38 : 87. [c]13 : 40

2653. In v. 19 disbelievers were stated as scornfully rejecting the very idea of a life after death and defiantly demanded its speedy coming, but the believers being conscious of their great responsibilities were mentioned as being afraid of facing it. In the present verse it is stated that on the Day of Judgment the tables will be turned upon disbelievers. They will be afraid of confronting the consequences of their evil deeds while believers will be happy in the Gardens of Bliss, basking in the sun of God's love.

2654. The words may also mean : (1) I ask of you no reward for calling you to the way of God except that, being related to you by ties of kinship, my solicitude for your spiritual well-being impels me to do so. (2) I ask of you no reward for the great work I am doing for your spiritual benefit except that you should learn to live and behave like blood relations. (3) I ask no reward or return for my solicitude and love for you except that in offering opposition to me you should at least have some regard for the ties of relationship that I have with you. (4) I want no reward from you except that you should learn to develop a liking for attaining nearness to God (the word, *Qurbā* meaning *Qurbah*, nearness). This last meaning agrees with 25 : 58 where the Holy Prophet is depicted as saying : *I ask of you naught in return for it except that he, who will, may take a way to his Lord.*

2655. The words may mean, 'If God had willed that your enemies should have been punished for calling you a liar and a forger, He would have sealed your heart, *i.e.*, He would have made your heart devoid of all mercy and solicitude for them, so that instead of being

26. [a]And He it is Who accepts repentance from His servants and forgives sins. And He knows what you do.

وَهُوَ الَّذِيْ يَقْبَلُ التَّوْبَةَ عَنْ عِبَادِهٖ وَيَعْفُوْا عَنِ السَّيِّاٰتِ وَيَعْلَمُ مَا تَفْعَلُوْنَ ﴿۲۶﴾

27. [b]And He accepts *the prayers of* those who believe and do good works, and gives them more *than their due reward,* out of His grace; and the disbelievers will have a severe punishment.

وَيَسْتَجِيْبُ الَّذِيْنَ اٰمَنُوْا وَعَمِلُوا الصّٰلِحٰتِ وَيَزِيْدُهُمْ مِّنْ فَضْلِهٖ ۚ وَالْكٰفِرُوْنَ لَهُمْ عَذَابٌ شَدِيْدٌ ﴿۲۷﴾

28. And if Allāh should *greatly* enlarge the provision for His servants, they would rebel in the earth; [c]but He sends down according to *a proper* measure as He pleases. Indeed, He is All-Aware *and* All-Seeing of *the condition of* His servants.

وَلَوْ بَسَطَ اللّٰهُ الرِّزْقَ لِعِبَادِهٖ لَبَغَوْا فِي الْاَرْضِ وَلٰكِنْ يُّنَزِّلُ بِقَدَرٍ مَّا يَشَآءُ ۭ اِنَّهٗ بِعِبَادِهٖ خَبِيْرٌۢ بَصِيْرٌ ﴿۲۸﴾

29. [d]And He it is Who sends down rain after they have despaired *of it* and spreads out his mercy. And He is the Protector, the Praiseworthy.

وَهُوَ الَّذِيْ يُنَزِّلُ الْغَيْثَ مِنْۢ بَعْدِ مَا قَنَطُوْا وَيَنْشُرُ رَحْمَتَهٗ ۭ وَهُوَ الْوَلِيُّ الْحَمِيْدُ ﴿۲۹﴾

30. [e]And among His Signs is the creation of the heavens and the earth, and *of* whatever living creatures He has spread forth in both. And He has the power to gather them together whenever He pleases.[2656]

وَمِنْ اٰيٰتِهٖ خَلْقُ السَّمٰوٰتِ وَالْاَرْضِ وَمَا بَثَّ فِيْهِمَا مِنْ دَآبَّةٍ ۭ وَهُوَ عَلٰى جَمْعِهِمْ اِذَا يَشَآءُ قَدِيْرٌ ﴿۳۰﴾

[a]9 : 104; 33 : 74. [b]2 : 187. [c]15 : 22. [d]31 : 35. [e]30 : 23.

solicitous for their spiritual well-being, you would have invoked God's curses upon them, but He has chosen not to do so.' Or, the meaning is, that had the Holy Prophet forged a lie against Allāh, his conduct thereafter would have been that of a man who had rebelled against Allāh. But the Holy Prophet advances continuously towards higher grades of virtue and righteousness which shows that he is under the care and protection of Allāh and is kept immune from error.

2656. The verse embodies a unique testimony to the Divine origin of the Qur'ān. It was not possible for any human being, much less for an unlettered son of the desert, to say, as far back as 1400 years, when the science of astronomy was yet in its infancy, that apart from our planet, life in some form or other existed in heavenly bodies. It was reserved for the Qur'ān to disclose this great and marvellous scientific truth as the words of this verse, *of whatever living creatures He has spread forth in both*, show. The reference in the words, *He has the power to gather them together* may be to the possibility of the creatures living on earth and in the heavenly bodies becoming united in some future time. Recent archaeological investigations have revealed that "Dropas" or visitors from the heaven came down upon this earth 12,000 years ago' (The Pakistan Times, dated 13.8.67).

R. 4 31. [a]And whatever misfortune befalls you is *the consequence of* what your *own* hands have wrought. And He forgives many *of your sins.*

وَمَآ اَصَابَكُمْ مِّنْ مُّصِيْبَةٍ فَبِمَا كَسَبَتْ اَيْدِيْكُمْ
وَيَعْفُوْا عَنْ كَثِيْرٍ ﴿٣١﴾

32. And you cannot frustrate *God's* purpose in the earth;[2657] [b]nor have you any friend or helper beside Allāh.

وَمَآ اَنْتُمْ بِمُعْجِزِيْنَ فِي الْاَرْضِ ۚ وَمَا لَكُمْ
مِّنْ دُوْنِ اللّٰهِ مِنْ وَّلِيٍّ وَّلَا نَصِيْرٍ ﴿٣٢﴾

33. [c]And of His Signs are the sailing ships on the sea, *tall* like mountains.[2658]

وَمِنْ اٰيٰتِهِ الْجَوَارِ فِي الْبَحْرِ كَالْاَعْلَامِ ﴿٣٣﴾

34. If He *so* desires He can cause the wind to become still so that they become motionless upon the surface thereof—in that, surely, are Signs for every patient and grateful person—

اِنْ يَّشَاْ يُسْكِنِ الرِّيْحَ فَيَظْلَلْنَ رَوَاكِدَ عَلٰى ظَهْرِهٖ ۚ
اِنَّ فِيْ ذٰلِكَ لَاٰيٰتٍ لِّكُلِّ صَبَّارٍ شَكُوْرٍ ﴿٣٤﴾

35. Or, He can destroy *those who are in* them because of that which they have earned—but He forgives many *of their sins*—

اَوْ يُوْبِقْهُنَّ بِمَا كَسَبُوْا وَيَعْفُ عَنْ كَثِيْرٍ ﴿٣٥﴾

36. [d]And *He destroys them so that* those who dispute concerning Our Signs may know that they have no refuge.

وَّيَعْلَمَ الَّذِيْنَ يُجَادِلُوْنَ فِيْٓ اٰيٰتِنَا ۗ مَا لَهُمْ مِّنْ
مَّحِيْصٍ ﴿٣٦﴾

37. [e]And whatever you have been given is only a temporary provision of this life, but that which is with Allāh is better and more lasting for those who believe and put their trust in their Lord,

فَمَآ اُوْتِيْتُمْ مِّنْ شَيْءٍ فَمَتَاعُ الْحَيٰوةِ الدُّنْيَا ۚ
وَمَا عِنْدَ اللّٰهِ خَيْرٌ وَّاَبْقٰى لِلَّذِيْنَ اٰمَنُوْا وَعَلٰى
رَبِّهِمْ يَتَوَكَّلُوْنَ ﴿٣٧﴾

38. [f]And those who eschew the more grievous sins and indecencies, and, when they are wroth,[2659] they forgive,

وَالَّذِيْنَ يَجْتَنِبُوْنَ كَبٰٓئِرَ الْاِثْمِ وَالْفَوَاحِشَ وَاِذَا
مَا غَضِبُوْا هُمْ يَغْفِرُوْنَ ﴿٣٨﴾

---

[a]4 : 80. [b]6 : 135; 11 : 34; 29 : 23. [c]31 : 32; 55 : 25. [d]22 : 4; 40 : 5. [e]28 : 61. [f]4 : 32; 53 : 33.

2657. Disbelievers are told that God has decreed that Islām shall become victorious and they will not be able to frustrate Divine decree and that no osbtacle or impediment will be allowed to stand in the way of its onward march.

2658. In this and several other verses the Qur'ān points to the great part that ships were to play in international intercourse. This truth, revealed to a son of the desert, as far back as fourteen hundred years ago, speaks volumes for the Divine origin of the Qur'ān.

2659. These words comprise all kinds of sins and moral lapses, but a separate mention is made of anger because many sins spring from anger when it exceeds legitimate bounds.

39. And those, who hearken to their Lord, and observe Prayer, [a]and whose affairs are *decided* by mutual consultation,[2660] and who spend out of what We have provided for them,

وَالَّذِينَ اسْتَجَابُوا لِرَبِّهِمْ وَأَقَامُوا الصَّلٰوةَ وَأَمْرُهُمْ شُورٰى بَيْنَهُمْ وَمِمَّا رَزَقْنٰهُمْ يُنْفِقُونَ ﴿٣٩﴾

40. And those who, when a wrong is done to them, defend themselves.

وَالَّذِينَ إِذَآ أَصَابَهُمُ الْبَغْيُ هُمْ يَنْتَصِرُونَ ﴿٤٠﴾

41. [b]*Remember that* the recompense of an injury is an injury the like thereof; but whoso forgives and *thereby* brings about an improvement, his reward is with Allāh.[2661] Surely, He loves not the wrongdoers.

وَجَزٰٓؤُا سَيِّئَةٍ سَيِّئَةٌ مِّثْلُهَا ۚ فَمَنْ عَفَا وَأَصْلَحَ فَأَجْرُهُ عَلَى اللّٰهِ ۚ إِنَّهُ لَا يُحِبُّ الظّٰلِمِينَ ﴿٤١﴾

42. There is no blame on those who defend themselves after they have been wronged.[2662]

وَلَمَنِ انْتَصَرَ بَعْدَ ظُلْمِهِ فَأُولٰٓئِكَ مَا عَلَيْهِمْ مِّنْ سَبِيلٍ ﴿٤٢﴾

43. The blame is only on those who wrong men and transgress in the earth without justification. Such will have a grievous punishment.

إِنَّمَا السَّبِيلُ عَلَى الَّذِينَ يَظْلِمُونَ النَّاسَ وَيَبْغُونَ فِي الْأَرْضِ بِغَيْرِ الْحَقِّ ۚ أُولٰٓئِكَ لَهُمْ عَذَابٌ أَلِيمٌ ﴿٤٣﴾

44. [c]And he who is patient and forgives—that, surely, is a matter of high resolve.

وَلَمَنْ صَبَرَ وَغَفَرَ إِنَّ ذٰلِكَ لَمِنْ عَزْمِ الْأُمُورِ ﴿٤٤﴾ ع

[a]3 : 160. [b]2 : 195; 16 : 127. [c]16 : 127.

2660. The verse lays down *Shūrā* (mutual consultation) as the basic principle which should guide Muslims in the transaction of their national affairs. This simple word contains the nucleus of a representative form of government of which the West is so proud. The *Khalifah* or Head of an Islamic State is bound to take counsel with the representatives of the people when he is to take a decision of vital national importance. See also 621 and 622.

2661. The verse forms the basis of the penal laws of Islām. The real object underlying the awarding of punishment to the guilty person according to Islamic teaching, is his moral reformation. If forgiveness is calculated to do him some moral good, he should be forgiven. But he should be punished, if punishment is likely to lead to his reformation; the punishment, however, should in no case be disproportionate to the offence committed. Islām does not believe in the monastic teaching of turning the other cheek, nor in the Jewish doctrine of "an eye for an eye," under all conditions It adopts the golden mean.

2662. Islamic principles about punishing an offender may not appeal to visionaries and unpractical idealists, but as a practical religion, Islām has laid down most wholesome and practical solutions for problems of law, economics and morals. It regards self-defence as the moral duty of a Muslim. The Holy Prophet is reported to have said, 'He who is killed in defence of his property and honour is a martyr' (Bukhārī, *Kitāb al-Maẓālim Wa'l-Ghaṣab*).

R. 5 45. [a]And he whom Allāh adjudges astray—there is no protector for him thereafter. And thou wilt find the wrongdoers, when they see the punishment, saying, 'Is there any way of return?'

وَمَنْ يُّضْلِلِ اللّٰهُ فَمَا لَهٗ مِنْ وَّلِيٍّ مِّنْۢ بَعْدِهٖ ؕ
وَتَرَى الظّٰلِمِيْنَ لَمَّا رَاَوُا الْعَذَابَ يَقُوْلُوْنَ هَلْ
اِلٰى مَرَدٍّ مِّنْ سَبِيْلٍ ﴿۴۵﴾

46. And thou wilt see them brought before *the Fire*, casting down *their* eyes in humiliation, looking *at it* with a furtive glance.[2663] And those who believe will say, 'The losers, indeed, are those who ruin themselves and their families on the Day of Resurrection.' Behold! the wrongdoers will *remain* in a lasting punishment.

وَتَرٰىهُمْ يُعْرَضُوْنَ عَلَيْهَا خٰشِعِيْنَ مِنَ الذُّلِّ
يَنْظُرُوْنَ مِنْ طَرْفٍ خَفِيٍّ ؕ وَقَالَ الَّذِيْنَ اٰمَنُوْٓا
اِنَّ الْخٰسِرِيْنَ الَّذِيْنَ خَسِرُوْٓا اَنْفُسَهُمْ وَاَهْلِيْهِمْ
يَوْمَ الْقِيٰمَةِ ؕ اَلَآ اِنَّ الظّٰلِمِيْنَ فِيْ عَذَابٍ مُّقِيْمٍ ﴿۴۶﴾

47. And they have no helpers to help them against Allāh. And for him, whom Allāh leaves in error, there is no way *of guidance*.

وَمَا كَانَ لَهُمْ مِّنْ اَوْلِيَآءَ يَنْصُرُوْنَهُمْ مِّنْ دُوْنِ
اللّٰهِ ؕ وَمَنْ يُّضْلِلِ اللّٰهُ فَمَا لَهٗ مِنْ سَبِيْلٍ ؕ ﴿۴۷﴾

48. Hearken ye to your Lord before there comes a day for which there will be no averting contrary to *the decree of* Allāh. There will be no refuge for you on that day, nor will there be for you any *chance of* denial.

اِسْتَجِيْبُوْا لِرَبِّكُمْ مِّنْ قَبْلِ اَنْ يَّاْتِيَ يَوْمٌ لَّا مَرَدَّ
لَهٗ مِنَ اللّٰهِ ؕ مَا لَكُمْ مِّنْ مَّلْجَاٍ يَّوْمَئِذٍ وَّمَا لَكُمْ
مِّنْ نَّكِيْرٍ ﴿۴۸﴾

49. But if they turn away, We have not sent thee as a guardian over them. Thy duty is only to convey *the Message*. [b]And truly when We cause man to taste of mercy from Us, he rejoices therein. But if an evil befalls them because of what their hands have sent forth, then lo! man is ungrateful.

فَاِنْ اَعْرَضُوْا فَمَآ اَرْسَلْنٰكَ عَلَيْهِمْ حَفِيْظًا ؕ اِنْ عَلَيْكَ
اِلَّا الْبَلٰغُ ؕ وَاِنَّآ اِذَآ اَذَقْنَا الْاِنْسَانَ مِنَّا رَحْمَةً فَرِحَ
بِهَا ۚ وَاِنْ تُصِبْهُمْ سَيِّئَةٌ ۢ بِمَا قَدَّمَتْ اَيْدِيْهِمْ
فَاِنَّ الْاِنْسَانَ كَفُوْرٌ ﴿۴۹﴾

[a]4 : 144; 17 : 98; 18 : 18. [b]11 : 11.

2663. The furtive glance is the glance of a guilty person who is hauled up for his crimes and is waiting to hear the sentence passed against him.

50. [a]To Allāh belongs the Kingdom of the heavens and the earth. He creates what He pleases. He bestows daughters upon whom He pleases and He bestows sons upon whom He pleases;

لِلّٰهِ مُلْكُ السَّمٰوٰتِ وَالْاَرْضِ ۭ يَخْلُقُ مَا يَشَآءُ ۭ
يَهَبُ لِمَنْ يَّشَآءُ اِنَاثًا وَّيَهَبُ لِمَنْ يَّشَآءُ
الذُّكُوْرَ ۝٥٠

51. Or, He mixes them, males and females; and He makes whom He pleases barren.[2664] Surely, He is All-Knowing, Powerful.

اَوْ يُزَوِّجُهُمْ ذُكْرَانًا وَّاِنَاثًا ۚ وَيَجْعَلُ مَنْ يَّشَآءُ
عَقِيْمًا ۭ اِنَّهٗ عَلِيْمٌ قَدِيْرٌ ۝٥١

52. And it is not for a man that Allāh should speak to him except by *direct* revelation, or from behind a veil, or by sending a messenger to reveal by His command[2665] what He pleases. Surely, He is High, Wise.

وَمَا كَانَ لِبَشَرٍ اَنْ يُّكَلِّمَهُ اللّٰهُ اِلَّا وَحْيًا اَوْ مِنْ
وَّرَآئِ حِجَابٍ اَوْ يُرْسِلَ رَسُوْلًا فَيُوْحِيَ بِاِذْنِهٖ
مَا يَشَآءُ ۭ اِنَّهٗ عَلِيٌّ حَكِيْمٌ ۝٥٢

53. And thus have We revealed to thee the Word[2666] by Our command. Thou didst not know what the Book was, nor what the faith. But We have made *the revelation* a light, whereby We guide such of Our servants as We please. And, truly, thou guidest *mankind* to the right path,

وَكَذٰلِكَ اَوْحَيْنَآ اِلَيْكَ رُوْحًا مِّنْ اَمْرِنَا ۭ مَا كُنْتَ
تَدْرِيْ مَا الْكِتٰبُ وَلَا الْاِيْمَانُ وَلٰكِنْ جَعَلْنٰهُ
نُوْرًا نَّهْدِيْ بِهٖ مَنْ نَّشَآءُ مِنْ عِبَادِنَا ۭ وَاِنَّكَ
لَتَهْدِيْٓ اِلٰى صِرَاطٍ مُّسْتَقِيْمٍ ۝٥٣

54. The[2667] path of Allāh, to Whom belongs whatever is in the heavens and whatever is in the earth. Remember, to Allāh do all things return.[2668]

صِرَاطِ اللّٰهِ الَّذِيْ لَهٗ مَا فِي السَّمٰوٰتِ وَمَا فِي الْاَرْضِ
اَلَآ اِلَى اللّٰهِ تَصِيْرُ الْاُمُوْرُ ۝٥٤ ع

[a]5 : 41; 39 : 45; 57 : 3.

2664. In this and the preceding verse the disbelievers have been warned that God has decreed that whereas the followers of Islām will increase and multiply, they will decrease and become barren—their children joining the fold of Islām.

2665. The verse makes mention of the three ways in which God speaks to His servants and reveals Himself to them : (*a*) He speaks to them direct without the aid of an intermediary. (*b*) He makes them see a vision which may or may not be interpretable, or, sometimes makes them hear words in a state of wakefulness, when they are not seeing the person speaking to them. This is the significance of the words, 'from behind the veil.' (*c*) God sends down a messenger—an angel who delivers the Divine Message.

2666. The Qur'ān has been called here *Rūḥ*, (breath of life, Lane), because through it a morally and spiritually dead people received a new life.

2667. Islām is the Life and the Light and the Way that leads to God and to the realization by man of the great and sublime object of his creation.

2668. The beginning and the end of all things is in the hand of Allāh.

CHAPTER 43

AL-ZUKHRUF

(*Revealed before Hijrah*)

Date of Revelation and Context

According to Qurṭubī there exists complete unanimity of opinion among scholars that this *Sūrah* was revealed at Mecca. Ibn 'Abbās also lends his powerful support to this view. It is, however, difficult to assign an exact date to its revelation. Scholarly opinion generally is inclined to place it towards the end of the fourth or the beginning of the fifth year of the Call. The previous *Sūrah* had ended on the note that the revelation which descends on Heavenly Messengers and Prophets by Divine command possesses an element of mystery. It was further stated that before revelation actually descended upon the Holy Prophet, he was not conversant with its nature and significance. The present *Sūrah* opens with the affirmation that because the Qur'ān has been revealed in a most clear and eloquent language and because also it deals with all basic truths and its teaching is easily comprehensible, therefore, in spite of the element of mystery in its revelation, there is no reasonable ground for anyone to reject it. It further says that God would not stop sending fresh revelation whenever there was genuine need for it, just as Prophets of God did not cease to come because they were mocked and jeered at. The phenomenon of the advent of Divine Reformers will continue despite anything the disbelievers might say or do.

Subject-Matter

The *Sūrah* like the three preceding Chapters opens with the declaration that the Qur'ān has been revealed by God, the Lord of all Honour and Praise, and proceeds to deal with the subject of Divine Unity—its basic theme—in a way and form different from that in which it has been dealt with in other Chapters of the Ḥā Mīm group. It says that God, in order to establish His Unity, has been sending, from time immemorial, His Messengers and Prophets. They preached and taught that God is One. They were rejected and opposed and persecuted. But this did not cause God to stop sending new Prophets and new revelations. Prophets continued to appear in the fulness of time, and the greatest of them came in the person of the Holy Prophet Muḥammad. The *Sūrah* develops this argument and says that God has created the heavens and the earth for the service of man and has made full provision for his physical needs. When He has taken so much care to provide for his material needs and physical comforts, it is inconceivable that He should have neglected or ignored to make similar provision for his moral and spiritual requirements. It is to meet man's moral needs that God sends a new revelation. But in their ignorance and folly disbelievers set up equals to God in various shapes and forms; and even go so far as to shift the responsibility for their idolatrous practices to God, brazenly saying that if God had so willed they would not have worshipped idols. The plea is against human intelligence and common sense, and no Divine Scripture supports it. The real cause of the disbelief of disbelievers lies in their pride and conceit because the Qur'ān, as they say, has not been revealed to a great man. In answer to this arrogant assumption of superiority the disbelievers receive a severe rebuke that what they call greatness carries no weight in the sight of God. Were it not that the obliteration of disparity of wealth, position and status would have rendered social order impossible and would have created chaos, God would have given to disbelievers tons of gold and silver so much so that even the staircases of their houses would have been made of gold, because these things are nothing in God's sight. As stated above the main theme of the *Sūrah* is the unsparing denunciation of idolatry. But while the Qur'ān condemns idol-worship it respects Jesus who, according to Christians, is an object of worship, as a great and noble Messenger of God, adding that he invited his people to the worship of One God, but they ignored his teachings and deified him. So the fault lay with them and not with him. The *Sūrah* ends on a brief but most clear and convincing discourse on Divine Unity.

سُوْرَةُ الزُّخْرُفِ مَكِّيَّةٌ (٤٣)

1. [a]In the name of Allāh, the Gracious, the Merciful.

بِسْمِ اللّٰهِ الرَّحْمٰنِ الرَّحِيْمِ ۝١

2. [b]Ḥā Mīm.[2668A]

حٰمٓ ۝٢

3. We cite as evidence this perspicuous Book,

وَالْكِتٰبِ الْمُبِيْنِ ۝٣

4. [c]We have made it *a Book* to be oft read in clear, eloquent language that you may understand.

اِنَّا جَعَلْنٰهُ قُرْءٰنًا عَرَبِيًّا لَّعَلَّكُمْ تَعْقِلُوْنَ ۝٤

5. And, surely, it is *safe* with Us in the Mother of the Book,[2669] exalted *and* full of wisdom.

وَاِنَّهٗ فِيْٓ اُمِّ الْكِتٰبِ لَدَيْنَا لَعَلِيٌّ حَكِيْمٌ ۝٥

6. Shall We then take away the Reminder from you, leaving you *without guidance*[2670] because you are an extravagant people?[2671]

اَفَنَضْرِبُ عَنْكُمُ الذِّكْرَ صَفْحًا اَنْ كُنْتُمْ قَوْمًا مُّسْرِفِيْنَ ۝٦

7. [d]And how many a Prophet did We send among the earlier peoples!

وَكَمْ اَرْسَلْنَا مِنْ نَّبِيٍّ فِي الْاَوَّلِيْنَ ۝٧

8. [e]But there never came to them a Prophet but they mocked at him.

وَمَا يَاْتِيْهِمْ مِّنْ نَّبِيٍّ اِلَّا كَانُوْا بِهٖ يَسْتَهْزِءُوْنَ ۝٨

9. And We destroyed *those* who were mightier in power than these, and the example of the earlier peoples has gone before.

فَاَهْلَكْنَآ اَشَدَّ مِنْهُمْ بَطْشًا وَّمَضٰى مَثَلُ الْاَوَّلِيْنَ ۝٩

[a]1:1. [b]44:2; 45:2. [c]39:29; 42:8; 46:13. [d]15:11. [e]15:12; 36:31.

2668A. See 2592 and 2643.

2669. *Umm al-Kitāb*, meaning sources of the commandments (Lane), the expression signifies that the Qur'ān existed in the knowledge of God—the Original Source—as the basis of the *Sharī'ah*, or it may signify that it was eternally decreed that the Qur'ān would form the basis of the last Divine Law.

2670. *Daraba 'an-hu* means, he left him and turned away from him. *Ṣafaḥa 'an-hu* also means, he turned away from him and left him. The Quranic expression means, 'Shall We take away the Reminder from you and turn Ourselves away from you and leave you without guidance' (Lane)?

2671. Heavenly Reminders in the form of Divine Signs will never cease to come. If rejection of Heavenly Signs had been a reasonable ground that they should discontinue to appear, then no Prophet would have come after the first one. But Prophets continued to appear.

10. And if thou ask them, 'Who created the heavens and the earth?' they will, surely, say, 'The Mighty, the All-Knowing *God* created them,'

وَلَئِنْ سَأَلْتَهُمْ مَّنْ خَلَقَ السَّمٰوٰتِ وَالْاَرْضَ
لَيَقُوْلُنَّ خَلَقَهُنَّ الْعَزِيْزُ الْعَلِيْمُ ﴿١٠﴾

11. [a]*He*, Who has made the earth for you a cradle and has made pathways for you therein, that you may follow the right way;

الَّذِيْ جَعَلَ لَكُمُ الْاَرْضَ مَهْدًا وَّجَعَلَ لَكُمْ
فِيْهَا سُبُلًا لَّعَلَّكُمْ تَهْتَدُوْنَ ﴿١١﴾

12. And Who sends down water from the clouds in proper measure, and We, thereby, quicken a dead land—even so will you be raised[2672]—

وَالَّذِيْ نَزَّلَ مِنَ السَّمَآءِ مَآءًۢ بِقَدَرٍ فَاَنْشَرْنَا
بِهٖ بَلْدَةً مَّيْتًا كَذٰلِكَ تُخْرَجُوْنَ ﴿١٢﴾

13. And Who has created pairs of all *things*, and has made for you ships and cattle whereon you ride,

وَالَّذِيْ خَلَقَ الْاَزْوَاجَ كُلَّهَا وَجَعَلَ لَكُمْ مِّنَ
الْفُلْكِ وَالْاَنْعَامِ مَا تَرْكَبُوْنَ ﴿١٣﴾

14. That you may sit firmly upon their backs, *and*, then, when you are firmly seated thereon, you may remember the favour of your Lord, and say, 'Holy is He Who has subjected these to us, and we were not capable of subduing them *ourselves*,

لِتَسْتَوٗا عَلٰى ظُهُوْرِهٖ ثُمَّ تَذْكُرُوْا نِعْمَةَ رَبِّكُمْ
اِذَا اسْتَوَيْتُمْ عَلَيْهِ وَتَقُوْلُوْا سُبْحٰنَ الَّذِيْ سَخَّرَ
لَنَا هٰذَا وَمَا كُنَّا لَهٗ مُقْرِنِيْنَ ﴿١٤﴾

15. 'And to our Lord, surely, shall we return.'

وَاِنَّآ اِلٰى رَبِّنَا لَمُنْقَلِبُوْنَ ﴿١٥﴾

16. And they assign to Him a part of His servants *as His children*.[2672A] Indeed man is manifestly ungrateful.

وَجَعَلُوْا لَهٗ مِنْ عِبَادِهٖ جُزْءًا اِنَّ الْاِنْسَانَ لَكَفُوْرٌ
مُّبِيْنٌ ﴿١٦﴾ ع ٢

R. 2 17. [b]Has He taken daughters from what He has created, and favoured you with sons?

اَمِ اتَّخَذَ مِمَّا يَخْلُقُ بَنٰتٍ وَّاَصْفٰكُمْ بِالْبَنِيْنَ ﴿١٧﴾

[a]20 : 54. [b]6 : 101; 16 : 58; 52 : 40; 53 : 22.

2672. The words signify that even as dry and parched earth blooms and blossoms into new life when rain falls on it, so do a morally and spiritually dead people receive a new life through Divine revelation.

2672A. The reference is to the Christian doctrine of Jesus being God's son.

18. [a]Yet when tidings are given to one of them of that the like of which he ascribes to the Gracious *God*, his face becomes dark and he is choked with inward grief.

وَإِذَا بُشِّرَ أَحَدُهُم بِمَا ضَرَبَ لِلرَّحْمَٰنِ مَثَلًا ظَلَّ وَجْهُهُ مُسْوَدًّا وَهُوَ كَظِيمٌ ﴿١٨﴾

19. *Do they assign to Allāh* one who is nurtured among ornaments,[2673] and who is not able to give clear expression *to an argument* in disputation?

أَوَمَن يُنَشَّأُ فِي الْحِلْيَةِ وَهُوَ فِي الْخِصَامِ غَيْرُ مُبِينٍ ﴿١٩﴾

20. [b]And they regard as females the angels who are the servants of the Gracious *God*. Did they witness their creation? Then their testimony will be recorded, and they will be questioned.

وَجَعَلُوا الْمَلَائِكَةَ الَّذِينَ هُمْ عِبَادُ الرَّحْمَٰنِ إِنَاثًا ۚ أَشَهِدُوا خَلْقَهُمْ ۚ سَتُكْتَبُ شَهَادَتُهُمْ وَيُسْأَلُونَ ﴿٢٠﴾

21. And they say, [c]'If the Gracious *God* had *so* willed, we should not have worshipped them.' They have no knowledge whatsoever of that. They do nothing but conjecture.

وَقَالُوا لَوْ شَاءَ الرَّحْمَٰنُ مَا عَبَدْنَاهُم ۗ مَّا لَهُم بِذَٰلِكَ مِنْ عِلْمٍ ۖ إِنْ هُمْ إِلَّا يَخْرُصُونَ ﴿٢١﴾

22. [d]Have We given them a Scripture before this, so that they are holding fast[2674] to it?

أَمْ آتَيْنَاهُمْ كِتَابًا مِّن قَبْلِهِ فَهُم بِهِ مُسْتَمْسِكُونَ ﴿٢٢﴾

23. Nay, but they say, [e]'We found our fathers following a *certain* course, and we are guided by their footsteps.'

بَلْ قَالُوا إِنَّا وَجَدْنَا آبَاءَنَا عَلَىٰ أُمَّةٍ وَإِنَّا عَلَىٰ آثَارِهِم مُّهْتَدُونَ ﴿٢٣﴾

[a]16 : 59. [b]17 : 41; 37 : 151; 52 : 40. [c]6 : 149; 16 : 36. [d]37 : 157-158; 68 : 38. [e]2 : 171; 7 : 29.

2673. The reference may be to the idols which were bedecked and bejewelled with ornaments. The verse administers a subtle rebuke to idol-worshippers that they worship idols which can neither speak nor answer their prayers or defend themselves against attacks made upon them.

2674. Idol-worshippers not only do not possess any reason or argument to uphold their irrational doctrines, they cannot even adduce the evidence of any Divine Scripture in their support.

24. Even so We never sent any Warner before thee to any township, but the wealthy ones among them said, [a]'We found our fathers following a *certain* course, and we are following in their footsteps.'

وَكَذٰلِكَ مَآ اَرْسَلْنَا مِنْ قَبْلِكَ فِيْ قَرْيَةٍ مِّنْ نَّذِيْرٍ
اِلَّا قَالَ مُتْرَفُوْهَآ ۙ اِنَّا وَجَدْنَآ اٰبَآءَنَا عَلٰٓى اُمَّةٍ وَّ
اِنَّا عَلٰٓى اٰثٰرِهِمْ مُّقْتَدُوْنَ ﴿۲۴﴾

25. *Their Messenger* said, 'What! even though I bring you a better guidance than that which you found your fathers following?' They said, 'Certainly we disbelieve in that which you are sent with.'

قٰلَ اَوَلَوْ جِئْتُكُمْ بِاَهْدٰى مِمَّا وَجَدْتُّمْ عَلَيْهِ
اٰبَآءَكُمْ ۭ قَالُوْٓا اِنَّا بِمَآ اُرْسِلْتُمْ بِهٖ كٰفِرُوْنَ ﴿۲۵﴾

26. [b]So We exacted retribution from them. Then see what was the end of those who rejected *the Prophets!*

فَانْتَقَمْنَا مِنْهُمْ فَانْظُرْ كَيْفَ كَانَ عَاقِبَةُ
الْمُكَذِّبِيْنَ ﴿۲۶﴾ ع النصف

R. 3 27. And *call to mind* when Abraham said to his father and his people, [c]'I do, indeed, disown what you worship,

وَاِذْ قَالَ اِبْرٰهِيْمُ لِاَبِيْهِ وَقَوْمِهٖٓ اِنَّنِيْ بَرَآءٌ
مِّمَّا تَعْبُدُوْنَ ﴿۲۷﴾

28. 'Except Him Who created me, and He will, surely, guide me.'

اِلَّا الَّذِيْ فَطَرَنِيْ فَاِنَّهٗ سَيَهْدِيْنِ ﴿۲۸﴾

29. And He left this *as* a permanent legacy among his posterity,[2675] that they might turn *to God*.

وَجَعَلَهَا كَلِمَةًۢ بَاقِيَةً فِيْ عَقِبِهٖ لَعَلَّهُمْ يَرْجِعُوْنَ ﴿۲۹﴾

30. Nay, but I bestowed upon these *disbelievers* and their fathers worldly provision until there came to them the truth and a Messenger who makes *his Message* clear.

بَلْ مَتَّعْتُ هٰٓؤُلَآءِ وَاٰبَآءَهُمْ حَتّٰى جَآءَهُمُ الْحَقُّ
وَرَسُوْلٌ مُّبِيْنٌ ﴿۳۰﴾

31. But when the truth came to them they said, [d]'This is sorcery and we do reject it.'

وَلَمَّا جَآءَهُمُ الْحَقُّ قَالُوْا هٰذَا سِحْرٌ وَّاِنَّا بِهٖ
كٰفِرُوْنَ ﴿۳۱﴾

[a]21 : 54; 26 : 75. [b]7 : 137; 43 : 56. [c]6 : 79; 9 : 114; 60 : 5. [d]27 : 14.

2675. Abraham was such a firm believer in Divine Unity and he preached it to his posterity with such sincerity and persistence that this belief came to stay among them for a long time.

32. And they say, 'Why has not this Qur'ān been sent to some great man of the two[2676] towns?'

وَقَالُوْا لَوْلَا نُزِّلَ هٰذَا الْقُرْاٰنُ عَلٰى رَجُلٍ مِّنَ الْقَرْيَتَيْنِ
عَظِيْمٍ ﴿۳۲﴾

33. Are they *then* the distributors[2677] of the mercy of thy Lord? It is We Who distribute among them their livelihood in the present life, and We exalt some of them above others in degrees *of rank*, so that some of them may make others subservient *to themselves*. And the mercy of thy Lord is better than that which they amass.

اَهُمْ يَقْسِمُوْنَ رَحْمَتَ رَبِّكَ ۭ نَحْنُ قَسَمْنَا بَيْنَهُمْ
مَّعِيْشَتَهُمْ فِي الْحَيٰوةِ الدُّنْيَا وَرَفَعْنَا بَعْضَهُمْ
فَوْقَ بَعْضٍ دَرَجٰتٍ لِّيَتَّخِذَ بَعْضُهُمْ بَعْضًا سُخْرِيًّا ۭ
وَرَحْمَتُ رَبِّكَ خَيْرٌ مِّمَّا يَجْمَعُوْنَ ﴿۳۳﴾

34. And were it not that all mankind would have become one type of people, We would have given to those who disbelieve in the Gracious *God* roofs *of silver* for their houses, and *silver* stairways by which they could ascend;

وَلَوْلَآ اَنْ يَّكُوْنَ النَّاسُ اُمَّةً وَّاحِدَةً لَّجَعَلْنَا لِمَنْ
يَّكْفُرُ بِالرَّحْمٰنِ لِبُيُوْتِهِمْ سُقُفًا مِّنْ فِضَّةٍ وَّمَعَارِجَ
عَلَيْهَا يَظْهَرُوْنَ ﴿۳۴﴾

35. And doors *of silver* to their houses, and couches *of silver*, on which they could recline,

وَلِبُيُوْتِهِمْ اَبْوَابًا وَّسُرُرًا عَلَيْهَا يَتَّكِـُٔوْنَ ﴿۳۵﴾

36. And *even* of gold. But all that is nothing but a *temporary* provision of the present life.[2678] And the *comfort of the* Hereafter with thy Lord is for the righteous.

وَزُخْرُفًا ۭ وَاِنْ كُلُّ ذٰلِكَ لَمَّا مَتَاعُ الْحَيٰوةِ الدُّنْيَا ۭ
وَالْاٰخِرَةُ عِنْدَ رَبِّكَ لِلْمُتَّقِيْنَ ﴿۳۶﴾

2676. The "two towns" are generally understood to mean Mecca and Ṭā'if. They were two important centres of Arab social and political life in the Holy Prophet's time.

2677. The verse administers a severe rebuke to disbelievers saying to them, 'Since when have they arrogated to themselves the role of being the distributors of God's grace and mercy, or the privilege of deciding who is deserving of it and who not?

2678. Were it not that by the obliteration of disparity of means, wealth and position, all men would have become of one type, and human society would have ceased to function. God would have provided disbelievers with houses made of silver, having doors and stairways made of gold, because these things possess no value or worth in His sight.

R. 4 37. [a]And he who turns away from the remembrance of the Gracious *God*, We appoint for him a satan, who *becomes* his intimate companion.

وَمَنْ يَّعْشُ عَنْ ذِكْرِ الرَّحْمٰنِ نُقَيِّضْ لَهٗ شَيْطٰنًا فَهُوَ لَهٗ قَرِيْنٌ ﴿۳۷﴾

38. [b]And, surely, these *companions* hinder them from the way *of God*, but they think that they are rightly guided;

وَاِنَّهُمْ لَيَصُدُّوْنَهُمْ عَنِ السَّبِيْلِ وَيَحْسَبُوْنَ اَنَّهُمْ مُّهْتَدُوْنَ ﴿۳۸﴾

39. Till when, such a one comes to Us, he says *to his companion*, "Would that between me and thee were the distance of the East and the West![2679]" What an evil companion is he!

حَتّٰٓى اِذَا جَآءَنَا قَالَ يٰلَيْتَ بَيْنِيْ وَبَيْنَكَ بُعْدَ الْمَشْرِقَيْنِ فَبِئْسَ الْقَرِيْنُ ﴿۳۹﴾

40. [d]And *it will be said to them*, 'Your being partners in punishment will not profit you this day, for you had acted wrongfully.'

وَلَنْ يَّنْفَعَكُمُ الْيَوْمَ اِذْ ظَّلَمْتُمْ اَنَّكُمْ فِي الْعَذَابِ مُشْتَرِكُوْنَ ﴿۴۰﴾

41. [e]Canst thou, then, make the deaf hear, or guide the blind and him who is in manifest error?[2680]

اَفَاَنْتَ تُسْمِعُ الصُّمَّ اَوْ تَهْدِي الْعُمْيَ وَمَنْ كَانَ فِيْ ضَلٰلٍ مُّبِيْنٍ ﴿۴۱﴾

42. [f]And if We take thee away *from this world*, We shall *nevertheless* take vengeance upon them;

فَاِمَّا نَذْهَبَنَّ بِكَ فَاِنَّا مِنْهُمْ مُّنْتَقِمُوْنَ ﴿۴۲﴾

43. Or, [g]We shall show thee that which We have promised them; for, surely, We have complete power over them.

اَوْ نُرِيَنَّكَ الَّذِيْ وَعَدْنٰهُمْ فَاِنَّا عَلَيْهِمْ مُّقْتَدِرُوْنَ ﴿۴۳﴾

44. So [h]hold thou fast to that which has been revealed to thee; for thou art on the right path.

فَاسْتَمْسِكْ بِالَّذِيْٓ اُوْحِيَ اِلَيْكَ ۚ اِنَّكَ عَلٰى صِرَاطٍ مُّسْتَقِيْمٍ ﴿۴۴﴾

[a]20 : 100, 101; 72 : 18. [b]8 : 35; 16 : 89; [c]3 : 31. [d]37 : 34. [e]10 : 43; 27 : 81. [f]13 : 41; 40 : 78. [g]10 : 47; 13 : 41; 40 : 78. [h]11 : 113.

2679. When man is confronted with the evil consequences of his wicked deeds, he seeks to avoid and shun his erstwhile companions as if he never knew them.

2680. When disbelievers deliberately shut their eyes and ears to the message of truth, they sink deeper and deeper into sin till they are completely lost.

45. And, truly, [a]this *Qur'ān* is *a source of* eminence[2681] for thee and for thy people; and you will, surely, be questioned.

وَاِنَّهٗ لَذِكْرٌ لَّكَ وَلِقَوْمِكَ ۚ وَسَوْفَ تُسْـَٔلُوْنَ ﴿٤٥﴾

46. [b]And ask those of Our Messengers whom We sent before thee, 'Did We appoint any deities beside the Gracious *God*, to be worshipped?'

وَسْـَٔلْ مَنْ اَرْسَلْنَا مِنْ قَبْلِكَ مِنْ رُّسُلِنَآ اَجَعَلْنَا
مِنْ دُوْنِ الرَّحْمٰنِ اٰلِهَةً يُّعْبَدُوْنَ ﴿٤٦﴾ ع

R. 5 47. And, indeed, [c]We sent Moses with Our Signs to Pharaoh and his chiefs and he said, 'I am, truly, a Messenger of the Lord of the worlds.'

وَلَقَدْ اَرْسَلْنَا مُوْسٰى بِاٰيٰتِنَآ اِلٰى فِرْعَوْنَ وَمَلَا۟ئِهٖ
فَقَالَ اِنِّيْ رَسُوْلُ رَبِّ الْعٰلَمِيْنَ ﴿٤٧﴾

48. But when he came to them with Our Signs, lo! they laughed at them.

فَلَمَّا جَآءَهُمْ بِاٰيٰتِنَآ اِذَا هُمْ مِّنْهَا يَضْحَكُوْنَ ﴿٤٨﴾

49. And We showed them no Sign but it was greater than its *preceding* sister *Sign*, and We seized them with punishment, that they might turn *to Us*.

وَمَا نُرِيْهِمْ مِّنْ اٰيَةٍ اِلَّا هِيَ اَكْبَرُ مِنْ اُخْتِهَا ۫ وَ
اَخَذْنٰهُمْ بِالْعَذَابِ لَعَلَّهُمْ يَرْجِعُوْنَ ﴿٤٩﴾

50. And *each time* they said, 'O thou sorcerer, [d]pray for us to thy Lord, according to the promise He made with thee *that if* He *avert this evil from us*, then we will, surely, follow guidance.'

وَقَالُوْا يٰٓاَيُّهَ السّٰحِرُ ادْعُ لَنَا رَبَّكَ بِمَا عَهِدَ عِنْدَكَ ۚ
اِنَّنَا لَمُهْتَدُوْنَ ﴿٥٠﴾

51. But [e]when We removed the punishment from them, behold! they broke their pledge.

فَلَمَّا كَشَفْنَا عَنْهُمُ الْعَذَابَ اِذَا هُمْ يَنْكُثُوْنَ ﴿٥١﴾

52. And Pharaoh made a proclamation among his people: 'O my people! does not the kingdom of Egypt belong to me and these streams flowing beneath me? Do you not then see?

وَنَادٰى فِرْعَوْنُ فِيْ قَوْمِهٖ قَالَ يٰقَوْمِ اَلَيْسَ لِيْ
مُلْكُ مِصْرَ وَهٰذِهِ الْاَنْهٰرُ تَجْرِيْ مِنْ تَحْتِيْ ۚ اَفَلَا
تُبْصِرُوْنَ ﴿٥٢﴾

[a]21 : 11; 38 : 2. [b]21 : 26. [c]11 : 97; 14 : 6; 23 : 46; 40 : 24.
[d]7 : 135. [e]7 : 136.

2681. The word *Dhikr* meaning eminence (Lane), the verse purports to say that through the Qur'ān the Holy Prophet and his followers will acquire great eminence and honour.

53. 'Nay, I am better than this despicable fellow who can scarcely express *himself* clearly.

اَمْ اَنَا خَيْرٌ مِّنْ هٰذَا الَّذِيْ هُوَ مَهِيْنٌ ۙ وَّلَا يَكَادُ يُبِيْنُ ﴿۵۳﴾

54. 'And why have not bracelets of gold been bestowed on him, or [a]angels accompanied him in serried ranks?'

فَلَوْلَآ اُلْقِيَ عَلَيْهِ اَسْوِرَةٌ مِّنْ ذَهَبٍ اَوْ جَآءَ مَعَهُ الْمَلٰٓئِكَةُ مُقْتَرِنِيْنَ ﴿۵۴﴾

55. Thus did he make light of his people, and they obeyed him. Indeed, they were a wicked people.

فَاسْتَخَفَّ قَوْمَهٗ فَاَطَاعُوْهُ ؕ اِنَّهُمْ كَانُوْا قَوْمًا فٰسِقِيْنَ ﴿۵۵﴾

56. So, when they excited Our anger, [b]We took vengeance upon them, and drowned them all.

فَلَمَّآ اٰسَفُوْنَا انْتَقَمْنَا مِنْهُمْ فَاَغْرَقْنٰهُمْ اَجْمَعِيْنَ ﴿۵۶﴾

57. And We made them a precedent, and an example for the coming generations.

فَجَعَلْنٰهُمْ سَلَفًا وَّمَثَلًا لِّلْاٰخِرِيْنَ ﴿۵۷﴾ ع

R. 6 58. And when the son of Mary is mentioned as an example, lo! thy people raise a clamour[2682] thereat;

وَلَمَّا ضُرِبَ ابْنُ مَرْيَمَ مَثَلًا اِذَا قَوْمُكَ مِنْهُ يَصِدُّوْنَ ﴿۵۸﴾

59. And they say, 'Are our gods better, or he?' They mention not this to thee but for *the sake of* disputation. Nay, but they are a contentious people.[2683]

وَقَالُوْٓا ءَاٰلِهَتُنَا خَيْرٌ اَمْ هُوَ ؕ مَا ضَرَبُوْهُ لَكَ اِلَّا جَدَلًا ؕ بَلْ هُمْ قَوْمٌ خَصِمُوْنَ ﴿۵۹﴾

60. He was only *Our* servant, on whom We bestowed *Our* favour, and We made him an example for the Children of Israel.

اِنْ هُوَ اِلَّا عَبْدٌ اَنْعَمْنَا عَلَيْهِ وَجَعَلْنٰهُ مَثَلًا لِّبَنِيْٓ اِسْرَآءِيْلَ ﴿۶۰﴾

[a]6 : 9; 11 : 13; 25 : 8. [b]43 : 26.

2682. *Ṣadda* (*Yaṣuddu*) means, he hindered him from a thing; and *Ṣadda* (*Yaṣiddu*) means, he raised a clamour (Aqrab).

2683. The advent of the Messiah was a sign that the Jews were going to be disgraced and humiliated and were about to be deprived of Prophethood for all time. *Mathal* signifying anything similar or equal to another (6 : 39), the verse, besides the meaning given in the text, may also signify that when the people of the Holy Prophet—the Muslims—are told that another person, who would be like Jesus and would be his counterpart, would be raised from among them to regenerate them and restore their lost spiritual glory, instead of being glad over this good tidings, they raise a clamour. The verse may thus be taken as referring to the Second Coming of Jesus.

61. And if We *so* willed, We could make from among you angels to be *your* successors in the earth.[2684]

وَلَوْ نَشَآءُ لَجَعَلْنَا مِنْكُمْ مَّلٰٓئِكَةً فِي الْاَرْضِ يَخْلُفُوْنَ ﴿٦١﴾

62. But, verily, he was a sign of the Hour.[2685] So entertain no doubt about it, but follow me. This is the right path.

وَاِنَّهٗ لَعِلْمٌ لِّلسَّاعَةِ فَلَا تَمْتَرُنَّ بِهَا وَاتَّبِعُوْنِ ۭ هٰذَا صِرَاطٌ مُّسْتَقِيْمٌ ﴿٦٢﴾

63. And let not Satan hinder you. Surely, he is to you an open enemy.

وَلَا يَصُدَّنَّكُمُ الشَّيْطٰنُ ۚ اِنَّهٗ لَكُمْ عَدُوٌّ مُّبِيْنٌ ﴿٦٣﴾

64. And when Jesus came with clear proofs, he said, 'Truly, I have come to you with wisdom, and to make clear to you some of that about which you differ. So fear Allāh and obey me.

وَلَمَّا جَآءَ عِيْسٰى بِالْبَيِّنٰتِ قَالَ قَدْ جِئْتُكُمْ بِالْحِكْمَةِ وَلِاُبَيِّنَ لَكُمْ بَعْضَ الَّذِيْ تَخْتَلِفُوْنَ فِيْهِ ۚ فَاتَّقُوا اللّٰهَ وَاَطِيْعُوْنِ ﴿٦٤﴾

65. 'Verily, [a]Allāh—He is my Lord and your Lord. So worship Him. This is the right path.'

اِنَّ اللّٰهَ هُوَ رَبِّيْ وَرَبُّكُمْ فَاعْبُدُوْهُ ۭ هٰذَا صِرَاطٌ مُّسْتَقِيْمٌ ﴿٦٥﴾

66. But [b]the parties differed among themselves. So woe to the wrongdoers because of the punishment of a painful day!

فَاخْتَلَفَ الْاَحْزَابُ مِنْۢ بَيْنِهِمْ ۚ فَوَيْلٌ لِّلَّذِيْنَ ظَلَمُوْا مِنْ عَذَابِ يَوْمٍ اَلِيْمٍ ﴿٦٦﴾

67. [c]They wait not but for the Hour to come suddenly upon them, while they perceive *it* not.

هَلْ يَنْظُرُوْنَ اِلَّا السَّاعَةَ اَنْ تَاْتِيَهُمْ بَغْتَةً وَّهُمْ لَا يَشْعُرُوْنَ ﴿٦٧﴾

68. Friends on that day will be foes to one another, [d]except the righteous;[2686]

اَلْاَخِلَّآءُ يَوْمَئِذٍۢ بَعْضُهُمْ لِبَعْضٍ عَدُوٌّ اِلَّا الْمُتَّقِيْنَ ﴿٦٨﴾

[a]3 : 52; 19 : 37. [b]19 : 38. [c]10 : 51; 12 : 108; 22 : 56; 47 : 19. [d]2 : 256.

2684. Angels could not serve as an example and model for men, therefore God always commissioned men to convey His Will to, and to serve as model and pattern for, men.

2685. "Hour" may denote the time of the end of the Mosaic Dispensation and the pronoun *hū* in *inna hū* may refer either to Jesus or to the Qur'ān and the verse would mean, that after Jesus the Israelites will be deprived of the gift of Prophethood, or that another Dispensation—Quranic Dispensation—will take the place of Mosaic Dispensation.

2686. In the hour of distress all friendships are forgotten. Friends desert each other, even turn into enemies. Elsewhere, the Qur'ān gives a graphic description of the condition of sinners when they are confronted with the evil consequences of their wicked deeds (70 : 11-15; 80 : 35-38).

R. 7 69. *To them Allāh will say*, 'O My servants, there is [a]no fear for you this day, nor shall you grieve;

يٰعِبَادِ لَا خَوْفٌ عَلَيْكُمُ الْيَوْمَ وَلَآ اَنْتُمْ تَحْزَنُوْنَ ﴿٦٩﴾

70. '*You* who believed in Our Signs and submitted,

الَّذِيْنَ اٰمَنُوْا بِاٰيٰتِنَا وَكَانُوْا مُسْلِمِيْنَ ﴿٧٠﴾

71. [b]"Enter ye the Garden, you and your wives, honoured and happy.'

اُدْخُلُوا الْجَنَّةَ اَنْتُمْ وَاَزْوَاجُكُمْ تُحْبَرُوْنَ ﴿٧١﴾

72. There will be passed round to them [c]dishes of gold and cups, and therein will be all that the souls desire and *in which* the eyes delight. And therein you will dwell for ever.

يُطَافُ عَلَيْهِمْ بِصِحَافٍ مِّنْ ذَهَبٍ وَّاَكْوَابٍ ۚ وَفِيْهَا مَا تَشْتَهِيْهِ الْاَنْفُسُ وَتَلَذُّ الْاَعْيُنُ ۚ وَاَنْتُمْ فِيْهَا خٰلِدُوْنَ ﴿٧٢﴾

73. 'And [d]this is the Garden to which you have been made heirs because of what you did.

وَتِلْكَ الْجَنَّةُ الَّتِيْٓ اُوْرِثْتُمُوْهَا بِمَا كُنْتُمْ تَعْمَلُوْنَ ﴿٧٣﴾

74. [e]"Therein for you is fruit in abundance, of which you will eat.'

لَكُمْ فِيْهَا فَاكِهَةٌ كَثِيْرَةٌ مِّنْهَا تَاْكُلُوْنَ ﴿٧٤﴾

75. [f]The guilty will, certainly, abide in the punishment of Hell.

اِنَّ الْمُجْرِمِيْنَ فِيْ عَذَابِ جَهَنَّمَ خٰلِدُوْنَ ﴿٧٥﴾

76. [g]It will not be lightened for them, and they will be seized therein with despair.

لَا يُفَتَّرُ عَنْهُمْ وَهُمْ فِيْهِ مُبْلِسُوْنَ ﴿٧٦﴾

77. And We wronged them not, but it was they themselves who were the wrongdoers.

وَمَا ظَلَمْنٰهُمْ وَلٰكِنْ كَانُوْا هُمُ الظّٰلِمِيْنَ ﴿٧٧﴾

78. And they will cry, 'O Mālik![2687] let thy Lord make an end of us.' He will say, 'You must stay *here*.'

وَنَادَوْا يٰمٰلِكُ لِيَقْضِ عَلَيْنَا رَبُّكَ ۚ قَالَ اِنَّكُمْ مّٰكِثُوْنَ ﴿٧٨﴾

79. *Allāh will say*, 'We, certainly, brought you the truth; but most of you were averse to the truth.'

لَقَدْ جِئْنٰكُمْ بِالْحَقِّ وَلٰكِنَّ اَكْثَرَكُمْ لِلْحَقِّ كٰرِهُوْنَ ﴿٧٩﴾

---

[a]10 : 63; 39 : 62. [b]30 : 16. [c]56 : 19; 76 : 16. [d]7 : 44; 19 : 64. [e]55 : 53; 77 : 43. [f]20 : 75. [g]2 : 87; 40 : 50-51.

2687. *Mālik*, meaning master, is generally considered to be the angel in charge of Hell.

80. Have they determined upon a course *to compass thy end?* Then We, *too*, have determined *their destruction*.

أَمْ أَبْرَمُوٓا أَمْرًا فَإِنَّا مُبْرِمُونَ ﴿٨٠﴾

81. Do they think that We hear not their secrets and their private counsels? Yea! [a]And Our messengers *remain* with them recording *everything*.

أَمْ يَحْسَبُونَ أَنَّا لَا نَسْمَعُ سِرَّهُمْ وَنَجْوٰىهُمْ ۚ بَلٰى
وَرُسُلُنَا لَدَيْهِمْ يَكْتُبُونَ ﴿٨١﴾

82. Say, 'If the Gracious *God* had a son, I would have been the first of worshippers.'[2688]

قُلْ إِنْ كَانَ لِلرَّحْمٰنِ وَلَدٌ ۖ فَأَنَا أَوَّلُ الْعٰبِدِينَ ﴿٨٢﴾

83. Holy is *Allāh*, the Lord of the heavens and the earth, the Lord of the Throne, far above that which they attribute *to Him*.

سُبْحٰنَ رَبِّ السَّمٰوٰتِ وَالْأَرْضِ رَبِّ الْعَرْشِ
عَمَّا يَصِفُونَ ﴿٨٣﴾

84. [b]So leave them alone to indulge in vain discourse and to amuse themselves until they meet that Day of theirs which they have been promised.

فَذَرْهُمْ يَخُوضُوا وَيَلْعَبُوا حَتّٰى يُلٰقُوا يَوْمَهُمُ الَّذِي
يُوعَدُونَ ﴿٨٤﴾

85. [c]He it is Who is God in heaven, and God on earth; and He is the Wise, the All-Knowing.

وَهُوَ الَّذِي فِي السَّمَآءِ إِلٰهٌ وَّفِي الْأَرْضِ إِلٰهٌ ۚ وَ
هُوَ الْحَكِيمُ الْعَلِيمُ ﴿٨٥﴾

86. And blessed is He to Whom belongs the Kingdom of the heavens and the earth and all that is between them, and with Him is the knowledge of the Hour, and to Him shall you *all* be brought back.

وَتَبٰرَكَ الَّذِي لَهُ مُلْكُ السَّمٰوٰتِ وَالْأَرْضِ وَ
مَا بَيْنَهُمَا ۚ وَعِنْدَهُ عِلْمُ السَّاعَةِ ۚ وَإِلَيْهِ تُرْجَعُونَ ﴿٨٦﴾

---

[a]50 : 19; 82 : 11-12. [b]23 : 55; 52 : 46; 70 : 43. [c]6 : 4.

2688. '*Ābid* is active participle from '*Abada* which means, he worshipped; and from *Abida* which means, he was angry; he denied; he was sorrowful for having been remiss; he was disdainful (Lane). The verse thus means: (*a*) If the Gracious God had a son, I would have been the first to worship him (the son) because, being God's most obedient and faithful servant, I would not have been remiss in my duty to him (the son). (*b*) If it could be possible that the Gracious God should have a son, I am most entitled to this position because I have worshipped God most and have served Him most. (*c*) The Gracious God, certainly, has no son (*in* meaning 'not') and I am the first to bear witness to this fact, the word '*Ābidīn* signifying *Shāhidīn*, *i.e.*, witnesses. (*d*) The Gracious God has no son, and I am the first disdainful denier of the assertion that He has one.

87. And [a]those on whom they call beside Him possess no power of intercession but *only* he *may intercede* who bears witness to the truth,[2689] and they know *this well.*

وَلَا يَمْلِكُ الَّذِينَ يَدْعُونَ مِنْ دُونِهِ الشَّفَاعَةَ إِلَّا مَنْ شَهِدَ بِالْحَقِّ وَهُمْ يَعْلَمُونَ ﴿٨٧﴾

88. And [b]if thou ask them, 'Who created them?' They will, surely, say, 'Allah.' How, then, are they being turned away?

وَلَئِنْ سَأَلْتَهُمْ مَنْ خَلَقَهُمْ لَيَقُولُنَّ اللَّهُ فَأَنَّىٰ يُؤْفَكُونَ ﴿٨٨﴾

89. We call to witness *the Prophet's repeated* cry: 'O my Lord! [c]these are a people who will not believe.'[2690]

وَقِيلِهِ يَارَبِّ إِنَّ هَٰؤُلَاءِ قَوْمٌ لَا يُؤْمِنُونَ ﴿٨٩﴾

90. And *Our reply was,* "So turn aside from them, and say, 'Peace;'" and soon shall they know.[2691]

فَاصْفَحْ عَنْهُمْ وَقُلْ سَلَامٌ فَسَوْفَ يَعْلَمُونَ ﴿٩٠﴾ ع

[a]19 : 88. [b]29 : 62; 31 : 26; 39 : 39. [c]84 : 21.

2689. The Holy Prophet.

2690. There could be no greater testimony to the Holy Prophet's solicitude and concern for the spiritual well-being of his people than the fact that God Himself swears by it. The Holy Prophet's grief over the denial of his people and their opposition to it was so deep and agonizing that it had almost killed him (18 : 7).

2691. The Holy Prophet is consoled and comforted that though he is now being opposed and persecuted, yet the time was fast approaching when his enemies would come under his power, and Islām would spread all over Arabia and peace would reign throughout the land. When that time comes, he should forgive his enemies.

CHAPTER 44

AL-DUKHĀN

(*Revealed before Hijrah*)

Date of Revelation and Context

All authorities including Ibn 'Abbās and Ibn Zubair agree that the *Sūrah* belongs to the Middle Meccan period. Noldeke assigns its revelation to the sixth or seventh year of the Call. In its closing verses, the preceding *Sūrah* had made a pathetic reference to the agonized out-pourings of the Holy Prophet's lacerated heart that, in spite of his best efforts his Message had failed to evoke adequate response in his people. In answer to his cries of agony, the Holy Prophet was told to overlook their faults and invoke God's mercy on them, for, thus his prayer would draw Divine grace and would make them realize their mistake and listen to him. The present *Sūrah* opens with the declaration that the Qur'ān which fully explains the truths and realities of life has been revealed in a period of spiritual darkness to eclaim mankind from sin. The *Sūrah* is the fifth of the *Ḥā Mīm* group. Like the preceding Chapter it opens with the subject of revelation of the Qur'ān, though in a different form and context. It commences with the theme that whenever darkness enshrouds the face of the earth and humanity is stuck fast in the quagmire of moral turpitude, God raises a Messenger and gives him a new Message to reclaim and regenerate the world. Prophets of God had been appearing at such times of decadence, and now that the moral need of humanity was greatest and spiritual darkness was most intense and overwhelming, God has raised the greatest of His Messengers and has given him the last and most perfect Law—the Qur'ān. The advent of the Holy Prophet is not a novel phenomenon. Divine Messengers had appeared before him in the fulness of time, most prominent among them being Moses. The *Sūrah* then gives a pathetic description of the dreadful fate that overtook Pharaoh and his people. They went to their doom in disgrace and ignominy, and God chose the Israelites for the bestowal of His special favours. This is how God brings about transformation in the life of a people. It further says that human life has a great mission. It is for the fulfilment of this great mission that God raises His Messengers in the world. The *Sūrah* ends on the note that the principles and ideals of Islām have been taught in a most clear and convincing manner.

سُورَةُ الدُّخَانِ مَكِّيَّةٌ (٤٤)

1. [a]In the name of Allāh, the Gracious, the Merciful.

بِسۡمِ اللّٰہِ الرَّحۡمٰنِ الرَّحِیۡمِ ﴿۱﴾

2. [b]Ḥā Mīm.[2691A]

حٰمٓ ﴿۲﴾

3. By this perspicuous Book.

وَ الۡکِتٰبِ الۡمُبِیۡنِ ﴿۳﴾

4. Truly, [c]We revealed it in a blessed night.[2692] Truly, We have *ever* been warning.

اِنَّاۤ اَنۡزَلۡنٰہُ فِیۡ لَیۡلَۃٍ مُّبٰرَکَۃٍ اِنَّا کُنَّا مُنۡذِرِیۡنَ ﴿۴﴾

5. [d]Therein are decided all matters of wisdom[2693]

فِیۡہَا یُفۡرَقُ کُلُّ اَمۡرٍ حَکِیۡمٍ ﴿۵﴾

6. *By* Our *own* command. Verily, We have ever been sending *Messengers,*

اَمۡرًا مِّنۡ عِنۡدِنَا ؕ اِنَّا کُنَّا مُرۡسِلِیۡنَ ﴿۶﴾

7. *As* a mercy from thy Lord. Verily, He is the All-Hearing, the All-Knowing,

رَحۡمَۃً مِّنۡ رَّبِّکَ ؕ اِنَّہٗ ہُوَ السَّمِیۡعُ الۡعَلِیۡمُ ﴿۷﴾

8. [e]The Lord of the heavens and the earth and all that is between them, if you would only *be inclined to* believe.

رَبِّ السَّمٰوٰتِ وَ الۡاَرۡضِ وَ مَا بَیۡنَہُمَا ۘ اِنۡ کُنۡتُمۡ مُّوۡقِنِیۡنَ ﴿۸﴾

9. There is no god but He. [f]He gives life and He causes death. He is your Lord and the Lord of your forefathers.

لَاۤ اِلٰہَ اِلَّا ہُوَ یُحۡیٖ وَ یُمِیۡتُ ؕ رَبُّکُمۡ وَ رَبُّ اٰبَآئِکُمُ الۡاَوَّلِیۡنَ ﴿۹﴾

---

[a]1 : 1. [b]40 : 2. [c]97 : 2. [d]97 : 5. [e]19 : 66; 37 : 6; 44 : 8. [f]10 : 57; 57 : 3.

2691A. See 2592 and 2643.

2692. Elsewhere in the Qur'ān, it is called the "Night of Destiny" (97:2). According to authentic traditions of the Holy Prophet, the "Night of Destiny" generally falls in the last ten nights of Ramaḍān, the month in which the Qur'ān began to be revealed (2 : 186), to be exact, on its 24th night (Musnad & Jarīr). The blessed night, or the "Night of Destiny," is the Quranic metaphor for a period of time when spiritual darkness enshrouds the entire face of the earth and a Divine Reformer is raised to reclaim and regenerate corrupt humanity. The night which gave to humanity its greatest Teacher and the last and most perfect Divine Law was, indeed the "Night of Destiny" for it. This night may also be taken as covering the whole period in which the Qur'ān continued to be revealed.

2693. The "Night of Destiny" or the time of the advent of a great Reformer heralds a new era, a new order of things, when, in fact, the future of humanity is decreed and decided. The time when the Qur'ān was revealed was humanity's greatest "Night of Destiny," for it was then that the foundations were laid of man's destiny for all time to come.

10. Yet they play about in doubt.

بَلْ هُمْ فِيْ شَكٍّ يَّلْعَبُوْنَ ۞

11. So watch thou for the day when the sky will bring forth a visible smoke,[2694]

فَارْتَقِبْ يَوْمَ تَأْتِي السَّمَآءُ بِدُخَانٍ مُّبِيْنٍ ۞

12. That will envelop the people. This will be a painful torment.

يَّغْشَى النَّاسَ هٰذَا عَذَابٌ أَلِيْمٌ ۞

13. *On seeing it the people will cry,* "Our Lord, remove from us the torment; truly, we are believers."

رَبَّنَا اكْشِفْ عَنَّا الْعَذَابَ إِنَّا مُؤْمِنُوْنَ ۞

14. How can they *benefit* by admonition, when there has already come to them a Messenger explaining *things* clearly,

أَنّٰى لَهُمُ الذِّكْرٰى وَقَدْ جَآءَهُمْ رَسُوْلٌ مُّبِيْنٌ ۞

15. And yet they turned away from him and said, 'He is [b]tutored, *a man* possessed !'

ثُمَّ تَوَلَّوْا عَنْهُ وَقَالُوْا مُعَلَّمٌ مَّجْنُوْنٌ ۞

16. 'We shall remove the punishment for a little while, *but* you will certainly revert *to mischief.*[2695]

إِنَّا كَاشِفُوا الْعَذَابِ قَلِيْلًا إِنَّكُمْ عَآئِدُوْنَ ۞

17. On the day when We shall seize *you* with the great seizure,[2696] *you will know* that We will, certainly, exact retribution.

يَوْمَ نَبْطِشُ الْبَطْشَةَ الْكُبْرٰى إِنَّا مُنْتَقِمُوْنَ ۞

---

[a]7 : 135;   43 : 51.   [b]37 : 37;   68 : 52.   [c]7 : 136;   43 : 51.

2694. The reference may be to the severe famine that overtook Mecca and lasted for several years till Abū Sufyān, then a great leader of disbelief, came to the Holy Prophet and begged him to pray for deliverance from that terrible scourge. The famine is said to have been so severe that the Meccans ate hides, bones and even dead bodies (Bukhārī, *Kitāb al-Istisqā'*). The famine has been described by the word *Dukhān* (smoke), because, as the tradition goes, the hunger was so severe that people felt a sort of smoke hanging before their eyes. Or, the word may have been used because there was no rain for a long time in Mecca, and the whole atmosphere had become dusty, for, *Dukhān* also means dust (Lane). The verse may also be taken as referring to the last two World Wars in which towns and cities were burnt down to rubble and the smoke that rose from their ruins filled the whole atmosphere with smoke and dust.

2695. According to reliable tradition the Holy Prophet prayed and the famine was removed. But the Quraish did not benefit by it and continued to oppose the Holy Prophet.

2696. The 'great seizure' may refer to the defeat of the Quraish at the Battle of Badr, or to the Fall of Mecca.

18. And We tried the people of Pharaoh before them, and there came to them a noble Messenger,

وَلَقَدْ فَتَنَّا قَبْلَهُمْ قَوْمَ فِرْعَوْنَ وَجَآءَهُمْ رَسُوْلٌ كَرِيْمٌ ۙ ۱۸

19. *Who said to them*, 'Deliver to me the servants of Allāh. Truly, I am to you a Messenger, faithful to *my* trust;

اَنْ اَدُّوْۤا اِلَيَّ عِبَادَ اللّٰهِ ؕ اِنِّيْ لَكُمْ رَسُوْلٌ اَمِيْنٌ ۙ ۱۹

20. 'And exalt not yourselves in defiance of Allāh. Surely, I come to you with a clear authority,

وَّاَنْ لَّا تَعْلُوْا عَلَى اللّٰهِ ؕ اِنِّيْ اٰتِيْكُمْ بِسُلْطٰنٍ مُّبِيْنٍ ۚ ۲۰

21. *a*"And I seek refuge in my Lord and your Lord, lest you stone me to death,

وَاِنِّيْ عُذْتُ بِرَبِّيْ وَرَبِّكُمْ اَنْ تَرْجُمُوْنِ ۙ ۲۱

22. 'And if you believe me not, then leave me alone.'

وَاِنْ لَّمْ تُؤْمِنُوْا لِيْ فَاعْتَزِلُوْنِ ۲۲

23. Then *Moses* prayed unto his Lord, 'These are, indeed, a sinful people.'

فَدَعَا رَبَّهٗۤ اَنَّ هٰۤؤُلَآءِ قَوْمٌ مُّجْرِمُوْنَ ۲۳

24. *Allāh said*, 'Take My servants away by night; *b*for you will surely, be pursued.

فَاَسْرِ بِعِبَادِيْ لَيْلًا اِنَّكُمْ مُّتَّبَعُوْنَ ۙ ۲۴

25. 'And leave thou the sea behind when it is calm,[2697] *crossing over the dunes*. Surely, they are a host that are *doomed* to be drowned.'

وَاتْرُكِ الْبَحْرَ رَهْوًا ؕ اِنَّهُمْ جُنْدٌ مُّغْرَقُوْنَ ۲۵

26. *c*'How many were the gardens and the springs that they left behind,

كَمْ تَرَكُوْا مِنْ جَنّٰتٍ وَّعُيُوْنٍ ۙ ۲۶

27. And the cornfields and the noble places,

وَّزُرُوْعٍ وَّمَقَامٍ كَرِيْمٍ ۙ ۲۷

28. And the comforts and luxuries wherein they took delight!

وَّنَعْمَةٍ كَانُوْا فِيْهَا فٰكِهِيْنَ ۲۸

---

*a*40 : 28.   *b*10 : 91; 20 : 79; 26 : 61.   *c*26 : 59.

2697. *Rahw* is derived from *Rahā*. They say, *Rahā Baina Rijlaihi, i.e.,* he parted his legs and made an opening between them; *Rahā al-Baḥru* means, the sea became still and calm. *Rahw* means calm; motionless; depressed place where water collects; an elevated and plain tract of ground (Lane). When Moses and the Israelites arrived at the northern extremity of the Red Sea, the ebb of the tide had begun. As the water receded, it left behind dunes, the tops of which were gradually uncovered, leaving the intervening depressions full of water. The Israelites crossed over at that moment. See also 20 : 78.

29. Thus *it happened.* [a]And We made another people inherit these things.

كَذٰلِكَ وَاَوْرَثْنٰهَا قَوْمًا اٰخَرِيْنَ ﴿۲۹﴾

30. And the heaven and the earth wept not for them, nor were they respited.[2698]

فَمَا بَكَتْ عَلَيْهِمُ السَّمَآءُ وَالْاَرْضُ وَمَا كَانُوْا مُنْظَرِيْنَ ﴿۳۰﴾

R. 2 31. [b]And We delivered the Children of Israel from the abasing torment

وَلَقَدْ نَجَّيْنَا بَنِيْٓ اِسْرَآءِيْلَ مِنَ الْعَذَابِ الْمُهِيْنِ ﴿۳۱﴾

32. *Inflicted* by Pharaoh. He was, surely, haughty *even* among the extravagant.

مِنْ فِرْعَوْنَ ۭ اِنَّهٗ كَانَ عَالِيًا مِّنَ الْمُسْرِفِيْنَ ﴿۳۲﴾

33. And We chose them above the peoples *of their time,* knowingly.[2699]

وَلَقَدِ اخْتَرْنٰهُمْ عَلٰى عِلْمٍ عَلَى الْعٰلَمِيْنَ ﴿۳۳﴾

34. And We gave them Signs wherein was a clear trial.

وَاٰتَيْنٰهُمْ مِّنَ الْاٰيٰتِ مَا فِيْهِ بَلٰٓؤٌا مُّبِيْنٌ ﴿۳۴﴾

35. These *people* do say,

اِنَّ هٰٓؤُلَآءِ لَيَقُوْلُوْنَ ﴿۳۵﴾

36. [c]"There is only one death for us, and we shall not be raised up again,

اِنْ هِيَ اِلَّا مَوْتَتُنَا الْاُوْلٰى وَمَا نَحْنُ بِمُنْشَرِيْنَ ﴿۳۶﴾

37. 'So bring *back* our fathers, if you speak the truth.'

فَاْتُوْا بِاٰبَآئِنَآ اِنْ كُنْتُمْ صٰدِقِيْنَ ﴿۳۷﴾

38. Are they better or the people of Tubba'[2700] and those before them ? We destroyed them because they were sinful.

اَهُمْ خَيْرٌ اَمْ قَوْمُ تُبَّعٍ ۙ وَّالَّذِيْنَ مِنْ قَبْلِهِمْ ۭ اَهْلَكْنٰهُمْ ۡ اِنَّهُمْ كَانُوْا مُجْرِمِيْنَ ﴿۳۸﴾

[a]7 : 138; 26 : 60; 28 : 7. [b]2 : 50; 14 : 7; 20 : 81. [c]6 : 30; 23 : 38; 37 : 60; 45 : 25.

2698. They went to their doom in disgrace and ignominy unwept, unhonoured and unsung. The ill-fated monarch who, in his conceit and arrogance, called himself god, went to the depths of the sea (10 : 91), with the memorable words, 'I believe that there is no god but He in Whom the Children of Israel believe,' on his lips.

2699. God chose the Israelites for His favours because in the Divine scheme of things they were found to be most suited to carry on the Divine mission at that time. The expression, '*Alā 'Ilmin,* may also signify, in view of their special circumstances.

2700. Tubba' is said to be the royal title of the Kings of Ḥimyar in Yemen. The Kings of Yemen were known by this title when they also held sway over Ḥimyar, Ḥaḍaramaut and Saba'. From ancient inscriptions it appears that the Tubba's ruled over these territories from 270 A.D. to 525 A.D. Historical records speak of their glory

39. [a]And We created not the heavens and the earth and all that is between them in sport.[2701]

وَمَا خَلَقْنَا السَّمٰوٰتِ وَالْاَرْضَ وَمَا بَيْنَهُمَا لٰعِبِيْنَ ﴿۳۹﴾

40. We created them not but for an eternal purpose, but most of them understand not.

مَا خَلَقْنٰهُمَآ اِلَّا بِالْحَقِّ وَلٰكِنَّ اَكْثَرَهُمْ لَا يَعْلَمُوْنَ ﴿۴۰﴾

41. Verily, the Day of Decision[2702] is the appointed time for all of them.

اِنَّ يَوْمَ الْفَصْلِ مِيْقَاتُهُمْ اَجْمَعِيْنَ ﴿۴۱﴾

42. [b]The day when a friend shall not avail a friend at all, nor shall they be helped,

يَوْمَ لَا يُغْنِيْ مَوْلًى عَنْ مَّوْلًى شَيْـًٔا وَّلَا هُمْ يُنْصَرُوْنَ ﴿۴۲﴾

43. Save those to whom Allāh shows mercy. Surely, He is the Mighty, the Merciful.

اِلَّا مَنْ رَّحِمَ اللّٰهُ ؕ اِنَّهٗ هُوَ الْعَزِيْزُ الرَّحِيْمُ ﴿۴۳﴾

R. 3 44. Verily, [c]the tree of *Zaqqūm*

اِنَّ شَجَرَتَ الزَّقُّوْمِ ﴿۴۴﴾

45. Will be the food of the sinful;

طَعَامُ الْاَثِيْمِ ﴿۴۵﴾

46. Like molten copper [d]it will boil in *their* bellies,

كَالْمُهْلِ ۚ يَغْلِيْ فِي الْبُطُوْنِ ﴿۴۶﴾

47. As the boiling of scalding water.

كَغَلْيِ الْحَمِيْمِ ﴿۴۷﴾

48. *We* shall *command the angels*: 'Seize him and drag him into the midst of the blazing Fire;

خُذُوْهُ فَاعْتِلُوْهُ اِلٰى سَوَآءِ الْجَحِيْمِ ﴿۴۸﴾

49. 'Then [e]pour upon his head the torment of boiling water.'

ثُمَّ صُبُّوْا فَوْقَ رَاْسِهٖ مِنْ عَذَابِ الْحَمِيْمِ ﴿۴۹﴾

[a]21 : 17; 38 : 28. [b]2 : 124; 70 : 11; 80 : 35-37. [c]37 : 63; 56 : 53. [d]22 : 21. [e]22 : 20; 55 : 45.

and despotism. They seemed to have extended their rule over all Arabia, even to East Africa (Enc. of Islām). The particular Tubba' referred to in the verse under comment is mentioned in some traditions as a Prophet of God. The Qur'ān seems to support this view (50 : 15).

2701. Human life has a grim purpose and a great mission. The great faculties and inborn powers of man are a sure indication that life is real and earnest. It is to this great principle that the creation of the heavens and the earth emphatically draws our attention.

2702. Besides the final Day of Decision when all secrets of the unknown will be laid bare and human actions weighed in the balance and finally judged, there is a day of decision in the time of every Prophet in this very life when truth triumphs and falsehood is defeated.

50. *And shall say to him,* 'Taste it. Thou *didst consider thyself* the mighty, the honourable one ;'²⁷⁰³

ذُقْ اِنَّكَ اَنْتَ الْعَزِيْزُ الْكَرِيْمُ ۝

51. 'This, indeed, is what you doubted.'

اِنَّ هٰذَا مَا كُنْتُمْ بِهٖ تَمْتَرُوْنَ ۝

52. Verily, ªthe righteous will be in a place of security,

اِنَّ الْمُتَّقِيْنَ فِيْ مَقَامٍ اَمِيْنٍ ۝

53. ᵇAmid gardens and springs,

فِيْ جَنّٰتٍ وَّعُيُوْنٍ ۝

54. ᶜAttired in fine silk and heavy brocade, facing one another.

يَّلْبَسُوْنَ مِنْ سُنْدُسٍ وَّاِسْتَبْرَقٍ مُّتَقٰبِلِيْنَ ۝

55. Thus *will it be.* And ᵈWe shall give them as companions fair maidens, having large, black eyes.

كَذٰلِكَ وَزَوَّجْنٰهُمْ بِحُوْرٍ عِيْنٍ ۝

56. They will call therein for ᵉevery *kind of* fruit, in *peace and* security.

يَدْعُوْنَ فِيْهَا بِكُلِّ فَاكِهَةٍ اٰمِنِيْنَ ۝

57. They will not taste death²⁷⁰⁴ therein, save the first death; ᶠand God will save them from the punishment of the blazing Fire,

لَا يَذُوْقُوْنَ فِيْهَا الْمَوْتَ اِلَّا الْمَوْتَةَ الْاُوْلٰى وَوَقٰهُمْ عَذَابَ الْجَحِيْمِ ۝

58. As an act of grace²⁷⁰⁵ from thy Lord. ᵍThat is the supreme achievement.

فَضْلًا مِّنْ رَّبِّكَ ذٰلِكَ هُوَ الْفَوْزُ الْعَظِيْمُ ۝

59. ʰAnd We have made *the* Qur'ān easy in thy tongue that they may take heed.

فَاِنَّمَا يَسَّرْنٰهُ بِلِسَانِكَ لَعَلَّهُمْ يَتَذَكَّرُوْنَ ۝

60. So wait thou; they, *too,* are waiting.

فَارْتَقِبْ اِنَّهُمْ مُّرْتَقِبُوْنَ ۝

ª30 : 16; 52 : 18. ᵇ68 : 35; 78 : 32. ᶜ18 : 32; 76 : 22. ᵈ55 : 71, 73; 56 : 23.
ᵉ55 : 53; 56 : 21. ᶠ52 : 28. ᵍ37 : 61. ʰ19 : 98; 54 : 18.

2703. The words have been spoken in irony.

2704. The verse unmistakably shows that life in the next world would be eternal and continuously progressive, and not a life of inaction.

2705 Salvation depends on the grace and mercy of God.

CHAPTER 45

AL-JĀTHIYAH

(*Revealed before Hijrah*)

Date of Revelation and Context

Like the other Chapters of the *Ḥā Mīm* group, this *Sūrah* was revealed at Mecca. But no exact date can be assigned to its revelation, though Noldeke places it immediately after 41st *Sūrah*. It opens with the statement that just as timely rain gives new life to dead earth, similarly a Divine Prophet is raised when men become morally corrupt. As men had become corrupt, so God now has raised the Holy Prophet Muḥammad to regenerate them.

Subject-Matter

Like the preceding five Chapters the present *Sūrah* also opens with the subject of the Quranic revelation and Divine Unity which constitute its main themes, and adduces the creation of man and of all animal and vegetable life on earth, the coming down of timely rain from the clouds which quickens the dead earth, the marvellous creation of the universe and the complete and consummate design and order that pervade and permeate it as great Signs to establish the existence of an Unerring and All-Powerful Being behind all this, and proceeds to invite disbelievers to consider how the Wise Being, Who has made such wonderful provision for man's short and temporary life on earth, could have failed to make similar provision for his eternal life. This provision for man's spiritual sustenance has been made in the revelation that descends upon God's Messengers to lead him to the achievement of the great goal of his life. The *Sūrah* then says that God does not allow the arrangement which He has made for the moral and spiritual regeneration of man to be interfered with, and so He does not allow a forger of lies to prosper. Sooner or later the impostor comes to grief. But the Holy Prophet's mission is making uniform progress. This is proof positive of the fact that he is not a liar but a true Messenger of God. The *Sūrah* then gives one more argument to prove and substantiate the claim of the Holy Prophet, *viz.*, that all the forces of nature are working in support and furtherance of his cause It is, therefore, bound to succeed. Next, a brief reference is made to the Mosaic Dispensation and it is stated that the Qur'ān has been revealed because the Torah had failed to satisfy the spiritual needs of man. It also fulfils the prophecies made in the Torah about the advent of a Prophet from among the brethren of the Israelites (Deut. 18 : 18). The *Sūrah* further tells disbelievers that God has created man to achieve a great and noble goal; therefore a better and fuller life which knows no end awaits him in the next world. It is only in this way that the creation of man can be justified. The *Sūrah* closes with a brief but very effective description of the Day of Judgment. But before that day comes, the disbelievers will have to give an explanation in this very life, why they disobeyed and defied the Prophets of God. They are warned that if they did not repent and mend their ways, they will be doomed to a life of failure and frustration.

سُوْرَةُ الْجَاثِيَةِ مَكِّيَّةٌ (٤٥)

1. [a]In the name of Allāh, the Gracious, the Merciful.

بِسْمِ اللّٰهِ الرَّحْمٰنِ الرَّحِيْمِ ①

2. [b]Ḥā Mīm.[2705A]

حٰمٓ ②

3. [c]The revelation of this Book is from Allāh, the Mighty, the Wise.

تَنْزِيْلُ الْكِتٰبِ مِنَ اللّٰهِ الْعَزِيْزِ الْحَكِيْمِ ③

4. [d]Verily, in the heavens and the earth are Signs for those who believe.

اِنَّ فِي السَّمٰوٰتِ وَالْاَرْضِ لَاٰيٰتٍ لِّلْمُؤْمِنِيْنَ ④

5. And in your own creation and *in* that of all the creatures which He spreads *in the earth* are Signs for a people who possess firm faith.

وَفِيْ خَلْقِكُمْ وَمَا يَبُثُّ مِنْ دَآبَّةٍ اٰيٰتٌ لِّقَوْمٍ يُّوْقِنُوْنَ ⑤

6. And *in* [e]the alternation of night and day, and the provision that Allāh sends down from the heaven, whereby [f]He quickens the earth after its death, and in the changing of the winds,[2706] are Signs for a people who would use their understanding.

وَاخْتِلَافِ الَّيْلِ وَالنَّهَارِ وَمَآ اَنْزَلَ اللّٰهُ مِنَ السَّمَآءِ مِنْ رِّزْقٍ فَاَحْيَا بِهِ الْاَرْضَ بَعْدَ مَوْتِهَا وَتَصْرِيْفِ الرِّيٰحِ اٰيٰتٌ لِّقَوْمٍ يَّعْقِلُوْنَ ⑥

7. These are the Signs of Allāh which We rehearse unto thee with truth. In what word, then, after[2707] *rejecting the Word of* Allāh and His Signs, will they believe?

تِلْكَ اٰيٰتُ اللّٰهِ نَتْلُوْهَا عَلَيْكَ بِالْحَقِّ فَبِاَيِّ حَدِيْثٍ بَعْدَ اللّٰهِ وَاٰيٰتِهٖ يُؤْمِنُوْنَ ⑦

8. Woe to every sinful liar,

وَيْلٌ لِّكُلِّ اَفَّاكٍ اَثِيْمٍ ⑧

---

[a]1 : 1. [b]41 : 2. [c]32 : 3; 36 : 6; 40 : 3; 41 : 3. [d]2 : 165; 42 : 30. [e]2 : 165; 3 : 191; 10 : 7. [f]16 : 66; 30 : 51;

2705A. See. 2592.

2706. Just as light follows darkness, similarly when spiritual darkness spreads over the entire earth, God creates a new light in the form of a Prophet or Divine Reformer to whom He reveals Himself. And just as winds carry pollen from male to female trees in order to fecundate them, in the same way the spiritually elevating ideas that emanate from a Divine Reformer impregnate the minds of believers and bring about spiritual revolution in them.

2707. *Ba'd* means, after; in spite of; contrary to or against; in addition to (Lane).

9. Who hears the Signs of Allāh recited unto him, and then proudly persists *in disbelief*, as though he heard them not. So give him the tidings of a painful punishment.

يَسْمَعُ اٰيٰتِ اللّٰهِ تُتْلٰى عَلَيْهِ ثُمَّ يُصِرُّ مُسْتَكْبِرًا كَاَنْ
لَّمْ يَسْمَعْهَا ۚ فَبَشِّرْهُ بِعَذَابٍ اَلِيْمٍ ﴿٩﴾

10. And when he learns something of Our Signs, [a]he makes a jest of them. For such there is an humiliating punishment.

وَاِذَا عَلِمَ مِنْ اٰيٰتِنَا شَيْـًٔا اتَّخَذَهَا هُزُوًا ؕ اُولٰٓئِكَ
لَهُمْ عَذَابٌ مُّهِيْنٌ ﴿١٠﴾

11. [b]Before them is Hell; and that which they have earned shall not avail them aught, nor shall those whom they have taken for protectors beside Allāh. And they will have a dreadful punishment.

مِنْ وَّرَآئِهِمْ جَهَنَّمُ ۚ وَلَا يُغْنِيْ عَنْهُمْ مَّا كَسَبُوْا
شَيْـًٔا وَّلَا مَا اتَّخَذُوْا مِنْ دُوْنِ اللّٰهِ اَوْلِيَآءَ ۚ وَلَهُمْ
عَذَابٌ عَظِيْمٌ ﴿١١﴾

12. This is *true* guidance. [c]And for those who disbelieve in the Signs of their Lord is the torture of a painful punishment.

هٰذَا هُدًى ۚ وَالَّذِيْنَ كَفَرُوْا بِاٰيٰتِ رَبِّهِمْ لَهُمْ عَذَابٌ
مِّنْ رِّجْزٍ اَلِيْمٌ ﴿١٢﴾ ع

R. 2 13. Allāh is He [d]Who has subjected the sea to you that ships may sail thereon by His command, and that you may seek of His bounty, and that you may be grateful.

اَللّٰهُ الَّذِيْ سَخَّرَ لَكُمُ الْبَحْرَ لِتَجْرِيَ الْفُلْكُ فِيْهِ بِاَمْرِهٖ
وَلِتَبْتَغُوْا مِنْ فَضْلِهٖ وَلَعَلَّكُمْ تَشْكُرُوْنَ ﴿١٣﴾

14. [e]And He has subjected to you whatsoever is in the heavens and whatsoever is in the earth; all *this* is from Him. In that, surely, are Signs for a people who reflect.[2708]

وَسَخَّرَ لَكُمْ مَّا فِي السَّمٰوٰتِ وَمَا فِي الْاَرْضِ جَمِيْعًا
مِّنْهُ ؕ اِنَّ فِيْ ذٰلِكَ لَاٰيٰتٍ لِّقَوْمٍ يَّتَفَكَّرُوْنَ ﴿١٤﴾

15. Tell those who believe to forgive those who *persecute them and* fear not the Days of Allāh,[2709] that He may requite a people for what they earn.

قُلْ لِّلَّذِيْنَ اٰمَنُوْا يَغْفِرُوْا لِلَّذِيْنَ لَا يَرْجُوْنَ اَيَّامَ اللّٰهِ
لِيَجْزِيَ قَوْمًا بِمَا كَانُوْا يَكْسِبُوْنَ ﴿١٥﴾

[a]31 : 7. [b]14 : 17-18. [c]2 : 40; 22 : 58. [d]16 : 15; 17 : 67. 35 : 13; [e]22 : 66.

2708. The whole universe has been created to serve man. This shows that he has a great mission to fulfil.

2709. See 1454.

16. [a]Whoso does good, does it for his own soul; and whoso does wrong, does so to its detriment. Then to your Lord will you *all* be brought back.

مَنْ عَمِلَ صَالِحًا فَلِنَفْسِهٖ ۚ وَمَنْ اَسَآءَ فَعَلَيْهَا ۫ ثُمَّ
اِلٰى رَبِّكُمْ تُرْجَعُوْنَ ﴿۱۶﴾

17. And verily, [b]We gave the Children of Israel the Book and sovereignty and Prophethood;[2710] and [c]We provided them with *good and* pure things, and We exalted them over the peoples *of their time*.

وَلَقَدْ اٰتَيْنَا بَنِيْٓ اِسْرَآءِيْلَ الْكِتٰبَ وَالْحُكْمَ وَالنُّبُوَّةَ
وَرَزَقْنٰهُمْ مِّنَ الطَّيِّبٰتِ وَفَضَّلْنٰهُمْ عَلَى الْعٰلَمِيْنَ ﴿۱۷﴾

18. And We gave them clear Signs regarding *this* Affair.[2711] [d]And they did not differ but after *true* knowledge had come to them, through mutual envy. Verily, thy Lord will judge between them on the Day of Resurrection concerning that wherein they differed.

وَاٰتَيْنٰهُمْ بَيِّنٰتٍ مِّنَ الْاَمْرِ ۚ فَمَا اخْتَلَفُوْٓا اِلَّا مِنْۢ
بَعْدِ مَا جَآءَهُمُ الْعِلْمُ ۙ بَغْيًا بَيْنَهُمْ ۚ اِنَّ رَبَّكَ
يَقْضِيْ بَيْنَهُمْ يَوْمَ الْقِيٰمَةِ فِيْمَا كَانُوْا فِيْهِ
يَخْتَلِفُوْنَ ﴿۱۸﴾

19. Then We set thee on a clear path concerning the Affair; so follow it, [e]and follow not the vain desires of those who do not know.[2712]

ثُمَّ جَعَلْنٰكَ عَلٰى شَرِيْعَةٍ مِّنَ الْاَمْرِ فَاتَّبِعْهَا وَ
لَا تَتَّبِعْ اَهْوَآءَ الَّذِيْنَ لَا يَعْلَمُوْنَ ﴿۱۹﴾

20. Verily, they will not avail thee aught against Allāh. Surely, the wrongdoers are friends, one of another; but Allāh is the friend of the righteous.

اِنَّهُمْ لَنْ يُّغْنُوْا عَنْكَ مِنَ اللّٰهِ شَيْـًٔا ۗ وَاِنَّ الظّٰلِمِيْنَ
بَعْضُهُمْ اَوْلِيَآءُ بَعْضٍ ۚ وَاللّٰهُ وَلِيُّ الْمُتَّقِيْنَ ﴿۲۰﴾

[a]29 : 7. [b]6 : 90. [c]10 : 94. [d]42 : 15; 98 : 5. [e]5 : 49; 6 : 151.

2710. Mention of Prophethood, separate from "the Book" (which means the Law or the *Sharī'ah*) shows that while Moses was given the Law, the Prophets who came after him brought no new Law but followed the Torah—the Book of Moses (5 : 45).

2711. "The Affair" signifies "the Affair of the Holy Prophet" and the verse purports to say that the Book of Moses contains many clear prophecies about the advent of the Holy Prophet and that the Israelites did not reject him because there was any dearth of arguments and Signs and Divine prophecies to support and establish his claim but because of 'mutual envy,' *i.e.*, they did not like the very idea that a Prophet should have appeared from among the non-Israelites.

2712. It is clear from the verse that "the Affair" referred to in the preceding verse signifies the advent of the Holy Prophet and the Quranic revelation.

21. [a]This *Book contains* clear evidences for mankind and is a guidance and a mercy for a people who possess firm faith.

هٰذَا بَصَآئِرُ لِلنَّاسِ وَهُدًى وَّرَحْمَةٌ لِّقَوْمٍ يُّوْقِنُوْنَ ۝٢١

22. [b]Do those who commit evil deeds imagine that We shall make them like those who believe and do righteous deeds, so that their life and their death shall be equal? Evil, *indeed*, is what they judge.

اَمْ حَسِبَ الَّذِيْنَ اجْتَرَحُوا السَّيِّاٰتِ اَنْ نَّجْعَلَهُمْ كَالَّذِيْنَ اٰمَنُوْا وَعَمِلُوا الصّٰلِحٰتِ سَوَآءً مَّحْيَاهُمْ وَمَمَاتُهُمْ سَآءَ مَا يَحْكُمُوْنَ ۝٢٢

R. 3 23. And Allāh has created the heavens and the earth *in accordance* with an eternal law, so that [c]every soul may be requited for that which it earns; and they shall not be wronged.

وَخَلَقَ اللّٰهُ السَّمٰوٰتِ وَالْاَرْضَ بِالْحَقِّ وَلِتُجْزٰى كُلُّ نَفْسٍ بِمَا كَسَبَتْ وَهُمْ لَا يُظْلَمُوْنَ ۝٢٣

24. Hast thou considered *the case of* him [d]who has taken his *own* low desire for his god, and whom Allāh has adjudged *as having gone* astray on the basis of *His perfect* knowledge, [e]and whose ears and whose heart He has sealed, up, and on whose eyes He has put a covering. Who, then, will guide him after Allāh *has so decreed concerning him?* Will you not then take heed?

اَفَرَءَيْتَ مَنِ اتَّخَذَ اِلٰهَهٗ هَوٰىهُ وَاَضَلَّهُ اللّٰهُ عَلٰى عِلْمٍ وَّخَتَمَ عَلٰى سَمْعِهٖ وَقَلْبِهٖ وَجَعَلَ عَلٰى بَصَرِهٖ غِشٰوَةً فَمَنْ يَّهْدِيْهِ مِنْۢ بَعْدِ اللّٰهِ اَفَلَا تَذَكَّرُوْنَ ۝٢٤

25. And they say, [f]"There is nothing *for us* but this our present life; we die and we live; and nothing but Time[2713] destroys us.' But they have no *real* knowledge of it; they do nothing but conjecture.

وَقَالُوْا مَا هِيَ اِلَّا حَيَاتُنَا الدُّنْيَا نَمُوْتُ وَنَحْيَا وَمَا يُهْلِكُنَآ اِلَّا الدَّهْرُ وَمَا لَهُمْ بِذٰلِكَ مِنْ عِلْمٍ اِنْ هُمْ اِلَّا يَظُنُّوْنَ ۝٢٥

---

[a]7 : 204. [b]32 : 19; 38 : 29. [c]14 : 52; 40 : 18. [d]25 : 44.
[e]2 : 8; 6 : 47; 16 : 109. [f]6 : 30; 23 : 38.

2713. *Dahr* means : (*a*) Time from the beginning of the world to its end; any period or portion of time; (*b*) fate; (*c*) an epoch; (*d*) vicissitudes of time, calamity; (*e*) custom, etc. (Lane). The verse purports to say that when disbelievers are told that they will have to render an account of their deeds before God in the next life, they refuse to believe that there is or can be any such life. On the contrary, they allege that one people die and another people take their place and this process goes on till with the passage of time matter becomes dissolved and is thus utterly destroyed. This is the be-all and end-all of human existence and there is no life hereafter.

26. And when Our clear Signs are recited unto them, their only contention[2714] is that they say, 'Bring *back* our fathers, if you are truthful.'

وَإِذَا تُتْلَىٰ عَلَيْهِمْ آيَاتُنَا بَيِّنَاتٍ مَّا كَانَ حُجَّتَهُمْ إِلَّا أَن قَالُوا ائْتُوا بِآبَائِنَا إِن كُنتُمْ صَادِقِينَ ۝٢٦

27. Say, 'It is Allāh Who gives you life, then [a]causes you to die; then He will gather you together unto the Day of Resurrection about which there is no doubt. But most men do not know.'

قُلِ اللَّهُ يُحْيِيكُمْ ثُمَّ يُمِيتُكُمْ ثُمَّ يَجْمَعُكُمْ إِلَىٰ يَوْمِ الْقِيَامَةِ لَا رَيْبَ فِيهِ وَلَٰكِنَّ أَكْثَرَ النَّاسِ لَا يَعْلَمُونَ ۝٢٧ ع ٣ ١٩

R. 4 28. To Allāh belongs the Kingdom of the heavens and the earth; and on the day when the Hour shall come, on that day those who follow falsehood shall be the losers.

وَلِلَّهِ مُلْكُ السَّمَاوَاتِ وَالْأَرْضِ ۚ وَيَوْمَ تَقُومُ السَّاعَةُ يَوْمَئِذٍ يَخْسَرُ الْمُبْطِلُونَ ۝٢٨

29. And thou wilt see every people on *their* knees. Every people will be [b]summoned to its Book,[2714A] *and it shall be said to them*, 'This day shall you be requited for that which you did.

وَتَرَىٰ كُلَّ أُمَّةٍ جَاثِيَةً ۚ كُلُّ أُمَّةٍ تُدْعَىٰ إِلَىٰ كِتَابِهَا الْيَوْمَ تُجْزَوْنَ مَا كُنتُمْ تَعْمَلُونَ ۝٢٩

30. [c]'This is Our Book;[2715] it speaks against you with truth. We caused *all* that you did to be *fully* recorded.'

هَٰذَا كِتَابُنَا يَنطِقُ عَلَيْكُم بِالْحَقِّ ۚ إِنَّا كُنَّا نَسْتَنسِخُ مَا كُنتُمْ تَعْمَلُونَ ۝٣٠

31. Now, [d]as for those who believed and did righteous deeds, their Lord will admit them into His mercy. That is the manifest achievement.

فَأَمَّا الَّذِينَ آمَنُوا وَعَمِلُوا الصَّالِحَاتِ فَيُدْخِلُهُمْ رَبُّهُمْ فِي رَحْمَتِهِ ۚ ذَٰلِكَ هُوَ الْفَوْزُ الْمُبِينُ ۝٣١

[a]2 : 29; 22 : 67. [b]17 : 14. [c]17 : 15; 83 : 21. [d]83 : 23.

2714. *Ḥujjah* means, argument; plea; excuse; contention (Lane).

2714A. The words, 'every people will be summoned to its Book,' suggest that the "Hour" referred to in the previous verse signifies the hour of the reckoning of a people in this very life, because in this life also nations are judged by their deeds and are punished or rewarded accordingly.

2715. The expression 'its Book' mentioned in the previous verse has been substituted by the expression, 'Our Book,' in the present verse, because the record of the deeds or actions of nations and individuals is preserved by God and they are judged and requited by Him accordingly.

32. But as to those who disbelieved, *it will be said to them,* *a*"Were not My Signs recited unto you? But you were arrogant and were a guilty people.

وَ اَمَّا الَّذِيْنَ كَفَرُوْا اَفَلَمْ تَكُنْ اٰيٰتِىْ تُتْلٰى عَلَيْكُمْ فَاسْتَكْبَرْتُمْ وَ كُنْتُمْ قَوْمًا مُّجْرِمِيْنَ ۞

33. "And when it was said *to you,* 'The promise of Allāh is certainly true, and *b*as to the Hour, there is no doubt about its *coming,*' you said, 'We know not what the Hour is; we think it to be nothing but a conjecture, and we have no certainty *concerning it.*"

وَ اِذَا قِيْلَ اِنَّ وَعْدَ اللّٰهِ حَقٌّ وَّ السَّاعَةُ لَا رَيْبَ فِيْهَا قُلْتُمْ مَّا نَدْرِىْ مَا السَّاعَةُ اِنْ نَّظُنُّ اِلَّا ظَنًّا وَّ مَا نَحْنُ بِمُسْتَيْقِنِيْنَ ۞

34. *c*And the evil *consequences* of their deeds will become apparent to them, and that which they used to mock at shall encompass them.

وَ بَدَا لَهُمْ سَيِّاٰتُ مَا عَمِلُوْا وَ حَاقَ بِهِمْ مَّا كَانُوْا بِهٖ يَسْتَهْزِءُوْنَ ۞

35. And it will be said *to them,* *d*"This day shall We abandon you *without help,* even as you forgot the meeting of this your day.2716 And your resort is the Fire, and you will have no helpers;

وَ قِيْلَ الْيَوْمَ نَنْسٰكُمْ كَمَا نَسِيْتُمْ لِقَآءَ يَوْمِكُمْ هٰذَا وَ مَأْوٰىكُمُ النَّارُ وَ مَا لَكُمْ مِّنْ نّٰصِرِيْنَ ۞

36. 'This is *so,* because *e*you made a jest of the Signs of Allāh, and the life of the world deceived you.' Therefore that day they will not be taken out of it, nor will they be taken back into favour.

ذٰلِكُمْ بِاَنَّكُمُ اتَّخَذْتُمْ اٰيٰتِ اللّٰهِ هُزُوًا وَّ غَرَّتْكُمُ الْحَيٰوةُ الدُّنْيَا فَالْيَوْمَ لَا يُخْرَجُوْنَ مِنْهَا وَ لَا هُمْ يُسْتَعْتَبُوْنَ ۞

37. All praise, then, belongs to Allāh, Lord of the Heavens and Lord of the earth, Lord of *all* the worlds.

فَلِلّٰهِ الْحَمْدُ رَبِّ السَّمٰوٰتِ وَ رَبِّ الْاَرْضِ رَبِّ الْعٰلَمِيْنَ ۞

38. *f*And His is the Majesty in the heavens and the earth, and He is the Mighty, the Wise.

وَ لَهُ الْكِبْرِيَآءُ فِى السَّمٰوٰتِ وَ الْاَرْضِ وَ هُوَ الْعَزِيْزُ الْحَكِيْمُ ۞

---

*a*23 : 106;　67 : 9-10.　*b*18 : 22;　20 : 16;　22 : 8.　*c*16 : 35;　21 : 42;　39 : 49.
*d*7 : 52　*e*5 : 58-59.　*f*30 : 28.

2716. This day of your promised punishment.

CHAPTER 46

AL-AḤQĀF

(Revealed before Hijrah)

Date of Revelation and Context

This is the last *Sūrah* of the Ḥā Mīm group. Like other Chapters of this group it was revealed at Mecca towards the middle of the Holy Prophet's ministry before *Hijrah*. Noldeke places its revelation immediately after Chapter 7. The *Sūrah* seems to resemble its sister *Sūrahs* of the Ḥā Mīm group in tone and tenor. The preceding *Sūrah* had ended on the solemn declaration that 'God is the Mighty, the Wise.' In the present *Sūrah* the claim made in these words is sought to be justified. The *Sūrah* claims that the Qur'ān has been revealed by the Wise and Mighty God. God is Wise in the sense that the Quranic teaching is based on sound and solid foundations, and is supported by reason, common sense and accumulated human experience; and He is Mighty in the sense that by living up to its ideals and principles Muslims will gain ascendancy and predominance over their opponents.

Subject-Matter

Like the preceding six Chapters this *Sūrah* opens with the subject of the Quranic revelation and Divine Unity which constitutes its main theme, and gives the following arguments in refutation of idolatry: (*a*) Only that Being can command and demand of us that we should adore and worship Him Who, besides being our Creator and Sustainer, is Almighty and All-Powerful and can therefore compel obedience to His laws and commandments (*b*) Idolatry finds no support in any revealed Scripture. (*c*) Human knowledge, reason and experience repel it and revolt against it. (*d*) A deity which cannot, and does not, answer our prayers is of no use and the so-called gods of idolaters are incapable of responding to the prayers of their votaries. The *Sūrah* next says that the Holy Prophet's claim to Prophethood is no new phenomenon. Divine Messengers have been appearing at all times and among all peoples to teach them Unity of God and their duty to their fellow-beings. It then dismisses as foolish and unfounded the plea which the disbelievers generally put forward as an excuse for rejecting the Divine Revelation, *viz*., 'If there had been any good in the revelation presented to us, we, being better informed and better placed in life, would have been the first to accept it.' The *Sūrah* further says that whereas disbelievers, being proud of their great material resources and social status, reject the Divine Message, others who are endowed with faith and spiritual wealth, accept it and stick to it under the severest trials and tribulations. It then refers to the fate of 'Ād, a people who had flourished in the neighbourhood of the Meccans, to show that disbelief never prospers. The Adites were so completely destroyed that not a vestige of their great and glorious civilization remained. Towards its end the *Sūrah* sounds a note of warning to the people of the Holy Prophet that they should not be misled by their wealth and prosperity and by the present poverty and weakness of Muslims, and that if they persisted in rejecting the Divine Message, their prosperity itself would prove to be their ruin. The *Sūrah* ends with an exhortation to the Holy Prophet and his followers, calling upon them, that as brave votaries of Truth they should bear with patience and fortitude all the suffering and persecution to which they are being subjected, as the time was fast approaching, when their cause will triumph and their persecutors will stand before them in utter disgrace and humiliation, begging for forgiveness and mercy.

ركوعاتها ٤ سُوْرَةُ الْاَحْقَافِ مَكِّيَّةٌ (٤٦) اٰياتها ٣٦

الجزء ٢٦

PART XXVI

1. [a]In the name of Allāh, the Gracious, the Merciful.

بِسْمِ اللّٰهِ الرَّحْمٰنِ الرَّحِيْمِ ①

2. [b]Ḥā Mīm.

حٰمٓ ②

3. [c]The revelation of this Book is from Allāh, the Mighty, the Wise.

تَنْزِيْلُ الْكِتٰبِ مِنَ اللّٰهِ الْعَزِيْزِ الْحَكِيْمِ ③

4. [d]We have not created the heavens and the earth, and all that is between them, but with an eternal purpose and for an appointed term,[2717] but those who disbelieve turn away from that of which they have been warned.

مَا خَلَقْنَا السَّمٰوٰتِ وَالْاَرْضَ وَمَا بَيْنَهُمَآ اِلَّا
بِالْحَقِّ وَاَجَلٍ مُّسَمًّى ۗ وَالَّذِيْنَ كَفَرُوْا عَمَّآ اُنْذِرُوْا
مُعْرِضُوْنَ ④

5. Say *to them,* [e]'Do you know what it is you call upon beside Allāh? Show me what they have created of the earth. Or, have they a share in the *creation of the* heavens?[2718] Bring me a Book *revealed* before this or some vestige of knowledge *in your support,*[2719] if you, *indeed,* speak the truth.'

قُلْ اَرَءَيْتُمْ مَّا تَدْعُوْنَ مِنْ دُوْنِ اللّٰهِ اَرُوْنِيْ
مَاذَا خَلَقُوْا مِنَ الْاَرْضِ اَمْ لَهُمْ شِرْكٌ فِي السَّمٰوٰتِ ۗ
اِيْتُوْنِيْ بِكِتٰبٍ مِّنْ قَبْلِ هٰذَآ اَوْ اَثٰرَةٍ مِّنْ عِلْمٍ
اِنْ كُنْتُمْ صٰدِقِيْنَ ⑤

---

[a]1 : 1. [b]40 : 2; 41 : 2; 42 : 2; 43 : 2; 44 : 2; 45 : 2. [c]20 : 5; 32 : 3; 36 : 6; 40 : 3; 45 : 3. [d]21 : 17; 38 : 28; 44 : 39. [e]35 : 41.

2717. The universe had a beginning and will also have an end. 'All that is on it will pass away. And there will remain only the Person of thy Lord, Master of Glory and Honour' (55 : 27-28).

2718. Only that Being can command adoration and is fit to be worshipped Who as the Architect and Creator of the universe controls our destinies. But the false gods of idolaters not only have not created anything but themselves have been created (25 : 4).

2719. In reality no authority except that of a revealed Scripture and also human science and reason can form the basis for determining whether a certain belief is right or wrong.

6. And who is in greater error than those who, instead of Allāh, pray unto such as will not answer them till the Day of Resurrection,[2720] and [a]they are not even aware of their prayer?

وَمَنْ اَضَلُّ مِمَّنْ يَّدْعُوْا مِنْ دُوْنِ اللّٰهِ مَنْ
لَّا يَسْتَجِيْبُ لَهٗٓ اِلٰى يَوْمِ الْقِيٰمَةِ وَهُمْ عَنْ دُعَآئِهِمْ
غٰفِلُوْنَ ﴿٦﴾

7. [b]And when mankind are raised up *after death*, the *false deities* will be enemies *of their worshippers* and will deny their worship.

وَاِذَا حُشِرَ النَّاسُ كَانُوْا لَهُمْ اَعْدَآءً وَّكَانُوْا
بِعِبَادَتِهِمْ كٰفِرِيْنَ ﴿٧﴾

8. [c]And when Our clear Signs are recited unto them, those who disbelieve say of the truth when it comes to them, 'This is manifest sorcery.'

وَاِذَا تُتْلٰى عَلَيْهِمْ اٰيٰتُنَا بَيِّنٰتٍ قَالَ الَّذِيْنَ كَفَرُوْا
لِلْحَقِّ لَمَّا جَآءَهُمْ ۙ هٰذَا سِحْرٌ مُّبِيْنٌ ﴿٨﴾

9. Do they say, 'He has forged it?' [d]Say, 'If I have forged it, you cannot avail me aught against[2721] Allāh. He knows best what *idle* talk you indulge in. Sufficient is He for a witness between me and you. And He is the Most Forgiving, the Merciful.'

اَمْ يَقُوْلُوْنَ افْتَرٰىهُ ۭ قُلْ اِنِ افْتَرَيْتُهٗ فَلَا تَمْلِكُوْنَ
لِيْ مِنَ اللّٰهِ شَيْئًا ۭ هُوَ اَعْلَمُ بِمَا تُفِيْضُوْنَ فِيْهِ ۭ
كَفٰى بِهٖ شَهِيْدًا بَيْنِيْ وَبَيْنَكُمْ ۭ وَهُوَ الْغَفُوْرُ
الرَّحِيْمُ ﴿٩﴾

10. Say, 'I am no innovation among Messengers, nor do I know what will be done with me or with you. [e]I only follow what is revealed to me; and I am but a plain Warner.'

قُلْ مَا كُنْتُ بِدْعًا مِّنَ الرُّسُلِ وَمَآ اَدْرِيْ مَا يُفْعَلُ
بِيْ وَلَا بِكُمْ ۭ اِنْ اَتَّبِعُ اِلَّا مَا يُوْحٰٓى اِلَيَّ وَمَآ اَنَا
اِلَّا نَذِيْرٌ مُّبِيْنٌ ﴿١٠﴾

[a]10 : 30. [b]6 : 23; 10 : 29. [c]34 : 44; 61 : 7. [d]11 : 36. [e]6 : 51; 7 : 204.

2720. Islām presents a Living God Who reveals Himself to His votaries by accepting their prayers and consoles them in the hour of distress by speaking to them words of comfort and consolation (2 : 187).

2721. The expression, *min Allāh*, means, (*a*) in opposition to Allāh; (*b*) from the punishment of Allāh.

11, Say, 'Tell me, if this *Qur'ān* is from Allāh and you disbelieve therein, and a [a]witness from among the Children of Israel[2722] bears witness to *the advent of* one like him, and he believed, but you are too proud *to believe, how should you fare?*' Verily, Allāh guides not the wrongdoing people.

قُلْ اَرَءَيْتُمْ اِنْ كَانَ مِنْ عِنْدِ اللّٰهِ وَكَفَرْتُمْ بِهٖ
وَشَهِدَ شَاهِدٌ مِّنْ بَنِيْٓ اِسْرَآءِيْلَ عَلٰى مِثْلِهٖ
فَاٰمَنَ وَاسْتَكْبَرْتُمْ ۭ اِنَّ اللّٰهَ لَا يَهْدِي الْقَوْمَ الظّٰلِمِيْنَ ﴿۱۱﴾ ع

R. 2 12. And those who disbelieve say of those who believe, [b]'If *the Qur'ān* were any good, they could not have been ahead of us in *believing in* it.' And since they have not been guided thereby, they will say, 'It is an old lie.'

وَقَالَ الَّذِيْنَ كَفَرُوْا لِلَّذِيْنَ اٰمَنُوْا لَوْ كَانَ خَيْرًا مَّا
سَبَقُوْنَآ اِلَيْهِ ۭ وَاِذْ لَمْ يَهْتَدُوْا بِهٖ فَسَيَقُوْلُوْنَ
هٰذَآ اِفْكٌ قَدِيْمٌ ﴿۱۲﴾

13. And before it there was [c]the Book of Moses, a guide and a mercy; and [d]this is a Book in the Arabic language, fulfilling *previous prophecies*[2723] that it may warn those who do wrong, and *give* glad tidings to those who do good.

وَمِنْ قَبْلِهٖ كِتٰبُ مُوْسٰٓى اِمَامًا وَّرَحْمَةً ۭ وَهٰذَا
كِتٰبٌ مُّصَدِّقٌ لِّسَانًا عَرَبِيًّا لِّيُنْذِرَ الَّذِيْنَ ظَلَمُوْا ۤ
وَبُشْرٰى لِلْمُحْسِنِيْنَ ﴿۱۳﴾

---

[a]11 : 18; 61 : 7. [b]11 : 28. [c]28 : 44. [d]20 : 114; 42 : 8; 43 : 4.

2722. The witness from among the Children of Israel is Moses. It is to his prophecy concerning the advent of the Holy Prophet that reference has been made in this verse. The prophecy is to this effect : 'I will raise them up a Prophet from among their brethren like unto thee, and will put My words in his mouth; and he shall speak unto them all that I shall command him. And it shall come to pass that whosoever will not hearken unto My words, which he shall speak in My name, I will require it of him' (Deut. 18 : 18-19).

2723. Verse 11 supported by Deut. 18 : 18 referred to the appearance of a Prophet among the Ishmaelites. The present verse refers to Arabia as the scene of the advent of the Prophet who was to be the like of Moses and also to the Book (the Qur'ān) which was to fulfil the prophecies contained in the Book of Moses and which also was to supersede it. The relevant prophecy is as follows : 'The burden upon Arabia. In the forest in Arabia shall ye lodge, O ye travelling companies of Dedanim. The inhabitants of the land of Tema brought water to him that was thirsty, they presented with their bread him that fled (Isa. 21 : 13-15).

14. 'Verily, those who say, 'Our Lord is Allāh,' *and* then are steadfast—no fear *shall come* upon them, nor shall they grieve.[2724]

إِنَّ الَّذِيْنَ قَالُوْا رَبُّنَا اللّٰهُ ثُمَّ اسْتَقَامُوْا فَلَا خَوْفٌ عَلَيْهِمْ وَلَاهُمْ يَحْزَنُوْنَ ۝

15. These are the dwellers of the Garden; they shall abide therein—a recompense for what they did.

أُولٰٓئِكَ أَصْحٰبُ الْجَنَّةِ خٰلِدِيْنَ فِيْهَا ۚ جَزَآءًۢ بِمَا كَانُوْا يَعْمَلُوْنَ ۝

16. ^bAnd We have enjoined on man to be good to his parents. His mother bears him with pain, and brings him forth with pain, and the bearing of him and his weaning *takes* thirty months[2725] till, when he attains his full maturity[2726] and reaches *the age of* forty years, he says, ^c'My Lord, grant me that I may be grateful for Thy favour which Thou hast bestowed upon me and upon my parents, and I may do such righteous deeds as may please Thee. And establish righteousness among my progeny for me. I do turn to Thee; and, truly, I am of those who are obedient *to Thee.*'

وَوَصَّيْنَا الْإِنْسَانَ بِوَالِدَيْهِ إِحْسٰنًا ۚ حَمَلَتْهُ أُمُّهُ كُرْهًا وَّوَضَعَتْهُ كُرْهًا ۗ وَحَمْلُهُ وَفِصٰلُهُ ثَلٰثُوْنَ شَهْرًا ۗ حَتّٰى إِذَا بَلَغَ أَشُدَّهُ وَبَلَغَ أَرْبَعِيْنَ سَنَةً ۙ قَالَ رَبِّ أَوْزِعْنِيْ أَنْ أَشْكُرَ نِعْمَتَكَ الَّتِيْ أَنْعَمْتَ عَلَيَّ وَعَلٰى وَالِدَيَّ وَأَنْ أَعْمَلَ صَالِحًا تَرْضٰهُ وَأَصْلِحْ لِيْ فِيْ ذُرِّيَّتِيْ ۚ إِنِّيْ تُبْتُ إِلَيْكَ وَإِنِّيْ مِنَ الْمُسْلِمِيْنَ ۝

17. These are they from whom We accept the best of what they do and overlook their evil deeds. *They shall be* among the inmates of the Garden, *in fulfilment of* the true promise which was made to ^dthem.

أُولٰٓئِكَ الَّذِيْنَ نَتَقَبَّلُ عَنْهُمْ أَحْسَنَ مَا عَمِلُوْا وَنَتَجَاوَزُ عَنْ سَيِّاٰتِهِمْ فِيْ أَصْحٰبِ الْجَنَّةِ ۗ وَعْدَ الصِّدْقِ الَّذِيْ كَانُوْا يُوْعَدُوْنَ ۝

---

^a29 : 70; 41 : 31.   ^b6 : 152; 17 : 24; 29 : 9.   ^c27 : 20.   ^d17 : 109; 19 : 62; 73 : 19.

2724. What fear or grief, even under the severest trial, can possibly disturb the equanimity and mental poise of a true believer, who possesses an invincible faith that Allāh, the Creator and Lord of the whole universe, is at his back?

2725. In 31 : 15, it was stated that the weaning of a child takes two years, but in this verse the combined period of pregnancy and suckling is given as thirty months which leaves six months as the period of gestation; and that seems to be the period during which a pregnant woman feels the burden of pregnancy, the fourth month being the time from which she begins to have such a feeling.

2726. The word *Ashudd* seems to have been used in the sense of spiritual maturity here and in 12 : 23, and in the sense of intellectual and physical maturity in 6 : 153 and 18 : 83.

18. But the one who says to his parents, 'Fie on you both; do you threaten me that I shall be brought forth *again*, when generations have already passed away before me?' And they both cry unto Allah for help *and say to him*, 'Woe unto thee! believe, for the promise of Allāh is true.' But he says, 'This is nothing but the fables of the ancients.'

وَالَّذِي قَالَ لِوَالِدَيْهِ أُفٍّ لَّكُمَا أَتَعِدَانِنِي أَنْ
أُخْرَجَ وَقَدْ خَلَتِ الْقُرُونُ مِن قَبْلِي وَهُمَا
يَسْتَغِيثَانِ اللَّهَ وَيْلَكَ آمِنْ إِنَّ وَعْدَ اللَّهِ حَقٌّ
فَيَقُولُ مَا هَٰذَا إِلَّا أَسَاطِيرُ الْأَوَّلِينَ ﴿١٨﴾

19. These are they against whom the sentence *of punishment* was fulfilled [a]along with the communities of the jinn and men that had gone before them. Indeed, they were the losers.

أُولَٰئِكَ الَّذِينَ حَقَّ عَلَيْهِمُ الْقَوْلُ فِي أُمَمٍ قَدْ
خَلَتْ مِن قَبْلِهِم مِّنَ الْجِنِّ وَالْإِنسِ إِنَّهُمْ
كَانُوا خَاسِرِينَ ﴿١٩﴾

20. And for all are degrees *of rank* according to what they [b]did, and *this will be so* that *Allāh* may fully repay them for their *deeds*;[2727] and they shall not be wronged.

وَلِكُلٍّ دَرَجَاتٌ مِّمَّا عَمِلُوا وَلِيُوَفِّيَهُمْ أَعْمَالَهُمْ
وَهُمْ لَا يُظْلَمُونَ ﴿٢٠﴾

21. And on the day when those who disbelieve will be brought before the Fire, *it will be said to them*, 'You exhausted your good things in the life of the world, and you *fully* enjoyed them. [c]Now this day you shall be requited with ignominious punishment because you were arrogant in the earth[2728] without justification, and because you acted rebelliously.'

وَيَوْمَ يُعْرَضُ الَّذِينَ كَفَرُوا عَلَى النَّارِ أَذْهَبْتُمْ
طَيِّبَاتِكُمْ فِي حَيَاتِكُمُ الدُّنْيَا وَاسْتَمْتَعْتُم بِهَا
فَالْيَوْمَ تُجْزَوْنَ عَذَابَ الْهُونِ بِمَا كُنتُمْ تَسْتَكْبِرُونَ
فِي الْأَرْضِ بِغَيْرِ الْحَقِّ وَبِمَا كُنتُمْ تَفْسُقُونَ ﴿٢١﴾ ع

[a]7 : 39; 41 : 26. [b]6 : 133. [c]6 : 94.

2727. All the works of men will be properly judged and weighed, and all relevant circumstances will be taken into consideration beforc judgment is pronounced. The Divine law of compensation works in this way that whereas the reward of a good deed is many times greater than the deed itself, the punishment of the evil deed is proportionate to the deed committed.

2728. When confronted with the consequences of their evil deeds the disbelievers will be told on the day of Reckoning that as they had fully exploited and drained to the dregs the material gifts that God had bestowed upon them and had used them not in the service of good causes but to further their own sordid ends, they should now be prepared to suffer disgrace and ignominy as a fit requital for their misdeeds.

R. 3 22. And remember [a]the brother of ʻĀd, when he warned his people among the sand-hills—and Warners there have been before him and after him—*saying*, 'Worship none but Allāh. I fear for you the punishment of a great day.'

وَاذْكُرْ أَخَا عَادٍ إِذْ أَنْذَرَ قَوْمَهُ بِالْأَحْقَافِ وَقَدْ خَلَتِ النُّذُرُ مِنْ بَيْنِ يَدَيْهِ وَمِنْ خَلْفِهِ أَلَّا تَعْبُدُوا إِلَّا اللّٰهَ إِنِّيْ أَخَافُ عَلَيْكُمْ عَذَابَ يَوْمٍ عَظِيمٍ ﴿٢٢﴾

23. They said, 'Hast thou come to us to turn us away from our gods? Bring us then that with which thou dost threaten us, if, *indeed*, thou art of the [b]truthful.'

قَالُوا أَجِئْتَنَا لِتَأْفِكَنَا عَنْ آلِهَتِنَا فَأْتِنَا بِمَا تَعِدُنَا إِنْ كُنْتَ مِنَ الصّٰدِقِينَ ﴿٢٣﴾

24. He said, 'The knowledge[2729] *thereof* is only with Allāh. And I convey to you what I have been sent with, but I see that you are a *very* ignorant people.'

قَالَ إِنَّمَا الْعِلْمُ عِنْدَ اللّٰهِ وَأُبَلِّغُكُمْ مَا أُرْسِلْتُ بِهِ وَلٰكِنِّيْ أَرٰكُمْ قَوْمًا تَجْهَلُونَ ﴿٢٤﴾

25. Then, when they saw *the punishment* coming towards their valleys *in the form of* a cloud, they said, 'This is a cloud which will give us rain.' *We said*, 'Nay, but it is that which you sought to hasten—a [c]wind wherein is a grievous punishment;

فَلَمَّا رَأَوْهُ عَارِضًا مُسْتَقْبِلَ أَوْدِيَتِهِمْ قَالُوا هٰذَا عَارِضٌ مُمْطِرُنَا بَلْ هُوَ مَا اسْتَعْجَلْتُمْ بِهِ رِيحٌ فِيهَا عَذَابٌ أَلِيمٌ ﴿٢٥﴾

26. 'It will destroy everything by the command of its Lord.' By morning there was nothing to be seen, except their dwellings. Thus do We requite the guilty people.

تُدَمِّرُ كُلَّ شَيْءٍ بِأَمْرِ رَبِّهَا فَأَصْبَحُوا لَا يُرٰى إِلَّا مَسٰكِنُهُمْ كَذٰلِكَ نَجْزِي الْقَوْمَ الْمُجْرِمِينَ ﴿٢٦﴾

[a]7 : 66; 11 : 51. [b]7 : 71. [c]41 : 17.

2729. As God alone knows the circumstances under which a man does his actions, good or bad, therefore only He knows whether or not he has incurred Divine punishment; and the knowledge of the time, manner and form of the punishment also rests with Him.

27. And [a]We had established them in that wherein We have not established you; and We gave them ears and eyes and hearts.[2730] But their ears and their eyes and their hearts availed them naught, since they denied the Signs of Allāh; and [b]that at which they used to mock encompassed them.

وَلَقَدْ مَكَّنّٰهُمْ فِيْمَآ اِنْ مَّكَّنّٰكُمْ فِيْهِ وَجَعَلْنَا لَهُمْ سَمْعًا وَّاَبْصَارًا وَّاَفْـِٕدَةً ۖ فَمَآ اَغْنٰى عَنْهُمْ سَمْعُهُمْ وَلَآ اَبْصَارُهُمْ وَلَآ اَفْـِٕدَتُهُمْ مِّنْ شَيْءٍ اِذْ كَانُوْا يَجْحَدُوْنَ ۙ بِاٰيٰتِ اللّٰهِ وَحَاقَ بِهِمْ مَّا كَانُوْا بِهٖ يَسْتَهْزِءُوْنَ ﴿٢٧﴾

R. 4 28. And, certainly, We destroyed townships round about you[2731] and We have explained *Our* Signs in various ways,[2732] that they might turn *to Us*.

وَلَقَدْ اَهْلَكْنَا مَا حَوْلَكُمْ مِّنَ الْقُرٰى وَصَرَّفْنَا الْاٰيٰتِ لَعَلَّهُمْ يَرْجِعُوْنَ ﴿٢٨﴾

29. Why, [c]then, did not those help them whom they had taken for gods beside Allāh that they might bring *them* near *to Him?* Nay, they were lost to them. That was *the consequence of* their lie, and of what they fabricated.

فَلَوْلَا نَصَرَهُمُ الَّذِيْنَ اتَّخَذُوْا مِنْ دُوْنِ اللّٰهِ قُرْبَانًا اٰلِهَةً ۖ بَلْ ضَلُّوْا عَنْهُمْ ۚ وَذٰلِكَ اِفْكُهُمْ وَمَا كَانُوْا يَفْتَرُوْنَ ﴿٢٩﴾

---

[a]6 : 7. [b]21 : 42. [c]42 : 47.

2730. '*Af'idah* (hearts) is the plural of *Fu'ād* which is synonymous with *Qalb*, both meaning heart, mind or intellect. In the Qur'ān both these words have been used synonymously. In 28 : 11 they have been used together, signifying the heart. It is the context which determines, where any of these words is used as signifying the heart and where as signifying the mind. Some authors, however, make a distinction between *Fu'ād* and *Qalb;* the latter is said to have a more special signification than the former which is said to be the *Ghisha*' or the *Wi'ā*' of the *Qalb*, or the middle or the interior thereof. *Ṭāra Fu'ādu-hū* means, his mind, or intellect, or courage fled (Lane).

2731. The peoples of 'Ād and Tubba' held sway over vast territories in the south of Arabia; and the tribe of Thamūd lived in its north-west, and on the shores of the Dead Sea were situated the towns of Sodom and Gomorrah. The destruction of these places constituted an eye opener for the Meccans. The words, 'round about you' may also signify the whole world.

2732. The Qur'ān reverts again and again to the fundamental problems of faith, morals and other kindred subjects, and deals with them from different angles and points of view in order to satisfy doubts and misgivings of men of varied attitudes, mental make-ups and outlooks on life. People of shallow thinking and prejudiced minds may call it a repetition, but in fact it is the right approach to different human problems.

30. And *call to mind* when [a]We turned towards thee a party of the jinn[2733] who wished to hear the Qur'ān and, when they were present *at its recitation*, they said *to one another*, 'Be silent and listen,' and when it was finished, they went back to their people, warning them.

وَإِذْ صَرَفْنَآ إِلَيْكَ نَفَرًا مِّنَ الْجِنِّ يَسْتَمِعُونَ الْقُرْاٰنَ
فَلَمَّا حَضَرُوْهُ قَالُوْٓا اَنْصِتُوْا فَلَمَّا قُضِيَ وَلَّوْا اِلٰى
قَوْمِهِمْ مُّنْذِرِيْنَ ﴿٣٠﴾

31. They said, 'O our people, [b]we have heard a Book, which has been sent down afte Moses,[2734] fulfilling that which is before it; it guides to the truth and to the right path;

قَالُوْا يٰقَوْمَنَآ اِنَّا سَمِعْنَا كِتٰبًا اُنْزِلَ مِنْ بَعْدِ مُوْسٰى
مُصَدِّقًا لِّمَا بَيْنَ يَدَيْهِ يَهْدِيْٓ اِلَى الْحَقِّ وَاِلٰى
طَرِيْقٍ مُّسْتَقِيْمٍ ﴿٣١﴾

32. 'O our people, respond to Allāh's summoner and believe in Him. He will forgive you your sins, and protect you from a painful punishment,

يٰقَوْمَنَآ اَجِيْبُوْا دَاعِيَ اللّٰهِ وَاٰمِنُوْا بِهٖ يَغْفِرْ لَكُمْ
مِّنْ ذُنُوْبِكُمْ وَيُجِرْكُمْ مِّنْ عَذَابٍ اَلِيْمٍ ﴿٣٢﴾

33. 'And whoso does not respond to Allāh's summoner, he cannot escape *Him* in the earth, nor can he have any protector beside Him. Such are in manifest error.'

وَمَنْ لَّا يُجِبْ دَاعِيَ اللّٰهِ فَلَيْسَ بِمُعْجِزٍ فِي الْاَرْضِ
وَلَيْسَ لَهٗ مِنْ دُوْنِهٖٓ اَوْلِيَآءُ ۚ اُولٰٓئِكَ فِيْ ضَلٰلٍ مُّبِيْنٍ ﴿٣٣﴾

34. Do they not realize that Allāh, Who created the heavens and the earth and was not wearied by their creation,[2735] [c]has the power to bring the dead to life? Yea, verily, He has power over all things.

اَوَلَمْ يَرَوْا اَنَّ اللّٰهَ الَّذِيْ خَلَقَ السَّمٰوٰتِ وَالْاَرْضَ
وَلَمْ يَعْيَ بِخَلْقِهِنَّ بِقٰدِرٍ عَلٰٓى اَنْ يُّحْيِيَ الْمَوْتٰى ۭ
بَلٰٓى اِنَّهٗ عَلٰى كُلِّ شَيْءٍ قَدِيْرٌ ﴿٣٤﴾

[a]72 : 2. [b]72 : 2-3. [c]17 : 100; 36 : 82; 86 : 9.

2733. The party of jinn referred to in this verse were the Jews of Naṣībīn, or, as some say, of Mauṣal or Nineveh in Iraq. Being apprehensive of the Meccans' opposition they met the Holy Prophet at night and after listening to the Qur'ān and to the Holy Prophet's discourse, they became converted to Islām and carried the new Message to their people who also readily accepted it (Bayān, vol. 8). See also 72 : 2.

2734. The verse shows that the party of jinn mentioned in the previous verse were Jews because they spoke of the Qur'ān as 'the Book which has been sent down after Moses.'

2735. The process of the creation of new heavens and earth has not ceased. Neither is it an empty and unsubstantiated claim. With the coming of a great Divine Reformer the old order dies and a new one takes its place. This signifies the coming into being of a new heaven and a new earth.

35. And on the day when those who disbelieve will be brought before the Fire, *it will be said to them*, 'Is not this the truth?' They will say, 'Aye, by our Lord, *it is the truth*.' He will say, 'Then taste the punishment, because you disbelieved.'

وَيَوْمَ يُعْرَضُ الَّذِيْنَ كَفَرُوْا عَلَى النَّارِ أَلَيْسَ هٰذَا
بِالْحَقِّ قَالُوْا بَلٰى وَرَبِّنَا قَالَ فَذُوْقُوا الْعَذَابَ
بِمَا كُنْتُمْ تَكْفُرُوْنَ ۝٣٥

36. Have patience, then, as the Messengrs, *possessed* of high resolve, had patience; and be in no haste concerning them. On the day when they see that with which they are threatened, *it will appear to them* [a]as though they had not tarried in this world save for an hour[2736] of a day. *This warning* has been conveyed; and none but the disobedient people shall be destroyed.

فَاصْبِرْ كَمَا صَبَرَ أُولُوا الْعَزْمِ مِنَ الرُّسُلِ وَلَا
تَسْتَعْجِلْ لَّهُمْ كَأَنَّهُمْ يَوْمَ يَرَوْنَ مَا يُوْعَدُوْنَ
لَمْ يَلْبَثُوْٓا إِلَّا سَاعَةً مِّنْ نَّهَارٍ بَلٰغٌ فَهَلْ يُهْلَكُ
إِلَّا الْقَوْمُ الْفٰسِقُوْنَ ۝٣٦ ع

[a]10 : 46; 30 : 56; 79 : 47.

2736. So severe, swift and overwhelming will be God's punishment for disbelievers that compared to it a whole life, spent in comfort and ease, would seem to them 'but an hour.'

CHAPTER 47

MUḤAMMAD

(*Revealed after Hijrah*)

Date of Revelation and Context

The *Sūrah* is also known as *Qitāl* (war) because it devotes a large portion of its text to the subject of war—its causes, ethics and consequences. Baiḍāwī, Zamakhsharī, Sayūṭī and others hold that the *Sūrah* was revealed after the *Hijrah*—a large part of it having been revealed probably before the Battle of Badr, in the early days of the Holy Prophet's life at Medina. Towards the end of the last *Sūrah* it was unambiguously and emphatically stated that opposition to the Divine Message, however powerful, organized and persistent, can never succeed and that Truth must prevail in the long run. The subject assumes a certain definiteness in this *Sūrah* and disbelievers are told that the cause of Islām will, after overcoming all difficulties and impediments, triumph.

Subject-Matter

The *Sūrah* opens with the challenging statement that all the efforts of disbelievers to retard and arrest the progress of Islām will come to naught and the condition of the Prophet's followers will improve day by day, and then proceeds to say that since disbelievers have drawn the sword against the Holy Prophet they shall perish by the sword. After holding out to Muslims a definite promise of success against their enemies, the *Sūrah* briefly lays down important rules of war, as, for instance, prisoners can be taken only after regular fighting in which the enemy is decisively beaten (v. 5), and that after the war is over, they are to be set free either as an act of favour, or, after taking proper ransom. Thus the *Sūrah* in a short verse, has struck most effectively at the evil practice of slavery. It is further stated that falsehood eventually must suffer defeat. This is a lesson writ large on the pages of history; and the evil fate of peoples nearer home such as 'Ād, Thamūd, Midian and the people of Lot should open the eyes of the Meccans. Next, the *Sūrah* says a few words of comfort and good cheer to the Holy Prophet, telling him that though he is being driven out of his native place, friendless and apparently helpless, to seek refuge in a distant place among alien people, yet his cause will triumph. Then it briefly mentions the aims and objects of war according to Islām and closes with an exhortation to Muslims to be prepared to spend whatever they possess for the cause they hold so dear, because not to spend when the cause requires its votaries to spend with both hands, is calculated not only to injure the common cause but also the individual himself.

سُوْرَةُ مُحَمَّدٍ مَدَنِيَّةٌ (٤٧)

1. [a]In the name of Allāh, the Gracious, the Merciful.

بِسْمِ اللّٰهِ الرَّحْمٰنِ الرَّحِيْمِ ①

2. [b]Those who disbelieve and hinder *men* from the way of Allāh—He renders their works vain.[2737]

اَلَّذِيْنَ كَفَرُوْا وَصَدُّوْا عَنْ سَبِيْلِ اللّٰهِ اَضَلَّ
اَعْمَالَهُمْ ②

3. But *as for* those who believe and do righteous deeds and believe in that which has been revealed to Muḥammad—and it is the truth from their Lord—He removes from them their sins and sets right their affairs.

وَالَّذِيْنَ اٰمَنُوْا وَعَمِلُوا الصّٰلِحٰتِ وَاٰمَنُوْا بِمَا نُزِّلَ
عَلٰى مُحَمَّدٍ وَّهُوَ الْحَقُّ مِنْ رَّبِّهِمْ ۙ كَفَّرَ عَنْهُمْ
سَيِّاٰتِهِمْ وَاَصْلَحَ بَالَهُمْ ③

4. That is because those who disbelieve follow falsehood while those who believe follow the truth from their Lord. Thus does Allāh set forth for men their *lessons by* similitudes.

ذٰلِكَ بِاَنَّ الَّذِيْنَ كَفَرُوا اتَّبَعُوا الْبَاطِلَ وَاَنَّ الَّذِيْنَ
اٰمَنُوا اتَّبَعُوا الْحَقَّ مِنْ رَّبِّهِمْ ۭ كَذٰلِكَ يَضْرِبُ اللّٰهُ
لِلنَّاسِ اَمْثَالَهُمْ ④

5. [c]And when you meet *in regular battle* those who disbelieve, smite *their* necks; and, when *you have overcome them,*[2738] by causing great slaughter among them, bind fast the fetters—then afterwards either *release them as a* favour or *by taking* ransom—until the war lays down its burdens. That *is the ordinance.*[2739]

فَاِذَا لَقِيْتُمُ الَّذِيْنَ كَفَرُوْا فَضَرْبَ الرِّقَابِ ۭ حَتّٰٓى اِذَآ
اَثْخَنْتُمُوْهُمْ فَشُدُّوا الْوَثَاقَ ۙ فَاِمَّا مَنًّۢا بَعْدُ وَاِمَّا
فِدَاۗءً حَتّٰى تَضَعَ الْحَرْبُ اَوْزَارَهَا ڔ ذٰلِكَ ڔ وَلَوْ يَشَاۗءُ

---

[a]1 : 1. [b]4 : 168; 16 : 89. [c]8 : 46, 68.

2737. Works of disbelievers are rendered vain in that their efforts to arrest the progress of Islām produce no results.

2738. *Athkhana fi'l Arḍi* means, he caused much slaughter in the land.

2739. The verse, in a nutshell, lays down some important rules about the ethics of war and its conduct and incidentally deals a death blow to slavery. Briefly, these are: (*a*) When they are engaged in regular battle in defence of their faith, honour, lives or property, Muslims are enjoined to fight bravely and relentlessly (8 : 13-17). (*b*) When war is once started, it should continue till peace is established and freedom of conscience secured (8 : 40). (*c*) Prisoners are to be taken from the enemy only after regular and pitched battle has been fought, and the enemy is decidedly and positively beaten. Thus regular war is declared to be the only reason for taking prisoners; for no other reason free

And if Allāh had *so* pleased, He could have punished them *Himself*, but *He has willed* that He may try[2740] some of you by others. And those who are killed in the way of Allāh—He will never render their works vain.[2741]

اللّٰهُ لَانْتَصَرَ مِنْهُمْ وَلٰكِنْ لِّيَبْلُوَا۟ بَعْضَكُمْ بِبَعْضٍ ؕ وَ
الَّذِيْنَ قُتِلُوْا فِيْ سَبِيْلِ اللّٰهِ فَلَنْ يُّضِلَّ اَعْمَالَهُمْ ۝٥

6. He will guide[2742] them *to success* and will improve their condition.

سَيَهْدِيْهِمْ وَيُصْلِحُ بَالَهُمْ ۚ ۝٦

7. [a]And will admit them into the Garden which He has made known[2743] to them.

وَيُدْخِلُهُمُ الْجَنَّةَ عَرَّفَهَا لَهُمْ ۝٧

8. O ye who believe! if you help *the cause of* Allāh, He will help you and will make your steps firm.

يٰۤاَيُّهَا الَّذِيْنَ اٰمَنُوْۤا اِنْ تَنْصُرُوا اللّٰهَ يَنْصُرْكُمْ وَ
يُثَبِّتْ اَقْدَامَكُمْ ۝٨

[a]3 : 196; 9 : 111.

men can be deprived of their liberty. (*d*) When war is over, prisoners should be released, either as an act of favour, or on taking ransom from them or by negotiating mutual exchange. They should not be held permanently in captivity or treated as slaves. The Holy Prophet set at liberty about a hundred families of Banī Muṣṭaliq and several thousand prisoners of Hawāzin after both these tribes had been decisively beaten in battle. After the Battle of Badr ransom was accepted from the prisoners, and those who could not pay their ransom in money but were literate, were required to teach reading and writing to Muslims. The verse thus has struck very effectively at the roots of slavery, abolishing it completely and for ever

2740. Allāh got the believers engaged in fighting with disbelievers so that on the one hand their own good qualities of character should have an opportunity to come into play, and on the other, the bad qualities of disbelievers should become exposed. Perhaps in no other aspect of life was the moral superiority of the Companions of the Holy Prophet so clearly demonstrated as in their treatment of their fallen foes.

2741. The sacrifice of Muslims slain in the field of battle will not be wasted. In fact, it was their sacrifice that firmly laid the foundation of Islām in Arabia.

2742. Since *Hidāyah* means, to follow the right path till one reaches one's destination and achieves the object of one's quest (Lane), the verse purports to say that by their death the martyred Muslims achieved the object for which they gave their lives which was the triumph of the cause of Islām.

2743. The believers had a foretaste of the blessings of Paradise in this life in the sense that they enjoyed in their physical form all those spiritual blessings and favours which are mentioned in the Qur'ān as having been promised to them in the next world. Or the verse may mean that the believers had a spiritual foretaste of "the Garden" because they saw with their own eyes the promise made to them in the Qur'ān about Paradise being fulfilled in this very life.

9. But those who disbelieve, perdition is their *lot;* and He will make their works vain.[2744]

وَالَّذِينَ كَفَرُوا فَتَعْسًا لَّهُمْ وَأَضَلَّ أَعْمَالَهُمْ ﴿٩﴾

10. That is because they hate what Allāh has revealed; so He has made their works vain.

ذَٰلِكَ بِأَنَّهُمْ كَرِهُوا مَا أَنزَلَ اللَّهُ فَأَحْبَطَ أَعْمَالَهُمْ ﴿١٠﴾

11. [a]Have they not travelled in the earth and seen what was the end of those who were before them?[2745] Allāh *utterly* destroyed them, and for the disbelievers there will be the like thereof.

أَفَلَمْ يَسِيرُوا فِي الْأَرْضِ فَيَنظُرُوا كَيْفَ كَانَ
عَاقِبَةُ الَّذِينَ مِن قَبْلِهِمْ دَمَّرَ اللَّهُ عَلَيْهِمْ وَ
لِلْكَافِرِينَ أَمْثَالُهَا ﴿١١﴾

12. That is because [b]Allāh is the Protector of those who believe, and the disbelievers have no protector.

ذَٰلِكَ بِأَنَّ اللَّهَ مَوْلَى الَّذِينَ آمَنُوا وَأَنَّ الْكَافِرِينَ
لَا مَوْلَىٰ لَهُمْ ﴿١٢﴾ ع

R. 2 13. Verily, Allāh will cause those who believe and do good works to enter the Gardens underneath which streams flow; [c]while those who disbelieve enjoy themselves and eat *even* as the cattle[2746] eat, and the Fire will be their *last* resort.

إِنَّ اللَّهَ يُدْخِلُ الَّذِينَ آمَنُوا وَعَمِلُوا الصَّالِحَاتِ
جَنَّاتٍ تَجْرِي مِن تَحْتِهَا الْأَنْهَارُ وَالَّذِينَ كَفَرُوا
يَتَمَتَّعُونَ وَيَأْكُلُونَ كَمَا تَأْكُلُ الْأَنْعَامُ وَالنَّارُ
مَثْوًى لَّهُمْ ﴿١٣﴾

14. And how many a township, mightier than thy town which has driven thee out,[2747] have We destroyed, and they had no helper.

وَكَأَيِّن مِّن قَرْيَةٍ هِيَ أَشَدُّ قُوَّةً مِّن قَرْيَتِكَ
الَّتِي أَخْرَجَتْكَ أَهْلَكْنَاهُمْ فَلَا نَاصِرَ لَهُمْ ﴿١٤﴾

[a]12 : 110; 22 : 47; 30 : 10; 35 : 45; 40 : 22. [b]3 : 151; 8 : 41. [c]14 : 31; 77 : 47.

2744. Three times in the few previous verses it is stated that 'God has made the works of disbelievers vain.' This signifies that disbelievers had bent all their energies of mind and body to the achievement of one supreme desire—to see Islām fail and come to naught. But Islām triumphed. It progressed and prospered and the disbelievers failed to see their desire fulfilled.

2745. As many as fifteen times, the disbelievers of the Holy Prophet have been told in the Qur'ān to travel in the earth and see for themselves the sad end to which the disbelievers of former Prophets had come. How can they, the verse warns them, expect to escape a similar fate? Divine punishment will, surely, overtake them in various forms and shapes.

2746. Whereas believers eat to live in order to serve God and man, the disbelievers live to eat and have no nobler objects to pursue. They do not rise above the level of animals as their whole concept of life is materialistic.

2747. The verse was revealed while the Holy Prophet was on his way from Mecca to Medina, having been driven out of his beloved native place, with a price on his head. He was hourly in fear of being caught, as Medina was far away and the country side swarmed with adventurers who sought to bring him dead or alive to get the much-coveted prize. The Holy Prophet was Divinely promised a safe journey.

15. Then, [a]is he who *takes* his *stand* upon a clear proof from his Lord like those to whom the evil of their deeds is made *to look* attractive and who follow their low desires?

أَفَمَنْ كَانَ عَلٰى بَيِّنَةٍ مِّنْ رَّبِّهٖ كَمَنْ زُيِّنَ لَهٗ سُوْٓءُ
عَمَلِهٖ وَاتَّبَعُوْٓا أَهْوَآءَهُمْ ۝١٥

16. [b]A description of the Garden promised to the righteous: Therein are streams of water which corrupts not; and streams of milk of which the taste changes not; and streams of wine, a delight to those who drink; and streams of clarified[2748] honey. And in it will they have all *kinds of* fruit, and forgiveness from their Lord. Can *those who enjoy such bliss* be like those who abide in the Fire and who are given boiling water to drink so that it tears their bowels?

مَثَلُ الْجَنَّةِ الَّتِيْ وُعِدَ الْمُتَّقُوْنَ ۭ فِيْهَآ أَنْهٰرٌ
مِّنْ مَّآءٍ غَيْرِ اٰسِنٍ ۚ وَأَنْهٰرٌ مِّنْ لَّبَنٍ لَّمْ يَتَغَيَّرْ
طَعْمُهٗ ۚ وَأَنْهٰرٌ مِّنْ خَمْرٍ لَّذَّةٍ لِّلشّٰرِبِيْنَ ۚ وَأَنْهٰرٌ
مِّنْ عَسَلٍ مُّصَفًّى ۭ وَلَهُمْ فِيْهَا مِنْ كُلِّ الثَّمَرٰتِ
وَمَغْفِرَةٌ مِّنْ رَّبِّهِمْ ۭ كَمَنْ هُوَ خَالِدٌ فِي النَّارِ
وَسُقُوْا مَآءً حَمِيْمًا فَقَطَّعَ أَمْعَآءَهُمْ ۝١٦

17. And among them are some who *seem to* listen to thee till, when they go forth from thy presence, they say to those who have been given knowledge, 'What has he been talking about just now?'[2749] [c]These are they upon whose hearts Allāh has set a seal, and who follow their own evil desires.

وَمِنْهُمْ مَّنْ يَّسْتَمِعُ إِلَيْكَ ۚ حَتّٰٓى إِذَا خَرَجُوْا مِنْ
عِنْدِكَ قَالُوْا لِلَّذِيْنَ أُوْتُوا الْعِلْمَ مَاذَا قَالَ اٰنِفًا ۣ
أُولٰٓئِكَ الَّذِيْنَ طَبَعَ اللّٰهُ عَلٰى قُلُوْبِهِمْ وَاتَّبَعُوْٓا
أَهْوَآءَهُمْ ۝١٧

[a]11 : 29. [b]13 : 36. [c]16 : 109; 63 : 4.

2748. Believers are promised, in this and the next life, rivers of pure water, rivers of milk of which the taste does not change, rivers of wine which gives delight and rivers of clarified honey. The word, *Anhār*, which has been used four times in the verse, besides other senses, signifies light and amplitude; and *'Asal*, among other things, means a good or righteous deed which wins for the doer the love and esteem of men. In view of this signification of these two words the verse may mean that the four things mentioned will be given to the righteous in plenty. Water is the source of all life (21 : 31); milk gives health and vigour to the body; wine gives pleasant sensations and forgetfulness of worries, and honey cures many a disease. Taken in the physical sense, the verse would signify that in the present life the believers will have in plenty all those things which make life pleasant, delightful and useful; and taken symbolically and in a spiritual sense, it would mean that believers will have a full life—they will be endowed with spiritual knowledge, will drink the wine of God's love and will do deeds that will win for them love and esteem of men.

2749. A hypocrite being a double-faced person generally uses language susceptible of double meaning. This he does in order to extricate himself from an awkward position, so that, should one construction of his speech land him in trouble, he might be able to avoid its consequences by putting quite a different construction on it. The above

18. But *as for* those who follow guidance, [a]He adds to their guidance, and bestows on them righteousness *suited to their condition*.[2750]

وَالَّذِيْنَ اهْتَدَوْا زَادَهُمْ هُدًى وَّ اٰتٰهُمْ
تَقْوٰىهُمْ ﴿۱۸﴾

19. The *disbelievers* wait not but for the Hour, that it should come upon them [b]suddenly. The signs[2751] thereof have already come. But *of* what *avail* will their admonition be to them when it has *actually* come upon them.

فَهَلْ يَنْظُرُوْنَ اِلَّا السَّاعَةَ اَنْ تَاْتِيَهُمْ بَغْتَةً
فَقَدْ جَآءَ اَشْرَاطُهَا فَاَنّٰى لَهُمْ اِذَا جَآءَتْهُمْ
ذِكْرٰىهُمْ ﴿۱۹﴾

20. Know, therefore, that there is no god other than Allāh, and ask protection for thy *human* frailties,[2752] and for believing men and believing women. And Allāh knows the place where you move about and the place where you stay.[2753]

فَاعْلَمْ اَنَّهٗ لَآ اِلٰهَ اِلَّا اللّٰهُ وَاسْتَغْفِرْ لِذَنْۢبِكَ وَ
لِلْمُؤْمِنِيْنَ وَالْمُؤْمِنٰتِ وَاللّٰهُ يَعْلَمُ مُتَقَلَّبَكُمْ وَ
مَثْوٰىكُمْ ﴿۲۰﴾ ع

R. 3 21. And those who believe say, 'Why is not a *Sūrah* revealed?' But when a decisive *Sūrah* is revealed and fighting is mentioned therein, thou seest those in whose hearts is a disease, looking towards thee like the look of one who is fainting on account of *approaching* death. So woe to them!

وَيَقُوْلُ الَّذِيْنَ اٰمَنُوْا لَوْلَا نُزِّلَتْ سُوْرَةٌ فَاِذَآ
اُنْزِلَتْ سُوْرَةٌ مُّحْكَمَةٌ وَّ ذُكِرَ فِيْهَا الْقِتَالُ رَاَيْتَ
الَّذِيْنَ فِيْ قُلُوْبِهِمْ مَّرَضٌ يَّنْظُرُوْنَ اِلَيْكَ نَظَرَ
الْمَغْشِيِّ عَلَيْهِ مِنَ الْمَوْتِ فَاَوْلٰى لَهُمْ ﴿۲۱﴾

[a]8 : 3; [b]22 : 56; 43 : 67.

expression is an appropriate instance of the equivocal language used by the Hypocrites of Medina. If one of them, after a meeting with the Holy Prophet, happened to meet a Muslim, he would say, 'What was it that the Prophet said just now,' meaning what beautiful and highly useful things the Prophet had said. But if he chanced to meet a Hypocrite like himself he would use the same expression but meaning 'what nonsense talk the Prophet had indulged in.'

2750. The Quranic expression may mean: (*a*) God makes them righteous; (*b*) He discloses to them the ways and means by employing which they could attain righteousness. (*c*) Allāh bestows upon believers favours and blessings which are the result of a life of righteousness.

2751. The reference in the word, *Ashrāṭ* (signs), seems to be to the Holy Prophet's flight from Mecca which proved to be the prelude to the appearance of many other Signs.

2752. See 2612 and 2765.

2753. The words, *Mutaqallabakum* and *Mathwākum*, may mean, 'When you move about transacting your affairs and when you take rest, or the former word may apply to this world and the latter to the next.

22. *Their attitude should have been one of* obedience [a]and of calling *people* to good. And when the matter was determined upon, it was good for them if they were true to Allāh.

طَاعَةٌ وَّقَوْلٌ مَّعْرُوْفٌ فَإِذَا عَزَمَ الْأَمْرُ فَلَوْ صَدَقُوا اللّٰهَ لَكَانَ خَيْرًا لَّهُمْ ﴿٢٢﴾

23. Would you not then, if you are placed in authority, create disorder in the land and sever your ties of kinship?[2754]

فَهَلْ عَسَيْتُمْ إِنْ تَوَلَّيْتُمْ أَنْ تُفْسِدُوْا فِي الْأَرْضِ وَتُقَطِّعُوْٓا أَرْحَامَكُمْ ﴿٢٣﴾

24. It is these whom Allāh has cursed, so that He has made them deaf and has made their eyes blind.

أُولٰٓئِكَ الَّذِيْنَ لَعَنَهُمُ اللّٰهُ فَأَصَمَّهُمْ وَأَعْمٰٓى أَبْصَارَهُمْ ﴿٢٤﴾

25. [b]Will they not, then, ponder over the Qur'ān, or, is it that there are locks on their hearts?

أَفَلَا يَتَدَبَّرُوْنَ الْقُرْاٰنَ أَمْ عَلٰى قُلُوْبٍ أَقْفَالُهَا ﴿٢٥﴾

26. Surely, [c]those who turn their backs after guidance has become manifest to them, Satan has seduced them and holds out false hopes to them.

إِنَّ الَّذِيْنَ ارْتَدُّوْا عَلٰٓى أَدْبَارِهِمْ مِّنْ بَعْدِ مَا تَبَيَّنَ لَهُمُ الْهُدَى الشَّيْطٰنُ سَوَّلَ لَهُمْ وَأَمْلٰى لَهُمْ ﴿٢٦﴾

27. That is because they said to those who hate what Allāh has revealed, 'We will obey you in some matters,'[2755] and Allāh knows their secrets.

ذٰلِكَ بِأَنَّهُمْ قَالُوْا لِلَّذِيْنَ كَرِهُوْا مَا نَزَّلَ اللّٰهُ سَنُطِيْعُكُمْ فِيْ بَعْضِ الْأَمْرِ وَاللّٰهُ يَعْلَمُ إِسْرَارَهُمْ ﴿٢٧﴾

28. But how *will they fare* when the angels will cause them to [d]die, smiting their faces and their backs?

فَكَيْفَ إِذَا تَوَفَّتْهُمُ الْمَلٰٓئِكَةُ يَضْرِبُوْنَ وُجُوْهَهُمْ وَأَدْبَارَهُمْ ﴿٢٨﴾

29. That is because they followed that which displeased Allāh, and disliked *the seeking of* His pleasure. So he rendered their works vain.

ذٰلِكَ بِأَنَّهُمُ اتَّبَعُوْا مَآ أَسْخَطَ اللّٰهَ وَكَرِهُوْا رِضْوَانَهُ فَأَحْبَطَ أَعْمَالَهُمْ ﴿٢٩﴾

---

[a]2 : 264. [b]4 : 83. [c]3 : 87. [d]4 : 98; 8 : 51; 16 : 29.

2754. Muslims were allowed to fight, because if the power of disbelievers had not been broken they would have created disorder in the land and have severed all ties of kinship and trampled under foot all rightful claims.

2755. The Hypocrites of Medina would not side with disbelievers openly and unreservedly. A hypocrite is too wily a person to burn his boats. He faces both ways.

R. 4　30. Do those in whose hearts is a disease suppose that Allāh will not bring to light their malice?

اَمْ حَسِبَ الَّذِيْنَ فِيْ قُلُوْبِهِمْ مَّرَضٌ اَنْ لَّنْ يُّخْرِجَ اللّٰهُ اَضْغَانَهُمْ ۝

31. And if We pleased, We could show them to thee so that thou shouldst know them by their marks. And thou shalt, surely, recognize them by the tone of *their* speech.[2756] And Allāh knows your deeds.

وَلَوْ نَشَآءُ لَاَرَيْنٰكَهُمْ فَلَعَرَفْتَهُمْ بِسِيْمٰهُمْ وَلَتَعْرِفَنَّهُمْ فِيْ لَحْنِ الْقَوْلِ وَاللّٰهُ يَعْلَمُ اَعْمَالَكُمْ ۝

32. And We will, surely, try you until We make manifest those among you who strive *for the cause of Allāh* and those who are [a]steadfast.. And We will make known[2757] the *true* facts about you.

وَلَنَبْلُوَنَّكُمْ حَتّٰى نَعْلَمَ الْمُجٰهِدِيْنَ مِنْكُمْ وَالصّٰبِرِيْنَ وَنَبْلُوَاْ اَخْبَارَكُمْ ۝

33. Those, who disbelieve and hinder *men* from the way of Allāh and oppose the Messenger after guidance has become manifest to them, shall not harm Allāh in the least; and He will make their works fruitless.

اِنَّ الَّذِيْنَ كَفَرُوْا وَصَدُّوْا عَنْ سَبِيْلِ اللّٰهِ وَشَآقُّوا الرَّسُوْلَ مِنْ بَعْدِ مَا تَبَيَّنَ لَهُمُ الْهُدٰى لَنْ يَّضُرُّوا اللّٰهَ شَيْئًا وَسَيُحْبِطُ اَعْمَالَهُمْ ۝

34. O ye who believe! obey Allāh and obey the Messenger and make not your works vain.

يٰاَيُّهَا الَّذِيْنَ اٰمَنُوْا اَطِيْعُوا اللّٰهَ وَاَطِيْعُوا الرَّسُوْلَ وَلَا تُبْطِلُوْا اَعْمَالَكُمْ ۝

35. [b]Verily, those who disbelieve and hinder *people* from the way of Allāh, *and* then die while they are disbelievers—Allāh certainly, will not forgive them.

اِنَّ الَّذِيْنَ كَفَرُوْا وَصَدُّوْا عَنْ سَبِيْلِ اللّٰهِ ثُمَّ مَاتُوْا وَهُمْ كُفَّارٌ فَلَنْ يَّغْفِرَ اللّٰهُ لَهُمْ ۝

---

[a]3 : 141-143; 29 : 4, 12.　[b]3 : 92; 4 : 19.

2756. A hypocrite never talks straight. He always indulges in ambiguous and equivocal speech in order that it should convey one sense to one person and quite another sense to another person. It is to this crooked manner of speech of the hypocrites that reference has also been made in 2 : 105.

2757. *'Arafa* is synonymous with *'Alima*, but *'Ilm* is wider and more general in signification than *Ma'rifah*. The root meaning of *'Ilm* is that of a mark or sign by which one thing is distinguished from another (Lane). Knowledge or *'Ilm* is of two kinds: (*a*) knowledge about a thing before its occurrence; and (*b*) knowledge about it after it has actually happened. The knowledge referred to in the verse under comment belongs to the latter category.

36. [a]So be not slack and sue not for peace,[2758] for you will, *certainly*, have the upper hand. And Allāh is with you, and He will not deprive you *of the reward* of your actions.

فَلَا تَهِنُوا وَتَدْعُوا إِلَى السَّلْمِ ۖ وَأَنتُمُ الْأَعْلَوْنَ ۖ وَاللَّهُ مَعَكُمْ وَلَن يَتِرَكُمْ أَعْمَالَكُمْ ﴿٣٦﴾

37. [b]The life of *this* world is but a sport and a pastime, and if you believe and be righteous, He will give you your rewards, and will not ask of you your wealth.[2759]

إِنَّمَا الْحَيٰوةُ الدُّنْيَا لَعِبٌ وَلَهْوٌ ۚ وَإِن تُؤْمِنُوا وَتَتَّقُوا يُؤْتِكُمْ أُجُورَكُمْ وَلَا يَسْأَلْكُمْ أَمْوَالَكُمْ ﴿٣٧﴾

38. Were He to ask it of you and press you, you would be niggardly, and He would bring to light your malice.[2760]

إِن يَسْأَلْكُمُوهَا فَيُحْفِكُمْ تَبْخَلُوا وَيُخْرِجْ أَضْغَانَكُمْ ﴿٣٨﴾

39. Behold ! you are those who are called upon to spend in the way of Allāh; but of you there are some who are niggardly. And whoso is niggardly, is niggardly only against his own soul.[2761] And Allāh is Self-Sufficient, and it is you who are needy. [c]And if you turn your backs, He will bring in your place another people; then they will not be like you.[2762]

هَا أَنتُمْ هٰؤُلَاءِ تُدْعَوْنَ لِتُنفِقُوا فِي سَبِيلِ اللَّهِ فَمِنكُم مَّن يَبْخَلُ ۖ وَمَن يَبْخَلْ فَإِنَّمَا يَبْخَلُ عَن نَّفْسِهِ ۚ وَاللَّهُ الْغَنِيُّ وَأَنتُمُ الْفُقَرَاءُ ۚ وَإِن تَتَوَلَّوْا يَسْتَبْدِلْ قَوْمًا غَيْرَكُمْ ثُمَّ لَا يَكُونُوا أَمْثَالَكُمْ ﴿٣٩﴾ ع

[a]3 : 140. [b]6 : 33; 29 : 65; 57 : 21. [c]5 : 55.

2758. Muslims are enjoined here that once fighting has started, they should never sue for peace, whatever form or shape the fortunes of war may take. They are to win either victory or martyrdom. No other choice is left to them.

2759. The verse purports to say that as Muslims have been enjoined to fight in the cause of Allāh, they will have to bear the expenses of war also and for that purpose they will have to make sacrifice of money. But Allāh does not need their money. It is for their own benefit that sacrifice of life and money is demanded of them because no success is possible without such sacrifice. True believers must understand and realize this supreme lesson.

2760. The verse particularly applies to the hypocrites.

2761. Miserliness is a deadly moral disease that eats into the vitals of man's moral and spiritual well-being. Elsewhere, the Qur'ān has used very strong language about such people (9 : 35).

2762. When the Holy Prophet was once asked as to whom the words 'He will bring instead a people other than you,' referred, he is reported to have said, 'If Faith were to go up to the Pleiades, a man of Persian descent will bring it back to the earth' (Rūḥ al-Ma'ānī).

CHAPTER 48

AL-FATḤ

(*Revealed after Hijrah*)

Date of Revelation and Context

According to consensus of scholarly opinion the *Sūrah* was revealed when, after signing the Treaty of Ḥudaibiyah, the Holy Prophet was on his way back to Medina, in the 6th year of *Hijrah* in the month of Dhu'l-Qa'dah (Bukhārī). The Treaty being an epoch-making event, all incidents connected with it have been carefully preserved in Islamic history. So, complete agreement exists concerning the date and place of the revelation of this *Sūrah*. It bears the title Al-Fatḥ (The Victory). The title is appropriate in that a seemingly diplomatic defeat eventually proved to be a master-stroke of strategy on the part of the Holy Prophet and led to the Fall of Mecca, and consequently to the conquest of the whole of Arabia. Towards the close of the preceding *Sūrah*, believers were given definite promise of victory over their opponents. The present *Sūrah* declares in clear and unequivocal terms that the promised victory is not a thing of some indefinite distant future, but is quite near. It is so near that it may be said to have actually arrived; and it will be so decisive and overwhelming that even the most sceptic person will find it hard to deny it.

Subject-Matter

The *Sūrah* opens with a firm declaration that the promised victory has actually arrived and that it would be clear, definite, and overwhelming. The Holy Prophet is further told that as a result of it people will join the fold of Islām in such large numbers that it would prove a formidable task for him adequately to train and educate the new converts into the tenets and principles of the Faith. He should, therefore, implore God's help in the discharge of his onerous duty, and ask for His forgiveness and mercy lest, due to human limitations, some defects should remain in its full execution. The *Sūrah* proceeds to say that because of lack of proper realization of the full import of the Treaty the believers were downcast, God would send down solace and tranquillity on them and their faith would increase, while the false satisfaction and delight of disbelievers would prove to be short-lived. The believers are further told that they should not have doubted the wisdom of the Holy Prophet's action in signing the Treaty since he was God's Messenger and all his actions were done under Divine direction and guidance. Their duty was 'to believe in him, help him, and honour him.' The *Sūrah* further says that believers earned the pleasure of God when they swore allegiance to the Holy Prophet under 'The Tree' that they would stand by him through thick and thin, even unto death. It was God's own plan that fighting did not take place at that time because in Mecca there lived some true and sincere Muslims whom believers did not know and who would have unwittingly been killed, if fighting had taken place. Next, the Hypocrites and those, who lagged behind, receive a severe rebuke and their hypocrisy is exposed. Whenever they are invited to fight in the cause of God, the *Sūrah* says, they invent false excuses to justify their staying behind, but by their foolish subterfuges and false excuses they deceive no one but themselves. Towards its close, the *Sūrah* reverts to the subject that not only would the Treaty of Ḥudaibiyah prove to be a great victory but that other victories would follow in its wake, and the neighbouring countries would fall to the victorious arms of Muslims.

سُوْرَةُ الْفَتْحِ مَدَنِيَّةٌ

1. [a]In the name of Allāh, the Gracious, the Merciful.

بِسْمِ اللّٰهِ الرَّحْمٰنِ الرَّحِيْمِ ﴿١﴾

2. Verily, We have given thee a clear Victory,[2763]

إِنَّا فَتَحْنَا لَكَ فَتْحًا مُّبِيْنًا ﴿٢﴾

---

[a] 1 : 1.

2763. The reference in the words 'a clear victory' seems to be to the Treaty of Ḥudaibiyah. It is remarkable that though, during the early brief six years of his life at Medina, the Holy Prophet had gained great victories over his enemies which had crippled and crushed their fighting power, yet none of them is called 'a clear victory' in the Qur'ān. It was reserved for the Treaty of Ḥudaibiyah to receive this signal honour, despite the fact that its terms were seemingly very humiliating, and the Muslims were greatly perturbed over this apparently rude rebuff to the prestige of Islām, so much so that even a stalwart like 'Umar exclaimed in extreme grief and indignation that if the terms had been settled by any other person than the Holy Prophet, he would have scorned to listen to them (Hishām). The Treaty was, indeed, a great victory in that it opened the way to the expansion and spread of Islām and led to the Fall of Mecca and ultimately to the conquest of the whole of Arabia. It proved to be a master-stroke of strategy on the Holy Prophet's part as his 'political status as an equal and independent Power was acknowledged by the Quraish' ("Mohammad at Medina" by Montgomery Watt).

The Holy Prophet had seen a vision that he was making a circuit of the Ka'bah along with a party of his followers. In order to fulfil his vision he started for Mecca with about 1500 Muslims to perform the Lesser Pilgrimage ('*Umrah*) in the Sacred Months in which, according to Arab tradition and usage, fighting was forbidden, and this was so even before Islām. When he reached '*Usfān*, a place, a few miles away from Mecca, he was informed by an advance party whom he had sent under the command of 'Abbād bin Bishr that the Quraish were bent upon barring his entry into the town. In order to avoid armed clash the Holy Prophet changed his route and, 'after a fatiguing march through devious and rugged pathways, reached Ḥudaibiyah' where he encamped. The Holy Prophet had declared that he would accept all the demands of the Quraish for the honour of the Holy Place (Hishām), but the Quraish were firmly resolved not to allow him to enter Mecca, whatever he might say. Messages were exchanged in an attempt to find a solution of the *impasse*. After heated and protracted parleys in which the Holy Prophet left no stone unturned, even at the cost of his prestige, to arrive at a reasonable compromise with the Quraish, a treaty was signed of which the terms were: 'War shall be suspended for ten years. Whosoever would like to join the Holy Prophet or enter into treaty with him, shall have liberty to do so, and likewise whosoever would like to join the Quraish or enter into treaty with them shall have liberty to do so. If a believing man goes over to the Prophet from Mecca without the permission of his guardian, he shall be sent back to his guardian; but should any of the followers of the Prophet return to the Quraish, he shall not be sent back. The Prophet shall go back this year without entering the city. Next year he and his Companions may visit Mecca only for three days to perform '*Umrah* (Lesser Pilgrimage), but they shall carry no arms save sheathed swords' (Bukhārī).

The terms were seemingly very humiliating. The Muslims were greatly upset. No words could adequately describe their anguish and sense of humiliation and injured pride. The third term was particularly galling. But the Holy Prophet was quite calm and tranquil. Being convinced of the moral force of Islām, he knew that 'a believer who had once tasted the sweetness of faith would prefer to be cast into fire rather than to revert to disbelief' (Bukhārī); and that he would prove to be a source of strength to his religion wherever he might happen to be. The Treaty subsequently proved to be 'a clear Victory.' The Companions of the Holy Prophet were rightly proud of being present on the occasion, and quite justified in regarding the Treaty and not the conquest of Mecca as 'the victory referred to in the present verse' (Bukhārī). According to them no victory was greater and more far-reaching in its results and effects than this Treaty (Hishām). And the

3. That Allāh may cover up[2764] for thee thy shortcomings,[2765] past and future,[2766] and that He may complete His favour upon thee, and may guide thee on a right path;

لِيَغْفِرَ لَكَ اللّٰهُ مَا تَقَدَّمَ مِنْ ذَنْۢبِكَ وَمَا تَأَخَّرَ وَيُتِمَّ نِعْمَتَهٗ عَلَيْكَ وَيَهْدِيَكَ صِرَاطًا مُّسْتَقِيْمًا ۝۳

Holy Prophet himself called it a great victory (Baihaquī). The Qur'ān calls it *a clear victory* (v. 2), *the supreme achievement* (v. 6); *a great reward* (v. 11) and the completion and perfection of God's favour upon the Holy Prophet (v. 3), because it opened the flood-gates of the spiritual and political conquests of Islām.

2764. The verse has been deliberately misrepresented, or, through lack of knowledge of Arabic idiom and phrase, misinterpreted by some Christian writers as signifying that the Holy Prophet was guilty of moral lapses. It is an article of faith with Muslims, as enjoined by the Qur'ān, that God's Prophets are born sinless and they remain sinless throughout their lives. They do not say or do anything contrary to Divine commandments (21 : 28). As they are commissioned by God to purge men of sins, so they cannot possibly commit sins themselves. And of Divine Messengers the Holy Prophet was the noblest and the purest. The Qur'ān abounds in verses which speak in glowing terms of the purity and spotlessness of his life (2 : 130; 3 : 32; 3 : 165; 6 : 163; 7 : 158; 8 : 25; 33 : 22; 48 : 11; 53 : 3-4; 68 : 5 & 81 : 20-22). For the expression *li-Yaghfira*, see 2612.

2765. A man of such high moral stature as the Holy Prophet, who raised a whole people, sunk into the lowest depths of moral turpitude, to the highest pinnacle of spiritual eminence, could not possibly be guilty of such moral lapses as his detractors have vainly sought to impute to him. A quite simple and harmless word, *Dhanb*, has been taken advantage of to malign him. The word signifies such frailties as adhere to human nature, and to errors as are calculated to bring about harmful results. The verse signifies that God would protect the Holy Prophet from the harmful results that would follow in the wake of the promised victory referred to in the preceding verse, inasmuch as large masses of people would enter the fold of Islām, and naturally their moral and spiritual training and upbringing would not be of the desired standard. That is why wherever in the Qur'ān success and victories are promised to the Holy Prophet, he is enjoined to seek protection of God from his *Dhanb*, *i.e.*, human weaknesses which might stand in the way of the realization of his great mission. The fact that of the four words, *Junāḥ*, *Jurm*, *Ithm* and *Dhanb*, which possess almost similar connotations, none of the first three words has been used in the Qur'ān with regard to God's Prophets, shows that *Dhanb* does not possess the sinister significance which the other three words possess. Besides, according to the Quranic idiom, the expression *Dhanbaka*, if at all *Dhanb* be taken to signify a sin or crime, would mean 'the sins alleged to have been committed by thee ; or the sins committed against thee.' According to the last meaning of *Dhanb* the Arabic word *laka* in the verse would mean 'for thy sake.' Elsewhere in the Qur'ān (5 : 30) a similar expression *Ithmī* (my sin) signifies 'the sin committed against me.' Thus the verse under comment would mean that as a result of the great victory—the Treaty of Hudaibiyah, all the sins and crimes and faults which his enemies imputed to the Holy Prophet, *viz.*, that he was a cheat, an impostor or a forger of lies against God and man, etc., would prove to be false, inasmuch as all sorts of people by coming into contact with his followers would find out the truth about him. Or the meaning is that 'the sins committed against thee by thine enemies will be pardoned for thy sake.' And so it happened. When Mecca fell and the Arabs accepted Islām, their sins were forgiven. The context also supports this meaning because grant of a clear victory and the completion of Divine favour upon the Holy Prophet, referred to in this and the preceding verse do not seem to possess any relevance to the forgiveness of sins, if *Dhanb* be taken to mean a sin.

2766. The words 'past and present' signify that the charges, that were levelled against the Holy Prophet in the past by the Quraish, and those that will be levelled against him in future by his enemies, will all be dispelled and he will stand completely vindicated.

وَّ يَنْصُرَكَ اللّٰهُ نَصْرًا عَزِيْزًا ﴿٤﴾

4. And that Allāh may help thee with a mighty help.[2767]

هُوَ الَّذِيْٓ اَنْزَلَ السَّكِيْنَةَ فِيْ قُلُوْبِ الْمُؤْمِنِيْنَ
لِيَزْدَادُوْٓا اِيْمَانًا مَّعَ اِيْمَانِهِمْ ؕ وَ لِلّٰهِ جُنُوْدُ
السَّمٰوٰتِ وَالْاَرْضِ ؕ وَ كَانَ اللّٰهُ عَلِيْمًا حَكِيْمًا ۙ﴿٥﴾

5. He it is Who sent down tranquillity[2768] into the hearts of the believers that they might add faith to their faith—and to Allāh belong the hosts of the heavens and the earth, and Allāh is All-Knowing, Wise—

لِّيُدْخِلَ الْمُؤْمِنِيْنَ وَ الْمُؤْمِنٰتِ جَنّٰتٍ تَجْرِيْ
مِنْ تَحْتِهَا الْاَنْهٰرُ خٰلِدِيْنَ فِيْهَا وَ يُكَفِّرَ عَنْهُمْ
سَيِّاٰتِهِمْ ؕ وَ كَانَ ذٰلِكَ عِنْدَ اللّٰهِ فَوْزًا عَظِيْمًا ۙ﴿٦﴾

6. That He may cause the believing men and the believing women to enter the Gardens beneath which streams flow, wherein they will abide, and *that* [a]He may remove their evils from them—and that, in the sight of Allāh, is the supreme achievement;

وَّ يُعَذِّبَ الْمُنٰفِقِيْنَ وَ الْمُنٰفِقٰتِ وَ الْمُشْرِكِيْنَ وَ
الْمُشْرِكٰتِ الظَّآنِّيْنَ بِاللّٰهِ ظَنَّ السَّوْءِ ؕ عَلَيْهِمْ دَآئِرَةُ
السَّوْءِ ۚ وَ غَضِبَ اللّٰهُ عَلَيْهِمْ وَ لَعَنَهُمْ وَ اَعَدَّ لَهُمْ
جَهَنَّمَ ؕ وَ سَآءَتْ مَصِيْرًا ﴿٧﴾

7. And *that* [b]He may punish the hypocritical men and the hypocritical women, and the idolatrous men and the idolatrous women, who entertain evil thoughts concerning Allāh. [c]On them *shall fall* an evil calamity, and the wrath of Allāh is upon them. And He has cursed them, and has prepared Hell for them. And that, indeed, is an evil destination.

وَ لِلّٰهِ جُنُوْدُ السَّمٰوٰتِ وَ الْاَرْضِ ؕ وَ كَانَ اللّٰهُ عَزِيْزًا
حَكِيْمًا ﴿٨﴾

8. And to Allāh belong the hosts of the heavens and the earth and Allāh is Mighty, Wise.

[a]8 : 30; 64 : 10; 66 : 9. [b]33 : 25. [c]9 : 98.

2767. Allāh's help came in the form of the rapid spread of Islām in Arabia after the signing of the Treaty of Ḥudaibiyah, and the Holy Prophet was acknowledged as the Head of an independent sovereign State.

2768. The expression shows that though, due to a misunderstanding about the terms of the Treaty of Ḥudaibiyah the believers were temporarily perturbed, they never lost peace of mind so far as fighting in the cause of Allāh was concerned, and were fully convinced that Divine hosts were with them. That is why when a false news reached Ḥudaibiyah that 'Uthmān, the Prophet's envoy to the Meccans, had been killed, and the Holy Prophet invited Muslims to take a solemn oath at his hand that they would avenge the death of 'Uthmān and would fight under his banner to the bitter end, all of them took the oath without evincing the least hesitation.

9. We have sent thee as a witness and [a]a bearer of glad tidings and a Warner,

إِنَّآ أَرْسَلْنٰكَ شَاهِدًا وَّمُبَشِّرًا وَّنَذِيرًا ﴿٩﴾

10. That you should believe in Allāh and His Messenger, and may help him, and honour [b]him, and *that* you may glorify *Allāh* morning and evening.

لِّتُؤْمِنُوا بِاللّٰهِ وَرَسُولِهٖ وَتُعَزِّرُوهُ وَتُوَقِّرُوهُ ۚ وَ
تُسَبِّحُوهُ بُكْرَةً وَّأَصِيلًا ﴿١٠﴾

11. Verily, those who swear allegiance to thee,[2769] indeed, swear allegiance to Allāh. The hand of Allāh is over their hands. So whoever breaks *his oath*, breaks *it* to his own loss; and whoever fulfils the covenant that he has made with Allāh, He will, surely, give him a great reward.

إِنَّ الَّذِينَ يُبَايِعُونَكَ إِنَّمَا يُبَايِعُونَ اللّٰهَ ۖ يَدُ اللّٰهِ
فَوْقَ أَيْدِيهِمْ ۚ فَمَن نَّكَثَ فَإِنَّمَا يَنكُثُ عَلٰى
نَفْسِهٖ ۖ وَمَنْ أَوْفٰى بِمَا عٰهَدَ عَلَيْهُ اللّٰهَ فَسَيُؤْتِيهِ
أَجْرًا عَظِيمًا ﴿١١﴾ ع

R. 2 12. Those of the desert Arabs, *who contrived to be* left behind,[2770] will say to thee, 'Our possessions and our families kept us occupied, so ask forgiveness for us.' [c]They say with their tongues that which is not in their hearts. Say, 'Who can avail you aught against Allāh, if He should intend you some harm, or if He should intend you some benefit? Nay, Allāh is Well-Aware of what you do.'

سَيَقُولُ لَكَ الْمُخَلَّفُونَ مِنَ الْأَعْرَابِ شَغَلَتْنَآ
أَمْوٰلُنَا وَأَهْلُونَا فَاسْتَغْفِرْ لَنَا ۚ يَقُولُونَ بِأَلْسِنَتِهِم
مَّا لَيْسَ فِي قُلُوبِهِمْ ۚ قُلْ فَمَن يَمْلِكُ لَكُم مِّنَ اللّٰهِ
شَيْئًا إِنْ أَرَادَ بِكُمْ ضَرًّا أَوْ أَرَادَ بِكُمْ نَفْعًا ۚ بَلْ
كَانَ اللّٰهُ بِمَا تَعْمَلُونَ خَبِيرًا ﴿١٢﴾

[a]25 : 57; 33 : 46; 35 : 25. [b]5 : 13. [c]3 : 168.

2769. The reference is to the oath taken by the believers at the hand of the Holy Prophet under a tree at Ḥudaibiyah (Bukhārī).

2770. Bedouin tribes around Medina, who apparently had friendly relations with the Muslims, were also invited to join the party of 1500 Muslims who went to Mecca to perform the Lesser Pilgrimage. Though the Holy Prophet went on a mission of peace, they thought that the Quraish would not allow his entry into Mecca and that in all likelihood there would be a clash of arms and Muslims not being properly armed would be defeated, and, therefore, going with the Holy Prophet was tantamount to marching on into the jaws of death (Muir & Kathīr). The verse may equally apply to those tribes who had remained behind in the expedition to Tabūk because analogous words have been used in *Sūrah* Al-Taubah about them.

13. 'Nay, you thought that the Messenger and the believers would never return to their families,[2771] and that was made *to appear* pleasing to your hearts, and you thought an evil thought, and you were a ruined people.'

بَلْ ظَنَنْتُمْ أَنْ لَّنْ يَّنْقَلِبَ الرَّسُوْلُ وَالْمُؤْمِنُوْنَ إِلٰٓى أَهْلِيْهِمْ أَبَدًا وَّزُيِّنَ ذٰلِكَ فِيْ قُلُوْبِكُمْ وَظَنَنْتُمْ ظَنَّ السَّوْءِ ۚ وَكُنْتُمْ قَوْمًا بُوْرًا ﴿١٣﴾

14. *And as for* those who believe not in Allāh and His Messenger—[a]We have, surely, prepared for the disbelievers a blazing fire.

وَمَنْ لَّمْ يُؤْمِنْ بِاللّٰهِ وَرَسُوْلِهٖ فَإِنَّآ أَعْتَدْنَا لِلْكٰفِرِيْنَ سَعِيْرًا ﴿١٤﴾

15. [b]And to Allāh belongs the Kingdom of the heavens and the earth. [c]He forgives whom He pleases, and punishes whom He pleases. And Allāh is Most Forgiving, ever Merciful.

وَلِلّٰهِ مُلْكُ السَّمٰوٰتِ وَالْأَرْضِ ۚ يَغْفِرُ لِمَنْ يَّشَآءُ وَيُعَذِّبُ مَنْ يَّشَآءُ ۚ وَكَانَ اللّٰهُ غَفُوْرًا رَّحِيْمًا ﴿١٥﴾

16. Those, *who contrived to be* left behind, will say, when you go forth to the spoils to take them, 'Let us follow you.' They seek to change the decree of Allāh. Say, 'You shall not follow us.[2772] Thus has Allāh said beforehand.' Then they will say, 'Nay, but you envy us.' *That is not so;* in fact they understand not except a little.

سَيَقُوْلُ الْمُخَلَّفُوْنَ إِذَا انْطَلَقْتُمْ إِلٰى مَغَانِمَ لِتَأْخُذُوْهَا ذَرُوْنَا نَتَّبِعْكُمْ ۚ يُرِيْدُوْنَ أَنْ يُّبَدِّلُوْا كَلٰمَ اللّٰهِ ۚ قُلْ لَّنْ تَتَّبِعُوْنَا كَذٰلِكُمْ قَالَ اللّٰهُ مِنْ قَبْلُ ۚ فَسَيَقُوْلُوْنَ بَلْ تَحْسُدُوْنَنَا ۚ بَلْ كَانُوْا لَا يَفْقَهُوْنَ إِلَّا قَلِيْلًا ﴿١٦﴾

[a]18 : 103; 29 : 69; 33 : 9; 76 : 5. [b]40 : 17. [c]3 : 130; 5 : 19.

2771. Wish being father to the thought, the Hypocrites, whenever invited by the Holy Prophet to join him in an expedition, entertained the fond hope that Muslims being very weak would never return safe to their families. Therefore, on one pretext or another, they asked to be excused. But their wishful thinking always ended in frustration and severe disappointment, and the Muslims returned successful from almost every expedition.

2772. The reference is to the booty which fell into the hands of Muslims in the Khaibar expedition. The *Sūrah* was revealed when the Holy Prophet was on his way back from Ḥudaibiyah. In v. 20, the Muslims were promised great spoils. It is to these spoils that the present verse refers. Shortly after his return from Ḥudaibiyah, the Holy Prophet marched against the Jews of Khaibar to punish them for their repeated acts of treachery. Those Bedouin tribes, who had contrived to remain behind when the Holy Prophet went to Mecca for the Lesser Pilgrimage, finding that his cause had prospered and that they would have a good share of the booty if they joined the expedition to Khaibar, requested him to allow them to accompany the Muslim army. They were told that they could not do so as the promise of booty was made only to those sincere Muslims who were with the Holy Prophet at Ḥudaibiyah.

17. Say to the desert Arabs *who contrived to be* left behind, 'You shall be called *to fight* against a people of mighty valour;[2773] you shall fight them until they surrender. Then, if you obey, Allāh will give you a good reward, but if you turn your backs, as you turned your backs before, He will punish you with a painful punishment.'

قُلْ لِّلْمُخَلَّفِيْنَ مِنَ الْاَعْرَابِ سَتُدْعَوْنَ اِلٰى قَوْمٍ اُولِيْ بَاْسٍ شَدِيْدٍ تُقَاتِلُوْنَهُمْ اَوْ يُسْلِمُوْنَ ۚ فَاِنْ تُطِيْعُوْا يُؤْتِكُمُ اللّٰهُ اَجْرًا حَسَنًا ۚ وَاِنْ تَتَوَلَّوْا كَمَا تَوَلَّيْتُمْ مِّنْ قَبْلُ يُعَذِّبْكُمْ عَذَابًا اَلِيْمًا ﴿١٦﴾

18. [a]There is no blame on the blind, nor is there blame on the lame, nor is there blame on the sick, *if they go not forth to fight.* [b]And whoso obeys Allāh and His Messenger, He will cause him to enter the Gardens beneath which streams flow; but whoso turns his back, him will He punish with a grievous punishment.

لَيْسَ عَلَى الْاَعْمٰى حَرَجٌ وَّلَا عَلَى الْاَعْرَجِ حَرَجٌ وَّلَا عَلَى الْمَرِيْضِ حَرَجٌ ؕ وَمَنْ يُّطِعِ اللّٰهَ وَرَسُوْلَهٗ يُدْخِلْهُ جَنّٰتٍ تَجْرِيْ مِنْ تَحْتِهَا الْاَنْهٰرُ ۚ وَمَنْ يَّتَوَلَّ يُعَذِّبْهُ عَذَابًا اَلِيْمًا ﴿١٧﴾ ع

R. 3 19. Surely, Allāh was well-pleased with the believers when they were swearing allegiance to thee under the Tree,[2774] and He knew what was in their hearts,[2775]

لَقَدْ رَضِيَ اللّٰهُ عَنِ الْمُؤْمِنِيْنَ اِذْ يُبَايِعُوْنَكَ تَحْتَ الشَّجَرَةِ فَعَلِمَ مَا فِيْ قُلُوْبِهِمْ فَاَنْزَلَ السَّكِيْنَةَ

[a]9 : 91. [b]4 : 14; 24 : 53; 33 : 72.

2773. The words, 'a people of mighty valour,' may refer to the mighty forces of the Byzantine and Iranian Empires which were far superior in material means and numbers than any other enemy, the Muslims had met so far. The verse constituted a warning that the Muslims would come into conflict with those mighty foes and would have to wage prolonged wars with them till the latter would be completely defeated and brought to their knees. The laggards are here told that though they cannot be allowed to march against the Jews of Khaibar and partake of the booty, yet in the near future they would be called upon to fight against a much more powerful enemy and that, if they then responded to the call, they would receive a good reward. The verse also signifies that wars with the Byzantine and Iranian Empires would be fierce and long.

2774. The swearing of allegiance took place at Ḥudaibiyah under an acacia tree after a report had reached the Holy Prophet that in breach of ambassadorial usage and etiquette his envoy, 'Uthmān, had been assassinated by the Meccans. It was, perhaps, not so much the reported murder of 'Uthmān as the violation of a sacred and time-honoured usage that exhausted the Holy Prophet's patience. The oath came to be known as *Bai'at al- Riḍwān*, which signified that those lucky people who had taken the oath had obtained God's pleasure.

2775. What greater proof could there be that God had sent down tranquillity on Muslims than that, being only about 1500 in number and being far away from home and being friendless and surrounded by hostile tribes and faced by a powerful enemy who was entrenched in his citadel, they were prepared to fight rather than agree to the proposed terms of the Treaty.

and He sent down tranquillity on them, and He rewarded them with a victory at hand;[2776]

عَلَيْهِمْ وَأَثَابَهُمْ فَتْحًا قَرِيبًا ﴿١٩﴾

20. And great spoils[2777] that they will take. Allāh is Mighty, Wise.

وَمَغَانِمَ كَثِيرَةً يَأْخُذُونَهَا ۗ وَكَانَ اللَّهُ عَزِيزًا
حَكِيمًا ﴿٢٠﴾

21. Allāh has promised you great spoils[2778] that you will take, and He has given you this in advance, and has [a]restrained the hands of men from you, that it may be a Sign for the believers, and that He may guide you on a right path;

وَعَدَكُمُ اللَّهُ مَغَانِمَ كَثِيرَةً تَأْخُذُونَهَا فَعَجَّلَ
لَكُمْ هَٰذِهِ وَكَفَّ أَيْدِيَ النَّاسِ عَنْكُمْ ۚ وَلِتَكُونَ
آيَةً لِلْمُؤْمِنِينَ وَيَهْدِيَكُمْ صِرَاطًا مُسْتَقِيمًا ﴿٢١﴾

22. And *He has promised you* another *victory*[2779] which you have not been able to achieve *yet, but* Allāh has, surely, compassed it. And Allāh has power over all things.

وَأُخْرَىٰ لَمْ تَقْدِرُوا عَلَيْهَا قَدْ أَحَاطَ اللَّهُ بِهَا ۚ
وَكَانَ اللَّهُ عَلَىٰ كُلِّ شَيْءٍ قَدِيرًا ﴿٢٢﴾

23. And if those who disbelieve should fight you, they would, certainly, turn their backs; then they would find neither protector nor helper.

وَلَوْ قَاتَلَكُمُ الَّذِينَ كَفَرُوا لَوَلَّوُا الْأَدْبَارَ ثُمَّ لَا
يَجِدُونَ وَلِيًّا وَلَا نَصِيرًا ﴿٢٣﴾

24. [b]*Such* has ever been the law of Allāh; and thou shalt not find any change in the law of Allāh.

سُنَّةَ اللَّهِ الَّتِي قَدْ خَلَتْ مِنْ قَبْلُ ۖ وَلَنْ تَجِدَ
لِسُنَّةِ اللَّهِ تَبْدِيلًا ﴿٢٤﴾

[a]5 : 12. [b]17 : 78; 33 : 63; 35 : 44.

2776. The words 'victory at hand' refer to the victory at Khaibar. On his return from Ḥudaibiyah the Holy Prophet led an expedition against the Jews of Khaibar (a great hot-bed of Jewish intrigue and conspiracy) with those Muslims who were with him at Ḥudaibiyah.

2777. 'Great spoils' may refer to the great gains which the Muslims got as a result of the 'near victory' promised in the preceding verse.

2778. 'Great spoils' mentioned in this verse may refer to the great booty which fell into the hands of Muslims in the conquests, which followed the victory at Khaibar in the rest of Arabia and the neighbouring countries, but the words, 'He has given you this in advance,' evidently refer to the spoils gained at Khaibar. The words, 'has restrained the hands of men from you,' mean that the Treaty of Ḥudaibiyah had ushered in a period of peace for Muslims.

2779. The verse embodies a prophecy that Muslims will achieve other great victories after the victory at Khaibar.

25. And He it is Who withheld their hands from you and your hands from them in the Valley of Mecca, after He had given you victory over them.[2780] And Allāh sees all that you do.

وَهُوَ الَّذِىۡ كَفَّ اَيۡدِيَهُمۡ عَنۡكُمۡ وَاَيۡدِيَكُمۡ عَنۡهُمۡ بِبَطۡنِ مَكَّةَ مِنۡۢ بَعۡدِ اَنۡ اَظۡفَرَكُمۡ عَلَيۡهِمۡ وَكَانَ اللّٰهُ بِمَا تَعۡمَلُوۡنَ بَصِيۡرًا ۞

26. It is they who disbelieved and *debarred you from the Sacred Mosque and also prevented the dedicated offerings from reaching their place of sacrifice. And had it not been for *some believing men and believing women who were then in Mecca and whom, not having known, you might have trampled down, and thus might have, on their account, incurred an unwitting guilt,[2781] He would have permitted you to fight, but He withheld you that He might admit into His mercy whom He will. If they had been clearly separated from the disbelievers, We would have, surely, punished those of them who disbelieved with a grievous punishment.

هُمُ الَّذِيۡنَ كَفَرُوۡا وَصَدُّوۡكُمۡ عَنِ الۡمَسۡجِدِ الۡحَرَامِ وَالۡهَدۡىَ مَعۡكُوۡفًا اَنۡ يَّبۡلُغَ مَحِلَّهٗ وَلَوۡلَا رِجَالٌ مُّؤۡمِنُوۡنَ وَنِسَآءٌ مُّؤۡمِنَاتٌ لَّمۡ تَعۡلَمُوۡهُمۡ اَنۡ تَطَئُوۡهُمۡ فَتُصِيۡبَكُمۡ مِّنۡهُمۡ مَّعَرَّةٌۢ بِغَيۡرِ عِلۡمٍ لِيُدۡخِلَ اللّٰهُ فِىۡ رَحۡمَتِهٖ مَنۡ يَّشَآءُ لَوۡ تَزَيَّلُوۡا لَعَذَّبۡنَا الَّذِيۡنَ كَفَرُوۡا مِنۡهُمۡ عَذَابًا اَلِيۡمًا ۞

---

*8 : 35; 22 : 26.

2780. In view of the circumstances in which the Muslims were then placed and of the far-reaching results it produced, the Treaty of Ḥudaibiyah was, indeed, a great victory. The words may also refer to the victories that God had granted to Muslims before they came to Ḥudaibiyah—the victory at Badr, the safe return from Uḥud to Medina of Muslims and the Holy Prophet, after they had been placed in a very dangerous and delicate situation, and the complete frustration of the Meccans in their evil designs to destroy Islām in the Battle of the Trench when they were repulsed with severe loss, etc. In a sense these were all victories of believers over disbelievers.

2781. There was a nucleus of Muslims in Mecca and if the fight had taken place, Muslim army would have unknowingly killed their own brethren in Faith, thereby causing great injury to their own cause, and earning obloquy and opprobrium in addition.

27. When those who disbelieved harboured in their hearts prideful indignation —indignation of *the Days of* Ignorance, *a*Allāh sent down His tranquillity on His Messenger and on the believers, and made them adhere firmly to the principle of righteousness, and they were better entitled to it and more worthy of it.[2782] And Allāh knows everything well.

اِذْ جَعَلَ الَّذِيْنَ كَفَرُوْا فِيْ قُلُوْبِهِمُ الْحَمِيَّةَ حَمِيَّةَ الْجَاهِلِيَّةِ فَاَنْزَلَ اللّٰهُ سَكِيْنَتَهٗ عَلٰى رَسُوْلِهٖ وَ عَلَى الْمُؤْمِنِيْنَ وَ اَلْزَمَهُمْ كَلِمَةَ التَّقْوٰى وَكَانُوْٓا اَحَقَّ بِهَا وَاَهْلَهَا ۚ وَكَانَ اللّٰهُ بِكُلِّ شَيْءٍ عَلِيْمًا ۟

R. 4　28. Allāh, indeed, fulfilled for His Messenger the Vision:[2783] You shall, certainly, enter the Sacred Mosque, if Allāh will, in security, some of you having their heads shaven and *others* having *their* hair cut short, you will have no fear. But He knew what you knew not. He has, in fact, ordained for you, besides that, a victory near at hand.

لَقَدْ صَدَقَ اللّٰهُ رَسُوْلَهُ الرُّءْيَا بِالْحَقِّ ۚ لَتَدْخُلُنَّ الْمَسْجِدَ الْحَرَامَ اِنْ شَآءَ اللّٰهُ اٰمِنِيْنَ ۙ مُحَلِّقِيْنَ رُءُوْسَكُمْ وَ مُقَصِّرِيْنَ ۙ لَا تَخَافُوْنَ ؕ فَعَلِمَ مَا لَمْ تَعْلَمُوْا فَجَعَلَ مِنْ دُوْنِ ذٰلِكَ فَتْحًا قَرِيْبًا ۟

29. *b*He it is Who has sent His Messenger with guidance and the true Religion, that He may cause it to prevail over *all other* religions.[2784] And *c*Sufficient is Allāh as a Witness.

هُوَ الَّذِيْٓ اَرْسَلَ رَسُوْلَهٗ بِالْهُدٰى وَدِيْنِ الْحَقِّ لِيُظْهِرَهٗ عَلَى الدِّيْنِ كُلِّهٖ ؕ وَكَفٰى بِاللّٰهِ شَهِيْدًا ۟

---

*a*9 : 26.　*b*61 : 10.　*c*4 : 167; 13 : 44; 29 : 53.

2782. Against their own tradition and usage that access to and circuit of the Ka'bah was not to be prevented in the four Sacred Months, the pagans of Mecca, from a false sense of dignity and national pride, had made it a point of honour with them not to allow Muslims to enter Mecca and perform the '*Umrah* (Lesser Pilgrimage). But 'Allāh sent His tranquillity' upon the Muslims and though they were greatly upset over the seemingly humiliating terms of the Treaty, yet in deference to the wish and command of their beloved Master they bore all this with becoming restraint and patience and did not abandon the path of rectitude and righteousness under the most severe provocation. The Companions of the Holy Prophet alone were capable of setting such a noble example.

2783. The verse refers to the Vision which the Holy Prophet had seen that he was performing the circuit of the Ka'bah with his Companions (Bukhārī). He set out for Mecca with about 1500 of his Companions to perform the Lesser Pilgrimage. He was not allowed access to the Ka'bah by the Quraish though the *Sūrah* was clear and emphatic that the Prophet's Vision was true and that the Muslims would most certainly enter the Ka'bah and perform the ceremonies of the Lesser Pilgrimage. The Holy Prophet's journey, besides serving other useful purposes to which reference is already made, established an important precedent that sometimes even great Prophets of God are liable to place seemingly erroneous interpretations on their visions.

2784. The verse makes a very bold prophecy that Islam would eventually triumph over all other religions.

مُحَمَّدٌ رَّسُوْلُ اللّٰهِ ؕ وَالَّذِيْنَ مَعَهٗۤ اَشِدَّآءُ عَلَى الْكُفَّارِ
رُحَمَآءُ بَيْنَهُمْ تَرٰىهُمْ رُكَّعًا سُجَّدًا يَّبْتَغُوْنَ فَضْلًا
مِّنَ اللّٰهِ وَرِضْوَانًا ؗ سِيْمَاهُمْ فِيْ وُجُوْهِهِمْ مِّنْ
اَثَرِ السُّجُوْدِ ؕ ذٰلِكَ مَثَلُهُمْ فِي التَّوْرٰىةِ ۖۛ وَمَثَلُهُمْ
فِي الْاِنْجِيْلِ ۛ كَزَرْعٍ اَخْرَجَ شَطْـَٔهٗ فَاٰزَرَهٗ فَاسْتَغْلَظَ
فَاسْتَوٰى عَلٰى سُوْقِهٖ يُعْجِبُ الزُّرَّاعَ لِيَغِيْظَ بِهِمُ
الْكُفَّارَ ؕ وَعَدَ اللّٰهُ الَّذِيْنَ اٰمَنُوْا وَعَمِلُوا الصّٰلِحٰتِ
مِنْهُمْ مَّغْفِرَةً وَّاَجْرًا عَظِيْمًا ٣٠ ع

30. Muḥammad is the Messenger of Allāh. And those who are with him are [a]hard against the disbelievers but tender[2785] among themselves. Thou seest them bowing and prostrating themselves *in Prayer*, [b]seeking Allāh's grace and pleasure. Their marks are upon their faces, being the traces of prostrations. This is their description in the Torah.[2786] And their description in the Gospel is like unto a seed-produce that sends forth its sprout, then makes it strong; it then becomes stout, and stands firm on its stem, delighting the sowers—that He may cause the disbelievers to boil with rage *at the sight* of them. Allāh has promised, unto those of them, who believe and do good works, forgiveness and a great reward.

[a]9 : 123. [b]59 : 9.

2785. These are the two essential characteristics of a progressive and prosperous people who seek to leave their mark on the course of world events. Elsewhere in the Qur'ān (5 : 55), the true and good Muslims have been described as kind and humble towards believers and hard and firm against disbelievers.

2786. The words, '*This is their description in the Torah*,' may refer to the biblical description, *viz*., 'he shined forth from mount Paran and he came with ten thousands of saints' (Deut. 33 : 2). And the expression, *And their description in the Gospel is like unto a seed-produce*, may refer to another biblical parable, *viz*., 'Behold, a sower went forth to sow; and when he sowed seeds; some fell into good ground and brought forth fruit, some hundredfold, some sixtyfold, some thirtyfold' (Matt. 13 : 3-8). The former description seems to apply to the Companions of the Holy Prophet and the latter parable to the followers of Jesus's counterpart, the Promised Messiah, who, from a very small and insignificant beginning, are destined to develop into a mighty organization and gradually but progressively to carry the Message of Islām to the ends of the earth till it will prevail and triumph over all religions, and its opponents will wonder at, and be jealous of, its power and prestige.

CHAPTER 49

AL-ḤUJURĀT

(*Revealed after Hijrah*)

Date of Revelation and Context

The *Sūrah* was revealed in the 9th year of the *Hijrah*, after the Fall of Mecca. When with the Fall of Mecca Islām had become a great political power and large masses of people had entered its fold, it was in the fitness of time that the newly initiated people should have been taught good manners and morals. The *Sūrah* teaches Muslims those good manners and morals. It also deals with some social evils which find their way into a materially-advanced and wealthy society (the Muslims had become such a society after the conquest of Arabia) and speaks of the accession to Islām of great political power and material wealth. Naturally, and quite appropriately, it embodies regulations for the settlement of international disputes. It opens with strict injunctions to Muslims to show full regard and respect to the Holy Prophet which befits his status as a great Divine Messenger. They are further enjoined not to anticipate his decisions but to give unquestioning obedience to him. They should not raise their voices above his voice; this not only constitutes bad manners but also shows lack of proper respect for the Leader which is calculated to undermine discipline in the Muslim Community. The *Sūrah*, then, warns Muslims to be on their guard against giving credence to false rumours, as such rumours are calculated to land Muslims into very awkward situations and lays down, in brief words, rules on which a League of Nations, or a United Nations Organization, can be built on sound and solid foundations. Next, it mentions some social evils which, if not guarded against and effectively checked in time, are calculated to eat into the vitals of a community and undermine its whole social structure. Of these social evils the common ones are suspicion, false accusation, spying, back-biting; and most pronounced and far-reaching in their evil consequences are conceit and pride born of a false sense of racial superiority. The Qur'ān recognizes no basis of superiority save that of piety and righteous conduct.

سُوْرَةُ الْحُجُرٰتِ مَدَنِيَّةٌ (٤٩)

1. [a]In the name of Allāh, the Gracious, the Merciful.

بِسْمِ اللّٰهِ الرَّحْمٰنِ الرَّحِيْمِ ۝١

2. O ye who believe! be not forward[2787] in the presence of Allāh and His Messenger, but fear Allāh. Verily, Allāh is All-Hearing, All-Knowing.

يٰٓاَيُّهَا الَّذِيْنَ اٰمَنُوْا لَا تُقَدِّمُوْا بَيْنَ يَدَيِ اللّٰهِ
وَرَسُوْلِهٖ وَاتَّقُوا اللّٰهَ اِنَّ اللّٰهَ سَمِيْعٌ عَلِيْمٌ ۝٢

3. O ye who believe! raise not your voices above the voice of the Prophet,[2788] nor speak loudly to him as you speak loudly to one another, lest your works come to naught while you perceive not.

يٰٓاَيُّهَا الَّذِيْنَ اٰمَنُوْا لَا تَرْفَعُوْٓا اَصْوَاتَكُمْ فَوْقَ
صَوْتِ النَّبِيِّ وَلَا تَجْهَرُوْا لَهٗ بِالْقَوْلِ كَجَهْرِ
بَعْضِكُمْ لِبَعْضٍ اَنْ تَحْبَطَ اَعْمَالُكُمْ وَاَنْتُمْ
لَا تَشْعُرُوْنَ ۝٣

4. Verily, those who lower their voices in the presence of the Messenger of Allāh—those are they whose hearts Allāh has purified for righteousness.[2789] For them is forgiveness and a great reward.

اِنَّ الَّذِيْنَ يَغُضُّوْنَ اَصْوَاتَهُمْ عِنْدَ رَسُوْلِ اللّٰهِ
اُولٰٓئِكَ الَّذِيْنَ امْتَحَنَ اللّٰهُ قُلُوْبَهُمْ لِلتَّقْوٰى
لَهُمْ مَّغْفِرَةٌ وَّاَجْرٌ عَظِيْمٌ ۝٤

5. Those who call out to thee from without *thy* private apartments—most of them have no sense.[2790]

اِنَّ الَّذِيْنَ يُنَادُوْنَكَ مِنْ وَّرَآءِ الْحُجُرٰتِ
اَكْثَرُهُمْ لَا يَعْقِلُوْنَ ۝٥

6. And if they had waited patiently until thou camest out to them, it would be better for them. But Allāh is Most Forgiving, Merciful.

وَلَوْ اَنَّهُمْ صَبَرُوْا حَتّٰى تَخْرُجَ اِلَيْهِمْ لَكَانَ
خَيْرًا لَّهُمْ وَاللّٰهُ غَفُوْرٌ رَّحِيْمٌ ۝٦

---

[a]1 : 1.

2787. Believers are enjoined to show proper respect to, and regard for, the Holy Prophet and to give him unqualified obedience and not to anticipate his commands or to prefer their own wishes to his.

2788. The verse lays great stress on observing an attitude of utmost respectfulness towards the Holy Prophet. The Muslims should not talk loudly in his presence or address him aloud which not only constitutes bad manners, but is calculated to do moral injury to one so rude as not to show due respect to the Leader.

2789. To speak in low tones in the presence of the Holy Prophet is indicative of respect for him and of one's own humility of heart, while the raising of voice unnecessarily smacks of conceit and arrogance.

2790. Calling out to the Prophet in a loud voice from outside his house amounts to intruding upon his privacy and shows lack of respect for his person and his valuable time; and only an ill-mannered person would be guilty of such foolish behaviour.

7. O ye who believe! if an unrighteous person brings you any news, [a]investigate[2791] it fully, lest you harm a people in ignorance, and then you repent of what you did.

يٰۤاَيُّهَا الَّذِيۡنَ اٰمَنُوۡۤا اِنۡ جَآءَكُمۡ فَاسِقٌۢ بِنَبَاٍ فَتَبَيَّنُوۡۤا اَنۡ تُصِيۡبُوۡا قَوۡمًۢا بِجَهَالَةٍ فَتُصۡبِحُوۡا عَلٰى مَا فَعَلۡتُمۡ نٰدِمِيۡنَ ﴿۷﴾

8. And know that among you is the Messenger of Allāh; if he were to follow your wishes in many matters, you would, surely, come to trouble;[2792] but Allāh has endeared the faith to you and has made it *look* beautiful to your hearts, and He has made disbelief, wickedness and disobedience hateful to you. Such, indeed, are those who follow the right course

وَاعۡلَمُوۡۤا اَنَّ فِيۡكُمۡ رَسُوۡلَ اللّٰهِ ؕ لَوۡ يُطِيۡعُكُمۡ فِىۡ كَثِيۡرٍ مِّنَ الۡاَمۡرِ لَعَنِتُّمۡ وَلٰكِنَّ اللّٰهَ حَبَّبَ اِلَيۡكُمُ الۡاِيۡمَانَ وَزَيَّنَهٗ فِىۡ قُلُوۡبِكُمۡ وَكَرَّهَ اِلَيۡكُمُ الۡكُفۡرَ وَالۡفُسُوۡقَ وَالۡعِصۡيَانَ ؕ اُولٰٓئِكَ هُمُ الرّٰشِدُوۡنَ ﴿۸﴾

9. By Allāh's grace and His favour. And Allāh is All-Knowing, Wise.

فَضۡلًا مِّنَ اللّٰهِ وَنِعۡمَةً ؕ وَاللّٰهُ عَلِيۡمٌ حَكِيۡمٌ ﴿۹﴾

10. And if two parties of believers fight each other, [b]make peace between them;[2793] then if *after that* one of them transgresses against the other, fight the party that transgresses until it returns to the command of Allāh. Then if it returns, make peace between them with equity, and act justly. Verily, Allāh loves the just.

وَاِنۡ طَآئِفَتٰنِ مِنَ الۡمُؤۡمِنِيۡنَ اقۡتَتَلُوۡا فَاَصۡلِحُوۡا بَيۡنَهُمَا ۚ فَاِنۡۢ بَغَتۡ اِحۡدٰىهُمَا عَلَى الۡاُخۡرٰى فَقَاتِلُوا الَّتِىۡ تَبۡغِىۡ حَتّٰى تَفِىۡٓءَ اِلٰٓى اَمۡرِ اللّٰهِ ۚ فَاِنۡ فَآءَتۡ فَاَصۡلِحُوۡا بَيۡنَهُمَا بِالۡعَدۡلِ وَاَقۡسِطُوۡا ؕ اِنَّ اللّٰهَ يُحِبُّ الۡمُقۡسِطِيۡنَ ﴿۱۰﴾

[a]4 : 95. [b]8 : 2.

2791. Though after the Fall of Mecca almost the whole of Arabia had entered the fold of Islām, some tribes had still refused to accept the new order of things and were determined upon fighting the Muslims to the bitter end. Moreover, the neighbouring Byzantine and Iranian Empires were also awakening to a realization of the challenge to their power and prestige, which challenge they thought had arisen in Arabia, and war with Islām seemed inevitable. So this injunction was necessary. The Muslims are told that even when the exigencies of war necessitate prompt action to forestal a military move on the enemy's part, rumours which are naturally very rife in time of war should not be given ready credence. They should be fully examined and tested and their correctness ascertained before action is taken upon them.

2792. Muslims are here told that the Holy Prophet might seek counsel in matters concerning them, but he should not be expected necessarily to follow their advice as he receives guidance from on High and because also his is the final responsibility.

2793. A great danger to the security and solidarity of a Muslim State are the disputes and quarrels that haply might arise between different Muslim groups or parties. This verse provides an effective remedy to compose such differences. Primarily, it deals with the settlement of disputes between Muslim parties, but it equally embodies a sound basis on which a really effective League of Nations or a United Nations Organization, can be built. The verse lays down a sound principle for the maintenance of international peace.

11. Surely, *all* believers are brothers. So make peace between your brothers,[2794] and fear Allāh that mercy may be shown to you.

إِنَّمَا الْمُؤْمِنُونَ إِخْوَةٌ فَأَصْلِحُوا بَيْنَ أَخَوَيْكُمْ
وَاتَّقُوا اللّٰهَ لَعَلَّكُمْ تُرْحَمُونَ ١١

R. 2 12. O ye who believe! let not one people deride *another* people, haply they may be better than they, nor let *one group of* women *deride other* women, haply they may be better than they. [a]And do not defame your people nor call *one another* by nick-names. It is *an* evil *thing to be called* by bad name after having believed; and those who repent not, such are the wrongdoers.

يٰۤاَيُّهَا الَّذِيْنَ اٰمَنُوْا لَا يَسْخَرْ قَوْمٌ مِّنْ قَوْمٍ عَسٰۤى
اَنْ يَّكُوْنُوْا خَيْرًا مِّنْهُمْ وَلَا نِسَآءٌ مِّنْ نِّسَآءٍ عَسٰۤى
اَنْ يَّكُنَّ خَيْرًا مِّنْهُنَّ ۚ وَلَا تَلْمِزُوْۤا اَنْفُسَكُمْ وَلَا
تَنَابَزُوْا بِالْاَلْقَابِ ؕ بِئْسَ الِاسْمُ الْفُسُوْقُ بَعْدَ
الْاِيْمَانِ ۚ وَمَنْ لَّمْ يَتُبْ فَاُولٰٓئِكَ هُمُ الظّٰلِمُوْنَ ١٢

13. O ye who believe! avoid much suspicion;[2795] [b]for suspicion in some *cases* is a sin. And spy not on one another, neither backbite one another. Would any of you like to eat the flesh of his dead brother? Certainly, you would loathe it. And fear Allāh, surely, Allāh is Oft-Returning *with compassion and* is Merciful.

يٰۤاَيُّهَا الَّذِيْنَ اٰمَنُوا اجْتَنِبُوْا كَثِيْرًا مِّنَ الظَّنِّ ۚ اِنَّ
بَعْضَ الظَّنِّ اِثْمٌ وَّلَا تَجَسَّسُوْا وَلَا يَغْتَبْ
بَّعْضُكُمْ بَعْضًا ؕ اَيُحِبُّ اَحَدُكُمْ اَنْ يَّاْكُلَ لَحْمَ
اَخِيْهِ مَيْتًا فَكَرِهْتُمُوْهُ ؕ وَاتَّقُوا اللّٰهَ ؕ اِنَّ اللّٰهَ
تَوَّابٌ رَّحِيْمٌ ١٣

[a]68 : 12; 104 : 2. [b]53 : 29.

2794. The verse lays special stress on Islamic brotherhood. If there happens to arise a quarrel or dispute between two Muslim individuals or groups, other Muslims are enjoined to take immediate steps to bring about reconciliation between them. Islām's real strength lies in this ideal of brotherhood which transcends all barriers of caste, colour or clime.

2795. The principal theme of the *Sūrah* being the establishment of concord, amity and goodwill among Muslim individuals and groups, this and the preceding verse mention some of those social evils which cause discord, dissensions and differences; and corrode, corrupt and contaminate a society and eat into its vitals; and enjoins Muslims to be on their guard against them. Ridiculing and taunting others, spying, and calling by nick-names, and suspicion and back-biting, are some of these social evils. Women have been particularly mentioned in this connection in that they are more prone to fall a victim to them. The main cause which lies at the root of these evils are conceit and a false sense of superiority, which the next verse expressly deals with. By removing these basic causes of disharmony and disagreement among Muslims the *Sūrah* has laid the foundation of a firm and solid brotherhood of Islām.

14. O mankind, We have created you from a male and a female; and We have made you tribes and sub-tribes that you may know one another.[2796] Verily, the most honourable[2797] among you, in the sight of Allāh, is he who is the most righteous among you. Surely, Allāh is All-Knowing, All-Aware.

يٰٓاَيُّهَا النَّاسُ اِنَّا خَلَقْنٰكُمْ مِّنْ ذَكَرٍ وَّاُنْثٰى وَجَعَلْنٰكُمْ شُعُوْبًا وَّقَبَآئِلَ لِتَعَارَفُوْا ؕ اِنَّ اَكْرَمَكُمْ عِنْدَ اللّٰهِ اَتْقٰىكُمْ ؕ اِنَّ اللّٰهَ عَلِيْمٌ خَبِيْرٌ ﴿۱۴﴾

15. The Arabs of the desert say, "We believe.' Say, 'You have not *truly* believed *yet*, but rather say, 'We have submitted, for *true* faith has not yet entered into your hearts."[2798] But if you obey Allāh and His Messenger, He will not detract anything from your deeds. Surely, Allāh is Most Forgiving, Merciful.

قَالَتِ الْاَعْرَابُ اٰمَنَّا ؕ قُلْ لَّمْ تُؤْمِنُوْا وَلٰكِنْ قُوْلُوْٓا اَسْلَمْنَا وَلَمَّا يَدْخُلِ الْاِيْمَانُ فِيْ قُلُوْبِكُمْ ؕ وَاِنْ تُطِيْعُوا اللّٰهَ وَرَسُوْلَهٗ لَا يَلِتْكُمْ مِّنْ اَعْمَالِكُمْ شَيْـًٔا ؕ اِنَّ اللّٰهَ غَفُوْرٌ رَّحِيْمٌ ﴿۱۵﴾

2796. *Shu'ūb* is the plural of *Sha'b* which means, a great tribe; the parent of the tribes called *Qabīlah* to which they refer their origin and which comprises them; a nation (Lane).

2797. After having dealt with the subject of Islamic brotherhood in the preceding two verses, the present verse lays down the basis of an all-comprehensive, all-pervading brotherhood of man. The verse, in fact, constitutes the Magna Carta of human fraternity and equality. It lays the axe at the false and foolish notions of superiority, born of racial arrogance or national conceit. Having been created from a male and a female as human beings all men have been declared equal in the sight of God. The worth of a man is not to be judged by the pigment of his skin, the amount of wealth he possesses, or by his rank or social status, descent or pedigree, but by his moral greatness and by the way in which he discharges his obligations to God and man. The whole human race is but one family. Division into tribes, nations, and races is meant to give them better knowledge of one another, in order that they might benefit from one another's national characteristics and good qualities. On the occasion of the Last Pilgrimage at Mecca, a short time before his death, the Holy Prophet addressing a vast concourse of Muslims said, 'O ye men! your God is One and your ancestor is one. An Arab possesses no superiority over a non-Arab, nor does a non-Arab over an Arab. A white is in no way superior to a red, nor, for that matter, a red to a white, but only to the extent to which he discharges his duty to God and man. The most honoured among you in the sight of God is the most righteous among you (Baihaquī). These noble words epitomize one of Islām's loftiest ideals and strongest principles. In a society riven with class distinctions the Holy Prophet preached a principle intensely democratic.

2798. All Muslims form an integral part of the Islamic brotherhood. Islām confers as equal rights on the unlettered and uncultured sons of the desert as it does on the civilized and cultured dwellers of cities and towns; only it exhorts the former to make greater efforts to learn and assimilate the teachings of Islām and make them the rule of their lives.

16. ᵃThe believers are only those who *truly* believe in Allāh and His Messenger, and then doubt not, but strive with their possessions and their persons in the cause of Allāh. It is they who are truthful.

اِنَّمَا الْمُؤْمِنُوْنَ الَّذِيْنَ اٰمَنُوْا بِاللّٰهِ وَرَسُوْلِهٖ ثُمَّ لَمْ يَرْتَابُوْا وَجَاهَدُوْا بِاَمْوَالِهِمْ وَاَنْفُسِهِمْ فِيْ سَبِيْلِ اللّٰهِ اُولٰٓئِكَ هُمُ الصّٰدِقُوْنَ ۞

17. Say, 'Would you acquaint Allāh with your faith, while ᵇAllāh knows whatever is in the heavens and whatever is in the earth, and Allāh knows all things full well?'

قُلْ اَتُعَلِّمُوْنَ اللّٰهَ بِدِيْنِكُمْ وَاللّٰهُ يَعْلَمُ مَا فِي السَّمٰوٰتِ وَمَا فِي الْاَرْضِ وَاللّٰهُ بِكُلِّ شَيْءٍ عَلِيْمٌ ۞

18. They presume to regard it as a favour to thee that they have embraced Islām. Say, 'Deem not your *embracing* Islām as a favour unto me. On the contrary, ᶜAllāh has bestowed a favour upon you in that He has guided you to the *true* Faith, if you are truthful.'

يَمُنُّوْنَ عَلَيْكَ اَنْ اَسْلَمُوْا قُلْ لَّا تَمُنُّوْا عَلَيَّ اِسْلَامَكُمْ بَلِ اللّٰهُ يَمُنُّ عَلَيْكُمْ اَنْ هَدٰىكُمْ لِلْاِيْمَانِ اِنْ كُنْتُمْ صٰدِقِيْنَ ۞

19. Verily, Allāh knows the secrets of the heavens and the earth. And Allāh sees all what you do.'

اِنَّ اللّٰهَ يَعْلَمُ غَيْبَ السَّمٰوٰتِ وَالْاَرْضِ وَاللّٰهُ بَصِيْرٌ بِمَا تَعْمَلُوْنَ ۞

ᵃ9 : 20; 61 : 12.   ᵇ20 : 8; 22 : 71; 27 : 66.   ᶜ3 : 165.

CHAPTER 50

QĀF

(*Revealed before Hijrah*)

Date of Revelation and Context

All competent authorities assign the revelation of this *Sūrah* to the early Meccan period. Its tenor and contents support this view. The preceding two *Sūrahs* had dealt with the prospects of a great and glorious future for Islām, and also with the social and political problems that arise when power and wealth come to a people. The present *Sūrah*, having the abbreviated letter *Qāf* in its beginning, points to the fact that the Almighty God has the power to make the weak and disorganized Arabs into a powerful nation, and that He will certainly bring about this consummation, using the Qur'ān as the means and instrument for achieving this purpose.

Subject-Matter

The *Sūrah* is the first of a group of seven Chapters which end with *Sūrah* Al-Wāqi'ah. Like all Meccan Chapters it lays special stress, in emphatic and prophetic language, on the Qur'ān being the revealed Word of God, on Resurrection being an undoubted reality, and particularly on the ultimate triumph of the cause of Islām. The *Sūrah* points to the phenomena of nature and to the histories of the past Prophets as guides which lead to this inevitable conclusion. It opens to deal with the all-important subject of Resurrection, and in order to prove the truth of this primal fact, uses as an argument the phenomenon that a people, who for long centuries had remained spiritually dead and defunct, will receive a new and vigorous life through the Qur'ān. The *Sūrah* further says that disbelievers cannot bring themselves to accept the fact that a Warner can appear from among them to tell them that they will be raised to life after 'they are dead and have become dust.' They are told to study the wonderful creation of the celestial firmament with the beautiful stars and planets which adorn it and which work with a regularity and punctuality that knows no deviation, and to ponder over the creation of the vast expanse of the earth which grows all sorts of fruits and foods for its dwellers. They will then realize that the Author and Architect of this great and complex universe possesses the power and wisdom to give man a new life after his physical habitat has disintegrated. The *Sūrah* then points to the purposefulness of the creation of man—God's supreme creature and His noblest handiwork—and to his discretion and complete responsibility and accountability for his actions. The *Sūrah* ends on the note that the creation of the universe and of man, its apex and acme, shows that the wise Creator could not have brought into existence this complex universe without a great purpose behind its creation. This leads to the conclusion that there must be and there is a life beyond the grave.

سُوْرَةُ قٓ مَكِّيَّةٌ (٥٠)

المنزل

1. [a]In the name of Allāh, the Gracious, the Merciful.

بِسْمِ اللّٰهِ الرَّحْمٰنِ الرَّحِيْمِ ﴿١﴾

2. Qāf.[2799] We cite the glorious Qur'ān[2800] *as a proof that the great Resurrection is sure to take place.*

قٓ وَالْقُرْاٰنِ الْمَجِيْدِ ﴿٢﴾

3. But they wonder that there has come to them a Warner from among themselves. And the disbelievers say, 'This is a strange thing.

بَلْ عَجِبُوْٓا اَنْ جَآءَهُمْ مُّنْذِرٌ مِّنْهُمْ فَقَالَ الْكٰفِرُوْنَ هٰذَا شَيْءٌ عَجِيْبٌ ﴿٣﴾

4. 'What! when we are dead and have become dust, *shall we be raised up again?* [b]That is a return far *from possible.*'

ءَاِذَا مِتْنَا وَكُنَّا تُرَابًا ۚ ذٰلِكَ رَجْعٌ ۢ بَعِيْدٌ ﴿٤﴾

5. We know how much the earth diminishes of them *and how much it adds to them*, and with Us is a Book that preserves *everything.*[2801]

قَدْ عَلِمْنَا مَا تَنْقُصُ الْاَرْضُ مِنْهُمْ ۚ وَعِنْدَنَا كِتٰبٌ حَفِيْظٌ ﴿٥﴾

6. Nay, they rejected the truth when it came to them, and so they are in a state of confusion.

بَلْ كَذَّبُوْا بِالْحَقِّ لَمَّا جَآءَهُمْ فَهُمْ فِيْٓ اَمْرٍ مَّرِيْجٍ ﴿٦﴾

7. Do they not look at the sky above them, how We have made it and [c]adorned it, and there are no flaws[2802] in it?

اَفَلَمْ يَنْظُرُوْٓا اِلَى السَّمَآءِ فَوْقَهُمْ كَيْفَ بَنَيْنٰهَا وَزَيَّنّٰهَا وَمَا لَهَا مِنْ فُرُوْجٍ ﴿٧﴾

[a]1 : 1. [b]13 : 6; 23 : 37. [c]37 : 7; 41 : 13; 67 : 6.

2799. The letter *Qāf* may stand for the Divine Attribute *Qādir* meaning, the Mighty God, or for the expression, *Al-Qiyāmatu Ḥaqqun, i.e.*, the Resurrection is an undoubted reality.

2800. The Qur'ān is cited as an evidence that the Great Resurrection will, certainly, take place.

2801. The verse refutes the disbelievers' objection mentioned in the preceding verse, *viz.*, how when they are dead and reduced to broken bones and particles of dust they would be raised again. It is the physical body, it says, that disintegrates and perishes. The soul is imperishable and will be given a new body in the next world to account for the deeds done in this world which are recorded in 'a Book that preserves everything.' The verse may also mean that even the particles of objects which the earth disintegrates are well preserved in God's knowledge. It may also signify that as complete knowledge about all the details of a thing presupposes the power to create it, and God is the Possessor of full knowledge of human anatomy and of the process of its disintegration, He, therefore, could and would recreate it after it had perished.

2802. This and the following few verses draw attention to the marvels of creation—the wonderful design in the universe, the celestial firmament with its countless beautiful planets and stars, the earth and its wide expanse teeming with human and animal life—and then points to the inevitable inference that the Great and Wise Designer, the Architect and the Controller, Who could bring into being this wonderful universe and Who placed man at its centre, does possess the power to recreate it after its disintegration and to give man a new life after he is dead.

8. And the earth—We have spread it out, and placed therein firm mountains; and We have made to grow therein [a]every *kind of* beautiful species,

وَالْاَرْضَ مَدَدْنٰهَا وَاَلْقَيْنَا فِيْهَا رَوَاسِيَ وَاَنْۢبَتْنَا فِيْهَا مِنْ كُلِّ زَوْجٍۭ بَهِيْجٍ ۙ﴿۸﴾

9. As *a means of* enlightenment and as a reminder[2803] to every servant that turns *to Us*.

تَبْصِرَةً وَّذِكْرٰى لِكُلِّ عَبْدٍ مُّنِيْبٍ ﴿۹﴾

10. [b]And We send down from the clouds water which is full of blessings, and We produce therewith gardens and crops,

وَنَزَّلْنَا مِنَ السَّمَآءِ مَآءً مُّبٰرَكًا فَاَنْۢبَتْنَا بِهٖ جَنّٰتٍ وَّحَبَّ الْحَصِيْدِ ۙ﴿۱۰﴾

11. And tall palm-trees with spathes piled one above the other,

وَالنَّخْلَ بٰسِقٰتٍ لَّهَا طَلْعٌ نَّضِيْدٌ ۙ﴿۱۱﴾

12. As a provision for *Our* servants; [c]and We quicken thereby a dead land. Even so shall be the Resurrection.[2804]

رِّزْقًا لِّلْعِبَادِ ۙ وَاَحْيَيْنَا بِهٖ بَلْدَةً مَّيْتًا ؕ كَذٰلِكَ الْخُرُوْجُ ﴿۱۲﴾

13. [d]The people of Noah rejected *the Truth* before them and *so did* the People of the Well and *the tribe of* Thamūd,

كَذَّبَتْ قَبْلَهُمْ قَوْمُ نُوْحٍ وَّاَصْحٰبُ الرَّسِّ وَثَمُوْدُ ۙ﴿۱۳﴾

14. And *the tribe of* 'Ād, and Pharaoh and the brethren of Lot,

وَعَادٌ وَّفِرْعَوْنُ وَاِخْوَانُ لُوْطٍ ۙ﴿۱۴﴾

15. [e]And the Dwellers of the Wood, and the People of Tubba'. All *of them* rejected the Messengers with the result that My threatened punishment befell *them*.

وَّاَصْحٰبُ الْاَيْكَةِ وَقَوْمُ تُبَّعٍ ؕ كُلٌّ كَذَّبَ الرُّسُلَ فَحَقَّ وَعِيْدِ ﴿۱۵﴾

---

[a]31 : 11. [b]25 : 49. [c]25 : 50; 43 : 12. [d]9 : 70; 14 : 10; 38 : 13. [e]15 : 79; 26 : 177; 38 : 14.

2803. It is logical to assume a purpose behind physical nature. The concept of God as Designer and Creator of all things gives a coherent and complete picture of origin, design and purpose. And the existence of a purpose behind the creation implies the existence of a Life after death because the very idea, that with the dissolution of its physical tabernacle the human soul suffers death, militates against the whole design and wisdom of God and against His purpose in creating the universe.

2804. Just as God sends down rain from heaven and causes a dry, dead land to bloom and blossom and pulsate with a new vigorous life, and brings forth from the earth all sorts of flowers and fruits, similarly He can and will give a new life to man after he is dead.

16. [a]Were We then wearied by the first creation?[2805] Nay, but they are in confusion about the new creation.

اَفَعَيِيْنَا بِالْخَلْقِ الْاَوَّلِ ؕ بَلْ هُمْ فِيْ لَبْسٍ مِّنْ خَلْقٍ جَدِيْدٍ ﴿۱۶﴾

R. 2 17. And assuredly, We have created man and We know what his mind whispers *to him*, and We are nearer to him than *even his* jugular vein.

وَلَقَدْ خَلَقْنَا الْاِنْسَانَ وَنَعْلَمُ مَا تُوَسْوِسُ بِهٖ نَفْسُهٗ ۚۖ وَنَحْنُ اَقْرَبُ اِلَيْهِ مِنْ حَبْلِ الْوَرِيْدِ ﴿۱۷﴾

18. When the two Recording *angels* record *everything*, sitting on *his* right and on *his* left;[2806]

اِذْ يَتَلَقَّى الْمُتَلَقِّيٰنِ عَنِ الْيَمِيْنِ وَعَنِ الشِّمَالِ قَعِيْدٌ ﴿۱۸﴾

19. He utters not a word but [b]there is by him a guardian *angel* ready *to record it*,

مَا يَلْفِظُ مِنْ قَوْلٍ اِلَّا لَدَيْهِ رَقِيْبٌ عَتِيْدٌ ﴿۱۹﴾

20. [c]And the stupor of death, certainly, comes. 'This is what thou wast striving to run from.'

وَجَآءَتْ سَكْرَةُ الْمَوْتِ بِالْحَقِّ ؕ ذٰلِكَ مَا كُنْتَ مِنْهُ تَحِيْدُ ﴿۲۰﴾

21. [d]And the trumpet shall be blown. That will be the Day of Promise.

وَنُفِخَ فِي الصُّوْرِ ؕ ذٰلِكَ يَوْمُ الْوَعِيْدِ ﴿۲۱﴾

22. And every soul shall come forth *and* along with it there will be *an angel* to drive it and *an angel* to bear witness.[2807]

وَجَآءَتْ كُلُّ نَفْسٍ مَّعَهَا سَآئِقٌ وَّشَهِيْدٌ ﴿۲۲﴾

[a]50 : 39. [b]43 : 81; 82 : 11-12; 86 : 5. [c]6 : 94; 23 : 100. [d]18 : 100; 23 : 102; 36 : 52; 39 : 69; 69 : 14.

2805. In all these verses 'creation,' besides its ordinary meaning, signifies spiritual awakening or revolution which is brought about by a Prophet among his people.

2806. According to some Commentators the angel sitting on man's right records his good actions and that on his left his bad actions—the words 'on the right' standing for his good actions and 'on the left' for his bad actions. Every deed or spoken word leaves its impress in the atmosphere and thus is preserved. Elsewhere in the Qur'ān (24 : 25 & 36 : 66) it is stated that the limbs of man—his hands, feet and tongue—will bear witness against him on the Judgment Day. Thus the different parts of a man's body may also be 'the recorders' referred to in the present verse as the Recording Angels.

2807. *Sā'iq* may be the angel that sits on man's left and records his bad deeds and as a punishment for them will drive him to Hell, and *Shahīd* may be the angel that sits on his right and records his good actions and will bear witness in his favour. Or, the two words metaphorically may stand respectively for man's misused limbs and faculties and those well and properly used.

23. *Then We shall say,* 'Thou wast heedless of this; now We have removed from thee thy veil, and keen is thy sight this day.' [2808]

لَقَدْ كُنْتَ فِى غَفْلَةٍ مِّنْ هٰذَا فَكَشَفْنَا عَنْكَ غِطَآءَكَ فَبَصَرُكَ الْيَوْمَ حَدِيْدٌ ۝

24. And his companion will say, 'This is what I have ready *of his record.'*

وَقَالَ قَرِيْنُهُ هٰذَا مَا لَدَىَّ عَتِيْدٌ ۝

25. *We shall say to his two companions,* 'Cast ye twain[2809] into Hell every disbelieving enemy *of Truth,*

اَلْقِيَا فِىْ جَهَنَّمَ كُلَّ كَفَّارٍ عَنِيْدٍ ۝

26. "Hinderer of good, transgressor, doubter;

مَّنَّاعٍ لِّلْخَيْرِ مُعْتَدٍ مُّرِيْبٍ ۝

27. 'Who sets up another god beside Allāh, so do, ye twain, cast him into the severe torment.'

اِلَّذِىْ جَعَلَ مَعَ اللّٰهِ اِلٰهًا اٰخَرَ فَاَلْقِيٰهُ فِى الْعَذَابِ الشَّدِيْدِ ۝

28. *His associate will say,* 'O our Lord, it was not I that caused him to rebel; but he *himself* was too far gone in error.'[2810]

قَالَ قَرِيْنُهُ رَبَّنَا مَا اَطْغَيْتُهُ وَلٰكِنْ كَانَ فِىْ ضَلٰلٍ بَعِيْدٍ ۝

29. *Allāh will say,* 'Quarrel not in My presence; I gave you the warning beforehand,

قَالَ لَا تَخْتَصِمُوْا لَدَىَّ وَقَدْ قَدَّمْتُ اِلَيْكُمْ بِالْوَعِيْدِ ۝

30. 'The sentence *passed* by Me cannot be changed, *and I am not* in the least unjust to *My* servants.'

مَا يُبَدَّلُ الْقَوْلُ لَدَىَّ وَمَا اَنَا بِظَلَّامٍ لِّلْعَبِيْدِ ۝

---

a68 : 13.   b14 : 23.   c3 : 183; 8 : 52; 22 : 11; 41 : 47.

2808. In the next world the veil will be lifted from the eyes of man and his vision and mental perception will become clearer and sharper. He will see the consequences of his actions in an embodied form which were hidden from his eyes in this world and will realize that, which he used to regard merely as an illusion, was a hard and stark reality.

2809. The dual form of *Alqiyā* is used either because the command is given to the two angels—the *Sā'iq* and the *Shahīd*, or, in order to impart emphasis to the command. This form of expression is also used in 23 : 100 where a plural verb is used for the subject in the singular. This is quite in consonance with the rules of Arabic grammar.

2810. It is human nature that when an evil-doer is confronted with the evil consequences of his deeds, he seeks to shift his responsibility to others. It is this state of mind of the disbeliever which is depicted in this verse. He will hold Satan responsible for his own transgressions and sins.

R. 3 31. On *that* day We will say to Hell, 'Art thou filled up?' And it will answer,[2811] 'Are there any more?'[2812]

يَوْمَ نَقُولُ لِجَهَنَّمَ هَلِ امْتَلَأْتِ وَتَقُولُ هَلْ مِن مَّزِيدٍ ﴿٣١﴾

32. [a]And Heaven will be brought near[2813] to the righteous, no longer remote.

وَأُزْلِفَتِ الْجَنَّةُ لِلْمُتَّقِينَ غَيْرَ بَعِيدٍ ﴿٣٢﴾

33. *And it will be said*, 'This is what was promised to you—to everyone who constantly turned *to God* and was watchful *of his actions*,

هَٰذَا مَا تُوعَدُونَ لِكُلِّ أَوَّابٍ حَفِيظٍ ﴿٣٣﴾

34. 'Who feared the Gracious *God* in private and came *to Him* with a penitent heart.

مَنْ خَشِيَ الرَّحْمَٰنَ بِالْغَيْبِ وَجَاءَ بِقَلْبٍ مُّنِيبٍ ﴿٣٤﴾

35. [b]'Enter ye therein in peace. This is the Day of Eternity.'[2814]

ادْخُلُوهَا بِسَلَامٍ ذَٰلِكَ يَوْمُ الْخُلُودِ ﴿٣٥﴾

36. They will have therein whatever they desire, and with Us is [c]*a good deal* more.[2815]

لَهُم مَّا يَشَاءُونَ فِيهَا وَلَدَيْنَا مَزِيدٌ ﴿٣٦﴾

[a]26 : 91; 81 : 14. [b]14 : 24; 15 : 47; 36 : 59. [c]10 : 27.

2811. The dialogue is metaphorical. Hell has been personified here and words are put in its mouth to express its state or condition and not that it will actually speak, or, for that matter, it can speak. The word, *Qāla*, has also been used in this sense in 41 : 12 where the heaven and the earth have been described as saying that they obey Divine laws willingly. It is one of the peculiarities and beauties of the Arabic language that it uses words and expressions for inanimate things which are used for human beings. See also 57 and 18 : 78.

2812. The expression, in fact, points to man's unlimited capacity for committing sins and his inordinate desire for worldly comforts by which he paves his way to Hell.

2813. Whereas in the preceding verse, it is mentioned that more and more persons will be thrown into Hell in order to be purged and purified of their spiritual maladies, the present verse says that Heaven will also be brought near for the righteous and the God-fearing.

2814. However dreadful its punishments may appear, Hell, according to the Qur'ān, is a temporary penitentiary, while Heaven is an eternal abode; its blessings know no limit or end (11 : 109).

2815. The righteous will have in Paradise what they desire to their heart's content, but as man's desires at best are limited, they will be given much more than what they desire or deserve, much more than what they would even contemplate or conceive.

37. [a]And how many a generation, who were mightier than they in prowess, have We destroyed before them! *But when the punishment came*, they went about in the lands, *devising plans to escape it*.[2815A] But was there any place of refuge *for them?*

وَكَمْ أَهْلَكْنَا قَبْلَهُم مِّن قَرْنٍ هُمْ أَشَدُّ مِنْهُم بَطْشًا فَنَقَّبُوا فِي الْبِلَادِ هَلْ مِن مَّحِيصٍ ﴿٣٧﴾

38. Therein, verily, is a reminder for him who has *an understanding* heart,[2816] or, who gives ear and is attentive.

إِنَّ فِي ذَٰلِكَ لَذِكْرَىٰ لِمَن كَانَ لَهُ قَلْبٌ أَوْ أَلْقَى السَّمْعَ وَهُوَ شَهِيدٌ ﴿٣٨﴾

39. And, verily, We created the heavens and the earth and all that is between them [b]in six periods[2817] and [c]no weariness touched Us.[2818]

وَلَقَدْ خَلَقْنَا السَّمَاوَاتِ وَالْأَرْضَ وَمَا بَيْنَهُمَا فِي سِتَّةِ أَيَّامٍ وَمَا مَسَّنَا مِن لُّغُوبٍ ﴿٣٩﴾

40. So bear with patience what they say, and celebrate the praises of thy Lord, before the rising of the sun and before its setting;

فَاصْبِرْ عَلَىٰ مَا يَقُولُونَ وَسَبِّحْ بِحَمْدِ رَبِّكَ قَبْلَ طُلُوعِ الشَّمْسِ وَقَبْلَ الْغُرُوبِ ﴿٤٠﴾

41. And in *parts of* the night also do thou glorify Him, and after *prescribed* prostrations.

وَمِنَ اللَّيْلِ فَسَبِّحْهُ وَأَدْبَارَ السُّجُودِ ﴿٤١﴾

[a]19 : 75; 47 : 14. [b]7 : 55; 10 : 4; 11 : 8; 25 : 60. [c]50 : 16.

2815A. The words in the text literally mean: 'Burrowed into the earth to save themselves,' and seem to refer to the present day underground trenches as protection against bombing attacks.

2816. *Qalb*, means, the heart; the soul; the conscience; the mind; and signifies the best part of a thing. They say *ma la-hū Qalbun*, *i.e.*, he has no intellect or intelligence (Lane).

2817. See 984 and 41 : 10-13.

2818. It is characteristic of the Qur'ān that not only does it exonerate God's noble Prophets from all the vices and immoralities imputed to them in the Bible but also clears the Divine Being of the flaws and defects which are inconsistent with His Majesty and Holiness. The Bible depicts God as 'having rested on the seventh day from all His work which He had made' (Gen. 2 : 2), but according to the Qur'ān no weariness can touch Him.

وَاسْتَمِعْ يَوْمَ يُنَادِ الْمُنَادِ مِنْ مَّكَانٍ قَرِيبٍ ﴿٤٢﴾

42. Hearken ! On the day when the caller[2819] will call from a place nearby,[2820]

يَوْمَ يَسْمَعُونَ الصَّيْحَةَ بِالْحَقِّ ذٰلِكَ يَوْمُ الْخُرُوجِ ﴿٤٣﴾

43. The day when they will hear the inevitable blast;[2821] that will be the day of coming forth *from the graves.*

إِنَّا نَحْنُ نُحْيِي وَنُمِيتُ وَإِلَيْنَا الْمَصِيرُ ﴿٤٤﴾

44. Verily, it is We Who give life and cause death, and to Us is the *final* return.

يَوْمَ تَشَقَّقُ الْأَرْضُ عَنْهُمْ سِرَاعًا ذٰلِكَ حَشْرٌ عَلَيْنَا يَسِيرٌ ﴿٤٥﴾

45. On the day when the earth will cleave asunder *and in consequence of their misdeeds they will come forth* hastening—that will be a raising up *of the dead* easy for Us.

نَحْنُ أَعْلَمُ بِمَا يَقُولُونَ وَمَا أَنْتَ عَلَيْهِمْ بِجَبَّارٍ فَذَكِّرْ بِالْقُرْاٰنِ مَنْ يَّخَافُ وَعِيدِ ﴿٤٦﴾

46. We know best what they say; and [a]thou art not to compel them *in any way.* So admonish, by means of the Qur'ān,[2822] him who fears My warning.

[a]39 : 42; 42 : 7.

2819. The 'crier' may refer to the Holy Prophet. The context supports this, as the next few verses seem to refer to the spiritual resurrection brought about by him among his people who at his call rose, as it were, from their graves.

2820. The words 'from a place nearby' may also signify that the call of the Holy Prophet will not remain a call in the wilderness, a distant cry, but will be listened to and accepted.

2821. 'The blast may also signify the stentorian call of the Holy Prophet.

2822. The resurrection to which reference has been made in the *Sūrah* has been brought about by the Qur'ān.

CHAPTER 51

AL-DHĀRIYĀT

(Revealed before Hijrah)

Date of Revelation and Context

Like the preceding one this *Sūrah* was revealed early in the Holy Prophet's ministry at Mecca. Noldeke assigns its revelation to the fourth year of the Call. The preceding *Sūrah* had dealt with two resurrections—a spiritual resurrection which was to be brought about by the teachings of the Qur'ān and the Final Resurrection in the Life after death, the former resurrection having been cited as an argument in support of the latter The *Sūrah* opens with an important prophecy that a body of highly righteous men would come into existence through the influence of the Quranic teaching. Like moisture-laden clouds which give rain to vast areas of parched and burnt land and make them blossom into new life, this holy band of righteous believers, having themselves awakened to a new spiritual life, would carry the Quranic Message to the ends of the earth, sweeping all opposition before their onward march. The prediction, seemingly impossible of fulfilment, would constitute, when turned into a palpable reality, an invincible argument in support of the fact of the Final Resurrection. The *Sūrah*, further, says that whenever a Divine Messenger appears in the world to tell his people that there is a life beyond the grave in which they will have to account for their deeds they laugh him to scorn, and oppose and persecute him; and cites the case of the people of Lot who were punished for their iniquities and unnatural and immoral practices. It also briefly refers to the punishment that overtook Pharaoh 'Ād, Thamūd and the people of Noah, and towards the end draws pointed attention to the supreme object of man's creation which is that he should cultivate and demonstrate in himself Divine attributes and should discharge fully and faithfully his obligations to God and his fellow-beings.

سُوْرَةُ الذّٰرِيٰتِ مَكِّيَّةٌ (٥١)

1. [a]In the name of Allāh, the Gracious, the Merciful.
بِسْمِ اللّٰهِ الرَّحْمٰنِ الرَّحِيْمِ ۝١

2. By[2823] those that scatter *with a true* scattering,[2823A]
وَالذّٰرِيٰتِ ذَرْوًا ۝٢

3. Then carry the load,
فَالْحٰمِلٰتِ وِقْرًا ۝٣

4. Then speed lightly along,
فَالْجٰرِيٰتِ يُسْرًا ۝٤

5. *And* then distribute *by Our* command,[2824]
فَالْمُقَسِّمٰتِ اَمْرًا ۝٥

6. Surely, that which you are promised is [b]true,
اِنَّمَا تُوْعَدُوْنَ لَصَادِقٌ ۝٦

7. And Judgment will, surely, come to pass.
وَّاِنَّ الدِّيْنَ لَوَاقِعٌ ۝٧

8. And by the heaven *full* of tracks,[2825]
وَالسَّمَآءِ ذَاتِ الْحُبُكِ ۝٨

---

[a]1 : 1. [b]52 : 8.

2823. See 2465.

2823A. For a collective note on this and the next three verses see 2824.

2824. From a phenomenon in physical nature, the four verses (2-5) draw attention to a parallel spiritual phenomenon. The parallelism is very striking. The four words—*al-Dhāriyāt* (those that scatter), *al-Ḥāmilāt* (those that carry), *al-Jāriyāt* (those that speed lightly along) and *al-Muqassimāt* (those that distribute) —when pointing to the physical phenomenon, may stand for winds that scatter far and wide, the vapours that rise from the oceans, carry the clouds laden with rain-water, blow gently and then cause rain to fall on dry, parched and burnt land and turn it into a smiling, blooming and blossoming piece of earth, full of verdure, beautiful flowers and sweet fruits. Spiritually speaking, these four words may stand for that band of righteous men, who drinking deep at the spiritual fountain that the Holy Prophet caused to flow, and who, after assimilating and being impregnated with the beautiful and life-giving Quranic teaching, went forth to the remote corners of Arabia and afterwards to far-off lands, carrying their blessed load and scattering the revealed Word of God in countries, reeking with polytheistic beliefs and immoral practices, not with the sword but with love and peace, like winds that blow gently and carry rain to withered lands.

2825. Tracks or paths of heaven are the orbits of planets, comets, and stars with which the vault of heaven is strewn. These celestial bodies float in their respective orbits performing their allotted tasks regularly, punctually and unerringly, without trespassing on one another's sphere of action and all united forming a glorious harmony of structure and motion. That the heaven is full of such tracks on which planets and stars travel, was a discovery made to the world by the Qur'ān, at a time when it was believed that the heavens were solid in their formation.

9. Truly, you are at variance²⁸²⁶ in what you say.

اِنَّكُمْ لَفِىْ قَوْلٍ مُّخْتَلِفٍ ۙ ۹

10. He *alone* is turned away from *the truth* who is *decreed*²⁸²⁷ *to be* turned away.

يُّؤْفَكُ عَنْهُ مَنْ اُفِكَ ۙ ۱۰

11. Cursed be the liars,

قُتِلَ الْخَرّٰصُوْنَ ۙ ۱۱

12. Who are heedless *of truth* in the depths *of ignorance.*²⁸²⁸

الَّذِيْنَ هُمْ فِىْ غَمْرَةٍ سَاهُوْنَ ۙ ۱۲

13. They ask, "When will the Day of Judgment be?'

يَسْـَٔلُوْنَ اَيَّانَ يَوْمُ الدِّيْنِ ؕ ۱۳

14. *Say,* 'It *will be* the day when they will be tormented with *the* torment *of* the Fire.'

يَوْمَ هُمْ عَلَى النَّارِ يُفْتَنُوْنَ ۱۴

15. *And it will be said to them,* 'Taste ye your torment. ᵇThis is what you asked to be hastened.'

ذُوْقُوْا فِتْنَتَكُمْ ؕ هٰذَا الَّذِىْ كُنْتُمْ بِهٖ تَسْتَعْجِلُوْنَ ۱۵

16. But, surely, the righteous will be in the midst of ᶜgardens and springs,

اِنَّ الْمُتَّقِيْنَ فِىْ جَنّٰتٍ وَّعُيُوْنٍ ۙ ۱۶

17. Taking what their Lord will bestow upon them; for they used to do good before that;²⁸²⁹

اٰخِذِيْنَ مَآ اٰتٰهُمْ رَبُّهُمْ ؕ اِنَّهُمْ كَانُوْا قَبْلَ ذٰلِكَ مُحْسِنِيْنَ ؕ ۱۷

18. They slept but ᵈa little of the night;

كَانُوْا قَلِيْلًا مِّنَ الَّيْلِ مَا يَهْجَعُوْنَ ۱۸

ᵃ7 : 188; 79 : 43.   ᵇ26 : 205; 27 : 72-73; 29 : 54,55.   ᶜ15 : 46; 52 : 18; 68 : 35; 77 : 42; 78 : 32.   ᵈ32 : 17.

2826. The great astronomical truth revealed in the preceding verse leads to the inference that the Qur'ān is God's own revealed Word and that there exists a unity of purpose and harmony in Divine work, and yet the materialistic philosophers coin far-fetched theories, groping and floundering in ill-founded surmises and conjectures, not believing in God's Word and in His Prophet.

2827. The words may also mean, 'he who himself would turn away.'

2828. *Ghamrah* means, depth of ignorance; error; obstinacy and perplexity; over-whelming heedlessness; a state of obstinate perseverance in a vain and false thing (Lane).

2829. A *Muttaqī* is one who discharges his obligations faithfully and fully to God and man, and a *Muḥsin* is he who does more good to others than the good he receives from them and acts and behaves as though he is actually seeing God, or, in a lesser degree, he is conscious of God watching over him. Thus a *Muḥsin* is a person of higher spiritual stature and calibre than a *Muttaqī.*

19. And at dawn they prayed for [a]*Divine* pardon;

وَبِالْأَسْحَارِ هُمْ يَسْتَغْفِرُونَ ⑲

20. And in their wealth was a [b]share for those who asked for help and for those who could not.[2830]

وَفِي أَمْوَالِهِمْ حَقٌّ لِّلسَّائِلِ وَالْمَحْرُومِ ⑳

21. And in the earth are Signs for those who have certainty of faith,

وَفِي الْأَرْضِ آيَاتٌ لِّلْمُوقِنِينَ ㉑

22. And *also* in your ownselves. Will you not then see?

وَفِي أَنفُسِكُمْ أَفَلَا تُبْصِرُونَ ㉒

23. And in heaven is your [c]sustenance, and *also* that which you are promised.[2831]

وَفِي السَّمَاءِ رِزْقُكُمْ وَمَا تُوعَدُونَ ㉓

24. And by the Lord of the heaven and the earth it is certainly the truth, just as *it is true that* you speak.[2832]

فَوَرَبِّ السَّمَاءِ وَالْأَرْضِ إِنَّهُ لَحَقٌّ مِّثْلَ مَا أَنَّكُمْ تَنطِقُونَ ㉔ ع

R. 2 25. Has the story of Abraham's honoured [d]guests reached thee?

هَلْ أَتَاكَ حَدِيثُ ضَيْفِ إِبْرَاهِيمَ الْمُكْرَمِينَ ㉕

26. When they came to him and said, [e]"Peace!' he said *in reply*, '*On you be* peace.' *He thought that* they were strangers.[2833]

إِذْ دَخَلُوا عَلَيْهِ فَقَالُوا سَلَامًا قَالَ سَلَامٌ قَوْمٌ مُّنكَرُونَ ㉖

[a]3 : 18. [b]70 : 25-26. [c]40 : 14; 45 : 6. [d]11 : 70, 71; 15 : 52. [e]11 : 70

2830. In the wealth of a rich Muslim, according to Islām, those who can express their needs, as also those who cannot, have a share, as of right. Thus a Muslim's wealth is a trust to the benefit of which the poor are also entitled. So when he satisfies the need of a poor brother, he, in fact, does him no favour but only discharges the obligation he owes to him and returns to him what was his due. The word, *al-Mahrūm*, not only includes in its connotation those poor people who, from a sense of self-respect or a feeling of shame, do not ask for alms (2 : 274), but also dumb animals. The word has been taken here as signifying a person who is debarred from earning his livelihood due to physical infirmity or some other similar cause.

2831. Promises of triumph and prosperity to believers and warnings to disbelievers.

2832. The fact mentioned in the preceding verse is neither wishful thinking on the Holy Prophet's part, nor is it a figment of his imagination, but is solid and hard truth as sure and true as it is true 'that you speak.' Or, the verse may mean that the Qur'ān is as undoubtedly God's own revealed Word as 'you speak.'

2833. See 11 : 70-71.

27. And he went quietly to his household, and brought a [a]fatted calf,

فَرَاغَ إِلَىٰٓ أَهْلِهِۦ فَجَآءَ بِعِجْلٍ سَمِينٍ ﴿٢٧﴾

28. And he placed it before them *and* said, 'Will you not eat?'

فَقَرَّبَهُۥٓ إِلَيْهِمْ قَالَ أَلَا تَأْكُلُونَ ﴿٢٨﴾

29. [b]And he conceived a fear of them. [c]They said, 'Fear not.' And they gave him glad tidings of *the birth of* a son *who would be blessed* with knowledge.[2834]

فَأَوْجَسَ مِنْهُمْ خِيفَةً ۖ قَالُوا۟ لَا تَخَفْ ۖ وَبَشَّرُوهُ بِغُلَٰمٍ عَلِيمٍ ﴿٢٩﴾

30. Then his wife came forward extremely embarrassed[2835] and smote her face and said, '*I am but* a barren old woman!'

فَأَقْبَلَتِ ٱمْرَأَتُهُۥ فِى صَرَّةٍ فَصَكَّتْ وَجْهَهَا وَقَالَتْ عَجُوزٌ عَقِيمٌ ﴿٣٠﴾

31. They said, 'Even so has thy Lord said. Surely, He is the Wise, the All-Knowing.'

قَالُوا۟ كَذَٰلِكِ قَالَ رَبُّكِ ۖ إِنَّهُۥ هُوَ ٱلْحَكِيمُ ٱلْعَلِيمُ ﴿٣١﴾

PART XXVII

32. *Abraham* said, [d]Now what is your errand, O ye who have been sent?'

الجزء ٢٧ قَالَ فَمَا خَطْبُكُمْ أَيُّهَا ٱلْمُرْسَلُونَ ﴿٣٢﴾

33. They said, 'We have been sent to a [e]sinful people,

قَالُوٓا۟ إِنَّآ أُرْسِلْنَآ إِلَىٰ قَوْمٍ مُّجْرِمِينَ ﴿٣٣﴾

34. 'That we may send down upon them [f]stones of clay,

لِنُرْسِلَ عَلَيْهِمْ حِجَارَةً مِّن طِينٍ ﴿٣٤﴾

35. [g]'Marked, with thy Lord, for those guilty of excesses.'

مُّسَوَّمَةً عِندَ رَبِّكَ لِلْمُسْرِفِينَ ﴿٣٥﴾

---

[a]11 : 70. [b]11 : 71; 15 : 53. [c]11 : 71, 72; 15 : 54. [d]15 : 57. [e]15 : 58. [f]11 : 83. [g]11 : 84.

2834. In the present verse as also in 15: 54 'the promised son,' has been described as 'a son endowed with knowledge,' while in 37 : 102 he has been called 'a forbearing son.' In the former verse the reference is to Isaac and in the latter to Ishmael.

2835. *Ṣarrah* means a most vehement clamour of crying; vehemence of grief, heat or anxiety; a contraction and moroseness of the face by reason of dislike or hatred or shame; a fit (Lane).

36. And We brought forth *therefrom* such of the believers as were there.

فَأَخْرَجْنَا مَنْ كَانَ فِيهَا مِنَ الْمُؤْمِنِينَ ﴿٣٦﴾

37. And We found there only one house of those who were obedient *to Us*.

فَمَا وَجَدْنَا فِيهَا غَيْرَ بَيْتٍ مِنَ الْمُسْلِمِينَ ﴿٣٧﴾

38. And We left therein a Sign [a]for those who fear painful punishment.

وَتَرَكْنَا فِيهَا آيَةً لِلَّذِينَ يَخَافُونَ الْعَذَابَ الْأَلِيمَ ﴿٣٨﴾

39. And in *the story of* Moses *also there was a Sign* when We sent him to Pharaoh with clear authority.

وَفِي مُوسَىٰ إِذْ أَرْسَلْنَاهُ إِلَىٰ فِرْعَوْنَ بِسُلْطَانٍ مُبِينٍ ﴿٣٩﴾

40. But he turned away *from Moses* in *the pride of* his might,[2836] and said, 'A sorcerer, or a madman.'

فَتَوَلَّىٰ بِرُكْنِهِ وَقَالَ سَاحِرٌ أَوْ مَجْنُونٌ ﴿٤٠﴾

41. [b]So We seized him and his hosts and threw them into the sea; and he was to blame.

فَأَخَذْنَاهُ وَجُنُودَهُ فَنَبَذْنَاهُمْ فِي الْيَمِّ وَهُوَ مُلِيمٌ ﴿٤١﴾

42. And *there was a Sign* in *the story of the tribe of* 'Ād, when We sent against them the destructive [c]wind;

وَفِي عَادٍ إِذْ أَرْسَلْنَا عَلَيْهِمُ الرِّيحَ الْعَقِيمَ ﴿٤٢﴾

43. [d]It spared nothing whatever that it came upon but made it like a rotten bone.

مَا تَذَرُ مِنْ شَيْءٍ أَتَتْ عَلَيْهِ إِلَّا جَعَلَتْهُ كَالرَّمِيمِ ﴿٤٣﴾

44. And *a Sign there was* in *the story of the tribe of* Thamūd when it was said to them, "Enjoy yourselves for a while.'

وَفِي ثَمُودَ إِذْ قِيلَ لَهُمْ تَمَتَّعُوا حَتَّىٰ حِينٍ ﴿٤٤﴾

---

[a]15 : 76; 29 : 36. [b]10 : 91; 28 : 41. [c]46 : 25. [d]46 : 26.

2836. *Rukn* means, a stay or support; power, might and resistance; a man's kinsfolk or clan, his people or party; persons by whom he is aided and strengthened; a noble or high person (Lane & Mufradāt).

45. But they rebelled against the command of their Lord. So the thunderbolt overtook them *while they gazed;

فَعَتَوْا عَنْ اَمْرِ رَبِّهِمْ فَاَخَذَتْهُمُ الصّٰعِقَةُ وَهُمْ يَنْظُرُوْنَ ۝

46. And they were not able to rise up, nor were they able to defend themselves.

فَمَا اسْتَطَاعُوْا مِنْ قِيَامٍ وَّمَا كَانُوْا مُنْتَصِرِيْنَ ۝

47. And *We destroyed* the people of Noah before *them;* they were a disobedient people.

وَقَوْمَ نُوْحٍ مِّنْ قَبْلُ ۫ اِنَّهُمْ كَانُوْا قَوْمًا فٰسِقِيْنَ ۝

R. 3 48. And We have built the heaven with *Our own* hands,[2837] and, verily, We have vast powers.[2837A]

وَالسَّمَآءَ بَنَيْنٰهَا بِاَيْدٍ وَّاِنَّا لَمُوْسِعُوْنَ ۝

49. *And the earth We have spread out, and how excellently do We spread *it* out !

وَالْاَرْضَ فَرَشْنٰهَا فَنِعْمَ الْمٰهِدُوْنَ ۝

50. And of everything have We created *pairs[2838] that you may reflect.

وَمِنْ كُلِّ شَيْءٍ خَلَقْنَا زَوْجَيْنِ لَعَلَّكُمْ تَذَكَّرُوْنَ ۝

51. Flee ye, therefore, unto Allāh. Surely, I am a plain Warner unto you from Him.

فَفِرُّوْا اِلَى اللّٰهِ ۫ اِنِّيْ لَكُمْ مِّنْهُ نَذِيْرٌ مُّبِيْنٌ ۝

52. And do not set up another god along with Allāh. Surely, I am a plain Warner unto you from Him.

وَلَا تَجْعَلُوْا مَعَ اللّٰهِ اِلٰهًا اٰخَرَ ۫ اِنِّيْ لَكُمْ مِّنْهُ نَذِيْرٌ مُّبِيْنٌ ۝

---

*11 : 68. *2 : 23; 20 : 54; 78 : 7. *13 : 4; 36 : 37.

2837. *Yad* signifies, (1) favour; (2) power; dignity; (3) protection; (4) wealth; (5) arm; etc. (Aqrab). Thus the expression in the text means : 'We have created the heaven with power and might,' or 'We have made the heaven as a manifestation of Our power and might,' *i.e.*, in the creation of the heavens and the earth there is proof of many Divine attributes, the prominent being God's Glory, Might and Majesty.

2837A. *Mūsi'ūn* also means, 'We go on expanding.'

2838. God has created all things in pairs. There are pairs not only in animal life, but also in vegetables, and even in inanimate things. There are pairs also in spiritual things. Even heaven and earth together make a pair.

53. Even so there came no Messenger to those before them, but they said, 'A sorcerer or a madman.'

كَذٰلِكَ مَآ اَتَى الَّذِيْنَ مِنْ قَبْلِهِمْ مِّنْ رَّسُوْلٍ اِلَّا
قَالُوْا سَاحِرٌ اَوْ مَجْنُوْنٌ ﴿۵۳﴾

54. Have they bequeathed[2839] this *attitude* to one another? Nay, they are all a rebellious people.

اَتَوَاصَوْا بِهٖ ۚ بَلْ هُمْ قَوْمٌ طَاغُوْنَ ﴿۵۴﴾

55. So turn away from them; and thou will not be to blame *for what they do*.

فَتَوَلَّ عَنْهُمْ فَمَآ اَنْتَ بِمَلُوْمٍ ﴿۵۵﴾

56. And keep on exhorting; for, verily, exhortation benefits those who would believe.

وَّذَكِّرْ فَاِنَّ الذِّكْرٰى تَنْفَعُ الْمُؤْمِنِيْنَ ﴿۵۶﴾

57. And I have not created the jinn and the men but that they may worship[2840] Me.

وَمَا خَلَقْتُ الْجِنَّ وَالْاِنْسَ اِلَّا لِيَعْبُدُوْنِ ﴿۵۷﴾

58. [a]I desire of them no provision, neither do I desire that they should feed[2841] Me.

مَآ اُرِيْدُ مِنْهُمْ مِّنْ رِّزْقٍ وَّمَآ اُرِيْدُ اَنْ يُّطْعِمُوْنِ ﴿۵۸﴾

59. Surely, it is Allāh *Himself* Who is the Great Sustainer, the Lord of Power, the Strong.

اِنَّ اللّٰهَ هُوَ الرَّزَّاقُ ذُو الْقُوَّةِ الْمَتِيْنُ ﴿۵۹﴾

---

[a]6 : 15; 20 : 133.

2839. So strikingly similar are the charges levelled against Divine Reformers by their opponents in all ages that it seems that the disbelievers of one age bequeath it as a legacy to their successors to go on repeating those accusations.

2840. The primary signification of the word *'Ibādah* is to subject oneself to a rigorous spiritual discipline, working with all one's inherent powers and capacities to their fullest scope, in perfect harmony with and in obedience to Divine commandments, so as to receive God's impress and thus to be able to assimilate and manifest in oneself His attributes. This is, as stated in the verse, the great and noble aim and object of man's creation and this is exactly what worship of God means. The external and internal endowments of human nature give us clearly to understand that of God-given faculties the highest is the one which awakens in man the urge to search after God and incites in him the noble desire completely to submit himself to His Will.

2841. If the spiritual wayfarer pursues his course towards the noble object of his life steadfastly and with perseverance, he does no good to God, or to anybody else, but himself profits by it and attains the object of his quest.

60. So the fate of those who do wrong shall, surely, be like the fate[2842] of their fellows *of old;* so let them not challenge Me to hasten on *the punishment.*

فَإِنَّ لِلَّذِيْنَ ظَلَمُوْا ذَنُوْبًا مِّثْلَ ذَنُوْبِ أَصْحٰبِهِمْ فَلَا يَسْتَعْجِلُوْنِ ۝٦٠

61. [a]Woe, then, to those who disbelieve, because of that day of theirs which they have been promised.

فَوَيْلٌ لِّلَّذِيْنَ كَفَرُوْا مِنْ يَّوْمِهِمُ الَّذِيْ يُوْعَدُوْنَ ۝٦١ ع

[a]14 : 3; 19 : 38; 38 : 28

2842. *Dhanūb* means, fate, lot, share or portion; requital; a day of prolonged evil (Lane).

CHAPTER 52

AL-ṬŪR

(Revealed before Hijrah)

Date of Revelation and Context

This *Sūrah* was revealed at Mecca in the early years of the Call. Noldeke places it after Chapter 51, while according to Muir it was revealed somewhat later. In the preceding *Sūrah* attention was drawn to the great spiritual revolution which was brought about by the Qur'ān. It was in the fitness of things and quite in accordance with the laws of nature (the *Sūrah* stated) that because men had become corrupt and had forgotten God, a new Revelation should have come. The *Sūrah* had ended on the note that like the former Prophets the Holy Prophet will meet with severe opposition, but the cause of Truth will triumph and disbelievers will be punished. The present *Sūrah* refers to the biblical prophecies about the Holy Prophet and warns disbelievers that if they persisted in their opposition Divine punishment will overtake them.

Subject-Matter

The *Sūrah* opens with a direct and emphatic reference to the prophecies about the Qur'ān and the Holy Prophet in the Bible and states that the Bible, the Qur'ān and the Ka'bah all bear witness to the truth of Islām and the Holy Prophet, and warns disbelievers that opposition to Truth is never productive of good results. But those righteous servants of God, who accept the Divine Teaching and mould their lives in accordance with it, would receive Divine favours. Next, the *Sūrah* declares that the Holy Prophet is neither a soothsayer nor a madman nor a poet but a true Messenger of God, because the great moral and spiritual revolution brought about by him could not be the work of a madman or a poet; nor could the great Divine Book—the Qur'ān—that has been revealed to him, be the work of a forger of lies. It has been revealed by the Great Creator of the heavens and the earth. The Holy Prophet seeks no reward nor will disbelievers' plans against him succeed, because he is under God's protection. But Divine punishment, which is fast approaching, will overtake the disbelievers.

سُوۡرَۃُ الطُّوۡرِ مَکِّیَّۃٌ (۵۲)

1. [a]In the name of Allāh, the Gracious, the Merciful. بِسۡمِ اللّٰہِ الرَّحۡمٰنِ الرَّحِیۡمِ ﴿۱﴾

2. By[2843] the [b]Mount; وَ الطُّوۡرِ ۙ﴿۲﴾

3. And *by* the Book[2844] inscribed وَ کِتٰبٍ مَّسۡطُوۡرٍ ۙ﴿۳﴾

4. On parchment unfolded; فِیۡ رَقٍّ مَّنۡشُوۡرٍ ۙ﴿۴﴾

5. And *by* the ever Frequented House;[2845] وَّ الۡبَیۡتِ الۡمَعۡمُوۡرِ ۙ﴿۵﴾

6. And *by* the Elevated Roof;[2846] وَ السَّقۡفِ الۡمَرۡفُوۡعِ ۙ﴿۶﴾

---

[a]1 : 1. [b]95 : 3.

2843. For the philosophy, importance and significance of oaths see 2465.

2844. The Qur'ān or the Book of Moses, preferably the former.

2845. The Temple at Jerusalem, or any sacred house of worship. Preferably the word may refer to the Ka'bah which is described in the Qur'ān as "a Resort" (2 : 126); "the Sacred House" (5 : 3); "the Sacred Mosque" (17 : 2); "the Ancient House" (22 : 30); and "the Town of Security" (95 : 4); etc.

2846. The tabernacle which Moses set up in the wilderness, in the form of a canopy under which the Israelites worshipped, or the Ka'bah; or the sky, the last reference being more appropriate and relevant.

It is characteristic of the Qur'ān that when it has to make a firm declaration and impart emphasis and certainty to that declaration it swears by, or cites as witnesses, certain beings or objects or natural laws or phenomena. In the first few verses the *Sūrah* swears by certain things intimately connected with Moses—the counterpart of the Holy Prophet. It was on Ṭūr that the revelation was vouchsafed to Moses which embodied his Law and the prophecies which spoke about the appearance of a great Divine Prophet from among the brethren of the Israelites (Deut. 18 : 18 & 33 : 2). Evidently, the Holy Prophet was the Divine Messenger spoken of in the prophecy. His advent is likened in the Qur'ān to the advent of Moses (73 : 16). The *Sūrah* then cites, as evidence, the "Inscribed Book" (the Bible or the Qur'ān, preferably the latter) which stands as a standing and incontrovertible testimony to the truth of the claims of the Holy Prophet. "The Frequented House"—the Ka'bah—more than anything else, shows that the religion of which it forms the citadel and the centre is God's Final Dispensation. Here, long centuries ago, a holy man of God, the Patriarch Abraham, assisted by his son, Ishmael, while raising its foundations, had prayed to God that the place might become a haven of safety and security and might constitute the centre from where God's Unity and Oneness might be proclaimed and preached. The reference in the words "the Elevated Roof," being to heaven, the verse (v. 6) signifies that the disbelievers are so unwise as not to see this simple fact that whereas the Holy Prophet continuously receives Divine help and his cause continues to progress and prosper, failure dogs their footsteps and all their designs and plans against him prove abortive.

7. And *by* the Swollen [a]Sea;[2847]

وَالْبَحْرِ الْمَسْجُورِ ﴿٧﴾

8. The punishment of thy Lord shall, certainly, come to [b]pass.

إِنَّ عَذَابَ رَبِّكَ لَوَاقِعٌ ﴿٨﴾

9. There is none to avert it.

مَا لَهُ مِنْ دَافِعٍ ﴿٩﴾

10. On the day[2848] when the heaven will be in *a state of terrific* commotion,

يَوْمَ تَمُورُ السَّمَاءُ مَوْرًا ﴿١٠﴾

11. [c]And the mountains shall move fast,[2849]

وَتَسِيرُ الْجِبَالُ سَيْرًا ﴿١١﴾

12. Then woe that day to those who reject the Truth,

فَوَيْلٌ يَوْمَئِذٍ لِلْمُكَذِّبِينَ ﴿١٢﴾

13. Who sportingly indulge in idle talk;

الَّذِينَ هُمْ فِي خَوْضٍ يَلْعَبُونَ ﴿١٣﴾

14. The day when they shall be thrust into the fire of Hell[2850] with a *violent* thrust.

يَوْمَ يُدَعُّونَ إِلَىٰ نَارِ جَهَنَّمَ دَعًّا ﴿١٤﴾

15. *And they will be told:* 'This is the Fire which you denied as a lie,

هَٰذِهِ النَّارُ الَّتِي كُنْتُمْ بِهَا تُكَذِّبُونَ ﴿١٥﴾

16. 'Is this then magic, or do you *still* not see?

أَفَسِحْرٌ هَٰذَا أَمْ أَنْتُمْ لَا تُبْصِرُونَ ﴿١٦﴾

---

[a]81 : 7. [b]51 : 6. [c]18 : 48; 78 : 21; 81 : 4.

2847. The words, "the Swollen Sea," may refer to the Red Sea where Pharaoh and his mighty hosts were drowned while pursuing the Israelites, or to the battle-field of Badr where all the great leaders of the Quraish were killed, as it was known as *Al-Bahr*, *i.e.*, the sea (Nihāyah).

2848. On that day all the heavenly forces will operate in favour of the Holy Prophet. So did it happen on the Day of Badr.

2849. On the day of retribution the leaders of disbelievers will meet with a terrible end. They will be blown away like chaff before the wind. Or, the verse may signify that the great Empires of the time will be broken and shattered. This and the preceding verse make a subtle allusion to the new order of things before which the old, decrepit and decayed systems will be swept away. These verses may equally apply to the Day of Judgment.

2850. The verse depicts the disbelievers' condition after their guilt will have been fully established and the time for repentance will have passed.

17. 'Burn ye therein; and whether you show patience or you show *it* not, it will be the same for [a]you. You are requited *only* for what you used to do.'

اِصْلَوْهَا فَاصْبِرُوْٓا اَوْ لَا تَصْبِرُوْا سَوَآءٌ عَلَيْكُمْ اِنَّمَا تُجْزَوْنَ مَا كُنْتُمْ تَعْمَلُوْنَ ﴿١٧﴾

18. [b]Verily, the righteous will, surely, be in Gardens and in bliss,

اِنَّ الْمُتَّقِيْنَ فِيْ جَنّٰتٍ وَّ نَعِيْمٍ ﴿١٨﴾

19. Rejoicing in what their Lord will have bestowed on them; and their Lord will save them from the torment of the Fire,

فٰكِهِيْنَ بِمَآ اٰتٰهُمْ رَبُّهُمْ وَوَقٰهُمْ رَبُّهُمْ عَذَابَ الْجَحِيْمِ ﴿١٩﴾

20. *And He will say to them*, 'Eat and drink with happy enjoyment because of what you used to do.'

كُلُوْا وَ اشْرَبُوْا هَنِيْٓـًٔا بِمَا كُنْتُمْ تَعْمَلُوْنَ ﴿٢٠﴾

21. *On that day they will be* [c]reclining on couches arranged in rows. [d]And We shall give[2851] them as companions fair maidens, having wide, *beautiful* eyes.[2851A]

مُتَّكِـِٕيْنَ عَلٰى سُرُرٍ مَّصْفُوْفَةٍ ۚ وَزَوَّجْنٰهُمْ بِحُوْرٍ عِيْنٍ ﴿٢١﴾

[a]14 : 22; 41 : 25. [b]15 : 46; 77 : 42-43; 78 : 32-33. [c]18 : 32; 55 : 55; 76 : 14. [d]44 : 55; 56 : 23.

2851. *Zawwaja Shai'an bi Shai'in* means, he paired or coupled a thing with a thing; he united it as its fellow or like. *Ḥūr* is the plural of *Ahwar* (masc.) and *Ḥaurā'* (fem.) and means, a person whose eyes are characterized by the quality termed *Ḥawar*, *i.e.*, intense whiteness of the white of the eye and intense blackness of the black thereof, with intense whiteness or fairness of the rest of the person. *Aḥwar* also means, pure or clear intellect.

2851A. *'In* is the plural of both *A'yan* and *Aina'* which respectively mean, man and woman having black wide large eyes, the latter word also meaning, a good or beautiful saying or word (Lane, Mufradāt & Tāj). Thus the two words *Ḥūr* and *'In* signify beauty and purity of person and character.

Life after death is only an image and manifestation of the present life, and the rewards and punishments of the next world would be only so many embodiments and images of the actions done in this life. Heaven and Hell are no new material worlds which come from outside. It is true that they shall be visible and palpable, call them material if you please, but they are only embodiments of the spiritual facts of this life. The entanglements of this world shall be seen as fetters on the feet in the next. The heart-burning of this world shall likewise be clearly seen as flames of burning fire, and the love, which a believer feels for his Lord and Creator, will appear embodied as wine in the life to come, etc. Thus there will be gardens, streams, milk, honey, flesh of birds, wine, fruits, thrones, companions and many other things in Paradise; but they will not be the things of this world, but will be the embodiments of spiritual facts of the life of this world. The words *Zawwajnā*, *Ḥūr* and *'In*, as explained above, show that in Paradise the righteous servants of God will be made to live with pure and clean companions whose faces will be shining with radiant spiritual beauty; or, they will have as companions fair maidens, *i.e.*, their own wives.

22. And those, who believe and whose children follow them in faith —with them will We [a]join their children.[2852] And We will not diminish anything from *the reward of* their works. Every man stands pledged[2853] for what he has earned.

وَالَّذِيْنَ اٰمَنُوْا وَاتَّبَعَتْهُمْ ذُرِّيَّتُهُمْ بِاِيْمَانٍ اَلْحَقْنَا بِهِمْ ذُرِّيَّتَهُمْ وَمَآ اَلَتْنٰهُمْ مِّنْ عَمَلِهِمْ مِّنْ شَيْءٍ ؕ كُلُّ امْرِئٍۢ بِمَا كَسَبَ رَهِيْنٌ ﴿۲۲﴾

23. And We shall bestow upon them *every kind of* [b]fruit and meat such as they will wish for.

وَاَمْدَدْنٰهُمْ بِفَاكِهَةٍ وَّلَحْمٍ مِّمَّا يَشْتَهُوْنَ ﴿۲۳﴾

24. There they will pass[2854] from one to another a cup wherein is neither levity nor [c]sin.

يَتَنَازَعُوْنَ فِيْهَا كَاْسًا لَّا لَغْوٌ فِيْهَا وَلَا تَاْثِيْمٌ ﴿۲۴﴾

25. [d]And there will wait upon them youths[2855] of their own, *pure* as though they were pearls well-preserved.

وَيَطُوْفُ عَلَيْهِمْ غِلْمَانٌ لَّهُمْ كَاَنَّهُمْ لُؤْلُؤٌ مَّكْنُوْنٌ ﴿۲۵﴾

[a]40 : 9. [b]55 : 12; 56 : 21. [c]19 : 63; 56 : 26; 78 : 36. [d]56 : 18; 76 : 20.

To understand and realize the nature of the rewards and punishments of the Life after death it should be borne in mind that that life is the continuation of the life which one leads in this world. As soon as the human soul leaves this tabernacle of clay, it is given a new body, because the soul can make no progress or enjoy no bliss or feel no pain without a body. The new body is as fine and delicate as the soul was in this world. As the form and nature of the new body will be incomprehensibly different from that of our present physical body, the nature of the rewards and punishments of the next world also are beyond our comprehension. This is why the Qur'ān says, *And no soul knows what joy of the eyes is hidden for them, as a reward for their good works* (32 : 18). And the Holy Prophet is reported to have said, 'No eye has seen the blessings of Paradise, nor has any ear heard of them, nor can human mind conceive of them' (Bukhārī). The fact that there will be no sin, levity or vain talk in Paradise, no pleasure of the flesh as we understand them, but all pervading peace and pleasure of God (56 : 26-27), sheds a flood of light on Paradise as conceived and promised to the righteous by the Qur'ān. See also 2326.

2852. Whereas in the former verse it was stated that the righteous will be made to live with their pure, beautiful wives, this verse explains that their children will also be united with them, thus making their joy complete.

2853. The mere fact of being related to a righteous man would do the believer no good. It is his own good works that will earn him his place in Paradise.

2854. *Tanāza'ū al-Ka'sa* means, they took the cup from one another's hand (Aqrab).

2855. *Ghilmān* (youths) is plural of *Ghulām* which means, a youth; servant; son; etc. (Lane). The word has also been used in the Qur'ān synonymously with *Walad* in the sense of son (3 : 41; 15 : 54; 19 : 8; 37 :102; 51 : 29). Elsewhere in the Qur'ān (76:20), the word *Wildān* (sons) has been substituted for *Ghilman* which shows that the youths who will move about in the company of the righteous in Paradise will be their own sons. The verse may also refer to the Divine promise of great wealth and power which was to fall into the possession of the Muslims and to the hosts of servants who were to wait upon them.

26. And they will turn one to another, asking questions.

وَأَقْبَلَ بَعْضُهُمْ عَلَىٰ بَعْضٍ يَتَسَاءَلُونَ ﴿٢٦﴾

27. They will say, 'Before this, when *we were* among our families, we were very much afraid *of Allāh's Judgment*;[2856]

قَالُوا إِنَّا كُنَّا قَبْلُ فِي أَهْلِنَا مُشْفِقِينَ ﴿٢٧﴾

28. 'But Allāh has been gracious unto us and has saved us from the torment of the scorching blast;

فَمَنَّ اللَّهُ عَلَيْنَا وَوَقَانَا عَذَابَ السَّمُومِ ﴿٢٨﴾

29. 'We used to pray to Him before. Surely, He is the Beneficent, the Merciful.'

إِنَّا كُنَّا مِن قَبْلُ نَدْعُوهُ إِنَّهُ هُوَ الْبَرُّ الرَّحِيمُ ﴿٢٩﴾

R. 2 30. So keep on admonishing. By the grace of thy Lord thou art neither a [a]soothsayer, nor a madman.

فَذَكِّرْ فَمَا أَنتَ بِنِعْمَتِ رَبِّكَ بِكَاهِنٍ وَلَا مَجْنُونٍ ﴿٣٠﴾

31. Do they say, '*He is* a [b]poet; we are waiting for some calamity[2857] which time *will bring* upon him?'

أَمْ يَقُولُونَ شَاعِرٌ نَّتَرَبَّصُ بِهِ رَيْبَ الْمَنُونِ ﴿٣١﴾

32. Say, [c]'Await ye[2858] then, I am, *too*, with you among those who are waiting.'

قُلْ تَرَبَّصُوا فَإِنِّي مَعَكُم مِّنَ الْمُتَرَبِّصِينَ ﴿٣٢﴾

33. Does their reason enjoin this upon them or are they a rebellious people?[2859]

أَمْ تَأْمُرُهُمْ أَحْلَامُهُم بِهَٰذَا أَمْ هُمْ قَوْمٌ طَاغُونَ ﴿٣٣﴾

[a]69 : 43. [b]21 : 6; 69 : 42. [c]9 : 52; 32 : 31.

2856. Besides the meanings given in the text the verse may also signify, 'Being surrounded by enemies, their threats would sometimes frighten and terrify us. But now we enjoy perfect peace and security.'

2857. *Raib* means, disquietude of mind; doubt combined with evil opinion; calamity (Lane); *Manūn* means, death; destiny or fate; time (Aqrab).

2858. The verse purports to say that the disbelievers call the Holy Prophet a poet, who indulges in building castles in the air about his great future, a soothsayer who plays upon the credulity of simple-minded folk, a raving maniac, and as such naturally they expect that sooner or later he will come to a sad end. But they will have to wait till doomsday for the realization of their futile expectations. Time alone will decide the issue between them and the Holy Prophet.

2859. Is it their reason that has misled them, or have they thrown all restraint and moderation to the winds, and in rejecting the Divine Message have transgressed all legitimate bounds?

34. Do they say, 'He has forged[2860] it ?' Nay, but they have no faith.

أَمْ يَقُولُونَ تَقَوَّلَهُ ۚ بَل لَّا يُؤْمِنُونَ ﴿٣٤﴾

35. Let them, then, produce a discourse like this,[2861] if they speak the truth.

فَلْيَأْتُوا بِحَدِيثٍ مِّثْلِهِ إِن كَانُوا صَادِقِينَ ﴿٣٥﴾

36. Have they been created without a purpose, or, are they themselves the creators ?

أَمْ خُلِقُوا مِنْ غَيْرِ شَيْءٍ أَمْ هُمُ الْخَالِقُونَ ﴿٣٦﴾

37. Did they create the heavens and the earth? Nay, but they have no faith *in the Creator*.

أَمْ خَلَقُوا السَّمَاوَاتِ وَالْأَرْضَ ۚ بَل لَّا يُوقِنُونَ ﴿٣٧﴾

38. Do they have the treasures of thy Lord with them, or, are they the guardians *thereof ?*

أَمْ عِندَهُمْ خَزَائِنُ رَبِّكَ أَمْ هُمُ الْمُصَيْطِرُونَ ﴿٣٨﴾

39. Have they a ladder by means of which they can *ascend into heaven*[2862] *and* overhear *the Divine words?* Then let their listener bring a manifest proof.

أَمْ لَهُمْ سُلَّمٌ يَسْتَمِعُونَ فِيهِ ۖ فَلْيَأْتِ مُسْتَمِعُهُم بِسُلْطَانٍ مُّبِينٍ ﴿٣٩﴾

40. Has He *only* daughters[2863] and you have sons?

أَمْ لَهُ الْبَنَاتُ وَلَكُمُ الْبَنُونَ ﴿٤٠﴾

2860. *Taqawwala* means, he lied; he attributed to a person a thing which he did not say (Aqrab).

2861. The verse refutes the disbelievers' allegation of forgery against the Holy Prophet. If the Holy Prophet, it seems to hold out a challenge to them, receives no revelations from God and the Qur'ān is his own fabrication, then let them produce a book like it, couched in such beautiful style and inapproachably exquisite diction as the Qur'ān, and should, like the Qur'ān, deal thoroughly and effectively with all the complex and difficult moral and spiritual human problems and satisfy the multitudinous and multifarious needs of man, and exert such powerful influence on the lives of its followers, and above all, should be the repository of all eternal truths and imperishable teachings. The disbelievers are further challenged to produce a book like the Qur'ān with their combined and concerted effort, calling in "all the men and jinn" to help and assist them in its composition. The Qur'ān emphatically declares that they will not be able to produce such a book because the Qur'ān is God's own revealed word. See also 2 : 24; 14 : 25 and 17 : 89.

2862. If disbelievers have access to the secrets of the heavens, then let them produce proofs for the allegation that the Holy Prophet is not the appointed Messenger of God.

2863. It is repugnant, says the verse, to God's Unity that He should have even a son, and yet the disbelievers have the hardihood to assign to Him daughters whose birth is considered as a mark of humiliation and disgrace for them.

41. [a]Dost thou ask a reward[2864] from them, so that they are weighed down with *a load of* debt?

أَمْ تَسْـَٔلُهُمْ أَجْرًا فَهُم مِّن مَّغْرَمٍ مُّثْقَلُونَ ﴿٤١﴾

42. Do they possess *knowledge of* the unseen, so that they write *it* down?

أَمْ عِندَهُمُ الْغَيْبُ فَهُمْ يَكْتُبُونَ ﴿٤٢﴾

43. Do they intend *to devise* a plot? But the disbelievers themselves will be the victims of their plot.

أَمْ يُرِيدُونَ كَيْدًا فَالَّذِينَ كَفَرُوا هُمُ الْمَكِيدُونَ ﴿٤٣﴾

44. Have they a god other than Allāh? Exalted is Allāh above *all* that which they associate *with Him*.

أَمْ لَهُمْ إِلٰهٌ غَيْرُ اللّٰهِ سُبْحٰنَ اللّٰهِ عَمَّا يُشْرِكُونَ ﴿٤٤﴾

45. And if they should see a fragment of the sky falling down, they would say, *just* clouds piled up.[2865]

وَإِن يَرَوْا كِسْفًا مِّنَ السَّمَاءِ سَاقِطًا يَقُولُوا سَحَابٌ مَّرْكُومٌ ﴿٤٥﴾

46. So leave them until they meet that day of theirs, on which they will be thunder-struck;

فَذَرْهُمْ حَتّٰى يُلٰقُوا يَوْمَهُمُ الَّذِي فِيهِ يُصْعَقُونَ ﴿٤٦﴾

47. The day when their scheming shall avail them naught, nor shall they be helped.

يَوْمَ لَا يُغْنِي عَنْهُمْ كَيْدُهُمْ شَيْئًا وَّلَا هُمْ يُنصَرُونَ ﴿٤٧﴾

---

[a]68 : 47.

2864. The verse seems to appeal to the good sense of disbelievers and purports to say to them that when, out of a sincere solicitude for their moral and spiritual well-being the Holy Prophet calls them to the ways of righteousness and asks for no reward for his labours, then why do they not accept him ?

2865. Such is the state of utter heedlessness and false sense of security of disbelievers that they do not benefit by the timely Divine warning, so much so that even if they see a piece of the sky actually falling down upon them, they would deceive themselves by considering it as a piece of God's mercy in the form of 'piled up clouds.'

48. And, verily, for those, who do wrong, there is a punishment besides that.[2866] But most of them know not.

وَإِنَّ لِلَّذِينَ ظَلَمُوا عَذَابًا دُونَ ذٰلِكَ وَلٰكِنَّ أَكْثَرَهُمْ لَا يَعْلَمُونَ ﴿٤٨﴾

49. So wait patiently for the judgment of thy Lord; for, assuredly, thou art before Our eyes;[2867] and [a]celebrate the praises of thy Lord when thou risest up *for prayer*,

وَاصْبِرْ لِحُكْمِ رَبِّكَ فَإِنَّكَ بِأَعْيُنِنَا وَسَبِّحْ بِحَمْدِ رَبِّكَ حِينَ تَقُومُ ﴿٤٩﴾

50. [b]And for part of the night *also* do thou glorify Him and at the setting of the stars.

وَمِنَ اللَّيْلِ فَسَبِّحْهُ وَإِدْبَارَ النُّجُومِ ﴿٥٠﴾ ع

[a]73 : 3-5; 76 : 27.

2866. *Dūn* means, before and behind in respect of place or time; nearby; present with; other; besides (Lane).

2867. Under Our protection (5 : 68).

CHAPTER 53

AL-NAJM

(Revealed before Hijrah)

Date of Revelation and Context

According to overwhelming scholarly opinion the *Sūrah* was revealed in the 5th year of the Call, shortly after the first Emigration to Abyssinia which took place in the month of Rajab of that year. In the preceding *Sūrah* the truth of the Quranic revelation and that of the Divine claim of the Holy Prophet was sought to be established by a fleeting reference to biblical prophecies and natural phenomena. In this *Sūrah* the same subject has been dealt with in a very exquisite and forceful style. It is stated that the Holy Prophet is a Divine Messenger *par excellence* and that he has been commissioned by God as humanity's last and infallible guide and preceptor.

Subject-Matter

The *Sūrah* opens with citing the falling of *al-Najm* as an evidence in support of the Divine claim of the Holy Prophet. The Prophet, having been initiated into Divine mysteries, and having drunk deep at the fountain of Divine grace and knowledge and of Divine realization, attained to the highest peak of spiritual eminence to which a human being can conceivably rise. Then he became filled to the fullest extent with the milk of human kindness, love and sympathy, and having been thus spiritually equipped, was appointed to preach Divine Unity to a world given to the worship of gods, made of wood and stone. The *Sūrah* then gives very strong, solid and sound arguments from human reason and history and from the insignificant beginnings of man, in support of the doctrine of the Oneness of God, and condemns idolatry in forceful terms. This foolish practice, it declares, is born of lack of true knowledge and rests on baseless conjecture which 'avails naught against truth.' Next, it says that idolaters should have learnt from the life-stories of Abraham, Moses and other Prophets that idolatrous beliefs and practices have always landed the idolaters into moral and spiritual ruin. It further says that every man will have to bear his own cross and to render account of his actions to God Who is the Final Goal of all. The *Sūrah* closes on a note of warning to disbelievers that if they persisted in rejecting the Divine Message, they would meet with a sad fate as did the people of Noah and 'Ād and Thamūd tribes, and that it was inevitable that falsehood will perish and nothing could avert it.

سُورَةُ النَّجۡمِ مَكِّيَّةٌ (٥٣)

1. [a]In the name of Allāh, the Gracious, the Merciful.

بِسۡمِ اللّٰهِ الرَّحۡمٰنِ الرَّحِيۡمِ ①

2. By the star[2868] when it falls,

وَالنَّجۡمِ اِذَا هَوٰى ②

3. Your Companion has neither erred, nor has he gone astray,[2869]

مَا ضَلَّ صَاحِبُكُمۡ وَمَا غَوٰى ③

4. Nor does he speak out of *his own* desire.

وَمَا يَنۡطِقُ عَنِ الۡهَوٰى ④

5. It is nothing but *pure* revelation, revealed *by God*.[2870]

اِنۡ هُوَ اِلَّا وَحۡىٌ يُّوۡحٰى ⑤

6. *The Lord* of Mighty Powers has taught him.[2871]

عَلَّمَهٗ شَدِيۡدُ الۡقُوٰى ⑥

---

[a]1 : 1.

2868. *Al-Najm* means, a star; or a stemless plant. But when used as proper noun it signifies "the Pleiades." The word is also taken by some scholars to signify the gradual revelation of the Qur'ān in pieces, and by some other authorities it refers to the Holy Prophet himself. Its plural *al-Nujūm* also means, chiefs of a people, or small states or principalities (Kashshāf, Tāj & Gharāi'b al-Qur'ān). In view of its different meanings the word *Al-Najm* in the verse may be explained (1) by a well-known saying of the Holy Prophet which is to the effect : 'When spiritual darkness will spread over the entire face of the earth and there will remain nothing of Islām but its name, and of the Qur'ān but its letters, and faith will go up to heaven, a man of the Persian descent will bring it back to earth (Bukhārī). (2) It may signify that the Quranic revelation bears witness to its own truth. (3) The tender plant of Islām, which now seems to be going down before the strong and adverse winds of opposition which are fiercely blowing against it, will very shortly rise and develop into a mighty tree under whose cool shade great nations will take rest. (4) As the Arabs are used to determine the course and direction of, and are guided in, their travels by the movements of the stars in the sandy waste of Arabia (16 : 17), so will they now be led to their spiritual goal by the star *par excellence*, *i.e.*, the Holy Prophet. (5) The verse may also embody a prophecy about the fall of the ramshakle State of Arabia, a prophecy much more explicitly stated in 54 : 2.

2869. The ideals and principles presented by the Holy Prophet are not wrong (he has neither erred), nor has he in the least deviated from those principles (nor has he gone astray). Thus both as regards his great and noble ideals and the way he lives upto them he is a sure and safe guide. The argument is reinforced in the next few verses.

2870. Whereas the present verse speaks of the Divine source of the Holy Prophet's revelation, the preceding two verses allude to the hallucinations of a deranged mind and to the ideas that proceed from one's own desires and the promptings of the Evil Spirit.

2871. The Qur'ān is a mighty and powerful Revelation before which all former revealed Scriptures pale into insignificance.

7. The *One* Possessor of Powers[2872] *which manifest themselves repeatedly*. So He settled[2873] Himself *on the throne*.

ذُوْمِرَّةٍ ۭ فَاسْتَوٰى ۙ﴿۷﴾

8. And *He revealed His Word* when he was on the uppermost [a]horizon.[2874]

وَهُوَ بِالْاُفُقِ الْاَعْلٰى ؕ﴿۸﴾

9. Then *the Prophet* drew near *to Allāh;* then *Allāh* leaned down *towards him*.[2875]

ثُمَّ دَنَا فَتَدَلّٰى ۙ﴿۹﴾

10. So that he became, *as it were*, one chord to two bows,[2876] or closer still.

فَكَانَ قَابَ قَوْسَيْنِ اَوْ اَدْنٰى ۚ﴿۱۰﴾

---

[a]81 : 24

2872. *Mirrah* means, strength of make or intellect; sound judgment; firmness, (Aqrab). *Dhū Mirrah* may also mean, one whose powers perpetually manifest themselves.

2873. The expression, *Istawā ʻalā al-Shaiʼi* means, he gained or had the mastery or complete ascendancy over the thing. If applied to the Holy Prophet, the expression would mean that his physical and intellectual powers have attained their fullest vigour and maturity.

2874. The Holy Prophet had attained to the highest point in his spiritual ascension when God revealed Himself to him in full Glory and Majesty. Or, the verse may mean that the light of Islām was set on a very high place from where it could illumine the whole world. The pronoun, *huwa*, may refer both to God and the Holy Prophet. See also verse 10.

2875. *Dallā al-Dalwa* means, he sent down the bucket in the well; he pulled up or out the bucket from the well. *Tadallā* means, he or it lowered or came down; he drew near or approached or increased in nearness (Lane & Lisān). The verse signifies that the Holy Prophet drew near to God and God leaned towards him. It may also mean that the Prophet attained the utmost nearness to God, and after having drunk deep at the Divine fountain of spiritual knowledge, he came down to impart that knowledge to mankind.

2876. *Qāb* means, the portion of a bow that is between the part which is grasped by the hand and the curved extremity; (2) from one extremity of the bow to the other; (3) measure or space. The Arabs say, *Bainahumā Qaba Qausaini, i.e.*, between them two is the measure of a bow, which means that there is very close relationship between them. The Arab proverb, *Ramauna ʻan Qausin Wāḥidin, i.e.*, they shot at us from one bow, signifies that they were unanimous against us. The word thus denotes complete agreement (Lane, Lisān & Zamakhsharī). Whatever may be the significance of the word *Qāb*, the expression, *Qāba Qausaini*, indicates very close union between two persons. The verse purports to say that the Holy Prophet continued to scale the heights of Spiritual Ascension and to approach near God till all distance between them disappeared and the Holy Prophet became, as it were, "one chord to two bows." The proverb reminds us of an ancient Arab custom according to which when two persons pledged themselves to firm friendship they would join their bows in such a way that they appeared as one, and then they would shoot an arrow from that combined bow, thus indicating that they had become, as it were, one person, and that an attack on one would be an attack on the other. If the word, *Tadallā*, be taken to apply to God, the verse would mean that the Holy Prophet went up to God and God came down to him till they both became, as it were,

11. Then *Allāh* revealed to His servant that which He revealed.[2877]

فَأَوْحٰٓى إِلٰى عَبْدِهٖ مَآ أَوْحٰى ﴿١١﴾

12. The heart *of the Prophet* lied not *in seeing* what he saw.[2878]

مَا كَذَبَ الْفُؤَادُ مَا رَاٰى ﴿١٢﴾

13. Will you, then, dispute with him about what he saw?

أَفَتُمٰرُوْنَهٗ عَلٰى مَا يَرٰى ﴿١٣﴾

14. And, certainly, he saw Him a second time,[2879]

وَلَقَدْ رَاٰهُ نَزْلَةً أُخْرٰى ﴿١٤﴾

15. Near the farthest Lote-tree,[2880]

عِنْدَ سِدْرَةِ الْمُنْتَهٰى ﴿١٥﴾

---

united into one person. The expression possesses yet another very beautiful and subtle significance, *viz*., that while on the one hand the Holy Prophet became so completely merged in his Lord and Creator that he became, as it were, His very image, on the other, he came down to mankind and became so full of love, sympathy and solicitude for them that Divinity and Humanity became united in him, and he became the central point of the chord of the two bows of Divinity and Humanity. The words, "or closer still," signify that the relationship between the Holy Prophet and God became closer and more intimate than could be conceived.

Verses 8-18 describe the *Mi'rāj* or the Spiritual Ascension of the Holy Propnet, when he was spiritually transported to heavens and was vouchsafed the view of a spiritual manifestation of God, and ascended spiritually very close to his Maker. It was, in fact, a double spiritual experience, comprising the spiritual ascent of the Holy Prophet, and the descent towards him of God's manifestation. The *Mi'rāj* (Spiritual Ascension) has become confused in popular mind with *Isrā'* (Spiritual Night Journey of the Holy Prophet to Jerusalem), from which it is quite distinct and separate. The *Isrā'* took place in the eleventh or twelfth year of the Call (Zurqānī), while the Holy Prophet had the experience of the *Mi'rāj* (Spiritual Ascension to Heavens) in its 5th year, shortly after the first Emigration to Abyssinia, six or seven years earlier. A careful and minute study of the details of these two incidents mentioned in the Ḥadīth also supports this view. For a somewhat detailed exposition of the two incidents—the *Mi'rāj* and the *Isrā'*—being separate and distinct from each other see 1590.

2877. *Mā* is sometimes used to denote honour, surprise or for emphasis (Aqrab). The verse signifies that God revealed to His servant, and what an excellent and mighty revelation it was !

2878. The implication is that what the Holy Prophet had seen was a real experience; it was veritable truth and no figment of his imagination.

2879. The Holy Prophet's vision was a double spiritual experience.

2880. In his Spiritual Ascension the Holy Prophet had reached such a high stage of nearness to God as was beyond human mind to conceive; or, the verse may signify that at that stage a sea of endless vistas of Divine knowledge and eternal realities and verities opened out before him; *Sadir* which is derived from the same root meaning the sea (Lane). Or, the verse may possess a symbolic allusion to the fact that Divine knowledge vouchsafed to the Holy Prophet would, like the lote-tree, give comfort and shelter to the tired and jaded limbs of the spiritual wayfarers. Moreover, as the leaves of the lote-tree possess the quality of safeguarding a dead body from becoming corrupt, the verse may signify that the Teaching revealed to the Holy Prophet not only is itself immune to, but is eminently fitted to save and preserve mankind from, corruption. Or, it may possess a prophetic reference to the tree under which the Companions of the Holy Prophet took the oath of fealty at his hand at the time of the Truce of Ḥudaibiyah.

16. Near which is the Garden of Eternal Abode.

عِنْدَهَا جَنَّةُ الْمَاْوٰى ﴿١٦﴾

17. *This was* when that, which covers,[2881] covered the Lote-tree.

اِذْ يَغْشَى السِّدْرَةَ مَا يَغْشٰى ﴿١٧﴾

18. The eye deviated not, nor did *it* wander.

مَا زَاغَ الْبَصَرُ وَمَا طَغٰى ﴿١٨﴾

19. Surely, he saw the greatest of the Signs of his Lord.

لَقَدْ رَاٰى مِنْ اٰيٰتِ رَبِّهِ الْكُبْرٰى ﴿١٩﴾

20. Now tell me about Lāt and 'Uzzā;

اَفَرَءَيْتُمُ اللّٰتَ وَالْعُزّٰى ﴿٢٠﴾

21. And Manāt, the third one,[2882] another *goddess*.

وَمَنٰوةَ الثَّالِثَةَ الْاُخْرٰى ﴿٢١﴾

22. 'What ! for you the males and for Him the [a]females?'

اَلَكُمُ الذَّكَرُ وَلَهُ الْاُنْثٰى ﴿٢٢﴾

23. That, indeed, is an unfair division.

تِلْكَ اِذًا قِسْمَةٌ ضِيْزٰى ﴿٢٣﴾

---

[a]6 : 101; 43 : 17; 52 : 40.

2881. The words, '*that which covers*,' signify Divine manifestation.

2882. Some prejudiced critics of the Holy Prophet have woven quite a fantastic story of his having once fallen a victim to the machinations of Satan. It is stated that one day at Mecca, when the Holy Prophet recited this *Sūrah* before a mixed assembly of Muslims and disbelievers and during the recitation he came to these verses, Satan contrived to put in his mouth the words : *Tilka al-Gharānīq al-'ulā wa inna Shafā 'atahunna Laturtajā*, *i.e.*, these are exalted goddesses and their intercession is hoped for (Zurqānī). The critics call it the "lapse of Muḥammad" or his "compromise with idolatry" and seem to rely for this entirely baseless story upon Wāqidī, that inveterate liar and fabricator of reports, and on Ṭabarī, who is generally regarded as a credulous and indiscriminate narrator of events. These gentlemen have the audacity to attribute this blasphemous utterance to that great iconoclast (the Holy Prophet) whose entire life was spent in denouncing and condemning idolatry and who carried out his noble mission with unremitting vigour and fearless devotion, spurning all offers of compromise with idol-worship, and whom blandishments, bribes cajolery or intimidation failed to move an inch from his set purpose, and to whose unshakable firmness against idolatry the Almighty Himself has borne testimony (18 : 7; 68 : 10). Moreover, the whole context belies this baseless assertion. Not only do the verses that follow but the entire *Sūrah* contains an unsparing condemnation of idolatry and an uncompromising insistence on Divine Unity. It is strange that this patent fact should have escaped the notice of the Holy Prophet's critics and carpers. Historical data, too, lend no support whatever to this so-called "lapse." The story has been rejected as completely unreliable by all the learned Commentators of the Qur'ān, Ibn Kathīr and Rāzī among them. The renowned leaders of Muslim religious thought, well-versed in the science of Ḥadīth, such as 'Ainī, Qādī 'Ayyāḍ and Nawawī, have regarded it as pure invention. No trace of this story is to be found in the Six Reliable Collections of Ḥadīth. Imām Bukhārī, whose collection, the Ṣaḥīḥ Bukhārī, is regarded by Muslim scholars as the most reliable book of Ḥadīth and who himself was a contemporary of Waqidī to whom goes the unenviable credit of

24. "These are but names which you have named—you and your fathers—for which Allāh has sent down no authority. They follow naught but conjecture[2883] and what *their* souls desire, while there has *already* come to them guidance from their Lord.

اِنْ هِيَ اِلَّا اَسْمَآءٌ سَمَّيْتُمُوْهَاۤ اَنْتُمْ وَ اٰبَآؤُكُمْ مَّاۤ اَنْزَلَ اللّٰهُ بِهَا مِنْ سُلْطٰنٍ ؕ اِنْ يَّتَّبِعُوْنَ اِلَّا الظَّنَّ وَ مَا تَهْوَى الْاَنْفُسُ ۚ وَ لَقَدْ جَآءَهُمْ مِّنْ رَّبِّهِمُ الْهُدٰى ؕ ۝

25. Can man have whatever he desires?

اَمْ لِلْاِنْسَانِ مَا تَمَنّٰى ۫ ۝

26. Nay, to Allāh belong the Hereafter and this *world*.

فَلِلّٰهِ الْاٰخِرَةُ وَ الْاُوْلٰى ع ۝

R. 2   27. And how many an angel is there in the heavens, but their intercession shall be of no avail, except after Allāh gives permission to whomsoever He wills and pleases.[2884]

وَ كَمْ مِّنْ مَّلَكٍ فِى السَّمٰوٰتِ لَا تُغْنِيْ شَفَاعَتُهُمْ شَيْئًا اِلَّا مِنْ بَعْدِ اَنْ يَّاْذَنَ اللّٰهُ لِمَنْ يَّشَآءُ وَ يَرْضٰى ۝

28. Those, who believe not in the Hereafter, give the angels female names;

اِنَّ الَّذِيْنَ لَا يُؤْمِنُوْنَ بِالْاٰخِرَةِ لَيُسَمُّوْنَ الْمَلٰٓئِكَةَ تَسْمِيَةَ الْاُنْثٰى ۝

29. But they have no knowledge thereof. They follow nothing but conjecture; and *b*conjecture avails naught against truth.

وَ مَا لَهُمْ بِهٖ مِنْ عِلْمٍ ؕ اِنْ يَّتَّبِعُوْنَ اِلَّا الظَّنَّ ۚ وَ اِنَّ الظَّنَّ لَا يُغْنِيْ مِنَ الْحَقِّ شَيْئًا ۝

---

*a*7 : 72; 12 : 41.   *b*6 : 117; 10 : 37.

forging and reporting this story, makes no mention of it, nor does the great historian, Ibn Isḥāq, who was born more than 40 years before him. It may be, as stated by Qastalāni and Zurqāni and supported by some other eminent scholars, that when the Holy Prophet, during the recital of the present *Sūrah* before a mixed assembly of Muslims and disbelievers, recited these verses, some evil-minded person from among the disbelievers might have loudly interjected the above-mentioned words, as was the disbelievers' wont to create confusion by resorting to such low tactics when the Qur'ān was being recited (41 : 27). It is also on record that in the "Days of Ignorance," the Quraish, when making a circuit of the Ka'bah used to recite these words (Mu'jam al-Buldān, vol. 5, under 'Uzzā). It is further alleged that the 53rd verse of *Sūrah* Al-Ḥajj was revealed in connection with this incident. The fact that the present *Sūrah* was revealed in the 5th year of the Call and *Sūrah* Al-Ḥajj in the 12th or 13th year, takes the bottom completely from under this baseless assertion. See also 1962.

2883. Whereas a true believer stands on the bed-rock of certainty and sure knowledge (12 : 109), an idolater possesses no rational argument and no revealed authority for his false beliefs and doctrines. He falls a helpless victim to conjecture and superstition and is a slave to his own desires and fancies. This verse, as also v. 29, speak of the utter untenability of an idolater's position, who stands on a broken reed.

2884. Besides the meaning given in the text the expression means, 'except regarding one who conforms to Allāh's will and with whom He is pleased.

30. So turn away from him who turns his back upon Our remembrance, and seeks nothing but the life of this world.

فَأَعْرِضْ عَنْ مَّنْ تَوَلّٰى ۙ عَنْ ذِكْرِنَا وَلَمْ يُرِدْ إِلَّا الْحَيٰوةَ الدُّنْيَا ﴿٣٠﴾

31. That is the utmost limit of their knowledge. Verily, thy Lord knows best him who strays away from His way, and He knows best him [a]who follows guidance.

ذٰلِكَ مَبْلَغُهُمْ مِّنَ الْعِلْمِ ۭ إِنَّ رَبَّكَ هُوَ أَعْلَمُ بِمَنْ ضَلَّ عَنْ سَبِيْلِهٖ ۙ وَهُوَ أَعْلَمُ بِمَنِ اهْتَدٰى ﴿٣١﴾

32. And to Allāh belongs whatever is in the heavens and whatever is in the earth, that He may requite those who do evil according to what they have wrought and reward those who do good with what is best;

وَلِلّٰهِ مَا فِي السَّمٰوٰتِ وَمَا فِي الْأَرْضِ ۙ لِيَجْزِيَ الَّذِيْنَ أَسَآءُوْا بِمَا عَمِلُوْا وَيَجْزِيَ الَّذِيْنَ أَحْسَنُوْا بِالْحُسْنٰى ﴿٣٢﴾

33. Those who [b]shun the grave sins and *all* indecencies except minor faults.[2885] Verily, thy Lord is Master of vast forgiveness. [c]He knows you well *from the time* when He created you from the earth, and when you were embryos in the bellies of your mothers. So ascribe not purity to yourselves. He knows him best who is *truly* righteous.

الَّذِيْنَ يَجْتَنِبُوْنَ كَبٰٓئِرَ الْإِثْمِ وَالْفَوَاحِشَ إِلَّا اللَّمَمَ ۭ إِنَّ رَبَّكَ وَاسِعُ الْمَغْفِرَةِ ۭ هُوَ أَعْلَمُ بِكُمْ إِذْ أَنْشَأَكُمْ مِّنَ الْأَرْضِ وَإِذْ أَنْتُمْ أَجِنَّةٌ فِيْ بُطُوْنِ أُمَّهٰتِكُمْ ۚ فَلَا تُزَكُّوْٓا أَنْفُسَكُمْ ۭ هُوَ أَعْلَمُ بِمَنِ اتَّقٰى ﴿٣٣﴾

R. 3 34. Seest thou him who turns away *from guidance*,

أَفَرَءَيْتَ الَّذِيْ تَوَلّٰى ﴿٣٤﴾

[a]16 : 126; 28 : 57; 68 : 8. [b]4 : 32; 42 : 38 [c]13 : 8.

2885. *Lamam* means, a chance leaning towards evil; a temporary and light lapse; a passing evil idea which flashes across the mind and leaves no impression on it; a chance, unintentional look at a woman. The root-word possesses the sense of temporariness, haste and infrequency and of doing a thing unintentionally (Lane).

35. And gives a little, and does it grudgingly?[2886]

وَأَعْطَىٰ قَلِيلًا وَّأَكْدَىٰ ﴿٣٥﴾

36. Has he the knowledge of the unseen, so that he can see *his own end?*

أَعِنْدَهُ عِلْمُ الْغَيْبِ فَهُوَ يَرَىٰ ﴿٣٦﴾

37. Has he not been informed of what is in the Scriptures of Moses,

أَمْ لَمْ يُنَبَّأْ بِمَا فِي صُحُفِ مُوسَىٰ ﴿٣٧﴾

38. And of Abraham who fulfilled *the Divine commandments?*—

وَإِبْرَاهِيمَ الَّذِي وَفَّىٰ ﴿٣٨﴾

39. [a]That no bearer of burden shall bear the burden of another,[2887]

أَلَّا تَزِرُ وَازِرَةٌ وِّزْرَ أُخْرَىٰ ﴿٣٩﴾

40. And that man will have nothing but what he strives for;[2888]

وَأَنْ لَّيْسَ لِلْإِنْسَانِ إِلَّا مَا سَعَىٰ ﴿٤٠﴾

41. And that *the result of* his striving shall soon be known;

وَأَنَّ سَعْيَهُ سَوْفَ يُرَىٰ ﴿٤١﴾

42. Then will he be rewarded for it with the fullest reward,

ثُمَّ يُجْزَاهُ الْجَزَاءَ الْأَوْفَىٰ ﴿٤٢﴾

43. And that with thy Lord is the final judgment;[2889]

وَأَنَّ إِلَىٰ رَبِّكَ الْمُنْتَهَىٰ ﴿٤٣﴾

44. And that it is He Who makes people laugh and makes *them* weep;

وَأَنَّهُ هُوَ أَضْحَكَ وَأَبْكَىٰ ﴿٤٤﴾

---

[a]6 : 165; 17 : 16; 35 : 19; 39 : 8.

2886. When used about a person *Akdā* means, he gave niggardly or grudgingly; he did not succeed in getting what he wanted. When used about a mine it means, it refused to bring out diamonds and jewels, but when used about a digger it means, in the course of digging he came across a hard or stony piece of ground or clod and could dig no further (Aqrab).

2887. Every man shall have to carry his own cross and bear his own burden.

2888. It is after unremitting, incessant and persistent striving, accompanied by noble ideals and sublime principles, that one can achieve the object of one's quest. The verse also signifies that one should earn one's livelihood by the sweat of one's brow.

2889. The whole system of cause and effect ends with God. He is the Cause of all causes or the First Cause. A natural order of cause and effect pervades the whole universe. Every cause, which is not itself primary, is traceable to some other cause and this to another, and so on.

45. And that it is He Who [a]causes death and gives life;

وَأَنَّهُ هُوَ أَمَاتَ وَأَحْيَا ﴿٤٥﴾

46. And that He creates the pairs, [b]male and female,

وَأَنَّهُ خَلَقَ الزَّوْجَيْنِ الذَّكَرَ وَالْأُنْثَىٰ ﴿٤٦﴾

47. [c]From a sperm-drop when it is emitted;

مِنْ نُطْفَةٍ إِذَا تُمْنَىٰ ﴿٤٧﴾

48. And that it is for Him to bring forth the second creation;

وَأَنَّ عَلَيْهِ النَّشْأَةَ الْأُخْرَىٰ ﴿٤٨﴾

49. And that it is He Who enriches and gives contentment;[2889A]

وَأَنَّهُ هُوَ أَغْنَىٰ وَأَقْنَىٰ ﴿٤٩﴾

50. And that He is the Lord of Sirius;[2890]

وَأَنَّهُ هُوَ رَبُّ الشِّعْرَىٰ ﴿٥٠﴾

51. And that He destroyed the first *tribe of* 'Ād,[2891]

وَأَنَّهُ أَهْلَكَ عَادًا الْأُولَىٰ ﴿٥١﴾

52. And *the tribe of* Thamūd, and He spared no one,

وَثَمُودَا فَمَا أَبْقَىٰ ﴿٥٢﴾

53. And *He destroyed* the people of Noah before them—verily, they were most unjust and most rebellious—

وَقَوْمَ نُوحٍ مِنْ قَبْلُ إِنَّهُمْ كَانُوا هُمْ أَظْلَمَ وَأَطْغَىٰ ﴿٥٣﴾

54. And He overthrew the subverted cities *of the people of Lot*,

وَالْمُؤْتَفِكَةَ أَهْوَىٰ ﴿٥٤﴾

55. So that there covered them that which covered.[2892]

فَغَشَّاهَا مَا غَشَّىٰ ﴿٥٥﴾

[a]2 : 29; 30 : 41. [b]4 : 2; 7 : 190; 30 : 22. [c]56 : 59-60; 75 : 38; 86 : 7.

2889A. *Aqnā Allāh Fulānan* means, Allāh made such a one rich and gave him so much as made him contented (Lane).

2890. The Arabs worshipped Sirius because they regarded it as a great source of good or bad luck for them.

2891. After having given arguments in support of Divine Unity from human reason and from the insignificant beginning of man, the *Sūrah*, from this verse, introduces history to prove the same thesis.

2892. The particle *mā* has been used here to denote respect or dignity, meaning that an overwhelming punishment enveloped them.

56. Which, then, *O man*, of the bounties of thy Lord wilt thou dispute?[2893]

فَبِاَيِّ اٰلَآءِ رَبِّكَ تَتَمَارٰى ﴿٥٦﴾

57. This *Messenger of Ours* is a Warner like the Warners of old.

هٰذَا نَذِيْرٌ مِّنَ النُّذُرِ الْاُوْلٰى ﴿٥٧﴾

58. *The Hour of Judgment*[2894] which was to come has drawn nigh,

اَزِفَتِ الْاٰزِفَةُ ﴿٥٨﴾

59. None but Allāh can avert it.

لَيْسَ لَهَا مِنْ دُوْنِ اللّٰهِ كَاشِفَةٌ ﴿٥٩﴾

60. Do you, then, wonder at this announcement?

اَفَمِنْ هٰذَا الْحَدِيْثِ تَعْجَبُوْنَ ﴿٦٠﴾

61. And do you laugh and weep not,

وَتَضْحَكُوْنَ وَلَا تَبْكُوْنَ ﴿٦١﴾

62. While you make merry?

وَاَنْتُمْ سٰمِدُوْنَ ﴿٦٢﴾

63. So prostrate yourselves before Allāh and [a]worship[2895] *Him*

السجدة

ع فَاسْجُدُوْا لِلّٰهِ وَاعْبُدُوْا ﴿٦٣﴾

[a]7 : 206; 22 : 78; 41 : 38; 96 : 20.

2893. After having seen so many and so clear and invincible arguments and Signs that support and substantiate the claims of the Holy Prophet, the verse says to the obstinate disbelievers, in words full of pathos mixed with irony, how long will they continue to deny Truth and wander in the wilderness of disbelief ?

2894. *Āzifah* means, the Hour of Judgment; the Resurrection ; the near event; death (Lane). The *Sūrah* was revealed very early in the Holy Prophet's ministry, in the fifth year of the Call, when in the midst of mockery, threats and persecution, the fate of Islām hung in the balance. It was at that time that the prophecy was made about the overthrow of the Quraishite power in this *Sūrah* and in much more forceful accents in the next (54 : 46).

2895. It seems that as the Holy Prophet finished reciting the *Sūrah* before the mixed gathering of Muslims and disbelievers, and along with his followers prostrated himself on the ground, the disbelievers too, being deeply impressed with the solemnity of the recitation of the Quranic words as well as with God's Majesty and Glory, might have fallen in prostration. This was not unlikely since they regarded God as the Supreme Lord and Creator and their own deities as mere intercessors with Him (10 : 19). By connecting this plausible incident, however, with the baseless legend woven round vv. 20-22 by some "inventive minds," the traducers of the Holy Prophet have persuaded themselves to detect in it a "lapse" on his part.

CHAPTER 54

AL-QAMAR

(*Revealed before Hijrah*)

Date of Revelation and Context

The *Sūrah* was revealed about the same time as the preceding one, Al-Najm, which was revealed in the 5th year of the Call. *Sūrah* Al-Najm had ended on a note of warning to disbelievers that the Hour of their doom had drawn near, and the present *Sūrah* opens with the expression that the threatened Hour has almost arrived—it is at their very door. This is the fifth of the group of seven Quranic Chapters which begin with *Sūrah* Qāf and end with Al-Wāqi'ah. All these Chapters were revealed very early in the Holy Prophet's ministry and deal with the basic doctrines of Islām—Existence and Unity of God, Resurrection and Revelation; and adduce laws of nature, human reason, commonsense and histories of the past Prophets as arguments to prove these theses. In some of them special emphasis is laid on one kind of arguments with a fleeting reference to other kinds and *vice versa*. In the present Chapter the Holy Prophet's Divine claim and Resurrection have been dealt with, with special reference to the histories of the past Prophets, particularly to those of Noah, the tribes of 'Ād and Thamūd and Lot's people. Towards its end the Chapter makes a pointed reference to the fulfilment of the prophecy about the destruction and overthrow of the power of pagan Arabs about which a warning had been given in the preceding *Sūrah* (53 : 58).

سُورَةُ الْقَمَرِ مَكِّيَّةٌ

1. [a]In the name of Allāh, the Gracious, the Merciful.

بِسْمِ اللّٰهِ الرَّحْمٰنِ الرَّحِيْمِ ①

2. [b]The Hour has drawn nigh, and the moon is rent asunder.[2896]

اِقْتَرَبَتِ السَّاعَةُ وَانْشَقَّ الْقَمَرُ ②

[a]1 : 1 [b]21 : 2.

2896. Whether or not "splitting of the moon" into two parts, observable by the naked eye, had contravened any physical law of nature, it is difficult to deny that the event seems to lack unimpeachable historical evidence. On the other hand nobody can presume to have fathomed all Divine mysteries or fully comprehended or encompassed all the secrets of nature. It is not possible to imagine that such an event, affecting a considerable area of the globe, should have remained unnoticed in the observatories of the world, or that it should have remained unrecorded in books of history. But the incident, having found a mention in such reliable collections of Ḥadīth as Bukhārī and Muslim and having been narrated successively in traditions of reliable authority and reported by such a learned Companion of the Holy Prophet as Ibn Mas'ūd, does show that some natural phenomenon of unusual importance must have taken place in the time of the Holy Prophet. Some Commentators of the Qur'ān—Rāḍī among them—have sought to solve the difficult problem by declaring the incident to be a lunar eclipse. Imām Ghazālī and Shah Wali Allāh also hold the view that the moon had not, in fact, been rent asunder, but that God has so designed that it appeared to the beholders as such. According to Ibn 'Abbās and Shah 'Abd al-'Azīz it was a kind of lunar eclipse. However, taking into consideration the forceful language in which it has been mentioned in the Qur'ān, the incident appears to be something more than a mere lunar eclipse. It indeed constituted a great miracle shown by the Holy Prophet at the insistent demand of disbelievers (Bukhārī & Muslim). It seems that it was a vision of the Holy Prophet in which some of his Companions and some of the disbelievers also were made to share—just as the rod turning into a serpent was a vision of Moses, in which the sorcerers were made to share. Or, it may be that just as the striking of sea-water by Moses with his rod coincided with the ebb of the tide and thus assumed the character of a miracle, similarly God may have commanded the Holy Prophet to show the miracle of the cleaving asunder of the moon at a time when some heavenly body was to take such a position in front of the moon that it caused the moon to appear to the beholders as being split into two parts. But the most plausible explanation, which is also possessed of very deep spiritual significance, lies in the fact that the moon was the national emblem of the Arabs and the symbol of their political power, just as the sun was the national ensign of the Persians. When Ṣafiyyah, the daughter of Ḥuyay ibn Akhṭab, a leader of the Jews of Khaibar, mentioned to her father that she had seen in a dream that the moon had fallen into her lap, he slapped her face saying that she wanted to marry the leader of the Arabs. After the fall of Khaibar Ṣafiyyah's dream was fulfilled when she was married to the Holy Prophet (Zurqānī & Usud al-Ghābbah). Similarly, 'Ā'ishah had seen in a dream that three moons had fallen in her private apartment which saw its fulfilment when the Holy Prophet, Abū Bakr and Umar were buried there one after the other (Mu'aṭṭa', *Kitāb al-Janā'iz*). According to this symbolical significance of *Qamar*, the verse would signify that the hour of the destruction of their political power with which the disbelieving Arabs had been threatened in 53 : 58 has already arrived. The word "Hour" in this case would refer to the Battle of Badr in which almost all the chiefs and leaders of the Quraish were killed and the foundations of the complete destruction of their power were laid. Thus the verse constituted a mighty prophecy which met with remarkable fulfilment, nearly eight or nine years after its announcement. Moreover, according to some writers the Arabic expression, *Inshaqqa al-Qamaru*, means, the affair has become manifest. In this sense of the word the verse would mean that the hour of the destruction of the Quraishite power has arrived and it would then become manifest that the Holy Prophet is a true Divine Messenger. See also 1023.

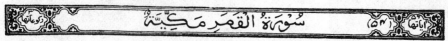

3. [a]And if they see a Sign, they turn away and say, 'An oft-repeated[2897] sorcery.'

وَاِنْ يَّرَوْا اٰيَةً يُّعْرِضُوْا وَ يَقُوْلُوْا سِحْرٌ مُّسْتَمِرٌّ ۝٣

4. They have rejected *the Truth* and follow their own fancies. But for everything there is an appointed time.[2898]

وَكَذَّبُوْا وَاتَّبَعُوْٓا اَهْوَآءَهُمْ وَكُلُّ اَمْرٍ مُّسْتَقِرٌّ ۝٤

5. And there has already come to them *accounts of* events containing warnings—

وَلَقَدْ جَآءَهُمْ مِّنَ الْاَنْۢبَآءِ مَا فِيْهِ مُزْدَجَرٌ ۝٥

6. Consummate wisdom; but the [b]warnings profit them not.

حِكْمَةٌۢ بَالِغَةٌ فَمَا تُغْنِ النُّذُرُ ۝٦

7. Therefore, turn thou away from them *and await* the day when the Summoner will summon *them* to a disagreeable thing,

فَتَوَلَّ عَنْهُمْ يَوْمَ يَدْعُ الدَّاعِ اِلٰى شَيْءٍ نُّكُرٍ ۝٧

8. [c]While their eyes will be cast down and they will come forth from *their* graves[2899] as though they were locusts scattered about,

خُشَّعًا اَبْصَارُهُمْ يَخْرُجُوْنَ مِنَ الْاَجْدَاثِ كَاَنَّهُمْ جَرَادٌ مُّنْتَشِرٌ ۝٨

9. [d]Hastening towards the Summoner.[2900] The disbelievers will say, 'This is a hard day.'

مُّهْطِعِيْنَ اِلَى الدَّاعِ ۭ يَقُوْلُ الْكٰفِرُوْنَ هٰذَا يَوْمٌ عَسِرٌ ۝٩

[a]21 : 3. [b]10 : 102. [c]70 : 45. [d]14 : 44; 36 : 52.

2897. *Mustamirr* means, (1) passing, fleeting, transient; (2) continuous; (3) strong, firm (Aqrab).

2898. The desctruction of the political power of the Quraish has been decreed by God, and the Divine decree must come to pass.

2899. "Graves" here signifies the houses of disbelievers. At several places in the Qur'ān disbelievers have been likened to the dead because of their being completely devoid of spiritual life (27 : 81; 35 : 23).

2900. This and the preceding two verses give a graphic picture of the utter confusion, consternation and bewilderment of the Quraish when they saw the Summoner—the Holy Prophet—whom they had driven out of Mecca and upon whose head they had laid a price only a few years earlier—at the very gates of their capital city.

10. The people of Noah[2901] [a]rejected *the Truth* before them; they called Our servant a liar and said, '*He is* a [b]madman, afflicted *by our idols*.'

كَذَّبَتْ قَبْلَهُمْ قَوْمُ نُوحٍ فَكَذَّبُوا عَبْدَنَا وَقَالُوا مَجْنُونٌ وَّازْدُجِرَ ﴿١٠﴾

11. So he prayed to his Lord: 'I am overcome, so *come* Thou *to my* [c]help!'

فَدَعَا رَبَّهُ أَنِّي مَغْلُوبٌ فَانْتَصِرْ ﴿١١﴾

12. Thereupon We opened the gates of heaven with water *which fell* in torrents;

فَفَتَحْنَا أَبْوَابَ السَّمَاءِ بِمَاءٍ مُّنْهَمِرٍ ﴿١٢﴾

13. [d]And We caused the earth to burst forth with springs, so the *two* waters[2902] met for a purpose that was decreed.

وَّفَجَّرْنَا الْأَرْضَ عُيُونًا فَالْتَقَى الْمَاءُ عَلَى أَمْرٍ قَدْ قُدِرَ ﴿١٣﴾

14. And [e]We carried him upon that *which was made* of planks and nails.

وَحَمَلْنٰهُ عَلَى ذَاتِ أَلْوَاحٍ وَّدُسُرٍ ﴿١٤﴾

15. It floated on under Our [f]eyes; a reward for him who had been denied.

تَجْرِي بِأَعْيُنِنَا جَزَاءً لِّمَنْ كَانَ كُفِرَ ﴿١٥﴾

16. [g]And We left it as a Sign *for the succeeding generations*. But is there anyone who would take heed?

وَلَقَدْ تَّرَكْنٰهَا آيَةً فَهَلْ مِنْ مُّدَّكِرٍ ﴿١٦﴾

17. How *terrible*, then, was My punishment and *how true* My warning!

فَكَيْفَ كَانَ عَذَابِي وَنُذُرِ ﴿١٧﴾

[a]6 : 35; 22 : 43; 35 : 26; 40 : 6. [b]23 : 26. [c]23 : 27; 26 : 118-119. [d]11 : 41. [e]26 : 120; 29 : 16. [f]11 : 42-43. [g]29 : 16.

2901. The cases of the people of Noah, of the tribes of 'Ād and Thamūd and that of the people of Lot have received repeated and somewhat detailed mention in the Qur'ān because these peoples lived on the confines of the Ḥijāz, and the Quraish were quite familiar with their histories and also had commercial relations with them. Noah's people lived in Iraq which lies to the north-east of Arabia, and the tribe of 'Ād lived in Yemen and Ḥaḍaramaut which form the southern part of it, while the tribe of Thamūd throve and flourished in the north-west of Arabia which extends from the Ḥijāz to Palestine, and the ill-fated people of Lot lived in Sodom and Gommorah in Palestine.

2902. The rain-water pouring down in torrents from the skies and the water gushing forth from under the earth—the two waters—caused a huge flood which engulfed the entire land and thus the Divine decree was fulfilled, destroying the people of Noah.

18. And, indeed, We have made the Qur'ān [a]easy to remember.[2903] Is there anyone who would take heed ?

وَلَقَدْ يَسَّرْنَا الْقُرْاٰنَ لِلذِّكْرِ فَهَلْ مِنْ مُّدَّكِرٍ ﴿۱۸﴾

19. The *tribe of* 'Ād [b]rejected *the Truth.* How *terrible*, then, was My punishment and *how true* My warning !

كَذَّبَتْ عَادٌ فَكَيْفَ كَانَ عَذَابِيْ وَ نُذُرِ ﴿۱۹﴾

20. We [c]sent against them a furious wind on a day of unending ill-luck,[2904]

اِنَّآ اَرْسَلْنَا عَلَيْهِمْ رِيْحًا صَرْصَرًا فِيْ يَوْمِ نَحْسٍ مُّسْتَمِرٍّ ﴿۲۰﴾

21. Tearing people away as though they were the *hollow* trunks [d]of uprooted palm-trees.

تَنْزِعُ النَّاسَ كَاَنَّهُمْ اَعْجَازُ نَخْلٍ مُّنْقَعِرٍ ﴿۲۱﴾

22. How *terrible*, then, was My punishment and *how true* My warning !

فَكَيْفَ كَانَ عَذَابِيْ وَ نُذُرِ ﴿۲۲﴾

23. And, indeed, We have made the Qur'ān easy to remember. But is there anyone who would take heed?

وَلَقَدْ يَسَّرْنَا الْقُرْاٰنَ لِلذِّكْرِ فَهَلْ مِنْ مُّدَّكِرٍ ﴿۲۳﴾ ع

R. 2 24. *The tribe of* Thamūd *also* [e]rejected the Warners.[2905]

كَذَّبَتْ ثَمُوْدُ بِالنُّذُرِ ﴿۲۴﴾

[a]19 : 98; 44 : 59. [b]26 : 124. [c]41 : 17; 69 : 7. [d]69 : 8. [e]69 : 5.

2903. The Qur'ān has been made easy in this sense also that it comprehends all those permanent and imperishable teachings that are found in other revealed Scriptures, with a great deal more that is indispensible for the guidance of man till the end of time (98 : 4). The treasures of Divine realization and deep mysteries of the unknown, which lie hidden in the Qur'ān are accessible only to those few righteous men of God who are endowed with a special spiritual insight and who have scaled the dizzy heights of communion with the Divine Being and have been purified by Him (56 : 80).

2904. The verse does not mean that any particular time is auspicious or inauspicious, lucky or unlucky. The meaning is that for the tribe of 'Ād the day proved unlucky.

2905. As all Prophets are commissioned by God and their revelation proceeds from the same Divine Source and it also contains analogous eternal basic truths, the rejection of one Prophet amounts to the rejection of all of them. That is why the verse describes the 'Ād and the Thamūd, the people of Noah and those of Lot as having rejected all Divine Messengers while, in fact, they had rejected only their own particular Prophets.

25. And they said, 'What! shall we follow a mortal, one out of ourselves? Then, indeed, we would be in manifest error, and *suffering from* madness.[2906]

فَقَالُوْٓا اَبَشَرًا مِّنَّا وَاحِدًا نَّتَّبِعُهٗٓ ۙ اِنَّآ اِذًا لَّفِيْ ضَلٰلٍ وَّسُعُرٍ ﴿۲۵﴾

26. [a]Has the Reminder been revealed to him *alone* of all of us? Nay, he is an impudent liar.'

ءَاُلْقِيَ الذِّكْرُ عَلَيْهِ مِنْۢ بَيْنِنَا بَلْ هُوَ كَذَّابٌ اَشِرٌ ﴿۲۶﴾

27. Tomorrow will they know who is the impudent liar.

سَيَعْلَمُوْنَ غَدًا مَّنِ الْكَذَّابُ الْاَشِرُ ﴿۲۷﴾

28. We will send the [b]she-camel as a trial for them. So watch them, *O Ṣaliḥ*, and have patience,

اِنَّا مُرْسِلُوا النَّاقَةِ فِتْنَةً لَّهُمْ فَارْتَقِبْهُمْ وَاصْطَبِرْ ﴿۲۸﴾

29. 'And tell them that the water is shared between *her and* them, every drinking time[2907] shall be attended.'

وَنَبِّئْهُمْ اَنَّ الْمَآءَ قِسْمَةٌۢ بَيْنَهُمْ ۚ كُلُّ شِرْبٍ مُّحْتَضَرٌ ﴿۲۹﴾

30. But they called their comrade and he seized *a sword* and [c]hamstrung *her*.

فَنَادَوْا صَاحِبَهُمْ فَتَعَاطٰى فَعَقَرَ ﴿۳۰﴾

31. How *terrible*, then, was My punishment and *how true* My warning!

فَكَيْفَ كَانَ عَذَابِيْ وَنُذُرِ ﴿۳۱﴾

32. We sent against them a single blast, and they became like the dry stubble, whittled down by a maker of hedges.[2908]

اِنَّآ اَرْسَلْنَا عَلَيْهِمْ صَيْحَةً وَّاحِدَةً فَكَانُوْا كَهَشِيْمِ الْمُحْتَظِرِ ﴿۳۲﴾

[a]38 : 9. [b]7 : 74; 11 : 65; 17 : 60. [c]7 : 78; 11 : 66; 26 : 158; 91 : 15.

2906. *Su'ira* means, he was smitten by hot wind; he was or became mad. *Su'r* means, madness, insanity, demoniacal possession; punishment; vehemence of heat, hunger or thirst; fury; pain (Lane).

2907. *Shirb* is infinitive noun from *Shariba* and means, water that one drinks; a draught of water; a share or portion of water which falls to one's lot; the right to use water for watering fields and beasts; a watering place; a turn or time of drinking. *Shurb* means, the act of drinking (Lane).

2908. The disbelievers were completely crushed, or they were as worthless in the sight of God as whittled down and crushed stubble, collected by a maker of hedges.

33. And, indeed, We have made the Qur'ān easy to remember. But is there anyone who will take heed?

وَلَقَدْ يَسَّرْنَا الْقُرْاٰنَ لِلذِّكْرِ فَهَلْ مِنْ مُّدَّكِرٍ ﴿٣٣﴾

34. [a]Lot's people *also* rejected the Warners.

كَذَّبَتْ قَوْمُ لُوْطٍ بِالنُّذُرِ ﴿٣٤﴾

35. [b]We sent a storm of stones upon them except the family of Lot, whom We delivered by early dawn,

اِنَّآ اَرْسَلْنَا عَلَيْهِمْ حَاصِبًا اِلَّآ اٰلَ لُوْطٍ نَجَّيْنٰهُمْ بِسَحَرٍ ﴿٣٥﴾

36. *As* a favour from Us. Thus do We reward him who is grateful.

نِّعْمَةً مِّنْ عِنْدِنَا كَذٰلِكَ نَجْزِيْ مَنْ شَكَرَ ﴿٣٦﴾

37. And he, indeed, had warned them of Our severe punishment, but they doubted the warning.

وَلَقَدْ اَنْذَرَهُمْ بَطْشَتَنَا فَتَمَارَوْا بِالنُّذُرِ ﴿٣٧﴾

38. And they *deceitfully* sought to turn him away from his guests. So We blinded their eyes,[2909] *and said*, 'Taste ye now My punishment and My warning.'

وَلَقَدْ رَاوَدُوْهُ عَنْ ضَيْفِهٖ فَطَمَسْنَآ اَعْيُنَهُمْ فَذُوْقُوْا عَذَابِيْ وَنُذُرِ ﴿٣٨﴾

39. And there came upon them early in the morning a lasting punishment.

وَلَقَدْ صَبَّحَهُمْ بُكْرَةً عَذَابٌ مُّسْتَقِرٌّ ﴿٣٩﴾

40. 'Now taste ye My punishment and My warning.'

فَذُوْقُوْا عَذَابِيْ وَنُذُرِ ﴿٤٠﴾

41. And, indeed, We have made the Qur'ān easy to remember. But is there anyone who would take heed?

وَلَقَدْ يَسَّرْنَا الْقُرْاٰنَ لِلذِّكْرِ فَهَلْ مِنْ مُّدَّكِرٍ ﴿٤١﴾

R. 3 42. And, surely, to the people of Pharaoh *also* came Warners.

وَلَقَدْ جَآءَ اٰلَ فِرْعَوْنَ النُّذُرُ ﴿٤٢﴾

[a]26 : 161. [b]25 : 41; 26 : 174.

2909. Lot's people sought to take hold of his guests but it seems the latter went into hiding and thus could not be found out. Or, the meaning is that God so arranged that attention of Lot's people became diverted from them.

43. [a]They rejected all Our Signs. So We seized them like the seizing of the Mighty, the Powerful.[2910]

كَذَّبُوا بِآيَاتِنَا كُلِّهَا فَأَخَذْنَاهُمْ أَخْذَ عَزِيزٍ مُّقْتَدِرٍ ﴿٤٣﴾

44. Are your disbelievers better than those? Or, have you an [b]immunity in the Scriptures?[2911]

أَكُفَّارُكُمْ خَيْرٌ مِّنْ أُولَٰئِكُمْ أَمْ لَكُم بَرَاءَةٌ فِي الزُّبُرِ ﴿٤٤﴾

45. Do they say, 'We are a victorious host?'

أَمْ يَقُولُونَ نَحْنُ جَمِيعٌ مُّنتَصِرٌ ﴿٤٥﴾

46. [c]The hosts shall soon be routed[2912] and shall turn their backs *in flight*.

سَيُهْزَمُ الْجَمْعُ وَيُوَلُّونَ الدُّبُرَ ﴿٤٦﴾

47. Aye, the Hour is their promised time; and the Hour will be most calamitous *for them* and most bitter.

بَلِ السَّاعَةُ مَوْعِدُهُمْ وَالسَّاعَةُ أَدْهَىٰ وَأَمَرُّ ﴿٤٧﴾

48. Surely, the guilty are in *manifest* error and *suffer from* madness.

إِنَّ الْمُجْرِمِينَ فِي ضَلَالٍ وَسُعُرٍ ﴿٤٨﴾

---

[a]20 : 57. [b]2 : 81. [c]3 : 13; 8 : 37; 38 : 12.

2910. Pharaoh was a very powerful monarch. He regarded himself as "the most high lord of the Israelites" (79 : 25). So the might of the real Omnipotent, Lord of Moses and Aaron was pitted against that self-designated lord, who was completely annihilated.

2911. The verse repeats a warning to the pagan Quraish in another form. 'Are you in any way better,' it asks them, 'than those who rejected Noah, Hūd, Lot or Moses? Or, have you received a Divine promise recorded in Divine Scriptures that you will not be punished for your rejection of the Holy Prophet?'

2912. The emphatic prophecy embodied in the verse is definitely about the crushing defeat which the Meccan army suffered in the Battle of Badr. The odds were so heavy against the Muslims that when fighting began the Holy Prophet prayed to God in utmost humility and extreme agony in a tent set up for him for this purpose in the memorable words : 'O Lord, I humbly beseech Thee to fulfil Thy covenant and Thy promise. If this small band of Muslims were destroyed, Thou wilt never be worshipped again on this earth' (Bukhārī). After having finished the prayer, the Holy Prophet came out of the tent and facing the field of battle recited the verse, "The hosts shall soon be routed and shall turn their backs in flight."

49. On the day when they will be dragged into the Fire[2913] on their faces, *it will be said to them*, 'Taste ye the touch of Hell.'

يَوْمَ يُسْحَبُونَ فِي النَّارِ عَلَىٰ وُجُوهِهِمْ ذُوقُوا مَسَّ سَقَرَ ﴿٤٩﴾

50. Verily, We have created everything [a]in *due* measure.[2914]

إِنَّا كُلَّ شَيْءٍ خَلَقْنَاهُ بِقَدَرٍ ﴿٥٠﴾

51. And Our command is *carried out by* only one *word* as the [b]twinkling of an eye.[2915]

وَمَا أَمْرُنَا إِلَّا وَاحِدَةٌ كَلَمْحٍ بِالْبَصَرِ ﴿٥١﴾

52. And, indeed, We have destroyed people like you *before*. But is there anyone who would take heed ?

وَلَقَدْ أَهْلَكْنَا أَشْيَاعَكُمْ فَهَلْ مِن مُّدَّكِرٍ ﴿٥٢﴾

53. [c]And everything they have done is *recorded* in the Books.[2916]

وَكُلُّ شَيْءٍ فَعَلُوهُ فِي الزُّبُرِ ﴿٥٣﴾

54. And every matter, small and great, is written down.

وَكُلُّ صَغِيرٍ وَكَبِيرٍ مُّسْتَطَرٌ ﴿٥٤﴾

55. Verily, the righteous will be in the midst of Gardens and streams,[2917]

إِنَّ الْمُتَّقِينَ فِي جَنَّاتٍ وَنَهَرٍ ﴿٥٥﴾

56. In an eternal and honoured abode in the presence of the Omnipotent King.

فِي مَقْعَدِ صِدْقٍ عِندَ مَلِيكٍ مُّقْتَدِرٍ ﴿٥٦﴾ ع ٣ ١٥

[a]15 : 22; 25 : 3. [b]7 : 188; 16 : 78. [c]18 : 50; 45 : 30.

2913. The defeat at Badr was, indeed, a most formidable and calamitous misfortune for the Quraish. Their power and prestige sustained a crushing blow. Most of their leaders were killed and their dead bodies were dragged along and thrown into a pit. The Holy Prophet went up to its brink and, addressing the dead bodies is reported to have said, 'Have you found true what your Lord had promised you ? I have, indeed, found true what my Lord had promised me' (Bukhārī, *Kitāb al-Maghāzī*). The prophecy was fulfilled to the very letter.

2914. There is a determined measure for everything. It has an appointed time and place.

2915. The defeat of the Meccans at the battle-field of Badr came like a bolt from the blue, so sudden and swift it was and so complete and overwhelming. The glory of Kedar departed, as if in the twinkling of an eye.

2916. The smallest action of man, good or bad, produces its inevitable result according to the laws of cause and effect and its indelible impress is preserved.

2917. *Nahar*, besides the meaning given in the text, means, amplitude; light (Aqrab).

CHAPTER 55

AL-RAḤMĀN

(*Revealed before Hijrah*)

Date of Revelation and Context

Being the 6th of the special group of the *Sūrahs*, which begin with Qāf and end with Al-Wāqi'ah, and which were revealed, more or less at the same time at Mecca, in the early years of the Call, this *Sūrah* has close resemblance with other members of the group in the subject-matter, and deals like them with the basic principles of Islām—Divine attributes, particularly with God's Unity, with Resurrection and Revelation. In *Sūrah* Al-Qamar instances were given of the peoples of some Prophets of antiquity with whom the Arabs were quite familiar and who were punished for rejecting the Divine Message, and then the pagan Quraish were asked, would they not benefit from the sad fate of those peoples and accept the Quranic Message which was so easy to understand and to follow? The present *Sūrah* also gives the reasons why the Qur'ān was revealed.

Subject-Matter

The *Sūrah* opens with the Divine attribute—*Al-Raḥmān*, signifying that after having created the universe, God created man, the apex and crown of all creation, and that his creation was the result of God's *Raḥmāniyyah* (Beneficence). After man's creation God revealed Himself to him through His Prophets and Messengers, because he could not attain the sublime object of his creation and fulfil his high destiny without being guided to his great goal by Divine revelation. Prophethood found its most complete and perfect manifestation in the person of the Holy Prophet Muḥammad to whom God gave the Qur'ān, the last and final code of Divine Laws for the guidance of the whole of humanity for all time. But God's gifts to man did not end with his creation. He made the whole universe subservient to him. The heavens with all the celestial bodies, and the earth with all its treasures, the deep seas and high mountains, were all created for his sake. Over and above all that God endowed him with great intellectual and discretionary powers so that by sifting the right from the wrong he might follow Divine guidance and thus attain the object of his creation. But man seems to be so constituted that, instead of benefiting from the endless vistas of spiritual progress and development opened up to him by the Gracious, Beneficent and Merciful Providence, in his conceit and arrogance he ignores and defies Divine Laws and consequently brings down upon himself God's displeasure. The disobedience and defiance of Divine Laws, the *Sūrah* hints, will assume a most heinous form in sometime to come (which seems to be the present time) and man will then be visited with such destructive and annihilating Divine punishment as he had not known before. But whereas punishment which will be meted out to the guilty and the iniquitous will be most grievous and frightful, the Divine favours which will be bestowed upon the righteous and the God-fearing in that age of Mammon-worship and hankering after pleasures of the flesh will also be beyond measure or count, and thus both Divine punishment and favours would show that whereas God is 'Swift at reckoning. He is also the Master of glory and honour.' The *Sūrah* seems to deal particularly with the time when the power and prestige of Western nations will be at their highest.

سُوۡرَةُ الرَّحۡمٰنِ مَكِّيَّةٌ

1. [a]In the name of Allāh, the Gracious, the Merciful.

بِسۡمِ اللّٰہِ الرَّحۡمٰنِ الرَّحِیۡمِ ﴿۱﴾

2. The Gracious *God.*

اَلرَّحۡمٰنُ ﴿۲﴾

3. He taught the Qur'ān.[2918]

عَلَّمَ الۡقُرۡاٰنَ ﴿۳﴾

4. [b]He created man,[2919]

خَلَقَ الۡاِنۡسَانَ ﴿۴﴾

5. *And* taught him plain speech.

عَلَّمَہُ الۡبَیَانَ ﴿۵﴾

6. [c]The sun and the moon *run their courses* according to a fixed reckoning.

اَلشَّمۡسُ وَ الۡقَمَرُ بِحُسۡبَانٍ ﴿۶﴾

7. And the stemless plants and the trees *humbly* submit *to His Will.*[2920]

وَّ النَّجۡمُ وَ الشَّجَرُ یَسۡجُدٰنِ ﴿۷﴾

8. And the heaven He has raised high and set up the [d]measure,[2921]

وَ السَّمَآءَ رَفَعَہَا وَ وَضَعَ الۡمِیۡزَانَ ﴿۸﴾

---

[a]1 : 1. [b]96 : 3. [c]6 : 97; 36 : 39-40. [d]42 : 18; 57 : 26.

2918. God revealed Himself through His Prophets and Messengers to whom He gave His Word. The Qur'ān constituted the culmination of Divine revelation. This revelation of God to man through His Word was not due to any good act on his part. It was a sheer Divine gift flowing from God's beneficence.

2919. The word, 'man,' besides its general connotation, may here signify 'the perfect man,' *i.e.*, the Holy Prophet, in whom Divine attributes found their most perfect and complete manifestation. The verse thus signifies that, out of beneficence, God created man in order that he may rise to the highest peaks of spiritual development and may reflect in his person Divine attributes.

2920. The verse, read along with the preceding one, shows that from the largest celestial body to the smallest stemless plant, all things are subject to certain laws, and they perform regularly, punctually and unerringly their allotted tasks. In the huge solar system which is but one of millions of such systems, every orb proceeds safely on its destined course and never deviates from it.

2921. The whole universe is subject to one uniform law and all its constituent parts unite to form a glorious harmony of structure and motion. If this harmony or equilibrium between different things is in the least disturbed, the whole universe would fall to pieces. But God has kept all the laws that regulate the world under His exclusive control, beyond the reach of man.

9. That you may not exceed the measure.[2922] — أَلَّا تَطْغَوْا فِي الْمِيزَانِ ﴿٩﴾

10. So weigh all things with justice and [a]fall not short of the measure. — وَأَقِيمُوا الْوَزْنَ بِالْقِسْطِ وَلَا تُخْسِرُوا الْمِيزَانَ ﴿١٠﴾

11. And He has set the earth for *His* creatures; — وَالْأَرْضَ وَضَعَهَا لِلْأَنَامِ ﴿١١﴾

12. Therein are *all kinds of* [b]fruit and palm-tree with sheaths, — فِيهَا فَاكِهَةٌ وَالنَّخْلُ ذَاتُ الْأَكْمَامِ ﴿١٢﴾

13. And grain with *its* husk and fragrant plants. — وَالْحَبُّ ذُو الْعَصْفِ وَالرَّيْحَانُ ﴿١٣﴾

14. Which, then, of the favours of your Lord will ye twain,[2923] *O men and jinn*, deny? — فَبِأَيِّ آلَاءِ رَبِّكُمَا تُكَذِّبَانِ ﴿١٤﴾

15. He created man of dry ringing clay *which is* [c]like baked[2924] pottery. — خَلَقَ الْإِنْسَانَ مِنْ صَلْصَالٍ كَالْفَخَّارِ ﴿١٥﴾

[a]11 : 85-86; 17 : 36; 26 : 182. [b]50 : 10-11. [c]15 : 27, 29.

2922. As there is an all-comprehensive harmony in the whole universe, so is man—the crown and object of creation—enjoined to maintain a just balance and to treat with equity and justice his fellow beings, giving everyone his due, and to avoid extremes and follow the golden mean in the discharge of his duties towards his Creator.

2923. The dual form in *Tukadhdhibān* may have been used for the two classes of jinn and men referred to in v. 34, or it may signify two classes of men, *viz*., believers and disbelievers, leaders and their followers, the rich and the poor, or the white and the coloured races. Or, the dual form may have been used to impart emphasis in order to denote the dignity of the commandment embodied in the various verses. Such dual form is generally used in the Arabic language. See also 50 : 25. The Holy Prophet is reported to have said that when this verse is recited the believers present should respond by uttering the words 'None of Thy favours, Our Lord, do we deny and for Thee is all praise' (Kathīr).

2924. After having mentioned the creation of the celestial firmament and the placing in it of the sun and the moon, followed by a mention of the spreading of the earth and of the vegetables that grow on it, the *Sūrah*, in this verse, refers to the coming into existence of man. Man's creation from dry ringing clay may signify that man has been created from matter in which the faculty and attribute of speech lies latent. As *Ṣalṣāl* emits a sound only when struck with something extraneous, the word is used here to hint that man's power to respond is subject to his being able to receive the Divine Call. Three words have been used in the Qur'ān to express the different stages of the creation and spiritual development of man. The first stage is expressed by the words, 'God created him out of dust' (3 : 60). The second stage is described by the expression, 'He created you from clay' (6 : 3), which means that after having received a sprinkling of Divine Word man attained the power of discrimination by which he could distinguish between right and wrong. At the third stage, which is called the stage of "baked pottery," man is tested and tried and is made to pass through the fire of trials and tribulations. It is after he has successfully passed all the tests and has attained spiritual maturity that he is received into Divine Presence.

16. [a]And the jinn He created of the flame of Fire.[2925]

وَخَلَقَ الْجَآنَّ مِنْ مَّارِجٍ مِّنْ نَّارٍ ﴿١٦﴾

17. Which, then, of the favours of your Lord will ye twain deny ?

فَبِاَيِّ اٰلَآءِ رَبِّكُمَا تُكَذِّبٰنِ ﴿١٧﴾

18. [b]The Lord of the two Easts and the Lord of the two Wests.[2926]

رَبُّ الْمَشْرِقَيْنِ وَرَبُّ الْمَغْرِبَيْنِ ﴿١٨﴾

19. Which, then, of the favours of your Lord will ye twain deny ?

فَبِاَيِّ اٰلَآءِ رَبِّكُمَا تُكَذِّبٰنِ ﴿١٩﴾

20. He has made the two bodies of water flow. They will *one day* meet ;[2927]

مَرَجَ الْبَحْرَيْنِ يَلْتَقِيٰنِ ﴿٢٠﴾

21. Between them there is *at present* a [c]barrier; they cannot encroach one upon the other.

بَيْنَهُمَا بَرْزَخٌ لَّا يَبْغِيٰنِ ﴿٢١﴾

22. Which, then, of the favours of your Lord will ye twain deny ?

فَبِاَيِّ اٰلَآءِ رَبِّكُمَا تُكَذِّبٰنِ ﴿٢٢﴾

23. There come out from both of them pearls and coral.[2928]

يَخْرُجُ مِنْهُمَا اللُّؤْلُؤُ وَالْمَرْجَانُ ﴿٢٣﴾

24. Which, then, of the favours of your Lord will ye twain deny ?

فَبِاَيِّ اٰلَآءِ رَبِّكُمَا تُكَذِّبٰنِ ﴿٢٤﴾

---

[a]7 : 13; 15 : 28; 38 : 77. [b]2 : 116; 26 : 29. [c]25 : 54; 27 : 62.

2925. See 15 : 28.

2926. Every spot on earth, in relation to other spots, is an East and a West. This phenomenon is described as the two Easts and the two Wests. Moreover, the earth being round, the East of the Eastern Hemisphere is the West of the Western Hemisphere and the West of the Western Hemisphere is the East of the Eastern Hemisphere, and thus there are two Easts and two Wests. In the modern political parlance the two Easts may be the Near East and the Far East, and the two Wests, Europe and America. The verse seems to signify that, God being the Lord of the whole world, the light of the Qur'ān will first spread in the East and then will illumine the West, and thus the 'whole earth will shine with the light of her Lord' (39 : 70).

2927. 'The two bodies of water' may be the Red Sea and the Mediterranean Sea, or the Atlantic Ocean and the Pacific Ocean, particularly the former two seas. The verse embodies a great prophecy which was remarkably fulfilled by the construction of the Suez and the Panama canals, the former linking the first two seas and the latter the mighty Atlantic and Pacific Oceans. The world had to wait for thirteen long centuries to see the fulfilment of this prophecy. Or, 'the two bodies of water' may signify the physical and spiritual sciences. Or, the natural laws and Divine revelation, which mistakenly considered to be mutually antagonistic, are corroborative of each other, the one being the Work of God and the other His Word.

2928. Curiously enough pearls and coral are found in both the Suez and Panama canals.

25. And His are the lofty ^aships reared aloft on the sea like mountains.[2929]

وَلَهُ الْجَوَارِ الْمُنْشَئَاتُ فِي الْبَحْرِ كَالْأَعْلَامِ ۝

26. Which, then, of the favours of your Lord will ye twain deny ?

فَبِأَيِّ آلَاءِ رَبِّكُمَا تُكَذِّبَانِ ۝

R. 2   27. ^bAll that is on *earth* will pass away ;[2930]

كُلُّ مَنْ عَلَيْهَا فَانٍ ۝

28. And there will abide for ever *only* the Person[2931] of thy Lord, Master of Glory and Honour.

وَيَبْقَى وَجْهُ رَبِّكَ ذُو الْجَلَالِ وَالْإِكْرَامِ ۝

29. Which, then, of the favours of your Lord will ye twain deny ?

فَبِأَيِّ آلَاءِ رَبِّكُمَا تُكَذِّبَانِ ۝

30. Of Him do beg all that are in the heavens and the earth. Every day He *reveals Himself* in a different state.[2932]

يَسْأَلُهُ مَنْ فِي السَّمَوَاتِ وَالْأَرْضِ كُلَّ يَوْمٍ هُوَ فِي شَأْنٍ ۝

31. Which, then, of the favours of your Lord will ye twain deny ?

فَبِأَيِّ آلَاءِ رَبِّكُمَا تُكَذِّبَانِ ۝

---

^a42 : 33.   ^b28 : 89.

2929. The reference seems to be to modern "leviathans," which ride the seas like mountains. The *Sūrah* may be dealing with the progress and prosperity of the Western nations which are the result of their making proper use of the great sea-routes for extending their commerce and trade.

2930. The whole universe is subject to decay and death and eventually is destined to perish. God alone will abide because He is Self-Subsisting, All-Sustaining, Independent and Besought of all.

2931. *Wajh*, among other things, means, that which is under one's care, or, 'to which one directs one's attention (28 : 89); the thing itself; favour; countenance (Aqrab). Since the earth will be reduced to nothing and heavenly bodies all brought to naught and the whole material universe made non-existent, still human reason demands that there should be a Being Who should never die nor be subject to change or decay. Such a Being is God Who created the whole universe and Who is the First and Final Cause of all things. The present and the previous verses point to two immutable laws of nature which work simultaneously, *viz.*, (1) everything is subject to decline, decadence and death; and (2) compliance with Divine laws ensures continuity of life.

2932. All creatures depend for their life and sustenance on God Who is their Creator, Sustainer and Nourisher. His attributes know no limit or count, and they keep finding their manifestation in diverse ways all the time.

32. Soon shall We attend to you, O ye two big *groups!*[2933]

سَنَفْرُغُ لَكُمْ اَيُّهَ الثَّقَلٰنِ ﴿٣٢﴾

33. Which, then, of the favours of your Lord will ye twain deny?

فَبِاَيِّ اٰلَآءِ رَبِّكُمَا تُكَذِّبٰنِ ﴿٣٣﴾

34. O company of jinn and men! if you have power to break through the confines of the heavens and the earth, then break *through them.* But you cannot break[2934] through save with authority.

يٰمَعْشَرَ الْجِنِّ وَ الْاِنْسِ اِنِ اسْتَطَعْتُمْ اَنْ تَنْفُذُوْا مِنْ اَقْطَارِ السَّمٰوٰتِ وَ الْاَرْضِ فَانْفُذُوْا ؕ لَا تَنْفُذُوْنَ اِلَّا بِسُلْطٰنٍ ﴿٣٤﴾

35. Which, then, of the favours of your Lord will ye twain deny?

فَبِاَيِّ اٰلَآءِ رَبِّكُمَا تُكَذِّبٰنِ ﴿٣٥﴾

36. There shall be sent against you a flame of fire, and molten copper;[2935] and you shall not be able to help yourselves.

يُرْسَلُ عَلَيْكُمَا شُوَاظٌ مِّنْ نَّارٍ ۬ۙ وَّ نُحَاسٌ فَلَا تَنْتَصِرٰنِ ﴿٣٦﴾

37. Which, then, of the favours of your Lord will ye twain deny?

فَبِاَيِّ اٰلَآءِ رَبِّكُمَا تُكَذِّبٰنِ ﴿٣٧﴾

2933. *Al-Thaqalān* meaning two weighty things (Lane), may signify "the men" and "the jinn" as the context shows, or the Arabs and the non-Arabs, or in the present political parlance the two main blocs—Russia or China and their allies on one side and the United States of America and its allies on the other; or the word may signify the Capitalist and the Labour classes. From the way in which these two great blocs are behaving, it seems that any day they may become locked into mortal conflict, completely destroying man's accumulated labour of centuries, spent in developing arts and sciences, and may render life on earth almost extinct. The verse seems to embody a warning to that effect.

2934. The verse has been variously interpreted. According to one interpretation the scientists and philosophers, who are proud of the great advance they have made in the material sciences, have been told that they cannot, however great advance they might make in knowledge and science, so completely comprehend all the laws of nature governing the universe as to acquire their complete mastery. Try as they might, they will fail in their quest. According to another interpretation, the verse warns sinners : 'Let them dare break through the confines of the heavens and earth, they shall not be able to defy Divine laws with impunity and escape Divine punishment. The verse may also point to the making of rockets, sputniks, etc., by means of which the Russians and the Americans are seeking to reach heavenly bodies. They are told that at best they may reach only some of the planets which are nearest to the earth, but God's universe is unfathomable.

2935. The verse points to the most destructive and dreadful punishment which might overtake the two hostile camps. The world seems to stand on the brink of a terrible conflagration which threatens to consume in its flames the entire human civilization.

38. [a]And when the heaven is rent asunder and becomes red like red hide.[2936]

فَاِذَا انْشَقَّتِ السَّمَآءُ فَكَانَتْ وَرْدَةً كَالدِّهَانِ ﴿۳۸﴾

39. Which, then, of the favours of your Lord will ye twain deny?

فَبِاَيِّ اٰلَآءِ رَبِّكُمَا تُكَذِّبٰنِ ﴿۳۹﴾

40. On that day neither man nor jinn will be asked about his sin.[2937]

فَيَوْمَئِذٍ لَّا يُسْـَٔلُ عَنْ ذَنْۢبِهٖۤ اِنْسٌ وَّلَا جَآنٌّ ﴿۴۰﴾

41. Which, then, of the favours of your Lord will ye twain deny?

فَبِاَيِّ اٰلَآءِ رَبِّكُمَا تُكَذِّبٰنِ ﴿۴۱﴾

42. The guilty will be known by their marks, and they will be seized by their forelocks and their feet.

يُعْرَفُ الْمُجْرِمُوْنَ بِسِيْمٰهُمْ فَيُؤْخَذُ بِالنَّوَاصِيْ وَ
الْاَقْدَامِ ﴿۴۲﴾

43. Which, then, of the favours of your Lord will ye twain deny?

فَبِاَيِّ اٰلَآءِ رَبِّكُمَا تُكَذِّبٰنِ ﴿۴۳﴾

44. [b]*And they will be told*: 'This is the Hell which the guilty deny,

هٰذِهٖ جَهَنَّمُ الَّتِيْ يُكَذِّبُ بِهَا الْمُجْرِمُوْنَ ﴿۴۴﴾

45. 'Between it and the fierce boiling water[2938] will they go round.'

يَطُوْفُوْنَ بَيْنَهَا وَبَيْنَ حَمِيْمٍ اٰنٍ ﴿۴۵﴾

46. Which, then, of the favours of your Lord will ye twain deny?

فَبِاَيِّ اٰلَآءِ رَبِّكُمَا تُكَذِّبٰنِ ﴿۴۶﴾

[a]69 : 17; 84 : 2. [b]52 : 15.

2936. What a graphic picture of the threatened punishment!

2937. The misdeeds of the guilty will be writ large on their faces so that they will not be asked whether or not they had committed them. As mentioned elsewhere in the Qur'ān (41 : 21), the very organs of the bodies of disbelievers will bear witness against them.

2938. The foregoing few verses together with the present one seem to point to the state of restlessness which will seize mankind when the two blocs referred to above are pitted against each other and the fear of atomic war will, like the Sword of Democles, hang over their heads. The present international groupings and tensions are bound to lead to an armed conflict of un-paralleled destructiveness. The conflict itself would be a veritable Hell; but preparations for it have brought about conditions which are not far removed from perpetual torment of one kind or other.

R. 3 47. And for him who fears to stand before his Lord there are two gardens[2939]—

وَلِمَنْ خَافَ مَقَامَ رَبِّهٖ جَنَّتٰنِ ﴿٤٧﴾

48. Which, then, of the favours of your Lord will ye twain deny?

فَبِاَيِّ اٰلَآءِ رَبِّكُمَا تُكَذِّبٰنِ ﴿٤٨﴾

49. Having many varieties[2940] *of trees*.

ذَوَاتَآ اَفْنَانٍ ﴿٤٩﴾

50. Which, then, of the favours of your Lord will ye twain deny?

فَبِاَيِّ اٰلَآءِ رَبِّكُمَا تُكَذِّبٰنِ ﴿٥٠﴾

51. In each of them there are two fountains[2941] flowing *freely*.

فِيْهِمَا عَيْنٰنِ تَجْرِيٰنِ ﴿٥١﴾

52. Which, then, of the favours of your Lord will ye twain deny?

فَبِاَيِّ اٰلَآءِ رَبِّكُمَا تُكَذِّبٰنِ ﴿٥٢﴾

53. Therein will be [a]every *kind of* fruit in pairs.[2942]

فِيْهِمَا مِنْ كُلِّ فَاكِهَةٍ زَوْجٰنِ ﴿٥٣﴾

54. Which, then, of the favours of your Lord will ye twain deny?

فَبِاَيِّ اٰلَآءِ رَبِّكُمَا تُكَذِّبٰنِ ﴿٥٤﴾

---

[a]44 : 56; 52 : 23; 56 : 21.

2939. The "two gardens" may signify, (1) peace of mind which is the result of leading a good life, and (2) freedom from gnawing cares and anxieties which come in the wake of life spent in the pursuit of material pleasures and comforts. One "garden" consists in giving up one's desires for the sake of God in this world and the other in being blessed with God's pleasure in the next. A true believer perpetually basks in the sun of God's grace in this life which cares cannot disturb. This is Paradise upon earth which is granted to a God-fearing man and in which he constantly dwells; the promised heaven in the next world is only an image of the present Paradise, being an embodiment of the spiritual blessings which such a one enjoys in this life. It is to this paradisiacal state of a true believer that the Qur'ān refers in 10 : 65 and 41 : 32 The "two gardens" may also be the two fertile valleys watered by two sets of rivers—Jaihān and Saihān; and Furāt and Nīl, which according to the Ḥadīth are the rivers of Paradise (Muslim). These two valleys fell into the hands of Muslims in the caliphate of 'Umar.

2940. Just as in the present life true believers undergo various kinds of tribulations for the sake of their Lord and do all sorts of good and righteous deeds, so in the next life those tribulations and good works will assume the form of flowers and fruits of various hues and tastes.

2941. The *two fountains flowing freely* may be the spiritual embodiments of *Ḥuqūq Allāh* (the obligations owed to God) and *Ḥuqūq al-'Ibād* (the obligations a Muslim owes to his fellow-beings) which the believers fully and faithfully discharge in this life. The discharge of these two obligations would assume the form of two fountains in the Hereafter. As a true believer ceaselessly continues to discharge these obligations, the fountains have been depicted as constantly flowing.

2942. Again the word "pairs" may metaphorically represent two kinds of righteous works of the believers—(1) those they do for their own spiritual advancement and (2) those services which they render to their fellow-beings.

55. *The inmates thereof* will [a]recline *on couches* over carpets, the linings of which will be of thick brocade. And the fruit of the two Gardens[2943] will be within *their easy* reach.

مُتَّكِـِٔيْنَ عَلٰى فُرُشٍۭ بَطَآئِنُهَا مِنْ اِسْتَبْرَقٍ ؕ وَ جَنَا الْجَنَّتَيْنِ دَانٍ ﴿۵۵﴾

56. Which, then, of the favours of your Lord will ye twain deny?

فَبِاَيِّ اٰلَآءِ رَبِّكُمَا تُكَذِّبٰنِ ﴿۵۶﴾

57. Therein will *also* be *chaste maidens* [b]restraining their glances,[2944] whom neither man nor jinn will have touched[2945] before them—

فِيْهِنَّ قٰصِرٰتُ الطَّرْفِ ۙ لَمْ يَطْمِثْهُنَّ اِنْسٌ قَبْلَهُمْ وَلَا جَآنٌّ ﴿۵۷﴾

58. Which, then, of the favours of your Lord will ye twain deny?

فَبِاَيِّ اٰلَآءِ رَبِّكُمَا تُكَذِّبٰنِ ﴿۵۸﴾

59. As if they were rubies and small [c]pearls;[2946].

كَاَنَّهُنَّ الْيَاقُوْتُ وَالْمَرْجَانُ ﴿۵۹﴾

60. Which, then, of the favours of your Lord will ye twain deny?

فَبِاَيِّ اٰلَآءِ رَبِّكُمَا تُكَذِّبٰنِ ﴿۶۰﴾

61. Is the reward of goodness anything but[2947] goodness?

هَلْ جَزَآءُ الْاِحْسَانِ اِلَّا الْاِحْسَانُ ﴿۶۱﴾

[a]38 : 52. [b]37 : 49; 38 : 53 [c]56 : 24.

2943. Three times the words "two gardens" have been used in this *Sūrah*. This is to emphasize that apart from the great blessings and boons of Paradise in the next world, believers will have all the good things of this world also.

2944. The expression, 'restraining their glances,' signifies that their whole attention would be devoted to God and they would not even cast a look at any other thing besides their Lord and Creator.

2945. Far from their bodies being touched by any man, even impure thoughts will not have found access to their hearts, the word *jinn* also signifying those invisible things that excite carnal passions in the mind. It is relevant to state here again that according to Islamic conception the blessings of Paradise would resemble the pleasures of the life on earth. There will be palaces, gardens, rivers, trees, fruits, wives, children, friends, etc., in Paradise, only the nature of these things will be different from that of the things of this world. In fact, they will be the spiritual representations of the good deeds the righteous will have done in this life.

2946. Whereas in v. 57 purity of mind and heart of the consorts of believers in Paradise has been mentioned, the verse under comment speaks of the beauty of their persons.

2947. *Iḥsān* means to worship God as if the worshipper is seeing Him, or at least God is seeing the worshipper (Bukhārī). This means that in all his deeds and actions God is constantly before the eyes of a believer and as a reward he receives God's pleasure—the sum total of all the blessings of Heaven.

62. Which, then, of the favours of your Lord will ye twain deny?

فَبِاَيِّ اٰلَاۗءِ رَبِّكُمَا تُكَذِّبٰنِ ﴿۶۲﴾

63. And besides these two, there are two[2948] *other* gardens—

وَمِنْ دُوْنِهِمَا جَنَّتٰنِ ﴿۶۳﴾

64. Which, then, of the favours of your Lord will ye twain deny?

فَبِاَيِّ اٰلَاۗءِ رَبِّكُمَا تُكَذِّبٰنِ ﴿۶۴﴾

65. Dark green with foliage[2949]—

مُدْهَاۗمَّتٰنِ ﴿۶۵﴾

66. Which, then, of the favours of your Lord will ye twain deny?

فَبِاَيِّ اٰلَاۗءِ رَبِّكُمَا تُكَذِّبٰنِ ﴿۶۶﴾

67. Therein also will be two springs,[2950] gushing forth *with water.*

فِيْهِمَا عَيْنٰنِ نَضَّاخَتٰنِ ﴿۶۷﴾

68. Which, then, of the favours of your Lord will ye twain deny?

فَبِاَيِّ اٰلَاۗءِ رَبِّكُمَا تُكَذِّبٰنِ ﴿۶۸﴾

69. [a]In both of them there will be *all kinds of* fruit, and dates and pomegranates.

فِيْهِمَا فَاكِهَةٌ وَّنَخْلٌ وَّرُمَّانٌ ﴿۶۹﴾

70. Which, then, of the favours of your Lord will ye twain deny?

فَبِاَيِّ اٰلَاۗءِ رَبِّكُمَا تُكَذِّبٰنِ ﴿۷۰﴾

[a]36 : 58; 38 : 52; 43 : 74.

2948. The "two gardens" mentioned in v. 47, may be the gardens of Paradise, and the "two gardens" referred to in this verse may be the gardens of this world. The Muslims were promised gardens in the next world and as a proof of the fulfilment of this Divine promise they were also promised the gardens of this world which indeed they came to possess when they conquered the fertile vallies of Egypt and Iraq. But the description of the "two gardens" mentioned in v. 47 is different from that in the present verse. This shows that two categories of believers have been mentioned in this *Sūrah*. The believers to whom "gardens" mentioned in v. 47 have been promised seem to be of a higher spiritual status than those to whom "gardens" mentioned in the verse under comment have been promised. A careful study of the relevant verses brings out this fact. These two classes of believers have been mentioned in the next *Sūrah* in vv. 11 and 28 respectively.

2949. Whereas in v. 49 above the "gardens" are described as having many varieties of trees which points to the vast variety of the good works of the believers to whom they are promised, the "gardens" mentioned in the verse under comment are described as "dark green with foliage" which indicates the intensity of the goodness of their works.

2950. In the present verse and in v. 51 above, two different descriptions of the fountains and springs promised to believers have been given. In v. 51 the fountains promised are described as flowing freely and ceaselessly (*Tajriyāni*). This signifies that believers to whom springs mentioned in that verse have been promised are of a higher spiritual status than the believers to whom springs mentioned in the present verse have been promised, since the believers of former category are engaged in doing good to others ceaselessly and freely without any idea or expectation of reward while those of the latter class do good works out of natural impulse but their doing of good is mainly confined to themselves. The qualifying word used is *Naḍḍākhatān* (gushing forth).

71. Therein will be *maidens*, good *and* beautiful.[2951]—

فِيْهِنَّ خَيْرٰتٌ حِسَانٌ ﴿٧١﴾

72. Which, then, of the favours of your Lord will ye twain deny?—

فَبِاَيِّ اٰلَآءِ رَبِّكُمَا تُكَذِّبٰنِ ﴿٧٢﴾

73. Fair maidens with lovely black eyes, guarded in[2952] pavilions—

حُوْرٌ مَّقْصُوْرٰتٌ فِي الْخِيَامِ ﴿٧٣﴾

74. Which, then, of the favours of your Lord will ye twain deny?—

فَبِاَيِّ اٰلَآءِ رَبِّكُمَا تُكَذِّبٰنِ ﴿٧٤﴾

75. Whom neither man nor jinn will have touched before them—

لَمْ يَطْمِثْهُنَّ اِنْسٌ قَبْلَهُمْ وَلَا جَآنٌّ ﴿٧٥﴾

76. Which, then, of the favours of your Lord will ye twain deny?—

فَبِاَيِّ اٰلَآءِ رَبِّكُمَا تُكَذِّبٰنِ ﴿٧٦﴾

77. [a]Reclining on green cushions and beautiful carpets.[2953]

مُتَّكِـِٕيْنَ عَلٰى رَفْرَفٍ خُضْرٍ وَّعَبْقَرِيٍّ حِسَانٍ ﴿٧٧﴾

78. Which, then, of the favours of your Lord will ye twain deny?[2954]

فَبِاَيِّ اٰلَآءِ رَبِّكُمَا تُكَذِّبٰنِ ﴿٧٨﴾

79. Blessed is the name of thy Lord, Master of glory and honour.

تَبٰرَكَ اسْمُ رَبِّكَ ذِي الْجَلٰلِ وَالْاِكْرَامِ ﴿٧٩﴾

---

[a]55 : 55.

2851. As compared with the words "good and beautiful" used with regard to the maidens in the present verse which possess only a general connotation, the words "rubies and small pearls" used in v. 59 have a particular significance and are expressive of beauty of special excellence.

2952. The words 'restraining their glances' in v. 57 evidently are expressive of chastity and modesty of a higher degree than the expression "guarded in pavilions" in the verse under comment.

2953. Again the words used in v. 55 about believers show that they possess greater dignity, respect and authority than those to whom the present verse refers. With this verse the comparison between these two categories of believers specifically mentioned in the next *Sūrah, i.e.*, "the foremost" (56 : 11) and "those on the right hand" (56 : 28) comes to an end.

2954. It is not without significance that this verse has been used as many as 31 times in the present *Sūrah*. The *Sūrah* seems particularly to refer to the great favours and blessings which God has bestowed upon man. In view of these multifarious and multitudinous favours, the repeated use of the verse seems quite appropriate. But then the *Sūrah* also speaks of the unprecedentedly destructive Divine punishment in the form of atomic wars which will overtake man if he does not repent and mend his ways. This fore-warning of an imminent danger also constitutes a blessing in disguise.

CHAPTER 56

AL-WĀQI'AH

(*Revealed before Hijrah*)

Date of Revelation and Context

This is the last of the group of seven Chapters which begin with *Sūrah* Qāf. These seven Chapters were revealed at Mecca, more or less at the same time, in the early years of the Holy Prophet's ministry. Naturally, therefore, they are very much similar in tone and tenor; but in no other case perhaps, is this similarity so marked as it is between this *Sūrah* and its predecessor, *Sūrah* Al-Raḥmān. The subject in *Sūrah* Al-Raḥmān is completed in this *Sūrah* and thus it forms a befitting sequel to *Sūrah* Al-Raḥmān. In *Sūrah* Al-Raḥmān, for instance, three groups of people — (*a*) those fortunate ones who are granted special nearness to God, (*b*) the general body of believers who have achieved Divine pleasure, and (*c*) the rejectors of Divine Messengers—were referred to only by implication. In the present *Sūrah*, however, they have been expressly mentioned. The *Sūrah* dealing particularly with the important subjects of the Resurrection, Revelation and the repudiation of idolatry, was quite appropriately revealed early at Mecca where the preaching of the Quranic Message was directed exclusively to the idolatrous Quraish, who believed neither in Resurrection nor in Revelation. The seven Chapters also contain certain prophecies about the great and glorious future of Islām, side by side with direct and emphatic mention of the inevitability of the Resurrection, thus drawing attention to the inescapable conclusion that the fulfilment of those prophecies about the progress of Islām would prove that the Resurrection was also an undeniable fact.

Subject-Matter

The *Sūrah* opens with a firm and emphatic declaration that the great and Inevitable Event, which was foretold in the preceding *Sūrah*, will most surely come to pass, and when it came to pass it will shake the earth to its depths, and the mountains shall be shattered, causing a new world to emerge from the ashes of the old. Further, as a result of this Great Event people will become sorted out into three groups: (*a*) The fortunate ones who will enjoy God's special nearness, (*b*) the true and righteous believers who will receive handsome rewards for their good deeds and (*c*) the unfortunate disbelievers who will be punished for their evil deeds. The *Sūrah* then gives a graphic description of the Divine blessings and favours in store for the first two classes, following with a description of the punishment to be meted out to the deniers of the Divine Message. Next, it advances the usual argument of the creation of man and of his development from a seminal drop into a full-fledged human being, to prove his second birth after death. Towards its close the *Sūrah* reverts to the subject with which it had begun, and explains that the great reformation to which it refers in its opening verses will be brought about by the Qur'ān which is indubitably the revealed Word of God, and which is protected and guarded like a precious treasure. The *Sūrah* closes with a beautiful homily that when the inevitable end of all life is death, from which there is no escape, then why should people be neglectful of this hard fact and consign God to oblivion?

آیاتها ۹۷ ‏(۵۶) سُوۡرَۃُ الۡوَاقِعَۃِ مَکِّیَّۃٌ رکوعاتها ۳

1. [a]In the name of Allāh, the Gracious, the Merciful.[2955]
بِسۡمِ اللّٰہِ الرَّحۡمٰنِ الرَّحِیۡمِ ﴿۱﴾

2. When [b]the Inevitable Event[2956] comes to pass—
اِذَا وَقَعَتِ الۡوَاقِعَۃُ ﴿۲﴾

3. There is [c]no denying its coming to pass—
لَیۡسَ لِوَقۡعَتِہَا کَاذِبَۃٌ ﴿۳﴾

4. *Some* it will bring low, *others* it will exalt.[2957]
خَافِضَۃٌ رَّافِعَۃٌ ﴿۴﴾

5. [d]When the earth will be shaken *with* a *terrible* [d]shaking;[2958]
اِذَا رُجَّتِ الۡاَرۡضُ رَجًّا ﴿۵﴾

6. And the mountains will be shattered—a *complete* [e]shattering.
وَّ بُسَّتِ الۡجِبَالُ بَسًّا ﴿۶﴾

7. *They* shall *all* become like dust particles scattered about.
فَکَانَتۡ ہَبَآءً مُّنۡۢبَثًّا ﴿۷﴾

8. And you shall be *divided into* three groups:
وَّ کُنۡتُمۡ اَزۡوَاجًا ثَلٰثَۃً ﴿۸﴾

9. Those on the right hand—how *lucky* are those on the right hand![2959]
فَاَصۡحٰبُ الۡمَیۡمَنَۃِ ۬ۙ مَاۤ اَصۡحٰبُ الۡمَیۡمَنَۃِ ﴿۹﴾

10. And those on the left hand—how *unlucky* are those on the left hand![2960]
وَ اَصۡحٰبُ الۡمَشۡـَٔمَۃِ ۬ۙ مَاۤ اَصۡحٰبُ الۡمَشۡـَٔمَۃِ ﴿۱۰﴾

---

[a]1 : 1. [b]52 : 8. [c]52 : 9; 70 : 3. [d]50 : 45; 99 : 2. [e]20 : 106; 70 : 10: 101 : 6.

2955. See 4.

2956. (*a*) The Final Resurrection; (*b*) total annihilation of idolatry from Arabia and complete defeat and discomfiture of the idolatrous Quraish; (*c*) appearance of a great religious Reformer—the Holy Prophet.

2957. The "Inevitable Event" will bring about a great revolution in the lives of men. A new world will come into being; the high and the mighty will be laid low and the oppressed and down-trodden will be exalted.

2958. The whole of Arabia will be shaken to its foundations. Old beliefs, ideas, moral values, customs, ways of life etc., will undergo a complete change. In fact, the old order will die, giving place to a completely new one. The verse along with the one preceding it and those that follow it may equally apply to the Resurrection after death.

2959. Elsewhere (75 : 3) the Qur'ān applies the term "self-accusing soul" to this group of believers.

2960. The soul prone to evil (12 : 54).

11. And the foremost;[2961] they are *truly* the foremost;

وَالسّٰبِقُوْنَ السّٰبِقُوْنَ ﴿۱۱﴾

12. They will be *those* near *to God;*

اُولٰٓئِكَ الْمُقَرَّبُوْنَ ﴿۱۲﴾

13. *And will be* in the Gardens of Bliss—

فِيْ جَنّٰتِ النَّعِيْمِ ﴿۱۳﴾

14. A large party from among the first *believers,*

ثُلَّةٌ مِّنَ الْاَوَّلِيْنَ ﴿۱۴﴾

15. And a few from among the later ones,

وَقَلِيْلٌ مِّنَ الْاٰخِرِيْنَ ﴿۱۵﴾

16. *Seated* on couches inwrought *with gold and jewels,*[2962]

عَلٰى سُرُرٍ مَّوْضُوْنَةٍ ﴿۱۶﴾

17. [a]Reclining thereon, facing each other.

مُّتَّكِئِيْنَ عَلَيْهَا مُتَقٰبِلِيْنَ ﴿۱۷﴾

18. [b]There will wait on them youths who will not age,[2963]

يَطُوْفُ عَلَيْهِمْ وِلْدَانٌ مُّخَلَّدُوْنَ ﴿۱۸﴾

19. *Carrying* [c]goblets and ewers and cups *filled* out of a flowing spring—

بِاَكْوَابٍ وَّاَبَارِيْقَ وَكَاْسٍ مِّنْ مَّعِيْنٍ ﴿۱۹﴾

20. No headache will they get therefrom, [d]nor will they be intoxicated—

لَّا يُصَدَّعُوْنَ عَنْهَا وَلَا يُنْزِفُوْنَ ﴿۲۰﴾

21. And *carrying* [e]such fruits as they choose,

وَفَاكِهَةٍ مِّمَّا يَتَخَيَّرُوْنَ ﴿۲۱﴾

22. And flesh of birds as they may desire.

وَلَحْمِ طَيْرٍ مِّمَّا يَشْتَهُوْنَ ﴿۲۲﴾

---

[a]37 : 45; 55 : 55; 76 : 14. [b]76 : 20. [c]43 : 72; 76 : 16. [d]37 : 48. [e]52 : 23.

2961. The soul at rest (89 : 28).

2962. The blessings of Paradise to be bestowed upon *al-Sābiqūn* (those lucky believers who will be favoured with special Divine nearness, mentioned in vv. 11-27 of the present *Sūrah*), closely resemble those Divine gifts which have been mentioned in vv. 47-62 of *Sūrah* Al-Raḥmān. This shows that the believers referred to in vv. 47-62 of *Sūrah* Al-Raḥmān are of the class of *Al-Sābiqūn* (those who have been granted special nearness to God) of this *Sūrah*.

2963. The verse points to the innocence and perpetual freshness of the servants who will wait upon believers.

23. And *there will be* fair maidens with [a]wide, lovely eyes,

وَحُوْرٌ عِيْنٌ ﴿٢٣﴾

24. Like pearls, well-preserved,

كَاَمْثَالِ اللُّؤْلُؤِ الْمَكْنُوْنِ ﴿٢٤﴾

25. As a reward for what they did.

جَزَآءًۢ بِمَا كَانُوْا يَعْمَلُوْنَ ﴿٢٥﴾

26. They will not hear therein any vain or sinful [b]talk,

لَا يَسْمَعُوْنَ فِيْهَا لَغْوًا وَّلَا تَاْثِيْمًا ﴿٢٦﴾

27. Except *only* the word *of salutation*—'Peace, peace.'[2964]

اِلَّا قِيْلًا سَلٰمًا سَلٰمًا ﴿٢٧﴾

28. Those on the right hand—how lucky are those on the right hand !—

وَاَصْحٰبُ الْيَمِيْنِ ۙ مَآ اَصْحٰبُ الْيَمِيْنِ ﴿٢٨﴾

29. *They will be* amidst thornless lote-trees,[2965]

فِيْ سِدْرٍ مَّخْضُوْدٍ ﴿٢٩﴾

30. And clustered bananas,[2966]

وَّطَلْحٍ مَّنْضُوْدٍ ﴿٣٠﴾

31. And [c]extended shade,

وَّظِلٍّ مَّمْدُوْدٍ ﴿٣١﴾

32. And flowing water,

وَّمَآءٍ مَّسْكُوْبٍ ﴿٣٢﴾

33. And abundant fruit,

وَّفَاكِهَةٍ كَثِيْرَةٍ ﴿٣٣﴾

[a]44 : 55; 52 : 21. [b]19 : 63; 78 : 36; 88 : 12. [c]4 : 58; 13 : 36.

2964. This and the preceding verse, like many other verses of the Qur'ān, most effectively repudiate all those foolish notions about a sensual Paradise which ignorant and evil-minded carpers and critics of Islām pretend to find in it; and give an insight into its nature, essence and reality. The Heaven as conceived and promised to Muslims by the Qur'ān would be a place of spiritual bliss where no sin, vain or idle talk or lying will find access (78 : 36). All its blessings would find their culmination and consummation in peace—complete peace of the mind and soul than which there could be no greater blessing. The Paradise promised to a Muslim has been designated as the "abode of peace" in the Qur'ān (6 : 128); the highest stage of spiritual development to which a believer can rise is that of the "soul at peace" (89 : 28) and the greatest gift which the dwellers of Paradise will receive from God will be "peace" (36 : 59), because God Himself is the Author of peace (59 : 24). Such is the sublime Quranic conception of Paradise.

2965. When the shade of lote-tree becomes dense and crowded, it is very pleasant, and in the hot and dry climate of Arabia the tired and fatigued travellers take shelter and find rest under it. The word *Sidr* having been qualified by *Makhdūd* signifies that the trees of Paradise will not only give pleasant and plenteous shade but will also bend down on account of the abundance of their fruit, *i.e.*, the blessings of Paradise will both be pleasant and plentiful.

2966. Whereas lote-tree mentioned in the preceding verse grows in dry climate, bananas require plenty of water for their growth. The mentioning together of these two fruits signifies that the fruits of Paradise will not only be plentiful and delightful but will also be found in all climatic conditions.

34. Neither failing, nor forbidden.[2967]

لَّا مَقْطُوْعَةٍ وَّلَا مَمْنُوْعَةٍ ﴿٣٤﴾

35. And *they will have* noble spouses.[2967A]—

وَّفُرُشٍ مَّرْفُوْعَةٍ ﴿٣٥﴾

36. Verily, We have created them a *good* creation,

إِنَّآ أَنْشَأْنٰهُنَّ إِنْشَآءً ﴿٣٦﴾

37. And made them virgins,

فَجَعَلْنٰهُنَّ أَبْكَارًا ﴿٣٧﴾

38. Loving, [a]of equal age;[2968]

عُرُبًا أَتْرَابًا ﴿٣٨﴾

39. For those on the right hand.

لِّأَصْحٰبِ الْيَمِيْنِ ﴿٣٩﴾

R. 2 40. A large party from among the first *believers*.

ثُلَّةٌ مِّنَ الْأَوَّلِيْنَ ﴿٤٠﴾

41. And a large party from the later ones.

وَثُلَّةٌ مِّنَ الْآخِرِيْنَ ﴿٤١﴾

42. And those on the left hand —how *unlucky* are those on the left hand!—

وَأَصْحٰبُ الشِّمَالِ ۙ مَآ أَصْحٰبُ الشِّمَالِ ﴿٤٢﴾

43. *They will be* in the midst of scorching winds and scalding water,[2969]

فِيْ سَمُوْمٍ وَّحَمِيْمٍ ﴿٤٣﴾

44. And under the shadow of pitch-black smoke;

وَّظِلٍّ مِّنْ يَّحْمُوْمٍ ﴿٤٤﴾

---

[a]78 : 34.

2967. The blessings promised to the dwellers of Paradise in this and other *Sūrahs* of the Qur'ān possess the following qualities: (*a*) They will be abundant; (*b*) will be easily accessible and at the entire disposal of the believers; (*c*) will know no diminution or end; and (*d*) they will cause no discomfort or disease.

2967A. *Furush* (spouses) is the plural of *Firāsh* which means, a bed; a man's wife; a woman's husband (Lane). In order to complete their happiness and peace of mind, the believers will have for their companions pure, beautiful spouses of noble descent and high dignity.

2968. '*Urub* is the plural of '*Arub* which means, a woman who loves her husband passionately and is obedient to him (Lane). *Atrāb* is the plural of *Tirb*, which means, one equal in age; a peer; one having similar tastes, habits, views, etc. (Lane). A beautiful, chaste and faithful wife, having views and tastes and outlook on life similar to that of her husband, is the greatest Divine blessing a person possibly can have. There will be good and virtuous women in Paradise, says the Qur'ān, as there will be good and righteous men. It is good companionship that makes human life happy and complete.

2969. The disbelievers in the heat of their passions indulged in all sorts of evil activities. That heat of passions will take the form of hot water and scorching heat.

45. Neither cool nor wholesome.

لَا بَارِدٍ وَّلَا كَرِيْمٍ ﴿٤٥﴾

46. Before this they lived a life of ease and plenty,

اِنَّهُمْ كَانُوْا قَبْلَ ذٰلِكَ مُتْرَفِيْنَ ﴿٤٦﴾

47. And persisted in extreme sinfulness

وَكَانُوْا يُصِرُّوْنَ عَلَى الْحِنْثِ الْعَظِيْمِ ﴿٤٧﴾

48. And they were wont to say, 'What! when we are dead and have become dust and bones, shall we, indeed, [a]be raised again,[2970]

وَكَانُوْا يَقُوْلُوْنَ اَئِذَا مِتْنَا وَكُنَّا تُرَابًا وَّ
عِظَامًا ءَاِنَّا لَمَبْعُوْثُوْنَ ﴿٤٨﴾

49. [b]'And our fathers of yore *too?*'

اَوَ اٰبَآؤُنَا الْاَوَّلُوْنَ ﴿٤٩﴾

50. Say, '*Yes,* the earlier ones and the later ones

قُلْ اِنَّ الْاَوَّلِيْنَ وَالْاٰخِرِيْنَ ﴿٥٠﴾

51. 'Will *all* be gathered together unto the fixed time of an appointed day.

لَمَجْمُوْعُوْنَ اِلٰى مِيْقَاتِ يَوْمٍ مَّعْلُوْمٍ ﴿٥١﴾

52. 'Then, O ye that have gone astray and have rejected *the truth,*

ثُمَّ اِنَّكُمْ اَيُّهَا الضَّآلُّوْنَ الْمُكَذِّبُوْنَ ﴿٥٢﴾

53. 'You will, surely, eat of the tree of [c]Zaqqūm,

لَاٰكِلُوْنَ مِنْ شَجَرٍ مِّنْ زَقُّوْمٍ ﴿٥٣﴾

54. [d]'And will fill *your* bellies therewith,

فَمَالِـُٔوْنَ مِنْهَا الْبُطُوْنَ ﴿٥٤﴾

55. 'And will drink boiling water, on *top of* that,

فَشٰرِبُوْنَ عَلَيْهِ مِنَ الْحَمِيْمِ ﴿٥٥﴾

56. 'Drinking as the insatiably thirsty camels drink.'[2971]

فَشٰرِبُوْنَ شُرْبَ الْهِيْمِ ﴿٥٦﴾

---

[a]17 : 50; 23 : 83; 37 : 17; 56 : 48. [b]37 : 18. [c]37 : 63; 44 : 44-45. [d]37 : 67.

2970. Denial of Resurrection and the Hereafter, whether by word of mouth or conduct, is at the root of all sin and crime in the world. There can be no real and effective check on sin, or incentive to good works, without a true and real belief in the Life after death.

2971. This and the preceding verses describe the punishment that will be meted out to the guilty in the after-life in a language which suits the enormity of their sins in the present life. They devoured what other people had earned with the sweat of their brows and suffered from an insatiable lust for wealth, amassing it by fair means and foul and, being proud of it, rejected the Divine Message. As a punishment, they will be given the tree of *Zaqqūm* to eat, which will burn their inside, and they will have scalding water to quench their thirst, and like sick thirsty camels their thirst will remain unsatisfied.

57. This will be their entertainment on the Day of Judgment.

هٰذَا نُزُلُهُمْ يَوْمَ الدِّيْنِ ﴿٥٧﴾

58. We have created you. Why, then, do you not accept *the truth?*

نَحْنُ خَلَقْنٰكُمْ فَلَوْلَا تُصَدِّقُوْنَ ﴿٥٨﴾

59. What think ye *of the sperm-drop* [a]that you emit?

اَفَرَءَيْتُمْ مَّا تُمْنُوْنَ ﴿٥٩﴾

60. Is it you who have created it, or are We the Creator?

ءَاَنْتُمْ تَخْلُقُوْنَهٗٓ اَمْ نَحْنُ الْخٰلِقُوْنَ ﴿٦٠﴾

61. We have ordained death for *all of* you; and [b]We cannot be hindered,

نَحْنُ قَدَّرْنَا بَيْنَكُمُ الْمَوْتَ وَمَا نَحْنُ بِمَسْبُوْقِيْنَ ﴿٦١﴾

62. From bringing in your place others like you, and *from* developing you into a form which you know not.[2972]

عَلٰٓى اَنْ نُّبَدِّلَ اَمْثَالَكُمْ وَنُنْشِئَكُمْ فِيْ مَا لَا تَعْلَمُوْنَ ﴿٦٢﴾

63. And you have, certainly, known the first creation. Why, then, do you not reflect?

وَلَقَدْ عَلِمْتُمُ النَّشْاَةَ الْاُوْلٰى فَلَوْلَا تَذَكَّرُوْنَ ﴿٦٣﴾

64. Do you see what you sow?[2973]

اَفَرَءَيْتُمْ مَّا تَحْرُثُوْنَ ﴿٦٤﴾

65. Is it you who cause it to grow, or are We the Grower?

ءَاَنْتُمْ تَزْرَعُوْنَهٗٓ اَمْ نَحْنُ الزّٰرِعُوْنَ ﴿٦٥﴾

66. If We *so* pleased, We could reduce it *all* to withered [c]stubble, then you would keep lamenting:

لَوْ نَشَآءُ لَجَعَلْنٰهُ حُطٰمًا فَظَلْتُمْ تَفَكَّهُوْنَ ﴿٦٦﴾

67. 'We are laden with debt!

اِنَّا لَمُغْرَمُوْنَ ﴿٦٧﴾

68. 'Nay, we are *totally* deprived *of everything*.'

بَلْ نَحْنُ مَحْرُوْمُوْنَ ﴿٦٨﴾

[a]75 : 38. [b]71 : 5. [c]57 : 21.

2972. The disintegration of man's physical tabernacle does not mean the end of his life. Death is only a change of state or form. After its flight from the physical habitat human soul is given another body, which grows and develops and takes forms which it is not possible for man to know or even to conceive of.

2973. Verses 64-72 give a brief account of things upon which man's life on earth depends. The three principal things are food, water and fire.

69. Have you considered the water which you drink?

أَفَرَءَيْتُمُ الْمَآءَ الَّذِي تَشْرَبُونَ ﴿٦٩﴾

70 Do you send it down from the clouds, or are We the Sender?

ءَأَنْتُمْ أَنْزَلْتُمُوهُ مِنَ الْمُزْنِ أَمْ نَحْنُ الْمُنْزِلُونَ ﴿٧٠﴾

71. If We so pleased, We could make it bitter. Why, then, do you not give thanks?

لَوْ نَشَآءُ جَعَلْنٰهُ أُجَاجًا فَلَوْلَا تَشْكُرُونَ ﴿٧١﴾

72. Have you considered the [a]fire[2974] which you kindle?

أَفَرَءَيْتُمُ النَّارَ الَّتِي تُورُونَ ﴿٧٢﴾

73. Is it you who produce the tree for it, or are We the Producer?

ءَأَنْتُمْ أَنْشَأْتُمْ شَجَرَتَهَآ أَمْ نَحْنُ الْمُنْشِـُٔونَ ﴿٧٣﴾

74. We have made it a reminder and benefit for the wayfarers.[2975]

نَحْنُ جَعَلْنٰهَا تَذْكِرَةً وَّمَتَاعًا لِّلْمُقْوِينَ ﴿٧٤﴾

75. [b]So glorify the name of thy Lord, the Great.

فَسَبِّحْ بِاسْمِ رَبِّكَ الْعَظِيمِ ﴿٧٥﴾

R. 3 76. Nay,[2976] I cite as proof the shooting of the stars[2977]—

فَلَآ أُقْسِمُ بِمَوٰقِعِ النُّجُومِ ﴿٧٦﴾

77. And, indeed, that is a grand testimony, if you only knew—

وَإِنَّهُ لَقَسَمٌ لَّوْ تَعْلَمُونَ عَظِيمٌ ﴿٧٧﴾

78. This is, indeed, a [c]noble Qur'ān,

إِنَّهُ لَقُرْءَانٌ كَرِيمٌ ﴿٧٨﴾

[a]36 : 81. [b]69 : 53; 87 : 2. [c]50 : 2.

2974. Fire plays a most important part in the life of man. Much of his physical comfort depends upon it. It is a thing of very great utility, also of destruction if not used properly. In this mechanistic age life is inconceivable without the use of fire. No industry, trade or travel is possible without it.

2975. Needy and hungry people; wayfarers in a desert or those who alight at a desolate place (Aqrab).

2976. The particle *lā* is generally used to impart emphasis to an oath, meaning that the thing which is going to be explained next is so self-evident that it does not need calling anything else to bear witness to its truth. When the refutation of a certain hypothesis is intended *lā* is used to signify that which is said before is not correct and the right thing is that which follows.

2977. The verse swears by, and holds forth, *Nujūm* which means, portions of the Qur'ān (Lane), as evidence to support the claim that the Qur'ān is eminently fitted to fulfil the grand object of man's creation, as well as to establish its own Divine origin. Taking the word *Mawāqi'* as meaning, the places and times of the falling of stars, the verse signifies that it is an unfailing Divine Law that, at the time of the appearance of a great Divine Reformer or Prophet, stars fall in unusually large numbers, and that this has happened in the time of the Holy Prophet also.

79. In [a] a well-preserved Book,[2978]
فِي كِتٰبٍ مَّكْنُوْنٍ ﴿٧٩﴾

80. Which none shall touch except those who are purified.[2979]
لَّا يَمَسُّهٗٓ اِلَّا الْمُطَهَّرُوْنَ ﴿٨٠﴾

81. [b] *It is* a revelation from the Lord of the worlds.
تَنْزِيْلٌ مِّنْ رَّبِّ الْعٰلَمِيْنَ ﴿٨١﴾

82. Is it this *Divine* discourse that you would reject,
اَفَبِهٰذَا الْحَدِيْثِ اَنْتُمْ مُّدْهِنُوْنَ ﴿٨٢﴾

83. And do you make the denial thereof your *means of* livelihood?[2980]
وَتَجْعَلُوْنَ رِزْقَكُمْ اَنَّكُمْ تُكَذِّبُوْنَ ﴿٨٣﴾

84. Why, then, when *the soul of the dying man* reaches the throat,
فَلَوْلَآ اِذَا بَلَغَتِ الْحُلْقُوْمَ ﴿٨٤﴾

85. And you are at that moment looking on—
وَاَنْتُمْ حِيْنَئِذٍ تَنْظُرُوْنَ ﴿٨٥﴾

86. [c] And We are nearer to him than you, but you see not—
وَنَحْنُ اَقْرَبُ اِلَيْهِ مِنْكُمْ وَلٰكِنْ لَّا تُبْصِرُوْنَ ﴿٨٦﴾

87. Why, then, if you are not to be called to account,
فَلَوْلَآ اِنْ كُنْتُمْ غَيْرَ مَدِيْنِيْنَ ﴿٨٧﴾

[a] 85 : 23. [b] 20 : 5; 26 : 193. [c] 50 : 17.

2978. That the Qur'ān is a well-preserved and well-protected Divinely revealed Book is an open challenge to the whole world which has remained unaccepted during the past fourteen centuries. No effort has been spared by its hostile critics to find fault with the purity of its text. But all efforts in this direction have led to but one inevitable—albeit unpalatable for its enemies—result that the Book which the Holy Prophet Muḥammad gave to the world fourteen hundred years ago has come down to us without the change of a single vowel (Muir). The Qur'ān is also a well-preserved Book in the sense that only those believers who are pure of heart can have access to its spiritual treasures as the next verse signifies. The verse may also signify that the ideals and principles embodied in the Qur'ān are inscribed in the book of nature, *i.e.*, they are in complete harmony with natural laws. Like the laws of nature they are immutable and unalterable and cannot be defied with impunity. Or, the verse may mean that the Qur'ān is preserved in 'the nature which God has bestowed upon man' (30 : 31). Human nature is based upon fundamental truths and has been endowed with the faculty to arrive at right judgment. A person who honestly calls human nature into action can easily recognize the truth of the Qur'ān.

2979. Only those lucky ones who by leading righteous lives achieve purity of the heart are granted true understanding of, and insight into, the real meanings of the Qur'ān, and are initiated into those spiritual mysteries of Divine knowledge to which the impure of heart are denied access. Incidentally, one should not touch or read the Qur'ān while one is not physically clean.

2980. The disbelievers are afraid lest by accepting truth they might be deprived of their means of livelihood. So it is for the sake of filthy lucre that they reject the Divine Message; or, the verse may mean that disbelievers have made rejection of truth something on which, as it were, their very lives depend. They will not accept it at any cost.

88. You cannot bring it back, if you are truthful?

تَرْجِعُوْنَهَآ اِنْ كُنْتُمْ صٰدِقِيْنَ ﴿٨٨﴾

89. Now if he be of those who are near *to God*,

فَاَمَّآ اِنْ كَانَ مِنَ الْمُقَرَّبِيْنَ ﴿٨٩﴾

90. Then *for him* is comfort and fragrance *of happiness* and Garden of Bliss;

فَرَوْحٌ وَّرَيْحَانٌ ۙ وَّجَنَّتُ نَعِيْمٍ ﴿٩٠﴾

91. And if he be of those of the right hand,

وَاَمَّآ اِنْ كَانَ مِنْ اَصْحٰبِ الْيَمِيْنِ ﴿٩١﴾

92. Then 'Peace be *ever* on thee, *O thou*, of those of the right hand!'

فَسَلٰمٌ لَّكَ مِنْ اَصْحٰبِ الْيَمِيْنِ ﴿٩٢﴾

93. But if he be of those who reject *the truth* and are in error,

وَاَمَّآ اِنْ كَانَ مِنَ الْمُكَذِّبِيْنَ الضَّآلِّيْنَ ﴿٩٣﴾

94. Then *for him will be* an entertainment of boiling water,

فَنُزُلٌ مِّنْ حَمِيْمٍ ﴿٩٤﴾

95. And burning in Hell.

وَّتَصْلِيَةُ جَحِيْمٍ ﴿٩٥﴾

96. Verily, [a]this is the certain truth.

اِنَّ هٰذَا لَهُوَ حَقُّ الْيَقِيْنِ ﴿٩٦﴾

97. So glorify the name of thy Lord, [b]the Incomparably Great.

فَسَبِّحْ بِاسْمِ رَبِّكَ الْعَظِيْمِ ﴿٩٧﴾

[a]35 : 32. [b]56 : 75.

CHAPTER 57

AL-ḤADĪD

(*Revealed after Hijrah*)

Date of Revelation and Context

This is the first of the last ten Medinite Chapters of the Qur'ān which end with Chapter 66. It seems to have been revealed after the conquest of Mecca or the Treaty of Ḥudaibiyah, as is clear from the mention of *al-Fatḥ* (the Victory) in v. 11 which refers to the Fall of Mecca or, according to some, more appropriately to the Treaty of Ḥudaibiyah. The series of the Meccan Chapters which began with Al-Saba' and which, with the exception of the three intervening Medinite Chapters—Muḥammad, Al-Fatḥ and Al-Ḥujurāt—had continued without interruption, ended with the preceding Chapter and had completed the subject matter of the Meccan *Sūrahs*. With the present *Sūrah*, however, begins a new series of Medinite Chapters which end with Al-Taḥrīm. In the preceding *Sūrah* it is stated that the Qur'ān is a well-preserved Book (v. 79) which among other things signifies that its teachings are in perfect harmony with natural laws and with the dictates and demands of human nature, reason and commonsense. The present *Sūrah* opens with the Divine attributes: the Mighty, the Wise. And quite naturally, the Being Who is Wise and Mighty must have revealed a Book whose teachings are consistent with the laws of nature and with human reason and conscience.

Subject-Matter

In the previous seven Meccan *Sūrahs*, especially in the three immediately preceding ones—Al-Qamar, Al-Raḥmān and Al-Wāqi'ah—it was repeatedly declared, in a forceful though metaphorical language, that a great reformation, a veritable resurrection, was about to be brought about by the Holy Prophet among a people who for long centuries had grovelled in moral dust and dirt; and who, because they had no living relations with civilized society, were looked down upon as pariahs among nations. The present *Sūrah* points out that the great day of the phenomenal progress and power of that pariah nation—the Arabs—has already dawned and that the eventual victory of truth over falsehood is in sight. But there are essential conditions to be fulfilled before that consummation takes place. There must be on the part of Muslims a firm and invincible faith in the truth of Islamic ideals and a preparedness to make necessary sacrifice of life and property for the furtherance of its cause. The believers then are told that after they have acquired power and prosperity they should not neglect moral ideals and indulge in the pursuit of transitory material pleasures. The *Sūrah* continues the theme, namely, that from time immemorial God's Messengers have been appearing in the world to lead men to the goal of their lives which is to win the pleasure of God, and which cannot be attained by leading a life of complete renunciation or flight from the world, as Jesus's followers mistakenly had thought and practised, but by making proper use of natural powers and faculties, bestowed by God on man and of the things He has created for his use.

سُوْرَةُ الْحَدِيْدِ مَدَنِيَّةٌ (٥٧)

1. [a]In the name of Allāh, the Gracious, the Merciful.

بِسْمِ اللّٰهِ الرَّحْمٰنِ الرَّحِيْمِ ①

2. Whatever is in the heavens and the earth [b]glorifies[2981] Allāh; and He is the Mighty, the Wise.

سَبَّحَ لِلّٰهِ مَا فِي السَّمٰوٰتِ وَالْاَرْضِ ۚ وَهُوَ الْعَزِيْزُ الْحَكِيْمُ ②

3. His is the Kingdom of the heavens and the earth; He gives life and [c]He causes death,[2982] and He has power over all things.

لَهٗ مُلْكُ السَّمٰوٰتِ وَالْاَرْضِ ۚ يُحْيٖ وَيُمِيْتُ ۚ وَهُوَ عَلٰى كُلِّ شَيْءٍ قَدِيْرٌ ③

4. He is the First[2983] and the Last,[2984] and the Manifest[2985] and the Hidden,[2986] and He has full knowledge of all things.

هُوَ الْاَوَّلُ وَالْاٰخِرُ وَالظَّاهِرُ وَالْبَاطِنُ ۚ وَهُوَ بِكُلِّ شَيْءٍ عَلِيْمٌ ④

---

[a]1 : 1. [b]17 : 45; 24 : 42; 61 : 2; 62 : 2; 64 : 2. [c]3 : 157; 7 : 159; 44 : 9.

2981. *Sabaḥa Fi Ḥawā'ijihī* means, he busied himself in earning his subsistence or in his affairs. *Sabḥ* signifies doing one's work or doing it with utmost effort and quickly, and the expression *Subḥān Allāh* denotes quickness in betaking oneself to God and agility in serving or obeying Him. In view of the root-meaning of this word, the Infinitive Noun *Tasbīḥ* from *Sabbaḥa* means, declaring God to be far from every imperfection or defect or betaking oneself quickly to God's service and to be prompt in obeying Him saying *Subḥān Allāh* (Lane). The verse thus means that everything in the universe is doing its allotted task punctually and regularly, and by making use of the faculties and powers bestowed upon it by God is fulfilling the object of its creation in such a wonderful manner that one is irresistibly drawn to the conclusion that the Designer and Architect of the universe is, indeed, Mighty and Wise and that the whole world collectively and every created thing individually and in its own limited sphere, bears testimony to the undeniable truth that God's handiwork is absolutely free from every flaw, defect or imperfection in all its multifarious and multitudinous aspects. This is the significance of *Tasbīḥ*.

2982. The process of construction and destruction is in operation simultaneously every moment in everything in the universe.

2983. God is the First Cause of all things.

2984. He is the Last and Final Cause.

2985. He is manifest in His works; or is more manifest than anything else.

2986. There is nothing hidden from God; or whereas He comprehends everything He Himself is Incomprehensible.

5. He it is Who created the heavens and the earth [a]in six periods, then He settled Himself on the Throne. He knows what enters the earth and [b]what comes out of it, and what comes down from heaven and what goes up into it.[2987] And He is with you wheresoever you may be. And Allāh sees all that you do.

هُوَ الَّذِي خَلَقَ السَّمٰوٰتِ وَالْاَرْضَ فِي سِتَّةِ اَيَّامٍ ثُمَّ اسْتَوٰى عَلَى الْعَرْشِ ۚ يَعْلَمُ مَا يَلِجُ فِي الْاَرْضِ وَمَا يَخْرُجُ مِنْهَا وَمَا يَنْزِلُ مِنَ السَّمَآءِ وَمَا يَعْرُجُ فِيْهَا ۚ وَهُوَ مَعَكُمْ اَيْنَ مَا كُنْتُمْ ۚ وَاللّٰهُ بِمَا تَعْمَلُوْنَ بَصِيْرٌ ﴿٥﴾

6. His is the [c]Kingdom of the heavens and the earth; and to Allāh are all affairs returned *for final judgment*.

لَهٗ مُلْكُ السَّمٰوٰتِ وَالْاَرْضِ ۚ وَاِلَى اللّٰهِ تُرْجَعُ الْاُمُوْرُ ﴿٦﴾

7. [d]He causes the night to pass into the day and causes the day to pass into the night; and He knows well all that is in the breasts.

يُوْلِجُ الَّيْلَ فِي النَّهَارِ وَيُوْلِجُ النَّهَارَ فِي الَّيْلِ ۚ وَهُوَ عَلِيْمٌۢ بِذَاتِ الصُّدُوْرِ ﴿٧﴾

8. Believe in Allāh and His Messenger, and spend *in the way of Allāh* out of that to which He has made you heirs. And those of you who believe and spend will have a great reward.

اٰمِنُوْا بِاللّٰهِ وَرَسُوْلِهٖ وَاَنْفِقُوْا مِمَّا جَعَلَكُمْ مُّسْتَخْلَفِيْنَ فِيْهِ ۚ فَالَّذِيْنَ اٰمَنُوْا مِنْكُمْ وَاَنْفَقُوْا لَهُمْ اَجْرٌ كَبِيْرٌ ﴿٨﴾

9. Why is it that you believe not in Allāh, while the Messenger calls you to believe in your Lord, and He has already taken a covenant[2988] from you, if indeed you are believers?

وَمَا لَكُمْ لَا تُؤْمِنُوْنَ بِاللّٰهِ ۚ وَالرَّسُوْلُ يَدْعُوْكُمْ لِتُؤْمِنُوْا بِرَبِّكُمْ وَقَدْ اَخَذَ مِيْثَاقَكُمْ اِنْ كُنْتُمْ مُّؤْمِنِيْنَ ﴿٩﴾

[a]7 : 55; 11 : 8; 25 : 60; 32 : 5. [b]34 : 3. [c]2 : 108; 7 : 159.
[d]22 : 62; 31 : 30; 35 : 14.

2987. The meaning is that God alone knows when a particular Divine Teaching is needed for a particular people; also when to take it back to heaven, *i.e.*, to abrogate it, when it is corrupted and ceases to fulfil the spiritual needs of the people to whom it is given. And He alone knows when to reveal a new Teaching.

2988. "The covenant" spoken of in the verse signifies the faith in God implanted in human nature and the longing to achieve His nearness.

10. He it is Who ᵃsends down clear Signs to His servant, that He ᵇmay bring you out of every kind of darkness into light. And, verily, Allāh is Compassionate and Merciful to you.

هُوَ الَّذِىۡ يُنَزِّلُ عَلٰى عَبۡدِهٖۤ اٰيٰتٍۭ بَيِّنٰتٍ لِّيُخۡرِجَكُمۡ مِّنَ الظُّلُمٰتِ اِلَى النُّوۡرِؕ وَاِنَّ اللّٰهَ بِكُمۡ لَرَءُوۡفٌ رَّحِيۡمٌ ۝

11. And why is it that you spend not in the way of Allāh, while to Allāh belongs the heritage²⁹⁸⁹ of the heavens and the earth? Those of you who spent and fought before the Victory²⁹⁹⁰ are not equal *to those who did so later* They are greater in rank than those who spent and fought ᶜafterwards. And to all has Allāh promised good. And Allāh is Well-Aware of what you do.

وَمَا لَكُمۡ اَلَّا تُنۡفِقُوۡا فِىۡ سَبِيۡلِ اللّٰهِ وَلِلّٰهِ مِيۡرَاثُ السَّمٰوٰتِ وَالۡاَرۡضِؕ لَا يَسۡتَوِىۡ مِنۡكُمۡ مَّنۡ اَنۡفَقَ مِنۡ قَبۡلِ الۡفَتۡحِ وَقٰتَلَؕ اُولٰٓئِكَ اَعۡظَمُ دَرَجَةً مِّنَ الَّذِيۡنَ اَنۡفَقُوۡا مِنۡۢ بَعۡدُ وَقٰتَلُوۡاؕ وَكُلًّا وَّعَدَ اللّٰهُ الۡحُسۡنٰىؕ وَاللّٰهُ بِمَا تَعۡمَلُوۡنَ خَبِيۡرٌ ۝

R. 2

12. ᵈWho is he who will lend to Allāh a goodly loan? So He will increase it manifold for him, and he will have a noble reward.

مَنۡ ذَا الَّذِىۡ يُقۡرِضُ اللّٰهَ قَرۡضًا حَسَنًا فَيُضٰعِفَهٗ لَهٗ وَلَهٗۤ اَجۡرٌ كَرِيۡمٌ ۝

13. And *think of* the day when thou wilt see the believing men and the believing women, their light running before ᵉthem and on their right hands, *and angels will say to them*, 'Glad tidings for you this day of Gardens through which streams flow, wherein you will abide. That is the supreme triumph.'

يَوۡمَ تَرَى الۡمُؤۡمِنِيۡنَ وَالۡمُؤۡمِنٰتِ يَسۡعٰى نُوۡرُهُمۡ بَيۡنَ اَيۡدِيۡهِمۡ وَبِاَيۡمَانِهِمۡ بُشۡرٰىكُمُ الۡيَوۡمَ جَنّٰتٌ تَجۡرِىۡ مِنۡ تَحۡتِهَا الۡاَنۡهٰرُ خٰلِدِيۡنَ فِيۡهَاؕ ذٰلِكَ هُوَ الۡفَوۡزُ الۡعَظِيۡمُ ۝

ᵃ22 : 17; 24 : 35; 58 : 6. ᵇ14 : 6; 33 : 44. ᶜ4 : 96; 9 : 20.
ᵈ2 : 246; 64 : 18; 73 : 21. ᵉ66 : 9.

2989. Man will have to leave behind in this world all his material possessions which in truth belong to God.

2990. Fall of Mecca or the Treaty of Ḥudaibiyah.

14. *That is* the day when the hypocritical men and the hypocritical women will say to those who believe, 'Wait for us *a while* that we may borrow some of your light,'[2991] it will be said *to them*, 'Go back[2992] *if you can*, and seek for light.' Then there will be set up between them a wall[2993] with a door in it. The inside of it will be *all* mercy and outside of it, in front, will be torment.

يَوْمَ يَقُوْلُ الْمُنٰفِقُوْنَ وَالْمُنٰفِقٰتُ لِلَّذِيْنَ اٰمَنُوا
انْظُرُوْنَا نَقْتَبِسْ مِنْ نُّوْرِكُمْ ۚ قِيْلَ ارْجِعُوْا
وَرَآءَكُمْ فَالْتَمِسُوْا نُوْرًا ۗ فَضُرِبَ بَيْنَهُمْ بِسُوْرٍ
لَّهٗ بَابٌ ۗ بَاطِنُهٗ فِيْهِ الرَّحْمَةُ وَظَاهِرُهٗ مِنْ قِبَلِهِ
الْعَذَابُ ۗ ﴿١٤﴾

15. *The hypocrites* will call out to *believers saying*, 'Were we not with you?' The *believers* will answer, 'Yea, but you let yourselves fall into temptation and you hesitated and doubted and your vain desires deceived you till the decree of Allāh[2994] came to pass. And the deceiver deceived you concerning Allāh.

يُنَادُوْنَهُمْ اَلَمْ نَكُنْ مَّعَكُمْ ۗ قَالُوْا بَلٰى وَلٰكِنَّكُمْ
فَتَنْتُمْ اَنْفُسَكُمْ وَتَرَبَّصْتُمْ وَارْتَبْتُمْ وَغَرَّتْكُمُ
الْاَمَانِيُّ حَتّٰى جَآءَ اَمْرُ اللّٰهِ وَغَرَّكُمْ بِاللّٰهِ الْغَرُوْرُ ﴿١٥﴾

16. 'So this day no ransom shall be accepted from you, nor from those who disbelieved. Your final abode is the Fire; that is your comrade;[2995] and an evil destination it is.'

فَالْيَوْمَ لَا يُؤْخَذُ مِنْكُمْ فِدْيَةٌ وَّلَا مِنَ الَّذِيْنَ
كَفَرُوْا ۗ مَاْوٰىكُمُ النَّارُ ۗ هِيَ مَوْلٰىكُمْ ۗ وَبِئْسَ
الْمَصِيْرُ ﴿١٦﴾

2991. "Your light" may mean the light of your faith and good actions or, the light of Divine realization and of the capacity to seek and achieve the pleasure of God in this very life.

2992. The word *Warā'akum* may signify the present life.

2993. "A wall" might signify the wall of Islām or of the Qur'ān. As the disbelievers remain outside this wall so this action of theirs will take the form of a wall in the Hereafter.

2994. Divine punishment.

2995. The words, 'that is your comrade,' seem to have been used ironically. Or, they may mean that only the fire of Hell will purify them of the impurities and dross of sins committed by disbelievers in this life and will make them fit for spiritual progress and thus will be a "friend" to them.

17. Has not the time *yet* arrived for those who believe that their hearts should feel humbled at the remembrance of Allāh and at the truth which has come down *to them*, and *that* they should not become like those who were given the Book before them, but *because* the period *of the bestowal of Allāh's grace upon* [a]*them* was prolonged for them, their [b]hearts became hardened, and many of them became rebellious?

اَلَمْ يَاْنِ لِلَّذِيْنَ اٰمَنُوْٓا اَنْ تَخْشَعَ قُلُوْبُهُمْ لِذِكْرِ
اللّٰهِ وَمَا نَزَلَ مِنَ الْحَقِّ وَلَا يَكُوْنُوْا كَالَّذِيْنَ اُوْتُوا
الْكِتٰبَ مِنْ قَبْلُ فَطَالَ عَلَيْهِمُ الْاَمَدُ فَقَسَتْ
قُلُوْبُهُمْ وَكَثِيْرٌ مِّنْهُمْ فٰسِقُوْنَ ﴿۱۷﴾

18. Know, then, that Allāh [c]quickens the earth after its death. We have made the Signs manifest to you, that you may understand.

اِعْلَمُوْٓا اَنَّ اللّٰهَ يُحْيِ الْاَرْضَ بَعْدَ مَوْتِهَا قَدْ
بَيَّنَّا لَكُمُ الْاٰيٰتِ لَعَلَّكُمْ تَعْقِلُوْنَ ﴿۱۸﴾

19. Surely, the men who give alms, and the women who give alms, and those who lend to Allāh a [d]goodly loan—it will be increased manifold for them, and theirs will *also* be a honourable reward—

اِنَّ الْمُصَّدِّقِيْنَ وَالْمُصَّدِّقٰتِ وَاَقْرَضُوا اللّٰهَ
قَرْضًا حَسَنًا يُّضٰعَفُ لَهُمْ وَلَهُمْ اَجْرٌ كَرِيْمٌ ﴿۱۹﴾

20. Those who believe in Allāh and His Messengers, they are the Truthful and the Witnesses in the sight of their Lord. They will have their *full* reward and their light. But those who disbelieve and reject Our Signs, these are the inmates of Hell.

وَالَّذِيْنَ اٰمَنُوْا بِاللّٰهِ وَرُسُلِهٖٓ اُولٰٓئِكَ هُمُ الصِّدِّيْقُوْنَ
وَالشُّهَدَآءُ عِنْدَ رَبِّهِمْ لَهُمْ اَجْرُهُمْ وَنُوْرُهُمْ
وَالَّذِيْنَ كَفَرُوْا وَكَذَّبُوْا بِاٰيٰتِنَآ اُولٰٓئِكَ اَصْحٰبُ
الْجَحِيْمِ ﴿۲۰﴾ ع ٢ ٩ ١٨

[a]21 : 45. [b]2 : 75; 6 : 44. [c]35 : 10. [d]2 : 246.

R. 3 21. Know that [a]the life of this world is only a sport and a pastime, and an adornment, and *a source of* boasting among yourselves, and *of* rivalry in multiplying riches and children. *It is* like the rain, the vegetation produced whereby rejoices the tillers. Then it dries up and thou seest it turn yellow; then [b]it becomes *worthless* stubble. And in the Hereafter there is severe punishment *for the wicked* and *also* forgiveness from Allāh, and *His* pleasure *for the righteous.* And the life of this world is nothing but *temporary* enjoyment of delucive things.

اِعْلَمُوْٓا اَنَّمَا الْحَيٰوةُ الدُّنْيَا لَعِبٌ وَّلَهْوٌ وَّزِيْنَةٌ
وَّتَفَاخُرٌۢ بَيْنَكُمْ وَتَكَاثُرٌ فِي الْاَمْوَالِ وَالْاَوْلَادِ
كَمَثَلِ غَيْثٍ اَعْجَبَ الْكُفَّارَ نَبَاتُهٗ ثُمَّ يَهِيْجُ
فَتَرٰىهُ مُصْفَرًّا ثُمَّ يَكُوْنُ حُطٰمًا ۭ وَفِي الْاٰخِرَةِ
عَذَابٌ شَدِيْدٌ ۙ وَّمَغْفِرَةٌ مِّنَ اللّٰهِ وَرِضْوَانٌ ۭ
وَمَا الْحَيٰوةُ الدُّنْيَآ اِلَّا مَتَاعُ الْغُرُوْرِ ﴿٢١﴾

22. [c]Vie, *then*, with one another in seeking forgiveness from your Lord and for a Garden the value[2996] whereof is equal to the value of the heaven and the earth; it has been prepared for those who believe in Allāh and His Messengers. That is Allāh's grace; He bestows it upon whomsoever He pleases, and Allāh is the Lord of immense grace.

سَابِقُوْٓا اِلٰى مَغْفِرَةٍ مِّنْ رَّبِّكُمْ وَجَنَّةٍ عَرْضُهَا
كَعَرْضِ السَّمَآءِ وَالْاَرْضِ ۙ اُعِدَّتْ لِلَّذِيْنَ اٰمَنُوْا
بِاللّٰهِ وَرُسُلِهٖ ۭ ذٰلِكَ فَضْلُ اللّٰهِ يُؤْتِيْهِ مَنْ يَّشَآءُ ۭ
وَاللّٰهُ ذُو الْفَضْلِ الْعَظِيْمِ ﴿٢٢﴾

23. There befalls not any calamity either in the earth or in your *own* persons, but it is *recorded* in a Book[2996A] before We bring it into being—surely, that is easy for Allāh—

مَآ اَصَابَ مِنْ مُّصِيْبَةٍ فِي الْاَرْضِ وَلَا فِيْٓ اَنْفُسِكُمْ
اِلَّا فِيْ كِتٰبٍ مِّنْ قَبْلِ اَنْ نَّبْرَاَهَا ۭ اِنَّ ذٰلِكَ عَلَى
اللّٰهِ يَسِيْرٌ ﴿٢٣﴾

[a]6 : 33; 29 : 65; 47 : 37. [b]56 : 66. [c]3 : 134.

2996. *'Arḍ* meaning value and vastness, the verse signifies that (*a*) the reward of the righteous in the Hereafter will be beyond measure or count. (*b*) Paradise being as extensive as both the heavens and the earth—the whole space—it comprises Hell also. This shows that Paradise and Hell are not two distinct and separate places but two conditions or states of mind. A well-known saying of the Holy Prophet gives an insight into the Quranic conception of Paradise and Hell. Once on being asked by some of his Companions: 'If Paradise comprises in its vastness heavens and earth, where is Hell,' the Holy Prophet is reported to have replied, 'Where is the night when the day comes' (Kathīr).

2996A. *Kitāb* may signify Divine Law or knowledge, or the Qur'ān, and the verse may mean that everything is subject to a certain law of nature or that the causes and cures of miseries befalling nations and individuals have been mentioned in the Qur'ān.

24. [a]That you may not grieve over what is lost to you nor exult because of that which He has bestowed upon you. And Allāh loves not any conceited boaster,

لِّكَيْلَا تَأْسَوْا عَلٰى مَا فَاتَكُمْ وَلَا تَفْرَحُوْا بِمَآ اٰتٰكُمْ ؕ
وَاللّٰهُ لَا يُحِبُّ كُلَّ مُخْتَالٍ فَخُوْرِۙ ﴿۲۴﴾

25. [b]Such as are niggardly and *also* enjoin upon men to be niggardly. And whoso turns his back, then surely, Allāh is Self-Sufficient, Worthy of all praise.

الَّذِيْنَ يَبْخَلُوْنَ وَيَاْمُرُوْنَ النَّاسَ بِالْبُخْلِ ؕ وَمَنْ
يَّتَوَلَّ فَاِنَّ اللّٰهَ هُوَ الْغَنِيُّ الْحَمِيْدُ ﴿۲۵﴾

26. Verily, We sent Our Messengers with [c]manifest Signs and sent down with them the Book and [d]the Balance[2997] that people may act with justice; and We sent down iron,[2998] wherein is *material for* violent warfare and diverse uses for mankind, and that Allāh may know those who help Him and His Messengers without having seen *Him*. Surely, Allāh is Powerful, Mighty.

لَقَدْ اَرْسَلْنَا رُسُلَنَا بِالْبَيِّنٰتِ وَاَنْزَلْنَا مَعَهُمُ
الْكِتٰبَ وَالْمِيْزَانَ لِيَقُوْمَ النَّاسُ بِالْقِسْطِ ۚ وَاَنْزَلْنَا
الْحَدِيْدَ فِيْهِ بَاْسٌ شَدِيْدٌ وَّمَنَافِعُ لِلنَّاسِ
وَلِيَعْلَمَ اللّٰهُ مَنْ يَّنْصُرُهٗ وَرُسُلَهٗ بِالْغَيْبِ ؕ اِنَّ
اللّٰهَ قَوِيٌّ عَزِيْزٌ ﴿۲۶﴾ ع ٣ ١٩

R. 4 27. And indeed We sent Noah and Abraham, and We placed among their seed Prophethood and the [e]Book. So some of them followed the guidance, but many of them were rebellious.

وَلَقَدْ اَرْسَلْنَا نُوْحًا وَّاِبْرٰهِيْمَ وَجَعَلْنَا فِيْ
ذُرِّيَّتِهِمَا النُّبُوَّةَ وَالْكِتٰبَ فَمِنْهُمْ مُّهْتَدٍ ۚ وَ
كَثِيْرٌ مِّنْهُمْ فٰسِقُوْنَ ﴿۲۷﴾

---

[a]3 : 154. [b]4 : 38. [c]7 : 102; 14 : 10; 35 : 26. [d]42 : 18; 55 : 8. [e]29 : 28.

2997. *Mīzān* may mean, (*a*) Principles of equity which people are enjoined to observe in their dealings with others. (*b*) Standards by which human actions are measured, weighed, appraised and judged. (*c*) Balance which pervades the whole universe maintaining just equilibrium among all things. (*d*) Practice of the Holy Prophet and right use of the Book of God. (*e*) Following the golden mean and avoiding extremes. (*f*) Reasons and arguments based on observation and experience.

2998. *Al-Ḥadīd* (iron) is the metal which perhaps has played the greatest and most useful part in the growth and development of human civilization. The word may also signify the power to compel obedience to the laws upon which the whole existence of human society depends. Thus the verse means that God has sent down three things: (*a*) Divine Laws; (*b*) the system which maintains just equilibrium in human social relations and (*c*) political power which compels obedience to Divine Laws.

28. Then [a]We caused Our Messengers to follow in their footsteps; and We caused Jesus, son of Mary, to follow *them*, and we gave him the Gospel. [b]And We put compassion and mercy in the hearts of those who followed him. And monasticism they invented—We did not prescribe it for them—for the seeking of Allāh's pleasure;[2999] but they observed it not as it should be observed. Yet We gave those of them, who believed, their *due* reward, but many of them are rebellious.

ثُمَّ قَفَّيْنَا عَلٰٓى اٰثَارِهِمْ بِرُسُلِنَا وَقَفَّيْنَا بِعِيْسَى
ابْنِ مَرْيَمَ وَاٰتَيْنٰهُ الْاِنْجِيْلَ ۵ وَجَعَلْنَا فِيْ
قُلُوْبِ الَّذِيْنَ اتَّبَعُوْهُ رَاْفَةً وَّرَحْمَةً ؕ وَرَهْبَانِيَّةَ
ۨابْتَدَعُوْهَا مَا كَتَبْنٰهَا عَلَيْهِمْ اِلَّا ابْتِغَآءَ
رِضْوَانِ اللّٰهِ فَمَا رَعَوْهَا حَقَّ رِعَايَتِهَا ۚ فَاٰتَيْنَا
الَّذِيْنَ اٰمَنُوْا مِنْهُمْ اَجْرَهُمْ ۚ وَكَثِيْرٌ مِّنْهُمْ
فٰسِقُوْنَ ﴿۲۸﴾

29. O ye who believe! fear Allāh and believe in His Messenger. He will give you a double portion of His mercy, and will provide for you a light wherein you will walk, and will grant you forgiveness—verily, Allāh is Most Forgiving, Merciful—

يٰۤاَيُّهَا الَّذِيْنَ اٰمَنُوا اتَّقُوا اللّٰهَ وَاٰمِنُوْا بِرَسُوْلِهٖ
يُؤْتِكُمْ كِفْلَيْنِ مِنْ رَّحْمَتِهٖ وَيَجْعَلْ لَّكُمْ
نُوْرًا تَمْشُوْنَ بِهٖ وَيَغْفِرْ لَكُمْ ؕ وَاللّٰهُ غَفُوْرٌ
رَّحِيْمٌ ۙ ﴿۲۹﴾

[a]2 : 88; 5 : 47. [b]5 : 83.

2999. The verse may mean that the followers of Jesus invented monasticism in order to seek Allāh's pleasure but Allāh had not prescribed it for them; or the meaning is that they invented monasticism which God had not prescribed for them—He had only prescribed for them the seeking of His pleasure. In v. 26 it was stated that God had sent down *al-Mīzān* in order that by avoiding extremes people should adopt the golden mean in all their affairs and actions. In the present verse the example of a people—the Christians—has been cited to show that the adoption of an extreme course by them, with howsoever good intentions, led them away from the goal they had sought to attain. They invented the institution of monkery in order, as they mistakenly thought, to seek the pleasure of God, and in conformity with, according to them, Jesus's own teaching and practice, but it proved to be a source of many social evils. They started with adopting monasticism and ended by giving themselves up to the worship of Mammon. Islām, however, has decried and deplored monasticism as repugnant to human nature. The Holy Prophet is reported to have said: "There is no monasticism in Islām" (Athīr). Islām is not a religion of visionaries who live in a world of their own conception or creation, entirely divorced from the hard realities of life. There is no place in Islām for such an impracticable teaching as "take no thought for the morrow" (Matt. 6 : 34). It emphatically enjoins a Muslim "to look to what he sends forth for the morrow" (59 : 19). A true Muslim is one who discharges equally and completely all his obligations to God and man.

30. *Thus it is* that the People of the Book may know that they have no power over anything of the grace[3000] of Allāh; [a]and that grace is *entirely* in the hands of Allāh, He gives it to whomsoever He pleases. And Allāh is the Master of immense grace.

لِّئَلَّا يَعْلَمَ اَهْلُ الْكِتٰبِ اَلَّا يَقْدِرُوْنَ عَلٰى شَيْءٍ
مِّنْ فَضْلِ اللّٰهِ وَاَنَّ الْفَضْلَ بِيَدِ اللّٰهِ يُؤْتِيْهِ
مَنْ يَّشَآءُ ؕ وَاللّٰهُ ذُو الْفَضْلِ الْعَظِيْمِ ۝٣٠ ع

[a]2 : 106; 3 : 74.

3000. Let the People of the Book disabuse their minds of the false notion that Divine grace is their monopoly and know that now God had transferred it to another people—the followers of Islām.

CHAPTER 58

AL-MUJĀDILAH

(*Revealed after Hijrah*)

Date of Revelation and Context

The *Sūrah* is the second of the last seven Medinite Chapters of the Qur'ān. It contains a somewhat detailed reference to the evil custom of *Ẓihār* (calling one's wife one's mother) which was only cursorily dealt with in *Sūrah* Al-Aḥzāb which shows that this *Sūrah* was revealed before Al-Aḥzāb. But as Al-Aḥzāb was revealed between 5th and 7th year of the *Hijrah*, the present *Sūrah*, therefore, must have been revealed earlier; very likely between the 3rd and the 4th year. In the immediately preceding *Sūrah*—*Sūrah* Al-Ḥadīd—"the People of the Book" were sternly told that Divine grace was not their monopoly and that since they had repeatedly defied and opposed and persecuted God's Messengers, it would now be transferred for all time to the House of Ishmael. In the present *Sūrah* Muslims are warned that as their material prosperity would excite the enmity of their external and internal foes, they should be on their guard against their evil designs and machinations. And, it is an invariable practice of the Qur'ān that whenever it deals with the machinations of the enemies of Islām, it also makes a pointed reference to some social evils. This method was adopted in *Sūrahs*, Al-Nūr and Al-Aḥzāb, and it has been adopted in the present *Sūrah* also.

Subject-Matter

The *Sūrah* opens with a sharp denunciation of the evil custom of *Ẓihār* and by citing the case of Khaulah, a Muslim lady, lays down the ordinance that if anyone calls his wife "mother," he has to atone for this heinous moral lapse by either freeing a slave, if he has one, or by fasting for two successive months, and failing that by feeding sixty needy persons. The *Sūrah* then proceeds to deal with the plots and conspiracies of the internal enemies of Islām and condemns the formation of secret societies and holding secret conferences to injure its cause. Then with befitting relevance it lays down some rules of conduct about social gatherings; and towards its close it sternly warns the enemies of Islām that by their opposition to it they will incur God's wrath but will never be able to arrest or impede its progress. This warning to disbelievers is followed by an equally strong warning to believers, that under no circumstances should they make friends with the enemies of their Faith, however closely related the latter might be to them, as by opposing Islām they have waged a veritable war against God, and friendship with God's enemies is inconsistent with true faith.

سُورَةُ الْمُجَادَلَةِ مَدَنِيَّةٌ (٥٨)

PART XXVIII

1. In the name of Allāh, the Gracious, the Merciful.

بِسۡمِ اللّٰهِ الرَّحۡمٰنِ الرَّحِيۡمِ ①

2. Allāh has, indeed, heard the talk of her who pleads with thee concerning her husband, and complains unto Allāh. And Allāh has heard the two of you conversing together.[3001] Verily, Allāh is All-Hearing, All-Seeing.

قَدۡ سَمِعَ اللّٰهُ قَوۡلَ الَّتِيۡ تُجَادِلُكَ فِيۡ زَوۡجِهَا وَ
تَشۡتَكِيۡۤ اِلَى اللّٰهِ ۖ وَاللّٰهُ يَسۡمَعُ تَحَاوُرَكُمَا ؕ اِنَّ اللّٰهَ
سَمِيۡعٌۢ بَصِيۡرٌ ②

3. Those among you who put away their wives by calling them mothers—they do not *thereby* become their mothers; their mothers are only those who gave them birth. They certainly utter words that are manifestly evil and untrue; but, surely, Allāh is the Effacer of sins, Most Forgiving.

اَلَّذِيۡنَ يُظٰهِرُوۡنَ مِنۡكُمۡ مِّنۡ نِّسَآئِهِمۡ مَّا هُنَّ
اُمَّهٰتِهِمۡ ؕ اِنۡ اُمَّهٰتُهُمۡ اِلَّا الّٰٓـىِٔۡ وَلَدۡنَهُمۡ ؕ وَ
اِنَّهُمۡ لَيَقُوۡلُوۡنَ مُنۡكَرًا مِّنَ الۡقَوۡلِ وَزُوۡرًا ؕ
وَاِنَّ اللّٰهَ لَعَفُوٌّ غَفُوۡرٌ ③

4. Those who put away their wives by calling them mothers, and then would go back[3002] on what they have said, must free a slave before they touch one another. This is what you are admonished with. And Allāh is Well-Aware of what you do.

وَالَّذِيۡنَ يُظٰهِرُوۡنَ مِنۡ نِّسَآئِهِمۡ ثُمَّ يَعُوۡدُوۡنَ
لِمَا قَالُوۡا فَتَحۡرِيۡرُ رَقَبَةٍ مِّنۡ قَبۡلِ اَنۡ يَّتَمَآسَّا ؕ
ذٰلِكُمۡ تُوۡعَظُوۡنَ بِهٖ ؕ وَاللّٰهُ بِمَا تَعۡمَلُوۡنَ خَبِيۡرٌ ④

3001. Khaulah, wife of Aus bin Ṣāmit and daughter of Tha'labah had become separated from her husband because the latter had called her "mother," the exact words used by him being, 'thou art to me as the back of my mother;' and thus according to an old Arab custom all conjugal relations had ceased between her and her husband. The unfortunate woman could neither demand divorce in order to contract a second marriage, nor could she enjoy conjugal rights and thus remained a suspended woman, uncared for. She came to the Holy Prophet and complained to him of the awkward situation in which she was placed, and sought his advice and help in the matter. The Holy Prophet pleaded his inability to do anything for her, as it was his wont that he would not give a decision in matters of this nature unless he was guided by revelation. The revelation came, and the custom of *Ẓihār* was declared unlawful.

3002. The words, "they would go back on what they have said," may signify that after calling their wives "mothers" they seek to re-establish conjugal relations with them, or they may mean that after having once called their wives "mothers" they repeat what they have said. According to this meaning, it is deliberate repetition of the obnoxious words and not their casual or inadvertent utterance that renders the utterer liable to the punishment prescribed in this and the following verse.

5. But he who does not find *a slave*, he must fast for two successive months, before they touch one another. And he who is not able to do so shall feed sixty poor people.[3003] This *is enjoined on you* so that you may have faith in Allāh and His Messenger. And these are the limits *prescribed* by Allāh; and for the disbelievers is a painful punishment.

فَمَنْ لَّمْ يَجِدْ فَصِيَامُ شَهْرَيْنِ مُتَتَابِعَيْنِ مِنْ قَبْلِ اَنْ يَّتَمَآسَّا ۚ فَمَنْ لَّمْ يَسْتَطِعْ فَاِطْعَامُ سِتِّيْنَ مِسْكِيْنًا ۗ ذٰلِكَ لِتُؤْمِنُوْا بِاللّٰهِ وَرَسُوْلِهٖ ۗ وَتِلْكَ حُدُوْدُ اللّٰهِ ۗ وَلِلْكٰفِرِيْنَ عَذَابٌ اَلِيْمٌ ۝٥

6. [a]Those who oppose Allāh[3004] and His Messenger will, surely, be abased even as those before them were abased; and We have already sent down clear Signs. And the disbelievers will have an humiliating punishment,

اِنَّ الَّذِيْنَ يُحَآدُّوْنَ اللّٰهَ وَرَسُوْلَهٗ كُبِتُوْا كَمَا كُبِتَ الَّذِيْنَ مِنْ قَبْلِهِمْ وَقَدْ اَنْزَلْنَآ اٰيٰتٍۭ بَيِّنٰتٍ ۗ وَلِلْكٰفِرِيْنَ عَذَابٌ مُّهِيْنٌ ۚ ۝٦

7. *On* the Day when Allāh will raise them all together. And He will inform them of what they did. Allāh has kept account of it, while they have forgotten it. And Allāh is Witness over all things.

يَوْمَ يَبْعَثُهُمُ اللّٰهُ جَمِيْعًا فَيُنَبِّئُهُمْ بِمَا عَمِلُوْا ۗ اَحْصٰىهُ اللّٰهُ وَنَسُوْهُ ۗ وَاللّٰهُ عَلٰى كُلِّ شَيْءٍ شَهِيْدٌ ۝٧ ع

R. 2 8. Seest thou not that Allāh knows all that is in the heavens and all that is in the earth? There is no secret counsel of three, but He is their fourth, nor of five but He is their sixth, nor of less than that, nor of more, but He is with them wheresoever they may be. Then on the Day of Resurrection He will inform them of what they did. Surely, Allāh has full knowledge of all things.

اَلَمْ تَرَ اَنَّ اللّٰهَ يَعْلَمُ مَا فِي السَّمٰوٰتِ وَمَا فِي الْاَرْضِ ۗ مَا يَكُوْنُ مِنْ نَّجْوٰى ثَلٰثَةٍ اِلَّا هُوَ رَابِعُهُمْ وَلَا خَمْسَةٍ اِلَّا هُوَ سَادِسُهُمْ وَلَآ اَدْنٰى مِنْ ذٰلِكَ وَلَآ اَكْثَرَ اِلَّا هُوَ مَعَهُمْ اَيْنَ مَا كَانُوْا ۚ ثُمَّ يُنَبِّئُهُمْ بِمَا عَمِلُوْا يَوْمَ الْقِيٰمَةِ ۗ اِنَّ اللّٰهَ بِكُلِّ شَيْءٍ عَلِيْمٌ ۝٨

[a]9 : 63.

3003. The drastic punishment mentioned in these verses indicates the extreme seriousness of the crime of calling one's wife "mother." The relationship with "mother" is too sacred to be trifled with.

3004. Calling one's wife "mother" is tantamount to opposing God—so hideous is the offence. Befittingly the subject of opposition to truth by the Jews and the Hypocrites is introduced in this verse.

9. Seest thou not those who were forbidden *to hold* secret counsels, then they return to that which they were forbidden, and confer in secret for sin and transgression and disobedience to the Messenger?[3005] And when they come to thee, they greet thee *with a* [a]*greeting* with which Allāh, has not greeted thee;[3006] but among themselves they say, 'Why does not Allāh punish us for what we say?' Sufficient for them is Hell, wherein they will burn; and a most evil destination it is!

أَلَمْ تَرَ إِلَى الَّذِينَ نُهُوا عَنِ النَّجْوٰى ثُمَّ يَعُودُونَ
لِمَا نُهُوا عَنْهُ وَيَتَنٰجَوْنَ بِالْإِثْمِ وَالْعُدْوَانِ
وَمَعْصِيَتِ الرَّسُولِ وَإِذَا جَاءُوكَ حَيَّوْكَ بِمَا
لَمْ يُحَيِّكَ بِهِ اللّٰهُ وَيَقُولُونَ فِي أَنْفُسِهِمْ لَوْلَا
يُعَذِّبُنَا اللّٰهُ بِمَا نَقُولُ حَسْبُهُمْ جَهَنَّمُ يَصْلَوْنَهَا
فَبِئْسَ الْمَصِيرُ ⑨

10. O ye who believe! when you confer together in private, confer not for *the purpose of promoting* sin and transgression and disobedience to the Messenger, but confer for *the purpose of promoting* virtue and righteousness,[3007] and fear Allāh unto Whom you shall *all* be gathered.

يٰٓأَيُّهَا الَّذِينَ اٰمَنُوٓا إِذَا تَنَاجَيْتُمْ فَلَا تَتَنَاجَوْا
بِالْإِثْمِ وَالْعُدْوَانِ وَمَعْصِيَتِ الرَّسُولِ وَتَنَاجَوْا
بِالْبِرِّ وَالتَّقْوٰى وَاتَّقُوا اللّٰهَ الَّذِيٓ إِلَيْهِ تُحْشَرُونَ ⑩

11. *Holding of* secret counsels *for evil purposes* is only of Satan, that he may cause grief to those who believe; but it cannot harm them in the least, except by Allāh's leave. And in Allāh should the believers put their trust.

إِنَّمَا النَّجْوٰى مِنَ الشَّيْطٰنِ لِيَحْزُنَ الَّذِينَ اٰمَنُوا
وَلَيْسَ بِضَآرِّهِمْ شَيْـًٔا إِلَّا بِإِذْنِ اللّٰهِ وَعَلَى اللّٰهِ
فَلْيَتَوَكَّلِ الْمُؤْمِنُونَ ⑪

[a]4 : 47

3005. The verse refers to the secret plots and conspiracies against Islām of the Jews and the Hypocrites of Medina and condemns this evil practice. The expulsion of the three Jewish tribes from Medina was the result of their repeated acts of defection and infidelity and their secret plots against Islām and the life of the Holy Prophet.

3006. The meaning is that they go beyond proper limits in hypocritically praising thee; or they invoke death and destruction upon thee. The words seem to refer to the evil practice of some of the Jews of Medina that when they came to the Holy Prophet they, with a little twist of the tongue, would invoke curses upon him by saying *Al-Sā'mu Alaika* (death to thee), instead of saluting him with the usual *Al-Salāmu 'Alaika, i.e.*, 'peace be upon thee' (Bukhārī).

3007. In this and the preceding two verses secret societies have been condemned, but the condmenation is not unqualified. The believers have been allowed to hold secret conferences to promote good and righteous causes.

12. O ye who believe! when it is said to you, 'Make room in *your* assemblies,' then do make room, Allāh will make ample room for you. And when it is said, 'Rise up'[3008] then rise up; Allāh will raise those who believe from among you, and those whom knowledge is given, to degrees *of rank*. And Allāh is Well-Aware of what you do.

يٰۤاَيُّهَا الَّذِيْنَ اٰمَنُوْۤا اِذَا قِيْلَ لَكُمْ تَفَسَّحُوْا فِي الْمَجٰلِسِ فَافْسَحُوْا يَفْسَحِ اللّٰهُ لَكُمْ ۚ وَاِذَا قِيْلَ انْشُزُوْا فَانْشُزُوْا يَرْفَعِ اللّٰهُ الَّذِيْنَ اٰمَنُوْا مِنْكُمْ ۙ وَالَّذِيْنَ اُوْتُوا الْعِلْمَ دَرَجٰتٍ ۗ وَاللّٰهُ بِمَا تَعْمَلُوْنَ خَبِيْرٌ ﴿١٢﴾

13. O ye who believe! when you consult the Messenger in private, give alms before your consultation.[3009] That is better for you and purer. But if you find not *anything to give* then Allāh is Most Forgiving, Merciful.

يٰۤاَيُّهَا الَّذِيْنَ اٰمَنُوْۤا اِذَا نَاجَيْتُمُ الرَّسُوْلَ فَقَدِّمُوْا بَيْنَ يَدَيْ نَجْوٰىكُمْ صَدَقَةً ۗ ذٰلِكَ خَيْرٌ لَّكُمْ وَاَطْهَرُ ۗ فَاِنْ لَّمْ تَجِدُوْا فَاِنَّ اللّٰهَ غَفُوْرٌ رَّحِيْمٌ ﴿١٣﴾

14. Are you afraid of giving alms before your consultation?[3010] So, when you do not do so and Allāh has been Merciful to you, then observe Prayer and pay the *Zakāt* and obey Allāh and His Messenger. And Allāh is Well-Aware of what you do.

ءَاَشْفَقْتُمْ اَنْ تُقَدِّمُوْا بَيْنَ يَدَيْ نَجْوٰىكُمْ صَدَقٰتٍ ۗ فَاِذْ لَمْ تَفْعَلُوْا وَتَابَ اللّٰهُ عَلَيْكُمْ فَاَقِيْمُوا الصَّلٰوةَ وَاٰتُوا الزَّكٰوةَ وَاَطِيْعُوا اللّٰهَ وَرَسُوْلَهٗ ۗ وَاللّٰهُ خَبِيْرٌۢ بِمَا تَعْمَلُوْنَ ﴿١٤﴾

R. 3 15. Seest thou not those who take for friends a people [a]with whom Allāh is wroth? They are neither of you nor of them, and they swear to falsehood knowingly.

اَلَمْ تَرَ اِلَى الَّذِيْنَ تَوَلَّوْا قَوْمًا غَضِبَ اللّٰهُ عَلَيْهِمْ ۗ مَا هُمْ مِّنْكُمْ وَلَا مِنْهُمْ ۙ وَيَحْلِفُوْنَ عَلَى الْكَذِبِ وَهُمْ يَعْلَمُوْنَ ﴿١٥﴾

---

[a]60 : 14.

3008. As in the preceding verses the subject of holding an assembly was dealt with, it was in the fitness of things that its ethics and etiquette should also have been pointed out and this has been done in the present verse.

3009. The believers should have due regard for the precious time of the Holy Prophet and as a compensation for taking his time to spend some money in charity before going to him for consultation. The Holy Prophet has been called "Counseller" in the Bible (Isa. 9 : 6).

3010. The commandment about the giving of alms before seeking the Holy Prophet's consultation is not obligatory but optional, though preferable. The apprehension of the Companions of the Holy Prophet was whether they had given enough in alms to have complied with God's commandment.

16. Allāh has prepared for them a severe punishment. Evil, indeed, is that which they used to do.

اَعَدَّ اللّٰهُ لَهُمْ عَذَابًا شَدِيْدًا ۭ اِنَّهُمْ سَاۗءَ مَا
كَانُوْا يَعْمَلُوْنَ ﴿١٦﴾

17. They have made their oaths a shield[3011] *for their falsehoods*, and *thereby* they seek to turn *men* away from the path of Allāh; for them, therefore, will be an humiliating punishment.

اِتَّخَذُوْٓا اَيْمَانَهُمْ جُنَّةً فَصَدُّوْا عَنْ سَبِيْلِ
اللّٰهِ فَلَهُمْ عَذَابٌ مُّهِيْنٌ ﴿١٧﴾

18. [a]Neither their wealth nor their children will avail them aught against Allāh. They are the inmates of the Fire wherein they will abide.

لَنْ تُغْنِيَ عَنْهُمْ اَمْوَالُهُمْ وَلَآ اَوْلَادُهُمْ مِّنَ
اللّٰهِ شَيْـًٔا ۭ اُولٰۗىِٕكَ اَصْحٰبُ النَّارِ ۭ هُمْ فِيْهَا خٰلِدُوْنَ ﴿١٨﴾

19. On the day when Allāh will raise them all together, they will swear to Him,[3012] even as they *now* swear to you, and they will think that they have something *to stand upon*. Now, surely, it is they who are the liars.

يَوْمَ يَبْعَثُهُمُ اللّٰهُ جَمِيْعًا فَيَحْلِفُوْنَ لَهٗ كَمَا
يَحْلِفُوْنَ لَكُمْ وَيَحْسَبُوْنَ اَنَّهُمْ عَلٰي شَيْءٍ ۭ اَلَآ
اِنَّهُمْ هُمُ الْكٰذِبُوْنَ ﴿١٩﴾

20. Satan has gained mastery over them, and has made them forget the remembrance of Allāh. They are Satan's party. Now, surely, it is Satan's party that are the losers.

اِسْتَحْوَذَ عَلَيْهِمُ الشَّيْطٰنُ فَاَنْسٰىهُمْ ذِكْرَ اللّٰهِ ۭ
اُولٰۗىِٕكَ حِزْبُ الشَّيْطٰنِ ۭ اَلَآ اِنَّ حِزْبَ الشَّيْطٰنِ
هُمُ الْخٰسِرُوْنَ ﴿٢٠﴾

21. [b]Certainly those who oppose Allāh and His Messenger are among the most abject.

اِنَّ الَّذِيْنَ يُحَاۗدُّوْنَ اللّٰهَ وَرَسُوْلَهٗٓ اُولٰۗىِٕكَ فِي
الْاَذَلِّيْنَ ﴿٢١﴾

[a]3 : 11 : 92 : 12 : 111 : 3. [b]9 : 63.

3011. The hypocrites protest loudly the sincerity of their faith by swearing and seek to take shelter behind their false oaths.

3012. When a person becomes an habitual or hardened liar, he regards his falsehood as truth. The hypocrites will protest their innocence even before God on the Day of Reckoning.

22. Allāh has decreed: 'Most [a]surely, I will prevail,[3013] I and My Messengers.' Verily, Allāh is Powerful, Mighty.

كَتَبَ اللّٰهُ لَاَغْلِبَنَّ اَنَا وَرُسُلِيْ ؕ اِنَّ اللّٰهَ قَوِيٌّ
عَزِيْزٌ ﴿۲۲﴾

23. [b]Thou wilt not find any people who believe in Allāh and the Last Day *and yet they* love those who oppose Allāh and His Messenger,[3014] even though they be their fathers, or their sons, or their brethren, or their kindred. These are they in whose hearts *Allāh* has inscribed *true* faith and whom He has strengthened with inspiration from Himself. And He will admit them into Gardens through which streams flow. Therein they will abide; [c]Allāh is well-pleased with them and they are well-pleased with Him. They are Allāh's party. Hearken! it is Allāh's party who are the successful.

لَا تَجِدُ قَوْمًا يُّؤْمِنُوْنَ بِاللّٰهِ وَالْيَوْمِ الْاٰخِرِ
يُوَآدُّوْنَ مَنْ حَآدَّ اللّٰهَ وَرَسُوْلَهٗ وَلَوْ كَانُوْٓا اٰبَآءَهُمْ
اَوْ اَبْنَآءَهُمْ اَوْ اِخْوَانَهُمْ اَوْ عَشِيْرَتَهُمْ ؕ اُولٰٓئِكَ
كَتَبَ فِيْ قُلُوْبِهِمُ الْاِيْمَانَ وَاَيَّدَهُمْ بِرُوْحٍ
مِّنْهُ ؕ وَيُدْخِلُهُمْ جَنّٰتٍ تَجْرِيْ مِنْ تَحْتِهَا
الْاَنْهٰرُ خٰلِدِيْنَ فِيْهَا ؕ رَضِيَ اللّٰهُ عَنْهُمْ وَرَضُوْا
عَنْهُ ؕ اُولٰٓئِكَ حِزْبُ اللّٰهِ ؕ اَلَآ اِنَّ حِزْبَ اللّٰهِ هُمُ
الْمُفْلِحُوْنَ ﴿۲۳﴾ ع

[a]5 : 57; 37 : 172-173. [b]3 : 29; 4 : 145; 9 : 23. [c]5 : 120; 9 : 100; 98 : 9.

3013. It is writ large on the face of History that eventually Truth has always prevailed against falsehood.

3014. Obviously, there could be no true or sincere friendship or relationship of love between the believers and the disbelievers. The ideals, principles and religious beliefs of the two being poles apart, and the community of interests which is the *sine qua non* of real intimate relationship being non-existent, believers are required not to have intimate and affectionate friendship with disbelievers. The bonds of Faith transcend all other bonds, even the close ties of blood. The verse seems to be of general application. But it applies specially to disbelievers who are at war with Muslims.

CHAPTER 59

AL-ḤASHR

(Revealed after Hijrah)

Date of Revelation and Context

The *Sūrah* is the third of the seven last Medinite Chapters of the Qur'ān. The preceding *Surah* had dealt with the secret plots and machinations against Islām of the Jews of Medina. The present one, however, deals with their punishment, particularly with the expulsion from Medina of the Banū Naḍir, one of the three Jewish tribes—Banū Qainuquā' Banū Naḍir and Banū Quraiẓah—a few months after the Battle of Uḥud in the fourth year of the *Hijrah.* The expulsion was an act of great wisdom and political foresight on the Holy Prophet's part. Because, if the Jews had been allowed to remain in Medina they would have proved, on account of their conspiracies and secret plots, a source of constant danger to Islām. Next, the *Sūrah* deals with the Hypocrites of Medina who were neither true to Muslims nor to Jews. A hypocrite is essentially a coward, and a cowardly person is never sincere or honest to anyone. The Hypocrites of Medina proved dishonest even to the Jews in the latter's hour of peril. The *Sūrah* opens with Divine glorification and ends with an exhortation to Muslims to sing the praises of the Beneficent and Merciful Lord, Who had nipped the wicked designs of their enemies in the bud and had opened out endless vistas of progress and prosperity for them. The *Surah* has close resemblance with *Surah* Al-Anfāl.

سُوْرَةُ الْحَشْرِ مَدَنِيَّةٌ (٥٩)

1. [a]In the name of Allāh, the Gracious, the Merciful.	بِسْمِ اللّٰهِ الرَّحْمٰنِ الرَّحِيْمِ ①
2. [b]All that is in the heavens and all that is in the earth glorifies[3015] Allāh; and He is the Mighty, the Wise.	سَبَّحَ لِلّٰهِ مَا فِي السَّمٰوٰتِ وَمَا فِي الْاَرْضِ وَهُوَ الْعَزِيْزُ الْحَكِيْمُ ②
3. He it is Who caused the disbelievers of the People of the Book to go forth from their homes at *the time of* the first banishment.[3016] You did not think that they would go forth and they thought that their	هُوَ الَّذِيْٓ اَخْرَجَ الَّذِيْنَ كَفَرُوْا مِنْ اَهْلِ الْكِتٰبِ مِنْ دِيَارِهِمْ لِاَوَّلِ الْحَشْرِ مَا ظَنَنْتُمْ اَنْ يَّخْرُجُوْا وَظَنُّوْٓا اَنَّهُمْ مَّانِعَتُهُمْ حُصُوْنُهُمْ مِّنَ اللّٰهِ فَاَتٰهُمُ

[a]1 : 1. [b]17 : 45; 24 : 42 ; 61 : 2; 62: 2; 64 : 2.

3015. See 2981. Whereas *Tasbīḥ* (glorifying) is used with regard to God's attributes, *Taqdīs* (extolling His holiness) is used concerning His actions.

3016. There lived in Medina three Jewish tribes—Banū Qainuquā', Banū Naḍīr and Banū Quraiẓah. The verse refers to the banishment from Medina of the Banū Naḍīr. This tribe like Banū Qainuquā' before them had acted treacherously towards Muslims on several occasions. They had hatched plots and entered into secret alliances against them, with their enemies. They had repeatedly broken their plighted word and had repudiated the solemn agreement that they would remain neutral between the Holy Prophet and his enemies, and even had conspired to take his life. Their leader Ka'b bin Ashraf had gone to Mecca to enlist the help of the Quraish and of other pagan tribes around Mecca to drive out the Muslims from Medina. After the temporary reverse suffered by Muslims at Uḥud, their machinations and defiance of the Holy Prophet had greatly increased. It was when the cup of their iniquities had become full to the brim and their presence in Medina had proved to be a constant source of mortal danger to Muslims and the Islamic State that the Holy Prophet had to take action against them. He laid siege to their fortresses and, after vainly holding out for about 21 days, they surrendered. They were told to leave Medina upon which they all left for Syria, only two families choosing to remain behind at Khaibar. The Holy Prophet was exceptionally kind and considerate to them. He allowed them to carry their goods and chattels with them. They departed from Medina in perfect safety, but not until they had despaired of the help they expected from their Meccan allies and from the Hypocrites of Medina, and had also found that their fortresses, which they thought were impregnable, could not save them. In view of their evil designs and machinations, their conspiracies and secret plots, their repeated acts of treachery and infidelity and the breach of their plighted word every now and then. the punishment meted out to them was extremely light.

The reference in the words, *at the time of the first banishment*, may be to the banishment of Banū Qainuquā' from Medina after the Battle of Badr, or the words may refer to the banishment by the Holy Prophet from Medina of all the three above-mentioned Jewish tribes. That was their first banishment. 'Umar, the Holy Prophet's Second Successor, however, banished all the Jews from the rest of Arabia for the second and last time. Thus the words may be taken as embodying a prophecy that after the Jewish tribes of Medina will have been banished by the Holy Prophet, all the Jews of Arabia would suffer the same fate at some later time.

fortresses would defend them against Allāh.[3017] But [a]Allāh came upon them whence they did not expect, and [b]cast terror into their hearts, so that they demolished their houses with their own hands[3018] and *with* the hands of the believers. So take a lesson, O ye who have eyes.

اللّٰهُ مِنْ حَيْثُ لَمْ يَحْتَسِبُوْا وَقَذَفَ فِيْ قُلُوْبِهِمُ الرُّعْبَ يُخْرِبُوْنَ بُيُوْتَهُمْ بِاَيْدِيْهِمْ وَاَيْدِي الْمُؤْمِنِيْنَ فَاعْتَبِرُوْا يٰاُولِي الْاَبْصَارِ ③

4. And had it not been that Allāh had decreed exile for them, He would have, surely, punished them *otherwise* in this world.[3019] And in the Hereafter they will, certainly, have the punishment of the Fire.

وَلَوْلَاۤ اَنْ كَتَبَ اللّٰهُ عَلَيْهِمُ الْجَلَاۤءَ لَعَذَّبَهُمْ فِي الدُّنْيَا وَلَهُمْ فِي الْاٰخِرَةِ عَذَابُ النَّارِ ④

5. That is because they opposed Allāh and His Messenger; and [c]whoso opposes Allāh—then, surely, Allāh is Severe in retribution.

ذٰلِكَ بِاَنَّهُمْ شَآقُّوا اللّٰهَ وَرَسُوْلَهٗ وَمَنْ يُّشَآقِّ اللّٰهَ فَاِنَّ اللّٰهَ شَدِيْدُ الْعِقَابِ ⑤

6. Whatever palm trees you cut down,[3020] or left standing on their roots, it was by Allāh's leave that He might humiliate the transgressors.

مَا قَطَعْتُمْ مِّنْ لِّيْنَةٍ اَوْ تَرَكْتُمُوْهَا قَآئِمَةً عَلٰۤى اُصُوْلِهَا فَبِاِذْنِ اللّٰهِ وَلِيُخْزِيَ الْفٰسِقِيْنَ ⑥

[a]16 : 27; 39 : 26. [b]3 : 152; 8 : 13. [c]4 : 116; 8 : 14; 47 : 33.

3017. In view of the material resources, political alliances and organization of the Jews of Medina, the Muslims could never think that the Jews could be driven out of Medina so easily and without any loss of human life on either side.

3018. Before departing from Medina the Banū Naḍīr had destroyed, with their own hands, their houses and other movable property before the very eyes of Muslims. The Holy Prophet had given them ten days to dispose of their affairs as they liked. Thus the Jews of Medina were the originators of the scorched earth policy, centuries before the Russians had adopted it in World War II.

3019. The exile of the Banū Naḍīr from Medina was a very light punishment. They deserved a much heavier punishment, and had they not been exiled they would have been severely punished in some other way.

3020. The reference is to the cutting, by orders of the Holy Prophet, of the palm trees of the Banū Naḍīr who, as stated in v. 3, had shut themselves up in their fortresses in defiance of the Holy Prophet's orders to surrender. After the siege had lasted for some days, the Holy Prophet, in order to compel them to surrender, ordered that some of their palm trees of the *līnah* kind, of which the dates are of very inferior quality and quite unfit for human consumption, (Al-Rauḍ al-Unuf), should be cut down. It was after only six trees had been cut down, that they surrendered (Zurqānī). The orders of the Holy Prophet were extremely light and lenient and quite in conformity with the laws of civilized warfare.

وما افاء الله على رسوله منهم فما اوجفتم
عليه من خيل ولا ركاب ولكن الله يسلط
رسله على من يشاء والله على كل شيء قدير ⑦

7. And whatever Allāh has given to His Messenger as spoils from them, *is of Allāh's grace*. You urged neither horse nor camel for that; but Allāh gives authority to His Messengers over whomsoever He pleases; and Allāh has power over all things.

ما افاء الله على رسوله من اهل القرى فلله
وللرسول ولذي القربى واليتمى والمسكين
وابن السبيل كي لا يكون دولة بين الاغنياء
منكم وما اتىكم الرسول فخذوه وما نهىكم
عنه فانتهوا واتقوا الله ان الله شديد العقاب ⑧

8. Whatever Allāh has given to His Messenger as spoils[3021] from the people of the towns, it is for Allāh and for the Messenger and for the near of kin and the orphans and the needy and the wayfarer, in order that it may not circulate *only* among those of you who are rich. And whatsoever the Messenger gives you, take it,[3022] and whatsoever he forbids you, abstain from *it*. And fear Allāh; surely, Allāh is Severe in retribution.

للفقراء المهجرين الذين اخرجوا من ديارهم
واموالهم يبتغون فضلا من الله ورضوانا
وينصرون الله ورسوله اولئك هم الصدقون ⑨

9. *And it is also* for the poor Refugees who have been driven out from their homes and their possessions; they seek the grace of Allāh and *His* pleasure; and help Allāh and His Messenger. These it is who are true *in their faith*;

3021. As *Fai'* consists of such booty as is attained without difficulty or labour and accrues to Muslims without war, the soldiers have no share in it, and the whole of it goes to the public treasury. The verse may have special reference to the spoils the Muslims got from the Jews of Khaibar. It lays down the principle that the circulation of wealth should not remain confined to the privileged and propertied class. As an individual's health requires that his physical needs be reasonably met, the health of the society requires that material goods be widely distributed and wealth be in easy circulation. This is the basic principle of Muslim economics. Finding humanity ground down under the tyranny of vested interests, Islām propounded measures that broke the barriers of economic caste and enormously reduced the injustice of special privilege. It does not, however, oppose the profit motive or economic competition, but only insists that acquisitiveness and competition be balanced by fair-play and compassion. Since human nature automatically takes care for the former, it falls to social laws to safeguard the latter. The *Zakāt* is Islām's basic device for institutionalizing regard for the need of others, but it is supplemented by a number of other measures.

3022. The words, *whatsoever the Messenger gives you, take it,* show that the *Sunnah* forms an integral part of the Islamic Law.

وَالَّذِيْنَ تَبَوَّؤُ الدَّارَ وَالْاِيْمَانَ مِنْ قَبْلِهِمْ يُحِبُّوْنَ
مَنْ هَاجَرَ اِلَيْهِمْ وَلَا يَجِدُوْنَ فِيْ صُدُوْرِهِمْ
حَاجَةً مِّمَّآ اُوْتُوْا وَيُؤْثِرُوْنَ عَلٰٓى اَنْفُسِهِمْ وَلَوْ
كَانَ بِهِمْ خَصَاصَةٌ ؕ وَمَنْ يُّوْقَ شُحَّ نَفْسِهٖ
فَاُولٰٓئِكَ هُمُ الْمُفْلِحُوْنَ ﴿١٠﴾

10. And *for* those who had established *their* home *in this City* and *had accepted* the Faith before them. They love those who come to them for refuge, and find not in their breasts any desire for that which is given them (the Refugees), but give preference *to the Refugees* above themselves, even though poverty be their *own lot*.[3023] Whoso is rid of the covetousness of his own soul—it is these [a]who will be successful;

وَالَّذِيْنَ جَآءُوْ مِنْۢ بَعْدِهِمْ يَقُوْلُوْنَ رَبَّنَا اغْفِرْ
لَنَا وَلِاِخْوَانِنَا الَّذِيْنَ سَبَقُوْنَا بِالْاِيْمَانِ وَلَا
تَجْعَلْ فِيْ قُلُوْبِنَا غِلًّا لِّلَّذِيْنَ اٰمَنُوْا رَبَّنَآ اِنَّكَ
رَءُوْفٌ رَّحِيْمٌ ﴿١١﴾

11. And *for* those who came after them.[3024] They say, 'Our Lord, forgive us and our brothers who preceded us in the Faith, and leave not any rancour in our hearts against those who believe. Our Lord! Thou art, indeed, Compassionate, Merciful.

اَلَمْ تَرَ اِلَى الَّذِيْنَ نَافَقُوْا يَقُوْلُوْنَ لِاِخْوَانِهِمُ الَّذِيْنَ
كَفَرُوْا مِنْ اَهْلِ الْكِتٰبِ لَئِنْ اُخْرِجْتُمْ لَنَخْرُجَنَّ
مَعَكُمْ وَلَا نُطِيْعُ فِيْكُمْ اَحَدًا اَبَدًا ۙ وَّاِنْ قُوْتِلْتُمْ
لَنَنْصُرَنَّكُمْ ؕ وَاللّٰهُ يَشْهَدُ اِنَّهُمْ لَكٰذِبُوْنَ ﴿١٢﴾

R. 2 12. Seest thou not the Hypocrites? They say to their brethren who disbelieve from among the People of the Book, 'If you are turned out *of Medina*, we will, surely, go out with you and we will never obey any one against you, and if you are fought against, we will, certainly, help you.[3025] But Allāh bears witness that, surely, they are liars.

[a]64 : 17.

3023. The words constitute a great testimonial to the spirit of self-sacrifice, hospitality and goodwill of the *Anṣār* (Helpers). The Refugees (*Muhājirīn*) from Mecca came to them, deprived and denuded of all their possessions, and they received them with open arms and made them equal partners in their belongings. The bond of love and brotherhood which the Holy Prophet established between the Refugees from Mecca and the Helpers of Medina and to which this verse bears an eloquent testimony, stands unrivalled in the whole history of human relationships.

3024. The words may apply to the Refugees who came later to Medina, or to all the coming generations of Muslims.

3025. The Hypocrites had urged the Jews of Medina to defy the Holy Prophet and break their plighted word with him, holding out to them false promises of help and succour in time of need. But when relying upon their promises the Jews defied the Holy Prophet and marched against him, they left them in the lurch.

13. If they are turned out, they will never go out with them; and if they are fought against, they will never help them. And even if they help them, they will, certainly, ^aturn *their* backs, and then they *themselves* shall not be helped.

لَئِنۡ اُخۡرِجُوۡا لَا يَخۡرُجُوۡنَ مَعَهُمۡۚ وَ لَئِنۡ قُوۡتِلُوۡا لَا يَنۡصُرُوۡنَهُمۡۚ وَ لَئِنۡ نَّصَرُوۡهُمۡ لَيُوَلُّنَّ الۡاَدۡبَارَ ثُمَّ لَا يُنۡصَرُوۡنَ ۝

14. Assuredly, they have greater ^bfear of you in their hearts than of Allāh. That is because they are a people who understand not.

لَاَنۡتُمۡ اَشَدُّ رَهۡبَةً فِىۡ صُدُوۡرِهِمۡ مِّنَ اللّٰهِۚ ذٰلِكَ بِاَنَّهُمۡ قَوۡمٌ لَّا يَفۡقَهُوۡنَ ۝

15. They will not fight you in a body except in strongly fortified towns or from behind the walls. Their fighting among themselves is severe. Thou thinkest them to be united, but their hearts are divided.[3026] That is because they are a people who have no sense.

لَا يُقَاتِلُوۡنَكُمۡ جَمِيۡعًا اِلَّا فِىۡ قُرًى مُّحَصَّنَةٍ اَوۡ مِنۡ وَّرَآءِ جُدُرٍؕ بَاۡسُهُمۡ بَيۡنَهُمۡ شَدِيۡدٌؕ تَحۡسَبُهُمۡ جَمِيۡعًا وَّ قُلُوۡبُهُمۡ شَتّٰىؕ ذٰلِكَ بِاَنَّهُمۡ قَوۡمٌ لَّا يَعۡقِلُوۡنَ ۝

16. *Their case is* like *the case of* those *people who passed away* only a short time before them. They tasted the evil consequences of their *evil* conduct.[3027] And for them is a painful punishment.

كَمَثَلِ الَّذِيۡنَ مِنۡ قَبۡلِهِمۡ قَرِيۡبًا ذَاقُوۡا وَبَالَ اَمۡرِهِمۡۚ وَ لَهُمۡ عَذَابٌ اَلِيۡمٌ ۝

---

^a3 : 112. ^b4 : 78.

3026. The verse means that the disbelievers, particularly the Jews and the Hypocrites of Medina, present a false *facade* of unity against Islām, but as they have no common cause to fight for, and as their interests are diverse and divergent, there can possibly exist no real unity among them. There were three parties in Arabia who appeared to be united against the Islamic State—the Jews, the Hypocrites of Medina and the pagan Quraish of Mecca. The Quraish saw in the rising power of Islām a great danger to their all-round supremacy, the Hypocrites (of whom 'Abd Allāh bin Ubayy was the leader) to their domination in Medina, and the Jews to their organization and racial superiority. Having no common objective their seeming unity had no real basis and it never materialized in time of danger.

3027. The reference may be to the Quraish of Mecca who sustained ignominious defeat at Badr, or to Banū Qainuqā' who were punished for their mischiefs and machinations after Badr. The latter were the first of the three Jewish tribes who were banished from Medina one month after the Battle of Badr because they had broken their pledged word with the Holy Prophet. Eventually they settled in Syria.

17. [a]*Or it is* like that of Satan, when he says to man, 'Disbelieve,' but when he disbelieves, he says, I have nothing to do with thee, I fear Allāh, the Lord of the worlds.'

كَمَثَلِ الشَّيْطٰنِ اِذْ قَالَ لِلْاِنْسَانِ اكْفُرْ ۚ فَلَمَّا كَفَرَ
قَالَ اِنِّيْ بَرِيْٓءٌ مِّنْكَ اِنِّيْٓ اَخَافُ اللّٰهَ رَبَّ الْعٰلَمِيْنَ ﴿١٧﴾

18. The end of both is that they are both in the Fire, abiding therein. Such is the reward of the wrongdoers.

فَكَانَ عَاقِبَتَهُمَآ اَنَّهُمَا فِي النَّارِ خَالِدَيْنِ فِيْهَا ۗ وَ
ذٰلِكَ جَزٰٓؤُا الظّٰلِمِيْنَ ﴿١٨﴾ ع

R. 3 19. O ye who believe! be mindful of your duty to Allāh and let *every* soul look to what it sends forth for the morrow. And fear Allāh, verily, Allāh is Well-Aware of what you do.

يٰٓاَيُّهَا الَّذِيْنَ اٰمَنُوا اتَّقُوا اللّٰهَ وَلْتَنْظُرْ نَفْسٌ مَّا قَدَّمَتْ
لِغَدٍ ۚ وَاتَّقُوا اللّٰهَ ۭ اِنَّ اللّٰهَ خَبِيْرٌۢ بِمَا تَعْمَلُوْنَ ﴿١٩﴾

20. And be not like those who [b]forgot Allāh, so He caused them to forget their own souls. It is they that are the transgressors.

وَلَا تَكُوْنُوْا كَالَّذِيْنَ نَسُوا اللّٰهَ فَاَنْسٰهُمْ اَنْفُسَهُمْ ۭ
اُولٰٓئِكَ هُمُ الْفٰسِقُوْنَ ﴿٢٠﴾

21. The inmates of the Fire and the inmates of the Garden are not equal. It is the inmates of the Garden that are the triumphant.

لَا يَسْتَوِيْٓ اَصْحٰبُ النَّارِ وَاَصْحٰبُ الْجَنَّةِ ۭ اَصْحٰبُ
الْجَنَّةِ هُمُ الْفَآئِزُوْنَ ﴿٢١﴾

22. [c]If We had sent down this Qur'ān on a mountain, thou wouldst, certainly, have seen it humbled and rent asunder[3027A] for fear of Allāh. And these are similitudes that We set forth for mankind that they may reflect.

لَوْ اَنْزَلْنَا هٰذَا الْقُرْاٰنَ عَلٰى جَبَلٍ لَّرَاَيْتَهٗ خَاشِعًا
مُّتَصَدِّعًا مِّنْ خَشْيَةِ اللّٰهِ ۭ وَتِلْكَ الْاَمْثَالُ
نَضْرِبُهَا لِلنَّاسِ لَعَلَّهُمْ يَتَفَكَّرُوْنَ ﴿٢٢﴾

---

[a]8 : 49; 14 : 23. [b]9 : 67. [c]13 : 32.

3027A. The verse may signify that the proud pagan Arabs whom no pre-Islamic teaching could wean from their polytheistic beliefs and idolatrous practices and who, like a strong rock, remained unmoved and firmly wedded to their Bedouin usages, unaffected by the corrosive influence of the glamour and glitter of the neighbouring Christian civilization, would be humbled before the sublime and powerful Message of Islām, and from their erstwhile stony hearts would gush forth fountains of light and learning.

23. He is Allāh, and there is no god beside Him, [a]the Knower of the unseen and the seen. He is the Gracious, the Merciful.

هُوَ اللّٰهُ الَّذِيْ لَآ اِلٰهَ اِلَّا هُوَ ۚ عٰلِمُ الْغَيْبِ وَالشَّهَادَةِ ۚ
هُوَ الرَّحْمٰنُ الرَّحِيْمُ ﴿٢٣﴾

24. He is Allāh, and there is no god beside Him, the Sovereign, the Holy One, the Source of peace, the Bestower of security, the Protector, the Mighty, the Subduer, the Exalted. Holy is Allāh, *far* above that which they associate *with Him*.

هُوَ اللّٰهُ الَّذِيْ لَآ اِلٰهَ اِلَّا هُوَ ۚ اَلْمَلِكُ الْقُدُّوْسُ
السَّلٰمُ الْمُؤْمِنُ الْمُهَيْمِنُ الْعَزِيْزُ الْجَبَّارُ الْمُتَكَبِّرُ ۗ
سُبْحٰنَ اللّٰهِ عَمَّا يُشْرِكُوْنَ ﴿٢٤﴾

25. He is Allāh, the Creator, the Maker, the Fashioner. [b]His are the most beautiful names. All that is in the heavens and the earth [c]glorifies Him, and He is the Mighty, the Wise.

هُوَ اللّٰهُ الْخَالِقُ الْبَارِئُ الْمُصَوِّرُ لَهُ الْاَسْمَآءُ الْحُسْنٰى ۗ
يُسَبِّحُ لَهٗ مَا فِي السَّمٰوٰتِ وَالْاَرْضِ ۚ وَهُوَ الْعَزِيْزُ
الْحَكِيْمُ ﴿٢٥﴾ ع

[a]6 : 74; 9 : 94; 13 : 10. [b]7 : 181. [c]17 : 45; 24 : 42; 61 : 2; 62 : 2; 64 : 2.

CHAPTER 60

AL-MUMTAḤANAH

(*Revealed after Hijrah*)

Date of Revelation and Context

Like the preceding three Chapters, this *Sūrah* was revealed, as its contents show, at Medina, in the 7th or 8th year of *Hijrah*, sometime during the interval between the Treaty of Ḥudaibiyah and the Fall of Mecca. The preceding *Sūrah* had dealt with the intrigues and machinations of the Hypocrites and the Jews of Medina and with the punishment which was meted out to them. The present *Sūrah* deals with the believers' social relations with disbelievers in general, and with those at war with Islām in particular. It opens with an emphatic prohibitory injunction to Muslims against having intimate friendly relations with those disbelievers who are at war with and are bent upon extirpating Islām. The injunction is so strict and comprehensive that even very near blood relations have not been exempted from it. The prohibitory injunction is followed by an implied prophecy that very soon the implacable enemies of Islām would become its devoted followers. The injunction, however, has its exception. It does not apply to those disbelievers who have good neighbourly relations with Muslims. Such disbelievers are to be treated equitably and with kindness. The *Sūrah* then lays down some important injunctions with regard to believing women who migrated to Medina, and also with regard to those women who left Medina and went over to disbelievers. In order to bring home to Muslims the seriousness of the matter, the *Sūrah* closes with repeating the injunction that Muslims are not to make friends with those people, who, by adopting an openly hostile attitude towards Islām, have incurred God's wrath.

سُورَةُ الْمُمْتَحِنَةِ مَدَنِيَّةٌ (٦٠)

1. [a]In the name of Allāh, the Gracious, the Merciful.

بِسْمِ اللّٰهِ الرَّحْمٰنِ الرَّحِيْمِ ①

2 O ye who believe! take not My enemy and your enemy for [b]friends. Would you offer them love,[3028] while they have disbelieved in the Truth which has come to you *and* [c]have driven out the Messenger and yourselves *from your homes, merely* because you believe in Allāh, your Lord? When you go forth to strive in My cause and to seek My pleasure, *some of* you send them *messages* of love in secret, while I know best what you conceal and what you reveal. And whoever of you does it has, indeed, strayed away from the right path.

يٰۤاَيُّهَا الَّذِيْنَ اٰمَنُوْا لَا تَتَّخِذُوْا عَدُوِّيْ وَعَدُوَّكُمْ
اَوْلِيَآءَ تُلْقُوْنَ اِلَيْهِمْ بِالْمَوَدَّةِ وَقَدْ كَفَرُوْا بِمَا
جَآءَكُمْ مِّنَ الْحَقِّ ۚ يُخْرِجُوْنَ الرَّسُوْلَ وَاِيَّاكُمْ اَنْ
تُؤْمِنُوْا بِاللّٰهِ رَبِّكُمْ ؕ اِنْ كُنْتُمْ خَرَجْتُمْ جِهَادًا
فِيْ سَبِيْلِيْ وَابْتِغَآءَ مَرْضَاتِيْ ٭ۖ تُسِرُّوْنَ اِلَيْهِمْ
بِالْمَوَدَّةِ ٭ۖ وَاَنَا اَعْلَمُ بِمَاۤ اَخْفَيْتُمْ وَمَاۤ اَعْلَنْتُمْ ؕ
وَمَنْ يَّفْعَلْهُ مِنْكُمْ فَقَدْ ضَلَّ سَوَآءَ السَّبِيْلِ ②

3. If they get the upper hand of you, they will be your *active* enemies, and will stretch forth their hands and their tongues *towards* you to do you harm; and they ardently desire that you should become disbelievers.

اِنْ يَّثْقَفُوْكُمْ يَكُوْنُوْا لَكُمْ اَعْدَآءً وَّيَبْسُطُوْۤا اِلَيْكُمْ
اَيْدِيَهُمْ وَاَلْسِنَتَهُمْ بِالسُّوْٓءِ وَوَدُّوْا لَوْ
تَكْفُرُوْنَ ؕ ③

---

[a]1 : 1. [b]3 : 119; 4 : 145; 5 : 58. [c]17 : 77.

3028. The prohibitory injunction is of very strict character. Muslims are not to have friendly relations with the avowed enemies of God—those who drove out the Prophet and the Muslims from their hearths and homes and sought to destroy Islām. It is all-comprehensive in this respect that no consideration of bonds or ties of even the nearest blood relationship is allowed to interfere with it. The enemy of Islām is God's enemy, whosoever he may be.

The immediate occasion of the revelation of this verse seems to be when the Quraish dishonoured the Treaty of Ḥudaibiyah, and the Holy Prophet had to take stern punitive action against them, Ḥāṭib bin Abi Balta'ah had written a secret letter to the Meccans informing them of the Holy Prophet's intended march on Mecca. The Prophet, informed by revelation about it, sent 'Alī, Zubair and Miqdād in search of the bearer of the letter. They overtook the Messenger—she was a woman—on the way to Mecca and the letter was brought back to Medina. Ḥāṭib's offence was extremely grave. He had sought to divulge an important State secret. He deserved exemplary punishment, but he was forgiven because he had committed the offence inadvertently, not realizing its grave consequences. Incidentally, the episode of the letter fixes the date of the revelation of the *Sūrah*.

4. [a]Neither your ties of kindred, nor your children will avail you aught on the Day of Resurrection. *Allāh* will decide between you. And Allāh sees all what you do.

لَنْ تَنْفَعَكُمْ أَرْحَامُكُمْ وَلَآ أَوْلَادُكُمْ ۚ يَوْمَ الْقِيٰمَةِ ۚ
يَفْصِلُ بَيْنَكُمْ ۚ وَاللّٰهُ بِمَا تَعْمَلُوْنَ بَصِيْرٌ ﴿٤﴾

5. [b]Indeed there is a good example for you in Abraham[3029] and those with him when they said to their people, [c]"We have nothing to do with you and with that which you worship beside Allāh. We disbelieve *all that* you *believe in*. There has become manifest enmity and hatred between us and you for ever, until you believe in Allāh alone—except that Abraham said to his father, [d]"I will, surely, ask forgiveness for thee, though I have no power to do aught for thee against Allāh.' *Their prayer* was: 'Our Lord, in Thee do we put our trust and to Thee do we turn in repentance, and towards Thee is the *final* return;

قَدْ كَانَتْ لَكُمْ أُسْوَةٌ حَسَنَةٌ فِيْٓ إِبْرٰهِيْمَ وَالَّذِيْنَ
مَعَهٗ ۚ إِذْ قَالُوْا لِقَوْمِهِمْ إِنَّا بُرَءٰٓؤُا مِنْكُمْ وَمِمَّا
تَعْبُدُوْنَ مِنْ دُوْنِ اللّٰهِ ۫ كَفَرْنَا بِكُمْ وَبَدَا بَيْنَنَا
وَبَيْنَكُمُ الْعَدَاوَةُ وَالْبَغْضَآءُ أَبَدًا حَتّٰى تُؤْمِنُوْا
بِاللّٰهِ وَحْدَهٗٓ إِلَّا قَوْلَ إِبْرٰهِيْمَ لِأَبِيْهِ لَأَسْتَغْفِرَنَّ
لَكَ وَمَآ أَمْلِكُ لَكَ مِنَ اللّٰهِ مِنْ شَيْءٍ ۗ رَبَّنَا عَلَيْكَ
تَوَكَّلْنَا وَإِلَيْكَ أَنَبْنَا وَإِلَيْكَ الْمَصِيْرُ ﴿٥﴾

6. 'Our Lord, make us not a [e]trial for those who disbelieve, and forgive us, our Lord; for, Thou alone art the Mighty, the Wise.'

رَبَّنَا لَا تَجْعَلْنَا فِتْنَةً لِّلَّذِيْنَ كَفَرُوْا وَاغْفِرْ لَنَا
رَبَّنَا ۚ إِنَّكَ أَنْتَ الْعَزِيْزُ الْحَكِيْمُ ﴿٦﴾

7. [f]Surely, there is a good example in them for you—for *all* who have hope *to see* Allāh and the Last Day. And whosoever turns away—truly, Allāh is Self-Sufficient, Worthy of all praise.

لَقَدْ كَانَ لَكُمْ فِيْهِمْ أُسْوَةٌ حَسَنَةٌ لِّمَنْ كَانَ
يَرْجُوا اللّٰهَ وَالْيَوْمَ الْاٰخِرَ ۚ وَمَنْ يَّتَوَلَّ فَإِنَّ اللّٰهَ
ع هُوَ الْغَنِيُّ الْحَمِيْدُ ﴿٧﴾

[a]3 : 11; 31 : 34. [b]60 : 7. 6 : 79; 43 : 27. [d]19 : 48. [e]10 : 86. [f]60 : 5.

3029. Abraham's example has been mentioned here to emphasize that whenever it becomes clear that a certain person or persons are inimically disposed towards truth and are bent upon extirpating it, all friendly relations with them are to be given up. The expression, *Kafarnā Bikum*, which is generally translated as 'we disbelieve all that you believe in' may also mean, *We have nothing to do with you*; the expression, *Kafara Bikadhā*, meaning, he declared himself to be clear or quit of such a thing (Lane).

R. 2 8. It may be that Allāh will bring about love between you and those of them with whom you are *now* at enmity,[3030] and Allāh is All-Powerful; and Allāh is Most Forgiving, Merciful.

عَسَى اللّٰهُ اَنْ يَّجْعَلَ بَيْنَكُمْ وَبَيْنَ الَّذِيْنَ عَادَيْتُمْ مِّنْهُمْ مَّوَدَّةً ۭ وَاللّٰهُ قَدِيْرٌ ۭ وَاللّٰهُ غَفُوْرٌ رَّحِيْمٌ ۝

9. Allāh forbids you not respecting those who have not fought against you on account of *your* religion, and who have not driven you out from your homes, that you be kind to them and deal equitably with them; surely, Allāh loves those who are equitable.

لَا يَنْهٰىكُمُ اللّٰهُ عَنِ الَّذِيْنَ لَمْ يُقَاتِلُوْكُمْ فِي الدِّيْنِ وَلَمْ يُخْرِجُوْكُمْ مِّنْ دِيَارِكُمْ اَنْ تَبَرُّوْهُمْ وَتُقْسِطُوْٓا اِلَيْهِمْ ۭ اِنَّ اللّٰهَ يُحِبُّ الْمُقْسِطِيْنَ ۝

10. Allāh only forbids you respecting those who have fought against you on account of *your* religion and have driven you out of your homes, and have helped *others* in driving you out, that you make friends with them, and whosoever makes friends with them—it is these that are the transgressors.

اِنَّمَا يَنْهٰىكُمُ اللّٰهُ عَنِ الَّذِيْنَ قٰتَلُوْكُمْ فِي الدِّيْنِ وَاَخْرَجُوْكُمْ مِّنْ دِيَارِكُمْ وَظٰهَرُوْا عَلٰٓي اِخْرَاجِكُمْ اَنْ تَوَلَّوْهُمْ ۚ وَمَنْ يَّتَوَلَّهُمْ فَاُولٰۗىِٕكَ هُمُ الظّٰلِمُوْنَ ۝

3030. The verse implied a prophecy. The Companions of the Holy Prophet were told that though they had been enjoined to renounce all friendly relations with the enemies of their Faith, even though the latter might be their very near blood relations, the prohibition was destined to be very short-lived. The time was fast approaching when the erstwhile enemies would become their loving friends. The commandment applies only to such disbelievers, as the next verse shows, who are at war with Muslims. Friendly relations with all non-Muslims as such are not forbidden.

11. O ye who believe! when believing women come to you as Refugees, examine[3031] them. Allāh knows best their faith. Then, if you find them *true* believers, send them not back to the disbelievers. These *women* are not lawful for them, nor are they lawful for these *women*. But give *their disbelieving husbands* what they have spent *on them*. *Thereafter* it is no sin for you to marry them, when you have given them their [a]dowries. And hold not to *your* matrimonial ties of the disbelieving [b]women, but *should they join the disbelievers*, then demand *the return* of that which you have spent; and let *the disbelieving husbands of believing women* demand that which they have spent. That is the judgment of Allāh. He judges between you. And Allāh is All-Knowing, Wise

يٰۤاَيُّهَا الَّذِيْنَ اٰمَنُوْۤا اِذَا جَآءَكُمُ الْمُؤْمِنٰتُ مُهٰجِرٰتٍ
فَامْتَحِنُوْهُنَّ اَللّٰهُ اَعْلَمُ بِاِيْمَانِهِنَّ فَاِنْ عَلِمْتُمُوْهُنَّ
مُؤْمِنٰتٍ فَلَا تَرْجِعُوْهُنَّ اِلَى الْكُفَّارِ لَا هُنَّ حِلٌّ
لَّهُمْ وَلَا هُمْ يَحِلُّوْنَ لَهُنَّ وَاٰتُوْهُمْ مَّاۤ اَنْفَقُوْا
وَلَا جُنَاحَ عَلَيْكُمْ اَنْ تَنْكِحُوْهُنَّ اِذَاۤ اٰتَيْتُمُوْهُنَّ
اُجُوْرَهُنَّ وَلَا تُمْسِكُوْا بِعِصَمِ الْكَوَافِرِ وَسْئَلُوْا
مَاۤ اَنْفَقْتُمْ وَلْيَسْئَلُوْا مَاۤ اَنْفَقُوْا ذٰلِكُمْ حُكْمُ اللّٰهِ
يَحْكُمُ بَيْنَكُمْ وَاللّٰهُ عَلِيْمٌ حَكِيْمٌ ﴿١١﴾

[a]4: 5, 25. [b]2 : 222.

3031. Though when Muslims were being bitterly persecuted and it was not safe to leave Mecca and join the Muslim Community at Medina, a continuous stream of believers was pouring into Medina, leaving behind in Mecca their dear and near ones. These Refugees contained a fair number of women among them. The verse refers to such refugee Muslim women. It constitutes an eloquent commentary on the Holy Prophet's anxiety not to accept into the Muslim Community any woman who had fled from Mecca unless there was proof available, after subjecting her to searching examination, that she was sincere and honest in her faith and was accepting Islām from no ulterior or otherwise objectionable motives. The verse further states that the marriage-tie between a refugee believing woman and her disbelieving husband becomes automatically dissolved when she joins the Muslim Community; and a believer is allowed to marry her provided he fulfils two conditions: (*a*) He should have paid back to her disbelieving husband what the latter had spent on her, and (*b*) he should also have fixed and paid her dowry. Similarly, the marriage-tie between a Muslim and his wife who gives up Islām could not continue and the same procedure would be adopted if such an apostate woman marries a disbeliever as in the case of marriage between a Muslim and a refugee believing woman. The reciprocal arrangement prescribed in this verse is not the private affair of the individuals concerned but is to be carried out by the State, as is the practice in time of war, to which these verses particularly apply. There could not and should not then continue any social relations between individual believers and individual disbelievers.

12. And if any of your wives goes away from you to the disbelievers, and afterwards you retaliate *and get some spoils from the disbelievers*, then give to those believers whose wives have gone away the like of that which they had spent on them.[3032] And fear Allāh in Whom you believe.

وَإِنْ فَاتَكُمْ شَيْءٌ مِّنْ أَزْوَاجِكُمْ إِلَى الْكُفَّارِ
فَعَاقَبْتُمْ فَآتُوا الَّذِينَ ذَهَبَتْ أَزْوَاجُهُم مِّثْلَ
مَا أَنفَقُوا ۚ وَاتَّقُوا اللَّهَ الَّذِي أَنتُم بِهِ مُؤْمِنُونَ ﴿١٢﴾

13. O Prophet! when believing women come to thee, taking the oath of allegiance *at thy hands* that they will not associate anything *with Allāh*, and that they will not steal, and will not commit adultery, nor kill their children, nor bring forth a scandalous charge which they themselves have deliberately forged, nor disobey thee in what is right, then accept their allegiance and ask Allāh to forgive them. Verily, Allāh is Most Forgiving, Merciful.

يَا أَيُّهَا النَّبِيُّ إِذَا جَاءَكَ الْمُؤْمِنَاتُ يُبَايِعْنَكَ عَلَىٰ
أَن لَّا يُشْرِكْنَ بِاللَّهِ شَيْئًا وَلَا يَسْرِقْنَ وَلَا يَزْنِينَ
وَلَا يَقْتُلْنَ أَوْلَادَهُنَّ وَلَا يَأْتِينَ بِبُهْتَانٍ يَفْتَرِينَهُ
بَيْنَ أَيْدِيهِنَّ وَأَرْجُلِهِنَّ وَلَا يَعْصِينَكَ فِي مَعْرُوفٍ
فَبَايِعْهُنَّ وَاسْتَغْفِرْ لَهُنَّ اللَّهَ ۖ إِنَّ اللَّهَ غَفُورٌ
رَّحِيمٌ ﴿١٣﴾

14. O ye who believe! take not for friends a people with whom [a]Allāh is wroth; they have, indeed, despaired of the Hereafter[3033] just as have the disbelievers despaired of those who are in the graves.

يَا أَيُّهَا الَّذِينَ آمَنُوا لَا تَتَوَلَّوْا قَوْمًا غَضِبَ اللَّهُ عَلَيْهِمْ
قَدْ يَئِسُوا مِنَ الْآخِرَةِ كَمَا يَئِسَ الْكُفَّارُ مِنْ أَصْحَابِ الْقُبُورِ ﴿١٤﴾

[a]58 : 15.

3032. If the wife of a Muslim deserts to disbelievers and thereafter a woman from among disbelievers is taken prisoner by the Muslims, or she flees from disbelievers and joins the Muslim Community, then the believing husband is to be compensated from the loss of the dowry paid by him to his deserting wife from the sum due to the disbelieving husband whose wife has joined the Muslim Community if the dowries are equal, but the deficiency, if any, is to be made up collectively by Muslims, or, as some authorities say, from the booty acquired by the State, the word '*Āqabtum* also meaning *Ghanimtum*, *i.e.*, you have acquired booty. This arrangement was necessary as disbelievers would refuse to return the dowries paid by their believing husbands to the women who had deserted to the former.

3033. The words, *they* (*disbelievers*) *have indeed despaired of the Hereafter*, mean that they have no faith in the Hereafter, just as they have no faith that dead will ever come to life. The word "they" may particularly apply to the Jews, since the expression, *with whom Allāh is wroth*, has been used about the Jews in several verses of the Qur'ān.

CHAPTER 61

AL-ṢAFF

(*Revealed after Hijrah*)

Date of Revelation and Context

The *Sūrah* was revealed at Medina, probably in the third or fourth year of the *Hijrah*, after the Battle of Uḥud, as v. 5 seems to possess an implied reference to the lack of discipline or unquestioning obedience to the Holy Prophet of which some of the Muslims were guilty in that battle. The preceding two Chapters had dealt with the subject of war against disbelievers, and with social and political problems arising out of it. The present *Sūrah* emphasizes the importance of giving unqualified and unquestioning obedience to the Leader, and of presenting, under his guidance, a solid, compact and united front to disbelievers.

Subject-Matter

The *Sūrah* opens with the glorification of God's wisdom and might, and proceeds to admonish believers that when they glorify God and extol His holiness with their tongues, they should give a practical proof of their profession with their actions, thus making their actions harmonize with their verbal declarations. And when they are called upon to fight in the cause of Truth, they should present a firm and solid front to disbelievers, and should give unqualified obedience to their Leader. The *Sūrah* then makes a brief reference to the misbehaviour of the followers of Moses who, by maligning and defying him, caused him much vexation and mental anguish, and, by implication, warns Muslims never to behave like them. Next, mention is made of the prophecy of Jesus about the advent of the Prophet Aḥmad, followed by a firm declaration that all the attempts of the votaries of darkness to extinguish the Light of Allāh will come to naught. The Light will continue to shine in all its glory and effulgence and Islām will prevail over all religions. But before this eventually comes to pass, the Muslims will have to 'strive with their wealth and persons in the cause of Allāh.' Only then will they deserve to be blessed with God's pleasure and material glory, 'with gardens through which streams flow.' The *Sūrah* closes with exhorting Muslims to help God's cause, as did the disciples of Jesus by undergoing all manner of sacrifice and suffering for it.

سُوۡرَۃُ الصَّفِّ مَدَنِیَّۃٌ (۶۱)

بِسۡمِ اللّٰہِ الرَّحۡمٰنِ الرَّحِیۡمِ ﴿۱﴾

1. [a]In the name of Allāh, the Gracious, the Merciful.

سَبَّحَ لِلّٰہِ مَا فِی السَّمٰوٰتِ وَ مَا فِی الۡاَرۡضِ ۚ وَ ہُوَ
الۡعَزِیۡزُ الۡحَکِیۡمُ ﴿۲﴾

2. [b]Whatever is in the heavens and whatever is in the earth glorifies Allāh; and He is the Mighty, the Wise.

یٰۤاَیُّہَا الَّذِیۡنَ اٰمَنُوۡا لِمَ تَقُوۡلُوۡنَ مَا لَا تَفۡعَلُوۡنَ ﴿۳﴾

3. O ye who believe! Why do you say what you do not?[3034]

کَبُرَ مَقۡتًا عِنۡدَ اللّٰہِ اَنۡ تَقُوۡلُوۡا مَا لَا تَفۡعَلُوۡنَ ﴿۴﴾

4. It is most hateful in the sight of Allāh that you say what you do not.

اِنَّ اللّٰہَ یُحِبُّ الَّذِیۡنَ یُقَاتِلُوۡنَ فِیۡ سَبِیۡلِہٖ صَفًّا
کَاَنَّہُمۡ بُنۡیَانٌ مَّرۡصُوۡصٌ ﴿۵﴾

5. Verily, Allāh loves those who fight in His cause arrayed in *solid* ranks, as though they were a *strong* structure[3035] cemented with *molten* lead.

وَ اِذۡ قَالَ مُوۡسٰی لِقَوۡمِہٖ یٰقَوۡمِ لِمَ تُؤۡذُوۡنَنِیۡ وَ قَدۡ
تَّعۡلَمُوۡنَ اَنِّیۡ رَسُوۡلُ اللّٰہِ اِلَیۡکُمۡ ؕ فَلَمَّا زَاغُوۡۤا اَزَاغَ
اللّٰہُ قُلُوۡبَہُمۡ ؕ وَ اللّٰہُ لَا یَہۡدِی الۡقَوۡمَ الۡفٰسِقِیۡنَ ﴿۶﴾

6. And *call to mind* when Moses said to his people, 'O my people, why do you malign[3036] me and you know that I am Allāh's Messenger unto you?' So when they deviated *from the right course*, Allāh caused their hearts to deviate; for Allāh guides not the rebellious people.

---

[a]1 : 1. [b]17 : 45; 24 : 42; 57 : 2; 62 : 2; 64 : 2.

3034. The actions of a Muslim should correspond to his professions. Boastful, empty talk carries one nowhere and verbal professions not accompanied by actual deeds smack of hypocrisy and insincerity.

3035. Muslims are expected to present a firm, compact and solid front to the forces of evil, under the command of their Leader whom they should give full and unqualified obedience. But a people who seek to become united into a solid and strong community, must possess one code of life, one ideal, one objective and one goal and one programme to achieve that objective.

3036. Perhaps no Prophet of God suffered so much mental agony at the hands of his followers as did Moses. Moses's people had seen the mighty hosts of Pharoah drown before their very eyes and yet they had hardly crossed the sea when they sought to revert to idolatry, and seeing some people worshipping idols asked Moses to set up one such idol for them also (7 : 139). When asked to march into Canaan which God had

7. And *call to mind* when Jesus, son of Mary, said, 'O Children of Israel, surely, I am Allāh's Messenger unto you, fulfilling that which is before me *of the prophecies* of the Torah, and giving glad tidings of a Messenger who will come after me, his name being Aḥmad.[3037] And when he came to them with clear proofs, they said, 'This is manifest [a]sorcery.'

وَاِذْ قَالَ عِيْسَى ابْنُ مَرْيَمَ يٰبَنِيْٓ اِسْرَآءِيْلَ اِنِّيْ
رَسُوْلُ اللّٰهِ اِلَيْكُمْ مُّصَدِّقًا لِّمَا بَيْنَ يَدَيَّ مِنَ
التَّوْرٰىةِ وَمُبَشِّرًا بِرَسُوْلٍ يَّأْتِيْ مِنْۢ بَعْدِي
اسْمُهٗٓ اَحْمَدُ ؕ فَلَمَّا جَآءَهُمْ بِالْبَيِّنٰتِ قَالُوْا هٰذَا
سِحْرٌ مُّبِيْنٌ ۝

[a]27 : 14; 43 : 31.

promised to give them, they scornfully and brazen-facedly told Moses to go with his Lord upon Whom he had relied so much; they were not going to budge an inch from the place where they had settled (5 : 25). Thus Moses was repeatedly insulted by, and baulked in his efforts to reclaim from idolatory the very people whom he had delivered from the crushing bondage of Pharoah. They even slandered and defamed him.

3037. For the prophecy of Jesus about the coming of Paraclete or the Comforter or the Spirit of Truth see John, 12 : 13; 14 : 16-17; 15 : 26; 16 : 7, from which the following inferences are clearly deducible :—

(*a*) Paraclete or the Comforter or the Spirit of Truth could not come unless Jesus should have departed from the world. (*b*) He was to abide in the world for ever; and was to say many things which Jesus himself could not say because the world could not then bear them. (*c*) He would guide men unto all truth. (*d*) He would not speak of himself, but whatever he would hear that would he speak. (*e*) He would glorify Jesus and testify to his truth. This description of Paraclete or the Comforter or the Spirit of Truth is in complete harmony with the status and mission of the Holy Prophet as given in the Qur'ān. The Holy Prophet appeared after Jesus had departed from this world; he was the last Law-giving Prophet and the Qur'ān the last revealed Divine Law for the whole of mankind till the end of time (5 : 4). He did not speak of himself but whatever he heard from God that did he spake (53 : 4). He glorified Jesus (2 : 254 ; 3 : 56). The above prophecy in the Gospel of John closely resembles the prophecy mentioned in the verse under comment except that instead of Aḥmad the name stated therein is Paraclete. Christian writers challenge the correctness of the Quranic version of the prophecy, basing their contention on this difference of the two names, irrespective of the otherwise identical features of the biblical and Quranic versions. In fact, Jesus spoke both Aramaic and Hebrew. Aramaic was his mother tongue and Hebrew his religious language. The present biblical version is the translation of Aramaic and Hebrew into Greek. A translation naturally cannot fully convey the beauty of the original text. Languages have their limitations. The same is true of the people who speak them. Their limitations are reflected in their works. The Greek language has another word, *i.e.*, Periklutos, with a similar meaning as Aḥmad in Arabic. Jack Finegan, the renowned Christian theologian, in his book, "The Archaeology of World Relgions," says: 'Where in Greek the word Parakletos (Comforter) is very similar to Periklutos (renowned), the latter word being the meaning of the names Aḥmad and Muḥammad.' Moreover, "The Damascus Document", a scripture discovered towards the end of the nineteenth century in Ezra synagogue, Old Cairo (p. 2), describes Jesus as having foretold the advent of a "Holy.Spirit," named Emeth: *And by His Messiah, He has made them know His Holy Spirit. For it is he who is Emeth, i.e., the Truthful One, and in accordance with His name are also theirs.....* "Emeth" in Hebrew means "the Truth", or "the Truthful One and a person of constant goodness" (Strachan's Fourth Gospel, p. 141). This word was interpreted by the Jews as "God's Seal." Naturally, though Jesus must have used the name Aḥmad, the phonetic resemblance between the two words (Aḥmad and Emeth) led later writers to substitute "Emeth" for Aḥmad, its Hebrew synonym. Thus the

8. [a]But who does greater wrong than he who forges a lie against Allāh while he is invited to Islām?[3038] Allāh guides not the wrongdoing people.

وَمَنْ اَظْلَمُ مِمَّنِ افْتَرٰى عَلَى اللّٰهِ الْكَذِبَ وَهُوَ يُدْعٰٓى اِلَى الْاِسْلَامِ ۭ وَاللّٰهُ لَا يَهْدِي الْقَوْمَ الظّٰلِمِيْنَ ⑧

9. [b]They desire to extinguish the Light of Allāh[3039] with *the breath of* their mouths, but Allāh will perfect His light, however much the disbelievers may dislike *it*.

يُرِيْدُوْنَ لِيُطْفِـُٔوْا نُوْرَ اللّٰهِ بِاَفْوَاهِهِمْ وَاللّٰهُ مُتِمُّ نُوْرِهٖ وَلَوْ كَرِهَ الْكٰفِرُوْنَ ⑨

10. [c]He it is Who has sent His Messenger with the guidance and the Religion of truth, that He may cause it to prevail over all religions,[3040] however much those who associate partners *with Allāh* may dislike *it*.

هُوَ الَّذِيْٓ اَرْسَلَ رَسُوْلَهٗ بِالْهُدٰى وَدِيْنِ الْحَقِّ لِيُظْهِرَهٗ عَلَى الدِّيْنِ كُلِّهٖ وَلَوْ كَرِهَ الْمُشْرِكُوْنَ ⑩

[a]6 : 22; 10 : 18; 11 : 19. [b]9 : 32. [c]9 : 33; 48 : 29.

prophecy mentioned in the verse applies to the Holy Prophet, but as a corollary it may also apply to the Promised Messiah, Founder of the Aḥmadiyya Movement, because he has also been called Aḥmad in Divine revelation (Barāhīn Aḥmadiyyah) and because also in his person the Second Manifestation or Second Advent of the Holy Prophet took place. To this Second Manifestation of the Holy Prophet, the third verse of *Sūrah* Al-Jumu'ah pointedly refers. It may be mentioned in passing that a prophecy about the Holy Prophet is also clearly stated in the Gospel of Barnabas which is treated by the Church as apocryphal, but which has as much claim to be accepted as authentic as any of the four Gospels.

3038. The verse refers to disbelievers to whom the Holy Prophet addressed his Message, since he was the inviter and they the invitees (20 : 109 & 33 : 47.) Moreover, they have been stigmatised in the Qur'ān as forgers of lies against God (6 : 138, 141). But if the prophecy be taken to apply to the Promised Messiah the expression, 'he is invited to Islām,' would signify that the Promised Messiah would be invited by the so-called defenders of Islām to recant, repent and be a Muslim like them, for, according to them, by his claim to be the Promised Messiah and Mahdī he would cease to be one.

3039. The Holy Prophet has been repeatedly called the "Light of Allāh," in the Qur'ān (4 : 175; 5 : 17; 64 : 9).

3040. Most Commentators of the Qur'ān are agreed that this verse applies to the Promised Messiah, because in his time all religions will have made their appearance and the superiority of Islām over all of them will become established.

R. 2 11. O ye who believe! shall I point out to you a commerce[3041] which will deliver you from a painful punishment?

يَٰٓأَيُّهَا الَّذِيْنَ اٰمَنُوْا هَلْ اَدُلُّكُمْ عَلٰى تِجَارَةٍ تُنْجِيْكُمْ مِّنْ عَذَابٍ اَلِيْمٍ ﴿١١﴾

12. [a]That you believe in Allāh and His Messenger, and strive in the cause of Allāh with your wealth and your persons. That is better for you, if you did but know.

تُؤْمِنُوْنَ بِاللّٰهِ وَرَسُوْلِهٖ وَتُجَاهِدُوْنَ فِيْ سَبِيْلِ اللّٰهِ بِاَمْوَالِكُمْ وَاَنْفُسِكُمْ ۭ ذٰلِكُمْ خَيْرٌ لَّكُمْ اِنْ كُنْتُمْ تَعْلَمُوْنَ ﴿١٢﴾

13. He will forgive you your sins, and admit you to Gardens through which streams flow, and to pure and pleasant dwellings in [b]Gardens of Eternity. That is the supreme triumph,

يَغْفِرْ لَكُمْ ذُنُوْبَكُمْ وَيُدْخِلْكُمْ جَنّٰتٍ تَجْرِيْ مِنْ تَحْتِهَا الْاَنْهٰرُ وَمَسٰكِنَ طَيِّبَةً فِيْ جَنّٰتِ عَدْنٍ ۭ ذٰلِكَ الْفَوْزُ الْعَظِيْمُ ﴿١٣﴾

14. And *He will bestow upon you* another *favour* which you love: help from Allāh and a nigh victory. So give **glad tidings** to the believers.

وَاُخْرٰى تُحِبُّوْنَهَا ۭ نَصْرٌ مِّنَ اللّٰهِ وَفَتْحٌ قَرِيْبٌ ۭ وَبَشِّرِ الْمُؤْمِنِيْنَ ﴿١٤﴾

15. O ye who believe! be helpers of Allāh, as said Jesus, son of Mary, to *his*[c]disciples, 'Who are my helpers in *the cause of* Allāh?' The disciples said, 'We are helpers of Allāh. So a party of the Children of Israel believed, while a party disbelieved. Then We aided those who believed against their enemy, and they became predominant.[3042]

يٰٓاَيُّهَا الَّذِيْنَ اٰمَنُوْا كُوْنُوْٓا اَنْصَارَ اللّٰهِ كَمَا قَالَ عِيْسَى ابْنُ مَرْيَمَ لِلْحَوَارِيّٖنَ مَنْ اَنْصَارِيْٓ اِلَى اللّٰهِ ۭ قَالَ الْحَوَارِيُّوْنَ نَحْنُ اَنْصَارُ اللّٰهِ فَاٰمَنَتْ طَّاۗىِٕفَةٌ مِّنْۢ بَنِيْٓ اِسْرَاۗءِيْلَ وَكَفَرَتْ طَّاۗىِٕفَةٌ ۚ فَاَيَّدْنَا الَّذِيْنَ اٰمَنُوْا عَلٰى عَدُوِّهِمْ فَاَصْبَحُوْا ظٰهِرِيْنَ ﴿١٥﴾ ع

[a]9 : 20, 41. [b]9 : 72; 19 : 62; 20 : 77. [c]3 : 53; 5 : 112.

3041. This verse also seems to refer to the time of the Promised Messiah when trade and commerce were to flourish and there was to be a mad rush for striking profitable bargains.

3042. Of the three religious groups among the Jews to whom Jesus preached his Message—the Pharisees, the Sadducees and the Essenes—Jesus belonged to the last, while he had not yet been commissioned as a Divine Preacher. The Essenes were a highly righteous people who lived away from the world's hustle and bustle, passing their time in meditation and prayer and in the service of humanity. It was from these people that most of Jesus's early followers came ("The Dead Sea Community" by Kurt Schubert & "The Crucifixion by An Eye-Witness"). They have been called "Helpers" by Eusephus. The concluding words of the *Sūrah* are indeed very prophetic. Throughout the ages the followers of Jesus have enjoyed power and predominance over their eternal enemies—the Jews. They have founded and ruled over vast and powerful empires while the Jews have remained a dispersed people so much so that "The Wandering Jew" has become a by-word.

CHAPTER 62

AL-JUMU'AH

(Revealed after Hijrah

Date of Revelation and Context

This *Sūrah* seems to have been revealed several years after *Hijrah* (see v. 4). In the preceding *Sūrah* Jesus's prophecy about the advent of the Prophet Aḥmad was mentioned. The present *Sūrah* further deals with that prophecy. Like the preceding *Sūrah* it opens with the glorification of the might and wisdom of God, and, as a proof and demonstration of these two Divine attributes, points to the appearance of the Holy Prophet among the unlettered Arabs, who from an uncivilized, uncultured and unlettered people, became, through the teaching of the Qur'ān and the Prophet's noble example, the teachers and leaders of mankind, spreading light and learning wherever they went. The *Sūrah* then refers to the same spiritual phenomenon which will take place at some later time through a great Deputy of the Holy Prophet, the Promised Messiah, and proceeds to condemn the Jewish people for their rejection of the Holy Prophet, in spite of the fact that their Scriptures abound in prophecies concerning him. Thus by implication the *Sūrah* warns Muslims against behaving like Jews when the Great Deputy of the Holy Prophet appears among them. Towards its close, importance of the Friday Prayer is emphasized and an implied hint is made that at the time of the Second Advent of the Holy Prophet which has been likened to the Friday Prayer, there would be a mad craze for trade, commerce and worldly gains and many other diversions to amuse and turn men away from God; and Muslims are exhorted not to let these things distract their attention in the midst of their religious duties.

ركوعاتها ٢ سُوْرَةُ الْجُمُعَةِ مَدَنِيَّةٌ (٦٢) اٰياتها ١٢

1. [a]In the name of Allāh, the Gracious, the Merciful.

بِسْمِ اللّٰهِ الرَّحْمٰنِ الرَّحِيْمِ ①

2. Whatever is in the heavens and whatever is in the earth [b]glorifies Allāh, the Sovereign, the Holy, the Mighty, the Wise.[3043]

يُسَبِّحُ لِلّٰهِ مَا فِي السَّمٰوٰتِ وَمَا فِي الْاَرْضِ الْمَلِكِ الْقُدُّوْسِ الْعَزِيْزِ الْحَكِيْمِ ②

3. He it is Who has raised among the unlettered[3044] *people* a [c]Messenger from among themselves who recites unto them His Signs, and purifies them, and teaches them the Book and Wisdom[3045] though before that they were in manifest error;

هُوَ الَّذِيْ بَعَثَ فِي الْاُمِّيّٖنَ رَسُوْلًا مِّنْهُمْ يَتْلُوْا عَلَيْهِمْ اٰيٰتِهٖ وَيُزَكِّيْهِمْ وَيُعَلِّمُهُمُ الْكِتٰبَ وَالْحِكْمَةَ ۗ وَاِنْ كَانُوْا مِنْ قَبْلُ لَفِيْ ضَلٰلٍ مُّبِيْنٍ ③

4. And *He will raise him among* others of them who have not *yet* joined them.[3046] He is the Mighty, the Wise.

وَّاٰخَرِيْنَ مِنْهُمْ لَمَّا يَلْحَقُوْا بِهِمْ ۭ وَهُوَ الْعَزِيْزُ الْحَكِيْمُ ④

---

[a]1 : 1. [b]61 : 2. [c]3 : 165; 7 : 158; 9 : 128.

3043. The four Divine attributes concern the fourfold mission of the Holy Prophet, mentioned in the next verse.

3044. See 3 : 76 and 7 : 158.

3045. The Divine mission of the Holy Prophet consisted in the performance of the fourfold sacred duty referred to in this verse. This was the great and noble task which was entrusted to him; because it was to his appearance among the unlettered Arabs that the Patriarch Abraham had prayed several thousand years ago, when in company with his son, Ishmael, he was raising the foundations of the Ka'bah (2 : 130). In fact, no Reformer can truly succeed in his mission unless he prepares, by his noble and purifying example, a community of sincere, devoted and righteous followers, whom he first teaches the ideals and the principles of his Message and their philosophy, significance and importance, and then sends them abroad to preach that Message to other people. The training he imparts to his followers refines their intellect, and the philosophy of his teaching engenders in them certainty of faith, and his noble example creates in them purity of heart. It is to this basic fact of religion that the verse refers.

3046. The Message of the Holy Prophet was meant not only for the Arabs among whom he was raised but for all non-Arabs as well, and not only for his contemporaries but also for the generations to come till the end of time. Or, the verse may signify that the Holy Prophet will be raised among another people who have not yet joined his immediate followers. The reference in the verse and in a well-known saying of the Holy Prophet is to the Second Advent of the Holy Prophet himself in the person of the Promised Messiah in the Latter Days. Says Abū Hurairah: "One Day we were sitting with the Holy Prophet when *Sūrah* Jumu'ah was revealed. I enquired from the Holy Prophet, 'Who are the people to whom the words, 'And among others of them who have not yet joined them,' refer." Salmān, the Persian, was sitting among us. Upon my repeatedly asking him the same

5. That is Allāh's grace; He bestows it on whom He pleases; and Allāh is the Lord of immense grace.

ذٰلِكَ فَضۡلُ اللّٰهِ يُؤۡتِيۡهِ مَنۡ يَّشَآءُ ‌ؕ وَاللّٰهُ ذُو الۡفَضۡلِ الۡعَظِيۡمِ ۝٥

6. The likeness of those who were charged with the *Law of* Torah, but did not carry out *its commandments*, is as the likeness of an ass carrying *a load of* books. Evil is the likeness of the people who reject the Signs of Allāh. And Allāh guides not the wrongdoing people.

مَثَلُ الَّذِيۡنَ حُمِّلُوا التَّوۡرٰٮةَ ثُمَّ لَمۡ يَحۡمِلُوۡهَا كَمَثَلِ الۡحِمَارِ يَحۡمِلُ اَسۡفَارًا‌ ؕ بِئۡسَ مَثَلُ الۡقَوۡمِ الَّذِيۡنَ كَذَّبُوۡا بِاٰيٰتِ اللّٰهِ‌ ؕ وَاللّٰهُ لَا يَهۡدِى الۡقَوۡمَ الظّٰلِمِيۡنَ ۝٦

7. Say, 'O ye who are Jews, if you claim that you are the friends of Allāh to the exclusion of *all other* peoples, then wish for death,[3047] [a]if, *indeed*, you are truthful.

قُلۡ يٰۤاَيُّهَا الَّذِيۡنَ هَادُوۡۤا اِنۡ زَعَمۡتُمۡ اَنَّكُمۡ اَوۡلِيَآءُ لِلّٰهِ مِنۡ دُوۡنِ النَّاسِ فَتَمَنَّوُا الۡمَوۡتَ اِنۡ كُنۡتُمۡ صٰدِقِيۡنَ ۝٧

8. [b]But they will never wish for it, because of that which their hands have sent on *before them*. And Allāh knows well those who do wrong.

وَلَا يَتَمَنَّوۡنَهٗۤ اَبَدًاۢ بِمَا قَدَّمَتۡ اَيۡدِيۡهِمۡ‌ ؕ وَاللّٰهُ عَلِيۡمٌۢ بِالظّٰلِمِيۡنَ ۝٨

9. Say, "[c]The death from which you flee will, surely, overtake you. Then you will be returned unto Him Who knows the unseen and the seen, and He will inform you of what you had been doing.'

قُلۡ اِنَّ الۡمَوۡتَ الَّذِىۡ تَفِرُّوۡنَ مِنۡهُ فَاِنَّهٗ مُلٰقِيۡكُمۡ‌ ثُمَّ تُرَدُّوۡنَ اِلٰى عٰلِمِ الۡغَيۡبِ وَالشَّهَادَةِ فَيُنَبِّئُكُمۡ بِمَا كُنۡتُمۡ تَعۡمَلُوۡنَ ۝٩ ع

[a]2 : 95. [b]2 : 96. [c]2 : 97; 4 : 79; 33 : 17.

question, the Holy Prophet put his hand on Salmān and said, 'If Faith were to go up to the Pleiades, a man from these would, surely, find it' (Bukhārī). This saying of the Holy Prophet shows that the verse applies to a man of Persian descent. The Promised Messiah, the Founder of the Aḥmadiyya Movement, was of Persian descent. Other sayings of the Holy Prophet speak of the appearance of the Messiah at a time when there would remain nothing of the Qur'ān but its words and of Islām but its name, *i.e.*, the true spirit of Islamic teaching will have been lost (Baihaquī). Thus the Qur'ān and the Ḥadith both agree that the present verse refers to the Second Advent of the Holy Prophet in the person of the Promised Messiah.

3047. The Promised Messiah will challenge the so-called Muslim Ulema, who will reject his claim, to *Mubahalah*, *i.e.*, prayer-contest by which Divine curse is invoked upon those who forge lies against God (3 : 62).

R. 2 10. O ye who believe! when the call is made for Prayer on Friday,[3047A] hasten to the remembrance of Allāh, and leave off *all* business. That is best for you, if you only knew.

يٰۤاَيُّهَا الَّذِيْنَ اٰمَنُوْۤا اِذَا نُوْدِيَ لِلصَّلٰوةِ مِنْ يَّوْمِ
الْجُمُعَةِ فَاسْعَوْا اِلٰى ذِكْرِ اللّٰهِ وَذَرُوا الْبَيْعَ ؕ ذٰلِكُمْ
خَيْرٌ لَّكُمْ اِنْ كُنْتُمْ تَعْلَمُوْنَ ۝١٠

11. And when the Prayer is finished, then disperse in the land and seek of Allāh's grace,[3048] and remember Allāh much that [a]you may prosper.

فَاِذَا قُضِيَتِ الصَّلٰوةُ فَانْتَشِرُوْا فِي الْاَرْضِ
وَابْتَغُوْا مِنْ فَضْلِ اللّٰهِ وَاذْكُرُوا اللّٰهَ كَثِيْرًا
لَّعَلَّكُمْ تُفْلِحُوْنَ ۝١١

12. But when they see some merchandise or amusement, they break up for it, and leave thee standing. Say, 'That which is with Allāh is better than amusement and merchandise, and Allāh is the Best of providers.'

وَاِذَا رَاَوْا تِجَارَةً اَوْ لَهْوَا ۨانْفَضُّوْۤا اِلَيْهَا وَتَرَكُوْكَ
قَآئِمًا ؕ قُلْ مَا عِنْدَ اللّٰهِ خَيْرٌ مِّنَ اللَّهْوِ وَمِنَ
التِّجَارَةِ ؕ وَاللّٰهُ خَيْرُ الرّٰزِقِيْنَ ۝١٢ ع

3047A. In the preceding verses mention was made of the Jews who rejected the Holy Prophet's Message and who profaned their Sabbath and consequently incurred God's displeasure. In the present verse, however, Muslims have been enjoined to be particularly careful about the obligatory Friday Prayer. Every people has a Sabbath and the Muslim Sabbath is Friday. As the *Sūrah* seems particularly to deal with the time of the Promised Messiah, the call for Friday Prayer may also signify his clarion call to Muslims to listen to his Message.

3048. Unlike the Jewish or Christian Sabbath, the Muslim Sabbath is not a day of rest. Before the Friday Prayer and after it Muslims may as usual pursue their daily avocations. The words 'of Allah's grace,' have generally been understood to mean 'doing business and earning one's livelihood.'

CHAPTER 63

AL-MUNĀFIQŪN

(Revealed after Hijrah)

Date of Revelation and Context

This also is a Medinite *Sūrah*, having been revealed, as its subject-matter shows, sometime after the Battle of Uḥud. Whereas the preceding *Sūrah* had specifically dealt with the Jews of Medina, this *Sūrah* deals with other enemies of Islām—the Hypocrites, and exposes their evil designs, their infidelity and dishonesty, and condemns their loud professions of faith as false and treacherous. They are the real enemies of Islām, says the *Sūrah*, since they try to deceive Muslims by their oaths and their false professions of faith, using them as a screen for that purpose. They have, by their evil designs and nefarious activities, condemned themselves beyond redemption. They mistakenly think that, like themselves, the Companions of the Holy Prophet are a band of self-seekers who will leave him when their material interests so demanded. The *Sūrah* closes with the exhortation to Muslims that they should spend their wealth in the cause of God, before the time comes when Islām will no longer need their money.

سُورَةُ الْمُنٰفِقُوْنَ مَدَنِيَّةٌ

(٦٣) آياتها ١٢ — ركوعاتها ٢

1. [a]In the name of Allāh, the Gracious, the Merciful.

بِسْمِ اللّٰهِ الرَّحْمٰنِ الرَّحِيْمِ ﴿١﴾

2. When the Hypocrites[3049] come to thee, they say, 'We bear witness that thou art the Messenger of Allāh.' And Allāh knows that thou art indeed His Messenger, but Allāh *also* bears witness that the Hypocrites certainly are liars.

إِذَا جَآءَكَ الْمُنٰفِقُوْنَ قَالُوْا نَشْهَدُ إِنَّكَ لَرَسُوْلُ
اللّٰهِ ۘ وَاللّٰهُ يَعْلَمُ إِنَّكَ لَرَسُوْلُهٗ ۗ وَاللّٰهُ يَشْهَدُ
إِنَّ الْمُنٰفِقِيْنَ لَكٰذِبُوْنَ ﴿٢﴾

3. They have made their oaths a cloak; thus [b]they hinder *men* from the way of Allāh. Surely, evil is that which they have been doing.

اِتَّخَذُوْٓا أَيْمَانَهُمْ جُنَّةً فَصَدُّوْا عَنْ سَبِيْلِ اللّٰهِ ۗ
إِنَّهُمْ سَآءَ مَا كَانُوْا يَعْمَلُوْنَ ﴿٣﴾

4. That is because they *first* believed *and* then [c]disbelieved. So a seal was set upon their hearts and *consequently* they understand not.[3050]

ذٰلِكَ بِأَنَّهُمْ اٰمَنُوْا ثُمَّ كَفَرُوْا فَطُبِعَ عَلٰى قُلُوْبِهِمْ
فَهُمْ لَا يَفْقَهُوْنَ ﴿٤﴾

5. And when thou seest them, their figures please thee; [d]and when they speak, thou listenest to their speech. They are as though they were *blocks of* wood propped up.[3051] They think that every cry is against them. They are the enemy, so beware of them. Allāh's curse be upon them, how are they being turned away *from the truth !*

وَإِذَا رَأَيْتَهُمْ تُعْجِبُكَ أَجْسَامُهُمْ ۗ وَإِنْ يَّقُوْلُوْا
تَسْمَعْ لِقَوْلِهِمْ ۗ كَأَنَّهُمْ خُشُبٌ مُّسَنَّدَةٌ ۗ يَحْسَبُوْنَ
كُلَّ صَيْحَةٍ عَلَيْهِمْ ۗ هُمُ الْعَدُوُّ فَاحْذَرْهُمْ ۗ قٰتَلَهُمُ
اللّٰهُ ۖ أَنّٰى يُؤْفَكُوْنَ ﴿٥﴾

---

[a]1 : 1. [b]9 : 9. [c]3 : 91 ; 4 : 138; 16 : 107. [d]2 : 205.

3049. It is characteristic of a hypocrite that he makes loud profession of his faith and thereby seeks to conceal the treachery and infidelity of his heart.

3050. The hypocrites seem to have lost all reason and understanding since they labour under the misconception that by their wiles and glib talk they can deceive Allāh and His Prophet.

3051. A hypocrite lacks self-reliance. He is always in search of some one upon whom to lean. Or, the verse may signify that his interior does not correspond to his exterior. He so conducts himself that while outwardly he appears to be a reasonable, dignified and honest person, inwardly he is quite hollow and rotten to the core. He seeks to please people with his glib talk but, being a coward, he suspects and sees danger everywhere.

6. And when it is said to them, 'Come, *a*that the Messenger of Allāh may ask forgiveness for you,' they turn their heads aside, and thou seest them holding back *disdainfully* while they are big with pride.

وَاِذَا قِيۡلَ لَهُمۡ تَعَالَوۡا يَسۡتَغۡفِرۡ لَكُمۡ رَسُوۡلُ اللّٰهِ لَوَّوۡا رُءُوۡسَهُمۡ وَرَاَيۡتَهُمۡ يَصُدُّوۡنَ وَهُمۡ مُّسۡتَكۡبِرُوۡنَ ۝

7. For them it is equal whether thou ask forgiveness for them, or ask not forgiveness for them. *b*Allāh will never forgive them. Surely, Allāh guides not the rebellious people.

سَوَآءٌ عَلَيۡهِمۡ اَسۡتَغۡفَرۡتَ لَهُمۡ اَمۡ لَمۡ تَسۡتَغۡفِرۡ لَهُمۡ لَنۡ يَّغۡفِرَ اللّٰهُ لَهُمۡ اِنَّ اللّٰهَ لَا يَهۡدِى الۡقَوۡمَ الۡفٰسِقِيۡنَ ۝

8. They it is who say, 'Spend not on those who are with the Messenger of Allāh that they may disperse *and leave him*;[3052] while to Allāh belong the treasures of the heavens and the earth; but the Hypocrites understand not.

هُمُ الَّذِيۡنَ يَقُوۡلُوۡنَ لَا تُنۡفِقُوۡا عَلٰى مَنۡ عِنۡدَ رَسُوۡلِ اللّٰهِ حَتّٰى يَنۡفَضُّوۡا وَلِلّٰهِ خَزَآئِنُ السَّمٰوٰتِ وَالۡاَرۡضِ وَلٰكِنَّ الۡمُنٰفِقِيۡنَ لَا يَفۡقَهُوۡنَ ۝

9. They say, 'If we return to Medina, the one most exalted will, surely, drive out therefrom the one most mean,'[3053] while *true* honour belongs to Allāh and to His Messenger and the believers; but the Hypocrites know not.

يَقُوۡلُوۡنَ لَئِنۡ رَّجَعۡنَاۤ اِلَى الۡمَدِيۡنَةِ لَيُخۡرِجَنَّ الۡاَعَزُّ مِنۡهَا الۡاَذَلَّ وَلِلّٰهِ الۡعِزَّةُ وَلِرَسُوۡلِهٖ وَلِلۡمُؤۡمِنِيۡنَ وَلٰكِنَّ الۡمُنٰفِقِيۡنَ لَا يَعۡلَمُوۡنَ ۝

---

*a*4 : 62.   *b*9 : 80.

3052. Insincere and dishonest himself, a hypocrite considers others to be like him. The Hypocrites of Medina had made an entirely foolish and wrong estimate of the sincerity of purpose of the Holy Prophet's Companions in that they thought that they (his Companions) had gathered round him from considerations of their material interests, and that the moment they found that their expectations had not materialized, they would desert him. Time completely belied their fond and futile expectations.

3053. In the course of a campaign (probably the one against Banū Muṣṭaliq) 'Abd Allāh bin Ubayy, leader of the Medina Hypocrites whose fond expectations to become the Chief of Medina were shattered by the Holy Prophet's arrival on the scene is reported to have said that on his return to Medina he, 'the most honourable of its inhabitants' meaning himself, would drive out therefrom 'the meanest of them,' meaning the Holy Prophet. 'Abd Allah's son heard of this vile boast of his father, and as the party reached Medina, he drew his sword and barred his father's entry into the town until he had confessed and declared that he himself was the meanest of the citizens of Medina and the Holy Prophet the most honourable of them. Thus his boast recoiled on his head.

R. 2

10. [a]O ye who believe! let not your wealth and your children divert you from the remembrance of Allāh. And whoever does so—it is they who are the losers.

يٰٓاَيُّهَا الَّذِيْنَ اٰمَنُوْا لَا تُلْهِكُمْ اَمْوَالُكُمْ وَلَآ اَوْلَادُكُمْ
عَنْ ذِكْرِ اللّٰهِ ۚ وَمَنْ يَّفْعَلْ ذٰلِكَ فَاُولٰٓئِكَ هُمُ
الْخٰسِرُوْنَ ﴿١٠﴾

11. [b]And spend out of that which We have given you before death comes upon one of you and he says, [c]'My Lord! if only Thou wouldst respite me for a little while, then I would give alms and be among the righteous.'

وَاَنْفِقُوْا مِنْ مَّا رَزَقْنٰكُمْ مِّنْ قَبْلِ اَنْ يَّاْتِيَ اَحَدَكُمُ
الْمَوْتُ فَيَقُوْلَ رَبِّ لَوْلَآ اَخَّرْتَنِيْٓ اِلٰٓى اَجَلٍ
قَرِيْبٍ ۙ فَاَصَّدَّقَ وَاَكُنْ مِّنَ الصّٰلِحِيْنَ ﴿١١﴾

12. [d]And Allāh will not grant respite to a soul when its appointed time has come;[3054] and Allāh is Well-Aware of what you do.

وَلَنْ يُّؤَخِّرَ اللّٰهُ نَفْسًا اِذَا جَآءَ اَجَلُهَا ۗ وَاللّٰهُ
خَبِيْرٌ ۢ بِمَا تَعْمَلُوْنَ ﴿١٢﴾

[a]8 : 29; 24 : 38; 64 : 16; 102 : 2. [b]2 : 196; 9 : 34. [c]14 : 45. [d]71 : 5.

3054. When it loses the God-given opportunity to serve a good cause.

CHAPTER 64

AL-TAGHĀBUN

(*Revealed after Hijrah*)

Introductory Remarks

The *Sūrah* was revealed at Medina. The previous *Sūrah* had closed on an exhortation to believers to spend liberally in the cause of Truth before the day arrived when they would have to render an account of their actions before God. In the present *Sūrah* some description is given of that awful day, which is called '*the day of losses and gains*.' The believers are exhorted again with greater emphasis not to allow any consideration of ties of relationship to stand in the way of their resolve to spend their wealth in Allāh's way. The *Sūrah* further says that God had brought into existence the entire universe for man's service and had endowed him with great natural powers and faculties in order that he should achieve the object of his creation. Unfortunately, ungrateful men defy God's commandments. They are warned that they should make preparation for the day when the realization of the loss resulting from disobedience of Heavenly Messnegers will be brought home to them. Towards the close of the *Sūrah* the believers are told that they can make up for remissness, if any, in the discharge of their obligations to God and their fellow beings, by giving unquestioning obedience to the commandments of God, and by spending liberally in the cause of Truth.

سُورَةُ التَّغَابُنِ مَدَنِيَّةٌ

1. [a]In the name of Allāh, the Gracious, the Merciful.

بِسۡمِ اللّٰہِ الرَّحۡمٰنِ الرَّحِیۡمِ ۝۱

2. [b]Whatever is in the heavens and whatever is in the earth glorifies[3055] Allāh. His is the Kingdom and His is the praise, and He has power over all things.

یُسَبِّحُ لِلّٰہِ مَا فِی السَّمٰوٰتِ وَمَا فِی الۡاَرۡضِ ۚ لَہُ الۡمُلۡکُ وَلَہُ الۡحَمۡدُ ۫ وَھُوَ عَلٰی کُلِّ شَیۡءٍ قَدِیۡرٌ ۝۲

3. It is He Who has created you, but *some* of you are disbelievers and *some* of you are believers.[3056] And Allāh sees what you do.

ھُوَ الَّذِیۡ خَلَقَکُمۡ فَمِنۡکُمۡ کَافِرٌ وَّمِنۡکُمۡ مُّؤۡمِنٌ ؕ وَاللّٰہُ بِمَا تَعۡمَلُوۡنَ بَصِیۡرٌ ۝۳

4. He created the heavens and the earth with an eternal purpose and [c]He gave you shape and made your shapes beautiful, and to Him is the *ultimate* return.[3057]

خَلَقَ السَّمٰوٰتِ وَالۡاَرۡضَ بِالۡحَقِّ وَصَوَّرَکُمۡ فَاَحۡسَنَ صُوَرَکُمۡ ۚ وَاِلَیۡہِ الۡمَصِیۡرُ ۝۴

5. He knows whatever is in the heavens and the earth, and He knows [d]what you hide and what you disclose;[3058] and Allāh knows full well *all* that which is *hidden* in the breasts.

یَعۡلَمُ مَا فِی السَّمٰوٰتِ وَالۡاَرۡضِ وَیَعۡلَمُ مَا تُسِرُّوۡنَ وَمَا تُعۡلِنُوۡنَ ؕ وَاللّٰہُ عَلِیۡمٌۢ بِذَاتِ الصُّدُوۡرِ ۝۵

[a]1 : 1. [b]17 : 45; 24 : 42; 59 : 25; 61 : 2; 62 : 2. [c]3 : 7; 7 : 12. [d]2 : 78; 16 : 20; 27 : 26.

3055. Every creature, by discharging its allotted task punctually and regularly and thus by fulfilling the object for which it has been created, declares God to be free from every defect, imperfection or impurity and to be its Master, Creator and Controller. This is the real significance of *Tasbīḥ*.

3056. God has bestowed upon men great natural powers and has provided for them opportunities for their moral and spiritual progress but while some of them, by failing to make proper use of them, practically refuse to acknowledge God's beneficence, others employ them in the service of their fellow beings and thus win the pleasure of Allāh. This is the significance of the words *Kāfir* and *Mu'min*.

3057. The universe is governed and controlled by certain fixed natural laws and man is not the victim of chance; on the contrary, he has been endowed with such powers and faculties as are suited to his exalted position as God's vicegerent on earth. He shall have to render to God an account of his deeds and actions.

3058. God being the Creator and Controller of the universe, nothing is hidden from Him or can escape His notice. It is, therefore, futile on man's part to think that he can avoid or escape responsibility for his actions.

6. ªHas there not come to you the account of those who disbelieved before? They tasted the evil consequences of their conduct, and for them is *decreed* painful punishment.

اَلَمۡ یَاۡتِکُمۡ نَبَؤُا الَّذِیۡنَ کَفَرُوۡا مِنۡ قَبۡلُ فَذَاقُوۡا وَبَالَ اَمۡرِهِمۡ وَلَهُمۡ عَذَابٌ اَلِیۡمٌ ۝

7. That was because their Messengers came to them with manifest Signs, but they said, 'Shall *mere* mortals guide us?' So they disbelieved and turned away, but Allāh had no need of them; and Allāh is Self-Sufficient, Worthy of all praise.

ذٰلِکَ بِاَنَّهٗ کَانَتۡ تَّاۡتِیۡهِمۡ رُسُلُهُمۡ بِالۡبَیِّنٰتِ فَقَالُوۡۤا اَبَشَرٌ یَّهۡدُوۡنَنَا فَکَفَرُوۡا وَتَوَلَّوۡا وَّاسۡتَغۡنَی اللّٰهُ وَاللّٰهُ غَنِیٌّ حَمِیۡدٌ ۝

8. Those who disbelieve think³⁰⁵⁹ that ᵇthey will not be raised up.³⁰⁵⁹ᴬ Say, 'Yea, by my Lord, you shall, surely, be raised up; then you shall, certainly, be informed of what you did. And that is easy for Allāh.'

زَعَمَ الَّذِیۡنَ کَفَرُوۡۤا اَنۡ لَّنۡ یُّبۡعَثُوۡا قُلۡ بَلٰی وَرَبِّیۡ لَتُبۡعَثُنَّ ثُمَّ لَتُنَبَّؤُنَّ بِمَا عَمِلۡتُمۡ وَذٰلِکَ عَلَی اللّٰهِ یَسِیۡرٌ ۝

9. Believe, therefore, ın Allāh and His Messenger, and in the ᶜLight³⁰⁶⁰ which We have sent down. And Allāh is Well-Aware of *all* that you do.

فَاٰمِنُوۡا بِاللّٰهِ وَرَسُوۡلِهٖ وَالنُّوۡرِ الَّذِیۡۤ اَنۡزَلۡنَا وَاللّٰهُ بِمَا تَعۡمَلُوۡنَ خَبِیۡرٌ ۝

ª40 : 22-23.   ᵇ36 : 79-80; 46 : 18; 50 : 4.   ᶜ4 : 175; 7 : 158.

3059. *Za'ama* means, he thought; claimed; believed; asserted (Lane).

3059A. Does man think that there is no future life or that he has been endowed with great natural powers, attributes and faculties for nothing, or, does he imagine that he can escape responsibility for his actions? He is sadly mistaken if he so imagines. There is certainly a life after death wherein *you shall certainly be informed of what you did*

3060. The light of revelation, wisdom, spiritual enlightenment and insight and Divine knowledge and discernment, with which the Holy Prophet was specially gifted.

10. The day when He shall gather you for the Day of Gathering; that will be the day *of the determination* of losses *and gains*.[3061] And whoso believes in Allāh and acts righteously —[a]He will remove from them the evil *consequences of their* deeds, and He will admit them into Gardens through which streams flow, to abide therein for ever. That is the supreme achievement.

يَوْمَ يَجْمَعُكُمْ لِيَوْمِ الْجَمْعِ ذٰلِكَ يَوْمُ التَّغَابُنِ ۗ
وَمَنْ يُّؤْمِنْ بِاللّٰهِ وَيَعْمَلْ صَالِحًا يُّكَفِّرْ عَنْهُ
سَيِّاٰتِهٖ وَيُدْخِلْهُ جَنّٰتٍ تَجْرِيْ مِنْ تَحْتِهَا الْاَنْهٰرُ
خٰلِدِيْنَ فِيْهَآ اَبَدًا ۗ ذٰلِكَ الْفَوْزُ الْعَظِيْمُ ﴿۱۰﴾

11. [b]But those who disbelieve and reject Our Signs, these shall be the inmates of the Fire, wherein they shall abide; and an evil destination it is !

وَالَّذِيْنَ كَفَرُوْا وَكَذَّبُوْا بِاٰيٰتِنَآ اُولٰٓئِكَ اَصْحٰبُ النَّارِ
خٰلِدِيْنَ فِيْهَا ۗ وَبِئْسَ الْمَصِيْرُ ﴿۱۱﴾

R. 2 12. [c]There befalls not any affliction but by the leave[3062] of Allāh. And whosoever believes in Allāh—He guides his heart aright. And Allāh knows all things well.

مَآ اَصَابَ مِنْ مُّصِيْبَةٍ اِلَّا بِاِذْنِ اللّٰهِ ۗ وَمَنْ
يُّؤْمِنْ بِاللّٰهِ يَهْدِ قَلْبَهٗ ۗ وَاللّٰهُ بِكُلِّ شَيْءٍ
عَلِيْمٌ ﴿۱۲﴾

13. [d]And obey Allāh and obey the Messenger. But if you turn away, then Our Messenger is responsible only for conveying *the Message* clearly

وَاَطِيْعُوا اللّٰهَ وَاَطِيْعُوا الرَّسُوْلَ ۚ فَاِنْ تَوَلَّيْتُمْ فَاِنَّمَا
عَلٰى رَسُوْلِنَا الْبَلٰغُ الْمُبِيْنُ ﴿۱۳﴾

14. Allāh! there is no god but He; so in Allāh let the believers put their trust.

اَللّٰهُ لَآ اِلٰهَ اِلَّا هُوَ ۗ وَعَلَى اللّٰهِ فَلْيَتَوَكَّلِ الْمُؤْمِنُوْنَ ﴿۱۴﴾

---

[a]8 : 30; 48 : 6; 66 : 9. [b]2 : 40; 7 : 37; 22 : 58. [c]30 : 17; 78 : 29. 4 : 79. [d]5 : 93; 24 : 55.

3061. The expression, *Yaum al-Taghābun*, has been variously interpreted as : (1) The day of losses and gains, *i.e.*, when believers will know what they had gained and disbelievers what they had lost. (2) The day of the manifestation of loss, *i.e.*, on that day disbelievers will realize how much they had been deficient in the discharge of their duties to God and man and thus their loss will become manifest to them. (3) The day when believers will attribute defect or deficiency to lack of wisdom of disbelievers in that they had preferred disbelief to belief (Mufradāt).

3062. God governs the universe according to certain laws. When man contravenes any of those laws he involves himself in trouble. But as God is the Creator of all natural laws and man's affliction is due to the contravention of one or other of these laws, or to one of God's special decrees, the trouble may be said to have emanated from Him, or to have come into being by His leave.

15. O ye who believe! surely, among your wives and your children are *some who are* your enemies, so beware of them. And if you overlook and forgive and pardon, then, surely, Allāh is Most Forgiving, *ever* Merciful.

يَا أَيُّهَا الَّذِينَ آمَنُوا إِنَّ مِنْ أَزْوَاجِكُمْ وَأَوْلَادِكُمْ عَدُوًّا لَكُمْ فَاحْذَرُوهُمْ ۚ وَإِنْ تَعْفُوا وَتَصْفَحُوا وَتَغْفِرُوا فَإِنَّ اللَّهَ غَفُورٌ رَحِيمٌ ﴿١٥﴾

16. Verily, your wealth and [a]your children are but a trial; but with Allāh is an immense reward.

إِنَّمَا أَمْوَالُكُمْ وَأَوْلَادُكُمْ فِتْنَةٌ ۚ وَاللَّهُ عِنْدَهُ أَجْرٌ عَظِيمٌ ﴿١٦﴾

17. So be mindful of your duty to Allāh as best you can, and listen and obey, and spend *in His cause*, it will be good for yourselves. [b]And whoso is rid of the covetousness of his own soul—it is they who shall succeed.

فَاتَّقُوا اللَّهَ مَا اسْتَطَعْتُمْ وَاسْمَعُوا وَأَطِيعُوا وَأَنْفِقُوا خَيْرًا لِأَنْفُسِكُمْ ۗ وَمَنْ يُوقَ شُحَّ نَفْسِهِ فَأُولَٰئِكَ هُمُ الْمُفْلِحُونَ ﴿١٧﴾

18. [c]If you lend to Allāh a goodly loan,[3063] He will multiply it for you, and will forgive you; and Allāh is Most Appreciating, Forbearing;

إِنْ تُقْرِضُوا اللَّهَ قَرْضًا حَسَنًا يُضَاعِفْهُ لَكُمْ وَيَغْفِرْ لَكُمْ ۚ وَاللَّهُ شَكُورٌ حَلِيمٌ ﴿١٨﴾

19. [d]The Knower of the unseen and the seen,[3063A] the Mighty, the Wise.

ع عَالِمُ الْغَيْبِ وَالشَّهَادَةِ الْعَزِيزُ الْحَكِيمُ ﴿١٩﴾

---

[a]8 : 29; 63 : 10. [b]59 : 10. [c]2 : 246; 57 : 12; 73 : 21.
[d]6 : 74; 9 : 94; 13 : 10; 59 : 23.

3063. Spending one's wealth in the cause of Truth is tantamount to giving a loan to the Bountiful and Appreciating God which He pays back manifold.

3063A. The invisible and the visible.

CHAPTER 65

AL-ṬALĀQ

(*Revealed after Hijrah*)

Date of Revelation and Context

The *Sūrah* was revealed at Medina, sometime in the fifth or sixth year of the *Hijrah*. The immediate cause of its revelation seems to be the divorce pronounced by 'Abd Allāh bin 'Umar against his wife during her monthly course, a procedure which the *Sūrah* is intended to prohibit (Bukhārī). In the preceding *Sūrah* a note of warning was sounded against some of the wives and children of believers, as sometime they tend to become an impediment in the way of men wishing to make monetary sacrifice in the cause of Truth. This may possibly lead to estrangement between the husband and the wife and ultimately to divorce, or the divorce may result from incompatibility of dispositions, or from some other cause. It was, therefore, necessary to lay down the correct procedure for divorce. This may be regarded as the immediate connection of this *Sūrah* with the preceding one. But there also runs a deeper connection in the subject matter of the Qur'ān as a whole. It is characteristic of the style of the Qur'ān that when any of its *Sūrahs* deals with a particular subject in its opening verses, then in order to emphasize its importance it briefly, but pointedly, reverts to the same subject in its closing verses. The same procedure has been adopted in the Qur'ān as regards the whole *Sūrahs*. Thus some of the social and political problems which were dealt with in detail in the opening Medinite Chapters such as Al-Baqarah, Āl 'Imrān, Al-Nisā', have again been briefly treated in the last ten Medinite Chapters. The subject of divorce with which this *Sūrah* briefly deals has already been dealt with in detail in *Sūrah* Al-Baqarah.

Subject-Matter

The *Sūrah* opens with the procedure to be adopted when a man intends to divorce his wife, and also with the treatment to be extended to her after the divorce has been pronounced and she is waiting for her *'Iddah* (period of waiting) to expire. It is enjoined that during this period she should be provided with all the necessities of life, commensurate with the financial means of the husband. It is significant that four times in the course of five brief verses of the *Sūrah* believers have been exhorted to observe fear of God in their dealings. This shows that in the matter of divorce husbands are generally tempted to treat their divorced wives unjustly. Hence the repeated injunction to observe fear of God.

سُورَةُ الطَّلَاقِ مَدَنِيَّةٌ (٦٥)

بِسْمِ اللّٰهِ الرَّحْمٰنِ الرَّحِيْمِ ①

1. [a]In the name of Allāh, the Gracious, the Merciful.

يٰٓاَيُّهَا النَّبِيُّ اِذَا طَلَّقْتُمُ النِّسَآءَ فَطَلِّقُوْهُنَّ
لِعِدَّتِهِنَّ وَاَحْصُوا الْعِدَّةَ ۚ وَاتَّقُوا اللّٰهَ رَبَّكُمْ ۚ
لَا تُخْرِجُوْهُنَّ مِنْۢ بُيُوْتِهِنَّ وَلَا يَخْرُجْنَ اِلَّآ اَنْ
يَّاْتِيْنَ بِفَاحِشَةٍ مُّبَيِّنَةٍ ۗ وَتِلْكَ حُدُوْدُ اللّٰهِ ۗ وَ
مَنْ يَّتَعَدَّ حُدُوْدَ اللّٰهِ فَقَدْ ظَلَمَ نَفْسَهٗ ۗ لَا تَدْرِيْ
لَعَلَّ اللّٰهَ يُحْدِثُ بَعْدَ ذٰلِكَ اَمْرًا ②

2. O Prophet! [b]when you divorce women,[3064] divorce them for the *prescribed* period, and *thereafter* reckon the period; and fear Allāh, your Lord. Turn them not out of their houses,[3064A] nor should they *themselves* leave unless they commit manifest indecency. [c]These are the limits *set* by Allāh; and whoso transgresses the limits of Allāh, he, indeed, wrongs his own soul. Thou knowest not; it may be that thereafter Allāh will bring something[3065] *new* to pass.

فَاِذَا بَلَغْنَ اَجَلَهُنَّ فَاَمْسِكُوْهُنَّ بِمَعْرُوْفٍ اَوْ
فَارِقُوْهُنَّ بِمَعْرُوْفٍ وَّاَشْهِدُوْا ذَوَيْ عَدْلٍ
مِّنْكُمْ وَاَقِيْمُوا الشَّهَادَةَ لِلّٰهِ ۗ ذٰلِكُمْ يُوْعَظُ بِهٖ مَنْ
كَانَ يُؤْمِنُ بِاللّٰهِ وَالْيَوْمِ الْاٰخِرِ ۬ وَمَنْ يَّتَّقِ اللّٰهَ
يَجْعَلْ لَّهٗ مَخْرَجًا ③

3. Then, [d]when they *are about to* reach *the limit* of their *prescribed* term, retain them with kindness, or part with them in a suitable manner, and call to witness two just persons from among you; and bear *true* witness for Allāh. Thus is admonished he who believes in Allāh and the Last Day. And he who fears Allāh—He will make for him a way out;[3066]

---

[a]1 : 1. [b]2 : 232-233. [c]2 : 230. [d]2 : 232.

3064. This is one of those verses of the Qur'ān in which the address made to the Holy Prophet is, in reality, meant for the believers. Since the Holy Prophet was debarred from divorcing any of his wives (33 : 53), the injunction is meant clearly for his followers.

3064A. The pronouncement of divorce should be made in the interval between two monthly courses, during which the husband and wife should not have conjugal relations. This ensures that the decision to divorce has not been taken hastily in a fit of anger or under the influence of some other momentary impulse but after cool and deliberate reflection. Moreover, a divorced wife is to remain in her house till the expiry of '*Iddah* (period of waiting). This procedure of divorce is enjoined because it is possible that during the period of waiting the causes of friction may wear out and reconciliation may take place between the estranged parties.

3065. *Amr* here signifies reconciliation between the estranged husband and wife.

3066. If differences between husband and wife are due to the poverty of the husband, God will provide for him from sources he never could imagine, provided he fears Allāh and makes an honest effort to tide over the difficult situation.

4. And will provide for him from whence he expects not. And he who puts his trust in Allāh—He is sufficient for him. Verily, Allāh will accomplish His purpose. For everything has Allāh appointed a measure.

وَّيَرْزُقْهُ مِنْ حَيْثُ لَا يَحْتَسِبُ ۭ وَمَنْ يَّتَوَكَّلْ عَلَى
اللّٰهِ فَهُوَ حَسْبُهٗ ۭ اِنَّ اللّٰهَ بَالِغُ اَمْرِهٖ ۭ قَدْ جَعَلَ
اللّٰهُ لِكُلِّ شَيْءٍ قَدْرًا ④

5. And if you are in doubt[3067] *as to the prescribed period* for such of your women as have despaired of monthly courses, then *know that* the prescribed period for them is [a]three months, and *also for* such as do not have their monthly courses *yet*. And *as for* those who are with child, their period shall be until they are delivered of their burden. And whoso fears Allāh, He will provide facilities for him in his affair.

وَالّٰۗـِٔيْ يَىِٕسْنَ مِنَ الْمَحِيْضِ مِنْ نِّسَاۗىِٕكُمْ اِنِ ارْتَبْتُمْ
فَعِدَّتُهُنَّ ثَلٰثَةُ اَشْهُرٍ ۙ وَّالّٰۗـِٔيْ لَمْ يَحِضْنَ ۭ وَاُولَاتُ
الْاَحْمَالِ اَجَلُهُنَّ اَنْ يَّضَعْنَ حَمْلَهُنَّ ۭ وَمَنْ يَّتَّقِ
اللّٰهَ يَجْعَلْ لَّهٗ مِنْ اَمْرِهٖ يُسْرًا ⑤

6. That is the command of Allāh which He has sent down to you. And whoso fears[3068] Allāh—He will remove the evil *effects* of his deeds and will enlarge his reward.

ذٰلِكَ اَمْرُ اللّٰهِ اَنْزَلَهٗٓ اِلَيْكُمْ ۭ وَمَنْ يَّتَّقِ اللّٰهَ يُكَفِّرْ
عَنْهُ سَيِّاٰتِهٖ وَيُعْظِمْ لَهٗٓ اَجْرًا ⑥

[a]2 : 229.

3067. The words ' if you are in doubt ' have been added because the stoppage of monthly course may be due to some disorder in the womb or to some other cause, thaugh menopause may not yet have arrived.

3068. In the preceding five verses the believers have been repeatedly enjoined to fear God. This shows that in the matter of divorce men are generally tempted to deal unjustly with their divorced wives and to deprive them of their just rights.

7. Lodge *the divorced women during the prescribed period* in the houses wherein you dwell, according to your means,[3068A] and harass them not that you may create hardships for them *and thus force them to leave*. And if they be with child, spend on them until they are delivered of their burden. [a]And if they give suck *to the child* for you, give them their due recompense, *to be fixed* in consultation with one another according to what is customary; but if you meet with difficulty from each other, then let another *woman* suckle *the child* for *the father*.

أَسْكِنُوهُنَّ مِنْ حَيْثُ سَكَنْتُمْ مِّنْ وُّجْدِكُمْ وَ
لَا تُضَآرُّوْهُنَّ لِتُضَيِّقُوْا عَلَيْهِنَّ ۗ وَإِنْ كُنَّ أُولَاتِ
حَمْلٍ فَأَنْفِقُوْا عَلَيْهِنَّ حَتّٰى يَضَعْنَ حَمْلَهُنَّ ۚ فَإِنْ
أَرْضَعْنَ لَكُمْ فَاٰتُوْهُنَّ أُجُوْرَهُنَّ ۚ وَأْتَمِرُوْا بَيْنَكُمْ
بِمَعْرُوْفٍ ۚ وَإِنْ تَعَاسَرْتُمْ فَسَتُرْضِعُ لَهٗٓ أُخْرٰى ﴿٧﴾

8. [b]Let him who has abundance *of means* spend out of his abundance. And let him whose means of subsistence are straitened spend out of what Allāh has given him. Allāh burdens not any soul beyond that which He has bestowed upon it. Allāh will soon bring about ease after hardship.

لِيُنْفِقْ ذُوْ سَعَةٍ مِّنْ سَعَتِهٖ ۗ وَمَنْ قُدِرَ عَلَيْهِ
رِزْقُهٗ فَلْيُنْفِقْ مِمَّآ اٰتٰىهُ اللّٰهُ ۗ لَا يُكَلِّفُ اللّٰهُ نَفْسًا
ع إِلَّا مَآ اٰتٰىهَا ۗ سَيَجْعَلُ اللّٰهُ بَعْدَ عُسْرٍ يُّسْرًا ﴿٨﴾

R.2 9. [c]How many a city rebelled against the command of its Lord[3069] and His Messengers, and We called it to severe account and punished it with dire punishment!

وَكَأَيِّنْ مِّنْ قَرْيَةٍ عَتَتْ عَنْ أَمْرِ رَبِّهَا وَرُسُلِهٖ
فَحَاسَبْنٰهَا حِسَابًا شَدِيْدًا ۙ وَّعَذَّبْنٰهَا عَذَابًا نُّكْرًا ﴿٩﴾

[a]2 : 234. [b]2 : 234. [c]7 : 5-6; 17 : 18; 21 : 12; 22 : 46.

3068A. In her *'Iddah* a divorced woman is to be looked after by the husband with the same care and consideration as when she was the mistress of his house, accordng to the best of his means, till she leaves the house and is free to adopt the way of life she chooses.

3069. From the subject of divorce dealt with in the preceding verses, the present verse passes on to the defiance of Divine commandments because those who defy Divine commandments, in fact, divorce themselves from God's grace.

10. So it tasted the evil consequences[3070] of its conduct, and the end of its affair was ruin.

فَذَاقَتْ وَبَالَ اَمْرِهَا وَكَانَ عَاقِبَةُ اَمْرِهَا
خُسْرًا ⑩

11. Allāh has prepared for them a severe punishment; so fear Allāh, O ye men of understanding who have believed. [a]Allāh has, indeed, sent down to you a Reminder—

اَعَدَّ اللّٰهُ لَهُمْ عَذَابًا شَدِيْدًا ۙ فَاتَّقُوا اللّٰهَ يٰۤاُولِي
الْاَلْبَابِ ۚۖ الَّذِيْنَ اٰمَنُوْا ۛ قَدْ اَنْزَلَ اللّٰهُ اِلَيْكُمْ
ذِكْرًا ۙ ⑪

12. A Messenger, who recites unto you the clear Signs of Allāh, [b]that he may bring those who believe and do good deeds out of every kind of darkness into light. And whoso believes in Allāh and does righteous deeds—He will make him enter Gardens, through which streams flow, to abide therein for ever. Allāh has, indeed, made excellent provision for him.

رَّسُوْلًا يَّتْلُوْا عَلَيْكُمْ اٰيٰتِ اللّٰهِ مُبَيِّنٰتٍ لِّيُخْرِجَ
الَّذِيْنَ اٰمَنُوْا وَعَمِلُوا الصّٰلِحٰتِ مِنَ الظُّلُمٰتِ اِلَى
النُّوْرِ ؕ وَمَنْ يُّؤْمِنْۢ بِاللّٰهِ وَيَعْمَلْ صَالِحًا يُّدْخِلْهُ
جَنّٰتٍ تَجْرِيْ مِنْ تَحْتِهَا الْاَنْهٰرُ خٰلِدِيْنَ فِيْهَاۤ اَبَدًا ؕ
قَدْ اَحْسَنَ اللّٰهُ لَهٗ رِزْقًا ⑫

13. Allāh is He Who created [c]seven heavens, and of the earth the like thereof.[3070A] The *Divine* command comes down in their midst, that you may know that Allāh has power over all things, and that Allāh encompasses all things in *His* knowledge.

اَللّٰهُ الَّذِيْ خَلَقَ سَبْعَ سَمٰوٰتٍ وَّمِنَ الْاَرْضِ مِثْلَهُنَّ ؕ
يَتَنَزَّلُ الْاَمْرُ بَيْنَهُنَّ لِتَعْلَمُوْۤا اَنَّ اللّٰهَ عَلٰى كُلِّ
ع شَيْءٍ قَدِيْرٌ ۙ وَّاَنَّ اللّٰهَ قَدْ اَحَاطَ بِكُلِّ شَيْءٍ عِلْمًا ⑬

[a]15 : 10; 36 : 70. [b]2 : 258; 5 : 17.
[c]67 : 4; 71 : 16.

3070. *Wabāl* means, injury; sin; punishment of sin. *Wabīl* means, dangerous, pernicious, violent (Aqrab).

3070A. 'Seven earths' may be the seven major planets of the solar system and seven heavens their orbits or ways as elsewhere so called in the Qur'ān (23 : 18). Or, spiritually speaking ' seven heavens ' may signify seven stages of the spiritual development of man and 'seven earths' those of his physical growth.

CHAPTER 66

AL-TAḤRĪM

(*Revealed after Hijrah*)

Date of Revelation and Context

With this Chapter ends the series of Medinite *Sūrahs* which began with *Sūrah* Al-Ḥadīd. A part of it may be assigned to the 7th or 8th year of *Hijrah* and a part of it to a later period, as the incident mentioned therein shows. The preceding *Sūrah* had dealt with some aspects of *Ṭalāq*—permanent separation between husband and wife. The present *Sūrah*, however, deals with the subject of temporary separation, that is to say, with cases wherein a man, due to some disagreement or conflict in domestic affairs, temporarily gives up conjugal relations with his wife, or swears not to use a lawful thing. The *Sūrah* opens with an injunction addressed personally to the Holy Prophet not to forbid himself the use of things which God has made lawful for him. The specific incident referred to in the opening verse indicates that due to misunderstanding or disagreement that may disturb, though temporarily, domestic harmony and peace, friction might sometimes arise in the otherwise most peaceful atmosphere of even a Prophet's household. The injunction, which applies to the Holy Prophet as much as to his followers, signifies that in such a case of temporary disharmony extreme measures should not be resorted to. The Holy Prophet's wives are further warned that they should never lose sight of his very exalted position as God's Messenger and should not make demands from him which are inconsistent with it. The *Sūrah* then tells believers to take care that members of their household do not deviate from the path of rectitude lest they might land themselves into trouble. As the *Sūrah* opens with mentioning an incident concerning relationship of the Holy Prophet with his wives, it ends fittingly with a simile, comparing disbelievers to the wives of the Prophets Noah and Lot; and believers to the wife of Pharaoh, and the highly and righteous ones among them, to Mary, mother of Jesus.

سُورَةُ التَّحْرِيمِ مَدَنِيَّةٌ (٦٦)

1. [a]In the name of Allāh, the Gracious, the Merciful.

بِسْمِ اللّٰهِ الرَّحْمٰنِ الرَّحِيْمِ ①

2. O Prophet! why dost thou forbid *thyself* that which Allāh has made lawful to thee. Thou seekest the pleasure of thy wives?[3071] And Allāh is Most Forgiving, Merciful.

يٰۤاَيُّهَا النَّبِيُّ لِمَ تُحَرِّمُ مَاۤ اَحَلَّ اللّٰهُ لَكَ ۚ تَبْتَغِيْ مَرْضَاتَ اَزْوَاجِكَ ؕ وَاللّٰهُ غَفُوْرٌ رَّحِيْمٌ ②

---

[a]1 : 1.

3071. It is related that one day one of the wives of the Holy Prophet gave him a drink made from honey, which he appeared to like. Some of his other wives, out of pique, pointed out to him that his breath smelt of *Maghāfīr*, a shrub the taste of which resembles that of honey but which gives out a bad smell. The Holy Prophet, because of his delicate nature, promised not to take honey any more (Buldān). It is to this incident that the verse under comment is generally taken to refer. But it seems improbable that the Holy Prophet, merely to satisfy the pique of his wife or wives, should have taken such a drastic step as to have permanently forbidden himself the use of something which was lawful, particularly of a thing in which, according to the Qur'ān, 'there is cure for men' (16 : 70). It appears that the narrator or narrators of this incident had suffered from some misunderstanding or mental confusion, particularly when, according to one tradition, the Holy Prophet took honey from the house of Zainab, and 'Ā'ishah and Ḥafṣah contrived to draw him into making the aforesaid promise, while, according to another tradition, it was at the house of Ḥafṣah herself that he was served with honey and that the wives who objected were 'Ā'ishah, Zainab and Ṣafiyyah. Moreover, according to the Ḥadīth, two, or at the most three, of the Holy Prophet's wives were concerned in the affair, but according to vv. 2 and 6 of the *Sūrah*, all of them were connected with it, two of them taking a leading part (v. 5). These facts show that the *Sūrah* refers to some incident of much greater significance than the mere taking of honey by the Holy Prophet at the house of one of his wives. In the commentary on this *Sūrah*, Bukhārī (*Kitāb al-Maẓālim wa'l Ghaṣb*) quotes Ibn 'Abbās as relating that he was always on the look-out to enquire of 'Umar as to who were the two wives to whom reference is made in the verse: *Now, if you two turn unto Allāh, it will be better for you, and your hearts are already so inclined.* One day, finding 'Umar alone, he sought to satisfy his curiosity. He had hardly finished his question, says Ibn 'Abbās, when 'Umar said that they were 'Ā'ishah and Ḥafṣah, and then proceeded to relate the story thus: "One day, when my wife offered me her advice concerning some domestic affair, I curtly told her that it was no business of hers to advise me, for in those days we did not hold our women-folk in much respect. My wife sternly replied: 'Your daughter Ḥafṣah takes so much liberty with the Prophet that she retorts back when he says something which she does not like till he feels offended, and you do not allow me to speak to you even about our domestic affairs.' Upon this I went to Ḥafṣah and warned her that she should not be misled by 'Ā'ishah in this matter as she was nearer to the Prophet's heart. Then I went to Ummi Salmah and had hardly broached the matter with her when she also curtly told me not to interfere in affairs concerning the Prophet and his wives. A short time after this the Holy Prophet separated himself from his wives and decided not to go to the house of any of them for sometime. The news went round that the Holy Prophet had divorced his wives. I went to him and asked him if it was true that he had divorced his wives to which he replied in the negative."

3. Allāh has, indeed, enjoined on you the expiation of *such* of your oaths *as would occasion trouble*,[3072] and Allāh is your Friend; and He is All-Knowing, Wise.

قَدْ فَرَضَ اللّٰهُ لَكُمْ تَحِلَّةَ اَيْمَانِكُمْ ۚ وَاللّٰهُ مَوْلٰىكُمْ ۚ وَهُوَ الْعَلِيْمُ الْحَكِيْمُ ۝٣

4. And when the Prophet confided a matter unto one of his wives and she divulged it, and Allāh informed him of it, he made known *to her* part thereof, and avoided *mentioning* part *of it*. And when he informed her of it, she said, 'Who has informed[3073] thee of it?' He said, 'The All-Knowing, the All-Aware *God* has informed me.'

وَاِذْ اَسَرَّ النَّبِيُّ اِلٰى بَعْضِ اَزْوَاجِهٖ حَدِيْثًا ۚ فَلَمَّا نَبَّاَتْ بِهٖ وَاَظْهَرَهُ اللّٰهُ عَلَيْهِ عَرَّفَ بَعْضَهٗ وَاَعْرَضَ عَنْۢ بَعْضٍ ۚ فَلَمَّا نَبَّاَهَا بِهٖ قَالَتْ مَنْ اَنْۢبَاَكَ هٰذَا ۗ قَالَ نَبَّاَنِيَ الْعَلِيْمُ الْخَبِيْرُ ۝٤

This incident shows that 'Umar, and Ibn 'Abbās were of the view that the relevant verses of the *Sūrah* referred to this temporary separation of the Holy Prophet from his wives. The fact that the preceding *Sūrah* mentions the subject of *Ṭalāq* which is separation of a permanent character, lends weight to the inference that these verses relate to the Prophet's separation from his wives which, however, was of a temporary nature. Besides, as reported by 'Ā'ishah in the above-mentioned tradition, immediately after the period of separation was over, v. 33 : 29 was revealed and the Prophet's wives were given the choice between the Prophet's companionship with a life of poverty and austere simplicity on the one hand, and separation from him with a life of ease and comfort and all sorts of material benefits on the other. The choice was given to all the wives and the verse under comment speaks of all the wives, as also v. 4. This shows that the incident referred to in these verses concerns *all the wives* in which two of them took a prominent part. And it is on record that the incident occurred when the Prophet's wives, led by 'Ā'ishah and Ḥafṣah, demanded of him that since the financial condition of the Muslims had greatly improved they, like other Muslim ladies, may be allowed to enjoy amenities of life and comfortable living (Fatḥ al-Qadīr). In this context the words 'thou seekest the pleasure of thy wives' would seem to signify something like this : 'Since thou always desirest to please thy wives and meet their wishes, they have become so emboldened by this loving attitude of thine as to lose sight of thy high position as a great Prophet of God and to make excessive demands from thee.'

The alleged incident of Mary, the copt, being too foolish and fantastic, a concoction of Christian writers and lacking all reliable historical evidence, does not merit serious notice. Incidentally, Mary was the Holy Prophet's wedded consort and the respected Mother of the Faithful. The Holy Prophet never kept a slave girl.

3072. The Holy Prophet had severely taken to heart his wives' demand for amenities of life, and in order to show his extreme displeasure had sworn to keep away from them for one month. The present verse describes that a lawful thing does not become unlawful for a person merely by his swearing not to use it. In such a contingency he is required only to expiate his broken oath.

3073. It is difficult to say to what particular incident the present verse, in fact, refers. The reference which seems to be supported by the context may be to the incident described by 'Ā'ishah herself, which is to this effect: When verse 33 : 29 was revealed, giving the Holy Prophet's wives the choice between his companionship and separation from him in reply to their demand for a life of comfort and ease, the Prophet first of all broached the matter with 'Ā'ishah (Bukhārī, *Kitāb al-Maẓālim wa'l-Ghaṣb*). The Holy Prophet

5. *Now* if you two[3074] turn unto Allāh repentant—and your hearts are *already so* inclined—*it will be better for you.* But if you back up one another against him, surely, Allāh is his helper and Gabriel and the righteous among the believers, and *all* the angels besides are *his* helpers.

إِنْ تَتُوبَآ إِلَى اللّٰهِ فَقَدْ صَغَتْ قُلُوبُكُمَا ۚ وَإِنْ
تَظٰهَرَا عَلَيْهِ فَإِنَّ اللّٰهَ هُوَ مَوْلٰهُ وَجِبْرِيلُ وَ
صَالِحُ الْمُؤْمِنِينَ ۚ وَالْمَلٰٓئِكَةُ بَعْدَ ذٰلِكَ ظَهِيرٌ ﴿۵﴾

6. Maybe, His Lord, if he divorces you, will give him instead wives better than you—resigned, believing, obedient, always turning *to God*, devout in worship, given to fasting, *both* widows and virgins.

عَسٰى رَبُّهٗٓ إِنْ طَلَّقَكُنَّ أَنْ يُّبْدِلَهٗٓ أَزْوَاجًا خَيْرًا
مِّنْكُنَّ مُسْلِمٰتٍ مُّؤْمِنٰتٍ قٰنِتٰتٍ تٰٓئِبٰتٍ عٰبِدٰتٍ
سٰٓئِحٰتٍ ثَيِّبٰتٍ وَّأَبْكَارًا ﴿۶﴾

7. O ye who believe! save yourselves and your families from a [a]Fire whose fuel is men and stones over which are appointed angels, stern *and* severe, who disobey not Allāh in what He commands them and do as they are commanded.

يٰٓأَيُّهَا الَّذِينَ اٰمَنُوا قُوٓا أَنْفُسَكُمْ وَأَهْلِيكُمْ نَارًا
وَّقُودُهَا النَّاسُ وَالْحِجَارَةُ عَلَيْهَا مَلٰٓئِكَةٌ غِلَاظٌ
شِدَادٌ لَّا يَعْصُونَ اللّٰهَ مَآ أَمَرَهُمْ وَيَفْعَلُونَ
مَا يُؤْمَرُونَ ﴿۷﴾

[a]2 : 25.

appears to have taken that course because it was 'A'ishah who had led the demand along with Ḥafṣah, and it is not unlikely that 'Ā'ishah should have passed on the Holy Prophet's secret communication to Ḥafṣah. Whatever the actual facts of the case may be, the verse emphasizes the obligation of a person to whom a secret is confided not to divulge it, particularly when the parties concerned are husband and wife and the secret relates to a private domestic affair ; or for that matter, when the parties are a Prophet of God and one of his followers.

3074. The words, "you two," seem to refer to 'Ā'ishah and Ḥafṣah who had led the demand for worldly comforts in their domestic lives. All the other wives of the Holy Prophet had, however, joined in the demand, though the leading part was taken by these two, and this, perhaps because they were the daughters respectively of Abū Bakr and 'Umar, the two most respected among the Holy Prophet's Companions. The phraseology of the verse indicates that the matter referred to in these verses was of a very serious nature, but taking honey from the house of one's wife evidently is not so serious an affair as to have led to separation of the Holy Prophet from all his wives for about a month. Nor was the admonition to the Prophet's wives implied in the words, 'Allāh is his helper and Gabriel and righteous among the believers' called for in such a case.

8. [a]O ye who disbelieve! make no excuses this day. You are requited for what you did.

يٰۤاَيُّهَا الَّذِيۡنَ كَفَرُوۡا لَا تَعۡتَذِرُوا الۡيَوۡمَ ؕ اِنَّمَا
تُجۡزَوۡنَ مَا كُنۡتُمۡ تَعۡمَلُوۡنَ ⑧ ع 1 19

R. 2 9. O ye who believe! turn to Allāh in sincere repentance. It may be that your Lord will remit the evil *effects* of your *deeds* and admit you into [b]Gardens through which streams flow, on the day when Allāh will not abase the Prophet nor those who have believed with him. Their light will run before them and on their right hands. They will say, 'Our Lord, perfect our light for us[3075] and forgive us;[3076] surely, Thou hast power over all things.'

يٰۤاَيُّهَا الَّذِيۡنَ اٰمَنُوۡا تُوۡبُوۡۤا اِلَى اللّٰهِ تَوۡبَةً نَّصُوۡحًا ؕ
عَسٰى رَبُّكُمۡ اَنۡ يُّكَفِّرَ عَنۡكُمۡ سَيِّاٰتِكُمۡ وَيُدۡخِلَكُمۡ
جَنّٰتٍ تَجۡرِىۡ مِنۡ تَحۡتِهَا الۡاَنۡهٰرُ ۙ يَوۡمَ لَا يُخۡزِى
اللّٰهُ النَّبِىَّ وَالَّذِيۡنَ اٰمَنُوۡا مَعَهٗ ۚ نُوۡرُهُمۡ يَسۡعٰى
بَيۡنَ اَيۡدِيۡهِمۡ وَبِاَيۡمَانِهِمۡ يَقُوۡلُوۡنَ رَبَّنَاۤ اَتۡمِمۡ
لَنَا نُوۡرَنَا وَاغۡفِرۡ لَنَا ۚ اِنَّكَ عَلٰى كُلِّ شَىۡءٍ قَدِيۡرٌ ⑨

10. O Prophet! strive hard[3077] against the disbelievers and the Hypocrites; and be stern with them; their resort is Hell, and an evil destination it is!

يٰۤاَيُّهَا النَّبِىُّ جَاهِدِ الۡكُفَّارَ وَالۡمُنٰفِقِيۡنَ وَاغۡلُظۡ
عَلَيۡهِمۡ ؕ وَمَاۡوٰٮهُمۡ جَهَنَّمُ ؕ وَبِئۡسَ الۡمَصِيۡرُ ⑩

---

[a]9 : 66. [b]48 : 6; 64 : 10.

3075. The never-ceasing desire for perfection on the part of believers in Paradise as expressed in the words, 'Our Lord perfect our light for us,' shows that life in Paradise will not be one of inaction. On the contrary, spiritual advance in Paradise will know no end, for as the believers will attain excellence, characteristic of a certain stage, they will not stop at that, but seeing in front of it a higher stage of excellence and finding that the stage at which they had arrived was not the highest stage will proceed further, and so on without end.

3076. It further appears that after entering Paradise, the believers will seek *Maghfirah, i.e.*, suppression of defects (Lane). They will be continually praying to God for the attainment of perfection and complete immersion in Divine Light and will be continually going upwards regarding each state as defective in comparison with a higher one, to which they will aspire, and will therefore pray to God to suppress the defective state that they may be able to get to the higher one. This is the true significance of *Istighfār* of which the literal meaning is, 'asking forgiveness for one's lapses.'

3077. No advance is possible unless the disbelievers and the Hypocrites are strenuously striven against. Incidentally, the verse explains the real significance of *Jihād* which means, 'striving hard.' Since the Hyprocrites were regarded as part of the Muslim Community, *Jihād* in the sense of fighting with the sword was never waged against them.

11. Allāh sets forth as an example, for those who disbelieve, the wife of Noah and the wife of Lot. They were under two righteous servants of Ours, but they acted treacherously[3078] to them. So they availed them naught against Allāh, and it was said *to them*, 'Enter the Fire, ye twain, along with those who enter *it*.'

ضَرَبَ اللّٰهُ مَثَلًا لِّلَّذِيْنَ كَفَرُوا امْرَاَتَ نُوْحٍ وَّ
امْرَاَتَ لُوْطٍ ؕ كَانَتَا تَحْتَ عَبْدَيْنِ مِنْ عِبَادِنَا
صَالِحَيْنِ فَخَانَتٰهُمَا فَلَمْ يُغْنِيَا عَنْهُمَا مِنَ اللّٰهِ
شَيْـًٔا وَّقِيْلَ ادْخُلَا النَّارَ مَعَ الدّٰخِلِيْنَ ﴿۱۱﴾

12. And Allāh holds forth as an example, for those who believe, the wife of Pharaoh when she said, 'My Lord ! build for me a house with Thee in the Garden; and deliver me from Pharaoh and his work, and deliver me from the wrongdoing people;

وَضَرَبَ اللّٰهُ مَثَلًا لِّلَّذِيْنَ اٰمَنُوا امْرَاَتَ فِرْعَوْنَ
اِذْ قَالَتْ رَبِّ ابْنِ لِيْ عِنْدَكَ بَيْتًا فِي الْجَنَّةِ وَ
نَجِّنِيْ مِنْ فِرْعَوْنَ وَعَمَلِهٖ وَنَجِّنِيْ مِنَ الْقَوْمِ
الظّٰلِمِيْنَ ۙ﴿۱۲﴾

13. And *sets forth as an example* Mary, the daughter of 'Imrān, [a]who guarded her chastity—so We breathed into him of Our Spirit[3078]—and she fulfilled *the prophecy conveyed to her in* the words of her Lord *contained in* His Books and she was *one* of the obedient.

وَمَرْيَمَ ابْنَتَ عِمْرٰنَ الَّتِيْٓ اَحْصَنَتْ فَرْجَهَا
فَنَفَخْنَا فِيْهِ مِنْ رُّوْحِنَا وَصَدَّقَتْ بِكَلِمٰتِ رَبِّهَا
ع وَكُتُبِهٖ وَكَانَتْ مِنَ الْقٰنِتِيْنَ ﴿۱۳﴾

---

[a]21 : 92.

3078. The disbelievers are compared to the wives of Noah and Lot in order to show that the companionship of a righteous man, even a Prophet of God, does not benefit an evilly-inclined person who is bent upon rejecting truth. The wife of Pharaoh represents those believers, who though passionately desiring and praying to get rid of sin, cannot fully dissociate themselves from evil influences which are represented by Pharaoh, and having arrived at the stage of the "self-accusing soul" sometimes fail and falter. Mary, the mother of Jesus, represents those righteous servants of God who, having closed all avenues of sin and having made peace with God, are blessed with Divine inspiration; the pronoun *hi* in *fīhi* standing for such fortunate believers. Or, the pronoun may stand for *Farj* which, literally meaning a cleft or fissure, signifies an opening through which sin can find access.

CHAPTER 67

AL-MULK

(*Revealed before Hijrah*)

Date of Revelation and Context

With this *Sūrah* begins a series of Chapters, extending to the end of the Qur'ān, which were revealed before *Hijrah* with the solitary exception of *Sūrah* Al-Naṣr which, though belonging to the Medinite period, was actually revealed at Mecca on the occasion of the Holy Prophet's Last Pilgrimage. The whole of the Qur'ān being God's own revealed Word is simply inimitable and inapproachable in subject-matter, style and diction but the Chapters revealed at Mecca in the early years of the Prophet's Call possess a majesty and grandeur, all their own. The beauty of rhythm and the charm of cadence of the revelations of this period are beyond human power adequately to describe. As these Chapters generally deal with matters of belief and doctrine, *e.g.*, prophecies about the great and glorious future of Islām, Existence of God and His attributes, Revelation, Resurrection and Life after death, much symbolism has necessarily been used to describe the mystical and the spiritual in terms of what we can perceive by our physical senses. This *Sūrah* belongs to the middle Meccan period—8th year of the Call being the approximate time when, according to competent authorities, it was revealed.

Subject-Matter

As stated above, the Meccan *Sūrahs* generally deal with matters of belief. The present *Sūrah* naturally opens with proclaiming the Lordship, Sovereignty and Almightiness of God, and as proof of these Divine attributes adduces the fact that God is the Creator of life and death and of the whole universe through whose component parts, from the smallest atom to the largest plannet, there runs a wonderful and flawless design and arrangement. The creation of the universe and the beautiful order that pervades the cosmos are proofs positive of the fact that God *is* and that He has created man to serve a sublime object and to achieve a noble goal. But man in his perversity and ingratitude has always rejected God's Message and consequently has incurred His displeasure. The *Sūrah* recounts the manifold Divine blessings and favours without which man cannot exist for a single moment and, by implication, calls upon him to make proper use of them for the realization of the purpose for which he has been created. It closes with a beautiful homily, thereby bringing home to man the supreme truth that just as no physical life can exist without water, so spiritual life, too, needs for its sustenance the heavenly water of Divine revelation.

سُوْرَةُ الْمُلْكِ مَكِّيَّةٌ (٦٧) آياتها ٣١ ركوعاتها ٢

الجزء ٢٩

PART XXIX

1. [a]In the name of Allāh, the Gracious, the Merciful.

بِسْمِ اللّٰهِ الرَّحْمٰنِ الرَّحِيْمِ ①

2. [b]Blessed is He in Whose hand is the Kingdom, and He has power over all things;

تَبٰرَكَ الَّذِيْ بِيَدِهِ الْمُلْكُ وَهُوَ عَلٰى كُلِّ شَيْءٍ
قَدِيْرُ ②

3. Who has created death[3079] and life [c]that He might try you—which of you is best in deeds; and He is the Mighty, the Most Forgiving;

الَّذِيْ خَلَقَ الْمَوْتَ وَالْحَيٰوةَ لِيَبْلُوَكُمْ اَيُّكُمْ
اَحْسَنُ عَمَلًا وَهُوَ الْعَزِيْزُ الْغَفُوْرُ ③

4. [d]Who has created seven heavens in harmony.[3079A] No incongruity canst thou see in the creation of the Gracious *God*. Then look again. Seest thou any flaw?

الَّذِيْ خَلَقَ سَبْعَ سَمٰوٰتٍ طِبَاقًا مَا تَرٰى فِيْ
خَلْقِ الرَّحْمٰنِ مِنْ تَفٰوُتٍ فَارْجِعِ الْبَصَرَ هَلْ
تَرٰى مِنْ فُطُوْرٍ ④

5. Aye, look again, and yet again, thy sight will *only* return unto thee confused and fatigued,[3080] *having seen no incongruity.*

ثُمَّ ارْجِعِ الْبَصَرَ كَرَّتَيْنِ يَنْقَلِبْ اِلَيْكَ الْبَصَرُ
خَاسِئًا وَّهُوَ حَسِيْرٌ ⑤

---

[a]1 : 1. [b]25 : 2-3 [c]5 : 49; 11 : 8; 18 : 8. [d]65 : 13; 67 : 4; 71 : 16.

3079. The law of life and death works in all nature. Every living creature is subject to decay and death. "Death", as also in vv. 2 : 29 and 53 : 45, has been mentioned in this verse before "life." The reason seems to be that death or non-existence is the state before life or perhaps because "death" is more important and is of greater significance than life," since it opens to man the portals of everlasting life and unending spiritual progress, while life on earth is only a temporary sojourn and a preparation for permanent and everlasting life beyond the grave.

3079A. *Ṭibāq* is synonymous with *Ṭabaq* and with its plural, *Aṭbāq*. They say such a thing is the *Ṭabāq* or *Ṭibāq* of that, *i.e.*, this thing is the match of that or the like of that in measure, size or quality, etc. *Ṭibāq* also means, a stage (Lane).

3080. Wonderful indeed is God's creation. The solar system of which our earth is but a small member is vast, varied and orderly and yet it is but one of hundreds of millions of systems, some of which are incalculably larger than it, yet the countless millions of suns and stars are so arranged and distributed in relation to one another as to produce everywhere harmony and beauty. The order that covers and pervades the universe is obvious to the ordinary naked eye and is spread far beyond the range of disciplined vision, assisted by all the instruments and appliances which science and art have been able to invent.

6. And verily, [a]We have adorned the lowest heaven with lamps, and [b]We have made them *the means of* driving away satans, and We have prepared for them the punishment of the blazing Fire.

وَلَقَدْ زَيَّنَّا السَّمَآءَ الدُّنْيَا بِمَصَابِيْحَ وَجَعَلْنٰهَا رُجُوْمًا لِّلشَّيٰطِيْنِ وَاَعْتَدْنَا لَهُمْ عَذَابَ السَّعِيْرِ ﴿٦﴾

7. And for those who disbelieve in their Lord, is the punishment of Hell, and an evil resort it is.

وَلِلَّذِيْنَ كَفَرُوْا بِرَبِّهِمْ عَذَابُ جَهَنَّمَ ۗ وَبِئْسَ الْمَصِيْرُ ﴿٧﴾

8. When they are cast therein, [c]they will hear it roaring as it boils up.

اِذَآ اُلْقُوْا فِيْهَا سَمِعُوْا لَهَا شَهِيْقًا وَّهِيَ تَفُوْرُ ﴿٨﴾

9. It would almost burst with fury. [d]Whenever a host *of wrong-doers* is cast into it the wardens thereof will ask them, 'Did no Warner come to you?'

تَكَادُ تَمَيَّزُ مِنَ الْغَيْظِ ۗ كُلَّمَآ اُلْقِيَ فِيْهَا فَوْجٌ سَاَلَهُمْ خَزَنَتُهَآ اَلَمْ يَاْتِكُمْ نَذِيْرٌ ﴿٩﴾

10. They will say, "Yea, indeed, a Warner did come to us, but we treated *him* as a liar, and we said, 'Allāh has not revealed anything; you are but in manifest error.''

قَالُوْا بَلٰى قَدْ جَآءَنَا نَذِيْرٌ ۙ فَكَذَّبْنَا وَقُلْنَا مَا نَزَّلَ اللّٰهُ مِنْ شَيْءٍ ۚ اِنْ اَنْتُمْ اِلَّا فِيْ ضَلٰلٍ كَبِيْرٍ ﴿١٠﴾

11. And they will say, 'Had we but listened or had sense,[3080A] we should not have been among the inmates of the blazing Fire.

وَقَالُوْا لَوْ كُنَّا نَسْمَعُ اَوْ نَعْقِلُ مَا كُنَّا فِيْٓ اَصْحٰبِ السَّعِيْرِ ﴿١١﴾

12. Thus will they confess their sins; but far removed *from God's mercy* are the inmates of the blazing Fire.

فَاعْتَرَفُوْا بِذَنْۢبِهِمْ ۚ فَسُحْقًا لِّاَصْحٰبِ السَّعِيْرِ ﴿١٢﴾

13. [e]Verily, those who fear their Lord in secret—for them is forgiveness and a great reward.

اِنَّ الَّذِيْنَ يَخْشَوْنَ رَبَّهُمْ بِالْغَيْبِ لَهُمْ مَّغْفِرَةٌ وَّاَجْرٌ كَبِيْرٌ ﴿١٣﴾

[a]15 : 17; 37 : 7; 41 : 13; 50 : 7. [b]15 : 18; 37 : 11. [c]11 : 107; 21 : 101; 25 : 13. [d]39 : 72; 40 : 51. [e]21 : 50; 55 : 47; 79 : 41-43.

3080A. If we had followed the dictates of the *Sharī'ah*, or of conscience.

14. [a]And whether you conceal what you say or say it openly, He knows well *all* that which is in *your* breasts.

وَأَسِرُّوا قَوْلَكُمْ أَوِ اجْهَرُوا بِهِ ۖ إِنَّهُ عَلِيمٌ بِذَاتِ الصُّدُورِ ﴿١٤﴾

15. Does He, Who has created *you*, not know *it?* He is the Knower of all subtleties, the All-Aware.

أَلَا يَعْلَمُ مَنْ خَلَقَ ۖ وَهُوَ اللَّطِيفُ الْخَبِيرُ ﴿١٥﴾

R. 2 16. He it is Who has made the earth even *and smooth* [b]for you; so walk[3081] in the spacious paths thereof, and eat of His provision. And unto Him will be the resurrection.

هُوَ الَّذِي جَعَلَ لَكُمُ الْأَرْضَ ذَلُولًا فَامْشُوا فِي مَنَاكِبِهَا وَكُلُوا مِنْ رِزْقِهِ ۖ وَإِلَيْهِ النُّشُورُ ﴿١٦﴾

17. [c]Do you feel secure from Him Who is in the heaven[3082] that He will not cause the earth to sink with you? When lo! it begins to shake.

أَأَمِنْتُمْ مَنْ فِي السَّمَاءِ أَنْ يَخْسِفَ بِكُمُ الْأَرْضَ فَإِذَا هِيَ تَمُورُ ﴿١٧﴾

18. Do you feel secure from Him Who is in the heaven that He will not send against you a heavy sand-storm? Then will you know how *terrible* was My warning!

أَمْ أَمِنْتُمْ مَنْ فِي السَّمَاءِ أَنْ يُرْسِلَ عَلَيْكُمْ حَاصِبًا ۖ فَسَتَعْلَمُونَ كَيْفَ نَذِيرِ ﴿١٨﴾

19. And, indeed, those before them also rejected *My Messengers*, then how *grievous* was My punishment!

وَلَقَدْ كَذَّبَ الَّذِينَ مِنْ قَبْلِهِمْ فَكَيْفَ كَانَ نَكِيرِ ﴿١٩﴾

[a]2 : 78; 6 : 4; 11 : 6; 20 : 8. [b]2 : 23; 20 : 54.
[c]16 : 46; 17 : 69; 34 : 10.

3081. Journeying in the earth is recommended again and again in the Qur'ān because leaving one's home and travelling to other lands and countries greatly helps to add to one's knowledge and experience.

3082. It is because punishment is generally spoken of in the Qur'ān as coming down from heaven that God is referred to here and in the next verse as being in heaven; otherwise God is here, there and everywhere.

20. [a]"Do they not see the birds above them, spreading out their wings in flight and then drawing *them* in *to swoop down upon the prey?*[3083] None withholds them but the Gracious *God*. He sees all things well.

أَوَلَمْ يَرَوْا إِلَى الطَّيْرِ فَوْقَهُمْ صٰٓفّٰتٍ وَّيَقْبِضْنَ ؔ مَا يُمْسِكُهُنَّ إِلَّا الرَّحْمٰنُ ؕ إِنَّهٗ بِكُلِّ شَيْءٍۭ بَصِيْرٌ ﴿٢٠﴾

21. Can those, who are *counted* your hosts, help you against the Gracious *God?* The disbelievers are only *the victims of* self-deception.

أَمَّنْ هٰذَا الَّذِيْ هُوَ جُنْدٌ لَّكُمْ يَنْصُرُكُمْ مِّنْ دُوْنِ الرَّحْمٰنِ ؕ إِنِ الْكٰفِرُوْنَ إِلَّا فِيْ غُرُوْرٍ ﴿٢١﴾

22. Or, [b]who is he that will provide for you, if He should withhold His provision?[3084] Nay, but they obstinately persist in rebellion and aversion.

أَمَّنْ هٰذَا الَّذِيْ يَرْزُقُكُمْ إِنْ أَمْسَكَ رِزْقَهٗ ۚ بَلْ لَّجُّوْا فِيْ عُتُوٍّ وَّنُفُوْرٍ ﴿٢٢﴾

23. What! is he who walks grovelling upon his face[3085] better guided, or he who walks upright on the straight path?

أَفَمَنْ يَّمْشِيْ مُكِبًّا عَلٰى وَجْهِهٖٓ أَهْدٰٓى أَمَّنْ يَّمْشِيْ سَوِيًّا عَلٰى صِرَاطٍ مُّسْتَقِيْمٍ ﴿٢٣﴾

24. Say, 'He it is Who brought you into being, and [c]made for you ears and eyes and hearts; *but* little thanks do you give.'

قُلْ هُوَ الَّذِيْٓ أَنْشَاَكُمْ وَجَعَلَ لَكُمُ السَّمْعَ وَالْأَبْصَارَ وَالْأَفْئِدَةَ ؕ قَلِيْلًا مَّا تَشْكُرُوْنَ ﴿٢٤﴾

25. Say, [d]'He it is who multiplied you in the earth, and unto Him will you all be gathered.'

قُلْ هُوَ الَّذِيْ ذَرَاَكُمْ فِي الْأَرْضِ وَإِلَيْهِ تُحْشَرُوْنَ ﴿٢٥﴾

[a]16 : 80. [b]10 : 32; 34 : 25. [c]16 : 79; 23 : 79. [d]23 : 80.

3083. If the disbelievers continue to oppose Truth, they will be destroyed by famines, earthquakes; particularly by wars, and the birds of the skies will feast upon their dead bodies (16 : 80). See also note 1880 in "The Larger Edition of the Commentary"

3084. The reference may be to the terrible famine that held Mecca in its grip for several years till the Meccans begged the Holy Prophet to pray for their deliverance from the scourge. See also 2694.

3085. The disbelievers walk on the wrong path, hanging down their heads and grovelling in the darkness of doubt and disbelief, while believers, in the certainty of faith, go straight on the path of Truth, holding their heads high. Can the two be equal?

26. [a]And they say, 'When will this promise *come to pass*, if, *indeed*, you are truthful?'

وَيَقُولُونَ مَتَىٰ هَٰذَا الْوَعْدُ إِنْ كُنْتُمْ صَادِقِينَ ٢٦

27. Say, 'The knowledge *of it* is with Allāh, and [b]I am but a plain Warner.'

قُلْ إِنَّمَا الْعِلْمُ عِنْدَ اللَّهِ وَإِنَّمَا أَنَا نَذِيرٌ مُبِينٌ ٢٧

28. But when they see it nigh, the faces of those who disbelieve will be grief-stricken,[3086] and it will be said, 'This is what you repeatedly asked for.'

فَلَمَّا رَأَوْهُ زُلْفَةً سِيئَتْ وُجُوهُ الَّذِينَ كَفَرُوا وَقِيلَ هَٰذَا الَّذِي كُنْتُمْ بِهِ تَدَّعُونَ ٢٨

29. Say, 'Tell me, if Allāh should destroy me and those who are with me, or have mercy upon us, who will protect the disbelievers from a painful torment?'

قُلْ أَرَأَيْتُمْ إِنْ أَهْلَكَنِيَ اللَّهُ وَمَنْ مَعِيَ أَوْ رَحِمَنَا فَمَنْ يُجِيرُ الْكَافِرِينَ مِنْ عَذَابٍ أَلِيمٍ ٢٩

30. Say, 'He is the Beneficent[3087] *God*, in Him have we believed and in Him have we put our trust. And you will soon know who is in manifest error.'

قُلْ هُوَ الرَّحْمَٰنُ آمَنَّا بِهِ وَعَلَيْهِ تَوَكَّلْنَا فَسَتَعْلَمُونَ مَنْ هُوَ فِي ضَلَالٍ مُبِينٍ ٣٠

31. Say, 'Tell me, if *all* your water were to disappear *in the depths of the earth*, who, then, will bring you *pure* running water?[3088]

قُلْ أَرَأَيْتُمْ إِنْ أَصْبَحَ مَاؤُكُمْ غَوْرًا فَمَنْ يَأْتِيكُمْ بِمَاءٍ مَعِينٍ ٣١ ع

[a]21 : 39; 34 : 30; 36 : 49. [b]22 : 50; 26 : 116; 29 : 51.

3086. It is characteristic of disbelievers that as long as punishment does not overtake them, they boast and brag and hurl jibes and railleries at believers, but when they are face to face with it, they are seized with a sense of extreme frustration, dismay and dejection.

3087. The Divine attribute *Al-Raḥmān* (the Beneficent) has been repeatedly mentioned in this *Sūrah*, as at many other places in the Qur'ān, because all the Divine bounties and favours mentioned in it, whether pertaining to man's physical sustenance or his spiritual development, are the direct result of God's beneficence (*Raḥmāniyyah*).

3088. All life, whether physical or spiritual, depends on water—the former on rain-water and the latter on the water of Divine revelation.

CHAPTER 68

AL-QALAM

(*Revealed before Hijrah*)

Date of Revelation, Context and Subject-Matter

This is one of the first four or five Chapters which were revealed at Mecca in the very beginning of the Call. According to some authorities it was revealed just after *Sūrah* Al-'Alaq, which was the first Quranic *Sūrah* to have been revealed, but some other authorities place it after *Sūrahs*, Al-Muzzammil and Al-Muddaththir. There is, however, no doubt about it that all these Chapters were revealed more or less in consecutive order, because there exists a strong likeness in their subject-matter. The present *Sūrah* deals principally with the Holy Prophet's claim as a Divine Messenger. Like all the Meccan *Sūrahs* which mainly deal with matters of doctrine and belief, it deals with the truth of the Holy Prophet's claim, and gives sound and solid arguments to support it. A large part of the *Sūrah* is also devoted to a discussion of the fight of disbelievers against Truth, and to the evil end to which they ultimately come, and gives reasons why they reject Truth and strive and struggle against it and how, when their efforts appear to be on the point of bearing fruit they come to naught, and Truth, which seems to be going under, begins to prosper, prevail and predominate. Towards the close of the *Sūrah*, the Holy Prophet is enjoined to bear with patience and fortitude all the mockery, opposition and persecution to which he is subjected, because his cause is bound to succeed.

سُورَةُ القَلَمِ مَكِّيَّةٌ (٦٨)

1. [a]In the name of Allāh, the Gracious, the Merciful.	بِسْمِ اللّٰهِ الرَّحْمٰنِ الرَّحِيْمِ ①
2. *By* the inkstand and the pen and *by* that which they write;[3089]	نٓ وَ الْقَلَمِ وَمَا يَسْطُرُوْنَ ②
3. [b]Thou are not, by the grace of thy Lord, a madman.[3089A]	مَآ اَنْتَ بِنِعْمَةِ رَبِّكَ بِمَجْنُوْنٍ ③
4. And for thee, most surely, there is an unending reward.[3090]	وَاِنَّ لَكَ لَاَجْرًا غَيْرَ مَمْنُوْنٍ ④
5. And thou dost, surely, possess sublime moral excellences.[3091]	وَاِنَّكَ لَعَلٰى خُلُقٍ عَظِيْمٍ ⑤
6. And thou wilt soon see and they, *too*, will see.	فَسَتُبْصِرُ وَيُبْصِرُوْنَ ⑥

[a]1 : 1. [b]34 : 47; 52 : 30.

3089. In this verse the inkstand and the pen and all the written material are cited as evidence to support and substantiate the statement made in the next three verses.

3089A. The verse means that by whatever test of knowledge and learning the claim of the Holy Prophet is examined, he will be found to be not a maniac, as the disbelievers say, but the sanest and the wisest of men. The next verse gives the reason why this charge is not only unfounded but is also foolish and fantastic.

3090. This verse, along with the next one, most effectively exposes the absurdity of the charge of madness. It purports to say that the actions of a mad man produce no abiding and useful result, but the Holy Prophet is eminently succeeding in fulfilling the object of his Divine mission and in bringing about a wonderful revolution in the lives of his degenerate people. And this revolution will not end with his death. Whenever in future his followers will deviate from the path of rectitude, God will raise among them Reformers who will regenerate them and will infuse in them a new life. And this process will continue till the end of time.

3091. This verse constitutes a further eloquent commentary on the charge of madness, imputed to the Holy Prophet, as being foolish. The Prophet, it says, not only is not a maniac but is the noblest and sublimest of men, possessing in full measure all those moral excellences that combine to make their possessor a perfect image of his Creator. He is a complete embodiment of all good moral qualities that a man is capable of possessing. All the high moral qualities are blended in his person in a perfect and harmonious whole. 'Ā'ishah, the Prophet's talented spouse, when once asked to shed some light on the Prophet's morals, said, 'He possessed all those moral excellences which are mentioned in the Qur'ān as the special marks of a true servant of God' (Bukhārī).

7. Which of you is afflicted *with madness*.[3092]

بِاَيِّكُمُ الْمَفْتُوْنُ ۞

8. Surely, thy Lord knows best [a]those who go astray from His way, and He knows best those who follow guidance.

اِنَّ رَبَّكَ هُوَ اَعْلَمُ بِمَنْ ضَلَّ عَنْ سَبِيْلِهٖ وَهُوَ اَعْلَمُ بِالْمُهْتَدِيْنَ ۞

9. So comply not with the wishes of those who reject *the Truth*.

فَلَا تُطِعِ الْمُكَذِّبِيْنَ ۞

10. [b]They wish that thou shouldst compromise[3093] so that they may *also* compromise.

وَدُّوْا لَوْ تُدْهِنُ فَيُدْهِنُوْنَ ۞

11. Yield thou not to any mean swearer,

وَلَا تُطِعْ كُلَّ حَلَّافٍ مَّهِيْنٍ ۞

12. [c]Backbiter, one who goes about slandering.[3094]

هَمَّازٍ مَّشَّآءٍۢ بِنَمِيْمٍ ۞

13. [d]Forbidder of good, transgressor, sinful,

مَّنَّاعٍ لِّلْخَيْرِ مُعْتَدٍ اَثِيْمٍ ۞

14. Ill-mannered and, in addition to that, of doubtful birth,

عُتُلٍّۢ بَعْدَ ذٰلِكَ زَنِيْمٍ ۞

15. [e]Only because he possesses riches and children,[3095]

اَنْ كَانَ ذَا مَالٍ وَّبَنِيْنَ ۞

[a]16 : 126; 53 : 31. [b]17 : 74. [c]104 : 2. [d]50 : 26. [e]23 :56; 74 : 13-14.

3092. The verse turns the tables upon the accusers of the Holy Prophet, and tells them in challenging words that time will show whether it was he or they who suffered from madness, or whether his claim to be God's Messenger was the outpouring of a heated brain, or they themselves were so demented as not to read the signs of time and so refused to believe in him.

3093. The verse may have special reference to the offers which the Quraish of Mecca made to the Holy Prophet in order to tempt him away from his fixed purpose; or it may possess general application, since Truth is as firm as rock while falsehood has no legs to stand upon and gives way to pressure or temptation and is ready to make compromises.

3094. The reference in this and the preceding three verses may particularly be to Walīd bin Mughirah or Abū Jahl; or, for that matter, to every leader of falsehood.

3095. All sins, vices and opposition to Truth are born of conceit or false pride and are the moral maladies of one who manages to amass great wealth by questionable means, and wields great power and influence. Or, the verse may mean that a base and vile man should not be shown consideration or respect simply because he happens to possess wealth and influence.

16. "When Our Signs are recited unto him, he says, 'Tales of the ancients.'

اِذَا تُتْلٰى عَلَيْهِ اٰيٰتُنَا قَالَ اَسَاطِيْرُ الْاَوَّلِيْنَ ۝

17. We will brand him on the snout.[3096]

سَنَسِمُهٗ عَلَى الْخُرْطُوْمِ ۝

18. We will, surely, try them as We tried the owners of the garden when they vowed *to each other* that they would, certainly, gather *all its fruit* in the morning.[3097]

اِنَّا بَلَوْنٰهُمْ كَمَا بَلَوْنَاۤ اَصْحٰبَ الْجَنَّةِ ۚ اِذْ اَقْسَمُوْا لَيَصْرِمُنَّهَا مُصْبِحِيْنَ ۝

19. And they made no exception[3098] *and said not, 'If God please.'*

وَلَا يَسْتَثْنُوْنَ ۝

20. [b]Then a visitation from thy Lord visited it while they were asleep;

فَطَافَ عَلَيْهَا طَآئِفٌ مِّنْ رَّبِّكَ وَهُمْ نَآئِمُوْنَ ۝

21. And the morning found it *like a garden* cut down.

فَاَصْبَحَتْ كَالصَّرِيْمِ ۝

22. So they called to one another at *the break of* dawn,

فَتَنَادَوْا مُصْبِحِيْنَ ۝

23. *Saying,* 'Go forth early in the morning to your field, if you would gather the fruit.'

اَنِ اغْدُوْا عَلٰى حَرْثِكُمْ اِنْ كُنْتُمْ صٰرِمِيْنَ ۝

24. And they set out talking to one another in low tones,

فَانْطَلَقُوْا وَهُمْ يَتَخَافَتُوْنَ ۝

---

[a]8 : 32; 16 : 25; 83 : 14.   [b]3 : 118; 18 : 43.

3096. "Branding on the snout" is a metaphor for disgracing a person.

3097. Here the base, greedy and conceited disbelievers have been compared to the owner of a garden who would devour all its fruit and would not share it with those who had also put in their labour in developing it and would defraud them of their just rights in it.

3098. The owners of the "garden" greedily devoured the fruit of the labour of others and fed fat on it, excluding the latter from sharing it with them. They were so sure of the successful outcome of their labours and so certain of gathering in their harvest without any mishap that they consigned God to complete oblivion, failing to seek Divine protection by uttering the words, 'If God please.'

25. *Saying*, 'Let no poor man today enter it while you are there.'[3099]

أَن لَّا يَدْخُلَنَّهَا الْيَوْمَ عَلَيْكُم مِّسْكِينٌ ﴿٢٥﴾

26. *Thus* they went forth early in the morning, determined to be niggardly,[3100]

وَغَدَوْا عَلَىٰ حَرْدٍ قَادِرِينَ ﴿٢٦﴾

27. But when they saw it, they said, 'Surely, we have lost our way!

فَلَمَّا رَأَوْهَا قَالُوا إِنَّا لَضَالُّونَ ﴿٢٧﴾

28. 'Nay, we have been deprived *of all our fruits*.'

بَلْ نَحْنُ مَحْرُومُونَ ﴿٢٨﴾

29. The best among them said, 'Did I not say to you, why do you not glorify *God?*'

قَالَ أَوْسَطُهُمْ أَلَمْ أَقُل لَّكُمْ لَوْلَا تُسَبِّحُونَ ﴿٢٩﴾

30. *Thereupon*, they said, 'Glory be to our Lord! Surely, we have been wrongdoers.'

قَالُوا سُبْحَانَ رَبِّنَا إِنَّا كُنَّا ظَالِمِينَ ﴿٣٠﴾

31. Then some of them turned to the others, reproaching one another.

فَأَقْبَلَ بَعْضُهُمْ عَلَىٰ بَعْضٍ يَتَلَاوَمُونَ ﴿٣١﴾

32. They said, 'Woe to us! We were, indeed, rebellious,

قَالُوا يَا وَيْلَنَا إِنَّا كُنَّا طَاغِينَ ﴿٣٢﴾

33. 'May be, *if we repent*, our Lord will give us instead *a* better *garden* than this; we do humbly entreat our Lord.'

عَسَىٰ رَبُّنَا أَن يُبْدِلَنَا خَيْرًا مِّنْهَا إِنَّا إِلَىٰ رَبِّنَا رَاغِبُونَ ﴿٣٣﴾

3099. The rich owners of the "garden" in the parable are compared to those selfish, cruel and greedy persons who, besides exploiting the labour of others, are so stingy that they would not spend any part of their ill-gotten gains to meet the needs of the needy and the poor.

3100. The exploiters of the labour of others are a class by themselves. They seek and scheme to debar the latter from the benefits of what they earn by the sweat of their brow. They revel in wealth, while their poor brethren grovel in dirt and squalor before their very eyes.

34. Such is the punishment *of this world*. And, surely, [a]the punishment of the Hereafter is greater.[3101] Did they but know!

كَذٰلِكَ الْعَذَابُ ۖ وَلَعَذَابُ الْاٰخِرَةِ اَكْبَرُ ۘ لَوْ كَانُوْا يَعْلَمُوْنَ ۝ ع

R. 2 35. [b]For the righteous, indeed, there are Gardens of Bliss with their Lord.

اِنَّ لِلْمُتَّقِيْنَ عِنْدَ رَبِّهِمْ جَنّٰتِ النَّعِيْمِ ۝

36. [c]Shall We, then, treat those who submit *to Us* as *We treat* the guilty?

اَفَنَجْعَلُ الْمُسْلِمِيْنَ كَالْمُجْرِمِيْنَ ۝

37. What is the matter with you? How judge ye?

مَا لَكُمْ ۫ كَيْفَ تَحْكُمُوْنَ ۝

38. Have you a Book wherein you read,

اَمْ لَكُمْ كِتٰبٌ فِيْهِ تَدْرُسُوْنَ ۝

39. That you shall, surely, have in it whatever you choose?

اِنَّ لَكُمْ فِيْهِ لَمَا تَخَيَّرُوْنَ ۝

40. Or, have you *taken* any covenant binding on Us till the Day of Resurrection that you shall, surely, have whatever you judge?[3102]

اَمْ لَكُمْ اَيْمَانٌ عَلَيْنَا بَالِغَةٌ اِلٰى يَوْمِ الْقِيٰمَةِ ۙ اِنَّ لَكُمْ لَمَا تَحْكُمُوْنَ ۝

41. Ask them, which of them will vouch for that.

سَلْهُمْ اَيُّهُمْ بِذٰلِكَ زَعِيْمٌ ۝

42. Or, have they any associate-gods? Let them, then, produce their associate-gods, if they are truthful.

اَمْ لَهُمْ شُرَكَآءُ ۚ فَلْيَاْتُوْا بِشُرَكَآئِهِمْ اِنْ كَانُوْا صٰدِقِيْنَ ۝

[a]13 : 35; 39 : 27. [b]30 : 16; 68 : 35; 78 : 32. [c]32 : 19; 38 : 29; 45 : 22.

3101. Sooner or later nemesis overtakes the exploiters and their contrivances to deprive others of the fruit of their labour fail altogether in their evil purpose.

3102. The verse asks the disbelievers, "Have they any authority in any revealed Scripture that they will be allowed to choose a way of life of their own liking and will also escape the consequences of their evil deeds? Or, have they taken a covenant from God which will remain in force till the Day of Judgment that they will have whatever they like and do whatever they like and yet will not suffer the consequences flowing from their actions?

43. On the day when the truth shall be laid bare[3103] and they will be called upon to prostrate themselves, they will not be able *to do so* ;

يَوْمَ يُكْشَفُ عَنْ سَاقٍ وَّيُدْعَوْنَ إِلَى السُّجُوْدِ فَلَا يَسْتَطِيْعُوْنَ ﴿٤٣﴾

44. [a]Their eyes will be cast down, *and* humiliation will cover them; and they were, indeed, called upon to prostrate themselves when they were safe and sound, *but they did not*.

خَاشِعَةً أَبْصَارُهُمْ تَرْهَقُهُمْ ذِلَّةٌ ۖ وَقَدْ كَانُوْا يُدْعَوْنَ إِلَى السُّجُوْدِ وَهُمْ سٰلِمُوْنَ ﴿٤٤﴾

45. [b]So leave Me *to deal* with those who reject this word *of Ours*. [c]We shall draw them *near to destruction* step by step[3104] whence they know not.

فَذَرْنِيْ وَمَنْ يُّكَذِّبُ بِهٰذَا الْحَدِيْثِ ۖ سَنَسْتَدْرِجُهُمْ مِّنْ حَيْثُ لَا يَعْلَمُوْنَ ﴿٤٥﴾

46. [d]And I shall grant them long respite; for My plan is sure.

وَأُمْلِيْ لَهُمْ ۚ إِنَّ كَيْدِيْ مَتِيْنٌ ﴿٤٦﴾

47. [e]Dost thou ask a reward of them that they feel weighed down by *its* burden?

أَمْ تَسْـَٔلُهُمْ أَجْرًا فَهُمْ مِّنْ مَّغْرَمٍ مُّثْقَلُوْنَ ﴿٤٧﴾

48. [f]Have they *the knowledge* of the unseen so that they write *it* down?

أَمْ عِنْدَهُمُ الْغَيْبُ فَهُمْ يَكْتُبُوْنَ ﴿٤٨﴾

49. So be thou steadfast in *carrying out* the command of thy Lord, and [g]be not like the Man of the Fish when he called *to his Lord* and he was full of grief.

فَاصْبِرْ لِحُكْمِ رَبِّكَ وَلَا تَكُنْ كَصَاحِبِ الْحُوْتِ ۘ إِذْ نَادٰى وَهُوَ مَكْظُوْمٌ ﴿٤٩﴾

[a]75 : 25; 88 : 3-4. [b]73 : 12; 74 : 12. [c]7 : 183. [d]7 : 184.
[e]23 : 73; 52 : 41. [f]52 : 42. [g]21 : 88.

3103. The verse may refer to the hardness and severity of the Day of Resurrection, or to the lifting of the veil from all mysteries and coming to light of all secrets on the Judgment Day. See 2177.

3104. Divine punishment will overtake disbelievers by degrees and in stages and thus they will have ample opportunities to repent and make amends by accepting the Quranic Message.

50. [a]Had it not been that a favour from his Lord had reached him, he would have, surely, been cast upon a barren waste[3105] to be blamed *by his people*.

لَوْلَآ اَنْ تَدٰرَكَهٗ نِعْمَةٌ مِّنْ رَّبِّهٖ لَنُبِذَ بِالْعَرَآءِ وَهُوَ مَذْمُوْمٌ ۝۵۰

51. But his Lord chose him and placed him among the righteous.

فَاجْتَبٰهُ رَبُّهٗ فَجَعَلَهٗ مِنَ الصّٰلِحِيْنَ ۝۵۱

52. And those who disbelieve would fain have dislodged thee *from thy God-given station* with their *angry*[3106] looks when they heard the Reminder; and they keep saying, 'He is, certainly, mad.'

وَاِنْ يَّكَادُ الَّذِيْنَ كَفَرُوْا لَيُزْلِقُوْنَكَ بِاَبْصَارِهِمْ لَمَّا سَمِعُوا الذِّكْرَ وَيَقُوْلُوْنَ اِنَّهٗ لَمَجْنُوْنٌ ۝۵۲

53. Nay, it is naught but *a source of* honour for all the worlds.

وَمَا هُوَ اِلَّا ذِكْرٌ لِّلْعٰلَمِيْنَ ۝۵۳ ع

[a]37 : 144-146.

3105. The verse may also imply a subtle hint to the Holy Prophet's *Hijrah* (Emigration) to Medina.

3106. The disbelievers cast severe looks at the Holy Prophet that might frighten a person of lesser calibre into giving up his mission, but the Prophet has a Divine Message to deliver and so he can hardly be intimidated, cajoled or bribed into yielding to such pressure tactics.

CHAPTER 69

AL-ḤĀQQAH

(*Revealed before Hijraḥ*)

General Remarks

The *Sūrah*, like the preceding one, was, as its subject-matter shows, among the earliest Chapters to be revealed at Mecca. It is almost wholly devoted to the subject of the inevitability of the Resurrection; and adduces the sure and certain success of the Holy Prophet against heavy odds as an argument in support of this hypothesis. As the Holy Prophet's ultimate success and the Resurrection were regarded by disbelievers as impossible, the coming to pass of the one did indeed, constitute an incontrovertible proof that the other will also take place. Thus the *Sūrah* opens with a firm and emphatic declaration that enemies of Truth shall be routed. It then proceeds to draw a parallel between the destruction of the deniers of the Divine Message and the Resurrection, and says that for disbelievers the "hour" of punishment will be most distressful and agonizing and for the believers it will be a time of perennial joy and happiness. The *Sūrah* closes with a firm and emphatic declaration that both these events—the Resurrection and the success of the Prophet's cause, against very heavy odds and under the most unfavourable circumstances—will, most surely, come to pass, because what the Prophet says is God's own revealed Word and not the bragging of a poet, nor the idle conjectures of a soothsayer, nor a fabrication, for, if he had forged a lie against God, he would have met with certain and violent death, because a forger is never allowed to prosper

سُورَةُ الْحَاقَّةِ مَكِّيَّةٌ (٦٩)

1. [a]In the name of Allāh, the Gracious, the Merciful.

بِسْمِ اللّٰهِ الرَّحْمٰنِ الرَّحِيْمِ ﴿١﴾

2. The Inevitable ![3107]

اَلْحَآقَّةُ ﴿٢﴾

3. What is the Inevitable?

مَا الْحَآقَّةُ ﴿٣﴾

4. And what should make thee know what the Inevitable is?

وَمَآ اَدْرٰىكَ مَا الْحَآقَّةُ ﴿٤﴾

5. The *tribes of* Thamūd and 'Ād treated as a lie the *sudden* calamity.

كَذَّبَتْ ثَمُوْدُ وَعَادٌۢ بِالْقَارِعَةِ ﴿٥﴾

6. [b]Then, as for Thamūd, they were destroyed with a blast of the utmost fury.

فَاَمَّا ثَمُوْدُ فَاُهْلِكُوْا بِالطَّاغِيَةِ ﴿٦﴾

7. [c]And as for 'Ād, they were destroyed by a fierce howling wind,

وَاَمَّا عَادٌ فَاُهْلِكُوْا بِرِيْحٍ صَرْصَرٍ عَاتِيَةٍ ﴿٧﴾

8. Which *God* caused to blow against them for seven nights and eight days continuously, so that thou mightest have seen the people therein lying prostrate, as though [d]they were trunks of palm trees fallen down.

سَخَّرَهَا عَلَيْهِمْ سَبْعَ لَيَالٍ وَّثَمٰنِيَةَ اَيَّامٍ حُسُوْمًا فَتَرَى الْقَوْمَ فِيْهَا صَرْعٰى كَاَنَّهُمْ اَعْجَازُ نَخْلٍ خَاوِيَةٍ ﴿٨﴾

9. Dost thou see any trace of them?

فَهَلْ تَرٰى لَهُمْ مِّنْۢ بَاقِيَةٍ ﴿٩﴾

10. [e]And Pharaoh, and those who were before him, and the overthrown cities *persistently* committed sins.

وَجَآءَ فِرْعَوْنُ وَمَنْ قَبْلَهٗ وَالْمُؤْتَفِكٰتُ بِالْخَاطِئَةِ ﴿١٠﴾

11. They disobeyed the Messenger of their Lord, therefore, He [f]seized them—a severe seizing.

فَعَصَوْا رَسُوْلَ رَبِّهِمْ فَاَخَذَهُمْ اَخْذَةً رَّابِيَةً ﴿١١﴾

---

[a]1 : 1. [b]41 : 18; 54 : 32. [c]41 : 17; 54 : 20. [d]54 : 21. [e]28 : 9. [f]73 : 17

3107. An established or inevitable fact; a catastrophe which is sure to happen; the final overthrow of disbelief.

12. [a]Verily, when the waters[3108] rose high, We bore you in the boat,

إِنَّا لَمَّا طَغَا الْمَآءُ حَمَلْنٰكُمْ فِي الْجَارِيَةِ ﴿١٢﴾

13. That We might make it a reminder for you, and that retaining ears might retain it.

لِنَجْعَلَهَا لَكُمْ تَذْكِرَةً وَّتَعِيَهَآ أُذُنٌ وَّاعِيَةٌ ﴿١٣﴾

14. [b]So that when a single blast is sounded on the trumpet,[3109]

فَإِذَا نُفِخَ فِي الصُّوْرِ نَفْخَةٌ وَّاحِدَةٌ ﴿١٤﴾

15. And the earth and the mountains are heaved up and then are crushed in a single crash,[3110]

وَّحُمِلَتِ الْاَرْضُ وَالْجِبَالُ فَدُكَّتَا دَكَّةً وَّاحِدَةً ﴿١٥﴾

16. On that day will the *great* Event come to pass.

فَيَوْمَئِذٍ وَّقَعَتِ الْوَاقِعَةُ ﴿١٦﴾

17. And the heaven will cleave asunder, [c]and it will be very frail that day.

وَانْشَقَّتِ السَّمَآءُ فَهِيَ يَوْمَئِذٍ وَّاهِيَةٌ ﴿١٧﴾

18. [d]And the angels will be *standing* on its borders, and above them on that day eight *angels* will bear the Throne of thy Lord.[3111]

وَّالْمَلَكُ عَلٰٓى اَرْجَآئِهَا ۗ وَيَحْمِلُ عَرْشَ رَبِّكَ فَوْقَهُمْ
يَوْمَئِذٍ ثَمٰنِيَةٌ ﴿١٨﴾

---

[a]11 : 41; 54 : 14. [b]18 : 100; 23 : 102; 36 : 52; 39 : 69; 50 : 21.
[c]55 : 38; 84 : 2. [d]39 : 76; 40 : 8.

3108. The reference in the verse is to Noah's Flood.

3109. The Holy Prophet's march on Mecca was so swift and sudden that the Meccans were taken completely by surprise. It came, as it were, a bolt from the blue for them. The verse may also apply to the Day of Resurrection, when with the blowing of the trumpet both the righteous and the guilty will stand before God's Great Judgment Seat to render an account of their deeds.

3110. The whole of Arabia was shaken from one end to the other; the leaders of Arab aristocracy and the common folk felt the strong impact of the conquests of Islām and of the great and violent change it brought about in their lives—*al-Jibāl* signifying leaders of men, and *al-Arḍ* common folk.

3111. '*Arsh* (Throne) represents God's transcendent attributes which are His exclusive prerogative. These attributes are manifested through God's attributes of similitude which have been described in the verse as the bearers of His Throne ('*Arsh*) These latter attributes are Rabb, Raḥmān, Raḥīm and Mālik Yaum al-Dīn and are the basic Divine attributes by which the world subsists and which mainly concern man's life and destiny. In view of their majesty, awfulness and greatness these four Divine attributes will have double manifestation on the Day of Judgment. Or, the words may mean that on that day, along with these four attributes of similitude, the four corresponding transcendent attributes will also come into operation. And as Divine attributes are manifested through angels, therefore eight angels are mentioned, as being the bearers of the Throne of God on that Great Day.

19. On that day you will be presented *before God; and* [a]none of your secrets will remain hidden.[3112]

يومئذ تعرضون لا تخفى منكم خافية ۝١٩

20. [b]Then, as for him who is given his record in his right hand,[3113] he will say, 'Come, read my record.'

فأما من أوتي كتابه بيمينه فيقول هاؤم اقرءوا كتابيه ۝٢٠

21. 'Surely, I knew that I would meet my reckoning.'

إني ظننت أني ملق حسابيه ۝٢١

22. [c]So he will *enjoy* a delightful life,

فهو في عيشة راضية ۝٢٢

23. [d]In a lofty Garden,

في جنة عالية ۝٢٣

24. [e]Whereof clusters of fruit will be within easy reach.

قطوفها دانية ۝٢٤

25. *It will be said to him*, [f]'Eat and drink joyfully because of the *good* deeds you did in days gone by.'

كلوا واشربوا هنيئا بما أسلفتم في الأيام الخالية ۝٢٥

[a]4 : 43; 41 : 21. [b]17 : 72; 84 : 8-9. [c]88 : 10; 101 : 8.
[d]43 : 73; 88 : 11. [e]55 : 55; 76 : 15. [f]77 : 44.

It is a mistaken view that because *'Arsh* is stated in the verse as being "borne" by angels, it must be something material. But the word *Hamala* is used in the Qur'ān not merely to denote the bearing of a thing in the physical sense but also figuratively. In 33: 73 man is spoken of as 'bearing the Law' or the *Sharī'ah*, but the *Sharī'ah* is not a material thing. Similarly, the bearing of the *'Arsh* by angels signifies that the reality of Divine attributes is disclosed and manifested through them. We cannot understand and realize the transcendent attributes of God (His *'Arsh*) except through His attributes of similitude. Thus God's attributes of similitude are, as it were, the bearers of His transcendent attributes (His *'Arsh*). Again it is said that *'Arsh* is spoken of as 'being on water' (11 : 8), which is a created element, therefore it must also be a created thing. But "water" in the language of revealed Scriptures often signifies the Word of God. In this sense the verse (11 : 8) signifies that the 'Throne of God' rests on the 'Word of God, which means that man cannot fully comprehend and realize the majesty and glory of God except with the help of the Word of God. That the *'Arsh* represents the transcendent attributes of God is also clear from 23 : 117. See also 986.

3112. Besides the meaning given in the text, the verse signifies that on the day of the Fall of Mecca, falsity of the idolatrous beliefs and practices of the Meccans will stand completely exposed.

3113. To be given one's record in one's right hand is a Quranic metaphor for passing the test successfully.

26. [a]But as for him who is given his record in his left hand,[3114] he will say, 'O, would that I had not been given my record !

وَأَمَّا مَنْ أُوتِيَ كِتَٰبَهُۥ بِشِمَالِهِۦ فَيَقُولُ يَٰلَيْتَنِي لَمْ أُوتَ كِتَٰبِيَهْ ۝٢٦

27. 'Nor known what my reckoning was !

وَلَمْ أَدْرِ مَا حِسَابِيَهْ ۝٢٧

28. 'O, would that *death* had made an end *of me !*[3115]

يَٰلَيْتَهَا كَانَتِ ٱلْقَاضِيَةَ ۝٢٨

29. 'My wealth has been of no avail to me;

مَآ أَغْنَىٰ عَنِّي مَالِيَهْ ۝٢٩

30. 'My authority is gone from me.'

هَلَكَ عَنِّي سُلْطَٰنِيَهْ ۝٣٠

31. *The angels will be commanded :* [b]'Seize him and fetter him,

خُذُوهُ فَغُلُّوهُ ۝٣١

32. 'Then cast him into Hell ;

ثُمَّ ٱلْجَحِيمَ صَلُّوهُ ۝٣٢

33. 'Then bind him with a chain, the length of which is seventy[3116] cubits,

ثُمَّ فِي سِلْسِلَةٍ ذَرْعُهَا سَبْعُونَ ذِرَاعًا فَٱسْلُكُوهُ ۝٣٣

34. 'Verily, he did not believe in Allāh, the Great,

إِنَّهُۥ كَانَ لَا يُؤْمِنُ بِٱللَّهِ ٱلْعَظِيمِ ۝٣٤

[a]56 : 42-43 ; 84 : 11 13. [b]76 : 5.

3114. To be given one's record in one's left hand, in Quranic terminology, signifies failure in the test.

3115. Disbelievers would wish death to be the end of all things so that there should be no other life and no rendering of account of their actions before God.

3116. It has repeatedly been explained in the Qur'ān that Life after death is not a new life but only an image and representation of the facts of the present life. In these verses the spiritual torture of the present world has been represented as the physical punishment in the next. The chain to be put round the neck, for instance, represents the desires of this world and it is these desires that will assume the form of fetters in the life to come. Similarly, the entanglements of this world will be seen as chains on the feet. The heart-burning of this world will, likewise, appear as the flames of burning fire. The limit of man's age may generally be fixed at seventy, excluding the periods of childhood and decrepitude. These seventy years, the wicked disbeliever wastes away in the entanglements of the world and in satisfying his sensual passions. He does not try to free himself from the chain of desires, and, therefore, in the next world the chain of desires, which he indulged in for seventy years, shall be embodied in a chain of the length of seventy cubits, every cubit representing a year, with which the wicked shall be fettered.

35. ^a"And he did not urge the feeding of the poor.

وَلَا يَحُضُّ عَلٰى طَعَامِ الْمِسْكِيْنِ ۗ

36. ^b"No friend, therefore, has he here this day;

فَلَيْسَ لَهُ الْيَوْمَ هٰهُنَا حَمِيْمٌ ۙ

37. 'Nor any food save the ^cwashing of wounds,

وَّلَا طَعَامٌ اِلَّا مِنْ غِسْلِيْنٍ ۙ

38. 'Which none but the sinners eat.'

لَّا يَأْكُلُهٗۤ اِلَّا الْخَاطِئُوْنَ ۗ

R. 2   39. But nay, I swear by that which you see,

فَلَاۤ اُقْسِمُ بِمَا تُبْصِرُوْنَ ۙ

40. And that which you see not.³¹¹⁷

وَمَا لَا تُبْصِرُوْنَ ۙ

41. That it is, surely, the word *brought* by a noble Messenger,

اِنَّهٗ لَقَوْلُ رَسُوْلٍ كَرِيْمٍ ۚ

42. ^dAnd not the word of a poet ; little is it that you believe!

وَّمَا هُوَ بِقَوْلِ شَاعِرٍ ۚ قَلِيْلًا مَّا تُؤْمِنُوْنَ ۙ

43. 'Nor is it the word of a soothsayer; little is it that you heed !

وَلَا بِقَوْلِ كَاهِنٍ ۚ قَلِيْلًا مَّا تَذَكَّرُوْنَ ۗ

44. *It is* a revelation from the Lord of the worlds.

تَنْزِيْلٌ مِّنْ رَّبِّ الْعٰلَمِيْنَ ۗ

45. ^fAnd if he had forged *and attributed* any sayings to Us,

وَلَوْ تَقَوَّلَ عَلَيْنَا بَعْضَ الْاَقَاوِيْلِ ۙ

46. We would, surely, have seized him by the right hand,

لَاَخَذْنَا مِنْهُ بِالْيَمِيْنِ ۙ

---

^a74 : 45; 89 : 19; 107 : 4.   ^b43 : 68; 70 : 11; 80 : 38.   ^c14 : 17;   78 : 25, 26. ^d36 : 70; 52 : 31.   ^e52 : 30.   ^f40 : 29.

3117. The things which we see working in the physical world, *i.e.,* the visible facts of life and the things which are hidden from our view, *i.e.,* human reason and conscience, have been cited in the verses (39-40) as evidences to establish the Divine origin of the Qur'ān. Or, the verses may mean that the great Signs which disbelievers in the Holy Prophet's time witnessed with their own eyes, and the prophecies about the bright future of Islām which yet await fulfilment constitute an irrefutable argument that the Qur'ān is God's own Word which He has revealed to His noble Prophet Muḥammad. It deals with the hard facts of life and is not a poet's fond dream, nor the groping in the dark of a soothsayer.

47. And then, surely, We would have cut his life-vein,	ثُمَّ لَقَطَعْنَا مِنْهُ الْوَتِيْنَ ﴿٤٧﴾
48. And not one of you could have held *Our punishment* off from him.[3118]	فَمَا مِنْكُمْ مِّنْ اَحَدٍ عَنْهُ حٰجِزِيْنَ ﴿٤٨﴾
49. And, verily, it is a reminder for the righteous,	وَاِنَّهٗ لَتَذْكِرَةٌ لِّلْمُتَّقِيْنَ ﴿٤٩﴾
50. And, surely, We know that there are some among you who reject *Our Signs*.	وَاِنَّا لَنَعْلَمُ اَنَّ مِنْكُمْ مُّكَذِّبِيْنَ ﴿٥٠﴾
51. And, verily, it will be *a source of* regret for the disbelievers.	وَاِنَّهٗ لَحَسْرَةٌ عَلَى الْكٰفِرِيْنَ ﴿٥١﴾
52. And, surely, it is the absolute truth.	وَاِنَّهٗ لَحَقُّ الْيَقِيْنِ ﴿٥٢﴾
53. [a]So glorify the name of thy Lord, the Great.	فَسَبِّحْ بِاسْمِ رَبِّكَ الْعَظِيْمِ ﴿٥٣﴾

[a]56 : 75; 87 : 2.

3118. In this and in the preceding three verses the argument is given that if the Holy Prophet had been a forger of lies, God's strong hand would have seized him by the throat and he would, certainly, have met with a violent death and his whole work and mission would have gone to pieces, as such is the fate of a false prophet. The claim and the arguments contained in these verses seem to be an exact reproduction of the biblical statement in Deut. 18 : 20.

CHAPTER 70

AL-MA'ĀRIJ

(*Revealed before Hijrah*)

Introductory Remarks

The *Sūrah* was revealed at Mecca about the 5th year of the Call, not later than the close of the early Meccan period. Noldeke, Muir and some other eminent authorities, assign this date to its revelation. In the preceding *Sūrah* the disbelievers were warned that *Al-Ḥāqqah* (The Great Calamity) would soon overtake them if they did not repent of their sins and accept the Divine Message. The present *Sūrah* opens with mentioning the disbelievers' demand: 'When will the threatened punishment come?' They are told that it would soon be upon them, nay, it is at their very door. But when it came, it would be so overwhelming and devastating that it would cause the mountains to fly like flakes of wool, and disbelievers would wish to part with their near and dear ones—their wives, children and brothers—as ransom for themselves. But then it will be too late. Towards its close the *Sūrah* warns disbelievers again that they consider prophecies about the glorious future of Islām as only the dream of a visionary, but the time was fast approaching when, with their eyes cast down, they will hasten to the Holy Prophet to accept Islām. Then they will realize to their shame and sorrow that what the Holy Prophet had foretold about their ultimate defeat was only too true.

سُوْرَةُ الْمَعَارِجِ مَكِّيَّةٌ (٧٠)

1. [a]In the name of Allāh, the Gracious, the Merciful.

بِسْمِ اللّٰهِ الرَّحْمٰنِ الرَّحِيْمِ ﴿١﴾

2. An inquirer[3119] inquires concerning [b]the punishment about to befall

سَاَلَ سَآئِلٌۢ بِعَذَابٍ وَّاقِعٍ ﴿٢﴾

3. The disbelievers, *and* which [c]none can repel.

لِّلْكٰفِرِيْنَ لَيْسَ لَهٗ دَافِعٌ ﴿٣﴾

4. *It is* from Allāh, Lord of *great* ascents.[3119A]

مِّنَ اللّٰهِ ذِي الْمَعَارِجِ ﴿٤﴾

5. The angels and the Spirit ascend to Him in a day, the measure of which is fifty thousand years.[3120]

تَعْرُجُ الْمَلٰٓئِكَةُ وَالرُّوْحُ اِلَيْهِ فِيْ يَوْمٍ كَانَ مِقْدَارُهٗ خَمْسِيْنَ اَلْفَ سَنَةٍ ﴿٥﴾

6. [d]So be patient with admirable patience.

فَاصْبِرْ صَبْرًا جَمِيْلًا ﴿٦﴾

7. They see it to be far off,

اِنَّهُمْ يَرَوْنَهٗ بَعِيْدًا ﴿٧﴾

8. But We see it to be nigh.

وَّنَرٰىهُ قَرِيْبًا ﴿٨﴾

9. The day when the heaven will become like molten copper,

يَوْمَ تَكُوْنُ السَّمَآءُ كَالْمُهْلِ ﴿٩﴾

10. [e]And the mountains will become like flakes of wool,[3121]

وَتَكُوْنُ الْجِبَالُ كَالْعِهْنِ ﴿١٠﴾

---

[a]1 : 1. [b]52 : 8; 56 : 2. [c]52 : 9; 56 : 3. [d]15 : 86.
[e]20 : 106; 70 : 10; 101 : 6.

3119. "The inquirer" in the verse is taken by some Commentators to refer to Nadr bin Al-Ḥārith, or Abū Jahl. But it need not refer to any particular person. It may refer to all disbelievers because all of them repeatedly challenged the Holy Prophet to bring down upon them the threatened punishment (8 : 33; 21 : 39; 27 : 72; 32 : 29; 34 : 30; 36 : 49; 67 : 26).

3119A. God grants to His votaries very exalted ranks.

3120. *Al-Rūḥ* meaning human soul, the verse may signify that the development and progress of the human soul will know no end. Or, the verse may mean that Divine plans and programmes take thousands of years to mature. Or, the reference may be to a specific cycle of fifty thousand years in which some particular great change is decreed to take place, because Divine prophecies have their fixed periods, epochs and cycles in which they are fulfilled.

3121. In this age of atom and hydrogen bombs the flying of mountains like flakes of wool is quite a possible occurrence.

11. [a]And a friend will not inquire after a friend,

وَلَا يَسْـَٔلُ حَمِيمٌ حَمِيمًا ﴿١١﴾

12. *Though* they will be placed in sight of one another. [b]The guilty one would fain ransom himself from the punishment of that day by *offering* his children,

يُبَصَّرُونَهُمْ يَوَدُّ الْمُجْرِمُ لَوْ يَفْتَدِي مِنْ عَذَابِ يَوْمِئِذٍ بِبَنِيهِ ﴿١٢﴾

13. [c]And his wife and his brother,

وَصَاحِبَتِهِ وَأَخِيهِ ﴿١٣﴾

14. And his kinsfolk who gave him shelter,

وَفَصِيلَتِهِ الَّتِي تُؤْوِيهِ ﴿١٤﴾

15. And *by offering all* those who are on the earth, if *only* thus he might save himself.[3122]

وَمَنْ فِي الْأَرْضِ جَمِيعًا ثُمَّ يُنْجِيهِ ﴿١٥﴾

16. But no ! surely, it is a flame of Fire,

كَلَّا إِنَّهَا لَظَىٰ ﴿١٦﴾

17. [d]Stripping off the skin *even* to the extremities *of the body*.

نَزَّاعَةً لِلشَّوَىٰ ﴿١٧﴾

18. It shall call him who turned his back and retreated,

تَدْعُو مَنْ أَدْبَرَ وَتَوَلَّىٰ ﴿١٨﴾

19. [e]And hoarded *wealth* and withheld *it*.

وَجَمَعَ فَأَوْعَىٰ ﴿١٩﴾

20. Verily, man is created[3123] impatient and miserly.

إِنَّ الْإِنْسَانَ خُلِقَ هَلُوعًا ﴿٢٠﴾

21. [f]When evil touches him, he is full of lamentations,

إِذَا مَسَّهُ الشَّرُّ جَزُوعًا ﴿٢١﴾

22. But when good falls to his *lot*, he is niggardly,

وَإِذَا مَسَّهُ الْخَيْرُ مَنُوعًا ﴿٢٢﴾

---

[a]44 : 42; 69 : 36. [b]5 : 37; 13 : 19; 39 : 48. [c]31 : 34; 80 ; 37. [d]74 : 30. [e]9 : 34; 53 : 35; 104 : 3. [f]11 : 10.

3122. What an awe-inspiring picture of the Day of Judgment is given in these verse. ! Face to face with a calamity man is prepared to part with everything, even to sacrifice his dearest and nearest ones, if only by doing so he can save his own skin.

3123. Man, by nature, is impatient and miserly. For this meaning of *Khuliqa* see 21 : 38; 30 : 55.

23. Except those who pray,

إِلَّا الْمُصَلِّيْنَ ۙ

24. "Those who are constant in their Prayer;

الَّذِيْنَ هُمْ عَلٰى صَلَاتِهِمْ دَآئِمُوْنَ ۙ

25. ᵇAnd those in whose wealth there is a known right—³¹²⁴

وَالَّذِيْنَ فِيْ اَمْوَالِهِمْ حَقٌّ مَّعْلُوْمٌ ۙ

26. For those who ask *for help* and those who do not *ask*—³¹²⁵

لِّلسَّآئِلِ وَالْمَحْرُوْمِ ۙ

27. And those who believe in the Day of Judgment³¹²⁵·ᴬ to be a reality;

وَالَّذِيْنَ يُصَدِّقُوْنَ بِيَوْمِ الدِّيْنِ ۙ

28. And those who are fearful of the punishment of their Lord—

وَالَّذِيْنَ هُمْ مِّنْ عَذَابِ رَبِّهِمْ مُّشْفِقُوْنَ ۙ

29. Verily, from the punishment of their Lord none can feel secure—

اِنَّ عَذَابَ رَبِّهِمْ غَيْرُ مَأْمُوْنٍ ۙ

30. ᶜAnd those who guard their private parts—

وَالَّذِيْنَ هُمْ لِفُرُوْجِهِمْ حٰفِظُوْنَ ۙ

31. ᵈExcept from their wives and *from* those whom their right hand spossess; such, indeed, are not to blame;

اِلَّا عَلٰۤى اَزْوَاجِهِمْ اَوْ مَا مَلَكَتْ اَيْمَانُهُمْ فَاِنَّهُمْ غَيْرُ مَلُوْمِيْنَ ۙ

32. ᵉBut those who seek to go beyond that, it is these who are transgressors—

فَمَنِ ابْتَغٰى وَرَآءَ ذٰلِكَ فَاُولٰٓئِكَ هُمُ الْعٰدُوْنَ ۚ

33. ᶠAnd those who are watchful of their trusts and their covenants;

وَالَّذِيْنَ هُمْ لِاَمٰنٰتِهِمْ وَعَهْدِهِمْ رٰعُوْنَ ۙ

ᵃ23 : 10.   ᵇ51 : 20.   ᶜ23 : 7.   ᵈ23 : 7.   ᵉ23 : 8.   ᶠ23 : 9.

3124. All things in the universe being the common property of the whole of mankind, there can be no absolute ownership of anything vesting in any individual; the poor have a share in the wealth of the rich as of right.

3125. The word *Maḥrūm* means, those who, because of some physical infirmity or from a sense of dignity, would not ask for alms. It includes animals also.

3125A. There could be no real sense of responsibility without a true and living belief in the Hereafter. This belief is the second cardinal belief of Islām, next to belief in the existence of God.

34. And those who are upright in their testimonies.

وَالَّذِينَ هُم بِشَهَادَاتِهِمْ قَائِمُونَ ﴿٣٤﴾

35. And those who are strict in the observance of their Prayer.

وَالَّذِينَ هُمْ عَلَىٰ صَلَاتِهِمْ يُحَافِظُونَ ﴿٣٥﴾

36. [a]These will be in the Gardens, *duly* honoured.

أُولَٰئِكَ فِي جَنَّاتٍ مُّكْرَمُونَ ﴿٣٦﴾

R. 2 37. But what is the matter with those who disbelieve that [b]they come hurrying on towards thee,

فَمَالِ الَّذِينَ كَفَرُوا قِبَلَكَ مُهْطِعِينَ ﴿٣٧﴾

38. From the right hand and from the left, in different parties?[3126]

عَنِ الْيَمِينِ وَعَنِ الشِّمَالِ عِزِينَ ﴿٣٨﴾

39. Does every man among them hope to enter the Garden of Bliss?

أَيَطْمَعُ كُلُّ امْرِئٍ مِّنْهُمْ أَن يُدْخَلَ جَنَّةَ نَعِيمٍ ﴿٣٩﴾

40. Never! We have created them of that which[3127] they know.

كَلَّا إِنَّا خَلَقْنَاهُم مِّمَّا يَعْلَمُونَ ﴿٤٠﴾

41. But nay! I swear by the Lord of the Easts and of the Wests that We have the power

فَلَا أُقْسِمُ بِرَبِّ الْمَشَارِقِ وَالْمَغَارِبِ إِنَّا لَقَادِرُونَ ﴿٤١﴾

42. To bring in their place *others* better than they,[3128] and We cannot be frustrated *in Our plans*.

عَلَىٰ أَن نُّبَدِّلَ خَيْرًا مِّنْهُمْ وَمَا نَحْنُ بِمَسْبُوقِينَ ﴿٤٢﴾

[a]18 : 108; 23 : 12. [b]14 : 43-44.

3126. This and the preceding verse give a prophetic description of the coming triumph of Islām when the pogan tribes of Arabia, from every part of the country, hastened to wait in deputations upon the Holy Prophet, begging to be taken into the fold of Islām. Or, the verses may refer to the highly alluring offers made by the leaders of the Quraish to the Holy Prophet, if only he should give up preaching against their idols. By some authorities, however, the verses have been taken to refer to the dangerous attacks that were made on the Holy Prophet in different forms and from different directions by his opponents.

3127. The word *Mimma* signifies, natural powers and faculties with which God has endowed man.

3128. The opponents of the Holy Prophet are told that old order will vanish and from its ruins will emerge a new and better order and other people will take their place.

43. So leave them alone to indulge in idle talk and to sport until they meet that day of theirs which they are promised,

فَذَرْهُمْ يَخُوضُوا وَيَلْعَبُوا حَتّٰى يُلٰقُوا يَوْمَهُمُ الَّذِيْ يُوْعَدُوْنَ ﴿٤٣﴾

44. [b]The day when they will come forth from their graves hastening, as though they were racing to a target,

يَوْمَ يَخْرُجُوْنَ مِنَ الْاَجْدَاثِ سِرَاعًا كَاَنَّهُمْ اِلٰى نُصُبٍ يُّوْفِضُوْنَ ﴿٤٤﴾

45. Their eyes cast down; and humiliation covering [c]them.[3129] Such is the Day which they are promised.

خَاشِعَةً اَبْصَارُهُمْ تَرْهَقُهُمْ ذِلَّةٌ ؕ ذٰلِكَ الْيَوْمُ الَّذِيْ كَانُوْا يُوْعَدُوْنَ ﴿٤٥﴾

[a]23 : 55; 43 : 84; 52 : 46. [b]36 : 52; 54 : 8-9.
[c]10 : 28; 54 : 8.

3129. This verse and the preceding one contain a graphic picture of the leaders of the Quraish, after the Fall of Mecca, when they came to the Holy Prophet completely dejected, dispirited and dismayed, their eyes cast down, and disappointment and a sense of guilt and regret writ large on their faces.

CHAPTER 71

NŪḤ

(Revealed before Hijrah)

Date of Revelation, Context and Subject-Matter

As the *Sūrah* records the spiritual experiences of the Prophet Noah, it has fittingly been named after him. Wherry gives 7th year of the Call as the date of its revelation, while Noldeke places it in the 5th year, but according to other authorities it was revealed in the first Meccan period, about the time when some of the immediately preceding Chapters were revealed. Towards the end of the preceding *Sūrah* it was stated that wicked people invariably reject the Divine Message; they oppose and persecute God's Messengers till the hour of punishment arrives and they meet their deserved end. The present *Sūrah* gives a brief account of the missionary activities of one of the greatest Prophets of antiquity —Noah, and depicts him as pouring out the agony of his heart before his Lord and Creator in words full of extreme pathos. He preached to his people day and night, he says, and spoke to them in public and in private. He reminded them of the great favours and bounties that God had bestowed upon them. He warned them of the evil consequences of the rejection of the Divine Message. But all his preaching and warning, his sympathy with and solicitude for, their well-being only met with ridicule, opposition and abuse; and instead of following him whose heart was full of love for them, they chose to follow those false leaders who led them to destruction. When Noah's exhortation and preaching of a whole lifetime proved a voice in the wilderness, he prayed to God to destroy the enemies of Truth. The *Sūrah* closes with this prayer of Noah.

سُورَةُ نُوحٍ مَكِّيَّةٌ

آياتها ٢٩ (٧١) ركوعاتها ٢

1. In the name of Allāh, the Gracious, the Merciful.

بِسْمِ اللّٰهِ الرَّحْمٰنِ الرَّحِيْمِ ①

2. We sent Noah to his people, *with the commandment*: 'Warn thy people before there comes upon them a grievous punishment.'

إِنَّآ أَرْسَلْنَا نُوحًا إِلَى قَوْمِهٖٓ أَنْ أَنْذِرْ قَوْمَكَ مِنْ قَبْلِ أَنْ يَّأْتِيَهُمْ عَذَابٌ أَلِيمٌ ②

3. He said, 'O my people! surely, I am a plain Warner unto you,

قَالَ يٰقَوْمِ إِنِّي لَكُمْ نَذِيرٌ مُّبِينٌ ③

4. 'That you serve Allāh and be mindful of your duty to Him and obey me,

أَنِ اعْبُدُوا اللّٰهَ وَاتَّقُوْهُ وَأَطِيعُوْنِ ④

5. 'He will forgive you your sins and grant you respite till an appointed time.' Verily, the [a]time appointed by Allāh cannot be put off when it comes,[3130] if only you knew.'

يَغْفِرْ لَكُمْ مِّنْ ذُنُوْبِكُمْ وَيُؤَخِّرْكُمْ إِلَىٰٓ أَجَلٍ مُّسَمًّى إِنَّ أَجَلَ اللّٰهِ إِذَا جَآءَ لَا يُؤَخَّرُ لَوْ كُنْتُمْ تَعْلَمُوْنَ ⑤

6. He said, 'My Lord, I have called my people night and day,

قَالَ رَبِّ إِنِّي دَعَوْتُ قَوْمِي لَيْلًا وَّنَهَارًا ⑥

7. 'But my calling *them* has only made them flee *from me all* the more;

فَلَمْ يَزِدْهُمْ دُعَآءِيٓ إِلَّا فِرَارًا ⑦

8. 'And every time I called them that Thou mightest forgive them, they put their fingers into their ears, [b]and drew close their garments,[3131] and persisted *in their iniquities* and were disdainfully proud;

وَإِنِّي كُلَّمَا دَعَوْتُهُمْ لِتَغْفِرَ لَهُمْ جَعَلُوْٓا أَصَابِعَهُمْ فِيْٓ اٰذَانِهِمْ وَاسْتَغْشَوْا ثِيَابَهُمْ وَأَصَرُّوْا وَاسْتَكْبَرُوا اسْتِكْبَارًا ⑧

---

[a]63 : 12. [b]11 : 6.

3130. When a Divine decree actually comes in operation, repentance is of no use.

3131. The words *Istaghshau Thiyābahum* metaphorically mean: 'They refused to listen to the Divine Message. They closed all the avenues of their hearts against it, *Thiyāb* meaning 'hearts' (Lane).

9. 'Then, I called them *to righteousness* openly,

ثُمَّ اِنِّيْ دَعَوْتُهُمْ جِهَارًا ﴿٩﴾

10. 'Then preached to them in public, and *appealed* to them in private.'[3132]

ثُمَّ اِنِّيْ اَعْلَنْتُ لَهُمْ وَاَسْرَرْتُ لَهُمْ اِسْرَارًا ﴿١٠﴾

11. [a]'And I said, 'Seek forgiveness of your Lord; for He is the Great Forgiver;

فَقُلْتُ اسْتَغْفِرُوْا رَبَّكُمْ اِنَّهٗ كَانَ غَفَّارًا ﴿١١﴾

12. 'He will send down rain for you in abundance,

يُّرْسِلِ السَّمَآءَ عَلَيْكُمْ مِّدْرَارًا ﴿١٢﴾

13. 'And He will grant you increase of wealth and children, and will cause gardens *to grow* for you and will cause rivers *to flow* for you.

وَّيُمْدِدْكُمْ بِاَمْوَالٍ وَّبَنِيْنَ وَيَجْعَلْ لَّكُمْ جَنّٰتٍ وَّيَجْعَلْ لَّكُمْ اَنْهٰرًا ﴿١٣﴾

14. 'What is the matter with you that you hope not for greatness *and wisdom* from Allāh?[3133]

مَا لَكُمْ لَا تَرْجُوْنَ لِلّٰهِ وَقَارًا ﴿١٤﴾

15. [b]'And He has created you in *different forms and* different conditions.[3133]

وَقَدْ خَلَقَكُمْ اَطْوَارًا ﴿١٥﴾

16. [c]'See you not how Allāh has created seven heavens in *perfect* harmony,

اَلَمْ تَرَوْا كَيْفَ خَلَقَ اللّٰهُ سَبْعَ سَمٰوٰتٍ طِبَاقًا ﴿١٦﴾

---

[a]11 : 4, 53. [b]23 : 13-15. [c]65 : 13; 67 : 4.

3132. Noah employed all the means at his disposal to make his people listen to the Divine Message. But they were equally determined not to listen to it.

3133. God has endowed different men with different natural capacities and capabilities, and on this disparity of aptitudes and physical conditions depend the existence, growth and development of human society. *Aṭwār* is plural of *Ṭaur* which means, a time; state; condition; quality; mode or manner; form or appearance. The verse means, God has created men of different forms and different conditions; of various aspects and dispositions, or He has created them by stages (Lane).

17. [a]"And has placed the moon, therein a light, and made the sun a lamp?

وَجَعَلَ الْقَمَرَ فِيهِنَّ نُورًا وَجَعَلَ الشَّمْسَ سِرَاجًا ﴿١٧﴾

18. [b]And Allāh has caused you to grow out of the earth as *a good* growth.

وَاللَّهُ أَنْبَتَكُمْ مِنَ الْأَرْضِ نَبَاتًا ﴿١٨﴾

19. "Then will He cause you to return thereto, and He will bring you forth a *new* bringing forth.

ثُمَّ يُعِيدُكُمْ فِيهَا وَيُخْرِجُكُمْ إِخْرَاجًا ﴿١٩﴾

20. [d]"And Allāh has made the earth for you a wide expanse,

وَاللَّهُ جَعَلَ لَكُمُ الْأَرْضَ بِسَاطًا ﴿٢٠﴾

21. "That you may traverse the spacious ways thereof.'

لِتَسْلُكُوا مِنْهَا سُبُلًا فِجَاجًا ﴿٢١﴾ ع

R. 2 22. *Then* Noah said, 'My Lord, they have disobeyed me, and followed one whose wealth and children have only added to his loss.

قَالَ نُوحٌ رَبِّ إِنَّهُمْ عَصَوْنِي وَاتَّبَعُوا مَنْ لَمْ يَزِدْهُ مَالُهُ وَوَلَدُهُ إِلَّا خَسَارًا ﴿٢٢﴾

23. 'And they have planned a mighty plan.'

وَمَكَرُوا مَكْرًا كُبَّارًا ﴿٢٣﴾

24. "And they say *to one another* [f]'Forsake not your gods, and forsake neither Wadd nor Suwā', nor Yaghūth and Ya'ūq and Nasr.'"[3134]

وَقَالُوا لَا تَذَرُنَّ آلِهَتَكُمْ وَلَا تَذَرُنَّ وَدًّا وَلَا سُوَاعًا وَلَا يَغُوثَ وَيَعُوقَ وَنَسْرًا ﴿٢٤﴾

---

[a]10 : 6; 25 : 62. [b]7 : 26; 20 : 56. [c]7 : 26; 20 : 56. [d]67 : 16; 78 : 7. [e]67 : 16. [f]38 : 7.

3134. Wadd was an idol worshipped by Banū Kalb in Daumat al-Jandal. It was in a man's figure representing manly power. Suwā' was an idol of Banū Hudhail. It was in a woman's shape, representing female beauty. Yaghūth belonged to the tribe of Murād, and Ya'ūq in the shape of horse was worshipped by Hamdān. Nasr, an idol of the Dhu'l-Kilā' tribe, was in the shape of an eagle or vulture, representing long life or insight. Noah's people were steeped in idol-worship. They had many idols, the five mentioned in the verse under comment being the most popular. The Arabs, several centuries afterwards, are supposed to have brought them from Iraq. Hubul, their most famous idol, was brought from Syria by 'Āmir bin Loḥayy; their own principal idols being Lāt, Manāt and 'Uzzā. Or, they might have named their own idols after the idols of the tribe of Noah as the two peoples lived not very distant from each other and there was general intercourse between them. There is nothing impossible or improbable in the two neighbouring idolatrous peoples having identical names for their idols.

25. [a]"And they have led many astray; so increase Thou not the wrongdoers *in aught* but error.'

وَقَدْ أَضَلُّوا كَثِيرًا ۚ وَلَا تَزِدِ الظّٰلِمِينَ إِلَّا ضَلٰلًا ﴿٢٥﴾

26. [b]Because of their sins they were drowned and made to enter Fire. And they found no helpers for themselves against Allāh.

مِمَّا خَطِيْٓـٰٔتِهِمْ أُغْرِقُوا فَأُدْخِلُوا نَارًا ۙ فَلَمْ يَجِدُوا لَهُمْ مِّنْ دُونِ اللّٰهِ أَنْصَارًا ﴿٢٦﴾

27. And Noah said, 'My Lord, leave not of the disbelievers even one dweller in the land;

وَقَالَ نُوحٌ رَّبِّ لَا تَذَرْ عَلَى الْأَرْضِ مِنَ الْكٰفِرِينَ دَيَّارًا ﴿٢٧﴾

28. 'For, if Thou dost leave them, they will *only* lead astray Thy servants and will beget none but sinners *and* disbelievers,

إِنَّكَ إِنْ تَذَرْهُمْ يُضِلُّوا عِبَادَكَ وَلَا يَلِدُوٓا إِلَّا فَاجِرًا كَفَّارًا ﴿٢٨﴾

29. [c]"My Lord! forgive me and my parents, and him who enters my house as a believer, and the believing men and the believing women; and increase Thou not the wrongdoers *in aught* but in ruin.'[3135]

رَبِّ اغْفِرْ لِي وَلِوَالِدَيَّ وَلِمَنْ دَخَلَ بَيْتِيَ مُؤْمِنًا وَّلِلْمُؤْمِنِينَ وَالْمُؤْمِنٰتِ ۖ وَلَا تَزِدِ الظّٰلِمِينَ إِلَّا تَبَارًا ﴿٢٩﴾

[a]14 : 37. [b]21 : 78; 26 : 121; 37 : 83. [c]14 : 42.

3135. God's Prophets are full of the milk of human kindness. Noah's prayer shows that opposition to him must have been long, persistent and unremitting, and that all his efforts to bring his people to the right path must have proved abortive, and there must have remained no possibility for any further addition to his small following, and also that his opponents must have exceeded all legitimate bounds in opposing and persecuting him and his followers, and in indulging in evil pursuits. Matters must have come to such a pass that a man of a most compassionate disposition like Noah was constrained to pray against his people. In an identical situation the Holy Prophet's attitude to his opponents presents a vivid contrast. In the battle of Uḥud, when his two teeth were broken and he was badly wounded and bled profusely, the only words that escaped his lips were, 'How will a people get salvation who have wounded their Prophet and have smeared his face with blood for no fault, but that he calls them to God. My Lord! forgive my people, for they know not what they do' (Zurqānī & Hishām).

CHAPTER 72

AL-JINN

(Revealed before Hijrah)

Date of Revelation, Context and Subject-Matter

This *Sūrah* is generally considered to have been revealed on the Holy Prophet's return from Ṭā'if, where, after he had almost despaired of the Meccans from whom he had received nothing but ridicule, opposition and persecution, he had gone to preach his Message. The visit to Ṭā'if took place two years before *Hijrah* when the opposition to the new Faith had taken an ugly turn and the condition of the Holy Prophet and his followers had become desperate in the extreme. If, as some authorities are of the view, the *Sūrah* relates to an incident other than the one mentioned in *Sūrah* Al-Aḥqāf (46 : 30-33), then it might have been revealed much earlier. The context and contents of the *Sūrah* seem to lend some weight to the latter view. In the preceding *Sūrah* it was stated that the lifelong preaching of Noah had met with only jibs and jeers, and that only a few persons other than his near relatives had given him their allegiance—even his son and wife taking an active part in opposition to him. In order to show that there existed a similarity between the circumstances of Noah and those of the Holy Prophet it is stated that a party of the jinn—a people not known to the Holy Prophet before—visited him, listened to the Qur'ān and at once believed in him. The *Sūrah* gives a fairly long account of the beliefs and doctrines of these people, their conduct and outlook on life, and emphatically affirms that it is impossible for anyone to distort or tamper with the revealed Word of God because, like a precious treasure, it is strongly guarded by Divine sentinels. Towards the end, it is stated that whenever a Divine Teacher calls men to God, the forces of evil try to stifle his voice, but the Teacher carries on his mission, undeterred by the machinations of evilly-disposed people. The *Sūrah* closes with an infallible criterion to test the Divine Source of the Message of a Prophet, *viz.*, that it contains prophecies about great world events which human knowledge cannot foresee or foretell, and also that the Prophet succeeds in delivering his Message and fulfils his mission.

ركوعاتها ٢ سُوْرَةُ الْجِنِّ مَكِّيَّةٌ (٧٢) اٰياتها ٢٩

1. [a]In the name of Allāh, the Gracious, the Merciful.

بِسْمِ اللّٰهِ الرَّحْمٰنِ الرَّحِيْمِ ①

2. Say, "It has been revealed to me that a company[3136] of the jinn listened *to the Qur'ān* and they said: 'Truly, we have heard a [b]wonderful Qur'ān,[3137]

قُلْ اُوْحِيَ اِلَيَّ اَنَّهُ اسْتَمَعَ نَفَرٌ مِّنَ الْجِنِّ فَقَالُوْٓا
اِنَّا سَمِعْنَا قُرْاٰنًا عَجَبًا ②

3. [c]'It guides to the right way; so we have believed in it, and we will not associate anyone with our Lord.[3138]

يَّهْدِيْٓ اِلَى الرُّشْدِ فَاٰمَنَّا بِهٖ ۗ وَلَنْ نُّشْرِكَ بِرَبِّنَآ
اَحَدًا ③

4. '*The truth is that*—exalted be the majesty of our Lord—[d]He has taken unto Himself neither wife nor son,

وَّاَنَّهٗ تَعٰلٰى جَدُّ رَبِّنَا مَا اتَّخَذَ صَاحِبَةً وَّلَا وَلَدًا ④

5. 'And that the foolish amongst us used to utter extravagant lies concerning Allāh,

وَّاَنَّهٗ كَانَ يَقُوْلُ سَفِيْهُنَا عَلَى اللّٰهِ شَطَطًا ⑤

6. 'And we thought that men and jinn would never utter a lie concerning Allāh,

وَّاَنَّا ظَنَنَّآ اَنْ لَّنْ تَقُوْلَ الْاِنْسُ وَالْجِنُّ عَلَى اللّٰهِ
كَذِبًا ⑥

---

[a]1 : 1. [b]46 : 31. [c]46 : 32. [d]17 : 112; 18 : 5; 25 : 3.

3136. See 2733.

3137. The reference may be to a party of the Jews of Naṣībin. They were non-Arabs and being strangers they have been called "jinn" which word among other things means, a stranger (Lane). The incident mentioned in this verse seems to be different from the one referred to in 46 : 30-33, though the verse is taken by some authorities to refer to those verses, because the words put in the mouth of 'a company of the jinn' in the present verse possess a seeming resemblance with the words spoken by a party of the jinn referred to in 46 : 30-33.

3138. The verse shows that 'a company of the jinn' were either Unitarian Christians, or such Jews as were closely associated with them or, being under their influence, were conversant with Christian beliefs.

7. [a]"And, indeed, some men[3139] from among the common folk used to seek the protection of some men from among the jinn, and thus they increased *the jinn* in arrogance,

وَّاَنَّهٗ كَانَ رِجَالٌ مِّنَ الْاِنْسِ يَعُوْذُوْنَ بِرِجَالٍ مِّنَ الْجِنِّ فَزَادُوْهُمْ رَهَقًا ۝٧

8. 'And, indeed, they thought, even as you think that Allāh would never raise any *Messenger*,[3140]

وَّاَنَّهُمْ ظَنُّوْا كَمَا ظَنَنْتُمْ اَنْ لَّنْ يَّبْعَثَ اللّٰهُ اَحَدًا ۝٨

9. 'And we sought to reach heaven,[3141] but we found it filled with strong guards and [b]shooting stars,

وَّاَنَّا لَمَسْنَا السَّمَآءَ فَوَجَدْنٰهَا مُلِئَتْ حَرَسًا شَدِيْدًا وَّشُهُبًا ۝٩

10. 'And we used to sit in some of its seats to listen. But whoso listens now finds a shooting star in ambush[3142] for him,

وَّاَنَّا كُنَّا نَقْعُدُ مِنْهَا مَقَاعِدَ لِلسَّمْعِ فَمَنْ يَّسْتَمِعِ الْاٰنَ يَجِدْ لَهٗ شِهَابًا رَّصَدًا ۝١٠

11. 'And we know not whether evil is intended for those who are in the earth, or whether their Lord intends to bestow guidance upon them,

وَّاَنَّا لَا نَدْرِيْٓ اَشَرٌّ اُرِيْدَ بِمَنْ فِي الْاَرْضِ اَمْ اَرَادَ بِهِمْ رَبُّهُمْ رَشَدًا ۝١١

[a]6 : 129. [b]15 : 17-19 ; 37 : 7-9.

3139. As the word *Rijāl* is used only with regard to human beings, the verse shows that 'a company of the jinn,' mentioned in this and in *Sūrah* Al-Aḥqāf were human beings and not any other species of creation. The Arabic word *Jinn* here may signify big or influential men and *Ins* lowly and humble ones who, by following the former and seeking their protection, increase their conceit and arrogance.

3140. The Jews had ceased to believe as early as in the time of the Prophet Joseph that any Divine Messenger would ever appear after him (40 : 35).

3141. The expression, 'Seeking to reach heaven,' means, trying to steal the secrets of the unknown. When a Divine Reformer is about to make his appearance in the world, an unusual shooting of stars takes place. It is to this exceptional natural phenomenon that reference seems to have been made in this verse.

3142. Before the appearance of a Divine Reformer, soothsayers and diviners dabble in occult sciences, and with the help of their questionable practices seek to hood-wink simple folk by posing to be able to have access to the secrets of the unknown and, being adept in the art of cheating, succeed in playing upon their credulity. But with the advent of a Heavenly Reformer their deceit is exposed and their counterfeit knowledge of the unseen becomes unmasked as only a superficial and fragmentary acquaintance with astrology. The word "now" is used here particularly with respect to the time of the Holy Prophet, but it may also signify the time of every great Divine Reformer. See also 37 : 7-10.

12. 'And some of us are righteous and some of us are otherwise—we are sects following different paths,

وَأَنَّا مِنَّا الصّٰلِحُونَ وَمِنَّا دُونَ ذٰلِكَ كُنَّا طَرَآئِقَ قِدَدًا ۝١٢

13. 'And we know that [a]we cannot frustrate *the plan of* Allāh in the earth, nor can we escape Him by flight,

وَأَنَّا ظَنَنَّآ أَنْ لَّنْ نُّعْجِزَ اللّٰهَ فِي الْأَرْضِ وَلَنْ نُّعْجِزَهٗ هَرَبًا ۝١٣

14. [b]'So when we heard *the call to* guidance, we believed in it. And he, who believes in his Lord, has no fear of loss or of injustice,

وَأَنَّا لَمَّا سَمِعْنَا الْهُدٰٓى اٰمَنَّا بِهٖ فَمَنْ يُّؤْمِنْ بِرَبِّهٖ فَلَا يَخَافُ بَخْسًا وَّلَا رَهَقًا ۝١٤

15. 'And some of us submit *to God* and some of us have deviated *from the right course*.' And those who submit *to God*—it is they who seek the right course,

وَأَنَّا مِنَّا الْمُسْلِمُونَ وَمِنَّا الْقٰسِطُونَ فَمَنْ أَسْلَمَ فَأُولٰٓئِكَ تَحَرَّوْا رَشَدًا ۝١٥

16. And those who deviate *from the right course*, they are the fuel of Hell.

وَأَمَّا الْقٰسِطُونَ فَكَانُوا لِجَهَنَّمَ حَطَبًا ۝١٦

17. And if the *Meccan disbelievers* keep to the *right* path, We shall, certainly, provide them with abundant water to drink,[3143]

وَّأَنْ لَّوِ اسْتَقَامُوا عَلَى الطَّرِيقَةِ لَأَسْقَيْنٰهُمْ مَّآءً غَدَقًا ۝١٧

18. That We may try them thereby. [c]And whoso turns away from the remembrance of his Lord—He will drive him into an overwhelmingly severe punishment.

لِّنَفْتِنَهُمْ فِيهِ وَمَنْ يُّعْرِضْ عَنْ ذِكْرِ رَبِّهٖ يَسْلُكْهُ عَذَابًا صَعَدًا ۝١٨

[a]55 : 34. [b]46 : 32. [c]20 : 101; 43 : 37.

3143. Water being the source of all life, "abundant water" signifies abundance of wealth and other material gains.

19. [a]And *all* places of worship[3144] belong to Allāh; so call not on anyone beside Allāh.

وَّاَنَّ الْمَسٰجِدَ لِلّٰهِ فَلَا تَدْعُوْا مَعَ اللّٰهِ اَحَدًا ﴿۱۹﴾

20. [b]And when the Servant of Allāh[3145] stands up praying to Him, they crowd upon him, well-nigh stifling him *to death.*

وَّاَنَّهٗ لَمَّا قَامَ عَبْدُ اللّٰهِ يَدْعُوْهُ كَادُوْا يَكُوْنُوْنَ عَلَيْهِ لِبَدًا ﴿۲۰﴾

R. 2 21. Say, 'I pray to my Lord only, [c]and I associate no one with Him.

قُلْ اِنَّمَآ اَدْعُوْا رَبِّيْ وَلَآ اُشْرِكُ بِهٖٓ اَحَدًا ﴿۲۱﴾

22. Say, 'I have no power to do you either harm or good.'

قُلْ اِنِّيْ لَآ اَمْلِكُ لَكُمْ ضَرًّا وَّلَا رَشَدًا ﴿۲۲﴾

23. Say, 'Surely, none can protect me against *the punishment of* Allāh, [d]nor can I find any place of refuge beside Him.'

قُلْ اِنِّيْ لَنْ يُّجِيْرَنِيْ مِنَ اللّٰهِ اَحَدٌ ۙ وَّلَنْ اَجِدَ مِنْ دُوْنِهٖ مُلْتَحَدًا ﴿۲۳﴾

24. '*My responsibility is* only to convey *what is revealed to me* from Allāh and His Messages.' And those who disobey Allāh and His Messenger, surely, for them is the fire of Hell, wherein they will abide for a long period.[3146]

اِلَّا بَلٰغًا مِّنَ اللّٰهِ وَرِسٰلٰتِهٖ ۭ وَمَنْ يَّعْصِ اللّٰهَ وَرَسُوْلَهٗ فَاِنَّ لَهٗ نَارَ جَهَنَّمَ خٰلِدِيْنَ فِيْهَآ اَبَدًا ﴿۲۴﴾

25. [e]*They will continue to disbelieve* until they see that which they are promised, but soon they will know who is weaker in helpers and fewer in numbers.

حَتّٰٓى اِذَا رَاَوْا مَا يُوْعَدُوْنَ فَسَيَعْلَمُوْنَ مَنْ اَضْعَفُ نَاصِرًا وَّاَقَلُّ عَدَدًا ﴿۲۵﴾

---

[a]2 : 115; 22 : 41. [b]96 : 10-11. [c]13 : 37; 18 : 39. [d]18 : 28. [e]19 : 76.

3144. In the foregoing verses it is declared that with the advent of the Holy Prophet God's plan with regard to the establishment of Divine Unity has become manifest. The verse under comment states that mosques would henceforth be the centres from which the light of Truth will emanate and spread throughout the world.

3145. The epithet, 'The Servant of Allāh,' refers to the Holy Prophet, he being God's servant *par excellence,* but it may also be applied to every Divine Messenger or Reformer.

3146. The difference between *Amad* and *Abad* is that whereas the former word means time limited in duration, the latter means time everlasting (Lane).

26. [a]Say, 'I know not whether that which you are promised is nigh, or whether my Lord has fixed for it a distant term.'

قُلْ إِنْ أَدْرِيْٓ أَقَرِيْبٌ مَّا تُوْعَدُوْنَ أَمْ يَجْعَلُ لَهٗ رَبِّيْٓ أَمَدًا ﴿٢٦﴾

27. *He is* the Knower of the unseen; and He reveals[3147] not His secrets to anyone,

عٰلِمُ الْغَيْبِ فَلَا يُظْهِرُ عَلٰى غَيْبِهٖٓ أَحَدًا ﴿٢٧﴾

28. Except to a Messenger *of His* whom He chooses. And then He causes an escort *of guarding angels* to go before him and behind him,[3148]

إِلَّا مَنِ ارْتَضٰى مِنْ رَّسُوْلٍ فَإِنَّهٗ يَسْلُكُ مِنْۢ بَيْنِ يَدَيْهِ وَمِنْ خَلْفِهٖ رَصَدًا ﴿٢٨﴾

29. That He may know that *His Messengers* have delivered the Messages of their Lord.[3149] And He encompasses *all* that is with them and He keeps count of all things.

لِيَعْلَمَ أَنْ قَدْ أَبْلَغُوْا رِسٰلٰتِ رَبِّهِمْ وَأَحَاطَ بِمَا لَدَيْهِمْ وَأَحْصٰى كُلَّ شَيْءٍ عَدَدًا ﴿٢٩﴾

[a]21 : 110.

3147. The expression, *Iẓhār 'alā al-Ghaib*, means, to be given knowledge frequently and in abundance of the secrets of the unknown that relate to and concern events of the greatest import.

3148. The verse embodies an incontestable criterion to distinguish between the nature and scope of the secrets of the unknown that are revealed to a Divine Messenger and those that are disclosed to other righteous believers. The distinction lies in the fact that whereas God's Messengers are granted *Iẓhār 'alā al-Ghaib*, *i.e.*, predominance over the unseen, secrets revealed to other righteous and holy men of God do not enjoy this distinction. Moreover, revelation granted to God's Messengers, being under special Divine protection, is secure against being distorted or tampered with by evil spirits, while secrets revealed to other righteous men are not so safe.

3149. The revelation of Divine Messengers is granted security against being distorted or tampered with, because they have a great Divine mission to fulfil and a great Heavenly Message to deliver.

CHAPTER 73

AL-MUZZAMMIL

(*Revealed before Hijrah*)

Date of Revelation and Context

Consensus of scholarly opinion assigns the revelation of this *Sūrah* to the earliest period of the Call; some scholars consider that it was the third Chapter to be revealed. In the preceding *Sūrah* (Al-Jinn) it was stated that angels descend upon Divine Messengers to guard the Word of God revealed to them from being distorted or tampered with. In the present *Sūrah* the Holy Prophet is enjoined to devote a part of the night to Prayer and remembrance of God so that angels may desçend upon him to help him against evil plots and machinations of his enemies. Like all Meccan *Sūrahs*, this *Sūrah* also deals mainly with the Divine mission of the Holy Prophet and with the truth of the Quranic revelation. It foretells in brief but very forceful words the eventual triumph of the Holy Prophet and adduces the fulfilment of this prophecy as an argument in support of Life after death and Resurrection. Particular emphasis has been laid on Prayer and remembrance of God which is a most effective means to draw Divine help and succour to prepare the Prophet for the mighty task that lies ahead of him.

سُورَةُ الْمُزَّمِّلِ مَكِّيَّةٌ

1. [a]In the name of Allāh, the Gracious, the Merciful.

بِسْمِ اللّٰهِ الرَّحْمٰنِ الرَّحِيْمِ ①

2. O thou wrapped up in *thy* mantle,[3150]

يٰۤاَيُّهَا الْمُزَّمِّلُ ②

3. Stand up *in Prayer* at night except a small portion thereof—

قُمِ الَّيْلَ اِلَّا قَلِيْلًا ③

4. Half of it, or reduce from it a little,

نِّصْفَهٗۤ اَوِ انْقُصْ مِنْهُ قَلِيْلًا ④

5. Or, add to it *a little*—and [b]recite the Qur'ān a good recital.

اَوْ زِدْ عَلَيْهِ وَرَتِّلِ الْقُرْاٰنَ تَرْتِيْلًا ⑤

6. Verily, We are about to charge thee with a weighty Word.[3151]

اِنَّا سَنُلْقِيْ عَلَيْكَ قَوْلًا ثَقِيْلًا ⑥

[a]1 : 1. [b]17 : 107; 25 : 33.

3150. *Zamala-hū* means, he carried him behinb his back. *Zammala*, besides the meaning given in the text, means, he ran and went along quickly. *Tazammala, Izzammala* or *Izdamala* means, he wrapped himself ; he bore, or carried it, namely a load at one time. *Muzzammil* (or *Mutazammil*) means, a man wrapped in his garments ; one bearing a heavy responsibility (Aqrab, Qadīr, Ma'ānī). After his first spiritual experience when the angel of God came to the Holy Prophet with Divine revelation in the Cave Ḥirā', he rushed home very much frightened. The fright was quite natural because the experience was quite novel. The Holy Prophet asked to be wrapped up in a mantle. As wrapping up also implies the sense of joining together and uniting, the meaning of the verse may be something like this, 'O thou who hast been commissioned to unite all the nations of the world under one banner !' The Holy Prophet has been described in the Ḥadith as *Al-Ḥāshir, i.e.*, joiner and uniter of the nations of the world (Bukhārī). The verse may also signify: (1) The Holy Prophet is one who has to go a long distance on the road to awaken humanity to the realization of its high destiny, and, therefore, he has to go fast, *i.e.*, work hard, incessantly and fast. (2) He is one who is to carry a heavy load, a very great responsibility of preaching the Divine Message to the world. The Holy Prophet may have been reminded of his onerous task of preparing a community of God-fearing followers, who, imbued with the same noble ideals and fired with the same unflagging zeal as himself, should help him to convey to mankind the Message of Islām. It is to the onerous duties and responsibilities of the Holy Prophet that reference is made here and not to his being wrapped up in his mantle.

3151. The expression, 'a weighty Word', may signify: 'The Quranic teaching is pregnant with the highest import. It is too weighty to be displaced or dislocated.' No word or letter of the Qur'ān can be changed, altered or amended. According to an oft-quoted *ḥadīth*, whenever a revelation descended upon the Holy Prophet, he went into a trance and felt a peculiar sensation so that even on an extremely cold day large drops of sweat fell from his forehead and he felt a dead-weight of his body (Bukhārī). The Quranic revelation being 'a weighty Word,' the Holy Prophet's paroxysm was due to this sensation.

7. Verily, getting up at night *for Prayer* is the most potent means of subduing *the self* and most effective in speech.[3152]

إِنَّ نَاشِئَةَ اللَّيْلِ هِيَ أَشَدُّ وَطْئًا وَأَقْوَمُ قِيلًا ۝٧

8. Thou hast, indeed, during the day *a* long *chain of* engagements.[3153]

إِنَّ لَكَ فِي النَّهَارِ سَبْحًا طَوِيلًا ۝٨

9. So remember the name of thy Lord and devote *thyself* to Him with full devotion.

وَاذْكُرِ اسْمَ رَبِّكَ وَتَبَتَّلْ إِلَيْهِ تَبْتِيلًا ۝٩

10. [a]*He is* the Lord of the East and the West; there is no god but He; so take him for *thy* Guardian.

رَبُّ الْمَشْرِقِ وَالْمَغْرِبِ لَا إِلٰهَ إِلَّا هُوَ فَاتَّخِذْهُ وَكِيلًا ۝١٠

11. And bear patiently all that they say; and withdraw from them in a decent manner.

وَاصْبِرْ عَلٰى مَا يَقُولُونَ وَاهْجُرْهُمْ هَجْرًا جَمِيلًا ۝١١

12. [b]And leave Me alone with those who reject *the truth*, possessors of ease and plenty; and give them a little respite.

وَذَرْنِي وَالْمُكَذِّبِينَ أُولِي النَّعْمَةِ وَمَهِّلْهُمْ قَلِيلًا ۝١٢

13. Surely, with Us are *heavy* fetters and a raging fire,

إِنَّ لَدَيْنَا أَنْكَالًا وَّجَحِيمًا ۝١٣

14. And food that chokes, and a painful punishment—

وَّطَعَامًا ذَا غُصَّةٍ وَّعَذَابًا أَلِيمًا ۝١٤

[a]26 : 29; 37 : 6. [b]68 : 45; 74 : 12.

3152. Getting up at night for Prayer is a potent means of subduing one's self and bringing under effective control one's evil propensities and inclinations. It is the proved experience of all holy men of God that nothing conduces to one's spiritual development so much as Prayer at night. In the stillness and solitude of night a peculiar sort of peace prevails and all nature is quiet, and man, being all alone with his Creator, enjoys special communion with Him and becomes illumined with a special heavenly light which he imparts to others. The time is eminently suited for one to develop strength of character and to make one's speech sane, solid and sound. Effective speech and infinite capacity for hard work are two very necessary qualifications for a Reformer in order to succeed in his mission. Prayer at night helps in the development of these two qualities. Having acquired control over one's mind and tongue one comes to exercise control over others.

3153. Reference in the verse is to the multifarious duties of the Holy Prophet which he performed with alacrity and in doing which he took great pleasure; this being the significance of the word *Sabḥan* (Lane).

15. On the day when the earth [a]and the mountains shall quake, and the mountains will become like crumbling sand-hills.

يَوْمَ تَرْجُفُ الْأَرْضُ وَالْجِبَالُ وَكَانَتِ الْجِبَالُ كَثِيبًا مَّهِيلًا ﴿١٥﴾

16. Verily, We have sent to you a Messenger, [b]who is a witness over you, even as We sent a Messenger to Pharaoh;[3154]

إِنَّا أَرْسَلْنَا إِلَيْكُمْ رَسُولًا شَاهِدًا عَلَيْكُمْ كَمَا أَرْسَلْنَا إِلَىٰ فِرْعَوْنَ رَسُولًا ﴿١٦﴾

17. But Pharaoh disobeyed the Messenger, [c]so We seized him with a terrible seizing.

فَعَصَىٰ فِرْعَوْنُ الرَّسُولَ فَأَخَذْنَاهُ أَخْذًا وَبِيلًا ﴿١٧﴾

18. How will you then, if you disbelieve, guard yourselves against a day which will turn children grey-headed?[3155]

فَكَيْفَ تَتَّقُونَ إِن كَفَرْتُمْ يَوْمًا يَجْعَلُ الْوِلْدَانَ شِيبًا ﴿١٨﴾

19. [d]The day when the heaven will be rent asunder; *and* His [3156]promise is bound to be fulfilled.

السَّمَاءُ مُنفَطِرٌ بِهِ ۚ كَانَ وَعْدُهُ مَفْعُولًا ﴿١٩﴾

20 This, surely, is a [e]reminder. So let him, who will, take a way unto his Lord.

إِنَّ هَٰذِهِ تَذْكِرَةٌ ۖ فَمَن شَاءَ اتَّخَذَ إِلَىٰ رَبِّهِ سَبِيلًا ﴿٢٠﴾

---

[a]56 : 5-6 ; 79 : 7. [b]33 : 46; 48 : 9. [c]20 : 79; 26 : 67; 28 : 41. [d]82 : 2. [e]20 : 4; 74 : 55; 76 : 30; 80 : 12.

3154. The verse refers to the biblical prophecy: 'I will raise them up a Prophet from among their brethren, like unto thee, and will put My word in his mouth; and he shall speak unto them all that I shall command. And it shall come to pass, that whosoever will not hearken unto My words which he shall speak in My name, I will require it of him' (Deut. 18 : 18-19).

3155. 'Turn children grey-headed' in the present verse, 'being rent asunder of the heaven' in the next, 'rolling up of heaven' in 21 : 105, and similar other expressions used in the Qur'ān (82 : 2 & 84 : 2) are metaphors for most calamitous happenings which bring about disastrous changes.

3156. The promise referred to in the verse was the total defeat and destruction of the forces of evil with the Fall of Mecca.

R. 2 21. Surely, thy Lord knows that [a]thou standest up *praying* for nearly two-thirds of the night, and *sometimes* half or a third thereof [b]and also a party of those who are with thee.[3157] And Allāh determines the measure[3158] of the night and the day. He knows that you cannot calculate the time accurately, so He has turned to you in mercy. Recite, then, as much of the Qur'ān as is easy *for you.* He knows that there will be some among you who may be sick, and others who may travel in the land, seeking Allāh's bounty, and others who may fight in the cause of Allāh. So recite of it that which is easy *for you*, and observe Prayer and pay the *Zakāt* [c]and lend to Allāh a goodly loan. And whatever good you may send on before you for your souls, you will find it with Allāh. *It will be* better and greater in reward. And seek forgiveness of Allāh. Surely, Allāh is Most Forgiving, Merciful.

إِنَّ رَبَّكَ يَعْلَمُ أَنَّكَ تَقُومُ أَدْنَىٰ مِن ثُلُثَيِ الَّيْلِ
وَنِصْفَهُ وَثُلُثَهُ وَطَآئِفَةٌ مِّنَ الَّذِينَ مَعَكَ
وَاللّٰهُ يُقَدِّرُ الَّيْلَ وَالنَّهَارَ عَلِمَ أَن لَّن تُحْصُوهُ
فَتَابَ عَلَيْكُمْ فَاقْرَءُوا مَا تَيَسَّرَ مِنَ الْقُرْآنِ
عَلِمَ أَن سَيَكُونُ مِنكُم مَّرْضَىٰ وَآخَرُونَ يَضْرِبُونَ
فِي الْأَرْضِ يَبْتَغُونَ مِن فَضْلِ اللّٰهِ وَآخَرُونَ
يُقَاتِلُونَ فِي سَبِيلِ اللّٰهِ فَاقْرَءُوا مَا تَيَسَّرَ مِنْهُ وَ
أَقِيمُوا الصَّلٰوةَ وَآتُوا الزَّكٰوةَ وَأَقْرِضُوا اللّٰهَ قَرْضًا
حَسَنًا وَمَا تُقَدِّمُوا لِأَنفُسِكُم مِّنْ خَيْرٍ تَجِدُوهُ
عِندَ اللّٰهِ هُوَ خَيْرًا وَأَعْظَمَ أَجْرًا وَاسْتَغْفِرُوا
اللّٰهَ إِنَّ اللّٰهَ غَفُورٌ رَّحِيمٌ ﴿٢١﴾

[a]26 : 219. [b]25 : 65; 41 : 39. [c]2 : 246; 57 : 12; 64 : 18.

3157. In the opening verse of the *Sūrah* the Holy Prophet was enjoined constantly to pray at night, for, that would give him the necessary strength to discharge the grave responsibility of preaching the Divine Message that was shortly going to devolve on him. In this verse he is assured of Divine pleasure, and is told that he has faithfully carried out God's command about Night-Prayer—not only he, but a party of believers also. The command was not specifically directed to the followers of the Holy Prophet, but being always desirous of following in his footsteps, they copied his example in this respect also.

3158. The sentence, 'Allāh determines the measure of the night and the day,' signifies that sometimes nights are long and sometimes they are short and sometimes they are equal. The words, 'you cannot calculate the time accurately,' may apply to Muslims in general. They are told that all of them would not be able to say the Night-Prayer regularly and punctually.

CHAPTER 74

AL-MUDDATHTHIR

(Revealed before Hijrah)

Date of Revelation and Context

By common consent this *Sūrah* was one of the first two or three *Sūrahs* which were revealed at Mecca. This and the preceding *Sūrah* (Al-Muzzammil) seem to be "twins" as they are so closely linked as regards the time of their revelation and their tone and tenor. The present *Sūrah*, in fact, complements the subject-matter of the preceding one. The Muzzammil of the previous *Sūrah*, immersed in devotional prayers and contemplation and passing through a period of intense preparation for the attainment of spiritual perfection, has become developed into the Muddaththir (destroyer of sin and vanquisher of the forces of evil, deliverer of mankind, their leader, guide and warner) of the present *Sūrah*. From that time onward, the Holy Prophet's life was no more his own. It was given to God. He preached the Divine Message with unswerving purpose, in the face of insult, opposition and persecution. The *Sūrah* opens with a firm command to the Holy Prophet to stand up, proclaim the Truth he has and warn those who would not accept it—those whom wealth, power and position have rendered spiritually blind and deaf—that they would suffer punishment because they did not offer Prayers and did not feed the poor and because also that they indulged in vain pursuits. The *Sūrah* ends on the note that the Qur'ān is but a reminder and an exhortation. He, who accepts its Message, accepts it for the good of his own soul and he, who rejects it, does so to his own detriment.

سُورَةُ الْمُدَّثِّرِ مَكِّيَّةٌ

1. [a]In the name of Allāh, the Gracious, the Merciful.

بِسْمِ اللّٰهِ الرَّحْمٰنِ الرَّحِيْمِ ۝

2. O thou who hast covered thyself with *thy* cloak,[3159]

يٰۤاَيُّهَا الْمُدَّثِّرُ ۝

3. Arise and warn,

قُمْ فَاَنْذِرْ ۝

4. And thy Lord do thou magnify,

وَرَبَّكَ فَكَبِّرْ ۝

5. And thy clothes[3160] do thou purify,

وَثِيَابَكَ فَطَهِّرْ ۝

6. And uncleanliness[3161] do thou shun,

وَالرُّجْزَ فَاهْجُرْ ۝

7. And bestow not favours seeking to get more *in return*,

وَلَا تَمْنُنْ تَسْتَكْثِرُ ۝

8. And for the sake of thy Lord do thou endure *trials* patiently.

وَلِرَبِّكَ فَاصْبِرْ ۝

---

[a]1 : 1.

3159. *Tadaththara* or *Iddaththara* means, he wrapped himself with a garment. *Daththara-hū* means, he destroyed or obliterated him or it; he covered him with a warm garment. *Daththara al-Ṭairu* means, the bird adjusted, or put in order its nest; *Tadaththara al-Farasa* means, he leaped upon and rode the horse. *Ṭadaththar al-'Aduwwa* means, he vanquished the enemy (Lane). According to the different meanings of the root-word, *Al-Muddaththir* would mean, the effacer or obliterator; the reformer or the one who adjusts or puts things in order; the vanquisher; the one who is about to leap upon and ride the horse. The word has also been interpreted as one entrusted with bearing the heavy load of the responsibilities of a Prophet (Qadīr). The word also means, one adorned with the best natural powers and qualities and prophetical dignity (Rūḥ al-Ma'ānī). All these epithets quite fitly apply to the Holy Prophet.

3160. *Thiyāb* means, clothes; dependents or followers of a person; the wearer's body or self (Lane & Steingass). The Holy Prophet is enjoined that before entering upon his great mission he should prepare a body of followers, pure of heart, conduct and reputation. Or, the verse may mean that he should himself become paragon of piety, righteousness and of pure conduct.

3161. *Al-Rujz* also meaning idol-worship (Lane), the verse may be taken as enjoining the Holy Prophet to spare no pains to exterminate idolatry

9. [a]And when the trumpet is sounded,[3162]

فَإِذَا نُقِرَ فِي النَّاقُورِ ﴿٩﴾

10. [b]That day will be a hard day,[3163]

فَذٰلِكَ يَوْمَئِذٍ يَوْمٌ عَسِيرٌ ﴿١٠﴾

11. For the disbelievers it will not be easy.

عَلَى الْكٰفِرِينَ غَيْرُ يَسِيرٍ ﴿١١﴾

12. [c]Leave Me alone[3164] *to deal* with him whom I created.

ذَرْنِي وَمَنْ خَلَقْتُ وَحِيدًا ﴿١٢﴾

13. [d]And I gave him abundant wealth,

وَّجَعَلْتُ لَهُ مَالًا مَّمْدُودًا ﴿١٣﴾

14. [e]And sons, dwelling in *his* presence,[3165]

وَّبَنِينَ شُهُودًا ﴿١٤﴾

15. And equipped him with all *necessary* things,

وَّمَهَّدْتُّ لَهُ تَمْهِيدًا ﴿١٥﴾

16. Yet he desires that I should give *him* more.

ثُمَّ يَطْمَعُ أَنْ أَزِيدَ ﴿١٦﴾

17. Certainly not![3166] for he was stubbornly opposed to Our Signs.

كَلَّا إِنَّهُ كَانَ لِآيٰتِنَا عَنِيدًا ﴿١٧﴾

[a]23 : 102; 50 : 21; 69 : 14. [b]25 : 27. [c]68 : 45; 73 : 12. [d]68 : 15. [e]68 : 15.

3162. The verse means, when a Divine Reformer—God's bugle—by which God summons men to Himself—makes his appearance and calls men to God.' Or, the verse may refer to the Holy Prophet's own call to his people.

3163. 'A hard day' signifies the Day of Resurrection or, the day of the final defeat of disbelief and the complete triumph of Truth.

3164. The words also mean: 'Leave Me to deal alone with him whom I created,' or 'Leave Me to deal with him who, on account of the great wealth, power and position, God has bestowed upon him, thinks himself to be peerless among his compatriots, *Waḥīd* also meaning unique, incomparable' (Lane).

Though this and the following several verses apply to every arrogant and conceited disbeliever, they may particularly apply to Walīd bin Mughīrah, who was an outstanding personality among the Quraish, and was known among his fellow citizens by such high sounding titles as "unique" and "fragrance of the Quraish." He was extremely handsome and was well-known for his elegant poems and other accomplishments. He had ten to thirteen sons and was a very rich man.

3165. The verse may mean that Walīd's sons also commanded respect like him. They, too, were offered a distinguished place in the assemblies which he attended. Or, Walīd was so rich that his sons always kept company with him, not wanting to go anywhere to earn their living.

3166. See next page.

18. I shall inflict on him an increasingly overwhelming torment.

سَأُرْهِقُهُ صَعُودًا ﴿۱۸﴾

19. Lo! he reflected and calculated!

إِنَّهُ فَكَّرَ وَقَدَّرَ ﴿۱۹﴾

20. Ruin seize him! how he calculated!

فَقُتِلَ كَيْفَ قَدَّرَ ﴿۲۰﴾

21. Ruin seize him[3167] again! how he calculated!

ثُمَّ قُتِلَ كَيْفَ قَدَّرَ ﴿۲۱﴾

22. Then he looked *around him*,

ثُمَّ نَظَرَ ﴿۲۲﴾

23. [a]Then he frowned and scowled,[3168]

ثُمَّ عَبَسَ وَبَسَرَ ﴿۲۳﴾

24. Then he turned away and was disdainful,

ثُمَّ أَدْبَرَ وَاسْتَكْبَرَ ﴿۲۴﴾

25. And said, [b]"This is nothing but magic handed down;

فَقَالَ إِنْ هَٰذَا إِلَّا سِحْرٌ يُؤْثَرُ ﴿۲۵﴾

26. 'This is nothing but the word of a man.

إِنْ هَٰذَا إِلَّا قَوْلُ الْبَشَرِ ﴿۲۶﴾

27. Soon shall I cast him into [c]the fire of Hell.

سَأُصْلِيهِ سَقَرَ ﴿۲۷﴾

28. And what will make thee know what Hell-fire is?

وَمَا أَدْرَاكَ مَا سَقَرُ ﴿۲۸﴾

29. It spares not and it leaves naught.

لَا تُبْقِي وَلَا تَذَرُ ﴿۲۹﴾

30. [d]It scorches the face.

لَوَّاحَةٌ لِلْبَشَرِ ﴿۳۰﴾

[a]80 : 2. [b]34 : 44; 37 : 16. [c]37 : 24. [d]70 : 17.

3166. The word, *Kallā*, is used to reject the request of a person and to reprimand him for making it (Lane).

3167. The reference is particularly to Walīd bin Mughīrah. Ruin continued to dog his footsteps. Three of his sons—Walīd, Khālid and Hishām accepted Islām, others perished before his eyes. He suffered heavy financial losses and ultimately died in poverty and disgrace.

3168. When the Qur'ān was read to him Walīd frowned and scowled in disdain and went away in high huff.

31. Over it are nineteen[3169] *angels.*

عَلَيْهَا تِسْعَةَ عَشَرَ ۝٣١

32. And none but angels have We made wardens of the Fire. And We have not fixed their number except as a trial for those who disbelieve, so that those, who have been given the Book, may attain certainty and those who believe may increase in faith, and those, who have been given the Book as well as the believers, may not doubt, and that those in whose hearts is disease and the disbelievers may say, 'What does Allāh mean by such an [a]illustration?' Thus does Allāh leave to go astray whom He pleases and guide whom He pleases. [b]And none knows the hosts of thy Lord but He. And this is nothing but a Reminder for man.

وَمَا جَعَلْنَآ أَصْحٰبَ النَّارِ إِلَّا مَلٰٓئِكَةً وَّمَا جَعَلْنَا
عِدَّتَهُمْ إِلَّا فِتْنَةً لِّلَّذِيْنَ كَفَرُوْا لِيَسْتَيْقِنَ الَّذِيْنَ
أُوْتُوا الْكِتٰبَ وَيَزْدَادَ الَّذِيْنَ اٰمَنُوْٓا إِيْمَانًا وَّلَا يَرْتَابَ
الَّذِيْنَ أُوْتُوا الْكِتٰبَ وَالْمُؤْمِنُوْنَ وَلِيَقُوْلَ الَّذِيْنَ فِيْ
قُلُوْبِهِمْ مَّرَضٌ وَّالْكٰفِرُوْنَ مَاذَآ أَرَادَ اللّٰهُ بِهٰذَا
مَثَلًا كَذٰلِكَ يُضِلُّ اللّٰهُ مَنْ يَّشَآءُ وَيَهْدِيْ مَنْ
يَّشَآءُ وَمَا يَعْلَمُ جُنُوْدَ رَبِّكَ إِلَّا هُوَ وَمَا هِيَ إِلَّا
ذِكْرٰى لِلْبَشَرِ ۝٣٢

R. 2 33. Nay, by the moon,

كَلَّا وَالْقَمَرِ ۝٣٣

34. And *by* the night when it departs,

وَالَّيْلِ إِذْ أَدْبَرَ ۝٣٤

35. [c]And *by* the dawn[3170] when it shines forth,

وَالصُّبْحِ إِذَآ أَسْفَرَ ۝٣٥

[a]2 : 27. [b]33 : 10; 48 : 5. [c]81 : 19.

3169. Man has been endowed with nine major senses, *i.e.*, the seven exteroceptive senses, one proprioceptive sense of position in space and one enteroceptive sense arising from internal organs relating to sensations of hunger, thirst, etc. These coupled with their nine spiritual counterparts together with the guardian or the controlling sense, *i.e.*, the will power which dominates and controls all these different faculties of human nature, are the nineteen guardians of Hell. Or, the number "nineteen" may be a great Divine secret specially concerning the People of the Book of which the significance and reality will be disclosed in God's own time and will make them acknowledge the truth of the Quranic teaching and will add greatly to the certainty of faith of the believers. Who dare claim to know all the Divine secrets ?

3170. 'The dawn' may also signify the Holy Prophet's great Deputy, the Promised Messiah and the 'departing night' may mean the night of spiritual darkness that would begin to depart after his appearance.

36. [a]Verily, it is one of the greatest calamities.

إِنَّهَا لَإِحْدَى الْكُبَرِ ﴿٣٦﴾

37. A warning to man,

نَذِيرًا لِّلْبَشَرِ ﴿٣٧﴾

38. To him among you who wishes to advance *in virtue* or hang back.

لِمَن شَآءَ مِنكُمْ أَن يَتَقَدَّمَ أَوْ يَتَأَخَّرَ ﴿٣٨﴾

39. [b]Every soul is pledged[3171] for what it has earned;

كُلُّ نَفْسٍ بِمَا كَسَبَتْ رَهِينَةٌ ﴿٣٩﴾

40. Except [c]those on the right hand.

إِلَّآ أَصْحٰبَ الْيَمِينِ ﴿٤٠﴾

41. *They will be* in Gardens enquiring

فِي جَنّٰتٍ يَتَسَآءَلُونَ ﴿٤١﴾

42. From the guilty ones,

عَنِ الْمُجْرِمِينَ ﴿٤٢﴾

43. 'What has brought you into Hell ?'

مَا سَلَكَكُمْ فِي سَقَرَ ﴿٤٣﴾

44. They will say, [d]'We were not of those who offered Prayer,

قَالُوا لَمْ نَكُ مِنَ الْمُصَلِّينَ ﴿٤٤﴾

45. [e]'Nor did we feed the poor,

وَلَمْ نَكُ نُطْعِمُ الْمِسْكِينَ ﴿٤٥﴾

46. 'And we indulged in idle talk with those who indulge therein.

وَكُنَّا نَخُوضُ مَعَ الْخَآئِضِينَ ﴿٤٦﴾

47. 'And we continued to deny the [f]Day of Judgment,

وَكُنَّا نُكَذِّبُ بِيَوْمِ الدِّينِ ﴿٤٧﴾

48. 'Until death[3172] [g]overtook us.'

حَتّٰى أَتٰنَا الْيَقِينُ ﴿٤٨﴾

[a]79 : 35. [b]14 : 52; 40 : 18; 45 : 23. [c]56 : 28. 90 : 19. [d]75 : 32. [e]69 : 35; 89 : 19; 107 : 4. [f]75 : 33. [g]15 : 100.

3171. Every soul shall remain in pledge unless it will have paid for the sins it had committed, *i.e.*, unless it will have been cleansed of sins after having suffered punishment for them.

3172. *Yaqīn* means, certainty; security; death (Aqrab).

49. So [a]the intercession of intercessors will not avail them.

فَمَا تَنفَعُهُمْ شَفَاعَةُ الشَّافِعِينَ ﴿٤٩﴾

50. Now what is the matter with them that they are turning away from the Exhortation,

فَمَا لَهُمْ عَنِ التَّذْكِرَةِ مُعْرِضِينَ ﴿٥٠﴾

51. As if they were frightened asses,

كَأَنَّهُمْ حُمُرٌ مُّسْتَنفِرَةٌ ﴿٥١﴾

52. Fleeing from a lion?

فَرَّتْ مِن قَسْوَرَةٍ ﴿٥٢﴾

53. Nay, every man among them desires to be given an open book.[3173]

بَلْ يُرِيدُ كُلُّ امْرِئٍ مِّنْهُمْ أَن يُؤْتَىٰ صُحُفًا مُّنَشَّرَةً ﴿٥٣﴾

54. This cannot be! Verily, they fear not the Hereafter.

كَلَّا بَل لَّا يَخَافُونَ الْآخِرَةَ ﴿٥٤﴾

55. Never! for, this *Qur'ān* is an exhortation *enough.*

كَلَّا إِنَّهُ تَذْكِرَةٌ ﴿٥٥﴾

56. Let him, then, who will, remember it.

فَمَن شَاءَ ذَكَرَهُ ﴿٥٦﴾

57. And they will not remember unless Allāh *so* [b]pleases.[3174] He *alone* is worthy to be feared and He *alone* is worthy to forgive.

وَمَا يَذْكُرُونَ إِلَّا أَن يَشَاءَ اللَّهُ هُوَ أَهْلُ التَّقْوَىٰ وَأَهْلُ الْمَغْفِرَةِ ﴿٥٧﴾

[a]20 : 110; 34 : 24. [b]76 : 31; 81 : 30.

3173. The reference here may be to the impudent demand of disbelievers mentioned elsewhere in the Qur'ān that they would not believe unless the Holy Prophet should bring down a Book for them from Heaven which they should read (17 : 94).

3174. The disbelievers will not benefit by the Qur'ān unless they make their own will conform to the Will of God, *i.e.*, unless they subordinate all their desires to the Divine Will (76 : 31).

CHAPTER 75

AL-QIYĀMAH

(*Revealed before Hijrah*)

Date of Revelation, Context and Subject-Matter

'The *Sūrah* is entitled, "The Resurrection," because it almost wholly deals with the subject of Resurrection. It is decidedly one of the earliest Chapters which were revealed at Mecca, because the Meccan Chapters specifically deal with God's Unity, Resurrection and Revelation. Towards the end of the preceding *Sūrah* it was emphatically declared that those people, who will accept the Quranic Message, will rise to great eminence and will enjoy an honoured place among the comity of powerful nations. The present *Sūrah* opening with a discussion of the subject of Resurrection, throws a broad hint that a great moral resurrection is going to be brought about among a morally degraded and degenerate people —the Arabs—through the ennobling teachings of the Qur'ān and the purifying company and example of the Holy Prophet Muḥammad.

The *Sūrah* opens with a solemn affirmation that the Resurrection undoubtedly will take place, and significantly enough adduces man's spiritual resurrection as evidence in support of this affirmation. As a further proof, it swears by *Nafs Lawwāmah* (the Self-Accusing Spirit) which in action is the first stage of the process of moral regeneration of man. Then an oft-repeated objection of disbelievers is mentioned that when they are dead and reduced to dust, how will they be raised again to life? The *Sūrah* refutes this objection by saying that in their heart of hearts they know that man's sins never go unpunished and, therefore, there must be a day when they will be called to account for all their actions. Next, the collection of the Qur'ān and the Divine protection of its text are offered as further arguments in the same connection, since of all revealed Scriptures the Qur'ān has laid the greatest emphasis on the inevitability of Resurrection. Then, a brief but graphic description is given of the agony of death and man's intense desire to be spared of it. This shows that at the moment of death the fear that one will have to render an account of one's actions gnaws at one's heart. Towards its close disbelievers are admonished that man has not been created without purpose or responsibility and that he will have to account for his failure to discharge it. The disbelievers are further reminded that man's physical development from a sperm-drop into a full-fledged human being, endowed with unique powers and faculties, constitutes an irrebuttable argument that his life is intended to serve a sublime purpose and that it will not end with the departure of the soul from its physical tabernacle.

سُوْرَةُ الْقِيٰمَةِ مَكِّيَّةٌ

1. [a]In the name of Allāh, the Gracious, the Merciful.[3175]

بِسْمِ اللّٰهِ الرَّحْمٰنِ الرَّحِيْمِ ۝١

2. Nay,[3176] I swear by the Day of Resurrection.

لَآ اُقْسِمُ بِيَوْمِ الْقِيٰمَةِ ۝٢

3. Nay, I swear by the self-accusing soul,[3177] *that the Day of Judgment is a certainty*.

وَلَآ اُقْسِمُ بِالنَّفْسِ اللَّوَّامَةِ ۝٣

4. Does man think that We shall not [b]assemble his bones?

اَيَحْسَبُ الْاِنْسَانُ اَلَّنْ نَّجْمَعَ عِظَامَهٗ ۝٤

5. Yea, We have the power to restore his very finger-tips.[3178]

بَلٰى قٰدِرِيْنَ عَلٰٓى اَنْ نُّسَوِّيَ بَنَانَهٗ ۝٥

6. But man desires to continue to send forth evil deeds in front of him.

بَلْ يُرِيْدُ الْاِنْسَانُ لِيَفْجُرَ اَمَامَهٗ ۝٦

7. He [c]enquires, 'When will be the Day of Resurrection?

يَسْـَٔلُ اَيَّانَ يَوْمُ الْقِيٰمَةِ ۝٧

8. When the eye is dazzled,

فَاِذَا بَرِقَ الْبَصَرُ ۝٨

9. And the moon is eclipsed,

وَخَسَفَ الْقَمَرُ ۝٩

---

[a]1 : 1. [b]23 : 83; 37 : 54; 56 : 48; 79 : 11-13. [c]78 : 2; 79 : 43.

3175. See 1 : 1

3176. *Lā* here may signify, 'It is not like what they think.' Sometimes it is used as an answer to some objection or in repudiation of what is said before (Lane).

3177. The Qur'ān has mentioned three stages of development of the human soul. The first stage is called *Nafs Ammārah* (the uncontrollable spirit), when the animal in man is predominant. The second stage is that of *Nafs Lawwāmah* (the self-accusing spirit), when man's awakened conscience upbraids him for doing bad deeds and restrains his passions and appetites. At this stage the human in man gets the upper hand. It is the beginning of his moral resurrection and therefore has been cited here in evidence of the Final Resurrection. If man has no responsibility, and if he is not to account for his actions in an after-life, then why this pricking of conscience at the doing of an evil deed? The third and the highest stage of development of the human soul, however, is that of *Nafs Muṭma'innah* (the soul at rest). At this stage the human soul becomes practically immune to failure or faltering and is at peace with its Creator.

3178. *Banān* represents man's power and strength, as by means of his fingers he grasps an object and defends himself. The word may stand also for the whole human body as part of a thing sometimes represents the whole. The verse signifies that God has the power to restore all the powers of man, or even of a whole people when, to all intents and purposes, they are dead and defunct.

وَجُمِعَ الشَّمْسُ وَالْقَمَرُ ﴿١٠﴾

10. And the sun and the moon are brought together,[3179]

يَقُولُ الْإِنسَانُ يَوْمَئِذٍ أَيْنَ الْمَفَرُّ ﴿١١﴾

11. On that day man will say, 'Whither to [a]flee?'

كَلَّا لَا وَزَرَ ﴿١٢﴾

12. Not at all; there is no refuge!

إِلَىٰ رَبِّكَ يَوْمَئِذٍ الْمُسْتَقَرُّ ﴿١٣﴾

13. With thy Lord *alone* will be the place of rest that day.

يُنَبَّأُ الْإِنسَانُ يَوْمَئِذٍ بِمَا قَدَّمَ وَأَخَّرَ ﴿١٤﴾

14. On that day will man be informed of that which he has sent forward and of that which he has left behind.[3180]

بَلِ الْإِنسَانُ عَلَىٰ نَفْسِهِ بَصِيرَةٌ ﴿١٥﴾

15. In truth man is a witness against himself,

وَلَوْ أَلْقَىٰ مَعَاذِيرَهُ ﴿١٦﴾

16. Even though he puts forward his excuses.

لَا تُحَرِّكْ بِهِ لِسَانَكَ لِتَعْجَلَ بِهِ ﴿١٧﴾

17. Move not thy tongue, *O Prophet*, with *the revelation of the Qur'ān* that thou mayest hasten *to preserve* it.

[a]80 : 35.

3179. The expression, 'the sun and the moon are brought together,' may signify that the whole solar system will be completely disrupted. Or, the verse may signify the destruction of the political power of the Arabs and of the Iranian empire, the moon being the symbol of the political power of the former and the sun that of the latter. Or, the reference may be to the lunar and solar eclipses which, according to a *ḥadīth*, were to occur in the time of the Promised Mahdī in the month of Ramaḍān (Baihaqui), it being quite an unusual natural phenomenon. Strangely enough, both the sun and the moon were eclipsed in the month of Ramaḍān in 1894 when the Founder of the Aḥmadiyya Movement had already made the claim that he was the Promised Messiah and Mahdī.

3180. The words mean: The evil actions which man did but which he should not have done, and the good ones which he should have done but failed to do, *i.e.*, his sins of omission and commission.

18. [a]Surely, upon Us *rests* its collection and its recital.[3181]

إِنَّ عَلَيْنَا جَمْعَهُ وَقُرْآنَهُ ﴿١٧﴾

19. So when We recite it, then follow thou its recital.

فَإِذَا قَرَأْنَاهُ فَاتَّبِعْ قُرْآنَهُ ﴿١٨﴾

20. Then upon Us *rests* the expounding thereof.

ثُمَّ إِنَّ عَلَيْنَا بَيَانَهُ ﴿١٩﴾

21. Hearken! [b]you love the present life;

كَلَّا بَلْ تُحِبُّونَ الْعَاجِلَةَ ﴿٢٠﴾

22. And you neglect the Hereafter.

وَتَذَرُونَ الْآخِرَةَ ﴿٢١﴾

23. [c]*Some* faces on that day will be radiant,

وُجُوهٌ يَوْمَئِذٍ نَاضِرَةٌ ﴿٢٢﴾

24. Looking *eagerly*[3182] towards their Lord;

إِلَىٰ رَبِّهَا نَاظِرَةٌ ﴿٢٣﴾

25. [d]And *some* faces on that day will be dismal,

وَوُجُوهٌ يَوْمَئِذٍ بَاسِرَةٌ ﴿٢٤﴾

---

[a]15 : 10. [b]87 : 17. [c]88 : 9. [d]68 : 44; 80 : 41; 88 : 3-4.

3181. Bukhārī reports that in the beginning when a certain portion of the Qur'ān was revealed to the Holy Prophet, in his anxiety lest he should forget it, he would start hurriedly repeating it. It is this practice that the Prophet was enjoined in the preceding verse to give up, since as stated in the following three verses, God has taken upon Himself not only to safeguard the text of the Qur'ān from being tampered with, but also to see that it was collected in the form of an immaculately arranged Book (see "Introduction to the Study of the Holy Qur'ān") and also that its Message was conveyed and explained to the whole world (15 : 10). Or, the significance of the verses may be that, because the preceding verses referred to a day of reckoning for disbelievers, the Holy Prophet was naturally anxious that the revelation bearing upon the promised punishment should come soon. He is here told that he need have no anxiety on that score, as it was God's responsibility when a relevant revelation should come and what form the punishment should take, and also that the Qur'ān should be collected, read and explained to the world. Besides the meaning given in the text, the verse has also been interpreted as follows: 'It is Our responsibility that We should explain the Quranic revelation through your tongue' (Rūḥ al-Ma'āni). This stresses the inviolability of the Holy Prophet's *Sunnah* and its indispensability as a safe and sure guide, next only to the Qur'ān itself.

3182. The righteous believers will look to their Lord, expecting to be rewarded for their good deeds, or they will be endowed with special spiritual eyes to see God. The sight of God will be a special Divine manifestation which will be unfolded to the human soul, untrammelled by its earthly raiment.

26. Knowing that a back-breaking calamity[3183] will befall them.

تَظُنُّ أَنْ يُفْعَلَ بِهَا فَاقِرَةٌ ﴿٢٦﴾

27. Hearken! [a]when *the soul of the dying man* comes up to the throat,

كَلَّا إِذَا بَلَغَتِ التَّرَاقِيَ ﴿٢٧﴾

28. And it is said, 'Who is the wizard[3184] *to save him?*'

وَقِيلَ مَنْ رَاقٍ ﴿٢٨﴾

29. And he is sure that it is the parting;

وَظَنَّ أَنَّهُ الْفِرَاقُ ﴿٢٩﴾

30. And one shank rubs against the other shank[3185] *in death-agony;*

وَالْتَفَّتِ السَّاقُ بِالسَّاقِ ﴿٣٠﴾

31. Unto thy Lord that day will be the driving.

إِلَىٰ رَبِّكَ يَوْمَئِذٍ الْمَسَاقُ ﴿٣١﴾

R. 2 32. For, he neither accepted *the Truth*[3186] [b]nor observed Prayer;

فَلَا صَدَّقَ وَلَا صَلَّىٰ ﴿٣٢﴾

33. [c]But he rejected *the Truth* and turned his back *on it;*

وَلَٰكِنْ كَذَّبَ وَتَوَلَّىٰ ﴿٣٣﴾

34. Then he went to his kinsfolk, strutting along *in pride*.

ثُمَّ ذَهَبَ إِلَىٰ أَهْلِهِ يَتَمَطَّىٰ ﴿٣٤﴾

35. 'Woe unto thee! and woe again!

أَوْلَىٰ لَكَ فَأَوْلَىٰ ﴿٣٥﴾

[a]56 : 84. [b]74 : 44. [c]74 : 47.

3183. The Arabs say, *Faqarat-hu al-Dāhiyatu*, *i.e.*, the calamity broke the vertebrae of his back (Lane).

3184. The verse means, (*a*) who will ascend with the soul of the dying man, the angel of mercy, who will take him to Paradise, or the angel of punishment, who will drag him to Hell ? (*b*) Where is the wizard or charmer who will avert the approaching death, or relieve the dying man of his agony?

3185. The word, *Sāq*, literally meaning shank, metaphorically signifies a calamity or affliction. See 2177. The verse signifies that one affliction will be joined to another for the departed soul—the agony of leaving his near and dear ones behind will be joined to the agony of death and the punishment awaiting the disbeliever in the next world.

3186. *Ṣaddaqa* stands for right belief and *Ṣallā* for good conduct, the two basic principles of Islām. Prayer is the essence of *'Ibādah* which is total submission and conforming one's conduct to Divine laws. Thus the verse means that both the mind and the body of disbelievers rebelled against God.

36. 'Then woe unto thee! and woe again!'[3187]	ثُمَّ اَوْلٰى لَكَ فَاَوْلٰى ۝
37. Does man think that he is to be left alone without purpose?[3188]	اَيَحْسَبُ الْاِنْسَانُ اَنْ يُّتْرَكَ سُدًى ۝
38. [a]Was he not a drop of fluid, emitted forth?	اَلَمْ يَكُ نُطْفَةً مِّنْ مَّنِيٍّ يُّمْنٰى ۝
39. [b]Then he became a clot, then *Allāh* gave him shape and perfected *him*.	ثُمَّ كَانَ عَلَقَةً فَخَلَقَ فَسَوّٰى ۝
40. [c]Then He made of him a pair, the male and female.	فَجَعَلَ مِنْهُ الزَّوْجَيْنِ الذَّكَرَ وَالْاُنْثٰى ۝
41. Has not such a One the power [d]to raise the dead to life?[3189]	اَلَيْسَ ذٰلِكَ بِقٰدِرٍ عَلٰٓى اَنْ يُّحْيِۦَ الْمَوْتٰى ۝

[a]18 : 38; 36 : 78; 80 : 20. [b]23 : 15; 40 : 68; 96 : 3. [c]92 : 4.
[d]17 : 51-52; 36 : 80; 46 : 34.

3187. The repetition of the words, 'woe unto thee,' signifies mental agony and physical punishment, or punishment in this world and in the next. Or, the words are used for the purpose of intensification.

3188. The whole idea is inconsistent with God's wisdom that He should have created man from an insignificant thing—from a sperm-drop—and should have endowed him with such great natural powers and faculties as to make him the centre and pivot of all His creation and then should have left him alone to eat, drink and be merry.

3189. The Lord, Who created man from such an insignificant beginning, possesses the power to give him a new life, when he is dead and is reduced to crumbled bones and dust, to make spiritual progress which will know no end.

CHAPTER 76

AL-DAHR

(Revealed before Hijrah)

Date of Revelation, Context and Subject-Matter

This *Sūrah*, like the preceding one, belongs to the early Meccan period. It is also called Al-Insān. Towards the end of the preceding *Sūrah* it was stated that man's creation from an insignificant fluid and his development into a full-fledged human being, endowed with great natural powers, leads to the inescapable inference that his life has a Divine purpose to serve and that the Great God Who created him from a sperm-drop possesses the power to give him a new life after he is dead. The present *Sūrah* constitutes an extension of the same theme, *viz.*, that man has been gifted with wonderful natural capabilities to rise to great spiritual heights. Its opening verses remind him of his insignificant beginning and of his having been endowed with reason and understanding, in order that, following the path shown to him by God's Prophets, he may make interminable spiritual progress and thus achieve the object for which he has been created. But when Divine Teachers appear to guide men to God, some of them reject God's Message and incur His displeasure, while others, more fortunate, respond to the Divine Call and earn Heavenly blessings. The *Sūrah*, then, gives a beautiful description of the Divine favours which are bestowed upon the righteous believers in this world and in the Hereafter, referring briefly also to the kind of punishment which the disbelievers receive here and will receive in the Hereafter for their wilful rejection of the Divine Message. It fittingly closes with the observation that God has revealed the Qur'ān, to guide man to the path which leads to the Lord and Creator of all creation, but he can derive no benefit from it unless he conforms his will to the Will of God.

ركوعاتها ٢ سُورَةُ الدَّهْرِ مَكِّيَّةٌ (٧٦) آياتها ٣١

1. [a]In the name of Allāh, the Gracious, the Merciful.

بِسْمِ اللّٰهِ الرَّحْمٰنِ الرَّحِيْمِ ۝١

2. There has, certainly, come upon man a period of time when he was not a [b]thing worth mentioning.

هَلْ أَتٰى عَلَى الْإِنْسَانِ حِيْنٌ مِّنَ الدَّهْرِ لَمْ يَكُنْ شَيْئًا مَّذْكُوْرًا ۝٢

3. [c]We have created man from a mingled sperm-drop[3190] that We might try him; so We made him hearing, seeing.

إِنَّا خَلَقْنَا الْإِنْسَانَ مِنْ نُّطْفَةٍ أَمْشَاجٍ نَّبْتَلِيْهِ فَجَعَلْنٰهُ سَمِيْعًا بَصِيْرًا ۝٣

4. [d]We have shown him the way, whether he be grateful or ungrateful.

إِنَّا هَدَيْنٰهُ السَّبِيْلَ إِمَّا شَاكِرًا وَّإِمَّا كَفُوْرًا ۝٤

5. [e]Verily, We have prepared for the disbelievers chains and iron-collars and blazing Fire.[3191]

إِنَّا أَعْتَدْنَا لِلْكٰفِرِيْنَ سَلٰسِلَا۟ وَأَغْلٰلًا وَّسَعِيْرًا ۝٥

6. *But* the virtuous shall drink of a cup, tempered with camphor—[3192]

إِنَّ الْأَبْرَارَ يَشْرَبُوْنَ مِنْ كَأْسٍ كَانَ مِزَاجُهَا كَافُوْرًا ۝٦

7. *From* a spring[3112A] wherefrom the servants of Allāh will drink—they make it gush forth—a forceful gushing forth.

عَيْنًا يَّشْرَبُ بِهَا عِبَادُ اللّٰهِ يُفَجِّرُوْنَهَا تَفْجِيْرًا ۝٧

---

[a]1 : 1. [b]19 : 68. [c]18 : 38; 35 : 12; 36 : 78; 40 : 68; 80 : 20.
[d]90 : 11. [e]18 : 103; 29 : 69; 33 : 9; 48 : 14.

3190. Man is created from a sperm-drop which itself is a mixture of several things, the implication being that he has been endowed with various natural powers, faculties and attributes which are meant for his moral and spiritual advance. This process points only to a general rule of man's creation; not that in no case could it be otherwise.

3191. Every action which a man does is followed by a corresponding act of God. The entanglements of disbelievers in worldly affairs will take the form of chains in the next world; cares of the world will take the form of iron-collars, and greed and carnal desires that of hell-fire and so on. See also 3116.

3192. *Kāfūr* is derived from *Kafara* which means, to cover or to suppress. The significance of the verse is that the quaffing of camphor-drink will have the effect of cooling down animal passions. The heart of righteous believers will be cleansed of all impure thoughts and they will be refrigerated with the coolness of deep Divine knowledge.

3192A. The righteous believers will drink of cups which will be filled from springs that they will have dug with great labour, this being the meaning of the word *Tafjīr*. The deeds, which they had done in the earthly life, would appear in the next world in the form of springs.

8. They fulfil *their* vow,[3193] and fear a day the evil of which is widespread.

يُوۡفُوۡنَ بِالنَّذۡرِ وَيَخَافُوۡنَ يَوۡمًا كَانَ شَرُّهٗ مُسۡتَطِيۡرًا ۝

9. [a]And they feed, for love of Him,[3194] the poor, the orphan and the prisoner;

وَيُطۡعِمُوۡنَ الطَّعَامَ عَلٰى حُبِّهٖ مِسۡكِيۡنًا وَّيَتِيۡمًا وَّاَسِيۡرًا ۝

10. *Assuring them:* 'We feed you to win Allāh's pleasure *only*. We desire no reward nor thanks from you.

اِنَّمَا نُطۡعِمُكُمۡ لِوَجۡهِ اللّٰهِ لَا نُرِيۡدُ مِنۡكُمۡ جَزَآءً وَّلَا شُكُوۡرًا ۝

11. 'Verily, we fear from our Lord a frowning, distressful[3195] day.'

اِنَّا نَخَافُ مِنۡ رَّبِّنَا يَوۡمًا عَبُوۡسًا قَمۡطَرِيۡرًا ۝

12. So Allāh will save them from the evil of that day, and will grant them joy and happiness.

فَوَقٰهُمُ اللّٰهُ شَرَّ ذٰلِكَ الۡيَوۡمِ وَلَقّٰهُمۡ نَضۡرَةً وَّسُرُوۡرًا ۝

13. [b]And He will reward them, for their steadfastness, with a Garden and *raiments of* silk,

وَجَزٰهُمۡ بِمَا صَبَرُوۡا جَنَّةً وَّحَرِيۡرًا ۝

---

[a]90 : 15-17.   [b]22 : 24.

This is the first stage of spiritual evolution which requires hard and continuous striving on the part of believers, because unless man brings under control and suppresses his evil propensities, he cannot make any spiritual progress. "The spring" mentioned in the verse is the spring of God's love and Divine realization.

3193. 'Fulfilling the vow' signifies discharging of man's duties to God. Man's obligations to his fellow-beings are mentioned in the next verse.

3194. The verse may mean, (1) because the righteous believers love God, so in order to win His pleasure they feed the poor and the captives. (2) They feed the poor for the sake of feeding them, *i.e.*, they do the good act of feeding the poor for the sake of doing good, seeking no reward, appreciation or approbation for what they do. (3) They feed the poor while they themselves love the money which they spend on them. (4) They feed the poor with wholesome and agreeable food, *Ṭa'ām* meaning agreeable and wholesome food (Lane).

3195. *Yaumun 'Abūsun* means, a distressful or calamitous day, or a day that makes one distressful, and *Yaumun Qamṭarīrun* means, a distressful or calamitous day, or a day that makes one knit the brow or contract the skin between the eyes (Lane).

14. [a]Reclining therein upon couches, they will experience therein [b]neither excessive heat nor bitter cold.

مُتَّكِـِٔينَ فِيهَا عَلَى الْأَرَآئِكِ لَا يَرَوْنَ فِيهَا شَمْسًا وَّلَا زَمْهَرِيرًا ﴿١٤﴾

15. And [b]its shades will be close over them, and its clustered fruits will be brought within *their* easy reach.

وَدَانِيَةً عَلَيْهِمْ ظِلٰلُهَا وَذُلِّلَتْ قُطُوفُهَا تَذْلِيلًا ﴿١٥﴾

16. [c]And vessels of silver will be passed round among them, and goblets

وَيُطَافُ عَلَيْهِم بِاٰنِيَةٍ مِّن فِضَّةٍ وَّاَكْوَابٍ كَانَتْ قَوَارِيرَا۟ ﴿١٦﴾

17. *Bright as* glass *but made* of silver, which they will measure according to *their own* measure.

قَوَارِيرَا۟ مِن فِضَّةٍ قَدَّرُوهَا تَقْدِيرًا ﴿١٧﴾

18. And therein will they be given to drink a cup tempered with ginger,[3196]

وَيُسْقَوْنَ فِيهَا كَأْسًا كَانَ مِزَاجُهَا زَنجَبِيلًا ﴿١٨﴾

19. *From* a spring named Salsabīl.[3197]

عَيْنًا فِيهَا تُسَمّٰى سَلْسَبِيلًا ﴿١٩﴾

[a]18 : 32; 36 : 57; 83 : 24. [b]20 : 120. [c]43 : 72.

3196. The word *Zanjabīl*, being a compound of *Zanā* (to ascend) and *Jabal* (mountain) signifies, he ascended the mountain. *Zanjabīl* or ginger is very useful in promoting the natural heat of the body. It gives strength to and generates heat in the weak body so as to enable a person to ascend precipitous heights. The two verses, in which *Kāfūr* (camphor) and *Zanjabīl* (ginger) are mentioned, are meant to call attention to the two stages through which a believer has to pass in order to make spiritual advance from the low position of slavery to passions to the heights of virtue and righteousness. The first stage in which poisonous matter is suppressed and the flood of passions begins to subside is termed the *Kāfūr* (camphor) stage; for in this stage only the suppression of poisonous matter is effected just as camphor has the property of nullifying the strong effect of passion. But the spiritual power which is required to overcome all difficulties is acquired in the second stage which is called the *Zanjabīl* stage. The spiritual ginger which has the effect of a tonic on the spiritual system is the manifestation of Divine Beauty and Glory which affords nourishment to the soul. Braced with this manifestation the spiritual wayfarer is able to traverse the dreary deserts and to climb the steep heights to be met with on his spiritual journey.

3197. The word, *Salsabīl*, literally meaning, 'enquire about the way,' the verse signifies that at the *Zanjabīl* stage the spiritual wayfarer becomes so much intoxicated with Divine love that, in his overbearing anxiety to meet God, he enquires everywhere and of everyone about the nearest and speediest approach to the Divine threshold.

20. [a]And there will wait upon them youths who will not age. When thou seest them, thou thinkest them to be pearls scattered about.

وَيَطُوفُ عَلَيْهِمْ وِلْدَانٌ مُّخَلَّدُونَ ۚ إِذَا رَأَيْتَهُمْ حَسِبْتَهُمْ لُؤْلُؤًا مَّنثُورًا ﴿٢٠﴾

21. And when thou seest, thou wilt see there a bliss and a vast kingdom.[3198]

وَإِذَا رَأَيْتَ ثَمَّ رَأَيْتَ نَعِيمًا وَمُلْكًا كَبِيرًا ﴿٢١﴾

22. On them will be garments of [b]fine green silk and thick brocade. And they will be made to wear [c]bracelets of silver. And their Lord will give them to drink a pure beverage.[3199]

عَالِيَهُمْ ثِيَابُ سُندُسٍ خُضْرٌ وَإِسْتَبْرَقٌ ۖ وَحُلُّوا أَسَاوِرَ مِن فِضَّةٍ وَسَقَاهُمْ رَبُّهُمْ شَرَابًا طَهُورًا ﴿٢٢﴾

23. *They will be told :* [d]"This is your reward, and your effort is appreciated.'

إِنَّ هَٰذَا كَانَ لَكُمْ جَزَاءً وَكَانَ سَعْيُكُم مَّشْكُورًا ﴿٢٣﴾

R. 2 24. Surely, We have revealed unto thee the Qur'ān piecemeal.[3200]

إِنَّا نَحْنُ نَزَّلْنَا عَلَيْكَ الْقُرْآنَ تَنزِيلًا ﴿٢٤﴾

[a]52 : 25; 56 : 18. [b]18 : 32; 44 : 54. [c]18 : 32; 22 : 24; 35 : 34. [d]32 : 18; 43 : 73.

3198. In addition to the spiritual kingdom that the righteous believers are promised in the Hereafter, the Companions of the Holy Prophet were given mastery of the great empires of the time in this very life.

3199. While at the *Kāfūr* stage of spiritual journey the God-intoxicated wayfarer is described as himself seeking to drink the wine of God's love (v. 6) and at the *Zanjabīl* stage he is served by others with the life-giving beverage (v. 18), at the last or *Salsabīl* stage God Himself gives him to drink the elixir of everlasting life. This is a significant graduation in the three knds of drink. Camphor has a cooling and ginger a warming effect, and *Salsabīl* means to pursue naturally the appointed course. The first drink is tempered with camphor. It helps to cool desires and passions. The second drink, tempered with ginger, stimulates the pursuit of righteousness and *Salsabīl* marks the stage in which the believer will naturally follow the righteous course.

3200. The Qur'ān was revealed gradually and piecemeal. Its revelation spread over a period of 23 years. This gradual process served a double purpose. It helped believers to learn, remember and assimilate it and to mould their lives in accordance with its teachings. The gradual process was also intended to meet the increasing needs of changing circumstances and to strengthen the belief and conviction of Muslims, since, during the interval they had the opportunities to witness fulfilment of prophecies made earlier in the Qur'ān. The piecemeal revelation of the Qur'ān also fulfilled the following biblical prophecy :

> "For, it is precept upon precept; line upon line, here a little and there a little; for, with strange lips and another tongue will he speak to this people" (Isa. 28 : 10).

25. So wait patiently for the judgment of thy Lord and yield not to any sinful or ungrateful one among them,

فَاصْبِرْ لِحُكْمِ رَبِّكَ وَلَا تُطِعْ مِنْهُمْ اٰثِمًا اَوْ
كَفُوْرًا ﴿٢٥﴾

26. [a]And remember the name of thy Lord morning and evening,

وَاذْكُرِ اسْمَ رَبِّكَ بُكْرَةً وَّاَصِيْلًا ﴿٢٦﴾

27. [b]And during the night prostrate thyself before Him, and extol His glory for *a* long *part of the* night.

وَمِنَ الَّيْلِ فَاسْجُدْ لَهٗ وَسَبِّحْهُ لَيْلًا طَوِيْلًا ﴿٢٧﴾

28. [c]Verily, these *people* love the present life, and they neglect a very hard day ahead.

اِنَّ هٰٓؤُلَآءِ يُحِبُّوْنَ الْعَاجِلَةَ وَيَذَرُوْنَ وَرَآءَهُمْ
يَوْمًا ثَقِيْلًا ﴿٢٨﴾

29. We have created them and have strengthened their make; and when We will, [d]We can replace them by others like them.[3201]

نَحْنُ خَلَقْنٰهُمْ وَشَدَدْنَآ اَسْرَهُمْ وَاِذَا شِئْنَا بَدَّلْنَآ
اَمْثَالَهُمْ تَبْدِيْلًا ﴿٢٩﴾

30. [e]Verily, this is a Reminder. So whoever wishes, may take a way unto his Lord.

اِنَّ هٰذِهٖ تَذْكِرَةٌ فَمَنْ شَآءَ اتَّخَذَ اِلٰى رَبِّهٖ سَبِيْلًا ﴿٣٠﴾

31. [f]But you cannot *so* wish unless Allāh so wills. Verily, Allāh is All-Knowing, Wise.

وَمَا تَشَآءُوْنَ اِلَّآ اَنْ يَّشَآءَ اللّٰهُ اِنَّ اللّٰهَ كَانَ
عَلِيْمًا حَكِيْمًا ﴿٣١﴾

32. [g]He admits into His mercy[3202] whom He pleases[3203] and for the wrongdoers He has prepared a painful punishment.

يُّدْخِلُ مَنْ يَّشَآءُ فِيْ رَحْمَتِهٖ وَالظّٰلِمِيْنَ اَعَدَّ
لَهُمْ عَذَابًا اَلِيْمًا ﴿٣٢﴾

---

[a]3 : 42; 48 : 10. [b]17 : 80; 50 : 41; 52 : 50. [c]17 : 19. [d]56 : 62. [e]73 : 20; 74 : 55; 80 : 12. [f]18 : 25; 74 : 57; 81 : 30. [g]48 : 26.

3201. God has created man in the best make (95 : 5) that he may develop and manifest in himself Divine attributes. So if the disbelievers refused to benefit by the Quranic teaching they will be replaced by another people who will.

3202. Besides the meaning given in the text, the verse may mean: (1) It is God's wish that you should exercise your will to take a way unto your Lord and so be admitted into His mercy. (2) You cannot take the way unto your Lord unless you subordinate and conform your will to the Will of God. (3) You should have subordinated your will to the Will of God, but you seem not to have done so.

3203. The verse may also mean that God admits into His mercy him who himself wishes to be admitted into His mercy by obeying Divine commandments.

CHAPTER 77

AL-MURSALĀT

(*Revealed before Hijrah*)

Date of Revelation and Context

Noldeke and Muir assign the revelation of this *Sūrah*, probably correctly, to the 4th year of the Call. Like other early Meccan Chapters, this *Sūrah* also deals with the subject of Resurrection, and as an argument in support of it, adduces the great spiritual revolution that is brought about by Divine Messengers among their peoples, especially the marvellous moral change which the Holy Prophet wrought in the lives of the degenerate and decadent Arabs. The advent of Divine Prophets has been compared in the *Sūrah* to the Day of Decision when bad men are separated from good men or, to use a beautiful metaphor, when grain becomes sifted from chaff. On that Day of Decision the guilty are punished and the righteous receive the rewards of their good deeds. The *Sūrah* gives very apt and adequate description of the punishment—fittingly corresponding to their evil deeds —that will be meted out in the Hereafter to the defiers and violators of Divine laws, and goes on to describe the blessings and boons of Paradise which will be bestowed upon those who regulate their lives and conduct in accordance with them. In support of the doctrine of the Resurrection the *Sūrah* also alludes, quite convincingly, to the development of the sperm-drop into a properly shaped human being, equipped with great natural powers —in itself a wonder of creation. Towards the end, the *Sūrah* brings home to disbelievers the untenability of their rejection of the Quranic revelation.

سُورَةُ الْمُرْسَلٰتِ مَكِّيَّةٌ (٧٧)

1. [a]In the name of Allāh, the Gracious, the Merciful. بِسْمِ اللّٰهِ الرَّحْمٰنِ الرَّحِيْمِ ﴿١﴾

2. By those sent forth[3204] *to spread* goodness, وَالْمُرْسَلٰتِ عُرْفًا ﴿٢﴾

3. Then they push on with a forceful pushing,[3205] فَالْعٰصِفٰتِ عَصْفًا ﴿٣﴾

4. And *by* those who spread *the Truth,* a good spreading,[3206] وَّالنّٰشِرٰتِ نَشْرًا ﴿٤﴾

5. Then they distinguish[3207] fully *between good and evil;* فَالْفٰرِقٰتِ فَرْقًا ﴿٥﴾

6. Then they carry the Exhortation *far and wide,* فَالْمُلْقِيٰتِ ذِكْرًا ﴿٦﴾

7. To excuse *some* and warn *others,*[3208] عُذْرًا اَوْ نُذْرًا ﴿٧﴾

8. [b]Verily, that which you are promised must come to pass. اِنَّمَا تُوْعَدُوْنَ لَوَاقِعٌ ﴿٨﴾

---

[a]1 : 1. [b]51 : 6.

3204. The things, agencies or beings, mentioned in this and the following four verses, have been taken by various authorities to refer to winds; angels; God's Messengers and their followers; and particularly and very appropriately, to the Companions of the Holy Prophet. As referring to the Companions of the Holy Prophet the verse would mean that in the beginning the Companions of the Holy Prophet would spread the Message of Islām slowly and gently.

3205. After the initial difficulties in the work of the preaching having been overcome, the Companions of the Holy Prophet would proceed much faster and carry on the Message of Islām with greater vigour; or, the verse may mean that with the help of the Quranic teaching, they would scatter before them falsehood and the forces of evil as broken straw is carried before the wind.

3206. They would proclaim and spread the Message of Truth far and wide; or scatter the seeds of goodness everywhere.

3207. With the dissemination of the Quranic Message, Truth will become distinguished from falsehood and good men from bad men.

3208. The verse signifies that the fact will become established that they had conveyed and fully discharged the duty entrusted to them.

9. [a]So when the stars are made to lose *their* light,[3209]

فَإِذَا النُّجُومُ طُمِسَتْ ۝٩

10. [b]And when the heaven is rent asunder,[3210]

وَإِذَا السَّمَآءُ فُرِجَتْ ۝١٠

11. And when the mountains are blown away[3211] *like dust,*

وَإِذَا الْجِبَالُ نُسِفَتْ ۝١١

12. And when the Messengers are made to appear[3212] at the appointed time—

وَإِذَا الرُّسُلُ أُقِّتَتْ ۝١٢

13. To what day have *these portents* been deferred ?

لِأَيِّ يَوْمٍ أُجِّلَتْ ۝١٣

14. To the Day of Decision.

لِيَوْمِ الْفَصْلِ ۝١٤

15. And what should make thee know what the Day of Decision is—

وَمَآ أَدْرٰىكَ مَا يَوْمُ الْفَصْلِ ۝١٥

16. Woe on that day unto those who reject *the Truth !*

وَيْلٌ يَّوْمَئِذٍ لِّلْمُكَذِّبِيْنَ ۝١٦

17. Did We not destroy the earlier peoples ?

أَلَمْ نُهْلِكِ الْأَوَّلِيْنَ ۝١٧

18. [c]We will *now* cause the later ones to follow them.

ثُمَّ نُتْبِعُهُمُ الْاٰخِرِيْنَ ۝١٨

19. Thus do We deal with the guilty.

كَذٰلِكَ نَفْعَلُ بِالْمُجْرِمِيْنَ ۝١٩

20. Woe on that day unto those who reject *the Truth !*

وَيْلٌ يَّوْمَئِذٍ لِّلْمُكَذِّبِيْنَ ۝٢٠

[a]82 : 3 [b]78 : 21 ; 82 : 2. [c]6 : 134.

3209. The verse means, when diverse calamities are about to befall people. The Arabs regarded the disappearance of stars as a sign of impending calamities.

3210. When great calamities and miseries come upon the world.

3211. When great changes take place, or when powerful and influential men are laid low ; or when old and time-honoured institutions are destroyed, root and branch. In short, when the whole corrupt order dies out.

3212. When a great Heavenly Reformer will appear with the power and spirit of God's Messengers, clad, as it were, in the mantles of all of them.

21. Did We not create you from [a]an insignificant fluid,

أَلَمْ نَخْلُقكُّم مِّن مَّآءٍ مَّهِينٍ ﴿٢١﴾

22. And placed it in a safe resting place,

فَجَعَلْنٰهُ فِى قَرَارٍ مَّكِينٍ ﴿٢٢﴾

23. For a known measure *of time?*

إِلٰى قَدَرٍ مَّعْلُومٍ ﴿٢٣﴾

24. Thus did We determine;[3213] and how excellent Determiner *are We!*

فَقَدَرْنَا فَنِعْمَ الْقٰدِرُوْنَ ﴿٢٤﴾

25. Woe on that day unto those who reject *the Truth!*

وَيْلٌ يَّوْمَئِذٍ لِّلْمُكَذِّبِيْنَ ﴿٢٥﴾

26. [b]Have We not made the earth so as to hold

أَلَمْ نَجْعَلِ الْأَرْضَ كِفَاتًا ﴿٢٦﴾

27. The living and the dead?[3214]

أَحْيَآءً وَّأَمْوٰتًا ﴿٢٧﴾

28. [c]And We placed therein high mountains, and gave you sweet water to drink.[3215]

وَّجَعَلْنَا فِيْهَا رَوٰسِىَ شٰمِخٰتٍ وَّأَسْقَيْنٰكُمْ مَّآءً فُرَاتًا ﴿٢٨﴾

29. Woe on that day unto those who reject *the Truth!*

وَيْلٌ يَّوْمَئِذٍ لِّلْمُكَذِّبِيْنَ ﴿٢٩﴾

30. *They will be commanded:* '*Now* move on towards that which you treated as a lie,

اِنْطَلِقُوْٓا إِلٰى مَا كُنْتُمْ بِهٖ تُكَذِّبُوْنَ ﴿٣٠﴾

[a]32 : 9. [b]7 : 26. [c]13 : 4; 15 : 20; 21 : 32; 31 : 11.

3213. This and the preceding three verses refer to the extremely subtle process of the development of sperm-drop in the womb, into a full-fledged human being, which indeed is a marvel of creation. This process of creation is advanced as an argument in support of the Resurrection, for there exists a beautiful parallelism between the two, the mother's womb being likened to man's life on earth and his birth to Resurrection.

3214. All mortals live on earth, and when they are dead, their remains, in one form or other, abide in the earth. The verse may also refer to the law of gravitation or to earth's motion on its axis or round the sun. The word, *Kifāt*, may also signify that all the physical needs of man have been met in the earth.

3215. Mountains serve as great natural reservoirs of water.

31. 'Aye, move on towards a three-pronged shadow,[3216]

انْطَلِقُوٓا اِلٰى ظِلٍّ ذِى ثَلٰثِ شُعَبٍ ﴿٣١﴾

32. 'Neither affording shade, nor protecting from the flame.'[3217]

لَّا ظَلِيْلٍ وَّ لَا يُغْنِىْ مِنَ اللَّهَبِ ﴿٣٢﴾

33. It throws up sparks like *huge* castles,[3218]

اِنَّهَا تَرْمِىْ بِشَرَرٍ كَالْقَصْرِ ﴿٣٣﴾

34. As if they were tawny camels.[3218A]

كَاَنَّهٗ جِمٰلَتٌ صُفْرٌ ﴿٣٤﴾

35. Woe on that day unto those who reject *the Truth!*

وَيْلٌ يَّوْمَئِذٍ لِّلْمُكَذِّبِيْنَ ﴿٣٥﴾

36. This is a day when they [a]shall not *be able to* speak,[3219]

هٰذَا يَوْمُ لَا يَنْطِقُوْنَ ﴿٣٦﴾

37. [b]Nor shall they be permitted to offer excuses.[3220]

وَ لَا يُؤْذَنُ لَهُمْ فَيَعْتَذِرُوْنَ ﴿٣٧﴾

38. Woe on that day unto those who reject *the Truth!*

وَيْلٌ يَّوْمَئِذٍ لِّلْمُكَذِّبِيْنَ ﴿٣٨﴾

---

[a]78 : 39. [b]9 : 66; 66 : 8.

3216. The wrong beliefs, foolish usages and practices, of disbelievers will take the form of three-pronged shadow in the next world. Or, according to Ibn 'Abbās the reference is to the Christian doctrine of the Trinity. Or, the verse may mean that disbelievers will be punished from the right, the left and from above. Moreover, teachers of moral wisdom point to three factors which operate against the development of proper awareness of one's duties—lack of sensitivity, lack of thought and lack of judgment. Similarly, three factors are said to operate against moral impulses having their course—fear, arrogance and sensual desires. In the language of psychology we could say that three factors are responsible for sending a man to Hell—errors of perception and reasoning, delinquencies of sex and weaknesses of will.

3217. See 56 : 43-45.

3218. As disbelievers sought ease and comfort and took pride in castles and stately buildings, their sins and transgressions will take the form of flames of fire rising high like huge castles.

3218A. The Arabs took pride in their camels which formed their greatest source of wealth.

3219. See 2457.

3220. The guilt of disbelievers having been fully established, they will not be allowed to offer any excuse or explanation.

39. [a]"This is the Day of Decision. We have gathered you and all the earlier peoples together;

هٰذَا يَوْمُ الْفَصْلِ جَمَعْنٰكُمْ وَالْاَوَّلِيْنَ ﴿٤٠﴾

40. 'If now you have any stratagem, try *your* stratagem against me.[3221]

فَاِنْ كَانَ لَكُمْ كَيْدٌ فَكِيْدُوْنِ ﴿٤١﴾

41. Woe on that day unto those who reject *the Truth!*

وَيْلٌ يَّوْمَئِذٍ لِّلْمُكَذِّبِيْنَ ﴿٤٢﴾ ع

R. 2 42. [b]The righteous will be in *the midst of* shades and springs,

اِنَّ الْمُتَّقِيْنَ فِيْ ظِلٰلٍ وَّعُيُوْنٍ ﴿٤٣﴾

43. [c]And fruits, such as they will desire.

وَّفَوَاكِهَ مِمَّا يَشْتَهُوْنَ ﴿٤٤﴾

44. *It will be said to them,* 'Eat and drink pleasantly as a reward for what you did'—

كُلُوْا وَاشْرَبُوْا هَنِيْٓـًٔا بِمَا كُنْتُمْ تَعْمَلُوْنَ ﴿٤٥﴾

45. Thus, surely, do We reward those who do good.

اِنَّا كَذٰلِكَ نَجْزِي الْمُحْسِنِيْنَ ﴿٤٦﴾

46. Woe on that day unto those who reject *the Truth*—

وَيْلٌ يَّوْمَئِذٍ لِّلْمُكَذِّبِيْنَ ﴿٤٧﴾

47. [d]"Eat and enjoy yourselves for a little while *in this world, O rejectors of Truth*, surely, you are the guilty ones.'

كُلُوْا وَتَمَتَّعُوْا قَلِيْلًا اِنَّكُمْ مُّجْرِمُوْنَ ﴿٤٨﴾

48. Woe on that day unto those who reject *the Truth!*

وَيْلٌ يَّوْمَئِذٍ لِّلْمُكَذِّبِيْنَ ﴿٤٩﴾

49. And when it is said unto them, 'Bow down,' they bow not down.

وَاِذَا قِيْلَ لَهُمُ ارْكَعُوْا لَا يَرْكَعُوْنَ ﴿٥٠﴾

[a]37 : 22. [b]56 : 31. [c]52 : 23; 55 : 53; 56 : 33. [d]14 : 31.

3221. The Holy Prophet's enemies have been challenged to do their worst against him.

50. Woe on that day unto those who reject *the Truth!*

وَيۡلٌ يَّوۡمَئِذٍ لِّلۡمُكَذِّبِيۡنَ ﴿۵۰﴾

51. In what discourse[3222] then, after this, will they believe?

فَبِاَيِّ حَدِيۡثٍۭ بَعۡدَهٗ يُؤۡمِنُوۡنَ ﴿۵۱﴾

3222. As these ill-fated disbelievers have refused to accept such an infallible Book as the Qur'ān, they will never listen to Truth and find the right path.

CHAPTER 78

AL-NABA'

(*Revealed before Hijrah*)

Date of Revelation and Context

The *Sūrah* is entitled Al-Naba' because it deals with subjects of exceptional importance *i.e.*, certainty of Resurrection, predominance of the Qur'ān over all other revealed Scriptures, and of Islām over all other Faiths. The Day of Decision, *i.e.*, the day when this Quranic claim will become an established fact, is mentioned twice in the preceding *Sūrah* and is repeated here. According to Muslim Commentators the *Sūrah* was revealed very early in the Holy Prophet's ministry at Mecca. Noldeke agrees with this Muslim scholarly opinion. It opens with enumerating the great Divine gifts bestowed upon man, and directs his attention to the implied suggestions that he has been placed upon this earth to serve a certain object and his life here is the seed-bed of an eternal future and it will be followed by a Day of Reckoning. The *Sūrah* then gives a brief but an awe-inspiring picture of that Day, and a graphic description of the heavenly blessings that await the righteous and of the terrible punishment which will be meted out to the rejectors of Truth in this life and in the next.

سُوْرَةُ النَّبَاِ مَكِّيَّةٌ (٧٨)

PART XXX

1. In the name of Allāh, the Gracious, the Merciful.

بِسْمِ اللّٰهِ الرَّحْمٰنِ الرَّحِيْمِ ①

2. What do they question one another about?

عَمَّ يَتَسَآءَلُوْنَ ②

3. About the mighty Event,[3223]

عَنِ النَّبَاِ الْعَظِيْمِ ③

4. Concerning which they differ.[3224]

الَّذِيْ هُمْ فِيْهِ مُخْتَلِفُوْنَ ④

5. Nay, [a]soon they will come to know.

كَلَّا سَيَعْلَمُوْنَ ⑤

6. Nay, *We say it* again, they will soon come to know.

ثُمَّ كَلَّا سَيَعْلَمُوْنَ ⑥

7. [b]Have We not made the earth as a bed,

اَلَمْ نَجْعَلِ الْاَرْضَ مِهٰدًا ⑦

8. And the mountains as pegs?

وَّالْجِبَالَ اَوْتَادًا ⑧

9. [c]And We have created you in pairs,

وَّخَلَقْنٰكُمْ اَزْوَاجًا ⑨

10. And have made your sleep for rest,

وَّجَعَلْنَا نَوْمَكُمْ سُبَاتًا ⑩

11. [d]And have made the night as a covering,

وَّجَعَلْنَا الَّيْلَ لِبَاسًا ⑪

12. [e]And have made the day for the pursuits of life.

وَّجَعَلْنَا النَّهَارَ مَعَاشًا ⑫

13. [f]And We have built above you seven strong *ones*;[3225]

وَّبَنَيْنَا فَوْقَكُمْ سَبْعًا شِدَادًا ⑬

---

[a]102 : 4-5. [b]2 : 23 ; 20 : 54 ; 51 : 49. [c]36 : 37 ; 51 : 50 ; 75 : 40 ; 92 : 4. [d]6 : 97 ; 25 : 48 ; 28 : 74. [e]17 : 13 ; 28 : 74. [f]23 : 18.

3223. The addition of the qualifying word, *Al-'Aẓīm* (mighty) to *Al-Naba'* which itself means a great news or event, suggests the tremendous import of the event referred to here.

3224. The disbelievers do not believe that there will ever be a Day of Reckoning.

3225. Seven major planets of the solar system of which the sun is the centre, or seven stages of spiritual development of man mentioned in *Sūrah* Al-Mu'minūn.

14. And have made *the sun* a bright lamp.

وَّجَعَلْنَا سِرَاجًا وَّهَّاجًا ﴿۱۴﴾

15. [a]And We send down from the dripping clouds water pouring forth abundantly.

وَّاَنْزَلْنَا مِنَ الْمُعْصِرٰتِ مَآءً ثَجَّاجًا ﴿۱۵﴾

16. [b]That We may bring forth thereby grain and vegetation,

لِّنُخْرِجَ بِهٖ حَبًّا وَّنَبَاتًا ﴿۱۶﴾

17. [c]And gardens of luxuriant growth.[3226]

وَّجَنّٰتٍ اَلْفَافًا ﴿۱۷﴾

18. Surely, the Day of Decision is an appointed time—

اِنَّ يَوْمَ الْفَصْلِ كَانَ مِيْقَاتًا ﴿۱۸﴾

19. [d]The day when the trumpet will be blown, and you will come in large groups.[3227]

يَّوْمَ يُنْفَخُ فِي الصُّوْرِ فَتَاْتُوْنَ اَفْوَاجًا ﴿۱۹﴾

20. And the heaven shall be opened and shall become *all* doors.[3228]

وَّفُتِحَتِ السَّمَآءُ فَكَانَتْ اَبْوَابًا ﴿۲۰﴾

21. [e]And the mountains shall be set in motion and shall become, *as if they were*, a mirage.[3229]

وَّسُيِّرَتِ الْجِبَالُ فَكَانَتْ سَرَابًا ﴿۲۱﴾

22. Surely, Hell lies in ambush,

اِنَّ جَهَنَّمَ كَانَتْ مِرْصَادًا ﴿۲۲﴾

23. A resort for the rebellious,

لِّلطّٰغِيْنَ مَاٰبًا ﴿۲۳﴾

---

[a]6 : 7; 71 : 12; 78 : 15; 80 : 26. [b]80 : 28-29. [c]80 : 31. [d]18 : 100; 20 : 103; 27 : 88; 36 : 52. [e]18 : 48; 52 : 11; 81 : 4.

3226. In these verses (7-17) some of the basic Divine bounties on which man's physical sustenance mainly depends have been mentioned, the implication being that God Who has made such adequate arrangement for the physical sustenance of man could not have neglected to make a similar provision for his spiritual sustenance.

3227. On the Day of Decision—the day of the Fall of Mecca—the Quraish, as if by the blowing of the trumpet, were gathered before the Holy Prophet, requesting him that their tyrannies and transgressions might be forgiven.

3228. At that time heavenly Signs will be shown in large numbers in support of the righteous and to the confusion of the wrongdoers.

3229. The verse means that (1) men of power and position will lose their authority and influence. (2) Before the onrush of the conquests of Islām great and firmly-founded empires will crumble like mounds of loose sand and will disappear so completely that it would seem that their erstwhile existence was only an optical illusion.

24. [a]Who will tarry therein for ages.

لّٰبِثِيْنَ فِيْهَآ اَحْقَابًا ﴿٢٤﴾

25. They will taste therein neither coolness,[3230] nor drink,

لَا يَذُوْقُوْنَ فِيْهَا بَرْدًا وَّلَا شَرَابًا ﴿٢٥﴾

26. [b]Save boiling water and a stinking fluid, intensely cold[3230A]—

اِلَّا حَمِيْمًا وَّغَسَّاقًا ﴿٢٦﴾

27. A meet requital.

جَزَآءً وِّفَاقًا ﴿٢٧﴾

28. Verily, they feared not the reckoning,

اِنَّهُمْ كَانُوْا لَا يَرْجُوْنَ حِسَابًا ﴿٢٨﴾

29. [c]And rejected Our Signs totally.

وَّكَذَّبُوْا بِاٰيٰتِنَا كِذَّابًا ﴿٢٩﴾

30. [d]And everything have We recorded in a Book.[3231]

وَكُلَّ شَيْءٍ اَحْصَيْنٰهُ كِتٰبًا ﴿٣٠﴾

31. 'Taste ye, therefore, *the punishment;* We will give you no increase except in torment.'

فَذُوْقُوْا فَلَنْ نَّزِيْدَكُمْ اِلَّا عَذَابًا ﴿٣١﴾

R. 2 32. Verily, for the righteous is *decreed* a triumph—

اِنَّ لِلْمُتَّقِيْنَ مَفَازًا ﴿٣٢﴾

33. Walled gardens and grape-vines,[3232]

حَدَآئِقَ وَاَعْنَابًا ﴿٣٣﴾

[a]11 : 108. [b]6 : 71; 69 : 37. [c]2 : 40; 7 : 37. [d]36 : 13.

3230. *Bard* means, coolness; pleasantness; comfort; sleep (Lane).

3230A. The turbulent pursuit of evil and cold indifference towards virtue and righteousness of wrongdoers will take the form of boiling water and intensely cold and stinking drink.

3231. Invention of television, wireless, tape-record and other kindred instruments has established the fact that not only man's actions but even his spoken words can be preserved and are, in fact, reproduced. See also 2456.

3232. Among the paradisiacal blessings grape-vines finds very frequent mention in the Qur'ān. This is because grape is a delicious and substantial food. It can be preserved for a long time, and causes intoxication. *Taqwā* (righteousness) also possesses all these three characteristics. So grape-vine is a fit reward for the righteous.

34. [a]And young maidens of equal age,[3233]

وَّكَوَاعِبَ اَتْرَابًا ﴿٣٤﴾

35. And over-flowing cups.[3234]

وَّكَاْسًا دِهَاقًا ﴿٣٥﴾

36. [b]Therein they will hear no vain discourse nor lying;

لَا يَسْمَعُوْنَ فِيْهَا لَغْوًا وَّلَا كِذّٰبًا ﴿٣٦﴾

37. A recompense from thy Lord —a gift amply sufficient—

جَزَآءً مِّنْ رَّبِّكَ عَطَآءً حِسَابًا ﴿٣٧﴾

38. [c]Lord of the heavens and the earth and all that is between them, the Gracious *God*. They shall not have the power to address Him.

رَّبِّ السَّمٰوٰتِ وَالْاَرْضِ وَمَا بَيْنَهُمَا الرَّحْمٰنِ لَا يَمْلِكُوْنَ مِنْهُ خِطَابًا ﴿٣٨﴾

39. On the day when the Spirit[3234A] and the angels will stand in rows, [d]they shall not speak, except he whom the Gracious *God* will grant leave, and who will speak *only* what is right.

يَوْمَ يَقُوْمُ الرُّوْحُ وَالْمَلٰٓئِكَةُ صَفًّا ۙ لَّا يَتَكَلَّمُوْنَ اِلَّا مَنْ اَذِنَ لَهُ الرَّحْمٰنُ وَقَالَ صَوَابًا ﴿٣٩﴾

40. That day is sure to come. So let him, who will, seek recourse unto his Lord.

ذٰلِكَ الْيَوْمُ الْحَقُّ ۚ فَمَنْ شَآءَ اتَّخَذَ اِلٰى رَبِّهٖ مَاٰبًا ﴿٤٠﴾

41. Verily, We have warned you of a punishment which is near at hand[3235]—a day when man will see what his hands have sent on before and the disbeliever will say, [e]"Would that I were mere dust !'

اِنَّآ اَنْذَرْنٰكُمْ عَذَابًا قَرِيْبًا ۚ يَّوْمَ يَنْظُرُ الْمَرْءُ مَا قَدَّمَتْ يَدٰهُ وَيَقُوْلُ الْكٰفِرُ يٰلَيْتَنِيْ كُنْتُ تُرٰبًا ﴿٤١﴾ ع

[a]56 : 38. [b]19 : 63; 52 : 24; 56 : 26. [c]19 : 66. [d]11 : 106. [e]4 : 43.

3233. The righteous will have companions or wives possessing freshness and vigour of youth and enjoying eminent position. They will be of noble descent and will be fired with high and noble ambitions, *Kā'ib* of which the plural is *Kawā'ib* meaning nobility; glory; eminence (Lane). Elsewhere (56 : 35) in the Qur'ān, companions of the righteous believers have been described as *Furushun Marfū'atun*, *i.e.*, noble spouses. For a full discussion of the nature and significance of heavenly blessings, see Chapters Al-Ṭūr, Al-Raḥmān and Al-Wāqi'ah.

3234. The God-intoxicated pilgrim, whose heart is so full of the love of God as to overflow with it, will deservedly be given to drink cups full of beverage that will add to their spiritual intoxication which will not abate.

3234A. "The Spirit" here may signify the perfect spirit—the Holy Prophet; and "the day" may mean the Day of Resurrection.

3235. "The punishment" may be the punishment which is meted out to the sinful disbelievers in this world. Elsewhere in the Qur'ān (32 : 22) this punishment has been described as nearer punishment as against the greater punishment which is punishment in the Hereafter.

CHAPTER 79

AL-NĀZI'ĀT

(Revealed before Hijrah)

General Remarks

All competent authorities, including Ibn 'Abbās and Ibn Zubair agree that, like the preceding Chapter this is a very early Meccan *Sūrah*. In that *Sūrah*, the Muslims were promised power, prosperity and predominance in the world. In the present *Sūrah* light is shed on the ways and means by which they could achieve these things, as well as on the signs and marks that point towards the imminent fulfilment of that promise. The *Sūrah* opens with a description of some of the special traits of character of the Holy Prophet's Companions and of other groups of righteous men who, by bringing into play these characteristics, achieved glory, power and victory. The *Sūrah* then points out that power will come to Muslims as a result of wars which will break the power of the enemies of Islām. The case of Pharaoh is cited to show that opposition to Truth never goes unpunished. Next, we are told that in the extremely weak condition of early Muslims, prophecies about a glorious future of Islām seemed impossible of fulfilment, but the Great God Who created the vast heavens and earth and Who placed on it rivers and mountains and high ways, had the power to make the impossible possible, and also that He can give a new life to the dead in the next world. Towards the close of the *Sūrah* it is stated that when the great Event—the complete triumph of Islām or the Final Resurrection—takes place, the guilty will burn in the fire of Hell, but those, who had lived a life of righteousness, will enjoy the blessings of Paradise.

سُوۡرَةُ النّٰزِعٰتِ مَکِّیَّۃٌ (۷۹)

1. [a]In the name of Allāh, the Gracious, the Merciful.

بِسۡمِ اللّٰہِ الرَّحۡمٰنِ الرَّحِیۡمِ ﴿۱﴾

2. By those who draw[3236] *people to* the *true Faith* vigorously,[3237]

وَ النّٰزِعٰتِ غَرۡقًا ﴿۲﴾

3. And *by* those who tie *their* knots firmly,[3238]

وَّ النّٰشِطٰتِ نَشۡطًا ﴿۳﴾

4. And *by* those who glide along swiftly,

وَّ السّٰبِحٰتِ سَبۡحًا ﴿۴﴾

5. Then they *advance and* greatly excel[3239] *others,*

فَالسّٰبِقٰتِ سَبۡقًا ﴿۵﴾

6. Then they administer affairs[3240] *in an excellent manner;*

فَالۡمُدَبِّرٰتِ اَمۡرًا ﴿۶﴾

---

[a]1 : 1.

3236. *Nāzi'āt* is derived from *Naza'a* and means, those beings or groups of people that pluck a thing; depose high officials ; resemble; draw with vigour; invite others to truth (Aqrab), the root-word possessing all these senses.

3237. *Gharq* is used here in the sense of *Ighrāq* which signifies the sending of the arrow to the utmost extent, or falling upon a person and overcoming him; or exerting oneself to the utmost extent (Lane).

3238. *Nāshiṭāt* means, those beings or groups of people who exert themselves vigorously in the discharge of their duties (Aqrab).

3239. *Sābiḥāt* means, (1) those beings or groups of people who go far into the country in the pursuit of their quest. (2) Who try to excel one another in carrying out their mission (Lane).

3240. *Mudabbirāt* means, those beings or groups of people who plan, manage and conduct the affairs entrusted to them in an excellent manner.

The verses (2-6) are taken to apply to angels by some scholars and Commentators of the Qur'ān and have been understood to signify that angels bear witness to the occurrence of the great event mentioned in vv. 7-8. But the evidence of angels is beyond human knowledge or comprehension. The verses, therefore, as the context shows, seem to refer to the Companions of the Holy Prophet and may be taken as embodying a prophecy about the spread of Islām far and wide through their selfless and vigorous efforts and a further prophecy that they would be entrusted with the responsibility of conducting and administering public affairs of great importance with ability and justice. Briefly, the verses mention some of the prominent qualities of the Holy Prophet's Companions. See also "The Larger Edition of the Commentary."

7. *This will be* on the day when [a]the quaking *earth* shall quake,[3241]

يَوْمَ تَرْجُفُ الرَّاجِفَةُ ۙ ﴿٧﴾

8. *And* a second *quaking* shall follow[3242] it.

تَتْبَعُهَا الرَّادِفَةُ ۗ ﴿٨﴾

9. On that day hearts will tremble,

قُلُوْبٌ يَّوْمَىِٕذٍ وَّاجِفَةٌ ۙ ﴿٩﴾

10. [b]*And* their eyes will be cast down.[3243]

اَبْصَارُهَا خَاشِعَةٌ ۘ ﴿١٠﴾

11. They say, 'Shall we *really* be restored to our former state?

يَقُوْلُوْنَ ءَ اِنَّا لَمَرْدُوْدُوْنَ فِى الْحَافِرَةِ ۗ ﴿١١﴾

12. [c]'What! even when we are rotten bones?'

ءَ اِذَا كُنَّا عِظَامًا نَّخِرَةً ۗ ﴿١٢﴾

13. They say, 'Then that, indeed, would be a losing return.'

قَالُوْا تِلْكَ اِذًا كَرَّةٌ خَاسِرَةٌ ۘ ﴿١٣﴾

14. It will only be a single cry,

فَاِنَّمَا هِىَ زَجْرَةٌ وَّاحِدَةٌ ۙ ﴿١٤﴾

15. And behold! they will *all come out* in the open.

فَاِذَا هُمْ بِالسَّاهِرَةِ ۗ ﴿١٥﴾

16. Has the story of Moses reached thee?

هَلْ اَتٰىكَ حَدِيْثُ مُوْسٰى ۘ ﴿١٦﴾

17. When his Lord called him in the holy Valley of Ṭuwā,

اِذْ نَادٰىهُ رَبُّهٗ بِالْوَادِ الْمُقَدَّسِ طُوًى ۚ ﴿١٧﴾

18. *And directed him:* 'Go thou to Pharaoh; he has rebelled,'

اِذْهَبْ اِلٰى فِرْعَوْنَ اِنَّهٗ طَغٰى ۖ ﴿١٨﴾

---

[a]56 : 5-6; 73 : 15. [b]70 : 45. [c]17 : 50; 36 : 79.

3241. The verse means that the prophecy, proclaimed in the foregoing verses, will be fulfilled as a result of fighting that will take place between God's righteous servants and the forces of evil in which the latter shall be routed, *Rajafa* meaning to perpare for war (Lane).

3242. Once the fighting starts between Muslims and infidels, it will not cease till the forces of evil are fully and finally crushed as a result of the successive blows they will receive.

3243. When disbelievers will suffer defeats in quick succession and will see Islām prevailing and predominating, then will a feeling of disquietude seize them, and apprehension about the possibility of the Resurrection will begin to assail their minds.

19. "And say *to him*, 'Wouldst thou be purified?

فَقُلْ هَلْ لَّكَ اِلٰٓى اَنْ تَزَكّٰى ﴿۱۹﴾

20. 'And I will guide thee to thy Lord so that thou mayest fear Him."

وَاَهْدِيَكَ اِلٰى رَبِّكَ فَتَخْشٰى ﴿۲۰﴾

21. [a]So he showed him the great Sign,[3244]

فَاَرٰىهُ الْاٰيَةَ الْكُبْرٰى ﴿۲۱﴾

22. But he rejected *him* and disobeyed;

فَكَذَّبَ وَعَصٰى ﴿۲۲﴾

23. Then he turned away *from the Truth*, devising schemes;

ثُمَّ اَدْبَرَ يَسْعٰى ﴿۲۳﴾

24. And he gathered *his people*, and proclaimed,

فَحَشَرَ فَنَادٰى ﴿۲۴﴾

25. Saying, 'I am your [b]Lord, the Most High.'

فَقَالَ اَنَا رَبُّكُمُ الْاَعْلٰى ﴿۲۵﴾

26. So Allāh seized him for the punishment of the Hereafter and the present world.

فَاَخَذَهُ اللّٰهُ نَكَالَ الْاٰخِرَةِ وَالْاُوْلٰى ﴿۲۶﴾

27. Therein, surely, is a lesson for him who fears *his Lord*.

اِنَّ فِيْ ذٰلِكَ لَعِبْرَةً لِّمَنْ يَّخْشٰى ﴿۲۷﴾

R. 2 28. Are you harder to create or the heaven that *Allāh* has made?[3245]

ءَاَنْتُمْ اَشَدُّ خَلْقًا اَمِ السَّمَآءُ بَنٰىهَا ﴿۲۸﴾

29. [c]He has raised the height[3245A] thereof and has made it perfect.

رَفَعَ سَمْكَهَا فَسَوّٰىهَا ﴿۲۹﴾

---

[a]20 : 57. [b]26 : 30; 28 : 39. [c]21 : 33.

3244. 'The great Sign' was the Sign of the Rod, which had precedence over all other Signs shown by Moses (20 : 21).

3245. The complex, but flawless and consummate, creation of the solar system, does indeed constitute an invincible argument in support of Life after death, *viz.*, that the Great God, Who could bring into being from nothing such a vast universe, could also give man, who is but a mere speck in it, a new life after he is dead. This is the purport of the present and the following six verses.

3245A. *Samk* means, the roof; the ceiling of a house; height, depth and thickness of a thing (Lane).

30. And [a]He has made its night dark; and has brought forth the morn thereof;[3246]

وَأَغْطَشَ لَيْلَهَا وَأَخْرَجَ ضُحٰهَا ٣٠

31. [b]And the earth, along with it, He has spread forth.[3247]

وَالْأَرْضَ بَعْدَ ذٰلِكَ دَحٰهَا ٣١

32. [c]He produced therefrom its water and its pasture,

أَخْرَجَ مِنْهَا مَآءَهَا وَمَرْعٰهَا ٣٢

33. [d]And the mountains, He made them firm.

وَالْجِبَالَ أَرْسٰهَا ٣٣

34. [e]*All this is* a provision for you and for your cattle.

مَتَاعًا لَّكُمْ وَلِأَنْعَامِكُمْ ٣٤

35. [f]But when the great calamity comes,

فَإِذَا جَآءَتِ الطَّآمَّةُ الْكُبْرٰى ٣٥

36. [g]The day when man will call to mind *all* that he strove for,

يَوْمَ يَتَذَكَّرُ الْإِنْسَانُ مَا سَعٰى ٣٦

37. [h]And Hell will be made manifest to him who sees.

وَبُرِّزَتِ الْجَحِيمُ لِمَنْ يَّرٰى ٣٧

38. Then, as for him who rebels,

فَأَمَّا مَنْ طَغٰى ٣٨

39. And prefers the life of this world,

وَاٰثَرَ الْحَيٰوةَ الدُّنْيَا ٣٩

40. The fire of Hell shall, surely, be *his* abode.

فَإِنَّ الْجَحِيمَ هِيَ الْمَأْوٰى ٤٠

41. [i]But as for him who fears to stand[3248] before his Lord, and restrains his soul from evil desires,

وَأَمَّا مَنْ خَافَ مَقَامَ رَبِّهٖ وَنَهَى النَّفْسَ عَنِ الْهَوٰى ٤١

---

[a]78 : 11-12. [b]20 : 54; 51 : 49. [c]20 : 54; 50 : 8. [d]50 : 8. [e]80 : 33. [f]74 : 36; 80 : 34. [g]89 : 24. [h]26 : 92. [i]55 : 47.

3246. The phenomenon of night and day, which pertains to the earth, has been attributed to the heaven in this verse because it is due to the working of the solar system that we have day and night.

3247. Besides the meaning given in the text, the verse signifies that the earth became castaway from a bigger mass.

3248. Who fears to stand before his Lord as a guilty person; or (2) who fears the Majesty of his Lord.

42. The Garden shall, surely, be *his* abode.

فَإِنَّ الْجَنَّةَ هِيَ الْمَأْوٰى ﴿٤٢﴾

43. [a]They ask thee concerning the Hour: 'When will it take place?'

يَسْـَٔلُوْنَكَ عَنِ السَّاعَةِ اَيَّانَ مُرْسٰهَا ﴿٤٣﴾

44. Wherein art thou *concerned* with the talk *of its coming?*

فِيْمَ اَنْتَ مِنْ ذِكْرٰىهَا ﴿٤٤﴾

45. The ultimate *knowledge* of it *rests* with thy Lord.

اِلٰى رَبِّكَ مُنْتَهٰهَا ﴿٤٥﴾

46. Thou art only a Warner unto him who fears it.

اِنَّمَآ اَنْتَ مُنْذِرُ مَنْ يَّخْشٰهَا ﴿٤٦﴾

47. [b]On the day when they see it, *it will be* as if they had not tarried *in the world* but an evening or a morn thereof.[3249]

كَاَنَّهُمْ يَوْمَ يَرَوْنَهَا لَمْ يَلْبَثُوْٓا اِلَّا عَشِيَّةً اَوْ ضُحٰهَا ﴿٤٧﴾ ع ٢

[a]7 : 188; 33 : 64; 51 : 13. [b]10 : 46; 30 : 56; 46 : 36.

3249. It is not the time, the place, the manner or the form of the punishment that matters. What matters is that disbelievers should realize that when Divine punishment comes, it will be so swift, sudden and severe that they will feel as if the period of their prosperity and enjoyment in the world was of a very short duration—only an evening or a morning.

CHAPTER 80

'ABASA

(*Revealed before Hijrah*)

Context and Subject-Matter

This *Sūrah*, like the two preceding it, is among those Chapters which were revealed at Mecca in the very early years of the Call. Noldeke and Muir, besides Muslim scholars, subscribe to this view. Towards the end of the preceding Chapter, the Holy Prophet was told that his duty was confined to conveying the Divine Message to his people. The present *Sūrah* opens to deal with the incident of 'Abd Allāh ibn Umm Maktūm, and proceeds to teach the moral lesson that it is not worldly riches and social status which determine the real worth of a person, but the goodness of his heart and willingness on his part to listen to truth and accept it. It also constitutes an eloquent commentary on the Holy Prophet's regard for the susceptibilities of the poor and oppressed people. It further says that being the last Divine Message for mankind the Qur'ān will be respected and read all over the world and will be protected and preserved. The *Sūrah* ends on a note of warning to disbelievers that if they rejected its Message and persisted in opposing the Holy Prophet they will have to face a day of reckoning when misery, shame and ignominy will be their lot. The righteous believers, however, will reside in the 'Gardens of Bliss,' their faces beaming with Divine joy and happiness.

سُوْرَةُ عَبَسَ مَكِّيَّةٌ (٨٠)

1. In the name of Allāh, the Gracious, the Merciful.

بِسْمِ اللّٰهِ الرَّحْمٰنِ الرَّحِيْمِ ۝١

2. He frowned[3250] and turned aside,

عَبَسَ وَتَوَلّٰٓى ۝٢

3. Because there came to him the blind man;

اَنْ جَآءَهُ الْاَعْمٰى ۝٣

4. And what would make thee know that he would purify himself,[3251]

وَمَا يُدْرِيْكَ لَعَلَّهٗ يَزَّكّٰٓى ۝٤

5. Or, that he would take heed and the taking of heed would benefit him?

اَوْ يَذَّكَّرُ فَتَنْفَعَهُ الذِّكْرٰى ۝٥

6. *How could it be* that he who is disdainfully indifferent *to the Truth*,

اَمَّا مَنِ اسْتَغْنٰى ۝٦

3250. The verse refers to a well-known historical incident. As the Holy Prophet was engaged one day in a talk with some of the Quraish chiefs about some matters of belief, there came up 'Abd Allāh ibn Umm Maktūm and, thinking that the Holy Prophet's precious time and energy were being wasted on the confirmed leaders of disbelief, he sought to divert his attention and asked to be enlightened on some religious questions. The Holy Prophet disliked the intrusion, and showed his displeasure by turning aside from 'Abd Allāh (Ṭabarī & Bayān). While it showed the Holy Prophet's solicitude for the spiritual well-being of the Quraish leaders in that he continued his discourse with them and paid no heed to 'Abd Allāh's interruption, the incident constituted also an evidence of his great regard for the tender susceptibilities of the blind man, because he merely turned his face away from him—an act which the latter could not see—and did not say even a word of reproach or disapprobation to him for his inopportune and rash interruption, thus taking scrupulous care not to wound his self-respect and tender susceptibilities. The verse thus throws a flood of light on the very high moral stature of the Holy Prophet; and instead of implying any Divine reproach or rebuke, as some Commentators seem to think, enjoins him and, in reality through him, his followers, to have due regard for the tender susceptibilities of the poor and the humble.

3251. The pronoun "thee" in the verse may be applied, as is done in the text, to the Holy Prophet and the pronoun "he" to the Quraish leader.

7. Unto him thou shouldst pay attention[3252]—	فَاَنْتَ لَهٗ تَصَدّٰى ۝٧
8. Though thou art not responsible if he does not become purified[3253]—	وَمَا عَلَيْكَ اَلَّا يَزَّكّٰى ۝٨
9. But he who comes to thee hastening,	وَاَمَّا مَنْ جَآءَكَ يَسْعٰى ۝٩
10. And he fears *God*,	وَهُوَ يَخْشٰى ۝١٠
11. Him shouldst thou neglect,[3254]	فَاَنْتَ عَنْهُ تَلَهّٰى ۝١١
12. *That should not be!* Surely, it is a [a]Reminder[3255]—	كَلَّآ اِنَّهَا تَذْكِرَةٌ ۝١٢
13. So let him who desires pay heed to it—	فَمَنْ شَآءَ ذَكَرَهٗ ۝١٣

[a]20 : 4 ; 73 : 20 ; 74 : 55.

3252. *Taṣadda la-hū* means, he addressed or applied or directed himself or his regard or attention or mind to him or it; he wanted; he inclined towards him or it (Lane).

3253. The verse constitutes an effective justification of the Holy Prophet's attitude towards 'Abd Allāh ibn Umm Maktūm. It purports to say that the Holy Prophet was not responsible if the Quraish leader did not benefit by his talk. His attitude of seeming indifference towards 'Abd Allāh or of deference towards the Quraish leader proceeded from no consideration of any personal interest. It was solely dictated by the commandments of the *Sharī'ah* about behaving kindly and courteously towards one's visitors.

3254. Verses 6-11 are applied to the Holy Prophet, the particle *Ammā* in the 6th verse signifies "how could it be that," *i. e.*, 'it cannot be;' and these verses would be interpreted as : 'How could it be possible that thou shouldst pay attention to him who is disdainfully indifferent and should neglect him who fears God and comes to thee hastening.' But these verses may also be applied to the Quraish leader who, as some Commentators are of the view, frowned and turned aside because there came to the Prophet the blind man. In this case these verses would be understood as having been used ironically and as bringing home to the critics of the Holy Prophet their own state of mind, and not referring to any weakness imputed to the Holy Prophet.

3255. The verse means that the charge of indifference is not correct. Why at all the Holy Prophet should have adopted an attitude of sullen indifference towards a blind man when the Qur'ān was meant equally for the rich and the poor? It was not only inconsistent with his own high moral stature but also against human reason to do so. What the Holy Prophet did on the specific occasion was demanded by the situation and, therefore was the right thing for him to do.

14. *Contained* in honoured Books,[3256]

فِيْ صُحُفٍ مُّكَرَّمَةٍ ﴿۱۴﴾

15. Exalted, purified,

مَّرْفُوْعَةٍ مُّطَهَّرَةٍ ﴿۱۵﴾

16. In the hands of writers,

بِاَيْدِيْ سَفَرَةٍ ﴿۱۶﴾

17. Noble *and* virtuous.[3257]

كِرَامٍۭ بَرَرَةٍ ﴿۱۷﴾

18. Woe unto man ! How ungrateful he is ![3258]

قُتِلَ الْاِنْسَانُ مَآ اَكْفَرَهٗ ﴿۱۸﴾

19. *Does he not consider*, from what thing did *God* create him?

مِنْ اَيِّ شَيْءٍ خَلَقَهٗ ﴿۱۹﴾

20. [a]From a sperm-drop! He creates him and proportions him;

مِنْ نُّطْفَةٍ ؕ خَلَقَهٗ فَقَدَّرَهٗ ﴿۲۰﴾

21. Then He makes the way easy for him,

ثُمَّ السَّبِيْلَ يَسَّرَهٗ ﴿۲۱﴾

22. Then *in due course* He causes him to die and assigns a grave[3259] to him;

ثُمَّ اَمَاتَهٗ فَاَقْبَرَهٗ ﴿۲۲﴾

23. Then, when He pleases, He will raise him up again.

ثُمَّ اِذَا شَآءَ اَنْشَرَهٗ ﴿۲۳﴾

24. Nay! he has not yet carried out what *God* commanded him *to do*.

كَلَّا لَمَّا يَقْضِ مَآ اَمَرَهٗ ﴿۲۴﴾

25. Now let man look at his food;

فَلْيَنْظُرِ الْاِنْسَانُ اِلٰى طَعَامِهٖٓ ﴿۲۵﴾

[a]18 : 38; 35 : 12; 36 : 78; 40 : 68.

3256. The Qur'ān, being a compendium of all permanent and imperishable teachings embodied in various revealed Scriptures, constitutes, as it were, a collection of all heavenly Books. This is the significance of the words *Contained in honoured Books.* The verse further says that the Qur'ān will be written in the form of a Book; it will be honoured and respected and will be protected and preserved against every kind of interpolation and interference.

3257. As against three prominent characteristics of the Qur'ān mentioned in the preceding verses (14-15) three equally marked qualities of the bearers of its Message have been mentioned in this and the preceding verse. The bearers of the Quranic Message are not only noble and virtuous but they travel far and wide to explain and spread it.

3258. How ungrateful are disbelievers that they should reject such a great and noble Book as the Qur'ān, which has been revealed to raise them from the dust and squalor of moral turpitude to the heights of spiritual glory, if only they should accept its Message.

3259. See next page.

26. [a]How We pour down water in abundance,

أَنَّا صَبَبْنَا الْمَاءَ صَبًّا ﴿٢٧﴾

27. Then We cleave the earth—a *proper* cleaving,

ثُمَّ شَقَقْنَا الْأَرْضَ شَقًّا ﴿٢٨﴾

28. [b]Then We cause to grow therein grain,

فَأَنْبَتْنَا فِيهَا حَبًّا ﴿٢٩﴾

29. And grapes and vegetables,

وَعِنَبًا وَقَضْبًا ﴿٣٠﴾

30. And the olive and the date-palm,

وَزَيْتُونًا وَنَخْلًا ﴿٣١﴾

31. [c]And walled gardens thickly planted,

وَحَدَائِقَ غُلْبًا ﴿٣٢﴾

32. And fruits and herbage,

وَفَاكِهَةً وَأَبًّا ﴿٣٣﴾

33. A [d]provision for you and your cattle.

مَتَاعًا لَكُمْ وَلِأَنْعَامِكُمْ ﴿٣٤﴾

34. [e]But when the deafening shout comes,

فَإِذَا جَاءَتِ الصَّاخَّةُ ﴿٣٥﴾

35. [f]On the day when a man will flee from his brother,

يَوْمَ يَفِرُّ الْمَرْءُ مِنْ أَخِيهِ ﴿٣٦﴾

36. And *from* his mother and his father,

وَأُمِّهِ وَأَبِيهِ ﴿٣٧﴾

37. And *from* his [g]wife and his sons,[3259A]

وَصَاحِبَتِهِ وَبَنِيهِ ﴿٣٨﴾

[a]71 : 12 ; 78 : 15. [b]78 : 16. [c]78 : 17. [d]79 : 34. [e]79 : 35. [f]44 : 42. [g]70 : 13.

3259. After its departure from its physical habitat the human soul acquires a new body and an abode according to the nature of the actions which man might have done during his life on earth. That is man's real sepulchre. It is not the pit in which his body is placed by his relatives but an abode of happiness or misery according to his spiritual condition.

3259A. What an alarming picture of the Day of Reckoning !

38. Every man among them that day will have concern enough *of his own* to make him indifferent[3260] *to others*.

لِكُلِّ امْرِئٍ مِّنْهُمْ يَوْمَئِذٍ شَأْنٌ يُّغْنِيْهِ ﴿٣٨﴾

39. [a]On that day *some* faces will be bright,

وُجُوْهٌ يَّوْمَئِذٍ مُّسْفِرَةٌ ﴿٣٩﴾

40. Laughing, joyous.

ضَاحِكَةٌ مُّسْتَبْشِرَةٌ ﴿٤٠﴾

41. [b]And *some* faces, on that day, will have dust upon them,

وَ وُجُوْهٌ يَّوْمَئِذٍ عَلَيْهَا غَبَرَةٌ ﴿٤١﴾

42. [c]Darkness covering them.

تَرْهَقُهَا قَتَرَةٌ ﴿٤٢﴾

43. Those will be the disbelievers, the doers of evil.

أُولٰٓئِكَ هُمُ الْكَفَرَةُ الْفَجَرَةُ ﴿٤٣﴾

[a]3 : 107 ; 10 : 27. [b]68 : 44 ; 75 : 25; 88 : 3-4. [c]14 : 51; 23 : 105.

3260. In time of tribulation and sorrow a man is apt to forget even his nearest relations. He has his own enough troubles to keep him busy.

CHAPTER 81

AL-TAKWĪR

(*Revealed before Hijrah*)

Date of Revelation and Context

The *Sūrah* was revealed early at Mecca, very probably in the 6th year of the Call or even earlier. The preceding Chapters had dealt with the subject of Resurrection and the great and marvellous revolution which was brought about by the Holy Prophet among his people and which has also been called "resurrection" in the Qur'ān. This "resurrection" was to take place twice, first by the advent of the Holy Prophet himself and then by his Second Advent in the person of a great Deputy of his—the Promised Messiah and Mahdī—to which a clear reference is made in 62 : 4. It is this second renaissance of Islām at the hands of the Promised Messiah and the great changes which were to take place in his time which this *Sūrah* speaks of. It opens with a description of those changes and follows it up with a fleeting reference to the moral degeneration of Muslims at that time and to the causes thereof, and ends by striking a note of optimism and cheerfulness to them, holding out to them the promise that eventually the night of the degradation of Muslims will give place to the dawn of their success, because Islām, being God's last Message for the whole of mankind, has come to stay.

سُوْرَةُ التَّكْوِيْرِ مَكِّيَّةٌ (٨١) آياتها ٣٠ ركوعها ١

1. [a]In the name of Allāh, the Gracious, the Merciful. — بِسْمِ اللّٰهِ الرَّحْمٰنِ الرَّحِيْمِ ①

2. When the sun is folded up,[3261] — إِذَا الشَّمْسُ كُوِّرَتْ ②

3. And when the stars are obscured,[3262] — وَإِذَا النُّجُوْمُ انْكَدَرَتْ ③

4. And [b]when the mountains are made to move,[3263] — وَإِذَا الْجِبَالُ سُيِّرَتْ ④

5. And when the she-camels, ten-month pregnant are abandoned,[3264] — وَإِذَا الْعِشَارُ عُطِّلَتْ ⑤

---

[a]1 : 1. [b]18 : 48; 52 : 11; 78 : 21.

3261. It is generally said that the *Sūrah* deals with the Final Resurrection, when the laws and processes of nature as we know them will cease to operate. But its whole trend and tenor speak so clearly of the conditions which obtain in the physical world that some of the verses will lose all sense if they are taken as referring only to the Final Resurrection. In fact, the *Sūrah* speaks of the great changes that have already taken place in the material world and in human life since the time of the Holy Prophet, particularly in our own time. The verse may mean: When there will be spiritual darkness all over the world—the light of the Spiritual Sun (the Holy Prophet) having become dim or disappeared altogether. Or, it may refer to the eclipses of the sun and the moon, which according to a well-known saying of the Holy Prophet, were to take place in the time of the Mahdī, in the month of Ramaḍān, a phenomenon which the world had never witnessed before (Quṭnī, p. 188) These eclipses of the sun and the moon took place in 1894 exactly as foretold.

3262. *Al-Nujūm* (stars) signifies religious Ulema. This meaning is supported by a well-known saying of the Holy Prophet: 'My Companions are like stars, whomsoever you will follow, you will receive right guidance' (Baihaqui). So the verse may mean : When religious leaders will become corrupt and will cease to exercise any influence. The reference may also be to the falling of the stars in exceptionally large numbers in the time of a Divine Reformer.

3263. When mountains will be blown away by dynamite and roads will be made through them; or metaphorically, when the authority of rulers will become undermined; the word *Jabal* meaning, the chief of a people (Lane).

3264. *'Ishār* is the plural of *'Usharā'* which means, a she-camel that has been ten-months with young. *'Ishār* is applied to she-camels until some of them have brought forth and others are expected to bring forth (Lane). The verse means that when she-camels will lose their importance even in Arabia The reference seems to be to the replacement of camels by better and swifter means of transport—railway trains, steamships, motor cars, aeroplanes, etc. There is a pointed reference to camels being replaced by other means of transport in a saying of the Holy Prophet which is to the effect: 'The camels will be abandoned and will not be used for going from one place to another' (Muslim).

6. And when the wild beasts are gathered together,[3265]

وَإِذَا الْوُحُوشُ حُشِرَتْ ۝٦

7. [a]And when the rivers are drained away,[3266]

وَإِذَا الْبِحَارُ سُجِّرَتْ ۝٧

8. And when *various* people are brought together,[3267]

وَإِذَا النُّفُوسُ زُوِّجَتْ ۝٨

9. And when the female-infant buried alive is questioned about—

وَإِذَا الْمَوْءُدَةُ سُئِلَتْ ۝٩

10. 'For what crime was she killed?'[3268]—

بِأَيِّ ذَنْبٍ قُتِلَتْ ۝١٠

11. And when books are spread *abroad*,[3269]

وَإِذَا الصُّحُفُ نُشِرَتْ ۝١١

12. And when the heaven is laid bare,[3270]

وَإِذَا السَّمَآءُ كُشِطَتْ ۝١٢

13. And when Hell-fire is set ablaze,[3271]

وَإِذَا الْجَحِيمُ سُعِّرَتْ ۝١٣

---

[a]52 : 7; 82 : 4.

3265. In view of the different meanings of the root-word *Ḥushira* (Lane), the verse would signify: When animals will be collected in zoos, or when primitive people will be settled in organized civil communities; or, when they will be compelled to leave their homelands.

3266. The verse signifies: When the waters of rivers will be drained away for irrigation and other purposes; or, when in sea-fights very large ships will be set on fire and it would seem as if the seas had caught fire; or, when large oceans will be joined together by means of canals; or, when rural population will go into towns and cities will overflow with their inhabitants. The word, *Sujjira*, possesses all these meanings (Lane).

3267. When means of transport and communication will become so developed, and intercourse between peoples living in far off lands become so easy and frequent as to make them unite into one people. The verse may also signify that people holding analogous social or political views will form themselves into parties.

3268. The burying or burning alive of girls will be made a capital crime.

3269. The reference seems to be to the vast circulation of newspapers, journals and books and to the system of libraries and reading rooms and such other places and means of spreading knowledge in the Latter Days.

3270. The verse may refer to the vast strides that the science of astronomy will make in the Latter Days. The advance in this branch of science during the past decade has startled the world.

3271. On account of the sinful and iniquitous conduct of man, God's wrath will be kindled and a veritable hell will be let loose upon the world in the form of destructive wars.

14. [a]And when Paradise is brought nigh,[3272]

وَإِذَا الْجَنَّةُ أُزْلِفَتْ ﴿١٤﴾

15. [b]Then every soul will know what it has produced.[3273]

عَلِمَتْ نَفْسٌ مَّا أَحْضَرَتْ ﴿١٥﴾

16. Nay! I call to witness those that recede *while advancing*,

فَلَا أُقْسِمُ بِالْخُنَّسِ ﴿١٦﴾

17. Rush ahead *and then* hide.[3274]

الْجَوَارِ الْكُنَّسِ ﴿١٧﴾

18. And I call to witness the night as it draws to a close,

وَاللَّيْلِ إِذَا عَسْعَسَ ﴿١٨﴾

19. [c]And the dawn as it begins to breathe,[3275]

وَالصُّبْحِ إِذَا تَنَفَّسَ ﴿١٩﴾

20. [d]That this is, surely, the word *revealed* to a noble Messenger,[3276]

إِنَّهُ لَقَوْلُ رَسُولٍ كَرِيمٍ ﴿٢٠﴾

21. Possessor of strength, established in the presence of the Lord of the Throne,

ذِي قُوَّةٍ عِندَ ذِي الْعَرْشِ مَكِينٍ ﴿٢١﴾

22. Entitled to obedience and faithful to *his* trust.[3277]

مُّطَاعٍ ثَمَّ أَمِينٍ ﴿٢٢﴾

---

[a]50 : 32. [b]3 : 31; 82 : 6. [c]74 : 35. [d]69 : 41.

3272. As in the Latter Days evil will abound and man will abandon himself to vice and the worship of Mammon, even a small act of righteousness will make him deserving of great reward and will draw him closer to Heaven.

3273. God's special decree will come into force and the punishment of man's evil deeds will take the form of widespread natural calamities.

3274. In the Latter Days Muslims will begin to decline from their position of eminence, as they will either rush forward headlong thoughtlessly to carry out their contemplated programmes; or will give up all creative and contsructive efforts in despair.

3275. With the advent of the Reformer of the Latter Days the night of moral decline and degradation of Muslims will begin to depart, giving place to the dawn of a great and glorious future for Islām.

3276. The words, 'a noble Messenger,' refer to the Holy Prophet and not to Archangel Gabriel as generally misunderstood.

3277. All the five attributes—noble Messenger, possessor of power, enjoying a high rank before the Lord of the Throne, the one entitled to obedience, and faithful to his trust in the Sight of God, quite fittingly apply to the Holy Prophet.

23. [a]And your companion is not mad.

وَمَا صَاحِبُكُمْ بِمَجْنُوْنٍ ۚ ﴿٢٣﴾

24. [b]And he, assuredly, saw him[2378] on the clear horizon.

وَلَقَدْ رَاٰهُ بِالْاُفُقِ الْمُبِيْنِ ۚ ﴿٢٤﴾

25. And he is not niggardly with respect to the unseen.[3279]

وَمَا هُوَ عَلَى الْغَيْبِ بِضَنِيْنٍ ۚ ﴿٢٥﴾

26. [c]Nor is this the word of Satan, the rejected.

وَمَا هُوَ بِقَوْلِ شَيْطٰنٍ رَّجِيْمٍ ۙ ﴿٢٦﴾

27. Whither, then, are you going?

فَاَيْنَ تَذْهَبُوْنَ ؕ ﴿٢٧﴾

28. [d]It is nothing but a Reminder unto all the worlds,

اِنْ هُوَ اِلَّا ذِكْرٌ لِّلْعٰلَمِيْنَ ۙ ﴿٢٨﴾

29. Unto such among you as desire to go straight.

لِمَنْ شَآءَ مِنْكُمْ اَنْ يَّسْتَقِيْمَ ؕ ﴿٢٩﴾

30. [e]And you desire not *a thing* except that Allāh, the Lord of the worlds, desires *it*.[3280]

وَمَا تَشَآءُوْنَ اِلَّآ اَنْ يَّشَآءَ اللّٰهُ رَبُّ الْعٰلَمِيْنَ ﴿٣٠﴾ ع

[a]52 : 30; 68 : 3. [b]53 : 13. [c]26 : 211 [d]12 : 105; 38 : 88.
[e]74 : 57; 76 : 31.

3278. The pronoun *hu* meaning "it" (glorious future of Islām). or "him" (the Holy Prophet), may signify in the first place the fulfilment of the prophecy about the glorious future of Islām and in the second place it may mean that the Holy Prophet saw himself in the distant East in the person of the Promised Messiah.

3279. God has disclosed to the world great secrets of the unknown from the mouth of the Holy Prophet.

3280. He alone would be guided to the right path who makes an attempt to find it and conforms his will to the Will of God.

CHAPTER 82

AL-INFIṬĀR

(*Revealed before Hijrah*)

Introductory Remarks

The *Sūrah* is so similar in style and subject-matter to the one preceding it that it forms, as it were, its counterpart, but with a separate name. It is characteristic of the Qur'ān that, in view of their importance, it takes out certain parts of the text of a particular *Sūrah* and in order to draw pointed attention to the subject dealt with in the separated parts and in order also that the separated parts may be easily committed to memory, it gives them a distinct name and individuality. The *Sūrah* deals particularly with the conditions that were to prevail in the Latter Days when Christian doctrines and ways of life will have impressed very deeply the conduct and concepts of non-Christian peoples, especially the Muslims. All the prophecies mentioned in the *Sūrah* have been literally fulfilled. It was revealed at Mecca in the early years of the Call about the time of the revelation of the preceding Chapter.

رُكُوْعُهَا ١ سُوْرَةُ الْاِنْفِطَارِ مَكِّيَّةٌ (٨٢) اٰيَاتُهَا ٢٠

1. [a]In the name of Allāh, the Gracious, the Merciful.

بِسْمِ اللّٰهِ الرَّحْمٰنِ الرَّحِيْمِ ①

2. [b]When the heaven is cleft asunder,[3281]

اِذَا السَّمَآءُ انْفَطَرَتْ ②

3. And when the stars are scattered,[3282]

وَاِذَا الْكَوَاكِبُ انْتَثَرَتْ ③

4. [c]And when the oceans are made to flow forth[3283] *and joined together*,

وَاِذَا الْبِحَارُ فُجِّرَتْ ④

5. [d]And when the graves are laid open,[3284]

وَاِذَا الْقُبُوْرُ بُعْثِرَتْ ⑤

6. [e]Every soul shall then know what it has sent forth and what it has kept back.[3285]

عَلِمَتْ نَفْسٌ مَّا قَدَّمَتْ وَاَخَّرَتْ ⑥

---

[a]1 : 1. [b]73 : 19. [c]81 : 7. [d]100 : 10. [e]3 : 31; 81 : 15.

3281. As mentioned in the "Introductory Remarks" the *Sūrah* deals particularly with the time when Christianity will be very much in the ascendant and the Christian doctrines of trinity, the sonship of Jesus and atonement will reign supreme. To this dominance of the false Christian doctrines the Qur'ān has referred in very strong words; 'The heavens might well-nigh be rent thereat, and the earth cleave asunder, and the mountains fall down into pieces because they ascribe a son to Allāh' (19 : 91-92) The verse under comment refers to these two verses and signifies that at that time false doctrines of Christianity will dominate the world, and as a result of it God's wrath, will be excited and Divine punishment will overtake the world in various forms.

3282. Metaphorically speaking the verse means that in the Latter Days men possessing true spiritual knowledge and guidance will disappear or become rare.

3283. At that time great seas and oceans will be made to flow into one another by means of canals; or their mouths will be dug wide open so as to make large ships ply in them. The reference may be to the Panama and Suez Canals.

3284. In the Latter Days graves will be dug open as has been done in the case of the tombs of the ancient Kings of Egypt; or, the verse may mean that towns and monuments, submerged and long forgotten, will be dug out.

3285. In this and the next few verses the address is to the protagonists and propagandists of the false Christian doctrines. They will come to realize the enormity and heinousness of their false teachings.

7. O man! what has deceived thee concerning thy Gracious Lord.

يٰٓاَيُّهَا الْاِنْسَانُ مَا غَرَّكَ بِرَبِّكَ الْكَرِيْمِ ۙ﴿۷﴾

8. Who created thee, then perfected thee, then proportioned thee [a]aright?[3286]

الَّذِيْ خَلَقَكَ فَسَوّٰىكَ فَعَدَلَكَ ۙ﴿۸﴾

9. In whatever form He pleased. He fashioned thee.

فِيْٓ اَيِّ صُوْرَةٍ مَّا شَآءَ رَكَّبَكَ ؕ﴿۹﴾

10. Nay, but you deny the Judgment.

كَلَّا بَلْ تُكَذِّبُوْنَ بِالدِّيْنِ ۙ﴿۱۰﴾

11. [b]Surely, there are guardians over you,

وَاِنَّ عَلَيْكُمْ لَحٰفِظِيْنَ ۙ﴿۱۱﴾

12. [c]Noble Recorders,[3287]

كِرَامًا كَاتِبِيْنَ ۙ﴿۱۲﴾

13. Who know *all* that you do.

يَعْلَمُوْنَ مَا تَفْعَلُوْنَ ﴿۱۳﴾

14. [d]Verily, the virtuous will be in bliss;

اِنَّ الْاَبْرَارَ لَفِيْ نَعِيْمٍ ۚ﴿۱۴﴾

15. [e]And the wicked will be in Hell;

وَاِنَّ الْفُجَّارَ لَفِيْ جَحِيْمٍ ۚۖ﴿۱۵﴾

16. [f]They will burn therein on the Day of Judgment;

يَّصْلَوْنَهَا يَوْمَ الدِّيْنِ ﴿۱۶﴾

17. And they will not *be able to* escape therefrom.

وَمَا هُمْ عَنْهَا بِغَآئِبِيْنَ ؕ﴿۱۷﴾

---

[a]87 : 3; 91 : 8. [b]6 : 62. [c]43 : 81; 50 : 19. [d]45 : 31; 83 : 23. [e]83 : 8. [f]23 : 104; 83 : 17.

3286. God has endowed man with great natural powers and faculties in order that he may rise to the highest peaks of spiritual eminence.

3287. Man is born a free agent and is responsible for the decisions he takes and the deeds he does, which are recorded by "Noble Recorders."

18. And what should make thee know what the Day of Judgment is !

وَمَآ أَدْرٰىكَ مَا يَوْمُ الدِّيْنِ ۝١٨

19. Again, what should make thee know what the Day of Jugdment is !

ثُمَّ مَآ أَدْرٰىكَ مَا يَوْمُ الدِّيْنِ ۝١٩

20. [a]The day when a soul shall have no power to do aught for another soul ! [b]And the command on that day will be Allāh's.

يَوْمَ لَا تَمْلِكُ نَفْسٌ لِّنَفْسٍ شَيْئًا ۗ وَالْأَمْرُ يَوْمَئِذٍ لِّلّٰهِ ۝٢٠

[a]2 : 124; 31 : 34. [b]18 : 45; 40 : 17.

CHAPTER 83

AL-TAṬFĪF

(Revealed before Hijrah)

Date of Revelation and Context

The *Sūrah* opens with a severe condemnation of the use of false measures and weights to defraud people. According to scholarly opinion, it was revealed early in the Meccan period. Noldeke and Muir assign its revelation to about the fourth year of the Call. The preceding *Sūrah* had ended with a warning to disbelievers that they will have to render account of their deeds and to make up their spiritual loss themselves, the sacrifice or intercession of no one else being of any use to them on the Day of Judgment. In that *Sūrah* man's relations with his Creator were discussed. In the present *Sūrah*, however, stress has been laid on man's dealings with his fellow-beings with special reference to the cruel exploitation by powerful nations of weaker and less developed peoples after depriving them of their liberty of action. It ends on a note of stern warning to the unjust and dishonest people that they will not be allowed to go unpunished. The Day of Reckoning awaits them in all its frightfulness and severity.

سُوْرَةُ التَّطْفِيْفِ مَكِّيَّةٌ (٨٣)

آياتها ٣٦ — ركوعها ١

1. [a]In the name of Allāh, the Gracious, the Merciful.

بِسْمِ اللّٰهِ الرَّحْمٰنِ الرَّحِيْمِ ﴿١﴾

2. [b]Woe unto those who give short measure;

وَيْلٌ لِّلْمُطَفِّفِيْنَ ﴿٢﴾

3. Those who, when they take by measure from other people, take it full;

الَّذِيْنَ اِذَا اكْتَالُوْا عَلَى النَّاسِ يَسْتَوْفُوْنَ ﴿٣﴾

4. [c]But when they give by measure to others or weigh to them, they give *them* less.

وَاِذَا كَالُوْهُمْ اَوْ وَّزَنُوْهُمْ يُخْسِرُوْنَ ﴿٤﴾

5. Do not such *people* know that they will be raised again

اَلَا يَظُنُّ اُولٰٓئِكَ اَنَّهُمْ مَّبْعُوْثُوْنَ ﴿٥﴾

6. *To witness the judgment of* a mighty day?[3288]

لِيَوْمٍ عَظِيْمٍ ﴿٦﴾

7. The day when mankind will stand before the Lord of the worlds.

يَّوْمَ يَقُوْمُ النَّاسُ لِرَبِّ الْعٰلَمِيْنَ ﴿٧﴾

8. Nay, the record of the wicked is in Sijjīn.[3289]

كَلَّآ اِنَّ كِتٰبَ الْفُجَّارِ لَفِيْ سِجِّيْنٍ ﴿٨﴾

9. And what should make thee know what Sijjīn is?

وَمَآ اَدْرٰىكَ مَا سِجِّيْنٌ ﴿٩﴾

---

[a]1 : 1. [b]11 : 85; 26 : 182-184; 55 : 9. [c]55 : 10.

3288. There is a Day of Reckoning in the after-life when men shall have to render account of their actions to their Lord and Master, but a day of reckoning also comes upon a people in this very life when their evil doings exceed legitimate bounds and they meet their Nemesis.

3289. *Sijjīn* is wrongly considered by some Commentators of the Qur'ān as a non-Arabic word, but according to such eminent authorities as Farrā', Zajjāj, Abū 'Ubaidah and Mubarrad, it is an Arabic word derived from *Sajana*. Lisān considers it as equivalent to *Sijn* (prison) *Sijjīn* is a Register or Book in which the record of evil deeds of the wicked is said to be kept in the next world. The word also means, anything hard, vehement and severe; continuous, lasting or everlasting (Lane).

10. *It is* a written Book *since eternity*.[3290]

كِتٰبٌ مَّرْقُوْمٌ ﴿١٠﴾

11. Woe on that day unto those who reject,

وَيْلٌ يَّوْمَئِذٍ لِّلْمُكَذِّبِيْنَ ﴿١١﴾

12. Who deny the Day of Judgment.

الَّذِيْنَ يُكَذِّبُوْنَ بِيَوْمِ الدِّيْنِ ﴿١٢﴾

13. And none denies it save every sinful transgressor,

وَمَا يُكَذِّبُ بِهٖٓ اِلَّا كُلُّ مُعْتَدٍ اَثِيْمٍ ﴿١٣﴾

14. [a]*Who*, when Our Signs are recited unto him, says, 'Tales of the ancient !'

اِذَا تُتْلٰى عَلَيْهِ اٰيٰتُنَا قَالَ اَسَاطِيْرُ الْاَوَّلِيْنَ ﴿١٤﴾

15. Nay, but that which they have earned is rust upon their hearts.

كَلَّا بَلْ سكتة رَانَ عَلٰى قُلُوْبِهِمْ مَّا كَانُوْا يَكْسِبُوْنَ ﴿١٥﴾

16. [b]Nay, they will, surely, be debarred from *seeing*[3291] their Lord on that day.

كَلَّآ اِنَّهُمْ عَنْ رَّبِّهِمْ يَوْمَئِذٍ لَّمَحْجُوْبُوْنَ ﴿١٦﴾

17. [c]Then, verily, they will burn in Hell,

ثُمَّ اِنَّهُمْ لَصَالُوا الْجَحِيْمِ ﴿١٧﴾

18. Then it will be said *to them*, 'This is what you used to [d]reject.'

ثُمَّ يُقَالُ هٰذَا الَّذِيْ كُنْتُمْ بِهٖ تُكَذِّبُوْنَ ﴿١٨﴾

[a]8 : 32; 16 : 25; 68 : 16. [b]3 : 78. [c]23 : 104; 82 : 16. [d]52 : 15.

3290. The name *Sijjīn* signifies that the punishment for the wicked disbelievers will be severe and lasting. Or, the verse may mean that the wicked will be kept in a place of disgrace and ignominy and this is an irrevocable decision. Or, *Sijjīn* and *'Illiyyīn* may be the names of two portions of the Qur'ān, the former dealing with the rejectors of the Divine Message and the punishments to be meted out to them, and the latter with the righteous servants of God and the rewards which will be bestowed upon them. Thus the meaning of the verse would be that the verdicts recorded in these two portions cannot be altered or changed.

3291. The sight of God is granted to a believer in two stages. The initial stage is that of belief, when he acquires firm faith in Divine attributes. The second or the higher stage consists in his being granted realization of the Divine Being. The sinners, on account of their sins, will remain deprived of the realization of the Divine Being on the Day of Judgment—they will not see the face of God.

19. Nay, but the record of the righteous is, surely, in 'Illiyyīn.[3292]

كَلَّآ إِنَّ كِتٰبَ الْأَبْرَارِ لَفِيْ عِلِّيِّيْنَ ﴿١٩﴾

20. And what should make thee know what 'Illiyyūn[3293] is?

وَمَآ أَدْرٰىكَ مَا عِلِّيُّوْنَ ﴿٢٠﴾

21. It is a written Book.

كِتٰبٌ مَّرْقُوْمٌ ﴿٢١﴾

22. The chosen ones *of God* will witness it.

يَّشْهَدُهُ الْمُقَرَّبُوْنَ ﴿٢٢﴾

23. [a]Surely, the righteous *will be* in bliss,

إِنَّ الْأَبْرَارَ لَفِيْ نَعِيْمٍ ﴿٢٣﴾

24. [b]*Seated* on couches, looking *at everything*.

عَلَى الْأَرَآئِكِ يَنْظُرُوْنَ ﴿٢٤﴾

25. Thou wilt find in their faces the freshness of bliss.

تَعْرِفُ فِيْ وُجُوْهِهِمْ نَضْرَةَ النَّعِيْمِ ﴿٢٥﴾

26. They will be given to drink of a pure beverage,[3294] sealed.

يُسْقَوْنَ مِنْ رَّحِيْقٍ مَّخْتُوْمٍ ﴿٢٦﴾

27. The sealing of it will be *with* musk—for this let the aspirants aspire—

خِتٰمُهٗ مِسْكٌ ۚ وَفِيْ ذٰلِكَ فَلْيَتَنَافَسِ الْمُتَنَافِسُوْنَ ﴿٢٧﴾

28. And it will be tempered with *the water of* Tasnīm,

وَمِزَاجُهٗ مِنْ تَسْنِيْمٍ ﴿٢٨﴾

29. A spring of which the chosen ones will drink.

عَيْنًا يَّشْرَبُ بِهَا الْمُقَرَّبُوْنَ ﴿٢٩﴾

[a]45 : 31; 82 : 14. [b]15 : 48; 18 : 32; 36 : 57; 76 : 14.

3292. *'Illiyyūn*, considered by some to have been derived from *'Alā*, which means, it was or became high, signifies the most exalted ranks which the righteous believers will enjoy. According to Mufradāt *'Illiyyūn* are those select righteous believers who will enjoy spiritual precedence over others. The word may also stand for those parts of the Qur'ān which contain prophecies about the great progress and prosperity of believers. According to Ibn 'Abbās the word signifies Paradise (Kathīr), while Imām Rāghib considers it to be the name of the dwellers thereof.

3293. *Sijjīn*, being singular and *'Illiyyūn* plural, it appears that while the punishment of evil-doers will be static, *i.e.*, stationary in one place, the spiritual progress of the righteous will be continuous without interruption, assuming different forms. They will go from one rank to another higher rank.

3294. If 'pure beverage' may refer to the Qur'ān, *Tasnīm* may be considered as revelations vouchsafed to the chosen ones of God—the righteous followers of the Holy Prophet.

30. [a]Those who were guilty used to laugh[3295] at those who believed,

إِنَّ الَّذِينَ أَجْرَمُوا كَانُوا مِنَ الَّذِينَ آمَنُوا يَضْحَكُونَ ۝٣٠

31. And when they passed by them, they winked at one another,

وَإِذَا مَرُّوا بِهِمْ يَتَغَامَزُونَ ۝٣١

32. [b]And when they returned to their families they returned exulting;

وَإِذَا انْقَلَبُوا إِلَىٰ أَهْلِهِمُ انْقَلَبُوا فَكِهِينَ ۝٣٢

33. And when they saw them they said, 'These, indeed, have gone astray.'

وَإِذَا رَأَوْهُمْ قَالُوا إِنَّ هَٰؤُلَاءِ لَضَالُّونَ ۝٣٣

34. But they were not sent as keepers over them.

وَمَا أُرْسِلُوا عَلَيْهِمْ حَافِظِينَ ۝٣٤

35. This day, then, it is the believers who will laugh at the disbelievers,

فَالْيَوْمَ الَّذِينَ آمَنُوا مِنَ الْكُفَّارِ يَضْحَكُونَ ۝٣٥

36. *Seated* on couches,[3296] gazing *around*.

عَلَى الْأَرَائِكِ يَنْظُرُونَ ۝٣٦

37. *They will say to one another*, 'Are not the disbelievers *fully* requited for what they used to do?'

هَلْ ثُوِّبَ الْكُفَّارُ مَا كَانُوا يَفْعَلُونَ ۝٣٧

[a]23 : 111. [b]84 : 14.

3295. Disbelievers used to laugh in their sleeves at the prophecies about the rapid spread and triumph of Islām, made at a time when it was fighting a seemingly losing battle for its very existence.

3296. The words mean : (1) Seated on the thrones of dignity the believers will witness the sad fate of the arrogant disbelievers; or, (2) seated on the thrones of authority they will administer justice to men; or, (3) they will pay due regard to the needs of others, this also being the meaning of *Naẓara* (Lane).

CHAPTER 84

AL-INSHIQĀQ

(Revealed before Hijrah)

Date of Revelation and Context

Like the preceding three Chapters, the present one was revealed early at Mecca. These four Chapters very much resemble one another in style, composition and subject-matter. Noldeke and Muir agree with Muslim scholars about the early date of the revelation of this *Sūrah*. In fact, it completes the chain of *Sūrahs* of which the preceding three Chapters form the component parts. Towards the end of the last Chapter disbelievers were warned in emphatic terms that their power would break and their glory depart. In the present Chapter, however, it is stated that belief will take the place of disbelief and from the ruins of the old decadent and decrepit order a new, vigorous and vibrant order would emerge. The *Surah* continues the theme of *Sūrah* Al-Infiṭār, the intervening *Sūrah* Al-Taṭfīf being merely its extension. *Sūrah* Al-Infiṭār had opened with the subject of the cleaving asunder of the heaven; and the present *Sūrah* begins with an analogous expression, with this difference that whereas in *Sūrah* Al-Infiṭār 'the cleaving asunder of the heaven' was connected with the false doctrines of Christianity, in the present *Sūrah* by 'the bursting asunder of the heaven' is meant the descent of Divine revelation and the emergence and spread of spiritual sciences. Thus along with the three preceding Chapters, this *Sūrah* forms a chain of Chapters which deal with the subject of the renaissance of Islām in the Latter Days and with the sins and iniquities of the preceding period. It specifically deals with the renaissance of Islām while the preceding Chapters deal especially with Christian corruption and immorality.

ركوعها ١ سُوْرَةُ الْاِنْشِقَاقِ مَكِّيَّةٌ (٨٤) اٰياتها ٢٦

1. [a]In the name of Allāh, the Gracious, the Merciful.

بِسْمِ اللّٰهِ الرَّحْمٰنِ الرَّحِيْمِ ۝١

2. When [b]the heaven bursts asunder,[3297]

اِذَا السَّمَآءُ انْشَقَّتْ ۝٢

3. And [c]hearkens unto her Lord[3298]—and *this* is incumbent upon her—

وَاَذِنَتْ لِرَبِّهَا وَحُقَّتْ ۝٣

4. And when [d]the earth is spread out[3299]

وَاِذَا الْاَرْضُ مُدَّتْ ۝٤

5. And casts out *all* that is in her, and *appears to* become empty,[3300]

وَاَلْقَتْ مَا فِيْهَا وَتَخَلَّتْ ۝٥

6. And hearkens unto her Lord—and *this* is incumbent upon her—

وَاَذِنَتْ لِرَبِّهَا وَحُقَّتْ ۝٦

7. Verily, thou, O man, art toiling along towards thy Lord, a hard toiling; until [e]thou meet Him.

يٰۤاَيُّهَا الْاِنْسَانُ اِنَّكَ كَادِحٌ اِلٰى رَبِّكَ كَدْحًا فَمُلٰقِيْهِ ۝٧

8. Then as for him [f]who is given his record in his right hand,

فَاَمَّا مَنْ اُوْتِيَ كِتٰبَهٗ بِيَمِيْنِهٖ ۝٨

---

[a]1 : 1. [b]55 : 38; 69 : 17. [c]41 : 12. [d]78 : 7. [e]2 : 224; 11 : 30; 18 : 111. [f]17 : 72; 69 : 20.

3297. The verse refers to the time when the gates of heaven will be thrown open and heavenly Signs in support of Islām will appear in large numbers and highly placed persons will begin to give serious thought to the revealed guidance.

3298. A new Adam will be born and the angels of the heaven will take their stand on his side, ready to help him in the furtherance and propagation of his Divine mission (69 : 18), because that is mainly the object of their creation and is their duty and obligation.

3299. The earth will get a new lease of life and the destruction which it had deserved on account of men's sins will be deferred; and new means will be provided for the spiritual progress of its dwellers. The verse may also signify that some planets which appear to pertain to the heaven will be discovered to form a part of the earth and men will try to reach them by means of rockets, etc. The word *Mudda* possesses all these meanings (Lane).

3300. The earth will throw out its hidden treasures so abundantly that it would appear as if it was going to empty itself out.

9. He will, surely, have an easy reckoning,

فَسَوْفَ يُحَاسَبُ حِسَابًا يَّسِيْرًا ٩

10. And he will return to his family, rejoicing.

وَّيَنْقَلِبُ اِلٰٓى اَهْلِهٖ مَسْرُوْرًا ١٠

11. But as for him who will have [a]his record given to him behind his back,[3301]

وَاَمَّا مَنْ اُوْتِيَ كِتٰبَهٗ وَرَآءَ ظَهْرِهٖ ١١

12. He will soon call for destruction,[3302]

فَسَوْفَ يَدْعُوْا ثُبُوْرًا ١٢

13. And he will burn in a blazing Fire.

وَّيَصْلٰى سَعِيْرًا ١٣

14. Verily, *before this* he used *to pass his time* [b]joyfully among his people.

اِنَّهٗ كَانَ فِيْٓ اَهْلِهٖ مَسْرُوْرًا ١٤

15. He, indeed, thought that he would never return *to God*.

اِنَّهٗ ظَنَّ اَنْ لَّنْ يَّحُوْرَ ١٥

16. Yea! surely, his Lord was ever Watchful of him.

بَلٰٓى اِنَّ رَبَّهٗ كَانَ بِهٖ بَصِيْرًا ١٦

17. But nay! I call to witness the glow of sunset,

فَلَآ اُقْسِمُ بِالشَّفَقِ ١٧

18. And the night and *all* that it envelops,

وَالَّيْلِ وَمَا وَسَقَ ١٨

19. And the moon when it becomes full,[3303]

وَالْقَمَرِ اِذَا اتَّسَقَ ١٩

[a]69 : 26. [b]83 : 32.

3301. Those who had treated the Qur'ān as a discarded thing (25 : 31).

3302. When a man is in extreme distress, he desires that death might end his life.

3303. The verses (17-19) contain a prophecy about the temporary decline of Muslims and their renaissance through the Great Deputy of the Holy Prophet—the Promised Messiah—who like the full moon was to reflect in his person fully and faithfully the glorious light of the Sun (the Holy Prophet).

20. That you shall, assuredly, pass on from one stage to another.[3304]

لَتَرۡكَبُنَّ طَبَقًا عَنۡ طَبَقٍ ﴿۲۰﴾

21. So [a]what is the matter with them that they believe not,[3305]

فَمَا لَهُمۡ لَا يُؤۡمِنُوۡنَ ﴿۲۱﴾

22. And when the Qur'ān is recited unto them, they do not bow in submission;

وَ اِذَا قُرِئَ عَلَيۡهِمُ الۡقُرۡاٰنُ لَا يَسۡجُدُوۡنَ ﴿۲۲﴾

23. On the contrary, those who disbelieve [b]reject *it*.

بَلِ الَّذِيۡنَ كَفَرُوۡا يُكَذِّبُوۡنَ ﴿۲۳﴾

24. And Allāh knows best what they keep hidden *in their hearts*.[3306]

وَ اللّٰهُ اَعۡلَمُ بِمَا يُوۡعُوۡنَ ﴿۲۴﴾

25. [c]So give them tidings of a painful punishment.

فَبَشِّرۡهُمۡ بِعَذَابٍ اَلِيۡمٍ ﴿۲۵﴾

26. But *as to* [d]those who believe and do good works, theirs is an unending reward.

اِلَّا الَّذِيۡنَ اٰمَنُوۡا وَ عَمِلُوا الصّٰلِحٰتِ لَهُمۡ اَجۡرٌ غَيۡرُ مَمۡنُوۡنٍ ﴿۲۶﴾

[a]43 : 89. [b]85 : 20. [c]9 : 34. [d]11 : 12; 41 : 9; 95 : 7.

3304. Muslims will pass through all the conditions referred to in the preceding verses.

3305. Why have the disbelievers, after having witnessed the fulfilment of the first two parts of the prophecy, despaired of the fulfilment of the third part? They have seen the ruddy glow of the sunset of Islām, followed by the darkness of spiritual night, and yet they do not believe that the moon of the 14th night will appear to dispel that darkness.

3306. Disbelievers are warned that God knows well the animosity and malice they harbour in their hearts against God's Messenger; He also knows the secret plots they hatch to bring to naught his mission and his efforts to promote the cause of Truth.

CHAPTER 85

AL-BURŪJ

(*Revealed before Hijrah*)

Date of Revelation and Context

This *Sūrah* was revealed at Mecca in the first few years of the Call. Its connection with the preceding *Sūrah*, Al-Inshiqāq, is indicated by the fact that in that *Sūrah* the full moon was invoked as a witness, and in the present *Sūrah* 'mansions of stars' and 'the promised day' have been invoked to serve the same purpose. The "Burūj" or 'mansions of stars' may represent the twelve Divine Reformers (*Mujaddids*), each of whom was raised at the beginning of every century of the *Hijrah*, and the Promised Day stands for the 14th century of the *Hijrah*. The *Sūrah* seems to point to the severe persecution to which the followers of the Promised Messiah would be subjected, ending appropriately on the note that because in his time the integrity of the Qur'ān as God's revealed Word would be assailed from all quarters, particularly by Christian writers, he would devote all his energies and his great God-given powers to rebut their attacks and to prove its infallibility and inviolability.

سُوْرَةُ الْبُرُوْجِ مَكِّيَّةٌ (٨٥)

1. [a]In the name of Allāh, the Gracious, the Merciful.

بِسۡمِ اللّٰہِ الرَّحۡمٰنِ الرَّحِیۡمِ ﴿۱﴾

2. By the heaven having [b]mansions *of stars*,[3307]

وَ السَّمَآءِ ذَاتِ الۡبُرُوۡجِ ﴿۲﴾

3. And the Promised Day,[3308]

وَ الۡیَوۡمِ الۡمَوۡعُوۡدِ ﴿۳﴾

4. And the witness[3309] and he to whom witness is borne,

وَ شَاہِدٍ وَّ مَشۡہُوۡدٍ ﴿۴﴾

5. Cursed be the Fellows of the Trench[3310]—

قُتِلَ اَصۡحٰبُ الۡاُخۡدُوۡدِ ﴿۵﴾

[a]1 : 1. [b]15 : 17; 25 : 62.

3307. *Mujaddids*, or twelve mansions in the spiritual firmament of Islām, who will keep its light burning after the Spiritual Sun will have set, *i.e.*, after the first three best centuries of Islām will have passed, resulting in the spread of spiritual darkness over the whole world. These Reformers will bear witness to the truth of Islām, and of the Qur'ān and to that of the Holy Prophet.

3308. "The Promised Day" may signify the day when the Promised Messiah will be raised to bring about the renaissance of Islām. In fact, there have been many such days in the history of Islām which could be called the promised day namely, the day of the Battle of Badr, the day when the Battle of the Trench came to a glorious end and the day of the Fall of Mecca. But the Promised Day *par excellence* is the time of the Second Advent of the Holy Prophet in the person of his Deputy in the 14th century A.H., when Islām is to receive a new life and to prevail over all other religions. The "Promised Day" may also mean the day when the righteous will enjoy the bliss of meeting with their Lord.

3309. Every Prophet or Divine Reformer is a *Shāhid, i.e.*, bearer of witness, because he is a living witness to the existence of God, and he is also *Mashhūd* (to whom witness is borne) because God bears witness to his truth by showing Signs and miracles at his hands. But here, as the text shows, the *Shāhid* is the Promised Messiah and *Mashhūd* is the Holy Prophet, and the verse signifies that the Promised Messiah will bear witness to the truth of the Holy Prophet by his speeches, discourses and writings and by the Signs that God will show at his hands. He will also bear witness in the sense that in his person the prophecy of the Holy Prophet about the appearance of the Promised Messiah and Mahdī in the 14th century A.H. will be fulfilled. The Promised Messiah is also *Mashhūd* in the sense that the Holy Prophet himself has borne witness to his truth. Thus the Holy Prophet and the Promised Messiah are both *Shāhids* (bearers of witness) and *Mashhūds* (to whom witness is borne).

3310. By some Commentators of the Qur'ān the verse is taken to refer to the burning to death of some Christians by the Jewish King, Dhū Nuwās of Yemen; by some others to the casting into a burning furnace of some Israelite leaders by King Nebuchadnezzar of Babylon (Dan. 3 : 19-22). The verse may more fittingly apply to those enemies of truth, who in the time of every Divine Reformer bitterly oppose and persecute believers. It is not intended here to refer to any past incident of doubtful authenticity. Nowhere in the Qur'ān has God sworn by past incidents. In v. 3 God swears by the "Promised Day." In the present and the next few verses it seems to be hinted that the followers of the Promised Messiah will have to suffer great hardships to usher in that great day.

6. The fire *fed* with fuel—

النَّارِ ذَاتِ الْوَقُودِ ۝٦

7. When they sat[3311] by it,

إِذْ هُمْ عَلَيْهَا قُعُودٌ ۝٧

8. And they were the witnesses of what they did to the believers.[3312]

وَهُمْ عَلَىٰ مَا يَفْعَلُونَ بِالْمُؤْمِنِينَ شُهُودٌ ۝٨

9. [a]And they hated them not but *only* because they believed in Allāh,[3313] the Almighty, the Praiseworthy,

وَمَا نَقَمُوا مِنْهُمْ إِلَّا أَنْ يُؤْمِنُوا بِاللَّهِ الْعَزِيزِ الْحَمِيدِ ۝٩

10. [b]To Whom belongs the Kingdom of the heavens and the earth; and Allāh is Witness over all things.

الَّذِي لَهُ مُلْكُ السَّمَاوَاتِ وَالْأَرْضِ ۚ وَاللَّهُ عَلَىٰ كُلِّ شَيْءٍ شَهِيدٌ ۝١٠

11. Those who persecute the believing men and the believing women and then repent not, for them is, surely, the punishment of Hell, and for them is the torment of heart-burning.

إِنَّ الَّذِينَ فَتَنُوا الْمُؤْمِنِينَ وَالْمُؤْمِنَاتِ ثُمَّ لَمْ يَتُوبُوا فَلَهُمْ عَذَابُ جَهَنَّمَ وَلَهُمْ عَذَابُ الْحَرِيقِ ۝١١

12. But those who believe and do good works, for them are Gardens through which streams flow. That is, indeed, the supreme achievement.

إِنَّ الَّذِينَ آمَنُوا وَعَمِلُوا الصَّالِحَاتِ لَهُمْ جَنَّاتٌ تَجْرِي مِنْ تَحْتِهَا الْأَنْهَارُ ۚ ذَٰلِكَ الْفَوْزُ الْكَبِيرُ ۝١٢

13. Surely, [c]the seizing of thy Lord is severe.

إِنَّ بَطْشَ رَبِّكَ لَشَدِيدٌ ۝١٣

14. [d]He it is Who originates and reproduces;[3314]

إِنَّهُ هُوَ يُبْدِئُ وَيُعِيدُ ۝١٤

---

[a]7 : 127. [b]14 : 3. [c]11 : 103; 22 : 3. [d]29 : 20; 30 : 12

3311. In vv. 5-9 mention is made of those enemies of truth who kindle the fire of persecution against righteous believers in all ages and constantly keep it ablaze. Their end is predicted in v. 11.

3312. The enemies of truth know in their heart of hearts that their opposition is cruel and unjustified and that the victims of their tyranny are innocent.

3313. The verse is full of pathos. Is belief in God really such a heinous crime, it asks, that its holders should be subjected to cruel persecution?

3314. God will punish the cruel and tyrannical persecutors of believers in this world and in the life to come.

15. And He is the Most Forgiving, the Loving;

وَهُوَ الْغَفُوْرُ الْوَدُوْدُ ۙ

16. The Lord of the Throne, the Lord of honour;

ذُو الْعَرْشِ الْمَجِيْدُ ۙ

17. Doer of what He wills.

فَعَّالٌ لِّمَا يُرِيْدُ ؕ

18. Has *not* the story of the hosts come to thee?

هَلْ اَتٰىكَ حَدِيْثُ الْجُنُوْدِ ۙ

19. Of Pharaoh and Thamūd?

فِرْعَوْنَ وَ ثَمُوْدَ ۬ؕ

20. Nay, but those who disbelieve *persist* in rejecting *the truth*.

بَلِ الَّذِيْنَ كَفَرُوْا فِيْ تَكْذِيْبٍ ۙ

21. And Allāh encompasses *them* *from before them and* from behind them.

وَّاللّٰهُ مِنْ وَّرَآئِهِمْ مُّحِيْطٌ ۚ

22. *Nay*, but it is a glorious Qur'ān.

بَلْ هُوَ قُرْاٰنٌ مَّجِيْدٌ ۙ

23. *In a well-guarded tablet.*3315

فِيْ لَوْحٍ مَّحْفُوْظٍ ۠

---

*17 : 60. *50 : 2; 56 : 78. *41 : 43; 56 : 79.

3315. The verse constitutes a challenging prophecy about the Qur'ān being guarded against every kind of interference and distortion. See also 1482. For Chapters 81—85 see "The Larger Edition of the Commentary."

CHAPTER 86

AL-ṬĀRIQ

(*Revealed before Hijrah*)

Date of Revelation and Context

Consensus of Muslim scholarly opinion assigns the *Sūrah* to the early period of the Holy Prophet's ministry. Noldeke and Muir among European scholars agree with this view. It is the last of the series of Chapters which started with *Sūrah* Al-Infiṭār. In all these Chapters the opening verse, in one form or another, furnishes an argument in support of the claim of the Reformer of the Latter Days. The intervening *Sūrah* Al-Taṭfīf, which has a different opening is, in fact, a part of *Sūrah* Al-Infiṭār. The present *Sūrah* continues and completes the topics which were dealt with in *Sūrah* Al-Infiṭār and in the following Chapters, and serves as a sort of *barzakh* between the Chapters that precede and those that follow it. From this *Sūrah*, however, begins a new subject.

سُورَةُ الطَّارِقِ مَكِّيَّةٌ (٨٦)

1. In the name of Allāh, the Gracious, the Merciful.

بِسْمِ اللّٰهِ الرَّحْمٰنِ الرَّحِيْمِ ①

2. By the heaven and the Morning Star[3316]—

وَالسَّمَآءِ وَالطَّارِقِ ②

3. And what should make thee know what the Morning Star is?

وَمَآ اَدْرٰىكَ مَا الطَّارِقُ ③

4. *It is* the Star of piercing brightness—

النَّجْمُ الثَّاقِبُ ④

5. There is not a soul but has a guardian[3317] over it.

اِنْ كُلُّ نَفْسٍ لَّمَّا عَلَيْهَا حَافِظٌ ⑤

6. So let man consider of what he is created.

فَلْيَنْظُرِ الْاِنْسَانُ مِمَّ خُلِقَ ⑥

7. He is created of gushing fluid,[3318]

خُلِقَ مِنْ مَّآءٍ دَافِقٍ ⑦

8. Which issues forth from between the loins and the breast-bones.[3318A]

يَّخْرُجُ مِنْ بَيْنِ الصُّلْبِ وَالتَّرَآئِبِ ⑧

3316. The reference in the verse may be to the Holy Prophet's Deputy whose advent like the morning star was to herald the dawn of the triumph and spread of Islām, after the night of spiritual darkness, which had come over Islām will have passed. According to some Commentators, however, the verse refers to the Holy Prophet himself who appeared when the night of spiritual darkness had spread over the entire world, it being pitch dark in Arabia, the land where he made his appearance.

3317. God will protect the Morning Star—the Holy Prophet's Deputy and the Star of piercing brightness—the Holy Prophet.

3318. Man's spiritual development is subject to alternate periods of progression and retrogression, like the seminal fluid that gushes forth and falls.

3318A. It is characteristic of the Quranic style that it substitutes mild or vague words of expressions for harsh and blunt ones. 'From between the loins and the breast-bones,' is one of such euphemisms used by the Qur'ān. The verse may signify that man is born of the water that comes out of the loins of his father and is fed by the breast of his mother. The fact that man has been created from a fluid which gushes forth and then falls may signify that he has been endowed with great natural faculties to make rapid progress but he is also likely to fall to the lowest depths of degradation, if he does not make proper use of those God-given powers. The verse signifies that man's spiritual development is subject to alternate periods of progression and retrogression, like the seminal fluid which gushes forth and then falls.

9. [a]Surely, *Allāh* has the Power to bring him back *to life*,

إِنَّهٗ عَلٰى رَجْعِهٖ لَقَادِرٌ ۝٩

10. [b]*On* the day when secrets shall be disclosed.

يَوْمَ تُبْلَى السَّرَآئِرُ ۝١٠

11. And he shall have no strength and no helper.

فَمَا لَهٗ مِنْ قُوَّةٍ وَّلَا نَاصِرٍ ۝١١

12. By the cloud which gives rain repeatedly,

وَالسَّمَآءِ ذَاتِ الرَّجْعِ ۝١٢

13. And *by* the earth which opens out *with herbage*.[3319]

وَالْاَرْضِ ذَاتِ الصَّدْعِ ۝١٣

14. Surely, *the Qur'ān* is a decisive word.

إِنَّهٗ لَقَوْلٌ فَصْلٌ ۝١٤

15. And it is not a vain talk.

وَّمَا هُوَ بِالْهَزْلِ ۝١٥

16. Surely, [c]they plan a plan,

إِنَّهُمْ يَكِيْدُوْنَ كَيْدًا ۝١٦

17. And I *also* plan a plan.

وَّاَكِيْدُ كَيْدًا ۝١٧

18. [d]So give respite to the disbelievers. *Aye* respite them for a little while.[3319A]

فَمَهِّلِ الْكٰفِرِيْنَ اَمْهِلْهُمْ رُوَيْدًا ۝١٨

---

[a]46 : 34. [b]10 : 31. [c]52 : 43. [d]68 : 46; 73 : 12.

3319. This and the preceding verse mean that just as the rain on which depends very largely the greenness and vegetation of the earth comes down from heaven and with its cessation earthly water begins gradually to dry up, similarly human reason loses its purity and strength without heavenly revelation.

3319A. The verse purports to say that disbelievers are granted respite that they may try all their evil plans and employ all the strength and resources they possess against Islām and the Holy Prophet. The triumph of Islām, despite all their planning and boasted strength, will be an irrefutable proof that it is from Allāh and has His support.

CHAPTER 87

AL-A'LĀ

(Revealed before Hijrah)

Date of Revelation and Context

The *Sūrah* was revealed very early in the Holy Prophet's ministry at Mecca. Besides most Commentators of the Qur'ān, Muir and Noldeke hold this view; the latter (Noldeke) places its revelation after Chapter 78, while some Muslim scholars assign it the eighth place in the chronological order of revelation of the Qur'ān. The preceding *Sūrah* had ended on the note that the Qur'ān is a complete and perfect code of Divine laws, fully capable of meeting the needs and requirements of all mankind; and that at no time will it be subject to change, abrogation or interpolation. This Quranic claim gives rise to the natural and inevitable question, *viz.*, where was the need of a new Reformer to whom reference has been made in the preceding several Chapters in the presence of such a complete and perfect revelation? The present *Sūrah* answers this important question. It was further stated in *Sūrah* Al-Ṭāriq that the development of man is subject to alternate periods of rise and fall. This fact again gives rise to another equally important question, *viz.*, that after the revelation of a Law, complete in all respects, man's progress should naturally become uniform and uninterrupted and immune against all possibility of retrogression. This being so, why was a complete *Sharī'ah* not revealed in the beginning of the world; why was it deferred till the time of the Holy Prophet? The *Sūrah* supplies an answer to this question also. It possesses another intimate connection with the preceding Chapter. In that *Sūrah* it was stated that man is born of a fluid which issues forth from the loins of his father and gets his sustenance from the breast of his mother. This constituted a subtle hint about the gradual process of man's physical development. We are told that like his physical development man's spiritual development is also gradual. The Holy Prophet generally recited this and the next *Sūrah* in the Friday and 'Īd Prayers.

سُوۡرَةُ الۡاَعۡلٰى مَكِّيَّةٌ (٨٧)

1. [a]In the name of Allāh, the Gracious, the Merciful.

بِسۡمِ اللّٰہِ الرَّحۡمٰنِ الرَّحِیۡمِ ۝۱

2. [b]Glorify the name of thy Lord,[3320] the Most High,

سَبِّحِ اسۡمَ رَبِّکَ الۡاَعۡلَی ۝۲

3. [c]Who creates *man* and perfects[3321] *him*.

الَّذِیۡ خَلَقَ فَسَوّٰی ۝۳

4. [d]And Who determines *his capacities* and furnishes him with *appropriate* guidance.

وَ الَّذِیۡ قَدَّرَ فَہَدٰی ۝۴

5. And Who brings forth the pasturage,

وَ الَّذِیۡۤ اَخۡرَجَ الۡمَرۡعٰی ۝۵

6. Then turns it into black [e]stubble.[3322]

فَجَعَلَہٗ غُثَآءً اَحۡوٰی ۝۶

[a]1 : 1. [b]56 : 75; 69 : 53. [c]82 : 8; 91 : 8. [d]80 : 20. [e]18 : 46; 57 : 21.

3320. The Divine attribute *Rabb* (Lord Who makes things grow and develop by stages) disposes of the objection: Why was the perfect Law not revealed in the begining of creation? The word implies that perfect Law should have been revealed when man's intellect and reason had attained their fullest development which could and did take place after a long and gradual process of evolution.

3321. A high destiny awaits man. He can attain the highest spiritual stature and can reflect in his person Divine attributes so as to become the mirror of his Creator.

3322. The verse constitutes a subtle answer to the objection: Why did God first reveal incomplete Laws, suited only to the needs of the peoples and the periods in which they were revealed, and then towards the end revealed the last and most perfect *Sharī'ah* in the form of the Qur'ān? The answer is that God has created two kinds of things: (*a*) Those that like herbage and pasture satisfy man's temporary needs and thus have a limited tenure of life. The former Scriptures, like these things, fulfilled only man's temporary needs and, therefore, were subject to decay and death. (*b*) Those things such as the sun, the moon, the earth, etc., which are of permanent use for man. They will last till the universe lasts. The Qur'ān is like the universe and is meant to be man's unerring guide till the end of time; hence it is immune to change, replacement and the wasting effect of time.

7. We shall teach thee *the Qur'ān*, and thou shalt not forget *it*,[3323]

سَنُقْرِئُكَ فَلَا تَنْسٰٓى ۝٧

8. Except as what Allāh wills.[3324] Surely, [a]He knows *what is* manifest and what is hidden.

اِلَّا مَا شَآءَ اللّٰهُ ۭ اِنَّهٗ يَعْلَمُ الْجَهْرَ وَمَا يَخْفٰى ۝٨

9. [b]And We shall provide thee with *every* facility.[3325]

وَنُيَسِّرُكَ لِلْيُسْرٰى ۝٩

10. So keep on admonishing *people*. Surely, admonition is, indeed, profitable.

فَذَكِّرْ اِنْ نَّفَعَتِ الذِّكْرٰى ۝١٠

11. [c]He who fears will heed;

سَيَذَّكَّرُ مَنْ يَّخْشٰى ۝١١

12. But the most wretched will turn aside from it,

وَيَتَجَنَّبُهَا الْاَشْقَى ۝١٢

13. He who will enter the great [d]Fire.

الَّذِيْ يَصْلَى النَّارَ الْكُبْرٰى ۝١٣

14. [e]Then he will neither die therein nor live.

ثُمَّ لَا يَمُوْتُ فِيْهَا وَلَا يَحْيٰى ۝١٤

[a]2 : 34; 20 : 8; 21 : 111; 24 : 30. [b]92 : 8. [c]51 : 56. [d]88 : 5. [e]14 : 18; 20 : 75.

3323. The Holy Prophet was human and as such was apt to forget and he did forget things as far as the affairs of life were concerned. But God in His infallible wisdom had so arranged that though the Holy Prophet was not literate and that sometimes long Chapters were revealed to him in one piece, the revelation remained so indelibly imprinted on his mind that he was never found to forget or falter in reciting the revealed portions. It is marvellous, indeed, that very long Chapters such as Al-Baqarah, Āl'Imrān and Al-Nisā', were revealed piecemeal, and a period of several years had intervened between the revelation of one piece and another and yet the Holy Prophet never, for a moment, fumbled or faltered in putting the revealed verses in their proper places. This is a fact which has not been disputed by even the most hostile critics of the Qur'ān.

3324. The expression, 'as what Allāh wills,' pertains only to matters of everyday life.

3325. The verse signifies: (*a*) That it is easy to commit the Qur'ān to memory; (*b*) that its teachings possess an adaptability all their own which makes them conform to, and meet, the exigencies of changing conditions and circumstances and also the needs and requirements of men of different temperaments and dispositions; and (*c*) that Quranic injunctions are not arbitrary but wise and rational. These factors combined make the Qur'ān a book easy to learn and to act upon. These, among others, are some of the means which God has provided for the eternal protection and preservation of the Quranic text and its meaning.

15. [a]Verily, he, indeed, will prosper who purifies himself,

قَدْ اَفْلَحَ مَنْ تَزَكّٰى ﴿١٥﴾

16. And remembers the name of his Lord and offers Prayers.

وَذَكَرَ اسْمَ رَبِّهٖ فَصَلّٰى ﴿١٦﴾

17. [b]But you prefer the life of this world,

بَلْ تُؤْثِرُوْنَ الْحَيٰوةَ الدُّنْيَا ﴿١٧﴾

18. [c]Whereas the Hereafter is better and more lasting.

وَالْاٰخِرَةُ خَيْرٌ وَّاَبْقٰى ﴿١٨﴾

19. [d]This, indeed, is *what is taught* in the former Scriptures—

اِنَّ هٰذَا لَفِى الصُّحُفِ الْاُوْلٰى ﴿١٩﴾

20. The Scriptures of Abraham and Moses.[3326]

صُحُفِ اِبْرٰهِيْمَ وَمُوْسٰى ﴿٢٠﴾

[a]91 : 10. [b]75 : 21. [c]93 : 5. [d]20 : 134.

3326. Because the essential principles of all religions are basically identical, the teachings mentioned in the foregoing verses are also found in the Scriptures of Moses and Abraham. The verse may also signify that the prophecy about the appearance of a great Prophet who was to give to the world the last Divine Message and the most perfect Teaching is found in the Scriptures of Moses and Abraham (Deut. 18 : 18-19 & 33 : 2).

CHAPTER 88

AL-GHĀSHIYAH

(*Revealed before Hijrah*)

Dated of Revelation and Context

The *Sūrah*, like the preceding one, was revealed early at Mecca. Eminent early Muslim scholars such as Ibn 'Abbās and Ibn Zubair hold this view. The famous German Orientalist Noldeke places it in the fourth year of the Call. This and some of the preceding Chapters deal with the collective life of the Muslim Community in the time of the Holy Prophet and also in the Latter Days. This is why the Holy Prophet generally used to recite it in the Friday and the 'Id Prayers. In some previous Chapters it was stated that Islām will never prosper by the employment only of material means. When Muslims will decline and decay and the Qur'ān will, as it were, go upto Heaven, a Divine Reformer will appear who will bring it back to earth and will make its ideals and principles shine in resplendent glory. It was also stated that Islām will continue to have, in every age, sincere and devoted followers who will preach and propagate its Message, and that other unpredictable circumstances will also arise which will greatly contribute to its progress and prosperity. In the present *Sūrah*, it is stated that Muslims will have to face severe opposition and cruel persecution, and after they will have patiently stood the test, success will come to them. Though the *Sūrah* deals primarily with the vicissitudes through which Muslims have to pass in this life, it also refers, as its name shows, to the Day of Resurrection. On the Day of Reckoning whether in this or in the next life, when the scales are set up, some faces are downcast, covered with disgrace and ignominy, and some others beam with joy being pleased with the results of their labour.

سُوْرَةُ الْغَاشِيَةِ مَكِّيَّةٌ (٨٨)

1. [a]In the name of Allāh, the Gracious, the Merciful.

بِسْمِ اللّٰهِ الرَّحْمٰنِ الرَّحِيْمِ ①

2. Has there come to thee [b]the news of the overwhelming *calamity* ?[3327]

هَلْ اَتٰىكَ حَدِيْثُ الْغَاشِيَةِ ②

3. *Some* [c]faces on that day will be downcast;

وُجُوْهٌ يَّوْمَئِذٍ خَاشِعَةٌ ③

4. Toiling, weary.

عَامِلَةٌ نَّاصِبَةٌ ④

5. *They* shall enter a blazing [d]Fire,

تَصْلٰى نَارًا حَامِيَةً ⑤

6. *And* will be made to drink from a boiling [e]spring.

تُسْقٰى مِنْ عَيْنٍ اٰنِيَةٍ ⑥

7. They will have no food save that of dry, bitter and thorny herbage,

لَيْسَ لَهُمْ طَعَامٌ اِلَّا مِنْ ضَرِيْعٍ ⑦

8. Which will neither nourish nor satisfy hunger.

لَّا يُسْمِنُ وَلَا يُغْنِيْ مِنْ جُوْعٍ ⑧

9. *And some* [f]faces on that day will be joyful;

وُجُوْهٌ يَّوْمَئِذٍ نَّاعِمَةٌ ⑨

10. Well-pleased with their *past* striving,[3328]

لِّسَعْيِهَا رَاضِيَةٌ ⑩

11. In a [g]lofty Garden,

فِيْ جَنَّةٍ عَالِيَةٍ ⑪

12. Wherein thou wilt hear no vain talk.

لَّا تَسْمَعُ فِيْهَا لَاغِيَةً ⑫

---

[a]1 : 1. [b]12 : 108. [c]68 : 44; 75 : 25; 80 : 41-42. [d]87 : 13; 101 : [e]55 : 45. [f]75 : 23. [g]69 : 23

3327. (*a*) The Judgment Day or a terrific calamity. (*b*) The severe famine that held Mecca in its grip for about seven years in the time of the Holy Prophet has also been referred to in the Qur'ān as Ghāshiyah (44 : 11-12).

3328. The righteous believers will be well-pleased with the marvellous results of the sacrifices they will have made for the cause of Islām.

13. Therein is a running spring,[3329]

فِيْهَا عَيْنٌ جَارِيَةٌ ﴿١٣﴾

14. Therein are raised couches,

فِيْهَا سُرُرٌ مَّرْفُوْعَةٌ ﴿١٤﴾

15. [a]And goblets properly placed,

وَّاَكْوَابٌ مَّوْضُوْعَةٌ ﴿١٥﴾

16. And cushions *beautifully* ranged in rows,

وَّنَمَارِقُ مَصْفُوْفَةٌ ﴿١٦﴾

17. And carpets *tastefully* spread.

وَّزَرَابِيُّ مَبْثُوْثَةٌ ﴿١٧﴾

18. Do they not then look at the camels,[3330] how they are created?

اَفَلَا يَنْظُرُوْنَ اِلَى الْاِبِلِ كَيْفَ خُلِقَتْ ﴿١٨﴾

19. [b]And at the heaven, how it is raised high?

وَاِلَى السَّمَآءِ كَيْفَ رُفِعَتْ ﴿١٩﴾

20. [c]And at the mountains, how they are fixed?

وَاِلَى الْجِبَالِ كَيْفَ نُصِبَتْ ﴿٢٠﴾

21. [d]And at the earth, how it is spread out?[3331]

وَاِلَى الْاَرْضِ كَيْفَ سُطِحَتْ ﴿٢١﴾

22. Admonish, therefore, for thou art but an admonisher;

فَذَكِّرْ اِنَّمَآ اَنْتَ مُذَكِّرٌ ﴿٢٢﴾

23. [e]Thou art not *appointed* a keeper over them.

لَسْتَ عَلَيْهِمْ بِمُصَيْطِرٍ ﴿٢٣﴾

24. But whoever turns away and disbelieves,

اِلَّا مَنْ تَوَلّٰى وَكَفَرَ ﴿٢٤﴾

25. Allāh will punish him with the greatest punishment.

فَيُعَذِّبُهُ اللّٰهُ الْعَذَابَ الْاَكْبَرَ ﴿٢٥﴾

26. Unto Us, surely, is their return.

اِنَّ اِلَيْنَآ اِيَابَهُمْ ﴿٢٦﴾

27. Then, surely, it is for Us to call them to account.

ثُمَّ اِنَّ عَلَيْنَا حِسَابَهُمْ ﴿٢٧﴾ ع ١٤ النصف

[a]43 : 72. [b]13 : 3; 55 : 8. [c]50 : 8. [d]50 : 8; 79 : 31. [e]6 : 108; 39 : 42; 42 : 7.

3329. Like a running spring their beneficence and goodness will flow unceasingly.

3330. Believers, like camels going straight in a line, all behind the one that leads them, give unquestioning obedience to their Leader. Or, like camels which can go on for days without water in a hot, sandy desert, they have infinite patience under trials and hardships and continue their spiritual journey without complaining, *Ibil* also meaning clouds (Lane), the verse may signify that God will spread the teachings of the Qur'ān which is spiritual water over the entire earth.

3331. The four verses (vv. 18—21) teach a Muslim the supreme moral lesson that (1) he should be generous like the clouds, (2) exalted like the heaven, (3) of fixed resolve like the mountains, and (4) soft and humble like the earth.

CHAPTER 89

AL-FAJR

Date of Revelation and Context

This Chapter was among the earliest *Sūrahs* which were revealed at Mecca. From historical data it appears to have been revealed sometime in the fourth year of the Call. Noldeke places it immediately after Al-Ghāshiyah, which was also revealed in the fourth year. The *Sūrah* contains a double prophecy which primarily applies to the Holy Prophet and secondarily to the Promised Messiah. In a beautiful allegory the *Sūrah* alludes to the last ten years of the Holy Prophet's life of hardship at Mecca and his Emigration to Medina, accompanied by his most faithful Companion, Abū Bakr, and to the first year of his life at Medina which was also full of strains and stresses. The *Sūrah* may also be taken as referring to the decline of Islām during the ten centuries after its first three hundred years of uniform success, and to the appearance of the Promised Messiah, as well as to the first century of trials and hardships for his mission and his followers. After this brief allegorical description of the vicissitudes and fluctuations of the fortunes of Islām in the time of the Holy Prophet and that of the Promised Messiah, the *Sūrah* mentions the case of Pharaoh as representing the opposition which the cause of Truth always encounters. Opposition to Truth (the *Sūrah* further states) springs from accumulation of power and wealth in the hands of a particular class, and the misuse of riches and authority by them brings about their decline and destruction. The *Sūrah* ends on the note that only a few fortunate people accept the Divine Message and by walking in the ways of righteousness succeed in winning God's pleasure, and consequently enjoy complete immunity from fear of failure or faltering, and after joining the company of His Elect, enter Heaven.

سُورَةُ الْفَجْرِ مَكِّيَّةٌ (٨٩)

1. [a]In the name of Allāh, the Gracious, the Merciful.	بِسْمِ اللّٰهِ الرَّحْمٰنِ الرَّحِيْمِ ①
2. By the Dawn,[3332]	وَالْفَجْرِ ②
3. And the Ten Nights,[3333]	وَلَيَالٍ عَشْرٍ ③
4. And the Even and the Odd,[3334]	وَّالشَّفْعِ وَالْوَتْرِ ④
5. And the Night when it moves on *to its close*,[3335]	وَالَّيْلِ اِذَا يَسْرِ ⑤
6. Is there *not* in it strong evidence for one possessed *of* understanding ?	هَلْ فِيْ ذٰلِكَ قَسَمٌ لِّذِيْ حِجْرٍ ⑥

[a]1 : 1.

3332. "The Dawn" may signify the Holy Prophet's Emigration to Medina with which ended the dark night of persecution at Mecca. It may also signify the advent of the Promised Messiah who was to bring a message of hope and of a bright future for Muslims after centuries of their decline and decadence.

3333. "The Ten Nights" may represent the last ten dark years of severe persecution to which Muslims were subjected at Mecca, or the ten centuries of the decline and decadence of Muslims before the advent of the Promised Messiah, with which would end the dark period of their spiritual and political degradation, and which would usher in the dawn of a glorious future for Islām. An implied reference to these "Ten Nights" or ten centuries of the decline of Islām is also to be found elsewhere in the Qur'ān (32 : 6). These ten centuries (or a thousand years) of the moral decadence of Muslims came after the first three centuries of the heyday of their glory and grandeur. which have been called the best three centuries of Islām by the Holy Prophet (Bukhārī, *Kitāb Al-Riqāq*), had passed. The decline of Islām began towards the end of the third century A.H., when, on the one hand, an Umayyad Caliph of Spain signed a pact of mutual assistance with the Pope against the Abbaside Empire of Baghdad and, on the other, the Caliph of Baghdad entered into a treaty of friendship with the Caesar of Rome against the Umayyad Caliph of Spain.

3334. Continuing the allegory the word *Al-Shaf'* (the Even) may allude to the Holy Prophet and Abū Bakr—his ever faithful Companion. The two of them made the number even, and God Who was with them in the hour of tribulation was *Al-Watr* (the Odd). To this "Even and Odd" number, a pointed reference is to be found in 9 : 40. Or, the Holy Prophet and the Promised Messiah may be taken as making an even number and Allāh an odd number, or "the Even and the Odd" may signify that whereas the Holy Prophet and the Promised Messiah were two separate individuals, the Promised Messiah was so completely lost in the Holy Prophet as to have become one with him.

3335. "The Night" may represent the first year of the *Hijrah* which did not see any abatement of the Holy Prophet's worries. Though after the Emigration to Medina the "Morning" had dawned for the Muslims, yet they were not completely out of the wood; they had to suffer hardships for another night, *i.e.*, another year of hardships after which in the Battle of Badr the Quraish suffered a crushing defeat and the Prophet Isaiah's prophecy (21 : 16) was literally fulfilled: 'For thus hath the Lord said unto me, within a year, according to the years of an hireling and all the glory of Kedar shall fail.'

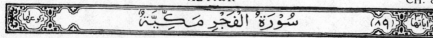

7. Hast thou not seen how thy Lord dealt with 'Ād[3336]—

أَلَمْ تَرَ كَيْفَ فَعَلَ رَبُّكَ بِعَادٍ ﴿٧﴾

8. *The tribe of* Iram, *possessors* of lofty buildings?

إِرَمَ ذَاتِ الْعِمَادِ ﴿٨﴾

9. The like of whom have not been created in *these* parts—

الَّتِي لَمْ يُخْلَقْ مِثْلُهَا فِي الْبِلَادِ ﴿٩﴾

10. [a]And *with* Thamūd who hewed out rocks in the valley,

وَثَمُودَ الَّذِينَ جَابُوا الصَّخْرَ بِالْوَادِ ﴿١٠﴾

11. And *with* Pharaoh, lord of *vast* hosts,

وَفِرْعَوْنَ ذِي الْأَوْتَادِ ﴿١١﴾

12. [b]Who committed excesses in the cities,

الَّذِينَ طَغَوْا فِي الْبِلَادِ ﴿١٢﴾

13. [c]And wrought much corruption therein?

فَأَكْثَرُوا فِيهَا الْفَسَادَ ﴿١٣﴾

14. Thy Lord, then, let loose on them the scourge[3337] of punishment.

فَصَبَّ عَلَيْهِمْ رَبُّكَ سَوْطَ عَذَابٍ ﴿١٤﴾

15. Surely, thy Lord is *ever* on the watch.

إِنَّ رَبَّكَ لَبِالْمِرْصَادِ ﴿١٥﴾

16. As for man, when his Lord tries him and honours him and [d]bestows favours[3338] on him, he says, 'My Lord has honoured me.'

فَأَمَّا الْإِنْسَانُ إِذَا مَا ابْتَلَاهُ رَبُّهُ فَأَكْرَمَهُ وَ
نَعَّمَهُ فَيَقُولُ رَبِّي أَكْرَمَنِ ﴿١٦﴾

[a]7 : 75; 26 : 150. [b]28 : 5. [c]28 : 5. [d]17 : 84.

3336. 'Ād were a very powerful people in their time: They excelled their contemporary nations in material means and resources.

3337. *Saut* means a whip; scourge; vehemence (Lane).

3338. Favours are bestowed upon man, sometimes to test his mettle; at other times to reward him for his good actions. Similarly, he is involved in troubles that he may be tried and rewarded or punished according to his desert. But man is so constituted that when he is in ease and affluence, he regards these things as the fruits of his own labour and superior intelligence (28 : 79); but when misfortunes overtake him, he attributes them to God.

17. But when He tries and straitens for him his *means of* [a]subsistence, he says 'My Lord has disgraced me.'

وَ اَمَّآ اِذَا مَا ابْتَلٰىهُ فَقَدَرَ عَلَيْهِ رِزْقَهٗ فَيَقُوْلُ رَبِّيْٓ اَهَانَنِ ﴿۱۷﴾

18. [b]Nay, but you honour not the orphan,

كَلَّا بَلْ لَّا تُكْرِمُوْنَ الْيَتِيْمَ ﴿۱۸﴾

19. [c]And urge not *one another* to feed the poor;

وَلَا تَحٰٓضُّوْنَ عَلٰى طَعَامِ الْمِسْكِيْنِ ﴿۱۹﴾

20. And devour the heritage *of other people*, devouring *greedily and* wholly;

وَتَاْكُلُوْنَ التُّرَاثَ اَكْلًا لَّمًّا ﴿۲۰﴾

21. [d]And you love wealth with exceeding love.[3339]

وَّتُحِبُّوْنَ الْمَالَ حُبًّا جَمًّا ﴿۲۱﴾

22. Hearken! when the earth is completely broken into pieces;

كَلَّآ اِذَا دُكَّتِ الْاَرْضُ دَكًّا دَكًّا ﴿۲۲﴾

23. [e]And thy Lord comes,[3340] *attended by* the angels, rank on rank;

وَّجَآءَ رَبُّكَ وَالْمَلَكُ صَفًّا صَفًّا ﴿۲۳﴾

24. And Hell is [f]brought *near* that day; on that day man will remember, [g]but of what avail shall that remembrance be to him?

وَجِايْٓءَ يَوْمَئِذٍۭ بِجَهَنَّمَ ۙ يَوْمَئِذٍ يَّتَذَكَّرُ الْاِنْسَانُ وَاَنّٰى لَهُ الذِّكْرٰى ﴿۲۴﴾

25. He will say, 'O, would that I had sent on *some good works* for my life *here !*'

يَقُوْلُ يٰلَيْتَنِيْ قَدَّمْتُ لِحَيَاتِيْ ﴿۲۵﴾

[a]17 : 84. [b]107 : 3. [c]69 : 35. [d]104 : 3. [e]2 : 110; 6 : 159; 16 : 34. [f]26 : 92. [g]79 : 36.

3339. The verse drives home to hoarders of wealth the evils of hoarding. Inordinate love of money creates in man an excessive desire to keep on adding to his wealth, without spending it for the furtherance of good causes. It makes him regardless of the means he employs to acquire it, which leads to his moral ruin. Islām takes as much care of the moral health of society as it takes of that of the individual; and society's health requires that material goods be widely distributed and wealth kept in easy circulation.

3340. The 'coming of the Lord' attended by the angels is a Quranic idiom for imminent and destructive Divine punishment.

26. So on that day none can punish like unto His punishment.

فَيَوْمَئِذٍ لَّا يُعَذِّبُ عَذَابَهُ أَحَدٌ ﴿٢٦﴾

27. And none can bind like unto His binding.[3341]

وَلَا يُوثِقُ وَثَاقَهُ أَحَدٌ ﴿٢٧﴾

28. O, thou soul at peace !

يَا أَيَّتُهَا النَّفْسُ الْمُطْمَئِنَّةُ ﴿٢٨﴾

29. Return to thy Lord, thou well-pleased *with Him* [a]*and* He well-pleased with thee.[3342]

ارْجِعِي إِلَى رَبِّكِ رَاضِيَةً مَّرْضِيَّةً ﴿٢٩﴾

30. So enter thou among My chosen servants,

فَادْخُلِي فِي عِبَادِي ﴿٣٠﴾

31. And enter thou My Garden.

وَادْخُلِي جَنَّتِي ﴿٣١﴾

3341. The mill of God grinds slowly, but it grinds exceeding small. God is slow to punish but when His punishment comes, it is most destructive. 'It spares not and it leaves naught' (74 : 29).

3342. This is the highest stage of spiritual development when man is well-pleased with his Lord and his Lord is well-pleased with him (58 : 23). At this stage which is called the heavenly stage, he becomes immune to all moral weaknesses and frailties and is braced with a peculiar spiritual strength. He is "united" with God and cannot exist without Him. It is in this life and not after death that this great spiritual transformation takes place in him and it is in this world and not elsewhere that access to Paradise is granted to him.

CHAPTER 90

AL-BALAD

(*Revealed before Hijrah*)

Date of Revelation and Context

This *Sūrah* is among the earliest Chapters to have been revealed at Mecca. According to Christian writers it was revealed in the first year of the Call. If not as early as that, it certainly was revealed towards the end of the third or the beginning of the fourth year. In *Sūrah* Al-Fajr it was stated that jibes, mockery and taunts, to which the Holy Prophet had been subjected in the first three years of his mission, were about to give place to determined, persistent and organized opposition and persecution, and that this persecution would continue for ten long years which allegorically were mentioned as "Ten Nights." In the *Sūrah* under comment, however, the Holy Prophet is told that it is in Mecca, his beloved native town, and by his own kith and kin, that he and his followers will be persecuted. It is further implied that centuries ago, in pursuance of Divine command, the Patriarch Abraham and his righteous son, Ishmael, had laid the foundations of this sacred town of Mecca and had prayed to God that it should become the Centre from where should emanate the light which should illumine the whole world. Both the father and the son made great sacrifices in carrying out the commands of God. Abraham's prayer was heard and the Holy Prophet appeared in the fulness of time and gave to the world the perfect Teaching in the form of the Qur'ān. The *Sūrah* further says that man chooses the easy path and refuses to attempt "the ascent" that leads to the achievement of his great goal. It ends on the note that only those, who place before them high ideals and live up to them, achieve their goal, while those, who possess no noble ideals and make no sacrifice for good causes, are condemned to a life of failure and frustration.

سُورَةُ الْبَلَدِ مَكِّيَّةٌ

(٩٠) آياتها ٢١ — ركوعها ١

1. [a]In the name of Allāh, the Gracious, the Merciful.

بِسْمِ اللّٰهِ الرَّحْمٰنِ الرَّحِيْمِ ①

2. [b]Nay, I cite as witness this City[3343]—

لَآ أُقْسِمُ بِهٰذَا الْبَلَدِ ②

3. And *affirm that* thou wilt, surely, alight[3344] in this City—

وَأَنْتَ حِلٌّۢ بِهٰذَا الْبَلَدِ ③

4. And *I cite as witness* the father and the son,[3345]

وَوَالِدٍ وَّمَا وَلَدَ ④

5. We have, surely, created man [c]to *toil and* struggle.[3346]

لَقَدْ خَلَقْنَا الْإِنْسَانَ فِيْ كَبَدٍ ⑤

---

[a]1 : 1. [b]52 : 5; 95 : 4. [c]84 : 7.

3343. The particle *lā* is used here to draw pointed attention to the subject which is about to be introduced and to signify that it is so clear and obvious that it needs no swearing to support it. Or, it may be intended to refute an understood objection. In that case the meaning would be: 'Not that thou art not a forger, as the disbelievers think, thou art a true Prophet of God and this City is called to bear witness to this fact.' But more appropriately the verse means something like this: 'You harbour evil designs about Islām. O disbelievers, I know what is in your minds, but I tell you that it would never happen as you desire, and I cite this City as a witness to this fact.

3344. *Ḥill* means: (1) A thing the doing of which is lawful; (2) target; (3) one free from obligation; (4) one alighting or dwelling in a place (Lane). The root-word *Ḥalla* possessing all these meanings, the verse signifies: (1) It is considered lawful by your enemies to do you any harm, even to kill you, in this City of Mecca which is so sacred that what to say of killing a living creature, it is strictly forbidden to do it the slightest harm in its precincts. (2) Thou alone art the target of every conceivable abuse, harm, injury, cruelty or violence against life, property or honour in this sacred City. (3) Thou wilt alight as a conqueror in this City from where thou art now being driven out as a fugitive. (4) For a short while thou wilt be freed from the obligation to observe the sacredness of this City when thou wilt enter it as a victor and those wicked people, who had placed themselves outside the pale of law by perpetrating unutterable cruelties on innocent Muslims, will be at your mercy.

3345. While raising the foundations of the Ka'bah, the Patriarch Abraham and his son Ishmael had prayed to God to raise among the Meccans a Messenger (2 : 129-130). Thus 'the father and the son' bear witness to the truth of the Holy Prophet.

3346. The prophecy, that the Holy Prophet will be expelled from Mecca and will come back to it as a conqueror and Mecca will submit to him and its inhabitants will enter the fold of Islām, will be fulfilled only after he and his followers will have gone through great hardships, that is to say, great toil and incessant struggle will be demanded of them to achieve their great goal.

6. [a]Does he think that no one has power over him?[3347]

أَيَحْسَبُ أَنْ لَّنْ يَّقْدِرَ عَلَيْهِ أَحَدٌ ۝٦

7. He says, 'I have wasted enormous wealth.'[3348]

يَقُوْلُ أَهْلَكْتُ مَالًا لُّبَدًا ۝٧

8. Does he think that no one sees him?

أَيَحْسَبُ أَنْ لَّمْ يَرَهٗٓ أَحَدٌ ۝٨

9. Have We not given him two eyes,

أَلَمْ نَجْعَلْ لَّهٗ عَيْنَيْنِ ۝٩

10. And a tongue and two lips?

وَلِسَانًا وَّشَفَتَيْنِ ۝١٠

11. [b]And We have pointed out to him the two highways[3349] *of good and evil*

وَهَدَيْنٰهُ النَّجْدَيْنِ ۝١١

12. But he attempted not the steep ascent;[3350]

فَلَا اقْتَحَمَ الْعَقَبَةَ ۝١٢

13. And what should make thee know what the steep ascent is?

وَمَآ أَدْرٰىكَ مَا الْعَقَبَةُ ۝١٣

14. *It is* the freeing of a slave,

فَكُّ رَقَبَةٍ ۝١٤

[a]96:15 [b]76:4.

3347. God is aware of the evil designs of disbelievers and He has the power to, and will bring them to naught.

3348. Let the opponents of Islām use all their means (the verse purports to say) and spend heaps of wealth to prevent Islām from spreading, they will not succeed in their evil designs and Islām will continue to make both spiritual and political conquests.

3349. *Al-Najdain* means the two highways of good and evil, of truth and falsehood, of spiritual and material progress. God has provided man with all those means by which he can find out the right path, can sift right from wrong and truth from falsehood. He has been endowed with both spiritual and physical eyes by which he can distinguish good from evil and has been given a tongue and two lips that he might ask for guidance, and above all God has placed before him a supreme object that he may devote all his faculties and energies to achieve it.

3350. Through the Holy Prophet God had opened up all the ways and means by using which man could make unlimited spiritual and material progress, but he refused to make the necessary sacrifices to achieve this object.

15. [a]Or, feeding on a day of hunger

أَوْ إِطْعَامٌ فِي يَوْمٍ ذِي مَسْغَبَةٍ ﴿١٥﴾

16. An orphan near of kin,

يَتِيمًا ذَا مَقْرَبَةٍ ﴿١٦﴾

17. Or, a poor man *lying* in the dust.[3351]

أَوْ مِسْكِينًا ذَا مَتْرَبَةٍ ﴿١٧﴾

18. Then, he should have been of those who believe and exhort one another to [b]perseverance and exhort one another to mercy.[3352]

ثُمَّ كَانَ مِنَ الَّذِينَ آمَنُوا وَتَوَاصَوْا بِالصَّبْرِ وَتَوَاصَوْا بِالْمَرْحَمَةِ ﴿١٨﴾

19. These are the people of the [c]right hand.

أُولَٰئِكَ أَصْحَابُ الْمَيْمَنَةِ ﴿١٩﴾

20. But those who reject Our Signs, they are the people of the left [d]hand.

وَالَّذِينَ كَفَرُوا بِآيَاتِنَا هُمْ أَصْحَابُ الْمَشْأَمَةِ ﴿٢٠﴾

21. On them will be Fire [e]closed over.[3353]

عَلَيْهِمْ نَارٌ مُؤْصَدَةٌ ﴿٢١﴾

[a]76 : 9; 89 : 19. [b]103 : 4. [c]56 ; 28. [d]56 : 42. [e]104 : 9.

3351. Verses 14-17 speak of the two methods which can raise the moral stature of a people : (*a*) Freeing of the slaves, *i.e.*, raising the suppressed, oppressed and depressed sections of the community to an equal partnership in life. (*b*) Helping the orphans and the poor to stand on their own legs and to become useful members of the community.

3352. Good actions mentioned in the foregoing verses are not enough to raise the all round stature of a community. Good ideals and right principles, combined with continuous and sustained adherence to the path of moral rectitude and the teaching of virtues to others, are equally essential for the attainment of the above-mentioned high aim.

3353. Fire when closed on all sides becomes most destructive.

CHAPTER 91

AL-SHAMS

(*Revealed before Hijrah*)

Date of Revelation and Context

The *Sūrah* admittedly belongs to the very early Meccan period. Some scholars regard it as having been revealed in the first year of the Call; others assign it to the second or the third year. The five *Sūrahs* (89-93) possess a striking similarity in the subject-matter. In all of them great stress has been laid on the development of good morals, specially those that intimately concern and affect the collective progress and prosperity of a community. Muslims have been exhorted to create an atmosphere and environment which should help to raise the standard and stature of the poor, depressed and suppressed section of their community and should enable them to take their proper share in its activities. The immediately preceding Chapter contained a hint about the supreme object for which Abraham and his son Ishmael had built the Ka'bah. That supreme object is explained in 2 : 130. It is on the Prophet referred to in that verse (the Holy Prophet) and on his great moral qualities that some light is shed in the present *Sūrah*. Towards its close the *Sūrah* points out that moral greatness can be achieved by anyone who eschews evil and walks in the path of righteousness. It ends on the note that those, who choose to defy Divine laws and adopt evil ways, bring about their ruin with their own hands.

سُوۡرَۃُ الشَّمۡسِ مَکِّیَّۃٌ (٩١)

1. [a]In the name of Allāh, the Gracious, the Merciful.

بِسۡمِ اللّٰہِ الرَّحۡمٰنِ الرَّحِیۡمِ ﴿۱﴾

2. By[3354] the sun and its[3355] brightness,

وَ الشَّمۡسِ وَ ضُحٰہَا ﴿۲﴾

3. *And* by the moon[3356] when it follows *the sun*,

وَ الۡقَمَرِ اِذَا تَلٰىہَا ﴿۳﴾

4. *And* by the day[3357] when it reveals *the sun*'s glory,

وَ النَّہَارِ اِذَا جَلّٰىہَا ﴿۴﴾

5. *And* by the night[3358] when it draws a veil over *the light of the sun*.

وَ الَّیۡلِ اِذَا یَغۡشٰىہَا ﴿۵﴾

---

[a]1 : 1.

3354. The Quranic oaths have deep meaning underlying them. Divine laws reveal two aspects of the works of God *viz*., the obvious and the inferential. The former are easily comprehensible; in the comprehension of the latter there is room for error. In His oaths God has called attention to what may be inferred from what is obvious. In the oaths mentioned in verses, 2—7, the sun and the moon, the day and the night, the heavens and the earth belong to the "obvious"— their properties, referred to in these verses being universally known and acknowledged. But the same properties found in man's soul are not obvious. To lead to an inference of the existence of these properties in the human soul God has called to witness His obvious works. See also 2465.

3355. "The sun" in the verse may refer to the sun of the spiritual universe—the Holy Prophet—who is the source of all spiritual light and who will continue to enlighten the world till the end of time.

3356. "The moon" may also refer to the Holy Prophet, because he received light from God and transmitted it to the spiritually dark world. Or it may refer to those religious Divines and Reformers—particularly his Great Deputy, the Promised Messiah—who would borrow the light of truth from the Holy Prophet and transmit it to the world to remove the darkness of moral and spiritual turpitude.

3357 "The day" may signify the time during which the Message of Islām and the truth of its Founder were established and foundations were laid for their propagation in the world. The reference in the verse may particularly be to the time of the Holy Prophet's 'rightly-guided Caliphs' when the light of Islām shone in all its glory and splendour.

3358. "The night" may refer to the period of decline and decadence of Muslims when the light of Islām had become veiled from the eyes of the world. These four verses (2—5) refer to four periods in the eventful career of Islām, *viz*., the time of the Holy Prophet himself when the Spiritual Sun (the Holy Prophet) was shining in full splendour in the spiritual heaven; (2) the time of his Great Deputy the Promised Messiah when the light derived from the Holy Prophet was being reflected on to a dark world; (3) the time of the Holy Prophet's immediate Successors when the light of Islām was still shining and, (4) the period when spiritual darkness had spread over the world after the first three centuries of Islām which was its most glorious period.

6. *And* by the heaven[3359] and its *wonderful* structure,

وَالسَّمَآءِ وَمَا بَنٰهَا ۝٦

7. *And* by the earth and its expanse,

وَالْاَرْضِ وَمَا طَحٰهَا ۝٧

8. *And* by the soul and its perfection[3459A]—

وَنَفْسٍ وَّمَا سَوّٰىهَا ۝٨

9. And He revealed to it *the ways of* evil and *the ways of* righteousness[3360]—

فَاَلْهَمَهَا فُجُوْرَهَا وَتَقْوٰىهَا ۝٩

10. He, indeed, prospers who purifies it,

قَدْ اَفْلَحَ مَنْ زَكّٰىهَا ۝١٠

11. And he is ruined who corrupts it.

وَقَدْ خَابَ مَنْ دَسّٰىهَا ۝١١

12. The *tribe of* Thamūd rejected *the Divine Messenger* because of their rebelliousness,

كَذَّبَتْ ثَمُوْدُ بِطَغْوٰىهَآ ۝١٢

13. When the most wretched among them got up.

اِذِ انْۢبَعَثَ اَشْقٰىهَا ۝١٣

3359. The particle *mā* in this and the next two verses is either *Maṣdariyyah,* or it signifies *Alladhī, i.e.,* 'he who.' Thus in these verses attention is focussed on the great Designer and Architect of the universe, or on its perfection and complete freedom from every flaw and defect.

3359A. The verse means that all the properties which the great heavenly bodies such as the sun and the moon, etc., devote to the service of God's creatures and to which an implied reference has been made in verses 10, bear witness to man having been endowed with similar qualities in a high degree. In fact, man is a universe in miniature and in him is represented, on a small scale, all that exists in the external universe. Like the sun he sheds his lustre over the world and enlightens it with the light of wisdom and knowledge. Like the moon he transmits to those who are in the dark the light of vision, inspiration and revelation which he borrows from the Great Original Source. He is bright like the day and shows the ways of truth and virtue. Like the night he draws the veil over the faults and misdeeds of others, lightens their burdens and gives rest to the tired and the weary. Like the heavens he takes every distressed soul under his shelter and revives the lifeless earth with salubrious rain. Like the earth he submits in all humility and lowliness to be trampled under the feet by others as a trial for them, and from his purified soul various sorts of trees of knowledge and truth grow up in abundance, and with their shade, flowers and fruits he regales the world. Such are the great Divines and heavenly Reformers, of whom the greatest and the most perfect was the Holy Prophet Muhammad (may eternal Divine blessings be upon him).

3360. God has implanted in man's nature a feeling or sense of what is good and bad and has revealed to him that he could achieve spiritual perfection by eschewing what is bad and wrong and adopting what is right and good.

14. Then the Messenger of Allāh said, '*Leave alone* the she-camel of Allāh[3361] and *obstruct not* her drink.'

فَقَالَ لَهُمْ رَسُولُ اللّٰهِ نَاقَةَ اللّٰهِ وَسُقْيٰهَا ﴿١٤﴾

15. But they called him a liar and hamstrung her, so their Lord destroyed them completely because of their sin, and made *destruction overtake all of them* alike.

فَكَذَّبُوْهُ فَعَقَرُوْهَا فَدَمْدَمَ عَلَيْهِمْ رَبُّهُمْ بِذَنْۢبِهِمْ فَسَوّٰىهَا ﴿١٥﴾

16. And He cared not for the consequences[3361A] thereof.

وَلَا يَخَافُ عُقْبٰهَا ﴿١٦﴾ ع

3361. The Prophet Ṣāliḥ rode on his she-camel from place to place to preach the Divine Message. Putting obstacles in the way of the camel's free movements was tantamount to placing impediments in the way of Ṣāliḥ himself and preventing him from discharging the sacred duty entrusted to him by God. In a sense Ṣāliḥ, like every Divine Reformer, was God's she-camel.

3361A. When a people incur Divine punishment and are destroyed, God does not care for those who survive the destruction; or the meaning is that God does not care to what utterly miserable state they are reduced.

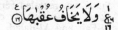

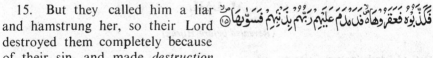

CHAPTER 92

AL-LAIL

(Revealed before Hijrah)

Date of Revelation and Context

Prominent Muslim scholars like Ibn 'Abbās and Ibn Zubair hold the view that the *Sūrah* was revealed very early at Mecca. William Muir agrees with their opinion. The *Sūrah* possesses very close resemblance with some previous Chapters, especially with Al-Fajr and Al-Balad. In the immediately preceding *Sūrah*, Al-Shams, it was hinted that the supreme object of the building of the Ka'bah, which was the principal theme of *Sūrah* Al-Balad, could not have been achieved without a great Divine Messenger—the Spirit *par excellence*. In the present *Sūrah*, however, it is stated that when an ideal Teacher like the Holy Prophet is blessed with ideal disciples like his Companions, progress of the cause of Truth becomes doubly accelerated. It also mentions some of the prominent moral qualities that marked the Companions of the Holy Prophet. In contrast, two glaring bad qualities that lead to the undoing of a people are also mentioned.

آیاتہا ۲۲ (۹۲) سُوْرَۃُ الَّیْلِ مَکِّیَّۃٌ رکوعہا ۱

1. [a]In the name of Allāh, the Gracious, the Merciful.

بِسۡمِ اللّٰہِ الرَّحۡمٰنِ الرَّحِیۡمِ ﴿۱﴾

2. [b]By the night[3362] when it covers up;

وَ الَّیۡلِ اِذَا یَغۡشٰی ﴿۲﴾

3. [c]And *by* the day when it shines forth,[3363]

وَ النَّہَارِ اِذَا تَجَلّٰی ﴿۳﴾

4. [d]And *by* the creation of the male and the female,[3363A]

وَ مَا خَلَقَ الذَّکَرَ وَ الۡاُنۡثٰۤی ﴿۴﴾

5. Surely, your strivings are diverse.[3364]

اِنَّ سَعۡیَکُمۡ لَشَتّٰی ﴿۵﴾

---

[a]1 : 1. [b]91 : 5. [c]91 : 4. [d]36 : 37; 51 : 50; 78 : 9.

3362. In the preceding *Sūrah* the principal subject of discussion was Al-Shams, *i.e.*, the Holy Prophet, who is the source and spring of all light. This is why mention of the sun and the day precedes that of the moon and the night. But in the present *Sūrah* a contrast is instituted between believers and disbelievers, and as the latter are generally larger in number and wield greater power and influence, mention of the night which represents disbelievers precedes that of the day which represents believers.

3363. By the substitution of the word *Tajallā* (shines forth) in this verse for *Jallā* (reveals its glory) in the corresponding verse in the preceding *Sūrah*, it is hinted that whereas in the preceding *Sūrah* the emphasis was on the high spiritual stature of the Teacher, in the present *Sūrah* it is on the great ability of the pupils to learn and assimilate the Divine Teaching.

3363A. Procreation of man depends upon the coming together of two individuals of opposite sexes. The characteristic quality of the one (the male) is to give and of the other (the female) is to receive. Like the physical world, there are in the spiritual world males—God's great Prophets and Divine Reformers who teach and guide; and spiritual females—their followers, who receive and benefit by the Divine Teaching. The verse embodies a hint that by the coming together of the perfect Teacher—the Holy Prophet—and the ideal pupils—his Companions—a new world is about to be born.

3364. The verse draws attention to the widely divergent goals of believers and disbelievers, and also to the disparity in the endeavours they make to achieve their respective goals. Whereas the efforts of believers are devoted to the dissemination of Truth, those of disbelievers are directed towards opposing it and putting obstacles and impediments in its way. The results of the two efforts must inevitably be different.

6. Then as for him who gives *for the cause of Allāh* and is righteous,

فَاَمَّا مَنْ اَعْطٰى وَاتَّقٰىۙ ۶

7. And testifies to *the truth of* what is right,[3365]

وَصَدَّقَ بِالْحُسْنٰىۙ ۷

8. "We will provide for him *every* facility[3366] *for good.*

فَسَنُيَسِّرُهٗ لِلْيُسْرٰىؕ ۸

9. But as for him who is niggardly and is *disdainfully* indifferent,

وَاَمَّا مَنْۢ بَخِلَ وَاسْتَغْنٰىۙ ۹

10. And rejects what is right,[3367]

وَكَذَّبَ بِالْحُسْنٰىۙ ۱۰

11. We will make easy for him *the path to* distress.[3368]

فَسَنُيَسِّرُهٗ لِلْعُسْرٰىؕ ۱۱

12. *b*And his wealth shall not avail him when he perishes.

وَمَا يُغْنِيْ عَنْهُ مَالُهٗۤ اِذَا تَرَدّٰىؕ ۱۲

13. *c*Surely, it is for Us to guide;

اِنَّ عَلَيْنَا لَلْهُدٰىۖ ۱۳

14. And to Us belongs the Hereafter as well as the present world.[3369]

وَاِنَّ لَنَا لَلْاٰخِرَةَ وَالْاُوْلٰى ۱۴

15. So I warn you of a blazing Fire.

فَاَنْذَرْتُكُمْ نَارًا تَلَظّٰىۚ ۱۵

---

*a*87 : 9.   *b*3 : 11; 58 : 18; 111 : 3.   *c*2 : 273; 28 : 57.

3365. This and the preceding verse mention three characteristics of those persons who are successful in life. Briefly, these are right action, right feeling and right thinking and these characteristics the believers possess in ample measure.

3366. He, who possesses the three characteristic qualities mentioned in the preceding two verses, will find that his actions are productive of the desired good results. Or, the verse may mean that the doing of good deeds becomes easy for such a person and he also enjoys doing them.

3367. In contrast to the three good qualities mentioned in the preceding two verses (6-7), three bad qualities that cause the moral undoing of a man are mentioned in these two verses (9-10).

3368. The actions of the person referred to in the preceding verse miss their mark and produce results contrary to what he expects or desires. Or, the verse may mean that the doing of good deeds becomes difficult for such a person.

3369. The wicked disbeliever faces failure in this life and will suffer punishment in the Hereafter because both the worlds are under God's control. The verse may also mean, 'to Us belongs the end and the beginning of all things.'

16. [a]None shall enter it but the most wicked one,

لَا يَصْلٰهَآ اِلَّا الْاَشْقَى ﴿۱۶﴾

17. [b]Who rejects *the Truth* and turns his back *on it*.[3370]

الَّذِىْ كَذَّبَ وَ تَوَلّٰى ﴿۱۷﴾

18. But the righteous one shall be kept away from it,

وَ سَيُجَنَّبُهَا الْاَتْقَى ﴿۱۸﴾

19. Who gives his wealth that he may be purified,

الَّذِىْ يُؤْتِىْ مَالَهٗ يَتَزَكّٰى ﴿۱۹﴾

20. And not *because* he owes a favour to anyone, which is to be repaid,

وَ مَا لِاَحَدٍ عِنْدَهٗ مِنْ نِّعْمَةٍ تُجْزٰٓى ﴿۲۰﴾

21. But solely to seek the pleasure of his Lord, the Most High.[3371]

اِلَّا ابْتِغَآءَ وَجْهِ رَبِّهِ الْاَعْلٰى ﴿۲۱﴾

22. Surely, will He be well-pleased *with him*.

وَ لَسَوْفَ يَرْضٰى ﴿۲۲﴾

[a]20 : 75; 87 : 12-13. [b]20 : 49.

3370. The word, *Kadhdhaba,* signifies that the sinful disbeliever holds wrong beliefs, and *Tawallā* implies that he does not do right actions.

3371. The righteous believer does good to others, not in return for any good received from them but only actuated by a desire to be of use to God's creatures and to win the pleasure of his Heavenly Lord and Master.

CHAPTER 93

AL-ḌUḤĀ

(*Revealed before Hijrah*)

Date of Revelation and Context

After the first two or three Chapters had been revealed, Revelation ceased to come to the Holy Prophet for some time. The present *Sūrah* is among those Chapters which were revealed soon after Revelation had started coming again. Thus it should be deemed to have been revealed very early at Mecca. Nöldeke places it after *Sūrah* Al-Balad, and Muir puts it near *Sūrah* Al-Inshirāḥ in chronological order. The *Sūrah* embodies a great prophecy that every morrow of the Holy Prophet will be better than his yesterday and this process will continue till his cause will meet with complete success. The prophecy was remarkably fulfilled by the mounting triumphs of the Holy Prophet. In subject-matter the *Sūrah* much resembles some of the previous ones. Like them it lays stress on the evils to which the Meccans were specially addicted, with this difference that whereas in this *Sūrah* the Holy Prophet and his followers have been enjoined to make proper use of their money, in the preceding *Sūrah* a contrast was instituted between the believers' and the disbelievers' treatment of the orphans and the needy. Moreover, in the preceding *Sūrah* it was briefly stated that the righteous believer spends his wealth in the way of God; in this *Sūrah* mention is made of the blessings which God bestows upon His chosen servants with particular reference to the Holy Prophet. Thus the *Sūrah* serves as a sequel to the one preceding it.

سُورَةُ الضُّحٰى مَكِّيَّةٌ

1. In the name of Allāh, the Gracious, the Merciful.

بِسۡمِ اللّٰهِ الرَّحۡمٰنِ الرَّحِيۡمِ ﴿۱﴾

2. By the brightness of the forenoon,[3372]

وَالضُّحٰى ﴿۲﴾

3. [a]And *by* the night when its darkness spreads out,[3373]

وَالَّيۡلِ اِذَا سَجٰى ﴿۳﴾

4. Thy Lord has not forsaken thee, nor is He displeased *with thee.*[3374]

مَا وَدَّعَكَ رَبُّكَ وَمَا قَلٰى ﴿۴﴾

5. Surely, thy latter state is better for thee than the former,[3375]

وَلَلۡاٰخِرَةُ خَيۡرٌ لَّكَ مِنَ الۡاُوۡلٰى ﴿۵﴾

6. And thy Lord will soon give thee, and thou wilt be well-pleased.

وَلَسَوۡفَ يُعۡطِيۡكَ رَبُّكَ فَتَرۡضٰى ﴿۶﴾

7. Did He not find thee an orphan and take thee under *His* care,[3376]

اَلَمۡ يَجِدۡكَ يَتِيۡمًا فَاٰوٰى ﴿۷﴾

---

[a]81 : 18

3372. 'The brightness of the forenoon' may signify the rise and progress of Islām. It may also refer to the particular "forenoon" when the Holy Prophet entered Mecca at the head of an army of ten thousand holy warriors and the Ka'bah was cleared of idols.

3373. 'The Night' may signify the prolonged period of the decline of Islām. It may also refer to that particular night when after the fall of darkness the Holy Prophet went out of his house and took refuge in Cave Thaur along with Abū Bakr. In fact, the night, when the Holy Prophet left Mecca and the day, when it fell, give in a nutshell the various ups and downs of the Holy Prophet's whole career.

3374. Every day and night of the Holy Prophet, his great successes and temporary set-backs, his joys and tribulations, his devotions at night and activities in the day, all bear out that God was with him

3375. Every moment of the Holy Prophet's life was better than the one preceding it.

3376. The Holy Prophet was an orphan in fact as well as figuratively. His orphanhood was of the extreme kind. His father died before he was born and his mother died when he was hardly six years old and his grand-father 'Abd al-Muṭṭalib, who took charge of him after his mother's death, died two years later, leaving him under the care of his uncle, a man of scanty means. Thus the Prophet was deprived of parental care and love in his early childhood. Yet he received love and affection from his juniors and seniors, his Companions and compatriots, from his followers in the later centuries, in such a large measure that no woman-born had ever received the like of it before, or is likely to receive it in future.

8. And found thee lost *in love for thy people*[3377] and provided thee with guidance *for them*,

وَوَجَدَكَ ضَآلًّا فَهَدٰى ﴿٨﴾

9. And found thee in want and enriched *thee* ?[3378]

وَوَجَدَكَ عَآئِلًا فَاَغْنٰى ﴿٩﴾

10. So the orphan, oppress not,

فَاَمَّا الْيَتِيْمَ فَلَا تَقْهَرْ ﴿١٠﴾

11. And him, who seeks *thy help*, chide not,

وَاَمَّا السَّآئِلَ فَلَا تَنْهَرْ ﴿١١﴾

12. And the bounty of thy Lord, proclaim.[3379]

وَاَمَّا بِنِعْمَةِ رَبِّكَ فَحَدِّثْ ﴿١٢﴾

3377. *Dalla* (lost in love) means, he was perplexed and was unable to see the course; he was entirely engrossed or lost in love or wandered in search of a thing and persevered in the search (Lane). In view of the different meanings of *Dalla*, the verse may be interpreted as: (1) The Holy Prophet wandered in search of the ways and means to attain to God, and God revealed to him the Law which guided him to the desired goal. (2) He was perplexed and did not know how to find the path that led to the attainment of his quest and God guided him to it (3) He was entirely lost in the love of his people and God provided him with perfect guidance for them. (4) He was hidden from the eyes of the world and God discovered him and chose him for the task of leading men to Him. Thus the word *Dalla* has not been used in disapprobation but in praise of the Holy Prophet. In the sense of 'gone astray' the word does not and cannot apply to the Holy Prophet, since according to another Quranic verse (53 : 3) he was immune to error or going astray. Moreover, the six concluding verses of the *Sūrah* reveal a certain sequence—vv. 7, 8 and 9 stand in close relationship with and correspond to vv. 10, 11 and 12 respectively. *Dalla* of verse 8 being substituted by *Sā'il* of verse 11, explains the significance of the former word which is, "one who sought God's help to be guided to Him, or to be provided with guidance.' The verse may also mean: 'God found thee lost in search of Him and guided thee unto Himself.'

3378. The Holy Prophet started his life as a poor orphan and ended it by being the undisputed master of the whole of Arabia.

3379. Verses 7, 8 and 9, speak of God's favours on the Holy Prophet and in vv. 10, 11 and 12 he is enjoined to show his gratitude by doing similar favours to his fellow-beings. The commandment applies equally to his followers.

CHAPTER 94

AL-INSHIRĀḤ

(*Revealed before Hijrah*)

Date of Revelation and Context

Since the *Sūrah* is closely connected with the one preceding it so as to form an extension of its subject-matter, it was obviously revealed at Mecca, most probably in the second or third year of the Call. While the preceding *Sūrah* spoke of the increasing prosperity of the Holy Prophet's cause, the present *Sūrah* alludes to some distinguishing features and marks which constitute a sure guarantee of the ultimate triumph of one's mission and for that matter of the mission of every preacher of Truth : (*a*) First of all, he should be firmly convinced of the truth of his claim and should possess necessary means for propagating it ; (*b*) he should be able to attract people's attention, and (*c*) the Divine decree should be working in his favour. In this *Sūrah* the Holy Prophet is described as being in possession of all these means in full measure. His cause is, therefore, bound to prevail.

ركوعها ١ سُوْرَةُ الْاِنْشِرَاحِ مَكِّيَّةٌ (٩٤) اٰياتها ٩

1. In the name of Allāh, the Gracious, the Merciful.

بِسْمِ اللّٰهِ الرَّحْمٰنِ الرَّحِيْمِ ①

2. Have We not opened for thee thy bosom,

اَلَمْ نَشْرَحْ لَكَ صَدْرَكَ ②

3. And removed from thee thy burden,

وَوَضَعْنَا عَنْكَ وِزْرَكَ ③

4. Which had *well-nigh* broken thy back?[3380]

الَّذِيْٓ اَنْقَضَ ظَهْرَكَ ④

5. And We have exalted thy name.[3881]

وَرَفَعْنَا لَكَ ذِكْرَكَ ⑤

6. Surely, there is ease after hardship.[3382]

فَاِنَّ مَعَ الْعُسْرِ يُسْرًا ⑥

7. *Aye*, surely, there is ease after hardship.

اِنَّ مَعَ الْعُسْرِ يُسْرًا ⑦

8. So when thou art free *from thy immediate task*, strive hard,

فَاِذَا فَرَغْتَ فَانْصَبْ ⑧

3380. The Holy Prophet had been saddled with such nerve-racking and back-breaking task as had never been entrusted to any human being, *i.e.*, first to raise a degenerate people from the depths of moral turpitude to the pinnacle of spiritual excellence and, then through them to cleanse and purify the whole of mankind of the dross of iniquity, ignorance and superstition. This was. indeed, a very heavy responsibility which had almost crushed him under its weight, but God lightened his burden.

3381. The *Sūrah* was revealed in the second or third year of the Call, at a time when the Holy Prophet was hardly known outside his immediate neighbourhood, but very soon he rose to be the best known and most loved, respected and successful of all religious Teachers. No leader, religious or temporal, has so much commanded the love and respect of his followers as has the Holy Prophet.

3382. The expression, 'Surely, there is ease after hardship,' has been repeated twice. This signifies that Islām will have to pass through very hard times, but on two occasions it will have to face a challenge to its very existence—first in the first few years of its life and then in the Latter Days—and on both these occasions it will emerge from the ordeal with renewed strength. These verses also indicate that the hardships with which the Holy Prophet and Muslims are faced are temporary, but their successes will be permanent and ever-expanding.

9. [a]And to thy Lord do thou turn *with full attention.*[3382A]

وَإِلَىٰ رَبِّكَ فَارْغَبْ ﴿٩﴾ ع ١٩

[a]73 : 9; 110 : 4.

3382A. The Holy Prophet is comforted with the assurance that endless vistas of spiritual progress lie before him and that after he has conquered the difficulties that bar his way he should not rest contented with the success achieved, but having scaled one peak he should strive to climb the next, and his attention should be wholly directed towards regenerating a fallen humanity and towards establishing God's Kingdom on earth. The verse may also signify that when the Holy Prophet has finished his day's work of teaching and training his followers and disposing of other temporal affairs he should turn to God with all his heart, for his spiritual journey knows no end.

CHAPTER 95

AL-TĪN

(*Revealed before Hijrah*)

Date of Revelation and Context

The *Sūrah* was revealed very early at Mecca. This is the view of Ibn 'Abbās and Ibn Zubair. Noldeke places it after Chapter 85. In the preceding *Sūrah* arguments based on reason and commonsense were given in support of the claim that the Holy Prophet will have a glorious future as he possesses all those qualities which are necessary for making a success of one's mission. In the present *Sūrah* examples of some Divine Messengers have been cited to show that as the Holy Prophet's own circumstances resembled their circumstances, so, like them, he, too, will achieve success. In Chapters 89-94 the Holy Prophet's Emigration to Medina and his subsequent success were hinted at in one form or another—in some by implication, in others by oblique reference and in yet others in clear words. In the *Sūrah* under comment, it is implied that like the Holy Prophet the former Prophets also had to leave their homes for the sake of their missions.

سُوْرَةُ التِّيْنِ مَكِّيَّةٌ (٩٥)

1. [a]In the name of Allāh, the Gracious, the Merciful.

بِسْمِ اللّٰهِ الرَّحْمٰنِ الرَّحِيْمِ ①

2. By[3383] the Fig and the Olive,

وَالتِّيْنِ وَالزَّيْتُوْنِ ②

3. And [b]Mount Sinai,[3383A]

وَطُوْرِ سِيْنِيْنَ ③

4. And this [c]Town of Security,

وَهٰذَا الْبَلَدِ الْاَمِيْنِ ④

5. Surely, We have created man in [d]the best make;

لَقَدْ خَلَقْنَا الْاِنْسَانَ فِيْٓ اَحْسَنِ تَقْوِيْمٍ ⑤

---

[a]1 : 1. [b]52 : 2. [c]90 : 2. [d]23 : 12-15.

3383. "The Fig," "the Olive," "Mount Sinai" and "this Town of Security" have been invoked as witnesses to support and substantiate the claim made in the *Sūrah* that the Holy Prophet shall succeed in his mission. "The Fig" and "the Olive" are symbolic of Jesus; "Mount Sinai" of Moses; and "this Town of Security" of the Holy Prophet. These three verses together point to the well-known biblical reference, 'The Lord came from Sinai, and rose up from Seir with them; and He shined forth from Mount Paran' (Deut. 33 : 2). According to some Commentators, however, "the Fig" stands for Buddhism, "the Olive" for Christianity, "Mount Sinai" for Judaism and "the City of Security" for the Holy Prophet of Islām. But perhaps the best explanation of the symbolism used in these verses is the one according to which the four words represent four periods in the history of human moral evolution, "the Fig" representing the era of Adam, "the Olive" that of Noah, "Mount Sinai" that of Moses and "this Town of Security" symbolising the Islamic epoch. This explanation finds ample support from the Bible and the Qur'ān. When Adam and Eve ate of the forbidden fruit and found themselves naked, they sewed fig leaves together, and made themselves aprons (Gen. 3 : 7). About Noah we read : 'And the dove came unto him in the evening; and lo! in her mouth was an olive leaf plucked off; so Noah knew that the waters were abated from off the earth' (Gen. 8 : 11). And it is an accepted fact that Moses received the Divine Law on Mount Sinai and that Mecca, the birth-place of Islām was, from time immemorial, regarded as, and proved to be, "the Town of Security." These four periods represent the four cycles through which man has passed to reach the stage of his complete development. In the cycle of Adam the foundations of human civilization were laid. Noah was the founder of the *Sharī'ah*. In the cycle of Moses the details of the *Sharī'ah* were revealed, while with the advent of the Holy Prophet the Divine Law became complete and perfect in all its manifold aspects, and man attained his complete intellectual, social, moral and spiritual development. "The Fig" may also be symbolic of Mosaic Dispensation and "the Olive" of the Islamic Dispensation. This simile has been further expressed in a more concrete form by the words "Mount Sinai" and "This City of Security."

3383A. The word *Sīnīn* being in the plural shows that there are several mountains of this name in that region. On one of them God manifested Himself to Moses.

6. Then, *if he does evil deeds*, We degrade him as the lowest of the low,[3384]

ثُمَّ رَدَدْنٰهُ اَسْفَلَ سٰفِلِيْنَ ﴿۶﴾

7. [a]Save those who believe and do good works; so for them is an unfailing reward.

اِلَّا الَّذِيْنَ اٰمَنُوْا وَعَمِلُوا الصّٰلِحٰتِ فَلَهُمْ اَجْرٌ غَيْرُ مَمْنُوْنٍ ﴿۷﴾

8. Then what is there to give the lie to thee after *this*, with regard to the judgment ?[3385]

فَمَا يُكَذِّبُكَ بَعْدُ بِالدِّيْنِ ﴿۸﴾

9. Is not Allāh the Most Just of judges ?

اَلَيْسَ اللّٰهُ بِاَحْكَمِ الْحٰكِمِيْنَ ﴿۹﴾

[a]11 : 12; 41 : 9; 84 : 26.

3384. Man is born with a pure and unsullied nature, with a natural tendency to do good, but he has also been given a large measure of freedom of will and action to mould himself as he chooses. He has been endowed with great natural powers and creative qualities to make unlimited moral progress and to rise spiritually so high as to become the mirror in which Divine attributes are reflected. But if he misuses God-given powers and attributes, he sinks lower than even beasts and brutes and becomes Devil incarnate as the next verse shows. Briefly, he is blessed with great potentialities for doing good and evil.

3385. When man has been created to achieve a very high spiritual destiny and God had sent His Messengers such as Adam, Noah, Moses and the Holy Prophet, to help him achieve his great goal, and if he does not make proper use of his natural faculties and rejects the Divine Message and opposes God's Messengers, he is punished, then, who can, with reason, deny that there is a Day of Judgment in this life and also in the Hereafter and that the commandments of God Who is the Best Judge cannot be defied with impunity and man's actions will not go unrequited ?

CHAPTER 96

AL-'ALAQ

(*Revealed before Hijrah*)

Date of Revelation and Context

The first five verses of the *Sūrah* are universally admitted to be the first revelation which descended upon the Holy Prophet in Cave Ḥirā' in a night in the month of Ramaḍān, 13 years before Hijrah. This date corresponds to 610 A.D. On that "Night of Destiny" when the Holy Prophet lay on the floor of the Cave, his mind locked in deep contemplation, these verses were revealed and the words became branded on his soul. 'These verses are the first act of mercy with which God blessed His servants' (Kathīr). The connection of this *Sūrah*, with the one preceding it, consists in the fact that in that *Sūrah* it was stated that from time immemorial God had been sending His Messengers and Prophets to whom He revealed His Will. First came Adam who was followed by Noah, and after a succession of Prophets appeared Moses, the greatest of the Israelite Prophets, and last of all came the Holy Prophet. In this *Sūrah* it is stated that just as the birth of man is the result of a gradual process of development, so is his spiritual evolution. The Prophets whose examples were cited in the preceding *Sūrah* attained to different stages of spiritual development, but the Holy Prophet represents in his person the best specimen of man's complete spiritual evolution.

سُوۡرَةُ الۡعَلَقِ مَكِّيَّةٌ (٩٦)

1. [a]In the name of Allāh, the Gracious, the Merciful,	بِسۡمِ اللّٰہِ الرَّحۡمٰنِ الرَّحِیۡمِ ①
2. Proclaim[3386] thou in the name of thy Lord Who created,	اِقۡرَاۡ بِاسۡمِ رَبِّکَ الَّذِیۡ خَلَقَ ②
3. Created man[3387] from a [b]clot of blood.	خَلَقَ الۡاِنۡسَانَ مِنۡ عَلَقٍ ③
4. Proclaim! And thy Lord is the Most Bounteous;[3388]	اِقۡرَاۡ وَ رَبُّکَ الۡاَکۡرَمُ ④
5. Who taught by the pen,[3389]	الَّذِیۡ عَلَّمَ بِالۡقَلَمِ ⑤
6. [c]Taught man what he knew not.	عَلَّمَ الۡاِنۡسَانَ مَا لَمۡ یَعۡلَمۡ ⑥
7. Nay! man, indeed, transgresses,	کَلَّاۤ اِنَّ الۡاِنۡسَانَ لَیَطۡغٰۤی ⑦
8. Because he thinks himself to be independent.	اَنۡ رَّاٰہُ اسۡتَغۡنٰی ⑧

[a]1 : 1. [b]23 : 15; 40 : 68; 75 : 39. [c]4 : 114; 55 : 5.

3386. The word *Iqra'* meaning read, recite, convey, proclaim or collect, the verse signifies that the Qur'ān was meant to be read and proclaimed, to be collected and put together and then conveyed to the whole world. The mention of the Divine attribute *Rabb*, (Nourisher, Sustainer and Developer, Who sustains man through all the stages of his development), shows that man's moral development was to be gradual till it was to find full consummation in the Holy Prophet.

3387. The verse signifies that love of God is ingrained in the nature of man, and that it was natural that there should have been someone in whom this instinctive impulse should have found its complete manifestation. He was the Holy Prophet who loved his Creator with all his mind, heart and soul, *Insān* in the verse besides the meaning given in the text signifies the perfect man—the Holy Prophet.

3388. The more the Qur'ān is read and proclaimed to the world, the more the Holiness of God and the dignity of man are recognised and appreciated.

3389. This verse seems to embody a prophecy that "pen" would play a very important part in committing the Qur'ān to writing and in preserving and protecting it from being lost or interfered with. It further refers to the great contribution which "pen" was to make towards the propagation and dissemination of the spiritual sciences and Divine secrets revealed by the Qur'ān and of the physical sciences to which the study of the Qur'ān was to impart a great stimulus. It is really very significant that frequent mention should have been made of "pen" in a Book which was revealed among a people who had no respect for, and had made rare use of, it and which was revealed to a person who himself did not know how to read and write.

9. Surely, [a]unto thy Lord is the return.

إِنَّ إِلَىٰ رَبِّكَ الرُّجْعَىٰ ٩

10. Hast thou seen him who [b]forbids

أَرَأَيْتَ الَّذِي يَنْهَىٰ ١٠

11. A servant *of Ours*[3390] when he prays ?

عَبْدًا إِذَا صَلَّىٰ ١١

12. Tell me if *Our servant* follows the guidance,

أَرَأَيْتَ إِنْ كَانَ عَلَى الْهُدَىٰ ١٢

13. Or enjoins righteousness.

أَوْ أَمَرَ بِالتَّقْوَىٰ ١٣

14. *And* tell me if *the forbidder* rejects *the Truth* and turns his back *on it, how shall he fare ?*

أَرَأَيْتَ إِنْ كَذَّبَ وَتَوَلَّىٰ ١٤

15. Does he not know that Allāh sees *all* ?

أَلَمْ يَعْلَمْ بِأَنَّ اللَّهَ يَرَىٰ ١٥

16. Nay, if he desist not, We will, assuredly, *seize and* drag him by the forelock[3391]—

كَلَّا لَئِنْ لَمْ يَنْتَهِ لَنَسْفَعًا بِالنَّاصِيَةِ ١٦

17. A forelock, lying, sinful.

نَاصِيَةٍ كَاذِبَةٍ خَاطِئَةٍ ١٧

18. Then let him call his associates.

فَلْيَدْعُ نَادِيَهُ ١٨

19. We, *too*, will call *Our* angels of punishment.[3392]

سَنَدْعُ الزَّبَانِيَةَ ١٩

20. Nay, yield not thou to him, but prostrate thyself and draw near *to Allāh*.

كَلَّا لَا تُطِعْهُ وَاسْجُدْ وَاقْتَرِبْ ٢٠ السجدة ع ١

[a]21 : 36; 53 : 43. [b]2 : 115; 72 : 20.

3390. The reference is to every Muslim, who prays, particularly to the Holy Prophet.

3391. The verses (10-18) though generally applying to every haughty and hardened disbeliever, have been taken by some Commentators to refer particularly to Abū Jahl, leader of the Quraish of Mecca. He was in the forefront to annoy, oppose and persecute the Holy Prophet and the Muslims. Some of the slaves, who had embraced Islām, at his instance were dragged by the forelock in the streets of Mecca. After the defeat at Badr, the dead bodies of some of the leaders of the Quraish, Abū Jahl among them, were dragged by their forelocks and thrown into a pit dug for that purpose. That was a fit punishment for the treatment they had meted out to the helpless Muslims years before at Mecca.

3392. *Zabāniyah* means, armed officers or the prefect of police; angels or guards of Hell; angels of punishment (Lane).

CHAPTER 97

AL-QADR

(Revealed before Hijrah)

Date of Revelation and Context

Some Commentators of the Qur'ān think that this *Sūrah* was revealed at Medina. This, however, is a mistaken view, being against all historical data. It is definitely a Meccan *Sūrah* and belongs to the very early years of the Call. Such eminent and respected authorities as Ibn 'Abbās, Ibn Zubair and 'Ā'ishah subscribe to this view. Noldeke places it after Chapter 93, which was one of the earliest Chapters to have been revealed at Mecca. The preceding *Sūrah* had opened with the Divine command to the Holy Prophet to recite the Qur'ān and preach and proclaim its Message to the world. The present *Sūrah* deals with the high status, dignity and excellence of the Qur'ān itself which is declared in the opening verse to have been revealed in *Lailat al-Qadr*, *i.e.*, the Night of Decree (or Dignity). This Night of Decree or Destiny has been described elsewhere in the Qur'ān, as the "Blessed Night" (44 : 4). The *Sūrah* has only five little verses, excluding the *Bismillāh* and yet its meaning and contents are of very deep spiritual significance.

آياتها ٦ (٩٧) سُورَةُ الْقَدْرِ مَكِّيَّةٌ ركوعها ١

1. In the name of Allāh, the Gracious, the Merciful.

بِسْمِ اللّٰهِ الرَّحْمٰنِ الرَّحِيْمِ ①

2. Surely, We sent it down during the Night[3393] of Decree.[3394]

إِنَّآ أَنْزَلْنٰهُ فِيْ لَيْلَةِ الْقَدْرِ ②

3. And what shall make thee know what the Night of Decree is ?[3395]

وَمَآ أَدْرٰىكَ مَا لَيْلَةُ الْقَدْرِ ③

4. The Night of Decree is better than a thousand months.[3396]

لَيْلَةُ الْقَدْرِ ۙ خَيْرٌ مِّنْ أَلْفِ شَهْرٍ ④

3393. Generally *Lail* and *Lailah* both mean night, but according to the famous lexicographer, Marzūquī, *Lail* is used as opposed to *Nahār* and *Lailah* as opposed to *Yaum*. *Lailah* possesses a wider and more extensive meaning than *Lail*, as *Yaum*, which is its opposite, has a wider sense than *Nahār* which is the opposite of *Lail*. *Lailah* has been used as many as eight times in the Qur'ān (2 : 52; 2 : 188; 44 : 4; twice in 7 : 143 and three times in the verses under comment), and everywhere it has been used in connection with the revelation of the Qur'ān and other kindred subjects. The word thus refers to the dignity, majesty and greatness of those nights in which the Qur'ān was revealed.

3394. *Qadr* means worth; sufficiency; dignity; decree; destiny; power (Lane). In view of the different meanings of *Qadr* and *Lailah* the verse may be interpreted as follows : The Qur'ān has been revealed in a night which had been specifically set apart for the manifestation of special Divine powers; or in a night which is equal in worth to all the other nights put together, or in a night of dignity, majesty and honour; or, in a night of sufficiency, *i.e.*, the Qur'ān fully meets all moral and spiritual human needs and requirements. Or, the meaning is that God has revealed it in the Night of Decree or Destiny, *i.e.*, the Qur'ān was revealed at a time when man's destiny was decreed, the future pattern of the universe was settled, and the right principles of guidance for humanity were laid down for all time to come. The time of the appearance of a great Divine Reformer is also called *Lailat al-Qadr* because at that time sin and vice hold widespread sway and the powers of darkness reign supreme. It has also been taken to mean the particular night among the odd nights in the last ten days of Ramaḍān when the Qur'ān first began to be revealed. Or, it may signify the whole period of 23 years of the Holy Prophet's ministry when the Qur'ān gradually was being revealed.

3395. The blessings of the Night of Decree are beyond count or calculation.

3396. *Alf* (a thousand), being the highest number of count in Arabic, signifies a number beyond count, and the verse means that the Night of Decree or Destiny is better than countless number of months. *i.e.*, the period of the Holy Prophet is infinitely better than and superior to all other periods put together. The verse embodies an allusion to the appearance of Divine Reformers among the Muslims when the latter would stand in need of them. One thousand months roughly make one century and the Holy Prophet is reported to have said that God will continue to raise from among His followers, at the head of every century, a Divine Reformer who would regenerate Islām and give it a new life and new vigour (Mājah).

5. Therein descend [a]angels and the Spirit[3397] by the command of their Lord *with Divine decree* [b]concerning every matter.

تَنَزَّلُ الْمَلٰٓئِكَةُ وَالرُّوْحُ فِيْهَا بِاِذْنِ رَبِّهِمْ ۚ مِنْ كُلِّ اَمْرٍ ۙ﴿۵﴾

6. *It is all* peace[3398] till the rising of the dawn.[3398A]

سَلٰمٌ ۛ هِيَ حَتّٰى مَطْلَعِ الْفَجْرِ ﴿۶﴾

[a]16 : 3; 40 : 16. [b]44 : 5.

3397. *Al-Rūḥ* here signifies a new spirit, awakening, zeal or determination. In the Night of Decree the angels of God descend to help the Divine Messenger or Reformer to promote and further the cause of Truth and his followers are inspired with a new life, and a new awakening to spread and propagate the Divine Message.

3398. In the time of a Prophet or Divine Reformer a peculiar kind of mental peace descends upon the believers amidst hardships and privations. The heavenly happiness, which inspires them at that time, transcends all material and sensuous joys.

3398A. 'Rising of the dawn' signifies the passing of the night of hardships and the rising of the dawn of predominance and ascendancy of the cause of Truth.

CHAPTER 98

AL-BAYYINAH

(Revealed before Hijrah)

Date of Revelation and Context

Scholars differ about the time of the revelation of this *Sūrah*. Ibn Mardawaih reports 'Ā'ishah as saying that it was revealed at Mecca, while according to Ibn 'Abbās, it was revealed in the early Medinite period. After taking all relevant facts into consideration, the majority of scholars have adhered to the view attributed to 'Ā'ishah. The preceding several Chapters had dealt with the important subject of revelation of the Qur'ān and its incomparable beauty and excellence. The present *Sūrah* deals with the change that the Qur'ān was intended to bring about. At the very outset it states that the people of the Book and the idolaters would have continued to grope in the dark and to lead a life of sin and iniquity if the Qur'ān had not been revealed. It is the Holy Prophet who brought them out of the darkness of doubt and disbelief and led them to the path of right beliefs and righteous conduct.

1. In the name of Allāh, the Gracious, the Merciful.

بِسْمِ اللّٰهِ الرَّحْمٰنِ الرَّحِيْمِ ①

2. Those, who disbelieve from among the People of the Book and the idolaters,[3399] would not desist *from disbelief* until there should come to them the clear evidence—

لَمْ يَكُنِ الَّذِيْنَ كَفَرُوْا مِنْ اَهْلِ الْكِتٰبِ وَالْمُشْرِكِيْنَ مُنْفَكِّيْنَ حَتّٰى تَاْتِيَهُمُ الْبَيِّنَةُ ②

3. [a]A Messenger from Allāh, reciting *unto them the* pure Scriptures,

رَسُوْلٌ مِّنَ اللّٰهِ يَتْلُوْا صُحُفًا مُّطَهَّرَةً ③

4. Wherein are lasting commandments.[3400]

فِيْهَا كُتُبٌ قَيِّمَةٌ ④

5. And those to whom the Book was given [b]did not become divided until after clear evidence had come to them.

وَمَا تَفَرَّقَ الَّذِيْنَ اُوْتُوا الْكِتٰبَ اِلَّا مِنْۢ بَعْدِ مَا جَآءَتْهُمُ الْبَيِّنَةُ ⑤

6. And they were not commanded but to serve Allāh, being sincere to Him in obedience, [c]*and* being upright, and to observe Prayer and pay the *Zakāt*. And that is the right religion.[3400A]

وَمَآ اُمِرُوْٓا اِلَّا لِيَعْبُدُوا اللّٰهَ مُخْلِصِيْنَ لَهُ الدِّيْنَ ۙ حُنَفَآءَ وَيُقِيْمُوا الصَّلٰوةَ وَيُؤْتُوا الزَّكٰوةَ وَذٰلِكَ دِيْنُ الْقَيِّمَةِ ⑥

[a]3 : 165; 62 : 3. [b]42 : 15; 45 : 18. [c]40 : 15.

3399. The Qur'ān has divided all disbelievers into two categories—the People of the Book and the idolaters (those who do not believe in any revealed Scripture).

3400 The Qur'ān is a compendium of all that is good, lasting and imperishable in the teachings of former revealed Scriptures, with a good deal more which those Scriptures lacked, but which man sorely needed for his moral and spiritual development. All those right ideals and principles and ordinances and commandments which were of permanent utility to man have been incorporated in it. The Qur'ān stands, as it were, as a guardian over those Books and has steered clear of all those defects and impurities which were found in them.

3400A. *Dīn* means, obedience; mastery; command; plan; righteousness; habit or custom; behaviour or conduct (Lane).

7. Verily, those, who disbelieve from among the People of the Book and the idolaters, will be in the fire of Hell, abiding therein. They are the worst of creatures.

إِنَّ الَّذِينَ كَفَرُوا مِنْ أَهْلِ الْكِتٰبِ وَالْمُشْرِكِينَ
فِي نَارِ جَهَنَّمَ خٰلِدِينَ فِيهَا ۚ أُولٰٓئِكَ هُمْ شَرُّ
الْبَرِيَّةِ ﴿٧﴾

8. Verily, those who believe and do righteous deeds—they are the best of creatures.

إِنَّ الَّذِينَ اٰمَنُوا وَعَمِلُوا الصّٰلِحٰتِ ۙ أُولٰٓئِكَ هُمْ
خَيْرُ الْبَرِيَّةِ ﴿٨﴾

9. Their reward is with their Lord—[a]Gardens of Eternity, through which streams flow; they will abide therein for ever. Allāh is well-pleased with them and they are well-pleased with Him.[3401] [b]That is for him who fears his Lord.

جَزَآؤُهُمْ عِنْدَ رَبِّهِمْ جَنّٰتُ عَدْنٍ تَجْرِي مِنْ
تَحْتِهَا الْأَنْهٰرُ خٰلِدِينَ فِيهَآ أَبَدًا ۖ رَضِيَ اللّٰهُ
ع عَنْهُمْ وَرَضُوا عَنْهُ ۚ ذٰلِكَ لِمَنْ خَشِيَ رَبَّهُ ﴿٩﴾ ١ ٩ ٢٣

[a]9 : 72; 13 : 24; 16 : 32; 35 : 34. [b]36 : 12; 55 : 47.

3401. The highest stage of spiritual development is reached when man's will becomes completely identified with the Divine Will.

CHAPTER 99

AL-ZILZĀL

(*Revealed before Hijrah*)

Date of Revelation and Context

There exists some difference of opinion about the time and place of the revelation of this *Sūrah*. Scholars like Mujāhid, 'Aṭā' and Ibn 'Abbās are of the view that it was revealed at Mecca; some others think that it was revealed at Medina. The latter view is evidently not based on sound historical data. Whereas in the preceding *Sūrah* mention was made of the great moral revolution that was to be brought about by the Holy Prophet, in this *Sūrah* it is stated that a similar change will take place at a later date, in the time of the Great Deputy of the Holy Prophet, the Promised Messiah and Mahdī, when all human institutions will be shaken to their foundations, and new discoveries and inventions in the domain of science and knowledge will change the entire shape of things, and the ideals and ideas of men will acquire a new orientation.

سُورَةُ الزِّلْزَالِ مَكِّيَّةٌ (٩٩) آياتها ٩ ركوعها ١

1. [a]In the name of Allāh, the Gracious, the Merciful.

بِسْمِ اللّٰهِ الرَّحْمٰنِ الرَّحِيْمِ ①

2. When the earth is shaken with her *violent* shaking,[3402]

إِذَا زُلْزِلَتِ الْأَرْضُ زِلْزَالَهَا ②

3. And the earth throws up her burdens,[3403]

وَأَخْرَجَتِ الْأَرْضُ أَثْقَالَهَا ③

4. And man says, 'What is the matter with her?'[3404]

وَقَالَ الْإِنْسَانُ مَا لَهَا ④

5. On that day will she tell her news,[3405]

يَوْمَئِذٍ تُحَدِّثُ أَخْبَارَهَا ⑤

6. For, thy Lord will have commanded[3406] her.

بِأَنَّ رَبَّكَ أَوْحٰى لَهَا ⑥

7. On that day will men issue forth in scattered groups[3407] that they may be shown *the results of* their works.[3408]

يَوْمَئِذٍ يَّصْدُرُ النَّاسُ أَشْتَاتًا لِّيُرَوْا أَعْمَالَهُمْ ⑦

8. [b]Then whoso does an atom's weight of good will see it,

فَمَنْ يَّعْمَلْ مِثْقَالَ ذَرَّةٍ خَيْرًا يَّرَهُ ⑧

9. And whoso does an atom's weight of evil will *also* see it.[3409]

وَمَنْ يَّعْمَلْ مِثْقَالَ ذَرَّةٍ شَرًّا يَّرَهُ ⑨

[a]1 : 1. [b]4 : 124-125; 17 : 8; 28 : 85; 41 : 47.

3402. The whole earth will experience all manner of internal as well as external commotions and upheavals.

3403. (*a*) The bowels of the earth will be ripped open and it will throw up its treasures of mineral wealth; (*b*) there will be a vast release and upsurge of knowledge of all kinds relating to physical as well as spiritual sciences, especially to the sciences of geology and archaeology.

3404. The changes will be so many and so far-reaching and the discoveries made so great that men will exclaim in wonder and bewilderment, 'What is the matter with the earth?'

3405. When asked about the meaning of the verse, the Holy Prophet is reported to have said that every action done in secret will come to light (Tirmidhī).

3406. The earth will throw out its treasures because God had commanded her to do so, the word *Auḥā* meaning, he commanded (Aqrab).

3407. In the Latter Days, in order to protect and safeguard their political, social and economic interests, people will form themselves into parties, companies and groups on political and economic bases; and powerful guilds, cartels and syndicates will come into existence.

3408. Individuals will pool their resources and collective efforts will take the place of individual efforts in order that they might make their weight felt and their labours to produce good result.

3409. No action of man, good or bad, is wasted. It must and does produce its result.

CHAPTER 100

AL-'ĀDIYĀT

(*Revealed before Hijrah*)

Date of Revelation and Context

Jābir, 'Ikrimah and Ibn Mas'ūd, one of the earliest Companions of the Holy Prophet and a great authority on Quranic chronology, are of the view that the *Sūrah* was revealed very early at Mecca. It takes its place in point of time next to the preceding one. In some of the foregoing Chapters conditions obtaining both in the time of the Holy Prophet and in the Latter Days were simultaneously mentioned. *Sūrah* Al-Zilzāl had dealt with the great advances that were to be made in science and knowledge, especially in the science of geology, and also with the vast changes that were to take place in the political, social and economic spheres in the Latter Days. The present *Sūrah* deals with the zeal and enthusiasm of the Companions of the Holy Prophet and with the great sacrifices they made and the battles they fought against heavy odds in the way of God. Some mystics take the *Sūrah* to refer to the constant war that the righteous believers have to wage against their evil passions and propensities, and to the heavenly light they receive as a result of the successful outcome of that fight.

سُورَةُ الْعٰدِيٰتِ مَكِّيَّةٌ (١٠٠)

1. In the name of Allāh, the Gracious, the Merciful.	بِسۡمِ اللّٰہِ الرَّحۡمٰنِ الرَّحِیۡمِ ﴿۱﴾
2. By the snorting chargers[3410]	وَ الۡعٰدِیٰتِ ضَبۡحًا ﴿۲﴾
3. Which strike sparks[3411] of fire *with their hoofs*,	فَالۡمُوۡرِیٰتِ قَدۡحًا ﴿۳﴾
4. Making raids at dawn,[3412]	فَالۡمُغِیۡرٰتِ صُبۡحًا ﴿۴﴾
5. And raising clouds of dust[3413] thereby,	فَاَثَرۡنَ بِہٖ نَقۡعًا ﴿۵﴾
6. And *thus* penetrate into the centre[3414] of *the enemy* ranks.	فَوَسَطۡنَ بِہٖ جَمۡعًا ﴿۶﴾
7. Surely, man is ungrateful to his Lord.	اِنَّ الۡاِنۡسَانَ لِرَبِّہٖ لَکَنُوۡدٌ ﴿۷﴾

3410. How dear to God must be those fighters who wage relentless war against the forces of evil that He has sworn by them or even by their horses, the word *'Ādiyāt* meaning, both the companies of warriors and their chargers. The verse speaks volumes for the zeal and enthusiasm of the Companions of the Holy Prophet to fight and lay down their lives in the way of God. It says that they march on to the field of battle with extreme delight and zeal to score a victory or be killed in the way of Allāh; and also refers admiringly to the swiftness of the movement of their chargers and the suddenness of their assault. It was revealed at Mecca at a time when Muslims had no horses. In the Battle of Badr, there were only two horses with the Muslim army, one belonging to Miqdād and the other to Zubair. The verse, in fact, constituted a prophecy that soon the Muslims will possess horses. The three words, *'Adiyāt, Muriyat, Mughırāt*, have been differently interpreted by different scholars. According to Ibn 'Abbas they refer to camels that run on the occasion of the Pilgrimage, but according to the author of Rūḥ al-Ma'ānī the reference is to the horses of the Muslim warriors. Some writers of mystical bent of mind, however, take them as a description of the spiritual wayfarers who run fast on their spiritual journey to meet their Lord and Master.

3411. The chargers of Muslim warriors run so fast that they produce sparks of fire when they strike their hoofs against the ground. The allusion is to the eagerness and zeal of the Muslim warriors to fight in the way of God.

3412. The brave Muslim warriors do not take undue advantage of the neglect and unawareness of the enemy by attacking them at night. They attack them in the full glare of the dawn. They are brave and clean fighters.

3413. The assault of the Muslim forces is so fierce and overwhelming that the whole horizon becomes dark with the dust raised by the quick steps of their horses.

3414. Muslim warriors do not attack individuals or weak helpless women, children and old men ; they attack in a body the whole enemy force and penetrate far into the heart of their ranks.

8. And, surely, he bears witness to it *by his conduct*.

وَإِنَّهُ عَلَىٰ ذَٰلِكَ لَشَهِيدٌ ۝٨

9. And, surely, he is passionate in his [a]love for wealth.

وَإِنَّهُ لِحُبِّ الْخَيْرِ لَشَدِيدٌ ۝٩

10. Does not such a one know that when those in the graves are raised,[3415]

أَفَلَا يَعْلَمُ إِذَا بُعْثِرَ مَا فِي الْقُبُورِ ۝١٠

11. And that which is *hidden* in the breasts is brought forth?[3416]

وَحُصِّلَ مَا فِي الصُّدُورِ ۝١١

12. Surely, their Lord will, on that day, be fully Aware of them.[3417]

إِنَّ رَبَّهُم بِهِمْ يَوْمَئِذٍ لَّخَبِيرٌ ۝١٢ ع

---

[a]89 : 21.

3415. There seems to be no life left in the disbelievers. They are lying dead in their graves—their houses. But soon they will rise in opposition to Islām and will march many miles to attack the Holy Prophet in Medina.

3416. The evil designs of the enemies of Islām will come to light.

3417. God is Well-Aware of their evil designs and He will punish them for their evil deeds.

CHAPTER 101

AL-QĀRI'AH

(*Revealed before Hijrah*)

Date of Revelation and Context

The *Sūrah* was revealed early at Mecca. All Commentators of the Qur'ān agree on this point. Noldeke and Muir, too, subscribe to this view. Like *Sūrah* Al-Zilzāl it primarily gives a brief but lucid description of the tremendous convulsions and catastrophic upheavals that would shake the foundations of the world in the Latter Days; the immediately preceding *Sūrah* having dealt with the great fight that the Companions of the Holy Prophet had put up against the forces of darkness. The *Sūrah* equally may apply to the Day of Judgment greater than which there could be no calamity for disbelievers.

سُوۡرَةُ الۡقَارِعَةِ مَكِّيَّةٌ

1. In the name of Allāh, the Gracious, the Merciful.	بِسۡمِ اللّٰہِ الرَّحۡمٰنِ الرَّحِیۡمِ ۱
2. The Great Calamity!	اَلۡقَارِعَۃُ ۲
3. What[3418] is the Great Calamity?	مَا الۡقَارِعَۃُ ۳
4. And what should make thee know what the Great Calamity[3419] is?	وَ مَاۤ اَدۡرٰىکَ مَا الۡقَارِعَۃُ ۴
5. The day when men will be like scattered moths,	یَوۡمَ یَکُوۡنُ النَّاسُ کَالۡفَرَاشِ الۡمَبۡثُوۡثِ ۵
6. And the mountains will be like carded wool.[3420]	وَ تَکُوۡنُ الۡجِبَالُ کَالۡعِہۡنِ الۡمَنۡفُوۡشِ ۶
7. Then, as for him [a]whose scales are heavy,[3421]	فَاَمَّا مَنۡ ثَقُلَتۡ مَوَازِیۡنُہٗ ۷
8. He will have a pleasant life.	فَہُوَ فِیۡ عِیۡشَۃٍ رَّاضِیَۃٍ ۸
9. But as for him [b]whose scales are light,	وَ اَمَّا مَنۡ خَفَّتۡ مَوَازِیۡنُہٗ ۹

[a]7 : 9; 23 : 103. [b]7 : 10; 23 : 104.

3418. Whereas the particle *al* added to *Qāri'ah* has particularized the calamity and heightened its dreadfulness, the addition of the particle *mā* (what) makes it all the more severe and destructive.

3419. The calamity would be so catastrophic that it is impossible to conceive of its dreadfulness, much less to describe it in words. See also 69 : 2-5 where an identical expression to produce an analogous effect has been used. *Qāri'ah*, besides a great calamity, signifies punishment that comes suddenly.

3420. Because it is beyond human mind to conceive of the dreadfulness of that calamity, a few only of its horrible effects have been pointed out. This and the next verse give some idea of the confusion and distress it will cause. The terrific and cataclysmic happening will scatter the people like flakes of carded wool and they will find refuge nowhere.

3421. When used in relation to an individual, *Mawāzīn* means his works; but when used in relation to a nation it signifies, its material means and resources. According to the present-day terminology of war, 'tonnage' seems to be an appropriate rendering of the word. In the latter sense the verse would mean that a nation, whose material resources are great or whose tonnage of steamships or aeroplanes is heavy, will predominate over its adversaries, and this fact will add to its prestige and power and consequently to its happiness.

10. Hell will be a *nursing* mother[3422] to him.	فَاُمُّهٗ هَاوِيَةٌ ؕ﴿۱۰﴾
11. And what should make thee know what that is?	وَمَآ اَدۡرٰىكَ مَا هِيَهۡ ؕ﴿۱۱﴾
12. *It is* a blazing Fire.	نَارٌ حَامِيَةٌ ﴿۱۲﴾

3422. The connection of the sinful people with Hell will be like that of a baby with its mother. Just as the embryo goes through various stages of development in the womb till it is born in the form of a full-fledged human being, so will the guilty people pass through different stages of spiritual torture, till their souls are completely cleansed of the taint of sin and they receive a new birth. Thus, the punishment of Hell is intended to make the wicked repent of their sins and to reform themselves. According to Islamic concept Hell is a penitentiary.

CHAPTER 102

AL-TAKĀTHUR

(*Revealed before Hijrah*)

Date of Revelation and Context

By common consent it is one of the earliest Chapters which were revealed at Mecca. In the preceding Chapters mention was made of the punishment that was to overtake disbelievers in the Holy Prophet's own time and in the subsequent long career of Islām, including the age of his Second Advent. The present *Sūrah* deals with the factors which engender in man an inclination to, or a liking for, disbelief and which divert his attention away from God. It deals with a very common but very deadly spiritual malady *viz.*, vying with one another in amassing worldly goods and taking pride in their abundance. The Holy Prophet is reported to have said that the *Sūrah* was equal in weight and worth a thousand verses (Baihaqī & Dailamī), thus stressing its great importance.

سُوۡرَةُ التَّکَاثُرِ مَکِّیَّةٌ

(١٠٢)

1. In the name of Allāh, the Gracious, the Merciful.

بِسۡمِ اللّٰہِ الرَّحۡمٰنِ الرَّحِیۡمِ ﴿١﴾

2. Mutual rivalry in *seeking* increase *in worldly possessions* diverts you[3423] *from God,*

اَلۡهٰکُمُ التَّکَاثُرُ ﴿٢﴾

3. Till you reach the graves.

حَتّٰی زُرۡتُمُ الۡمَقَابِرَ ﴿٣﴾

4. Nay! you will soon come to know *the Truth.*

کَلَّا سَوۡفَ تَعۡلَمُوۡنَ ﴿٤﴾

5. Nay again! you will soon come to know.[3424]

ثُمَّ کَلَّا سَوۡفَ تَعۡلَمُوۡنَ ﴿٥﴾

6. Nay! if you only knew with certain knowledge;

کَلَّا لَوۡ تَعۡلَمُوۡنَ عِلۡمَ الۡیَقِیۡنِ ﴿٦﴾

7. You will, surely, see Hell[3425] *in this very life.*

لَتَرَوُنَّ الۡجَحِیۡمَ ﴿٧﴾

3423. Acquisitiveness and man's inordinate desire to outstrip others in wealth, position and prestige lie at the root of all human troubles and of the neglect of higher values of life. It is man's great misfortune that his passion for acquiring worldly things knows no limit and leaves him no time to think of God or the Hereafter. He remains entirely engrossed in these things till death comes upon him, and then he finds that he had wasted his precious life in idle pursuits.

3424. Repetition of the verse is intended to add emphasis to and render more effective the warning contained in the *Sūrah*. Or, the *Sūrah* may refer to the nemesis that will come in the wake of blind engrossment by man in the acquisition of worldly things in this life.

3425. Had man used common sense and what little amount of knowledge he possesses, then, surely, he would have seen a veritable Hell yawning before his eyes in this very life, *i.e.*, he would have realized that his engrossment in the pursuit of pomp, circumstance and the material advantages of this temporary existence causes his total moral ruin.

8. Aye, you will, surely, see it with the eye of certainty *Hereafter*.[3426]

ثُمَّ لَتَرَوُنَّهَا عَيْنَ الْيَقِينِ ۝٨

9. Then, on that day you shall be called to account for the favours *bestowed upon you.*

ثُمَّ لَتُسْـَٔلُنَّ يَوْمَئِذٍ عَنِ النَّعِيمِ ۝٩

3426. Verses 5—8 leave no doubt as to the commencement of a hellish life in this very world. The Hell of next life is prepared in this life, hidden from the human eye, but can be recognised with the knowledge of certainty by those who reflect upon it. These verses describe three stages of certainty of human knowledge with regard to Hell, *viz.*, *'Ilm al-Yaqīn* or certainty by inference; *'Ain al-Yaqīn* or certainty by sight and *Haqq al-Yaqīn* or certainty by realization. The certainty of knowledge can be had in this very life by inference by those who reflect upon the nature of evil, but after death man will see Hell with his own eyes, while on the Day of Resurrection he shall have a full realization of the truth of certainty by actually entering into Hell.

CHAPTER 103

AL-'AṢR

(Revealed before Hijrah)

Date of Revelation and Context

By general agreement the *Sūrah* was revealed in the early years of the Call. Western writers, besides Muslim Commentators of the Qur'ān, assign it to that period. The preceding *Sūrah* had dealt with man's strong passion for amassing wealth and worldly goods, and with its evil consequences. In the present *Sūrah* we are told that a purposeless life, having no good ideals to pursue goes waste; and that material progress and prosperity cannot save a people if they do not possess faith and do not lead clean and pure lives. This is the unfailing testimony of Time. Drunk with their great material resources and power. prestige and prosperity, disbelievers, especially the Western Christian nations, labour under the misconception that these things will never see decline or diminution. On the other hand, Muslims seem to have despaired of their future. The *Sūrah* relates particularly to the present time. It may, however, be taken to relate also to the Holy Prophet's own time, since by *Al-'Aṣr* is meant his time also.

ركوعها سُورَةُ الْعَصْرِ مَكِّيَّةٌ (١٠٣) اٰياتها

1. [a]In the name of Allāh, the Gracious, the Merciful.

بِسْمِ اللّٰهِ الرَّحْمٰنِ الرَّحِيْمِ ①

2. By the Time,[3427]

وَالْعَصْرِ ②

3. Surely, man[3428] is *ever* in *a state of* [b]loss,[3429]

إِنَّ الْإِنْسَانَ لَفِيْ خُسْرٍ ③

4. Except those who believe and do righteous deeds, and [c]exhort one another to *preach* Truth, and exhort[3430] one another to be steadfast.

إِلَّا الَّذِيْنَ اٰمَنُوْا وَعَمِلُوا الصّٰلِحٰتِ وَتَوَاصَوْا
بِالْحَقِّ ۙ وَتَوَاصَوْا بِالصَّبْرِ ④ ع

[a]1 : 1. [b]10 : 46. [c]90 : 18.

3427. *'Aṣr* means, time; history; succession of ages; the afternoon; or the evening. *Al-Aṣrān* means, the night and the day; the morning and the evening (Lane).

3428. *Al-Insān* (man) here signifies man as mentioned in 17 : 12; 18 : 55; 36 : 78; and 70 : 20, *viz.*, the hasty, the contentious man, or the man who opposes Divine Messengers.

3429. It is History's infallible testimony that those individuals or nations, who do not make proper use of the opportunities that come to them in life, and who defy the eternal natural laws which determine human destiny, inevitably come to grief. It is such individuals and nations who are the losers in the race against Time and it is to these that the word *Al-Insān* in the *Sūrah* particularly refers. Divine laws cannot be defied with impunity.

3430. In this *Sūrah* and at several other places in the Qur'ān, believers have been enjoined not only to adopt right and good principles and right ideals themselves but also to preach them to others and thus to help in the creation of a healthy atmosphere around them. They are further enjoined not to be discouraged or dismayed by opposition or persecution they might have to face in the discharge of their very difficult task but to bear it with patience and fortitude. Thus, the *Sūrah* in one brief verse has laid down rules of conduct by observing which one can lead a happy, contented, prosperous and progressive life.

CHAPTER 104

AL-HUMAZAH

(*Revealed before Hijrah*)

Date of Revelation and Context

The *Sūrah* was revealed very early at Mecca. It was, in fact, among the earliest *Sūrahs* to have been revealed. There is complete unanimity of opinion among the Commentators of the Qur'ān on this point, and Western Orientalists also agree with this view. In *Sūrah* Al-Ṭakāthur a warning was held out that unhealthy competition in amassing wealth and taking pride in it, is calculated to divert man's attention from God and true values of life; and in *Sūrah* Al-'Aṣr it was stated that only by adopting noble ideals and righteous conduct can man save himself from a life of "loss." In this *Sūrah* mention is made of the dreadful end of those disbelievers who, instead of spending their hoarded wealth in promoting good causes, indulge in finding fault with and in slandering good and righteous believers.

سُوْرَةُ الْهُمَزَةِ مَكِّيَّةٌ

ركوعها ١ (١٠٤) اياتها

1. [a]In the name of Allāh, the Gracious, the Merciful.

بِسْمِ اللّٰهِ الرَّحْمٰنِ الرَّحِيْمِ ﴿١﴾

2. [b]Woe to every back-biter,[3431] slanderer,

وَيْلٌ لِّكُلِّ هُمَزَةٍ لُّمَزَةِ ﴿٢﴾

3. Who amasses wealth and [c]counts it over and over.[3432]

الَّذِيْ جَمَعَ مَالًا وَّعَدَّدَهٗ ﴿٣﴾

4. He thinks that his wealth will make him immortal.[3433]

يَحْسَبُ اَنَّ مَالَهٗۤ اَخْلَدَهٗ ﴿٤﴾

5. Nay! he shall, surely, be cast into the crushing torment.[3434]

كَلَّا لَيُنْۢبَذَنَّ فِي الْحُطَمَةِ ﴿٥﴾

6. And what should make thee know what the crushing torment[3434A] is?

وَمَاۤ اَدْرٰىكَ مَا الْحُطَمَةُ ﴿٦﴾

7. *It is* Allāh's kindled fire,

نَارُ اللّٰهِ الْمُوْقَدَةُ ﴿٧﴾

8. Which rises over the hearts.

الَّتِيْ تَطَّلِعُ عَلَى الْاَفْـِٕدَةِ ﴿٨﴾

9. It will be [d]closed[3435] in on them

اِنَّهَا عَلَيْهِمْ مُّؤْصَدَةٌ ﴿٩﴾

10. In outstretched columns.[3435A]

فِيْ عَمَدٍ مُّمَدَّدَةٍ ﴿١٠﴾

[a]1 : 1. [b]49 : 13 ; 68 : 12. [c]9 : 34; 89 : 21. [d]90 ; 21.

3431. *Humazah* means, one who finds fault with others behind their backs and *Lumazah* is he who finds fault with them behind their backs or before their eyes (Aqrab). As against two basic good qualities—goodness and patience mentioned in the preceding *Sūrah*, two bad qualities which cut at the root of all social peace and harmony have been mentioned in this *Sūrah*. Backbiting and slander-mongering are the two main evils from which the so-called civilized society badly suffers today.

3432. The verse constitutes a sad commentary on man's passion for worldly riches. Worship of Mammon is the bane of the materialistic civilization of the day.

3433 The ill-fated miser goes on earning wealth by all sorts of means, good or bad, and amassing and hoarding it, taking pride in it and refraining from spending it on good causes, thinking that this will immortalize him, will rescue his name from oblivion and will render his prosperity abiding. But he labours under a serious misconception.

3434. There could be no greater humiliation or mental agony for a person than that he should see that the cause against which he had fought tooth and nail and which he had tried with might and main to crush, was progressing and prospering before his very eyes. It is this sense of burning anguish of the heart which the leaders of the Quraish felt when they saw the tender plant of Islām growing into a mighty tree before their very eyes.

3434A. The Arabs say, *Ḥaṭamat-hu al-Sinnu, i.e.*, old age broke him (Lane).

3435. The intensity of the heat of enclosed fire becomes increased manifold.

3435A. The "outstretched columns" are bad habits, evil customs and usages which would not let disbelievers conform their lives to beneficent standards and values.

CHAPTER 105

AL-FĪL

(Revealed before Hijrah)

Date of Revelation and Context

The *Sūrah* was revealed very early at Mecca. Its title is taken from the expression *Aṣḥāb al-Fīl* (Owners of the Elephant), occurring in 2nd verse; Abraha's army was so called because there were one or more elephants in it. The *Sūrah* refers to the invasion of Mecca by Abraha Ashram—the viceroy in Yemen of the Christian King of Abyssinia—who came with the intention of destroying the Ka'bah. In order to curry favour with the Negus, the King of Abyssinia, and to break the national unity of the Arabs, or, as tradition goes, to stem the apprehended tide of Arab nationalism under a great Prophet whose appearance was eagerly awaited and was expected to take place very soon, and in order also to divert the attention of the Arabs from the Ka'bah and to preach and disseminate Christianity in Arabia, Abraha built a church at Ṣan'ā', capital of Yemen. When, however, he failed to cajole or coerce the Arabs into accepting the church at Ṣan'ā' in place of the Ka'bah as their central place of worship, he was stung with rage; and being intoxicated with great military power, he marched on Mecca with an army of 20,000 strong, in order to raze the Ka'bah to the ground. Arriving at a place, a few miles from Mecca, he sent for the leaders of the Quraish in order to negotiate with them about the fate of the Ka'bah. The Quraish deputation, led by the venerable 'Abd al-Muṭṭalib, grandfather of the Holy Prophet, met Abraha who treated him with great honour. But to Abraha's great surprise and contempt, 'Abd al-Muṭṭalib, instead of beseeching that the Ka'bah be spared, only requested that his two hundred camels, which Abraha's men had seized, be restored. 'Abd al-Muṭṭalib, on being told by Abraha that he had not expected such a paltry request from him when he had come to destroy their holy House of Worship, poured out the anguish of his heart and expressed his firm faith in the invulnerability of the Ka'bah in the words: "I am the master of the camels and the Ka'bah has a Master of its own Who will protect it" (Al-Kāmil, vol. I). Naturally, the negotiations broke down, and finding that they were too weak to offer effective resistance to Abraha, 'Abd al-Muṭṭalib advised his compatriots to repair to the surrounding hills. Before leaving the city, 'Abd al-Muṭṭalib, holding the skirts of the Ka'bah, prayed to God in words, full of extreme pathos, of which the rendering in English is something like this: 'Just as a man protects his house and property from plunder, so do Thou, O Lord, defend Thine own House and suffer not the Cross to triumph over the Ka'bah' (Al-Kāmil & Muir). Abraha's army had hardly moved when Divine scourge overtook them. 'A pestilential distemper,' says Muir, 'had shown itself in the camp of Abraha. It broke out with deadly pustules and blains which was probably an aggravated form of small-pox. In confusion and dismay his army commenced retreat. Abandoned by their guides, they perished among the valleys, and a flood swept multitudes into the sea. Scarcely any one recovered who had once been smitten by it. And Abraha himself, a mass of malignant and putrid sores, died miserably on his return to Ṣan'ā'.' It is particularly to this incident that the *Sūrah* refers. The fact that the disease which destroyed Abraha's army was small-pox in a virulently epidemic form is supported by the great historian Ibn Isḥāq. He quotes 'Ā'isha, the Holy Prophet's very noble and talented wife, as saying that she saw two blind beggars in Mecca and on enquiring who they were, she was told that they were the drivers of Abraha's elephants (Manthūr).

سُوْرَةُ الْفِيْلِ مَكِّيَّةٌ (١٠٥) اٰيَاتُهَا ٦ رُكُوْعُهَا ١

1. In the name of Allāh, the Gracious, the Merciful.

بِسْمِ اللّٰهِ الرَّحْمٰنِ الرَّحِيْمِ ۝١

2. Knowest thou not how thy Lord dealt with the Owners of the Elephant ?[3436]

اَلَمْ تَرَ كَيْفَ فَعَلَ رَبُّكَ بِاَصْحٰبِ الْفِيْلِ ۝٢

3. Did He not cause [a]their design to miscarry?

اَلَمْ يَجْعَلْ كَيْدَهُمْ فِيْ تَضْلِيْلٍ ۝٣

4. And He sent against them swarms of birds,[3437]

وَّاَرْسَلَ عَلَيْهِمْ طَيْرًا اَبَابِيْلَ ۝٤

5. *Which ate their dead bodies*, striking them against stones of clay.[3438]

تَرْمِيْهِمْ بِحِجَارَةٍ مِّنْ سِجِّيْلٍ ۝٥

6. And *thus* made them like broken straw, eaten up.

فَجَعَلَهُمْ كَعَصْفٍ مَّاْكُوْلٍ ۝٦ ع

---

[a]27 : 51-52.

3436. Abraha, the viceroy in Yemen of the Negus, marched on Mecca with a large army in 570 A.D., the year of the Holy Prophet's birth, in order to destroy the Ka'bah. He had a number of elephants with him. A plague or epidemic of the nature of small-pox, completely destroyed his army and their rotting bodies were eaten up by swarms of birds. See Introduction to the *Sūrah*.

3437. According to some authorities *Abābīl* is the plural of *Ibbaul* which means, a separate or distinct portion of a number of birds or horses or camels following one another. The words, *Ṭairan Abābīl*, means, birds in separate flocks or bevies, or birds in companies from this or that quarter, or following one another, flock after flock (Lane).

3438. Swarms of birds feasted themselves upon dead bodies of the invaders, striking the severed pieces against stones, as birds generally do when eating the small and severed pieces of the dead body of an animal; the particle *ba* meaning *'alā, i.e.*, upon or against (Lane).

CHAPTER 106

AL-QURAISH

(*Revealed before Hijrah*)

Date of Revelation and Context

This *Sūrah*, like the preceding one, was revealed at Mecca in the early years of the Call. Though an independent *Sūrah*, complete in all respects, its subject-matter is so closely related to *Sūrah* Al-Fīl that it has been wrongly regarded by some Commentators as its component part. In *Sūrah* Al-Fīl a brief but graphic and forceful description was given of the utter annihilation of Abraha's army (who had come to destroy the Ka'bah) by a heavenly scourge which took the form of a virulent variety of small-pox. In the present *Sūrah* God reminds the Quraish that it behoved them to worship 'the Lord of the House'—the House to serve which they were granted security from fear and hunger. In the preceding *Sūrah* mention was made of an enemy of the Ka'bah and of the Divine punishment that overtook him for his audacity to launch an attack on it. In this *Sūrah* it is stated, how in the utterly bleak and arid valley of Mecca God provided the custodians of this House with every kind of food and made them secure against fear and danger.

رکوعها ١ — سُوْرَةُ الْقُرَيْشِ مَكِّيَّةٌ — (١٠٦) آیاتها ٥

1. [a]In the name of Allāh, the Gracious, the Merciful.

بِسْمِ اللّٰهِ الرَّحْمٰنِ الرَّحِيْمِ ①

2. *Thy Lord destroyed the Owners of the Elephant* in order to attach[3439] *the hearts of* the Quraish[3440]—

لِاِيْلٰفِ قُرَيْشٍ ②

3. To make them attached to their journeys[3441] in winter and summer.—

اٖلٰفِهِمْ رِحْلَةَ الشِّتَآءِ وَالصَّيْفِ ③

4. So they should worship the Lord of [b]this House,

فَلْيَعْبُدُوْا رَبَّ هٰذَا الْبَيْتِ ④

---

[a]1 : 1. [b]3 : 97; 27 : 92.

3439. *Īlāf*, being noun-infinitive from *Ālafa*, means, sticking or making one stick to a thing; loving and making one love a person or thing; providing a person with a thing; a covenant or an obligation involving responsibility for safety; protection (Lane).

3440. The word *Quraish* being derived from the root-word *Qarasha* which means, he collected it from here and there and attached one part of it to another (Aqrab), the Quraish tribe were so called because one of their ancestors, Quṣayy ibn Kilāb bin Naḍr, had prevailed upon them to migrate from all parts of Arabia where they had lived a nomadic life, and to settle in Mecca. Of Banū Kanānah, only the progeny of Naḍr settled in Mecca and as they were a small group, they were called Quraish which means, a small group gathered from here and there.

3441. As *lām* is a particle and in Arabic a new sentence never begins with a particle, a sentence or clause or expression, therefore, must be taken as understood before this verse. The verse prefixed by the understood expression may read something like this: 'Dost thou wonder, O Muḥammad, at God's great favour upon the Quraish that He has created in their hearts love for journey in winter and summer.' The Divine favour consisted in the fact that by taking trade caravans in winter to Yemen and in summer to Syria and Palestine, the Quraish brought necessities of life to Mecca. By this trading activity, they developed a certain prestige, added to the prosperity of their town and also became acquainted with the prophecies about the appearance of a great Prophet in Arabia by coming into contact with the Jews of Yemen and the Christians of Syria who knew those prophecies. The Quraish were so rooted in the soil and had such great attachment for the Ka'bah that they would rather starve than leave it even temporarily. It was by the exhortation of Hāshim, the Holy Prophet's great grandfather, that they took to this calling. Thus it constituted a great Divine favour upon them that by their journeys to these places they, besides other advantages accruing from these journeys, were being prepared to accept the Holy Prophet whose appearance was expected to take place very soon. There is another explanation of the verses which fits in, perhaps more appropriately, with the context. The explanation is something like this: 'O Muḥammad! thy Lord destroyed the Owners of the Elephant in order to attach the hearts of the Quraish to their journeying freely in winter and summer, which constituted a great Divine favour upon them.' It seems to be very plausible because if Abraha had not been destroyed, the Quraish would not have loved journeying to these places and their journeys would not have been safe. The destruction of Abraha thus, besides opening the way for trade-journeys for the Quraish, made the Ka'bah all the more sacred in the eyes of the Arabs for whom it was already a place of pilgrimage. This, in turn, gave added impetus to the trade of the Quraish. The verse may also mean, 'Thy Lord destroyed the Owners of the Elephant for the protection of the Quraish'.

5. Who has fed them against hunger, and has given them security against fear.[3442]

ع الَّذِيٓ اَطْعَمَهُمْ مِّنْ جُوْعٍ ۙ وَّاٰمَنَهُمْ مِّنْ خَوْفٍ ۝

3442. The Quraish were granted security from fear, while all around them raged fear and insecurity. Besides, they were provided, round the year, with every kind of fruit and food. All this was not due to mere chance. It was in pursuance of a Divine plan and in fulfilment of a prophecy made by the Patriarch Abraham 2500 years age (2 : 127, 130 & 14 : 36, 38). The verse drives home to the disbelieving Quraish their guilt of ingratitude by telling them that they had taken to the worship of gods made of wood and stone in preference to the Gracious and Merciful God Who had bestowed great favours upon them and had granted them security against fear and hunger.

CHAPTER 107

AL-MĀ'ŪN

(Revealed before Hijrah)

Date of Revelation and Context

This *Sūrah* is among those Chapters which were revealed very early at Mecca. In the preceding *Sūrah* the Quraish were told that God had granted them peace and security from danger and had provided them with all necessities of life, purely out of His special grace and mercy and not due to any effort on their part or because they deserved these favours. They were told, therefore, that as an act of gratitude they should have rendered sincere and devoted service to their Gracious Creator. Instead, they became engrossed in the pursuit of worldly affairs and took to idol-worship. In this *Sūrah* it is stated that love of the world caused nations to lose faith in the Hereafter and to consign God to oblivion. It also deals with the two basic principles of Islām whose neglect constitutes denial of Religion itself—worship of God and service of fellow human beings.

ركوعها ١ سُوْرَةُ الْمَاعُوْنِ مَكِّيَّةٌ (١٠٧) اٰياتها ٨

1. [a]In the name of Allāh, the Gracious, the Merciful.

بِسْمِ اللّٰهِ الرَّحْمٰنِ الرَّحِيْمِ ﴿١﴾

2. Hast thou seen him who denies the [b]Judgment ?[3443]

اَرَءَيْتَ الَّذِيْ يُكَذِّبُ بِالدِّيْنِ ﴿٢﴾

3. That is he who drives away the orphan,[3444]

فَذٰلِكَ الَّذِيْ يَدُعُّ الْيَتِيْمَ ﴿٣﴾

4. And [c]urges not the feeding of the poor.

وَلَا يَحُضُّ عَلٰى طَعَامِ الْمِسْكِيْنِ ﴿٤﴾

5. So woe to those who pray,[3445]

فَوَيْلٌ لِّلْمُصَلِّيْنَ ﴿٥﴾

6. But are unmindful of their Prayer.

الَّذِيْنَ هُمْ عَنْ صَلَاتِهِمْ سَاهُوْنَ ﴿٦﴾

7. They like *only* [d]to be seen[3446] *of men*,

الَّذِيْنَ هُمْ يُرَآءُوْنَ ﴿٧﴾

8. And withhold *legal* alms.

وَيَمْنَعُوْنَ الْمَاعُوْنَ ﴿٨﴾ ع ١ ٣٢

[a]1 : 1. [b]82 : 10. [c]69 : 35; 89 : 19. [d]4 : 143.

3443. He, indeed, is a very bad man who has no faith in Divine reckoning, or who does not believe in Religion which is the source and basis of all morals.

3444. This and the next verse speak of two very deadly social ills which, if not scrupulously guarded against, are calculated to bring about the total decline and disintegration of a community. The failure to take proper care of the orphans kills in a people the spirit of sacrifice; and neglect of the poor and the needy deprives a useful section of the community of all initiative and the will to improve their lot.

3445. Prayer represents the duties and obligations we owe to God, and the Prayers of those hypocritical pharisees, who do not discharge the obligations they owe to God's creatures, are a body without soul, a shell without substance.

3446. The hypocritical pharisees make only a show of soulless acts of goodness and charity.

3447. *Al-Mā'ūn* means, small household articles of common use, such as axe, cooking pot, etc.; an act of kindness; any useful thing; *Zakāt* (Aqrab).

CHAPTER 108

AL-KAUTHAR

(*Revealed before Hijrah*)

Date of Revelation and Context

Being one of the earliest revelations the *Sūrah* constitutes a strong proof of the Qur'ān being the revealed Word of God, and also of the serial arrangement of its Chapters as having been adopted under Divine direction. For, while the *Sūrah* was revealed very early at Mecca, sometime in the first four years of the Call, it has been placed almost at the end of the Qur'ān. The order in which the Qur'ān exists today is different from the order in which it was revealed. It is, indeed, a miracle of the Qur'ān that the order in which the various Chapters were revealed was best suited to the needs of the period during which they were revealed, but they were arranged as its component parts in the order which was best suited to human needs for all time to come. The promise contained in this *Sūrah* was made at a time when the Holy Prophet was hardly known outside Mecca and his claim that he was the last Deliverer of humanity was looked upon by his compatriots as unworthy even of serious consideration. The promise was in emphatic terms. The words, 'We have bestowed upon thee abundance of good,' show that the promised good had already been given to the Holy Prophet. It was in the fitness of things that, in order to prove the Divine origin of the Qur'ān, the *Sūrah* should have been revealed at a time when, humanly speaking, there was hardly any possibility of the fulfilment of the promise and should have been placed at its end when the promise had already been fulfilled.

The connection of the *Sūrah* with the preceding one consists in the fact that whereas in that *Sūrah* some prominent moral sins of the hypocrites were mentioned, in this *Surah* some corresponding virtues of the righteous believers have been referred to, *viz*., generosity, observance of daily Prayers, devotion to God, and willingness to make sacrifice for national causes.

سُورَةُ الْكَوْثَرِ مَكِّيَّةٌ

1. In the name of Allāh, the Gracious, the Merciful.	بِسْمِ اللّٰهِ الرَّحْمٰنِ الرَّحِيْمِ ۝١
2. Surely, We have [a]bestowed upon thee abundance *of good*;[3448]	إِنَّآ أَعْطَيْنٰكَ الْكَوْثَرَ ۝٢
3. So pray to thy Lord, and offer sacrifice.	فَصَلِّ لِرَبِّكَ وَانْحَرْ ۝٣
4. Surely, it is thy enemy [b]who shall be without issue.[3449]	إِنَّ شَانِئَكَ هُوَ الْأَبْتَرُ ۝٤

[a]93 : 6. [b]111 : 2.

3448. *Kauthar* among other things means, abundance of good. It also means, a person possessing much good and one who gives much and often (Mufradāt & Jarīr). The *Sūrah* refers to the Holy Prophet as one upon whom God had bestowed abundant good. It was revealed at a time when the Holy Prophet did not possess anything and had nothing to give. He was then a very poor man and his claim to Prophethood was looked upon with contempt and as unworthy of serious consideration. For years after the *Sūrah* had been revealed he was mocked and jeered at, opposed and persecuted and at last he had to leave his native town as a fugitive, a price having been laid on his head. For several years at Medina, too, his life was in constant peril and his enemies were eagerly waiting to see (humanly speaking quite justifiably) the tragic and early end of Islām. Then towards the end of his life abundance of good in every shape and form began to pour down upon him like a cataract, and the promise contained in the *Sūrah* was literally fulfilled. The "outlaw" of Mecca became the arbiter of the destinies of the whole of Arabia, and the unlettered son of the desert proved to be the eternal Teacher for all mankind. God gave him a Book which is humanity's infallible guide for all time to come and by imbibing Divine attributes he rose to such high degree of nearness to his Creator as is possible for any human being to attain. He was blessed with a company of devoted followers whose loyalty and devotion have never been equalled; and when the Call came to him from his Creator to leave the world he was satisfied that he had fully discharged the sacred task entrusted to him. In short, all manner of good, material and moral, was bestowed upon the Holy Prophet in full measure. He, therefore, eminently deserved to be called, 'the most successful of all Prophets' (Enc. Brit.).

3449. It is very significant that in this verse enemies of the Holy Prophet have been emphatically referred to as *Abtar* (having no male issue), while the historical fact is that all the sons of the Holy Prophet himself born before and after the revelation of this *Sūrah* died and he left no male issue after him. This shows that the word *Abtar* here only means, 'one deprived of spiritual issues and not of sons commonly so called.' In fact, it was God's own design that the Holy Prophet should have left no male issue as he was destined to be the spiritual father of a multitude of sons in all ages to the end of time—sons who were to be far more faithful, obedient and loving than the physical sons of any father. Thus, it was not the Holy Prophet but his enemies who died issueless, since by joining the fold of Islām their sons had become the spiritual sons of the Holy Prophet, and they felt sense of shame and humiliation at their pedigree being attributed to their own fathers.

CHAPTER 109

AL-KĀFIRŪN

(*Revealed before Hijrah*)

Date of Revelation and Context

It is generally agreed that this *Sūrah* was revealed at Mecca. Ḥasan, 'Ikrimah and Ibn Mas'ūd are of this opinion. Noldeke places it in the beginning of the fourth year of the Call. The *Sūrah* has a deep connection with *Sūrah* Al-Kauthar. In that *Sūrah* it was stated that spiritual and material blessings will be bestowed upon the Holy Prophet such as have no parallel or precedent in human history. In this *Sūrah*, however, those disbelievers, against whom a Divine decree had gone forth that they would not accept Islām, are warned that when after having seen such manifest Signs in support of the Holy Prophet they had refused to accept him, how could they expect Muslims to give up their Faith and accept their foolish and fantastic beliefs? He is reported to have said that *Sūrah* Ikhlāṣ 112th *Sūrah* was equal to 1/3 of the Qur'ān, and this *Sūrah* to 1/4 of it, and whosoever would frequenly recite these two *Sūrahs* and give serious thought to their subject-matter would command great respect and prestige (Ibn Mardwaih), meaning that as *Sūrah* Ikhlāṣ deals with a basic principle of Islām—Divine Unity—and as in the present *Sūrah* believers are enjoined courageously to stick to their Faith in an hostile environment and under adverse circumstances, so he, who will comprehend and realize the significance and importance of these two Chapters, will necessarily command great respect.

سُوْرَةُ الْكَافِرُوْنَ مَكِّيَّةٌ (١٠٩)

1. In the name of Allāh, the Gracious, the Merciful.	بِسْمِ اللّٰهِ الرَّحْمٰنِ الرَّحِيْمِ ①
2. Say,[3450] 'O ye[3451] disbelievers ![3452]	قُلْ يٰۤاَيُّهَا الْكٰفِرُوْنَ ②
3. 'I worship not as you worship,	لَاۤ اَعْبُدُ مَا تَعْبُدُوْنَ ③
4. 'Nor do you worship as I worship.	وَلَاۤ اَنْتُمْ عٰبِدُوْنَ مَاۤ اَعْبُدُ ④
5. 'Nor do I worship *those* that you worship,	وَلَاۤ اَنَا عَابِدٌ مَّا عَبَدْتُّمْ ⑤
6. 'Nor do you worship Him[3453] Whom I worship.	وَلَاۤ اَنْتُمْ عٰبِدُوْنَ مَاۤ اَعْبُدُ ⑥

3450. The Divine command, expressed by the word *Qul*, applies to every Muslim. Besides the present *Sūrah*, the word is placed at the beginning of Chapters 72, 112, 113 and 114, and is used in about 306 verses of the Qur'ān; and wherever it is used it emphasizes the importance of the subject-matter governed by it. Thus believers are enjoined to proclaim loudly and repeatedly, and to convey to disbelievers in clear and definite terms, the great principles of Islām enunciated and emphasized in this *Sūrah*.

3451. The expression "O ye" is intended to draw pointed attention to the subject-matter of the *Sūrah* and to emphasize its importance. The expression has frequently been used in the Qur'ān to serve this purpose.

3452. "The disbelievers" may refer to those confirmed disbelievers who, by their persistent and defiant rejection of the Truth, rule out all possibility of accepting it, and disbelief becomes, as it were, part of their being.

3453. Various explanations have been given of the present and the preceding three verses by the Commentators. Some say that as the pagan Meccans had put their question in two forms, therefore, two forms have been adopted in answer to their question. Others say that the repetition is for the sake of emphasis. Yet some others like Zajjāj are of the opinion that the first two sentences signify denial of worship in the present time and the last two sentences denial of it in the future. As against this Zamakhsharī says that the first two sentences stand for denial of worship in future while the last two for that in the past. Be that as it may, when the particle *lā* (no; not) governs an aorist, it signifies the future tense. According to this use of the particle the expression *lā A'budu* would mean: 'I will never worship.'

The particle *mā* is used in two forms. As *Maṣdariyyah* it transforms into infinitive the verb which it governs and as *Mauṣūlah* it means *Alladhī* (that which). Sometimes it is also used for rational beings and means "he who." *Mā* may be taken as *Maṣdariyyah* in the former two verses and as *Mauṣūlah* in the latter two, and the four verses would be interpreted something like this: 'I will never adopt your mode or manner of worship, nor will you adopt the manner in which I worship. And I shall not worship those things (idols) or rational or irrational beings whom you worship, nor will you worship Him (Allāh) Whom I worship.'

7. 'For you your religion, and for me my religion.'3454

ع لَكُمْ دِينُكُمْ وَلِيَ دِينِ ۝

3454. The verse signifies that as there is absolutely no meeting ground between the believers' way of life and that of the disbelievers and as they are in complete disagreement not only with regard to the basic concepts of Religion but also with regard to its details and other aspects, therefore, there can possibly be no compromise between the two.

CHAPTER 110

AL-NAṢR

(Revealed at Mecca after Hijrah)

Date of Revelation and Context

This is a Medinite *Sūrah* in the sense that it was revealed after *Hijrah* in the Medinite period, but is a Meccan *Sūrah* in the sense that it was revealed at Mecca on the occasion of the Last Pilgrimage, only about 70 or 80 days before the Holy Prophet's death. All relevant historical data, coupled with reliable traditions and supported by such eminent authority as 'Abd Allāh bin 'Umar, one of the very early and distinguished Companions of the Holy Prophet, have assigned this date to its revelation. This was the last whole *Sūrah* to be revealed, though the last verse with which the Quranic revelation came to an end was the 4th verse of *Sūrah* Al-Mā'idah. In the preceding *Sūrah*, disbelievers were plainly told that as their outlook on life, their ideals and principles, their religious practices and mode and manner of worship were quite different from those of believers, there was absolutely no possibility of a compromise between the two. They shall reap the consequences of their deeds while the Muslims will enjoy the fruits of their labour. In the present *Sūrah* believers are told that the victory promised to them has already come and people have begun to join the fold of Islām in large numbers. Therefore, they, particularly the Holy Prophet, should give thanks to his Lord, extol His praises and seek protection from Him against the short-comings and moral weaknesses that generally find their way into a new Movement at a time when large groups of people join its fold, because, in view of the vast number of new converts and owing to lack of adequate number of experienced teachers to teach them the essentials of the new Movement, they fail to comprehend and assimilate properly its teachings and imbibe its spirit.

سُوْرَةُ النَّصْرِ مَدَنِيَّةٌ (١١٠)

1. In the name of Allāh, the Gracious, the Merciful.

بِسْمِ اللّٰهِ الرَّحْمٰنِ الرَّحِيْمِ ①

2. When the help of Allāh comes and the Victory,[3455]

إِذَا جَآءَ نَصْرُ اللّٰهِ وَالْفَتْحُ ②

3. And thou seest men entering the religion of Allāh in troops,

وَرَأَيْتَ النَّاسَ يَدْخُلُوْنَ فِيْ دِيْنِ اللّٰهِ أَفْوَاجًا ③

4. [a]Glorify thy Lord with *His* praise[3456] and seek His forgiveness.[3457] Surely He is Oft-returning with mercy.

فَسَبِّحْ بِحَمْدِ رَبِّكَ وَاسْتَغْفِرْهُ ۚ إِنَّهُ كَانَ تَوَّابًا ④

[a]15 : 99; 20 : 131; 50 : 40.

3455. The promised victory.

3456. The Holy Prophet is here enjoined that since God's promise has been fulfilled and large masses of people have begun to enter the fold of Islām, he should give thanks to his Lord for fulfilling His promise and should sing His praises.

3457. The Holy Prophet is here told that since victory has come to him and Islām has become predominant in the land and his erstwhile enemies have become his devoted followers, he should pray to God to forgive them the grave wrongs they had done to him in the past. This seems to be the meaning and significance of the injunction to the Holy Prophet to seek God's forgiveness. Or, the meaning is that the Holy Prophet is enjoined to ask God's protection against the weaknesses and short-comings that might find their way into the Muslim Community on account of lack of adequate training or education of the new converts. It is very significant that wherever in the Qur'ān mention is made of victory or some other great success coming to the Holy Prophet, he is told to ask God's forgiveness and to seek His protection. This clearly shows that in the present verse also he is enjoined to ask God's forgiveness and seek His protection not for himself but for others, *i.e.*, he is enjoined to pray that whenever there was any danger of his followers deviating from Islamic principles or precepts, God may save them from such a crisis. Thus there is no question here of the Holy Prophet's asking forgiveness for any of his own actions. According to the Qur'ān he enjoyed complete immunity from every moral lapse or deviation from the right course. See also 2612 and 2765.

CHAPTER 111

AL-LAHAB

(*Revealed before Hijrah*)

Date of Revelation and Context

There is complete unanimity of opinion among Muslim scholars and Commentators of the Qur'ān that this *Sūrah* was revealed at Mecca during the early years of the Call. Noldeke and Muir also subscribe to this view. Some scholars, however, are of the opinion that the *Sūrah* was the fifth to be revealed, the four *Sūrahs* Al-'Alaq, Al-Qalam, Al-Muzzammil and Al-Muddaththir preceding it. It seems to deal with the people having red-faces and fiery tempers; hence its title. In *Sūrah* Al-Kauthar the Holy Prophet was given a twofold promise about the great and rapid increase of his followers and about the failure of the machinations of his enemies against Islām. In the immediately preceding *Sūrah*—Al-Naṣr—reference was made to the first part of the promise, the present *Sūrah* refers to its second part.

سُوْرَةُ اللَّهَبِ مَكِّيَّةٌ (١١١)

1. In the name of Allāh, the Gracious, the Merciful.	بِسْمِ اللّٰهِ الرَّحْمٰنِ الرَّحِيْمِ ﴿١﴾
2. [a]Perish the two hands of Abū Lahab,[3458] and perish he !	تَبَّتْ يَدَآ اَبِيْ لَهَبٍ وَّتَبَّ ﴿٢﴾
3. [b]His wealth and what he has earned[3459] shall avail him naught,	مَآ اَغْنٰى عَنْهُ مَالُهٗ وَمَا كَسَبَ ﴿٣﴾
4. Soon shall he burn in a flaming fire;[3460]	سَيَصْلٰى نَارًا ذَاتَ لَهَبٍ ﴿٤﴾
5. And his wife, *too*, bearer of slander,[3461]	وَّامْرَاَتُهٗ حَمَّالَةَ الْحَطَبِ ﴿٥﴾

---

[a]108 : 4. [b]3 : 11; 58 : 18.

3458. Abū Lahab (Father of Flame) was the nickname of 'Abd Al-'Uzzā, the Holy Prophet's uncle and his inveterate enemy and persecutor. He was so called either because his complexion and hair were ruddy or also because he had a fiery temper. The *Sūrah* recalls an incident during the early preaching of the Holy Prophet. On being commanded by God to call together his relatives and to deliver to them the Divine Message, the Holy Prophet, one day, stood on mount Ṣafā and called the different Meccan tribes by name—the tribes of Luwayy, Murrah, Kilāb and Quṣayy—and his near relatives, and told them that he was God's Messenger, and that if they did not accept his Message and did not give up their evil ways, Divine punishment would overtake them. The Holy Prophet had hardly finished his speech, when Abū Lahab stood up and said, 'Ruin seize thee, is it for this that thou hast called us together' (Bukhārī)? The nickname 'Father of Flame' may either refer particularly to Abū Lahab or to any hot-tempered enemy of Islām or better still it may apply to Western nations of the Latter Days who own and control atomic and nuclear weapons—one group of them repudiating God altogether and the other denying Divine Unity, but both being equally opposed to Islām. In this sense 'the two hands' would mean these two groups, and the verse would signify that all endeavours and machinations of the enemies of Islām, particularly of the two groups of Western Powers and their satellites, would utterly fail and all their nefarious designs would recoil on their own heads; they would burn with rage at seeing Islām progressing and their own wealth, power and possessions perishing before their very eyes.

3459. The words his wealth' may mean, the wealth produced in their own countries, and 'what he has earned' may signify the riches they amass by exploiting weaker nations and despoiling them of their natural resources.

3460. The expression, Abū Lahab, may also mean, one who invents things which produce fire and flames, or one who himself is consumed in the flames of fire. In the latter sense, the verse may be interpreted as predicting the destruction of the two major political Blocs of the Latter Days by their own fire-producing weapons, such as atom bombs and other nuclear weapons. The verse also shows that the day of reckoning for these nations is not far off.

3461. The reference in the verse seems to be to Abū Lahab's wife, Umm Jamīl who strew the Holy Prophet's path with thorns and would go about spreading calumnies against him; *Ḥaṭab* also meaning calumny (Lane). The verse may also apply to those people who spread calumnies and false accusations against Islām and the Holy Prophet.

6. Round her neck shall be a halter of twisted palm-fibre.[3462]	فِيْ جِيْدِهَا حَبْلٌ مِّنْ مَّسَدٍ ﴿٦﴾ ع

3462. Though apparently free, these nations will be so strongly tied to their respective political ideologies and systems that the,' will not be able to break away from them. Or, like Umm Jamīl, who is said to have become strangled by the very rope by which she carried fire-wood, these nations will perish by the very means by which they would seek to destroy others.

CHAPTER 112

AL-IKHLĀṢ

(*Revealed before Hijrah*)

Date of Revelation and Context

That this is one of the earliest Meccan Chapters is the view of Ḥasan, 'Ikrimah and above all Ibn Mas'ūd, one of the earliest Companions of the Holy Prophet. But Ibn 'Abbās, though much younger than Ibn Mas'ūd, and regarded as one of the most learned of the Companions, thinks that the *Sūrah* was revealed at Medina. In view of these conflicting opinions of the two very respected Companions of the Holy Prophet, some Commentators of the Qur'ān are inclined to think that the *Sūrah* was revealed twice, first at Mecca and then at Medina. Among Orientalists Muir places it among the earliest Meccan Chapters while Noldeke assigns it to the end of the first period—about the fourth year of the Call. In view of the importance of its subject-matter, the *Sūrah* has come to be known by several names, of which more important are: Al-Tafrīd; Al-Tajrīd; Al-Tauḥīd; Al-Ikhlāṣ; Al-Ma'rifah; Al-Ṣamad; Al-Aḥad; Al-Nūr, etc. Because it deals with the basic belief of Islām—Unity of God—the *Sūrah* has the distinction of being called by the Holy Prophet as the greatest of all the Quranic *Sūrahs* (Ma'ānī). 'Ā'ishah is reported to have said that before going to bed the Holy Prophet used to recite this and the last two Chapters at least thrice (Dawūd). The *Sūrah* is entitled Ikhlāṣ, because its recitation and deliberation over its subject-matter is calculated to foster in the reader a deep attachment to God. What adds to its great importance is the fact that while Al-Fātiḥah is considered to be the resume of the whole of the Qur'ān, the present *Sūrah*, together with the two following Chapters, repeats and rehearses the subject-matter of Al-Fātiḥah. It deals with the four principal transcendent Divine attributes while *Sūrah* Al-Fatiḥah deals with the four main attributes of similitude.

سُورَةُ الْإِخْلَاصِ مَكِّيَّةٌ (١١٢)

1. In the name of Allāh, the Gracious, the Merciful.

بِسْمِ اللّٰهِ الرَّحْمٰنِ الرَّحِيْمِ ①

2. Say,[3463] 'He[3464] is Allāh,[3465] the [a]One ![3466]

قُلْ هُوَ اللّٰهُ اَحَدٌ ②

3. 'Allāh, the Independent and Besought of all.[3467]

اَللّٰهُ الصَّمَدُ ③

[a]16 : 23; 22 : 35; 59 : 23.

3463. The word, *Qul* (say), here embodies a permanent command to Muslims to keep proclaiming, 'God is One.'

3464. *Huwa* (He) used as *Damīr al-Sha'n* and meaning, 'the truth is,' signifies that the truth is embedded in human nature that God *is* and that He is One and Alone.

3465. *Allāh* is a distinctive name used in the Qur'ān for the Supreme Being. In the Arabic language the word is never used for any other thing or being. It is the substantive name of God, neither attributive nor descriptive. See also 3.

3466. *Aḥad* is an epithet applied to God alone and signifies, the One; the Sole; He Who has been and will ever be One and Alone; Who has no second to share in His Lordship nor in His Essence (Lane). Whereas *Aḥad* signifies Oneness of God in His Person—the idea of a second being inconceivable — *Wāḥid* signifies uniqueness of God in His attributes. Thus the expression, *Allāhu Wāḥidun*, would signify that God is that Supreme Being Who is the Source and Fountain-head from Whom all creation had emanated ; and *Allāhu Aḥadun* means that Allāh is that Being Who is One and Alone in the sense that when we think of Him, the very idea that there is any other being or thing is absent from our minds. He is One and Alone in every sense. He is neither the starting link of any chain, nor its last link. Nothing is like Him, nor is He like anything else. This is Allāh as conceived and presented by the Qur'ān.

3467. *Ṣamad* means, one to whom recourse is had; or to whom obedience is rendered; without whom no affair is accomplished; a person or place above whom or which there is no one. *Al-Ṣamad* being a Divine attribute means, the Supreme Being to Whom recourse is had for the accomplishment of needs; Who is Independent of all and upon Whom all depend for their needs; Who will continue to exist for ever after all creation has ceased to exist; above Whom there is no one (Lane). In the preceding verse the claim was made that God is One, Alone, and Unique. The present verse substantiates that claim. It says that all things and beings depend upon God but He Himself is Independent and Besought of all. All have need of Him but He has need of none. He needed the help of no being or matter to create the universe. In fact, nothing in the universe is complete in itself, not even the smallest atom. Nothing is self-subsisting; everything depends on some other thing for its existence. God alone is such a Being Who depends on no being or thing; He is above conception and conjecture. His attributes know no bound or limit.

4. [a]"He begets not, nor is He begotten;[3468]

لَمْ يَلِدْ ۙ وَلَمْ يُوْلَدْ ۝

5. 'And there is none like unto Him.'[3469]

وَلَمْ يَكُنْ لَّهٗ كُفُوًا اَحَدٌ ۝

[a]17 : 112; 19 : 93; 25 : 3; 37 : 153. [b]42 : 12.

3468. The Divine attribute *Al-Ṣamad* (Independent and Besought of all) was mentioned in the previous verse to establish the claim that Allāh is *Aḥad* (One, Alone, Unique) and now in the present verse the Divine attribute 'He begets not, nor is He begotten' is mentioned to show that He is *Al-Ṣamad* (He is above need), because the presence of need in Him presupposes that He requires the assistance of someone without whom He cannot carry on His work, and who should continue His work after He is dead, inasmuch as all those beings that succeed, or are succeeded by, others are subject to death. Allāh has succeeded no one and will be succeeded by no one. He is complete in all His attributes and is Eternal, Everlasting and Absolute.

3469. This verse disposes of a possible doubt to which the previous verses might have given rise. Granted that Allāh is One, Alone, Absolute and Independent of all, and granted that He neither begets nor is He begotten, but there might be in existence another being who, like Him, might also be possessing all the attributes He possesses. The verse removes this misgiving. It says that there is none like Allāh. Human reason also demands that there should be only One Creator and Controller of the whole universe. The perfect order that pervades and permeates it leads to the inevitable result that one uniform law must govern it, and the unity and uniformity of the law and the design proves and proclaims the Unity of the Maker (21 : 23). Thus the *Sūrah* cuts at the root of all polytheistic beliefs that are to be found in one form or other in other Faiths—belief in two, three or more gods, or the belief that soul and matter co-exist with Allāh. This is the sublime definition of the Supreme Being as given in the Qur'ān, and nothing in any other revealed Scripture touches even the fringes of the beauty, sublimity and majesty of this definition

CHAPTER 113

AL-FALAQ

(Revealed before Hijrah)

Date of Revelation and Context

This and the next *Sūrah* are so closely linked together that though they are complete in themselves and independent of each other, yet the following *Sūrah* (Al-Nās) may be regarded as complementary to the present *Sūrah*. The present *Sūrah* deals with one aspect of the same subject while the next *Sūrah* deals with the other. Both the *Sūrahs* together are called *Mu'awwidhatān* meaning, 'the two that afford protection,' because both of them open with the expression, 'I seek refuge in the Lord.' There is a wide divergence of opinion among scholars regarding the time when these *Sūrahs* were revealed. Some scholars, including Ibn 'Abbās and Qatādah, assign them to Medina, while according to Ḥasan, 'Ikrimah, 'Aṭā' and Jābir, they were revealed at Mecca. Taking all relevant facts and historical data into consideration, the majority of Muslim scholars and Commentators are inclined to place them among the Meccan *Sūrahs*.

Subject-Matter

The connection of these two *Sūrahs* with *Sūrah* Al-Ikhlāṣ consists in the fact that in Al-Ikhlāṣ believers were enjoined to proclaim to the world that God is One and Unique, that He is far above anything or any person being a partner in His Divinity. In these two *Sūrahs* believers are told that they should not be afraid of any tyrant, dictator or ruler in the discharge of this sacred duty and should hold the firm belief that God is the Sole Director and Controller of the whole universe and that He has the power to protect His votaries from any harm or injury that the forces of darkness might seek to do them. Though constituting an integral part of the Qur'ān these two *Sūrahs* may be regarded as forming a sort of epilogue to it. The main body of the Qur'ān seems to end with *Sūrah* Al-Ikhlāṣ, which recapitulates, as it were, in a nutshell, the basic Quranic principles; and in these two *Sūrahs* believers are enjoined to seek Divine protection against deviating from the right path and against the mischiefs and evils which might adversely affect their material well-being and spiritual development. The Holy Prophet used to recite them regularly before going to bed.

سُوْرَةُ الْفَلَقِ مَدَنِيَّةٌ

(١١٣) آياتها ٦ — ركوعها ١

1. In the name of Allāh, the Gracious, the Merciful.

بِسْمِ اللّٰهِ الرَّحْمٰنِ الرَّحِيْمِ ①

2. Say, 'I seek refuge in [a]the Lord of the dawn,[3470]

قُلْ اَعُوْذُ بِرَبِّ الْفَلَقِ ②

3. 'From the evil of that which He has created,

مِنْ شَرِّ مَا خَلَقَ ③

4. 'And from the evil of darkness[3471] when it overspreads,

وَمِنْ شَرِّ غَاسِقٍ اِذَا وَقَبَ ④

5. 'And from the evil of those who blow upon the knots[3472] *of mutual relationships to undo them*,

وَمِنْ شَرِّ النَّفّٰثٰتِ فِي الْعُقَدِ ⑤

6. 'And from the evil of the envier when he envies.'

وَمِنْ شَرِّ حَاسِدٍ اِذَا حَسَدَ ⑥ ع

---

[a]6 : 97.

3470. *Falaq* meaning dawn; Hell; whole creation (Lane), a Muslim is enjoined to pray that (1) when the night of darkness over Islām has passed away and the morning of its bright future dawns, its sun should continue to shine till it reaches the Meridian ; (2) that God might protect him from the hidden and manifest evil of all that He has created, including the evil influences of heredity, bad environment, defective education, etc., and (3) that God should save him from the torments of Hell in this life and in the Hereafter.

3471. The verse may refer to the evils of the time when the light of Truth becomes extinguished and the darkness of sin and iniquity spreads over the entire face of the earth. Or, it may refer to the evils of the time when one is overwhelmed by distress and privation, and it is darkness all around him and the last ray of hope disappears.

3472. The reference in the verse seems to be to those whisperers of evil suggestions who cause solemn contracts and friendships to break down and inspire people with a spirit of defiance of the established authority, or with violating the oath of fealty, and thus seek to create discord and dissension among the Muslim Community and encourage fissiparous tendencies among them. This *Sūrah* deals with the material side of man's life as the next does with its spiritual side. Man is confronted with various kinds of dangers and difficulties in life. When he is engaged in an undertaking of a serious import, particularly when he takes it upon himself to spread the light of Truth, forces of darkness surround him on all sides; and when he appears to succeed, men of evil designs bar his way and create all sorts of impediments and difficulties for him. But when at last success dawns on him, persons of jealous nature seek to deprive him of the fruits of his labour. As protection against all these obstacles, difficulties and perils in life, a believer is enjoined to invoke the help and assistance of the Lord of *Falaq* to give him light when darkness is all round; and to protect him from the evil designs of mischief-makers and the nefarious machinations of jealous persons.

CHAPTER 114

AL-NĀS

(Revealed before Hijrah)

Date of Revelation and Context

This *Sūrah*, the second of the *Mu'awwidhatān*, constitutes an extension of the subject-matter of the preceding one and is, in a way, complementary to it, in that in *Sūrah* Al-Falaq the believers were enjoined to seek protection from God against the hardships and privations of the physical life, in the present *Sūrah* protection is sought from trials and tribulations that hamper man's spiritual development, and the protection is to be invoked not only by verbal solicitation but by deeds and actions that may draw God's grace. This is the real significance of the commandment conveyed by the word *Qul* (say). The *Sūrah* is quite fittingly entitled *Al-Nās*, since protection has been solicited from the Lord, King and God of mankind (*al-Nās*) against the mischief of whisperers from among jinn and men (*al-Nās*), who whisper evil thoughts into the hearts of men (*al-Nās*). The *Sūrah*, having been revealed at the same time as *Sūrah* Al-Falaq, constitutes, along with it, appropriate end of the Qur'ān.

سُوْرَةُ النَّاسِ مَدَنِيَّةٌ (۱۱۴)

1. In the name of Allāh, the Gracious, the Merciful.

بِسْمِ اللّٰهِ الرَّحْمٰنِ الرَّحِيْمِ ۝١

2. Say, 'I seek refuge in the Lord of mankind,

قُلْ اَعُوْذُ بِرَبِّ النَّاسِ ۝٢

3. [a]"The King of mankind,

مَلِكِ النَّاسِ ۝٣

4. 'The God of mankind,[3473]

اِلٰهِ النَّاسِ ۝٤

5. **'From the evil *whisperings* of the sneaking whisperer;**

مِنْ شَرِّ الْوَسْوَاسِ ۙ الْخَنَّاسِ ۝٥

6. Who whispers into the hearts of men,

الَّذِيْ يُوَسْوِسُ فِيْ صُدُوْرِ النَّاسِ ۝٦

7. 'From among jinn and men.'[3474]

مِنَ الْجِنَّةِ وَالنَّاسِ ۝٧ ع ١ ٣٩

---

[a]59 : 24; 62 : 2.

3473. In the present *Sūrah* three Divine attributes—*Rabb* (Lord of mankind), *Malik* (King of mankind), and *Ilāh* (God of mankind), have been invoked as against one attribute, *viz.*, *Rabb al-Falaq* (Lord of the dawn) in the preceding *Sūrah*, because this one attribute comprises all the three above-mentioned attributes. Whereas one Divine attribute —Lord of the dawn—has been invoked against four kinds of mischief in the previous *Sūrah*, in the present *Sūrah* three Divine attributes have been invoked against one mischief, *i.e.*, whispering of the Evil One. This is because the promptings or insinuations of Satan cover all conceivable evils.

The three Divine attributes have a subtle connection with the physical, moral and spiritual conditions of man. Man's physical and moral developments take place under the attribute *Rabb*, and his thoughts, words and actions are punished or rewarded by *Malik*; and the attribute *Ilāh* signifies that God is the object of his love and adoration and is his aim and object. Mention of three Divine attributes in this *Sūrah* implies that all sins proceed from three causes, *viz.*, when a person looks upon another person as his Lord or King or God, that is to say, when he regards him as the main prop or support of his life, or slavishly surrenders to his undue authority or makes him the object of his love and adoration. A believer is enjoined here to look up to God alone as the real support of his life, to render Him alone true and unconditional obedience and to make Him alone the real object of his love and adoration. Or, he may have been enjoined in these verses constantly to seek protection against the ravages of exploiting capitalists, tyrannical rulers and the crafty priestly class who, taking undue advantage of the unwary and simple-minded folk, exploit them mercilessly.

3474. The Evil One whispers evil thoughts into the hearts of jinn (big men) and *Nās* (common men), sparing no one. Or, the verse may mean that whisperers of evil thoughts are to be found both among jinn and common men.

ARABIC WORDS AND EXPRESSIONS

EXPLAINED IN THE COMMENTARY

The number in the brackets indicates the number of the footnote

Ab (150).
Abābīl (3437).
(mā) A'ba'u bi-hī (2093).
Abraṣ (420F).
Abṣār (887).
Abtar (3449).
Abū Lahab (3458, 3460).
Adam (425).
Aḍ'āfan Muḍā'afah (477).
Aḍalla-hū Allāh (49).
Adhā (331); Ādhā-hu (2373).
Adhān (1153); Udhun (1194).
Ad'iyā' (2331).
Āfāq (2642).
Af'idah (2730).
Aḥad (1432, 3466).
Aḥbār (750, 1177).
Aḥkama-hū (1293A).
Ahl al-Dhimmah (1161);
—al-Bait (1333, 2353).
Aḥzāb (1448).
Ajal (1041, 1348); Balagha al-Ajala (283A).
Akdā (2886).
Akhfā (1810); Akhfa al-Shai'a (1815).
al-Ākhirah (25).
Akmah (420E).
Al (5, 17A).
Āl (88).
Alf (3396).
Alif Lām Mīm (16);—Ṣād (942).
Allāh (3, 3465).
Alladhāni (577); Alladhīna (2028).
Alqā (2303); Alqiyā (2809).
Amad (3146).
Amānah (355); Ḥamala al-Amānata (2374).
al-Amīn (2133).
Ammā (3254).
Amr (3065);—Jāmi' (2059A).
Amr & Khalq (987, 1647).
Amwāt (50, 527).
An (524).
A'nāq (2095).
al-An'ām (2419); Bahīmat al-An'ām (716).
Anbā' (822, 2227).
Anfus (95); Anfusa-kum (665); Anfusa-hum (95).
Anfāl (1092).
Anhār (2748).
Annā (271).
Anzala (2563).
Aqāma (21); Muqīmīn (705).
Aqnā (2889A).
A'rāf (978).
al-Arḍ (1802, 3110).
Asarrū (1270).
Āṣāl (1091).
Ashhur al-Ḥurum (1155A).
Aṣḥāb al-Aikah (1516);
—al-Kahf (1666A);
— al-Qaryah (2432).
Ashrāṭ (2751).
Ashudd (2726).
Asmā' (62A).
Atā al-Shai'a (1835A).
Athar (1847).
Athkhana fi'l-Arḍi (2738).
Aṭwār (3133).
Auḥā (1745, 3406); mā Yūḥā (1821).
Aulayān (802).
Ausaṭ (790).
Autād (2520).
Āyah (131A, 132, 1133);
Āyat al-Kursiyy (318).
Ayāmā (2045).
A'yun (1314).
Ayyām (984); Ayyām Allāh (1454).
Ayyūb (869).
Āzar (864).
Āzifah (2894).
'Ābid (2668, 2830).
'Abūs (3195).
'Ād (995, 1323).
'Adhāb al-Khuld (1269).
'Ādiyāt (3410).
'Adl (86, 1570).
'Aḍud (2216).
'Afw (265, 480, 481);
'Afā Allāhu 'anka (213, 1189);
Ya'fū (294A).
'Āhada (1151).
'Aīn Sīn Qāf (2643A).
'Ain (1822);
'Ain al-Yaqīn (3426).

Furush (2967A).
Fuṣṣilat (1294).
Ghafarnā la-hū (2526, 3076); Ghafara al-Matā'a (2612); Maghfirah (332); Istighfār (664, 1320, 2612).
Ghāfilāt (2038).
al-Ghaib (20); Iẓhār 'ala al-Ghaib (3147, 3148); bi'l Ghaib (1787).
Ghair Musma'in (613);—Ṣāliḥ (1318).
Ghamrah (2828).
Ghamām (251).
Ghanam al-Qaum (1905).
Gharq (3236).
Ghasaq (1641).
Ghulām (408, 1716); Ghilmān (2855).
Ghuthā' (1996).
Hady (720); Hidāyah (13, 2742); Hudā (1933).
Hai'ah (420B).
Haihāta (1995).
Haita (1371).
Hal (762).
Hāmān (2198).
Hārūt & Mārūt (130).
Hudhud (2160).
Huwa (3464); Hum (62B).
Humazah (3431).
Ḥā Mīm (2592, 2643).
Ḥadīd (2998).
Ḥafiyy (1083).
Ḥājah (2619).
Ḥama' (1493).
Ḥamala al-Amānata (2374); Taḥmilu-hū (1761); al-Ḥāmilāt (2824).
Ḥaraḍ (1404).
Ḥaraj (2059).
Ḥarf (1935).
al-Ḥarth (1905).
Ḥaram (2267) ; Ashhur al-Ḥurum (1155A).
Ḥāsha lillāhi (1388).
Ḥasharnā (1697); Ḥushira (3265).
Ḥaṭab (3461).
Ḥaṭamat-hu al-Sinnu (3434A).
Ḥattā (1417A).
Ḥijran Maḥjūran (2072).
Ḥujjah (2714).
Ḥuqub (1704A).
Ḥūr (2851).
Ḥusnā (1254).
Ḥūt (1705).
Ibil (3330).
Iblīs (67).
Ibn Maryam (417, 1767).
Ibtilā' (142A).
Ibyaḍḍa & Iswadda Wajhu-hū (455, 1552A).
Ibyaḍḍat 'Ainā-hu (1403).
Idrīs (1783).
Iḥsān (1570, 2947).
Ikmāl (721).
Iktasaba (360).
Īlā' (275).
Īlāf (3439).
Ilāh (3473).
Ilḥāf (348).
Ill (1160).
Illā (66); Illa Nafsa-ka (641).
Ilyāsīn (2503).
Imām (143, 2431).
Īmān (1282).
In (486).
Ināth (671).
Injīl (366).
al-Insān (1788, 3428, 3429).
Inṭalaqā (1713).
Iqra' (3386).
Islām (383, 1282).
Ism (2); Asmā' (62A); Bismillāh (1).
Iṣr (362).
Isrā' & Mi'rāj (1590).
Israel (*Isrā'īl* (75).
Istamta'a (590).
Istawā (54, 2873).
Istaghshau Thiyāba-hum (3131).
Ītā'i Dhi'l-Qurbā (1570), Āti (2288).
Ithm (199, 263, 766); Ithmī (738).
I'tikāf (215).
Iṭmi'nān (327).
Iẓhār 'alā al-Ghaib (3147, 3148).
'Ibādah (11, 1774, 2840); 'Ābid (2668, 2830).
'Ibrah (1555, 1991).
'Īd (809).
'Iddah (278, 289, 3064A, 3068A).
'Iḍīn (1525).
'Ifrīt (2172, 2173).
'Illiyyin (3290, 3292, 3293).
'Ilm (1933, 2237); 'Alā 'Ilmin (2699). 'Ilm al-Yaqīn (3426);
'Imrān (399, 400); Imra'at 'Imrān (401).
'Īn (2482, 2851A).
'Īsā (416).
'Ishār (3264).
Ja'ala (424B, 817, 1393).
Jabal (1317, 3263); Jibāl (1441, 1697. 1802, 1851, 1907, 3110).
Jahannam (246, 1790,)
Jāhil (844); Jahālah (1585); Jahūl (2374).
Jalābīb (2044, 2369).

Jālūt (310A, 311).
Jamal (974).
Jama'a Kaida-hū (1830); Amr Jāmi' (2059A).
Jannah (68, 1857).
Jānn (1023).
Al-Jāriyāt (2824); Tajriyān (2950).
Jibrīl (123).
al-Jibt (617).
Jidāl (233).
Jihād (1199, 1580, 1956, 1976, 2084, 2239, 2268, 3077).
Jinn (885, 900, 2153, 2945, 3139).
Jiyād (2528A).
Jizya (1175).
Al-Jūdī (1317A).
Juz' (329).
Ka'bah (145, 163, 1943, 1943A).
Kabā'ir (594) ; Kabīr (1400).
Kadhdhaba (3370); Tukadhdhibān (2923).
Kāfir (3056); Kafarnā bi-kum (3029); Kafūr (3192).
Kāf Hā Yā 'Ain Ṣād (1738).
Kāffah (249).
Kahl (418B); Kuhūlah (418A).
Kalālah (575, 715).
Kalimah (414, 712); Kalimāt (142B).
Kallā (1797, 3166).
Kamā (1093).
Kashafa 'an Sāqihī (2177).
Kasaba; Iktasaba (360).
Katabnā (1049); Mukātabah (2046).
Kauthar (3448).
Kawā'ib (3233).
Kibr (2613); Mustakbirīn (2007).
Kifāt (3214).
Kifl (642).
Kitāb (2996A); al-Kitāb (2222); Kiṭāban Mutashābihan (2572);
Kun (1546, 1770); mā Kāna la-hū (432).
Kurh & Karh (2625).
Kursiyy ; Āyat al-Kursiyy (318).
Khabāl (462).
Khabīthāt (2041).
Khāda'a-hū (29).
Khair (344, 348A, 452, 1242).
Khālidīn (1351).
Khalq (987); Khalaqa (420); Khuliqa al-Insānu min 'Ajal (1888).
Khamr (261).
Khalīfah (61).
Kharajta (172).
Khāsi'īn (107).
Khaṭb (1846).
Khātam (2359).
Khaṭa' & Khiṭ' (1614); Khaṭī'ah (361, 667).
Khauf (72); Takhawwuf (1549).
Khawālif (1205).
Khimār (2044).
Khinzīr (198).
(min) Khilāfin (1835B).
Khul' (282).
Khuluq (2127).
Lā (2976, 3176, 3343).
La'alla (1301).
(Abū) Lahab (3458, 3460).
Lail (3393).
Lām (534, 1075, 1629, 2200, 3441).
Lamam (2885).
Lāta (2516).
Lawāqiḥ (1491).
Līnah (3020).
Lisān Ṣidqin (1779).
Mā (628, 1821, 1895, 2877, 2892, 3359, 3418, 3453).
Ma'ārib (1816).
Madadnā (1489).
Mafāzah (545).
Mafātiḥ (2232).
Maghfirah (332).
Mahd (418A).
Maḥrūm (2830).
Maisir (262).
Majma' al-Baḥrain (1704A).
Majnūn (1480).
Makānah (1355).
Makhḍūd (2965).
Mala' (1003).
(mā) Malakat Aimānu-kum (561, 589).
Malik (3473); Mālik (8, 2687).
Malā'ikah (57A).
Man (2474).
Mann (98, 331).
Mansak (1952).
Manṭiq (2152).
Maqbūḥ (2217A).
al-Marwah (184).
Marratān (280).
Maryam (402B); Ibn Maryam (417).
Ma'shar (908).
Mash'ar al-Ḥarām (236).
Mashhūd (3209).
al-Masīḥ (415).
Masnūn (1493).
Mathal (2299).
Mathābah (144).

Mathānī (2572); al-Sab' al-Mathānī (1522).
Mau'iẓah (1271).
Ma'ūn (3447).
Mautā (110A, 844A); Amwāt (50,527).
Maulūdun la-hū (287).
Mawaddata baini-kum (2248).
Mawālī (596).
Mīkāl (124).
Min (343, 1891, 2721); Min-kum (1793A); Mimmā (3127); Min Khilāfin (1935B).
Minhāj (753).
Mīrāth (537).
Mirrah (2872).
Mi'rāj & Isrā' (1590, 2876).
Miṣbāḥ (2047).
Mi'shār (2402).
Mishkāt (2046B).
Mīthāq al-Nabiyyīn (433).
Mīzān (2650, 2997, 2999); Mawāzīn (3421).
Mu'adhdhir (1207).
al-Mu'aqqibāt (1427).
Mubārak (932, 1894, 2047); Tabāraka (2062).
Mubīn (1281).
Mudabbirāt (3239); Tadbīr (1258).
Mudda (3299).
Muḍghah (2565).
Mughīrāt (3410).
Muḥkam (369); Muḥkamāt & Mutashābihāt (373); Aḥkama-hū (1293A).
Muḥarrar (401).
Muḥṣanāt (588, 2028).
Muhaimin (752).
Muḥsin (989, 1589, 2203, 2829); Iḥsān (1570); Ḥusnā (1254).
Mujāhid (654).
Mukātabah (2046).
Mu'min (3056).
Munāfiq (1196).
Munkar (1570).
al-Muqaṭṭa'āt (16, 2094).
al-Muqassimāt (2824).
Muqīm (1515); Muqīmīn (705).
Muqtasimīn (1524).
Mursā (1081).
Mūriyāt (3410).
Mūsi'ūn (2837A).
Musaddiq (77, 433A).
Musawwimīn (473).
Mushawarah (515).
Mustakbirīn (2007).
Mustaqarr & Mustauda' (883, 1298).
Mutaqallab & Mathwā (2753).
Mutawaffī (424).
Mutawaṣṣimīn (1514).
Muttaqī (19, 1589, 2829).
Mutashābih (371); Kitāban Mutashābihan (2572); Mutashābihāt (373).
Muwallī (171).
Naba' (2551, 3223).
al-Nabī (784, 2329); Rasūl & Nabī (1780).
Naḍḍākhatān (2950).
Nafs (109A, 397); Nafs Lawwāmah (3177); Anfus (95); Anfusa-kum (665).
Nāfilah (1642).
Nahār (1969); al-Nahār & al-Lail (2413).
al-Najdain (3349).
Najiyy (1399).
Nakkara-hū (2175); Munkar (1570).
Naml (2156).
Naṣīb (642).
Nashazat al-Mar'atu (599).
al-Nās (46, 2419, 2614).
Nāshiṭāt (3238).
Naẓara (3296); Unẓurnā (131).
Nāzi'āt (3236).
Nidd (189).
Nikāḥ (2026A).
Nisyān (361, 1197).
Nujūm (2977, 3262); al-Najm (2868).
Nūr (1236, 2046A).
Nuṭfah (2565).
Nuzul (552).
Nuwalliyannaka (165).
Qāb; Qāba Qausain (2876).
Qabḍ & Basṭ (2053).
Qabīlah (2796).
Qadam (1231).
Qadr (3394).
Qadar & Qaḍā' (1754); lan-Naqdira 'alai-hi (1913).
Qāf (2799).
Al-Qāhir (832, 857).
Qāla (57); Qul (3450, 3463); la-Yaqūlunna (2314).
Qalā'id (720).
Qalb (2816); Mutaqallab (2753).
Qārūn (2231).
Qarn (823).
Qāri'ah (3418, 3419).
Qāt' (744); Qaṭa'a al-Ṭarīqa (2249).
Qatl (103, 506B, 646); Qataltum (109); Uqtulū Anfusa-kum (627); Nuqattilu (1036); ma Qatalū-hu Yaqīnan (699).
Qawwāmūn (598); Qayyim (1662); Ummatun Qā'imatun (459).
Qawā'id (2058A).
Qiblah (159, 162, 168).

Qibal (2170).
Qissīs (785).
Qiṭmīr (2413A).
Quraish (3440).
al-Qur'ān (207B).
al-Qurā (911); Qaryah (1063, 1401, 1603, 2432).
Qurbā (2654).
Qurū' (277).
Quwwah (1137).
Rabb (6, 3220, 3473).
Rabbāniyyīn (432A).
Rābiṭū (554, 555).
Rafath (233).
Raf' (424A).
al-Raḥmān (4, 3087); al-Raḥīm (4); Raḥmah (106, 990).
Rahw (2697).
Raib (2857).
Rā'inā (131).
Rajīm (402D); Rajama-hū (1776, 2129A, 2435).
Rajul (2437); Rijāl (3139).
Rajafa (3241).
Rāki' (79).
Ramaḍān (207A).
Ramz (1745).
Rasūl (2100); Rasūl & Nabī (1780).
Rāwada-hū (1370).
Ribā (350).
Ribbiyyūn (495).
Rid' (2215).
Rifd (1344).
Rīḥ (1128, 2185, 2380).
Rijs (924).
Rizq (22).
Ruhbān (786).
Rūḥ (712, 1529, 1647, 2324, 2666, 3120);
—al-Qudus (119):
al-Rūh, 3397);
—al-Amīn (2133);
Rujz (3161).
Rukn (2836).
Rass (2078).
al-Sā'ah (1929, 2069).
Saba' (2383A).
Sabaḥa (2981, 3015, 3115); Sābiḥāt (3239); Tasbīḥ (60, 3015, 3055); Nusabbiḥu (59).
Sābiqūn (2962).
al-Sab' al-Mathānī (1522).
Sadir (2880).
Safiha (148).
al-Ṣafā & al-Marwah (184).
Sā'ibah (798A).
Sā'iq (2807).
Sakhkhara-hū (2020).
Salām (1253, 2456).
Salsabīl (3197).
Salwā (99).
Samk (3245A).
Samā' (39, 1937); al-Samāwāt (1802).
Samiyy (1742).
Sāmirī (1841).
Sanah (1038); Sanah & 'Ām (2243).
Sāq (3185).
al-Sāriq (744).
Sauṭ (3337).
Sawā' (1136).
Sawwā (55); Istawā (54).
Sayyi'ah (958); Sayyi'āt (548).
Siḥr (128, 1281); Sāḥir (1025); Musaḥḥar (2129).
Sijjīn (3289, 3290).
Sīmā (347);
Sirr (1810); Asarrū (1270).
Subul (1538).
Sujjira (3266).
Sukārā (609).
Sunan (484).
Suqiṭa fī yadi-hī (1054).
Sha'ā'ir Allāh (242).
Shadda al-Shai'a (1283B).
Shafā'ah (85); al-Shaf' (3334).
Shāhid; Mashhūd (3209); Shahīd (445, 2807).
Shahīq (1349).
Shai (41A, 136).
Shaiṭān (70, 964, 1102, 1910); Shayāṭīn (32, 2534, 2535).
Shajarah (69).
Shākilah (1646).
Shighāf (1379).
Shirk (615, 1247, 1606).
Shir'ah (753).
Shu'aib (1011).
Shubbiha la-hum (698).
Shukr (690, 1455); Shukr & Kufr (2566).
Shuḥḥ (2341).
Shūrā (2660); Mushāwarah (515).
Shurra'an (1064).
Shu'ūb (2796).
Shu'ūr (2125).
Ṣa'aara Khadda-hū (2309).
Ṣabr (82, 179).
Ṣadaqah (349); Ṣadaqāt (1193); Ṣaduqāt (563); Ṣaddaqa (3186).
Ṣād (2513).
Ṣadda (2682).

Ṣafaḥa 'an-hu (2670).
Ṣāfināt (2528).
Ṣāghirūn (1175).
Ṣāḥib (1078).
Ṣaiḥah (1328).
Ṣakhrah (1707).
Ṣalṣāl (1493, 2924).
Ṣalaba (697).
Ṣāliḥ (999); Ṣāliḥāt (1235).
Ṣalāt (2051); Ṣallā (3186); Yuṣallī (2359A).
al-Ṣamad (3467, 3468).
Ṣarrah (2835).
Ṣibghah (156).
Ṣur-hunna (328).
Ta'affuf (348).
Tābūt (308).
Tadaththara (3159).
Tafaqqada (2159).
Tafjīr (3192A).
Taḥt (1240, 1758).
lā Taḥnath (2539).
Tajallā (3363).
Tajriyān (2950).
Takhawwuf (1549).
Talautu-hū (126); Yatlūna (142); Utlu (2256).
Tamattu' (230); Tamatta'a (590).
Tamīda bi-him (1885).
Tanāza'ū al-Ka'sa (2854).
Taqawwala (2860).
Tasbīḥ (60).
Tasnīm (3294).
Taṣaddā lahū (3252).
Taubah (85, 631, 1295, 2091); Tāba (1221).
Taurāt (365).
Ta'ūlū (562).
Ta'wīl (372, 983).
Tilka (1228).
lā Tuḍārra (286).
Tubba' (2700).
Tukadhdhibān (2923).
Turāb (2277).
Thamūd (998, 1326, 2128).
al-Thaqalān (2933).
Thiyāb (3160); Istaghshau Thiyāba-hum (3131).
Thu'bān (1023).
Thumma (1791).
Ṭa'ana (1163).
Ṭā Hā (1807); Ṭā Sīn (2143).
Ṭāghūt (320).
Ṭair (420C, 1907, 2153, 2154); Ṭā'ir (1039, 1599); Taṭayyara bi-hī (2177A).
Ṭālūt (307, 312).
Ṭamasa 'alaihi (1284A).
Ṭarf (2174); Aṭrāf (1451).
Ṭarīqah (1831A); Ṭarīqat al-Qaum (1850A).
Ṭaul (2593).
Ṭayyib (192, 722); Ṭayyibāt (197); Ṭibtum (2590).
Ṭibāq (3079A).
Ṭīn (420A).
Ubri'u (420D).
Udhun (1194).
Uff (1608).
Ukht (1763); Ukht Hārūn (401).
Umm, (370, 1450); —al-Kitāb (2645; 2669); Ummī (1058); Ummiyyūn, (113A, 384).
Ummah(1586).
Unẓurnā (131).
Urīdu (737).
Ushriba (122).
'Udwān (223).
'Umrah (228).
'Umyun (34).
'Urḍah (273).
'Urf (1087A).
'Urub (2968).
'Uzair (1176).
Wabāl (3070).
Wāḥid (1432 ; 3466); Waḥīd (3164).
Wajh (135, 2236, 2931); Wujūh (1854A, 2077A, 2372); Ibyaḍḍa & Iswadda Wajhu-hū (455).
Walad (574, 677A, 886).
Waliyy (2178A).
Waqa'a al-Qaulu (2190).
Warā' (2992).
Waraq (959, 1861).
Wasaṭ (160); Ausaṭ (790).
Wasīlah (743).
Waṣīlah (798B).
al-Watr (3334).
Waṭar (2357A).
Waw (2465).
Waza'a (2155).
Wird (1343B, 1801).
Yā Sīn (2426).
Yad (744, 1817, 2540, 2837); 'an Yadin (1175); Yad Baiḍā' (1818).
Ya'fu (294A).
Yaghlibūn (2271).

Yaḥyā (406).
Ya'jūj & Ma'jūj (1728).
Yalhath (1074).
Yamīn (2478A, 2495, 2587).
Yaqīn (3172); 'Ain al-Yaqīn (3426).
Ya'qilūn (1535).
Yaqnut (2351).
Ya'rifūna-hū (170).
Yarjū (2238).
Yastahzi'u (33).
Yas'ā (2438).
Ya'ṣirūn (1386).
Yataṭahharūn (2180).
Yatafakkarūn (1535).
Yatlūna (142).
Yaum (9, 323A, 2622); —al-Dīn (9); —al-Taghābun (3061); —'Abūs & —Qamtarīr (3195); Ayyām (984).
Yughāthu (1385).
Yuṭīqūna (207).
Za'ama (3059).
Zabāniyah (3392).
Zabūr (540).
Zafīr (1349).
Zahaqa (1645).
Zakāt (349, 1981, 2288, 2289).
Zakariah (403).
Zammala (3150).
al-Zānī (2025A).
Zanjabīl (3196).
Zaqqūm (2486, 2971).
Zawwajā Shai'an bi-Shai'in (2851).
Zayyanna (895); Zīnah (2044).
Ziyādah (1255).
Zujājah (2046C).
Zūr (2092).
Ẓahīrah (2058).
Ẓihār (2330).
Ẓulm (948, 1020); Ẓalūm (2374); Ẓalama-hū (2206); Ẓulumāt (37, 858).

INDEX

The first number in the reference indicates the page. The numbers of the relevant Chapter and verse follow The number in the brackets represents the number of the foot-note.

Aaron, commissioned to Pharaoh, 445, 10 : 76; 670, 20 : 44; 794, 26 : 16; favours of God on, 969, 37 : 115—121; Moses' subordinate and deputy, 355, 7 : 143 (1045) ; 668,20: 30-37 (1820); 783, 25; 36 ; 794, 26 : 14-16 (2098); 843, 28 : 35-36 (2215); prayer of Moses for, 358, 7 : 152; Prophethood of, 235, 4 : 164; 298, 6 : 85; 445, 10 : 76; 654, 19 : 54; 698, 21 : 49; 741, 23 : 46; 783, 25 : 36; reprimanded by Moses and excuse of, 358, 7 : 151 (1055); 679, 20 : 93-94; vindication of, 679, 20 : 91 (1845)

Abbreviations (Muqaṭṭa'āt), meanings of, 12, 2 : 2 (16); 324, 7 : 2 (942); 641, 19 : 2 (1738); 664, 20 : 2 (1807); 793, 26 : 2 (2094); 816, 27 : 2 (2143); 836, 28 : 2 (2195); 856, 29 : 2 (2236A); 870, 30 : 2 (2269); 884, 31 : 2; 1006, 40 : 2 (2592)

'Abd Allāh ibn Jubair, bravery of, 168, 3 : 153 (502-503)

'Abd al-Muṭṭalib, 1402, Ch. 105

'Abd Allāh ibn 'Ubayy, boastfulness of, 1216, 63 : 9 (3053); defection of, at the battle of Uḥud, 159, 3 : 122-123 (467-468); ignominy of, 759, 24 : 12 (2033)

'Abd Allāh ibn Umme Maktūm, and the Holy Prophet, 1315, 80 : 2 (3250)

'Abd al-'Uzzā, 1417, 111 : 2 (3458)

Ablution, and Tayammum before offering Prayers, 203, 4 : 44 (610-612); 244, 5 : 7 (725-725A)

Abraha, invasion of Mecca by, 64, 2 : 151 (176); 1403, 105 : 2-6 (3436-3438)

Abraham, cooling of the fire for, 701, 21 : 69-71 (1902); 860, 29 : 25; 967, 37 : 98-99 (2496); covenant made with, 54, 2 : 126; dissociation of, from disbelievers, 422, 9:114 (1220); 1201, 60 : 5-6 (3029); dispute with a king of, 107, 2 : 259 (321); emigration of, 701, 21 : 72 (1903); enjoined to keep the Sacred House clean, 54, 2 : 126; 719, 22 : 27 (1944); enjoins upon his progeny complete submission to God, 58, 2 : 133 (149) ; 1049, 43 : 29 (2675); exaltation of the progeny of, 132, 3 : 34; as exampler, 578, 16 : 121 (1586); 1201, 60 : 5 (3029); firm believer in Divine Unity, 1049, 43 : 28-29 (2675); friend of God, 224, 4 : 126 (675); given Isaac and Jacob, 298, 6 : 85; glad tidings of a son to, 545, 15 : 54—57; 1120, 51 : 29-31 (2834); good name of, 969, 37 : 109 (2499); granted knowledge of laws, 296, 6 : 76 (865); guided by God, 699, 21 : 52; hospitality of, 470, 11 : 70-74 (1330-1332); 545, 15 : 52-61 (1505-1506); 1119, 51 : 25-35 (2833-2835); iconoclasm of, 699, 21 : 58-68 (1897-1901); 966, 37 : 92-97 (2494-2495); identity of the father of, 296, 6 : 75 (864); and Ishmael pray for a Messenger to be raised among their offspring, 56, 2 :130 (147); with Ishmael rebuilds the Ka'bah, 55, 2 : 128 (146); and Ishmael testify to the truth of the Holy Prophet, 1358, 90 : 4 (3345); national renaissance and, 108, 2 : 260-261 (327-329); people of, idol-worshippers and, 699, 21 : 53 (1895); 800, 26 : 72 ; Pilgrimage instituted by, 719,

22 : 28 (1946); pleads for Lot's people, 471, 11 : 75-76 (1334); prayers of : for the forgiveness of his father, 422, 9 : 114; 653, 19 : 48, for the grant of a son accepted, 967, 37 : 101-102; for the grant of lasting reputation, 801, 26 : 85 (2121); for the security and prosperity of Mecca, 530, 14 : 36 (1468); 531, 14 : 38 (1470-1471); for his progeny to be submissive to God, 56, 2 : 129; Prophethood of, 54, 2 : 125 (142A); 57, 2 : 131; 578, 16 : 121-123; 652, 19 : 42; 701, 21 : 72-74 (1903); 985, 38 : 46-48; Prophethood in the descendants of, 861, 29 : 28; 969, 37 : 114 (2500); 985, 38 : 46-48; 1181, 57 : 27; rise and fall of the posterity of, 109, 2 : 261 (329); story of, 652, 19 : 42-49 (1774-1776); 699, 21 : 53-59 (1895-1896); 700, 21 : 63-65 (1900); 800, 26 : 70-83 (2118-2120); 966, 37 : 86-97 (2491-2495)

Abrogation, of Scriptures, 49, 2 : 107 (132); in Qur'ān, 74, 2 : 181 (205); 270, 5 : 98 (794); 574, 16 : 102 (1577)

Abstinence, from conjugal relations, 77, 2 : 188 (215); 91, 2 : 223 (268); see "Food"

Abū 'Āmir, arch-enemy of Islām, 420, 9 : 107 (1217)

Abū Bakr, spiritual eminence of, 405, 9 : 40 (1185-1186)

Abū Jahl, punishment meted out to, 383, 8 : 33 (1117)

Abū Lahab, 1417, 111 : 2 (3458); wife of, 1417, 111 : 5-6 (3461-3462)

Abyssinia, Muslim refugees into, 266, 5 : 84 (788)

Actions, effects of, 243, 5 : 6; 934, 35 : 9; 1152, 54 : 53 (2916); faith and, 574, 16 : 98 (1576); 587, 17 : 20 (1604); record of, 1070, 45 : 30 (2715); 1327, 82 : 11-13 (3287); requital of, 181, 3 : 196 (549); 202, 4 : 41 (606); 921, 34 : 3-6 (2376-2377); 1077, 46 : 20 (2727); 1083, 47 : 5 (2741); reward of, 320, 6 : 161 (938); 853, 28 : 85 (2234); 1141, 53 : 40 (2888); weighing of, 325, 7 : 9, 10 (947-948)

Accountability, of human thoughts and actions, 118, 2 : 285 (356); 293, 6 : 63; 698, 21 : 48; 1219, 64 : 5, 8 (3058-3059); 1245, 68 : 40 (3102); 1388, 99 : 8-9 (3409); individual nature of, 60, 2 : 140; 438, 10 : 42; 1037, 42 : 16; of Messengers and people, 324, 7 : 7 (946)

'Ād, destruction of, 862, 29 : 39 (2252); 1148, 54 : 19-22 (2904); 1249, 69 : 5, 7-8; great civilization of, 805, 26 : 129-131 (2126); heirs of Noah's people, 340, 7 : 70 (997); Hūd deputed to, 465, 11 : 51; identity of, 339, 7 : 66 (995); 465, 11 : 50-61 (1322-1324); rejection of the Truth by, 1110, 50 : 13-14; story of, 339, 7 : 66-73 (995-997A)

Adam, angels submit to, 25, 2 : 35 (65); 325, 7 : 12 (950); 541, 15 : 29-30 (1495); 596, 17 : 62 (1629); 988, 38 : 72-74 (2553); beguiled by Satan, 26, 2 : 37 (70); 328, 7 : 23 (959); 684, 20 : 121-122 (1860); the chosen one, 132, 3 : 34; and the concomitants of civilized life, 683, 20 : 119-120 (1858); creation of, 143, 3 : 60 (425A); as image of Allāh, 988, 38 : 76 (2555); dwelling place of, 26, 2 : 36 (68); emigration of, 26, 2 : 37, 39 ; 328, 7 : 25 (961); 685, 20 : 124 (1863); and Eve and the forbidden tree, 26, 2 : 36 (69); 327, 7 : 20 (957-957A), 683, 20 : 118-122 (1857—1859); Iblīs refuses to submit to, 542, 15 : 32 (1496); 596, 17 : 62 (1629); identity of, 23, 2 : 31 (61); and Jesus, 143, 3 : 60 (425); knowledge of God and, 24, 2 : 32 (62A); lapse of, and remedy adopted by, 684, 20 : 121-123 (1859-1862); necessity of, 25, 2 : 34(64); repentance of, 27, 2 : 38; 328, 7 : 24 (960); shame of, 327,

Bestower, 126, 3 : 9 ; choosing of Messengers by, 57, 2: 131; 132, 3 : 34; 356, 7 : 145; 731, 22 : 76; as Compassionate, 61, 2 : 144; 132, 3 : 31; as Controller, 427, 10 : 4 (1234); 436, 10 : 32; 509, 13 : 3; 892, 32 : 6; as Creator, 282, 6 : 15 (829); 302, 6 : 96 (879); 651, 19 : 36 (1770); enthronement of, 336, 7 : 55 (985-986); 427, 10 : 4 (1233); 664, 20 : 6 (1809); 892, 35 : 5 (2322); 1009, 40 : 16 (2600); as Encompasser, 17, 2 : 20; existence of, 22, 2: 29; 68, 2 : 165 (188); 77, 2 : 187; 295, 6 : 74 (863); 365, 7 : 173 (1070); 436, 10 : 32 (1258); 777, 25 : 3-4 (2064-2065); 829, 27 : 61-67 (2182-2187); 873, 30 : 21-28 (2277-2282); favours of, 587, 17 : 21 (1605); 889, 31 : 32 (2317); 1170, 56 : 64-74 (2973-2975); 1304, 78 : 7-17 (3225-3226); fear of, 526, 14 : 15; 938, 35 : 29-30 (2419-2420); 1160, 55: 47; 1312, 79 : 41 (3248); as the First and the Final cause, 1141, 53 : 43-55 (2889); 1157, 55 : 27-28 (2930-2931); 1175, 57 : 3-4 (2982—2986); as Forbearing, 92, 2 : 226; forgiveness and, 92, 2 : 226 ; and the repentant, 419, 9 : 104; forgers of lies against, 284, 6 : 22 (835); 431, 10 : 18 (1246); 457, 11 : 19; 1208, 61 : 8; freedom of, from : forgetfulness, 656, 19 : 65; 671, 20 : 53 (1827); sleep, 106, 2 : 256; weariness, 106, 2 : 256; 1114, 50 : 39 (2818); friendship of, 107, 2 : 258; grace of, 3, 1 : 1 (4); 451, 10 : 108 (1292); glorification of, 592, 17 : 45 (1622); 769, 24 : 42 (2051); 1198, 59 : 25; 1206, 61 : 2; 1211, 62 : 2; 1219, 64 : 2 (3055); grief of, 948, 36 : 31 (2442); as Guardian, 467, 11 : 58; 554; 16 : 3 ; 582, 17 : 3; 597, 17 : 69; 732, 22 : 79; 926, 34 : 22; 1034, 42 : 7 (2644); guidance of, 60, 2 : 143 ; 437, 10 : 36 ; 525, 14 : 11 (1458); 727, 22 : 55; 899, 33 : 5; holiness of, 24, 2 : 33; 304, 6 : 101; 592, 17 : 44; 1003, 39 : 68; human urge for recognition of, 517, 13 : 29 (1440); immanènce of, 325, 7 : 8; indecencies and, 329, 7 : 29; incomparably great, 511, 13 : 10; 1036, 42 : 12 (2647); incomprehensibleness of, 304, 6 : 104 (887); intermediaries between man and, 252, 5 : 36 (743); as Light, 767, 24 : 36 (2046A-2047); the Living, 106, 2 : 256; 123, 3 : 3 (363); as the Lord, 4, 1 : 2 (6); love of, 80, 2 : 196; 91, 2 : 223; 132, 3 : 32; 148, 3 : 77; 167, 3:147; 171, 3 : 160; 254, 5 : 43; 258, 5 : 55; 396, 9 : 7; 475, 11 : 91; 1206, 61 : 5; loyalty to, 857, 29 : 9 (2240); majesty of, 921, 34 : 2-4 (2375-2377); as the Maker, 282, 6 : 15 (829); 505, 12 : 102; 525, 14 : 11; 933, 35 : 2; manifestations of, 455, 11 : 8 (1300); as Master, 5, 1 : 4 (8-10); 7, 1 : 7 (15); mercy of, 3, 1 : 1 (4); 282, 6 : 13 (828); 441, 10 : 59; 481, 11 : 120; 686, 20 : 130 (1866); 1034, 42 : 6 (2643B); omniscience of, 25, 2 : 34; 40, 2 : 78; 106, 2 : 256 (318); 132, 3: 30; 442, 10 : 62 (1273); 665, 20 : 8 (1810) 682, 20 : 111 (1854); as Originator, 52, 2 : 118 (140); 282, 6: 15 (829); 933, 35 : 2; 999, 39 : 47; 1035, 42 : 12; partners with, 201, 4 : 37; 204, 4 : 49 (615); 317, 6 : 152; 520, 13: 37; 621, 18 : 39; 719, 22 : 27; 777, 25 : 3 ; 875, 30 : 29-31 (2283-2284); 885, 31 : 14 (2305); 886, 31 : 16 (2307); perfection of, 554, 16 : 4 (1530); power of, 17, 2 : 21; 213, 4 : 86; 487, 12 : 22; 567, 16 : 71; 716, 22 : 15; 717, 22 : 19; quickening of the dead by, 565, 16 : 66; 714, 22 : 7; 880, 30 : 51 (2293); 1066, 45 : 6; reckoning by, 213, 4 : 87; 521, 13 : 42; remembrance of, 180, 3 : 192; 220, 4 : 104 (662); 386, 8 : 46 ; 643, 19 : 11-12 (1744); 1213, 62 : 11; sealing of hearts by, 14, 2 : 8 (27); 231, 4 : 156 (695); 284, 6 : 26; 289, 6 : 47; 346, 7 : 102 (1018); 445, 10:75 (1280); 576, 16: 109 ; 1069, 45 : 24; 1331, 83:15; as Self-Subsisting, 106, 2 : 256; 123, 3 : 3 (363); as Self-Sufficient, 112, 2 : 268; Signs of, 182, 3 : 200; 353, 7 : 134 (1040); 639, 18 : 110 (1736); 873, 30 : 21-28 (2277-2282); 888, 31 : 28 (2315); mockery of the Signs of, 228, 4 : 141; slow in punishing, 430, 10 : 12 (1242); 625, 18 : 59; 942, 35 : 46 (2425); Source : of good and evil, 211, 4 : 79-80 (636-637); of laws, 520, 13 : 40 (1449); of life, 867, 29 : 62 (2265); 1157, 55: 28 (2931); sovereignty of, 131, 3: 27; 682, 20: 115; 777, 25: 3 (2064); submission

INDEX

Anṣārs, brotherhood between Meccan refugees and, 1195, 59 : 10-11 (3023-3024)

Apostasy, forgiven through repentance, 151, 3 : 90-91 (436A-437); harmless to the cause of Faith, 166, 3 : 145 (494); 258, 5 : 55 (760); punishment for, 88, 2 : 218; 151, 3 : 87 -89 (436); 227, 4 : 138 (684); 575, 16 : 107 (1579)

Arabia, and spiritual knowledge, 949, 36 : 35 (2444)

Arabic, beauty of, 1113, 50 : 31 (2811); peculiarities of, 483, 12 : 3 (1357); 1046, 43 : 4

Arabs, before the Holy Prophet, 154, 3 : 104 (450); idols of, 1264, 71 : 24 (3134); married step-mothers, 196, 4 : 23 (585); rise of, 1018, 40 : 69 (2616); superstitious customs of, 271, 5 : 104 (798-798D); 313, 6 : 138-141 (915-921); 404, 9 : 37 (1183)

Ark, Noah's, 339, 7 : 65; 445, 10 : 74; 461, 11: 38-39; 739, 23: 28

Arrows, divination by, 242, 5 : 4; 268, 5 : 91

Ascension, of Jesus, 26, 2 : 37 (71); 329, 7 : 26 (962); 671, 20 : 56; see Jesus

Atheism, see Allāh, existence of

Atonement, refutation of, 119, 2 : 287 (359) ; 123, 3 : 3 (363); 130, 3 : 26 (391); 199, 4 : 29 (593); 264, 5 : 75 (779); 320, 6 : 165 (940); 586, 17 : 16 (1601); 1141, 53 : 39 (2887)

Ayyūb, (Job), history of, 704, 21 : 84-85 (1911); paragon of patience, 298, 6 : 85 (869)

Āzar, Abraham's father, 296, 6 : 75 (864)

Badr, aversion of believers to fight at, 376, 8 : 6 (1095); disposition of opposing forces at, 385, 8 : 43-45 (1124-1126); loss of Muslims at, 173, 3 : 166 (521) ; Second Expedition of, 175, 3 : 173 (529); significance of, 781, 25 : 27 (2074); victory of believers at, 86, 2 : 211 (252); 127, 3 : 14 (377-378); 160, 3 : 124 (469); 377, 8 : 8-13 (1097-1098); 379, 8 : 18 (1107); 896, 32 : 30 (2328)

Bal'am ibn Ba'ūra, abasement of, 366, 7 : 176-177 (1072-1074)

Bequests, charitable objects and, 74, 2 : 181 (205)

Belief, in After-life, 14, 2 : 5 (25); 301, 6 : 93 (876); 816, 27 : 4; 884, 31 : 5; 1258, 70 : 27 (3125A); basis of, 506, 12 : 109 (1417); 790, 25 : 74; (2092A); elements of, 35, 2 : 63 (104); 118, 2 : 286 (358); 262, 5 : 70 (775); 515, 13: 22 (1434); in God and human nature, 365, 7 : 173 (1070); 1176, 57 : 9 (2988); and observance of Divine laws, 450, 10 : 101 (1290); and practice, 224, 4 : 125; 876, 30 : 32 (2285); 1013, 40 : 41; 1206, 61 : 3-4 (3034); in all Prophets, 14, 2 : 5 (24-25); 59, 2:137 (154); 118, 2 : 286; 864, 29 : 47; and right acts and rewards, 20, 2 : 26 (46A-47); and disbelief compared, 458, 11 : 25 (1308); 514, 13 : 17; 937, 35 : 20-23 (2415-2416); 1016, 40 : 59; 1238, 67 : 23 (3085)

Believers, categories of, 217, 4 : 96 (654); 857, 29: 11 (2241); 1177, 57 : 11 (2990); conditions for emigration of, 217, 4 : 98 (655); 218, 4 : 101 (658); as friends of Allāh, 107, 2 : 258; 145, 3 : 69; 1068, 45 : 20; fruitfulness of endeavours of, 224, 4 : 125 (674); help of Allāh for, 450, 10 : 104; 1015, 40 : 52 (2611); 1190, 58 : 22 (3013); honoured by Allāh, 238, 4 : 176; 873, 30 : 16 (2275); increase in faith of, 376, 8 : 3; 425, 9 : 124; marks of true, 128, 3 : 18 (381); 163, 3 : 135-137 (481-483); 376,

8 : 3-5; 392, 8 : 75; 693, 21 : 20-21 (1877); 735, 23 : 2-12 (1978-1983); 768, 24 : 38 (2048); 771, 24 : 52 (2056); 775, 24 : 63 (2060); 1292, 76 : 8-11 (3193-3194); 1200, 60 : 2-5, 9-10 (3028-3029); no fear and grief for, 35, 2 : 63; 262, 5 : 70; 290, 6 : 49; 442, 10 : 63 (1274); 1076, 46 : 14 (2724); observance of golden means by, 1155, 55 : 9-10 (2922); rewards for, 20, 2 : 26; 162, 3 : 134 (479A); 182, 3 : 199 (552); 194, 4 : 14; 206, 4 : 58 (620); 245, 5 : 13; 267, 5 : 86; 330, 7 : 33 (968); 333, 7 : 44 (976); 334, 7 : 47 (978); 392, 8 : 75; 400, 9 : 20; 416, 9 : 89; 429, 10 : 10 (1240); 540, 15 : 24 (1492); 559, 16 : 31-32 (1542); 584, 17 : 10 (1596); 780, 25 : 16-17 (2071); 867, 29 : 59 (2263); 879, 30 : 46; 1007, 40 : 9 (2596); 1086, 47 : 16 (2748); 1160, 55 : 47-59 (2939-2946); 1162, 55 : 63-79 (2948-2954); 1166, 56 : 16-41 (2962-2968); 1291, 76:6-7 (3192-3192A); 1292, 76 : 12-23 (3196-3199); sale of Paradise to, 210, 4 : 75; 421, 9 : 111-112; 1209, 61 : 11-12; stand on sure knowledge, 291, 6 : 58; 506, 12 : 109 (1417); trials of, 856, 29 : 3-4 (2237); 993, 39 : 11 (2567); will triumph, 258, 5 : 57; 400, 9 : 20; worship of Allāh by, 991, 39 : 3, 4, 12, 15 (2568); see Paradise

Bible, abrogation of, by the Qur'ān, 49, 2 : 107 (132); different versions in, and Qur'ān regarding : Abraham's father, 296, 6 : 75 (864); Abraham's truthfulness, 652, 19 : 42 (1773); Aaron, 679, 20 : 91 (1845); the death and birth of Jesus, 647, 19 : 26 (1759); the forbidden tree, 26, 2 : 36 (69); 327, 7 : 20-23 (957-958); gold given by Egyptians to Israelites, 678, 20 : 88 (1842); Jālūt, 104, 2 : 251-252 (310A-312); Joseph, 484, 12 : 5 (1360); Mary, 644, 19 : 17 (1747); mutual killing of Israelites, 32, 2 : 55 (95); number of Israelites on Exodus, 101, 2 : 244 (301); Pharaoh, 448, 10 : 93 (1286); punishment for worshipping calf, 32, 2 : 55 (95); sister of Aaron, 649, 19 : 29 (1763); Tābūt, 103, 2 : 249 (308-309); Ṭālūt (Gideon), 102, 2 : 248 (307); interpolations in, 40, 2 : 76; 41, 2 : 80 (114); 148, 3 : 79 (431); 204, 4 : 47; 253, 5 : 42; prophecies about Islām in the, 63, 2 : 150 (173); 360, 7 : 158 (1059); 421, 9 : 111 (1219); 738, 23 : 21 (1990); 1101, 48 : 30 (2786); 1207, 61 : 7 (3037)

Birth-control, forbidden, 317, 6 : 152; 589, 17 : 32 (1613-1614)

Bondwomen, idolatrous women and believing, 91, 2 : 222 (267); punishment for adultery by, 198, 4 : 26 (592); status and marriage of, 187, 4 : 4 (561); 766, 24 : 33

Bribery, condemned, 78, 2 : 189 (216)

Brotherhood, factors to promote real spirit of, 447, 10 : 88 (1284); Muslim, 392, 8 : 73 (1147); 393, 8 : 76 (1149); 412, 9 : 71-72; 1105, 49 : 11-13 (2794-2795); 1106, 49 : 15 (2798)

Burnt-offering, and the Holy Prophet, 178, 3 : 184 (539)

Book, qualities of a revealed, 528, 14 : 25-27 (1465-1466)

Barnabas, prophecy about the Holy Prophet in the Gospel of, 1207, 61 : 7 (3037)

Ba'l, name of an idol, 970, 37 : 126 (2502)

Barzakh (barrier), punishment in, 750, 23 : 101 (2017); 786, 25 : 54 (2085); 1014, 40 : 47 (2609)

Calamities, foretold, 595, 17 : 59 (1626); law of God about, 311, 6 : 132 (912); 345, 7 : 95 (1015); 812 , 26 : 209 (2137)

INDEX

INDEX

Creation, diversity in, 556, 16 : 14 (1534); of earth, 1023, 41 : 10-11 (2622-2623); of new heaven and earth, 1080, 46 : 34 (2735); pairs in, 510, 13 : 4 (1421); 949, 36 : 37 (2445); 1122, 51 : 50 (2838); process of, 561, 16 : 41 (1546); purpose of, 1219, 64 : 4(3057); of the universe in six periods, 336, 7 : 55 (984-986)

Crucifixion, of Jesus, 232, 4 : 158 (697-699); in the time of Moses, 351, 7 : 125 (1033); see Jesus

Cyrus, and the Jews of Babylon, 47, 2 : 103 (130A); rebuilding of Jerusalem by, 108, 2 : 260 (323)

Covenant, taken from Prophets, 149, 3 : 82 (433); 901, 33 : 8 (2334)

Customs, of Meccan disbelievers, 271, 5 : 104 (798-798D)

Commerce, fair dealing in, 591, 17 : 36 (1618)

David, attempt to murder, 979, 38 : 22-25 (2523-2525); favours of God on, 105, 2 : 252 (312); 235, 4 : 164 (706); Israelites cursed by Jesus and, 265, 5 : 79 (782); policies of, 703, 21 : 79 (1905); power and glory of, 703, 21 : 80-81 (1907-1908); 818, 27 : 16 (2151); 923, 34 : 11-12 (2379); 979, 38 : 18-21 (2522); progeny of Noah, 298, 6 : 85; vindication of, 981, 38 : 26 (2526)

Dajjāl, identity of, 639, 18 : 111 (1737); time of punishment of, 725, 22 : 48 (1961A)

Dead, return of the, 707, 21 : 96 (1917); 750, 23 : 100-101; spiritual regeneration of the, 33, 2 : 57 (96); 287, 6 : 37 (844A-845); testify to the truth of Prophets, 306, 6 : 112 (898)

Death, blessings of, 801, 26 : 82 (2120); inevitability of, 179, 3 : 186 (542); 211, 4 : 79 (635); 737, 23 : 16 (1986); significance of, 1235, 67 : 3 (3079); twofold birth and, 1008, 40 : 12 (2598)

Death-penalty, remedy for murder, 590, 17 : 34 (1616)

Debts, payment of, 193, 4 : 13 (575A)

Deism, denounced, 304, 6 : 104 (887)

Destiny, man maker of his, 998, 39 : 42 (2579); 1041, 42 : 31; 1068, 45 : 16; the night or, 1059, 44 : 4-5 (2692-2693); 1382, 97 : 2-6 (3393-3398A)

Devil, see Satan.

Dhūl Qarnain, identity and works of, 632, 18 : 84-99 (1719-1732)

Disbelievers, aggressiveness of, 858, 29 : 13-14 (2242); apathy towards guidance of, 1022, 41 : 6 (2621); attitude towards Islām of, 310, 6 : 126 (907); blindness and deafness of, 458, 11 : 25 (1308); 598, 17 : 73 (1637); consternation of, 996, 39 : 25 (2573); 1039, 42 : 23 (2653); and continuity of Prophethood, 1012, 40 : 35 (2605); coverings on the eyes and ears of, 593, 17 : 47 (1623); decadence of, 538, 15 : 15-16 (1484-1485); defeat of, 507, 12 : 111 (1418); 560, 16 : 34-35 (1543-1544); false sense of security of, 1132, 52 : 45 (2865); no favours to be shown to, 1026, 41 : 25-26 (2631-2632); fruitlessness of the works of, 325, 7 : 9-10 (948); 1083, 47 : 2 (2737); 1085, 47 : 9-10 (2744); frustration of, 929, 34 : 39 (2401); harmlessness to Faith of, 284, 6 : 22 (835); humiliation of, 559, 16 : 28-29 (1541); 561, 16 : 40 (1545); accusation of

Prophets by, 445, 10 : 77 (1281); inability to bring the likeness of the Holy Qur'ān of, 18, 2 : 24 (44); 382, 8 : 32 (1116); 438, 10 : 39 (1262); 456, 11 : 14-15 (1303); likeness to animals of, 478, 11 : 107 (1349); 1085, 47 : 13 (2746); marks of, 230, 4 : 151-153 (692); 334, 7 : 46, 52 (977, 982); obliviousness to Divine call of, 951, 36 : 53 (2452); perceptive understanding of, 438, 10 : 44 (1263); pessimism of, 426, 10 : 3 (1231A); prejudices of, 945, 36 : 9-11 (2428-2430); punishment of, 289, 6 : 43-48 (849-851); 332, 7 : 41 (974); 458, 11 : 20, 23 (1306); 779, 25 : 12-15 (2068-2070); 866, 29 : 54-55 (2261-2261A); 1077, 46 : 21 (2728); rejection of Truth by, 454, 11 : 6 (1296); 1027, 41 : 27 (2633); slaves of passion, 568, 16 : 76 (1562); state of mind of, 1112, 50 : 28 (2810); superiority complex of, 738, 23 : 25 (1992); torments of, 604, 17 : 98 (1654); transgression of, 625, 18 : 58 (1703); wish they were Muslims, 536, 15 : 3 (1477); witness against themselves, 953, 36 : 66 (2457)

Divinity, test of, 437, 10 : 35—37 (1259-1260)

Divorce, hatefulness of, 226, 4 : 131 (681); and 'Iddah, 93, 2 : 229 (277); 98, 2 : 235 (289); Islamic Law of, 93, 2 : 228-233; (276-278, 280 285); 1224, 65:2-8 (3064-3068A); kind treatment on giving, 100, 2 : 242 (299); 196, 4 : 21-22 (582-583); 913, 33 : 50 (2361); obstacles put in the way of, 93, 2 : 227 (275)

Doomsday, arguments in support of, 1377, 95 : 8 (3385); disbelievers' lot on, 1127, 52 : 10-17 (2848-2850); and salvation. 106, 2 : 255 (315-317); significance of, 288, 6 : 41-42 (847-848)

Dowry, of a divorcee before consummation of marriage, 99, 2 : 237-238 (292-294A); forfeiture of, 94, 2 : 230 (282); meanings of, 94, 2 : 230 (281); payment and settlement of, 189, 4 : 5 (563-564); 197, 4 : 25; taking back of, 196, 4 : 21-22 (582-583)

Dualism, refuted, 211, 4 : 79; 280, 6 : 2 (817)

Earth, food producing capacity of, 1023, 41 : 11 (2623-2624); number of, 1227, 65 : 13 (3070A); ownership of, 352, 7 : 129

Egyptians, punishment of, 353, 7 : 134-135 (1040)

Elias, identity of, 299, 6 : 86

Elisha, identity of, 299, 6 : 87 (870)

Emigration, in the cause of Allāh, 218, 4 : 101 (658); of the Holy Prophet, 405, 9 : 40 (1185-1186)

Environment, human actions and, 516, 13 : 24-25 (1436-1437); reforming of, 381, 8 : 26 (1111)

Equality, of all mankind, 598, 17 : 71 (1635); 1106, 49 : 14 (2797); of men and women, 200, 4 : 33 (595)

Eve, see Adam

Evidence, about adultery, 759, 24 : 14 (2034); law of, 116, 2 : 283; 190, 4 : 7 (569); 194, 4 : 16 (576); 227, 4 : 136 (682); 272, 5 : 107-109 (800-802)

INDEX

Evil(s), causes of, 195, 4 : 18 (578); 578, 16 : 120 (1585); consequences of, 41, 2 : 82; 224, 4:124; disbelievers persist in, 329, 7:29; evil-doers and, 816, 27:5 (2145); forgiveness of, 132, 3 : 32; 163, 3 : 136 (482); 221, 4 : 111; friendship based on, 571, 16 : 87 (1569); man himself cause of, 211, 4 : 80 (637); open and secret, 309, 6 : 121; 317, 6 : 152; 331, 7 : 34; punishment of, 320, 6 : 161; 435, 10 : 28 (1256); 853, 28 : 85 (2234); redemption of, 480, 11 : 115; 515, 13 : 23 (1435); 578, 16 : 120 (1585); reward of good and, 853, 28 : 85 (2234); social, 1105, 49 : 13 (2795)

Evolution, and belief in God, 4, 1 : 2 (6A)

Ezekiel, identity of, 705, 21 : 86 (1912); Vision of, 108, 2 : 260 (323-326)

Ezra, sonship of God of, 402, 9 : 30 (1176)

Education, of children, 589, 17 : 32 (1613)

Economy, Muslim, 1194, 59 : 8 (3021)

Exploitation, consequences of, 1330, 83 : 2-6 (3288)

Faith, and blood relations, 400, 9 : 23-24 (1171-1172); concealment of, 1011, 40 : 29 (2603); elements of, 59, 2 : 137; 177, 3 : 180; 236, 4 : 171; 362, 7 : 159; increases, 176, 3 : 174; judgment on, 308, 6 : 117-118 (903); light treatment of, 228, 4 : 141 (686); 294, 6 : 69, 71; marks of, 13, 2 : 4-6; 68, 2 : 166 (190); 118, 2 : 286; 230, 4 : 151-153 (692) ; recantation of, 575, 16 : 107 (1579); 576, 16 : 111 (1580); as source of light, 107, 2 : 258; see Belief and Believers

Fasting, concessions in, 76, 2 : 186, 188, (209, 214-215); prescription of, 75, 2 : 184-187 (206-207A, 209-210); revelation of the Qur'ān in the month of, 76, 2 : 186 (208)

Food, forbidden and lawful, 69, 2 : 169 (192-193); 70, 2 : 173-174 (197-199); 241, 5 : 2 (716-717); 243, 5:5-6 (722-723); 267, 5 : 88-89; 268, 5 : 94 (791); 308, 6 : 119-120 (904); 309, 6 : 122 (905); 314, 6 : 143-147 (922-926); 330, 7 : 33 (968); and human actions, 330, 7 : 32; 577, 16 : 116-119; 743, 23 : 52 (2001); sufficiency of, 1023, 41 : 11 (2624)

Forgiveness, meaning of asking, 1015, 40 : 56 (2612-2612A); mercy of God drawn by asking, 208, 4 : 65; 383, 8 : 34; 453, 11 : 4 (1295); 466, 11 : 53; not to be sought for idolaters, 422, 9 : 113

Force, use of, 107, 2 : 257 (319); 344, 7 : 89 (1013); see Compulsion

Freedom, significance of, 513, 13 : 16 (1431)

Freud, on Moses, 665, 20 : 10 (1812)

Friendship, in distress, 1054, 43 : 68 (2686)

Gabriel, chief angel, 46, 2 : 98 (123)

Gambling, 89, 2 : 220 (262); 268, 5 : 91-92 (790A)

God(s), abusing false, 306, 6 : 109 (894); stages in realization of, 51, 2 : 113 (135) : theory of son of, 52, 2 : 117 (139); 661, 19 : 91-93 (1802-1803); see Allāh

INDEX

Gog and Magog, identity of, 635, 18 : 95 (1728-1729); 637, 18 : 98-100 (1732-1734); material glory and destruction of, 621, 18 : 41-43 (1692-1695); 623, 18 : 48-49 (1697-1698); 707, 21 : 97-98 (1919-1920A); prayer against machinations of, 710, 21 : 113 (1928); see Christians

Good, definition of, 427, 10 : 5 (1235); 656, 19 : 61 (1786); and evil emanate from Allāh, 1221, 64 : 12 (3062); man endowed with knowledge of evil and, 1359, 90 : 11 (3349); reward of evil and, 435, 10 : 28 (1256)

Gospel(s), description of Muslims in, 1101, 48: 30 (2786); guidance in, 123, 3 : 4 (366); 255, 5 : 47-48; prophecies in, 1; 360, 7 : 158 (1059); 1207, 61 : 7 (3037)

Government, Islamic form of, 206, 4 : 59-60 (621-623) ; 1042, 42 : 39 (2660); obligations of, 683, 20 : 119-120 (1858)

Guidance, law pertaining to, 516, 13 : 28 (1439)

Ḥadīth, authenticity of, 144, (426A)

Hagar, identity of, 968, 37 : 103 (2497);

Hārūt and Mārūt, descriptive names, 47, 2 : 103 (129-130)

Heaven, expansion of, 1122, 51 : 48 (2837-2837A); functions of, 18, 2 : 23 (43); 695, 21 : 33-34 (1886-1886A); orbits of planets in, 1117, 51:8 (2825); purpose of creation of, 554, 16:4 (1530); source of guidance and life, 525, 14:11 (1458); 1008, 40 : 14 (2599); spiritual, 788, 25 : 62 (2087-2087A); supportlessness of, 509, 13 : 3 (1420); time of creation of, 336, 7 : 55 (984); 427, 10 : 4; 455, 11 : 8

Hell, believers and, 658, 19 : 72 (1793A); 708, 21 : 102-103 (1922); eternity of, 27, 2 : 40 (74); 478, 11 : 107-108 (1349-1350); 698, 21 : 48 (1893); fuel of, 19, 2: 25 (45); inmates of, 69, 2 : 168, punishment in, 206, 4 : 57 (619); roaring and raging of, 478, 11 : 107 (1349); wretchedness in, 515, 13 : 19

Ḥijāz, purging of, 394, 9 : 3 (1154)

Hoarding, condemned, 1401, 104 : 3-5 (3432-3434); punishment for, 403, 9 : 34-35 (1180)

Holy land, blissfulness of, 354, 7 : 138 (1042-1043); inheritors of, 709, 21 : 106-113 (1925, 1928); and Israelites, 248, 5 : 22 (731); 352, 7 : 130 (1037)

Homicide, 215, 4 : 93-94 (649-651)

Honey, as cure for men, 566, 16 : 70

Hūd, fate of the rejectors of, 339, 7 : 66-73 (997-997A); 465, 11 : 51-61 (1323-1325); and his people, 805, 26 : 124-140 (2126)

Hudaibiyah, oath of allegiance at, 1097, 48 : 19 (2774-2775); Treaty of, 1092, 48:2 (2763); 1099, 48 : 25 (2780); 1100, 48 : 27 (2782)

Human honour, sanctity of, 591, 17 : 37 (1619)

Human nature, laws of, 306, 6 : 109-111 (895, 897); purity of, 543, 15 : 43 (1500)

Human progress, bound up with hope and fear, 429, 10 : 8 (1239)

INDEX

Human reason, and comprehension of God, 304, 6 : 104 (887); and religion, 69, 2 : 171-172 (195-196); 271, 5 : 105; 367, 7 : 180; and revelation, 556, 16 : 12 (1533); 566, 16 : 67 (1555)

Human soul, creation of, 893, 32 : 10 (2324); eternity of, 52, 2 : 118 (140); evolution of, 1170, 56 : 61-62 (2972); 1256, 70 : 5 (3120); immortality of, 999, 39 : 43 (2580); nature of, 430, 10 : 13; responsibility of, 937, 35 : 19; stages of development of, 1285, 75 : 3 (3177); 1291, 76 : 6-7 (3192-3192A); 1293, 76 : 18-19 (3196-3197); 1294, 76 : 22 (3199); 1356, 89 : 28-29 (3342); warned, 999, 39 : 44 (2581)

Ḥunain, victory of Muslims at, 401, 9 : 25 (1173)

Hunting, training of beasts and birds for, 243, 5 : 5 (722A)

Hypocrites, and the battle of Tabūk, 407, 9 : 45—59 (1191-1192); boastfulness of, 1216, 63 : 9 (3053); condition of, 413, 9 : 74-87, 90 (1204); contradictory leanings of, 1088, 47 : 27, 31 (2755-2756); denunciation of, 229, 4 : 143-144, 146 (687-689); disunity among, 1196, 59 : 15 (3026); equivocal language of, 1086, 47 : 17 (2749); evil wishes of, 1096, 48 : 13 (2771); and Expedition of Khaibar, 1096, 48 : 16 (2772); exposed, 16, 2 : 18 (37); false estimations of, 1216, 63 : 8 (3052); false promises of, 1195, 59 : 12 (3025); increase in their disease, 16, 2 : 16 (33A); kinds of, 17, 2 : 20-21 (40-41); lack self-reliance, 1215, 63 : 5 (3051); are liars, 1215, 63 : 2 (3049); loss of, 411, 9 : 67-69 (1197); machinations of, 420, 9: 107-108 (1217); mock at the Holy Prophet, 410, 9 : 64 (1195); punishment of, 1178, 57 : 14-16 (2991-2995); rebellion of, 959, 37 : 8 (2472); treatment of, 208, 4 : 64 (624); 214, 4 : 89(644); and Uḥud, 169, 3 : 155 (506A); 174, 3 : 168 (525)

Iblīs, dialogue between God and, 326, 7 : 13—19 (952—955); identity of, 25, 2 : 35 (67); 325, 7 : 12 (951); 542, 15 : 31-42 (1496-1499); 596, 17 : 62 (1629); 623, 18 : 51; 683, 20 : 117; see Satan

Idolatry (Idols, Idolators), arguments against, 107, 2 : 259 (321); 168, 3 : 152 (498); 280, 6 : 2 (817); 283, 6 : 20 (833); 652, 19 : 45 (1775); 678, 20 : 90 (1844); 699, 21 : 53 (1895); 716, 22 : 14 (1936); 717, 22 : 19 (1940) ; 720, 22 : 31-32 (1949); 730, 22 : 72 (1973); 731, 22 : 74-75 (1974-1975); 863, 29 : 42 (2254); 877, 30 : 36 (2287); 878, 30 : 41 (2290); 887, 31 : 21 (2310-2311); 966, 37 : 87 (2491); 967, 37 : 93 (2494); 972, 37 : 150 (2507); 991, 39 : 4 (2562); 996, 39 : 30 (2575); 1003, 39 : 68 (2587); 1048, 43 : 19, 22 (2673-2674) ; 1073, 46 : 5-6 (2718-2720); 1139, 53 : 24 (2883); basis of, 432, 10 : 19 (1247); declaration of absolution regarding, 394, 9: 1-4 (1150-1155); and forgiveness, 422, 9 : 113-114 (1220); helplessness of, 731, 22 : 74 (1974); impotence of, 295, 6 : 72; mosques and, 399, 9 : 17-19 (1168-1170); reappearance in Arabia of, 931, 34 : 50 (2404); and the Sacred Mosque, 401, 9 : 28 (1174)

Idrīs, identity of, 655, 19 : 57 (1783)

'Imrān, identity of, 132, 3 : 34 (399); 133, 3: 36 (400-401)

Inheritance, Islamic law of, 74, 2 : 181-183 (205-205B); 191, 4 : 8-14 (570-575A); 900, 33 : 7 (2333); of Kalālah, 238, 4 : 177 (715)

Intercession, acceptance of, 30, 2 : 49 (85); accountability of, 213, 4 : 86 (642); and disbelievers, 290, 6 : 52 ; permission for, 106, 2 : 256; 926, 34 : 24 (2389A-2392)

INDEX

Khulʻ, obtaining of, 95, 2 : 230 (282)

Knowledge, seeking of, 424, 9 : 122 (1224); soothsayers and, 1268, 72 : 9-13 (3142); value of, 113, 2 : 270 (340)

Korah, (Qārūn), ruin of, 851, 28 : 77-83 (2231-2232); 863, 29 : 40

Labour, exploitation of, 1243, 68 : 18-28, 34 (3098, 3100-3101)

Law, fundamentals of, 271, 5 : 104 (798D); miracles and natural, 348, 7 : 108-109 (1023-1024); nature of, 286, 6 : 35 (843); 308, 6 : 116 (902); 942, 35 : 44-45 (2424-2425); 1098, 48 : 24; of nature and of Sharīʻah, 717, 22 : 19 (1940); need of Divine, 199, 4 : 29 (593); penal, 1042, 42 : 41 (2661); spirit and form of, 399, 9 : 19 (1170)

Life, dependence on water of, 1239, 67 : 31 (3088); similitude of, 622, 18 : 46-47 (1696); transitoriness of, 1081, 46 : 36 (2736); vanity of, 751, 23 : 114-115 (2021)

Loans, record of, 116, 2 : 283-284 (354-354B); respite in payment of, 116, 2 : 281 (353)

Lot, belief of, 860, 29 : 27; daughters of, 472, 11: 79-80 (1336-1338); destruction of the people of, 342, 7 : 81-85 (1005-1009); 475, 11 : 90; 547, 15 : 74-75; emigration of, 701, 21 : 72 (1903); entertainment of strangers by, 547, 15 : 71 (1512); messengers to, 472, 11 : 78, 82 (1335, 1339); 546, 15 : 62-71 (1507-1512); and his people, 472, 11 : 78-84 (1335-1339A); 828, 27 : 55-59 (2179A-2180); 861, 29 : 31-35 (2251); 1150, 54 : 34-40 (2909); vices of the people of, 861, 29 : 30 (2249-2250)

Luqmān, moral precepts of, 885, 31 : 13-20 (2304-2308)

Man, relation of Allāh with, 381, 8 : 25 (1110A); angels subservient to, 325, 7 : 12 (950); communion with God of, 541, 15 : 27 (1493); 542, 15 : 30 (1495); connection with earth of, 329, 7 : 26 (962); creation of, 143, 3 : 60 (425A); 280, 6 : 3 (818); 325, 7 : 12-13 (949, 953); 541, 15 : 27-28 (1493-1494); 692, 21 : 17-18 (1875A-1876); 736, 23 : 13-15 (1984-1985); 752, 23 : 116 (2022); 1123, 51 : 57 (2840); 1155, 55 : 15 (2924); 1376, 95 : 5-6 (3384); destiny of, 586, 17 : 16 (1600); 880, 30 : 54 (2294); 998, 39 : 42 (2579); 1051, 43 : 39 (2679); 1129, 52 : 22 (2853); 1141, 53 : 39-42 (2887-2888); 1346, 87 : 3 (3321); Divine mercy on, 479, 11 : 111 (1352); exaltation of, 598, 17 : 71 (1635B); 655, 19 : 59 (1784); and evil, 327, 7 : 20 (957); freedom of, 305, 6 : 108 (892); 316, 6 : 150 (927); 325, 7 : 12 (949); growth of, 268, 5 : 94 (791); 302, 6 : 96 (879); guardian over woman, 93, 2 : 229 (279); 200, 4 : 35 (598); kinds of, 287, 6 : 37, 39 (845-846); nature of, 876, 30 : 31 (2284); 877, 30 : 37; 918, 33 : 68 (2372); 928, 34 : 32 (2397); 986, 38 : 61-62 (2547-2548); 1000, 39 : 50 (2583); 1008, 40 : 11 (2597); arrogance of : 1031, 41 : 51-52 (2641); contentiousness, 554, 16 : 5 (1531); 624, 18:55 (1702); frivolity, 884, 31: 7 (2302); hastiness, 696, 21 : 38 (1888); immortal, 964, 37 : 59-61 (2484-2485); miserliness of, 605, 17 : 101; 1257, 70 : 20-22 (3123); mortal, 696, 21 : 35 (1887); superstitious, 887, 31 : 22 (2312); ungratefulness, of 430, 10 : 13; 455, 11 : 10-12; 597, 17 : 68 (1634); power of, 919, 33 : 73 (2374); 1219, 64 : 3 (3056); 1363, 91 : 9 (3360); rise and fall of, 1180, 57 : 23 (2996A); superiority of, 598, 17 : 71 (1635B); universe in miniature, 1363, 91 : 8 (3359A); volition of, 1024, 41 : 12 (2625-2626); as witness against himself, 1025, 41 : 21-23 (2628-2629); works of, 585, 17 : 14-15 (1599)

Mankind, as one community, 743, 23 : 53 (2002)

Mountains, functions of, 885, 31 : 11 (2303), and earthquakes, 557, 16 : 16 (1537-1538)

Morals, constituents of; chastity, 735, 23 : 6-8 (1981A); 763, 24 : 31-32 (2043-2043A); 766, 24 : 34; 774, 24 : 61; cleanliness, 91, 2 : 223; 720, 22 : 30; co-operativeness, 241, 5 : 3 (720); doing good, 63, 2 : 149 (171); 80, 2 : 196; 156, 3 : 111 (457); 749, 23 : 97 (2015); forgiveness, 761, 24 : 23 (2037); frugality, 588, 17:27, 28, 30 (1610, 1612); fulfilment of promises, 72, 2 : 178; 590, 17 : 35; 736, 23 : 9; gratefulness, 166, 3 : 145; hospitality, 470, 11 : 70; 546, 15 : 69, 70 (1511); 588, 17 : 27; humility, 788, 25 : 64 (2089); 887, 31 : 19 (2309); justice, 317, 6 : 153 (929); 571, 16 : 91 (1570); kindness, 42, 2 : 84; 201, 4 : 37 (604); 587, 17 : 24-25 (1607-1609); 589, 17 : 29 (1611); 877, 30 : 39 (2288); moderation, 330, 7 : 32; 788, 25 : 68; peace-making, 92, 2 : 225; 222, 4 : 115; perseverance, 29, 2 : 46 (82); 65, 2 : 154 (179); 66, 2 : 156 (182); 480, 11 : 113; 515, 13 : 23; philanthropy, 72, 2 : 178 (203); retaliation, 728, 22 : 61; spirit of sacrifice, 152, 3 : 93 (438); steadfastness, 72, 2 : 178; 179, 3 : 187; 455, 11 : 12; suppression of anger, 163, 3:135 (480-481); trust in God, 526, 14 : 13; 787, 25:59; trustworthiness, 118, 2 : 284 (355); 206, 4 : 59; 736, 23 : 9; truthfulness, 720, 22 : 31; 789, 25 : 73 (2092); unity, 154, 3 : 104 (450); development of, 556, 16 : 12-14 (1535); spiritual development and, 571, 16 : 91 (1570); reward of, 434 , 10 : 27 (1254-1255)

Morality, stages of, 556, 16 : 12-14 (1535)

Mortgage, 118, 2 : 284 (355)

Moses, accomplishments of, 839, 28 : 15 (2203); and Aaron, 668, 20 : 30-31 (1820); Ascension of, 626, 18 : 61-83 (1704-1718); aspirations of, 355, 7:144 (1046); charges against, 918, 33 : 70 (2373A); communion with God of, 842, 28 : 30-36 (2212-2216); Exodus of, 31, 2 : 51 (89); 354, 7 : 139; 448, 10 : 91; 675, 20 : 78; Freud on, 665, 20 : 10 (1812); and the Holy Land, 352, 7 : 129-130(1037); and the Holy Prophet, 457, 11 : 18 (1304); 1075, 46 : 11 (2722); and Israelites, 446, 10 : 84-94; marriage of, 842, 28 : 28 (2211); kills a man, 839, 28 : 16 (2205); meeting with God of, 32, 2 : 52 (90-92); 355, 7 : 143 (1044); 817, 27 : 8-10 (2147-2148); in Midian, 669, 20 : 41 (1823); miracles of, 34, 2 : 61 (101); 348, 7 : 108-109 (1023-1024); 350, 7 : 118 (1029); 353, 7 : 134 (1040); 605, 17 : 102 (1657); 667, 20 : 19-24 (1816A-1819); 818, 27 : 13 (2149); and Pharaoh, 30, 2 : 50 (87); 347, 7 : 105-119 (1022-1024); 445, 10 : 76-83; 476, 11 : 97-98; 447, 10 : 89 (1284A, 1284B); 605, 17 : 102-103 (1657); 669, 20 : 40, 43-62 (1822, 1825-1831); 794, 26 : 11-68; 1121, 51 : 39-41 (2836); Prophets subordinate to, 43, 2 : 88; revelation of, 32, 2354 (93-94); 300, 6 : 92 (874); 318, 6 : 155 (931); 742, 23 : 50; rod of, 817, 27 : 11 (2148); scope of the Message of, 347, 7:106 (1022); and the sorcerers, 350, 7:114-127 (1027-1033); 674, 20 : 71; slandering by Jews of, 1206, 61 : 6 (3036); status of, 356, 7 : 145 (1048); story of, 837, 28 : 8-47 (2200-2220); Vision of , 666, 20 : 11 (1813)

Mosques, outrages against, 51, 2 : 115 (137)

Muḥammad (The Holy Prophet), and ‘Abd Allāh ibn Maktūm, 1315, 80 : 2 (3250); advent of, 43, 2 : 90 (120); 56, 2 : 130 (147); 530, 14 : 36-38 (1468-1471); Ascension of, 581, 17 : 2 (1590-1591); 595, 17 : 61 (1627A); 1136, 53 : 8-19 (2874-2880); authority of, 771, 24 : 52-55 (2056); 909, 33 : 37 (2356); challenge of prayer-contest by, 144, 3 : 62(426); Companions of, 248, 5 : 23 (733); 418, 9 : 100 (1212); 423, 9 : 117; 768, 24 : 38-39 (2048); 814, 26 : 220 (2141); 905, 33 : 24 (2345); 1083, 47 : 5 (2740); 1297, 77 : 2-7 (3204-3208); 1309, 79 : 2-6 (3236-3240); 1366, 92 : 4 (721);

INDEX

INDEX

Power, transitoriness of, 1006, 40 : 5 (2594)

Plague, prophecy about, 832, 27 : 83 (2190-2191)

Prayer, ablution before, 244, 5 : 7 (725-725A); benefits of, chastening power of, 864, 29 : 46 (2256-2256A); of disbelievers, 735, 23 : 2-3 (1978-1979); 1259, 70 : 35-36; 1015, 40 : 51 (2610); in fear, 100, 2 : 240 (297); insincere, 1408, 107 : 5-7 (3445-3446); naturalness to man of, 430, 10 : 13; need of, 790, 25 : 78 (2093); night, 600, 17 : 80 (1642-1643); 1274, 73 : 7 (3152); negligence in, 655, 19 : 60 (1785); observance of, 13, 2 : 4 (21); 99, 2 : 239 (295-296); 607, 17 : 111; prohibition of, 203, 4 : 44 (609-612); shortening of, 218, 4 : 102-103 (659-660); times of, 600, 17 : 79 (1641); 686, 20 : 131 (1867)

Preaching, methods of, 579, 16 : 126 (1588); 670, 20 : 45 (1824); 813, 26 : 215 (2140); 864, 29 : 47 (2257); 1028, 41 : 35 (2636); 1123, 51 : 56

Pre-destination, significance of, 477, 11 : 102 (1345); 741, 23 : 44 (1998); 777, 25 : 3 (2064); 801, 26 : 81 (2119); 1141, 53 : 40 (2888)

Prisoners of war, emancipation of, 187, 4 : 4 (561); 766, 24 : 34 (2046); marriage with, 766, 24 : 33 taking of, 391, 8 : 68-69 (1144-1145A); treatment of, 1083, 47 : 5(2739)

Property, acquisition of, 78, 2 : 189 (215A-216); 199, 4 : 30; benefits of, 190, 4 : 6 (566); disposal of, 190, 4 : 6-7 (565-569); ownership of , 567, 16 : 72 (1558); as a trial, 382, 8 : 29

Prophecies, cancellation of, 439, 10 : 47 (1265); fulfilment of, 294, 6 : 68 (861); 460, 11 : 34 (1311); 520, 13 : 39, 41; 1019, 40 : 78 (2617); kinds of, 125, 3 : 8 (373); nature of, 308, 6 : 116 (902); object of, 595, 17 : 60; about: great changes, 713, 22 : 2-3 (1929-1930); Christians, 611, 18 : 9 (1666); The Holy Prophet, 444, 10 : 72 (1278); 854, 28 : 86 (2235); 978, 38 : 11-12 (2518-2519); 1075, 46 : 11-13 (2722-2723); linking of two seas, 1156, 55 : 20, 21, 23 (2927-2928); pen, 1379, 96 : 5 (3389); Persians, 870, 30 : -35 (2271); 1151, 54 : 46-49 (2912-2913); plague, 832, 27 : 83 (2191); transport, 555, 16 : 9 (1532A); 950, 36 : 43 (2447); triumph of Islām, 52, 2 : 116 (138); 601, 17 : 82 (1645); 905, 33 : 23 (2344); 935, 35 : 12 (2411); 977, 38:2 (2514); 1032, 41 : 54 (2642); 1098, 48 : 22 (2779); 1100, 48 : 29 (2784); 1310, 79 : 7-10 (3241-3243); 1336, 84 : 17-21 (3303-3305); 1358, 90 : 2-3 (3343, 3346); World Wars, 623, 18 : 48 (1697)

Prophethood, bestowal of, 310, 6 : 125 (906A); categories of, 105, 2 : 254 (314); 208, 4 : 65 (625); 209, 4 : 70 (629); 300, 6: 90 (871); claimants to, 284, 6 : 22 (835); 1254, 69 : 45-48 (3118); continuity of, 331, 7 : 36 (970); 731, 22 : 76; functions of, 654, 19 : 52 (1780); need of, 687, 20 : 135; 846, 28 : 48

Prophets, belief in, 230, 4:151 (692); brotherhood of, 743, 23 : 53 (2002); deference due to, 48, 2 : 105 (131); enemies of, 307, 6 : 113; as exemplars, 526, 14 : 12 (1459); falsehood and, 431, 10 : 18 (1246); 446, 10 : 83 (1281A); 694, 21:30 (1883); functions of, 270, 5 : 100; 290, 6 : 49; 444, 10 : 73 (1279); 654, 19 : 52, 55 (1780); 695, 21 : 31 (1884); 779, 25 : 11 (2068); forgiveness of, 532, 14 : 42 (1472); humanity of, 520, 13 : 39; 603, 17 : 94 (1652); 639, 18 :111; 691, 21 : 8-9 (1873); honesty of, 172, 3 : 162 (517); and inmates of Hell, 334, 7 : 47-50 (978-980); among all peoples, 439, 10 : 48 (1266); 511, 13 : 8; 525, 14 : 10 (1456); 560, 16 : 37; 570, 16 : 85 (1568); 937, 35 : 25 (2417); language of, 523, 14 : 5 (1453); manifestation of God by, 1007, 40 : 8 (2595);

INDEX

INDEX

Transport, new means of, 555, 16 : 9 (1532A)

Trench (Battle of), and Hypocrites, 902, 33 : 11, 14-15 (2337-2339); 903, 33 : 20-21 (2341-2342); significance of, 901, 33 : 10 (2335-2336); 905, 33 : 26 (2346)

Trinity, denunciation of, 236, 4 : 172; 263, 5 : 74 (778)

Trusts, treatment of, 118, 2 : 284 (355)

Truth, triumph of, 377, 8 : 8-9 (1098); 514, 13 : 18 (1433); Unity and, 445, 10 : 77 (1281)

Tourism, and Muslims, 1237, 67 : 16 (3081)

Uḥud, Battle of, 159, 3 : 122, 125-127 (467, 468, 470, 472, 474); 164, 3 : 141 (488); 168, 3 : 153-155 (500-506A); 172, 3 : 162 (517); 174, 3 : 168 (525)

Universe, creation of, 67, 2 : 165 (188); 304, 6 : 102; 336, 7 : 55 (984); 530, 14 : 33-34; 695, 21 : 31 (1884); 892, 32 : 5 (2321); 1024, 41 : 13 (2627); destruction of, 1073, 46:4 (2717); 1157, 55 : 27 (2930); glorification of Allāh by, 1175, 57 : 2 (2981); 1192, 59 : 2 (3015); 1219, 64 : 2 (3055); laws governing the, 1024, 41 : 12 (2625-2626); 1154, 55 : 6-8 (2920-2921); as pointer to Allāh, 864, 29 : 45 (2255); 888, 31 : 26 (2314); 949, 36 : 41 (2446); 1235, 67 : 4-5 (3080); unfathomableness of, 1158, 55 : 34 (2934); vanity of, 180, 3 : 191-192 (546-547); 692, 21 : 17 (1875A); 981, 38 : 28; 1063, 44 : 39-40 (2701); 1067, 45 : 14 (2708)

U.N.O., principles of, 1104, 49 : 10 (2793)

Unseen, the knowledge of the, 830, 27 : 66-67 (2187)

Vices, adultery, 590, 17 : 33 (1615); 789, 25 : 69 (2090); dishonesty, 220, 4 : 108; murder, 789, 25 : 69 (2090); niggardliness, 202, 4 : 38; pride, 977, 38 : 3 (2515); 1016, 40 : 57 (2613); prodigality, 588, 17 : 27 28 (1610); robbery, 252, 5 : 39 (744); suspicion, 591, 17 : 37 (1619); telling lies, 720, 22 : 31; vain talk, 735, 23 : 4 (1980)

Vision, erroneous interpretation of, 1100, 48 : 28 (2783); sharpening of, 1112, 50 : 23 (2808)

Wāqidī, narrations of, 1138 (2882)

Wealth, share of the poor in, 1119, 51 : 20 (2830); and spiritual progress, 929, 34 : 38 (2400); 1396, 102 : 2-9 (3423-3425)

West, destruction of the, 1417, 111 : 2-6 (3458-3462)

Widows, maintenance of, 100, 2 : 241 (298); remarriage of, 98, 2 : 235-236 (289-291)

Will, altering of, 74, 2 : 182, 183 (205A, 205B)

Woman, equality with man of, 181, 3 : 196 (549); 224, 4 : 125 (674); 574, 16 : 98 (1576); 908, 33 : 36 (2355); functions of, 77, 2 : 188 (212); treatment of, 195, 4 : 20 (580-581)

Zacharia, birth of a son to, 641, 19 : 3-12 (1739-1745); identity of, 135, 3 : 38 (403): prayer of, 135, 3 : 39-42 (405-410); 642, 19 : 6-7 (1741)

Zakāt, see Alms

Ẕihār, denunciation of, 899, 33 : 5 (2330-2331); 1185, 58 : 2-6 (3001-3004)

Zoroastrianism, refutation of, 280, 6 : 2 (817)

Ahmadiyya Movement In Islam
10610 JANE ST., MAPLE (ONT.)
CANADA L6A 1S1 (416) 832-2669